D1087412

PR 2645 .B3
Bates, Steven L.
A concordance to the poems
of Ben Jonson /

A Concordance to the Poems of
Ben Jonson

Compiled by Steven L. Bates
and Sidney D. Orr

OHIO UNIVERSITY PRESS: ATHENS

RITTER LIBRARY
BALDWIN-WALLACE COLLEGE

©Copyright 1978 Steven L. Bates and Sidney D. Orr
ISBN 0-8214-0359-1
Library of Congress Catalog Number: 76 25613
Printed in the United States of America
All rights reserved

Contents

1. The Poems Concorded

This volume supplies an alphabetical index of the words, with their contexts, in Ben Jonson's non-dramatic English poetry. We base the concordance on the poems as they have been collected and edited by C. H. Herford and Percy and Evelyn Simpson. Although their edition appeared nearly thirty years ago — as volume VIII of their edition of Jonson's completed works[1] — it remains "the standard text today."[2] Volume VIII contains the two collections that Jonson printed as part of the 1616 Folio, *Epigrammes* and *The Forrest* (VIII, 27-89, 93-122), and a third, *The Vnder-wood* (VIII, 127-295), that he may have had a hand in formulating but did not live to see in print. (This collection first appeared in the second volume of the folio *Works* of 1640-41.) It also contains the modern editors' assemblage of Jonson's Ungathered Verse (VIII, 361-423), including a few translations; a collection of his Inscriptions, one wholly and one partly in English verse (VIII, 662, 666); two versions of Horace's Art of Poetry (VIII, 305-37, 338-55); and one other poem, lines that appeared over the entrance to the Apollo Room of the Old Devil tavern (VIII, 657), which the editors pair with a Latin poem, "Leges Convivales," under the general heading of the latter. We add two isolable poems from earlier volumes of Herford and Simpson: the Ode to Himself, "Come leaue the lothed stage," printed with *The New Inne* in 1631 and included with that play in volume VI (1938), pages 492-94; and "A Panegyre" to King James, printed in 1604 with two royal entertainments and included with them in volume VII (1941), pages 113-17. This body of 307 poems and translations is concorded here.

Included in volume VIII but not concorded are Jonson's Latin verse and non-dramatic prose, the Greek and Latin quotations that sometimes preface or conclude a poem in English, and a few titles of poems supplied by Herford and Simpson. The dramatic verse — prologues, epilogues, songs and poems from the masques and plays — is not represented here.[3] It is to be hoped that the plays and masques will soon have their own concordances.[4] Herford and Simpson print in volume VIII a number of poems ascribed to Jonson. We omit them and follow the conservative canon that the editors establish.[5] We do not concord, for example, the poem beginning "To make the Doubt cleare that no Woman's true" (VIII, 194-97), claimed variously for Jonson, Donne, and others. The more reliable the canon, the more reliable the relative frequency of a word's occurrences in Jonson's poetry, a figure computed and supplied for each word in the concordance.

When Herford and Simpson edit and print two versions of the same set of lines, we concord one set fully and concord non-duplicative words from the other. The letters of omitted words appear as ellipses in the few lines in question. Two poems — "And must I sing?" (VIII, 107-108) and *"Proludium"* (VIII, 108) — share a line and a half introducing a third poem ("Epode," VIII, 109-13). We omit duplicative words from lines 15-16 of *"Proludium,"* which overlap with lines 29-30 of "And must I sing?" Fifteen lines in each of two poems that Jonson wrote to anonymous friends — *"An Epistle to a friend,"* lines 19-33 (VIII, 190), and "Censure, not sharplye then, but mee advise," lines 12-26 (VIII, 421-22) — are closely similar. We concord the former in full and the non-duplicative words from the latter. Herford and Simpson print two versions of a rhyming grace (VIII, 418-19); we concord the first fully and omit duplicative words from the second. We concord all of the words in Jonson's later version of Horace's Art of Poetry (VIII, 305-37) and the non-duplicative words from an earlier version (VIII, 338-55). Jonson cancelled the ending of the printed version of *"Epistle* To Elizabeth Covntesse of Rvtland" (VIII, 113-16), and Herford and Simpson supply the missing eight lines from manuscripts. We pick up the conclusion at line 93, omit an overlapping half-line from the printed version, and follow the continuous lineation of the modern editors.

We follow Herford and Simpson exactly in lineation, spelling, and punctuation, including editorial brackets. But with the computer's encouragement we depart from their text in minor ways. We expand the ligatures æ and œ, omit diacritical marks (as in *poême*), lower superscript letters (M^r. becomes *Mr.*), raise subscript quotation marks to their usual place, transcribe dashes (~ and —) as two unspaced hyphens, and expand one other sign (-*e* becomes -*es*). Herford and Simpson draw attention to two acrostics by setting apart the first letter in each line (VIII, 39, 378). We close up the space. (The computer of course does not read the acrostic words.) We print capital letters of all types and sizes in a uniform upper case, although we usually avoid Herford and Simpson's practice, in the first line of each poem, of capitalizing not only the first letter but the second (and sometimes more letters). We transliterate four Greek words — ἀλληγορική, ΑΠΟΘΕΩΣΙΣ, ἐνθουσιαστική , Σκευοποιός — and indicate the transliteration, when each appears, by a prior #-sign:

> #allegorike
> #APOTHEOSIS
> #enthousiastike
> #Skeuopoios

Italic type in Herford and Simpson is not indicated in these pages. A computer print-train with italic characters was not available to us and the expense of other methods was prohibitive.

2. Index Words

Each word — and each different spelling of the same word — receives a separate entry in the alphabetical index. Apart from words added as cross-references, each word is followed on the same line by two numbers. The first is a simple count of the word's occurrences in Jonson's poetry. (In the Appendix words are listed in order of frequency: from "the" occurring 2787 times to "zodiackes," occurring once.) The second, a computed figure, tells the relative frequency with which the word occurs. If a word occurs on an average of once per thousand words, its relative frequency is listed as 0.00100. A typical entry looks like this:

> name   frequency: 90   relative frequency: 0.00130

When a word is out of its normal place in the alphabet because of abbreviation, bracketing, compounding, contraction, or old spelling, a standard spelling with a "See" reference to the other spelling(s) is added at the expected place:

> eternal. See "aeternall," "eternall," "th'aeternall," "th'eternall."

When a word occurs in both a standard spelling and one or more other spellings, a "See also" reference directs the reader from the modern spelling, usually unabbreviated and uncontracted, to the other(s):

> all   frequency: 569   relative frequency: 0.00823
>   See also "all's," "farre-all-seeing," "t⟨o⟩ 'all," "woo-all."

Alphabetizing. A word containing an apostrophe comes in its expected place in the alphabet: "admiration," "admir'd," "admired." But *hyphens and internal brackets are sorted as if they precede the letter* a: "a-fire" precedes "aarons," "the⟨e⟩" precedes "theatre" and "thee." This departure from convention causes compound words that share a first term to come together in the alphabet. For example, directly after the index entry for "court" come the entries for "court-bred-fillie," "court-durt," "court-hobby-horse," and "court-pucell." Such words, quickly apparent, are not ordinarily cross-indexed at the entry preceding them. (Second and third terms — here "bred," "fillie," "durt," etc. — are cross-indexed.) When brackets enclose an entire word, that word appears in the alphabet after the same word without brackets: first "the," then "⟨the⟩." A bracket before the first letter of a word drops away when that word occurs in the alphabetical index: "the⟩," "y⟩our," but it appears in the word's context lines: "⟨the⟩," "⟨y⟩our." The index entry for "&" follows that for "and." The entry for "&c." follows that for "etcetera." Numerals are concorded at the end of the alphabet.

Bracketed words and letters. In Herford and Simpson's text conical brackets enclose a letter or word inserted "to supply an omission of the original." Square brackets enclose "a letter, a word, or a poem wrongly inserted in the original" (VIII, xv). Since we accept their boundaries for Jonson's canon, we do not concord whole poems wrongly inserted. But each word in either kind of brackets and each word containing one or more bracketed letters receives a separate entry in the concordance and, when necessary, is cross-indexed. We list these words separately in the note below (in usual alphabetical order) and retain their context lines in the concordance so that the changes they indicate may easily be seen.[6] To get a sense of the original, visualize the text without conical brackets and their contents, and without square brackets but *with* their contents.

3. Context Lines

Beneath each index word is a listing of the lines in which the word appears. Exceptions to this rule are "See" entries — words entered merely as cross-references — and a few index words for which context lines are omitted. Three pieces of information precede each line and locate it exactly: a page number, a designation of a poem, and a line number. Here is a sample context line:

p. 93   FOREST 2   1   Thou art not, PENSHVRST, built to
                                  enuious show,

A single asterisk before a page number ("*p. 492") refers the reader to Herford and Simpson, volume VI. Two asterisks ("**p. 117") refer him to volume VII. A page number without asterisk(s) — by far the most common form in these columns — refers him to volume VIII.

        *p. 492 = Herford and Simpson, volume VI
       **p. 117 = Herford and Simpson, volume VII
         p. 253 = Herford and Simpson, volume VIII

The second item preceding a context line is a shorthand designation of the poem in which the line occurs (see below, pp. *xiii-xliii*). The third item is the number of the line in the designated poem. When the letter "t" precedes a line number the line is from the poem's title:

> t1 = first line of title
> t2 = second line of title
> t3 = third line of title, etc.[7]

A plus-sign *after* a line number indicates that the line in question is unnumbered in Herford and Simpson but follows directly the line whose number appears:

> 48+ = an unnumbered line following line 48
> 48++ = the second of two unnumbered lines following line 48, etc.

Unnumbered lines indicated in this way are usually speakers' names or internal titles. In "On the famovs Voyage" (VIII, 84), for instance, an unnumbered subtitle, "The Voyage it selfe," comes after twenty introductory lines and is listed here as line "20+."

No compiler of a concordance happily omits context lines, but limited space has required us to omit the contexts of a few words. We retain an index entry for each word, including the frequency, relative frequency, and cross-references, if any. A machine-readable copy of the concordance containing all contexts of all words is available on tape at UCLA; the interested scholar can retrieve omitted contexts at minimal expense. Context lines are omitted for the following words:

&	bene (been)	ffor
&c.	be'st (beest *verb*)	for
a	bin (been)	for'his
am	but	from
an	bvt	
and	by	ha' (have)
are		had
as	can	hadst
as't (as it)	cann	had'st
at	cannot	has
at's (at his)	canst	ha's (has)
att	could	hath
	couldst	haue
be	could'st	haue'hem (have them)
been		hauing
beene	durst	have
beest (*verb*)		

xi

have't (have it)
having
he
hee
hee'd (he would)
hee'ld
hee'll
heere
hee's
he'had
he'le (he will)
he'll
hem (them)
'hem (them)
her
here
here's
hers
he's
h'had
h'has
h'hath
him
hir (her)
his
how
howe
hym (him)
hyme (him)

I
i' (in)
I'am
if
if't (if it)
I'had
I'haue
I'ld
I'le (I will)
I'll
I'm
in
in's (in his)

in't (in it)
into
is
is't (is it)
it
it' (its)
i'th' (in the)
i'the
its
it's

ma' (may *verb*)
maist
mayst
may'st
me
mee
mightst
mought
  (*cf.* might *verb*)
must (*verb*)
my

no
no' (no)
noe
nor
not

o' (of)
of
on
on't (on it)
or
o'th' (of the)
o'the
our
ours
out
ovr

's (is)
shall
shalt

she
shee
shee'll
shee's
she'hath
sh'had
sh'hath
should
should'st
so
soe
so't (so it)
such

't (it)
th' (the)
than
th'are (they are)
th'art (thou art)
that
that's
t'haue (to have)
t'have (to have)
the
thee
their
theire
theirs
them
then
there
there's
these
they
they'
they'are
they'd (they
  would)
they'haue
theyr (their)
theyre (their)
they're
th'hast (thou hast)

th'haue (they
  have)
th'how (the how)
thie (thy)
thine
this
this's
those
thou
thou'ast
thou'hast
thou'ldst
thou'lt
thou'rt
tho'wert
th'were (they were)
thy
thyne
tis
t'is (it is)
'tis
to
to'a
too
to't (to it)
'twas
'twere
t'will (it will)
'twill

unto
upon
us

vnto
vpon
vppon
vs

w'are (we are)
was
was't (was it)
wch (which)
we
we'are
wee
wee'l
wee'll
were
wert
wer't (wert)
what
what's
when
where
where's
where't (where it)
which
who
who'd
whoe
who'had
who'haue
who'in
who'it
who'll
whom

whome
who's
whose
why
wil (cf. will
  aux. verb)
wilt (aux. verb)
with
wi'the
wou'd
would
wouldst
would'st
wth (with)
wull (cf. will
  aux. verb)

yf (if)
yff (if)
yo'are
yo'had
yo'haue
yo'have
yo'in
yor (your)
you
you'haue
you'l
you'ld
you'll
your
yours

4. Titles

The titles of many of the poems are too long to appear in full in the reference columns of the concordance. Listed below are the shorthand designations used here, together with their equivalent titles, first lines, and locations in Herford and Simpson. We designate two poems, those from volumes VI and VII, by short title ("To Himself," "Panegyre"). The remaining poems, all from volume VIII, are designated by editorial collection and number. For example, "Underwood 77" stands for *"To the right Honourable, the Lord Treasurer of* England. *An Epigram."* Many titles, like this one, are not easily pointed to fit in the reference columns. Several poems are untitled. Others, sometimes as many as five or six, share a single unilluminating title ("An Elegie") or depend on context for meaning ("To the same") or both. In any case, the sheer number of poems concorded would make improbable the reader's unhesitating association of all titles, however designated, with the poems they head. (We share the reader's gloom at the absence from these pages of titles like "To Sir Annval Tilter," "To Penshvrst," and "To . . . Shakespeare" — here "Epigrams 29," "Forest 2," and "Ungathered 26," respectively.)

To indicate a series of poems that share an inclusive title and editorial number we reserve the usual formula for the comprehensive heading ("Underwood 2" for "A Celebration of Charis in ten Lyrick Peeces" — VIII, 131). For each poem in the series, following the practice of Herford and Simpson, we add a point and a numeral to the formula ("Underwood 2.3" stands for *"What hee suffered,"* the third poem in "A Celebration of Charis" — VIII, 133). The earlier version of Horace's Art of Poetry is here "Horace 1" (VIII, 338-55), the later version "Horace 2" (VIII, 305-37). Occasionally Herford and Simpson print two versions of the same poem under a single editorial number. We designate an early version of "Forest 10" as "Forest 10A" (VIII, 108), a second version of "Ungathered 47" as "Ungathered 47A" (VIII, 419).

Some Jonson editions index the poems by first line only. To make the concordance usable with texts other than Herford and Simpson's, we include in the list below the first line of each poem in quotation marks following its title.[8] Untitled poems are represented by first lines alone. The poems from volumes VI and VII of Herford and Simpson appear first in the list. Thereafter the collections in volume VIII appear in alphabetical order: Epigrams, Forest, Horace, Inscripts. (Inscriptions), L. Convivales (Leges Convivales), Underwood, and Ungathered (Ungathered Verse). For ease of reference, titles and first lines are here lightly regularized (as they are not in the concordance). Ellipses indicate a few shortened titles.

Volume Six

Designation in concordance	Title and first line in Herford and Simpson	Page number(s) in Herford and Simpson
TO HIMSELF	. . . Ode to himselfe "Come leave the lothed stage"	492-94

5. Acknowledgements

Vinton Dearing wrote the basic program for this concordance. George Guffey's concordances to the poems of Andrew Marvell and Thomas Traherne were before us as we compiled this one. We are indebted to Professor Dearing and Professor Guffey, who are not to be held liable for our departures from their precept and example. Grants from the Research Committee of the UCLA Academic Senate and from the Campus Computing Network helped to underwrite our expenses, and we are similarly obliged to Dean John Burke, Dean Philip Levine, and Dean Robert Kinsman. Lois North, Frances Reed, Tony Sheehan, and Mark Watanabe assisted us in a variety of tasks. We are grateful to them. The Clarendon edition of Jonson's poems by C. H. Herford and Percy and Evelyn Simpson has been a source of continuing wonder and delight, and the authors gratefully acknowledge the permission of Clarendon Press for the use of this edition.

Notes

[1] *Ben Jonson*, vols. I-XI (Oxford: Clarendon Press, 1925-52). Vol. VIII appeared in 1947. The copy used to make this concordance was reprinted lithographically in 1970 "from corrected sheets of the first edition" (VIII, iv).

[2] True now as in 1963 when William B. Hunter, Jr., so described it in his edition, *The Complete Poetry of Ben Jonson* (1963; New York: Norton, 1968), p. 445.

[3] One exception. A song, "Come my Celia, let vs proue," appeared in *Volpone* in 1605 (3.7.166-83). Jonson incorporated it with minor changes as the fifth poem in *The Forrest* (VIII, 102). Odd lines do otherwise appear in both plays and poems; see the notes *passim* in Ian Donaldson's recent edition, Ben Jonson, *Poems* (London: Oxford University Press, 1975).

[4] See T. H. Howard-Hill, "Towards a Jonson Concordance: A Discussion of Texts and Problems," *Research Opportunities in Renaissance Drama*, XV-XVI (1972-73), 17-32.

[5] One uncertainty. Herford and Simpson (XI, 146) doubt Jonson's authorship of a poem of twenty short lines, "Truth is the triall of it selfe," but print it as Jonson's (Ungathered 27, VIII, 393). George Parfitt in his recent edition — Ben Jonson, *The Complete Poems* (Harmondsworth: Penguin, 1975), p. 555n. — mentions their reservations but also lets it stand. Donaldson, pp. 379-80, demotes it to a collection of Jonson's *dubia*. It is concorded here.

[6] ⟨a⟩

aelian⟨'s⟩	⟨but⟩	grea⟨t⟩est
als⟨o⟩'her	b⟨y⟩'imputed	heav'n⟨s⟩
b⟨e⟩'asham'd	c⟨h⟩loe	h⟨e⟩'offend
b⟨e⟩'embrac'd	chronicle⟨r⟩s	⟨her⟩
be'⟨i⟩n	circumvol⟨v⟩d	⟨hidden⟩
⟨benn⟩	⟨come⟩	hold⟨s⟩
b⟨ess⟩	co⟨u⟩nsellors	i'⟨h⟩ad
bewail⟨e⟩d	creat[t]es	⟨im⟩mortall
brit[t]aine	dip⟨h⟩thera	⟨in⟩
b⟨roughton⟩s	el⟨izabeths⟩	k⟨ing⟩
burl⟨eigh⟩	⟨ever⟩	light[s]
	fil⟨l⟩ed	mad⟨e⟩

n⟨e⟩'re

⟨not⟩

⟨of⟩

⟨oft⟩

on[e]

⟨other⟩

pamp⟨h⟩lets

pas⟨s⟩e

p⟨avy⟩

phao⟨n⟩s

phoeb⟨e⟩'s

p⟨l⟩ace

ra⟨n⟩ging

s⟨alomon⟩

scandero⟨o⟩ne

s⟨c⟩urrile

so'⟨e⟩xceed

⟨still⟩

s⟨tr⟩ow

[that]

⟨the⟩

⟨thee⟩

the⟨e⟩

the⟨ir⟩

then⟨ce⟩

th⟨e⟩y

th⟨ey⟩'are

they'⟨h⟩ave

th⟨ey⟩'were

th⟨o⟩rough

thou'⟨h⟩ast

th⟨ou⟩'have

t⟨o⟩'a

t⟨o⟩'accuse

t⟨o⟩'admire

t⟨o⟩'adore

t⟨o⟩'aduance

t⟨o⟩'advance

t⟨o⟩'all

t⟨o⟩'alledge

t⟨o⟩'allow

t⟨o⟩'amend

t⟨o⟩'appeare

t⟨o⟩'approue

t⟨o⟩'approve

t⟨o⟩'aquit

t⟨o⟩'assist

t⟨o⟩'attire

t⟨o⟩'effect

t⟨o⟩'enjoy

t⟨o⟩'escape

t⟨o⟩'exact

t⟨o⟩'exchange

t⟨o⟩'expect

t⟨o⟩'expresse

t⟨o⟩'extract

to'⟨h⟩ave

t⟨o⟩'himselfe

t⟨o⟩'idolatrie

t⟨o⟩'increase

t⟨o⟩'indite

t⟨o⟩'inflict

t⟨o⟩'inhabit

t⟨o⟩'inherit

t⟨o⟩'inlive

t⟨o⟩'instruct

t⟨o⟩'inueigh

to⟨o⟩

t⟨o⟩'obay

t⟨o⟩'obey

t⟨o⟩'observe

t⟨o⟩'obtaine

t⟨o⟩'offend

t⟨o⟩'our

t⟨o⟩'out-strip

t⟨o⟩'usher

watch'⟨d⟩

we'⟨h⟩ave

well[s]

will⟨i⟩am

world⟨s⟩

⟨you⟩

⟨y⟩our

[7] The first four lines of Underwood 76, beginning *"The humble Petition of poore* Ben." (VIII, 259), serve both as title lines set off from the poem and (in rhyme, meter, and editorial lineation) as the poem's opening lines. They appear in the concordance as lines 1-4 without "t" designation.

[8] Donaldson's modern-spelling text is especially easy to use with this concordance. It retains exactly Herford and Simpson's major collections, poem numbers, and line numbers, and helpfully takes the names of the collections for its page heads.

a   frequency: 1116   relative frequency: 0.01615
      See also "a>," "studie'a," "t<o>'a," "to'a."

a-bed   frequency: 1   relative frequency: 0.00001
      p. 97 FOREST 3   22 A-bed canst heare the loud stag speake,

a-farre   frequency: 2   relative frequency: 0.00002
      p. 169 UNDERWOOD 18   5 Or was she gracious a-farre off? but neere
      p. 290 UNDERWOOD 85   13 Or in the bending Vale beholds a-farre

a-fire   frequency: 1   relative frequency: 0.00001
      p. 189 UNDERWOOD 36   9 A Sparke to set whole world<s> a-fire,

a-iax   frequency: 1   relative frequency: 0.00001
      p. 89 EPIGRAMS 133   196 My Muse had plough'd with his, that sung
                               A-IAX.

a-life   frequency: 1   relative frequency: 0.00001
      p. 232 UNDERWOOD 58   13 If they goe on, and that thou lov'st a-life

a-new   frequency: 1   relative frequency: 0.00001
      p. 67 EPIGRAMS 105   5 But euen their names were to be made a-new,

a-while   frequency: 2   relative frequency: 0.00002
      p. 252 UNDERWOOD 75   2 A-while with us, bright Sun, and helpe our
                               light;
      p. 257 UNDERWOOD 75   153 Th'Ignoble never liv'd, they were a-while

a>   frequency: 2   relative frequency: 0.00002
      p. 183 UNDERWOOD 29   27 Worth <a> crowning.
      p. 191 UNDERWOOD 38   14 Looke forth, but cannot last in such <a> forme.

aarons   frequency: 1   relative frequency: 0.00001
      p. 361 UNGATHERED 1   14 how lyke the Carbuncle in Aarons brest

ab   frequency: 1   relative frequency: 0.00001
      p. 86 EPIGRAMS 133   95 Had burst with storme, and downe fell, ab
                               excelsis,

abandon'd   frequency: 1   relative frequency: 0.00001
      p. 117 FOREST 13   17 Or so my selfe abandon'd, as because

abate   frequency: 1   relative frequency: 0.00001
      p. 327 HORACE 2   488 The publike, from the private; to abate

abbeuile   frequency: 2   relative frequency: 0.00002
      p. 374 UNGATHERED 10   13 Hee's carried 'twixt Montrell and Abbeuile.
      p. 380 UNGATHERED 12   53 In a Cart twixt Montrell and Abbeuile.

abbeville. See "abbeuile."

abed. See "a-bed."

abhord   frequency: 1   relative frequency: 0.00001
      p. 48 EPIGRAMS 65   1 Away, and leaue me, thou thing most abhord,

abhorred. See "abhord."

abhorres   frequency: 1   relative frequency: 0.00001
      p. 311 HORACE 2   123 Abhorres low numbers, and the private straine

abhors. See "abhorres."

abide   frequency: 2   relative frequency: 0.00002
      p. 114 FOREST 12   48 That had no Muse to make their fame abide.
      p. 128 UNDERWOOD 1.1   45 12. Among thy Saints elected to abide,

able   frequency: 4   relative frequency: 0.00005
      p. 84 EPIGRAMS 133   23 One was; and he, for brawne, and braine, right
                               able
      p. 257 UNDERWOOD 75   136 With all corroding Arts, be able to untie!
      p. 402 UNGATHERED 34   4 Able to talk of Euclide, and correct
      p. 407 UNGATHERED 36   4 Able to eat into his bones & pierce

abler   frequency: 2   relative frequency: 0.00002
     p. 80 EPIGRAMS 127   11 And, than this same, I know no abler way
     p. 362 UNGATHERED 1   29 my abler faculties; and thus brake foorth

aboue   frequency: 8   relative frequency: 0.00011
     p. 88 EPIGRAMS 133   160 And, now, aboue the poole, a face right fat
     p. 95 FOREST 2   58 Adde to thy free prouisions, farre aboue
     p. 115 FOREST 12   85 Aboue your vnder-carued ornaments,
     p. 119 FOREST 13   95 Of your blest wombe, made fruitfull from aboue,
     p. 367 UNGATHERED 6   55 Whose strength is aboue strength;
     p. 384 UNGATHERED 18   t1 To the most noble, and aboue his Titles,
     p. 391 UNGATHERED 26   16 Aboue th'ill fortune of them, or the need.
     p. 400 UNGATHERED 32   2 Aboue his Reader, or his Prayser, is.

abound   frequency: 1   relative frequency: 0.00001
     p. 230 UNDERWOOD 56   12 And that's made up as doth the purse abound.

abounds   frequency: 1   relative frequency: 0.00001
     p. 260 UNDERWOOD 76   28 Let their spite (which now abounds)

about   frequency: 32   relative frequency: 0.00046
     See also "aboute," "'bout."
   **p. 116 PANEGYRE   131 About the streets, as it would force a spring
     p. 53 EPIGRAMS 79   3 Or then, or since, about our Muses springs,
     p. 63 EPIGRAMS 97   19 About his forme. What then so swells each lim?
     p. 74 EPIGRAMS 115   6 About the towne; and knowne too, at that price.
     p. 87 EPIGRAMS 133   125 About the shore, of farts, but late departed,
     p. 94 FOREST 2   47 There's none, that dwell about them, wish them
                               downe;
     p. 105 FOREST 8   17 Liuers, round about the towne.
     p. 119 FOREST 13   100 Heare, what the Muses sing about thy roote,
     p. 132 UNDERWOOD 2.2   12 Every Cloud about his eye;
     p. 186 UNDERWOOD 31   8 Still flie about the Odour of your Name;
     p. 191 UNDERWOOD 38   24 Or goe about to countenance the vice,
     p. 193 UNDERWOOD 38   75 About in Cloudes, and wrapt in raging weather,
     p. 211 UNDERWOOD 43   185 Or in small Fagots have him blaze about
     p. 225 UNDERWOOD 51   2 How comes it all things so about the<e> smile?
     p. 236 UNDERWOOD 64   5 And as it turnes our joyfull yeare about,
     p. 242 UNDERWOOD 70   5 Thou, looking then about,
     p. 248 UNDERWOOD 71   6 Have cast a trench about mee, now, five yeares;
     p. 271 UNDERWOOD 83   85 If you can cast about your either eye,
     p. 271 UNDERWOOD 83   86 And see all dead here, or about to dye!
     p. 283 U'WOOD 84.9   32 Whoorles me about, and to blaspheme in fashion!
     p. 291 UNDERWOOD 85   67 These thoughts when Usurer Alphius, now about
     p. 307 HORACE 2   29 Was meant at first. Why, forcing still about
     p. 307 HORACE 2   45 The worst of Statuaries, here about
     p. 319 HORACE 2   305 In his train'd Gowne about the Stage: So grew
     p. 319 HORACE 2   312 The Tragedie, and carried it about,
     p. 333 HORACE 2   604 Of an entangling suit; and bring 't about:
     p. 335 HORACE 2   650 And stalketh, like a Fowler, round about,
     p. 395 UNGATHERED 29   3 Of Fortunes wheele by Lucan driu'n about,
     p. 396 UNGATHERED 30   9 About the towne: this reck'ning I will pay,
     p. 396 UNGATHERED 30   14 Hot from thy trumpet, round, about the world.
     p. 397 UNGATHERED 30   49 And flight about the Ile, well neare, by this,
     p. 405 UNGATHERED 34   80 Vp & about? Dyue into Cellars too

aboute   frequency: 1   relative frequency: 0.00001
     p. 421 UNGATHERED 48   39 Aboute this Isle, and Charme the rounde, as
                               when

above   frequency: 14   relative frequency: 0.00020
     See also "aboue," "'boue," "'bove," "so'above."
     p. 136 UNDERWOOD 2.5   16 Just above her sparkling eyes,
     p. 136 UNDERWOOD 2.5   24 And, above her even chin,
     p. 171 UNDERWOOD 20   6 That ne're was knowne to last above a fit!
     p. 176 UNDERWOOD 25   6 Her upright head, above the reach of Chance,
     p. 187 UNDERWOOD 33   38 And (which doth all Atchievements get above)
     p. 218 UNDERWOOD 47   19 That to speake well, thinke it above all sinne,
     p. 221 UNDERWOOD 48   37 That when King James, above here,
     p. 234 UNDERWOOD 60   10 Of Vertue, got above his name?
     p. 240 UNDERWOOD 67   31 6. ERAT. Shee showes so farre above
     p. 243 UNDERWOOD 70   24 Above his fact?
     p. 253 UNDERWOOD 75   38 Above the rest
     p. 270 UNDERWOOD 83   60 Made her friends joyes to get above their feares!
     p. 272 UNDERWOOD 83   99 The Serpents head: Gets above Death, and
                               Sinne,
     p. 285 U'WOOD 84.9   100 Whom her Redeemer, honour'd hath above

abroad   frequency: 6   relative frequency: 0.00008
     See also "abro'd."

abroad (cont.)
**p. 115 PANEGYRE   82 "Though hid at home, abroad is search'd into:
  p. 87 EPIGRAMS 133   138 And, after, swom abroad in ample flakes,
  p. 146 UNDERWOOD 6   2 That talke abroad of Womans change,
  p. 164 UNDERWOOD 15   74 To be abroad chanting some baudie song,
  p. 411 UNGATHERED 39   11 Thy blatant Muse abroad, and teach it rather
  p. 413 UNGATHERED 41   36 How are thy gifts, and graces blaz'd abroad!

abro'd   frequency: 1   relative frequency: 0.00001
  p. 414 UNGATHERED 41   53 How are thy gifts and graces blaz'd abro'd,

absence   frequency: 4   relative frequency: 0.00005
  p. 107 FOREST 10   21 His absence in my verse, is all I aske.
  p. 194 UNDERWOOD 38   116 Absence, or Distance, shall not breed decay.
  p. 197 UNDERWOOD 40   8 Shortly againe: and make our absence sweet.
  p. 212 UNDERWOOD 43   209 We aske your absence here, we all love peace,

absent   frequency: 1   relative frequency: 0.00001
  p. 218 UNDERWOOD 47   17 On all Soules that are absent; even the dead;

absolute   frequency: 2   relative frequency: 0.00002
  p. 53 EPIGRAMS 79   11 He should those rare, and absolute numbers view,
  p. 272 UNDERWOOD 84   t7 A Gentleman absolute in all Numbers;

absolv'd   frequency: 1   relative frequency: 0.00001
  p. 228 UNDERWOOD 53   14 Before, I thinke my wish absolv'd had beene.

abstain. See "abstaine," "abstayne."

abstaine   frequency: 1   relative frequency: 0.00001
  p. 333 HORACE 2   590 And both from Wine, and Women did abstaine.

abstayne   frequency: 1   relative frequency: 0.00001
  p. 112 FOREST 11   85 Though we acknowledge, who can so abstayne,

abstinence   frequency: 1   relative frequency: 0.00001
  p. 111 FOREST 11   84 Haue fill'd with abstinence:

abstruse   frequency: 1   relative frequency: 0.00001
  p. 307 HORACE 2   69 Yet, if by chance, in utt'ring things abstruse,

absurdity   frequency: 1   relative frequency: 0.00001
  p. 405 UNGATHERED 34   82 Discouer Vice? Commit Absurdity?

abus'd   frequency: 2   relative frequency: 0.00002
  p. 86 EPIGRAMS 133   97 And all his followers, that had so abus'd him:
  p. 192 UNDERWOOD 38   66 In man, because man hath the flesh abus'd.

abuse   frequency: 10   relative frequency: 0.00014
  p. 48 EPIGRAMS 65   6 And, as thou'hast mine, his houres, and youth
                             abuse.
  p. 68 EPIGRAMS 107   2 That's, sit, and eate: doe not my eares abuse.
  p. 84 EPIGRAMS 133   4 With tales of Troyes iust knight, our faiths
                             abuse:
  p. 101 FOREST 4   42 Thou did'st abuse, and then betray;
  p. 161 UNDERWOOD 14   83 On whom I could take up, and ne're abuse
  p. 171 UNDERWOOD 19   21 To use the present, then, is not abuse,
  p. 187 UNDERWOOD 33   17 Dar'st not abuse thy wisdome, in the Lawes,
  p. 190 UNDERWOOD 37   24 Will unto Licence that faire leave abuse.
  p. 194 UNDERWOOD 38   107 I will no more abuse my vowes to you,
  p. 361 UNGATHERED 1   11 Whilst other soules conuert to base abuse

abused   frequency: 1   relative frequency: 0.00001
  See also "abus'd."
  p. 184 UNDERWOOD 29   46 Tyran Rime hath so abused,

abuses   frequency: 2   relative frequency: 0.00002
  p. 85 EPIGRAMS 133   53 And art a god, if Fame thee not abuses,
  p. 657 L. CONVIVALES   9 He the half of Life abuses,

academie   frequency: 1   relative frequency: 0.00001
  p. 215 UNDERWOOD 44   89 The Academie, where the Gallants meet --

academy. See "academie."

accents   frequency: 1   relative frequency: 0.00001
  p. 249 UNDERWOOD 72   7 Adding her owne glad accents, to this Day,

accept   frequency: 3   relative frequency: 0.00004
  p. 31 EPIGRAMS 14   14 But for their powers, accept my pietie.

accept (cont.)
    p. 231 UNDERWOOD 56   26 Accept his Muse; and tell, I know you can,
    p. 245 UNDERWOOD 70   77 Accept this garland, plant it on thy head,

acceptable   frequency: 1   relative frequency: 0.00001
    p. 293 UNDERWOOD 87   3 His armes more acceptable free,

acceptably   frequency: 1   relative frequency: 0.00001
    p. 321 HORACE 2   327 With something that was acceptably new.

acceptance   frequency: 2   relative frequency: 0.00002
    p. 64 EPIGRAMS 101   7 It is the faire acceptance, Sir, creates
    p. 127 UNDERWOOD 1.1   13 4. For thy acceptance. O, behold me right,

accepted   frequency: 1   relative frequency: 0.00001
    p. 259 UNDERWOOD 76   14 And that this so accepted summe,

access. See "accesse."

accesse   frequency: 2   relative frequency: 0.00002
  **p. 117 PANEGYRE   145 The lesser fiers dim) in his accesse
    p. 401 UNGATHERED 32   17 This Fort of so impregnable accesse,

accession   frequency: 1   relative frequency: 0.00001
    p. 47 EPIGRAMS 64   t2 Vpon the accession of the Treasurer-ship to him.

accite   frequency: 1   relative frequency: 0.00001
    p. 206 UNDERWOOD 43   85 But in my Deske, what was there to accite

accius   frequency: 2   relative frequency: 0.00002
    p. 323 HORACE 2   382 Of Accius, and Ennius, rare appeares:
    p. 391 UNGATHERED 26   35 Paccuuius, Accius, him of Cordoua dead,

accomplish   frequency: 1   relative frequency: 0.00001
    p. 157 UNDERWOOD 13   136 We must accomplish; 'Tis the last Key-stone

accompt   frequency: 2   relative frequency: 0.00002
    p. 140 UNDERWOOD 2.8   29 Make accompt, unlesse you can,
    p. 237 UNDERWOOD 64   21 Are lost upon accompt! And none will know

accompted   frequency: 1   relative frequency: 0.00001
    p. 201 UNDERWOOD 42   49 Of race accompted, that no passion have

according   frequency: 3   relative frequency: 0.00004
    p. 213 UNDERWOOD 44   t1 A speach according to Horace.
    p. 284 U'WOOD 84.9   83 And give her place, according to her blood,
    p. 335 HORACE 2   647 According to the Moone. But, then the boyes

account   frequency: 1   relative frequency: 0.00001
    See also "accompt," "th'accompt."
    p. 115 FOREST 12   69 (Or Poet, in the court account) then I,

accounted   frequency: 2   relative frequency: 0.00002
    See also "accompted."
    p. 102 FOREST 5   18 These haue crimes accounted beene.
    p. 657 L. CONVIVALES   13 And the Poets' Horse accounted.

accounts. See "'counts."

accumulated   frequency: 1   relative frequency: 0.00001
    p. 285 U'WOOD 84.9   111 Accumulated on her, by the Lord

accursed   frequency: 1   relative frequency: 0.00001
    p. 209 UNDERWOOD 43   147 And that accursed ground, the Parish-Garden:

accusations   frequency: 1   relative frequency: 0.00001
    p. 75 EPIGRAMS 115   32 That seeming prayses, are, yet accusations.

accuse. See "t<o>'accuse."

ache. See "ake."

acheron   frequency: 2   relative frequency: 0.00002
    p. 84 EPIGRAMS 133   7 All, that they boast of STYX, of
                             ACHERON,
    p. 88 EPIGRAMS 133   141 And so they did, from STYX, to
                             ACHERON:

achievements. See "atchievements."

achilles   frequency: 2 relative frequency: 0.00002
    p. 114 FOREST 12   51 ACHILLES was not first, that valiant was,
    p. 313 HORACE 2   171 Honour'd Achilles chance by thee be seiz'd,

acknowledge   frequency: 1 relative frequency: 0.00001
    p. 112 FOREST 11   85 Though we acknowledge, who can so abstayne,

acornes   frequency: 1 relative frequency: 0.00001
   *p. 492 TO HIMSELF   12 And they will acornes eat:

acorns. See "acornes."

acquaintance   frequency: 2 relative frequency: 0.00002
    p. 51 EPIGRAMS 73   6 I lent you, on meere acquaintance, at a feast.
    p. 398 UNGATHERED 30 85 And Gossip-got acquaintance, as, to vs

acquainted   frequency: 1 relative frequency: 0.00001
    p. 87 EPIGRAMS 133 134 Nor thumbe, nor finger to the stop acquainted,

acquit. See "t<o>'aquit."

acrostichs   frequency: 1 relative frequency: 0.00001
    p. 204 UNDERWOOD 43   39 Acrostichs, and Telestichs, on jumpe names,

acrostics. See "acrostichs."

act   frequency: 20 relative frequency: 0.00028
    p. 47 EPIGRAMS 63   5 And that thou seek'st reward of thy each act,
    p. 57 EPIGRAMS 89   12 As others speake, but onely thou dost act.
    p. 77 EPIGRAMS 120   13 And did act (what now we mone)
    p. 84 EPIGRAMS 133   6 Had power to act, what they to faine had not.
    p. 85 EPIGRAMS 133   57 Act a braue worke, call it thy last aduentry:
    p. 93 FOREST 1   1 Some act of Loue's bound to reherse,
    p. 115 FOREST 12   77 Will proue old ORPHEVS act no tale to be:
    p. 153 UNDERWOOD 13   11 And in the Act did so my blush prevent,
    p. 190 UNDERWOOD 37   25 It is an Act of tyrannie, not love,
    p. 218 UNDERWOOD 47   7 And shewing so weake an Act to vulgar eyes,
    p. 224 UNDERWOOD 50   5 Not only shunning by your act, to doe
    p. 243 UNDERWOOD 70   22 Not by the act?
    p. 255 UNDERWOOD 75   87 Who the whole Act expresse:
    p. 261 UNDERWOOD 77   16 And act the businesse, which they paint, or
                             carve.
    p. 270 UNDERWOOD 83   46 Could summe to a perfection, was her Act!
    p. 270 UNDERWOOD 83   61 And, in her last act, taught the Standers-by,
    p. 288 U'WOOD 84.9   215 In that great Act of judgement: which the
                             Father
    p. 315 HORACE 2   239 Lookes after honours, and bewares to act
    p. 319 HORACE 2   314 Those that did sing, and act: their faces dy'd
    p. 398 UNGATHERED 30 63 The Poets act! and for his Country's sake

acted   frequency: 3 relative frequency: 0.00004
    p. 156 UNDERWOOD 13   95 Or feats of darknesse acted in Mid-Sun,
    p. 214 UNDERWOOD 44   41 So acted to the life, as Maurice might,
    p. 317 HORACE 2   256 Or acted told. But, ever, things that run

acteth   frequency: 1 relative frequency: 0.00001
    p. 423 UNGATHERED 50 14 the sword, but that it acteth what it list.

action   frequency: 10 relative frequency: 0.00014
    p. 71 EPIGRAMS 110   20 Action, or engine, worth a note of thine,
    p. 72 EPIGRAMS 111   5 And that, in action, there is nothing new,
    p. 78 EPIGRAMS 121   6 If onely loue should make the action pris'd:
    p. 84 EPIGRAMS 133   26 But, in the action, greater man then hee:
    p. 89 EPIGRAMS 133 191 They tooke 'hem all to witnesse of their action:
    p. 162 UNDERWOOD 15   6 That gaspe for action, and would yet revive
    p. 180 UNDERWOOD 26   17 In one full Action; nor have you now more
    p. 234 UNDERWOOD 60   12 No love of action, and high Arts,
    p. 262 UNDERWOOD 78   13 Witnesse his Action done at Scandero<o>ne;
    p. 280 U'WOOD 84.4   65 In action, winged as the wind,

actions   frequency: 16 relative frequency: 0.00023
  **p. 117 PANEGYRE   149 Of his great actions, first to see, and do
    p. 40 EPIGRAMS 43   2 Whose actions so themselues doe celebrate;
    p. 55 EPIGRAMS 85   12 What would his serious actions me haue learned?
    p. 62 EPIGRAMS 95   32 The councells, actions, orders, and euents
    p. 70 EPIGRAMS 108   7 And did not shame it with my actions, then,
    p. 142 UNDERWOOD 2.9 45 All his actions to be such,
    p. 152 UNDERWOOD 12   19 And adde his Actions unto these,
    p. 156 UNDERWOOD 13   98 That men such reverence to such actions show!
    p. 197 UNDERWOOD 40   20 In all his Actions rarified to spright;

actions (cont.)
```
    p. 201 UNDERWOOD 42      60 In at a hole, and see these Actions creepe
    p. 245 UNDERWOOD 70      59 Not liv'd; for Life doth her great actions
                                spell,
    p. 250 UNDERWOOD 73       3 In his great Actions: view whom his large hand
    p. 284 U'WOOD 84.9       77 Have all his actions wondred at, and view'd
    p. 287 U'WOOD 84.9      177 In all her petite actions, so devote,
    p. 397 UNGATHERED 30     44 That Rebells actions, are but valiant crimes!
    p. 422 UNGATHERED 50      1 Just and fit actions Ptolemey (he saith)
```

actiue   frequency: 2   relative frequency: 0.00002
```
    p.  49 EPIGRAMS 68        4 Actiue in's braine, and passiue in his bones.
    p. 107 FOREST 10          3 For the more countenance to my actiue Muse?
```

active   frequency: 4   relative frequency: 0.00005
    See also "actiue."
```
    p. 200 UNDERWOOD 42       6 As light, and active as the youngest hee
    p. 240 UNDERWOOD 67      37 7. CALLI. See, see our active King
    p. 256 UNDERWOOD 75     116 And by his Rise, in active men, his Name
    p. 313 HORACE 2         172 Keepe him still active, angry, un-appeas'd,
```

actors   frequency: 1   relative frequency: 0.00001
```
    p. 317 HORACE 2         276 An Actors parts, and Office too, the Quire
```

acts   frequency: 16   relative frequency: 0.00023
```
  *p. 494 TO HIMSELF        59 In tuning forth the acts of his sweet raigne:
 **p. 115 PANEGYRE          88 "In publique acts what face and forme they beare.
 **p. 115 PANEGYRE          95 "She shewd him, who made wise, who honest acts;
 **p. 116 PANEGYRE         101 "Where acts gaue licence to impetuous lust
   p.  58 EPIGRAMS 91        9 I leaue thy acts, which should I prosequute
   p.  71 EPIGRAMS 110       6 To haue engrau'd these acts, with his owne stile,
   p.  74 EPIGRAMS 115      27 Acts old Iniquitie, and in the fit
   p. 128 UNDERWOOD 1.1     28 For acts of grace.
   p. 128 UNDERWOOD 1.1     29 8. Increase those acts, o glorious Trinitie
   p. 162 UNDERWOOD 15       9 All other Acts of Worldlings, are but toyle
   p. 213 UNDERWOOD 44      19 And comming home, to tell what acts were done
   p. 244 UNDERWOOD 70      39 To sordid flatteries, acts of strife,
   p. 313 HORACE 2         185 Of Homers, forth in acts, then of thine owne,
   p. 317 HORACE 2         272 Have more or lesse then just five Acts: nor
                                laid,
   p. 317 HORACE 2         278 Betweene the Acts, a quite cleane other thing
   p. 367 UNGATHERED 6      59 His farre-admired Acts,
```

actuate   frequency: 1   relative frequency: 0.00001
```
    p. 341 HORACE 1         120 Of ....... noyses, borne to actuate things.
```

ad   frequency: 1   relative frequency: 0.00001
```
    p. 662 INSCRIP1S. 2      t2 ad Librum.
```

adam   frequency: 2   relative frequency: 0.00002
```
    p. 274 U'WOOD 84.2       15 Into the Kindred, whence thy Adam drew
    p. 405 UNGATHERED 34     79 How would he firke? lyke Adam ouerdooe
```

add   frequency: 2   relative frequency: 0.00002
    See also "adde."
```
    p. 385 UNGATHERED 19      4 What can one witnesse, and a weake one, add
    p. 416 UNGATHERED 45      2 I am come to Add, and speake,
```

adde   frequency: 9   relative frequency: 0.00013
```
    p.  58 EPIGRAMS 92        2 Vnto the cryes of London Ile adde one;
    p.  61 EPIGRAMS 95       13 O, would'st thou adde like hand, to all the rest!
    p.  95 FOREST 2          58 Adde to thy free prouisions, farre aboue
    p. 103 FOREST 6          11 Adde a thousand, and so more:
    p. 152 UNDERWOOD 12      19 And adde his Actions unto these,
    p. 157 UNDERWOOD 13     132 Profit in ought; each day some little adde,
    p. 169 UNDERWOOD 17      10 I adde that (but) because I understand
    p. 172 UNDERWOOD 21       8 That thought can adde, unthankfull, the lay-stall
    p. 327 HORACE 2         470 He cries, Good boy, thou'lt keepe thine owne.
                                Now, adde
```

added   frequency: 2   relative frequency: 0.00002
```
 **p. 117 PANEGYRE         157 Nor to her blisse, could ought now added bee,
   p. 189 UNDERWOOD 37       4 You have unto my Store added a booke,
```

adding   frequency: 2   relative frequency: 0.00002
```
    p.  41 EPIGRAMS 43        8 Of adding to thy fame: thine may to me,
    p. 249 UNDERWOOD 72       7 Adding her owne glad accents, to this Day,
```

adjuncts   frequency: 1   relative frequency: 0.00001
```
    p. 317 HORACE 2         254 In fitting proper adjuncts to each day.
```

admirable   frequency: 1   relative frequency: 0.00001
     p. 333 HORACE 2   594 An admirable Verse. The great Scurfe take

admiracon   frequency: 1   relative frequency: 0.00001
     p. 361 UNGATHERED 1   4 I could not but in admiracon stand.

admiration   frequency: 3   relative frequency: 0.00004
     See also "admiracon."
     p. 163 UNDERWOOD 15   50 In admiration, stretch'd upon the rack
     p. 270 UNDERWOOD 83   62 With admiration, and applause to die!
     p. 323 HORACE 2   400 And jests; and both to admiration raise

admir'd   frequency: 2   relative frequency: 0.00002
     p. 112 FOREST 11   107 In the full floud of her admir'd perfection?
     p. 361 UNGATHERED 1   9 Then I admir'd, the rare and prescious vse

admire   frequency: 4   relative frequency: 0.00005
     See also "may'admire," "t<o>'admire."
     p. 83 EPIGRAMS 132   1 If to admire were to commend, my praise
     p. 269 UNDERWOOD 83   31 To touch these Mysteries! We may admire
     p. 371 UNGATHERED 8   16 Or moathes shall eate, what all these Fooles
                              admire.
     p. 383 UNGATHERED 17 10 To vnderstand, hee may at length admire.

admired   frequency: 2   relative frequency: 0.00002
     See also "admir'd," "farre-admired,"
               "th'admir'd."
     p. 397 UNGATHERED 30 50 In thy admired Periegesis,
     p. 414 UNGATHERED 41 46 And most to be admired of thy Sexe,

admiring   frequency: 1   relative frequency: 0.00001
     p. 366 UNGATHERED 6   5 Besides the other Swannes admiring him,

admit   frequency: 2   relative frequency: 0.00002
     p. 224 UNDERWOOD 50   25 For you admit no companie, but good,
     p. 385 UNGATHERED 19   6 If Praises, when th'are full, heaping admit,

admitted   frequency: 1   relative frequency: 0.00001
     p. 305 HORACE 2   6 Admitted to the sight, although his friends,

ado. See "adoe."

adoe   frequency: 1   relative frequency: 0.00001
     p. 403 UNGATHERED 34 38 And Goody Sculpture, brought wth much adoe

adopt   frequency: 1   relative frequency: 0.00001
     p. 286 U'WOOD 84.9   140 Adopt us Heires, by grace, who were of those

adoration   frequency: 1   relative frequency: 0.00001
     p. 254 UNDERWOOD 75   48 With Modestie so crown'd, and Adoration seene.

ador'd   frequency: 2   relative frequency: 0.00002
     p. 61 EPIGRAMS 95   8 Where NERO falls, and GALBA is ador'd,
     p. 413 UNGATHERED 41 28 As if they' ador'd the Head, wheron th'are fixt.

adore   frequency: 4   relative frequency: 0.00005
     See also "t<o>'adore."
     p. 79 EPIGRAMS 125   10 I could adore, almost t<o>'idolatrie.
     p. 149 UNDERWOOD 9   4 Whom I adore so much, should so slight me,
     p. 201 UNDERWOOD 42   55 He did lay up, and would adore the shooe,
     p. 276 U'WOOD 84.3   20 May rather yet adore, then spy.

adorn. See "adorne."

adornd   frequency: ' 1   relative frequency: 0.00001
     p. 365 UNGATHERED 5   9 Iudgement (adornd with Learning)

adorne   frequency: 2   relative frequency: 0.00002
     p. 75 EPIGRAMS 116   11 That bloud not mindes, but mindes did bloud
                              adorne:
     p. 284 U'WOOD 84.9   71 Nothing can more adorne it, then the seat

adorned. See "adornd."

adornes   frequency: 1   relative frequency: 0.00001
     p. 30 EPIGRAMS 12   18 Calls for his stoole, adornes the stage: god
                              payes.

adorns. See "adornes."

adria   frequency: 1   relative frequency: 0.00001
    p. 294 UNDERWOOD 87   23 And then rough Adria, angrier, farre;

aduanc'd   frequency: 1   relative frequency: 0.00001
    p. 392 UNGATHERED 26   76 Aduanc'd, and made a Constellation there!

aduance   frequency: 1   relative frequency: 0.00001
    p. 391 UNGATHERED 26   9 Or blinde Affection, which doth ne're aduance

aduanced   frequency: 2   relative frequency: 0.00002
    p. 28 EPIGRAMS 3   8 Or in cleft-sticks, aduanced to make calls
    p. 67 EPIGRAMS 104   11 Were you aduanced, past those times, to be

aduentry   frequency: 1   relative frequency: 0.00001
    p. 85 EPIGRAMS 133   57 Act a braue worke, call it thy last aduentry:

aduenture   frequency: 1   relative frequency: 0.00001
    p. 84 EPIGRAMS 133   21 I sing the braue aduenture of two wights,

aduise   frequency: 1   relative frequency: 0.00001
    p. 38 EPIGRAMS 38   2 And to conceale your vlcers, did aduise,

adulterate   frequency: 1   relative frequency: 0.00001
    p. 204 UNDERWOOD 43   45 Adulterate moneys, such as might not goe:

adulterer's. See "adult'rers."

adulteries   frequency: 1   relative frequency: 0.00001
    p. 165 UNDERWOOD 15   85 Adulteries, now, are not so hid, or strange,

adulters. See "he'adulters."

adult'rers   frequency: 1   relative frequency: 0.00001
    p. 369 UNGATHERED 6   104 Or thought they, Leda's white Adult'rers place

aduocate   frequency: 1   relative frequency: 0.00001
    p. 122 FOREST 15   12 My iudge, my witnesse, and my aduocate.

advanc'd   frequency: 3   relative frequency: 0.00004
    p. 210 UNDERWOOD 43   164 More then advanc'd the houses, and their rites?
    p. 244 UNDERWOOD 70   36 And had his noble name advanc'd with men:
    p. 416 UNGATHERED 44   5 Vpon this obeliske, advanc'd for it,

advance   frequency: 5   relative frequency: 0.00007
    See also "aduance," "re-aduance,"
             "t<o>'aduance," "t<o>'advance."
    p. 156 UNDERWOOD 13   123 No! he must feele and know, that will advance.
    p. 176 UNDERWOOD 25   5 High, as his mind, that doth advance
    p. 209 UNDERWOOD 43   151 If that were so, thou rather would'st advance
    p. 286 U'WOOD 84.9   143 Yet have all debts forgiven us, and advance
    p. 416 UNGATHERED 43   7 How they advance true Love, and neighbourhood,

advanced. See "aduanc'd," "aduanced," "advanc'd."

advances   frequency: 1   relative frequency: 0.00001
    p. 222 UNDERWOOD 48   49 Or else a health advances,

advantage   frequency: 2   relative frequency: 0.00002
    See also "th'advantage."
    p. 229 UNDERWOOD 54   11 But rather with advantage to be found
    p. 421 UNGATHERED 49   6 I haue, wth strict advantage of ffree tyme

adventure. See "aduentry," "aduenture," "th'aduenter."

adventures. See "th'adventures."

adversaries   frequency: 1   relative frequency: 0.00001
    p. 187 UNDERWOOD 33   33 Thy Adversaries fall, as not a word

advise   frequency: 2   relative frequency: 0.00002
    See also "aduise."
    p. 223 UNDERWOOD 49   35 Shall I advise thee, Pucell? steale away
    p. 421 UNGATHERED 49   1 Censure, not sharplye then, but mee advise

adviseth   frequency: 1   relative frequency: 0.00001
    p. 421 UNGATHERED 49   4 Hee that soe Censureth, or adviseth synns,

advocate. See "aduocate."

aeacvs   frequency: 1   relative frequency: 0.00001
     p.   89 EPIGRAMS 133   188 A sope-boyler; and AEACVS him nigh,

aelian<'s>   frequency: 1   relative frequency: 0.00001
     p. 214 UNDERWOOD 44   35 Translated Aelian<'s> tactickes to be read,

aemilian. See "th'aemilian."

aemulate   frequency: 1   relative frequency: 0.00001
     p. 387 UNGATHERED 22   10 And teach your nephewes it to aemulate:

aemulation   frequency: 1   relative frequency: 0.00001
     p. 389 UNGATHERED 24   22 Faire Aemulation, and no Enuy is;

aeneas   frequency: 1   relative frequency: 0.00001
     p.   81 EPIGRAMS 128   12 This is that good AENEAS, past through
                                 fire,

aerie   frequency: 2   relative frequency: 0.00002
     p. 222 UNDERWOOD 49   10 As aerie light, and as like wit as those?
     p. 249 UNDERWOOD 72   11 Three Kingdomes Mirth, in light, and aerie man,

aeschilus   frequency: 1   relative frequency: 0.00001
     p. 391 UNGATHERED 26   33 For names; but call forth thund'ring Aeschilus,

aeschylus. See "aeschilus," "eschylus."

aescvlape   frequency: 1   relative frequency: 0.00001
     p.   31 EPIGRAMS 13   2 Of old, they gaue a cock to AESCVLAPE;

aesop. See "aesope."

aesope   frequency: 2   relative frequency: 0.00002
     p.   56 EPIGRAMS 89   3 As skilfull ROSCIVS, and graue
                                 AESOPE, men,
     p. 213 UNDERWOOD 44   5 Old Aesope Gundomar: the French can tell,

aeternall   frequency: 1   relative frequency: 0.00001
     p. 394 UNGATHERED 28   26 This second marriage, will aeternall make.

aeternities   frequency: 1   relative frequency: 0.00001
     p. 400 UNGATHERED 31   35 Aeternities great charter; which became

aetna   frequency: 3   relative frequency: 0.00004
     p. 212 UNDERWOOD 43   197 Would you had kept your Forge, at Aetna still,
     p. 335 HORACE 2   663 Conceipt, and into burning Aetna leap'd.
     p. 363 UNGATHERED 3   10 Were they as strong ram'd vp as Aetna gates.

aetnean   frequency: 1   relative frequency: 0.00001
     p. 179 UNDERWOOD 25   44 And, after all the Aetnean Ire,

afar. See "a-farre."

afeard   frequency: 2   relative frequency: 0.00002
     See also "affeard."
     p. 141 UNDERWOOD 2.9   24 And make Love or me afeard.
     p. 414 UNGATHERED 42   4 You know, I never was of Truth afeard,

affaires   frequency: 3   relative frequency: 0.00004
     p. 194 UNDERWOOD 38   114 Publike affaires command me now to goe
     p. 214 UNDERWOOD 44   60 In Politique, and Militar Affaires.
     p. 253 UNDERWOOD 75   15 Or were Affaires in tune,

affairs. See "affaires," "th'affaires."

affeard   frequency: 2   relative frequency: 0.00002
     p.   84 EPIGRAMS 133   18 Lash'd by their consciences, to die, affeard.
     p.   87 EPIGRAMS 133   106 Touching this cause, where they will be affeard

affect   frequency: 1   relative frequency: 0.00001
     p. 366 UNGATHERED 6   13 Smiles in his Sphaere, to see the rest affect,

affected   frequency: 1   relative frequency: 0.00001
     See also "ill-affected."
     p. 193 UNDERWOOD 38   83 Be not affected with these markes too much

affection   frequency: 8   relative frequency: 0.00011
     p.   34 EPIGRAMS 23   6 And which no' affection praise enough can giue!
     p.   51 EPIGRAMS 74   4 That no affection in thy voyce commands;
     p. 112 FOREST 11   108 What sauage, brute affection,

affection (cont.)
    p. 158 UNDERWOOD 14   10 Chance that the Friends affection proves Allay
    p. 177 UNDERWOOD 25   15 On these darke rymes; that my affection
    p. 200 UNDERWOOD 42   13 Sooner then my affection from the faire.
    p. 270 UNDERWOOD 83   49 From all affection! when they urg'd the Cure
    p. 391 UNGATHERED 26   9 Or blinde Affection, which doth ne're aduance

affections   frequency: 7   relative frequency: 0.00010
  **p. 117 PANEGYRE   141 That wan affections, ere his steps wan ground;
    p. 40 EPIGRAMS 42   15 In all affections shee concurreth still.
    p. 74 EPIGRAMS 115   7 A subtle thing, that doth affections win
    p. 109 FOREST 11   13 To wakefull reason, our affections king:
    p. 109 FOREST 11   21 For either our affections doe rebell,
    p. 119 FOREST 13   118 This makes, that your affections still be new,
    p. 150 UNDERWOOD 10   11 What my Affections were.

affects   frequency: 2   relative frequency: 0.00002
    p. 78 EPIGRAMS 123   3 But both th'hast so, as who affects the state
    p. 339 HORACE 1   42 So he that varying still affects .. draw

affoards   frequency: 1   relative frequency: 0.00001
    p. 406 UNGATHERED 34   94 Vermilion, Lake, or Cinnopar affoards

affoord   frequency: 1   relative frequency: 0.00001
    p. 404 UNGATHERED 34   43 Court Hieroglyphicks! & all Artes affoord

afford   frequency: 3   relative frequency: 0.00004
  See also "affoord."
    p. 37 EPIGRAMS 32   3 That selfe-diuided Belgia did afford:
    p. 163 UNDERWOOD 15   52 I, that's a Charme and halfe! She must afford
    p. 315 HORACE 2   198 Afford? The Mountaines travail'd, and brought
                              forth

affords   frequency: 3   relative frequency: 0.00004
  See also "affoards."
  **p. 114 PANEGYRE   38 But, when their speech so poore a helpe affords
    p. 98 FOREST 3   55 Thy noblest spouse affords them welcome grace;
    p. 311 HORACE 2   140 'Tis not enough, th'elaborate Muse affords

affraid   frequency: 1   relative frequency: 0.00001
    p. 107 FOREST 10   14 That, at thy birth, mad'st the poore Smith
                              affraid,

affricke   frequency: 1   relative frequency: 0.00001
    p. 398 UNGATHERED 30   88 Then Affricke knew, or the full Grecian store!

affright   frequency: 2   relative frequency: 0.00002
    p. 65 EPIGRAMS 101   41 Shall make vs sad next morning: or affright
    p. 100 FOREST 3   104 That neither want doe thee affright,

affrighted. See "th'affrighted."

affrights   frequency: 2   relative frequency: 0.00002
    p. 46 EPIGRAMS 62   5 Is it the paine affrights? that's soone forgot.
    p. 191 UNDERWOOD 38   10 As light breakes from you, that affrights
                              despaire,

affront. See "afront."

afire. See "a-fire."

afore   frequency: 1   relative frequency: 0.00001
    p. 171 UNDERWOOD 20   9 Knew I all this afore? had I perceiv'd,

afraid   frequency: 6   relative frequency: 0.00008
  See also "affraid."
    p. 130 UNDERWOOD 1.3   5 Who saw the light, and were afraid,
    p. 151 UNDERWOOD 11   13 And sleepe so guiltie and afraid,
    p. 186 UNDERWOOD 32   4 Then to make falshood blush, and fraud afraid:
    p. 207 UNDERWOOD 43   95 With all th'adventures; Three bookes not afraid
    p. 217 UNDERWOOD 46   8 Thy just defences made th'oppressor afraid.
    p. 307 HORACE 2   39 Creepes on the ground; too safe, too afraid of
                              storme.

afric. See "affricke."

afront   frequency: 1   relative frequency: 0.00001
    p. 203 UNDERWOOD 43   7 Or in remembrance of thy afront, and scorne,

after   frequency: 29   relative frequency: 0.00041
  p.   51 EPIGRAMS 73   7 Item, a tale or two, some fortnight after;
  p.   87 EPIGRAMS 133   138 And, after, swom abroad in ample flakes,
  p.   88 EPIGRAMS 133   150 And, after mouldie growne, againe were tosted,
  p. 113 FOREST 12   11 Though neuer after; whiles it gaynes the voyce
  p. 118 FOREST 13   66 And after varyed, as fresh obiects goes,
  p. 118 FOREST 13   75 And almost, all dayes after, while they liue;
  p. 118 FOREST 13   81 Let 'hem waste body, and state; and after all,
  p. 122 FOREST 15   7 And iudge me after: if I dare pretend
  p. 122 FOREST 15   20 And destin'd vnto iudgement, after all.
  p. 133 UNDERWOOD 2.3   1 After many scornes like these,
  p. 137 UNDERWOOD 2.5   36 After flight; and put new stings
  p. 155 UNDERWOOD 13   62 Like Money-brokers, after Names, and hire
  p. 165 UNDERWOOD 15   104 Those thousands on his back, shall after blow
  p. 179 UNDERWOOD 25   44 And, after all the Aetnean Ire,
  p. 197 UNDERWOOD 40   5 And take some sirrup after; so doe I,
  p. 201 UNDERWOOD 42   57 Court every hanging Gowne, and after that,
  p. 207 UNDERWOOD 43   103 After the Fathers, and those wiser Guides
  p. 229 UNDERWOOD 54   19 To goe out after ----- till when take this letter
  p. 247 UNDERWOOD 70   108 You lik'd, then after, to apply
  p. 258 UNDERWOOD 75   168 (After the last child borne;) This is our
                            wedding day.
  p. 293 UNDERWOOD 87   6 Nor after C<h>loe did his Lydia sound;
  p. 309 HORACE 2   108 After, mens Wishes, crown'd in their events,
  p. 311 HORACE 2   156 And tortures us: and, after, by the tongue
  p. 315 HORACE 2   201 Speake to me, Muse, the Man, who, after Troy
                            was sack't,
  p. 315 HORACE 2   205 Wonders forth after: As Antiphates,
  p. 315 HORACE 2   239 Lookes after honours, and bewares to act
  p. 319 HORACE 2   320 For the vile Goat, soone after, forth did send
  p. 364 UNGATHERED 4   1 Now, after all, let no man
  p. 666 INSCRIPTS. 11   10 To make these good, and what comes after,
                            better./

after-state   frequency: 1   relative frequency: 0.00001
  p.   43 EPIGRAMS 51   8 Doe beg thy care vnto thy after-state.

after-thoughts   frequency: 1   relative frequency: 0.00001
  p.   48 EPIGRAMS 65   13 Shee shall instruct my after-thoughts to write

after-times   frequency: 2   relative frequency: 0.00002
  p.   45 EPIGRAMS 56   11 He markes not whose 'twas first: and after-times
  p.   61 EPIGRAMS 95   20 Thou need'st not shrinke at voyce of after-times;

afternoones   frequency: 1   relative frequency: 0.00001
  p. 230 UNDERWOOD 56   22 A mornings, and at afternoones, to foole

afterwards   frequency: 1   relative frequency: 0.00001
  p.   31 EPIGRAMS 15   3 Where, afterwards, it grew a butter-flye:

again. See "againe," "agen."

againe   frequency: 40   relative frequency: 0.00057
 **p. 113 PANEGYRE   3 Againe, the glory of our Westerne world
 **p. 117 PANEGYRE   160 With a twice louder shoute againe they cry'd,
  p.   49 EPIGRAMS 68   2 Takes priuate beatings, and begins againe.
  p.   56 EPIGRAMS 87   6 Since when, hee's sober againe, and all play's
                            made.
  p.   72 EPIGRAMS 111   14 They murder him againe, that enuie thee.
  p.   78 EPIGRAMS 122   10 Who prou'st, all these were, and againe may bee.
  p.   88 EPIGRAMS 133   150 And, after mouldie growne, againe were tosted,
  p.   93 FOREST 1   8 With which he fled me: and againe,
  p. 101 FOREST 4   32 Render his head in there againe?
  p. 102 FOREST 5   6 Sunnes, that set, may rise againe:
  p. 103 FOREST 6   5 Kisse againe: no creature comes.
  p. 139 UNDERWOOD 2.7   1 For Loves-sake, kisse me once againe,
  p. 144 UNDERWOOD 3   23 To fall againe; at such a feast,
  p. 147 UNDERWOOD 7   1 I love, and he loves me againe,
  p. 151 UNDERWOOD 11   12 Of sleepe againe, who was his Aid;
  p. 159 UNDERWOOD 14   38 Of Gathering? Bountie' in pouring out againe?
  p. 167 UNDERWOOD 15   152 Give me but that againe, that I must wast
  p. 168 UNDERWOOD 15   184 But what she gives, thou dar'st give her againe;
  p. 175 UNDERWOOD 23   29 To give the world againe:
  p. 184 UNDERWOOD 29   37 Scarce the Hill againe doth flourish,
  p. 184 UNDERWOOD 29   40 Phoebus to his Crowne againe;
  p. 192 UNDERWOOD 38   55 Could you demand the gifts you gave, againe?
  p. 192 UNDERWOOD 38   63 But to exact againe what once is given,
  p. 197 UNDERWOOD 40   8 Shortly againe: and make our absence sweet.
  p. 271 UNDERWOOD 83   80 T'have paid againe a blessing was but lent,
  p. 291 UNDERWOOD 85   60 Or Kid forc't from the Wolfe againe.

againe (cont.)
p.	291	UNDERWOOD 85	70	At th'Calends, puts all out againe.
p.	292	UNDERWOOD 86	1	Venus, againe thou mov'st a warre
p.	305	HORACE 2	13	And both doe crave, and give againe, this leave.
p.	313	HORACE 2	170	Things in themselves agreeing: If againe
p.	313	HORACE 2	194	Forbids thee forth againe thy foot to draw.
p.	317	HORACE 2	271	Once seene, to be againe call'd for, and plaid,
p.	333	HORACE 2	589	While he was young; he sweat; and freez'd againe:
p.	367	UNGATHERED 6	41	From thence, display thy wing againe
p.	368	UNGATHERED 6	77	And vp againe, in skies, and aire to vent
p.	391	UNGATHERED 26	36	To life againe, to heare thy Buskin tread,
p.	395	UNGATHERED 29	7	But when againe I veiw the parts so peiz'd,
p.	397	UNGATHERED 30	55	But that I heare, againe, thy Drum to beate
p.	401	UNGATHERED 33	8	Againe hath brought the Lillie to the Rose;
p.	406	UNGATHERED 34	102	Againe, thy Architect to ashes turne!

against   frequency: 29   relative frequency: 0.00041
See also "gainst," "'gainst."
p.	49	EPIGRAMS 66	9	Against thy fortune: when no foe, that day,
p.	58	EPIGRAMS 91	12	Against my graue, and time could not forgiue.
p.	60	EPIGRAMS 93	16	Wherewith, against thy bloud, they'offenders bee.
p.	66	EPIGRAMS 102	3	Against the bad, but of, and to the good:
p.	70	EPIGRAMS 109	11	To make thy lent life, good against the Fates:
p.	87	EPIGRAMS 133	124	Against their breasts. Here, seu'rall ghosts did flit
p.	150	UNDERWOOD 10	t1	Against Iealousie.
p.	153	UNDERWOOD 13	26	Against his will that do's 'hem? that hath weav'd
p.	160	UNDERWOOD 14	63	A banke against it. Nothing but the round
p.	163	UNDERWOOD 15	33	Against his Maker; high alone with weeds,
p.	173	UNDERWOOD 22	12	Against or Faith, or honours lawes.
p.	183	UNDERWOOD 29	t1	A Fit of Rime against Rime.
p.	187	UNDERWOOD 33	31	Against a multitude; and (with thy Stile
p.	208	UNDERWOOD 43	119	Squire of the Squibs, against the Pageant day,
p.	208	UNDERWOOD 43	125	Against thy furie, when to serve their needs,
p.	208	UNDERWOOD 43	132	Against the Globe, the Glory of the Banke.
p.	210	UNDERWOOD 43	175	Against this Vulcan? No Injunction?
p.	283	U'WOOD 84.9	33	I murmure against God, for having ta'en
p.	284	U'WOOD 84.9	59	Who will be there, against that day prepar'd,
p.	284	U'WOOD 84.9	75	Against the Nature he would worship. Hee
p.	291	UNDERWOOD 85	44	Against the Husband comes home tir'd;
p.	325	HORACE 2	444	There words will follow, not against their will.
p.	331	HORACE 2	574	Wilt nothing against nature speake, or doe:
p.	335	HORACE 2	665	Hee that preserves a man, against his will,
p.	391	UNGATHERED 26	15	But thou art proofe against them, and indeed
p.	396	UNGATHERED 30	8	Hanch against Hanch, or raise a riming Club
p.	397	UNGATHERED 30	40	Drums against Drums, the neighing of the Horse,
p.	401	UNGATHERED 32	14	A Trench against it, nor a Battry plac't?
p.	408	UNGATHERED 37	10	By barking against mee. Thou look'st at least,

ag'd   frequency: 1   relative frequency: 0.00001
| **p. | 115 | PANEGYRE | 67 | To bring them forth: Whil'st riper ag'd, and apt |

age   frequency: 41   relative frequency: 0.00059
See also "th'age."
*p.	492	TO HIMSELF	2	And the more lothsome age:
**p.	114	PANEGYRE	58	No age, nor sex, so weake, or strongly dull,
p.	31	EPIGRAMS 14	5	Then thee the age sees not that thing more graue,
p.	41	EPIGRAMS 45	8	And, if no other miserie, yet age?
p.	47	EPIGRAMS 64	3	Of loue, and what the golden age did hold
p.	56	EPIGRAMS 89	1	If Rome so great, and in her wisest age,
p.	57	EPIGRAMS 90	6	And, finding good securitie in his age,
p.	66	EPIGRAMS 102	5	Nor could the age haue mist thee, in this strife
p.	67	EPIGRAMS 104	10	Of former age, or glorie of our one,
p.	71	EPIGRAMS 110	13	For, where his person liu'd scarce one iust age,
p.	75	EPIGRAMS 116	4	That age, when thou stood'st vp the master-braine:
p.	75	EPIGRAMS 117	1	GROYNE, come of age, his state sold out of hand
p.	76	EPIGRAMS 119	15	He, that, but liuing halfe his age, dyes such;
p.	78	EPIGRAMS 122	2	The aged SATVRNE'S age, and rites to know:
p.	84	EPIGRAMS 133	19	Then let the former age, with this content her,
p.	96	FOREST 2	92	A fortune, in this age, but rarely knowne.
p.	98	FOREST 3	63	Such, and no other was that age, of old,
p.	98	FOREST 3	70	That they may sleepe with scarres in age.
p.	100	FOREST 4	2	That houre vpon my morne of age,
p.	102	FOREST 4	62	To age, misfortune, sicknesse, griefe:
p.	105	FOREST 8	12	And this age will build no more:
p.	114	FOREST 12	22	Then this, our guilt, nor golden age can deeme,
p.	131	UNDERWOOD 2.1	21	Keepe the middle age at stay,

age (cont.)
```
p. 166 UNDERWOOD 15   135 He that no more for Age, Cramps, Palsies, can
p. 175 UNDERWOOD 23    31 And since our Daintie age,
p. 183 UNDERWOOD 29    26 Not a Poet in an Age,
p. 188 UNDERWOOD 34     2 One beautie in an Age, and free from thee?
p. 200 UNDERWOOD 42    27 It is a ryming Age, and Verses swarme
p. 205 UNDERWOOD 43    55 And so, have kept me dying a whole age,
p. 223 UNDERWOOD 49    42 This Age would lend no faith to Dorrels Deed;
p. 244 UNDERWOOD 70    51 As though his age imperfect might appeare,
p. 244 UNDERWOOD 70    56 To swell thine age;
p. 245 UNDERWOOD 70    79 Hee leap'd the present age,
p. 254 UNDERWOOD 75    75 In all thy age of Journals thou hast tooke,
p. 315 HORACE 2       223 The customes of each age thou must observe,
p. 317 HORACE 2       252 The parts of age to youth be given; or men
p. 391 UNGATHERED 26   17 I, therefore will begin. Soule of the Age!
p. 391 UNGATHERED 26   43 He was not of an age, but for all time!
p. 404 UNGATHERED 34   52 This is ye money-gett, Mechanick Age!
p. 409 UNGATHERED 38    8 Which I, your Master, first did teach the Age.
p. 420 UNGATHERED 48   27 And in this Age, canst hope no <other> grace.
```

aged   frequency: 3   relative frequency: 0.00004
See also "ag'd."
```
p.  78 EPIGRAMS 122     2 The aged SATVRNE'S age, and rites to
                         know;
p.  94 FOREST 2        33 Fat, aged carps, that runne into thy net.
p. 309 HORACE 2        87 The first-borne dying; so the aged state
```

agen   frequency: 4   relative frequency: 0.00005
```
p. 131 UNDERWOOD 2.1    6 Some have lov'd as old agen.
p. 173 UNDERWOOD 22    14 In whom alone Love lives agen?
p. 199 UNDERWOOD 41    22 Till I may see both it and you agen.
p. 212 UNDERWOOD 43   212 That have good places: therefore once agen,
```

agents   frequency: 1   relative frequency: 0.00001
```
p.  69 EPIGRAMS 107    23 Your Arch-Dukes Agents, and your Beringhams,
```

ages   frequency: 2   relative frequency: 0.00002
```
p. 242 UNDERWOOD 69    23 Then knew the former ages: yet to life,
p. 379 UNGATHERED 12   11 Which, vnto all Ages, for his will be knowne,
```

agile   frequency: 1   relative frequency: 0.00001
```
p. 180 UNDERWOOD 26     4 A gentler, and more agile hand, to tend
```

agincourt   frequency: 2   relative frequency: 0.00002
```
p. 398 UNGATHERED 30   70 An Agincourt, an Agincourt, or dye.
```

agree   frequency: 2   relative frequency: 0.00002
```
p.  40 EPIGRAMS 42     18 I know no couple better can agree!
p. 305 HORACE 2         8 This peece, my Piso's, and that booke agree,
```

agreeing   frequency: 1   relative frequency: 0.00001
```
p. 313 HORACE 2       170 Things in themselves agreeing: If againe
```

agrees   frequency: 1   relative frequency: 0.00001
See also "'grees."
```
p. 345 HORACE 1       279 .... .. ... ........ ..... ... ..... agrees
```

aiax   frequency: 1   relative frequency: 0.00001
```
p. 114 FOREST 12       54 AIAX, or IDOMEN, or all the store,
```

aid   frequency: 2   relative frequency: 0.00002
See also "aide."
```
p. 151 UNDERWOOD 11    12 Of sleepe againe, who was his Aid;
p. 291 UNDERWOOD 85    40 For houshold aid, and Children sweet;
```

aide   frequency: 6   relative frequency: 0.00008
```
p.  85 EPIGRAMS 133    54 Alwayes at hand, to aide the merry Muses.
p. 176 UNDERWOOD 25     2 Thy present Aide: Arise Invention,
p. 186 UNDERWOOD 32     3 Without the pompe of Counsell; or more Aide,
p. 217 UNDERWOOD 46     7 When, being the Strangers helpe, the poore mans
                         aide,
p. 217 UNDERWOOD 46    24 Needs lend an aide, to thine she had her eyes.
p. 275 U'WOOD 84.3      5 Send these suspected helpes, to aide
```

aided   frequency: 3   relative frequency: 0.00004
```
p. 175 UNDERWOOD 23    30 Who aided him, will thee, the issue of Joves
                         braine.
p. 217 UNDERWOOD 46     4 Whom Fortune aided lesse, or Vertue more.
p. 217 UNDERWOOD 46    22 None Fortune aided lesse, or Vertue more.
```

aides   frequency: 2   relative frequency: 0.00002
    p. 248 UNDERWOOD 71   3 Of Princes aides, or good mens Charities.
    p. 268 UNDERWOOD 82   6 Great aides to Empire, as they are great care

aids. See "aides," "aydes."

ail. See "aile."

aile   frequency: 1   relative frequency: 0.00001
    p. 192 UNDERWOOD 38   45 An ill-affected limbe (what e're it aile)

aim. See "aime," "ayme."

aime   frequency: 3   relative frequency: 0.00004
    p. 234 UNDERWOOD 60   13 No aime at glorie, or, in warre,
    p. 269 UNDERWOOD 83   25 I durst not aime at that: The dotes were such
    p. 313 HORACE 2   173 Sharpe, and contemning lawes, at him should aime,

aimed. See "aymd," "aymed."

aims. See "aymes."

air. See "aire," "ayre," "lady-aire."

aire   frequency: 6   relative frequency: 0.00008
  **p. 114 PANEGYRE   60 Of hearts, and voices. All the aire was rent,
    p. 230 UNDERWOOD 56   13 Marrie the Muse is one, can tread the Aire,
    p. 321 HORACE 2   335 Or, whilst he shuns the Earth, to catch at Aire
    p. 367 UNGATHERED 6   37 But proue the Aire, and saile from Coast to
                             Coast:
    p. 368 UNGATHERED 6   77 And vp againe, in skies, and aire to vent
    p. 401 UNGATHERED 33   6 French Aire and English Verse here Wedded
                             lie.

airising   frequency: 1   relative frequency: 0.00001
    p. 87 EPIGRAMS 133   131 Airising in that place, through which, who goes,

airs. See "ayres."

airy. See "aerie," "ayrie."

ajax. See "a-iax," "aiax."

ake   frequency: 1   relative frequency: 0.00001
    p. 250 UNDERWOOD 73   12 T<o>'effect it, feele, thou'ast made thine owne
                             heart ake.

alarm. See "larum."

alarmes   frequency: 2   relative frequency: 0.00002
    p. 289 UNDERWOOD 85   5 Nor Souldier-like started with rough alarmes,
    p. 398 UNGATHERED 30   66 How do his trumpets breath! What loud alarmes!

alarms. See "alarmes."

alas   frequency: 10   relative frequency: 0.00014
    See also "'lasse."
    p. 77 EPIGRAMS 120   19 But viewing him since (alas, too late)
    p. 86 EPIGRAMS 133   90 Row close then, slaues. Alas, they will beshite
                             vs.
    p. 101 FOREST 4   37 Yes, threaten, doe. Alas I feare
    p. 107 FOREST 10   4 HERCVLES? alas his bones are yet sore,
    p. 137 UNDERWOOD 2.5   43 But alas, thou seest the least
    p. 199 UNDERWOOD 41   11 Alas I ha' lost my heat, my blood, my prime,
    p. 244 UNDERWOOD 70   43 Alas, but Morison fell young:
    p. 269 UNDERWOOD 83   13 Alas, I am all Marble! write the rest
    p. 319 HORACE 2   300 And in their numbers; For, alas, what knew
    p. 365 UNGATHERED 5   17 Alas: then whither wade I,

alba   frequency: 1   relative frequency: 0.00001
    p. 292 UNDERWOOD 86   20 Beneath a Sweet-wood Roofe, neere Alba Lake:

albin's   frequency: 1   relative frequency: 0.00001
    p. 327 HORACE 2   467 There's Albin's sonne will say, Substract an
                             ounce

alcaic. See "alcaick."

alcaick   frequency: 1   relative frequency: 0.00001
   *p. 493 TO HIMSELF   42 And take the Alcaick Lute;

alchemist. See "alchimist."

alchemists. See "alchymists."

alchimist   frequency: 1   relative frequency: 0.00001
     p. 208 UNDERWOOD 43 118 Some Alchimist there may be yet, or odde

alchymists   frequency: 1   relative frequency: 0.00001
     p. 29 EPIGRAMS 6   t1 TO ALCHYMISTS.

alcides   frequency: 2   relative frequency: 0.00002
     p. 85 EPIGRAMS 133   50 ALCIDES, be thou succouring to my song.
     p. 89 EPIGRAMS 133 182 Were you IOVE'S sonnes, or had
                              ALCIDES might.

alcoran   frequency: 1   relative frequency: 0.00001
     p. 205 UNDERWOOD 43   65 The Talmud, and the Alcoran had come,

alde-legh   frequency: 1   relative frequency: 0.00001
     p. 274 U'WOOD 84.2   13 And tell thou, ALDE-LEGH, None can tell
                              more true

alderley. See "alde-legh."

alderman   frequency: 1   relative frequency: 0.00001
     p. 117 FOREST 13   38 Doe I reflect. Some alderman has power,

aldermanitie   frequency: 1   relative frequency: 0.00001
     p. 214 UNDERWOOD 44   46 The Battells of thy Aldermanitie;

aldermanity. See "aldermanitie."

ale   frequency: 4   relative frequency: 0.00005
     p. 193 UNDERWOOD 38   95 The wit of Ale, and Genius of the Malt
     p. 407 UNGATHERED 35   9 Or Ale! He build a pallace! Thou a shopp
     p. 417 UNGATHERED 45 39 at Pem Wakers good ale Tapp,
     p. 418 UNGATHERED 45 42 or theire Ale, they break the peace,

ale-house   frequency: 1   relative frequency: 0.00001
     p. 89 EPIGRAMS 133 189 Who kept an ale-house; with my little MINOS,

alexandria   frequency: 1   relative frequency: 0.00001
     p. 211 UNDERWOOD 43 195 Or Alexandria; and though a Divine

alfius. See "alphius."

alice   frequency: 2   relative frequency: 0.00002
     p. 411 UNGATHERED 40   t2 Mrs. Alice Sutcliffe, on
     p. 412 UNGATHERED 40   24 the Anagram of ALICE.

alife. See "a-life."

alight   frequency: 1   relative frequency: 0.00001
     p. 368 UNGATHERED 6   79 Till thou at Tames alight,

alike   frequency: 5   relative frequency: 0.00007
    **p. 114 PANEGYRE   57 The ioy of either was alike, and full;
     p. 46 EPIGRAMS 61   1 Thy praise, or dispraise is to me alike,
     p. 60 EPIGRAMS 93   3 Who did, alike with thee, thy house vp-beare,
     p. 176 UNDERWOOD 24   8 When Vice alike in time with vertue dur'd.
     p. 413 UNGATHERED 41   34 Alike of kin, to that most blessed Trine,

alike-stated   frequency: 1   relative frequency: 0.00001
     p. 295 UNDERWOOD 90   7 A wise simplicity; freindes alike-stated;

aliue   frequency: 4   relative frequency: 0.00005
    **p. 115 PANEGYRE   70 The Nobles zeale, yet either kept aliue
     p. 47 EPIGRAMS 64   10 Where merit is not sepulcher'd aliue.
     p. 81 EPIGRAMS 129   10 Whose noyse shall keepe thy miming most aliue,
     p. 391 UNGATHERED 26   23 And art aliue still, while thy Booke doth liue,

alive   frequency: 10   relative frequency: 0.00014
     See also "aliue," "'live."
     p. 162 UNDERWOOD 15   5 It is a call to keepe the spirits alive
     p. 172 UNDERWOOD 21   9 Of putrid flesh alive! of blood, the sinke!
     p. 214 UNDERWOOD 44   56 Alive yet, in the noise; and still the same;
     p. 234 UNDERWOOD 61   5 That scarce you heare a publike voyce alive,
     p. 257 UNDERWOOD 75   151 Alive, which else would die,
     p. 257 UNDERWOOD 75   163 Be kept alive those Sweet, and Sacred fires
     p. 273 U'WOOD 84.1   6 Their names of being kept alive,

alive (cont.)
    p. 329 HORACE 2   509 It would, must be: lest it alive would draw
    p. 412 UNGATHERED 41   8 As Love, here studied to keep Grace alive.
    p. 416 UNGATHERED 43   5 How they doe keepe alive his memorie;

all   frequency: 569   relative frequency: 0.00823
   See also "all's," "farre-all-seeing,"
          "t<o>'all," "woo-all."
  **p. 113 PANEGYRE   16 Those dampes, that so offend all good mens eyes,
  **p. 114 PANEGYRE   34 Vpon his face all threw their couetous eyes,
  **p. 114 PANEGYRE   44 All, as vnwearied, as vnsatisfied:
  **p. 114 PANEGYRE   60 Of hearts, and voices. All the aire was rent,
  **p. 114 PANEGYRE   63 Walls, windores, roofes, towers, steeples, all
                      were set
  **p. 115 PANEGYRE   81 "As they are men, then men. That all they doe,
  **p. 115 PANEGYRE   93 "And all so iustly, as his eare was ioy'd
  **p. 115 PANEGYRE   96 "Who both, who neither: all the cunning tracts,
  **p. 116 PANEGYRE   104 "When, publique iustice borrow'd all her powers
  **p. 116 PANEGYRE   107 "All this she told, and more, with bleeding eyes;
  **p. 116 PANEGYRE   128 In all these knowing artes our prince excell'd.
  **p. 117 PANEGYRE   146 Brighter then all, hath yet made no one lesse;
  **p. 117 PANEGYRE   150 What all mens wishes did aspire vnto.
    p. 29 EPIGRAMS 6   1 If all you boast of your great art be true;
    p. 29 EPIGRAMS 9   t1 TO ALL, TO WHOM I WRITE.
    p. 31 EPIGRAMS 12   20 His onely answere is to all, god payes.
    p. 31 EPIGRAMS 14   2 All that I am in arts, all that I know,
    p. 31 EPIGRAMS 14   12 Which conquers all, be once ouer-come by thee.
    p. 31 EPIGRAMS 15   1 All men are wormes: But this no man. In silke
    p. 32 EPIGRAMS 16   8 Make good what thou dar'st doe in all the rest.
    p. 32 EPIGRAMS 18   10 Thy faith is all the knowledge that thou hast.
    p. 33 EPIGRAMS 22   3 Yet, all heauens gifts, being heauens due,
    p. 34 EPIGRAMS 23   2 Who, to thy one, all other braines refuse;
    p. 34 EPIGRAMS 23   9 All which I meant to praise, and, yet, I would;
    p. 35 EPIGRAMS 28   3 Makes serious vse of all great trade he knowes.
    p. 36 EPIGRAMS 29   4 All braines, at times of triumph, should runne
                      wit.
    p. 37 EPIGRAMS 32   2 Could not effect, not all the furies doe,
    p. 37 EPIGRAMS 32   10 Seas, serenes, swords, shot, sicknesse, all are
                      there.
    p. 39 EPIGRAMS 39   1 For all night-sinnes, with others wiues,
                      vnknowne,
    p. 39 EPIGRAMS 40   5 All the gazers on the skies
    p. 39 EPIGRAMS 41   2 And get more gold, then all the colledge can:
    p. 40 EPIGRAMS 42   11 All this doth IONE. Or that his long-yearn'd
                      life
    p. 40 EPIGRAMS 42   15 In all affections shee concurreth still.
    p. 41 EPIGRAMS 44   2 And rich in issue to inherit all,
    p. 41 EPIGRAMS 44   4 Saw all his race approch the blacker floods:
    p. 41 EPIGRAMS 45   5 O, could I loose all father, now. For why
    p. 41 EPIGRAMS 45   11 For whose sake, hence-forth, all his vowes be
                      such,
    p. 45 EPIGRAMS 56   8 He takes vp all, makes each mans wit his owne.
    p. 47 EPIGRAMS 63   7 Who can behold all enuie so declin'd
    p. 47 EPIGRAMS 63   10 Without his, thine, and all times iniurie?
    p. 48 EPIGRAMS 65   9 Make him loose all his friends; and, which is
                      worse,
    p. 48 EPIGRAMS 65   10 Almost all wayes, to any better course.
    p. 49 EPIGRAMS 67   2 Most thinke all praises flatteries. But truth
                      brings
    p. 49 EPIGRAMS 67   8 As all thy honors were by them first sought:
    p. 50 EPIGRAMS 72   3 At MADAMES table, where thou mak'st all
                      wit
    p. 53 EPIGRAMS 78   2 To draw thee custome: but her selfe gets all.
    p. 53 EPIGRAMS 79   8 Nature, they thought, in all, that he would
                      faine.
    p. 54 EPIGRAMS 81   5 For all thou hear'st, thou swear'st thy selfe
                      didst doo.
    p. 56 EPIGRAMS 87   6 Since when, hee's sober againe, and all play's
                      made.
    p. 56 EPIGRAMS 88   12 By which his damme conceiu'd him, clothes and
                      all?
    p. 57 EPIGRAMS 89   10 Out-strip, then they did all that went before:
    p. 57 EPIGRAMS 89   11 And present worth in all dost so contract,
    p. 59 EPIGRAMS 92   25 They all get Porta, for the sundrie wayes
    p. 59 EPIGRAMS 92   31 With England. All forbidden bookes they get.
    p. 60 EPIGRAMS 93   4 Stand'st thou, to shew the times what you all
                      were?
    p. 60 EPIGRAMS 93   9 Thou, that art all their valour, all their
                      spirit,
    p. 60 EPIGRAMS 93   12 Nor could I, had I seene all Natures roule,

all (cont.)

p.	61	EPIGRAMS 95	5 So hast thou rendred him in all his bounds,
p.	61	EPIGRAMS 95	6 And all his numbers, both of sense, and sounds.
p.	61	EPIGRAMS 95	13 O, would'st thou adde like hand, to all the rest!
p.	62	EPIGRAMS 95	35 But most we need his faith (and all haue you)
p.	62	EPIGRAMS 96	7 Reade all I send: and, if I find but one
p.	65	EPIGRAMS 101	34 Are all but LVTHERS beere, to this I sing.
p.	66	EPIGRAMS 102	2 It is an Epigramme, on all man-kind;
p.	66	EPIGRAMS 102	6 Of vice, and vertue; wherein all great life
p.	66	EPIGRAMS 103	8 And glorie of them all, but to repeate!
p.	67	EPIGRAMS 105	1 MADAME, had all antiquitie beene lost,
p.	67	EPIGRAMS 105	2 All historie seal'd vp, and fables crost;
p.	67	EPIGRAMS 105	6 Who could not but create them all, from you?
p.	68	EPIGRAMS 105	11 If dancing, all would cry th'Idalian Queene,
p.	68	EPIGRAMS 105	20 I' your selfe, all treasure lost of th'age before.
p.	68	EPIGRAMS 106	4 Truth might spend all her voyce, Fame all her art.
p.	68	EPIGRAMS 106	10 And yet, they, all together, lesse then thee.
p.	69	EPIGRAMS 107	15 And, in some yeere, all these together heap'd,
p.	70	EPIGRAMS 109	4 Where all is faire, beside thy pedigree.
p.	71	EPIGRAMS 110	1 Not CAESARS deeds, nor all his honors wonne,
p.	71	EPIGRAMS 110	5 All yeelding to his fortune, nor, the while,
p.	71	EPIGRAMS 110	11 Not all these, EDMONDS, or what else put too,
p.	72	EPIGRAMS 111	7 Which all, but ignorant Captaynes, will confesse:
p.	72	EPIGRAMS 112	5 Thy all, at all: and what so ere I doe,
p.	74	EPIGRAMS 114	8 But, in your loue, made all his seruants wise.
p.	74	EPIGRAMS 115	12 Doe all, that longs to the anarchy of drinke,
p.	74	EPIGRAMS 115	17 Tell's of him, all the tales, it selfe then makes;
p.	74	EPIGRAMS 115	19 It will deny all; and forsweare it too:
p.	75	EPIGRAMS 115	31 An inginer, in slanders, of all fashions,
p.	75	EPIGRAMS 116	2 All gentrie, yet, owe part of their best flame!
p.	76	EPIGRAMS 118	1 GVT eates all day, and lechers all the night,
p.	76	EPIGRAMS 118	2 So all his meate he tasteth ouer, twise:
p.	76	EPIGRAMS 119	7 No, SHELTON, giue me thee, canst want all these,
p.	77	EPIGRAMS 120	1 Weepe with me all you that read
p.	77	EPIGRAMS 120	18 They all consented;
p.	78	EPIGRAMS 122	10 Who prou'st, all these were, and againe may bee.
p.	79	EPIGRAMS 124	7 If, at all, shee had a fault,
p.	79	EPIGRAMS 124	12 Then that it liu'd at all. Farewell.
p.	80	EPIGRAMS 127	9 So, all reward, or name, that growes to mee
p.	80	EPIGRAMS 128	3 T<o>'extract, and choose the best of all these knowne,
p.	81	EPIGRAMS 128	6 Attend thee hence: and there, may all thy ends,
p.	81	EPIGRAMS 129	8 The very call, to make all others come:
p.	82	EPIGRAMS 130	14 Including all, were thence call'd harmonie:
p.	82	EPIGRAMS 130	17 But when I haue said, The proofes of all these bee
p.	82	EPIGRAMS 131	3 For, then, all mouthes will iudge, and their owne way:
p.	83	EPIGRAMS 131	5 And though we could all men, all censures heare,
p.	83	EPIGRAMS 132	4 And vtter stranger to all ayre of France)
p.	84	EPIGRAMS 133	7 All, that they boast of STYX, of ACHERON,
p.	85	EPIGRAMS 133	43 All, that are readers: but, me thinkes 'tis od,
p.	85	EPIGRAMS 133	44 That all this while I haue forgot some god,
p.	85	EPIGRAMS 133	51 Thou hast seene hell (some say) and know'st all nookes there,
p.	85	EPIGRAMS 133	64 Of all your night-tubs, when the carts doe cluster,
p.	86	EPIGRAMS 133	78 Ploughing the mayne. When, see (the worst of all lucks)
p.	86	EPIGRAMS 133	97 And all his followers, that had so abus'd him:
p.	87	EPIGRAMS 133	110 Vanish'd away: as you must all presume
p.	87	EPIGRAMS 133	127 Then all those Atomi ridiculous,
p.	87	EPIGRAMS 133	135 But open, and vn-arm'd encounter'd all:
p.	88	EPIGRAMS 133	140 All was to them the same, they were to passe,
p.	89	EPIGRAMS 133	191 They tooke 'hem all to witnesse of their action:
p.	94	FOREST 2	14 At his great birth, where all the Muses met.
p.	94	FOREST 2	48 But all come in, the farmer, and the clowne:
p.	95	FOREST 2	60 With all, that hospitalitie doth know!
p.	95	FOREST 2	73 For fire, or lights, or liuorie: all is there;
p.	95	FOREST 2	81 With all their zeale, to warme their welcome here.

all (cont.)

p.	96 FOREST 2	86	To haue her linnen, plate, and all things nigh,
p.	96 FOREST 2	89	These, PENSHVRST, are thy praise, and yet not all.
p.	97 FOREST 3	25	Or with thy friends, the heart of all the yeere,
p.	97 FOREST 3	31	While all, that follow, their glad eares apply
p.	100 FOREST 4	8	From all the nets that thou canst spread.
p.	100 FOREST 4	16	And all thy good is to be sold.
p.	101 FOREST 4	28	With all my powers, my selfe to loose?
p.	101 FOREST 4	44	When all the causes were away.
p.	101 FOREST 4	55	That, what to all may happen here,
p.	101 FOREST 4	59	From all my kinde: that, for my sake,
p.	103 FOREST 6	4	All your bounties will betray.
p.	103 FOREST 6	13	All the grasse that Rumney yeelds,
p.	104 FOREST 8	9	Liue not we, as, all thy stalls,
p.	105 FOREST 8	35	Them, and all their officers.
p.	105 FOREST 8	36	That, to make all pleasure theirs,
p.	107 FOREST 10	21	His absence in my verse, is all I aske.
p.	108 FOREST 10	25	Nor all the ladies of the Thespian lake,
p.	108 FOREST 10 A	14	and Coniures all my faculties t<o>'approue
p.	109 FOREST 11	1	Not to know vice at all, and keepe true state,
p.	110 FOREST 11	56	The'Elixir of all ioyes?
p.	111 FOREST 11	65	Of all his happinesse? But soft: I heare
p.	112 FOREST 11	97	All taste of bitternesse, and makes the ayre
p.	112 FOREST 11	101	All her best symmetrie in that one feature!
p.	113 FOREST 12	1	Whil'st that, for which, all vertue now is sold,
p.	113 FOREST 12	7	Well, or ill, onely, all the following yeere,
p.	113 FOREST 12	18	Or perhaps lesse: whil'st gold beares all this sway,
p.	114 FOREST 12	39	The world hath seene, which all these had in trust,
p.	114 FOREST 12	54	AIAX, or IDOMEN, or all the store,
p.	115 FOREST 12	66	Of all LVCINA'S traine; LVCY the bright,
p.	115 FOREST 12	79	Then all, that haue but done my Muse least grace,
p.	117 FOREST 13	31	And so doe many more. All which can call
p.	117 FOREST 13	36	And, in those outward formes, all fooles are wise.
p.	118 FOREST 13	50	Without which, all the rest were sounds, or lost.
p.	118 FOREST 13	70	For truthes complexion, where they all weare maskes.
p.	118 FOREST 13	75	And almost, all dayes after, while they liue;
p.	118 FOREST 13	81	Let 'hem waste body, and state; and after all,
p.	119 FOREST 13	92	Into your harbor, and all passage shut
p.	120 FOREST 14	5	And all doe striue t<o>'aduance
p.	120 FOREST 14	17	When all the noyse
p.	121 FOREST 14	25	Striue all right wayes it can,
p.	122 FOREST 15	6	And hearts of all, if I be sad for show,
p.	122 FOREST 15	9	As thou art all, so be thou all to mee,
p.	122 FOREST 15	20	And destin'd vnto iudgement, after all.
p.	127 UNDERWOOD 1.1	7	As my heart lies in peeces, all confus'd,
p.	127 UNDERWOOD 1.1	18	This All of nothing, gavest it forme, and fate,
p.	128 UNDERWOOD 1.1	38	All coeternall in your Majestie,
p.	129 UNDERWOCD 1.2	22	With all since bought.
p.	130 UNDERWOOD 1.3	8	That did us all salvation bring,
p.	130 UNDERWOOD 1.3	22	To see this Babe, all innocence;
p.	131 UNDERWOOD 2.1	24	All the world for love may die.
p.	132 UNDERWOOD 2.2	4	All the Pride the fields than have:
p.	132 UNDERWOOD 2.2	28	Mock'd of all: and call'd of one
p.	133 UNDERWOCD 2.3	21	Looser-like, now, all my wreake
p.	134 UNDERWOOD 2.4	5	As she goes, all hearts doe duty
p.	134 UNDERWOOD 2.4	12	All that Loves world compriseth!
p.	134 UNDERWOOD 2.4	20	All the Gaine, all the Good, of the Elements strife.
p.	137 UNDERWOOD 2.5	39	I confesse all, I replide,
p.	137 UNDERWOOD 2.5	42	All is Venus: save unchaste.
p.	138 UNDERWOOD 2.6	15	Of the Court, to day, then all
p.	138 UNDERWOOD 2.6	26	As might all the Graces lead,
p.	138 UNDERWOOD 2.6	33	To have left all sight for you:
p.	139 UNDERWOOD 2.7	10	And all your bountie wrong:
p.	139 UNDERWOOD 2.8	6	All that heard her, with desire.
p.	140 UNDERWOOD 2.8	12	We all feare, she loveth none.
p.	140 UNDERWOOD 2.8	28	All your sweet of life is past,
p.	141 UNDERWOOD 2.9	30	All his blood should be a flame
p.	141 UNDERWOOD 2.9	33	'Twere to<o> long, to speake of all:
p.	142 U'WOOD 2.10	6	All I wish is understood.
p.	142 UNDERWOOD 2.9	45	All his actions to be such,
p.	143 UNDERWOOD 3	2	And challenge all the Spheares,
p.	143 UNDERWOOD 3	4	And all the world turne Eares.

all (cont.)

p. 145	UNDERWOOD 5	10	So going thorow all your straine,
p. 147	UNDERWOOD 7	24	Where Love may all his Torches light,
p. 150	UNDERWOOD 10	8	On all mens Fruit, and flowers, as well as mine.
p. 150	UNDERWOOD 9	18	And all these through her eyes, have stopt her eares.
p. 151	UNDERWOOD 11	11	In all my wild desire,
p. 151	UNDERWOOD 12	14	All order, and Disposure, still.
p. 153	UNDERWOOD 13	1	If, Sackvile, all that have the power to doe
p. 154	UNDERWOOD 13	33	All this corrupts the thankes; lesse hath he wonne,
p. 155	UNDERWOOD 13	72	All the Towne-curs take each their snatch at me.
p. 155	UNDERWOOD 13	81	All as their prize, turne Pyrats here at Land,
p. 158	UNDERWOOD 13	164	Find you to reckon nothing, me owe all.
p. 158	UNDERWOOD 14	11	Unto the Censure. Yours all need doth flie
p. 159	UNDERWOOD 14	30	Ever at home: yet, have all Countries seene:
p. 160	UNDERWOOD 14	59	In sharpnesse of all Search, wisdome of Choise,
p. 162	UNDERWOOD 15	3	All that dare rowse: or are not loth to quit
p. 162	UNDERWOOD 15	9	All other Acts of Worldlings, are but toyle
p. 162	UNDERWOOD 15	26	For all their spight, be like him if they could:
p. 163	UNDERWOOD 15	34	And impious ranknesse of all Sects and seeds:
p. 163	UNDERWOOD 15	40	And shamefastnesse together! All lawes dead,
p. 163	UNDERWOOD 15	46	All which he makes the servants of the Groine,
p. 163	UNDERWOOD 15	53	That all respect; She must lie downe: Nay more,
p. 164	UNDERWOOD 15	76	Doe all the tricks of a saut Lady Bitch;
p. 165	UNDERWOOD 15	91	Or use all arts, or haunt all Companies
p. 167	UNDERWOOD 15	175	Goe, quit 'hem all. And take along with thee,
p. 168	UNDERWOOD 15	179	That thou dost all things more for truth, then glory,
p. 168	UNDERWOOD 16	4	All that is left of PHILIP GRAY,
p. 169	UNDERWOOD 17	16	All is not barren land, doth fallow lie.
p. 169	UNDERWOOD 18	6	A terror? or is all this but my feare?
p. 171	UNDERWOOD 19	23	Of all that can be done him; Such a one
p. 171	UNDERWOOD 19	26	His Issue, and all Circumstance of life,
p. 171	UNDERWOOD 20	9	Knew I all this afore? had I perceiv'd,
p. 172	UNDERWOOD 20	13	Knew I, that all their Dialogues, and discourse,
p. 172	UNDERWOOD 20	18	Then all Ingredients made into one curse,
p. 172	UNDERWOOD 20	20	Thinke but the Sin of all her sex, 'tis she!
p. 172	UNDERWOOD 20	24	The Divell; and be the damning of us all.
p. 172	UNDERWOOD 21	6	Of all vice hurld together, there he was,
p. 172	UNDERWOOD 21	7	Proud, false, and trecherous, vindictive, all
p. 173	UNDERWOOD 22	7	And draw, and conquer all mens love,
p. 173	UNDERWOOD 22	26	To whom all Lovers are design'd,
p. 174	UNDERWOOD 23	7	Are all th'Aonian springs
p. 179	UNDERWOOD 25	44	And, after all the Aetnean Ire,
p. 180	UNDERWOOD 25	65	As farre from all revolt, as you are now from Fortune.
p. 181	UNDERWOOD 27	20	Which all the world then styl'd divine?
p. 181	UNDERWOOD 27	24	Which all the Fate of Troy foretold?
p. 182	UNDERWOOD 27	29	Have all these done (and yet I misse
p. 182	UNDERWOOD 27	34	Come short of all this learned throng,
p. 182	UNDERWOOD 28	9	For in your verse all Cupids Armorie,
p. 183	UNDERWOOD 29	14	All good Poetrie hence was flowne,
p. 183	UNDERWOOD 29	17	All Parnassus Greene did wither,
p. 183	UNDERWOOD 29	24	All light failed!
p. 185	UNDERWOOD 30	2	Read here in one, what thou in all canst find,
p. 185	UNDERWOOD 30	10	That in all tempests, never quit the helme,
p. 185	UNDERWOOD 30	19	Of all the Land. Who now at such a Rate,
p. 185	UNDERWOOD 31	1	So, justest Lord, may all your Judgements be
p. 186	UNDERWOOD 31	5	So, from all sicknesse, may you rise to health,
p. 187	UNDERWOOD 33	11	All mouthes, that dare entitle them (from hence)
p. 187	UNDERWOOD 33	30	Arm'd at all peeces, as to keepe a Fort
p. 187	UNDERWOOD 33	38	And (which doth all Atchievements get above)
p. 187	UNDERWOOD 33	40	Alone, but all thy ranke a reverend Name.
p. 188	UNDERWOOD 34	16	Make all hereafter, had'st thou ruin'd this?
p. 188	UNDERWOOD 35	3	What wonder perfect, all were fil'd,
p. 189	UNDERWOOD 36	6	All light[s] into his one doth run;
p. 189	UNDERWOOD 36	7	Without which all the world were darke;
p. 191	UNDERWOOD 38	1	'Tis true, I'm broke! Vowes, Oathes, and all I had
p. 192	UNDERWOOD 38	46	We cut not off, till all Cures else doe faile:
p. 192	UNDERWOOD 38	59	That were to wither all, and make a Grave
p. 193	UNDERWOOD 38	71	He cannot angrie be, but all must quake,
p. 193	UNDERWOOD 38	72	It shakes even him, that all things else doth shake.
p. 193	UNDERWOOD 38	76	As all with storme and tempest ran together.
p. 193	UNDERWOOD 38	88	Streight puts off all his Anger, and doth kisse
p. 193	UNDERWOOD 38	94	What Fooles, and all their Parasites can apply;
p. 194	UNDERWOOD 38	111	How all my Fibres by your Spirit doe move,

all (cont.)

p. 194	UNDERWOOD 38	121	Till then 'tis all but darknesse, that I have;
p. 197	UNDERWOOD 40	6	To put all relish from my memorie
p. 197	UNDERWOOD 40	20	In all his Actions rarified to spright;
p. 197	UNDERWOOD 40	22	And turning all he toucheth into pelfe,
p. 198	UNDERWOOD 40	28	'Bove all your standing waters, choak'd with weedes.
p. 200	UNDERWOOD 42	12	In all that is call'd lovely: take my sight
p. 202	UNDERWOOD 42	80	And all the originall riots of the place:
p. 203	UNDERWOOD 43	13	That since thou tak'st all envious care and paine,
p. 205	UNDERWOOD 43	30	Th'Esplandians, Arthurs, Palmerins, and all
p. 205	UNDERWOOD 43	56	Not ravish'd all hence in a minutes rage.
p. 205	UNDERWOOD 43	64	Thou should'st have cry'd, and all beene proper stuffe.
p. 206	UNDERWOOD 43	70	All the madde Rolands, and sweet Oliveers;
p. 206	UNDERWOOD 43	81	The weekly Corrants, with Pauls Seale; and all
p. 207	UNDERWOOD 43	89	All the old Venusine, in Poetrie,
p. 207	UNDERWOOD 43	95	With all th'adventures; Three bookes not afraid
p. 207	UNDERWOOD 43	106	All soote, and embers! odious, as thy worke!
p. 209	UNDERWOOD 43	153	O no, cry'd all, Fortune, for being a whore,
p. 210	UNDERWOOD 43	171	In those Records, which, were all Chronicle<r>s gone,
p. 210	UNDERWOOD 43	173	But say, all sixe good men, what answer yee?
p. 211	UNDERWOOD 43	190	But I'le conclude all in a civill curse.
p. 211	UNDERWOOD 43	192	To all as fatall as 't hath beene to me,
p. 211	UNDERWOOD 43	194	'Bove all your Fire-workes, had at Ephesus,
p. 212	UNDERWOOD 43	206	Make your Petards, and Granats, all your fine
p. 212	UNDERWOOD 43	209	We aske your absence here, we all love peace,
p. 212	UNDERWOOD 43	214	And all the Evils that flew out of her box
p. 213	UNDERWOOD 44	11	All Ensignes of a Warre, are not yet dead,
p. 213	UNDERWOOD 44	27	These ten yeares day; As all may sweare that looke
p. 215	UNDERWOOD 44	70	All licence in our lives? What need we know,
p. 215	UNDERWOOD 44	91	All that they doe at Playes. O, but first here
p. 215	UNDERWOOD 44	93	But why are all these Irons i' the fire
p. 217	UNDERWOOD 46	1	He that should search all Glories of the Gowne,
p. 217	UNDERWOOD 46	2	And steps of all rais'd servants of the Crowne,
p. 217	UNDERWOOD 46	3	He could not find, then thee, of all that store
p. 217	UNDERWOOD 46	19	No lesse of praise, then readers in all kinds
p. 217	UNDERWOOD 46	21	Such is thy All; that (as I sung before)
p. 218	UNDERWOOD 47	1	Men that are safe, and sure, in all they doe,
p. 218	UNDERWOOD 47	17	On all Soules that are absent; even the dead;
p. 218	UNDERWOOD 47	19	That to speake well, thinke it above all sinne,
p. 218	UNDERWOOD 47	23	That censure all the Towne, and all th'affaires,
p. 219	UNDERWOOD 47	37	I wish all well, and pray high heaven conspire
p. 219	UNDERWOOD 47	52	Lose all my credit with my Christmas Clay,
p. 219	UNDERWOOD 47	62	With reverence using all the gifts then<ce> given.
p. 220	UNDERWOOD 47	69	But all so cleare, and led by reasons flame,
p. 220	UNDERWOOD 47	72	And free it from all question to preserve.
p. 220	UNDERWOOD 48	8	Of all to the great Master.
p. 221	UNDERWOOD 48	19	By all the Arts of Gladnesse,
p. 221	UNDERWOOD 48	34	Pursue thee in all places,
p. 222	UNDERWOOD 48	51	And set us all on skipping,
p. 222	UNDERWOOD 49	12	Make State, Religion, Bawdrie, all a theame?
p. 224	UNDERWOOD 50	11	By all oblique Degrees, that killing height
p. 224	UNDERWOOD 50	13	And though all praise bring nothing to your name,
p. 224	UNDERWOOD 50	16	A cheerefull worke to all good eyes, to see
p. 225	UNDERWOOD 51	2	How comes it all things so about the<e> smile?
p. 225	UNDERWOOD 51	6	For whose returnes, and many, all these pray:
p. 227	UNDERWOOD 52	9	My Superficies: that was all you saw.
p. 227	UNDERWOOD 52	14	An Archetype, for all the world to see,
p. 227	UNDERWOOD 52	24	To all posteritie; I will write Burlase.
p. 228	UNDERWOOD 53	3	To all the uses of the field, and race,
p. 230	UNDERWOOD 56	16	Run all the Rounds in a soft Ladyes eare,
p. 232	UNDERWOOD 58	1	Thou, Friend, wilt heare all censures; unto thee
p. 232	UNDERWOOD 58	2	All mouthes are open, and all stomacks free:
p. 232	UNDERWOOD 59	6	As all defence, or offence, were a chime!
p. 233	UNDERWOOD 59	19	All this (my Lord) is Valour! This is yours!
p. 233	UNDERWOOD 59	20	And was your Fathers! All your Ancestours!
p. 233	UNDERWOOD 59	21	Who durst live great, 'mongst all the colds, and heates,
p. 233	UNDERWOOD 59	22	Of humane life! as all the frosts, and sweates
p. 234	UNDERWOOD 61	2	And all the games of Fortune, plaid at Court;
p. 234	UNDERWOOD 61	11	T<o>'obtaine of God, what all the Land should aske?
p. 235	UNDERWOOD 63	1	Who dares denie, that all first-fruits are due
p. 236	UNDERWOOD 63	10	And thinke all still the best, that he will doe.
p. 237	UNDERWOOD 64	13	When all your life's a president of dayes,

all (cont.)

p. 239 UNDERWOOD 67	t1 An Ode, or Song, by all the Muses.
p. 240 UNDERWOOD 67	29 Of all her Brothers storie,
p. 240 UNDERWOOD 67	40 Whilst all the ravish'd rout
p. 240 UNDERWOOD 67	49 9. POLY. Sweet! happy Mary! All
p. 241 UNDERWOOD 69	12 All live dogs from the lane, and his shops sight,
p. 242 UNDERWOOD 69	15 At a Friends freedome, proves all circling meanes
p. 242 UNDERWOOD 69	20 To judge; So all men comming neere can spie.
p. 242 UNDERWOOD 69	24 All is but web, and painting; be the strife
p. 243 UNDERWOOD 70	18 And all on utmost ruine set;
p. 243 UNDERWOOD 70	20 No doubt all Infants would returne like thee.
p. 244 UNDERWOOD 70	38 Hee stoop'd in all mens sight
p. 244 UNDERWOOD 70	48 All Offices were done
p. 247 UNDERWOOD 70	114 And titles, by which all made claimes
p. 249 UNDERWOOD 72	6 Repeating all Great Britain's joy, and more,
p. 249 UNDERWOOD 72	12 Made lighter with the Wine. All noises else,
p. 251 UNDERWOOD 74	15 As all the wealth of Season, there was spread;
p. 251 UNDERWOOD 74	20 Bring all your friends, (faire Lord) that burne
p. 251 UNDERWOOD 74	23 With all the fruit shall follow it,
p. 252 UNDERWOOD 75	11 Hath fil<l>ed, with Caroches, all the way,
p. 253 UNDERWOOD 75	16 By all the Spheares consent, so in the heart of June?
p. 253 UNDERWOOD 75	20 As they came all to see, and to be seene!
p. 253 UNDERWOOD 75	23 In all her bloome, and flower;
p. 253 UNDERWOOD 75	26 The Month of youth, which calls all Creatures forth
p. 253 UNDERWOOD 75	32 Through which not only we, but all our Species are.
p. 253 UNDERWOOD 75	36 And all did ring th'approches of the Bride;
p. 253 UNDERWOOD 75	39 Of all the Maidens faire;
p. 253 UNDERWOOD 75	44 On all that come her Simplesse to rebuke!
p. 254 UNDERWOOD 75	50 The choisest Virgin-troup of all the Land!
p. 254 UNDERWOOD 75	68 And all the Ground were Garden, where she led!
p. 254 UNDERWOOD 75	72 With all the pompe of Youth, and all our Court beside.
p. 254 UNDERWOOD 75	73 Our Court, and all the Grandees; now, Sun, looke,
p. 254 UNDERWOOD 75	75 In all thy age of Journals thou hast tooke,
p. 255 UNDERWOOD 75	78 Who, in all they doe,
p. 255 UNDERWOOD 75	88 All else we see beside, are Shadowes, and goe lesse.
p. 255 UNDERWOOD 75	91 All is a story of the King and Queene!
p. 255 UNDERWOOD 75	101 In all the prov'd assayes,
p. 257 UNDERWOOD 75	136 With all corroding Arts, be able to untie!
p. 257 UNDERWOOD 75	147 All that their Fathers, and their Mothers might
p. 258 UNDERWOOD 75	192 The longing Couple, all that elder Lovers know.
p. 259 UNDERWOOD 76	8 To make all the MUSES debters
p. 259 UNDERWOOD 76	18 All the envie of the Rymes,
p. 260 UNDERWOOD 76	30 This would all their envie burst:
p. 262 UNDERWOOD 78	3 In honour, courtesie, and all the parts
p. 262 UNDERWOOD 78	6 In him all vertue is beheld in State:
p. 262 UNDERWOOD 78	10 Where all heroique ample thoughts doe meet:
p. 263 UNDERWOOD 78	32 Being sent to one, they will be read of all.
p. 263 UNDERWOOD 79	2 Lute, Lyre, Theorbo, all are call'd to day.
p. 263 UNDERWOOD 79	10 And shuts the old. Haste, haste, all loyall Swaines,
p. 264 UNDERWOOD 79	15 2. To him we owe all profits of our grounds.
p. 264 UNDERWOOD 79	33 Of all that Nature, yet, to life did bring;
p. 265 UNDERWOOD 79	46 Haste, haste you hither, all you gentler Swaines,
p. 265 UNDERWOOD 79	49 To whom you owe all duties of your grounds;
p. 265 UNDERWOOD 79	56 Hee gives all plentie, and encrease,
p. 269 UNDERWOOD 83	8 A horrour in mee! all my blood is steele!
p. 269 UNDERWOOD 83	13 Alas, I am all Marble! write the rest
p. 270 UNDERWOOD 83	42 And pietie the Center, where all met.
p. 270 UNDERWOOD 83	49 From all affection! when they urg'd the Cure
p. 270 UNDERWOOD 83	56 And I, into the world, all Soule, was sent!
p. 271 UNDERWOOD 83	74 What the beginnings of all beauties be;
p. 271 UNDERWOOD 83	75 And all beatitudes, that thence doe flow:
p. 271 UNDERWOOD 83	86 And see all dead here, or about to dye!
p. 271 UNDERWOOD 83	90 Whole Nations! nay, Mankind! the World, with all
p. 271 UNDERWOOD 83	94 When we were all borne, we began to die;
p. 272 UNDERWOOD 84	t7 A Gentleman absolute in all Numbers;
p. 273 U'WOOD 84.1	13 That all Posteritie, as wee,
p. 273 U'WOOD 84.1	32 Of ord'ring all.
p. 276 U'WOOD 84.3	13 Draw first a Cloud: all save her neck;
p. 276 U'WOOD 84.3	16 And Men may thinke, all light rose there.
p. 276 U'WOOD 84.3	22 With all that Youth, or it can bring:

all (cont.)

p. 278	U'WOOD 84.4	23	That all may say, that see the frame,
p. 279	U'WOOD 84.4	31	It moveth all; and makes a flight
p. 280	U'WOOD 84.4	51	In all the bounds of beautie fit
p. 280	U'WOOD 84.4	61	Smooth, soft, and sweet, in all a floud
p. 281	U'WOOD 84.8	17	Which all men doe, that urge not their owne deeds
p. 282	U'WOOD 84.8	20	Hang all your roomes, with one large Pedigree:
p. 282	U'WOOD 84.8	23	Study illustrious Him and you have all.
p. 282	U'WOOD 84.9	2	Who was my Muse, and life of all I sey'd,
p. 282	U'WOOD 84.9	4	All that was good, or great in me she weav'd,
p. 283	U'WOOD 84.9	17	With all her aydes, to save her from the seize
p. 283	U'WOOD 84.9	26	I summe up mine owne breaking, and wish all.
p. 284	U'WOOD 84.9	60	T<o>'accuse, or quit all Parties to be heard!
p. 284	U'WOOD 84.9	64	To Body, and Soule! where Love is all the guest!
p. 284	U'WOOD 84.9	67	All other gladnesse, with the thought is barr'd;
p. 284	U'WOOD 84.9	76	Will honour'd be in all simplicitie!
p. 284	U'WOOD 84.9	77	Have all his actions wondred at, and view'd
p. 285	U'WOOD 84.9	84	Amongst her Peeres, those Princes of all good!
p. 285	U'WOOD 84.9	110	By all the wealth of blessings, and the store
p. 285	U'WOOD 84.9	113	There, all the happy soules, that ever were,
p. 286	U'WOOD 84.9	119	But all of God; They still shall have to say,
p. 286	U'WOOD 84.9	120	But make him All in All, their Theme, that Day:
p. 286	U'WOOD 84.9	122	Where Hee will be, all Beautie to the Sight;
p. 286	U'WOOD 84.9	127	Hee will all Glory, all Perfection be,
p. 286	U'WOOD 84.9	143	Yet have all debts forgiven us, and advance
p. 286	U'WOOD 84.9	150	Who knowes the hearts of all, and can dissect
p. 287	U'WOOD 84.9	152	Find all our Atomes from a point t<o>'a span!
p. 287	U'WOOD 84.9	159	Of title in her! All Nobilitie
p. 287	U'WOOD 84.9	168	She swaid all bus'nesse in the Familie!
p. 287	U'WOOD 84.9	171	He run; and all did strive with diligence
p. 287	U'WOOD 84.9	177	In all her petite actions, so devote,
p. 287	U'WOOD 84.9	182	Of sorrow, then all pompe of gaudy daies:
p. 288	U'WOOD 84.9	189	And hers were all Humilitie! they beat
p. 288	U'WOOD 84.9	201	On all the world! She saw him on the Crosse
p. 288	U'WOOD 84.9	207	Of raising, judging, and rewarding all
p. 288	U'WOOD 84.9	209	All this by Faith she saw, and fram'd a Plea,
p. 289	U'WOOD 84.9	219	The last of houres, and shutter up of all;
p. 289	U'WOOD 84.9	221	Of all are dead to life! His Wisdome show
p. 289	U'WOOD 84.9	224	And giving dues to all Mankinds deserts!
p. 289	UNDERWOOD 85	1	Happie is he, that from all Businesse cleere,
p. 290	UNDERWOOD 85	28	And all invite to easie sleepe.
p. 291	UNDERWOOD 85	70	At th'Calends, puts all out againe.
p. 292	UNDERWOOD 86	18	With thee 'bove all his Rivals gifts take place,
p. 293	UNDERWOOD 87	7	In name, I went all names before,
p. 294	UNDERWOOD 89	1	Liber, of all thy friends, thou sweetest care,
p. 305	HORACE 2	12	Of daring all, hath still beene given; we know it:
p. 307	HORACE 2	57	His matter to his power, in all he makes,
p. 309	HORACE 2	72	Of the Cethegi; And all men will grace,
p. 309	HORACE 2	90	Our selves, and all that's ours, to death we owe:
p. 309	HORACE 2	98	Being taught a better way. All mortall deeds
p. 309	HORACE 2	111	All the Grammarians strive; and yet in Court
p. 311	HORACE 2	114	To chant the Gods, and all their God-like race,
p. 311	HORACE 2	155	With weightie sorrow hurles us all along,
p. 317	HORACE 2	244	Or do's all businesse coldly, and with feare;
p. 317	HORACE 2	260	Yet, to the Stage, at all thou maist not tender
p. 317	HORACE 2	275	Any fourth man, to speake at all, aspire.
p. 321	HORACE 2	330	And so to turne all earnest into jest,
p. 321	HORACE 2	344	Quite from all face of Tragedie to goe,
p. 323	HORACE 2	374	But meere Iambicks all, from first to last.
p. 323	HORACE 2	392	Or rather, thinking all my faults may spie,
p. 323	HORACE 2	394	Within the hope of having all forgiven?
p. 325	HORACE 2	421	Exclude all sober Poets, from their share
p. 327	HORACE 2	459	And better stayes them there, then all fine noise
p. 329	HORACE 2	497	All way of life was shewen; the grace of Kings
p. 329	HORACE 2	501	All which I tell, lest when Apollo's nam'd,
p. 331	HORACE 2	568	Or trundling Wheele, he can sit still, from all;
p. 331	HORACE 2	584	Can; or all toile, without a wealthie veine:
p. 333	HORACE 2	627	Hee'd bid, blot all: and to the anvile bring
p. 335	HORACE 2	637	They're darke, bid cleare this: all that's doubtfull wrote
p. 337	HORACE 2	676	All; So this grievous Writer puts to flight
p. 364	UNGATHERED 4	1	Now, after all, let no man
p. 364	UNGATHERED 5	2	For other formes come short all
p. 365	UNGATHERED 5	16	All Nature of commending.
p. 367	UNGATHERED 6	51	Hath all beene Harmony:
p. 367	UNGATHERED 6	56	And conquers all things, yea it selfe, at length.
p. 368	UNGATHERED 6	89	All which, when they but heare a straine

all (cont.)

p. 369	UNGATHERED 6	112	Conceal'd from all but cleare Propheticke eyes.
p. 369	UNGATHERED 6	118	With all the race
p. 370	UNGATHERED 7	4	All which are parts commend the cunning hand;
p. 370	UNGATHERED 7	5	And all your Booke (when it is throughly scan'd)
p. 371	UNGATHERED 8	12	And wish that all the Muses blood were spilt,
p. 371	UNGATHERED 8	16	Or moathes shall eate, what all these Fooles admire.
p. 372	UNGATHERED 9	11	Wth Rites not bound, but conscience. Wouldst thou All?
p. 374	UNGATHERED 10	11	All sorts of fish with Musicke of his maw.
p. 379	UNGATHERED 12	3	Who, because his matter in all should be meete,
p. 379	UNGATHERED 12	11	Which, vnto all Ages, for his will be knowne,
p. 380	UNGATHERED 12	28	Horse, foote, and all but flying in the ayre:
p. 382	UNGATHERED 16	2	hath armde att all poyntes; charge mee humblye kneele
p. 384	UNGATHERED 18	25	That all, yt view you then, and late; may say,
p. 385	UNGATHERED 19	7	My suffrage brings thee all increase, to crowne
p. 387	UNGATHERED 22	4	will all turne dust, & may not make me swell.
p. 387	UNGATHERED 22	5	Let such as iustly haue out=liu'd all prayse,
p. 388	UNGATHERED 23	7	If all the vulgar Tongues, that speake this day,
p. 389	UNGATHERED 23	11	As, now, of all men, it is call'd thy Trade:
p. 389	UNGATHERED 24	20	Had cloath'd him so. Here's all I can supply
p. 390	UNGATHERED 25	8	All, that was euer writ in brasse.
p. 390	UNGATHERED 26	5	'Tis true, and all mens suffrage. But these wayes
p. 391	UNGATHERED 26	10	The truth, but gropes, and vrgeth all by chance;
p. 391	UNGATHERED 26	39	Of all, that insolent Greece, or haughtie Rome
p. 391	UNGATHERED 26	42	To whom all Scenes of Europe homage owe.
p. 391	UNGATHERED 26	43	He was not of an age, but for all time!
p. 391	UNGATHERED 26	44	And all the Muses still were in their prime,
p. 392	UNGATHERED 26	55	Yet must I not giue Nature all: Thy Art,
p. 393	UNGATHERED 27	12	All false-hood vnder feete.
p. 395	UNGATHERED 29	11	Calme Brutus tenor start; but all along
p. 396	UNGATHERED 30	2	A Friend at all; or, if at all, to thee:
p. 396	UNGATHERED 30	16	That all Earth look'd on; and that earth, all Eyes!
p. 397	UNGATHERED 30	31	Did all so strike me, as I cry'd, who can
p. 397	UNGATHERED 30	52	Of all that reade thy Poly-Olbyon.
p. 398	UNGATHERED 30	90	To all thy vertuous, and well chosen Friends,
p. 399	UNGATHERED 31	8	Code, Digests, Pandects of all faemale glory!
p. 399	UNGATHERED 31	10	Vpon her selfe) to all her sexe!
p. 399	UNGATHERED 31	14	All Circles had their spring and end
p. 399	UNGATHERED 31	17	All that was solid, in the name
p. 400	UNGATHERED 31	38	Of Angells, and all witnesses of light,
p. 400	UNGATHERED 32	9	And doth deserue all muniments of praise,
p. 402	UNGATHERED 34	15	By all your Titles, & whole style at ones
p. 403	UNGATHERED 34	30	And all men eccho you haue made a Masque.
p. 404	UNGATHERED 34	43	Court Hieroglyphicks! & all Artes affoord
p. 404	UNGATHERED 34	60	His name is #Skeuopoios wee all knowe,
p. 404	UNGATHERED 34	65	All in ye Worke! And soe shall still for Ben:
p. 406	UNGATHERED 34	99	Of all ye Worthyes hope t'outlast thy one,
p. 406	UNGATHERED 34	104	Wth all Remonstrance make an honest man.
p. 406	UNGATHERED 35	4	All kings to doe ye self same deeds wth some!
p. 407	UNGATHERED 35	21	An Earle of show: for all thy worke is showe:
p. 408	UNGATHERED 36	12	Will well designe thee, to be viewd of all
p. 410	UNGATHERED 38	12	Both learned, and vnlearned, all write Playes.
p. 410	UNGATHERED 39	5	All which thou hast incurr'd deseruedly:
p. 411	UNGATHERED 40	6	to all good Nations.
p. 412	UNGATHERED 41	6	The gladdest ground to all the numbred-five,
p. 413	UNGATHERED 41	21	But, that which summes all, is the Eglantine,
p. 413	UNGATHERED 41	31	All, pouring their full showre of graces downe,
p. 414	UNGATHERED 41	42	Most venerable. Cause of all our ioy.
p. 414	UNGATHERED 41	47	Who mad'st us happy all, in thy reflexe,
p. 414	UNGATHERED 41	54	Through all the lines of this circumference,
p. 414	UNGATHERED 41	55	T'imprint in all purg'd hearts this virgin sence,
p. 415	UNGATHERED 42	9	Or why to like; they found, it all was new,
p. 415	UNGATHERED 42	26	A Say-master, hath studied all the tricks
p. 415	UNGATHERED 42	28	Yo'haue all the Mysteries of Wits new Mint,
p. 416	UNGATHERED 45	5	And I sweare by all the light
p. 417	UNGATHERED 45	15	morts, and mirkins that wagg all,
p. 419	UNGATHERED 47	7	God blesse them all, and keepe them safe:
p. 419	UNGATHERED 48	8	And better Blason them, then all their Coates,
p. 423	UNGATHERED 50	15	Yet ware; thou mayst do all things cruellie:
p. 657	L. CONVIVALES	1	Welcome all, who lead or follow,
p. 657	L. CONVIVALES	5	All his Answers are Divine,
p. 657	L. CONVIVALES	7	Hang up all the poor Hop-Drinkers,
p. 657	L. CONVIVALES	14	Ply it, and you all are mounted;
p. 657	L. CONVIVALES	17	Pays all Debts, cures all Diseases,
p. 657	L. CONVIVALES	19	Welcome all, who lead or follow,

all-gracious   frequency: 1   relative frequency: 0.00001
    p. 127 UNDERWOOD 1.1   9 3. All-gracious God, the Sinners sacrifice,

all-vertuous   frequency: 1   relative frequency: 0.00001
    p. 68 EPIGRAMS 106   3 All-vertuous HERBERT! on whose euery part

allay   frequency: 3   relative frequency: 0.00004
    p. 158 UNDERWOOD 14   10 Chance that the Friends affection proves Allay
    p. 173 UNDERWOOD 22   5 A vertue, like Allay, so gone
    p. 204 UNDERWOOD 43   42 There were some pieces of as base allay,

allege. See "t<o>'alledge."

allegorike   frequency: 1   relative frequency: 0.00001
    p. 360 UNGATHERED 6   t1 Ode. allegorike.

allen   frequency: 2   relative frequency: 0.00002
    p. 56 EPIGRAMS 89   t1 TO EDWARD ALLEN.
    p. 57 EPIGRAMS 89   8 That ALLEN, I should pause to publish thee?

alley. See "popes-head-alley."

alleyn. See "allen."

allied   frequency: 1   relative frequency: 0.00001
    p. 215 UNDERWOOD 44   66 Borne, bred, allied? what's he dare tutor us?

allies   frequency: 2   relative frequency: 0.00002
    p. 224 UNDERWOOD 50   27 Or your Allies, you make your bookes your
                             friends,
    p. 399 UNGATHERED 31   3 Transmitt it to your Nephewes, ffreinds,
                             Allies,

allmighty   frequency: 1   relative frequency: 0.00001
    p. 406 UNGATHERED 34 92 Allmighty. Architecture? who noe less

allotted   frequency: 1   relative frequency: 0.00001
    p. 311 HORACE 2   125 The place allotted it, with decent thewes.

allow   frequency: 4   relative frequency: 0.00005
    See also "t<o>'allow."
    p. 41 EPIGRAMS 43   7 Yet dare not, to my thought, lest hope allow
    p. 75 EPIGRAMS 116   14 Vertuously practise must at least allow
    p. 309 HORACE 2   77 A Roman to Caecilius will allow,
    p. 379 UNGATHERED 12   9 And allow you for each particular mile,

allowance   frequency: 1   relative frequency: 0.00001
    p. 241 UNDERWOOD 68   10 So, the allowance from the King to use,

allow'd   frequency: 4   relative frequency: 0.00005
    p. 95 FOREST 2   61 Where comes no guest, but is allow'd to eate,
    p. 138 UNDERWOOD 2.6   8 That the Bride (allow'd a Maid)
    p. 164 UNDERWOOD 15   84 Great, brave, and fashion'd folke, these are
                             allow'd
    p. 414 UNGATHERED 42   6 How well I lov'd Truth: I was scarce allow'd

allowed   frequency: 1   relative frequency: 0.00001
    See also "allow'd," "alow'd."
    p. 253 UNDERWOOD 75   31 And the allowed warre:

allowes   frequency: 1   relative frequency: 0.00001
    p. 263 UNDERWOOD 78   29 Allowes them? Then, what copies shall be had,

allows. See "allowes."

alloy   frequency: 1   relative frequency: 0.00001
    See also "allay."
    p. 415 UNGATHERED 42 27 Of Finenesse, and alloy: follow his hint,

all's   frequency: 2   relative frequency: 0.00002
    p. 128 UNDERWOOD 1.1 24 All's done in me.
    p. 189 UNDERWOOD 37   3 Then to your love, and gift. And all's but due.

allures   frequency: 1   relative frequency: 0.00001
    p. 39 EPIGRAMS 41   3 Such her quaint practise is, so it allures,

almanacks   frequency: 1   relative frequency: 0.00001
    p. 59 EPIGRAMS 92   13 And vnto whom: They are the almanacks

almanacs. See "almanacks."

almes   frequency: 1   relative frequency: 0.00001
     p. 288 U'WOOD 84.9   192 Her solemne houres she spent, or giving Almes,

almes-basket   frequency: 1   relative frequency: 0.00001
    *p. 493 TO HIMSELF   30 Needs set them, but, the almes-basket of wit.

almightie   frequency: 1   relative frequency: 0.00001
     p. 113 FOREST 12   2 And almost euery vice, almightie gold,

almighties   frequency: 1   relative frequency: 0.00001
     p. 236 UNDERWOOD 63   8 That the Almighties will to you is such:

almighty. See "allmighty," "almightie."

almond   frequency: 1   relative frequency: 0.00001
     p. 412 UNGATHERED 41   9 The second string is the sweet Almond bloome

almonds   frequency: 1   relative frequency: 0.00001
     p. 412 UNGATHERED 41   3 The M. the Myrtle, A. the Almonds clame,

almost   frequency: 11   relative frequency: 0.00015
     p. 48 EPIGRAMS 65   10 Almost all wayes, to any better course.
     p. 48 EPIGRAMS 66   6 Durst valour make, almost, but not a crime.
     p. 66 EPIGRAMS 102   7 Almost, is exercis'd: and scarse one knowes,
     p. 79 EPIGRAMS 125   10 I could adore, almost t<o>'idolatrie.
     p. 113 FOREST 12   2 And almost euery vice, almightie gold,
     p. 114 FOREST 12   34 Almost you haue, or may haue, when you will?
     p. 116 FOREST 13   1 'Tis growne almost a danger to speake true
     p. 118 FOREST 13   75 And almost, all dayes after, while they liue;
     p. 156 UNDERWOOD 13   99 And almost deifie the Authors! make
     p. 171 UNDERWOOD 20   5 At fifty yeares, almost, to value it,
     p. 269 UNDERWOOD 83   11 Hee's good, as great. I am almost a stone!

alms. See "almes," "almes-basket."

aloft   frequency: 1   relative frequency: 0.00001
     p. 157 UNDERWOOD 13   152 Aloft, grow lesse and streightned, full of knot;

alone   frequency: 32   relative frequency: 0.00046
    See also "diana'alone," "so'alone."
   **p. 113 PANEGYRE   1 Heau'n now not striues, alone, our brests to fill
     p. 35 EPIGRAMS 28   12 He doth, at meales, alone, his pheasant eate,
     p. 46 EPIGRAMS 60   10 But sauer of my countrey thee alone.
     p. 60 EPIGRAMS 93   1 How like a columne, RADCLIFFE, left
                               alone
     p. 62 EPIGRAMS 96   3 That so alone canst iudge, so'alone dost make:
     p. 104 FOREST 7   4 Let her alone, shee will court you.
     p. 114 FOREST 12   41 It is the Muse, alone, can raise to heauen,
     p. 118 FOREST 13   55 Of vertue, which you tread? what if alone?
     p. 120 FOREST 14   20 And he, with his best Genius left alone.
     p. 134 UNDERWOOD 2.4   19 As alone there triumphs to the life
     p. 146 UNDERWOOD 6   20 In love, doth not alone help forth
     p. 157 UNDERWOOD 13   134 Alone in money, but in manners too.
     p. 163 UNDERWOOD 15   33 Against his Maker; high alone with weeds,
     p. 171 UNDERWOOD 19   24 As would make shift, to make himselfe alone,
     p. 173 UNDERWOOD 22   14 In whom alone Love lives agen?
     p. 187 UNDERWOOD 33   40 Alone, but all thy ranke a reverend Name.
     p. 191 UNDERWOOD 38   8 Alone lend succours, and this furie stay,
     p. 192 UNDERWOOD 38   52 As not alone the Cure, but scarre be faire.
     p. 216 UNDERWOOD 45   12 'Tis vertue alone, or nothing, that knits
                               friends:
     p. 237 UNDERWOOD 64   19 'T is not alone the Merchant, but the Clowne,
     p. 257 UNDERWOOD 75   157 Alone, and such a race,
     p. 258 UNDERWOOD 75   184 So great; his Body now alone projects the shade.
     p. 277 U'WOOD 84.4   3 This worke I can performe alone;
     p. 282 U'WOOD 84.8   21 'Tis Vertue alone, is true Nobilitie.
     p. 321 HORACE 2   342 Plaine phrase, my Piso's, as alone, t<o>'approve
     p. 335 HORACE 2   632 Alone, without a rivall, by his will.
     p. 339 HORACE 1   25 .... alone .. ..
     p. 367 UNGATHERED 6   36 Thy tunes alone;
     p. 368 UNGATHERED 6   63 When him alone we sing)
     p. 371 UNGATHERED 9   4 That durst be that in Court: a vertu' alone
     p. 391 UNGATHERED 26   38 Leaue thee alone, for the comparison
     p. 412 UNGATHERED 41   11 As it, alone, (and onely it) had roome,

along   frequency: 7   relative frequency: 0.00010
   **p. 114 PANEGYRE   46 Along with him, and the same trouble proue.
   **p. 117 PANEGYRE   154 Of heauen is discharg'd along the skie:
     p. 85 EPIGRAMS 133   49 Or magick sacrifice, they past along!
     p. 167 UNDERWOOD 15   175 Goe, quit 'hem all. And take along with thee,

along (cont.)
       p. 264 UNDERWOOD 79   26 Who walkes on Earth as May still went along,
       p. 311 HORACE 2   155 With weightie sorrow hurles us all along,
       p. 395 UNGATHERED 29   11 Calme Brutus tenor start; but all along

along'st   frequency: 1 relative frequency: 0.00001
       p. 97 FOREST 3   17 Along'st the curled woods, and painted meades,

aloof. See "aloofe."

aloofe   frequency: 1 relative frequency: 0.00001
       p. 175 UNDERWOOD 23   35 But sing high and aloofe,

aloud   frequency: 5 relative frequency: 0.00007
       p. 62 EPIGRAMS 97   7 He wont was to encounter me, aloud,
       p. 74 EPIGRAMS 115   2 Him not, aloud, that boasts so good a fame:
       p. 261 UNDERWOOD 77   28 Aloud; and (happ'ly) it may last as long.
       p. 319 HORACE 2   285 Hide faults, pray to the Gods, and wish aloud
       p. 335 HORACE 2   653 And cry aloud, Helpe, gentle Countrey-men,

alow'd   frequency: 1 relative frequency: 0.00001
       p. 155 UNDERWOOD 13   88 Carryed and wrapt, I only am alow'd

alpes   frequency: 1 relative frequency: 0.00001
       p. 374 UNGATHERED 10   16 Here, vp the Alpes (not so plaine as to
                                  Dunstable)

alphius   frequency: 1 relative frequency: 0.00001
       p. 291 UNDERWOOD 85   67 These thoughts when Usurer Alphius, now about

alphonso   frequency: 3 relative frequency: 0.00004
       p. 82 EPIGRAMS 130   1 To vrge, my lou'd ALPHONSO, that bold
                                  fame
       p. 82 EPIGRAMS 130   t1 TO ALPHONSO FERRABOSCO, on his
                                  Booke.
       p. 82 EPIGRAMS 131   1 When we doe giue, ALPHONSO, to the light,

alps. See "alpes."

already   frequency: 2 relative frequency: 0.00002
       p. 115 FOREST 12   74 I haue already vs'd some happy houres,
       p. 368 UNGATHERED 6   65 Who (see) already hath ore-flowne

als<o>'her   frequency: 1 relative frequency: 0.00001
       p. 274 U'WOOD 84.1   37 Is sung: as als<o>'her getting up

also   frequency: 3 relative frequency: 0.00004
    See also "als<o>'her."
       p. 95 FOREST 2   64 That is his Lordships, shall be also mine.
       p. 307 HORACE 2   65 In using also of new words, to be
       p. 309 HORACE 2   109 Were also clos'd: But, who the man should be,

altar   frequency: 2 relative frequency: 0.00002
    See also "alter."
       p. 292 UNDERWOOD 86   28 Thrice 'bout thy Altar with their Ivory feet.
       p. 305 HORACE 2   20 Diana's Grove, or Altar, with the bor-

altars   frequency: 3 relative frequency: 0.00004
       p. 104 FOREST 8   4 To thy altars, by their nights
       p. 173 UNDERWOOD 22   19 His Altars kept from the Decay,
       p. 288 U'WOOD 84.9   188 The holy Altars, when it least presumes.

alter   frequency: 5 relative frequency: 0.00007
       p. 315 HORACE 2   237 These studies alter now, in one, growne man;
       p. 367 UNGATHERED 6   30 Or alter kinde.
       p. 382 UNGATHERED 16   6 presentes a Royall Alter of fayre peace,
       p. 383 UNGATHERED 16   9 hee freely bringes; and on[e] this Alter layes
       p. 403 UNGATHERED 34   26 Noe veluet Sheath you weare, will alter kynde.

alter'd   frequency: 1 relative frequency: 0.00001
       p. 117 FOREST 13   16 Of Fortune, haue not alter'd yet my looke,

alternate   frequency: 1 relative frequency: 0.00001
       p. 246 UNDERWOOD 70   95 But fate doth so alternate the designe,

although   frequency: 12 relative frequency: 0.00017
       p. 61 EPIGRAMS 95   25 Although to write be lesser then to doo,
       p. 97 FOREST 3   36 Although the coldest of the yeere!
       p. 167 UNDERWOOD 15   149 Although, perhaps it has, what's that to me,
       p. 200 UNDERWOOD 42   18 When he is furious, love, although not lust.

although (cont.)
    p. 219 UNDERWOOD 47   49 Although my Fame, to his, not under-heares,
    p. 231 UNDERWOOD 56   25 By this, although you fancie not the man,
    p. 245 UNDERWOOD 70   71 Although it fall, and die that night;
    p. 254 UNDERWOOD 75   56 Although that thou, O Sun, at our intreaty
                              stay!
    p. 305 HORACE 2   6 Admitted to the sight, although his friends,
    p. 335 HORACE 2   652 Into a pit, or hole; although he call,
    p. 335 HORACE 2   658 Not thence be sav'd, although indeed he could?
    p. 418 UNGATHERED 46   7 Although the gate were hard, the gayne is sweete.

alwayes   frequency: 11   relative frequency: 0.00015
    p. 52 EPIGRAMS 74   8 As is thy conscience, which is alwayes one:
    p. 63 EPIGRAMS 98   9 Be alwayes to thy gather'd selfe the same:
    p. 81 EPIGRAMS 128   8 And perfect in a circle alwayes meet.
    p. 85 EPIGRAMS 133   54 Alwayes at hand, to aide the merry Muses.
    p. 99 FOREST 3   98 He alwayes giues what he knowes meet;
    p. 131 UNDERWOOD 2.1   7 And it is not alwayes face,
    p. 168 UNDERWOOD 15   186 Thou shrinke or start not, but be alwayes one;
    p. 264 UNDERWOOD 79   37 The fairest flowers are alwayes found;
    p. 317 HORACE 2   253 To children; we must alwayes dwell, and stay
    p. 329 HORACE 2   524 Nor alwayes doth the loosed Bow, hit that
    p. 339 HORACE 1   32 .. .. alwayes ...

always. See "alwayes."

am   frequency: 60   relative frequency: 0.00086
    See also "i'am," "i'm."

amadis   frequency: 1   relative frequency: 0.00001
    p. 203 UNDERWOOD 43   29 Had I compil'd from Amadis de Gaule,

amaze   frequency: 1   relative frequency: 0.00001
    p. 169 UNDERWOOD 18   4 Then like, then love; and now would they amaze?

amazed   frequency: 1   relative frequency: 0.00001
  **p. 114 PANEGYRE   35 As on a wonder: some amazed stood,

amazement   frequency: 2   relative frequency: 0.00002
    p. 284 U'WOOD 84.9   78 With silence, and amazement! not with rude,
    p. 361 UNGATHERED 1   25 till giddie with amazement I fell downe

ambassadour   frequency: 1   relative frequency: 0.00001
    p. 213 UNDERWOOD 44   4 T'have wak'd, if sleeping, Spaines Ambassadour,

amber   frequency: 2   relative frequency: 0.00002
    p. 57 EPIGRAMS 90   9 Not though that haire grew browne, which once was
                              amber,
    p. 105 FOREST 8   32 Lying for the spirit of amber.

ambition   frequency: 4   relative frequency: 0.00005
    p. 66 EPIGRAMS 102   15 Of what ambition, faction, pride can raise;
    p. 73 EPIGRAMS 113   12 Who'in such ambition can but follow thee.
    p. 234 UNDERWOOD 60   14 Ambition to become a Starre,
    p. 395 UNGATHERED 29   10 Caesar's ambition, Cato's libertie,

ambitious   frequency: 7   relative frequency: 0.00010
    See also "th'ambitious."
  **p. 114 PANEGYRE   52 As our ambitious dames, when they make feast,
    p. 96 FOREST 2   101 Those proud, ambitious heaps, and nothing else,
    p. 96 FOREST 3   5 That at great times, art no ambitious guest
    p. 167 UNDERWOOD 15   168 Ambitious, factious, superstitious, lowd
    p. 333 HORACE 2   587 Hee, that's ambitious in the race to touch
    p. 403 UNGATHERED 34   19 Or are you soe ambitious 'boue your peers!
    p. 408 UNGATHERED 36   6 Thou'rt too ambitious: and dost fear in vaine!

ambitiously   frequency: 1   relative frequency: 0.00001
    p. 218 UNDERWOOD 47   6 To speake my selfe out too ambitiously,

ambling   frequency: 1   relative frequency: 0.00001
    p. 396 UNGATHERED 30   4 Those ambling visits, passe in verse, betweene

ambrosiac. See "ambrosiack."

ambrosiack   frequency: 1   relative frequency: 0.00001
    p. 182 UNDERWOOD 27   27 Or Constables Ambrosiack Muse

amen   frequency: 1   relative frequency: 0.00001
    p. 256 UNDERWOOD 75   128 The Solemne Quire cryes, Joy; and they
                              returne, Amen.

amend. See "t<o>'amend."

amends   frequency: 2   relative frequency: 0.00002
    p. 46 EPIGRAMS 62   8 To make amends, yo'are thought a wholesome
                              creature.
    p. 384 UNGATHERED 18   14 Hymens amends, to make it worth his fault.

amiable   frequency: 2   relative frequency: 0.00002
    p. 364 UNGATHERED 4   3 If a Bird so amiable,
    p. 662 INSCRIPTS. 2   2 vnto the bright, and amiable

amid'   frequency: 1   relative frequency: 0.00001
    p. 307 HORACE 2   42 A Dolphin, and a Boare amid' the floods.

amidst   frequency: 2   relative frequency: 0.00002
    See also "amid'."
    p. 65 EPIGRAMS 101   23 Of which wee'll speake our minds, amidst our
                              meate;
    p. 339 HORACE 1   44 . ... amidst ... .

amiss. See "amisse."

amisse   frequency: 2   relative frequency: 0.00002
    p. 188 UNDERWOOD 34   15 That heaven should make no more; or should
                              amisse,
    p. 315 HORACE 2   200 Who nought assaies unaptly, or amisse?

amitie   frequency: 2   relative frequency: 0.00002
    p. 190 UNDERWOOD 37   19 Little know they, that professe Amitie,
    p. 283 U'WOOD 84.9   36 I envie it the Angels amitie!

amity. See "amitie."

among   frequency: 12   relative frequency: 0.00017
    See also "amonge."
    p. 30 EPIGRAMS 12   1 SHIFT, here, in towne, not meanest among
                              squires,
    p. 128 UNDERWOOD 1.1   45 12. Among thy Saints elected to abide,
    p. 161 UNDERWOOD 14   80 Among my commings in, and see it mount,
    p. 173 UNDERWOOD 22   28 Among which faithful troope am I.
    p. 181 UNDERWOOD 27   12 Shine more, then she, the Stars among?
    p. 207 UNDERWOOD 43   93 The puritie of Language; and among
    p. 214 UNDERWOOD 44   51 Up among Nations. In the stead of bold
    p. 224 UNDERWOOD 50   17 Among the daily Ruines that fall foule,
    p. 235 UNDERWOOD 62   1 Great CHARLES, among the holy gifts of
                              grace
    p. 291 UNDERWOOD 85   61 Among these Cates how glad the sight doth come
    p. 293 UNDERWOOD 86   35 Or why, my well-grac'd words among,
    p. 369 UNGATHERED 6   105 Among the starres should be resign'd

amonge   frequency: 1   relative frequency: 0.00001
    p. 387 UNGATHERED 22   1 Sonnes, seeke not me amonge these polish'd
                              stones:

amongst   frequency: 6   relative frequency: 0.00008
    See also "mongst," "'mongst," "'mong'st."
    p. 34 EPIGRAMS 22   9 Hath plac'd amongst her virgin-traine:
    p. 167 UNDERWOOD 15   171 (Because th'are every where amongst Man-kind
    p. 171 UNDERWOOD 20   3 Amongst my many other, that I may
    p. 199 UNDERWOOD 41   21 Or like a Ghost walke silent amongst men,
    p. 284 U'WOOD 84.9   84 Amongst her Peeres, those Princes of all good!
    p. 290 UNDERWOOD 85   37 Who (amongst these delights) would not forget

amorous   frequency: 2   relative frequency: 0.00002
  **p. 114 PANEGYRE   50 The amorous Citie spar'd no ornament,
    p. 108 FOREST 10A   3 Thy thoughtes did neuer melt in amorous fire,

amphion   frequency: 1   relative frequency: 0.00001
    p. 327 HORACE 2   483 Amphion, too, that built the Theban towres,

ample   frequency: 6   relative frequency: 0.00008
    p. 87 EPIGRAMS 133   138 And, after, swom abroad in ample flakes,
    p. 141 UNDERWOOD 2.9   18 Front, an ample field of snow;
    p. 244 UNDERWOOD 70   49 By him, so ample, full, and round,
    p. 262 UNDERWOOD 78   10 Where all heroique ample thoughts doe meet:
    p. 390 UNGATHERED 26   2 Am I thus ample to thy Booke, and Fame:
    p. 395 UNGATHERED 29   12 Keepe due proportion in the ample song,

an   frequency: 159   relative frequency: 0.00230

anacreon   frequency: 4   relative frequency: 0.00005
    p.   65 EPIGRAMS 101   31 Of which had HORACE, or ANACREON
                             tasted,
    p. 136 UNDERWOOD 2.5   14 So, Anacreon drawne the Ayre
    p. 181 UNDERWOOD 27   6 In whom Anacreon once did joy,
    p. 199 UNDERWOOD 42   2 As Horace fat; or as Anacreon old;

anacreons   frequency: 1   relative frequency: 0.00001
   *p. 493 TO HIMSELF   43 Or thine owne Horace, or Anacreons Lyre;

anagram   frequency: 2   relative frequency: 0.00002
    p.   51 EPIGRAMS 73   16 Item, your mistris anagram, i' your hilt.
    p. 412 UNGATHERED 40   24 the Anagram of ALICE.

anagrams   frequency: 1   relative frequency: 0.00001
    p. 204 UNDERWOOD 43   35 Or pomp'd for those hard trifles, Anagrams,

analysde   frequency: 1   relative frequency: 0.00001
    p. 364 UNGATHERED 4   t1 The Phoenix Analysde.

analysed. See "analysde."

anarchie   frequency: 1   relative frequency: 0.00001
    p. 218 UNDERWOOD 47   10 That live in the wild Anarchie of Drinke,

anarchy   frequency: 1   relative frequency: 0.00001
    See also "anarchie."
    p.   74 EPIGRAMS 115   12 Doe all, that longs to the anarchy of drinke,

anatomie   frequency: 1   relative frequency: 0.00001
    p. 179 UNDERWOOD 25   37 When her dead essence (like the Anatomie

anatomy. See "anatomie."

ancestors   frequency: 5   relative frequency: 0.00007
    See also "ancestours."
    p. 121 FOREST 14   40 With dust of ancestors, in graues but dwell.
    p. 215 UNDERWOOD 44   78 Our Ancestors impos'd on Prince and State.
    p. 281 U'WOOD 84.8   10 Boast not these Titles of your Ancestors;
    p. 281 U'WOOD 84.8   18 Up to their Ancestors; the rivers side,
    p. 323 HORACE 2   399 Our Ancestors did Plautus numbers praise,

ancestours   frequency: 1   relative frequency: 0.00001
    p. 233 UNDERWOOD 59   20 And was your Fathers! All your Ancestours!

ancient   frequency: 4   relative frequency: 0.00005
    See also "antient."
    p.   89 EPIGRAMS 133 190 An ancient pur-blinde fletcher, with a high nose;
    p.   93 FOREST 2   5 Or stayre, or courts; but stand'st an ancient
                             pile,
    p. 228 UNDERWOOD 53   4 Me thought I read the ancient Art of Thrace,
    p. 290 UNDERWOOD 85   23 Then now beneath some ancient Oke he may,

and   frequency: 2674   relative frequency: 0.03870
    See also "&" (which follows this entry),
             "&c." (which follows "etcetera"),
             "foot-and-halfe-foot."

&   frequency: 29   relative frequency: 0.00041

anenst   frequency: 1   relative frequency: 0.00001
    p.   86 EPIGRAMS 133   75 And many a sinke pour'd out her rage anenst 'hem;

anent. See "anenst."

anew. See "a-new."

angel. See "angell."

angell   frequency: 1   relative frequency: 0.00001
    p. 238 UNDERWOOD 66   2 And by an Angell, to the blessed'st Maid,

angells   frequency: 2   relative frequency: 0.00002
    p. 144 UNDERWOOD 3   17 They say the Angells marke each Deed,
    p. 400 UNGATHERED 31   38 Of Angells, and all witnesses of light,

angelo   frequency: 1   relative frequency: 0.00001
    p. 260 UNDERWOOD 77   7 Titian, or Raphael, Michael Angelo,

angels   frequency: 9   relative frequency: 0.00013
    See also "angells," "arch-angels."
    p. 128 UNDERWOOD 1.1   46 And with thy Angels, placed side, by side,
    p. 130 UNDERWOOD 1.3   3 The Angels so did sound it,
    p. 144 UNDERWOOD 3   22 Of Angels should be driven
    p. 239 UNDERWOOD 67   21 The Angels from their Spheares:
    p. 255 UNDERWOOD 75   84 With Angels, Muse, to speake these: Nothing
                             can
    p. 270 UNDERWOOD 83   63 Let Angels sing her glories, who did call
    p. 283 U'WOOD 84.9   36 I envie it the Angels amitie!
    p. 285 U'WOOD 84.9   86 Angels, Arch-angels, Principalities,
    p. 286 U'WOOD 84.9   146 Equall with Angels, and Co-heires of it?

anger   frequency: 4   relative frequency: 0.00005
    p. 82 EPIGRAMS 130   5 Declineth anger, perswades clemencie,
    p. 164 UNDERWOOD 15   62 Not make a verse; Anger; or laughter would,
    p. 193 UNDERWOOD 38   88 Streight puts off all his Anger, and doth kisse
    p. 311 HORACE 2   154 Or urgeth us to anger; and anon

angle   frequency: 1   relative frequency: 0.00001
 **p. 113 PANEGYRE   6 To euery nooke and angle of his realme.

angles   frequency: 2   relative frequency: 0.00002
    p. 232 UNDERWOOD 59   5 To hit in angles, and to clash with time:
    p. 399 UNGATHERED 31   16 Or without angles, it was shee!

angrie   frequency: 2   relative frequency: 0.00002
    p. 69 EPIGRAMS 107   31 Come, be not angrie, you are HVNGRY; eate;
    p. 193 UNDERWOOD 38   71 He cannot angrie be, but all must quake,

angrier   frequency: 1   relative frequency: 0.00001
    p. 294 UNDERWOOD 87   23 And then rough Adria, angrier, farre;

angry   frequency: 9   relative frequency: 0.00013
    See also "angrie."
    p. 70 EPIGRAMS 108   10 But 's angry for the Captayne, still: is such.
    p. 144 UNDERWOOD 4   5 O, be not angry with those fires,
    p. 311 HORACE 2   133 Her voyce, and angry Chremes chafes out-right
    p. 311 HORACE 2   150 The angry brow; the sportive, wanton things;
    p. 313 HORACE 2   172 Keepe him still active, angry, un-appeas'd,
    p. 315 HORACE 2   227 Soone angry, and soone pleas'd, is sweet, or
                             sowre,
    p. 317 HORACE 2   282 The angry, and love those that feare t<o>'offend.
    p. 329 HORACE 2   536 Angry. Sometimes, I heare good Homer snore.
    p. 354 HORACE 1   647 Under ... angry ....

animated   frequency: 1   relative frequency: 0.00001
    p. 219 UNDERWOOD 47   53 And animated Porc'lane of the Court,

anne   frequency: 1   relative frequency: 0.00001
    p. 405 UNGATHERED 34   68 Swim wthout Corke! Why, thank ye good Queen
                             Anne.

annexed   frequency: 1   relative frequency: 0.00001
    p. 235 UNDERWOOD 62   2 Annexed to thy Person, and thy place,

anniversarie   frequency: 1   relative frequency: 0.00001
    p. 249 UNDERWOOD 72   t2 An Epigram Anniversarie.

anniversary   frequency: 1   relative frequency: 0.00001
    See also "anniversarie."
    p. 236 UNDERWOOD 64   t3 On his Anniversary Day.

annoy'd   frequency: 1   relative frequency: 0.00001
    p. 101 FOREST 4   34 The engines, that haue them annoy'd;

annual. See "annval."

annuitie   frequency: 1   relative frequency: 0.00001
    p. 259 UNDERWOOD 76   11 A large hundred Markes annuitie,

annuity. See "annuitie."

annval   frequency: 1   relative frequency: 0.00001
    p. 36 EPIGRAMS 29   t1 TO SIR ANNVAL TILTER.

anon   frequency: 1   relative frequency: 0.00001
    See also "anone."
    p. 311 HORACE 2   154 Or urgeth us to anger; and anon

anone   frequency: 1   relative frequency: 0.00001
    p. 317 HORACE 2   263 Present anone: Medea must not kill

another   frequency: 20   relative frequency: 0.00028
  **p. 116 PANEGYRE   119 One wickednesse another must defend;
    p. 39 EPIGRAMS 40   17 Earth, thou hast not such another.
    p. 103 FOREST 6   9 Then a thousand, then another
    p. 122 FOREST 15   22 Vpon my flesh t<o>'inflict another wound.
    p. 138 UNDERWOOD 2.6 36 May not claime another kisse.
    p. 139 UNDERWOOD 2.7 t1 Begging another, on colour of mending
    p. 142 U'WOOD 2.10   t1 Another Ladyes exception present at the hearing.
    p. 146 UNDERWOOD 6   t1 Another.
    p. 166 UNDERWOOD 15 125 Tilt one upon another, and now beare
    p. 186 UNDERWOOD 32   t1 Another to him.
    p. 193 UNDERWOOD 38   90 Upon the hope to have another sin
    p. 197 UNDERWOOD 40   10 Under another Name, I take your health;
    p. 202 UNDERWOOD 42   74 Another answers, 'Lasse, those Silkes are none,
    p. 254 UNDERWOOD 75   69 See, at another doore,
    p. 257 UNDERWOOD 75 140 Doe long to make themselves, so, another way:
    p. 269 UNDERWOOD 83   9 Stiffe! starke! my joynts 'gainst one another
                             knock!
    p. 279 U'WOOD 84.4   30 As it another Nature were,
    p. 287 U'WOOD 84.9   170 To another, Move; he went; To a third, Go,
    p. 339 HORACE 1   37 .... Another ....
    p. 380 UNGATHERED 12 51 Or any thing else that another should hide,

anothers   frequency: 4   relative frequency: 0.00005
    p. 27 EPIGRAMS 2   10 Made from the hazard of anothers shame:
    p. 36 EPIGRAMS 28   15 He keepes anothers wife, which is a spice
    p. 165 UNDERWOOD 15   87 He that will follow but anothers wife,
    p. 285 U'WOOD 84.9   115 And each shall know, there, one anothers face,

answer   frequency: 2   relative frequency: 0.00002
  See also "answere."
    p. 210 UNDERWOOD 43 173 But say, all sixe good men, what answer yee?
    p. 226 UNDERWOOD 52   t1 My Answer.

answer'd   frequency: 3   relative frequency: 0.00004
    p. 80 EPIGRAMS 126   6 I answer'd, DAPHNE now no paine can proue.
    p. 154 UNDERWOOD 13   59 Are they not worthy to be answer'd so,
    p. 245 UNDERWOOD 70   63 Each syllab'e answer'd, and was form'd, how
                             faire;

answere   frequency: 2   relative frequency: 0.00002
    p. 31 EPIGRAMS 12   20 His onely answere is to all, god payes.
    p. 87 EPIGRAMS 133 107 To answere me. And sure, it was th'intent

answering   frequency: 1   relative frequency: 0.00001
    p. 218 UNDERWOOD 47   t1 An Epistle answering to one that

answers   frequency: 2   relative frequency: 0.00002
    p. 202 UNDERWOOD 42   74 Another answers, 'Lasse, those Silkes are none,
    p. 657 L. CONVIVALES   5 All his Answers are Divine,

anticks   frequency: 1   relative frequency: 0.00001
    p. 402 UNGATHERED 34 13 Vizors or Anticks? or it comprhend

antics. See "anticks."

anticyra's   frequency: 1   relative frequency: 0.00001
    p. 325 HORACE 2   428 Their heads, which three Anticyra's cannot
                             heale.

antient   frequency: 3   relative frequency: 0.00004
    p. 225 UNDERWOOD 51   1 Haile, happie Genius of this antient pile!
    p. 274 U'WOOD 84.1   33 This, utter'd by an antient BARD,
    p. 319 HORACE 2   303 Thus, to his antient Art the Piper lent

antipathy   frequency: 1   relative frequency: 0.00001
    p. 52 EPIGRAMS 75   1 I Cannot thinke there's that antipathy

antiphates   frequency: 1   relative frequency: 0.00001
    p. 315 HORACE 2   205 Wonders forth after: As Antiphates,

antiquated   frequency: 1   relative frequency: 0.00001
    p. 392 UNGATHERED 26 53 But antiquated, and deserted lye

antique   frequency: 2   relative frequency: 0.00002
  See also "th'antique."
    p. 31 EPIGRAMS 14   8 What sight in searching the most antique springs!

antique (cont.)
    p. 413 UNGATHERED 41   19 Preserved, in her antique bed of Vert,

antiquitie   frequency: 3   relative frequency: 0.00004
    p. 67 EPIGRAMS 105   1 MADAME, had all antiquitie beene lost,
    p. 160 UNDERWOOD 14   60 Newnesse of Sense, Antiquitie of voyce!
    p. 176 UNDERWOOD 24   17 Times witnesse, herald of Antiquitie,

antiquities   frequency: 1   relative frequency: 0.00001
    p. 160 UNDERWOOD 14   40 Antiquities search'd! Opinions dis-esteem'd!

antiquity. See "antiquitie."

antwerp. See "antwerpe."

antwerpe   frequency: 1   relative frequency: 0.00001
    p. 85 EPIGRAMS 133   40 Or his to Antwerpe. Therefore, once more, list
    ho'.

anuile   frequency: 1   relative frequency: 0.00001
    p. 392 UNGATHERED 26   61 Vpon the Muses anuile: turne the same,

anvil. See "anuile," "anvile."

anvile   frequency: 1   relative frequency: 0.00001
    p. 333 HORACE 2   627 Hee'd bid, blot all: and to the anvile bring

any   frequency: 65   relative frequency: 0.00094
See also "may'any."
    p. 35 EPIGRAMS 27   3 If any sword could saue from Fates, ROE'S
    could;
    p. 35 EPIGRAMS 27   4 If any Muse out-liue their spight, his can;
    p. 35 EPIGRAMS 27   5 If any friends teares could restore, his would;
    p. 35 EPIGRAMS 27   6 If any pious life ere lifted man
    p. 38 EPIGRAMS 38   4 Any man else, you clap your hands, and rore,
    p. 48 EPIGRAMS 65   10 Almost all wayes, to any better course.
    p. 53 EPIGRAMS 77   2 That, any way, my booke should speake thy name:
    p. 58 EPIGRAMS 91   11 To any one, were enuie: which would liue
    p. 63 EPIGRAMS 97   14 Of any Madames, hath neadd squires, and must.
    p. 65 EPIGRAMS 101 37 Nor shall our cups make any guiltie men:
    p. 66 EPIGRAMS 103   6 Need any Muses praise to giue it fame?
    p. 76 EPIGRAMS 119   9 Dar'st breath in any ayre; and with safe skill,
    p. 81 EPIGRAMS 129   5 That scarse the Towne designeth any feast
    p. 93 FOREST 1   10 By any arte. Then wonder not,
    p. 105 FOREST 8   27 Any paines; yea, thinke it price,
    p. 105 FOREST 8   39 Dare entayle their loues on any,
    p. 109 FOREST 11   20 By many? scarse by any.
    p. 116 FOREST 13   2 Of any good minde, now: There are so few.
    p. 132 UNDERWOOD 2.2 18 Nor for any threat, or call,
    p. 138 UNDERWOOD 2.6 30 Whether any would up-braid
    p. 141 UNDERWOOD 2.9 27 Skin as smooth as any rush,
    p. 145 UNDERWOOD 5   14 In any curious peece you see
    p. 153 UNDERWOOD 13   24 Where any Deed is forc't, the Grace is mard.
    p. 154 UNDERWOOD 13   55 As farre as any poore Sword i' the Land.
    p. 155 UNDERWOOD 13   76 Of any, is a great and generous Deed:
    p. 168 UNDERWOOD 15 182 Thy person fit for any charge thou tak'st;
    p. 172 UNDERWOOD 21   2 His name in any mettall, it would breake.
    p. 188 UNDERWOOD 34   10 Any beliefe, in Madam Baud-bees bath,
    p. 194 UNDERWOOD 38 103 There is not any punishment, or paine,
    p. 198 UNDERWOOD 40   45 Weaknesse of braine, or any charme of Wine,
    p. 200 UNDERWOOD 42   31 As any Mercer; or the whale-bone man
    p. 201 UNDERWOOD 42   62 He would have done in verse, with any of those
    p. 202 UNDERWOOD 42   76 Any Comparison had with his Cheap-side.
    p. 202 UNDERWOOD 42   84 Or a Close-stoole so cas'd; or any fat
    p. 203 UNDERWOOD 43   14 To ruine any issue of the braine?
    p. 203 UNDERWOOD 43   20 Any, least loose, or s<c>urrile paper, lie
    p. 210 UNDERWOOD 43 154 Scap'd not his Justice any jot the more:
    p. 215 UNDERWOOD 44   83 Past any need of vertue. Let them care,
    p. 218 UNDERWOOD 47   20 Of any Companie but that they are in,
    p. 220 UNDERWOOD 47   63 'Mongst which, if I have any friendships sent,
    p. 221 UNDERWOOD 48   20 From any thought like sadnesse.
    p. 222 UNDERWOOD 49   5 And that as any are strooke, her breath creates
    p. 223 UNDERWOOD 49   23 I never stood for any place: my wit
    p. 227 UNDERWOOD 52   7 You were not tied, by any Painters Law,
    p. 228 UNDERWOOD 53   16 Nor any of their houshold, halfe so well.
    p. 231 UNDERWOOD 57   18 Nor any least fit
    p. 232 UNDERWOOD 57   27 nor any quick-warming-pan helpe him to bed,
    p. 278 U'WOOD 84.4   27 And so disdaining any tryer;
    p. 280 U'WOOD 84.4   62 Where it may run to any good;
    p. 291 UNDERWOOD 85   52 Into our Seas send any such:

any (cont.)
    p. 294 UNDERWOOD 87   22 Thou lighter then the barke of any tree,
    p. 317 HORACE 2   275 Any fourth man, to speake at all, aspire.
    p. 321 HORACE 2   331 As neither any God, were brought in there,
    p. 323 HORACE 2   379 Provided, ne're to yeeld, in any case
    p. 331 HORACE 2   561 So, any Poeme, fancied, or forth-brought
    p. 347 HORACE 1   356 .... any Crowne ... .
    p. 348 HORACE 1   388 .. .. any ...
    p. 379 UNGATHERED 12   15 He sayes to the world, let any man mend it,
    p. 380 UNGATHERED 12   51 Or any thing else that another should hide,
    p. 394 UNGATHERED 28   9 No stone in any wall here, but can tell
    p. 402 UNGATHERED 34   18 Will any of these express yor place? or witt?
    p. 404 UNGATHERED 34   58 Of any Art, besyde what he calls his!
    p. 417 UNGATHERED 45   33 Or if any strife bety'de
    p. 423 UNGATHERED 50   20 shall never dare do any thing but feare./
    p. 662 INSCRIPTS. 2   8 if any way she do rewarde thee

aonian. See "th'aonian."

apart   frequency: 1   relative frequency: 0.00001
    p. 234 UNDERWOOD 61   10 To see you set apart, thus, from the rest,

ape   frequency: 1   relative frequency: 0.00001
    See also "poet-ape."
    p. 132 UNDERWOOD 2.2   31 Or else one that plaid his Ape,

apollo   frequency: 7   relative frequency: 0.00010
    See also "apollo's."
    p. 55 EPIGRAMS 85   4 And why that bird was sacred to APOLLO,
    p. 221 UNDERWOOD 48   26 Thee still, and leave Apollo,
    p. 353 HORACE 1   579 .... of the singer Apollo, and Muses fam'd
    p. 366 UNGATHERED 6   12 Whil'st pleas'd Apollo
    p. 392 UNGATHERED 26   45 When like Apollo he came forth to warme
    p. 657 L. CONVIVALES   2 To the Oracle of Apollo.
    p. 657 L. CONVIVALES   20 To the Oracle of Apollo.

apollo's   frequency: 4   relative frequency: 0.00005
    p. 98 FOREST 3   51 APOLLO'S harpe, and HERMES lyre
                                resound,
    p. 149 UNDERWOOD 9   10 That sits in shadow of Apollo's tree.
    p. 183 UNDERWOOD 29   23 And Apollo's Musique die,
    p. 329 HORACE 2   501 All which I tell, lest when Apollo's nam'd,

apologetic. See "apologetique."

apologetique   frequency: 1   relative frequency: 0.00001
    p. 145 UNDERWOOD 5   t2 A Song Apologetique.

apostacie   frequency: 1   relative frequency: 0.00001
    p. 363 UNGATHERED 3   15 Straines fancie vnto foule Apostacie,

apostasy. See "apostacie."

apostle   frequency: 1   relative frequency: 0.00001
    p. 262 UNDERWOOD 78   15 When the Apostle Barnabee the bright

apostrophe   frequency: 1   relative frequency: 0.00001
    p. 288 U'WOOD 84.9   210 In manner of a daily Apostrophe,

apothecary. See "'pothecarie."

#apotheosis   frequency: 1   relative frequency: 0.00001
    p. 282 U'WOOD 84.9   t5 Her #APOTHEOSIS, or Relation to the Saints.

appear. See "appeare," "t<o>'appeare."

appear'd   frequency: 2   relative frequency: 0.00002
    p. 85 EPIGRAMS 133   61 In the first lawes appear'd that vgly monster,
    p. 233 UNDERWOOD 59   23 Of fortune! when, or death appear'd, or bands!

appeare   frequency: 11   relative frequency: 0.00015
    p. 65 EPIGRAMS 101   25 To this, if ought appeare, which I not know of,
    p. 170 UNDERWOOD 18   8 Crooked appeare; so that doth my conceipt:
    p. 174 UNDERWOOD 22   34 Appeare, and that to shortest view,
    p. 244 UNDERWOOD 70   51 As though his age imperfect might appeare,
    p. 254 UNDERWOOD 75   53 Whose Majesties appeare,
    p. 276 U'WOOD 84.3   15 Till, like her face, it doe appeare,
    p. 286 U'WOOD 84.9   138 What love with mercy mixed doth appeare?
    p. 289 U'WOOD 84.9   220 Where first his Power will appeare, by call

appeare (cont.)
    p. 315 HORACE 2   218 The last doth from the midst dis-joyn'd appeare.
    p. 392 UNGATHERED 26   72 To see thee in our waters yet appeare,
    p. 421 UNGATHERED 48   44 And by their takeinge, lett it once appeare

appeares   frequency: 3   relative frequency: 0.00004
    p. 186 UNDERWOOD 32   15 When this appeares, just Lord, to your sharp
                              sight,
    p. 309 HORACE 2   85 Stamp'd to the time. As woods whose change
                              appeares
    p. 323 HORACE 2   382 Of Accius, and Ennius, rare appeares:

appears.   See "appeares."

appetite   frequency: 3   relative frequency: 0.00004
    p. 57 EPIGRAMS 90   4 At last, ease, appetite, and example wan
    p. 156 UNDERWOOD 13   107 Or appetite of offending, but a skill,
    p. 206 UNDERWOOD 43   86 So ravenous, and vast an appetite?

appetites   frequency: 1   relative frequency: 0.00001
   *p. 492 TO HIMSELF   16 Whose appetites are dead!

applaud   frequency: 1   relative frequency: 0.00001
    p. 167 UNDERWOOD 15   157 That watch, and catch, at what they may applaud,

applause   frequency: 8   relative frequency: 0.00011
    p. 43 EPIGRAMS 52   3 When I am read, thou fain'st a weake applause,
    p. 49 EPIGRAMS 66   15 Though euery fortitude deserues applause,
    p. 174 UNDERWOOD 23   18 'Tis crowne enough to vertue still, her owne
                              applause.
    p. 270 UNDERWOOD 83   62 With admiration, and applause to die!
    p. 315 HORACE 2   220 If such a ones applause thou dost require,
    p. 321 HORACE 2   364 Receive, or give it an applause, the more.
    p. 391 UNGATHERED 26   18 The applause! delight! the wonder of our Stage!
    p. 409 UNGATHERED 38   5 And you doe doe them well, with good applause,

apple   frequency: 1   relative frequency: 0.00001
    p. 137 UNDERWOOD 2.5   47 For the Apple, and those three

apple-haruest   frequency: 1   relative frequency: 0.00001
    p. 98 FOREST 3   43 The apple-haruest, that doth longer last;

apples   frequency: 2   relative frequency: 0.00002
    p. 95 FOREST 2   52 Some nuts, some apples; some that thinke they
                              make
    p. 290 UNDERWOOD 85   18 His head, with mellow Apples crown'd,

applie   frequency: 1   relative frequency: 0.00001
    p. 176 UNDERWOOD 25   8 Cynthius, I applie

apply   frequency: 10   relative frequency: 0.00014
    See also "applie," "mis-apply."
    p. 76 EPIGRAMS 119   11 That to the vulgar canst thy selfe apply,
    p. 97 FOREST 3   31 While all, that follow, their glad eares apply
    p. 99 FOREST 3   91 But thou, my WROTH, if I can truth apply,
    p. 155 UNDERWOOD 13   65 Still, still, the hunters of false fame apply
    p. 182 UNDERWOOD 28   12 But then his Mothers sweets you so apply,
    p. 192 UNDERWOOD 38   53 That is, if still your Favours you apply;
    p. 193 UNDERWOOD 38   94 What Fooles, and all their Parasites can apply;
    p. 247 UNDERWOOD 70   108 You lik'd, then after, to apply
    p. 279 U'WOOD 84.4   42 So swift, so pure, should yet apply
    p. 329 HORACE 2   514 But he hath every suffrage, can apply

apprehension   frequency: 1   relative frequency: 0.00001
    p. 231 UNDERWOOD 57   11 To take Apprehension

apprenticeship. See "prentise-ship."

approach   frequency: 2   relative frequency: 0.00002
    See also "approch."
    p. 230 UNDERWOOD 56   9 Laden with Bellie, and doth hardly approach
    p. 247 UNDERWOOD 70   109 That liking; and approach so one the tother,

approaches   frequency: 3   relative frequency: 0.00004
    See also "approches," "th'approches."
    p. 191 UNDERWOOD 38   4 This sadnesse makes no approaches, but to kill.
    p. 232 UNDERWOOD 59   4 Of making just approaches, how to kill,
    p. 248 UNDERWOOD 71   7 And made those strong approaches, by False
                              braies,

approaching   frequency: 1   relative frequency: 0.00001
    p. 291 UNDERWOOD 85   62 Of the fed flocks approaching home!

approch   frequency: 1   relative frequency: 0.00001
    p. 41 EPIGRAMS 44   4 Saw all his race approch the blacker floods:

approches   frequency: 1   relative frequency: 0.00001
    p. 401 UNGATHERED 32   15 Stay, till she make her vaine Approches. Then

appropriates   frequency: 1   relative frequency: 0.00001
    p. 662 INSCRIPTS. 2   4 appropriates still vnto that County:

approve   frequency: 1   relative frequency: 0.00001
    See also "t<o>'approue," "t<o>'approve."
    p. 161 UNDERWOOD 14   74 Embrace, and cherish; but he can approve

apricot   frequency: 1   relative frequency: 0.00001
    p. 94 FOREST 2   43 The blushing apricot, and woolly peach

april   frequency: 2   relative frequency: 0.00002
  **p. 116 PANEGYRE   130 When, like an April Iris, flew her shine
    p. 268 UNDERWOOD 83   1 What gentle Ghost, besprent with April deaw,

apt   frequency: 3   relative frequency: 0.00004
  **p. 115 PANEGYRE   67 To bring them forth: Whil'st riper ag'd, and apt
    p. 61 EPIGRAMS 95   28 Of historie, and how to apt their places;
    p. 368 UNGATHERED 6   62 (But this more apt

apteth   frequency: 1   relative frequency: 0.00001
    p. 113 FOREST 12   10 And some one apteth to be trusted, then,

apulians   frequency: 1   relative frequency: 0.00001
    p. 291 UNDERWOOD 85   42 Some lustie quick Apulians spouse,

arar   frequency: 1   relative frequency: 0.00001
    p. 369 UNGATHERED 6   117 Slow Arar, nor swift Rhone; the Loyre, nor
                             Seine,

arbiter   frequency: 1   relative frequency: 0.00001
    p. 189 UNDERWOOD 36   8+ ARBITER.

arch   frequency: 1   relative frequency: 0.00001
    p. 157 UNDERWOOD 13   137 That makes the Arch. The rest that there were
                             put

arch-angels   frequency: 1   relative frequency: 0.00001
    p. 285 U'WOOD 84.9   86 Angels, Arch-angels, Principalities,

arch-dukes   frequency: 1   relative frequency: 0.00001
    p. 69 EPIGRAMS 107   23 Your Arch-Dukes Agents, and your Beringhams,

arched   frequency: 1   relative frequency: 0.00001
    p. 134 UNDERWOOD 2.4   17 And from her arched browes, such a grace

archetype   frequency: 1   relative frequency: 0.00001
    p. 227 UNDERWOOD 52   14 An Archetype, for all the world to see,

archilochus   frequency: 1   relative frequency: 0.00001
    p. 311 HORACE 2   117 Th'Iambick arm'd Archilochus to rave,

archimede   frequency: 1   relative frequency: 0.00001
    p. 402 UNGATHERED 34   5 Both him & Archimede; damne Architas

architas   frequency: 1   relative frequency: 0.00001
    p. 402 UNGATHERED 34   5 Both him & Archimede; damne Architas

architect   frequency: 5   relative frequency: 0.00007
    p. 75 EPIGRAMS 115   30 From friendship, is it's owne fames architect.
    p. 261 UNDERWOOD 77   25 Which, though I cannot as an Architect
    p. 402 UNGATHERED 34   3 you are; from them leapt forth an Architect,
    p. 405 UNGATHERED 34   85 Oh wise Surueyor! wyser Architect!
    p. 406 UNGATHERED 34 102 Againe, thy Architect to ashes turne!

architectonice   frequency: 1   relative frequency: 0.00001
    p. 402 UNGATHERED 34   10 How much Architectonice is your owne!

architectonike. See "architectonice."

architects   frequency: 1   relative frequency: 0.00001
    p. 404 UNGATHERED 34   56 Terme of ye Architects is called Designe!

architecture   frequency: 2   relative frequency: 0.00002
    p. 403 UNGATHERED 34 37 Dame History, Dame Architecture too,
    p. 406 UNGATHERED 34 92 Allmighty Architecture? who noe less

archytas. See "architas."

arden   frequency: 2   relative frequency: 0.00002
    p. 87 EPIGRAMS 133 118 Stunke not so ill; nor, when shee kist, KATE
                             ARDEN.
    p. 209 UNDERWOOD 43 148 Nay, sigh'd a Sister, 'twas the Nun, Kate
                             Arden,

ardor   frequency: 2   relative frequency: 0.00002
    p. 131 UNDERWOOD 2.1 11 With the Ardor, and the Passion,
    p. 413 UNGATHERED 41 23 Inflam'd with ardor to that mystick Shine,

are   frequency: 267   relative frequency: 0.00386
    See also "th<ey>'are," "th'are," "they'are,"
          "they're," "w'are," "we'are," "yo'are."

argiue   frequency: 1   relative frequency: 0.00001
    p. 114 FOREST 12 49 How many equall with the Argiue Queene,

argive. See "argiue."

argo   frequency: 1   relative frequency: 0.00001
    p. 115 FOREST 12 59 Who placed IASONS ARGO in the skie?

argos. See "argus."

argue   frequency: 2   relative frequency: 0.00002
    p. 35 EPIGRAMS 28 9 He will both argue, and discourse in oathes,
    p. 210 UNDERWOOD 43 165 I will not argue thee, from those, of guilt,

argument   frequency: 1   relative frequency: 0.00001
    p. 187 UNDERWOOD 33 27 Of Argument, still drawing forth the best,

argus   frequency: 1   relative frequency: 0.00001
    p. 313 HORACE 2 168 Or, with the milke of Thebes; or Argus, fed.

ariadnes   frequency: 1   relative frequency: 0.00001
    p. 115 FOREST 12 60 Or set bright ARIADNES crowne so high?

aright   frequency: 1   relative frequency: 0.00001
    p. 146 UNDERWOOD 6 10 If ever we will love aright.

arion   frequency: 1   relative frequency: 0.00001
    p. 374 UNGATHERED 10 10 Here, like Arion, our Coryate doth draw

arise   frequency: 2   relative frequency: 0.00002
  **p. 113 PANEGYRE 15 From whose foule reeking cauernes first arise
    p. 176 UNDERWOOD 25 2 Thy present Aide: Arise Invention,

arising. See "airising."

aristarchus   frequency: 1   relative frequency: 0.00001
    p. 335 HORACE 2 639 Become an Aristarchus. And, not say,

aristophanes   frequency: 1   relative frequency: 0.00001
    p. 392 UNGATHERED 26 51 The merry Greeke, tart Aristophanes,

aristotle   frequency: 1   relative frequency: 0.00001
    p. 402 UNGATHERED 34 9 Drawne Aristotle on vs! & thence showne

arm. See "arme."

arm'd   frequency: 4   relative frequency: 0.00005
    p. 110 FOREST 11 38 Arm'd with bow, shafts, and fire;
    p. 186 UNDERWOOD 32 8 Both arm'd with wealth, and slander to oppose,
    p. 187 UNDERWOOD 33 30 Arm'd at all peeces, as to keepe a Fort
    p. 311 HORACE 2 117 Th'Iambick arm'd Archilochus to rave,

armde   frequency: 1   relative frequency: 0.00001
    p. 382 UNGATHERED 16 2 hath armde att all poyntes; charge mee humblye
                          kneele

arme   frequency: 1   relative frequency: 0.00001
    p. 258 UNDERWOOD 75 179 But like an Arme of Eminence, 'mongst them,

armed   frequency: 1   relative frequency: 0.00001
    See also "arm'd," "armde."
    p. 68 EPIGRAMS 105   13 And, armed to the chase, so bare her bow

armes   frequency: 16   relative frequency: 0.00023
    p. 42 EPIGRAMS 48   1 His bought armes MVNG' not lik'd; for his
                             first day
    p. 60 EPIGRAMS 93   6 Vpbraiding rebells armes, and barbarous pride:
    p. 96 FOREST 2   98 The mysteries of manners, armes, and arts.
    p. 98 FOREST 3   67 Let others watch in guiltie armes, and stand
    p. 114 FOREST 12   42 And, at her strong armes end, hold vp, and euen,
    p. 177 UNDERWOOD 25   19 Breake the knit Circle of her Stonie Armes,
    p. 212 UNDERWOOD 43 198 And there made Swords, Bills, Glaves, and
                             Armes your fill;
    p. 214 UNDERWOOD 44   44 Of bearing Armes! most civill Soldierie!
    p. 215 UNDERWOOD 44   85 To serve the State by Councels, and by Armes:
    p. 216 UNDERWOOD 44 102 Her broken Armes up, to their emptie moulds.
    p. 232 UNDERWOOD 59   1 They talke of Fencing, and the use of Armes,
    p. 293 UNDERWOOD 87   3 His armes more acceptable free,
    p. 325 HORACE 2   412 In vertue, and renowne of armes, then in
    p. 331 HORACE 2   566 His armes in Mars his field, he doth refuse;
    p. 375 UNGATHERED 10 27 And louse-dropping Case, are the Armes of his
                             trauell.
    p. 398 UNGATHERED 30 65 And when he ships them where to vse their Armes,

armies   frequency: 1   relative frequency: 0.00001
    See also "armyes."
    p. 114 FOREST 12   52 Or, in an armies head, that, lockt in brasse,

armorie   frequency: 1   relative frequency: 0.00001
    p. 182 UNDERWOOD 28   9 For in your verse all Cupids Armorie,

armory. See "armorie."

armour   frequency: 2   relative frequency: 0.00002
    p. 179 UNDERWOOD 25   48 No Armour to the mind! he is shot-free
    p. 213 UNDERWOOD 44   7 That we have Trumpets, Armour, and great
                             Horse,

arms. See "armes."

armyes   frequency: 1   relative frequency: 0.00001
    p. 423 UNGATHERED 50 11 whole armyes fall, swayd by those nyce respects.

aromatic. See "aromatique."

aromatique   frequency: 1   relative frequency: 0.00001
    p. 251 UNDERWOOD 74   18 In making soft her aromatique bed.

arraign'd   frequency: 2   relative frequency: 0.00002
    p. 29 EPIGRAMS 8   2 RIDWAY was tane, arraign'd, condemn'd to
                             dye;
    p. 191 UNDERWOOD 38   27 No, I will stand arraign'd, and cast, to be

arraigning   frequency: 1   relative frequency: 0.00001
   *p. 492 TO HIMSELF   5 Indicting, and arraigning euery day

arrantest. See "errant'st."

arras   frequency: 1   relative frequency: 0.00001
    p. 260 UNDERWOOD 77   4 Not with the Arras, but the Persian Loomes.

arrayes   frequency: 1   relative frequency: 0.00001
    p. 30 EPIGRAMS 12   5 By that one spell he liues, eates, drinkes,
                             arrayes

arrays. See "arrayes."

arrearage. See "arrerage."

arrerage   frequency: 1   relative frequency: 0.00001
    p. 32 EPIGRAMS 16   5 So, in short time, th'art in arrerage growne

arrest   frequency: 1   relative frequency: 0.00001
    p. 252 UNDERWOOD 75   4 Betweene thy Tropicks, to arrest thy sight,

arriue   frequency: 2   relative frequency: 0.00002
    p. 109 FOREST 11   11 Obiect arriue there, but the heart (our spie)
    p. 388 UNGATHERED 23   5 Still, still, dost thou arriue with, at our
                             shore,

arrive
    See also "arriue."   frequency: 1   relative frequency: 0.00001
    p. 157 UNDERWOOD 13 131 'Tis by degrees that men arrive at glad

arrow   frequency: 3   relative frequency: 0.00004
    p. 132 UNDERWOOD 2.2 17 Letting Bow and Arrow fall,
    p. 132 UNDERWOOD 2.2 21 Both the Arrow he had quit,
    p. 133 UNDERWOOD 2.3 14 But the Arrow home did draw

arrowes   frequency: 1   relative frequency: 0.00001
    p. 170 UNDERWOOD 19   4 His double Bow, and round his Arrowes sends;

arrows. See "arrowes."

arse. See "divels-arse."

arsenic. See "arsenike."

arsenike   frequency: 1   relative frequency: 0.00001
    p. 42 EPIGRAMS 50   3 Arsenike would thee fit for societie make.

arses   frequency: 1   relative frequency: 0.00001
    p. 84 EPIGRAMS 133 13 Arses were heard to croake, in stead of frogs;

art   frequency: 83 relative frequency: 0.00120
    See also "arte," "arte's," "th'art," "thou'rt."
    p. 28 EPIGRAMS 4   7 And such a Prince thou art, wee daily see,
    p. 29 EPIGRAMS 6   1 If all you boast of your great art be true;
    p. 37 EPIGRAMS 33   2 Glad-mention'd ROE: thou art but gone before.
    p. 44 EPIGRAMS 53   8 Thou art the father, and the witnesse too.
    p. 44 EPIGRAMS 55   8 What is thine, that so thy friend deceiues?
    p. 47 EPIGRAMS 64   4 A treasure, art: contemn'd in th'age of gold.
    p. 49 EPIGRAMS 67   9 And thou design'd to be the same thou art,
    p. 50 EPIGRAMS 69   1 COB, thou nor souldier, thiefe, nor fencer art,
    p. 52 EPIGRAMS 74   7 Whil'st thou art certaine to thy words, once
                          gone,
    p. 58 EPIGRAMS 91   5 Which thou art to thy selfe: whose fame was wonne
    p. 60 EPIGRAMS 93   9 Thou, that art all their valour, all their
                          spirit,
    p. 66 EPIGRAMS 102 17 That art so reuerenc'd, as thy comming in,
    p. 68 EPIGRAMS 106   2 What man art thou, that art so many men,
    p. 68 EPIGRAMS 106   4 Truth might spend all her voyce, Fame all her
                          art.
    p. 70 EPIGRAMS 109 13 To be the same in roote, thou art in height;
    p. 71 EPIGRAMS 110 17 Thy learned hand, and true Promethean art
    p. 72 EPIGRAMS 112   1 With thy small stocke, why art thou ventring
                          still,
    p. 72 EPIGRAMS 112   6 Art still at that, and think'st to blow me'vp
                          too?
    p. 73 EPIGRAMS 112 19 And neuer art encounter'd, I confesse:
    p. 82 EPIGRAMS 130 16 When these were but the praises of the Art.
    p. 85 EPIGRAMS 133 53 And art a god, if Fame thee not abuses,
    p. 93 FOREST 2   1 Thou art not, PENSHVRST, built to
                          enuious show,
    p. 93 FOREST 2   6 And these grudg'd at, art reuerenc'd the while.
    p. 93 FOREST 2   8 Of wood, of water: therein thou art faire.
    p. 96 FOREST 3   1 How blest art thou, canst loue the countrey,
                          WROTH,
    p. 96 FOREST 3   4 Art tane with neithers vice, nor sport:
    p. 96 FOREST 3   5 That at great times, art no ambitious guest
    p. 100 FOREST 4   14 Yet art thou both shrunke vp, and old,
    p. 100 FOREST 4   17 I know thou whole art but a shop
    p. 100 FOREST 4   20 Yet art thou falser then thy wares.
    p. 111 FOREST 11 69 Peace, Luxurie, thou art like one of those
    p. 122 FOREST 15   9 As thou art all, so be thou all to mee,
    p. 132 UNDERWOOD 2.2 10 Here's a shaft, thou art to slow!
    p. 133 UNDERWOOD 2.3 15 And (to gaine her by his Art)
    p. 145 UNDERWOOD 5   17 And having pleas'd our art, wee'll try
    p. 158 UNDERWOOD 14   3 Lesse shall I for the Art or dressing care,
    p. 160 UNDERWOOD 14 48 Forme, Art or Ensigne, that hath scap'd your
                          sight?
    p. 176 UNDERWOOD 25   1 Where art thou, Genius? I should use
    p. 183 UNDERWOOD 29 15 And Art banish'd.
    p. 187 UNDERWOOD 33 13 Thou art my Cause: whose manners since I knew,
    p. 188 UNDERWOOD 34   7 Art, her false servant; Nor, for Sir Hugh
                          Plat,
    p. 202 UNDERWOOD 42 87 Thou art jealous of thy Wifes, or Daughters
                          Case:
    p. 206 UNDERWOOD 43 76 The art of kindling the true Coale, by Lungs:
    p. 214 UNDERWOOD 44 43 O happie Art! and wise Epitome

art (cont.)
      p. 216 UNDERWOOD 45   5 I neither am, nor art thou one of those
      p. 220 UNDERWOOD 48   1 Since, Bacchus, thou art father
      p. 220 UNDERWOOD 48   4 Where now, thou art made Dweller;
      p. 221 UNDERWOOD 48   13 For, Bacchus, thou art freer
      p. 227 UNDERWOOD 52   10 Which if in compasse of no Art it came
      p. 228 UNDERWOOD 53   4 Me thought I read the ancient Art of Thrace,
      p. 232 UNDERWOOD 59   2 The art of urging, and avoyding harmes,
      p. 237 UNDERWOOD 65   1 And art thou borne, brave Babe? Blest be thy
                                 birth,
      p. 237 UNDERWOOD 65   6 The same that thou art promis'd, but be slow,
      p. 268 UNDERWOOD 82   1 That thou art lov'd of God, this worke is done,
      p. 272 U'WOOD 84.1   1 Faire FAME, who art ordain'd to crowne
      p. 277 U'WOOD 84.4   5 Not, that your Art I doe refuse:
      p. 281 U'WOOD 84.4   70 Yet know, with what thou art possest,
      p. 282 U'WOOD 84.9   16 With such a Raritie, and not rowse Art
      p. 283 U'WOOD 84.9   22 (For so thou art with me) now shee is gone.
      p. 295 UNDERWOOD 90   8 Thy table without art, and easy-rated:
      p. 295 UNDERWOOD 90   12 Will to bee, what thou art; and nothing more:
      p. 305 HORACE 2   t3 THE ART
      p. 319 HORACE 2   303 Thus, to his antient Art the Piper lent
      p. 323 HORACE 2   386 Or a worse Crime, the ignorance of art.
      p. 325 HORACE 2   420 Happier then wretched art, and doth, by it,
      p. 327 HORACE 2   456 A Poeme, of no grace, weight, art, in rimes,
      p. 331 HORACE 2   582 Nature, or Art. My Judgement will not pierce
      p. 341 HORACE 1   104 ..... Art ... .
      p. 370 UNGATHERED 7   8 So bold, as shewes your Art you can command.
      p. 385 UNGATHERED 20   6 The art of vttring wares, if they were bad;
      p. 391 UNGATHERED 26   15 But thou art proofe against them, and indeed
      p. 391 UNGATHERED 26   22 Thou art a Moniment, without a tombe,
      p. 391 UNGATHERED 26   23 And art aliue still, while thy Booke doth liue,
      p. 392 UNGATHERED 26   55 Yet must I not giue Nature all: Thy Art,
      p. 392 UNGATHERED 26   58 His Art doth giue the fashion. And, that he,
      p. 398 UNGATHERED 30   59 There, thou art Homer! Pray thee, vse the stile
      p. 398 UNGATHERED 30   68 With bold Tyrtaeus verse, when thou art nam'd,
      p. 400 UNGATHERED 32   10 That Art, or Ingine, on the strength can raise.
      p. 404 UNGATHERED 34   58 Of any Art, besyde what he calls his!
      p. 408 UNGATHERED 37   9 To be knowne what thou art, a blatant beast,
      p. 409 UNGATHERED 37   13 Thou art not worth it. Who will care to knowe
      p. 414 UNGATHERED 41   44 And art the spotlesse Mirrour to Mans eyes.

arte   frequency: 3   relative frequency: 0.00004
      p. 93 FOREST 1   10 By any arte. Then wonder not,
      p. 361 UNGATHERED 1   15 The seauen-fold flower of Arte (more rich then
                                 gold)
      p. 420 UNGATHERED 48   14 That hath not Countrye impudence enough to
                                 laughe att Arte,

artes   frequency: 2   relative frequency: 0.00002
    **p. 116 PANEGYRE   128 In all these knowing artes our prince excell'd.
      p. 404 UNGATHERED 34   43 Court Hieroglyphicks! & all Artes affoord

arte's   frequency: 1   relative frequency: 0.00001
      p. 383 UNGATHERED 16   15 shall looke, & on hyme soe, then arte's a
                                 lyer

arth: frequency: 1   relative frequency: 0.00001
      p. 216 UNDERWOOD 45   t2 Arth: Squib.

arthur   frequency: 4   relative frequency: 0.00005
      See also "arth:."
      p. 215 UNDERWOOD 44   81 From Guy, or Bevis, Arthur, or from whom
      p. 216 UNDERWOOD 45   3 My gentle Arthur; that it might be said
      p. 229 UNDERWOOD 54   t2 To Mr. ARTHUR SQUIB.
      p. 229 UNDERWOOD 54   16 Lend me, deare Arthur, for a weeke five more,

arthurs   frequency: 1   relative frequency: 0.00001
      See also "arthvrs."
      p. 203 UNDERWOOD 43   30 Th'Esplandians, Arthurs, Palmerins, and all

arthvrs   frequency: 1   relative frequency: 0.00001
      p. 84 EPIGRAMS 133   24 To haue beene stiled of King ARTHVRS
                                 table.

artichokes   frequency: 1   relative frequency: 0.00001
      p. 88 EPIGRAMS 133   166 When euery clerke eates artichokes, and peason,

article   frequency: 1   relative frequency: 0.00001
      p. 198 UNDERWOOD 40   48 That Article, may not become <y>our lover:

artillerie   frequency: 1   relative frequency: 0.00001
     p. 213 UNDERWOOD 44   23 Well, I say, thrive, thrive brave Artillerie
                                yard,

artillery. See "artillerie," "th'artillery."

artlesse   frequency: 2   relative frequency: 0.00002
     p. 307 HORACE 2   44 When in a wrong, and artlesse way we tread.
     p. 335 HORACE 2   634 On artlesse Verse; the hard ones he will blame;

arts   frequency: 30   relative frequency: 0.00043
     See also "artes."
     p. 28 EPIGRAMS 3   11 If, without these vile arts, it will not sell,
     p. 31 EPIGRAMS 14   2 All that I am in arts, all that I know,
     p. 34 EPIGRAMS 23   7 To it, thy language, letters, arts, best life,
     p. 36 EPIGRAMS 28   21 SVRLY, vse other arts, these only can
     p. 75 EPIGRAMS 116   13 These were thy knowing arts: which who doth now
     p. 78 EPIGRAMS 122   9 I need no other arts, but studie thee:
     p. 96 FOREST 2   98 The mysteries of manners, armes, and arts.
     p. 100 FOREST 4   9 I know thy formes are studyed arts,
     p. 101 FOREST 4   47 Where enuious arts professed be,
     p. 117 FOREST 13   12 By arts, and practise of the vicious,
     p. 165 UNDERWOOD 15   91 Or use all arts, or haunt all Companies
     p. 167 UNDERWOOD 15   164 Informers, Masters both of Arts and lies;
     p. 174 UNDERWOOD 23   6 That eats on wits, and Arts, and <oft> destroyes
                                them both.
     p. 206 UNDERWOOD 43   88 There were of search, and mastry in the Arts.
     p. 208 UNDERWOOD 43   110 'Cause thou canst halt, with us, in Arts, and
                                Fire!
     p. 215 UNDERWOOD 44   74 Their Sonnes to studie Arts, the Lawes, the
                                Creed:
     p. 221 UNDERWOOD 48   19 By all the Arts of Gladnesse,
     p. 234 UNDERWOOD 60   12 No love of action, and high Arts,
     p. 244 UNDERWOOD 70   34 Got up and thriv'd with honest arts:
     p. 251 UNDERWOOD 74   17 Have multipli'd their arts, and powers,
     p. 257 UNDERWOOD 75   136 With all corroding Arts, be able to untie!
     p. 261 UNDERWOOD 77   11 Catch'd with these Arts, wherein the Judge is
                                wise
     p. 261 UNDERWOOD 77   17 What you have studied are the arts of life;
     p. 262 UNDERWOOD 78   4 Court can call hers, or Man could call his
                                Arts.
     p. 292 UNDERWOOD 86   15 Child of a hundred Arts, and farre
     p. 325 HORACE 2   449 Can tell a States-mans dutie, what the arts
     p. 327 HORACE 2   466 A pound, or piece, by their long compting arts:
     p. 395 UNGATHERED 29   16 What godds but those of arts, and eloquence?
     p. 396 UNGATHERED 30   22 As it had beene the circle of the Arts!
     p. 409 UNGATHERED 38   4 Of Fellowship, professing my old Arts.

arundell   frequency: 1   relative frequency: 0.00001
     p. 228 UNDERWOOD 53   10 Of bold Sir Bevis, and his Arundell:

as   frequency: 608   relative frequency: 0.00880
     See also "as't," "aswell."

ascend   frequency: 1   relative frequency: 0.00001
     p. 288 U'WOOD 84.9   205 Shee saw him too, in glory to ascend

ascent. See "th'ascent."

ascribe   frequency: 1   relative frequency: 0.00001
     p. 61 EPIGRAMS 95   9 To thine owne proper I ascribe then more;

asham'd   frequency: 6   relative frequency: 0.00008
     p. 53 EPIGRAMS 77   4 I'am more asham'd to haue thee thought my foe.
     p. 82 EPIGRAMS 130   9 T<o>'alledge, that greatest men were not asham'd,
     p. 182 UNDERWOOD 28   5 Nor is my Muse, or I asham'd to owe it
     p. 194 UNDERWOOD 38   106 And let your mercie make me asham'd t<o>'offend.
     p. 353 HORACE 1   580 .... to be asham'd
     p. 414 UNGATHERED 42   5 And lesse asham'd; not when I told the crowd

ashamed   frequency: 1   relative frequency: 0.00001
     See also "asham'd," "b<e>'asham'd."
     p. 83 EPIGRAMS 131   11 And would (being ask'd the truth) ashamed say,

ashes   frequency: 3   relative frequency: 0.00004
     p. 149 UNDERWOOD 8   11 Even ashes of lovers find no rest.
     p. 391 UNGATHERED 26   40 Sent forth, or since did from their ashes come.
     p. 406 UNGATHERED 34   102 Againe, thy Architect to ashes turne!

ashore   frequency: 1   relative frequency: 0.00001
     p.   94 FOREST 2   26 Fertile of wood, ASHORE, and
                              SYDNEY'S copp's,

ashour. See "ashore."

aside   frequency: 2   relative frequency: 0.00002
   **p. 115 PANEGYRE   73 Meane while, the reuerend THEMIS drawes
                              aside
     p. 307 HORACE 2   64 Lay that aside, the Epicks office is.

asinigo   frequency: 1   relative frequency: 0.00001
     p. 403 UNGATHERED 34 20 you would be an Asinigo, by your ears?

ask. See "aske."

ask'd   frequency: 5   relative frequency: 0.00007.
     p.   30 EPIGRAMS 11   4 It made me a great face, I ask'd the name.
     p.   41 EPIGRAMS 45   9 Rest in soft peace, and, ask'd, say here doth lye
     p.   54 EPIGRAMS 84   2 I ask'd a lord a buck, and he denyed me;
     p.   66 EPIGRAMS 102   4 Both which are ask'd, to haue thee vnderstood.
     p.   83 EPIGRAMS 131 11 And would (being ask'd the truth) ashamed say,

aske   frequency: 26   relative frequency: 0.00037
   **p. 117 PANEGYRE   161 Yet, let blest Brit[t]aine aske (without your
                              wrong)
     p.   54 EPIGRAMS 84   3 And, ere I could aske you, I was preuented:
     p.   59 EPIGRAMS 92   18 Nay, aske you, how the day goes, in your eare.
     p.   60 EPIGRAMS 94   6 Crowne with their owne. Rare poemes aske rare
                              friends
     p.   60 EPIGRAMS 94   12 Dare for these poemes, yet, both aske, and read,
     p.   68 EPIGRAMS 105 15 There's none so dull, that for your stile would
                              aske,
     p. 106 FOREST 9   6 Doth aske a drinke diuine:
     p. 107 FOREST 10   21 His absence in my verse, is all I aske.
     p. 139 UNDERWOOD 2.7 8 Can he that loues, aske lesse then one?
     p. 158 UNDERWOOD 14   7 To aske it: though in most of workes it be
     p. 159 UNDERWOOD 14 24 Upon my selfe, and aske to whom? and why?
     p. 171 UNDERWOOD 19 15 I'le therefore aske no more, but bid you love;
     p. 172 UNDERWOOD 20 17 Doe not you aske to know her, she is worse
     p. 172 UNDERWOOD 21   1 Aske not to know this Man. If fame should
                              speake
     p. 192 UNDERWOOD 38 56 Why was't? did e're the Cloudes aske back their
                              raine?
     p. 192 UNDERWOOD 38 65 Should aske the blood, and spirits he hath
                              infus'd
     p. 202 UNDERWOOD 42 86 None of their pleasures! nor will aske thee, why
     p. 212 UNDERWOOD 43 209 We aske your absence here, we all love peace,
     p. 234 UNDERWOOD 61 11 T<o>'obtaine of God, what all the Land should
                              aske?
     p. 257 UNDERWOOD 75 160 But dare not aske our wish in Language
                              fescennine:
     p. 269 UNDERWOOD 83 12 And e're I can aske more of her, shee's gone!
     p. 278 U'WOOD 84.4   14 Would aske a Heavens Intelligence;
     p. 383 UNGATHERED 17 4 May aske, what Author would conceale his name?
     p. 403 UNGATHERED 34 29 What is ye cause you pompe it soe? I aske,
     p. 404 UNGATHERED 34 45 You aske noe more then certeyne politique Eyes,
     p. 409 UNGATHERED 37 18 To aske thy name, if he haue half his Nose!

asked   frequency: 2   relative frequency: 0.00002
     See also "ask'd," "askt."
     p. 218 UNDERWOOD 47 t2 asked to be Sealed of the
     p. 220 UNDERWOOD 47 75 Are asked to climbe. First give me faith, who
                              know

askes   frequency: 4   relative frequency: 0.00005
     p. 108 FOREST 10 A   1 An elegie? no, muse; yt askes a straine
     p. 117 FOREST 13   35 That askes but to be censur'd by the eyes:
     p. 118 FOREST 13   69 Your conscience, and not wonder, if none askes
     p. 256 UNDERWOOD 75 124 Askes first, Who gives her (I Charles) then he
                              plights

asks. See "askes."

askt   frequency: 1   relative frequency: 0.00001
     p. 388 UNGATHERED 23 8 Were askt of thy Discoueries; They must say,

asleep   frequency: 1   relative frequency: 0.00001
     See also "asleepe."
     p. 413 UNGATHERED 41 18 But lowlie laid, as on the earth asleep,

asleepe   frequency: 1   relative frequency: 0.00001
    p. 113 FOREST 12   14 When his proud patrons fauours are asleepe;

aspire   frequency: 7   relative frequency: 0.00010
 **p. 117 PANEGYRE   150 What all mens wishes did aspire vnto.
    p.   35 EPIGRAMS 28   1 DON SVRLY, to aspire the glorious name
    p. 157 UNDERWOOD 13   148 Nor fashion; if they chance aspire to height,
    p. 175 UNDERWOOD 23   27 With Japhets lyne, aspire
    p. 208 UNDERWOOD 43   109 Thou woo Minerva! or to wit aspire!
    p. 307 HORACE 2   49 Not to designe the whole. Should I aspire
    p. 317 HORACE 2   275 Any fourth man, to speake at all, aspire.

asquint   frequency: 1   relative frequency: 0.00001
    p. 362 UNGATHERED 2   7 If they seeme wry, to such as looke asquint,

ass   frequency: 1   relative frequency: 0.00001
    See also "asse."
    p. 408 UNGATHERED 36   8 He makes ye Camell & dull Ass his prize.

assaies   frequency: 1   relative frequency: 0.00001
    p. 315 HORACE 2   200 Who nought assaies unaptly, or amisse?

assay. See "say-master."

assay'd   frequency: 1   relative frequency: 0.00001
    p. 354 HORACE 1   626 ... . assay'd .. but .. ....

assayes   frequency: 1   relative frequency: 0.00001
    p. 255 UNDERWOOD 75   101 In all the prov'd assayes,

assays. See "assayes," "ssayes."

asse   frequency: 2   relative frequency: 0.00002
    p. 164 UNDERWOOD 15   64 How they may make some one that day an Asse;
    p. 198 UNDERWOOD 40   32 But the grave Lover ever was an Asse;

assembly. See "th'assembly."

asses   frequency: 2   relative frequency: 0.00002
    p.   62 EPIGRAMS 96   11 And, till they burst, their backs, like asses
                               load:
    p. 175 UNDERWOOD 23   36 Safe from the wolves black jaw, and the dull
                               Asses hoofe.

assiduous   frequency: 1   relative frequency: 0.00001
    p. 236 UNDERWOOD 64   11 When your assiduous practise doth secure

assign'd   frequency: 3   relative frequency: 0.00004
    p.   67 EPIGRAMS 103   12 For euery part a character assign'd.
    p. 283 U'WOOD 84.9   20 Beene trusted to thee: not to't selfe assign'd.
    p. 331 HORACE 2   548 This saying: To some things there is assign'd

assignes   frequency: 1   relative frequency: 0.00001
    p. 170 UNDERWOOD 18   23 That I must send one first, my Choyce assignes,

assigns. See "assignes."

assist. See "t<o>'assist."

assisted   frequency: 1   relative frequency: 0.00001
    p. 176 UNDERWOOD 24   14 Assisted by no strengths, but are her owne,

assurance   frequency: 2   relative frequency: 0.00002
    p.   43 EPIGRAMS 53   6 To giue the world assurance thou wert both;
    p. 198 UNDERWOOD 40   49 Which in assurance to your brest I tell,

assur'd   frequency: 1   relative frequency: 0.00001
    p. 159 UNDERWOOD 14   27 So that my Reader is assur'd, I now

assure   frequency: 1   relative frequency: 0.00001
    p. 270 UNDERWOOD 83   50 Of her disease, how did her soule assure

assyria   frequency: 1   relative frequency: 0.00001
    p. 313 HORACE 2   167 Of Colchis borne; or in Assyria bred;

assyrian. See "'syrian."

as't   frequency: 1   relative frequency: 0.00001

asterism. See "asterisme."

asterisme   frequency: 1   relative frequency: 0.00001
    p. 246 UNDERWOOD 70   89 In this bright Asterisme:

astraea. See "astrea."

astrea   frequency: 1   relative frequency: 0.00001
    p. 114 FOREST 12   24 Or put to flight ASTREA, when her ingots

asunder   frequency: 1   relative frequency: 0.00001
    p. 239 UNDERWOOD 67   12 Their guarded gates asunder?

aswell   frequency: 2   relative frequency: 0.00002
    p. 146 UNDERWOOD 6   9 Which we in love must doe aswell,
    p. 265 UNDERWOOD 79   51 Your teeming Ewes, aswell as mounting Rammes.

at   frequency: 259   relative frequency: 0.00374
    See also "at's," "att."

atchievements   frequency: 1   relative frequency: 0.00001
    p. 187 UNDERWOOD 33   38 And (which doth all Atchievements get above)

athenian   frequency: 1   relative frequency: 0.00001
    p. 397 UNGATHERED 30   34 Pearch'd ouer head, the wise Athenian Owle:

atomes   frequency: 2   relative frequency: 0.00002
    p. 148 UNDERWOOD 8   3 By Atomes mov'd;
    p. 287 U'WOOD 84.9   152 Find all our Atomes from a point t<o>'a span!

atomi   frequency: 1   relative frequency: 0.00001
    p. 87 EPIGRAMS 133   127 Then all those Atomi ridiculous,

atoms. See "atomes."

atreus   frequency: 1   relative frequency: 0.00001
    p. 317 HORACE 2   265 Natur'd, and wicked Atreus cooke, to th'eye,

at's   frequency: 1   relative frequency: 0.00001

att   frequency: 2   relative frequency: 0.00002

attain. See "attaine."

attaine   frequency: 1   relative frequency: 0.00001
    p. 128 UNDERWOOD 1.1   31 Till I attaine the long'd-for mysterie

attempt   frequency: 2   relative frequency: 0.00002
    p. 80 EPIGRAMS 127   10 By her attempt, shall still be owing thee.
    p. 151 UNDERWOOD 11   6 Whom never yet he durst attempt awake;

attempted   frequency: 2   relative frequency: 0.00002
    p. 202 UNDERWOOD 43   5 I ne're attempted, Vulcan, 'gainst thy life;
    p. 329 HORACE 2   498 Attempted by the Muses tunes, and strings;

attend   frequency: 2   relative frequency: 0.00002
    p. 81 EPIGRAMS 128   6 Attend thee hence; and there, may all thy ends,
    p. 221 UNDERWOOD 48   17 See then thou dost attend him,

attending   frequency: 1   relative frequency: 0.00001
    p. 55 EPIGRAMS 86   6 Attending such a studie, such a choice.

attent. See "tent."

attir'd   frequency: 1   relative frequency: 0.00001
    p. 362 UNGATHERED 2   2 And see a minde attir'd in perfect straines;

attire. See "attyre," "t<o>'attire," "tire-man," "tyre," "tyre-man."

attires. See "attyres," "tires."

attributes   frequency: 1   relative frequency: 0.00001
    p. 394 UNGATHERED 28   6 And number Attributes vnto a flood:

attyre   frequency: 1   relative frequency: 0.00001
    p. 404 UNGATHERED 34   54 Attyre ye Persons as noe thought can teach

attyres   frequency: 1   relative frequency: 0.00001
    p. 118 FOREST 13   71 Let who will follow fashions, and attyres,

auailes   frequency: 1   relative frequency: 0.00001
     p. 64 EPIGRAMS 99   7 But much it now auailes, what's done, of whom:

aubigny. See "avbigny," "'avbigny."

auditor   frequency: 1   relative frequency: 0.00001
     p. 45 EPIGRAMS 56   10 The sluggish gaping auditor deuoures;

audleys   frequency: 1   relative frequency: 0.00001
     p. 214 UNDERWOOD 44   52 Beauchamps, and Nevills, Cliffords, Audleys
                              old;

auert   frequency: 1   relative frequency: 0.00001
  **p. 113 PANEGYRE   30 (Which Fates auert) should force her from her
                              right.

aught. See "ought."

augure   frequency: 1   relative frequency: 0.00001
     p. 364 UNGATHERED 4   5 Or (by our Turtles Augure)

augury. See "augure."

aulus   frequency: 1   relative frequency: 0.00001
     p. 331 HORACE 2   553 Or knowes not what Cassellius Aulus can;

auon   frequency: 1   relative frequency: 0.00001
     p. 392 UNGATHERED 26   71 Sweet Swan of Auon! what a sight it were

auoyd   frequency: 1   relative frequency: 0.00001
     p. 101 FOREST 4   36 If I could not thy ginnes auoyd.

auspice   frequency: 1   relative frequency: 0.00001
     p. 213 UNDERWOOD 44   20 Under the Auspice of young Swynnerton.

auspicious   frequency: 1   relative frequency: 0.00001
     p. 361 UNGATHERED 1   2 (so well dispos'd by thy auspicious hand)

auspiciously. See "auspitiously."

auspitiously   frequency: 1   relative frequency: 0.00001
     p. 179 UNDERWOOD 25   57 If I auspitiously divine,

austere   frequency: 1   relative frequency: 0.00001
     p. 190 UNDERWOOD 37   17 Rigid, and harsh, which is a Drug austere

author   frequency: 14   relative frequency: 0.00020
     See also "avthor."
    *p. 492 TO HIMSELF   t1 The iust indignation the Author
     p. 130 UNDERWOOD 1.3   2 The Author both of Life, and light;
     p. 265 UNDERWOOD 79   57 Hee is the author of our peace.
     p. 329 HORACE 2   519 With honour make the farre-knowne Author live.
     p. 329 HORACE 2   538 May, with some right, upon an Author creepe.
     p. 370 UNGATHERED 7   t1 To the Author.
     p. 370 UNGATHERED 8   t1 To the worthy Author M.
     p. 378 UNGATHERED 11   87 Of Tom of Odcombe that odde Iouiall Author,
     p. 383 UNGATHERED 17   4 May aske, what Author would conceale his name?
     p. 383 UNGATHERED 17   t2 friend the Author.
     p. 385 UNGATHERED 19   t1 To his friend the Author vpon
     p. 385 UNGATHERED 20   t1 To the worthy Author on
     p. 389 UNGATHERED 24   t1 On the Author, Worke, and Translator.
     p. 409 UNGATHERED 38   t3 the Author of this Work, M. RICH.
                              BROME.

authorem   frequency: 1   relative frequency: 0.00001
     p. 362 UNGATHERED 2   t1 In Authorem.

authoritie   frequency: 5   relative frequency: 0.00007
     p. 31 EPIGRAMS 14   9 What weight, and what authoritie in thy speech!
     p. 49 EPIGRAMS 67   3 That sound, and that authoritie with her name,
     p. 62 EPIGRAMS 96   6 As thou hast best authoritie, t<o>'allow.
     p. 191 UNDERWOOD 38   26 As I would urge Authoritie for sinne.
     p. 217 UNDERWOOD 46   10 And skill in thee, now, grew Authoritie;

authorities   frequency: 1   relative frequency:.0.00001
     p. 160 UNDERWOOD 14   41 Impostures branded! and Authorities urg'd!

authority. See "authoritie."

authoriz'd   frequency: 1   relative frequency: 0.00001
    p. 397 UNGATHERED 30   46 A wild, and an authoriz'd wickednesse!

authors   frequency: 8   relative frequency: 0.00011
    See also "th'authors."
    p. 43 EPIGRAMS 53   3 Thou wert content the authors name to loose:
    p. 120 FOREST 14   10 Both loue the cause, and authors of the feast?
    p. 156 UNDERWOOD 13   99 And almost deifie the Authors! make
    p. 160 UNDERWOOD 14   43 Records, and Authors of! how rectified
    p. 362 UNGATHERED 2   12 So with this Authors Readers will it thriue:
    p. 380 UNGATHERED 21   9 And, where the most reade bookes, on Authors
                             fames,
    p. 389 UNGATHERED 24   1 Who tracks this Authors, or Translators Pen,
    p. 401 UNGATHERED 32 19 Nor flatt'ry! but secur'd, by the Authors Name,

autumn. See "autumne."

autumne   frequency: 2   relative frequency: 0.00002
    p. 97 FOREST 3   27 In autumne, at the Partrich makes a flight,
    p. 290 UNDERWOOD 85   17 Or when that Autumne, through the fields, lifts
                             round

avails. See "auailes."

avbigny   frequency: 2   relative frequency: 0.00002
    p. 80 EPIGRAMS 127   3 To whom I am so bound, lou'd AVBIGNY?
    p. 116 FOREST 13   t2 TO KATHERINE, LADY AVBIGNY.

'avbigny   frequency: 2   relative frequency: 0.00002
    p. 80 EPIGRAMS 127   t1 TO ESME, LORD 'AVBIGNY.
    p. 119 FOREST 13   105 T<o>'expect the honors of great 'AVBIGNY:

avernvs   frequency: 1   relative frequency: 0.00001
    p. 85 EPIGRAMS 133   41 A Docke there is, that called is AVERNVS,

avert   frequency: 1   relative frequency: 0.00001
    See also "auert."
    p. 235 UNDERWOOD 61   19 And doe their penance, to avert Gods rod,

avoid   frequency: 1   relative frequency: 0.00001
    See also "auoyd."
    p. 325 HORACE 2   424 Retire themselves, avoid the publike baths;

avoiding. See "avoyding."

avon. See "auon."

avow. See "dis-auow."

avoyding   frequency: 1   relative frequency: 0.00001
    p. 232 UNDERWOOD 59   2 The art of urging, and avoyding harmes,

avthor   frequency: 2   relative frequency: 0.00002
    p. 390 UNGATHERED 26 t2 The AVTHOR
    p. 662 INSCRIPTS. 2   t1 AVTHOR

awake   frequency: 4   relative frequency: 0.00005
    p. 151 UNDERWOOD 11   6 Whom never yet he durst attempt awake;
    p. 239 UNDERWOOD 67   10 As fearfull to awake
    p. 283 U'WOOD 84.9   46 In earth, till the last Trumpe awake the Sheepe
    p. 396 UNGATHERED 30 11 It was no Dreame! I was awake, and saw!

away   frequency: 33   relative frequency: 0.00047
    p. 42 EPIGRAMS 48   2 Of bearing them in field, he threw 'hem away:
    p. 45 EPIGRAMS 59   3 Stinke, and are throwne away. End faire enough.
    p. 48 EPIGRAMS 65   1 Away, and leaue me, thou thing most abhord,
    p. 49 EPIGRAMS 66   18 That vertuous is, when the reward 's away.
    p. 52 EPIGRAMS 75   3 Though LIPPE, at PAVLS, ranne from his
                             text away,
    p. 60 EPIGRAMS 93   8 The Belgick feuer rauished away.
    p. 69 EPIGRAMS 107   9 Tell them, what parts yo'haue tane, whence run
                             away,
    p. 87 EPIGRAMS 133 110 Vanish'd away: as you must all presume
    p. 89 EPIGRAMS 133 179 Tempt not his furie, PLVTO is away:
    p. 93 FOREST 1   3 Which when he felt, Away (quoth hee)
    p. 95 FOREST 2   66 At great mens tables) and yet dine away.
    p. 100 FOREST 4   22 Like such as blow away their liues,
    p. 101 FOREST 4   44 When all the causes were away.
    p. 105 FOREST 8   42 Play away, health, wealth, and fame.
    p. 118 FOREST 13   73 Melt downe their husbands land, to poure away

away (cont.)

p.	132 UNDERWOOD 2.2	15	Or his courage; for away
p.	139 UNDERWOOD 2.7	6	That doth but touch his flower, and flies away.
p.	146 UNDERWOOD 6	5	Take that away, you take our lives,
p.	147 UNDERWOOD 7	23	As make away my doubt,
p.	154 UNDERWOOD 13	42	A Benefit; or that doth throw 't away:
p.	173 UNDERWOOD 22	18	The withered Garlands tane away;
p.	183 UNDERWOOD 29	19	Pegasus did flie away,
p.	194 UNDERWOOD 38	115	Out of your eyes, and be awhile away;
p.	199 UNDERWOOD 41	6	Or that the Sun was here, but forc't away;
p.	215 UNDERWOOD 44	97	This other for his eye-browes; hence, away,
p.	223 UNDERWOOD 49	35	Shall I advise thee, Pucell? steale away
p.	228 UNDERWOOD 53	19	And cri'd, Away with the Caesarian bread,
p.	231 UNDERWOOD 56	23	Away ill company, and helpe in rime
p.	236 UNDERWOOD 63	6	What (at his liking) he will take away.
p.	257 UNDERWOOD 75	138	Now, Sun, and post away the rest of day:
p.	270 UNDERWOOD 83	51	Her suffrings, as the body had beene away!
p.	282 U'WOOD 84.9	8	Till swept away, th<ey>'were cancell'd with a broome!
p.	363 UNGATHERED 3	17	Then why should we dispaire? Dispaire, away:

awde   frequency: 1   relative frequency: 0.00001
    p. 215 UNDERWOOD 44   67 Are we by Booke-wormes to be awde? must we

awe   frequency: 2   relative frequency: 0.00002
  *p. 494 TO HIMSELF   53 His zeale to God, and his iust awe o're men;
    p. 367 UNGATHERED 6   48 "Where neither Force can bend, nor Feare can awe.

awed. See "awde."

awfull   frequency: 2   relative frequency: 0.00002
    p. 270 UNDERWOOD 83   43 A reverend State she had, an awfull Eye,
    p. 287 U'WOOD 84.9   167 And by the awfull manage of her Eye

awhile   frequency: 1   relative frequency: 0.00001
  See also "a-while."
    p. 194 UNDERWOOD 38   115 Out of your eyes, and be awhile away;

awl. See "nail."

axe   frequency: 1   relative frequency: 0.00001
    p. 107 FOREST 10   15 Who, with his axe, thy fathers mid-wife plaid.

aydes   frequency: 3   relative frequency: 0.00004
    p.   38 EPIGRAMS 35   7 Like aydes gainst treasons who hath found before?
    p. 283 U'WOOD 84.9   17 With all her aydes, to save her from the seize
    p. 398 UNGATHERED 30   62 Thy list of aydes, and force, for so it is:

aye   frequency: 1   relative frequency: 0.00001
  See also "i" (p. 163, Underwood 15, line 52;
          p. 188, Underwood 34, line 17;
          p. 219, Underwood 47, line 54).
    p. 164 UNDERWOOD 15   63 To see 'hem aye discoursing with their Glasse,

aymd   frequency: 1   relative frequency: 0.00001
    p. 406 UNGATHERED 34   96 Aymd at in thy omnipotent Designe!

ayme   frequency: 4   relative frequency: 0.00005
    p. 122 FOREST 15   8 To ought but grace, or ayme at other end.
    p. 188 UNDERWOOD 34   17 I, that thy Ayme was; but her fate prevail'd:
    p. 259 UNDERWOOD 76   21 When their pot-guns ayme to hit,
    p. 368 UNGATHERED 6   64 Now must we plie our ayme; our Swan's on wing.

aymed   frequency: 1   relative frequency: 0.00001
    p. 133 UNDERWOOD 2.3   12 Aymed with that selfe-same shaft.

aymes   frequency: 2   relative frequency: 0.00002
    p. 407 UNGATHERED 35   15 Thy Canvas Gyant, at some Channell aymes,
    p. 422 UNGATHERED 50   8 are distant, so is proffitt from iust aymes.

ayre   frequency: 30   relative frequency: 0.00043
  **p. 117 PANEGYRE   152 Their bursting ioyes; but through the ayre was rol'd
    p.   37 EPIGRAMS 32   5 The cold of Mosco, and fat Irish ayre,
    p.   76 EPIGRAMS 119   9 Dar'st breath in any ayre; and with safe skill,
    p.   83 EPIGRAMS 132   4 And vtter stranger to all ayre of France)
    p.   85 EPIGRAMS 133   63 Belch'd forth an ayre, as hot, as at the muster
    p.   93 FOREST 2   7 Thou ioy'st in better markes, of soyle, of ayre,
    p.   94 FOREST 2   40 Fresh as the ayre, and new as are the houres.

ayre (cont.)
```
     p. 101 FOREST 4        31 And tasting ayre, and freedome, wull
     p. 112 FOREST 11       97 All taste of bitternesse, and makes the ayre
     p. 113 FOREST 12       12 Of some grand peere, whose ayre doth make reioyce
     p. 136 UNDERWOOD 2.5   14 So, Anacreon drawne the Ayre
     p. 137 UNDERWOOD 2.6    3 From your lips, and suck'd an ayre
     p. 147 UNDERWOOD 7     17 As Summers sky, or purged Ayre,
     p. 154 UNDERWOOD 13    45 Lest Ayre, or Print, but flies it: Such men
                               would
     p. 192 UNDERWOOD 38    51 You may so place me, and in such an ayre,
     p. 192 UNDERWOOD 38    57 The Sunne his heat, and light, the ayre his dew?
     p. 200 UNDERWOOD 42    14 No face, no hand, proportion, line, or Ayre
     p. 227 UNDERWOOD 52    17 Your Power of handling shadow, ayre, and
                               spright,
     p. 233 UNDERWOOD 59    10 Of bodies, meet like rarified ayre!
     p. 234 UNDERWOOD 60     7 Of honour, nor no ayre of good?
     p. 239 UNDERWOOD 67    14 And cleave both ayre and ground,
     p. 245 UNDERWOOD 70    64 These make the lines of life, and that's her
                               ayre.
     p. 251 UNDERWOOD 74     9 The rudest Winds obey the calmest Ayre:
     p. 274 U'WOOD 84.2      4 That ever Nature, or the later Ayre
     p. 275 U'WOOD 84.3      8 Needs nought to cloath it but the ayre.
     p. 279 U'WOOD 84.4     38 As some soft chime had stroak'd the ayre;
     p. 380 UNGATHERED 12   28 Horse, foote, and all but flying in the ayre:
     p. 389 UNGATHERED 24   15 For though Spaine gaue him his first ayre and
                               Vogue,
     p. 397 UNGATHERED 30   36 Like him, to make the ayre, one volary:
     p. 420 UNGATHERED 48   23 Whose ayre will sooner Hell, then their dull
                               senses peirce,
```

ayres   frequency: 1   relative frequency: 0.00001
```
     p. 397 UNGATHERED 30   26 Heard the soft ayres, between our swaynes &
                               thee,
```

ayrie   frequency: 2   relative frequency: 0.00002
```
     p. 197 UNDERWOOD 40    19 Yet should the Lover still be ayrie and light,
     p. 254 UNDERWOOD 75    67 As if her ayrie steps did spring the flowers,
```

b<e>'asham'd   frequency: 1   relative frequency: 0.00001
```
     p. 329 HORACE 2       502 Or Muse, upon the Lyre, thou chance
                               b<e>'asham'd.
```

b<e>'embrac'd   frequency: 1   relative frequency: 0.00001
```
     p. 226 UNDERWOOD 52     3 But there are lines, wherewith I might
                               b<e>'embrac'd.
```

b<ess>   frequency: 1   relative frequency: 0.00001
```
     p. 212 UNDERWOOD 43   216 Thy Wives pox on thee, and B<ess> B<roughton>s
                               too.
```

b<roughton>s   frequency: 1   relative frequency: 0.00001
```
     p. 212 UNDERWOOD 43   216 Thy Wives pox on thee, and B<ess> B<roughton>s
                               too.
```

b<y>'imputed   frequency: 1   relative frequency: 0.00001
```
     p. 286 U'WOOD 84.9    144 B<y>'imputed right to an inheritance
```

babe   frequency: 3   relative frequency: 0.00004
```
     p. 130 UNDERWOOD 1.3   22 To see this Babe, all innocence;
     p. 237 UNDERWOOD 65     1 And art thou borne, brave Babe? Blest be thy
                               birth,
     p. 268 UNDERWOOD 82    11 Grow up, sweet Babe, as blessed, in thy Name,
```

babes   frequency: 1   relative frequency: 0.00001
```
     p. 223 UNDERWOOD 49    44 Both for the Mothers, and the Babes of grace,
```

babion   frequency: 1   relative frequency: 0.00001
```
     p.  81 EPIGRAMS 129    12 Out-dance the Babion, or out-boast the Braue;
```

baboon. See "babion."

babylonian   frequency: 1   relative frequency: 0.00001
```
     p.  51 EPIGRAMS 73      9 Item, the babylonian song you sing;
```

bacchus   frequency: 5   relative frequency: 0.00007
```
     See also "bacchvs."
     p. 220 UNDERWOOD 48     1 Since, Bacchus, thou art father
     p. 220 UNDERWOOD 48    t2 To Bacchus.
     p. 221 UNDERWOOD 48    13 For, Bacchus, thou art freer
     p. 321 HORACE 2       348 Or old Silenus, Bacchus guard, and Nurse.
```

bacchus (cont.)
  p. 378 UNGATHERED 11 91 To be his Bacchus as his Pallas: bee

bacchvs   frequency: 1   relative frequency: 0.00001
  p. 93 FOREST 2   11 Where PAN, and BACCHVS their high
                    feasts haue made,

back   frequency: 10   relative frequency: 0.00014
  See also "backe."
  p. 132 UNDERWOOD 2.2 19 Could be brought once back to looke.
  p. 163 UNDERWOOD 15   49 His Lace and Starch: And fall upon her back
  p. 165 UNDERWOOD 15 104 Those thousands on his back, shall after blow
  p. 187 UNDERWOOD 33   22 Thou hast the brave scorne, to put back the fee!
  p. 192 UNDERWOOD 38   56 Why was't? did e're the Cloudes aske back their
                    raine?
  p. 219 UNDERWOOD 47   40 And force back that, which will not be restor'd,
  p. 243 UNDERWOOD 70   11 Did wiser Nature draw thee back,
  p. 254 UNDERWOOD 75   45 Her tresses trim her back,
  p. 292 UNDERWOOD 86   8 Goe where Youths soft intreaties call thee back.
  p. 416 UNGATHERED 45   6 at my back, I am no spright,

back-slides   frequency: 1   relative frequency: 0.00001
  p. 412 UNGATHERED 40   15 From fearefull back-slides;

backe   frequency: 16   relative frequency: 0.00023
  p. 78 EPIGRAMS 122   3 If I would striue to bring backe times, and trie
  p. 81 EPIGRAMS 128   14 Came backe vntouch'd. This man hath trauail'd
                    well.
  p. 85 EPIGRAMS 133   55 Great Club-fist, though thy backe, and bones be
                    sore,
  p. 86 EPIGRAMS 133   87 Backe, cry'd their brace of CHARONS: they
                    cry'd, no,
  p. 86 EPIGRAMS 133   88 No going backe; on still you rogues, and row.
  p. 88 EPIGRAMS 133 173 Cannot the Plague-bill keepe you backe? nor
                    bells
  p. 89 EPIGRAMS 133 192 And so went brauely backe, without protraction.
  p. 106 FOREST 9   14 And sent'st it backe to mee:
  p. 109 FOREST 11   25 Backe the intelligence, and falsely sweares,
  p. 118 FOREST 13   62 Not looking by, or backe (like those, that waite
  p. 121 FOREST 14   28 Of going backe
  p. 227 UNDERWOOD 52   4 'Tis true, as my wombe swells, so my backe
                    stoupes,
  p. 228 UNDERWOOD 53   1 When first, my Lord, I saw you backe your
                    horse,
  p. 355 HORACE 1   668 Now, bring ... backe, he'le .. ..
  p. 374 UNGATHERED 10   14 A Horse here is sadled, but no Tom him to
                    backe,
  p. 413 UNGATHERED 41 997 on the backe side.

backes   frequency: 1   relative frequency: 0.00001
  p. 368 UNGATHERED 6   69 To vtmost Thule: whence, he backes the Seas

backs   frequency: 1   relative frequency: 0.00001
  See also "backes."
  p. 62 EPIGRAMS 96   11 And, till they burst, their backs, like asses
                    load:

backward   frequency: 1   relative frequency: 0.00001
  p. 85 EPIGRAMS 133   35 Or him that backward went to Berwicke, or which

bacon   frequency: 1   relative frequency: 0.00001
  p. 225 UNDERWOOD 51   8 Since Bacon, and thy Lord was borne, and here;

bacons   frequency: 1   relative frequency: 0.00001
  p. 225 UNDERWOOD 51   t1 Lord BACONS Birth-day.

bad   frequency: 12   relative frequency: 0.00017
  p. 27 EPIGRAMS 3   2 Call'st a booke good, or bad, as it doth sell,
  p. 38 EPIGRAMS 38   1 GVILTIE, because I bad you late be wise,
  p. 50 EPIGRAMS 70   5 Delay is bad, doubt worse, depending worst;
  p. 52 EPIGRAMS 76   18 My Muse bad, Bedford write, and that was shee.
  p. 66 EPIGRAMS 102   3 Against the bad, but of, and to the good:
  p. 66 EPIGRAMS 102   11 And are so good, and bad, iust at a price,
  p. 80 EPIGRAMS 126   4 And bad me lay th'vsurped laurell downe:
  p. 87 EPIGRAMS 133 115 And bad her fare-well sough, vnto the lurden:
  p. 116 FOREST 13   3 The bad, by number, are so fortified,
  p. 146 UNDERWOOD 6   17 The good, from bad, is not describe,
  p. 250 UNDERWOOD 73   6 Who seldome sleepes! whom bad men only hate!
  p. 385 UNGATHERED 20   6 The art of vttring wares, if they were bad;

bade. See "bid."

bag   frequency: 1   relative frequency: 0.00001
    p. 135 UNDERWOOD 2.4   29 Or have tasted the bag o'the Bee?

bags   frequency: 1   relative frequency: 0.00001
    p. 165 UNDERWOOD 15   112 Sweet bags, sweet Powders, nor sweet words will
                             passe

baies   frequency: 1   relative frequency: 0.00001
    p. 183 UNDERWOOD 29   28 Not a worke deserving Baies,

baits   frequency: 1   relative frequency: 0.00001
    See also "baytes."
    p. 100 FOREST 4   12 And what thou call'st thy gifts are baits.

bake   frequency: 1   relative frequency: 0.00001
    p. 42 EPIGRAMS 50   2 Or fumie clysters, thy moist lungs to bake:

balance. See "ballance."

bald   frequency: 2   relative frequency: 0.00002
    p. 105 FOREST 8   40 Bald, or blinde, or nere so many:
    p. 245 UNDERWOOD 70   68 To fall a logge at last, dry, bald, and seare:

ball   frequency: 3   relative frequency: 0.00004
    p. 141 UNDERWOOD 2.9   20 Smooth as is the Billiard Ball:
    p. 206 UNDERWOOD 43   82 Th'admir'd discourses of the Prophet Ball:
    p. 331 HORACE 2   567 Or, who's unskilfull at the Coit, or Ball,

balladrie   frequency: 1   relative frequency: 0.00001
    p. 175 UNDERWOOD 23   21 Of worded Balladrie,

balladry. See "balladrie."

ballads   frequency: 1   relative frequency: 0.00001
    p. 411 UNGATHERED 39   12 A Tune to drown the Ballads of thy Father:

ballance   frequency: 2   relative frequency: 0.00002
    p. 188 UNDERWOOD 34   6 Quarrell with Nature, or in ballance brought
    p. 229 UNDERWOOD 54   10 Within the ballance; and not want a mite;

balm. See "balme."

balme   frequency: 3   relative frequency: 0.00004
    p. 187 UNDERWOOD 33   36 Thy Hearers Nectar, and thy Clients Balme,
    p. 280 U'WOOD 84.4   60 As showers; and sweet as drops of Balme.
    p. 286 U'WOOD 84.9   125 Unto the Sent, a Spicerie, or Balme;

balmes   frequency: 1   relative frequency: 0.00001
    p. 180 UNDERWOOD 26   2 I send nor Balmes, nor Cor'sives to your wound,

balms. See "balmes."

banck   frequency: 3   relative frequency: 0.00004
    p. 36 EPIGRAMS 31   1 BANCK feeles no lamenesse of his knottie
                             gout,
    p. 36 EPIGRAMS 31   t1 ON BANCK THE VSVRER.
    p. 209 UNDERWOOD 43   143 Bred on the Banck, in time of Poperie,

banck-side   frequency: 1   relative frequency: 0.00001
    p. 84 EPIGRAMS 133   30 Makes the poore Banck-side creature wet it'
                             shoone,

bancke   frequency: 1   relative frequency: 0.00001
    p. 416 UNGATHERED 44   3 Bred by your breath, on this low bancke of ours;

bancks   frequency: 1   relative frequency: 0.00001
    p. 41 EPIGRAMS 44   t1 ON CHVFFE, BANCKS THE
                             VSVRER'S

banckside   frequency: 1   relative frequency: 0.00001
    p. 208 UNDERWOOD 43   123 Well fare the wise-men yet, on the Banckside,

band   frequency: 7   relative frequency: 0.00010
    p. 42 EPIGRAMS 46   3 'Tis LVCKLESSE he, that tooke vp one on
                             band
    p. 140 UNDERWOOD 2.8   19 And pronounce, which band, or lace,
    p. 142 U'WOOD 2.10   4 His Clothes rich, and band sit neat,
    p. 164 UNDERWOOD 15   69 Ready to cast, at one, whose band sits ill,
    p. 169 UNDERWOOD 17   9 And their words too; where I but breake my
                             Band.

band (cont.)
    p. 169 UNDERWOOD 17   12 Simply my Band, his trust in me forsakes,
    p. 215 UNDERWOOD 44   95 His Lordship. That is for his Band, his haire

bands   frequency: 3   relative frequency: 0.00004
    p. 233 UNDERWOOD 59   23 Of fortune! when, or death appear'd, or bands!
    p. 256 UNDERWOOD 75   129 O happy bands! and thou more happy place,
    p. 289 UNDERWOOD 85   4 And is not in the Usurers bands:

banish'd   frequency: 2   relative frequency: 0.00002
    p. 183 UNDERWOOD 29   15 And Art banish'd.
    p. 311 HORACE 2   138 When they are poore, and banish'd, must throw by

bank. See "banck," "bancke," "banke."

banke   frequency: 8   relative frequency: 0.00011
    p. 94 FOREST 2   25 Each banke doth yeeld thee coneyes; and the topps
    p. 136 UNDERWOOD 2.5   25 Have you plac'd the banke of kisses,
    p. 160 UNDERWOOD 14   63 A banke against it. Nothing but the round
    p. 170 UNDERWOOD 19   9 And lastly by your lips, the banke of kisses,
    p. 208 UNDERWOOD 43   132 Against the Globe, the Glory of the Banke.
    p. 215 UNDERWOOD 44   76 In so much land a yeare, or such a Banke,
    p. 251 UNDERWOOD 74   10 Rare Plants from ev'ry banke doe rise,
    p. 280 U'WOOD 84.4   67 Upon a banke, or field of flowers,

banke-rupt   frequency: 1   relative frequency: 0.00001
    p. 237 UNDERWOOD 64   20 Is Banke-rupt turn'd! the Cassock, Cloake, and
                             Gowne,

bankes   frequency: 5   relative frequency: 0.00007
    p. 88 EPIGRAMS 133   142 The euer-boyling floud. Whose bankes vpon
    p. 88 EPIGRAMS 133   156 Old BANKES the iuggler, our
                             PYTHAGORAS,
    p. 89 EPIGRAMS 133   183 They cry'd out PVSSE. He told them he was
                             BANKES,
    p. 290 UNDERWOOD 85   25 Whilst from the higher Bankes doe slide the
                             floods;
    p. 392 UNGATHERED 26   73 And make those flights vpon the bankes of
                             Thames,

bankrupt. See "banke-rupt."

banks. See "bancks," "bankes."

bankside. See "banck-side," "banckside."

banquet   frequency: 1   relative frequency: 0.00001
    p. 284 U'WOOD 84.9   65 And the whole Banquet is full sight of God!

baphyre   frequency: 1   relative frequency: 0.00001
    p. 367 UNGATHERED 6   57 Who euer sipt at Baphyre riuer,

baptism. See "baptisme."

baptisme   frequency: 2   relative frequency: 0.00002
    p. 44 EPIGRAMS 53   7 And that, as puritanes at baptisme doo,
    p. 268 UNDERWOOD 82   10 This day, by Baptisme, and his Saviours crosse:

bar. See "barre."

barbarous   frequency: 2   relative frequency: 0.00002
  **p. 115 PANEGYRE   98 "The bloody, base, and barbarous she did quote;
    p. 60 EPIGRAMS 93   6 Vpbraiding rebells armes, and barbarous pride:

barber   frequency: 1   relative frequency: 0.00001
    p. 325 HORACE 2   427 And from the Barber Licinus conceale

barbican   frequency: 1   relative frequency: 0.00001
    p. 256 UNDERWOOD 75   112 He had so highly set; and, in what Barbican.

bard   frequency: 2   relative frequency: 0.00002
    p. 241 UNDERWOOD 68   11 As the old Bard, should no Canary lack.
    p. 274 U'WOOD 84.1   33 This, utter'd by an antient BARD,

bare   frequency: 4   relative frequency: 0.00005
    p. 68 EPIGRAMS 105   13 And, armed to the chase, so bare her bow
    p. 160 UNDERWOOD 14   51 And then of times (besides the bare Conduct
    p. 291 UNDERWOOD 85   63 To view the weary Oxen draw, with bare
    p. 364 UNGATHERED 4   8 But a bare Type and Figure.

bark. See "barke."

barke   frequency: 2   relative frequency: 0.00002
     p.   94 FOREST 2   15 There, in the writhed barke, are cut the names
     p. 294 UNDERWOOD 87   22 Thou lighter then the barke of any tree,

barking   frequency: 2   relative frequency: 0.00002
     p. 408 UNGATHERED 37   10 By barking against mee. Thou look'st at least,
     p. 410 UNGATHERED 39   8 Keep in thy barking Wit, thou bawling Fool?

barnabee   frequency: 1   relative frequency: 0.00001
     p. 262 UNDERWOOD 78   15 When the Apostle Barnabee the bright

barnaby. See "barnabee."

baronet   frequency: 1   relative frequency: 0.00001
     p. 400 UNGATHERED 32   t2 Friend, Sir Iohn Beaumont, Baronet.

barons   frequency: 1   relative frequency: 0.00001
     p. 397 UNGATHERED 30   42 I saw, and read, it was thy Barons Warres!

barr'd   frequency: 1   relative frequency: 0.00001
     p. 284 U'WOOD 84.9   67 All other gladnesse, with the thought is barr'd;

barre   frequency: 5   relative frequency: 0.00007
     p.   44 EPIGRAMS 54   2 And threatens the starre-chamber, and the barre:
     p.   99 FOREST 3   73 Let this man sweat, and wrangle at the barre,
     p. 186 UNDERWOOD 33   1 That I, hereafter, doe not thinke the Barre,
     p. 289 UNDERWOOD 85   7 But flees the Barre and Courts, with the proud
                                bords,
     p. 331 HORACE 2   551 Or Pleader at the Barre, that may come short

barrel. See "barrell."

barrell   frequency: 1   relative frequency: 0.00001
     p. 221 UNDERWOOD 48   32 Have issue from the Barrell;

barren   frequency: 5   relative frequency: 0.00007
     p.   46 EPIGRAMS 62   3 The world reputes you barren: but I know
     p. 169 UNDERWOOD 17   16 All is not barren land, doth fallow lie.
     p. 237 UNDERWOOD 64   15 How is she barren growne of love! or broke!
     p. 295 UNDERWOOD 90   4 A Soyle, not barren; a continewall fire;
     p. 309 HORACE 2   93 A kingly worke; or that long barren fen

bartas   frequency: 2   relative frequency: 0.00002
     p.   83 EPIGRAMS 132   7 Behold! the reuerend shade of BARTAS stands
     p.   83 EPIGRAMS 132   10 BARTAS doth wish thy English now were his.

base   frequency: 7   relative frequency: 0.00010
   **p. 115 PANEGYRE   98 "The bloody, base, and barbarous she did quote;
     p.   45 EPIGRAMS 59   1 SPIES, you are lights in state, but of base
                                stuffe,
     p. 109 FOREST 11   26 Th'are base, and idle feares
     p. 204 UNDERWOOD 43   42 There were some pieces of as base allay,
     p. 319 HORACE 2   302 Clowne, Towns-man, base, and noble, mix'd, to
                                judge?
     p. 321 HORACE 2   334 With poore base termes, through every baser shop:
     p. 361 UNGATHERED 1   11 Whilst other soules conuert to base abuse

basenesse   frequency: 1   relative frequency: 0.00001
     p. 142 UNDERWOOD 2.9   51 And from basenesse to be free,

baser   frequency: 1   relative frequency: 0.00001
     p. 321 HORACE 2   334 With poore base termes, through every baser shop:

basest   frequency: 1   relative frequency: 0.00001
     p. 101 FOREST 4   46 Where breathe the basest of thy fooles;

basket. See "almes-basket."

baskets   frequency: 1   relative frequency: 0.00001
     p.   95 FOREST 2   55 This way to husbands; and whose baskets beare

bastard   frequency: 1   relative frequency: 0.00001
     p. 223 UNDERWOOD 49   46 Will cal't a Bastard, when a Prophet's borne.

bastinado   frequency: 2   relative frequency: 0.00002
     p.   33 EPIGRAMS 21   6 The late tane bastinado. So I thought.
     p. 375 UNGATHERED 10   23 A Rabbin confutes him with the Bastinado.

bath   frequency: 2   relative frequency: 0.00002
     p. 136 UNDERWOOD 2.5   21 As the Bath your verse discloses

bath (cont.)
    p. 188 UNDERWOOD 34   10 Any beliefe, in Madam Baud-bees bath,

bathes   frequency: 2   relative frequency: 0.00002
    p. 77 EPIGRAMS 120   22 In bathes to steepe him;
    p. 170 UNDERWOOD 19   7 By those pure bathes your either cheeke
                                discloses,

baths   frequency: 1   relative frequency: 0.00001
    See also "bathes."
    p. 325 HORACE 2   424 Retire themselves, avoid the publike baths:

battaile   frequency: 1   relative frequency: 0.00001
    p. 60 EPIGRAMS 93   5 Two brauely in the battaile fell, and dy'd,

battells   frequency: 1   relative frequency: 0.00001
    p. 214 UNDERWOOD 44   46 The Battells of thy Aldermanitie;

battery. See "battry."

battle. See "battaile."

battles. See "battells."

battry   frequency: 1   relative frequency: 0.00001
    p. 401 UNGATHERED 32   14 A Trench against it, nor a Battry plac't?

baud   frequency: 5   relative frequency: 0.00007
    p. 31 EPIGRAMS 12   23 But see! th'old baud hath seru'd him in his trim,
    p. 39 EPIGRAMS 41   1 GYPSEE, new baud, is turn'd physitian,
    p. 39 EPIGRAMS 41   4 For what shee gaue, a whore; a baud, shee cures.
    p. 167 UNDERWOOD 15   158 As a poore single flatterer, without Baud,
    p. 391 UNGATHERED 26   13 These are, as some infamous Baud, or Whore,

baud-bees   frequency: 1   relative frequency: 0.00001
    p. 188 UNDERWOOD 34   10 Any beliefe, in Madam Baud-bees bath,

baudie   frequency: 2   relative frequency: 0.00002
    p. 63 EPIGRAMS 97   10 Nor baudie stock, that trauells for encrease,
    p. 164 UNDERWOOD 15   74 To be abroad chanting some baudie song,

baudrie'   frequency: 1   relative frequency: 0.00001
    p. 45 EPIGRAMS 57   2 Baudrie', and vsurie were one kind of game.

baudy   frequency: 1   relative frequency: 0.00001
    p. 74 EPIGRAMS 115   9 Talkes loud, and baudy, has a gather'd deale

bavdes   frequency: 1   relative frequency: 0.00001
    p. 45 EPIGRAMS 57   t1 ON BAVDES, AND VSVRERS.

bawd   frequency: 1   relative frequency: 0.00001
    See also "baud."
    p. 202 UNDERWOOD 42   85 Bawd, in a Velvet scabberd! I envy

bawd-be's. See "baud-bees."

bawdie   frequency: 1   relative frequency: 0.00001
    p. 321 HORACE 2   359 Or crack out bawdie speeches, and uncleane.

bawdrie   frequency: 2   relative frequency: 0.00002
    p. 42 EPIGRAMS 49   3 I haue no salt: no bawdrie he doth meane.
    p. 222 UNDERWOOD 49   12 Make State, Religion, Bawdrie, all a theame?

bawdry   frequency: 1   relative frequency: 0.00001
    See also "baudrie'," "bawdrie."
    p. 223 UNDERWOOD 49   26 For bawdry, 'tis her language, and not mine.

bawds   frequency: 1   relative frequency: 0.00001
    See also "bavdes."
    p. 118 FOREST 13   78 Till that no vsurer, nor his bawds dare lend

bawdy. See "baudie," "baudy," "bawdie."

bawl. See "bawle."

bawle   frequency: 1   relative frequency: 0.00001
    p. 408 UNGATHERED 37   7 But bawle thou on; I pitty thee, poore Curre,

bawling   frequency: 1   relative frequency: 0.00001
    p. 410 UNGATHERED 39   8 Keep in thy barking Wit, thou bawling Fool?

bayes   frequency: 5   relative frequency: 0.00007
 p.   32 EPIGRAMS 17   5 And, but a sprigge of bayes, giuen by thee,
 p.   73 EPIGRAMS 113   1 So PHOEBVS makes me worthy of his bayes,
 p.   80 EPIGRAMS 126   2 'Mongst Hampton shades, and PHOEBVS groue
         of bayes,
 p. 232 UNDERWOOD 58   6 Thanke him: if other, hee can give no Bayes.
 p. 420 UNGATHERED 48   26 And come fforth worthie Ivye, or the Bayes,

bays. See "baies," "bayes."

baytes   frequency: 1   relative frequency: 0.00001
 p. 175 UNDERWOOD 23   20 Be taken with false Baytes

be   frequency: 469   relative frequency: 0.00678
 See also "b<e>'asham'd," "b<e>'embrac'd,"
   "be'<i>n," "bee," "out-bee,"
   "wovld-bee"; also "baud-bees."

be'<i>n   frequency: 1   relative frequency: 0.00001
 p. 155 UNDERWOOD 13   64 Or stands to be'<i>n Commission o' the blade?

beadle   frequency: 1   relative frequency: 0.00001
 p.   86 EPIGRAMS 133   81 One said, it was bold BRIAREVS, or the
         beadle,

beam. See "beame."

beame   frequency: 2   relative frequency: 0.00002
 p. 177 UNDERWOOD 25   14 Rich beame of honour, shed your light
 p. 396 UNGATHERED 30   17 It cast a beame as when the chear=full Sun

beames   frequency: 2   relative frequency: 0.00002
 p. 276 U'WOOD 84.3   17 Then let the beames of that, disperse
 p. 366 UNGATHERED 6   24 From Zephyr's rape would close him with his
         beames.

beamie   frequency: 1   relative frequency: 0.00001
 p. 176 UNDERWOOD 24   9 Which makes that (lighted by the beamie hand

beams   frequency: 1   relative frequency: 0.00001
 See also "beames."
**p. 113 PANEGYRE   8 But these his searching beams are cast, to prie

beamy. See "beamie."

bear. See "beare," "vp-beare."

beard   frequency: 2   relative frequency: 0.00002
 p. 132 UNDERWOOD 2.2   30 Cupids Statue with a Beard,
 p. 141 UNDERWOOD 2.9   23 Till he cherish'd too much beard,

beards   frequency: 3   relative frequency: 0.00004
 p.   58 EPIGRAMS 92   6 Ripe are their ruffes, their cuffes, their
         beards, their gate,
 p. 325 HORACE 2   423 Their nailes, nor shave their beards, but to
         by-paths
 p. 417 UNGATHERED 45   13 To the merry beards in Hall,

beare   frequency: 22   relative frequency: 0.00031
**p. 113 PANEGYRE   27 Her third, IRENE, help'd to beare his
         traine;
**p. 114 PANEGYRE   59 That did not beare a part in this consent
**p. 115 PANEGYRE   88 "In publique acts what face and forme they beare.
 p.   28 EPIGRAMS 4   1 How, best of Kings, do'st thou a scepter beare!
 p.   46 EPIGRAMS 62   2 That loue to make so well, a child to beare?
 p.   55 EPIGRAMS 84   10 Make it your gift. See whither that will beare
         mee.
 p.   57 EPIGRAMS 90   18 First bearing him a calfe, beare him a bull.
 p.   95 FOREST 2   55 This way to husbands; and whose baskets beare
 p. 101 FOREST 4   39 I know thou canst nor shew, nor beare
 p. 101 FOREST 4   53 But, what we'are borne for, we must beare:
 p. 102 FOREST 4   63 But I will beare these, with that scorne,
 p. 113 FOREST 12   8 Iust to the waight their this dayes-presents
         beare;
 p. 116 FOREST 12   100 My best of wishes, may you beare a sonne.
 p. 166 UNDERWOOD 15   119 What reputation to beare one Glasse more?
 p. 166 UNDERWOOD 15   125 Tilt one upon another, and now beare
 p. 232 UNDERWOOD 58   11 Like a rung Beare, or Swine: grunting out wit
 p. 269 UNDERWOOD 83   18 At least may beare th'inscription to her Tombe.
 p. 307 HORACE 2   55 Upon your shoulders. Prove what they will beare,

beare (cont.)
    p. 323 HORACE 2   377 The steadie Spondaees; so themselves to beare
    p. 337 HORACE 2   674 And, as a Beare, if he the strength but had
    p. 417 UNGATHERED 45   28 the Moone will beare it.
    p. 423 UNGATHERED 50   19 That prince that shames a tyrants name to beare,

bearer   frequency: 1   relative frequency: 0.00001
    p. 166 UNDERWOOD 15   120 When oft the Bearer, is borne out of dore?

beares   frequency: 9   relative frequency: 0.00013
    p. 33 EPIGRAMS 22   7 Whose soule heauens Queene, (whose name shee
                              beares)
    p. 58 EPIGRAMS 91   1 Which of thy names I take, not onely beares
    p. 63 EPIGRAMS 97   12 Nor 'bout the beares, nor noyse to make lords
                              sport.
    p. 87 EPIGRAMS 133   117 The meate-boate of Beares colledge,
                              Paris-garden,
    p. 110 FOREST 11   51 In equall knots: This beares no brands, nor
                              darts,
    p. 113 FOREST 12   18 Or perhaps lesse: whil'st gold beares all this
                              sway,
    p. 176 UNDERWOOD 24   15 Some note of which each varied Pillar beares,
    p. 209 UNDERWOOD 43   146 And cry'd, it was a threatning to the beares;
    p. 219 UNDERWOOD 47   50 That guides the Motions, and directs the beares.

bearing   frequency: 5   relative frequency: 0.00007
    p. 42 EPIGRAMS 48   2 Of bearing them in field, he threw 'hem away:
    p. 57 EPIGRAMS 90   18 First bearing him a calfe, beare him a bull.
    p. 214 UNDERWOOD 44   44 Of bearing Armes! most civill Soldierie!
    p. 215 UNDERWOOD 44   65 Us, in our bearing, that are thus, and thus,
    p. 252 UNDERWOOD 75   10 (Bearing the promise of some better fate)

bears. See "beares."

beast   frequency: 9   relative frequency: 0.00013
    p. 34 EPIGRAMS 25   1 While BEAST instructs his faire, and
                              innocent wife,
    p. 34 EPIGRAMS 25   t1 ON SIR VOLVPTVOVS BEAST.
    p. 35 EPIGRAMS 26   1 Then his chast wife, though BEAST now know
                              no more,
    p. 35 EPIGRAMS 26   t1 ON THE SAME BEAST.
    p. 101 FOREST 4   29 What bird, or beast, is knowne so dull,
    p. 143 UNDERWOOD 3   5 At such a Call, what beast or fowle,
    p. 156 UNDERWOOD 13   117 And feeles it; Else he tarries by the Beast.
    p. 403 UNGATHERED 34   21 Why much good doo't you! Be what beast you will,
    p. 408 UNGATHERED 37   9 To be knowne what thou art, a blatant beast,

beastly   frequency: 1   relative frequency: 0.00001
    p. 27 EPIGRAMS 2   11 Much lesse with lewd, prophane, and beastly
                              phrase,

beasts   frequency: 2   relative frequency: 0.00002
    p. 82 EPIGRAMS 130   2 Of building townes, and making wilde beasts tame,
    p. 294 UNDERWOOD 88   4 Like lustfull beasts, that onely know to doe it:

beat   frequency: 3   relative frequency: 0.00004
    See also "beate."
    p. 36 EPIGRAMS 28   17 Blaspheme god, greatly. Or some poore hinde
                              beat,
    p. 288 U'WOOD 84.9   189 And hers were all Humilitie! they beat
    p. 333 HORACE 2   613 Out at his friendly eyes, leape, beat the groun'.

beate   frequency: 2   relative frequency: 0.00002
    p. 88 EPIGRAMS 133   170 Vrine, and plaisters? when the noise doth beate
    p. 397 UNGATHERED 30   55 But that I heare, againe, thy Drum to beate

beaten   frequency: 2   relative frequency: 0.00002
    p. 375 UNGATHERED 10   24 Here, by a Boore too, hee's like to be beaten
    p. 380 UNGATHERED 12   35 He was in his trauaile, how like to be beaten,

beates   frequency: 1   relative frequency: 0.00001
    p. 162 UNDERWOOD 15   2 Beates brave, and loude in Europe, and bids come

beatific. See "beatifick."

beatifick   frequency: 1   relative frequency: 0.00001
    p. 285 U'WOOD 84.9   116 By beatifick vertue of the Place.

beating   frequency: 2   relative frequency: 0.00002
    p. 179 UNDERWOOD 25   41 Sweat at the forge, their hammers beating;

beating (cont.)
    p. 239 UNDERWOOD 67   15 With beating of our Drums:

                         frequency: 1   relative frequency: 0.00001
beatings
    p. 49 EPIGRAMS 68   2 Takes priuate beatings, and begins againe.

                         frequency: 1   relative frequency: 0.00001
beatitude
    p. 286 U'WOOD 84.9   137 What fulnesse of beatitude is here?

                         frequency: 1   relative frequency: 0.00001
beatitudes
    p. 271 UNDERWOOD 83   75 And all beatitudes, that thence doe flow:

beats. See "beates."

                         frequency: 1   relative frequency: 0.00001
beauchamps
    p. 214 UNDERWOOD 44   52 Beauchamps, and Nevills, Cliffords, Audleys
                      old;

                         frequency: 2   relative frequency: 0.00002
beaumont
    See also "beavmont."
    p. 391 UNGATHERED 26   20 Chaucer, or Spenser, or bid Beaumont lye
    p. 400 UNGATHERED 32   t2 Friend, Sir Iohn Beaumont, Baronet.

                         frequency: 1   relative frequency: 0.00001
beaumonts
    p. 400 UNGATHERED 32   7 Though I confesse a Beaumonts Booke to bee

                         frequency: 1   relative frequency: 0.00001
beauteous
    p. 414 UNGATHERED 41   49 Thou Throne of glory, beauteous as the Moone,

                         frequency: 27 relative frequency: 0.00039
beautie
    p. 39 EPIGRAMS 40   2 A dead beautie vnder-neath thee,
    p. 74 EPIGRAMS 114   6 Where finding so much beautie met with vertue,
    p. 79 EPIGRAMS 124   4 As much beautie, as could dye:
    p. 108 FOREST 10   27 A beautie of that merit, that should take
    p. 112 FOREST 11   93 A beautie of that cleere, and sparkling light,
    p. 114 FOREST 12   37 Beautie, I know, is good, and bloud is more;
    p. 114 FOREST 12   50 Haue beautie knowne, yet none so famous seene?
    p. 117 FOREST 13   30 Your beautie; for you see that euery day:
    p. 117 FOREST 13   37 Nor that your beautie wanted not a dower,
    p. 131 UNDERWOOD 2.1 19 Of whose Beautie it was sung,
    p. 169 UNDERWOOD 18   1 Can Beautie that did prompt me first to write,
    p. 171 UNDERWOOD 19 20 I know no beautie, nor no youth that will.
    p. 173 UNDERWOOD 22   1 Though Beautie be the Marke of praise,
    p. 188 UNDERWOOD 34   2 One beautie in an Age, and free from thee?
    p. 188 UNDERWOOD 34 14 Of Beautie, so to nullifie a face,
    p. 188 UNDERWOOD 35   1 What Beautie would have lovely stilde,
    p. 200 UNDERWOOD 42 15 Of beautie; but the Muse hath interest in:
    p. 215 UNDERWOOD 44 96 This, and that box his Beautie to repaire;
    p. 245 UNDERWOOD 70 73 In small proportions, we just beautie see:
    p. 251 UNDERWOOD 74   6 Of the prime beautie of the yeare, the Spring.
    p. 251 UNDERWOOD 74 30 And both a strength, and Beautie to his Land!
    p. 252 UNDERWOOD 75   8 The bountie of a King, and beautie of his
                      Queene!
    p. 269 UNDERWOOD 83   5 I doe obey you, Beautie! for in death,
    p. 275 U'WOOD 84.3   7 This beautie without falshood fayre,
    p. 280 U'WOOD 84.4 51 In all the bounds of beautie fit
    p. 286 U'WOOD 84.9 122 Where Hee will be, all Beautie to the Sight;
    p. 311 HORACE 2   141 Her Poem's beautie, but a sweet delight

                         frequency: 10 relative frequency: 0.00014
beauties
  **p. 114 PANEGYRE   51 That might her beauties heighten; but so drest,
    p. 117 FOREST 13   44 And takes, and giues the beauties of the mind.
    p. 133 UNDERWOOD 2.3   2 Which the prouder Beauties please,
    p. 181 UNDERWOOD 27   2 Thy beauties, yet could write of thee?
    p. 200 UNDERWOOD 42 33 Have eaten with the Beauties, and the wits,
    p. 228 UNDERWOOD 53 11 Nay, so your Seate his beauties did endorse,
    p. 253 UNDERWOOD 75 17 What Beavie of beauties, and bright youths at
                      charge
    p. 264 UNDERWOOD 79 38 2. As if the beauties of the yeare,
    p. 271 UNDERWOOD 83 74 What the beginnings of all beauties be;
    p. 277 U'WOOD 84.3 28 And thou hast painted beauties world.

                         frequency: 4   relative frequency: 0.00005
beauty
    See also "beautie."
    p. 108 FOREST 10A   8 in whom the flame of euery beauty raignes,
    p. 134 UNDERWOOD 2.4   6 Unto her beauty;
    p. 137 UNDERWOOD 2.5 49 For this Beauty yet doth hide
    p. 396 UNGATHERED 30 15 I saw a Beauty from the Sea to rise,

beaver. See "bever."

beavie   frequency: 1   relative frequency: 0.00001
    p. 253 UNDERWOOD 75   17 What Beavie of beauties, and bright youths at
                              charge

beavmont   frequency: 2   relative frequency: 0.00002
    p. 44 EPIGRAMS 55   1 How I doe loue thee BEAVMONT, and thy
                              Muse,
    p. 44 EPIGRAMS 55   t1 TO FRANCIS BEAVMONT.

became   frequency: 4   relative frequency: 0.00005
    p. 254 UNDERWOOD 75   76 Saw'st thou that Paire, became these Rites so
                              well,
    p. 271 UNDERWOOD 83   68 Became her Birth-day to Eternitie!
    p. 287 U'WOOD 84.9   161 She had, and it became her! she was fit
    p. 400 UNGATHERED 31   35 Aeternities great charter; which became

becam'st   frequency: 1   relative frequency: 0.00001
    p. 128 UNDERWOOD 1.1   22 To take our nature; becam'st man, and dyd'st,

because   frequency: 24   relative frequency: 0.00034
    See also "by-cause," "cause," "'cause."
    p. 34 EPIGRAMS 23   10 But leaue, because I cannot as I should!
    p. 38 EPIGRAMS 38   1 GVILTIE, because I bad you late be wise,
    p. 67 EPIGRAMS 104   5 Or, because some scarce thinke that storie true,
    p. 111 FOREST 11   71 Because they moue, the continent doth so:
    p. 111 FOREST 11   78 Because lust's meanes are spent:
    p. 115 FOREST 12   56 Because they lack'd the sacred pen, could giue
    p. 117 FOREST 13   17 Or so my selfe abandon'd, as because
    p. 118 FOREST 13   65 Because that studies spectacles, and showes,
    p. 120 FOREST 13   124 Because nor it can change, nor such a minde.
    p. 167 UNDERWOOD 15   171 (Because th'are every where amongst Man-kind
    p. 169 UNDERWOOD 17   10 I adde that (but) because I understand
    p. 170 UNDERWOOD 18   18 Because they would free Justice imitate,
    p. 171 UNDERWOOD 19   27 As in his place, because he would not varie,
    p. 173 UNDERWOOD 22   9 Wherein you triumph yet: because
    p. 192 UNDERWOOD 38   66 In man, because man hath the flesh abus'd.
    p. 203 UNDERWOOD 43   11 Was it because thou wert of old denied
    p. 234 UNDERWOOD 60   18 Because it durst have noblier dy'd.
    p. 251 UNDERWOOD 74   12 Because the order of the whole is faire!
    p. 279 U'WOOD 84.4   45 Is it because it sees us dull,
    p. 317 HORACE 2   242 Either because he seekes, and, having found,
    p. 319 HORACE 2   323 How he could jest, because he mark'd and saw,
    p. 325 HORACE 2   419 Because Democritus beleeves a wit
    p. 379 UNGATHERED 12   3 Who, because his matter in all should be meete,
    p. 396 UNGATHERED 30   3 Because, who make the question, haue not seene

beckning   frequency: 1   relative frequency: 0.00001
    p. 268 UNDERWOOD 83   3 And beckning wooes me, from the fatall tree

beckoning. See "beckning."

become   frequency: 19   relative frequency: 0.00027
    See also "becum."
    p. 27 EPIGRAMS 2   5 Become a petulant thing, hurle inke, and wit,
    p. 29 EPIGRAMS 8   6 The courtier is become the greater thiefe.
    p. 44 EPIGRAMS 56   3 From brocage is become so bold a thiefe,
    p. 58 EPIGRAMS 91   17 And best become the valiant man to weare,
    p. 105 FOREST 8   28 To become thy sacrifice.
    p. 117 FOREST 13   21 I, Madame, am become your praiser. Where,
    p. 152 UNDERWOOD 12   37 Reader, whose life, and name, did e're become
    p. 162 UNDERWOOD 15   14 Till he become both their, and his owne curse!
    p. 182 UNDERWOOD 28   3 Since I exscribe your Sonnets, am become
    p. 192 UNDERWOOD 38   39 I am regenerate now, become the child
    p. 198 UNDERWOOD 40   48 That Article, may not become <y>our lover:
    p. 199 UNDERWOOD 41   19 And so I spare it. Come what can become
    p. 201 UNDERWOOD 42   52 That from the Foot-man, when he was become
    p. 215 UNDERWOOD 44   82 The Herald will. Our blood is now become
    p. 234 UNDERWOOD 60   14 Ambition to become a Starre,
    p. 269 UNDERWOOD 83   17 When I, who would her Poet have become,
    p. 287 U'WOOD 84.9   178 As her whole life was now become one note
    p. 335 HORACE 2   639 Become an Aristarchus. And, not say,
    p. 406 UNGATHERED 35   3 Our Charles should make thee such? T'will not
                              become

becomes   frequency: 5   relative frequency: 0.00007
    p. 67 EPIGRAMS 103   14 Becomes none more then you, who need it least.
    p. 154 UNDERWOOD 13   40 So each, that's done, and tane, becomes a Brace.
    p. 280 U'WOOD 84.4   63 And where it stayes, it there becomes
    p. 329 HORACE 2   533 So he that flaggeth much, becomes to me
    p. 421 UNGATHERED 49   9 And though yor virtue (as becomes it) still

becometh.   See "becommeth."

becommeth   frequency: 1   relative frequency: 0.00001
    p. 325 HORACE 2   438 The Poet, what becommeth, and what not:

becum   frequency: 1   relative frequency: 0.00001
    p. 362 UNGATHERED 1   30 Palmer thy trauayles well becum thy name,

bed   frequency: 10   relative frequency: 0.00014
    See also "a-bed."
    p. 157 UNDERWOOD 13   127 Sydney e're night! or that did goe to bed
    p. 232 UNDERWOOD 57   27 nor any quick-warming-pan helpe him to bed,
    p. 237 UNDERWOOD 65   3 The bed of the chast Lilly, and the Rose!
    p. 248 UNDERWOOD 71   11 Fix'd to the bed, and boords, unlike to win
    p. 251 UNDERWOOD 74   18 In making soft her aromatique bed.
    p. 257 UNDERWOOD 75   162 (The holy perfumes of the Mariage bed.)
    p. 258 UNDERWOOD 75   185 They both are slip'd to Bed; Shut fast the
                               Doore,
    p. 283 U'WOOD 84.9   43 From off her pillow, and deluded bed;
    p. 295 UNDERWOOD 89   6 And heat, with softest love, thy softer bed.
    p. 413 UNGATHERED 41   19 Preserved, in her antique bed of Vert,

bed-mate   frequency: 1   relative frequency: 0.00001
    p. 295 UNDERWOOD 90   10 No sowre, or sollen bed-mate, yet a Chast;

bed-rid   frequency: 1   relative frequency: 0.00001
    p. 248 UNDERWOOD 71   15 A Bed-rid Wit, then a besieged Towne.

bedew'd   frequency: 1   relative frequency: 0.00001
    p. 254 UNDERWOOD 75   66 Have they bedew'd the Earth, where she doth
                               tread,

bedford   frequency: 6   relative frequency: 0.00008
    p. 52 EPIGRAMS 76   t1 ON LVCY COVNTESSE OF
                               BEDFORD.
    p. 52 EPIGRAMS 76   18 My Muse bad, Bedford write, and that was shee.
    p. 54 EPIGRAMS 84   t1 TO LVCY COVNTESSE OF
                               BEDFORD.
    p. 60 EPIGRAMS 94   t1 TO LVCY, COVNTESSE OF
                               BEDFORD,
    p. 419 UNGATH'D 47A   7 ... . vs ... Bedford ....
    p. 662 INSCRIPTS. 2   3 LVCY of BEDFORD; she, that Bounty

beds   frequency: 1   relative frequency: 0.00001
    p. 100 FOREST 8   45 On their beds, most prostitute,

bee   frequency: 57   relative frequency: 0.00082
  **p. 117 PANEGYRE   157 Nor to her blisse, could ought now added bee,
    p. 28 EPIGRAMS 4   8 As chiefe of those still promise they will bee.
    p. 38 EPIGRAMS 35   9 First thou preserued wert, our king to bee,
    p. 38 EPIGRAMS 36   4 Thou flattered'st thine, mine cannot flatter'd
                               bee.
    p. 47 EPIGRAMS 64   5 Nor glad as those, that old dependents bee,
    p. 49 EPIGRAMS 66   13 Loue honors, which of best example bee,
    p. 56 EPIGRAMS 88   5 And land on one, whose face durst neuer bee
    p. 60 EPIGRAMS 93   16 Wherewith, against thy bloud, they'offenders bee.
    p. 60 EPIGRAMS 94   7 Yet, Satyres, since the most of mankind bee
    p. 62 EPIGRAMS 96   1 Who shall doubt, DONNE, where I a Poet
                               bee,
    p. 64 EPIGRAMS 99   11 Well, though thy name lesse then our great ones
                               bee,
    p. 65 EPIGRAMS 101   27 Digestiue cheese, and fruit there sure will bee;
    p. 67 EPIGRAMS 104   2 Euen in the dew of grace, what you would bee?
    p. 68 EPIGRAMS 106   9 Their latter praise would still the greatest bee,
    p. 72 EPIGRAMS 111   2 What th'antique souldiers were, the moderne bee?
    p. 73 EPIGRAMS 114   1 I must beleeue some miracles still bee,
    p. 78 EPIGRAMS 122   10 Who prou'st, all these were, and againe may bee.
    p. 80 EPIGRAMS 127   1 Is there a hope, that Man would thankefull bee,
    p. 82 EPIGRAMS 130   17 But when I haue said, The proofes of all these
                               bee
    p. 106 FOREST 9   12 It could not withered bee.
    p. 117 FOREST 13   24 In my character, what your features bee,
    p. 118 FOREST 13   68 Right, the right way: yet must your comfort bee
    p. 119 FOREST 13   112 What your try'd manners are, what theirs should
                               bee.
    p. 122 FOREST 15   2 But it must, straight, my melancholy bee?
    p. 122 FOREST 15   25 Of discontent; or that these prayers bee
    p. 135 UNDERWOOD 2.4   29 Or have tasted the bag o'the Bee?
    p. 139 UNDERWOOD 2.7   5 I'le taste as lightly as the Bee,
    p. 144 UNDERWOOD 3   25 Nay, rather both our soules bee strayn'd

bee (cont.)

p. 184 UNDERWOOD 29	50 May his joynts tormented bee,
p. 189 UNDERWOOD 36	12 And waste still, that they still might bee.
p. 200 UNDERWOOD 42	5 Who shall forbid me then in Rithme to bee
p. 232 UNDERWOOD 58	3 Bee thou my Bookes intelligencer, note
p. 238 UNDERWOOD 65	8 Thee quickly <come> the gardens eye to bee,
p. 245 UNDERWOOD 70	66 In bulke, doth make man better bee;
p. 245 UNDERWOOD 70	74 And in short measures, life may perfect bee.
p. 273 U'WOOD 84.1	14 Who read what the CREPUNDIA bee,
p. 283 U'WOOD 84.9	39 Dare I prophane, so irreligious bee
p. 293 UNDERWOOD 86	39 Whether in Mars his field thou bee,
p. 295 UNDERWOOD 90	12 Will to bee, what thou art; and nothing more:
p. 309 HORACE 2	84 And ever will, to utter termes that bee
p. 313 HORACE 2	166 Of some small thankfull land: whether he bee
p. 329 HORACE 2	526 Much in the Poeme shine, I will not bee
p. 375 UNGATHERED 10	29 F. shewes what he was, K. what he will bee.
p. 378 UNGATHERED 11	91 To be his Bacchus as his Pallas: bee
p. 384 UNGATHERED 18	8 And pray, thy ioyes as lasting bee, as great.
p. 384 UNGATHERED 18	22 Mortality, till you <im>mortall bee.
p. 386 UNGATHERED 21	4 And, if thou list thy selfe, what thou canst bee.
p. 389 UNGATHERED 24	19 Will bee receiu'd in Court; If not, would I
p. 396 UNGATHERED 30	1 It hath beene question'd, MICHAEL, if I bee
p. 399 UNGATHERED 31	15 In her! and what could perfect bee,
p. 399 UNGATHERED 31	21 What was proportion, or could bee
p. 400 UNGATHERED 31	31 Vntill the dust retorned bee
p. 400 UNGATHERED 32	7 Though I confesse a Beaumonts Booke to bee
p. 412 UNGATHERED 40	23 Must CELIA bee,
p. 417 UNGATHERED 45	31 or hir quarters lighter bee,
p. 421 UNGATHERED 48	45 Whoe worthie wine, whoe not, to bee wyse Pallas guests.
p. 421 UNGATHERED 49	2 before, I wryte more verse, to bee more wyse.

beech   frequency: 1   relative frequency: 0.00001
    p. 93 FOREST 2   12 Beneath the broad beech, and the chest-nut shade;

beeing   frequency: 1   relative frequency: 0.00001
    p. 375 UNGATHERED 10 35 Beeing in feare to be robd, he most learnedly begs.

been   frequency: 1   relative frequency: 0.00001
    See also "beene," "bene," "bin."

beene   frequency: 31   relative frequency: 0.00044

beer. See "beere."

beere   frequency: 3   relative frequency: 0.00004
    p. 63 EPIGRAMS 101 34 Are all but LVTHERS beere, to this I sing.
    p. 95 FOREST 2   63 Where the same beere, and bread, and selfe-same wine,
    p. 167 UNDERWOOD 15 153 In Sugar Candide, or in butter'd beere,

beest   frequency: 1   relative frequency: 0.00001
    See also "be'st."

befall   frequency: 1   relative frequency: 0.00001
    p. 263 UNDERWOOD 78 31 Wilt thou be, Muse, when this shall them befall?

before   frequency: 48   relative frequency: 0.00069
    See also "'fore."
  **p. 114 PANEGYRE   47 They that had seene, but foure short daies before,
  **p. 117 PANEGYRE   143 Before mens hearts had crown'd him. Who (vnlike
    p. 37 EPIGRAMS 33   2 Glad-mention'd ROE: thou art but gone before,
    p. 38 EPIGRAMS 35   7 Like aydes gainst treasons who hath found before?
    p. 38 EPIGRAMS 38   3 You laugh when you are touch'd, and long before
    p. 49 EPIGRAMS 67   10 Before thou wert it, in each good mans heart.
    p. 53 EPIGRAMS 79   2 Your noblest father prou'd: like whom, before,
    p. 57 EPIGRAMS 89   10 Out-strip't, then they did all that went before:
    p. 61 EPIGRAMS 95   10 And gratulate the breach, I grieu'd before:
    p. 68 EPIGRAMS 105 20 I' your selfe, all treasure lost of th'age before.
    p. 83 EPIGRAMS 132   8 Before my thought, and (in thy right) commands
    p. 94 FOREST 2   38 Before the fisher, or into his hand.
    p. 114 FOREST 12   53 Gaue killing strokes. There were braue men, before
    p. 116 FOREST 12   99 Before his swift and circled race be run,
    p. 119 FOREST 13   102 Before the moones haue fill'd their tripple trine,

before (cont.)
```
  p. 129 UNDERWOOD 1.2    29 Before my losse
  p. 134 UNDERWOOD 2.4    22 Before rude hands have touch'd it?
  p. 134 UNDERWOOD 2.4    24 Before the soyle hath smutch'd it?
  p. 146 UNDERWOOD 6      15 (By searching) what before was strange,
  p. 151 UNDERWOOD 12      4 Before me here, the Friend and Sonne;
  p. 158 UNDERWOOD 14     14 Pernitious enemie; we see, before
  p. 159 UNDERWOOD 14     26 Before men get a verse: much lesse a Praise;
  p. 184 UNDERWOOD 29     42 As before.
  p. 185 UNDERWOOD 30     16 Rather than meet him: And, before his eyes
  p. 191 UNDERWOOD 38     30 Your honour now, then your disgrace before.
  p. 192 UNDERWOOD 38     50 Before you prove a medicine, is unjust.
  p. 203 UNDERWOOD 43     28 A cause before; or leave me one behind.
  p. 217 UNDERWOOD 46     21 Such is thy All; that (as I sung before)
  p. 221 UNDERWOOD 48     30 Before his braine doe know it;
  p. 228 UNDERWOOD 53     14 Before, I thinke my wish absolv'd had beene.
  p. 250 UNDERWOOD 73     11 Dreame thou could'st hurt it; but before thou
                             wake
  p. 251 UNDERWOOD 74      8 The Clowdes rack cleare before the Sun,
  p. 257 UNDERWOOD 75    146 Some houres before it should, that these may know
  p. 268 UNDERWOOD 82     13 Me thought, Great Britaine in her Sea, before,
  p. 285 U'WOOD 84.9      89 That, planted round, there sing before the Lamb,
  p. 285 U'WOOD 84.9     109 Much more desir'd, and dearer then before,
  p. 293 UNDERWOOD 87      7 In name, I went all names before,
  p. 309 HORACE 2        112 Before the Judge, it hangs, and waites report.
  p. 317 HORACE 2        264 Her Sonnes before the people; nor the ill-
  p. 371 UNGATHERED 8      7 That may iudge for his six-pence) had, before
  p. 375 UNGATHERED 10    25 For Grapes he had gather'd before they were
                             eaten.
  p. 380 UNGATHERED 12    36 For grapes he had gather'd, before they were
                             eaten.
  p. 386 UNGATHERED 20     9 That went before, a Husband. Shee, Ile sweare,
  p. 388 UNGATHERED 23     3 Who hadst before wrought in rich Homers Mine?
  p. 397 UNGATHERED 30    37 And I had stil'd thee, Orpheus, but before
  p. 401 UNGATHERED 32    13 Before this worke? where Enuy hath not cast
  p. 406 UNGATHERED 34    91 And not fall downe before it? and confess
  p. 421 UNGATHERED 49     2 before, I wryte more verse, to bee more wyse.
```

beg   frequency: 3   relative frequency: 0.00004
```
  p.  43 EPIGRAMS 51       8 Doe beg thy care vnto thy after-state.
  p. 107 FOREST 10        10 Nor will I beg of thee, Lord of the vine,
  p. 139 UNDERWOOD 2.7     2 I long, and should not beg in vaine,
```

began   frequency: 4   relative frequency: 0.00005
  See also "begann."
```
**p. 116 PANEGYRE        134 To heare her speech; which still began in him
  p.  88 EPIGRAMS 133    164 And, in a pittious tune, began. How dare
  p. 228 UNDERWOOD 53     12 As I began to wish my selfe a horse.
  p. 271 UNDERWOOD 83     94 When we were all borne, we began to die;
```

begann   frequency: 1   relative frequency: 0.00001
```
  p. 402 UNGATHERED 34     1 Mr Surueyr, you yt first begann
```

began'st   frequency: 1   relative frequency: 0.00001
```
  p. 368 UNGATHERED 6     80 From whose prowde bosome, thou began'st thy
                             flight.
```

begat   frequency: 2   relative frequency: 0.00002
```
 *p. 492 TO HIMSELF      t4 begat this following Ode to
  p.  55 EPIGRAMS 86       8 It was a knowledge, that begat that loue.
```

beg'd   frequency: 1   relative frequency: 0.00001
```
  p.  29 EPIGRAMS 8        4 Beg'd RIDWAYES pardon: DVNCOTE,
                             now, doth crye,
```

beget   frequency: 2   relative frequency: 0.00002
  See also "get."
```
  p. 208 UNDERWOOD 43    130 Made thee beget that cruell Stratagem,
  p. 212 UNDERWOOD 43    202 Who from the Divels-Arse did Guns beget;
```

begetting   frequency: 1   relative frequency: 0.00001
```
  p.  40 EPIGRAMS 42      14 Of his begetting. And so sweares his IONE.
```

begg'd   frequency: 2   relative frequency: 0.00002
  See also "beg'd."
```
  p. 162 UNDERWOOD 15     12 His unjust hopes, with praises begg'd, or (worse)
  p. 263 UNDERWOOD 78     30 What transcripts begg'd? how cry'd up, and how
                             glad,
```

begging   frequency: 1   relative frequency: 0.00001
     p. 139 UNDERWOOD 2.7   t1 Begging another, on colour of mending

begin   frequency: 9   relative frequency: 0.00013
     See also "begyn."
     p. 50 EPIGRAMS 70   2 Then to begin, my ROE: He makes a state
     p. 207 UNDERWOOD 43   107 I now begin to doubt, if ever Grace,
     p. 313 HORACE 2   195 Nor so begin, as did that Circler late,
     p. 369 UNGATHERED 6   93 Yet, looking in thy face, they shall begin
     p. 391 UNGATHERED 26   17 I, therefore will begin. Soule of the Age!
     p. 394 UNGATHERED 28   1 I could begin with that graue forme, Here lies,
     p. 395 UNGATHERED 29   4 And the world in it, I begin to doubt,
     p. 396 UNGATHERED 30   7 And, though I now begin, 'tis not to rub
     p. 416 UNGATHERED 44   7 To Crowne the years, which you begin, great
                                  king,

beginners   frequency: 1   relative frequency: 0.00001
     p. 141 UNDERWOOD 2.9   31 Quickly fir'd, as in beginners

beginning   frequency: 2   relative frequency: 0.00002
     p. 271 UNDERWOOD 83   91 That ever had beginning there, to'<h>ave end!
     p. 294 UNDERWOOD 88   10 Can this decay, but is beginning ever.

beginnings   frequency: 5   relative frequency: 0.00007
     p. 81 EPIGRAMS 128   7 As the beginnings here, proue purely sweet,
     p. 160 UNDERWOOD 14   46 And noted the beginnings and decayes!
     p. 217 UNDERWOOD 46   5 Such, Coke, were thy beginnings, when thy good
     p. 271 UNDERWOOD 83   74 What the beginnings of all beauties be;
     p. 305 HORACE 2   17 In grave beginnings, and great things profest,

beginns   frequency: 1   relative frequency: 0.00001
     p. 421 UNGATHERED 49   3 Soe ended yor Epistle, myne beginns

begins   frequency: 2   relative frequency: 0.00002
     See also "beginns."
     p. 49 EPIGRAMS 68   2 Takes priuate beatings, and begins againe.
     p. 315 HORACE 2   209 Of Diomede; nor Troyes sad Warre begins

begin'st   frequency: 1   relative frequency: 0.00001
     p. 221 UNDERWOOD 48   16 And still begin'st the greeting:

begot   frequency: 4   relative frequency: 0.00005
     See also "begat," "got."
     p. 80 EPIGRAMS 127   8 Lent timely succours, and new life begot:
     p. 204 UNDERWOOD 43   32 And so some goodlier monster had begot:
     p. 241 UNDERWOOD 69   5 Freedome, and Truth; with love from those begot:
     p. 325 HORACE 2   437 What nourisheth, what formed, what begot

begotten   frequency: 1   relative frequency: 0.00001
     See also "onely-gotten."
     p. 280 U'WOOD 84.4   68 Begotten by that wind, and showers.

begs   frequency: 1   relative frequency: 0.00001
     p. 375 UNGATHERED 10   35 Beeing in feare to be robd, he most learnedly
                                  begs.

beguil'd   frequency: 1   relative frequency: 0.00001
     p. 339 HORACE 1   35 ... . beguil'd

beguile   frequency: 1   relative frequency: 0.00001
     p. 102 FOREST 5   13 Or his easier eares beguile,

beguiles   frequency: 1   relative frequency: 0.00001
     p. 137 UNDERWOOD 2.5   51 Outward Grace weake love beguiles:

begun   frequency: 3   relative frequency: 0.00004
     See also "begunne."
     p. 63 EPIGRAMS 98   1 Thou hast begun well, ROE, which stand well
                                  too,
     p. 162 UNDERWOOD 15   10 In dreames, begun in hope, and end in spoile.
     p. 396 UNGATHERED 30   18 Is fayre got vp, and day some houres begun!

begunne   frequency: 1   relative frequency: 0.00001
     p. 121 FOREST 14   46 When well begunne:

begyn   frequency: 1   relative frequency: 0.00001
     p. 422 UNGATHERED 50   10 if it begyn religious thoughts to cherish;

behalf. See "behalfe."

behalfe   frequency: 1   relative frequency: 0.00001
    p. 382 UNGATHERED 16   t2 behalfe of the two noble Brothers sr Robert
                              & sr Henrye

beheld   frequency: 5   relative frequency: 0.00007
    p. 132 UNDERWOOD 2.2   1 I beheld her, on a day,
    p. 133 UNDERWOOD 2.3   17 Which when she beheld to bleed,
    p. 133 UNDERWOOD 2.6   23 Of your Peeres, you were beheld,
    p. 234 UNDERWOOD 61   1 That you have seene the pride, beheld the sport,
    p. 262 UNDERWOOD 78   6 In him all vertue is beheld in State:

behind   frequency: 6   relative frequency: 0.00008
    p. 149 UNDERWOOD 9   5 And cast my love behind:
    p. 203 UNDERWOOD 43   28 A cause before; or leave me one behind.
    p. 231 UNDERWOOD 57   13 And more is behind:
    p. 257 UNDERWOOD 75 141 There is a Feast behind,
    p. 280 U'WOOD 84.4   66 In rest, like spirits left behind
    p. 333 HORACE 2   595 Him that is last, I scorne to come behind,

behold   frequency: 13   relative frequency: 0.00018
    See also "behould."
    p. 47 EPIGRAMS 63   7 Who can behold all enuie so declin'd
    p. 51 EPIGRAMS 74   3 Whil'st I behold thee liue with purest hands;
    p. 55 EPIGRAMS 86   3 Then doe I loue thee, and behold thy ends
    p. 67 EPIGRAMS 104   3 Or did our times require it, to behold
    p. 83 EPIGRAMS 132   7 Behold! the reuerend shade of BARTAS stands
    p. 89 EPIGRAMS 133 176 Behold where CERBERVS, rear'd on the wall
    p. 127 UNDERWOOD 1.1 13 4. For thy acceptance. O, behold me right,
    p. 164 UNDERWOOD 15   60 Who can behold their Manners, and not clowd-
    p. 240 UNDERWOOD 67   25 5. TERP. Behold the royall Mary,
    p. 258 UNDERWOOD 75 169 Till you behold a race to fill your Hall,
    p. 361 UNGATHERED 1   13 Next, that which rapt mee, was: I might behold
    p. 366 UNGATHERED 6   3 Behold, where one doth swim:
    p. 389 UNGATHERED 24 23 When you behold me wish my selfe, the man

beholder   frequency: 1   relative frequency: 0.00001
    p. 317 HORACE 2   259 And the beholder to himselfe doth render.

beholders   frequency: 1   relative frequency: 0.00001
    p. 166 UNDERWOOD 15 140 To be beholders, when their powers are spent.

beholding   frequency: 2   relative frequency: 0.00002
    p. 72 EPIGRAMS 111   4 Beholding, to this master of the warre;
    p. 128 UNDERWOOD 1.1 33 9. Beholding one in three, and three in one,

beholds   frequency: 3   relative frequency: 0.00004
    p. 251 UNDERWOOD 74   27 When he beholds a graft of his owne hand,
    p. 271 UNDERWOOD 83   73 Beholds her Maker! and, in him, doth see
    p. 290 UNDERWOOD 85   13 Or in the bending Vale beholds a-farre

behould   frequency: 1   relative frequency: 0.00001
    p. 383 UNGATHERED 16 12 made prospectiue, behould hym, hee must pas<s>e

being   frequency: 56   relative frequency: 0.00081
    See also "beeing."
  **p. 115 PANEGYRE   83 "And, being once found out, discouer'd lies
    p. 33 EPIGRAMS 22   3 Yet, all heauens gifts, being heauens due,
    p. 60 EPIGRAMS 93   2 For the great marke of vertue, those being gone
    p. 66 EPIGRAMS 103   5 And, being nam'd, how little doth that name
    p. 74 EPIGRAMS 115   5 Being no vitious person, but the vice
    p. 77 EPIGRAMS 120   23 But, being so much too good for earth,
    p. 83 EPIGRAMS 131   11 And would (being ask'd the truth) ashamed say,
    p. 88 EPIGRAMS 133 158 Being, beyond sea, burned for one witch:
    p. 99 FOREST 3   86 By being organes to great sinne,
    p. 111 FOREST 11   70 Who, being at sea, suppose,
    p. 119 FOREST 13   117 Vnto himselfe, by being so deare to you.
    p. 122 FOREST 15   15 Dwell, dwell here still: O, being euery-where,
    p. 132 UNDERWOOD 2.2   5 Farre I was from being stupid,
    p. 138 UNDERWOOD 2.6 27 And was worthy (being so seene)
    p. 144 UNDERWOOD 4   4 Lest shame destroy their being.
    p. 146 UNDERWOOD 6   22 From being forsaken, then doth worth:
    p. 155 UNDERWOOD 13   87 If it were cleare, but being so in cloud
    p. 157 UNDERWOOD 13 151 But few and faire Divisions: but being got
    p. 159 UNDERWOOD 14   23 Since, being deceiv'd, I turne a sharper eye
    p. 163 UNDERWOOD 15   32 And being a thing, blowne out of nought, rebells
    p. 166 UNDERWOOD 15 124 But being in Motion still (or rather in race)
    p. 172 UNDERWOOD 20   21 I could forgive her being proud! a whore!
    p. 187 UNDERWOOD 33   28 And not being borrow'd by thee, but possest.
    p. 189 UNDERWOOD 36   11 And have their being, their waste to see;
    p. 190 UNDERWOOD 37   11 And which you (being the worthier) gave me leave

being (cont.)

p. 190 UNDERWOOD 37	22	And lesse they know, who being free to use
p. 193 UNDERWOOD 38	99	I number these as being of the Chore
p. 201 UNDERWOOD 42	42	Being, the best clothes still to praeoccupie.
p. 209 UNDERWOOD 43	153	O no, cry'd all, Fortune, for being a whore,
p. 217 UNDERWOOD 46	7	When, being the Strangers helpe, the poore mans aide,
p. 230 UNDERWOOD 56	7	And you may justly, being a tardie, cold,
p. 233 UNDERWOOD 59	16	Valour! to sleight it, being done to you!
p. 263 UNDERWOOD 78	32	Being sent to one, they will be read of all.
p. 272 UNDERWOOD 84	t13	Her being chosen a MUSE.
p. 273 U'WOOD 84.1	6	Their names of being kept alive,
p. 282 U'WOOD 84.9	t4	Being
p. 284 U'WOOD 84.9	69	This being thus: why should my tongue, or pen
p. 288 U'WOOD 84.9	213	(As being Redeemer, and Repairer too
p. 288 U'WOOD 84.9	217	As being the Sonne of Man) to shew his Power,
p. 309 HORACE 2	73	And give, being taken modestly, this leave,
p. 309 HORACE 2	98	Being taught a better way. All mortall deeds
p. 313 HORACE 2	189	For, being a Poet, thou maist feigne, create,
p. 315 HORACE 2	214	What he despaires, being handled, might not show.
p. 315 HORACE 2	229	Th'unbearded Youth, his Guardian once being gone,
p. 319 HORACE 2	293	They might with ease be numbred, being a few
p. 319 HORACE 2	325	Having well eat, and drunke (the rites being done)
p. 327 HORACE 2	457	With specious places, and being humour'd right,
p. 327 HORACE 2	463	Being men were covetous of nought, but praise.
p. 339 HORACE 1	41	Being over-safe, and fearing .. the flaw:
p. 352 HORACE 1	547	... ... being honest ... . doth ....
p. 361 UNGATHERED 1	23	which thoughts being circumvol<v>d in gyerlyk mocion
p. 362 UNGATHERED 2	13	Which being eyed directly, I diuine,
p. 370 UNGATHERED 7	14	Being tould there, Reason cannot, Sense may erre.
p. 380 UNGATHERED 12	54	And being at Flushing enforced to feele
p. 381 UNGATHERED 12	57	Which he not denies. Now being so free,
p. 414 UNGATHERED 41	56	Of being Daughter, Mother, Spouse of GOD!

belch'd   frequency: 1   relative frequency: 0.00001
    p. 85 EPIGRAMS 133   63 Belch'd forth an ayre, as hot, as at the muster

belcheth   frequency: 1   relative frequency: 0.00001
    p. 335 HORACE 2   649 The while he belcheth loftie Verses out,

beleeu'd   frequency: 2   relative frequency: 0.00002
    p. 69 EPIGRAMS 107   17 If but to be beleeu'd you haue the hap,
    p. 101 FOREST 4   50 But, as 'tis rumor'd, so beleeu'd:

beleeue   frequency: 7   relative frequency: 0.00010
    p. 32 EPIGRAMS 18   9 Pr'y thee beleeue still, and not iudge so fast,
    p. 38 EPIGRAMS 38   7 Beleeue it, GVILTIE, if you loose your shame,
    p. 56 EPIGRAMS 88   1 Would you beleeue, when you this MOVNSIEVR see,
    p. 61 EPIGRAMS 95   3 I should beleeue, the soule of TACITVS
    p. 64 EPIGRAMS 100   3 And I must now beleeue him: for, to day,
    p. 73 EPIGRAMS 114   1 I must beleeue some miracles still bee,
    p. 379 UNGATHERED 12   17 But who will beleeue this, that chanceth to looke

beleeve   frequency: 4   relative frequency: 0.00005
    p. 148 UNDERWOOD 8   4 Could you beleeve, that this,
    p. 187 UNDERWOOD 33   5 That, henceforth, I beleeve nor bookes, nor men,
    p. 215 UNDERWOOD 44   75 We will beleeve, like men of our owne Ranke,
    p. 317 HORACE 2   269 What so is showne, I not beleeve, and hate.

beleeved   frequency: 1   relative frequency: 0.00001
    p. 127 UNDERWOOD 1.1   3 The faithfull mans beleeved Mysterie,

beleeves   frequency: 1   relative frequency: 0.00001
    p. 325 HORACE 2   419 Because Democritus beleeves a wit

belgia   frequency: 1   relative frequency: 0.00001
    p. 37 EPIGRAMS 32   3 That selfe-diuided Belgia did afford;

belgic. See "belgick."

belgick   frequency: 1   relative frequency: 0.00001
    p. 60 EPIGRAMS 93   8 The Belgick feuer rauished away.

belgicus. See "gallo-belgicvs."

belie   frequency: 2   relative frequency: 0.00002
  See also "belye."
    p. 157 UNDERWOCD 13 146 As if they would belie their stature; those
    p. 198 UNDERWOOD 40   38 Farre from the Nest, and so himselfe belie

belief. See "beliefe."

beliefe   frequency: 1   relative frequency: 0.00001
    p. 188 UNDERWOOD 34   10 Any beliefe, in Madam Baud-bees bath,

believe   frequency: 1   relative frequency: 0.00001
  See also "beleeue," "beleeve."
    p. 198 UNDERWOOD 40   40 Due to that one, that doth believe him just.

believed. See "beleeu'd," "beleeved."

believes. See "beleeves."

belike   frequency: 1   relative frequency: 0.00001
    p. 219 UNDERWOOD 47   33 Or the States Ships sent forth belike to meet

bell-mans   frequency: 1   relative frequency: 0.00001
    p. 211 UNDERWOOD 43 187 Or in the Bell-Mans Lanthorne, like a spie,

bellie   frequency: 1   relative frequency: 0.00001
    p. 230 UNDERWOOD 56   9 Laden with Bellie, and doth hardly approach

bells   frequency: 3   relative frequency: 0.00004
    p. 88 EPIGRAMS 133 173 Cannot the Plague-bill keepe you backe? nor
                            bells
    p. 249 UNDERWOOD 72   10 The Poetrie of Steeples, with the Bells,
    p. 253 UNDERWOOD 75   33 Harke how the Bells upon the waters play

belly   frequency: 6   relative frequency: 0.00008
  See also "bellie."
    p. 46 EPIGRAMS 62   11 In a great belly. Write, then on thy wombe,
    p. 54 EPIGRAMS 81   6 Thy wit liues by it, PROVLE, and belly too.
    p. 76 EPIGRAMS 118   5 Thus, in his belly, can he change a sin,
    p. 150 UNDERWOOD 9   17 My mountaine belly, and my rockie face,
    p. 162 UNDERWOOD 15   17 To gaine upon his belly; and at last
    p. 291 UNDERWOCD 85   54 Could not goe downe my belly then

beloued   frequency: 1   relative frequency: 0.00001
    p. 390 UNGATHERED 26 t1 To the memory of my beloued,

belov'd   frequency: 2   relative frequency: 0.00002
    p. 167 UNDERWOOD 15 161 And be belov'd, while the Whores last. O times,
    p. 268 UNDERWOOD 82   4 How much they are belov'd of God, in thee;

beloved. See "beloued," "belov'd," "truly-belou'd."

below   frequency: 2   relative frequency: 0.00002
    p. 95 FOREST 2   70 He knowes, below, he shall finde plentie of
                            meate,
    p. 144 UNDERWOCD 3   18 And exercise below,

belye   frequency: 1   relative frequency: 0.00001
    p. 51 EPIGRAMS 73   11 With which a learned Madame you belye.

ben   frequency: 11   relative frequency: 0.00015
    p. 41 EPIGRAMS 45   10 BEN. IONSON his best piece of poetrie.
    p. 140 UNDERWOOD 2.9   1 Of your Trouble, Ben, to ease me,
    p. 218 UNDERWOOD 47   t3 Tribe of BEN.
    p. 220 UNDERWOOD 47   78 Sir, you are Sealed of the Tribe of Ben.
    p. 231 UNDERWOOD 57   7 Tell him his Ben
    p. 246 UNDERWOOD 70   84 And there he lives with memorie; and Ben
    p. 259 UNDERWOOD 76   1 The humble Petition of poore Ben.
    p. 395 UNGATHERED 29 26 BEN: IONSON.
    p. 396 UNGATHERED 30 t2 BEN. IONSON, ON THE
    p. 404 UNGATHERED 34 65 All in ye Worke! And soe shall still for Ben:
    p. 418 UNGATHERED 46   5 Il may Ben Johnson slander so his feete,

bench   frequency: 1   relative frequency: 0.00001
    p. 370 UNGATHERED 8   1 The wise, and many-headed Bench, that sits

bend   frequency: 5   relative frequency: 0.00007
    p. 132 UNDERWOOD 2.2   9 Where's thy Quiver? bend thy Bow:
    p. 233 UNDERWOOD 59   18 To bend, to breake, provoke,or suffer it!
    p. 292 UNDERWOOD 86   6 To bend a man, now at his fiftieth yeare
    p. 317 HORACE 2   281 Be wonne a friend; it must both sway, and bend

bend (cont.)
    p. 367 UNGATHERED 6   48 "Where neither Force can bend, nor Feare can
        awe.

bending   frequency: 1   relative frequency: 0.00001
    p. 290 UNDERWOOD 85   13 Or in the bending Vale beholds a-farre

bends   frequency: 3   relative frequency: 0.00004
    p. 94 FOREST 2   22 The lower land, that to the riuer bends,
    p. 170 UNDERWOOD 19   3 By that faire Stand, your forehead, whence he
        bends
    p. 363 UNGATHERED 3   11 It bends the hams of Gossip Vigilance,

bene   frequency: 1   relative frequency: 0.00001

beneath   frequency: 6   relative frequency: 0.00008
**p. 114 PANEGYRE   62 The ground beneath did seeme a mouing floud:
    p. 43 EPIGRAMS 51   4 And farre beneath least pause of such a king,
    p. 93 FOREST 2   12 Beneath the broad beech, and the chest-nut shade;
    p. 177 UNDERWOOD 25   30 Sinke not beneath these terrors:
    p. 290 UNDERWOOD 85   23 Then now beneath some ancient Oke he may,
    p. 292 UNDERWOOD 86   20 Beneath a Sweet-wood Roofe, neere Alba Lake:

benefit   frequency: 1   relative frequency: 0.00001
  See also "benefite."
    p. 154 UNDERWOOD 13   42 A Benefit; or that doth throw 't away:

benefite   frequency: 1   relative frequency: 0.00001
**p. 116 PANEGYRE   111 For though by right, and benefite of Times,

benefits   frequency: 3   relative frequency: 0.00004
    p. 80 EPIGRAMS 127   12 To thanke thy benefits: which is, to pay.
    p. 153 UNDERWOOD 13   5 For benefits are ow'd with the same mind
    p. 153 UNDERWOOD 13   19 They are the Noblest benefits, and sinke

beniamin   frequency: 1   relative frequency: 0.00001
    p. 78 EPIGRAMS 121   t1 TO BENIAMIN RVDYERD.

benjamin. See "ben," "beniamin."

benn>   frequency: 1   relative frequency: 0.00001
    p. 187 UNDERWOOD 33   6 Who 'gainst the Law, weave Calumnies, my
        <BENN:>

bent   frequency: 3   relative frequency: 0.00004
    p. 129 UNDERWOOD 1.2   13 As minds ill bent
    p. 136 UNDERWOOD 2.5   17 Both her Browes, bent like my Bow.
    p. 141 UNDERWOOD 2.9   17 Eye-brows bent like Cupids bow,

bequeath   frequency: 1   relative frequency: 0.00001
    p. 39 EPIGRAMS 40   3 Rich, as nature could bequeath thee:

bereaues   frequency: 1   relative frequency: 0.00001
    p. 44 EPIGRAMS 55   7 What fate is mine, that so it selfe bereaues?

bereaves. See "bereaues."

berenices   frequency: 1   relative frequency: 0.00001
    p. 115 FOREST 12   61 Who made a lampe of BERENICES hayre?

bergamo   frequency: 1   relative frequency: 0.00001
    p. 380 UNGATHERED 12   38 And lay in straw with the horses at Bergamo,

bergen. See "berghen."

berghen   frequency: 1   relative frequency: 0.00001
    p. 214 UNDERWOOD 44   40 The Berghen siege, and taking in Breda,

beringhams   frequency: 1   relative frequency: 0.00001
    p. 69 EPIGRAMS 107   23 Your Arch-Dukes Agents, and your Beringhams,

bermudas   frequency: 1   relative frequency: 0.00001
    p. 155 UNDERWOOD 13   82 Ha' their Bermudas, and their streights i'th'
        Strand:

berries. See "straw-berries."

berwick. See "berwicke."

berwicke   frequency: 1   relative frequency: 0.00001
     p. 85 EPIGRAMS 133   35 Or him that backward went to Berwicke, or which

beshit. See "beshite."

beshite   frequency: 1   relative frequency: 0.00001
     p. 86 EPIGRAMS 133   90 Row close then, slaues. Alas, they will beshite
                              vs.

beside   frequency: 6   relative frequency: 0.00008
     See also "besyde."
  **p. 113 PANEGYRE   23 Beside her, stoup't on either hand, a maid,
     p. 70 EPIGRAMS 109   4 Where all is faire, beside thy pedigree.
     p. 207 UNDERWOOD 43   99 Wherein was oyle, beside the succour spent,
     p. 254 UNDERWOOD 75   72 With all the pompe of Youth, and all our Court
                              beside.
     p. 255 UNDERWOOD 75   88 All else we see beside, are Shadowes, and goe
                              lesse.
     p. 277 U'WOOD 84.4   7 Beside, your hand will never hit,

besides   frequency: 5   relative frequency: 0.00007
     See also "besydes."
     p. 160 UNDERWOOD 14   51 And then of times (besides the bare Conduct
     p. 366 UNGATHERED 6   5 Besides the other Swannes admiring him,
     p. 370 UNGATHERED 7   2 Require (besides the likenesse of the thing)
     p. 380 UNGATHERED 12   27 Besides he tried Ship, Cart, Waggon, and
                              Chayre,
     p. 420 UNGATHERED 48   33 As shall besides delyght

besieg'd   frequency: 1   relative frequency: 0.00001
     p. 66 EPIGRAMS 102   14 And one true posture, though besieg'd with ill

besieged   frequency: 1   relative frequency: 0.00001
     See also "besieg'd."
     p. 248 UNDERWOOD 71   15 A Bed-rid Wit, then a besieged Towne.

bespoke   frequency: 1   relative frequency: 0.00001
     p. 81 EPIGRAMS 129   6 To which thou'rt not a weeke, bespoke a guest;

besprent   frequency: 1   relative frequency: 0.00001
     p. 268 UNDERWOOD 83   1 What gentle Ghost, besprent with April deaw,

bess. See "b<ess>," "besse."

besse   frequency: 1   relative frequency: 0.00001
     p. 418 UNGATHERED 47   2 The Paltzgrave, and the Lady Besse,

best   frequency: 57   relative frequency: 0.00082
     See also "best-best," "th'best."
   *p. 493 TO HIMSELF   28 As the best order'd meale.
  **p. 117 PANEGYRE   147 Though many greater: and the most, the best.
     p. 28 EPIGRAMS 4   1 How, best of Kings, do'st thou a scepter beare!
     p. 28 EPIGRAMS 4   2 How, best of Poets, do'st thou laurell weare!
     p. 28 EPIGRAMS 4   9 Whom should my Muse then flie to, but the best
     p. 32 EPIGRAMS 18   4 DAVIS, and WEEVER, and the best haue
                              beene,
     p. 34 EPIGRAMS 23   7 To it, thy language, letters, arts, best life,
     p. 41 EPIGRAMS 45   10 BEN. IONSON his best piece of poetrie.
     p. 49 EPIGRAMS 66   13 Loue honors, which of best example bee,
     p. 50 EPIGRAMS 70   6 Each best day of our life escapes vs, first.
     p. 58 EPIGRAMS 91   17 And best become the valiant man to weare,
     p. 61 EPIGRAMS 94   14 Be of the best: and 'mongst those, best are you.
     p. 62 EPIGRAMS 96   6 As thou hast best authoritie, t<o>'allow.
     p. 75 EPIGRAMS 116   2 All gentrie, yet, owe part of their best flame!
     p. 75 EPIGRAMS 116   10 In men, but euery brauest was the best:
     p. 76 EPIGRAMS 119   10 Till thou canst finde the best, choose the least
                              ill.
     p. 78 EPIGRAMS 123   4 Of the best writer, and iudge, should emulate.
     p. 80 EPIGRAMS 128   3 T<o>'extract, and choose the best of all these
                              knowne,
     p. 85 EPIGRAMS 133   52 Canst tell me best, how euery Furie lookes
                              there,
     p. 104 FOREST 8   2 Ladies? and of them the best?
     p. 112 FOREST 11   101 All her best symmetrie in that one feature!
     p. 116 FOREST 12   100 My best of wishes, may you beare a sonne.
     p. 120 FOREST 14   20 And he, with his best Genius left alone.
     p. 129 UNDERWOOD 1.2   3 Is my best part:
     p. 137 UNDERWOOD 2.5   44 Of her good, who is the best
     p. 144 UNDERWOOD 3   21 O sing not you then lest the best
     p. 158 UNDERWOOD 14   4 Truth, and the Graces best, when naked are.

best (cont.)

p.	166 UNDERWOOD 15	144	That scratching now's our best Felicitie?
p.	169 UNDERWOOD 17	18	And I will bring a Crop, if not the best.
p.	170 UNDERWOOD 18	14	And then the best are, still, the blindest friends!
p.	182 UNDERWOOD 27	35	Yet sure my tunes will be the best,
p.	182 UNDERWOOD 28	8	Both braines and hearts; and mine now best doe know it:
p.	187 UNDERWOOD 33	27	Of Argument, still drawing forth the best,
p.	189 UNDERWOOD 36	2	For Love in shadow best is made.
p.	198 UNDERWOOD 40	29	They looke at best like Creame-bowles, and you soone
p.	201 UNDERWOOD 42	42	Being, the best clothes still to praeoccupie.
p.	208 UNDERWOOD 43	113	When thou wert borne, and that thou look'st at best,
p.	217 UNDERWOOD 46	6	In others evill best was understood:
p.	222 UNDERWOOD 49	9	Equall with that, which for the best newes goes,
p.	236 UNDERWOOD 63	10	And thinke all still the best, that he will doe.
p.	253 UNDERWOOD 75	13	When look'd the yeare, at best,
p.	254 UNDERWOOD 75	74	And looking with thy best Inquirie, tell,
p.	263 UNDERWOOD 79	7	We sing the best of Monarchs, Masters, Men;
p.	263 UNDERWOOD 79	13	Best Kings expect first-fruits of your glad gaines.
p.	264 UNDERWOOD 79	20	Shep. Of PAN wee sing, the best of Hunters, PAN,
p.	264 UNDERWOOD 79	34	And were shee lost, could best supply her place,
p.	265 UNDERWOOD 79	45	In truth of colours, both are best.
p.	287 U'WOOD 84.9	155	And best he knew her noble Character,
p.	288 U'WOOD 84.9	214	Of lapsed Nature) best know what to doe,
p.	309 HORACE 2	106	What number best can fit, Homer declares.
p.	321 HORACE 2	329	And so their prating to present was best,
p.	325 HORACE 2	442	Which the Socratick writings best can show:
p.	325 HORACE 2	447	What height of love, a Parent will fit best,
p.	379 UNGATHERED 12	5	And that, say Philosophers, is the best modell.
p.	390 UNGATHERED 26	8	Which, when it sounds at best, but eccho's right;
p.	399 UNGATHERED 31	11	The best of Woemen! her whole life

be'st   frequency: 1   relative frequency: 0.00001

best-best   frequency: 1   relative frequency: 0.00001
     p. 180 UNDERWOOD 25   63 O then (my best-best lov'd) let me importune,

bestowes   frequency: 1   relative frequency: 0.00001
     p. 112 FOREST 11   104 How onely shee bestowes

bestowing   frequency: 1   relative frequency: 0.00001
     p. 39 EPIGRAMS 40   11 Till time, strong by her bestowing,

bestows. See "bestowes."

bestride. See "bestryde."

bestryde   frequency: 1   relative frequency: 0.00001
     p. 407 UNGATHERED 35   13 He some Colossus to bestryde ye Seas,

besyde   frequency: 1   relative frequency: 0.00001
     p. 404 UNGATHERED 34   58 Of any Art, besyde what he calls his!

besydes   frequency: 1   relative frequency: 0.00001
     p. 406 UNGATHERED 35   5 Besydes, his Man may merit it, and be

bet   frequency: 1   relative frequency: 0.00001
     p. 76 EPIGRAMS 119   3 Cryes out 'gainst cocking, since he cannot bet,

betide. See "bety'de."

betraid   frequency: 1   relative frequency: 0.00001
  **p. 115 PANEGYRE   87 "Betraid to fame, should take more care, and feare

betray   frequency: 11   relative frequency: 0.00015
     p. 36 EPIGRAMS 30   3 'Twere madnesse in thee, to betray thy fame,
     p. 43 EPIGRAMS 52   6 Would both thy folly, and thy spite betray.
     p. 49 EPIGRAMS 66   10 Could conquer thee, but chance, who did betray.
     p. 87 EPIGRAMS 133   116 Neuer did bottome more betray her burden;
     p. 94 FOREST 2   36 Officiously, at first, themselues betray.
     p. 101 FOREST 4   42 Thou did'st abuse, and then betray;
     p. 103 FOREST 6   4 All your bounties will betray.
     p. 145 UNDERWOOD 4   12 Mine owne enough betray me.
     p. 190 UNDERWOOD 37   33 Her furie, yet no friendship to betray.

betray (cont.)
   p. 198 UNDERWOOD 40   36 Doth, while he keepes his watch, betray his
                                stand.
   p. 366 UNGATHERED 6   6 Betray it true:

betray'd   frequency: 2   relative frequency: 0.00002
   See also "betraid."
   p.   48 EPIGRAMS 65   2 That hast betray'd me to a worthlesse lord;
   p. 101 FOREST 4   51 Where euery freedome is betray'd,

betrayes   frequency: 1   relative frequency: 0.00001
   p.   31 EPIGRAMS 12   21 Not his poore cocatrice but he betrayes

betrays. See "betrayes."

better   frequency: 53   relative frequency: 0.00076
 **p. 114 PANEGYRE   32 Breath'd in his way; and soules (their better
                                parts)
 **p. 115 PANEGYRE   77 "With better pompe. She tells him first, that
                                Kings
   p.   28 EPIGRAMS 5   1 When was there contract better driuen by Fate?
   p.   31 EPIGRAMS 14   13 Many of thine this better could, then I,
   p.   35 EPIGRAMS 27   2 Take better ornaments, my teares, and verse.
   p.   40 EPIGRAMS 42   18 I know no couple better can agree!
   p.   44 EPIGRAMS 55   10 For writing better, I must enuie thee.
   p.   48 EPIGRAMS 65   10 Almost all wayes, to any better course.
   p.   52 EPIGRAMS 74   5 That still th'art present to the better cause;
   p.   53 EPIGRAMS 79   12 As he would burne, or better farre his booke.
   p.   61 EPIGRAMS 95   14 Or, better worke! were thy glad countrey blest,
   p.   62 EPIGRAMS 96   8 Mark'd by thy hand, and with the better stone,
   p.   64 EPIGRAMS 101 10 An oliue, capers, or some better sallade
   p.   65 EPIGRAMS 101 22 LIVIE, or of some better booke to vs,
   p.   66 EPIGRAMS 102 10 To morrow vice, if shee giue better pay:
   p.   75 EPIGRAMS 116 12 And to liue great, was better, then great borne.
   p.   76 EPIGRAMS 119 12 Treading a better path, not contrary;
   p.   78 EPIGRAMS 121   3 Whose better studies while shee emulates,
   p.   93 FOREST 2   7 Thou ioy'st in better markes, of soyle, of ayre,
   p.   95 FOREST 2   53 The better cheeses, bring 'hem; or else send
   p.   96 FOREST 3   7 Nor com'st to view the better cloth of state;
   p.   99 FOREST 3   94 'Tis better, if he there can dwell.
   p. 114 FOREST 12   25 Were yet vnfound, and better plac'd in earth,
   p. 115 FOREST 12   68 Who, though shee haue a better verser got,
   p. 118 FOREST 13   53 Wherewith, then, Madame, can you better pay
   p. 140 UNDERWOOD 2.8 20 Better fits him, then his face;
   p. 146 UNDERWOOD 6   14 For what is better, or to make
   p. 166 UNDERWOOD 15 145 Well, let it goe. Yet this is better, then
   p. 173 UNDERWOOD 22 27 That would their better objects find:
   p. 182 UNDERWOOD 28   4 A better lover, and much better Poet.
   p. 194 UNDERWOOD 38 110 How much you are the better part of me;
   p. 210 UNDERWOOD 43 166 For they were burnt, but to be better built.
   p. 224 UNDERWOOD 50 23 Only your time you better entertaine,
   p. 229 UNDERWOOD 54 20 For your securitie. I can no better.
   p. 241 UNDERWOOD 68 12 'T were better spare a Butt, then spill his
                                  Muse.
   p. 245 UNDERWOOD 70 66 In bulke, doth make man better bee;
   p. 252 UNDERWOOD 75 10 (Bearing the promise of some better fate)
   p. 264 UNDERWOOD 79 30 To better Pastures then great PALES can:
   p. 265 UNDERWOOD 79 59 The better grasse, and flowers are found.
   p. 277 U'WOOD 84.4   2 Now I have better thought thereon,
   p. 284 U'WOOD 84.9   73 Better be dumbe, then superstitious!
   p. 309 HORACE 2   98 Being taught a better way. All mortall deeds
   p. 313 HORACE 2   184 And thou maist better bring a Rhapsody
   p. 315 HORACE 2   199 A scorned Mouse! O, how much better this,
   p. 325 HORACE 2   431 Out better Poems? But I cannot buy
   p. 327 HORACE 2   459 And better stayes them there, then all fine noise
   p. 333 HORACE 2   611 For hee'll cry, Good, braue, better, excellent!
   p. 333 HORACE 2   625 If you denied, you had no better straine,
   p. 384 UNGATHERED 18 10 Wth the same looke, or wth a better, shine.
   p. 397 UNGATHERED 30 56 A better cause, and strike the brauest heate
   p. 419 UNGATHERED 48   8 And better Blason them, then all their Coates,
   p. 666 INSCRIPTS. 11 10 To make these good, and what comes after,
                                  better./

better'd   frequency: 2   relative frequency: 0.00002
   p.   63 EPIGRAMS 99   2 Better'd thy trust to letters; that thy skill;
   p. 315 HORACE 2   238 His better'd mind seekes wealth, and friendship:
                                  than

bettering. See "bettring."

bettring   frequency: 1   relative frequency: 0.00001
        p. 331 HORACE 2   562 To bettring of the mind of man, in ought,

between   frequency: 2   relative frequency: 0.00002
        See also "betweene," "'tweene."
        p. 397 UNGATHERED 30   26 Heard the soft ayres, between our swaynes &
                                   thee,
        p. 412 UNGATHERED 41   7 Is so implexed, and laid in, between,

betweene   frequency: 11   relative frequency: 0.00015
        p. 86 EPIGRAMS 133   67 Betweene two walls; where, on one side, to scar
                                   men,
        p. 87 EPIGRAMS 133   114 The well-greas'd wherry now had got betweene,
        p. 113 FOREST 12   16 Runs betweene man, and man; 'tweene dame, and
                                   dame;
        p. 137 UNDERWOOD 2.5   33 And betweene each rising breast,
        p. 149 UNDERWOOD 9   12 That flie my thoughts betweene,
        p. 252 UNDERWOOD 75   4 Betweene thy Tropicks, to arrest thy sight,
        p. 257 UNDERWOOD 75   164 Of Love betweene you, and your Lovely-head:
        p. 261 UNDERWOOD 77   14 Discerne betweene a Statue, and a Man;
        p. 317 HORACE 2   278 Betweene the Acts, a quite cleane other thing
        p. 370 UNGATHERED 7   12 Betweene the doubtfull sway of Reason', and
                                   sense;
        p. 396 UNGATHERED 30   4 Those ambling visits, passe in verse, betweene

betwixt   frequency: 1   relative frequency: 0.00001
        See also "twixt," "'twixt."
        p. 284 U'WOOD 84.9   54 Of Body and Spirit together, plac'd betwixt

bety'de   frequency: 1   relative frequency: 0.00001
        p. 417 UNGATHERED 45   33 Or if any strife bety'de

bever   frequency: 1   relative frequency: 0.00001
        p. 135 UNDERWOOD 2.4   25 Have you felt the wooll o' the Bever?

bevis   frequency: 2   relative frequency: 0.00002
        p. 215 UNDERWOOD 44   81 From Guy, or Bevis, Arthur, or from whom
        p. 228 UNDERWOOD 53   10 Of bold Sir Bevis, and his Arundell:

bevy. See "beavie."

bewail<e>d   frequency: 1   relative frequency: 0.00001
        See also "bewaild."
        p. 183 UNDERWOOD 29   21 But bewail<e>d

bewaild   frequency: 1   relative frequency: 0.00001
        p. 313 HORACE 2   176 Ino bewaild; Ixion false, forsworne;

beware   frequency: 2   relative frequency: 0.00002
        See also "ware."
        p. 321 HORACE 2   355 But, let the Faunes, drawne from their Groves,
                                   beware,
        p. 333 HORACE 2   607 But you, my Piso, carefully beware,

bewares   frequency: 1   relative frequency: 0.00001
        p. 315 HORACE 2   239 Lookes after honours, and bewares to act

beyond   frequency: 2   relative frequency: 0.00002
        p. 88 EPIGRAMS 133   158 Being, beyond sea, burned for one witch:
        p. 161 UNDERWOOD 14   71 But nought beyond. He thou hast given it to,

bid   frequency: 10   relative frequency: 0.00014
        p. 163 UNDERWOOD 15   28 But there are objects, bid him to be gone
        p. 166 UNDERWOOD 15   129 I'le bid thee looke no more, but flee, flee
                                   friend,
        p. 171 UNDERWOOD 19   15 I'le therefore aske no more, but bid you love;
        p. 199 UNDERWOOD 41   1 Since you must goe, and I must bid farewell,
        p. 307 HORACE 2   31 In short; I bid, Let what thou work'st upon,
        p. 325 HORACE 2   453 And I still bid the learned Maker looke
        p. 333 HORACE 2   627 Hee'd bid, blot all: and to the anvile bring
        p. 335 HORACE 2   637 They're darke, bid cleare this: all that's
                                   doubtfull wrote
        p. 384 UNGATHERED 18   6 That bid, God giue thee ioy, and haue no endes.
        p. 391 UNGATHERED 26   20 Chaucer, or Spenser, or bid Beaumont lye

bide   frequency: 2   relative frequency: 0.00002
        p. 187 UNDERWOOD 33   23 But in a businesse, that will bide the Touch,
        p. 281 U'WOOD 84.8   19 By which yo'are planted, shew's your fruit shall
                                   bide.

bids   frequency: 4   relative frequency: 0.00005
    p.   50 EPIGRAMS 70   1 When Nature bids vs leaue to liue, 'tis late
    p. 155 UNDERWOOD 13   68 And hurt seeks Cure, the Surgeon bids take
                              bread,
    p. 162 UNDERWOOD 15   2 Beates brave, and loude in Europe, and bids come
    p. 375 UNGATHERED 10   20 Religiously here he bids, row from the stewes,

big   frequency: 1   relative frequency: 0.00001
    p. 157 UNDERWOOD 13   149 'Tis like light Canes, that first rise big and
                              brave,

bilbao.   See "bilbo," "bilbo-smith."

bilbo   frequency: 1   relative frequency: 0.00001
    p. 212 UNDERWOOD 43   199 Maintain'd the trade at Bilbo, or else-where;

bilbo-smith   frequency: 1   relative frequency: 0.00001.
    p. 410 UNGATHERED 38   15 An honest Bilbo-Smith would make good blades,

bill   frequency: 2   relative frequency: 0.00002
    See also "plague-bill."
    p.   29 EPIGRAMS 7   2 A purging bill, now fix'd vpon the dore,
    p.   30 EPIGRAMS 12   10 Lookes o're the bill, likes it: and say's, god
                              payes.

billiard   frequency: 1   relative frequency: 0.00001
    p. 141 UNDERWOOD 2.9   20 Smooth as is the Billiard Ball:

billow   frequency: 1   relative frequency: 0.00001
    p. 214 UNDERWOOD 44   63 Should he <not> heare of billow, wind, and
                              storme,

bills   frequency: 1   relative frequency: 0.00001
    See also "bils."
    p. 212 UNDERWOOD 43   198 And there made Swords, Bills, Glaves, and
                              Armes your fill;

bils   frequency: 1   relative frequency: 0.00001
    p.   59 EPIGRAMS 92   24 Or BILS, and there he buyes the names of
                              books.

bin   frequency: 5   relative frequency: 0.00007

bind   frequency: 2   relative frequency: 0.00002
    See also "binde."
    p. 157 UNDERWOOD 13   138 Are nothing till that comes to bind and shut.
    p. 401 UNGATHERED 33   2 That, while they bind the senses, doe so please?

binde   frequency: 1   relative frequency: 0.00001
    p.   93 FOREST 1   2 I thought to binde him, in my verse:

bird   frequency: 5   relative frequency: 0.00007
    See also "black-bird."
    p.   55 EPIGRAMS 85   4 And why that bird was sacred to APOLLO,
    p. 101 FOREST 4   29 What bird, or beast, is knowne so dull,
    p. 364 UNGATHERED 4   3 If a Bird so amiable,
    p. 366 UNGATHERED 6   7 A gentler Bird, then this,
    p. 369 UNGATHERED 6   96 So blacke a Bird, so bright a Qualitie.

birds   frequency: 1   relative frequency: 0.00001
    p. 290 UNDERWOOD 85   26 The soft birds quarrell in the Woods,

birth   frequency: 20   relative frequency: 0.00028
    p.   34 EPIGRAMS 22   11 This graue partakes the fleshly birth.
    p.   67 EPIGRAMS 104   8 Of birth, of match, of forme, of chastitie?
    p.   77 EPIGRAMS 120   21 And haue sought (to giue new birth)
    p.   94 FOREST 2   14 At his great birth, where all the Muses met.
    p. 107 FOREST 10   14 That, at thy birth, mad'st the poore Smith
                              affraid,
    p. 114 FOREST 12   26 Then, here, to giue pride fame, and peasants
                              birth.
    p. 118 FOREST 13   49 Of so great title, birth, but vertue most,
    p. 130 UNDERWOOD 1.3   1 I sing the birth, was borne to night,
    p. 142 UNDERWOOD 2.9   44 And as honest as his Birth.
    p. 177 UNDERWOOD 25   32 Where only a mans birth is his offence,
    p. 197 UNDERWOOD 40   17 And must be bred, so to conceale his birth,
    p. 237 UNDERWOOD 65   1 And art thou borne, brave Babe? Blest be thy
                              birth,
    p. 237 UNDERWOOD 65   t1 An Epigram on the Princes birth.
    p. 250 UNDERWOOD 74   2 Doth take in easie Natures birth,

birth (cont.)
    p. 257 UNDERWOOD 75   156 Of Life, that fall so; Christians know their
                              birth
    p. 321 HORACE 2   360 The Roman Gentrie, men of birth, and meane,
    p. 384 UNGATHERED 18   20 And eu'ry birth encrease the heate of Loue.
    p. 394 UNGATHERED 28   4 In blood, in birth, by match, and by her seate;
    p. 398 UNGATHERED 30   83 Yet giue mee leaue, to wonder at the birth
    p. 417 UNGATHERED 45   19 she desires of euery birth

birth-day   frequency: 7   relative frequency: 0.00010
    p. 120 FOREST 14   t3 BIRTH-DAY.
    p. 121 FOREST 14   60 The Birth-day shines, when logs not burne, but
                              men.
    p. 225 UNDERWOOD 51   t1 Lord BACONS Birth-day.
    p. 239 UNDERWOOD 67   t2 In celebration of her Majesties birth-day.
    p. 249 UNDERWOOD 72   t1 To the King. On his Birth-day.
    p. 262 UNDERWOOD 78   14 Upon my Birth-day the eleventh of June;
    p. 271 UNDERWOOD 83   68 Became her Birth-day to Eternitie!

birth-right   frequency: 1   relative frequency: 0.00001
    p. 323 HORACE 2   376 Into their birth-right, and for fitnesse sake,

births   frequency: 1   relative frequency: 0.00001
    p. 53 EPIGRAMS 79   1 That Poets are far rarer births then kings,

bishop   frequency: 2   relative frequency: 0.00002
    p. 256 UNDERWOOD 75   122 And Bishop stay, to consummate the Rites:
    p. 256 UNDERWOOD 75   132 And this their chosen Bishop celebrate,

bishops   frequency: 2   relative frequency: 0.00002
    p. 59 EPIGRAMS 92   35 Or 'gainst the Bishops, for the Brethren,
                              raile,
    p. 234 UNDERWOOD 61   13 Fit for a Bishops knees! O bow them oft,

bitch   frequency: 1   relative frequency: 0.00001
    p. 164 UNDERWOOD 15   76 Doe all the tricks of a saut Lady Bitch;

bite   frequency: 1   relative frequency: 0.00001
    p. 155 UNDERWOOD 13   70 Then give it to the Hound that did him bite;

bitten   frequency: 1   relative frequency: 0.00001
    p. 155 UNDERWOOD 13   67 But one is bitten by the Dog he fed,

bitter   frequency: 1   relative frequency: 0.00001
    p. 197 UNDERWOOD 40   1 That Love's a bitter sweet, I ne're conceive

bitternesse   frequency: 1   relative frequency: 0.00001
    p. 112 FOREST 11   97 All taste of bitternesse, and makes the ayre

black   frequency: 7   relative frequency: 0.00010
    See also "blacke," "blacke-springing."
    p. 87 EPIGRAMS 133   126 White, black, blew, greene, and in more formes
                              out-started,
    p. 141 UNDERWOOD 2.9   14 Gold, upon a ground of black.
    p. 175 UNDERWOOD 23   36 Safe from the wolves black jaw, and the dull
                              Asses hoofe.
    p. 179 UNDERWOOD 25   40 Let Brontes, and black Steropes,
    p. 227 UNDERWOOD 52   20 A Poet hath no more but black and white,
    p. 285 U'WOOD 84.9   98 Put black, and mourning on? and say you misse
    p. 307 HORACE 2   52 With faire black eyes, and haire; and a wry nose.

black-bird   frequency: 1   relative frequency: 0.00001
    p. 335 HORACE 2   651 Busie to catch a Black-bird; if he fall

blacke   frequency: 6   relative frequency: 0.00008
  **p. 113 PANEGYRE   10 Where men commit blacke incest with their faults;
    p. 109 FOREST 11   4 And her blacke spight expell.
    p. 338 HORACE 1   5 .... a blacke foule ....
    p. 366 UNGATHERED 6   2 Produce vs a blacke Swan?
    p. 369 UNGATHERED 6   96 So blacke a Bird, so bright a Qualitie.
    p. 380 UNGATHERED 12   48 Iest, he saies. Item one sute of blacke taffata

blacke-springing   frequency: 1   relative frequency: 0.00001
    p. 368 UNGATHERED 6   72 To Loumond lake, and Twedes blacke-springing
                              fountaine.

blackenesse   frequency: 1   relative frequency: 0.00001
    p. 366 UNGATHERED 6   16 And Phoebus loue cause of his blackenesse is.

blacker   frequency: 1   relative frequency: 0.00001
     p. 41 EPIGRAMS 44   4 Saw all his race approch the blacker floods:

blackest   frequency: 1   relative frequency: 0.00001
     p. 112 FOREST 11   95 And turne the blackest sorrowes to bright ioyes:

blackness. See "blackenesse."

blacks   frequency: 1   relative frequency: 0.00001
     p. 41 EPIGRAMS 44   3 Ere blacks were bought for his owne funerall,

blade   frequency: 1   relative frequency: 0.00001
     p. 155 UNDERWOOD 13   64 Or stands to be'<i>n Commission o' the blade?

blades   frequency: 1   relative frequency: 0.00001
     p. 410 UNGATHERED 38   15 An honest Bilbo-Smith would make good blades,

blame   frequency: 3   relative frequency: 0.00004
     p. 148 UNDERWOOD 7   33 But so exempt from blame,
     p. 323 HORACE 2   395 'Tis cleare, this way I have got off from blame,
     p. 335 HORACE 2   634 On artlesse Verse; the hard ones he will blame;

blanched. See "blanch't."

blanch't   frequency: 1   relative frequency: 0.00001
     p. 321 HORACE 2   362 Him that buyes chiches blanch't, or chance to
                              like

blason   frequency: 1   relative frequency: 0.00001
     p. 419 UNGATHERED 48   8 And better Blason them, then all their Coates,

blaspheme   frequency: 3   relative frequency: 0.00004
     p. 36 EPIGRAMS 28   17 Blaspheme god, greatly. Or some poore hinde
                              beat,
     p. 168 UNDERWOOD 15   191 And last, blaspheme not, we did never heare
     p. 283 U'WOOD 84.9   32 Whoorles me about, and to blaspheme in fashion!

blasphemie   frequency: 1   relative frequency: 0.00001
     p. 203 UNDERWOOD 43   16 Imposture, witchcraft, charmes, or blasphemie,

blasphemy   frequency: 1   relative frequency: 0.00001
     See also "blasphemie."
     p. 286 U'WOOD 84.9   147 Nor dare we under blasphemy conceive

blast   frequency: 1   relative frequency: 0.00001
     p. 58 EPIGRAMS 91   7 When on thy trumpet shee did sound a blast,

blatant   frequency: 2   relative frequency: 0.00002
     p. 408 UNGATHERED 37   9 To be knowne what thou art, a blatant beast,
     p. 411 UNGATHERED 39   11 Thy blatant Muse abroad, and teach it rather

blaz'd   frequency: 2   relative frequency: 0.00002
     p. 413 UNGATHERED 41   36 How are thy gifts, and graces blaz'd abroad!
     p. 414 UNGATHERED 41   53 How are thy gifts and graces blaz'd abro'd,

blaze   frequency: 4   relative frequency: 0.00005
     p. 211 UNDERWOOD 43   185 Or in small Fagots have him blaze about
     p. 233 UNDERWOOD 59   8 That trembles in the blaze, but (then) mounts
                              higher!
     p. 269 UNDERWOOD 83   32 The blaze, and splendor, but not handle fire!
     p. 420 UNGATHERED 48   15 Whilest lyke a blaze of strawe,

blazon   frequency: 1   relative frequency: 0.00001
     See also "blason."
     p. 197 UNDERWOOD 40   13 But ever without blazon, or least shade

bleed   frequency: 1   relative frequency: 0.00001
     p. 133 UNDERWOOD 2.3   17 Which when she beheld to bleed,

bleeding   frequency: 2   relative frequency: 0.00002
   **p. 116 PANEGYRE   107 "All this she told, and more, with bleeding eyes;
     p. 363 UNGATHERED 3   2 Seldome descend but bleeding to their graue.

bleeds   frequency: 1   relative frequency: 0.00001
     p. 168 UNDERWOOD 15   178 Not wound thy conscience, when thy body bleeds;

bless. See "blesse."

blesse   frequency: 7   relative frequency: 0.00010
     p. 256 UNDERWOOD 75   131 To have thy God to blesse, thy King to grace,

blesse (cont.)
```
    p. 418 UNGATHERED 47    1 Our King and Queen the Lord-God blesse,
    p. 418 UNGATHERED 47    3 And God blesse every living thing,
    p. 419 UNGATHERED 47    5 God blesse the Councell of Estate,
    p. 419 UNGATHERED 47    7 God blesse them all, and keepe them safe:
    p. 419 UNGATHERED 47    8 And God blesse me, and God blesse Raph.
```

blessed   frequency: 12   relative frequency: 0.00017
See also "blest."
```
    p. 112 FOREST 11         86 Makes a most blessed gayne.
    p. 127 UNDERWOOD 1.1     1 1. O holy, blessed, glorious Trinitie
    p. 259 UNDERWOOD 76      6 JAMES the blessed, pleas'd the rather,
    p. 268 UNDERWOOD 82     11 Grow up, sweet Babe, as blessed, in thy Name,
    p. 283 U'WOOD 84.9      34 Her blessed Soule, hence, forth this valley vane
    p. 393 UNGATHERED 27    17 This, blessed Warre, thy blessed Booke
    p. 412 UNGATHERED 41     1 Here, are five letters in this blessed Name,
    p. 412 UNGATHERED 41    t2 of the blessed Virgin
    p. 413 UNGATHERED 41    34 Alike of kin, to that most blessed Trine,
    p. 413 UNGATHERED 41    37 Most holy, & pure Virgin, blessed Mayd,
    p. 415 UNGATHERED 43     4 Renew the Glories of our blessed Ieames:
```

blessed'st   frequency: 1   relative frequency: 0.00001
```
    p. 238 UNDERWOOD 66      2 And by an Angell, to the blessed'st Maid,
```

blessing   frequency: 4   relative frequency: 0.00005
```
    p. 118 FOREST 13        54 This blessing of your starres, then by that way
    p. 185 UNDERWOOD 30     20 Of divine blessing, would not serve a State?
    p. 268 UNDERWOOD 82      3 And by thy blessing, may thy People see
    p. 271 UNDERWOOD 83     80 T'have paid againe a blessing was but lent,
```

blessings   frequency: 3   relative frequency: 0.00004
```
    p. 236 UNDERWOOD 64      4 If he but weigh'd the blessings of this day?
    p. 261 UNDERWOOD 77     20 What worlds of blessings to good Kings they owe:
    p. 285 U'WOOD 84.9     110 By all the wealth of blessings, and the store
```

blest   frequency: 15   relative frequency: 0.00021
```
  **p. 116 PANEGYRE        133 She blest the people, that in shoales did swim
  **p. 117 PANEGYRE        161 Yet, let blest Brit[t]aine aske (without your
                              wrong)
    p.  37 EPIGRAMS 32       8 Was his blest fate, but our hard lot to find.
    p.  61 EPIGRAMS 95      14 Or, better worke! were thy glad countrey blest,
    p.  81 EPIGRAMS 128      9 So, when we, blest with thy returne, shall see
    p.  96 FOREST 3          1 How blest art thou, canst loue the countrey,
                               WROTH,
    p.  97 FOREST 3         14 Liue, with vn-bought prouision blest;
    p. 111 FOREST 11        62 Who (blest with such high chance)
    p. 119 FOREST 13        95 Of your blest wombe, made fruitfull from aboue,
    p. 128 UNDERWOOD 1.1    44 O, then how blest,
    p. 188 UNDERWOOD 35      4 Upon record, in this blest child.
    p. 234 UNDERWOOD 61      9 Your happinesse, and doth not speake you blest,
    p. 236 UNDERWOOD 63     12 With a long, large, and blest posteritie!
    p. 237 UNDERWOOD 65      1 And art thou borne, brave Babe? Blest be thy
                               birth,
    p. 270 UNDERWOOD 83     57 Then comforted her Lord! and blest her Sonne!
```

blew   frequency: 2   relative frequency: 0.00002
```
    p.  87 EPIGRAMS 133    126 White, black, blew, greene, and in more formes
                               out-started,
    p. 241 UNDERWOOD 68      8 Would make the very Greene-cloth to looke blew:
```

blind   frequency: 7   relative frequency: 0.00010
See also "blinde," "pur-blinde."
```
    p.  40 EPIGRAMS 42      10 Harsh sights at home, GILES wisheth he were
                               blind.
    p.  53 EPIGRAMS 80       3 How wilfull blind is he then, that would stray,
    p. 149 UNDERWOOD 9       1 I now thinke, Love is rather deafe, then blind,
    p. 170 UNDERWOOD 18     11 But which shall lead me on? both these are blind:
    p. 170 UNDERWOOD 18     16 Or Love, or Fortune blind, when they but winke
    p. 250 UNDERWOOD 73     10 To vertue, and true worth, be ever blind.
    p. 383 UNGATHERED 17     6 Yet may as blind men sometimes hit the marke.
```

blinde   frequency: 5   relative frequency: 0.00007
```
    p. 105 FOREST 8         40 Bald, or blinde, or nere so many:
    p. 110 FOREST 11        30 And strike our reason blinde.
    p. 110 FOREST 11        37 The thing, they here call Loue, is blinde
                               Desire,
    p. 363 UNGATHERED 3     16 And strikes the quickest-sighted Iudgement
                               blinde.
    p. 391 UNGATHERED 26     9 Or blinde Affection, which doth ne're aduance
```

blindest   frequency: 1   relative frequency: 0.00001
    p. 170 UNDERWOOD 18   14 And then the best are, still, the blindest
                               friends!

blindly   frequency: 1   relative frequency: 0.00001
    p. 294 UNDERWOOD 88   3 Let us not then rush blindly on unto it,

bliss. See "blisse."

blisse   frequency: 3   relative frequency: 0.00004
  **p. 117 PANEGYRE   157 Nor to her blisse, could ought now added bee,
    p. 271 UNDERWOOD 83   83 If you can envie your owne Daughters blisse,
    p. 283 U'WOOD 84.9   41 So sweetly taken to the Court of blisse,

blisses   frequency: 2   relative frequency: 0.00002
    p. 136 UNDERWOOD 2.5   26 Where, you say, men gather blisses,
    p. 170 UNDERWOOD 19   10 Where men at once may plant, and gather blisses:

block   frequency: 1   relative frequency: 0.00001
    p. 202 UNDERWOOD 42   82 A Goat in Velvet; or some block could move

block'd   frequency: 1   relative frequency: 0.00001
    See also "blockt."
    p. 248 UNDERWOOD 71   10 But lyes block'd up, and straightned, narrow'd
                               in,

blocks   frequency: 2   relative frequency: 0.00002
   *p. 493 TO HIMSELF   38 Wrought vpon twenty blocks:
    p. 216 UNDERWOOD 44   99 These Carkasses of honour; Taylors blocks,

blockt   frequency: 1   relative frequency: 0.00001
    p. 191 UNDERWOOD 38   5 It is a Darknesse hath blockt up my sense,

blood   frequency: 30   relative frequency: 0.00043
    See also "bloud."
   *p. 493 TO HIMSELF   45 And though thy nerues be shrunke, and blood be
                               cold,
    p. 30 EPIGRAMS 11   5 A lord, it cryed, buried in flesh, and blood,
    p. 105 FOREST 8   23 Sleeked limmes, and finest blood?
    p. 121 FOREST 14   33 Your blood
    p. 136 UNDERWOOD 2.5   3 And doe governe more my blood,
    p. 140 UNDERWOOD 2.9   4 Noble; or of greater Blood:
    p. 141 UNDERWOOD 2.9   30 All his blood should be a flame
    p. 155 UNDERWOOD 13   69 And spunge-like with it dry up the blood quite:
    p. 164 UNDERWOOD 15   55 Hee's one of blood, and fashion! and with these
    p. 167 UNDERWOOD 15   165 Lewd slanderers, soft whisperers that let blood
    p. 172 UNDERWOOD 21   9 Of putrid flesh alive! of blood, the sinke!
    p. 185 UNDERWOOD 30   6 What is there more that can ennoble blood?
    p. 192 UNDERWOOD 38   65 Should aske the blood, and spirits he hath
                               infus'd
    p. 199 UNDERWOOD 41   11 Alas I ha' lost my heat, my blood, my prime,
    p. 214 UNDERWOOD 44   47 Without the hazard of a drop of blood,
    p. 215 UNDERWOOD 44   82 The Herald will. Our blood is now become
    p. 224 UNDERWOOD 50   26 And when you want those friends, or neere in
                               blood,
    p. 234 UNDERWOOD 60   8 But crept like darknesse through his blood?
    p. 246 UNDERWOOD 70   106 That kni' brave minds, and manners, more then
                               blood.
    p. 268 UNDERWOOD 82   7 To pious parents, who would have their blood
    p. 269 UNDERWOOD 83   8 A horrour in mee! all my blood is steele!
    p. 270 UNDERWOOD 83   36 From the inherent Graces in her blood!
    p. 274 U'WOOD 84.2   12 The wonder of her Sexe, and of your Blood.
    p. 284 U'WOOD 84.9   83 And give her place, according to her blood,
    p. 287 U'WOOD 84.9   157 And to that forme, lent two such veines of blood
    p. 337 HORACE 2   680 Till he drop off, a Horse-leech, full of blood.
    p. 363 UNGATHERED 3   1 Those that in blood such violent pleasure haue,
    p. 371 UNGATHERED 8   12 And wish that all the Muses blood were spilt,
    p. 394 UNGATHERED 28   4 In blood, in birth, by match, and by her seate;
    p. 397 UNGATHERED 30   57 That euer yet did fire the English blood!

blood-shaken   frequency: 1   relative frequency: 0.00001
   *p. 494 TO HIMSELF   54 They may, blood-shaken, then,

bloody   frequency: 1   relative frequency: 0.00001
  **p. 115 PANEGYRE   98 "The bloody, base, and barbarous she did quote;

bloom. See "bloome."

bloome   frequency: 2   relative frequency: 0.00002
    p. 253 UNDERWOOD 75   23 In all her bloome, and flower;

bloome (cont.)
    p. 412 UNGATHERED 41   9 The second string is the sweet Almond bloome

bloomed   frequency: 1   relative frequency: 0.00001
    p. 247 UNDERWOOD 70 127 Who, e're the first downe bloomed on the chin,

blooming   frequency: 1   relative frequency: 0.00001
    p. 251 UNDERWOOD 74   22 The bus'nesse of your blooming wit,

blot   frequency: 4   relative frequency: 0.00005
    See also "blott."
    p. 227 UNDERWOOD 52   12 With one great blot, yo'had form'd me as I am.
    p. 325 HORACE 2   416 To taxe that Verse, which many a day, and blot
    p. 333 HORACE 2   627 Hee'd bid, blot all: and to the anvile bring
    p. 335 HORACE 2   635 Blot out the carelesse, with his turned pen;

blots   frequency: 1   relative frequency: 0.00001
    p. 160 UNDERWOOD 14   42 What blots and errours, have you watch'd and
                            purg'd

blott   frequency: 1   relative frequency: 0.00001
    p. 420 UNGATHERED 48   19 Breake then thie quills, blott out

bloud   frequency: 11   relative frequency: 0.00015
  **p. 113 PANEGYRE   13 Carowsing humane bloud in yron bowles,
    p. 49 EPIGRAMS 67   6 High in thy bloud, thy place, but highest then,
    p. 52 EPIGRAMS 76   6 Of greatest bloud, and yet more good then great;
    p. 60 EPIGRAMS 93   16 Wherewith, against thy bloud, they'offenders bee.
    p. 75 EPIGRAMS 116   11 That bloud not mindes, but mindes did bloud
                            adorne:
    p. 80 EPIGRAMS 128   4 And those to turne to bloud, and make thine owne:
    p. 114 FOREST 12   37 Beautie, I know, is good, and bloud is more;
    p. 117 FOREST 13   46 As bloud, and match. Wherein, how more then much
    p. 119 FOREST 13   98 To CLIPTON'S bloud, that is deny'd their
                            name.
    p. 188 UNDERWOOD 34   9 Her owne bloud gave her: Shee ne're had, nor
                            hath

blow   frequency: 8   relative frequency: 0.00011
    See also "ouer-blow."
    p. 72 EPIGRAMS 112   6 Art still at that, and think'st to blow me'vp
                            too?
    p. 99 FOREST 3   79 To blow vp orphanes, widdowes, and their states;
    p. 100 FOREST 4   22 Like such as blow away their liues,
    p. 162 UNDERWOOD 15   22 Till envie wound, or maime it at a blow!
    p. 165 UNDERWOOD 15 104 Those thousands on his back, shall after blow
    p. 198 UNDERWOOD 40   47 (Made to blow up loves secrets) to discover
    p. 212 UNDERWOOD 43 205 Blow up, and ruine, myne, and countermyne,
    p. 219 UNDERWOOD 47   51 But that's a blow, by which in time I may

blowes   frequency: 1   relative frequency: 0.00001
    p. 283 U'WOOD 84.9   27 Thou hast no more blowes, Fate, to drive at one:

blown. See "blowne," "ore-blowne."

blowne   frequency: 5   relative frequency: 0.00007
    p. 57 EPIGRAMS 90   14 Blowne vp; and he (too'vnwieldie for that place)
    p. 83 EPIGRAMS 131   14 For fame, with breath soone kindled, soone blowne
                            out.
    p. 108 FOREST 10A   4 like glasse, blowne vp, and fashion'd by desire.
    p. 147 UNDERWOOD 7   19 That were this morning blowne;
    p. 163 UNDERWOOD 15   32 And being a thing, blowne out of nought, rebells

blows. See "blowes."

blowze. See "sun-burnt-blowse."

blue. See "blew."

bluntly   frequency: 1   relative frequency: 0.00001
    p. 383 UNGATHERED 17   3 Who bluntly doth but looke vpon the same,

blurt   frequency: 1   relative frequency: 0.00001
    p. 321 HORACE 2   337 And farre unworthy to blurt out light rimes;

blush   frequency: 7   relative frequency: 0.00010
    p. 117 FOREST 13   22 If it may stand with your soft blush to heare
    p. 119 FOREST 13   111 Other great wiues may blush at: when they see
    p. 141 UNDERWOOD 2.9 28 And so thin, to see a blush
    p. 153 UNDERWOOD 13   11 And in the Act did so my blush prevent,

blush (cont.)
  p. 171 UNDERWOOD 19   13 You blush, but doe not: friends are either none,
  p. 186 UNDERWOOD 32   4 Then to make falshood blush, and fraud afraid:
  p. 386 UNGATHERED 20 12 Shee need not blush vpon the Mariage-Day.

blushed   frequency: 1   relative frequency: 0.00001
  p. 214 UNDERWOOD 44 42 And Spinola have blushed at the sight.

blushes   frequency: 1   relative frequency: 0.00001
  p. 136 UNDERWOOD 2.5 20 Such my Mothers blushes be,

                     frequency: 2   relative frequency: 0.00002
blushing
  *p. 493 TO HIMSELF   50 May, blushing, sweare no palsey's in thy braine.
  p. 94 FOREST 2   43 The blushing apricot, and woolly peach

boar. See "boare."

board   frequency: 1   relative frequency: 0.00001
  See also "boord," "bord."
  p. 404 UNGATHERED 34 44 In ye mere perspectiue of an Inch board!

boardes   frequency: 1   relative frequency: 0.00001
  p. 404 UNGATHERED 34 49 Oh, to make Boardes to speake! There is a taske

boards. See "boardes," "boords," "bords," "deal-boards."

boare   frequency: 1   relative frequency: 0.00001
  p. 307 HORACE 2   42 A Dolphin, and a Boare amid' the floods.

boars. See "bores."

boast   frequency: 17   relative frequency: 0.00024
  See also "out-boast."
  p. 29 EPIGRAMS 6   1 If all you boast of your great art be true;
  p. 56 EPIGRAMS 89   2 Fear'd not to boast the glories of her stage,
  p. 61 EPIGRAMS 95   12 Onely to boast thy merit in supply.
  p. 83 EPIGRAMS 132 13 Thine the originall; and France shall boast,
  p. 84 EPIGRAMS 133   7 All, that they boast of STYX, of
                      ACHERON,
  p. 93 FOREST 2   2 Of touch, or marble; nor canst boast a row
  p. 99 FOREST 3   78 And each where boast it as his merit,
  p. 115 FOREST 12   80 Shall thronging come, and boast the happy place
  p. 119 FOREST 13   84 Boast, but how oft they haue gone wrong to man:
  p. 186 UNDERWOOD 32 12 Thinke, yea and boast, that they have done it so
  p. 198 UNDERWOOD 40 46 The sinne of Boast, or other countermine
  p. 205 UNDERWOOD 43 57 But that's a marke, wherof thy Rites doe boast,
  p. 242 UNDERWOOD 69 26 Rather to boast rich hangings, then rare friends.
  p. 253 UNDERWOOD 75 19 Doe boast their Loves, and Brav'ries so at
                      large,
  p. 281 U'WOOD 84.8   10 Boast not these Titles of your Ancestors;
  p. 339 HORACE 1   33 The greater part, that boast the Muses fire,
  p. 367 UNGATHERED 6   35 Nor let one Riuer boast

boasted   frequency: 1   relative frequency: 0.00001
  p. 225 UNDERWOOD 50 32 Not boasted in your life, but practis'd true,

boasters   frequency: 1   relative frequency: 0.00001
  p. 167 UNDERWOOD 15 169 Boasters, and perjur'd, with the infinite more

boasting. See "selfe-boasting."

boasts   frequency: 2   relative frequency: 0.00002
  p. 74 EPIGRAMS 115 2 Him not, aloud, that boasts so good a fame:
  p. 98 FOREST 3   64 Which boasts t'haue had the head of gold.

boat. See "meate-boate."

boates   frequency: 4   relative frequency: 0.00005
  p. 155 UNDERWOOD 13 83 Man out their Boates to th' Temple, and not
                      shift
  p. 205 UNDERWOOD 43 68 The<ir> charmed Boates, and the<ir> inchanted
                      Wharfes;
  p. 208 UNDERWOOD 43 128 And safely trust to dresse, not burne their
                      Boates.
  p. 273 U'WOOD 84.1   22 Their painted Maskes, their paper Boates,

boats. See "boates."

bodies   frequency: 4   relative frequency: 0.00005
  See also "bodyes."

bodies (cont.)

**p.	117	PANEGYRE	144 Those greater bodies of the sky, that strike
p.	33	EPIGRAMS 21	8 The bodies stripes, I see, the soule may saue.
p.	200	UNDERWOOD 42	32 That quilts those bodies, I have leave to span:
p.	233	UNDERWOOD 59	10 Of bodies, meet like rarified ayre!

body   frequency: 29   relative frequency: 0.00041

p.	56	EPIGRAMS 88	2 That his whole body should speake french, not he?
p.	57	EPIGRAMS 90	13 MILL was the same. Since, both his body and face
p.	79	EPIGRAMS 125	4 Restored in thy body, and thy minde!
p.	79	EPIGRAMS 125	5 Who sees a soule, in such a body set,
p.	82	EPIGRAMS 130	7 And is t<o>' a body, often, ill inclin'd,
p.	99	FOREST 3	102 A body sound, with sounder minde;
p.	112	FOREST 11	99 A body so harmoniously compos'd,
p.	118	FOREST 13	81 Let 'hem waste body, and state; and after all,
p.	141	UNDERWOOD 2.9	35 In a body, should be there.
p.	148	UNDERWOOD 8	5 The body <ever> was
p.	165	UNDERWOOD 15	105 His body to the Counters, or the Fleete?
p.	166	UNDERWOOD 15	133 And whilst our states, strength, body, and mind we waste,
p.	168	UNDERWOOD 15	178 Not wound thy conscience, when thy body bleeds;
p.	206	UNDERWOOD 43	87 I dare not say a body, but some parts
p.	219	UNDERWOOD 47	41 I have a body, yet, that spirit drawes
p.	223	UNDERWOOD 49	33 Not he, that should the body have, for Case
p.	224	UNDERWOOD 50	18 Of State, of fame, of body, and of soule,
p.	234	UNDERWOOD 60	16 That spread his body o're, to kill:
p.	258	UNDERWOOD 75	184 So great; his Body now alone projects the shade.
p.	270	UNDERWOOD 83	51 Her suffrings, as the body had beene away!
p.	270	UNDERWOOD 83	55 'Tis but a body which you can torment,
p.	274	U'WOOD 84.2	3 For Mind, and Body, the most excellent
p.	275	U'WOOD 84.3	t1 The Picture of the BODY.
p.	283	U'WOOD 84.9	44 And left her lovely body unthought dead!
p.	284	U'WOOD 84.9	54 Of Body and Spirit together, plac'd betwixt
p.	284	U'WOOD 84.9	64 To Body, and Soule! where Love is all the guest!
p.	284	U'WOOD 84.9	82 Out of her noble body, to this Feast:
p.	295	UNDERWOOD 90	6 A quiet mind; free powers; and body sound;
p.	394	UNGATHERED 28	10 Such things, of euery body, and as well.

bodyes   frequency: 2   relative frequency: 0.00002

p.	171	UNDERWOOD 19	14 (Though they may number bodyes) or but one.
p.	291	UNDERWOOD 85	58 Or Mallowes loosing bodyes ill:

bogg'd   frequency: 1   relative frequency: 0.00001

p.	163	UNDERWOOD 15	30 Rather then here so bogg'd in vices stay.

boiler. See "sope-boyler."

boiling. See "euer-boyling."

boils. See "boyles."

bold   frequency: 14   relative frequency: 0.00020

p.	27	EPIGRAMS 2	3 Thou should'st be bold, licentious, full of gall,
p.	44	EPIGRAMS 56	3 From brocage is become so bold a thiefe,
p.	80	EPIGRAMS 126	7 PHOEBVS replyed. Bold head, it is not shee:
p.	82	EPIGRAMS 130	1 To vrge, my lou'd ALPHONSO, that bold fame
p.	86	EPIGRAMS 133	81 One said, it was bold BRIAREVS, or the beadle,
p.	120	FOREST 13	122 Madame, be bold to vse this truest glasse:
p.	214	UNDERWOOD 44	34 Supplant bold Panton; and brought there to view
p.	214	UNDERWOOD 44	51 Up among Nations. In the stead of bold
p.	228	UNDERWOOD 53	10 Of bold Sir Bevis, and his Arundell:
p.	274	U'WOOD 84.2	7 Speake it, you bold PENATES, you that stand
p.	321	HORACE 2	346 And the bold Pythias, having cheated weake
p.	342	HORACE 1	174 .. .. so 'bove ... ... bold ....
p.	370	UNGATHERED 7	8 So bold, as shewes your Art you can command.
p.	398	UNGATHERED 30	68 With bold Tyrtaeus verse, when thou art nam'd,

bolder   frequency: 2   relative frequency: 0.00002

p.	84	EPIGRAMS 133	1 No more let Greece her bolder fables tell
p.	177	UNDERWOOD 25	9 My bolder numbers to thy golden Lyre:

boldnesse   frequency: 1   relative frequency: 0.00001

p.	170	UNDERWOOD 18	9 I can helpe that with boldnesse; And Love sware,

bombard-phrase   frequency: 1   relative frequency: 0.00001
    p. 311 HORACE 2   139 Their bombard-phrase, and foot-and-halfe-foot
                    words.

bombard-stile   frequency: 1   relative frequency: 0.00001
    p. 85 EPIGRAMS 133   46 And with both bombard-stile, and phrase, rehearse

bond   frequency: 1   relative frequency: 0.00001
    See also "band."
    p. 30 EPIGRAMS 12   14 Signes to new bond, forfeits: and cryes, god
                    payes.

bondmen   frequency: 1   relative frequency: 0.00001
    p. 291 UNDERWOOD 85 65 The wealthy houshold swarme of bondmen met,

bonds. See "bands."

bone   frequency: 1   relative frequency: 0.00001
    See also "whale-bone."
    p. 393 UNGATHERED 27 14 The Marrow from the Bone,

bone-fires   frequency: 1   relative frequency: 0.00001
    p. 121 FOREST 14   59 Of bone-fires. Then

bonefires   frequency: 1   relative frequency: 0.00001
    p. 249 UNDERWOOD 72 13 At Bonefires, Rockets, Fire-workes, with the
                    Shoutes

bones   frequency: 7   relative frequency: 0.00010
    p. 49 EPIGRAMS 68   4 Actiue in's braine, and passiue in his bones.
    p. 85 EPIGRAMS 133   55 Great Club-fist, though thy backe, and bones be
                    sore,
    p. 107 FOREST 10   4 HERCVLES? alas his bones are yet sore,
    p. 151 UNDERWOOD 12   6 Of him whose bones this Grave doth gather:
    p. 166 UNDERWOOD 15 136 Now use the bones, we see doth hire a man
    p. 387 UNGATHERED 22 2 these only hide part of my flesh, and bones:
    p. 407 UNGATHERED 36 4 Able to eat into his bones & pierce

bonfires. See "bone-fires," "bonefires."

bonnie   frequency: 1   relative frequency: 0.00001
    p. 378 UNGATHERED 11 86 Come forth thou bonnie bouncing booke then,
                    daughter

bonny. See "bonnie."

book   frequency: 1   relative frequency: 0.00001
    See also "booke," "debt-booke."
    p. 338 HORACE 1   t2 his book .. ..

book-seller   frequency: 1   relative frequency: 0.00001
    p. 232 UNDERWOOD 58 t1 Epigram, to my Book-seller.

booke   frequency: 44   relative frequency: 0.00063
    p. 27 EPIGRAMS 1   1 Pray thee, take care, that tak'st my booke in
                    hand,
    p. 27 EPIGRAMS 2   1 It will be look'd for, booke, when some but see
    p. 27 EPIGRAMS 2   t1 TO MY BOOKE.
    p. 27 EPIGRAMS 3   2 Call'st a booke good, or bad, as it doth sell,
    p. 29 EPIGRAMS 9   1 May none, whose scatter'd names honor my booke,
    p. 41 EPIGRAMS 43   9 When, in my booke, men reade but CECILL'S
                    name,
    p. 42 EPIGRAMS 49   6 In my chast booke: professe them in thine owne.
    p. 43 EPIGRAMS 53   2 When hauing pill'd a booke, which no man buyes,
    p. 53 EPIGRAMS 77   2 That, any way, my booke should speake thy name:
    p. 53 EPIGRAMS 79   12 As he would burne, or better farre his booke.
    p. 54 EPIGRAMS 83   2 Throughout my booke. 'Troth put out woman too.
    p. 60 EPIGRAMS 94   4 Whose poemes would not wish to be your booke?
    p. 65 EPIGRAMS 101 22 LIVIE, or of some better booke to vs,
    p. 72 EPIGRAMS 111   1 Who EDMONDS, reades thy booke, and doth
                    not see
    p. 82 EPIGRAMS 130 t1 TO ALPHONSO FERRABOSCO, on his
                    Booke.
    p. 158 UNDERWOOD 14 5 Your Booke, my Selden, I have read, and much
    p. 175 UNDERWOOD 24 t1 The mind of the Frontispice to a Booke.
    p. 189 UNDERWOOD 37   4 You have unto my Store added a booke,
    p. 213 UNDERWOOD 44 28 But on thy practise, and the Posture booke:
    p. 230 UNDERWOOD 56   3 A booke to a few lynes: but, it was fit
    p. 263 UNDERWOOD 78 24 Upon them, (next to Spenser's noble booke,)
    p. 292 UNDERWOOD 86 t1 Ode the first. The fourth Booke.

booke (cont.)
```
   p. 293 UNDERWOOD 87    t1 Ode IX. 3 Booke, to Lydia.
   p. 305 HORACE 2         8 This peece, my Piso's, and that booke agree,
   p. 325 HORACE 2       454 On life, and manners, and make those his booke,
   p. 329 HORACE 2       517 This booke will get the Sosii money; This
   p. 370 UNGATHERED 7     5 And all your Booke (when it is throughly scan'd)
   p. 378 UNGATHERED 11   t3 and his Booke now going to
   p. 378 UNGATHERED 11   86 Come forth thou bonnie bouncing booke then,
                             daughter
   p. 379 UNGATHERED 12   10 By the scale of his booke, a yard of his stile?
   p. 379 UNGATHERED 12   18 The Mappe of his iourney, and sees in his booke,
   p. 380 UNGATHERED 12   43 Yes. And thanks God in his Pistle or his
                             Booke
   p. 385 UNGATHERED 20    1 It fits not onely him that makes a Booke,
   p. 389 UNGATHERED 24    7 And hath the noblest marke of a good Booke,
   p. 390 UNGATHERED 25   10 Not on his Picture, but his Booke.
   p. 390 UNGATHERED 26    2 Am I thus ample to thy Booke, and Fame:
   p. 391 UNGATHERED 26   23 And art aliue still, while thy Booke doth liue,
   p. 393 UNGATHERED 27   17 This, blessed Warre, thy blessed Booke
   p. 398 UNGATHERED 30   71 This booke! it is a Catechisme to fight,
   p. 399 UNGATHERED 31    6 With pause vpon it; make this page your booke;
   p. 399 UNGATHERED 31    7 Your booke? your volume! Nay, the state, and
                             story!
   p. 400 UNGATHERED 32    1 This Booke will liue; It hath a Genius: This
   p. 400 UNGATHERED 32    7 Though I confesse a Beaumonts Booke to bee
   p. 662 INSCRIPTS. 2     1 Goe little Booke, Goe little Fable
```

booke-seller   frequency: 1   relative frequency: 0.00001
```
   p.  27 EPIGRAMS 3     t1 TO MY BOOKE-SELLER.
```

booke-wormes   frequency: 1   relative frequency: 0.00001
```
   p. 215 UNDERWOOD 44   67 Are we by Booke-wormes to be awde? must we
```

bookes   frequency: 18   relative frequency: 0.00026
```
   p.  55 EPIGRAMS 86     2 Vpon thy wel-made choise of friends, and bookes;
   p.  55 EPIGRAMS 86     4 In making thy friends bookes, and thy bookes
                             friends:
   p.  59 EPIGRAMS 92    31 With England. All forbidden bookes they get.
   p.  71 EPIGRAMS 110   15 His deedes too dying, but in bookes (whose good
   p. 159 UNDERWOOD 14   15 A many'of bookes, even good judgements wound
   p. 187 UNDERWOOD 33    5 That, henceforth, I beleeve nor bookes, nor men,
   p. 187 UNDERWOOD 33   25 Of Bookes, of Presidents, hast thou at hand!
   p. 203 UNDERWOOD 43   18 Perhaps, to have beene burned with my bookes.
   p. 207 UNDERWOOD 43   95 With all th'adventures; Three bookes not afraid
   p. 224 UNDERWOOD 50   27 Or your Allies, you make your bookes your
                             friends,
   p. 232 UNDERWOOD 58    3 Bee thou my Bookes intelligencer, note
   p. 259 UNDERWOOD 76   15 Or dispenc'd in bookes, or bread,
   p. 271 UNDERWOOD 83   70 On Natures secrets, there, as her owne bookes:
   p. 386 UNGATHERED 21   1 Some men, of Bookes or Freinds not speaking
                             right,
   p. 386 UNGATHERED 21   9 And, where the most reade bookes, on Authors
                             fames,
   p. 389 UNGATHERED 24   2 Shall finde, that either hath read Bookes, and
                             Men:
   p. 389 UNGATHERED 24  11 Such Bookes deserue Translators, of like coate
```

books   frequency: 1   relative frequency: 0.00001
See alsc "bookes."
```
   p.  59 EPIGRAMS 92    24 Or BILS, and there he buyes the names of
                             books.
```

bookseller. See "book-seller," "booke-seller."

bookworms. See "booke-wormes."

boor. See "boore."

boord   frequency: 3   relative frequency: 0.00004
```
   p.  35 EPIGRAMS 28    13 Which is maine greatnesse. And, at his still
                             boord,
   p.  65 EPIGRAMS 101   40 That shall be vtter'd at our mirthfull boord,
   p.  95 FOREST 2       59 The neede of such? whose liberall boord doth
                             flow,
```

boords   frequency: 1   relative frequency: 0.00001
```
   p. 248 UNDERWOOD 71   11 Fix'd to the bed, and boords, unlike to win
```

boore   frequency: 1   relative frequency: 0.00001
```
   p. 375 UNGATHERED 10  24 Here, by a Boore too, hee's like to be beaten
```

boot   frequency: 1   relative frequency: 0.00001
    See also "boote."
    p. 291 UNDERWOOD 85   39 But if, to boot with these, a chaste Wife meet

boote   frequency: 4   relative frequency: 0.00005
    p. 71 EPIGRAMS 110   4 CATO'S to boote, Rome, and her libertie,
    p. 113 FOREST 12   3 That which, to boote with hell, is thought worth
                              heauen,
    p. 141 UNDERWOOD 2.9   7 French to boote, at least in fashion,
    p. 167 UNDERWOOD 15   160 But he that's both, and slave to boote, shall
                              live,

bor-   frequency: 1   relative frequency: 0.00001
    p. 305 HORACE 2   20 Diana's Grove, or Altar, with the bor-

bord   frequency: 1   relative frequency: 0.00001
    p. 263 UNDERWOOD 78   27 When hee shall read them at the Treasurers bord,

bordering. See "bor-."

borders   frequency: 1   relative frequency: 0.00001
    p. 218 UNDERWOOD 47   16 Or th'other on their borders, that will jeast

bords   frequency: 1   relative frequency: 0.00001
    p. 289 UNDERWOOD 85   7 But flees the Barre and Courts, with the proud
                              bords,

bore. See "bare."

bores   frequency: 1   relative frequency: 0.00001
    p. 290 UNDERWOOD 85   32 Wild Bores into his toyles pitch'd round:

borlase. See "burlase."

born. See "borne," "first-borne," "free-borne,"
           "home-borne," "street-borne," "town-born."

borne   frequency: 26   relative frequency: 0.00037
    p. 46 EPIGRAMS 62   12 Of the not borne, yet buried, here's the tombe.
    p. 67 EPIGRAMS 104   9 Or, more then borne for the comparison
    p. 75 EPIGRAMS 116   12 And to liue great, was better, then great borne.
    p. 99 FOREST 3   72 And brag, that they were therefore borne.
    p. 101 FOREST 4   53 But, what we'are borne for, we must beare:
    p. 101 FOREST 4   61 No, I doe know, that I was borne
    p. 110 FOREST 11   39 Inconstant, like the sea, of whence 't' borne,
    p. 114 FOREST 12   47 That bred them, graues: when they were borne,
                              they di'd,
    p. 115 FOREST 12   84 Borne vp by statues, shall I reare your head,
    p. 122 FOREST 15   18 Conceiu'd in sinne, and vnto labour borne,
    p. 130 UNDERWOOD 1.3   1 I sing the birth, was borne to night,
    p. 130 UNDERWOOD 1.3   23 A Martyr borne in our defence;
    p. 166 UNDERWOOD 15   120 When oft the Bearer, is borne out of dore?
    p. 197 UNDERWOOD 40   16 And free societie, hee's borne else-where,
    p. 208 UNDERWOOD 43   113 When thou wert borne, and that thou look'st at
                              best,
    p. 215 UNDERWOOD 44   66 Borne, bred, allied? what's he dare tutor us?
    p. 223 UNDERWOOD 49   46 Will cal't a Bastard, when a Prophet's borne.
    p. 225 UNDERWOOD 51   8 Since Bacon, and thy Lord was borne, and here;
    p. 237 UNDERWOOD 65   1 And art thou borne, brave Babe? Blest be thy
                              birth,
    p. 258 UNDERWOOD 75   168 (After the last child borne;) This is our
                              wedding day.
    p. 271 UNDERWOOD 83   94 When we were all borne, we began to die;
    p. 309 HORACE 2   88 Of words decay, and phrases borne but late
    p. 313 HORACE 2   167 Of Colchis borne; or in Assyria bred;
    p. 341 HORACE 1   120 Of .... noyses, borne to actuate things.
    p. 378 UNGATHERED 11   89 Yes thou wert borne out of his trauelling thigh
    p. 392 UNGATHERED 26   64 For a good Poet's made, as well as borne.

borrow'd   frequency: 4   relative frequency: 0.00005
  **p. 116 PANEGYRE   104 "When, publique iustice borrow'd all her powers
    p. 30 EPIGRAMS 12   12 At dice his borrow'd money: which, god payes.
    p. 165 UNDERWOOD 15   110 His deare and borrow'd Bravery he must cast?
    p. 187 UNDERWOOD 33   28 And not being borrow'd by thee, but possest.

borrowers   frequency: 2   relative frequency: 0.00002
    p. 51 EPIGRAMS 73   3 As't were a challenge, or a borrowers letter?
    p. 154 UNDERWOOD 13   48 Well knowne, and practiz'd borrowers on their
                              word,

borrowing   frequency: 1   relative frequency: 0.00001
     p. 155 UNDERWOOD 13   80 Is borrowing; that but stopt, they doe invade

bosom.   See "bosome."

bosome   frequency: 5   relative frequency: 0.00007
     p. 52 EPIGRAMS 76   12 Fit in that softer bosome to reside.
     p. 102 FOREST 4   68 Here in my bosome, and at home.
     p. 179 UNDERWOOD 25   55 Though many Gems be in your bosome stor'd,
     p. 230 UNDERWOOD 56   15 Sleepe in a Virgins bosome without feare,
     p. 368 UNGATHERED 6   80 From whose prowde bosome, thou began'st thy
                                flight.

both   frequency: 100   relative frequency: 0.00144
 **p. 115 PANEGYRE   96 "Who both, who neither: all the cunning tracts,
     p. 28 EPIGRAMS 4   4 And gaue thee both, to shew they could no more.
     p. 29 EPIGRAMS 8   5 Rob'd both of money, and the lawes reliefe,
     p. 32 EPIGRAMS 18   2 When both it is the old way, and the true.
     p. 35 EPIGRAMS 28   9 He will both argue, and discourse in oathes,
     p. 35 EPIGRAMS 28   10 Both which are great. And laugh at ill-made
                                clothes;
     p. 38 EPIGRAMS 37   2 But as they come, on both sides he takes fees,
     p. 38 EPIGRAMS 37   3 And pleaseth both. For while he melts his greace
     p. 39 EPIGRAMS 40   12 Conquer'd hath both life and it.
     p. 43 EPIGRAMS 52   6 Would both thy folly, and thy spite betray.
     p. 43 EPIGRAMS 53   6 To giue the world assurance thou wert both;
     p. 46 EPIGRAMS 62   10 And there's both losse of time, and losse of
                                sport
     p. 48 EPIGRAMS 66   4 In onely thee, might be both great, and glad.
     p. 54 EPIGRAMS 81   8 I must a libell make, and cosen both.
     p. 55 EPIGRAMS 85   3 Where I both learn'd, why wise-men hawking
                                follow,
     p. 57 EPIGRAMS 89   9 Who both their graces in thy selfe hast more
     p. 57 EPIGRAMS 90   13 MILL was the same. Since, both his body and
                                face
     p. 60 EPIGRAMS 94   12 Dare for these poemes, yet, both aske, and read,
     p. 61 EPIGRAMS 95   6 And all his numbers, both of sense, and sounds.
     p. 63 EPIGRAMS 98   11 Though both be good, the latter yet is worst,
     p. 64 EPIGRAMS 101   1 To night, graue sir, both my poore house, and I
     p. 66 EPIGRAMS 102   4 Both which are ask'd, to haue thee vnderstood.
     p. 70 EPIGRAMS 109   3 Where vertue makes them both, and that's in thee:
     p. 73 EPIGRAMS 112   18 That both for wit, and sense, so oft dost plucke,
     p. 78 EPIGRAMS 123   3 But both th'hast so, as who affects the state
     p. 79 EPIGRAMS 125   3 Both whose dimensions, lost, the world might
                                finde
     p. 83 EPIGRAMS 132   2 Might then both thee, thy worke and merit raise:
     p. 85 EPIGRAMS 133   46 And with both bombard-stile, and phrase, rehearse
     p. 88 EPIGRAMS 133   157 Graue tutor to the learned horse. Both which,
     p. 96 FOREST 3   2 Whether by choice, or fate, or both;
     p. 100 FOREST 4   14 Yet art thou both shrunke vp, and old,
     p. 116 FOREST 13   5 So both the prais'd, and praisers suffer: Yet,
     p. 118 FOREST 13   76 (They finde it both so wittie, and safe to giue.)
     p. 120 FOREST 14   10 Both loue the cause, and authors of the feast?
     p. 122 FOREST 15   17 I know my state, both full of shame, and scorne,
     p. 128 UNDERWOOD 1.1   25 7. Eternall Spirit, God from both proceeding,
     p. 130 UNDERWOOD 1.3   2 The Author both of Life, and light;
     p. 130 UNDERWOOD 1.3   15 Both wills were in one stature;
     p. 132 UNDERWOOD 2.2   21 Both the Arrow he had quit,
     p. 133 UNDERWOOD 2.3   8 Both the Bow, and shaft I held,
     p. 136 UNDERWOOD 2.5   2 Both my fortune, and my Starre!
     p. 136 UNDERWOOD 2.5   17 Both her Browes, bent like my Bow.
     p. 144 UNDERWOOD 3   25 Nay, rather both our soules bee strayn'd
     p. 145 UNDERWOOD 5   5 Wee have both wits, and fancies too,
     p. 151 UNDERWOOD 11   5 Hath both my heart and me surpriz'd,
     p. 151 UNDERWOOD 12   3 Would say as much, as both have done
     p. 151 UNDERWOOD 12   5 For I both lost a friend and Father,
     p. 152 UNDERWOOD 12   40 Who makes the one, so't be first, makes both.
     p. 161 UNDERWOOD 14   86 You both are modest. So am I. Farewell.
     p. 162 UNDERWOOD 15   14 Till he become both their, and his owne curse!
     p. 166 UNDERWOOD 15   128 But both fell prest under the load they make.
     p. 167 UNDERWOOD 15   160 But he that's both, and slave to boote, shall
                                live,
     p. 167 UNDERWOOD 15   164 Informers, Masters both of Arts and lies;
     p. 170 UNDERWOOD 18   11 But which shall lead me on? both these are blind:
     p. 171 UNDERWOOD 19   25 That which we can, who both in you, his Wife,
     p. 174 UNDERWOOD 23   6 That eats on wits, and Arts, and <oft> destroyes
                                them both.
     p. 176 UNDERWOOD 24   7 But both might know their wayes were understood,
     p. 182 UNDERWOOD 28   8 Both braines and hearts; and mine now best doe
                                know it:

both (cont.)

p. 186 UNDERWOOD 32	8	Both arm'd with wealth, and slander to oppose,
p. 199 UNDERWOOD 41	22	Till I may see both it and you agen.
p. 202 UNDERWOOD 42	77	And vouches both the Pageant, and the Day,
p. 212 UNDERWOOD 43	204	On both sides doe your mischiefes with delight;
p. 216 UNDERWOOD 45	4	One lesson we have both learn'd, and well read;
p. 220 UNDERWOOD 48	11	That both, their odour take him,
p. 223 UNDERWOOD 49	44	Both for the Mothers, and the Babes of grace,
p. 228 UNDERWOOD 53	6	So seem'd your horse and you, both of a peece!
p. 239 UNDERWOOD 67	14	And cleave both ayre and ground,
p. 243 UNDERWOOD 70	28	Troubled both foes, and friends;
p. 251 UNDERWOOD 74	24	Both to the honour of the King and State.
p. 251 UNDERWOOD 74	30	And both a strength, and Beautie to his Land!
p. 254 UNDERWOOD 75	52	Both Crownes, and Kingdomes in their either hand;
p. 256 UNDERWOOD 75	126	Whilst they both stand,
p. 258 UNDERWOOD 75	165	That when you both are old,
p. 258 UNDERWOOD 75	185	They both are slip'd to Bed; Shut fast the Doore,
p. 259 UNDERWOOD 76	16	(For with both the MUSE was fed)
p. 264 UNDERWOOD 79	29	That leades our flocks and us, and calls both forth
p. 265 UNDERWOOD 79	45	In truth of colours, both are best.
p. 273 U'WOOD 84.1	7	By THEE, and CONSCIENCE, both who thrive
p. 292 UNDERWOOD 86	13	For he's both noble, lovely, young,
p. 305 HORACE 2	13	And both doe crave, and give againe, this leave.
p. 309 HORACE 2	97	His course so hurtfull both to graine, and seedes,
p. 311 HORACE 2	135	Complaines in humble phrase. Both Telephus,
p. 313 HORACE 2	159	In sound, quite from his fortune; both the rout,
p. 317 HORACE 2	281	Be wonne a friend; it must both sway, and bend
p. 319 HORACE 2	299	Both in their tunes, the licence greater grew,
p. 323 HORACE 2	400	And jests; and both to admiration raise
p. 333 HORACE 2	588	The wished goale, both did, and suffer'd much
p. 333 HORACE 2	590	And both from Wine, and Women did abstaine.
p. 341 HORACE 1	103	.. .. with whom both choyse, and ....
p. 341 HORACE 1	132	... . both ... . raise
p. 367 UNGATHERED 6	33	Be then both Rare, and Good; and long
p. 375 UNGATHERED 10	30	Here France, and Italy both to him shed
p. 395 UNGATHERED 29	2	And see both climing vp the slippery staire
p. 398 UNGATHERED 30	84	Of thy strange Moon-Calfe, both thy straine of mirth,
p. 400 UNGATHERED 31	39	Both Saints, and Martyrs, by her loued Lord.
p. 402 UNGATHERED 34	5	Both him & Archimede; damne Architas
p. 410 UNGATHERED 38	12	Both learned, and vnlearned, all write Playes.
p. 416 UNGATHERED 43	8	And doe both Church, and Common-wealth the good,
p. 419 UNGATHERED 48	3	As when they both were greate, and both knewe howe

bottle   frequency: 1   relative frequency: 0.00001
p. 657 L. CONVIVALES   4 Or the Tripos, his Tower Bottle:

bottom. See "bottome."

bottome   frequency: 2   relative frequency: 0.00002
p. 87 EPIGRAMS 133 116 Neuer did bottome more betray her burden;
p. 197 UNDERWOOD 40   4 In hast the bottome of a med'cin'd Cup,

'boue   frequency: 2   relative frequency: 0.00002
*p. 494 TO HIMSELF   60 And raysing Charles his chariot, 'boue his Waine.
p. 403 UNGATHERED 34 19 Or are you soe ambitious 'boue your peers!

bough   frequency: 1   relative frequency: 0.00001
p. 85 EPIGRAMS 133   48 Sans helpe of SYBIL, or a golden bough,

boughes   frequency: 1   relative frequency: 0.00001
p. 98 FOREST 3   45 The trees cut out in log; and those boughes made

boughs   frequency: 1   relative frequency: 0.00001
See also "boughes."
p. 285 U'WOOD 84.9   96 With boughs of Palme, a crowned Victrice stand!

bought   frequency: 12   relative frequency: 0.00017
p. 28 EPIGRAMS 3   6 Not offer'd, as it made sute to be bought;
p. 41 EPIGRAMS 44   3 Ere blacks were bought for his owne funerall,
p. 42 EPIGRAMS 46   2 A knight-hood bought, to goe a wooing in?
p. 42 EPIGRAMS 48   1 His bought armes MVNG' not lik'd; for his first day

bought (cont.)
   p. 59 EPIGRAMS 92   9 Yet haue they seene the maps, and bought 'hem
                            too,
   p. 129 UNDERWOOD 1.2   22 With all since bought.
   p. 162 UNDERWOOD 15   13 Bought Flatteries, the issue of his purse,
   p. 180 UNDERWOOD 26   19 Thinke but how deare you bought
   p. 273 U'WOOD 84.1   27 With Gold, or Claspes, which might be bought
   p. 380 UNGATHERED 12   49 Except a dublet, and bought of the Iewes:
   p. 384 UNGATHERED 18   4 Do wayte vpon thee: and theyre Loue not bought.
   p. 398 UNGATHERED 30   72 And will be bought of euery Lord, and Knight,

boulstred   frequency: 1   relative frequency: 0.00001
   p. 372 UNGATHERED 9   12 She was 'Sell Boulstred. In wch name, I call

bouncing   frequency: 1   relative frequency: 0.00001
   p. 378 UNGATHERED 11   86 Come forth thou bonnie bouncing booke then,
                            daughter

bound   frequency: 8   relative frequency: 0.00011
   See also "wind-bound."
   p. 80 EPIGRAMS 127   3 To whom I am so bound, lou'd AVBIGNY?
   p. 93 FOREST 1   1 Some act of Loue's bound to reherse,
   p. 160 UNDERWOOD 14   64 Large claspe of Nature, such a wit can bound.
   p. 183 UNDERWOOD 29   12 They were bound!
   p. 319 HORACE 2   287 The Hau'-boy, not as now with latten bound,
   p. 319 HORACE 2   295 But, as they conquer'd, and enlarg'd their bound,
   p. 372 UNGATHERED 9   11 Wth Rites not bound, but conscience. Wouldst
                            thou All?
   p. 400 UNGATHERED 32   8 The Bound, and Frontire of our Poetrie;

bounds   frequency: 6   relative frequency: 0.00008
   p. 61 EPIGRAMS 95   5 So hast thou rendred him in all his bounds,
   p. 230 UNDERWOOD 64   10 And what are bounds to her, you make your owne?
   p. 264 UNDERWOOD 79   14 1. PAN is the great Preserver of our bounds.
   p. 265 UNDERWOOD 79   48 This is the great Preserver of our bounds,
   p. 280 U'WOOD 84.4   51 In all the bounds of beautie fit
   p. 291 UNDERWOOD 85   59 Or at the Feast of Bounds, the Lambe then
                            slaine,

bounteous   frequency: 1   relative frequency: 0.00001
   p. 142 UNDERWOOD 2.9   43 Bounteous as the clouds to earth;

bountie   frequency: 5   relative frequency: 0.00007
   p. 139 UNDERWOOD 2.7   10 And all your bountie wrong:
   p. 201 UNDERWOOD 42   45 When by thy sordid bountie she hath on
   p. 235 UNDERWOOD 62   12 O bountie! so to difference the rates!
   p. 252 UNDERWOOD 75   8 The bountie of a King, and beautie of his
                            Queene!
   p. 259 UNDERWOOD 76   9 To his bountie; by extension

bountie'   frequency: 1   relative frequency: 0.00001
   p. 159 UNDERWOOD 14   38 Of Gathering? Bountie' in pouring out againe?

bounties   frequency: 4   relative frequency: 0.00005
   p. 103 FOREST 6   4 All your bounties will betray.
   p. 155 UNDERWOOD 13   63 Their bounties forth, to him that last was made,
   p. 192 UNDERWOOD 38   54 And not the bounties you ha' done, deny.
   p. 255 UNDERWOOD 75   90 And wonder'd at, the bounties of this day:

bounty   frequency: 1   relative frequency: 0.00001
   See also "bountie," "bountie'."
   p. 662 INSCRIPTS. 2   3 LVCY of BEDFORD; she, that Bounty

'bout   frequency: 8   relative frequency: 0.00011
   p. 63 EPIGRAMS 97   12 Nor 'bout the beares, nor noyse to make lords
                            sport.
   p. 137 UNDERWOOD 2.5   41 And the Girdle 'bout her waste,
   p. 249 UNDERWOOD 72   3 Discharge it 'bout the Iland, in an houre,
   p. 270 UNDERWOOD 83   41 Were like a ring of Vertues, 'bout her set,
   p. 277 U'WOOD 84.3   27 Of Constellations 'bout her horld;
   p. 291 UNDERWOOD 85   66 And 'bout the steeming Chimney set!
   p. 292 UNDERWOOD 86   28 Thrice 'bout thy Altar with their Ivory feet.
   p. 293 UNDERWOOD 87   2 And ('bout thy Ivory neck,) no youth did fling

boutersheim   frequency: 1   relative frequency: 0.00001
   p. 69 EPIGRAMS 107   26 Hans-spiegle, Rotteinberg, and Boutersheim,

bouts   frequency: 1   relative frequency: 0.00001
   p. 338 HORACE 1   21 Bouts .. fleet .... doe intertwine

'bove   frequency: 8   relative frequency: 0.00011
   p. 127 UNDERWOOD 1.1   11 But 'bove the fat of rammes, or bulls, to prize
   p. 147 UNDERWOOD 7   12 It were a plague 'bove scorne,
   p. 181 UNDERWOOD 27   23 His new Cassandra, 'bove the old;
   p. 198 UNDERWOOD 40   28 'Bove all your standing waters, choak'd with
               weedes.
   p. 211 UNDERWOOD 43   194 'Bove all your Fire-workes, had at Ephesus,
   p. 273 U'WOOD 84.1   16 'Bove rattling Rime.
   p. 292 UNDERWOOD 86   18 With thee 'bove all his Rivals gifts take place,
   p. 342 HORACE 1   174 .. .. so 'bove ... ... bold ....

bow   frequency: 13   relative frequency: 0.00018
   p.   68 EPIGRAMS 105   13 And, armed to the chase, so bare her bow
   p.   81 EPIGRAMS 129   4 To Braynford, Hackney, Bow, but thou mak'st
               one;
   p. 110 FOREST 11   38 Arm'd with bow, shafts, and fire;
   p. 132 UNDERWOOD 2.2   9 Where's thy Quiver? bend thy Bow:
   p. 132 UNDERWOOD 2.2   17 Letting Bow and Arrow fall,
   p. 132 UNDERWOOD 2.2   22 And the Bow: with thought to hit
   p. 133 UNDERWOOD 2.3   8 Both the Bow, and shaft I held,
   p. 136 UNDERWOOD 2.5   17 Both her Browes, bent like my Bow.
   p. 141 UNDERWOOD 2.9   17 Eye-brows bent like Cupids bow,
   p. 170 UNDERWOOD 19   4 His double Bow, and round his Arrowes sends;
   p. 182 UNDERWOOD 28   10 His flames, his shafts, his Quiver, and his
               Bow,
   p. 234 UNDERWOOD 61   13 Fit for a Bishops knees! O bow them oft,
   p. 329 HORACE 2   524 Nor alwayes doth the loosed Bow, hit that

bower   frequency: 1   relative frequency: 0.00001
   p. 253 UNDERWOOD 75   24 To welcome home a Paire, and deck the nuptiall
               bower?

bowers   frequency: 4   relative frequency: 0.00005
**p. 116 PANEGYRE   103 "And with their ruines raise the panders bowers:
   p. 111 FOREST 11   57 A forme more fresh, then are the Eden bowers,
   p. 174 UNDERWOOD 23   12 To see their Seats and Bowers by chattring
               Pies defac't?
   p. 285 U'WOOD 84.9   88 The Thrones, the Cherube, and Seraphick
               bowers,

bowl. See "bowle," "deep-crown'd-bowle."

bowle   frequency: 1   relative frequency: 0.00001
   p. 167 UNDERWOOD 15   147 To flatter my good Lord, and cry his Bowle

bowles   frequency: 1   relative frequency: 0.00001
**p. 113 PANEGYRE   13 Carowsing humane bloud in yron bowles,

bowls. See "bowles," "creame-bowles."

box   frequency: 3   relative frequency: 0.00004
   p. 166 UNDERWOOD 15   137 To take the box up for him; and pursues
   p. 212 UNDERWOOD 43   214 And all the Evils that flew out of her box
   p. 215 UNDERWOOD 44   96 This, and that box his Beautie to repaire;

boxes   frequency: 1   relative frequency: 0.00001
   p. 327 HORACE 2   476 And in smooth Cypresse boxes to be keep'd?

boy   frequency: 7   relative frequency: 0.00010
   p.   41 EPIGRAMS 45   2 My sinne was too much hope of thee, lou'd boy,
   p. 107 FOREST 10   19 Let the old boy, your sonne, ply his old taske,
   p. 181 UNDERWOOD 27   5 Of Phao<n>s forme? or doth the Boy
   p. 241 UNDERWOOD 69   11 Was, t'have a Boy stand with a Club, and fright
   p. 293 UNDERWOOD 86   29 Me now, nor Wench, nor wanton Boy,
   p. 293 UNDERWOOD 87   16 So Fates would let the Boy a long thred run.
   p. 327 HORACE 2   470 He cries, Good boy, thou'lt keepe thine owne.
               Now, adde

boy'd   frequency: 1   relative frequency: 0.00001
   p. 244 UNDERWOOD 70   42 But that the Corke of Title boy'd him up.

boyes   frequency: 4   relative frequency: 0.00005
   p. 259 UNDERWOOD 76   20 Of the lesse-Poetique boyes;
   p. 273 U'WOOD 84.1   19 As prop'rest gifts, to Girles, and Boyes,
   p. 335 HORACE 2   647 According to the Moone. But, then the boyes
   p. 407 UNGATHERED 35   17 And stradling shews ye Boyes Brown paper fleet,

boyles   frequency: 1   relative frequency: 0.00001
   p. 110 FOREST 11   42 And boyles, as if he were

boys. See "boyes."

brace   frequency: 2   relative frequency: 0.00002
    p.   86 EPIGRAMS 133   87 Backe, cry'd their brace of CHARONS: they
                                 cry'd, no,
    p.   154 UNDERWOOD 13   40 So each, that's done, and tane, becomes a Brace.

brag   frequency: 1   relative frequency: 0.00001
    p.   99 FOREST 3   72 And brag, that they were therefore borne.

braies   frequency: 1   relative frequency: 0.00001
    p.   248 UNDERWOOD 71   7 And made those strong approaches, by False
                                 braies,

brain. See "braine," "brayne-hardie," "master-braine."

braine   frequency: 19   relative frequency: 0.00027
   *p.   492 TO HIMSELF   8 Commission of the braine
   *p.   493 TO HIMSELF   50 May, blushing, sweare no palsey's in thy braine.
    p.   32 EPIGRAMS 16   1 HARDIE, thy braine is valiant, 'tis confest,
    p.   49 EPIGRAMS 68   4 Actiue in's braine, and passiue in his bones.
    p.   53 EPIGRAMS 79   6 (Saue that most masculine issue of his braine)
    p.   56 EPIGRAMS 87   4 Of what shee had wrought came in, and wak'd his
                                 braine,
    p.   84 EPIGRAMS 133   23 One was: and he, for brawne, and braine, right
                                 able
    p.   136 UNDERWOOD 2.5   10 Sure, said he, if I have Braine,
    p.   175 UNDERWOOD 23   30 Who aided him, will thee, the issue of Joves
                                 braine.
    p.   177 UNDERWOOD 25   11 Thy Priest in this strange rapture: heat my
                                 braine
    p.   184 UNDERWOOD 29   41 And the Muses to their braine:
    p.   198 UNDERWOOD 40   45 Weaknesse of braine, or any charme of Wine,
    p.   203 UNDERWOOD 43   14 To ruine any issue of the braine?
    p.   221 UNDERWOOD 48   30 Before his braine doe know it:
    p.   230 UNDERWOOD 55   5 But since the Wine hath steep'd my braine,
    p.   331 HORACE 2   583 Into the Profits, what a meere rude braine
    p.   361 UNGATHERED 1   21 So in my braine; the strônge impression
    p.   380 UNGATHERED 12   32 Of his foote, or his penne, his braine or his
                                 hoofe,
    p.   391 UNGATHERED 26   25 That I not mixe thee so, my braine excuses:

braines   frequency: 10   relative frequency: 0.00014
    p.   34 EPIGRAMS 23   2 Who, to thy one, all other braines refuse:
    p.   36 EPIGRAMS 29   4 All braines, at times of triumph, should runne
                                 wit.
    p.   108 FOREST 10A   7 Then, leaue these lighter numbers, to light
                                 braines
    p.   116 FOREST 12   90 From braines entranc'd, and fill'd with extasies:
    p.   182 UNDERWOOD 28   8 Both braines and hearts: and mine now best doe
                                 know it:
    p.   208 UNDERWOOD 43   122 As th'other may his braines with Quicksilver.
    p.   362 UNGATHERED 2   4 In these pide times, only to shewe their braines,
    p.   378 UNGATHERED 11   90 As well as from his braines, and claimest thereby
    p.   378 UNGATHERED 11   92 Euer his thighes Male then, and his braines
                                 Shee.
  ⸗ p.   409 UNGATHERED 37   22 Thy Dirty braines, Men smell thy want of worth.

brains   frequency: 1   relative frequency: 0.00001
    See also "braines."
  . p.   657 L. CONVIVALES   16 Clears the Brains, makes Wit the Quicker:

brake   frequency: 2   relative frequency: 0.00002
    p.   142 UNDERWOOD 2.9   40 Or were set up in a Brake.
    p.   362 UNGATHERED 1   29 my abler faculties; and thus brake foorth

brakes   frequency: 1   relative frequency: 0.00001
    p.   162 UNDERWOOD 15   18 Crush'd in the snakie brakes, that he had past!

branch   frequency: 1   relative frequency: 0.00001
    p.   80 EPIGRAMS 126   3 I pluck'd a branch; the iealous god did frowne,

branches   frequency: 3   relative frequency: 0.00004
    p.   139 FOREST 13   99 Grow, grow, faire tree, and as thy branches
                                 shoote,
   .p.   185 UNDERWOOD 30   17 Clos'd to their peace, he saw his branches shoot,
    p.   291 UNDERWOOD 85   56 From fattest branches of the Tree:

branching   frequency: 1   relative frequency: 0.00001
    p.   276 U'WOOD 84.3   23 Foure Rivers branching forth like Seas,

brand   frequency: 3   relative frequency: 0.00004
  p. 203 UNDERWOOD 43   25 Itch to defame the State? or brand the Times?
  p. 315 HORACE 2   207 Nor from the brand, with which the life did burne
  p. 408 UNGATHERED 36   14 Thy Forehead is too narrow for my Brand.

branded   frequency: 2   relative frequency: 0.00002
  p. 160 UNDERWOOD 14   41 Impostures branded! and Authorities urg'd!
  p. 411 UNGATHERED 39   16 Cropt, branded, slit, neck-stockt; go, you are
                                    stript.

brandish'd   frequency: 1   relative frequency: 0.00001
  See also "brandish't."
  p. 187 UNDERWOOD 33   32 So brightly brandish'd) wound'st, defend'st! the
                                    while

brandish't   frequency: 1   relative frequency: 0.00001
  p. 392 UNGATHERED 26   70 As brandish't at the eyes of Ignorance.

brands   frequency: 1   relative frequency: 0.00001
  p. 110 FOREST 11   51 In equall knots: This beares no brands, nor
                                    darts,

brass. See "brasse."

brasse   frequency: 5   relative frequency: 0.00007
  p. 46 EPIGRAMS 60   4 Thy fact, in brasse or marble writ the same)
  p. 114 FOREST 12   52 Or, in an armies head, that, lockt in brasse,
  p. 307 HORACE 2   46 Th'Aemilian Schoole, in brasse can fashion out
  p. 390 UNGATHERED 25   6 As well in brasse, as he hath hit
  p. 390 UNGATHERED 25   8 All, that was euer writ in brasse.

brauado   frequency: 1   relative frequency: 0.00001
  p. 375 UNGATHERED 10   22 And there, while he giues the zealous Brauado,

braue   frequency: 14   relative frequency: 0.00020
 *p. 493 TO HIMSELF   32 Braue plush, and veluet-men;
  p. 30 EPIGRAMS 11   1 At court I met it, in clothes braue enough,
  p. 37 EPIGRAMS 32   1 What two braue perills of the priuate sword
  p. 81 EPIGRAMS 129   12 Out-dance the Babion, or out-boast the Braue;
  p. 84 EPIGRAMS 133   21 I sing the braue aduenture of two wights,
  p. 85 EPIGRAMS 133   57 Act a braue worke, call it thy last aduentry:
  p. 86 EPIGRAMS 133   77 And, on they went, like CASTOR braue, and
                                 POLLVX:
  p. 88 EPIGRAMS 133   163 Our braue Heroes with a milder glare,
  p. 95 FOREST 2   77 With his braue sonne, the Prince, they saw thy
                                  fires
  p. 114 FOREST 12   53 Gaue killing strokes. There were braue men,
                                  before
  p. 116 FOREST 12   92 And your braue friend, and mine so well did loue.
  p. 119 FOREST 13   85 And call it their braue sinne. For such there be
  p. 371 UNGATHERED 8   6 With the shops Foreman, or some such braue
                                  sparke,
  p. 398 UNGATHERED 30   64 Braue are the Musters, that the Muse will make.

brauely   frequency: 2   relative frequency: 0.00002
  p. 60 EPIGRAMS 93   5 Two brauely in the battaile fell, and dy'd,
  p. 89 EPIGRAMS 133   192 And so went brauely backe, without protraction.

brauerie   frequency: 1   relative frequency: 0.00001
  p. 96 FOREST 3   10 Of the short brauerie of the night;

brauest   frequency: 2   relative frequency: 0.00002
  p. 75 EPIGRAMS 116   10 In men, but euery brauest was the best:
  p. 397 UNGATHERED 30   56 A better cause, and strike the brauest heate

braules   frequency: 1   relative frequency: 0.00001
  p. 32 EPIGRAMS 16   3 Thy selfe into fresh braules: when, call'd vpon,

bravado. See "brauado."

brave   frequency: 21   relative frequency: 0.00030
  See also "braue," "out-brave."
  p. 157 UNDERWOOD 13   149 'Tis like light Canes, that first rise big and
                                  brave,
  p. 162 UNDERWOOD 15   2 Beates brave, and loude in Europe, and bids come
  p. 164 UNDERWOOD 15   84 Great, brave, and fashion'd folke, these are
                                  allow'd
  p. 187 UNDERWOOD 33   22 Thou hast the brave scorne, to put back the fee!
  p. 201 UNDERWOOD 42   50 But when thy Wife (as thou conceiv'st) is brave?
  p. 213 UNDERWOOD 44   23 Well, I say, thrive, thrive brave Artillerie
                                  yard,

brave (cont.)
    p. 224 UNDERWOOD 50   7 Is of so brave example, as he were
    p. 225 UNDERWOOD 51   17 'Tis a brave cause of joy, let it be knowne,
    p. 227 UNDERWOOD 52   15 You made it a brave piece, but not like me.
    p. 233 UNDERWOCD 60   3 Henry, the brave young Lord La-ware,
    p. 237 UNDERWOOD 65   1 And art thou borne, brave Babe? Blest be thy
                                birth,
    p. 239 UNDERWOOD 67   3 Some brave un-common way:
    p. 242 UNDERWOOD 70   1 Brave Infant of Saguntum, cleare
    p. 246 UNDERWOOD 70   106 That knits brave minds, and manners, more then
                                blood.
    p. 262 UNDERWOOD 78   9 His brest is a brave Palace, a broad Street,
    p. 271 UNDERWOOD 83   95 And, but for that Contention, and brave strife
    p. 278 U'WOOD 84.4   18 As you goe on, by what brave way
    p. 281 U'WOOD 84.8   11 (Brave Youths) th<ey>'are their possessions,
                                none of yours:
    p. 313 HORACE 2   175 Medea make brave with impetuous scorne;
    p. 325 HORACE 2   451 Of a brave Chiefe sent to the warres: He can,
    p. 333 HORACE 2   611 For hee'll cry, Good, brave, better, excellent!

bravely. See "brauely."

braveries   frequency: 1   relative frequency: 0.00001
    See also "brav'ries."
    p. 200 UNDERWOOD 42   34 And braveries of Court, and felt their fits

bravery   frequency: 3   relative frequency: 0.00004
    See also "brauerie."
    p. 163 UNDERWOOD 15   45 In bravery, or gluttony, or coyne,
    p. 164 UNDERWOOD 15   56 The bravery makes, she can no honour leese:
    p. 165 UNDERWOOD 15   110 His deare and borrow'd Bravery he must cast?

bravest. See "brauest."

brav'ries   frequency: 1   relative frequency: 0.00001
    p. 253 UNDERWOOD 75   19 Doe boast their Loves, and Brav'ries so at
                                large,

brawls. See "braules."

brawn. See "brawne."

brawne   frequency: 1   relative frequency: 0.00001
    p. 84 EPIGRAMS 133   23 One was; and he, for brawne, and braine, right
                                able

bray   frequency: 1   relative frequency: 0.00001
    p. 403 UNGATHERED 34   23 What makes your Wretchednes to bray soe loud

brayes   frequency: 1   relative frequency: 0.00001
    See also "braies."
    p. 31 EPIGRAMS 12   19 To euery cause he meets, this voyce he brayes:

brayne-hardie   frequency: 1   relative frequency: 0.00001
    p. 32 EPIGRAMS 16   t1 TO BRAYNE-HARDIE.

braynford   frequency: 1   relative frequency: 0.00001
    p. 81 EPIGRAMS 129   4 To Braynford, Hackney, Bow, but thou mak'st
                                one;

brays. See "brayes."

brazen   frequency: 2   relative frequency: 0.00002
    p. 269 UNDERWOOD 83   24 And voyce to raise them from my brazen Lungs,
    p. 294 UNDERWOOD 87   18 And us dis-joyn'd force to her brazen yoke,

breach   frequency: 3   relative frequency: 0.00004
    p. 61 EPIGRAMS 95   10 And gratulate the breach, I grieu'd before:
    p. 169 UNDERWOOD 17   11 That as the lesser breach: for he that takes
    p. 323 HORACE 2   388 To note, in Poemes, breach of harmonie;

breaches   frequency: 1   relative frequency: 0.00001
    p. 98 FOREST 3   69 Goe enter breaches, meet the cannons rage,

bread   frequency: 6   relative frequency: 0.00008
   *p. 492 TO HIMSELF   15 To offer them a surfet of pure bread,
    p. 95 FOREST 2   63 Where the same beere, and bread, and selfe-same
                                wine,
    p. 155 UNDERWOOD 13   68 And hurt seeks Cure, the Surgeon bids take
                                bread,

bread (cont.)
p. 228 UNDERWOOD 53   19 And cri'd, Away with the Caesarian bread,
p. 259 UNDERWOOD 76   15 Or dispenc'd in bookes, or bread,
p. 408 UNGATHERED 36   10 Seek out some hungry painter, yt for bread

bread-streets   frequency: 1   relative frequency: 0.00001
p. 85 EPIGRAMS 133   37 At Bread-streets Mermaid, hauing din'd, and
                          merry,

break   frequency: 1   relative frequency: 0.00001
See also "breake."
p. 418 UNGATHERED 45   42 or theire Ale, they break the peace,

breake   frequency: 14   relative frequency: 0.00020
p. 59 EPIGRAMS 92   29 To breake vp seales, and close 'hem. And they
                          know,
p. 97 FOREST 3   21 Or, if thou list the night in watch to breake,
p. 99 FOREST 3   88 The secrets, that shall breake their sleepe:
p. 169 UNDERWOOD 17   2 Debts when they can: good men may breake their
                          day,
p. 169 UNDERWOOD 17   9 And their words too; where I but breake my
                          Band.
p. 172 UNDERWOOD 21   2 His name in any mettall, it would breake.
p. 177 UNDERWOOD 25   19 Breake the knit Circle of her Stonie Armes,
p. 215 UNDERWOOD 44   72 The Hawking language? or our Day to breake
p. 230 UNDERWOOD 56   10 His friends, but to breake Chaires, or cracke a
                          Coach.
p. 233 UNDERWOOD 59   18 To bend, to breake, provoke, or suffer it!
p. 269 UNDERWOOD 83   27 Their Carract was! I, or my trump must breake,
p. 276 U'WOOD 84.3   14 And, out of that, make Day to breake;
p. 416 UNGATHERED 45   3 or as some would say to breake
p. 420 UNGATHERED 48   19 Breake then thie quills, blott out

breakes   frequency: 2   relative frequency: 0.00002
p. 63 EPIGRAMS 98   5 Fortune vpon him breakes her selfe, if ill,
p. 191 UNDERWOOD 38   10 As light breakes from you, that affrights
                          despaire,

breaking   frequency: 2   relative frequency: 0.00002
p. 213 UNDERWOOD 44   8 Launces, and men, and some a breaking force.
p. 283 U'WOOD 84.9   26 I summe up mine owne breaking, and wish all.

breaks. See "breakes."

breast   frequency: 2   relative frequency: 0.00002
See also "brest."
p. 137 UNDERWOOD 2.5   33 And betweene each rising breast,
p. 366 UNGATHERED 6   8 Did neuer dint the breast of Tamisis.

breastes   frequency: 1   relative frequency: 0.00001
p. 421 UNGATHERED 48   43 Throughout their generall breastes,

breasts   frequency: 1   relative frequency: 0.00001
See also "breastes," "brests."
p. 87 EPIGRAMS 133   124 Against their breasts. Here, seu'rall ghosts did
                          flit

breath   frequency: 20   relative frequency: 0.00028
p. 57 EPIGRAMS 89   6 Then CICERO, whose euery breath was fame:
p. 76 EPIGRAMS 119   9 Dar'st breath in any ayre; and with safe skill,
p. 81 EPIGRAMS 128   5 May windes as soft as breath of kissing friends,
p. 83 EPIGRAMS 131   14 For fame, with breath soone kindled, soone blowne
                          out.
p. 99 FOREST 3   75 And change possessions, oftner with his breath,
p. 103 FOREST 6   8 While you breath. First giue a hundred,
p. 106 FOREST 9   13 But thou thereon did'st onely breath,
p. 112 FOREST 11   96 Whose od'rous breath destroyes
p. 122 FOREST 15   24 With holy PAVL, lest it be thought the breath
p. 137 UNDERWOOD 2.5   27 Rip'ned with a breath more sweet,
p. 139 UNDERWOOD 2.7   16 Each suck <the> others breath.
p. 222 UNDERWOOD 49   5 And that as any are strooke, her breath creates
p. 248 UNDERWOOD 71   12 Health, or scarce breath, as she had never bin,
p. 269 UNDERWOOD 83   6 You seeme a faire one! O that you had breath,
p. 285 U'WOOD 84.9   92 What 'tis t<o>'enjoy an everlasting breath!
p. 286 U'WOOD 84.9   136 The safetie of our soules, and forfeit breath!
p. 288 U'WOOD 84.9   204 To justifie, and quicken us in breath!
p. 365 UNGATHERED 5   13 Her breath for sweete exceeding
p. 398 UNGATHERED 30   66 How do his trumpets breath! What loud alarmes!
p. 416 UNGATHERED 44   3 Bred by your breath, on this low bancke of ours;

breath'd   frequency: 2   relative frequency: 0.00002
  **p. 114 PANEGYRE   32 Breath'd in his way; and soules (their better
                             parts)
    p. 319 HORACE 2   289 But soft, and simple, at few holes breath'd time

breathe   frequency: 2   relative frequency: 0.00002
  See also "breath."
    p. 37 EPIGRAMS 33   4 Breathe to expect my when, and make my how.
    p. 101 FOREST 4   46 Where breathe the basest of thy fooles;

breathes   frequency: 1   relative frequency: 0.00001
  See also "breath's."
    p. 36 EPIGRAMS 28   18 That breathes in his dogs way: and this is great.

breath's   frequency: 1   relative frequency: 0.00001
    p. 418 UNGATHERED 47   4 That lives, and breath's, and loves the King.

breath'st   frequency: 1   relative frequency: 0.00001
    p. 127 UNDERWOOD 1.1   19 And breath'st into it, life, and light, with
                             state

bred   frequency: 12   relative frequency: 0.00017
  See also "court-bred-fillie."
    p. 60 EPIGRAMS 94   11 They, then, that liuing where the matter is bred,
    p. 114 FOREST 12   47 That bred them, graues: when they were borne,
                             they di'd,
    p. 146 UNDERWOOD 6   3 We were not bred to sit on stooles,
    p. 173 UNDERWOOD 22   16 And kept, and bred, and brought up true.
    p. 197 UNDERWOOD 40   17 And must be bred, so to conceale his birth,
    p. 209 UNDERWOOD 43   143 Bred on the Banck, in time of Poperie,
    p. 215 UNDERWOOD 44   66 Borne, bred, allied? what's he dare tutor us?
    p. 237 UNDERWOOD 64   17 O Times! O Manners! Surfet bred of ease,
    p. 313 HORACE 2   167 Of Colchis borne; or in Assyria bred;
    p. 367 UNGATHERED 6   40 The Vale, that bred thee pure, as her Hills
                             Snow.
    p. 410 UNGATHERED 38   14 That knew the Crafts they had bin bred in,
                             right:
    p. 416 UNGATHERED 44   3 Bred by your breath, on this low bancke of ours;

breda   frequency: 1   relative frequency: 0.00001
    p. 214 UNDERWOOD 44   40 The Berghen siege, and taking in Breda,

breeches   frequency: 1   relative frequency: 0.00001
    p. 417 UNGATHERED 45   34 for the breeches with the bride,

breed   frequency: 4   relative frequency: 0.00005
    p. 94 FOREST 2   24 The middle grounds thy mares, and horses breed.
    p. 146 UNDERWOOD 6   12 Is that which doth perfection breed.
    p. 194 UNDERWOOD 38   116 Absence, or Distance, shall not breed decay.
    p. 215 UNDERWOOD 44   73 With Citizens? let Clownes, and Tradesmen
                             breed

breedes   frequency: 1   relative frequency: 0.00001
    p. 198 UNDERWOOD 40   27 Keepe secret in his Channels what he breedes,

breeding   frequency: 1   relative frequency: 0.00001
    p. 365 UNGATHERED 5   14 The Phoenix place of breeding,

breeds   frequency: 2   relative frequency: 0.00002
  See also "breedes."
    p. 50 EPIGRAMS 72   5 'Tis not thy iudgement breeds the preiudice,
    p. 187 UNDERWOOD 33   39 Thy sincere practise, breeds not thee a fame

breeze. See "brize."

brentford. See "braynford."

brest   frequency: 9   relative frequency: 0.00013
    p. 61 EPIGRAMS 95   19 That hast thy brest so cleere of present crimes,
    p. 109 FOREST 11   5 Which to effect (since no brest is so sure,
    p. 198 UNDERWOOD 40   49 Which in assurance to your brest I tell,
    p. 208 UNDERWOOD 43   114 She durst not kisse, but flung thee from her
                             brest.
    p. 262 UNDERWOOD 78   9 His brest is a brave Palace, a broad Street,
    p. 269 UNDERWOOD 83   14 Thou wouldst have written, Fame, upon my brest:
    p. 281 U'WOOD 84.4   71 Thou entertaining in thy brest,
    p. 361 UNGATHERED 1   14 how lyke the Carbuncle in Aarons brest
    p. 366 UNGATHERED 6   27 And still is in the Brest:

brests   frequency: 5   relative frequency: 0.00007
  **p. 113 PANEGYRE   1 Heau'n now not striues, alone, our brests to fill
  **p. 115 PANEGYRE   76 How he may triumph in his subiects brests,
    p. 110 FOREST 11   34 In our enflamed brests:
    p. 155 UNDERWOOD 13   91 Such a religious horrour in the brests
    p. 329 HORACE 2   506 But flowes out, that ore-swelleth in full brests.

brethren   frequency: 4   relative frequency: 0.00005
    p. 59 EPIGRAMS 92   35 Or 'gainst the Bishops, for the Brethren,
                             raile,
    p. 59 EPIGRAMS 92   36 Much like those Brethren; thinking to preuaile
    p. 209 UNDERWOOD 43   139 The Brethren, they streight nois'd it out for
                             Newes,
    p. 325 HORACE 2   448 What brethren, what a stranger, and his guest,

bretons   frequency: 1   relative frequency: 0.00001
    p. 362 UNGATHERED 2   5 Looke here on Bretons worke, the master print:

breuitie   frequency: 1   relative frequency: 0.00001
    p. 62 EPIGRAMS 95   29 Where breuitie, where splendor, and where height,

brevity. See "breuitie."

brew-houses   frequency: 1   relative frequency: 0.00001
    p. 211 UNDERWOOD 43   179 But to confine him to the Brew-houses,

briar. See "brier."

briarevs   frequency: 1   relative frequency: 0.00001
    p. 86 EPIGRAMS 133   81 One said, it was bold BRIAREVS, or the
                             beadle,

brick-kills   frequency: 1   relative frequency: 0.00001
    p. 211 UNDERWOOD 43   183 Condemne him to the Brick-kills, or some Hill-

bride   frequency: 7   relative frequency: 0.00010
    p. 138 UNDERWOOD 2.6   8 That the Bride (allow'd a Maid)
    p. 138 UNDERWOOD 2.6   18 Wisht the Bride were chang'd to night,
    p. 203 UNDERWOOD 43   12 By Jove to have Minerva for thy Bride,
    p. 253 UNDERWOOD 75   36 And all did ring th'approches of the Bride;
    p. 254 UNDERWOOD 75   71 The Bridegroome meets the Bride
    p. 394 UNGATHERED 28   24 To lay her here, inclos'd, his second Bride.
    p. 417 UNGATHERED 45   34 for the breeches with the bride,

bride-well   frequency: 1   relative frequency: 0.00001
    p. 85 EPIGRAMS 133   42 Of some Bride-well, and may, in time, concerne
                             vs

bridegroome   frequency: 1   relative frequency: 0.00001
    p. 254 UNDERWOOD 75   71 The Bridegroome meets the Bride

brides   frequency: 1   relative frequency: 0.00001
    p. 254 UNDERWOOD 75   59 The bright Brides paths, embelish'd more then
                             thine

bridewell. See "bride-well."

brief. See "briefe."

briefe   frequency: 1   relative frequency: 0.00001
    p. 329 HORACE 2   503 Be briefe, in what thou wouldst command, that so

brier   frequency: 2   relative frequency: 0.00002
    p. 135 UNDERWOOD 2.4   27 Or have smelt o'the bud o'the Brier?
    p. 413 UNGATHERED 41   22 Which, of the field is clep'd the sweetest brier,

bright   frequency: 35   relative frequency: 0.00050
  **p. 113 PANEGYRE   18 And in their vapor her bright mettall drowne.
    p. 39 EPIGRAMS 40   8 Then they might in her bright eyes.
    p. 68 EPIGRAMS 105   10 You were the bright OENONE, FLORA, or
                             May?
    p. 94 FOREST 2   37 Bright eeles, that emulate them, and leape on
                             land, .
    p. 95 FOREST 2   78 Shine bright on euery harth as the desires
    p. 110 FOREST 11   48 Whose linkes are bright, and euen,
    p. 112 FOREST 11   95 And turne the blackest sorrowes to bright ioyes:
    p. 115 FOREST 12   60 Or set bright ARIADNES crowne so high?
    p. 115 FOREST 12   66 Of all LVCINA'S traine; LVCY the
                             bright,
    p. 121 FOREST 14   57 Of loue be bright,

bright (cont.)

p.	134	UNDERWOOD 2.4	13 Doe but looke on her Haire, it is bright
p.	134	UNDERWOOD 2.4	21 Have you seene but a bright Lillie grow,
p.	147	UNDERWOOD 7	22 But he hath eyes so round, and bright,
p.	170	UNDERWOOD 19	1 By those bright Eyes, at whose immortall fires
p.	179	UNDERWOOD 25	54 (Whose heart in that bright Sphere flames clearest,
p.	181	UNDERWOOD 27	15 With bright Lycoris, Gallus choice,
p.	206	UNDERWOOD 43	74 Their Jemme of Riches, and bright Stone, that brings
p.	245	UNDERWOOD 70	81 To see that bright eternall Day:
p.	246	UNDERWOOD 70	89 In this bright Asterisme:
p.	252	UNDERWOOD 75	2 A-while with us, bright Sun, and helpe our light;
p.	253	UNDERWOOD 75	17 What Beavie of beauties, and bright youths at charge
p.	254	UNDERWOOD 75	59 The bright Brides paths, embelish'd more then thine
p.	262	UNDERWOOD 78	15 When the Apostle Barnabee the bright
p.	285	U'WOOD 84.9	101 Her fellowes, with the oyle of gladnesse, bright
p.	288	U'WOOD 84.9	200 Incarnate in the Manger, shining bright
p.	291	UNDERWOOD 85	50 Nor Turbot, nor bright Golden-eyes:
p.	291	UNDERWOOD 85	51 If with bright floods, the Winter troubled much,
p.	292	UNDERWOOD 86	10 With thy bright Swans, of Paulus Maximus:
p.	294	UNDERWOOD 87	19 That I bright C<h>loe off should shake;
p.	315	HORACE 2	204 But light from smoake; that he may draw his bright
p.	368	UNGATHERED 6	61 With entheate rage, to publish their bright tracts?
p.	369	UNGATHERED 6	96 So blacke a Bird, so bright a Qualitie.
p.	397	UNGATHERED 30	23 When, by thy bright Ideas standing by,
p.	420	UNGATHERED 48	28 Yett: since the bright, and wyse,
p.	662	INSCRIPTS. 2	2 vnto the bright, and amiable

brighter   frequency: 3   relative frequency: 0.00004

**p.	117	PANEGYRE	146 Brighter then all, hath yet made no one lesse;
p.	52	EPIGRAMS 76	7 I meant the day-starre should not brighter rise,
p.	181	UNDERWOOD 27	26 Where never Star shone brighter yet?

brightest   frequency: 3   relative frequency: 0.00004

**p.	114	PANEGYRE	54 Her brightest tyre; and, in it, equall shone
p.	264	UNDERWOOD 79	24 Nym. Of brightest MIRA, doe we raise our Song,
p.	264	UNDERWOOD 79	32 Nymp. Of brightest MIRA, is our Song; the grace

brightly   frequency: 2   relative frequency: 0.00002

p.	187	UNDERWOOD 33	32 So brightly brandish'd) wound'st, defend'st! the while
p.	392	UNGATHERED 26	67 Of Shakespeares minde, and manners brightly shines

brightnesse   frequency: 3   relative frequency: 0.00004

p.	60	EPIGRAMS 94	1 LVCY, you brightnesse of our spheare, who are
p.	61	EPIGRAMS 94	15 LVCY, you brightnesse of our spheare, who are
p.	364	UNGATHERED 5	3 Of her illustrate brightnesse,

brill   frequency: 1   relative frequency: 0.00001

p.	213	UNDERWOOD 44	30 Would thinke no more of Vlushing, or the Brill:

bring   frequency: 32   relative frequency: 0.00046
See also "bring't."

**p.	115	PANEGYRE	67 To bring them forth: Whil'st riper ag'd, and apt
**p.	117	PANEGYRE	140 The temp'rance of a priuate man did bring,
p.	47	EPIGRAMS 64	2 With thy new place, bring I these early fruits
p.	47	EPIGRAMS 64	11 Where good mens vertues them to honors bring,
p.	69	EPIGRAMS 108	1 Strength of my Countrey, whilst I bring to view
p.	78	EPIGRAMS 122	3 If I would striue to bring backe times, and trie
p.	95	FOREST 2	51 Some bring a capon, some a rurall cake,
p.	95	FOREST 2	53 The better cheeses, bring 'hem; or else send
p.	108	FOREST 10	28 My Muse vp by commission: No, I bring
p.	115	FOREST 12	75 To her remembrance; which when time shall bring
p.	130	UNDERWOOD 1.3	8 That did us all salvation bring,
p.	167	UNDERWOOD 15	173 Then once to number, or bring forth to hand,
p.	169	UNDERWOOD 17	18 And I will bring a Crop, if not the best.
p.	182	UNDERWOOD 27	31 And shall not I my Celia bring,
p.	213	UNDERWOOD 44	25 Powder, or paper, to bring up the youth
p.	216	UNDERWOOD 45	9 Much lesse a name would we bring up, or nurse,
p.	224	UNDERWOOD 50	13 And though all praise bring nothing to your name,
p.	250	UNDERWOOD 73	1 Looke up, thou seed of envie, and still bring

bring (cont.)
```
  p. 251 UNDERWOOD 74    20 Bring all your friends, (faire Lord) that burne
  p. 256 UNDERWOOD 75   107 To day, the Fathers service; who could bring
  p. 264 UNDERWOOD 79    33 Of all that Nature, yet, to life did bring;
  p. 276 U'WOOD 84.3     22 With all that Youth, or it can bring:
  p. 313 HORACE 2       184 And thou maist better bring a Rhapsody
  p. 317 HORACE 2       250 Mans comming yeares much good with them doe
                            bring:
  p. 325 HORACE 2       430 For choller! If I did not, who could bring
  p. 325 HORACE 2       439 Whether truth may, and whether error bring.
  p. 333 HORACE 2       604 Of an entangling suit; and bring 't about:
  p. 333 HORACE 2       609 You doe not bring, to judge your Verses, one,
  p. 333 HORACE 2       627 Hee'd bid, blot all: and to the anvile bring
  p. 355 HORACE 1       668 Now, bring ... backe, he'le .. .. .... . ...
  p. 394 UNGATHERED 28    2 And pray thee Reader, bring thy weepinge Eyes
  p. 415 UNGATHERED 43    1 I cannot bring my Muse to dropp <her> Vies
```

bringes   frequency: 1   relative frequency: 0.00001
```
  p. 383 UNGATHERED 16    9 hee freely bringes; and on[e] this Alter layes
```

bringing   frequency: 1   relative frequency: 0.00001
```
  p. 414 UNGATHERED 41   48 By bringing forth GOD's onely Son, no other.
```

brings   frequency: 8   relative frequency: 0.00011
See also "bringes."
```
  p.  30 EPIGRAMS 12      9 The taylor brings a suite home; he it ssayes,
  p.  32 EPIGRAMS 16      4 Scarse thy weekes swearing brings thee of, of
                            one.
  p.  49 EPIGRAMS 67      2 Most thinke all praises flatteries. But truth
                            brings
  p. 206 UNDERWOOD 43    74 Their Jemme of Riches, and bright Stone, that
                            brings
  p. 222 UNDERWOOD 48    54 And Charles brings home the Ladie.
  p. 256 UNDERWOOD 75   114 It brings Friends Joy, Foes Griefe,
                            Posteritie Fame;
  p. 315 HORACE 2       208 Of Meleager, brings he the returne
  p. 385 UNGATHERED 19    7 My suffrage brings thee all increase, to crowne
```

bringst   frequency: 1   relative frequency: 0.00001
```
  p. 313 HORACE 2       179 Unto the Scene thou bringst, and dar'st create
```

bring'st   frequency: 1   relative frequency: 0.00001
See also "bringst."
```
  p. 263 UNDERWOOD 78    21 He will cleare up his forehead, thinke thou
                            bring'st
```

bring't   frequency: 1   relative frequency: 0.00001
```
  p. 353 HORACE 1       604 .. .. ........... .... or bring't .....
```

bristo'   frequency: 1   relative frequency: 0.00001
```
  p.  85 EPIGRAMS 133    39 A harder tasque, then either his to Bristo',
```

bristol. See "bristo'."

brit[t]aine   frequency: 1   relative frequency: 0.00001
```
**p. 117 PANEGYRE       161 Yet, let blest Brit[t]aine aske (without your
                            wrong)
```

britain. See "brit[t]aine," "britaine."

britaine   frequency: 3   relative frequency: 0.00004
```
  p. 236 UNDERWOOD 64     7 Indeed, when had great Britaine greater cause
  p. 268 UNDERWOOD 82    13 Me thought, Great Britaine in her Sea, before,
  p. 391 UNGATHERED 26   41 Triumph, my Britaine, thou hast one to showe,
```

britain's   frequency: 1   relative frequency: 0.00001
```
  p. 249 UNDERWOOD 72     6 Repeating all Great Britain's joy, and more,
```

brize   frequency: 1   relative frequency: 0.00001
```
  p. 164 UNDERWOOD 15    71 As if a Brize were gotten i' their tayle;
```

broad   frequency: 3   relative frequency: 0.00004
```
  p.  62 EPIGRAMS 96     12 A man should seeke great glorie, and not broad.
  p.  93 FOREST 2        12 Beneath the broad beech, and the chest-nut shade;
  p. 262 UNDERWOOD 78     9 His brest is a brave Palace, a broad Street,
```

broad-seales   frequency: 1   relative frequency: 0.00001
```
  p. 385 UNGATHERED 19    3 Or, to so many, and so Broad-seales had,
```

broad-troden   frequency: 1   relative frequency: 0.00001
    p. 313 HORACE 2   188 If thou the vile, broad-troden ring forsake.

broader   frequency: 1   relative frequency: 0.00001
    p. 366 UNGATHERED 6   23 To brookes, and broader streames,

broadest   frequency: 1   relative frequency: 0.00001
    p. 99 FOREST 3   83 And brooding o're it sit, with broadest eyes,

brocage   frequency: 1   relative frequency: 0.00001
    p. 44 EPIGRAMS 56   3 From brocage is become so bold a thiefe,

broeck   frequency: 1   relative frequency: 0.00001
    p. 49 EPIGRAMS 66   12 To liue when Broeck not stands, nor Roor doth
                                runne.

broick. See "broeck."

brokage. See "brocage."

broke   frequency: 5   relative frequency: 0.00007
    See also "brake."
    p. 101 FOREST 4   30 That fled his cage, or broke his chaine,
    p. 151 UNDERWOOD 12   10 Yet he broke them, e're they could him,
    p. 169 UNDERWOOD 17   8 But that some greater names have broke with me,
    p. 191 UNDERWOOD 38   1 'Tis true, I'm broke! Vowes, Oathes, and all
                                I had
    p. 237 UNDERWOOD 64   15 How is she barren growne of love! or broke!

broken   frequency: 5   relative frequency: 0.00007
    p. 127 UNDERWOOD 1.1   10 A broken heart thou wert not wont despise,
    p. 129 UNDERWOOD 1.2   2 A broken heart,
    p. 216 UNDERWOOD 44   102 Her broken Armes up, to their emptie moulds.
    p. 288 U'WOOD 84.9   185 Her broken sighes did never misse whole sense:
    p. 398 UNGATHERED 30   74 Get broken peeces, and fight well by those.

brokers. See "money-brokers."

brome   frequency: 2   relative frequency: 0.00002
    p. 409 UNGATHERED 38   1 I had you for a Seruant, once, Dick Brome;
    p. 409 UNGATHERED 38   t3 the Author of this Work, M. RICH.
                                BROME.

brontes   frequency: 1   relative frequency: 0.00001
    p. 179 UNDERWOOD 25   40 Let Brontes, and black Steropes,

brooding   frequency: 2   relative frequency: 0.00002
    p. 99 FOREST 3   83 And brooding o're it sit, with broadest eyes,
    p. 400 UNGATHERED 31   29 And howrely brooding ore the same,

brookes   frequency: 2   relative frequency: 0.00002
    p. 189 UNDERWOOD 36   4 None brookes the Sun-light worse then he.
    p. 366 UNGATHERED 6   23 To brookes, and broader streames,

brooks. See "brookes."

broom. See "broome."

broome   frequency: 1   relative frequency: 0.00001
    p. 282 U'WOOD 84.9   8 Till swept away, th<ey>'were cancell'd with a
                                broome!

brother   frequency: 4   relative frequency: 0.00005
    p. 39 EPIGRAMS 40   15 Fate, in a brother. To conclude,
    p. 165 UNDERWOOD 15   93 The brother trades a sister; and the friend
    p. 285 U'WOOD 84.9   117 There shall the Brother, with the Sister walke,
    p. 331 HORACE 2   545 You Sir, the elder brother, though you are

brothers   frequency: 3   relative frequency: 0.00004
    p. 240 UNDERWOOD 67   29 Of all her Brothers storie,
    p. 382 UNGATHERED 16   t2 behalfe of the two noble Brothers sr Robert
                                & sr Henrye
    p. 383 UNGATHERED 16   10 As true oblations; his Brothers Embleme sayes,

brought   frequency: 31   relative frequency: 0.00044
    See also "forth-brought."
    p. 31 EPIGRAMS 15   2 'Twas brought to court first wrapt, and white as
                                milke;
    p. 81 EPIGRAMS 128   10 Thy selfe, with thy first thoughts, brought home
                                by thee,

brought (cont.)
p.   84 EPIGRAMS 133   20 Shee brought the Poets forth, but ours
                            th'aduenter.
p. 100 FOREST 4   1 False world, good-night: since thou hast brought
p. 115 FOREST 12   55 That HOMER brought to Troy; yet none so
                            liue:
p. 132 UNDERWOOD 2.2   19 Could be brought once back to looke.
p. 161 UNDERWOOD 14   76 In the same Mines of knowledge; and thence
                            brought
p. 166 UNDERWOOD 15   122 Brought on us, and will every houre increase.
p. 170 UNDERWOOD 18   20 Be brought by us to meet our Destinie.
p. 173 UNDERWOOD 22   16 And kept, and bred, and brought up true.
p. 188 UNDERWOOD 34   6 Quarrell with Nature, or in ballance brought
p. 198 UNDERWOOD 40   44 And never be by time, or folly brought,
p. 214 UNDERWOOD 44   34 Supplant bold Panton; and brought there to view
p. 223 UNDERWOOD 49   19 And spangled Petticotes brought forth to eye,
p. 238 UNDERWOOD 66   7 (Except the joy that the first Mary brought,
p. 240 UNDERWOOD 67   53 Hath brought the Land an Heire!
p. 245 UNDERWOOD 70   61 In season, and so brought
p. 257 UNDERWOOD 75   144 One to the other, long e're these to light were
                            brought.
p. 264 UNDERWOOD 79   41 2. Shee, to the Crowne, hath brought encrease.
p. 273 U'WOOD 84.1   25 Yet, here are no such Trifles brought,
p. 309 HORACE 2   82 And wealth unto our language; and brought forth
p. 315 HORACE 2   198 Afford? The Mountaines travail'd, and brought
                            forth
p. 315 HORACE 2   232 To every vice, as hardly to be brought
p. 319 HORACE 2   307 The rash, and head-long eloquence brought forth
p. 319 HORACE 2   316 Brought in the Visor, and the robe of State,
p. 321 HORACE 2   331 As neither any God, were brought in there,
p. 388 UNGATHERED 23   4 What treasure hast thou brought vs! and what
                            store
p. 395 UNGATHERED 29   19 But who hath them interpreted, and brought
p. 398 UNGATHERED 30   86 Thou hadst brought Lapland, or old Cobalus,
p. 401 UNGATHERED 33   8 Againe hath brought the Lillie to the Rose;
p. 403 UNGATHERED 34   38 And Goody Sculpture, brought wth much adoe

broughton's. See "b<roughton>s."

brought'st   frequency: 1   relative frequency: 0.00001
p.   48 EPIGRAMS 65   12 And which thou brought'st me, welcome pouertie.

brow   frequency: 1   relative frequency: 0.00001
p. 311 HORACE 2   150 The angry brow; the sportive, wanton things;

browes   frequency: 2   relative frequency: 0.00002
p. 134 UNDERWOOD 2.4   17 And from her arched browes, such a grace
p. 136 UNDERWOOD 2.5   17 Both her Browes, bent like my Bow.

brown   frequency: 1   relative frequency: 0.00001
  See also "browne."
p. 407 UNGATHERED 35   17 And stradling shews ye Boyes Brown paper fleet,

browne   frequency: 2   relative frequency: 0.00002
p.   57 EPIGRAMS 90   9 Not though that haire grew browne, which once was
                            amber,
p. 386 UNGATHERED 21   t2 Mr. BROWNE:

brows. See "browes," "eye-browes," "eye-brows."

bruis'd   frequency: 1   relative frequency: 0.00001
p. 127 UNDERWOOD 1.1   5 2. My selfe up to thee, harrow'd, torne, and
                            bruis'd

bruised   frequency: 1   relative frequency: 0.00001
  See also "bruis'd."
p. 288 U'WOOD 84.9   186 Nor can the bruised heart want eloquence:

bruiseth   frequency: 1   relative frequency: 0.00001
p. 272 UNDERWOOD 83   98 But as he soares at that, he bruiseth then

brunsfield   frequency: 1   relative frequency: 0.00001
p. 219 UNDERWOOD 47   44 Brunsfield, and Mansfield doe this yeare, my
                            fates

brush'd   frequency: 1   relative frequency: 0.00001
p. 201 UNDERWOOD 42   54 To ev'ry Petticote he brush'd, and Glove

brute   frequency: 1   relative frequency: 0.00001
p. 112 FOREST 11   108 What sauage, brute affection,

brutus   frequency: 1   relative frequency: 0.00001
    p. 395 UNGATHERED 29   11 Calme Brutus tenor start; but all along

buck   frequency: 1   relative frequency: 0.00001
    p.   54 EPIGRAMS 84   2 I ask'd a lord a buck, and he denyed me;

buckingham   frequency: 1   relative frequency: 0.00001
    p. 419 UNGATHERED 47   6 And Buckingham the fortunate.

bucklers-bury   frequency: 1   relative frequency: 0.00001
    p.   28 EPIGRAMS 3   12 Send it to Bucklers-bury, there 'twill, well.

bud   frequency: 1   relative frequency: 0.00001
    p. 135 UNDERWOOD 2.4   27 Or have smelt o'the bud o'the Brier?

buds   frequency: 1   relative frequency: 0.00001
    p. 309 HORACE 2   89 Like tender buds shoot up, and freshly grow.

build   frequency: 4   relative frequency: 0.00005
    p. 105 FOREST 8   12 And this age will build no more:
    p. 210 UNDERWOOD 43   162 Did not she save from thence, to build a Rome?
    p. 327 HORACE 2   490 Build Townes, and carve the Lawes in leaves of
                              wood.
    p. 407 UNGATHERED 35   9 Or Ale! He build a pallace! Thou a shopp

builders   frequency: 1   relative frequency: 0.00001
    p. 380 UNGATHERED 12   30 Or builders of Story haue oft imputation

building   frequency: 1   relative frequency: 0.00001
    See also "buylding."
    p.   82 EPIGRAMS 130   2 Of building townes, and making wilde beasts tame,

built   frequency: 8   relative frequency: 0.00011
    p.   93 FOREST 2   1 Thou art not, PENSHVRST, built to
                              enuious show,
    p.   96 FOREST 2   102 May say, their lords haue built, but thy lord
                              dwells.
    p. 210 UNDERWOOD 43   166 For they were burnt, but to be better built.
    p. 220 UNDERWOOD 47   65 Not built with Canvasse, paper, and false
                              lights,
    p. 256 UNDERWOOD 75   130 Which to this use, wert built and consecrate!
    p. 262 UNDERWOOD 78   7 And he is built like some imperiall roome
    p. 319 HORACE 2   317 Built a small-timbred Stage, and taught them
                              talke
    p. 327 HORACE 2   483 Amphion, too, that built the Theban towres,

bulk. See "bulke."

bulke   frequency: 1   relative frequency: 0.00001
    p. 245 UNDERWOOD 70   66 In bulke, doth make man better bee;

bull   frequency: 2   relative frequency: 0.00002
    p.   57 EPIGRAMS 90   18 First bearing him a calfe, beare him a bull.
    p.   69 EPIGRAMS 107   8 Of your Morauian horse, Venetian bull.

bullocks   frequency: 1   relative frequency: 0.00001
    p.   94 FOREST 2   23 Thy sheepe, thy bullocks, kine, and calues doe
                              feed:

bulls   frequency: 1   relative frequency: 0.00001
    p. 127 UNDERWOOD 1.1   11 But 'bove the fat of rammes, or bulls, to prize

bulstrode. See "boulstred."

bulwarkes   frequency: 1   relative frequency: 0.00001
    p. 400 UNGATHERED 32   4 In Bulwarkes, Rau'lins, Ramparts, for defense,

bulwarks. See "bulwarkes."

buoyed. See "boy'd."

burden   frequency: 2   relative frequency: 0.00002
    See also "burthen."
    p.   87 EPIGRAMS 133 116 Neuer did bottome more betray her burden;
    p. 249 UNDERWOOD 72   17 And ever close the burden of the Song,

burges   frequency: 4   relative frequency: 0.00005
    p. 229 UNDERWOOD 55   1 Would God, my Burges, I could thinke
    p. 229 UNDERWOOD 55   t2 Mr. IOHN BURGES.
    p. 231 UNDERWOOD 57   1 Father John Burges,

burges (cont.)
    p. 231 UNDERWOOD 57   t1 To Master Iohn Burges.

burgess. See "burges."

burghley. See "burl<eigh>."

buried   frequency: 4   relative frequency: 0.00005
    See also "buryed."
    p. 30 EPIGRAMS 11   5 A lord, it cryed, buried in flesh, and blood,
    p. 46 EPIGRAMS 62   12 Of the not borne, yet buried, here's the tombe.
    p. 162 UNDERWOOD 15   7 Mans buried honour, in his sleepie life:
    p. 174 UNDERWOOD 23   2 Buried in ease and sloth?

burl<eigh>   frequency: 1   relative frequency: 0.00001
    p. 185 UNDERWOOD 30   t2 On WILL<I>AM Lord Burl<eigh,>

burlase   frequency: 1   relative frequency: 0.00001
    p. 227 UNDERWOOD 52   24 To all posteritie; I will write Burlase.

burn. See "burne."

burne   frequency: 12   relative frequency: 0.00017
    p. 53 EPIGRAMS 79   12 As he would burne, or better farre his booke.
    p. 101 FOREST 4   27 From whence, so lately, I did burne,
    p. 121 FOREST 14   60 The Birth-day shines, when logs not burne, but
                             men.
    p. 173 UNDERWOOD 22   21 And on them burne so chaste a flame,
    p. 189 UNDERWOOD 36   10 Who more they burne, they more desire,
    p. 208 UNDERWOOD 43 128 And safely trust to dresse, not burne their
                             Boates.
    p. 209 UNDERWOOD 43 150 No Foole would his owne harvest spoile, or
                             burne!
    p. 211 UNDERWOOD 43 188 Burne to a snuffe, and then stinke out, and die:
    p. 251 UNDERWOOD 74   20 Bring all your friends, (faire Lord) that burne
    p. 270 UNDERWOOD 83   54 Your hottest Causticks to, burne, lance, or cut:
    p. 315 HORACE 2   207 Nor from the brand, with which the life did burne
    p. 406 UNGATHERED 34 101 Lyue long ye ffeasting Roome. And ere thou
                             burne

burned   frequency: 2   relative frequency: 0.00002
    See also "burnt."
    p. 88 EPIGRAMS 133 158 Being, beyond sea, burned for one witch:
    p. 203 UNDERWOOD 43   18 Perhaps, to have beene burned with my bookes.

burning   frequency: 2   relative frequency: 0.00002
    p. 335 HORACE 2   663 Conceipt, and into burning Aetna leap'd.
    p. 413 UNGATHERED 41 25 Thus, Love, and Hope, and burning Charitie,

burnt   frequency: 4   relative frequency: 0.00005
    See also "burned," "sun-burnt-blowse."
    p. 42 EPIGRAMS 50   1 Leaue COD, tabacco-like, burnt gummes to take,
    p. 45 EPIGRAMS 59   2 Who, when you'haue burnt your selues downe to the
                             snuffe,
    p. 210 UNDERWOOD 43 155 He burnt that Idoll of the Revels too:
    p. 210 UNDERWOOD 43 166 For they were burnt, but to be better built.

burst   frequency: 5   relative frequency: 0.00007
    p. 62 EPIGRAMS 96   11 And, till they burst, their backs, like asses
                             load:
    p. 86 EPIGRAMS 133   95 Had burst with storme, and downe fell, ab
                             excelsis,
    p. 260 UNDERWOOD 76   30 This would all their envie burst:
    p. 415 UNGATHERED 42 22 A Master-worker call'd, th'old standerd burst
    p. 416 UNGATHERED 43 10 Of Subiects; Let such envie, till they burst.

bursting   frequency: 1   relative frequency: 0.00001
  **p. 117 PANEGYRE   152 Their bursting ioyes; but through the ayre was
                             rol'd

burthen   frequency: 1   relative frequency: 0.00001
    p. 119 FOREST 13   103 To crowne the burthen which you goe withall,

bury   frequency: 2   relative frequency: 0.00002
  **p. 116 PANEGYRE   102 "To bury churches, in forgotten dust,
    p. 158 UNDERWOOD 13 160 Which you will bury; but therein, the strife

buryed   frequency: 1   relative frequency: 0.00001
    p. 79 EPIGRAMS 124   8 Leaue it buryed in this vault.

bush   frequency: 2   relative frequency: 0.00002
    p.   97 FOREST 3   33 Or hauking at the riuer, or the bush,
    p. 413 UNGATHERED 41   24 In Moses bush, un-wasted in the fire.

busie   frequency: 3   relative frequency: 0.00004
    p. 262 UNDERWOOD 78   20 Busie, or frowne at first; when he sees thee,
    p. 284 U'WOOD 84.9   80 Have busie search made in his mysteries!
    p. 335 HORACE 2   651 Busie to catch a Black-bird; if he fall

busied   frequency: 1   relative frequency: 0.00001
    p. 243 UNDERWOOD 70   27 He vexed time, and busied the whole State;

business. See "businesse," "bus'nesse."

businesse   frequency: 8   relative frequency: 0.00011
    p.   35 EPIGRAMS 28   7 H'has tympanies of businesse, in his face,
    p. 187 UNDERWOOD 33   23 But in a businesse, that will bide the Touch,
    p. 261 UNDERWOOD 77   16 And act the businesse, which they paint, or
                              carve.
    p. 289 UNDERWOOD 85   1 Happie is he, that from all Businesse cleere,
    p. 311 HORACE 2   116 Fresh Lovers businesse, and the Wines free
                              source.
    p. 311 HORACE 2   120 On popular noise with, and doe businesse in.
    p. 317 HORACE 2   244 Or do's all businesse coldly, and with feare;
    p. 317 HORACE 2   255 The businesse either on the Stage is done,

buskin   frequency: 2   relative frequency: 0.00002
    p. 319 HORACE 2   318 Loftie, and grave; and in the buskin stalke.
    p. 391 UNGATHERED 26   36 To life againe, to heare thy Buskin tread,

buskins   frequency: 1   relative frequency: 0.00001
    p. 311 HORACE 2   118 This foot the socks tooke up, and buskins grave,

bus'nesse   frequency: 2   relative frequency: 0.00002
    p. 251 UNDERWOOD 74   22 The bus'nesse of your blooming wit,
    p. 287 U'WOOD 84.9   168 She swaid all bus'nesse in the Familie!

busy. See "busie."

but   frequency: 668   relative frequency: 0.00967
    See also "but>," "butt," "bvt."

but>   frequency: 1   relative frequency: 0.00001
    p. 227 UNDERWOOD 52   11 To be describ'd <but> by a Monogram,

butt   frequency: 2   relative frequency: 0.00002
    p. 241 UNDERWOOD 68   12 'T were better spare a Butt, then spill his
                              Muse.
    p. 420 UNGATHERED 48   10 Butt, Clownishe pride hath gott

butter   frequency: 1   relative frequency: 0.00001
    p. 408 UNGATHERED 36   7 The Lybian Lion hunts noe butter flyes,

butter-flye   frequency: 1   relative frequency: 0.00001
    p.   31 EPIGRAMS 15   3 Where, afterwards, it grew a butter-flye:

butter'd   frequency: 1   relative frequency: 0.00001
    p. 167 UNDERWOOD 15   153 In Sugar Candide, or in butter'd beere,

butterfly. See "butter-flye."

buttock   frequency: 1   relative frequency: 0.00001
    p.   88 EPIGRAMS 133   169 Is fill'd with buttock? And the walls doe sweate

buy   frequency: 4   relative frequency: 0.00005
    p.   27 EPIGRAMS 2   14 For vulgar praise, doth it too dearely buy.
    p.   45 EPIGRAMS 56   6 Buy the reuersion of old playes; now growne
    p. 223 UNDERWOOD 49   28 To stuffes and Laces, those my Man can buy.
    p. 325 HORACE 2   431 Out better Poems? But I cannot buy

buyer   frequency: 1   relative frequency: 0.00001
    p. 333 HORACE 2   598 That to the sale of Wares calls every Buyer;

buyes   frequency: 4   relative frequency: 0.00005
    p.   43 EPIGRAMS 53   2 When hauing pill'd a booke, which no man buyes,
    p.   59 EPIGRAMS 92   24 Or BILS, and there he buyes the names of
                              books.
    p. 113 FOREST 12   15 While thus it buyes great grace, and hunts poore
                              fame;
    p. 321 HORACE 2   362 Him that buyes chiches blanch't, or chance to
                              like

buylding   frequency: 1   relative frequency: 0.00001
     p. 402 UNGATHERED 34   11 Whether ye buylding of ye Stage or Scene!

buys. See "buyes."

bvt   frequency: 2   relative frequency: 0.00002

by   frequency: 301   relative frequency: 0.00435
     See also "b<y>'imputed," "by'example,"
            "hard-by," "passer-by," "standers-by."

by-cause   frequency: 1   relative frequency: 0.00001
     p. 415 UNGATHERED 42   10 And newer, then could please them, by-cause trew.

by-paths   frequency: 1   relative frequency: 0.00001
     p. 325 HORACE 2   423 Their nailes, nor shave their beards, but to
                             by-paths

by'example   frequency: 1   relative frequency: 0.00001
     p. 37 EPIGRAMS 35   2 A Prince, that rules by'example, more than sway?

c<h>loe   frequency: 2   relative frequency: 0.00002
     p. 293 UNDERWOOD 87   6 Nor after C<h>loe did his Lydia sound;
     p. 294 UNDERWOOD 87   19 That I bright C<h>loe off should shake;

caballs   frequency: 1   relative frequency: 0.00001
     p. 206 UNDERWOOD 43   71 To Merlins Marvailes, and his Caballs losse,

cabal's. See "caballs."

cabinet   frequency: 1   relative frequency: 0.00001
     p. 79 EPIGRAMS 125   6 Might loue the treasure for the cabinet.

cadmus   frequency: 1   relative frequency: 0.00001
     p. 317 HORACE 2   267 Into a Swallow there; Nor Cadmus take,

caecilius   frequency: 1   relative frequency: 0.00001
     p. 309 HORACE 2   77 A Roman to Caecilius will allow,

caesar   frequency: 4   relative frequency: 0.00005
     p. 71 EPIGRAMS 110   12 Can so speake CAESAR, as thy labours doe.
     p. 72 EPIGRAMS 111   8 Nor to giue CAESAR this, makes ours the
                             lesse.
     p. 72 EPIGRAMS 111   12 CAESAR stands vp, as from his vrne late
                             rose,
     p. 89 EPIGRAMS 133 180 And MADAME CAESAR, great
                             PROSERPINA,

caesarian   frequency: 1   relative frequency: 0.00001
     p. 228 UNDERWOOD 53   19 And cri'd, Away with the Caesarian bread,

caesars   frequency: 3   relative frequency: 0.00004
     p. 71 EPIGRAMS 110   1 Not CAESARS deeds, nor all his honors
                             wonne,
     p. 71 EPIGRAMS 110   t2 CAESARS Commentaries obserued, and
                             translated.
     p. 181 UNDERWOOD 27   19 Of Caesars Daughter, and the line

caesar's   frequency: 1   relative frequency: 0.00001
     See also "caesars."
     p. 395 UNGATHERED 29 10 Caesar's ambition, Cato's libertie,

caesura. See "ceasure."

cage   frequency: 1   relative frequency: 0.00001
     p. 101 FOREST 4   30 That fled his cage, or broke his chaine,

cake   frequency: 1   relative frequency: 0.00001
     p. 95 FOREST 2   51 Some bring a capon, some a rurall cake,

calais   frequency: 1   relative frequency: 0.00001
     p. 293 UNDERWOOD 87   14 With gentle Calais, Thurine Orniths Sonne;

calamitie   frequency: 1   relative frequency: 0.00001
     p. 283 U'WOOD 84.9   35 Of teares, and dungeon of calamitie!

calamity. See "calamitie."

cal'd   frequency: 2   relative frequency: 0.00002
     p. 137 UNDERWOOD 2.5 34 Lyes the Valley, cal'd my nest,

cal'd (cont.)
   p. 378 UNGATHERED 11 88 Rather his sonne, I should haue cal'd thee, why?

caledon   frequency: 1   relative frequency: 0.00001
   p. 368 UNGATHERED 6   70 To Caledon,

calends. See "th'calends."

calf. See "calfe," "moon-calfe."

calfe   frequency: 1   relative frequency: 0.00001
   p. 57 EPIGRAMS 90   18 First bearing him a calfe, beare him a bull.

call   frequency: 47   relative frequency: 0.00068
   See also "cal't," "mis-call't."
  *p. 492 TO HIMSELF   6 Something they call a Play.
   p. 68 EPIGRAMS 105   8 Would call you more then CERES, if not that:
   p. 80 EPIGRAMS 127   4 No, I doe, therefore, call Posteritie
   p. 81 EPIGRAMS 129   8 The very call, to make all others come:
   p. 84 EPIGRAMS 133   22 And pitty 'tis, I cannot call 'hem knights:
   p. 85 EPIGRAMS 133   57 Act a braue worke, call it thy last aduentry:
   p. 86 EPIGRAMS 133   68 Were seene your vgly Centaures, yee call
                  Car-men,
   p. 95 FOREST 2   69 But giues me what I call, and lets me eate,
   p. 96 FOREST 2   91 His children thy great lord may call his owne:
   p. 107 FOREST 10   13 PALLAS, nor thee I call on, mankinde maid,
   p. 110 FOREST 11   37 The thing, they here call Loue, is blinde
                  Desire,
   p. 117 FOREST 13   31 And so doe many more. All which can call
   p. 119 FOREST 13   85 And call it their braue sinne. For such there be
   p. 132 UNDERWOOD 2.2   18 Nor for any threat, or call,
   p. 136 UNDERWOOD 2.5   19 Which you call my Shafts. And see!
   p. 137 UNDERWOOD 2.5   46 Call to mind the formes, that strove
   p. 141 UNDERWOOD 2.9   34 What we harmonie doe call
   p. 142 U'WOOD 2.10   7 What you please, you parts may call,
   p. 143 UNDERWOOD 3   5 At such a Call, what beast or fowle,
   p. 143 UNDERWOOD 3   12 And call the walking woods.
   p. 154 UNDERWOOD 13   35 Or that doth sound a Trumpet, and doth call
   p. 162 UNDERWOOD 15   5 It is a call to keepe the spirits alive
   p. 163 UNDERWOOD 15   38 And even our sports are dangers! what we call
   p. 169 UNDERWOOD 18   3 Did her perfections call me on to gaze,
   p. 202 UNDERWOOD 43   2 What had I done that might call on thine ire?
   p. 218 UNDERWOOD 47   21 Call every night to Supper in these fitts,
   p. 219 UNDERWOOD 47   45 Shall carry me at Call; and I'le be well,
   p. 220 UNDERWOOD 47   74 I would call mine, to which not many Staires
   p. 240 UNDERWOOD 67   50 The People her doe call.
   p. 245 UNDERWOOD 70   75 Call, noble Lucius, then for Wine,
   p. 258 UNDERWOOD 75   171 Upon a Thomas, or a Francis call;
   p. 262 UNDERWOOD 78   4 Court can call hers, or Man could call his
                  Arts.
   p. 270 UNDERWOOD 83   63 Let Angels sing her glories, who did call
   p. 273 U'WOOD 84.1   30 And Call to the high Parliament
   p. 278 U'WOOD 84.4   21 I call you Muse; now make it true:
   p. 282 U'WOOD 84.9   t3 Who living, gave me leave to call her so.
   p. 284 U'WOOD 84.9   51 For, as there are three Natures, Schoolemen
                  call
   p. 284 U'WOOD 84.9   81 Hee knowes, what worke h'hath done, to call this
                  Guest,
   p. 289 U'WOOD 84.9   220 Where first his Power will appeare, by call
   p. 292 UNDERWOOD 86   8 Goe where Youths soft intreaties call thee back.
   p. 335 HORACE 2   652 Into a pit, or hole; although he call,
   p. 372 UNGATHERED 9   12 She was 'Sell Boulstred. In wch name, I call
   p. 383 UNGATHERED 17   5 Who reads may roaue, and call the passage darke,
   p. 391 UNGATHERED 26   33 For names; but call forth thund'ring Aeschilus,
   p. 394 UNGATHERED 28   19 To call on Sicknes still, to be her Guest,
   p. 398 UNGATHERED 30   93 I call the world, that enuies mee, to see

call'd   frequency: 20   relative frequency: 0.00028
   p. 32 EPIGRAMS 16   3 Thy selfe into fresh braules: when, call'd vpon,
   p. 57 EPIGRAMS 90   10 And he growne youth, was call'd to his ladies
                  chamber.
   p. 82 EPIGRAMS 130   14 Including all, were thence call'd harmonie:
   p. 132 UNDERWOOD 2.2   6 For I ran and call'd on Cupid;
   p. 132 UNDERWOOD 2.2   28 Mock'd of all: and call'd of one
   p. 139 UNDERWOOD 2.7   11 This could be call'd but halfe a kisse.
   p. 162 UNDERWOOD 15   23 See him, that's call'd, and thought the happiest
                  man,
   p. 165 UNDERWOOD 15   89 The Husband now's call'd churlish, or a poore
   p. 200 UNDERWOOD 42   12 In all that is call'd lovely: take my sight
   p. 235 UNDERWOOD 62   4 To cure the call'd Kings Evill with thy touch;

call'd (cont.)
  p. 241 UNDERWOOD 69   1 Sonne, and my Friend, I had not call'd you so
  p. 263 UNDERWOOD 79   2 Lute, Lyre, Theorbo, all are call'd to day.
  p. 271 UNDERWOOD 83   82 At pleasure, to be call'd for, every day!
  p. 311 HORACE 2   129 Am I call'd Poet? wherefore with wrong shame,
  p. 317 HORACE 2   271 Once seene, to be againe call'd for, and plaid,
  p. 389 UNGATHERED 23 11 As, now, of all men, it is call'd thy Trade:
  p. 389 UNGATHERED 24 16 He would be call'd, henceforth, the
                             English-Rogue,
  p. 397 UNGATHERED 30 32 With vs be call'd, the Naso, but this man?
  p. 399 UNGATHERED 31 22 By warrant call'd iust Symetry,
  p. 415 UNGATHERED 42 22 A Master-worker call'd, th'old standerd burst

called   frequency: 2   relative frequency: 0.00002
     See also "cal'd," "call'd," "misse-call'd."
  p. 85 EPIGRAMS 133   41 A Docke there is, that called is AVERNVS,
  p. 404 UNGATHERED 34 56 Terme of ye Architects is called Designe!

calli.   frequency: 1   relative frequency: 0.00001
  p. 240 UNDERWOOD 67   37 7. CALLI. See, see our active King

calling   frequency: 4   relative frequency: 0.00005
  p. 33 EPIGRAMS 21   7 What seuerall wayes men to their calling haue!
  p. 89 EPIGRAMS 133 187 Calling for RADAMANTHVS, that dwelt
                             by,
  p. 183 UNDERWOOD 29   7 Wresting words, from their true calling;
  p. 270 UNDERWOOD 83   35 And, calling truth to witnesse, make that good

calliope. See "calli."

calls   frequency: 9   relative frequency: 0.00013
  p. 28 EPIGRAMS 3   8 Or in cleft-sticks, aduanced to make calls
  p. 30 EPIGRAMS 12   18 Calls for his stoole, adornes the stage: god
                             payes.
  p. 70 EPIGRAMS 109   1 Who now calls on thee, NEVIL, is a Muse,
  p. 97 FOREST 3   19 To some coole, courteous shade, which he calls
                             his,
  p. 193 UNDERWOOD 38   78 That makes us live, not that which calls to die.
  p. 253 UNDERWOOD 75   26 The Month of youth, which calls all Creatures
                             forth
  p. 264 UNDERWOOD 79   29 That leades our flocks and us, and calls both
                             forth
  p. 333 HORACE 2   598 That to the sale of Wares calls every Buyer;
  p. 404 UNGATHERED 34 58 Of any Art, besyde what he calls his!

call's   frequency: 1   relative frequency: 0.00001
  p. 273 U'WOOD 84.1   26 No cobweb Call's; no Surcoates wrought

call'st   frequency: 3   relative frequency: 0.00004
  p. 27 EPIGRAMS 3   2 Call'st a booke good, or bad, as it doth sell,
  p. 29 EPIGRAMS 10   1 Thou call'st me Poet, as a terme of shame:
  p. 100 FOREST 4   12 And what thou call'st thy gifts are baits.

calm. See "calme."

calme   frequency: 5   relative frequency: 0.00007
  p. 110 FOREST 11   53 But, in a calme, and god-like vnitie,
  p. 193 UNDERWOOD 38   74 In a calme skie, then when the heaven is horl'd
  p. 280 U'WOOD 84.4   59 As smooth as Oyle pour'd forth, and calme
  p. 287 U'WOOD 84.9   163 She had a mind as calme, as she was faire;
  p. 395 UNGATHERED 29 11 Calme Brutus tenor start; but all along

calmest   frequency: 1   relative frequency: 0.00001
  p. 251 UNDERWOOD 74   9 The rudest Winds obey the calmest Ayre:

cal't   frequency: 1   relative frequency: 0.00001
  p. 223 UNDERWOOD 49   46 Will cal't a Bastard, when a Prophet's borne.

calues   frequency: 1   relative frequency: 0.00001
  p. 94 FOREST 2   23 Thy sheepe, thy bullocks, kine, and calues doe
                             feed:

calumnies   frequency: 1   relative frequency: 0.00001
  p. 187 UNDERWOOD 33   6 Who 'gainst the Law, weave Calumnies, my
                             <BENN:>

calves. See "calues."

camden   frequency: 2   relative frequency: 0.00002
  p. 31 EPIGRAMS 14   1 CAMDEN, most reuerend head, to whom I owe

camden (cont.)
p. 31 EPIGRAMS 14   t1 TO WILLIAM CAMDEN.

came   frequency: 26   relative frequency: 0.00037
**p. 113 PANEGYRE   26 On earth, till now, they came to grace his
                              throne.
**p. 117 PANEGYRE   138 That came to saue, what discord would destroy:
p. 30 EPIGRAMS 11   3 To seeme a statesman: as I neere it came,
p. 34 EPIGRAMS 23   4 Came forth example, and remaines so, yet:
p. 53 EPIGRAMS 79   4 Came not that soule exhausted so their store.
p. 56 EPIGRAMS 87   4 Of what shee had wrought came in, and wak'd his
                              braine,
p. 57 EPIGRAMS 90   1 When MILL first came to court, the
                              vnprofiting foole,
p. 81 EPIGRAMS 128   14 Came backe vntouch'd. This man hath trauail'd
                              well.
p. 95 FOREST 2   80 To entertayne them; or the countrey came,
p. 141 UNDERWOOD 2.9   29 Rising through it e're it came;
p. 142 UNDERWOOD 2.9   55 But of one, if short he came,
p. 152 UNDERWOOD 12   18 That never came ill odour thence:
p. 157 UNDERWOOD 13   130 Were the Rack offer'd them, how they came so;
p. 165 UNDERWOOD 15   100 Ne're came to taste the plenteous Mariage-horne.
p. 200 UNDERWOOD 42   35 Of love, and hate: and came so nigh to know
p. 227 UNDERWOOD 52   10 Which if in compasse of no Art it came
p. 253 UNDERWOOD 75   20 As they came all to see, and to be seene!
p. 278 U'WOOD 84.4   16 But what's of kinne to whence it came.
p. 287 U'WOOD 84.9   183 And came forth ever cheered, with the rod
p. 319 HORACE 2   294 Chaste, thriftie, modest folke, that came to
                              view.
p. 327 HORACE 2   492 To divine Poets, and their Verses came.
p. 333 HORACE 2   596 Or, of the things, that ne're came in my mind,
p. 366 UNGATHERED 6   22 And, when they came
p. 371 UNGATHERED 8   10 With vices, which they look'd for, and came to.
p. 380 UNGATHERED 12   25 He went out at each place, and at what he came
                              in,
p. 392 UNGATHERED 26   45 When like Apollo he came forth to warme

camel. See "camell."

camell   frequency: 1   relative frequency: 0.00001
p. 408 UNGATHERED 36   8 He makes ye Camell & dull Ass his prize.

cam'st   frequency: 2   relative frequency: 0.00002
p. 150 UNDERWOOD 10   2 How cam'st thou thus to enter me?
p. 150 UNDERWOOD 10   10 Thou sai'st, thou only cam'st to prove

can   frequency: 209   relative frequency: 0.00302
   See also "cann."

canary   frequency: 1   relative frequency: 0.00001
p. 241 UNDERWOOD 68   11 As the old Bard, should no Canary lack.

canary-wine   frequency: 1   relative frequency: 0.00001
p. 65 EPIGRAMS 101   29 Is a pure cup of rich Canary-wine,

cancell'd   frequency: 1   relative frequency: 0.00001
p. 282 U'WOOD 84.9   8 Till swept away, th<ey>'were cancell'd with a
                              broome!

candidates   frequency: 1   relative frequency: 0.00001
p. 222 UNDERWOOD 49   6 New in their stead, out of the Candidates?

candide   frequency: 1   relative frequency: 0.00001
p. 167 UNDERWOOD 15   153 In Sugar Candide, or in butter'd beere,

candied. See "candide."

candle   frequency: 1   relative frequency: 0.00001
p. 223 UNDERWOOD 49   32 Her face there's none can like by Candle light.

candor   frequency: 1   relative frequency: 0.00001
p. 78 EPIGRAMS 123   2 I know not which th'hast most, candor, or wit:

canes   frequency: 1   relative frequency: 0.00001
p. 157 UNDERWOOD 13   149 'Tis like light Canes, that first rise big and
                              brave,

canker'd   frequency: 2   relative frequency: 0.00002
p. 257 UNDERWOOD 75   135 Or canker'd Jealousie,
p. 327 HORACE 2   472 Sixe ounces. O, when once the canker'd rust,

cann   frequency: 1   relative frequency: 0.00001

cannons   frequency: 1   relative frequency: 0.00001
    p. 98 FOREST 3   69 Goe enter breaches, meet the cannons rage,

cannot   frequency: 38   relative frequency: 0.00055

canon   frequency: 1   relative frequency: 0.00001
    p. 151 UNDERWOOD 12   11 With the just Canon of his life,

canst   frequency: 24   relative frequency: 0.00034

canuas   frequency: 1   relative frequency: 0.00001
    p. 407 UNGATHERED 35   15 Thy Canuas Gyant, at some Channell aymes,

canvas. See "canuas," "canvasse."

canvasse   frequency: 1   relative frequency: 0.00001
    p. 220 UNDERWOOD 47   65 Not built with Canvasse, paper, and false
                             lights,

cap   frequency: 1   relative frequency: 0.00001
    See also "capp," "cap's."
    p. 371 UNGATHERED 8   5 Veluet, or Taffata cap, rank'd in the darke

caparison   frequency: 1   relative frequency: 0.00001
    p. 201 UNDERWOOD 42   46 A Gowne of that, was the Caparison?

capering. See "cap'ring."

capers   frequency: 1   relative frequency: 0.00001
    p. 64 EPIGRAMS 101   10 An oliue, capers, or some better sallade

capital. See "capitall," "cap'tall."

capitall   frequency: 1   relative frequency: 0.00001
    p. 163 UNDERWOOD 15   37 Our Delicacies are growne capitall,

capon   frequency: 1   relative frequency: 0.00001
    p. 95 FOREST 2   51 Some bring a capon, some a rurall cake,

capons   frequency: 1   relative frequency: 0.00001
    p. 205 UNDERWOOD 43   53 Sindge Capons, or poore Pigges, dropping their
                             eyes;

capp   frequency: 1   relative frequency: 0.00001
    p. 417 UNGATHERED 45   38 each to pawne hir husbands capp,

cap'ring   frequency: 1   relative frequency: 0.00001
    p. 108 FOREST 10A   2 to loose, and Cap'ring, for thy stricter veyne.

cap's   frequency: 1   relative frequency: 0.00001
    p. 200 UNDERWOOD 42   28 At every stall; The Cittie Cap's a charme.

capt.   frequency: 1   relative frequency: 0.00001
    p. 54 EPIGRAMS 82   t1 ON CASHIERD CAPT. SVRLY.

captain. See "capt.," "captaine," "captayne."

captaine   frequency: 4   relative frequency: 0.00005
    p. 56 EPIGRAMS 87   t1 ON CAPTAINE HAZARD THE
                             CHEATER.
    p. 206 UNDERWOOD 43   79 Or Captaine Pamp<h>lets horse, and foot, that
                             sallie
    p. 214 UNDERWOOD 44   39 Were now the greater Captaine? for they saw
    p. 370 UNGATHERED 8   3 (Compos'd of Gamester, Captaine, Knight,
                             Knight's man,

captaines   frequency: 2   relative frequency: 0.00002
    p. 213 UNDERWOOD 44   29 He that but saw thy curious Captaines drill,
    p. 309 HORACE 2   105 The gests of Kings, great Captaines, and sad
                             Warres,

captains. See "captaines," "captaynes."

cap'tall   frequency: 1   relative frequency: 0.00001
    p. 117 FOREST 13   14 For their owne cap'tall crimes, t<o>'indite my
                             wit;

captayne   frequency: 5   relative frequency: 0.00007
    p.   62 EPIGRAMS 97   2 Nor Captayne POD, nor yet the Eltham-thing;
    p.   68 EPIGRAMS 107   1 Doe what you come for, Captayne, with your
                              newes;
    p.   68 EPIGRAMS 107   t1 TO CAPTAYNE HVNGRY.
    p.   69 EPIGRAMS 107   32 Doe what you come for Captayne, There's your
                              meate.
    p.   70 EPIGRAMS 108   10 But 's angry for the Captayne, still: is such.

captaynes   frequency: 2   relative frequency: 0.00002
    p.   69 EPIGRAMS 108   2 Such as are misse-call'd Captaynes, and wrong
                              you;
    p.   72 EPIGRAMS 111   7 Which all, but ignorant Captaynes, will
                              confesse:

captiv'd   frequency: 1   relative frequency: 0.00001
    p. 285 U'WOOD 84.9   93 To have her captiv'd spirit freed from flesh,

car. See "carre."

car-men   frequency: 1   relative frequency: 0.00001
    p.   86 EPIGRAMS 133   68 Were seene your vgly Centaures, yee call
                              Car-men,

carat. See "carract."

carbuncle   frequency: 1   relative frequency: 0.00001
    p. 361 UNGATHERED 1   14 how lyke the Carbuncle in Aarons brest

carcass. See "carkasse."

carcasses. See "carkasses."

care   frequency: 23   relative frequency: 0.00033
    See also "'care."
  **p. 115 PANEGYRE   87 "Betraid to fame, should take more care, and
                              feare
    p.   27 EPIGRAMS 1   1 Pray thee, take care, that tak'st my booke in
                              hand,
    p.   43 EPIGRAMS 51   8 Doe beg thy care vnto thy after-state.
    p. 111 FOREST 11   60 Sober, as saddest care:
    p. 142 U'WOOD 2.10   1 For his Mind, I doe not care,
    p. 145 UNDERWOOD 5   8 If wee would search with care, and paine,
    p. 158 UNDERWOOD 14   3 Lesse shall I for the Art or dressing care,
    p. 186 UNDERWOOD 31   6 The Care, and wish still of the publike wealth:
    p. 203 UNDERWOOD 43   13 That since thou tak'st all envious care and
                              paine,
    p. 210 UNDERWOOD 43   160 Troy, though it were so much his Venus care.
    p. 215 UNDERWOOD 44   83 Past any need of vertue. Let them care,
    p. 218 UNDERWOOD 47   2 Care not what trials they are put unto;
    p. 233 UNDERWOOD 60   4 Minerva's and the Muses care!
    p. 234 UNDERWOOD 60   5 What could their care doe 'gainst the spight
    p. 268 UNDERWOOD 82   6 Great aides to Empire, as they are great care
    p. 293 UNDERWOOD 86   31 Nor care I now healths to propound;
    p. 294 UNDERWOOD 89   1 Liber, of all thy friends, thou sweetest care,
    p. 313 HORACE 2   190 Not care, as thou wouldst faithfully translate,
    p. 325 HORACE 2   413 Her language, if the Stay, and Care t'have
                              mended,
    p. 327 HORACE 2   473 And care of getting, thus, our minds hath
                              stain'd,
    p. 331 HORACE 2   546 Informed rightly, by your Fathers care,
    p. 335 HORACE 2   654 There's none will take the care, to helpe him
                              then;
    p. 409 UNGATHERED 37   13 Thou art not worth it. Who will care to knowe

'care   frequency: 1   relative frequency: 0.00001
    p. 238 UNDERWOOD 65   10 And interpose thy selfe, ('care not how soone.)

care=full   frequency: 1   relative frequency: 0.00001
    p. 387 UNGATHERED 22   6 trust in the tombes, their care=full freinds do
                              rayse;

carefully   frequency: 1   relative frequency: 0.00001
    p. 333 HORACE 2   607 But you, my Piso, carefully beware,

carelesse   frequency: 4   relative frequency: 0.00005
    p. 174 UNDERWOOD 23   1 Where do'st thou carelesse lie,
    p. 313 HORACE 2   234 For his owne good, a carelesse letter-goe
    p. 335 HORACE 2   635 Blot out the carelesse, with his turned pen;
    p. 354 HORACE 1   648 .... carelesse ....

cares   frequency: 7   relative frequency: 0.00010
   p. 56 EPIGRAMS 87   3 Each night, to drowne his cares: But when the
                             gaine
   p. 82 EPIGRAMS 130   4 That shee remoueth cares, sadnesse eiects,
   p. 98 FOREST 3   60 And in their cups, their cares are drown'd:
   p. 221 UNDERWOOD 48   14 Of cares, and over-seer
   p. 290 UNDERWOOD 85   38 Loves cares so evil, and so great?
   p. 295 UNDERWOOD 90   9 Thy night not dronken, but from cares layd wast;
   p. 368 UNGATHERED 6   87 Their cares in wine; with sure

carew   frequency: 1   relative frequency: 0.00001
   p. 207 UNDERWOOD 43   100 Which noble Carew, Cotton, Selden lent:

caried   frequency: 1   relative frequency: 0.00001
   p. 397 UNGATHERED 30   45 And caried, though with shoute, and noyse,
                             confesse

caring   frequency: 1   relative frequency: 0.00001
   p. 27 EPIGRAMS 2   6 As mad-men stones: not caring whom they hit.

carkasse   frequency: 1   relative frequency: 0.00001
   p. 219 UNDERWOOD 47   42 To live, or fall a Carkasse in the cause.

carkasses   frequency: 1   relative frequency: 0.00001
   p. 216 UNDERWOOD 44   99 These Carkasses of honour; Taylors blocks,

caroches   frequency: 1   relative frequency: 0.00001
   p. 252 UNDERWOOD 75   11 Hath fil<l>ed, with Caroches, all the way,

caroline   frequency: 1   relative frequency: 0.00001
   p. 240 UNDERWOOD 67   54 And CHARLES a Caroline!

carousing. See "carowsing."

carowsing   frequency: 1   relative frequency: 0.00001
 **p. 113 PANEGYRE   13 Carowsing humane bloud in yron bowles,

carpentry   frequency: 1   relative frequency: 0.00001
   p. 404 UNGATHERED 34   50 Painting & Carpentry are ye Soule of
                             Masque.

carper   frequency: 1   relative frequency: 0.00001
   p. 421 UNGATHERED 49   5 The emptye Carper, scorne, not Creditt wynns.

carpets   frequency: 1   relative frequency: 0.00001
   p. 398 UNGATHERED 30   81 As, on two flowry Carpets, that did rise,

carps   frequency: 1   relative frequency: 0.00001
   p. 94 FOREST 2   33 Fat, aged carps, that runne into thy net.

carract   frequency: 3   relative frequency: 0.00004
   p. 255 UNDERWOOD 75   100 But doth his Carract, and just Standard keepe
   p. 269 UNDERWOOD 83   27 Their Carract was! I, or my trump must breake,
   p. 415 UNGATHERED 42   30 Concluded from a Carract to a dramme.

carre   frequency: 1   relative frequency: 0.00001
   p. 134 UNDERWOOD 2.4   4 And well the Carre Love guideth.

carriage   frequency: 1   relative frequency: 0.00001
   p. 215 UNDERWOOD 44   88 Carriage, and dressing. There is up of late

carried   frequency: 4   relative frequency: 0.00005
   See also "caried," "carryed."
   p. 186 UNDERWOOD 33   t2 pleaded, and carried the Cause.
   p. 319 HORACE 2   312 The Tragedie, and carried it about,
   p. 374 UNGATHERED 10   13 Hee's carried 'twixt Montrell and Abbeuile.
   p. 374 UNGATHERED 10   17 Hee's carried like a Cripple, from Constable to
                             Constable.

carries   frequency: 1   relative frequency: 0.00001
   p. 363 UNGATHERED 3   6 It carries Palme with it, (where e're it goes)

carry   frequency: 6   relative frequency: 0.00008
   p. 59 EPIGRAMS 92   15 They carry in their pockets TACITVS,
   p. 114 FOREST 12   27 But let this drosse carry what price it will
   p. 187 UNDERWOOD 33   18 Or skill, to carry out an evill cause!
   p. 194 UNDERWOOD 38   102 To carry noble danger in the face:
   p. 219 UNDERWOOD 47   45 Shall carry me at Call; and I'le be well,
   p. 270 UNDERWOOD 83   66 To carry, and conduct the Complement

carryed   frequency: 1   relative frequency: 0.00001
     p. 155 UNDERWOOD 13   88 Carryed and wrapt, I only am alow'd

cart   frequency: 3   relative frequency: 0.00004
     p. 107 FOREST 10   7 PHOEBVS. No? tend thy cart still. Enuious
                                 day
     p. 380 UNGATHERED 12   27 Besides he tried Ship, Cart, Waggon, and
                                 Chayre,
     p. 380 UNGATHERED 12   53 In a Cart twixt Montrell and Abbeuile.

carts   frequency: 2   relative frequency: 0.00002
     p.   85 EPIGRAMS 133   64 Of all your night-tubs, when the carts doe
                                 cluster,
     p. 319 HORACE 2   313 Till then unknowne, in Carts, wherein did ride

caru'd   frequency: 1   relative frequency: 0.00001
     p. 114 FOREST 12   45 Painted, or caru'd vpon our great-mens tombs,

carve   frequency: 2   relative frequency: 0.00002
     p. 261 UNDERWOOD 77   16 And act the businesse, which they paint, or
                                 carve.
     p. 327 HORACE 2   490 Build Townes, and carve the Lawes in leaves of
                                 wood.

carved. See "caru'd," "vnder-carued."

cary   frequency: 6   relative frequency: 0.00008
     p.   48 EPIGRAMS 66   2 To greatnesse, CARY, I sing that, and thee.
     p.   48 EPIGRAMS 66   t1 TO SIR HENRIE CARY.
     p.   80 EPIGRAMS 126   8 CARY my loue is, DAPHNE but my tree.
     p.   80 EPIGRAMS 126   t1 TO HIS LADY, THEN Mrs. CARY.
     p. 242 UNDERWOOD 70   t2 that noble paire, Sir LVCIVS CARY,
     p. 247 UNDERWOOD 70   116 But as a CARY, or a MORISON.

cascellius. See "cassellius."

cas'd   frequency: 1   relative frequency: 0.00001
     p. 202 UNDERWOOD 42   84 Or a Close-stoole so cas'd; or any fat

case   frequency: 5   relative frequency: 0.00007
     p.   62 EPIGRAMS 97   3 But one more rare, and in the case so new:
     p. 202 UNDERWOOD 42   87 Thou art jealous of thy Wifes, or Daughters
                                 Case:
     p. 223 UNDERWOOD 49   33 Not he, that should the body have, for Case
     p. 323 HORACE 2   379 Provided, ne're to yeeld, in any case
     p. 375 UNGATHERED 10   27 And louse-dropping Case, are the Armes of his
                                 trauell.

cashierd   frequency: 1   relative frequency: 0.00001
     p.   54 EPIGRAMS 82   t1 ON CASHIERD CAPT. SVRLY.

cashiered. See "cashierd."

caske   frequency: 1   relative frequency: 0.00001
     p.   68 EPIGRAMS 105   16 That saw you put on PALLAS plumed caske:

casque. See "caske."

cassandra   frequency: 1   relative frequency: 0.00001
     p. 181 UNDERWOOD 27   23 His new Cassandra, 'bove the old;

cassellius   frequency: 1   relative frequency: 0.00001
     p. 331 HORACE 2   553 Or knowes not what Cassellius Aulus can;

cassiopea   frequency: 1   relative frequency: 0.00001
     p. 115 FOREST 12   62 Or lifted CASSIOPEA in her chayre?

cassock   frequency: 1   relative frequency: 0.00001
     p. 237 UNDERWOOD 64   20 Is Banke-rupt turn'd! the Cassock, Cloake, and
                                 Gowne,

cast   frequency: 21   relative frequency: 0.00030
   **p. 113 PANEGYRE   8 But these his searching beams are cast, to prie
     p.   54 EPIGRAMS 82   2 He cast, yet keeps her well! No, shee keeps him.
     p.   94 FOREST 2   35 As loth, the second draught, or cast to stay,
     p. 111 FOREST 11   64 Cast himselfe from the spire
     p. 141 UNDERWOOD 2.9   11 Cast in thousand snares, and rings
     p. 144 UNDERWOOD 4   3 Nor cast them downe, but let them rise,
     p. 149 UNDERWOOD 9   5 And cast my love behind:
     p. 164 UNDERWOOD 15   69 Ready to cast, at one, whose band sits ill,

cast (cont.)
```
     p. 165 UNDERWOOD 15  110 His deare and borrow'd Bravery he must cast?
     p. 166 UNDERWOOD 15  134 Goe make our selves the Usurers at a cast.
     p. 167 UNDERWOOD 15  151 When I am hoarse, with praising his each cast,
     p. 191 UNDERWOOD 38   27 No, I will stand arraign'd, and cast, to be
     p. 224 UNDERWOOD 50   12 From whence they fall, cast downe with their owne
                              weight.
     p. 248 UNDERWOOD 71    6 Have cast a trench about mee, now, five yeares;
     p. 271 UNDERWOOD 83   85 If you can cast about your either eye,
     p. 329 HORACE 2      512 Cast out by voyces; want they pleasure, then
     p. 335 HORACE 2      656 To let it downe, who knowes, if he did cast
     p. 361 UNGATHERED 1   17 thus, as a ponderous thinge in water cast
     p. 396 UNGATHERED 30  17 It cast a beame as when the chear=full Sun
     p. 401 UNGATHERED 32  13 Before this worke? where Enuy hath not cast
     p. 420 UNGATHERED 48  30 Vppon soe humbled earth to cast hir eyes:
```

castor   frequency: 2   relative frequency: 0.00002
```
     p.  80 EPIGRAMS 133   77 And, on they went, like CASTOR braue, and
                              POLLVX:
     p. 228 UNDERWOOD 53    8 Or Castor mounted on his Cyllarus:
```

casts   frequency: 1   relative frequency: 0.00001
```
     p. 392 UNGATHERED 26  59 Who casts to write a liuing line, must sweat,
```

cat   frequency: 1   relative frequency: 0.00001
```
     p.  88 EPIGRAMS 133  159 Their spirits transmigrated to a cat:
```

catalogue   frequency: 2   relative frequency: 0.00002
```
     p.  59 EPIGRAMS 92    22 Are sure to con the catalogue by hart;
     p. 398 UNGATHERED 30  61 Thy Catalogue of Ships, exceeding his,
```

cataplasmes   frequency: 1   relative frequency: 0.00001
```
     p.  86 EPIGRAMS 133  102 Suppositories, cataplasmes, and lotions.
```

cataplasms. See "cataplasmes."

catch   frequency: 6   relative frequency: 0.00008
```
     p.  27 EPIGRAMS 2     12 To catch the worlds loose laughter, or vaine
                              gaze.
     p. 164 UNDERWOOD 15   67 To catch the flesh in, and to pound a Prick.
     p. 167 UNDERWOOD 15  157 That watch, and catch, at what they may applaud,
     p. 206 UNDERWOOD 43   78 And the strong lines, that so the time doe catch:
     p. 321 HORACE 2      335 Or, whilst he shuns the Earth, to catch at Aire
     p. 335 HORACE 2      651 Busie to catch a Black-bird; if he fall
```

catch'd   frequency: 2   relative frequency: 0.00002
```
     p. 118 FOREST 13      58 Contagion in the prease is soonest catch'd.
     p. 261 UNDERWOOD 77   11 Catch'd with these Arts, wherein the Judge is
                              wise
```

catches   frequency: 1   relative frequency: 0.00001
```
     p.  74 EPIGRAMS 115   13 Except the duell. Can sing songs, and catches;
```

catechism. See "catechisme."

catechisme   frequency: 1   relative frequency: 0.00001
```
     p. 398 UNGATHERED 30  71 This booke! it is a Catechisme to fight,
```

cater-piller   frequency: 1   relative frequency: 0.00001
```
     p.  31 EPIGRAMS 15     4 Which was a cater-piller. So't will dye.
```

cates   frequency: 2   relative frequency: 0.00002
```
     p.  64 EPIGRAMS 101    8 The entertaynment perfect: not the cates.
     p. 291 UNDERWOOD 85   61 Among these Cates how glad the sight doth come
```

cato's   frequency: 3   relative frequency: 0.00004
```
     p.  71 EPIGRAMS 110    4 CATO'S to boote, Rome, and her libertie,
     p. 309 HORACE 2       81 Cato's and Ennius tongues have lent much worth,
     p. 395 UNGATHERED 29  10 Caesar's ambition, Cato's libertie,
```

cats   frequency: 1   relative frequency: 0.00001
```
     p.  88 EPIGRAMS 133  149 Cats there lay diuers had beene flead, and
                              rosted,
```

cattell   frequency: 1   relative frequency: 0.00001
```
     p. 257 UNDERWOOD 75  154 Like Swine, or other Cattell here on earth:
```

cattle. See "cattell."

catullus   frequency: 1   relative frequency: 0.00001
     p. 181 UNDERWOOD 27   9 Was Lesbia sung by learn'd Catullus?

caue   frequency: 1   relative frequency: 0.00001
     p. 406 UNGATHERED 35   8 Cittyes & Temples! thou a Caue for Wyne,

cauendish   frequency: 1   relative frequency: 0.00001
     p. 387 UNGATHERED 22   t1 Charles Cauendish to his posteritie.

cauernes   frequency: 1   relative frequency: 0.00001
  **p. 113 PANEGYRE   15 From whose foule reeking cauernes first arise

caught   frequency: 1   relative frequency: 0.00001
     p. 180 UNDERWOOD 26   20 This same which you have caught,

cauls. See "call's."

caus'd   frequency: 1   relative frequency: 0.00001
     p. 61 EPIGRAMS 95   11 Which Fate (it seemes) caus'd in the historie,

cause   frequency: 41   relative frequency: 0.00059
     See also "by-cause."
  **p. 116 PANEGYRE   124 To offer cause of iniurie, or feare.
     p. 31 EPIGRAMS 12   19 To euery cause he meets, this voyce he brayes:
     p. 33 EPIGRAMS 19   2 I sent the cause: Hee wooes with an ill sprite.
     p. 38 EPIGRAMS 35   5 Hast purg'd thy realmes, as we haue now no cause
     p. 38 EPIGRAMS 37   1 No cause, nor client fat, will CHEV'RILL
                                leese,
     p. 43 EPIGRAMS 52   4 As if thou wert my friend, but lack'dst a cause.
     p. 44 EPIGRAMS 54   4 That quit'st the cause so oft, and rayl'st at
                                men?
     p. 46 EPIGRAMS 62   9 What should the cause be? Oh, you liue at court:
     p. 49 EPIGRAMS 66   16 It may be much, or little, in the cause.
     p. 52 EPIGRAMS 74   5 That still th'art present to the better cause;
     p. 61 EPIGRAMS 95   24 As, then, his cause, his glorie emulate.
     p. 63 EPIGRAMS 97   9 Know you the cause? H'has neither land, nor
                                lease,
     p. 87 EPIGRAMS 133   106 Touching this cause, where they will be affeard
     p. 87 EPIGRAMS 133   130 These be the cause of those thicke frequent mists
     p. 98 FOREST 3   61 They thinke not, then, which side the cause shall
                                leese,
     p. 109 FOREST 11   16 Close, the close cause of it.
     p. 120 FOREST 14   10 Both loue the cause, and authors of the feast?
     p. 171 UNDERWOOD 20   4 No more, I am sorry for so fond cause, say,
     p. 174 UNDERWOOD 23   14 As 'tis too just a cause;
     p. 186 UNDERWOOD 31   10 You favour Truth, and me, in this mans Cause.
     p. 186 UNDERWOOD 32   2 When a good Cause is destitute of friends,
     p. 186 UNDERWOOD 33   t2 pleaded, and carried the Cause.
     p. 187 UNDERWOOD 33   13 Thou art my Cause: whose manners since I knew,
     p. 187 UNDERWOOD 33   18 Or skill, to carry out an evill cause!
     p. 188 UNDERWOOD 34   13 What was the cause then? Thought'st thou in
                                disgrace
     p. 203 UNDERWOOD 43   28 A cause before; or leave me one behind.
     p. 217 UNDERWOOD 46   12 More for thy Patronage, then for their Cause,
     p. 219 UNDERWOOD 47   42 To live, or fall a Carkasse in the cause.
     p. 225 UNDERWOOD 51   17 'Tis a brave cause of joy, let it be knowne,
     p. 236 UNDERWOOD 64   7 Indeed, when had great Britaine greater cause
     p. 241 UNDERWOOD 68   1 What can the cause be, when the K<ing> hath
                                given
     p. 317 HORACE 2   284 Peace, and the open ports, that peace doth cause.
     p. 335 HORACE 2   670 His cause of making Verses none knowes why:
     p. 366 UNGATHERED 6   16 And Phoebus loue cause of his blackenesse is.
     p. 381 UNGATHERED 12   58 Poore Tom haue we cause to suspect iust thee?
     p. 397 UNGATHERED 30   56 A better cause, and strike the brauest heate
     p. 403 UNGATHERED 34   29 What is ye cause you pompe it soe? I aske,
     p. 406 UNGATHERED 35   1 But cause thou hearst ye mighty k. of Spaine
     p. 414 UNGATHERED 41   42 Most venerable. Cause of all our ioy.
     p. 420 UNGATHERED 48   35 Give cause to some of wonnder, some despite,
     p. 421 UNGATHERED 48   42 Cause Reverence, yf not ffeare,

'cause   frequency: 5   relative frequency: 0.00007
     p. 117 FOREST 13   20 Or feare to draw true lines, 'cause others paint:
     p. 168 UNDERWOOD 15   192 Man thought the valianter, 'cause he durst
                                sweare,
     p. 168 UNDERWOOD 15   194 More honour in him, 'cause we'<h>ave knowne him
                                mad:
     p. 208 UNDERWOOD 43   110 'Cause thou canst halt, with us, in Arts, and
                                Fire!
     p. 331 HORACE 2   559 As Poppie, and Sardane honey; 'cause without

causes   frequency: 5   relative frequency: 0.00007
     p.   50 EPIGRAMS 70   4 On the true causes, ere they grow too old.
     p.   62 EPIGRAMS 95   34 Can write the things, the causes, and the men.
     p.   76 EPIGRAMS 119   4 Shuns prease, for two maine causes, poxe, and
                               debt,
     p. 101 FOREST 4   44 When all the causes were away.
     p. 221 UNDERWOOD 48   39 The causes and the Guests too,

causticks   frequency: 1   relative frequency: 0.00001
     p. 270 UNDERWOOD 83   54 Your hottest Causticks to, burne, lance, or cut:

caustics. See "causticks."

cave. See "caue."

cavendish. See "cauendish."

caverns. See "cauernes."

ceas'd   frequency: 1   relative frequency: 0.00001
   **p. 117 PANEGYRE   135 And ceas'd in them. She told them, what a fate

cease   frequency: 1   relative frequency: 0.00001
     p. 323 HORACE 2   370 His power of foulely hurting made to cease.

ceasure   frequency: 1   relative frequency: 0.00001
     p. 184 UNDERWOOD 29   48 Other ceasure.

cecil   frequency: 1   relative frequency: 0.00001
     See also "cecill."
     p.   48 EPIGRAMS 64   15 These (noblest CECIL) labour'd in my
                              thought,

cecilia. See "'sell."

cecill   frequency: 1   relative frequency: 0.00001
     p. 185 UNDERWOOD 30   5 Cecill, the grave, the wise, the great, the good,

cecill's   frequency: 1   relative frequency: 0.00001
     p.   41 EPIGRAMS 43   9 When, in my booke, men reade but CECILL'S
                              name,

cecil's. See "cecill's."

cedar   frequency: 1   relative frequency: 0.00001
     p. 327 HORACE 2   475 In juyce of Cedar worthy to be steep'd,

celebrate   frequency: 3   relative frequency: 0.00004
     p.   40 EPIGRAMS 43   2 Whose actions so themselues doe celebrate;
     p. 253 UNDERWOOD 75   28 And celebrate (perfection at the worth)
     p. 256 UNDERWOOD 75 132 And this their chosen Bishop celebrate,

celebrated   frequency: 1   relative frequency: 0.00001
     p.   28 EPIGRAMS 5   2 Or celebrated with more truth of state?

celebrating   frequency: 2   relative frequency: 0.00002
     p. 252 UNDERWOOD 75   t4 CELEBRATING THE NVPTIALS
     p. 323 HORACE 2   408 And celebrating our owne home-borne facts;

celebration   frequency: 2   relative frequency: 0.00002
     p. 131 UNDERWOOD 2   t1 A Celebration of CHARIS in
     p. 239 UNDERWOOD 67   t2 In celebration of her Majesties birth-day.

celestial. See "celestiall."

celestiall   frequency: 1   relative frequency: 0.00001
     p. 279 U'WOOD 84.4   47 Us forth, by some Celestiall slight

celia   frequency: 5   relative frequency: 0.00007
     p. 102 FOREST 5   1 Come my CELIA, let vs proue,
     p. 102 FOREST 5   t2 TO CELIA.
     p. 106 FOREST 9   t2 TO CELIA.
     p. 182 UNDERWOOD 27   31 And shall not I my Celia bring,
     p. 412 UNGATHERED 40 23 Must CELIA bee,

cellar   frequency: 2   relative frequency: 0.00002
     p. 220 UNDERWOCD 48   3 We dedicate this Cellar,
     p. 220 UNDERWOCD 48   t1 The Dedication of the Kings new Cellar.

cellars   frequency: 1   relative frequency: 0.00001
    p. 405 UNGATHERED 34   80 Vp & about? Dyue into Cellars too

censoriovs   frequency: 1   relative frequency: 0.00001
    p.   43 EPIGRAMS 52   t1 TO CENSORIOVS COVRTLING.

censur'd   frequency: 2   relative frequency: 0.00002
    p. 117 FOREST 13   35 That askes but to be censur'd by the eyes:
    p. 411 UNGATHERED 39   15 A Rogue by Statute, censur'd to be whipt,

censure   frequency: 12   relative frequency: 0.00017
   *p. 492 TO HIMSELF   9 Run on, and rage, sweat, censure, and condemn:
   *p. 492 TO HIMSELF   t2 tooke at the vulgar censure of his
    p.   32 EPIGRAMS 17   4 Charge them, for crowne, to thy sole censure hye.
    p.   32 EPIGRAMS 18   8 When thou wert wont t<o>'admire, not censure men.
    p.   62 EPIGRAMS 95   33 Of state, and censure them: we need his pen
    p. 158 UNDERWOOD 14   11 Unto the Censure. Yours all need doth flie
    p. 218 UNDERWOOD 47   23 That censure all the Towne, and all th'affaires,
    p. 222 UNDERWOOD 49   1 Do's the Court-Pucell then so censure me,
    p. 362 UNGATHERED 2   11 Wants facultie to make a censure true:
    p. 414 UNGATHERED 42   8 That sit to censure Playes, yet know not when,
    p. 415 UNGATHERED 42   19 This is my censure. Now there is a new
    p. 421 UNGATHERED 49   1 Censure, not sharplye then, but mee advise

censurer. See "censvrer."

censures   frequency: 3   relative frequency: 0.00004
    p.   62 EPIGRAMS 96   4 And, in thy censures, euenly, dost take
    p.   83 EPIGRAMS 131   5 And though we could all men, all censures heare,
    p. 232 UNDERWOOD 58   1 Thou, Friend, wilt heare all censures: unto thee

censureth   frequency: 1   relative frequency: 0.00001
    p. 421 UNGATHERED 49   4 Hee that soe Censureth, or adviseth synns,

censuring   frequency: 1   relative frequency: 0.00001
    p. 317 HORACE 2   249 And still correcting youth, and censuring.

censvrer   frequency: 1   relative frequency: 0.00001
    p.   32 EPIGRAMS 18   t1 TO MY MEERE ENGLISH
                               CENSVRER.

centaur. See "centaure."

centaure   frequency: 1   relative frequency: 0.00001
    p. 228 UNDERWOOD 53   5 And saw a Centaure, past those tales of Greece;

centaures   frequency: 1   relative frequency: 0.00001
    p.   86 EPIGRAMS 133   68 Were seene your vgly Centaures, yee call
                               Car-men,

centaurs. See "centaures."

center   frequency: 5   relative frequency: 0.00007
    p. 159 UNDERWOOD 14   32 Upon your Center, doe your Circle fill
    p. 219 UNDERWOOD 47   60 And dwell as in my Center, as I can,
    p. 243 UNDERWOOD 70   10 Of deepest lore, could we the Center find!
    p. 270 UNDERWOOD 83   42 And pietie the Center, where all met.
    p. 361 UNGATHERED 1   16 did sparcle foorth in Center of the rest:

cerbervs   frequency: 2   relative frequency: 0.00002
    p.   84 EPIGRAMS 133   14 And for one CERBERVS, the whole coast was
                               dogs.
    p.   89 EPIGRAMS 133   176 Behold where CERBERVS, rear'd on the wall

ceremonies   frequency: 1   relative frequency: 0.00001
    p. 197 UNDERWOOD 40   11 And turne the Ceremonies of those Nights

ceres   frequency: 1   relative frequency: 0.00001
    p.   68 EPIGRAMS 105   8 Would call you more then CERES, if not that:

certain. See "certaine," "certeyne."

certaine   frequency: 3   relative frequency: 0.00004
    p.   52 EPIGRAMS 74   7 Whil'st thou art certaine to thy words, once
                               gone,
    p. 156 UNDERWOOD 13   102 Unto their praise, in certaine swearing rites!
    p. 337 HORACE 2   673 (Defiled) touch'd; but certaine he was mad,

certainly   frequency: 1   relative frequency: 0.00001
    p. 355 HORACE 1   673 Polluted .... certainly he's ...

certeyne   frequency: 1   relative frequency: 0.00001
     p. 404 UNGATHERED 34   45 You aske noe more then certeyne politique Eyes,

ceston   frequency: 2   relative frequency: 0.00002
     p. 182 UNDERWOOD 28   14 For Venus Ceston, every line you make.
     p. 240 UNDERWOOD 67   36 Had got the Ceston on!

cestrian   frequency: 1   relative frequency: 0.00001
     p. 274 U'WOOD 84.2   16 Maschines honour with the Cestrian fame

cethegi   frequency: 1   relative frequency: 0.00001
     p. 309 HORACE 2   72 Of the Cethegi; And all men will grace,

chafes   frequency: 1   relative frequency: 0.00001
     p. 311 HORACE 2   133 Her voyce, and angry Chremes chafes out-right

chain. See "chaine."

chaine   frequency: 5   relative frequency: 0.00007
  **p. 113 PANEGYRE   21 Vpon his state; let downe in that rich chaine,
     p. 69 EPIGRAMS 107   30 Twirle the poore chaine you run a feasting in.
     p. 101 FOREST 4   30 That fled his cage, or broke his chaine,
     p. 110 FOREST 11   47 It is a golden chaine let downe from heauen,
     p. 137 UNDERWOOD 2.5   32 Lovers, made into a Chaine!

chained   frequency: 1   relative frequency: 0.00001
     p. 401 UNGATHERED 33   9 And, with their Chained dance,

chainge   frequency: 2   relative frequency: 0.00002
     p. 108 FOREST 10 A   10 only pursewinge Constancy, in Chainge;
     p. 417 UNGATHERED 45   29 Though shee chainge as oft as shee,

chains. See "gold-chaines."

chair. See "chaire," "chayre."

chaire   frequency: 4   relative frequency: 0.00005
   *p. 492 TO HIMSELF   4 Vsurpe the chaire of wit!
     p. 57 EPIGRAMS 90   15 Hath got the stewards chaire; he will not tarry
     p. 223 UNDERWOOD 49   45 For there the wicked in the Chaire of scorne,
     p. 225 UNDERWOOD 51   14 In his soft Cradle to his Fathers Chaire,

chaires   frequency: 2   relative frequency: 0.00002
     p. 201 UNDERWOOD 42   47 So I might dote upon thy Chaires, and Stooles,
     p. 230 UNDERWOOD 56   10 His friends, but to breake Chaires, or cracke a
                               Coach.

chairs. See "chaires."

chalice   frequency: 1   relative frequency: 0.00001
     p. 412 UNGATHERED 40   22 of this sweet Chalice,

chalk   frequency: 1   relative frequency: 0.00001
     See also "chalke."
     p. 408 UNGATHERED 36   11 Wth rotten chalk, or Cole vpon a wall,

chalke   frequency: 1   relative frequency: 0.00001
     p. 193 UNDERWOOD 38   97 Produce; though threatning with a coale, or
                               chalke

challenge   frequency: 2   relative frequency: 0.00002
     p. 51 EPIGRAMS 73   3 As't were a challenge, or a borrowers letter?
     p. 143 UNDERWOOD 3   2 And challenge all the Spheares,

chamber   frequency: 4   relative frequency: 0.00005
     See also "star-chamber," "starre-chamber."
     p. 30 EPIGRAMS 12   15 That lost, he keepes his chamber, reades
                               Essayes,
     p. 57 EPIGRAMS 90   10 And he growne youth, was call'd to his ladies
                               chamber.
     p. 105 FOREST 8   31 With ten Emp'ricks, in their chamber,
     p. 222 UNDERWOOD 49   3 What though her Chamber be the very pit

chamber-critick   frequency: 1   relative frequency: 0.00001
     p. 50 EPIGRAMS 72   2 A chamber-critick, and dost dine, and sup

chamber-fellow   frequency: 1   relative frequency: 0.00001
     p. 161 UNDERWOOD 14   72 Thy learned Chamber-fellow, knowes to doe

chambers   frequency: 3   relative frequency: 0.00004
**p. 116 PANEGYRE   105 "From priuate Chambers; that could then create
  p. 209 UNDERWOOD 43 135 I saw with two poore Chambers taken in,
  p. 289 UNDERWOOD 85   8 And waiting Chambers of great Lords.

champion   frequency: 2   relative frequency: 0.00002
  p. 161 UNDERWOOD 14   78 And strength to be a Champion, and defend
  p. 311 HORACE 2   115 The conqu'ring Champion, the prime Horse in
                           course,

chanc'd   frequency: 1   relative frequency: 0.00001
    See also "chanc't."
  p. 201 UNDERWOOD 42   66 That chanc'd the lace, laid on a Smock, to see,

chance   frequency: 22   relative frequency: 0.00031
  p.   46 EPIGRAMS 60   5 I, that am glad of thy great chance, here doo!
  p.   49 EPIGRAMS 66   10 Could conquer thee, but chance, who did betray.
  p.   64 EPIGRAMS 100   1 PLAY-WRIGHT, by chance, hearing some
                           toyes I'had writ,
  p. 101 FOREST 4   56 If't chance to me, I must not grutch.
  p. 111 FOREST 11   62 Who (blest with such high chance)
  p. 117 FOREST 13   41 A Princes fortune: These are gifts of chance,
  p. 118 FOREST 13   51 'Tis onely that can time, and chance defeat:
  p. 154 UNDERWOOD 13   30 But by meere Chance? for interest? or to free
  p. 156 UNDERWOOD 13 124 Men have beene great, but never good by chance,
  p. 157 UNDERWOOD 13 148 Nor fashion; if they chance aspire to height,
  p. 158 UNDERWOOD 14   10 Chance that the Friends affection proves Allay
  p. 176 UNDERWOOD 25   6 Her upright head, above the reach of Chance,
  p. 190 UNDERWOOD 37   23 That friendship which no chance but love did
                           chuse,
  p. 217 UNDERWOOD 46   23 Of if Chance must, to each man that doth rise,
  p. 241 UNDERWOOD 69   3 Profit, or Chance had made us: But I know
  p. 246 UNDERWOOD 70   99 Of hearts the union. And those not by chance
  p. 307 HORACE 2   69 Yet, if by chance, in utt'ring things abstruse,
  p. 313 HORACE 2   171 Honour'd Achilles chance by thee be seiz'd,
  p. 321 HORACE 2   362 Him that buyes chiches blanch't, or chance to
                           like
  p. 329 HORACE 2   502 Or Muse, upon the Lyre, thou chance
                           b<e>'asham'd.
  p. 391 UNGATHERED 26 10 The truth, but gropes, and vrgeth all by chance;
  p. 418 UNGATHERED 45 41 Or by chance if in their grease

chancellor   frequency: 2   relative frequency: 0.00002
    See also "chancelor."
  p. 185 UNDERWOOD 31   t3 the last Terme he sate Chancellor.
  p. 225 UNDERWOOD 51   13 Englands high Chancellor: the destin'd heire

chancelor   frequency: 1   relative frequency: 0.00001
  p.   51 EPIGRAMS 74   t1 TO THOMAS LORD CHANCELOR.

chancerie   frequency: 1   relative frequency: 0.00001
  p. 210 UNDERWOOD 43 174 Lyes there no Writ, out of the Chancerie,

chancery. See "chancerie."

chanceth   frequency: 1   relative frequency: 0.00001
  p. 379 UNGATHERED 12 17 But who will beleeue this, that chanceth to looke

chanc't   frequency: 1   relative frequency: 0.00001
  p. 136 UNDERWOOD 2.5   8 Where he chanc't your name to see

chang'd   frequency: 7   relative frequency: 0.00010
  p.   33 EPIGRAMS 21   1 Lord, how is GAM'STER chang'd! his haire
                           close cut!
  p.   74 EPIGRAMS 114   5 Hath chang'd his soule, and made his obiect you:
  p. 133 UNDERWOOD 2.3 19 And would faine have chang'd the fate,
  p. 138 UNDERWOOD 2.6 18 Wisht the Bride were chang'd to night,
  p. 165 UNDERWOOD 15 107 Coach'd, or on foot-cloth, thrice chang'd every
                           day,
  p. 200 UNDERWOOD 42   23 Curst in their Cradles, or there chang'd by
                           Elves,
  p. 412 UNGATHERED 41   2 Which, chang'd, a five-fold mysterie designe,

change   frequency: 18   relative frequency: 0.00026
    See also "chainge."
  p.   34 EPIGRAMS 25   8 Iust wife, and, to change me, make womans hast?
  p.   37 EPIGRAMS 32   6 His often change of clime (though not of mind)
  p.   76 EPIGRAMS 118   5 Thus, in his belly, can he change a sin,
  p.   99 FOREST 3   75 And change possessions, oftner with his breath,
  p. 106 FOREST 9   8 I would not change for thine.

change (cont.)
```
     p. 118 FOREST 13        67 Giddie with change, and therefore cannot see
     p. 120 FOREST 13       124 Because nor it can change, nor such a minde.
     p. 146 UNDERWOOD 6       2 That talke abroad of Womans change,
     p. 146 UNDERWOOD 6       8 Doe change, though man, and often fight,
     p. 146 UNDERWOOD 6      13 Nor is't inconstancie to change
     p. 185 UNDERWOOD 31      2 Lawes, and no change e're come to one decree:
     p. 199 UNDERWOOD 41      9 What fate is this, to change mens dayes and
                                houres,
     p. 263 UNDERWOOD 79      3 Your change of Notes, the flat, the meane, the
                                sharpe,
     p. 309 HORACE 2         85 Stamp'd to the time. As woods whose change
                                appeares
     p. 331 HORACE 2        579 To change, and mend, what you not forth doe set.
     p. 335 HORACE 2        630 Then change; no word, or worke, more would he
                                spend
     p. 403 UNGATHERED 34    25 your Trappings will not change you. Change yor
                                mynd.
```

changed   frequency: 2   relative frequency: 0.00002
```
     See also "chang'd," "change'd."
     p. 309 HORACE 2         96 Or the wilde river, who hath changed now
     p. 335 HORACE 2        638 Reprove; and, what is to be changed, note:
```

change'd   frequency: 1   relative frequency: 0.00001
```
     p. 366 UNGATHERED 6     25 This change'd his Downe; till this, as white
```

changes   frequency: 2   relative frequency: 0.00002
```
     p. 253 UNDERWOOD 75     35 As they had learn'd new changes, for the day,
     p. 341 HORACE 1        121 .. ... ... changes ... ... severall ....
```

changeth   frequency: 1   relative frequency: 0.00001
```
     p. 315 HORACE 2        228 He knowes not why, and changeth every houre.
```

changing   frequency: 1   relative frequency: 0.00001
```
     p. 238 UNDERWOOD 65      7 And long in changing. Let our Nephewes see
```

channel. See "channell."

channell   frequency: 1   relative frequency: 0.00001
```
     p. 407 UNGATHERED 35    15 Thy Canuas Gyant, at some Channell aymes,
```

channels   frequency: 1   relative frequency: 0.00001
```
     p. 198 UNDERWOOD 40     27 Keepe secret in his Channels what he breedes,
```

chant   frequency: 2   relative frequency: 0.00002
```
     p. 274 U'WOOD 84.1      36 To chant her 'gree,
     p. 311 HORACE 2        114 To chant the Gods, and all their God-like race,
```

chanting   frequency: 1   relative frequency: 0.00001
```
     p. 164 UNDERWOOD 15     74 To be abroad chanting some baudie song,
```

chapel. See "chappel," "chappell."

chaplaines   frequency: 1   relative frequency: 0.00001
```
     p. 198 UNDERWOOD 40     31 They may say Grace, and for Loves Chaplaines
                                passe;
```

chaplains. See "chaplaines."

chapman   frequency: 2   relative frequency: 0.00002
```
     p. 388 UNGATHERED 23     1 Whose worke could this be, Chapman, to refine
     p. 388 UNGATHERED 23    t2 Mr George Chapman, on his Translation
```

chapmen   frequency: 1   relative frequency: 0.00001
```
     p.  59 EPIGRAMS 92      10 And vnderstand 'hem, as most chapmen doe.
```

chappel   frequency: 1   relative frequency: 0.00001
```
     p.  77 EPIGRAMS 120     t2 OF Q. EL<IZABETHS> CHAPPEL.
```

chappell   frequency: 2   relative frequency: 0.00002
```
     p. 256 UNDERWOOD 75    121 See, now the Chappell opens; where the King
     p. 257 UNDERWOOD 75    137 The Chappell empties, and thou may'st be gone
```

character   frequency: 5   relative frequency: 0.00007
```
     See also "carract."
     p.  59 EPIGRAMS 92      27 To ope' the character. They'haue found the
                                sleight
     p.  67 EPIGRAMS 103     12 For euery part a character assign'd.
     p. 117 FOREST 13        24 In my character, what your features bee,
```

character (cont.)
```
    p. 220 UNDERWOOD 47      73 So short you read my Character, and theirs
    p. 287 U'WOOD 84.9      155 And best he knew her noble Character,
```

characters   frequency: 1   relative frequency: 0.00001
```
    p. 206 UNDERWOOD 43      73 Their Seales, their Characters, Hermetique
                               rings,
```

charg'd   frequency: 1   relative frequency: 0.00001
```
    p. 138 UNDERWOOD 2.6     32 Or have charg'd his sight of Crime,
```

charge   frequency: 12   relative frequency: 0.00017
```
    p.  30 EPIGRAMS 12        4 The charge of that state, with this charme, god
                               payes.
    p.  32 EPIGRAMS 17        4 Charge them, for crowne, to thy sole censure hye.
    p.  83 EPIGRAMS 131       8 They should be fooles, for me, at their owne
                               charge.
    p. 119 FOREST 13         93 'Gainst stormes, or pyrats, that might charge
                               your peace;
    p. 168 UNDERWOOD 15     182 Thy person fit for any charge thou tak'st;
    p. 214 UNDERWOOD 44      32 For that unnecessarie Charge they were.
    p. 235 UNDERWOOD 62       8 As thou dost cure our Evill, at thy charge.
    p. 253 UNDERWOOD 75      17 What Beavie of beauties, and bright youths at
                               charge
    p. 256 UNDERWOOD 75     127 Hearing their charge, and then
    p. 325 HORACE 2         436 Their Charge, and Office, whence their wealth
                               to fet,
    p. 378 UNGATHERED 11     83 Marry he sets it out at his owne charge;
    p. 382 UNGATHERED 16      2 hath armde att all poyntes; charge mee humblye
                               kneele
```

chariot   frequency: 3   relative frequency: 0.00004
```
   *p. 494 TO HIMSELF        60 And raysing Charles his chariot, 'boue his
                               Waine.
    p. 134 UNDERWOOD 2.4      1 See the Chariot at hand here of Love,
    p. 175 UNDERWOOD 23      28 Sols Chariot for new fire,
```

charis   frequency: 5   relative frequency: 0.00007
```
    p. 131 UNDERWOOD 2       t1 A Celebration of CHARIS in
    p. 136 UNDERWOOD 2.5      1 Noblest Charis, you that are
    p. 137 UNDERWOOD 2.6      1 Charis, guesse, and doe not misse,
    p. 139 UNDERWOOD 2.8      1 Charis one day in discourse
    p. 140 UNDERWOOD 2.8     13 Therefore, Charis, you must do't,
```

charitable   frequency: 1   relative frequency: 0.00001
```
    p. 287 U'WOOD 84.9      176 So charitable, to religious end,
```

charitie   frequency: 3   relative frequency: 0.00004
```
    p. 186 UNDERWOOD 32       6 Are there for Charitie, and not for fee.
    p. 288 U'WOOD 84.9      193 Or doing other deeds of Charitie,
    p. 413 UNGATHERED 41     25 Thus, Love, and Hope, and burning Charitie,
```

charities   frequency: 1   relative frequency: 0.00001
```
    p. 248 UNDERWOOD 71       3 Of Princes aides, or good mens Charities.
```

charity. See "charitie."

charles   frequency: 21   relative frequency: 0.00030
```
   *p. 494 TO HIMSELF        60 And raysing Charles his chariot, 'boue his
                               Waine.
    p. 222 UNDERWOOD 48      54 And Charles brings home the Ladie.
    p. 235 UNDERWOOD 62       1 Great CHARLES, among the holy gifts of
                               grace
    p. 235 UNDERWOOD 62      t2 To K. CHARLES
    p. 235 UNDERWOOD 62      t1 To K. CHARLES, and Q. MARY.
    p. 236 UNDERWOOD 63       7 Then, Royall CHARLES, and MARY, doe
                               not grutch
    p. 236 UNDERWOOD 64       3 How many times, Live long, CHARLES, would
                               he say,
    p. 236 UNDERWOOD 64      t2 To our great and good K. CHARLES
    p. 237 UNDERWOOD 64      22 How much to heaven for thee, great
                               CHARLES, they owe!
    p. 238 UNDERWOOD 65      12 Sol will re-shine. If not, CHARLES hath a
                               Sonne.
    p. 240 UNDERWOOD 67      54 And CHARLES a Caroline!
    p. 249 UNDERWOOD 72       1 This is King CHARLES his Day. Speake
                               it, thou Towre,
    p. 249 UNDERWOOD 72      18 Still to have such a CHARLES, but this
                               CHARLES long.
    p. 251 UNDERWOOD 74      26 To see great Charles of Travaile eas'd,
```

charles (cont.)
   p. 256 UNDERWOOD 75 124 Askes first, Who gives her (I Charles) then he
                           plights
   p. 259 UNDERWOCD 76 2+ King CHARLES.
   p. 263 UNDERWOOD 79 8++ CHARLES, 1635.
   p. 367 UNGATHERED 6 50 (Charles Montioy) whose command
   p. 387 UNGATHERED 22 t1 Charles Cauendish to his posteritie.
   p. 406 UNGATHERED 35 3 Our Charles should make thee such? T'will not
                           become

charm. See "Charme."

charme   frequency: 9 relative frequency: 0.00013
   p. 30 EPIGRAMS 12 4 The charge of that state, with this charme, god
                           payes.
   p. 51 EPIGRAMS 73 12 Item, a charme surrounding fearefully
   p. 163 UNDERWOOD 15 52 I, that's a Charme and halfe! She must afford
   p. 182 UNDERWOOD 28 7 But charme the Senses, others over-come
   p. 198 UNDERWOOD 40 45 Weaknesse of braine, or any charme of Wine,
   p. 200 UNDERWOOD 42 28 At every stall; The Cittie Cap's a charme.
   p. 367 UNGATHERED 6 44 There charme the rout
   p. 392 UNGATHERED 26 46 Our eares, or like a Mercury to charme!
   p. 421 UNGATHERED 48 39 Aboute this Isle, and Charme the rounde, as
                           when

charmed   frequency: 1 relative frequency: 0.00001
   p. 205 UNDERWOOD 43 68 The<ir> charmed Boates, and the<ir> inchanted
                           Wharfes;

charmes   frequency: 2 relative frequency: 0.00002
   p. 177 UNDERWOOD 25 18 Then shall my Verses, like strong Charmes,
   p. 203 UNDERWOOD 43 16 Imposture, witchcraft, charmes, or blasphemie,

charming   frequency: 1 relative frequency: 0.00001
   p. 401 UNGATHERED 33 1 What charming Peales are these,

charms. See "charmes."

charon   frequency: 1 relative frequency: 0.00001
   p. 84 EPIGRAMS 133 12 And in it, two more horride knaues, then
                           CHARON.

charons   frequency: 1 relative frequency: 0.00001
   p. 86 EPIGRAMS 133 87 Backe, cry'd their brace of CHARONS: they
                           cry'd, no,

charter   frequency: 1 relative frequency: 0.00001
   p. 400 UNGATHERED 31 35 Aeternities great charter; which became

charybdis   frequency: 1 relative frequency: 0.00001
   p. 315 HORACE 2 206 Scylla, Charybdis, Polypheme, with these.

chase   frequency: 2 relative frequency: 0.00002
   p. 68 EPIGRAMS 105 13 And, armed to the chase, so bare her bow
   p. 264 UNDERWOOD 79 22 And in the chase, more then SYLVANUS can,

chast   frequency: 10 relative frequency: 0.00014
   p. 32 EPIGRAMS 17 6 Shall out-liue gyrlands, stolne from the chast
                           tree.
   p. 34 EPIGRAMS 25 7 What doth he else, but say, leaue to be chast,
   p. 35 EPIGRAMS 26 1 Then his chast wife, though BEAST now know
                           no more,
   p. 42 EPIGRAMS 49 6 In my chast booke: professe them in thine owne.
   p. 119 FOREST 13 96 To pay your lord the pledges of chast loue:
   p. 230 UNDERWOOD 56 14 And stroke the water, nimble, chast, and faire,
   p. 237 UNDERWOOD 65 3 The bed of the chast Lilly, and the Rose!
   p. 257 UNDERWOOD 75 161 Yet, as we may, we will, with chast desires,
   p. 295 UNDERWOOD 90 10 No sowre, or sollen bed-mate, yet a Chast;
   p. 394 UNGATHERED 28 5 Religious, wise, chast, louing, gratious, good;

chaste   frequency: 5 relative frequency: 0.00007
   See also "chast."
   p. 96 FOREST 2 90 Thy lady's noble, fruitfull, chaste withall.
   p. 111 FOREST 11 68 As this chaste loue we sing.
   p. 173 UNDERWOOD 22 21 And on them burne so chaste a flame,
   p. 291 UNDERWOOD 85 39 But if, to boot with these, a chaste Wife meet
   p. 319 HORACE 2 294 Chaste, thriftie, modest folke, that came to
                           view.

chastely. See "chastly."

chastetye   frequency: 1   relative frequency: 0.00001
     p. 108 FOREST 10 A   6 Could ne'er make prize of thy white Chastetye.

chastitie   frequency: 2   relative frequency: 0.00002
     p. 67 EPIGRAMS 104   8 Of birth, of match, of forme, of chastitie?
     p. 111 FOREST 11   81 Cannot so safely sinne. Their chastitie

chastity. See "chastetye," "chastitie."

chastly   frequency: 1   relative frequency: 0.00001
     p. 111 FOREST 11   74 Turtles can chastly dye;

chattel. See "chattell."

chattell   frequency: 1   relative frequency: 0.00001
     p. 230 UNDERWOOD 56   8 Unprofitable Chattell, fat and old,

chattels   frequency: 1   relative frequency: 0.00001
     p. 41 EPIGRAMS 44   1 CHVFFE, lately rich in name, in chattels,
                                   goods,

chattering. See "chattring."

chattring   frequency: 1   relative frequency: 0.00001
     p. 174 UNDERWOOD 23   12 To see their Seats and Bowers by chattring
                                   Pies defac't?

chaucer   frequency: 1   relative frequency: 0.00001
     p. 391 UNGATHERED 26   20 Chaucer, or Spenser, or bid Beaumont lye

chayre   frequency: 2   relative frequency: 0.00002
     p. 115 FOREST 12   62 Or lifted CASSIOPEA in her chayre?
     p. 380 UNGATHERED 12   27 Besides he tried Ship, Cart, Waggon, and
                                   Chayre,

cheap. See "cheape."

cheap-side   frequency: 1   relative frequency: 0.00001
     p. 202 UNDERWOOD 42   76 Any Comparison had with his Cheap-side.

cheape   frequency: 2   relative frequency: 0.00002
     p. 167 UNDERWOOD 15   155 Pardon his Lordship. Flattry's growne so cheape
     p. 408 UNGATHERED 37   6 Is to make cheape, the Lord, the lines, the
                                   price.

cheapside. See "cheap-side."

chear=full   frequency: 1   relative frequency: 0.00001
     p. 396 UNGATHERED 30   17 It cast a beame as when the chear=full Sun

chear'd   frequency: 1   relative frequency: 0.00001
     p. 270 UNDERWOOD 83   58 Chear'd her faire Sisters in her race to runne!

cheare   frequency: 3   relative frequency: 0.00004
     p. 95 FOREST 2   82 What (great, I will not say, but) sodayne cheare
     p. 197 UNDERWOOD 40   15 For though Love thrive, and may grow up with
                                   cheare,
     p. 231 UNDERWOOD 57   16 And neither good Cheare,

chearfull   frequency: 1   relative frequency: 0.00001
     p. 414 UNGATHERED 41   43 Whose chearfull look our sadnesse doth destroy,

chearfully   frequency: 1   relative frequency: 0.00001
     p. 176 UNDERWOOD 24   13 Shee chearfully supporteth what she reares,

cheated   frequency: 2   relative frequency: 0.00002
     p. 42 EPIGRAMS 46   5 The knight-wright's cheated then: Hee'll neuer
                                   pay.
     p. 321 HORACE 2   346 And the bold Pythias, having cheated weake

cheater   frequency: 2   relative frequency: 0.00002
     p. 56 EPIGRAMS 87   t1 ON CAPTAINE HAZARD THE
                                   CHEATER.
     p. 107 FOREST 10   22 HERMES, the cheater, shall not mixe with vs,

check. See "checke."

checke   frequency: 1   relative frequency: 0.00001
  **p. 116 PANEGYRE   123 Sustaine the reynes, and in the checke forbeare

checked. See "checkt."

checkt   frequency: 1   relative frequency: 0.00001
    p. 163 UNDERWOOD 15   35 Not to be checkt, or frighted now with fate,

cheek. See "cheeke."

cheeke   frequency: 2   relative frequency: 0.00002
    p. 141 UNDERWOOD 2.9   19 Even nose, and cheeke (withall)
    p. 170 UNDERWOOD 19   7 By those pure bathes your either cheeke
                             discloses,

cheekes   frequency: 1   relative frequency: 0.00001
    p. 136 UNDERWOOD 2.5 22 In her cheekes, of Milke, and Roses;

cheeks   frequency: 1   relative frequency: 0.00001
    See also "cheekes."
    p. 293 UNDERWOOD 86   34 Flow my thin teares, downe these pale cheeks of
                             mine?

cheer. See "cheare," "cheere."

cheere   frequency: 2   relative frequency: 0.00002
    p. 98 FOREST 3   49 And fills thy open hall with mirth, and cheere,
    p. 392 UNGATHERED 26 78 Or influence, chide, or cheere the drooping
                             Stage;

cheered   frequency: 1   relative frequency: 0.00001
    See also "chear'd."
    p. 287 U'WOOD 84.9   183 And came forth ever cheered, with the rod

cheerefull   frequency: 2   relative frequency: 0.00002
    p. 154 UNDERWOOD 13   39 No! Gifts and thankes should have one cheerefull
                             face,
    p. 224 UNDERWOOD 50   16 A cheerefull worke to all good eyes, to see

cheerful. See "chear=full," "chearfull," "cheerefull."

cheerfully. See "chearfully."

cheese   frequency: 1   relative frequency: 0.00001
    p. 65 EPIGRAMS 101   27 Digestiue cheese, and fruit there sure will bee;

cheeses   frequency: 1   relative frequency: 0.00001
    p. 95 FOREST 2   53 The better cheeses, bring 'hem; or else send

chelsea. See "chelsey."

chelsey   frequency: 1   relative frequency: 0.00001
    p. 103 FOREST 6   14 Or the sands in Chelsey fields,

chequer   frequency: 1   relative frequency: 0.00001
    p. 666 INSCRIPTS. 11   8 Wth Chequer Inke, vpon his guift, my paper,

cherish   frequency: 3   relative frequency: 0.00004
    p. 161 UNDERWOOD 14   74 Embrace, and cherish; but he can approve
    p. 192 UNDERWOOD 38   61 Her order is to cherish, and preserve,
    p. 422 UNGATHERED 50 10 if it begyn religious thoughts to cherish;

cherish'd   frequency: 1   relative frequency: 0.00001
    p. 141 UNDERWOOD 2.9 23 Till he cherish'd too much beard,

cherishing   frequency: 1   relative frequency: 0.00001
    See also "cherissheinge."
    p. 128 UNDERWOOD 1.1 43 With grace, with love, with cherishing intire:

cherissheinge   frequency: ' 1   relative frequency: 0.00001
    p. 419 UNGATHERED 48   5 By Cherissheinge the Spirrites yt gaue their
                             greatnesse grace:

cherries   frequency: 1   relative frequency: 0.00001
    p. 58 EPIGRAMS 92   1 Ere cherries ripe, and straw-berries be gone,

cherry   frequency: 1   relative frequency: 0.00001
    p. 94 FOREST 2   41 The earely cherry, with the later plum,

cherub. See "cherube."

cherube   frequency: 1   relative frequency: 0.00001
    p. 285 U'WOOD 84.9   88 The Thrones, the Cherube, and Seraphick
                             bowers,

chest-nut   frequency: 1   relative frequency: 0.00001
     p. 93 FOREST 2   12 Beneath the broad beech, and the chest-nut shade;

chestnut   frequency: 1   relative frequency: 0.00001
     See also "chest-nut."
     p. 141 UNDERWOOD 2.9   13 Chestnut colour, or more slack

chev-ril   frequency: 1   relative frequency: 0.00001
     p. 44 EPIGRAMS 54   3 What are thy petulant pleadings, CHEV-RIL,
                                 then,

cheverel. See "chev-ril," "chev'ril," "chev'rill."

chev'ril   frequency: 2   relative frequency: 0.00002
     p. 44 EPIGRAMS 54   1 CHEV'RIL cryes out, my verses libells are;
     p. 44 EPIGRAMS 54   t1 ON CHEV'RIL.

chev'rill   frequency: 2   relative frequency: 0.00002
     p. 38 EPIGRAMS 37   1 No cause, nor client fat, will CHEV'RILL
                                 leese,
     p. 38 EPIGRAMS 37   t1 ON CHEV'RILL THE LAWYER.

chiches   frequency: 1   relative frequency: 0.00001
     p. 321 HORACE 2   362 Him that buyes chiches blanch't, or chance to
                                 like

chid   frequency: 1   relative frequency: 0.00001
     p. 152 UNDERWOOD 12   28 It chid the vice, yet not the Men.

chide   frequency: 1   relative frequency: 0.00001
     p. 392 UNGATHERED 26   78 Or influence, chide, or cheere the drooping
                                 Stage;

chief. See "chiefe."

chiefe   frequency: 7   relative frequency: 0.00010
     p. 28 EPIGRAMS 4   6 Thou wert, as chiefe of them are said t'haue
                                 beene.
     p. 28 EPIGRAMS 4   8 As chiefe of those still promise they will bee.
     p. 44 EPIGRAMS 56   1 Poore POET-APE, that would be thought our
                                 chiefe,
     p. 187 UNDERWOOD 33   29 So comm'st thou like a Chiefe into the Court,
     p. 217 UNDERWOOD 46   t2 Lord chiefe Iustice of England.
     p. 264 UNDERWOOD 79   28 Shep. Of PAN wee sing, the Chiefe of
                                 Leaders, PAN,
     p. 325 HORACE 2   451 Of a brave Chiefe sent to the warres: He can,

chiefes   frequency: 1   relative frequency: 0.00001
     p. 58 EPIGRAMS 91   16 As noble in great chiefes, as they are rare.

chiefly   frequency: 1   relative frequency: 0.00001
     p. 112 FOREST 11   103 Who could be false to? chiefly, when he knowes

chiefs. See "chiefes."

child   frequency: 17   relative frequency: 0.00024
     See also "grand-child."
     p. 41 EPIGRAMS 45   1 Farewell, thou child of my right hand, and ioy;
     p. 46 EPIGRAMS 62   2 That loue to make so well, a child to beare?
     p. 77 EPIGRAMS 120   5 'Twas a child, that so did thriue
     p. 77 EPIGRAMS 120   t1 EPITAPH ON S<ALOMON> P<AVY> A
                                 CHILD
     p. 79 EPIGRAMS 125   7 But I, no child, no foole, respect the kinde,
     p. 83 EPIGRAMS 132   3 But, as it is (the Child of Ignorance,
     p. 94 FOREST 2   44 Hang on thy walls, that euery child may reach.
     p. 188 UNDERWOOD 35   4 Upon record, in this blest child.
     p. 189 UNDERWOOD 36   16 The eldest God, yet still a Child.
     p. 192 UNDERWOOD 38   39 I am regenerate now, become the child
     p. 242 UNDERWOOD 70   7 Wise child, did'st hastily returne,
     p. 258 UNDERWOOD 75   168 (After the last child borne;) This is our
                                 wedding day.
     p. 271 UNDERWOOD 83   78 If you not understand, what Child you had.
     p. 292 UNDERWOOD 86   15 Child of a hundred Arts, and farre
     p. 315 HORACE 2   225 Fit rites. The Child, that now knowes how to
                                 say,
     p. 329 HORACE 2   510 The Child, when Lamia'has din'd, out of her
                                 maw.
     p. 389 UNGATHERED 24   14 More then the Foster-father of this Child;

children   frequency: 5   relative frequency: 0.00007
     See alsc "grand=children."
     p.   40 EPIGRAMS 42   13 The children, that he keepes, GILES sweares
                                are none
     p.   96 FOREST 2   91 His children thy great lord may call his owne:
     p. 291 UNDERWOOD 85   40 For houshold aid, and Children sweet;
     p. 317 HORACE 2   253 To children; we must alwayes dwell, and stay
     p. 399 UNGATHERED 31   2 Her Children, and Grand=children, reed it
                                heere!

chimaera   frequency: 2   relative frequency: 0.00002
     p.   86 EPIGRAMS 133   80 Man, that had neuer heard of a Chimaera.
     p. 206 UNDERWOOD 43   72 With the Chimaera of the Rosie-Crosse,

chime   frequency: 4   relative frequency: 0.00005
     See alsc "chyme."
     p. 232 UNDERWOOD 59   6 As all defence, or offence, were a chime!
     p. 246 UNDERWOOD 70   102 No pleasures vaine did chime,
     p. 253 UNDERWOOD 75   27 To doe their Offices in Natures Chime,
     p. 279 U'WOOD 84.4   38 As some soft chime had stroak'd the ayre;

chimes   frequency: 1   relative frequency: 0.00001
     p. 389 UNGATHERED 24   3 To say but one, were single. Then it chimes,

chimney   frequency: 1   relative frequency: 0.00001
     p. 291 UNDERWOOD 85   66 And 'bout the steeming Chimney set!

chin   frequency: 4   relative frequency: 0.00005
     p.   69 EPIGRAMS 107   29 Nay, now you puffe, tuske, and draw vp your chin,
     p. 136 UNDERWOOD 2.5   24 And, above her even chin,
     p. 141 UNDERWOOD 2.9   21 Chin, as woolly as the Peach;
     p. 247 UNDERWOOD 70   127 Who, e're the first downe bloomed on the chin,

chincke   frequency: 1   relative frequency: 0.00001
     p. 177 UNDERWOOD 25   16 May shine (through every chincke) to every sight

chink. See "chincke."

chinnes   frequency: 1   relative frequency: 0.00001
     p.   87 EPIGRAMS 133   123 Of worship, they their nodding chinnes doe hit

chins. See "chinnes."

chloe. See "C<h>loe."

chloes   frequency: 1   relative frequency: 0.00001
     p. 293 UNDERWOOD 87   9 HOR. 'Tis true, I'am Thracian Chloes, I,

choak'd   frequency: 1   relative frequency: 0.00001
     p. 198 UNDERWOOD 40   28 'Bove all your standing waters, choak'd with
                                weedes.

choake   frequency: 1   relative frequency: 0.00001
     p. 211 UNDERWOOD 43   182 Or lest that vapour might the Citie choake,

choerilus   frequency: 1   relative frequency: 0.00001
     p. 329 HORACE 2   534 A Choerilus, in whom if I but see

choice   frequency: 6   relative frequency: 0.00008
     See also "choise," "choyce," "choyse."
   **p. 117 PANEGYRE   148 Wherein, his choice was happie with the rest
     p.   49 EPIGRAMS 67   11 Which, by no lesse confirm'd, then thy kings
                                choice,
     p.   55 EPIGRAMS 86   6 Attending such a studie, such a choice.
     p.   96 FOREST 3   2 Whether by choice, or fate, or both;
     p. 181 UNDERWOOD 27   15 With bright Lycoris, Gallus choice,
     p. 307 HORACE 2   56 And what they will not. Him, whose choice doth
                                reare

choicest   frequency: 1   relative frequency: 0.00001
     See alsc "choisest," "choysest."
     p. 401 UNGATHERED 33   4 Of two, the choicest Paire of Mans delights,

choir. See "quire."

choise   frequency: 4   relative frequency: 0.00005
     p.   55 EPIGRAMS 86   2 Vpon thy wel-made choise of friends, and bookes;
     p. 160 UNDERWOOD 14   59 In sharpnesse of all Search, wisdome of Choise,
     p. 368 UNGATHERED 6   83 The choise of Europes pride;
     p. 395 UNGATHERED 29   25 Your true freind in Iudgement and Choise

choisest   frequency: 1   relative frequency: 0.00001
     p. 254 UNDERWOOD 75   50 The choisest Virgin-troup of all the Land!

choke. See "choake."

choked. See "choak'd."

choler. See "choller."

choller   frequency: 1   relative frequency: 0.00001
     p. 325 HORACE 2   430 For choller! If I did not, who could bring

choose   frequency: 4   relative frequency: 0.00005
     See also "chuse."
     p. 43 EPIGRAMS 53   4 But when (in place) thou didst the patrons
                               choose,
     p. 76 EPIGRAMS 119   10 Till thou canst finde the best, choose the least
                               ill.
     p. 80 EPIGRAMS 128   3 T<o>'extract, and choose the best of all these
                               knowne,
     p. 157 UNDERWOOD 13   154 Their difference, cannot choose which you will
                               be.

chor.   frequency: 5   relative frequency: 0.00007
     p. 264 UNDERWOOD 79   19 Chor. Sound, sound his praises loud, and with
                               his, hers divide.
     p. 264 UNDERWOOD 79   23 Chor. Heare, o you Groves, and, Hills, resound
                               his praise.
     p. 264 UNDERWOOD 79   27 Chor. Rivers, and Vallies, Eccho what wee
                               sing.
     p. 264 UNDERWOOD 79   31 Chor. Heare, O you Groves, and, Hills,
                               resound his worth.
     p. 264 UNDERWOOD 79   35 Chor. Rivers, and Valleys, Eccho what wee
                               sing.

chore   frequency: 1   relative frequency: 0.00001
     p. 193 UNDERWOOD 38   99 I number these as being of the Chore

chori   frequency: 1   relative frequency: 0.00001
     p. 263 UNDERWOOD 79   9 Rector Chori. To day old Janus opens the new
                               yeare,

chorus   frequency: 3   relative frequency: 0.00004
     See also "chor.," "chorvs."
     p. 265 UNDERWOOD 79   44 Chorus Our great, our good. Where one's so
                               drest
     p. 319 HORACE 2   290 And tune too, fitted to the Chorus rime,
     p. 323 HORACE 2   369 Which law receiv'd, the Chorus held his peace,

chorvs   frequency: 1   relative frequency: 0.00001
     p. 189 UNDERWOOD 36   12+ CHORVS.

chose   frequency: 1   relative frequency: 0.00001
     p. 255 UNDERWOOD 75   94 Whom they have chose,

chosen   frequency: 4   relative frequency: 0.00005
     p. 256 UNDERWOOD 75   132 And this their chosen Bishop celebrate,
     p. 272 UNDERWOOD 84   t13 Her being chosen a MUSE.
     p. 395 UNGATHERED 29   t1 To my chosen Friend,
     p. 398 UNGATHERED 30   90 To all thy vertuous, and well chosen Friends,

choyce   frequency: 2   relative frequency: 0.00002
     p. 153 UNDERWOOD 13   17 Yet choyce from whom I take them; and would
                               shame
     p. 170 UNDERWOOD 18   23 That I must send one first, my Choyce assignes,

choyse   frequency: 1   relative frequency: 0.00001
     p. 341 HORACE 1   103 .. .. with whom both choyse, and ....

choysest   frequency: 1   relative frequency: 0.00001
     p. 225 UNDERWOOD 51   16 Out of their Choysest, and their whitest wooll.

chremes   frequency: 1   relative frequency: 0.00001
     p. 311 HORACE 2   133 Her voyce, and angry Chremes chafes out-right

christ   frequency: 1   relative frequency: 0.00001
     p. 288 U'WOOD 84.9   212 Jesus, the onely-gotten Christ! who can

christ-masse   frequency: 1   relative frequency: 0.00001
     p. 45 EPIGRAMS 58   7 So haue I seene at CHRIST-masse sports one
                               lost,

christall   frequency: 1   relative frequency: 0.00001
     p. 365 UNGATHERED 5   12 Closde in an orbe of Christall.

christendom. See "christendome."

christendome   frequency: 2   relative frequency: 0.00002
     p. 59 EPIGRAMS 92   8 They know the states of Christendome, not the
                             places:
     p. 157 UNDERWOOD 13   129 Of Christendome! And neither of these know,

christening. See "christning."

christian   frequency: 2   relative frequency: 0.00002
     p. 271 UNDERWOOD 83   96 The Christian hath t<o>'enjoy the future life,
     p. 394 UNGATHERED 28   12 And Christian name too, with a Heralds witt.

christians   frequency: 2   relative frequency: 0.00002
     p. 257 UNDERWOOD 75   156 Of Life, that fall so; Christians know their
                             birth
     p. 411 UNGATHERED 40   13 The comfort of weake Christians,

christmas   frequency: 2   relative frequency: 0.00002
     See also "christ-masse," "christmasse."
     p. 219 UNDERWOOD 47   52 Lose all my credit with my Christmas Clay,
     p. 231 UNDERWOOD 57   15 Christmas is neere;

christmasse   frequency: 1   relative frequency: 0.00001
     p. 190 UNDERWOOD 37   8 Their vice of loving for a Christmasse fit;

christning   frequency: 1   relative frequency: 0.00001
     p. 268 UNDERWOOD 82   t2 On the Christning

chronicle<r>s   frequency: 1   relative frequency: 0.00001
     p. 210 UNDERWOOD 43   171 In those Records, which, were all Chronicle<r>s
                             gone,

chrystall   frequency: 1   relative frequency: 0.00001
     p. 421 UNGATHERED 48   38 Thie Chrystall sheild

chuff. See "chvffe."

church   frequency: 5   relative frequency: 0.00007
     p. 203 UNDERWOOD 43   24 Or taxe the Glories of the Church, and Gowne?
     p. 222 UNDERWOOD 49   16 To Church, as others doe to Feasts and Playes,
     p. 257 UNDERWOOD 75   139 These two, now holy Church hath made them one,
     p. 394 UNGATHERED 28   7 But euery Table in this Church can say,
     p. 416 UNGATHERED 43   8 And doe both Church, and Common-wealth the
                             good,

church-yard   frequency: 1   relative frequency: 0.00001
     p. 378 UNGATHERED 11   85 Shewes he dares more then Paules Church-yard
                             durst do.

churches   frequency: 1   relative frequency: 0.00001
  **p. 116 PANEGYRE   102 "To bury churches, in forgotten dust,

churlish   frequency: 1   relative frequency: 0.00001
     p. 165 UNDERWOOD 15   89 The Husband now's call'd churlish, or a poore

chuse   frequency: 4   relative frequency: 0.00005
     p. 70 EPIGRAMS 109   2 That serues nor fame, nor titles; but doth chuse
     p. 107 FOREST 10   1 And must I sing? what subiect shall I chuse?
     p. 173 UNDERWOOD 22   11 The noblest freedome, not to chuse
     p. 190 UNDERWOOD 37   23 That friendship which no chance but love did
                             chuse,

chvffe   frequency: 2   relative frequency: 0.00002
     p. 41 EPIGRAMS 44   1 CHVFFE, lately rich in name, in chattels,
                             goods,
     p. 41 EPIGRAMS 44   t1 ON CHVFFE, BANCKS THE
                             VSVRER'S

chyme   frequency: 1   relative frequency: 0.00001
     p. 403 UNGATHERED 34   31 I chyme that too: And I haue mett wth those

cicero   frequency: 1   relative frequency: 0.00001
     p. 57 EPIGRAMS 89   6 Then CICERO, whose euery breath was fame:

cinara. See "cynara."

cinders   frequency: 1   relative frequency: 0.00001
     p. 149 UNDERWOOD 8   8 Turn'd to cinders by her eye?

cinnabar. See "cinnopar."

cinnopar   frequency: 1   relative frequency: 0.00001
     p. 406 UNGATHERED 34   94 Vermilion, Lake, or Cinnopar affoards

cinthia. See "cynthia."

cinthius. See "cynthius."

cipher. See "cypher."

cipresse   frequency: 1   relative frequency: 0.00001
     p. 305 HORACE 2   25 Know'st only well to paint a Cipresse tree.

circle   frequency: 12   relative frequency: 0.00017
     p. 55 EPIGRAMS 85   9 To former height, and there in circle tarrie,
     p. 81 EPIGRAMS 128   8 And perfect in a circle alwayes meet.
     p. 107 FOREST 10   12 In the greene circle of thy Iuy twine.
     p. 159 UNDERWOOD 14   32 Upon your Center, doe your Circle fill
     p. 177 UNDERWOOD 25   19 Breake the knit Circle of her Stonie Armes,
     p. 185 UNDERWOOD 30   3 And goe no farther: let this Circle be
     p. 227 UNDERWOOD 52   8 To square my Circle, I confesse; but draw
     p. 243 UNDERWOOD 70   9 How summ'd a circle didst thou leave man-kind
     p. 284 U'WOOD 84.9   66 Of joy the Circle, and sole Period!
     p. 396 UNGATHERED 30   22 As it had beene the circle of the Arts!
     p. 416 UNGATHERED 44   6 We offer as a Circle the most fit
     p. 417 UNGATHERED 45   30 and of Circle be as free,

circled   frequency: 1   relative frequency: 0.00001
     p. 116 FOREST 12   99 Before his swift and circled race be run,

circler   frequency: 1   relative frequency: 0.00001
     p. 313 HORACE 2   195 Nor so begin, as did that Circler late,

circles   frequency: 4   relative frequency: 0.00005
     p. 276 U'WOOD 84.3   25 Last, draw the circles of this Globe,
     p. 305 HORACE 2   21 Dring Circles of swift waters that intwine
     p. 361 UNGATHERED 1   18 extendeth circles into infinits,
     p. 399 UNGATHERED 31   14 All Circles had their spring and end

circling   frequency: 2   relative frequency: 0.00002
     p. 242 UNDERWOOD 69   15 At a Friends freedome, proves all circling
                              meanes
     p. 413 UNGATHERED 41   30 On the reverse of this your circling crowne,

circuits   frequency: 1   relative frequency: 0.00001
     p. 221 UNDERWOOD 48   41 Thy Circuits, and thy Rounds free,

circular   frequency: 2   relative frequency: 0.00002
     p. 279 U'WOOD 84.4   32 As circular, as infinite.
     p. 396 UNGATHERED 30   19 And fill'd an Orbe as circular, as heauen!

circumduction   frequency: 1   relative frequency: 0.00001
     p. 397 UNGATHERED 30   51 Or vniuersall circumduction

circumference   frequency: 1   relative frequency: 0.00001
     p. 414 UNGATHERED 41   54 Through all the lines of this circumference,

circumfused   frequency: 1   relative frequency: 0.00001
     p. 271 UNDERWOOD 83   69 And now, through circumfused light, she lookes

circumstance   frequency: 1   relative frequency: 0.00001
     p. 171 UNDERWOOD 19   26 His Issue, and all Circumstance of life,

circumvol<v>d   frequency: 1   relative frequency: 0.00001
     p. 361 UNGATHERED 1   23 which thoughts being circumvol<v>d in gyerlyk
                              mocion

circumvolved. See "circumvol<v>d."

cis. See "sis."

citie   frequency: 6   relative frequency: 0.00008
  **p. 114 PANEGYRE   50 The amorous Citie spar'd no ornament,
     p. 89 EPIGRAMS 133   194 The citie since hath rais'd a Pyramide.
     p. 96 FOREST 3   3 And, though so neere the citie, and the court,
     p. 211 UNDERWOOD 43   182 Or lest that vapour might the Citie choake,

citie (cont.)
    p. 239 UNDERWOOD 67   11 This Citie, or to shake
    p. 319 HORACE 2   296 That wider Walls embrac'd their Citie round,

cities. See "cittyes."

citizens   frequency: 3   relative frequency: 0.00004
    p. 105 FOREST 8   34 More then citizens dare lend
    p. 213 UNDERWOOD 44   15 Withall, the dirtie paines those Citizens take,
    p. 215 UNDERWOOD 44   73 With Citizens? let Clownes, and Tradesmen
                       breed

cittie   frequency: 1   relative frequency: 0.00001
    p. 200 UNDERWOOD 42   28 At every stall; The Cittie Cap's a charme.

cittie-question   frequency: 1   relative frequency: 0.00001
    p. 214 UNDERWOOD 44   38 The Cittie-Question, whether Tilly, or he,

cittyes   frequency: 1   relative frequency: 0.00001
    p. 406 UNGATHERED 35   8 Cittyes & Temples! thou a Caue for Wyne,

city. See "citie," "cittie," "cittie-question."

civil. See "civill."

civilitie   frequency: 1   relative frequency: 0.00001
    p. 163 UNDERWOOD 15   54 'Tis there civilitie to be a whore;

civility. See "civilitie."

civill   frequency: 4   relative frequency: 0.00005
    p. 186 UNDERWOOD 33   2 The Seat made of a more then civill warre;
    p. 211 UNDERWOOD 43   190 But I'le conclude all in a civill curse.
    p. 214 UNDERWOOD 44   44 Of bearing Armes! most civill Soldierie!
    p. 420 UNGATHERED 48   12 Of Civill virtue, that hee now is not

claim. See "claime," "clame."

claime   frequency: 4   relative frequency: 0.00005
    p. 138 UNDERWOOD 2.6   36 May not claime another kisse.
    p. 200 UNDERWOOD 42   11 Fathers, and Husbands, I doe claime a right
    p. 216 UNDERWOOD 45   10 That could but claime a kindred from the purse.
    p. 313 HORACE 2   174 Be nought so'above him but his sword let claime.

claimed. See "claym'd."

claimes   frequency: 2   relative frequency: 0.00002
    p. 247 UNDERWOOD 70   114 And titles, by which all made claimes
    p. 274 U'WOOD 84.1   34 Who claimes (of reverence) to be heard,

claimest   frequency: 1   relative frequency: 0.00001
    p. 378 UNGATHERED 11   90 As well as from his braines, and claimest thereb.

claimeth. See "claymeth."

claiming. See "clayming."

claims. See "claimes."

clame   frequency: 1   relative frequency: 0.00001
    p. 412 UNGATHERED 41   3 The M. the Myrtle, A. the Almonds clame,

clap   frequency: 2   relative frequency: 0.00002
    p. 38 EPIGRAMS 38   4 Any man else, you clap your hands, and rore,
    p. 315 HORACE 2   222 And sits, till th'Epilogue saies Clap, or
                       Crowne:

claps   frequency: 1   relative frequency: 0.00001
    p. 62 EPIGRAMS 96   9 My title's seal'd. Those that for claps doe
                       write,

clarius   frequency: 1   relative frequency: 0.00001
    p. 174 UNDERWOOD 23   9 Doth Clarius Harp want strings,

clarke-like   frequency: 1   relative frequency: 0.00001
    p. 28 EPIGRAMS 3   9 For termers, or some clarke-like seruing-man,

clarkes   frequency: 1   relative frequency: 0.00001
    p. 65 EPIGRAMS 101   15 And, though fowle, now, be scarce, yet there are
                       clarkes,

clash   frequency: 1   relative frequency: 0.00001
     p. 232 UNDERWOOD 59   5 To hit in angles, and to clash with time:

clasp. See "claspe."

claspe   frequency: 1   relative frequency: 0.00001
     p. 160 UNDERWOOD 14   64 Large claspe of Nature, such a wit can bound.

claspes   frequency: 1   relative frequency: 0.00001
     p. 273 U'WOOD 84.1   27 With Gold, or Claspes, which might be bought

clasps. See "claspes."

clay   frequency: 2   relative frequency: 0.00002
     p. 219 UNDERWOOD 47   52 Lose all my credit with my Christmas Clay,
     p. 279 U'WOOD 84.4   46 And stuck in clay here, it would pull

claym'd   frequency: 1   relative frequency: 0.00001
     p. 371 UNGATHERED 9   6 She might haue claym'd t'have made the Graces
                                foure;

claymeth   frequency: 1   relative frequency: 0.00001
     p. 61 EPIGRAMS 95   21 Whose knowledge claymeth at the helme to stand;

clayming   frequency: 1   relative frequency: 0.00001
     p. 137 UNDERWOOD 2.6   t1 Clayming a second kisse by Desert.

clean. See "cleane."

cleane   frequency: 1   relative frequency: 0.00001
     p. 317 HORACE 2   278 Betweene the Acts, a quite cleane other thing

cleans'd   frequency: 2   relative frequency: 0.00002
     p. 268 UNDERWOOD 82   9 As hath thy JAMES; cleans'd from originall
                                drosse,
     p. 346 HORACE 1   339 .... cleans'd ... .

cleanse. See "clense."

clear. See "cleare," "cleere."

cleare   frequency: 17   relative frequency: 0.00024
   **p. 113 PANEGYRE   7 His former rayes did onely cleare the skie;
   **p. 113 PANEGYRE   19 To this so cleare and sanctified an end,
     p. 111 FOREST 11   75 And yet (in this t<o>'expresse our selues more
                                cleare)
     p. 155 UNDERWOOD 13   87 If it were cleare, but being so in cloud
     p. 220 UNDERWOOD 47   69 But all so cleare, and led by reasons flame,
     p. 234 UNDERWOOD 61   7 Yet are got off thence, with cleare mind, and
                                hands
     p. 242 UNDERWOOD 70   1 Brave Infant of Saguntum, cleare
     p. 251 UNDERWOOD 74   8 The Clowdes rack cleare before the Sun,
     p. 254 UNDERWOOD 75   54 To make more cleare
     p. 263 UNDERWOOD 78   21 He will cleare up his forehead, thinke thou
                                bring'st
     p. 295 UNDERWOOD 89   5 Darke thy cleare glasse with old Falernian
                                Wine;
     p. 323 HORACE 2   395 'Tis cleare, this way I have got off from blame,
     p. 335 HORACE 2   637 They're darke, bid cleare this: all that's
                                doubtfull wrote
     p. 365 UNGATHERED 5   11 Cleare as a naked vestall
     p. 366 UNGATHERED 6   19 The cleare Dircaean Fount
     p. 369 UNGATHERED 6   112 Conceal'd from all but cleare Propheticke eyes.
     p. 421 UNGATHERED 49   8 As Cleare, and distant, as yor: selfe from
                                Cryme;

clearest   frequency: 1   relative frequency: 0.00001
     p. 179 UNDERWOOD 25   54 (Whose heart in that bright Sphere flames
                                clearest,

clearly. See "cleerely."

clearnesse   frequency: 1   relative frequency: 0.00001
     p. 363 UNGATHERED 3   14 Muffles the clearnesse of Election,

clears   frequency: 1   relative frequency: 0.00001
     p. 657 L. CONVIVALES   16 Clears the Brains, makes Wit the Quicker:

cleave   frequency: 2   relative frequency: 0.00002
     p. 239 UNDERWOOD 67   14 And cleave both ayre and ground,

cleave (cont.)
   p. 305 HORACE 2   14 Yet, not as therefore wild, and tame should
                               cleave

cleere   frequency: 6   relative frequency: 0.00008
   p. 41 EPIGRAMS 43   12 As thou stand'st cleere of the necessitie.
   p. 61 EPIGRAMS 95   19 That hast thy brest so cleere of present crimes,
   p. 112 FOREST 11   93 A beautie of that cleere, and sparkling light,
   p. 117 FOREST 13   43 My mirror is more subtile, cleere, refin'd,
   p. 289 UNDERWOOD 85   1 Happie is he, that from all Businesse cleere,
   p. 307 HORACE 2   58 Nor language, nor cleere order ere forsakes.

cleerely   frequency: 1   relative frequency: 0.00001
   p. 47 EPIGRAMS 63   3 And not thy fortune; who can cleerely see

clees. See "cleies."

cleft. See "hoofe-cleft."

cleft-sticks   frequency: 1   relative frequency: 0.00001
   p. 28 EPIGRAMS 3   8 Or in cleft-sticks, aduanced to make calls

cleies   frequency: 1   relative frequency: 0.00001
   p. 283 U'WOOD 84.9   18 Of Vulture death, and those relentlesse cleies?

clemencie   frequency: 1   relative frequency: 0.00001
   p. 82 EPIGRAMS 130   5 Declineth anger, perswades clemencie,

clemency. See "clemencie."

clement   frequency: 1   relative frequency: 0.00001
   p. 71 EPIGRAMS 110   t1 TO CLEMENT EDMONDS, ON HIS

clense   frequency: 1   relative frequency: 0.00001
   p. 187 UNDERWOOD 33   20 Thou prov'st the gentler wayes, to clense the
                               wound,

clep'd   frequency: 1   relative frequency: 0.00001
   p. 413 UNGATHERED 41   22 Which, of the field is clep'd the sweetest brier,

cleped. See "clep'd," "ycleped."

clerk. See "clarke-like," "clerke."

clerke   frequency: 2   relative frequency: 0.00002
   p. 88 EPIGRAMS 133   166 When euery clerke eates artichokes, and peason,
   p. 214 UNDERWOOD 44   33 Well did thy craftie Clerke, and Knight, Sir
                               Hugh,

clerkes   frequency: 1   relative frequency: 0.00001
   p. 210 UNDERWOOD 43   172 Will be remembred by Six Clerkes, to one.

clerks. See "clarkes," "clerkes."

client   frequency: 1   relative frequency: 0.00001
   See also "clyent."
   p. 38 EPIGRAMS 37   1 No cause, nor client fat, will CHEV'RILL
                               leese,

clients   frequency: 3   relative frequency: 0.00004
   p. 119 FOREST 13   88 Eate on her clients, and some one deuoure.
   p. 187 UNDERWOOD 33   36 Thy Hearers Nectar, and thy Clients Balme,
   p. 217 UNDERWOOD 46   11 That Clients strove, in Question of the Lawes,

cliffords   frequency: ' 1   relative frequency: 0.00001
   p. 214 UNDERWOOD 44   52 Beauchamps, and Nevills, Cliffords, Audleys
                               old;

clifton's   frequency: 1   relative frequency: 0.00001
   p. 119 FOREST 13   98 To CLIFTON'S bloud, that is deny'd their
                               name.

climb. See "climbe."

climbe   frequency: 2   relative frequency: 0.00002
   p. 220 UNDERWOOD 47   75 Are asked to climbe. First give me faith, who
                               know
   p. 224 UNDERWOOD 50   10 Are growne so fruitfull, and false pleasures
                               climbe,

climbing. See "climing."

clime   frequency: 1   relative frequency: 0.00001
       p.   37 EPIGRAMS 32   6 His often change of clime (though not of mind)

climes   frequency: 2   relative frequency: 0.00002
       p.   80 EPIGRAMS 128   2 Countries, and climes, manners, and men to know,
       p. 224 UNDERWOOD 50   22 Countries, and Climes, manners, and men to know.

climing   frequency: 1   relative frequency: 0.00001
       p. 395 UNGATHERED 29   2 And see both climing vp the slippery staire

cling   frequency: 1   relative frequency: 0.00001
       p. 223 UNDERWOOD 49   38 You cling to Lords, and Lords, if them you
                                       leave

clio   frequency: 1   relative frequency: 0.00001
       p. 239 UNDERWOOD 67   1 1. CLIO. Up publike joy, remember

cloak. See "cloake," "cloke."

cloake   frequency: 1   relative frequency: 0.00001
       p. 237 UNDERWOOD 64   20 Is Banke-rupt turn'd! the Cassock, Cloake, and
                                       Gowne,

cloath   frequency: 2   relative frequency: 0.00002
       p. 275 U'WOOD 84.3   8 Needs nought to cloath it but the ayre.
       p. 288 U'WOOD 84.9   194 To cloath the naked, feed the hungry. Shee

cloath'd   frequency: 2   relative frequency: 0.00002
       p. 201 UNDERWOOD 42   48 That are like cloath'd: must I be of those
                                       fooles
       p. 389 UNGATHERED 24   20 Had cloath'd him so. Here's all I can supply

clock. See "clocke."

clocke   frequency: 1   relative frequency: 0.00001
       p. 380 UNGATHERED 12   24 The truth of his heart there, and tell's what a
                                       clocke

cloke   frequency: 1   relative frequency: 0.00001
       p.   62 EPIGRAMS 97   4 His cloke with orient veluet quite lin'd through,

clos'd   frequency: 3   relative frequency: 0.00004
    See also "closde."
       p. 185 UNDERWOOD 30   17 Clos'd to their peace, he saw his branches shoot,
       p. 203 UNDERWOOD 43   8 With Clownes, and Tradesmen, kept thee clos'd
                                       in horne.
       p. 309 HORACE 2   109 Were also clos'd: But, who the man should be,

closde   frequency: 1   relative frequency: 0.00001
       p. 365 UNGATHERED 5   12 Closde in an orbe of Christall.

close   frequency: 14   relative frequency: 0.00020
       p.   33 EPIGRAMS 21   1 Lord, how is GAM'STER chang'd! his haire
                                       close cut!
       p.   59 EPIGRAMS 92   19 Keepe a starre-chamber sentence close, twelue
                                       dayes:
       p.   59 EPIGRAMS 92   29 To breake vp seales, and close 'hem. And they
                                       know,
       p.   86 EPIGRAMS 133   90 Row close then, slaues. Alas, they will beshite
                                       vs.
       p. 109 FOREST 11   16 Close, the close cause of it.
       p. 118 FOREST 13   74 On the close groome, and page, on new-yeeres day,
       p. 149 UNDERWOOD 9   7 And every close did meet
       p. 198 UNDERWOOD 40   42 The Jewell of your name, as close as sleepe
       p. 229 UNDERWOOD 54   9 And hold me to it close; to stand upright
       p. 248 UNDERWOOD 71   8 Reduicts, Halfe-moones, Horne-workes, and such
                                       close wayes,
       p. 249 UNDERWOOD 72   17 And ever close the burden of the Song,
       p. 339 HORACE 1   40 Downe close .. shore, this other creeping
                                       steales,
       p. 366 UNGATHERED 6   24 From Zephyr's rape would close him with his
                                       beames.

close-stoole   frequency: 1   relative frequency: 0.00001
       p. 202 UNDERWOOD 42   84 Or a Close-stoole so cas'd; or any fat

closely   frequency: 1   relative frequency: 0.00001
       p. 294 UNDERWOOD 88   7 Let us together closely lie, and kisse,

closer   frequency: 1   relative frequency: 0.00001
   p. 69 EPIGRAMS 1C7   20 And then lye with you, closer, then a punque,

closest   frequency: 1   relative frequency: 0.00001
   p. 287 U'WOOD 84.9   153 Our closest Creekes, and Corners, and can trace

cloth   frequency: 5   relative frequency: 0.00007
  See also "cloth's," "foot-cloth."
   p. 96 FOREST 3   7 Nor com'st to view the better cloth of state;
   p. 164 UNDERWOOD 15   57 To do't with Cloth, or Stuffes, lusts name
                       might merit;
   p. 230 UNDERWOOD 55   8 But Scarlet-like out-lasts the Cloth.
   p. 389 UNGATHERED 24   17 But that hee's too well suted, in a cloth,
   p. 406 UNGATHERED 34   93 A Goddess is, then paynted Cloth, Deal-boards,

clothe. See "cloath."

clothed. See "cloath'd."

clothes   frequency: 11   relative frequency: 0.00015
  See also "stage-clothes."
   p. 30 EPIGRAMS 11   1 At court I met it, in clothes braue enough,
   p. 33 EPIGRAMS 21   3 His clothes two fashions of, and poore! his sword
   p. 35 EPIGRAMS 28   10 Both which are great. And laugh at ill-made
                       clothes;
   p. 56 EPIGRAMS 88   12 By which his damme conceiu'd him, clothes and
                       all?
   p. 63 EPIGRAMS 97   20 Onely his clothes haue ouer-leauen'd him.
   p. 76 EPIGRAMS 119   1 Not he that flies the court for want of clothes,
   p. 131 UNDERWOOD 2.1   8 Clothes, or Fortune gives the grace;
   p. 141 UNDERWOOD 2.9   36 Well he should his clothes to<o> weare;
   p. 142 U'WOOD 2.10   4 His Clothes rich, and band sit neat,
   p. 201 UNDERWOOD 42   42 Being, the best clothes still to praeoccupie.
   p. 384 UNGATHERED 18   2 And clothes, and guifts, that only do thee grace

cloth's   frequency: 1   relative frequency: 0.00001
   p. 74 EPIGRAMS 115   24 The cloth's no sooner gone, but it gets vp

cloud   frequency: 7   relative frequency: 0.00010
   p. 86 EPIGRAMS 133   94 Crack did report it selfe, as if a cloud
   p. 110 FOREST 11   35 But this doth from the<ir> cloud of error grow,
   p. 132 UNDERWOOD 2.2   12 Every Cloud about his eye;
   p. 155 UNDERWOOD 13   87 If it were cleare, but being so in cloud
   p. 276 U'WOOD 84.3   13 Draw first a Cloud: all save her neck;
   p. 276 U'WOOD 84.3   18 The Cloud, and show the Universe;
   p. 280 U'WOOD 84.4   58 But stooping gently, as a Cloud,

cloud-like. See "clowd-."

cloudes   frequency: 3   relative frequency: 0.00004
   p. 192 UNDERWOOD 38   56 Why was't? did e're the Cloudes aske back their
                       raine?
   p. 193 UNDERWOOD 38   75 About in Cloudes, and wrapt in raging weather,
   p. 403 UNGATHERED 34   33 The majesty of Iuno in ye Cloudes,

clouds   frequency: 1   relative frequency: 0.00001
  See also "cloudes," "clowdes."
   p. 142 UNDERWOOD 2.9   43 Bounteous as the clouds to earth;

clowd-   frequency: 1   relative frequency: 0.00001
   p. 164 UNDERWOOD 15   60 Who can behold their Manners, and not clowd-

clowdes   frequency: 2   relative frequency: 0.00002
   p. 251 UNDERWOOD 74   8 The Clowdes rack cleare before the Sun,
   p. 321 HORACE 2   336 And emptie Clowdes. For Tragedie is faire,

clown. See "clowne."

clownage   frequency: 1   relative frequency: 0.00001
   p. 163 UNDERWOOD 15   43 As they are made! Pride, and stiffe Clownage
                       mixt

clowne   frequency: 3   relative frequency: 0.00004
   p. 94 FOREST 2   48 But all come in, the farmer, and the clowne:
   p. 237 UNDERWOOD 64   19 'T is not alone the Merchant, but the Clowne,
   p. 319 HORACE 2   302 Clowne, Towns-man, base, and noble, mix'd, to
                       judge?

clownes   frequency: 4   relative frequency: 0.00005
   p. 155 UNDERWOOD 13   89 My wonder, why the taking a Clownes purse,

clownes (cont.)
    p. 203 UNDERWOOD 43   8 With Clownes, and Tradesmen, kept thee clos'd
                                  in horne.
    p. 208 UNDERWOOD 43   116 No mar'le the Clownes of Lemnos tooke thee up,
    p. 215 UNDERWOOD 44   73 With Citizens? let Clownes, and Tradesmen
                                  breed

clownish. See "clownishe."

clownishe   frequency: 1   relative frequency: 0.00001
    p. 420 UNGATHERED 48   10 Butt, Clownishe pride hath gott

clowns. See "clownes."

club   frequency: 2   relative frequency: 0.00002
    See also "clubb," "play-club."
    p. 241 UNDERWOOD 69   11 Was, t'have a Boy stand with a Club, and fright
    p. 396 UNGATHERED 30   8 Hanch against Hanch, or raise a riming Club

club-fist   frequency: 1   relative frequency: 0.00001
    p. 85 EPIGRAMS 133   55 Great Club-fist, though thy backe, and bones be
                                    sore,

clubb   frequency: 1   relative frequency: 0.00001
    p. 409 UNGATHERED 37   21 Thy Noddle, with his clubb; and dashing forth

cluid   frequency: 1   relative frequency: 0.00001
    p. 367 UNGATHERED 6   39 But first to Cluid stoope low,

cluster   frequency: 1   relative frequency: 0.00001
    p. 85 EPIGRAMS 133   64 Of all your night-tubs, when the carts doe
                                    cluster,

clwyd. See "cluid."

clyent   frequency: 1   relative frequency: 0.00001
    p. 292 UNDERWOOD 86   14 And for the troubled Clyent fyl's his tongue,

clysters   frequency: 1   relative frequency: 0.00001
    p. 42 EPIGRAMS 50   2 Or fumie clysters, thy moist lungs to bake:

co<u>nsellors   frequency: 1   relative frequency: 0.00001
 **p. 116 PANEGYRE   106 "Lawes, iudges, co<u>nsellors, yea prince, and
                                  state.

co-heire   frequency: 1   relative frequency: 0.00001
    p. 274 U'WOOD 84.2   6 And STANLEY, to the which shee was
                                  Co-heire.

co-heires   frequency: 1   relative frequency: 0.00001
    p. 286 U'WOOD 84.9   146 Equall with Angels, and Co-heires of it?

coach   frequency: 2   relative frequency: 0.00002
    p. 105 FOREST 8   37 Will by coach, and water goe,
    p. 230 UNDERWOOD 56   10 His friends, but to breake Chaires, or cracke a
                                  Coach.

coach-man   frequency: 1   relative frequency: 0.00001
    p. 164 UNDERWOOD 15   72 And firke, and jerke, and for the Coach-man
                                  raile,

coach-mare   frequency: 1   relative frequency: 0.00001
    p. 201 UNDERWOOD 42   43 Put a Coach-mare in Tissue, must I horse

coach'd   frequency: 2   relative frequency: 0.00002
    p. 156 UNDERWOOD 13   121 Ride, saile, am coach'd, know I how farre I
                                  have gone,
    p. 165 UNDERWOOD 15   107 Coach'd, or on foot-cloth, thrice chang'd every
                                  day,

coal. See "coale," "cole," "sea-coale."

coale   frequency: 2   relative frequency: 0.00002
    p. 193 UNDERWOOD 38   97 Produce; though threatning with a coale, or
                                  chalke
    p. 206 UNDERWOOD 43   76 The art of kindling the true Coale, by Lungs:

coarse. See "course."

coarser. See "courser."

coast   frequency: 5   relative frequency: 0.00007
    p.   84 EPIGRAMS 133   14 And for one CERBERVS, the whole coast was
                              dogs.
    p. 116 FOREST 12   93 Who, wheresoere he be, on what dear coast,
    p. 367 UNGATHERED 6   37 But proue the Aire, and saile from Coast to
                              Coast:
    p. 388 UNGATHERED 23   9 To the Greeke coast thine onely knew the way.

coat   frequency: 1   relative frequency: 0.00001
    See also "coate."
    p. 232 UNDERWOOD 58   4 What each man sayes of it, and of what coat

coate   frequency: 1   relative frequency: 0.00001
    p. 389 UNGATHERED 24   11 Such Bookes deserue Translators, of like coate

coates   frequency: 3   relative frequency: 0.00004
    p. 208 UNDERWOOD 43   127 Whom they durst handle in their holy-day coates,
    p. 273 U'WOOD 84.1   21 Their Corrals, Whistles, and prime Coates,
    p. 419 UNGATHERED 48   8 And better Blason them, then all their Coates,

coats. See "coates," "cotes."

cob   frequency: 2   relative frequency: 0.00002
    p.   50 EPIGRAMS 69   1 COB, thou nor souldier, thiefe, nor fencer art,
    p.   50 EPIGRAMS 69   t1 TO PERTINAX COB.

cob-web-lawne   frequency: 1   relative frequency: 0.00001
    p.   51 EPIGRAMS 73   14 In solemne cypres, the other cob-web-lawne.

cobalus   frequency: 1   relative frequency: 0.00001
    p. 398 UNGATHERED 30   86 Thou hadst brought Lapland, or old Cobalus,

cobbled. See "cobled."

cobbler. See "cobler."

cobled   frequency: 1   relative frequency: 0.00001
    p. 380 UNGATHERED 12   42 From Venice to Flushing, were not they well
                              cobled?

cobler   frequency: 1   relative frequency: 0.00001
    p. 410 UNGATHERED 38   17 The Cobler kept him to his nall; but, now

cobweb   frequency: 1   relative frequency: 0.00001
    See also "cob-web-lawne."
    p. 273 U'WOOD 84.1   26 No cobweb Call's; no Surcoates wrought

cobwebs   frequency: 1   relative frequency: 0.00001
    p. 282 U'WOOD 84.9   5 And set it forth; the rest were Cobwebs fine,

cocatrice   frequency: 1   relative frequency: 0.00001
    p.   31 EPIGRAMS 12   21 Not his poore cocatrice but he betrayes

cock   frequency: 2   relative frequency: 0.00002
    See also "wood-cock."
    p.   31 EPIGRAMS 13   2 Of old, they gaue a cock to AESCVLAPE;
    p.   51 EPIGRAMS 73   18 Item, an epitaph on my lords cock,

cockatrice. See "cocatrice."

cocking   frequency: 1   relative frequency: 0.00001
    p.   76 EPIGRAMS 119   3 Cryes out 'gainst cocking, since he cannot bet,

cocks   frequency: 1   relative frequency: 0.00001
    p. 222 UNDERWOOD 49   4 Where fight the prime Cocks of the Game, for
                              wit?

cocytvs   frequency: 2   relative frequency: 0.00002
    p.   84 EPIGRAMS 133   8 COCYTVS, PHLEGETON, our haue
                              prou'd in one;
    p.   86 EPIGRAMS 133   89 How hight the place? a voyce was heard,
                              COCYTVS.

cod   frequency: 6   relative frequency: 0.00008
    p.   33 EPIGRAMS 19   1 That COD can get no widdow, yet a knight,
    p.   33 EPIGRAMS 19   t1 ON SIR COD THE PERFVMED.
    p.   33 EPIGRAMS 20   2 Except thou could'st, Sir COD, weare them
                              within.
    p.   33 EPIGRAMS 20   t1 TO THE SAME SIR COD.
    p.   42 EPIGRAMS 50   1 Leaue COD, tabacco-like, burnt gummes to take,

cod (cont.)
          p.   42 EPIGRAMS 50   t1 TO SIR COD.

code   frequency: 1   relative frequency: 0.00001
          p. 399 UNGATHERED 31   8 Code, Digests, Pandects of all faemale glory!

coeternal. See "coeternall."

coeternall   frequency: 1   relative frequency: 0.00001
          p. 128 UNDERWOOD 1.1   38 All coeternall in your Majestie,

coheir. See "co-heire."

coheirs. See "co-heires."

coin. See "coyne."

coined. See "late-coyn'd."

coit   frequency: 1   relative frequency: 0.00001
          p. 331 HORACE 2   567 Or, who's unskilfull at the Coit, or Ball,

coke   frequency: 2   relative frequency: 0.00002
          p. 217 UNDERWOOD 46   5 Such, Coke, were thy beginnings, when thy good
          p. 217 UNDERWOOD 46   t1 An Epigram on Sir Edward Coke, when he was

cokely   frequency: 1   relative frequency: 0.00001
          p. 81 EPIGRAMS 129   16 Thou dost out-zany COKELY, POD; nay,
                                      GVE:

colby   frequency: 1   relative frequency: 0.00001
          p. 167 UNDERWOOD 15   176 Thy true friends wishes, Colby, which shall be,

colchis   frequency: 1   relative frequency: 0.00001
          p. 313 HORACE 2   167 Of Colchis borne; or in Assyria bred;

cold   frequency: 10   relative frequency: 0.00014
         *p. 493 TO HIMSELF   45 And though thy nerues be shrunke, and blood be
                                      cold,
          p. 37 EPIGRAMS 32   5 The cold of Mosco, and fat Irish ayre,
          p. 93 FOREST 1   11 That since, my numbers are so cold,
          p. 140 UNDERWOOD 2.8   9 But we find that cold delay,
          p. 177 UNDERWOOD 25   22 Lock't in her cold embraces, from the view
          p. 184 UNDERWOOD 29   56 The cold tumor in his feet,
          p. 189 UNDERWOOD 36   15 Now hot, now cold, now fierce, now mild.
          p. 199 UNDERWOOD 42   1 Let me be what I am, as Virgil cold;
          p. 230 UNDERWOOD 56   7 And you may justly, being a tardie, cold,
          p. 258 UNDERWOOD 75   166 You find no cold

coldest   frequency: 1   relative frequency: 0.00001
          p. 97 FOREST 3   36 Although the coldest of the yeere!

coldly   frequency: 1   relative frequency: 0.00001
          p. 317 HORACE 2   244 Or do's all businesse coldly, and with feare;

colds   frequency: 2   relative frequency: 0.00002
          p. 220 UNDERWOOD 47   67 And that there be no fev'ry heats, nor colds,
          p. 233 UNDERWOOD 59   21 Who durst live great, 'mongst all the colds, and
                                      heates,

cole   frequency: 1   relative frequency: 0.00001
          p. 408 UNGATHERED 36   11 Wth rotten chalk, or Cole vpon a wall,

colledge   frequency: 2   relative frequency: 0.00002
          p. 39 EPIGRAMS 41   2 And get more gold, then all the colledge can:
          p. 87 EPIGRAMS 133   117 The meate-boate of Beares colledge,
                                      Paris-garden,

college. See "colledge."

colossus   frequency: 1   relative frequency: 0.00001
          p. 407 UNGATHERED 35   13 He some Colossus to bestryde ye Seas,

colour   frequency: 4   relative frequency: 0.00005
          p. 73 EPIGRAMS 112   20 Nor scarce dost colour for it, which is lesse.
          p. 139 UNDERWOOD 2.7   t1 Begging another, on colour of mending
          p. 141 UNDERWOOD 2.9   13 Chestnut colour, or more slack
          p. 204 UNDERWOOD 43   40 Thou then hadst had some colour for thy flames,

colouring. See "culloring."

```
colours                          frequency:    6   relative frequency: 0.00008
      See also "coulors," "cullors."
      p. 160 UNDERWOOD 14    58 But to the Subject, still the Colours fit
      p. 171 UNDERWOOD 20    11 Of many Colours; outward, fresh from spots,
      p. 227 UNDERWOOD 52    21 Ne knowes he flatt'ring Colours, or false light.
      p. 265 UNDERWOOD 79    45 In truth of colours, both are best.
      p. 277 U'WOOD 84.4      6 But here I may no colours use.
      p. 311 HORACE 2       126 If now the turnes, the colours, and right hues


colt                             frequency:    2   relative frequency: 0.00002
      p.  39 EPIGRAMS 39      2 COLT, now, doth daily penance in his owne.
      p.  39 EPIGRAMS 39     t1 ON OLD COLT.


column.  See "columne."


columne                          frequency:    2   relative frequency: 0.00002
      p.  46 EPIGRAMS 60      2 An obeliske, or columne to thy name,
      p.  60 EPIGRAMS 93      1 How like a columne, RADCLIFFE, left
                                alone


comaund                          frequency:    1   relative frequency: 0.00001
      p. 422 UNGATHERED 50     9 The mayne comaund of scepters, soone doth perishe


comb.  See "combe."


combe                            frequency:    1   relative frequency: 0.00001
      p. 204 UNDERWOOD 43    38 A paire of Scisars, and a Combe in verse;


combes                           frequency:    1   relative frequency: 0.00001
      p. 165 UNDERWOOD 15   111 When not his Combes, his Curling-irons, his
                                Glasse,


combines                         frequency:    1   relative frequency: 0.00001
      p. 110 FOREST 11       49 That falls like sleepe on louers, and combines


combs.  See "combes."


come                             frequency:   68   relative frequency: 0.00098
      See also "come>," "new-come," "ouer-come,"
                "over-come."
     *p. 492 TO HIMSELF       1 Come leaue the lothed stage,
      p.  30 EPIGRAMS 12      7 The quarter day is come; the hostesse sayes,
      p.  32 EPIGRAMS 18      5 And mine come nothing like. I hope so. Yet,
      p.  38 EPIGRAMS 37      2 But as they come, on both sides he takes fees,
      p.  56 EPIGRAMS 88      4 And shooe, and tye, and garter should come
                                hether,
      p.  59 EPIGRAMS 92     14 For twelue yeeres yet to come, what each state
                                lacks.
      p.  64 EPIGRAMS 101     5 With those that come; whose grace may make that
                                seeme
      p.  64 EPIGRAMS 99      8 The selfe-same deeds, as diuersly they come,
      p.  65 EPIGRAMS 101    17 Ile tell you of more, and lye, so you will come:
      p.  68 EPIGRAMS 107     1 Doe what you come for, Captayne, with your
                                newes;
      p.  69 EPIGRAMS 107    31 Come, be not angrie, you are HVNGRY; eate;
      p.  69 EPIGRAMS 107    32 Doe what you come for Captayne, There's your
                                meate.
      p.  74 EPIGRAMS 115    11 Can come from Tripoly, leape stooles, and winke,
      p.  75 EPIGRAMS 117     1 GROYNE, come of age, his state sold out of
                                hand
      p.  81 EPIGRAMS 129     8 The very call, to make all others come:
      p.  89 EPIGRAMS 133   178 And stayes but till you come vnto the dore!
      p.  94 FOREST 2        42 Fig, grape, and quince, each in his time doth
                                come:
      p.  94 FOREST 2        48 But all come in, the farmer, and the clowne:
      p.  98 FOREST 3        53 The rout of rurall folke come thronging in,
      p. 102 FOREST 5         1 Come my CELIA, let vs proue,
      p. 115 FOREST 12       80 Shall thronging come, and boast the happy place
      p. 129 UNDERWOOD 1.2   28 But, I'le come in,
      p. 132 UNDERWOOD 2.2    8 Marke of glorie, come with me;
      p. 143 UNDERWOOD 3      1 Come, with our Voyces, let us warre,
      p. 151 UNDERWOOD 11    14 As since he dares not come within my sight.
      p. 162 UNDERWOOD 15     2 Beates braue, and loude in Europe, and bids come
      p. 170 UNDERWOOD 18    21 If it be thus; Come Love, and Fortune goe,
      p. 179 UNDERWOOD 25    42 Pyracmon's houre will come to give them ease,
      p. 182 UNDERWOOD 27    34 Come short of all this learned throng,
      p. 185 UNDERWOOD 31     2 Lawes, and no change e're come to one decree:
      p. 186 UNDERWOOD 32    14 They will come of, and scape the Punishment.
      p. 189 UNDERWOOD 36     1 Come, let us here enjoy the shade,
      p. 198 UNDERWOOD 40    33 Is fix'd upon one leg, and dares not come
```

come (cont.)
p. 198	UNDERWOOD 40	35	Like the dull wearied Crane that (come on land)
p. 199	UNDERWOOD 41	12	Winter is come a Quarter e're his Time,
p. 199	UNDERWOOD 41	19	And so I spare it. Come what can become
p. 205	UNDERWOOD 43	65	The Talmud, and the Alcoran had come,
p. 210	UNDERWOOD 43	161	Foole, wilt thou let that in example come?
p. 214	UNDERWOOD 44	58	Come to their Schooles,) show 'hem the use of Guns;
p. 229	UNDERWOOD 54	15	It doe not come: One piece I have in store,
p. 231	UNDERWOOD 57	20	Will come at the Court,
p. 232	UNDERWOOD 57	23	will come to the Table,
p. 241	UNDERWOOD 69	8	Nor dares he come in the comparison.
p. 242	UNDERWOOD 69	17	Some of his formes, he lets him not come neere
p. 253	UNDERWOOD 75	44	On all that come her Simplesse to rebuke!
p. 259	UNDERWOOD 76	13	For done service, and to come:
p. 277	U'WOOD 84.4	1	Painter, yo'are come, but may be gone,
p. 279	U'WOOD 84.4	43	It selfe to us, and come so nigh
p. 283	U'WOOD 84.9	47	And Goates together, whither they must come
p. 284	U'WOOD 84.9	57	Must come to take a sentence, by the sense
p. 285	U'WOOD 84.9	103	Thither, you hope to come; and there to find
p. 291	UNDERWOOD 85	61	Among these Cates how glad the sight doth come
p. 309	HORACE 2	76	And come not too much wrested. What's that thing,
p. 317	HORACE 2	246	With sloth, yet greedy still of what's to come:
p. 317	HORACE 2	273	To have a God come in; except a knot
p. 323	HORACE 2	378	More slow, and come more weightie to the eare:
p. 325	HORACE 2	426	But fame of Poets, they thinke, if they come forth,
p. 331	HORACE 2	551	Or Pleader at the Barre, that may come short
p. 333	HORACE 2	595	Him that is last, I scorne to come behind,
p. 364	UNGATHERED 5	2	For other formes come short all
p. 378	UNGATHERED 11	86	Come forth thou bonnie bouncing booke then, daughter
p. 391	UNGATHERED 26	40	Sent forth, or since did from their ashes come.
p. 397	UNGATHERED 30	28	Or Rurall Virgil come, to pipe to vs!
p. 401	UNGATHERED 32	16	If, maymed, she come off, 'tis not of men
p. 404	UNGATHERED 34	62	The Scene! the Engyne! but he now is come
p. 416	UNGATHERED 45	2	I am come to Add, and speake,
p. 420	UNGATHERED 48	26	And come fforth worthie Ivye, or the Bayes,
p. 422	UNGATHERED 50	4	whom fortune hath deprest; come nere the fates

come>   frequency: 1   relative frequency: 0.00001
| p. 238 | UNDERWOOD 65 | 8 | Thee quickly <come> the gardens eye to bee, |

comedie   frequency: 1   relative frequency: 0.00001
| p. 311 | HORACE 2 | 132 | Yet, sometime, doth the Comedie excite |

comedy. See "comedie," "ccmcedie," "comoedy."

comelie   frequency: 1   relative frequency: 0.00001
| p. 190 | UNDERWOOD 37 | 20 | And seeke to scant her comelie libertie, |

comely   frequency: 2   relative frequency: 0.00002
See also "comelie."
| p. 157 | UNDERWOOD 13 | 150 | Shoot forth in smooth and comely spaces; have |
| p. 287 | U'WOOD 84.9 | 166 | Mov'd by the wind, so comely moved she. |

comends   frequency: 1   relative frequency: 0.00001
| p. 417 | UNGATHERED 45 | 12 | The Moone comends hir |

comes   frequency: 14   relative frequency: 0.00020
p. 76	EPIGRAMS 118	6	Lust it comes out, that gluttony went in.
p. 78	EPIGRAMS 121	2	My lighter comes, to kisse thy learned Muse;
p. 95	FOREST 2	61	Where comes no guest, but is allow'd to eate,
p. 103	FOREST 6	5	Kisse againe: no creature comes.
p. 133	UNDERWOOD 2.3	20	But the Pittie comes too late.
p. 157	UNDERWOOD 13	138	Are nothing till that comes to bind and shut.
p. 164	UNDERWOOD 15	81	And comes by these Degrees, the Stile t<o>'inherit
p. 197	UNDERWOOD 40	2	Till the sower Minute comes of taking leave,
p. 225	UNDERWOOD 51	2	How comes it all things so about the<e> smile?
p. 240	UNDERWOOD 67	28	Comes in the pompe, and glorie
p. 291	UNDERWOOD 85	44	Against the Husband comes home tir'd;
p. 307	HORACE 2	30	Thy labouring wheele, comes scarce a Pitcher out?
p. 321	HORACE 2	354	There comes sometimes to things of meanest place.
p. 666	INSCRIPTS. 11	10	To make these good, and what comes after, better./

comest. See "comm'st," "com'st."

comfort   frequency: 6   relative frequency: 0.00008
     p.   33 EPIGRAMS 22   8 In comfort of her mothers teares,
     p. 118 FOREST 13   68 Right, the right way: yet must your comfort bee
     p. 130 UNDERWOOD 1.3   19 What comfort by him doe wee winne,
     p. 286 U'WOOD 84.9   131 By light, and comfort of spirituall Grace,
     p. 287 U'WOOD 84.9   184 Of divine Comfort, when sh'had talk'd with God.
     p. 411 UNGATHERED 40   13 The comfort of weake Christians,

comforted   frequency: 1   relative frequency: 0.00001
     p. 270 UNDERWOOD 83   57 Then comforted her Lord! and blest her Sonne!

comforter   frequency: 1   relative frequency: 0.00001
     p. 128 UNDERWOOD 1.1   26 Father and Sonne; the Comforter, inbreeding

comforts   frequency: 1   relative frequency: 0.00001
     p. 384 UNGATHERED 18   19 So, may those Mariage-Pledges, comforts proue:

comic. See "Comick."

comick   frequency: 4   relative frequency: 0.00005
    *p. 493 TO HIMSELF   37 With their foule comick socks;
     p.   72 EPIGRAMS 112   8 Tragick, or Comick; but thou writ'st the play.
     p. 311 HORACE 2   121 The Comick matter will not be exprest
     p. 409 UNGATHERED 38   7 By obseruation of those Comick Lawes

coming. See "comming."

comings. See "commings."

command   frequency: 13   relative frequency: 0.00018
     See also "comaund."
   **p. 116 PANEGYRE   121 He knew, that those, who would, with loue,
                                    command,
     p.   98 FOREST 3   68 The furie of a rash command,
     p. 154 UNDERWOOD 13   53 Now dam'mee, Sir, if you shall not command
     p. 155 UNDERWOOD 13   84 Now, but command; make tribute, what was gift;
     p. 180 UNDERWOOD 25   62 Doth now command;
     p. 180 UNDERWOOD 26   16 True valour doth her owne renowne command
     p. 187 UNDERWOOD 33   26 As if the generall store thou didst command
     p. 194 UNDERWOOD 38   114 Publike affaires command me now to goe
     p. 228 UNDERWOOD 53   2 Provoke his mettall, and command his force
     p. 329 HORACE 2   503 Be briefe, in what thou wouldst command, that so
     p. 333 HORACE 2   600 Or great in money's out at use, command
     p. 367 UNGATHERED 6   50 (Charles Montioy) whose command
     p. 370 UNGATHERED 7   8 So bold, as shewes your Art you can command.

commandements   frequency: 1   relative frequency: 0.00001
     p. 287 U'WOOD 84.9   172 T<o>'obey, and serve her sweet Commandements.

commanding   frequency: 1   relative frequency: 0.00001
     p. 168 UNDERWOOD 15   181 That by commanding first thy selfe, thou mak'st

commandments. See "commandements."

commands   frequency: 4   relative frequency: 0.00005
     p.   51 EPIGRAMS 74   4 That no affection in thy voyce commands;
     p.   83 EPIGRAMS 132   8 Before my thought, and (in thy right) commands
     p. 192 UNDERWOOD 38   38 Your just commands; yet those, not I, be lost.
     p. 292 UNDERWOOD 86   7 Too stubborne for Commands so slack:

commend   frequency: 6   relative frequency: 0.00008
     p.   83 EPIGRAMS 132   1 If to admire were to commend, my praise
     p.   95 FOREST 2   54 By their ripe daughters, whom they would commend
     p. 163 UNDERWOOD 15   48 To have his Court-bred-fillie there commend
     p. 230 UNDERWOOD 56   20 And can for other Graces her commend,
     p. 370 UNGATHERED 7   4 All which are parts commend the cunning hand;
     p. 386 UNGATHERED 20   8 And therefore I commend vnto the Wife,

commended   frequency: 2   relative frequency: 0.00002
     p. 201 UNDERWOOD 42   69 Commended the French-hood, and Scarlet gowne
     p. 408 UNGATHERED 37   1 My verses were commended, thou dar'st say,

commender   frequency: 1   relative frequency: 0.00001
     p. 317 HORACE 2   247 Froward, complaining, a commender glad

commending   frequency: 1   relative frequency: 0.00001
     p. 365 UNGATHERED 5   16 All Nature of commending.

commends   frequency: 1   relative frequency: 0.00001
     See also "comends."

commends (cont.)
    p. 386 UNGATHERED 21   8 This thy worke forth: that iudgment mine
                              commends.

commentaries   frequency: 1   relative frequency: 0.00001
    p. 71 EPIGRAMS 110   t2 CAESARS Commentaries obserued, and
                              translated.

comming   frequency: 13   relative frequency: 0.00018
    p. 66 EPIGRAMS 102   17 That art so reuerenc'd, as thy comming in,
    p. 73 EPIGRAMS 113   5 I thinke, the Fate of court thy comming crau'd,
    p. 86 EPIGRAMS 133   85 But, comming neere, they found it but a liter,
    p. 153 UNDERWOOD 13   23 They are so long a comming, and so hard;
    p. 188 UNDERWOOD 35   5 And, till the comming of the Soule
    p. 213 UNDERWOOD 44   19 And comming home, to tell what acts were done
    p. 242 UNDERWOOD 69   20 To judge; So all men comming neere can spie.
    p. 242 UNDERWOOD 70   2 Thy comming forth in that great yeare,
    p. 249 UNDERWOOD 72   16 On th'often comming of this Holy-day:
    p. 274 U'WOOD 84.1   35 As comming with his Harpe, prepar'd
    p. 317 HORACE 2   250 Mans comming yeares much good with them doe
                              bring:
    p. 362 UNGATHERED 2   9 For, as one comming with a laterall viewe,
    p. 375 UNGATHERED 10   28 Here, finer then comming from his Punke you him
                              see,

commings   frequency: 1   relative frequency: 0.00001
    p. 161 UNDERWOOD 14   80 Among my commings in, and see it mount,

commission   frequency: 4   relative frequency: 0.00005
   *p. 492 TO HIMSELF   8 Commission of the braine
    p. 108 FOREST 10   28 My Muse vp by commission: No, I bring
    p. 155 UNDERWOOD 13   64 Or stands to be'<i>n Commission o' the blade?
    p. 220 UNDERWOOD 48   5 And seale thee thy Commission:

commit   frequency: 7   relative frequency: 0.00010
  **p. 113 PANEGYRE   10 Where men commit blacke incest with their faults;
    p. 48 EPIGRAMS 65   3 Made me commit most fierce idolatrie
    p. 75 EPIGRAMS 116   15 Them in, if not, from thee; or must commit
    p. 109 FOREST 11   15 Will quickly taste the treason, and commit
    p. 190 UNDERWOOD 37   7 Not like your Countrie-neighbours, that commit
    p. 391 UNGATHERED 26   28 I should commit thee surely with thy peeres,
    p. 405 UNGATHERED 34   82 Discouer Vice? Commit Absurdity?

commixt   frequency: 1   relative frequency: 0.00001
    p. 284 U'WOOD 84.9   53 Like single; so, there is a third, commixt,

commoditie   frequency: 4   relative frequency: 0.00005
    p. 30 EPIGRAMS 12   13 Then takes vp fresh commoditie, for dayes;
    p. 165 UNDERWOOD 15   86 They're growne Commoditie upon Exchange;
    p. 229 UNDERWOOD 54   6 An ill commoditie! 'T must make good weight.
    p. 241 UNDERWOOD 69   7 His is more safe commoditie, or none:

commodity. See "commoditie."

common   frequency: 16   relative frequency: 0.00023
See also "comon."
   *p. 493 TO HIMSELF   25 Throwne forth, and rak't into the common tub,
    p. 41 EPIGRAMS 43   11 From seruile flatterie (common Poets shame)
    p. 46 EPIGRAMS 60   6 And proud, my worke shall out-last common deeds,
    p. 103 FOREST 6   3 When the common courting iay
    p. 105 FOREST 8   41 And, for thee, at common game,
    p. 111 FOREST 11   79 Or those, who doubt the common mouth of fame,
    p. 116 FOREST 12   88 Or common places, filch'd, that take these times,
    p. 121 FOREST 14   31 Nor can a little of the common store,
    p. 174 UNDERWOOD 23   5 It is the common Moath,
    p. 194 UNDERWOOD 38   119 Others by common Stars their courses run,
    p. 214 UNDERWOOD 44   31 But give them over to the common eare
    p. 271 UNDERWOOD 83   93 T<o>'escape this common knowne necessitie,
    p. 307 HORACE 2   67 Most worthie praise, when words that common grew,
    p. 313 HORACE 2   183 'Tis hard, to speake things common, properly:
    p. 313 HORACE 2   187 Yet common matter thou thine owne maist make,
    p. 400 UNGATHERED 32   5 Such, as the creeping common Pioners vse

common-law   frequency: 1   relative frequency: 0.00001
    p. 211 UNDERWOOD 43   177 At Common-Law: me thinkes in his despight

common-wealth   frequency: 3   relative frequency: 0.00004
    p. 66 EPIGRAMS 102   20 The common-wealth still safe, must studie thee.
    p. 210 UNDERWOOD 43   170 And didst invade part of the Common-wealth,
    p. 416 UNGATHERED 43   8 And doe both Church, and Common-wealth the
                              good,

comm'st   frequency: 1   relative frequency: 0.00001
    p. 187 UNDERWOOD 33   29 So comm'st thou like a Chiefe into the Court,

communion   frequency: 1   relative frequency: 0.00001
    p. 221 UNDERWOOD 48   43 Be it he hold Communion

communitie   frequency: 1   relative frequency: 0.00001
    p. 110 FOREST 11   54 Preserues communitie.

community. See "communitie."

comoedie   frequency: 1   relative frequency: 0.00001
    p. 321 HORACE 2   365 To these succeeded the old Comoedie,

comoedy   frequency: 1   relative frequency: 0.00001
    p. 323 HORACE 2   410 Or 'twere the gowned Comoedy they taught.

comon   frequency: 1   relative frequency: 0.00001
    p. 408 UNGATHERED 36 13 That sit vpon ye Comon Draught: or Strand!

companie   frequency: 6   relative frequency: 0.00008
    p. 56 EPIGRAMS 88   8 As french-men in his companie, should seeme
                             dutch?
    p. 64 EPIGRAMS 101   2 Doe equally desire your companie:
    p. 164 UNDERWOOD 15   79 For these with her young Companie shee'll enter,
    p. 191 UNDERWOOD 38   25 By naming in what companie 'twas in,
    p. 218 UNDERWOOD 47   20 Of any Companie but that they are in,
    p. 224 UNDERWOOD 50   25 For you admit no companie, but good,

companies   frequency: 1   relative frequency: 0.00001
    p. 165 UNDERWOOD 15   91 Or use all arts, or haunt all Companies

companions   frequency: 1   relative frequency: 0.00001
    p. 118 FOREST 13   56 Without companions? 'Tis safe to haue none.

company   frequency: 2   relative frequency: 0.00002
    See also "companie," "company'."
    p. 40 EPIGRAMS 42   5 By his free will, be in IONES company.
    p. 231 UNDERWOOD 56   23 Away ill company, and helpe in rime

company'   frequency: 1   relative frequency: 0.00001
    p. 74 EPIGRAMS 115   8 By speaking well o' the company' it 's in.

compar'd   frequency: 1   relative frequency: 0.00001
    p. 285 U'WOOD 84.9   106 Compar'd unto that long eternitie,

compare   frequency: 2   relative frequency: 0.00002
    p. 238 UNDERWOOD 66   12 To compare small with great, as still we owe
    p. 406 UNGATHERED 34 98 That might compare wth thee? what story shall

comparison   frequency: 4   relative frequency: 0.00005
    p. 67 EPIGRAMS 104   9 Or, more then borne for the comparison
    p. 202 UNDERWOOD 42   76 Any Comparison had with his Cheap-side.
    p. 241 UNDERWOOD 69   8 Nor dares he come in the comparison.
    p. 391 UNGATHERED 26 38 Leaue thee alone, for the comparison

compass. See "compasse."

compasse   frequency: 2   relative frequency: 0.00002
    p. 159 UNDERWOOD 14   31 And like a Compasse keeping one foot still
    p. 227 UNDERWOOD 52   10 Which if in compasse of no Art it came

compassed. See "well-compass'd."

compassion   frequency: 2   relative frequency: 0.00002
    p. 127 UNDERWOOD 1.1 14 And take compassion on my grievous plight.
    p. 192 UNDERWOOD 38   40 Of your compassion; Parents should be mild:

compassionate   frequency: 1   relative frequency: 0.00001
  **p. 116 PANEGYRE   108 "For Right is as compassionate as wise.

compeeres   frequency: 1   relative frequency: 0.00001
    p. 248 UNDERWOOD 71   5 Want, with the rest of his conceal'd compeeres,

compeers. See "compeeres."

compell'd   frequency: 1   relative frequency: 0.00001
  **p. 116 PANEGYRE   127 When they are led, then when they are compell'd.

compil'd   frequency: 1   relative frequency: 0.00001
     p. 203 UNDERWOOD 43   29 Had I compil'd from Amadis de Gaule,

complain. See "complaine."

complaine   frequency: 2   relative frequency: 0.00002
     p. 122 FOREST 15   23 Yet dare I not complaine, or wish for death
     p. 168 UNDERWOOD 15   183 That fortune never make thee to complaine,

complaines   frequency: 2   relative frequency: 0.00002
     p. 110 FOREST 11   27 Whereof the loyall conscience so complaines.
     p. 311 HORACE 2   135 Complaines in humble phrase. Both Telephus,

complaining   frequency: 1   relative frequency: 0.00001
     p. 317 HORACE 2   247 Froward, complaining, a commender glad

complains. See "complaines."

compleat   frequency: 1   relative frequency: 0.00001
     p. 284 U'WOOD 84.9   72 That she is in, or, make it more compleat?

complement   frequency: 1   relative frequency: 0.00001
     p. 270 UNDERWOOD 83   66 To carry, and conduct the Complement

complete. See "compleat."

complexion   frequency: 1   relative frequency: 0.00001
     p. 118 FOREST 13   70 For truthes complexion, where they all weare
                              maskes.

complexions   frequency: 1   relative frequency: 0.00001
     p. 46 EPIGRAMS 62   6 Or your complexions losse? you haue a pot,

compos'd   frequency: 2   relative frequency: 0.00002
     p. 112 FOREST 11   99 A body so harmoniously compos'd,
     p. 370 UNGATHERED 8   3 (Compos'd of Gamester, Captaine, Knight,
                              Knight's man,

compose   frequency: 2   relative frequency: 0.00002
     p. 261 UNDERWOOD 77   18 To compose men, and manners; stint the strife
     p. 401 UNGATHERED 33   7 Who did this Knot compose,

comprehend. See "comprhend."

comprhend   frequency: 1   relative frequency: 0.00001
     p. 402 UNGATHERED 34   13 Vizors or Anticks? or it comprhend

compriseth   frequency: 1   relative frequency: 0.00001
     p. 134 UNDERWOOD 2.4   12 All that Loves world compriseth!

compromise   frequency: 1   relative frequency: 0.00001
     p. 218 UNDERWOOD 47   8 Put conscience and my right to compromise.

compting   frequency: 1   relative frequency: 0.00001
     p. 327 HORACE 2   466 A pound, or piece, by their long compting arts:

comptroller   frequency: 1   relative frequency: 0.00001
     p. 415 UNGATHERED 42   24 And a Comptroller, two most rigid men

com'st   frequency: 2   relative frequency: 0.00002
     p. 96 FOREST 3   7 Nor com'st to view the better cloth of state;
     p. 187 UNDERWOOD 33   35 Then com'st thou off with Victorie and Palme,

comvs   frequency: 1   relative frequency: 0.00001
     p. 98 FOREST 3   48 COMVS puts in, for new delights;

con   frequency: 1   relative frequency: 0.00001
     p. 59 EPIGRAMS 92   22 Are sure to con the catalogue by hart;

conceal. See "conceale."

conceal'd   frequency: 3   relative frequency: 0.00004
     p. 203 UNDERWOOD 43   21 Conceal'd, or kept there, that was fit to be,
     p. 248 UNDERWOOD 71   5 Want, with the rest of his conceal'd compeeres,
     p. 369 UNGATHERED 6   112 Conceal'd from all but cleare Propheticke eyes.

conceale   frequency: 4   relative frequency: 0.00005
     p. 38 EPIGRAMS 38   2 And to conceale your vlcers, did aduise,
     p. 197 UNDERWOOD 40   17 And must be bred, so to conceale his birth,
     p. 325 HORACE 2   427 And from the Barber Licinus conceale

conceale (cont.)
     p. 383 UNGATHERED 17   4 May aske, what Author would conceale his name?

concealed   frequency: 1   relative frequency: 0.00001
     See also "conceal'd."
  **p. 113 PANEGYRE   9 Into those darke and deepe concealed vaults,

conceales   frequency: 1   relative frequency: 0.00001
     p. 333 HORACE 2   622 For praises, where the mind conceales a foxe.

conceals. See "conceales."

conceipt   frequency: 4   relative frequency: 0.00005
     p. 170 UNDERWOOD 18   8 Crooked appeare; so that doth my conceipt:
     p. 183 UNDERWOOD 29   3 True Conceipt,
     p. 209 UNDERWOOD 43   145 But, others fell with that conceipt by the eares,
     p. 335 HORACE 2   663 Conceipt, and into burning Aetna leap'd.

conceit. See "conceipt."

conceits   frequency: 1   relative frequency: 0.00001
     p. 175 UNDERWOOD 23   23 They die with their conceits,

conceiu'd   frequency: 2   relative frequency: 0.00002
     p. 56 EPIGRAMS 88   12 By which his damme conceiu'd him, clothes and
                                     all?
     p. 122 FOREST 15   18 Conceiu'd in sinne, and vnto labour borne,

conceiv'd   frequency: 2   relative frequency: 0.00002
     See also "conceiu'd," "conceyud."
     p. 208 UNDERWOOD 43   112 With lust conceiv'd thee; Father thou hadst
                                     none:
     p. 282 U'WOOD 84.9   3 The Spirit that I wrote with, and conceiv'd;

conceive   frequency: 4   relative frequency: 0.00005
     p. 152 UNDERWOOD 12   32 Now I conceive him by my want,
     p. 187 UNDERWOOD 33   14 Have made me to conceive a Lawyer new.
     p. 197 UNDERWOOD 40   1 That Love's a bitter sweet, I ne're conceive
     p. 286 U'WOOD 84.9   147 Nor dare we under blasphemy conceive

conceiv'st   frequency: 1   relative frequency: 0.00001
     p. 201 UNDERWOOD 42   50 But when thy Wife (as thou conceiv'st) is brave?

concern. See "concerne."

concerne   frequency: 1   relative frequency: 0.00001
     p. 85 EPIGRAMS 133   42 Of some Bride-well, and may, in time, concerne
                                     vs

conceyud   frequency: 1   relative frequency: 0.00001
     p. 405 UNGATHERED 34   90 Thy twice conceyud, thrice payd for Imagery?

conclude   frequency: 4   relative frequency: 0.00005
     p. 39 EPIGRAMS 40   15 Fate, in a brother. To conclude,
     p. 177 UNDERWOOD 25   24 Who would with judgement search, searching
                                     conclude
     p. 211 UNDERWOOD 43   190 But I'le conclude all in a civill curse.
     p. 339 HORACE 1   31 Heare me conclude ... .

concluded   frequency: 2   relative frequency: 0.00002
     p. 229 UNDERWOOD 54   5 Who, when shee heard the match, concluded
                                     streight,
     p. 415 UNGATHERED 42   30 Concluded from a Carract to a dramme.

conclusion   frequency: 1   relative frequency: 0.00001
     p. 323 HORACE 2   396 But, in conclusion, merited no fame.

concord   frequency: 2   relative frequency: 0.00002
     p. 40 EPIGRAMS 42   17 The selfe-same things, a note of concord be:
     p. 384 UNGATHERED 18   17 So, be yor Concord, still, as deepe, as mute;

concurreth   frequency: 1   relative frequency: 0.00001
     p. 40 EPIGRAMS 42   15 In all affections shee concurreth still.

condemn   frequency: 1   relative frequency: 0.00001
     See also "condemne."
    *p. 492 TO HIMSELF   9 Run on, and rage, sweat, censure, and condemn:

condemn'd   frequency: 2   relative frequency: 0.00002
     p. 29 EPIGRAMS 8   2 RIDWAY was tane, arraign'd, condemn'd to
                                     dye;

condemn'd (cont.)
    p. 205 UNDERWOOD 43   54 Condemn'd me to the Ovens with the pies;

condemne   frequency: 2   relative frequency: 0.00002
    p. 142 UNDERWOOD 2.9 47 Nor o're-praise, nor yet condemne;
    p. 211 UNDERWOOD 43 183 Condemne him to the Brick-kills, or some Hill-

condition   frequency: 2   relative frequency: 0.00002
    p. 101 FOREST 4   54 Our fraile condition it is such,
    p. 220 UNDERWOOD 48   6 But 'tis with a condition,

conditions   frequency: 1   relative frequency: 0.00001
    p. 133 UNDERWOOD 2.3   5 And would on Conditions, be

conduct   frequency: 2   relative frequency: 0.00002
    p. 160 UNDERWOOD 14 51 And then of times (besides the bare Conduct
    p. 270 UNDERWOOD 83 66 To carry, and conduct the Complement

conduits. See "water-conduits."

coney   frequency: 2   relative frequency: 0.00002
    p. 65 EPIGRAMS 101 13 Limons, and wine for sauce: to these, a coney
    p. 231 UNDERWOOD 57 22 No Plover, or Coney

coneyes   frequency: 1   relative frequency: 0.00001
    p. 94 FOREST 2   25 Each banke doth yeeld thee coneyes; and the topps

confer. See "conferre."

conferre   frequency: 1   relative frequency: 0.00001
    p. 83 EPIGRAMS 132   6 Since they can only iudge, that can conferre.

conferring   frequency: 1 relative frequency: 0.00001
    p. 396 UNGATHERED 30 10 Without conferring symboles. This's my day.

confess   frequency: 1   relative frequency: 0.00001
    See also "confesse."
    p. 406 UNGATHERED 34 91 And not fall downe before it? and confess

confesse   frequency: 13   elative frequency: 0.00018
    p. 72 EPIGRAMS 111   7 Which all, but ignorant Captaynes, will
                             confesse:
    p. 73 EPIGRAMS 112 19 And neuer art encounter'd, I confesse:
    p. 137 UNDERWOOD 2.5 39 I confesse all, I replide,
    p. 140 UNDERWOOD 2.9   5 Titles, I confesse, doe take me;
    p. 159 UNDERWOOD 14 19 Though I confesse (as every Muse hath err'd,
    p. 189 UNDERWOOD 37   6 But must confesse from whom what gift I tooke.
    p. 190 UNDERWOOD 37 18 In friendship, I confesse: But, deare friend,
                             heare.
    p. 227 UNDERWOOD 52   8 To square my Circle, I confesse; but draw
    p. 329 HORACE 2   537 But, I confesse, that, in a long worke, sleepe
    p. 370 UNGATHERED 7   6 Will well confesse; presenting, limiting,
    p. 390 UNGATHERED 26   3 While I confesse thy writings to be such,
    p. 397 UNGATHERED 30 45 And caried, though with shoute, and noyse,
                             confesse
    p. 400 UNGATHERED 32   7 Though I confesse a Beaumonts Booke to bee

confessed. See "confest."

confessing   frequency: 1   relative frequency: 0.00001
    p. 191 UNDERWOOD 38 23 Or in confessing of the Crime be nice,

confession   frequency: 1   relative frequency: 0.00001
   **p. 117 PANEGYRE   155 And this confession flew from euery voyce:

confest   frequency: 1   relative frequency: 0.00001
    p. 32 EPIGRAMS 16   1 HARDIE, thy braine is valiant, 'tis confest,

confident   frequency: 1   relative frequency: 0.00001
    p. 194 UNDERWOOD 38 113 You would be then most confident, that tho

confine   frequency: 1   relative frequency: 0.00001
    p. 211 UNDERWOOD 43 179 But to confine him to the Brew-houses,

confining   frequency: 1   relative frequency: 0.00001
    p. 276 U'WOOD 84.3 24 And Paradise confining these.

confirm'd   frequency: 1   relative frequency: 0.00001
    p. 49 EPIGRAMS 67 11 Which, by no lesse confirm'd, then thy kings
                             choice,

confus'd   frequency: 1   relative frequency: 0.00001
    p. 127 UNDERWOOD 1.1   7 As my heart lies in peeces, all confus'd,

confused   frequency: 1   relative frequency: 0.00001
    See also "confus'd."
    p. 84 EPIGRAMS 133   10 Subtly distinguish'd, was confused here.

confutes   frequency: 1   relative frequency: 0.00001
    p. 375 UNGATHERED 10   23 A Rabbin confutes him with the Bastinado.

conies. See "coneyes."

coniures   frequency: 1   relative frequency: 0.00001
    p. 108 FOREST 10 A   14 and Coniures all my faculties t<o>'approue

coniuring   frequency: 1   relative frequency: 0.00001
    p. 107 FOREST 10   11 To raise my spirits with thy coniuring wine,

conjectures   frequency: 1   relative frequency: 0.00001
    p. 160 UNDERWOOD 14   50 Conjectures retriv'd! And a Storie now

conjures. See "coniures."

conjuring. See "coniuring."

connexion   frequency: 1   relative frequency: 0.00001
    p. 321 HORACE 2   353 Of Order, and Connexion; so much grace

conquer   frequency: 3   relative frequency: 0.00004
    p. 49 EPIGRAMS 66   10 Could conquer thee, but chance, who did betray.
    p. 173 UNDERWOOD 22   7 And draw, and conquer all mens love,
    p. 224 UNDERWOOD 50   4 To conquer rumour, and triumph on spight;

conquer'd   frequency: 2   relative frequency: 0.00002
    p. 39 EPIGRAMS 40   12 Conquer'd hath both life and it.
    p. 319 HORACE 2   295 But, as they conquer'd, and enlarg'd their bound,

conquering. See "conqu'ring."

conquers   frequency: 2   relative frequency: 0.00002
    p. 31 EPIGRAMS 14   12 Which conquers all, be once ouer-come by thee.
    p. 367 UNGATHERED 6   56 And conquers all things, yea it selfe, at length.

conqu'ring   frequency: 1   relative frequency: 0.00001
    p. 311 HORACE 2   115 The conqu'ring Champion, the prime Horse in
                             course,

conscience   frequency: 18   relative frequency: 0.00026
    p. 48 EPIGRAMS 64   14 As her owne conscience, still, the same reward.
    p. 52 EPIGRAMS 74   8 As is thy conscience, which is alwayes one:
    p. 63 EPIGRAMS 98   10 And studie conscience, more then thou would'st
                             fame.
    p. 76 EPIGRAMS 119   14 Which is to liue to conscience, not to show.
    p. 110 FOREST 11   27 Whereof the loyall conscience so complaines.
    p. 111 FOREST 11   83 Nor meane we those, whom vowes and conscience
    p. 113 FOREST 12   4 And, for it, life, conscience, yea, soules are
                             giuen,
    p. 118 FOREST 13   69 Your conscience, and not wonder, if none askes
    p. 154 UNDERWOOD 13   46 Run from the Conscience of it, if they could.
    p. 168 UNDERWOOD 15   178 Not wound thy conscience, when thy body bleeds;
    p. 185 UNDERWOOD 31   3 So, may the King proclaime your Conscience is
    p. 218 UNDERWOOD 47   8 Put conscience and my right to compromise.
    p. 224 UNDERWOOD 50   14 Who (herein studying conscience, and not fame)
    p. 273 U'WOOD 84.1   7 By THEE, and CONSCIENCE, both who
                             thrive
    p. 284 U'WOOD 84.9   58 Of that great Evidence, the Conscience!
    p. 289 U'WOOD 84.9   222 In the discerning of each conscience, so!
    p. 372 UNGATHERED 9   11 Wth Rites not bound, but conscience. Wouldst
                             thou All?
    p. 411 UNGATHERED 40   7 The Peace of Conscience,

consciences   frequency: 1   relative frequency: 0.00001
    p. 84 EPIGRAMS 133   18 Lash'd by their consciences, to die, affeard.

conscious   frequency: 1   relative frequency: 0.00001
    p. 149 UNDERWOOD 9   11 Oh, but my conscious feares,

consecrate   frequency: 1   relative frequency: 0.00001
    p. 256 UNDERWOOD 75   130 Which to this use, wert built and consecrate!

consent
                              frequency: 4   relative frequency: 0.00005
  **p. 114 PANEGYRE   59 That did not beare a part in this consent
    p. 200 UNDERWOOD 42   19 But then consent, your Daughters and your
                             Wives,
    p. 253 UNDERWOOD 75   16 By all the Spheares consent, so in the heart of
                             June?
    p. 411 UNGATHERED 40   12 by Consent.

consented
                              frequency: 1   relative frequency: 0.00001
    p. 77 EPIGRAMS 120   18 They all consented;

consider
                              frequency: 2   relative frequency: 0.00002
    p. 47 EPIGRAMS 63   1 Who can consider thy right courses run,
    p. 148 UNDERWOOD 8   1 Doe but consider this small dust,

consisting
                              frequency: 2   relative frequency: 0.00002
    p. 272 UNDERWOOD 84   t8 Consisting of these Ten Pieces.

consists
                              frequency: 1   relative frequency: 0.00001
    p. 87 EPIGRAMS 133   129 One said, the other swore, the world consists.

consolatorie
                              frequency: 1   relative frequency: 0.00001
    p. 235 UNDERWOOD 63   t3 An Epigram Consolatorie.

consolatory. See "consolatorie."

consort
                              frequency: 1   relative frequency: 0.00001
    p. 423 UNGATHERED 50   18 Virtue, and Soveraigntie, they not consort./

conspicuous
                              frequency: 1   relative frequency: 0.00001
  **p. 115 PANEGYRE   78 "Are here on earth the most conspicuous things:

conspire
                              frequency: 3   relative frequency: 0.00004
    p. 119 FOREST 13   119 And that your soules conspire, as they were gone
    p. 219 UNDERWOOD 47   37 I wish all well, and pray high heaven conspire
    p. 333 HORACE 2   586 And friendly should unto one end conspire.

constable
                              frequency: 2   relative frequency: 0.00002
    p. 374 UNGATHERED 10   17 Hee's carried like a Cripple, from Constable to
                             Constable.

constables
                              frequency: 1   relative frequency: 0.00001
    p. 182 UNDERWOOD 27   27 Or Constables Ambrosiack Muse

constancy
                              frequency: 1   relative frequency: 0.00001
    p. 108 FOREST 10A   10 only pursewinge Constancy, in Chainge;

constant
                              frequency: 2   relative frequency: 0.00002
    p. 47 EPIGRAMS 63   8 By constant suffring of thy equall mind;
    p. 171 UNDERWOOD 19   28 Is constant to be extraordinarie.

constellation
                              frequency: 1   relative frequency: 0.00001
    p. 392 UNGATHERED 26   76 Aduanc'd, and made a Constellation there!

constellations
                              frequency: 1   relative frequency: 0.00001
    p. 277 U'WOOD 84.3   27 Of Constellations 'bout her horld;

constrain. See "constraine."

constraine
                              frequency: 1   relative frequency: 0.00001
    p. 37 EPIGRAMS 35   3 Whose manners draw, more than thy powers
                             constraine.

consult
                              frequency: 1   relative frequency: 0.00001
    p. 140 UNDERWOOD 2.8   26 To consult, if Fucus this

consuming
                              frequency: 1   relative frequency: 0.00001
    p. 203 UNDERWOOD 43   17 I had deserv'd, then, thy consuming lookes,

consummate
                              frequency: 1   relative frequency: 0.00001
    p. 256 UNDERWOOD 75   122 And Bishop stay, to consummate the Rites:

consumption
                              frequency: 2   relative frequency: 0.00002
    p. 205 UNDERWOOD 43   58 To make consumption, ever, where thou go'st;
    p. 235 UNDERWOOD 61   17 Of riot, and consumption, knowes the way

consumptions
                              frequency: 1   relative frequency: 0.00001
    p. 192 UNDERWOOD 38   62 Consumptions nature to destroy, and sterve.

contagion   frequency: 1   relative frequency: 0.00001
    p. 118 FOREST 13   58 Contagion in the prease is soonest catch'd.

contain. See "containe."

containe   frequency: 1   relative frequency: 0.00001
    p. 305 HORACE 2   7 Could you containe your laughter? Credit mee,

contemn. See "contemne."

contemn'd   frequency: 1   relative frequency: 0.00001
    p. 47 EPIGRAMS 64   4 A treasure, art: contemn'd in th'age of gold.

contemne   frequency: 2   relative frequency: 0.00002
    p. 59 EPIGRAMS 92   39 Others more modest, but contemne vs too,
    p. 142 UNDERWOOD 2.9   48 Nor out-valew, nor contemne;

contemning   frequency: 1   relative frequency: 0.00001
    p. 313 HORACE 2   173 Sharpe, and contemning lawes, at him should aime,

contempt   frequency: 1   relative frequency: 0.00001
    p. 270 UNDERWOOD 83   47 How did she leave the world? with what contempt?

contend   frequency: 1   relative frequency: 0.00001
    p. 319 HORACE 2   319 Hee too, that did in Tragick Verse contend

contends   frequency: 1   relative frequency: 0.00001
    p. 48 EPIGRAMS 64   13 Contends t'haue worth enioy, from his regard,

content   frequency: 6   relative frequency: 0.00008
    p. 43 EPIGRAMS 53   3 Thou wert content the authors name to loose:
    p. 84 EPIGRAMS 133   19 Then let the former age, with this content her,
    p. 98 FOREST 3   65 And such since thou canst make thine owne
                               content,
    p. 133 UNDERWOOD 2.3   3 She content was to restore
    p. 166 UNDERWOOD 15   139 Of what he throwes: Like letchers growne content
    p. 407 UNGATHERED 35   20 Content thee to be Pancridge Earle ye whyle;

contented   frequency: 1   relative frequency: 0.00001
    p. 105 FOREST 8   13 'Pray thee, feed contented, then,

contention   frequency: 1   relative frequency: 0.00001
    p. 271 UNDERWOOD 83   95 And, but for that Contention, and brave strife

continent   frequency: 2   relative frequency: 0.00002
    p. 111 FOREST 11   71 Because they moue, the continent doth so:
    p. 111 FOREST 11   77 Such spirits as are onely continent,

continewall   frequency: 1   relative frequency: 0.00001
    p. 295 UNDERWOOD 90   4 A Soyle, not barren; a continewall fire;

continual. See "continewall," "continuall."

continuall   frequency: 1   relative frequency: 0.00001
    p. 110 FOREST 11   43 In a continuall tempest. Now, true Loue

continu'd   frequency: 2   relative frequency: 0.00002
    p. 57 EPIGRAMS 90   11 Still MILL continu'd: Nay, his face growing
                               worse,
    p. 409 UNGATHERED 38   t2 his continu'd Vertue) my louing Friend:

continue   frequency: 1   relative frequency: 0.00001
    p. 367 UNGATHERED 6   34 Continue thy sweete Song.

contract   frequency: 3   relative frequency: 0.00004
    p. 28 EPIGRAMS 5   1 When was there contract better driuen by Fate?
    p. 57 EPIGRAMS 89   11 And present worth in all dost so contract,
    p. 223 UNDERWOOD 49   30 In Contract twice, what can shee perjure more?

contrary   frequency: 1   relative frequency: 0.00001
    p. 76 EPIGRAMS 119   12 Treading a better path, not contrary;

contrite   frequency: 2   relative frequency: 0.00002
    p. 127 UNDERWOOD 1.1   15 What odour can be, then a heart contrite,
    p. 193 UNDERWOOD 38   89 The contrite Soule, who hath no thought to win

control. See "controll," "controule."

controll   frequency: 1   relative frequency: 0.00001
    p. 402 UNGATHERED 34   7 Controll Ctesibius: ouerbearing vs

controls. See "controules."

controule   frequency: 1   relative frequency: 0.00001
    p. 52 EPIGRAMS 76   15 The rock, the spindle, and the sheeres controule

controules   frequency: 1   relative frequency: 0.00001
    p. 108 FOREST 10 A   12 A farther fury my ray'sd spirit Controoules,

contumelie   frequency: 1   relative frequency: 0.00001
    p. 193 UNDERWOOD 38   100 Of Contumelie, and urge a good man more

contumely. See "contumelie."

conuert   frequency: 1   relative frequency: 0.00001
    p. 361 UNGATHERED 1   11 Whilst other soules conuert to base abuse

conuerted   frequency: 1   relative frequency: 0.00001
    p. 122 FOREST 15   10 First, midst, and last, conuerted one, and three;

conuerting   frequency: 1   relative frequency: 0.00001
    p. 375 UNGATHERED 10   21 He will expiate this sinne with conuerting the
                              Iewes.

conuict   frequency: 1   relative frequency: 0.00001
    p. 49 EPIGRAMS 68   1 PLAY-WRIGHT conuict of publike wrongs to
                              men,

conuince   frequency: 1   relative frequency: 0.00001
    p. 88 EPIGRAMS 133   152 But still, it seem'd, the ranknesse did conuince
                              'hem.

convert. See "conuert."

converted. See "conuerted."

converting. See "conuerting."

convict. See "conuict."

convince. See "conuince."

cony. See "coney."

coockold   frequency: 1   relative frequency: 0.00001
    p. 417 UNGATHERED 45   25 If there be a Coockold Maior,

cook. See "cooke."

cooke   frequency: 1   relative frequency: 0.00001
    p. 317 HORACE 2   265 Natur'd, and wicked Atreus cooke, to th'eye,

cookes   frequency: 1   relative frequency: 0.00001
    p. 88 EPIGRAMS 133   143 Your Fleet-lane Furies; and hot cookes doe
                              dwell,

cooks. See "cookes."

cool. See "coole."

coole   frequency: 2   relative frequency: 0.00002
    p. 97 FOREST 3   19 To some coole, courteous shade, which he calls
                              his,
    p. 368 UNGATHERED 6   76 There coole thy Plumes,

cop'ces   frequency: 1   relative frequency: 0.00001
    p. 97 FOREST 3   38 Of flowrie fields, of cop'ces greene,

copie   frequency: 2   relative frequency: 0.00002
    p. 247 UNDERWOOD 70   112 The Copie of his friend.
    p. 277 U'WOOD 84.3   30 A Copie of this peece; nor tell

copies   frequency: 1   relative frequency: 0.00001
    p. 263 UNDERWOOD 78   29 Allowes them? Then, what copies shall be had,

coppie   frequency: 1   relative frequency: 0.00001
    p. 400 UNGATHERED 31   40 And this a coppie is of the Record.

copp's   frequency: 2   relative frequency: 0.00002
    p. 94 FOREST 2   19 Thy copp's, too, nam'd of GAMAGE, thou hast
                              there,

copp's (cont.)
    p. 94 FOREST 2   26 Fertile of wood, ASHORE, and
                              SYDNEY'S copp's,

copse. See "copp's."

copses. See "cop'ces."

copy. See "copie," "coppie."

corals. See "corrals."

corbet   frequency: 2   relative frequency: 0.00002
    p. 151 UNDERWOOD 12   7 Deare Vincent Corbet, who so long
    p. 151 UNDERWOOD 12   t2 VINCENT CORBET.

cordoua   frequency: 1   relative frequency: 0.00001
    p. 391 UNGATHERED 26   35 Paccuuius, Accius, him of Cordoua dead,

cordova. See "cordoua."

coriat   frequency: 2   relative frequency: 0.00002
    p. 81 EPIGRAMS 129   17 And thine owne CORIAT too. But (would'st
                              thou see)
    p. 157 UNDERWOOD 13   128 Coriat, should rise the most sufficient head

corinna. See "corynna."

cork. See "corke."

corke   frequency: 2   relative frequency: 0.00002
    p. 244 UNDERWOOD 70   42 But that the Corke of Title boy'd him up.
    p. 405 UNGATHERED 34   68 Swim wthout Corke! Why, thank ye good Queen
                              Anne.

corner   frequency: 1   relative frequency: 0.00001
    p. 163 UNDERWOOD 15   27 No part or corner man can looke upon,

corners   frequency: 2   relative frequency: 0.00002
    p. 154 UNDERWOOD 13   44 Nought but in corners; and is loath to leave
    p. 287 U'WOOD 84.9   153 Our closest Creekes, and Corners, and can trace

corollary   frequency: 1   relative frequency: 0.00001
    p. 406 UNGATHERED 35   t2 A Corollary.

corporal. See "corporall."

corporall   frequency: 3   relative frequency: 0.00004
    p. 180 UNDERWOOD 26   5 The Cure of that, which is but corporall,
    p. 229 UNDERWOOD 54   7 So that upon the point, my corporall feare
    p. 284 U'WOOD 84.9   52 One corporall, only; th'other spirituall,

corpse. See "corse."

corrals   frequency: 1   relative frequency: 0.00001
    p. 273 U'WOOD 84.1   21 Their Corrals, Whistles, and prime Coates,

corrants   frequency: 1   relative frequency: 0.00001
    p. 206 UNDERWOOD 43   81 The weekly Corrants, with Pauls Seale; and all

correct   frequency: 2   relative frequency: 0.00002
    p. 152 UNDERWOOD 12   27 His lookes would so correct it, when
    p. 402 UNGATHERED 34   4 Able to talk of Euclide, and correct

corrected   frequency: 1   relative frequency: 0.00001
    p. 325 HORACE 2   418 Not, ten times o're, corrected to the naile.

correcting   frequency: 1   relative frequency: 0.00001
    p. 317 HORACE 2   249 And still correcting youth, and censuring.

corroding   frequency: 1   relative frequency: 0.00001
    p. 257 UNDERWOOD 75   136 With all corroding Arts, be able to untie!

corrosives. See "cor'sives."

corrupt   frequency: 2   relative frequency: 0.00002
    p. 165 UNDERWOOD 15   92 That may corrupt her, even in his eyes.
    p. 218 UNDERWOOD 47   18 Like flies, or wormes, which mans corrupt parts
                              fed:

corrupts   frequency: 1   relative frequency: 0.00001
     p. 154 UNDERWOOD 13   33 All this corrupts the thankes; lesse hath he
                              wonne,

corse   frequency: 1   relative frequency: 0.00001
     p. 282 U'WOOD 84.9   11 O! had I seene her laid out a faire Corse,

cor'sives   frequency: 1   relative frequency: 0.00001
     p. 180 UNDERWOOD 26   2 I send nor Balmes, nor Cor'sives to your wound,

coryate   frequency: 4   relative frequency: 0.00005
     See also "coriat."
     p. 374 UNGATHERED 10 10 Here, like Arion, our Coryate doth draw
     p. 378 UNGATHERED 11 t2 his trauailes, the Coryate of Odcombe,
     p. 379 UNGATHERED 12   2 The height, let him learne of Mr. Tom.
                              Coryate;
     p. 381 UNGATHERED 12 60 The height, let him learne of Mr. Tom Coryate.

corynna   frequency: 1   relative frequency: 0.00001
     p. 181 UNDERWOOD 27   17 Or hath Corynna, by the name

cosen   frequency: 2   relative frequency: 0.00002
     p. 54 EPIGRAMS 81   8 I must a libell make, and cosen both.
     p. 86 EPIGRAMS 133   72 The least of which was to the plague a cosen.

cosening   frequency: 1   relative frequency: 0.00001
     p. 183 UNDERWOOD 29   5 Cosening Judgement with a measure,

cos'ning   frequency: 1   relative frequency: 0.00001
     p. 117 FOREST 13   39 Or cos'ning farmer of the customes so,

cossen'd   frequency: 1   relative frequency: 0.00001
     p. 386 UNGATHERED 21 11 On credit, and are cossen'd; see, that thou

cost   frequency: 3   relative frequency: 0.00004
     p. 49 EPIGRAMS 66   14 When they cost dearest, and are done most free,
     p. 51 EPIGRAMS 73   19 In most vile verses, and cost me more paine,
     p. 160 UNDERWOOD 14   54 To see the workmanship so'<e>xceed the cost!

cotes   frequency: 1   relative frequency: 0.00001
     p. 114 FOREST 12   44 Inscrib'd in touch or marble, or the cotes

cotswold   frequency: 2   relative frequency: 0.00002
     p. 415 UNGATHERED 43   2 Twixt Cotswold, and the Olimpicke exercise:
     p. 415 UNGATHERED 43 t4 At Cotswold.

cotton   frequency: 1   relative frequency: 0.00001
     p. 207 UNDERWOOD 43 100 Which noble Carew, Cotton, Selden lent:

couer   frequency: 3   relative frequency: 0.00004
     p. 34 EPIGRAMS 22   12 Which couer lightly, gentle earth.
     p. 39 EPIGRAMS 40   1 Marble, weepe, for thou dost couer
     p. 103 FOREST 6   2 Can your fauours keepe, and couer,

couers   frequency: 2   relative frequency: 0.00002
     p. 365 UNGATHERED 5   8 When night their meeting couers.
     p. 371 UNGATHERED 9   3 It couers, first, a Virgin; and then, one

couetous   frequency: 4   relative frequency: 0.00005
   **p. 114 PANEGYRE   34 Vpon his face all threw their couetous eyes,
   **p. 117 PANEGYRE   142 And was not hot, or couetous to be crown'd
     p. 27 EPIGRAMS 2   9 Thou are not couetous of least selfe-fame,
     p. 40 EPIGRAMS 43   6 I, not the worst, am couetous of thee.

could   frequency: 122   relative frequency: 0.00176

couldst   frequency: 1   relative frequency: 0.00001
     See also "could'st."

could'st   frequency: 3   relative frequency: 0.00004

coulors   frequency: 2   relative frequency: 0.00002
     p. 404 UNGATHERED 34 47 Of many Coulors! read them! & reueale
     p. 405 UNGATHERED 34 88 Reuiuing wth fresh coulors ye pale Ghosts

councell   frequency: 1   relative frequency: 0.00001
     p. 419 UNGATHERED 47   5 God blesse the Councell of Estate,

councellour   frequency: 1   relative frequency: 0.00001
     p. 186 UNDERWOOD 33   t1 An Epigram to the Councellour that

councells   frequency: 1   relative frequency: 0.00001
    p. 62 EPIGRAMS 95   32 The councells, actions, orders, and euents

councels   frequency: 2   relative frequency: 0.00002
    p. 59 EPIGRAMS 92   11 The councels, proiects, practises they know,
    p. 215 UNDERWOOD 44   85 To serve the State by Councels, and by Armes:

council. See "councell."

councils. See "councels."

counsel. See "counsell."

counsell   frequency: 3   relative frequency: 0.00004
    p. 71 EPIGRAMS 110   19 In euery counsell, stratageme, designe,
    p. 186 UNDERWOOD 32   3 Without the pompe of Counsell; or more Aide,
    p. 315 HORACE 2   233 To endure counsell: a Provider slow

counsellor. See "councellour."

counsellors. See "co<u>nsellors."

counsells   frequency: 2   relative frequency: 0.00002
    p. 234 UNDERWOOD 61   6 But whisper'd Counsells, and those only thrive;
    p. 255 UNDERWOOD 75   98 That Mine of Wisdome, and of Counsells deep,

counsels. See "councells," "councels," "counsells."

count   frequency: 1   relative frequency: 0.00001
    p. 161 UNDERWOOD 14   79 Thy gift 'gainst envie. O how I doe count

countenance   frequency: 2   relative frequency: 0.00002
    p. 107 FOREST 10   3 For the more countenance to my actiue Muse?
    p. 191 UNDERWOOD 38   24 Or goe about to countenance the vice,

countenances. See "ccunt'nances."

counter-turne   frequency: 4   relative frequency: 0.00005
    p. 243 UNDERWOOD 70   10+ The Counter-turne.
    p. 244 UNDERWOOD 70   42+ The Counter-turne.
    p. 245 UNDERWOOD 70   74+ The Counter-turne.
    p. 247 UNDERWOOD 70 106+ The Counter-turne.

counterfeits   frequency: 1   relative frequency: 0.00001
    p. 216 UNDERWOOD 45   17 For there are many slips, and Counterfeits.

countermine   frequency: 1   relative frequency: 0.00001
    See also "countermyne."
    p. 198 UNDERWOOD 40   46 The sinne of Boast, or other countermine

countermyne   frequency: 1   relative frequency: 0.00001
    p. 212 UNDERWOOD 43 205 Blow up, and ruine, myne, and countermyne,

counters   frequency: 1   relative frequency: 0.00001
    p. 165 UNDERWOOD 15 105 His body to the Counters, or the Fleete?

countess. See "countesse," "covntesse."

countesse   frequency: 3   relative frequency: 0.00004
    p. 224 UNDERWOOD 50   t3 ---- Countesse of ----
    p. 394 UNGATHERED 28   3 To see (who' it is?) A noble Countesse, greate,
    p. 394 UNGATHERED 28 t3 and Countesse of Shrewsbury:--

counting. See "compting."

count'nances   frequency: 1   relative frequency: 0.00001
    p. 342 HORACE 1   143 .... count'nances ....

countrey   frequency: 11   relative frequency: 0.00015
    p. 31 EPIGRAMS 14   3 (How nothing's that?) to whom my countrey owes
    p. 46 EPIGRAMS 60   1 Loe, what my countrey should haue done (haue
                             rais'd
    p. 46 EPIGRAMS 60   10 But sauer of my countrey thee alone.
    p. 61 EPIGRAMS 95   14 Or, better worke! were thy glad countrey blest,
    p. 69 EPIGRAMS 108   1 Strength of my Countrey, whilst I bring to view
    p. 94 FOREST 2   45 And though thy walls be of the countrey stone,
    p. 95 FOREST 2   80 To entertayne them; or the countrey came,
    p. 96 FOREST 3   1 How blest art thou, canst loue the countrey,
                             WROTH,
    p. 100 FOREST 3   103 To doe thy countrey seruice, thy selfe right;

countrey (cont.)
    p. 325 HORACE 2   446 What to his Countrey, what his friends he owes,
    p. 416 UNGATHERED 43   6 With the Glad Countrey, and Posteritie:

countrey-men   frequency: 1   relative frequency: 0.00001
    p. 335 HORACE 2   653 And cry aloud, Helpe, gentle Countrey-men,

countrie   frequency: 1   relative frequency: 0.00001
    p. 289 UNDERWOOD 85   t2 The praises of a Countrie life.

countrie-neighbours   frequency: 1   relative frequency: 0.00001
    p. 190 UNDERWOOD 37   7 Not like your Countrie-neighbours, that commit

countries   frequency: 5   relative frequency: 0.00007
    See also "low-countrey's," "low-countries."
    p. 40 EPIGRAMS 43   3 Which should thy countries loue to speake refuse,
    p. 46 EPIGRAMS 60   9 My countries parents I haue many knowne;
    p. 80 EPIGRAMS 128   2 Countries, and climes, manners, and men to know,
    p. 159 UNDERWOOD 14   30 Ever at home: yet, have all Countries seene:
    p. 224 UNDERWOOD 50   22 Countries, and Climes, manners, and men to know.

country. See "countrey," "countrie,"
           "countrie-neighbours," "countrye."

countrye   frequency: 1   relative frequency: 0.00001
    p. 420 UNGATHERED 48   14 That hath not Countrye impudence enough to
              laughe att Arte,

countrymen. See "countrey-men."

country's   frequency: 1   relative frequency: 0.00001
    See also "countries."
    p. 398 UNGATHERED 30   63 The Poets act! and for his Country's sake

'counts   frequency: 1   relative frequency: 0.00001
    p. 290 UNDERWOOD 85   36 And 'counts them sweet rewards so ta'en.

county   frequency: 1   relative frequency: 0.00001
    p. 662 INSCRIPTS. 2   4 appropriates still vnto that County:

couple   frequency: 2   relative frequency: 0.00002
    p. 40 EPIGRAMS 42   18 I know no couple better can agree!
    p. 258 UNDERWOOD 75   192 The longing Couple, all that elder Lovers know.

coupled   frequency: 1   relative frequency: 0.00001
    p. 305 HORACE 2   16 With Doves; or Lambes, with Tygres coupled be.

courage   frequency: 1   relative frequency: 0.00001
    p. 132 UNDERWOOD 2.2   15 Or his courage; for away

courants. See "corrants."

course   frequency: 12   relative frequency: 0.00017
    p. 48 EPIGRAMS 65   10 Almost all wayes, to any better course.
    p. 63 EPIGRAMS 98   8 With thine owne course the iudgement of thy
              friend,
    p. 109 FOREST 11   19 But this true course is not embrac'd by many:
    p. 119 FOREST 13   91 And, keeping a iust course, haue earely put
    p. 165 UNDERWOOD 15   98 A fellow of course Letcherie, is nam'd,
    p. 233 UNDERWOOD 59   12 As they out-did the lightning in the<ir> course;
    p. 309 HORACE 2   97 His course so hurtfull both to graine, and
              seedes,
    p. 311 HORACE 2   115 The conqu'ring Champion, the prime Horse in
              course,
    p. 313 HORACE 2   163 Or some hot youth, yet in his flourishing course:
    p. 399 UNGATHERED 31   20 Or sweet, or various, in the course!
    p. 414 UNGATHERED 41   51 Who like a Giant hasts his course to run,
    p. 422 UNGATHERED 49   19 .. Course of ....

courser   frequency: 1   relative frequency: 0.00001
    p. 219 UNDERWOOD 47   54 I, and for this neglect, the courser sort

courses   frequency: 2   relative frequency: 0.00002
    p. 47 EPIGRAMS 63   1 Who can consider thy right courses run,
    p. 194 UNDERWOOD 38   119 Others by common Stars their courses run,

court   frequency: 43   relative frequency: 0.00062
    See also words beginning "covrt-."
  **p. 113 PANEGYRE   91 "Of kings, praeceding him in that high court;

court (cont.)
```
p.  30 EPIGRAMS 11      1 At court I met it, in clothes braue enough,
p.  31 EPIGRAMS 15      2 'Twas brought to court first wrapt, and white as
                          milke;
p.  46 EPIGRAMS 62      9 What should the cause be? Oh, you liue at court:
p.  57 EPIGRAMS 90      1 When MILL first came to court, the
                          vnprofiting foole,
p.  63 EPIGRAMS 97     11 Nor office in the towne, nor place in court,
p.  73 EPIGRAMS 113     5 I thinke, the Fate of court thy comming crau'd,
p.  76 EPIGRAMS 119     1 Not he that flies the court for want of clothes,
p.  96 FOREST 3         3 And, though so neere the citie, and the court,
p.  97 FOREST 3        24 Who, for it, makes thy house his court;
p. 104 FOREST 7         3 So court a mistris, shee denyes you;
p. 104 FOREST 7         4 Let her alone, shee will court you.
p. 113 FOREST 12        5 Toyles, by graue custome, vp and downe the court,
p. 115 FOREST 12       69 (Or Poet, in the court account) then I,
p. 119 FOREST 13      115 Not fashion'd for the court, or strangers eyes;
p. 138 UNDERWOOD 2.6   15 Of the Court, to day, then all
p. 186 UNDERWOOD 32    13 As though the Court pursues them on the sent,
p. 187 UNDERWOOD 33    29 So comm'st thou like a Chiefe into the Court,
p. 200 UNDERWOOD 42    34 And braveries of Court, and felt their fits
p. 201 UNDERWOOD 42    57 Court every hanging Gowne, and after that,
p. 211 UNDERWOOD 43   178 A Court of Equitie should doe us right,
p. 213 UNDERWOOD 44    16 To see the Pride at Court, their Wives doe
                          make:
p. 219 UNDERWOOD 47    53 And animated Porc'lane of the Court,
p. 222 UNDERWOOD 48    50 To put his Court in dances,
p. 222 UNDERWOOD 49    t3 The Court Pucell.
p. 223 UNDERWOOD 49    36 From Court, while yet thy fame hath some small
                          day;
p. 223 UNDERWOOD 49    43 Or if it would, the Court is the worst place,
p. 231 UNDERWOOD 57    20 Will come at the Court,
p. 234 UNDERWOOD 61     2 And all the games of Fortune, plaid at Court;
p. 240 UNDERWOOD 67    43 8. URA. This day the Court doth measure
p. 251 UNDERWOOD 74    25 O how will then our Court be pleas'd,
p. 254 UNDERWOOD 75    72 With all the pompe of Youth, and all our Court
                          beside.
p. 254 UNDERWOOD 75    73 Our Court, and all the Grandees; now, Sun,
                          looke,
p. 262 UNDERWOOD 78     4 Court can call hers, or Man could call his
                          Arts.
p. 283 U'WOOD 84.9     41 So sweetly taken to the Court of blisse,
p. 309 HORACE 2       111 All the Grammarians strive; and yet in Court
p. 331 HORACE 2       552 Of eloquent Messalla's power in Court,
p. 371 UNGATHERED 9     4 That durst be that in Court: a vertu' alone
p. 389 UNGATHERED 24   19 Will bee receiu'd in Court; If not, would I
p. 398 UNGATHERED 30   79 But then refreshed, with thy Fayerie Court,
p. 403 UNGATHERED 34   24 In Towne & Court? Are you growne rich?
                          & proud?
p. 404 UNGATHERED 34   43 Court Hieroglyphicks! & all Artes affoord
p. 423 UNGATHERED 50   17 he that will honest be, may quitt the Court,
```

court-bred-fillie   frequency: 1   relative frequency: 0.00001
```
p. 163 UNDERWOOD 15    48 To have his Court-bred-fillie there commend
```

court-durt   frequency: 1   relative frequency: 0.00001
```
p. 172 UNDERWOOD 21     5 A parcell of Court-durt, a heape, and masse
```

court-hobby-horse   frequency: 1   relative frequency: 0.00001
```
p. 410 UNGATHERED 38   11 Now each Court-Hobby-horse will wince in rime;
```

court-pucell   frequency: 1   relative frequency: 0.00001
```
p. 222 UNDERWOOD 49     1 Do's the Court-Pucell then so censure me,
```

courted   frequency: 1   relative frequency: 0.00001
```
**p. 114 PANEGYRE      53 And would be courted: so this Towne put on
```

courteous   frequency: 1   relative frequency: 0.00001
See also "curteous."
```
p.  97 FOREST 3        19 To some coole, courteous shade, which he calls
                          his,
```

courtesie   frequency: 2   relative frequency: 0.00002
```
p. 262 UNDERWOOD 78     3 In honour, courtesie, and all the parts
p. 270 UNDERWOOD 83    39 Her Sweetnesse, Softnesse, her faire
                          Courtesie,
```

courtesies   frequency: 1   relative frequency: 0.00001
See also "curtesies."
```
p. 153 UNDERWOOD 13    16 The smallest courtesies with thankes, I make
```

courtesy. See "courtesie," "curtesie."

courtier   frequency: 3   relative frequency: 0.00004
    p. 29 EPIGRAMS 8   3 But, for this money was a courtier found,
    p. 29 EPIGRAMS 8   6 The courtier is become the greater thiefe.
    p. 30 EPIGRAMS 11   2 To be a courtier; and lookes graue enough,

courtiers   frequency: 1   relative frequency: 0.00001
    p. 213 UNDERWOOD 44   17 And the returne those thankfull Courtiers yeeld,

courting   frequency: 1   relative frequency: 0.00001
    p. 103 FOREST 6   3 When the common courting iay

courtling. See "covrt-ling," "covrtling."

courts   frequency: 4   relative frequency: 0.00005
    p. 48 EPIGRAMS 65   7 Get him the times long grudge, the courts ill
                             will;
    p. 93 FOREST 2   5 Or stayre, or courts; but stand'st an ancient
                             pile,
    p. 187 UNDERWOOD 33   37 The Courts just honour, and thy Judges love.
    p. 289 UNDERWOOD 85   7 But flees the Barre and Courts, with the proud
                             bords,

cousin. See "cosen."

covell   frequency: 1   relative frequency: 0.00001
    p. 230 UNDERWOOD 56   t2 To my Lady COVELL.

cover   frequency: 2   relative frequency: 0.00002
    See also "couer."
    p. 202 UNDERWOOD 42   83 Under that cover; an old Mid-wives hat!
    p. 209 UNDERWOOD 43 138 Left! and wit since to cover it with Tiles.

cover'd   frequency: 1   relative frequency: 0.00001
    p. 216 UNDERWOOD 44 100 Cover'd with Tissue, whose prosperitie mocks

covers. See "couers."

covetous   frequency: 2   relative frequency: 0.00002
    See also "couetous."
    p. 180 UNDERWOOD 26   13 Your covetous hand,
    p. 327 HORACE 2   463 Being men were covetous of nought, but praise.

covey   frequency: 1   relative frequency: 0.00001
    p. 218 UNDERWOOD 47   22 And are received for the Covey of Witts;

covntesse   frequency: 6   relative frequency: 0.00008
    p. 52 EPIGRAMS 76   t1 ON LVCY COVNTESSE OF
                             BEDFORD.
    p. 53 EPIGRAMS 79   t1 TO ELIZABETH COVNTESSE OF
                             RVTLAND.
    p. 54 EPIGRAMS 84   t1 TO LVCY COVNTESSE OF
                             BEDFORD.
    p. 60 EPIGRAMS 94   t1 TO LVCY, COVNTESSE OF
                             BEDFORD,
    p. 67 EPIGRAMS 104   t1 TO SVSAN COVNTESSE OF
                             MONTGOMERY.
    p. 113 FOREST 12   t2 TO ELIZABETH COVNTESSE OF
                             RVTLAND.

covrt-ling   frequency: 1   relative frequency: 0.00001
    p. 50 EPIGRAMS 72   t1 TO COVRT-LING.

covrt-parrat   frequency: 1   relative frequency: 0.00001
    p. 50 EPIGRAMS 71   t1 ON COVRT-PARRAT.

covrt-worme   frequency: 1   relative frequency: 0.00001
    p. 31 EPIGRAMS 15   t1 ON COVRT-WORME.

covrtling   frequency: 4   relative frequency: 0.00005
    p. 43 EPIGRAMS 52   1 COVRTLING, I rather thou should'st
                             vtterly
    p. 43 EPIGRAMS 52   t1 TO CENSORIOVS COVRTLING.
    p. 50 EPIGRAMS 72   1 I grieue not, COVRTLING, thou are
                             started vp
    p. 50 EPIGRAMS 72   6 Thy person only, COVRTLING, is the vice.

coyne   frequency: 2   relative frequency: 0.00002
    p. 68 EPIGRAMS 107   3 I oft looke on false coyne, to know't from true:

coyne (cont.)
    p. 163 UNDERWOOD 15   45 In bravery, or gluttony, or coyne,

cozen. See "cosen."

cozened. See "cossen'd."

cozening. See "cosening," "cos'ning."

crack   frequency: 2   relative frequency: 0.00002
   See also "cracke."
    p. 86 EPIGRAMS 133   94 Crack did report it selfe, as if a cloud
    p. 321 HORACE 2   359 Or crack out bawdie speeches, and uncleane.

crack'd   frequency: 1   relative frequency: 0.00001
   See also "crackt."
    p. 219 UNDERWOOD 47   58 Lest it be justled, crack'd, made nought, or
                 lesse:

cracke   frequency: 2   relative frequency: 0.00002
    p. 230 UNDERWOOD 56   10 His friends, but to breake Chaires, or cracke a
                 Coach.
    p. 395 UNGATHERED 29   6 At least, if not the generall Engine cracke.

crackers. See "nut-crackers."

crackt   frequency: 1   relative frequency: 0.00001
    p. 113 FOREST 12   17 Solders crackt friendship; makes loue last a day;

cradle   frequency: 5   relative frequency: 0.00007
    p. 192 UNDERWOOD 38   60 Of that wise Nature would a Cradle have.
    p. 215 UNDERWOOD 44   84 That in the Cradle of their Gentrie are;
    p. 225 UNDERWOOD 51   14 In his soft Cradle to his Fathers Chaire,
    p. 272 U'WOOD 84.1   t1 The Dedication of her CRADLE.
    p. 273 U'WOOD 84.1   10 This CRADLE, and for Goodnesse sake,

cradles   frequency: 2   relative frequency: 0.00002
    p. 200 UNDERWOOD 42   23 Curst in their Cradles, or there chang'd by
                 Elves,
    p. 204 UNDERWOOD 43   37 Of Egges, and Halberds, Cradles, and a Herse,

craftie   frequency: 1   relative frequency: 0.00001
    p. 214 UNDERWOOD 44   33 Well did thy craftie Clerke, and Knight, Sir
                 Hugh,

crafts   frequency: 1   relative frequency: 0.00001
   See also "wise-crafts."
    p. 410 UNGATHERED 38   14 That knew the Crafts they had bin bred in,
                 right:

crafty   frequency: 1   relative frequency: 0.00001
   See also "craftie."
    p. 391 UNGATHERED 26   11 Or crafty Malice, might pretend this praise,

cramp. See "crampe."

cramp-ring   frequency: 1   relative frequency: 0.00001
    p. 232 UNDERWOOD 58   8 Thy Wife a fit of laughter; a Cramp-ring

cramp'd   frequency: 1   relative frequency: 0.00001
    p. 184 UNDERWOOD 29   51 Cramp'd for ever;

crampe   frequency: 1   relative frequency: 0.00001
    p. 107 FOREST 10   16 Goe, crampe dull MARS, light VENVS, when
                 he snorts,

cramps   frequency: 1   relative frequency: 0.00001
    p. 166 UNDERWOOD 15   135 He that no more for Age, Cramps, Palsies, can

crane   frequency: 2   relative frequency: 0.00002
    p. 198 UNDERWOOD 40   35 Like the dull wearied Crane that (come on land)
    p. 290 UNDERWOOD 85   35 And snares the fearfull Hare, and new-come
                 Crane,

crau'd   frequency: 1   relative frequency: 0.00001
    p. 73 EPIGRAMS 113   5 I thinke, the Fate of court thy comming crau'd,

craue   frequency: 3   relative frequency: 0.00004
    p. 27 EPIGRAMS 3   3 Vse mine so, too: I giue thee leaue. But craue
    p. 31 EPIGRAMS 14   6 More high, more holy, that shee more would craue.

craue (cont.)
    p. 380 UNGATHERED 12   55 Some want, they say in a sort he did craue:

crave   frequency: 2   relative frequency: 0.00002
    See alsc "craue."
    p. 129 UNDERWOOD 1.2   17 Who more can crave
    p. 305 HORACE 2   13 And both doe crave, and give againe, this leave.

craved. See "crau'd."

craves   frequency: 1   relative frequency: 0.00001
    p. 186 UNDERWOOD 32   16 He do's you wrong, that craves you to doe right.

cream. See "Creame-bowles."

creame-bowles   frequency: 1   relative frequency: 0.00001
    p. 198 UNDERWOOD 40   29 They looke at best like Creame-bowles, and you
            soone

creat[t]es   frequency: 1   relative frequency: 0.00001
    p. 383 UNGATHERED 16   14 your Royal Eye which still creat[t]es new men

create   frequency: 5   relative frequency: 0.00007
**p. 116 PANEGYRE   105 "From priuate chambers; that could then create
    p. 67 EPIGRAMS 105   6 Who could not but create them all, from you?
    p. 127 UNDERWOOD 1.1   17 5. Eternall Father, God, who did'st create
    p. 313 HORACE 2   179 Unto the Scene thou bringst, and dar'st create
    p. 313 HORACE 2   189 For, being a Poet, thou maist feigne, create,

created   frequency: 1   relative frequency: 0.00001
    p. 361 UNGATHERED 1   22 of thy rich labors worlds of thoughts created,

creates   frequency: 2   relative frequency: 0.00002
    See alsc "creat[t]es."
    p. 64 EPIGRAMS 101   7 It is the faire acceptance, Sir, creates
    p. 222 UNDERWOOD 49   5 And that as any are strooke, her breath creates

creation   frequency: 1   relative frequency: 0.00001
    p. 71 EPIGRAMS 110   18 (As by a new creation) part by part,

creature   frequency: 10   relative frequency: 0.00014
    p. 46 EPIGRAMS 62   8 To make amends, yo'are thought a wholesome
            creature.
    p. 52 EPIGRAMS 76   3 What kinde of creature I could most desire,
    p. 77 EPIGRAMS 120   8 Which own'd the creature.
    p. 84 EPIGRAMS 133   30 Makes the poore Banck-side creature wet it'
            shoone,
    p. 103 FOREST 6   5 Kisse againe: no creature comes.
    p. 112 FOREST 11   102 O, so diuine a creature
    p. 191 UNDERWOOD 38   29 And (stil'd your mercies Creature) will live
            more
    p. 255 UNDERWOOD 75   82 Of Sex, to rob the Creature; but from Man,
    p. 305 HORACE 2   3 On every limbe, ta'en from a severall creature,
    p. 364 UNGATHERED 4   6 That Natures fairest Creature,

creatures   frequency: 2   relative frequency: 0.00002
    p. 253 UNDERWOOD 75   26 The Month of youth, which calls all Creatures
            forth
    p. 255 UNDERWOOD 75   83 The king of Creatures, take his paritie

credit   frequency: 9   relative frequency: 0.00013
    See alsc "creditt."
    p. 32 EPIGRAMS 18   6 As theirs did with thee, mine might credit get:
    p. 45 EPIGRAMS 56   7 To'a little wealth, and credit in the scene,
    p. 69 EPIGRAMS 107   24 That are your wordes of credit. Keepe your
            Names
    p. 161 UNDERWOOD 14   84 The Credit, what would furnish a tenth Muse!
    p. 191 UNDERWOOD 38   2 Of Credit lost. And I am now run madde:
    p. 219 UNDERWOOD 47   52 Lose all my credit with my Christmas Clay;
    p. 229 UNDERWOOD 54   14 Stinketh my credit, if into the Pocket
    p. 305 HORACE 2   7 Could you containe your laughter? Credit mee,
    p. 386 UNGATHERED 21   11 On credit, and are cossen'd; see, that thou

creditt   frequency: 1   relative frequency: 0.00001
    p. 421 UNGATHERED 49   5 The emptye Carper, scorne, not Creditt wynns.

credulous   frequency: 1   relative frequency: 0.00001
    p. 293 UNDERWOOD 86   30 Delights, nor credulous hope of mutuall Joy,

creed   frequency: 1   relative frequency: 0.00001
    p. 215 UNDERWOOD 44   74 Their Sonnes to studie Arts, the Lawes, the
                              Creed:

creekes   frequency: 2   relative frequency: 0.00002
    p. 160 UNDERWOOD 14   45 Sought out the Fountaines, Sources, Creekes,
                              paths, wayes,
    p. 287 U'WOOD 84.9   153 Our closest Creekes, and Corners, and can trace

creeks. See "creekes."

creep   frequency: 1   relative frequency: 0.00001
    See also "creepe."
    p. 413 UNGATHERED 41   20 No faith's more firme, or flat, then where't doth
                              creep.

creepe   frequency: 3   relative frequency: 0.00004
    p. 201 UNDERWOOD 42   60 In at a hole, and see these Actions creepe
    p. 290 UNDERWOOD 85   27 The Fountaines murmure as the streames doe
                              creepe,
    p. 329 HORACE 2   538 May, with some right, upon an Author creepe.

creepes   frequency: 1   relative frequency: 0.00001
    p. 307 HORACE 2   39 Creepes on the ground; too safe, too afraid of
                              storme.

creeping   frequency: 2   relative frequency: 0.00002
    p. 339 HORACE 1   40 Downe close .. shore, this other creeping
                              steales,
    p. 400 UNGATHERED 32   5 Such, as the creeping common Pioners vse

creeps. See "creepes."

crept   frequency: 2   relative frequency: 0.00002
    p. 166 UNDERWOOD 15   117 What furie of late is crept into our Feasts?
    p. 234 UNDERWOOD 60   8 But crept like darknesse through his blood?

crepundia   frequency: 1   relative frequency: 0.00001
    p. 273 U'WOOD 84.1   14 Who read what the CREPUNDIA bee,

crest   frequency: 1   relative frequency: 0.00001
    p. 412 UNGATHERED 41   10 Ymounted high upon Selinis crest:

cri'd   frequency: 1   relative frequency: 0.00001
    p. 228 UNDERWOOD 53   19 And cri'd, Away with the Caesarian bread,

crie   frequency: 5   relative frequency: 0.00007
    p. 35 EPIGRAMS 28   11 That's greater, yet: to crie his owne vp neate.
    p. 38 EPIGRAMS 38   5 And crie good! good! This quite peruerts my
                              sense,
    p. 58 EPIGRAMS 92   t1 THE NEW CRIE.
    p. 231 UNDERWOOD 57   3 My wofull crie,
    p. 380 UNGATHERED 12   37 How faine for his venery he was to crie (Tergum
                              o)

cried. See "cri'd," "cry'd," "cryed."

criedest. See "cryd'st."

crier   frequency: 1   relative frequency: 0.00001
    p. 333 HORACE 2   597 To say, I'm ignorant. Just as a Crier

cries   frequency: 2   relative frequency: 0.00002
    See also "cryes," "out-cryes."
    p. 327 HORACE 2   470 He cries, Good boy, thou'lt keepe thine owne.
                              Now, adde
    p. 657 L. CONVIVALES   8 Cries Old Sym, the King of Skinkers;

criest. See "cry'st."

crime   frequency: 6   relative frequency: 0.00008
    See also "cryme."
    p. 48 EPIGRAMS 66   6 Durst valour make, almost, but not a crime.
    p. 138 UNDERWOOD 2.6   32 Or have charg'd his sight of Crime,
    p. 159 UNDERWOOD 14   18 Not flie the Crime, but the Suspition too:
    p. 169 UNDERWOOD 17   4 'Tis then a crime, when the Usurer is Judge.
    p. 191 UNDERWOOD 38   23 Or in confessing of the Crime be nice,
    p. 323 HORACE 2   386 Or a worse Crime, the ignorance of art.

crimes   frequency: 10   relative frequency: 0.00014
  **p. 116 PANEGYRE   112 He ownde their crownes, he would not so their
                                crimes.
    p.   36 EPIGRAMS 30   1 GVILTIE, be wise; and though thou know'st
                                the crimes
    p.   38 EPIGRAMS 35   6 Left vs of feare, but first our crimes, then
                                lawes.
    p.   45 EPIGRAMS 56   9 And, told of this, he slights it. Tut, such
                                crimes
    p.   61 EPIGRAMS 95   19 That hast thy brest so cleere of present crimes,
    p. 102 FOREST 5   18 These haue crimes accounted beene.
    p. 117 FOREST 13   14 For their owne cap'tall crimes, t<o>'indite my
                                wit;
    p. 186 UNDERWOOD 32   10 A right by the prosperitie of their Crimes;
    p. 187 UNDERWOOD 33   16 Mak'st it religion to grow rich by Crimes!
    p. 397 UNGATHERED 30   44 That Rebells actions, are but valiant crimes!

cringe   frequency: 1   relative frequency: 0.00001
    p.   56 EPIGRAMS 88   14 And stoupe, and cringe. O then, it needs must
                                proue

cripple   frequency: 1   relative frequency: 0.00001
    p. 374 UNGATHERED 10   17 Hee's carried like a Cripple, from Constable to
                                Constable.

crips   frequency: 1   relative frequency: 0.00001
    p. 214 UNDERWOOD 44   54 As Stiles, Dike, Ditchfield, Millar, Crips,
                                and Fen:

crispe. See "crips."

crisped   frequency: 1   relative frequency: 0.00001
    p. 141 UNDERWOOD 2.9   10 Yet a man; with crisped haire

crispeth   frequency: 1   relative frequency: 0.00001
    p. 170 UNDERWOOD 19   6 He flying curles, and crispeth, with his wings;

critic. See "chamber-critick," "critick."

critical. See "criticall."

criticall   frequency: 1   relative frequency: 0.00001
    p. 180 UNDERWOOD 26   6 And doubtfull Dayes (which were nam'd
                                Criticall,)

critick   frequency: 1   relative frequency: 0.00001
    p.   32 EPIGRAMS 17   t1 TO THE LEARNED CRITICK.

croak. See "croake."

croake   frequency: 1   relative frequency: 0.00001
    p.   84 EPIGRAMS 133   13 Arses were heard to croake, in stead of frogs;

croaking   frequency: 1   relative frequency: 0.00001
    p.   86 EPIGRAMS 133   91 No matter, stinkards, row. What croaking sound

crooked   frequency: 1   relative frequency: 0.00001
    p. 170 UNDERWOOD 18   8 Crooked appeare; so that doth my conceipt:

crop   frequency: 1   relative frequency: 0.00001
    p. 169 UNDERWOOD 17   18 And I will bring a Crop, if not the best.

cropped. See "cropt."

cropt   frequency: 1   relative frequency: 0.00001
    p. 411 UNGATHERED 39   16 Cropt, branded, slit, neck-stockt; go, you are
                                stript.

cross. See "Crosse," "rosie-crosse."

crosse   frequency: 5   relative frequency: 0.00007
    p. 128 UNDERWOOD 1.1   23 To pay our debts, upon thy Crosse, and cryd'st,
    p. 130 UNDERWOOD 1.2   32 Under his Crosse.
    p. 268 UNDERWOOD 82   10 This day, by Baptisme, and his Saviours crosse:
    p. 288 U'WOOD 84.9   201 On all the world! She saw him on the Crosse
    p. 401 UNGATHERED 32   20 Defies, what's crosse to Piety, or good Fame.

crossed. See "crost."

crost   frequency: 2   relative frequency: 0.00002
     p.   67 EPIGRAMS 105   2 All historie seal'd vp, and fables crost;
     p. 192 UNDERWOOD 38   37 Errour and folly in me may have crost

crowd   frequency: 1   relative frequency: 0.00001
     p. 414 UNGATHERED 42   5 And lesse asham'd; not when I told the crowd

crown   frequency: 1   relative frequency: 0.00001
     See also "crowne," "crowne-plate,"
            "crowne-worthy."
     p. 412 UNGATHERED 40   20 th'aeternall Crown to win.

crown'd   frequency: 9   relative frequency: 0.00013
   **p. 117 PANEGYRE   142 And was not hot, or couetous to be crown'd
   **p. 117 PANEGYRE   143 Before mens hearts had crown'd him. Who (vnlike
     p.   56 EPIGRAMS 89   4 Yet crown'd with honors, as with riches, then;
     p. 120 FOREST 14   1 Now that the harth is crown'd with smiling fire,
     p. 237 UNDERWOOD 65   2 That so hath crown'd our hopes, our spring, and
                               earth,
     p. 254 UNDERWOOD 75   48 With Modestie so crown'd, and Adoration seene.
     p. 284 U'WOOD 84.9   55 Those other two; which must be judg'd, or
                               crown'd:
     p. 290 UNDERWOOD 85   18 His head, with mellow Apples crown'd,
     p. 309 HORACE 2   108 After, mens Wishes, crown'd in their events,

crowne   frequency: 34   relative frequency: 0.00049
   **p. 113 PANEGYRE   17 And would (if not dispers'd) infect the Crowne,
     p.   32 EPIGRAMS 17   4 Charge them, for crowne, to thy sole censure lye.
     p.   60 EPIGRAMS 94   6 Crowne with their owne. Rare poemes aske rare
                               friends
     p.   66 EPIGRAMS 103   1 How well, faire crowne of your faire sexe, might
                               hee,
     p.   94 FOREST 2   27 To crowne thy open table, doth prouide
     p. 105 FOREST 8   18 But, forgiue me, with thy crowne
     p. 115 FOREST 12   60 Or set bright ARIADNES crowne so high?
     p. 119 FOREST 13   103 To crowne the burthen which you goe withall,
     p. 174 UNDERWOOD 23   18 'Tis crowne enough to vertue still, her owne
                               applause.
     p. 184 UNDERWOOD 29   40 Phoebus to his Crowne againe;
     p. 203 UNDERWOOD 43   10 And Mars, that gave thee a Lanthorne for a
                               Crowne.
     p. 203 UNDERWOOD 43   23 Did I there wound the honour of the Crowne?
     p. 217 UNDERWOOD 46   2 And steps of all rais'd servants of the Crowne,
     p. 242 UNDERWOOD 70   3 When the Prodigious Hannibal did crowne
     p. 248 UNDERWOOD 71   13 Unlesse some saving-Honour of the Crowne,
     p. 255 UNDERWOOD 75   104 Mens Loves unto the Lawes, and Lawes to love
                               the Crowne.
     p. 264 UNDERWOOD 79   41 2. Shee, to the Crowne, hath brought encrease.
     p. 271 UNDERWOOD 83   76 Which they that have the Crowne are sure to
                               know!
     p. 272 U'WOOD 84.1   1 Faire FAME, who art ordain'd to crowne
     p. 272 UNDERWOOD 84   t18 Her Inscription, or CROWNE.
     p. 283 U'WOOD 84.9   37 The joy of Saints! the Crowne for which it
                               lives,
     p. 294 UNDERWOOD 89   4 Thy locks, and rosie garlands crowne thy head;
     p. 315 HORACE 2   222 And sits, till th'Epilogue saies Clap, or
                               Crowne:
     p. 321 HORACE 2   333 A royall Crowne, and purple, be made hop,
     p. 323 HORACE 2   406 Nor did they merit the lesse Crowne to weare,
     p. 329 HORACE 2   499 Playes were found out; and rest, the end, and
                               crowne
     p. 347 HORACE 1   356 .... any Crowne ... .
     p. 361 UNGATHERED 1   27 When loe to crowne thy worth
     p. 371 UNGATHERED 8   14 Do crowne thy murdred Poeme: which shall rise
     p. 385 UNGATHERED 19   7 My suffrage brings thee all increase, to crowne
     p. 400 UNGATHERED 31   34 To gaine the Crowne of immortalitye,
     p. 412 UNGATHERED 41   12 To knit thy Crowne, and glorifie the rest.
     p. 413 UNGATHERED 41   30 On the reverse of this your circling crowne,
     p. 416 UNGATHERED 44   7 To Crowne the years, which you begin, great
                               king,

crowne-plate   frequency: 1   relative frequency: 0.00001
     p.   96 FOREST 3   8 The richer hangings, or crowne-plate;

crowne-worthy   frequency: 1   relative frequency: 0.00001
     p. 112 FOREST 11   88 Is more crowne-worthy still,

crowned   frequency: 2   relative frequency: 0.00002
     See also "crown'd," "deep-crown'd-bowle."
     p. 240 UNDERWOOD 67   47 Summe up this crowned day,

crowned (cont.)
     p. 285 U'WOOD 84.9   96 With boughs of Palme, a crowned Victrice stand!

crownes   frequency: 3   relative frequency: 0.00004
   **p. 116 PANEGYRE   112 He ownde their crownes, he would not so their
                                    crimes.
     p. 217 UNDERWOOD 46   14 Stood up thy Nations fame, her Crownes defence.
     p. 254 UNDERWOOD 75   52 Both Crownes, and Kingdomes in their either
                                    hand;

crowning   frequency: 1   relative frequency: 0.00001
     p. 183 UNDERWOOD 29   27 Worth <a> crowning.

crowns. See "crownes."

cruel. See "cruell."

cruell   frequency: 4   relative frequency: 0.00005
     p. 77 EPIGRAMS 120   10 When Fates turn'd cruell,
     p. 193 UNDERWOOD 38   82 The name of Cruell weather, storme, and raine?
     p. 208 UNDERWOOD 43   130 Made thee beget that cruell Stratagem,
     p. 338 HORACE 1   14 ... ... cruell things ....

cruellie   frequency: 1   relative frequency: 0.00001
     p. 423 UNGATHERED 50   15 Yet ware; thou mayst do all things cruellie:

cruelly. See "cruellie."

crueltie   frequency: 2   relative frequency: 0.00002
     p. 193 UNDERWOOD 38   84 Of crueltie, lest they doe make you such.
     p. 204 UNDERWOOD 43   49 Thou mightst have yet enjoy'd thy crueltie

cruelty. See "crueltie."

crush'd   frequency: 1   relative frequency: 0.00001
   See also "crusht."
     p. 162 UNDERWOOD 15   18 Crush'd in the snakie brakes, that he had past!

crusht   frequency: 1   relative frequency: 0.00001
     p. 108 FOREST 10   26 (Though they were crusht into one forme) could
                                    make

crusts   frequency: 1   relative frequency: 0.00001
    *p. 493 TO HIMSELF   23 As the Shrieues crusts, and nasty as his fish-

cry   frequency: 18   relative frequency: 0.00026
   See also "crie," "crye."
    *p. 494 TO HIMSELF   56 As they shall cry, like ours
   **p. 114 PANEGYRE   41 Some cry from tops of houses; thinking noise
     p. 52 EPIGRAMS 75   2 'Twixt puritanes, and players, as some cry;
     p. 68 EPIGRAMS 105   11 If dancing, all would cry th'Idalian Queene,
     p. 68 EPIGRAMS 105   17 Or, keeping your due state, that would not cry,
     p. 97 FOREST 3   32 To the full greatnesse of the cry:
     p. 155 UNDERWOOD 13   66 Their thoughts and meanes to making loude the
                                    cry;
     p. 167 UNDERWOOD 15   147 To flatter my good Lord, and cry his Bowle
     p. 236 UNDERWOOD 64   6 For safetie of such Majestie, cry out?
     p. 238 UNDERWOOD 66   4 (Without prophanenesse) yet, a Poet, cry,
     p. 249 UNDERWOOD 72   14 That cry that gladnesse, which their hearts would
                                    pray,
     p. 333 HORACE 2   611 For hee'll cry, Good, brave, better, excellent!
     p. 333 HORACE 2   615 Cry, and doe more then the true Mourners: so
     p. 335 HORACE 2   633 A wise, and honest man will cry out shame
     p. 335 HORACE 2   653 And cry aloud, Helpe, gentle Countrey-men,
     p. 395 UNGATHERED 29   13 It makes me rauish'd with iust wonder, cry
     p. 398 UNGATHERED 30   69 So shall our English Youth vrge on, and cry
     p. 403 UNGATHERED 34   32 That doe cry vp ye Machine, & ye Showes!

cry'd   frequency: 11   relative frequency: 0.00015
   **p. 117 PANEGYRE   160 With a twice louder shoute againe they cry'd,
     p. 64 EPIGRAMS 100   2 Cry'd to my face, they were th'elixir of wit:
     p. 86 EPIGRAMS 133   87 Backe, cry'd their brace of CHARONS: they
                                    cry'd, no,
     p. 89 EPIGRAMS 133   183 They cry'd out PVSSE. He told them he was
                                    BANKES,
     p. 205 UNDERWOOD 43   64 Thou should'st have cry'd, and all beene proper
                                    stuffe.
     p. 209 UNDERWOOD 43   146 And cry'd, it was a threatning to the beares:
     p. 209 UNDERWOOD 43   153 O no, cry'd all, Fortune, for being a whore,
     p. 263 UNDERWOOD 78   30 What transcripts begg'd? how cry'd up, and how
                                    glad,

cry'd (cont.)
p. 397 UNGATHERED 30   31 Did all so strike me, as I cry'd, who can
p. 415 UNGATHERED 42   21 Cry'd up of late: whereto there must be first

cryd'st   frequency: 1   relative frequency: 0.00001
p. 123 UNDERWOOD 1.1   23 To pay our debts, upon thy Crosse, and cryd'st,

crye   frequency: 1   relative frequency: 0.00001
p.   29 EPIGRAMS 8   4 Beg'd RIDWAYES pardon: DVNCOTE,
                          now, doth crye,

cryed   frequency: 1   relative frequency: 0.00001
p.   30 EPIGRAMS 11   5 A lord, it cryed, buried in flesh, and blood,

cryes   frequency: 9   relative frequency: 0.00013
**p. 114 PANEGYRE   33 Hasting to follow forth in shouts, and cryes.
p.   30 EPIGRAMS 12   14 Signes to new bond, forfeits: and cryes, god
                          payes.
p.   44 EPIGRAMS 54   1 CHEV'RIL cryes out, my verses libells are;
p.   58 EPIGRAMS 92   2 Vnto the cryes of London Ile adde one;
p.   76 EPIGRAMS 119   3 Cryes out 'gainst cocking, since he cannot bet,
p.   84 EPIGRAMS 133   16 And, for the cryes of Ghosts, women, and men,
p. 111 FOREST 11   67 That cryes, we dreame, and sweares, there's no
                          such thing,
p. 256 UNDERWOOD 75   128 The Solemne Quire cryes, Joy; and they
                          returne, Amen.
p. 397 UNGATHERED 30   41 The Fights, the Cryes, and wondring at the
                          Iarres

crying   frequency: 1   relative frequency: 0.00001
p.   86 EPIGRAMS 133   96 Poore MERCVRY, crying out on
                          PARACELSVS,

cryme   frequency: 1   relative frequency: 0.00001
p. 421 UNGATHERED 49   8 As Cleare, and distant, as your selfe from
                          Cryme;

cry'st   frequency: 1   relative frequency: 0.00001
p.   73 EPIGRAMS 112   16 O, (thou cry'st out) that is thy proper game.

crystal. See "christall," "chrystall."

ctesibius   frequency: 1   relative frequency: 0.00001
p. 402 UNGATHERED 34   7 Controll Ctesibius: ouerbearing vs

cuckold. See "coockold."

cuckquean. See "cucqueane."

cucqueane   frequency: 1   relative frequency: 0.00001
p.   34 EPIGRAMS 25   5 And now, her (hourely) her owne cucqueane makes,

cuffes   frequency: 1   relative frequency: 0.00001
p.   58 EPIGRAMS 92   6 Ripe are their ruffes, their cuffes, their
                          beards, their gate,

cuffs. See "cuffes."

cull'd   frequency: 1   relative frequency: 0.00001
p. 413 UNGATHERED 41   13 The third, is from the garden cull'd, the Rose,

culloring   frequency: 1   relative frequency: 0.00001
p. 370 UNGATHERED 7   3 Light, Posture, Height'ning, Shadow,
                          Culloring,

cullors   frequency: 1   relative frequency: 0.00001
p.   98 FOREST 3   71 And shew their feathers shot, and cullors torne,

cunning   frequency: 8   relative frequency: 0.00011
See also "cunninge."
**p. 115 PANEGYRE   96 "Who both, who neither: all the cunning tracts,
p. 145 UNDERWOOD 5   13 And as a cunning Painter takes
p. 162 UNDERWOOD 15   15 Looke on the false, and cunning man, that loves
p. 242 UNDERWOOD 69   14 So doth the flatt'rer with faire cunning strike
p. 293 UNDERWOOD 87   10 Who sings so sweet, and with such cunning plaies,
p. 307 HORACE 2   68 Are, by thy cunning placing, made meere new.
p. 362 UNGATHERED 2   10 Vnto a cunning piece wrought perspectiue,
p. 370 UNGATHERED 7   4 All which are parts commend the cunning hand;

cunninge   frequency: 1   relative frequency: 0.00001
    p. 420 UNGATHERED 48   34 And Cunninge of their grownde

cunningly   frequency: 1   relative frequency: 0.00001
    p. 315 HORACE 2   215 And so well faines, so mixeth cunningly

cup   frequency: 5   relative frequency: 0.00007
    p. 65 EPIGRAMS 101   29 Is a pure cup of rich Canary-wine,
    p. 106 FOREST 9   3 Or leaue a kisse but in the cup,
    p. 120 FOREST 14   11 Giue me my cup, but from the Thespian well,
    p. 197 UNDERWOOD 40   4 In hast the bottome of a med'cin'd Cup,
    p. 208 UNDERWOOD 43   115 And so did Jove, who ne're meant thee his Cup:

cupid   frequency: 3   relative frequency: 0.00004
    See also "cvpid."
    p. 132 UNDERWOOD 2.2   6 For I ran and call'd on Cupid;
    p. 136 UNDERWOOD 2.5   t1 His discourse with Cupid.
    p. 221 UNDERWOOD 48   36 Then Cupid, and his Mother.

cupids   frequency: 4   relative frequency: 0.00005
    p. 132 UNDERWOOD 2.2   30 Cupids Statue with a Beard,
    p. 141 UNDERWOOD 2.9   17 Eye-brows bent like Cupids bow,
    p. 182 UNDERWOOD 28   9 For in your verse all Cupids Armorie,
    p. 369 UNGATHERED 6   100 With Cupids wing;

cupping-glasses   frequency: 1   relative frequency: 0.00001
    p. 270 UNDERWOOD 83   53 Stick on your Cupping-glasses, feare not, put

cups   frequency: 4   relative frequency: 0.00005
    p. 65 EPIGRAMS 101   37 Nor shall our cups make any guiltie men:
    p. 95 FOREST 2   67 Here no man tells my cups; nor, standing by,
    p. 98 FOREST 3   60 And in their cups, their cares are drown'd:
    p. 333 HORACE 2   617 Rich men are said with many cups to plie,

cur. See "curre."

cure   frequency: 12   relative frequency: 0.00017
    p. 82 EPIGRAMS 130   8 No lesse a sou'raigne cure, then to the mind;
    p. 155 UNDERWOOD 13   68 And hurt seeks Cure, the Surgeon bids take
                                 bread,
    p. 156 UNDERWOOD 13   115 Looke to and cure; Hee's not a man hath none,
    p. 180 UNDERWOOD 26   5 The Cure of that, which is but corporall,
    p. 192 UNDERWOOD 38   52 As not alone the Cure, but scarre be faire.
    p. 221 UNDERWOOD 48   24 And cure the Worlds diseases:
    p. 235 UNDERWOOD 62   4 To cure the call'd Kings Evill with thy touch;
    p. 235 UNDERWOOD 62   6 To cure the Poets Evill, Povertie:
    p. 235 UNDERWOOD 62   8 As thou dost cure our Evill, at thy charge.
    p. 235 UNDERWOOD 62   14 But, that he cure the Peoples Evill too?
    p. 270 UNDERWOOD 83   49 From all affection! when they urg'd the Cure
    p. 411 UNGATHERED 39   13 For thou hast nought <in thee> to cure his Fame,

cures   frequency: 4   relative frequency: 0.00005
    p. 39 EPIGRAMS 41   4 For what shee gaue, a whore; a baud, shee cures.
    p. 192 UNDERWOOD 38   46 We cut not off, till all Cures else doe faile:
    p. 235 UNDERWOOD 62   7 And, in these Cures, do'st so thy selfe enlarge,
    p. 657 I. CONVIVALES   17 Pays all Debts, cures all Diseases,

curious   frequency: 8   relative frequency: 0.00011
   *p. 493 TO HIMSELF   49 As curious fooles, and enuious of thy straine,
    p. 103 FOREST 6   19 That the curious may not know
    p. 115 FOREST 12   76 To curious light, the notes, I then shall sing,
    p. 145 UNDERWOOD 5   14 In any curious peece you see
    p. 204 UNDERWOOD 43   34 Of Logogriphes, and curious Palindromes,
    p. 213 UNDERWOOD 44   29 He that but saw thy curious Captaines drill,
    p. 227 UNDERWOOD 52   13 But whilst you curious were to have it be
    p. 260 UNDERWOOD 77   2 I would present you now with curious plate

curl. See "curle."

curle   frequency: 1   relative frequency: 0.00001
    p. 140 UNDERWOOD 2.8   24 There; or to reforme a curle;

curled   frequency: 2   relative frequency: 0.00002
    p. 97 FOREST 3   17 Along'st the curled woods, and painted meades,
    p. 307 HORACE 2   47 The nailes, and every curled haire disclose;

curles   frequency: 2   relative frequency: 0.00002
    p. 164 UNDERWOOD 15   65 Planting their Purles, and Curles spread forth
                                 like Net,

curles (cont.)
   p. 170 UNDERWOOD 19   6 He flying curles, and crispeth, with his wings;

curling-irons   frequency: 1   relative frequency: 0.00001
   p. 165 UNDERWOOD 15   111 When not his Combes, his Curling-irons, his
                         Glasse,

curls. See "curles."

curre   frequency: 2   relative frequency: 0.00002
   p. 408 UNGATHERED 37   7 But bawle thou on; I pitty thee, poore Curre,
   p. 409 UNGATHERED 37   15 A Mungrel Curre? Thou should'st stinck forth,
                         and dye

curs. See "towne-curs."

curse   frequency: 3   relative frequency: 0.00004
   p. 162 UNDERWOOD 15   14 Till he become both their, and his owne curse!
   p. 172 UNDERWOOD 20   18 Then all Ingredients made into one curse,
   p. 211 UNDERWOOD 43   190 But I'le conclude all in a civill curse.

cursed. See "curst."

curst   frequency: 3   relative frequency: 0.00004
   p. 47 EPIGRAMS 63   11 Curst be his Muse, that could lye dumbe, or hid
   p. 146 UNDERWOOD 6   23 For were the worthiest woman curst
   p. 200 UNDERWOOD 42   23 Curst in their Cradles, or there chang'd by
                         Elves,

curteous   frequency: 1   relative frequency: 0.00001
   p. 52 EPIGRAMS 76   9 I meant shee should be curteous, facile, sweet,

curtesie   frequency: 2   relative frequency: 0.00002
   p. 100 FOREST 4   11 Thy curtesie but sodaine starts,
   p. 158 UNDERWOOD 13   159 By thanking thus the curtesie to life,

curtesies   frequency: 1   relative frequency: 0.00001
   p. 153 UNDERWOOD 13   25 Can I owe thankes, for Curtesies receiv'd

custom. See "custome."

custome   frequency: 4   relative frequency: 0.00005
   p. 53 EPIGRAMS 78   2 To draw thee custome: but her selfe gets all.
   p. 113 FOREST 12   5 Toyles, by graue custome, vp and downe the court,
   p. 118 FOREST 13   60 Farre from the maze of custome, error, strife,
   p. 309 HORACE 2   103 If Custome please; at whose disposing will

customer   frequency: 1   relative frequency: 0.00001
   p. 201 UNDERWOOD 42   41 Home to the Customer: his Letcherie

customes   frequency: 3   relative frequency: 0.00004
   p. 117 FOREST 13   39 Or cos'ning farmer of the customes so,
   p. 160 UNDERWOOD 14   44 Times, manners, customes! Innovations spide!
   p. 315 HORACE 2   223 The customes of each age thou must observe,

customs. See "customes."

cut   frequency: 12   relative frequency: 0.00017
   p. 33 EPIGRAMS 21   1 Lord, how is GAM'STER chang'd! his haire
                         close cut!
   p. 86 EPIGRAMS 133   84 Made of the trull, that cut her fathers lock:
   p. 94 FOREST 2   15 There, in the writhed barke, are cut the names
   p. 98 FOREST 3   45 The trees cut out in log; and those boughes made
   p. 114 FOREST 12   23 When gold was made no weapon to cut throtes,
   p. 192 UNDERWOOD 38   46 We cut not off, till all Cures else doe faile:
   p. 270 UNDERWOOD 83   54 Your hottest Causticks to, burne, lance, or cut:
   p. 325 HORACE 2   434 On steele, though 't selfe be dull, and cannot
                         cut.
   p. 335 HORACE 2   636 Cut off superfluous ornaments; and when
   p. 390 UNGATHERED 25   2 It was for gentle Shakespeare cut;
   p. 396 UNGATHERED 30   20 The Orbe was cut forth into Regions seauen.
   p. 401 UNGATHERED 32   12 To cut a Dike? or sticke a Stake vp, here,

cuthbert   frequency: 1   relative frequency: 0.00001
   p. 394 UNGATHERED 28   t2 eldest Daughter, to Cuthbert Lord Ogle:

cutlers   frequency: 1   relative frequency: 0.00001
   p. 212 UNDERWOOD 43   200 Strooke in at Millan with the Cutlers there;

cvpid   frequency: 1   relative frequency: 0.00001
      p.   73 EPIGRAMS 114   3 For CVPID, who (at first) tooke vaine
                                delight,

cycnvs   frequency: 1   relative frequency: 0.00001
      p. 369 UNGATHERED 6   99 Were CYCNVS, once high flying

cygnus. See "cycnvs."

cyllarus   frequency: 1   relative frequency: 0.00001
      p. 228 UNDERWOOD 53   8 Or Castor mounted on his Cyllarus:

cynara   frequency: 1   relative frequency: 0.00001
      p. 292 UNDERWOOD 86   4 Of the good Cynara I was: Refraine,

cynthia   frequency: 3   relative frequency: 0.00004
      p. 181 UNDERWOOD 27   11 Doth Cynthia, in Propertius song
      p. 371 UNGATHERED 9   7 Taught Pallas language; Cynthia modesty;
      p. 398 UNGATHERED 30   80 I looke on Cynthia, and Sirenas sport,

cynthias   frequency: 1   relative frequency: 0.00001
      p. 662 INSCRIPTS. 2   6 to CYNTHIAS fayrest Nymph hath sent thee,

cynthius   frequency: 1   relative frequency: 0.00001
      p. 176 UNDERWOOD 25   8 Cynthius, I applie

cypher   frequency: 1   relative frequency: 0.00001
      p.   59 EPIGRAMS 92   26 To write in cypher, and the seuerall keyes,

cypres   frequency: 1   relative frequency: 0.00001
      p.   51 EPIGRAMS 73   14 In solemne cypres, the other cob-web-lawne.

cypress. See "cipresse," "cypres," "cypresse."

cypresse   frequency: 1   relative frequency: 0.00001
      p. 327 HORACE 2   476 And in smooth Cypresse boxes to be keep'd?

d.   frequency: 1   relative frequency: 0.00001
      p. 252 UNDERWOOD 75   t10 Daughter of ESME D. of Lenox deceased,

dagger   frequency: 2   relative frequency: 0.00002
      p. 403 UNGATHERED 34   27 A wodden Dagger, is a Dagger of wood

daies   frequency: 3   relative frequency: 0.00004
    **p. 114 PANEGYRE   47 They that had seene, but foure short daies
                                before,
      p. 287 U'WOOD 84.9   182 Of sorrow, then all pompe of gaudy daies:
      p. 293 UNDERWOOD 87   12 So Fate would give her life, and longer daies.

daily   frequency: 5   relative frequency: 0.00007
    See also "dayly."
      p.   28 EPIGRAMS 4   7 And such a Prince thou art, wee daily see,
      p.   39 EPIGRAMS 39   2 COLT, now, doth daily penance in his owne.
      p.   56 EPIGRAMS 88   16 Daily to turne in PAVLS, and helpe the
                                trade.
      p. 224 UNDERWOOD 50   17 Among the daily Ruines that fall foule,
      p. 288 U'WOOD 84.9   210 In manner of a daily Apostrophe,

daintie   frequency: 3   relative frequency: 0.00004
      p.   88 EPIGRAMS 133   165 Your daintie nostrills (in so hot a season,
      p. 175 UNDERWOOD 23   31 And since our Daintie age,
      p. 239 UNDERWOOD 67   18 With touch of daintie thum's!

daintinesse   frequency: 1   relative frequency: 0.00001
      p. 103 FOREST 8   22 Daintinesse, and softer ease,

dainty   frequency: 1   relative frequency: 0.00001
    See also "daintie."
      p. 292 UNDERWOOD 86   21 There shall thy dainty Nostrill take

dale   frequency: 1   relative frequency: 0.00001
      p. 367 UNGATHERED 6   43 To the Fugenian dale;

dam. See "damme."

damd   frequency: 1   relative frequency: 0.00001
      p. 371 UNGATHERED 8   8 They saw it halfe, damd thy whole play, and more;

dame   frequency: 10   relative frequency: 0.00014
    **p. 116 PANEGYRE   129 And now the dame had dried her dropping eyne,

dame (cont.)
p. 112 FOREST 11   109 Would not be fearefull to offend a dame
p. 113 FOREST 12   16 Runs betweene man, and man; 'tweene dame, and
                           dame;
p. 164 UNDERWOOD 15   78 That payes, or what he will: The Dame is
                           steele.
p. 229 UNDERWOOD 54   8 Is, she will play Dame Justice, too severe;
p. 274 U'WOOD 84.2   2 Of Dame VENETIA DIGBY, styl'd The
                           Faire:
p. 403 UNGATHERED 34   36 Not they that sided her, Dame Poetry,
p. 403 UNGATHERED 34   37 Dame History, Dame Architecture too,

dames   frequency: 4   relative frequency: 0.00005
    See also "grand-dames."
**p. 114 PANEGYRE   52 As our ambitious dames, when they make feast,
  p. 78 EPIGRAMS 121   1 RVDYERD, as lesser dames, to great ones
                           vse,
  p. 205 UNDERWOOD 43   67 Of errant Knight-hood, with the<ir> Dames, and
                           Dwarfes,
  p. 213 UNDERWOOD 44   14 Lent by the London Dames, to the Lords men;

damme   frequency: 1   relative frequency: 0.00001
  p. 50 EPIGRAMS 88   12 By which his damme conceiu'd him, clothes and
                           all?

dam'mee   frequency: 1   relative frequency: 0.00001
  p. 154 UNDERWOOD 13   53 Now dam'mee, Sir, if you shall not command

damn. See "dam'mee," "damne."

damnation   frequency: 1   relative frequency: 0.00001
  p. 166 UNDERWOOD 15   116 Or by Damnation voids it? or by stealth?

damn'd   frequency: 1   relative frequency: 0.00001
  p. 154 UNDERWOOD 13   57 Dam's whom he damn'd to, as the veriest Gull,

damne   frequency: 2   relative frequency: 0.00002
  p. 32 EPIGRAMS 16   10 He that dares damne himselfe, dares more then
                           fight.
  p. 402 UNGATHERED 34   5 Both him & Archimede; damne Architas

damned   frequency: 1   relative frequency: 0.00001
    See also "damd," "damn'd."
  p. 88 EPIGRAMS 133   172 And out-cryes of the damned in the Fleet?

damnes   frequency: 1   relative frequency: 0.00001
  p. 42 EPIGRAMS 49   1 PLAY-WRIGHT me reades, and still my
                           verses damnes,

damning   frequency: 1   relative frequency: 0.00001
  p. 172 UNDERWOOD 20   24 The Divell; and be the damning of us all.

damns. See "damnes," "dam's."

dampes   frequency: 1   relative frequency: 0.00001
**p. 113 PANEGYRE   16 Those dampes, that so offend all good mens eyes;

damps. See "dampes."

dam's   frequency: 1   relative frequency: 0.00001
  p. 154 UNDERWOOD 13   57 Dam's whom he damn'd to, as the veriest Gull,

dance   frequency: 4   relative frequency: 0.00005
    See also "daunce," "out-dance."
  p. 85 EPIGRAMS 133   36 Did dance the famous Morrisse, vnto Norwich)
  p. 120 FOREST 14   2 And some doe drinke, and some doe dance,
  p. 321 HORACE 2   339 To Dance, so she should, shamefac'd, differ
                           farre
  p. 401 UNGATHERED 33   9 And, with their Chained dance,

dances   frequency: 1   relative frequency: 0.00001
    See also "daunces."
  p. 222 UNDERWOOD 48   50 To put his Court in dances,

dancing   frequency: 1   relative frequency: 0.00001
    See also "dauncing."
  p. 68 EPIGRAMS 105   11 If dancing, all would cry th'Idalian Queene,

danes   frequency: 1   relative frequency: 0.00001
  p. 368 UNGATHERED 6   86 The Danes that drench

danger   frequency: 7   relative frequency: 0.00010
    p.   31 EPIGRAMS 13   4 From my diseases danger, and from thee.
    p. 116 FOREST 13   1 'Tis growne almost a danger to speake true
    p. 130 UNDERWOOD 1.3   9 And freed the soule from danger;
    p. 142 UNDERWOOD 2.9   42 Shewing danger more then ire.
    p. 194 UNDERWOOD 38   102 To carry noble danger in the face:
    p. 233 UNDERWOOD 59   17 To know the heads of danger! where 'tis fit
    p. 411 UNGATHERED 40   9 The Danger of delaying

dangerous   frequency: 2   relative frequency: 0.00002
    p.   31 EPIGRAMS 13   1 When men a dangerous disease did scape,
    p. 117 FOREST 13   11 And, in this name, am giuen out dangerous

dangers   frequency: 4   relative frequency: 0.00005
    p.   43 EPIGRAMS 51   10 Looke not vpon thy dangers, but our feares.
    p.   47 EPIGRAMS 64   12 And not to dangers. When so wise a king
    p. 118 FOREST 13   57 In single paths, dangers with ease are watch'd:
    p. 163 UNDERWOOD 15   38 And even our sports are dangers! what we call

daphne   frequency: 2   relative frequency: 0.0000
    p.   80 EPIGRAMS 126   6 I answer'd, DAPHNE now no paine can prove.
    p.   80 EPIGRAMS 126   8 CARY my loue is, DAPHNE but my tree.

dapper   frequency: 1   relative frequency: 0.00001
    p. 309 HORACE 2   110 That first sent forth the dapper Elegie,

darby   frequency: 1   relative frequency: 0.00001
    p. 417 UNGATHERED 45   21 Specially the newes of Darby;

dare   frequency: 31   relative frequency: 0.00044
   *p. 493 TO HIMSELF   34 Dare quit, vpon your oathes,
    p.   30 EPIGRAMS 11   8 For I will dare none. Good Lord, walke dead
                              still.
    p.   41 EPIGRAMS 43   7 Yet dare not, to my thought, lest hope allow
    p.   60 EPIGRAMS 94   12 Dare for these poemes, yet, both aske, and read,
    p.   62 EPIGRAMS 96   2 When I dare send my Epigrammes to thee?
    p.   70 EPIGRAMS 108   8 No more, then I dare now doe, with my pen.
    p.   88 EPIGRAMS 133   164 And, in a pittious tune, began. How dare
    p. 105 FOREST 8   33 That for th'oyle of Talke, dare spend
    p. 105 FOREST 8   34 More then citizens dare lend
    p. 105 FOREST 8   39 Dare entayle their loues on any,
    p. 116 FOREST 13   4 As what th'haue lost t<o>'expect, they dare
                              deride.
    p. 118 FOREST 13   78 Till that no vsurer, nor his bawds dare lend
    p. 122 FOREST 15   7 And iudge me after: if I dare pretend
    p. 122 FOREST 15   23 Yet dare I not complaine, or wish for death
    p. 147 UNDERWOOD 7   2 Yet dare I not tell who;
    p. 155 UNDERWOOD 13   86 And superstition I dare scarce reveale,
    p. 162 UNDERWOOD 15   3 All that dare rowse: or are not loth to quit
    p. 170 UNDERWOOD 18   10 And Fortune once, t<o>'assist the spirits that
                              dare.
    p. 187 UNDERWOOD 33   11 All mouthes, that dare entitle them (from hence)
    p. 206 UNDERWOOD 43   87 I dare not say a body, but some parts
    p. 215 UNDERWOOD 44   66 Borne, bred, allied? what's he dare tutor us?
    p. 215 UNDERWOOD 44   68 Live by their Scale, that dare doe nothing free?
    p. 222 UNDERWOOD 49   2 And thinkes I dare not her? let the world see.
    p. 248 UNDERWOOD 71   14 Dare thinke it, to relieve, no lesse renowne,
    p. 257 UNDERWOOD 75   160 But dare not aske our wish in Language
                              fescennine:
    p. 271 UNDERWOOD 83   79 If you dare grudge at Heaven, and repent
    p. 283 U'WOOD 84.9   39 Dare I prophane, so irreligious bee
    p. 286 U'WOOD 84.9   147 Nor dare we under blasphemy conceive
    p. 321 HORACE 2   356 Be I their Judge, they doe at no time dare
    p. 423 UNGATHERED 50   20 shall never dare do any thing but feare./
    p. 662 INSCRIPTS. 2   9 But with a Kisse, (if thou canst dare it)

dares   frequency: 14   relative frequency: 0.00020
    p.   32 EPIGRAMS 16   10 He that dares damne himselfe, dares more then
                              fight.
    p.   36 EPIGRAMS 28   16 Of solemne greatnesse. And he dares, at dice,
    p.   49 EPIGRAMS 66   17 Hee's valiant'st, that dares fight, and not for
                              pay;
    p.   62 EPIGRAMS 95   36 That dares nor write things false, nor hide
                              things true.
    p. 151 UNDERWOOD 11   14 As since he dares not come within my sight.
    p. 198 UNDERWOOD 40   33 Is fix'd upon one leg, and dares not come
    p. 235 UNDERWOOD 63   1 Who dares denie, that all first-fruits are due
    p. 241 UNDERWOOD 69   8 Nor dares he come in the comparison.
    p. 331 HORACE 2   570 Yet who's most ignorant, dares Verses make.
    p. 378 UNGATHERED 11   85 Shewes he dares more then Paules Church-yard
                              durst do.

dares (cont.)
    p. 380 UNGATHERED 12   33 That he dares to informe you, but somewhat
                                         meticulous,
    p. 389 UNGATHERED 24   8 That an ill man dares not securely looke
    p. 401 UNGATHERED 32   11 Yet, who dares offer a redoubt to reare?

darest. See "dar'st."

daring   frequency: 3   relative frequency: 0.00004
    p. 233 UNDERWOOD 59   15 Of daring not to doe a wrong, is true
    p. 305 HORACE 2   12 Of daring all, hath still beene given; we know
                                         it:
    p. 323 HORACE 2   407 In daring to forsake the Grecian tracts,

dark. See "darke."

dark-lanterne   frequency: 1   relative frequency: 0.00001
    p. 198 UNDERWOOD 40   23 Keepe in reserv'd in his Dark-lanterne face,

darke   frequency: 13   relative frequency: 0.00018
**p. 113 PANEGYRE   9 Into those darke and deepe concealed vaults,
    p. 128 UNDERWOOD 1.1   35 The gladdest light, darke man can thinke upon;
    p. 175 UNDERWOOD 24   1 From Death, and darke oblivion, neere the same,
    p. 177 UNDERWOOD 25   15 On these darke rymes; that my affection
    p. 189 UNDERWOOD 36   7 Without which all the world were darke;
    p. 193 UNDERWOOD 38   79 In darke, and sullen mornes, doe we not say,
    p. 199 UNDERWOOD 41   8 Where we must feele it Darke for halfe a yeare.
    p. 282 U'WOOD 84.9   7 To hang a window, or make darke the roome,
    p. 295 UNDERWOOD 89   5 Darke thy cleare glasse with old Falernian
                                         Wine;
    p. 331 HORACE 2   541 As some the farther off: This loves the darke;
    p. 335 HORACE 2   637 They're darke, bid cleare this: all that's
                                         doubtfull wrote
    p. 371 UNGATHERED 8   5 Veluet, or Taffata cap, rank'd in the darke
    p. 383 UNGATHERED 17   5 Who reads may roaue, and call the passage darke,

darkest   frequency: 1   relative frequency: 0.00001
    p. 295 UNDERWOOD 90   11 Sleepe, that will make the darkest howres
                                         swift-pac't;

darknesse   frequency: 6   relative frequency: 0.00008
    p. 156 UNDERWOOD 13   95 Or feats of darknesse acted in Mid-Sun,
    p. 180 UNDERWOOD 25   61 Where darknesse with her gloomie-sceptred hand,
    p. 191 UNDERWOOD 38   5 It is a Darknesse hath blockt up my sense,
    p. 194 UNDERWOOD 38   121 Till then 'tis all but darknesse, that I have;
    p. 234 UNDERWOOD 60   8 But crept like darknesse through his blood?
    p. 273 U'WOOD 84.1   5 Of Death, and Darknesse; and deprive

darrel's. See "dorrels."

dar'st   frequency: 8   relative frequency: 0.00011
    p. 32 EPIGRAMS 16   2 Thou more; that with it euery day, dar'st iest
    p. 32 EPIGRAMS 16   8 Make good what thou dar'st doe in all the rest.
    p. 72 EPIGRAMS 112   4 Or thy ranke setting? that thou dar'st put in
    p. 76 EPIGRAMS 119   9 Dar'st breath in any ayre; and with safe skill,
    p. 168 UNDERWOOD 15   184 But what she gives, thou dar'st give her againe;
    p. 187 UNDERWOOD 33   17 Dar'st not abuse thy wisdome, in the Lawes,
    p. 313 HORACE 2   179 Unto the Scene thou bringst, and dar'st create
    p. 408 UNGATHERED 37   1 My verses were commended, thou dar'st say,

darting   frequency: 1   relative frequency: 0.00001
    p. 253 UNDERWOOD 75   43 And Sister: darting forth a dazling light

darts   frequency: 1   relative frequency: 0.00001
    p. 110 FOREST 11   51 In equall knots: This beares no brands, nor
                                         darts,

dashing   frequency: 1   relative frequency: 0.00001
    p. 409 UNGATHERED 37   21 Thy Noddle, with his clubb; and dashing forth

date   frequency: 1   relative frequency: 0.00001
    p. 309 HORACE 2   100 Or grace of speech, should hope a lasting date.

daughter   frequency: 11   relative frequency: 0.00015
See also "davghter."
    p. 33 EPIGRAMS 22   2 MARY, the daughter of their youth:
    p. 181 UNDERWOOD 27   19 Of Caesars Daughter, and the line
    p. 240 UNDERWOOD 67   26 The Daughter of great Harry!
    p. 252 UNDERWOOD 75   t10 Daughter of ESME D. of Lenox deceased,
    p. 253 UNDERWOOD 75   42 Like what she is, the Daughter of a Duke,

daughter (cont.)
```
   p. 269 UNDERWOOD 83    10 Whose Daughter? ha? Great Savage of the Rock?
   p. 378 UNGATHERED 11   86 Come forth thou bonnie bouncing booke then,
                             daughter
   p. 394 UNGATHERED 28   t2 eldest Daughter, to Cuthbert Lord Ogle:
   p. 402 UNGATHERED 33   12 The faire French Daughter to learne English
                             in;
   p. 413 UNGATHERED 41   33 Daughter, and Mother, and the Spouse of GOD,
   p. 414 UNGATHERED 41   56 Of being Daughter, Mother, Spouse of GOD!
```

daughters   frequency: 6   relative frequency: 0.00008
```
 **p. 113 PANEGYRE        25 To be her daughters: and but faintly knowne
   p.  95 FOREST 2        54 By their ripe daughters, whom they would commend
   p. 200 UNDERWOOD 42    19 But then consent, your Daughters and your
                             Wives,
   p. 202 UNDERWOOD 42    87 Thou art jealous of thy Wifes, or Daughters
                             Case:
   p. 271 UNDERWOOD 83    83 If you can envie your owne Daughters blisse,
   p. 285 U'WOOD 84.9    118 And Sons, and Daughters, with their Parents
                             talke;
```

daunce   frequency: 1   relative frequency: 0.00001
```
   p. 108 FOREST 10A      11 Let these in wanton feete daunce out their
                             soules.
```

daunces   frequency: 2   relative frequency: 0.00002
```
   p. 138 UNDERWOOD 2.6   22 In the Daunces, with what spight
   p. 210 UNDERWOOD 43   157 Though but in daunces, it shall know his power;
```

dauncing   frequency: 1   relative frequency: 0.00001
```
   p. 415 UNGATHERED 43   t3 Instauration of his Hunting, and Dauncing
```

davghter   frequency: 1   relative frequency: 0.00001
```
   p.  33 EPIGRAMS 22     t1 ON MY FIRST DAVGHTER.
```

davids   frequency: 1   relative frequency: 0.00001
```
   p. 413 UNGATHERED 41   38 Sweet Tree of Life, King Davids Strength and
                             Tower,
```

davies. See "davis."

davis   frequency: 1   relative frequency: 0.00001
```
   p.  32 EPIGRAMS 18      4 DAVIS, and WEEVER, and the best haue
                             beene,
```

davus   frequency: 1   relative frequency: 0.00001
```
   p. 321 HORACE 2       345 As not make difference, whether Davus speake,
```

day   frequency: 106   relative frequency: 0.00153
     See also "birth-day," "holy-day," "mariage-day,"
              "noone-day."
```
  *p. 492 TO HIMSELF       5 Indicting, and arraigning euery day
 **p. 113 PANEGYRE         5 (To day) a thousand radiant lights, that stream
   p.  30 EPIGRAMS 12      7 The quarter day is come: the hostesse sayes,
   p.  32 EPIGRAMS 16      2 Thou more; that with it euery day, dar'st iest
   p.  36 EPIGRAMS 31      3 And though the soundest legs goe euery day,
   p.  41 EPIGRAMS 45      4 Exacted by thy fate, on the iust day.
   p.  42 EPIGRAMS 46      4 To pay at's day of marriage. By my hand
   p.  42 EPIGRAMS 46      6 Yes, now he weares his knight-hood euery day.
   p.  42 EPIGRAMS 48      1 His bought armes MVNG' not lik'd; for his
                             first day
   p.  43 EPIGRAMS 51     t3 and twentieth day of March,
   p.  49 EPIGRAMS 66      9 Against thy fortune: when no foe, that day,
   p.  50 EPIGRAMS 70      6 Each best day of our life escapes vs, first.
   p.  57 EPIGRAMS 90      7 Went on: and prouing him still, day by day,
   p.  57 EPIGRAMS 90     16 Longer a day, but with his MILL will marry.
   p.  59 EPIGRAMS 92     18 Nay, aske you, how the day goes, in your eare.
   p.  59 EPIGRAMS 92     23 Or, euery day, some one at RIMEE'S looks,
   p.  60 EPIGRAMS 94      2 Life of the Muses day, their morning-starre!
   p.  64 EPIGRAMS 100     3 And I must now beleeue him: for, to day,
   p.  66 EPIGRAMS 102     9 They follow vertue, for reward, to day;
   p.  76 EPIGRAMS 118     1 GVT eates all day, and lechers all the night,
   p.  83 EPIGRAMS 131    12 They were not to be nam'd on the same day.
   p.  84 EPIGRAMS 133    29 It was the day, what time the powerfull Moone
   p.  87 EPIGRAMS 133   119 Yet, one day in the yeere, for sweet 'tis voyc't,
   p.  95 FOREST 2        65 And I not faine to sit (as some, this day,
   p.  95 FOREST 2        71 Thy tables hoord not vp for the next day,
   p.  96 FOREST 2        96 With the whole houshold, and may, euery day,
   p.  97 FOREST 3        35 Thou dost with some delight the day out-weare,
   p. 100 FOREST 4        23 And neuer will redeeme a day,
```

day (cont.)

p. 107	FOREST 10	7	PHOEBVS. No? tend thy cart still. Enuious day
p. 112	FOREST 11	94	Would make a day of night,
p. 113	FOREST 12	17	Solders crackt friendship; makes loue last a day;
p. 117	FOREST 13	30	Your beautie; for you see that euery day:
p. 118	FOREST 13	74	On the close groome, and page, on new-yeeres day,
p. 120	FOREST 14	13	This day
p. 120	FOREST 14	21	This day sayes, then, the number of glad yeeres
p. 121	FOREST 14	54	This day
p. 132	UNDERWOOD 2.2	1	I beheld her, on a day,
p. 138	UNDERWOOD 2.6	15	Of the Court, to day, then all
p. 139	UNDERWOOD 2.8	1	Charis one day in discourse
p. 140	UNDERWOOD 2.8	10	And excuse spun every day,
p. 156	UNDERWOOD 13	116	But like to be, that every day mends one,
p. 157	UNDERWOOD 13	132	Profit in ought; each day some little adde,
p. 163	UNDERWOOD 15	29	As farre as he can flie, or follow day,
p. 164	UNDERWOOD 15	64	How they may make some one that day an Asse;
p. 165	UNDERWOOD 15	107	Coach'd, or on foot-cloth, thrice chang'd every day,
p. 166	UNDERWOOD 15	131	Or side, but threatens Ruine. The whole Day
p. 168	UNDERWOOD 16	3	But here doth lie, till the last Day,
p. 169	UNDERWOOD 17	2	Debts when they can: good men may breake their day,
p. 186	UNDERWOOD 32	7	Such shall you heare to day, and find great foes,
p. 193	UNDERWOOD 38	80	This looketh like an Execution day?
p. 202	UNDERWOOD 42	77	And vouches both the Pageant, and the Day,
p. 204	UNDERWOOD 43	44	Fitter to see the fire-light, then the day;
p. 208	UNDERWOOD 43	119	Squire of the Squibs, against the Pageant day,
p. 213	UNDERWOOD 44	2	But we have Powder still for the Kings Day,
p. 213	UNDERWOOD 44	10	If they stay here, but till Saint Georges Day.
p. 213	UNDERWOOD 44	27	These ten yeares day; As all may sweare that looke
p. 214	UNDERWOOD 44	48	More then the surfets, in thee, that day stood.
p. 215	UNDERWOOD 44	72	The Hawking language? or our Day to breake
p. 223	UNDERWOOD 49	36	From Court, while yet thy fame hath some small day;
p. 225	UNDERWOOD 51	5	Pardon, I read it in thy face, the day
p. 231	UNDERWOOD 56	29	I gaine, in having leave to keepe my Day,
p. 236	UNDERWOOD 64	4	If he but weigh'd the blessings of this day?
p. 236	UNDERWOOD 64	t3	On his Anniversary Day.
p. 240	UNDERWOOD 67	43	8. URA. This day the Court doth measure
p. 240	UNDERWOOD 67	47	Summe up this crowned day,
p. 245	UNDERWOOD 70	69	A Lillie of a Day,
p. 245	UNDERWOOD 70	81	To see that bright eternall Day:
p. 249	UNDERWOOD 72	1	This is King CHARLES his Day. Speake it, thou Towre,
p. 249	UNDERWOOD 72	7	Adding her owne glad accents, to this Day,
p. 250	UNDERWOOD 73	t3	Vpon the Day,
p. 252	UNDERWOOD 75	5	Then thou shalt see to day:
p. 252	UNDERWOOD 75	9	See, the Procession! what a Holy day
p. 253	UNDERWOOD 75	35	As they had learn'd new changes, for the day,
p. 254	UNDERWOOD 75	55	This Feast, then can the Day,
p. 255	UNDERWOOD 75	86	Themselves to day,
p. 255	UNDERWOOD 75	90	And wonder'd at, the bounties of this day:
p. 256	UNDERWOOD 75	107	To day, the Fathers service; who could bring
p. 257	UNDERWOOD 75	138	Now, Sun, and post away the rest of day:
p. 258	UNDERWOOD 75	168	(After the last child borne;) This is our wedding day.
p. 258	UNDERWOOD 75	190	Will last till day;
p. 263	UNDERWOOD 79	2	Lute, Lyre, Theorbo, all are call'd to day.
p. 263	UNDERWOOD 79	9	Rector Chori. To day old Janus opens the new yeare,
p. 268	UNDERWOOD 82	10	This day, by Baptisme, and his Saviours crosse:
p. 271	UNDERWOOD 83	82	At pleasure, to be call'd for, every day!
p. 271	UNDERWOOD 83	88	And Day, deceasing with the Prince of light,
p. 276	U'WOOD 84.3	14	And, out of that, make Day to breake;
p. 284	U'WOOD 84.9	59	Who will be there, against that day prepar'd,
p. 284	U'WOOD 84.9	61	O Day of joy, and suretie to the just!
p. 286	U'WOOD 84.9	120	But make him All in All, their Theme, that Day:
p. 286	U'WOOD 84.9	121	That happy Day, that never shall see night!
p. 292	UNDERWOOD 86	25	There twice a day in sacred Laies,
p. 295	UNDERWOOD 90	13	Nor feare thy latest day, nor wish therfore.
p. 317	HORACE 2	254	In fitting proper adjuncts to each day.
p. 323	HORACE 2	398	In hand, and turne them over, day, and night.
p. 325	HORACE 2	416	To taxe that Verse, which many a day, and blot
p. 384	UNGATHERED 18	9	Not only this, but every day of thine,
p. 384	UNGATHERED 18	11	May she, whome thou for spouse, to day, dost take,

day (cont.)
p. 384 UNGATHERED 18   26 Sure, this glad payre were married, but this day.
p. 388 UNGATHERED 23   7 If all the vulgar Tongues, that speake this day,
p. 392 UNGATHERED 26   80 And despaires day, but for thy Volumes light.
p. 396 UNGATHERED 30   10 Without conferring symboles. This's my day.
p. 396 UNGATHERED 30   18 Is fayre got vp, and day some houres begun!
p. 400 UNGATHERED 31   27 And when the flesh, here, shut vp day,
p. 416 UNGATHERED 44   1 Fresh as the Day, and new as are the flowers,
p. 417 UNGATHERED 45   11 I shall think on't ere't be day.

day-starre   frequency: 1   relative frequency: 0.00001
p. 52 EPIGRAMS 76   7 I meant the day-starre should not brighter rise,

dayes   frequency: 19   relative frequency: 0.00027
p. 28 EPIGRAMS 4   5 For such a Poet, while thy dayes were greene,
p. 30 EPIGRAMS 12   13 Then takes vp fresh commoditie, for dayes;
p. 55 EPIGRAMS 85   2 My selfe a witnesse of thy few dayes sport:
p. 59 EPIGRAMS 92   19 Keepe a starre-chamber sentence close, twelue
                             dayes:
p. 104 FOREST 8   5 Spent in surfets: and their dayes,
p. 118 FOREST 13   75 And almost, all dayes after, while they liue;
p. 121 FOREST 14   50 To liue vntill to morrow' hath lost two dayes.
p. 159 UNDERWOOD 14   25 And what I write? and vexe it many dayes
p. 180 UNDERWOOD 26   6 And doubtfull Dayes (which were nam'd
                             Criticall,)
p. 199 UNDERWOOD 41   9 What fate is this, to change mens dayes and
                             houres,
p. 237 UNDERWOOD 64   13 When all your life's a president of dayes,
p. 244 UNDERWOOD 70   53 Goe now, and tell out dayes summ'd up with
                             feares,
p. 248 UNDERWOOD 71   9 The Muse not peepes out, one of hundred dayes;
p. 288 U'WOOD 84.9   195 Would sit in an Infirmery, whole dayes
p. 295 UNDERWOOD 89   7 Hee, that but living halfe his dayes, dies such,
p. 319 HORACE 2   298 Steepe the glad Genius in the Wine, whole
                             dayes,
p. 388 UNGATHERED 23   t3 of Hesiods Works, & Dayes.
p. 410 UNGATHERED 38   10 A Prentise-ship: which few doe now a dayes.
p. 420 UNGATHERED 48   24 Thou that doest spend thie dayes

dayes-presents   frequency: 1   relative frequency: 0.00001
p. 113 FOREST 12   8 Iust to the waight their this dayes-presents
                             beare;

dayly   frequency: 1   relative frequency: 0.00001
p. 369 UNGATHERED 6   101 Though, now by Loue transform'd, & dayly
                             dying:

days. See "daies," "dayes," "dayes-presents,"
          "log-daies," "holy-dayes."

dazeling   frequency: 2   relative frequency: 0.00002
p. 233 UNDERWOOD 59   9 A quick, and dazeling motion when a paire
p. 234 UNDERWOOD 60   9 Offended with the dazeling flame

dazling   frequncy: 2   relative frequency: 0.00002
p. 253 UNDERWOOD 75   43 And Sister: darting forth a dazling light
p. 270 UNDERWOOD 83   44 A dazling, yet inviting, Majestie:

dazzling. See "dazeling," "dazling."

de   frequency: 1   relative frequency: 0.00001
p. 203 UNDERWOOD 43   29 Had I compil'd from Amadis de Gaule,

dead   frequency: 24   relative frequency: 0.00034
*p. 492 TO HIMSELF   16 Whose appetites are dead!
p. 30 EPIGRAMS 11   8 For I will dare none. Good Lord, walke dead
                             still.
p. 39 EPIGRAMS 40   2 A dead beautie vnder-neath thee,
p. 80 EPIGRAMS 127   6 How full of want, how swallow'd vp, how dead
p. 139 UNDERWOOD 2.7   18 Let who will thinke us dead, or wish our death.
p. 152 UNDERWOOD 12   36 I feele, I'm rather dead than he!
p. 162 UNDERWOOD 15   8 Quickning dead Nature, to her noblest strife.
p. 163 UNDERWOOD 15   40 And shamefastnesse together! All lawes dead,
p. 168 UNDERWOOD 15   189 So, 'live or dead, thou wilt preserve a fame
p. 179 UNDERWOOD 25   37 When her dead essence (like the Anatomie
p. 213 UNDERWOOD 44   11 All Ensignes of a Warre, are not yet dead,
p. 218 UNDERWOOD 47   17 On all Soules that are absent; even the dead;
p. 233 UNDERWOOD 60   2 Stay, drop a teare for him that's dead,
p. 244 UNDERWOOD 70   40 And sunke in that dead sea of life

dead (cont.)
```
    p. 245 UNDERWOOD 70    78 And thinke, nay know, thy Morison's not dead.
    p. 271 UNDERWOOD 83    86 And see all dead here, or about to dye!
    p. 282 U'WOOD 84.9      1 'Twere time that I dy'd too, now shee is dead,
    p. 283 U'WOOD 84.9     29 Sure, I am dead, and know it not! I feele
    p. 283 U'WOOD 84.9     44 And left her lovely body unthought dead!
    p. 283 U'WOOD 84.9     45 Indeed, she is not dead! but laid to sleepe
    p. 289 U'WOOD 84.9    221 Of all are dead to life! His Wisdome show
    p. 309 HORACE 2       101 Much phrase that now is dead, shall be reviv'd;
    p. 391 UNGATHERED 26   35 Paccuuius, Accius, him of Cordoua dead,
    p. 405 UNGATHERED 34   89 Of thy dead Standards: or (wth miracle) see
```

deadly   frequency: 1   relative frequency: 0.00001
```
    p. 171 UNDERWOOD 20     2 Forgive me this one foolish deadly sin,
```

deaf. See "deafe."

deafe   frequency: 1   relative frequency: 0.00001
```
    p. 149 UNDERWOOD 9      1 I now thinke, Love is rather deafe, then blind,
```

deal. See "deale."

deal-boards   frequency: 1   relative frequency: 0.00001
```
    p. 406 UNGATHERED 34   93 A Goddess is, then paynted Cloth, Deal-boards,
```

deale   frequency: 4   relative frequency: 0.00005
```
    p.  74 EPIGRAMS 115     9 Talkes loud, and baudy, has a gather'd deale
    p. 217 UNDERWOOD 46    15 And now such is thy stand; while thou dost deale
    p. 218 UNDERWOOD 47    27 I have no portion in them, nor their deale
    p. 404 UNGATHERED 34   48 Mythology there painted on slit deale!
```

dear   frequency: 1   relative frequency: 0.00001
```
    See also "deare."
    p. 116 FOREST 12       93 Who, wheresoere he be, on what dear coast,
```

deare   frequency: 12   relative frequency: 0.00017
```
  **p. 117 PANEGYRE       137 How deare a father they did now enioy
    p.  51 EPIGRAMS 73     21 Fortie things more, deare GRAND, which you
                              know true,
    p.  63 EPIGRAMS 97     13 He is no fauourites fauourite, no deare trust
    p. 119 FOREST 13      117 Vnto himselfe, by being so deare to you.
    p. 151 UNDERWOOD 12     7 Deare Vincent Corbet, who so long
    p. 165 UNDERWOOD 15   110 His deare and borrow'd Bravery he must cast?
    p. 180 UNDERWOOD 26    19 Thinke but how deare you bought
    p. 190 UNDERWOOD 37    18 In friendship, I confesse: But, deare friend,
                              heare.
    p. 198 UNDERWOOD 40    50 If I had writ no word, but Deare, farewell.
    p. 229 UNDERWOOD 54    16 Lend me, deare Arthur, for a weeke five more,
    p. 285 U'WOOD 84.9    107 That shall re-joyne yee. Was she, then, so
                              deare,
    p. 414 UNGATHERED 42   t1 To my deare Sonne, and right-learned Friend,
```

dearely   frequency: 1   relative frequency: 0.00001
```
    p.  27 EPIGRAMS 2      14 For vulgar praise, doth it too dearely buy.
```

dearer   frequency: 3   relative frequency: 0.00004
```
    p.  99 FOREST 3        96 To him, man's dearer, then t<o>'himselfe.
    p. 119 FOREST 13      116 But to please him, who is the dearer prise
    p. 285 U'WOOD 84.9    109 Much more desir'd, and dearer then before,
```

dearest   frequency: 2   relative frequency: 0.00002
```
    p.  49 EPIGRAMS 66     14 When they cost dearest, and are done most free,
    p. 179 UNDERWOOD 25    56 Unknowne which is the Dearest)
```

dearly. See "dearely."

death   frequency: 32   relative frequency: 0.00046
```
    p.  37 EPIGRAMS 32      9 Which shewes, where euer death doth please
                              t<o>'appeare,
    p.  37 EPIGRAMS 34      1 He that feares death, or mournes it, in the iust,
    p.  37 EPIGRAMS 34     t1 OF DEATH.
    p.  43 EPIGRAMS 51     t2 Vpon the happy false rumour of his death, the two
    p.  53 EPIGRAMS 80      1 The ports of death are sinnes; of life, good
                              deeds:
    p.  53 EPIGRAMS 80     t1 OF LIFE, AND DEATH.
    p.  54 EPIGRAMS 80      7 So to front death, as men might iudge vs past it.
    p.  54 EPIGRAMS 80      8 For good men but see death, the wicked tast it.
    p.  79 EPIGRAMS 124    10 Th'other let it sleepe with death:
    p.  99 FOREST 3        76 Then either money, warre, or death:
    p. 100 FOREST 3       105 Nor death; but when thy latest sand is spent,
```

death (cont.)

p.	122 FOREST 15	23	Yet dare I not complaine, or wish for death
p.	129 UNDERWOOD 1.2	23	Sinne, Death, and Hell,
p.	139 UNDERWOOD 2.7	18	Let who will thinke us dead, or wish our death.
p.	149 UNDERWOOD 8	9	Yes; and in death, as life, unblest,
p.	175 UNDERWOOD 24	1	From Death, and darke oblivion, neere the same,
p.	233 UNDERWOOD 59	23	Of fortune! when, or death appear'd, or bands!
p.	243 UNDERWOOD 70	14	Lay trampled on; the deeds of death, and night,
p.	269 UNDERWOOD 83	5	I doe obey you, Beautie! for in death,
p.	271 UNDERWOOD 83	67	'Twixt death and life! Where her mortalitie
p.	272 UNDERWOOD 83	99	The Serpents head: Gets above Death, and Sinne,
p.	273 U'WOOD 84.1	5	Of Death, and Darknesse; and deprive
p.	282 U'WOOD 84.9	12	By Death, on Earth, I should have had remorse
p.	283 U'WOOD 84.9	18	Of Vulture death, and those relentlesse cleies?
p.	285 U'WOOD 84.9	91	And she doth know, out of the shade of Death,
p.	286 U'WOOD 84.9	135	Through his inherent righteousnesse, in death,
p.	288 U'WOOD 84.9	203	Shee saw him rise, triumphing over Death
p.	309 HORACE 2	90	Our selves, and all that's ours, to death we owe:
p.	335 HORACE 2	659	I'le tell you but the death, and the disease
p.	335 HORACE 2	669	Or love of this so famous death lay by.
p.	370 UNGATHERED 8	2	Vpon the Life, and Death of Playes, and Wits,
p.	394 UNGATHERED 28	25	Where spight of Death, next Life, for her Loues sake,

deaths   frequency: 2   relative frequency: 0.00002
     p. 54 EPIGRAMS 80   5 This world deaths region is, the other lifes:
     p. 394 UNGATHERED 28   21 Then entertaine, and as Deaths Harbinger;

death's   frequency: 2   relative frequency: 0.00002
     See also "deaths."
     p. 77 EPIGRAMS 120   4 Death's selfe is sorry.
     p. 244 UNDERWOOD 70   41 So deep, as he did then death's waters sup;

deaw   frequency: 1   relative frequency: 0.00001
     p. 268 UNDERWOOD 83   1 What gentle Ghost, besprent with April deaw,

debentur   frequency: 1   relative frequency: 0.00001
     p. 231 UNDERWOOD 57   6 To send my Debentur.

debenture. See "debentur."

debt   frequency: 4   relative frequency: 0.00005
     p. 76 EPIGRAMS 119   4 Shuns prease, for two maine causes, poxe, and debt,
     p. 80 EPIGRAMS 127   5 Into the debt; and reckon on her head,
     p. 325 HORACE 2   445 Hee, that hath studied well the debt, and knowes
     p. 412 UNGATHERED 40   16 And the debt we'are in,

debt-booke   frequency: 1   relative frequency: 0.00001
     p. 154 UNDERWOOD 13   34 That puts it in his Debt-booke e're't be done;

debter   frequency: 1   relative frequency: 0.00001
     p. 51 EPIGRAMS 73   4 The world must know your greatnesse is my debter.

debters   frequency: 1   relative frequency: 0.00001
     p. 259 UNDERWOOD 76   8 To make all the MUSES debters

debtor. See "debter."

debtors. See "debters."

debts   frequency: 4   relative frequency: 0.00005
     p. 128 UNDERWOOD 1.1   23 To pay our debts, upon thy Crosse, and cryd'st,
     p. 169 UNDERWOOD 17   2 Debts when they can: good men may breake their day,
     p. 286 U'WOOD 84.9   143 Yet have all debts forgiven us, and advance
     p. 657 L. CONVIVALES   17 Pays all Debts, cures all Diseases,

decay   frequency: 6   relative frequency: 0.00008
     p. 131 UNDERWOOD 2.1   22 And let nothing high decay,
     p. 173 UNDERWOOD 22   19 His Altars kept from the Decay,
     p. 194 UNDERWOOD 38   116 Absence, or Distance, shall not breed decay.
     p. 294 UNDERWOOD 88   5 For lust will languish, and that heat decay.
     p. 294 UNDERWOOD 88   10 Can this decay, but is beginning ever.
     p. 309 HORACE 2   88 Of words decay, and phrases borne but late

decay'd   frequency: 2   relative frequency: 0.00002
     p. 259 UNDERWOOD 76   23 Parts of me (they judg'd) decay'd,
     p. 275 U'WOOD 84.3   6 Some Forme defective, or decay'd;

decayes   frequency: 1   relative frequency: 0.00001
    p. 160 UNDERWOOD 14   46 And noted the beginnings and decayes!

decays. See "decayes."

deceased   frequency: 1   relative frequency: 0.00001
    See also "deceast."
    p. 252 UNDERWOOD 75   t10 Daughter of ESME D. of Lenox deceased,

deceasing   frequency: 1   relative frequency: 0.00001
    p. 271 UNDERWOOD 83   88 And Day, deceasing with the Prince of light,

deceast   frequency: 1   relative frequency: 0.00001
    p. 121 FOREST 14   38 On what's deceast.

deceipt   frequency: 1   relative frequency: 0.00001
    p. 411 UNGATHERED 40 11 And the deceipt of pleasures,

deceit   frequency: 1   relative frequency: 0.00001
    See also "deceipt."
    p. 216 UNDERWOOD 45   18 Deceit is fruitfull. Men have Masques and nets,

deceiue   frequency: 1   relative frequency: 0.00001
    p. 27 EPIGRAMS 2   7 Deceiue their malice, who could wish it so.

deceiues   frequency: 1   relative frequency: 0.00001
    p. 44 EPIGRAMS 55   8 What art is thine, that so thy friend deceiues?

deceiv'd   frequency: 2   relative frequency: 0.00002
    p. 159 UNDERWOOD 14   23 Since, being deceiv'd, I turne a sharper eye
    p. 307 HORACE 2   60 Or I am much deceiv'd, shall be to place

deceive. See "deceiue."

deceives. See "deceiues."

decent   frequency: 1   relative frequency: 0.00001
    p. 311 HORACE 2   125 The place allotted it, with decent thewes.

deck   frequency: 3   relative frequency: 0.00004
    See also "decke."
    p. 137 UNDERWOOD 2.5   30 With the Lace that doth it deck,
    p. 253 UNDERWOOD 75   24 To welcome home a Paire, and deck the nuptiall
                              bower?
    p. 291 UNDERWOOD 85   43 To deck the hallow'd Harth with old wood fir'd

decke   frequency: 1   relative frequency: 0.00001
    p. 35 EPIGRAMS 27   1 In place of scutcheons, that should decke thy
                              herse,

declares   frequency: 1   relative frequency: 0.00001
    p. 309 HORACE 2   106 What number best can fit, Homer declares.

declin'd   frequency: 1   relative frequency: 0.00001
    p. 47 EPIGRAMS 63   7 Who can behold all enuie so declin'd

decline   frequency: 2   relative frequency: 0.00002
    p. 118 FOREST 13   59 This makes, that wisely you decline your life,
    p. 368 UNGATHERED 6   74 Humber, or Owse, decline;

declineth   frequency: 1   relative frequency: 0.00001
    p. 82 EPIGRAMS 130   5 Declineth anger, perswades clemencie,

decoctions   frequency: 1   relative frequency: 0.00001
    p. 105 FOREST 8   30 In decoctions; and are mann'd

decreased. See "decreast."

decreast   frequency: 1   relative frequency: 0.00001
    p. 156 UNDERWOOD 13 118 Can I discerne how shadowes are decreast,

decree   frequency: 2   relative frequency: 0.00002
    p. 185 UNDERWOOD 31   2 Lawes, and no change e're come to one decree:
    p. 211 UNDERWOOD 43 176 No order? no Decree? Though we be gone

decreed   frequency: 3   relative frequency: 0.00004
    p. 53 EPIGRAMS 79   5 Hence was it, that the destinies decreed
    p. 130 UNDERWOOD 1.3 16 And as that wisedome had decreed,
    p. 219 UNDERWOOD 47   57 I have decreed; keepe it from waves, and presse;

dedicate   frequency: 2   relative frequency: 0.00002
    p.   44 EPIGRAMS 53   10 Could saue that line to dedicate to thee?
    p. 220 UNDERWOOD 48   3 We dedicate this Cellar,

dedicated   frequency: 1   relative frequency: 0.00001
    p. 273 U'WOOD 84.1   11 A dedicated Ensigne make

dedication   frequency: 2   relative frequency: 0.00002
    p. 220 UNDERWOOD 48   t1 The Dedication of the Kings new Cellar.
    p. 272 U'WOOD 84.1   t1 The Dedication of her CRADLE.

deed   frequency: 11   relative frequency: 0.00015
    p.   49 EPIGRAMS 66   7 Which deed I know not, whether were more high,
    p.   55 EPIGRAMS 86   5 Now, I must giue thy life, and deed, the voice
    p.   61 EPIGRAMS 95   26 It is the next deed, and a great one too.
    p.   89 EPIGRAMS 133   193 In memorie of which most liquid deed,
    p. 133 UNDERWOOD 2.3   18 She repented of the deed,
    p. 144 UNDERWOOD 3   17 They say the Angells marke each Deed,
    p. 146 UNDERWOOD 6   11 The frequent varying of the deed,
    p. 153 UNDERWOOD 13   24 Where any Deed is forc't, the Grace is mard.
    p. 155 UNDERWOOD 13   76 Of any, is a great and generous Deed:
    p. 223 UNDERWOOD 49   42 This Age would lend no faith to Dorrels Deed;
    p. 247 UNDERWOOD 70   123 Friendship, in deed, was written, not in words:

deedes   frequency: 2   relative frequency: 0.00002
    p.   70 EPIGRAMS 109   17 Thy deedes, vnto thy name, will proue new wombes,
    p.   71 EPIGRAMS 110   15 His deedes too dying, but in bookes (whose good

deeds   frequency: 13   relative frequency: 0.00018
    See also "deedes."
    p.   46 EPIGRAMS 60   6 And proud, my worke shall out-last common deeds,
    p.   53 EPIGRAMS 80   1 The ports of death are sinnes; of life, good
                                    deeds:
    p.   58 EPIGRAMS 91   6 In th'eye of Europe, where thy deeds were done,
    p.   64 EPIGRAMS 99   8 The selfe-same deeds, as diuersly they come,
    p.   71 EPIGRAMS 110   1 Not CAESARS deeds, nor all his honors
                                    wonne,
    p. 167 UNDERWOOD 15   177 That thine be just, and honest; that thy Deeds
    p. 185 UNDERWOOD 30   11 But stood unshaken in his Deeds, and Name,
    p. 243 UNDERWOOD 70   14 Lay trampled on; the deeds of death, and night,
    p. 281 U'WOOD 84.8   17 Which all men doe, that urge not their owne deeds
    p. 288 U'WOOD 84.9   193 Or doing other deeds of Charitie,
    p. 309 HORACE 2   98 Being taught a better way. All mortall deeds
    p. 341 HORACE 1   105 ... deeds .. ..
    p. 406 UNGATHERED 35   4 All kings to doe ye self same deeds wth some!

deem. See "deeme."

deeme   frequency: 1   relative frequency: 0.00001
    p. 114 FOREST 12   22 Then this, our guilt, nor golden age can deeme,

deep   frequency: 2   relative frequency: 0.00002
    See also "deepe," "deepe-grounded."
    p. 244 UNDERWOOD 70   41 So deep, as he did then death's waters sup;
    p. 255 UNDERWOOD 75   98 That Mine of Wisdome, and of Counsells deep,

deep-crown'd-bowle   frequency: 1   relative frequency: 0.00001
    p. 225 UNDERWOOD 51   19 Give me a deep-crown'd-Bowle, that I may sing

deepe   frequency: 6   relative frequency: 0.00008
  **p. 113 PANEGYRE   9 Into those darke and deepe concealed vaults,
    p.   71 EPIGRAMS 110   7 And that so strong and deepe, as 't might be
                                    thought,
    p. 108 FOREST 10   30 And now an Epode to deepe eares I sing.
    p. 361 UNGATHERED 1   26 in a deepe trance;
    p. 384 UNGATHERED 18   17 So, be yor Concord, still, as deepe, as mute;
    p. 412 UNGATHERED 40   21 I sayd, who'had supp'd so deepe

deepe-grounded   frequency: 1   relative frequency: 0.00001
    p. 414 UNGATHERED 42   7 By those deepe-grounded, understanding men,

deeper   frequency: 1   relative frequency: 0.00001
    p. 365 UNGATHERED 5   22 Are deeper then their Faces:

deepest   frequency: 2   relative frequency: 0.00002
    p. 153 UNDERWOOD 13   20 Deepest in Man, of which when he doth thinke,
    p. 243 UNDERWOOD 70   10 Of deepest lore, could we the Center find!

deer. See "deere."

deere   frequency: 2   relative frequency: 0.00002
    p. 94 FOREST 2   20 That neuer failes to serue thee season'd deere,
    p. 97 FOREST 3   26 Diuid'st, vpon the lesser Deere;

defaced. See "defac't."

defac't   frequency: 1   relative frequency: 0.00001
    p. 174 UNDERWOOD 23 12 To see their Seats and Bowers by chattring
                             Pies defac't?

defame   frequency: 1   relative frequency: 0.00001
    p. 203 UNDERWOOD 43 25 Itch to defame the State? or brand the Times?

defeat   frequency: 2   relative frequency: 0.00002
    See also "defeate."
    p. 118 FOREST 13   51 'Tis only that can time, and chance defeat:
    p. 191 UNDERWOOD 38 18 In will and power, only to defeat.

defeate   frequency: 1   relative frequency: 0.00001
    *p. 493 TO HIMSELF   48 Throughout, to their defeate:

defect   frequency: 1   relative frequency: 0.00001
    p. 75 EPIGRAMS 115 29 Executes men in picture. By defect,

defective   frequency: 1   relative frequency: 0.00001
    p. 275 U'WOOD 84.3   6 Some Forme defective, or decay'd;

defence   frequency: 4   relative frequency: 0.00005
    See also "defense."
    p. 130 UNDERWOOD 1.3 23 A Martyr borne in our defence;
    p. 146 UNDERWOOD 6   t2 In defence of their Inconstancie.
    p. 217 UNDERWOOD 46 14 Stood up thy Nations fame, her Crownes defence.
    p. 232 UNDERWOOD 59   6 As all defence, or offence, were a chime!

defences   frequency: 1   relative frequency: 0.00001
    p. 217 UNDERWOOD 46   8 Thy just defences made th'oppressor afraid.

defend   frequency: 6   relative frequency: 0.00008
    **p. 116 PANEGYRE   110 As once defend, what THEMIS did reproue.
    **p. 116 PANEGYRE   119 One wickednesse another must defend;
    p. 63 EPIGRAMS 98   7 That thou at once, then, nobly maist defend
    p. 161 UNDERWOOD 14 78 And strength to be a Champion, and defend
    p. 221 UNDERWOOD 48 18 Lyaeus, and defend him,
    p. 335 HORACE 2   629 Then: If your fault you rather had defend

defenders   frequency: 1   relative frequency: 0.00001
    p. 186 UNDERWOOD 32   5 When those good few, that her Defenders be,

defend'st   frequency: 1   relative frequency: 0.00001
    p. 187 UNDERWOOD 33 32 So brightly brandish'd) wound'st, defend'st! the
                             while

defense   frequency: 1   relative frequency: 0.00001
    p. 400 UNGATHERED 32 4 In Bulwarkes, Rau'lins, Ramparts, for defense,

defer. See "deferre."

deferre   frequency: 1   relative frequency: 0.00001
    p. 102 FOREST 5   9 Why should we deferre our ioyes?

deferrer   frequency: 1   relative frequency: 0.00001
    See also "differrer."
    p. 317 HORACE 2   245 A great deferrer, long in hope, growne numbe

defies   frequency: 1   relative frequency: 0.00001
    p. 401 UNGATHERED 32 20 Defies, what's crosse to Piety, or good Fame.

defiled   frequency: 1   relative frequency: 0.00001
    p. 337 HORACE 2   673 (Defiled) touch'd; but certaine he was mad,

defin'd   frequency: 1   relative frequency: 0.00001
    p. 75 EPIGRAMS 115 33 Describ'd, it 's thus: Defin'd would you it
                             haue?

defineth   frequency: 1   relative frequency: 0.00001
    p. 393 UNGATHERED 27 8 That Faith and Loue defineth.

deform'd   frequency: 1   relative frequency: 0.00001
    p. 227 UNDERWOOD 52   5 And the whole lumpe growes round, deform'd, and
                             droupes,

deformed   frequency: 2   relative frequency: 0.00002
    See also "deform'd."
    p. 200 UNDERWOOD 42   22 Wish, you had fowle ones, and deformed got;
    p. 389 UNGATHERED 24   10 As a deformed face doth a true glasse.

defrauded   frequency: 1   relative frequency: 0.00001
    p. 176 UNDERWOOD 24   6 Might be defrauded, nor the great secur'd,

defrayes   frequency: 1   relative frequency: 0.00001
    p. 30 EPIGRAMS 12   3 Keepes himselfe, with halfe a man, and defrayes

defrays. See "defrayes."

degenerate   frequency: 1   relative frequency: 0.00001
    p. 367 UNGATHERED 6   32 "For stile of rarenesse, to degenerate.

degradation   frequency: 1   relative frequency: 0.00001
    p. 410 UNGATHERED 39   6 Nor Degradation from the Ministry,

degree   frequency: 5   relative frequency: 0.00007
    See also "'gree."
    p. 73 EPIGRAMS 113   11 Nor may'any feare, to loose of their degree,
    p. 84 EPIGRAMS 133   25 The other was a squire, of faire degree;
    p. 96 FOREST 3   58 Freedome doth with degree dispense.
    p. 225 UNDERWOOD 51   12 Now with a Title more to the Degree;
    p. 399 UNGATHERED 31   23 In number, measure, or degree

degrees   frequency: 4   relative frequency: 0.00005
    p. 29 EPIGRAMS 9   2 For strict degrees of ranke, or title looke:
    p. 157 UNDERWOOD 13   131 'Tis by degrees that men arrive at glad
    p. 164 UNDERWOOD 15   81 And comes by these Degrees, the Stile
                                 t<o>'inherit
    p. 224 UNDERWOOD 50   11 By all oblique Degrees, that killing height

deifie   frequency: 1   relative frequency: 0.00001
    p. 156 UNDERWOOD 13   99 And almost deifie the Authors! make

deify. See "deifie."

deignes   frequency: 2   relative frequency: 0.00002
    p. 420 UNGATHERED 48   29 Mynerva deignes
    p. 421 UNGATHERED 49   10 deignes myne the power to ffinde, yett want I
                                 will

deigns. See "deignes."

deity. See "dietie."

delated   frequency: 1   relative frequency: 0.00001
    p. 361 UNGATHERED 1   24 wear spent with wonder as they weare delated,

delay   frequency: 4   relative frequency: 0.00005
    p. 50 EPIGRAMS 70   5 Delay is bad, doubt worse, depending worst;
    p. 140 UNDERWOOD 2.8   9 But we find that cold delay,
    p. 154 UNDERWOOD 13   41 He neither gives, or do's, that doth delay
    p. 258 UNDERWOOD 75   189 Strifes, murmures, or delay,

delayes   frequency: 1   relative frequency: 0.00001
    p. 153 UNDERWOOD 13   27 Excuses, or Delayes? or done 'hem scant,

delaying   frequency: 1   relative frequency: 0.00001
    p. 411 UNGATHERED 40   9 The Danger of delaying

delays. See "delayes."

delia's   frequency: 1   relative frequency: 0.00001
    p. 181 UNDERWOOD 27   10 Or Delia's Graces, by Tibullus?

delicacies   frequency: 1   relative frequency: 0.00001
    p. 163 UNDERWOOD 15   37 Our Delicacies are growne capitall,

delicious   frequency: 1   relative frequency: 0.00001
    p. 286 U'WOOD 84.9   123 Wine, or delicious fruits, unto the Taste;

delight   frequency: 16   relative frequency: 0.00023
    See also "delyght."
    p. 34 EPIGRAMS 23   1 DONNE, the delight of PHOEBVS, and
                                 each Muse,
    p. 62 EPIGRAMS 96   10 Let pui'nees, porters, players praise delight,
    p. 73 EPIGRAMS 114   3 For CVPID, who (at first) tooke vaine
                                 delight,

delight (cont.)
      p. 76 EPIGRAMS 118   3 And, striuing so to double his delight,
      p. 97 FOREST 3   35 Thou dost with some delight the day out-weare,
      p. 151 UNDERWOOD 11   8 He did me the Delight,
      p. 212 UNDERWOOD 43   204 On both sides doe your mischiefes with delight;
      p. 223 UNDERWOOD 49   31 Indeed, her Dressing some man might delight,
      p. 227 UNDERWOOD 52   18 How I would draw, and take hold and delight.
      p. 311 HORACE 2   141 Her Poem's beautie, but a sweet delight
      p. 327 HORACE 2   458 More strongly takes the people with delight,
      p. 327 HORACE 2   477 Poets would either profit, or delight,
      p. 329 HORACE 2   516 As doctrine, and delight together go.
      p. 331 HORACE 2   544 Doth please; this, ten times over, will delight.
      p. 369 UNGATHERED 6   103 With more delight, and grace)
      p. 391 UNGATHERED 26   18 The applause! delight! the wonder of our Stage!

delightfull   frequency: 1   relative frequency: 0.00001
      p. 365 UNGATHERED 5   6 As fire; and more delightfull

delights   frequency: 6   relative frequency: 0.00008
      p. 98 FOREST 3   48 COMVS puts in, for new delights;
      p. 103 FOREST 6   18 When youths ply their stolne delights.
      p. 153 UNDERWOOD 13   21 The memorie delights him more, from whom
      p. 290 UNDERWOOD 85   37 Who (amongst these delights) would not forget
      p. 293 UNDERWOOD 86   30 Delights, nor credulous hope of mutuall Joy,
      p. 401 UNGATHERED 33   4 Of two, the choicest Paire of Mans delights,

deliuer   frequency: 1   relative frequency: 0.00001
      p. 367 UNGATHERED 6   58 That heard but Spight deliuer

deliuer'd   frequency: 1   relative frequency: 0.00001
      p. 400 UNGATHERED 31   37 Seal'd, and deliuer'd to her, in the sight

deliver. See "deliuer."

deliver'd   frequency: 1   relative frequency: 0.00001
   See also "deliuer'd."
      p. 251 UNDERWOOD 74   5 Shee lies deliver'd, without paine,

delphic. See "delphick."

delphick   frequency: 2   relative frequency: 0.00002
      p. 177 UNDERWOOD 25   12 With Delphick fire:
      p. 319 HORACE 2   310 Now differ'd not from Delphick riddling.

delude   frequency: 1   relative frequency: 0.00001
      p. 102 FOREST 5   11 Cannot we delude the eyes

deluded   frequency: 1   relative frequency: 0.00001
      p. 283 U'WOOD 84.9   43 From off her pillow, and deluded bed;

delyght   frequency: 1   relative frequency: 0.00001
      p. 420 UNGATHERED 48   33 As shall besides delyght

demand   frequency: 1   relative frequency: 0.00001
      p. 192 UNDERWOOD 38   55 Could you demand the gifts you gave, againe?

demerit   frequency: 1   relative frequency: 0.00001
      p. 192 UNDERWOOD 38   41 There is no Father that for one demerit,

democrite   frequency: 1   relative frequency: 0.00001
      p. 87 EPIGRAMS 133   128 Whereof old DEMOCRITE, and HILL
                                   NICHOLAS,

democritus   frequency: 1   relative frequency: 0.00001
   See also "democrite."
      p. 325 HORACE 2   419 Because Democritus beleeves a wit

den. See "denne."

denie   frequency: 2   relative frequency: 0.00002
      p. 235 UNDERWOOD 63   1 Who dares denie, that all first-fruits are due
      p. 241 UNDERWOOD 68   14 The Kings fame lives. Go now, denie his
                                   Teirce.

denied   frequency: 2   relative frequency: 0.00002
   See also "deny'd," "denyed."
      p. 203 UNDERWOOD 43   11 Was it because thou wert of old denied
      p. 333 HORACE 2   625 If you denied, you had no better straine,

deniedest. See "denyd'st."

denies   frequency: 2   relative frequency: 0.00002
    See also "denyes."
    p. 235 UNDERWOOD 63   2 To God, denies the God-head to be true:
    p. 381 UNGATHERED 12   57 Which he not denies. Now being so free,

denis   frequency: 1   relative frequency: 0.00001
    p. 410 UNGATHERED 39   7 To be the Denis of thy Father's School,

denmark. See "denmarke."

denmarke   frequency: 1   relative frequency: 0.00001
    p. 63 EPIGRAMS 97   15 Nor did the king of Denmarke him salute,

denne   frequency: 1   relative frequency: 0.00001
  **p. 113 PANEGYRE   14 And make their denne the slaughter-house of
                              soules:

deny   frequency: 3   relative frequency: 0.00004
    See also "denie."
    p. 74 EPIGRAMS 115   19 It will deny all; and forsweare it too:
    p. 155 UNDERWOOD 13   75 I not deny it, but to helpe the need
    p. 192 UNDERWOOD 38   54 And not the bounties you ha' done, deny.

deny'd   frequency: 2   relative frequency: 0.00002
  **p. 117 PANEGYRE   159 Which when time, nature, and the fates deny'd,
    p. 119 FOREST 13   98 To CLIFTON'S bloud, that is deny'd their
                              name.

denyd'st   frequency: 1   relative frequency: 0.00001
    p. 128 UNDERWOOD 1.1   21 6. Eternall God the Sonne, who not denyd'st

denyed   frequency: 1   relative frequency: 0.00001
    p. 54 EPIGRAMS 84   2 I ask'd a lord a buck, and he denyed me;

denyes   frequency: 1   relative frequency: 0.00001
    p. 104 FOREST 7   3 So court a mistris, shee denyes you;

depart   frequency: 3   relative frequency: 0.00004
    p. 194 UNDERWOOD 38   118 I may dilate my selfe, but not depart.
    p. 199 UNDERWOOD 41   13 My health will leave me; and when you depart,
    p. 331 HORACE 2   563 If ne're so little it depart the first,

departed   frequency: 2   relative frequency: 0.00002
    p. 87 EPIGRAMS 133   125 About the shore, of farts, but late departed,
    p. 283 U'WOOD 84.9   108 When shee departed? you will meet her there,

departing   frequency: 2   relative frequency: 0.00002
    p. 199 UNDERWOOD 41   2 Heare, Mistris, your departing servant tell
    p. 317 HORACE 2   251 As his departing take much thence: lest, then,

departs   frequency: 1   relative frequency: 0.00001
    p. 27 EPIGRAMS 2   13 He that departs with his owne honesty

depend   frequency: 1   relative frequency: 0.00001
    p. 216 UNDERWOOD 45   11 Those are poore Ties, depend on those false
                              ends,

dependents   frequency: 1   relative frequency: 0.00001
    p. 47 EPIGRAMS 64   5 Nor glad as those, that old dependents bee,

depending   frequency: 2   relative frequency: 0.00002
    p. 50 EPIGRAMS 70   5 Delay is bad, doubt worse, depending worst;
    p. 119 FOREST 13   114 You are depending on his word, and will;

deposited   frequency: 1   relative frequency: 0.00001
    p. 271 UNDERWOOD 83   81 And trusted so, as it deposited lay

depraue   frequency: 1   relative frequency: 0.00001
    p. 72 EPIGRAMS 111   11 And thence, depraue thee, and thy worke. To
                              those

deprave. See "depraue."

depressed. See "deprest."

deprest   frequency: 1   relative frequency: 0.00001
    p. 422 UNGATHERED 50   4 Whom fortune hath deprest; come nere the fates

deprive   frequency: 1   relative frequency: 0.00001
    p. 273 U'WOOD 84.1   5 Of Death, and Darknesse; and deprive

depth   frequency: 2   relative frequency: 0.00002
   p. 176 UNDERWOOD 24   12 Doth mete, whose lyne doth sound the depth of
                    things:)
   p. 198 UNDERWOOD 40   30 Shall find their depth: they're sounded with a
                    spoone.

derby. See "darby."

deride   frequency: 2   relative frequency: 0.00002
   p. 116 FOREST 13   4 As what th'haue lost t<o>'expect, they dare
                    deride.
   p. 202 UNDERWOOD 42   75 In smiling L'envoye, as he would deride

descend   frequency: 2   relative frequency: 0.00002
**p. 113 PANEGYRE   20 I saw, when reuerend THEMIS did descend
   p. 363 UNGATHERED 3   2 Seldome descend but bleeding to their graue.

descended   frequency: 1   relative frequency: 0.00001
   p. 215 UNDERWOOD 44   80 Descended in a rope of Titles, be

descent   frequency: 4   relative frequency: 0.00005
   p. 273 U'WOOD 84.1   29 But, here's a Song of her DESCENT;
   p. 274 U'WOOD 84.2   1 I sing the just, and uncontrol'd Descent
   p. 274 U'WOOD 84.2   t1 The Song of her DESCENT.
   p. 394 UNGATHERED 28   11 Nay they will venter ones Descent to hitt,

describ'd   frequency: 5   relative frequency: 0.00007
   p. 75 EPIGRAMS 115   33 Describ'd, it 's thus: Defin'd would you it
                    haue?
   p. 227 UNDERWOOD 52   11 To be describ'd <but> by a Monogram,
   p. 269 UNDERWOOD 83   30 To be describ'd! Fames fingers are too foule
   p. 305 HORACE 2   23 Or Rainbow is describ'd. But here was now
   p. 311 HORACE 2   127 Of Poems here describ'd, I can, nor use,

describe   frequency: 1   relative frequency: 0.00001
   p. 85 EPIGRAMS 133   58 But hold my torch, while I describe the entry

described   frequency: 1   relative frequency: 0.00001
   See also "describ'd."
   p. 140 UNDERWOOD 2.9   t1 Her man described by her owne Dictamen.

descride   frequency: 1   relative frequency: 0.00001
   p. 146 UNDERWOOD 6   17 The good, from bad, is not descride,

descried. See "descride."

description   frequency: 2   relative frequency: 0.00002
   p. 74 EPIGRAMS 115   4 Suffers no name, but a description:
   p. 136 UNDERWOOD 2.5   12 By description, but my Mother!

desert   frequency: 3   relative frequency: 0.00004
   p. 137 UNDERWOOD 2.6   t1 Clayming a second kisse by Desert.
   p. 389 UNGATHERED 24   21 To your desert, who'haue done it, Friend. And
                    this
   p. 420 UNGATHERED 48   13 nor cann be of desert,

deserted   frequency: 1   relative frequency: 0.00001
   p. 392 UNGATHERED 26   53 But antiquated, and deserted lye

deserts   frequency: 1   relative frequency: 0.00001
   p. 289 U'WOOD 84.9   224 And giving dues to all Mankinds deserts!

deseru'd   frequency: 1   relative frequency: 0.00001
   p. 398 UNGATHERED 30   60 Thou hast deseru'd: And let me reade the while

deserue   frequency: 3   relative frequency: 0.00004
   p. 106 FOREST 8   43 These, disease, will thee deserue:
   p. 389 UNGATHERED 24   11 Such Bookes deserue Translators, of like coate
   p. 400 UNGATHERED 32   9 And doth deserue all muniments of praise,

deseruedly   frequency: 1   relative frequency: 0.00001
   p. 410 UNGATHERED 39   5 All which thou hast incurr'd deseruedly:

deserues   frequency: 1   relative frequency: 0.00001
   p. 49 EPIGRAMS 66   15 Though euery fortitude deserues applause,

deserv'd   frequency: 3   relative frequency: 0.00004
   See also "deseru'd."
   p. 152 UNDERWOOD 12   38 An Epitaph, deserv'd a Tombe:
   p. 203 UNDERWOOD 43   17 I had deserv'd, then, thy consuming lookes,

deserv'd (cont.)
p. 415 UNGATHERED 42   13 (You have deserv'd it from me) I have read,

deserve   frequency: 2   relative frequency: 0.00002
See also "deserue."
p. 198 UNDERWOOD 40   39 To others, as he will deserve the Trust
p. 261 UNDERWOOD 77   15 Can doe the things that Statues doe deserve,

deservedly. See "deseruedly."

deserves   frequency: 1   relative frequency: 0.00001
See also "deserues."
p. 329 HORACE 2   531 Deserves no pardon; or who'd play, and sing

deserving   frequency: 2   relative frequency: 0.00002
p. 183 UNDERWOOD 29   28 Not a worke deserving Baies,
p. 183 UNDERWOOD 29   29 Nor a lyne deserving praise,

design. See "designe."

design'd   frequency: 3   relative frequency: 0.00004
p. 49 EPIGRAMS 67   9 And thou design'd to be the same thou art,
p. 173 UNDERWOOD 22   26 To whom all Lovers are design'd,
p. 276 U'WOOD 84.3   21 The Heaven design'd, draw next a Spring,

designe   frequency: 9   relative frequency: 0.00013
p. 71 EPIGRAMS 110   19 In euery counsell, stratageme, designe,
p. 219 UNDERWOOD 47   31 What is't to me whether the French Designe
p. 246 UNDERWOOD 70   95 But fate doth so alternate the designe,
p. 307 HORACE 2   49 Not to designe the whole. Should I aspire
p. 404 UNGATHERED 34   56 Terme of ye Architects is called Designe!
p. 406 UNGATHERED 34   96 Aymd at in thy omnipotent Designe!
p. 406 UNGATHERED 35   7 He may haue skill & iudgment to designe
p. 408 UNGATHERED 36   12 Will well designe thee, to be viewd of all
p. 412 UNGATHERED 41   2 Which, chang'd, a five-fold mysterie designe,

designed   frequency: 1   relative frequency: 0.00001
See also "design'd."
p. 288 U'WOOD 84.9 __ 206 For his designed worke, the perfect end

designes   frequency: 1   relative frequency: 0.00001
p. 392 UNGATHERED 26   47 Nature her selfe was proud of his designes,

designeth   frequency: 1   relative frequency: 0.00001
p. 81 EPIGRAMS 129   5 That scarse the Towne designeth any feast

designs. See "designes."

desir'd   frequency: 4   relative frequency: 0.00005
p. 60 EPIGRAMS 94   5 But these, desir'd by you, the makers ends
p. 121 FOREST 14   55 Be more, and long desir'd:
p. 285 U'WOOD 84.9   109 Much more desir'd, and dearer then before,
p. 394 UNGATHERED 28   17 But Sorrow, she desir'd no other ffriend:

desire   frequency: 21   relative frequency: 0.00030
p. 52 EPIGRAMS 76   3 What kinde of creature I could most desire,
p. 64 EPIGRAMS 101   2 Doe equally desire your companie:
p. 69 EPIGRAMS 108   3 And your high names: I doe desire, that thence
p. 108 FOREST 10A   4 like glasse, blowne vp, and fashion'd by desire.
p. 110 FOREST 11   37 The thing, they here call Loue, is blinde
                          Desire,
p. 111 FOREST 11   63 Would, at suggestion of a steepe desire,
p. 128 UNDERWOOD 1.1   42 To heare, to mediate, sweeten my desire,
p. 139 UNDERWOOD 2.8   6 All that heard her, with desire.
p. 144 UNDERWOOD 3   26 To meet their high desire;
p. 150 UNDERWOOD 10   5 To vent that poore desire,
p. 151 UNDERWOOD 11   11 In all my wild desire,
p. 153 UNDERWOOD 13   7 You then, whose will not only, but desire
p. 189 UNDERWOOD 36   10 Who more they burne, they more desire,
p. 205 UNDERWOOD 43   59 Had I fore-knowne of this thy least desire
p. 219 UNDERWOOD 47   38 My Princes safetie, and my Kings desire,
p. 307 HORACE 2   50 To forme a worke, I would no more desire
p. 315 HORACE 2   219 Heare, what it is the People, and I desire:
p. 315 HORACE 2   235 Of money, haughtie, to desire soon mov'd,
p. 345 HORACE 1   275 ... . desire.
p. 382 UNGATHERED 16   1 Two noble knightes, whome true desire and zeale,
p. 383 UNGATHERED 17   9 Who cannot reade, but onely doth desire

desired   frequency: 2   relative frequency: 0.00002
See also "desir'd."

desired (cont.)
```
    p.  53 EPIGRAMS 77     t1 TO ONE THAT DESIRED ME NOT
                              TO
    p. 217 UNDERWOOD 46     16 Desired Justice to the publique Weale,
```

desires   frequency: 5 relative frequency: 0.00007
```
    p.  95 FOREST 2         78 Shine bright on euery harth as the desires
    p. 144 UNDERWOOD 4       7 Nor looke too kind on my desires,
    p. 170 UNDERWOOD 19      2 Love lights his torches to inflame desires;
    p. 257 UNDERWOOD 75    161 Yet, as we may, we will, with chast desires,
    p. 417 UNGATHERED 45    19 she desires of euery birth
```

desirous. See "desyrous."

desk. See "deske."

deske   frequency: 1 relative frequency: 0.00001
```
    p. 206 UNDERWOOD 43     85 But in my Deske, what was there to accite
```

desmond   frequency: 1 relative frequency: 0.00001
```
    p. 176 UNDERWOOD 25     t1 An Ode to IAMES Earle of Desmond,
```

despair. See "despaire," "dispaire," "dispayre."

despair'd   frequency: 1 relative frequency: 0.00001
```
    p.  65 EPIGRAMS 101     14 Is not to be despair'd of, for our money;
```

despaire   frequency: 2 relative frequency: 0.00002
```
    p. 191 UNDERWOOD 38     10 As light breakes from you, that affrights
                              despaire,
    p. 192 UNDERWOOD 38     49 Doe not despaire my mending; to distrust
```

despaires   frequency: 2 relative frequency: 0.00002
```
    p. 315 HORACE 2        214 What he despaires, being handled, might not show.
    p. 392 UNGATHERED 26    80 And despaires day, but for thy Volumes light.
```

despairs. See "despaires."

desperate   frequency: 3 relative frequency: 0.00004
```
    p.  75 EPIGRAMS 116     16 A desperate soloecisme in truth and wit.
    p. 163 UNDERWOOD 15     36 But more licentious made, and desperate!
    p. 191 UNDERWOOD 38      3 Or doe upon my selfe some desperate ill;
```

despight   frequency: 2 relative frequency: 0.00002
```
    p. 201 UNDERWOOD 42     63 Wrung on the Withers, by Lord Loves despight,
    p. 211 UNDERWOOD 43    177 At Common-Law: me thinkes in his despight
```

despis'd   frequency: 1 relative frequency: 0.00001
```
    p.  78 EPIGRAMS 121      5 Yet is the office not to be despis'd,
```

despise   frequency: 1 relative frequency: 0.00001
```
    p. 127 UNDERWOOD 1.1    10 A broken heart thou wert not wont despise,
```

despised. See "despis'd," "dispised."

despite   frequency: 1 relative frequency: 0.00001
   See also "despight."
```
    p. 420 UNGATHERED 48    35 Give cause to some of wonnder, some despite,
```

destin'd   frequency: 2 relative frequency: 0.00002
```
    p. 122 FOREST 15        20 And destin'd vnto iudgement, after all.
    p. 225 UNDERWOOD 51     13 Englands high Chancellor: the destin'd heire
```

destinie   frequency: 2 relative frequency: 0.00002
```
    p.  52 EPIGRAMS 76      16 Of destinie, and spin her owne free houres.
    p. 170 UNDERWOOD 18     20 Be brought by us to meet our Destinie.
```

destinies   frequency: 1 relative frequency: 0.00001
```
    p.  53 EPIGRAMS 79       5 Hence was it, that the destinies decreed
```

destiny. See "destinie."

destitute   frequency: 1 relative frequency: 0.00001
```
    p. 186 UNDERWOOD 32      2 When a good Cause is destitute of friends,
```

destroy   frequency: 6 relative frequency: 0.00008
```
  **p. 117 PANEGYRE       138 That came to saue, what discord would destroy:
    p. 144 UNDERWOOD 4       4 Lest shame destroy their being.
    p. 191 UNDERWOOD 38     12 That you should be too noble to destroy.
    p. 192 UNDERWOOD 38     62 Consumptions nature to destroy, and sterve.
```

destroy (cont.)
  p. 199 UNDERWOOD 41   10 To shift their seasons, and destroy their powers!
  p. 414 UNGATHERED 41   43 Whose chearfull look our sadnesse doth destroy,

destroy'd   frequency: 1   relative frequency: 0.00001
  p. 210 UNDERWOOD 43 167 'Tis true, that in thy wish they were destroy'd,

destroyes   frequency: 2   relative frequency: 0.00002
  p. 112 FOREST 11   96 Whose od'rous breath destroyes
  p. 174 UNDERWOOD 23   6 That eats on wits, and Arts, and <oft> destroyes
                           them both.

destroys. See "destroyes."

destruction   frequency: 1   relative frequency: 0.00001
  p. 404 UNGATHERED 34 57 But in ye practisd truth Destruction is

desyrous   frequency: 1   relative frequency: 0.00001
  p. 408 UNGATHERED 36   9 If thou be soe desyrous to be read,

detractor   frequency: 1   relative frequency: 0.00001
  p. 408 UNGATHERED 37 t1 To my Detractor:--

deuice   frequency: 1   relative frequency: 0.00001
  p. 36 EPIGRAMS 29   3 For thy late sharpe deuice. I say 'tis fit

deuoure   frequency: 2   relative frequency: 0.00002
  p. 105 FOREST 8   16 Woman-kinde; deuoure the wast
  p. 119 FOREST 13   88 Eate on her clients, and some one deuoure.

deuoures   frequency: 1   relative frequency: 0.00001
  p. 45 EPIGRAMS 56   10 The sluggish gaping auditor deuoures;

deuout   frequency: 1   relative frequency: 0.00001
  p. 43 EPIGRAMS 51   7 No lesse than if from perill; and deuout,

device. See "deuice."

devil. See "divell."

devil's. See "divels-arse."

devote   frequency: 1   relative frequency: 0.00001
  p. 287 U'WOOD 84.9 177 In all her petite actions, so devote,

devotion   frequency: 1   relative frequency: 0.00001
  p. 127 UNDERWOOD 1   t2 OF DEVOTION.

devotions   frequency: 1   relative frequency: 0.00001
  p. 287 U'WOOD 84.9 181 For her devotions, and those sad essayes

devour. See "deuoure," "devoure."

devoure   frequency: 1   relative frequency: 0.00001
  p. 202 UNDERWOOD 43   3 Or urge thy Greedie flame, thus to devoure

devours. See "deuoures."

devout. See "deuout."

dew   frequency: 4   relative frequency: 0.00005
  See also "deaw."
  p. 67 EPIGRAMS 104   2 Euen in the dew of grace, what you would bee?
  p. 192 UNDERWOOD 38 57 The Sunne his heat, and light, the ayre his dew?
  p. 251 UNDERWOOD 74   4 And in a dew of sweetest Raine,
  p. 353 HORACE 1   612 .... dew ... .

dexterously   frequency: 1   relative frequency: 0.00001
  p. 133 UNDERWOOD 2.3 25 Which how Dexterously I doe,

dialogue   frequency: 2   relative frequency: 0.00002
  p. 143 UNDERWOOD 3   t1 The Musicall strife; In a Pastorall Dialogue.
  p. 293 UNDERWOOD 87 t2 Dialogue of Horace, and Lydia.

dialogues   frequency: 1   relative frequency: 0.00001
  p. 172 UNDERWOOD 20 13 Knew I, that all their Dialogues, and
                           discourse,

dian   frequency: 1   relative frequency: 0.00001
  p. 182 UNDERWOOD 27 28 Made Dian, not his notes refuse?

diana. See "dian," "diana'alone."

diana'alone   frequency: 1   relative frequency: 0.00001
    p. 68 EPIGRAMS 105   14 DIANA'alone, so hit, and hunted so.

diana's   frequency: 1   relative frequency: 0.00001
    p. 305 HORACE 2   20 Diana's Grove, or Altar, with the bor-

dice   frequency: 5   relative frequency: 0.00007
  **p. 113 PANEGYRE   24 Faire DICE, and EVNOMIA; who were said
    p. 30 EPIGRAMS 12   12 At dice his borrow'd money: which, god payes.
    p. 36 EPIGRAMS 28   16 Of solemne greatnesse. And he dares, at dice,
    p. 76 EPIGRAMS 119   6 Whose dice not doing well, to'a pulpit ran.
    p. 166 UNDERWOOD 15   138 The Dice with glassen eyes, to the glad viewes

dick   frequency: 1   relative frequency: 0.00001
    p. 409 UNGATHERED 38   1 I had you for a Seruant, once, Dick Brome;

dictamen   frequency: 1   relative frequency: 0.00001
    p. 140 UNDERWOOD 2.9   t1 Her man described by her owne Dictamen.

did   frequency: 176   relative frequency: 0.00254
    See also "out-did."
  **p. 113 PANEGYRE   7 His former rayes did onely cleare the skie;
  **p. 113 PANEGYRE   20 I saw, when reuerend THEMIS did descend
  **p. 114 PANEGYRE   59 That did not beare a part in this consent
  **p. 114 PANEGYRE   62 The ground beneath did seeme a mouing floud:
  **p. 114 PANEGYRE   65 Old men were glad, their fates till now did last;
  **p. 115 PANEGYRE   69 This was the peoples loue, with which did striue
  **p. 115 PANEGYRE   92 "Their lawes, their endes; the men she did
                              report:
  **p. 115 PANEGYRE   98 "The bloody, base, and barbarous she did quote;
  **p. 116 PANEGYRE   109 Nor did he seeme their vices so to loue,
  **p. 116 PANEGYRE   110 As once defend, what THEMIS did reproue.
  **p. 116 PANEGYRE   133 She blest the people, that in shoales did swim
  **p. 117 PANEGYRE   137 How deare a father they did now enioy
  **p. 117 PANEGYRE   140 The temp'rance of a priuate man did bring,
  **p. 117 PANEGYRE   150 What all mens wishes did aspire vnto.
    p. 31 EPIGRAMS 13   1 When men a dangerous disease did scape,
    p. 32 EPIGRAMS 18   6 As theirs did with thee, mine might credit get:
    p. 37 EPIGRAMS 32   3 That selfe-diuided Belgia did afford;
    p. 38 EPIGRAMS 38   2 And to conceale your vlcers, did aduise,
    p. 43 EPIGRAMS 51   2 Great heau'n did well, to giue ill fame free
                              wing;
    p. 43 EPIGRAMS 51   3 Which though it did but panick terror proue,
    p. 43 EPIGRAMS 53   1 Long-gathering OLD-END, I did feare thee
                              wise,
    p. 47 EPIGRAMS 64   3 Of loue, and what the golden age did hold
    p. 49 EPIGRAMS 66   10 Could conquer thee, but chance, who did betray.
    p. 52 EPIGRAMS 75   4 T<o>'inueigh 'gainst playes: what did he then but
                              play?
    p. 55 EPIGRAMS 84   9 O Madame, if your grant did thus transferre mee,
    p. 56 EPIGRAMS 88   9 Or had his father, when he did him get,
    p. 57 EPIGRAMS 89   10 Out-strip, then they did all that went before:
    p. 57 EPIGRAMS 89   13 Weare this renowne. 'Tis iust, that who did giue
    p. 58 EPIGRAMS 91   7 When on thy trumpet shee did sound a blast,
    p. 60 EPIGRAMS 93   3 Who did, alike with thee, thy house vp-beare,
    p. 63 EPIGRAMS 97   15 Nor did the king of Denmarke him salute,
    p. 66 EPIGRAMS 103   2 That but the twi-light of your sprite did see,
    p. 67 EPIGRAMS 104   1 Were they that nam'd you, prophets? Did they
                              see,
    p. 67 EPIGRAMS 104   3 Or did our times require it, to behold
    p. 67 EPIGRAMS 104   6 To make those faithfull, did the Fates send you?
    p. 69 EPIGRAMS 107   14 What at Ligorne, Rome, Florence you did doe:
    p. 70 EPIGRAMS 108   6 Your great profession; which I once, did proue:
    p. 70 EPIGRAMS 108   7 And did not shame it with my actions, then,
    p. 75 EPIGRAMS 116   3 So did thy vertue'enforme, thy wit sustaine
    p. 75 EPIGRAMS 116   11 That bloud not mindes, but mindes did bloud
                              adorne:
    p. 77 EPIGRAMS 120   5 'Twas a child, that so did thriue
    p. 77 EPIGRAMS 120   13 And did act (what now we mone)
    p. 79 EPIGRAMS 124   5 Which in life did harbour giue
    p. 80 EPIGRAMS 126   3 I pluck'd a branch; the iealous god did frowne,
    p. 85 EPIGRAMS 133   36 Did dance the famous Morrisse, vnto Norwich)
    p. 85 EPIGRAMS 133   62 Ycleped Mud, which, when their oares did once
                              stirre,
    p. 86 EPIGRAMS 133   94 Crack did report it selfe, as if a cloud
    p. 87 EPIGRAMS 133 111 Their MERCVRY did now. By this, the
                              stemme
    p. 87 EPIGRAMS 133 116 Neuer did bottome more betray her burden;

did (cont.)

p.	87	EPIGRAMS 133	124	Against their breasts. Here, seu'rall ghosts did flit
p.	87	EPIGRAMS 133	133	And that ours did. For, yet, no nare was tainted,
p.	88	EPIGRAMS 133	141	And so they did, from STYX, to ACHERON:
p.	88	EPIGRAMS 133	152	But still, it seem'd, the ranknesse did conuince 'hem.
p.	88	EPIGRAMS 133	162	Thrise did it spit: thrise diu'd. At last, it view'd
p.	93	FOREST 1	5	It is enough, they once did get
p.	101	FOREST 4	27	From whence, so lately, I did burne,
p.	108	FOREST 10 A	3	Thy thoughtes did neuer melt in amorous fire,
p.	116	FOREST 12	91	Moodes, which the god-like SYDNEY oft did proue,
p.	116	FOREST 12	92	And your braue friend, and mine so well did loue.
p.	130	UNDERWOOD 1.3	3	The Angels so did sound it,
p.	130	UNDERWOOD 1.3	8	That did us all salvation bring,
p.	130	UNDERWOOD 1.3	11	The Word, which heaven, and earth did make:
p.	132	UNDERWOOD 2.2	3	And her dressing did out-brave
p.	132	UNDERWOOD 2.2	11	And (withall) I did untie
p.	133	UNDERWOOD 2.3	14	But the Arrow home did draw
p.	138	UNDERWOOD 2.6	12	Of th'Assembly, as did you!
p.	138	UNDERWOOD 2.6	13	Or, that did you sit, or walke,
p.	138	UNDERWOOD 2.6	19	And did thinke, such Rites were due
p.	138	UNDERWOOD 2.6	21	Or, if you did move to night
p.	140	UNDERWOOD 2.9	6	And a woman God did make me:
p.	149	UNDERWOOD 9	7	And every close did meet
p.	151	UNDERWOOD 11	8	He did me the Delight,
p.	151	UNDERWOOD 12	9	That though they did possesse each limbe,
p.	152	UNDERWOOD 12	37	Reader, whose life, and name, did e're become
p.	153	UNDERWOOD 13	11	And in the Act did so my blush prevent,
p.	153	UNDERWOOD 13	12	As I did feele it done, as soone as meant:
p.	154	UNDERWOOD 13	29	Or if he did it not to succour me,
p.	155	UNDERWOOD 13	70	Then give it to the Hound that did him bite;
p.	157	UNDERWOOD 13	127	Sydney e're night! or that did goe to bed
p.	163	UNDERWOOD 15	47	Thither it flowes. How much did Stallion spend
p.	168	UNDERWOOD 15	191	And last, blaspheme not, we did never heare
p.	169	UNDERWOOD 18	1	Can Beautie that did prompt me first to write,
p.	169	UNDERWOOD 18	2	Now threaten, with those meanes she did invite?
p.	169	UNDERWOOD 18	3	Did her perfections call me on to gaze,
p.	181	UNDERWOOD 27	1	Helen, did Homer never see
p.	181	UNDERWOOD 27	3	Did Sappho on her seven-tongu'd Lute,
p.	181	UNDERWOOD 27	6	In whom Anacreon once did joy,
p.	181	UNDERWOOD 27	8	As he whom Maro did rehearse?
p.	183	UNDERWOOD 29	17	All Parnassus Greene did wither,
p.	183	UNDERWOOD 29	19	Pegasus did flie away,
p.	183	UNDERWOOD 29	20	At the Well[s] no Muse did stay,
p.	183	UNDERWOOD 29	25	Starveling rimes did fill the Stage,
p.	185	UNDERWOOD 30	15	Whose Offices, and honours did surprize,
p.	188	UNDERWOOD 34	3	What did she worth thy spight? were there not store
p.	188	UNDERWOOD 34	5	Then this did by her true? She never sought
p.	190	UNDERWOOD 37	23	That friendship which no chance but love did chuse,
p.	192	UNDERWOOD 38	56	Why was't? did e're the Cloudes aske back their raine?
p.	199	UNDERWOOD 42	3	No Poets verses yet did ever move,
p.	199	UNDERWOOD 42	4	Whose Readers did not thinke he was in love.
p.	201	UNDERWOOD 42	53	An Officer there, did make most solemne love,
p.	201	UNDERWOOD 42	55	He did lay up, and would adore the shooe,
p.	203	UNDERWOOD 43	23	Did I there wound the honour of the Crowne?
p.	208	UNDERWOOD 43	115	And so did Jove, who ne're meant thee his Cup:
p.	209	UNDERWOOD 43	149	Kindled the fire! But then, did one returne,
p.	210	UNDERWOOD 43	159	Hae is true Vulcan still! He did not spare
p.	210	UNDERWOOD 43	162	Did not she save from thence, to build a Rome?
p.	212	UNDERWOOD 43	202	Who from the Divels-Arse did Guns beget;
p.	213	UNDERWOOD 44	6	For they did see it the last tilting well,
p.	214	UNDERWOOD 44	33	Well did thy craftie Clerke, and Knight, Sir Hugh,
p.	218	UNDERWOOD 47	14	That never yet did friend, or friendship seeke
p.	228	UNDERWOOD 53	11	Nay, so your Seate his beauties did endorse,
p.	230	UNDERWOOD 56	4	You won them too, your oddes did merit it.
p.	242	UNDERWOOD 70	3	When the Prodigious Hannibal did crowne
p.	243	UNDERWOOD 70	11	Did wiser Nature draw thee back,
p.	243	UNDERWOOD 70	30	What did this Stirrer, but die late?
p.	243	UNDERWOOD 70	32	For three of his foure-score, he did no good.
p.	244	UNDERWOOD 70	41	So deep, as he did then death's waters sup;
p.	246	UNDERWOOD 70	102	No pleasures vaine did chime,

did (cont.)

p. 253	UNDERWOOD 75	22	Or so did shine,
p. 253	UNDERWOOD 75	36	And all did ring th'approches of the Bride;
p. 254	UNDERWOOD 75	46	As she did lack
p. 254	UNDERWOOD 75	67	As if her ayrie steps did spring the flowers,
p. 264	UNDERWOOD 79	33	Of all that Nature, yet, to life did bring;
p. 269	UNDERWOOD 83	33	What she did here, by great example, well,
p. 270	UNDERWOOD 83	47	How did she leave the world? with what contempt?
p. 270	UNDERWOOD 83	50	Of her disease, how did her soule assure
p. 270	UNDERWOOD 83	63	Let Angels sing her glories, who did call
p. 282	U'WOOD 84.9	13	On Nature, for her: who did let her lie,
p. 287	U'WOOD 84.9	169	To one she said, Doe this, he did it; So
p. 287	U'WOOD 84.9	171	He run; and all did strive with diligence
p. 288	U'WOOD 84.9	185	Her broken sighes did never misse whole sense:
p. 293	UNDERWOOD 87	2	And ('bout thy Ivory neck,) no youth did fling
p. 293	UNDERWOOD 87	6	Nor after C<h>loe did his Lydia sound;
p. 313	HORACE 2	195	Nor so begin, as did that Circler late,
p. 315	HORACE 2	207	Nor from the brand, with which the life did burne
p. 315	HORACE 2	210	From the two Egges, that did disclose the twins.
p. 319	HORACE 2	313	Till then unknowne, in Carts, wherein did ride
p. 319	HORACE 2	314	Those that did sing, and act: their faces dy'd
p. 319	HORACE 2	319	Hee too, that did in Tragick Verse contend
p. 319	HORACE 2	320	For the vile Goat, soone after, forth did send
p. 323	HORACE 2	375	Nor is't long since, they did with patience take
p. 323	HORACE 2	399	Our Ancestors did Plautus numbers praise,
p. 323	HORACE 2	406	Nor did they merit the lesse Crowne to weare,
p. 325	HORACE 2	430	For choller! If I did not, who could bring
p. 327	HORACE 2	494	On edge the Masculine spirits, and did whet
p. 329	HORACE 2	495	Their minds to Warres, with rimes they did rehearse;
p. 333	HORACE 2	588	The wished goale, both did, and suffer'd much
p. 333	HORACE 2	590	And both from Wine, and Women did abstaine.
p. 333	HORACE 2	592	Did learne them first, and once a Master fear'd.
p. 335	HORACE 2	656	To let it downe, who knowes, if he did cast
p. 335	HORACE 2	667	Nor did he doe this once; for if you can
p. 361	UNGATHERED 1	5	ffirst: thy successe did strike my sence with wonder;
p. 361	UNGATHERED 1	16	did sparcle foorth in Center of the rest:
p. 362	UNGATHERED 1	28	I struggled with this passion that did drowne
p. 366	UNGATHERED 6	8	Did neuer dint the breast of Tamisis.
p. 374	UNGATHERED 10	15	It should rather haue bene Tom that a horse did lack.
p. 375	UNGATHERED 10	19	For he did but kisse her, and so let her go.
p. 375	UNGATHERED 10	33	To lie at Liuory, while the Horses did stand.
p. 380	UNGATHERED 12	26	How long he did stay, at what signe he did Inne.
p. 380	UNGATHERED 12	52	Doth he once dissemble, but tels he did ride
p. 380	UNGATHERED 12	55	Some want, they say in a sort he did craue:
p. 380	UNGATHERED 12	56	I writ he onely his taile there did waue;
p. 384	UNGATHERED 18	12	Out-bee yt Wife, in worth, thy freind did make:
p. 387	UNGATHERED 22	3	which, did they neere so neate, or proudly dwell,
p. 391	UNGATHERED 26	40	Sent forth, or since did from their ashes come.
p. 392	UNGATHERED 26	74	That so did take Eliza, and our Iames?
p. 394	UNGATHERED 28	20	Whom shee, with Sorrow first did lodge, then feast,
p. 397	UNGATHERED 30	31	Did all so strike me, as I cry'd, who can
p. 397	UNGATHERED 30	57	That euer yet did fire the English blood!
p. 398	UNGATHERED 30	81	As, on two flowry Carpets, that did rise,
p. 400	UNGATHERED 31	28	Fames heate vpon the graue did stay:
p. 400	UNGATHERED 31	33	For this did Katherine, Ladie Ogle, die
p. 401	UNGATHERED 33	7	Who did this Knot compose,
p. 409	UNGATHERED 38	8	Which I, your Master, first did teach the Age.
p. 662	INSCRIPTS. 2	5	Tell her, his Muse that did inuent thee

di'd   frequency: 1   relative frequency: 0.00001

p. 114	FOREST 12	47	That bred them, graues: when they were borne, they di'd,

didst   frequency: 9   relative frequency: 0.00013

See also "did'st."

p. 32	EPIGRAMS 18	7	If thou'ldst but vse thy faith, as thou didst then,
p. 43	EPIGRAMS 53	4	But when (in place) thou didst the patrons choose,
p. 54	EPIGRAMS 81	5	For all thou hear'st, thou swear'st thy selfe didst doo.
p. 187	UNDERWOOD 33	26	As if the generall store thou didst command
p. 201	UNDERWOOD 42	59	Thou didst tell me; and wert o're-joy'd to peepe
p. 203	UNDERWOOD 43	19	But, on thy malice, tell me, didst thou spie
p. 210	UNDERWOOD 43	170	And didst invade part of the Common-wealth,
p. 243	UNDERWOOD 70	9	How summ'd a circle didst thou leave man-kind

didst (cont.)
    p. 391 UNGATHERED 26   29 And tell, how farre thou didst our Lily
                               out-shine,

did'st   frequency: 7 relative frequency: 0.00010
    p. 45 EPIGRAMS 58   6 Then thou did'st late my sense, loosing my
                             points.
    p. 95 FOREST 2   83 Did'st thou, then, make 'hem! and what praise was
                             heap'd
    p. 101 FOREST 4   42 Thou did'st abuse, and then betray;
    p. 106 FOREST 9   13 But thou thereon did'st onely breath,
    p. 127 UNDERWOOD 1.1 17 5. Eternall Father, God, who did'st create
    p. 225 UNDERWOOD 51   4 Thou stand'st as if some Mysterie thou did'st!
    p. 242 UNDERWOOD 70   7 Wise child, did'st hastily returne,

die   frequency: 19 relative frequency: 0.00027
    See also "dye."
    p. 84 EPIGRAMS 133   18 Lash'd by their consciences, to die, affeard.
    p. 131 UNDERWOOD 2.1 24 All the world for love may die.
    p. 168 UNDERWOOD 16   6 For, if such men as he could die,
    p. 174 UNDERWOOD 23   3 Knowledge, that sleepes, doth die;
    p. 175 UNDERWOOD 23   23 They die with their conceits,
    p. 181 UNDERWOOD 27   14 Rap't from the Earth, as not to die?
    p. 183 UNDERWOOD 29   23 And Apollo's Musique die,
    p. 193 UNDERWOOD 38   78 That makes us live, not that which calls to die.
    p. 193 UNDERWOOD 38   92 Rather then once displease you more, to die
    p. 211 UNDERWOOD 43 188 Burne to a snuffe, and then stinke out, and die:
    p. 243 UNDERWOOD 70   30 What did this Stirrer, but die late?
    p. 245 UNDERWOOD 70   71 Although it fall, and die that night;
    p. 257 UNDERWOOD 75 151 Alive, which else would die,
    p. 270 UNDERWOOD 83   62 With admiration, and applause to die!
    p. 271 UNDERWOOD 83   94 When we were all borne, we began to die;
    p. 282 U'WOOD 84.9   14 And saw that portion of her selfe to die.
    p. 293 UNDERWOOD 87   11 As, for her, I'ld not feare to die,
    p. 294 UNDERWOOD 87   24 Yet would I wish to love, live, die with thee.
    p. 400 UNGATHERED 31 33 For this did Katherine, Ladie Ogle, die

died. See "di'd," "die'd," "dy'd," "dyed."

die'd   frequency: 1 relative frequency: 0.00001
    p. 387 UNGATHERED 22 12 not when I die'd, but how I liud. Farewell.

diedest. See "dyd'st."

dies   frequency: 1 relative frequency: 0.00001
    See also "dyes."
    p. 295 UNDERWOOD 89   7 Hee, that but living halfe his dayes, dies such,

diet   frequency: 1 relative frequency: 0.00001
    p. 317 HORACE 2   283 Praise the spare diet, wholsome justice, lawes,

dietie   frequency: 1 relative frequency: 0.00001
    p. 173 UNDERWOOD 22   25 And you are he: the Dietie

differ   frequency: 3 relative frequency: 0.00004
    p. 307 HORACE 2   61 Invention. Now, to speake; and then differ
    p. 313 HORACE 2   161 It much will differ, if a God speake, than,
    p. 321 HORACE 2   339 To Dance, so she should, shamefac'd, differ
                             farre

differ'd   frequency: 1 relative frequency: 0.00001
    p. 319 HORACE 2   310 Now differ'd not from Delphick riddling.

difference   frequency: 6 relative frequency: 0.00008
    p. 57 EPIGRAMS 90   8 Discern'd no difference of his yeeres, or play,
    p. 75 EPIGRAMS 116   9 That Nature no such difference had imprest
    p. 78 EPIGRAMS 121   4 Shee learnes to know long difference of their
                             states.
    p. 157 UNDERWOOD 13 154 Their difference, cannot choose which you will
                             be.
    p. 235 UNDERWOOD 62   12 O bountie! so to difference the rates!
    p. 321 HORACE 2   345 As not make difference, whether Davus speake,

different   frequency: 1 relative frequency: 0.00001
    p. 110 FOREST 11   52 To murther different hearts,

differing   frequency: 1 relative frequency: 0.00001
    p. 407 UNGATHERED 35 19 your workes thus differing, troth let soe yor
                             style:

differrer   frequency: 1   relative frequency: 0.00001
    p. 344 HORACE 1   245 . ..... differrer ....

differs   frequency: 1   relative frequency: 0.00001
    p. 315 HORACE 2   217 Where the midst differs from the first: or where

digby   frequency: 7   relative frequency: 0.00010
    p. 262 UNDERWOOD 78   1 Tho', happy Muse, thou know my Digby well,
    p. 262 UNDERWOOD 78   t2 To my MVSE, the Lady Digby, on her
    p. 262 UNDERWOOD 78   t3 Husband, Sir KENELME DIGBY.
    p. 272 UNDERWOOD 84   t5 Of that truly-noble Lady, the Lady
                             VENETIA DIGBY,
    p. 272 UNDERWOOD 84   t6 late Wife of Sir KENELME DIGBY,
                             Knight:
    p. 274 U'WOOD 84.2   2 Of Dame VENETIA DIGBY, styl'd The
                             Faire:
    p. 282 U'WOOD 84.9   t2 The truly honoured Lady, the Lady
                             VENETIA DIGBY;

digestiue   frequency: 1   relative frequency: 0.00001
    p. 65 EPIGRAMS 101   27 Digestiue cheese, and fruit there sure will bee;

digestive. See "digestiue."

digests   frequency: 1   relative frequency: 0.00001
    p. 399 UNGATHERED 31   8 Code, Digests, Pandects of all faemale glory!

dignifie   frequency: 1   relative frequency: 0.00001
    p. 64 EPIGRAMS 101   4 But that your worth will dignifie our feast,

dignify. See "dignifie."

dignitie   frequency: 2   relative frequency: 0.00002
    p. 67 EPIGRAMS 104   7 And to your Scene lent no lesse dignitie
    p. 255 UNDERWOOD 75   92 And what of Dignitie, and Honour may

dignities   frequency: 2   relative frequency: 0.00002
    p. 70 EPIGRAMS 109   6 Wrestlest with dignities, or fain'st a scope
    p. 166 UNDERWOOD 15   146 To lose the formes, and dignities of men,

dignity. See "dignitie."

dike   frequency: 2   relative frequency: 0.00002
    p. 214 UNDERWOOD 44   54 As Stiles, Dike, Ditchfield, Millar, Crips,
                             and Fen:
    p. 401 UNGATHERED 32   12 To cut a Dike? or sticke a Stake vp, here,

dilate   frequency: 1   relative frequency: 0.00001
    p. 194 UNDERWOOD 38   118 I may dilate my selfe, but not depart.

dilated. See "delated."

diligence   frequency: 1   relative frequency: 0.00001
    p. 287 U'WOOD 84.9   171 He run; and all did strive with diligence

diligent   frequency: 1   relative frequency: 0.00001
    p. 313 HORACE 2   164 Where some great Lady, or her diligent Nourse;

dim   frequency: 1   relative frequency: 0.00001
    See also "dimme."
  **p. 117 PANEGYRE   145 The lesser fiers dim) in his accesse

dimensions   frequency: 1   relative frequency: 0.00001
    p. 79 EPIGRAMS 125   3 Both whose dimensions, lost, the world might
                             finde

dimme   frequency: 1   relative frequency: 0.00001
    p. 369 UNGATHERED 6   108 To dimme and drowne

dimmed. See "dimn'd."

dimn'd   frequency: 1   relative frequency: 0.00001
    p. 181 UNDERWOOD 27   18 Her Ovid gave her, dimn'd the fame

din'd   frequency: 2   relative frequency: 0.00002
    p. 85 EPIGRAMS 133   37 At Bread-streets Mermaid, hauing din'd, and
                             merry,
    p. 329 HORACE 2   510 The Child, when Lamia'has din'd, out of her
                             maw.

dine   frequency: 5   relative frequency: 0.00007
    p.   50 EPIGRAMS 72   2 A chamber-critick, and dost dine, and sup
    p.   74 EPIGRAMS 115   23 At euery meale, where it doth dine, or sup,
    p.   95 FOREST 2   66 At great mens tables) and yet dine away.
    p. 206 UNDERWOOD 43   83 These, had'st thou pleas'd either to dine, or
                               sup,
    p. 229 UNDERWOOD 54   1 I am to dine, Friend, where I must be weigh'd

dinner   frequency: 1   relative frequency: 0.00001
    p.   96 FOREST 3   6 Of Sheriffes dinner, or Maiors feast.

dint   frequency: 1   relative frequency: 0.00001
    p. 366 UNGATHERED 6   8 Did neuer dint the breast of Tamisis.

diomede   frequency: 1   relative frequency: 0.00001
    p. 315 HORACE 2   209 Of Diomede; nor Troyes sad Warre begins

dioscuri   frequency: 1   relative frequency: 0.00001
    p. 246 UNDERWOOD 70   93 Lights, the Dioscuri;

dip<h>thera   frequency: 1   relative frequency: 0.00001
    p. 399 UNGATHERED 31   8+ Dip<h>thera Iouis:--

dircaean   frequency: 1   relative frequency: 0.00001
    p. 366 UNGATHERED 6   19 The cleare Dircaean Fount

dire   frequency: 1   relative frequency: 0.00001
    p.   85 EPIGRAMS 133   59 To this dire passage. Say, thou stop thy nose:

direct   frequency: 1   relative frequency: 0.00001
    p. 366 UNGATHERED 6   11 How vpward, and direct!

directly   frequency: 1   relative frequency: 0.00001
    p. 362 UNGATHERED 2   13 Which being eyed directly, I diuine,

directs   frequency: 1   relative frequency: 0.00001
    p. 219 UNDERWOOD 47   50 That guides the Motions, and directs the beares.

dirt. See "court-durt."

dirtie   frequency: 1   relative frequency: 0.00001
    p. 213 UNDERWOOD 44   15 Withall, the dirtie paines those Citizens take,

dirty   frequency: 1   relative frequency: 0.00001
    See also "dirtie," "durtie."
    p. 409 UNGATHERED 37   22 Thy Dirty braines, Men smell thy want of worth.

dis-auow   frequency: 1   relative frequency: 0.00001
    p.   62 EPIGRAMS 96   5 As free simplicitie, to dis-auow,

dis-esteem'd   frequency: 1   relative frequency: 0.00001
    p. 160 UNDERWOOD 14   40 Antiquities search'd! Opinions dis-esteem'd!

dis-esteeme   frequency: 1   relative frequency: 0.00001
    p. 118 FOREST 13   64 Which though the turning world may dis-esteeme,

dis-favour   frequency: 1   relative frequency: 0.00001
    p. 177 UNDERWOOD 25   33 Or the dis-favour

dis-inherit   frequency: 1   relative frequency: 0.00001
    p. 192 UNDERWOOD 38   42 Or two, or three, a Sonne will dis-inherit,

dis-ioynts   frequency: 1   relative frequency: 0.00001
    p.   45 EPIGRAMS 58   5 And so my sharpnesse thou no lesse dis-ioynts,

dis-joyn'd   frequency: 2   relative frequency: 0.00002
    p. 294 UNDERWOOD 87   18 And us dis-joyn'd force to her brazen yoke,
    p. 315 HORACE 2   218 The last doth from the midst dis-joyn'd appeare.

disavow   frequency: 1   relative frequency: 0.00001
    See also "dis-auow."
    p. 309 HORACE 2   78 Or Plautus, and in Virgil disavow,

discard   frequency: 1   relative frequency: 0.00001
    p. 662 INSCRIPTS. 2   7 And sworne, that he will quite discard thee

discern. See "discerne."

discern'd   frequency: 1   relative frequency: 0.00001
    p.   57 EPIGRAMS 90   8 Discern'd no difference of his yeeres, or play,

discerne   frequency: 2   relative frequency: 0.00002
    p. 156 UNDERWOOD 13 118 Can I discerne how shadowes are decreast,
    p. 261 UNDERWOOD 77   14 Discerne betweene a Statue, and a Man;

discerned   frequency: 1   relative frequency: 0.00001
    See also "discern'd."
    p. 55 EPIGRAMS 85   11 Now, in whose pleasures I haue this discerned,

discernes   frequency: 1   relative frequency: 0.00001
    p. 66 EPIGRAMS 102   12 As nothing else discernes the vertue' or vice.

discerning   frequency: 4   relative frequency: 0.00005
    p. 156 UNDERWOOD 13 108 Or Science of discerning Good and Ill.
    p. 289 U'WOOD 84.9   222 In the discerning of each conscience, so!
    p. 365 UNGATHERED 5   10 Doth shine in her discerning,
    p. 412 UNGATHERED 40 18 by our owne discerning

discerns. See "discernes."

discharg'd   frequency: 1   relative frequency: 0.00001
  **p. 117 PANEGYRE   154 Of heauen is discharg'd along the skie:

discharge   frequency: 2   relative frequency: 0.00002
    p. 85 EPIGRAMS 133   65 Who shall discharge first his merd-vrinous load:
    p. 249 UNDERWOOD 72   3 Discharge it 'bout the Iland, in an houre,

discipline   frequency: 1   relative frequency: 0.00001
    p. 214 UNDERWOOD 44   36 And the Greeke Discipline (with the moderne)
                             shed

disclos'd   frequency: 1   relative frequency: 0.00001
    p. 112 FOREST 11   100 As if Nature disclos'd

disclose   frequency: 3   relative frequency: 0.00004
    p. 237 UNDERWOOD 65   4 What Month then May, was fitter to disclose
    p. 307 HORACE 2   47 The nailes, and every curled haire disclose;
    p. 315 HORACE 2   210 From the two Egges, that did disclose the twins.

discloses   frequency: 2   relative frequency: 0.00002
    p. 136 UNDERWOOD 2.5 21 As the Bath your verse discloses
    p. 170 UNDERWOOD 19   7 By those pure bathes your either cheeke
                             discloses,

discontent   frequency: 2   relative frequency: 0.00002
    p. 122 FOREST 15   25 Of discontent; or that these prayers bee
    p. 384 UNGATHERED 18 15 So, be there neuer discontent, or sorrow,

discord   frequency: 2   relative frequency: 0.00002
  **p. 117 PANEGYRE   138 That came to saue, what discord would destroy:
    p. 40 EPIGRAMS 42   1 Who sayes that GILES and IONE at discord
                             he?

discords   frequency: 1   relative frequency: 0.00001
    p. 88 EPIGRAMS 133   171 Vpon your eares, of discords so vn-sweet?

discouer   frequency: 1   relative frequency: 0.00001
    p. 405 UNGATHERED 34 82 Discouer Vice? Commit Absurdity?

discouer'd   frequency: 1   relative frequency: 0.00001
  **p. 115 PANEGYRE   83 "And, being once found out, discouer'd lies

discoueries   frequency: 1   relative frequency: 0.00001
    p. 388 UNGATHERED 23   8 Were askt of thy Discoueries; They must say,

discourse   frequency: 6   relative frequency: 0.00008
    p. 35 EPIGRAMS 28   9 He will both argue, and discourse in oathes,
    p. 136 UNDERWOOD 2.5   5 Heare, what late Discourse of you,
    p. 136 UNDERWOOD 2.5 t1 His discourse with Cupid.
    p. 139 UNDERWOOD 2.8   1 Charis one day in discourse
    p. 172 UNDERWOOD 20   13 Knew I, that all their Dialogues, and
                             discourse,
    p. 311 HORACE 2   119 As fit t<o>'exchange discourse; a Verse to win

discourses   frequency: 1   relative frequency: 0.00001
    p. 206 UNDERWOOD 43   82 Th'admir'd discourses of the Prophet Ball:

discourseth   frequency: 2   relative frequency: 0.00002
    p. 271 UNDERWOOD 83   71 Speakes Heavens Language! and discourseth free
    p. 378 UNGATHERED 11 82 Of trauell he discourseth so at large,

discoursing   frequency: 1   relative frequency: 0.00001
    p. 104 UNDERWOOD 15   63 To see 'hem dye discoursing with their Glasse,

discover   frequency: 1   relative frequency: 0.00001
    See also "discouer."
    p. 198 UNDERWOOD 40   47 (Made to blow up loves secrets) to discover

discovered. See "discouer'd."

discoveries. See "discoueries."

discreeter   frequency: 1   relative frequency: 0.00001
    p. 287 U'WOOD 84.9   174 A tender Mother, a discreeter Wife,

disdain. See "disdaine."

disdaine   frequency: 3   relative frequency: 0.00004
    p. 194 UNDERWOOD 38   104 A man should flie from, as he would disdaine.
    p. 208 UNDERWOOD 43   129 But, O those Reeds! thy meere disdaine of them,
    p. 363 UNGATHERED 3   13 It thawes the frostiest, and most stiffe
                             disdaine:

disdaine-full   frequency: 1   relative frequency: 0.00001
   *p. 493 TO HIMSELF   47 Strike that disdaine-full heate

disdained   frequency: 1   relative frequency: 0.00001
    p. 375 UNGATHERED 10   32 And here he disdained not, in a forraine land

disdainful. See "disdaine-full."

disdaining   frequency: 1   relative frequency: 0.00001
    p. 278 U'WOOD 84.4   27 And so disdaining any tryer;

disease   frequency: 14   relative frequency: 0.00020
    p. 31 EPIGRAMS 13   1 When men a dangerous disease did scape,
    p. 56 EPIGRAMS 88   10 The french disease, with which he labours yet?
    p. 76 EPIGRAMS 119   8 But dost it out of iudgement, not disease;
    p. 104 FOREST 8   1 Why, Disease, dost thou molest
    p. 106 FOREST 8   43 These, disease, will thee deserue:
    p. 122 FOREST 15   3 Is it interpreted in me disease,
    p. 150 UNDERWOOD 10   16 I ne're will owe my health to a disease.
    p. 165 UNDERWOOD 15 114 Is it that man pulls on himselfe Disease?
    p. 188 UNDERWOOD 34   1 Envious and foule Disease, could there not be
    p. 234 UNDERWOOD 60   6 Of a Disease, that lov'd no light
    p. 237 UNDERWOOD 64   18 The truly Epidemicall disease!
    p. 248 UNDERWOOD 71   4 Disease, the Enemie, and his Ingineeres,
    p. 270 UNDERWOOD 83   50 Of her disease, how did her soule assure
    p. 335 HORACE 2   659 I'le tell you but the death, and the disease

diseases   frequency: 7   relative frequency: 0.00010
    p. 31 EPIGRAMS 13   4 From my diseases danger, and from thee.
    p. 86 EPIGRAMS 133   70 Hung stench, diseases, and old filth, their
                             mother,
    p. 105 FOREST 8   20 And haue more diseases made.
    p. 151 UNDERWOOD 12   8 Had wrestled with Diseases strong,
    p. 221 UNDERWOOD 48   24 And cure the Worlds diseases:
    p. 265 UNDERWOOD 79   62 Hee drives diseases from our Folds,
    p. 657 L. CONVIVALES 17 Pays all Debts, cures all Diseases,

disesteem. See "dis-esteeme."

disesteemed. See "dis-esteem'd."

disfavour. See "dis-favour."

disgrace   frequency: 2   relative frequency: 0.00002
    p. 188 UNDERWOOD 34   13 What was the cause then? Thought'st thou in
                             disgrace
    p. 191 UNDERWOOD 38   30 Your honour now, then your disgrace before.

disgraced. See "disgrac't."

disgrac't   frequency: 1   relative frequency: 0.00001
    p. 174 UNDERWOOD 23   11 Or droop they as disgrac't,

disguisd   frequency: 1   relative frequency: 0.00001
    p. 405 UNGATHERED 34 81 Disguisd? and thence drag forth Enormity?

disguis'd   frequency: 1   relative frequency: 0.00001
    See also "disguisd."

disguis'd (cont.)
    p. 151 UNDERWOOD 11   4 Love in a subtile Dreame disguis'd,

disguise   frequency: 1   relative frequency: 0.00001
    p. 150 UNDERWOOD 10   9 But under the Disguise of love,

dish   frequency: 3   relative frequency: 0.00004
   *p. 493 TO HIMSELF   24 scraps, out <of> euery dish,
    p. 88 EPIGRAMS 133   151 Then, selling not, a dish was tane to mince 'hem,
    p. 94 FOREST 2   31 And if the high-swolne Medway faile thy dish,

disinherit   frequency: 1   relative frequency: 0.00001
    See also "dis-inherit."
    p. 99 FOREST 3   77 Let him, then hardest sires, more disinherit,

disjoined. See "dis-joyn'd."

disjoints. See "dis-ioynts."

dispaire   frequency: 2   relative frequency: 0.00002
    p. 363 UNGATHERED 3   17 Then why should we dispaire? Dispaire, away:

dispayre   frequency: 1   relative frequency: 0.00001
    p. 420 UNGATHERED 48   36 But vnto more dispayre to Imitate their sounde.

dispenc'd   frequency: 1   relative frequency: 0.00001
    p. 259 UNDERWOOD 76   15 Or dispenc'd in bookes, or bread,

dispensation   frequency: 1   relative frequency: 0.00001
    p. 219 UNDERWOOD 47   35 Whether the Dispensation yet be sent,

dispense   frequency: 2   relative frequency: 0.00002
    p. 86 EPIGRAMS 133   100 And subtiltie of mettalls) they dispense
    p. 98 FOREST 3   58 Freedome doth with degree dispense.

dispensed. See "dispenc'd."

dispers'd   frequency: 1   relative frequency: 0.00001
  **p. 113 PANEGYRE   17 And would (if not dispers'd) infect the Crowne,

disperse   frequency: 1   relative frequency: 0.00001
    p. 276 U'WOOD 84.3   17 Then let the beames of that, disperse

dispised   frequency: 1   relative frequency: 0.00001
    p. 361 UNGATHERED 1   10 Thy skill hath made of ranck dispised weedes;

display   frequency: 3   relative frequency: 0.00004
    p. 202 UNDERWOOD 42   78 When not the Shops, but windowes doe display
    p. 292 UNDERWOOD 86   16 Will he display the Ensignes of thy warre.
    p. 367 UNGATHERED 6   41 From thence, display thy wing againe

displeas'd   frequency: 1   relative frequency: 0.00001
    p. 53 EPIGRAMS 79   9 At which, shee happily displeas'd, made you:

displease   frequency: 1   relative frequency: 0.00001
    p. 193 UNDERWOOD 38   92 Rather then once displease you more, to die

dispos'd   frequency: 1   relative frequency: 0.00001
    p. 361 UNGATHERED 1   2 (so well dispos'd by thy auspicious hand)

disposing   frequency: 1   relative frequency: 0.00001
    p. 309 HORACE 2   103 If Custome please; at whose disposing will

disposure   frequency: 2   relative frequency: 0.00002
    p. 151 UNDERWOOD 12   14 All order, and Disposure, still.
    p. 269 UNDERWOOD 83   16 And the disposure will be something new,

dispraise   frequency: 2   relative frequency: 0.00002
    p. 43 EPIGRAMS 52   2 Dispraise my worke, then praise it frostily:
    p. 46 EPIGRAMS 61   1 Thy praise, or dispraise is to me alike,

disproportion'd   frequency: 1   relative frequency: 0.00001
    p. 391 UNGATHERED 26   26 I meane with great, but disproportion'd Muses:

dispute   frequency: 1   relative frequency: 0.00001
    p. 354 HORACE 1   638 Dispute ... .

dissect   frequency: 1   relative frequency: 0.00001
    p. 286 U'WOOD 84.9   150 Who knowes the hearts of all, and can dissect

dissection   frequency: 1   relative frequency: 0.00001
     p. 194 UNDERWOOD 38   109 O, that you could but by dissection see

dissemble   frequency: 1   relative frequency: 0.00001
     p. 380 UNGATHERED 12   52 Doth he once dissemble, but tels he did ride

distance   frequency: 3   relative frequency: 0.00004
     p. 194 UNDERWOOD 38   116 Absence, or Distance, shall not breed decay.
     p. 242 UNDERWOOD 69   19 For as at distance, few have facultie
     p. 276 U'WOOD 84.3   19 But at such distance, as the eye

distant   frequency: 2   relative frequency: 0.00002
     p. 421 UNGATHERED 49   8 As Cleare, and distant, as yor: selfe from
                               Cryme;
     p. 422 UNGATHERED 50   8 are distant, so is proffitt from iust aymes.

distill   frequency: 2   relative frequency: 0.00002
     p. 105 FOREST 8   29 That distill their husbands land
     p. 333 HORACE 2   612 Looke pale, distill a showre (was never meant)

distinct   frequency: 1   relative frequency: 0.00001
     p. 128 UNDERWOOD 1.1   39 Distinct in persons, yet in Unitie

distinctions   frequency: 1   relative frequency: 0.00001
     p. 242 UNDERWOOD 69   18 Where he would fixe, for the distinctions feare.

distinguish'd   frequency: 1   relative frequency: 0.00001
     p. 84 EPIGRAMS 133   10 Subtly distinguish'd, was confused here.

distract   frequency: 1   relative frequency: 0.00001
     p. 145 UNDERWOOD 4   11 Nor spread them as distract with feares,

distrust   frequency: 2   relative frequency: 0.00002
     p. 192 UNDERWOOD 38   49 Doe not despaire my mending; to distrust
     p. 235 UNDERWOOD 63   4 Doth by his doubt, distrust his promise more.

ditch   frequency: 1   relative frequency: 0.00001
   See also "new-ditch."
     p. 209 UNDERWOOD 43   134 Flanck'd with a Ditch, and forc'd out of a
                               Marish,

ditchfield   frequency: 1   relative frequency: 0.00001
     p. 214 UNDERWOOD 44   54 As Stiles, Dike, Ditchfield, Millar, Crips,
                               and Fen:

dittie   frequency: 1   relative frequency: 0.00001
     p. 239 UNDERWOOD 67   24 Whilst it the Dittie heares.

ditties   frequency: 1   relative frequency: 0.00001
     p. 241 UNDERWOOD 68   7 Hee'ld frame such ditties of their store, and
                               want,

ditty. See "dittie."

diu'd   frequency: 1   relative frequency: 0.00001
     p. 88 EPIGRAMS 133   162 Thrise did it spit: thrise diu'd. At last, it
                               view'd

diuers   frequency: 1   relative frequency: 0.00001
     p. 88 EPIGRAMS 133   149 Cats there lay diuers had beene flead, and
                               rosted,

diuersly   frequency: 1   relative frequency: 0.00001
     p. 64 EPIGRAMS 99   8 The selfe-same deeds, as diuersly they come,

diuide   frequency: 2   relative frequency: 0.00002
     p. 368 UNGATHERED 6   85 The Dutch whom Wealth (not Hatred) doth
                               diuide;
     p. 393 UNGATHERED 27   13 It is the Sword that doth diuide

diuided   frequency: 1   relative frequency: 0.00001
     p. 101 FOREST 4   58 To harbour a diuided thought

diuid'st   frequency: 1   relative frequency: 0.00001
     p. 97 FOREST 3   26 Diuid'st, vpon the lesser Deere;

diuine   frequency: 6   relative frequency: 0.00008
     p. 106 FOREST 9   6 Doth aske a drinke diuine:
     p. 110 FOREST 11   46 Pure, perfect, nay diuine;
     p. 112 FOREST 11   102 O, so diuine a creature

diuine (cont.)
```
     p. 115 FOREST 12       63 But onely Poets, rapt with rage diuine?
     p. 119 FOREST 13      101 By me, their priest (if they can ought diuine)
     p. 362 UNGATHERED 2    13 Which being eyed directly, I diuine,
```

dive. See "dyue."

dived. See "diu'd."

divell   frequency: 1   relative frequency: 0.00001
```
     p. 172 UNDERWOOD 20    24 The Divell; and be the damning of us all.
```

divels-arse   frequency: 1   relative frequency: 0.00001
```
     p. 212 UNDERWOOD 43   202 Who from the Divels-Arse did Guns beget;
```

divers   frequency: 1   relative frequency: 0.00001
     See also "diuers."
```
     p. 305 HORACE 2        2 Set a Horse-neck, and divers feathers fold
```

diversely. See "diuersly."

divide   frequency: 2   relative frequency: 0.00002
     See also "diuide."
```
     p. 264 UNDERWOOD 79    19 Chor. Sound, sound his praises loud, and with
                               his, hers divide.
     p. 327 HORACE 2       465 How to divide, into a hundred parts,
```

divided. See "diuided," "selfe-diuided."

dividest. See "diuid'st."

divine   frequency: 13   relative frequency: 0.00018
     See also "diuine."
```
     p. 131 UNDERWOOD 2.1    5 Poets, though divine, are men:
     p. 179 UNDERWOOD 25    57 If I auspitiously divine,
     p. 181 UNDERWOOD 27    20 Which all the world then styl'd divine?
     p. 185 UNDERWOOD 30    20 Of divine blessing, would not serve a State?
     p. 211 UNDERWOOD 43   195 Or Alexandria; and though a Divine
     p. 223 UNDERWOOD 49    25 I am no States-man, and much lesse Divine,
     p. 240 UNDERWOOD 67    51 And this the wombe divine,
     p. 278 U'WOOD 84.4     26 As 'tis not radiant, but divine:
     p. 287 U'WOOD 84.9    184 Of divine Comfort, when sh'had talk'd with God.
     p. 327 HORACE 2       492 To divine Poets, and their Verses came.
     p. 411 UNGATHERED 40   t3 her divine Meditations.
     p. 413 UNGATHERED 41   35 Of Persons, yet in Vnion (ONE) divine.
     p. 657 L. CONVIVALES    5 All his Answers are Divine,
```

diviner   frequency: 1   relative frequency: 0.00001
```
     p. 174 UNDERWOOD 22    31 One sparke of your Diviner heat
```

divinest   frequency: 1   relative frequency: 0.00001
```
     p. 413 UNGATHERED 41   26 (Divinest graces) are so entermixt,
```

divinitie   frequency: 1   relative frequency: 0.00001
```
     p. 207 UNDERWOOD 43   102 With humble Gleanings in Divinitie,
```

divinity. See "divinitie."

divisions   frequency: 1   relative frequency: 0.00001
```
     p. 157 UNDERWOOD 13   151 But few and faire Divisions: but being got
```

do   frequency: 17   relative frequency: 0.00024
     See also "doe," "doo," "doo't," "do't,"
             "do'you," "out-doo."
```
   **p. 117 PANEGYRE        149 Of his great actions, first to see, and do
     p. 333 HORACE 2        620 When you write Verses, with your judge do so:
     p. 364 UNGATHERED 4      4 Do turne into a Woman.
     p. 371 UNGATHERED 8      9 Their motiues were, since it had not to do
     p. 371 UNGATHERED 8     14 Do crowne thy murdred Poeme: which shall rise
     p. 378 UNGATHERED 11    85 Shewes he dares more then Paules Church-yard
                                durst do.
     p. 384 UNGATHERED 18     2 And clothes, and guifts, that only do thee grace
     p. 384 UNGATHERED 18     4 Do wayte vpon thee: and theyre Loue not bought.
     p. 384 UNGATHERED 18     7 Wch I do, early, vertuous Somerset,
     p. 385 UNGATHERED 20     4 Least a false praise do make theyr dotage his.
     p. 385 UNGATHERED 20     5 I do not feele that euer yet I had
     p. 387 UNGATHERED 22     6 trust in the tombes, their care=full freinds do
                                rayse;
     p. 398 UNGATHERED 30    66 How do his trumpets breath! What loud alarmes!
     p. 413 UNGATHERED 41    29 These Mysteries do point to three more great,
```

do (cont.)
```
       p.  423 UNGATHERED 50   15 Yet ware; thou mayst do all things cruellie:
       p.  423 UNGATHERED 50   20 shall never dare do any thing but feare./
       p.  662 INSCRIPTS. 2     8 if any way she do rewarde thee
```

docile   frequency: 1   relative frequency: 0.00001
```
       p.  329 HORACE 2        504 The docile mind may soone thy precepts know,
```

dock. See "docke," "dock's."

docke   frequency: 1   relative frequency: 0.00001
```
       p.  85 EPIGRAMS 133     41 A Docke there is, that called is AVERNVS,
```

dock's   frequency: 1   relative frequency: 0.00001
```
       p.  85 EPIGRAMS 133     60 'Tis but light paines: Indeede this Dock's no
                                   rose.
```

doctor   frequency: 1   relative frequency: 0.00001
```
       p.  31 EPIGRAMS 13      t1 TO DOCTOR EMPIRICK.
```

doctors   frequency: 1   relative frequency: 0.00001
See also "o'th'doctors."
```
       p.  270 UNDERWOOD 83    52 And to the Torturers (her Doctors) say,
```

doctrine   frequency: 2   relative frequency: 0.00002
```
       p.  61 EPIGRAMS 95       2 That stranger doctrine of PYTHAGORAS,
       p.  329 HORACE 2        516 As doctrine, and delight together go.
```

doe   frequency: 230   relative frequency: 0.00332
```
     *p.  493 TO HIMSELF       27 There, sweepings doe as well
    **p.  113 PANEGYRE         12 Where Murder, Rapine, Lust, doe sit within,
    **p.  115 PANEGYRE         81 "As they are men, then men. That all they doe,
    **p.  116 PANEGYRE        118 Who once haue got the habit to doe ill.
    **p.  116 PANEGYRE        125 That kings, by their example, more doe sway
    **p.  116 PANEGYRE        126 Then by their power; and men doe more obay
      p.  30 EPIGRAMS 11        7 For I will doe none: and as little ill,
      p.  32 EPIGRAMS 16        8 Make good what thou dar'st doe in all the rest.
      p.  32 EPIGRAMS 17        2 As guiltie men doe magistrates: glad I,
      p.  34 EPIGRAMS 28        5 Longer a knowing, then most wits doe liue.
      p.  35 EPIGRAMS 28        6 And, that is done, as he saw great men doe.
      p.  36 EPIGRAMS 29        5 For then, our water-conduits doe runne wine;
      p.  36 EPIGRAMS 30        2 Be thine, I taxe, yet doe not owne my rimes:
      p.  37 EPIGRAMS 32        2 Could not effect, not all the furies doe,
      p.  40 EPIGRAMS 43        2 Whose actions so themselues doe celebrate;
      p.  43 EPIGRAMS 51        8 Doe beg thy care vnto thy after-state.
      p.  44 EPIGRAMS 55        1 How I doe loue thee BEAVMONT, and thy
                                  Muse,
      p.  44 EPIGRAMS 55        3 How I doe feare my selfe, that am not worth
      p.  49 EPIGRAMS 67        1 Since men haue left to doe praise-worthy things,
      p.  55 EPIGRAMS 86        3 Then doe I loue thee, and behold thy ends
      p.  59 EPIGRAMS 92       10 And vnderstand 'hem, as most chapmen doe.
      p.  59 EPIGRAMS 92       38 On them: And therefore doe not onely shunne
      p.  60 EPIGRAMS 93       11 Then whose I doe not know a whiter soule,
      p.  62 EPIGRAMS 96        9 My title's seal'd. Those that for claps doe
                                  write,
      p.  64 EPIGRAMS 101       2 Doe equally desire your companie:
      p.  65 EPIGRAMS 101      32 Their liues, as doe their lines, till now had
                                  lasted.
      p.  66 EPIGRAMS 102       1 I doe but name thee PEMBROKE, and I find
      p.  68 EPIGRAMS 107       1 Doe what you come for, Captayne, with your
                                  newes;
      p.  68 EPIGRAMS 107       2 That's, sit, and eate: doe not my eares abuse.
      p.  69 EPIGRAMS 107      14 What at Ligorne, Rome, Florence you did doe:
      p.  69 EPIGRAMS 107      32 Doe what you come for Captayne, There's your
                                  meate.
      p.  69 EPIGRAMS 108       3 And your high names: I doe desire, that thence
      p.  70 EPIGRAMS 108       8 No more, then I dare now doe, with my pen.
      p.  71 EPIGRAMS 110      12 Can so speake CAESAR, as thy labours doe.
      p.  72 EPIGRAMS 112       5 Thy all, at all: and what so ere I doe,
      p.  74 EPIGRAMS 115      12 Doe all, that longs to the anarchy of drinke,
      p.  74 EPIGRAMS 115      26 Parts, then th'Italian could doe, with his dore.
      p.  80 EPIGRAMS 127       4 No, I doe, therefore, call Posteritie
      p.  82 EPIGRAMS 131       1 When we doe giue, ALPHONSO, to the light,
      p.  83 EPIGRAMS 131      10 Euen those for whom they doe this, know they
                                  erre:
      p.  85 EPIGRAMS 133      64 Of all your night-tubs, when the carts doe
                                  cluster,
      p.  87 EPIGRAMS 133     123 Of worship, they their nodding chinnes doe hit
      p.  88 EPIGRAMS 133     143 Your Fleet-lane Furies; and hot cookes doe
                                  dwell,
```

doe (cont.)

p.	88	EPIGRAMS 133	169	Is fill'd with buttock? And the walls doe sweate
p.	93	FOREST 2	10	Thy Mount, to which the Dryads doe resort,
p.	94	FOREST 2	23	Thy sheepe, thy bullocks, kine, and calues doe feed:
p.	100	FOREST 3	103	To doe thy countrey seruice, thy selfe right;
p.	100	FOREST 3	104	That neither want doe thee affright,
p.	100	FOREST 4	5	Doe not once hope, that thou canst tempt
p.	101	FOREST 4	37	Yes, threaten, doe. Alas I feare
p.	101	FOREST 4	61	No, I doe know, that I was borne
p.	102	FOREST 4	66	As wandrers doe, that still doe rome,
p.	104	FOREST 8	3	Doe not men, ynow of rites
p.	104	FOREST 8	7	Take heed, Sicknesse, what you doe,
p.	105	FOREST 8	26	Doe enough; and who would take
p.	109	FOREST 11	21	For either our affections doe rebell,
p.	110	FOREST 11	29	Doe seuerall passions <still> inuade the minde,
p.	111	FOREST 11	73	Though thy wild thoughts with sparrowes wings doe flye,
p.	111	FOREST 11	76	We doe not number, here,
p.	114	FOREST 12	46	Or in their windowes; doe but proue the wombs,
p.	117	FOREST 13	31	And so doe many more. All which can call
p.	117	FOREST 13	38	Doe I reflect. Some alderman has power,
p.	119	FOREST 13	86	That doe sinne onely for the infamie:
p.	120	FOREST 13	121	Liue that one, still; and as long yeeres doe passe,
p.	120	FOREST 14	2	And some doe drinke, and some doe dance,
p.	120	FOREST 14	5	And all doe striue t<o>'aduance
p.	120	FOREST 14	16	Which I doe tell:
p.	130	UNDERWOOD 1.3	19	What comfort by him doe wee winne,
p.	133	UNDERWOOD 2.3	25	Which how Dexterously I doe,
p.	134	UNDERWOOD 2.4	5	As she goes, all hearts doe duty
p.	134	UNDERWOOD 2.4	7	And enamour'd, doe wish, so they might
p.	134	UNDERWOOD 2.4	11	Doe but looke on her eyes, they doe light
p.	134	UNDERWOOD 2.4	13	Doe but looke on her Haire, it is bright
p.	134	UNDERWOOD 2.4	15	Doe but marke, her forehead's smoother
p.	136	UNDERWOOD 2.5	3	And doe governe more my blood,
p.	136	UNDERWOOD 2.5	18	By her lookes I doe her know,
p.	137	UNDERWOOD 2.6	1	Charis, guesse, and doe not misse,
p.	139	UNDERWOOD 2.7	4	Why doe you doubt, or stay?
p.	139	UNDERWOOD 2.7	12	What w'are but once to doe, we should doe long.
p.	140	UNDERWOOD 2.9	5	Titles, I confesse, doe take me;
p.	141	UNDERWOOD 2.9	34	What we harmonie doe call
p.	142	U'WOOD 2.10	1	For his Mind, I doe not care,
p.	142	UNDERWOOD 2.9	46	As to doe no thing too much.
p.	142	UNDERWOOD 2.9	49	Nor doe wrongs, nor wrongs receaue;
p.	143	UNDERWOOD 3	13	What need of mee? doe you but sing,
p.	143	UNDERWOOD 3	16	But what those lips doe make.
p.	144	UNDERWOOD 4	1	Oh doe not wanton with those eyes,
p.	145	UNDERWOOD 4	9	O, doe not steepe them in thy Teares,
p.	145	UNDERWOOD 5	7	Nor doe we doubt, but that we can,
p.	146	UNDERWOOD 6	8	Doe change, though man, and often fight,
p.	146	UNDERWOOD 6	9	Which we in love must doe aswell,
p.	147	UNDERWOOD 7	18	And lookes as Lillies doe,
p.	148	UNDERWOOD 8	1	Doe but consider this small dust,
p.	153	UNDERWOOD 13	1	If, Sackvile, all that have the power to doe
p.	153	UNDERWOOD 13	18	To have such doe me good, I durst not name:
p.	155	UNDERWOOD 13	80	Is borrowing; that but stopt, they doe invade
p.	157	UNDERWOOD 13	157	That I may love your Person (as I doe)
p.	159	UNDERWOOD 14	17	But I on yours farre otherwise shall doe,
p.	159	UNDERWOOD 14	32	Upon your Center, doe your Circle fill
p.	159	UNDERWOOD 14	34	Heard what times past have said, seene what ours doe:
p.	161	UNDERWOOD 14	72	Thy learned Chamber-fellow, knowes to doe
p.	161	UNDERWOOD 14	79	Thy gift 'gainst envie. O how I doe count
p.	164	UNDERWOOD 15	76	Doe all the tricks of a saut Lady Bitch;
p.	165	UNDERWOOD 15	101	Thus they doe talke. And are these objects fit
p.	166	UNDERWOOD 15	123	Our vices doe not tarry in a place,
p.	169	UNDERWOOD 17	1	They are not, Sir, worst Owers, that doe pay
p.	170	UNDERWOOD 19	11	Tell me (my lov'd Friend) doe you love, or no,
p.	171	UNDERWOOD 19	13	You blush, but doe not: friends are either none,
p.	171	UNDERWOOD 19	18	Others, in time may love, as we doe now.
p.	172	UNDERWOOD 20	15	Knew I this Woman? yes: And you doe see,
p.	172	UNDERWOOD 20	17	Doe not you aske to know her, she is worse
p.	180	UNDERWOOD 26	18	To doe, then be a husband of that store.
p.	182	UNDERWOOD 27	32	Where men may see whom I doe sing?
p.	182	UNDERWOOD 28	8	Both braines and hearts; and mine now best doe know it:
p.	186	UNDERWOOD 32	16	He do's you wrong, that craves you to doe right.
p.	186	UNDERWOOD 33	1	That I, hereafter, doe not thinke the Barre,
p.	187	UNDERWOOD 33	10	Upon the reverend Pleaders; doe now shut

doe (cont.)

p.	191	UNDERWOOD 38	3 Or doe upon my selfe some desperate ill;
p.	192	UNDERWOOD 38	46 We cut not off, till all Cures else doe faile:
p.	192	UNDERWOOD 38	49 Doe not despaire my mending; to distrust
p.	193	UNDERWOOD 38	79 In darke, and sullen mornes, doe we not say,
p.	193	UNDERWOOD 38	84 Of crueltie, lest they doe make you such.
p.	194	UNDERWOOD 38	111 How all my Fibres by your Spirit doe move,
p.	194	UNDERWOOD 38	120 When I see you, then I doe see my Sun,
p.	197	UNDERWOOD 40	5 And take some sirrup after; so doe I,
p.	197	UNDERWOOD 40	18 As neither wine doe rack it out, or mirth.
p.	199	UNDERWOOD 41	3 What it is like: And doe not thinke they can
p.	199	UNDERWOOD 41	14 How shall I doe, sweet Mistris, for my heart?
p.	200	UNDERWOOD 42	11 Fathers, and Husbands, I doe claime a right
p.	200	UNDERWOOD 42	24 So to be sure you doe injoy your selves.
p.	201	UNDERWOOD 42	40 To doe her Husbands rites in, e're 'twere gone
p.	201	UNDERWOOD 42	58 Lift up some one, and doe, I tell not what.
p.	202	UNDERWOOD 42	78 When not the Shops, but windowes doe display
p.	205	UNDERWOOD 43	57 But that's a marke, wherof thy Rites doe boast,
p.	206	UNDERWOOD 43	78 And the strong lines, that so the time doe catch:
p.	207	UNDERWOOD 43	92 To teach some that, their Nurses could <not> doe,
p.	210	UNDERWOOD 43	156 Nay, let White-Hall with Revels have to doe,
p.	211	UNDERWOOD 43	178 A Court of Equitie should doe us right,
p.	212	UNDERWOOD 43	204 On both sides doe your mischiefes with delight;
p.	213	UNDERWOOD 44	16 To see the Pride at Court, their Wives doe make:
p.	215	UNDERWOOD 44	68 Live by their Scale, that dare doe nothing free?
p.	215	UNDERWOOD 44	91 All that they doe at Playes. O, but first here
p.	216	UNDERWOOD 45	13 And as within your Office, you doe take
p.	216	UNDERWOOD 45	15 Inquirie of the worth: So must we doe,
p.	218	UNDERWOOD 47	1 Men that are safe, and sure, in all they doe,
p.	219	UNDERWOOD 47	44 Brunsfield, and Mansfield doe this yeare, my fates
p.	219	UNDERWOOD 47	46 Though I doe neither heare these newes, nor tell
p.	219	UNDERWOOD 47	56 Well, with mine owne fraile Pitcher, what to doe
p.	221	UNDERWOOD 48	30 Before his braine doe know it;
p.	222	UNDERWOOD 49	16 To Church, as others doe to Feasts and Playes,
p.	223	UNDERWOOD 49	21 What though she hath won on Trust, as many doe,
p.	224	UNDERWOOD 50	5 Not only shunning by your act, to doe
p.	225	UNDERWOOD 51	7 And so doe I. This is the sixtieth yeare
p.	229	UNDERWOOD 54	3 If I doe lose it: And, without a Tale,
p.	229	UNDERWOOD 54	15 It doe not come: One piece I have in store,
p.	230	UNDERWOOD 56	19 Such, (if her manners like you) I doe send:
p.	233	UNDERWOOD 59	15 Of daring not to doe a wrong, is true
p.	234	UNDERWOOD 60	5 What could their care doe 'gainst the spight
p.	234	UNDERWOOD 61	15 And wee doe weepe, to water, for our sinne.
p.	235	UNDERWOOD 61	19 And doe their penance, to avert Gods rod,
p.	235	UNDERWOOD 62	13 What can the Poet wish his King may doe,
p.	236	UNDERWOOD 63	7 Then, Royall CHARLES, and MARY, doe not grutch
p.	236	UNDERWOOD 63	10 And thinke all still the best, that he will doe.
p.	240	UNDERWOOD 67	41 Doe mingle in a shout,
p.	240	UNDERWOOD 67	50 The People her doe call.
p.	250	UNDERWOOD 73	7 Why doe I irritate, or stirre up thee,
p.	251	UNDERWOOD 74	7 The Rivers in their shores doe run,
p.	251	UNDERWOOD 74	10 Rare Plants from ev'ry banke doe rise,
p.	253	UNDERWOOD 75	19 Doe boast their Loves, and Brav'ries so at large,
p.	253	UNDERWOOD 75	27 To doe their Offices in Natures Chime,
p.	254	UNDERWOOD 75	49 Stay, thou wilt see what rites the Virgins doe!
p.	255	UNDERWOOD 75	78 Who, in all they doe,
p.	256	UNDERWOOD 75	108 Him up, to doe the same himselfe had done.
p.	257	UNDERWOOD 75	140 Doe long to make themselves, so, another way:
p.	260	UNDERWOOD 76	29 Then goe on, and doe its worst;
p.	260	UNDERWOOD 77	10 This I would doe, could I thinke Weston one
p.	261	UNDERWOOD 77	15 Can doe the things that Statues doe deserve,
p.	262	UNDERWOOD 78	10 Where all heroique ample thoughts doe meet:
p.	264	UNDERWOOD 79	24 Nym. Of brightest MIRA, doe we raise our Song,
p.	269	UNDERWOOD 83	5 I doe obey you, Beautie! for in death,
p.	271	UNDERWOOD 83	75 And all beatitudes, that thence doe flow:
p.	276	U'WOOD 84.3	15 Till, like her face, it doe appeare,
p.	277	U'WOOD 84.3	29 But, Painter, see thou doe not sell
p.	277	U'WOOD 84.4	5 Not, that your Art I doe refuse:
p.	278	U'WOOD 84.4	19 Our sense you doe with knowledge fill,
p.	281	U'WOOD 84.8	17 Which all men doe, that urge not their owne deeds
p.	283	U'WOOD 84.9	30 Nothing I doe; but, like a heavie wheele,
p.	287	U'WOOD 84.9	169 To one she said, Doe this, he did it; So
p.	288	U'WOOD 84.9	214 Of lapsed Nature) best know what to doe,
p.	290	UNDERWOOD 85	25 Whilst from the higher Bankes doe slide the floods;

doe (cont.)
p. 290 UNDERWOOD 85   27 The Fountaines murmure as the streames doe
                          creepe,
p. 294 UNDERWOOD 88   4 Like lustfull beasts, that onely know to doe it:
p. 305 HORACE 2   13 And both doe crave, and give againe, this leave.
p. 311 HORACE 2   120 On popular noise with, and doe businesse in.
p. 315 HORACE 2   241 The old man many evils doe girt round;
p. 317 HORACE 2   250 Mans comming yeares much good with them doe
                          bring:
p. 317 HORACE 2   257 In at the eare, doe stirre the mind more slow
p. 321 HORACE 2   356 Be I their Judge, they doe at no time dare
p. 331 HORACE 2   571 Why not? I'm gentle, and free-borne, doe hate
p. 331 HORACE 2   574 Wilt nothing against nature speake, or doe:
p. 331 HORACE 2   579 To change, and mend, what you not forth doe set.
p. 333 HORACE 2   609 You doe not bring, to judge your Verses, one,
p. 333 HORACE 2   615 Cry, and doe more then the true Mourners: so
p. 335 HORACE 2   667 Nor did he doe this once; for if you can
p. 338 HORACE 1   21 Bouts .. fleet .... doe intertwine
p. 362 UNGATHERED 2   3 Not wearing moodes, as gallants doe a fashion,
p. 362 UNGATHERED 2   6 Where, such perfections to the life doe rise.
p. 389 UNGATHERED 24   4 When the old words doe strike on the new times,
p. 399 UNGATHERED 31   5 To veiw the truth and owne it. Doe but looke
p. 400 UNGATHERED 32   6 When they doe sweat to fortifie a Muse.
p. 401 UNGATHERED 33   2 That, while they bind the senses, doe so please?
p. 402 UNGATHERED 34   17 I doe salute you! Are you fitted yet?
p. 403 UNGATHERED 34   32 That doe cry vp ye Machine, & ye Showes!
p. 404 UNGATHERED 34   64 He is, or would be ye mayne Dominus doe
p. 405 UNGATHERED 34   70 To be worth Enuy. Henceforth I doe meane
p. 405 UNGATHERED 34   75 What would he doe now, gi'ng his mynde yt waye
p. 406 UNGATHERED 35   4 All kings to doe ye self same deeds wth some!
p. 408 UNGATHERED 37   5 ffoole, doe not rate my Rymes; I'haue found thy
                          Vice
p. 409 UNGATHERED 38   5 And you doe doe them well, with good applause,
p. 410 UNGATHERED 38   10 A Prentise-ship: which few doe now a dayes.
p. 416 UNGATHERED 43   5 How they doe keepe alive his memorie;
p. 416 UNGATHERED 43   8 And doe both Church, and Common-wealth the
                          good,
p. 417 UNGATHERED 45   32 yet doe not feare it.
p. 423 UNGATHERED 50   12 It is a lycense to doe ill, protectes

does   frequency: 1   relative frequency: 0.00001
    See also "do's."
    p. 331 HORACE 2   549 A meane, and toleration, which does well:

doest   frequency: 1   relative frequency: 0.00001
    p. 420 UNGATHERED 48   24 Thou that doest spend thie dayes

dog   frequency: 3   relative frequency: 0.00004
    p. 155 UNDERWOOD 13   67 But one is bitten by the Dog he fed,
    p. 215 UNDERWOOD 44   71 More then to praise a Dog? or Horse? or speake
    p. 241 UNDERWOOD 69   10 Painted a Dog, that now his subtler skill

dog-daies   frequency: 1   relative frequency: 0.00001
    p. 409 UNGATHERED 37   20 Out in the Dog-daies, least the killer meete

dogges   frequency: 1   relative frequency: 0.00001
    p. 315 HORACE 2   230 Loves Dogges, and Horses; and is ever one

dogs   frequency: 5   relative frequency: 0.00007
    See also "dogges."
    p. 36 EPIGRAMS 28   18 That breathes in his dogs way: and this is great.
    p. 84 EPIGRAMS 133   14 And for one CERBERVS, the whole coast was
                              dogs.
    p. 88 EPIGRAMS 133   146 The heads, houghs, entrailes, and the hides of
                              dogs:
    p. 187 UNDERWOOD 33   12 To the Wolves studie, or Dogs eloquence;
    p. 241 UNDERWOOD 69   12 All live dogs from the lane, and his shops sight,

doing   frequency: 5   relative frequency: 0.00007
    p. 76 EPIGRAMS 119   6 Whose dice not doing well, to'a pulpit ran.
    p. 99 FOREST 3   84 Not doing good, scarce when he dyes.
    p. 168 UNDERWOOD 15   180 And never but for doing wrong be sory;
    p. 288 U'WOOD 84.9   193 Or doing other deeds of Charitie,
    p. 294 UNDERWOOD 88   1 Doing, a filthy pleasure is, and short;

dolphin   frequency: 1   relative frequency: 0.00001
    p. 307 HORACE 2   42 A Dolphin, and a Boare amid' the floods.

dominations   frequency: 1   relative frequency: 0.00001
    p. 285 U'WOOD 84.9   87 The Dominations, Vertues, and the Powers,

dominus   frequency: 1   relative frequency: 0.00001
    p. 404 UNGATHERED 34   64 He is, or would be ye mayne Dominus doe

domitian   frequency: 1   relative frequency: 0.00001
    p.   38 EPIGRAMS 36   2 To thy DOMITIAN, than I can my
                                 IAMES:

don   frequency: 3   relative frequency: 0.00004
    p.   35 EPIGRAMS 28   1 DON SVRLY, to aspire the glorious name
    p.   35 EPIGRAMS 28   t1 ON DON SVRLY.
    p. 204 UNDERWOOD 43   31 The learned Librarie of Don Quixote;

done   frequency: 49   relative frequency: 0.00070
    See also "donne."
    p.   35 EPIGRAMS 28   6 And, that is done, as he saw great men doe.
    p.   46 EPIGRAMS 60   1 Loe, what my countrey should haue done (haue
                                 rais'd
    p.   49 EPIGRAMS 66   14 When they cost dearest, and are done most free,
    p.   58 EPIGRAMS 91   6 In th'eye of Europe, where thy deeds were done,
    p.   59 EPIGRAMS 92   37 With ignorance on vs, as they haue done
    p.   64 EPIGRAMS 99   7 But much it now auailes, what's done, of whom:
    p.   71 EPIGRAMS 110   2 In these west-parts, nor when that warre was
                                 done,
    p. 101 FOREST 4   35 Little, for me, had reason done,
    p. 115 FOREST 12   71 Yet, for the timely fauours shee hath done,
    p. 115 FOREST 12   79 Then all, that haue but done my Muse least
                                 grace,
    p. 128 UNDERWOOD 1.1   24 All's done in me.
    p. 129 UNDERWOOD 1.2   18 Then thou hast done?
    p. 138 UNDERWOOD 2.6   5 What my Muse and I have done:
    p. 151 UNDERWOOD 12   3 Would say as much, as both have done
    p. 152 UNDERWOOD 12   30 And more, and more, I should have done,
    p. 153 UNDERWOOD 13   6 As they are done, and such returnes they find:
    p. 153 UNDERWOOD 13   12 As I did feele it done, as soone as meant:
    p. 153 UNDERWOOD 13   27 Excuses, or Delayes? or done 'hem scant,
    p. 154 UNDERWOOD 13   34 That puts it in his Debt-booke e're't be done;
    p. 154 UNDERWOOD 13   40 So each, that's done, and tane, becomes a Brace.
    p. 156 UNDERWOOD 13   96 And told of with more Licence then th'were done!
    p. 169 UNDERWOOD 17   6 Is done for gaine: If't be, 'tis not sincere.
    p. 171 UNDERWOOD 14   23 Of all that can be done him; Such a one
    p. 182 UNDERWOOD 27   29 Have all these done (and yet I misse
    p. 186 UNDERWOOD 32   12 Thinke, yea and boast, that they have done it so
    p. 192 UNDERWOOD 38   54 And not the bounties you ha' done, deny.
    p. 201 UNDERWOOD 42   62 He would have done in verse, with any of those
    p. 202 UNDERWOOD 43   2 What had I done that might call on thine ire?
    p. 210 UNDERWOOD 43   163 And what hast thou done in these pettie spights,
    p. 213 UNDERWOOD 44   19 And comming home, to tell what acts were done
    p. 214 UNDERWOOD 44   61 But he that should perswade, to have this done
    p. 233 UNDERWOOD 59   16 Valour! to sleight it, being done to you!
    p. 244 UNDERWOOD 70   48 All Offices were done
    p. 245 UNDERWOOD 70   60 By what was done and wrought
    p. 247 UNDERWOOD 70   115 Unto the Vertue. Nothing perfect done,
    p. 255 UNDERWOOD 75   93 Be duly done to those
    p. 256 UNDERWOOD 75   108 Him up, to doe the same himselfe had done.
    p. 259 UNDERWOOD 76   13 For done service, and to come:
    p. 262 UNDERWOOD 78   13 Witnesse his Action done at Scandero<o>ne;
    p. 268 UNDERWOOD 82   1 That thou art lov'd of God, this worke is done,
    p. 284 U'WOOD 84.9   81 Hee knowes, what worke h'hath done, to call this
                                 Guest,
    p. 294 UNDERWOOD 88   2 And done, we straight repent us of the sport:
    p. 317 HORACE 2   255 The businesse either on the Stage is done,
    p. 317 HORACE 2   261 Things worthy to be done within, but take
    p. 319 HORACE 2   325 Having well eat, and drunke (the rites being
                                 done)
    p. 339 HORACE 1   38 Wants strength, and .... as his spirits were
                                 done;
    p. 370 UNGATHERED 7   9 But now, your Worke is done, if they that view
    p. 389 UNGATHERED 24   21 To your desert, who'haue done it, Friend. And
                                 this
    p. 389 UNGATHERED 24   24 That would haue done, that, which you onely can.

donees.   See "donnee's."

donne   frequency: 5   relative frequency: 0.00007
    p.   34 EPIGRAMS 23   1 DONNE, the delight of PHOEBVS, and
                                 each Muse,
    p.   34 EPIGRAMS 23   t1 TO IOHN DONNE.
    p.   62 EPIGRAMS 96   1 Who shall doubt, DONNE, where I a Poet
                                 bee,
    p.   62 EPIGRAMS 96   t1 TO IOHN DONNE.

donne (cont.)
      p. 367 UNGATHERED 6   54 Then Time hath donne,

donnee's   frequency: 1   relative frequency: 0.00001
      p. 158 UNDERWOOD 13   163 Donnor's or Donnee's, to their practise shall

donnes   frequency: 1   relative frequency: 0.00001
      p. 60 EPIGRAMS 94   t2 WITH Mr. DONNES SATYRES.

donnor's   frequency: 1   relative frequency: 0.00001
      p. 158 UNDERWOOD 13   163 Donnor's or Donnee's, to their practise shall

donors. See "donnor's."

doo   frequency: 8   relative frequency: 0.00011
      p. 44 EPIGRAMS 53   7 And that, as puritanes at baptisme doo,
      p. 46 EPIGRAMS 60   5 I, that am glad of thy great chance, here doo!
      p. 54 EPIGRAMS 81   5 For all thou hear'st, thou swear'st thy selfe
                                  didst doo.
      p. 59 EPIGRAMS 92   40 That know not so much state, wrong, as they doo.
      p. 61 EPIGRAMS 95   25 Although to write be lesser then to doo,
      p. 63 EPIGRAMS 98   2 And I know nothing more thou hast to doo.
      p. 74 EPIGRAMS 115   20 Not that it feares, but will not haue to doo
      p. 212 UNDERWOOD 43   215 Light on thee: Or if those plagues will not doo,

doom. See "doome."

doome   frequency: 2   relative frequency: 0.00002
      p. 283 U'WOOD 84.9   48 To heare their Judge, and his eternall doome;
      p. 288 U'WOOD 84.9   208 The kind of Man, on whom his doome should fall!

door. See "doore," "dore."

doore   frequency: 3   relative frequency: 0.00004
      p. 254 UNDERWOOD 75   69 See, at another doore,
      p. 258 UNDERWOOD 75   185 They both are slip'd to Bed; Shut fast the
                                  Doore,
      p. 288 U'WOOD 84.9   190 The doore of Grace, and found the Mercy-Seat.

doores   frequency: 2   relative frequency: 0.00002
      p. 40 EPIGRAMS 42   7 And hauing got him out of doores is glad.
      p. 363 UNGATHERED 3   9 Enforcing yron doores to yeeld it way,

doors. See "doores."

doo't   frequency: 2   relative frequency: 0.00002
      p. 46 EPIGRAMS 60   8 But thine, for which I doo't, so much exceeds!
      p. 403 UNGATHERED 34   21 Why much good doo't you! Be what beast you will,

dor. See "dore."

dore   frequency: 4   relative frequency: 0.00005
      p. 29 EPIGRAMS 7   2 A purging bill, now fix'd vpon the dore,
      p. 74 EPIGRAMS 115   26 Parts, then th'Italian could doe, with his dore.
      p. 89 EPIGRAMS 133   178 And stayes but till you come vnto the dore!
      p. 166 UNDERWOOD 15   120 When oft the Bearer, is borne out of dore?

dorrels   frequency: 1   relative frequency: 0.00001
      p. 223 UNDERWOOD 49   42 This Age would lend no faith to Dorrels Deed;

dorset   frequency: 1   relative frequency: 0.00001
      p. 153 UNDERWOOD 13   t2 now Earle of Dorset.

do's   frequency: 5   relative frequency: 0.00007
      p. 153 UNDERWOOD 13   26 Against his will that do's 'hem? that hath weav'd
      p. 154 UNDERWOOD 13   41 He neither gives, or do's, that doth delay
      p. 186 UNDERWOOD 32   16 He do's you wrong, that craves you to doe right.
      p. 222 UNDERWOOD 49   1 Do's the Court-Pucell then so censure me,
      p. 317 HORACE 2   244 Or do's all businesse coldly, and with feare;

dose   frequency: 1   relative frequency: 0.00001
      p. 74 EPIGRAMS 115   14 Giue euery one his dose of mirth: and watches

dosen   frequency: 1   relative frequency: 0.00001
      p. 86 EPIGRAMS 133   71 With famine, wants, and sorrowes many a dosen,

dost   frequency: 32   relative frequency: 0.00046
      See also "doest," "dc'st."
      p. 32 EPIGRAMS 16   6 Some hundred quarrells, yet dost thou fight none;
      p. 39 EPIGRAMS 40   1 Marble, weepe, for thou dost couer

dost (cont.)

	p.			
	p.	44	EPIGRAMS 55	2 That vnto me dost such religion vse!
	p.	50	EPIGRAMS 72	2 A chamber-critick, and dost dine, and sup
	p.	57	EPIGRAMS 89	11 And present worth in all dost so contract,
	p.	57	EPIGRAMS 89	12 As others speake, but onely thou dost act.
	p.	62	EPIGRAMS 96	3 That so alone canst iudge, so'alone dost make:
	p.	62	EPIGRAMS 96	4 And, in thy censures, euenly, dost take
	p.	73	EPIGRAMS 112	14 To Satyres; and thou dost pursue me. Where,
	p.	73	EPIGRAMS 112	18 That both for wit, and sense, so oft dost plucke,
	p.	73	EPIGRAMS 112	20 Nor scarce dost colour for it, which is lesse.
	p.	76	EPIGRAMS 119	8 But dost it out of iudgement, not disease;
	p.	81	EPIGRAMS 129	11 Whil'st thou dost rayse some Player, from the graue,
	p.	81	EPIGRAMS 129	16 Thou dost out-zany COKELY, POD; nay, GVE:
	p.	97	FOREST 3	35 Thou dost with some delight the day out-weare,
	p.	104	FOREST 8	1 Why, Disease, dost thou molest
	p.	122	FOREST 15	5 O, be thou witnesse, that the reynes dost know,
	p.	168	UNDERWOOD 15	179 That thou dost all things more for truth, then glory,
	p.	187	UNDERWOOD 33	15 So dost thou studie matter, men, and times,
	p.	187	UNDERWOOD 33	19 But first dost vexe, and search it! If not sound,
	p.	207	UNDERWOOD 43	105 How in these ruines, Vulcan, thou dost lurke,
	p.	217	UNDERWOOD 46	15 And now such is thy stand; while thou dost deale
	p.	221	UNDERWOOD 48	17 See then thou dost attend him,
	p.	235	UNDERWOOD 62	8 As thou dost cure our Evill, at thy charge.
	p.	292	UNDERWOOD 86	12 If a fit livor thou dost seeke to toast;
	p.	313	HORACE 2	169 Or follow fame, thou that dost write, or faine
	p.	315	HORACE 2	220 If such a ones applause thou dost require,
	p.	384	UNGATHERED 18	11 May she, whome thou for spouse, to day, dost take,
	p.	388	UNGATHERED 23	5 Still, still, dost thou arriue with, at our shore,
	p.	397	UNGATHERED 30	43 O, how in those, dost thou instruct these times,
	p.	408	UNGATHERED 36	6 Thou'rt too ambitious: and dost fear in vaine!
	p.	423	UNGATHERED 50	16 not safe; but when thou dost them thoroughlie:

do'st   frequency: 5   relative frequency: 0.00007

	p.	28	EPIGRAMS 4	1 How, best of Kings, do'st thou a scepter beare!
	p.	28	EPIGRAMS 4	2 How, best of Poets, do'st thou laurell weare!
	p.	54	EPIGRAMS 83	1 To put out the word, whore, thou do'st me woo,
	p.	174	UNDERWOOD 23	1 Where do'st thou carelesse lie,
	p.	235	UNDERWOOD 62	7 And, in these Cures, do'st so thy selfe enlarge,

do't   frequency: 3   relative frequency: 0.00004

	*p.	493	TO HIMSELF	31 And much good do't you then:
	p.	140	UNDERWOOD 2.8	13 Therefore, Charis, you must do't,
	p.	164	UNDERWOOD 15	57 To do't with Cloth, or Stuffes, lusts name might merit;

dotage   frequency: 1   relative frequency: 0.00001

	p.	385	UNGATHERED 20	4 Least a false praise do make theyr dotage his.

dote   frequency: 1   relative frequency: 0.00001

	p.	201	UNDERWOOD 42	47 So I might dote upon thy Chaires, and Stooles,

dotes   frequency: 1   relative frequency: 0.00001

	p.	269	UNDERWOOD 83	25 I durst not aime at that: The dotes were such

doth   frequency: 194   relative frequency: 0.00280

	**p.	115	PANEGYRE	71 The others flame, as doth the wike and waxe.
	p.	27	EPIGRAMS 2	14 For vulgar praise, doth it too dearely buy.
	p.	27	EPIGRAMS 3	2 Call'st a booke good, or bad, as it doth sell,
	p.	29	EPIGRAMS 8	4 Beg'd RIDWAYES pardon: DVNCOTE, now, doth crye,
	p.	34	EPIGRAMS 22	10 Where, while that seuer'd doth remaine,
	p.	34	EPIGRAMS 25	7 What doth he else, but say, leaue to be chast,
	p.	35	EPIGRAMS 28	12 He doth, at meales, alone, his pheasant eate,
	p.	37	EPIGRAMS 32	9 Which shewes, where euer death doth please t<o>'appeare,
	p.	39	EPIGRAMS 39	2 COLT, now, doth daily penance in his owne.
	p.	40	EPIGRAMS 42	4 But that his IONE doth too. And GILES would neuer,
	p.	40	EPIGRAMS 42	9 And so is IONE. Oft-times, when GILES doth find
	p.	40	EPIGRAMS 42	11 All this doth IONE. Or that his long-yearn'd life
	p.	41	EPIGRAMS 45	9 Rest in soft peace, and, ask'd, say here doth lye
	p.	42	EPIGRAMS 49	3 I haue no salt: no bawdrie he doth meane.

doth (cont.)

p.	46 EPIGRAMS 61	2	One doth not stroke me, nor the other strike.
p.	49 EPIGRAMS 66	12	To liue when Broeck not stands, nor Roor doth runne.
p.	49 EPIGRAMS 68	3	Two kindes of valour he doth shew, at ones;
p.	54 EPIGRAMS 82	1	SVRLY'S old whore in her new silkes doth swim:
p.	55 EPIGRAMS 85	5	Shee doth instruct men by her gallant flight,
p.	55 EPIGRAMS 86	7	Where, though 't be loue, that to thy praise doth moue,
p.	56 EPIGRAMS 88	13	Or is it some french statue? No: 'T doth moue,
p.	59 EPIGRAMS 92	12	And what each prince doth for intelligence owe,
p.	65 EPIGRAMS 101	28	But that, which most doth take my Muse, and mee,
p.	66 EPIGRAMS 102	18	But in the view, doth interrupt their sinne;
p.	66 EPIGRAMS 103	5	And, being nam'd, how little doth that name
p.	70 EPIGRAMS 109	2	That serues nor fame, nor titles; but doth chuse
p.	71 EPIGRAMS 110	21	T<o>'all future time, not onely doth restore
p.	72 EPIGRAMS 111	1	Who EDMONDS, reades thy booke, and doth not see
p.	72 EPIGRAMS 111	13	By thy great helpe: and doth proclaime by mee,
p.	73 EPIGRAMS 113	4	Where, what makes others great, doth keepe thee good!
p.	74 EPIGRAMS 115	7	A subtle thing, that doth affections win
p.	74 EPIGRAMS 115	23	At euery meale, where it doth dine, or sup,
p.	74 EPIGRAMS 115	25	And, shifting of it's faces, doth play more
p.	75 EPIGRAMS 116	13	These were thy knowing arts: which who doth now
p.	75 EPIGRAMS 117	2	For'his whore: GROYNE doth still occupy his land.
p.	79 EPIGRAMS 124	3	Vnder-neath this stone doth lye
p.	79 EPIGRAMS 124	6	To more vertue, then doth liue.
p.	81 EPIGRAMS 129	13	Or (mounted on a stoole) thy face doth hit
p.	82 EPIGRAMS 130	6	Doth sweeten mirth, and heighten pietie,
p.	83 EPIGRAMS 132	10	BARTAS doth wish thy English now were his.
p.	86 EPIGRAMS 133	82	(Who hath the hundred hands when he doth meddle)
p.	88 EPIGRAMS 133	170	Vrine, and plaisters? when the noise doth beate
p.	94 FOREST 2	25	Each banke doth yeeld thee coneyes; and the topps
p.	94 FOREST 2	27	To crowne thy open table, doth prouide
p.	94 FOREST 2	42	Fig, grape, and quince, each in his time doth come:
p.	95 FOREST 2	59	The neede of such? whose liberall boord doth flow,
p.	95 FOREST 2	60	With all, that hospitalitie doth know!
p.	95 FOREST 2	68	A waiter, doth my gluttony enuy:
p.	98 FOREST 3	43	The apple-haruest, that doth longer last;
p.	98 FOREST 3	58	Freedome doth with degree dispense.
p.	99 FOREST 3	80	And thinke his power doth equall Fates.
p.	106 FOREST 9	5	The thirst, that from the soule doth rise,
p.	106 FOREST 9	6	Doth aske a drinke diuine:
p.	109 FOREST 11	23	(That should ring larum to the heart) doth sleepe,
p.	109 FOREST 11	24	Or some great thought doth keepe
p.	110 FOREST 11	35	But this doth from the<ir> cloud of error grow,
p.	110 FOREST 11	44	No such effects doth proue;
p.	111 FOREST 11	71	Because they moue, the continent doth so:
p.	113 FOREST 12	12	Of some grand peere, whose ayre doth make reioyce
p.	115 FOREST 12	70	And, who doth me (though I not him) enuy,
p.	117 FOREST 13	34	As I, can say, and see it doth excell.
p.	119 FOREST 13	87	And neuer thinke, how vice doth euery houre,
p.	120 FOREST 14	14	Doth say,
p.	121 FOREST 14	27	Since he doth lacke
p.	121 FOREST 14	30	Doth vrge him to runne wrong, or to stand still.
p.	137 UNDERWOOD 2.5	30	With the Lace that doth it deck,
p.	137 UNDERWOOD 2.5	49	For this Beauty yet doth hide
p.	139 UNDERWOOD 2.7	6	That doth but touch his flower, and flies away.
p.	143 UNDERWOOD 3	7	What Tree or stone doth want a soule?
p.	146 UNDERWOOD 6	12	Is that which doth perfection breed.
p.	146 UNDERWOOD 6	20	In love, doth not alone help forth
p.	146 UNDERWOOD 6	22	From being forsaken, then doth worth:
p.	148 UNDERWOOD 7	31	One un-becomming thought doth move
p.	151 UNDERWOOD 12	6	Of him whose bones this Grave doth gather:
p.	153 UNDERWOOD 13	20	Deepest in Man, of which when he doth thinke,
p.	154 UNDERWOOD 13	35	Or that doth sound a Trumpet, and doth call
p.	154 UNDERWOOD 13	41	He neither gives, or do's, that doth delay
p.	154 UNDERWOOD 13	42	A Benefit; or that doth throw 't away:
p.	154 UNDERWOOD 13	43	No more then he doth thanke, that will receive
p.	158 UNDERWOOD 14	9	Rather then Office, when it doth or may
p.	158 UNDERWOOD 14	11	Unto the Censure. Yours all need doth flie
p.	166 UNDERWOOD 15	136	Now use the bones, we see doth hire a man
p.	168 UNDERWOOD 16	3	But here doth lie, till the last Day,
p.	169 UNDERWOOD 17	16	All is not barren land, doth fallow lie.

doth (cont.)

p. 170	UNDERWOOD 18	8	Crooked appeare; so that doth my conceipt:
p. 170	UNDERWOOD 19	8	Where he doth steepe himselfe in Milke and Roses;
p. 174	UNDERWOOD 23	3	Knowledge, that sleepes, doth die;
p. 174	UNDERWOOD 23	9	Doth Clarius Harp want strings,
p. 175	UNDERWOOD 24	4	Doth vindicate it to eternitie.
p. 176	UNDERWOOD 24	12	Doth mete, whose lyne doth sound the depth of things:)
p. 176	UNDERWOOD 25	5	High, as his mind, that doth advance
p. 180	UNDERWOOD 25	62	Doth now command;
p. 180	UNDERWOOD 26	9	Yet doth some wholsome Physick for the mind,
p. 180	UNDERWOOD 26	16	True valour doth her owne renowne command
p. 181	UNDERWOOD 27	5	Of Phao<n>s forme? or doth the Boy
p. 181	UNDERWOOD 27	11	Doth Cynthia, in Propertius song
p. 184	UNDERWOOD 29	37	Scarce the Hill againe doth flourish,
p. 184	UNDERWOOD 29	38	Scarce the world a Wit doth nourish,
p. 187	UNDERWOOD 33	38	And (which doth all Atchievements get above)
p. 189	UNDERWOOD 36	5	Where Love doth shine, there needs no Sunne,
p. 189	UNDERWOOD 36	6	All light[s] into his one doth run;
p. 192	UNDERWOOD 38	33	Where weaknesse doth offend, and vertue grieve,
p. 193	UNDERWOOD 38	72	It shakes even him, that all things else doth shake.
p. 193	UNDERWOOD 38	81	And with the vulgar doth it not obtaine
p. 193	UNDERWOOD 38	88	Streight puts off all his Anger, and doth kisse
p. 198	UNDERWOOD 40	36	Doth, while he keepes his watch, betray his stand.
p. 198	UNDERWOOD 40	40	Due to that one, that doth believe him just.
p. 200	UNDERWOOD 42	7	That from the Muses fountaines doth indorse
p. 212	UNDERWOOD 43	211	So doth the King, and most of the Kings men
p. 217	UNDERWOOD 46	23	Of if Chance must, to each man that doth rise,
p. 222	UNDERWOOD 49	14	Doth labour with the Phrase more then the sense?
p. 230	UNDERWOOD 56	9	Laden with Bellie, and doth hardly approach
p. 230	UNDERWOOD 56	12	And that's made up as doth the purse abound.
p. 234	UNDERWOOD 61	9	Your happinesse, and doth not speake you blest,
p. 235	UNDERWOOD 63	4	Doth by his doubt, distrust his promise more.
p. 236	UNDERWOOD 64	11	When your assiduous practise doth secure
p. 240	UNDERWOOD 67	43	8. URA. This day the Court doth measure
p. 242	UNDERWOOD 69	14	So doth the flatt'rer with faire cunning strike
p. 245	UNDERWOOD 70	59	Not liv'd; for Life doth her great actions spell,
p. 245	UNDERWOOD 70	66	In bulke, doth make man better bee;
p. 246	UNDERWOOD 70	95	But fate doth so alternate the designe,
p. 250	UNDERWOOD 74	2	Doth take in easie Natures birth,
p. 251	UNDERWOOD 74	16	Doth show, the Graces, and the Houres,
p. 251	UNDERWOOD 74	19	Such joyes, such sweet's doth your Returne
p. 254	UNDERWOOD 75	60	With light of love, this Paire doth intertexe!
p. 254	UNDERWOOD 75	66	Have they bedew'd the Earth, where she doth tread,
p. 255	UNDERWOOD 75	100	But doth his Carract, and just Standard keepe
p. 256	UNDERWOOD 75	117	Doth Emulation stirre;
p. 259	UNDERWOOD 76	3	Doth most humbly show it,
p. 262	UNDERWOOD 78	2	Yet read him in these lines: He doth excell
p. 262	UNDERWOOD 78	16	Unto our yeare doth give the longest light.
p. 263	UNDERWOOD 78	23	For he doth love my Verses, and will looke
p. 270	UNDERWOOD 83	37	Else, who doth praise a person by a new,
p. 270	UNDERWOOD 83	38	But a fain'd way, doth rob it of the true.
p. 271	UNDERWOOD 83	73	Beholds her Maker! and, in him, doth see
p. 285	U'WOOD 84.9	91	And she doth know, out of the shade of Death,
p. 286	U'WOOD 84.9	138	What love with mercy mixed doth appeare?
p. 290	UNDERWOOD 85	9	The Poplar tall, he then doth marrying twine
p. 290	UNDERWOOD 85	15	Or the prest honey in pure pots doth keepe
p. 291	UNDERWOOD 85	46	Their swelling udders doth draw dry:
p. 291	UNDERWOOD 85	61	Among these Cates how glad the sight doth come
p. 294	UNDERWOOD 88	9	This hath pleas'd, doth please, and long will please; never
p. 307	HORACE 2	43	So, shunning faults, to greater fault doth lead,
p. 307	HORACE 2	56	And what they will not. Him, whose choice doth reare
p. 309	HORACE 2	92	That from the North, the Navie safe doth store,
p. 309	HORACE 2	94	Once rowable, but now doth nourish men
p. 311	HORACE 2	132	Yet, sometime, doth the Comedie excite
p. 311	HORACE 2	152	For Nature, first, within doth fashion us
p. 313	HORACE 2	197	What doth this Promiser such gaping worth
p. 315	HORACE 2	218	The last doth from the midst dis-joyn'd appeare.
p. 317	HORACE 2	243	Doth wretchedly the use of things forbeare,
p. 317	HORACE 2	259	And the beholder to himselfe doth render.
p. 317	HORACE 2	284	Peace, and the open ports, that peace doth cause.
p. 323	HORACE 2	383	So rare, as with some taxe it doth ingage
p. 325	HORACE 2	420	Happier then wretched art, and doth, by it,

doth (cont.)

p. 329 HORACE 2	521	For, neither doth the String still yeeld that sound
p. 329 HORACE 2	524	Nor alwayes doth the loosed Bow, hit that
p. 329 HORACE 2	525	Which it doth threaten. Therefore, where I see
p. 331 HORACE 2	544	Doth please; this, ten times over, will delight.
p. 331 HORACE 2	557	As jarring Musique doth, at jolly feasts,
p. 331 HORACE 2	566	His armes in Mars his field, he doth refuse;
p. 333 HORACE 2	585	So doth the one, the others helpe require,
p. 333 HORACE 2	599	So doth the Poet, who is rich in land,
p. 333 HORACE 2	616	The Scoffer, the true Praiser doth out-goe.
p. 335 HORACE 2	666	Doth the same thing with him, that would him kill.
p. 351 HORACE 1	525	. ... doth ....
p. 352 HORACE 1	547	... ... being honest ... . doth ....
p. 365 UNGATHERED 5	10	Doth shine in her discerning,
p. 366 UNGATHERED 6	3	Behold, where one doth swim;
p. 367 UNGATHERED 6	31	"So much doth Virtue hate,
p. 368 UNGATHERED 6	85	The Dutch whom Wealth (not Hatred) doth diuide;
p. 374 UNGATHERED 10	10	Here, like Arion, our Coryate doth draw
p. 380 UNGATHERED 12	23	Each leafe of his iournall, and line doth vnlocke
p. 380 UNGATHERED 12	46	He there doth protest he saw of the eleuen.
p. 380 UNGATHERED 12	52	Doth he once dissemble, but tels he did ride
p. 383 UNGATHERED 17	3	Who bluntly doth but looke vpon the same,
p. 383 UNGATHERED 17	9	Who cannot reade, but onely doth desire
p. 389 UNGATHERED 24	10	As a deformed face doth a true glasse.
p. 391 UNGATHERED 26	9	Or blinde Affection, which doth ne're aduance
p. 391 UNGATHERED 26	23	And art aliue still, while thy Booke doth liue,
p. 392 UNGATHERED 26	58	His Art doth giue the fashion. And, that he,
p. 393 UNGATHERED 27	13	It is the Sword that doth diuide
p. 393 UNGATHERED 27	16	Doth shew the Holy one.
p. 393 UNGATHERED 27	18	Vnto the world doth proue.
p. 400 UNGATHERED 32	9	And doth deserue all muniments of praise,
p. 402 UNGATHERED 34	14	Something your Surship doth not yet intend!
p. 407 UNGATHERED 36	1	Sr Inigo doth feare it as I heare
p. 413 UNGATHERED 41	20	No faith's more firme, or flat, then where't doth creep.
p. 414 UNGATHERED 41	43	Whose chearfull look our sadnesse doth destroy,
p. 418 UNGATHERED 46	6	for when the profitt with the payne doth meete,
p. 422 UNGATHERED 50	9	The mayne comaund of scepters, soone doth perishe
p. 657 L. CONVIVALES	6	Truth itself doth flow in Wine.

double   frequency: 2   relative frequency: 0.00002

p. 76 EPIGRAMS 118	3	And, striuing so to double his delight,
p. 170 UNDERWOOD 19	4	His double Bow, and round his Arrowes sends;

doublet. See "dublet."

doubly   frequency: 2   relative frequency: 0.00002

p. 31 EPIGRAMS 13	3	Let me giue two: that doubly am got free,
p. 293 UNDERWOOD 87	15	For whom I doubly would expire,

doubt   frequency: 17   relative frequency: 0.00024

*p. 492 TO HIMSELF	21	No doubt some mouldy tale,
p. 31 EPIGRAMS 14	10	Man scarse can make that doubt, but thou canst teach.
p. 43 EPIGRAMS 51	5	Yet giue thy iealous subiects leaue to doubt:
p. 50 EPIGRAMS 70	5	Delay is bad, doubt worse, depending worst;
p. 62 EPIGRAMS 96	1	Who shall doubt, DONNE, where I a Poet bee,
p. 70 EPIGRAMS 109	15	Goe on, and doubt not, what posteritie,
p. 111 FOREST 11	79	Or those, who doubt the common mouth of fame,
p. 122 FOREST 15	16	How can I doubt to finde thee euer, here?
p. 139 UNDERWOOD 2.7	4	Why doe you doubt, or stay?
p. 145 UNDERWOOD 5	7	Nor doe we doubt, but that we can,
p. 147 UNDERWOOD 7	20	Yet, yet I doubt he is not knowne,
p. 147 UNDERWOOD 7	23	As make away my doubt,
p. 153 UNDERWOOD 13	13	You cannot doubt, but I, who freely know
p. 207 UNDERWOOD 43	107	I now begin to doubt, if ever Grace,
p. 235 UNDERWOOD 63	4	Doth by his doubt, distrust his promise more.
p. 243 UNDERWOOD 70	20	No doubt all Infants would returne like thee.
p. 395 UNGATHERED 29	4	And the world in it, I begin to doubt,

doubtfull   frequency: 4   relative frequency: 0.00005

p. 117 FOREST 13	40	T<o>'aduance his doubtfull issue, and ore-flow
p. 180 UNDERWOOD 26	6	And doubtfull Dayes (which were nam'd Criticall,)
p. 335 HORACE 2	637	They're darke, bid cleare this: all that's doubtfull wrote

doubtfull (cont.)
    p. 370 UNGATHERED 7   12 Betweene the doubtfull sway of Reason', and
                                  sense;

doubting   frequency: 1   relative frequency: 0.00001
    p. 150 UNDERWOOD 10   15 Seeke doubting Men to please,

doubts   frequency: 1   relative frequency: 0.00001
    p. 235 UNDERWOOD 63   3 Who doubts, those fruits God can with gaine
                                    restore,

doue   frequency: 1   relative frequency: 0.00001
    p. 112 FOREST 11   91 But we propose a person like our Doue,

dove   frequency: 1   relative frequency: 0.00001
    See also "doue."
    p. 134 UNDERWOOD 2.4   3 Each that drawes, is a Swan, or a Dove,

dover   frequency: 2   relative frequency: 0.00002
    p. 415 UNGATHERED 43   3 But I can tell thee, Dover, how thy Games
    p. 415 UNGATHERED 43   t2 Good Freind Mr. Robert Dover, on his great

doves   frequency: 1   relative frequency: 0.00001
    p. 305 HORACE 2   16 With Doves; or Lambes, with Tygres coupled be.

dower   frequency: 1   relative frequency: 0.00001
    p. 117 FOREST 13   37 Nor that your beautie wanted not a dower,

dowgate   frequency: 1   relative frequency: 0.00001
    p. 407 UNGATHERED 35   16 Or Dowgate Torrent falling into Thames,

down. See "downe."

downe   frequency: 35   relative frequency: 0.00050
**p. 113 PANEGYRE   21 Vpon his state; let downe in that rich chaine,
    p. 45 EPIGRAMS 59   2 Who, when you'haue burnt your selues downe to the
                                    snuffe,
    p. 50 EPIGRAMS 71   1 To plucke downe mine, POLL sets vp new wits
                                    still,
    p. 80 EPIGRAMS 126   4 And bad me lay th'vsurped laurell downe:
    p. 86 EPIGRAMS 133   95 Had burst with storme, and downe fell, ab
                                    excelsis,
    p. 87 EPIGRAMS 133   137 Or were precipitated downe the jakes,
    p. 94 FOREST 2   47 There's none, that dwell about them, wish them
                                    downe;
    p. 110 FOREST 11   47 It is a golden chaine let downe from heauen,
    p. 113 FOREST 12   5 Toyles, by graue custome, vp and downe the court,
    p. 118 FOREST 13   73 Melt downe their husbands land, to poure away
    p. 135 UNDERWOOD 2.4   26 Or Swans Downe ever?
    p. 141 UNDERWOOD 2.9   26 As the Downe, and shew it oft;
    p. 144 UNDERWOOD 4   3 Nor cast them downe, but let them rise,
    p. 163 UNDERWOOD 15   53 That all respect; She must lie downe: Nay more,
    p. 200 UNDERWOOD 42   37 It is not likely I should now looke downe
    p. 203 UNDERWOOD 43   9 'Twas Jupiter that hurl'd thee headlong downe,
    p. 219 UNDERWOOD 47   47 Of Spaine or France; or were not prick'd downe
                                      one
    p. 224 UNDERWOOD 50   12 From whence they fall, cast downe with their owne
                                    weight.
    p. 247 UNDERWOOD 70   127 Who, e're the first downe bloomed on the chin,
    p. 255 UNDERWOOD 75   103 Of Tryals, to worke downe
    p. 272 U'WOOD 84.1   3 Their Heads, that ENVY would hold downe
    p. 291 UNDERWOOD 85   54 Could not goe downe my belly then
    p. 293 UNDERWOOD 86   34 Flow my thin teares, downe these pale cheeks of
                                      mine?
    p. 315 HORACE 2   221 That tarries till the hangings be ta'en downe,
    p. 329 HORACE 2   500 Of their long labours, was in Verse set downe:
    p. 335 HORACE 2   656 To let it downe, who knowes, if he did cast
    p. 339 HORACE 1   40 Downe close .. shore, this other creeping
                                      steales,
    p. 361 UNGATHERED 1   25 till giddie with amazement I fell downe
    p. 366 UNGATHERED 6   25 This change'd his Downe; till this, as white
    p. 374 UNGATHERED 10   12 Here, not vp Holdborne, but downe a steepe hill,
    p. 378 UNGATHERED 11   81 Honest Tom Tell-Troth puts downe Roger, How?
    p. 385 UNGATHERED 19   8 Thy Richard, rais'd in song, past pulling downe.
    p. 406 UNGATHERED 34   91 And not fall downe before it? and confess
    p. 407 UNGATHERED 35   18 yearly set out there, to sayle downe ye Street,
    p. 413 UNGATHERED 41   31 All, pouring their full showre of graces downe,

dowrie   frequency: 1   relative frequency: 0.00001
    p. 114 FOREST 12   35 Wherein wise Nature you a dowrie gaue,

dowry.   See "dowrie."

do'you   frequency: 1   relative frequency: 0.00001
    p.   88 EPIGRAMS 133   155 But 'mong'st these Tiberts, who do'you thinke
                               there was?

dozen.   See "dosen."

draff.   See "draffe."

draffe   frequency: 1   relative frequency: 0.00001
  *p. 492 TO HIMSELF   18 Huskes, draffe to drinke, and swill.

drag   frequency: 1   relative frequency: 0.00001
    p. 405 UNGATHERED 34   81 Disguisd? and thence drag forth Enormity?

dram.   See "dramme."

drama   frequency: 1   relative frequency: 0.00001
    p.   72 EPIGRAMS 112   7 I cannot for the stage a Drama lay,

dramme   frequency: 1   relative frequency: 0.00001
    p. 415 UNGATHERED 42   30 Concluded from a Carract to a dramme.

draught   frequency: 3   relative frequency: 0.00004
    p.   94 FOREST 2   35 As loth, the second draught, or cast to stay,
    p. 133 UNDERWOOD 2.3 11 Mee, the scope of his next draught,
    p. 408 UNGATHERED 36 13 That sit vpon ye Comon Draught: or Strand!

draw   frequency: 33   relative frequency: 0.00047
    p.   37 EPIGRAMS 35   3 Whose manners draw, more than thy powers
                               constraine.
    p.   53 EPIGRAMS 78   2 To draw thee custome: but her selfe gets all.
    p.   66 EPIGRAMS 102   19 Thou must draw more: and they, that hope to see
    p.   69 EPIGRAMS 107   29 Nay, now you puffe, tuske, and draw vp your chin,
    p. 111 FOREST 11   66 Some vicious foole draw neare,
    p. 117 FOREST 13   20 Or feare to draw true lines, 'cause others paint:
    p. 133 UNDERWOOD 2.3 14 But the Arrow home did draw
    p. 173 UNDERWOOD 22   7 And draw, and conquer all mens love,
    p. 200 UNDERWOOD 42   26 For Silke will draw some sneaking Songster
                               thither.
    p. 214 UNDERWOOD 44   45 Thou canst draw forth thy forces, and fight drie
    p. 219 UNDERWOOD 47   39 But if, for honour, we must draw the Sword,
    p. 227 UNDERWOOD 52   8 To square my Circle, I confesse; but draw
    p. 227 UNDERWOOD 52   18 How I would draw, and take hold and delight.
    p. 227 UNDERWOOD 52   22 Yet when of friendship I would draw the face,
    p. 233 UNDERWOOD 59   13 This were a spectacle! A sight to draw
    p. 243 UNDERWOOD 70   11 Did wiser Nature draw thee back,
    p. 276 U'WOOD 84.3   13 Draw first a Cloud: all save her neck;
    p. 276 U'WOOD 84.3   21 The Heaven design'd, draw next a Spring,
    p. 276 U'WOOD 84.3   25 Last, draw the circles of this Globe,
    p. 277 U'WOOD 84.3   32 Next sitting we will draw her mind.
    p. 277 U'WOOD 84.4   8 To draw a thing that cannot sit.
    p. 291 UNDERWOOD 85   46 Their swelling udders doth draw dry:
    p. 291 UNDERWOOD 85   63 To view the weary Oxen draw, with bare
    p. 313 HORACE 2   194 Forbids thee forth againe thy foot to draw.
    p. 315 HORACE 2   204 But light from smoake; that he may draw his
                               bright
    p. 327 HORACE 2   455 Thence draw forth true expressions. For,
                               sometimes,
    p. 329 HORACE 2   509 It would, must be: lest it alive would draw
    p. 339 HORACE 1   42 So he that varying still affects .. draw
    p. 367 UNGATHERED 6   47 "Musicke hath power to draw,
    p. 374 UNGATHERED 10 10 Here, like Arion, our Coryate doth draw
    p. 390 UNGATHERED 26   1 To draw no enuy (Shakespeare) on thy name,
    p. 396 UNGATHERED 30 12 Lend me thy voyce, O FAME, that I may draw
    p. 407 UNGATHERED 35 11 He draw a Forum, wth quadriuiall Streets!

drawer   frequency: 1   relative frequency: 0.00001
    p. 156 UNDERWOOD 13   94 Or swaggering with the Watch, or Drawer,
                               drunke;

drawes   frequency: 5   relative frequency: 0.00007
  **p. 115 PANEGYRE   73 Meane while, the reuerend THEMIS drawes
                               aside
    p. 134 UNDERWOOD 2.4   3 Each that drawes, is a Swan, or a Dove,
    p. 217 UNDERWOOD 46   18 With endlesse labours, whilst thy learning drawes
    p. 219 UNDERWOOD 47   41 I have a body, yet, that spirit drawes
    p. 337 HORACE 2   679 Not letting goe his hold, where he drawes food,

drawing   frequency: 1   relative frequency: 0.00001
    p. 187 UNDERWOOD 33   27 Of Argument, still drawing forth the best,

drawn. See "drawne."

drawne   frequency: 15 relative frequency: 0.00021
    p. 51 EPIGRAMS 73   13 Your partie-per-pale picture, one halfe drawne
    p. 136 UNDERWOOD 2.5   14 So, Anacreon drawne the Ayre
    p. 181 UNDERWOOD 27   7 Lie drawne to life, in his soft Verse,
    p. 188 UNDERWOOD 34   8 Was drawne to practise other hue, then that
    p. 207 UNDERWOOD 43   104 Whom Faction had not drawne to studie sides.
    p. 213 UNDERWOOD 44   18 To have their Husbands drawne forth to the
                               field,
    p. 242 UNDERWOOD 69   13 Till he had sold his Piece, drawne so unlike:
    p. 259 UNDERWOOD 76   17 Hath drawne on me, from the times,
    p. 275 U'WOOD 84.3   1 Sitting, and ready to be drawne,
    p. 321 HORACE 2   338 But, as a Matrone drawne at solemne times
    p. 321 HORACE 2   355 But, let the Faunes, drawne from their Groves,
                               beware,
    p. 331 HORACE 2   560 These, the free meale might have beene well
                               drawne out:
    p. 380 UNGATHERED 12   44 How many learned men he haue drawne with his
                               hooke
    p. 390 UNGATHERED 25   5 O, could he but haue drawne his wit
    p. 402 UNGATHERED 34   9 Drawne Aristotle on vs! & thence showne

draws. See "drawes."

drayton   frequency: 1   relative frequency: 0.00001
    p. 396 UNGATHERED 30   t4 M. DRAYTON.

dreads   frequency: 1   relative frequency: 0.00001
    p. 289 UNDERWOOD 85   6 Nor dreads the Seas inraged harmes:

dream. See "dreame."

dreame   frequency: 6   relative frequency: 0.00008
    p. 111 FOREST 11   67 That cryes, we dreame, and sweares, there's no
                               such thing,
    p. 150 UNDERWOOD 11   t1 The Dreame.
    p. 151 UNDERWOOD 11   4 Love in a subtile Dreame disguis'd,
    p. 250 UNDERWOOD 73   11 Dreame thou could'st hurt it; but before thou
                               wake
    p. 293 UNDERWOOD 86   37 Hard-hearted, I dreame every Night
    p. 396 UNGATHERED 30   11 It was no Dreame! I was awake, and saw!

dreames   frequency: 2   relative frequency: 0.00002
    p. 162 UNDERWOOD 15   10 In dreames, begun in hope, and end in spoile.
    p. 305 HORACE 2   9 Whose shapes, like sick-mens dreames, are fain'd
                               so vaine,

dreams. See "dreames."

drench   frequency: 1   relative frequency: 0.00001
    p. 368 UNGATHERED 6   86 The Danes that drench

dress. See "dresse."

dresse   frequency: 3   relative frequency: 0.00004
    p. 70 EPIGRAMS 109   10 And elements of honor, then the dresse;
    p. 208 UNDERWOOD 43   128 And safely trust to dresse, not burne their
                               Boates.
    p. 287 U'WOOD 84.9   180 She spent more time in teares her selfe to dresse

dressed. See "drest."

dressing   frequency: 7   relative frequency: 0.00010
    p. 132 UNDERWOOD 2.2   3 And her dressing did out-brave
    p. 158 UNDERWOOD 14   3 Lesse shall I for the Art or dressing care,
    p. 164 UNDERWOOD 15   66 And every Dressing for a Pitfall set
    p. 215 UNDERWOOD 44   88 Carriage, and dressing. There is up of late
    p. 223 UNDERWOOD 49   31 Indeed, her Dressing some man might delight,
    p. 230 UNDERWOOD 56   21 To make you merry on the Dressing stoole,
    p. 392 UNGATHERED 26   48 And ioy'd to weare the dressing of his lines!

drest   frequency: 8   relative frequency: 0.00011
  **p. 114 PANEGYRE   51 That might her beauties heighten; but so drest,
    p. 53 EPIGRAMS 78   1 HORNET, thou hast thy wife drest, for the
                               stall,
    p. 68 EPIGRAMS 105   9 And, drest in shepheards tyre, who would not say:

drest (cont.)
```
    p.  96 FOREST 2       87 When shee was farre: and not a roome, but drest,
    p. 141 UNDERWOOD 2.9  38 Drest, you still for man should take him;
    p. 251 UNDERWOOD 74   14 Wherein she sits so richly drest,
    p. 253 UNDERWOOD 75   37 The Lady Frances, drest
    p. 265 UNDERWOOD 79   44 Chorus Our great, our good. Where one's so
                             drest
```

drew   frequency: 3 relative frequency: 0.00004
```
    p. 132 UNDERWOOD 2.2  24 Such a Lightning (as I drew)
    p. 137 UNDERWOOD 2.6   2 Since I drew a Morning kisse
    p. 274 U'WOOD 84.2    15 Into the Kindred, whence thy Adam drew
```

dri'd   frequency: 1 relative frequency: 0.00001
```
    p. 174 UNDERWOOD 23    8 Dri'd up? lyes Thespia wast?
```

drie   frequency: 2 relative frequency: 0.00002
```
    p. 183 UNDERWOOD 29   22 So to see the Fountaine drie,
    p. 214 UNDERWOOD 44   45 Thou canst draw forth thy forces, and fight drie
```

dried   frequency: 1 relative frequency: 0.00001
    See also "dri'd."
```
  **p. 116 PANEGYRE      129 And now the dame had dried her dropping eyne,
```

drill   frequency: 1 relative frequency: 0.00001
```
    p. 213 UNDERWOOD 44   29 He that but saw thy curious Captaines drill,
```

dring   frequency: 1 relative frequency: 0.00001
```
    p. 305 HORACE 2       21 Dring Circles of swift waters that intwine
```

drink. See "drinke," "drrinke."

drinke   frequency: 9 relative frequency: 0.00013
```
   *p. 492 TO HIMSELF     18 Huskes, draffe to drinke, and swill.
    p.  74 EPIGRAMS 115   12 Doe all, that longs to the anarchy of drinke,
    p. 106 FOREST 9        6 Doth aske a drinke diuine:
    p. 120 FOREST 14       2 And some doe drinke, and some doe dance,
    p. 156 UNDERWOOD 13  100 Lowd sacrifice of drinke, for their health-sake!
    p. 167 UNDERWOOD 15  159 Is nothing, such scarce meat and drinke he'le
                             give,
    p. 197 UNDERWOOD 40    3 And then I taste it. But as men drinke up
    p. 218 UNDERWOOD 47   10 That live in the wild Anarchie of Drinke,
    p. 246 UNDERWOOD 70  104 Orgies of drinke, or fain'd protests:
```

drinkers. See "hop-drinkers."

drinkes   frequency: 3 relative frequency: 0.00004
```
    p.  30 EPIGRAMS 12     5 By that one spell he lives, eates, drinkes,
                             arrayes
    p.  35 EPIGRAMS 28    14 He drinkes to no man: that's, too, like a lord.
    p. 166 UNDERWOOD 15  115 Surfet? and Quarrel? drinkes the tother health?
```

drinking   frequency: 1 relative frequency: 0.00001
```
    p. 418 UNGATHERED 45  43 forfeitinge their drinking lease,
```

drinks. See "drinkes."

driuen   frequency: 1 relative frequency: 0.00001
```
    p.  28 EPIGRAMS 5      1 When was there contract better driuen by Fate?
```

driu'n   frequency: 1 relative frequency: 0.00001
```
    p. 395 UNGATHERED 29   3 Of Fortunes wheele by Lucan driu'n about,
```

drive   frequency: 1 relative frequency: 0.00001
```
    p. 283 U'WOOD 84.9    27 Thou hast no more blowes, Fate, to drive at one:
```

driven   frequency: 2 relative frequency: 0.00002
    See also "driuen," "driu'n," "warie-driven."
```
    p. 144 UNDERWOOD 3    22 Of Angels should be driven
    p. 241 UNDERWOOD 68    3 Are they so scanted in their store? or driven
```

drives   frequency: 4 relative frequency: 0.00005
```
    p. 191 UNDERWOOD 38    6 And drives it in to eat on my offence,
    p. 264 UNDERWOOD 79   21 That drives the Hart to seeke unused wayes,
    p. 265 UNDERWOOD 79   62 Hee drives diseases from our Folds,
    p. 290 UNDERWOOD 85   31 Or hence, or thence, he drives with many a Hound
```

dronken   frequency: 1 relative frequency: 0.00001
```
    p. 295 UNDERWOOD 90    9 Thy night not dronken, but from cares layd wast;
```

droop   frequency: 1   relative frequency: 0.00001
    p. 174 UNDERWOOD 23   11 Or droop they as disgrac't,

drooping   frequency: 1   relative frequency: 0.00001
    p. 392 UNGATHERED 26   78 Or influence, chide, or cheere the drooping
                                Stage;

droops. See "droupes."

drop   frequency: 4   relative frequency: 0.00005
    See also "dropp."
    p. 214 UNDERWOOD 44   47 Without the hazard of a drop of blood,
    p. 233 UNDERWOOD 60   2 Stay, drop a teare for him that's dead,
    p. 337 HORACE 2   680 Till he drop off, a Horse-leech, full of blood.
    p. 666 INSCRIPTS. 11   9 Shall powre forth many a line, drop many a
                                letter,

dropp   frequency: 1   relative frequency: 0.00001
    p. 415 UNGATHERED 43   1 I cannot bring my Muse to dropp <her> Vies

dropping   frequency: 2   relative frequency: 0.00002
    See also "louse-dropping."
 **p. 116 PANEGYRE   129 And now the dame had dried her dropping eyne,
    p. 205 UNDERWOOD 43   53 Sindge Capons, or poore Pigges, dropping their
                                eyes;

drops   frequency: 3   relative frequency: 0.00004
    p. 44 EPIGRAMS 55   4 The least indulgent thought thy pen drops forth!
    p. 103 FOREST 6   15 Or the drops in siluer Thames,
    p. 280 U'WOOD 84.4   60 As showers; and sweet as drops of Balme.

dross. See "drosse."

drosse   frequency: 2   relative frequency: 0.00002
    p. 114 FOREST 12   27 But let this drosse carry what price it will
    p. 268 UNDERWOOD 82   9 As hath thy JAMES; cleans'd from originall
                                drosse,

droupes   frequency: 1   relative frequency: 0.00001
    p. 227 UNDERWOOD 52   5 And the whole lumpe growes round, deform'd, and
                                droupes,

drown   frequency: 1   relative frequency: 0.00001
    See also "drowne."
    p. 411 UNGATHERED 39   12 A Tune to drown the Ballads of thy Father:

drownd   frequency: 1   relative frequency: 0.00001
    p. 361 UNGATHERED 1   20 till th'one hath drownd the other in our sightes,

drown'd   frequency: 3   relative frequency: 0.00004
    See also "drownd."
    p. 88 EPIGRAMS 133   154 Yet drown'd they not. They had fiue liues in
                                future.
    p. 98 FOREST 3   60 And in their cups, their cares are drown'd:
    p. 311 HORACE 2   145 If thou would'st have me weepe, be thou first
                                drown'd

drowne   frequency: 5   relative frequency: 0.00007
 **p. 113 PANEGYRE   18 And in their vapor her bright mettall drowne.
    p. 56 EPIGRAMS 87   3 Each night, to drowne his cares: But when the
                                gaine
    p. 197 UNDERWOOD 40   7 Of parting, drowne it in the hope to meet
    p. 362 UNGATHERED 1   28 I struggled with this passion that did drowne
    p. 369 UNGATHERED 6   108 To dimme and drowne

drownes   frequency: 1   relative frequency: 0.00001
    p. 182 UNDERWOOD 27   36 So much my Subject drownes the rest.

drowning   frequency: 2   relative frequency: 0.00002
    p. 183 UNDERWOOD 29   10 Joynting Syllabes, drowning Letters,
    p. 365 UNGATHERED 5   20 My selfe am so neare drowning?

drowns. See "drownes."

drrinke   frequency: 1   relative frequency: 0.00001
    p. 106 FOREST 9   1 Drrinke to me, onely, with thine eyes,

drudge   frequency: 1   relative frequency: 0.00001
    p. 319 HORACE 2   301 The Idiot, keeping holy-day, or drudge,

drug   frequency: 2   relative frequency: 0.00002
  p. 46 EPIGRAMS 62   4 Your 'pothecarie, and his drug sayes no.
  p. 190 UNDERWOOD 37   17 Rigid, and harsh, which is a Drug austere

drum   frequency: 3   relative frequency: 0.00004
  p. 81 EPIGRAMS 129   7 That still th'art made the suppers flagge, the
                                     drum,
  p. 162 UNDERWOOD 15   1 Wake, friend, from forth thy Lethargie: the
                                     Drum
  p. 397 UNGATHERED 30   55 But that I heare, againe, thy Drum to beate

drums   frequency: 4   relative frequency: 0.00005
  p. 239 UNDERWOOD 67   15 With beating of our Drums:
  p. 249 UNDERWOOD 72   9 What Drums or Trumpets, or great Ord'nance
                                     can,
  p. 397 UNGATHERED 30   40 Drums against Drums, the neighing of the Horse,

drunk. See "drunke."

drunkards   frequency: 1   relative frequency: 0.00001
  p. 211 UNDERWOOD 43   186 Vile Tavernes, and the Drunkards pisse him out;

drunke   frequency: 4   relative frequency: 0.00005
  p. 56 EPIGRAMS 87   2 HAZARD a month forsware his; and grew
                                     drunke,
  p. 69 EPIGRAMS 107   19 Giue your yong States-men, (that first make you
                                     drunke,
  p. 156 UNDERWOOD 13   94 Or swaggering with the Watch, or Drawer,
                                     drunke;
  p. 319 HORACE 2   325 Having well eat, and drunke (the rites being
                                     done)

drunken. See "dronken."

drunkennest   frequency: 1   relative frequency: 0.00001
  p. 166 UNDERWOOD 15   118 What honour given to the drunkennest Guests?

dry   frequency: 3   relative frequency: 0.00004
  See also "drie."
  p. 155 UNDERWOOD 13   69 And spunge-like with it dry up the blood quite:
  p. 245 UNDERWOOD 70   68 To fall a logge at last, dry, bald, and seare:
  p. 291 UNDERWOOD 85   46 Their swelling udders doth draw dry:

dryads   frequency: 1   relative frequency: 0.00001
  p. 93 FOREST 2   10 Thy Mount, to which the Dryads doe resort,

dublet   frequency: 1   relative frequency: 0.00001
  p. 380 UNGATHERED 12   49 Except a dublet, and bought of the Iewes:

due   frequency: 11   relative frequency: 0.00015
  p. 33 EPIGRAMS 22   3 Yet, all heauens gifts, being heauens due,
  p. 68 EPIGRAMS 105   17 Or, keeping your due state, that would not cry,
  p. 81 EPIGRAMS 129   15 O, runne not proud of this. Yet, take thy due.
  p. 138 UNDERWOOD 2.6 19 And did thinke, such Rites were due
  p. 155 UNDERWOOD 13   93 Such worship due to kicking of a Punck!
  p. 189 UNDERWOOD 37   3 Then to your love, and gift. And all's but due.
  p. 198 UNDERWOOD 40   40 Due to that one, that doth believe him just.
  p. 231 UNDERWOOD 56   27 How many verses, Madam, are your Due!
  p. 235 UNDERWOOD 63   1 Who dares denie, that all first-fruits are due
  p. 395 UNGATHERED 29   12 Keepe due proportion in the ample song,
  p. 415 UNGATHERED 42   12 Now, for mine owne part, and it is but due,

duel. See "duell."

duelists. See "due'llists."

duell   frequency: 1   relative frequency: 0.00001
  p. 74 EPIGRAMS 115   13 Except the duell. Can sing songs, and catches;

due'llists   frequency: 1   relative frequency: 0.00001
  p. 42 EPIGRAMS 48   3 And hath no honor lost, our Due'llists say.

duely   frequency: 1   relative frequency: 0.00001
  p. 77 EPIGRAMS 120   14 Old men so duely,

dues   frequency: 3   relative frequency: 0.00004
  p. 289 U'WOOD 84.9   224 And giving dues to all Mankinds deserts!
  p. 325 HORACE 2   452 Indeed, give fitting dues to every man.
  p. 344 HORACE 1   225 ... dues ... .

duke   frequency: 2   relative frequency: 0.00002
    See also "d."
    p. 252 UNDERWOOD 75   t11 and Sister of the Surviving Duke
    p. 253 UNDERWOOD 75   42 Like what she is, the Daughter of a Duke,

duke's. See "arch-dukes."

dull   frequency: 16   relative frequency: 0.00023
  **p. 114 PANEGYRE   58 No age, nor sex, so weake, or strongly dull,
    p. 57 EPIGRAMS 90   3 Was dull, and long, ere shee would goe to man:
    p. 68 EPIGRAMS 105   15 There's none so dull, that for your stile would
                              aske,
    p. 101 FOREST 4   29 What bird, or beast, is knowne so dull,
    p. 107 FOREST 10   6 Of his dull god-head, were sinne. Ile implore
    p. 107 FOREST 10   16 Goe, crampe dull MARS, light VENVS, when
                              he snorts,
    p. 146 UNDERWOOD 6   1 Hang up those dull, and envious fooles,
    p. 175 UNDERWOOD 23   36 Safe from the wolves black jaw, and the dull
                              Asses hoofe.
    p. 198 UNDERWOOD 40   35 Like the dull wearied Crane that (come on land)
    p. 256 UNDERWOOD 75   118 To th' dull, a Spur
    p. 279 U'WOOD 84.4   45 Is it because it sees us dull,
    p. 284 U'WOOD 84.9   79 Dull, and prophane, weake, and imperfect eyes,
    p. 325 HORACE 2   434 On steele, though 't selfe be dull, and cannot
                              cut.
    p. 408 UNGATHERED 36   8 He makes ye Camell & dull Ass his prize.
    p. 420 UNGATHERED 48   23 Whose ayre will sooner Hell, then their dull
                              senses peirce,
    p. 657 L. CONVIVALES   11 Those dull Girls, no good can mean us,

dullness. See "dulnesse."

dulnesse   frequency: 1   relative frequency: 0.00001
    p. 198 UNDERWOOD 40   24 As if that ex'lent Dulnesse were Loves grace;

duly   frequency: 1   relative frequency: 0.00001
    See also "duely."
    p. 255 UNDERWOOD 75   93 Be duly done to those

dumb. See "dumbe."

dumbe   frequency: 4   relative frequency: 0.00005
    p. 47 EPIGRAMS 63   11 Curst be his Muse, that could lye dumbe, or hid
    p. 62 EPIGRAMS 97   8 Where ere he met me; now hee's dumbe, or proud.
    p. 182 UNDERWOOD 28   2 Though not in these, in rithmes not wholly dumbe,
    p. 284 U'WOOD 84.9   73 Better be dumbe, then superstitious!

duncote. See "dvncote."

dungeon   frequency: 1   relative frequency: 0.00001
    p. 283 U'WOOD 84.9   35 Of teares, and dungeon of calamitie!

dunstable   frequency: 1   relative frequency: 0.00001
    p. 394 UNGATHERED 10   16 Here, vp the Alpes (not so plaine as to
                              Dunstable)

dur'd   frequency: 1   relative frequency: 0.00001
    p. 176 UNDERWOOD 24   8 When Vice alike in time with vertue dur'd.

durst   frequency: 17   relative frequency: 0.00024

durtie   frequency: 1   relative frequency: 0.00001
    p. 220 UNDERWOOD 47   68 Oylie Expansions, or shrunke durtie folds,

dust   frequency: 6   relative frequency: 0.00008
  **p. 116 PANEGYRE   102 "To bury churches, in forgotten dust,
    p. 114 FOREST 12   40 And now lye lost in their forgotten dust.
    p. 121 FOREST 14   40 With dust of ancestors, in graues but dwell.
    p. 148 UNDERWOOD 8   1 Doe but consider this small dust,
    p. 387 UNGATHERED 22   4 Will all turne dust, & may not make me swell.
    p. 400 UNGATHERED 31   31 Vntill the dust retorned bee

dutch   frequency: 3   relative frequency: 0.00004
    p. 56 EPIGRAMS 88   8 As french-men in his companie, should seeme
                              dutch?
    p. 68 EPIGRAMS 107   5 Tell the grosse Dutch those grosser tales of
                              yours,
    p. 368 UNGATHERED 6   85 The Dutch whom Wealth (not Hatred) doth
                              diuide;

dutie   frequency: 1   relative frequency: 0.00001
    p. 325 HORACE 2   449 Can tell a States-mans dutie, what the arts

duties   frequency: 1   relative frequency: 0.00001
    p. 265 UNDERWOOD 79   49 To whom you owe all duties of your grounds;

duty   frequency: 1   relative frequency: 0.00001
   See also "dutie."
    p. 134 UNDERWOOD 2.4   5 As she goes, all hearts doe duty

dvncote   frequency: 2   relative frequency: 0.00002
    p.   29 EPIGRAMS 8   1 RIDWAY rob'd DVNCOTE of three hundred
                               pound,
    p.   29 EPIGRAMS 8   4 Beg'd RIDWAYES pardon: DVNCOTE,
                               now, doth crye,

dwarfes   frequency: 2   relative frequency: 0.00002
    p. 157 UNDERWOOD 13   147 Are Dwarfes of Honour, and have neither weight
    p. 205 UNDERWOOD 43   67 Of errant Knight-hood, with the<ir> Dames, and
                               Dwarfes,

dwarfs. See "dwarfes."

dwell   frequency: 12   relative frequency: 0.00017
    p.   88 EPIGRAMS 133   143 Your Fleet-lane Furies; and hot cookes doe
                               dwell,
    p.   94 FOREST 2   47 There's none, that dwell about them, wish them
                               downe;
    p.   99 FOREST 3   94 'Tis better, if he there can dwell.
    p. 121 FOREST 14   40 With dust of ancestors, in graues but dwell.
    p. 122 FOREST 15   15 Dwell, dwell here still: O, being euery-where,
    p. 219 UNDERWOOD 47   60 And dwell as in my Center, as I can,
    p. 228 UNDERWOOD 53   15 For never saw I yet the Muses dwell,
    p. 262 UNDERWOOD 78   8 For that to dwell in, and be still at home.
    p. 262 UNDERWOOD 78   12 As other soules, to his, dwell in a Lane:
    p. 317 HORACE 2   253 To children; we must alwayes dwell, and stay
    p. 387 UNGATHERED 22   3 Which, did they neere so neate, or proudly dwell,

dweller   frequency: 1   relative frequency: 0.00001
    p. 220 UNDERWOOD 48   4 Where now, thou art made Dweller;

dwells   frequency: 1   relative frequency: 0.00001
    p.   96 FOREST 2   102 May say, their lords haue built, but thy lord
                               dwells.

dwelt   frequency: 1   relative frequency: 0.00001
    p.   89 EPIGRAMS 133   187 Calling for RADAMANTHVS, that dwelt
                               by,

dy'd   frequency: 4   relative frequency: 0.00005
    p.   60 EPIGRAMS 93   5 Two brauely in the battaile fell, and dy'd,
    p. 234 UNDERWOOD 60   18 Because it durst have noblier dy'd.
    p. 282 U'WOOD 84.9   1 'Twere time that I dy'd too, now shee is dead,
    p. 319 HORACE 2   314 Those that did sing, and act: their faces dy'd

dyd'st   frequency: 1   relative frequency: 0.00001
    p. 128 UNDERWOOD 1.1   22 To take our nature; becam'st man, and dyd'st,

dye   frequency: 12   relative frequency: 0.00017
    p.   29 EPIGRAMS 8   2 RIDWAY was tane, arraign'd, condemn'd to
                               dye;
    p.   31 EPIGRAMS 15   4 Which was a cater-piller. So't will dye.
    p.   57 EPIGRAMS 89   7 How can so great example dye in mee,
    p.   71 EPIGRAMS 110   22 His life, but makes, that he can dye no more.
    p.   79 EPIGRAMS 124   4 As much beautie, as could dye:
    p. 111 FOREST 11   74 Turtles can chastly dye;
    p. 230 UNDERWOOD 55   7 Yet with a Dye, that feares no Moth,
    p. 271 UNDERWOOD 83   86 And see all dead here, or about to dye!
    p. 309 HORACE 2   102 And much shall dye, that now is nobly liv'd,
    p. 397 UNGATHERED 30   54 With euery song, I sweare, and so would dye:
    p. 398 UNGATHERED 30   70 An Agincourt, an Agincourt, or dye.
    p. 409 UNGATHERED 37   15 A Mungrel Curre? Thou should'st stinck forth,
                               and dye

dye-fats   frequency: 1   relative frequency: 0.00001
    p. 211 UNDERWOOD 43   180 The Glasse-house, Dye-fats, and their
                               Fornaces;

dyed   frequency: 1   relative frequency: 0.00001
   See also "dy'd."

dyed (cont.)
       p.   79 EPIGRAMS 124   11 Fitter, where it dyed, to tell,

dyes   frequency: 4   relative frequency: 0.00005
       p.   76 EPIGRAMS 119   15 He, that, but liuing halfe his age, dyes such;
       p.   99 FOREST 3   84 Not doing good, scarce when he dyes.
       p. 382 UNGATHERED 16   8 his life, his loue, his honour, which ne'r dyes,
       p. 420 UNGATHERED 48   16 Hee dyes wth an Ill sent,

dying   frequency: 5   relative frequency: 0.00007
       p.   71 EPIGRAMS 110   15 His deedes too dying, but in bookes (whose good
       p. 205 UNDERWOOD 43   55 And so, have kept me dying a whole age,
       p. 288 U'WOOD 84.9   202 Suffring, and dying to redeeme our losse!
       p. 309 HORACE 2   87 The first-borne dying; so the aged state
       p. 369 UNGATHERED 6   101 Though, now by Loue transform'd, & dayly
                                    dying:

dyke. See "like."

dyue   frequency: 1   relative frequency: 0.00001
       p. 405 UNGATHERED 34   80 Vp & about? Dyue into Cellars too

e.   frequency: 1   relative frequency: 0.00001
       p. 412 UNGATHERED 41   4 R. Rose, I. Ivy, E. sweet Eglantine.

each   frequency: 62   relative frequency: 0.00089
       p.   33 EPIGRAMS 22   1 Here lyes to each her parents ruth,
       p.   34 EPIGRAMS 23   1 DONNE, the delight of PHOEBVS, and
                                    each Muse,
       p.   34 EPIGRAMS 25   3 Telling the motions of each petticote,
       p.   45 EPIGRAMS 56   8 He takes vp all, makes each mans wit his owne.
       p.   47 EPIGRAMS 63   5 And that thou seek'st reward of thy each act,
       p.   49 EPIGRAMS 67   10 Before thou wert it, in each good mans heart.
       p.   50 EPIGRAMS 70   6 Each best day of our life escapes vs, first.
       p.   52 EPIGRAMS 76   11 I meant each softest vertue, there should meet,
       p.   56 EPIGRAMS 87   3 Each night, to drowne his cares: But when the
                                    gaine
       p.   59 EPIGRAMS 92   12 And what each prince doth for intelligence owe,
       p.   59 EPIGRAMS 92   14 For twelue yeeres yet to come, what each state
                                    lacks.
       p.   62 EPIGRAMS 97   6 By his each glorious parcell to be knowne!
       p.   63 EPIGRAMS 97   19 About his forme. What then so swells each lim?
       p.   81 EPIGRAMS 128   11 We each to other may this voyce enspire;
       p.   81 EPIGRAMS 129   1 That, not a paire of friends each other see,
       p.   84 EPIGRAMS 133   15 Furies there wanted not: each scold was ten.
       p.   88 EPIGRAMS 133   168 Tempt such a passage? when each priuies seate
       p.   94 FOREST 2   25 Each banke doth yeeld thee coneyes; and the topps
       p.   94 FOREST 2   42 Fig, grape, and quince, each in his time doth
                                    come:
       p.   96 FOREST 2   95 Each morne, and euen, they are taught to pray,
       p.   99 FOREST 3   78 And each where boast it as his merit,
       p. 120 FOREST 13   120 Each into other, and had now made one.
       p. 134 UNDERWOOD 2.4   3 Each that drawes, is a Swan, or a Dove,
       p. 137 UNDERWOOD 2.5   33 And betweene each rising breast,
       p. 139 UNDERWOOD 2.7   16 Each suck <the> others breath.
       p. 143 UNDERWOOD 3   3 Till each of us be made a Starre,
       p. 144 UNDERWOOD 3   17 They say the Angells marke each Deed,
       p. 148 UNDERWOOD 7   34 As it would be to each a fame:
       p. 151 UNDERWOOD 12   9 That though they did possesse each limbe,
       p. 154 UNDERWOOD 13   40 So each, that's done, and tane, becomes a Brace.
       p. 155 UNDERWOOD 13   72 All the Towne-curs take each their snatch at me.
       p. 157 UNDERWOOD 13   132 Profit in ought; each day some little adde,
       p. 164 UNDERWOOD 15   73 And jealous each of other, yet thinke long
       p. 165 UNDERWOOD 15   108 To teach each suit he has, the ready way
       p. 167 UNDERWOOD 15   151 When I am hoarse, with praising his each cast,
       p. 176 UNDERWOOD 24   15 Some note of which each varied Pillar beares,
       p. 181 UNDERWOOD 27   13 Is Horace his each love so high
       p. 190 UNDERWOOD 37   28 From each of which I labour to be free,
       p. 193 UNDERWOOD 38   68 God lightens not at mans each fraile offence,
       p. 217 UNDERWOOD 46   23 Of if Chance must, to each man that doth rise,
       p. 222 UNDERWOOD 49   13 And as lip-thirstie, in each words expence,
       p. 232 UNDERWOOD 58   4 What each man sayes of it, and of what coat
       p. 239 UNDERWOOD 67   22 And each intelligence
       p. 241 UNDERWOOD 69   4 What, by that name, wee each to other owe,
       p. 245 UNDERWOOD 70   63 Each syllab'e answer'd, and was form'd, how
                                    faire;
       p. 247 UNDERWOOD 70   111 Each stiled, by his end,
       p. 258 UNDERWOOD 75   176 How each one plays his part, of the large
                                    Pedigree.
       p. 285 U'WOOD 84.9   115 And each shall know, there, one anothers face,

each (cont.)
```
  p. 287 U'WOOD 84.9    154 Each line, as it were graphick, in the face!
  p. 289 U'WOOD 84.9    222 In the discerning of each conscience, so!
  p. 311 HORACE 2       124 Fit for the sock: Each subject should retaine
  p. 313 HORACE 2       157 Her truch-man, she reports the minds each throw.
  p. 315 HORACE 2       223 The customes of each age thou must observe,
  p. 317 HORACE 2       254 In fitting proper adjuncts to each day.
  p. 319 HORACE 2       309 That found out profit, and foretold each thing,
  p. 370 UNGATHERED 7     7 Each subt'lest Passion, with her source, and
                            spring,
  p. 379 UNGATHERED 12    9 And allow you for each particular mile,
  p. 380 UNGATHERED 12   23 Each leafe of his iournall, and line doth vnlocke
  p. 380 UNGATHERED 12   25 He went out at each place, and at what he came
                            in,
  p. 392 UNGATHERED 26   69 In each of which, he seemes to shake a Lance,
  p. 410 UNGATHERED 38   11 Now each Court-Hobby-horse will wince in rime;
  p. 417 UNGATHERED 45   38 each to pawne hir husbands capp,
```

eagle   frequency: 1   relative frequency: 0.00001
```
  p. 278 U'WOOD 84.4     10 An Eagle towring in the skye,
```

ear. See "eare," "th'eare."

eare   frequency: 15   relative frequency: 0.00021
```
**p. 115 PANEGYRE       93 "And all so iustly, as his eare was ioy'd
  p.  59 EPIGRAMS 92     18 Nay, aske you, how the day goes, in your eare.
  p.  74 EPIGRAMS 115    15 Whose name's vn-welcome to the present eare,
  p.  83 EPIGRAMS 131     6 We ought not giue them taste, we had an eare.
  p. 109 FOREST 11        9 At th'eye and eare (the ports vnto the minde)
  p. 154 UNDERWOOD 13    49 Give thankes by stealth, and whispering in the
                            eare,
  p. 172 UNDERWOOD 21     4 Out of his Grave, and poyson every eare.
  p. 214 UNDERWOOD 44    31 But give them over to the common eare
  p. 230 UNDERWOOD 56    16 Run all the Rounds in a soft Ladyes eare,
  p. 279 U'WOOD 84.4     35 Of grace, and Musique to the eare,
  p. 317 HORACE 2       257 In at the eare, doe stirre the mind more slow
  p. 323 HORACE 2       378 More slow, and come more weightie to the eare:
  p. 331 HORACE 2       576 To send it to be judg'd by Metius eare,
  p. 404 UNGATHERED 34   53 To plant ye Musick where noe eare can reach!
  p. 420 UNGATHERED 48   32 And once more stryke the eare of tyme wth those
                            ffresh straynes:
```

earely   frequency: 3   relative frequency: 0.00004
```
  p.  34 EPIGRAMS 23      3 Whose euery worke, of thy most earely wit,
  p.  94 FOREST 2        41 The earely cherry, with the later plum,
  p. 119 FOREST 13       91 And, keeping a iust course, haue earely put
```

eares   frequency: 15   relative frequency: 0.00021
```
 *p. 493 TO HIMSELF     36 Of larding your large eares
  p.  43 EPIGRAMS 51      9 For we, that haue our eyes still in our eares,
  p.  68 EPIGRAMS 107     2 That's, sit, and eate: doe not my eares abuse.
  p.  88 EPIGRAMS 133   171 Vpon your eares, of discords so vn-sweet?
  p.  97 FOREST 3        31 While all, that follow, their glad eares apply
  p.  98 FOREST 3        41 The ripened eares, yet humble in their height,
  p. 102 FOREST 5        13 Or his easier eares beguile,
  p. 108 FOREST 10       30 And now an Epode to deepe eares I sing.
  p. 143 UNDERWOOD 3      4 And all the world turne Eares.
  p. 148 UNDERWOOD 7     28 Will be my Rivall, though she have but eares.
  p. 150 UNDERWOOD 9     18 And all these through her eyes, have stopt her
                            eares.
  p. 209 UNDERWOOD 43   145 But, others fell with that conceipt by the eares,
  p. 286 U'WOOD 84.9    124 A Musique in the Eares, will ever last;
  p. 292 UNDERWOOD 86    22 In many a Gumme, and for thy soft eares sake
  p. 392 UNGATHERED 26   46 Our eares, or like a Mercury to charme!
```

earl. See "earle."

earle   frequency: 13   relative frequency: 0.00018
```
  p.  40 EPIGRAMS 43     t1 TO ROBERT EARLE OF
                            SALISBVRIE.
  p.  47 EPIGRAMS 63     t1 TO ROBERT EARLE OF
                            SALISBVRIE.
  p.  49 EPIGRAMS 67     t1 TO THOMAS EARLE OF
                            SVFFOLKE.
  p.  66 EPIGRAMS 102    t1 TO WILLIAM EARLE OF
                            PEMBROKE.
  p. 153 UNDERWOOD 13    t2 now Earle of Dorset.
  p. 176 UNDERWOOD 25    t1 An Ode to IAMES Earle of Desmond,
  p. 228 UNDERWOOD 53    t3 WILLIAM, Earle of Newcastle.
  p. 232 UNDERWOOD 59    t2 To WILLIAM Earle of Newcastle.
```

earle (cont.)
  p. 250 UNDERWOOD 73   t4 Hee was made Earle of Portland,
  p. 269 UNDERWOOD 83   21 Earle Rivers Grand-Child -- serve not formes,
                            good Fame,
  p. 384 UNGATHERED 18   t2 Robert, Earle of Somerset,
  p. 407 UNGATHERED 35   20 Content thee to be Pancridge Earle ye whyle;
  p. 407 UNGATHERED 35   21 An Earle of show: for all thy worke is showe:

earles   frequency: 1   relative frequency: 0.00001
  p. 382 UNGATHERED 16   t3 Rich, now Earles of Warwick and Hollande.

earls. See "earles."

early   frequency: 7   relative frequency: 0.00010
  See also "earely."
  p. 40 EPIGRAMS 42   6 No more would IONE he should. GILES
                            riseth early,
  p. 47 EPIGRAMS 64   2 With thy new place, bring I these early fruits
  p. 247 UNDERWOOD 70   125 Of two so early men,
  p. 258 UNDERWOOD 75   180 Extend a reaching vertue, early and late:
  p. 288 U'WOOD 84.9   199 Shee saw her Saviour, by an early light,
  p. 384 UNGATHERED 18   7 Wch I do, early, vertuous Somerset,
  p. 386 UNGATHERED 21   5 For, though but early in these pathes thou tread,

earnest   frequency: 2   relative frequency: 0.00002
  p. 99 FOREST 3   101 Be thankes to him, and earnest prayer, to finde
  p. 321 HORACE 2   330 And so to turne all earnest into jest,

ears   frequency: 2   relative frequency: 0.00002
  See also "eares," "th'eares."
  p. 403 UNGATHERED 34   20 you would be an Asinigo, by your ears?
  p. 410 UNGATHERED 39   4 Pillory nor Whip, nor want of Ears,

earth   frequency: 29   relative frequency: 0.00041
**p. 113 PANEGYRE   26 On earth, till now, they came to grace his
                            throne.
**p. 115 PANEGYRE   78 "Are here on earth the most conspicuous things:
  p. 34 EPIGRAMS 22   12 Which couer lightly, gentle earth.
  p. 39 EPIGRAMS 40   17 Earth, thou hast not such another.
  p. 52 EPIGRAMS 74   9 The Virgin, long-since fled from earth, I see,
  p. 77 EPIGRAMS 120   23 But, being so much too good for earth,
  p. 114 FOREST 12   25 Were yet vnfound, and better plac'd in earth,
  p. 130 UNDERWOOD 1.3   11 The Word, which heaven, and earth did make;
  p. 142 UNDERWOOD 2.9   43 Bounteous as the clouds to earth;
  p. 144 UNDERWOOD 3   24 Mistaking earth for heaven.
  p. 167 UNDERWOOD 15   163 Light thee from hell on earth: where flatterers,
                            spies,
  p. 181 UNDERWOOD 27   14 Rap't from the Earth, as not to die?
  p. 237 UNDERWOOD 65   2 That so hath crown'd our hopes, our spring, and
                            earth,
  p. 246 UNDERWOOD 70   96 Whilst that in heav'n, this light on earth must
                            shine.
  p. 250 UNDERWOOD 74   1 Such pleasure as the teeming Earth
  p. 253 UNDERWOOD 75   21 When look'd the Earth so fine,
  p. 254 UNDERWOOD 75   66 Have they bedew'd the Earth, where she doth
                            tread,
  p. 257 UNDERWOOD 75   154 Like Swine, or other Cattell here on earth:
  p. 264 UNDERWOOD 79   26 Who walkes on Earth as May still went along,
  p. 282 U'WOOD 84.9   12 By Death, on Earth, I should have had remorse
  p. 283 U'WOOD 84.9   46 In earth, till the last Trumpe awake the Sheepe
  p. 290 UNDERWOOD 85   16 Of Earth, and sheares the tender Sheepe:
  p. 321 HORACE 2   335 Or, whilst he shuns the Earth, to catch at Aire
  p. 396 UNGATHERED 30   16 That all Earth look'd on; and that earth, all
                            Eyes!
  p. 413 UNGATHERED 41   18 But lowlie laid, as on the earth asleep,
  p. 417 UNGATHERED 45   18 rise or fall vppon the earth,
  p. 420 UNGATHERED 48   30 Vppon soe humbled earth to cast hir eyes:
  p. 422 UNGATHERED 50   7 Looke how the starres from earth, or seas from
                            flames

earthen   frequency: 1   relative frequency: 0.00001
  p. 219 UNDERWOOD 47   55 Of earthen Jarres, there may molest me too:

earthes   frequency: 1   relative frequency: 0.00001
  p. 372 UNGATHERED 9   9 Of Spheares, as light of starres; She was
                            earthes Eye:

earthly   frequency: 2   relative frequency: 0.00002
**p. 113 PANEGYRE   22 That fastneth heauenly power to earthly raigne:
  p. 107 FOREST 10   5 With his old earthly labours. T<o>'exact more,

earths   frequency: 1   relative frequency: 0.00001
    See also "earthes."
    p. 279 U'WOOD 84.4   44 Earths grossnesse; There's the how, and why.

eas'd   frequency: 1   relative frequency: 0.00001
    p. 251 UNDERWOOD 74   26 To see great Charles of Travaile eas'd,

ease   frequency: 11   relative frequency: 0.00015
    p. 57 EPIGRAMS 90   4 At last, ease, appetite, and example wan
    p. 105 FOREST 8   22 Daintinesse, and softer ease,
    p. 118 FOREST 13   57 In single paths, dangers with ease are watch'd:
    p. 122 FOREST 15   4 That, laden with my sinnes, I seeke for ease?
    p. 140 UNDERWOOD 2.9   1 Of your Trouble, Ben, to ease me,
    p. 162 UNDERWOOD 15   4 Their vitious ease, and be o'rewhelm'd with it.
    p. 174 UNDERWOOD 23   2 Buried in ease and sloth?
    p. 179 UNDERWOOD 25   42 Pyracmon's houre will come to give them ease,
    p. 237 UNDERWOOD 64   17 O Times! O Manners! Surfet bred of ease,
    p. 295 UNDERWOOD 90   2 Most pleasant Martial; Substance got with ease,
    p. 319 HORACE 2   293 They might with ease be numbred, being a few

eased   frequency: 1   relative frequency: 0.00001
    See also "eas'd."
    p. 417 UNGATHERED 45   40 hir minde is eased.

eases   frequency: 1   relative frequency: 0.00001
    p. 221 UNDERWOOD 48   23 To give mankind their eases,

easie   frequency: 2   relative frequency: 0.00002
    p. 250 UNDERWOOD 74   2 Doth take in easie Natures birth,
    p. 290 UNDERWOOD 85   28 And all invite to easie sleepe.

easier   frequency: 2   relative frequency: 0.00002
    p. 102 FOREST 5   13 Or his easier eares beguile,
    p. 167 UNDERWOOD 15   172 Spread through the World) is easier farre to
                              find,

easy. See "easie."

easy-rated   frequency: 1   relative frequency: 0.00001
    p. 295 UNDERWOOD 90   8 Thy table without art, and easy-rated:

eat   frequency: 7   relative frequency: 0.00010
    See also "eate."
   *p. 492 TO HIMSELF   12 And they will acornes eat:
    p. 94 FOREST 2   34 And pikes, now weary their owne kinde to eat,
    p. 140 UNDERWOOD 2.8   15 You shall neither eat, nor sleepe,
    p. 142 UNDERWOOD 2.9   39 And not thinke h'had eat a stake,
    p. 191 UNDERWOOD 38   6 And drives it in to eat on my offence,
    p. 319 HORACE 2   325 Having well eat, and drunke (the rites being
                              done)
    p. 407 UNGATHERED 36   4 Able to eat into his bones & pierce

eate   frequency: 8   relative frequency: 0.00011
    p. 35 EPIGRAMS 28   12 He doth, at meales, alone, his pheasant eate,
    p. 68 EPIGRAMS 107   2 That's, sit, and eate: doe not my eares abuse.
    p. 69 EPIGRAMS 107   31 Come, be not angrie, you are HVNGRY; eate;
    p. 95 FOREST 2   61 Where comes no guest, but is allow'd to eate,
    p. 95 FOREST 2   69 But giues me what I call, and lets me eate,
    p. 99 FOREST 3   89 And, so they ride in purple, eate in plate,
    p. 119 FOREST 13   88 Eate on her clients, and some one deuoure.
    p. 371 UNGATHERED 8   16 Or moathes shall eate, what all these Fooles
                              admire.

eaten   frequency: 3   relative frequency: 0.00004
    p. 200 UNDERWOOD 42   33 Have eaten with the Beauties, and the wits,
    p. 375 UNGATHERED 10   25 For Grapes he had gather'd before they were
                              eaten.
    p. 380 UNGATHERED 12   36 For grapes he had gather'd, before they were
                              eaten.

eates   frequency: 3   relative frequency: 0.00004
    p. 30 EPIGRAMS 12   5 By that one spell he liues, eates, drinkes,
                              arrayes
    p. 76 EPIGRAMS 118   1 GVT eates all day, and lechers all the night,
    p. 88 EPIGRAMS 133   166 When euery clerke eates artichokes, and peason,

eating   frequency: 1   relative frequency: 0.00001
    See also "th'eating."
    p. 55 EPIGRAMS 84   8 And PHOEBVS-selfe should be at eating it.

eats   frequency: 1   relative frequency: 0.00001
    See also "eates."
    p. 174 UNDERWOOD 23   6 That eats on wits, and Arts, and <oft> destroyes
                               them both.

eccho   frequency: 6   relative frequency: 0.00008
    p. 249 UNDERWOOD 72   8 Like Eccho playing from the other shore.
    p. 264 UNDERWOOD 79   27 Chor. Rivers, and Vallies, Eccho what wee
                               sing.
    p. 264 UNDERWOOD 79   35 Chor. Rivers, and Valleys, Eccho what wee
                               sing.
    p. 279 U'WOOD 84.4   40 Still left an Eccho in the sense.
    p. 403 UNGATHERED 34   30 And all men eccho you haue made a Masque.
    p. 411 UNGATHERED 39   14 But Tune and Noise the Eccho of thy Shame.

eccho'd   frequency: 1   relative frequency: 0.00001
    p. 265 UNDERWOOD 79   53 That they may take it eccho'd by the Floods.

eccho's   frequency: 1   relative frequency: 0.00001
    p. 390 UNGATHERED 26   8 Which, when it sounds at best, but eccho's right;

echo. See "eccho."

echoed. See "eccho'd."

echoes. See "eccho's."

eclipse   frequency: 1   relative frequency: 0.00001
    p. 238 UNDERWOOD 65   11 And threat' the great Eclipse. Two houres but
                               runne,

ecstasies. See "extasies."

ecstasy. See "extasie."

eden   frequency: 1   relative frequency: 0.00001
    p. 111 FOREST 11   57 A forme more fresh, then are the Eden bowers,

edge   frequency: 2   relative frequency: 0.00002
    p. 325 HORACE 2   433 Be like a Whet-stone, that an edge can put
    p. 327 HORACE 2   494 On edge the Masculine spirits, and did whet

edifices   frequency: 1   relative frequency: 0.00001
    p. 96 FOREST 2   100 With other edifices, when they see

edmondes. See "edmonds."

edmonds   frequency: 3   relative frequency: 0.00004
    p. 71 EPIGRAMS 110   t1 TO CLEMENT EDMONDS, ON HIS
    p. 71 EPIGRAMS 110   11 Not all these, EDMONDS, or what else put
                               too,
    p. 72 EPIGRAMS 111   1 Who EDMONDS, reades thy booke, and doth
                               not see

education   frequency: 1   relative frequency: 0.00001
    p. 214 UNDERWOOD 44   62 For education of our Lordings; soone

edward   frequency: 5   relative frequency: 0.00007
    p. 56 EPIGRAMS 89   t1 TO EDWARD ALLEN.
    p. 68 EPIGRAMS 106   t1 TO SIR EDWARD HERBERT.
    p. 153 UNDERWOOD 13   t1 An Epistle to Sir EDWARD SACVILE,
    p. 217 UNDERWOOD 46   t1 An Epigram on Sir Edward Coke, when he was
    p. 401 UNGATHERED 33   t1 To my worthy Friend, Master Edward Filmer,

eeke   frequency: 1   relative frequency: 0.00001
    p. 86 EPIGRAMS 133   101 His spirits, now, in pills, and eeke in potions,

eeles   frequency: 1   relative frequency: 0.00001
    p. 94 FOREST 2   37 Bright eeles, that emulate them, and leape on
                               land,

eels. See "eeles."

eene   frequency: 1   relative frequency: 0.00001
    p. 44 EPIGRAMS 56   2 Whose workes are eene the tripperie of wit,

effect   frequency: 3   relative frequency: 0.00004
    See also "t<o>'effect."
    p. 37 EPIGRAMS 32   2 Could not effect, not all the furies doe,
    p. 109 FOREST 11   5 Which to effect (since no brest is so sure,

effect (cont.)
    p. 393 UNGATHERED 27   15 And in effect of Heauenly loue

effected   frequency: 1   relative frequency: 0.00001
    p. 140 UNDERWOOD 2.8   8 When the worke would be effected:

effects   frequency: 2   relative frequency: 0.00002
    p. 82 EPIGRAMS 130   3 Which Musick had; or speake her knowne effects,
    p. 110 FOREST 11   44 No such effects doth proue;

egerton   frequency: 1   relative frequency: 0.00001
    p. 51 EPIGRAMS 74   1 Whil'st thy weigh'd iudgements, EGERTON,
                               I heare,

egges   frequency: 2   relative frequency: 0.00002
    p. 204 UNDERWOOD 43   37 Of Egges, and Halberds, Cradles, and a Herse,
    p. 315 HORACE 2   210 From the two Egges, that did disclose the twins.

eggs. See "egges," "egs."

eglantine   frequency: 2   relative frequency: 0.00002
    p. 412 UNGATHERED 41   4 R. Rose, I. Ivy, E. sweet Eglantine.
    p. 413 UNGATHERED 41   21 But, that which summes all, is the Eglantine,

egs   frequency: 2   relative frequency: 0.00002
    p. 64 EPIGRAMS 101   12 If we can get her, full of egs, and then,
    p. 375 UNGATHERED 10   18 A Punke here pelts him with egs. How so?

eiects   frequency: 1   relative frequency: 0.00001
    p. 82 EPIGRAMS 130   4 That shee remoueth cares, sadnesse eiects,

eight   frequency: 2   relative frequency: 0.00002
    p. 82 EPIGRAMS 130   12 That the eight spheare, no lesse, then planets
                              seauen,
    p. 207 UNDERWOOD 43   98 Of our fift Henry, eight of his nine yeare;

eighth. See "eight."

either   frequency: 31   relative frequency: 0.00044
    See also "ayther."
**p. 113 PANEGYRE   23 Beside her, stoup't on either hand, a maid,
**p. 114 PANEGYRE   57 The ioy of either was alike, and full;
**p. 115 PANEGYRE   70 The Nobles zeale, yet either kept aliue
    p. 85 EPIGRAMS 133   39 A harder tasque, then either his to Bristo',
    p. 97 FOREST 3   40 And feasts, that either shearers keepe;
    p. 99 FOREST 3   76 Then either money, warre, or death:
    p. 109 FOREST 11   21 For either our affections doe rebell,
    p. 131 UNDERWOOD 2.1   16 Either whom to love, or how:
    p. 133 UNDERWOOD 2.3   23 And in either Prose, or Song,
    p. 148 UNDERWOOD 7   32 From either heart, I know;
    p. 158 UNDERWOOD 13   162 (As their true rule or lesson) either men,
    p. 170 UNDERWOOD 19   7 By those pure bathes your either cheeke
                              discloses,
    p. 171 UNDERWOOD 19   13 You blush, but doe not: friends are either none,
    p. 171 UNDERWOOD 19   16 And so that either may example prove
    p. 206 UNDERWOOD 43   83 These, had'st thou pleas'd either to dine, or
                              sup,
    p. 230 UNDERWOOD 56   18 Of either Suitor, or a Servant by.
    p. 247 UNDERWOOD 70   110 Till either grew a portion of the other:
    p. 253 UNDERWOOD 75   34 Their Sister-tunes, from Thames his either
                              side,
    p. 254 UNDERWOOD 75   52 Both Crownes, and Kingdomes in their either
                              hand;
    p. 254 UNDERWOOD 75   58 (Lillies and Roses, Flowers of either Sexe)
    p. 271 UNDERWOOD 83   85 If you can cast about your either eye,
    p. 274 U'WOOD 84.2   8 At either Stemme, and know the veines of good
    p. 307 HORACE 2   33 Most Writers, noble Sire, and either Sonne,
    p. 311 HORACE 2   131 To ignorance still, then either learne, or know?
    p. 317 HORACE 2   242 Either because he seekes, and, having found,
    p. 317 HORACE 2   255 The businesse either on the Stage is done,
    p. 323 HORACE 2   402 If either you, or I, know the right way
    p. 327 HORACE 2   477 Poets would either profit, or delight,
    p. 338 HORACE 1   19 . purple .... either
    p. 389 UNGATHERED 24   2 Shall finde, that either hath read Bookes, and
                              Men:
    p. 417 UNGATHERED 45   17 And as either newes or mirth

eithers   frequency: 2   relative frequency: 0.00002
    p. 190 UNDERWOOD 37   29 Yet if with eithers vice I teynted be,
    p. 202 UNDERWOOD 42   88 More then of eithers manners, wit, or face!

ejects. See "eiects."

eke. See "eeke."

el<izabeths>   frequency: 1   relative frequency: 0.00001
     p. 77 EPIGRAMS 120   t2 OF Q. EL<IZABETHS> CHAPPEL.

elaborate. See "th'elaborate."

elder   frequency: 4   relative frequency: 0.00005
     p. 113 FOREST 12   20 A present, which (if elder writs reherse
     p. 258 UNDERWOOD 75   192 The longing Couple, all that elder Lovers know.
     p. 331 HORACE 2   545 You Sir, the elder brother, though you are
     p. 382 UNGATHERED 16   5 The elder of these two, riche hopes Increase,

elders   frequency: 1   relative frequency: 0.00001
     p. 72 EPIGRAMS 111   6 More, then to varie what our elders knew:

eldest   frequency: 2   relative frequency: 0.00002
     p. 189 UNDERWOOD 36   16 The eldest God, yet still a Child.
     p. 394 UNGATHERED 28   t2 eldest Daughter, to Cuthbert Lord Ogle:

elect   frequency: 1   relative frequency: 0.00001
     p. 286 U'WOOD 84.9   149 Himselfe so un-inform'd of his elect,

elected   frequency: 1   relative frequency: 0.00001
     p. 128 UNDERWOOD 1.1   45 12. Among thy Saints elected to abide,

election   frequency: 2   relative frequency: 0.00002
     p. 288 U'WOOD 84.9   198 By sure Election, and predestin'd grace!
     p. 363 UNGATHERED 3   14 Muffles the clearnesse of Election,

elegie   frequency: 11   relative frequency: 0.00015
     p. 108 FOREST 10A   1 An elegie? no, muse; yt askes a straine
     p. 169 UNDERWOOD 18   t1 An Elegie.
     p. 170 UNDERWOOD 19   t1 An Elegie.
     p. 173 UNDERWOOD 22   t1 An Elegie.
     p. 191 UNDERWOOD 38   t1 An Elegie.
     p. 197 UNDERWOOD 40   t1 An Elegie.
     p. 199 UNDERWOOD 41   t1 An Elegie.
     p. 199 UNDERWOOD 42   t1 An Elegie.
     p. 268 UNDERWOOD 83   t1 An Elegie
     p. 282 U'WOOD 84.9   t1 Elegie on my Muse.
     p. 309 HORACE 2   110 That first sent forth the dapper Elegie,

elegies   frequency: 1   relative frequency: 0.00001
     p. 73 EPIGRAMS 112   13 I passe to Elegies; Thou meet'st me there:

elegy. See "elegie."

elements   frequency: 2   relative frequency: 0.00002
     p. 70 EPIGRAMS 109   10 And elements of honor, then the dresse;
     p. 134 UNDERWOOD 2.4   20 All the Gaine, all the Good, of the Elements
                              strife.

eleuen   frequency: 1   relative frequency: 0.00001
     p. 380 UNGATHERED 12   46 He there doth protest he saw of the eleuen.

eleven. See "eleuen."

eleventh   frequency: 1   relative frequency: 0.00001
     p. 262 UNDERWOOD 78   14 Upon my Birth-day the eleventh of June;

elf. See "elfe."

elfe   frequency: 1   relative frequency: 0.00001
     p. 379 UNGATHERED 12   7 Of our Odcombian, that literate Elfe?

elixir. See "the'elixir," "th'elixir."

eliza   frequency: 1   relative frequency: 0.00001
     p. 392 UNGATHERED 26   74 That so did take Eliza, and our Iames!

elizabeth   frequency: 4   relative frequency: 0.00005
     See also "eliza."
     p. 53 EPIGRAMS 79   t1 TO ELIZABETH COVNTESSE OF
                              RVTLAND.
     p. 79 EPIGRAMS 124   9 One name was ELIZABETH,
     p. 79 EPIGRAMS 124   t1 EPITAPH ON ELIZABETH, L. H.
     p. 113 FOREST 12   t2 TO ELIZABETH COVNTESSE OF
                              RVTLAND.

elizabeths   frequency: 1   relative frequency: 0.00001
    See also "el<izabeths>."
    p. 176 UNDERWOOD 25   t2 writ in Queene ELIZABETHS time,

ellesmere. See "elsmere."

elocution   frequency: 1   relative frequency: 0.00001
    p. 160 UNDERWOOD 14   56 And manly elocution, not one while

eloquence   frequency: 7   relative frequency: 0.00010
    p. 86 EPIGRAMS 133   99 For (where he was the god of eloquence,
    p. 187 UNDERWOOD 33   12 To the Wolves studie, or Dogs eloquence;
    p. 217 UNDERWOOD 46   13 And that thy strong and manly Eloquence
    p. 288 U'WOOD 84.9   186 Nor can the bruised heart want eloquence:
    p. 319 HORACE 2   307 The rash, and head-long eloquence brought forth
    p. 395 UNGATHERED 29 16 What godds but those of arts, and eloquence?
    p. 403 UNGATHERED 34 40 The Eloquence of Masques! What need of prose

eloquent   frequency: 1   relative frequency: 0.00001
    p. 331 HORACE 2   552 Of eloquent Messalla's power in Court,

else   frequency: 29   relative frequency: 0.00041
    p. 30 EPIGRAMS 12   17 Or else by water goes, and so to playes;
    p. 34 EPIGRAMS 25   7 What doth he else, but say, leaue to be chast,
    p. 38 EPIGRAMS 38   4 Any man else, you clap your hands, and rore,
    p. 64 EPIGRAMS 101   6 Something, which, else, could hope for no
                             esteeme.
    p. 66 EPIGRAMS 102   12 As nothing else discernes the vertue' or vice.
    p. 71 EPIGRAMS 110   11 Not all these, EDMONDS, or what else put
                             too,
    p. 95 FOREST 2   53 The better cheeses, bring 'hem; or else send
    p. 96 FOREST 2   101 Those proud, ambitious heaps, and nothing else,
    p. 101 FOREST 4   57 Else, I my state should much mistake,
    p. 109 FOREST 11   22 Or else the sentinell
    p. 132 UNDERWOOD 2.2 31 Or else one that plaid his Ape,
    p. 138 UNDERWOOD 2.6 16 Else that glister'd in White-hall;
    p. 149 UNDERWOOD 9   2 For else it could not be,
    p. 154 UNDERWOOD 13   36 His Groomes to witnesse; or else lets it fall
    p. 156 UNDERWOOD 13 117 And feeles it; Else he tarries by the Beast.
    p. 170 UNDERWOOD 18   17 To see men feare: or else for truth, and State,
    p. 192 UNDERWOOD 38   46 We cut not off, till all Cures else doe faile:
    p. 193 UNDERWOOD 38   72 It shakes even him, that all things else doth
                             shake.
    p. 218 UNDERWOOD 47   11 Subject to quarrell only; or else such
    p. 219 UNDERWOOD 47   30 Then these can ever be; or else wish none.
    p. 222 UNDERWOOD 48   49 Or else a health advances,
    p. 249 UNDERWOOD 72   12 Made lighter with the Wine. All noises else,
    p. 255 UNDERWOOD 75   88 All else we see beside, are Shadowes, and goe
                             lesse.
    p. 257 UNDERWOOD 75 151 Alive, which else would die,
    p. 270 UNDERWOOD 83   37 Else, who doth praise a person by a new,
    p. 380 UNGATHERED 12 51 Or any thing else that another should hide,
    p. 389 UNGATHERED 23 12 And who make thither else, rob, or inuade.
    p. 399 UNGATHERED 31 19 Or else Magnetique in the force,
    p. 417 UNGATHERED 45   9 I had somwhat else to say,

else-where   frequency: 2   relative frequency: 0.00002
    p. 197 UNDERWOOD 40   16 And free societie, hee's borne else-where,
    p. 212 UNDERWOOD 43 199 Maintain'd the trade at Bilbo, or else-where;

elsmere   frequency: 1   relative frequency: 0.00001
    p. 185 UNDERWOOD 31   t2 To THOMAS Lo: ELSMERE,

eltham-thing   frequency: 1   relative frequency: 0.00001
    p. 62 EPIGRAMS 97   2 Nor Captayne POD, nor yet the Eltham-thing;

elves   frequency: 1   relative frequency: 0.00001
    p. 200 UNDERWOOD 42   23 Curst in their Cradles, or there chang'd by
                             Elves,

embarked. See "imbarqu'd."

embassage   frequency: 2   relative frequency: 0.00002
    p. 85 EPIGRAMS 133   34 Of sixe times to, and fro, without embassage,
    p. 221 UNDERWOOD 48   46 Of some wel-wrought Embassage:

embassie   frequency: 1   relative frequency: 0.00001
    p. 250 UNDERWOOD 74   t3 For his Returne from his Embassie.

embassies   frequency: 1   relative frequency: 0.00001
     p. 69 EPIGRAMS 107   11 Giue them your seruices, and embassies

embassy. See "embassie."

embelish'd   frequency: 1   relative frequency: 0.00001
     p. 254 UNDERWOOD 75   59 The bright Brides paths, embelish'd more then
                              thine

embellished. See "embelish'd."

embers   frequency: 1   relative frequency: 0.00001
     p. 207 UNDERWOOD 43   106 All scote, and embers! odious, as thy worke!

emblem. See "embleme."

embleme   frequency: 2   relative frequency: 0.00002
     p. 95 FOREST 2   56 An embleme of themselues, in plum, or peare.
     p. 383 UNGATHERED 16   10 As true oblations; his Brothers Embleme sayes,

emblemes   frequency: 1   relative frequency: 0.00001
     p. 254 UNDERWOOD 75   63 The Emblemes of their way.

emblems. See "emblemes."

embrac'd   frequency: 2   relative frequency: 0.00002
     See also "b<e>'embrac'd."
     p. 109 FOREST 11   19 But this true course is not embrac'd by many:
     p. 319 HORACE 2   296 That wider Walls embrac'd their Citie round,

embrace   frequency: 4   relative frequency: 0.00005
     See also "imbrace."
     p. 45 EPIGRAMS 58   8 And, hood-wink'd, for a man, embrace a post.
     p. 61 EPIGRAMS 95   1 If, my religion safe, I durst embrace
     p. 161 UNDERWOOD 14   74 Embrace, and cherish; but he can approve
     p. 220 UNDERWOOD 47   71 These I will honour, love, embrace, and serve:

embraces   frequency: 1   relative frequency: 0.00001
     p. 177 UNDERWOOD 25   22 Lock't in her cold embraces, from the view

embrions   frequency: 1   relative frequency: 0.00001
     p. 165 UNDERWOOD 15   96 If it be thought, kild like her Embrions; for,

embroderies   frequency: 1   relative frequency: 0.00001
     p. 275 U'WOOD 84.3   3 Embroderies, Feathers, Fringes, Lace,

embroideries. See "embroderies."

embryons. See "embrions."

eminence   frequency: 1   relative frequency: 0.00001
     p. 258 UNDERWOOD 75   179 But like an Arme of Eminence, 'mongst them,

emissarie   frequency: 1   relative frequency: 0.00001
     p. 140 UNDERWOOD 2.8   17 With your emissarie eye,

emissary. See "emissarie."

empedocles   frequency: 1   relative frequency: 0.00001
     p. 335 HORACE 2   660 Of the Sicilian Poet Empedocles,

emperours   frequency: 1   relative frequency: 0.00001
     p. 63 EPIGRAMS 107   6 How great you were with their two Emperours;

empire   frequency: 1   relative frequency: 0.00001
     p. 268 UNDERWOOD 82   6 Great aides to Empire, as they are great care

empiric. See "empirick."

empirick   frequency: 1   relative frequency: 0.00001
     p. 31 EPIGRAMS 13   t1 TO DOCTOR EMPIRICK.

empirics. See "emp'ricks."

employ   frequency: 2   relative frequency: 0.00002
     p. 50 EPIGRAMS 70   3 In life, that can employ it; and takes hold
     p. 405 UNGATHERED 34   77 Should but ye king his Iustice-hood employ

employd   frequency: 1   relative frequency: 0.00001
     p. 385 UNGATHERED 19   1 When these, and such, their voices haue employd;

employed. See "emplcyd."

emp'ricks   frequency: 1   relative frequency: 0.00001
       p. 10ɔ FOREST 8   31 With ten Emp'ricks, in their chamber,

emptie   frequency: 4   relative frequency: 0.00005
       p. 143 UNDERWOCD 3   6 Of reason emptie is?
       p. 21ɓ UNJ3RWOOD 44   102 Her broken Armes up, to their emptie moulds.
       p. 232 UNDERWOOD 57   28 it the'Chequer be emptie, so will be his Head.
       p. 321 HORACE 2   336 And emptie Clowdes. For Tragedie is faire,

empties   frequency: 1   relative frequency: 0.00001
       p. 257 UNDERWOOD 75   137 The Chappell empties, and thou may'st be jone

empty   frequency: 1   relative frequency: 0.00001
       See alsc "emptie," "emptye."
       p. 349 HORACE 1   460 .. empty Verses ... meere ....

empty-handed   frequency: 1   relative frequency: 0.00001
       p. 95 FOREST 2   49 And no one empty-handed, to salute

emptye   frequency: 1   relative frequency: 0.00001
       p. 421 UNJATHERED 49   5 The emptye Carper, scorne, not Creditt wynns.

empusa   frequency: 1   relative frequency: 0.00001
       p. 398 UNJATHERED 30   87 Empusa, Lamia, or some Monster, more

empyrean   frequency: 1   relative frequency: 0.00001
       p. 285 U'WOOD 84.9   102 In Heav'n<s> Empyrean, with a robe of light?

emulate   frequency: 4   relative frequency: 0.00005
       See alsc "aemulate."
       p. 61 EPIGRAMS 95   24 As, then, his cause, his glorie emulate.
       p. 78 EPIGRAMS 123   4 Of the best writer, and iudge, should emulate.
       p. 94 FOREST 2   37 Bright eeles, that emulate them, and leape on
                                  land,
       p. 193 UNDERWOOD 38   86 As I the penitents here emulate:

emulates   frequency: 1   relative frequency: 0.00001
       p. 7d EPIGRAMS 121   3 Whose better studies while shee emulates,

emulation   frequency: 1   relative frequency: 0.00001
       See alsc "aemulaticn."
       p. 25ɓ UNDERWOOD 75   117 Doth Emulation stirre;

enable   frequency: 1   relative frequency: 0.00001
       p. 232 UNDERWOOD 57   24 or Wine to enable

enamor'd   frequency: 1   relative frequency: 0.00001
       p. 100 FOREST 4   24 Enamor'd of their golden gyues?

enamour'd   frequency: 1   relative frequency: 0.00001
       See alsc "enamor'd," "th'enamour'd."
       p. 134 UNDERWOOD 2.4   7 And enamour'd, doe wish, so they might

enchanted. See "inchanted."

enclosed. See "inclos'd."

encounter   frequency: 1   relative frequency: 0.00001
       p. 62 EPIGRAMS 97   7 He wont was to encounter me, aloud,

encounter'd   frequency: 2   relative frequency: 0.00002
       p. 73 EPIGRAMS 112   19 And neuer art encounter'd, I confesse:
       p. 87 EPIGRAMS 133   135 But open, and vn-arm'd encounter'd all:

encourage   frequency: 1   relative frequency: 0.00001
       p. 64 EPIGRAMS 99   12 Thy fact is more: let truth encourage thee.

encreas'd   frequency: 1   relative frequency: 0.00001
       p. 371 UNGATHEREC 9   8 As fit to haue encreas'd the harmony

encrease   frequency: 6   relative frequency: 0.00008
       p. 60 EPIGRAMS 93   10 And thine owne goodnesse to encrease thy merit,
       p. 63 EPIGRAMS 97   10 Nor baudie stock, that trauells for encrease,
       p. 119 FOREST 13   94 For which you worthy are the glad encrease
       p. 264 UNDERWOOD 79   41 2. Shee, to the Crowne, hath brought encrease.
       p. 265 UNJERWOCD 79   56 Hee gives all plentie, and encrease,
       p. 384 UNGATHERED 18   20 And eu'ry birth encrease the heate of Loue.

encreast   frequency: 1   relative frequency: 0.00001
    p. 63 EPIGRAMS 99   1 That thou hast kept thy loue, encreast thy will,

end   frequency: 26   relative frequency: 0.00037
    See also "old-end."
  **p. 113 PANEGYRE   19 To this so cleare and sanctified an end,
    p. 27 EPIGRAMS 3   1 Thou, that mak'st gaine thy end, and wisely well,
    p. 33 EPIGRAMS 22   5 At sixe moneths end, shee parted hence
    p. 45 EPIGRAMS 59   3 Stinke, and are throwne away. End faire enough.
    p. 70 EPIGRAMS 109   7 Of seruice to the publique, when the end
    p. 72 EPIGRAMS 112   10 An Epick poeme; thou hast the same end.
    p. 114 FOREST 12   42 And, at her strong armes end, hold vp, and euen,
    p. 122 FOREST 15   8 To ought but grace, or ayme at other end.
    p. 162 UNDERWOOD 15   10 In dreames, begun in hope, and end in spoile.
    p. 165 UNDERWOOD 15   94 Lives to the Lord, but to the Ladies end.
    p. 166 UNDERWOOD 15   130 This Praecipice, and Rocks that have no end,
    p. 194 UNDERWOOD 38   105 Then Mistris, here, here let your rigour end,
    p. 244 UNDERWOOD 70   45 Hee stood, a Souldier to the last right end,
    p. 247 UNDERWOOD 70   111 Each stiled, by his end,
    p. 253 UNDERWOOD 75   29 Mariage, the end of life,
    p. 271 UNDERWOOD 83   91 That ever had beginning there, to'<h>ave end!
    p. 284 U'WOOD 84.9   68 Hope, hath her end! and Faith hath her reward!
    p. 287 U'WOOD 84.9   176 So charitable, to religious end,
    p. 288 U'WOOD 84.9   206 For his designed worke, the perfect end
    p. 315 HORACE 2   211 He ever hastens to the end, and so
    p. 329 HORACE 2   499 Playes were found out; and rest, the end, and
                               crowne
    p. 333 HORACE 2   586 And friendly should unto one end conspire.
    p. 337 HORACE 2   678 And, there an end of him, reciting makes:
    p. 394 UNGATHERED 28   18 And her, she made her Inmate, to the End,
    p. 399 UNGATHERED 31   14 All Circles had their spring and end
    p. 410 UNGATHERED 39   9 Thinking to stir me, thou hast lost thy End,

ended   frequency: 2   relative frequency: 0.00002
    p. 100 FOREST 4   4 My part is ended on thy stage.
    p. 421 UNGATHERED 49   3 Soe ended yor Epistle, myne beginns

endes   frequency: 2   relative frequency: 0.00002
  **p. 115 PANEGYRE   92 "Their lawes, their endes; the men she did
                               report:
    p. 384 UNGATHERED 18   6 That bid, God giue thee ioy, and haue no endes.

endew'd   frequency: 1   relative frequency: 0.00001
    p. 116 FOREST 13   10 With sinne and vice, though with a throne
                               endew'd;

endlesse   frequency: 2   relative frequency: 0.00002
    p. 217 UNDERWOOD 46   18 With endlesse labours, whilst thy learning drawes
    p. 294 UNDERWOOD 88   6 But thus, thus, keeping endlesse Holy-day,

endorse   frequency: 1   relative frequency: 0.00001
    See also "indorse."
    p. 228 UNDERWOOD 53   11 Nay, so your Seate his beauties did endorse,

ends   frequency: 15   relative frequency: 0.00021
    See also "endes."
    p. 45 EPIGRAMS 57   1 If, as their ends, their fruits were so, the
                               same,
    p. 55 EPIGRAMS 86   3 Then doe I loue thee, and behold thy ends
    p. 60 EPIGRAMS 94   5 But these, desir'd by you, the makers ends
    p. 68 EPIGRAMS 106   7 Thy standing vpright to thy selfe, thy ends
    p. 81 EPIGRAMS 128   6 Attend thee hence; and there, may all thy ends,
    p. 145 UNDERWOOD 5   4 Our owne false praises, for your ends:
    p. 156 UNDERWOOD 13   111 Her ends are honestie, and publike good!
    p. 170 UNDERWOOD 18   13 Except the way be errour to those ends:
    p. 171 UNDERWOOD 20   12 But their whole inside full of ends, and knots?
    p. 216 UNDERWOOD 45   11 Those are poore Ties, depend on those false
                               ends,
    p. 224 UNDERWOOD 50   28 And studie them unto the noblest ends,
    p. 242 UNDERWOOD 69   25 Never so great to get them: and the ends,
    p. 243 UNDERWOOD 70   29 But ever to no ends:
    p. 305 HORACE 2   5 Which in some swarthie fish uncomely ends:
    p. 398 UNGATHERED 30   89 I gratulate it to thee, and thy Ends,

endued. See "endew'd," "indu'd."

endure   frequency: 1   relative frequency: 0.00001
    See also "indure."
    p. 315 HORACE 2   233 To endure counsell: a Provider slow

endures   frequency: 1   relative frequency: 0.00001
    p. 387 UNGATHERED 22   8 to which there's no materiall that endures;

enemie   frequency: 3   relative frequency: 0.00004
    p. 71 EPIGRAMS 110   3 The name of POMPEY for an enemie,
    p. 158 UNDERWOOD 14   14 Pernitious enemie; we see, before
    p. 248 UNDERWOOD 71   4 Disease, the Enemie, and his Ingineeres,

enemies   frequency: 1   relative frequency: 0.00001
    p. 185 UNDERWOOD 31   4 Law, to his Law; and thinke your enemies his:

enemy. See "enemie."

enflamed   frequency: 1   relative frequency: 0.00001
    p. 110 FOREST 11   34 In our enflamed brests:

enforced   frequency: 1   relative frequency: 0.00001
    p. 380 UNGATHERED 12   54 And being at Flushing enforced to feele

enforcing   frequency: 1   relative frequency: 0.00001
    p. 363 UNGATHERED 3   9 Enforcing yron doores to yeeld it way,

engage   frequency: 1   relative frequency: 0.00001
    See also "ingage."
    p. 417 UNGATHERED 45   27 as the standerd shall engage hir,

engaged   frequency: 1   relative frequency: 0.00001
    p. 118 FOREST 13   47 Are you engaged to your happy fate,

engine   frequency: 2   relative frequency: 0.00002
    See also "engyne," "ingine."
    p. 71 EPIGRAMS 110   20 Action, or engine, worth a note of thine,
    p. 395 UNGATHERED 29   6 At least, if not the generall Engine cracke.

engineer. See "ingenyre," "inginer."

engineers. See "ingineeres."

engines   frequency: 2   relative frequency: 0.00002
    See also "ginnes."
    p. 101 FOREST 4   34 The engines, that haue them annoy'd;
    p. 212 UNDERWOOD 43   207 Engines of Murder, and receive the praise

england   frequency: 8   relative frequency: 0.00011
    p. 59 EPIGRAMS 92   31 With England. All forbidden bookes they get.
    p. 116 FOREST 12   94 Now thincking on you, though to England lost,
    p. 185 UNDERWOOD 30   t3 Lo: high Treasurer of England.
    p. 217 UNDERWOOD 46   t2 Lord chiefe Iustice of England.
    p. 248 UNDERWOOD 71   t2 the Lord high Treasurer of England.
    p. 250 UNDERWOOD 73   t2 Weston, L. high Treasurer of England,
    p. 252 UNDERWOOD 75   t7 Lord high Treasurer of England,
    p. 260 UNDERWOOD 77   t2 of England.

englands   frequency: 1   relative frequency: 0.00001
    p. 225 UNDERWOOD 51   13 Englands high Chancellor: the destin'd heire

english   frequency: 12   relative frequency: 0.00017
    p. 32 EPIGRAMS 18   t1 TO MY MEERE ENGLISH
                              CENSVRER.
    p. 56 EPIGRAMS 88   t1 ON ENGLISH MOVNSIEVR
    p. 83 EPIGRAMS 132   10 BARTAS doth wish thy English now were his.
    p. 115 FOREST 12   82 Had not their forme touch'd by an English wit.
    p. 207 UNDERWOOD 43   91 Was there mad<e> English: with a Grammar too,
    p. 214 UNDERWOOD 44   50 And keepe the Glorie of the English name,
    p. 214 UNDERWOOD 44   59 And there instruct the noble English heires
    p. 225 UNDERWOOD 51   10 Fame, and foundation of the English Weale.
    p. 397 UNGATHERED 30   57 That euer yet did fire the English blood!
    p. 398 UNGATHERED 30   69 So shall our English Youth vrge on, and cry
    p. 401 UNGATHERED 33   6 French Aire and English Verse here Wedded
                              lie.
    p. 402 UNGATHERED 33   12 The faire French Daughter to learne English
                              in;

english-rogue   frequency: 1   relative frequency: 0.00001
    p. 389 UNGATHERED 24   16 He would be call'd, henceforth, the
                              English-Rogue,

engrau'd   frequency: 1   relative frequency: 0.00001
    p. 71 EPIGRAMS 110   6 To haue engrau'd these acts, with his owne stile,

engraved. See "engrau'd."

engyne   frequency: 1   relative frequency: 0.00001
    p. 404 UNGATHERED 34   62 The Scene! the Engyne! but he now is come

enhance   frequency: 1   relative frequency: 0.00001
    p. 117 FOREST 13   42 And raise not vertue; they may vice enhance.

enioy   frequency: 4   relative frequency: 0.00005
  **p. 117 PANEGYRE   137 How deare a father they did now enioy
    p. 48 EPIGRAMS 64   13 Contends t'haue worth enioy, from his regard,
    p. 65 EPIGRAMS 101   42 The libertie, that wee'll enioy to night.
    p. 392 UNGATHERED 26 56 My gentle Shakespeare, must enioy a part.

enioyes   frequency: 1   relative frequency: 0.00001
    p. 110 FOREST 11   55 O, who is he, that (in this peace) enioyes

enjoy   frequency: 4   relative frequency: 0.00005
    See also "enioy," "irjoy," "t<o>'enjoy."
    p. 134 UNDERWOOD 2.4   8 But enjoy such a sight,
    p. 160 UNDERWOOD 14   66 Of others honours, thus, enjoy thine owne.
    p. 189 UNDERWOOD 36   1 Come, let us here enjoy the shade,
    p. 202 UNDERWOOD 42   81 Let the poore fooles enjoy their follies, love

enjoy'd   frequency: 3   relative frequency: 0.00004
    p. 204 UNDERWOOD 43   49 Thou mightst have yet enjoy'd thy crueltie
    p. 210 UNDERWOOD 43 168 Which thou hast only vented, not enjoy'd.
    p. 285 U'WOOD 84.9   105 You once enjoy'd: A short space severs yee,

enjoys. See "enioyes."

enlarg'd   frequency: 1   relative frequency: 0.00001
    p. 319 HORACE 2   295 But, as they conquer'd, and enlarg'd their bound,

enlarge   frequency: 1   relative frequency: 0.00001
    p. 235 UNDERWOOD 62   7 And, in these Cures, do'st so thy selfe enlarge,

enlive. See "t<o>'inlive."

ennius   frequency: 2   relative frequency: 0.00002
    p. 309 HORACE 2   81 Cato's and Ennius tongues have lent much worth,
    p. 323 HORACE 2   382 Of Accius, and Ennius, rare appeares:

ennoble   frequency: 1   relative frequency: 0.00001
    p. 185 UNDERWOOD 30   6 What is there more that can ennoble blood?

enormity   frequency: 1   relative frequency: 0.00001
    p. 405 UNGATHERED 34 81 Disguisd? and thence drag forth Enormity?

enough   frequency: 22   relative frequency: 0.00031
    See also "inough," "inoughe," "inow," "ynow."
   *p. 493 TO HIMSELF   39 Which, if they are torne, and turn'd, &
                             patch't enough,
    p. 30 EPIGRAMS 11   1 At court I met it, in clothes braue enough,
    p. 30 EPIGRAMS 11   2 To be a courtier; and lookes graue enough,
    p. 34 EPIGRAMS 23   6 And which no' affection praise enough can giue!
    p. 40 EPIGRAMS 43   4 Her foes enough would fame thee, in their hate.
    p. 45 EPIGRAMS 59   3 Stinke, and are throwne away. End faire enough.
    p. 93 FOREST 1   5 It is enough, they once did get
    p. 105 FOREST 8   26 Doe enough; and who would take
    p. 145 UNDERWOOD 4   12 Mine owne enough betray me.
    p. 145 UNDERWOOD 5   12 One good enough for a songs sake.
    p. 161 UNDERWOOD 14   77 Humanitie enough to be a friend,
    p. 166 UNDERWOOD 15 132 Is not enough now, but the Nights to play:
    p. 172 UNDERWOOD 21   3 Two letters were enough the plague to teare
    p. 174 UNDERWOOD 23   18 'Tis crowne enough to vertue still, her owne
                             applause.
    p. 205 UNDERWOOD 43   63 To redeeme mine, I had sent in; Enough,
    p. 232 UNDERWOOD 58   9 Will be reward enough: to weare like those,
    p. 235 UNDERWOOD 62   3 'T is not enough (thy pietie is such)
    p. 268 UNDERWOOD 82   14 Sate safe enough, but now secured more.
    p. 311 HORACE 2   140 'Tis not enough, th'elaborate Muse affords
    p. 319 HORACE 2   291 As loud enough to fill the seates, not yet
    p. 333 HORACE 2   593 But, now, it is enough to say; I make
    p. 420 UNGATHERED 48 14 That hath not Countrye impudence enough to
                             laughe att Arte,

enquire   frequency: 1   relative frequency: 0.00001
    p. 155 UNDERWOOD. 13 61 And seeke not wants to succour: but enquire,

enraged. See "inraged."

enshrin'd   frequency: 1   relative frequency: 0.00001
       p. 79 EPIGRAMS 125   8 The full, the flowing graces there enshrin'd;

ensign. See "ensigne."

ensigne   frequency: 2   relative frequency: 0.00002
       p. 160 UNDERWOOD 14   48 Forme, Art or Ensigne, that hath scap'd your
                                  sight?
       p. 273 U'WOOD 84.1   11 A dedicated Ensigne make

ensignes   frequency: 3   relative frequency: 0.00004
       p. 213 UNDERWOOD 44   11 All Ensignes of a Warre, are not yet dead,
       p. 254 UNDERWOOD 75   51 Porting the Ensignes of united Two,
       p. 292 UNDERWOOD 86   16 Will he display the Ensignes of thy warre.

ensigns. See "ensignes."

enspire   frequency: 1   relative frequency: 0.00001
       p. 81 EPIGRAMS 128   11 We each to other may this voyce enspire;

entail. See "entayle."

entailed. See "entayl'd."

entangling   frequency: 1   relative frequency: 0.00001
       p. 333 HORACE 2   604 Of an entangling suit; and bring 't about:

entayl'd   frequency: 1   relative frequency: 0.00001
       p. 75 EPIGRAMS 116   7 'Twas not entayl'd on title. That some word

entayle   frequency: 1   relative frequency: 0.00001
       p. 105 FOREST 8   39 Dare entayle their loues on any,

entend   frequency: 1   relative frequency: 0.00001
       p. 72 EPIGRAMS 112   9 I leaue thee there, and giuing way, entend

enter   frequency: 3   relative frequency: 0.00004
       p. 98 FOREST 3   69 Goe enter breaches, meet the cannons rage,
       p. 150 UNDERWOOD 10   2 How cam'st thou thus to enter me?
       p. 164 UNDERWOOD 15   79 For these with her young Companie shee'll enter,

entered. See "entred."

entering. See "entring."

entermixt   frequency: 1   relative frequency: 0.00001
       p. 413 UNGATHERED 41   26 (Divinest graces) are so entermixt,

entertain. See "entertaine," "entertayne."

entertaine   frequency: 2   relative frequency: 0.00002
       p. 224 UNDERWOOD 50   23 Only your time you better entertaine,
       p. 394 UNGATHERED 28   21 Then entertaine, and as Deaths Harbinger;

entertaining   frequency: 2   relative frequency: 0.00002
       p. 281 U'WOOD 84.4   71 Thou entertaining in thy brest,
       p. 368 UNGATHERED 6   82 In entertaining late

entertainment. See "entertaynment."

entertayne   frequency: 1   relative frequency: 0.00001
       p. 95 FOREST 2   80 To entertayne them; or the countrey came,

entertaynment   frequency: 1   relative frequency: 0.00001
       p. 64 EPIGRAMS 101   8 The entertaynment perfect: not the cates.

entheate   frequency: 1   relative frequency: 0.00001
       p. 368 UNGATHERED 6   61 With entheate rage, to publish their bright
                                  tracts?

#enthousiastike   frequency: 1   relative frequency: 0.00001
       p. 364 UNGATHERED 5   t1 Ode #enthousiastike.

entire. See "intire."

entitle   frequency: 1   relative frequency: 0.00001
       p. 187 UNDERWOOD 33   11 All mouthes, that dare entitle them (from hence)

entrailes   frequency: 2   relative frequency: 0.00002
       p. 88 EPIGRAMS 133 146 The heads, houghs, entrailes, and the hides of
                                  dogs:

entrailes (cont.)
    p. 317 HORACE 2   266 His Nephews entrailes; nor must Progne flie

entrails. See "entrailes."

entranc'd   frequency: 1 relative frequency: 0.00001
    p. 116 FOREST 12   90 From braines entranc'd, and fill'd with extasies;

entrance   frequency: 2 relative frequency: 0.00002
  **p. 112 PANEGYRE   t5 ENTRANCE OF IAMES,
    p. 109 FOREST 11   7 Some way of entrance) we must plant a guard

entreat. See "intreat."

entreaties. See "intreaties."

entreaty. See "intreaty."

entred   frequency: 1 relative frequency: 0.00001
    p. 244 UNDERWOOD 70   33 Hee entred well, by vertuous parts,

entrenchment. See "intrenchmt."

entring   frequency: 1 relative frequency: 0.00001
  **p. 117 PANEGYRE   139 And entring with the power of a king,

entry   frequency: 1 relative frequency: 0.00001
    p. 85 EPIGRAMS 133   58 But hold my torch, while I describe the entry

entwine. See "intwine."

enuie   frequency: 8 relative frequency: 0.00011
    p. 37 EPIGRAMS 32   4 What not the enuie of the seas reach'd too,
    p. 41 EPIGRAMS 45   6 Will man lament the state he should enuie?
    p. 44 EPIGRAMS 55   10 For writing better, I must enuie thee.
    p. 47 EPIGRAMS 63   7 Who can behold all enuie so declin'd
    p. 58 EPIGRAMS 91   11 To any one, were enuie: which would liue
    p. 66 EPIGRAMS 102   16 Whose life, eu'n they, that enuie it, must
                               praise;
    p. 72 EPIGRAMS 111   14 They murder him againe, that enuie thee.
    p. 369 UNGATHERED 6   95 And (in the place) enuie

enuies   frequency: 2 relative frequency: 0.00002
  **p. 115 PANEGYRE   84 "Vnto as many enuies, there, as eyes.
    p. 398 UNGATHERED 30   93 I call the world, that enuies mee, to see

enuious   frequency: 5 relative frequency: 0.00007
  *p. 493 TO HIMSELF   49 As curious fooles, and enuious of thy straine,
    p. 93 FOREST 2   1 Thou art not, PENSHVRST, built to
                               enuious show,
    p. 101 FOREST 4   47 Where enuious arts professed be,
    p. 103 FOREST 6   21 And the enuious, when they find
    p. 107 FOREST 10   7 PHOEBVS. No? tend thy cart still. Enuious
                               day

enuy   frequency: 9 relative frequency: 0.00013
  *p. 492 TO HIMSELF   20 Enuy them not, their palate's with the swine.
    p. 67 EPIGRAMS 104   16 If not, 'tis fit for you, some should enuy.
    p. 95 FOREST 2   68 A waiter, doth my gluttony enuy:
    p. 99 FOREST 3   92 Shalt neither that, nor this enuy:
    p. 115 FOREST 12   70 And, who doth me (though I not him) enuy,
    p. 389 UNGATHERED 24   22 Faire Aemulation, and no Enuy is;
    p. 390 UNGATHERED 26   1 To draw no enuy (Shakespeare) on thy name,
    p. 401 UNGATHERED 32   13 Before this worke? where Enuy hath not cast
    p. 405 UNGATHERED 34   70 To be worth Enuy. Henceforth I doe meane

enuy'   frequency: 1 relative frequency: 0.00001
    p. 71 EPIGRAMS 110   14 And that, midst enuy' and parts; then fell by
                               rage:

enuyous   frequency: 1 relative frequency: 0.00001
    p. 361 UNGATHERED 1   8 Vnseason'd ffrostes, or the most enuyous weather.

envi'd   frequency: 3 relative frequency: 0.00004
    See also "envy'd," "th'enuy'd."
    p. 138 UNDERWOOD 2.6   28 To be envi'd of the Queene.
    p. 162 UNDERWOOD 15   24 Honour'd at once, and envi'd (if it can
    p. 309 HORACE 2   79 Or Varius? Why am I now envi'd so,

envie   frequency: 12   relative frequency: 0.00017
    p. 147 UNDERWOOD 7   9 They yet may envie me:
    p. 161 UNDERWOOD 14   79 Thy gift 'gainst envie. O how I doe count
    p. 162 UNDERWOOD 15   22 Till envie wound, or maime it at a blow!
    p. 173 UNDERWOOD 22   20 That envie wish'd, and Nature fear'd.
    p. 176 UNDERWOOD 25   7 Or the times envie:
    p. 189 UNDERWOOD 36   3 Though Envie oft his shadow be,
    p. 250 UNDERWOOD 73   1 Looke up, thou seed of envie, and still bring
    p. 259 UNDERWOOD 76   18 All the envie of the Rymes,
    p. 260 UNDERWOOD 76   30 This would all their envie burst:
    p. 271 UNDERWOOD 83   83 If you can envie your owne Daughters blisse,
    p. 283 U'WOOD 84.9   36 I envie it the Angels amitie!
    p. 416 UNGATHERED 43   10 Of Subiects; Let such envie, till they burst.

envies. See "enuies."

envious   frequency: 7   relative frequency: 0.00010
    See also "enuious," "enuyous."
    p. 146 UNDERWOOD 6   1 Hang up those dull, and envious fooles,
    p. 167 UNDERWOOD 15   167 Of the poore sufferers) where the envious, proud,
    p. 188 UNDERWOOD 34   1 Envious and foule Disease, could there not be
    p. 203 UNDERWOOD 43   13 That since thou tak'st all envious care and
                             paine,
    p. 238 UNDERWOOD 65   9 And there to stand so. Hast now, envious Moone,
    p. 250 UNDERWOOD 73   t5 To the Envious.
    p. 256 UNDERWOOD 75   119 It is: to th' envious meant

envoy. See "l'envoye."

envy   frequency: 3   relative frequency: 0.00004
    See also "enuie," "enuy," "enuy'," "envie,"
        "envye," "t'enuy."
    p. 202 UNDERWOOD 42   85 Bawd, in a Velvet scabberd! I envy
    p. 272 U'WOOD 84.1   3 Their Heads, that ENVY would hold downe
    p. 287 U'WOOD 84.9   162 T'have knowne no envy, but by suffring it!

envy'd   frequency: 1   relative frequency: 0.00001
    p. 234 UNDERWOOD 60   17 And only, his great Soule envy'd,

envye   frequency: 1   relative frequency: 0.00001
    p. 421 UNGATHERED 48   41 The Rebell Gyantes stoope, and Gorgon Envye
                             yeild,

ephesus   frequency: 1   relative frequency: 0.00001
    p. 211 UNDERWOOD 43   194 'Bove all your Fire-workes, had at Ephesus,

epic. See "epick."

epicene. See "epicoene."

epick   frequency: 1   relative frequency: 0.00001
    p. 72 EPIGRAMS 112   10 An Epick poeme; thou hast the same end.

epicks   frequency: 1   relative frequency: 0.00001
    p. 307 HORACE 2   64 Lay that aside, the Epicks office is.

epicoene   frequency: 1   relative frequency: 0.00001
    p. 222 UNDERWOOD 49   8 And in an Epicoene fury can write newes

epic's. See "epicks."

epidemical. See "epidemicall."

epidemicall   frequency: 1   relative frequency: 0.00001
    p. 237 UNDERWOOD 64   18 The truly Epidemicall disease!

epigram   frequency: 24   relative frequency: 0.00034
    See also "epigramme."
    p. 29 EPIGRAMS 9   3 'Tis 'gainst the manners of an Epigram:
    p. 185 UNDERWOOD 30   t1 An Epigram
    p. 185 UNDERWOOD 31   t1 An Epigram.
    p. 186 UNDERWOOD 33   t1 An Epigram to the Councellour that
    p. 188 UNDERWOOD 34   t1 An Epigram.
    p. 217 UNDERWOOD 46   t1 An Epigram on Sir Edward Coke, when he was
    p. 222 UNDERWOOD 49   t1 An Epigram
    p. 224 UNDERWOOD 50   t1 An Epigram.
    p. 228 UNDERWOOD 53   t1 An Epigram.
    p. 232 UNDERWOOD 58   t1 Epigram, to my Book-seller.
    p. 232 UNDERWOOD 59   t1 An Epigram.
    p. 234 UNDERWOOD 61   t1 An Epigram.

epigram (cont.)
    p. 235 UNDERWOOD 62   t1 An Epigram.
    p. 235 UNDERWOOD 63   t3 An Epigram Consolatorie.
    p. 236 UNDERWOOD 64   t1 An Epigram.
    p. 237 UNDERWOOD 65   t1 An Epigram on the Princes birth.
    p. 238 UNDERWOOD 66   t1 An Epigram to the Queene, then lying in.
    p. 241 UNDERWOOD 68   t1 An Epigram,
    p. 241 UNDERWOOD 69   t1 Epigram.
    p. 249 UNDERWOOD 72   t2 An Epigram Anniversarie.
    p. 260 UNDERWOOD 77   t3 An Epigram.
    p. 262 UNDERWOOD 78   t1 An Epigram
    p. 407 UNGATHERED 36   t1 To a ffreind an Epigram
    p. 415 UNGATHERED 43   t1 AN EPIGRAM TO MY IOVIALL

epigramme   frequency: 3   relative frequency: 0.00004
    p. 51 EPIGRAMS 73   2 Or take an Epigramme so fearefully:
    p. 66 EPIGRAMS 102   2 It is an Epigramme, on all man-kind;
    p. 73 EPIGRAMS 112   15 Where shall I scape thee? in an Epigramme?

epigrammes   frequency: 7   relative frequency: 0.00010
    p. 27 EPIGRAMS 2   2 Thy title, Epigrammes, and nam'd of mee,
    p. 27 GENERAL TITLE   t1 EPIGRAMMES.
    p. 32 EPIGRAMS 18   1 To thee, my way in Epigrammes seemes new,
    p. 36 EPIGRAMS 28   20 May heare my Epigrammes, but like of none.
    p. 38 EPIGRAMS 36   1 MARTIAL, thou gau'st farre nobler
                              Epigrammes
    p. 42 EPIGRAMS 49   2 He sayes, I want the tongue of Epigrammes;
    p. 62 EPIGRAMS 96   2 When I dare send my Epigrammes to thee?

epigrams. See "epigrammes."

epilogue   frequency: 1   relative frequency: 0.00001
    See also "th'epilogue."
    p. 344 HORACE 1   222 ... . the Epilogue ....

epistle   frequency: 13   relative frequency: 0.00018
    See also "pistle."
    p. 113 FOREST 12   t1 Epistle
    p. 116 FOREST 13   t1 Epistle.
    p. 153 UNDERWOOD 13   t1 An Epistle to Sir EDWARD SACVILE,
    p. 158 UNDERWOOD 14   t1 An Epistle to Master
    p. 162 UNDERWOOD 15   t1 An Epistle to a Friend, to perswade
    p. 169 UNDERWOOD 17   t1 Epistle
    p. 189 UNDERWOOD 37   t1 An Epistle to a friend.
    p. 216 UNDERWOOD 45   t1 An Epistle to Master
    p. 218 UNDERWOOD 47   t1 An Epistle answering to one that
    p. 229 UNDERWOOD 54   t1 Epistle
    p. 230 UNDERWOOD 56   t1 Epistle.
    p. 248 UNDERWOOD 71   t3 An Epistle Mendicant.
    p. 421 UNGATHERED 49   3 Soe ended yor Epistle, myne beginns

epistolar. See "thy'epistolar."

epitaph   frequency: 10   relative frequency: 0.00014
    p. 51 EPIGRAMS 73   18 Item, an epitaph on my lords cock,
    p. 77 EPIGRAMS 120   t1 EPITAPH ON S<ALOMON> P<AVY> A
                              CHILD
    p. 79 EPIGRAMS 124   t1 EPITAPH ON ELIZABETH, L. H.
    p. 151 UNDERWOOD 12   t1 An Epitaph on Master
    p. 152 UNDERWOOD 12   38 An Epitaph, deserv'd a Tombe:
    p. 168 UNDERWOOD 16   t1 An Epitaph on Master
    p. 188 UNDERWOOD 35   t1 An Epitaph.
    p. 233 UNDERWOOD 60   t1 An Epitaph, on HENRY
    p. 371 UNGATHERED 9   5 To fill an Epitaph. But she had more.
    p. 371 UNGATHERED 9   t1 Epitaph.

epithalamion   frequency: 1   relative frequency: 0.00001
    p. 252 UNDERWOOD 75   t1 EPITHALAMION;

epithets. See "epithites."

epithites   frequency: 1   relative frequency: 0.00001
    p. 394 UNGATHERED 28   8 A list of Epithites: And prayse this way.

epitome   frequency: 2   relative frequency: 0.00002
    p. 185 UNDERWOOD 30   4 Thy Universe, though his Epitome.
    p. 214 UNDERWOOD 44   43 O happie Art! and wise Epitome

epode   frequency: 2   relative frequency: 0.00002
    p. 108 FOREST 10   30 And now an Epode to deepe eares I sing.

epode (cont.)
   p. 109 FOREST 11   t1 EPODE.

equal. See "equall."

equall   frequency: 12   relative frequency: 0.00017
  **p. 114 PANEGYRE   54 Her brightest tyre; and, in it, equall shone
    p. 47 EPIGRAMS 63   8 By constant suffring of thy equall mind;
    p. 67 EPIGRAMS 104   4 A new SVSANNA, equall to that old?
    p. 99 FOREST 3   80 And thinke his power doth equall Fates.
    p. 103 FOREST 6   12 Till you equall with the store,
    p. 110 FOREST 11   51 In equall knots: This beares no brands, nor
                          darts,
    p. 114 FOREST 12   49 How many equall with the Argiue Queene,
    p. 181 UNDERWOOD 27 22 Equall with her? or Ronsart prais'd
    p. 222 UNDERWOOD 49   9 Equall with that, which for the best newes goes,
    p. 260 UNDERWOOD 77   8 Have left in fame to equall, or out-goe
    p. 286 U'WOOD 84.9 146 Equall with Angels, and Co-heires of it?
    p. 305 HORACE 2   11 But equall power, to Painter, and to Poet,

equall'd   frequency: 1   relative frequency: 0.00001
    p. 281 U'WOOD 84.8 12 When your owne Vertues, equall'd have their
                         Names,

equally   frequency: 2   relative frequency: 0.00002
    p. 64 EPIGRAMS 101   2 Doe equally desire your companie:
    p. 67 EPIGRAMS 104 15 And like it too; if they looke equally:

equitie   frequency: 1   relative frequency: 0.00001
    p. 211 UNDERWOOD 43 178 A Court of Equitie should doe us right,

equity. See "equitie."

erat.   frequency: 1   relative frequency: 0.00001
    p. 240 UNDERWOOD 67 31 6. ERAT. Shee showes so farre above

erato. See "erat."

ere   frequency: 22   relative frequency: 0.00031
    See also "e're," "ere't," "e're't."
   *p. 493 TO HIMSELF   46 Ere yeares haue made thee old;
   *p. 494 TO HIMSELF   58 No Harpe ere hit the starres;
  **p. 117 PANEGYRE   141 That wan affections, ere his steps wan ground;
    p. 35 EPIGRAMS 27   6 If any pious life ere lifted man
    p. 36 EPIGRAMS 30   4 And person to the world; ere I thy name.
    p. 41 EPIGRAMS 44   3 Ere blacks were bought for his owne funerall,
    p. 50 EPIGRAMS 70   4 On the true causes, ere they grow too old.
    p. 54 EPIGRAMS 84   3 And, ere I could aske you, I was preuented:
    p. 57 EPIGRAMS 90   3 Was dull, and long, ere shee would goe to man:
    p. 58 EPIGRAMS 92   1 Ere cherries ripe, and straw-berries be gone,
    p. 60 EPIGRAMS 94   9 For none ere tooke that pleasure in sinnes sense,
    p. 62 EPIGRAMS 97   8 Where ere he met me; now hee's dumbe, or proud.
    p. 65 EPIGRAMS 101 20 Knat, raile, and ruffe too. How so ere, my man
    p. 67 EPIGRAMS 103 13 My praise is plaine, and where so ere profest,
    p. 72 EPIGRAMS 112   5 Thy all, at all: and what so ere I doe,
    p. 72 EPIGRAMS 112 12 Next morne, an Ode: Thou mak'st a song ere
                          night.
    p. 74 EPIGRAMS 115 22 'Twill see it's sister naked, ere a sword.
    p. 106 FOREST 8   44 And will, long ere thou should'st starue,
    p. 264 UNDERWOOD 79 36 1. Where ere they tread th'enamour'd ground,
    p. 307 HORACE 2   58 Nor language, nor cleere order ere forsakes.
    p. 406 UNGATHERED 34 97 What Poesy ere was painted on a wall
    p. 406 UNGATHERED 34 101 Lyue long ye ffeasting Roome. And ere thou
                          burne

e're   frequency: 22   relative frequency: 0.00031
    p. 48 EPIGRAMS 65 15 But I repent me: Stay. Who e're is rais'd,
    p. 141 UNDERWOOD 2.9 29 Rising through it e're it came;
    p. 148 UNDERWOOD 7   27 What Nymph so e're his voyce but heares,
    p. 151 UNDERWOOD 12   10 Yet he broke them, e're they could him,
    p. 152 UNDERWOOD 12   37 Reader, whose life, and name, did e're become
    p. 157 UNDERWOOD 13 127 Sydney e're night! or that did goe to bed
    p. 185 UNDERWOOD 31   2 Lawes, and no change e're come to one decree:
    p. 192 UNDERWOOD 38 45 An ill-affected limbe (what e're it aile)
    p. 192 UNDERWOOD 38 56 Why was't? did e're the Cloudes aske back their
                         raine?
    p. 193 UNDERWOOD 38 98 On every wall, and sung where e're I walke.
    p. 199 UNDERWOOD 41 12 Winter is come a Quarter e're his Time,
    p. 201 UNDERWOOD 42 40 To doe her Husbands rites in, e're 'twere gone
    p. 209 UNDERWOOD 43 136 And raz'd, e're thought could urge, This might
                         have bin!

e're (cont.)
p. 242 UNDERWOOD 70   6 E're thou wert halfe got out,
p. 246 UNDERWOOD 70   85 Jonson, who sung this of him, e're he went
p. 247 UNDERWOOD 70 127 Who, e're the first downe bloomed on the chin,
p. 257 UNDERWOOD 75 144 One to the other, long e're these to light were
                           brought.
p. 265 UNDERWOOD 79   58 Where e're he goes upon the ground,
p. 269 UNDERWOOD 83   12 And e're I can aske more of her, shee's gone!
p. 329 HORACE 2   508 The truth; nor let thy Fable thinke, what e're
p. 363 UNGATHERED 3   6 It carries Palme with it, (where e're it goes)
p. 409 UNGATHERED 37 14 If such a Tyke as thou, er'e wer't, or noe?

erect   frequency: 1   relative frequency: 0.00001
p. 261 UNDERWOOD 77   26 In glorious Piles, or Pyramids erect

erected   frequency: 1   relative frequency: 0.00001
p. 157 UNDERWOOD 13 141 It was erected; and still walking under

ere't   frequency: 1   relative frequency: 0.00001
p. 417 UNGATHERED 45 11 I shall think on't ere't be day.

e're't   frequency: 1   relative frequency: 0.00001
p. 154 UNDERWOOD 13   34 That puts it in his Debt-booke e're't be done;

eridanus   frequency: 1   relative frequency: 0.00001
p. 369 UNGATHERED 6 109 In heau'n the Signe of old Eridanus:

err. See "erre."

errant   frequency: 1   relative frequency: 0.00001
p. 205 UNDERWOOD 43   67 Of errant Knight-hood, with the<ir> Dames, and
                           Dwarfes,

errant'st   frequency: 1   relative frequency: 0.00001
p. 75 EPIGRAMS 115   34 Then, The townes honest Man's her errant'st
                           knaue.

err'd   frequency: 1   relative frequency: 0.00001
p. 159 UNDERWOOD 14   19 Though I confesse (as every Muse hath err'd,

erre   frequency: 5   relative frequency: 0.00007
p. 83 EPIGRAMS 131   10 Euen those for whom they doe this, know they
                           erre:
p. 83 EPIGRAMS 132   5 How can I speake of thy great paines, but erre?
p. 139 UNDERWOOD 2.7   9 Nay, you may erre in this,
p. 255 UNDERWOOD 75   99 Great Say-Master of State, who cannot erre,
p. 370 UNGATHERED 7   14 Being tould there, Reason cannot, Sense may
                           erre.

error   frequency: 4   relative frequency: 0.00005
See also "errour."
p. 77 EPIGRAMS 120   17 So, by error, to his fate
p. 110 FOREST 11   35 But this doth from the<ir> cloud of error grow,
p. 118 FOREST 13   60 Farre from the maze of custome, error, strife,
p. 325 HORACE 2   439 Whether truth may, and whether error bring.

errors   frequency: 2   relative frequency: 0.00002
See also "errours."
p. 76 EPIGRAMS 119   13 And, in their errors maze, thine owne way know:
p. 177 UNDERWOOD 25   28 If subject to the jealous errors

errour   frequency: 2   relative frequency: 0.00002
p. 170 UNDERWOOD 18   13 Except the way be errour to those ends:
p. 192 UNDERWOOD 38   37 Errour and folly in me may have crost

errours   frequency: 1   relative frequency: 0.00001
p. 160 UNDERWOOD 14   42 What blots and errours, have you watch'd and
                           purg'd

escape. See "scape," "t<o>'escape," "th'escape."

escaped. See "scap'd."

escapes   frequency: 1   relative frequency: 0.00001
p. 50 EPIGRAMS 70   6 Each best day of our life escapes vs, first.

eschylus   frequency: 1   relative frequency: 0.00001
p. 319 HORACE 2   315 With lees of Wine. Next Eschylus, more late,

escutcheons. See "scutcheons."

esme   frequency: 2   relative frequency: 0.00002
    p. 80 EPIGRAMS 127   t1 TO ESME, LORD 'AVBIGNY.
    p. 252 UNDERWOOD 75   t10 Daughter of ESME D. of Lenox deceased,

especially   frequency: 1   relative frequency: 0.00001
    p. 205 UNDERWOOD 43   61 Especially in paper; that, that steame

espie   frequency: 2   relative frequency: 0.00002
    p. 256 UNDERWOOD 75   110 Could soone espie
    p. 315 HORACE 2   216 Falshood with truth, as no man can espie

esplandians. See "th'esplandians."

espy. See "espie."

esquire   frequency: 1   relative frequency: 0.00001
    See also "esqvire."
    p. 395 UNGATHERED 29   t4 Esquire.

esqvire   frequency: 1   relative frequency: 0.00001
    p. 42 EPIGRAMS 48   t1 ON MVNGRIL ESQVIRE.

essayed. See "assay'd," "'ssayd."

essayes   frequency: 2   relative frequency: 0.00002
    p. 30 EPIGRAMS 12   15 That lost, he keepes his chamber, reades
                              Essayes,
    p. 287 U'WOOD 84.9   181 For her devotions, and those sad essayes

essays. See "assaies," "essayes."

essence   frequency: 3   relative frequency: 0.00004
    p. 110 FOREST 11   45 That is an essence, farre more gentle, fine,
    p. 179 UNDERWOOD 25   37 When her dead essence (like the Anatomie
    p. 236 UNDERWOOD 63   13 For God, whose essence is so infinite,

estate   frequency: 3   relative frequency: 0.00004
    See also "state."
    p. 114 FOREST 12   36 Worth an estate, treble to that you haue.
    p. 331 HORACE 2   572 Vice, and, am knowne to have a Knights estate.
    p. 419 UNGATHERED 47   5 God blesse the Councell of Estate,

estates   frequency: 1   relative frequency: 0.00001
    p. 235 UNDERWOOD 62   11 O pietie! so to weigh the poores estates!

esteem. See "dis-esteeme," "esteeme."

esteeme   frequency: 2   relative frequency: 0.00002
    p. 64 EPIGRAMS 101   6 Something, which, else, could hope for no
                              esteeme.
    p. 114 FOREST 12   21 The truth of times) was once of more esteeme,

esteemed   frequency: 1   relative frequency: 0.00001
    See also "dis-esteem'd."
    p. 383 UNGATHERED 17   t1 To his much and worthily esteemed

estimate   frequency: 1   relative frequency: 0.00001
    p. 161 UNDERWOOD 14   75 And estimate thy Paines; as having wrought

etcetera. See "&c." (which follows).

&c.   frequency: 1   relative frequency: 0.00001

eteostichs   frequency: 1   relative frequency: 0.00001
    p. 204 UNDERWOOD 43   36 Or Eteostichs, or those finer flammes

eteostics. See "eteostichs."   +

eternal. See "aeternall," "eternall," "th'aeternall," "th'eternall."

eternall   frequency: 11   relative frequency: 0.00015
    p. 127 UNDERWOOD 1.1   17 5. Eternall Father, God, who did'st create
    p. 128 UNDERWOOD 1.1   21 6. Eternall God the Sonne, who not denyd'st
    p. 128 UNDERWOOD 1.1   25 7. Eternall Spirit, God from both proceeding,
    p. 181 UNDERWOOD 27   16 Whose fame hath an eternall voice?
    p. 245 UNDERWOOD 70   81 To see that bright eternall Day:
    p. 274 U'WOOD 84.1   39 Of that eternall Port kept ope'
    p. 283 U'WOOD 84.9   48 To heare their Judge, and his eternall doome;

eternall (cont.)
```
     p. 284 U'WOOD 84.9     63 That great eternall Holy-day of rest,
     p. 286 U'WOOD 84.9    145 In his eternall Kingdome, where we sit
     p. 288 U'WOOD 84.9    197 To that eternall Rest, where now sh'hath place
     p. 294 UNDERWOOD 89     2 Thou worthy in eternall Flower to fare,
```

eternitie   frequency: 4   relative frequency: 0.00005
```
     p.  58 EPIGRAMS 91      8 Whose rellish to eternitie shall last.
     p. 175 UNDERWOOD 24     4 Doth vindicate it to eternitie.
     p. 271 UNDERWOOD 83    68 Became her Birth-day to Eternitie!
     p. 285 U'WOOD 84.9    106 Compar'd unto that long eternitie,
```

eternity. See "eternitie."

eternity's. See "aeternities."

eterniz'd   frequency: 1   relative frequency: 0.00001
```
     p.  89 EPIGRAMS 133   195 And I could wish for their eterniz'd sakes,
```

ethnicism. See "ethnicisme."

ethnicisme   frequency: 1   relative frequency: 0.00001
```
     p. 401 UNGATHERED 32   22 Of Ethnicisme, makes his Muse a Saint.
```

etna. See "aetna."

etnean. See "aetnean."

euclid. See "euclide."

euclide   frequency: 1   relative frequency: 0.00001
```
     p. 402 UNGATHERED 34    4 Able to talk of Euclide, and correct
```

euen   frequency: 14   relative frequency: 0.00020
```
     p.  44 EPIGRAMS 55      9 When euen there, where most thou praysest mee,
     p.  52 EPIGRAMS 76     14 I purpos'd her; that should, with euen powers,
     p.  64 EPIGRAMS 99     10 And euen the praisers iudgement suffers so.
     p.  67 EPIGRAMS 104     2 Euen in the dew of grace, what you would bee?
     p.  67 EPIGRAMS 105     5 But euen their names were to be made a-new,
     p.  82 EPIGRAMS 130    10 Of old, euen by her practise, to be fam'd;
     p.  83 EPIGRAMS 131    10 Euen those for whom they doe this, know they
                               erre:
     p.  96 FOREST 2        95 Each morne, and euen, they are taught to pray,
     p. 104 FOREST 7         7 At morne, and euen, shades are longest;
     p. 110 FOREST 11       48 Whose linkes are bright, and euen,
     p. 114 FOREST 12       42 And, at her strong armes end, hold vp, and euen,
     p. 118 FOREST 13       61 And keepe an euen, and vnalter'd gaite;
     p. 392 UNGATHERED 26   66 Liues in his issue, euen so, the race
     p. 423 UNGATHERED 50   13 Euen states most hated, when no lawes resist
```

euening   frequency: 1   relative frequency: 0.00001
```
     p.  61 EPIGRAMS 94     16 The Muses euening, as their morning-starre.
```

euening's   frequency: 1   relative frequency: 0.00001
```
     p.  99 FOREST 3       100 Thy morning's, and thy euening's vow
```

euenly   frequency: 1   relative frequency: 0.00001
```
     p.  62 EPIGRAMS 96      4 And, in thy censures, euenly, dost take
```

euents   frequency: 1   relative frequency: 0.00001
```
     p.  62 EPIGRAMS 95     32 The councells, actions, orders, and euents
```

euer   frequency: 18   relative frequency: 0.00026
```
     p.  37 EPIGRAMS 32      9 Which shewes, where euer death doth please
                               t<o>'appeare,
     p.  39 EPIGRAMS 40     10 And like Nectar euer flowing:
     p.  40 EPIGRAMS 42      3 Indeed, poore GILES repents he married euer.
     p.  63 EPIGRAMS 98     12 And euer is ill got without the first.
     p.  78 EPIGRAMS 122     8 I would restore, and keepe it euer such;
     p. 102 FOREST 5         3 Time will not be ours, for euer:
     p. 113 FOREST 11      115 And to his sense obiect this sentence euer,
     p. 118 FOREST 13      52 For he, that once is good, is euer great.
     p. 122 FOREST 15      16 How can I doubt to finde thee euer, here?
     p. 367 UNGATHERED 6   57 Who euer sipt at Baphyre riuer,
     p. 378 UNGATHERED 11  92 Euer his thighes Male then, and his braines
                               Shee.
     p. 379 UNGATHERED 12   1 Who euer he be, would write a Story at
     p. 380 UNGATHERED 12  29 And therefore how euer the trauelling nation,
     p. 385 UNGATHERED 20   5 I do not feele that euer yet I had
     p. 390 UNGATHERED 25   8 All, that was euer writ in brasse.
```

euer (cont.)
    p. 393 UNGATHERED 27   6 The Sunne that euer shineth,
    p. 397 UNGATHERED 30   57 That euer yet did fire the English blood!
    p. 402 UNGATHERED 34   6 The noblest Ingenyre that euer was!

euer-boyling   frequency: 1   relative frequency: 0.00001
    p. 88 EPIGRAMS 133   142 The euer-boyling floud. Whose bankes vpon

euer-lasting   frequency: 1   relative frequency: 0.00001
    p. 382 UNGATHERED 16   7 And as an euer-lasting Sacrifice

euery   frequency: 48   relative frequency: 0.00069
  *p. 492 TO HIMSELF   5 Indicting, and arraigning euery day
  *p. 493 TO HIMSELF   24 scraps, out <of> euery dish,
 **p. 113 PANEGYRE   6 To euery nooke and angle of his realme.
 **p. 114 PANEGYRE   45 And euery windore grieu'd it could not moue
 **p. 117 PANEGYRE   155 And this confession flew from euery voyce:
   p. 31 EPIGRAMS 12   19 To euery cause he meets, this voyce he brayes:
   p. 32 EPIGRAMS 16   2 Thou more; that with it euery day, dar'st iest
   p. 34 EPIGRAMS 23   3 Whose euery worke, of thy most earely wit,
   p. 36 EPIGRAMS 31   3 And though the soundest legs goe euery day,
   p. 42 EPIGRAMS 46   6 Yes, now he weares his knight-hood euery day.
   p. 42 EPIGRAMS 47   2 Hee that wooes euery widdow, will get none.
   p. 49 EPIGRAMS 66   15 Though euery fortitude deserues applause,
   p. 55 EPIGRAMS 84   7 I would haue spent: how euery Muse should know
                            it,
   p. 57 EPIGRAMS 89   6 Then CICERO, whose euery breath was fame:
   p. 58 EPIGRAMS 92   3 Ripe statesmen, ripe: They grow in euery street.
   p. 59 EPIGRAMS 92   21 They meet in sixes, and at euery mart,
   p. 59 EPIGRAMS 92   23 Or, euery day, some one at RIMEE'S looks,
   p. 67 EPIGRAMS 103   12 For euery part a character assign'd.
   p. 68 EPIGRAMS 106   3 All-vertuous HERBERT! on whose euery part
   p. 71 EPIGRAMS 110   19 In euery counsell, stratageme, designe,
   p. 74 EPIGRAMS 115   14 Giue euery one his dose of mirth: and watches
   p. 74 EPIGRAMS 115   23 At euery meale, where it doth dine, or sup,
   p. 75 EPIGRAMS 116   10 In men, but euery brauest was the best:
   p. 85 EPIGRAMS 133   52 Canst tell me best, how euery Furie lookes
                            there,
   p. 88 EPIGRAMS 133   166 When euery clerke eates artichokes, and peason,
   p. 94 FOREST 2   29 The painted partrich lyes in euery field,
   p. 94 FOREST 2   44 Hang on thy walls, that euery child may reach.
   p. 95 FOREST 2   78 Shine bright on euery harth as the desires
   p. 96 FOREST 2   96 With the whole houshold, and may, euery day,
   p. 99 FOREST 3   74 For euery price, in euery iarre,
   p. 101 FOREST 4   51 Where euery freedome is betray'd,
   p. 101 FOREST 4   52 And euery goodnesse tax'd, or grieu'd.
   p. 105 FOREST 8   38 Euery stew in towne to know;
   p. 108 FOREST 10 A   8 in whom the flame of euery beauty raignes,
   p. 113 FOREST 12   2 And almost euery vice, almightie gold,
   p. 113 FOREST 12   6 To euery squire, or groome, that will report
   p. 116 FOREST 13   8 With euery vertue, wheresoere it moue,
   p. 117 FOREST 13   30 Your beautie; for you see that euery day:
   p. 119 FOREST 13   87 And neuer thinke, how vice doth euery houre,
   p. 384 UNGATHERED 18   9 Not only this, but euery day of thine,
   p. 394 UNGATHERED 28   7 But euery Table in this Church can say,
   p. 394 UNGATHERED 28   10 Such things, of euery body, and as well.
   p. 395 UNGATHERED 29   5 At euery line some pinn thereof should slacke
   p. 397 UNGATHERED 30   54 With euery song, I sweare, and so would dye:
   p. 398 UNGATHERED 30   72 And will be bought of euery Lord, and Knight,
   p. 398 UNGATHERED 30   78 And stop my sight, in euery line I goe.
   p. 417 UNGATHERED 45   19 she desires of euery birth

eue'ry   frequency: 1   relative frequency: 0.00001
    p. 384 UNGATHERED 18   18 And eue'ry ioy, in mariage, turne a fruite.

euery-where   frequency: 1   relative frequency: 0.00001
    p. 122 FOREST 15   15 Dwell, dwell here still: O, being euery-where,

eugenian   frequency: 1   relative frequency: 0.00001
    p. 367 UNGATHERED 6   43 To the Eugenian dale;

euill   frequency: 1   relative frequency: 0.00001
 **p. 116 PANEGYRE   117 An euill king: And so must such be still,

eu'n   frequency: 1   relative frequency: 0.00001
    p. 66 EPIGRAMS 102   16 Whose life, eu'n they, that enuie it, must
                            praise;

eunomia. See "evnomia."

eupheme   frequency: 1   relative frequency: 0.00001
    p. 272 UNDERWOOD 84   t1 EUPHEME;

euripides   frequency: 1   relative frequency: 0.00001
    p. 391 UNGATHERED 26   34 Euripides, and Sophocles to vs,

europe   frequency: 4   relative frequency: 0.00005
    p. 58 EPIGRAMS 91   6 In th'eye of Europe, where thy deeds were done,
    p. 162 UNDERWOOD 15   2 Beates brave, and loude in Europe, and bids come
    p. 222 UNDERWOOD 48   48 The wished Peace of Europe:
    p. 391 UNGATHERED 26   42 To whom all Scenes of Europe homage owe.

europes   frequency: 2   relative frequency: 0.00002
    p. 368 UNGATHERED 6   83 The choise of Europes pride;
    p. 369 UNGATHERED 6   119 Of Europes waters can

eu'ry   frequency: 1   relative frequency: 0.00001
    p. 384 UNGATHERED 18   20 And eu'ry birth encrease the heate of Loue.

euterpe. See "evt."

euthanasee   frequency: 1   relative frequency: 0.00001
    p. 283 U'WOOD 84.9   40 To 'greet, or grieve her soft Euthanasee?

euthanasy. See "euthanasee."

even   frequency: 15   relative frequency: 0.00021
    See also "eene," "euen," "eu'n."
    p. 136 UNDERWOOD 2.5   24 And, above her even chin,
    p. 141 UNDERWOOD 2.9   19 Even nose, and cheeke (withall)
    p. 149 UNDERWOOD 8   11 Even ashes of lovers find no rest.
    p. 152 UNDERWOOD 12   23 They were so even, grave, and holy;
    p. 159 UNDERWOOD 14   15 A many'of bookes, even good judgements wound
    p. 163 UNDERWOOD 15   38 And even! our sports are dangers! what we call
    p. 165 UNDERWOOD 15   92 That may corrupt her, even in his eyes.
    p. 181 UNDERWOOD 26   24 Even in youth.
    p. 193 UNDERWOOD 38   72 It shakes even him, that all things else doth
                              shake.
    p. 218 UNDERWOOD 47   17 On all Soules that are absent; even the dead;
    p. 225 UNDERWOOD 51   15 Whose even Thred the Fates spinne round, and
                              full,
    p. 280 U'WOOD 84.4   55 So polisht, perfect, round, and even,
    p. 287 U'WOOD 84.9   165 But, kept an even gate, as some streight tree
    p. 339 HORACE 1   61 Is ... . even now to ......
    p. 415 UNGATHERED 42   16 Where it runs round, and even: where so well,

evening. See "euening."

evening's. See "euening's."

evenly. See "euenly."

events   frequency: 1   relative frequency: 0.00001
    See also "euents."
    p. 309 HORACE 2   108 After, mens Wishes, crown'd in their events,

ever   frequency: 36   relative frequency: 0.00052
    See also "ere," "e're," "euer," "euer-boyling,"
             "ever>," "how-so-e're."
    p. 132 UNDERWOOD 2.2   7 Love, if thou wilt ever see
    p. 135 UNDERWOOD 2.4   26 Or Swans Downe ever?
    p. 146 UNDERWOOD 6   10 If ever we will love aright.
    p. 152 UNDERWOOD 12   25 To licence ever was so light,
    p. 155 UNDERWOOD 13   79 But these men ever want: their very trade
    p. 159 UNDERWOOD 14   30 Ever at home: yet, have all Countries seene:
    p. 184 UNDERWOOD 29   51 Cramp'd for ever;
    p. 188 UNDERWOOD 34   11 Or Turners oyle of Talck. Nor ever got
    p. 190 UNDERWOOD 37   13 Which, how most sacred I will ever keepe,
    p. 197 UNDERWOOD 40   13 But ever without blazon, or least shade
    p. 198 UNDERWOOD 40   32 But the grave Lover ever was an Asse;
    p. 199 UNDERWOOD 42   3 No Poets verses yet did ever move,
    p. 205 UNDERWOOD 43   58 To make consumption, ever, where thou go'st;
    p. 207 UNDERWOOD 43   107 I now begin to doubt, if ever Grace,
    p. 216 UNDERWOOD 45   7 Nor ever trusted to that friendship yet,
    p. 216 UNDERWOOD 45   20 They cannot last. No lie grew ever old.
    p. 219 UNDERWOOD 47   30 Then these can ever be; or else wish none.
    p. 219 UNDERWOOD 47   36 Or that the Match from Spaine was ever meant?
    p. 219 UNDERWOOD 47   61 Still looking to, and ever loving heaven;
    p. 243 UNDERWOOD 70   29 But ever to no ends:
    p. 249 UNDERWOOD 72   17 And ever close the burden of the Song,

ever (cont.)
```
  p. 250 UNDERWOOD 73    10 To vertue, and true worth, be ever blind.
  p. 265 UNDERWOOD 79    61 Then ever PALES could, or PAN;
  p. 271 UNDERWOOD 83    91 That ever had beginning there, to'<h>ave end!
  p. 274 U'WOOD 84.2      4 That ever Nature, or the later Ayre
  p. 285 U'WOOD 84.9    113 There, all the happy soules, that ever were,
  p. 286 U'WOOD 84.9    124 A Musique in the Eares, will ever last;
  p. 287 U'WOOD 84.9    183 And came forth ever cheered, with the rod
  p. 294 UNDERWOOD 88    10 Can this decay, but is beginning ever.
  p. 309 HORACE 2        83 New names of things. It hath beene ever free,
  p. 309 HORACE 2        84 And ever will, to utter termes that bee
  p. 311 HORACE 2       151 And the severe, speech ever serious.
  p. 315 HORACE 2       211 He ever hastens to the end, and so
  p. 315 HORACE 2       230 Loves Dogges, and Horses; and is ever one
  p. 317 HORACE 2       256 Or acted told. But, ever, things that run
  p. 331 HORACE 2       556 Poets should ever be indifferent.
```

ever-greene   frequency: 1   relative frequency: 0.00001
```
  p. 272 U'WOOD 84.1      2 With ever-greene, and great renowne,
```

ever>   frequency: 1   relative frequency: 0.00001
```
  p. 148 UNDERWOOD 8      5 The body <ever> was
```

everlasting   frequency: 1   relative frequency: 0.00001
  See also "euer-lasting."
```
  p. 285 U'WOOD 84.9     92 What 'tis t<o>'enjoy an everlasting breath!
```

every   frequency: 42   relative frequency: 0.00060
  See also "euery," "eue'ry," "eu'ry," "ev'ry."
```
  p. 132 UNDERWOOD 2.2   12 Every Cloud about his eye;
  p. 138 UNDERWOOD 2.6   24 That at every motion sweld
  p. 140 UNDERWOOD 2.8   10 And excuse spun every day,
  p. 140 UNDERWOOD 2.8   23 To say over every purle
  p. 142 UNDERWOOD 2.9   53 Such a man, with every part,
  p. 149 UNDERWOOD 9      7 And every close did meet
  p. 156 UNDERWOOD 13   116 But like to be, that every day mends one,
  p. 159 UNDERWOOD 14    19 Though I confesse (as every Muse hath err'd,
  p. 164 UNDERWOOD 15    66 And every Dressing for a Pitfall set
  p. 165 UNDERWOOD 15   107 Coach'd, or on foot-cloth, thrice chang'd every
                           day,
  p. 166 UNDERWOOD 15   122 Brought on us, and will every houre increase.
  p. 167 UNDERWOOD 15   171 (Because th'are every where amongst Man-kind
  p. 172 UNDERWOOD 21     4 Out of his Grave, and poyson every eare.
  p. 177 UNDERWOOD 25    16 May shine (through every chincke) to every sight
  p. 182 UNDERWOOD 28    14 For Venus Ceston, every line you make.
  p. 193 UNDERWOOD 38    98 On every wall, and sung where e're I walke.
  p. 200 UNDERWOOD 42    28 At every stall; The Cittie Cap's a charme.
  p. 201 UNDERWOOD 42    57 Court every hanging Gowne, and after that,
  p. 218 UNDERWOOD 47    21 Call every night to Supper in these fitts,
  p. 239 UNDERWOOD 67    16 Let every Lyre be strung,
  p. 271 UNDERWOOD 83    72 To every Order, ev'ry Hierarchie!
  p. 271 UNDERWOOD 83    82 At pleasure, to be call'd for, every day!
  p. 273 U'WOOD 84.1     28 On every Stall.
  p. 275 U'WOOD 84.3      4 Where every lim takes like a face?
  p. 278 U'WOOD 84.4     22 Hence-forth may every line be you;
  p. 293 UNDERWOOD 86    37 Hard-hearted, I dreame every Night
  p. 305 HORACE 2         3 On every limbe, ta'en from a severall creature,
  p. 307 HORACE 2        47 The nailes, and every curled haire disclose;
  p. 311 HORACE 2       153 To every state of fortune; she helpes on,
  p. 315 HORACE 2       228 He knowes not why, and changeth every houre.
  p. 315 HORACE 2       232 To every vice, as hardly to be brought
  p. 321 HORACE 2       334 With poore base termes, through every baser shop:
  p. 321 HORACE 2       350 And so, as every man may hope the same;
  p. 323 HORACE 2       387 But every Judge hath not the facultie
  p. 325 HORACE 2       414 Had not our every Poet like offended.
  p. 325 HORACE 2       429 O I left-witted, that purge every spring
  p. 325 HORACE 2       452 Indeed, give fitting dues to every man.
  p. 329 HORACE 2       514 But he hath every suffrage, can apply
  p. 333 HORACE 2       598 That to the sale of Wares calls every Buyer;
  p. 418 UNGATHERED 47    3 And God blesse every living thing,
  p. 420 UNGATHERED 48   17 To every sence, and scorne to those that sawe
```

everywhere. See "euery-where."

evidence   frequency: 1   relative frequency: 0.00001
```
  p. 284 U'WOOD 84.9     58 Of that great Evidence, the Conscience!
```

evil   frequency: 1   relative frequency: 0.00001
  See also "euill," "evill."
```
  p. 290 UNDERWOOD 85    38 Loves cares so evil, and so great?
```

evill   frequency: 7   relative frequency: 0.00010
    p. 175 UNDERWOOD 24   3 Raising the World to good or evill fame,
    p. 187 UNDERWOOD 33   18 Or skill, to carry out an evill cause!
    p. 217 UNDERWOOD 46   6 In others evill best was understood:
    p. 235 UNDERWOOD 62   4 To cure the call'd Kings Evill with thy touch;
    p. 235 UNDERWOOD 62   6 To cure the Poets Evill, Povertie:
    p. 235 UNDERWOOD 62   8 As thou dost cure our Evill, at thy charge.
    p. 235 UNDERWOOD 62   14 But, that he cure the Peoples Evill too?

evils   frequency: 2   relative frequency: 0.00002
    p. 212 UNDERWOOD 43   214 And all the Evils that flew out of her box
    p. 315 HORACE 2   241 The old man many evils doe girt round;

evnomia   frequency: 1   relative frequency: 0.00001
  **p. 113 PANEGYRE   24 Faire DICE, and EVNOMIA; who were said

ev'ry   frequency: 6   relative frequency: 0.00008
    p. 201 UNDERWOOD 42   54 To ev'ry Petticote he brush'd, and Glove
    p. 250 UNDERWOOD 74   3 When shee puts forth the life of ev'ry thing:
    p. 251 UNDERWOOD 74   10 Rare Plants from ev'ry banke doe rise,
    p. 251 UNDERWOOD 74   11 And ev'ry Plant the sense surprize,
    p. 271 UNDERWOOD 83   72 To every Order, ev'ry Hierarchie!
    p. 415 UNGATHERD 42   14 And weigh'd your Play: untwisted ev'ry thread,

evt.   frequency: 1   relative frequency: 0.00001
    p. 239 UNDERWOOd 67   19 4. EVT. That when the Quire is full,

ewes   frequency: 2   relative frequency: 0.00002
    p. 264 UNDERWOOD 79   17 7. Our teeming Ewes, 8. and lustie-mounting
                             Rammes.
    p. 265 UNDERWOOD 79   51 Your teeming Ewes, aswell as mounting Rammes.

exact   frequency: 1   relative frequency: 0.00001
    See also "t<o>'exact."
    p. 192 UNDERWOOD 38   63 But to exact againe what once is given,

exacted   frequency: 2   relative frequency: 0.00002
    p. 41 EPIGRAMS 45   4 Exacted by thy fate, on the iust day.
    p. 121 FOREST 14   41 'T will be exacted of your name, whose sonne,

exacts   frequency: 1   relative frequency: 0.00001
    p. 258 UNDERWOOD 75   188 Exacts then she is pleas'd to pay: no suits,

exalt   frequency: 1   relative frequency: 0.00001
    p. 384 UNGATHERED 18   13 And thou to her, that Husband, may exalt

exalted   frequency: 3   relative frequency: 0.00004
    p. 246 UNDERWOOD 70   97 And shine as you exalted are;
    p. 279 U'WOOD 84.4   29 There, high exalted in the Sphaere,
    p. 285 U'WOOD 84.9   104 That pure, that pretious, and exalted mind

examin'd   frequency: 3   relative frequency: 0.00004
    p. 101 FOREST 4   49 Where nothing is examin'd, weigh'd,
    p. 160 UNDERWOOD 14   49 How are Traditions there examin'd: how
    p. 421 UNGATHERED 49   7 O're read, examin'd, try'd, and prou'd yor: Ryme

examine   frequency: 1   relative frequency: 0.00001
    p. 307 HORACE 2   54 Unto your strength, and long examine it,

examining. See "th'examining."

example   frequency: 16   relative frequency: 0.00023
    See also "by'example."
  **p. 116 PANEGYRE   125 That kings, by their example, more doe sway
    p. 34 EPIGRAMS 23   4 Came forth example, and remaines so, yet:
    p. 49 EPIGRAMS 66   13 Loue honors, which of best example bee,
    p. 57 EPIGRAMS 89   7 How can so great example dye in mee,
    p. 57 EPIGRAMS 90   4 At last, ease, appetite, and example wan
    p. 64 EPIGRAMS 99   5 How much of great example wert thou, ROE,
    p. 133 UNDERWOOD 2.3   26 Heare and make Example too.
    p. 153 UNDERWOOD 13   161 May grow so great to be example, when
    p. 171 UNDERWOOD 19   16 And so that either may example prove
    p. 193 UNDERWOOD 38   67 O may your wisdome take example hence,
    p. 210 UNDERWOOD 43   161 Foole, wilt thou let that in example come?
    p. 224 UNDERWOOD 50   7 Is of so brave example, as he were
    p. 236 UNDERWOOD 64   9 When you that raigne, are her Example growne,
    p. 247 UNDERWOOD 70   117 And such a force the faire example had,
    p. 269 UNDERWOOD 83   33 What she did here, by great example, well,
    p. 399 UNGATHERED 31   12 Was the example of a wife!

exampled. See "th'exampled."

examples   frequency: 1   relative frequency: 0.00001
    p. 323 HORACE 2   397 Take you the Greeke Examples, for your light,

exceed   frequency: 1   relative frequency: 0.00001
    See also "so'<e>xceed."
    p.   53 EPIGRAMS 79   7 No male vnto him: who could so exceed

exceedeth   frequency: 1   relative frequency: 0.00001
    p. 265 UNDERWOOD 79   55 And hunting, PAN, exceedeth thee.

exceeding   frequency: 2   relative frequency: 0.00002
    p. 365 UNGATHERED 5   13 Her breath for sweete exceeding
    p. 398 UNGATHERED 30   61 Thy Catalogue of Ships, exceeding his,

exceeds   frequency: 1   relative frequency: 0.00001
    p.   46 EPIGRAMS 60   8 But thine, for which I doo't, so much exceeds!

excel. See "excell."

excell   frequency: 4   relative frequency: 0.00005
    p. 117 FOREST 13   34 As I, can say, and see it doth excell.
    p. 146 UNDERWOOD 6   7 Such as in valour would excell,
    p. 262 UNDERWOOD 78   2 Yet read him in these lines: He doth excell
    p. 331 HORACE 2   550 There may a Lawyer be, may not excell;

excell'd   frequency: 1   relative frequency: 0.00001
  **p. 116 PANEGYRE   128 In all these knowing artes our prince excell'd.

excellence   frequency: 2   relative frequency: 0.00002
    p. 173 UNDERWOOD 22   23 As Love, t<o>'aquit such excellence,
    p. 321 HORACE 2   352 And toile in vaine: the excellence is such

excellent   frequency: 3   relative frequency: 0.00004
    See also "ex'lent."
    p. 160 UNDERWOOD 14   55 To marke the excellent seas'ning of your Stile!
    p. 274 U'WOOD 84.2   3 For Mind, and Body, the most excellent
    p. 333 HORACE 2   611 For hee'll cry, Good, brave, better, excellent!

excelling   frequency: 1   relative frequency: 0.00001
    p. 112 FOREST 11   110 Of this excelling frame?

excelsis   frequency: 1   relative frequency: 0.00001
    p.   86 EPIGRAMS 133   95 Had burst with storme, and downe fell, ab
                              excelsis,

except   frequency: 8   relative frequency: 0.00011
    p.   33 EPIGRAMS 20   2 Except thou could'st, Sir COD, weare them
                              within.
    p.   74 EPIGRAMS 115   13 Except the duell. Can sing songs, and catches;
    p. 170 UNDERWOOD 18   13 Except the way be errour to those ends:
    p. 215 UNDERWOOD 44   69 Why are we rich, or great, except to show
    p. 238 UNDERWOOD 66   7 (Except the joy that the first Mary brought,
    p. 317 HORACE 2   273 To have a God come in; except a knot
    p. 380 UNGATHERED 12   49 Except a dublet, and bought of the Iewes:
    p. 383 UNGATHERED 16   11 Except your Gratious Eye as through a Glass

exception   frequency: 1   relative frequency: 0.00001
    p. 142 U'WOOD 2.10   t1 Another Ladyes exception present at the hearing.

excess. See "excesse."

excesse   frequency: 1   relative frequency: 0.00001
    p. 279 U'WOOD 84.4   34 In speech; it is with that excesse

exchange   frequency: 1   relative frequency: 0.00001
    See also "t<o>'exchange," "th'exchange."
    p. 165 UNDERWOOD 15   86 They're growne Commoditie upon Exchange;

exchequer. See "chequer," "the'chequer."

excite   frequency: 1   relative frequency: 0.00001
    See also "accite."
    p. 311 HORACE 2   132 Yet, sometime, doth the Comedie excite

exclude   frequency: 1   relative frequency: 0.00001
    p. 325 HORACE 2   421 Exclude all sober Poets, from their share

excuse   frequency: 6   relative frequency: 0.00008
    p. 131 UNDERWOOD 2.1   t1 His Excuse for loving.
    p. 140 UNDERWOOD 2.8   10 And excuse spun every day,

excuse (cont.)
    p. 166 UNDERWOOD 15   142 Is that the truer excuse? or have we got
    p. 171 UNDERWOOD 19   22 You have a Husband is the just excuse
    p. 191 UNDERWOCD 38   22 Or lay the excuse upon the Vintners vault;
    p. 307 HORACE 2   70 Thou need new termes; thou maist, without excuse,

excuses   frequency: 2   relative frequency: 0.00002
    p. 153 UNDERWOOD 13   27 Excuses, or Delayes? or done 'hem scant,
    p. 391 UNGATHERED 26   25 That I not mixe thee so, my braine excuses;

execration   frequency: 1   relative frequency: 0.00001
    p. 202 UNDERWOOD 43   t1 An Execration upon Vulcan.

executes   frequency: 1   relative frequency: 0.00001
    p. 75 EPIGRAMS 115   29 Executes men in picture. By defect,

execution   frequency: 1   relative frequency: 0.00001
    p. 193 UNDERWOOD 38   80 This looketh like an Execution day?

executioner   frequency: 1   relative frequency: 0.00001
    p. 204 UNDERWOOD 43   47 Shee is the Judge, Thou Executioner:

executor   frequency: 1   relative frequency: 0.00001
    p. 41 EPIGRAMS 44   6 When he made him executor, might be heire.

exempt   frequency: 3   relative frequency: 0.00004
    p. 100 FOREST 4   7 Vpon thy throate, and liue exempt
    p. 148 UNDERWOCD 7   33 But so exempt from blame,
    p. 270 UNDERWOOD 83   48 Just as she in it liv'd! and so exempt

exercis'd   frequency: 1   relative frequency: 0.00001
    p. 66 EPIGRAMS 102   7 Almost, is exercis'd: and scarse one knowes,

exercise   frequency: 4   relative frequency: 0.00005
    p. 94 FOREST 2   21 When thou would'st feast, or exercise thy
                              friends.
    p. 97 FOREST 3   30 More for thy exercise, then fare;
    p. 144 UNDERWOOD 3   18 And exercise below,
    p. 415 UNGATHERED 43   2 Twixt Cotswold, and the Olimpicke exercise:

exhausted   frequency: 1   relative frequency: 0.00001
    p. 53 EPIGRAMS 79   4 Came not that soule exhausted so their store.

exil'd   frequency: 1   relative frequency: 0.00001
    p. 122 FOREST 15   13 Where haue I beene this while exil'd from thee?

ex'lent   frequency: 1   relative frequency: 0.00001
    p. 198 UNDERWOOD 40   24 As if that ex'lent Dulnesse were Loves grace;

expansions   frequency: 1   relative frequency: 0.00001
    p. 220 UNDERWOOD 47   68 Oylie Expansions, or shrunke durtie folds,

expect   frequency: 6   relative frequency: 0.00008
    See alsc "t<o>'expect."
    p. 37 EPIGRAMS 33   4 Breathe to expect my when, and make my how.
    p. 173 UNDERWOOD 22   13 But who should lesse expect from you,
    p. 246 UNDERWOOD 70   83 Such truths, as we expect for happy men,
    p. 263 UNDERWOOD 79   1 New yeares, expect new gifts: Sister, your
                              Harpe,
    p. 263 UNDERWOOD 79   13 Best Kings expect first-fruits of your glad
                              gaines.
    p. 396 UNGATHERED 30   5 Thy Muse, and mine, as they expect. 'Tis true:

expected   frequency: 3   relative frequency: 0.00004
    p. 96 FOREST 2   88 As if it had expected such a guest!
    p. 140 UNDERWOOD 2.8   7 With the rest, I long expected,
    p. 283 U'WOOD 84.9   50 Expected with the fleshes restitution.

expel. See "expell."

expell   frequency: 1   relative frequency: 0.00001
    p. 109 FOREST 11   4 And her blacke spight expell.

expence   frequency: 4   relative frequency: 0.00005
    p. 173 UNDERWOCD 22   22 With so much Loyalties expence,
    p. 222 UNDERWOOD 49   13 And as lip-thirstie, in each words expence,
    p. 241 UNDERWOOD 68   9 And rather wish, in their expence of Sack,
    p. 273 U'WOOD 84.1   20 Of light expence;

expense   frequency: 2   relative frequency: 0.00002
    See also "expence," "th'expence."
    p. 400 UNGATHERED 32   3 Hence, then, prophane: Here needs no words
                              expense
    p. 666 INSCRIPTS. 11   7 Till I, at much expense of Time, and Taper

experience   frequency: 1   relative frequency: 0.00001
    p. 176 UNDERWOOD 24   11 And guided by Experience, whose straite wand

expiate   frequency: 2   relative frequency: 0.00002
    p. 60 EPIGRAMS 93   15 Willing to expiate the fault in thee,
    p. 375 UNGATHERED 10   21 He will expiate this sinne with conuerting the
                              Iewes.

expire   frequency: 1   relative frequency: 0.00001
    p. 293 UNDERWOOD 87   15 For whom I doubly would expire,

explaitest. See "explat'st."

explat'st   frequency: 1   relative frequency: 0.00001
    p. 217 UNDERWOOD 46   17 Like Solons selfe; explat'st the knottie Lawes

expostulacon   frequency: 1   relative frequency: 0.00001
    p. 402 UNGATHERED 34   t1 An Expostulacon wth Inigo Iones.

expostulaticn. See "expostulacon."

express   frequency: 1   relative frequency: 0.00001
    See also "expresse," "t<o>'expresse,"
            "t'express."
    p. 402 UNGATHERED 34   18 Will any of these express yor place? or witt?

expresse   frequency: 5   relative frequency: 0.00007
    p. 95 FOREST 2   57 But what can this (more then expresse their loue)
    p. 255 UNDERWOOD 75   87 Who the whole Act expresse;
    p. 269 UNDERWOOD 83   26 Thereof, no notion can expresse how much
    p. 278 U'WOOD 84.4   13 No, to expresse a Mind to sense,
    p. 279 U'WOOD 84.4   33 Whose Notions when it will expresse

expressed. See "exprest."

expresser   frequency: 1   relative frequency: 0.00001
    p. 39 EPIGRAMS 40   7 Expresser truth, or truer glorie,

expresseth   frequency: 1   relative frequency: 0.00001
    p. 183 UNDERWOOD 29   2 That expresseth but by fits,

expression   frequency: 2   relative frequency: 0.00002
   **p. 114 PANEGYRE   39 Vnto their zeales expression; they are mute:
    p. 406 UNGATHERED 34   95 Expression for! wth that vnbounded lyne

expressions   frequency: 1   relative frequency: 0.00001
    p. 327 HORACE 2   455 Thence draw forth true expressions. For,
                              sometimes,

exprest   frequency: 3   relative frequency: 0.00004
    p. 149 UNDERWOOD 8   10 To have't exprest,
    p. 246 UNDERWOOD 70   88 To have exprest,
    p. 311 HORACE 2   121 The Comick matter will not be exprest

exscribe   frequency: 1   relative frequency: 0.00001
    p. 182 UNDERWOOD 28   3 Since I exscribe your Sonnets, am become

extasie   frequency: 1   relative frequency: 0.00001
    p. 289 U'WOOD 84.9   225 In this sweet Extasie, she was rapt hence.

extasies   frequency: 1   relative frequency: 0.00001
    p. 116 FOREST 12   90 From braines entranc'd, and fill'd with extasies;

extend   frequency: 2   relative frequency: 0.00002
    p. 67 EPIGRAMS 103   10 A SYDNEY: but in that extend as farre
    p. 258 UNDERWOOD 75   180 Extend a reaching vertue, early and late:

extendeth   frequency: 1   relative frequency: 0.00001
    p. 361 UNGATHERED 1   18 extendeth circles into infinits,

extends   frequency: 1   relative frequency: 0.00001
    p. 186 UNDERWOOD 32   1 The Judge his favour timely then extends,

extension   frequency: 1   relative frequency: 0.00001
     p. 259 UNDERWOOD 76   9 To his bountie; by extension

extract. See "t<o>'extract."

extraordinarie   frequency: 1   relative frequency: 0.00001
     p. 171 UNDERWOOD 19   28 Is constant to be extraordinarie.

extraordinary. See "extraordinarie."

extremities   frequency: 1   relative frequency: 0.00001
     p. 248 UNDERWOOD 71   1 Poore wretched states, prest by extremities,

eye   frequency: 22   relative frequency: 0.00031
     See also "th'eye."
     p. 108 FOREST 10A   5 The skilfull mischife of a rovinge Eye
     p. 111 FOREST 11   61 A fixed thought, an eye vn-taught to glance;
     p. 132 UNDERWOOD 2.2 12 Every Cloud about his eye;
     p. 138 UNDERWOOD 2.6 14 You were more the eye, and talke
     p. 140 UNDERWOOD 2.8 17 With your emissarie eye,
     p. 149 UNDERWOOD 8   8 Turn'd to cinders by her eye?
     p. 159 UNDERWOOD 14   23 Since, being deceiv'd, I turne a sharper eye
     p. 223 UNDERWOOD 49   19 And spangled Petticotes brought forth to eye,
     p. 238 UNDERWOOD 65   8 Thee quickly <come> the gardens eye to bee,
     p. 250 UNDERWOOD 73   5 WESTON! That waking man! that Eye of
                              State!
     p. 256 UNDERWOOD 75 109 That farre-all-seeing Eye
     p. 261 UNDERWOOD 77   23 These I looke up at, with a reverent eye
     p. 270 UNDERWOOD 83   43 A reverend State she had, an awfull Eye,
     p. 271 UNDERWOOD 83   85 If you can cast about your either eye,
     p. 276 U'WOOD 84.3   19 But at such distance, as the eye
     p. 278 U'WOOD 84.4   9 You could make shift to paint an Eye,
     p. 287 U'WOOD 84.9   167 And by the awfull manage of her Eye
     p. 345 HORACE 1   265 .... the eye
     p. 372 UNGATHERED 9   9 Of Spheares, as light of starres; She was
                              earthes Eye:
     p. 383 UNGATHERED 16 11 Except your Gratious Eye as through a Glass
     p. 383 UNGATHERED 16 14 your Royal Eye which still creat[t]es new men
     p. 413 UNGATHERED 41 14 The Eye of flowers, worthy, for his scent,

eye-browes   frequency: 1   relative frequency: 0.00001
     p. 215 UNDERWOOD 44   97 This other for his eye-browes; hence, away,

eye-brows   frequency: 1   relative frequency: 0.00001
     See also "eye-browes."
     p. 141 UNDERWOOD 2.9 17 Eye-brows bent like Cupids bow,

eyed   frequency: 1   relative frequency: 0.00001
     p. 362 UNGATHERED 2   13 Which being eyed directly, I diuine,

eyes   frequency: 57   relative frequency: 0.00082
     See also "eyne."
   **p. 113 PANEGYRE   4 Vnfolds himself: & from his eyes are hoorl'd
   **p. 113 PANEGYRE   16 Those dampes, that so offend all good mens eyes;
   **p. 114 PANEGYRE   34 Vpon his face all threw their couetous eyes,
   **p. 114 PANEGYRE   64 With seuerall eyes, that in this obiect met.
   **p. 115 PANEGYRE   84 "Vnto as many enuies, there, as eyes.
   **p. 116 PANEGYRE   107 "All this she told, and more, with bleeding eyes;
     p. 33 EPIGRAMS 21   2 His neck fenc'd round with ruffe! his eyes halfe
                              shut!
     p. 39 EPIGRAMS 40   8 Then they might in her bright eyes.
     p. 43 EPIGRAMS 51   9 For we, that haue our eyes still in our eares,
     p. 45 EPIGRAMS 56   13 Foole, as if halfe eyes will not know a fleece
     p. 49 EPIGRAMS 67   5 Stand high, then, HOWARD, high in eyes of
                              men,
     p. 74 EPIGRAMS 114   7 He hath not onely gain'd himselfe his eyes,
     p. 88 EPIGRAMS 133 161 With great gray eyes, are lifted vp, and mew'd;
     p. 99 FOREST 3   83 And brooding o're it sit, with broadest eyes,
     p. 102 FOREST 5   11 Cannot we delude the eyes
     p. 106 FOREST 9   1 Drrinke to me, onely, with thine eyes,
     p. 117 FOREST 13   35 That askes but to be censur'd by the eyes:
     p. 119 FOREST 13   115 Not fashion'd for the court, or strangers eyes;
     p. 133 UNDERWOOD 2.3   4 Eyes and limbes; to hurt me more.
     p. 134 UNDERWOOD 2.4 11 Doe but looke on her eyes, they doe light
     p. 136 UNDERWOOD 2.5 16 Just above her sparkling eyes,
     p. 141 UNDERWOOD 2.9 15 Venus, and Minerva's eyes,
     p. 144 UNDERWOOD 4   1 Oh doe not wanton with those eyes,
     p. 147 UNDERWOOD 7   22 But he hath eyes so round, and bright,
     p. 150 UNDERWOOD 9   18 And all these through her eyes, have stopt her
                              eares.

eyes (cont.)

p. 165	UNDERWOOD 15	92 That may corrupt her, even in his eyes.
p. 166	UNDERWOOD 15	138 The Dice with glassen eyes, to the glad viewes
p. 170	UNDERWOOD 18	19 Vaile their owne eyes, and would impartially
p. 170	UNDERWOOD 19	1 By those bright Eyes, at whose immortall fires
p. 177	UNDERWOOD 25	23 Of eyes more true,
p. 182	UNDERWOOD 28	11 His very eyes are yours to overthrow.
p. 185	UNDERWOOD 30	16 Rather than meet him: And, before his eyes
p. 194	UNDERWOOD 38	115 Out of your eyes, and be awhile away;
p. 205	UNDERWOOD 43	53 Sindge Capons, or poore Pigges, dropping their eyes;
p. 208	UNDERWOOD 43	121 And for it lose his eyes with Gun-powder,
p. 217	UNDERWOOD 46	24 Needs lend an aide, to thine she had her eyes.
p. 218	UNDERWOOD 47	7 And shewing so weake an Act to vulgar eyes,
p. 224	UNDERWOOD 50	16 A cheerefull worke to all good eyes, to see
p. 250	UNDERWOOD 73	2 Thy faint, and narrow eyes, to reade the King
p. 261	UNDERWOOD 77	12 As farre as sense, and onely by the eyes.
p. 284	U'WOOD 84.9	79 Dull, and prophane, weake, and imperfect eyes,
p. 307	HORACE 2	52 With faire black eyes, and haire: and a wry nose.
p. 317	HORACE 2	258 Then those the faithfull eyes take in by show,
p. 333	HORACE 2	613 Out at his friendly eyes, leape, beat the groun'.
p. 362	UNGATHERED 2	8 The fault's not in the object, but their eyes.
p. 369	UNGATHERED 6	112 Conceal'd from all but cleare Propheticke eyes.
p. 371	UNGATHERED 8	13 In such a Martirdome; To vexe their eyes,
p. 392	UNGATHERED 26	70 As brandish't at the eyes of Ignorance.
p. 394	UNGATHERED 28	2 And pray thee Reader, bring thy weepinge Eyes
p. 396	UNGATHERED 30	16 That all Earth look'd on; and that earth, all Eyes!
p. 398	UNGATHERED 30	76 Of tender eyes will more be wept, then seene:
p. 398	UNGATHERED 30	82 And with their grassie greene restor'd mine eyes.
p. 399	UNGATHERED 31	4 Tenants, and Seruants, haue they harts, and eyes,
p. 404	UNGATHERED 34	45 You aske noe more then certeyne politique Eyes,
p. 404	UNGATHERED 34	46 Eyes yt can pierce into ye Misteryes
p. 414	UNGATHERED 41	44 And art the spotlesse Mirrour to Mans eyes.
p. 420	UNGATHERED 48	30 Vppon soe humbled earth to cast hir eyes:

eyne   frequency: 1   relative frequency: 0.00001
**p. 116 PANEGYRE   129 And now the dame had dried her dropping eyne,

eyther   frequency: 1   relative frequency: 0.00001
  p. 384 UNGATHERED 18   16 To rise wth eyther of you, on the morrow.

f.   frequency: 1   relative frequency: 0.00001
  p. 375 UNGATHERED 10   29 F. shewes what he was, K. what he will bee.

fa-ding   frequency: 1   relative frequency: 0.00001
  p. 62 EPIGRAMS 97   1 See you yond' Motion? Not the old Fa-ding,

fable   frequency: 7   relative frequency: 0.00010

p. 224	UNDERWOOD 50	20 As makes Penelopes old fable true,
p. 317	HORACE 2	270 Nor must the Fable, that would hope the Fate,
p. 321	HORACE 2	349 I can out of knowne geare, a fable frame,
p. 329	HORACE 2	508 The truth; nor let thy Fable thinke, what e're
p. 364	UNGATHERED 4	2 Receiue it for a Fable,
p. 372	UNGATHERED 9	14 Might make the Fable of Good Women true.
p. 662	INSCRIPTS. 2	1 Goe little Booke, Goe little Fable

fabler   frequency: 1   relative frequency: 0.00001
  p. 404 UNGATHERED 34   63 To be ye Musick Master! Fabler too!

fables   frequency: 3   relative frequency: 0.00004

p. 67	EPIGRAMS 105	2 All historie seal'd vp, and fables crost;
p. 84	EPIGRAMS 133	1 No more let Greece her bolder fables tell
p. 159	UNDERWOOD 14	39 What fables have you vext! what truth redeem'd!

face   frequency: 46   relative frequency: 0.00066
  See also "fface," "quarter-face."

**p. 114	PANEGYRE	34 Vpon his face all threw their couetous eyes,
**p. 115	PANEGYRE	88 "In publique acts what face and forme they beare.
p. 30	EPIGRAMS 11	4 It made me a great face, I ask'd the name.
p. 35	EPIGRAMS 28	7 H' has tympanies of businesse, in his face,
p. 56	EPIGRAMS 88	5 And land on one, whose face durst neuer bee
p. 57	EPIGRAMS 90	11 Still MILL continu'd: Nay, his face growing worse,
p. 57	EPIGRAMS 90	13 MILL was the same. Since, both his body and face
p. 64	EPIGRAMS 100	2 Cry'd to my face, they were th'elixir of wit:
p. 73	EPIGRAMS 114	2 When SYDNYES name I heare, or face I see:

face (cont.)
p.	81 EPIGRAMS 129	13 Or (mounted on a stoole) thy face doth hit
p.	88 EPIGRAMS 133	160 And, now, aboue the poole, a face right fat
p.	118 FOREST 13	80 Whether it be a face they weare, or no.
p.	128 UNDERWOOD 1.1	32 Of seeing your face,
p.	131 UNDERWOOD 2.1	7 And it is not alwayes face,
p.	132 UNDERWOOD 2.2	25 At my face, that tooke my sight,
p.	134 UNDERWOOD 2.4	18 Sheds it selfe through the face,
p.	136 UNDERWOOD 2.5	15 Of her face, and made to rise,
p.	140 UNDERWOOD 2.8	20 Better fits him, then his face;
p.	142 U'WOOD 2.10	5 Himselfe young, and face be good,
p.	150 UNDERWOOD 9	17 My mountaine belly, and my rockie face,
p.	154 UNDERWOOD 13	39 No! Gifts and thankes should have one cheerefull face,
p.	162 UNDERWOOD 15	20 In outward face, but inward, light as Furre,
p.	168 UNDERWOOD 15	185 That whatsoever face thy fate puts on,
p.	188 UNDERWOOD 34	14 Of Beautie, so to nullifie a face,
p.	191 UNDERWOOD 38	13 There may some face or menace of a storme
p.	194 UNDERWOOD 38	102 To carry noble danger in the face:
p.	198 UNDERWOOD 40	23 Keepe in reserv'd in his Dark-lanterne face,
p.	200 UNDERWOOD 42	14 No face, no hand, proportion, line, or Ayre
p.	202 UNDERWOOD 42	88 More then of eithers manners, wit, or face!
p.	207 UNDERWOOD 43	108 Or Goddesse, could be patient of thy face.
p.	223 UNDERWOOD 49	32 Her face there's none can like by Candle light.
p.	225 UNDERWOOD 51	5 Pardon, I read it in thy face, the day
p.	227 UNDERWOOD 52	22 Yet when of friendship I would draw the face,
p.	243 UNDERWOOD 70	23 Or masked man, if valu'd by his face,
p.	275 U'WOOD 84.3	4 Where every lim takes like a face?
p.	276 U'WOOD 84.3	15 Till, like her face, it doe appeare,
p.	285 U'WOOD 84.9	115 And each shall know, there, one anothers face,
p.	286 U'WOOD 84.9	132 The vision of our Saviour, face to face,
p.	287 U'WOOD 84.9	154 Each line, as it were graphick, in the face!
p.	321 HORACE 2	344 Quite from all face of Tragedie to goe,
p.	369 UNGATHERED 6	93 Yet, looking in thy face, they shall begin
p.	384 UNGATHERED 18	1 They are not those, are present wth theyre face,
p.	389 UNGATHERED 24	10 As a deformed face doth a true glasse.
p.	390 UNGATHERED 25	7 His face; the Print would then surpasse
p.	392 UNGATHERED 26	65 And such wert thou. Looke how the fathers face

faces   frequency: 9   relative frequency: 0.00013
p.	59 EPIGRAMS 92	7 And graue as ripe, like mellow as their faces.
p.	59 EPIGRAMS 92	34 And at the Pope, and Spaine slight faces make.
p.	74 EPIGRAMS 115	25 And, shifting of it's faces, doth play more
p.	188 UNDERWOOD 34	4 Of those that set by their false faces more
p.	200 UNDERWOOD 42	36 Whether their faces were their owne, or no:
p.	220 UNDERWOOD 48	9 And looke unto their faces,
p.	311 HORACE 2	143 Mens faces, still, with such as laugh, are prone
p.	319 HORACE 2	314 Those that did sing, and act: their faces dy'd
p.	365 UNGATHERED 5	22 Are deeper then their Faces:

facile   frequency: 1   relative frequency: 0.00001
| p. | 52 EPIGRAMS 76 | 9 I meant shee should be curteous, facile, sweet, |

fact   frequency: 5   relative frequency: 0.00007
p.	46 EPIGRAMS 60	4 Thy fact, in brasse or marble writ the same)
p.	47 EPIGRAMS 63	6 Not from the publike voyce, but priuate fact;
p.	64 EPIGRAMS 99	12 Thy fact is more: let truth encourage thee.
p.	243 UNDERWOOD 70	24 Above his fact?
p.	270 UNDERWOOD 83	45 What Nature, Fortune, Institution, Fact

faction   frequency: 4   relative frequency: 0.00005
*p.	492 TO HIMSELF	3 Where pride, and impudence (in faction knit)
p.	61 EPIGRAMS 95	18 That liu'st from hope, from feare, from faction free;
p.	66 EPIGRAMS 102	15 Of what ambition, faction, pride can raise;
p.	207 UNDERWOOD 43	104 Whom Faction had not drawne to studie sides.

factious   frequency: 1   relative frequency: 0.00001
| p. | 167 UNDERWOOD 15 | 168 Ambitious, factious, superstitious, lowd |

facts   frequency: 2   relative frequency: 0.00002
| p. | 64 EPIGRAMS 99 | 6 If time to facts, as vnto men would owe? |
| p. | 323 HORACE 2 | 408 And celebrating our owne home-borne facts; |

facultie   frequency: 4   relative frequency: 0.00005
p.	201 UNDERWOOD 42	64 Had he'had the facultie to reade, and write!
p.	242 UNDERWOOD 69	19 For as at distance, few have facultie
p.	323 HORACE 2	387 But every Judge hath not the facultie
p.	302 UNGATHERED 2	11 Wants facultie to make a censure true:

faculties   frequency: 2   relative frequency: 0.00002
    p. 108 FOREST 10A   14 and Coniures all my faculties t<o>'approue
    p. 362 UNGATHERED 1   29 my abler faculties; and thus brake foorth

faculty. See "facultie."

fading. See "fa-ding."

faemale   frequency: 1   relative frequency: 0.00001
    p. 399 UNGATHERED 31   8 Code, Digests, Pandects of all faemale glory!

faggots. See "fagots."

fagots   frequency: 1   relative frequency: 0.00001
    p. 211 UNDERWOOD 43   185 Or in small Fagots have him blaze about

fail. See "faile."

fail'd   frequency: 1   relative frequency: 0.00001
    p. 188 UNDERWOOD 34   18 And scorn'd, thou'<h>ast showne thy malice, but
                             hast fail'd.

faile   frequency: 5   relative frequency: 0.00007
    p. 80 EPIGRAMS 127   2 If I should faile, in gratitude, to thee,
    p. 94 FOREST 2   31 And if the high-swolne Medway faile thy dish,
    p. 115 FOREST 12   64 And such, or my hopes faile, shall make you
                             shine.
    p. 192 UNDERWOOD 38   46 We cut not off, till all Cures else doe faile:
    p. 325 HORACE 2   417 Have not kept in; and (lest perfection faile)

failed   frequency: 1   relative frequency: 0.00001
    See also "fail'd."
    p. 183 UNDERWOOD 29   24 All light failed!

failes   frequency: 2   relative frequency: 0.00002
    p. 94 FOREST 2   20 That neuer failes to serue thee season'd deere,
    p. 293 UNDERWOOD 86   36 With an uncomely silence failes my tongue?

fails. See "failes."

fain. See "faine," "fayne."

fain'd   frequency: 4   relative frequency: 0.00005
    p. 246 UNDERWOOD 70   104 Orgies of drinke, or fain'd protests:
    p. 270 UNDERWOOD 83   38 But a fain'd way, doth rob it of the true.
    p. 305 HORACE 2   9 Whose shapes, like sick-mens dreames, are fain'd
                             so vaine,
    p. 327 HORACE 2   474 Thinke wee, or hope, there can be Verses fain'd

faine   frequency: 12   relative frequency: 0.00017
  **p. 114 PANEGYRE   37 Others would faine haue shew'ne it in their
                             words:
    p. 52 EPIGRAMS 76   17 Such when I meant to faine, and wish'd to see,
    p. 53 EPIGRAMS 79   8 Nature, they thought, in all, that he would
                             faine.
    p. 84 EPIGRAMS 133   6 Had power to act, what they to faine had not.
    p. 95 FOREST 2   65 And I not faine to sit (as some, this day,
    p. 133 UNDERWOOD 2.3   19 And would faine have chang'd the fate,
    p. 216 UNDERWOOD 45   1 What I am not, and what I faine would be,
    p. 224 UNDERWOOD 50   24 Then the great Homers wit, for her, could faine;
    p. 248 UNDERWOOD 71   2 Are faine to seeke for succours, and supplies
    p. 309 HORACE 2   71 Faine words, unheard of to the well-truss'd race
    p. 313 HORACE 2   169 Or follow fame, thou that dost write, or faine
    p. 380 UNGATHERED 12   37 How faine for his venery he was to crie (Tergum
                             o)

fained   frequency: 1   relative frequency: 0.00001
    p. 240 UNDERWOOD 67   32 The fained Queene of Love,

faines   frequency: 1   relative frequency: 0.00001
    p. 315 HORACE 2   215 And so well faines, so mixeth cunningly

fain'st   frequency: 3   relative frequency: 0.00004
    p. 43 EPIGRAMS 52   3 When I am read, thou fain'st a weake applause,
    p. 70 EPIGRAMS 109   6 Wrestlest with dignities, or fain'st a scope
    p. 329 HORACE 2   507 Let what thou fain'st for pleasures sake, be
                             neere

faint   frequency: 2   relative frequency: 0.00002
    p. 117 FOREST 13   19 Of nature, and societie, I should faint;

faint (cont.)
    p. 250 UNDERWOOD 73   2 Thy faint, and narrow eyes, to reade the King

fainting   frequency: 1   relative frequency: 0.00001
    p. 291 UNDERWOOD 85   64 And fainting necks, the turned Share!

faintly   frequency: 1   relative frequency: 0.00001
  **p. 113 PANEGYRE   25 To be her daughters: and but faintly knowne

fair. See "faire," "fayre."

faire   frequency: 62   relative frequency: 0.00089
  **p. 113 PANEGYRE   24 Faire DICE, and EVNOMIA; who were said
    p. 34 EPIGRAMS 25   1 While BEAST instructs his faire, and
                             innocent wife,
    p. 39 EPIGRAMS 40   6 Read not in faire heauens storie,
    p. 45 EPIGRAMS 59   3 Stinke, and are throwne away. End faire enough.
    p. 51 EPIGRAMS 73   10 Item, a faire greeke poesie for a ring:
    p. 52 EPIGRAMS 76   5 I meant to make her faire, and free, and wise,
    p. 64 EPIGRAMS 101   7 It is the faire acceptance, Sir, creates
    p. 66 EPIGRAMS 103   1 How well, faire crowne of your faire sexe, might
                             hee,
    p. 70 EPIGRAMS 109   4 Where all is faire, beside thy pedigree.
    p. 73 EPIGRAMS 113   9 Repent thee not of thy faire precedent,
    p. 80 EPIGRAMS 126   1 Retyr'd, with purpose your faire worth to praise,
    p. 84 EPIGRAMS 133   25 The other was a squire, of faire degree;
    p. 93 FOREST 2   8 Of wood, of water: therein thou art faire.
    p. 119 FOREST 13   99 Grow, grow, faire tree, and as thy branches
                             shoote,
    p. 137 UNDERWOOD 2.6   4 Thence, as sweet, as you are faire,
    p. 138 UNDERWOOD 2.6   9 Look'd not halfe so fresh, and faire,
    p. 141 UNDERWOOD 2.9   9 Young I'ld have him to<o>, and faire,
    p. 147 UNDERWOOD 7   15 He is, if they can find him, faire,
    p. 157 UNDERWOOD 13   151 But few and faire Divisions: but being got
    p. 170 UNDERWOOD 19   3 By that faire Stand, your forehead, whence he
                             bends
    p. 179 UNDERWOOD 25   58 (As my hope tells) that our faire Phoeb<e>'s
                             shine,
    p. 180 UNDERWOOD 26   14 Happy in that faire honour it hath gain'd,
    p. 187 UNDERWOOD 33   21 And make the Scarre faire; If that will not be,
    p. 190 UNDERWOOD 37   24 Will unto Licence that faire leave abuse.
    p. 191 UNDERWOOD 38   9 Offended Mistris, you are yet so faire,
    p. 192 UNDERWOOD 38   52 As not alone the Cure, but scarre be faire.
    p. 193 UNDERWOOD 38   73 And how more faire, and lovely lookes the world
    p. 200 UNDERWOOD 42   13 Sooner then my affection from the faire.
    p. 200 UNDERWOOD 42   20 (If they be faire and worth it) have their lives
    p. 221 UNDERWOOD 48   42 As shall the feasts faire grounds be.
    p. 230 UNDERWOOD 56   14 And stroke the water, nimble, chast, and faire,
    p. 240 UNDERWOOD 67   52 So fruitfull, and so faire,
    p. 242 UNDERWOOD 69   14 So doth the flatt'rer with faire cunning strike
    p. 245 UNDERWOOD 70   63 Each syllab'e answer'd, and was form'd, how
                             faire;
    p. 247 UNDERWOOD 70   117 And such a force the faire example had,
    p. 251 UNDERWOOD 74   12 Because the order of the whole is faire!
    p. 251 UNDERWOOD 74   20 Bring all your friends, (faire Lord) that burne
    p. 251 UNDERWOOD 74   28 Shoot up an Olive fruitfull, faire,
    p. 253 UNDERWOOD 75   39 Of all the Maidens faire;
    p. 254 UNDERWOOD 75   64 O, now thou smil'st, faire Sun, and shin'st, as
                             thou wouldst stay!
    p. 269 UNDERWOOD 83   6 You seeme a faire one! O that you had breath,
    p. 269 UNDERWOOD 83   15 It is a large faire table, and a true,
    p. 270 UNDERWOOD 83   39 Her Sweetnesse, Softnesse, her faire
                             Courtesie,
    p. 270 UNDERWOOD 83   58 Chear'd her faire Sisters in her race to runne!
    p. 272 U'WOOD 84 1   1 Faire FAME, who art ordain'd to crowne
    p. 272 UNDERWOOD 84   t3 THE FAIRE FAME
    p. 272 UNDERWOOD 84   t14 Her faire OFFICES.
    p. 274 U'WOOD 84.2   2 Of Dame VENETIA DIGBY, styl'd The
                             Faire:
    p. 279 U'WOOD 84.4   37 The Voyce so sweet, the words so faire,
    p. 281 U'WOOD 84.4   69 In thee, faire Mansion, let it rest,
    p. 281 U'WOOD 84.8   13 'Twill be but faire, to leane upon their Fames;
    p. 282 U'WOOD 84.9   11 O! had I seene her laid out a faire Corse,
    p. 287 U'WOOD 84.9   163 She had a mind as calme, as she was faire;
    p. 305 HORACE 2   4 Presenting upwards, a faire female feature,
    p. 307 HORACE 2   52 With faire black eyes, and haire; and a wry nose.
    p. 317 HORACE 2   262 Much from the sight, which faire report will make
    p. 321 HORACE 2   336 And emptie Clowdes. For Tragedie is faire,
    p. 366 UNGATHERED 6   10 How faire a flight he makes!
    p. 389 UNGATHERED 24   22 Faire Aemulation, and no Enuy is;

faire (cont.)
p. 399 UNGATHERED 31   26 In faire freehould, not an Inmate:
p. 402 UNGATHERED 33   12 The faire French Daughter to learne English
                          in;

fairer   frequency: 2   relative frequency: 0.00002
p. 245 UNDERWOOD 70   70 Is fairer farre, in May,
p. 294 UNDERWOOD 87   21 LYD. Though he be fairer then a Starre;

fairest   frequency: 4   relative frequency: 0.00005
See also "fayrest."
p. 180 UNDERWOOD 26   7 Have made their fairest flight,
p. 264 UNDERWOOD 79   37 The fairest flowers are alwayes found;
p. 364 UNGATHERED 4   6 That Natures fairest Creature,
p. 413 UNGATHERED 41   15 To top the fairest Lillie, now, that growes,

fairy. See "fayerie."

faith   frequency: 18   relative frequency: 0.00026
See also "faith's."
p. 31 EPIGRAMS 14   7 What name, what skill, what faith hast thou in
                          things!
p. 32 EPIGRAMS 18   7 If thou'ldst but vse thy faith, as thou didst
                          then,
p. 32 EPIGRAMS 18   10 Thy faith is all the knowledge that thou hast.
p. 62 EPIGRAMS 95   35 But most we need his faith (and all haue you)
p. 122 FOREST 15   11 My faith, my hope, my loue: and in this state,
p. 139 UNDERWOOD 2.7   7 Once more, and (faith) I will be gone,
p. 159 UNDERWOOD 14   36 Or faith in things? or is't your wealth and will
p. 173 UNDERWOOD 22   12 Against or Faith, or honours lawes.
p. 220 UNDERWOOD 47   75 Are asked to climbe. First give me faith, who
                          know
p. 223 UNDERWOOD 49   42 This Age would lend no faith to Dorrels Deed;
p. 236 UNDERWOOD 64   12 That Faith, which she professeth to be pure?
p. 243 UNDERWOOD 70   13 Where shame, faith, honour, and regard of right
p. 284 U'WOOD 84.9   68 Hope, hath her end! and Faith hath her reward!
p. 288 U'WOOD 84.9   209 All this by Faith she saw, and fram'd a Plea,
p. 380 UNGATHERED 12   22 Pies on't, you haue his historicall faith.
p. 393 UNGATHERED 27   8 That Faith and Loue defineth.
p. 393 UNGATHERED 27   11 As giues a power to faith, to tread
p. 422 UNGATHERED 50   2 make many, hurt themselues; a praysed faith

faithful   frequency: 1   relative frequency: 0.00001
See also "faithfull."
p. 173 UNDERWOOD 22   28 Among which faithful troope am I.

faithfull   frequency: 6   relative frequency: 0.00008
p. 67 EPIGRAMS 104   6 To make those faithfull, did the Fates send you?
p. 127 UNDERWOOD 1.1   3 The faithfull mans beleeved Mysterie,
p. 185 UNDERWOOD 30   9 The only faithfull Watchman for the Realme,
p. 317 HORACE 2   258 Then those the faithfull eyes take in by show,
p. 409 UNGATHERED 38   2 And you perform'd a Seruants faithfull parts:
p. 409 UNGATHERED 38   t1 To my old Faithfull Seruant: and (by

faithfully   frequency: 2   relative frequency: 0.00002
p. 313 HORACE 2   190 Not care, as thou wouldst faithfully translate,
p. 329 HORACE 2   505 And hold them faithfully; For nothing rests,

faiths   frequency: 1   relative frequency: 0.00001
p. 84 EPIGRAMS 133   4 With tales of Troyes iust knight, our faiths
                          abuse:

faith's   frequency: 1   relative frequency: 0.00001
p. 413 UNGATHERED 41   20 No faith's more firme, or flat, then where't doth
                          creep.

fal   frequency: 1   relative frequency: 0.00001
p. 413 UNGATHERED 41   40 The Morning-star, whose light our Fal hath
                          stay'd.

falernian   frequency: 1   relative frequency: 0.00001
p. 295 UNDERWOOD 89   5 Darke thy cleare glasse with old Falernian
                          Wine;.

fall   frequency: 26   relative frequency: 0.00037
See also "fal."
p. 118 FOREST 13   82 When their owne Parasites laugh at their fall,
p. 119 FOREST 13   104 It shall a ripe and timely issue fall,
p. 122 FOREST 15   19 Standing with feare, and must with horror fall,
p. 132 UNDERWOOD 2.2   17 Letting Bow and Arrow fall,

fall (cont.)

p. 134	UNDERWOOD 2.4	23	Have you mark'd but the fall o'the Snow
p. 144	UNDERWOOD 3	23	To fall againe; at such a feast,
p. 154	UNDERWOOD 13	36	His Groomes to witnesse; or else lets it fall
p. 163	UNDERWOOD 15	49	His Lace and Starch; And fall upon her back
p. 179	UNDERWOOD 25	36	O vertues fall,
p. 187	UNDERWOOD 33	33	Thy Adversaries fall, as not a word
p. 219	UNDERWOOD 47	42	To live, or fall a Carkasse in the cause.
p. 224	UNDERWOOD 50	12	From whence they fall, cast downe with their owne weight.
p. 224	UNDERWOOD 50	17	Among the daily Ruines that fall foule,
p. 245	UNDERWOOD 70	68	To fall a logge at last, dry, bald, and seare:
p. 245	UNDERWOOD 70	71	Although it fall, and die that night;
p. 257	UNDERWOOD 75	156	Of Life, that fall so; Christians know their birth
p. 271	UNDERWOOD 83	89	The Sunne! great Kings, and mightiest Kingdomes fall!
p. 282	U'WOOD 84.8	22	Which Vertue from your Father, ripe, will fall;
p. 283	U'WOOD 84.9	25	The world to ruine with it; in her Fall,
p. 288	U'WOOD 84.9	208	The kind of Man, on whom his doome should fall!
p. 309	HORACE 2	75	So they fall gently from the Grecian spring,
p. 335	HORACE 2	651	Busie to catch a Black-bird; if he fall
p. 406	UNGATHERED 34	91	And not fall downe before it? and confess
p. 417	UNGATHERED 45	14	those turnd vp, and those that fall,
p. 417	UNGATHERED 45	18	rise or fall vppon the earth,
p. 423	UNGATHERED 50	11	whole armyes fall, swayd by those nyce respects.

fallen. See "falne."

falling   frequency: 4   relative frequency: 0.00005

p. 65	EPIGRAMS 101	16	The skie not falling, thinke we may haue larkes.
p. 173	UNDERWOOD 22	17	His falling Temples you have rear'd,
p. 183	UNDERWOOD 29	8	Propping Verse, for feare of falling
p. 407	UNGATHERED 35	16	Or Dowgate Torrent falling into Thames,

fallow   frequency: 1   relative frequency: 0.00001

p. 169	UNDERWOOD 17	16	All is not barren land, doth fallow lie.

falls   frequency: 3   relative frequency: 0.00004
See also "pit-falls."

p. 61	EPIGRAMS 95	8	Where NERO falls, and GALBA is ador'd,
p. 110	FOREST 11	49	That falls like sleepe on louers, and combines
p. 168	UNDERWOOD 15	196	Who falls for love of God, shall rise a Starre.

fall'st   frequency: 1   relative frequency: 0.00001

p. 244	UNDERWOOD 70	44	Hee never fell, thou fall'st, my tongue.

falne   frequency: 3   relative frequency: 0.00004

**p. 117	PANEGYRE	136	Was gently falne from heauen vpon this state;
p. 60	EPIGRAMS 93	7	And two, that would haue falne as great, as they,
p. 243	UNDERWOOD 70	31	How well at twentie had he falne, or stood!

false   frequency: 26   relative frequency: 0.00037

p. 43	EPIGRAMS 51	t2	Vpon the happy false rumour of his death, the two
p. 56	EPIGRAMS 87	1	Touch'd with the sinne of false play, in his punque,
p. 62	EPIGRAMS 95	36	That dares nor write things false, nor hide things true.
p. 68	EPIGRAMS 107	3	I oft looke on false coyne, to know't from true:
p. 100	FOREST 4	1	False world, good-night: since thou hast brought
p. 102	FOREST 4	64	As shall not need thy false reliefe.
p. 112	FOREST 11	103	Who could be false to? chiefly, when he knowes
p. 117	FOREST 13	27	And this shall be no false one, but as much
p. 145	UNDERWOOD 5	4	Our owne false praises, for your ends:
p. 155	UNDERWOOD 13	65	Still, still, the hunters of false fame apply
p. 162	UNDERWOOD 15	15	Looke on the false, and cunning man, that loves
p. 172	UNDERWOOD 21	7	Proud, false, and trecherous, vindictive, all
p. 175	UNDERWOOD 23	20	Be taken with false Baytes
p. 183	UNDERWOOD 29	6	But false weight.
p. 188	UNDERWOOD 34	4	Of those that set by their false faces more
p. 188	UNDERWOOD 34	7	Art, her false servant; Nor, for Sir Hugh Plat,
p. 204	UNDERWOOD 43	43	And as false stampe there; parcels of a Play,
p. 216	UNDERWOOD 45	11	Those are poore Ties, depend on those false ends,
p. 220	UNDERWOOD 47	65	Not built with Canvasse, paper, and false lights,
p. 224	UNDERWOOD 50	10	Are growne so fruitfull, and false pleasures climbe,
p. 227	UNDERWOOD 52	21	Ne knowes he flatt'ring Colours, or false light.

false (cont.)
    p. 248 UNDERWOOD 71   7 And made those strong approaches, by False
                            braies,
    p. 313 HORACE 2   176 Ino bewaild; Ixion false, forsworne;
    p. 370 UNGATHERED 7   11 To iudge which Passion's false, and which is
                            true,
    p. 385 UNGATHERED 20 4 Least a false praise do make theyr dotage his.
    p. 407 UNGATHERED 35 10 Wth slyding windowes, & false Lights a top!

false-hood   frequency: 1   relative frequency: 0.00001
    p. 393 UNGATHERED 27 12 All false-hood vnder feete.

falsehood. See "false-hood," "falshood."

falsely   frequency: 1   relative frequency: 0.00001
    p. 109 FOREST 11   25 Backe the intelligence, and falsely sweares,

falser   frequency: 1   relative frequency: 0.00001
    p. 100 FOREST 4   20 Yet art thou falser then thy wares.

falshood   frequency: 4   relative frequency: 0.00005
    p. 186 UNDERWOOD 32   4 Then to make falshood blush, and fraud afraid:
    p. 194 UNDERWOOD 38 108 Then I will studie falshood, to be true.
    p. 275 U'WOOD 84.3   7 This beautie without falshood fayre,
    p. 315 HORACE 2   216 Falshood with truth, as no man can espie

fam'd   frequency: 3   relative frequency: 0.00004
    p. 82 EPIGRAMS 130   10 Of old, euen by her practise, to be fam'd;
    p. 353 HORACE 1   579 .... of the singer Apollo, and Muses fam'd
    p. 407 UNGATHERED 35 14 From ye fam'd pillars of old Hercules!

fame   frequency: 70   relative frequency: 0.00101
    See also "selfe-fame."
  **p. 115 PANEGYRE   87 "Betraid to fame, should take more care, and
                            feare
  **p. 116 PANEGYRE   113 He knew that princes, who had sold their fame
    p. 32 EPIGRAMS 17   3 That wish my poemes a legitimate fame,
    p. 36 EPIGRAMS 30   3 'Twere madnesse in thee, to betray thy fame,
    p. 40 EPIGRAMS 43   4 Her foes enough would fame thee, in their hate.
    p. 41 EPIGRAMS 43   8 Of adding to thy fame; thine may to me,
    p. 43 EPIGRAMS 51   2 Great heau'n did well, to giue ill fame free
                            wing;
    p. 48 EPIGRAMS 66   1 That neither fame, nor loue might wanting be
    p. 49 EPIGRAMS 67   4 As, to be rais'd by her, is onely fame.
    p. 53 EPIGRAMS 77   1 Be safe, nor feare thy selfe so good a fame,
    p. 57 EPIGRAMS 89   6 Then CICERO, whose euery breath was fame:
    p. 58 EPIGRAMS 91   5 Which thou art to thy selfe: whose fame was wonne
    p. 63 EPIGRAMS 98   10 And studie conscience, more then thou would'st
                            fame.
    p. 66 EPIGRAMS 103   6 Need any Muses praise to giue it fame?
    p. 68 EPIGRAMS 106   4 Truth might spend all her voyce, Fame all her
                            art.
    p. 70 EPIGRAMS 109   2 That serues nor fame, nor titles; but doth chuse
    p. 71 EPIGRAMS 110 10 Vn-argued then, and yet hath fame from those;
    p. 74 EPIGRAMS 115   2 Him not, aloud, that boasts so good a fame:
    p. 82 EPIGRAMS 130   1 To vrge, my lou'd ALPHONSO, that bold
                            fame
    p. 83 EPIGRAMS 131 14 For fame, with breath soone kindled, soone blowne
                            out.
    p. 85 EPIGRAMS 133 53 And art a god, if Fame thee not abuses,
    p. 102 FOREST 5   10 Fame, and rumor are but toyes.
    p. 105 FOREST 8   42 Play away, health, wealth, and fame.
    p. 111 FOREST 11   79 Or those, who doubt the common mouth of fame,
    p. 113 FOREST 12   15 While thus it buyes great grace, and hunts poore
                            fame;
    p. 114 FOREST 12   26 Then, here, to giue pride fame, and peasants
                            birth.
    p. 114 FOREST 12   48 That had no Muse to make their fame abide.
    p. 119 FOREST 13   97 And raise a noble stemme, to giue the fame,
    p. 148 UNDERWOOD 7   34 As it would be to each a fame:
    p. 155 UNDERWOOD 13 65 Still, still, the hunters of false fame apply
    p. 168 UNDERWOOD 15 189 So, 'live or dead, thou wilt preserve a fame
    p. 172 UNDERWOOD 21   1 Aske not to know this Man. If fame should
                            speake
    p. 175 UNDERWOOD 24   3 Raising the World to good or evill fame,
    p. 181 UNDERWOOD 27 16 Whose fame hath an eternall voice?
    p. 181 UNDERWOOD 27 18 Her Ovid gave her, dimn'd the fame
    p. 185 UNDERWOOD 30 12 And labour'd in the worke; not with the fame:
    p. 186 UNDERWOOD 31   7 So may the gentler Muses, and good fame
    p. 187 UNDERWOOD 33 39 Thy sincere practise, breeds not thee a fame

fame (cont.)
```
    p. 190 UNDERWOOD 37      15 And Fame wake for me, when I yeeld to sleepe.
    p. 204 UNDERWOOD 43      46 Thou should'st have stay'd, till publike fame
                                said so.
    p. 214 UNDERWOOD 44      49 Goe on, increase in vertue; and in fame:
    p. 217 UNDERWOOD 46      14 Stood up thy Nations fame, her Crownes defence.
    p. 219 UNDERWOOD 47      49 Although my Fame, to his, not under-heares,
    p. 223 UNDERWOOD 49      36 From Court, while yet thy fame hath some small
                                day;
    p. 224 UNDERWOOD 50      14 Who (herein studying conscience, and not fame)
    p. 224 UNDERWOOD 50      18 Of State, of fame, of body, and of soule,
    p. 225 UNDERWOOD 51      10 Fame, and foundation of the English Weale.
    p. 241 UNDERWOOD 68      14 The Kings fame lives. Go now, denie his
                                Teirce.
    p. 244 UNDERWOOD 70      35 He purchas'd friends, and fame, and honours then,
    p. 256 UNDERWOOD 75     114 It brings Friends Joy, Foes Griefe,
                                Posteritie Fame;
    p. 257 UNDERWOOD 75     152 For Fame keepes Vertue up, and it Posteritie.
    p. 260 UNDERWOOD 77       8 Have left in fame to equall, or out-goe
    p. 263 UNDERWOOD 78      25 And praise them too. O! what a fame 't will be?
    p. 268 UNDERWOOD 82      12 As in renewing thy good Grandsires fame;
    p. 269 UNDERWOOD 83      14 Thou wouldst have written, Fame, upon my brest:
    p. 269 UNDERWOOD 83      21 Earle Rivers Grand-Child -- serve not formes,
                                good Fame,
    p. 269 UNDERWOOD 83      34 T<o>'inlive posteritie, her Fame may tell!
    p. 272 U'WOOD 84.1        1 Faire FAME, who art ordain'd to crowne
    p. 272 UNDERWOOD 84      t3 THE FAIRE FAME
    p. 274 U'WOOD 84.2       16 Meschines honour with the Cestrian fame
    p. 313 HORACE 2         169 Or follow fame, thou that dost write, or faine
    p. 323 HORACE 2         396 But, in conclusion, merited no fame.
    p. 325 HORACE 2         426 But fame of Poets, they thinke, if they come
                                forth,
    p. 362 UNGATHERED 1      31 And thou in them shalt liue as longe as Fame.
    p. 390 UNGATHERED 26      2 Am I thus ample to thy Booke, and Fame:
    p. 396 UNGATHERED 30     12 Lend me thy voyce, O FAME, that I may draw
    p. 401 UNGATHERED 32     20 Defies, what's crosse to Piety, or good Fame.
    p. 403 UNGATHERED 34     35 Th'ascent of Lady Fame which none could spy
    p. 409 UNGATHERED 37     12 Shall not worke out vnto it, such a fame.
    p. 411 UNGATHERED 39     13 For thou hast nought <in thee> to cure his Fame,
```

fame-vaynes   frequency: 1   relative frequency: 0.00001
```
    p. 167 UNDERWOOD 15     166 The life, and fame-vaynes (yet not understood
```

fames   frequency: 6   relative frequency: 0.00008
```
    p.  75 EPIGRAMS 115      30 From friendship, is it's owne fames architect.
    p. 257 UNDERWOOD 75     150 And keepe their Fames
    p. 269 UNDERWOOD 83      30 To be describ'd! Fames fingers are too foule
    p. 281 U'WOOD 84.8       13 'Twill be but faire, to leane upon their Fames;
    p. 386 UNGATHERED 21      9 And, where the most reade bookes, on Authors
                                fames,
    p. 400 UNGATHERED 31     28 Fames heate vpon the graue did stay;
```

familiar   frequency: 1   relative frequency: 0.00001
```
    p. 146 UNDERWOOD 6       16 Familiar, for the uses sake;
```

familie   frequency: 2   relative frequency: 0.00002
```
    p. 274 U'WOOD 84.2       17 Of the first Lupus, to the Familie
    p. 287 U'WOOD 84.9      168 She swaid all bus'nesse in the Familie!
```

families   frequency: 1   relative frequency: 0.00001
```
    p. 185 UNDERWOOD 30      18 And in the noblest Families tooke root
```

family   frequency: 1   relative frequency: 0.00001
See also "familie."
```
    p. 392 UNGATHERED 26     54 As they were not of Natures family.
```

famine   frequency: 2   relative frequency: 0.00002
```
    p.  86 EPIGRAMS 133      71 With famine, wants, and sorrowes many a dosen,
    p. 243 UNDERWOOD 70      17 Sword, fire, and famine, with fell fury met;
```

famous   frequency: 6   relative frequency: 0.00008
See also "famovs."
```
    p.  29 EPIGRAMS 7         1 Where lately harbour'd many a famous whore,
    p.  85 EPIGRAMS 133      36 Did dance the famous Morrisse, vnto Norwich)
    p.  85 EPIGRAMS 133      66 Thorough her wombe they make their famous road,
    p. 114 FOREST 12         50 Haue beautie knowne, yet none so famous seene?
    p. 323 HORACE 2         381 This foot yet, in the famous Trimeters
    p. 335 HORACE 2         669 Or love of this so famous death lay by.
```

famovs   frequency: 1   relative frequency: 0.00001
    p.   84 EPIGRAMS 133   t1 ON THE FAMOVS VOYAGE.

fan   frequency: 1   relative frequency: 0.00001
    p. 370 UNGATHERED 8   4 Lady, or Pusil, that weares maske, or fan,

fancie   frequency: 3   relative frequency: 0.00004
    p. 231 UNDERWOOD 56   25 By this, although you fancie not the man,
    p. 276 U'WOOD 84.3   12 Worke with my fancie, his owne hand.
    p. 363 UNGATHERED 3   15 Straines fancie vnto foule Apostacie,

fancied   frequency: 2   relative frequency: 0.00002
    p.   55 EPIGRAMS 84   6 I fancied to my selfe, what wine, what wit
    p. 331 HORACE 2   561 So, any Poeme, fancied, or forth-brought

fancies   frequency: 1   relative frequency: 0.00001
    p. 145 UNDERWOOD 5   5 Wee have both wits, and fancies too,

fancy. See "fancie."

far   frequency: 1   relative frequency: 0.00001
    See also "a-farre," "farre," "farre-admired,"
            "farre-all-seeing," "farre-knowne."
    p.   53 EPIGRAMS 79   1 That Poets are far rarer births then kings,

fare   frequency: 3   relative frequency: 0.00004
    See also "thorough-fare."
    p.   97 FOREST 3   30 More for thy exercise, then fare;
    p. 208 UNDERWOOD 43 123 Well fare the wise-men yet, on the Banckside,
    p. 294 UNDERWOOD 89   2 Thou worthy in eternall Flower to fare,

fare-well   frequency: 1   relative frequency: 0.00001
    p.   87 EPIGRAMS 133 115 And bad her fare-well sough, vnto the lurden:

farewell   frequency: 7   relative frequency: 0.00010
    See also "fare-well."
    p.   41 EPIGRAMS 45   1 Farewell, thou child of my right hand, and ioy;
    p.   79 EPIGRAMS 124   12 Then that it liu'd at all. Farewell.
    p. 100 FOREST 4   t2 A farewell for a Gentle-woman, vertuous
    p. 161 UNDERWOOD 14   86 You both are modest. So am I. Farewell.
    p. 198 UNDERWOOD 40   50 If I had writ no word, but Deare, farewell.
    p. 199 UNDERWOOD 41   1 Since you must goe, and I must bid farewell,
    p. 387 UNGATHERED 22 12 not when I die'd, but how I liud. Farewell.

farmer   frequency: 4   relative frequency: 0.00005
    p.   94 FOREST 2   48 But all come in, the farmer, and the clowne:
    p. 117 FOREST 13   39 Or cos'ning farmer of the customes so,
    p. 291 UNDERWOOD 85   68 To turne mere farmer, had spoke out,
    p. 313 HORACE 2   165 A ventring Merchant, or the Farmer free

farre   frequency: 33   relative frequency: 0.00047
    p.   38 EPIGRAMS 36   1 MARTIAL, thou gau'st farre nobler
                             Epigrammes
    p.   38 EPIGRAMS 38   6 And lyes so farre from wit, 'tis impudence.
    p.   41 EPIGRAMS 43   10 And what I write thereof find farre, and free
    p.   43 EPIGRAMS 51   4 And farre beneath least pause of such a king,
    p.   53 EPIGRAMS 79   12 As he would burne, or better farre his booke.
    p.   67 EPIGRAMS 103   10 A SYDNEY: but in that extend as farre
    p.   95 FOREST 2   58 Adde to thy free prouisions, farre aboue
    p.   96 FOREST 2   87 When shee was farre: and not a roome, but drest,
    p. 102 FOREST 4   65 Nor for my peace will I goe farre,
    p. 110 FOREST 11   45 That is an essence, farre more gentle, fine,
    p. 118 FOREST 13   60 Farre from the maze of custome, error, strife,
    p. 121 FOREST 14   45 Say you haue follow'd farre,
    p. 132 UNDERWOOD 2.2   5 Farre I was from being stupid,
    p. 154 UNDERWOOD 13   55 As farre as any poore Sword i' the Land.
    p. 156 UNDERWOOD 13 121 Ride, saile, am coach'd, know I how farre I
                             have gone,
    p. 159 UNDERWOOD 14   17 But I on yours farre otherwise shall doe,
    p. 163 UNDERWOOD 15   29 As farre as he can flie, or follow day,
    p. 167 UNDERWOOD 15 172 Spread through the World) is easier farre to
                             find,
    p. 180 UNDERWOOD 25   65 As farre from all revolt, as you are now from
                             Fortune.
    p. 198 UNDERWOOD 40   38 Farre from the Nest, and so himselfe belie
    p. 219 UNDERWOOD 47   43 So farre without inquirie what the States,
    p. 240 UNDERWOOD 67   31 6. ERAT. Shee showes so farre above
    p. 242 UNDERWOOD 69   22 More subtle workes, and finer pieces farre,
    p. 245 UNDERWOOD 70   70 Is fairer farre, in May,
    p. 261 UNDERWOOD 77   12 As farre as sense, and onely by the eyes.

farre (cont.)
```
     p. 292 UNDERWOOD 86    15 Child of a hundred Arts, and farre
     p. 294 UNDERWOOD 87    23 And then rough Adria, angrier, farre;
     p. 309 HORACE 2        99 Shall perish: so farre off it is, the state,
     p. 321 HORACE 2       337 And farre unworthy to blurt out light rimes;
     p. 321 HORACE 2       339 To Dance, so she should, shamefac'd, differ
                              farre
     p. 321 HORACE 2       367 Fell into fault so farre, as now they saw
     p. 364 UNGATHERED 5     4 As farre as Sinne's from lightnesse.
     p. 391 UNGATHERED 26   29 And tell, how farre thou didst our Lily
                              out-shine,
```

farre-admired   frequency: 1 relative frequency: 0.00001
```
     p. 367 UNGATHERED 6    59 His farre-admired Acts,
```

farre-all-seeing   frequency: 1 relative frequency: 0.00001
```
     p. 256 UNDERWOOD 75   109 That farre-all-seeing Eye
```

farre-knowne   frequency: 1 relative frequency: 0.00001
```
     p. 329 HORACE 2       519 With honour make the farre-knowne Author live.
```

fart   frequency: 1 relative frequency: 0.00001
```
     p.  87 EPIGRAMS 133   108 Of the graue fart, late let in parliament,
```

farther   frequency: 6 relative frequency: 0.00008
See also "further."
```
     p.  56 EPIGRAMS 88      6 Toward the sea, farther then halfe-way tree?
     p. 108 FOREST 10A      12 A farther fury my ray'sd spirit Controules,
     p. 129 UNDERWOOD 1.2   30 Me farther tosse
     p. 154 UNDERWOOD 13    31 Himselfe of farther trouble, or the weight
     p. 185 UNDERWOOD 30     3 And goe no farther: let this Circle be
     p. 331 HORACE 2       541 As some the farther off: This loves the darke;
```

farthest   frequency: 1 relative frequency: 0.00001
```
     p. 223 UNDERWOOD 49    27 Farthest I am from the Idolatrie
```

farts   frequency: 1 relative frequency: 0.00001
```
     p.  87 EPIGRAMS 133   125 About the shore, of farts, but late departed,
```

fashion   frequency: 15 relative frequency: 0.00021
```
     p.  39 EPIGRAMS 40     13 Life, whose griefe was out of fashion,
     p.  47 EPIGRAMS 64      7 Nor glad for fashion. Nor to shew a fit
     p. 131 UNDERWOOD 2.1   12 Gives the Lover weight, and fashion.
     p. 141 UNDERWOOD 2.9    7 French to boote, at least in fashion,
     p. 157 UNDERWOOD 13   148 Nor fashion; if they chance aspire to height,
     p. 164 UNDERWOOD 15    55 Hee's one of blood, and fashion! and with these
     p. 164 UNDERWOOD 15    82 Of woman of fashion, and a Lady of spirit:
     p. 171 UNDERWOOD 20     8 Put on for fashion, and take up on trust:
     p. 229 UNDERWOOD 54    17 And you shall make me good, in weight, and
                              fashion,
     p. 283 U'WOOD 84.9     32 Whoorles me about, and to blaspheme in fashion!
     p. 307 HORACE 2        46 Th'Aemilian Schoole, in brasse can fashion out
     p. 311 HORACE 2       152 For Nature, first, within doth fashion us
     p. 362 UNGATHERED 2     3 Not wearing moodes, as gallants doe a fashion,
     p. 392 UNGATHERED 26   58 His Art doth giue the fashion. And, that he,
     p. 399 UNGATHERED 31   24 Of weight, or fashion, it was shee.
```

fashion'd   frequency: 3 relative frequency: 0.00004
```
     p. 108 FOREST 10A       4 like glasse, blowne vp, and fashion'd by desire.
     p. 119 FOREST 13      115 Not fashion'd for the court, or strangers eyes;
     p. 164 UNDERWOOD 15    84 Great, brave, and fashion'd folke, these are
                              allow'd
```

fashions   frequency: 3 relative frequency: 0.00004
```
     p.  33 EPIGRAMS 21      3 His clothes two fashions of, and poore! his sword
     p.  75 EPIGRAMS 115    31 An inginer, in slanders, of all fashions,
     p. 118 FOREST 13       71 Let who will follow fashions, and attyres,
```

fast   frequency: 5 relative frequency: 0.00007
```
     p.  32 EPIGRAMS 18      9 Pr'y thee beleeue still, and not iudge so fast,
     p. 157 UNDERWOOD 13   143 Such Notes are vertuous men! they live as fast
     p. 235 UNDERWOOD 61    18 To teach the people, how to fast, and pray,
     p. 258 UNDERWOOD 75   185 They both are slip'd to Bed; Shut fast the
                              Doore,
     p. 293 UNDERWOOD 86    38 I hold thee fast! but fled hence, with the
                              Light,
```

fasteneth. See "fastneth."

fastening. See "fastning."

fastidious   frequency: 1   relative frequency: 0.00001
  *p. 492 TO HIMSELF   7 Let their fastidious, vaine

fastneth   frequency: 1   relative frequency: 0.00001
  **p. 113 PANEGYRE   22 That fastneth heauenly power to earthly raigne:

fastning   frequency: 1   relative frequency: 0.00001
  p. 183 UNDERWOOD 29   11 Fastning Vowells, as with fetters

fat   frequency: 10   relative frequency: 0.00014
  p. 37 EPIGRAMS 32   5 The cold of Mosco, and fat Irish ayre,
  p. 38 EPIGRAMS 37   1 No cause, nor client fat, will CHEV'RILL
                             leese,
  p. 88 EPIGRAMS 133   160 And, now, aboue the poole, a face right fat
  p. 94 FOREST 2   33 Fat, aged carps, that runne into thy net.
  p. 98 FOREST 3   44 The hogs return'd home fat from mast;
  p. 127 UNDERWOOD 1.1   11 But 'bove the fat of rammes, or bulls, to prize
  p. 199 UNDERWOOD 42   2 As Horace fat; or as Anacreon old;
  p. 202 UNDERWOOD 42   84 Or a Close-stoole so cas'd; or any fat
  p. 230 UNDERWOOD 56   8 Unprofitable Chattell, fat and old,
  p. 405 UNGATHERED 34   69 I am too fat t'enuy him. He too leane

fatal. See "fatall."

fatall   frequency: 2   relative frequency: 0.00002
  p. 211 UNDERWOOD 43   192 To all as fatall as 't hath beene to me,
  p. 268 UNDERWOOD 83   3 And beckning wooes me, from the fatall tree

fate   frequency: 34   relative frequency: 0.00049
  **p. 115 PANEGYRE   85 "That princes, since they know it is their fate,
  **p. 117 PANEGYRE   135 And ceas'd in them. She told them, what a fate
  p. 28 EPIGRAMS 5   1 When was there contract better driuen by Pate?
  p. 37 EPIGRAMS 32   8 Was his blest fate, but our hard lot to find.
  p. 39 EPIGRAMS 40   15 Fate, in a brother. To conclude,
  p. 41 EPIGRAMS 45   4 Exacted by thy fate, on the iust day.
  p. 44 EPIGRAMS 55   7 What fate is mine, that so it selfe bereaues?
  p. 61 EPIGRAMS 95   11 Which Fate (it seemes) caus'd in the historie,
  p. 73 EPIGRAMS 113   5 I thinke, the Fate of court thy comming crau'd,
  p. 77 EPIGRAMS 120   17 So, by error, to his fate
  p. 89 EPIGRAMS 133   185 They laugh't, at his laugh-worthy fate. And past
  p. 96 FOREST 3   2 Whether by choice, or fate, or both;
  p. 99 FOREST 3   90 Though poyson, thinke it a great fate.
  p. 109 FOREST 11   2 Is vertue, and not Fate:
  p. 118 FOREST 13   47 Are you engaged to your happy fate,
  p. 127 UNDERWOOD 1.1   18 This All of nothing, gavest it forme, and fate,
  p. 133 UNDERWOOD 2.3   19 And would faine have chang'd the fate,
  p. 163 UNDERWOOD 15   35 Not to be checkt, or frighted now with fate,
  p. 168 UNDERWOOD 15   185 That whatsoever face thy fate puts on,
  p. 170 UNDERWOOD 18   22 I'le lead you on; or if my fate will so,
  p. 180 UNDERWOOD 26   3 Your fate hath found
  p. 181 UNDERWOOD 27   24 Which all the Fate of Troy foretold?
  p. 188 UNDERWOOD 34   17 I, that thy Ayme was; but her fate prevail'd:
  p. 199 UNDERWOOD 41   9 What fate is this, to change mens dayes and
                             houres,
  p. 207 UNDERWOOD 43   96 To speake the fate of the Sicilian Maid
  p. 216 UNDERWOOD 44   101 The fate of things: whilst totter'd vertue holds
  p. 246 UNDERWOOD 70   95 But fate doth so alternate the designe,
  p. 252 UNDERWOOD 75   10 (Bearing the promise of some better fate)
  p. 283 U'WOOD 84.9   27 Thou hast no more blowes, Fate, to drive at one:
  p. 293 UNDERWOOD 87   12 So Fate would give her life, and longer daies.
  p. 313 HORACE 2   196 I sing a noble Warre, and Priam's Fate.
  p. 317 HORACE 2   270 Nor must the Fable, that would hope the Fate,
  p. 340 HORACE 1   87 ... . Fate
  p. 368 UNGATHERED 6   81 Tames, prowde of thee, and of his Fate

fates   frequency: 14   relative frequency: 0.00020
  **p. 113 PANEGYRE   30 (Which Fates auert) should force her from her
                             right.
  **p. 114 PANEGYRE   65 Old men were glad, their fates till now did last;
  **p. 117 PANEGYRE   159 Which when time, nature, and the fates deny'd,
  p. 28 EPIGRAMS 4   3 But two things, rare, the FATES had in their
                             store,
  p. 35 EPIGRAMS 27   3 If any sword could saue from Fates, ROE'S
                             could;
  p. 67 EPIGRAMS 104   6 To make those faithfull, did the Fates send you?
  p. 70 EPIGRAMS 109   11 To make thy lent life, good against the Fates:
  p. 77 EPIGRAMS 120   10 When Fates turn'd cruell,
  p. 99 FOREST 3   80 And thinke his power doth equall Fates.
  p. 119 FOREST 13   107 But which the Fates forbid me to reueale.
  p. 219 UNDERWOOD 47   44 Brunsfield, and Mansfield doe this yeare, my
                             fates

fates (cont.)
    p. 225 UNDERWOOD 51   15 Whose even Thred the Fates spinne round, and
                              full,
    p. 293 UNDERWOOD 87   16 So Fates would let the Boy a long thred run.
    p. 422 UNGATHERED 50   4 whom fortune hath deprest; come nere the fates

father   frequency: 23   relative frequency: 0.00033
    See also "foster-father."
  **p. 117 PANEGYRE   137 How deare a father they did now enioy
    p. 33 EPIGRAMS 22   4 It makes the father, lesse, to rue.
    p. 41 EPIGRAMS 45   5 O, could I loose all father, now. For why
    p. 44 EPIGRAMS 53   8 Thou art the father, and the witnesse too.
    p. 53 EPIGRAMS 79   2 Your noblest father prou'd: like whom, before,
    p. 56 EPIGRAMS 88   9 Or had his father, when he did him get,
    p. 127 UNDERWOOD 1.1   17 5. Eternall Father, God, who did'st create
    p. 128 UNDERWOOD 1.1   26 Father and Sonne; the Comforter, inbreeding
    p. 128 UNDERWOOD 1.1   37 10. Father, and Sonne, and Holy Ghost, you three
    p. 129 UNDERWOOD 1.2   t1 A Hymne to God the Father.
    p. 151 UNDERWOOD 12   5 For I both lost a friend and Father,
    p. 192 UNDERWOOD 38   41 There is no Father that for one demerit,
    p. 208 UNDERWOOD 43   112 With lust conceiv'd thee; Father thou hadst
                              none:
    p. 220 UNDERWOOD 48   1 Since, Bacchus, thou art father
    p. 225 UNDERWOOD 51   11 What then his Father was, that since is hee,
    p. 231 UNDERWOOD 57   1 Father John Burges,
    p. 259 UNDERWOOD 76   5 That whereas your royall Father,
    p. 264 UNDERWOOD 79   40 1. Hee is the Father of our peace;
    p. 282 U'WOOD 84.8   22 Which Vertue from your Father, ripe, will fall;
    p. 288 U'WOOD 84.9   215 In that great Act of judgement: which the
                              Father
    p. 339 HORACE 1   34 Father ... sons right worthy of your ....
    p. 411 UNGATHERED 39   12 A Tune to drown the Ballads of thy Father:
    p. 416 UNGATHERED 44   8 And you, with them, as Father of our spring.

fathers   frequency: 17   relative frequency: 0.00024
    p. 47 EPIGRAMS 64   6 To see thy fathers rites new laid on thee.
    p. 86 EPIGRAMS 133   84 Made of the trull, that cut her fathers lock:
    p. 107 FOREST 10   15 Who, with his axe, thy fathers mid-wife plaid.
    p. 114 FOREST 12   31 For what a sinne 'gainst your great fathers
                              spirit,
    p. 130 UNDERWOOD 1.3   13 The Fathers wisedome will'd it so,
    p. 200 UNDERWOOD 42   11 Fathers, and Husbands, I doe claime a right
    p. 207 UNDERWOOD 43   103 After the Fathers, and those wiser Guides
    p. 225 UNDERWOOD 51   14 In his soft Cradle to his Fathers Chaire,
    p. 233 UNDERWOOD 59   20 And was your Fathers! All your Ancestours!
    p. 240 UNDERWOOD 67   30 And of her Fathers prowesse!
    p. 256 UNDERWOOD 75   107 To day, the Fathers service; who could bring
    p. 257 UNDERWOOD 75   147 All that their Fathers, and their Mothers might
    p. 260 UNDERWOOD 76   27 Those your Fathers Markes, your Pounds;
    p. 331 HORACE 2   546 Informed rightly, by your Fathers care,
    p. 331 HORACE 2   577 And, to your Fathers, and to mine; though 't be
    p. 335 HORACE 2   671 Whether he piss'd upon his Fathers grave;
    p. 392 UNGATHERED 26   65 And such wert thou. Looke how the fathers face

father's   frequency: 1   relative frequency: 0.00001
    See also "fathers."
    p. 410 UNGATHERED 39   7 To be the Denis of thy Father's School,

fattest   frequency: 1   relative frequency: 0.00001
    p. 291 UNDERWOOD 85   56 From fattest branches of the Tree:

fault   frequency: 8   relative frequency: 0.00011
    See also "fault's."
    p. 60 EPIGRAMS 93   15 Willing to expiate the fault in thee,
    p. 79 EPIGRAMS 124   7 If, at all, shee had a fault,
    p. 191 UNDERWOOD 38   21 I will not stand to justifie my fault,
    p. 307 HORACE 2   43 So, shunning faults, to greater fault doth lead,
    p. 321 HORACE 2   367 Fell into fault so farre, as now they saw
    p. 335 HORACE 2   629 Then: If your fault you rather had defend
    p. 370 UNGATHERED 7   13 'Tis not your fault, if they shall sense
                              preferre,
    p. 384 UNGATHERED 18   14 Hymens amends, to make it worth his fault.

faults   frequency: 6   relative frequency: 0.00008
    See also "ffaultes."
  **p. 113 PANEGYRE   10 Where men commit blacke incest with their faults;
    p. 156 UNDERWOOD 13   114 I have the lyst of mine owne faults to know,
    p. 307 HORACE 2   43 So, shunning faults, to greater fault doth lead,
    p. 319 HORACE 2   285 Hide faults, pray to the Gods, and wish aloud

faults (cont.)
    p. 323 HORACE 2   392 Or rather, thinking all my faults may spie,
    p. 329 HORACE 2   520 There are yet faults, which we would well
                             forgive,

fault's   frequency: 1   relative frequency: 0.00001
    p. 362 UNGATHERED 2   8 The fault's not in the obiect, but their eyes.

faunes   frequency: 2   relative frequency: 0.00002
    p. 34 FOREST 2   18 The lighter Faunes, to reach the Ladies oke.
    p. 321 HORACE 2   355 But, let the Faunes, drawne from their Groves,
                             beware,

fauns. See "faunes."

fauors   frequency: 1   relative frequency: 0.00001
  **p. 113 PANEGYRE   2 With ioyes: but vrgeth his full fauors still.

fauour   frequency: 1   relative frequency: 0.00001
    p. 27 EPIGRAMS 3   4 For the lucks sake, it thus much fauour haue,

fauourite   frequency: 1   relative frequency: 0.00001
    p. 63 EPIGRAMS 97   13 He is no fauourites fauourite, no deare trust

fauourites   frequency: 1   relative frequency: 0.00001
    p. 63 EPIGRAMS 97   13 He is no fauourites fauourite, no deare trust

fauours   frequency: 3   relative frequency: 0.00004
    p. 103 FOREST 6   2 Can your fauours keepe, and couer,
    p. 113 FOREST 12   14 When his proud patrons fauours are asleepe;
    p. 115 FOREST 12   71 Yet, for the timely fauours shee hath done,

favorite   frequency: 1   relative frequency: 0.00001
    p. 235 UNDERWOOD 61   20 He is the Man, and Favorite of God.

favour   frequency: 5   relative frequency: 0.00007
    See also "dis-favour," "fauour."
    p. 186 UNDERWOOD 31   10 You favour Truth, and me, in this mans Cause.
    p. 186 UNDERWOOD 32   1 The Judge his favour timely then extends,
    p. 255 UNDERWOOD 75   89 It is their Grace, and favour, that makes seene,
    p. 277 U'WOOD 84.3   31 Whose 'tis: but if it favour find,
    p. 317 HORACE 2   280 It still must favour good men, and to these

favouring   frequency: 1   relative frequency: 0.00001
    p. 159 UNDERWOOD 14   16 Themselves through favouring what is there not
                             found:

favourite. See "fauourite," "favorite."

favourite's. See "fauourites."

favours   frequency: 1   relative frequency: 0.00001
    See also "fauors," "fauours."
    p. 192 UNDERWOOD 38   53 That is, if still your Favours you apply,

fayerie   frequency: 1   relative frequency: 0.00001
    p. 398 UNGATHERED 30 79 But then refreshed, with thy Fayerie Court,

fayne   frequency: 1   relative frequency: 0.00001
    p. 406 UNGATHERED 35   2 Hath made his Inigo Marquess, wouldst thou
                             fayne

fayre   frequency: 4   relative frequency: 0.00005
    p. 112 FOREST 11   98 As sweet, as shee is fayre.
    p. 275 U'WOOD 84.3   7 This beautie without falshood fayre,
    p. 382 UNGATHERED 16   6 presentes a Royall Alter of fayre peace,
    p. 396 UNGATHERED 30 18 Is fayre got vp, and day some houres begun!

fayrest   frequency: 1   relative frequency: 0.00001
    p. 662 INSCRIPTS. 2   6 to CYNTHIAS fayrest Nymph hath sent thee,

fear   frequency: 1   relative frequency: 0.00001
    See also "feare," "ffeare."
    p. 408 UNGATHERED 36   6 Thou'rt too ambitious: and dost fear in vaine!

fear'd   frequency: 3   relative frequency: 0.00004
    p. 56 EPIGRAMS 89   2 Fear'd not to boast the glories of her stage,
    p. 173 UNDERWOOD 22   20 That envie wish'd, and Nature fear'd.
    p. 333 HORACE 2   592 Did learne them first, and once a Master fear'd.

feare   frequency: 48   relative frequency: 0.00069
  **p. 115 PANEGYRE   87 "Betraid to fame, should take more care, and
                              feare
  **p. 116 PANEGYRE   124 To offer cause of iniurie, or feare.
    p.   32 EPIGRAMS 17   1 May others feare, flie, and traduce thy name,
    p.   38 EPIGRAMS 35   6 Left vs of feare, but first our crimes, then
                              lawes.
    p.   43 EPIGRAMS 53   1 Long-gathering OLD-END, I did feare thee
                              wise,
    p.   44 EPIGRAMS 55   3 How I doe feare my selfe, that am not worth
    p.   46 EPIGRAMS 62   1 Fine MADAME WOVLD-BEE, wherefore
                              should you feare,
    p.   53 EPIGRAMS 77   1 Be safe, nor feare thy selfe so good a fame,
    p.   58 EPIGRAMS 91   18 Who more should seeke mens reuerence, then feare.
    p.   59 EPIGRAMS 92   17 And talke reseru'd, lock'd vp, and full of feare,
    p.   61 EPIGRAMS 95   18 That liu'st from hope, from feare, from faction
                              free;
    p.   73 EPIGRAMS 113   11 Nor may'any feare, to loose of their degree,
    p.   86 EPIGRAMS 133   79 They met the second Prodigie, would feare a
    p.   95 FOREST 2   62 Without his feare, and of thy lords owne meate:
    p. 101 FOREST 4   37 Yes, threaten, doe. Alas I feare
    p. 104 FOREST 8   8 I shall feare, you'll surfet too.
    p. 110 FOREST 11   41 With whom who sailes, rides on the surge of
                              feare,
    p. 117 FOREST 13   20 Or feare to draw true lines, 'cause others paint:
    p. 122 FOREST 15   19 Standing with feare, and must with horror fall,
    p. 140 UNDERWOOD 2.8 12 We all feare, she loveth none.
    p. 147 UNDERWOOD 7   4 I feare they'd love him too;
    p. 147 UNDERWOOD 7   21 And feare much more, that more of him be showne.
    p. 148 UNDERWOOD 7   35 If Love, or feare, would let me tell his name.
    p. 150 UNDERWOOD 10   12 Think'st thou that love is help'd by feare?
    p. 156 UNDERWOOD 13 106 'Twixt feare and rashnesse: not a lust obscene,
    p. 169 UNDERWOOD 18   6 A terror? or is all this but my feare?
    p. 170 UNDERWOOD 18   17 To see men feare: or else for truth, and State,
    p. 183 UNDERWOOD 29   8 Propping Verse, for feare of falling
    p. 199 UNDERWOOD 41   15 You would restore it? No, that's worth a feare,
    p. 229 UNDERWOOD 54   7 So that upon the point, my corporall feare
    p. 230 UNDERWOOD 56   6 The first of which, I feare, you will refuse:
    p. 230 UNDERWOOD 56   15 Sleepe in a Virgins bosome without feare,
    p. 240 UNDERWOOD 67   45 And with a reverend feare,
    p. 242 UNDERWOOD 69   18 Where he would fixe, for the distinctions feare.
    p. 270 UNDERWOOD 83   53 Stick on your Cupping-glasses, feare not, put
    p. 293 UNDERWOOD 83   11 As, for her, I'ld not feare to die,
    p. 295 UNDERWOOD 90   13 Nor feare thy latest day, nor wish therfore.
    p. 317 HORACE 2   244 Or do's all businesse coldly, and with feare;
    p. 317 HORACE 2   282 The angry, and love those that feare t'offend.
    p. 331 HORACE 2   575 But, if hereafter thou shalt write, not feare
    p. 335 HORACE 2   643 Wise, sober folke, a frantick Poet feare,
    p. 367 UNGATHERED 6   48 "Where neither Force can bend, nor Feare can
                              awe.
    p. 369 UNGATHERED 6   94 To loose that feare;
    p. 375 UNGATHERED 10 35 Beeing in feare to be robd, he most learnedly
                              begs.
    p. 407 UNGATHERED 36   1 Sr Inigo doth feare it as I heare
    p. 407 UNGATHERED 36   2 (And labours to seem worthy of yt feare)
    p. 417 UNGATHERED 45 32 yet doe not feare it.
    p. 423 UNGATHERED 50 20 shall never dare do any thing but feare./

fearefull   frequency: 2   relative frequency: 0.00002
    p. 112 FOREST 11   109 Would not be fearefull to offend a dame
    p. 412 UNGATHERED 40 15 From fearefull back-slides;

fearefully   frequency: 2   relative frequency: 0.00002
    p.   51 EPIGRAMS 73   2 Or take an Epigramme so fearefully
    p.   51 EPIGRAMS 73   12 Item, a charme surrounding fearefully

feares   frequency: 14   relative frequency: 0.00020
    p.   37 EPIGRAMS 34   1 He that feares death, or mournes it, in the iust,
    p.   43 EPIGRAMS 51   10 Looke not vpon thy dangers, but our feares.
    p.   74 EPIGRAMS 115   20 Not that it feares, but will not haue to doo
    p. 101 FOREST 4   43 Since stird'st vp iealousies and feares,
    p. 109 FOREST 11   26 Th'are base, and idle feares
    p. 112 FOREST 11   90 His heart sinnes, though he feares.
    p. 145 UNDERWOOD 4   11 Nor spread them as distract with feares,
    p. 148 UNDERWOOD 7   26 But then t'increase my feares,
    p. 149 UNDERWOOD 9   11 Oh, but my conscious feares,
    p. 223 UNDERWOOD 49   22 And that her truster feares her? Must I too?
    p. 230 UNDERWOOD 55   7 Yet with a Dye, that feares no Moth,
    p. 244 UNDERWOOD 70   53 Goe now, and tell out dayes summ'd up with
                              feares,

feares (cont.)
    p. 270 UNDERWOOD 83   60 Made her friends joyes to get above their feares!
    p. 380 UNGATHERED 12   31 Of lying, he feares so much the reproofe

fearful. See "fearefull," "fearfull."

fearfull   frequency: 2   relative frequency: 0.00002
    p. 239 UNDERWOOD 67   10 As fearfull to awake
    p. 290 UNDERWOOD 85   35 And snares the fearfull Hare, and new-come
                            Crane,

fearfully. See "fearefully."

fearing   frequency: 2   relative frequency: 0.00002
    p. 331 HORACE 2   542 This, fearing not the subtlest Judges marke,
    p. 339 HORACE 1   41 Being over-safe, and fearing .. the flaw:

fears. See "feares."

feast   frequency: 20   relative frequency: 0.00028
**p. 114 PANEGYRE   52 As our ambitious dames, when they make feast,
    p. 51 EPIGRAMS 73   6 I lent you, on meere acquaintance, at a feast.
    p. 64 EPIGRAMS 101   4 But that your worth will dignifie our feast,
    p. 81 EPIGRAMS 129   5 That scarse the Towne designeth any feast
    p. 94 FOREST 2   21 When thou would'st feast, or exercise thy
                            friends.
    p. 96 FOREST 3   6 Of Sheriffes dinner, or Maiors feast.
    p. 120 FOREST 14   10 Both loue the cause, and authors of the feast?
    p. 144 UNDERWOOD 3   23 To fall againe; at such a feast,
    p. 205 UNDERWOOD 43 60 T'have held a Triumph, or a feast of fire,
    p. 221 UNDERWOOD 48 15 Of feast, and merry meeting,
    p. 221 UNDERWOOD 48 38 Shall feast it, thou maist love there
    p. 253 UNDERWOOD 75 14 So like a feast?
    p. 254 UNDERWOOD 75 55 This Feast, then can the Day,
    p. 257 UNDERWOOD 75 141 There is a Feast behind,
    p. 284 U'WOOD 84.9   62 Who in that feast of Resurrection trust!
    p. 284 U'WOOD 84.9   82 Out of her noble body, to this Feast:
    p. 291 UNDERWOOD 85 59 Or at the Feast of Bounds, the Lambe then
                            slaine,
    p. 292 UNDERWOOD 86 11 There jest, and feast, make him thine host,
    p. 311 HORACE 2   122 In tragick Verse; no lesse Thyestes feast
    p. 394 UNGATHERED 28 20 Whom shee, with Sorrow first did lodge, then
                            feast,

feasting   frequency: 1   relative frequency: 0.00001
    See also "ffeasting."
    p. 69 EPIGRAMS 107   30 Twirle the poore chaine you run a feasting in.

feasts   frequency: 8   relative frequency: 0.00011
    p. 93 FOREST 2   11 Where PAN, and BACCHVS their high
                            feasts haue made,
    p. 97 FOREST 3   40 And feasts, that either shearers keepe;
    p. 166 UNDERWOOD 15 117 What furie of late is crept into our Feasts?
    p. 221 UNDERWOOD 48 42 As shall the feasts faire grounds be.
    p. 222 UNDERWOOD 49 16 To Church, as others doe to Feasts and Playes,
    p. 246 UNDERWOOD 70 103 Of rimes, or ryots, at your feasts,
    p. 319 HORACE 2   297 And they uncensur'd might at Feasts, and Playes
    p. 331 HORACE 2   557 As jarring Musique doth, at jolly feasts,

feat. See "ffeat."

feather. See "fether."

feathers   frequency: 6   relative frequency: 0.00008
    p. 98 FOREST 3   71 And shew their feathers shot, and cullors torne,
    p. 154 UNDERWOOD 13 58 Ha's Feathers, and will serve a man to pull.
    p. 162 UNDERWOOD 15 21 Or Feathers: lay his fortune out to show,
    p. 213 UNDERWOOD 44   9 They saw too store of feathers, and more may,
    p. 275 U'WOOD 84.3   3 Embroderies, Feathers, Fringes, Lace,
    p. 305 HORACE 2   2 Set a Horse-neck, and divers feathers fold

feats   frequency: 1   relative frequency: 0.00001
    p. 156 UNDERWOOD 13 95 Or feats of darknesse acted in Mid-Sun,

feature   frequency: 7   relative frequency: 0.00010
    p. 39 EPIGRAMS 40   16 For wit, feature, and true passion,
    p. 46 EPIGRAMS 62   7 That can restore that. Will it hurt your
                          feature?
    p. 77 EPIGRAMS 120   6 In grace, and feature,
    p. 112 FOREST 11   101 All her best symmetrie in that one feature!

feature (cont.)
    p. 131 UNDERWOOD 2.1   9 Or the feature, or the youth:
    p. 305 HORACE 2   4 Presenting upwards, a faire female feature,
    p. 364 UNGATHERED 4   7 Proue of his Mistris Feature,

features   frequency: 1   relative frequency: 0.00001
    p. 117 FOREST 13   24 In my character, what your features bee,

fed   frequency: 6   relative frequency: 0.00008
    p. 155 UNDERWOOD 13   67 But one is bitten by the Dog he fed,
    p. 218 UNDERWOOD 47   18 Like flies, or wormes, which mans corrupt parts
                              fed:
    p. 228 UNDERWOOD 53   20 At these Immortall Mangers Virgil fed.
    p. 259 UNDERWOOD 76   16 (For with both the MUSE was fed)
    p. 291 UNDERWOOD 85   62 Of the fed flocks approaching home!
    p. 313 HORACE 2   168 Or, with the milke of Thebes; or Argus, fed.

fee   frequency: 2   relative frequency: 0.00002
    p. 186 UNDERWOOD 32   6 Are there for Charitie, and not for fee.
    p. 187 UNDERWOOD 33   22 Thou hast the brave scorne, to put back the fee!

feed   frequency: 7   relative frequency: 0.00010
  *p. 493 TO HIMSELF   33 Can feed on orts: And safe in your
                              stage-clothes,
    p. 94 FOREST 2   23 Thy sheepe, thy bullocks, kine, and calues doe
                              feed:
    p. 105 FOREST 8   13 'Pray thee, feed contented, then,
    p. 144 UNDERWOOD 3   19 And out of inward pleasure feed
    p. 155 UNDERWOOD 13   74 Feed those, at whom the Table points at still?
    p. 250 UNDERWOOD 73   9 Feed on thy selfe for spight, and shew thy Kind:
    p. 288 U'WOOD 84.9   194 To cloath the naked, feed the hungry. Shee

feeding   frequency: 1   relative frequency: 0.00001
    p. 128 UNDERWOOD 1.1   27 Pure thoughts in man: with fiery zeale them
                              feeding

feel. See "feele."

feele   frequency: 14   relative frequency: 0.00020
  *p. 494 TO HIMSELF   55 Feele such a flesh-quake to possesse their
                              powers:
    p. 122 FOREST 15   21 I feele my griefes too, and there scarce is
                              ground,
    p. 152 UNDERWOOD 12   36 I feele, I'm rather dead than he!
    p. 153 UNDERWOOD 13   12 As I did feele it done, as soone as meant:
    p. 156 UNDERWOOD 13   123 No! he must feele and know, that will advance.
    p. 164 UNDERWOOD 15   77 For t'other pound of sweet-meats, he shall feele
    p. 199 UNDERWOOD 41   8 Where we must feele it Darke for halfe a yeare.
    p. 250 UNDERWOOD 73   12 T<o>'effect it, feele, thou'ast made thine owne
                              heart ake.
    p. 261 UNDERWOOD 77   21 And mightiest Monarchs feele what large increase
    p. 269 UNDERWOOD 83   7 To give your shade a name! Stay, stay, I feele
    p. 283 U'WOOD 84.9   29 Sure, I am dead, and know it not! I feele
    p. 380 UNGATHERED 12   54 And being at Flushing enforced to feele
    p. 385 UNGATHERED 20   5 I do not feele that euer yet I had
    p. 398 UNGATHERED 30   77 I feele it by mine owne, that ouer flow,

feeles   frequency: 3   relative frequency: 0.00004
    p. 36 EPIGRAMS 31   1 BANCK feeles no lamenesse of his knottie
                              gout,
    p. 156 UNDERWOOD 13   117 And feeles it; Else he tarries by the Beast.
    p. 309 HORACE 2   95 In neighbour-townes, and feeles the weightie
                              plough;

feels. See "feeles."

fees   frequency: 2   relative frequency: 0.00002
    p. 38 EPIGRAMS 37   2 But as they come, on both sides he takes fees,
    p. 98 FOREST 3   62 Nor how to get the lawyer fees.

feet   frequency: 5   relative frequency: 0.00007
    See also "feete."
    p. 149 UNDERWOOD 9   8 In sentence, of as subtile feet,
    p. 184 UNDERWOOD 29   56 The cold tumor in his feet,
    p. 292 UNDERWOOD 86   28 Thrice 'bout thy Altar with their Ivory feet.
    p. 379 UNGATHERED 12   4 To his strength, hath measur'd it out with his
                              feet.
    p. 405 UNGATHERED 34   67 Hee's warme on his feet now he sayes, & can

feete   frequency: 4   relative frequency: 0.00005
   p. 108 FOREST 10 A   11 Let these in wanton feete daunce out their
                                  soules.
   p. 363 UNGATHERED 3   12 And makes her supple feete, as swift as winde.
   p. 393 UNGATHERED 27   12 All false-hood vnder feete.
   p. 418 UNGATHERED 46   5 Il may Ben Johnson slander so his feete,

feign. See "raine," "feigne."

feigne   frequency: 1   relative frequency: 0.00001
   p. 313 HORACE 2   189 For, being a Poet, thou maist feigne, create,

feigned. See "fain'd," "fained."

feignest. See "fain'st."

feigns. See "faines."

felicitie   frequency: 1   relative frequency: 0.00001
   p. 166 UNDERWOOD 15   144 That scratching now's our best Felicitie?

felicity. See "felicitie."

fell   frequency: 10   relative frequency: 0.00014
   p. 60 EPIGRAMS 93   5 Two brauely in the battaile fell, and dy'd,
   p. 71 EPIGRAMS 110   14 And that, midst enuy' and parts; then fell by
                                    rage:
   p. 86 EPIGRAMS 133   95 Had burst with storme, and downe fell, ab
                                    excelsis,
   p. 166 UNDERWOOD 15   128 But both fell prest under the load they make.
   p. 209 UNDERWOOD 43   145 But, others fell with that conceipt by the eares,
   p. 243 UNDERWOOD 70   17 Sword, fire, and famine, with fell fury met;
   p. 244 UNDERWOOD 70   43 Alas, but Morison fell young:
   p. 244 UNDERWOOD 70   44 Hee never fell, thou fall'st, my tongue.
   p. 321 HORACE 2   367 Fell into fault so farre, as now they saw
   p. 361 UNGATHERED 1   25 till giddie with amazement I fell downe

fellow   frequency: 2   relative frequency: 0.00002
   See alsc "chamber-fellow."
   p. 165 UNDERWOOD 15   98 A fellow of course Letcherie, is nam'd,
   p. 339 HORACE 1   53 .. .. fellow .... to be ..... out

fellowes   frequency: 1   relative frequency: 0.00001
   p. 285 U'WOOD 84.9   101 Her fellowes, with the oyle of gladnesse, bright

fellows. See "fellowes."

fellowship   frequency: 2   relative frequency: 0.00002
   p. 323 HORACE 2   380 Of fellowship, the fourth, or second place.
   p. 409 UNGATHERED 38   4 Of Fellowship, professing my old Arts.

fells   frequency: 2   relative frequency: 0.00002
   p. 264 UNDERWOOD 79   16 3. Our milke. 4. Our fells. 5. Our fleeces. 6.
                                    And first Lambs.
   p. 265 UNDERWOOD 79   50 Your Milkes, your Fells, your Fleeces, and
                                    first Lambes,

felt   frequency: 5   relative frequency: 0.00007
  **p. 114 PANEGYRE   36 As if they felt, but had not knowne their good:
   p. 93 FOREST 1   3 Which when he felt, Away (quoth hee)
   p. 135 UNDERWOOD 2.4   25 Have you felt the wooll o' the Bever?
   p. 200 UNDERWOOD 42   34 And braveries of Court, and felt their fits
   p. 234 UNDERWOOD 61   14 My Lord, till felt griefe make our stone hearts
                                    soft,

female   frequency: 1   relative frequency: 0.00001
   See alsc "faemale."
   p. 305 HORACE 2   4 Presenting upwards, a faire female feature,

fen   frequency: 2   relative frequency: 0.00002
   p. 214 UNDERWOOD 44   54 As Stiles, Dike, Ditchfield, Millar, Crips,
                                    and Fen:
   p. 309 HORACE 2   93 A kingly worke; or that long barren fen

fenc'd   frequency: 1   relative frequency: 0.00001
   See alsc "fenc't."
   p. 33 EPIGRAMS 21   2 His neck fenc'd round with ruffe! his eyes halfe
                                    shut!

fencer
                          frequency: 1   relative frequency: 0.00001
     p.   50 EPIGRAMS 69   1 COB, thou nor souldier, thiefe, nor fencer art,

fencing
                          frequency: 1   relative frequency: 0.00001
     p. 232 UNDERWOOD 59   1 They talke of Fencing, and the use of Armes,

fenc't
                          frequency: 1   relative frequency: 0.00001
     p.   36 EPIGRAMS 133   76 But still their valour, and their vertue fenc't
                               'hem,

fenn. See "fen."

ferrabosco
                          frequency: 1   relative frequency: 0.00001
     p.   82 EPIGRAMS 130   t1 TO ALPHONSO FERRABOSCO, on his
                               Booke.

fertile
                          frequency: 1   relative frequency: 0.00001
     p.   94 FOREST 2   26 Fertile of wood, ASHORE, and
                               SYDNEY'S copp's,

fescennine
                          frequency: 1   relative frequency: 0.00001
     p. 257 UNDERWOOD 75   160 But dare not aske our wish in Language
                               fescennine:

fet
                          frequency: 1   relative frequency: 0.00001
     p. 325 HORACE 2   436 Their Charge, and Office, whence their wealth
                               to fet,

fetch
                          frequency: 2   relative frequency: 0.00002
     p. 140 UNDERWOOD 2.8   18 To fetch in the Formes goe by:
     p. 188 UNDERWOOD 35   6 To fetch the flesh, we keepe the Rowle.

tether
                          frequency: 1   relative frequency: 0.00001
     p.   56 EPIGRAMS 88   3 That so much skarfe of France, and hat, and
                               fether,

fetter
                          frequency: 1   relative frequency: 0.00001
     p.   93 FOREST 1   4 Can Poets hope to fetter mee?

fetters
                          frequency: 1   relative frequency: 0.00001
     p. 183 UNDERWOOD 29   11 Fastning Vowells, as with fetters

feud. See "fewd."

feuer
                          frequency: 1   relative frequency: 0.00001
     p.   60 EPIGRAMS 93   8 The Belgick feuer rauished away.

fever. See "feuer."

fevery. See "fev'ry."

fev'ry
                          frequency: 1   relative frequency: 0.00001
     p. 220 UNDERWOOD 47   67 And that there be no fev'ry heats, nor colds,

few
                          frequency: 15   relative frequency: 0.00021
     p.   32 EPIGRAMS 16   7 Nor need'st thou: for those few, by oath releast,
     p.   39 EPIGRAMS 40   14 In these times. Few so haue ru'de
     p.   55 EPIGRAMS 85   2 My selfe a witnesse of thy few dayes sport:
     p.   61 EPIGRAMS 94   13 And like them too; must needfully, though few,
     p.   71 EPIGRAMS 110   16 How few haue read! how fewer vnderstood!)
     p. 102 FOREST 5   12 Of a few poore houshold spyes?
     p. 116 FOREST 13   2 Of any good minde, now: There are so few.
     p. 157 UNDERWOOD 13   151 But few and faire Divisions: but being got
     p. 186 UNDERWOOD 32   5 When those good few, that her Defenders be,
     p. 230 UNDERWOOD 56   3 A booke to a few lynes: but, it was fit
     p. 242 UNDERWOOD 69   19 For as at distance, few have facultie
     p. 319 HORACE 2   289 But soft, and simple, at few holes breath'd time
     p. 319 HORACE 2   293 They might with ease be numbred, being a few
     p. 329 HORACE 2   527 Offended with few spots, which negligence
     p. 410 UNGATHERED 38   10 A Prentise-ship: which few doe now a dayes.

fewd
                          frequency: 1   relative frequency: 0.00001
     p. 116 FOREST 13   9 And howsoeuer; as I am at fewd

fewer
                          frequency: 1   relative frequency: 0.00001
     p.   71 EPIGRAMS 110   16 How few haue read! how fewer vnderstood!)

fewest
                          frequency: 1   relative frequency: 0.00001
     p.   60 EPIGRAMS 94   8 Their vn-auoided subiect, fewest see:

fface   frequency: 2   relative frequency: 0.00002
   p. 419 UNGATHERED 48   2 Of that true fface
   p. 420 UNGATHERED 48   25 to gett the<e> a leane fface,

ffaultes   frequency: 1   relative frequency: 0.00001
   p. 421 UNGATHERED 49   11 or Malyce to make ffaultes, wch nowe is skill.

ffeare   frequency: 1   relative frequency: 0.00001
   p. 421 UNGATHERED 48   42 Cause Reverence, yf not ffeare,

ffeasting   frequency: 1   relative frequency: 0.00001
   p. 406 UNGATHERED 34 101 Lyue long ye ffeasting Roome. And ere thou
                             burne

ffeat   frequency: 1   relative frequency: 0.00001
   p. 405 UNGATHERED 34   71 To pitty him, as smiling at his ffeat

ffeild   frequency: 1   relative frequency: 0.00001
   p. 421 UNGATHERED 48   40 Thou mad'st in open ffeild

ffinde   frequency: 1   relative frequency: 0.00001
   p. 421 UNGATHERED 49   10 deignes myne the power to ffinde, yett want I
                             will

ffirst   frequency: 1   relative frequency: 0.00001
   p. 361 UNGATHERED 1   5 ffirst: thy successe did strike my sence with
                             wonder;

ffoole   frequency: 1   relative frequency: 0.00001
   p. 408 UNGATHERED 37   5 ffoole, doe not rate my Rymes; I'haue found thy
                             Vice

ffor   frequency: 1   relative frequency: 0.00001

fforth   frequency: 1   relative frequency: 0.00001
   p. 420 UNGATHERED 48   26 And come fforth worthie Ivye, or the Bayes,

ffortune   frequency: 1   relative frequency: 0.00001
   p. 419 UNGATHERED 48   4 that ffortune to imbrace,

ffree   frequency: 2   relative frequency: 0.00002
   p. 421 UNGATHERED 49   6 I haue, wth strict advantage of ffree tyme
   p. 422 UNGATHERED 49   17 .... ffree ....

ffreind   frequency: 1   relative frequency: 0.00001
   p. 407 UNGATHERED 36   t1 To a ffreind an Epigram

ffreinds   frequency: 1   relative frequency: 0.00001
   p. 399 UNGATHERED 31   3 Transmitt it to your Nephewes, ffreinds,
                             Allies,

ffresh   frequency: 1   relative frequency: 0.00001
   p. 420 UNGATHERED 48   32 And once more stryke the eare of tyme wth those
                             ffresh straynes:

ffriend   frequency: 1   relative frequency: 0.00001
   p. 394 UNGATHERED 28   17 But Sorrow, she desir'd no other ffriend:

ffrostes   frequency: 1   relative frequency: 0.00001
   p. 361 UNGATHERED 1   8 Vnseason'd ffrostes, or the most enuyous weather.

ffyre   frequency: 1   relative frequency: 0.00001
   p. 420 UNGATHERED 48   21 And rather to the ffyre, then to the Rowte

fibre   frequency: 1   relative frequency: 0.00001
   p. 286 U'WOOD 84.9   151 The smallest Fibre of our flesh; he can

fibres   frequency: 1   relative frequency: 0.00001
   p. 194 UNDERWOOD 38   111 How all my Fibres by your Spirit doe move,

field   frequency: 12   relative frequency: 0.00017
   See also "ffeild."
   p. 42 EPIGRAMS 48   2 Of bearing them in field, he threw 'hem away:
   p. 94 FOREST 2   29 The painted partrich lyes in euery field,
   p. 141 UNDERWOOD 2.9   18 Front, an ample field of snow;
   p. 185 UNDERWOOD 30   8 The poores full Store-house, and just servants
                             field.
   p. 186 UNDERWOOD 33   3 Or the great Hall at Westminster, the field
   p. 213 UNDERWOOD 44   18 To have their Husbands drawne forth to the
                             field,

field (cont.)
    p. 228 UNDERWOOD 53   3 To all the uses of the field, and race,
    p. 280 U'WOOD 84.4   67 Upon a banke, or field of flowers,
    p. 293 UNDERWOOD 86   39 Whether in Mars his field thou bee,
    p. 315 HORACE 2   231 I'the open field; is Waxe like to be wrought
    p. 331 HORACE 2   566 His armes in Mars his field, he doth refuse;
    p. 413 UNGATHERED 41   22 Which, of the field is clep'd the sweetest brier,

fields   frequency: 4   relative frequency: 0.00005
    p. 97 FOREST 3   38 Of flowrie fields, of cop'ces greene,
    p. 103 FOREST 6   14 Or the sands in Chelsey fields,
    p. 132 UNDERWOOD 2.2   4 All the Pride the fields than have:
    p. 290 UNDERWOOD 85   17 Or when that Autumne, through the fields, lifts
             round

fier   frequency: 1   relative frequency: 0.00001
    p. 383 UNGATHERED 16   16 yf from a little sparke hee rise not fier.

fierce   frequency: 4   relative frequency: 0.00005
    p. 48 EPIGRAMS 65   3 Made me commit most fierce idolatrie
    p. 189 UNDERWOOD 36   15 Now hot, now cold, now fierce, now mild.
    p. 327 HORACE 2   482 Was Tigers, said, and Lyons fierce, to tame.
    p. 342 HORACE 1   175 .... wild, fierce ....

fiers   frequency: 1   relative frequency: 0.00001
**p. 117 PANEGYRE   145 The lesser fiers dim) in his accesse

fiery   frequency: 1   relative frequency: 0.00001
    p. 128 UNDERWOOD 1.1   27 Pure thoughts in man: with fiery zeale them
             feeding

fift   frequency: 1   relative frequency: 0.00001
    p. 207 UNDERWOOD 43   98 Of our fift Henry, eight of his nine yeare;

fifth. See "fift."

fiftie   frequency: 2   relative frequency: 0.00002
    p. 131 UNDERWOOD 2.1   3 Though I now write fiftie yeares,
    p. 204 UNDERWOOD 43   33 Or spun out Riddles, and weav'd fiftie tomes

fiftieth   frequency: 1   relative frequency: 0.00001
    p. 292 UNDERWOOD 86   6 To bend a man, now at his fiftieth yeare

fifty   frequency: 1   relative frequency: 0.00001
    See also "fiftie."
    p. 171 UNDERWOOD 20   5 At fifty yeares, almost, to value it,

fig   frequency: 1   relative frequency: 0.00001
    p. 94 FOREST 2   42 Fig, grape, and quince, each in his time doth
             come:

fight   frequency: 8   relative frequency: 0.00011
    p. 32 EPIGRAMS 16   6 Some hundred quarrells, yet dost thou fight none;
    p. 32 EPIGRAMS 16   10 He that dares damne himselfe, dares more then
             fight.
    p. 49 EPIGRAMS 66   17 Hee's valiant'st, that dares fight, and not for
             pay;
    p. 146 UNDERWOOD 6   8 Doe change, though man, and often fight,
    p. 214 UNDERWOOD 44   45 Thou canst draw forth thy forces, and fight drie
    p. 222 UNDERWOOD 49   4 Where fight the prime Cocks of the Game, for
             wit?
    p. 398 UNGATHERED 30   71 This booke! it is a Catechisme to fight,
    p. 398 UNGATHERED 30   74 Get broken peeces, and fight well by those.

fights   frequency: 1   relative frequency: 0.00001
    p. 397 UNGATHERED 30   41 The Fights, the Cryes, and wondring at the
             Iarres

figure   frequency: 4   relative frequency: 0.00005
    p. 317 HORACE 2   268 Upon the Stage, the figure of a Snake.
    p. 339 HORACE 1   48 .... figure ...
    p. 364 UNGATHERED 4   8 But a bare Type and Figure.
    p. 390 UNGATHERED 25   1 This Figure, that thou here seest put,

figures   frequency: 1   relative frequency: 0.00001
    p. 370 UNGATHERED 7   10 The seuerall figures, languish in suspence,

fil<l>ed   frequency: 1   relative frequency: 0.00001
    p. 252 UNDERWOOD 75   11 Hath fil<l>ed, with Caroches, all the way,

filch'd   frequency: 1   relative frequency: 0.00001
   p. 116 FOREST 12   88 Or common places, filch'd, that take these times,

fil'd   frequency: 1   relative frequency: 0.00001
   p. 188 UNDERWOOD 35   3 What wonder perfect, all were fil'd,

file   frequency: 1   relative frequency: 0.00001
   p. 257 UNDERWOOD 75 155 Their names are not recorded on the File

filed. See "fil'd," "true-filed."

files. See "fyl's."

fill   frequency: 10   relative frequency: 0.00014
  *p. 492 TO HIMSELF   17 No, giue them graines their fill,
 **p. 113 PANEGYRE   1 Heau'n now not striues, alone, our brests to fill
   p.   69 EPIGRAMS 107   7 And yet are with their Princes: Fill them full
   p. 159 UNDERWOOD 14   32 Upon your Center, doe your Circle fill
   p. 183 UNDERWOOD 29   25 Starveling rimes did fill the Stage,
   p. 212 UNDERWOOD 43 198 And there made Swords, Bills, Glaves, and
                              Armes your fill;
   p. 258 UNDERWOOD 75 169 Till you behold a race to fill your Hall,
   p. 278 U'WOOD 84.4   19 Our sense you doe with knowledge fill,
   p. 319 HORACE 2   291 As loud enough to fill the seates, not yet
   p. 371 UNGATHERED 9   5 To fill an Epitaph. But she had more.

fill'd   frequency: 6   relative frequency: 0.00008
   p.   77 EPIGRAMS 120   11 Yet three fill'd Zodiackes had he beene
   p.   88 EPIGRAMS 133 169 Is fill'd with buttock? And the walls doe sweate
   p. 111 FOREST 11   84 Haue fill'd with abstinence:
   p. 116 FOREST 12   90 From braines entranc'd, and fill'd with extasies;
   p. 119 FOREST 13   102 Before the moones haue fill'd their tripple
                              trine,
   p. 396 UNGATHERED 30 19 And fill'd an Orbe as circular, as heauen!

filled. See "fil<l>ed," "fill'd," "fist-fill'd."

fills   frequency: 2   relative frequency: 0.00002
   p.   98 FOREST 3   49 And fills thy open hall with mirth, and cheere,
   p. 191 UNDERWOOD 38   11 And fills my powers with perswading joy,

filly. See "court-bred-fillie."

filmer   frequency: 1   relative frequency: 0.00001
   p. 401 UNGATHERED 33 t1 To my worthy Friend, Master Edward Filmer,

filth   frequency: 2   relative frequency: 0.00002
   p.   84 EPIGRAMS 133   9 The filth, stench, noyse: saue only what was
                              there
   p.   86 EPIGRAMS 133   70 Hung stench, diseases, and old filth, their
                              mother,

filthy   frequency: 1   relative frequency: 0.00001
   p. 294 UNDERWOOD 88   1 Doing, a filthy pleasure is, and short;

final. See "finall."

finall   frequency: 1   relative frequency: 0.00001
   p. 283 U'WOOD 84.9   49 To have that finall retribution,

find   frequency: 32   relative frequency: 0.00046
   See also "ffinde," "finde."
   p.   37 EPIGRAMS 32   8 Was his blest fate, but our hard lot to find.
   p.   40 EPIGRAMS 42   9 And so is IONE. Oft-times, when GILES
                              doth find
   p.   41 EPIGRAMS 43   10 And what I write thereof find farre, and free
   p.   62 EPIGRAMS 96   7 Reade all I send: and, if I find but one
   p.   66 EPIGRAMS 102   1 I doe but name thee PEMBROKE, and I find
   p.   67 EPIGRAMS 103   11 As lowdest praisers, who perhaps would find
   p. 103 FOREST 6   21 And the enuious, when they find
   p. 114 FOREST 12   30 With you, I know, my offring will find grace.
   p. 140 UNDERWOOD 2.8   9 But we find that cold delay,
   p. 145 UNDERWOOD 5   9 Find some one good, in some one man;
   p. 147 UNDERWOOD 7   15 He is, if they can find him, faire,
   p. 149 UNDERWOOD 8   11 Even ashes of lovers find no rest.
   p. 153 UNDERWOOD 13   6 As they are done, and such returnes they find:
   p. 158 UNDERWOOD 13 164 Find you to reckon nothing, me owe all.
   p. 167 UNDERWOOD 15 172 Spread through the World) is easier farre to
                              find,
   p. 170 UNDERWOOD 18   12 Such Guides men use not, who their way would
                              find,

find (cont.)
    p. 173 UNDERWOOD 22   27 That would their better objects find:
    p. 185 UNDERWOOD 30   2 Read here in one, what thou in all canst find,
    p. 186 UNDERWOOD 32   7 Such shall you heare to day, and find great foes,
    p. 198 UNDERWOOD 40   30 Shall find their depth: they're sounded with a
                               spoone.
    p. 203 UNDERWOOD 43   27 If none of these, then why this fire? Or find
    p. 217 UNDERWOOD 46   3 He could not find, then thee, of all that store
    p. 225 UNDERWOOD 50   35 For when they find so many meet in one,
    p. 243 UNDERWOOD 70   10 Of deepest lore, could we the Center find!
    p. 247 UNDERWOOD 70   122 Where they might read, and find
    p. 255 UNDERWOOD 75   79 Search, Sun, and thou wilt find,
    p. 258 UNDERWOOD 75   166 You find no cold
    p. 277 U'WOOD 84.3   31 Whose 'tis: but if it favour find,
    p. 285 U'WOOD 84.9   103 Thither, you hope to come; and there to find
    p. 287 U'WOOD 84.9   152 Find all our Atomes from a point t<o>'a span!
    p. 288 U'WOOD 84.9   196 Poring, as on a Map, to find the wayes
    p. 386 UNGATHERED 21   6 I find thee write most worthy to be read.

finde   frequency: 9   relative frequency: 0.00013
    p. 76 EPIGRAMS 119   10 Till thou canst finde the best, choose the least
                               ill.
    p. 79 EPIGRAMS 125   3 Both whose dimensions, lost, the world might
                               finde
    p. 95 FOREST 2   70 He knowes, below, he shall finde plentie of
                               meate,
    p. 99 FOREST 3   101 Be thankes to him, and earnest prayer, to finde
    p. 118 FOREST 13   76 (They finde it both so wittie, and safe to giue.)
    p. 120 FOREST 13   123 Wherein, your forme, you still the same shall
                               finde;
    p. 122 FOREST 15   16 How can I doubt to finde thee euer, here?
    p. 362 UNGATHERED 2   1 Thou, that wouldst finde the habit of true
                               passion,
    p. 389 UNGATHERED 24   2 Shall finde, that either hath read Bookes, and
                               Men:

finding   frequency: 3   relative frequency: 0.00004
    p. 57 EPIGRAMS 90   6 And, finding good securitie in his age,
    p. 74 EPIGRAMS 114   6 Where finding so much beautie met with vertue,
    p. 136 UNDERWOOD 2.5   7 'Mongst my Muses finding me,

finds   frequency: 1   relative frequency: 0.00001
    p. 292 UNDERWOOD 86   17 And when he smiling finds his Grace

fine   frequency: 10   relative frequency: 0.00014
    See also "fyne."
    p. 46 EPIGRAMS 62   1 Fine MADAME WOVLD-BEE, wherefore
                               should you feare,
    p. 46 EPIGRAMS 62   t1 TO FINE LADY WOVLD-BEE.
    p. 51 EPIGRAMS 73   1 What is't, fine GRAND, makes thee my
                               friendship flye,
    p. 51 EPIGRAMS 73   t1 TO FINE GRAND.
    p. 110 FOREST 11   45 That is an essence, farre more gentle, fine,
    p. 212 UNDERWOOD 43   206 Make your Petards, and Granats, all your fine
    p. 253 UNDERWOOD 75   21 When look'd the Earth so fine,
    p. 278 U'WOOD 84.4   25 A Mind so pure, so perfect fine,
    p. 282 U'WOOD 84.9   5 And set it forth; the rest were Cobwebs fine,
    p. 327 HORACE 2   459 And better stayes them there, then all fine noise

fine-man   frequency: 1   relative frequency: 0.00001
    p. 165 UNDERWOOD 15 106 Is it for these that Fine-man meets the street

finenesse   frequency: 1   relative frequency: 0.00001
    p. 415 UNGATHERED 42   27 Of Finenesse, and alloy: follow his hint,

finer   frequency: 4   relative frequency: 0.00005
    p. 204 UNDERWOOD 43   36 Or Eteostichs, or those finer flammes
    p. 242 UNDERWOOD 69   22 More subtle workes, and finer pieces farre,
    p. 375 UNGATHERED 10   28 Here, finer then comming from his Punke you him
                               see,
    p. 389 UNGATHERED 24   18 Finer then was his Spanish, if my Oath

finest   frequency: 2   relative frequency: 0.00002
    p. 105 FOREST 8   23 Sleeked limmes, and finest blood?
    p. 183 UNDERWOOD 29   1 Rime, the rack of finest wits,

finger   frequency: 2   relative frequency: 0.00002
    p. 87 EPIGRAMS 133 134 Nor thumbe, nor finger to the stop acquainted,
    p. 323 HORACE 2   404 A lawfull Verse, by th'eare, or finger scan.

fingers   frequency: 2   relative frequency: 0.00002
  p. 141 UNDERWOOD 2.9   12 For Loves fingers, and his wings:
  p. 269 UNDERWOOD 83   30 To be describ'd! Fames fingers are too foule

fir'd   frequency: 2   relative frequency: 0.00002
  p. 141 UNDERWOOD 2.9   31 Quickly fir'd, as in beginners
  p. 291 UNDERWOOD 85   43 To deck the hallow'd Harth with old wood fir'd

fire   frequency: 39   relative frequency: 0.00056
  See also "a-fire," "ffyre," "fier."
  *p. 493 TO HIMSELF   44 Warme thee, by Pindares fire:
  p. 52 EPIGRAMS 76   1 This morning, timely rapt with holy fire,
  p. 81 EPIGRAMS 128   12 This is that good AENEAS, past through
                               fire,
  p. 95 FOREST 2   73 For fire, or lights, or liuorie: all is there;
  p. 98 FOREST 3   46 A fire now, that lent a shade!
  p. 108 FOREST 10   29 My owne true fire. Now my thought takes wing,
  p. 108 FOREST 10 A   3 Thy thoughtes did neuer melt in amorous fire,
  p. 110 FOREST 11   38 Arm'd with bow, shafts, and fire;
  p. 120 FOREST 14   1 Now that the harth is crown'd with smiling fire,
  p. 135 UNDERWOOD 2.4   28 Or the Nard i' the fire?
  p. 139 UNDERWOOD 2.8   5 And that promise set on fire
  p. 142 UNDERWOOD 2.9   41 Valiant he should be as fire,
  p. 150 UNDERWOOD 10   6 That others should not warme them at my fire,
  p. 153 UNDERWOOD 13   8 To succour my necessities, tooke fire,
  p. 175 UNDERWOOD 23   28 Sols Chariot for new fire,
  p. 177 UNDERWOOD 25   12 With Delphick fire:
  p. 179 UNDERWOOD 25   45 Gold, that is perfect, will out-live the fire.
  p. 193 UNDERWOOD 38   101 Then sword, or fire, or what is of the race
  p. 202 UNDERWOOD 43   1 And why to me this, thou lame Lord of fire,
  p. 203 UNDERWOOD 43   27 If none of these, then why this fire? Or find
  p. 205 UNDERWOOD 43   60 T'have held a Triumph, or a feast of fire,
  p. 208 UNDERWOOD 43   110 'Cause thou canst halt, with us, in Arts, and
                               Fire!
  p. 209 UNDERWOOD 43   141 And this a Sparkle of that fire let loose
  p. 209 UNDERWOOD 43   149 Kindled the fire! But then, did one returne,
  p. 215 UNDERWOOD 44   93 But why are all these Irons i' the fire
  p. 218 UNDERWOOD 47   3 They meet the fire, the Test, as Martyrs would;
  p. 225 UNDERWOOD 51   3 The fire, the wine, the men! and in the midst,
  p. 233 UNDERWOOD 59   7 I hate such measur'd, give me mettall'd fire
  p. 243 UNDERWOOD 70   17 Sword, fire, and famine, with fell fury met;
  p. 249 UNDERWOOD 72   4 As lowd as Thunder, and as swift as fire.
  p. 269 UNDERWOOD 83   32 The blaze, and splendor, but not handle fire!
  p. 278 U'WOOD 84.4   28 'Tis got where it can try the fire.
  p. 293 UNDERWOOD 87   13 LYD. And I, am mutually on fire
  p. 295 UNDERWOOD 90   4 A Soyle, not barren; a continewall fire;
  p. 339 HORACE 1   33 The greater part, that boast the Muses fire,
  p. 365 UNGATHERED 5   6 As fire; and more delightfull
  p. 371 UNGATHERED 8   15 A glorified worke to Time, when Fire,
  p. 397 UNGATHERED 30   57 That euer yet did fire the English blood!
  p. 413 UNGATHERED 41   24 In Moses bush, un-wasted in the fire.

fire-light   frequency: 1   relative frequency: 0.00001
  p. 204 UNDERWOOD 43   44 Fitter to see the fire-light, then the day;

fire-workes   frequency: 2   relative frequency: 0.00002
  p. 211 UNDERWOOD 43   194 'Bove all your Fire-workes, had at Ephesus,
  p. 249 UNDERWOOD 72   13 At Bonefires, Rockets, Fire-workes, with the
                               Shoutes

fires   frequency: 4   relative frequency: 0.00005
  See also "bone-fires," "fiers," "fyres."
  p. 95 FOREST 2   77 With his braue sonne, the Prince, they saw thy
                               fires
  p. 144 UNDERWOOD 4   5 O, be not angry with those fires,
  p. 170 UNDERWOOD 19   1 By those bright Eyes, at whose immortall fires
  p. 257 UNDERWOOD 75   163 Be kept alive those Sweet, and Sacred fires

fireworks. See "fire-workes."

firk. See "firke."

firke   frequency: 2   relative frequency: 0.00002
  p. 164 UNDERWOOD 15   72 And firke, and jerke, and for the Coach-man
                               raile,
  p. 405 UNGATHERED 34   79 How would he firke? lyke Adam ouerdooe

firm. See "firme."

firme   frequency: 3   relative frequency: 0.00004
  p. 116 FOREST 12   95 For that firme grace he holdes in your regard,
  p. 315 HORACE 2   226 And can tread firme, longs with like lads to
                                        play;
 * p. 413 UNGATHERED 41   20 No faith's more firme, or flat, then where't doth
                                        creep.

first   frequency: 94   relative frequency: 0.00136
  See also "ffirst."
**p. 112 PANEGYRE   t8 His first high Session of PARLIAMENT
**p. 113 PANEGYRE   15 From whose foule reeking cauernes first arise
**p. 115 PANEGYRE   77 "With better pompe. She tells him first, that
                                        Kings
**p. 117 PANEGYRE   149 Of his great actions, first to see, and do
  p. 31 EPIGRAMS 15   2 'Twas brought to court first wrapt, and white as
                                        milke;
  p. 33 EPIGRAMS 22   t1 ON MY FIRST DAVGHTER.
  p. 38 EPIGRAMS 35   6 Left vs of feare, but first our crimes, then
                                        lawes.
  p. 38 EPIGRAMS 35   9 First thou preserued wert, our king to bee,
  p. 41 EPIGRAMS 45   t1 ON MY FIRST SONNE.
  p. 42 EPIGRAMS 48   1 His bought armes MVNG' not lik'd; for his
                                        first day
  p. 45 EPIGRAMS 56   5 At first he made low shifts, would picke and
                                        gleane,
  p. 45 EPIGRAMS 56   11 He markes not whose 'twas first: and after-times
  p. 49 EPIGRAMS 67   8 As all thy honors were by them first sought:
  p. 50 EPIGRAMS 70   6 Each best day of our life escapes vs, first.
  p. 54 EPIGRAMS 80   6 And here, it should be one of our first strifes,
  p. 57 EPIGRAMS 90   1 When MILL first came to court, the
                                        vnprofiting foole,
  p. 57 EPIGRAMS 90   18 First bearing him a calfe, beare him a bull.
  p. 63 EPIGRAMS 98   12 And euer is ill got without the first.
  p. 69 EPIGRAMS 107   19 Giue your yong States-men, (that first make you
                                        drunke,
  p. 70 EPIGRAMS 109   12 And first to know thine owne state, then the
                                        States.
  p. 73 EPIGRAMS 114   3 For CVPID, who (at first) tooke vaine
                                        delight,
  p. 75 EPIGRAMS 116   5 Thou wert the first, mad'st merit know her
                                        strength,
  p. 78 EPIGRAMS 122   6 And heare her speake with one, and her first
                                        tongue;
  p. 79 EPIGRAMS 125   1 VV'DALE, thou piece of the first times, a
                                        man
  p. 81 EPIGRAMS 128   10 Thy selfe, with thy first thoughts, brought home
                                        by thee,
  p. 81 EPIGRAMS 129   2 But the first question is, when one saw thee?
  p. 85 EPIGRAMS 133   61 In the first iawes appear'd that vgly monster,
  p. 85 EPIGRAMS 133   65 Who shall discharge first his merd-vrinous load:
  p. 94 FOREST 2   36 Officiously, at first, themselues betray.
  p. 101 FOREST 4   41 My tender, first, and simple yeeres
  p. 103 FOREST 6   8 While you breath. First giue a hundred,
  p. 110 FOREST 11   32 The first; as prone to moue
  p. 114 FOREST 12   51 ACHILLES was not first, that valiant was,
  p. 122 FOREST 15   10 First, midst, and last, conuerted one, and three;
  p. 129 UNDERWOOD 1.2   21 First made of nought;
  p. 131 UNDERWOOD 2.1   14 First, prepare you to be sorie,
  p. 133 UNDERWOOD 2.3   7 First, that I must kneeling yeeld
  p. 146 UNDERWOOD 6   24 To love one man, hee'd leave her first.
  p. 152 UNDERWOOD 12   40 Who makes the one, so't be first, makes both.
  p. 157 UNDERWOOD 13   149 'Tis like light Canes, that first rise big and
                                        brave,
  p. 159 UNDERWOOD 14   35 Which Grace shall I make love to first? your
                                        skill,
  p. 161 UNDERWOOD 14   67 I first salute thee so; and gratulate,
  p. 168 UNDERWOOD 15   181 That by commanding first thy selfe, thou mak'st
  p. 169 UNDERWOOD 18   1 Can Beautie that did prompt me first to write,
  p. 170 UNDERWOOD 18   23 That I must send one first, my Choyce assignes,
  p. 184 UNDERWOOD 29   49 He that first invented thee,
  p. 187 UNDERWOOD 33   19 But first dost vexe, and search it! If not
                                        sound,
  p. 189 UNDERWOOD 37   1 Sir, I am thankfull, first, to heaven, for you;
  p. 212 UNDERWOOD 43   201 Or stay'd but where the Fryar, and you first
                                        met,
  p. 215 UNDERWOOD 44   91 All that they doe at Playes. O, but first here
  p. 216 UNDERWOOD 45   16 First weigh a friend, then touch, and trie him
                                        too:
  p. 216 UNDERWOOD 45   23 For that is first requir'd, A man be his owne.
  p. 220 UNDERWOOD 47   75 Are asked to climbe. First give me faith, who
                                        know

first (cont.)
```
    p. 228 UNDERWOOD 53      1 When first, my Lord, I saw you backe your
                               horse,
    p. 230 UNDERWOOD 56      6 The first of which, I feare, you will refuse;
    p. 238 UNDERWOOD 66      7 (Except the joy that the first Mary brought,
    p. 247 UNDERWOOD 70    107 This made you first to know the Why
    p. 247 UNDERWOOD 70    127 Who, e're the first downe bloomed on the chin,
    p. 250 UNDERWOOD 75    124 Askes first, who gives her (I Charles) then he
                               plights
    p. 262 UNDERWOOD 78     20 Busie, or frowne at first; when he sees thee,
    p. 264 UNDERWOOD 79     16 3. Our milke. 4. Our fells. 5. Our fleeces. 6.
                               And first Lambs.
    p. 265 UNDERWOOD 79     50 Your Milkes, your Fells, your Fleeces, and
                               first Lambes,
    p. 268 UNDERWOOD 82      8 Should take first Seisin of the publique good,
    p. 273 U'WOOD 84.1      23 With Sayles of silke, as the first notes
    p. 274 U'WOOD 84.2      17 Of the first Lupus, to the Familie
    p. 276 U'WOOD 84.3      13 Draw first a Cloud: all save her neck;
    p. 289 U'WOOD 84.9     220 Where first his Power will appeare, by call
    p. 292 UNDERWOOD 86     t1 Ode the first. The fourth Booke.
    p. 307 HORACE 2         29 Was meant at first. Why, forcing still about
    p. 309 HORACE 2        107 In Verse unequall match'd, first sowre Laments,
    p. 309 HORACE 2        110 That first sent forth the dapper Elegie,
    p. 311 HORACE 2        145 If thou would'st have me weepe, be thou first
                               drown'd
    p. 311 HORACE 2        152 For Nature, first, within doth fashion us
    p. 313 HORACE 2        181 Unto the last, as when he first went forth,
    p. 313 HORACE 2        186 First publish things unspoken, and unknowne.
    p. 315 HORACE 2        217 Where the midst differs from the first: or where
    p. 319 HORACE 2        311 Thespis is said to be the first found out
    p. 323 HORACE 2        374 But meere Iambicks all, from first to last.
    p. 325 HORACE 2        441 Is to be wise; thy matter first to know;
    p. 327 HORACE 2        480 First frighted men, that wildly liv'd, at ods,
    p. 327 HORACE 2        491 And thus, at first, an honour, and a name
    p. 331 HORACE 2        563 If ne're so little it depart the first,
    p. 333 HORACE 2        592 Did learne them first, and once a Master fear'd.
    p. 366 UNGATHERED 6     17 He shew'd him first the hoofe-cleft Spring,
    p. 367 UNGATHERED 6     39 But first to Cluid stoope low,
    p. 371 UNGATHERED 9      3 It couers, first, a Virgin; and then, one
    p. 381 UNGATHERED 12    59 No: as I first said, who would write a story at
    p. 389 UNGATHERED 24    15 For though Spaine gaue him his first ayre and
                               Vogue,
    p. 394 UNGATHERED 28    20 Whom shee, with Sorrow first did lodge, then
                               feast,
    p. 402 UNGATHERED 34     1 Mr Surueyr, you yt first begann
    p. 409 UNGATHERED 38     8 Which I, your Master, first did teach the Age.
    p. 414 UNGATHERED 42     2 Unto the world, in praise of your first Play:
    p. 415 UNGATHERED 42    21 Cry'd up of late: Whereto there must be first
    p. 416 UNGATHERED 44     2 Our first of fruits, that is the prime of flowers
```

first-borne   frequency: 2   relative frequency: 0.00002
```
    p. 235 UNDERWOOD 63     t2 For the losse of their first-borne,
    p. 309 HORACE 2         87 The first-borne dying; so the aged state
```

first-fruits   frequency: 3   relative frequency: 0.00004
```
    p. 235 UNDERWOOD 63      1 Who dares denie, that all first-fruits are due
    p. 258 UNDERWOOD 75    186 And let him freely gather Loves First-fruits,
    p. 263 UNDERWOOD 79     13 Best Kings expect first-fruits of your glad
                               gaines.
```

fish   frequency: 3   relative frequency: 0.00004
```
    p.  94 FOREST 2         32 Thou hast thy ponds, that pay thee tribute fish,
    p. 305 HORACE 2          5 Which in some swarthie fish uncomely ends:
    p. 374 UNGATHERED 10    11 All sorts of fish with Musicke of his maw.
```

fish-   frequency: 1   relative frequency: 0.00001
```
   *p. 493 TO HIMSELF       23 As the Shrieues crusts, and nasty as his fish-
```

fish-scraps. See "fish-."

fisher   frequency: 1   relative frequency: 0.00001
```
    p.  94 FOREST 2         38 Before the fisher, or into his hand.
```

fist. See "club-fist."

fist-fill'd   frequency: 1   relative frequency: 0.00001
```
    p. 154 UNDERWOOD 13     52 But then, fist-fill'd, to put me off the sent.
```

fit   frequency: 40   relative frequency: 0.00057
```
   *p. 493 TO HIMSELF       29 For, who the relish of these ghests will fit,
```

fit (cont.)

p.	36 EPIGRAMS 29	3	For thy late sharpe deuice. I say 'tis fit
p.	42 EPIGRAMS 50	3	Arsenike would thee fit for societie make.
p.	47 EPIGRAMS 64	7	Nor glad for fashion. Nor to shew a fit
p.	51 EPIGRAMS 73	20	Then had I made 'hem good, to fit your vaine.
p.	52 EPIGRAMS 76	12	Fit in that softer bosome to reside.
p.	58 EPIGRAMS 91	3	Illustrous VERE, or HORACE; fit to be
p.	67 EPIGRAMS 104	16	If not, 'tis fit for you, some should enuy.
p.	74 EPIGRAMS 115	27	Acts old Iniquitie, and in the fit
p.	117 FOREST 13	13	Such as suspect them-selues, and thinke it fit
p.	160 UNDERWOOD 14	58	But to the Subject, still the Colours fit
p.	165 UNDERWOOD 15	101	Thus they doe talke. And are these objects fit
p.	168 UNDERWOOD 15	182	Thy person fit for any charge thou tak'st;
p.	171 UNDERWOOD 20	6	That ne're was knowne to last above a fit!
p.	183 UNDERWOOD 29	t1	A Fit of Rime against Rime.
p.	190 UNDERWOOD 37	8	Their vice of loving for a Christmasse fit;
p.	203 UNDERWOOD 43	21	Conceal'd, or kept there, that was fit to be,
p.	230 UNDERWOOD 56	3	A booke to a few lynes: but, it was fit
p.	231 UNDERWOOD 57	18	Nor any least fit
p.	232 UNDERWOOD 58	8	Thy Wife a fit of laughter; a Cramp-ring
p.	232 UNDERWOOD 58	12	As if that part lay for a [ ] most fit!
p.	233 UNDERWOOD 59	17	To know the heads of danger! where 'tis fit
p.	234 UNDERWOOD 61	13	Fit for a Bishops knees! O bow them oft,
p.	263 UNDERWOOD 79	6	To fit the softnesse of our Yeares-gift: when
p.	280 U'WOOD 84.4	51	In all the bounds of beautie fit
p.	282 U'WOOD 84.9	10	A sorrow in me, fit to wait to her!
p.	287 U'WOOD 84.9	161	She had, and it became her! she was fit
p.	292 UNDERWOOD 86	12	If a fit livor thou dost seeke to toast;
p.	307 HORACE 2	53	Take, therefore, you that write, still, matter fit
p.	309 HORACE 2	106	What number best can fit, Homer declares.
p.	311 HORACE 2	119	As fit t<o>'exchange discourse; a Verse to win
p.	311 HORACE 2	124	Fit for the sock: Each subject should retaine
p.	315 HORACE 2	225	Fit rites. The Child, that now knowes how to say,
p.	321 HORACE 2	368	Her licence fit to be restrain'd by law:
p.	325 HORACE 2	447	What height of love, a Parent will fit best,
p.	327 HORACE 2	478	Or mixing sweet, and fit, teach life the right.
p.	371 UNGATHERED 9	8	As fit to haue encreas'd the harmony
p.	392 UNGATHERED 26	49	Which were so richly spun, and wouen so fit,
p.	416 UNGATHERED 44	6	We offer as a Circle the most fit
p.	422 UNGATHERED 50	1	Just and fit actions Ptolemey (he saith)

fitly   frequency: 2   relative frequency: 0.00002
p.	275 U'WOOD 84.3	10	Were fitly interpos'd; so new:
p.	317 HORACE 2	279	Then to the purpose leades, and fitly 'grees.

fitnesse   frequency: 1   relative frequency: 0.00001
p.	323 HORACE 2	376	Into their birth-right, and for fitnesse sake,

fits   frequency: 6   relative frequency: 0.00008
See also "fitts."
p.	140 UNDERWOOD 2.8	20	Better fits him, then his face;
p.	183 UNDERWOOD 29	2	That expresseth but by fits,
p.	200 UNDERWOOD 42	34	And braveries of Court, and felt their fits
p.	223 UNDERWOOD 49	40	They say you weekly invite with fits o'th' Mother,
p.	311 HORACE 2	149	Sad language fits sad lookes; stuff'd menacings,
p.	385 UNGATHERED 20	1	It fits not onely him that makes a Booke,

fitted   frequency: 2   relative frequency: 0.00002
p.	319 HORACE 2	290	And tune too, fitted to the Chorus rime,
p.	402 UNGATHERED 34	17	I doe salute you! Are you fitted yet?

fitter   frequency: 4   relative frequency: 0.00005
p.	79 EPIGRAMS 124	11	Fitter, where it dyed, to tell,
p.	204 UNDERWOOD 43	44	Fitter to see the fire-light, then the day;
p.	237 UNDERWOOD 65	4	What Month then May, was fitter to disclose
p.	307 HORACE 2	63	Till fitter season. Now, to like of this,

fittest   frequency: 1   relative frequency: 0.00001
**p.	114 PANEGYRE	42	The fittest herald to proclaime true ioyes:

fitting   frequency: 3   relative frequency: 0.00004
p.	289 U'WOOD 84.9	223	And most his Justice, in the fitting parts,
p.	317 HORACE 2	254	In fitting proper adjuncts to each day.
p.	325 HORACE 2	452	Indeed, give fitting dues to every man.

fitts   frequency: 1   relative frequency: 0.00001
p.	218 UNDERWOOD 47	21	Call every night to Supper in these fitts,

```
fiue                          frequency:    4   relative frequency: 0.00005
    p.  64 EPIGRAMS 100    4 Fiue of my iests, then stolne, past him a play.
    p.  88 EPIGRAMS 133  154 Yet drown'd they not. They had fiue liues in
                              future.
    p. 379 UNGATHERED 12   16 In fiue monthes he went it, in fiue monthes he
                              pend it.

five                          frequency:    5   relative frequency: 0.00007
    See also "fiue," "numbred-five."
    p. 229 UNDERWOOD 54    16 Lend me, deare Arthur, for a weeke five more,
    p. 248 UNDERWOOD 71     6 Have cast a trench about mee, now, five yeares;
    p. 317 HORACE 2       272 Have more or lesse then just five Acts: nor
                              laid,
    p. 327 HORACE 2       468 From the five ounces; what remaines? pronounce
    p. 412 UNGATHERED 41    1 Here, are five letters in this blessed Name,

five-fold                     frequency:    1   relative frequency: 0.00001
    p. 412 UNGATHERED 41    2 Which, chang'd, a five-fold mysterie designe,

fix. See "fixe."

fix'd                         frequency:    4   relative frequency: 0.00005
    p.  29 EPIGRAMS 7       2 A purging bill, now fix'd vpon the dore,
    p. 163 UNDERWOOD 15    44 To make up Greatnesse! and mans whole good fix'd
    p. 198 UNDERWOOD 40    33 Is fix'd upon one leg, and dares not come
    p. 248 UNDERWOOD 71    11 Fix'd to the bed, and boords, unlike to win

fixe                          frequency:    1   relative frequency: 0.00001
    p. 242 UNDERWOOD 69    18 Where he would fixe, for the distinctions feare.

fixed                         frequency:    2   relative frequency: 0.00002
    See also "fix'd," "fixt."
    p. 111 FOREST 11       61 A fixed thought, an eye vn-taught to glance;
    p. 194 UNDERWOOD 38   117 Your forme shines here, here fixed in my heart:

fixt                          frequency:    2   relative frequency: 0.00002
    p. 212 UNDERWOOD 43   203 Or fixt in the Low-Countrey's, where you might
    p. 413 UNGATHERED 41   28 As if they' ador'd the Head, wheron th'are fixt.

flaccus                       frequency:    1   relative frequency: 0.00001
    p. 338 HORACE 1        t1 Quintus Horatius Flaccus

flag. See "flagge."

flagge                        frequency:    1   relative frequency: 0.00001
    p.  81 EPIGRAMS 129     7 That still th'art made the suppers flagge, the
                              drum,

flaggeth                      frequency:    1   relative frequency: 0.00001
    p. 329 HORACE 2       533 So he that flaggeth much, becomes to me

flakes                        frequency:    1   relative frequency: 0.00001
    p.  87 EPIGRAMS 133   138 And, after, swom abroad in ample flakes,

flame                         frequency:   13   relative frequency: 0.00018
  **p. 115 PANEGYRE        71 The others flame, as doth the wike and waxe,
    p.  75 EPIGRAMS 116     2 All gentrie, yet, owe part of their best flame!
    p.  95 FOREST 2        79 Of thy Penates had beene set on flame,
    p. 108 FOREST 10A       8 in whom the flame of euery beauty raignes,
    p. 121 FOREST 14       56 And with the flame
    p. 141 UNDERWOOD 2.9   30 All his blood should be a flame
    p. 149 UNDERWOOD 8      7 And in his Mrs. flame, playing like a flye,
    p. 173 UNDERWOOD 22    21 And on them burne so chaste a flame,
    p. 202 UNDERWOOD 43     3 Or urge thy Greedie flame, thus to devoure
    p. 220 UNDERWOOD 47    69 But all so cleare, and led by reasons flame,
    p. 233 UNDERWOOD 59    11 Their weapons shot out, with that flame, and
                              force,
    p. 234 UNDERWOOD 60     9 Offended with the dazeling flame
    p. 278 U'WOOD 84.4     15 Since nothing can report that flame,

flames                        frequency:    5   relative frequency: 0.00007
    p.  94 FOREST 2        16 Of many a SYLVANE, taken with his flames.
    p. 179 UNDERWOOD 25    54 (Whose heart in that bright Sphere flames
                              clearest,
    p. 182 UNDERWOOD 28    10 His flames, his shafts, his Quiver, and his
                              Bow,
    p. 204 UNDERWOOD 43    40 Thou then hadst had some colour for thy flames,
    p. 422 UNGATHERED 50    7 Looke how the starres from earth, or seas from
                              flames
```

flameship
          frequency: 1   relative frequency: 0.00001
    p. 211 UNDERWOOD 43   191 Pox on your flameship, Vulcan; if it be

flammes
          frequency: 1   relative frequency: 0.00001
    p. 204 UNDERWOOD 43   36 Or Eteostichs, or those finer flammes

flams. See "flammes."

flanck'd
          frequency: 1   relative frequency: 0.00001
    p. 209 UNDERWOOD 43   134 Flanck'd with a Ditch, and forc'd out of a
                              Marish,

flanked. See "flanck'd."

flat
          frequency: 3   relative frequency: 0.00004
    p. 263 UNDERWOOD 79   3 Your change of Notes, the flat, the meane, the
                              sharpe,
    p. 329 HORACE 2   523 Oft-times a Sharpe, when we require a Flat:
    p. 413 UNGATHERED 41   20 No faith's more firme, or flat, then where't doth
                              creep.

flatter
          frequency: 2   relative frequency: 0.00002
    p. 99 FOREST 3   85 Let thousands more goe flatter vice, and winne,
    p. 167 UNDERWOOD 15   147 To flatter my good Lord, and cry his Bowle

flatter'd
          frequency: 1   relative frequency: 0.00001
    p. 38 EPIGRAMS 36   4 Thou flattered'st thine, mine cannot flatter'd
                              bee.

flattered'st
          frequency: 1   relative frequency: 0.00001
    p. 38 EPIGRAMS 36   4 Thou flattered'st thine, mine cannot flatter'd
                              bee.

flatterer
    See also "flatt'rer."   frequency: 2   relative frequency: 0.00002
    p. 167 UNDERWOOD 15   158 As a poore single flatterer, without Baud,
    p. 241 UNDERWOOD 69   6 Wise-crafts, on which the flatterer ventures not.

flatterers
          frequency: 2   relative frequency: 0.00002
    p. 167 UNDERWOOD 15   163 Light thee from hell on earth: where flatterers,
                              spies,
    p. 333 HORACE 2   601 His flatterers to their gaine. But say, he can

flatterie
          frequency: 3   relative frequency: 0.00004
    p. 41 EPIGRAMS 43   11 From seruile flatterie (common Poets shame)
    p. 47 EPIGRAMS 64   8 Of flatterie to thy titles. Nor of wit.
    p. 79 EPIGRAMS 125   9 Which (would the world not mis-call't flatterie)

flatteries
          frequency: 3   relative frequency: 0.00004
    p. 49 EPIGRAMS 67   2 Most thinke all praises flatteries. But truth
                              brings
    p. 162 UNDERWOOD 15   13 Bought Flatteries, the issue of his purse,
    p. 244 UNDERWOOD 70   39 To sordid flatteries, acts of strife,

flattering. See "flatt'ring."

flattery
    See also "flatterie," "flatt'rie," "flatt'ry,"   frequency: 2   relative frequency: 0.00002
          "flattry's."
  **p. 115 PANEGYRE   94 "To heare the truth, from spight, or flattery
                              voyd.
    p. 242 UNDERWOOD 69   21 Though now of flattery, as of picture, are

flatt'rer
          frequency: 1   relative frequency: 0.00001
    p. 242 UNDERWOOD 69   14 So doth the flatt'rer with faire cunning strike

flatt'rie
          frequency: 1   relative frequency: 0.00001
    p. 58 EPIGRAMS 91   10 Throughout, might flatt'rie seeme; and to be mute

flatt'ring
          frequency: 2   relative frequency: 0.00002
    p. 157 UNDERWOOD 13   155 You know (without my flatt'ring you) too much
    p. 227 UNDERWOOD 52   21 Ne knowes he flatt'ring Colours, or false light.

flatt'ry
          frequency: 2   relative frequency: 0.00002
    p. 190 UNDERWOOD 37   27 As flatt'ry with friends humours still to move.
    p. 401 UNGATHERED 32   19 Nor flatt'ry! but secur'd, by the Authors Name,

flattry's
          frequency: 1   relative frequency: 0.00001
    p. 167 UNDERWOOD 15   155 Pardon his Lordship. Flattry's growne so cheape

flaw   frequency: 1   relative frequency: 0.00001
    p. 339 HORACE 1   41 Being over-safe, and fearing .. the flaw:

flayed. See "flead."

flea   frequency: 1   relative frequency: 0.0000⌐
    p. 69 EPIGRAMS 107   18 Then can a flea at twise skip i'the Map.

flead   frequency: 1   relative frequency: 0.0000⌐
    p. 88 EPIGRAMS 133   149 Cats there lay diuers had beene flead, and
                               rosted,

fled   frequency: 9   relative frequency: 0.0001⌐
    p. 52 EPIGRAMS 74   9 The Virgin, long-since fled from earth, I see,
    p. 73 EPIGRAMS 113   7 For since, what ignorance, what pride is fled!
    p. 93 FOREST 1   8 With which he fled me: and againe,
    p. 93 FOREST 1   12 When Loue is fled, and I grow old.
    p. 101 FOREST 4   30 That fled his cage, or broke his chaine,
    p. 120 FOREST 14   19 Are fled and gone,
    p. 163 UNDERWOOD 15   39 Friendship is now mask'd Hatred! Justice fled,
    p. 213 UNDERWOOD 44   12 Nor markes of wealth so from our Nation fled,
    p. 293 UNDERWOOD 86   38 I hold thee fast! but fled hence, with the
                               Light,

flee   frequency: 4   relative frequency: 0.00005
    p. 166 UNDERWOOD 15   129 I'le bid thee looke no more, but flee, flee
                               friend,
    p. 349 HORACE 1   424 In secret places, flee ... .
    p. 422 UNGATHERED 50   6 whom thou seest happy; wretches flee as foes:

fleece   frequency: 2   relative frequency: 0.00002
    p. 45 EPIGRAMS 56   13 Foole, as if halfe eyes will not know a fleece
    p. 415 UNGATHERED 42   18 As it were spun by nature, off the fleece:

fleeced   frequency: 1   relative frequency: 0.00001
    p. 97 FOREST 3   39 The mowed meddowes, with the fleeced sheepe,

fleeces   frequency: 2   relative frequency: 0.00002
    p. 264 UNDERWOOD 79   16 3. Our milke. 4. Our fells. 5. Our fleeces. 6.
                               And first Lambs.
    p. 265 UNDERWOOD 79   50 Your Milkes, your Fells, your Fleeces, and
                               first Lambes,

flees   frequency: 1   relative frequency: 0.00001
    p. 289 UNDERWOOD 85   7 But flees the Barre and Courts, with the proud
                               bords,

fleet   frequency: 5   relative frequency: 0.00007
    See also "fleete."
    p. 88 EPIGRAMS 133   172 And out-cryes of the damned in the Fleet?
    p. 219 UNDERWOOD 47   34 Some hopes of Spaine in their West-Indian
                               Fleet?
    p. 305 HORACE 2   28 The whole fleet wreck'd? A great jarre to be
                               shap'd,
    p. 338 HORACE 1   21 Bouts .. fleet .... doe intertwine
    p. 407 UNGATHERED 35   17 And stradling shews ye Boyes Brown paper fleet,

fleet-lane   frequency: 1   relative frequency: 0.00001
    p. 88 EPIGRAMS 133   143 Your Fleet-lane Furies; and hot cookes doe
                               dwell,

fleete   frequency: 1   relative frequency: 0.00001
    p. 165 UNDERWOOD 15   105 His body to the Counters, or the Fleete?

flesh   frequency: 14   relative frequency: 0.00020
    p. 30 EPIGRAMS 11   5 A lord, it cryed, buried in flesh, and blood,
    p. 66 EPIGRAMS 103   3 And noted for what flesh such soules were fram'd,
    p. 70 EPIGRAMS 109   14 And that thy soule should giue thy flesh her
                               weight.
    p. 122 FOREST 15   22 Vpon my flesh t<o>'inflict another wound.
    p. 127 UNDERWOOD 1.1   6 By sinne, and Sathan; and my flesh misus'd,
    p. 130 UNDERWOOD 1.3   17 The Word was now made Flesh indeed,
    p. 164 UNDERWOOD 15   67 To catch the flesh in, and to pound a Prick.
    p. 172 UNDERWOOD 21   9 Of putrid flesh alive! of blood, the sinke!
    p. 188 UNDERWOOD 35   6 To fetch the flesh, we keepe the Rowle.
    p. 192 UNDERWOOD 38   66 In man, because man hath the flesh abus'd.
    p. 285 U'WOOD 84.9   93 To have her captiv'd spirit freed from flesh,
    p. 286 U'WOOD 84.9   151 The smallest Fibre of our flesh; he can
    p. 387 UNGATHERED 22   2 these only hide part of my flesh, and bones:
    p. 400 UNGATHERED 31   27 And when the flesh, here, shut vp day,

flesh-quake   frequency: 1   relative frequency: 0.00001
   *p. 494 TO HIMSELF   55 Feele such a flesh-quake to possesse their
                                powers:

fleshes   frequency: 3   relative frequency: 0.00004
    p.   41 EPIGRAMS 45   7 To haue so soone scap'd worlds, and fleshes rage,
    p. 283 U'WOOD 84.9   50 Expected with the fleshes restitution.
    p. 399 UNGATHERED 31   25 Her soule possest her fleshes state

fleshly   frequency: 1   relative frequency: 0.00001
    p.   34 EPIGRAMS 22   11 This graue partakes the fleshly birth.

fletcher   frequency: 2   relative frequency: 0.00002
    p.   89 EPIGRAMS 133   190 An ancient pur-blinde fletcher, with a high nose;
    p. 370 UNGATHERED 8   t2 Iohn Fletcher.

flew   frequency: 3   relative frequency: 0.00004
  **p. 116 PANEGYRE   130 When, like an April Iris, flew her shine
  **p. 117 PANEGYRE   155 And this confession flew from euery voyce:
    p. 212 UNDERWOOD 43   214 And all the Evils that flew out of her box

flie   frequency: 13   relative frequency: 0.00018
    p.   28 EPIGRAMS 4   9 Whom should my Muse then flie to, but the best
    p.   32 EPIGRAMS 17   1 May others feare, flie, and traduce thy name,
    p. 149 UNDERWOOD 9   12 That flie my thoughts betweene,
    p. 158 UNDERWOOD 14   11 Unto the Censure. Yours all need doth flie
    p. 159 UNDERWOOD 14   18 Not flie the Crime, but the Suspition too:
    p. 163 UNDERWOOD 15   29 As farre as he can flie, or follow day,
    p. 167 UNDERWOOD 15   162 Friend, flie from hence; and let these kindled
                                rimes
    p. 183 UNDERWOOD 29   19 Pegasus did flie away,
    p. 186 UNDERWOOD 31   8 Still flie about the Odour of your Name;
    p. 194 UNDERWOOD 38   104 A man should flie from, as he would disdaine.
    p. 198 UNDERWOOD 40   37 Where he that knowes will, like a Lapwing, flie
    p. 218 UNDERWOOD 47   5 I could say more of such, but that I flie
    p. 317 HORACE 2   266 His Nephews entrailes; nor must Progne flie

flies   frequency: 7   relative frequency: 0.00010
   See also "flyes."
    p.   76 EPIGRAMS 119   1 Not he that flies the court for want of clothes,
    p. 104 FOREST 7   1 Follow a shaddow, it still flies you;
    p. 116 FOREST 12   89 But high, and noble matter, such as flies
    p. 139 UNDERWOOD 2.7   6 That doth but touch his flower, and flies away.
    p. 154 UNDERWOOD 13   45 Lest Ayre, or Print, but flies it: Such men
                                would
    p. 218 UNDERWOOD 47   18 Like flies, or wormes, which mans corrupt parts
                                fed:
    p. 283 U'WOOD 84.9   24 It rages, runs, flies, stands, and would provoke

flight   frequency: 12   relative frequency: 0.00017
    p.   55 EPIGRAMS 85   5 Shee doth instruct men by her gallant flight,
    p.   97 FOREST 3   27 In autumne, at the Partrich makes a flight,
    p. 114 FOREST 12   24 Or put to flight ASTREA, when her ingots
    p. 137 UNDERWOOD 2.5   36 After flight; and put new stings
    p. 180 UNDERWOOD 26   7 Have made their fairest flight,
    p. 244 UNDERWOOD 70   37 But weary of that flight,
    p. 279 U'WOOD 84.4   31 It moveth all; and makes a flight
    p. 337 HORACE 2   676 All; So this grievous Writer puts to flight
    p. 366 UNGATHERED 6   10 How faire a flight he makes!
    p. 368 UNGATHERED 6   80 From whose prowde bosome, thou began'st thy
                                flight.
    p. 392 UNGATHERED 26   79 Which, since thy flight from hence, hath mourn'd
                                like night,
    p. 397 UNGATHERED 30   49 And flight about the Ile, well neare, by this,

flights   frequency: 1   relative frequency: 0.00001
    p. 392 UNGATHERED 26   73 And make those flights vpon the bankes of
                                Thames,

fling   frequency: 1   relative frequency: 0.00001
    p. 293 UNDERWOOD 87   2 And ('bout thy Ivory neck,) no youth did fling

flit   frequency: 1   relative frequency: 0.00001
    p.   87 EPIGRAMS 133   124 Against their breasts. Here, seu'rall ghosts did
                                flit

flock   frequency: 2   relative frequency: 0.00002
    p. 265 UNDERWOOD 79   47 That have a Flock, or Herd, upon these plaines;
    p. 291 UNDERWOOD 85   45 That penning the glad flock in hurdles by,

flocks   frequency: 2   relative frequency: 0.00002
    p. 264 UNDERWOOD 79   29 That leades our flocks and us, and calls both
                              forth
    p. 291 UNDERWOOD 85   62 Of the fed flocks approaching home!

flood   frequency: 5   relative frequency: 0.00007
    See also "floud."
    p. 136 UNDERWOOD 2.5   4 Then the various Moone the flood!
    p. 234 UNDERWOOD 61   16 He, that in such a flood, as we are in
    p. 274 U'WOOD 84.2   10 Meeting of Graces, that so swell'd the flood
    p. 287 U'WOOD 84.9   158 As nature could not more increase the flood
    p. 394 UNGATHERED 28   6 And number Attributes vnto a flood:

floods   frequency: 6   relative frequency: 0.00008
    p. 41 EPIGRAMS 44   4 Saw all his race approch the blacker floods:
    p. 143 UNDERWOOD 3   10 To stay the running floods,
    p. 265 UNDERWOOD 79   53 That they may take it eccho'd by the Floods.
    p. 290 UNDERWOOD 85   25 Whilst from the higher Bankes doe slide the
                              floods;
    p. 291 UNDERWOOD 85   51 If with bright floods, the Winter troubled much,
    p. 307 HORACE 2   42 A Dolphin, and a Boare amid' the floods.

floor. See "floore."

floore   frequency: 2   relative frequency: 0.00002
    p. 228 UNDERWOOD 53   17 So well! as when I saw the floore, and Roome,
    p. 254 UNDERWOOD 75   70 On the same floore,

flora   frequency: 1   relative frequency: 0.00001
    p. 68 EPIGRAMS 105   10 You were the bright OENONE, FLORA, or
                              May?

florence   frequency: 1   relative frequency: 0.00001
    p. 69 EPIGRAMS 107   14 What at Ligorne, Rome, Florence you did doe:

floud   frequency: 4   relative frequency: 0.00005
  **p. 114 PANEGYRE   62 The ground beneath did seeme a mouing floud:
    p. 88 EPIGRAMS 133   142 The euer-boyling floud. Whose bankes vpon
    p. 112 FOREST 11   107 In the full floud of her admir'd perfection?
    p. 280 U'WOOD 84.4   61 Smooth, soft, and sweet, in all a floud

flourish   frequency: 1   relative frequency: 0.00001
    p. 184 UNDERWOOD 29   37 Scarce the Hill againe doth flourish,

flourished. See "cut-flourisht."

flourishing   frequency: 1   relative frequency: 0.00001
    p. 313 HORACE 2   163 Or some hot youth, yet in his flourishing course;

flow   frequency: 9   relative frequency: 0.00013
    See also "ore-flow."
    p. 95 FOREST 2   59 The neede of such? whose liberall boord doth
                              flow,
    p. 103 FOREST 6   20 How to tell' hem, as th<e>y flow,
    p. 154 UNDERWOOD 13   60 That to such Natures let their full hands flow,
    p. 271 UNDERWOOD 83   75 And all beatitudes, that thence doe flow:
    p. 293 UNDERWOOD 86   34 Flow my thin teares, downe these pale cheeks of
                              mine?
    p. 307 HORACE 2   36 Obscure. This, striving to run smooth, and flow,
    p. 313 HORACE 2   158 If now the phrase of him that speakes, shall
                              flow,
    p. 398 UNGATHERED 30   77 I feele it by mine owne, that ouer flow,
    p. 657 L. CONVIVALES   6 Truth itself doth flow in Wine.

flower   frequency: 6   relative frequency: 0.00008
    See also "flowre."
    p. 139 UNDERWOOD 2.7   6 That doth but touch his flower, and flies away.
    p. 192 UNDERWOOD 38   58 Or winds the Spirit, by which the flower so
                              grew?
    p. 253 UNDERWOOD 75   23 In all her bloome, and flower;
    p. 286 U'WOOD 84.9   126 And to the Touch, a Flower, like soft as
                              Palme.
    p. 294 UNDERWOOD 89   2 Thou worthy in eternall Flower to fare,
    p. 361 UNGATHERED 1   15 The seauen-fold flower of Arte (more rich then
                              gold)

flowers   frequency: 14   relative frequency: 0.00020
    p. 94 FOREST 2   39 Then hath thy orchard fruit, thy garden flowers,
    p. 111 FOREST 11   58 And lasting, as her flowers:
    p. 137 UNDERWOOD 2.5   28 Then when flowers, and West-winds meet.

flowers (cont.)
      p. 150 UNDERWOOD 10   8 On all mens Fruit, and flowers, as well as mine.
      p. 237 UNDERWOOD 65   5 This Prince of flowers? Soone shoot thou up,
                                 and grow
      p. 254 UNDERWOOD 75   58 (Lillies and Roses, Flowers of either Sexe)
      p. 254 UNDERWOOD 75   67 As if her ayrie steps did spring the flowers,
      p. 264 UNDERWOOD 79   37 The fairest flowers are alwayes found;
      p. 265 UNDERWOOD 79   59 The better grasse, and flowers are found.
      p. 280 U'WOOD 84.4   67 Upon a banke, or field of flowers,
      p. 293 UNDERWOOD 86   32 Or with fresh flowers to girt my temple round.
      p. 361 UNGATHERED 1   1 When late (graue Palmer) these thy graffs and
                                 flowers
      p. 413 UNGATHERED 41   14 The Eye of flowers, worthy, for his scent,
      p. 416 UNGATHERED 44   2 Our first of fruits, that is the prime of flowers

flowery. See "flowrie," "flowry."

flowes   frequency: 4   relative frequency: 0.00005
      p. 160 UNDERWOOD 14   62 Flowes in upon me, and I cannot raise
      p. 163 UNDERWOOD 15   47 Thither it flowes. How much did Stallion spend
      p. 329 HORACE 2   506 But flowes out, that ore-swelleth in full brests.
      p. 363 UNGATHERED 3   4 Flowes fro the surfets which we take in peace.

flowing   frequency: 2   relative frequency: 0.00002
      p. 39 EPIGRAMS 40   10 And like Nectar euer flowing:
      p. 79 EPIGRAMS 125   8 The full, the flowing graces there enshrin'd;

flown. See "flowne," "ore-flowne."

flowne   frequency: 1   relative frequency: 0.00001
      p. 183 UNDERWOOD 29   14 All good Poetrie hence was flowne,

flowre   frequency: 2   relative frequency: 0.00002
      p. 240 UNDERWOOD 67   42 Hay! for the flowre of France!
      p. 245 UNDERWOOD 70   72 It was the Plant, and flowre of light.

flowrie   frequency: 1   relative frequency: 0.00001
      p. 97 FOREST 3   38 Of flowrie fields, of cop'ces greene,

flowry   frequency: 1   relative frequency: 0.00001
      p. 398 UNGATHERED 30   81 As, on two flowry Carpets, that did rise,

flows. See "flowes."

flung   frequency: 1   relative frequency: 0.00001
      p. 208 UNDERWOOD 43   114 She durst not kisse, but flung thee from her
                                 brest.

flushing   frequency: 2   relative frequency: 0.00002
      See also "vlushing."
      p. 380 UNGATHERED 12   42 From Venice to Flushing, were not they well
                                 cobled?
      p. 380 UNGATHERED 12   54 And being at Flushing enforced to feele

flute   frequency: 1   relative frequency: 0.00001
      p. 292 UNDERWOOD 86   24 And Phrygian Hau'boy, not without the Flute.

fly   frequency: 1   relative frequency: 0.00001
      See also "butter-flye," "flie," "flye."
      p. 409 UNGATHERED 37   19 But fly thee, like the Pest! Walke not the
                                 street

flye   frequency: 5   relative frequency: 0.00007
      p. 51 EPIGRAMS 73   1 What is't, fine GRAND, makes thee my
                                 friendship flye,
      p. 104 FOREST 7   2 Seeme to flye it, it will pursue:
      p. 111 FOREST 11   73 Though thy wild thoughts with sparrowes wings doe
                                 flye,
      p. 149 UNDERWOOD 8   7 And in his Mrs. flame, playing like a flye,
      p. 354 HORACE 1   644 ... flye .. ..

flyes   frequency: 1   relative frequency: 0.00001
      p. 408 UNGATHERED 36   7 The Lybian Lion hunts noe butter flyes,

flying   frequency: 4   relative frequency: 0.00005
      p. 97 FOREST 3   29 And, in the winter, hunt'st the flying hare,
      p. 170 UNDERWOOD 19   6 He flying curles, and crispeth, with his wings;
      p. 369 UNGATHERED 6   99 Were CYCNVS, once high flying
      p. 380 UNGATHERED 12   28 Horse, foote, and all but flying in the ayre:

foam. See "foame."

foame   frequency: 1   relative frequency: 0.00001
    p. 408 UNGATHERED 37   8 That thou hast lost thy noyse, thy foame, thy
                                      stirre,

foe   frequency: 2   relative frequency: 0.00002
    p. 49 EPIGRAMS 66   9 Against thy fortune: when no foe, that day,
    p. 53 EPIGRAMS 77   4 I' am more asham'd to haue thee thought my foe.

foes   frequency: 8   relative frequency: 0.00011
    p. 40 EPIGRAMS 43   4 Her foes enough would fame thee, in their hate.
    p. 71 EPIGRAMS 110   9 Nor that his worke liu'd in the hands of foes,
    p. 186 UNDERWOOD 32   7 Such shall you heare to day, and find great foes,
    p. 243 UNDERWOOD 70   28 Troubled both foes, and friends;
    p. 256 UNDERWOOD 75 114 It brings Friends Joy, Foes Griefe,
                                        Posteritie Fame;
    p. 286 U'WOOD 84.9   139 To style us Friends, who were, by Nature,
                                        Foes?
    p. 386 UNGATHERED 21   2 May hurt them more with praise, then Foes with
                                        spight.
    p. 422 UNGATHERED 50   6 whom thou seest happy; wretches flee as foes:

foiled   frequency: 1   relative frequency: 0.00001
    p. 184 UNDERWOOD 29   36 But rests foiled.

foist   frequency: 1   relative frequency: 0.00001
    p. 87 EPIGRAMS 133 120 And that is when it is the Lord Maiors foist.

fold   frequency: 1   relative frequency: 0.00001
See also "ore-fold."
    p. 305 HORACE 2   2 Set a Horse-neck, and divers feathers fold

folds   frequency: 2   relative frequency: 0.00002
    p. 220 UNDERWOOD 47   68 Oylie Expansions, or shrunke durtie folds,
    p. 265 UNDERWOOD 79   62 Hee drives diseases from our Folds,

folk. See "folke."

folke   frequency: 5   relative frequency: 0.00007
    p. 98 FOREST 3   53 The rout of rurall folke come thronging in,
    p. 164 UNDERWOOD 15   84 Great, brave, and fashion'd folke, these are
                                        allow'd
    p. 235 UNDERWOOD 62   10 One Poet, then of other folke ten score.
    p. 319 HORACE 2   294 Chaste, thriftie, modest folke, that came to
                                        view.
    p. 335 HORACE 2   643 Wise, sober folke, a frantick Poet feare,

folks. See "market-folkes."

follies   frequency: 2   relative frequency: 0.00002
    p. 202 UNDERWOOD 42   81 Let the poore fooles enjoy their follies, love
    p. 204 UNDERWOOD 43   41 On such my serious follies; But, thou'lt say,

follow   frequency: 21   relative frequency: 0.00030
**p. 114 PANEGYRE   33 Hasting to follow forth in shouts, and cryes.
    p. 37 EPIGRAMS 33   3 Whither the world must follow. And I, now,
    p. 55 EPIGRAMS 85   3 Where I both learn'd, why wise-men hawking
                                        follow,
    p. 66 EPIGRAMS 102   9 They follow vertue, for reward, to day;
    p. 73 EPIGRAMS 113   12 Who'in such ambition can but follow thee.
    p. 97 FOREST 3   31 While all, that follow, their glad eares apply
    p. 104 FOREST 7   1 Follow a shaddow, it still flies you;
    p. 118 FOREST 13   71 Let who will follow fashions, and attyres,
    p. 163 UNDERWOOD 15   29 As farre as he can flie, or follow day,
    p. 165 UNDERWOOD 15   87 He that will follow but anothers wife,
    p. 221 UNDERWOOD 48   25 So may the Muses follow
    p. 251 UNDERWOOD 74   23 With all the fruit shall follow it,
    p. 293 UNDERWOOD 86   40 Or Tybers winding streames, I follow thee.
    p. 313 HORACE 2   169 Or follow fame, thou that dost write, or faine
    p. 325 HORACE 2   444 There words will follow, not against their will.
    p. 335 HORACE 2   648 They vexe, and follow him with shouts, and noise.
    p. 366 UNGATHERED 6   14 In vaine to follow:
    p. 412 UNGATHERED 40   17 To follow Goodnesse,
    p. 415 UNGATHERED 42   27 Of Finenesse, and alloy: follow his hint,
    p. 657 L. CONVIVALES   1 Welcome'all, who lead or follow,
    p. 657 L. CONVIVALES 19 Welcome all, who lead or follow,

follow'd   frequency: 2   relative frequency: 0.00002
    p. 121 FOREST 14   45 Say you haue follow'd farre,
    p. 167 UNDERWOOD 15 156 With him, for he is follow'd with that heape

followers   frequency: 1   relative frequency: 0.00001
     p.   86 EPIGRAMS 133   97 And all his followers, that had so abus'd him:

following   frequency: 2   relative frequency: 0.00002
    *p. 492 TO HIMSELF   t4 begat this following Ode to
     p. 113 FOREST 12   7 Well, or ill, onely, all the following yeere,

folly   frequency: 5   relative frequency: 0.00007
     p.   43 EPIGRAMS 52   6 Would both thy folly, and thy spite betray.
     p. 152 UNDERWOOD 12   24 No stubbornnesse so stiffe, nor folly
     p. 175 UNDERWOOD 23   24 And only pitious scorne, upon their folly waites.
     p. 192 UNDERWOOD 38   37 Errour and folly in me may have crost
     p. 198 UNDERWOOD 40   44 And never be by time, or folly brought,

fond   frequency: 1   relative frequency: 0.00001
     p. 171 UNDERWOOD 20   4 No more, I am sorry for so fond cause, say,

fondly   frequency: 1   relative frequency: 0.00001
     p. 323 HORACE 2   401 Too patiently, that I not fondly say;

food   frequency: 2   relative frequency: 0.00002
     p. 105 FOREST 8   24 If thy leanenesse loue such food,
     p. 337 HORACE 2   679 Not letting goe his hold, where he drawes food,

fool   frequency: 1   relative frequency: 0.00001
See also "ffoole," "foole."
     p. 410 UNGATHERED 39   8 Keep in thy barking Wit, thou bawling Fool?

foole   frequency: 12   relative frequency: 0.00017
     p.   36 EPIGRAMS 28   22 Stile thee a most great foole, but no great man.
     p.   45 EPIGRAMS 56   13 Foole, as if halfe eyes will not know a fleece
     p.   46 EPIGRAMS 61   t1 TO FOOLE, OR KNAVE.
     p.   55 EPIGRAMS 85   10 Till they be sure to make the foole their
                                  quarrie.
     p.   57 EPIGRAMS 90   1 When MILL first came to court, the
                                  vnprofiting foole,
     p.   79 EPIGRAMS 125   7 But I, no child, no foole, respect the kinde,
     p. 111 FOREST 11   66 Some vicious foole draw neare,
     p. 113 FOREST 12   13 The foole that gaue it; who will want, and weepe,
     p. 184 UNDERWOOD 29   58 And his Title be long foole,
     p. 209 UNDERWOOD 43   150 No Foole would his owne harvest spoile, or
                                  burne!
     p. 210 UNDERWOOD 43   161 Foole, wilt thou let that in example come?
     p. 230 UNDERWOOD 56   22 A mornings, and at afternoones, to foole

foole-hardie   frequency: 1   relative frequency: 0.00001
     p. 132 UNDERWOOD 2.2   20 I foole-hardie, there up-tooke

fooles   frequency: 14   relative frequency: 0.00020
    *p. 493 TO HIMSELF   49 As curious fooles, and enuious of thy straine,
     p.   43 EPIGRAMS 52   5 This but thy iudgement fooles: the other way
     p.   83 EPIGRAMS 131   8 They should be fooles, for me, at their owne
                                  charge.
     p. 100 FOREST 4   15 That onely fooles make thee a saint,
     p. 101 FOREST 4   46 Where breathe the basest of thy fooles;
     p. 117 FOREST 13   36 And, in those outward formes, all fooles are
                                  wise.
     p. 145 UNDERWOOD 5   2 The fooles, or Tyrants with your friends,
     p. 146 UNDERWOOD 6   1 Hang up those dull, and envious fooles,
     p. 179 UNDERWOOD 25   51 So fooles, we see,
     p. 191 UNDERWOOD 38   20 The ignorant, and fooles, no pittie have.
     p. 193 UNDERWOOD 38   94 What Fooles, and all their Parasites can apply;
     p. 201 UNDERWOOD 42   48 That are like cloath'd: must I be of those
                                  fooles
     p. 202 UNDERWOOD 42   81 Let the poore fooles enjoy their follies, love
     p. 371 UNGATHERED 8   16 Or moathes shall eate, what all these Fooles
                                  admire.

foolhardy.   See "foole-hardie."

fooling   frequency: 1   relative frequency: 0.00001
     p. 231 UNDERWOOD 57   17 Mirth, fooling, nor wit,

foolish   frequency: 2   relative frequency: 0.00002
     p. 150 UNDERWOOD 10   1 Wretched and foolish Jealousie,
     p. 171 UNDERWOOD 20   2 Forgive me this one foolish deadly sin,

fools.   See "fooles."

foorth   frequency: 2   relative frequency: 0.00002
    p. 361 UNGATHERED 1   16 did sparcle foorth in Center of the rest:
    p. 362 UNGATHERED 1   29 my abler faculties; and thus brake foorth

foot   frequency: 8   relative frequency: 0.00011
    See also "foote."
    p. 159 UNDERWOOD 14   31 And like a Compasse keeping one foot still
    p. 206 UNDERWOOD 43   79 Or Captaine Pamp<h>lets horse, and foot, that
                             sallie
    p. 211 UNDERWOOD 43 184 foot (out in Sussex) to an iron Mill;
    p. 305 HORACE 2   10 As neither head, nor foot, one forme retaine.
    p. 311 HORACE 2   118 This foot the socks tooke up, and buskins grave,
    p. 313 HORACE 2   194 Forbids thee forth againe thy foot to draw.
    p. 323 HORACE 2   372 A foot, whose swiftnesse gave the Verse the name
    p. 323 HORACE 2   381 This foot yet, in the famous Trimeters

foot-and-halfe-foot   frequency: 1   relative frequency: 0.00001
    p. 311 HORACE 2   139 Their bombard-phrase, and foot-and-halfe-foot
                             words.

foot-cloth   frequency: 1   relative frequency: 0.00001
    p. 165 UNDERWOOD 15 107 Coach'd, or on foot-cloth, thrice chang'd every
                             day,

foot-man   frequency: 1   relative frequency: 0.00001
    p. 201 UNDERWOOD 42   52 That from the Foot-man, when he was become

foote   frequency: 2   relative frequency: 0.00002
    p. 380 UNGATHERED 12 28 Horse, foote, and all but flying in the ayre:
    p. 380 UNGATHERED 12 32 Of his foote, or his penne, his braine or his
                             hoofe,

for   frequency: 478   relative frequency: 0.00691
    See also "ffor," "for'his," "long'd-for."

forbear. See "forbeare."

forbeare   frequency: 5   relative frequency: 0.00007
  **p. 116 PANEGYRE   123 Sustaine the reynes, and in the checke forbeare
    p. 45 EPIGRAMS 58   1 IDEOT, last night, I pray'd thee but
                             forbeare
    p. 54 EPIGRAMS 81   1 Forbeare to tempt me, PROVLE, I will not
                             show
    p. 292 UNDERWOOD 86   5 Sower Mother of sweet Loves, forbeare
    p. 317 HORACE 2   243 Doth wretchedly the use of things forbeare,

forbeares   frequency: 1   relative frequency: 0.00001
    p. 112 FOREST 11   89 Then he, which for sinnes penaltie forbeares.

forbears. See "forbeares."

forbid   frequency: 3   relative frequency: 0.00004
    p. 47 EPIGRAMS 63   12 To so true worth, though thou thy selfe forbid.
    p. 119 FOREST 13   107 But which the Fates forbid me to reueale.
    p. 200 UNDERWOOD 42   5 Who shall forbid me then in Rithme to bee

forbidd'   frequency: 1   relative frequency: 0.00001
    p. 33 EPIGRAMS 21   4 Forbidd' his side! and nothing, but the word

forbidden   frequency: 1   relative frequency: 0.00001
    See also "forbidd'."
    p. 59 EPIGRAMS 92   31 With England. All forbidden bookes they get.

forbids   frequency: 1   relative frequency: 0.00001
    p. 313 HORACE 2   194 Forbids thee forth againe thy foot to draw.

forborne   frequency: 1   relative frequency: 0.00001
    p. 147 UNDERWOOD 7   13 And yet it cannot be forborne,

forc'd   frequency: 2   relative frequency: 0.00002
    See also "forc't."
    p. 120 FOREST 14   18 Of these forc'd ioyes,
    p. 209 UNDERWOOD 43 134 Flanck'd with a Ditch, and forc'd out of a
                             Marish,

.force   frequency: 18   relative frequency: 0.00026
  **p. 113 PANEGYRE   30 (Which Fates auert) should force her from her
                             right.
  **p. 116 PANEGYRE   131 About the streets, as it would force a spring
    p. 139 UNDERWOOD 2.8   2 Had of Love, and of his force,

force (cont.)
```
    p. 201 UNDERWOOD 42    44 Her presently? Or leape thy Wife of force,
    p. 213 UNDERWOOD 44     8 Launces, and men, and some a breaking force.
    p. 219 UNDERWOOD 47    40 And force back that, which will not be restor'd,
    p. 222 UNDERWOOD 49     7 What though with Tribade lust she force a Muse,
    p. 228 UNDERWOOD 53     2 Provoke his mettall, and command his force
    p. 233 UNDERWOOD 59    11 Their weapons shot out, with that flame, and
                              force,
    p. 247 UNDERWOOD 70   117 And such a force the faire example had,
    p. 255 UNDERWOOD 75    81 Force from the Phoenix, then, no raritie
    p. 294 UNDERWOOD 87    18 And us dis-joyn'd force to her brazen yoke,
    p. 337 HORACE 2       675 To force the grates, that hold him in, would
                              fright
    p. 348 HORACE 1       402 ... force was ... .. .. .......... .. ...
    p. 367 UNGATHERED 6    48 "Where neither Force can bend, nor Feare can
                              awe.
    p. 397 UNGATHERED 30   39 And Rouze, the Marching of a mighty force,
    p. 398 UNGATHERED 30   62 Thy list of aydes, and force, for so it is:
    p. 399 UNGATHERED 31   19 Or else Magnetique in the force,
```

forces   frequency: 1   relative frequency: 0.00001
```
    p. 214 UNDERWOOD 44    45 Thou canst draw forth thy forces, and fight drie
```

forcing   frequency: 1   relative frequency: 0.00001
```
    p. 307 HORACE 2        29 Was meant at first. Why, forcing still about
```

forc't   frequency: 3   relative frequency: 0.00004
```
    p. 153 UNDERWOOD 13    24 Where any Deed is forc't, the Grace is mard.
    p. 199 UNDERWOOD 41     6 Or that the Sun was here, but forc't away;
    p. 291 UNDERWOOD 85    60 Or Kid forc't from the Wolfe againe.
```

'fore   frequency: 1   relative frequency: 0.00001
```
    p. 140 UNDERWOOD 2.8   22 'Fore your Idoll Glasse a whit,
```

fore-knowne   frequency: 1   relative frequency: 0.00001
```
    p. 205 UNDERWOOD 43    59 Had I fore-knowne of this thy least desire
```

fore-see   frequency: 1   relative frequency: 0.00001
```
    p. 243 UNDERWOOD 70    19 As, could they but lifes miseries fore-see,
```

forehead   frequency: 3   relative frequency: 0.00004
```
  See also "forehead's."
    p. 170 UNDERWOOD 19     3 By that faire Stand, your forehead, whence he
                              bends
    p. 263 UNDERWOOD 78    21 He will cleare up his forehead, thinke thou
                              bring'st
    p. 408 UNGATHERED 36   14 Thy Forehead is too narrow for my Brand.
```

forehead's   frequency: 1   relative frequency: 0.00001
```
    p. 134 UNDERWOOD 2.4   15 Doe but marke, her forehead's smoother
```

foreign. See "forraine."

foreknown. See "fore-knowne."

foreman   frequency: 1   relative frequency: 0.00001
```
    p. 371 UNGATHERED 8     6 With the shops Foreman, or some such braue
                              sparke,
```

foresee. See "fore-see."

forest. See "forrest."

forestall   frequency: 1   relative frequency: 0.00001
```
    p. 172 UNDERWOOD 20    23 But she is such, as she might, yet, forestall
```

foretold   frequency: 2   relative frequency: 0.00002
```
    p. 181 UNDERWOOD 27    24 Which all the Fate of Troy foretold?
    p. 319 HORACE 2       309 That found out profit, and foretold each thing,
```

forfeit   frequency: 2   relative frequency: 0.00002
```
    p. 169 UNDERWOOD 17    13 And lookes unto the forfeit. If you be
    p. 286 U'WOOD 84.9    136 The safetie of our soules, and forfeit breath!
```

forfeiting. See "forfeitinge."

forfeitinge   frequency: 1   relative frequency: 0.00001
```
    p. 418 UNGATHERED 45   43 forfeitinge their drinking lease,
```

forfeits   frequency: 1   relative frequency: 0.00001
     p. 30 EPIGRAMS 12   14 Signes to new bond, forfeits: and cryes, god
                               payes.

forge   frequency: 2   relative frequency: 0.00002
     p. 179 UNDERWOOD 25   41 Sweat at the forge, their hammers beating;
     p. 212 UNDERWOOD 43   197 Would you had kept your Forge, at Aetna still,

forget   frequency: 4   relative frequency: 0.00005
     p. 35 EPIGRAMS 28   8 And, can forget mens names, with a great grace.
     p. 116 FOREST 13   6 For others ill, ought none their good forget.
     p. 130 UNDERWOOD 1.3   24 Can man forget this Storie?
     p. 290 UNDERWOOD 85   37 Who (amongst these delights) would not forget

forgiue   frequency: 3   relative frequency: 0.00004
     p. 58 EPIGRAMS 91   12 Against my graue, and time could not forgiue.
     p. 67 EPIGRAMS 103   9 Forgiue me then, if mine but say you are
     p. 105 FOREST 8   18 But, forgiue me, with thy crowne

forgive   frequency: 6   relative frequency: 0.00008
     See also "forgiue."
     p. 171 UNDERWOOD 20   2 Forgive me this one foolish deadly sin,
     p. 172 UNDERWOOD 20   21 I could forgive her being proud! a whore!
     p. 190 UNDERWOOD 37   30 Forgive it, as my frailtie, and not me.
     p. 191 UNDERWOOD 38   19 God, and the good, know to forgive, and save.
     p. 192 UNDERWOOD 38   32 Thinke that your selfe like heaven forgive me
                               can:
     p. 329 HORACE 2   520 There are yet faults, which we would well
                               forgive,

forgiven   frequency: 3   relative frequency: 0.00004
     p. 193 UNDERWOOD 38   91 Forgiven him; And in that lyne stand I,
     p. 286 U'WOOD 84.9   143 Yet have all debts forgiven us, and advance
     p. 323 HORACE 2   394 Within the hope of having all forgiven?

forgot   frequency: 3   relative frequency: 0.00004
     p. 46 EPIGRAMS 62   5 Is it the paine affrights? that's soone forgot.
     p. 85 EPIGRAMS 133   44 That all this while I haue forgot some god,
     p. 129 UNDERWOOD 1.2   10 I had forgot

forgotten   frequency: 2   relative frequency: 0.00002
   **p. 116 PANEGYRE   102 "To bury churches, in forgotten dust,
     p. 114 FOREST 12   40 And now lye lost in their forgotten dust.

for'his   frequency: 1   relative frequency: 0.00001

fork. See "forke."

forke   frequency: 1   relative frequency: 0.00001
     p. 290 UNDERWOOD 85   33 Or straines on his small forke his subtill nets

forked   frequency: 1   relative frequency: 0.00001
     p. 366 UNGATHERED 6   21 The pale Pyrene, and the forked Mount:

form. See "forme."

form'd   frequency: 5   relative frequency: 0.00007
     p. 227 UNDERWOOD 52   12 With one great blot, yo'had form'd me as I am.
     p. 245 UNDERWOOD 70   63 Each syllab'e answer'd, and was form'd, how
                               faire;
     p. 287 U'WOOD 84.9   156 For 'twas himselfe who form'd, and gave it her.
     p. 338 HORACE 1   9 .... sick mens .... form'd ..
                               ....
     p. 389 UNGATHERED 24   6 But in one tongue, was form'd with the worlds
                               wit:

forme   frequency: 24   relative frequency: 0.00034
   **p. 115 PANEGYRE   88 "In publique acts what face and forme they beare.
     p. 52 EPIGRAMS 76   2 I thought to forme vnto my zealous Muse,
     p. 63 EPIGRAMS 97   19 About his forme. What then so swells each lim?
     p. 67 EPIGRAMS 104   8 Of birth, of match, of forme, of chastitie?
     p. 108 FOREST 10   26 (Though they were crusht into one forme) could
                               make .
     p. 111 FOREST 11   57 A forme more fresh, then are the Eden bowers,
     p. 115 FOREST 12   82 Had not their forme touch'd by an English wit.
     p. 116 FOREST 12   87 Your forme imprest there: not with tickling
                               rimes,
     p. 120 FOREST 13   123 Wherein, your forme, you still the same shall
                               finde;
     p. 127 UNDERWOOD 1.1   18 This All of nothing, gavest it forme, and fate,

forme (cont.)
    p. 160 UNDERWOOD 14   48 Forme, Art or Ensigne, that hath scap'd your
                                    sight?
    p. 173 UNDERWOOD 22   6 Throughout your forme; as though that move,
    p. 181 UNDERWOOD 27   5 Of Phao<n>s forme? or doth the Boy
    p. 191 UNDERWOOD 38   14 Looke forth, but cannot last in such <a> forme.
    p. 194 UNDERWOOD 38   117 Your forme shines here, here fixed in my heart:
    p. 275 U'WOOD 84.3   6 Some Forme defective, or decay'd;
    p. 280 U'WOOD 84.4   54 For this so loftie forme, so streight,
    p. 287 U'WOOD 84.9   157 And to that forme, lent two such veines of blood
    p. 305 HORACE 2   10 As neither head, nor foot, one forme retaine.
    p. 307 HORACE 2   40 This, seeking, in a various kind, to forme
    p. 307 HORACE 2   50 To forme a worke, I would no more desire
    p. 394 UNGATHERED 28   1 I could begin with that graue forme, Here lies,
    p. 397 UNGATHERED 30   38 My lippes could forme the voyce, I heard that
                                        Rore,
    p. 412 UNGATHERED 41   5 These forme thy Ghyrlond. Wherof Myrtle green,

formed   frequency: 1   relative frequency: 0.00001
  See also "form'd."
    p. 325 HORACE 2   437 What nourisheth, what formed, what begot

former   frequency: 7   relative frequency: 0.00010
 **p. 113 PANEGYRE   7 His former rayes did onely cleare the skie:
    p. 55 EPIGRAMS 85   9 To former height, and there in circle tarrie,
    p. 67 EPIGRAMS 104   10 Of former age, or glorie of our one,
    p. 84 EPIGRAMS 133   19 Then let the former age, with this content her,
    p. 85 EPIGRAMS 133   56 Still, with thy former labours; yet, once more,
    p. 139 UNDERWOOD 2.7   t2 the former.
    p. 242 UNDERWOOD 69   23 Then knew the former ages: yet to life,

formes   frequency: 9   relative frequency: 0.00013
    p. 87 EPIGRAMS 133   126 White, black, blew, greene, and in more formes
                                        out-started,
    p. 100 FOREST 4   9 I know thy formes are studyed arts,
    p. 117 FOREST 13   36 And, in those outward formes, all fooles are
                                        wise.
    p. 137 UNDERWOOD 2.5   46 Call to mind the formes, that strove
    p. 140 UNDERWOOD 2.8   18 To fetch in the Formes goe by:
    p. 166 UNDERWOOD 15   146 To lose the formes, and dignities of men,
    p. 242 UNDERWOOD 69   17 Some of his formes, he lets him not come neere
    p. 269 UNDERWOOD 83   21 Earle Rivers Grand-Child -- serve not formes,
                                        good Fame,
    p. 364 UNGATHERED 5   2 For other formes come short all

forms. See "formes," "out-formes."

fornaces   frequency: 1   relative frequency: 0.00001
    p. 211 UNDERWOOD 43   180 The Glasse-house, Dye-fats, and their
                                        Fornaces;

forraine   frequency: 3   relative frequency: 0.00004
 **p. 113 PANEGYRE   29 Till forraine malice, or vnnaturall spight
    p. 118 FOREST 13   72 Maintayne their liedgers forth, for forraine
                                        wyres,
    p. 375 UNGATHERED 10   32 And here he disdained not, in a forraine land

forrest   frequency: 2   relative frequency: 0.00002
    p. 93 GENERAL TITLE   t1 THE FORREST.
    p. 108 FOREST 10A   9 Such, as in lustes wilde forrest loue to rainge,

forsake   frequency: 3   relative frequency: 0.00004
    p. 313 HORACE 2   188 If thou the vile, broad-troden ring forsake.
    p. 323 HORACE 2   407 In daring to forsake the Grecian tracts,
    p. 339 HORACE 1   59 ... . will forsake:

forsaken   frequency: 1   relative frequency: 0.00001
    p. 146 UNDERWOOD 6   22 From being forsaken, then doth worth:

forsakes   frequency: 2   relative frequency: 0.00002
    p. 169 UNDERWOOD 17   12 Simply my Band, his trust in me forsakes,
    p. 307 HORACE 2   58 Nor language, nor cleere order ere forsakes.

forsook. See "forsocke."

forsooke   frequency: 1   relative frequency: 0.00001
    p. 117 FOREST 13   15 I, that haue suffer'd this; and, though forsooke

forsware   frequency: 1   relative frequency: 0.00001
    p. 56 EPIGRAMS 87   2 HAZARD a month forsware his; and grew
                                     drunke.

forswear. See "forsweare."

forsweare   frequency: 2   relative frequency: 0.00002
    p. 74 EPIGRAMS 115   19 It will deny all; and forsweare it too:
    p. 154 UNDERWOOD 13   50 For what they streight would to the world
                              forsweare;

forswore   frequency: 1   relative frequency: 0.00001
    See also "forsware."
    p. 223 UNDERWOOD 49   29 And trust her I would least, that hath forswore

forsworn. See "forsworne."

forsworne   frequency: 1   relative frequency: 0.00001
    p. 313 HORACE 2   176 Ino bewaild; Ixion false, forsworne;

fort   frequency: 4   relative frequency: 0.00005
    p. 187 UNDERWOOD 33   30 Arm'd at all peeces, as to keepe a Fort
    p. 209 UNDERWOOD 43   133 Which, though it were the Fort of the whole
                              Parish,
    p. 213 UNDERWOOD 44   21 What a strong Fort old Pimblicoe had bin!
    p. 401 UNGATHERED 32   17 This Fort of so impregnable accesse,

forth   frequency: 74   relative frequency: 0.00107
    See also "fforth," "foorth," "hence-forth."
   *p. 493 TO HIMSELF   25 Throwne forth, and rak't into the common tub,
   *p. 494 TO HIMSELF   59 In tuning forth the acts of his sweet raigne:
  **p. 114 PANEGYRE   33 Hasting to follow forth in shouts, and cryes.
  **p. 115 PANEGYRE   67 To bring them forth: Whil'st riper ag'd, and apt
    p. 34 EPIGRAMS 23   4 Came forth example, and remaines so, yet:
    p. 44 EPIGRAMS 55   4 The least indulgent thought thy pen drops forth!
    p. 61 EPIGRAMS 95   22 But, wisely, thrusts not forth a forward hand,
    p. 68 EPIGRAMS 105   12 Were leading forth the Graces on the greene:
    p. 84 EPIGRAMS 133   20 Shee brought the Poets forth, but ours
                              th'aduenter.
    p. 85 EPIGRAMS 133   63 Belch'd forth an ayre, as hot, as at the muster
    p. 118 FOREST 13   63 Times, and occasions, to start forth, and seeme)
    p. 118 FOREST 13   72 Maintayne their liedgers forth, for forraine
                              wyres,
    p. 140 UNDERWOOD 2.8 16 No, nor forth your window peepe,
    p. 146 UNDERWOOD 6   20 In love, doth not alone help forth
    p. 150 UNDERWOOD 10   13 Goe, get thee quickly forth,
    p. 155 UNDERWOOD 13   63 Their bounties forth, to him that last was made,
    p. 155 UNDERWOOD 13   77 Yea, of th'ingratefull: and he forth must tell
    p. 157 UNDERWOOD 13 150 Shoot forth in smooth and comely spaces; have
    p. 159 UNDERWOOD 14   29 Stand forth my Object, then, you that have beene
    p. 162 UNDERWOOD 15   1 Wake, friend, from forth thy Lethargie: the
                              Drum
    p. 164 UNDERWOOD 15   65 Planting their Purles, and Curles spread forth
                              like Net,
    p. 167 UNDERWOOD 15 173 Then once to number, or bring forth to hand,
    p. 187 UNDERWOOD 33   27 Of Argument, still drawing forth the best,
    p. 191 UNDERWOOD 38   14 Looke forth, but cannot last in such <a> forme.
    p. 211 UNDERWOOD 43 181 To live in Sea-coale, and goe forth in smoake;
    p. 213 UNDERWOOD 44   18 To have their Husbands drawne forth to the
                              field,
    p. 214 UNDERWOOD 44   45 Thou canst draw forth thy forces, and fight drie
    p. 219 UNDERWOOD 47   33 Or the States Ships sent forth belike to meet
    p. 223 UNDERWOOD 49   19 And spangled Petticotes brought forth to eye,
    p. 239 UNDERWOOD 67   9 Their noises forth in Thunder:
    p. 242 UNDERWOOD 70   2 Thy comming forth in that great yeare,
    p. 243 UNDERWOOD 70   15 Urg'd, hurried forth, and horld
    p. 243 UNDERWOOD 70   26 And told forth fourescore yeares;
    p. 250 UNDERWOOD 74   3 When shee puts forth the life of ev'ry thing:
    p. 253 UNDERWOOD 75   26 The Month of youth, which calls all Creatures
                              forth
    p. 253 UNDERWOOD 75   41 See, how she paceth forth in Virgin-white,
    p. 253 UNDERWOOD 75   43 And Sister: darting forth a dazling light
    p. 258 UNDERWOOD 75 175 Peepe forth a Gemme; to see
    p. 263 UNDERWOOD 79   4 To shew the rites, and t<o>'usher forth the way
    p. 264 UNDERWOOD 79   29 That leades our flocks and us, and calls both
                              forth
    p. 276 U'WOOD 84.3   23 Foure Rivers branching forth like Seas,
    p. 279 U'WOOD 84.4   47 Us forth, by some Celestiall slight
    p. 280 U'WOOD 84.4   59 As smooth as Oyle pour'd forth, and calme
    p. 282 U'WOOD 84.9   5 And set it forth; the rest were Cobwebs fine,
    p. 283 U'WOOD 84.9   34 Her blessed Soule, hence, forth this valley vane
    p. 287 U'WOOD 84.9   183 And came forth ever cheered, with the rod
    p. 309 HORACE 2   82 And wealth unto our language; and brought forth
    p. 309 HORACE 2   110 That first sent forth the dapper Elegie,

forth (cont.)
p. 313 HORACE 2	181	Unto the last, as when he first went forth,
p. 313 HORACE 2	185	Of Homers, forth in acts, then of thine owne,
p. 313 HORACE 2	194	Forbids thee forth againe thy foot to draw.
p. 315 HORACE 2	198	Afford? The Mountaines travail'd, and brought forth
p. 315 HORACE 2	205	Wonders forth after: As Antiphates,
p. 319 HORACE 2	307	The rash, and head-long eloquence brought forth
p. 319 HORACE 2	320	For the vile Goat, soone after, forth did send
p. 325 HORACE 2	426	But fame of Poets, they thinke, if they come forth,
p. 327 HORACE 2	455	Thence draw forth true expressions. For, sometimes,
p. 331 HORACE 2	579	To change, and mend, what you not forth doe set.
p. 378 UNGATHERED 11	86	Come forth thou bonnie bouncing booke then, daughter
p. 386 UNGATHERED 21	8	This thy worke forth: that iudgment mine commends.
p. 386 UNGATHERED 21	16	With the how much they set forth, but th'how well.
p. 391 UNGATHERED 26	33	For names; but call forth thund'ring Aeschilus,
p. 391 UNGATHERED 26	40	Sent forth, or since did from their ashes come.
p. 392 UNGATHERED 26	45	When like Apollo he came forth to warme
p. 392 UNGATHERED 26	77	Shine forth, thou Starre of Poets, and with rage,
p. 396 UNGATHERED 30	20	The Orbe was cut forth into Regions seauen.
p. 402 UNGATHERED 34	3	you are; from them leapt forth an Architect,
p. 403 UNGATHERED 34	34	And peering forth of Iris in ye Shrowdes!
p. 405 UNGATHERED 34	78	In setting forth of such a solemne Toye!
p. 405 UNGATHERED 34	81	Disguisd? and thence drag forth Enormity?
p. 409 UNGATHERED 37	15	A Mungrel Curre? Thou should'st stinck forth, and dye
p. 409 UNGATHERED 37	21	Thy Noddle, with his clubb; and dashing forth
p. 414 UNGATHERED 41	48	By bringing forth GOD's onely Son, no other.
p. 666 INSCRIPTS. 11	9	Shall powre forth many a line, drop many a letter,

forth-brought   frequency: 1   relative frequency: 0.00001
p. 331 HORACE 2	561	So, any Poeme, fancied, or forth-brought

fortie   frequency: 2   relative frequency: 0.00002
p. 51 EPIGRAMS 73	21	Fortie things more, deare GRAND, which you know true,
p. 150 UNDERWOOD 9	15	Told seven and fortie years,

fortifie   frequency: 1   relative frequency: 0.00001
p. 400 UNGATHERED 32	6	When they doe sweat to fortifie a Muse.

fortified   frequency: 1   relative frequency: 0.00001
p. 116 FOREST 13	3	The bad, by number, are so fortified,

fortify. See "fortifie."

fortitude   frequency: 2   relative frequency: 0.00002
p. 49 EPIGRAMS 66	15	Though euery fortitude deserues applause,
p. 156 UNDERWOOD 13	105	I thought that Fortitude had beene a meane

fortnight   frequency: 1   relative frequency: 0.00001
p. 51 EPIGRAMS 73	7	Item, a tale or two, some fortnight after;

fortunate   frequency: 1   relative frequency: 0.00001
p. 419 UNGATHERED 47	6	And Buckingham the fortunate.

fortune   frequency: 32   relative frequency: 0.00046
See also "ffortune," "fortvne."
p. 47 EPIGRAMS 63	3	And not thy fortune; who can cleerely see
p. 49 EPIGRAMS 66	9	Against thy fortune: when no foe, that day,
p. 63 EPIGRAMS 98	5	Fortune vpon him breakes her selfe, if ill,
p. 64 EPIGRAMS 99	9	From place, or fortune, are made high, or low,
p. 71 EPIGRAMS 110	5	All yeelding to his fortune, nor, the while,
p. 72 EPIGRAMS 112	3	Think'st thou it is meere fortune, that can win?
p. 96 FOREST 2	92	A fortune, in this age, but rarely knowne.
p. 117 FOREST 13	16	Of Fortune, haue not alter'd yet my looke,
p. 117 FOREST 13	41	A Princes fortune: These are gifts of chance,
p. 131 UNDERWOOD 2.1	8	Clothes, or Fortune gives the grace;
p. 136 UNDERWOOD 2.5	2	Both my fortune, and my Starre!
p. 153 UNDERWOOD 13	15	And though my fortune humble me, to take
p. 162 UNDERWOOD 15	21	Or Feathers: lay his fortune out to show,
p. 168 UNDERWOOD 15	183	That fortune never make thee to complaine,
p. 170 UNDERWOOD 18	10	And Fortune once, t<o>'assist the spirits that dare.

fortune (cont.)
```
  p. 170 UNDERWOOD 18    16 Or Love, or Fortune blind, when they but winke
  p. 170 UNDERWOOD 18    21 If it be thus; Come Love, and Fortune goe,
  p. 170 UNDERWOOD 18    24 Love to my heart, and Fortune to my lines.
  p. 174 UNDERWOOD 23    17 Should not on fortune pause,
  p. 180 UNDERWOOD 25    65 As farre from all revolt, as you are now from
                            Fortune.
  p. 181 UNDERWOOD 26    23 For men to use their fortune reverently,
  p. 209 UNDERWOOD 43   153 O no, cry'd all, Fortune, for being a whore,
  p. 217 UNDERWOOD 46     4 Whom Fortune aided lesse, or Vertue more.
  p. 217 UNDERWOOD 46    22 None Fortune aided lesse, or Vertue more.
  p. 233 UNDERWOOD 59    23 Of fortune! when, or death appear'd, or bands!
  p. 234 UNDERWOOD 61     2 And all the games of Fortune, plaid at Court;
  p. 270 UNDERWOOD 83    45 What Nature, Fortune, Institution, Fact
  p. 311 HORACE 2       153 To every state of fortune; she helpes on,
  p. 313 HORACE 2       159 In sound, quite from his fortune; both the rout,
  p. 319 HORACE 2       286 Fortune would love the poore, and leave the
                            proud.
  p. 391 UNGATHERED 26   16 Aboue th'ill fortune of them, or the need.
  p. 422 UNGATHERED 50    4 whom fortune hath deprest; come nere the fates
```

fortunes   frequency: 5   relative frequency: 0.00007
```
  p.  48 EPIGRAMS 64     18 I'haue sung the greater fortunes of our state.
  p.  60 EPIGRAMS 93     14 Though not vnprou'd: which shewes, thy fortunes
                            are
  p. 112 FOREST 11      106 Making his fortunes swim
  p. 342 HORACE 1       153 .. ...... Fortunes habit ... ...... ..
  p. 395 UNGATHERED 29    3 Of Fortunes wheele by Lucan driu'n about,
```

fortvne   frequency: 1   relative frequency: 0.00001
```
  p. 117 FOREST 13       45 Though it reiect not those of FORTVNE:
                            such
```

forty   frequency: 1   relative frequency: 0.00001
```
  See also "fortie."
  p. 408 UNGATHERED 37    4 Th'enuy'd returne, of forty pound in gold.
```

forum   frequency: 1   relative frequency: 0.00001
```
  p. 407 UNGATHERED 35   11 He draw a Forum, wth quadriuiall Streets!
```

forward   frequency: 1   relative frequency: 0.00001
```
  p.  61 EPIGRAMS 95     22 But, wisely, thrusts not forth a forward hand,
```

foster-father   frequency: 1   relative frequency: 0.00001
```
  p. 389 UNGATHERED 24   14 More then the Foster-father of this Child;
```

fought   frequency: 2   relative frequency: 0.00002
```
  p.  71 EPIGRAMS 110     8 He wrote, with the same spirit that he fought,
  p. 186 UNDERWOOD 33     4 Where mutuall frauds are fought, and no side
                            yeild;
```

foul. See "foule," "fowle."

foule   frequency: 9   relative frequency: 0.00013
```
 *p. 493 TO HIMSELF     37 With their foule comick socks;
**p. 113 PANEGYRE       15 From whose foule reeking cauernes first arise
  p. 188 UNDERWOOD 34    1 Envious and foule Disease, could there not be
  p. 224 UNDERWOOD 50   17 Among the daily Ruines that fall foule,
  p. 269 UNDERWOOD 83   30 To be describ'd! Fames fingers are too foule
  p. 327 HORACE 2      481 From slaughters, and foule life; and for the same
  p. 338 HORACE 1        5 ..... .. a blacke foule .... ......... ....
  p. 363 UNGATHERED 3   15 Straines fancie vnto foule Apostacie,
  p. 417 UNGATHERED 45  16 Tough, foule, or Tender.
```

foulely   frequency: 1   relative frequency: 0.00001
```
  p. 323 HORACE 2      370 His power of foulely hurting made to cease.
```

fouily. See "foulely."

found   frequency: 26   relative frequency: 0.00037
```
**p. 115 PANEGYRE       83 "And, being once found out, discouer'd lies
  p.  29 EPIGRAMS 8      3 But, for this money was a courtier found,
  p.  38 EPIGRAMS 35     7 Like aydes gainst treasons who hath found before?
  p.  59 EPIGRAMS 92    27 To ope' the character. They'haue found the
                           sleight
  p.  75 EPIGRAMS 116    8 Might be found out as good, and not my Lord.
  p.  86 EPIGRAMS 133   85 But, comming neere, they found it but a liter,
  p.  95 FOREST 2       76 That found King IAMES, when hunting late,
                           this way,
  p.  98 FOREST 3       52 Nor are the Muses strangers found:
```

found (cont.)
p. 130 UNDERWOOD 1.3   6 Yet search'd, and true they found it.
p. 159 UNDERWOOD 14   16 Themselves through favouring what is there not
                            found:
p. 180 UNDERWOOD 26   3 Your fate hath found
p. 229 UNDERWOOD 54   11 But rather with advantage to be found
p. 258 UNDERWOOD 75   181 Whilst the maine tree, still found
p. 264 UNDERWOOD 79   37 The fairest flowers are alwayes found;
p. 265 UNDERWOOD 79   59 The better grasse, and flowers are found.
p. 280 U'WOOD 84.4   50 Some Paradise, or Palace found
p. 284 U'WOOD 84.9   56 This as it guilty is, or guiltlesse found,
p. 288 U'WOOD 84.9   190 The doore of Grace, and found the Mercy-Seat.
p. 317 HORACE 2   242 Either because he seekes, and, having found,
p. 319 HORACE 2   309 That found out profit, and foretold each thing,
p. 319 HORACE 2   311 Thespis is said to be the first found out
p. 329 HORACE 2   499 Playes were found out; and rest, the end, and
                            crowne
p. 389 UNGATHERED 23   10 Such Passage hast thou found, such Returnes
                            made,
p. 397 UNGATHERED 30   24 I found it pure, and perfect Poesy,
p. 408 UNGATHERED 37   5 ffoole, doe not rate my Rymes; I'haue found thy
                            Vice
p. 415 UNGATHERED 42   9 Or why to like; they found, it all was new,

foundation   frequency: 1   relative frequency: 0.00001
p. 225 UNDERWOOD 51   10 Fame, and foundation of the English Weale.

founder   frequency: 1   relative frequency: 0.00001
p. 184 UNDERWOOD 29   60 Was the founder.

foundered. See "foundred."

foundred   frequency: 1   relative frequency: 0.00001
p. 107 FOREST 10   9 And foundred thy hot teame, to tune my lay.

fount   frequency: 1   relative frequency: 0.00001
p. 366 UNGATHERED 6   19 The cleare Dircaean Fount

fountain. See "fountaine."

fountaine   frequency: 2   relative frequency: 0.00002
p. 183 UNDERWOOD 29   22 So to see the Fountaine drie,
p. 368 UNGATHERED 6   72 To Loumond lake, and Twedes blacke-springing
                            fountaine.

fountaines   frequency: 3   relative frequency: 0.00004
p. 160 UNDERWOOD 14   45 Sought out the Fountaines, Sources, Creekes,
                            paths, wayes,
p. 200 UNDERWOOD 42   7 That from the Muses fountaines doth indorse
p. 290 UNDERWOOD 85   27 The Fountaines murmure as the streames doe
                            creepe,

fountains. See "fountaines."

four. See "foure."

foure   frequency: 4   relative frequency: 0.00005
**p. 114 PANEGYRE   47 They that had seene, but foure short daies
                            before,
p. 276 U'WOOD 84.3   23 Foure Rivers branching forth like Seas,
p. 327 HORACE 2   469 A third of twelve, you may: foure ounces. Glad,
p. 371 UNGATHERED 9   6 She might haue claym'd t'have made the Graces
                            foure;

foure-score   frequency: 1   relative frequency: 0.00001
p. 243 UNDERWOOD 70   32 For three of his foure-score, he did no good.

fourescore   frequency: 1   relative frequency: 0.00001
p. 243 UNDERWOOD 70   26 And told forth fourescore yeares;

fourescore. See "foure-score," "fourescore."

fourth   frequency: 4   relative frequency: 0.00005
p. 292 UNDERWOOD 86   t1 Ode the first. The fourth Booke.
p. 317 HORACE 2   275 Any fourth man, to speake at all, aspire.
p. 323 HORACE 2   380 Of fellowship, the fourth, or second place.
p. 413 UNGATHERED 41   17 The fourth is humble Ivy, intersert,

fowl. See "fowle."

fowle   frequency: 4   relative frequency: 0.00005
    p. 65 EPIGRAMS 101   15 And, though fowle, now, be scarce, yet there are
                             clarkes,
    p. 143 UNDERWOOD 3   5 At such a Call, what beast or fowle,
    p. 200 UNDERWOOD 42   22 Wish, you had fowle ones, and deformed got;
    p. 397 UNGATHERED 30   33 And looking vp, I saw Mineruas fowle,

fowler   frequency: 1   relative frequency: 0.00001
    p. 335 HORACE 2   650 And stalketh, like a Fowler, round about,

fox. See "foxe."

foxe   frequency: 1   relative frequency: 0.00001
    p. 333 HORACE 2   622 For praises, where the mind conceales a foxe.

fragrant   frequency: 1   relative frequency: 0.00001
    p. 147 UNDERWOOD 7   16 And fresh and fragrant too,

frail. See "fraile."

fraile   frequency: 3   relative frequency: 0.00004
    p. 101 FOREST 4   54 Our fraile condition it is such,
    p. 193 UNDERWOOD 38   68 God lightens not at mans each fraile offence,
    p. 219 UNDERWOOD 47   56 Well, with mine owne fraile Pitcher, what to doe

frailtie   frequency: 3   relative frequency: 0.00004
    p. 190 UNDERWOOD 37   30 Forgive it, as my frailtie, and not me.
    p. 192 UNDERWOOD 38   31 Thinke it was frailtie, Mistris, thinke me man,
    p. 329 HORACE 2   528 Hath shed, or humane frailtie not kept thence.

frailty. See "frailtie."

fram'd   frequency: 2   relative frequency: 0.00002
    p. 66 EPIGRAMS 103   3 And noted for what flesh such soules were fram'd,
    p. 288 U'WOOD 84.9   209 All this by Faith she saw, and fram'd a Plea,

frame   frequency: 9   relative frequency: 0.00013
    p. 112 FOREST 11   110 Of this excelling frame?
    p. 241 UNDERWOOD 68   7 Hee'ld frame such ditties of their store, and
                             want,
    p. 278 U'WOOD 84.4   23 That all may say, that see the frame,
    p. 321 HORACE 2   349 I can out of knowne geare, a fable frame,
    p. 323 HORACE 2   371 Two rests, a short and long, th'Iambick frame;
    p. 339 HORACE 1   52 .. frame . ...
    p. 392 UNGATHERED 26 62 (And himselfe with it) that he thinkes to frame;
    p. 395 UNGATHERED 29 20 Lucans whole frame vnto vs, and so wrought,
    p. 399 UNGATHERED 31 18 Of vertue, pretious in the frame:

france   frequency: 9   relative frequency: 0.00013
    p. 56 EPIGRAMS 88   3 That so much skarfe of France, and hat, and
                             fether,
    p. 83 EPIGRAMS 132   4 And vtter stranger to all ayre of France)
    p. 83 EPIGRAMS 132   13 Thine the originall; and France shall boast,
    p. 219 UNDERWOOD 47   47 Of Spaine or France; or were not prick'd downe
                             one
    p. 240 UNDERWOOD 67   42 Hay! for the flowre of France!
    p. 375 UNGATHERED 10 30 Here France, and Italy both to him shed
    p. 379 UNGATHERED 12 19 France, Sauoy, Italy, and Heluetia,
    p. 397 UNGATHERED 30 58 Our right in France! if ritely vnderstood.
    p. 401 UNGATHERED 33 10 Recelebrates the ioyfull Match with France.

frances   frequency: 2   relative frequency: 0.00002
    p. 252 UNDERWOOD 75   t9 FRANCES STUART,
    p. 253 UNDERWOOD 75   37 The Lady Frances, drest

francis   frequency: 2   relative frequency: 0.00002
    p. 44 EPIGRAMS 55   t1 TO FRANCIS BEAVMONT.
    p. 258 UNDERWOOD 75 171 Upon a Thomas, or a Francis call;

frank   frequency: 1   relative frequency: 0.00001
    p. 258 UNDERWOOD 75 172 A Kate, a Frank, to honour their Grand-dames,

frantic. See "frantick."

frantick   frequency: 1   relative frequency: 0.00001
    p. 335 HORACE 2   643 Wise, sober folke, a frantick Poet feare,

fraud   frequency: 1   relative frequency: 0.00001
    p. 186 UNDERWOOD 32   4 Then to make falshood blush, and fraud afraid:

frauds   frequency: 1   relative frequency: 0.00001
      p. 186 UNDERWOOD 33   4 Where mutuall frauds are fought, and no side
                                yeild;

free   frequency: 47 relative frequency: 0.00068
      See also "ffree," "shot-free."
      p. 31 EPIGRAMS 13   3 Let me giue two: that doubly am got free,
      p. 31 EPIGRAMS 14   11 Pardon free truth, and let thy modestie,
      p. 40 EPIGRAMS 42   5 By his free will, be in IONES company.
      p. 41 EPIGRAMS 43   10 And what I write thereof find farre, and free
      p. 43 EPIGRAMS 51   2 Great heau'n did well, to giue ill fame free
                                wing;
      p. 49 EPIGRAMS 66   14 When they cost dearest, and are done most free,
      p. 52 EPIGRAMS 76   5 I meant to make her faire, and free, and wise,
      p. 52 EPIGRAMS 76   16 Of destinie, and spin her owne free houres.
      p. 58 EPIGRAMS 91   4 Sung by a HORACE, or a Muse as free;
      p. 61 EPIGRAMS 95   18 That liu'st from hope, from feare, from faction
                                free;
      p. 62 EPIGRAMS 96   5 As free simplicitie, to dis-auow,
      p. 65 EPIGRAMS 101   35 Of this we will sup free, but moderately,
      p. 95 FOREST 2   58 Adde to thy free prouisions, farre aboue
      p. 97 FOREST 3   15 Free from proud porches, or their guilded roofes,
      p. 129 UNDERWOOD 1.2   9 But left me free,
      p. 129 UNDERWOOD 1.2   20 To free a slave,
      p. 142 UNDERWOOD 2.9   51 And from basenesse to be free,
      p. 154 UNDERWOOD 13   30 But by meere Chance? for interest? or to free
      p. 158 UNDERWOOD 14   8 A pennance, where a man may not be free,
      p. 170 UNDERWOOD 18   18 Because they would free Justice imitate,
      p. 174 UNDERWOOD 23   16 Minds that are great and free,
      p. 184 UNDERWOOD 29   31 Greeke was free from Rimes infection,
      p. 184 UNDERWOOD 29   35 Is not yet free from Rimes wrongs,
      p. 188 UNDERWOOD 34   2 One beautie in an Age, and free from thee?
      p. 190 UNDERWOOD 37   22 And lesse they know, who being free to use
      p. 190 UNDERWOOD 37   28 From each of which I labour to be free,
      p. 197 UNDERWOOD 40   16 And free societie, hee's borne else-where,
      p. 200 UNDERWOOD 42   30 Where I may handle Silke, as free, and neere,
      p. 215 UNDERWOOD 44   68 Live by their Scale, that dare doe nothing free?
      p. 220 UNDERWOOD 47   72 And free it from all question to preserve,
      p. 221 UNDERWOOD 48   41 Thy Circuits, and thy Rounds free,
      p. 230 UNDERWOOD 56   2 When you would play so nobly, and so free.
      p. 232 UNDERWOOD 58   2 All mouthes are open, and all stomacks free:
      p. 259 UNDERWOOD 76   10 Of a free Poetique Pension,
      p. 271 UNDERWOOD 83   71 Speakes Heavens Language! and discourseth free
      p. 293 UNDERWOOD 87   3 His armes more acceptable free,
      p. 295 UNDERWOOD 90   6 A quiet mind; free powers; and body sound;
      p. 309 HORACE 2   83 New names of things. It hath beene ever free,
      p. 311 HORACE 2   116 Fresh Lovers businesse, and the Wines free
                                source.
      p. 313 HORACE 2   165 A ventring Merchant, or the Farmer free
      p. 319 HORACE 2   324 The free spectators, subject to no Law,
      p. 331 HORACE 2   560 These, the free meale might have beene well
                                drawne out:
      p. 331 HORACE 2   578 Nine yeares kept in, your papers by, yo'are free
      p. 352 HORACE 1   545 .... rings .... free ....
                                ....
      p. 381 UNGATHERED 12   57 Which he not denies. Now being so free,
      p. 401 UNGATHERED 32   21 And like a hallow'd Temple, free from taint
      p. 417 UNGATHERED 45   30 and of Circle be as free,

free-borne   frequency: 1   relative frequency: 0.00001
      p. 331 HORACE 2   571 Why not? I'm gentle, and free-borne, doe hate

freed   frequency: 2   relative frequency: 0.00002
      p. 130 UNDERWOOD 1.3   9 And freed the soule from danger;
      p. 285 U'WOOD 84.9   93 To have her captiv'd spirit freed from flesh,

freedom. See "freedome."

freedome   frequency: 7   relative frequency: 0.00010
      p. 98 FOREST 3   58 Freedome doth with degree dispense.
      p. 101 FOREST 4   31 And tasting ayre, and freedome, wull
      p. 101 FOREST 4   51 Where euery freedome is betray'd,
      p. 166 UNDERWOOD 15   121 This hath our ill-us'd freedome, and soft peace
      p. 173 UNDERWOOD 22   11 The noblest freedome, not to chuse
      p. 241 UNDERWOOD 69   5 Freedome, and Truth; with love from those begot:
      p. 242 UNDERWOOD 69   15 At a Friends freedome, proves all circling
                                meanes

freehold. See "freehould."

freehould   frequency: 1   relative frequency: 0.00001
   p. 399 UNGATHERED 31   26 In faire freehould, not an Inmate:

freely   frequency: 4   relative frequency: 0.00005
   p. 153 UNDERWOOD 13   13 You cannot doubt, but I, who freely know
   p. 153 UNDERWOOD 13   14 This Good from you, as freely will it owe;
   p. 258 UNDERWOOD 75   186 And let him freely gather Loves First-fruits,
   p. 383 UNGATHERED 16   9 hee freely bringes; and on[e] this Alter layes

freer   frequency: 1   relative frequency: 0.00001
   p. 221 UNDERWOOD 48   13 For, Bacchus, thou art freer

freez'd   frequency: 1   relative frequency: 0.00001
   p. 333 HORACE 2   589 While he was young; he sweat; and freez'd againe:

freind   frequency: 5   relative frequency: 0.00007
   p. 384 UNGATHERED 18   12 Out-bee yt Wife, in worth, thy freind did make:
   p. 386 UNGATHERED 21   t1 To my truly-belou'd Freind,
   p. 395 UNGATHERED 29   25 Your true freind in Iudgement and Choise
   p. 399 UNGATHERED 31   13 Or of a parent! or a freind!
   p. 415 UNGATHERED 43   t2 Good Freind Mr. Robert Dover, on his great

freindes   frequency: 2   relative frequency: 0.00002
   p. 295 UNDERWOOD 90   7 A wise simplicity; freindes alike-stated;
   p. 384 UNGATHERED 18   5 Such weare true wedding robes, and are true
                             freindes,

freinds   frequency: 2   relative frequency: 0.00002
   p. 386 UNGATHERED 21   1 Some men, of Bookes or Freinds not speaking
                             right,
   p. 387 UNGATHERED 22   6 trust in the tombes, their care=full freinds do
                             rayse;

french   frequency: 11   relative frequency: 0.00015
   p. 56 EPIGRAMS 88   2 That his whole body should speake french, not he?
   p. 56 EPIGRAMS 88   7 That he, vntrauell'd, should be french so much,
   p. 56 EPIGRAMS 88   10 The french disease, with which he labours yet?
   p. 56 EPIGRAMS 88   13 Or is it some french statue? No: 'T doth moue,
   p. 59 EPIGRAMS 92   33 At naming the French King, their heads they
                             shake,
   p. 141 UNDERWOOD 2.9   7 French to boote, at least in fashion,
   p. 213 UNDERWOOD 44   5 Old Aesope Gundomar: the French can tell,
   p. 219 UNDERWOOD 47   31 What is't to me whether the French Designe
   p. 368 UNGATHERED 6   84 The nimble French;
   p. 401 UNGATHERED 33   6 French Aire and English Verse here Wedded
                             lie.
   p. 402 UNGATHERED 33   12 The faire French Daughter to learne English
                             in;

french-hood   frequency: 1   relative frequency: 0.00001
   p. 201 UNDERWOOD 42   69 Commended the French-hood, and Scarlet gowne

french-men   frequency: 1   relative frequency: 0.00001
   p. 56 EPIGRAMS 88   8 As french-men in his companie, should seeme
                             dutch?

french-taylors   frequency: 1   relative frequency: 0.00001
   p. 56 EPIGRAMS 88   15 The new french-taylors motion, monthly made,

frequent   frequency: 4   relative frequency: 0.00005
   p. 87 EPIGRAMS 133   130 These be the cause of those thicke frequent mists
   p. 110 FOREST 11   33 Most frequent tumults, horrors, and vnrests,
   p. 146 UNDERWOOD 6   11 The frequent varying of the deed,
   p. 288 U'WOOD 84.9   191 In frequent speaking by the pious Psalmes

fresh   frequency: 14   relative frequency: 0.00020
   See also "ffresh."
   p. 30 EPIGRAMS 12   13 Then takes vp fresh commoditie, for dayes;
   p. 32 EPIGRAMS 16   3 Thy selfe into fresh braules: when, call'd vpon,
   p. 94 FOREST 2   40 Fresh as the ayre, and new as are the houres.
   p. 111 FOREST 11   57 A forme more fresh, then are the Eden bowers,
   p. 118 FOREST 13   66 And after varyed, as fresh obiects goes,
   p. 138 UNDERWOOD 2.6   9 Look'd not halfe so fresh, and faire,
   p. 147 UNDERWOOD 7   16 And fresh and fragrant too,
   p. 171 UNDERWOOD 20   11 Of many Colours; outward, fresh from spots,
   p. 285 U'WOOD 84.9   94 And on her Innocence, a garment fresh
   p. 293 UNDERWOOD 86   32 Or with fresh flowers to girt my temple round.
   p. 311 HORACE 2   116 Fresh Lovers businesse, and the Wines free
                             source.
   p. 342 HORACE 1   178 .. .. fresh ....

fresh (cont.)
    p. 405 UNGATHERED 34   88 Reuiuing wth fresh coulors ye pale Ghosts
    p. 416 UNGATHERED 44   1 Fresh as the Day, and new as are the Howers,

freshly   frequency: 1   relative frequency: 0.00001
    p. 309 HORACE 2   89 Like tender buds shoot up, and freshly grow.

friar. See "fryar."

frie   frequency: 1   relative frequency: 0.00001
    p. 175 UNDERWOOD 23   19 What though the greedie Frie

friend   frequency: 56   relative frequency: 0.00081
    See also "ffreind," "ffriend," "freind."
**p. 116 PANEGYRE   120 For vice is safe, while she hath vice to friend.
  p. 37 EPIGRAMS 33   6 Who wets my graue, can be no friend of mine.
  p. 43 EPIGRAMS 52   4 As if thou wert my friend, but lack'dst a cause.
  p. 44 EPIGRAMS 55   8 What art is thine, that so thy friend deceiues?
  p. 54 EPIGRAMS 83   t1 TO A FRIEND.
  p. 63 EPIGRAMS 98   8 With thine owne course the iudgement of thy
              friend,
  p. 64 EPIGRAMS 101   t1 INVITING A FRIEND TO
              SVPPER.
  p. 70 EPIGRAMS 108   5 I sweare by your true friend, my Muse, I loue
  p. 70 EPIGRAMS 109   8 Is priuate gaine, which hath long guilt to
              friend.
  p. 116 FOREST 12   92 And your braue friend, and mine so well did loue.
  p. 151 UNDERWOOD 12   4 Before me here, the Friend and Sonne;
  p. 151 UNDERWOOD 12   5 For I both lost a friend and Father,
  p. 161 UNDERWOOD 14   77 Humanitie enough to be a friend,
  p. 162 UNDERWOOD 15   1 Wake, friend, from forth thy Lethargie: the
              Drum
  p. 162 UNDERWOOD 15   t1 An Epistle to a Friend, to perswade
  p. 165 UNDERWOOD 15   93 The brother trades a sister; and the friend
  p. 166 UNDERWOOD 15   129 I'le bid thee looke no more, but flee, flee
              friend,
  p. 167 UNDERWOOD 15   162 Friend, flie from hence; and let these kindled
              rimes
  p. 169 UNDERWOOD 17   t2 To a Friend.
  p. 169 UNDERWOOD 17   14 Now so much friend, as you would trust in me,
  p. 170 UNDERWOOD 19   11 Tell me (my lov'd Friend) doe you love, or no,
  p. 180 UNDERWOOD 26   1 High-spirited friend,
  p. 189 UNDERWOOD 37   t1 An Epistle to a friend.
  p. 190 UNDERWOOD 37   10 But, as a friend, which name your selfe receave,
  p. 190 UNDERWOOD 37   18 In friendship, I confesse: But, deare friend,
              heare.
  p. 216 UNDERWOOD 45   16 First weigh a friend, then touch, and trie him
              too:
  p. 216 UNDERWOOD 45   22 Friend to himselfe, that would be friend to thee.
  p. 216 UNDERWOOD 45   24 But he that's too-much that, is friend of none.
  p. 218 UNDERWOOD 47   14 That never yet did friend, or friendship seeke
  p. 224 UNDERWOOD 50   8 No friend to vertue, could be silent here.
  p. 229 UNDERWOOD 54   1 I am to dine, Friend, where I must be weigh'd
  p. 232 UNDERWOOD 58   1 Thou, Friend, wilt heare all censures; unto thee
  p. 241 UNDERWOOD 69   1 Sonne, and my Friend, I had not call'd you so
  p. 241 UNDERWOOD 69   t2 To a Friend, and Sonne.
  p. 244 UNDERWOOD 70   46 A perfect Patriot, and a noble friend,
  p. 247 UNDERWOOD 70   112 The Copie of his friend.
  p. 285 U'WOOD 84.9   99 A Wife, a Friend, a Lady, or a Love;
  p. 287 U'WOOD 84.9   175 A solemne Mistresse, and so good a Friend,
  p. 317 HORACE 2   281 Be wonne a friend; it must both sway, and bend
  p. 333 HORACE 2   606 Whether his soothing friend speake truth, or no.
  p. 333 HORACE 2   624 Hee'd say, Mend this, good friend, and this;
              'tis naught.
  p. 335 HORACE 2   640 Why should I grieve my friend, this trifling
              way?
  p. 383 UNGATHERED 17   t2 friend the Author.
  p. 385 UNGATHERED 19   t1 To his friend the Author vpon
  p. 388 UNGATHERED 23   t1 To my worthy and honour'd Friend,
  p. 389 UNGATHERED 24   21 To your desert, who'haue done it, Friend. And
              this
  p. 395 UNGATHERED 29   t1 To my chosen Friend,
  p. 396 UNGATHERED 30   2 A Friend at all; or, if at all, to thee:
  p. 396 UNGATHERED 30   t3 MUSES OF HIS FRIEND
  p. 398 UNGATHERED 30   94 If I can be a Friend, and Friend to thee.
  p. 400 UNGATHERED 32   t2 Friend, Sir Iohn Beaumont, Baronet.
  p. 401 UNGATHERED 33   t1 To my worthy Friend, Master Edward Filmer,
  p. 409 UNGATHERED 38   t2 his continu'd Vertue) my louing Friend:
  p. 414 UNGATHERED 42   t1 To my deare Sonne, and right-learned Friend,

friend-ship   frequency: 1   relative frequency: 0.00001
  p. 78 EPIGRAMS 122   7 If holiest friend-ship, naked to the touch,

friendly   frequency: 3   relative frequency: 0.00004
**p. 115 PANEGYRE   72 That friendly temper'd, one pure taper makes.
  p. 333 HORACE 2   586 And friendly should unto one end conspire.
  p. 333 HORACE 2   613 Out at his friendly ayes, leape, beat the groun'.

friends   frequency: 38   relative frequency: 0.00055
  See also "ffreinds," "freindes," "freinds."
  p. 35 EPIGRAMS 27   5 If any friends teares could restore, his would;
  p. 48 EPIGRAMS 65   9 Make him loose all his friends; and, which is
                  worse,
  p. 53 EPIGRAMS 77   3 For, if thou shame, ranck'd with my friends, to
                  goe,
  p. 55 EPIGRAMS 86   2 Vpon thy wel-made choise of friends, and bookes;
  p. 55 EPIGRAMS 86   4 In making thy friends bookes, and thy bookes
                  friends:
  p. 60 EPIGRAMS 94   6 Crowne with their owne. Rare poemes aske rare
                  friends
  p. 68 EPIGRAMS 106   8 Like straight, thy pietie to God, and friends:
  p. 81 EPIGRAMS 128   5 May windes as soft as breath of kissing friends,
  p. 81 EPIGRAMS 129   1 That, not a paire of friends each other see,
  p. 94 FOREST 2   21 When thou would'st feast, or exercise thy
                  friends.
  p. 97 FOREST 3   25 Or with thy friends, the heart of all the yeere,
  p. 145 UNDERWOOD 5   2 The fooles, or Tyrants with your friends,
  p. 158 UNDERWOOD 14   10 Chance that the Friends affection proves Allay
  p. 167 UNDERWOOD 15   176 Thy true friends wishes, Colby, which shall be,
  p. 170 UNDERWOOD 18   14 And then the best are, still, the blindest
                  friends!
  p. 171 UNDERWOOD 19   13 You blush, but doe not: friends are either none,
  p. 186 UNDERWOOD 32   2 When a good Cause is destitute of friends,
  p. 190 UNDERWOOD 37   27 As flatt'ry with friends humours still to move.
  p. 197 UNDERWOOD 40   12 I give, or owe my friends, into your Rites,
  p. 208 UNDERWOOD 43   124 My friends, the Watermen! They could provide
  p. 216 UNDERWOOD 45   12 'Tis vertue alone, or nothing, that knits
                  friends:
  p. 216 UNDERWOOD 45   25 Then rest, and a friends value understand,
  p. 224 UNDERWOOD 50   26 And when you want those friends, or neere in
                  blood,
  p. 224 UNDERWOOD 50   27 Or your Allies, you make your bookes your
                  friends,
  p. 230 UNDERWOOD 56   10 His friends, but to breake Chaires, or cracke a
                  Coach.
  p. 242 UNDERWOOD 69   15 At a Friends freedome, proves all circling
                  meanes
  p. 242 UNDERWOOD 69   26 Rather to boast rich hangings, then rare friends.
  p. 243 UNDERWOOD 70   28 Troubled both foes, and friends;
  p. 244 UNDERWOOD 70   35 He purchas'd friends, and fame, and honours then,
  p. 251 UNDERWOOD 74   20 Bring all your friends, (faire Lord) that burne
  p. 256 UNDERWOOD 75   114 It brings Friends Joy, Foes Griefe,
                  Posteritie Fame;
  p. 270 UNDERWOOD 83   60 Made her friends joyes to get above their feares!
  p. 286 U'WOOD 84.9   139 To style us Friends, who were, by Nature,
                  Foes?
  p. 294 UNDERWOOD 89   1 Liber, of all thy friends, thou sweetest care,
  p. 305 HORACE 2   6 Admitted to the sight, although his friends,
  p. 325 HORACE 2   446 What to his Countrey, what his friends he owes,
  p. 398 UNGATHERED 30   90 To all thy vertuous, and well chosen Friends,

friendship   frequency: 21   relative frequency: 0.00030
  See also "friend-ship."
  p. 51 EPIGRAMS 73   1 What is't, fine GRAND, makes thee my
                  friendship flye,
  p. 75 EPIGRAMS 115   30 From friendship, is it's owne fames architect.
  p. 78 EPIGRAMS 121   7 Nor he, for friendship, to be thought vnfit,
  p. 113 FOREST 12   17 Solders crackt friendship; makes loue last a day;
  p. 163 UNDERWOOD 15   39 Friendship is now mask'd Hatred! Justice fled,
  p. 169 UNDERWOOD 17   5 And he is not in friendship. Nothing there
  p. 171 UNDERWOOD 20   1 A Womans friendship! God whom I trust in,
  p. 190 UNDERWOOD 37   9 Which is indeed but friendship of the spit:
  p. 190 UNDERWOOD 37   18 In friendship, I confesse: But, deare friend,
                  heare.
  p. 190 UNDERWOOD 37   23 That friendship which no chance but love did
                  chuse,
  p. 190 UNDERWOOD 37   26 In practiz'd friendship wholly to reprove,
  p. 190 UNDERWOOD 37   33 Her furie, yet no friendship to betray.
  p. 216 UNDERWOOD 45   7 Nor ever trusted to that friendship yet,
  p. 218 UNDERWOOD 47   14 That never yet did friend, or friendship seeke

friendship (cont.)
p. 227 UNDERWOOD 52   22 Yet when of friendship I would draw the face,
p. 242 UNDERWOOD 70   t1 To the immortall memorie, and friendship of
p. 246 UNDERWOOD 70   98 Two names of friendship, but one Starre:
p. 247 UNDERWOOD 70   123 Friendship, in deed, was written, not in words:
p. 315 HORACE 2-   238 His better'd mind seekes wealth, and friendship:
                          than
p. 333 HORACE 2   619 If of their friendship he be worthy, or no:
p. 380 UNGATHERED 12   45 Of Latine and Greeke, to his friendship. And
                          seuen

friendships   frequency: 5   relative frequency: 0.00007
p. 161 UNDERWOOD 14   81 The Gaine of your two friendships! Hayward and
p. 219 UNDERWOOD 47   29 I studie other friendships, and more one,
p. 220 UNDERWOOD 47   63 'Mongst which, if I have any friendships sent,
p. 246 UNDERWOOD 70   90 Where it were friendships schisme,
p. 344 HORACE 1   238 ... . friendships ....

fright   frequency: 2   relative frequency: 0.00002
p. 241 UNDERWOOD 69   11 Was, t'have a Boy stand with a Club, and fright
p. 337 HORACE 2   675 To force the grates, that hold him in, would
                          fright

frighted   frequency: 2   relative frequency: 0.00002
p. 163 UNDERWOOD 15   35 Not to be checkt, or frighted now with fate,
p. 327 HORACE 2   480 First frighted men, that wildly liv'd, at ods,

frights   frequency: 1   relative frequency: 0.00001
p. 193 UNDERWOOD 38   70 And then his thunder frights more, then it kills.

fringes   frequency: 2   relative frequency: 0.00002
p. 202 UNDERWOOD 42   79 The Stuffes, the Velvets, Plushes, Fringes,
                          Lace,
p. 275 U'WOOD 84.3   3 Embroderies, Feathers, Fringes, Lace,

fripperie   frequency: 1   relative frequency: 0.00001
p. 44 EPIGRAMS 56   2 Whose workes are eene the fripperie of wit,

frippery. See "fripperie."

fro   frequency: 2   relative frequency: 0.00002
p. 85 EPIGRAMS 133   34 Of sixe times to, and fro, without embassage,
p. 363 UNGATHERED 3   4 Flowes fro the surfets which we take in peace.

frogs   frequency: 2   relative frequency: 0.00002
p. 84 EPIGRAMS 133   13 Arses were heard to croake, in stead of frogs;
p. 86 EPIGRAMS 133   92 Is this we heare? of frogs? No, guts wind-bound,

from   frequency: 230   relative frequency: 0.00332
  See also "fro."

front   frequency: 2   relative frequency: 0.00002
p. 54 EPIGRAMS 80   7 So to front death, as men might iudge vs past it.
p. 141 UNDERWOOD 2.9   18 Front, an ample field of snow;

frontier. See "frontire."

frontire   frequency: 1   relative frequency: 0.00001
p. 400 UNGATHERED 32   8 The Bound, and Frontire of our Poetrie;

frontispice   frequency: 1   relative frequency: 0.00001
p. 175 UNDERWOOD 24   t1 The mind of the Frontispice to a Booke.

frontispiece. See "frontispice."

frostiest   frequency: 1   relative frequency: 0.00001
p. 363 UNGATHERED 3   13 It thawes the frostiest, and most stiffe
                          disdaine:

frostily   frequency: 1   relative frequency: 0.00001
p. 43 EPIGRAMS 52   2 Dispraise my worke, then praise it frostily:

frosts   frequency: 1   relative frequency: 0.00001
  See also "ffrostes."
p. 233 UNDERWOOD 59   22 Of humane life! as all the frosts, and sweates

froward   frequency: 1   relative frequency: 0.00001
p. 317 HORACE 2   247 Froward, complaining, a commender glad

frown. See "frowne."

frowne   frequency: 3   relative frequency: 0.00004
     p. 80 EPIGRAMS 126   3 I pluck'd a branch; the iealous god did frowne,
     p. 262 UNDERWOOD 78   20 Busie, or frowne at first: when he sees thee,
     p. 369 UNGATHERED 6   110 How they would frowne!

frownes   frequency: 1   relative frequency: 0.00001
     p. 200 UNDERWOOD 42   10 Who frownes, who jealous is, who taxeth me.

frowning   frequency: 1   relative frequency: 0.00001
     p. 183 UNDERWOOD 29   30 Pallas frowning.

frowns. See "frownes."

fruit   frequency: 6   relative frequency: 0.00008
     See also "fruite."
     p. 65 EPIGRAMS 101   27 Digestiue cheese, and fruit there sure will bee;
     p. 94 FOREST 2   39 Then hath thy orchard fruit, thy garden flowers,
     p. 102 FOREST 5   15 'Tis no sinne, loues fruit to steale,
     p. 150 UNDERWOOD 10   8 On all mens Fruit, and flowers, as well as mine.
     p. 251 UNDERWOOD 74   23 With all the fruit shall follow it,
     p. 281 U'WOOD 84.8   19 By which yo'are planted, shew's your fruit shall
                               bide.

fruite   frequency: 1   relative frequency: 0.00001
     p. 384 UNGATHERED 18   18 And eue'ry ioy, in mariage, turne a fruite.

fruites   frequency: 1   relative frequency: 0.00001
     p. 212 UNDERWOOD 43   210 And pray the fruites thereof, and the increase;

fruitfull   frequency: 8   relative frequency: 0.00011
     p. 96 FOREST 2   90 Thy lady's noble, fruitfull, chaste withall.
     p. 119 FOREST 13   95 Of your blest wombe, made fruitfull from aboue,
     p. 190 UNDERWOOD 37   14 So may the fruitfull Vine my temples steepe,
     p. 216 UNDERWOOD 45   18 Deceit is fruitfull. Men have Masques and nets,
     p. 224 UNDERWOOD 50   10 Are growne so fruitfull, and false pleasures
                               climbe,
     p. 240 UNDERWOOD 67   52 So fruitfull, and so faire,
     p. 251 UNDERWOOD 74   28 Shoot up an Olive fruitfull, faire,
     p. 257 UNDERWOOD 75   159 Your fruitfull spreading Vine,

fruitlesse   frequency: 1   relative frequency: 0.00001
     p. 290 UNDERWOOD 85   11 And with his hooke lops off the fruitlesse race,

fruits   frequency: 6   relative frequency: 0.00008
     See also "first-fruits," "fruites."
     p. 45 EPIGRAMS 57   1 If, as their ends, their fruits were so, the
                               same,
     p. 47 EPIGRAMS 64   2 With thy new place, bring I these early fruits
     p. 235 UNDERWOOD 63   3 Who doubts, those fruits God can with gaine
                               restore,
     p. 247 UNDERWOOD 70   128 Had sow'd these fruits, and got the harvest in.
     p. 286 U'WOOD 84.9   123 Wine, or delicious fruits, unto the Taste;
     p. 416 UNGATHERED 44   2 Our first of fruits, that is the prime of flowers

fry. See "frie."

fryar   frequency: 1   relative frequency: 0.00001
     p. 212 UNDERWOOD 43   201 Or stay'd but where the Fryar, and you first
                               met,

fucus   frequency: 1   relative frequency: 0.00001
     p. 140 UNDERWOOD 2.8   26 To consult, if Fucus this

fuliginous   frequency: 1   relative frequency: 0.00001
     p. 405 UNGATHERED 34   72 Of Lanterne-lerry: wth fuliginous heat

full   frequency: 31   relative frequency: 0.00044
  **p. 113 PANEGYRE   2 With ioyes: but vrgeth his full fauors still.
  **p. 114 PANEGYRE   57 The ioy of either was alike, and full;
     p. 27 EPIGRAMS 2   3 Thou should'st be bold, licentious, full of gall,
     p. 59 EPIGRAMS 92   17 And talke reseru'd, lock'd vp, and full of feare,
     p. 64 EPIGRAMS 101   12 If we can get her, full of egs, and then,
     p. 69 EPIGRAMS 107   7 And yet are with their Princes: Fill them full
     p. 79 EPIGRAMS 125   8 The full, the flowing graces there enshrin'd;
     p. 80 EPIGRAMS 127   6 How full of want, how swallow'd vp, how dead
     p. 97 FOREST 3   32 To the full greatnesse of the cry:
     p. 112 FOREST 11   107 In the full floud of her admir'd perfection?
     p. 122 FOREST 15   17 I know my state, both full of shame, and scorne,
     p. 154 UNDERWOOD 13   60 That to such Natures let their full hands flow,
     p. 157 UNDERWOOD 13   152 Aloft, grow lesse and streightned, full of knot;

full (cont.)
    p. 171 UNDERWOOD 20   12 But their whole inside full of ends, and knots?
    p. 180 UNDERWOOD 26   17 In one full Action; nor have you now more
    p. 185 UNDERWOOD 30   8 The poores full Store-house, and just servants
                      field.
    p. 225 UNDERWOOD 51   15 Whose even Thred the Fates spinne round, and
                      full,
    p. 229 UNDERWOOD 54   12 Full twentie stone; of which I lack two pound:
    p. 238 UNDERWOOD 66   1 Haile Mary, full of grace, it once was said,
    p. 238 UNDERWOOD 66   5 Haile Mary, full of honours, to my Queene,
    p. 239 UNDERWOOD 67   19 4. EVT. That when the Quire is full,
    p. 244 UNDERWOOD 70   49 By him, so ample, full, and round,
    p. 246 UNDERWOOD 70   87 Or taste a part of that full joy he meant
    p. 254 UNDERWOOD 75   65 With what full hands, and in how plenteous
                      showers
    p. 284 U'WOOD 84.9   65 And the whole Banquet is full sight of God!
    p. 329 HORACE 2   506 But flowes out, that ore-swelleth in full brests.
    p. 337 HORACE 2   680 Till he drop off, a Horse-leech, full of blood.
    p. 375 UNGATHERED 10   26 Old Hat here, torne Hose, with Shoes full of
                      grauell,
    p. 385 UNGATHERED 19   6 If Praises, when th'are full, heaping admit,
    p. 398 UNGATHERED 30   88 Then Affricke knew, or the full Grecian store!
    p. 413 UNGATHERED 41   31 All, pouring their full showre of graces downe,

fullness. See "fulnesse."

fulnesse   frequency: 2   relative frequency: 0.00002
    p. 284 U'WOOD 84.9   70 Presume to interpell that fulnesse, when
    p. 286 U'WOOD 84.9   137 What fulnesse of beatitude is here?

fume   frequency: 1   relative frequency: 0.00001
    p. 87 EPIGRAMS 133   109 Had it beene seconded, and not in fume

fumes   frequency: 1   relative frequency: 0.00001
    p. 368 UNGATHERED 6   78 Their reeking fumes;

fumie   frequency: 1   relative frequency: 0.00001
    p. 42 EPIGRAMS 50   2 Or fumie clysters, thy moist lungs to bake:

fumy. See "fumie."

funeral. See "funerall."

funerall   frequency: 1   relative frequency: 0.00001
    p. 41 EPIGRAMS 44   3 Ere blacks were bought for his owne funerall,

funeralls   frequency: 1   relative frequency: 0.00001
    p. 333 HORACE 2   614 As those that hir'd to weepe at Funeralls,
                      swoune,

funerals. See "funeralls."

fur. See "furre."

furie   frequency: 7   relative frequency: 0.00010
    p. 85 EPIGRAMS 133   52 Canst tell me best, how euery Furie lookes
                      there,
    p. 89 EPIGRAMS 133   179 Tempt not his furie, PLVTO is away:
    p. 98 FOREST 3   68 The furie of a rash command,
    p. 166 UNDERWOOD 15   117 What furie of late is crept into our Feasts?
    p. 190 UNDERWOOD 37   33 Her furie, yet no friendship to betray.
    p. 191 UNDERWOOD 38   8 Alone lend succours, and this furie stay,
    p. 208 UNDERWOOD 43   125 Against thy furie, when to serve their needs,

furies   frequency: 3   relative frequency: 0.00004
    p. 37 EPIGRAMS 32   2 Could not effect, not all the furies doe,
    p. 84 EPIGRAMS 133   15 Furies there wanted not: each scold was ten.
    p. 88 EPIGRAMS 133   143 Your Fleet-lane Furies; and hot cookes doe
                      dwell,

furious   frequency: 3   relative frequency: 0.00004
    p. 200 UNDERWOOD 42   18 When he is furious, love, although not lust.
    p. 335 HORACE 2   646 The yellow Jaundies, or were furious mad
    p. 354 HORACE 1   643 Those that are .... . furious ....

furnaces. See "fornaces."

furnish   frequency: 1   relative frequency: 0.00001
    p. 161 UNDERWOOD 14   84 The Credit, what would furnish a tenth Muse!

furniture   frequency: 1   relative frequency: 0.00001
    p. 234 UNDERWOOD 60   11 No noble furniture of parts,

furre   frequency: 1   relative frequency: 0.00001
    p. 162 UNDERWOOD 15   20 In outward face, but inward, light as Furre,

furrowes   frequency: 1   relative frequency: 0.00001
    p. 98 FOREST 3   42 And furrowes laden with their weight;

furrows. See "furrowes."

further   frequency: 1   relative frequency: 0.00001
    See also "farther."
    p. 391 UNGATHERED 26 21 A little further, to make thee a roome:

furthest. See "farthest."

fury   frequency: 5   relative frequency: 0.00007
    See also "furie."
   *p. 492 TO HIMSELF   13 'Twere simple fury, still, thy selfe to waste
    p. 108 FOREST 10 A   12 A farther fury my ray'sd spirit Controules,
    p. 179 UNDERWOOD 25   46 For fury wasteth,
    p. 222 UNDERWOOD 49   8 And in an Epicoene fury can write newes
    p. 243 UNDERWOOD 70   17 Sword, fire, and famine, with fell fury met;

future   frequency: 3   relative frequency: 0.00004
    p. 71 EPIGRAMS 110   21 T<o>'all future time, not onely doth restore
    p. 88 EPIGRAMS 133 154 Yet drown'd they not. They had fiue liues in
                            future.
    p. 271 UNDERWOOD 83   96 The Christian hath t<o>'enjoy the future life,

fyl's   frequency: 1   relative frequency: 0.00001
    p. 292 UNDERWOOD 86   14 And for the troubled Clyent fyl's his tongue,

fyne   frequency: 1   relative frequency: 0.00001
    p. 404 UNGATHERED 34 55 Sense, what they are! which by a specious fyne

fyres   frequency: 1   relative frequency: 0.00001
    p. 406 UNGATHERED 34 103 Whom not ten fyres, nor a Parlyamt can

gain. See "gaine," "gayne."

gain'd   frequency: 5   relative frequency: 0.00007
    p. 74 EPIGRAMS 114   7 He hath not onely gain'd himselfe his eyes,
    p. 132 UNDERWOOD 2.2 13 But, he had not gain'd his sight
    p. 154 UNDERWOOD 13   37 In that proud manner, as a good so gain'd,
    p. 180 UNDERWOOD 26   14 Happy in that faire honour it hath gain'd,
    p. 230 UNDERWOOD 56   5 So have you gain'd a Servant, and a Muse:

gaine   frequency: 16   relative frequency: 0.00023
    p. 27 EPIGRAMS 3   1 Thou, that mak'st gaine thy end, and wisely well,
    p. 56 EPIGRAMS 87   3 Each night, to drowne his cares: But when the
                            gaine
    p. 70 EPIGRAMS 109   8 Is priuate gaine, which hath long guilt to
                            friend.
    p. 133 UNDERWOOD 2.3 15 And (to gaine her by his Art)
    p. 134 UNDERWOOD 2.4 20 All the Gaine, all the Good, of the Elements
                            strife.
    p. 161 UNDERWOOD 14   81 The Gaine of your two friendships! Hayward and
    p. 162 UNDERWOOD 15   17 To gaine upon his belly; and at last
    p. 169 UNDERWOOD 17   6 Is done for gaine: If't be, 'tis not sincere.
    p. 186 UNDERWOOD 32   9 Who thus long safe, would gaine upon the times
    p. 231 UNDERWOOD 56   29 I gaine, in having leave to keepe my Day,
    p. 235 UNDERWOOD 63   3 Who doubts, those fruits God can with gaine
                            restore,
    p. 283 U'WOOD 84.9   38 The glorie, and gaine of rest, which the place
                            gives!
    p. 325 HORACE 2   425 For so, they shall not only gaine the worth,
    p. 333 HORACE 2   601 His flatterers to their gaine. But say, he can
    p. 392 UNGATHERED 26 63 Or for the lawrell, he may gaine a scorne,
    p. 400 UNGATHERED 31 34 To gaine the Crowne of immortalitye,

gained   frequency: 1   relative frequency: 0.00001
    See also "gain'd."
    p. 409 UNGATHERED 38   6 Which you haue iustly gained from the Stage,

gaines   frequency: 1   relative frequency: 0.00001
    p. 263 UNDERWOOD 79   13 Best Kings expect first-fruits of your glad
                            gaines.

gains. See "gaines," "gaynes."

gainst   frequency: 1   relative frequency: 0.00001
    p.   38 EPIGRAMS 35   7 Like aydes gainst treasons who hath found before?

'gainst   frequency: 14   relative frequency: 0.00020
    p.   29 EPIGRAMS 9   3 'Tis 'gainst the manners of an Epigram:
    p.   50 EPIGRAMS 71   2 Still, 'tis his lucke to praise me 'gainst his
                                will.
    p.   52 EPIGRAMS 75   4 T<o>'inueigh 'gainst playes: what did he then but
                                play?
    p.   59 EPIGRAMS 92   35 Or 'gainst the Bishops, for the Brethren,
                                raile,
    p.   76 EPIGRAMS 119   3 Cryes out 'gainst cocking, since he cannot bet,
    p.   114 FOREST 12   31 For what a sinne 'gainst your great fathers
                                spirit,
    p.   119 FOREST 13   93 'Gainst stormes, or pyrats, that might charge
                                your peace;
    p.   161 UNDERWOOD 14   79 Thy gift 'gainst envie. O how I doe count
    p.   187 UNDERWOOD 33   6 Who 'gainst the Law, weave Calumnies, my
                                <BENN:>
    p.   202 UNDERWOOD 43   5 I ne're attempted, Vulcan, 'gainst thy life;
    p.   234 UNDERWOOD 60   5 What could their care doe 'gainst the spight
    p.   269 UNDERWOOD 83   9 Stiffe! starke! my joynts 'gainst one another
                                knock!
    p.   291 UNDERWOOD 85   69 'Gainst th'Ides, his moneys he gets in with
                                paine,
    p.   349 HORACE 1   444 .... never ...... 'gainst ....

gait. See "gaite," "gate."

gaite   frequency: 1   relative frequency: 0.00001
    p.   118 FOREST 13   61 And keepe an euen, and vnalter'd gaite;

galba   frequency: 1   relative frequency: 0.00001
    p.   61 EPIGRAMS 95   8 Where NERO falls, and GALBA is ador'd,

gall   frequency: 1   relative frequency: 0.00001
    p.   27 EPIGRAMS 2   3 Thou should'st be bold, licentious, full of gall,

gallant   frequency: 1   relative frequency: 0.00001
    p.   55 EPIGRAMS 85   5 Shee doth instruct men by her gallant flight,

gallantry   frequency: 1   relative frequency: 0.00001
    p.   155 UNDERWOOD 13   92 Of our Towne Gallantry! or why there rests

gallants   frequency: 3   relative frequency: 0.00004
    p.   215 UNDERWOOD 44   89 The Academie, where the Gallants meet --
    p.   329 HORACE 2   513 Our Gallants give them none, but passe them by:
    p.   362 UNGATHERED 2   3 Not wearing moodes, as gallants doe a fashion,

gallo-belgicvs   frequency: 1   relative frequency: 0.00001
    p.   59 EPIGRAMS 92   16 And the GAZETTI, or
                                GALLO-BELGICVS:

gallus   frequency: 1   relative frequency: 0.00001
    p.   181 UNDERWOOD 27   15 With bright Lycoris, Gallus choice,

gamage   frequency: 1   relative frequency: 0.00001
    p.   94 FOREST 2   19 Thy copp's, too, nam'd of GAMAGE, thou hast
                                there,

gambol   frequency: 1   relative frequency: 0.00001
    p.   231 UNDERWOOD 57   19 Of gambol, or sport

game   frequency: 4   relative frequency: 0.00005
    p.   45 EPIGRAMS 57   2 Baudrie', and vsurie were one kind of game.
    p.   73 EPIGRAMS 112   16 O, (thou cry'st out) that is thy proper game.
    p.   105 FOREST 8   41 And, for thee, at common game,
    p.   222 UNDERWOOD 49   4 Where fight the prime Cocks of the Game, for
                                wit?

games   frequency: 3   relative frequency: 0.00004
    p.   234 UNDERWOOD 61   2 And all the games of Fortune, plaid at Court;
    p.   331 HORACE 2   565 Hee, that not knowes the games, nor how to use
    p.   415 UNGATHERED 43   3 But I can tell thee, Dover, how thy Games

gamester   frequency: 1   relative frequency: 0.00001
    See also "gamster," "gam'ster."
    p.   370 UNGATHERED 8   3 (Compos'd of Gamester, Captaine, Knight,
                                Knight's man,

gamesters   frequency: 1   relative frequency: 0.00001
    *p. 493 TO HIMSELF   40 The gamesters share your guilt, and you their
                              stuffe.

gamster   frequency: 1   relative frequency: 0.00001
    p. 72 EPIGRAMS 112   t1 TO A WEAKE GAMSTER IN
                              POETRY.

gam'ster   frequency: 2   relative frequency: 0.00002
    p. 33 EPIGRAMS 21   1 Lord, how is GAM'STER chang'd! his haire
                              close cut!
    p. 33 EPIGRAMS 21   t1 ON REFORMED GAM'STER.

ganimede   frequency: 1   relative frequency: 0.00001
    p. 34 EPIGRAMS 25   4 And how his GANIMEDE mou'd, and how his
                              goate,

ganymede. See "ganimede."

gaping   frequency: 2   relative frequency: 0.00002
    p. 45 EPIGRAMS 56   10 The sluggish gaping auditor deuoures;
    p. 313 HORACE 2   197 What doth this Promiser such gaping worth

garden   frequency: 3   relative frequency: 0.00004
    See also "paris-garden," "parish-garden."
    p. 94 FOREST 2   39 Then hath thy orchard fruit, thy garden flowers,
    p. 254 UNDERWOOD 75   68 And all the Ground were Garden, where she led!
    p. 413 UNGATHERED 41   13 The third, is from the garden cull'd, the Rose,

gardens   frequency: 1   relative frequency: 0.00001
    p. 238 UNDERWOOD 65   8 Thee quickly <come> the gardens eye to bee,

garland   frequency: 5   relative frequency: 0.00007
    See also "ghyrlond."
    p. 200 UNDERWOOD 42   9 Put on my Ivy Garland, let me see
    p. 245 UNDERWOOD 70   77 Accept this garland, plant it in thy head,
    p. 253 UNDERWOOD 75   40 In gracefull Ornament of Garland, Gemmes, and
                              Haire.
    p. 268 UNDERWOOD 83   4 To pluck a Garland, for her selfe, or mee?
    p. 416 UNGATHERED 44   4 Now, in a garland by the graces knit:

garlands   frequency: 2   relative frequency: 0.00002
    See also "gyrlands."
    p. 173 UNDERWOOD 22   18 The withered Garlands tane away;
    p. 294 UNDERWOOD 89   4 Thy locks, and rosie garlands crowne thy head;

garment   frequency: 1   relative frequency: 0.00001
    p. 285 U'WOOD 84.9   94 And on her Innocence, a garment fresh

garter   frequency: 1   relative frequency: 0.00001
    p. 56 EPIGRAMS 88   4 And shooe, and tye, and garter should come
                              hether,

garters   frequency: 1   relative frequency: 0.00001
    p. 62 EPIGRAMS 97   5 His rosie tyes and garters so ore-blowne,

gasp. See "gaspe."

gaspe   frequency: 1   relative frequency: 0.00001
    p. 162 UNDERWOOD 15   6 That gaspe for action, and would yet revive

gate   frequency: 7   relative frequency: 0.00010
    p. 58 EPIGRAMS 92   6 Ripe are their ruffes, their cuffes, their
                              beards, their gate,
    p. 215 UNDERWOOD 44   87 What love you then? your whore. What study?
                              gate,
    p. 252 UNDERWOOD 75   12 From Greenwich, hither, to Row-hampton gate!
    p. 287 U'WOOD 84.9   165 But, kept an even gate, as some streight tree
    p. 294 UNDERWOOD 87   20 And to left-Lydia, now the gate stood ope.
    p. 413 UNGATHERED 41   39 The House of gold, the Gate of heavens power,
    p. 418 UNGATHERED 46   7 Although the gate were hard, the gayne is sweete.

gates   frequency: 2   relative frequency: 0.00002
    p. 239 UNDERWOOD 67   12 Their guarded gates asunder?
    p. 363 UNGATHERED 3   10 Were they as strong ram'd vp as Aetna gates.

gather   frequency: 4   relative frequency: 0.00005
    p. 136 UNDERWOOD 2.5   26 Where, you say, men gather blisses,
    p. 151 UNDERWOOD 12   6 Of him whose bones this Grave doth gather:
    p. 170 UNDERWOOD 19   10 Where men at once may plant, and gather blisses:

gather (cont.)
  p. 258 UNDERWOOD 75   186 And let him freely gather Loves First-fruits,

gather'd   frequency: 5   relative frequency: 0.00007
  p.   63 EPIGRAMS 98   9 Be alwayes to thy gather'd selfe the same:
  p.   74 EPIGRAMS 115   9 Talkes loud, and baudy, has a gather'd deale
  p. 291 UNDERWOOD 85   55 More sweet then Olives, that new gather'd be
  p. 375 UNGATHERED 10   25 For Grapes he had gather'd before they were
                                eaten.
  p. 380 UNGATHERED 12   36 For grapes he had gather'd, before they were
                                eaten.

gatherer   frequency: 1   relative frequency: 0.00001
  p.   43 EPIGRAMS 53   t1 TO OLD-END GATHERER.

gathering   frequency: 2   relative frequency: 0.00002
  See alsc "long-gathering."
  p. 159 UNDERWOOD 14   38 Of Gathering? Bountie' in pouring out againe?
  p. 290 UNDERWOOD 85   30 Are gathering by the Wintry houres;

gaudy   frequency: 1   relative frequency: 0.00001
  p. 287 U'WOOD 84.9   182 Of sorrow, then all pompe of gaudy daies:

gaue   frequency: 11   relative frequency: 0.00015
**p. 114 PANEGYRE   56 Her place, and yeares, gaue her precedencie.
**p. 116 PANEGYRE   101 "Where acts gaue licence to impetuous lust
  p.   28 EPIGRAMS 4   4 And gaue thee both, to shew they could no more.
  p.   31 EPIGRAMS 13   2 Of old, they gaue a cock to AESCVLAPE;
  p.   39 EPIGRAMS 41   4 For what shee gaue, a whore; a baud, shee cures.
  p.   84 EPIGRAMS 133   27 Who gaue, to take at his returne from Hell,
  p. 113 FOREST 12   13 The foole that gaue it; who will want, and weepe,
  p. 114 FOREST 12   35 Wherein wise Nature you a dowrie gaue,
  p. 114 FOREST 12   53 Gaue killing strokes. There were braue men,
                                before
  p. 389 UNGATHERED 24   15 For though Spaine gaue him his first ayre and
                                Vogue,
  p. 419 UNGATHERED 48   5 By Cherissheinge the Spirrites yt gaue their
                                greatnesse grace:

gaul. See "gaule."

gaule   frequency: 1   relative frequency: 0.00001
  p. 203 UNDERWOOD 43   29 Had I compil'd from Amadis de Gaule,

gau'st   frequency: 1   relative frequency: 0.00001
  p.   38 EPIGRAMS 36   1 MARTIAL, thou gau'st farre nobler
                                Epigrammes

gave   frequency: 11   relative frequency: 0.00015
  See alsc "gaue."
  p. 181 UNDERWOOD 27   18 Her Ovid gave her, dimn'd the fame
  p. 188 UNDERWOOD 34   9 Her owne bloud gave her: Shee ne're had, nor
                                hath
  p. 190 UNDERWOOD 37   11 And which you (being the worthier) gave me leave
  p. 192 UNDERWOOD 38   55 Could you demand the gifts you gave, againe?
  p. 203 UNDERWOOD 43   10 And Mars, that gave thee a Lanthorne for a
                                Crowne.
  p. 274 U'WOOD 84.2   5 Gave two such Houses as
                                NORTHUMBERLAND,
  p. 282 U'WOOD 84.9   t3 who living, gave me leave to call her so.
  p. 287 U'WOOD 84.9   156 For 'twas himselfe who form'd, and gave it her.
  p. 309 HORACE 2   113 Unto the Lyrick Strings, the Muse gave grace
  p. 323 HORACE 2   372 A foot, whose swiftnesse gave the Verse the name
  p. 327 HORACE 2   461 The Muse not only gave the Greek's a wit,

gavest   frequency: 1   relative frequency: 0.00001
  See also "gau'st," "gav'st."
  p. 127 UNDERWOOD 1.1   18 This All of nothing, gavest it forme, and fate,

gav'st   frequency: 2   relative frequency: 0.00002
  p. 129 UNDERWOOD 1.2   19 That gav'st a Sonne,
  p. 274 U'WOOD 84.2   14 Thy Neeces line, then thou that gav'st thy Name

gayne   frequency: 2   relative frequency: 0.00002
  p. 112 FOREST 11   86 Makes a most blessed gayne.
  p. 418 UNGATHERED 46   7 Although the gate were hard, the gayne is sweete.

gaynes   frequency: 1   relative frequency: 0.00001
  p. 113 FOREST 12   11 Though neuer after; whiles it gaynes the voyce

gaze   frequency: 2   relative frequency: 0.00002
    p.   27 EPIGRAMS 2   12 To catch the worlds loose laughter, or vaine
                              gaze.
    p. 169 UNDERWOOD 18   3 Did her perfections call me on to gaze,

gazers   frequency: 1   relative frequency: 0.00001
    p.   39 EPIGRAMS 40   5 All the gazers on the skies

gazetti   frequency: 1   relative frequency: 0.00001
    p.   59 EPIGRAMS 92   16 And the GAZETTI, or
                              GALLO-BELGICVS:

gazing   frequency: 1   relative frequency: 0.00001
  **p. 114 PANEGYRE   43 Others on ground runne gazing by his side,

gear. See "geare."

geare   frequency: 1   relative frequency: 0.00001
    p. 321 HORACE 2   349 I can out of knowne geare, a fable frame,

geese   frequency: 1   relative frequency: 0.00001
    p. 205 UNDERWOOD 43   52 To light Tobacco, or save roasted Geese,

gem. See "gemme," "jemme."

gemme   frequency: 1   relative frequency: 0.00001
    p. 258 UNDERWOOD 75   175 Peepe forth a Gemme; to see

gemmes   frequency: 1   relative frequency: 0.00001
    p. 253 UNDERWOOD 75   40 In gracefull Ornament of Garland, Gemmes, and
                              Haire.

gems   frequency: 1   relative frequency: 0.00001
    See also "gemmes."
    p. 179 UNDERWOOD 25   55 Though many Gems be in your bosome stor'd,

general. See "generall."

generall   frequency: 5   relative frequency: 0.00007
    p. 159 UNDERWOOD 14   33 Of generall knowledge; watch'd men, manners too,
    p. 187 UNDERWOOD 33   26 As if the generall store thou didst command
    p. 238 UNDERWOOD 66   9 So generall a gladnesse to an Isle,
    p. 395 UNGATHERED 29   6 At least, if not the generall Engine cracke.
    p. 421 UNGATHERED 48   43 Throughout their generall breastes,

generous   frequency: 2   relative frequency: 0.00002
    p. 112 FOREST 11   111 Much more a noble, and right generous mind
    p. 155 UNDERWOOD 13   76 Of any, is a great and generous Deed:

genius   frequency: 9   relative frequency: 0.00013
    p. 120 FOREST 14   20 And he, with his best Genius left alone.
    p. 176 UNDERWOOD 25   1 Where art thou, Genius? I should use
    p. 193 UNDERWOOD 38   95 The wit of Ale, and Genius of the Malt
    p. 225 UNDERWOOD 51   1 Haile, happie Genius of this antient pile!
    p. 241 UNDERWOOD 68   13 For in the Genius of a Poets Verse,
    p. 319 HORACE 2   298 Steepe the glad Genius in the Wine, whole
                              dayes,
    p. 389 UNGATHERED 24   12 As was the Genius wherewith they were wrote;
    p. 395 UNGATHERED 29   23 The selfe same Genius! so the worke will say.
    p. 400 UNGATHERED 32   1 This Booke will liue; It hath a Genius: This

gentle   frequency: 11   relative frequency: 0.00015
    p.   34 EPIGRAMS 22   12 Which couer lightly, gentle earth.
    p. 110 FOREST 11   45 That is an essence, farre more gentle, fine,
    p. 216 UNDERWOOD 45   3 My gentle Arthur; that it might be said
    p. 268 UNDERWOOD 83   1 What gentle Ghost, besprent with April deaw,
    p. 293 UNDERWOOD 87   14 With gentle Calais, Thurine Orniths Sonne;
    p. 331 HORACE 2   571 Why not? I'm gentle, and free-borne, doe hate
    p. 335 HORACE 2   653 And cry aloud, Helpe, gentle Countrey-men,
    p. 338 HORACE 1   15 To gentle ... .
    p. 339 HORACE 1   49 ... . gentle ....
    p. 390 UNGATHERED 25   2 It was for gentle Shakespeare cut;
    p. 392 UNGATHERED 26   56 My gentle Shakespeare, must enioy a part.

gentle-woman   frequency: 1   relative frequency: 0.00001
    p. 100 FOREST 4   t2 A farewell for a Gentle-woman, vertuous

gentleman   frequency: 2   relative frequency: 0.00002
    See also "gent'man."
    p. 252 UNDERWOOD 75   t5 of that Noble Gentleman, Mr. HIEROME
                              WESTON,

gentleman (cont.)
p. 272 UNDERWOOD 84   t7 A Gentleman absolute in all Numbers;

gentlemen   frequency: 1   relative frequency: 0.00001
p. 281 U'WOOD 84.8   15 The greatest are but growing Gentlemen.

gentler   frequency: 6   relative frequency: 0.00008
p. 96 FOREST 2   94 Their gentler spirits haue suck'd innocence.
p. 180 UNDERWOOD 26   4 A gentler, and more agile hand, to tend
p. 186 UNDERWOOD 31   7 So may the gentler Muses, and good fame
p. 187 UNDERWOOD 33   20 Thou prov'st the gentler wayes, to clense the
                          wound,
p. 265 UNDERWOOD 79   46 Haste, haste you hither, all you gentler
                          Swaines,
p. 366 UNGATHERED 6   7 A gentler Bird, then this,

gentlest   frequency: 1   relative frequency: 0.00001
p. 395 UNGATHERED 29   21 As not the smallest ioint, or gentlest word

gentlewoman. See "gentle-woman."

gently   frequency: 3   relative frequency: 0.00004
**p. 117 PANEGYRE   136 Was gently falne from heauen vpon this state;
p. 280 U'WOOD 84.4   58 But stooping gently, as a Cloud,
p. 309 HORACE 2   75 So they fall gently from the Grecian spring,

gent'man   frequency: 1   relative frequency: 0.00001
p. 57 EPIGRAMS 90   12 And he remou'd to gent'man of the horse,

gentrie   frequency: 4   relative frequency: 0.00005
p. 75 EPIGRAMS 116   2 All gentrie, yet, owe part of their best flame!
p. 215 UNDERWOOD 44   84 That in the Cradle of their Gentrie are;
p. 313 HORACE 2   160 And Roman Gentrie, jearing, will laugh out.
p. 321 HORACE 2   360 The Roman Gentrie, men of birth, and meane,

gentry. See "gentrie."

george   frequency: 2   relative frequency: 0.00002
p. 281 U'WOOD 84.8   t1 To KENELME, IOHN, GEORGE.
p. 388 UNGATHERED 23   t2 Mr George Chapman, on his Translation

georges   frequency: 2   relative frequency: 0.00002
p. 213 UNDERWOOD 44   10 If they stay here, but till Saint Georges Day.
p. 221 UNDERWOOD 48   44 In great Saint Georges Union;

germany   frequency: 2   relative frequency: 0.00002
p. 375 UNGATHERED 10   31 Their hornes, and Germany pukes on his head.
p. 379 UNGATHERED 12   20 The Low-countries, Germany and Rhetia

gests   frequency: 1   relative frequency: 0.00001
p. 309 HORACE 2   105 The gests of Kings, great Captaines, and sad
                          Warres,

gesture   frequency: 2   relative frequency: 0.00002
p. 81 EPIGRAMS 129   14 On some new gesture, that 's imputed wit?
p. 319 HORACE 2   304 Gesture, and riot, whilst he swooping went

get   frequency: 23   relative frequency: 0.00033
See also "gett," "money-gett."
p. 32 EPIGRAMS 18   6 As theirs did with thee, mine might credit get:
p. 33 EPIGRAMS 19   1 That COD can get no widdow, yet a knight,
p. 39 EPIGRAMS 41   2 And get more gold, then all the colledge can:
p. 42 EPIGRAMS 47   2 Hee that wooes euery widdow, will get none.
p. 48 EPIGRAMS 65   7 Get him the times long grudge, the courts ill
                          will;
p. 56 EPIGRAMS 88   9 Or had his father, when he did him get,
p. 59 EPIGRAMS 92   25 They all get Porta, for the sundrie wayes
p. 59 EPIGRAMS 92   31 With England. All forbidden bookes they get.
p. 64 EPIGRAMS 101   12 If we can get her, full of egs, and then,
p. 68 EPIGRAMS 106   1 If men get name, for some one vertue: Then,
p. 93 FOREST 1   5 It is enough, they once did get
p. 98 FOREST 3   62 Nor how to get the lawyer fees.
p. 99 FOREST 3   87 Get place, and honor, and be glad to keepe
p. 150 UNDERWOOD 10   13 Goe, get thee quickly forth,
p. 159 UNDERWOOD 14   26 Before men get a verse: much lesse a Praise;
p. 187 UNDERWOOD 33   38 And (which doth all Atchievements get above)
p. 218 UNDERWOOD 47   28 Of newes they get, to strew out the long meale,
p. 219 UNDERWOOD 47   32 Be, or be not, to get the Val-telline?
p. 242 UNDERWOOD 69   25 Never so great to get them: and the ends,
p. 260 UNDERWOOD 77   5 I would, if price, or prayer could them get,

get (cont.)
p. 270 UNDERWOOD 83   60 Made her friends joyes to get above their feares!
p. 329 HORACE 2   517 This booke will get the Sosii money; This
p. 398 UNGATHERED 30 74 Get broken peeces, and fight well by those.

gets   frequency: 5   relative frequency: 0.00007
p. 53 EPIGRAMS 78   2 To draw thee custome: but her selfe gets all.
p. 74 EPIGRAMS 115   24 The cloth's no sooner gone, but it gets vp
p. 74 EPIGRAMS 115   28 Of miming, gets th'opinion of a wit.
p. 272 UNDERWOOD 83   99 The Serpents head: Gets above Death, and
                         Sinne,
p. 291 UNDERWOOD 85   69 'Gainst th'Ides, his moneys he gets in with
                         paine,

gett   frequency: 1   relative frequency: 0.00001
p. 420 UNGATHERED 48 25 to gett the<e> a leane fface,

getting   frequency: 2   relative frequency: 0.00002
p. 274 U'WOOD 84.1   37 Is sung: as als<o>'her getting up
p. 327 HORACE 2   473 And care of getting, thus, our minds hath
                         stain'd,

ghest   frequency: 1   relative frequency: 0.00001
p. 64 EPIGRAMS 101   3 Not that we thinke vs worthy such a ghest,

ghests   frequency: 1   relative frequency: 0.00001
*p. 493 TO HIMSELF   29 For, who the relish of these ghests will fit,

ghost   frequency: 4   relative frequency: 0.00005
p. 38 EPIGRAMS 36   t1 TO THE GHOST OF MARTIAL.
p. 128 UNDERWOOD 1.1 37 10. Father, and Sonne, and Holy Ghost, you
                         three
p. 199 UNDERWOOD 41   21 Or like a Ghost walke silent amongst men,
p. 268 UNDERWOOD 83   1 What gentle Ghost, besprent with April deaw,

ghosts   frequency: 3   relative frequency: 0.00004
p. 84 EPIGRAMS 133   16 And, for the cryes of Ghosts, women, and men,
p. 87 EPIGRAMS 133 124 Against their breasts. Here, seu'rall ghosts did
                         flit
p. 405 UNGATHERED 34 88 Reuiuing wth fresh coulors ye pale Ghosts.

ghyrlond   frequency: 2   relative frequency: 0.00002
p. 412 UNGATHERED 41   5 These forme thy Ghyrlond. Wherof Myrtle green,
p. 412 UNGATHERED 41 t1 THE GHYRLOND

giant   frequency: 1   relative frequency: 0.00001
See also "gyant."
p. 414 UNGATHERED 41 51 Who like a Giant hasts his course to run,

giants. See "gyantes."

giddie   frequency: 2   relative frequency: 0.00002
p. 118 FOREST 13   67 Giddie with change, and therefore cannot see
p. 361 UNGATHERED 1   25 till giddie with amazement I fell downe

giddy. See "giddie."

gift   frequency: 9   relative frequency: 0.00013
See also "guift," "new-yeares-gift,"
         "yeares-gift."
p. 55 EPIGRAMS 84   10 Make it your gift. See whither that will beare
                         mee.
p. 127 UNDERWOOD 1.1   8 O take my gift.
p. 155 UNDERWOOD 13   84 Now, but command; make tribute, what was gift;
p. 157 UNDERWOOD 13 158 Without your gift, though I can rate that too,
p. 161 UNDERWOOD 14   79 Thy gift 'gainst envie. O how I doe count
p. 189 UNDERWOOD 37   3 Then to your love, and gift. And all's but due.
p. 189 UNDERWOOD 37   6 But must confesse from whom what gift I tooke.
p. 229 UNDERWOOD 55   2 Thoughts worthy of thy gift, this Inke,
p. 400 UNGATHERED 31 36 Her right, by gift, and purchase of the Lambe:

gifts   frequency: 13   relative frequency: 0.00018
See also "guifts."
p. 33 EPIGRAMS 22   3 Yet, all heauens gifts, being heauens due,
p. 100 FOREST 4   .12 And what thou call'st thy gifts are baits.
p. 117 FOREST 13   41 A Princes fortune: These are gifts of chance,
p. 153 UNDERWOOD 13   22 Then what he hath receiv'd. Gifts stinke from
                         some,
p. 154 UNDERWOOD 13   39 No! Gifts and thankes should have one cheerefull
                         face,

gifts (cont.)
p. 192 UNDERWOOD 38	55	Could you demand the gifts you gave, againe?
p. 219 UNDERWOOD 47	62	With reverence using all the gifts then<ce> given.
p. 235 UNDERWOOD 62	1	Great CHARLES, among the holy gifts of grace
p. 263 UNDERWOOD 79	1	New yeares, expect new gifts: Sister, your Harpe,
p. 273 U'WOOD 84.1	19	As prop'rest gifts, to Girles, and Boyes,
p. 292 UNDERWOOD 86	18	With thee 'bove all his Rivals gifts take place,
p. 413 UNGATHERED 41	36	How are thy gifts, and graces blaz'd abroad!
p. 414 UNGATHERED 41	53	How are thy gifts and graces blaz'd abro'd,

gild. See "guild."

gilded. See "guilded."

giles   frequency: 8   relative frequency: 0.00011
p. 40 EPIGRAMS 42	1	Who sayes that GILES and IONE at discord be?
p. 40 EPIGRAMS 42	3	Indeed, poore GILES repents he married euer.
p. 40 EPIGRAMS 42	4	But that his IONE doth too. And GILES would neuer,
p. 40 EPIGRAMS 42	6	No more would IONE he should. GILES riseth early,
p. 40 EPIGRAMS 42	9	And so is IONE. Oft-times, when GILES doth find
p. 40 EPIGRAMS 42	t1	ON GILES AND IONE.
p. 40 EPIGRAMS 42	10	Harsh sights at home, GILES wisheth he were blind.
p. 40 EPIGRAMS 42	13	The children, that he keepes, GILES sweares are none

gill   frequency: 1   relative frequency: 0.00001
p. 410 UNGATHERED 39	2	Secure thy railing Rhymes, infamous Gill,

gilt. See "guilt."

gi'ng   frequency: 1   relative frequency: 0.00001
p. 405 UNGATHERED 34	75	What would he doe now, gi'ng his mynde yt waye

ginnes   frequency: 1   relative frequency: 0.00001
p. 101 FOREST 4	36	If I could not thy ginnes auoyd.

ginny   frequency: 1   relative frequency: 0.00001
p. 291 UNDERWOOD 85	53	Th'Ionian God-wit, nor the Ginny hen

girded   frequency: 1   relative frequency: 0.00001
p. 340 HORACE 1	71	.... girded ....

girdle   frequency: 1   relative frequency: 0.00001
p. 137 UNDERWOOD 2.5	41	And the Girdle 'bout her waste,

girles   frequency: 1   relative frequency: 0.00001
p. 273 U'WOOD 84.1	19	As prop'rest gifts, to Girles, and Boyes,

girls   frequency: 1   relative frequency: 0.00001
See also "girles."
p. 657 L. CONVIVALES	11	Those dull Girls, no good can mean us,

girt   frequency: 2   relative frequency: 0.00002
See also "sea-girt."
p. 293 UNDERWOOD 86	32	Or with fresh flowers to girt my temple round.
p. 315 HORACE 2	241	The old man many evils doe girt round;

giue   frequency: 36   relative frequency: 0.00052
*p. 492 TO HIMSELF	17	No, giue them graines their fill,
p. 27 EPIGRAMS 3	3	Vse mine so, too: I giue thee leaue. But craue
p. 31 EPIGRAMS 13	3	Let me giue two: that doubly am got free,
p. 34 EPIGRAMS 23	6	And which no' affection praise enough can giue!
p. 43 EPIGRAMS 51	2	Great heau'n did well, to giue ill fame free wing;
p. 43 EPIGRAMS 51	5	Yet giue thy iealous subiects leaue to doubt:
p. 43 EPIGRAMS 53	6	To giue the world assurance thou wert both;
p. 55 EPIGRAMS 86	5	Now, I must giue thy life, and deed, the voice
p. 57 EPIGRAMS 89	13	Weare this renowne. 'Tis iust, that who did giue
p. 66 EPIGRAMS 102	10	To morrow vice, if shee giue better pay:
p. 66 EPIGRAMS 103	6	Need any Muses praise to giue it fame?
p. 69 EPIGRAMS 107	11	Giue them your seruices, and embassies
p. 69 EPIGRAMS 107	19	Giue your yong States-men, (that first make you drunke,

giue (cont.)
p.   70 EPIGRAMS 109   14 And that thy soule should giue thy flesh her
                                 weight.
p.   72 EPIGRAMS 111   8 Nor to giue CAESAR this, makes ours the
                                 lesse.
p.   73 EPIGRAMS 112   21 Pr'y thee, yet saue thy rest; giue ore in time:
p.   74 EPIGRAMS 115   14 Giue euery one his dose of mirth: giue the fame,
p.   76 EPIGRAMS 119   7 No, SHELTON, giue me thee, canst want all
                                 these,
p.   77 EPIGRAMS 120   21 And haue sought (to giue new birth)
p.   79 EPIGRAMS 124   5 Which in life did harbour giue
p.   82 EPIGRAMS 131   1 When we doe giue, ALPHONSO, to the light,
p.   83 EPIGRAMS 131   6 We ought not giue them taste, we had an eare.
p. 103 FOREST 6   8 While you breath. First giue a hundred,
p. 107 FOREST 10   8 Shall not giue out, that I haue made thee stay,
p. 109 FOREST 11   12 Giue knowledge instantly,
p. 114 FOREST 12   26 Then, here, to giue pride fame, and peasants
                                 birth.
p. 115 FOREST 12   56 Because they lack'd the sacred pen, could giue
p. 118 FOREST 13   76 (They finde it both so wittie, and safe to giue.)
p. 119 FOREST 13   97 And raise a noble stemme, to giue the fame,
p. 120 FOREST 14   11 Giue me my cup, but from the Thespian well,
p. 384 UNGATHERED 18   6 That bid, God giue thee ioy, and haue no endes.
p. 388 UNGATHERED 23   2 Olde Hesiods Ore, and giue it vs; but thine,
p. 391 UNGATHERED 26   24 And we haue wits to read, and praise to giue.
p. 392 UNGATHERED 26   55 Yet must I not giue Nature all: Thy Art,
p. 392 UNGATHERED 26   58 His Art doth giue the fashion. And, that he,
p. 398 UNGATHERED 30   83 Yet giue mee leaue, to wonder at the birth

giuen   frequency: 4 relative frequency: 0.00005
p.   32 EPIGRAMS 17   5 And, but a sprigge of bayes, giuen by thee,
p.   76 EPIGRAMS 119   16 Makes, the whole longer, then 'twas giuen him,
                                 much.
p. 113 FOREST 12   4 And, for it, life, conscience, yea, soules are
                                 giuen,
p. 117 FOREST 13   11 And, in this name, am giuen out dangerous

giues   frequency: 5 relative frequency: 0.00007
p.   95 FOREST 2   69 But giues me what I call, and lets me eate,
p.   99 FOREST 3   98 He alwayes giues what he knowes meet;
p. 117 FOREST 13   44 And takes, and giues the beauties of the mind.
p. 375 UNGATHERED 10   22 And there, while he giues the zealous Brauado,
p. 393 UNGATHERED 27   11 As giues a power to faith, to tread

giuing   frequency: 3 relative frequency: 0.00004
p.   44 EPIGRAMS 55   6 And giuing largely to me, more thou tak'st.
p.   72 EPIGRAMS 112   9 I leaue thee there, and giuing way, entend
p. 106 FOREST 9   11 As giuing it a hope, that there

giu'st   frequency: 1 relative frequency: 0.00001
p.   97 FOREST 3   28 And giu'st thy gladder guests the sight;

give   frequency: 35 relative frequency: 0.00050
See also "giue."
p. 142 UNDERWOOD 2.9   54 I could give my very heart;
p. 154 UNDERWOOD 13   49 Give thankes by stealth, and whispering in the
                                 eare,
p. 155 UNDERWOOD 13   70 Then give it to the Hound that did him bite;
p. 167 UNDERWOOD 15   152 Give me but that againe, that I must wast
p. 167 UNDERWOOD 15   159 Is nothing, such scarce meat and drinke he'le
                                 give,
p. 168 UNDERWOOD 15   184 But what she gives, thou dar'st give her againe;
p. 174 UNDERWOOD 22   35 Yet give me leave t<o>'adore in you
p. 175 UNDERWOOD 23   29 To give the world againe:
p. 179 UNDERWOOD 25   42 Pyracmon's houre will come to give them ease,
p. 197 UNDERWOOD 40   12 I give, or owe my friends, into your Rites,
p. 214 UNDERWOOD 44   31 But give them over to the common eare
p. 220 UNDERWOOD 47   75 Are asked to climbe. First give me faith, who
                                 know
p. 221 UNDERWOOD 48   23 To give mankind their eases,
p. 225 UNDERWOOD 51   19 Give me a deep-crown'd-Bowle, that I may sing
p. 229 UNDERWOOD 55   3 Then would I promise here to give
p. 232 UNDERWOOD 58   6 Thanke him: if other, hee can give no Bayes.
p. 233 UNDERWOOD 59   7 I hate such measur'd, give me mettall'd fire
p. 255 UNDERWOOD 75   96 To give a greater Name, and Title to! Their
                                 owne!
p. 262 UNDERWOOD 78   16 Unto our yeare doth give the longest light.
p. 262 UNDERWOOD 78   18 Which I have vow'd posteritie to give.
p. 269 UNDERWOOD 83   7 To give your shade a name! Stay, stay, I feele
p. 269 UNDERWOOD 83   22 Sound thou her Vertues, give her soule a Name.

give (cont.)

p. 277	U'WOOD 84.4	4	And give you reasons more then one.
p. 283	U'WOOD 84.9	21	Looke on thy sloth, and give thy selfe undone,
p. 284	U'WOOD 84.9	83	And give her place, according to her blood,
p. 293	UNDERWOOD 87	12	So Fate would give her life, and longer daies.
p. 305	HORACE 2-	13	And both doe crave, and give againe, this leave.
p. 309	HORACE 2	73	And give, being taken modestly, this leave,
p. 309	HORACE 2	80	If I can give some small increase? when, loe,
p. 315	HORACE 2	203	Hee thinkes not, how to give you smoake from light,
p. 315	HORACE 2	224	And give their yeares, and natures, as they swerve,
p. 321	HORACE 2	364	Receive, or give it an applause, the more.
p. 325	HORACE 2	452	Indeed, give fitting dues to every man.
p. 329	HORACE 2	513	Our Gallants give them none, but passe them by:
p. 420	UNGATHERED 48	35	Give cause to some of wonnder, some despite,

given   frequency: 15   relative frequency: 0.00021
    See also "giuen."

p. 161	UNDERWOOD 14	71	But nought beyond. He thou hast given it to,
p. 166	UNDERWOOD 15	118	What honour given to the drunkennest Guests?
p. 192	UNDERWOOD 38	63	But to exact againe what once is given,
p. 219	UNDERWOOD 47	62	With reverence using all the gifts then<ce> given.
p. 241	UNDERWOOD 68	1	What can the cause be, when the K<ing> hath given
p. 259	UNDERWOOD 76	12	To be given me in gratuitie
p. 288	U'WOOD 84.9	216	Hath given wholly to the Sonne (the rather
p. 295	UNDERWOOD 89	8	Makes his life longer then 'twas given him, much.
p. 305	HORACE 2	12	Of daring all, hath still beene given; we know it:
p. 317	HORACE 2	252	The parts of age to youth be given; or men
p. 323	HORACE 2	389	And there is given too unworthy leave
p. 329	HORACE 2	496	The Oracles, too, were given out in Verse;
p. 331	HORACE 2	554	Yet, there's a value given to this man.
p. 333	HORACE 2	608	(Whether yo'are given to, or giver are)
p. 333	HORACE 2	610	With joy of what is given him, over-gone:

giver   frequency: 1   relative frequency: 0.00001
| p. 333 | HORACE 2 | 608 | (Whether yo'are given to, or giver are) |

gives   frequency: 7   relative frequency: 0.00010
    See also "giues."

p. 131	UNDERWOOD 2.1	8	Clothes, or Fortune gives the grace;
p. 131	UNDERWOOD 2.1	12	Gives the Lover weight, and fashion.
p. 154	UNDERWOOD 13	41	He neither gives, or do's, that doth delay
p. 168	UNDERWOOD 15	184	But what she gives, thou dar'st give her againe;
p. 256	UNDERWOOD 75	124	Askes first, Who gives her (I Charles) then he plights
p. 265	UNDERWOOD 79	56	Hee gives all plentie, and encrease,
p. 283	U'WOOD 84.9	38	The glorie, and gaine of rest, which the place gives!

givest.   See "giu'st."

giving   frequency: 2   relative frequency: 0.00002
    See also "gi'ng," "giuing."

p. 288	U'WOOD 84.9	192	Her solemne houres she spent, or giving Almes,
p. 289	U'WOOD 84.9	224	And giving dues to all Mankinds deserts!

glad   frequency: 36   relative frequency: 0.00052

**p. 11	PANEGYRE	65	Old men were glad, their fates till now did last;
p. 32	EPIGRAMS 17	2	As guiltie men doe magistrates: glad I,
p. 40	EPIGRAMS 42	7	And hauing got him out of doores is glad.
p. 40	EPIGRAMS 43	5	'Tofore, great men were glad of Poets: Now,
p. 46	EPIGRAMS 60	5	I, that am glad of thy great chance, here doo!
p. 47	EPIGRAMS 64	1	Not glad, like those that haue new hopes, or sutes,
p. 47	EPIGRAMS 64	5	Nor glad as those, that old dependents bee,
p. 47	EPIGRAMS 64	7	Nor glad for fashion. Nor to shew a fit
p. 47	EPIGRAMS 64	9	But I am glad to see that time suruiue,
p. 48	EPIGRAMS 66	4	In onely thee, might be both great, and glad.
p. 55	EPIGRAMS 85	1	GOODYERE, I'am glad, and gratefull to report,
p. 61	EPIGRAMS 95	14	Or, better worke! were thy glad countrey blest,
p. 97	FOREST 3	31	While all, that follow, their glad eares apply
p. 99	FOREST 3	87	Get place, and honor, and be glad to keepe
p. 119	FOREST 13	94	For which you worthy are the glad encrease
p. 120	FOREST 14	21	This day sayes, then, the number of glad yeeres
p. 131	UNDERWOOD 2.1	17	But be glad, as soone with me,

glad (cont.)
    p. 147 UNDERWOOD 7   8 I'le tell, that if they be not glad,
    p. 157 UNDERWOOD 13   131 'Tis by degrees that men arrive at glad
    p. 166 UNDERWOOD 15   138 The Dice with glassen eyes, to the glad viewes
    p. 177 UNDERWOOD 25   31 But whisper; O glad Innocence,
    p. 247 UNDERWOOD 70   119 The good, and durst not practise it, were glad
    p. 249 UNDERWOOD 72   7 Adding her owne glad accents, to this Day,
    p. 257 UNDERWOOD 75   143 Which their glad Parents taught
    p. 263 UNDERWOOD 78   30 What transcripts begg'd? how cry'd up, and how
                                glad,
    p. 263 UNDERWOOD 79   13 Best Kings expect first-fruits of your glad
                                gaines.
    p. 290 UNDERWOOD 85   20 And purple-matching Grapes, hee's glad!
    p. 291 UNDERWOOD 85   45 That penning the glad flock in hurdles by,
    p. 291 UNDERWOOD 85   61 Among these Cates how glad the sight doth come
    p. 317 HORACE 2   247 Froward, complaining, a commender glad
    p. 319 HORACE 2   298 Steepe the glad Genius in the Wine, whole
                                dayes,
    p. 327 HORACE 2   469 A third of twelve, you may: foure ounces. Glad,
    p. 351 HORACE 1   536 .... glad ....
    p. 371 UNGATHERED 8   11 I, that am glad, thy Innocence was thy Guilt,
    p. 384 UNGATHERED 18   26 Sure, this glad payre were married, but this day.
    p. 416 UNGATHERED 43   6 With the Glad Countrey, and Posteritie:

glad-mention'd   frequency: 1   relative frequency: 0.00001
    p. 37 EPIGRAMS 33   2 Glad-mention'd ROE: thou art but gone before,

gladder   frequency: 1   relative frequency: 0.00001
    p. 97 FOREST 3   28 And giu'st thy gladder guests the sight;

gladdest   frequency: 2   relative frequency: 0.00002
    p. 128 UNDERWOOD 1.1   35 The gladdest light, darke man can thinke upon;
    p. 412 UNGATHERED 41   6 The gladdest ground to all the numbred-five,

gladding   frequency: 2   relative frequency: 0.00002
  **p. 114 PANEGYRE   48 His gladding looke, now long'd to see it more.
    p. 253 UNDERWOOD 75   18 Of Summers Liveries, and gladding greene;

gladnesse   frequency: 10   relative frequency: 0.00014
    p. 120 FOREST 14   6 The gladnesse higher:
    p. 221 UNDERWOOD 48   19 By all the Arts of Gladnesse,
    p. 225 UNDERWOOD 51   18 For 't were a narrow gladnesse, kept thine owne.
    p. 238 UNDERWOOD 66   9 So generall a gladnesse to an Isle,
    p. 245 UNDERWOOD 70   76 And let thy lookes with gladnesse shine:
    p. 249 UNDERWOOD 72   14 That cry that gladnesse, which their hearts would
                                pray,
    p. 270 UNDERWOOD 83   59 With gladnesse temper'd her sad Parents teares!
    p. 284 U'WOOD 84.9   67 All other gladnesse, with the thought is barr'd;
    p. 285 U'WOOD 84.9   101 Her fellowes, with the oyle of gladnesse, bright
    p. 285 U'WOOD 84.9   114 Shall meet with gladnesse in one Theatre;

glaives. See "glaves."

glance   frequency: 1   relative frequency: 0.00001
    p. 111 FOREST 11   61 A fixed thought, an eye vn-taught to glance;

glare   frequency: 1   relative frequency: 0.00001
    p. 88 EPIGRAMS 133   163 Our braue Heroes with a milder glare,

glass   frequency: 1   relative frequency: 0.00001
    See also "glasse," "glasse-house,"
              "glassen," "houre-glasse."
    p. 383 UNGATHERED 16   11 Except your Gratious Eye as through a Glass

glasse   frequency: 11   relative frequency: 0.00015
    p. 108 FOREST 10A   4 like glasse, blowne vp, and fashion'd by desire.
    p. 117 FOREST 13   26 No lady, but, at some time, loues her glasse.
    p. 120 FOREST 13   122 Madame, be bold to vse this truest glasse:
    p. 137 UNDERWOOD 2.5   40 And the Glasse hangs by her side,
    p. 140 UNDERWOOD 2.8   22 'Fore your Idoll Glasse a whit,
    p. 148 UNDERWOOD 8   2 Here running in the Glasse,
    p. 164 UNDERWOOD 15   63 To see 'hem aye discoursing with their Glasse,
    p. 165 UNDERWOOD 15   111 When not his Combes, his Curling-irons, his
                                Glasse,
    p. 166 UNDERWOOD 15   119 What reputation to beare one Glasse more?
    p. 295 UNDERWOOD 89   5 Darke thy cleare glasse with old Falernian
                                Wine;
    p. 389 UNGATHERED 24   10 As a deformed face doth a true glasse.

glasse-house   frequency: 1   relative frequency: 0.00001
     p. 211 UNDERWOOD 43   180 The Glasse-house, Dye-fats, and their
                               Fornaces;

glassen   frequency: 1   relative frequency: 0.00001
     p. 166 UNDERWOOD 15   138 The Dice with glassen eyes, to the glad viewes

glasses. See "cupping-glasses."

glaves   frequency: 1   relative frequency: 0.00001
     p. 212 UNDERWOOD 43   198 And there made Swords, Bills, Glaves, and
                               Armes your fill:

glean. See "gleane."

gleane   frequency: 1   relative frequency: 0.00001
     p. 45 EPIGRAMS 56   5 At first he made low shifts, would picke and
                               gleane,

gleanes   frequency: 1   relative frequency: 0.00001
     p. 242 UNDERWOOD 69   16 To keepe him off; and how-so-e're he gleanes

gleanings   frequency: 1   relative frequency: 0.00001
     p. 207 UNDERWOOD 43   102 With humble Gleanings in Divinitie,

gleans. See "gleanes."

glister'd   frequency: 1   relative frequency: 0.00001
     p. 138 UNDERWOOD 2.6   16 Else that glister'd in White-hall;

globe   frequency: 2   relative frequency: 0.00002
     p. 208 UNDERWOOD 43   132 Against the Globe, the Glory of the Banke.
     p. 276 U'WOOD 84.3   25 Last, draw the circles of this Globe,

globy   frequency: 1   relative frequency: 0.00001
     p. 170 UNDERWOOD 19   5 By that tall Grove, your haire; whose globy
                               rings

gloomie-sceptred   frequency: 1   relative frequency: 0.00001
     p. 180 UNDERWOOD 25   61 Where darknesse with her gloomie-sceptred hand,

gloomy. See "gloomie-sceptred."

glorie   frequency: 13   relative frequency: 0.00018
     p. 35 EPIGRAMS 27   8 Wee, sad for him, may glorie, and not sinne.
     p. 39 EPIGRAMS 40   7 Expresser truth, or truer glorie,
     p. 61 EPIGRAMS 95   24 As, then, his cause, his glorie emulate.
     p. 62 EPIGRAMS 96   12 A man should seeke great glorie, and not broad.
     p. 66 EPIGRAMS 103   8 And glorie of them all, but to repeate!
     p. 67 EPIGRAMS 104   10 Of former age, or glorie of our one,
     p. 132 UNDERWOOD 2.2   8 Marke of glorie, come with me;
     p. 192 UNDERWOOD 38   34 There greatnesse takes a glorie to relieve.
     p. 214 UNDERWOOD 44   50 And keepe the Glorie of the English name,
     p. 234 UNDERWOOD 60   13 No aime at glorie, or, in warre,
     p. 238 UNDERWOOD 66   13 Glorie to God. Then, Haile to Mary! spring
     p. 240 UNDERWOOD 67   28 Comes in the pompe, and glorie
     p. 283 U'WOOD 84.9   38 The glorie, and gaine of rest, which the place
                               gives!

glories   frequency: 8   relative frequency: 0.00011
    *p. 494 TO HIMSELF   52 The glories of thy King,
     p. 56 EPIGRAMS 89   2 Fear'd not to boast the glories of her stage,
     p. 83 EPIGRAMS 132   14 No more, those mayden glories shee hath lost.
     p. 108 FOREST 10A   15 the glories of yt ... or muse ....
     p. 203 UNDERWOOD 43   24 Or taxe the Glories of the Church, and Gowne?
     p. 217 UNDERWOOD 46   1 He that should search all Glories of the Gowne,
     p. 270 UNDERWOOD 83   63 Let Angels sing her glories, who did call
     p. 415 UNGATHERED 43   4 Renew the Glories of our blessed Ieames:

glorifie   frequency: 1   relative frequency: 0.00001
     p. 412 UNGATHERED 41   12 To knit thy Crowne, and glorifie the rest.

glorified   frequency: 2   relative frequency: 0.00002
     p. 128 UNDERWOOD 1.1   47 But in thy presence, truly glorified,
     p. 371 UNGATHERED 8   15 A glorified worke to Time, when Fire,

glorify. See "glorifie."

glorious   frequency: 11   relative frequency: 0.00015
     p. 35 EPIGRAMS 28   1 DON SVRLY, to aspire the glorious name

glorious (cont.)
p. 62 EPIGRAMS 97	6 By his each glorious parcell to be knowne!
p. 114 FOREST 12	43 The soules, shee loues. Those other glorio notes,
p. 127 UNDERWOOD 1.1	1 1. O holy, blessed, glorious Trinitie
p. 128 UNDERWOOD 1.1	29 8. Increase those acts, o glorious Trini
p. 129 UNDERWOOD 1.2	24 His glorious Name
p. 220 UNDERWOOD 47	66 As are the Glorious Scenes, at the great sights;
p. 261 UNDERWOOD 77	26 In glorious Piles, or Pyramids erect
p. 286 U'WOOD 84.9	129 That holy, great, and glorious Mysterie,
p. 325 HORACE 2	411 Nor had our Italie more glorious bin
p. 413 UNGATHERED 41	32 The glorious Trinity in Vnion met.

glory   frequency: 12   relative frequency: 0.00017
See also "glorie."
**p. 113 PANEGYRE	3 Againe, the glory of our Westerne world
p. 130 UNDERWOOD 1.3	21 To make us heires of glory!
p. 168 UNDERWOOD 15	179 That thou dost all things more for truth, then glory,
p. 192 UNDERWOOD 38	48 Would live his glory that could keepe it on;
p. 208 UNDERWOOD 43	132 Against the Globe, the Glory of the Banke.
p. 252 UNDERWOOD 75	3 Thou canst not meet more Glory, on the way,
p. 264 UNDERWOOD 79	25 Sister of PAN, and glory of the Spring:
p. 286 U'WOOD 84.9	127 Hee will all Glory, all Perfection be,
p. 288 U'WOOD 84.9	205 Shee saw him too, in glory to ascend
p. 367 UNGATHERED 6	49 Be proofe, the glory of his hand,
p. 399 UNGATHERED 31	8 Code, Digests, Pandects of all faemale glory!
p. 414 UNGATHERED 41	49 Thou Throne of glory, beauteous as the Moone,

glove   frequency: 1   relative frequency: 0.00001
| p. 201 UNDERWOOD 42 | 54 To ev'ry Petticote he brush'd, and Glove |

glutted   frequency: 1   relative frequency: 0.00001
| p. 218 UNDERWOOD 47 | 13 They'<h>ave glutted in, and letcher'd out that weeke, |

gluttony   frequency: 3   relative frequency: 0.00004
p. 76 EPIGRAMS 118	6 Lust it comes out, that gluttony went in.
p. 95 FOREST 2	68 A waiter, doth my gluttony enuy:
p. 163 UNDERWOOD 15	45 In bravery, or gluttony, or coyne,

go   frequency: 6   relative frequency: 0.00008
See also "goe," "letter-goe," "out-goe."
p. 241 UNDERWOOD 68	14 The Kings fame lives. Go now, denie his Teirce.
p. 287 U'WOOD 84.9	170 To another, Move; he went; To a third, Go,
p. 329 HORACE 2	516 As doctrine, and delight together go.
p. 375 UNGATHERED 10	19 For he did but kisse her, and so let her go.
p. 410 UNGATHERED 39	10 I'll laugh at thee poor wretched Tike, go send
p. 411 UNGATHERED 39	16 Cropt, branded, slit, neck-stockt; go, you are stript.

goal. See "goale."

goale   frequency: 1   relative frequency: 0.00001
| p. 333 HORACE 2 | 588 The wished goale, both did, and suffer'd much |

goat   frequency: 2   relative frequency: 0.00002
See also "goate."
| p. 202 UNDERWOOD 42 | 82 A Goat in Velvet; or some block could move |
| p. 319 HORACE 2 | 320 For the vile Goat, soone after, forth did send |

goate   frequency: 1   relative frequency: 0.00001
| p. 34 EPIGRAMS 25 | 4 And how his GANIMEDE mou'd, and how his goate, |

goates   frequency: 1   relative frequency: 0.00001
| p. 283 U'WOOD 84.9 | 47 And Goates together, whither they must come |

goats. See "goates."

god   frequency: 70   relative frequency: 0.00101
See also "lord-god," "semi-god."
*p. 494 TO HIMSELF	53 His zeale to God, and his iust awe o're men;
p. 30 EPIGRAMS 12	4 The charge of that state, with this charme, god payes.
p. 30 EPIGRAMS 12	6 Himselfe: his whole reuennue is, god payes.
p. 30 EPIGRAMS 12	8 Shee must haue money: he returnes, god payes.
p. 30 EPIGRAMS 12	10 Lookes o're the bill, likes it: and say's, god payes.

god (cont.)

p.	30	EPIGRAMS 12	12	At dice his borrow'd money: which, god payes.
p.	30	EPIGRAMS 12	14	Signes to new bond, forfeits: and cryes, god payes.
p.	30	EPIGRAMS 12	16	Takes physick, teares the papers: still god payes.
p.	30	EPIGRAMS 12	18	Calls for his stoole, adornes the stage: god payes.
p.	31	EPIGRAMS 12	20	His onely answere is to all, god payes.
p.	31	EPIGRAMS 12	22	Thus: and for his letcherie, scores, god payes.
p.	36	EPIGRAMS 28	17	Blaspheme god, greatly. Or some poore hinde beat,
p.	38	EPIGRAMS 35	8	And than in them, how could we know god more?
p.	68	EPIGRAMS 106	8	Like straight, thy pietie to God, and friends:
p.	80	EPIGRAMS 126	3	I pluck'd a branch; the iealous god did frowne,
p.	85	EPIGRAMS 133	44	That all this while I haue forgot some god,
p.	85	EPIGRAMS 133	53	And art a god, if Fame thee not abuses.
p.	86	EPIGRAMS 133	99	For (where he was the god of eloquence,
p.	99	FOREST 3	95	God wisheth, none should wracke on a strange shelfe.
p.	122	FOREST 15	1	Good, and great GOD, can I not thinke of thee,
p.	127	UNDERWOOD 1.1	2	Of persons, still one God, in Unitie,
p.	127	UNDERWOOD 1.1	9	3. All-gracious God, the Sinners sacrifice,
p.	127	UNDERWOOD 1.1	17	5. Eternall Father, God, who did'st create
p.	128	UNDERWOOD 1.1	21	6. Eternall God the Sonne, who not denyd'st
p.	128	UNDERWOOD 1.1	25	7. Eternall Spirit, God from both proceeding,
p.	128	UNDERWOOD 1.1	30	Of persons, still one God in Unitie;
p.	128	UNDERWOOD 1.1	40	One God to see,
p.	129	UNDERWOOD 1.2	1	Heare mee, O God!
p.	129	UNDERWOOD 1.2	t1	A Hymne to God the Father.
p.	130	UNDERWOOD 1.3	7	The Sonne of God, th'Eternall King,
p.	140	UNDERWOOD 2.9	6	And a woman God did make me:
p.	168	UNDERWOOD 15	196	Who falls for love of God, shall rise a Starre.
p.	171	UNDERWOOD 20	1	A Womans friendship! God whom I trust in,
p.	189	UNDERWOOD 36	16	The eldest God, yet still a Child.
p.	191	UNDERWOOD 38	19	God, and the good, know to forgive, and save.
p.	193	UNDERWOOD 38	68	God lightens not at mans each fraile offence,
p.	208	UNDERWOOD 43	117	For none but Smiths would have made thee a God.
p.	229	UNDERWOOD 55	1	Would God, my Burges, I could thinke
p.	234	UNDERWOOD 61	11	T<o>'obtaine of God, what all the Land should aske?
p.	235	UNDERWOOD 61	20	He is the Man, and Favorite of God.
p.	235	UNDERWOOD 63	2	To God, denies the God-head to be true:
p.	235	UNDERWOOD 63	3	Who doubts, those fruits God can with gaine restore,
p.	236	UNDERWOOD 63	13	For God, whose essence is so infinite,
p.	238	UNDERWOOD 66	13	Glorie to God. Then, Haile to Mary! spring
p.	256	UNDERWOOD 75	131	To have thy God to blesse, thy King to grace,
p.	268	UNDERWOOD 82	1	That thou art lov'd of God, this worke is done,
p.	268	UNDERWOOD 82	4	How much they are belov'd of God, in thee;
p.	281	U'WOOD 84.4	72	But such a Mind, mak'st God thy Guest.
p.	283	U'WOOD 84.9	33	I murmure against God, for having ta'en
p.	284	U'WOOD 84.9	65	And the whole Banquet is full sight of God!
p.	285	U'WOOD 84.9	112	Of life, and light, the Sonne of God, the Word!
p.	286	U'WOOD 84.9	119	But all of God; They still shall have to say,
p.	286	U'WOOD 84.9	128	God, in the Union, and the Trinitie!
p.	287	U'WOOD 84.9	184	Of divine Comfort, when sh'had talk'd with God.
p.	288	U'WOOD 84.9	211	To him should be her Judge, true God, true Man,
p.	313	HORACE 2	161	It much will differ, if a God speake, than,
p.	317	HORACE 2	273	To have a God come in; except a knot
p.	321	HORACE 2	331	As neither any God, were brought in there,
p.	335	HORACE 2	661	Hee, while they labour'd to be thought a God
p.	380	UNGATHERED 12	43	Yes. And thanks God in his Pistle or his Booke
p.	384	UNGATHERED 18	6	That bid, God giue thee ioy, and haue no endes.
p.	395	UNGATHERED 29	14	What Muse, or rather God of harmony
p.	413	UNGATHERED 41	33	Daughter, and Mother, and the Spouse of GOD,
p.	414	UNGATHERED 41	56	Of being Daughter, Mother, Spouse of GOD!
p.	418	UNGATHERED 47	3	And God blesse every living thing,
p.	419	UNGATH'D 47A	1	The ..... ye .... Prince god ......
p.	419	UNGATHERED 47	5	God blesse the Councell of Estate,
p.	419	UNGATHERED 47	7	God blesse them all, and keepe them safe:
p.	419	UNGATHERED 47	8	And God blesse me, and God blesse Raph.

god-head   frequency: 3   relative frequency: 0.00004

p.	107	FOREST 10	6	Of his dull god-head, were sinne. Ile implore
p.	235	UNDERWOOD 63	2	To God, denies the God-head to be true:

god-head (cont.)
   p. 284 U'WOOD 84.9   74 Who violates the God-head, is most vitious

god-like   frequency: 3   relative frequency: 0.00004
   p. 110 FOREST 11   53 But, in a calme, and god-like vnitie,
   p. 116 FOREST 12   91 Moodes, which the god-like SYDNEY oft did
                        proue,
   p. 311 HORACE 2   114 To chant the Gods, and all their God-like race,

god-wit   frequency: 1   relative frequency: 0.00001
   p. 291 UNDERWOOD 85   53 Th'Ionian God-wit, nor the Ginny hen

goddess   frequency: 1   relative frequency: 0.00001
   See also "goddesse."
   p. 406 UNGATHERED 34   93 A Goddess is, then paynted Cloth, Deal-boards,

goddesse   frequency: 2   relative frequency: 0.00002
   p. 85 EPIGRAMS 133   45 Or goddesse to inuoke, to stuffe my verse;
   p. 207 UNDERWOOD 43 108 Or Goddesse, could be patient of thy face.

godds   frequency: 2   relative frequency: 0.00002
   p. 395 UNGATHERED 29 16 What godds but those of arts, and eloquence?
   p. 395 UNGATHERED 29 18 Are still th'interpreters twixt godds, and men!

godhead. See "god-head."

godlike. See "god-like."

godly's   frequency: 1   relative frequency: 0.00001
   p. 411 UNGATHERED 40   8 and the Godly's strife,

gods   frequency: 7   relative frequency: 0.00010
   See also "godds."
   p. 49 EPIGRAMS 67   12 Proues, that is gods, which was the peoples
                        voice.
   p. 235 UNDERWOOD 61 19 And doe their penance, to avert Gods rod,
   p. 311 HORACE 2   114 To chant the Gods, and all their God-like race,
   p. 319 HORACE 2   285 Hide faults, pray to the Gods, and wish aloud
   p. 327 HORACE 2   479 Orpheus, a priest, and speaker for the Gods,
   p. 331 HORACE 2   555 But neither, Men, nor Gods, nor Pillars meant,
   p. 422 UNGATHERED 50   5 and the immortall gods; loue only those

god's   frequency: 1   relative frequency: 0.00001
   See also "gods."
   p. 414 UNGATHERED 41 48 By bringing forth GOD's onely Son, no other.

godwit   frequency: 1   relative frequency: 0.00001
   See also "god-wit."
   p. 65 EPIGRAMS 101 19 May yet be there; and godwit, if we can:

goe   frequency: 53   relative frequency: 0.00076
   p. 36 EPIGRAMS 31   3 And though the soundest legs goe euery day,
   p. 42 EPIGRAMS 46   2 A knight-hood bought, to goe a wooing in?
   p. 50 EPIGRAMS 72   4 Goe high, or low, as thou wilt value it.
   p. 53 EPIGRAMS 77   3 For, if thou shame, ranck'd with my friends, to
                        goe,
   p. 57 EPIGRAMS 90   3 Was dull, and long, ere shee would goe to man:
   p. 59 EPIGRAMS 92 30 If the States make peace, how it will goe
   p. 70 EPIGRAMS 109 15 Goe on, and doubt not, what posteritie,
   p. 80 EPIGRAMS 128   1 ROE (and my ioy to name) th'art now, to goe
   p. 85 EPIGRAMS 133 38 Propos'd to goe to Hol'borne in a wherry:
   p. 98 FOREST 3   69 Goe enter breaches, meet the cannons rage,
   p. 99 FOREST 3   81 Let that goe heape a masse of wretched wealth,
   p. 99 FOREST 3   85 Let thousands more goe flatter vice, and winne,
   p. 102 FOREST 4   65 Nor for my peace will I goe farre,
   p. 105 FOREST 8   37 Will by coach, and water goe,
   p. 107 FOREST 10   16 Goe, crampe dull MARS, light VENVS, when
                        he snorts,
   p. 119 FOREST 13 103 To crowne the burthen which you goe withall,
   p. 140 UNDERWOOD 2.8 18 To fetch in the Formes goe by:
   p. 150 UNDERWOOD 10 13 Goe, get thee quickly forth,
   p. 156 UNDERWOOD 13 113 No more are these of us, let them then goe,
   p. 157 UNDERWOOD 13 127 Sydney e're night! or that did goe to bed
   p. 157 UNDERWOOD 13 135 Yet we must more then move still, or goe on,
   p. 157 UNDERWOOD 13 153 And last, goe out in nothing: You that see
   p. 165 UNDERWOOD 15 103 His time? health? soule? will he for these goe
                        throw
   p. 166 UNDERWOOD 15 134 Goe make our selves the Usurers at a cast.
   p. 166 UNDERWOOD 15 145 Well, let it goe. Yet this is better, then
   p. 167 UNDERWOOD 15 175 Goe, quit 'hem all. And take along with thee,

goe (cont.)
 p. 168 UNDERWOOD 15 195 These take, and now goe seeke thy peace in
            Warre,
 p. 170 UNDERWOOD 18 21 If it be thus; Come Love, and Fortune goe,
 p. 185 UNDERWOOD 30   3 And goe no farther: let this Circle be
 p. 191 UNDERWOOD 38 24 Or goe about to countenance the vice,
 p. 194 UNDERWOOD 38 114 Publike affaires command me now to goe
 p. 199 UNDERWOOD 41   1 Since you must goe, and I must bid farewell,
 p. 204 UNDERWOOD 43 45 Adulterate moneys, such as might not goe:
 p. 211 UNDERWOOD 43 181 To live in Sea-coale, and goe forth in smoake;
 p. 214 UNDERWOOD 44 49 Goe on, increase in vertue; and in fame:
 p. 224 UNDERWOOD 50 21 Whilst your Ulisses hath ta'ne leave to goe,
 p. 229 UNDERWOOD 54 19 To goe out after ----- till when take this letter
 p. 232 UNDERWOOD 58 13 If they goe on, and that thou lov'st a-life
 p. 244 UNDERWOOD 70 53 Goe now, and tell out dayes summ'd up with
            feares,
 p. 254 UNDERWOOD 75 62 (Where she shall goe)
 p. 255 UNDERWOOD 75 88 All else we see beside, are Shadowes, and goe
            lesse.
 p. 260 UNDERWOOD 76 29 Then goe on, and doe its worst;
 p. 262 UNDERWOOD 78 19 Goe, Muse, in, and salute him. Say he be
 p. 271 UNDERWOOD 83 77 Goe now, her happy Parents, and be sad,
 p. 278 U'WOOD 84.4   18 As you goe on, by what brave way
 p. 291 UNDERWOOD 85 54 Could not goe downe my belly then
 p. 292 UNDERWOOD 86   8 Goe where Youths soft intreaties call thee back.
 p. 315 HORACE 2   213 The middle of his matter: letting goe
 p. 321 HORACE 2   344 Quite from all face of Tragedie to goe,
 p. 337 HORACE 2   679 Not letting goe his hold, where he drawes food,
 p. 398 UNGATHERED 30 78 And stop my sight, in euery line I goe.
 p. 662 INSCRIPTS. 2   1 Goe little Booke, Goe little Fable

goes   frequency: 12 relative frequency: 0.00017
 p. 30 EPIGRAMS 12 17 Or else by water goes, and so to playes;
 p. 31 EPIGRAMS 14 4 The great renowne, and name wherewith shee goes.
 p. 59 EPIGRAMS 92 18 Nay, aske you, how the day goes, in your eare.
 p. 87 EPIGRAMS 133 131 Airising in that place, through which, who goes,
 p. 118 FOREST 13   66 And after varyed, as fresh obiects goes,
 p. 134 UNDERWOOD 2.4   5 As she goes, all hearts doe duty
 p. 193 UNDERWOOD 38 69 He pardons slips, goes by a world of ills,
 p. 216 UNDERWOOD 45 6 That hearkens to a Jacks-pulse, when it goes.
 p. 222 UNDERWOOD 49 9 Equall with that, which for the best newes goes,
 p. 265 UNDERWOOD 79 58 Where e're he goes upon the ground,
 p. 363 UNGATHERED 3 6 It carries Palme with it, (where e're it goes)
 p. 409 UNGATHERED 37 17 No man will tarry by thee, as hee goes,

goest. See "go'st."

going   frequency: 6 relative frequency: 0.00008
**p. 115 PANEGYRE   90 "Where he was going; and the vpward race
 p. 84 EPIGRAMS 133 2 Of HERCVLES, or THESEVS going to
            hell,
 p. 86 EPIGRAMS 133 88 No going backe; on still you rogues, and row.
 p. 121 FOREST 14   28 Of going backe
 p. 145 UNDERWOOD 5 10 So going thorow all your straine,
 p. 378 UNGATHERED 11 t3 and his Booke now going to

gold   frequency: 18 relative frequency: 0.00026
 See also "gold's."
 p. 39 EPIGRAMS 41 2 And get more gold, then all the colledge can:
 p. 47 EPIGRAMS 64 4 A treasure, art: contemn'd in th'age of gold.
 p. 78 EPIGRAMS 122 4 The world's pure gold, and wise simplicitie;
 p. 93 FOREST 2   3 Of polish'd pillars, or a roofe of gold:
 p. 98 FOREST 3   64 Which boasts t'haue had the head of gold.
 p. 113 FOREST 12   2 And almost euery vice, almightie gold,
 p. 113 FOREST 12   18 Or perhaps lesse: whil'st gold beares all this
            sway,
 p. 114 FOREST 12   23 When gold was made no weapon to cut throtes,
 p. 141 UNDERWOOD 2.9 14 Gold, upon a ground of black.
 p. 179 UNDERWOOD 25 45 Gold, that is perfect, will out-live the fire.
 p. 218 UNDERWOOD 47 4 And though Opinion stampe them not, are gold.
 p. 273 U'WOOD 84.1 27 With Gold, or Claspes, which might be bought
 p. 361 UNGATHERED 1 15 The seauen-fold flower of Arte (more rich then
            gold)
 p. 363 UNGATHERED 3 5 Gold is a sutor, neuer tooke repulse,
 p. 393 UNGATHERED 27 3 And purer then the purest Gold,
 p. 403 UNGATHERED 34 28 Though gold or Iuory haftes would make it good.
 p. 408 UNGATHERED 37 4 Th'enuy'd returne, of forty pound in gold.
 p. 413 UNGATHERED 41 39 The House of gold, the Gate of heavens power,

gold-chaines   frequency: 1   relative frequency: 0.00001
  p. 213 UNDERWOOD 44   13 But they may see Gold-Chaines, and Pearle
                            worne then,

golden   frequency: 7   relative frequency: 0.00010
  p. 47 EPIGRAMS 64   3 Of loue, and what the golden age did hold
  p. 85 EPIGRAMS 133   48 Sans helpe of SYBIL, or a golden bough,
  p. 100 FOREST 4   24 Enamor'd of their golden gyues?
  p. 110 FOREST 11   47 It is a golden chaine let downe from heauen,
  p. 114 FOREST 12   22 Then this, our guilt, nor golden age can deeme,
  p. 115 FOREST 12   83 There like a rich, and golden pyramede,
  p. 177 UNDERWOOD 25   9 My bolder numbers to thy golden Lyre:

golden-eyes   frequency: 1   relative frequency: 0.00001
  p. 291 UNDERWOOD 85   50 Nor Turbot, nor bright Golden-eyes:

goldeneys. See "golden-eyes."

gold's   frequency: 1   relative frequency: 0.00001
  p. 363 UNGATHERED 3   18 Where Gold's the Motiue, women haue no Nay.

gon   frequency: 1   relative frequency: 0.00001
  p. 368 UNGATHERED 6   68 From thence is gon

gondomar. See "gundomar."

gone   frequency: 26   relative frequency: 0.00037
  See also "gon," "over-gone."
  p. 37 EPIGRAMS 33   2 Glad-mention'd ROE: thou art but gone before,
  p. 52 EPIGRAMS 74   7 Whil'st thou art certaine to thy words, once
                            gone,
  p. 58 EPIGRAMS 92   1 Ere cherries ripe, and straw-berries be gone,
  p. 60 EPIGRAMS 93   2 For the great marke of vertue, those being gone
  p. 63 EPIGRAMS 97   17 Since he was gone, more then the one he weares.
  p. 74 EPIGRAMS 115   24 The cloth's no sooner gone, but it gets vp
  p. 119 FOREST 13   84 Boast, but how oft they haue gone wrong to man:
  p. 119 FOREST 13   119 And that your soules conspire, as they were gone
  p. 120 FOREST 14   19 Are fled and gone,
  p. 139 UNDERWOOD 2.7   7 Once more, and (faith) I will be gone,
  p. 156 UNDERWOOD 13   121 Ride, saile, am coach'd, know I how farre I
                            have gone,
  p. 163 UNDERWOOD 15   28 But there are objects, bid him to be gone
  p. 173 UNDERWOOD 22   5 A vertue, like Allay, so gone
  p. 173 UNDERWOOD 22   24 Is gone himselfe into your Name.
  p. 192 UNDERWOOD 38   47 And then with pause; for sever'd once, that's
                            gone,
  p. 201 UNDERWOOD 42   40 To doe her Husbands rites in, e're 'twere gone
  p. 208 UNDERWOOD 43   111 Sonne of the Wind! for so thy mother gone
  p. 210 UNDERWOOD 43   171 In those Records, which, were all Chronicle<r>s
                            gone,
  p. 211 UNDERWOOD 43   176 No order? no Decree? Though we be gone
  p. 257 UNDERWOOD 75   137 The Chappell empties, and thou may'st be gone
  p. 269 UNDERWOOD 83   12 And e're I can aske more of her, shee's gone!
  p. 277 U'WOOD 84.4   1 Painter, yo'are come, but may be gone,
  p. 283 U'WOOD 84.9   22 (For so thou art with me) now shee is gone.
  p. 283 U'WOOD 84.9   28 What's left a Poet, when his Muse is gone?
  p. 289 U'WOOD 84.9   228 To publish her a Saint. My Muse is gone.
  p. 315 HORACE 2   229 Th'unbearded Youth, his Guardian once being
                            gone,

good   frequency: 136   relative frequency: 0.00196
 *p. 493 TO HIMSELF   31 And much good do't you then:
 **p. 113 PANEGYRE   16 Those dampes, that so offend all good mens eyes;
 **p. 114 PANEGYRE   36 As if they felt, but had not knowne their good:
 **p. 116 PANEGYRE   116 Whose necessary good 'twas now to be
  p. 27 EPIGRAMS 3   2 Call'st a booke good, or bad, as it doth sell,
  p. 30 EPIGRAMS 11   6 And such from whom let no man hope least good,
  p. 30 EPIGRAMS 11   8 For I will dare none. Good Lord, walke dead
                            still.
  p. 32 EPIGRAMS 16   8 Make good what thou dar'st doe in all the rest.
  p. 34 EPIGRAMS 24   1 There's reason good, that you good lawes should
                            make:
  p. 38 EPIGRAMS 38   5 And crie good! good! This quite peruerts my
                            sense,
  p. 47 EPIGRAMS 64   11 Where good mens vertues them to honors bring,
  p. 49 EPIGRAMS 67   10 Before thou wert it, in each good mans heart.
  p. 50 EPIGRAMS 69   2 Yet by thy weapon liu'st! Th'hast one good part.
  p. 51 EPIGRAMS 73   20 Then had I made 'hem good, to fit your vaine.
  p. 52 EPIGRAMS 76   6 Of greatest bloud, and yet more good then great;
  p. 53 EPIGRAMS 77   1 Be safe, nor feare thy selfe so good a fame,

good (cont.)

p.	53 EPIGRAMS 80	1 The ports of death are sinnes; of life, good deeds:
p.	54 EPIGRAMS 80	8 For good men but see death, the wicked tast it.
p.	54 EPIGRAMS 81	3 Or that I'haue by, two good sufficient men,
p.	57 EPIGRAMS 90	6 And, finding good securitie in his age,
p.	63 EPIGRAMS 98	11 Though both be good, the latter yet is worst,
p.	66 EPIGRAMS 102	3 Against the bad, but of, and to the good:
p.	66 EPIGRAMS 102	11 And are so good, and bad, iust at a price,
p.	70 EPIGRAMS 109	11 To make thy lent life, good against the Fates:
p.	71 EPIGRAMS 110	15 His deedes too dying, but in bookes (whose good
p.	73 EPIGRAMS 113	4 Where, what makes others great, doth keepe thee good!
p.	74 EPIGRAMS 115	2 Him not, aloud, that boasts so good a fame:
p.	75 EPIGRAMS 116	8 Might be found out as good, and not my Lord.
p.	76 EPIGRAMS 119	5 With me can merit more, then that good man,
p.	77 EPIGRAMS 120	23 But, being so much too good for earth,
p.	81 EPIGRAMS 128	12 This is that good AENEAS, past through fire,
p.	95 FOREST 2	84 On thy good lady, then! who, therein, reap'd
p.	99 FOREST 3	84 Not doing good, scarce when he dyes.
p.	100 FOREST 4	16 And all thy good is to be sold.
p.	102 FOREST 5	4 He, at length, our good will seuer.
p.	114 FOREST 12	37 Beautie, I know, is good, and bloud is more;
p.	116 FOREST 13	2 Of any good minde, now: There are so few.
p.	116 FOREST 13	6 For others ill, ought none their good forget.
p.	118 FOREST 13	52 For he, that once is good, is euer great.
p.	121 FOREST 14	34 So good
p.	122 FOREST 15	1 Good, and great GOD, can I not thinke of thee,
p.	134 UNDERWOOD 2.4	20 All the Gaine, all the Good, of the Elements strife.
p.	137 UNDERWOOD 2.5	44 Of her good, who is the best
p.	140 UNDERWOOD 2.8	27 Be as good, as was the last:
p.	142 U'WOOD 2.10	5 Himselfe young, and face be good,
p.	142 U'WOOD 2.10	8 'Tis one good part I'ld lie withall.
p.	145 UNDERWOOD 5	9 Find some one good, in some one man;
p.	145 UNDERWOOD 5	12 One good enough for a songs sake.
p.	146 UNDERWOOD 6	17 The good, from bad, is not describe,
p.	147 UNDERWOOD 7	6 The pleasure is as good as none,
p.	153 UNDERWOOD 13	2 Great and good turns, as wel could time them too,
p.	153 UNDERWOOD 13	14 This Good from you, as freely will it owe;
p.	153 UNDERWOOD 13	18 To have such doe me good, I durst not name:
p.	154 UNDERWOOD 13	37 In that proud manner, as a good so gain'd,
p.	156 UNDERWOOD 13	108 Or Science of discerning Good and Ill.
p.	156 UNDERWOOD 13	111 Her ends are honestie, and publike good!
p.	156 UNDERWOOD 13	124 Men have beene great, but never good by chance,
p.	159 UNDERWOOD 14	15 A many'of bookes, even good judgements wound
p.	163 UNDERWOOD 15	44 To make up Greatnesse! and mans whole good fix'd
p.	167 UNDERWOOD 15	147 To flatter my good Lord, and cry his Bowle
p.	168 UNDERWOOD 15	187 That thou thinke nothing great, but what is good,
p.	169 UNDERWOOD 17	2 Debts when they can: good men may breake their day,
p.	171 UNDERWOOD 20	7 Or have the least of Good, but what it must
p.	175 UNDERWOOD 24	3 Raising the World to good or evill fame,
p.	176 UNDERWOOD 24	5 Wise Providence would so; that nor the good
p.	183 UNDERWOOD 29	14 All good Poetrie hence was flowne,
p.	185 UNDERWOOD 30	5 Cecill, the grave, the wise, the great, the good,
p.	185 UNDERWOOD 30	13 That still was good for goodnesse sake, nor thought
p.	186 UNDERWOOD 31	7 So may the gentler Muses, and good fame
p.	186 UNDERWOOD 32	2 When a good Cause is destitute of friends,
p.	186 UNDERWOOD 32	5 When those good few, that her Defenders be,
p.	191 UNDERWOOD 38	19 God, and the good, know to forgive, and save.
p.	193 UNDERWOOD 38	100 Of Contumelie, and urge a good man more
p.	210 UNDERWOOD 43	173 But say, all sixe good men, what answer yee?
p.	212 UNDERWOOD 43	212 That have good places: therefore once agen,
p.	217 UNDERWOOD 46	5 Such, Coke, were thy beginnings, when thy good
p.	224 UNDERWOOD 50	16 A cheerefull worke to all good eyes, to see
p.	224 UNDERWOOD 50	25 For you admit no companie, but good,
p.	229 UNDERWOOD 54	6 An ill commoditie! 'T must make good weight.
p.	229 UNDERWOOD 54	17 And you shall make me good, in weight, and fashion,
p.	231 UNDERWOOD 57	16 And neither good Cheare,
p.	234 UNDERWOOD 60	7 Of honour, nor no ayre of good?
p.	236 UNDERWOOD 64	2 Most pious King, but his owne good in you!
p.	236 UNDERWOOD 64	t2 To our great and good K. CHARLES
p.	243 UNDERWOOD 70	32 For three of his foure-score, he did no good.
p.	246 UNDERWOOD 70	105 But simple love of greatnesse, and of good;
p.	247 UNDERWOOD 70	119 The good, and durst not practise it, were glad

good (cont.)
```
     p. 248 UNDERWOOD 71     3 Of Princes aides, or good mens Charities.
     p. 261 UNDERWOOD 77    20 What worlds of blessings to good Kings they owe:
     p. 263 UNDERWOOD 78    22 Good Omen to him, in the note thou sing'st,
     p. 265 UNDERWOOD 79    44 Chorus Our great, our good. Where one's so
                               drest
     p. 268 UNDERWOOD 82     8 Should take first Seisin of the publique good,
     p. 268 UNDERWOOD 82    12 As in renewing thy good Grandsires fame;
     p. 269 UNDERWOOD 83    11 Hee's good, as great. I am almost a stone!
     p. 269 UNDERWOOD 83    21 Earle Rivers Grand-Child -- serve not formes,
                               good Fame,
     p. 270 UNDERWOOD 83    35 And, calling truth to witnesse, make that good
     p. 274 U'WOOD 84.2      8 At either Stemme, and know the veines of good
     p. 280 U'WOOD 84.4     62 Where it may run to any good;
     p. 282 U'WOOD 84.9      4 All that was good, or great in me she weav'd,
     p. 284 U'WOOD 84.9     84 Amongst her Peeres, those Princes of all good!
     p. 287 U'WOOD 84.9    175 A solemne Mistresse, and so good a Friend,
     p. 292 UNDERWOOD 86     4 Of the good Cynara I was: Refraine,
     p. 315 HORACE 2       234 For his owne good, a carelesse letter-goe
     p. 317 HORACE 2       250 Mans comming yeares much good with them doe
                               bring:
     p. 317 HORACE 2       280 It still must favour good men, and to these
     p. 327 HORACE 2       470 He cries, Good boy, thou'lt keepe thine owne.
                               Now, adde
     p. 327 HORACE 2       489 Wild ra<n>ging lusts; prescribe the mariage good;
     p. 329 HORACE 2       535 Twice, or thrice good, I wonder: but am more
     p. 329 HORACE 2       536 Angry. Sometimes, I heare good Homer snore.
     p. 333 HORACE 2       611 For hee'll cry, Good, brave, better, excellent!
     p. 333 HORACE 2       624 Hee'd say, Mend this, good friend, and this;
                               'tis naught.
     p. 354 HORACE 1       633 . good ... ..... ... .... .... open .....
     p. 367 UNGATHERED 6    33 Be then both Rare, and Good; and long
     p. 372 UNGATHERED 9    14 Might make the Fable of Good Women true.
     p. 385 UNGATHERED 20    2 To see his worke be good; but that he looke
     p. 386 UNGATHERED 20   10 Was worthy of a Good one; And this, here,
     p. 386 UNGATHERED 21   13 Hold thyne owne worth vnbroke: which is so good
     p. 389 UNGATHERED 24    7 And hath the noblest marke of a good Booke,
     p. 392 UNGATHERED 26   64 For a good Poet's made, as well as borne.
     p. 394 UNGATHERED 28    5 Religious, wise, chast, louing, gratious, good;
     p. 400 UNGATHERED 31   30 Keeps warme the spice of her good name,
     p. 401 UNGATHERED 32   20 Defies, what's crosse to Piety, or good Fame.
     p. 403 UNGATHERED 34   21 Why much good doo't you! Be what beast you will,
     p. 403 UNGATHERED 34   28 Though gold or Iuory haftes would make it good.
     p. 405 UNGATHERED 34   68 Swim wthout Corke! Why, thank ye good Queen
                               Anne.
     p. 408 UNGATHERED 37    2 And they were very good: yet thou think'st nay.
     p. 409 UNGATHERED 38    5 And you doe doe them well, with good applause,
     p. 410 UNGATHERED 38   15 An honest Bilbo-Smith would make good blades,
     p. 411 UNGATHERED 40    6 to all good Nations.
     p. 415 UNGATHERED 43   t2 Good Freind Mr. Robert Dover, on his great
     p. 416 UNGATHERED 43    8 And doe both Church, and Common-wealth the
                               good,
     p. 417 UNGATHERED 45   39 at Pem Wakers good ale Tapp,
     p. 657 L. CONVIVALES   11 Those dull Girls, no good can mean us,
     p. 666 INSCRIPTS. 11   10 To make these good, and what comes after,
                               better./
```

good-night   frequency: 1   relative frequency: 0.00001
```
     p. 100 FOREST 4         1 False world, good-night: since thou hast brought
```

goodlier   frequency: 1   relative frequency: 0.00001
```
     p. 204 UNDERWOOD 43    32 And so some goodlier monster had begot:
```

goodnesse   frequency: 11   relative frequency: 0.00015
```
     p.  60 EPIGRAMS 93     10 And thine owne goodnesse to encrease thy merit,
     p. 101 FOREST 4        52 And euery goodnesse tax'd, or grieu'd.
     p. 112 FOREST 11       87 He that for loue of goodnesse hateth ill,
     p. 119 FOREST 13      109 Vnto your name, and goodnesse of your life,
     p. 185 UNDERWOOD 30    13 That still was good for goodnesse sake, nor
                               thought
     p. 191 UNDERWOOD 38    17 Spare your owne goodnesse yet; and be not great
     p. 236 UNDERWOOD 63     9 But thanke his greatnesse, and his goodnesse too;
     p. 260 UNDERWOOD 76    26 Of your .grace, for goodnesse sake,
     p. 273 U'WOOD 84.1      9 Of Goodnesse still: Vouchsafe to take
     p. 273 U'WOOD 84.1     10 This CRADLE, and for Goodnesse sake,
     p. 412 UNGATHERED 40   17 To follow Goodnesse,
```

goods   frequency: 1   relative frequency: 0.00001
```
     p.  41 EPIGRAMS 44      1 CHVFFE, lately rich in name, in chattels,
                               goods,
```

goody   frequency: 1   relative frequency: 0.00001
    p. 403 UNGATHERED 34   38 And Goody Sculpture, brought wth much adoe

goodyere   frequency: 3   relative frequency: 0.00004
    p. 55 EPIGRAMS 85   1 GOODYERE, I'am glad, and gratefull to
                             report,
    p. 55 EPIGRAMS 85   t1 TO SIR HENRY GOODYERE.
    p. 55 EPIGRAMS 86   1 When I would know thee GOODYERE, my
                             thought lookes

goose   frequency: 1   relative frequency: 0.00001
    p. 209 UNDERWOOD 43 142 That was rak'd up in the Winchestrian Goose

gorgon   frequency: 1   relative frequency: 0.00001
    p. 421 UNGATHERED 48   41 The Rebell Gyantes stoope, and Gorgon Envye
                             yeild,

gorgonian   frequency: 1   relative frequency: 0.00001
    p. 86 EPIGRAMS 133   69 Gorgonian scolds, and Harpyes: on the other

gossip   frequency: 1   relative frequency: 0.00001
    p. 363 UNGATHERED 3   11 It bends the hams of Gossip Vigilance,

gossip-got   frequency: 1   relative frequency: 0.00001
    p. 398 UNGATHERED 30   85 And Gossip-got acquaintance, as, to vs

gossipps   frequency: 1   relative frequency: 0.00001
    p. 417 UNGATHERED 45   37 Or if't be the Gossipps happ

gossips'. See "gossipps."

go'st   frequency: 1   relative frequency: 0.00001
    p. 205 UNDERWOOD 43   58 To make consumption, ever, where thou go'st;

got   frequency: 26   relative frequency: 0.00037
    See also "gossip-got," "gott."
  **p. 116 PANEGYRE   118 Who once haue got the habit to doe ill.
    p. 31 EPIGRAMS 13   3 Let me giue two: that doubly am got free,
    p. 40 EPIGRAMS 42   7 And hauing got him out of doores is glad.
    p. 57 EPIGRAMS 90   15 Hath got the stewards chaire; he will not tarry
    p. 63 EPIGRAMS 97   16 When he was here. Nor hath he got a sute,
    p. 63 EPIGRAMS 98   12 And euer is ill got without the first.
    p. 84 EPIGRAMS 133   5 We haue a SHELTON, and a HEYDEN got,
    p. 87 EPIGRAMS 133 114 The well-greas'd wherry now had got betweene,
    p. 93 FOREST 1   9 Into my ri'mes could ne're be got
    p. 115 FOREST 12   68 Who, though shee haue a better verser got,
    p. 157 UNDERWOOD 13 151 But few and faire Divisions: but being got
    p. 166 UNDERWOOD 15 142 Is that the truer excuse? or have we got
    p. 188 UNDERWOOD 34   11 Or Turners oyle of Talck. Nor ever got
    p. 200 UNDERWOOD 42   22 Wish, you had fowle ones, and deformed got;
    p. 234 UNDERWOOD 60   10 Of Vertue, got above his name?
    p. 234 UNDERWOOD 61   7 Yet are got off thence, with cleare mind, and
                             hands
    p. 234 UNDERWOOD 61   12 A Nations sinne got pardon'd! 'twere a taske
    p. 240 UNDERWOOD 67   36 Had got the Ceston on!
    p. 242 UNDERWOOD 70   6 E're thou wert halfe got out,
    p. 244 UNDERWOOD 70   34 Got up and thriv'd with honest arts:
    p. 247 UNDERWOOD 70 128 Had sow'd these fruits, and got the harvest in.
    p. 278 U'WOOD 84.4   28 'Tis got where it can try the fire.
    p. 295 UNDERWOOD 90   2 Most pleasant Martial; Substance got with ease,
    p. 323 HORACE 2   395 'Tis cleare, this way I have got off from blame,
    p. 396 UNGATHERED 30   18 Is fayre got vp, and day some houres begun!
    p. 409 UNGATHERED 38   3 Now, you are got into a nearer roome,

gott   frequency: 1   relative frequency: 0.00001
    p. 420 UNGATHERED 48   10 Butt, Clownishe pride hath gott

gotten   frequency: 1   relative frequency: 0.00001
    See also "onely-gotten."
    p. 164 UNDERWOOD 15   71 As if a Brize were gotten i' their tayle;

gout   frequency: 1   relative frequency: 0.00001
    p. 36 EPIGRAMS 31   1 BANCK feeles no lamenesse of his knottie
                             gout,

govern. See "joverne."

joverne   frequency: 1   relative frequency: 0.00001
    p. 136 UNDERWOOD 2.5   3 And doe governe more my blood,

governing   frequency: 1   relative frequency: 0.00001
    p. 415 UNGATHERED 42   25 For order, and for governing the pixe,

gown. See "gowne."

gown'd   frequency: 1   relative frequency: 0.00001
    p. 295 UNDERWOOD 90   5 Never at Law; seldome in office gown'd;

gowne   frequency: 8   relative frequency: 0.00011
    p. 200 UNDERWOOD 42   38 Upon a Velvet Petticote, or a Gowne,
    p. 201 UNDERWOOD 42   46 A Gowne of that, was the Caparison?
    p. 201 UNDERWOOD 42   57 Court every hanging Gowne, and after that,
    p. 201 UNDERWOOD 42   69 Commended the French-hood, and Scarlet gowne
    p. 203 UNDERWOOD 43   24 Or taxe the Glories of the Church, and Gowne?
    p. 217 UNDERWOOD 46   1 He that should search all Glories of the Gowne,
    p. 237 UNDERWOOD 64   20 Is Banke-rupt turn'd! the Cassock, Cloake, and
                             Gowne,
    p. 319 HORACE 2   305 In his train'd Gowne about the Stage: So grew

gowned   frequency: 2   relative frequency: 0.00002
    See also "gown'd."
    p. 187 UNDERWOOD 33   9 Hook-handed Harpies, gowned Vultures, put
    p. 323 HORACE 2   410 Or 'twere the gowned Comoedy they taught.

gownes   frequency: 1   relative frequency: 0.00001
    p. 222 UNDERWOOD 49   18 What though she be with Velvet gownes indu'd,

gowns. See "gownes."

grac'd   frequency: 1   relative frequency: 0.00001
    p. 112 FOREST 11   92 Grac'd with a Phoenix loue;

grace   frequency: 59   relative frequency: 0.00085
  **p. 113 PANEGYRE   26 On earth, till now, they came to grace his
                             throne.
    p. 28 EPIGRAMS 4   10 Of Kings for grace; of Poets for my test?
    p. 35 EPIGRAMS 28   8 And, can forget mens names, with a great grace.
    p. 45 EPIGRAMS 58   3 For offring, with thy smiles, my wit to grace,
    p. 60 EPIGRAMS 94   3 If workes (not th'authors) their owne grace
                             should looke,
    p. 64 EPIGRAMS 101   5 With those that come; whose grace may make that
                             seeme
    p. 67 EPIGRAMS 104   2 Euen in the dew of grace, what you would bee?
    p. 67 EPIGRAMS 105   4 Least mention of a Nymph, a Muse, a Grace,
    p. 77 EPIGRAMS 120   6 In grace, and feature,
    p. 98 FOREST 3   55 Thy noblest spouse affords them welcome grace;
    p. 113 FOREST 12   15 While thus it buyes great grace, and hunts poore
                             fame;
    p. 114 FOREST 12   30 With you, I know, my offring will find grace.
    p. 115 FOREST 12   79 Then all, that haue but done my Muse least
                             grace,
    p. 116 FOREST 12   95 For that firme grace he holdes in your regard,
    p. 122 FOREST 15   8 To ought but grace, or ayme at other end.
    p. 128 UNDERWOOD 1.1 28 For acts of grace.
    p. 128 UNDERWOOD 1.1 43 With grace, with love, with cherishing intire:
    p. 131 UNDERWOOD 2.1   8 Clothes, or Fortune gives the grace;
    p. 134 UNDERWOOD 2.4 17 And from her arched browes, such a grace
    p. 137 UNDERWOOD 2.5 51 Outward Grace weake love beguiles:
    p. 138 UNDERWOOD 2.6 20 To no other Grace but you!
    p. 144 UNDERWOOD 3   27 So they in state of Grace retain'd,
    p. 153 UNDERWOOD 13   24 Where any Deed is forc't, the Grace is mard.
    p. 159 UNDERWOOD 14   35 Which Grace shall I make love to first? your
                             skill,
    p. 191 UNDERWOOD 38   28 The Subject of your Grace in pardoning me,
    p. 198 UNDERWOOD 40   24 As if that ex'lent Dulnesse were Loves grace;
    p. 198 UNDERWOOD 40   31 They may say Grace, and for Loves Chaplaines
                             passe;
    p. 207 UNDERWOOD 43 107 I now begin to doubt, if ever Grace,
    p. 223 UNDERWOOD 49   34 To his poore Instrument, now out of grace.
    p. 223 UNDERWOOD 49   44 Both for the Mothers, and the Babes of grace,
    p. 235 UNDERWOOD 62   1 Great CHARLES, among the holy gifts of
                             grace
    p. 236 UNDERWOOD 63   14 Cannot but heape that grace, he will requite.
    p. 238 UNDERWOOD 66   1 Haile Mary, full of grace, it once was said,
    p. 249 UNDERWOOD 72   15 Had they but grace, of thinking, at these routes,
    p. 255 UNDERWOOD 75   89 It is their Grace, and favour, that makes seene,
    p. 256 UNDERWOOD 75 131 To have thy God to blesse, thy King to grace,
    p. 257 UNDERWOOD 75 158 We pray may grace
    p. 259 UNDERWOOD 76   7 Of his speciall grace to Letters,
    p. 260 UNDERWOOD 76   26 Of your grace, for goodnesse sake,

grace (cont.)
```
  p. 264 UNDERWOOD 79    32 Nymp. Of brightest MIRA, is our Song; the
                            grace
  p. 279 U'WOOD 84.4     35 Of grace, and Musique to the eare,
  p. 286 U'WOOD 84.9    131 By light, and comfort of spirituall Grace,
  p. 286 U'WOOD 84.9    140 Adopt us Heires, by grace, who were of those
  p. 288 U'WOOD 84.9    190 The doore of Grace, and found the Mercy-Seat.
  p. 288 U'WOOD 84.9    198 By sure Election, and predestin'd grace!
  p. 292 UNDERWOOD 86    17 And when he smiling finds his Grace
  p. 307 HORACE 2       59 The vertue of which order, and true grace,
  p. 309 HORACE 2       72 Of the Cethegi; And all men will grace,
  p. 309 HORACE 2      100 Or grace of speech, should hope a lasting date.
  p. 309 HORACE 2      113 Unto the Lyrick Strings, the Muse gave grace
  p. 321 HORACE 2      353 Of Order, and Connexion; so much grace
  p. 327 HORACE 2      456 A Poeme, of no grace, weight, art, in rimes,
  p. 329 HORACE 2      497 All way of life was shewen; the grace of Kings
  p. 369 UNGATHERED 6  103 With more delight, and grace)
  p. 384 UNGATHERED 18   2 And clothes, and guifts, that only do thee grace
  p. 393 UNGATHERED 27   7 And spirit of that speciall Grace,
  p. 412 UNGATHERED 41   8 As Love, here studied to keep Grace alive.
  p. 419 UNGATHERED 48   5 By Cherissheinge the Spirrites yt gaue their
                            greatnesse grace:
  p. 420 UNGATHERED 48  27 And in this Age, canst hope no <other> grace.
```

graced   frequency: 2   relative frequency: 0.00002
See also "grac'd," "well-grac'd."
```
  p. 177 UNDERWOOD 25    17 Graced by your Reflection!
  p. 402 UNGATHERED 33   13 And, graced with her song,
```

gracefull   frequency: 1   relative frequency: 0.00001
```
  p. 253 UNDERWOOD 75    40 In gracefull Ornament of Garland, Gemmes, and
                            Haire.
```

graces   frequency: 24   relative frequency: 0.00034
```
  p.  57 EPIGRAMS 89     9 Who both their graces in thy selfe hast more
  p.  58 EPIGRAMS 91    13 I speake thy other graces, not lesse showne,
  p.  61 EPIGRAMS 95    27 We need a man that knowes the seuerall graces
  p.  68 EPIGRAMS 105   12 Were leading forth the Graces on the greene:
  p.  79 EPIGRAMS 125    8 The full, the flowing graces there enshrin'd;
  p. 138 UNDERWOOD 2.6  26 As might all the Graces lead,
  p. 158 UNDERWOOD 14    4 Truth, and the Graces best, when naked are.
  p. 179 UNDERWOOD 25   60 With lustrous Graces,
  p. 181 UNDERWOOD 27   10 Or Delia's Graces, by Tibullus?
  p. 182 UNDERWOOD 28    6 To those true numerous Graces; whereof some,
  p. 191 UNDERWOOD 38   16 Of Graces, or your mercie here in me,
  p. 221 UNDERWOOD 48   33 But Venus and the Graces
  p. 225 UNDERWOOD 50   31 These Graces, when the rest of Ladyes view
  p. 230 UNDERWOOD 56   20 And can for other Graces her commend,
  p. 251 UNDERWOOD 74   16 Doth show, the Graces, and the Houres,
  p. 270 UNDERWOOD 83   36 From the inherent Graces in her blood!
  p. 274 U'WOOD 84.2    10 Meeting of Graces, that so swell'd the flood
  p. 365 UNGATHERED 5   21 Retire, and say; Her Graces
  p. 371 UNGATHERED 9    6 She might haue claym'd t'have made the Graces
                            foure;
  p. 413 UNGATHERED 41  26 (Divinest graces) are so entermixt,
  p. 413 UNGATHERED 41  31 All, pouring their full showre of graces downe,
  p. 413 UNGATHERED 41  36 How are thy gifts, and graces blaz'd abroad!
  p. 414 UNGATHERED 41  53 How are thy gifts and graces blaz'd abro'd,
  p. 416 UNGATHERED 44   4 Now, in a garland by the graces knit:
```

gracious   frequency: 2   relative frequency: 0.00002
See also "all-gracious," "gratious."
```
  p.  37 EPIGRAMS 33     5 Which if most gracious heauen grant like thine,
  p. 169 UNDERWOOD 18    5 Or was she gracious a-farre off? but neere
```

graffs   frequency: 1   relative frequency: 0.00001
```
  p. 361 UNGATHERED 1    1 When late (graue Palmer) these thy graffs and
                            flowers
```

graft   frequency: 1   relative frequency: 0.00001
```
  p. 251 UNDERWOOD 74   27 When he beholds a graft of his owne hand,
```

grafted   frequency: 1   relative frequency: 0.00001
```
  p. 290 UNDERWOOD 85   19 How plucking Peares, his owne hand grafted had,
```

grafts. See "graffs."

grain. See "graine."

graine   frequency: 1   relative frequency: 0.00001
    p. 309 HORACE 2   97 His course so hurtfull both to graine, and
                           seedes,

graines   frequency: 1   relative frequency: 0.00001
   *p. 492 TO HIMSELF   17 No, giue them graines their fill,

grains. See "graines."

grammar   frequency: 1   relative frequency: 0.00001
    p. 207 UNDERWOOD 43 91 Was there mad<e> English: with a Grammar too,

grammarians   frequency: 1   relative frequency: 0.00001
    p. 309 HORACE 2   111 All the Grammarians strive; and yet in Court

grampius   frequency: 1   relative frequency: 0.00001
    p. 368 UNGATHERED 6 71 And ouer Grampius mountaine,

granats   frequency: 1   relative frequency: 0.00001
    p. 212 UNDERWOOD 43 206 Make your Petards, and Granats, all your fine

grand   frequency: 6   relative frequency: 0.00008
    p. 51 EPIGRAMS 73   1 What is't, fine GRAND, makes thee my
                            friendship flye,
    p. 51 EPIGRAMS 73   5 In-primis, GRAND, you owe me for a iest,
    p. 51 EPIGRAMS 73 t1 TO FINE GRAND.
    p. 51 EPIGRAMS 73 21 Fortie things more, deare GRAND, which you
                            know true,
    p. 113 FOREST 12   12 Of some grand peere, whose ayre doth make reioyce
    p. 274 U'WOOD 84.2   9 Run from your rootes; Tell, testifie the grand

grand=children   frequency: 1   relative frequency: 0.00001
    p. 399 UNGATHERED 31 2 Her Children, and Grand=children, reed it
                            heere!

grand-child   frequency: 2   relative frequency: 0.00002
    p. 121 FOREST 14   42 Whose nephew, whose grand-child you are;
    p. 269 UNDERWOOD 83 21 Earle Rivers Grand-Child -- serve not formes,
                            good Fame,

grand-dames   frequency: 1   relative frequency: 0.00001
    p. 258 UNDERWOOD 75 172 A Kate, a Frank, to honour their Grand-dames,

grandees   frequency: 1   relative frequency: 0.00001
    p. 254 UNDERWOOD 75 73 Our Court, and all the Grandees; now, Sun,
                            looke,

grandlings   frequency: 1   relative frequency: 0.00001
    p. 215 UNDERWOOD 44 64 From the Tempestuous Grandlings, Who'll
                            informe

grandsires   frequency: 2   relative frequency: 0.00002
    p. 258 UNDERWOOD 75 173 And 'tweene their Grandsires thighes,
    p. 268 UNDERWOOD 82 12 As in renewing thy good Grandsires fame;

grant   frequency: 6   relative frequency: 0.00008
    p. 37 EPIGRAMS 33   5 Which if most gracious heauen grant like thine,
    p. 39 EPIGRAMS 40   4 Grant then, no rude hand remoue her.
    p. 55 EPIGRAMS 84   9 O Madame, if your grant did thus transferre mee,
    p. 104 FOREST 7   10 But grant vs perfect, they're not knowne.
    p. 128 UNDERWOOD 1.1 36 O grant it me!
    p. 241 UNDERWOOD 68 5 Well, they should know him, would the K<ing> but
                            grant

grape   frequency: 1   relative frequency: 0.00001
    p. 94 FOREST 2   42 Fig, grape, and quince, each in his time doth
                            come:

grapes   frequency: 3   relative frequency: 0.00004
    p. 290 UNDERWOOD 85 20 And purple-matching Grapes, hee's glad!
    p. 375 UNGATHERED 10 25 For Grapes he had gather'd before they were
                            eaten.
    p. 380 UNGATHERED 12 36 For grapes he had gather'd, before they were
                            eaten.

graphic. See "graphick."

graphick   frequency: 1   relative frequency: 0.00001
    p. 287 U'WOOD 84.9 154 Each line, as it were graphick, in the face!

grass. See "grasse."

grasse   frequency: 3   relative frequency: 0.00004
    p. 103 FOREST 6   13 All the grasse that Rumney yeelds,
    p. 265 UNDERWOOD 79   59 The better grasse, and flowers are found.
    p. 290 UNDERWOOD 85   24 Now in the rooted Grasse him lay,

grassie   frequency: 1   relative frequency: 0.00001
    p. 398 UNGATHERED 30   82 And with their grassie greene restor'd mine eyes.

grassy. See "grassie."

gratefull   frequency: 3   relative frequency: 0.00004
    p.   55 EPIGRAMS 85   1 GOODYERE, I'am glad, and gratefull to
                               report,
    p. 115 FOREST 12   73 My gratefull soule, the subiect of her powers,
    p. 116 FOREST 12   96 I, that am gratefull for him, haue prepar'd

grates   frequency: 1   relative frequency: 0.00001
    p. 337 HORACE 2   675 To force the grates, that hold him in, would
                               fright

gratious   frequency: 2   relative frequency: 0.00002
    p. 383 UNGATHERED 16. 11 Except your Gratious Eye as through a Glass
    p. 394 UNGATHERED 28   5 Religious, wise, chast, louing, gratious, good:

gratitude   frequency: 2   relative frequency: 0.00002
    p.   80 EPIGRAMS 127   2 If I should faile, in gratitude, to thee,
    p. 237 UNDERWOOD 64   16 That nothing can her gratitude provoke!

gratuitie   frequency: 1   relative frequency: 0.00001
    p. 259 UNDERWOOD 76   12 To be given me in gratuitie

gratuity. See "gratuitie."

gratulate   frequency: 6   relative frequency: 0.00008
  **p. 116 PANEGYRE   132 From out the stones, to gratulate the king.
    p.   43 EPIGRAMS 51   6 Who this thy scape from rumour gratulate,
    p.   48 EPIGRAMS 64   17 That whil'st I meant but thine to gratulate,
    p.   61 EPIGRAMS 95   10 And gratulate the breach, I grieu'd before:
    p. 161 UNDERWOOD 14   67 I first salute thee so; and gratulate,
    p. 398 UNGATHERED 30   89 I gratulate it to thee, and thy Ends,

gratulates   frequency: 1   relative frequency: 0.00001
    p. 221 UNDERWOOD 48   45 Or gratulates the passage

gratulatorie   frequency: 1   relative frequency: 0.00001
    p. 250 UNDERWOOD 74   t2 An Ode gratulatorie,

gratulatory. See "gratulatorie."

graue   frequency: 16   relative frequency: 0.00023
    p.   30 EPIGRAMS 11   2 To be a courtier; and lookes graue enough,
    p.   31 EPIGRAMS 14   5 Then thee the age sees not that thing more graue,
    p.   34 EPIGRAMS 22   11 This graue partakes the fleshly birth.
    p.   37 EPIGRAMS 33   6 Who wets my graue, can be no friend of mine.
    p.   56 EPIGRAMS 89   3 As skilfull ROSCIVS, and graue
                               AESOPE, men,
    p.   58 EPIGRAMS 91   12 Against my graue, and time could not forgiue.
    p.   59 EPIGRAMS 92   7 And graue as ripe, like mellow as their faces.
    p.   64 EPIGRAMS 101   1 To night, graue sir, both my poore house, and I
    p.   81 EPIGRAMS 129   11 Whil'st thou dost rayse some Player, from the
                               graue,
    p.   87 EPIGRAMS 133   108 Of the graue fart, late let in parliament,
    p.   88 EPIGRAMS 133   157 Graue tutor to the learned horse. Both which,
    p. 113 FOREST 12   5 Toyles, by graue custome, vp and downe the court,
    p. 361 UNGATHERED 1   1 When late (graue Palmer) these thy graffs and
                               flowers
    p. 363 UNGATHERED 3   2 Seldome descend but bleeding to their graue.
    p. 394 UNGATHERED 28   1 I could begin with that graue forme, Here lies,
    p. 400 UNGATHERED 31   28 Fames heate vpon the graue did stay;

grauell   frequency: 1   relative frequency: 0.00001
    p. 375 UNGATHERED 10   26 Old Hat here, torne Hose, with Shoes full of
                               grauell,

grauer   frequency: 1   relative frequency: 0.00001
    p. 390 UNGATHERED 25   3 Wherein the Grauer had a strife

graues   frequency: 2   relative frequency: 0.00002
    p. 114 FOREST 12   47 That bred them, graues: when they were borne,
                               they di'd,

graues (cont.)
   p. 121 FOREST 14   40 With dust of ancestors, in graues but dwell.

grave   frequency: 17   relative frequency: 0.00024
  See also "graue."
   p. 143 UNDERWOOD 3   14 Sleepe, and the Grave will wake.
   p. 151 UNDERWOOD 12   6 Of him whose bones this Grave doth gather:
   p. 152 UNDERWOOD 12   23 They were so even, grave, and holy;
   p. 162 UNDERWOOD 15   19 See the grave, sower, and supercilious Sir
   p. 172 UNDERWOOD 21   4 Out of his Grave, and poyson every eare.
   p. 175 UNDERWOOD 24   2 The Mistresse of Mans life, grave Historie,
   p. 185 UNDERWOOD 30   5 Cecill, the grave, the wise, the great, the good,
   p. 192 UNDERWOOD 38   59 That were to wither all, and make a Grave
   p. 194 UNDERWOOD 38   122 Rather then want your light, I wish a grave.
   p. 198 UNDERWOOD 40   32 But the grave Lover ever was an Asse;
   p. 225 UNDERWOOD 51   9 Sonne to the grave wise Keeper of the Seale,
   p. 305 HORACE 2   17 In grave beginnings, and great things profest,
   p. 311 HORACE 2   118 This foot the socks tooke up, and buskins grave,
   p. 319 HORACE 2   318 Loftie, and grave; and in the buskin stalke.
   p. 329 HORACE 2   511 The Poems void of profit, our grave men
   p. 335 HORACE 2   671 Whether he piss'd upon his Fathers grave;
   p. 346 HORACE 1   306 .. the grave Harp, and Violl voyces ...

gravel. See "grauell."

graver. See "grauer."

graves. See "graues."

gravitie   frequency: 1   relative frequency: 0.00001
   p. 319 HORACE 2   322 Though sower, with safetie of his gravitie,

gravity. See "gravitie."

gray   frequency: 4   relative frequency: 0.00005
   p.   88 EPIGRAMS 133   161 With great gray eyes, are lifted vp, and mew'd;
   p. 150 UNDERWOOD 9   14 My hundred of gray haires,
   p. 168 UNDERWOOD 16   4 All that is left of PHILIP GRAY,
   p. 168 UNDERWOOD 16   t2 PHILIP GRAY.

grazing   frequency: 1   relative frequency: 0.00001
   p. 290 UNDERWOOD 85   14 The lowing herds there grazing are:

grea<t>est   frequency: 1   relative frequency: 0.00001
   p. 363 UNGATHERED 3   3 Warres grea<t>est woes, and miseries increase,

greace   frequency: 1   relative frequency: 0.00001
   p.   38 EPIGRAMS 37   3 And pleaseth both. For while he melts his greace

grease   frequency: 2   relative frequency: 0.00002
  See also "greace."
   p.   88 EPIGRAMS 133   145 The sinkes ran grease, and haire of meazled hogs,
   p. 418 UNGATHERED 45   41 Or by chance if in their grease

greased. See "well-greas'd."

great   frequency: 157   relative frequency: 0.00227
  See also "greate."
**p. 114 PANEGYRE   55 To her great sister: saue that modestie,
**p. 117 PANEGYRE   149 Of his great actions, first to see, and do
   p.   29 EPIGRAMS 6   1 If all you boast of your great art be true;
   p.   30 EPIGRAMS 11   4 It made me a great face, I ask'd the name.
   p.   31 EPIGRAMS 14   4 The great renowne, and name wherewith shee goes.
   p.   35 EPIGRAMS 28   2 Of a great man, and to be thought the same,
   p.   35 EPIGRAMS 28   3 Makes serious vse of all great trade he knowes.
   p.   35 EPIGRAMS 28   5 Which hee thinkes great; and so reades verses,
                                 too:
   p.   35 EPIGRAMS 28   6 And, that is done, as he saw great men doe.
   p.   35 EPIGRAMS 28   8 And, can forget mens names, with a great grace.
   p.   35 EPIGRAMS 28   10 Both which are great. And laugh at ill-made
                                 clothes;
   p.   36 EPIGRAMS 28   18 That breathes in his dogs way: and this is great.
   p.   36 EPIGRAMS 28   22 Stile thee a most great foole, but no great man.
   p.   40 EPIGRAMS 43   5 'Tofore, great men were glad of Poets: Now,
   p.   43 EPIGRAMS 51   2 Great heau'n did well, to giue ill fame free
                                 wing;
   p.   46 EPIGRAMS 60   5 I, that am glad of thy great chance, here doo!
   p.   46 EPIGRAMS 60   7 Durst thinke it great, and worthy wonder too,
   p.   46 EPIGRAMS 62   11 In a great belly. Write, then on thy wombe,
   p.   48 EPIGRAMS 65   4 To a great image through thy luxurie.

great (cont.)

p.	48	EPIGRAMS 66	4	In onely thee, might be both great, and glad.
p.	49	EPIGRAMS 66	11	Loue thy great losse, which a renowne hath wonne,
p.	52	EPIGRAMS 76	6	Of greatest bloud, and yet more good then great;
p.	56	EPIGRAMS 89	1	If Rome so great, and in her wisest age,
p.	57	EPIGRAMS 89	7	How can so great example dye in mee,
p.	58	EPIGRAMS 91	16	As noble in great chiefes, as they are rare.
p.	60	EPIGRAMS 93	2	For the great marke of vertue, those being gone
p.	60	EPIGRAMS 93	7	And two, that would haue falne as great, as they,
p.	61	EPIGRAMS 95	17	For who can master those great parts like thee,
p.	61	EPIGRAMS 95	26	It is the next deed, and a great one too.
p.	62	EPIGRAMS 96	12	A man should seeke great glorie, and not broad.
p.	64	EPIGRAMS 99	5	How much of great example wert thou, ROE,
p.	64	EPIGRAMS 99	11	Well, though thy name lesse then our great ones bee,
p.	66	EPIGRAMS 102	6	Of vice, and vertue; wherein all great life
p.	66	EPIGRAMS 103	7	Which is, it selfe, the imprese of the great,
p.	68	EPIGRAMS 107	6	How great you were with their two Emperours;
p.	70	EPIGRAMS 108	6	Your great profession; which I once, did proue:
p.	72	EPIGRAMS 111	13	By thy great helpe: and doth proclaime by mee,
p.	73	EPIGRAMS 113	4	Where, what makes others great, doth keepe thee good!
p.	75	EPIGRAMS 116	12	And to liue great, was better, then great borne.
p.	78	EPIGRAMS 121	1	RVDYERD, as lesser dames, to great ones vse,
p.	81	EPIGRAMS 129	9	Think'st thou, MIME, this is great? or, that they striue
p.	83	EPIGRAMS 132	5	How can I speake of thy great paines, but erre?
p.	85	EPIGRAMS 133	55	Great Club-fist, though thy backe, and bones be sore,
p.	88	EPIGRAMS 133	161	With great gray eyes, are lifted vp, and mew'd;
p.	89	EPIGRAMS 133	180	And MADAME CAESAR, great PROSERPINA,
p.	94	FOREST 2	14	At his great birth, where all the Muses met.
p.	95	FOREST 2	66	At great mens tables) and yet dine away.
p.	95	FOREST 2	82	What (great, I will not say, but) sodayne cheare
p.	96	FOREST 2	91	His children thy great lord may call his owne:
p.	96	FOREST 3	5	That at great times, art no ambitious guest
p.	98	FOREST 3	56	And the great Heroes, of her race,
p.	99	FOREST 3	86	By being organes to great sinne,
p.	99	FOREST 3	90	Though poyson, thinke it a great fate.
p.	107	FOREST 10	2	Or whose great name in Poets heauen vse,
p.	109	FOREST 11	24	Or some great thought doth keepe
p.	113	FOREST 12	15	While thus it buyes great grace, and hunts poore fame;
p.	114	FOREST 12	31	For what a sinne 'gainst your great fathers spirit,
p.	118	FOREST 13	49	Of so great title, birth, but vertue most,
p.	118	FOREST 13	52	For he, that once is good, is euer great.
p.	119	FOREST 13	105	T<o>'expect the honors of great 'AVBIGNY:
p.	119	FOREST 13	111	Other great wiues may blush at: when they see
p.	121	FOREST 14	35	And great, must seeke for new,
p.	122	FOREST 15	1	Good, and great GOD, can I not thinke of thee,
p.	142	U'WOOD 2.10	3	Let his Title be but great,
p.	153	UNDERWOOD 13	2	Great and good turns, as wel could time them too,
p.	155	UNDERWOOD 13	76	Of any, is a great and generous Deed:
p.	156	UNDERWOOD 13	124	Men have beene great, but never good by chance,
p.	158	UNDERWOOD 13	161	May grow so great to be example, when
p.	161	UNDERWOOD 14	69	In offering this thy worke to no great Name,
p.	164	UNDERWOOD 15	84	Great, brave, and fashion'd folke, these are allow'd
p.	165	UNDERWOOD 15	97	Whom no great Mistresse hath as yet infam'd,
p.	168	UNDERWOOD 15	187	That thou thinke nothing great, but what is good,
p.	174	UNDERWOOD 23	16	Minds that are great and free,
p.	176	UNDERWOOD 24	6	Might be defrauded, nor the great secur'd,
p.	181	UNDERWOOD 27	25	Hath our great Sydney, Stella set,
p.	185	UNDERWOOD 30	5	Cecill, the grave, the wise, the great, the good,
p.	186	UNDERWOOD 32	7	Such shall you heare to day, and find great foes,
p.	186	UNDERWOOD 33	3	Or the great Hall at Westminster, the field
p.	191	UNDERWOOD 38	17	Spare your owne goodnesse yet; and be not great
p.	213	UNDERWOOD 44	7	That we have Trumpets, Armour, and great Horse,
p.	214	UNDERWOOD 44	57	And could (if our great men would let their Sonnes
p.	215	UNDERWOOD 44	69	Why are we rich, or great, except to show
p.	220	UNDERWOOD 47	66	As are the Glorious Scenes, at the great sights;
p.	220	UNDERWOOD 48	8	Of all to the great Master.
p.	221	UNDERWOOD 48	44	In great Saint Georges Union;

great (cont.)

p. 224	UNDERWOOD 50	19	So great a Vertue stand upright to view,
p. 224	UNDERWOOD 50	24	Then the great Homers wit, for her, could faine;
p. 227	UNDERWOOD 52	12	With one great blot, yo'had form'd me as I am.
p. 233	UNDERWOOD 59	21	Who durst live great, 'mongst all the colds, and heates,
p. 234	UNDERWOOD 60	17	And only, his great Soule envy'd,
p. 235	UNDERWOOD 62	1	Great CHARLES, among the holy gifts of grace
p. 236	UNDERWOOD 64	7	Indeed, when had great Britaine greater cause
p. 236	UNDERWOOD 64	t2	To our great and good K. CHARLES
p. 237	UNDERWOOD 64	22	How much to heaven for thee, great CHARLES, they owe!
p. 238	UNDERWOOD 65	11	And threat' the great Eclipse. Two houres but runne,
p. 238	UNDERWOOD 66	12	To compare small with great, as still we owe
p. 240	UNDERWOOD 67	26	The Daughter of great Harry!
p. 242	UNDERWOOD 69	25	Never so great to get them: and the ends,
p. 242	UNDERWOOD 70	2	Thy comming forth in that great yeare,
p. 245	UNDERWOOD 70	59	Not liv'd; for Life doth her great actions spell,
p. 247	UNDERWOOD 70	113	You liv'd to be the great surnames,
p. 249	UNDERWOOD 72	6	Repeating all Great Britain's joy, and more,
p. 249	UNDERWOOD 72	9	What Drums or Trumpets, or great Ord'nance can,
p. 249	UNDERWOOD 72	19	The wish is great; but where the Prince is such,
p. 250	UNDERWOOD 73	3	In his great Actions: view whom his large hand
p. 251	UNDERWOOD 74	26	To see great Charles of Travaile eas'd,
p. 255	UNDERWOOD 75	99	Great Say-Master of State, who cannot erre,
p. 258	UNDERWOOD 75	184	So great; his Body now alone projects the shade.
p. 260	UNDERWOOD 77	1	If to my mind, great Lord, I had a state,
p. 264	UNDERWOOD 79	14	1. PAN is the great Preserver of our bounds.
p. 264	UNDERWOOD 79	30	To better Pastures then great PALES can:
p. 265	UNDERWOOD 79	43	PAN only our great Shep'ard is,
p. 265	UNDERWOOD 79	44	Chorus Our great, our good. Where one's so drest
p. 265	UNDERWOOD 79	48	This is the great Preserver of our bounds,
p. 265	UNDERWOOD 79	65	This only the great Shep'ard is.
p. 268	UNDERWOOD 82	2	Great King, thy having of a second Sonne:
p. 268	UNDERWOOD 82	6	Great aides to Empire, as they are great care
p. 268	UNDERWOOD 82	13	Me thought, Great Britaine in her Sea, before,
p. 269	UNDERWOOD 83	10	Whose Daughter? ha? Great Savage of the Rock?
p. 269	UNDERWOOD 83	11	Hee's good, as great. I am almost a stone!
p. 269	UNDERWOOD 83	33	What she did here, by great example, well,
p. 271	UNDERWOOD 83	89	The Sunne! great Kings, and mightiest Kingdomes fall!
p. 272	U'WOOD 84.1	2	With ever-greene, and great renowne,
p. 282	U'WOOD 84.9	4	All that was good, or great in me she weav'd,
p. 284	U'WOOD 84.9	58	Of that great Evidence, the Conscience!
p. 284	U'WOOD 84.9	63	That great eternall Holy-day of rest,
p. 285	U'WOOD 84.9	90	A new Song to his praise, and great I AM:
p. 286	U'WOOD 84.9	129	That holy, great, and glorious Mysterie,
p. 288	U'WOOD 84.9	215	In that great Act of judgement: which the Father
p. 289	UNDERWOOD 85	8	And waiting Chambers of great Lords.
p. 290	UNDERWOOD 85	38	Loves cares so evil, and so great?
p. 305	HORACE 2	17	In grave beginnings, and great things profest,
p. 305	HORACE 2	28	The whole fleet wreck'd? A great jarre to be shap'd,
p. 309	HORACE 2	105	The gests of Kings, great Captaines, and sad Warres,
p. 313	HORACE 2	164	Where some great Lady, or her diligent Nourse;
p. 317	HORACE 2	245	A great deferrer, long in hope, growne numbe
p. 325	HORACE 2	422	In Helicon; a great sort will not pare
p. 327	HORACE 2	493	Next these great Homer and Tyrtaeus set
p. 333	HORACE 2	594	An admirable Verse. The great Scurfe take
p. 333	HORACE 2	600	Or great in money's out at use, command
p. 333	HORACE 2	602	Make a great Supper; or for some poore man
p. 343	HORACE 1	197	.... great ....
p. 348	HORACE 1	398	.... great ... . walk
p. 354	HORACE 1	617	Great ... ...
p. 384	UNGATHERED 18	8	And pray, thy ioyes as lasting bee, as great.
p. 391	UNGATHERED 26	26	I meane with great, but disproportion'd Muses:
p. 394	UNGATHERED 28	15	At least so great a Lady. She was wife
p. 395	UNGATHERED 29	22	In the great masse, or machine there is stirr'd?
p. 400	UNGATHERED 31	35	Aeternities great charter; which became
p. 412	UNGATHERED 40	19	Our great reward,
p. 413	UNGATHERED 41	29	These Mysteries do point to three more great,
p. 414	UNGATHERED 41	41	Great Queen of Queens, most mild, most meek, most wise,

great (cont.)
    p. 415 UNGATHERED 43   t2 Good Freind Mr. Robert Dover, on his great
    p. 416 UNGATHERED 44   7 To Crowne the years, which you begin, great
                                  king,

great-mens   frequency: 1   relative frequency: 0.00001
    p. 114 FOREST 12   45 Painted, or caru'd vpon our great-mens tombs,

greate   frequency: 2   relative frequency: 0.00002
    p. 394 UNGATHERED 28   3 To see (who'it is?) A noble Countesse, greate,
    p. 419 UNGATHERED 48   3 As when they both were greate, and both knewe
                                howe

greater   frequency: 15   relative frequency: 0.00021
**p. 117 PANEGYRE   144 Those greater bodies of the sky, that strike
**p. 117 PANEGYRE   147 Though many greater: and the most, the best.
    p. 29 EPIGRAMS 8   6 The courtier is become the greater thiefe.
    p. 35 EPIGRAMS 28   11 That's greater, yet: to crie his owne vp neate.
    p. 48 EPIGRAMS 64   18 I'haue sung the greater fortunes of our state.
    p. 84 EPIGRAMS 133   26 But, in the action, greater man then hee:
    p. 119 FOREST 13   106 And greater rites, yet writ in mysterie,
    p. 140 UNDERWOOD 2.9   4 Noble; or of greater Blood:
    p. 169 UNDERWOOD 17   8 But that some greater names have broke with me,
    p. 214 UNDERWOOD 44   39 Were now the greater Captaine? for they saw
    p. 236 UNDERWOOD 64   7 Indeed, when had great Britaine greater cause
    p. 255 UNDERWOOD 75   96 To give a greater Name, and Title to! Their
                                  owne!
    p. 307 HORACE 2   43 So, shunning faults, to greater fault doth lead,
    p. 319 HORACE 2   299 Both in their tunes, the licence greater grew,
    p. 339 HORACE 1   33 The greater part, that boast the Muses fire,

greatest   frequency: 5   relative frequency: 0.00007
See also "grea<t>est."
    p. 52 EPIGRAMS 76   6 Of greatest bloud, and yet more good then great;
    p. 68 EPIGRAMS 106   9 Their latter praise would still the greatest bee,
    p. 82 EPIGRAMS 130   9 T<o>'alledge, that greatest men were not asham'd,
    p. 281 U'WOOD 84.8   15 The greatest are but growing Gentlemen.
    p. 361 UNGATHERED 1   19 still making that the greatest that is last

greatly   frequency: 1   relative frequency: 0.00001
    p. 36 EPIGRAMS 28   17 Blaspheme god, greatly. Or some poore hinde
                                  beat,

greatnesse   frequency: 13   relative frequency: 0.00018
    p. 35 EPIGRAMS 28   13 Which is maine greatnesse. And, at his still
                                  boord,
    p. 36 EPIGRAMS 28   16 Of solemne greatnesse. And he dares, at dice,
    p. 36 EPIGRAMS 28   19 Nay more, for greatnesse sake, he will be one
    p. 48 EPIGRAMS 66   2 To greatnesse, CARY, I sing that, and thee.
    p. 51 EPIGRAMS 73   4 The world must know your greatnesse is my debter.
    p. 52 EPIGRAMS 76   10 Hating that solemne vice of greatnesse, pride;
    p. 97 FOREST 3   32 To the full greatnesse of the cry:
    p. 163 UNDERWOOD 15   44 To make up Greatnesse! and mans whole good fix'd
    p. 192 UNDERWOOD 38   34 There greatnesse takes a glorie to relieve.
    p. 236 UNDERWOOD 63   9 But thanke his greatnesse, and his goodnesse too;
    p. 246 UNDERWOOD 70   105 But simple love of greatnesse, and of good;
    p. 307 HORACE 2   38 Professing greatnesse, swells: That, low by lee
    p. 419 UNGATHERED 48   5 By Cherissheinge the Spirrites yt gaue their
                                  greatnesse grace:

grecian   frequency: 3   relative frequency: 0.00004
    p. 309 HORACE 2   75 So they fall gently from the Grecian spring,
    p. 323 HORACE 2   407 In daring to forsake the Grecian tracts,
    p. 398 UNGATHERED 30   88 Then Affricke knew, or the full Grecian store!

'gree   frequency: 1   relative frequency: 0.00001
    p. 274 U'WOOD 84.1   36 To chant her 'gree,

greece   frequency: 3   relative frequency: 0.00004
    p. 84 EPIGRAMS 133   1 No more let Greece her bolder fables tell
    p. 228 UNDERWOOD 53   5 And saw a Centaure, past those tales of Greece;
    p. 391 UNGATHERED 26   39 Of all, that insolent Greece, or haughtie Rome

greedie   frequency: 3   relative frequency: 0.00004
    p. 97 FOREST 3   34 Or shooting at the greedie thrush,
    p. 175 UNDERWOOD 23   19 What though the greedie Frie
    p. 202 UNDERWOOD 43   3 Or urge thy Greedie flame, thus to devoure

greedy   frequency: 1   relative frequency: 0.00001
See also "greedie."

greedy (cont.)
    p. 317 HORACE 2   246 With sloth, yet greedy still of what's to come:

greek. See "greeke."

greek-hands   frequency: 1   relative frequency: 0.00001
    p. 260 UNDERWOOD 77   9 The old Greek-hands in picture, or in stone.

greeke   frequency: 9   relative frequency: 0.00013
    p. 51 EPIGRAMS 73   10 Item, a faire greeke poesie for a ring:
    p. 184 UNDERWOOD 29   31 Greeke was free from Rimes infection,
    p. 184 UNDERWOOD 29   32 Happy Greeke, by this protection,
    p. 214 UNDERWOOD 44   36 And the Greeke Discipline (with the moderne)
                             shed
    p. 323 HORACE 2   397 Take you the Greeke Examples, for your light,
    p. 380 UNGATHERED 12 45 Of Latine and Greeke, to his friendship. And
                             seuen
    p. 388 UNGATHERED 23   9 To the Greeke coast thine onely knew the way.
    p. 391 UNGATHERED 26 31 And though thou hadst small Latine, and lesse
                             Greeke,
    p. 392 UNGATHERED 26 51 The merry Greeke, tart Aristophanes,

greeks   frequency: 1   relative frequency: 0.00001
    See also "greek's."
    p. 348 HORACE 1   383 .... Greeks ....

greek's   frequency: 1   relative frequency: 0.00001
    p. 327 HORACE 2   461 The Muse not only gave the Greek's a wit,

green   frequency: 1   relative frequency: 0.00001
    See also "ever-greene," "greene."
    p. 412 UNGATHERED 41   5 These forme thy Ghyrlond. Wherof Myrtle green,

greencloth. See "greene-cloth."

greene   frequency: 8   relative frequency: 0.00011
    p. 28 EPIGRAMS 4   5 For such a Poet, while thy dayes were greene,
    p. 68 EPIGRAMS 105   12 Were leading forth the Graces on the greene:
    p. 87 EPIGRAMS 133 126 White, black, blew, greene, and in more formes
                             out-started,
    p. 97 FOREST 3   38 Of flowrie fields, of cop'ces greene,
    p. 107 FOREST 10   12 In the greene circle of thy Iuy twine.
    p. 183 UNDERWOOD 29   17 All Parnassus Greene did wither,
    p. 253 UNDERWOOD 75   18 Of Summers Liveries, and gladding greene;
    p. 398 UNGATHERED 30 82 And with their grassie greene restor'd mine eyes.

greene-cloth   frequency: 1   relative frequency: 0.00001
    p. 241 UNDERWOOD 68   8 Would make the very Greene-cloth to looke blew:

greenwich   frequency: 1   relative frequency: 0.00001
    p. 252 UNDERWOOD 75   12 From Greenwich, hither, to Row-hampton gate!

'grees   frequency: 1   relative frequency: 0.00001
    p. 317 HORACE 2   279 Then to the purpose leades, and fitly 'grees.

'greet   frequency: 1   relative frequency: 0.00001
    p. 283 U'WOOD 84.9   40 To 'greet, or grieve her soft Euthanasee?

greeting   frequency: 1   relative frequency: 0.00001
    p. 221 UNDERWOOD 48   16 And still begin'st the greeting:

grenades. See "granats."

grew   frequency: 13   relative frequency: 0.00018
    p. 31 EPIGRAMS 15   3 Where, afterwards, it grew a butter-flye:
    p. 56 EPIGRAMS 87   2 HAZARD a month forsware his; and grew
                             drunke,
    p. 56 EPIGRAMS 87   5 Vpon th'accompt, hers grew the quicker trade.
    p. 57 EPIGRAMS 90   9 Not though that haire grew browne, which once was
                             amber,
    p. 192 UNDERWOOD 38   58 Or winds the Spirit, by which the flower so
                             grew?
    p. 214 UNDERWOOD 44   37 So, in that ground, as soone it grew to be
    p. 216 UNDERWOOD 45   20 They cannot last. No lie grew ever old.
    p. 217 UNDERWOOD 46   10 And skill in thee, now, grew Authoritie;
    p. 247 UNDERWOOD 70 110 Till either grew a portion of the other:
    p. 274 U'WOOD 84.2   11 Of vertues in her, as, in short, shee grew
    p. 307 HORACE 2   67 Most worthie praise, when words that common grew,
    p. 319 HORACE 2   299 Both in their tunes, the licence greater grew,
    p. 319 HORACE 2   305 In his train'd Gowne about the Stage: So grew

grief. See "griefe."

griefe   frequency: 7   relative frequency: 0.00010
    p.   39 EPIGRAMS 40   13 Life, whose griefe was out of fashion,
    p. 102 FOREST 4   62 To age, misfortune, sicknesse, griefe:
    p. 132 UNDERWOOD 2.2   29 (Which with griefe and wrath I heard)
    p. 234 UNDERWOOD 61   14 My Lord, till felt griefe make our stone hearts
                              soft,
    p. 256 UNDERWOOD 75   114 It brings Friends Joy, Foes Griefe,
                              Posteritie Fame;
    p. 256 UNDERWOOD 75   120 A meere upbraiding Griefe, and tort'ring
                              punishment.
    p. 369 UNGATHERED 6   113 It is inough, their griefe shall know

griefes   frequency: 1   relative frequency: 0.00001
    p. 122 FOREST 15   21 I feele my griefes too, and there scarce is
                              ground,

griefs. See "griefes."

grieu'd   frequency: 3   relative frequency: 0.00004
  **p. 114 PANEGYRE   45 And euery windore grieu'd it could not moue
    p.   61 EPIGRAMS 95   10 And gratulate the breach, I grieu'd before:
    p. 101 FOREST 4   52 And euery goodnesse tax'd, or grieu'd.

grieue   frequency: 1   relative frequency: 0.00001
    p.   50 EPIGRAMS 72   1 I grieue not, COVRTLING, thou are
                              started vp

griev'd   frequency: 2   relative frequency: 0.00002
  See also "grieu'd."
    p. 174 UNDERWOOD 22   36 What I, in her, am griev'd to want.
    p. 342 HORACE 1   177 .. still .... griev'd .... sad

grieve   frequency: 4   relative frequency: 0.00005
  See also "grieue."
    p. 192 UNDERWOOD 38   33 Where weaknesse doth offend, and vertue grieve,
    p. 283 U'WOOD 84.9   40 To 'greet, or grieve her soft Euthanasee?
    p. 311 HORACE 2   144 To laughter; so they grieve with those that mone.
    p. 335 HORACE 2   640 Why should I grieve my friend, this trifling
                              way?

grievous   frequency: 2   relative frequency: 0.00002
    p. 127 UNDERWOOD 1.1   14 And take compassion on my grievous plight.
    p. 337 HORACE 2   676 All; So this grievous Writer puts to flight

grisly   frequency: 1   relative frequency: 0.00001
    p.   89 EPIGRAMS 133   175 But you will visit grisly PLVTO'S hall?

groan. See "grone."

groin. See "groine," "groyne."

groine   frequency: 1   relative frequency: 0.00001
    p. 163 UNDERWOOD 15   46 All which he makes the servants of the Groine,

grone   frequency: 1   relative frequency: 0.00001
    p.   94 FOREST 2   46 They'are rear'd with no mans ruine, no mans
                              grone,

groom. See "groome."

groome   frequency: 5   relative frequency: 0.00007
    p.   45 EPIGRAMS 58   t1 TO GROOME IDEOT.
    p. 113 FOREST 12   6 To euery squire, or groome, that will report
    p. 118 FOREST 13   74 On the close groome, and page, on new-yeeres day,
    p. 201 UNDERWOOD 42   51 Then ope thy wardrobe, thinke me that poore
                              Groome
    p. 228 UNDERWOOD 53   18 I look'd for Hercules to be the Groome:

groomes   frequency: 2   relative frequency: 0.00002
    p. 154 UNDERWOOD 13   36 His Groomes to witnesse; or else lets it fall
    p. 303 UNGATHERED 3   8 The knottie heads of the most surly Groomes,

grooms. See "groomes."

gropes   frequency: 1   relative frequency: 0.00001
    p. 391 UNGATHERED 26   10 The truth, but gropes, and vrgeth all by chance;

gross. See "grosse."

grosse   frequency: 2   relative frequency: 0.00002
  p.   68 EPIGRAMS 107   5 Tell the grosse Dutch those grosser tales of
                             yours,
  p. 331 HORACE 2   558 Or thick grosse ointment, but offend the Guests:

grosser   frequency: 1   relative frequency: 0.00001
  p.   68 EPIGRAMS 107   5 Tell the grosse Dutch those grosser tales of
                             yours,

grossnesse   frequency: 1   relative frequency: 0.00001
  p. 279 U'WOOD 84.4   44 Earths grossnesse; There's the how, and why.

groue   frequency: 1   relative frequency: 0.00001
  p.   80 EPIGRAMS 126   2 'Mongst Hampton shades, and PHOEBVS groue
                             of bayes,

groun'   frequency: 1   relative frequency: 0.00001
  p. 333 HORACE 2   613 Out at his friendly eyes, leape, beat the groun'.

ground   frequency: 15   relative frequency: 0.00021
   See also "groun'," "grownde."
 **p. 114 PANEGYRE   43 Others on ground runne gazing by his side,
 **p. 114 PANEGYRE   62 The ground beneath did seeme a mouing floud:
 **p. 117 PANEGYRE   141 That wan affections, ere his steps wan ground;
   p. 122 FOREST 15   21 I feele my griefes too, and there scarce is
                             ground,
   p. 141 UNDERWOOD 2.9   14 Gold, upon a ground of black.
   p. 183 UNDERWOOD 29   9 To the ground.
   p. 209 UNDERWOOD 43   147 And that accursed ground, the Parish-Garden:
   p. 214 UNDERWOOD 44   37 So, in that ground, as soone it grew to be
   p. 239 UNDERWOOD 67   14 And cleave both ayre and ground,
   p. 254 UNDERWOOD 75   68 And all the Ground were Garden, where she led!
   p. 264 UNDERWOOD 79   36 1. Where ere they tread th'enamour'd ground,
   p. 265 UNDERWOOD 79   58 Where e're he goes upon the ground,
   p. 280 U'WOOD 84.4   49 Or hath she here, upon the ground,
   p. 307 HORACE 2   39 Creepes on the ground; too safe, too afraid of
                             storme.
   p. 412 UNGATHERED 41   6 The gladdest ground to all the numbred-five,

grounded. See "deepe-grounded."

grounds   frequency: 6   relative frequency: 0.00008
  p.   94 FOREST 2   24 The middle grounds thy mares, and horses breed.
  p. 169 UNDERWOOD 17   17 Some grounds are made the richer, for the Rest;
  p. 221 UNDERWOOD 48   42 As shall the feasts faire grounds be.
  p. 264 UNDERWOOD 79   15 2. To him we owe all profits of our grounds.
  p. 265 UNDERWOOD 79   49 To whom you owe all duties of your grounds;
  p. 305 HORACE 2   22 The pleasant grounds, or when the River Rhine,

grove   frequency: 2   relative frequency: 0.00002
   See also "groue."
  p. 170 UNDERWOOD 19   5 By that tall Grove, your haire; whose globy
                             rings
  p. 305 HORACE 2   20 Diana's Grove, or Altar, with the bor-

groves   frequency: 3   relative frequency: 0.00004
  p. 264 UNDERWOOD 79   23 Chor. Heare, o you Groves, and, Hills, resound
                             his praise.
  p. 264 UNDERWOOD 79   31 Chor. Heare, O you Groves, and, Hills,
                             resound his worth.
  p. 321 HORACE 2   355 But, let the Faunes, drawne from their Groves,
                             beware,

grow   frequency: 19   relative frequency: 0.00027
   See also "growe."
  p.   50 EPIGRAMS 70   4 On the true causes, ere they grow too old.
  p.   58 EPIGRAMS 92   3 Ripe statesmen, ripe: They grow in euery street.
  p.   93 FOREST 1   12 When Loue is fled, and I grow old.
  p. 110 FOREST 11   35 But this doth from the<ir> cloud of error grow,
  p. 119 FOREST 13   99 Grow, grow, faire tree, and as thy branches
                             shoote,
  p. 134 UNDERWOOD 2.4   21 Have you seene but a bright Lillie grow,
  p. 147 UNDERWOOD 7   10 But then if I grow jealous madde,
  p. 157 UNDERWOOD 13   152 Aloft, grow lesse and streightned, full of knot;
  p. 158 UNDERWOOD 13   161 May grow so great to be example, when
  p. 184 UNDERWOOD 29   57 Grow unsounder.
  p. 187 UNDERWOOD 33   16 Mak'st it religion to grow rich by Crimes!
  p. 197 UNDERWOOD 40   15 For though Love thrive, and may grow up with
                             cheare,
  p. 231 UNDERWOOD 56   30 And should grow rich, had I much more to pay.

grow (cont.)
    p. 237 UNDERWOOD 65   5 This Prince of flowers? Soone shoot thou up,
                           and grow
    p. 268 UNDERWOOD 82   11 Grow up, sweet Babe, as blessed, in thy Name,
    p. 307 HORACE 2   35 My selfe for shortnesse labour; and I grow
    p. 309 HORACE 2   89 Like tender buds shoot up, and freshly grow.
    p. 323 HORACE 2   393 Grow a safe Writer, and be warie-driven

growe   frequency: 1   relative frequency: 0.00001
    p. 404 UNGATHERED 34 59 Whither? oh whither will this Tire-man growe?

growes   frequency: 5   relative frequency: 0.00007
    p. 80 EPIGRAMS 127   9 So, all reward, or name, that growes to mee
    p. 106 FOREST 9   15 Since when it growes, and smells, I sweare,
    p. 177 UNDERWOOD 25   26 True noblesse. Palme growes straight, though
                           handled ne're so rude.
    p. 227 UNDERWOOD 52   5 And the whole lumpe growes round, deform'd, and
                           droupes,
    p. 413 UNGATHERED 41 15 To top the fairest Lillie, now, that growes,

growing   frequency: 4   relative frequency: 0.00005
    p. 57 EPIGRAMS 90   11 Still MILL continu'd: Nay, his face growing
                           worse,
    p. 172 UNDERWOOD 21   t1 A little Shrub growing by.
    p. 245 UNDERWOOD 70   65 It is not growing like a tree
    p. 281 U'WOOD 84.8   15 The greatest are but growing Gentlemen.

grown. See "growne."

grownde   frequency: 1   relative frequency: 0.00001
    p. 420 UNGATHERED 48 34 And Cunninge of their grownde

growne   frequency: 18   relative frequency: 0.00026
    p. 32 EPIGRAMS 16   5 So, in short time, th'art in arrerage growne
    p. 45 EPIGRAMS 56   6 Buy the reuersion of old playes; now growne
    p. 57 EPIGRAMS 90   10 And he growne youth, was call'd to his ladies
                           chamber.
    p. 88 EPIGRAMS 133 150 And, after mouldie growne, againe were tosted,
    p. 116 FOREST 13   1 'Tis growne almost a danger to speake true
    p. 156 UNDERWOOD 13 119 Or growne; by height or lownesse of the Sunne?
    p. 163 UNDERWOOD 15   37 Our Delicacies are growne capitall,
    p. 165 UNDERWOOD 15   86 They're growne Commoditie upon Exchange;
    p. 166 UNDERWOOD 15 139 Of what he throwes: Like letchers growne content
    p. 167 UNDERWOOD 15 155 Pardon his Lordship. Flattry's growne so cheape
    p. 214 UNDERWOOD 44   55 That keepe the warre, though now't be growne more
                           tame,
    p. 224 UNDERWOOD 50   10 Are growne so fruitfull, and false pleasures
                           climbe,
    p. 236 UNDERWOOD 64   9 When you that raigne, are her Example growne,
    p. 237 UNDERWOOD 64   15 How is she barren growne of love! or broke!
    p. 290 UNDERWOOD 85   10 With the growne issue of the Vine;
    p. 315 HORACE 2   237 These studies alter now, in one, growne man;
    p. 317 HORACE 2   245 A great deferrer, long in hope, growne numbe
    p. 403 UNGATHERED 34 24 In Towne & Court? Are you growne rich?
                           & proud?

grows. See "growes."

groyne   frequency: 3   relative frequency: 0.00004
    p. 75 EPIGRAMS 117   1 GROYNE, come of age, his state sold out of
                           hand
    p. 75 EPIGRAMS 117   2 For'his whore: GROYNE doth still occupy his
                           land.
    p. 75 EPIGRAMS 117   t1 ON GROYNE.

grudg'd   frequency: 1   relative frequency: 0.00001
    p. 93 FOREST 2   6 And these grudg'd at, art reuerenc'd the while.

grudge   frequency: 3   relative frequency: 0.00004
    See also "grutch."
    p. 48 EPIGRAMS 65   7 Get him the times long grudge, the courts ill
                           will;
    p. 169 UNDERWOOD 17   3 And yet the noble Nature never grudge;
    p. 271 UNDERWOOD 83   79 If you dare grudge at Heaven, and repent

grunting   frequency: 1   relative frequency: 0.00001
    p. 232 UNDERWOOD 58 11 Like a rung Beare, or Swine: grunting out wit

grutch   frequency: 3   relative frequency: 0.00004
    p. 72 EPIGRAMS 111   9 Yet thou, perhaps, shalt meet some tongues will
                           grutch,

grutch (cont.)
    p. 101 FOREST 4   56 If't chance to me, I must not grutch.
    p. 236 UNDERWOOD 63   7 Then, Royall CHARLES, and MARY, doe
                              not grutch

guard   frequency: 2   relative frequency: 0.00002
    p. 109 FOREST 11   7 Some way of entrance) we must plant a guard
    p. 321 HORACE 2   348 Or old Silenus, Bacchus guard, and Nurse.

guarded   frequency: 2   relative frequency: 0.00002
    p. 239 UNDERWOOD 67   12 Their guarded gates asunder?
    p. 323 HORACE 2   409 Whether the guarded Tragedie they wrought,

guardes   frequency: 1   relative frequency: 0.00001
    p. 270 UNDERWOOD 83   40 Her wary guardes, her wise simplicitie,

guardian   frequency: 1   relative frequency: 0.00001
    p. 315 HORACE 2   229 Th'unbearded Youth, his Guardian once being
                              gone,

guards. See "guardes."

gue. See "gve."

guess. See "guesse."

guesse   frequency: 2   relative frequency: 0.00002
    p. 137 UNDERWOOD 2.6   1 Charis, guesse, and doe not misse,
    p. 138 UNDERWOOD 2.6   34 Guesse of these, which is the true;

guest   frequency: 9   relative frequency: 0.00013
    See also "ghest."
    p. 81 EPIGRAMS 129   6 To which thou'rt not a weeke, bespoke a guest;
    p. 95 FOREST 2   61 Where comes no guest, but is allow'd to eate,
    p. 96 FOREST 2   88 As if it had expected such a guest!
    p. 96 FOREST 3   5 That at great times, art no ambitious guest
    p. 281 U'WOOD 84.4   72 But such a Mind, mak'st God thy Guest.
    p. 284 U'WOOD 84.9   64 To Body, and Soule! where Love is all the
                              guest!
    p. 284 U'WOOD 84.9   81 Hee knowes, what worke h'hath done, to call this
                              Guest,
    p. 325 HORACE 2   448 What brethren, what a stranger, and his guest,
    p. 394 UNGATHERED 28   19 To call on Sicknes still, to be her Guest,

guests   frequency: 5   relative frequency: 0.00007
    See also "ghests."
    p. 97 FOREST 3   28 And giu'st thy gladder guests the sight;
    p. 166 UNDERWOOD 15   118 What honour given to the drunkennest Guests?
    p. 221 UNDERWOOD 48   39 The causes and the Guests too,
    p. 331 HORACE 2   558 Or thick grosse ointment, but offend the Guests:
    p. 421 UNGATHERED 48   45 Whoe worthie wine, whoe not, to bee wyse Pallas
                              guests.

guide   frequency: 1   relative frequency: 0.00001
    p. 410 UNGATHERED 38   18 Hee'll be a Pilot, scarce can guide a Plough.

guided   frequency: 1   relative frequency: 0.00001
    p. 176 UNDERWOOD 24   11 And guided by Experience, whose straite wand

guides   frequency: 3   relative frequency: 0.00004
    p. 170 UNDERWOOD 18   12 Such Guides men use not, who their way would
                              find,
    p. 207 UNDERWOOD 43   103 After the Fathers, and those wiser Guides
    p. 219 UNDERWOOD 47   50 That guides the Motions, and directs the beares.

guideth   frequency: 1   relative frequency: 0.00001
    p. 134 UNDERWOOD 2.4   4 And well the Carre Love guideth.

guift   frequency: 2   relative frequency: 0.00002
    p. 76 EPIGRAMS 119   2 At hunting railes, hauing no guift in othes,
    p. 666 INSCRIPTS. 11   8 Wth Chequer Inke, vpon his guift, my paper,

guifts   frequency: 2   relative frequency: 0.00002
    p. 102 FOREST 5   5 Spend not then his guifts in vaine.
    p. 384 UNGATHERED 18   2 And clothes, and guifts, that only do thee grace

guild   frequency: 1   relative frequency: 0.00001
    p. 103 FOREST 6   16 Or the starres, that guild his streames,

guilded   frequency: 1   relative frequency: 0.00001
     p.   97 FOREST 3   15 Free from proud porches, or their guilded roofes,

guilt   frequency: 7   relative frequency: 0.00010
    *p. 493 TO HIMSELF   40 The gamesters share your guilt, and you their
                             stuffe.
     p.   70 EPIGRAMS 109   8 Is priuate gaine, which hath long guilt to
                             friend.
     p. 112 FOREST 11   113 That knowes the waight of guilt: He will
                             refraine
     p. 114 FOREST 12   22 Then this, our guilt, nor golden age can deeme,
     p. 186 UNDERWOOD 32 11 Who, though their guilt, and perjurie they know,
     p. 210 UNDERWOOD 43 165 I will not argue thee, from those, of guilt,
     p. 371 UNGATHERED 8 11 I, that am glad, thy Innocence was thy Guilt,

guiltie   frequency: 4   relative frequency: 0.00005
     p.   32 EPIGRAMS 17   2 As guiltie men doe magistrates: glad I,
     p.   65 EPIGRAMS 101 37 Nor shall our cups make any guiltie men:
     p.   98 FOREST 3   67 Let others watch in guiltie armes, and stand
     p. 151 UNDERWOOD 11 13 And sleepe so guiltie and afraid,

guiltlesse   frequency: 2   relative frequency: 0.00002
     p.   36 EPIGRAMS 29   2 And thou, right guiltlesse, may'st plead to it,
                             why?
     p. 284 U'WOOD 84.9   56 This as it guilty is, or guiltlesse found,

guilty   frequency: 1   relative frequency: 0.00001
     See also "guiltie," "gviltie."
     p. 284 U'WOOD 84.9   56 This as it guilty is, or guiltlesse found,

guinea. See "ginny."

gull   frequency: 1   relative frequency: 0.00001
     p. 154 UNDERWOOD 13 57 Dam's whom he damn'd to, as the veriest Gull,

gull'd   frequency: 1   relative frequency: 0.00001
     p.   69 EPIGRAMS 107 10 What States yo'haue gull'd, and which yet keepes
                             yo'in pay.

gulling   frequency: 1   relative frequency: 0.00001
     p.   51 EPIGRAMS 73   15 Item, a gulling imprese for you, at tilt.

gum. See "gumme."

gumme   frequency: 1   relative frequency: 0.00001
     p. 292 UNDERWOOD 86 22 In many a Gumme, and for thy soft eares sake

gummes   frequency: 2   relative frequency: 0.00002
     p.   42 EPIGRAMS 50   1 Leaue COD, tabacco-like, burnt gummes to take,
     p. 280 U'WOOD 84.4   64 A nest of odorous spice, and gummes.

gums. See "gummes."

gun-powder   frequency: 1   relative frequency: 0.00001
     p. 208 UNDERWOOD 43 121 And for it lose his eyes with Gun-powder,

gundomar   frequency: 1   relative frequency: 0.00001
     p. 213 UNDERWOOD 44   5 Old Aesope Gundomar: the French can tell,

gunnes   frequency: 1   relative frequency: 0.00001
     p. 239 UNDERWOOD 67   8 And Gunnes there, spare to poure

gunpowder. See "gun-powder."

guns   frequency: 2   relative frequency: 0.00002
     See also "gunnes," "pct-guns."
     p. 212 UNDERWOOD 43 202 Who from the Divels-Arse did Guns beget;
     p. 214 UNDERWOOD 44   58 Come to their Schooles,) show 'hem the use of
                             Guns;

gut. See "gvt."

guts   frequency: 1   relative frequency: 0.00001
     p.   86 EPIGRAMS 133 92 Is this we heare? of frogs? No, guts wind-bound,

guy   frequency: 1   relative frequency: 0.00001
     p. 215 UNDERWOOD 44 81 From Guy, or Bevis, Arthur, or from whom

gve   frequency: 1   relative frequency: 0.00001
     p.   81 EPIGRAMS 129 16 Thou dost out-zany COKELY, POD; nay,
                             GVE:

gviltie   frequency: 5   relative frequency: 0.00007
     p.   30 EPIGRAMS 30   1 GVILTIE, be wise; and though thou know'st
                                 the crimes
     p.   30 EPIGRAMS 30   t1 TO PERSON GVILTIE.
     p.   38 EPIGRAMS 38   1 GVILTIE, because I bad you late be wise,
     p.   38 EPIGRAMS 38   7 Beleeue it, GVILTIE, if you loose your
                                 shame,
     p.   38 EPIGRAMS 38   t1 TO PERSON GVILTIE.

gvt   frequency: 2   relative frequency: 0.00002
     p.   76 EPIGRAMS 118   1 GVT eates all day, and lechers all the night,
     p.   76 EPIGRAMS 118   t1 ON GVT.

gyant   frequency: 1   relative frequency: 0.00001
     p. 407 UNGATHERED 35   15 Thy Canuas Gyant, at some Channell aymes,

gyantes   frequency: 1   relative frequency: 0.00001
     p. 421 UNGATHERED 48   41 The Rebell Gyantes stoope, and Gorgon Envye
                                 yeild,

gyerlyk   frequency: 1   relative frequency: 0.00001
     p. 361 UNGATHERED 1   23 which thoughts being circumvol<v>d in gyerlyk
                                 mocion

gypsee   frequency: 2   relative frequency: 0.00002
     p.   39 EPIGRAMS 41   1 GYPSEE, new baud, is turn'd physitian,
     p.   39 EPIGRAMS 41   t1 ON GYPSEE.

gypsy. See "gypsee."

gyre-like. See "gyerlyk."

gyrlands   frequency: 1   relative frequency: 0.00001
     p.   32 EPIGRAMS 17   6 Shall out-liue gyrlands, stolne from the chast
                                 tree.

gyues   frequency: 1   relative frequency: 0.00001
     p. 100 FOREST 4   24 Enamor'd of their golden gyues?

gyves. See "gyues."

h.   frequency: 2   relative frequency: 0.00002
     p.   79 EPIGRAMS 124   t1 EPITAPH ON ELIZABETH, L. H.
     p. 242 UNDERWOOD 70   t3 and Sir H. MORISON.

h<e>'offend   frequency: 1   relative frequency: 0.00001
     p. 329 HORACE 2   529 How then? Why, as a Scrivener, if h<e>'offend

ha   frequency: 1   relative frequency: 0.00001
     p. 269 UNDERWOOD 83   10 Whose Daughter? ha? Great Savage of the Rock?

ha'   frequency: 3   relative frequency: 0.00004

habit   frequency: 3   relative frequency: 0.00004
   **p. 116 PANEGYRE   118 Who once haue got the habit to doe ill.
     p. 342 HORACE 1   153 .. .. Fortunes habit ... .
     p. 362 UNGATHERED 2   1 Thou, that wouldst finde the habit of true
                                 passion,

hackney   frequency: 1   relative frequency: 0.00001
     p.   81 EPIGRAMS 129   4 To Braynford, Hackney, Bow, but thou mak'st
                                 one;

had   frequency: 162   relative frequency: 0.00234
     See also "he'had," "h'had," "i'<h>ad," "i'had,"
           "sh'had," "who'had," "yo'had."

hadst   frequency: 7   relative frequency: 0.00010
     See also "had'st."

had'st   frequency: 3   relative frequency: 0.00004

haftes   frequency: 1   relative frequency: 0.00001
     p. 403 UNGATHERED 34   28 Though gold or Iuory haftes would make it good.

hafts. See "haftes."

hail. See "haile."

naile   frequency: 4   relative frequency: 0.00005
    p. 225 UNDERWOOD 51   1 Haile, happie Genius of this antient pile!
    p. 238 UNDERWOOD 66   1 Haile Mary, full of grace, it once was said,
    p. 238 UNDERWOOD 66   5 Haile Mary, full of honours, to my Queene,
    p. 238 UNDERWOOD 66   13 Glorie to God. Then, Haile to Mary! spring

nails. See "nayles."

hair. See "haire," "hayre."

haire   frequency: 12   relative frequency: 0.00017
    p.   33 EPIGRAMS 21   1 Lord, how is GAM'STER chang'd! his haire
                               close cut!
    p.   57 EPIGRAMS 90   9 Not though that haire grew browne, which once was
                               amber,
    p.   88 EPIGRAMS 133   145 The sinkes ran grease, and haire of meazled hogs,
    p. 134 UNDERWOOD 2.4   13 Doe but looke on her Haire, it is bright
    p. 136 UNDERWOOD 2.5   13 So hath Homer prais'd her haire;
    p. 138 UNDERWOOD 2.6   10 With th'advantage of her haire,
    p. 141 UNDERWOOD 2.9   10 Yet a man; with crisped haire
    p. 170 UNDERWOOD 19   5 By that tall Grove, your haire; whose globy
                               rings
    p. 215 UNDERWOOD 44   95 His Lordship. That is for his Band, his haire
    p. 253 UNDERWOOD 75   40 In gracefull Ornament of Garland, Gemmes, and
                               Haire.
    p. 307 HORACE 2   47 The nailes, and every curled haire disclose;
    p. 307 HORACE 2   52 With faire black eyes, and haire; and a wry nose.

haires   frequency: 1   relative frequency: 0.00001
    p. 150 UNDERWOOD 9   14 My hundred of gray haires,

hairs. See "haires."

halberds   frequency: 1   relative frequency: 0.00001
    p. 204 UNDERWOOD 43   37 Of Egges, and Halberds, Cradles, and a Herse,

half   frequency: 2   relative frequency: 0.00002
    See also "foot-and-halfe-foot," "halfe."
    p. 409 UNGATHERED 37   18 To aske thy name, if he haue half his Nose!
    p. 657 L. CONVIVALES   9 He the half of Life abuses,

half-moons. See "halfe-moones."

half-way. See "halfe-way."

halfe   frequency: 17   relative frequency: 0.00024
    p.   30 EPIGRAMS 12   3 Keepes himselfe, with halfe a man, and defrayes
    p.   33 EPIGRAMS 21   2 His neck fenc'd round with ruffe! his eyes halfe
                               shut!
    p.   34 EPIGRAMS 23   8 Which might with halfe mankind maintayne a
                               strife.
    p.   45 EPIGRAMS 56   13 Foole, as if halfe eyes will not know a fleece
    p.   51 EPIGRAMS 73   13 Your partie-per-pale picture, one halfe drawne
    p.   76 EPIGRAMS 119   15 He, that, but liuing halfe his age, dyes such;
    p. 138 UNDERWOOD 2.6   9 Look'd not halfe so fresh, and faire,
    p. 139 UNDERWOOD 2.7   11 This could be call'd but halfe a kisse.
    p. 163 UNDERWOOD 15   52 I, that's a Charme and halfe! She must afford
    p. 199 UNDERWOOD 41   8 Where we must feele it Darke for halfe a yeare.
    p. 228 UNDERWOOD 53   16 Nor any of their houshold, halfe so well.
    p. 242 UNDERWOOD 70   6 E're thou wert halfe got out,
    p. 246 UNDERWOOD 70   94 And keepe the one halfe from his Harry.
    p. 249 UNDERWOOD 72   5 Let Ireland meet it out at Sea, halfe way,
    p. 295 UNDERWOOD 89   7 Hee, that but living halfe his dayes, dies such,
    p. 327 HORACE 2   471 An ounce, what makes it then? The halfe pound
                               just:
    p. 371 UNGATHERED 8   8 They saw it halfe, damd thy whole play, and more;

halfe-moones   frequency: 1   relative frequency: 0.00001
    p. 248 UNDERWOOD 71   8 Reduicts, Halfe-moones, Horne-workes, and such
                               close wayes,

halfe-way   frequency: 1   relative frequency: 0.00001
    p.   56 EPIGRAMS 88   6 Toward the sea, farther then halfe-way tree?

hall   frequency: 8   relative frequency: 0.00011
    p.   85 EPIGRAMS 133   31 In it' owne hall; when these (in worthy scorne
    p.   89 EPIGRAMS 133   175 But you will visit grisly PLVTO'S hall?
    p.   98 FOREST 3   49 And fills thy open hall with mirth, and cheere,
    p. 179 UNDERWOOD 25   38 In Surgeons hall)
    p. 186 UNDERWOOD 33   3 Or the great Hall at Westminster, the field

hall (cont.)
       p. 258 UNDERWOOD 75   169 Till you behold a race to fill your Hall,
       p. 321 HORACE 2   357 Like men street-borne, and neere the Hall,
                                 reherse
       p. 417 UNGATHERED 45   13 To the merry beards in Hall,

hallow'd   frequency: 2   relative frequency: 0.00002
       p. 291 UNDERWOOD 85   43 To deck the hallow'd Harth with old wood fir'd
       p. 401 UNGATHERED 32   21 And like a hallow'd Temple, free from taint

halt   frequency: 1   relative frequency: 0.00001
       p. 208 UNDERWOOD 43   110 'Cause thou canst halt, with us, in Arts, and
                                 Fire!

hammering   frequency: 1   relative frequency: 0.00001
       p. 333 HORACE 2   628 Those ill-torn'd Verses, to new hammering.

hammers   frequency: 1   relative frequency: 0.00001
       p. 179 UNDERWOOD 25   41 Sweat at the forge, their hammers beating;

hampton   frequency: 1   relative frequency: 0.00001
       p. 80 EPIGRAMS 126   2 'Mongst Hampton shades, and PHOEBVS groue
                                 of bayes,

hams   frequency: 1   relative frequency: 0.00001
       p. 363 UNGATHERED 3   11 It bends the hams of Gossip Vigilance,

hanau. See "hannow."

hanch   frequency: 2   relative frequency: 0.00002
       p. 396 UNGATHERED 30   8 Hanch against Hanch, or raise a riming Club

hand   frequency: 42   relative frequency: 0.00060
  **p. 113 PANEGYRE   23 Beside her, stoup't on either hand, a maid,
  **p. 116 PANEGYRE   122 Must with a tender (yet a stedfast) hand
    p. 27 EPIGRAMS 1   1 Pray thee, take care, that tak'st my booke in
                                 hand,
    p. 39 EPIGRAMS 40   4 Grant then, no rude hand remoue her.
    p. 41 EPIGRAMS 45   1 Farewell, thou child of my right hand, and ioy;
    p. 42 EPIGRAMS 46   4 To pay at's day of marriage. By my hand
    p. 61 EPIGRAMS 95   13 O, would'st thou adde like hand, to all the rest!
    p. 61 EPIGRAMS 95   22 But, wisely, thrusts not forth a forward hand,
    p. 62 EPIGRAMS 96   8 Mark'd by thy hand, and with the better stone,
    p. 71 EPIGRAMS 110   17 Thy learned hand, and true Promethean art
    p. 75 EPIGRAMS 117   1 GROYNE, come of age, his state sold out of
                                 hand
    p. 85 EPIGRAMS 133   54 Alwayes at hand, to aide the merry Muses.
    p. 94 FOREST 2   38 Before the fisher, or into his hand.
    p. 133 UNDERWOOD 2.3   10 At her hand, with oath, to make
    p. 134 UNDERWOOD 2.4   1 See the Chariot at hand here of Love,
    p. 141 UNDERWOOD 2.9   25 He would have a hand as soft
    p. 154 UNDERWOOD 13   56 Then turning unto him is next at hand,
    p. 167 UNDERWOOD 15   173 Then once to number, or bring forth to hand,
    p. 175 UNDERWOOD 23   25 Then take in hand thy Lyre,
    p. 176 UNDERWOOD 24   9 Which makes that (lighted by the beamie hand
    p. 180 UNDERWOOD 25   61 Where darknesse with her gloomie-sceptred hand,
    p. 180 UNDERWOOD 26   4 A gentler, and more agile hand, to tend
    p. 180 UNDERWOOD 26   13 Your covetous hand,
    p. 187 UNDERWOOD 33   25 Of Bookes, of Presidents, hast thou at hand!
    p. 200 UNDERWOOD 42   14 No face, no hand, proportion, line, or Ayre
    p. 250 UNDERWOOD 73   3 In his great Actions: view whom his large hand
    p. 251 UNDERWOOD 74   27 When he beholds a graft of his owne hand,
    p. 254 UNDERWOOD 75   52 Both Crownes, and Kingdomes in their either
                                 hand;
    p. 256 UNDERWOOD 75   125 One in the others hand,
    p. 276 U'WOOD 84.3   12 Worke with my fancie, his owne hand.
    p. 277 U'WOOD 84.4   7 Beside, your hand will never hit,
    p. 285 U'WOOD 84.9   95 And white, as that, put on: and in her hand,
    p. 290 UNDERWOOD 85   19 How plucking Peares, his owne hand grafted had,
    p. 323 HORACE 2   398 In hand, and turne them over, day, and night.
    p. 329 HORACE 2   522 The hand, and mind would, but it will resound
    p. 329 HORACE 2   539 As Painting, so is Poesie. Some mans hand
    p. 361 UNGATHERED 1   2 (so well dispos'd by thy auspicious hand)
    p. 367 UNGATHERED 6   49 Be proofe, the glory of his hand,
    p. 370 UNGATHERED 7   4 All which are parts commend the cunning hand;
    p. 383 UNGATHERED 17   1 Who takes thy volume to his vertuous hand,
    p. 383 UNGATHERED 17   8 May take thy volume to his vertuous hand.
    p. 662 INSCRIPTS. 2   10 of her white Hand; or she can spare it.

handed. See "empty-handed," "hook-handed."

handle   frequency: 3   relative frequency: 0.00004
    p. 200 UNDERWOOD 42   30 Where I may handle Silke, as free, and neere,
    p. 208 UNDERWOOD 43   127 Whom they durst handle in their holy-day coates,
    p. 209 UNDERWOOD 83   32 The blaze, and splendor, but not handle fire!

handled   frequency: 2   relative frequency: 0.00002
    p. 177 UNDERWOOD 25   26 True noblesse. Palme growes straight, though
                               handled ne're so rude.
    p. 315 HORACE 2   214 What he despaires, being handled, might not show.

handles   frequency: 1   relative frequency: 0.00001
    p. 415 UNGATHERED 42   17 So soft, and smooth it handles, the whole piece,

handling   frequency: 1   relative frequency: 0.00001
    p. 227 UNDERWOOD 52   17 Your Power of handling shadow, ayre, and
                               spright,

hands   frequency: 11   relative frequency: 0.00015
    See also "greek-hands."
    p.   38 EPIGRAMS 38   4 Any man else, you clap your hands, and rore,
    p.   51 EPIGRAMS 74   3 Whil'st I behold thee liue with purest hands;
    p.   71 EPIGRAMS 110   9 Nor that his worke liu'd in the hands of foes,
    p.   86 EPIGRAMS 133   82 (Who hath the hundred hands when he doth meddle)
    p. 134 UNDERWOOD 2.4 22 Before rude hands have touch'd it?
    p. 154 UNDERWOOD 13   60 That to such Natures let their full hands flow,
    p. 233 UNDERWOOD 59   24 And valiant were, with, or without their hands.
    p. 234 UNDERWOOD 61   7 Yet are got off thence, with cleare mind, and
                               hands
    p. 254 UNDERWOOD 75   65 With what full hands, and in how plenteous
                               showers
    p. 290 UNDERWOOD 85   21 With which, Priapus, he may thanke thy hands,
    p. 375 UNGATHERED 10 34 Bvt here, neither trusting his hands, nor his
                               legs,

hang   frequency: 8   relative frequency: 0.00011
    p.   94 FOREST 2   44 Hang on thy walls, that euery child may reach.
    p. 145 UNDERWOOD 5   18 To make a new, and hang that by.
    p. 146 UNDERWOOD 6   1 Hang up those dull, and envious fooles,
    p. 232 UNDERWOOD 58   10 That hang their richest jewells i' their nose;
    p. 260 UNDERWOOD 77   3 Of Noremberg, or Turkie; hang your roomes
    p. 282 U'WOOD 84.8   20 Hang all your roomes, with one large Pedigree;
    p. 282 U'WOOD 84.9   7 To hang a window, or make darke the roome,
    p. 657 L. CONVIVALES   7 Hang up all the poor Hop-Drinkers,

hanging   frequency: 1   relative frequency: 0.00001
    p. 201 UNDERWOOD 42   57 Court every hanging Gowne, and after that,

hangings   frequency: 3   relative frequency: 0.00004
    p.   96 FOREST 3   8 The richer hangings, or crowne-plate;
    p. 242 UNDERWOOD 69   26 Rather to boast rich hangings, then rare friends.
    p. 315 HORACE 2   221 That tarries till the hangings be ta'en downe,

hangs   frequency: 2   relative frequency: 0.00002
    p. 137 UNDERWOOD 2.5 40 And the Glasse hangs by her side,
    p. 309 HORACE 2   112 Before the Judge, it hangs, and waites report.

hannibal   frequency: 1   relative frequency: 0.00001
    p. 242 UNDERWOOD 70   3 When the Prodigious Hannibal did crowne

hannow   frequency: 1   relative frequency: 0.00001
    p.   69 EPIGRAMS 107   25 Of Hannow, Shieter-huissen, Popenheim,

hans-spiegle   frequency: 1   relative frequency: 0.00001
    p.   69 EPIGRAMS 107   26 Hans-spiegle, Rotteinberg, and Boutersheim,

hap   frequency: 1   relative frequency: 0.00001
    See also "happ."
    p.   69 EPIGRAMS 107   17 If but to be beleeu'd you haue the hap,

haplesse   frequency: 1   relative frequency: 0.00001
    p. 307 HORACE 2   48 But in the maine worke haplesse: since he knowes

haply. See "hap'ly," "happ'ly."

hap'ly   frequency: 1   relative frequency: 0.00001
    p. 305 HORACE 2   24 No place for these. And, Painter, hap'ly, thou

happ   frequency: 1   relative frequency: 0.00001
    p. 417 UNGATHERED 45 37 Or if't be the Gossipps happ

happen   frequency: 2   relative frequency: 0.00002
    p. 101 FOREST 4   55 That, what to all may happen here,
    p. 317 HORACE 2   274 Worth his untying happen there: And not

happie   frequency: 11   relative frequency: 0.00015
  **p. 112 PANEGYRE   t4 THE HAPPIE
  **p. 117 PANEGYRE   148 Wherein, his choice was happie with the rest
    p.   44 EPIGRAMS 55   5 At once thou mak'st me happie, and vnmak'st;
    p.   49 EPIGRAMS 66   8 Or thou more happie, it to iustifie
    p. 214 UNDERWOOD 44   43 O happie Art! and wise Epitome
    p. 225 UNDERWOOD 51   1 Haile, happie Genius of this antient pile!
    p. 271 UNDERWOOD 83   84 And wish her state lesse happie then it is!
    p. 272 UNDERWOOD 84   t15 Her happie MATCH.
    p. 289 UNDERWOOD 85   1 Happie is he, that from all Businesse cleere,
    p. 333 HORACE 2   605 I wonder how this happie man should know,
    p. 419 UNGATHERED 48   9 That were the happie subiect of my songe.

happier   frequency: 3   relative frequency: 0.00004
    p.   48 EPIGRAMS 65   11 With me thou leau'st an happier Muse then thee,
    p. 295 UNDERWOOD 90   1 The Things that make the happier life, are
                                   these,
    p. 325 HORACE 2   420 Happier then wretched art, and doth, by it,

happiest   frequency: 2   relative frequency: 0.00002
    p.   37 EPIGRAMS 35   4 And in this short time of thy happiest raigne,
    p. 162 UNDERWOOD 15   23 See him, that's call'd, and thought the happiest
                                   man,

happily   frequency: 1   relative frequency: 0.00001
    p.   53 EPIGRAMS 79   9 At which, shee happily displeas'd, made you:

happinesse   frequency: 2   relative frequency: 0.00002
    p. 111 FOREST 11   65 Of all his happinesse? But soft: I heare
    p. 234 UNDERWOOD 61   9 Your happinesse, and doth not speake you blest,

happ'ly   frequency: 1   relative frequency: 0.00001
    p. 261 UNDERWOOD 77   28 Aloud; and (happ'ly) it may last as long.

happy   frequency: 21   relative frequency: 0.00030
    See also "happie."
    p.   35 EPIGRAMS 27   7 To heauen; his hath: O happy state! wherein
    p.   43 EPIGRAMS 51   t2 Vpon the happy false rumour of his death, the two
    p.   99 FOREST 3   99 Which who can vse is happy: Such be thou.
    p. 115 FOREST 12   74 I haue already vs'd some happy houres,
    p. 115 FOREST 12   80 Shall thronging come, and boast the happy place
    p. 118 FOREST 13   47 Are you engaged to your happy fate,
    p. 180 UNDERWOOD 26   14 Happy in that faire honour it hath gain'd,
    p. 184 UNDERWOOD 29   32 Happy Greeke, by this protection,
    p. 236 UNDERWOOD 64   1 How happy were the Subject, if he knew,
    p. 240 UNDERWOOD 67   49 9. POLY. Sweet! happy Mary! All
    p. 246 UNDERWOOD 70   83 Such truths, as we expect for happy men,
    p. 256 UNDERWOOD 75   129 O happy bands! and thou more happy place,
    p. 262 UNDERWOOD 78   1 Tho', happy Muse, thou know my Digby well,
    p. 271 UNDERWOOD 83   77 Goe now, her happy Parents, and be sad,
    p. 280 U'WOOD 84.4   53 Thrice happy house, that hast receipt
    p. 285 U'WOOD 84.9   113 There, all the happy soules, that ever were,
    p. 286 U'WOOD 84.9   121 That happy Day, that never shall see night!
    p. 290 UNDERWOOD 85   12 And sets more happy in the place:
    p. 414 UNGATHERED 41   47 Who mad'st us happy all, in thy reflexe,
    p. 422 UNGATHERED 50   6 whom thou seest happy; wretches flee as foes:

harbinger   frequency: 1   relative frequency: 0.00001
    p. 394 UNGATHERED 28   21 Then entertaine, and as Deaths Harbinger;

harbor   frequency: 1   relative frequency: 0.00001
    p. 119 FOREST 13   92 Into your harbor, and all passage shut

harbour   frequency: 2   relative frequency: 0.00002
    See also "harbor."
    p.   79 EPIGRAMS 124   5 Which in life did harbour giue
    p. 101 FOREST 4   58 To harbour a diuided thought

harbour'd   frequency: 1   relative frequency: 0.00001
    p.   29 EPIGRAMS 7   1 Where lately harbour'd many a famous whore,

harbours   frequency: 1   relative frequency: 0.00001
    p. 354 HORACE 1   622 ... . harbours . ....

hard   frequency: 8   relative frequency: 0.00011
    See also "th'hard."

hard (cont.)
  p.   37 EPIGRAMS 32   8 Was his blest fate, but our hard lot to find.
  p. 153 UNDERWOOD 13   4 Lesse list of proud, hard, or ingratefull Men.
  p. 153 UNDERWOOD 13   23 They are so long a comming, and so hard;
  p. 204 UNDERWOOD 43   35 Or pomp'd for those hard trifles, Anagrams,
  p. 225 UNDERWOOD 50   33 As they are hard, for them to make their owne,
  p. 313 HORACE 2   183 'Tis hard, to speake things common, properly:
  p. 335 HORACE 2   634 On artlesse Verse; the hard ones he will blame;
  p. 418 UNGATHERED 46   7 Although the gate were hard, the gayne is sweete.

hard-by   frequency: 1   relative frequency: 0.00001
  p. 417 UNGATHERED 45   23 to the Peake it is so hard-by,

hard-hearted   frequency: 1   relative frequency: 0.00001
  p. 293 UNDERWOOD 86   37 Hard-hearted, I dreame every Night

harder   frequency: 1   relative frequency: 0.00001
  p.   85 EPIGRAMS 133   39 A harder tasque, then either his to Bristo',

hardest   frequency: 1   relative frequency: 0.00001
  p.   99 FOREST 3   77 Let him, then hardest sires, more disinherit,

hardie   frequency: 1   relative frequency: 0.00001
  p.   32 EPIGRAMS 16   1 HARDIE, thy braine is valiant, 'tis confest,

hardly   frequency: 3   relative frequency: 0.00004
  p. 103 FOREST 6   7 On my lips, thus hardly sundred,
  p. 230 UNDERWOOD 56   9 Laden with Bellie, and doth hardly approach
  p. 315 HORACE 2   232 To every vice, as hardly to be brought

hardy. See "brayne-hardie," "foole-hardie," "hardie."

hare   frequency: 2   relative frequency: 0.00002
  p.   97 FOREST 3   29 And, in the winter, hunt'st the flying hare,
  p. 290 UNDERWOOD 85   35 And snares the fearfull Hare, and new-come
                            Crane,

hark. See "harke."

harke   frequency: 1   relative frequency: 0.00001
  p. 253 UNDERWOOD 75   33 Harke how the Bells upon the waters play

harmes   frequency: 3   relative frequency: 0.00004
  p. 215 UNDERWOOD 44   86 We neither love the Troubles, nor the harmes.
  p. 232 UNDERWOOD 59   2 The art of urging, and avoyding harmes,
  p. 289 UNDERWOOD 85   6 Nor dreads the Seas inraged harmes:

harmonie   frequency: 3   relative frequency: 0.00004
  p.   82 EPIGRAMS 130   14 Including all, were thence call'd harmonie:
  p. 141 UNDERWOOD 2.9   34 What we harmonie doe call
  p. 323 HORACE 2   388 To note, in Poemes, breach of harmonie;

harmoniously   frequency: 1   relative frequency: 0.00001
  p. 112 FOREST 11   99 A body so harmoniously compos'd,

harmony   frequency: 4   relative frequency: 0.00005
  See also "harmonie."
  p. 239 UNDERWOOD 67   20 The Harmony may pull
  p. 367 UNGATHERED 6   51 Hath all beene Harmony:
  p. 371 UNGATHERED 9   8 As fit to haue encreas'd the harmony
  p. 395 UNGATHERED 29   14 What Muse, or rather God of harmony

harms   frequency: 1   relative frequency: 0.00001
  See also "harmes."
  p. 342 HORACE 1   146 ... . harms ....

harp   frequency: 2   relative frequency: 0.00002
  See also "harpe."
  p. 174 UNDERWOOD 23   9 Doth Clarius Harp want strings,
  p. 340 HORACE 1   306 .. the grave Harp, and Violl voyces ...

harpe   frequency: 6   relative frequency: 0.00008
 *p. 494 TO HIMSELF   58 No Harpe ere hit the starres;
  p.   98 FOREST 3   51 APOLLO'S harpe, and HERMES lyre
                            resound,
  p. 239 UNDERWOOD 67   17 Harpe, Lute, Theorbo sprung,
  p. 263 UNDERWOOD 79   1 New yeares, expect new gifts: Sister, your
                            Harpe,
  p. 274 U'WOOD 84.1   35 As comming with his Harpe, prepar'd
  p. 292 UNDERWOOD 86   23 Shall Verse be set to Harpe and Lute,

harpies   frequency: 1   relative frequency: 0.00001
    See also "harpyes."
    p. 187 UNDERWOOD 33   9 Hook-handed Harpies, gowned Vultures, put

harpyes   frequency: 1   relative frequency: 0.00001
    p. 86 EPIGRAMS 133   69 Gorgonian scolds, and Harpyes: on the other

harrow'd   frequency: 1   relative frequency: 0.00001
    p. 127 UNDERWOOD 1.1   5 2. My selfe up to thee, harrow'd, torne, and
                             bruis'd

harry   frequency: 2   relative frequency: 0.00002
    p. 240 UNDERWOOD 67   26 The Daughter of great Harry!
    p. 246 UNDERWOOD 70   94 And keepe the one halfe from his Harry.

harsh   frequency: 2   relative frequency: 0.00002
    p. 40 EPIGRAMS 42   10 Harsh sights at home, GILES wisheth he were
                             blind.
    p. 190 UNDERWOOD 37   17 Rigid, and harsh, which is a Drug austere

hart   frequency: 2   relative frequency: 0.00002
    p. 59 EPIGRAMS 92   22 Are sure to con the catalogue by hart;
    p. 264 UNDERWOOD 79   21 That drives the Hart to seeke unused wayes,

hartes   frequency: 1   relative frequency: 0.00001
    p. 382 UNGATHERED 16   4 to tender thus, their liues, their loues, their
                             hartes!

harth   frequency: 3   relative frequency: 0.00004
    p. 95 FOREST 2   78 Shine bright on euery harth as the desires
    p. 120 FOREST 14   1 Now that the harth is crown'd with smiling fire,
    p. 291 UNDERWOOD 85   43 To deck the hallow'd Harth with old wood fir'd

harts   frequency: 1   relative frequency: 0.00001
    p. 399 UNGATHERED 31   4 Tenants, and Seruants, haue they harts, and
                             eyes,

harvest   frequency: 2   relative frequency: 0.00002
    See also "apple-haruest."
    p. 209 UNDERWOOD 43 150 No Foole would his owne harvest spoile, or
                             burne!
    p. 247 UNDERWOOD 70 128 Had sow'd these fruits, and got the harvest in.

has   frequency: 5   relative frequency: 0.00007
    See also "ha's," "h'has," "lamia'has."

ha's   frequency: 1   relative frequency: 0.00001

hast   frequency: 55   relative frequency: 0.00079
    See also "th'hast," "thou'<h>ast," "thou'ast,"
              "thou'hast."
  **p. 115 PANEGYRE   66 And infants, that the houres had made such hast
    p. 31 EPIGRAMS 14   7 What name, what skill, what faith hast thou in
                             things!
    p. 32 EPIGRAMS 18   3 Thou saist, that cannot be: for thou hast seene
    p. 32 EPIGRAMS 18   10 Thy faith is all the knowledge that thou hast.
    p. 34 EPIGRAMS 25   8 Iust wife, and, to change me, make womans hast?
    p. 38 EPIGRAMS 35   5 Hast purg'd thy realmes, as we haue now no cause
    p. 39 EPIGRAMS 40   17 Earth, thou hast not such another.
    p. 40 EPIGRAMS 43   1 What need hast thou of me? or of my Muse?
    p. 48 EPIGRAMS 65   2 That hast betray'd me to a worthlesse lord;
    p. 53 EPIGRAMS 78   1 HORNET, thou hast thy wife drest, for the
                             stall,
    p. 57 EPIGRAMS 89   9 Who both their graces in thy selfe hast more
    p. 61 EPIGRAMS 95   5 So hast thou rendred him in all his bounds,
    p. 61 EPIGRAMS 95   19 That hast thy brest so cleere of present crimes,
    p. 62 EPIGRAMS 96   6 As thou hast best authoritie, t<o>'allow.
    p. 63 EPIGRAMS 98   1 Thou hast begun well, ROE, which stand well
                             too,
    p. 63 EPIGRAMS 98   2 And I know nothing more thou hast to doo.
    p. 63 EPIGRAMS 99   1 That thou hast kept thy loue, encreast thy will,
    p. 63 EPIGRAMS 99   3 Hast taught thy selfe worthy thy pen to tread,
    p. 72 EPIGRAMS 112 10 An Epick poeme; thou hast the same end.
    p. 85 EPIGRAMS 133 51 Thou hast seene hell (some say) and know'st all
                             nookes there,
    p. 93 FOREST 2   4 Thou hast no lantherne, whereof tales are told;
    p. 93 FOREST 2   9 Thou hast thy walkes for health, as well as
                             sport:
    p. 94 FOREST 2   19 Thy copp's, too, nam'd of GAMAGE, thou hast
                             there,

hast (cont.)

p. 94 FOREST 2	32	Thou hast thy ponds, that pay thee tribute fish,
p. 97 FOREST 3	37	The whil'st, the seuerall seasons thou hast seene
p. 100 FOREST 4	1	False world, good-night: since thou hast brought
p. 101 FOREST 4	40	More hatred, then thou hast to mee.
p. 101 FOREST 4.	45	Then, in a soile hast planted me,
p. 129 UNDERWOOD 1.2	18	Then thou hast done?
p. 137 UNDERWOOD 2.5	50	Something more then thou hast spi'd.
p. 161 UNDERWOOD 14	71	But nought beyond. He thou hast given it to,
p. 187 UNDERWOOD 33	22	Thou hast the brave scorne, to put back the fee!
p. 187 UNDERWOOD 33	25	Of Bookes, of Presidents, hast thou at hand!
p. 188 UNDERWOOD 34	18	And scorn'd, thou'<h>ast showne thy malice, but hast fail'd.
p. 197 UNDERWOOD 40	4	In hast the bottome of a med'cin'd Cup,
p. 210 UNDERWOOD 43	163	And what hast thou done in these pettie spights,
p. 210 UNDERWOOD 43	168	Which thou hast only vented, not enjoy'd.
p. 213 UNDERWOOD 44	24	Thou Seed-plot of the warre, that hast not spar'd
p. 238 UNDERWOOD 65	9	And there to stand so. Hast now, envious Moone,
p. 245 UNDERWOOD 70	58	To shew thou hast beene long,
p. 252 UNDERWOOD 75	1	Though thou hast past thy Summer standing, stay
p. 254 UNDERWOOD 75	75	In all thy age of Journals thou hast tooke,
p. 277 U'WOOD 84.3	28	And thou hast painted beauties world.
p. 280 U'WOOD 84.4	53	Thrice happy house, that hast receipt
p. 283 U'WOOD 84.9	27	Thou hast no more blowes, Fate, to drive at one:
p. 388 UNGATHERED 23	4	What treasure hast thou brought vs! and what store
p. 389 UNGATHERED 23	10	Such Passage hast thou found, such Returnes made,
p. 391 UNGATHERED 26	41	Triumph, my Britaine, thou hast one to showe,
p. 397 UNGATHERED 30	48	Vnder one title. Thou hast made thy way
p. 398 UNGATHERED 30	60	Thou hast deseru'd: And let me reade the while
p. 408 UNGATHERED 37	3	ffor thou obiectest (as thou hast been told)
p. 408 UNGATHERED 37	8	That thou hast lost thy noyse, thy foame, thy stirre,
p. 410 UNGATHERED 39	5	All which thou hast incurr'd deseruedly:
p. 410 UNGATHERED 39	9	Thinking to stir me, thou hast lost thy End,
p. 411 UNGATHERED 39	13	For thou hast nought <in> <thee> to cure his Fame,

haste   frequency: 10   relative frequency: 0.00014
See also "hast."

p. 257 UNDERWOOD 75	145	Haste, haste, officious Sun, and send them Night
p. 263 UNDERWOOD 79	10	And shuts the old. Haste, haste, all loyall Swaines,
p. 265 UNDERWOOD 79	46	Haste, haste you hither, all you gentler Swaines,
p. 323 HORACE 2	385	Of too much haste, and negligence in part,
p. 335 HORACE 2	655	For, if one should, and with a rope make haste
p. 368 UNGATHERED 6	73	Haste, Haste, sweete Singer: Nor to Tine,

hastens   frequency: 1   relative frequency: 0.00001
   p. 315 HORACE 2   211 He ever hastens to the end, and so

hastes.   See "hasts."

hastily   frequency: 1   relative frequency: 0.00001
   p. 242 UNDERWOOD 70   7 Wise child, did'st hastily returne,

hasting   frequency: 1   relative frequency: 0.00001
 **p. 114 PANEGYRE   33 Hasting to follow forth in shouts, and cryes.

hasts   frequency: 1   relative frequency: 0.00001
   p. 414 UNGATHERED 41   51 Who like a Giant hasts his course to run,

hasty   frequency: 1   relative frequency: 0.00001
   p. 116 FOREST 12   97 This hasty sacrifice, wherein I reare

hat   frequency: 4   relative frequency: 0.00005
   p. 56 EPIGRAMS 88   3 That so much skarfe of France, and hat, and fether,
   p. 68 EPIGRAMS 105   7 He, that but saw you weare the wheaten hat,
   p. 202 UNDERWOOD 42   83 Under that cover; an old Mid-wives hat!
   p. 373 UNGATHERED 10   26 Old Hat here, torne Hose, with Shoes full of grauell,

hate   frequency: 8   relative frequency: 0.00011
   p. 40 EPIGRAMS 43   4 Her foes enough would fame thee, in their hate.
   p. 147 UNDERWOOD 7   25 Though hate had put them out;

hate (cont.)
   p. 200 UNDERWOOD 42   35 Of love, and hate: and came so nigh to know
   p. 233 UNDERWOOD 59   7 I hate such measur'd, give me mettall'd fire
   p. 250 UNDERWOOD 73   6 Who seldome sleepes! whom bad men only hate!
   p. 317 HORACE 2   269 What so is showne, I not beleeve, and hate.
   p. 331 HORACE 2   571 Why not? I'm gentle, and free-borne, doe hate
   p. 367 UNGATHERED 6   31 "So much doth Virtue hate,

hated   frequency: 1   relative frequency: 0.00001
   p. 423 UNGATHERED 50 13 Euen states most hated, when no lawes resist

hateth   frequency: 1   relative frequency: 0.00001
   p. 112 FOREST 11   87 He that for loue of goodnesse hateth ill,

hath   frequency: 126   relative frequency: 0.00182
   See also "h'hath," "she'hath," "sh'hath."

hating   frequency: 1   relative frequency: 0.00001
   p. 52 EPIGRAMS 76   10 Hating that solemne vice of greatnesse, pride;

hatred   frequency: 3   relative frequency: 0.00004
   p. 101 FOREST 4   40 More hatred, then thou hast to mee.
   p. 163 UNDERWOOD 15 39 Friendship is now mask'd Hatred! Justice fled,
   p. 368 UNGATHERED 6 85 The Dutch whom Wealth (not Hatred) doth
                              diuide;

hau'-boy   frequency: 1   relative frequency: 0.00001
   p. 319 HORACE 2   287 The Hau'-boy, not as now with latten bound,

hau'boy   frequency: 1   relative frequency: 0.00001
   p. 292 UNDERWOOD 86 24 And Phrygian Hau'boy, not without the Flute.

haue   frequency: 123   relative frequency: 0.00178

haue'hem   frequency: 1   relative frequency: 0.00001

haughtie   frequency: 2   relative frequency: 0.00002
   p. 315 HORACE 2   235 Of money, haughtie, to desire soon mov'd,
   p. 391 UNGATHERED 26 39 Of all, that insolent Greece, or haughtie Rome

haughty. See "haughtie."

hauing   frequency: 7   relative frequency: 0.00010

hauking   frequency: 1   relative frequency: 0.00001
   p. 97 FOREST 3   33 Or hauking at the riuer, or the bush,

haunch. See "hanch."

haunt   frequency: 2   relative frequency: 0.00002
   p. 30 EPIGRAMS 12   2 That haunt Pickt-hatch, Mersh-Lambeth, and
                             White-fryers,
   p. 165 UNDERWOOD 15 91 Or use all arts, or haunt all Companies

hautboy. See "hau'-boy," "hau'boy."

have   frequency: 163   relative frequency: 0.00235
   See also "ha'," "haue," "haue'hem," "have't,"
           "i'haue," "th<ou>'have," "t'haue,"
           "t'have," "they'<h>ave," "they'haue,"
           "th'haue," "to'<h>ave," "we'<h>ave,"
           "who'haue," "yo'haue," "yo'have,"
           "you'haue."

have't   frequency: 1   relative frequency: 0.00001

having   frequency: 9   relative frequency: 0.00013
   See also "hauing."

hawking   frequency: 2   relative frequency: 0.00002
   See also "hauking."
   p. 55 EPIGRAMS 85   3 Where I both learn'd, why wise-men hawking
                             follow,
   p. 215 UNDERWOOD 44 72 The Hawking language? or our Day to breake

hay   frequency: 1   relative frequency: 0.00001
   p. 240 UNDERWOOD 67 42 Hay! for the flowre of France!

hayles   frequency: 1   relative frequency: 0.00001
   p. 268 UNDERWOOD 83 2 Hayles me, so solemnly, to yonder Yewgh?

hayre   frequency: 1   relative frequency: 0.00001
    p. 115 FOREST 12   61 Who made a lampe of BERENICES hayre?

hayward   frequency: 1   relative frequency: 0.00001
    p. 161 UNDERWOOD 14   81 The Gaine of your two friendships! Hayward and

hazard   frequency: 4   relative frequency: 0.00005
    p.   27 EPIGRAMS 2   10 Made from the hazard of anothers shame:
    p.   56 EPIGRAMS 87   2 HAZARD a month forsware his; and grew
                                drunke,
    p.   56 EPIGRAMS 87   t1 ON CAPTAINE HAZARD THE
                                CHEATER.
    p. 214 UNDERWOOD 44   47 Without the hazard of a drop of blood,

he   frequency: 447   relative frequency: 0.00647
    See also "h<e>'offend," "he'adulters," "hee,"
             "hee'd," "hee'ld," "hee'll," "hee's,"
             "he'had," "he'le," "he'll," "he's,"
             "h'had," "h'has," "h'hath."

head   frequency: 21   relative frequency: 0.00030
    See also "popes-head-alley."
    p.   31 EPIGRAMS 14   1 CAMDEN, most reuerend head, to whom I owe
    p.   80 EPIGRAMS 126   7 PHOEBVS replyed. Bold head, it is not
                                shee:
    p.   80 EPIGRAMS 127   5 Into the debt; and reckon on her head,
    p.   89 EPIGRAMS 133   186 The tripple head without a sop. At last,
    p.   98 FOREST 3   64 Which boasts t'haue had the head of gold.
    p. 101 FOREST 4   32 Render his head in there againe?
    p. 114 FOREST 12   52 Or, in an armies head, that, lockt in brasse,
    p. 115 FOREST 12   84 Borne vp by statues, shall I reare your head,
    p. 157 UNDERWOOD 13   128 Coriat, should rise the most sufficient head
    p. 176 UNDERWOOD 25   6 Her upright head, above the reach of Chance,
    p. 232 UNDERWOOD 57   28 if the'Chequer be emptie, so will be his Head.
    p. 245 UNDERWOOD 70   77 Accept this garland, plant it on thy head,
    p. 272 UNDERWOOD 83   99 The Serpents head: Gets above Death, and
                                Sinne,
    p. 290 UNDERWOOD 85   18 His head, with mellow Apples crown'd,
    p. 294 UNDERWOOD 89   4 Thy locks, and rosie garlands crowne thy head;
    p. 305 HORACE 2   1 If to a Womans head a Painter would
    p. 305 HORACE 2   10 As neither head, nor foot, one forme retaine.
    p. 349 HORACE 1   428 The head that ....
    p. 375 UNGATHERED 10   31 Their hornes, and Germany pukes on his head.
    p. 397 UNGATHERED 30   34 Pearch'd ouer head, the wise Athenian Owle:
    p. 413 UNGATHERED 41   28 As if they' ador'd the Head, wheron th'are fixt.

head-long   frequency: 1   relative frequency: 0.00001
    p. 319 HORACE 2   307 The rash, and head-long eloquence brought forth

headed. See "many-headed."

heades   frequency: 1   relative frequency: 0.00001
    p. 417 UNGATHERED 45   26 that the wife heades for a wager

headlong   frequency: 1   relative frequency: 0.00001
    See also "head-long."
    p. 203 UNDERWOOD 43   9 'Twas Jupiter that hurl'd thee headlong downe,

heads   frequency: 8   relative frequency: 0.00011
    See also "heades."
    p.   59 EPIGRAMS 92   33 At naming the French King, their heads they
                                shake,
    p.   86 EPIGRAMS 133   93 Ouer your heads: Well, row. At this a loud
    p.   88 EPIGRAMS 133   146 The heads, houghs, entrailes, and the hides of
                                dogs:
    p.   89 EPIGRAMS 133   177 Of Hol'borne (<the> three sergeants heads)
                                lookes ore,
    p. 233 UNDERWOOD 59   17 To know the heads of danger! where 'tis fit
    p. 272 U'WOOD 84.1   3 Their Heads, that ENVY would hold downe
    p. 325 HORACE 2   428 Their heads, which three Anticyra's cannot
                                heale.
    p. 363 UNGATHERED 3   8 The knottie heads of the most surly Groomes,

he'adulters   frequency: 1   relative frequency: 0.00001
    p.   35 EPIGRAMS 26   2 He'adulters still: his thoughts lye with a whore.

heal. See "heale."

heale   frequency: 1   relative frequency: 0.00001
    p. 325 HORACE 2   428 Their heads, which three Anticyra's cannot
                                heale.

health   frequency: 10   relative frequency: 0.00014
    p. 93 FOREST 2   9 Thou hast thy walkes for health, as well as
                               sport:
    p. 105 FOREST 8   42 Play away, health, wealth, and fame.
    p. 150 UNDERWOOD 10   16 I ne're will owe my health to a disease.
    p. 165 UNDERWOOD 15   103 His time? health? soule? will he for these goe
                               throw
    p. 166 UNDERWOOD 15   115 Surfet? and Quarrel? drinkes the tother health?
    p. 186 UNDERWOOD 31   5 So, from all sicknesse, may you rise to health,
    p. 197 UNDERWOOD 40   10 Under another Name, I take your health;
    p. 199 UNDERWOOD 41   13 My health will leave me; and when you depart,
    p. 222 UNDERWOOD 48   49 Or else a health advances,
    p. 248 UNDERWOOD 71   12 Health, or scarce breath, as she had never bin,

health-sake   frequency: 1   relative frequency: 0.00001
    p. 156 UNDERWOOD 13   100 Lowd sacrifice of drinke, for their health-sake!

healths   frequency: 1   relative frequency: 0.00001
    p. 293 UNDERWOOD 86   31 Nor care I now healths to propound;

heap. See "heape."

heap'd   frequency: 3   relative frequency: 0.00004
    p. 69 EPIGRAMS 107   15 And, in some yeere, all these together heap'd,
    p. 88 EPIGRAMS 133   139 Or, that it lay, heap'd like an vsurers masse,
    p. 95 FOREST 2   83 Did'st thou, then, make 'hem! and what praise was
                               heap'd

heape   frequency: 5   relative frequency: 0.00007
    p. 99 FOREST 3   81 Let that goe heape a masse of wretched wealth,
    p. 157 UNDERWOOD 13   133 In time 'twill be a heape; This is not true
    p. 167 UNDERWOOD 15   156 With him, for he is follow'd with that heape
    p. 172 UNDERWOOD 21   5 A parcell of Court-durt, a heape, and masse
    p. 236 UNDERWOOD 63   14 Cannot but heape that grace, he will requite.

heapes   frequency: 1   relative frequency: 0.00001
    p. 331 HORACE 2   569 Lest the throng'd heapes should on a laughter
                               take:

heaping   frequency: 1   relative frequency: 0.00001
    p. 385 UNGATHERED 19   6 If Praises, when th'are full, heaping admit,

heaps   frequency: 1   relative frequency: 0.00001
    See also "heapes."
    p. 96 FOREST 2   101 Those proud, ambitious heaps, and nothing else,

hear. See "heare."

heard   frequency: 20   relative frequency: 0.00028
    p. 60 EPIGRAMS 94   10 But, when they heard it tax'd, tooke more
                               offence.
    p. 84 EPIGRAMS 133   13 Arses were heard to croake, in stead of frogs;
    p. 84 EPIGRAMS 133   17 Laden with plague-sores, and their sinnes, were
                               heard,
    p. 86 EPIGRAMS 133   80 Man, that had neuer heard of a Chimaera.
    p. 86 EPIGRAMS 133   89 How hight the place? a voyce was heard,
                               COCYTVS.
    p. 87 EPIGRAMS 133   105 But I will speake (and know I shall be heard)
    p. 132 UNDERWOOD 2.2   29 (Which with griefe and wrath I heard)
    p. 133 UNDERWOOD 2.3   13 He no sooner heard the Law,
    p. 139 UNDERWOOD 2.8   6 All that heard her, with desire.
    p. 159 UNDERWOOD 14   34 Heard what times past have said, seene what ours
                               doe:
    p. 229 UNDERWOOD 54   5 Who, when shee heard the match, concluded
                               streight,
    p. 274 U'WOOD 84.1   34 Who claimes (of reverence) to be heard,
    p. 284 U'WOOD 84.9   60 T<o>'accuse, or quit all Parties to be heard!
    p. 317 HORACE 2   277 Must maintaine manly; not be heard to sing,
    p. 333 HORACE 2   591 Who, since, to sing the Pythian rites is heard,
    p. 366 UNGATHERED 6   26 As the whole heard in sight,
    p. 367 UNGATHERED 6   58 That heard but Spight deliuer
    p. 397 UNGATHERED 30   26 Heard the soft ayres, between our swaynes &
                               thee,
    p. 397 UNGATHERED 30   38 My lippes could forme the voyce, I heard that
                               Rore,
    p. 414 UNGATHERED 42   3 And truely, so I would, could I be heard.

heards   frequency: 1   relative frequency: 0.00001
    p. 97 FOREST 3   16 'Mongst loughing heards, and solide hoofes:

```
heare                              frequency:    42   relative frequency: 0.00060
   *p.  494 TO HIMSELF        51 But, when they heare thee sing
  **p.  115 PANEGYRE          94 "To heare the truth, from spight, or flattery
                                  voyd.
  **p.  116 PANEGYRE         134 To heare her speech; which still began in him
    p.   36 EPIGRAMS 28       20 May heare my Epigrammes, but like of none.
    p.   45 EPIGRAMS 58        2 To reade my verses; now I must to heare:
    p.   51 EPIGRAMS 74        1 Whil'st thy weigh'd iudgements, EGERTON,
                                  I heare,
    p.   73 EPIGRAMS 114       2 When SYDNYES name I heare, or face I
                                  see:
    p.   78 EPIGRAMS 122       6 And heare her speake with one, and her first
                                  tongue;
    p.   79 EPIGRAMS 124       1 Would'st thou heare, what man can say
    p.   83 EPIGRAMS 131       5 And though we could all men, all censures heare,
    p.   86 EPIGRAMS 133      92 Is this we heare? of frogs? No, guts wind-bound,
    p.   97 FOREST 3          22 A-bed canst heare the loud stag speake,
    p.  111 FOREST 11         65 Of all his happinesse? But soft: I heare
    p.  117 FOREST 13         22 If it may stand with your soft blush to heare
    p.  119 FOREST 13        100 Heare, what the Muses sing about thy roote,
    p.  128 UNDERWOOD 1.1     42 To heare, to mediate, sweeten my desire,
    p.  129 UNDERWOOD 1.2      1 Heare mee, O God!
    p.  133 UNDERWOOD 2.3     26 Heare and make Example too.
    p.  136 UNDERWOOD 2.5      5 Heare, what late Discourse of you,
    p.  168 UNDERWOOD 15     191 And last, blaspheme not, we did never heare
    p.  186 UNDERWOOD 32       7 Such shall you heare to day, and find great foes,
    p.  187 UNDERWOOD 33       7 But when I read or heare the names so rife
    p.  190 UNDERWOOD 37      18 In friendship, I confesse: But, deare friend,
                                  heare.
    p.  199 UNDERWOOD 41       2 Heare, Mistris, your departing servant tell
    p.  214 UNDERWOOD 44      63 Should he <not> heare of billow, wind, and
                                  storme,
    p.  219 UNDERWOOD 47      46 Though I doe neither heare these newes, nor tell
    p.  228 UNDERWOOD 53       9 Or what we heare our home-borne Legend tell,
    p.  232 UNDERWOOD 58       1 Thou, Friend, wilt heare all censures; unto thee
    p.  234 UNDERWOOD 61       5 That scarce you heare a publike voyce alive,
    p.  251 UNDERWOOD 74      21 With love, to heare your modestie relate
    p.  264 UNDERWOOD 79      23 Chor. Heare, o you Groves, and, Hills, resound
                                  his praise.
    p.  264 UNDERWOOD 79      31 Chor. Heare, O you Groves, and, Hills,
                                  resound his worth.
    p.  283 U'WOOD 84.9       48 To heare their Judge, and his eternall doome;
    p.  286 U'WOOD 84.9      133 In his humanitie! To heare him preach
    p.  315 HORACE 2         219 Heare, what it is the People, and I desire:
    p.  329 HORACE 2         536 Angry. Sometimes, I heare good Homer snore.
    p.  333 HORACE 1          31 Heare me conclude ... .... .... .... ....
    p.  368 UNGATHERED 6      89 All which, when they but heare a straine
    p.  391 UNGATHERED 26     36 To life againe, to heare thy Buskin tread,
    p.  397 UNGATHERED 30     55 But that I heare, againe, thy Drum to beate
    p.  407 UNGATHERED 36      1 Sr Inigo doth feare it as I heare
    p.  417 UNGATHERED 45     24 shee soone will heare it.

hearer                             frequency:     1   relative frequency: 0.00001
    p.  315 HORACE 2         212 (As if he knew it) rapps his hearer to

hearers                            frequency:     2   relative frequency: 0.00002
    p.  187 UNDERWOOD 33      36 Thy Hearers Nectar, and thy Clients Balme,
    p.  311 HORACE 2         142 To worke the hearers minds, still, to their
                                  plight.

heares                             frequency:     2   relative frequency: 0.00002
    p.  148 UNDERWOOD 7       27 What Nymph so e're his voyce but heares,
    p.  239 UNDERWOOD 67      24 Whilst it the Dittie heares.

hearing                            frequency:     3   relative frequency: 0.00004
    p.   64 EPIGRAMS 100       1 PLAY-WRIGHT, by chance, hearing some
                                  toyes I'had writ,
    p.  142 U'WOOD 2.10       t1 Another Ladyes exception present at the hearing.
    p.  256 UNDERWOOD 75     127 Hearing their charge, and then

hearkens                           frequency:     1   relative frequency: 0.00001
    p.  216 UNDERWOOD 45       6 That hearkens to a Jacks-pulse, when it goes.

hears.  See "heares," "under-heares."

hearse.  See "herse."

hearst                             frequency:     1   relative frequency: 0.00001
    p.  406 UNGATHERED 35      1 But cause thou hearst ye mighty k. of Spaine
```

hear'st   frequency: 1   relative frequency: 0.00001
  See also "hearst."
  p.   54 EPIGRAMS 81   5 For all thou hear'st, thou swear'st thy selfe
                            didst doo.

heart   frequency: 26   relative frequency: 0.00037
  See also "hart."
  p.   49 EPIGRAMS 67   10 Before thou wert it, in each good mans heart.
  p.   97 FOREST 3   25 Or with thy friends, the heart of all the yeere,
  p. 109 FOREST 11   11 Obiect arriue there, but the heart (our spie)
  p. 109 FOREST 11   23 (That should ring larum to the heart) doth
                            sleepe,
  p. 112 FOREST 11   90 His heart sinnes, though he feares.
  p. 127 UNDERWOOD 1.1   7 As my heart lies in peeces, all confus'd,
  p. 127 UNDERWOOD 1.1   10 A broken heart thou wert not wont despise,
  p. 127 UNDERWOOD 1.1   15 What odour can be, then a heart contrite,
  p. 129 UNDERWOOD 1.2   2 A broken heart,
  p. 133 UNDERWOOD 2.3   16 Left it sticking in my heart:
  p. 142 UNDERWOOD 2.9   54 I could give my very heart;
  p. 147 UNDERWOOD 7   14 Unlesse my heart would as my thought be torne.
  p. 148 UNDERWOOD 7   32 From either heart, I know;
  p. 151 UNDERWOOD 11   5 Hath both my heart and me surpriz'd,
  p. 170 UNDERWOOD 18   24 Love to my heart, and Fortune to my lines.
  p. 179 UNDERWOOD 25   54 (Whose heart in that bright Sphere flames
                            clearest,
  p. 194 UNDERWOOD 38   117 Your forme shines here, here fixed in my heart:
  p. 198 UNDERWOOD 40   43 Can lock the Sense up, or the heart a thought,
  p. 199 UNDERWOOD 41   14 How shall I doe, sweet Mistris, for my heart?
  p. 227 UNDERWOOD 52   23 A letter'd mind, and a large heart would place
  p. 247 UNDERWOOD 70   124 And with the heart, not pen,
  p. 250 UNDERWOOD 73   12 T<o>'effect it, feele, thou'ast made thine owne
                            heart ake.
  p. 253 UNDERWOOD 75   16 By all the Spheares consent, so in the heart of
                            June?
  p. 288 U'WOOD 84.9   186 Nor can the bruised heart want eloquence:
  p. 380 UNGATHERED 12   24 The truth of his heart there, and tell's what a
                            clocke
  p. 384 UNGATHERED 18   3 At these thy Nuptials; but, whose heart, and
                            thought

heart-strike   frequency: 1   relative frequency: 0.00001
  p. 311 HORACE 2   136 And Peleus, if they seeke to heart-strike us

hearted. See "hard-hearted."

hearth. See "harth."

hearts   frequency: 15   relative frequency: 0.00021
  See also "hartes," "harts."
**p. 113 PANEGYRE   31 With these he pass'd, and with his peoples hearts
**p. 114 PANEGYRE   60 Of hearts, and voices. All the aire was rent,
**p. 117 PANEGYRE   143 Before mens hearts had crown'd him. Who (vnlike
  p. 110 FOREST 11   52 To murther different hearts,
  p. 122 FOREST 15   6 And hearts of all, if I be sad for show,
  p. 134 UNDERWOOD 2.4   5 As she goes, all hearts doe duty
  p. 137 UNDERWOOD 2.5   31 Is my Mothers! Hearts of slaine
  p. 182 UNDERWOOD 28   8 Both braines and hearts; and mine now best doe
                            know it:
  p. 213 UNDERWOOD 44   1 Why yet, my noble hearts, they cannot say,
  p. 234 UNDERWOOD 61   14 My Lord, till felt griefe make our stone hearts
                            soft,
  p. 238 UNDERWOOD 66   10 To make the hearts of a whole Nation smile,
  p. 246 UNDERWOOD 70   99 Of hearts the union. And those not by chance
  p. 249 UNDERWOOD 72   14 That cry that gladnesse, which their hearts would
                            pray,
  p. 286 U'WOOD 84.9   150 Who knowes the hearts of all, and can dissect
  p. 414 UNGATHERED 41   55 T'imprint in all purg'd hearts this virgin sence,

heat   frequency: 8   relative frequency: 0.00011
  See also "heate."
  p. 174 UNDERWOOD 22   31 One sparke of your Diviner heat
  p. 177 UNDERWOOD 25   11 Thy Priest in this strange rapture; heat my
                            braine
  p. 192 UNDERWOOD 38   57 The Sunne his heat, and light, the ayre his dew?
  p. 199 UNDERWOOD 41   11 Alas I ha' lost my heat, my blood, my prime,
  p. 294 UNDERWOOD 88   5 For lust will languish, and that heat decay.
  p. 295 UNDERWOOD 89   6 And heat, with softest love, thy softer bed.
  p. 392 UNGATHERED 26   60 (Such as thine are) and strike the second heat
  p. 405 UNGATHERED 34   72 Of Lanterne-lerry: wth fuliginous heat

heate
```
                              frequency:    4    relative frequency: 0.00005
  *p.  493 TO HIMSELF         47 Strike that disdaine-full heate
   p.  384 UNGATHERED 18      20 And eu'ry birth encrease the heate of Loue.
   p.  397 UNGATHERED 30      56 A better cause, and strike the brauest heate
   p.  400 UNGATHERED 31      28 Fames heate vpon the graue did stay;
```

heates
```
                              frequency:    1    relative frequency: 0.00001
   p.  233 UNDERWOOD 59       21 Who durst live great, 'mongst all the colds, and
                                 heates,
```

heating
```
                              frequency:    1    relative frequency: 0.00001
   p.  179 UNDERWOOD 25       43 Though but while mettal's heating:
```

heats
```
  See also "heates."          frequency:    1    relative frequency: 0.00001
   p.  220 UNDERWOOD 47       67 And that there be no fev'ry heats, nor colds,
```

heau'd
```
                              frequency:    1    relative frequency: 0.00001
   p.  115 FOREST 12          57 Like life vnto 'hem. Who heau'd HERCVLES
```

heauen
```
                              frequency:   17    relative frequency: 0.00024
 **p.  115 PANEGYRE           79 "That they, by Heauen, are plac'd vpon his
                                 throne,
 **p.  115 PANEGYRE           80 "To rule like Heauen; and haue no more, their
                                 owne,
 **p.  117 PANEGYRE          136 Was gently falne from heauen vpon this state;
 **p.  117 PANEGYRE          154 Of heauen is discharg'd along the skie:
   p.   35 EPIGRAMS 27         7 To heauen; his hath: O happy state! wherein
   p.   37 EPIGRAMS 33         5 Which if most gracious heauen grant like thine,
   p.   52 EPIGRAMS 74        10 T<o>'our times return'd, hath made her heauen in
                                 thee.
   p.   77 EPIGRAMS 120        7 As Heauen and Nature seem'd to striue
   p.   77 EPIGRAMS 120       24 Heauen vowes to keepe him.
   p.   82 EPIGRAMS 130       11 To say, indeed, shee were the soule of heauen,
   p.  107 FOREST 10           2 Or whose great name in Poets heauen vse,
   p.  110 FOREST 11          47 It is a golden chaine let downe from heauen,
   p.  113 FOREST 12           3 That which, to boote with hell, is thought worth
                                 heauen,
   p.  114 FOREST 12          41 It is the Muse, alone, can raise to heauen,
   p.  115 FOREST 12          67 Then which, a nobler heauen it selfe knowes not.
   p.  396 UNGATHERED 30      19 And fill'd an Orbe as circular, as heauen!
   p.  399 UNGATHERED 31       1 T'is a Record in heauen. You, that were
```

heau'en
```
                              frequency:    1    relative frequency: 0.00001
   p.  108 FOREST 10 A        13 wch rap's mee vp to the true heau'en of loue;
```

heauenly
```
                              frequency:    2    relative frequency: 0.00002
 **p.  113 PANEGYRE           22 That fastneth heauenly power to earthly raigne:
   p.  393 UNGATHERED 27      15 And in effect of Heauenly loue
```

heauens
```
                              frequency:    4    relative frequency: 0.00005
   p.   33 EPIGRAMS 22         3 Yet, all heauens gifts, being heauens due,
   p.   33 EPIGRAMS 22         7 Whose soule heauens Queene, (whose name shee
                                 beares)
   p.   39 EPIGRAMS 40         6 Read not in faire heauens storie,
```

heau'n
```
                              frequency:    3    relative frequency: 0.00004
 **p.  113 PANEGYRE            1 Heau'n now not striues, alone, our brests to fill
   p.   43 EPIGRAMS 51         2 Great heau'n did well, to giue ill fame free
                                 wing;
   p.  369 UNGATHERED 6      109 In heau'n the Signe of old Eridanus:
```

heaued. See "heau'd."

heaven
```
                              frequency:   18    relative frequency: 0.00026
  See also "heauen," "heau'en," "heau'n,"
            "heav'n."
   p.  122 FOREST 15          t1 TO HEAVEN.
   p.  130 UNDERWOOD 1.3      11 The Word, which heaven, and earth did make;
   p.  144 UNDERWOOD 3        24 Mistaking earth for heaven.
   p.  188 UNDERWOOD 34       15 That heaven should make no more; or should
                                 amisse,
   p.  189 UNDERWOOD 37        1 Sir, I am thankfull, first, to heaven, for you;
   p.  192 UNDERWOOD 38       32 Thinke that your selfe like heaven forgive me
                                 can:
   p.  192 UNDERWOOD 38       64 Is natures meere obliquitie! as Heaven
   p.  193 UNDERWOOD 38       74 In a calme skie, then when the heaven is horl'd
   p.  219 UNDERWOOD 47       37 I wish all well, and pray high heaven conspire
   p.  219 UNDERWOOD 47       61 Still looking to, and ever loving heaven;
   p.  234 UNDERWOOD 61        8 To lift to heaven: who is't not understands
```

heaven (cont.)
    p. 237 UNDERWOOD 64   22 How much to heaven for thee, great
                                        CHARLES, they owe!
    p. 269 UNDERWOOD 83   29 It is too neere of kin to Heaven, the Soule,
    p. 271 UNDERWOOD 83   79 If you dare grudge at Heaven, and repent
    p. 272 UNDERWOOD 83   100 And, sure of Heaven, rides triumphing in.
    p. 273 U'WOOD 84.1   31 Of Heaven; where SERAPHIM take tent
    p. 276 U'WOOD 84.3   21 The Heaven design'd, draw next a Spring,
    p. 280 U'WOOD 84.4   56 As it slid moulded off from Heaven.

heavenly. See "heauenly."

heavens   frequency: 3   relative frequency: 0.00004
    See also "heauens," "heav'n<s>."
    p. 271 UNDERWOOD 83   71 Speakes Heavens Language! and discourseth free
    p. 278 U'WOOD 84.4   14 Would aske a Heavens Intelligence;
    p. 413 UNGATHERED 41   39 The House of gold, the Gate of heavens power,

heavie   frequency: 2   relative frequency: 0.00002
    p. 283 U'WOOD 84.9   30 Nothing I doe; but, like a heavie wheele,
    p. 323 HORACE 2   384 Those heavie Verses, sent so to the Stage,

heav'n   frequency: 1   relative frequency: 0.00001
    p. 246 UNDERWOOD 70   96 Whilst that in heav'n, this light on earth must
                                         shine.

heav'n<s>   frequency: 1   relative frequency: 0.00001
    p. 285 U'WOOD 84.9   102 In Heav'n<s> Empyrean, with a robe of light?

heavy. See "heavie."

hebrid   frequency: 1   relative frequency: 0.00001
    p. 368 UNGATHERED 6   66 The Hebrid Isles, and knowne

hee   frequency: 62   relative frequency: 0.00089

heed   frequency: 2   relative frequency: 0.00002
    p. 104 FOREST 8   7 Take heed, Sicknesse, what you doe,
    p. 223 UNDERWOOD 49   41 And practise for a Miracle; take heed

hee'd   frequency: 3   relative frequency: 0.00004

hee'ld   frequency: 2   relative frequency: 0.00002

hee'll   frequency: 3   relative frequency: 0.00004

heere   frequency: 1   relative frequency: 0.00001

hee's   frequency: 16   relative frequency: 0.00023

he'had   frequency: 1   relative frequency: 0.00001

heidelberg   frequency: 1   relative frequency: 0.00001
    p. 227 UNDERWOOD 52   6 But yet the Tun at Heidelberg had houpes.

height   frequency: 13   relative frequency: 0.00018
    See also "hight."
    p. 55 EPIGRAMS 85   9 To former height, and there in circle tarrie,
    p. 62 EPIGRAMS 95   29 Where breuitie, where splendor, and where height,
    p. 63 EPIGRAMS 98   4 Need seeke no other strength, no other height;
    p. 70 EPIGRAMS 109   13 To be the same in roote, thou art in height;
    p. 98 FOREST 3   41 The ripened eares, yet humble in their height,
    p. 156 UNDERWOOD 13 119 Or growne; by height or lownesse of the Sunne?
    p. 157 UNDERWOOD 13 140 Observe the strength, the height, the why, and
                                     when,
    p. 157 UNDERWOOD 13 148 Nor fashion; if they chance aspire to height,
    p. 224 UNDERWOOD 50   11 By all oblique Degrees, that killing height
    p. 325 HORACE 2   447 What height of love, a Parent will fit best,
    p. 339 HORACE 1   39 His Muse .... height, and ....
                                         ......
    p. 379 UNGATHERED 12   2 The height, let him learne of Mr. Tom.
                                         Coryate;
    p. 381 UNGATHERED 12 60 The height, let him learne of Mr. Tom Coryate.

heighten   frequency: 2   relative frequency: 0.00002
  **p. 114 PANEGYRE   51 That might her beauties heighten; but so drest,
    p. 82 EPIGRAMS 130   6 Doth sweeten mirth, and heighten pietie,

heightening. See "height'ning."

height'ning   frequency: 1   relative frequency: 0.00001
     p. 370 UNGATHERED 7   3 Light, Posture, Height'ning, Shadow,
                                Culloring,

heir. See "co-heire," "heire."

heire   frequency: 5   relative frequency: 0.00007
     p. 41 EPIGRAMS 44   6 When he made him executor, might be heire.
     p. 225 UNDERWOOD 51   13 Englands high Chancellor: the destin'd heire
     p. 240 UNDERWOOD 67   53 Hath brought the Land an Heire!
     p. 251 UNDERWOOD 74   29 To be a shadow to his Heire,
     p. 252 UNDERWOOD 75   t6 Son, and Heire, of the Lord WESTON,

heires   frequency: 3   relative frequency: 0.00004
     p. 130 UNDERWOOD 1.3   21 To make us heires of glory!
     p. 214 UNDERWOOD 44   59 And there instruct the noble English heires
     p. 286 U'WOOD 84.9   140 Adopt us Heires, by grace, who were of those

heirs. See "co-heires," "heires."

held   frequency: 4   relative frequency: 0.00005
     p. 133 UNDERWOOD 2.3   8 Both the Bow, and shaft I held,
     p. 205 UNDERWOOD 43   60 T'have held a Triumph, or a feast of fire,
     p. 213 UNDERWOOD 44   22 How it held out! how (last) 'twas taken in!
     p. 323 HORACE 2   369 Which law receiv'd, the Chorus held his peace,

he'le   frequency: 2   relative frequency: 0.00002

helen   frequency: 1   relative frequency: 0.00001
     p. 181 UNDERWOOD 27   1 Helen, did Homer never see

helicon   frequency: 1   relative frequency: 0.00001
     p. 325 HORACE 2   422 In Helicon: a great sort will not pare

hell   frequency: 10   relative frequency: 0.00014
     p. 36 EPIGRAMS 31   4 He toyles to be at hell, as soone as they.
     p. 81 EPIGRAMS 128   13 Through seas, stormes, tempests: and imbarqu'd
                                for hell,
     p. 84 EPIGRAMS 133   2 Of HERCVLES, or THESEVS going to
                                hell,
     p. 84 EPIGRAMS 133   27 Who gaue, to take at his returne from Hell,
     p. 85 EPIGRAMS 133   51 Thou hast seene hell (some say) and know'st all
                                nookes there,
     p. 88 EPIGRAMS 133   144 That, with still-scalding steemes, make the place
                                hell.
     p. 113 FOREST 12   3 That which, to boote with hell, is thought worth
                                heauen,
     p. 129 UNDERWOOD 1.2   23 Sinne, Death, and Hell,
     p. 167 UNDERWOOD 15   163 Light thee from hell on earth: where flatterers,
                                spies,
     p. 420 UNGATHERED 48   23 Whose ayre will sooner Hell, then their dull
                                senses peirce,

he'll   frequency: 1   relative frequency: 0.00001

helm. See "helme."

helme   frequency: 2   relative frequency: 0.00002
     p. 61 EPIGRAMS 95   21 Whose knowledge claymeth at the helme to stand;
     p. 185 UNDERWOOD 30   10 That in all tempests, never quit the helme,

help   frequency: 2   relative frequency: 0.00002
See also "helpe."
     p. 141 UNDERWOOD 2.9   37 Yet no Taylor help to make him;
     p. 146 UNDERWOOD 6   20 In love, doth not alone help forth

help'd   frequency: 2   relative frequency: 0.00002
   **p. 113 PANEGYRE   27 Her third, IRENE, help'd to beare his
                                traine;
     p. 150 UNDERWOOD 10   12 Think'st thou that love is help'd by feare?

helpe   frequency: 17   relative frequency: 0.00024
   **p. 114 PANEGYRE   38 But, when their speech so poore a helpe affords
     p. 56 EPIGRAMS 88   16 Daily to turne in PAVLS, and helpe the
                                trade.
     p. 72 EPIGRAMS 111   13 By thy great helpe: and doth proclaime by mee,
     p. 85 EPIGRAMS 133   48 Sans helpe of SYBIL, or a golden bough,
     p. 127 UNDERWOOD 1.1   4 Helpe, helpe to lift
     p. 155 UNDERWOOD 13   75 I not deny it, but to helpe the need
     p. 170 UNDERWOOD 18   9 I can helpe that with boldnesse; And Love
                                sware,

helpe (cont.)
```
    p. 191 UNDERWOOD 38     7 Or there to sterve it. Helpe, O you that may
    p. 217 UNDERWOOD 46     7 When, being the Strangers helpe, the poore mans
                              aide,
    p. 231 UNDERWOOD 56    23 Away ill company, and helpe in rime
    p. 232 UNDERWOOD 57    27 nor any quick-warming-pan helpe him to bed,
    p. 252 UNDERWOOD 75     2 A-while with us, bright Sun, and helpe our
                              light;
    p. 333 HORACE 2       585 So doth the one, the others helpe require,
    p. 333 HORACE 2       603 Will be a suretie; or can helpe him out
    p. 335 HORACE 2       653 And cry aloud, Helpe, gentle Countrey-men,
    p. 335 HORACE 2       654 There's none will take the care, to helpe him
                              then;
```

helpes   frequency: 2   relative frequency: 0.00002
```
    p. 275 U'WOOD 84.3      5 Send these suspected helpes, to aide
    p. 311 HORACE 2       153 To every state of fortune; she helpes on,
```

helps   frequency: 2   relative frequency: 0.00002
    See also "helpes."
```
    p. 215 UNDERWOOD 44    94 Of severall makings? helps, helps, t<o>'attire
```

heluetia   frequency: 1   relative frequency: 0.00001
```
    p. 379 UNGATHERED 12   19 France, Sauoy, Italy, and Heluetia,
```

helvetia.   See "heluetia."

hem   frequency: 1   relative frequency: 0.00001

'hem   frequency: 29   relative frequency: 0.00041

hemisphere   frequency: 2   relative frequency: 0.00002
```
    p. 199 UNDERWOOD 41     7 And we were left under that Hemisphere,
    p. 392 UNGATHERED 26   75 But stay, I see thee in the Hemisphere
```

hen   frequency: 2   relative frequency: 0.00002
```
    p.  64 EPIGRAMS 101    11 Vshring the mutton; with a short-leg'd hen,
    p. 291 UNDERWOOD 85    53 Th'Ionian God-wit, nor the Ginny hen
```

hence   frequency: 16   relative frequency: 0.00023
```
    p.  33 EPIGRAMS 22      5 At sixe moneths end, shee parted hence
    p.  53 EPIGRAMS 79      5 Hence was it, that the destinies decreed
    p.  81 EPIGRAMS 128     6 Attend thee hence; and there, may all thy ends,
    p. 167 UNDERWOOD 15   162 Friend, flie from hence; and let these kindled
                              rimes
    p. 174 UNDERWOOD 23    13 If hence thy silence be,
    p. 183 UNDERWOOD 29    14 All good Poetrie hence was flowne,
    p. 187 UNDERWOOD 33    11 All mouthes, that dare entitle them (from hence)
    p. 193 UNDERWOOD 38    67 O may your wisdome take example hence,
    p. 205 UNDERWOOD 43    56 Not ravish'd all hence in a minutes rage.
    p. 215 UNDERWOOD 44    97 This other for his eye-browes; hence, away,
    p. 283 U'WOOD 84.9     34 Her blessed Soule, hence, forth this valley vane
    p. 289 U'WOOD 84.9    225 In this sweet Extasie, she was rapt hence.
    p. 290 UNDERWOOD 85    31 Or hence, or thence, he drives with many a Hound
    p. 293 UNDERWOOD 86    38 I hold thee fast! but fled hence, with the
                              Light,
    p. 392 UNGATHERED 26   79 Which, since thy flight from hence, hath mourn'd
                              like night,
    p. 400 UNGATHERED 32    3 Hence, then, prophane: Here needs no words
                              expense
```

hence-forth   frequency: 3   relative frequency: 0.00004
```
    p.  41 EPIGRAMS 45     11 For whose sake, hence-forth, all his vowes be
                              such,
    p. 100 FOREST 4         3 Hence-forth I quit thee from my thought,
    p. 278 U'WOOD 84.4     22 Hence-forth may every line be you;
```

henceforth   frequency: 3   relative frequency: 0.00004
    See also "hence-forth."
```
    p. 187 UNDERWOOD 33     5 That, henceforth, I beleeve nor bookes, nor men,
    p. 389 UNGATHERED 24   16 He would be call'd, henceforth, the
                              English-Rogue,
    p. 405 UNGATHERED 34   70 To be worth Enuy. Henceforth I doe meane
```

henrie   frequency: 2   relative frequency: 0.00002
```
    p.  48 EPIGRAMS 66     t1 TO SIR HENRIE CARY.
    p.  61 EPIGRAMS 95     t1 TO SIR HENRIE SAVILE.
```

henry   frequency: 5   relative frequency: 0.00007
    See also "h.," "henrie," "henrye."

henry (cont.)
    p. 55 EPIGRAMS 85   t1 TO SIR HENRY GOODYERE.
    p. 70 EPIGRAMS 109   t1 TO SIR HENRY NEVIL.
    p. 207 UNDERWOOD 43 98 Of our fift Henry, eight of his nine yeare;
    p. 233 UNDERWOOD 60   3 Henry, the brave young Lord La-ware,
    p. 233 UNDERWOOD 60 t1 An Epitaph, on HENRY

henrye   frequency: 1   relative frequency: 0.00001
    p. 382 UNGATHERED 16 t2 behalfe of the two noble Brothers sr Robert
                               & sr Henrye

her   frequency: 364   relative frequency: 0.00526
    See also "als<o>'her," "her>," "hir."

her>   frequency: 1   relative frequency: 0.00001
    p. 415 UNGATHERED 43 1 I cannot bring my Muse to dropp <her> Vies

herald   frequency: 4   relative frequency: 0.00005
 **p. 114 PANEGYRE   42 The fittest herald to proclaime true ioyes:
    p. 29 EPIGRAMS 9   4 And, I a Poet here, no Herald am.
    p. 176 UNDERWOOD 24 17 Times witnesse, herald of Antiquitie,
    p. 215 UNDERWOOD 44 82 The Herald will. Our blood is now become

heralds   frequency: 2   relative frequency: 0.00002
    p. 269 UNDERWOOD 83 20 Of Winchester; the Heralds can tell this:
    p. 394 UNGATHERED 28 12 And Christian name too, with a Heralds witt.

herb   frequency: 1   relative frequency: 0.00001
    p. 291 UNDERWOOD 85 57 Or the herb Sorrell, that loves Meadows still,

herbert   frequency: 2   relative frequency: 0.00002
    p. 68 EPIGRAMS 106   3 All-vertuous HERBERT! on whose euery part
    p. 68 EPIGRAMS 106 t1 TO SIR EDWARD HERBERT.

hercules   frequency: 2   relative frequency: 0.00002
    See also "hercvles."
    p. 228 UNDERWOOD 53 18 I look'd for Hercules to be the Groome:
    p. 407 UNGATHERED 35 14 From ye fam'd pillars of old Hercules!

hercules-his   frequency: 1   relative frequency: 0.00001
    p. 132 UNDERWOOD 2.2 32 In a Hercules-his shape.

hercvles   frequency: 3   relative frequency: 0.00004
    p. 84 EPIGRAMS 133   2 Of HERCVLES, or THESEVS going to
                             hell,
    p. 107 FOREST 10   4 HERCVLES? alas his bones are yet sore,
    p. 115 FOREST 12   57 Like life vnto 'hem. Who heau'd HERCVLES

herd   frequency: 1   relative frequency: 0.00001
    See also "heard."
    p. 265 UNDERWOOD 79 47 That have a Flock, or Herd, upon these plaines;

herds   frequency: 1   relative frequency: 0.00001
    See also "heards."
    p. 290 UNDERWOOD 85 14 The lowing herds there grazing are:

here   frequency: 96   relative frequency: 0.00138
    See also "heere," "here's."

hereafter   frequency: 3   relative frequency: 0.00004
    p. 186 UNDERWOOD 33   1 That I, hereafter, doe not thinke the Barre,
    p. 188 UNDERWOOD 34 16 Make all hereafter, had'st thou ruin'd this?
    p. 331 HORACE 2   575 But, if hereafter thou shalt write, not feare

hereat   frequency: 1   relative frequency: 0.00001
 **p. 117 PANEGYRE   151 Hereat, the people could no longer hold

herein   frequency: 1   relative frequency: 0.00001
    p. 224 UNDERWOOD 50 14 Who (herein studying conscience, and not fame)

here's   frequency: 8   relative frequency: 0.00011

heresie   frequency: 1   relative frequency: 0.00001
    p. 203 UNDERWOOD 43 15 Had I wrote treason there, or heresie,

heresy. See "heresie."

heretofore. See "'tofore."

hermes   frequency: 3   relative frequency: 0.00004
 p. 98 FOREST 3   51 APOLLO'S harpe, and HERMES lyre
  resound,
 p. 107 FOREST 10   22 HERMES, the cheater, shall not mixe with vs,
 p. 395 UNGATHERED 29 17 Phoebus, and Hermes? They whose tongue, or pen

hermetic. See "hermetique."

hermetique   frequency: 1   relative frequency: 0.00001
 p. 206 UNDERWOOD 43   73 Their Seales, their Characters, Hermetique
  rings,

hero. See "heroe."

heroe   frequency: 1   relative frequency: 0.00001
 p. 313 HORACE 2   162 Or an Heroe; if a ripe old man,

heroes   frequency: 2   relative frequency: 0.00002
 p. 88 EPIGRAMS 133 163 Our braue Heroes with a milder glare,
 p. 98 FOREST 3   56 And the great Heroes, of her race,

heroic. See "heroick," "heroique."

heroick   frequency: 1   relative frequency: 0.00001
 p. 397 UNGATHERED 30 29 But then, thy'epistolar Heroick Songs,

heroique   frequency: 1   relative frequency: 0.00001
 p. 262 UNDERWOOD 78   10 Where all heroique ample thoughts doe meet:

hers   frequency: 4   relative frequency: 0.00005

herse   frequency: 2   relative frequency: 0.00002
 p. 35 EPIGRAMS 27   1 In place of scutcheons, that should decke thy
  herse,
 p. 204 UNDERWOOD 43   37 Of Egges, and Halberds, Cradles, and a Herse,

he's   frequency: 2   relative frequency: 0.00002

hesiods   frequency: 2   relative frequency: 0.00002
 p. 388 UNGATHERED 23   2 Olde Hesiods Ore, and giue it vs; but thine,
 p. 388 UNGATHERED 23 t3 of Hesiods Works, & Dayes.

hether   frequency: 2   relative frequency: 0.00002
 p. 56 EPIGRAMS 88   4 And shooe, and tye, and garter should come
  hether,
 p. 361 UNGATHERED 1   6 that mongst so manie plants transplanted hether,

hey. See "hay."

heyden   frequency: 1   relative frequency: 0.00001
 p. 84 EPIGRAMS 133   5 We haue a SHELTON, and a HEYDEN got,

heydon. See "heyden."

heyward. See "hayward."

h'had   frequency: 1   relative frequency: 0.00001

h'has   frequency: 2   relative frequency: 0.00002

h'hath   frequency: 2   relative frequency: 0.00002

hid   frequency: 3   relative frequency: 0.00004
 **p. 115 PANEGYRE   82 "Though hid at home, abroad is search'd into:
 p. 47 EPIGRAMS 63   11 Curst be his Muse, that could lye dumbe, or hid
 p. 165 UNDERWOOD 15   85 Adulteries, now, are not so hid, or strange,

hidden>   frequency: 1   relative frequency: 0.00001
 p. 176 UNDERWOOD 24   10 Of Truth that searcheth the most <hidden>
  Springs,

hide   frequency: 5   relative frequency: 0.00007
 p. 62 EPIGRAMS 95   36 That dares nor write things false, nor hide
  things true.
 p. 137 UNDERWOOD 2.5   49 For this Beauty yet doth hide
 p. 319 HORACE 2   285 Hide faults, pray to the Gods, and wish aloud
 p. 380 UNGATHERED 12   51 Or any thing else that another should hide,
 p. 387 UNGATHERED 22   2 these only hide part of my flesh, and bones:

```
hide-parke                        frequency:   1   relative frequency: 0.00001
     p. 165 UNDERWOOD 15   109 From Hide-Parke to the Stage, where at the
                               last

hides                             frequency:   1   relative frequency: 0.00001
     p.  88 EPIGRAMS 133   146 The heads, houghs, entrailes, and the hides of
                               dogs:

hie                               frequency:   1   relative frequency: 0.00001
     See also "hye."
     p. 292 UNDERWOOD 86     9 More timely hie thee to the house,

hierarchie                        frequency:   1   relative frequency: 0.00001
     p. 271 UNDERWOOD 83    72 To every Order, ev'ry Hierarchie!

hierarchies                       frequency:   1   relative frequency: 0.00001
     p. 285 U'WOOD 84.9     85 Saints, Martyrs, Prophets, with those
                               Hierarchies,

hierarchy.  See "hierarchie."

hieroglyphicks                    frequency:   1   relative frequency: 0.00001
     p. 404 UNGATHERED 34   43 Court Hieroglyphicks! & all Artes affoord

hieroglyphics.  See "hieroglyphicks."

hierome                           frequency:   3   relative frequency: 0.00004
     p. 250 UNDERWOOD 74    t1 To the Right honble Hierome, L. Weston.
     p. 252 UNDERWOOD 75    t5 of that Noble Gentleman, Mr. HIEROME
                               WESTON,
     p. 258 UNDERWOOD 75   170 A Richard, and a Hierome, by their names

high                              frequency:  37   relative frequency: 0.00053
   **p. 112 PANEGYRE         t8 His first high Session of PARLIAMENT
   **p. 115 PANEGYRE         91 "Of kings, praeceding him in that high court;
     p.  31 EPIGRAMS 14       6 More high, more holy, that shee more would craue.
     p.  49 EPIGRAMS 66       7 Which deed I know not, whether were more high,
     p.  49 EPIGRAMS 67       5 Stand high, then, HOWARD, high in eyes of
                               men,
     p.  49 EPIGRAMS 67       6 High in thy bloud, thy place, but highest then,
     p.  50 EPIGRAMS 72       4 Goe high, or low, as thou wilt value it.
     p.  64 EPIGRAMS 99       9 From place, or fortune, are made high, or low,
     p.  69 EPIGRAMS 108      3 And your high names: I doe desire, that thence
     p.  82 EPIGRAMS 130     13 Mou'd by her order, and the ninth more high,
     p.  89 EPIGRAMS 133    190 An ancient pur-blinde fletcher, with a high nose;
     p.  93 FOREST 2         11 Where PAN, and BACCHVS their high
                               feasts haue made,
     p.  96 FOREST 2         85 The iust reward of her high huswifery:
     p. 111 FOREST 11        62 Who (blest with such high chance)
     p. 115 FOREST 12        60 Or set bright ARIADNES crowne so high?
     p. 116 FOREST 12        89 But high, and noble matter, such as flies
     p. 131 UNDERWOOD 2.1    22 And let nothing high decay,
     p. 144 UNDERWOOD 3      26 To meet their high desire;
     p. 157 UNDERWOOD 13    144 As they are high; are rooted, and will last.
     p. 163 UNDERWOOD 15     33 Against his Maker; high alone with weeds,
     p. 175 UNDERWOOD 23     35 But sing high and aloofe,
     p. 176 UNDERWOOD 25      5 High, as his mind, that doth advance
     p. 181 UNDERWOOD 26     22 'Tis wisdome, and that high,
     p. 181 UNDERWOOD 27     13 Is Horace his each love so high
     p. 185 UNDERWOOD 30     t3 Lo: high Treasurer of England.
     p. 219 UNDERWOOD 47     37 I wish all well, and pray high heaven conspire
     p. 225 UNDERWOOD 51     13 Englands high Chancellor: the destin'd heire
     p. 234 UNDERWOOD 60     12 No love of action, and high Arts,
     p. 248 UNDERWOOD 71     t2 the Lord high Treasurer of England.
     p. 250 UNDERWOOD 73     t2 Weston, L. high Treasurer of England,
     p. 252 UNDERWOOD 75     t7 Lord high Treasurer of England,
     p. 273 U'WOOD 84.1      30 And Call to the high Parliament
     p. 279 U'WOOD 84.4      29 There, high exalted in the Sphaere,
     p. 279 U'WOOD 84.4      41 But, that a Mind so rapt, so high,
     p. 369 UNGATHERED 6     99 Were CYCNVS, once high flying
     p. 412 UNGATHERED 41    10 Ymounted high upon Selinis crest:

high-spirited                     frequency:   1   relative frequency: 0.00001
     p. 180 UNDERWOOD 26      1 High-spirited friend,

high-swolne                       frequency:   1   relative frequency: 0.00001
     p.  94 FOREST 2         31 And if the high-swolne Medway faile thy dish,

higher                            frequency:   5   relative frequency: 0.00007
     p. 120 FOREST 14         6 The gladnesse higher:
```

higher (cont.)
p. 232 UNDERWOOD 58   7 If his wit reach no higher, but to spring
p. 233 UNDERWOOD 59   8 That trembles in the blaze, but (then) mounts
                            higher!
p. 290 UNDERWOOD 85   25 Whilst from the higher Bankes doe slide the
                            floods;
p. 401 UNGATHERED 32   18 But higher power, as spight could not make lesse,

highest   frequency: 2   relative frequency: 0.00002
p.   49 EPIGRAMS 67   6 High in thy bloud, thy place, but highest then,
p. 331 HORACE 2   564 And highest; sinketh to the lowest, and worst.

highly   frequency: 1   relative frequency: 0.00001
p. 256 UNDERWOOD 75   112 He had so highly set; and, in what Barbican.

hight   frequency: 2   relative frequency: 0.00002
p.   86 EPIGRAMS 133   89 How hight the place? a voyce was heard,
                            COCYTVS.
p. 279 U'WOOD 84.4   48 Up to her owne sublimed hight?

hill   frequency: 3   relative frequency: 0.00004
p.   87 EPIGRAMS 133   128 Whereof old DEMOCRITE, and HILL
                            NICHOLAS,
p. 184 UNDERWOOD 29   37 Scarce the Hill againe doth flourish,
p. 374 UNGATHERED 10   12 Here, not vp Holdborne, but downe a steepe hill,

hill-   frequency: 1   relative frequency: 0.00001
p. 211 UNDERWOOD 43   183 Condemne him to the Brick-kills, or some Hill-

hill-foot. See "hill-."

hills   frequency: 3   relative frequency: 0.00004
p. 264 UNDERWOOD 79   23 Chor. Heare, o you Groves, and, Hills, resound
                            his praise.
p. 264 UNDERWOOD 79   31 Chor. Heare, O you Groves, and, Hills,
                            resound his worth.
p. 367 UNGATHERED 6   40 The Vale, that bred thee pure, as her Hills
                            Snow.

hilt   frequency: 1   relative frequency: 0.00001
p.   51 EPIGRAMS 73   16 Item, your mistris anagram, i' your hilt.

him   frequency: 180   relative frequency: 0.00260
    See also "hym," "hyme."

himself   frequency: 1   relative frequency: 0.00001
    See also "himselfe," "t<o>'himselfe."
 **p. 113 PANEGYRE   4 Vnfolds himself: & from his eyes are hoorl'd

himselfe   frequency: 32   relative frequency: 0.00046
 *p. 492 TO HIMSELF   t5 himselfe.
p.   30 EPIGRAMS 12   3 Keepes himselfe, with halfe a man, and defrayes
p.   30 EPIGRAMS 12   6 Himselfe: his whole reuennue is, god payes.
p.   32 EPIGRAMS 16   10 He that dares damne himselfe, dares more then
                            fight.
p.   63 EPIGRAMS 98   3 He that is round within himselfe, and streight,
p.   66 EPIGRAMS 102   8 To which, yet, of the sides himselfe he owes.
p.   74 EPIGRAMS 114   7 He hath not onely gain'd himselfe his eyes,
p.   76 EPIGRAMS 118   4 He makes himselfe a thorough-fare of vice.
p. 111 FOREST 11   64 Cast himselfe from the spire
p. 119 FOREST 13   117 Vnto himselfe, by being so deare to you.
p. 130 UNDERWOOD 1.3   20 Who made himselfe the price of sinne,
p. 138 UNDERWOOD 2.6   31 To himselfe his losse of Time;
p. 142 U'WOOD 2.10   5 Himselfe young, and face be good,
p. 154 UNDERWOOD 13   31 Himselfe of farther trouble, or the weight
p. 165 UNDERWOOD 15   114 Is it that man pulls on himselfe Disease?
p. 170 UNDERWOOD 19   8 Where he doth steepe himselfe in Milke and
                            Roses;
p. 171 UNDERWOOD 19   24 As would make shift, to make himselfe alone,
p. 173 UNDERWOOD 22   24 Is gone himselfe into your Name.
p. 174 UNDERWOOD 23   t1 An Ode. To himselfe.
p. 189 UNDERWOOD 36   8 Yet he himselfe is but a sparke.
p. 197 UNDERWOOD 40   21 Not, like a Midas, shut up in himselfe,
p. 198 UNDERWOOD 40   38 Farre from the Nest, and so himselfe belie
p. 216 UNDERWOOD 45   22 Friend to himselfe, that would be friend to thee.
p. 246 UNDERWOOD 70   86 Himselfe to rest,
p. 256 UNDERWOOD 75   108 Him up, to doe the same himselfe had done.
p. 286 U'WOOD 84.9   149 Himselfe so un-inform'd of his elect,
p. 287 U'WOOD 84.9   156 For 'twas himselfe who form'd, and gave it her.
p. 313 HORACE 2   182 Still to be like himselfe, and hold his worth.

himselfe (cont.)
```
    p. 317 HORACE 2      259 And the beholder to himselfe doth render.
    p. 335 HORACE 2      657 Himselfe there purposely, or no; and would
    p. 379 UNGATHERED 12   8 To line out no stride, but pas'd by himselfe?
    p. 392 UNGATHERED 26  62 (And himselfe with it) that he thinkes to frame;
```

hind. See "hinde."

hinde   frequency: 1   relative frequency: 0.00001
```
    p.  30 EPIGRAMS 28    17 Blaspheme god, greatly. Or some poore hinde
                             beat,
```

hint   frequency: 1   relative frequency: 0.00001
```
    p. 415 UNGATHERED 42  27 Of Finenesse, and alloy: follow his hint,
```

hipocrites   frequency: 1   relative frequency: 0.00001
```
    p. 416 UNGATHERED 43   9 In spite of Hipocrites, who are the worst
```

hippocrenes   frequency: 1   relative frequency: 0.00001
```
    p. 221 UNDERWOOD 48   28 Then Hippocrenes liquor:
```

hir   frequency: 7   relative frequency: 0.00010

hir'd   frequency: 1   relative frequency: 0.00001
```
    p. 333 HORACE 2      614 As those that hir'd to weepe at Funeralls,
                             swoune,
```

hire   frequency: 2   relative frequency: 0.00002
```
    p. 155 UNDERWOOD 13   62 Like Money-brokers, after Names, and hire
    p. 160 UNDERWOOD 15  136 Now use the bones, we see doth hire a man
```

hirelings   frequency: 1   relative frequency: 0.00001
```
    p. 187 UNDERWOOD 33    8 Of hirelings, wranglers, stitchers-to of strife,
```

hireth   frequency: 1   relative frequency: 0.00001
```
    p. 305 HORACE 2       26 What's this? if he whose money hireth thee
```

his   frequency: 663   relative frequency: 0.00959
    See also "at's," "for'his," "hercules-his,"
              "in's."

historical. See "historicall."

historicall   frequency: 1   relative frequency: 0.00001
```
    p. 380 UNGATHERED 12  22 Pies on't, you haue his historicall faith.
```

historie   frequency: 4   relative frequency: 0.00005
```
    p.  61 EPIGRAMS 95    11 Which Fate (it seemes) caus'd in the historie,
    p.  61 EPIGRAMS 95    28 Of historie, and how to apt their places;
    p.  67 EPIGRAMS 105    2 All historie seal'd vp, and fables crost;
    p. 175 UNDERWOOD 24    2 The Mistresse of Mans life, grave Historie,
```

history   frequency: 1   relative frequency: 0.00001
    See also "historie."
```
    p. 403 UNGATHERED 34  37 Dame History, Dame Architecture too,
```

hit   frequency: 14   relative frequency: 0.00020
    See also "hitt."
```
   *p. 494 TO HIMSELF     58 No Harpe ere hit the starres;
    p.  27 EPIGRAMS 2      6 As mad-men stones: not caring whom they hit.
    p.  68 EPIGRAMS 105   14 DIANA'alone, so hit, and hunted so.
    p.  81 EPIGRAMS 129   13 Or (mounted on a stoole) thy face doth hit
    p.  87 EPIGRAMS 133  123 Of worship, they their nodding chinnes doe hit
    p. 132 UNDERWOOD 2.2  22 And the Bow: with thought to hit
    p. 179 UNDERWOOD 25   50 That is not hurt; not he, that is not hit;
    p. 232 UNDERWOOD 59    5 To hit in angles, and to clash with time:
    p. 259 UNDERWOOD 76   21 When their pot-guns ayme to hit,
    p. 277 U'WOOD 84.4     7 Beside, your hand will never hit,
    p. 329 HORACE 2      524 Nor alwayes doth the loosed Bow, hit that
    p. 379 UNGATHERED 12   6 Yet who could haue hit on't but the wise noddell
    p. 383 UNGATHERED 17   6 Yet may as blind men sometimes hit the marke.
    p. 390 UNGATHERED 25   6 As well in brasse, as he hath hit
```

hither   frequency: 2   relative frequency: 0.00002
    See also "hether."
```
    p. 252 UNDERWOOD 75   12 From Greenwich, hither, to Row-hampton gate!
    p. 265 UNDERWOOD 79   46 Haste, haste you hither, all you gentler
                             Swaines,
```

hitt   frequency: 1   relative frequency: 0.00001
    p. 394 UNGATHERED 28   11 Nay they will venter ones Descent to hitt,

ho'   frequency: 1   relative frequency: 0.00001
    p. 85 EPIGRAMS 133   40 Or his to Antwerpe. Therefore, once more, list
                             ho'.

hoard. See "hoord."

hoarse   frequency: 1   relative frequency: 0.00001
    p. 167 UNDERWOOD 15   151 When I am hoarse, with praising his each cast,

hobbled. See "hobled."

hobby-horse. See "court-hobby-horse."

hobled   frequency: 1   relative frequency: 0.00001
    p. 380 UNGATHERED 12   41 I meane that one paire, wherewith he so hobled

hodges   frequency: 1   relative frequency: 0.00001
    p. 214 UNDERWOOD 44   53 Insert thy Hodges, and those newer men,

hogs   frequency: 2   relative frequency: 0.00002
    p. 88 EPIGRAMS 133   145 The sinkes ran grease, and haire of meazled hogs,
    p. 98 FOREST 3   44 The hogs return'd home fat from mast;

holborn. See "hol'borne," "holdborne."

hol'borne   frequency: 2   relative frequency: 0.00002
    p. 85 EPIGRAMS 133   38 Propos'd to goe to Hol'borne in a wherry:
    p. 89 EPIGRAMS 133   177 Of Hol'borne (<the> three sergeants heads)
                             lookes ore,

hold   frequency: 20   relative frequency: 0.00028
  **p. 117 PANEGYRE   151 Hereat, the people could no longer hold
    p. 47 EPIGRAMS 64   3 Of loue, and what the golden age did hold
    p. 50 EPIGRAMS 70   3 In life, that can employ it; and takes hold
    p. 85 EPIGRAMS 133   58 But hold my torch, while I describe the entry
    p. 114 FOREST 12   42 And, at her strong armes end, hold vp, and euen,
    p. 115 FOREST 12   81 They hold in my strange poems, which, as yet,
    p. 167 UNDERWOOD 15   150 That may stand by, and hold my peace? will he,
    p. 221 UNDERWOOD 48   43 Be it he hold Communion
    p. 227 UNDERWOOD 52   18 How I would draw, and take hold and delight.
    p. 229 UNDERWOOD 54   9 And hold me to it close; to stand upright
    p. 272 U'WOOD 84.1   3 Their Heads, that ENVY would hold downe
    p. 293 UNDERWOOD 86   38 I hold thee fast! but fled hence, with the
                             Light,
    p. 313 HORACE 2   182 Still to be like himselfe, and hold his worth.
    p. 329 HORACE 2   505 And hold them faithfully; For nothing rests,
    p. 337 HORACE 2   675 To force the grates, that hold him in, would
                             fright
    p. 337 HORACE 2   679 Not letting goe his hold, where he drawes food,
    p. 367 UNGATHERED 6   45 With thy soft notes, and hold them within Pale
    p. 368 UNGATHERED 6   92 To hold them here:
    p. 386 UNGATHERED 21   13 Hold thyne owne worth vnbroke: which is so good
    p. 403 UNGATHERED 34   39 To hold her vp. O Showes! Showes! Mighty
                             Showes!

hold<s>   frequency: 1   relative frequency: 0.00001
    p. 177 UNDERWOOD 25   20 That hold<s> your spirit:

holdborne   frequency: 1   relative frequency: 0.00001
    p. 374 UNGATHERED 10   12 Here, not vp Holdborne, but downe a steepe hill,

holdes   frequency: 1   relative frequency: 0.00001
    p. 116 FOREST 12   95 For that firme grace he holdes in your regard,

holdeth   frequency: 1   relative frequency: 0.00001
    p. 355 HORACE 1   677 .... holdeth ....

holding   frequency: 1   relative frequency: 0.00001
    p. 337 HORACE 2   677 Learn'd and unlearn'd; holding, whom once he
                             takes;

holds   frequency: 3   relative frequency: 0.00004
    See also "hold<s>," "holdes."
    p. 38 EPIGRAMS 37   4 For this: that winnes, for whom he holds his
                             peace.
    p. 216 UNDERWOOD 44   101 The fate of things: whilst totter'd vertue holds
    p. 265 UNDERWOOD 79   63 The theefe from spoyle, his presence holds.

hole   frequency: 2   relative frequency: 0.00002
    p. 201 UNDERWOOD 42   60 In at a hole, and see these Actions creepe
    p. 335 HORACE 2   652 Into a pit, or hole; although he call,

holes   frequency: 1   relative frequency: 0.00001
    p. 319 HORACE 2_   289 But soft, and simple, at few holes breath'd time

holiday. See "holy-day."

holidays. See "holy-dayes."

holiest   frequency: 1   relative frequency: 0.00001
    p.   78 EPIGRAMS 122   7 If holiest friend-ship, naked to the touch,

holinesse   frequency: 1   relative frequency: 0.00001
    p. 287 U'WOOD 84.9   179 Of Pietie, and private holinesse.

holland   frequency: 1   relative frequency: 0.00001
    See also "hollande."
    p.   69 EPIGRAMS 107   12 In Ireland, Holland, Sweden, pompous lies,

hollande   frequency: 1   relative frequency: 0.00001
    p. 382 UNGATHERED 16   t3 Rich, now Earles of warwick and Hollande.

holy   frequency: 20   relative frequency: 0.00028
    See also "holye."
    p.   31 EPIGRAMS 14   6 More high, more holy, that shee more would craue.
    p.   52 EPIGRAMS 76   1 This morning, timely rapt with holy fire,
    p. 117 FOREST 13   18 Men are not iust, or keepe no holy lawes
    p. 122 FOREST 15   24 With holy PAVL, lest it be thought the breath
    p. 127 UNDERWOOD 1.1   1 1. O holy, blessed, glorious Trinitie
    p. 127 UNDERWOOD 1.1   t2 To the Holy Trinitie.
    p. 128 UNDERWOOD 1.1   37 10. Father, and Sonne, and Holy Ghost, you
                                   three
    p. 152 UNDERWOOD 12   23 They were so even, grave, and holy;
    p. 235 UNDERWOOD 62   1 Great CHARLES, among the holy gifts of
                                   grace
    p. 245 UNDERWOOD 70   80 Possest with holy rage,
    p. 252 UNDERWOOD 75   9 See, the Procession! what a Holy day
    p. 253 UNDERWOOD 75   30 That holy strife,
    p. 256 UNDERWOOD 75   123 The holy Prelate prayes, then takes the Ring,
    p. 257 UNDERWOOD 75   139 These two, now holy Church hath made them one,
    p. 257 UNDERWOOD 75   162 (The holy perfumes of the Mariage bed.)
    p. 286 U'WOOD 84.9   129 That holy, great, and glorious Mysterie,
    p. 288 U'WOOD 84.9   188 The holy Altars, when it least presumes.
    p. 393 UNGATHERED 27   16 Doth shew the Holy one.
    p. 411 UNGATHERED 40   2 your holy Meditations,
    p. 413 UNGATHERED 41   37 Most holy, & pure Virgin, blessed Mayd,

holy-day   frequency: 6   relative frequency: 0.00008
    p. 208 UNDERWOOD 43   127 Whom they durst handle in their holy-day coates,
    p. 239 UNDERWOOD 67   6 Ring thou it Holy-day.
    p. 249 UNDERWOOD 72   16 On th'often comming of this Holy-day:
    p. 284 U'WOOD 84.9   63 That great eternall Holy-day of rest,
    p. 294 UNDERWOOD 88   6 But thus, thus, keeping endlesse Holy-day,
    p. 319 HORACE 2   301 The Idiot, keeping holy-day, or drudge,

holy-dayes   frequency: 1   relative frequency: 0.00001
    p. 222 UNDERWOOD 49   15 What though she ride two mile on Holy-dayes

holye   frequency: 1   relative frequency: 0.00001
    p. 421 UNGATHERED 48   37 Throwe, Holye Virgin, then

homage   frequency: 1   relative frequency: 0.00001
    p. 391 UNGATHERED 26   42 To whom all Scenes of Europe homage owe.

home   frequency: 22   relative frequency: 0.00031
  **p. 115 PANEGYRE   82 "Though hid at home, abroad is search'd into:
    p.   30 EPIGRAMS 12   9 The taylor brings a suite home; he it ssayes,
    p.   37 EPIGRAMS 32   7 What could not worke; at home in his repaire
    p.   40 EPIGRAMS 42   8 The like is IONE. But turning home, is sad.
    p.   40 EPIGRAMS 42   10 Harsh sights at home, GILES wisheth he were
                                   blind.
    p.   55 EPIGRAMS 84   5 Straight went I home; and there most like a
                                   Poet,
    p.   81 EPIGRAMS 128   10 Thy selfe, with thy first thoughts, brought home
                                   by thee,
    p.   89 EPIGRAMS 133   181 Is now from home. You lose your labours quite,
    p.   97 FOREST 3   13 But canst, at home, in thy securer rest,
    p.   98 FOREST 3   44 The hogs return'd home fat from mast;

home (cont.)
```
     p. 102 FOREST 4        68 Here in my bosome, and at home.
     p. 133 UNDERWOOD 2.3   14 But the Arrow home did draw
     p. 159 UNDERWOOD 14    30 Ever at home: yet, have all Countries seene:
     p. 198 UNDERWOOD 40    34 Out with the other, for hee's still at home;
     p. 201 UNDERWOOD 42    41 Home to the Customer: his Letcherie
     p. 213 UNDERWOOD 44    19 And comming home, to tell what acts were done
     p. 222 UNDERWOOD 48    54 And Charles brings home the Ladie.
     p. 253 UNDERWOOD 75    24 To welcome home a Paire, and deck the nuptiall
                               bower?
     p. 262 UNDERWOOD 78     8 For that to dwell in, and be still at home.
     p. 270 UNDERWOOD 83    64 Her spirit home, to her originall!
     p. 291 UNDERWOOD 85    44 Against the Husband comes home tir'd;
     p. 291 UNDERWOOD 85    62 Of the fed flocks approaching home!
```

home-borne   frequency: 2   relative frequency: 0.00002
```
     p. 228 UNDERWOOD 53     9 Or what we heare our home-borne Legend tell,
     p. 323 HORACE 2       408 And celebrating our owne home-borne facts;
```

homer   frequency: 7   relative frequency: 0.00010
```
     p. 115 FOREST 12       55 That HOMER brought to Troy: yet none so
                               liue:
     p. 136 UNDERWOOD 2.5   13 So hath Homer prais'd her haire;
     p. 181 UNDERWOOD 27     1 Helen, did Homer never see
     p. 309 HORACE 2       106 What number best can fit, Homer declares.
     p. 327 HORACE 2       493 Next these great Homer and Tyrtaeus set
     p. 329 HORACE 2       536 Angry. Sometimes, I heare good Homer snore.
     p. 398 UNGATHERED 30   59 There, thou art Homer! Pray thee, vse the stile
```

homers   frequency: 3   relative frequency: 0.00004
```
     p. 224 UNDERWOOD 50    24 Then the great Homers wit, for her, could faine;
     p. 313 HORACE 2       185 Of Homers, forth in acts, then of thine owne,
     p. 388 UNGATHERED 23    3 Who hadst before wrought in rich Homers Mine?
```

honble   frequency: 1   relative frequency: 0.00001
```
     p. 250 UNDERWOOD 74    t1 To the Right honble Hierome, L. Weston.
```

honest   frequency: 13   relative frequency: 0.00018
```
   **p. 115 PANEGYRE        95 "She shewd him, who made wise, who honest acts;
     p.  74 EPIGRAMS 115    t1 ON THE TOWNES HONEST MAN.
     p.  75 EPIGRAMS 115    34 Then, The townes honest Man's her errant'st
                               knaue.
     p. 142 UNDERWOOD 2.9   44 And as honest as his Birth.
     p. 167 UNDERWOOD 15   177 That thine be just, and honest; that thy Deeds
     p. 244 UNDERWOCD 70    34 Got up and thriv'd with honest arts:
     p. 335 HORACE 2       633 A wise, and honest man will cry out shame
     p. 352 HORACE 1       547 ... ... being honest ... .......... doth ....
     p. 378 UNGATHERED 11   81 Honest Tom Tell-Troth puts downe Roger, How?
     p. 406 UNGATHERED 34  104 Wth all Remonstrance make an honest man.
     p. 406 UNGATHERED 35    6 A Noble honest Soule! what's this to thee?
     p. 410 UNGATHERED 38   15 An honest Bilbo-Smith would make good blades,
     p. 423 UNGATHERED 50   17 he that will honest be, may quitt the Court,
```

honestie   frequency: 2   relative frequency: 0.00002
```
     p. 156 UNDERWOOD 13   111 Her ends are honestie, and publike good!
     p. 163 UNDERWOOD 15    42 Honour and honestie, as poore things thought
```

honesty   frequency: 1   relative frequency: 0.00001
  See also "honestie."
```
     p.  27 EPIGRAMS 2      13 He that departs with his owne honesty
```

honey   frequency: 2   relative frequency: 0.00002
```
     p. 290 UNDERWOOD 85    15 Or the prest honey in pure pots doth keepe
     p. 331 HORACE 2       559 As Poppie, and Sardane honey; 'cause without
```

honor   frequency: 7   relative frequency: 0.00010
```
     p.  29 EPIGRAMS 9       1 May none, whose scatter'd names honor my booke,
     p.  42 EPIGRAMS 48      3 And hath no honor lost, our Due'llists say.
     p.  48 EPIGRAMS 66      3 Whose house, if it no other honor had,
     p.  52 EPIGRAMS 76      4 To honor, serue, and loue; as Poets vse.
     p.  70 EPIGRAMS 109    10 And elements of honor, then the dresse;
     p.  99 FOREST 3        87 Get place, and honor, and be glad to keepe
     p. 121 FOREST 14       51 So may you liue in honor, as in name,
```

honor'd   frequency: 2   relative frequency: 0.00002
```
     p.  63 EPIGRAMS 97     18 Nor are the Queenes most honor'd maides by
                               th'eares
     p. 400 UNGATHERED 32   t1 On the honor'd Poems of his honored
```

honored   frequency: 1   relative frequency: 0.00001
       p. 400 UNGATHERED 32   t1 On the honor'd Poems of his honored

honoring   frequency: 1   relative frequency: 0.00001
       p. 106 FOREST 9   10 Not so much honoring thee,

honors   frequency: 6   relative frequency: 0.00008
    p.   47 EPIGRAMS 64   11 Where good mens vertues them to honors bring,
    p.   49 EPIGRAMS 66   13 Loue honors, which of best example bee,
    p.   49 EPIGRAMS 67   8 As all thy honors were by them first sought:
    p.   55 EPIGRAMS 89   4 Yet crown'd with honors, as with riches, then;
    p.   71 EPIGRAMS 110   1 Not CAESARS deeds, nor all his honors
                                 wonne,
       p. 119 FOREST 13   105 T<o>'expect the honors of great 'AVBIGNY:

honour   frequency: 29   relative frequency: 0.00041
See also "honor," "saving-honour."
    p.   157 UNDERWOOD 13   147 Are Dwarfes of Honour, and have neither weight
    p.   162 UNDERWOOD 15   7 Mans buried honour, in his sleepie life:
    p.   162 UNDERWOOD 15   25 Be honour is so mixt) by such as would,
    p.   163 UNDERWOOD 15   42 Honour and honestie, as poore things thought
    p.   164 UNDERWOOD 15   56 The bravery makes, she can no honour leese:
    p.   166 UNDERWOOD 15   118 What honour given to the drunkennest Guests?
    p.   168 UNDERWOOD 15   194 More honour in him, 'cause we'<h>ave knowne him
                                 mad:
    p.   177 UNDERWOOD 25   14 Rich beame of honour, shed your light
    p.   180 UNDERWOOD 26   14 Happy in that faire honour it hath gain'd,
    p.   186 UNDERWOOD 31   9 As with the safetie, and honour of the Lawes,
    p.   187 UNDERWOOD 33   37 The Courts just honour, and thy Judges love.
    p.   191 UNDERWOOD 38   30 Your honour now, then your disgrace before.
    p.   203 UNDERWOOD 43   23 Did I there wound the honour of the Crowne?
    p.   216 UNDERWOOD 44   99 These Carkasses of honour; Taylors blocks,
    p.   219 UNDERWOOD 47   39 But if, for honour, we must draw the Sword,
    p.   220 UNDERWOOD 47   71 These I will honour, love, embrace, and serve:
    p.   234 UNDERWOOD 60   7 Of honour, nor no ayre of good?
    p.   243 UNDERWOOD 70   13 Where shame, faith, honour, and regard of right
    p.   251 UNDERWOOD 74   24 Both to the honour of the King and State.
    p.   255 UNDERWOOD 75   92 And what of Dignitie, and Honour may
    p.   258 UNDERWOOD 75   172 A Kate, a Frank, to honour their Grand-dames,
    p.   261 UNDERWOOD 77   27 Unto your honour: I can tune in song
    p.   262 UNDERWOOD 78   3 In honour, courtesie, and all the parts
    p.   274 U'WOOD 84.2   16 Meschines honour with the Cestrian fame
    p.   327 HORACE 2   491 And thus, at first, an honour, and a name
    p.   329 HORACE 2   519 With honour make the farre-knowne Author live.
    p.   382 UNGATHERED 16   8 his life, his loue, his honour, which ne'r dyes,
    p.   388 UNGATHERED 23   6 To make thy honour, and our wealth the more!
    p.   391 UNGATHERED 26   32 From thence to honour thee, I would not seeke

honourable   frequency: 3   relative frequency: 0.00004
See also "honble."
    p.   248 UNDERWOOD 71   t1 To the Right Honourable,
    p.   250 UNDERWOOD 73   t1 On the Right Honourable, and vertuous Lord
    p.   260 UNDERWOOD 77   t1 To the right Honourable, the Lord Treasurer

honour'd   frequency: 6   relative frequency: 0.00008
    p.   162 UNDERWOOD 15   24 Honour'd at once, and envi'd (if it can
    p.   224 UNDERWOOD 50   t2 To the honour'd
    p.   284 U'WOOD 84.9   76 Will honour'd be in all simplicitie!
    p.   285 U'WOOD 84.9   100 Whom her Redeemer, honour'd hath above
    p.   313 HORACE 2   171 Honour'd Achilles chance by thee be seiz'd,
    p.   388 UNGATHERED 23   t1 To my worthy and honour'd Friend,

honoured   frequency: 2   relative frequency: 0.00002
See also "honor'd," "honored," "honour'd."
    p.   282 U'WOOD 84.9   t2 The truly honoured Lady, the Lady
                                 VENETIA DIGBY:
    p.   394 UNGATHERED 28   t1 To ye memorye of that most honoured Ladie Jane,

honouring. See "honoring."

honours   frequency: 8   relative frequency: 0.00011
See also "honors."
    p.   160 UNDERWOOD 14   66 Of others honours, thus, enjoy thine owne.
    p.   173 UNDERWOOD 22   12 Against or Faith, or honours lawes.
    p.   179 UNDERWOOD 25   35 Nothing, but practise upon honours thrall.
    p.   185 UNDERWOOD 30   15 Whose Offices, and honours did surprize,
    p.   238 UNDERWOOD 66   5 Haile Mary, full of honours, to my Queene,
    p.   244 UNDERWOOD 70   35 He purchas'd friends, and fame, and honours then,
    p.   256 UNDERWOOD 75   106 To pay, with honours, to his noble Sonne,
    p.   315 HORACE 2   239 Lookes after honours, and bewares to act

hood. See "french-hood."

hood-wink'd   frequency: 1   relative frequency: 0.00001
    p. 45 EPIGRAMS 58   8 And, hood-wink'd, for a man, embrace a post.

hoof. See "hoofe," "hoofe-cleft."

hoofe   frequency: 2   relative frequency: 0.00002
    p. 175 UNDERWOOD 23   36 Safe from the wolves black jaw, and the dull
                               Asses hoofe.
    p. 380 UNGATHERED 12   32 Of his foote, or his penne, his braine or his
                               hoofe,

hoofe-cleft   frequency: 1   relative frequency: 0.00001
    p. 366 UNGATHERED 6   17 He shew'd him first the hoofe-cleft Spring,

hoofes   frequency: 1   relative frequency: 0.00001
    p. 97 FOREST 3   16 'Mongst loughing heards, and solide hoofes:

hoofs. See "hoofes."

hook. See "hooke."

hook-handed   frequency: 1   relative frequency: 0.00001
    p. 187 UNDERWOOD 33   9 Hook-handed Harpies, gowned Vultures, put

hooke   frequency: 2   relative frequency: 0.00002
    p. 290 UNDERWOOD 85   11 And with his hooke lops off the fruitlesse race,
    p. 380 UNGATHERED 12   44 How many learned men he haue drawne with his
                               hooke

hoops. See "houpes."

hoord   frequency: 1   relative frequency: 0.00001
    p. 95 FOREST 2   71 Thy tables hoord not vp for the next day,

hoorld   frequency: 1   relative frequency: 0.00001
    p. 396 UNGATHERED 30   13 Wonder to truth! and haue my Vision hoorld,

hoorl'd   frequency: 1   relative frequency: 0.00001
  **p. 113 PANEGYRE   4 Vnfolds himself: & from his eyes are hoorl'd

hop   frequency: 1   relative frequency: 0.00001
    p. 321 HORACE 2   333 A royall Crowne, and purple, be made hop,

hop-drinkers   frequency: 1   relative frequency: 0.00001
    p. 657 L. CONVIVALES   7 Hang up all the poor Hop-Drinkers,

hop'd   frequency: 1   relative frequency: 0.00001
    p. 57 EPIGRAMS 90   17 And it is hop'd, that shee, like MILO, wull,

hope   frequency: 31   relative frequency: 0.00044
    p. 30 EPIGRAMS 11   6 And such from whom let no man hope least good,
    p. 32 EPIGRAMS 18   5 And mine come nothing like. I hope so. Yet,
    p. 41 EPIGRAMS 43   7 Yet dare not, to my thought, lest hope allow
    p. 41 EPIGRAMS 45   2 My sinne was too much hope of thee, lou'd boy,
    p. 61 EPIGRAMS 95   18 That liu'st from hope, from feare, from faction
                               free;
    p. 64 EPIGRAMS 101   6 Something, which, else, could hope for no
                               esteeme.
    p. 66 EPIGRAMS 102   19 Thou must draw more: and they, that hope to see
    p. 70 EPIGRAMS 109   5 Thou are not one, seek'st miseries with hope,
    p. 80 EPIGRAMS 127   1 Is there a hope, that Man would thankefull bee,
    p. 93 FOREST 1   4 Can Poets hope to fetter mee?
    p. 100 FOREST 4   5 Doe not once hope, that thou canst tempt
    p. 101 FOREST 4   38 As little, as I hope from thee:
    p. 106 FOREST 9   11 As giuing it a hope, that there
    p. 122 FOREST 15   11 My faith, my hope, my loue: and in this state,
    p. 162 UNDERWOOD 15   10 In dreames, begun in hope, and end in spoile.
    p. 179 UNDERWOOD 25   58 (As my hope tells) that our faire Phoeb<e>'s
                               shine,
    p. 192 UNDERWOOD 38   44 No man inflicts that paine, till hope be spent:
    p. 193 UNDERWOOD 38   90 Upon the hope to have another sin
    p. 197 UNDERWOOD 40   7 Of parting, drowne it in the hope to meet
    p. 284 U'WOOD 84.9   68 Hope, hath her end! and Faith hath her reward!
    p. 285 U'WOOD 84.9   103 Thither, you hope to come; and there to find
    p. 293 UNDERWOOD 86   30 Delights, nor credulous hope of mutuall Joy,
    p. 309 HORACE 2   100 Or grace of speech, should hope a lasting date.
    p. 317 HORACE 2   245 A great deferrer, long in hope, growne numbe
    p. 317 HORACE 2   270 Nor must the Fable, that would hope the Fate,

hope (cont.)
```
      p. 321 HORACE 2       350 And so, as every man may hope the same;
      p. 323 HORACE 2       394 Within the hope of having all forgiven?
      p. 327 HORACE 2       474 Thinke wee, or hope, there can be Verses fain'd
      p. 406 UNGATHERED 34   99 Of all ye Worthyes hope t'outlast thy one,
      p. 413 UNGATHERED 41   25 Thus, Love, and Hope, and burning Charitie,
      p. 420 UNGATHERED 48   27 And in this Age, canst hope no <other> grace.
```

hopefull   frequency: 1   relative frequency: 0.00001
```
      p. 272 UNDERWOOD 84   t16 Her hopefull ISSUE.
```

hopelesse   frequency: 1   relative frequency: 0.00001
```
      p. 305 HORACE 2        27 To paint him, hath by swimming, hopelesse,
                                scap'd,
```

hopes   frequency: 8   relative frequency: 0.00011
```
      p.  47 EPIGRAMS 64      1 Not glad, like those that haue new hopes, or
                                sutes,
      p. 115 FOREST 12       64 And such, or my hopes faile, shall make you
                                shine.
      p. 144 UNDERWOOD 4      8 For then my hopes will spill me.
      p. 162 UNDERWOOD 15    12 His unjust hopes, with praises begg'd, or (worse)
      p. 219 UNDERWOOD 47    34 Some hopes of Spaine in their West-Indian
                                Fleet?
      p. 237 UNDERWOOD 65     2 That so hath crown'd our hopes, our spring, and
                                earth,
      p. 382 UNGATHERED 16    5 The elder of these two, riche hopes Increase,
      p. 383 UNGATHERED 17    7 Who reads, who roaues, who hopes to vnderstand,
```

hor.   frequency: 3   relative frequency: 0.00004
```
      p. 293 UNDERWOOD 87     1 HOR. Whilst, Lydia, I was lov'd of thee,
      p. 293 UNDERWOOD 87     9 HOR. 'Tis true, I'am Thracian Chloes, I,
      p. 294 UNDERWOOD 87    17 HOR. But, say old Love returne should make,
```

horace   frequency: 11   relative frequency: 0.00015
    See also "hor."
```
     *p. 493 TO HIMSELF      43 Or thine owne Horace, or Anacreons Lyre;
      p.  58 EPIGRAMS 91      3 Illustrous VERE, or HORACE; fit to be
      p.  58 EPIGRAMS 91      4 Sung by a HORACE, or a Muse as free;
      p.  58 EPIGRAMS 91     t1 TO SIR HORACE VERE.
      p.  65 EPIGRAMS 101    31 Of which had HORACE, or ANACREON
                                tasted,
      p. 181 UNDERWOOD 27    13 Is Horace his each love so high
      p. 199 UNDERWOOD 42     2 As Horace fat; or as Anacreon old;
      p. 213 UNDERWOOD 44    t1 A speach according to Horace.
      p. 293 UNDERWOOD 87     5 LYD. Whilst Horace lov'd no Mistres more,
      p. 293 UNDERWOOD 87    t2 Dialogue of Horace, and Lydia.
      p. 305 HORACE 2        t1 HORACE,
```

horatius   frequency: 1   relative frequency: 0.00001
```
      p. 338 HORACE 1        t1 Quintus Horatius Flaccus
```

horld   frequency: 2   relative frequency: 0.00002
```
      p. 243 UNDERWOOD 70    15 Urg'd, hurried forth, and horld
      p. 277 U'WOOD 84.3     27 Of Constellations 'bout her horld;
```

horl'd   frequency: 1   relative frequency: 0.00001
```
      p. 193 UNDERWOOD 38    74 In a calme skie, then when the heaven is horl'd
```

horn. See "horne," "mariage-horne."

horne   frequency: 1   relative frequency: 0.00001
```
      p. 203 UNDERWOOD 43     8 With Clownes, and Tradesmen, kept thee clos'd
                                in horne.
```

horne-workes   frequency: 1   relative frequency: 0.00001
```
      p. 248 UNDERWOOD 71     8 Reduicts, Halfe-moones, Horne-workes, and such
                                close wayes,
```

hornes   frequency: 1   relative frequency: 0.00001
```
      p. 375 UNGATHERED 10   31 Their hornes, and Germany pukes on his head.
```

hornet   frequency: 2   relative frequency: 0.00002
```
      p.  53 EPIGRAMS 78      1 HORNET, thou hast thy wife drest, for the
                                stall,
      p.  53 EPIGRAMS 78     t1 TO HORNET.
```

horns. See "hornes."

hornworks. See "horne-workes."

horrid. See "horride."

horride   frequency: 1   relative frequency: 0.00001
    p.   84 EPIGRAMS 133   12 And in it, two more horride knaues, then
                              CHARON.

horror   frequency: 1   relative frequency: 0.00001
    See also "horrour."
    p. 122 FOREST 15   19 Standing with feare, and must with horror fall,

horrors   frequency: 1   relative frequency: 0.00001
    p. 110 FOREST 11   33 Most frequent tumults, horrors, and vnrests,

horrour   frequency: 4   relative frequency: 0.00005
    p. 155 UNDERWOOD 13   91 Such a religious horrour in the brests
    p. 160 UNDERWOOD 14   57 With horrour rough, then rioting with wit!
    p. 243 UNDERWOOD 70   12 From out the horrour of that sack?
    p. 269 UNDERWOOD 83   8 A horrour in mee! all my blood is steele!

horse   frequency: 18   relative frequency: 0.00026
    See also "court-hobby-horse."
    p.   57 EPIGRAMS 90   12 And he remou'd to gent'man of the horse,
    p.   69 EPIGRAMS 107   8 Of your Morauian horse, Venetian bull.
    p.   88 EPIGRAMS 133   157 Graue tutor to the learned horse. Both which,
    p. 200 UNDERWOOD 42   8 His lynes, and hourely sits the Poets horse?
    p. 201 UNDERWOOD 42   43 Put a Coach-mare in Tissue, must I horse
    p. 206 UNDERWOOD 43   79 Or Captaine Pamp<h>lets horse, and foot, that
                              sallie
    p. 213 UNDERWOOD 44   7 That we have Trumpets, Armour, and great
                              Horse,
    p. 215 UNDERWOOD 44   71 More then to praise a Dog? or Horse? or speake
    p. 228 UNDERWOOD 53   1 When first, my Lord, I saw you backe your
                              horse,
    p. 228 UNDERWOOD 53   6 So seem'd your horse and you, both of a peece!
    p. 228 UNDERWOOD 53   12 As I began to wish my selfe a horse.
    p. 311 HORACE 2   115 The conqu'ring Champion, the prime Horse in
                              course,
    p. 338 HORACE 1   2 . horse neck joyn . sundry plumes ore-fold
    p. 374 UNGATHERED 10   14 A Horse here is sadled, but no Tom him to
                              backe,
    p. 374 UNGATHERED 10   15 It should rather haue bene Tom that a horse did
                              lack.
    p. 380 UNGATHERED 12   28 Horse, foote, and all but flying in the ayre:
    p. 397 UNGATHERED 30   40 Drums against Drums, the neighing of the Horse,
    p. 657 I. CONVIVALES   13 And the Poets' Horse accounted.

horse-leech   frequency: 1   relative frequency: 0.00001
    p. 337 HORACE 2   680 Till he drop off, a Horse-leech, full of blood.

horse-leech-like   frequency: 1   relative frequency: 0.00001
    p. 355 HORACE 1   680 .... horse-leech-like .. ..

horse-neck   frequency: 1   relative frequency: 0.00001
    p. 305 HORACE 2   2 Set a Horse-neck, and divers feathers fold

horses   frequency: 4   relative frequency: 0.00005
    p.   94 FOREST 2   24 The middle grounds thy mares, and horses breed.
    p. 315 HORACE 2   230 Loves Dogges, and Horses; and is ever one
    p. 375 UNGATHERED 10   33 To lie at Liuory, while the Horses did stand.
    p. 380 UNGATHERED 12   38 And lay in straw with the horses at Bergamo,

hose   frequency: 1   relative frequency: 0.00001
    p. 375 UNGATHERED 10   26 Old Hat here, torne Hose, with Shoes full of
                              grauell,

hospital. See "spittle."

hospitalitie   frequency: 1   relative frequency: 0.00001
    p.   95 FOREST 2   60 With all, that hospitalitie doth know!

hospitality. See "hospitalitie."

hospitalls   frequency: 1   relative frequency: 0.00001
    p. 104 FOREST 8   10 Spittles, pest-house, hospitalls,

hospitals. See "hospitalls," "spittles."

host   frequency: 1   relative frequency: 0.00001
    p. 292 UNDERWOOD 86   11 There jest, and feast, make him thine host,

hostess. See "hostesse."

hostesse   frequency: 1   relative frequency: 0.00001
      p.   30 EPIGRAMS 12   7 The quarter day is come; the hostesse sayes,

hot   frequency: 8   relative frequency: 0.00011
    **p. 117 PANEGYRE   142 And was not hot, or couetous to be crown'd
      p.   85 EPIGRAMS 133   63 Belch'd forth an ayre, as hot, as at the muster
      p.   88 EPIGRAMS 133   143 Your Fleet-lane Furies; and hot cookes doe
                                   dwell,
      p.   88 EPIGRAMS 133   165 Your daintie nostrills (in so hot a season,
      p. 107 FOREST 10   9 And foundred thy hot teame, to tune my lay.
      p. 189 UNDERWOOD 36   15 Now hot, now cold, now fierce, now mild.
      p. 313 HORACE 2   163 Or some hot youth, yet in his flourishing course;
      p. 396 UNGATHERED 30   14 Hot from thy trumpet, round, about the world.

hot-house   frequency: 1   relative frequency: 0.00001
      p.   29 EPIGRAMS 7   3 Tells you it is a hot-house: So it ma',

hot-hovse   frequency: 1   relative frequency: 0.00001
      p.   29 EPIGRAMS 7   t1 ON THE NEW HOT-HOVSE.

hottest   frequency: 1   relative frequency: 0.00001
      p. 270 UNDERWOOD 83   54 Your hottest Causticks to, burne, lance, or cut:

houghs   frequency: 1   relative frequency: 0.00001
      p.   88 EPIGRAMS 133   146 The heads, houghs, entrailes, and the hides of
                                   dogs:

hound   frequency: 2   relative frequency: 0.00002
      p. 155 UNDERWOOD 13   70 Then give it to the Hound that did him bite;
      p. 290 UNDERWOOD 85   31 Or hence, or thence, he drives with many a Hound

houpes   frequency: 1   relative frequency: 0.00001
      p. 227 UNDERWOOD 52   6 But yet the Tun at Heidelberg had houpes.

hour. See "houre."

hour-glass. See "houre-glasse."

houre   frequency: 9   relative frequency: 0.00013
      p. 100 FOREST 4   2 That houre vpon my morne of age,
      p. 119 FOREST 13   87 And neuer thinke, how vice doth euery houre,
      p. 166 UNDERWOOD 15   122 Brought on us, and will every houre increase.
      p. 179 UNDERWOOD 25   42 Pyracmon's houre will come to give them ease,
      p. 202 UNDERWOOD 43   4 So many my Yeares-labours in an houre?
      p. 210 UNDERWOOD 43   158 There was a Judgement shew'n too in an houre.
      p. 249 UNDERWOOD 72   3 Discharge it 'bout the Iland, in an houre,
      p. 288 U'WOOD 84.9   218 His Wisdome, and his Justice, in that houre,
      p. 315 HORACE 2   228 He knowes not why, and changeth every houre.

houre-glasse   frequency: 1   relative frequency: 0.00001
      p. 148 UNDERWOOD 8   t1 The Houre-glasse.

hourely   frequency: 3   relative frequency: 0.00004
      p.   34 EPIGRAMS 25   5 And now, her (hourely) her owne cucqueane makes,
      p.   89 EPIGRAMS 133   174 Of loud SEPVLCHRES with their hourely
                                   knells,
      p. 200 UNDERWOOD 42   8 His lynes, and hourely sits the Poets horse?

houres   frequency: 13   relative frequency: 0.00018
    **p. 115 PANEGYRE   66 And infants, that the houres had made such hast
      p.   48 EPIGRAMS 65   6 And, as thou'hast mine, his houres, and youth
                                   abuse.
      p.   52 EPIGRAMS 76   16 Of destinie, and spin her owne free houres.
      p.   94 FOREST 2   40 Fresh as the ayre, and new as are the houres.
      p. 115 FOREST 12   74 I haue already vs'd some happy houres,
      p. 199 UNDERWOOD 41   9 What fate is this, to change mens dayes and
                                   houres,
      p. 238 UNDERWOOD 65   11 And threat' the great Eclipse. Two houres but
                                   runne,
      p. 251 UNDERWOOD 74   16 Doth show, the Graces, and the Houres,
      p. 257 UNDERWOOD 75   146 Some houres before it should, that these may know
      p. 288 U'WOOD 84.9   192 Her solemne houres she spent, or giving Almes,
      p. 289 U'WOOD 84.9   219 The last of houres, and shutter up of all;
      p. 290 UNDERWOOD 85   30 Are gathering by the Wintry houres;
      p. 396 UNGATHERED 30   18 Is fayre got vp, and day some houres begun!

hourly. See "hourely," "howrely."

hours. See "houres," "howers," "howres."

house   frequency: 9   relative frequency: 0.00013
    See alsc "ale-house," "glasse-house,"
              "hot-house," "hot-hovse,"
              "pest-house," "slaughter-house,"
              "store-house," "whore-house."
    p.   48 EPIGRAMS 66   3 Whose house, if it no other honor had,
    p.   51 EPIGRAMS 73   8 That yet maintaynes you, and your house in
                      laughter.
    p.   60 EPIGRAMS 93   3 Who did, alike with thee, thy house vp-beare,
    p.   64 EPIGRAMS 101   1 To night, graue sir, both my poore house, and I
    p.   97 FOREST 3   24 Who, for it, makes thy house his court;
    p. 280 U'WOOD 84.4   53 Thrice happy house, that hast receipt
    p. 292 UNDERWOOD 86   9 More timely hie thee to the house,
    p. 372 UNGATHERED 9   10 The sole Religious house, and Votary,
    p. 413 UNGATHERED 41   39 The House of gold, the Gate of heavens power,

house-hold   frequency: 3   relative frequency: 0.00004
    p. 241 UNDERWOOD 68   2 His Poet Sack, the House-hold will not pay?
    p. 241 UNDERWOOD 68   6 His Poet leave to sing his House-hold true;
    p. 241 UNDERWOOD 68   t2 To the House-hold.

household. See "house-hcld," "houshold."

houses   frequency: 3   relative frequency: 0.00004
    See alsc "brew-houses."
  **p. 114 PANEGYRE   41 Some cry from tops of houses; thinking noise
    p. 210 UNDERWOOD 43   164 More then advanc'd the houses, and their rites?
    p. 274 U'WOOD 84.2   5 Gave two such Houses as
                      NORTHUMBERLAND,

housewifery. See "huswifery."

houshold   frequency: 5   relative frequency: 0.00007
    p.   96 FOREST 2   96 With the whole houshold, and may, euery day,
    p. 102 FOREST 5   12 Of a few poore houshold spyes?
    p. 228 UNDERWOOD 53   16 Nor any of their houshold, halfe so well.
    p. 291 UNDERWOOD 85   40 For houshold aid, and Children sweet;
    p. 291 UNDERWOOD 85   65 The wealthy houshold swarme of bondmen met,

how   frequency: 149   relative frequency: 0.00215
    See alsc "ho'," "howe," "th'how."

how-so-e're   frequency: 1   relative frequency: 0.00001
    p. 242 UNDERWOOD 69   16 To keepe him off; and how-so-e're he gleanes

howard   frequency: 1   relative frequency: 0.00001
    p.   49 EPIGRAMS 67   5 Stand high, then, HOWARD, high in eyes of
                      men,

howe   frequency: 2   relative frequency: 0.00002

howers   frequency: 1   relative frequency: 0.00001
    p. 416 UNGATHERED 44   1 Fresh as the Day, and new as are the Howers,

howrely   frequency: 1   relative frequency: 0.00001
    p. 400 UNGATHERED 31   29 And howrely brooding ore the same,

howres   frequency: 1   relative frequency: 0.00001
    p. 295 UNDERWOOD 90   11 Sleepe, that will make the darkest howres
                      swift-pac't;

howsoeuer   frequency: 2   relative frequency: 0.00002
    p.   99 FOREST 3   97 And, howsoeuer we may thinke things sweet,
    p. 116 FOREST 13   9 And howsoeuer; as I am at fewd

howsoever. See "how-so-e're," "howsoeuer."

hue   frequency: 2   relative frequency: 0.00002
    p. 188 UNDERWOOD 34   8 Was drawne to practise other hue, then that
    p. 366 UNGATHERED 6   4 Whose Note, and Hue,

hues   frequency: 1   relative frequency: 0.00001
    p. 311 HORACE 2   126 If now the turnes, the colours, and right hues

huge   frequency: 1   relative frequency: 0.00001
    p.   86 EPIGRAMS 133   86 So huge, it seem'd, they could by no meanes quite
                      her.

hugh   frequency: 2   relative frequency: 0.00002
    p. 188 UNDERWOOD 34   7 Art, her false servant; Nor, for Sir Hugh
                      Plat,

hugh (cont.)
    p. 214 UNDERWOOD 44   33 Well did thy craftie Clerke, and Knight, Sir
                    Hugh,

huishers   frequency: 1   relative frequency: 0.00001
    p. 113 FOREST 12   9 While it makes huishers seruiceable men,

hulk. See "hulke."

hulke   frequency: 1   relative frequency: 0.00001
    p. 87 EPIGRAMS 133 112 Of the hulke touch'd, and, as by
                    POLYPHEME

human. See "numane."

humane   frequency: 3   relative frequency: 0.00004
  **p. 113 PANEGYRE   13 Carowsing humane bloud in yron bowles,
    p. 233 UNDERWOOD 59   22 Of humane life! as all the frosts, and sweates
    p. 329 HORACE 2   528 Hath shed, or humane frailtie not kept thence.

humanitie   frequency: 7   relative frequency: 0.00010
    p. 58 EPIGRAMS 91   15 Humanitie, and pietie, which are
    p. 73 EPIGRAMS 113   8 And letters and humanitie in the stead!
    p. 158 UNDERWOOD 14   12 Of this so vitious Humanitie.
    p. 161 UNDERWOOD 14   77 Humanitie enough to be a friend,
    p. 207 UNDERWOOD 43 101 And twice-twelve-yeares stor'd up humanitie,
    p. 244 UNDERWOOD 70   52 His life was of Humanitie the Spheare.
    p. 286 U'WOOD 84.9   133 In his humanitie! To heare him preach

humanity. See "humanitie."

humber   frequency: 1   relative frequency: 0.00001
    p. 368 UNGATHERED 6   74 Humber, or Owse, decline;

humble   frequency: 6   relative frequency: 0.00008
    p. 98 FOREST 3   41 The ripened eares, yet humble in their height,
    p. 153 UNDERWOOD 13   15 And though my fortune humble me, to take
    p. 207 UNDERWOOD 43 102 With humble Gleanings in Divinitie,
    p. 259 UNDERWOOD 76   1 The humble Petition of poore Ben.
    p. 311 HORACE 2   135 Complaines in humble phrase. Both Telephus,
    p. 413 UNGATHERED 41 17 The fourth is humble Ivy, intersert,

humbled   frequency: 1   relative frequency: 0.00001
    p. 420 UNGATHERED 48 30 Vppon soe humbled earth to cast hir eyes:

humblest   frequency: 1   relative frequency: 0.00001
    p. 106 FOREST 8   46 Moue it, as their humblest sute,

humbly   frequency: 1   relative frequency: 0.00001
    See also "humblye."
    p. 259 UNDERWOOD 76   3 Doth most humbly show it,

humblye   frequency: 1   relative frequency: 0.00001
    p. 382 UNGATHERED 16   2 hath armde att all poyntes; charge mee humblye
                    kneele

humilitie   frequency: 2   relative frequency: 0.00002
    p. 288 U'WOOD 84.9   189 And hers were all Humilitie! they beat
    p. 413 UNGATHERED 41 27 With od'rous sweets and soft humilitie,

humility. See "humilitie."

humorous. See "hum'rous."

humour'd   frequency: 1   relative frequency: 0.00001
    p. 327 HORACE 2   457 With specious places, and being humour'd right,

humours   frequency: 1   relative frequency: 0.00001
    p. 190 UNDERWOOD 37   27 As flatt'ry with friends humours still to move.

hum'rous   frequency: 1   relative frequency: 0.00001
    p. 83 EPIGRAMS 131   7 For, if the hum'rous world will talke at large,

hundred   frequency: 11   relative frequency: 0.00015
    p. 29 EPIGRAMS 8   1 RIDWAY rob'd DVNCOTE of three hundred
                    pound,
    p. 32 EPIGRAMS 16   6 Some hundred quarrells, yet dost thou fight none;
    p. 86 EPIGRAMS 133   82 (Who hath the hundred hands when he doth meddle)
    p. 103 FOREST 6   8 While you breath. First giue a hundred,
    p. 103 FOREST 6   10 Hundred, then vnto the tother

hundred (cont.)
```
    p. 150 UNDERWOOD 9      14 My hundred of gray haires,
    p. 245 UNDERWOOD 70     67 Or standing long an Oake, three hundred yeare,
    p. 248 UNDERWOOD 71      9 The Muse not peepes out, one of hundred dayes;
    p. 259 UNDERWOOD 76     11 A large hundred Markes annuitie,
    p. 292 UNDERWOOD 86     15 Child of a hundred Arts, and farre
    p. 327 HORACE 2        465 How to divide, into a hundred parts,
```

hung   frequency: 2   relative frequency: 0.00002
```
    p.  56 EPIGRAMS 88      11 Or hung some MOVNSIEVRS picture on the
                              wall,
    p.  86 EPIGRAMS 133     70 Hung stench, diseases, and old filth, their
                              mother,
```

hungary   frequency: 1   relative frequency: 0.00001
```
    p.  69 EPIGRAMS 107     13 In Hungary, and Poland, Turkie too;
```

hungry   frequency: 2   relative frequency: 0.00002
See also "hvngry."
```
    p. 288 U'WOOD 84.9     194 To cloath the naked, feed the hungry. Shee
    p. 408 UNGATHERED 36    10 Seek out some hungry painter, yt for bread
```

hunted   frequency: 1   relative frequency: 0.00001
```
    p.  68 EPIGRAMS 105     14 DIANA'alone, so hit, and hunted so.
```

hunters   frequency: 2   relative frequency: 0.00002
```
    p. 155 UNDERWOOD 13     65 Still, still, the hunters of false fame apply
    p. 264 UNDERWOOD 79     20 Shep. Of PAN wee sing, the best of Hunters,
                              PAN,
```

hunting   frequency: 4   relative frequency: 0.00005
```
    p.  76 EPIGRAMS 119      2 At hunting railes, hauing no guift in othes,
    p.  95 FOREST 2         76 That found King IAMES, when hunting late,
                              this way,
    p. 265 UNDERWOOD 79     55 And hunting, PAN, exceedeth thee.
    p. 415 UNGATHERED 43    t3 Instauration of his Hunting, and Dauncing
```

hunts   frequency: 2   relative frequency: 0.00002
```
    p. 113 FOREST 12        15 While thus it buyes great grace, and hunts poore
                              fame;
    p. 408 UNGATHERED 36     7 The Lybian Lion hunts noe butter flyes,
```

hunt'st   frequency: 1   relative frequency: 0.00001
```
    p.  97 FOREST 3         29 And, in the winter, hunt'st the flying hare,
```

hurdles   frequency: 1   relative frequency: 0.00001
```
    p. 291 UNDERWOOD 85     45 That penning the glad flock in hurdles by,
```

hurl. See "hurle."

hurld   frequency: 1   relative frequency: 0.00001
```
    p. 172 UNDERWOOD 21      6 Of all vice hurld together, there he was,
```

hurl'd   frequency: 1   relative frequency: 0.00001
See also "hoorld," "hoorl'd," "horld," "horl'd,"
          "hurld."
```
    p. 203 UNDERWOOD 43      9 'Twas Jupiter that hurl'd thee headlong downe,
```

hurle   frequency: 1   relative frequency: 0.00001
```
    p.  27 EPIGRAMS 2        5 Become a petulant thing, hurle inke, and wit,
```

hurles   frequency: 1   relative frequency: 0.00001
```
    p. 311 HORACE 2        155 With weightie sorrow hurles us all along,
```

hurls. See "hurles."

hurried   frequency: 1   relative frequency: 0.00001
```
    p. 243 UNDERWOOD 70     15 Urg'd, hurried forth, and horld
```

hurt   frequency: 9   relative frequency: 0.00013
```
    p.  46 EPIGRAMS 62       7 That can restore that. Will it hurt your
                              feature?
    p.  63 EPIGRAMS 98       6 And what would hurt his vertue makes it still.
    p. 133 UNDERWOOD 2.3     4 Eyes and limbes; to hurt me more.
    p. 155 UNDERWOOD 13     68 And hurt seeks Cure, the Surgeon bids take
                              bread,
    p. 179 UNDERWOOD 25     50 That is not hurt; not he, that is not hit;
    p. 250 UNDERWOOD 73     11 Dreame thou could'st hurt it; but before thou
                              wake
    p. 386 UNGATHERED 21     2 May hurt them more with praise, then Poes with
                              spight.
```

hurt (cont.)
```
     p. 391 UNGATHERED 26   14 Should praise a Matron. What could hurt her
                                 more?
     p. 422 UNGATHERED 50    2 make many, hurt themselues; a praysed faith
```

hurtfull   frequency: 1   relative frequency: 0.00001
```
     p. 309 HORACE 2        97 His course so hurtfull both to graine, and
                                 seedes,
```

hurting   frequency: 1   relative frequency: 0.00001
```
     p. 323 HORACE 2       370 His power of foulely hurting made to cease.
```

husband   frequency: 10   relative frequency: 0.00014
```
     p. 165 UNDERWOOD 15    89 The Husband now's call'd churlish, or a poore
     p. 171 UNDERWOOD 19    22 You have a Husband is the just excuse
     p. 180 UNDERWOOD 26    18 To doe, then be a husband of that store.
     p. 262 UNDERWOOD 78    t3 Husband, Sir KENELME DIGBY.
     p. 291 UNDERWOOD 85    44 Against the Husband comes home tir'd;
     p. 342 HORACE 1       165 ........ ........ .. ... husband ....
     p. 384 UNGATHERED 18   13 And thou to her, that Husband, may exalt
     p. 385 UNGATHERED 20   t2 the Husband.
     p. 386 UNGATHERED 20    9 That went before, a Husband. Shee, Ile sweare,
     p. 394 UNGATHERED 28   16 But of one Husband; and since he left life,
```

husbands   frequency: 7   relative frequency: 0.00010
```
     p.  95 FOREST 2        55 This way to husbands; and whose baskets beare
     p. 105 FOREST 8        29 That distill their husbands land
     p. 118 FOREST 13       73 Melt downe their husbands land, to poure away
     p. 200 UNDERWOOD 42    11 Fathers, and Husbands, I doe claime a right
     p. 201 UNDERWOOD 42    40 To doe her Husbands rites in, e're 'twere gone
     p. 213 UNDERWOOD 44    18 To have their Husbands drawne forth to the
                                 field,
     p. 417 UNGATHERED 45   38 each to pawne hir husbands capp,
```

huskes   frequency: 1   relative frequency: 0.00001
```
    *p. 432 TO HIMSELF      18 Huskes, draffe to drinke, and swill.
```

husks. See "huskes."

huswifery   frequency: 1   relative frequency: 0.00001
```
     p.  96 FOREST 2        85 The iust reward of her high huswifery;
```

hvngry   frequency: 2   relative frequency: 0.00002
```
     p.  68 EPIGRAMS 107    t1 TO CAPTAYNE HVNGRY.
     p.  69 EPIGRAMS 107    31 Come, be not angrie, you are HVNGRY; eate;
```

hyde. See "hide-parke."

hydra   frequency: 1   relative frequency: 0.00001
```
     p.  86 EPIGRAMS 133    83 The other thought it HYDRA, or the rock
```

hye   frequency: 1   relative frequency: 0.00001
```
     p.  32 EPIGRAMS 17      4 Charge them, for crowne, to thy sole censure hye.
```

hym   frequency: 1   relative frequency: 0.00001

hyme   frequency: 1   relative frequency: 0.00001

hymens   frequency: 1   relative frequency: 0.00001
```
     p. 384 UNGATHERED 18   14 Hymens amends, to make it worth his fault.
```

hymn. See "hymne."

hymne   frequency: 3   relative frequency: 0.00004
```
     p. 129 UNDERWOOD 1.2   t1 A Hymne to God the Father.
     p. 130 UNDERWOOD 1.3   t1 A Hymne
     p. 174 UNDERWOOD 22    30 Have sung this Hymne, and here intreat
```

hypocrites. See "hipocrites."

i   frequency: 750   relative frequency: 0.01085
```
    See also "i'<h>ad," "i'am," "i'had," "i'haue,"
             "i'ld," "ile," "i'le," "i'll," "i'm."
```

i'<h>ad   frequency: 1   relative frequency: 0.00001
```
     p. 325 HORACE 2       432 My title, at the<ir> rate, I'<h>ad rather, I,
```

i'   frequency: 7   relative frequency: 0.00010

i'am   frequency: 3   relative frequency: 0.00004 iambic. See "iambicke," "th'iambick."

iambicke   frequency: 1   relative frequency: 0.00001
     p. 341 HORACE 1   117 The Iambicke ....

iambicks   frequency: 1   relative frequency: 0.00001
     p. 323 HORACE 2   374 But meere Iambicks all, from first to last.

iambics. See "iambicks."

iames   frequency: 10   relative frequency: 0.00014
  **p. 112 PANEGYRE   t5 ENTRANCE OF IAMES,
    p. 28 EPIGRAMS 4   t1 TO KING IAMES.
    p. 37 EPIGRAMS 35   1 Who would not be thy subiect, IAMES,
                              t<o>'obay
    p. 37 EPIGRAMS 35   t1 TO KING IAMES.
    p. 38 EPIGRAMS 36   2 To thy DOMITIAN, than I can my
                              IAMES:
    p. 43 EPIGRAMS 51   t1 TO KING IAMES.
    p. 95 FOREST 2   76 That found King IAMES, when hunting late,
                              this way,
    p. 176 UNDERWOOD 25   t1 An Ode to IAMES Earle of Desmond,
    p. 268 UNDERWOOD 82   t3 His second Sonne IAMES.
    p. 392 UNGATHERED 26   74 That so did take Eliza, and our Iames!

ianin's   frequency: 1   relative frequency: 0.00001
     p. 69 EPIGRAMS 107   22 Ianin's, your Nuncio's, and your Tuilleries,

iarre   frequency: 1   relative frequency: 0.00001
     p. 99 FOREST 3   74 For euery price, in euery iarre,

iarres   frequency: 1   relative frequency: 0.00001
     p. 397 UNGATHERED 30 41 The Fights, the Cryes, and wondring at the
                              Iarres

iasons   frequency: 1   relative frequency: 0.00001
     p. 115 FOREST 12   59 Who placed IASONS ARGO in the skie?

iawes   frequency: 1   relative frequency: 0.00001
     p. 85 EPIGRAMS 133   61 In the first Iawes appear'd that vgly monster,

iay   frequency: 1   relative frequency: 0.00001
     p. 103 FOREST 6   3 When the common courting iay

iberus   frequency: 1   relative frequency: 0.00001
     p. 369 UNGATHERED 6 115 Iberus, Tagus, Rheine,

idalian. See "th'idalian."

ideas   frequency: 1   relative frequency: 0.00001
     p. 397 UNGATHERED 30 23 When, by thy bright Ideas standing by,

ideot   frequency: 2   relative frequency: 0.00002
     p. 45 EPIGRAMS 58   1 IDEOT, last night, I pray'd thee but
                              forbeare
     p. 45 EPIGRAMS 58   t1 TO GROOME IDEOT.

ides. See "ta'ides."

idiot   frequency: 1   relative frequency: 0.00001
   See also "ideot."
     p. 319 HORACE 2   301 The Idiot, keeping holy-day, or drudge,

idle   frequency: 2   relative frequency: 0.00002
     p. 109 FOREST 11   26 Th'are base, and idle feares
     p. 199 UNDERWOOD 41   4 Be idle words, though of a parting Man;

idol. See "idoll."

idolatrie   frequency: 2   relative frequency: 0.00002
     p. 48 EPIGRAMS 65   3 Made me commit most fierce idolatrie
     p. 223 UNDERWOOD 49   27 Farthest I am from the Idolatrie

idolatrous   frequency: 1   relative frequency: 0.00001
     p. 156 UNDERWOOD 13 104 Of Valour, but at this Idolatrous rate?

idolatry. See "idolatrie," "t<o>'idolatrie."

idoll   frequency: 2   relative frequency: 0.00002
     p. 140 UNDERWOOD 2.8 22 'Fore your Idoll Glasse a whit,

idoll (cont.)
   p. 210 UNDERWOOD 43   155 He burnt that Idoll of the Revels too:

idomen   frequency: 1   relative frequency: 0.00001
   p. 114 FOREST 12   54 AIAX, or IDOMEN, or all the store,

iealous   frequency: 2   relative frequency: 0.00002
   p. 43 EPIGRAMS 51   5 Yet giue thy iealous subiects leaue to doubt:
   p. 80 EPIGRAMS 126   3 I pluck'd a branch; the iealous god did frowne,

iealousie   frequency: 1   relative frequency: 0.00001
   p. 150 UNDERWOOD 10   t1 Against Iealousie.

iealousies   frequency: 2   relative frequency: 0.00002
   p. 101 FOREST 4   43 Since stird'st vp iealousies and feares,
   p. 397 UNGATHERED 30 30 Their loues, their quarrels, iealousies, and
                         wrongs,

ieames   frequency: 1   relative frequency: 0.00001
   p. 415 UNGATHERED 43   4 Renew the Glories of our blessed Ieames:

iephson   frequency: 2   relative frequency: 0.00002
   p. 75 EPIGRAMS 116   1 IEPHSON, thou man of men, to whose lou'd
                         name
   p. 75 EPIGRAMS 116   t1 TO SIR WILLIAM IEPHSON.

ierna   frequency: 1   relative frequency: 0.00001
   p. 367 UNGATHERED 6   42 Ouer Ierna maine,

iest   frequency: 3   relative frequency: 0.00004
   p. 32 EPIGRAMS 16   2 Thou more; that with it euery day, dar'st iest
   p. 51 EPIGRAMS 73   5 In-primis, GRAND, you owe me for a iest,
   p. 380 UNGATHERED 12 48 Iest, he saies. Item one sute of blacke taffata

iests   frequency: 1   relative frequency: 0.00001
   p. 64 EPIGRAMS 100   4 Fiue of my iests, then stolne, past him a play.

iewell   frequency: 1   relative frequency: 0.00001
   p. 77 EPIGRAMS 120 12 The stages iewell;

iewells   frequency: 1   relative frequency: 0.00001
   p. 97 FOREST 3   11 To view the iewells, stuffes, the paines, the wit

iewes   frequency: 2   relative frequency: 0.00002
   p. 375 UNGATHERED 10 21 He will expiate this sinne with conuerting the
                         Iewes.
   p. 380 UNGATHERED 12 49 Except a dublet, and bought of the Iewes:

if   frequency: 260   relative frequency: 0.00376
   See also "if't," "yf," "yff."

if't   frequency: 3   relative frequency: 0.00004

ignoble. See "th'ignoble."

ignorance   frequency: 11   relative frequency: 0.00015
   p. 45 EPIGRAMS 58   4 Thy ignorance still laughs in the wrong place.
   p. 55 EPIGRAMS 85   7 And neuer stoupe, but to strike ignorance:
   p. 59 EPIGRAMS 92   37 With ignorance on vs, as they haue done
   p. 73 EPIGRAMS 113   7 For since, what ignorance, what pride is fled!
   p. 83 EPIGRAMS 132   3 But, as it is (the Child of Ignorance,
   p. 101 FOREST 4   48 And pride, and ignorance the schooles,
   p. 218 UNDERWOOD 47 24 And know whose ignorance is more then theirs;
   p. 311 HORACE 2   131 To ignorance still, then either learne, or know?
   p. 323 HORACE 2   386 Or a worse Crime, the ignorance of art.
   p. 390 UNGATHERED 26   7 For seeliest Ignorance on these may light,
   p. 392 UNGATHERED 26 70 As brandish't at the eyes of Ignorance.

ignorant   frequency: 6   relative frequency: 0.00008
   p. 29 EPIGRAMS 10   t1 TO MY LORD IGNORANT.
   p. 72 EPIGRAMS 111   7 Which all, but ignorant Captaynes, will
                         confesse:
   p. 164 UNDERWOOD 15 59 O, these so ignorant Monsters! light, as proud,
   p. 191 UNDERWOOD 38 20 The ignorant, and fooles, no pittie have.
   p. 331 HORACE 2   570 Yet who's most ignorant, dares Verses make.
   p. 333 HORACE 2   597 To say, I'm ignorant. Just as a Crier

ignorants   frequency: 1   relative frequency: 0.00001
   p. 114 FOREST 12   28 With noble ignorants, and let them still,

i'had   frequency: 1   relative frequency: 0.00001 i'haue   frequency: 3   relative frequency: 0.00004

il   frequency: 1   relative frequency: 0.00001
   p. 418 UNGATHERED 46   5 Il may Ben Johnson slander so his feete,

iland   frequency: 1   relative frequency: 0.00001
   p. 249 UNDERWOOD 72   3 Discharge it 'bout the Iland, in an houre,

i'ld   frequency: 3   relative frequency: 0.00004

ile   frequency: 9   relative frequency: 0.00013
   p. 37 EPIGRAMS 33   1 Ile not offend thee with a vaine teare more,
   p. 51 EPIGRAMS 73   22 For which, or pay me quickly', or Ile pay you.
   p. 58 EPIGRAMS 92   2 Vnto the cryes of London Ile adde one;
   p. 65 EPIGRAMS 101   17 Ile tell you of more, and lye, so you will come:
   p. 65 EPIGRAMS 101   24 And Ile professe no verses to repeate:
   p. 106 FOREST 9   4 And Ile not looke for wine.
   p. 107 FOREST 10   6 Of his dull god-head, were sinne. Ile implore
   p. 386 UNGATHERED 20   9 That went before, a Husband. Shee, Ile sweare,
   p. 397 UNGATHERED 30 49 And flight about the Ile, well neare, by this,

i'le   frequency: 12   relative frequency: 0.00017

ilia   frequency: 1   relative frequency: 0.00001
   p. 293 UNDERWOOD 87   8 The Roman Ilia was not more renown'd.

ill   frequency: 30   relative frequency: 0.00043
     See also "il," words beginning "ill-," "th'ill."
  **p. 116 PANEGYRE   118 Who once haue got the habit to doe ill.
   p. 30 EPIGRAMS 11   7 For I will doe none: and as little ill,
   p. 33 EPIGRAMS 19   2 I sent the cause: Hee wooes with an ill sprite.
   p. 43 EPIGRAMS 51   2 Great heau'n did well, to giue ill fame free
                            wing;
   p. 48 EPIGRAMS 65   7 Get him the times long grudge, the courts ill
                            will;
   p. 63 EPIGRAMS 98   5 Fortune vpon him breakes her selfe, if ill,
   p. 63 EPIGRAMS 98   12 And euer is ill got without the first.
   p. 66 EPIGRAMS 102   14 And one true posture, though besieg'd with ill
   p. 72 EPIGRAMS 112   2 At this so subtile sport: and play'st so ill?
   p. 73 EPIGRAMS 112   17 Troth, if it be, I pitty thy ill lucke;
   p. 76 EPIGRAMS 119   10 Till thou canst finde the best, choose the least
                            ill.
   p. 82 EPIGRAMS 130   7 And is t<o>'a body, often, ill inclin'd,
   p. 87 EPIGRAMS 133 118 Stunke not so ill; nor, when shee kist, KATE
                            ARDEN.
   p. 112 FOREST 11   87 He that for loue of goodnesse hateth ill,
   p. 113 FOREST 12   7 Well, or ill, onely, all the following yeere,
   p. 116 FOREST 13   6 For others ill, ought none their good forget.
   p. 129 UNDERWOOD 1.2 13 As minds ill bent
   p. 152 UNDERWOOD 12   18 That never came ill odour thence:
   p. 156 UNDERWOOD 13 108 Or Science of discerning Good and Ill.
   p. 164 UNDERWOOD 15   69 Ready to cast, at one, whose band sits ill,
   p. 191 UNDERWOOD 38   3 Or doe upon my selfe some desperate ill;
   p. 224 UNDERWOOD 50   6 Ought that is ill, but the suspition too,
   p. 229 UNDERWOOD 54   6 An ill commoditie! 'T must make good weight.
   p. 231 UNDERWOOD 56   23 Away ill company, and helpe in rime
   p. 234 UNDERWOOD 60   15 Could stop the malice of this ill,
   p. 241 UNDERWOOD 69   9 But as the wretched Painter, who so ill
   p. 291 UNDERWOOD 85   58 Or Mallowes loosing bodyes ill:
   p. 389 UNGATHERED 24   8 That an ill man dares not securely looke
   p. 420 UNGATHERED 48 16 Hee dyes wth an Ill sent,
   p. 423 UNGATHERED 50 12 It is a lycense to doe ill, protectes

i'll   frequency: 1   relative frequency: 0.00001

ill-   frequency: 1   relative frequency: 0.00001
   p. 317 HORACE 2   264 Her Sonnes before the people; nor the ill-

ill-affected   frequency: 1   relative frequency: 0.00001
   p. 192 UNDERWOOD 38 45 An ill-affected limbe (what e're it aile)

ill-made   frequency: 1   relative frequency: 0.00001
   p. 35 EPIGRAMS 28 10 Both which are great. And laugh at ill-made
                          clothes;

ill-natured. See "ill-."

ill-penn'd   frequency: 1   relative frequency: 0.00001
   p. 311 HORACE 2   148 And ill-penn'd things, I shall, or sleepe, or
                           smile.

ill-torn'd   frequency: 1   relative frequency: 0.00001
    p. 333 HORACE 2   628 Those ill-torn'd Verses, to new hammering.

ill-us'd   frequency: 1   relative frequency: 0.00001
    p. 166 UNDERWOOD 15   121 This hath our ill-us'd freedome, and soft peace

ills   frequency: 1   relative frequency: 0.00001
    p. 193 UNDERWOOD 38   69 He pardons slips, goes by a world of ills,

illustrate   frequency: 2   relative frequency: 0.00002
    p. 255 UNDERWOOD 75   85 Illustrate these, but they
    p. 364 UNGATHERED 5   3 Of her illustrate brightnesse,

illustrious   frequency: 1   relative frequency: 0.00001
    See also "illustrous."
    p. 282 U'WOOD 84.8   23 Study illustrious Him and you have all.

illustrous   frequency: 1   relative frequency: 0.00001
    p. 58 EPIGRAMS 91   3 Illustrous VERE, or HORACE; fit to be

i'm   frequency: 5   relative frequency: 0.00007

im>mortall   frequency: 1   relative frequency: 0.00001
    p. 384 UNGATHERED 18   22 Mortality, till you <im>mortall bee.

image   frequency: 1   relative frequency: 0.00001
    p. 48 EPIGRAMS 65   4 To a great image through thy luxurie.

imagery   frequency: 1   relative frequency: 0.00001
    p. 405 UNGATHERED 34   90 Thy twice conceyud, thrice payd for Imagery?

imbarqu'd   frequency: 1   relative frequency: 0.00001
    p. 81 EPIGRAMS 128   13 Through seas, stormes, tempests: and imbarqu'd
                              for hell,

imbrace   frequency: 2   relative frequency: 0.00002
    p. 150 UNDERWOOD 9   16 Read so much wast, as she cannot imbrace
    p. 419 UNGATHERED 48   4 that ffortune to imbrace,

imitate   frequency: 3   relative frequency: 0.00004
    p. 170 UNDERWOOD 18   18 Because they would free Justice imitate,
    p. 193 UNDERWOOD 38   77 O imitate that sweet Serenitie
    p. 420 UNGATHERED 48   36 But vnto more dispayre to Imitate their sounde.

imitation   frequency: 1   relative frequency: 0.00001
    p. 313 HORACE 2   192 Of imitation, leape into a streight,

immortal. See "im>mortall," "immortall."

immortalitye   frequency: 1   relative frequency: 0.00001
    p. 400 UNGATHERED 31   34 To gaine the Crowne of immortalitye,

immortall   frequency: 7   relative frequency: 0.00010
    p. 170 UNDERWOOD 19   1 By those bright Eyes, at whose immortall fires
    p. 228 UNDERWOOD 53   20 At these Immortall Mangers Virgil fed.
    p. 242 UNDERWOOD 70   4 His rage, with razing your immortall Towne.
    p. 242 UNDERWOOD 70   t1 To the immortall memorie, and friendship of
    p. 335 HORACE 2   662 Immortall, tooke a melancholique, odde
    p. 403 UNGATHERED 34   41 Or Verse, or Sense t'express Immortall you?
    p. 422 UNGATHERED 50   5 and the immortall gods; loue only those

impartially   frequency: 1   relative frequency: 0.00001
    p. 170 UNDERWOOD 18   19 Vaile their owne eyes, and would impartially

imperfect   frequency: 2   relative frequency: 0.00002
    p. 244 UNDERWOOD 70   51 As though his age imperfect might appeare,
    p. 284 U'WOOD 84.9   79 Dull, and prophane, weake, and imperfect eyes,

imperial. See "imperiall."

imperiall   frequency: 1   relative frequency: 0.00001
    p. 262 UNDERWOOD 78   7 And he is built like some imperiall roome

impetuous   frequency: 2   relative frequency: 0.00002
  **p. 116 PANEGYRE   101 "Where acts gaue licence to impetuous lust
    p. 313 HORACE 2   175 Medea make brave with impetuous scorne;

impious   frequency: 1   relative frequency: 0.00001
    p. 163 UNDERWOOD 15   34 And impious ranknesse of all Sects and seeds:

implexed   frequency: 1   relative frequency: 0.00001
    p. 412 UNGATHERED 41   7 Is so implexed, and laid in, between,

implore   frequency: 1   relative frequency: 0.00001
    p. 107 FOREST 10   6 Of his dull god-head, were sinne. Ile implore

importune   frequency: 2   relative frequency: 0.00002
    p. 180 UNDERWOOD 25   63 O then (my best-best lov'd) let me importune,
    p. 394 UNGATHERED 28   23 Importune wish; and by her lou'd Lords side

impos'd   frequency: 1   relative frequency: 0.00001
    p. 215 UNDERWOOD 44   78 Our Ancestors impos'd on Prince and State.

imposture   frequency: 1   relative frequency: 0.00001
    p. 203 UNDERWOOD 43   16 Imposture, witchcraft, charmes, or blasphemie,

impostures   frequency: 1   relative frequency: 0.00001
    p. 160 UNDERWOOD 14   41 Impostures branded! and Authorities urg'd!

impregnable   frequency: 1   relative frequency: 0.00001
    p. 401 UNGATHERED 32   17 This Fort of so impregnable accesse,

impresa. See "imprese."

imprese   frequency: 2   relative frequency: 0.00002
    p. 51 EPIGRAMS 73   15 Item, a gulling imprese for you, at tilt.
    p. 66 EPIGRAMS 103   7 Which is, it selfe, the imprese of the great,

impressed. See "imprest."

impression   frequency: 1   relative frequency: 0.00001
    p. 361 UNGATHERED 1   21 So in my braine; the stronge impression

imprest   frequency: 2   relative frequency: 0.00002
    p. 75 EPIGRAMS 116   9 That Nature no such difference had imprest
    p. 116 FOREST 12   87 Your forme imprest there: not with tickling
                               rimes,

imprimis. See "in-primis."

imprint. See "t'imprint."

imprison   frequency: 1   relative frequency: 0.00001
    p. 87 EPIGRAMS 133   104 (In the meane time, let 'hem imprison mee)

impudence   frequency: 3   relative frequency: 0.00004
   *p. 492 TO HIMSELF   3 Where pride, and impudence (in faction knit)
    p. 38 EPIGRAMS 38   6 And lyes so farre from wit, 'tis impudence.
    p. 420 UNGATHERED 48   14 That hath not Countrye impudence enough to
                               laughe att Arte,

imputation   frequency: 2   relative frequency: 0.00002
    p. 179 UNDERWOOD 25   52 Oft scape an Imputation, more through luck, then
                               wit.
    p. 380 UNGATHERED 12   30 Or builders of Story haue oft imputation

imputed   frequency: 1   relative frequency: 0.00001
    See also "b<y>'imputed."
    p. 81 EPIGRAMS 129   14 On some new gesture, that 's imputed wit?

in   frequency: 996   relative frequency: 0.01441
    See also "be'<i>n," "i'," "in>," "in's," "in't,"
             "i'th'," "i'the," "i'th'open,"
             "who'in," "yo'in."

in-land   frequency: 1   relative frequency: 0.00001
    p. 85 EPIGRAMS 133   33 From Venice, Paris, or some in-land passage

in-primis   frequency: 1   relative frequency: 0.00001
    p. 51 EPIGRAMS 73   5 In-primis, GRAND, you owe me for a iest,

in>   frequency: 1   relative frequency: 0.00001
    p. 411 UNGATHERED 39   13 For thou hast nought <in thee> to cure his Fame,

inbreeding   frequency: 1   relative frequency: 0.00001
    p. 128 UNDERWOOD 1.1   26 Father and Sonne; the Comforter, inbreeding

incarnate   frequency: 1   relative frequency: 0.00001
    p. 288 U'WOOD 84.9   200 Incarnate in the Manger, shining bright

incense   frequency: 1   relative frequency: 0.00001
     p. 288 U'WOOD 84.9   187 For, Prayer is the Incense most perfumes

incest   frequency: 1   relative frequency: 0.00001
   **p. 113 PANEGYRE   10 Where men commit blacke incest with their faults;

inch   frequency: 1   relative frequency: 0.00001
     p. 404 UNGATHERED 34   44 In ye mere perspectiue of an Inch board!

inchanted   frequency: 1   relative frequency: 0.00001
     p. 205 UNDERWOOD 43   68 The<ir> charmed Boates, and the<ir> inchanted
                              Wharfes;

incivilitie   frequency: 1   relative frequency: 0.00001
     p. 287 U'WOOD 84.9   160 (But pride, that schisme of incivilitie)

incivility. See "incivilitie."

inclin'd   frequency: 2   relative frequency: 0.00002
     p. 82 EPIGRAMS 130   7 And is t<o>'a body, often, ill inclin'd,
     p. 112 FOREST 11   112 (To vertuous moods inclin'd)

inclos'd   frequency: 1   relative frequency: 0.00001
     p. 394 UNGATHERED 28   24 To lay her here, inclos'd, his second Bride.

including   frequency: 1   relative frequency: 0.00001
     p. 82 EPIGRAMS 130   14 Including all, were thence call'd harmonie:

inconstancie   frequency: 2   relative frequency: 0.00002
     p. 146 UNDERWOOD 6   t2 In defence of their Inconstancie.
     p. 146 UNDERWOOD 6   13 Nor is't inconstancie to change

inconstancy. See "inconstacie."

inconstant   frequency: 1   relative frequency: 0.00001
     p. 110 FOREST 11   39 Inconstant, like the sea, of whence 'tis borne,

increase   frequency: 10   relative frequency: 0.00014
     See also "encrease," "t<o>'increase."
     p. 128 UNDERWOOD 1.1   29 8. Increase those acts, o glorious Trinitie
     p. 166 UNDERWOOD 15   122 Brought on us, and will every houre increase.
     p. 212 UNDERWOOD 43   210 And pray the fruites thereof, and the increase;
     p. 214 UNDERWOOD 44   49 Goe on, increase in vertue; and in fame:
     p. 261 UNDERWOOD 77   21 And mightiest Monarchs feele what large increase
     p. 287 U'WOOD 84.9   158 As nature could not more increase the flood
     p. 309 HORACE 2   80 If I can give some small increase? when, loe,
     p. 363 UNGATHERED 3   3 Warres grea<t>est woes, and miseries increase,
     p. 382 UNGATHERED 16   5 The elder of these two, riche hopes Increase,
     p. 385 UNGATHERED 19   7 My suffrage brings thee all increase, to crowne

increased. See "encreas'd," "encreast."

incurr'd   frequency: 1   relative frequency: 0.00001
     p. 410 UNGATHERED 39   5 All which thou hast incurr'd deseruedly:

indeed   frequency: 10   relative frequency: 0.00014
     See also "indeede."
     p. 40 EPIGRAMS 42   3 Indeed, poore GILES repents he married euer.
     p. 82 EPIGRAMS 130   11 To say, indeed, shee were the soule of heauen,
     p. 130 UNDERWOOD 1.3   17 The Word was now made Flesh indeed,
     p. 190 UNDERWOOD 37   9 Which is indeed but friendship of the spit:
     p. 223 UNDERWOOD 49   31 Indeed, her Dressing some man might delight,
     p. 236 UNDERWOOD 64   7 Indeed, when had great Britaine greater cause
     p. 283 U'WOOD 84.9   45 Indeed, she is not dead! but laid to sleepe
     p. 325 HORACE 2   452 Indeed, give fitting dues to every man.
     p. 335 HORACE 2   658 Not thence be sav'd, although indeed he could?
     p. 391 UNGATHERED 26   15 But thou art proofe against them, and indeed

indeede   frequency: 1   relative frequency: 0.00001
     p. 85 EPIGRAMS 133   60 'Tis but light paines: Indeede this Dock's no
                              rose.

indentur'd   frequency: 1   relative frequency: 0.00001
     p. 246 UNDERWOOD 70   100 Made, or indentur'd, or leas'd out t<o>'advance

index   frequency: 1   relative frequency: 0.00001
     p. 68 EPIGRAMS 105   19 So are you Natures Index, and restore,

indian. See "west-indian."

indice   frequency: 1   relative frequency: 0.00001
    p. 157 UNDERWOCD 13 156 For me to be your Indice. Keep you such,

indict. See "t<o>'indite."

indicting   frequency: 1   relative frequency: 0.00001
    *p. 492 TO HIMSELF   5 Indicting, and arraigning euery day

indifferent   frequency: 1   relative frequency: 0.00001
    p. 331 HORACE 2   556 Poets should ever be indifferent.

indignation   frequency: 1   relative frequency: 0.00001
    *p. 492 TO HIMSELF   t1 The iust indignation the Author

indorse   frequency: 1   relative frequency: 0.00001
    p. 200 UNDERWOOD 42   7 That from the Muses fountaines doth indorse

indu'd   frequency: 1   relative frequency: 0.00001
    p. 222 UNDERWOOD 49   18 What though she be with Velvet gownes indu'd,

indulgent   frequency: 1   relative frequency: 0.00001
    p. 44 EPIGRAMS 55   4 The least indulgent thought thy pen drops forth!

indure   frequency: 1   relative frequency: 0.00001
    p. 175 UNDERWOCD 23   32 Cannot indure reproofe,

infam'd   frequency: 1   relative frequency: 0.00001
    p. 165 UNDERWOCD 15   97 Whom no great Mistresse hath as yet infam'd,

infamie   frequency: 2   relative frequency: 0.00002
    p. 119 FOREST 13   86 That doe sinne onely for the infamie:
    p. 193 UNDERWOOD 38   93 To suffer tortures, scorne, and Infamie,

infamous   frequency: 2   relative frequency: 0.00002
    p. 391 UNGATHERED 26 13 These are, as some infamous Baud, or Whore,
    p. 410 UNGATHERED 39   2 Secure thy railing Rhymes, infamous Gill,

infamy   frequency: 1   relative frequency: 0.00001
    See alsc "infamie."
    p. 409 UNGATHERED 37 16 Nameless, and noysome, as thy infamy!

infant   frequency: 1   relative frequency: 0.00001
    p. 242 UNDERWOOD 70   1 Brave Infant of Saguntum, cleare

infants   frequency: 4   relative frequency: 0.00005
    **p. 115 PANEGYRE   66 And infants, that the houres had made such hast
    p. 154 UNDERWOOD 13   47 As I have seene some Infants of the Sword,
    p. 243 UNDERWOOD 70   20 No doubt all Infants would returne like thee.
    p. 273 U'WOOD 84.1   18 Take little Infants with their noyse,

infect   frequency: 1   relative frequency: 0.00001
    **p. 113 PANEGYRE   17 And would (if not dispers'd) infect the Crowne,

infected   frequency: 1   relative frequency: 0.00001
    p. 335 HORACE 2   645 Infected with the leprosie, or had

infection   frequency: 1   relative frequency: 0.00001
    p. 184 UNDERWOOD 29   31 Greeke was free from Rimes infection,

infinite   frequency: 3   relative frequency: 0.00004
    p. 167 UNDERWOOD 15 169 Boasters, and perjur'd, with the infinite more
    p. 236 UNDERWOOD 63   13 For God, whose essence is so infinite,
    p. 279 U'WOOD 84.4   32 As circular, as infinite.

infinites. See "infinits."

infinits   frequency: 1   relative frequency: 0.00001
    p. 361 UNGATHERED 1   18 extendeth circles into infinits,

infirmary. See "infirmery."

infirmery   frequency: 1   relative frequency: 0.00001
    p. 288 U'WOOD 84.9   195 Would sit in an Infirmery, whole dayes

inflam'd   frequency: 2   relative frequency: 0.00002
    p. 398 UNGATHERED 30 67 Looke, how we read the Spartans were inflam'd
    p. 413 UNGATHERED 41 23 Inflam'd with ardor to that mystick Shine,

inflame   frequency: 1   relative frequency: 0.00001
    p. 170 UNDERWOOD 19   2 Love lights his torches to inflame desires;

inflamed. See "enflamed," "inflam'd."

inflict. See "t<o>'inflict."

inflicts   frequency: 1   relative frequency: 0.00001
    p. 192 UNDERWOOD 38   44 No man inflicts that paine, till hope be spent:

influence   frequency: 2   relative frequency: 0.00002
    p. 52 EPIGRAMS 76   8 Nor lend like influence from his lucent seat.
    p. 392 UNGATHERED 26   78 Or influence, chide, or cheere the drooping
                              Stage;

inform. See "informe," "vertue'enforme."

informe   frequency: 3   relative frequency: 0.00004
    p. 215 UNDERWOOD 44   64 From the Tempestuous Grandlings, Who'll
                              informe
    p. 216 UNDERWOOD 45   2 Whilst I informe my selfe, I would teach thee,
    p. 380 UNGATHERED 12   33 That he dares to informe you, but somewhat
                              meticulous,

informed   frequency: 1   relative frequency: 0.00001
    p. 331 HORACE 2   546 Informed rightly, by your Fathers care,

informers   frequency: 1   relative frequency: 0.00001
    p. 167 UNDERWOOD 15   164 Informers, Masters both of Arts and lies;

infus'd   frequency: 1   relative frequency: 0.00001
    p. 192 UNDERWOOD 38   65 Should aske the blood, and spirits he hath
                              infus'd

ingage   frequency: 1   relative frequency: 0.00001
    p. 323 HORACE 2   383 So rare, as with some taxe it doth ingage

ingenyre   frequency: 1   relative frequency: 0.00001
    p. 402 UNGATHERED 34   6 The noblest Ingenyre that euer was!

ingine   frequency: 1   relative frequency: 0.00001
    p. 400 UNGATHERED 32   10 That Art, or Ingine, on the strength can raise.

ingineeres   frequency: 1   relative frequency: 0.00001
    p. 248 UNDERWOOD 71   4 Disease, the Enemie, and his Ingineeres,

inginer   frequency: 1   relative frequency: 0.00001
    p. 75 EPIGRAMS 115   31 An inginer, in slanders, of all fashions,

ingots   frequency: 1   relative frequency: 0.00001
    p. 114 FOREST 12   24 Or put to flight ASTREA, when her ingots

ingratefull   frequency: 1   relative frequency: 0.00001
    p. 153 UNDERWOOD 13   4 Lesse list of proud, hard, or ingratefull Men.

ingredients   frequency: 1   relative frequency: 0.00001
    p. 172 UNDERWOOD 20   18 Then all Ingredients made into one curse,

inhabit. See "t<o>'inhabit."

inherent   frequency: 2   relative frequency: 0.00002
    p. 270 UNDERWOOD 83   36 From the inherent Graces in her blood!
    p. 286 U'WOOD 84.9   135 Through his inherent righteousnesse, in death,

inherit   frequency: 2   relative frequency: 0.00002
    See also "dis-inherit," "t<o>'inherit."
    p. 41 EPIGRAMS 44   2 And rich in issue to inherit all,
    p. 114 FOREST 12   32 Were it to thinke, that you should not inherit

inheritance   frequency: 2   relative frequency: 0.00002
    p. 209 UNDERWOOD 43   152 The place, that was thy Wives inheritance.
    p. 286 U'WOOD 84.9   144 B<y>'imputed right to an inheritance

inigo   frequency: 8   relative frequency: 0.00011
    p. 402 UNGATHERED 34   t1 An Expostulacon wth Inigo Iones.
    p. 403 UNGATHERED 34   22 you'l be as Langley sayd, an Inigo still.
    p. 405 UNGATHERED 34   66 Be Inigo, ye Whistle, & his men!
    p. 405 UNGATHERED 34   86 But wisest Inigo! who can reflect
    p. 406 UNGATHERED 35   2 Hath made his Inigo Marquess, wouldst thou
                              fayne
    p. 406 UNGATHERED 35   t1 To Inigo Marquess Would be
    p. 407 UNGATHERED 35   22 But when thou turnst a Reall Inigo;
    p. 407 UNGATHERED 36   1 Sr Inigo doth feare it as I heare

iniquitie   frequency: 1   relative frequency: 0.00001
      p. 74 EPIGRAMS 115   27 Acts old Iniquitie, and in the fit

iniquity. See "iniquitie."

iniurie   frequency: 2   relative frequency: 0.00002
    **p. 116 PANEGYRE   124 To offer cause of iniurie, or feare.
      p. 47 EPIGRAMS 63   10 Without his, thine, and all times iniurie?

injoy   frequency: 1   relative frequency: 0.00001
      p. 200 UNDERWOOD 42   24 So to be sure you doe injoy your selves.

injunction   frequency: 1   relative frequency: 0.00001
      p. 210 UNDERWOOD 43   175 Against this Vulcan? No Injunction?

injurie   frequency: 1   relative frequency: 0.00001
      p. 179 UNDERWOOD 25   49 From injurie,

injury. See "iniurie," "injurie."

injustice   frequency: 1   relative frequency: 0.00001
      p. 271 UNDERWOOD 83   92 With what injustice should one soule pretend

ink. See "inke."

inke   frequency: 3   relative frequency: 0.00004
      p. 27 EPIGRAMS 2   5 Become a petulant thing, hurle inke, and wit,
      p. 229 UNDERWOOD 55   2 Thoughts worthy of thy gift, this Inke,
      p. 666 INSCRIPTS. 11   8 Wth Chequer Inke, vpon his guift, my paper,

inland. See "in-land."

inmate   frequency: 2   relative frequency: 0.00002
      p. 394 UNGATHERED 28   18 And her, she made her Inmate, to the End,
      p. 399 UNGATHERED 31   26 In faire freehould, not an Inmate:

inn. See "inne."

inne   frequency: 1   relative frequency: 0.00001
      p. 380 UNGATHERED 12   26 How long he did stay, at what signe he did Inne.

innocence   frequency: 6   relative frequency: 0.00008
      p. 33 EPIGRAMS 22   6 With safetie of her innocence;
      p. 96 FOREST 2   94 Their gentler spirits haue suck'd innocence.
      p. 130 UNDERWOOD 1.3   22 To see this Babe, all innocence;
      p. 177 UNDERWOOD 25   31 But whisper; O glad Innocence,
      p. 285 U'WOOD 84.9   94 And on her Innocence, a garment fresh
      p. 371 UNGATHERED 8   11 I, that am glad, thy Innocence was thy Guilt,

innocent   frequency: 2   relative frequency: 0.00002
      p. 34 EPIGRAMS 25   1 While BEAST instructs his faire, and
                                         innocent wife,
      p. 98 FOREST 3   66 Striue, WROTH, to liue long innocent.

innocently   frequency: 1   relative frequency: 0.00001
      p. 65 EPIGRAMS 101   39 We innocently met. No simple word,

innovations   frequency: 1   relative frequency: 0.00001
      p. 160 UNDERWOOD 14   44 Times, manners, customes! Innovations spide!

ino   frequency: 1   relative frequency: 0.00001
      p. 313 HORACE 2   176 Ino bewaild; Ixion false, forsworne;

inough   frequency: 1   relative frequency: 0.00001
      p. 369 UNGATHERED 6   113 It is inough, their griefe shall know

inoughe   frequency: 1   relative frequency: 0.00001
      p. 387 UNGATHERED 22   11 it will be matter lowd inoughe to tell

inow   frequency: 1   relative frequency: 0.00001
      p. 386 UNGATHERED 21   12 By offring not more sureties, then inow,

inquir'd   frequency: 1   relative frequency: 0.00001
      p. 331 HORACE 2   581 'Tis now inquir'd, which makes the nobler Verse,

inquire   frequency: 1   relative frequency: 0.00001
      See also "enquire."
      p. 151 UNDERWOOD 11   10 But leaves me to inquire,

inquirie   frequency: 3   relative frequency: 0.00004
    p. 216 UNDERWOOD 45   15 Inquirie of the worth: So must we doe,
    p. 219 UNDERWOOD 47   43 So farre without inquirie what the States,
    p. 254 UNDERWOOD 75   74 And looking with thy best Inquirie, tell,

inquiry. See "inquirie."

inraged   frequency: 1   relative frequency: 0.00001
    p. 289 UNDERWOOD 85   6 Nor dreads the Seas inraged harmes:

in's   frequency: 1   relative frequency: 0.00001

inscrib'd   frequency: 1   relative frequency: 0.00001
    p. 114 FOREST 12   44 Inscrib'd in touch or marble, or the cotes

inscription   frequency: 2   relative frequency: 0.00002
    See also "th'inscription."
    p. 272 UNDERWOOD 84   t18 Her Inscription, or CROWNE.
    p. 387 UNGATHERED 22   9 nor yet inscription like it. Write but that;

insert   frequency: 1   relative frequency: 0.00001
    p. 214 UNDERWOOD 44   53 Insert thy Hodges, and those newer men,

inside   frequency: 1   relative frequency: 0.00001
    p. 171 UNDERWOOD 20   12 But their whole inside full of ends, and knots?

insolent   frequency: 1   relative frequency: 0.00001
    p. 391 UNGATHERED 26   39 Of all, that insolent Greece, or haughtie Rome

inspir'd   frequency: 2   relative frequency: 0.00002
    p. 121 FOREST 14   52 If with this truth you be inspir'd,
    p. 225 UNDERWOOD 50   30 The same it was inspir'd, rich, and refin'd.

inspire   frequency: 1   relative frequency: 0.00001
    See also "enspire."
    p. 177 UNDERWOOD 25   10 O, then inspire

instantly   frequency: 1   relative frequency: 0.00001
    p. 109 FOREST 11   12 Giue knowledge instantly,

instauration   frequency: 1   relative frequency: 0.00001
    p. 415 UNGATHERED 43   t3 Instauration of his Hunting, and Dauncing

institution   frequency: 1   relative frequency: 0.00001
    p. 270 UNDERWOOD 83   45 What Nature, Fortune, Institution, Fact

instruct   frequency: 5   relative frequency: 0.00007
    See also "t<o>'instruct."
    p. 48 EPIGRAMS 65   13 Shee shall instruct my after-thoughts to write
    p. 55 EPIGRAMS 85   5 Shee doth instruct men by her gallant flight,
    p. 160 UNDERWOOD 14   52 Of what it tells us) weav'd in to instruct!
    p. 214 UNDERWOOD 44   59 And there instruct the noble English heires
    p. 397 UNGATHERED 30   43 O, how in those, dost thou instruct these times,

instructs   frequency: 1   relative frequency: 0.00001
    p. 34 EPIGRAMS 25   1 While BEAST instructs his faire, and
                              innocent wife,

instrument   frequency: 1   relative frequency: 0.00001
    p. 223 UNDERWOOD 49   34 To his poore Instrument, now out of grace.

in't   frequency: 1   relative frequency: 0.00001

integritie   frequency: 1   relative frequency: 0.00001
    p. 217 UNDERWOOD 46   9 Such was thy Processe, when Integritie,

integrity. See "integritie."

intelligence   frequency: 5   relative frequency: 0.00007
    p. 59 EPIGRAMS 92   12 And what each prince doth for intelligence owe,
    p. 109 FOREST 11   25 Backe the intelligence, and falsely sweares,
    p. 239 UNDERWOOD 67   22 And each intelligence
    p. 278 U'WOOD 84.4   14 Would aske a Heavens Intelligence;
    p. 289 U'WOOD 84.9   226 Who reades, will pardon my Intelligence,

intelligencer   frequency: 1   relative frequency: 0.00001
    p. 232 UNDERWOOD 58   3 Bee thou my Bookes intelligencer, note

intend   frequency: 1   relative frequency: 0.00001
    See also "entend."

intend (cont.)
    p. 402 UNGATHERED 34   14 Something your Surship doth not yet intend!

intended   frequency: 1   relative frequency: 0.00001
    p. 383 UNGATHERED 17   2 Must be intended still to vnderstand:

intent. See "th'intent."

intention   frequency: 1   relative frequency: 0.00001
    p. 176 UNDERWOOD 25   4 To towre with my intention

intents   frequency: 1   relative frequency: 0.00001
    p. 62 EPIGRAMS 95   31 We need a man, can speake of the intents,

interest   frequency: 2   relative frequency: 0.00002
    See also "int'rest."
    p. 154 UNDERWOOD 13   30 But by meere Chance? for interest? or to free
    p. 200 UNDERWOOD 42   15 Of beautie; but the Muse hath interest in:

intermitted   frequency: 1   relative frequency: 0.00001
    p. 292 UNDERWOOD 86   2 Long intermitted, pray thee, pray thee spare:

intermixed. See "entermixt."

interpel. See "interpell."

interpell   frequency: 1   relative frequency: 0.00001
    p. 284 U'WOOD 84.9   70 Presume to interpell that fulnesse, when

interpos'd   frequency: 1   relative frequency: 0.00001
    p. 275 U'WOOD 84.3   10 Were fitly interpos'd; so new:

interpose   frequency: 1   relative frequency: 0.00001
    p. 238 UNDERWOOD 65   10 And interpose thy selfe, ('care not how soone.)

interpreted   frequency: 2   relative frequency: 0.00002
    p. 122 FOREST 15   3 Is it interpreted in me disease,
    p. 395 UNGATHERED 29   19 But who hath them interpreted, and brought

interpreters. See "th'interpreters."

interrupt   frequency: 1   relative frequency: 0.00001
    p. 66 EPIGRAMS 102   18 But in the view, doth interrupt their sinne;

intersert   frequency: 1   relative frequency: 0.00001
    p. 413 UNGATHERED 41   17 The fourth is humble Ivy, intersert,

intertex. See "intertexe."

intertexe   frequency: 1   relative frequency: 0.00001
    p. 254 UNDERWOOD 75   60 With light of love, this Paire doth intertexe!

intertwind   frequency: 1   relative frequency: 0.00001
    p. 268 UNDERWOOD 82   16 Her Rose, and Lilly, intertwind, have made.

intertwine   frequency: 1   relative frequency: 0.00001
    p. 338 HORACE 1   21 Bouts .. fleet .... doe intertwine

intertwined. See "intertwind."

intire   frequency: 1   relative frequency: 0.00001
    p. 128 UNDERWOOD 1.1   43 With grace, with love, with cherishing intire:

into   frequency: 47   relative frequency: 0.00068

intreat   frequency: 1   relative frequency: 0.00001
    p. 174 UNDERWOOD 22   30 Have sung this Hymne, and here intreat

intreaties   frequency: 1   relative frequency: 0.00001
    p. 292 UNDERWOOD 86   8 Goe where Youths soft intreaties call thee back.

intreaty   frequency: 1   relative frequency: 0.00001
    p. 254 UNDERWOOD 75   56 Although that thou, O Sun, at our intreaty
                                  stay!

intrenchmt   frequency: 1   relative frequency: 0.00001
    p. 407 UNGATHERED 35   23 Or canst of truth ye least intrenchmt pitch,

int'rest   frequency: 1   relative frequency: 0.00001
    p. 236 UNDERWOOD 63   5 Hee can, he will, and with large int'rest pay,

intwine   frequency: 1   relative frequency: 0.00001
    p. 305 HORACE 2   21 Dring Circles of swift waters that intwine

inuade   frequency: 2   relative frequency: 0.00002
    p. 110 FOREST 11   29 Doe seuerall passions <still> inuade the minde,
    p. 389 UNGATHERED 23   12 And who make thither else, rob, or inuade.

inuent   frequency: 2   relative frequency: 0.00002
    p. 107 FOREST 10   17 Or, with thy Tribade trine, inuent new sports,
    p. 662 INSCRIPTS. 2   5 Tell her, his Muse that did inuent thee

inuentions   frequency: 1   relative frequency: 0.00001
    p. 83 EPIGRAMS 132   11 So well in that are his inuentions wrought,

inuoke   frequency: 1   relative frequency: 0.00001
    p. 85 EPIGRAMS 133   45 Or goddesse to inuoke, to stuffe my verse;

invade   frequency: 2   relative frequency: 0.00002
    See also "inuade."
    p. 155 UNDERWOOD 13   80 Is borrowing; that but stopt, they doe invade
    p. 210 UNDERWOOD 43   170 And didst invade part of the Common-wealth,

inveigh. See "t<o>'inueigh."

invent   frequency: 1   relative frequency: 0.00001
    See also "inuent."
    p. 211 UNDERWOOD 43   189 I could invent a sentence, yet were worse;

invented   frequency: 1   relative frequency: 0.00001
    p. 184 UNDERWOOD 29   49 He that first invented thee,

invention   frequency: 2   relative frequency: 0.00002
    p. 176 UNDERWOOD 25   2 Thy present Aide: Arise Invention,
    p. 307 HORACE 2   61 Invention. Now, to speake; and then differ

inventions. See "inuentions."

invisibilitie   frequency: 1   relative frequency: 0.00001
    p. 206 UNDERWOOD 43   75 Invisibilitie, and strength, and tongues:

invisibility. See "invisibilitie."

invite   frequency: 3   relative frequency: 0.00004
    p. 169 UNDERWOOD 18   2 Now threaten, with those meanes she did invite?
    p. 223 UNDERWOOD 49   40 They say you weekly invite with fits o'th'
                              Mother,
    p. 290 UNDERWOOD 85   28 And all invite to easie sleepe.

inviting   frequency: 2   relative frequency: 0.00002
    p. 64 EPIGRAMS 101   t1 INVITING A FRIEND TO
                              SVPPER.
    p. 270 UNDERWOOD 83   44 A dazling, yet inviting, Majestie:

invoke. See "inuoke."

inward   frequency: 2   relative frequency: 0.00002
    p. 144 UNDERWOOD 3   19 And out of inward pleasure feed
    p. 162 UNDERWOOD 15   20 In outward face, but inward, light as Furre,

io. See "jo."

iohn   frequency: 11   relative frequency: 0.00015
    p. 34 EPIGRAMS 23   t1 TO IOHN DONNE.
    p. 35 EPIGRAMS 27   t1 ON SIR IOHN ROE.
    p. 37 EPIGRAMS 32   t1 ON SIR IOHN ROE.
    p. 60 EPIGRAMS 93   t1 TO SIR IOHN RADCLIFFE.
    p. 62 EPIGRAMS 96   t1 TO IOHN DONNE.
    p. 158 UNDERWOOD 14   t2 IOHN SELDEN.
    p. 229 UNDERWOOD 55   t2 Mr. IOHN BURGES.
    p. 231 UNDERWOOD 57   t1 To Master Iohn Burges.
    p. 281 U'WOOD 84.8   t1 To KENELME, IOHN, GEORGE.
    p. 370 UNGATHERED 8   t2 Iohn Fletcher.
    p. 400 UNGATHERED 32   t2 Friend, Sir Iohn Beaumont, Baronet.

ioint   frequency: 1   relative frequency: 0.00001
    p. 395 UNGATHERED 29   21 As not the smallest ioint, or gentlest word

iolly   frequency: 1   relative frequency: 0.00001
    p. 98 FOREST 3   59 The iolly wassall walkes the often round,

ione			frequency: 8 relative frequency: 0.00011	
p.	40	EPIGRAMS 42	1	Who sayes that GILES and IONE at discord be?
p.	40	EPIGRAMS 42	4	But that his IONE doth too. And GILES would neuer,
p.	40	EPIGRAMS 42	6	No more would IONE he should. GILES riseth early,
p.	40	EPIGRAMS 42	8	The like is IONE. But turning home, is sad.
p.	40	EPIGRAMS 42	9	And so is IONE. Oft-times, when GILES doth find
p.	40	EPIGRAMS 42	t1	ON GILES AND IONE.
p.	40	EPIGRAMS 42	11	All this doth IONE. Or that his long-yearn'd life
p.	40	EPIGRAMS 42	14	Of his begetting. And so sweares his IONE.

iones			frequency: 3 relative frequency: 0.00004	
p.	40	EPIGRAMS 42	5	By his free will, be in IONES company.
p.	402	UNGATHERED 34	t1	An Expostulacon wth Inigo Iones.
p.	402	UNGATHERED 34	16	Of Tyre-man, Mounte-banck & Iustice Iones,

ionian. See "th'icnian."

ionson			frequency: 3 relative frequency: 0.00004	
p.	41	EPIGRAMS 45	10	BEN. IONSON his best piece of poetrie.
p.	395	UNGATHERED 29	26	BEN: IONSON.
p.	396	UNGATHERED 30	t2	BEN. IONSON, ON THE

iosvah			frequency: 1 relative frequency: 0.00001	
p.	83	EPIGRAMS 132	t1	TO Mr. IOSVAH SYLVESTER.

iouiall			frequency: 1 relative frequency: 0.00001	
p.	378	UNGATHERED 11	87	Of Tom of Odcombe that odde Iouiall Author,

iouis			frequency: 1 relative frequency: 0.00001	
p.	399	UNGATHERED 31	8+	Dip<h>thera Iouis:--

iournall			frequency: 1 relative frequency: 0.00001	
p.	380	UNGATHERED 12	23	Each leafe of his iournall, and line doth vnlocke

iourney			frequency: 2 relative frequency: 0.00002	
p.	81	EPIGRAMS 129	3	That there 's no iourney set, or thought vpon,
p.	379	UNGATHERED 12	18	The Mappe of his iourney, and sees in his booke,

iove's			frequency: 2 relative frequency: 0.00002	
p.	89	EPIGRAMS 133	182	Were you IOVE'S sonnes, or had ALCIDES might.
p.	106	FOREST 9	7	But might I of IOVE'S Nectar sup,

ioviall			frequency: 1 relative frequency: 0.00001	
p.	415	UNGATHERED 43	t1	AN EPIGRAM TO MY IOVIALL

ioy			frequency: 6 relative frequency: 0.00008	
**p.	114	PANEGYRE	57	The ioy of either was alike, and full;
p.	41	EPIGRAMS 45	1	Farewell, thou child of my right hand, and ioy;
p.	80	EPIGRAMS 128	1	ROE (and my ioy to name) th'art now, to goe
p.	384	UNGATHERED 18	6	That bid, God giue thee ioy, and haue no endes.
p.	384	UNGATHERED 18	18	And eue'ry ioy, in mariage, turne a fruite.
p.	414	UNGATHERED 41	42	Most venerable. Cause of all our ioy.

ioy'd			frequency: 2 relative frequency: 0.00002	
**p.	115	PANEGYRE	93	"And all so iustly, as his eare was ioy'd
p.	392	UNGATHERED 26	48	And ioy'd to weare the dressing of his lines!

ioyes			frequency: 8 relative frequency: 0.00011	
**p.	113	PANEGYRE	2	With ioyes: but vrgeth his full fauors still.
**p.	114	PANEGYRE	42	The fittest herald to proclaime true ioyes:
**p.	117	PANEGYRE	152	Their bursting ioyes; but through the ayre was rol'd
p.	102	FOREST 5	9	Why should we deferre our ioyes?
p.	110	FOREST 11	56	The'Elixir of all ioyes?
p.	112	FOREST 11	95	And turne the blackest sorrowes to bright ioyes:
p.	120	FOREST 14	18	Of these forc'd ioyes,
p.	384	UNGATHERED 18	8	And pray, thy ioyes as lasting bee, as great.

ioyfull			frequency: 1 relative frequency: 0.00001	
p.	401	UNGATHERED 33	10	Recelebrates the ioyfull Match with France.

ioy'st			frequency: 1 relative frequency: 0.00001	
p.	93	FOREST 2	7	Thou ioy'st in better markes, of soyle, of ayre,

ire   frequency: 3 relative frequency: 0.00004
 p. 142 UNDERWOOD 2.9 42 Shewing danger more then ire.
 p. 179 UNDERWOOD 25 44 And, after all the Aetnean Ire,
 p. 202 UNDERWOOD 43 2 What had I done that might call on thine ire?

ireland   frequency: 2 relative frequency: 0.00002
 p. 69 EPIGRAMS 107 12 In Ireland, Holland, Sweden, pompous lies,
 p. 249 UNDERWOOD 72 5 Let Ireland meet it out at Sea, halfe way,

irene   frequency: 1 relative frequency: 0.00001
**p. 113 PANEGYRE 27 Her third, IRENE, help'd to beare his
         traine;

iris   frequency: 2 relative frequency: 0.00002
**p. 116 PANEGYRE 130 When, like an April Iris, flew her shine
 p. 403 UNGATHERED 34 34 And peering forth of Iris in ye Shrowdes!

irish   frequency: 1 relative frequency: 0.00001
 p. 37 EPIGRAMS 32 5 The cold of Mosco, and fat Irish ayre,

irishry   frequency: 1 relative frequency: 0.00001
 p. 367 UNGATHERED 6 53 Vpon the Kerne, and wildest Irishry,

iron   frequency: 1 relative frequency: 0.00001
 See alsc "yron."
 p. 211 UNDERWOOD 43 184 foot (out in Sussex) to an iron Mill;

irons   frequency: 1 relative frequency: 0.00001
 See also "curling-ircns."
 p. 215 UNDERWOOD 44 93 But why are all these Irons i' the fire

irreligious   frequency: 1 relative frequency: 0.00001
 p. 283 U'WOOD 84.9 39 Dare I prophane, so irreligious bee

irritate   frequency: 1 relative frequency: 0.00001
 p. 250 UNDERWOOD 73 7 Why doe I irritate, or stirre up thee,

is   frequency: 468 relative frequency: 0.00677
 See also "all's," "apollo's," "arte's," "cap's,"
    "cloth's," "dock's," "faith's,"
    "fault's," "flattry's," "forehead's,"
    "gold's," "hee's," "here's," "he's,"
    "is't," "knight-wright's," "lady's,"
    "life's," "loue's," "love's," "man's,"
    "mettal's," "morison's," "name's,"
    "nature's," "nights," "noone-sted's,"
    "nothing's," "now's," "one's,"
    "palate's," "palsey's," "passion's,"
    "play's," "poet's," "prophet's," "'s,"
    "shee's," "sinne's," "sin's," "swan's,"
    "that's," "there's," "this's," "tis,"
    "t'is," "'tis," "title's," "what's,"
    "where's," "who's."

island. See "iland."

isle   frequency: 3 relative frequency: 0.00004
 See alsc "ile."
 p. 238 UNDERWOOD 66 9 So generall a gladnesse to an Isle,
 p. 240 UNDERWOOD 67 33 This sea-girt Isle upon:
 p. 421 UNGATHERED 48 39 Aboute this Isle, and Charme the rounde, as
         when

isles   frequency: 1 relative frequency: 0.00001
 p. 368 UNGATHERED 6 66 The Hebrid Isles, and knowne

issue   frequency: 14 relative frequency: 0.00020
 p. 41 EPIGRAMS 44 2 And rich in issue to inherit all,
 p. 53 EPIGRAMS 79 6 (Saue that most masculine issue of his braine)
 p. 117 FOREST 13 40 T<o>'aduance his doubtfull issue, and ore-flow
 p. 119 FOREST 13 104 It shall a ripe and timely issue fall,
 p. 162 UNDERWOOD 15 13 Bought Flatteries, the issue of his purse,
 p. 171 UNDERWOOD 19 26 His Issue, and all Circumstance of life,
 p. 175 UNDERWOOD 23 30 Who aided him, will thee, the issue of Joves
         braine.
 p. 203 UNDERWOOD 43 14 To ruine any issue of the braine?
 p. 216 UNDERWOOD 45 8 Was issue of the Taverne, or the Spit:
 p. 218 UNDERWOOD 47 26 To vent their Libels, and to issue rimes,
 p. 221 UNDERWOOD 48 32 Have issue from the Barrell;
 p. 272 UNDERWOOD 84 t16 Her hopefull ISSUE.

issue (cont.)
    p. 290 UNDERWOOD 85   10 With the growne issue of the Vine;
    p. 392 UNGATHERED 26   66 Liues in his issue, euen so, the race

is't   frequency: 7   relative frequency: 0.00010

it   frequency: 547   relative frequency: 0.00791
    See also "as't," "bring't," "cal't," "doo't,"
            "do't," "ere't," "e're't," "have't,"
            "if't," "in't," "is't," "know't,"
            "mis-call't," "now't," "on't," "so't,"
            "'t," "though't," "tis," "t'is,"
            "'tis," "to't," "'twas," "'twere,"
            "t'will," "'twill," "was't," "where't,"
            "who'it."

it'   frequency: 2   relative frequency: 0.00002

italian. See "th'italian."

italie   frequency: 1   relative frequency: 0.00001
    p. 325 HORACE 2   411 Nor had our Italie more glorious bin

italy   frequency: 3   relative frequency: 0.00004
    See also "italie."
    p. 368 UNGATHERED 6   88 Though slower Spaine; and Italy mature.
    p. 375 UNGATHERED 10   30 Here France, and Italy both to him shed
    p. 379 UNGATHERED 12   19 France, Sauoy, Italy, and Heluetia,

itch   frequency: 3   relative frequency: 0.00004
    p. 164 UNDERWOOD 15   75 And laugh, and measure thighes, then squeake,
                                 spring, itch,
    p. 166 UNDERWOOD 15   143 In this, and like, an itch of Vanitie,
    p. 203 UNDERWOOD 43   25 Itch to defame the State? or brand the Times?

item   frequency: 9   relative frequency: 0.00013
    p. 51 EPIGRAMS 73   7 Item, a tale or two, some fortnight after;
    p. 51 EPIGRAMS 73   9 Item, the babylonian song you sing;
    p. 51 EPIGRAMS 73   10 Item, a faire greeke poesie for a ring:
    p. 51 EPIGRAMS 73   12 Item, a charme surrounding fearefully
    p. 51 EPIGRAMS 73   15 Item, a gulling imprese for you, at tilt.
    p. 51 EPIGRAMS 73   16 Item, your mistris anagram, i' your hilt.
    p. 51 EPIGRAMS 73   17 Item, your owne, sew'd in your mistris smock.
    p. 51 EPIGRAMS 73   18 Item, an epitaph on my lords cock,
    p. 380 UNGATHERED 12 48 Iest, he saies. Item one sute of blacke taffata

i'th'   frequency: 1   relative frequency: 0.00001

i'the   frequency: 3   relative frequency: 0.00004

i'th'open   frequency: 1   relative frequency: 0.00001
    p. 344 HORACE 1   231 I'th'open .... waxe-like .. ..

its   frequency: 1   relative frequency: 0.00001
    See also "it'," "it's."

it's   frequency: 4   relative frequency: 0.00005

itself   frequency: 1   relative frequency: 0.00001
    p. 657 L. CONVIVALES   6 Truth itself doth flow in Wine.

iudge   frequency: 14   relative frequency: 0.00020
    p. 32 EPIGRAMS 18   9 Pr'y thee beleeue still, and not iudge so fast,
    p. 45 EPIGRAMS 56   12 May iudge it to be his, as well as ours.
    p. 51 EPIGRAMS 74   2 And know thee, then, a iudge, not of one yeare;
    p. 54 EPIGRAMS 80   7 So to front death, as men might iudge vs past it.
    p. 62 EPIGRAMS 96   3 That so alone canst iudge, so'alone dost make:
    p. 67 EPIGRAMS 104   13 Iudge they, that can: Here I haue rais'd to
                                 show
    p. 70 EPIGRAMS 109   16 Now I haue sung thee thus, shall iudge of thee.
    p. 78 EPIGRAMS 123   4 Of the best writer, and iudge, should emulate.
    p. 82 EPIGRAMS 131   3 For, then, all mouthes will iudge, and their owne
                                 way: .
    p. 83 EPIGRAMS 132   6 Since they can only iudge, that can conferre.
    p. 122 FOREST 15   7 And iudge me after: if I dare pretend
    p. 122 FOREST 15   12 My iudge, my witnesse, and my aduocate.
    p. 370 UNGATHERED 7   11 To iudge which Passion's false, and which is
                                 true,
    p. 371 UNGATHERED 8   7 That may iudge for his six-pence) had, before

iudgement   frequency: 13   relative frequency: 0.00018
    p.   43 EPIGRAMS 52   5 This but thy iudgement fooles: the other way
    p.   47 EPIGRAMS 63   4 The iudgement of the king so shine in thee;
    p.   50 EPIGRAMS 72   5 'Tis not thy iudgement breeds the preiudice,
    p.   63 EPIGRAMS 98   8 With thine owne course the iudgement of thy
                               friend,
    p.   64 EPIGRAMS 99   10 And euen the praisers iudgement suffers so.
    p.   68 EPIGRAMS 106   6 Or valour, or thy iudgement seasoning it,
    p.   76 EPIGRAMS 119   8 But dost it out of iudgement, not disease;
    p. 122 FOREST 15   20 And destin'd vnto iudgement, after all.
    p. 363 UNGATHERED 3   16 And strikes the quickest-sighted Iudgement
                               blinde.
    p. 365 UNGATHERED 5   9 Iudgement (adornd with Learning)
    p. 385 UNGATHERED 20   3 Who are his Test, and what their iudgement is:
    p. 391 UNGATHERED 26   27 For, if I thought my iudgement were of yeeres,
    p. 395 UNGATHERED 29   25 Your true freind in Iudgement and Choise

iudgements   frequency: 1   relative frequency: 0.00001
    p.   51 EPIGRAMS 74   1 Whil'st thy weigh'd iudgements, EGERTON,
                               I heare,

iudges   frequency: 1   relative frequency: 0.00001
  **p. 116 PANEGYRE   106 "Lawes, iudges, co<u>nsellors, yea prince, and
                               state.

iudging   frequency: 1   relative frequency: 0.00001
    p.   78 EPIGRAMS 123   1 Writing thy selfe, or iudging others writ,

iudgment   frequency: 3   relative frequency: 0.00004
    p. 386 UNGATHERED 21   7 It must be thine owne iudgment, yet, that sends
    p. 386 UNGATHERED 21   8 This thy worke forth: that iudgment mine
                               commends.
    p. 406 UNGATHERED 35   7 He may haue skill & iudgment to designe

iuggler   frequency: 1   relative frequency: 0.00001
    p.   88 EPIGRAMS 133   156 Old BANKES the iuggler, our
                               PYTHAGORAS,

iuno   frequency: 1   relative frequency: 0.00001
    p. 403 UNGATHERED 34   33 The majesty of Iuno in ye Cloudes,

iuory   frequency: 1   relative frequency: 0.00001
    p. 403 UNGATHERED 34   28 Though gold or Iuory haftes would make it good.

iust   frequency: 17   relative frequency: 0.00024
   *p. 492 TO HIMSELF   t1 The iust indignation the Author
   *p. 494 TO HIMSELF   53 His zeale to God, and his iust awe o're men;
    p.   34 EPIGRAMS 25   8 Iust wife, and, to change me, make womans hast?
    p.   37 EPIGRAMS 34   1 He that feares death, or mournes it, in the iust,
    p.   41 EPIGRAMS 45   4 Exacted by thy fate, on the iust day.
    p.   57 EPIGRAMS 89   13 Weare this renowne. 'Tis iust, that who did giue
    p.   66 EPIGRAMS 102   11 And are so good, and bad, iust at a price,
    p.   71 EPIGRAMS 110   13 For, where his person liu'd scarce one iust age,
    p.   84 EPIGRAMS 133   4 With tales of Troyes iust knight, our faiths
                               abuse:
    p.   96 FOREST 2   85 The iust reward of her high huswifery;
    p. 113 FOREST 12   8 Iust to the waight their this dayes-presents
                               beare;
    p. 117 FOREST 13   18 Men are not iust, or keepe no holy lawes
    p. 119 FOREST 13   91 And, keeping a iust course, haue earely put
    p. 381 UNGATHERED 12   58 Poore Tom haue we cause to suspect iust thee?
    p. 395 UNGATHERED 29   13 It makes me rauish'd with iust wonder, cry
    p. 399 UNGATHERED 31   22 By warrant call'd iust Symetry,
    p. 422 UNGATHERED 50   8 are distant, so is proffitt from iust aymes.

iustice   frequency: 4   relative frequency: 0.00005
  **p. 116 PANEGYRE   104 "When, publique iustice borrow'd all her powers
    p. 106 FOREST 8   47 In thy iustice to molest
    p. 217 UNDERWOOD 46   t2 Lord chiefe Iustice of England.
    p. 402 UNGATHERED 34   16 Of Tyre-man, Mounte-banck & Iustice
                               Iones,

iustice-hood   frequency: 1   relative frequency: 0.00001
    p. 405 UNGATHERED 34   77 Should but ye king his Iustice-hood employ

iustifie   frequency: 1   relative frequency: 0.00001
    p.   49 EPIGRAMS 66   8 Or thou more happie, it to iustifie

iustly   frequency: 4   relative frequency: 0.00005
  **p. 115 PANEGYRE   93 "And all so iustly, as his eare was ioy'd

iustly (cont.)
  p. 120 FOREST 14   22 Are iustly summ'd, that make you man;
  p. 387 UNGATHERED 22   5 Let such as iustly haue out=liu'd all prayse,
  p. 409 UNGATHERED 38   6 Which you haue iustly gained from the Stage,

iuy   frequency: 1   relative frequency: 0.00001
  p. 107 FOREST 10   12 In the greene circle of thy Iuy twine.

iuyce   frequency: 1   relative frequency: 0.00001
  p. 59 EPIGRAMS 92   28 With iuyce of limons, onions, pisse, to write,

ivno   frequency: 1   relative frequency: 0.00001
  p. 68 EPIGRAMS 105 18 There IVNO sate, and yet no Peacock by.

ivory   frequency: 2   relative frequency: 0.00002
  See also "iuory."
  p. 292 UNDERWOOD 86   28 Thrice 'bout thy Altar with their Ivory feet.
  p. 293 UNDERWOOD 87   2 And ('bout thy Ivory neck,) no youth did fling

ivy   frequency: 3   relative frequency: 0.00004
  See also "iuy," "ivye."
  p. 200 UNDERWOOD 42   9 Put on my Ivy Garland, let me see
  p. 412 UNGATHERED 41   4 R. Rose, I. Ivy, E. sweet Eglantine.
  p. 413 UNGATHERED 41 17 The fourth is humble Ivy, intersert,

ivye   frequency: 1   relative frequency: 0.00001
  p. 420 UNGATHERED 48 26 And come fforth worthie Ivye, or the Bayes,

ixion   frequency: 1   relative frequency: 0.00001
  p. 313 HORACE 2   176 Ino bewaild; Ixion false, forsworne;

jacks-pulse   frequency: 1   relative frequency: 0.00001
  p. 216 UNDERWOOD 45   6 That hearkens to a Jacks-pulse, when it goes.

jacobs   frequency: 1   relative frequency: 0.00001
  p. 274 U'WOOD 84.1   38 By JACOBS Ladder, to the top

jakes   frequency: 1   relative frequency: 0.00001
  p. 87 EPIGRAMS 133 137 Or were precipitated downe the jakes,

james   frequency: 4   relative frequency: 0.00005
  See also "iames," "ieames."
  p. 221 UNDERWOOD 48 37 That when King James, above here,
  p. 259 UNDERWOOD 76   6 JAMES the blessed, pleas'd the rather,
  p. 268 UNDERWOOD 82   9 As hath thy JAMES; cleans'd from originall
                         drosse,
  p. 382 UNGATHERED 16 t1 A speach presented vnto king James at a tylting
                         in the

jane   frequency: 3   relative frequency: 0.00004
  p. 268 UNDERWOOD 83 t2 On the Lady JANE PAWLET,
  p. 269 UNDERWOOD 83 19 Shee was the Lady Jane, and Marchionisse
  p. 394 UNGATHERED 28 t1 To ye memorye of that most honoured Ladie Jane,

janus   frequency: 1   relative frequency: 0.00001
  p. 263 UNDERWOOD 79   9 Rector Chori. To day old Janus opens the new
                         yeare,

japhets   frequency: 1   relative frequency: 0.00001
  p. 175 UNDERWOOD 23 27 With Japhets lyne, aspire

jar. See "iarre," "jarre."

jarre   frequency: 2   relative frequency: 0.00002
  p. 184 UNDERWOOD 29 52 Still may Syllabes jarre with time,
  p. 305 HORACE 2   28 The whole fleet wreck'd? A great jarre to be
                         shap'd,

jarres   frequency: 1   relative frequency: 0.00001
  p. 219 UNDERWOOD 47 55 Of earthen Jarres, there may molest me too:

jarreth   frequency: 1   relative frequency: 0.00001
  p. 329 HORACE 2   532 Is laugh'd at, that still jarreth on one string:

jarring   frequency: 1   relative frequency: 0.00001
  p. 331 HORACE 2   557 As jarring Musique doth, at jolly feasts,

jars. See "iarres," "jarres."

jason's. See "iasons."

jaundice. See "jaundies."

jaundies   frequency: 1   relative frequency: 0.00001
      p. 335 HORACE 2 ˙   646 The yellow Jaundies, or were furious mad

jaw   frequency: 1   relative frequency: 0.00001
      p. 175 UNDERWOOD 23   36 Safe from the wolves black jaw, and the dull
                               Asses hoofe.

jaws. See "iawes."

jay. See "iay."

jealous   frequency: 5   relative frequency: 0.00007
      See also "iealous."
      p. 147 UNDERWOOD 7   10 But then if I grow jealous madde,
      p. 164 UNDERWOOD 15   73 And jealous each of other, yet thinke long
      p. 177 UNDERWOOD 25   28 If subject to the jealous errors
      p. 200 UNDERWOOD 42   10 Who frownes, who jealous is, who taxeth me.
      p. 202 UNDERWOOD 42   87 Thou art jealous of thy Wifes, or Daughters
                               Case:

jealousie   frequency: 3   relative frequency: 0.00004
      p. 150 UNDERWOOD 10   1 Wretched and foolish Jealousie,
      p. 230 UNDERWOOD 56   17 Widow or Wife, without the jealousie
      p. 257 UNDERWOOD 75   135 Or canker'd Jealousie,

jealousies. See "iealousies."

jealousy. See "iealousie," "jealousie."

jeannins. See "ianin's."

jearing   frequency: 1   relative frequency: 0.00001
      p. 313 HORACE 2   160 And Roman Gentrie, jearing, will laugh out.

jeast   frequency: 1   relative frequency: 0.00001
      p. 218 UNDERWOOD 47   16 Or th'other on their borders, that will jeast

jeering. See "jearing."

jemme   frequency: 1   relative frequency: 0.00001
      p. 206 UNDERWOOD 43   74 Their Jemme of Riches, and bright Stone, that
                               brings

jephson. See "iephson."

jerk. See "jerke."

jerke   frequency: 1   relative frequency: 0.00001
      p. 164 UNDERWOOD 15   72 And firke, and jerke, and for the Coach-man
                               raile,

jerome. See "hiercme."

jest   frequency: 3   relative frequency: 0.00004
      See also "iest," "jeast."
      p. 292 UNDERWOOD 86   11 There jest, and feast, make him thine host,
      p. 319 HORACE 2   323 How he could jest, because he mark'd and saw,
      p. 321 HORACE 2   330 And so to turne all earnest into jest,

jests   frequency: 2   relative frequency: 0.00002
      See also "iests."
      p. 221 UNDERWOOD 48   40 And have thy tales and jests too,
      p. 323 HORACE 2   400 And jests; and both to admiration raise

jesus   frequency: 1   relative frequency: 0.00001
      p. 288 U'WOOD 84.9   212 Jesus, the onely-gotten Christ! who can

jewel. See "iewell," "jewell."

jewell   frequency: 1   relative frequency: 0.00001
      p. 198 UNDERWOOD 40   42 The Jewell of your name, as close as sleepe

jewells   frequency: 1   relative frequency: 0.00001
      p. 232 UNDERWOOD 58   10 That hang their richest jewells i' their nose;

jewels   frequency: 2   relative frequency: 0.00002
    See also "iewells," "jewells."
    p. 138 UNDERWOOD 2.6   11 And her Jewels, to the view
    p. 271 UNDERWOOD 83   87 The Starres, that are the Jewels of the Night,

jews. See "iewes."

jo   frequency: 1   relative frequency: 0.00001
    p. 313 HORACE 2   177 Poore Jo wandring; wild Orestes mad:

joan. See "ione," "joane."

joane   frequency: 1   relative frequency: 0.00001
    p. 231 UNDERWOOD 56   24 Your Joane to passe her melancholie time.

joan's. See "iones."

john   frequency: 1   relative frequency: 0.00001
    See also "iohn."
    p. 231 UNDERWOOD 57   1 Father John Burges,

johnson   frequency: 1   relative frequency: 0.00001
    p. 418 UNGATHERED 46   5 Il may Ben Johnson slander so his feete,

join. See "joyn," "joyne," "re-joyne."

joined. See "dis-joyn'd."

joint. See "ioint."

jointing. See "joynting."

joints. See "dis-ioynts," "joynts."

jolly   frequency: 1   relative frequency: 0.00001
    See also "iolly."
    p. 331 HORACE 2   557 As jarring Musique doth, at jolly feasts,

jones. See "iones."

jonson   frequency: 1   relative frequency: 0.00001
    See also "ionson," "johnson."
    p. 246 UNDERWOOD 70   85 Jonson, who sung this of him, e're he went

joseph   frequency: 2   relative frequency: 0.00002
    p. 414 UNGATHERED 42   1 You looke, my Joseph, I should something say
    p. 414 UNGATHERED 42   t2 Master JOSEPH RVTTER.

joshua. See "iosvah."

jostled. See "justled."

jot   frequency: 1   relative frequency: 0.00001
    p. 210 UNDERWOOD 43   154 Scap'd not his Justice any jot the more:

journal. See "iournall."

journals   frequency: 1   relative frequency: 0.00001
    p. 254 UNDERWOOD 75   75 In all thy age of Journals thou hast tooke,

journey   frequency: 1   relative frequency: 0.00001
    See also "iourney."
    p. 207 UNDERWOOD 43   94 The rest, my journey into Scotland song,

jove   frequency: 3   relative frequency: 0.00004
    p. 203 UNDERWOOD 43   12 By Jove to have Minerva for thy Bride,
    p. 208 UNDERWOOD 43   115 And so did Jove, who ne're meant thee his Cup:
    p. 290 UNDERWOOD 85   29 Then when the thundring Jove his Snow and
                             showres

joves   frequency: 1   relative frequency: 0.00001
    p. 175 UNDERWOOD 23   30 Who aided him, will thee, the issue of Joves
                             braine.

jove's. See "iove's," "joves."

jovial. See "iouiall," "ioviall."

jovis. See "iouis."

joy
  See also "ioy."   frequency: 16   relative frequency: 0.00023
  p. 147 UNDERWOOD 7   7 For that's a narrow joy is but our owne.
  p. 181 UNDERWOOD 27   6 In whom Anacreon once did joy,
  p. 191 UNDERWOOD 38   11 And fills my powers with perswading joy,
  p. 225 UNDERWOOD 51   17 'Tis a brave cause of joy, let it be knowne,
  p. 238 UNDERWOOD 66   7 (Except the joy that the first Mary brought,
  p. 239 UNDERWOOD 67   1 1. CLIO. Up publike joy, remember
  p. 240 UNDERWOOD 67   44 Her joy in state, and pleasure;
  p. 246 UNDERWOOD 70   87 Or taste a part of that full joy he meant
  p. 249 UNDERWOOD 72   6 Repeating all Great Britain's joy, and more,
  p. 256 UNDERWOOD 75   114 It brings Friends Joy, Foes Griefe,
                          Posteritie Fame;
  p. 256 UNDERWOOD 75   128 The Solemne Quire cryes, Joy; and they
                          returne, Amen.
  p. 283 U'WOOD 84.9   37 The joy of Saints! the Crowne for which it
                          lives,
  p. 284 U'WOOD 84.9   61 O Day of joy, and suretie to the just!
  p. 284 U'WOOD 84.9   66 Of joy the Circle, and sole Period!
  p. 293 UNDERWOOD 86   30 Delights, nor credulous hope of mutuall Joy,
  p. 333 HORACE 2   610 With joy of what is given him, over-gone:

joyed. See "ioy'd," "o're-joy'd."

joyes   frequency: 3   relative frequency: 0.00004
  p. 182 UNDERWOOD 28   13 Her joyes, her smiles, her loves, as readers take
  p. 251 UNDERWOOD 74   19 Such joyes, such sweet's doth your Returne
  p. 270 UNDERWOOD 83   60 Made her friends joyes to get above their feares!

joyest. See "ioy'st."

joyful. See "ioyfull," "joyfull."

joyfull   frequency: 1   relative frequency: 0.00001
  p. 236 UNDERWOOD 64   5 And as it turnes our joyfull yeare about,

joyn   frequency: 1   relative frequency: 0.00001
  p. 338 HORACE 1   2 . horse neck joyn . sundry plumes ore-fold

joyne   frequency: 1   relative frequency: 0.00001
  p. 139 UNDERWOOD 2.7 15 Joyne lip to lip, and try:

joynting   frequency: 1   relative frequency: 0.00001
  p. 183 UNDERWOOD 29   10 Joynting Syllabes, drowning Letters,

joynts   frequency: 2   relative frequency: 0.00002
  p. 184 UNDERWOOD 29   50 May his joynts tormented bee,
  p. 269 UNDERWOOD 83   9 Stiffe! starke! my joynts 'gainst one another
                          knock!

joys. See "ioyes," "joyes."

judg'd   frequency: 3   relative frequency: 0.00004
  p. 259 UNDERWOOD 76   23 Parts of me (they judg'd) decay'd,
  p. 284 U'WOOD 84.9   55 Those other two; which must be judg'd, or
                          crown'd:
  p. 331 HORACE 2   576 To send it to be judg'd by Metius eare,

judge   frequency: 15   relative frequency: 0.00021
  See also "iudge."
  p. 169 UNDERWOOD 17   4 'Tis then a crime, when the Usurer is Judge.
  p. 186 UNDERWOOD 32   1 The Judge his favour timely then extends,
  p. 204 UNDERWOOD 43   47 Shee is the Judge, Thou Executioner:
  p. 242 UNDERWOOD 69   20 To judge; So all men comming neere can spie.
  p. 261 UNDERWOOD 77   11 Catch'd with these Arts, wherein the Judge is
                          wise
  p. 283 U'WOOD 84.9   48 To heare their Judge, and his eternall doome;
  p. 286 U'WOOD 84.9 148 He that shall be our supreme Judge, should leave
  p. 288 U'WOOD 84.9 211 To him should be her Judge, true God, true
                          Man,
  p. 309 HORACE 2   112 Before the Judge, it hangs, and waites report.
  p. 319 HORACE 2   302 Clowne, Towns-man, base, and noble, mix'd, to
                          judge?
  p. 321 HORACE 2   356 Be I their Judge, they doe at no time dare
  p. 323 HORACE 2   387 But every Judge hath not the facultie
  p. 325 HORACE 2   450 And office of a Judge are, what the parts
  p. 333 HORACE 2   609 You doe not bring, to judge your Verses, one,
  p. 333 HORACE 2   620 When you write Verses, with your judge do so:

judgement   frequency: 9   relative frequency: 0.00013
   See also "iudgement," "iudgment."
   p. 158 UNDERWOOD 14   6 Was trusted, that you thought my judgement such
   p. 177 UNDERWOOD 25   24 Who would with judgement search, searching
                 conclude
   p. 183 UNDERWOOD 29   5 Cosening Judgement with a measure,
   p. 210 UNDERWOOD 43   158 There was a Judgement shew'n too in an houre.
   p. 232 UNDERWOOD 58   5 His judgement is; If he be wise, and praise,
   p. 256 UNDERWOOD 75   105 And this well mov'd the Judgement of the King
   p. 288 U'WOOD 84.9   215 In that great Act of judgement: which the
                 Father
   p. 331 HORACE 2   573 Thou, such thy judgement is, thy knowledge too,
   p. 331 HORACE 2   582 Nature, or Art. My Judgement will not pierce

judgements   frequency: 3   relative frequency: 0.00004
   See also "iudgements."
   p. 159 UNDERWOOD 14   15 A many'of bookes, even good judgements wound
   p. 185 UNDERWOOD 31   1 So, justest Lord, may all your Judgements be
   p. 232 UNDERWOOD 58   14 Their perfum'd judgements, let them kisse thy
                 Wife.

judges   frequency: 2   relative frequency: 0.00002
   See also "iudges."
   p. 187 UNDERWOOD 33   37 The Courts just honour, and thy Judges love.
   p. 331 HORACE 2   542 This, fearing not the subtlest Judges marke,

judging   frequency: 1   relative frequency: 0.00001
   See also "iudging."
   p. 288 U'WOOD 84.9   207 Of raising, judging, and rewarding all

juggler. See "iuggler."

juice. See "iuyce," "juyce."

jump. See "jumpe."

jumpe   frequency: 1   relative frequency: 0.00001
   p. 204 UNDERWOOD 43   39 Acrostichs, and Telestichs, on jumpe names,

june   frequency: 2   relative frequency: 0.00002
   p. 253 UNDERWOOD 75   16 By all the Spheares consent, so in the heart of
                 June?
   p. 262 UNDERWOOD 78   14 Upon my Birth-day the eleventh of June;

juno   frequency: 1   relative frequency: 0.00001
   See also "iuno," "ivno."
   p. 137 UNDERWOOD 2.5   53 But shee's Juno, when she walkes,

jupiter   frequency: 1   relative frequency: 0.00001
   p. 203 UNDERWOOD 43   9 'Twas Jupiter that hurl'd thee headlong downe,

just   frequency: 27   relative frequency: 0.00039
   See also "iust."
   p. 136 UNDERWOOD 2.5   16 Just above her sparkling eyes,
   p. 151 UNDERWOOD 12   11 With the just Canon of his life,
   p. 167 UNDERWOOD 15   177 That thine be just, and honest; that thy Deeds
   p. 171 UNDERWOOD 19   22 You have a Husband is the just excuse
   p. 174 UNDERWOOD 23   14 As 'tis too just a cause;
   p. 185 UNDERWOOD 30   8 The poores full Store-house, and just servants
                 field.
   p. 186 UNDERWOOD 32   15 When this appeares, just Lord, to your sharp
                 sight,
   p. 187 UNDERWOOD 33   37 The Courts just honour, and thy Judges love.
   p. 192 UNDERWOOD 38   38 Your just commands; yet those, not I, be lost.
   p. 198 UNDERWOOD 40   40 Due to that one, that doth believe him just.
   p. 217 UNDERWOOD 46   8 Thy just defences made th'oppressor afraid.
   p. 229 UNDERWOOD 54   2 For a just wager, and that wager paid
   p. 232 UNDERWOOD 59   4 Of making just approaches, how to kill,
   p. 240 UNDERWOOD 67   27 And Sister to just Lewis!
   p. 245 UNDERWOOD 70   73 In small proportions, we just beautie see:
   p. 255 UNDERWOOD 75   100 But doth his Carract, and just Standard keepe
   p. 262 UNDERWOOD 78   5 Hee's prudent, valiant, just, and temperate;
   p. 263 UNDERWOOD 79   12 And offer your just service on these plaines;
   p. 270 UNDERWOOD 83   48 Just as she in it liv'd! and so exempt
   p. 273 U'WOOD 84.1   8 By the just trade
   p. 274 U'WOOD 84.2   1 I sing the just, and uncontrol'd Descent
   p. 284 U'WOOD 84.9   61 O Day of joy, and suretie to the just!
   p. 317 HORACE 2   272 Have more or lesse then just five Acts: nor
                 laid,
   p. 327 HORACE 2   471 An ounce, what makes it then? The halfe pound
                 just;

just (cont.)
    p. 333 HORACE 2   597 To say, I'm ignorant. Just as a Crier
    p. 347 HORACE 1   353 .... just ....
    p. 422 UNGATHERED 50   1 Just and fit actions Ptolemey (he saith)

justest   frequency: 1   relative frequency: 0.00001
    p. 185 UNDERWOOD 31   1 So, justest Lord, may all your Judgements be

justice   frequency: 8   relative frequency: 0.00011
   See also "iustice."
    p. 163 UNDERWOOD 15   39 Friendship is now mask'd Hatred! Justice fled,
    p. 170 UNDERWOOD 18   18 Because they would free Justice imitate,
    p. 210 UNDERWOOD 43 154 Scap'd not his Justice any jot the more:
    p. 217 UNDERWOOD 46   16 Desired Justice to the publique Weale,
    p. 229 UNDERWOOD 54   8 Is, she will play Dame Justice, too severe;
    p. 288 U'WOOD 84.9 218 His Wisdome, and his Justice, in that houre,
    p. 289 U'WOOD 84.9 223 And most his Justice, in the fitting parts,
    p. 317 HORACE 2   283 Praise the spare diet, wholsome justice, lawes,

justicehood. See "iustice-hood."

justifie   frequency: 2   relative frequency: 0.00002
    p. 191 UNDERWOOD 38   21 I will not stand to justifie my fault,
    p. 288 U'WOOD 84.9 204 To justifie, and quicken us in breath!

justify. See "iustifie," "justifie."

justled   frequency: 1   relative frequency: 0.00001
    p. 219 UNDERWOOD 47   58 Lest it be justled, crack'd, made nought, or
                        lesse:

justly   frequency: 1   relative frequency: 0.00001
   See also "iustly."
    p. 230 UNDERWOOD 56   7 And you may justly, being a tardie, cold,

juyce   frequency: 1   relative frequency: 0.00001
    p. 327 HORACE 2   475 In juyce of Cedar worthy to be steep'd,

k.   frequency: 5   relative frequency: 0.00007
    p. 235 UNDERWOOD 62   t2 To K. CHARLES
    p. 235 UNDERWOOD 63   t1 To K. CHARLES, and Q. MARY.
    p. 236 UNDERWOOD 64   t2 To our great and good K. CHARLES
    p. 375 UNGATHERED 10 29 F. shewes what he was, K. what he will bee.
    p. 406 UNGATHERED 35   1 But cause thou hearst ye mighty k. of Spaine

k<ing>   frequency: 2   relative frequency: 0.00002
    p. 241 UNDERWOOD 68   1 What can the cause be, when the K<ing> hath
                        given
    p. 241 UNDERWOOD 68   5 Well, they should know him, would the K<ing> but
                        grant

kate   frequency: 3   relative frequency: 0.00004
    p. 87 EPIGRAMS 133 118 Stunke not so ill; nor, when shee kist, KATE
                        ARDEN.
    p. 209 UNDERWOOD 43 148 Nay, sigh'd a Sister, 'twas the Nun, Kate
                        Arden,
    p. 258 UNDERWOOD 75 172 A Kate, a Frank, to honour their Grand-dames,

katherine   frequency: 2   relative frequency: 0.00002
    p. 116 FOREST 13   t2 TO KATHERINE, LADY AVBIGNY.
    p. 400 UNGATHERED 31 33 For this did Katherine, Ladie Ogle, die

keep   frequency: 4   relative frequency: 0.00005
   See also "keepe."
    p. 157 UNDERWOOD 13 156 For me to be your Indice. Keep you such,
    p. 345 HORACE 1   277 .... keep, and ... .
    p. 410 UNGATHERED 39   8 Keep in thy barking Wit, thou bawling Fool?
    p. 412 UNGATHERED 41   8 As Love, here studied to keep Grace alive.

keep'd   frequency: 1   relative frequency: 0.00001
    p. 327 HORACE 2   476 And in smooth Cypresse boxes to be keep'd?

keepe   frequency: 45   relative frequency: 0.00065
   *p. 493 TO HIMSELF   26 May keepe vp the Play-club:
    p. 32 EPIGRAMS 16   9 Keepe thy selfe there, and thinke thy valure
                        right,
    p. 48 EPIGRAMS 65   8 And, reconcil'd, keepe him suspected still.
    p. 59 EPIGRAMS 92 19 Keepe a starre-chamber sentence close, twelue
                        dayes:
    p. 69 EPIGRAMS 107 24 That are your wordes of credit. Keepe your
                        Names

keepe (cont.)

p.	73 EPIGRAMS 113	4	Where, what makes others great, doth keepe thee good!
p.	77 EPIGRAMS 120	24	Heauen vowes to keepe him.
p.	78 EPIGRAMS 122	8	I would restore, and keepe it euer such;
p.	81 EPIGRAMS 129	10	Whose noyse shall keepe thy miming most aliue,
p.	88 EPIGRAMS 133	173	Cannot the Plague-bill keepe you backe? nor bells
p.	97 FOREST 3	40	And feasts, that either shearers keepe;
p.	99 FOREST 3	87	Get place, and honor, and be glad to keepe
p.	103 FOREST 6	2	Can your fauours keepe, and couer,
p.	109 FOREST 11	1	Not to know vice at all, and keepe true state,
p.	109 FOREST 11	24	Or some great thought doth keepe
p.	117 FOREST 13	18	Men are not iust, or keepe no holy lawes
p.	118 FOREST 13	61	And keepe an euen, and vnalter'd gaite;
p.	131 UNDERWOOD 2.1	21	Keepe the middle age at stay,
p.	159 UNDERWOOD 14	28	Meane what I speake: and still will keepe that Vow.
p.	162 UNDERWOOD 15	5	It is a call to keepe the spirits alive
p.	187 UNDERWOOD 33	30	Arm'd at all peeces, as to keepe a Fort
p.	188 UNDERWOOD 35	6	To fetch the flesh, we keepe the Rowle.
p.	190 UNDERWOOD 37	13	Which, how most sacred I will ever keepe,
p.	192 UNDERWOOD 38	48	Would live his glory that could keepe it on;
p.	198 UNDERWOOD 40	23	Keepe in reserv'd in his Dark-lanterne face,
p.	198 UNDERWOOD 40	27	Keepe secret in his Channels what he breedes,
p.	198 UNDERWOOD 40	41	And such your Servant is, who vowes to keepe
p.	199 UNDERWOOD 41	17	O, keepe it still; for it had rather be
p.	200 UNDERWOOD 42	25	Yet keepe those up in sackcloth too, or lether,
p.	214 UNDERWOOD 44	50	And keepe the Glorie of the English name,
p.	214 UNDERWOOD 44	55	That keepe the warre, though now't be growne more tame,
p.	219 UNDERWOOD 47	57	I have decreed; keepe it from waves, and presse;
p.	225 UNDERWOOD 50	29	Searching for knowledge, and to keepe your mind
p.	231 UNDERWOOD 56	29	I gaine, in having leave to keepe my Day,
p.	242 UNDERWOOD 69	16	To keepe him off; and how-so-e're he gleanes
p.	246 UNDERWOOD 70	94	And keepe the one halfe from his Harry.
p.	255 UNDERWOOD 75	100	But doth his Carract, and just Standard keepe
p.	257 UNDERWOOD 75	150	And keepe their Fames
p.	290 UNDERWOOD 85	15	Or the prest honey in pure pots doth keepe
p.	313 HORACE 2	172	Keepe him still active, angry, un-appeas'd,
p.	313 HORACE 2	180	A meere new person, looke he keepe his state
p.	327 HORACE 2	470	He cries, Good boy, thou'lt keepe thine owne. Now, adde
p.	395 UNGATHERED 29	12	Keepe due proportion in the ample song,
p.	416 UNGATHERED 43	5	How they doe keepe alive his memorie;
p.	419 UNGATHERED 47	7	God blesse them all, and keepe them safe:

keeper   frequency: 1   relative frequency: 0.00001

p.	225 UNDERWOOD 51	9	Sonne to the grave wise Keeper of the Seale,

keepes   frequency: 9   relative frequency: 0.00013

p.	30 EPIGRAMS 12	3	Keepes himselfe, with halfe a man, and defrayes
p.	30 EPIGRAMS 12	15	That lost, he keepes his chamber, reades Essayes,
p.	36 EPIGRAMS 28	15	He keepes anothers wife, which is a spice
p.	40 EPIGRAMS 42	13	The children, that he keepes, GILES sweares are none
p.	69 EPIGRAMS 107	10	What States yo'haue gull'd, and which yet keepes yo'in pay.
p.	74 EPIGRAMS 115	21	With such a one. And therein keepes it's word.
p.	177 UNDERWOOD 25	21	And keepes your merit
p.	198 UNDERWOOD 40	36	Doth, while he keepes his watch, betray his stand.
p.	257 UNDERWOOD 75	152	For Fame keepes Vertue up, and it Posteritie.

keeping   frequency: 6   relative frequency: 0.00008

p.	68 EPIGRAMS 105	17	Or, keeping your due state, that would not cry,
p.	119 FOREST 13	91	And, keeping a iust course, haue earely put
p.	159 UNDERWOOD 14	31	And like a Compasse keeping one foot still
p.	161 UNDERWOOD 14	68	With that thy Stile, thy keeping of thy State,
p.	294 UNDERWOOD 88	6	But thus, thus, keeping endlesse Holy-day,
p.	319 HORACE 2	301	The Idiot, keeping holy-day, or drudge,

keeps   frequency: 4   relative frequency: 0.00005
See also "keepes."

p.	54 EPIGRAMS 82	2	He cast, yet keeps her well! No, shee keeps him.
p.	66 EPIGRAMS 102	13	But thou, whose noblesse keeps one stature still,
p.	400 UNGATHERED 31	30	Keeps warme the spice of her good name,

kenelm. See "kenelme."

kenelme   frequency: 3   relative frequency: 0.00004
     p. 262 UNDERWOOD 78   t3 Husband, Sir KENELME DIGBY.
     p. 272 UNDERWOOD 84   t6 late Wife of Sir KENELME DIGBY,
                                    Knight:
     p. 281 U'WOOD 84.8   t1 To KENELME, IOHN, GEORGE.

kept   frequency: 21   relative frequency: 0.00030
     See also "keep'd."
  **p. 115 PANEGYRE   70 The Nobles zeale, yet either kept aliue
     p. 63 EPIGRAMS 99   1 That thou hast kept thy loue, encreast thy will,
     p. 89 EPIGRAMS 133   189 Who kept an ale-house; with my little MINOS,
     p. 151 UNDERWOOD 12   15 His Mind as pure, and neatly kept,
     p. 163 UNDERWOOD 15   41 That kept man living! Pleasures only sought!
     p. 173 UNDERWOOD 22   16 And kept, and bred, and brought up true.
     p. 173 UNDERWOOD 22   19 His Altars kept from the Decay,
     p. 203 UNDERWOOD 43   8 With Clownes, and Tradesmen, kept thee clos'd
                                   in horne.
     p. 203 UNDERWOOD 43   21 Conceal'd, or kept there, that was fit to be,
     p. 205 UNDERWOOD 43   55 And so, have kept me dying a whole age,
     p. 212 UNDERWOOD 43   197 Would you had kept your Forge, at Aetna still,
     p. 225 UNDERWOOD 51   18 For 't were a narrow gladnesse, kept thine owne.
     p. 257 UNDERWOOD 75   163 Be kept alive those Sweet, and Sacred fires
     p. 273 U'WOOD 84.1   6 Their names of being kept alive,
     p. 274 U'WOOD 84.1   39 Of that eternall Port kept ope'
     p. 287 U'WOOD 84.9   165 But, kept an even gate, as some streight tree
     p. 325 HORACE 2   417 Have not kept in; and (lest perfection faile)
     p. 329 HORACE 2   528 Hath shed, or humane frailtie not kept thence.
     p. 331 HORACE 2   578 Nine yeares kept in, your papers by, yo'are free
     p. 335 HORACE 2   664 Let Poets perish, that will not be kept.
     p. 410 UNGATHERED 38   17 The Cobler kept him to his nall; but, now

keptst   frequency: 1   relative frequency: 0.00001
     p. 290 UNDERWOOD 85   22 And, Sylvane, thine, that keptst his Lands!

kern. See "kerne."

kerne   frequency: 1   relative frequency: 0.00001
     p. 367 UNGATHERED 6   53 Vpon the Kerne, and wildest Irishry,

key-stone   frequency: 1   relative frequency: 0.00001
     p. 157 UNDERWOOD 13   136 We must accomplish; 'Tis the last Key-stone

keyes   frequency: 1   relative frequency: 0.00001
     p. 59 EPIGRAMS 92   26 To write in cypher, and the seuerall keyes,

keys. See "keyes."

kicking   frequency: 1   relative frequency: 0.00001
     p. 155 UNDERWOOD 13   93 Such worship due to kicking of a Punck!

kid   frequency: 2   relative frequency: 0.00002
     p. 291 UNDERWOOD 85   60 Or Kid forc't from the Wolfe againe.
     p. 391 UNGATHERED 26   30 Or sporting Kid, or Marlowes mighty line.

kild   frequency: 1   relative frequency: 0.00001
     p. 165 UNDERWOOD 15   96 If it be thought, kild like her Embrions; for,

kill   frequency: 7   relative frequency: 0.00010
  **p. 116 PANEGYRE   100 "Where sleeping they could saue, and waking kill;
     p. 144 UNDERWOOD 4   6 For then their threats will kill me;
     p. 191 UNDERWOOD 38   4 This sadnesse makes no approaches, but to kill.
     p. 232 UNDERWOOD 59   4 Of making just approaches, how to kill,
     p. 234 UNDERWOOD 60   16 That spread his body o're, to kill:
     p. 317 HORACE 2   263 Present anone: Medea must not kill
     p. 335 HORACE 2   666 Doth the same thing with him, that would him
                                   kill.

kill'd   frequency: 1   relative frequency: 0.00001
     See also "kild."
     p. 94 FOREST 2   30 And, for thy messe, is willing to be kill'd.

killer   frequency: 1   relative frequency: 0.00001
     p. 409 UNGATHERED 37   20 Out in the Dog-daies, least the killer meete

killing   frequency: 2   relative frequency: 0.00002
     p. 114 FOREST 12   53 Gaue killing strokes. There were braue men,
                                   before
     p. 224 UNDERWOOD 50   11 By all oblique Degrees, that killing height

kills   frequency: 1   relative frequency: 0.00001
    p. 193 UNDERWOOD 38   70 And then his thunder frights more, then it kills.

kilns. See "brick-kills."

kin   frequency: 2   relative frequency: 0.00002
    See also "kinne."
    p. 269 UNDERWOOD 83   29 It is too neere of kin to Heaven, the Soule,
    p. 413 UNGATHERED 41   34 Alike of kin, to that most blessed Trine,

kind   frequency: 10   relative frequency: 0.00014
    See also "kinde," "kynde," "man-kind,"
            "woman-kind," "woman-kinde."
    p. 45 EPIGRAMS 57   2 Baudrie', and vsurie were one kind of game.
    p. 144 UNDERWOOD 4   7 Nor looke too kind on my desires,
    p. 150 UNDERWOOD 10   3 I n<e>'re was of thy kind;
    p. 250 UNDERWOOD 73   9 Feed on thy selfe for spight, and shew thy Kind:
    p. 255 UNDERWOOD 75   80 They are th'exampled Paire, and mirrour of their
                              kind.
    p. 256 UNDERWOOD 75   111 What kind of waking Man
    p. 257 UNDERWOOD 75   142 To them of kind,
    p. 283 U'WOOD 84.9   19 Thou wouldst have lost the Phoenix, had the kind
    p. 288 U'WOOD 84.9   208 The kind of Man, on whom his doome should fall!
    p. 307 HORACE 2   40 This, seeking, in a various kind, to forme

kinde   frequency: 5   relative frequency: 0.00007
    p. 52 EPIGRAMS 76   3 What kinde of creature I could most desire,
    p. 79 EPIGRAMS 125   7 But I, no child, no foole, respect the kinde,
    p. 94 FOREST 2   34 And pikes, now weary their owne kinde to eat,
    p. 101 FOREST 4   59 From all my kinde: that, for my sake,
    p. 367 UNGATHERED 6   30 Or alter kinde.

kindes   frequency: 1   relative frequency: 0.00001
    p. 49 EPIGRAMS 68   3 Two kindes of valour he doth shew, at ones;

kindle   frequency: 1   relative frequency: 0.00001
    p. 174 UNDERWOOD 22   33 Which if it kindle not, but scant

kindled   frequency: 3   relative frequency: 0.00004
    p. 83 EPIGRAMS 131   14 For fame, with breath soone kindled, soone blowne
                              out.
    p. 167 UNDERWOOD 15   162 Friend, flie from hence; and let these kindled
                              rimes
    p. 209 UNDERWOOD 43   149 Kindled the fire! But then, did one returne,

kindling   frequency: 1   relative frequency: 0.00001
    p. 206 UNDERWOOD 43   76 The art of kindling the true Coale, by Lungs:

kindly   frequency: 1   relative frequency: 0.00001
    p. 253 UNDERWOOD 75   25 It is the kindly Season of the time,

kindred   frequency: 2   relative frequency: 0.00002
    p. 216 UNDERWOOD 45   10 That could but claime a kindred from the purse.
    p. 274 U'WOOD 84.2   15 Into the Kindred, whence thy Adam drew

kinds   frequency: 1   relative frequency: 0.00001
    See also "kindes."
    p. 217 UNDERWOOD 46   19 No lesse of praise, then readers in all kinds

kine   frequency: 1   relative frequency: 0.00001
    p. 94 FOREST 2   23 Thy sheepe, thy bullocks, kine, and calues doe
                              feed:

king   frequency: 52   relative frequency: 0.00075
    See also "k.," "k<ing>," "kinge."
  *p. 494 TO HIMSELF   52 The glories of thy King,
 **p. 116 PANEGYRE   117 An euill king: And so must such be still,
 **p. 116 PANEGYRE   132 From out the stones, to gratulate the king.
 **p. 117 PANEGYRE   139 And entring with the power of a king,
 **p. 117 PANEGYRE   162 Still to haue such a king, and this king long.
   p. 28 EPIGRAMS 4   t1 TO KING IAMES.
   p. 28 EPIGRAMS 5   3 The world the temple was, the priest a king,
   p. 37 EPIGRAMS 35   t1 TO KING IAMES.
   p. 38 EPIGRAMS 35   9 First thou preserued wert, our king to bee,
   p. 43 EPIGRAMS 51   4 And farre beneath least pause of such a king,
   p. 43 EPIGRAMS 51   t1 TO KING IAMES.
   p. 47 EPIGRAMS 63   4 The iudgement of the king so shine in thee;
   p. 47 EPIGRAMS 64   12 And not to dangers. When so wise a king
   p. 59 EPIGRAMS 92   33 At naming the French King, their heads they
                            shake,

king (cont.)

p.	63 EPIGRAMS 97	15 Nor did the king of Denmarke him salute,
p.	84 EPIGRAMS 133	24 To haue beene stiled of King ARTHVRS table,
p.	95 FOREST 2	76 That found King IAMES, when hunting late, this way,
p.	109 FOREST 11	13 To wakefull reason, our affections king:
p.	130 UNDERWOOD 1.3	7 The Sonne of God, th'Eternall King,
p.	185 UNDERWOOD 31	3 So, may the King proclaime your Conscience is
p.	212 UNDERWOOD 43	211 So doth the King, and most of the Kings men
p.	221 UNDERWOOD 48	37 That when King James, above here,
p.	225 UNDERWOOD 51	20 In raysing him the wisdome of my King.
p.	235 UNDERWOOD 62	13 What can the Poet wish his King may doe,
p.	236 UNDERWOOD 64	2 Most pious King, but his owne good in you!
p.	238 UNDERWOOD 66	14 Of so much safetie to the Realme, and King!
p.	240 UNDERWOOD 67	37 7. CALLI. See, see our active King
p.	241 UNDERWOOD 68	10 So, the allowance from the King to use,
p.	249 UNDERWOOD 72	1 This is King CHARLES his Day. Speake it, thou Towre,
p.	249 UNDERWOOD 72	t1 To the King. On his Birth-day.
p.	250 UNDERWOOD 73	2 Thy faint, and narrow eyes, to reade the King
p.	251 UNDERWOOD 74	24 Both to the honour of the King and State.
p.	252 UNDERWOOD 75	8 The bountie of a King, and beautie of his Queene!
p.	255 UNDERWOOD 75	83 The king of Creatures, take his paritie
p.	255 UNDERWOOD 75	91 All is a story of the King and Queene!
p.	256 UNDERWOOD 75	105 And this well mov'd the Judgement of the King
p.	256 UNDERWOOD 75	121 See, now the Chappell opens; where the King
p.	256 UNDERWOOD 75	131 To have thy God to blesse, thy King to grace,
p.	259 UNDERWOOD 76	2+ King CHARLES.
p.	263 UNDERWOOD 79	8+ A New-yeares-Gift sung to King
p.	268 UNDERWOOD 82	2 Great King, thy having of a second Sonne:
p.	268 UNDERWOOD 82	t1 To my L. the King,
p.	293 UNDERWOOD 87	4 I thought me richer then the Persian King.
p.	382 UNGATHERED 16	3 vnto thee, king of men; their noblest partes
p.	382 UNGATHERED 16	t1 A speach presented vnto king James at a tylting in the
p.	405 UNGATHERED 34	77 Should but ye king his Iustice-hood employ
p.	413 UNGATHERED 41	38 Sweet Tree of Life, King Davids Strength and Tower,
p.	416 UNGATHERED 44	7 To Crowne the years, which you begin, great king,
p.	418 UNGATHERED 47	1 Our King and Queen the Lord-God blesse,
p.	418 UNGATHERED 47	4 That lives, and breath's, and loves the King.
p.	657 L. CONVIVALES	8 Cries Old Sym, the King of Skinkers;

kingdom. See "kingdome."

kingdome   frequency: 2   relative frequency: 0.00002
**p. 112 PANEGYRE   t9 in this his Kingdome, the 19. of
   p. 286 U'WOOD 84.9   145 In his eternall Kingdome, where we sit

kingdomes   frequency: 3   relative frequency: 0.00004
   p. 249 UNDERWOOD 72   11 Three Kingdomes Mirth, in light, and aerie man,
   p. 254 UNDERWOOD 75   52 Both Crownes, and Kingdomes in their either hand;
   p. 271 UNDERWOOD 83   89 The Sunne! great Kings, and mightiest Kingdomes fall!

kingdoms. See "kingdomes."

kinge   frequency: 1   relative frequency: 0.00001
   p. 419 UNGATH'D 47A   6 .... the Kinge loues . ...

kinglier   frequency: 1   relative frequency: 0.00001
   p. 235 UNDERWOOD 62   5 But thou wilt yet a Kinglier mastrie trie,

kingly   frequency: 1   relative frequency: 0.00001
   p. 309 HORACE 2   93 A kingly worke; or that long barren fen

kings   frequency: 20   relative frequency: 0.00028
**p. 115 PANEGYRE   74 The Kings obeying will, from taking pride
**p. 115 PANEGYRE   77 "With better pompe. She tells him first, that Kings
**p. 115 PANEGYRE   91 "Of kings, praeceding him in that high court;
**p. 116 PANEGYRE   125 That kings, by their example, more doe sway
   p. 28 EPIGRAMS 4   1 How, best of Kings, do'st thou a scepter beare!
   p. 28 EPIGRAMS 4   10 Of Kings for grace; of Poets for my test?
   p. 49 EPIGRAMS 67   11 Which, by no lesse confirm'd, then thy kings choice,

kings (cont.)
```
     p.  53 EPIGRAMS 79       1 That Poets are far rarer births then kings,
     p. 212 UNDERWOOD 43     211 So doth the King, and most of the Kings men
     p. 213 UNDERWOOD 44       2 But we have Powder still for the Kings Day,
     p. 219 UNDERWOOD 47      38 My Princes safetie, and my Kings desire,
     p. 220 UNDERWOOD 48      t1 The Dedication of the Kings new Cellar.
     p. 235 UNDERWOOD 62       4 To cure the call'd Kings Evill with thy touch;
     p. 241 UNDERWOOD 68      14 The Kings fame lives. Go now, denie his
                                 Teirce.
     p. 261 UNDERWOOD 77      20 What worlds of blessings to good Kings they owe:
     p. 263 UNDERWOOD 79      13 Best Kings expect first-fruits of your glad
                                 gaines.
     p. 271 UNDERWOOD 83      89 The Sunne! great Kings, and mightiest
                                 Kingdomes fall!
     p. 309 HORACE 2         105 The gests of Kings, great Captaines, and sad
                                 Warres,
     p. 329 HORACE 2         497 All way of life was shewen; the grace of Kings
     p. 406 UNGATHERED 35      4 All kings to doe ye self same deeds wth some!
```

kinne   frequency: 1   relative frequency: 0.00001
```
     p. 278 U'WOOD 84.4       16 But what's of kinne to whence it came.
```

kinsman   frequency: 1   relative frequency: 0.00001
```
     p.  41 EPIGRAMS 44       t2 KINSMAN.
```

kiss. See "kisse."

kisse   frequency: 18   relative frequency: 0.00026
```
     p.  78 EPIGRAMS 121       2 My lighter comes, to kisse thy learned Muse;
     p. 103 FOREST 6           1 Kisse me, sweet: The warie louer
     p. 103 FOREST 6           5 Kisse againe: no creature comes.
     p. 103 FOREST 6           6 Kisse, and score vp wealthy summes
     p. 106 FOREST 9           3 Or leaue a kisse but in the cup,
     p. 137 UNDERWOOD 2.6      2 Since I drew a Morning kisse
     p. 137 UNDERWOOD 2.6     t1 Clayming a second kisse by Desert.
     p. 138 UNDERWOOD 2.6     36 May not claime another kisse.
     p. 139 UNDERWOOD 2.7      1 For Loves-sake, kisse me once againe,
     p. 139 UNDERWOOD 2.7     11 This could be call'd but halfe a kisse.
     p. 193 UNDERWOOD 38      88 Streight puts off all his Anger, and doth kisse
     p. 201 UNDERWOOD 42      56 Or slipper was left off, and kisse it too,
     p. 208 UNDERWOOD 43     114 She durst not kisse, but flung thee from her
                                 brest.
     p. 232 UNDERWOOD 58      14 Their perfum'd judgements, let them kisse thy
                                 Wife.
     p. 283 U'WOOD 84.9       42 As spirits had stolne her Spirit, in a kisse,
     p. 294 UNDERWOOD 88       7 Let us together closely lie, and kisse,
     p. 375 UNGATHERED 10     19 For he did but kisse her, and so let her go.
     p. 662 INSCRIPTS. 2       9 But with a Kisse, (if thou canst dare it)
```

kissed. See "kist."

kisses   frequency: 2   relative frequency: 0.00002
```
     p. 136 UNDERWOOD 2.5     25 Have you plac'd the banke of kisses,
     p. 170 UNDERWOOD 19       9 And lastly by your lips, the banke of kisses,
```

kissing   frequency: 2   relative frequency: 0.00002
```
     p.  81 EPIGRAMS 128       5 May windes as soft as breath of kissing friends,
     p. 141 UNDERWOOD 2.9     22 And his lip should kissing teach,
```

kist   frequency: 1   relative frequency: 0.00001
```
     p.  87 EPIGRAMS 133     118 Stunke not so ill; nor, when shee kist, KATE
                                 ARDEN.
```

knat   frequency: 1   relative frequency: 0.00001
```
     p.  65 EPIGRAMS 101      20 Knat, raile, and ruffe too. How so ere, my man
```

knaue   frequency: 1   relative frequency: 0.00001
```
     p.  75 EPIGRAMS 115      34 Then, The townes honest Man's her errant'st
                                 knaue.
```

knaues   frequency: 1   relative frequency: 0.00001
```
     p.  84 EPIGRAMS 133      12 And in it, two more horride knaues, then
                                 CHARON.
```

knave   frequency: 1   relative frequency: 0.00001
See also "knaue."
```
     p.  46 EPIGRAMS 61       t1 TO FOOLE, OR KNAVE.
```

knaves. See "knaues."

kneel. See "kneele."

kneele   frequency: 1   relative frequency: 0.00001
     p. 382 UNGATHERED 16   2 hath armde att all poyntes; charge mee humblye
                                 kneele

kneeling   frequency: 1   relative frequency: 0.00001
     p. 133 UNDERWOOD 2.3   7 First, that I must kneeling yeeld

knees   frequency: 1   relative frequency: 0.00001
     p. 234 UNDERWOOD 61   13 Fit for a Bishops knees! O bow them oft,

knells   frequency: 1   relative frequency: 0.00001
     p. 89 EPIGRAMS 133   174 Of loud SEPVLCHRES with their hourely
                                 knells,

knew   frequency: 20   relative frequency: 0.00028
     See also "knewe."
   **p. 116 PANEGYRE   113 He knew that princes, who had sold their fame
   **p. 116 PANEGYRE   121 He knew, that those, who would, with loue,
                                 command,
     p. 72 EPIGRAMS 111   6 More, then to varie what our elders knew:
     p. 130 UNDERWOOD 1.3   14 The Sonnes obedience knew no No,
     p. 131 UNDERWOOD 2.1   15 That you never knew till now,
     p. 151 UNDERWOOD 12   12 A life that knew nor noise, nor strife:
     p. 153 UNDERWOOD 13   3 And knew their how, and where: we should have,
                                 then,
     p. 171 UNDERWOOD 20   9 Knew I all this afore? had I perceiv'd,
     p. 172 UNDERWOOD 20   13 Knew I, that all their Dialogues, and
                                 discourse,
     p. 172 UNDERWOOD 20   15 Knew I this Woman? yes; And you doe see,
     p. 187 UNDERWOOD 33   13 Thou art my Cause: whose manners since I knew,
     p. 231 UNDERWOOD 57   8 Knew the time, when
     p. 236 UNDERWOOD 64   1 How happy were the Subject, if he knew,
     p. 242 UNDERWOOD 69   23 Then knew the former ages: yet to life,
     p. 287 U'WOOD 84.9   155 And best he knew her noble Character,
     p. 315 HORACE 2   212 (As if he knew it) rapps his hearer to
     p. 319 HORACE 2   300 And in their numbers; For, alas, what knew
     p. 388 UNGATHERED 23   9 To the Greeke coast thine onely knew the way.
     p. 398 UNGATHERED 30   88 Then Affricke knew, or the full Grecian store!
     p. 410 UNGATHERED 38   14 That knew the Crafts they had bin bred in,
                                 right:

knewe   frequency: 1   relative frequency: 0.00001
     p. 419 UNGATHERED 48   3 As when they both were greate, and both knewe
                                 howe

knight   frequency: 7   relative frequency: 0.00010
     p. 28 EPIGRAMS 3   10 Who scarse can spell th'hard names: whose knight
                                 lesse can.
     p. 33 EPIGRAMS 19   1 That COD can get no widdow, yet a knight,
     p. 84 EPIGRAMS 133   4 With tales of Troyes iust knight, our faiths
                                 abuse:
     p. 214 UNDERWOOD 44   33 Well did thy craftie Clerke, and Knight, Sir
                                 Hugh,
     p. 272 UNDERWOOD 84   t6 late Wife of Sir KENELME DIGBY,
                                 Knight:
     p. 370 UNGATHERED 8   3 (Compos'd of Gamester, Captaine, Knight,
                                 Knight's man,
     p. 398 UNGATHERED 30   72 And will be bought of euery Lord, and Knight,

knight-hood   frequency: 3   relative frequency: 0.00004
     p. 42 EPIGRAMS 46   2 A knight-hood bought, to goe a wooing in?
     p. 42 EPIGRAMS 46   6 Yes, now he weares his knight-hood euery day.
     p. 205 UNDERWOOD 43   67 Of errant Knight-hood, with the<ir> Dames, and
                                 Dwarfes,

knight-wright's   frequency: 1   relative frequency: 0.00001
     p. 42 EPIGRAMS 46   5 The knight-wright's cheated then: Hee'll neuer
                                 pay.

knightes   frequency: 1   relative frequency: 0.00001
     p. 382 UNGATHERED 16   1 Two noble knightes, whome true desire and zeale,

knighthood. See "knight-hood."

knights   frequency: 2   relative frequency: 0.00002
     See also "knightes."
     p. 84 EPIGRAMS 133   22 And pitty 'tis, I cannot call 'hem knights:
     p. 331 HORACE 2   572 Vice, and, am knowne to have a Knights estate.

knight's   frequency: 1   relative frequency: 0.00001
See alsc "knights."
  p. 370 UNGATHERED 8   3 (Compos'd of Gamester, Captaine, Knight,
                               Knight's man,

knit   frequency: 6   relative frequency: 0.00008
  *p. 492 TO HIMSELF   3 Where pride, and impudence (in faction knit)
  p. 177 UNDERWOOD 25   19 Breake the knit Circle of her Stonie Armes,
  p. 222 UNDERWOOD 48   47 Whereby he may knit sure up
  p. 257 UNDERWOOD 75   133 And knit the Nuptiall knot,
  p. 412 UNGATHERED 41   12 To knit thy Crowne, and glorifie the rest.
  p. 416 UNGATHERED 44   4 Now, in a garland by the graces knit:

knits   frequency: 2   relative frequency: 0.00002
  p. 216 UNDERWOOD 45   12 'Tis vertue alone, or nothing, that knits
                         friends:
  p. 246 UNDERWOOD 70   106 That knits brave minds, and manners, more then
                         blood.

knock   frequency: 1   relative frequency: 0.00001
  p. 269 UNDERWOOD 83   9 Stiffe! starke! my joynts 'gainst one another
                         knock!

knot   frequency: 5   relative frequency: 0.00007
see "knat."
  p. 157 UNDERWOOD 13   152 Aloft, grow lesse and streightned, full of knot;
  p. 200 UNDERWOOD 42   16 There is not worne that lace, purle, knot or pin,
  p. 257 UNDERWOOD 75   133 And knit the Nuptiall knot,
  p. 317 HORACE 2   273 To have a God come in; except a knot
  p. 401 UNGATHERED 33   7 Who did this Knot compose,

knots   frequency: 4   relative frequency: 0.00005
  p. 110 FOREST 11   51 In equall knots: This beares no brands, nor
                         darts,
  p. 142 UNDERWOOD 2.9   50 Nor tie knots, nor knots unweave;
  p. 171 UNDERWOOD 20   12 But their whole inside full of ends, and knots?

knottie   frequency: 3   relative frequency: 0.00004
  p. 36 EPIGRAMS 31   1 BANCK feeles no lamenesse of his knottie
                         gout,
  p. 217 UNDERWOOD 46   17 Like Solons selfe; explat'st the knottie Lawes
  p. 363 UNGATHERED 3   8 The knottie heads of the most surly Groomes,

knotty. See "knottie."

know   frequency: 128   relative frequency: 0.00185
See alsc "knowe," "know't."
  **p. 115 PANEGYRE   85 "That princes, since they know it is their fate,
  p. 27 EPIGRAMS 2   8 And by thy wiser temper, let men know
  p. 31 EPIGRAMS 14   2 All that I am in arts, all that I know,
  p. 35 EPIGRAMS 26   1 Then his chast wife, though BEAST now know
                         no more,
  p. 38 EPIGRAMS 35   8 And than in them, how could we know god more?
  p. 40 EPIGRAMS 42   18 I know no couple better can agree!
  p. 43 EPIGRAMS 51   1 That we thy losse might know, and thou our loue,
  p. 45 EPIGRAMS 56   13 Foole, as if halfe eyes will not know a fleece
  p. 46 EPIGRAMS 62   3 The world reputes you barren: but I know
  p. 49 EPIGRAMS 66   7 Which deed I know not, whether were more high,
  p. 50 EPIGRAMS 70   7 Then, since we (more then many) these truths
                         know:
  p. 51 EPIGRAMS 73   4 The world must know your greatnesse is my debter.
  p. 51 EPIGRAMS 73   21 Fortie things more, deare GRAND, which you
                         know true,
  p. 51 EPIGRAMS 74   2 And know thee, then, a iudge, not of one yeare;
  p. 54 EPIGRAMS 81   2 A line vnto thee, till the world it know;
  p. 55 EPIGRAMS 84   7 I would haue spent: how euery Muse should know
                         it,
  p. 55 EPIGRAMS 86   1 When I would know thee GOODYERE, my
                         thought lookes
  p. 59 EPIGRAMS 92   8 They know the states of Christendome, not the
                         places:
  p. 59 EPIGRAMS 92   11 The councels, proiects, practises they know,
  p. 59 EPIGRAMS 92   29 To breake vp seales, and close 'hem. And they
                         know,
  p. 59 EPIGRAMS 92   40 That know not so much state, wrong, as they doo.
  p. 60 EPIGRAMS 93   11 Then whose I doe not know a whiter soule,
  p. 63 EPIGRAMS 97   9 Know you the cause? H'has neither land, nor
                         lease,
  p. 63 EPIGRAMS 98   2 And I know nothing more thou hast to doo.
  p. 65 EPIGRAMS 101   25 To this, if ought appeare, which I not know of,

know (cont.)

p.	66	EPIGRAMS	103	4 Know you to be a SYDNEY, though vn-nam'd?
p.	67	EPIGRAMS	104	14 A picture, which the world for yours must know,
p.	70	EPIGRAMS	109	12 And first to know thine owne state, then the States.
p.	75	EPIGRAMS	116	5 Thou wert the first, mad'st merit know her strength,
p.	76	EPIGRAMS	119	13 And, in their errors maze, thine owne way know:
p.	77	EPIGRAMS	120	3 And know, for whom a teare you shed,
p.	78	EPIGRAMS	121	4 Shee learnes to know long difference of their states.
p.	78	EPIGRAMS	122	2 The aged SATVRNE'S age, and rites to know;
p.	78	EPIGRAMS	123	2 I know not which th'hast most, candor, or wit:
p.	80	EPIGRAMS	127	11 And, than this same, I know no abler way
p.	80	EPIGRAMS	128	2 Countries, and climes, manners, and men to know,
p.	83	EPIGRAMS	131	10 Euen those for whom they doe this, know they erre:
p.	87	EPIGRAMS	133	105 But I will speake (and know I shall be heard)
p.	95	FOREST	2	60 With all, that hospitalitie doth know!
p.	100	FOREST	4	9 I know thy formes are studyed arts,
p.	100	FOREST	4	13 I know too, though thou strut, and paint,
p.	100	FOREST	4	17 I know thou whole art but a shop
p.	101	FOREST	4	39 I know thou canst nor shew, nor beare
p.	101	FOREST	4	61 No, I doe know, that I was borne
p.	103	FOREST	6	19 That the curious may not know
p.	105	FOREST	8	38 Euery stew in towne to know;
p.	109	FOREST	11	1 Not to know vice at all, and keepe true state,
p.	109	FOREST	11	3 Next, to that vertue, is to know vice well,
p.	111	FOREST	11	72 No, vice, we let thee know,
p.	114	FOREST	12	30 With you, I know, my offring will find grace.
p.	114	FOREST	12	37 Beautie, I know, is good, and bloud is more;
p.	118	FOREST	13	79 Them, or their officers: and no man know,
p.	122	FOREST	15	5 O, be thou witnesse, that the reynes dost know,
p.	122	FOREST	15	17 I know my state, both full of shame, and scorne,
p.	131	UNDERWOOD	2.1	18 When you know, that this is she,
p.	136	UNDERWOOD	2.5	18 By her lookes I doe her know,
p.	144	UNDERWOOD	3	20 On what they viewing know.
p.	147	UNDERWOOD	7	3 For if the Nymphs should know my Swaine,
p.	148	UNDERWOOD	7	32 From either heart, I know;
p.	153	UNDERWOOD	13	13 You cannot doubt, but I, who freely know
p.	156	UNDERWOOD	13	97 Sure there is Misterie in it, I not know,
p.	156	UNDERWOOD	13	109 And you, Sir, know it well, to whom I write,
p.	156	UNDERWOOD	13	114 I have the lyst of mine owne faults to know,
p.	156	UNDERWOOD	13	121 Ride, saile, am coach'd, know I how farre I have gone,
p.	156	UNDERWOOD	13	123 No! he must feele and know, that will advance.
p.	157	UNDERWOOD	13	129 Of Christendome! And neither of these know,
p.	157	UNDERWOOD	13	155 You know (without my flatt'ring you) too much
p.	158	UNDERWOOD	14	1 I know to whom I write. Here, I am sure,
p.	171	UNDERWOOD	19	20 I know no beautie, nor no youth that will.
p.	172	UNDERWOOD	20	17 Doe not you aske to know her, she is worse
p.	172	UNDERWOOD	21	1 Aske not to know this Man. If fame should speake
p.	176	UNDERWOOD	24	7 But both might know their wayes were understood,
p.	182	UNDERWOOD	28	8 Both braines and hearts; and mine now best doe know it:
p.	185	UNDERWOOD	30	1 If thou wouldst know the vertues of Man-kind,
p.	186	UNDERWOOD	32	11 Who, though their guilt, and perjurie they know,
p.	190	UNDERWOOD	37	19 Little know they, that professe Amitie,
p.	190	UNDERWOOD	37	22 And lesse they know, who being free to use
p.	191	UNDERWOOD	38	19 God, and the good, know to forgive, and save.
p.	200	UNDERWOOD	42	35 Of love, and hate: and came so nigh to know
p.	210	UNDERWOOD	43	157 Though but in daunces, it shall know his power;
p.	215	UNDERWOOD	44	70 All licence in our lives? What need we know,
p.	216	UNDERWOOD	45	14 No piece of money, but you know, or make
p.	218	UNDERWOOD	47	24 And know whose ignorance is more then theirs;
p.	220	UNDERWOOD	47	75 Are asked to climbe. First give me faith, who know
p.	221	UNDERWOOD	48	30 Before his braine doe know it;
p.	224	UNDERWOOD	50	22 Countries, and Climes, manners, and men to know.
p.	231	UNDERWOOD	56	26 Accept his Muse; and tell, I know you can,
p.	232	UNDERWOOD	57	26 the Parish will know it.
p.	233	UNDERWOOD	59	17 To know the heads of danger! where 'tis fit
p.	237	UNDERWOOD	64	21 Are lost upon accompt! And none will know
p.	241	UNDERWOOD	68	5 Well, they should know him, would the K<ing> but grant
p.	241	UNDERWOOD	69	3 Profit, or Chance had made us: But I know
p.	245	UNDERWOOD	70	78 And thinke, nay know, thy Morison's not dead.
p.	247	UNDERWOOD	70	107 This made you first to know the Why

know (cont.)

p. 257	UNDERWOOD 75	146	Some houres before it should, that these may know
p. 257	UNDERWOOD 75	156	Of Life, that fall so; Christians know their birth
p. 258	UNDERWOOD 75	192	The longing Couple, all that elder Lovers know.
p. 261	UNDERWOOD 77	13	But you I know, my Lord; and know you can
p. 261	UNDERWOOD 77	19	Of murmuring Subjects; make the Nations know
p. 262	UNDERWOOD 78	1	Tho', happy Muse, thou know my Digby well,
p. 263	UNDERWOOD 79	11	That know the times, and seasons when t<o>'appeare,
p. 265	UNDERWOOD 79	42	1. Wee know no other power then his,
p. 271	UNDERWOOD 83	76	Which they that have the Crowne are sure to know!
p. 274	U'WOOD 84.2	8	At either Stemme, and know the veines of good
p. 281	U'WOOD 84.4	70	Yet know, with what thou art possest,
p. 283	U'WOOD 84.9	29	Sure, I am dead, and know it not! I feele
p. 285	U'WOOD 84.9	91	And she doth know, out of the shade of Death,
p. 285	U'WOOD 84.9	115	And each shall know, there, one anothers face,
p. 288	U'WOOD 84.9	214	Of lapsed Nature) best know what to doe,
p. 294	UNDERWOOD 88	4	Like lustfull beasts, that onely know to doe it:
p. 305	HORACE 2	12	Of daring all, hath still beene given; we know it:
p. 311	HORACE 2	128	Nor know t<o>'observe: why (i'the Muses name)
p. 311	HORACE 2	131	To ignorance still, then either learne, or know?
p. 323	HORACE 2	402	If either you, or I, know the right way
p. 325	HORACE 2	441	Is to be wise; thy matter first to know;
p. 329	HORACE 2	504	The docile mind may soone thy precepts know,
p. 333	HORACE 2	605	I wonder how this happie man should know,
p. 365	UNGATHERED 5	24	Nor takes she pride to know them.
p. 369	UNGATHERED 6	97	But should they know (as I) that this,
p. 369	UNGATHERED 6	113	It is inough, their griefe shall know
p. 371	UNGATHERED 9	2	Read here a little, that thou mayst know much.
p. 386	UNGATHERED 20	11	I know for such, as (if my word will waigh)
p. 386	UNGATHERED 21	3	But I haue seene thy worke, and I know thee:
p. 394	UNGATHERED 28	13	But, I would haue, thee, to know something new,
p. 414	UNGATHERED 42	4	You know, I never was of Truth afeard,
p. 414	UNGATHERED 42	8	That sit to censure Playes, yet know not when,
p. 415	UNGATHERED 42	15	And know the woofe, and warpe thereof; can tell

knowe   frequency: 2   relative frequency: 0.00002

p. 404	UNGATHERED 34	60	His name is #Skeuopoios wee all knowe,
p. 409	UNGATHERED 37	13	Thou art not worth it. Who will care to knowe

knowes   frequency: 24   relative frequency: 0.00034

p. 35	EPIGRAMS 28	3	Makes serious vse of all great trade he knowes.
p. 61	EPIGRAMS 95	27	We need a man that knowes the seuerall graces
p. 66	EPIGRAMS 102	7	Almost, is exercis'd: and scarse one knowes,
p. 95	FOREST 2	70	He knowes, below, he shall finde plentie of meate,
p. 99	FOREST 3	98	He alwayes giues what he knowes meet;
p. 112	FOREST 11	103	Who could be false to? chiefly, when he knowes
p. 112	FOREST 11	113	That knowes the waight of guilt: He will refraine
p. 115	FOREST 12	67	Then which, a nobler heauen it selfe knowes not.
p. 155	UNDERWOOD 13	73	O, is it so? knowes he so much? and will
p. 161	UNDERWOOD 14	72	Thy learned Chamber-fellow, knowes to doe
p. 198	UNDERWOOD 40	37	Where he that knowes will, like a Lapwing, flie
p. 227	UNDERWOOD 52	21	He knowes he flatt'ring Colours, or false light.
p. 235	UNDERWOOD 61	17	Of riot, and consumption, knowes the way
p. 265	UNDERWOOD 79	64	PAN knowes no other power then his,
p. 284	U'WOOD 84.9	81	Hee knowes, what worke h'hath done, to call this Guest,
p. 286	U'WOOD 84.9	150	Who knowes the hearts of all, and can dissect
p. 307	HORACE 2	48	But in the maine worke haplesse: since he knowes
p. 315	HORACE 2	225	Fit rites. The Child, that now knowes how to say,
p. 315	HORACE 2	228	He knowes not why, and changeth every houre.
p. 325	HORACE 2	445	Hee, that hath studied well the debt, and knowes
p. 331	HORACE 2	553	Or knowes not what Cassellius Aulus can;
p. 331	HORACE 2	565	Hee, that not knowes the games, nor how to use
p. 335	HORACE 2	656	To let it downe, who knowes, if he did cast
p. 335	HORACE 2	670	His cause of making Verses none knowes why:

knowing   frequency: 7   relative frequency: 0.00010

**p. 116	PANEGYRE	128	In all these knowing artes our prince excell'd.
p. 34	EPIGRAMS 23	5	Longer a knowing, then most wits doe liue.
p. 75	EPIGRAMS 116	13	These were thy knowing arts: which who doth now
p. 100	FOREST 4	21	And, knowing this, should I yet stay,
p. 241	UNDERWOOD 68	4	For want of knowing the Poet, to say him nay?
p. 263	UNDERWOOD 78	28	The knowing Weston, and that learned Lord

knowing (cont.)
    p. 285 U'WOOD 84.9   97 And will you, worthy Sonne, Sir, knowing this,

knowledge   frequency: 12   relative frequency: 0.00017
    p. 32 EPIGRAMS 18   10 Thy faith is all the knowledge that thou hast.
    p. 55 EPIGRAMS 85   6 That they to knowledge so should toure vpright,
    p. 55 EPIGRAMS 86   8 It was a knowledge, that begat that loue.
    p. 61 EPIGRAMS 95   21 Whose knowledge claymeth at the helme to stand;
    p. 109 FOREST 11   12 Giue knowledge instantly,
    p. 159 UNDERWOOD 14   33 Of generall knowledge; watch'd men, manners too,
    p. 161 UNDERWOOD 14   76 In the same Mines of knowledge; and thence
                             brought
    p. 174 UNDERWOOD 23   3 Knowledge, that sleepes, doth die;
    p. 217 UNDERWOOD 46   20 Of worthiest knowledge, that can take mens minds.
    p. 225 UNDERWOOD 50   29 Searching for knowledge, and to keepe your mind
    p. 273 U'WOOD 84.4   19 Our sense you doe with knowledge fill,
    p. 331 HORACE 2   573 Thou, such thy judgement is, thy knowledge too,

known. See "farre-knowne," "fore-knowne," "knowne."

knowne   frequency: 30   relative frequency: 0.00043
  **p. 113 PANEGYRE   25 To be her daughters: and but faintly knowne
  **p. 114 PANEGYRE   36 As if they felt, but had not knowne their good:
    p. 42 EPIGRAMS 49   5 PLAY-WRIGHT, I loath to haue thy
                             manners knowne
    p. 46 EPIGRAMS 60   9 My countries parents I haue many knowne;
    p. 58 EPIGRAMS 91   14 Nor lesse in practice; but lesse mark'd, lesse
                             knowne:
    p. 62 EPIGRAMS 97   6 By his each glorious parcell to be knowne!
    p. 74 EPIGRAMS 115   6 About the towne; and knowne too, at that price.
    p. 80 EPIGRAMS 128   3 T<o>'extract, and choose the best of all these
                             knowne,
    p. 82 EPIGRAMS 130   3 Which Musick had; or speake her knowne effects,
    p. 96 FOREST 2   92 A fortune, in this age, but rarely knowne.
    p. 101 FOREST 4   29 What bird, or beast, is knowne so dull,
    p. 104 FOREST 7   10 But grant vs perfect, they're not knowne.
    p. 114 FOREST 12   50 Haue beautie knowne, yet none so famous seene?
    p. 147 UNDERWOOD 7   5 Yet if it be not knowne,
    p. 147 UNDERWOOD 7   20 Yet, yet I doubt he is not knowne,
    p. 154 UNDERWOOD 13 48 Well knowne, and practiz'd borrowers on their
                             word,
    p. 168 UNDERWOOD 15 194 More honour in him, 'cause we'<h>ave knowne him
                             mad:
    p. 171 UNDERWOOD 20   6 That ne're was knowne to last above a fit!
    p. 176 UNDERWOOD 24 16 By which as proper titles, she is knowne
    p. 183 UNDERWOOD 29 13 Soone as lazie thou wert knowne,
    p. 201 UNDERWOOD 42 39 Whose like I have knowne the Taylors Wife put
                             on
    p. 225 UNDERWOOD 50 34 So are they profitable to be knowne:
    p. 225 UNDERWOOD 51 17 'Tis a brave cause of joy, let it be knowne,
    p. 271 UNDERWOOD 83 93 T<o>'escape this common knowne necessitie,
    p. 287 U'WOOD 84.9 162 T'have knowne no envy, but by suffring it!
    p. 321 HORACE 2   349 I can out of knowne geare, a fable frame,
    p. 331 HORACE 2   572 Vice, and, am knowne to have a Knights estate.
    p. 368 UNGATHERED 6 66 The Hebrid Isles, and knowne
    p. 379 UNGATHERED 12 11 Which, vnto all Ages, for his will be knowne,
    p. 408 UNGATHERED 37 9 To be knowne what thou art, a blatant beast,

knows. See "knowes."

know'st   frequency: 3   relative frequency: 0.00004
    p. 36 EPIGRAMS 30   1 GVILTIE, be wise; and though thou know'st
                             the crimes
    p. 85 EPIGRAMS 133 51 Thou hast seene hell (some say) and know'st all
                             nookes there,
    p. 305 HORACE 2   25 Know'st only well to paint a Cipresse tree.

know't   frequency: 1   relative frequency: 0.00001
    p. 68 EPIGRAMS 107   3 I oft looke on false coyne, to know't from true:

kyd. See "kii."

kynde   frequency: 1   relative frequency: 0.00001
    p. 403 UNGATHERED 34 26 Noe veluet Sheath you weare, will alter kynde.

l.   frequency: 5   relative frequency: 0.00007
    p. 79 EPIGRAMS 124 t1 EPITAPH ON ELIZABETH, L. H.
    p. 233 UNDERWOOD 60 t2 L. La-ware.
    p. 250 UNDERWOOD 73 t2 Weston, L. high Treasurer of England,
    p. 250 UNDERWOOD 74 t1 To the Right honble Hierome, L. Weston.

l. (cont.)
   p. 268 UNDERWOOD 82   t1 To my L. the King,

la-ware   frequency: 2   relative frequency: 0.00002
   p. 233 UNDERWOOD 60   3 Henry, the brave young Lord La-ware,
   p. 233 UNDERWOOD 60   t2 L. La-ware.

labors   frequency: 1   relative frequency: 0.00001
   p. 361 UNGATHERED 1   22 of thy rich labors worlds of thoughts created,

labour   frequency: 7   relative frequency: 0.00010
   p. 122 FOREST 15   18 Conceiu'd in sinne, and vnto labour borne,
   p. 190 UNDERWOOD 37   28 From each of which I labour to be free,
   p. 222 UNDERWOOD 49   14 Doth labour with the Phrase more then the sense?
   p. 294 UNDERWOOD 88   8 There is no labour, nor no shame in this;
   p. 307 HORACE 2   35 My selfe for shortnesse labour; and I grow
   p. 315 HORACE 2   240 What straight-way he must labour to retract.
   p. 321 HORACE 2   343 Meere raigning words: nor will I labour so

labour'd   frequency: 5   relative frequency: 0.00007
   p. 48 EPIGRAMS 64   15 These (noblest CECIL) labour'd in my
                             thought,
   p. 185 UNDERWOOD 30   12 And labour'd in the worke; not with the fame:
   p. 295 UNDERWOOD 90   3 Not labour'd for, but left thee by thy Sire;
   p. 335 HORACE 2   661 Hee, while he labour'd to be thought a God
   p. 420 UNGATHERED 48   22 Their labour'd tunes reherse,

labouring   frequency: 2   relative frequency: 0.00002
   p. 307 HORACE 2   30 Thy labouring wheele, comes scarce a Pitcher
                             out?
   p. 341 HORACE 1   140 ... ... the labouring ....

labours   frequency: 8   relative frequency: 0.00011
   See also "labors," "yeares-labours."
   p. 56 EPIGRAMS 88   10 The french disease, with which he labours yet?
   p. 71 EPIGRAMS 110   12 Can so speake CAESAR, as thy labours doe.
   p. 85 EPIGRAMS 133   56 Still, with thy former labours; yet, once more,
   p. 89 EPIGRAMS 133   181 Is now from home. You lose your labours quite,
   p. 107 FOREST 10   5 With his old earthly labours. T<o>'exact more,
   p. 217 UNDERWOOD 46   18 With endlesse labours, whilst thy learning drawes
   p. 329 HORACE 2   500 Of their long labours, was in Verse set downe:
   p. 407 UNGATHERED 36   2 (And labours to seem worthy of yt feare)

lace   frequency: 7   relative frequency: 0.00010
   p. 137 UNDERWOOD 2.5   30 With the Lace that doth it deck,
   p. 140 UNDERWOOD 2.8   19 And pronounce, which band, or lace,
   p. 163 UNDERWOOD 15   49 His Lace and Starch; And fall upon her back
   p. 200 UNDERWOOD 42   16 There is not worne that lace, purle, knot or pin,
   p. 201 UNDERWOOD 42   66 That chanc'd the lace, laid on a Smock, to see,
   p. 202 UNDERWOOD 42   79 The Stuffes, the Velvets, Plushes, Fringes,
                             Lace,
   p. 275 U'WOOD 84.3   3 Embroderies, Feathers, Fringes, Lace,

laces   frequency: 1   relative frequency: 0.00001
   p. 223 UNDERWOOD 49   28 To stuffes and Laces, those my Man can buy.

lack   frequency: 4   relative frequency: 0.00005
   See also "lacke."
   p. 229 UNDERWOOD 54   12 Full twentie stone; of which I lack two pound:
   p. 241 UNDERWOOD 68   11 As the old Bard, should no Canary lack.
   p. 254 UNDERWOOD 75   46 As she did lack
   p. 374 UNGATHERED 10   15 It should rather haue bene Tom that a horse did
                             lack.

lack'd   frequency: 2   relative frequency: 0.00002
   p. 75 EPIGRAMS 116   6 And those that lack'd it, to suspect at length,
   p. 115 FOREST 12   56 Because they lack'd the sacred pen, could giue

lack'dst   frequency: 1   relative frequency: 0.00001
   p. 43 EPIGRAMS 52   4 As if thou wert my friend, but lack'dst a cause.

lacke   frequency: 1   relative frequency: 0.00001
   p. 121 FOREST 14   27 Since he doth lacke

lacks   frequency: 1   relative frequency: 0.00001
   p. 59 EPIGRAMS 92   14 For twelue yeeres yet to come, what each state
                             lacks.

lad   frequency: 1   relative frequency: 0.00001
   p. 317 HORACE 2   248 Of the times past, when he was a young lad;

ladder   frequency: 1   relative frequency: 0.00001
    p. 274 U'WOOD 84.1   38 By JACOBS Ladder, to the top

laden   frequency: 4   relative frequency: 0.00005
    p.   84 EPIGRAMS 133   17 Laden with plague-sores, and their sinnes, were
                              heard,
    p.   98 FOREST 3   42 And furrowes laden with their weight;
    p. 122 FOREST 15   4 That, laden with my sinnes, I seeke for ease?
    p. 230 UNDERWOOD 56   9 Laden with Bellie, and doth hardly approach

ladie   frequency: 4   relative frequency: 0.00005
    p. 222 UNDERWOOD 48   54 And Charles brings home the Ladie.
    p. 365 UNGATHERED 5   18 In thought to praise this Ladie;
    p. 394 UNGATHERED 28   t1 To ye memorye of that most honoured Ladie Jane,
    p. 400 UNGATHERED 31   33 For this did Katherine, Ladie Ogle, die

ladies   frequency: 7   relative frequency: 0.00010
    See also "ladyes."
    p.   57 EPIGRAMS 90   5 The nicer thing to tast her ladies page;
    p.   57 EPIGRAMS 90   t1 ON MILL MY LADIES WOMAN.
    p.   57 EPIGRAMS 90   10 And he growne youth, was call'd to his ladies
                              chamber.
    p.   94 FOREST 2   18 The lighter Faunes, to reach the Ladies oke.
    p. 104 FOREST 8   2 Ladies? and of them the best?
    p. 108 FOREST 10   25 Nor all the ladies of the Thespian lake,
    p. 165 UNDERWOOD 15   94 Lives to the Lord, but to the Ladies end.

lads   frequency: 1   relative frequency: 0.00001
    p. 315 HORACE 2   226 And can tread firme, longs with like lads to
                              play;

lady   frequency: 32   relative frequency: 0.00046
    See also "ladie," "lady's."
    p.   46 EPIGRAMS 62   t1 TO FINE LADY WOVLD-BEE.
    p.   66 EPIGRAMS 103   t1 TO MARY LADY WRO"H.
    p.   67 EPIGRAMS 105   t1 TO MARY LADY WROTH.
    p.   80 EPIGRAMS 126   t1 TO HIS LADY, THEN Mrs. CARY.
    p.   95 FOREST 2   50 Thy lord, and lady, though they haue no sute.
    p.   95 FOREST 2   84 On thy good lady, then! who, therein, reap'd
    p. 116 FOREST 13   t2 TO KATHERINE, LADY AVBIGNY.
    p. 117 FOREST 13   26 No lady, but, at some time, loues her glasse.
    p. 134 UNDERWOOD 2.4   2 Wherein my Lady rideth!
    p. 138 UNDERWOOD 2.6   25 So to see a Lady tread,
    p. 164 UNDERWOOD 15   76 Doe all the tricks of a saut Lady Bitch;
    p. 164 UNDERWOOD 15   82 Of woman of fashion, and a Lady of spirit:
    p. 182 UNDERWOOD 28   t2 To the noble Lady, the Lady
    p. 201 UNDERWOOD 42   70 The Lady Mayresse pass'd in through the Towne,
    p. 230 UNDERWOOD 56   t2 To my Lady COVELL.
    p. 252 UNDERWOOD 75   t8 with the Lady
    p. 253 UNDERWOOD 75   37 The Lady Frances, drest
    p. 262 UNDERWOOD 78   t2 To my MVSE, the Lady Digby, on her
    p. 268 UNDERWOOD 83   t2 On the Lady JANE PAWLET,
    p. 269 UNDERWOOD 83   19 Shee was the Lady Jane, and Marchionisse
    p. 272 UNDERWOOD 84   t5 Of that truly-noble Lady, the Lady
                              VENETIA DIGBY,
    p. 282 U'WOOD 84.9   t2 The truly honoured Lady, the Lady
                              VENETIA DIGBY;
    p. 285 U'WOOD 84.9   99 A Wife, a Friend, a Lady, or a Love;
    p. 313 HORACE 2   164 Where some great Lady, or her diligent Nourse;
    p. 370 UNGATHERED 8   4 Lady, or Pusil, that weares maske, or fan,
    p. 394 UNGATHERED 28   14 Not vsuall in a Lady; and yet true:
    p. 394 UNGATHERED 28   15 At least so great a Lady. She was wife
    p. 403 UNGATHERED 34   35 Th'ascent of Lady Fame which none could spy
    p. 418 UNGATHERED 47   2 The Paltzgrave, and the Lady Besse,

lady-aire   frequency: 1   relative frequency: 0.00001
    p. 287 U'WOOD 84.9   164 Not tost or troubled with light Lady-aire;

ladyes   frequency: 4   relative frequency: 0.00005
    p. 142 U'WOOD 2.10   t1 Another Ladyes exception present at the hearing.
    p. 207 UNDERWOOD 43   97 To our owne Ladyes; and in storie there
    p. 225 UNDERWOOD 50   31 These Graces, when the rest of Ladyes view
    p. 230 UNDERWOOD 56   16 Run all the Rounds in a soft Ladyes eare,

lady's   frequency: 1   relative frequency: 0.00001
    See also "ladies," "ladyes."
    p.   96 FOREST 2   90 Thy lady's noble, fruitfull, chaste withall.

laid   frequency: 10   relative frequency: 0.00014
    See also "layd."

laid (cont.)
<table>
<tr><td>p.</td><td>47 EPIGRAMS 64</td><td>6</td><td>To see thy fathers rites new laid on thee.</td></tr>
<tr><td>p.</td><td>130 UNDERWOOD 1.3</td><td>12</td><td>Was now laid in a Manger.</td></tr>
<tr><td>p.</td><td>138 UNDERWOOD 2.6</td><td>7</td><td>If by us, the oddes were laid,</td></tr>
<tr><td>p.</td><td>153 UNDERWOOD 13</td><td>9</td><td>Not at my prayers, but your sense; which laid</td></tr>
<tr><td>p.</td><td>201 UNDERWOOD 42</td><td>66</td><td>That chanc'd the lace, laid on a Smock, to see,</td></tr>
<tr><td>p.</td><td>282 U'WOOD 84.9</td><td>11</td><td>O! had I seene her laid out a faire Corse,</td></tr>
<tr><td>p.</td><td>283 U'WOOD 84.9</td><td>45</td><td>Indeed, she is not dead! but laid to sleepe</td></tr>
<tr><td>p.</td><td>317 HORACE 2</td><td>272</td><td>Have more or lesse then just five Acts: nor laid,</td></tr>
<tr><td>p.</td><td>412 UNGATHERED 41</td><td>7</td><td>Is so implexed, and laid in, between,</td></tr>
<tr><td>p.</td><td>413 UNGATHERED 41</td><td>18</td><td>But lowlie laid, as on the earth asleep,</td></tr>
</table>

laies   frequency: 1   relative frequency: 0.00001
    p. 292 UNDERWOOD 86   25 There twice a day in sacred Laies,

lake   frequency: 4   relative frequency: 0.00005
    p. 108 FOREST 10   25 Nor all the ladies of the Thespian lake,
    p. 292 UNDERWOOD 86   20 Beneath a Sweet-wood Roofe, neere Alba Lake:
    p. 368 UNGATHERED 6   72 To Loumond lake, and Twedes blacke-springing
                             fountaine.
    p. 406 UNGATHERED 34 94 Vermilion, Lake, or Cinnopar affoards

lamb   frequency: 1   relative frequency: 0.00001
    See also "lambe."
    p. 285 U'WOOD 84.9   89 That, planted round, there sing before the Lamb,

lambe   frequency: 2   relative frequency: 0.00002
    p. 291 UNDERWOOD 85   59 Or at the Feast of Bounds, the Lambe then
                             slaine,
    p. 400 UNGATHERED 31 36 Her right, by gift, and purchase of the Lambe:

lambes   frequency: 2   relative frequency: 0.00002
    p. 265 UNDERWOOD 79   50 Your Milkes, your Fells, your Fleeces, and
                             first Lambes,
    p. 305 HORACE 2   16 With Doves; or Lambes, with Tygres coupled be.

lambeth. See "mersh-lambeth."

lambs   frequency: 1   relative frequency: 0.00001
    See also "lambes."
    p. 264 UNDERWOOD 79   16 3. Our milke. 4. Our fells. 5. Our fleeces. 6.
                             And first Lambs.

lame   frequency: 2   relative frequency: 0.00002
    p. 190 UNDERWOOD 37   21 How much they lame her in her propertie.
    p. 202 UNDERWOOD 43   1 And why to me this, thou lame Lord of fire,

lamenesse   frequency: 1   relative frequency: 0.00001
    p. 36 EPIGRAMS 31   1 BANCK feeles no lamenesse of his knottie
                             gout,

lament   frequency: 1   relative frequency: 0.00001
    p. 41 EPIGRAMS 45   6 Will man lament the state he should enuie?

laments   frequency: 1   relative frequency: 0.00001
    p. 309 HORACE 2   107 In Verse unequall match'd, first sowre Laments,

lamia   frequency: 1   relative frequency: 0.00001
    See also "lamia'has."
    p. 398 UNGATHERED 30 87 Empusa, Lamia, or some Monster, more

lamia'has   frequency: 1   relative frequency: 0.00001
    p. 329 HORACE 2   510 The Child, when Lamia'has din'd, out of her
                             maw.

lamp. See "lampe."

lampe   frequency: 1   relative frequency: 0.00001
    p. 115 FOREST 12   61 Who made a lampe of BERENICES hayre?

lance   frequency: 3   relative frequency: 0.00004
    p. 240 UNDERWOOD 67   39 Upon his pointed Lance:
    p. 270 UNDERWOOD 83   54 Your hottest Causticks to, burne, lance, or cut:
    p. 392 UNGATHERED 26 69 In each of which, he seemes to shake a Lance,

lancelots. See "lanc'lots."

lances. See "launces."

lanc'lots   frequency: 1   relative frequency: 0.00001
    p. 206 UNDERWOOD 43   69 The Tristrams, Lanc'lots, Turpins, and the
                                 Peers,

land   frequency: 28   relative frequency: 0.00040
    See also "in-land."
  **p. 117 PANEGYRE   156 Neuer had land more reason to reioyce.
    p. 38 EPIGRAMS 35   10 And since, the whole land was preseru'd for thee.
    p. 56 EPIGRAMS 88   5 And land on one, whose face durst neuer bee
    p. 63 EPIGRAMS 97   9 Know you the cause? H'has neither land, nor
                                 lease,
    p. 69 EPIGRAMS 107   16 For which there must more sea, and land be
                                 leap'd,
    p. 75 EPIGRAMS 117   2 For'his whore: GROYNE doth still occupy his
                                 land.
    p. 94 FOREST 2   22 The lower land, that to the riuer bends,
    p. 94 FOREST 2   37 Bright eeles, that emulate them, and leape on
                                 land,
    p. 105 FOREST 8   29 That distill their husbands land
    p. 118 FOREST 13   73 Melt downe their husbands land, to poure away
    p. 154 UNDERWOOD 13   55 As farre as any poore Sword i' the Land.
    p. 155 UNDERWOOD 13   81 All as their prize, turne Pyrats here at Land,
    p. 167 UNDERWOOD 15   174 Though thou wert Muster-master of the Land.
    p. 169 UNDERWOOD 17   16 All is not barren land, doth fallow lie.
    p. 185 UNDERWOOD 30   19 Of all the Land. Who now at such a Rate,
    p. 198 UNDERWOOD 40   35 Like the dull wearied Crane that (come on land)
    p. 215 UNDERWOOD 44   76 In so much land a yeare, or such a Banke,
    p. 216 UNDERWOOD 45   26 It is a richer Purchase then of land.
    p. 234 UNDERWOOD 61   11 T<o>'obtaine of God, what all the Land should
                                 aske?
    p. 240 UNDERWOOD 67   53 Hath brought the Land an Heire!
    p. 250 UNDERWOOD 73   4 Hath rais'd to be the Port unto his Land!
    p. 251 UNDERWOOD 74   30 And both a strength, and Beautie to his Land!
    p. 254 UNDERWOOD 75   50 The choisest Virgin-troup of all the Land!
    p. 268 UNDERWOOD 82   15 At land she triumphs in the triple shade,
    p. 313 HORACE 2   166 Of some small thankfull land: whether he bee
    p. 333 HORACE 2   599 So doth the Poet, who is rich in land,
    p. 368 UNGATHERED 6   75 But ouer Land to Trent:
    p. 375 UNGATHERED 10   32 And here he disdained not, in a forraine land

lands   frequency: 2   relative frequency: 0.00002
    p. 289 UNDERWOOD 85   3 With his owne Oxen tills his Sires left lands,
    p. 290 UNDERWOOD 85   22 And, Sylvane, thine, that keptst his Lands!

lane   frequency: 3   relative frequency: 0.00004
    See also "fleet-lane."
    p. 241 UNDERWOOD 69   12 All live dogs from the lane, and his shops sight,
    p. 262 UNDERWOOD 78   12 As other soules, to his, dwell in a Lane:
    p. 407 UNGATHERED 35   12 Thou paint a Lane, where Thumb ye Pygmy meets!

langley   frequency: 1   relative frequency: 0.00001
    p. 403 UNGATHERED 34   22 you'l be as Langley sayd, an Inigo still.

language   frequency: 16   relative frequency: 0.00023
    p. 34 EPIGRAMS 23   7 To it, thy language, letters, arts, best life,
    p. 42 EPIGRAMS 49   4 For wittie, in his language, is obscene.
    p. 131 UNDERWOOD 2.1   10 But the Language, and the Truth,
    p. 149 UNDERWOOD 9   6 I'm sure my language to her, was as sweet,
    p. 207 UNDERWOOD 43   93 The puritie of Language; and among
    p. 215 UNDERWOOD 44   72 The Hawking language? or our Day to breake
    p. 223 UNDERWOOD 49   26 For bawdry, 'tis her language, and not mine.
    p. 257 UNDERWOOD 75   160 But dare not aske our wish in Language
                                 fescennine:
    p. 271 UNDERWOOD 83   71 Speakes Heavens Language! and discourseth free
    p. 307 HORACE 2   58 Nor language, nor cleere order ere forsakes.
    p. 309 HORACE 2   82 And wealth unto our language; and brought forth
    p. 311 HORACE 2   149 Sad language fits sad lookes; stuff'd menacings,
    p. 319 HORACE 2   308 Unwonted language; and that sense of worth
    p. 325 HORACE 2   413 Her language, if the Stay, and Care t'have
                                 mended,
    p. 371 UNGATHERED 9   7 Taught Pallas language; Cynthia modesty;
    p. 402 UNGATHERED 33   14 To make the Language sweet vpon her tongue.

languages   frequency: 1   relative frequency: 0.00001
    p. 184 UNDERWOOD 29   43 Vulgar Languages that want

languish   frequency: 2   relative frequency: 0.00002
    p. 294 UNDERWOOD 88   5 For lust will languish, and that heat decay.
    p. 370 UNGATHERED 7   10 The seuerall figures, languish in suspence,

languishing   frequency: 1   relative frequency: 0.00001
    p. 87 EPIGRAMS 133   136 Whether it languishing stucke vpon the wall,

lantern.   See "dark-lanterne," "lanterne-lerry,"
           "lantherne," "lanthorne."

lanterne-lerry   frequency: 1   relative frequency: 0.00001
    p. 405 UNGATHERED 34   72 Of Lanterne-lerry: wth fuliginous heat

lantherne   frequency: 1   relative frequency: 0.00001
    p. 93 FOREST 2   4 Thou hast no lantherne, whereof tales are told;

lanthorne   frequency: 2   relative frequency: 0.00002
    p. 203 UNDERWOOD 43   10 And Mars, that gave thee a Lanthorne for a
                             Crowne.
    p. 211 UNDERWOOD 43 187 Or in the Bell-Mans Lanthorne, like a spie,

lapland   frequency: 1   relative frequency: 0.00001
    p. 398 UNGATHERED 30   86 Thou hadst brought Lapland, or old Cobalus,

lapsed   frequency: 1   relative frequency: 0.00001
    p. 288 U'WOOD 84.9   214 Of lapsed Nature) best know what to doe,

lapwing   frequency: 1   relative frequency: 0.00001
    p. 198 UNDERWOOD 40   37 Where he that knowes will, like a Lapwing, flie

larding   frequency: 1   relative frequency: 0.00001
   *p. 493 TO HIMSELF   36 Of larding your large eares

large   frequency: 16   relative frequency: 0.00023
   *p. 493 TO HIMSELF   36 Of larding your large eares
    p. 83 EPIGRAMS 131   7 For, if the hum'rous world will talke at large,
    p. 160 UNDERWOOD 14   64 Large claspe of Nature, such a wit can bound.
    p. 205 UNDERWOOD 43   62 Had tickled your large Nosthrill: many a Reame
    p. 227 UNDERWOOD 52   23 A letter'd mind, and a large heart would place
    p. 236 UNDERWOOD 63   5 Hee can, he will, and with large int'rest pay,
    p. 236 UNDERWOOD 63   12 With a long, large, and blest posteritie!
    p. 250 UNDERWOOD 73   3 In his great Actions: view whom his large hand
    p. 253 UNDERWOOD 75   19 Doe boast their Loves, and Brav'ries so at
                             large,
    p. 258 UNDERWOOD 75 176 How each one playes his part, of the large
                             Pedigree.
    p. 259 UNDERWOOD 76   11 A large hundred Markes annuitie,
    p. 261 UNDERWOOD 77   21 And mightiest Monarchs feele what large increase
    p. 262 UNDERWOOD 78   11 Where Nature such a large survey hath ta'en,
    p. 269 UNDERWOOD 83   15 It is a large faire table, and a true,
    p. 282 U'WOOD 84.8   20 Hang all your roomes, with one large Pedigree:
    p. 378 UNGATHERED 11 82 Of trauell he discourseth so at large,

largely   frequency: 1   relative frequency: 0.00001
    p. 44 EPIGRAMS 55   6 And giuing largely to me, more thou tak'st.

larkes   frequency: 1   relative frequency: 0.00001
    p. 65 EPIGRAMS 101   16 The skie not falling, thinke we may haue larkes.

larks.   See "larkes."

larum   frequency: 1   relative frequency: 0.00001
    p. 109 FOREST 11   23 (That should ring larum to the heart) doth
                             sleepe,

lash'd   frequency: 1   relative frequency: 0.00001
    p. 84 EPIGRAMS 133   18 Lash'd by their consciences, to die, affeard.

'lasse   frequency: 1   relative frequency: 0.00001
    p. 202 UNDERWOOD 42   74 Another answers, 'Lasse, those Silkes are none,

last   frequency: 46   relative frequency: 0.00066
    See also "out-last."
  **p. 114 PANEGYRE   65 Old men were glad, their fates till now did last;
    p. 45 EPIGRAMS 58   1 IDEOT, last night, I pray'd thee but
                             forbeare
    p. 57 EPIGRAMS 90   4 At last, ease, appetite, and example wan
    p. 58 EPIGRAMS 91   8 Whose rellish to eternitie shall last.
    p. 85 EPIGRAMS 133   57 Act a braue worke, call it thy last aduentry:
    p. 88 EPIGRAMS 133 162 Thrise did it spit: thrise diu'd. At last, it
                             view'd
    p. 89 EPIGRAMS 133 186 The tripple head without a sop. At last,
    p. 93 FOREST 3   43 The apple-haruest, that doth longer last;

last (cont.)

p. 113	FOREST 12	17	Solders crackt friendship; makes loue last a day;
p. 122	FOREST 15	10	First, midst, and last, conuerted one, and three;
p. 139	UNDERWOOD 2.7	13	I will but mend the last, and tell
p. 140	UNDERWOOD 2.8	27	Be as good, as was the last:
p. 145	UNDERWOOD 5	11	Wee shall, at last, of parcells make
p. 155	UNDERWOOD 13	63	Their bounties forth, to him that last was made,
p. 157	UNDERWOOD 13	136	We must accomplish; 'Tis the last Key-stone
p. 157	UNDERWOOD 13	144	As they are high; are rooted, and will last.
p. 157	UNDERWOOD 13	153	And last, goe out in nothing: You that see
p. 162	UNDERWOOD 15	17	To gaine upon his belly; and at last
p. 165	UNDERWOOD 15	109	From Hide-Parke to the Stage, where at the last
p. 167	UNDERWOOD 15	161	And be belov'd, while the Whores last. O times,
p. 168	UNDERWOOD 15	191	And last, blaspheme not, we did never heare
p. 168	UNDERWOOD 16	3	But here doth lie, till the last Day,
p. 171	UNDERWOOD 20	6	That ne're was knowne to last above a fit!
p. 185	UNDERWOOD 31	t3	the last Terme he sate Chancellor.
p. 191	UNDERWOOD 38	14	Looke forth, but cannot last in such <a> forme.
p. 192	UNDERWOOD 38	43	That as the last of punishments is meant;
p. 213	UNDERWOOD 44	6	For they did see it the last tilting well,
p. 213	UNDERWOOD 44	22	How it held out! how (last) 'twas taken in!
p. 216	UNDERWOOD 45	20	They cannot last. No lie grew ever old.
p. 244	UNDERWOOD 70	45	Hee stood, a Souldier to the last right end,
p. 245	UNDERWOOD 70	68	To fall a logge at last, dry, bald, and seare:
p. 258	UNDERWOOD 75	168	(After the last child borne;) This is our wedding day.
p. 258	UNDERWOOD 75	190	Will last till day;
p. 259	UNDERWOOD 76	24	But we last out, still unlay'd.
p. 261	UNDERWOOD 77	28	Aloud; and (happ'ly) it may last as long.
p. 270	UNDERWOOD 83	61	And, in her last act, taught the Standers-by,
p. 276	U'WOOD 84.3	25	Last, draw the circles of this Globe,
p. 283	U'WOOD 84.9	46	In earth, till the last Trumpe awake the Sheepe
p. 286	U'WOOD 84.9	124	A Musique in the Eares, will ever last;
p. 289	U'WOOD 84.9	219	The last of houres, and shutter up of all;
p. 313	HORACE 2	181	Unto the last, as when he first went forth,
p. 315	HORACE 2	218	The last doth from the midst dis-joyn'd appeare.
p. 323	HORACE 2	374	But meere Iambicks all, from first to last.
p. 333	HORACE 2	595	Him that is last, I scorne to come behind,
p. 361	UNGATHERED 1	19	still making that the greatest that is last
p. 394	UNGATHERED 28	22	So wood at last, that he was wonne to her

lasted   frequency: 1   relative frequency: 0.00001
    p. 65 EPIGRAMS 101   32 Their liues, as doe their lines, till now had
                              lasted.

lasteth   frequency: 1   relative frequency: 0.00001
    p. 179 UNDERWOOD 25   47 As patience lasteth.

lasting   frequency: 3   relative frequency: 0.00004
    See also "euer-lasting."
    p. 111 FOREST 11   58 And lasting, as her flowers:
    p. 309 HORACE 2   100 Or grace of speech, should hope a lasting date.
    p. 384 UNGATHERED 18   8 And pray, thy ioyes as lasting bee, as great.

lastly   frequency: 1   relative frequency: 0.00001
    p. 170 UNDERWOOD 19   9 And lastly by your lips, the banke of kisses,

lasts.   See "out-lasts."

late   frequency: 30   relative frequency: 0.00043
  **p. 114 PANEGYRE   49 And as of late, when he through London went,
    p. 33 EPIGRAMS 21   6 The late tane bastinado. So I thought.
    p. 36 EPIGRAMS 29   3 For thy late sharpe deuice. I say 'tis fit
    p. 38 EPIGRAMS 38   1 GVILTIE, because I bad you late be wise,
    p. 45 EPIGRAMS 58   6 Then thou did'st late my sense, loosing my
                              points.
    p. 50 EPIGRAMS 70   1 When Nature bids vs leaue to liue, 'tis late
    p. 54 EPIGRAMS 84   1 MADAME, I told you late how I repented,
    p. 72 EPIGRAMS 111   12 CAESAR stands vp, as from his vrne late
                              rose,
    p. 77 EPIGRAMS 120   19 But viewing him since (alas, too late)
    p. 87 EPIGRAMS 133   108 Of the graue fart, late let in parliament,
    p. 87 EPIGRAMS 133   125 About the shore, of farts, but late departed,
    p. 95 FOREST 2   76 That found King IAMES, when hunting late,
                              this way,
    p. 100 FOREST 9   9 I sent thee, late, a rosie wreath,
    p. 133 UNDERWOOD 2.3   20 But the Pittie comes too late.
    p. 136 UNDERWOOD 2.5   5 Heare, what late Discourse of you,
    p. 166 UNDERWOOD 15   117 What furie of late is crept into our Feasts?

late (cont.)
- p. 215 UNDERWOOD 44   88 Carriage, and dressing. There is up of late
- p. 219 UNDERWOOD 47   48 Of the late Mysterie of reception,
- p. 243 UNDERWOOD 70   30 What did this Stirrer, but die late?
- p. 258 UNDERWOOD 75   180 Extend a reaching vertue, early and late:
- p. 272 UNDERWOOD 84   t6 late Wife of Sir KENELME DIGBY,
                            Knight:
- p. 309 HORACE 2   88 Of words decay, and phrases borne but late
- p. 313 HORACE 2   195 Nor so begin, as did that Circler late,
- p. 319 HORACE 2   315 With lees of Wine. Next Eschylus, more late,
- p. 321 HORACE 2   332 Or Semi-god, that late was seene to weare
- p. 361 UNGATHERED 1   1 When late (graue Palmer) these thy graffs and
                            flowers
- p. 367 UNGATHERED 6   46 That late were out.
- p. 368 UNGATHERED 6   82 In entertaining late
- p. 384 UNGATHERED 18   25 That all, yt view you then, and late; may say,
- p. 415 UNGATHERED 42   21 Cry'd up of late: Whereto there must be first

late-coyn'd   frequency: 1   relative frequency: 0.00001
- p. 309 HORACE 2   74 And those thy new, and late-coyn'd words receive,

lately   frequency: 3   relative frequency: 0.00004
- p. 29 EPIGRAMS 7   1 Where lately harbour'd many a famous whore,
- p. 41 EPIGRAMS 44   1 CHVFFE, lately rich in name, in chattels,
                            goods,
- p. 101 FOREST 4   27 From whence, so lately, I did burne,

later   frequency: 2   relative frequency: 0.00002
- p. 94 FOREST 2   41 The earely cherry, with the later plum,
- p. 274 U'WOOD 84.2   4 That ever Nature, or the later Ayre

lateral. See "laterall."

laterall   frequency: 1   relative frequency: 0.00001
- p. 362 UNGATHERED 2   9 For, as one comming with a laterall viewe,

latest   frequency: 2   relative frequency: 0.00002
- p. 100 FOREST 3   105 Nor death; but when thy latest sand is spent,
- p. 295 UNDERWOOD 90   13 Nor feare thy latest day, nor wish therfore.

latin   frequency: 1   relative frequency: 0.00001
See also "latine."
- p. 184 UNDERWOOD 29   34 Whilst the Latin, Queene of Tongues,

latine   frequency: 3   relative frequency: 0.00004
- p. 84 EPIGRAMS 133   3 ORPHEVS, VLYSSES: or the Latine
                            Muse,
- p. 380 UNGATHERED 12   45 Of Latine and Greeke, to his friendship. And
                            seuen
- p. 391 UNGATHERED 26   31 And though thou hadst small Latine, and lesse
                            Greeke,

latten   frequency: 1   relative frequency: 0.00001
- p. 319 HORACE 2   287 The Hau'-boy, not as now with latten bound,

latter   frequency: 3   relative frequency: 0.00004
- p. 63 EPIGRAMS 98   11 Though both be good, the latter yet is worst,
- p. 68 EPIGRAMS 106   9 Their latter praise would still the greatest bee,
- p. 72 EPIGRAMS 111   3 Wherein thou shew'st, how much the latter are

laugh   frequency: 9   relative frequency: 0.00013
See also "laughe."
- p. 35 EPIGRAMS 28   10 Both which are great. And laugh at ill-made
                            clothes;
- p. 38 EPIGRAMS 38   3 You laugh when you are touch'd, and long before
- p. 81 EPIGRAMS 129   18 Men loue thee not for this: They laugh at thee.
- p. 118 FOREST 13   82 When their owne Parasites laugh at their fall,
- p. 164 UNDERWOOD 15   75 And laugh, and measure thighes, then squeake,
                            spring, itch,
- p. 311 HORACE 2   143 Mens faces, still, with such as laugh, are prone
- p. 313 HORACE 2   160 And Roman Gentrie, jearing, will laugh out.
- p. 380 UNGATHERED 12   47 Nay more in his wardrobe, if you will laugh at a
- p. 410 UNGATHERED 39   10 I'll laugh at thee poor wretched Tike, go send

laugh-worthy   frequency: 1   relative frequency: 0.00001
- p. 89 EPIGRAMS 133   185 They laugh't, at his laugh-worthy fate. And past

laugh'd   frequency: 1   relative frequency: 0.00001
See also "laugh't."
- p. 329 HORACE 2   532 Is laugh'd at, that still jarreth on one string:

laughe   frequency: 1   relative frequency: 0.00001
    p. 420 UNGATHERED 48   14 That hath not Countrye impudence enough to
                                  laughe att Arte,

laughs   frequency: 1   relative frequency: 0.00001
    p.   45 EPIGRAMS 58   4 Thy ignorance still laughs in the wrong place.

laugh't   frequency: 1   relative frequency: 0.00001
    p.   89 EPIGRAMS 133   185 They laugh't, at his laugh-worthy fate. And past

laughter   frequency: 9   relative frequency: 0.00013
    p.   27 EPIGRAMS 2   12 To catch the worlds loose laughter, or vaine
                                  gaze.
    p.   51 EPIGRAMS 73   8 That yet maintaynes you, and your house in
                                  laughter.
    p. 131 UNDERWOOD 2.1   2 Lesse your laughter; that I love.
    p. 164 UNDERWOOD 15   62 Not make a verse; Anger; or laughter would,
    p. 232 UNDERWOOD 58   8 Thy Wife a fit of laughter; a Cramp-ring
    p. 305 HORACE 2   7 Could you containe your laughter? Credit mee,
    p. 311 HORACE 2   144 To laughter; so they grieve with those that mone.
    p. 331 HORACE 2   569 Lest the throng'd heapes should on a laughter
                                  take:
    p. 342 HORACE 1   160 ... . with laughter shout.

launces   frequency: 1   relative frequency: 0.00001
    p. 213 UNDERWOOD 44   8 Launces, and men, and some a breaking force.

laura   frequency: 1   relative frequency: 0.00001
    p. 181 UNDERWOOD 27   21 Hath Petrarch since his Laura rais'd

laurel. See "laurell," "lawrell."

laurell   frequency: 2   relative frequency: 0.00002
    p.   28 EPIGRAMS 4   2 How, best of Poets, do'st thou laurell weare!
    p.   80 EPIGRAMS 126   4 And bad me lay th'vsurped laurell downe:

law   frequency: 12   relative frequency: 0.00017
    See also "common-law."
    p. 133 UNDERWOOD 2.3   13 He no sooner heard the Law,
    p. 185 UNDERWOOD 31   4 Law, to his Law; and thinke your enemies his:
    p. 187 UNDERWOOD 33   6 Who 'gainst the Law, weave Calumnies, my
                                  <BENN:>
    p. 227 UNDERWOOD 52   7 You were not tied, by any Painters Law,
    p. 233 UNDERWOOD 59   14 Wonder to Valour! No, it is the Law
    p. 247 UNDERWOOD 70   120 That such a Law
    p. 295 UNDERWOOD 90   5 Never at Law; seldome in office gown'd;
    p. 313 HORACE 2   193 From whence thy Modestie, or Poemes law
    p. 319 HORACE 2   324 The free spectators, subject to no Law,
    p. 321 HORACE 2   368 Her licence fit to be restrain'd by law:
    p. 323 HORACE 2   369 Which law receiv'd, the Chorus held his peace,

lawes   frequency: 24   relative frequency: 0.00034
  **p. 115 PANEGYRE   92 "Their lawes, their endes; the men she did
                                  report:
  **p. 115 PANEGYRE   99 "Where lawes were made to serue the tyran' will:
  **p. 116 PANEGYRE   106 "Lawes, iudges, co<u>nsellors, yea prince, and
                                  state.
    p.   29 EPIGRAMS 8   5 Rob'd both of money, and the lawes reliefe,
    p.   34 EPIGRAMS 24   1 There's reason good, that you good lawes should
                                  make:
    p.   38 EPIGRAMS 35   6 Left vs of feare, but first our crimes, then
                                  lawes.
    p.   52 EPIGRAMS 74   6 And no lesse wise, then skilfull in the lawes;
    p. 117 FOREST 13   18 Men are not iust, or keepe no holy lawes
    p. 163 UNDERWOOD 15   40 And shamefastnesse together! All lawes dead,
    p. 173 UNDERWOOD 22   12 Against or Faith, or honours lawes.
    p. 185 UNDERWOOD 31   2 Lawes, and no change e're come to one decree:
    p. 186 UNDERWOOD 31   9 As with the safetie, and honour of the Lawes,
    p. 187 UNDERWOOD 33   17 Dar'st not abuse thy wisdome, in the Lawes,
    p. 215 UNDERWOOD 44   74 Their Sonnes to studie Arts, the Lawes, the
                                  Creed:
    p. 217 UNDERWOOD 46   11 That Clients strove, in Question of the Lawes,
    p. 217 UNDERWOOD 46   17 Like Solons selfe; explat'st the knottie Lawes
    p. 236 UNDERWOOD 64   8 Then now, to love the Soveraigne, and the
                                  Lawes?
    p. 255 UNDERWOOD 75   104 Mens Loves unto the Lawes, and Lawes to love
                                  the Crowne.
    p. 313 HORACE 2   173 Sharpe, and contemning lawes, at him should aime,
    p. 317 HORACE 2   283 Praise the spare diet, wholsome justice, lawes,
    p. 327 HORACE 2   490 Build Townes, and carve the Lawes in leaves of
                                  wood.

lawes (cont.)
        p. 409 UNGATHERED 38   7 By obseruation of those Comick Lawes
        p. 423 UNGATHERED 50   13 Euen states most hated, when no lawes resist

lawfull   frequency: 2   relative frequency: 0.00002
        p. 238 UNDERWOOD 66   11 As in this Prince? Let it be lawfull, so
        p. 323 HORACE 2   404 A lawfull Verse, by th'eare, or finger scan.

lawn.   See "cob-web-lawne," "lawne."

lawne   frequency: 1   relative frequency: 0.00001
        p. 275 U'WOOD 84.3   2 What make these Velvets, Silkes, and Lawne,

lawrell   frequency: 1   relative frequency: 0.00001
        p. 392 UNGATHERED 26   63 Or for the lawrell, he may gaine a scorne,

laws.   See "liwes."

lawyer   frequency: 4   relative frequency: 0.00005
        p. 38 EPIGRAMS 37   t1 ON CHEV'RILL THE LAWYER.
        p. 98 FOREST 3   62 Nor how to get the lawyer fees.
        p. 187 UNDERWOOD 33   14 Have made me to conceive a Lawyer new.
        p. 331 HORACE 2   550 There may a Lawyer be, may not excell;

laxatiue   frequency: 1   relative frequency: 0.00001
        p. 88 EPIGRAMS 133   167 Laxatiue lettuce, and such windie meate)

laxative.   See "laxatiue."

lay   frequency: 17   relative frequency: 0.00024
        p. 72 EPIGRAMS 112   7 I cannot for the stage a Drama lay,
        p. 80 EPIGRAMS 126   4 And bad me lay th'vsurped laurell downe:
        p. 82 EPIGRAMS 131   4 The learn'd haue no more priuiledge, then the lay.
        p. 88 EPIGRAMS 133   139 Or, that it lay, heap'd like an vsurers masse,
        p. 88 EPIGRAMS 133   149 Cats there lay diuers had beene flead, and
                                   rosted,
        p. 107 FOREST 10   9 And foundred thy hot teame, to tune my lay.
        p. 162 UNDERWOOD 15   21 Or Feathers: lay his fortune out to show,
        p. 191 UNDERWOOD 38   22 Or lay the excuse upon the Vintners vault;
        p. 201 UNDERWOOD 42   55 He did lay up, and would adore the shooe,
        p. 232 UNDERWOOD 58   12 As if that part lay for a [   ] most fit!
        p. 243 UNDERWOOD 70   14 Lay trampled on; the deeds of death, and night,
        p. 271 UNDERWOOD 83   81 And trusted so, as it deposited lay
        p. 290 UNDERWOOD 85   24 Now in the rooted Grasse him lay,
        p. 307 HORACE 2   64 Lay that aside, the Epicks office is.
        p. 335 HORACE 2   669 Or love of this so famous death lay by.
        p. 380 UNGATHERED 12   38 And lay in straw with the horses at Bergamo,
        p. 394 UNGATHERED 28   24 To lay her here, inclos'd, his second Bride.

lay-stall   frequency: 1   relative frequency: 0.00001
        p. 172 UNDERWOOD 21   8 That thought can adde, unthankfull, the lay-stall

layd   frequency: 1   relative frequency: 0.00001
        p. 295 UNDERWOOD 90   9 Thy night not dronken, but from cares layd wast;

layes   frequency: 2   relative frequency: 0.00002
        p. 74 EPIGRAMS 115   16 And him it layes on; if he be not there.
        p. 383 UNGATHERED 16   9 hee freely bringes; and on[e] this Alter layes

lays.   See "laies," "layes."

lazie   frequency: 1   relative frequency: 0.00001
        p. 183 UNDERWOOD 29   13 Soone as lazie thou wert knowne,

lazy.   See "lazie."

le.   See "l'envoye."

lead   frequency: 9   relative frequency: 0.00013
        p. 138 UNDERWOOD 2.6   26 As might all the Graces lead,
        p. 170 UNDERWOOD 18   11 But which shall lead me on? both these me hold:
        p. 170 UNDERWOOD 18   22 I'le lead you on; or if my fate will so,
        p. 265 UNDERWOOD 79   60 To sweeter Pastures lead hee can,
        p. 307 HORACE 2   43 So, shunning faults, to greater fault doth lead,
        p. 327 HORACE 2   485 And lead them with soft songs, where that he
                                   would.
        p. 335 HORACE 2   641 These trifles into serious mischiefes lead
        p. 657 L. CONVIVALES   1 Welcome all, who lead or follow,
        p. 657 L. CONVIVALES   19 Welcome all, who lead or follow,

leaders   frequency: 1   relative frequency: 0.00001
    p. 264 UNDERWOOD 79   28 Shep. Of PAN wee sing, the Chiefe of
                                 Leaders, PAN,

leades   frequency: 3   relative frequency: 0.00004
    p. 97 FOREST 3.   18 Through which a serpent riuer leades
    p. 264 UNDERWOOD 79   29 That leades our flocks and us, and calls both
                                 forth
    p. 317 HORACE 2   279 Then to the purpose leades, and fitly 'grees.

leading   frequency: 1   relative frequency: 0.00001
    p. 68 EPIGRAMS 105   12 Were leading forth the Graces on the greene:

leads   frequency: 1   relative frequency: 0.00001
    See also "leades."
    p. 53 EPIGRAMS 80   2 Through which, our merit leads vs to our meeds.

leaf. See "leafe," "title-leafe."

leafe   frequency: 1   relative frequency: 0.00001
    p. 380 UNGATHERED 12   23 Each leafe of his iournall, and line doth vnlocke

lean. See "leane."

leane   frequency: 3   relative frequency: 0.00004
    p. 281 U'WOOD 84.8   13 'Twill be but faire, to leane upon their Fames;
    p. 405 UNGATHERED 34   69 I am too fat t'enuy him. He too leane
    p. 420 UNGATHERED 48   25 to gett the<e> a leane fface,

leanenesse   frequency: 1   relative frequency: 0.00001
    p. 105 FOREST 8   24 If thy leanenesse loue such food,

leanness. See "leanenesse."

leap. See "leape."

leap'd   frequency: 3   relative frequency: 0.00004
    See also "leapt."
    p. 69 EPIGRAMS 107   16 For which there must more sea, and land be
                                 leap'd,
    p. 245 UNDERWOOD 70   79 Hee leap'd the present age,
    p. 335 HORACE 2   663 Conceipt, and into burning Aetna leap'd.

leape   frequency: 6   relative frequency: 0.00008
    p. 74 EPIGRAMS 115   11 Can come from Tripoly, leape stooles, and winke,
    p. 94 FOREST 2   37 Bright eeles, that emulate them, and leape on
                                 land,
    p. 164 UNDERWOOD 15   70 And then, leape mad on a neat Pickardill,
    p. 201 UNDERWOOD 42   44 Her presently? Or leape thy Wife of force,
    p. 313 HORACE 2   192 Of imitation, leape into a streight,
    p. 333 HORACE 2   613 Out at his friendly eyes, leape, beat the groun'.

leapt   frequency: 1   relative frequency: 0.00001
    p. 402 UNGATHERED 34   3 you are; from them leapt forth an Architect,

learn. See "learne."

learn'd   frequency: 8   relative frequency: 0.00011
    p. 55 EPIGRAMS 85   3 Where I both learn'd, why wise-men hawking
                                 follow,
    p. 82 EPIGRAMS 131   4 The learn'd haue no more priuiledge, then the
                                 lay.
    p. 119 FOREST 13   89 You, Madame, yong haue learn'd to shunne these
                                 shelues,
    p. 181 UNDERWOOD 27   9 Was Lesbia sung by learn'd Catullus?
    p. 216 UNDERWOOD 45   4 One lesson we have both learn'd, and well read;
    p. 253 UNDERWOOD 75   35 As they had learn'd new changes, for the day,
    p. 337 HORACE 2   677 Learn'd and unlearn'd; holding, whom once he
                                 takes;
    p. 410 UNGATHERED 38   9 You learn'd it well; and for it, seru'd your time

learne   frequency: 7   relative frequency: 0.00010
    p. 215 UNDERWOOD 44   92 They learne and studie; and then practise there.
    p. 311 HORACE 2   131 To ignorance still, then either learne, or know?
    p. 327 HORACE 2   464 Our Roman Youths they learne the subtle wayes
    p. 333 HORACE 2   592 Did learne them first, and once a Master fear'd.
    p. 379 UNGATHERED 12   2 The height, let him learne of Mr. Tom.
                                 Coryate;
    p. 381 UNGATHERED 12   60 The height, let him learne of Mr. Tom Coryate.
    p. 402 UNGATHERED 33   12 The faire French Daughter to learne English
                                 in;

learned   frequency: 16   relative frequency: 0.00023
    See also "learn'd," "right-learned."
    p.   32 EPIGRAMS 17   t1 TO THE LEARNED CRITICK.
    p.   51 EPIGRAMS 73   11 With which a learned Madame you belye.
    p.   52 EPIGRAMS 76   13 Onely a learned, and a manly soule
    p.   55 EPIGRAMS 85   12 What would his serious actions me haue learned?
    p.   71 EPIGRAMS 110   17 Thy learned hand, and true Promethean art
    p.   78 EPIGRAMS 121   2 My lighter comes, to kisse thy learned Muse;
    p.   88 EPIGRAMS 133   157 Graue tutor to the learned horse. Both which,
    p. 161 UNDERWOOD 14   72 Thy learned Chamber-fellow, knowes to doe
    p. 182 UNDERWOOD 27   34 Come short of all this learned throng,
    p. 204 UNDERWOOD 43   31 The learned Librarie of Don Quixote;
    p. 263 UNDERWOOD 78   28 The knowing Weston, and that learned Lord
    p. 325 HORACE 2   453 And I still bid the learned Maker looke
    p. 380 UNGATHERED 12   44 How many learned men he haue drawne with his
                                    hooke
    p. 395 UNGATHERED 29   t2 The learned Translator of LVCAN,
    p. 397 UNGATHERED 30   25 There read I, streight, thy learned Legends
                                    three,
    p. 410·UNGATHERED 38   12 Both learned, and vnlearned, all write Playes.

learnedly   frequency: 1   relative frequency: 0.00001
    p. 375 UNGATHERED 10   35 Beeing in feare to be robd, he most learnedly
                                    begs.

learnes   frequency: 1   relative frequency: 0.00001
    p.   78 EPIGRAMS 121   4 Shee learnes to know long difference of their
                                    states.

learning   frequency: 3   relative frequency: 0.00004
    p.   68 EPIGRAMS 106   5 Whether thy learning they would take, or wit,
    p. 217 UNDERWOOD 46   18 With endlesse labours, whilst thy learning drawes
    p. 365 UNGATHERED 5   9 Iudgement (adornd with Learning)

learns. See "learnes."

leas'd   frequency: 1   relative frequency: 0.00001
    p. 246 UNDERWOOD 70   100 Made, or indentur'd, or leas'd out t<o>'advance

lease   frequency: 2   relative frequency: 0.00002
    p.   63 EPIGRAMS 97   9 Know you the cause? H'has neither land, nor
                                    lease,
    p. 418 UNGATHERED 45   43 forfeitinge their drinking lease,

least   frequency: 29   relative frequency: 0.00041
    See also "lest."
    p.   27 EPIGRAMS 2   9 Thou are not couetous of least selfe-fame,
    p.   30 EPIGRAMS 11   6 And such from whom let no man hope least good,
    p.   43 EPIGRAMS 51   4 And farre beneath least pause of such a king,
    p.   44 EPIGRAMS 55   4 The least indulgent thought thy pen drops forth!
    p.   67 EPIGRAMS 103   14 Becomes none more then you, who need it least.
    p.   67 EPIGRAMS 105   4 Least mention of a Nymph, a Muse, a Grace,
    p.   75 EPIGRAMS 116   14 Vertuously practise must at least allow
    p.   76 EPIGRAMS 119   10 Till thou canst finde the best, choose the least
                                    ill.
    p.   86 EPIGRAMS 133   72 The least of which was to the plague a cosen.
    p. 115 FOREST 12   79 Then all, that haue but done my Muse least
                                    grace,
    p. 120 FOREST 14   9 Who not the least,
    p. 137 UNDERWOOD 2.5   43 But alas, thou seest the least
    p. 141 UNDERWOOD 2.9   7 French to boote, at least in fashion,
    p. 159 UNDERWOOD 14   20 And mine not least) I have too oft preferr'd
    p. 171 UNDERWOOD 20   7 Or have the least of Good, but what it must
    p. 197 UNDERWOOD 40   13 But ever without blazon, or least shade
    p. 203 UNDERWOOD 43   6 Nor made least line of love to thy loose Wife;
    p. 203 UNDERWOOD 43   20 Any, least loose, or s<c>urrile paper, lie
    p. 205 UNDERWOOD 43   59 Had I fore-knowne of this thy least desire
    p. 223 UNDERWOOD 49   29 And trust her I would least, that hath forswore
    p. 231 UNDERWOOD 57   18 Nor any least fit
    p. 269 UNDERWOOD 83   18 At least may beare th'inscription to her Tombe.
    p. 288 U'WOOD 84.9   188 The holy Altars, when it least presumes.
    p. 385 UNGATHERED 20   4 Least a false praise do make theyr dotage his.
    p. 394 UNGATHERED 28   15 At least so great a Lady. She was wife
    p. 395 UNGATHERED 29   6 At least, if not the generall Engine cracke.
    p. 407 UNGATHERED 35   23 Or canst of truth ye least intrenchmt pitch,
    p. 408 UNGATHERED 37   10 By barking against mee. Thou look'st at least,
    p. 409 UNGATHERED 37   20 Out in the Dog-daies, least the killer meete

leather. See "lether."

leaue   frequency: 20   relative frequency: 0.00028
 *p. 492 TO HIMSELF   1 Come leaue the lothed stage,
 *p. 492 TO HIMSELF   19 If they loue lees, and leaue the lusty wine,
 *p. 493 TO HIMSELF   41 Leaue things so prostitute,
  p.   27 EPIGRAMS 3   3 Vse mine so, too: I giue thee leaue. But craue
  p.   34 EPIGRAMS 23   10 But leaue, because I cannot as I should!
  p.   34 EPIGRAMS 25   7 What doth he else, but say, leaue to be chast,
  p.   42 EPIGRAMS 50   1 Leaue COD, tabacco-like, burnt gummes to take,
  p.   43 EPIGRAMS 51   5 Yet giue thy iealous subiects leaue to doubt:
  p.   44 EPIGRAMS 56   4 As we, the rob'd, leaue rage, and pittie it.
  p.   48 EPIGRAMS 65   1 Away, and leaue me, thou thing most abhord,
  p.   50 EPIGRAMS 70   1 When Nature bids vs leaue to liue, 'tis late
  p.   54 EPIGRAMS 81   7 Which, if thou leaue not soone (though I am
                             loth)
  p.   58 EPIGRAMS 91   9 I leaue thy acts, which should I prosequute
  p.   72 EPIGRAMS 112   9 I leaue thee there, and giuing way, entend
  p.   79 EPIGRAMS 124   8 Leaue it buryed in this vault.
  p. 106 FOREST 8   48 None but them, and leaue the rest.
  p. 106 FOREST 9   3 Or leaue a kisse but in the cup,
  p. 108 FOREST 10 A   7 Then, leaue these lighter numbers, to light
                             braines
  p. 391 UNGATHERED 26   38 Leaue thee alone, for the comparison
  p. 398 UNGATHERED 30   83 Yet giue mee leaue, to wonder at the birth

leau'st   frequency: 1   relative frequency: 0.00001
  p.   48 EPIGRAMS 65   11 With me thou leau'st an happier Muse then thee,

leave   frequency: 27   relative frequency: 0.00039
  See also "leaue."
  p. 133 UNDERWOOD 2.3   22 Is, that I have leave to speake,
  p. 146 UNDERWOOD 6   24 To love one man, hee'd leave her first.
  p. 154 UNDERWOOD 13   44 Nought but in corners; and is loath to leave
  p. 166 UNDERWOOD 15   141 Can we not leave this worme? or will we not?
  p. 172 UNDERWOOD 21   10 And so I leave to stirre him, lest he stinke.
  p. 174 UNDERWOOD 22   35 Yet give me leave t<o>'adore in you
  p. 190 UNDERWOOD 37   11 And which you (being the worthier) gave me leave
  p. 190 UNDERWOOD 37   24 Will unto Licence that faire leave abuse.
  p. 197 UNDERWOOD 40   2 Till the sower Minute comes of taking leave,
  p. 199 UNDERWOOD 41   13 My health will leave me; and when you depart,
  p. 200 UNDERWOOD 42   32 That quilts those bodies, I have leave to span:
  p. 203 UNDERWOOD 43   28 A cause before; or leave me one behind.
  p. 221 UNDERWOOD 48   26 Thee still, and leave Apollo,
  p. 223 UNDERWOOD 49   37 The wits will leave you, if they once perceive
  p. 223 UNDERWOOD 49   38 You cling to Lords, and Lords, if them you
                             leave
  p. 224 UNDERWOOD 50   21 Whilst your Ulisses hath ta'ne leave to goe,
  p. 231 UNDERWOOD 56   29 I gaine, in having leave to keepe my Day,
  p. 241 UNDERWOOD 68   6 His Poet leave to sing his House-hold true;
  p. 243 UNDERWOOD 70   9 How summ'd a circle didst thou leave man-kind
  p. 270 UNDERWOOD 83   47 How did she leave the world? with what contempt?
  p. 282 U'WOOD 84.9   t3 who living, gave me leave to call her so.
  p. 286 U'WOOD 84.9   148 He that shall be our supreme Judge, should leave
  p. 305 HORACE 2   13 And both doe crave, and give againe, this leave.
  p. 309 HORACE 2   73 And give, being taken modestly, this leave,
  p. 315 HORACE 2   236 And then as swift to leave what he hath lov'd.
  p. 319 HORACE 2   286 Fortune would love the poore, and leave the
                             proud.
  p. 323 HORACE 2   389 And there is given too unworthy leave

leaven'd   frequency: 1   relative frequency: 0.00001
  See also "ouer-leauen'd."
  p. 163 UNDERWOOD 15   31 The whole world here leaven'd with madnesse
                             swells;

leaves   frequency: 3   relative frequency: 0.00004
  p. 151 UNDERWOOD 11   10 But leaves me to inquire,
  p. 309 HORACE 2   86 Still in their leaves, throughout the sliding
                             yeares,
  p. 327 HORACE 2   490 Build Townes, and carve the Lawes in leaves of
                             wood.

leavest. See "leau'st."

lechered. See "letcher'd."

lechers   frequency: 1   relative frequency: 0.00001
  See also "letchers."
  p.   76 EPIGRAMS 118   1 GVT eates all day, and lechers all the night,

lechery. See "letcherie."

led   frequency: 3   relative frequency: 0.00004
  **p. 116 PANEGYRE   127 When they are led, then when they are compell'd.
    p. 220 UNDERWOOD 47   69 But all so cleare, and led by reasons flame,
    p. 254 UNDERWOOD 75   68 And all the Ground were Garden, where she led!

leda's   frequency: 1   relative frequency: 0.00001
    p. 369 UNGATHERED 6 104 Or thought they, Leda's white Adult'rers place

lee   frequency: 1   relative frequency: 0.00001
    p. 307 HORACE 2   38 Professing greatnesse, swells: That, low by lee

leech. See "horse-leech," "horse-leech-like."

lees   frequency: 2   relative frequency: 0.00002
  *p. 492 TO HIMSELF   19 If they loue lees, and leaue the lusty wine,
    p. 319 HORACE 2   315 With lees of Wine. Next Eschylus, more late,

leese   frequency: 3   relative frequency: 0.00004
    p.   38 EPIGRAMS 37   1 No cause, nor client fat, will CHEV'RILL
                             leese,
    p.   98 FOREST 3   61 They thinke not, then, which side the cause shall
                             leese,
    p. 164 UNDERWOOD 15 56 The bravery makes, she can no honour leese:

left   frequency: 27   relative frequency: 0.00039
    p.   38 EPIGRAMS 35   6 Left vs of feare, but first our crimes, then
                             lawes.
    p.   49 EPIGRAMS 67   1 Since men haue left to doe praise-worthy things,
    p.   60 EPIGRAMS 93   1 How like a columne, RADCLIFFE, left
                             alone
    p.   67 EPIGRAMS 105   3 That we had left vs, nor by time, nor place,
    p. 118 FOREST 13   83 May they haue nothing left, whereof they can
    p. 120 FOREST 14   20 And he, with his best Genius left alone.
    p. 129 UNDERWOOD 1.2 9 But left me free,
    p. 133 UNDERWOOD 2.3 16 Left it sticking in my heart:
    p. 138 UNDERWOOD 2.6 33 To have left all sight for you:
    p. 149 UNDERWOOD 9   t1 My Picture left in Scotland.
    p. 152 UNDERWOOD 12 35 For truly, since he left to be,
    p. 168 UNDERWOOD 16   4 All that is left of PHILIP GRAY,
    p. 199 UNDERWOOD 41   7 And we were left under that Hemisphere,
    p. 201 UNDERWOOD 42 56 Or slipper was left off, and kisse it too,
    p. 209 UNDERWOOD 43 138 Left! and wit since to cover it with Tiles.
    p. 247 UNDERWOOD 70 121 Was left yet to Man-kind;
    p. 260 UNDERWOOD 77   8 Have left in fame to equall, or out-goe
    p. 272 UNDERWOOD 84 t4 LEFT TO POSTERITIE
    p. 279 U'WOOD 84.4   40 Still left an Eccho in the sense.
    p. 280 U'WOOD 84.4   66 In rest, like spirits left behind
    p. 283 U'WOOD 84.9   28 What's left a Poet, when his Muse is gone?
    p. 283 U'WOOD 84.9   44 And left her lovely body unthought dead!
    p. 289 UNDERWOOD 85   3 With his owne Oxen tills his Sires left lands,
    p. 295 UNDERWOOD 90   3 Not labour'd for, but left thee by thy Sire;
    p. 323 HORACE 2   405 Our Poets, too, left nought unproved here;
    p. 390 UNGATHERED 26 t5 what he hath left vs.
    p. 394 UNGATHERED 28 16 But of one Husband; and since he left life,

left-lydia   frequency: 1   relative frequency: 0.00001
    p. 294 UNDERWOOD 87 20 And to left-Lydia, now the gate stood ope.

left-witted   frequency: 1   relative frequency: 0.00001
    p. 325 HORACE 2   429 O I left-witted, that purge every spring

leg   frequency: 1   relative frequency: 0.00001
    p. 198 UNDERWOOD 40 33 Is fix'd upon one leg, and dares not come

legal. See "legall."

legall   frequency: 1   relative frequency: 0.00001
    p. 255 UNDERWOOD 75 102 And legall wayes

legend   frequency: 2   relative frequency: 0.00002
    p. 205 UNDERWOOD 43 66 With pieces of the Legend; The whole summe
    p. 228 UNDERWOOD 53   9 Or what we heare our home-borne Legend tell,

legends   frequency: 1   relative frequency: 0.00001
    p. 397 UNGATHERED 30 25 There read I, streight, thy learned Legends
                             three,

legged. See "short-leg'd."

leghorn. See "ligorne."

legitimate   frequency: 1   relative frequency: 0.00001
     p.   32 EPIGRAMS 17   3 That wish my poemes a legitimate fame,

legs   frequency: 3   relative frequency: 0.00004
     p.   36 EPIGRAMS 31   3 And though the soundest legs goe euery day,
     p. 215 UNDERWOOD 44   90 What, to make legs? yes, and to smell most sweet,
     p. 375 UNGATHERED 10   34 Bvt here, neither trusting his hands, nor his
                                 legs,

lemnos   frequency: 1   relative frequency: 0.00001
     p. 208 UNDERWOOD 43   116 No mar'le the Clownes of Lemnos tooke thee up,

lemons. See "limons."

lend   frequency: 8   relative frequency: 0.00011
     p.   52 EPIGRAMS 76   8 Nor lend like influence from his lucent seat.
     p. 105 FOREST 8   34 More then citizens dare lend
     p. 118 FOREST 13   78 Till that no vsurer, nor his bawds dare lend
     p. 191 UNDERWOOD 38   8 Alone lend succours, and this furie stay,
     p. 217 UNDERWOOD 46   24 Needs lend an aide, to thine she had her eyes.
     p. 223 UNDERWOOD 49   42 This Age would lend no faith to Dorrels Deed;
     p. 229 UNDERWOOD 54   16 Lend me, deare Arthur, for a weeke five more,
     p. 396 UNGATHERED 30   12 Lend me thy voyce, O FAME, that I may draw

length   frequency: 4   relative frequency: 0.00005
     p.   75 EPIGRAMS 116   6 And those that lack'd it, to suspect at length,
     p. 102 FOREST 5   4 He, at length, our good will seuer.
     p. 367 UNGATHERED 6   56 And conquers all things, yea it selfe, at length.
     p. 383 UNGATHERED 17   10 To vnderstand, hee may at length admire.

lengthened. See "length'ned."

length'ned   frequency: 1   relative frequency: 0.00001
  **p. 117 PANEGYRE   153 The length'ned showt, as when th'artillery

lennox. See "lenox."

lenox   frequency: 1   relative frequency: 0.00001
     p. 252 UNDERWOOD 75   t10 Daughter of ESME D. of Lenox deceased,

lent   frequency: 14   relative frequency: 0.00020
     p.   31 EPIGRAMS 12   24 Lent him a pockie whore. Shee hath paid him.
     p.   41 EPIGRAMS 45   3 Seuen yeeres tho'wert lent to me, and I thee
                                 pay,
     p.   51 EPIGRAMS 73   6 I lent you, on meere acquaintance, at a feast.
     p.   67 EPIGRAMS 104   7 And to your Scene lent no lesse dignitie
     p.   70 EPIGRAMS 109   11 To make thy lent life, good against the Fates:
     p.   80 EPIGRAMS 127   8 Lent timely succours, and new life begot:
     p.   98 FOREST 3   46 A fire now, that lent a shade!
     p. 100 FOREST 3   106 Thou maist thinke life, a thing but lent.
     p. 207 UNDERWOOD 43   100 Which noble Carew, Cotton, Selden lent:
     p. 213 UNDERWOOD 44   14 Lent by the London Dames, to the Lords men;
     p. 271 UNDERWOOD 83   80 T'have paid againe a blessing was but lent,
     p. 287 U'WOOD 84.9   157 And to that forme, lent two such veines of blood
     p. 309 HORACE 2   81 Cato's and Ennius tongues have lent much worth,
     p. 319 HORACE 2   303 Thus, to his antient Art the Piper lent

l'envoy. See "l'envoye."

l'envoye   frequency: 1   relative frequency: 0.00001
     p. 202 UNDERWOOD 42   75 In smiling L'envoye, as he would deride

leprosie   frequency: 1   relative frequency: 0.00001
     p. 335 HORACE 2   645 Infected with the leprosie, or had

leprosy. See "leprosie."

lesbia   frequency: 1   relative frequency: 0.00001
     p. 181 UNDERWOOD 27   9 Was Lesbia sung by learn'd Catullus?

less   frequency: 1   relative frequency: 0.00001
     See also "lesse," "lesse-poetique,"
          "meere-matter-lesse."
     p. 406 UNGATHERED 34   92 Allmighty Architecture? who noe less

lesse   frequency: 53   relative frequency: 0.00076
   *p. 492 TO HIMSELF   10 They were not made for thee, lesse, thou for
                                 them.
  **p. 117 PANEGYRE   146 Brighter then all, hath yet made no one lesse;
     p.   27 EPIGRAMS 2   11 Much lesse with lewd, prophane, and beastly
                                 phrase,

lesse (cont.)
p.   28 EPIGRAMS 3   10 Who scarse can spell th'hard names: whose knight
                           lesse can.
p.   33 EPIGRAMS 22   4 It makes the father, lesse, to rue.
p.   43 EPIGRAMS 51   7 No lesse than if from perill; and deuout,
p.   45 EPIGRAMS 58   5 And so my sharpnesse thou no lesse dis-ioynts,
p.   49 EPIGRAMS 67   11 Which, by no lesse confirm'd, then thy kings
                           choice,
p.   52 EPIGRAMS 74   6 And no lesse wise, then skilfull in the lawes;
p.   57 EPIGRAMS 89   5 Who had no lesse a trumpet of their name,
p.   58 EPIGRAMS 91   13 I speake thy other graces, not lesse showne,
p.   58 EPIGRAMS 91   14 Nor lesse in practice: but lesse mark'd, lesse
                           knowne:
p.   64 EPIGRAMS 99   11 Well, though thy name lesse then our great ones
                           bee,
p.   67 EPIGRAMS 104   7 And to your Scene lent no lesse dignitie
p.   68 EPIGRAMS 106   10 And yet, they, all together, lesse then thee.
p.   72 EPIGRAMS 111   8 Nor to giue CAESAR this, makes ours the
                           lesse.
p.   73 EPIGRAMS 112   20 Nor scarce dost colour for it, which is lesse.
p.   82 EPIGRAMS 130   8 No lesse a sou'raigne cure, then to the mind;
p.   82 EPIGRAMS 130   12 That the eight spheare, no lesse, then planets
                           seauen,
p. 113 FOREST 12   18 Or perhaps lesse: whil'st gold beares all this
                           sway,
p. 115 FOREST 12   72 To my lesse sanguine Muse, wherein she'hath
                           wonne
p. 115 FOREST 12   78 For I shall moue stocks, stones, no lesse then
                           he.
p. 131 UNDERWOOD 2.1   2 Lesse your laughter; that I love.
p. 139 UNDERWOOD 2.7   8 Can he that loves, aske lesse then one?
p. 153 UNDERWOOD 13   4 Lesse list of proud, hard, or ingratefull Men.
p. 154 UNDERWOOD 13   33 All this corrupts the thankes; lesse hath he
                           wonne,
p. 156 UNDERWOOD 13   120 And can I lesse of substance? When I runne,
p. 157 UNDERWOOD 13   152 Aloft, grow lesse and streightned, full of knot;
p. 158 UNDERWOOD 14   3 Lesse shall I for the Art or dressing care,
p. 159 UNDERWOOD 14   26 Before men get a verse: much lesse a Praise;
p. 165 UNDERWOOD 15   95 Lesse must not be thought on then Mistresse: or,
p. 165 UNDERWOOD 15   113 For lesse Securitie? O   for these
p. 173 UNDERWOOD 22   13 But who should lesse expect from you,
p. 190 UNDERWOOD 37   22 And lesse they know, who being free to use
p. 216 UNDERWOOD 45   9 Much lesse a name would we bring up, or nurse,
p. 217 UNDERWOOD 46   4 Whom Fortune aided lesse, or Vertue more.
p. 217 UNDERWOOD 46   19 No lesse of praise, then readers in all kinds
p. 217 UNDERWOOD 46   22 None Fortune aided lesse, or Vertue more.
p. 219 UNDERWOOD 47   58 Lest it be justled, crack'd, made nought, or
                           lesse:
p. 223 UNDERWOOD 49   25 I am no States-man, and much lesse Divine,
p. 248 UNDERWOOD 71   14 Dare thinke it, to relieve, no lesse renowne,
p. 255 UNDERWOOD 75   88 All else we see beside, are Shadowes, and goe
                           lesse.
p. 256 UNDERWOOD 75   115 In him the times, no lesse then Prince, are
                           prais'd,
p. 263 UNDERWOOD 79   8 For, had we here said lesse, we had sung nothing
                           then.
p. 271 UNDERWOOD 83   84 And wish her state lesse happie then it is!
p. 311 HORACE 2   122 In tragick Verse; no lesse Thyestes feast
p. 317 HORACE 2   272 Have more or lesse then just five Acts: nor
                           laid,
p. 323 HORACE 2   406 Nor did they merit the lesse Crowne to weare,
p. 391 UNGATHERED 26   31 And though thou hadst small Latine, and lesse
                           Greeke,
p. 401 UNGATHERED 32   18 But higher power, as spight could not make lesse,
p. 414 UNGATHERED 42   5 And lesse asham'd; not when I told the crowd

lesse-poetique   frequency: 1   relative frequency: 0.00001
p. 259 UNDERWOOD 76   20 Of the lesse-Poetique boyes;

lesser   frequency: 5   relative frequency: 0.00007
**p. 117 PANEGYRE   145 The lesser fiers dim) in his accesse
p.   61 EPIGRAMS 95   25 Although to write be lesser then to doo,
p.   78 EPIGRAMS 121   1 RVDYERD, as lesser dames, to great ones
                           vse,
p.   97 FOREST 3   26 Diuid'st, vpon the lesser Deere;
p. 169 UNDERWOOD 17   11 That as the lesser breach: for he that takes

lesson   frequency: 2   relative frequency: 0.00002
p. 158 UNDERWOOD 13   162 (As their true rule or lesson) either men,
p. 216 UNDERWOOD 45   4 One lesson we have both learn'd, and well read;

lest   frequency: 15   relative frequency: 0.00021
   See also "least."
    p. 41 EPIGRAMS 43   7 Yet dare not, to my thought, lest hope allow
    p. 122 FOREST 15   24 With holy PAVL, lest it be thought the breath
    p. 144 UNDERWOOD 3   21 O sing not you then lest the best
    p. 144 UNDERWOOD 4   2 Lest I be sick with seeing;
    p. 144 UNDERWOOD 4   4 Lest shame destroy their being.
    p. 154 UNDERWOOD 13   45 Lest Ayre, or Print, but flies it: Such men
                                      would
    p. 172 UNDERWOOD 21   10 And so I leave to stirre him, lest he stinke.
    p. 193 UNDERWOOD 38   84 Of crueltie, lest they doe make you such.
    p. 211 UNDERWOOD 43   182 Or lest that vapour might the Citie choake,
    p. 219 UNDERWOOD 47   58 Lest it be justled, crack'd, made nought, or
                                      lesse:
    p. 317 HORACE 2   251 As his departing take much thence: lest, then,
    p. 325 HORACE 2   417 Have not kept in; and (lest perfection faile)
    p. 329 HORACE 2   501 All which I tell, lest when Apollo's nam'd,
    p. 329 HORACE 2   509 It would, must be: lest it alive would draw
    p. 331 HORACE 2   569 Lest the throng'd heapes should on a laughter
                                      take:

let   frequency: 104   relative frequency: 0.00150
   See also "let's," "lett."
 *p. 492 TO HIMSELF   7 Let their fastidious, vaine
**p. 113 PANEGYRE   21 Vpon his state; let downe in that rich chaine,
**p. 117 PANEGYRE   161 Yet, let blest Brit[t]aine aske (without your
                                    wrong)
    p. 27 EPIGRAMS 2   8 And by thy wiser temper, let men know
    p. 30 EPIGRAMS 11   6 And such from whom let no man hope least good,
    p. 30 EPIGRAMS 13   3 Let me giue two: that doubly am got free,
    p. 31 EPIGRAMS 14   11 Pardon free truth, and let thy modestie,
    p. 50 EPIGRAMS 70   8 Though life be short, let vs not make it so.
    p. 62 EPIGRAMS 96   10 Let pui'nees, porters, players praise delight,
    p. 64 EPIGRAMS 99   12 Thy fact is more: let truth encourage thee.
    p. 79 EPIGRAMS 124   10 Th'other let it sleepe with death:
    p. 84 EPIGRAMS 133   1 No more let Greece her bolder fables tell
    p. 84 EPIGRAMS 133   19 Then let the former age, with this content her,
    p. 87 EPIGRAMS 133   104 (In the meane time, let 'hem imprison mee)
    p. 87 EPIGRAMS 133   108 Of the graue fart, late let in parliament,
    p. 98 FOREST 3   67 Let others watch in guiltie armes, and stand
    p. 99 FOREST 3   73 Let this man sweat, and wrangle at the barre,
    p. 99 FOREST 3   77 Let him, then hardest sires, more disinherit,
    p. 99 FOREST 3   81 Let that goe heape a masse of wretched wealth,
    p. 99 FOREST 3   85 Let thousands more goe flatter vice, and winne,
    p. 102 FOREST 5   1 Come my CELIA, let vs proue,
    p. 104 FOREST 7   4 Let her alone, shee will court you.
    p. 107 FOREST 10   19 Let the old boy, your sonne, ply his old taske,
    p. 108 FOREST 10A   11 Let these in wanton feete daunce out their
                                      soules.
    p. 110 FOREST 11   47 It is a golden chaine let downe from heauen,
    p. 111 FOREST 11   72 No, vice, we let thee know,
    p. 114 FOREST 12   27 But let this drosse carry what price it will
    p. 114 FOREST 12   28 With noble ignorants, and let them still,
    p. 118 FOREST 13   71 Let who will follow fashions, and attyres,
    p. 118 FOREST 13   77 Let 'hem on poulders, oyles, and paintings,
                                      spend,
    p. 118 FOREST 13   81 Let 'hem waste body, and state; and after all,
    p. 131 UNDERWOOD 2.1   1 Let it not your wonder move,
    p. 131 UNDERWOOD 2.1   22 And let nothing high decay,
    p. 139 UNDERWOOD 2.7   18 Let who will thinke us dead, or wish our death.
    p. 140 UNDERWOOD 2.8   21 Nay, I will not let you sit
    p. 142 U'WOOD 2.10   3 Let his Title be but great,
    p. 143 UNDERWOOD 3   1 Come, with our Voyces, let us warre,
    p. 144 UNDERWOOD 4   3 Nor cast them downe, but let them rise,
    p. 148 UNDERWOOD 7   35 If Love, or feare, would let me tell his name.
    p. 154 UNDERWOOD 13   60 That to such Natures let their full hands flow,
    p. 156 UNDERWOOD 13   113 No more are these of us, let them then goe,
    p. 165 UNDERWOOD 15   88 Is lov'd, though he let out his owne for life:
    p. 165 UNDERWOOD 15   90 Nature, that will not let his Wife be a whore;
    p. 166 UNDERWOOD 15   145 Well, let it goe. Yet this is better, then
    p. 167 UNDERWOOD 15   162 Friend, flie from hence; and let these kindled
                                      rimes
    p. 167 UNDERWOOD 15   165 Lewd slanderers, soft whisperers that let blood
    p. 174 UNDERWOOD 23   15 Let this thought quicken thee,
    p. 179 UNDERWOOD 25   40 Let Brontes, and black Steropes,
    p. 180 UNDERWOOD 25   63 O then (my best-best lov'd) let me importune,
    p. 185 UNDERWOOD 30   3 And goe no farther: let this Circle be
    p. 189 UNDERWOOD 36   1 Come, let us here enjoy the shade,
    p. 194 UNDERWOOD 38   105 Then Mistris, here, here let your rigour end,
    p. 194 UNDERWOOD 38   106 And let your mercie make me asham'd t<o>'offend.

let (cont.)

p. 199	UNDERWOOD 42	1	Let me be what I am, as Virgil cold;
p. 200	UNDERWOOD 42	9	Put on my Ivy Garland, let me see
p. 202	UNDERWOOD 42	81	Let the poore fooles enjoy their follies, love
p. 209	UNDERWOOD 43	141	And this a Sparkle of that fire let loose
p. 210	UNDERWOOD 43	156	Nay, let White-Hall with Revels have to doe,
p. 210	UNDERWOOD 43	161	Foole, wilt thou let that in example come?
p. 214	UNDERWOOD 44	57	And could (if our great men would let their Sonnes
p. 215	UNDERWOOD 44	73	With Citizens? let Clownes, and Tradesmen breed
p. 215	UNDERWOOD 44	79	Let poore Nobilitie be vertuous: Wee,
p. 215	UNDERWOOD 44	83	Past any need of vertue. Let them care,
p. 218	UNDERWOOD 47	9	Let those that meerely talke, and never thinke,
p. 218	UNDERWOOD 47	15	But for a Sealing: let these men protest.
p. 218	UNDERWOOD 47	25	Let these men have their wayes, and take their times
p. 222	UNDERWOOD 49	2	And thinkes I dare not her? let the world see.
p. 225	UNDERWOOD 51	17	'Tis a brave cause of joy, let it be knowne,
p. 232	UNDERWOOD 58	14	Their perfum'd judgements, let them kisse thy Wife.
p. 238	UNDERWOOD 65	7	And long in changing. Let our Nephewes see
p. 238	UNDERWOOD 66	11	As in this Prince? Let it be lawfull, so
p. 239	UNDERWOOD 67	13	3. THAL. Yet, let our Trumpets sound;
p. 239	UNDERWOOD 67	16	Let every Lyre be strung,
p. 245	UNDERWOOD 70	76	And let thy lookes with gladnesse shine:
p. 249	UNDERWOOD 72	5	Let Ireland meet it out at Sea, halfe way,
p. 258	UNDERWOOD 75	186	And let him freely gather Loves First-fruits,
p. 260	UNDERWOOD 76	28	Let their spite (which now abounds)
p. 270	UNDERWOOD 83	63	Let Angels sing her glories, who did call
p. 276	U'WOOD 84.3	17	Then let the beames of that, disperse
p. 276	U'WOOD 84.3	26	And let there be a starry Robe
p. 281	U'WOOD 84.4	69	In thee, faire Mansion, let it rest,
p. 282	U'WOOD 84.9	13	On Nature, for her: who did let her lie,
p. 293	UNDERWOOD 87	16	So Fates would let the Boy a long thred run.
p. 294	UNDERWOOD 88	3	Let us not then rush blindly on unto it,
p. 294	UNDERWOOD 88	7	Let us together closely lie, and kisse,
p. 294	UNDERWOOD 89	3	If thou be'st wise, with 'Syrian Oyle let shine
p. 307	HORACE 2	31	In short; I bid, Let what thou work'st upon,
p. 313	HORACE 2	174	Be nought so above him but his sword let claime.
p. 321	HORACE 2	355	But, let the Faunes, drawne from their Groves, beware,
p. 329	HORACE 2	507	Let what thou fain'st for pleasures sake, be neere
p. 329	HORACE 2	508	The truth; nor let thy Fable thinke, what e're
p. 335	HORACE 2	656	To let it downe, who knowes, if he did cast
p. 335	HORACE 2	664	Let Poets perish, that will not be kept.
p. 364	UNGATHERED 4	1	Now, after all, let no man
p. 367	UNGATHERED 6	35	Nor let one Riuer boast
p. 375	UNGATHERED 10	19	For he did but kisse her, and so let her go.
p. 379	UNGATHERED 12	2	The height, let him learne of Mr. Tom. Coryate;
p. 379	UNGATHERED 12	15	He sayes to the world, let any man mend it,
p. 381	UNGATHERED 12	60	The height, let him learne of Mr. Tom Coryate.
p. 387	UNGATHERED 22	5	Let such as iustly haue out=liu'd all prayse,
p. 389	UNGATHERED 24	9	Vpon it, but will loath, or let it passe,
p. 398	UNGATHERED 30	60	Thou hast deseru'd: And let me reade the while
p. 407	UNGATHERED 35	19	your workes thus differing, troth let soe yor style:
p. 416	UNGATHERED 43	10	Of Subiects; Let such envie, till they burst.

letcher'd   frequency: 1   relative frequency: 0.00001
| p. 218 | UNDERWOOD 47 | 13 | They'<h>ave glutted in, and letcher'd out that weeke, |

letcherie   frequency: 3   relative frequency: 0.00004
p. 31	EPIGRAMS 12	22	Thus: and for his letcherie, scores, god payes.
p. 165	UNDERWOOD 15	98	A fellow of course Letcherie, is nam'd,
p. 201	UNDERWOOD 42	41	Home to the Customer: his Letcherie

letchers   frequency: 1   relative frequency: 0.00001
| p. 166 | UNDERWOOD 15 | 139 | Of what he throwes: Like letchers growne content |

lethargie   frequency: 1   relative frequency: 0.00001
| p. 102 | UNDERWOOD 15 | 1 | Wake, friend, from forth thy Lethargie: the Drum |

lethargy. See "lethargie."

lether   frequency: 1   relative frequency: 0.00001
     p. 200 UNDERWOOD 42   25 Yet keepe those up in sackcloth too, or lether,

lets   frequency: 3   relative frequency: 0.00004
     p. 95 FOREST 2   69 But giues me what I call, and lets me eate,
     p. 154 UNDERWOOB 13   36 His Groomes to witnesse; or else lets it fall
     p. 242 UNDERWOOD 69   17 Some of his formes, he lets him not come neere

let's   frequency: 2   relative frequency: 0.00002
     p. 145 UNDERWOOD 5   6 And if wee must, let's sing of you.
     p. 265 UNDERWOOD 79   52 Whose praises let's report unto the Woods,

lett   frequency: 1   relative frequency: 0.00001
     p. 421 UNGATHERED 48   44 And by their takeinge, lett it once appeare

letter   frequency: 3   relative frequency: 0.00004
     p. 51 EPIGRAMS 73   3 As't were a challenge, or a borrowers letter?
     p. 229 UNDERWOOD 54   19 To goe out after ----- till when take this letter
     p. 666 INSCRIPTS. 11   9 Shall powre forth many a line, drop many a
                                letter,

letter-goe   frequency: 1   relative frequency: 0.00001
     p. 315 HORACE 2   234 For his owne good, a carelesse letter-goe

letter'd   frequency: 1   relative frequency: 0.00001
     p. 227 UNDERWOOD 52   23 A letter'd mind, and a large heart would place

letters   frequency: 10   relative frequency: 0.00014
     p. 34 EPIGRAMS 23   7 To it, thy language, letters, arts, best life,
     p. 63 EPIGRAMS 99   2 Better'd thy trust to letters; that thy skill;
     p. 73 EPIGRAMS 113   8 And letters and humanitie in the stead!
     p. 160 UNDERWOOD 14   65 Monarch in Letters! 'Mongst thy Titles showne
     p. 172 UNDERWOOD 21   3 Two letters were enough the plague to teare
     p. 183 UNDERWOOD 29   10 Joynting Syllabes, drowning Letters,
     p. 190 UNDERWOOD 37   12 In letters, that mixe spirits, thus to weave.
     p. 259 UNDERWOOD 76   7 Of his speciall grace to Letters,
     p. 386 UNGATHERED 21   14 Vpon th'Exchange of Letters, as I wou'd
     p. 412 UNGATHERED 41   1 Here, are five letters in this blessed Name,

letting   frequency: 3   relative frequency: 0.00004
     p. 132 UNDERWOOD 2.2   17 Letting Bow and Arrow fall,
     p. 315 HORACE 2   213 The middle of his matter: letting goe
     p. 337 HORACE 2   679 Not letting goe his hold, where he drawes food,

lettuce   frequency: 1   relative frequency: 0.00001
     p. 88 EPIGRAMS 133   167 Laxatiue lettuce, and such windie meate)

lewd   frequency: 2   relative frequency: 0.00002
     p. 27 EPIGRAMS 2   11 Much lesse with lewd, prophane, and beastly
                                phrase,
     p. 167 UNDERWOOD 15   165 Lewd slanderers, soft whisperers that let blood

lewis   frequency: 1   relative frequency: 0.00001
     p. 240 UNDERWOOD 67   27 And Sister to just Lewis!

liar. See "lyer."

libel. See "libell."

libell   frequency: 2   relative frequency: 0.00002
     p. 54 EPIGRAMS 81   8 I must a libell make, and cosen both.
     p. 193 UNDERWOOD 38   96 Can pumpe for; or a Libell without salt

libelling   frequency: 1   relative frequency: 0.00001
     p. 410 UNGATHERED 39   3 At libelling? Shall no Star-Chamber Peers,

libells   frequency: 1   relative frequency: 0.00001
     p. 44 EPIGRAMS 54   1 CHEV'RIL cryes out, my verses libells are;

libels   frequency: 1   relative frequency: 0.00001
     See also "libells."
     p. 218 UNDERWOOD 47   26 To vent their Libels, and to issue rimes,

liber   frequency: 1   relative frequency: 0.00001
     p. 294 UNDERWOOD 89   1 Liber, of all thy friends, thou sweetest care,

liberal. See "liberall."

liberall   frequency: 1   relative frequency: 0.00001
     p. 95 FOREST 2   59 The neede of such? whose liberall boord doth
                                flow,

libertie   frequency: 5   relative frequency: 0.00007
    p. 65 EPIGRAMS 101   42 The libertie, that wee'll enioy to night.
    p. 71 EPIGRAMS 110   4 CATO'S to boote, Rome, and her libertie,
    p. 190 UNDERWOOD 37   20 And seeke to scant her comelie libertie,
    p. 321 HORACE 2   366 And not without much praise; till libertie
    p. 395 UNGATHERED 29 10 Caesar's ambition, Cato's libertie,

liberty. See "libertie."

librarie   frequency: 1   relative frequency: 0.00001
    p. 204 UNDERWOOD 43   31 The learned Librarie of Don Quixote;

library. See "librarie."

librum   frequency: 1   relative frequency: 0.00001
    p. 662 INSCRIPTS. 2   t2 ad Librum.

libyan. See "lybian."

lice   frequency: 1   relative frequency: 0.00001
    p. 380 UNGATHERED 12 50 So that not them, his scabbes, lice, or the
                             stewes,

licence   frequency: 7   relative frequency: 0.00010
    See also "lycense."
 **p. 116 PANEGYRE   101 "Where acts gaue licence to impetuous lust
    p. 152 UNDERWOOD 12   25 To licence ever was so light,
    p. 156 UNDERWOOD 13   96 And told of with more Licence then th'were done!
    p. 190 UNDERWOOD 37   24 Will unto Licence that faire leave abuse.
    p. 215 UNDERWOOD 44   70 All licence in our lives? What need we know,
    p. 319 HORACE 2   299 Both in their tunes, the licence greater grew,
    p. 321 HORACE 2   368 Her licence fit to be restrain'd by law:

licentious   frequency: 2   relative frequency: 0.00002
    p. 27 EPIGRAMS 2   3 Thou should'st be bold, licentious, full of gall,
    p. 163 UNDERWOOD 15   36 But more licentious made, and desperate!

licentiously   frequency: 1   relative frequency: 0.00001
    p. 323 HORACE 2   391 My Verse at randome, and licentiously?

licinus   frequency: 1   relative frequency: 0.00001
    p. 325 HORACE 2   427 And from the Barber Licinus conceale

lick   frequency: 1   relative frequency: 0.00001
    p. 206 UNDERWOOD 43   84 Had made a meale for Vulcan to lick up.

lie   frequency: 14   relative frequency: 0.00020
    See also "lye."
    p. 139 UNDERWOOD 2.7 17 And whilst our tongues perplexed lie,
    p. 142 U'WOOD 2.10   8 'Tis one good part I'ld lie withall.
    p. 163 UNDERWOOD 15   53 That all respect; She must lie downe: Nay more,
    p. 168 UNDERWOOD 16   3 But here doth lie, till the last Day,
    p. 169 UNDERWOOD 17   16 All is not barren land, doth fallow lie.
    p. 174 UNDERWOOD 23   1 Where do'st thou carelesse lie,
    p. 180 UNDERWOOD 26   10 Wrapt in this paper lie,
    p. 181 UNDERWOOD 27   7 Lie drawne to life, in his soft Verse,
    p. 203 UNDERWOOD 43   20 Any, least loose, or s<c>urrile paper, lie
    p. 216 UNDERWOOD 45   20 They cannot last. No lie grew ever old.
    p. 282 U'WOOD 84.9   13 On Nature, for her: who did let her lie,
    p. 294 UNDERWOOD 88   7 Let us together closely lie, and kisse,
    p. 375 UNGATHERED 10 33 To lie at Liuory, while the Horses did stand.
    p. 401 UNGATHERED 33   6 French Aire and English Verse here Wedded
                             lie.

liedgers   frequency: 1   relative frequency: 0.00001
    p. 118 FOREST 13   72 Maintayne their liedgers forth, for forraine
                             wyres,

liegers. See "liedgers."

lies   frequency: 6   relative frequency: 0.00008
    See also "lyes."
 **p. 115 PANEGYRE   83 "And, being once found out, discouer'd lies
    p. 69 EPIGRAMS 107   12 In Ireland, Holland, Sweden, pompous lies,
    p. 127 UNDERWOOD 1.1   7 As my heart lies in peeces, all confus'd,
    p. 167 UNDERWOOD 15 164 Informers, Masters both of Arts and lies;
    p. 251 UNDERWOOD 74   5 Shee lies deliver'd, without paine,
    p. 394 UNGATHERED 28   1 I could begin with that graue forme, Here lies,

lieutenant. See "lievtenant."

lievtenant   frequency: 1   relative frequency: 0.00001
    p. 30 EPIGRAMS 12   t1 ON LIEVTENANT SHIFT.

life   frequency: 93   relative frequency: 0.00134
    See also "a-life," "life's," "lyfe."
    p. 34 EPIGRAMS 23   7 To it, thy language, letters, arts, best life,
    p. 34 EPIGRAMS 25   2 In the past pleasures of his sensuall life,
    p. 35 EPIGRAMS 27   6 If any pious life ere lifted man
    p. 39 EPIGRAMS 40   12 Conquer'd hath both life and it.
    p. 39 EPIGRAMS 40   13 Life, whose griefe was out of fashion,
    p. 40 EPIGRAMS 42   11 All this doth IONE. Or that his long-yearn'd
                               life
    p. 50 EPIGRAMS 70   3 In life, that can employ it; and takes hold
    p. 50 EPIGRAMS 70   6 Each best day of our life escapes vs, first.
    p. 50 EPIGRAMS 70   8 Though life be short, let vs not make it so.
    p. 53 EPIGRAMS 80   1 The ports of death are sinnes; of life, good
                               deeds:
    p. 53 EPIGRAMS 80   t1 OF LIFE, AND DEATH.
    p. 55 EPIGRAMS 86   5 Now, I must giue thy life, and deed, the voice
    p. 57 EPIGRAMS 89   14 So many Poets life, by one should liue.
    p. 60 EPIGRAMS 94   2 Life of the Muses day, their morning-starre!
    p. 66 EPIGRAMS 102   6 Of vice, and vertue; wherein all great life
    p. 66 EPIGRAMS 102   16 Whose life, eu'n they, that enuie it, must
                               praise;
    p. 70 EPIGRAMS 109   11 To make thy lent life, good against the Fates:
    p. 71 EPIGRAMS 110   22 His life, but makes, that he can dye no more.
    p. 73 EPIGRAMS 113   3 So, where thou liu'st, thou mak'st life
                               vnderstood!
    p. 79 EPIGRAMS ·124   5 Which in life did harbour giue
    p. 80 EPIGRAMS 127   8 Lent timely succours, and new life begot:
    p. 100 FOREST 3   106 Thou maist thinke life, a thing but lent.
    p. 113 FOREST 12   4 And, for it, life, conscience, yea, soules are
                               giuen,
    p. 115 FOREST 12   57 Like life vnto 'hem. Who heau'd HERCVLES
    p. 115 FOREST 12   86 And show, how, to the life, my soule presents
    p. 118 FOREST 13   59 This makes, that wisely you decline your life,
    p. 119 FOREST 13   109 Vnto your name, and goodnesse of your life,
    p. 122 FOREST 15   26 For wearinesse of life, not loue of thee.
    p. 127 UNDERWOOD 1.1   19 And breath'st into it, life, and light, with
                               state
    p. 130 UNDERWOOD 1.3   2 The Author both of Life, and light;
    p. 134 UNDERWOOD 2.4   19 As alone there triumphs to the life
    p. 140 UNDERWOOD 2.8   28 All your sweet of life is past,
    p. 149 UNDERWOOD 8   9 Yes; and in death, as life, unblest,
    p. 151 UNDERWOOD 12   11 With the just Canon of his life,
    p. 151 UNDERWOOD 12   12 A life that knew nor noise, nor strife:
    p. 152 UNDERWOOD 12   37 Reader, whose life, and name, did e're become
    p. 158 UNDERWOOD 13   159 By thanking thus the curtesie to life,
    p. 162 UNDERWOOD 15   7 Mans buried honour, in his sleepie life:
    p. 165 UNDERWOOD 15   88 Is lov'd, though he let out his owne for life:
    p. 167 UNDERWOOD 15   166 The life, and fame-vaynes (yet not understood
    p. 168 UNDERWOOD 16   7 What suretie of life have thou, and I?
    p. 171 UNDERWOOD 19   26 His Issue, and all Circumstance of life,
    p. 171 UNDERWOOD 20   10 That their whole life was wickednesse, though
                               weav'd
    p. 175 UNDERWOOD 24   2 The Mistresse of Mans life, grave Historie,
    p. 176 UNDERWOOD 24   18 The light of Truth, and life of Memorie.
    p. 181 UNDERWOOD 27   7 Lie drawne to life, in his soft Verse,
    p. 194 UNDERWOOD 38   112 And that there is no life in me, but love.
    p. 202 UNDERWOOD 43   5 I ne're attempted, Vulcan, 'gainst thy life;
    p. 214 UNDERWOOD 44   41 So acted to the life, as Maurice might,
    p. 224 UNDERWOOD 50   1 The Wisdome, Madam, of your private Life,
    p. 225 UNDERWOOD 50   32 Not boasted in your life, but practis'd true,
    p. 233 UNDERWOOD 59   22 Of humane life! as all the frosts, and sweates
    p. 242 UNDERWOOD 69   23 Then knew the former ages: yet to life,
    p. 243 UNDERWOOD 70   21 For, what is life, if measur'd by the space,
    p. 244 UNDERWOOD 70   40 And sunke in that dead sea of life
    p. 244 UNDERWOOD 70   52 His life was of Humanitie the Sphaere.
    p. 245 UNDERWOOD 70   59 Not liv'd; for Life doth her great actions
                               spell,
    p. 245 UNDERWOOD 70   64 These make the lines of life, and that's her
                               ayre.
    p. 245 UNDERWOOD 70   74 And in short measures, life may perfect bee.
    p. 250 UNDERWOOD 74   3 When shee puts forth the life of ev'ry thing:
    p. 253 UNDERWOOD 75   29 Mariage, the end of life,
    p. 257 UNDERWOOD 75   156 Of Life, that fall so; Christians know their
                               birth
    p. 261 UNDERWOOD 77   17 What you have studied are the arts of life;
    p. 264 UNDERWOOD 79   33 Of all that Nature, yet, to life did bring;
    p. 271 UNDERWOOD 83   67 'Twixt death and life! Where her mortalitie

life (cont.)
```
   p.  271 UNDERWOOD 83    96 The Christian hath t<o>'enjoy the future life,
   p.  282 U'WOOD 84.9      2 Who was my Muse, and life of all I sey'd,
   p.  285 U'WOOD 84.9    112 Of life, and light, the Sonne of God, the
                             Word!
   p.  287 U'WOOD 84.9    173 She was, in one, a many parts of life;
   p.  287 U'WOOD 84.9    178 As her whole life was now become one note
   p.  289 U'WOOD 84.9    221 Of all are dead to life! His Wisdome show
   p.  289 UNDERWOOD 85    t2 The praises of a Countrie life.
   p.  293 UNDERWOOD 87    12 So Fate would give her life, and longer daies.
   p.  295 UNDERWOOD 89     8 Makes his life longer then 'twas given him, much.
   p.  295 UNDERWOOD 90     1 The Things that make the happier life, are
                             these,
   p.  315 HORACE 2       207 Nor from the brand, with which the life did burne
   p.  325 HORACE 2       454 On life, and manners, and make those his booke.
   p.  327 HORACE 2       478 Or mixing sweet, and fit, teach life the right.
   p.  327 HORACE 2       481 From slaughters, and foule life; and for the same
   p.  329 HORACE 2       497 All way of life was shewen; the grace of Kings
   p.  362 UNGATHERED 2     6 Where, such perfections to the life doe rise.
   p.  370 UNGATHERED 8     2 Vpon the Life, and Death of Playes, and Wits,
   p.  382 UNGATHERED 16    8 his life, his loue, his honour, which ne'r dyes,
   p.  386 UNGATHERED 20    7 Or skill of making matches in my life:
   p.  390 UNGATHERED 25    4 With Nature, to out-doo the life:
   p.  391 UNGATHERED 26   36 To life againe, to heare thy Buskin tread,
   p.  393 UNGATHERED 27    5 It is the life and light of loue,
   p.  394 UNGATHERED 28   16 But of one Husband; and since he left life,
   p.  394 UNGATHERED 28   25 Where spight of Death, next Life, for her
                             Loues sake,
   p.  399 UNGATHERED 31   11 The best of Woemen! her whole life
   p.  411 UNGATHERED 40    4 th'uncertainty of Life,
   p.  413 UNGATHERED 41   38 Sweet Tree of Life, King Davids Strength and
                             Tower,
   p.  657 L. CONVIVALES    9 He the half of Life abuses,
```

```
lifes                        frequency:    2   relative frequency: 0.00002
   p.   54 EPIGRAMS 80      5 This world deaths region is, the other lifes:
   p.  243 UNDERWOOD 70    19 As, could they but lifes miseries fore-see,
```

```
life's                       frequency:    1   relative frequency: 0.00001
   See also "lifes."
   p.  237 UNDERWOOD 64    13 When all your life's a president of dayes,
```

```
lift                         frequency:    3   relative frequency: 0.00004
   p.  127 UNDERWOOD 1.1    4 Helpe, helpe to lift
   p.  201 UNDERWOOD 42    58 Lift up some one, and doe, I tell not what.
   p.  234 UNDERWOOD 61     8 To lift to heaven: who is't not understands
```

```
lifted                       frequency:    3   relative frequency: 0.00004
   p.   35 EPIGRAMS 27      6 If any pious life ere lifted man
   p.   88 EPIGRAMS 133   161 With great gray eyes, are lifted vp, and mew'd;
   p.  115 FOREST 12      62 Or lifted CASSIOPEA in her chayre?
```

```
lifts                        frequency:    1   relative frequency: 0.00001
   p.  290 UNDERWOOD 85    17 Or when that Autumne, through the fields, lifts
                             round
```

```
light                        frequency:   71   relative frequency: 0.00102
   See also "fire-light," "light[s]," "sun-light."
   p.   67 EPIGRAMS 104    12 The light, and marke vnto posteritie?
   p.   82 EPIGRAMS 131     1 When we doe giue, ALPHONSO, to the light,
   p.   85 EPIGRAMS 133    60 'Tis but light paines: Indeede this Dock's no
                             rose.
   p.  102 FOREST 5         7 But if once we loose this light,
   p.  107 FOREST 10       16 Goe, crampe dull MARS, light VENVS, when
                             he snorts,
   p.  108 FOREST 10A       7 Then, leaue these lighter numbers, to light
                             braines
   p.  112 FOREST 11       93 A beautie of that cleere, and sparkling light,
   p.  115 FOREST 12       65 You, and that other starre, that purest light,
   p.  115 FOREST 12       76 To curious light, the notes, I then shall sing,
   p.  121 FOREST 14       58 As with the light
   p.  127 UNDERWOOD 1.1   19 And breath'st into it, life, and light, with
                             state
   p.  128 UNDERWOOD 1.1   35 The gladdest light, darke man can thinke upon;
   p.  130 UNDERWOOD 1.3    2 The Author both of Life, and light;
   p.  130 UNDERWOOD 1.3    5 Who saw the light, and were afraid,
   p.  134 UNDERWOOD 2.4   11 Doe but looke on her eyes, they doe light
   p.  147 UNDERWOOD 7     24 Where Love may all his Torches light,
   p.  152 UNDERWOOD 12    25 To licence ever was so light,
   p.  156 UNDERWOOD 13   110 That with these mixtures we put out her light.
```

light (cont.)

p. 157 UNDERWOOD 13	149	'Tis like light Canes, that first rise big and brave,
p. 162 UNDERWOOD 15	20	In outward face, but inward, light as Furre,
p. 164 UNDERWOOD 15	59	O, these so ignorant Monsters! light, as proud,
p. 167 UNDERWOOB 15	163	Light thee from hell on earth: where flatterers, spies,
p. 174 UNDERWOOD 22	32	To light upon a Love of mine.
p. 176 UNDERWOCD 24	18	The light of Truth, and life of Memorie.
p. 177 UNDERWOOD 25	14	Rich beame of honour, shed your light
p. 179 UNDERWOOD 25	59	Shall light those places
p. 183 UNDERWOOD 29	24	All light failed!
p. 191 UNDERWOOD 38	10	As light breakes from you, that affrights despaire,
p. 192 UNDERWOOD 38	57	The Sunne his heat, and light, the ayre his dew?
p. 194 UNDERWOOD 38	122	Rather then want your light, I wish a grave.
p. 197 UNDERWOOD 40	19	Yet should the Lover still be ayrie and light,
p. 200 UNDERWOOD 42	6	As light, and active as the youngest hee
p. 205 UNDERWOOD 43	52	To light Tobacco, or save roasted Geese,
p. 212 UNDERWOOD 43	215	Light on thee: Or if those plagues will not doo,
p. 222 UNDERWOOD 49	10	As aerie light, and as like wit as those?
p. 223 UNDERWOCD 49	32	Her face there's none can like by Candle light.
p. 227 UNDERWOCD 52	21	Ne knowes he flatt'ring Colours, or false light.
p. 234 UNDERWOOD 60	6	Of a Disease, that lov'd no light
p. 245 UNDERWOOD 70	62	To light: her measures are, how well
p. 245 UNDERWOOD 70	72	It was the Plant, and flowre of light.
p. 246 UNDERWOOD 70	96	Whilst that in heav'n, this light on earth must shine.
p. 249 UNDERWOOD 72	11	Three Kingdomes Mirth, in light, and aerie man,
p. 252 UNDERWOOD 75	2	A-while with us, bright Sun, and helpe our light;
p. 253 UNDERWOOD 75	43	And Sister: darting forth a dazling light
p. 254 UNDERWOOD 75	60	With light of love, this Paire doth intertexe!
p. 257 UNDERWOOD 75	144	One to the other, long e're these to light were brought.
p. 262 UNDERWOOD 78	16	Unto our yeare doth give the longest light.
p. 271 UNDERWOOD 83	69	And now, through circumfused light, she lookes
p. 271 UNDERWOOD 83	88	And Day, deceasing with the Prince of light,
p. 273 U'WOOD 84.1	20	Of light expence;
p. 276 U'WOOD 84.3	16	And Men may thinke, all light rose there.
p. 285 U'WOOD 84.9	102	In Heav'n<s> Empyrean, with a robe of light?
p. 285 U'WOOD 84.9	112	Of life, and light, the Sonne of God, the Word!
p. 286 U'WOOD 84.9	131	By light, and comfort of spirituall Grace,
p. 287 U'WOOD 84.9	164	Not tost or troubled with light Lady-aire;
p. 288 U'WOOD 84.9	199	Shee saw her Saviour, by an early light,
p. 293 UNDERWOOD 86	38	I hold thee fast! but fled hence, with the Light,
p. 315 HORACE 2	203	Hee thinkes not, how to give you smoake from light,
p. 315 HORACE 2	204	But light from smoake; that he may draw his bright
p. 321 HORACE 2	337	And farre unworthy to blurt out light rimes;
p. 323 HORACE 2	397	Take you the Greeke Examples, for your light,
p. 331 HORACE 2	543	Will in the light be view'd: This, once, the sight
p. 370 UNGATHERED 7	3	Light, Posture, Height'ning, Shadow, Culloring,
p. 372 UNGATHERED 9	9	Of Spheares, as light of starres; She was earthes Eye:
p. 390 UNGATHERED 26	7	For seeliest Ignorance on these may light,
p. 392 UNGATHERED 26	80	And despaires day, but for thy Volumes light.
p. 393 UNGATHERED 27	5	It is the life and light of loue,
p. 399 UNGATHERED 31	9	Shee was the light (without reflexe
p. 400 UNGATHERED 31	38	Of Angells, and all witnesses of light,
p. 413 UNGATHERED 41	40	The Morning-star, whose light our Fal hath stay'd.
p. 416 UNGATHERED 45	5	And I sweare by all the light

light[s]   frequency: 1   relative frequency: 0.00001
    p. 189 UNDERWOOD 36   6 A'l light[s] into his one doth run;

lighted   frequency: 2   relative frequency: 0.00002
    p. 176 UNDERWOOD 24   9 Which makes that (lighted by the beamie hand
    p. 207 UNDERWOOD 43   90 And lighted by the Stagirite, could spie,

lighten   frequency: 1   relative frequency: 0.00001
    p. 164 UNDERWOOD 15   61 Like upon them lighten? If nature could

lightens   frequency: 1   relative frequency: 0.00001
  p. 193 UNDERWOOD 38   68 God lightens not at mans each fraile offence,

lighter   frequency: 6   relative frequency: 0.00008
See also "liter."
  p. 78 EPIGRAMS 121   2 My lighter comes, to kisse thy learned Muse;
  p. 94 FOREST 2   18 The lighter Faunes, to reach the Ladies oke.
  p. 108 FOREST 10A   7 Then, leaue these lighter numbers, to light
                                    braines
  p. 249 UNDERWOOD 72   12 Made lighter with the Wine. All noises else,
  p. 294 UNDERWOOD 87   22 Thou lighter then the barke of any tree,
  p. 417 UNGATHERED 45 31 Or hir quarters lighter bee,

lightly   frequency: 3   relative frequency: 0.00004
  p. 34 EPIGRAMS 22   12 Which couer lightly, gentle earth.
  p. 139 UNDERWOOD 2.7   5 I'le taste as lightly as the Bee,
  p. 139 UNDERWOOD 2.8   3 Lightly promis'd, she would tell

lightnesse   frequency: 1   relative frequency: 0.00001
  p. 364 UNGATHERED 5   4 As farre as Sinne's from lightnesse.

lightning   frequency: 2   relative frequency: 0.00002
  p. 132 UNDERWOOD 2.2 24 Such a Lightning (as I drew)
  p. 233 UNDERWOOD 59   12 As they out-did the lightning in the<ir> course;

lights   frequency: 7   relative frequency: 0.00010
**p. 113 PANEGYRE   5 (To day) a thousand radiant lights, that stream
  p. 45 EPIGRAMS 59   1 SPIES, you are lights in state, but of base
                                    stuffe,
  p. 95 FOREST 2   73 For fire, or lights, or liuorie: all is there;
  p. 170 UNDERWOOD 19   2 Love lights his torches to inflame desires;
  p. 220 UNDERWOOD 47   65 Not built with Canvasse, paper, and false
                                    lights,
  p. 246 UNDERWOOD 70   93 Lights, the Dioscuri;
  p. 407 UNGATHERED 35 10 Wth slyding windowes, & false Lights a top!

ligorne   frequency: 1   relative frequency: 0.00001
  p. 69 EPIGRAMS 107   14 What at Ligorne, Rome, Florence you did doe:

ligurine   frequency: 1   relative frequency: 0.00001
  p. 293 UNDERWOOD 86   33 But, why, oh why, my Ligurine,

lik'd   frequency: 2   relative frequency: 0.00002
  p. 42 EPIGRAMS 48   1 His bought armes MVNG' not lik'd; for his
                                    first day
  p. 247 UNDERWOOD 70 108 You lik'd, then after, to apply

like   frequency: 134   relative frequency: 0.00193
See also "clarke-like," "god-like," "gyerlyk,"
         "horse-leech-like," "looser-like,"
         "lyke," "scarlet-like,"
         "souldier-like," "spunge-like,"
         "tabacco-like," "waxe-like."
*p. 492 TO HIMSELF   22 Like Pericles; and stale
*p. 494 TO HIMSELF   56 As they shall cry, like ours
**p. 115 PANEGYRE   80 "To rule like Heauen; and haue no more, their
                                    owne,
**p. 116 PANEGYRE   130 When, like an April Iris, flew her shine
  p. 32 EPIGRAMS 18   5 And mine come nothing like. I hope so. Yet,
  p. 35 EPIGRAMS 28   14 He drinkes to no man: that's, too, like a lord.
  p. 36 EPIGRAMS 28   20 May heare my Epigrammes, but like of none.
  p. 37 EPIGRAMS 33   5 Which ·if most gracious heauen grant like thine,
  p. 38 EPIGRAMS 35   7 Like aydes gainst treasons who hath found before?
  p. 39 EPIGRAMS 40   10 And like Nectar euer flowing:
  p. 40 EPIGRAMS 42   8 The like is IONE. But turning home, is sad.
  p. 40 EPIGRAMS 42   12 Were quite out-spun. The like wish hath his
                                    wife.
  p. 41 EPIGRAMS 45   12 As what he loues may neuer like too much.
  p. 47 EPIGRAMS 64   1 Not glad, like those that haue new hopes, or
                                    sutes,
  p. 52 EPIGRAMS 76   8 Nor lend like influence from his lucent seat.
  p. 53 EPIGRAMS 79   2 Your noblest father prou'd: like whom, before,
  p. 55 EPIGRAMS 84   5 Straight went I home; and there most like a
                                    Poet,
  p. 57 EPIGRAMS 90   17 And it is hop'd, that shee, like MILO, wull,
  p. 59 EPIGRAMS 92   7 And graue as ripe, like mellow as their faces.
  p. 59 EPIGRAMS 92   36 Much like those Brethren; thinking to preuaile
  p. 60 EPIGRAMS 93   1 How like a columne, RADCLIFFE, left
                                    alone
  p. 61 EPIGRAMS 94   13 And like them too; must needfully, though few,

like (cont.)

p.	61	EPIGRAMS 95	13	O, would'st thou adde like hand, to all the rest!
p.	61	EPIGRAMS 95	17	For who can master those great parts like thee,
p.	62	EPIGRAMS 96	11	And, till they burst, their backs, like asses load:
p.	67	EPIGRAMS 104	15	And like it too; if they looke equally:
p.	68	EPIGRAMS 106	8	Like straight, thy pietie to God, and friends:
p.	86	EPIGRAMS 133	77	And, on they went, like CASTOR braue, and POLLVX:
p.	88	EPIGRAMS 133	139	Or, that it lay, heap'd like an vsurers masse,
p.	100	FOREST 4	22	Like such as blow away their liues,
p.	108	FOREST 10 A	4	like glasse, blowne vp, and fashion'd by desire.
p.	110	FOREST 11	39	Inconstant, like the sea, of whence 'tis borne,
p.	110	FOREST 11	40	Rough, swelling, like a storme:
p.	110	FOREST 11	49	That falls like sleepe on louers, and combines
p.	111	FOREST 11	69	Peace, Luxurie, thou art like one of those
p.	112	FOREST 11	91	But we propose a person like our Doue,
p.	115	FOREST 12	57	Like life vnto 'hem. Who heau'd HERCVLES
p.	115	FOREST 12	83	There like a rich, and golden pyramede,
p.	118	FOREST 13	62	Not looking by, or backe (like those, that waite
p.	130	UNDERWOOD 1.3	4	And like the ravish'd Sheep'erds said,
p.	133	UNDERWOOD 2.3	1	After many scornes like these,
p.	136	UNDERWOOD 2.5	17	Both her Browes, bent like my Bow.
p.	141	UNDERWOOD 2.9	17	Eye-brows bent like Cupids bow,
p.	149	UNDERWOOD 8	7	And in his Mrs. flame, playing like a flye,
p.	154	UNDERWOOD 13	32	Of pressure, like one taken in a streight?
p.	155	UNDERWOOD 13	62	Like Money-brokers, after Names, and hire
p.	156	UNDERWOOD 13	116	But like to be, that every day mends one,
p.	157	UNDERWOOD 13	149	'Tis like light Canes, that first rise big and brave,
p.	159	UNDERWOOD 14	31	And like a Compasse keeping one foot still
p.	162	UNDERWOOD 15	26	For all their spight, be like him if they could:
p.	164	UNDERWOOD 15	61	Like upon them lighten? If nature could
p.	164	UNDERWOOD 15	65	Planting their Purles, and Curles spread forth like Net,
p.	165	UNDERWOOD 15	96	If it be thought, kild like her Embrions; for,
p.	166	UNDERWOOD 15	139	Of what he throwes: Like letchers growne content
p.	166	UNDERWOOD 15	143	In this, and like, an itch of Vanitie,
p.	169	UNDERWOOD 18	4	Then like, then love; and now would they amaze?
p.	173	UNDERWOOD 22	5	A vertue, like Allay, so gone
p.	177	UNDERWOOD 25	18	Then shall my Verses, like strong Charmes,
p.	179	UNDERWOOD 25	37	When her dead essence (like the Anatomie
p.	187	UNDERWOOD 33	29	So comm'st thou like a Chiefe into the Court,
p.	190	UNDERWOOD 37	7	Not like your Countrie-neighbours, that commit
p.	192	UNDERWOOD 38	32	Thinke that your selfe like heaven forgive me can:
p.	193	UNDERWOOD 38	80	This looketh like an Execution day?
p.	197	UNDERWOOD 40	21	Not, like a Midas, shut up in himselfe,
p.	198	UNDERWOOD 40	26	Moves like a sprightly River, and yet can
p.	198	UNDERWOOD 40	29	They looke at best like Creame-bowles, and you soone
p.	198	UNDERWOOD 40	35	Like the dull wearied Crane that (come on land)
p.	198	UNDERWOOD 40	37	Where he that knowes will, like a Lapwing, flie
p.	199	UNDERWOOD 41	3	What it is like: And doe not thinke they can
p.	199	UNDERWOOD 41	21	Or like a Ghost walke silent amongst men,
p.	201	UNDERWOOD 42	39	Whose like I have knowne the Taylors Wife put on
p.	201	UNDERWOOD 42	48	That are like cloath'd: must I be of those fooles
p.	211	UNDERWOOD 43	187	Or in the Bell-Mans Lanthorne, like a spie,
p.	215	UNDERWOOD 44	75	We will beleeve, like men of our owne Ranke,
p.	217	UNDERWOOD 46	17	Like Solons selfe; explat'st the knottie Lawes
p.	218	UNDERWOOD 47	18	Like flies, or wormes, which mans corrupt parts fed:
p.	221	UNDERWOOD 48	20	From any thought like sadnesse.
p.	222	UNDERWOOD 49	10	As aerie light, and as like wit as those?
p.	223	UNDERWOOD 49	32	Her face there's none can like by Candle light.
p.	227	UNDERWOOD 52	15	You made it a brave piece, but not like me.
p.	228	UNDERWOOD 53	7	You shew'd like Perseus upon Pegasus;
p.	230	UNDERWOOD 56	19	Such, (if her manners like you) I doe send:
p.	232	UNDERWOOD 58	9	Will be reward enough: to weare like those,
p.	232	UNDERWOOD 58	11	Like a rung Beare, or Swine: grunting out wit
p.	233	UNDERWOOD 59	10	Of bodies, meet like rarified ayre!
p.	234	UNDERWOOD 60	8	But crept like darknesse through his blood?
p.	243	UNDERWOOD 70	20	No doubt all Infants would returne like thee.
p.	245	UNDERWOOD 70	65	It is not growing like a tree
p.	249	UNDERWOOD 72	8	Like Eccho playing from the other shore.
p.	253	UNDERWOOD 75	14	So like a feast?
p.	253	UNDERWOOD 75	42	Like what she is, the Daughter of a Duke,
p.	257	UNDERWOOD 75	154	Like Swine, or other Cattell here on earth:

like (cont.)
```
     p. 258 UNDERWOOD 75    174 Like pretty Spies,
     p. 258 UNDERWOOD 75    179 But like an Arme of Eminence, 'mongst them,
     p. 262 UNDERWOOD 78      7 And he is built like some imperiall roome
     p. 270 UNDERWOOD 83     41 Were like a ring of Vertues, 'bout her set,
     p. 275 U'WOOD 84.3       4 Where every lim takes like a face?
     p. 276 U'WOOD 84.3      15 Till, like her face, it doe appeare,
     p. 276 U'WOOD 84.3      23 Foure Rivers branching forth like Seas,
     p. 278 U'WOOD 84.4      12 But these are like a Mind, not it.
     p. 280 U'WOOD 84.4      57 Not swelling like the Ocean proud,
     p. 280 U'WOOD 84.4      66 In rest, like spirits left behind
     p. 283 U'WOOD 84.9      30 Nothing I doe; but, like a heavie wheele,
     p. 284 U'WOOD 84.9      53 Like single; so, there is a third, commixt,
     p. 286 U'WOOD 84.9     126 And to the Touch, a Flower, like soft as
                                Palme.
     p. 294 UNDERWOOD 88      4 Like lustfull beasts, that onely know to doe it:
     p. 305 HORACE 2          9 Whose shapes, like sick-mens dreames, are fain'd
                                so vaine,
     p. 307 HORACE 2         63 Till fitter season. Now, to like of this,
     p. 309 HORACE 2         89 Like tender buds shoot up, and freshly grow.
     p. 313 HORACE 2        182 Still to be like himselfe, and hold his worth.
     p. 315 HORACE 2        226 And can tread firme, longs with like lads to
                                play;
     p. 315 HORACE 2        231 I'the open field; is Waxe like to be wrought
     p. 321 HORACE 2        357 Like men street-borne, and neare the Hall,
                                reherse
     p. 321 HORACE 2        362 Him that buyes chiches blanch't, or chance to
                                like
     p. 325 HORACE 2        414 Had not our every Poet like offended.
     p. 325 HORACE 2        433 Be like a Whet-stone, that an edge can put
     p. 335 HORACE 2        650 And stalketh, like a Fowler, round about,
     p. 369 UNGATHERED 6    120 Set out a like, or second to our Swan.
     p. 374 UNGATHERED 10    10 Here, like Arion, our Coryate doth draw
     p. 374 UNGATHERED 10    17 Hee's carried like a Cripple, from Constable to
                                Constable.
     p. 375 UNGATHERED 10    24 Here, by a Boore too, hee's like to be beaten,
     p. 380 UNGATHERED 12    35 He was in his trauaile, how like to be beaten,
     p. 386 UNGATHERED 21    10 Or, like our Money-Brokers, take vp names
     p. 386 UNGATHERED 21    15 More of our writers would like thee, not swell
     p. 387 UNGATHERED 22     9 nor yet inscription like it. Write but that;
     p. 389 UNGATHERED 24    11 Such Bookes deserue Translators, of like coate
     p. 392 UNGATHERED 26    45 When like Apollo he came forth to warme
     p. 392 UNGATHERED 26    46 Our eares, or like a Mercury to charme!
     p. 392 UNGATHERED 26    79 Which, since thy flight from hence, hath mourn'd
                                like night,
     p. 397 UNGATHERED 30    36 Like him, to make the ayre, one volary:
     p. 401 UNGATHERED 32    21 And like a hallow'd Temple, free from taint
     p. 409 UNGATHERED 37    19 But fly thee, like the Pest! Walke not the
                                street
     p. 414 UNGATHERED 41    51 Who like a Giant hasts his course to run,
     p. 415 UNGATHERED 42     9 Or why to like; they found, it all was new,
```

likely   frequency: 1   relative frequency: 0.00001
```
     p. 200 UNDERWOOD 42     37 It is not likely I should now looke downe
```

likenesse   frequency: 2   relative frequency: 0.00002
```
     p. 307 HORACE 2         34 Are, with the likenesse of the truth, undone.
     p. 370 UNGATHERED 7      2 Require (besides the likenesse of the thing)
```

likes   frequency: 1   relative frequency: 0.00001
```
     p.  30 EPIGRAMS 12      10 Lookes o're the bill, likes it: and say's, god
                                payes.
```

liking   frequency: 2   relative frequency: 0.00002
```
     p. 236 UNDERWOOD 63      6 What (at his liking) he will take away.
     p. 247 UNDERWOOD 70    109 That liking; and approach so one the tother,
```

lilies.   See "lillies."

lillie   frequency: 4   relative frequency: 0.00005
```
     p. 134 UNDERWOOD 2.4    21 Have you seene but a bright Lillie grow,
     p. 245 UNDERWOOD 70     69 A Lillie of a Day,
     p. 401 UNGATHERED 33     8 Againe hath brought the Lillie to the Rose;
     p. 413 UNGATHERED 41    15 To top the fairest Lillie, now, that growes,
```

lillies   frequency: 3   relative frequency: 0.00004
```
     p. 147 UNDERWOOD 7      18 And lookes as Lillies doe,
     p. 254 UNDERWOOD 75     57 See, how with Roses, and with Lillies shine,
     p. 254 UNDERWOOD 75     58 (Lillies and Roses, Flowers of either Sexe)
```

lilly   frequency: 2   relative frequency: 0.00002
    p. 237 UNDERWOOD 65   3 The bed of the chast Lilly, and the Rose!
    p. 268 UNDERWOOD 82   16 Her Rose, and Lilly, intertwind, have made.

lily   frequency: 1   relative frequency: 0.00001
    See alsc "lillie," "lilly."
    p. 391 UNGATHERED 26   29 And tell, how farre thou didst our Lily
                               out-shine,

lim   frequency: 2   relative frequency: 0.00002
    p.   63 EPIGRAMS 97   19 About his forme. What then so swells each lim?
    p. 275 U'WOOD 84.3   4 Where every lim takes like a face?

limb. See "lim," "limbe."

limbe   frequency: 3   relative frequency: 0.00004
    p. 151 UNDERWOOD 12   9 That though they did possesse each limbe,
    p. 192 UNDERWOOD 38   45 An ill-affected limbe (what e're it aile)
    p. 305 HORACE 2   3 On every limbe, ta'en from a severall creature,

limbes   frequency: 1   relative frequency: 0.00001
    p. 133 UNDERWOOD 2.3   4 Eyes and limbes: to hurt me more.

limbs. See "limbes," "limmes."

limiting   frequency: 1   relative frequency: 0.00001
    p. 370 UNGATHERED 7   6 Will well confesse; presenting, limiting,

limmes   frequency: 1   relative frequency: 0.00001
    p. 105 FOREST 8   23 Sleeked limmes, and finest blood?

limons   frequency: 2   relative frequency: 0.00002
    p.   59 EPIGRAMS 92   28 With iuyce of limons, onions, pisse, to write,
    p.   65 EPIGRAMS 101   13 Limons, and wine for sauce: to these, a coney

lin'd   frequency: 1   relative frequency: 0.00001
    p.   62 EPIGRAMS 97   4 His cloke with orient veluet quite lin'd through,

line   frequency: 17   relative frequency: 0.00024
    See also "lyne."
    p.   44 EPIGRAMS 53   10 Could saue that line to dedicate to thee?
    p.   54 EPIGRAMS 81   2 A line vnto thee, till the world it know;
    p. 181 UNDERWOOD 27   19 Of Caesars Daughter, and the line
    p. 182 UNDERWOOD 28   14 For Venus Ceston, every line you make.
    p. 200 UNDERWOOD 42   14 No face, no hand, proportion, line, or Ayre
    p. 203 UNDERWOOD 43   6 Nor made least line of love to thy loose Wife;
    p. 274 U'WOOD 84.2   14 Thy Neeces line, then thou that gav'st thy Name
    p. 278 U'WOOD 84.4   22 Hence-forth may every line be you;
    p. 287 U'WOOD 84.9   154 Each line, as it were graphick, in the face!
    p. 362 UNGATHERED 2   14 His proofe their praise, will meete, as in this
                               line.
    p. 379 UNGATHERED 12   8 To line out no stride, but pas'd by himselfe?
    p. 380 UNGATHERED 12   23 Each leafe of his iournall, and line doth vnlocke
    p. 391 UNGATHERED 26   30 Or sporting Kid, or Marlowes mighty line.
    p. 392 UNGATHERED 26   59 Who casts to write a liuing line, must sweat,
    p. 395 UNGATHERED 29   5 At euery line some pinn thereof should slacke
    p. 398 UNGATHERED 30   78 And stop my sight, in euery line I goe.
    p. 666 INSCRIPTS. 11   9 Shall powre forth many a line, drop many a
                               letter,

linen. See "Linnen."

lines   frequency: 13   relative frequency: 0.00018
    See also "lynes."
    p.   65 EPIGRAMS 101   32 Their liues, as doe their lines, till now had
                               lasted.
    p. 117 FOREST 13   20 Or feare to draw true lines, 'cause others paint:
    p. 170 UNDERWOOD 18   24 Love to my heart, and Fortune to my lines.
    p. 200 UNDERWOOD 43   78 And the strong lines, that so the time doe catch:
    p. 226 UNDERWOOD 52   3 But there are lines, wherewith I might
                               b<e>'embrac'd.
    p. 245 UNDERWOOD 70   64 These make the lines of life, and that's her
                               ayre.
    p. 247 UNDERWOOD 70   126 Whose lines her rowles were, and records.
    p. 262 UNDERWOOD 78   2 Yet read him in these lines: He doth excell
    p. 263 UNDERWOOD 78   26 What reputation to my lines, and me,
    p. 392 UNGATHERED 26   48 And ioy'd to weare the dressing of his lines!
    p. 392 UNGATHERED 26   68 In his well torned, and true-filed lines:
    p. 408 UNGATHERED 37   6 Is to make cheape, the Lord, the lines, the
                               price.

lines (cont.)
    p. 414 UNGATHERED 41 54 Through all the lines of this circumference,

linkes   frequency: 1   relative frequency: 0.00001
    p. 110 FOREST 11   48 Whose linkes are bright, and euen,

links. See "linkes."

linnen   frequency: 1   relative frequency: 0.00001
    p. 96 FOREST 2   86 To haue her linnen, plate, and all things nigh,

lion   frequency: 1   relative frequency: 0.00001
    p. 408 UNGATHERED 36 7 The Lybian Lion hunts noe butter flyes,

lions. See "lyons."

lip   frequency: 3   relative frequency: 0.00004
  See also "lippe."
    p. 139 UNDERWOOD 2.7 15 Joyne lip to lip, and try:
    p. 141 UNDERWOOD 2.9 22 And his lip should kissing teach,

lip-thirstie   frequency: 1   relative frequency: 0.00001
    p. 222 UNDERWOOD 49 13 And as lip-thirstie, in each words expence,

lippe   frequency: 2   relative frequency: 0.00002
    p. 52 EPIGRAMS 75   3 Though LIPPE, at PAVLS, ranne from his
                         text away,
    p. 52 EPIGRAMS 75   t1 ON LIPPE, THE TEACHER.

lippes   frequency: 1   relative frequency: 0.00001
    p. 397 UNGATHERED 30 38 My lippes could forme the voyce, I heard that
                         Rore,

lips   frequency: 5   relative frequency: 0.00007
  See also "lippes."
    p. 33 EPIGRAMS 21   5 Quick in his lips! Who hath this wonder wrought?
    p. 103 FOREST 6   7 On my lips, thus hardly sundred,
    p. 137 UNDERWOOD 2.6 3 From your lips, and suck'd an ayre
    p. 143 UNDERWOOD 3   16 But what those lips doe make.
    p. 170 UNDERWOOD 19   9 And lastly by your lips, the banke of kisses,

liquid   frequency: 1   relative frequency: 0.00001
    p. 89 EPIGRAMS 133 193 In memorie of which most liquid deed,

liquor   frequency: 2   relative frequency: 0.00002
    p. 221 UNDERWOOD 48 28 Then Hippocrenes liquor:
    p. 657 L. CONVIVALES 15 Tis the true Phoebeian Liquor,

list   frequency: 7   relative frequency: 0.00010
  See also "lyst."
    p. 85 EPIGRAMS 133   40 Or his to Antwerpe. Therefore, once more, list
                         ho'.
    p. 97 FOREST 3   21 Or, if thou list the night in watch to breake,
    p. 153 UNDERWOOD 13   4 Lesse list of proud, hard, or ingratefull Men.
    p. 386 UNGATHERED 21 4 And, if thou list thy selfe, what thou canst bee.
    p. 394 UNGATHERED 28 8 A list of Epithites: And prayse this way.
    p. 398 UNGATHERED 30 62 Thy list of aydes, and force, for so it is:
    p. 423 UNGATHERED 50 14 the sword, but that it acteth what it list.

listen   frequency: 1   relative frequency: 0.00001
    p. 84 EPIGRAMS 133   28 His three for one. Now, lordings, listen well.

liter   frequency: 1   relative frequency: 0.00001
    p. 86 EPIGRAMS 133   85 But, comming neere, they found it but a liter,

literate   frequency: 1   relative frequency: 0.00001
    p. 379 UNGATHERED 12 7 Of our Odcombian, that literate Elfe?

little   frequency: 24   relative frequency: 0.00034
    p. 30 EPIGRAMS 11   7 For I will doe none: and as little ill,
    p. 37 EPIGRAMS 34   2 Shewes of the resurrection little trust.
    p. 45 EPIGRAMS 56   7 To'a little wealth, and credit in the scene,
    p. 49 EPIGRAMS 66   16 It may be much, or little, in the cause.
    p. 66 EPIGRAMS 103   5 And, being nam'd, how little doth that name
    p. 77 EPIGRAMS 120   2 This little storie?
    p. 79 EPIGRAMS 124   2 In a little? Reader, stay.
    p. 89 EPIGRAMS 133 189 Who kept an ale-house; with my little MINOS,
    p. 101 FOREST 4   35 Little, for me, had reason done,
    p. 101 FOREST 4   38 As little, as I hope from thee:
    p. 121 FOREST 14   29 Little, whose will

little (cont.)
      p. 121 FOREST 14   31 Nor can a little of the common store,
      p. 157 UNDERWOOD 13   132 Profit in ought; each day some little adde,
      p. 172 UNDERWOOD 21   t1 A little Shrub growing by.
      p. 190 UNDERWOOD 37   19 Little know they, that professe Amitie,
      p. 220 UNDERWOOD 47   76 My selfe a little. I will take you so,
      p. 273 U'WOOD 84.1   18 Take little Infants with their noyse,
      p. 331 HORACE 2   563 If ne're so little it depart the first,
      p. 371 UNGATHERED 9   2 Read here a little, that thou mayst know much.
      p. 383 UNGATHERED 16   13 still that same little poynte hee was; but when
      p. 383 UNGATHERED 16   16 yf from a little sparke hee rise not fier.
      p. 391 UNGATHERED 26   21 A little further, to make thee a roome:
      p. 662 INSCRIPTS. 2   1 Goe little Booke, Goe little Fable

liud   frequency: 1   relative frequency: 0.00001
      p. 387 UNGATHERED 22   12 not when I die'd, but how I liud. Farewell.

liu'd   frequency: 4   relative frequency: 0.00005
      p. 61 EPIGRAMS 95   4 In thee, most weighty SAVILE, liu'd to vs:
      p. 71 EPIGRAMS 110   9 Nor that his worke liu'd in the hands of foes,
      p. 71 EPIGRAMS 110   13 For, where his person liu'd scarce one iust age,
      p. 79 EPIGRAMS 124   12 Then that it liu'd at all. Farewell.

liue   frequency: 22   relative frequency: 0.00031
      p. 34 EPIGRAMS 23   5 Longer a knowing, then most wits doe liue.
      p. 46 EPIGRAMS 62   9 What should the cause be? Oh, you liue at court:
      p. 49 EPIGRAMS 66   12 To liue when Broeck not stands, nor Roor doth
                                 runne.
      p. 50 EPIGRAMS 70   1 When Nature bids vs leaue to liue, 'tis late
      p. 51 EPIGRAMS 74   3 Whil'st I behold thee liue with purest hands;
      p. 57 EPIGRAMS 89   14 So many Poets life, by one should liue.
      p. 58 EPIGRAMS 91   11 To any one, were enuie: which would liue
      p. 73 EPIGRAMS 116   12 And to liue great, was better, then great borne.
      p. 76 EPIGRAMS 119   14 Which is to liue to conscience, not to show.
      p. 79 EPIGRAMS 124   6 To more vertue, then doth liue.
      p. 97 FOREST 3   14 Liue, with vn-bought prouision blest;
      p. 98 FOREST 3   66 Striue, WROTH, to liue long innocent.
      p. 100 FOREST 4   7 Vpon thy throate, and liue exempt
      p. 104 FOREST 8   9 Liue not we, as, all thy stalls,
      p. 115 FOREST 12   55 That HOMER brought to Troy; yet none so
                                 liue:
      p. 118 FOREST 13   75 And almost, all dayes after, while they liue;
      p. 120 FOREST 13   121 Liue that one, still; and as long yeeres doe
                                  passe,
      p. 121 FOREST 14   50 To liue vntill to morrow' hath lost two dayes.
      p. 121 FOREST 14   51 So may you liue in honor, as in name,
      p. 362 UNGATHERED 1   31 And thou in them shalt liue as longe as Fame.
      p. 391 UNGATHERED 26   23 And art aliue still, while thy Booke doth liue,
      p. 400 UNGATHERED 32   1 This Booke will liue; It hath a Genius: This

liuers   frequency: 1   relative frequency: 0.00001
      p. 105 FOREST 8   17 Liuers, round about the towne.

liues   frequency: 8   relative frequency: 0.00011
      p. 29 EPIGRAMS 6   2 Sure, willing pouertie liues most in you.
      p. 30 EPIGRAMS 12   5 By that one spell he liues, eates, drinkes,
                                 arrayes
      p. 54 EPIGRAMS 81   6 Thy wit liues by it, PROVLE, and belly too.
      p. 65 EPIGRAMS 101   32 Their liues, as doe their lines, till now had
                                 lasted.
      p. 88 EPIGRAMS 133   154 Yet drown'd they not. They had fiue liues in
                                  future.
      p. 100 FOREST 4   22 Like such as blow away their liues,
      p. 382 UNGATHERED 16   4 to tender thus, their liues, their loues, their
                                hartes!
      p. 392 UNGATHERED 26   66 Liues in his issue, euen so, the race

liuing   frequency: 4   relative frequency: 0.00005
      p. 53 EPIGRAMS 79   10 On whom, if he were liuing now, to looke,
      p. 60 EPIGRAMS 94   11 They, then, that liuing where the matter is bred,
      p. 76 EPIGRAMS 119   15 He, that, but liuing halfe his age, dyes such;
      p. 392 UNGATHERED 26   59 Who casts to write a liuing line, must sweat,

liuorie   frequency: 1   relative frequency: 0.00001
      p. 95 FOREST 2   73 For fire, or lights, or liuorie: all is there;

liuory   frequency: 1   relative frequency: 0.00001
      p. 375 UNGATHERED 10   33 To lie at Liuory, while the Horses did stand.

liu'st   frequency: 3   relative frequency: 0.00004
  p. 50 EPIGRAMS 69   2 Yet by thy weapon liu'st! Th'hast one good part.
  p. 61 EPIGRAMS 95   18 That liu'st from hope, from feare, from faction
                  free;
  p. 73 EPIGRAMS 113   3 So, where thou liu'st, thou mak'st life
                  vnderstood!

liv'd   frequency: 7   relative frequency: 0.00010
  See alsc "liud," "liu'd," "out=liu'd,"
      "out-liv'd."
  p. 200 UNDERWOOD 42   29 But I who live, and have liv'd twentie yeare
  p. 245 UNDERWOOD 70   59 Not liv'd; for Life doth her great actions
                  spell,
  p. 247 UNDERWOOD 70   113 You liv'd to be the great surnames,
  p. 257 UNDERWOOD 75   153 Th'Ignoble never liv'd, they were a-while
  p. 270 UNDERWOOD 83   48 Just as she in it liv'd! and so exempt
  p. 309 HORACE 2   102 And much shall dye, that now is nobly liv'd,
  p. 327 HORACE 2   480 First frighted men, that wildly liv'd, at ods,

live   frequency: 20   relative frequency: 0.00028
  See alsc "liue," "lyue," "out-liue," "out-live."
  p. 157 UNDERWOOD 13   143 Such Notes are vertuous men! they live as fast
  p. 167 UNDERWOOD 15   160 But he that's both, and slave to boote, shall
                  live,
  p. 171 UNDERWOOD 19   17 Unto the other; and live patterns, how
  p. 191 UNDERWOOD 38   29 And (stil'd your mercies Creature) will live
                  more
  p. 192 UNDERWOOD 38   48 Would live his glory that could keepe it on;
  p. 193 UNDERWOOD 38   78 That makes us live, not that which calls to die.
  p. 200 UNDERWOOD 42   29 But I who live, and have liv'd twentie yeare
  p. 211 UNDERWOOD 43   181 To live in Sea-coale, and goe forth in smoake;
  p. 215 UNDERWOOD 44   68 Live by their Scale, that dare doe nothing free?
  p. 218 UNDERWOOD 47   10 That live in the wild Anarchie of Drinke,
  p. 219 UNDERWOOD 47   42 To live, or fall a Carkasse in the cause.
  p. 219 UNDERWOOD 47   59 Live to that point I will, for which I am man,
  p. 224 UNDERWOOD 50   2 Wherewith this while you live a widow'd wife,
  p. 233 UNDERWOOD 59   21 Who durst live great, 'mongst all the colds, and
                  heates,
  p. 236 UNDERWOOD 64   3 How many times, Live long, CHARLES, would
                  he say,
  p. 241 UNDERWOOD 69   12 All live dogs from the lane, and his shops sight,
  p. 262 UNDERWOOD 78   17 In signe the Subject, and the Song will live,
  p. 294 UNDERWOOD 87   24 Yet would I wish to love, live, die with thee.
  p. 307 HORACE 2   51 To be that Smith; then live, mark'd one of
                  those,
  p. 329 HORACE 2   519 With honour make the farre-knowne Author live.

'live   frequency: 1   relative frequency: 0.00001
  p. 168 UNDERWOOD 15   189 So, 'live or dead, thou wilt preserve a fame

liver. See "livor."

liveries   frequency: 1   relative frequency: 0.00001
  p. 253 UNDERWOOD 75   18 Of Summers Liveries, and gladding greene;

livers. See "liuers."

livery. See "liuorie," "liuery."

lives   frequency: 11   relative frequency: 0.00015
  See also "liues."
  p. 146 UNDERWOOD 6   5 Take that away, you take our lives,
  p. 165 UNDERWOOD 15   94 Lives to the Lord, but to the Ladies end.
  p. 166 UNDERWOOD 15   127 More then themselves, or then our lives could
                  take,
  p. 173 UNDERWOOD 22   14 In whom alone Love lives agen?
  p. 190 UNDERWOOD 37   31 For no man lives so out of passions sway,
  p. 200 UNDERWOOD 42   20 (If they be faire and worth it) have their lives
  p. 215 UNDERWOOD 44   70 All licence in our lives? What need we know,
  p. 241 UNDERWOOD 68   14 The Kings fame lives. Go now, denie his
                  Teirce.
  p. 246 UNDERWOOD 70   84 And there he lives with memorie; and Ben
  p. 283 U'WOOD 84.9   37 The joy of Saints! the Crowne for which it
                  lives,
  p. 418 UNGATHERED 47   4 That lives, and breath's, and loves the King.

livest. See "liu'st."

livie   frequency: 2   relative frequency: 0.00002
  p. 65 EPIGRAMS 101   22 LIVIE, or of some better booke to vs,

livie (cont.)
    p. 86 EPIGRAMS 133   74 Spake to 'hem louder, then the oxe in LIVIE;

living   frequency: 4   relative frequency: 0.00005
    See also "liuing."
    p. 163 UNDERWOOD 15   41 That kept man living! Pleasures only sought!
    p. 282 U'WOOD 84.9   t3 who living, gave me leave to call her so.
    p. 295 UNDERWOOD 89   7 Hee, that but living halfe his dayes, dies such,
    p. 418 UNGATHERED 47   3 And God blesse every living thing,

livor   frequency: 1   relative frequency: 0.00001
    p. 292 UNDERWOOD 86   12 If a fit livor thou dost seeke to toast;

livy. See "livie."

lo   frequency: 2   relative frequency: 0.00002
    See also "loe."
    p. 185 UNDERWOOD 30   t3 Lo: high Treasurer of England.
    p. 185 UNDERWOOD 31   t2 To THOMAS Lo: ELSMERE,

load   frequency: 3   relative frequency: 0.00004
    p. 62 EPIGRAMS 96   11 And, till they burst, their backs, like asses
                  load:
    p. 85 EPIGRAMS 133   65 Who shall discharge first his merd-vrinous load:
    p. 166 UNDERWOOD 15   128 But both fell prest under the load they make.

loath   frequency: 3   relative frequency: 0.00004
    See also "loth."
    p. 42 EPIGRAMS 49   5 PLAY-WRIGHT, I loath to haue thy
                   manners knowne
    p. 154 UNDERWOOD 13   44 Nought but in corners; and is loath to leave
    p. 389 UNGATHERED 24   9 Vpon it, but will loath, or let it passe,

loathe. See "loath."

loathed. See "lothed."

loathsome. See "lothsome."

lock   frequency: 2   relative frequency: 0.00002
    p. 86 EPIGRAMS 133   84 Made of the trull, that cut her fathers lock:
    p. 198 UNDERWOOD 40   43 Can lock the Sense up, or the heart a thought,

lock'd   frequency: 1   relative frequency: 0.00001
    See also "lockt," "lock't."
    p. 59 EPIGRAMS 92   17 And talke reseru'd, lock'd vp, and full of feare,

locks   frequency: 2   relative frequency: 0.00002
    p. 45 EPIGRAMS 56   14 From locks of wooll, or shreds from the whole
                   peece?
    p. 294 UNDERWOOD 89   4 Thy locks, and rosie garlands crowne thy head;

lockt   frequency: 1   relative frequency: 0.00001
    p. 114 FOREST 12   52 Or, in an armies head, that, lockt in brasse,

lock't   frequency: 1   relative frequency: 0.00001
    p. 177 UNDERWOOD 25   22 Lock't in her cold embraces, from the view

lodge   frequency: 2   relative frequency: 0.00002
    p. 391 UNGATHERED 26   19 My Shakespeare, rise; I will not lodge thee by
    p. 394 UNGATHERED 28   20 Whom shee, with Sorrow first did lodge, then
                   feast,

lodging   frequency: 1   relative frequency: 0.00001
    p. 95 FOREST 2   72 Nor, when I take my lodging, need I pray

loe   frequency: 3   relative frequency: 0.00004
    p. 46 EPIGRAMS 60   1 Loe, what my countrey should haue done (haue
                   rais'd
    p. 309 HORACE 2   80 If I can give some small increase? when, loe,
    p. 361 UNGATHERED 1   27 When loe to crowne thy worth

loftie   frequency: 4   relative frequency: 0.00005
    p. 280 U'WOOD 84.4   54 For this so loftie forme, so streight,
    p. 307 HORACE 2   37 Hath neither soule, nor sinewes. Loftie he
    p. 319 HORACE 2   318 Loftie, and grave; and in the buskin stalke.
    p. 335 HORACE 2   649 The while he belcheth loftie verses out,

lofty. See "loftie."

log   frequency: 1   relative frequency: 0.00001
    See also "logge."
    p. 98 FOREST 3   45 The trees cut out in log; and those boughes made

logge   frequency: 1   relative frequency: 0.00001
    p. 245 UNDERWOOD 70   68 To fall a logge at last, dry, bald, and seare:

logogriphes   frequency: 1   relative frequency: 0.00001
    p. 204 UNDERWOOD 43   34 Of Logogriphes, and curious Palindromes,

logographs. See "logogriphes."

logs   frequency: 1   relative frequency: 0.00001
    p. 121 FOREST 14   60 The Birth-day shines, when logs not burne, but
                                      men.

loire. See "loyre."

lomand. See "loumand."

london   frequency: 5   relative frequency: 0.00007
**p. 114 PANEGYRE   49 And as of late, when he through London went,
    p. 58 EPIGRAMS 92   2 Vnto the cryes of London Ile adde one;
    p. 213 UNDERWOOD 44   14 Lent by the London Dames, to the Lords men;
    p. 213 UNDERWOOD 44   26 Of London, in the Militarie truth,
    p. 379 UNGATHERED 12   t1 To the London Reader, on the Odcombian writer,

long   frequency: 50   relative frequency: 0.00072
    See also "longe."
**p. 117 PANEGYRE   162 Still to haue such a king, and this king long.
    p. 38 EPIGRAMS 38   3 You laugh when you are touch'd, and long before
    p. 48 EPIGRAMS 65   7 Get him the times long grudge, the courts ill
                                      will;
    p. 57 EPIGRAMS 90   3 Was dull, and long, ere shee would goe to man:
    p. 70 EPIGRAMS 109   8 Is priuate gaine, which hath long guilt to
                                      friend.
    p. 74 EPIGRAMS 115   10 Of newes, and noyse, to s<tr>ow out a long meale.
    p. 78 EPIGRAMS 121   4 Shee learnes to know long difference of their
                                      states.
    p. 86 EPIGRAMS 133   98 And, in so shitten sort, so long had vs'd him:
    p. 98 FOREST 3   66 Striue, WROTH, to liue long innocent.
    p. 106 FOREST 8   44 And will, long ere thou should'st starue,
    p. 120 FOREST 13   121 Liue that one, still; and as long yeeres doe
                                      passe,
    p. 121 FOREST 14   55 Be more, and long desir'd:
    p. 139 UNDERWOOD 2.7   2 I long, and should not beg in vaine,
    p. 139 UNDERWOOD 2.7   12 What w'are but once to doe, we should doe long.
    p. 140 UNDERWOOD 2.8   7 With the rest, I long expected,
    p. 141 UNDERWOOD 2.9   33 'Twere to<o> long, to speake of all:
    p. 151 UNDERWOOD 12   7 Deare Vincent Corbet, who so long
    p. 153 UNDERWOOD 13   23 They are so long a comming, and so hard;
    p. 164 UNDERWOOD 15   73 And jealous each of other, yet thinke long
    p. 184 UNDERWOOD 29   47 That they long since have refused
    p. 184 UNDERWOOD 29   58 And his Title be long foole,
    p. 186 UNDERWOOD 32   9 Who thus long safe, would gaine upon the times
    p. 218 UNDERWOOD 47   28 Of newes they get, to strew out the long meale,
    p. 236 UNDERWOOD 63   12 With a long, large, and blest posteritie!
    p. 236 UNDERWOOD 64   3 How many times, Live long, CHARLES, would
                                      he say,
    p. 238 UNDERWOOD 65   7 And long in changing. Let our Nephewes see
    p. 245 UNDERWOOD 70   58 To shew thou hast beene long,
    p. 245 UNDERWOOD 70   67 Or standing long an Oake, three hundred yeare,
    p. 246 UNDERWOOD 70   91 (Were not his Lucius long with us to tarry)
    p. 249 UNDERWOOD 72   18 Still to have such a CHARLES, but this
                                      CHARLES long.
    p. 257 UNDERWOOD 75   140 Doe long to make themselves, so, another way:
    p. 257 UNDERWOOD 75   144 One to the other, long e're these to light were
                                      brought.
    p. 261 UNDERWOOD 77   28 Aloud; and (happ'ly) it may last as long.
    p. 285 U'WOOD 84.9   106 Compar'd unto that long eternitie,
    p. 292 UNDERWOOD 86   2 Long intermitted, pray thee, pray thee spare:
    p. 293 UNDERWOOD 87   16 So Fates would let the Boy a long thred run.
    p. 294 UNDERWOOD 88   9 This hath pleas'd, doth please, and long will
                                      please; never
    p. 307 HORACE 2   54 Unto your strength, and long examine it,
    p. 309 HORACE 2   93 A kingly worke; or that long barren fen
    p. 317 HORACE 2   245 A great deferrer, long in hope, growne numbe
    p. 323 HORACE 2   371 Two rests, a short and long, th'Iambick frame;
    p. 323 HORACE 2   375 Nor is't long since, they did with patience take
    p. 327 HORACE 2   466 A pound, or piece, by their long compting arts:

long (cont.)
    p. 329 HORACE 2   500 Of their long labours, was in Verse set downe:
    p. 329 HORACE 2   518 Will passe the Seas, and long as nature is,
    p. 329 HORACE 2   537 But, I confesse, that, in a long worke, sleepe
    p. 367 UNGATHERED 6   33 Be then both Rare, and Good; and long
    p. 380 UNGATHERED 12 26 How long he did stay, at what signe he did Inne.
    p. 406 UNGATHERED 34 101 Lyue long ye ffeasting Roome. And ere thou
                             burne
    p. 420 UNGATHERED 48 20 Thie long watch'<d> verse

long-gathering   frequency: 1   relative frequency: 0.00001
    p. 43 EPIGRAMS 53   1 Long-gathering OLD-END, I did feare thee
                            wise,

long-since   frequency: 1   relative frequency: 0.00001
    p. 52 EPIGRAMS 74   9 The Virgin, long-since fled from earth, I see,

long-yearn'd   frequency: 1   relative frequency: 0.00001
    p. 40 EPIGRAMS 42   11 All this doth IONE. Or that his long-yearn'd
                            life

long'd   frequency: 1   relative frequency: 0.00001
  **p. 114 PANEGYRE   48 His gladding looke, now long'd to see it more.

long'd-for   frequency: 1   relative frequency: 0.00001
    p. 128 UNDERWOOD 1.1 31 Till I attaine the long'd-for mysterie

longe   frequency: 1   relative frequency: 0.00001
    p. 362 UNGATHERED 1 31 And thou in them shalt liue as longe as Fame.

longer   frequency: 10   relative frequency: 0.00014
  **p. 117 PANEGYRE   151 Hereat, the people could no longer hold
    p. 34 EPIGRAMS 23   5 Longer a knowing, then most wits doe liue.
    p. 57 EPIGRAMS 90   16 Longer a day, but with his MILL will marry.
    p. 76 EPIGRAMS 119 16 Makes, the whole longer, then 'twas giuen him,
                            much.
    p. 98 FOREST 3   43 The apple-haruest, that doth longer last;
    p. 169 UNDERWOOD 17 15 Venter a longer time, and willingly:
    p. 200 UNDERWOOD 42 21 Made longer by our praises. Or, if not,
    p. 216 UNDERWOOD 44 98 I may no longer on these pictures stay,
    p. 293 UNDERWOOD 87 12 So Fate would give her life, and longer daies.
    p. 295 UNDERWOOD 89   8 Makes his life longer then 'twas given him, much.

longest   frequency: 2   relative frequency: 0.00002
    p. 104 FOREST 7   7 At morne, and euen, shades are longest;
    p. 202 UNDERWOOD 78 16 Unto our yeare doth give the longest light.

longing   frequency: 1   relative frequency: 0.00001
    p. 258 UNDERWOOD 75 192 The longing Couple, all that elder Lovers know.

longs   frequency: 2   relative frequency: 0.00002
    p. 74 EPIGRAMS 115 12 Doe all, that longs to the anarchy of drinke,
    p. 315 HORACE 2   226 And can tread firme, longs with like lads to
                            play;

look   frequency: 1   relative frequency: 0.00001
    See also "looke."
    p. 414 UNGATHERED 41 43 Whose chearfull look our sadnesse doth destroy,

look'd   frequency: 7   relative frequency: 0.00010
    p. 27 EPIGRAMS 2   1 It will be look'd for, booke, when some but see
    p. 138 UNDERWOOD 2.6 9 Look'd not halfe so fresh, and faire,
    p. 228 UNDERWOOD 53 18 I look'd for Hercules to be the Groome:
    p. 253 UNDERWOOD 75 13 When look'd the yeare, at best,
    p. 253 UNDERWOOD 75 21 When look'd the Earth so fine,
    p. 371 UNGATHERED 8 10 With vices, which they look'd for, and came to.
    p. 396 UNGATHERED 30 16 That all Earth look'd on; and that earth, all
                            Eyes!

looke   frequency: 54   relative frequency: 0.00078
  **p. 114 PANEGYRE   48 His gladding looke, now long'd to see it more.
    p. 29 EPIGRAMS 9   2 For strict degrees of ranke, or title looke:
    p. 43 EPIGRAMS 51   10 Looke not vpon thy dangers, but our feares.
    p. 53 EPIGRAMS 79   10 On whom, if he were liuing now, to looke,
    p. 60 EPIGRAMS 94   3 If workes (not th'authors) their owne grace
                            should looke,
    p. 67 EPIGRAMS 104 15 And like it too; if they looke equally:
    p. 68 EPIGRAMS 107   3 I oft looke on false coyne, to know't from true:
    p. 106 FOREST 9   4 And Ile not looke for wine.
    p. 117 FOREST 13   16 Of Fortune, haue not alter'd yet my looke,

looke (cont.)

p. 117 FOREST 13	29	Looke then, and see your selfe. I will not say
p. 132 UNDERWOOD 2.2	2	When her looke out-flourisht May:
p. 132 UNDERWOOD 2.2	19	Could be brought once back to looke.
p. 134 UNDERWOOD 2.4	11	Doe but looke on her eyes, they doe light
p. 134 UNDERWOOD 2.4	13	Doe but looke on her Haire, it is bright
p. 141 UNDERWOOD 2.9	16	For he must looke wanton-wise.
p. 144 UNDERWOOD 4	7	Nor looke too kind on my desires,
p. 156 UNDERWOOD 13	115	Looke to and cure; Hee's not a man hath none,
p. 157 UNDERWOOD 13	142	Meet some new matter to looke up and wonder!
p. 162 UNDERWOOD 15	11	Looke on th'ambitious man, and see him nurse
p. 162 UNDERWOOD 15	15	Looke on the false, and cunning man, that loves
p. 163 UNDERWOOD 15	27	No part or corner man can looke upon,
p. 166 UNDERWOOD 15	129	I'le bid thee looke no more, but flee, flee friend,
p. 189 UNDERWOOD 37	5	On which with profit, I shall never looke,
p. 191 UNDERWOOD 38	14	Looke forth, but cannot last in such <a> forme.
p. 198 UNDERWOOD 40	29	They looke at best like Creame-bowles, and you soone
p. 200 UNDERWOOD 42	37	It is not likely I should now looke downe
p. 213 UNDERWOOD 44	27	These ten yeares day; As all may sweare that looke
p. 216 UNDERWOOD 45	21	Turne him, and see his Threds: looke, if he be
p. 220 UNDERWOOD 48	9	And looke unto their faces,
p. 241 UNDERWOOD 68	8	Would make the very Greene-cloth to looke blew:
p. 250 UNDERWOOD 73	1	Looke up, thou seed of envie, and still bring
p. 254 UNDERWOOD 75	73	Our Court, and all the Grandees; now, Sun, looke,
p. 261 UNDERWOOD 77	23	These I looke up at, with a reverent eye,
p. 263 UNDERWOOD 78	23	For he doth love my Verses, and will looke
p. 283 U'WOOD 84.9	21	Looke on thy sloth, and give thy selfe undone,
p. 313 HORACE 2	180	A meere new person, looke he keepe his state
p. 325 HORACE 2	453	And I still bid the learned Maker looke
p. 333 HORACE 2	612	Looke pale, distill a showre (was never meant)
p. 333 HORACE 2	621	Looke through him, and be sure, you take not mocks
p. 362 UNGATHERED 2	5	Looke here on Bretons worke, the master print:
p. 362 UNGATHERED 2	7	If they seeme wry, to such as looke asquint,
p. 379 UNGATHERED 12	17	But who will beleeue this, that chanceth to looke
p. 383 UNGATHERED 16	15	shall looke, & on hyme soe, then arte's a lyer
p. 383 UNGATHERED 17	3	Who bluntly doth but looke vpon the same,
p. 384 UNGATHERED 18	10	Wth the same looke, or wth a better, shine.
p. 385 UNGATHERED 20	2	To see his worke be good; but that he looke
p. 389 UNGATHERED 24	8	That an ill man dares not securely looke
p. 390 UNGATHERED 25	9	But, since he cannot, Reader, looke
p. 392 UNGATHERED 26	65	And such wert thou. Looke how the fathers face
p. 398 UNGATHERED 30	67	Looke, how we read the Spartans were inflam'd
p. 398 UNGATHERED 30	80	I looke on Cynthia, and Sirenas sport,
p. 399 UNGATHERED 31	5	To veiw the truth and owne it. Doe but looke
p. 414 UNGATHERED 42	1	You looke, my Joseph, I should something say
p. 422 UNGATHERED 50	7	Looke how the starres from earth, or seas from flames

lookes   frequency: 15   relative frequency: 0.00021

p. 30 EPIGRAMS 11	2	To be a courtier; and lookes graue enough,
p. 30 EPIGRAMS 12	10	Lookes o're the bill, likes it: and say's, god payes.
p. 55 EPIGRAMS 86	1	When I would know thee GOODYERE, my thought lookes
p. 85 EPIGRAMS 133	52	Canst tell me best, how euery Furie lookes there,
p. 89 EPIGRAMS 133	177	Of Hol'borne (<the> three sergeants heads) lookes ore,
p. 136 UNDERWOOD 2.5	18	By her lookes I doe her know,
p. 147 UNDERWOOD 7	18	And lookes as Lillies doe,
p. 152 UNDERWOOD 12	27	His lookes would so correct it, when
p. 169 UNDERWOOD 17	13	And lookes unto the forfeit. If you be
p. 193 UNDERWOOD 38	73	And how more faire, and lovely lookes the world
p. 203 UNDERWOOD 43	17	I had deserv'd, then, thy consuming lookes,
p. 245 UNDERWOOD 70	76	And let thy lookes with gladnesse shine:
p. 271 UNDERWOOD 83	69	And now, through circumfused light, she lookes
p. 311 HORACE 2	149	Sad language fits sad lookes; stuff'd menacings,
p. 315 HORACE 2	239	Lookes after honours, and bewares to act

looketh   frequency: 1   relative frequency: 0.00001
p. 193 UNDERWOOD 38   80 This looketh like an Execution day?

looking   frequency: 6   relative frequency: 0.00008
p. 118 FOREST 13   62 Not looking by, or backe (like those, that waite

looking (cont.)
      p. 219 UNDERWOOD 47   61 Still looking to, and ever loving heaven;
      p. 242 UNDERWOOD 70   5 Thou, looking then about,
      p. 254 UNDERWOOD 75   74 And looking with thy best Inquirie, tell,
      p. 369 UNGATHERED 6   93 Yet, looking in thy face, they shall begin
      p. 397 UNGATHERED 30   33 And looking vp, I saw Mineruas fowle,

looks   frequency: 1   relative frequency: 0.00001
      See also "lookes."
      p.   59 EPIGRAMS 92   23 Or, euery day, some one at RIMEE'S looks,

look'st   frequency: 2   relative frequency: 0.00002
      p. 208 UNDERWOOD 43   113 When thou wert borne, and that thou look'st at
                                  best,
      p. 408 UNGATHERED 37   10 By barking against mee. Thou look'st at least,

loom. See "loome."

loome   frequency: 1   relative frequency: 0.00001
      p.   61 EPIGRAMS 95   16 MINERVAES loome was neuer richer spred.

loomes   frequency: 1   relative frequency: 0.00001
      p. 260 UNDERWOOD 77   4 Not with the Arras, but the Persian Loomes.

looms. See "loomes."

loose   frequency: 14   relative frequency: 0.00020
      p.   27 EPIGRAMS 2   12 To catch the worlds loose laughter, or vaine
                                  gaze.
      p.   38 EPIGRAMS 38   7 Beleeue it, GVILTIE, if you loose your
                                  shame,
      p.   38 EPIGRAMS 38   8 I'le loose my modestie, and tell your name.
      p.   41 EPIGRAMS 45   5 O, could I loose all father, now. For why
      p.   43 EPIGRAMS 53   3 Thou wert content the authors name to loose:
      p.   48 EPIGRAMS 65   9 Make him loose all his friends; and, which is
                                  worse,
      p.   73 EPIGRAMS 113   11 Nor may'any feare, to loose of their degree,
      p. 101 FOREST 4   28 With all my powers, my selfe to loose?
      p. 102 FOREST 5   7 But if once we loose this light,
      p. 108 FOREST 10 A   2 to loose, and Cap'ring, for thy stricter veyne.
      p. 203 UNDERWOOD 43   6 Nor made least line of love to thy loose Wife;
      p. 203 UNDERWOOD 43   20 Any, least loose, or s<c>urrile paper, lie
      p. 209 UNDERWOOD 43   141 And this a Sparkle of that fire let loose
      p. 369 UNGATHERED 6   94 To loose that feare;

loosed   frequency: 1   relative frequency: 0.00001
      p. 329 HORACE 2   524 Nor alwayes doth the loosed Bow, hit that

loosenesse   frequency: 1   relative frequency: 0.00001
      p. 107 FOREST 10   18 Thou, nor thy loosenesse with my making sorts.

looser-like   frequency: 1   relative frequency: 0.00001
      p. 133 UNDERWOOD 2.3   21 Looser-like, now, all my wreake

loosing   frequency: 2   relative frequency: 0.00002
      p.   45 EPIGRAMS 58   6 Then thou did'st late my sense, loosing my
                                  points.
      p. 291 UNDERWOOD 85   58 Or Mallowes loosing bodyes ill:

lops   frequency: 1   relative frequency: 0.00001
      p. 290 UNDERWOOD 85   11 And with his hooke lops off the fruitlesse race,

lord   frequency: 51   relative frequency: 0.00073
      See also "l.," "lo."
      p.   29 EPIGRAMS 10   t1 TO MY LORD IGNORANT.
      p.   30 EPIGRAMS 11   5 A lord, it cryed, buried in flesh, and blood,
      p.   30 EPIGRAMS 11   8 For I will dare none. Good Lord, walke dead
                                  still.
      p.   33 EPIGRAMS 21   1 Lord, how is GAM'STER chang'd! his haire
                                  close cut!
      p.   35 EPIGRAMS 28   14 He drinkes to no man: that's, too, like a lord.
      p.   46 EPIGRAMS 60   t1 TO WILLIAM LORD MOVNTEAGLE.
      p.   48 EPIGRAMS 65   2 That hast betray'd me to a worthlesse lord;
      p.   51 EPIGRAMS 74   t1 TO THOMAS LORD CHANCELOR.
      p.   54 EPIGRAMS 84   2 I ask'd a lord a buck, and he denyed me;
      p.   75 EPIGRAMS 116   8 Might be found out as good, and not my Lord.
      p.   80 EPIGRAMS 127   t1 TO ESME, LORD 'AVBIGNY.
      p.   87 EPIGRAMS 133   120 And that is when it is the Lord Maiors foist.
      p.   95 FOREST 2   50 Thy lord, and lady, though they haue no sute.
      p.   96 FOREST 2   91 His children thy great lord may call his owne:

lord (cont.)
```
  p.  96 FOREST 2       102 May say, their lords haue built, but thy lord
                            dwells.
  p. 107 FOREST 10       10 Nor will I beg of thee, Lord of the vine,
  p. 119 FOREST 13       96 To pay your lord the pledges of chast loue:
  p. 163 UNDERWOOD 15    51 Of lust, to his rich Suit and Title, Lord?
  p. 165 UNDERWOOD 15    94 Lives to the Lord, but to the Ladies end.
  p. 167 UNDERWOOD 15   147 To flatter my good Lord, and cry his Bowle
  p. 168 UNDERWOOD 15   193 No more, then we should thinke a Lord had had
  p. 179 UNDERWOOD 25    53 But to your selfe, most loyal Lord,
  p. 185 UNDERWOOD 30    t2 On WILL<I>AM Lord Burl<eigh,>
  p. 185 UNDERWOOD 31     1 So, justest Lord, may all your Judgements be
  p. 186 UNDERWOOD 32    15 When this appeares, just Lord, to your sharp
                            sight,
  p. 201 UNDERWOOD 42    63 Wrung on the Withers, by Lord Loves despight,
  p. 202 UNDERWOOD 43     1 And why to me this, thou lame Lord of fire,
  p. 217 UNDERWOOD 46    t2 Lord chiefe Iustice of England.
  p. 225 UNDERWOOD 51     8 Since Bacon, and thy Lord was borne, and here;
  p. 225 UNDERWOOD 51    t1 Lord BACONS Birth-day.
  p. 228 UNDERWOOD 53     1 When first, my Lord, I saw you backe your
                            horse,
  p. 233 UNDERWOOD 59    19 All this (my Lord) is Valour! This is yours!
  p. 233 UNDERWOOD 60     3 Henry, the brave young Lord La-ware,
  p. 234 UNDERWOOD 61    14 My Lord, till felt griefe make our stone hearts
                            soft,
  p. 238 UNDERWOOD 66     3 The Mother of our Lord: why may not I
  p. 248 UNDERWOOD 71    t2 the Lord high Treasurer of England.
  p. 248 UNDERWOOD 71   t3+ MY LORD;
  p. 250 UNDERWOOD 73    t1 On the Right Honourable, and vertuous Lord
  p. 251 UNDERWOOD 74    20 Bring all your friends, (faire Lord) that burne
  p. 252 UNDERWOOD 75    t6 Son, and Heire, of the Lord WESTON,
  p. 252 UNDERWOOD 75    t7 Lord high Treasurer of England,
  p. 260 UNDERWOOD 77     1 If to my mind, great Lord, I had a state,
  p. 260 UNDERWOOD 77    t1 To the right Honourable, the Lord Treasurer
  p. 261 UNDERWOOD 77    13 But you I know, my Lord; and know you can
  p. 263 UNDERWOOD 78    28 The knowing Weston, and that learned Lord
  p. 270 UNDERWOOD 83    57 Then comforted her Lord! and blest her Sonne!
  p. 285 U'WOOD 84.9    111 Accumulated on her, by the Lord
  p. 394 UNGATHERED 28   t2 eldest Daughter, to Cuthbert Lord Ogle:
  p. 398 UNGATHERED 30   72 And will be bought of euery Lord, and Knight,
  p. 400 UNGATHERED 31   39 Both Saints, and Martyrs, by her loued Lord.
  p. 408 UNGATHERED 37    6 Is to make cheape, the Lord, the lines, the
                            price.
```

lord-god   frequency: 1   relative frequency: 0.00001
```
  p. 418 UNGATHERED 47    1 Our King and Queen the Lord-God blesse,
```

lordings   frequency: 2   relative frequency: 0.00002
```
  p.  84 EPIGRAMS 133    28 His three for one. Now, lordings, listen well.
  p. 214 UNDERWOOD 44    62 For education of our Lordings; soone
```

lords   frequency: 9   relative frequency: 0.00013
```
  p.  51 EPIGRAMS 73     18 Item, an epitaph on my lords cock,
  p.  63 EPIGRAMS 97     12 Nor 'bout the beares, nor noyse to make lords
                            sport.
  p.  95 FOREST 2        62 Without his feare, and of thy lords owne meate:
  p.  96 FOREST 2       102 May say, their lords haue built, but thy lord
                            dwells.
  p. 213 UNDERWOOD 44    14 Lent by the London Dames, to the Lords men;
  p. 223 UNDERWOOD 49    38 You cling to Lords, and Lords, if them you
                            leave
  p. 289 UNDERWOOD 85     8 And waiting Chambers of great Lords.
  p. 394 UNGATHERED 28   23 Importune wish; and by her lou'd Lords side
```

lordship   frequency: 2   relative frequency: 0.00002
```
  p. 167 UNDERWOOD 15   155 Pardon his Lordship. Flattry's growne so cheape
  p. 215 UNDERWOOD 44    95 His Lordship. That is for his Band, his haire
```

lordships   frequency: 2   relative frequency: 0.00002
```
  p.  95 FOREST 2        64 That is his Lordships, shall be also mine.
  p. 167 UNDERWOOD 15   148 Runs sweetly, as it had his Lordships Soule;
```

lore   frequency: 1   relative frequency: 0.00001
```
  p. 243 UNDERWOOD 70    10 Of deepest lore, could we the Center find!
```

lose   frequency: 7   relative frequency: 0.00010
```
  See also "loose."
  p.  89 EPIGRAMS 133   181 Is now from home. You lose your labours quite,
  p. 143 UNDERWOOD 3      8 What man but must lose his?
  p. 166 UNDERWOOD 15   146 To lose the formes, and dignities of men,
```

lose (cont.)
         p. 208 UNDERWOOD 43   121 And for it lose his eyes with Gun-powder,
         p. 219 UNDERWOOD 47   52 Lose all my credit with my Christmas Clay,
         p. 229 UNDERWOOD 54   3 If I doe lose it: And, without a Tale,
         p. 231 UNDERWOOD 56   28 I can lose none in tendring these to you.

loser. See "looser-like."

losing. See "loosing."

loss. See "losse."

losse   frequency: 15   relative frequency: 0.00021
         p.   43 EPIGRAMS 51   1 That we thy losse might know, and thou our loue,
         p.   46 EPIGRAMS 62   6 Or your complexions losse? you haue a pot,
         p.   46 EPIGRAMS 62   10 And there's both losse of time, and losse of
                                      sport
         p.   49 EPIGRAMS 66   11 Loue thy great losse, which a renowne hath wonne,
         p.   98 FOREST 3   57 Sit mixt with losse of state, or reuerence.
         p. 129 UNDERWOOD 1.2   29 Before my losse
         p. 138 UNDERWOOD 2.6   31 To himselfe his losse of Time;
         p. 206 UNDERWOOD 43   71 To Merlins Marvailes, and his Caballs losse,
         p. 211 UNDERWOOD 43   196 Losse, remaines yet, as unrepair'd as mine.
         p. 235 UNDERWOOD 63   t2 For the losse of their first-borne,
         p. 236 UNDERWOOD 63   11 That thought shall make, he will this losse
                                      supply
         p. 288 U'WOOD 84.9   202 Suffring, and dying to redeeme our losse!
         p. 311 HORACE 2   146 Thy selfe in teares, then me thy losse will
                                      wound,
         p. 398 UNGATHERED 30   91 Onely my losse is, that I am not there:

lost   frequency: 29   relative frequency: 0.00041
      **p. 116 PANEGYRE   114 To their voluptuous lustes, had lost their name;
         p.   30 EPIGRAMS 12   15 That lost, he keepes his chamber, reades
                                      Essayes,
         p.   42 EPIGRAMS 48   3 And hath no honor lost, our Due'llists say.
         p.   45 EPIGRAMS 58   7 So haue I seene at CHRIST-masse sports one
                                      lost,
         p.   67 EPIGRAMS 105   1 MADAME, had all antiquitie beene lost,
         p.   68 EPIGRAMS 105   20 I' your selfe, all treasure lost of th'age
                                      before.
         p.   73 EPIGRAMS 114   4 In meere out-formes, vntill he lost his sight,
         p.   79 EPIGRAMS 125   3 Both whose dimensions, lost, the world might
                                      finde
         p.   83 EPIGRAMS 132   14 No more, those mayden glories shee hath lost.
         p. 114 FOREST 12   40 And now lye lost in their forgotten dust.
         p. 116 FOREST 12   94 Now thincking on you, though to England lost,
         p. 116 FOREST 13   4 As what th'haue lost t<o>'expect, they dare
                                      deride.
         p. 118 FOREST 13   50 Without which, all the rest were sounds, or lost.
         p. 121 FOREST 14   50 To liue vntill to morrow' hath lost two dayes.
         p. 132 UNDERWOOD 2.2   14 Sooner, then he lost his might,
         p. 138 UNDERWOOD 2.6   6 Whether we have lost, or wonne,
         p. 151 UNDERWOOD 12   5 For I both lost a friend and Father,
         p. 160 UNDERWOOD 14   53 I wonder'd at the richnesse, but am lost,
         p. 176 UNDERWOOD 25   t3 since lost, and recovered.
         p. 191 UNDERWOOD 38   2 Of Credit lost. And I am now run madde:
         p. 192 UNDERWOOD 38   38 Your just commands; yet those, not I, be lost.
         p. 199 UNDERWOOD 41   11 Alas I ha' lost my heat, my blood, my prime,
         p. 237 UNDERWOOD 64   21 Are lost upon accompt! And none will know
         p. 264 UNDERWOOD 79   34 And were shee lost, could best supply her place,
         p. 283 U'WOOD 84.9   19 Thou wouldst have lost the Phoenix, had the kind
         p. 286 U'WOOD 84.9   141 Had lost our selves? and prodigally spent
         p. 408 UNGATHERED 37   8 That thou hast lost thy noyse, thy foame, thy
                                      stirre,
         p. 410 UNGATHERED 39   9 Thinking to stir me, thou hast lost thy End,
         p. 417 UNGATHERED 45   10 but haue lost it by the way,

lot   frequency: 2   relative frequency: 0.00002
         p.   37 EPIGRAMS 32   8 Was his blest fate, but our hard lot to find.
         p. 118 FOREST 13   48 For such a lot! that mixt you with a state

loth   frequency: 3   relative frequency: 0.00004
         p.   54 EPIGRAMS 81   7 Which, if thou leaue not soone (though I am
                                      loth)
         p.   94 FOREST 2   35 As loth, the second draught, or cast to stay,
         p. 162 UNDERWOOD 15   3 All that dare rowse: or are not loth to quit

lothed   frequency: 1   relative frequency: 0.00001
       *p. 492 TO HIMSELF   1 Come leaue the lothed stage,

lothsome   frequency: 1   relative frequency: 0.00001
  *p. 492 TO HIMSELF   2 And the more lothsome age:

lotions   frequency: 1   relative frequency: 0.00001
   p. 86 EPIGRAMS 133   102 Suppositories, cataplasmes, and lotions.

loud   frequency: 8   relative frequency: 0.00011
  See also "loude," "lowd."
   p. 74 EPIGRAMS 115   9 Talkes loud, and baudy, has a gather'd deale
   p. 86 EPIGRAMS 133   93 Ouer your heads: Well, row. At this a loud
   p. 89 EPIGRAMS 133   174 Of loud SEPVLCHRES with their hourely
                             knells,
   p. 97 FOREST 3   22 A-bed canst heare the loud stag speake,
   p. 264 UNDERWOOD 79   19 Chor. Sound, sound his praises loud, and with
                             his, hers divide.
   p. 319 HORACE 2   291 As loud enough to fill the seates, not yet
   p. 398 UNGATHERED 30   66 How do his trumpets breath! What loud alarmes!
   p. 403 UNGATHERED 34   23 What makes your Wretchednes to bray soe loud

lou'd   frequency: 5   relative frequency: 0.00007
   p. 41 EPIGRAMS 45   2 My sinne was too much hope of thee, lou'd boy,
   p. 75 EPIGRAMS 116   1 IEPHSON, thou man of men, to whose lou'd
                             name
   p. 80 EPIGRAMS 127   3 To whom I am so bound, lou'd AVBIGNY?
   p. 82 EPIGRAMS 130   1 To vrge, my lou'd ALPHONSO, that bold
                             fame
   p. 394 UNGATHERED 28   23 Importune wish; and by her lou'd Lords side

loude   frequency: 2   relative frequency: 0.00002
   p. 155 UNDERWOOD 13   66 Their thoughts and meanes to making loude the
                             cry;
   p. 162 UNDERWOOD 15   2 Beates brave, and loude in Europe, and bids come

louder   frequency: 2   relative frequency: 0.00002
 **p. 117 PANEGYRE   160 With a twice louder shoute againe they cry'd,
   p. 86 EPIGRAMS 133   74 Spake to 'hem louder, then the oxe in LIVIE;

loudest. See "lowdest."

loue   frequency: 59   relative frequency: 0.00085
  *p. 492 TO HIMSELF   19 If they loue lees, and leaue the lusty wine,
 **p. 115 PANEGYRE   69 This was the peoples loue, with which did striue
 **p. 116 PANEGYRE   109 Nor did he seeme their vices so to loue,
 **p. 116 PANEGYRE   121 He knew, that those, who would, with loue,
                             command,
   p. 40 EPIGRAMS 43   3 Which should thy countries loue to speake refuse,
   p. 43 EPIGRAMS 51   1 That we thy losse might know, and thou our loue,
   p. 44 EPIGRAMS 55   1 How I doe loue thee BEAVMONT, and thy
                             Muse,
   p. 46 EPIGRAMS 62   2 That loue to make so well, a child to beare?
   p. 47 EPIGRAMS 64   3 Of loue, and what the golden age did hold
   p. 48 EPIGRAMS 66   1 That neither fame, nor loue might wanting be
   p. 49 EPIGRAMS 66   11 Loue thy great losse, which a renowne hath wonne,
   p. 49 EPIGRAMS 66   13 Loue honors, which of best example bee,
   p. 52 EPIGRAMS 76   4 To honor, serue, and loue; as Poets vse.
   p. 55 EPIGRAMS 86   3 Then doe I loue thee, and behold thy ends
   p. 55 EPIGRAMS 86   7 Where, though 't be loue, that to thy praise doth
                             moue,
   p. 55 EPIGRAMS 86   8 It was a knowledge, that begat that loue.
   p. 63 EPIGRAMS 99   1 That thou hast kept thy loue, encreast thy will,
   p. 68 EPIGRAMS 107   4 Not that I loue it, more, then I will you.
   p. 70 EPIGRAMS 108   5 I sweare by your true friend, my Muse, I loue
   p. 74 EPIGRAMS 114   8 But, in your loue, made all his seruants wise.
   p. 78 EPIGRAMS 121   6 If onely loue should make the action pris'd:
   p. 79 EPIGRAMS 125   6 Might loue the treasure for the cabinet.
   p. 80 EPIGRAMS 126   5 Said I wrong'd him, and (which was more) his
                             loue.
   p. 80 EPIGRAMS 126   8 CARY my loue is, DAPHNE but my tree.
   p. 81 EPIGRAMS 129   18 Men loue thee not for this: They laugh at thee.
   p. 93 FOREST 1   12 When Loue is fled, and I grow old.
   p. 95 FOREST 2   57 But what can this (more then expresse their loue)
   p. 96 FOREST 3   1 How blest art thou, canst loue the countrey,
                             WROTH,
   p. 102 FOREST 5   2 While we may, the sports of loue;
   p. 105 FOREST 8   24 If thy leanenesse loue such food,
   p. 108 FOREST 10A   9 Such, as in lustes wilde forrest loue to rainge,
   p. 108 FOREST 10A   13 wch rap's mee vp to the true heau'en of loue;
   p. 110 FOREST 11   31 Of which vsurping rancke, some haue thought loue
   p. 110 FOREST 11   37 The thing, they here call Loue, is blinde
                             Desire,

loue (cont.)

p. 110 FOREST 11	43	In a continuall tempest. Now, true Loue
p. 111 FOREST 11	68	As this chaste loue we sing.
p. 112 FOREST 11	87	He that for loue of goodnesse hateth ill,
p. 112 FOREST 11	92	Grac'd with a Phoenix loue;
p. 112 FOREST 11	105	The wealthy treasure of her loue on him;
p. 113 FOREST 12	17	Solders crackt friendship; makes loue last a day;
p. 114 FOREST 12	33	His loue vnto the Muses, when his skill
p. 116 FOREST 12	92	And your braue friend, and mine so well did loue.
p. 116 FOREST 13	7	I, therefore, who professe my selfe in loue
p. 119 FOREST 13	96	To pay your lord the pledges of chast loue:
p. 119 FOREST 13	113	How you loue one, and him you should; how still
p. 120 FOREST 14	10	Both loue the cause, and authors of the feast?
p. 121 FOREST 14	57	Of loue be bright,
p. 122 FOREST 15	11	My faith, my hope, my loue: and in this state,
p. 122 FOREST 15	26	For wearinesse of life, not loue of thee.
p. 360 UNGATHERED 6	16	And Phoebus loue cause of his blackenesse is.
p. 369 UNGATHERED 6	101	Though, now by Loue transform'd, & dayly dying:
p. 382 UNGATHERED 16	8	his life, his loue, his honour, which ne'r dyes,
p. 384 UNGATHERED 18	4	Do wayte vpon thee: and theyre Loue not bought.
p. 384 UNGATHERED 18	20	And eu'ry birth encrease the heate of Loue.
p. 393 UNGATHERED 27	5	It is the life and light of loue,
p. 393 UNGATHERED 27	8	That Faith and Loue defineth.
p. 393 UNGATHERED 27	15	And in effect of Heauenly loue
p. 393 UNGATHERED 27	20	Of the most worthie loue.
p. 422 UNGATHERED 50	5	and the immortall gods; loue only those

loued   frequency: 1   relative frequency: 0.00001
    p. 400 UNGATHERED 31   39 Both Saints, and Martyrs, by her loued Lord.

louer   frequency: 1   relative frequency: 0.00001
    p. 103 FOREST 6   1 Kisse me, sweet: The warie louer

louers   frequency: 2   relative frequency: 0.00002
    p. 110 FOREST 11   49 That falls like sleepe on louers, and combines
    p. 365 UNGATHERED 5   7 Then the stolne sports of Louers,

loues   frequency: 9   relative frequency: 0.00013
    p. 41 EPIGRAMS 45   12 As what he loues may neuer like too much.
    p. 102 FOREST 5   15 'Tis no sinne, loues fruit to steale,
    p. 105 FOREST 8   39 Dare entayle their loues on any,
    p. 114 FOREST 12   43 The soules, shee loues. Those other glorious notes,
    p. 117 FOREST 13   26 No lady, but, at some time, loues her glasse.
    p. 382 UNGATHERED 16   4 to tender thus, their liues, their loues, their hartes!
    p. 394 UNGATHERED 28   25 Where spight of Death, next Life, for her Loues sake,
    p. 397 UNGATHERED 30   30 Their loues, their quarrels, iealousies, and wrongs,
    p. 419 UNJATH'D 47A   6 .... the Kinge loues . ...

loue's   frequency: 1   relative frequency: 0.00001
    p. 93 FOREST 1   1 Some act of Loue's bound to reherse,

loughing   frequency: 1   relative frequency: 0.00001
    p. 97 FOREST 3   16 'Mongst loughing heards, and solide hoofes:

louing   frequency: 2   relative frequency: 0.00002
    p. 394 UNGATHERED 28   5 Religious, wise, chast, louing, gratious, good;
    p. 409 UNGATHERED 38   t2 his continu'd Vertue) my louing Friend:

louis. See "lewis."

loumond   frequency: 1   relative frequency: 0.00001
    p. 368 UNGATHERED 6   72 To Loumond lake, and Twedes blacke-springing fountaine.

louse-dropping   frequency: 1   relative frequency: 0.00001
    p. 375 UNGATHERED 10   27 And louse-dropping Case, are the Armes of his trauell.

lov'd   frequency: 13   relative frequency: 0.00018
    p. 131 UNDERWOOD 2.1   6 Some have lov'd as old agen.
    p. 148 UNDERWOOD 8   6 Of one that lov'd?
    p. 162 UNDERWOOD 15   16 No person, nor is lov'd: what wayes he proves
    p. 165 UNDERWOOD 15   88 Is lov'd, though he let out his owne for life:
    p. 170 UNDERWOOD 19   11 Tell me (my lov'd Friend) doe you love, or no,
    p. 180 UNDERWOOD 25   63 O then (my best-best lov'd) let me importune,

lov'd (cont.)

p. 231	UNDERWOOD 57	9	He lov'd the Muses;
p. 234	UNDERWOOD 60	6	Of a Disease, that lov'd no light
p. 268	UNDERWOOD 82	1	That thou art lov'd of God, this worke is done,
p. 293	UNDERWOOD 87	1	HOR. Whilst, Lydia, I was lov'd of thee,
p. 293	UNDERWOOD 87	5	LYD. Whilst Horace lov'd no Mistres more,
p. 315	HORACE 2	236	And then as swift to leave what he hath lov'd.
p. 414	UNGATHERED 42	6	How well I lov'd Truth: I was scarce allow'd

love   frequency: 99   relative frequency: 0.00143
See also "loue," "loue's," "love's."

p. 93	FOREST 1	t1	WHY I WRITE NOT OF LOVE.
p. 128	UNDERWOOD 1.1	43	With grace, with love, with cherishing intire:
p. 129	UNDERWOOD 1.2	6	Therein, thy Love.
p. 131	UNDERWOOD 2.1	2	Lesse your laughter; that I love.
p. 131	UNDERWOOD 2.1	16	Either whom to love, or how:
p. 131	UNDERWOOD 2.1	24	All the world for love may die.
p. 132	UNDERWOOD 2.2	7	Love, if thou wilt ever see
p. 133	UNDERWOOD 2.3	6	Reconcil'd to Love, and me.
p. 133	UNDERWOOD 2.3	9	Unto her; which Love might take
p. 134	UNDERWOOD 2.4	1	See the Chariot at hand here of Love,
p. 134	UNDERWOOD 2.4	4	And well the Carre Love guideth.
p. 136	UNDERWOOD 2.5	6	Love, and I have had; and true.
p. 137	UNDERWOOD 2.5	45	Of her Sex; But could'st thou, Love,
p. 137	UNDERWOOD 2.5	51	Outward Grace weake love beguiles:
p. 139	UNDERWOOD 2.8	2	Had of Love, and of his force,
p. 139	UNDERWOOD 2.8	4	What a man she could love well:
p. 141	UNDERWOOD 2.9	24	And make Love or me afeard.
p. 142	UNDERWOOD 2.9	52	As he durst love Truth and me.
p. 145	UNDERWOOD 5	1	Men, if you love us, play no more
p. 146	UNDERWOOD 6	9	Which we in love must doe aswell,
p. 146	UNDERWOOD 6	10	If ever we will love aright.
p. 146	UNDERWOOD 6	20	In love, doth not alone help forth
p. 146	UNDERWOOD 6	24	To love one man, hee'd leave her first.
p. 147	UNDERWOOD 7	1	I love, and he loves me againe,
p. 147	UNDERWOOD 7	4	I feare they'd love him too;
p. 147	UNDERWOOD 7	24	Where Love may all his Torches light,
p. 148	UNDERWOOD 7	29	I'le tell no more, and yet I love,
p. 148	UNDERWOOD 7	35	If Love, or feare, would let me tell his name.
p. 149	UNDERWOOD 9	1	I now thinke, Love is rather deafe, then blind,
p. 149	UNDERWOOD 9	5	And cast my love behind:
p. 150	UNDERWOOD 10	9	But under the Disguise of love,
p. 150	UNDERWOOD 10	12	Think'st thou that love is help'd by feare?
p. 151	UNDERWOOD 11	4	Love in a subtile Dreame disguis'd,
p. 157	UNDERWOOD 13	157	That I may love your Person (as I doe)
p. 159	UNDERWOOD 14	35	Which Grace shall I make love to first? your skill,
p. 161	UNDERWOOD 14	73	It true respects. He will not only love,
p. 168	UNDERWOOD 15	196	Who falls for love of God, shall rise a Starre.
p. 169	UNDERWOOD 18	4	Then like, then love; and now would they amaze?
p. 170	UNDERWOOD 18	9	I can helpe that with boldnesse; And Love sware,
p. 170	UNDERWOOD 18	16	Or Love, or Fortune blind, when they but winke
p. 170	UNDERWOOD 18	21	If it be thus; Come Love, and Fortune goe,
p. 170	UNDERWOOD 18	24	Love to my heart, and Fortune to my lines.
p. 170	UNDERWOOD 19	2	Love lights his torches to inflame desires;
p. 170	UNDERWOOD 19	11	Tell me (my lov'd Friend) doe you love, or no,
p. 171	UNDERWOOD 19	15	I'le therefore aske no more, but bid you love;
p. 171	UNDERWOOD 19	18	Others, in time may love, as we doe now.
p. 173	UNDERWOOD 22	7	And draw, and conquer all mens love,
p. 173	UNDERWOOD 22	8	This subjects you to love of one.
p. 173	UNDERWOOD 22	14	In whom alone Love lives agen?
p. 173	UNDERWOOD 22	23	As Love, t<o>'aquit such excellence,
p. 174	UNDERWOOD 22	32	To light upon a Love of mine.
p. 181	UNDERWOOD 26	21	Such thoughts wil make you more in love with truth.
p. 181	UNDERWOOD 27	13	Is Horace his each love so high
p. 187	UNDERWOOD 33	37	The Courts just honour, and thy Judges love.
p. 189	UNDERWOOD 36	2	For Love in shadow best is made.
p. 189	UNDERWOOD 36	5	Where Love doth shine, there needs no Sunne,
p. 189	UNDERWOOD 37	2	Next to your selfe, for making your love true:
p. 189	UNDERWOOD 37	3	Then to your love, and gift. And all's but due.
p. 190	UNDERWOOD 37	23	That friendship which no chance but love did chuse,
p. 190	UNDERWOOD 37	25	It is an Act of tyrannie, not love,
p. 194	UNDERWOOD 38	112	And that there is no life in me, but love.
p. 197	UNDERWOOD 40	15	For though Love thrive, and may grow up with cheare,
p. 199	UNDERWOOD 42	4	Whose Readers did not thinke he was in love.
p. 200	UNDERWOOD 42	18	When he is furious, love, although not lust.

love (cont.)
```
    p. 200 UNDERWOOD 42     35 Of love, and hate: and came so nigh to know
    p. 201 UNDERWOOD 42     53 An Officer there, did make most solemne love,
    p. 202 UNDERWOOD 42     81 Let the poore fooles enjoy their follies, love
    p. 203 UNDERWOOD 43      6 Nor made least line of love to thy loose Wife;
    p. 212 UNDERWOOD 43    209 We aske your absence here, we all love peace,
    p. 215 UNDERWOOD 44     86 We neither love the Troubles, nor the harmes.
    p. 215 UNDERWOOD 44     87 What love you then? your whore. What study?
                               gate,
    p. 220 UNDERWOOD 47     71 These I will honour, love, embrace, and serve:
    p. 221 UNDERWOOD 48     38 Shall feast it, thou maist love there
    p. 234 UNDERWOOD 60     12 No love of action, and high Arts,
    p. 236 UNDERWOOD 64      8 Then now, to love the Soveraigne, and the
                               Lawes?
    p. 237 UNDERWOOD 64     15 How is she barren growne of love! or broke!
    p. 240 UNDERWOOD 67     32 The fained Queene of Love,
    p. 241 UNDERWOOD 69      5 Freedome, and Truth; with love from those begot:
    p. 246 UNDERWOOD 70    105 But simple love of greatnesse, and of good;
    p. 251 UNDERWOOD 74     21 With love, to heare your modestie relate
    p. 254 UNDERWOOD 75     60 With light of love, this Paire doth intertexe!
    p. 255 UNDERWOOD 75    104 Mens Loves unto the Lawes, and Lawes to love
                               the Crowne.
    p. 257 UNDERWOOD 75    164 Of Love betweene you, and your Lovely-head:
    p. 263 UNDERWOOD 78     23 For he doth love my Verses, and will looke
    p. 284 U'WOOD 84.9      64 To Body, and Soule! where Love is all the
                               guest!
    p. 285 U'WOOD 84.9      99 A Wife, a Friend, a Lady, or a Love;
    p. 286 U'WOOD 84.9     138 What love with mercy mixed doth appeare?
    p. 294 UNDERWOOD 87     17 HOR. But, say old Love returne should make,
    p. 294 UNDERWOOD 87     24 Yet would I wish to love, live, die with thee.
    p. 295 UNDERWOOD 89      6 And heat, with softest love, thy softer bed.
    p. 317 HORACE 2        282 The angry, and love those that feare t<o>'offend.
    p. 319 HORACE 2        286 Fortune would love the poore, and leave the
                               proud.
    p. 321 HORACE 2        341 Nor I, when I write Satyres, will so love
    p. 325 HORACE 2        447 What height of love, a Parent will fit best,
    p. 335 HORACE 2        631 In vaine, but you, and yours, you should love
                               still
    p. 335 HORACE 2        669 Or love of this so famous death lay by.
    p. 412 UNGATHERED 41     8 As Love, here studied to keep Grace alive.
    p. 413 UNGATHERED 41    25 Thus, Love, and Hope, and burning Charitie,
    p. 416 UNGATHERED 43     7 How they advance true Love, and neighbourhood,
```

loved. See "lou'd," "loued," "lov'd."

lovelihead. See "lovely-head."

lovely   frequency: 6   relative frequency: 0.00008
```
    p. 188 UNDERWOOD 35      1 What Beautie would have lovely stilde,
    p. 193 UNDERWOOD 38     73 And how more faire, and lovely lookes the world
    p. 200 UNDERWOOD 42     12 In all that is call'd lovely: take my sight
    p. 283 U'WOOD 84.9      44 And left her lovely body unthought dead!
    p. 292 UNDERWOOD 86     13 For he's both noble, lovely, young,
    p. 414 UNGATHERED 41    45 The Seat of Sapience, the most lovely Mother,
```

lovely-head   frequency: 1   relative frequency: 0.00001
```
    p. 257 UNDERWOOD 75    164 Of Love betweene you, and your Lovely-head:
```

lover   frequency: 8   relative frequency: 0.00011
    See also "louer."
```
    p. 131 UNDERWOOD 2.1    12 Gives the Lover weight, and fashion.
    p. 170 UNDERWOOD 18     15 Oh how a Lover may mistake! to thinke,
    p. 182 UNDERWOOD 28      1 I that have beene a lover, and could shew it,
    p. 182 UNDERWOOD 28      4 A better lover, and much better Poet.
    p. 189 UNDERWOOD 36    t1+ LOVER.
    p. 197 UNDERWOOD 40     19 Yet should the Lover still be ayrie and light,
    p. 198 UNDERWOOD 40     32 But the grave Lover ever was an Asse;
    p. 198 UNDERWOOD 40     48 That Article, may not become <y>our lover:
```

lovers   frequency: 5   relative frequency: 0.00007
    See also "louers."
```
    p. 137 UNDERWOOD 2.5    32 Lovers, made into a Chaine!
    p. 149 UNDERWOOD 8      11 Even ashes of lovers find no rest.
    p. 173 UNDERWOOD 22     26 To whom all Lovers are design'd,
    p. 258 UNDERWOOD 75    192 The longing Couple, all that elder Lovers know.
    p. 311 HORACE 2        116 Fresh Lovers businesse, and the Wines free
                               source.
```

loves   frequency: 23   relative frequency: 0.00033
    See also "loues."

loves (cont.)

p. 134	UNDERWOOD 2.4	12	All that Loves world compriseth!
p. 134	UNDERWOOD 2.4	14	As Loves starre when it riseth!
p. 139	UNDERWOOD 2.7	8	Can he that loves, aske lesse then one?
p. 141	UNDERWOOD 2.9	12	For Loves fingers, and his wings:
p. 141	UNDERWOOD 2.9	32	In loves schoole, and yet no sinners.
p. 147	UNDERWOOD 7	1	I love, and he loves me againe,
p. 148	UNDERWOOD 7	30	And he loves me; yet no
p. 150	UNDERWOOD 10	14	Loves sicknesse, and his noted want of worth,
p. 162	UNDERWOOD 15	15	Looke on the false, and cunning man, that loves
p. 182	UNDERWOOD 28	13	Her joyes, her smiles, her loves, as readers take
p. 198	UNDERWOOD 40	24	As if that ex'lent Dulnesse were Loves grace;
p. 198	UNDERWOOD 40	31	They may say Grace, and for Loves Chaplaines passe;
p. 198	UNDERWOOD 40	47	(Made to blow up loves secrets) to discover
p. 201	UNDERWOOD 42	63	Wrung on the Withers, by Lord Loves despight,
p. 253	UNDERWOOD 75	19	Doe boast their Loves, and Brav'ries so at large,
p. 255	UNDERWOOD 75	104	Mens Loves unto the Lawes, and Lawes to love the Crowne.
p. 258	UNDERWOOD 75	186	And let him freely gather Loves First-fruits,
p. 290	UNDERWOOD 85	38	Loves cares so evil, and so great?
p. 291	UNDERWOOD 85	57	Or the herb Sorrell, that loves Meadows still,
p. 292	UNDERWOOD 86	5	Sower Mother of sweet Loves, forbeare
p. 315	HORACE 2	230	Loves Dogges, and Horses; and is ever one
p. 331	HORACE 2	541	As some the farther off: This loves the darke;
p. 418	UNGATHERED 47	4	That lives, and breath's, and loves the King.

love's   frequency: 1   relative frequency: 0.00001
See also "loues," "loue's," "loves,"
            "loves-sake."
      p. 197 UNDERWOOD 40   1 That Love's a bitter sweet, I ne're conceive

loves-sake   frequency: 1   relative frequency: 0.00001
      p. 139 UNDERWOOD 2.7   1 For Loves-sake, kisse me once againe,

loveth   frequency: 1   relative frequency: 0.00001
      p. 140 UNDERWOOD 2.8 12 We all feare, she loveth none.

loving   frequency: 3   relative frequency: 0.00004
See also "louing."
      p. 131 UNDERWOOD 2.1 t1 His Excuse for loving.
      p. 190 UNDERWOOD 37   8 Their vice of loving for a Christmasse fit;
      p. 219 UNDERWOOD 47   61 Still looking to, and ever loving heaven;

lov'st   frequency: 1   relative frequency: 0.00001
      p. 232 UNDERWOOD 58   13 If they goe on, and that thou lov'st a-life

low   frequency: 7   relative frequency: 0.00010
      p. 45 EPIGRAMS 56   5 At first he made low shifts, would picke and gleane,
      p. 50 EPIGRAMS 72   4 Goe high, or low, as thou wilt value it.
      p. 64 EPIGRAMS 99   9 From place, or fortune, are made high, or low,
      p. 307 HORACE 2   38 Professing greatnesse, swells: That, low by lee
      p. 311 HORACE 2   123 Abhorres low numbers, and the private straine
      p. 367 UNGATHERED 6   39 But first to Cluid stoope low,
      p. 416 UNGATHERED 44   3 Bred by your breath, on this low bancke of ours;

low-countrey's   frequency: 1   relative frequency: 0.00001
      p. 212 UNDERWOOD 43 203 Or fixt in the Low-Countrey's, where you might

low-countries   frequency: 1   relative frequency: 0.00001
      p. 379 UNGATHERED 12 20 The Low-countries, Germany and Rhetia

lowd   frequency: 5   relative frequency: 0.00007
      p. 156 UNDERWOOD 13 100 Lowd sacrifice of drinke, for their health-sake!
      p. 167 UNDERWOOD 15 168 Ambitious, factious, superstitious, lowd
      p. 249 UNDERWOOD 72   4 As lowd as Thunder, and as swift as fire.
      p. 387 UNGATHERED 22 11 it will be matter lowd inoughe to tell
      p. 419 UNGATHERED 48   7 Lowd to the wondringe thronge

lowdest   frequency: 1   relative frequency: 0.00001
      p. 67 EPIGRAMS 103   11 As lowdest praisers, who perhaps would find

lower   frequency: 1   relative frequency: 0.00001
      p. 94 FOREST 2   22 The lower land, that to the riuer bends,

lowest   frequency: 1   relative frequency: 0.00001
      p. 331 HORACE 2   564 And highest; sinketh to the lowest, and worst.

lowing   frequency: 1   relative frequency: 0.00001
     See also "loughing."
     p. 290 UNDERWOOD 85   14 The lowing herds there grazing are:

lowlie   frequency: 1   relative frequency: 0.00001
     p. 413 UNGATHERED 41   18 But lowlie laid, as on the earth asleep,

lowly. See "lowlie."

lownesse   frequency: 1   relative frequency: 0.00001
     p. 156 UNDERWOOD 13   119 Or growne; by height or lownesse of the Sunne?

loyal   frequency: 1   relative frequency: 0.00001
     See also "loyall."
     p. 179 UNDERWOOD 25   53 But to your selfe, most loyal Lord,

loyall   frequency: 2   relative frequency: 0.00002
     p. 110 FOREST 11   27 Whereof the loyall conscience so complaines.
     p. 263 UNDERWOOD 79   10 And shuts the old. Haste, haste, all loyall
                              Swaines,

loyalties   frequency: 1   relative frequency: 0.00001
     p. 173 UNDERWOOD 22   22 With so much Loyalties expence,

loyre   frequency: 1   relative frequency: 0.00001
     p. 369 UNGATHERED 6   117 Slow Arar, nor swift Rhone; the Loyre, nor
                              Seine,

lucan   frequency: 3   relative frequency: 0.00004
     See also "lucane," "lvcan."
     p. 395 UNGATHERED 29   3 Of Fortunes wheele by Lucan driu'n about,
     p. 395 UNGATHERED 29   15 Taught Lucan these true moodes! Replyes my
                              sence
     p. 397 UNGATHERED 30   47 Sayst thou so, Lucan? But thou scornst to stay

lucane   frequency: 1   relative frequency: 0.00001
     p. 422 UNGATHERED 50   t1 A speech out of Lucane.

lucans   frequency: 1   relative frequency: 0.00001
     p. 395 UNGATHERED 29   20 Lucans whole frame vnto vs, and so wrought,

lucent   frequency: 1   relative frequency: 0.00001
     p. 52 EPIGRAMS 76   8 Nor lend like influence from his lucent seat.

lucina's. See "lvcina's."

lucius   frequency: 2   relative frequency: 0.00002
     See also "lvcius."
     p. 245 UNDERWOOD 70   75 Call, noble Lucius, then for Wine,
     p. 246 UNDERWOOD 70   91 (Were not his Lucius long with us to tarry)

luck   frequency: 1   relative frequency: 0.00001
     See also "lucke."
     p. 179 UNDERWOOD 25   52 Oft scape an Imputation, more through luck, then
                              wit.

lucke   frequency: 2   relative frequency: 0.00002
     p. 50 EPIGRAMS 71   2 Still, 'tis his lucke to praise me 'gainst his
                              will.
     p. 73 EPIGRAMS 112   17 Troth, if it be, I pitty thy ill lucke;

luckily   frequency: 1   relative frequency: 0.00001
     p. 379 UNGATHERED 12   13 And that you may see he most luckily ment

luckless. See "lvcklesse."

lucks   frequency: 3   relative frequency: 0.00004
     p. 27 EPIGRAMS 3   4 For the lucks sake, it thus much fauour haue,
     p. 42 EPIGRAMS 47   1 Sir LVCKLESSE, troth, for lucks sake
                              passe by one:
     p. 86 EPIGRAMS 133   78 Ploughing the mayne. When, see (the worst of all
                              lucks)

lucrine   frequency: 1   relative frequency: 0.00001
     p. 291 UNDERWOOD 85   49 Not Lucrine Oysters I could then more prize,

lucy. See "lvcy."

lump. See "lumpe."

lumpe   frequency: 1   relative frequency: 0.00001
    p. 227 UNDERWOOD 52   5 And the whole lumpe growes round, deform'd, and
                               droupes,

lungs   frequency: 3   relative frequency: 0.00004
    p.   42 EPIGRAMS 50   2 Or fumie clysters, thy moist lungs to bake:
    p. 206 UNDERWOOD 43   76 The art of kindling the true Coale, by Lungs:
    p. 269 UNDERWOOD 83   24 And voyce to raise them from my brazen Lungs,

lupus   frequency: 1   relative frequency: 0.00001
    p. 274 U'WOOD 84.2   17 Of the first Lupus, to the Familie

lurdan. See "lurden."

lurden   frequency: 1   relative frequency: 0.00001
    p.   87 EPIGRAMS 133   115 And bad her fare-well sough, vnto the lurden:

lurk. See "lurke."

lurke   frequency: 1   relative frequency: 0.00001
    p. 207 UNDERWOOD 43   105 How in these ruines, Vulcan, thou dost lurke,

lurry. See "lanterne-lerry."

lust   frequency: 11   relative frequency: 0.00015
  **p. 113 PANEGYRE   12 Where Murder, Rapine, Lust, doe sit within,
  **p. 116 PANEGYRE   101 "Where acts gaue licence to impetuous lust
    p.   34 EPIGRAMS 25   6 In varied shapes, which for his lust shee takes:
    p.   76 EPIGRAMS 118   6 Lust it comes out, that gluttony went in.
    p. 105 FOREST 8   15 Or if needs thy lust will tast
    p. 156 UNDERWOOD 13   106 'Twixt feare and rashnesse: not a lust obscene,
    p. 163 UNDERWOOD 15   51 Of lust, to his rich Suit and Title, Lord?
    p. 200 UNDERWOOD 42   18 When he is furious, love, although not lust.
    p. 208 UNDERWOOD 43   112 With lust conceiv'd thee; Father thou hadst
                               none:
    p. 222 UNDERWOOD 49   7 What though with Tribade lust she force a Muse,
    p. 294 UNDERWOOD 88   5 For lust will languish, and that heat decay.

lustes   frequency: 2   relative frequency: 0.00002
  **p. 116 PANEGYRE   114 To their voluptuous lustes, had lost their name;
    p. 108 FOREST 10A   9 Such, as in lustes wilde forrest loue to rainge,

lustfull   frequency: 1   relative frequency: 0.00001
    p. 294 UNDERWOOD 88   4 Like lustfull beasts, that onely know to doe it:

lustie   frequency: 1   relative frequency: 0.00001
    p. 291 UNDERWOOD 85   42 Some lustie quick Apulians spouse,

lustie-mounting   frequency: 1   relative frequency: 0.00001
    p. 264 UNDERWOOD 79   17 7. Our teeming Ewes, 8. and lustie-mounting
                               Rammes. .

lustrous   frequency: 1   relative frequency: 0.00001
    p. 179 UNDERWOOD 25   60 With lustrous Graces,

lusts   frequency: 2   relative frequency: 0.00002
    See also "lustes."
    p. 164 UNDERWOOD 15   57 To do't with Cloth, or Stuffes, lusts name
                               might merit;
    p. 327 HORACE 2   489 Wild ra<n>ging lusts; prescribe the mariage good;

lust's   frequency: 1   relative frequency: 0.00001
    See also "lustes," "lusts."
    p. 111 FOREST 11   78 Because lust's meanes are spent:

lusty   frequency: 1   relative frequency: 0.00001
    see "lustie," "lustie-mounting."
  *p. 492 TO HIMSELF   19 If they loue lees, and leaue the lusty wine,

lute   frequency: 5   relative frequency: 0.00007
  *p. 493 TO HIMSELF   42 And take the Alcaick Lute;
    p. 181 UNDERWOOD 27   3 Did Sappho on her seven-tongu'd Lute,
    p. 239 UNDERWOOD 67   17 Harpe, Lute, Theorbo sprung,
    p. 263 UNDERWOOD 79   2 Lute, Lyre, Theorbo, all are call'd to day.
    p. 292 UNDERWOOD 86   23 Shall Verse be set to Harpe and Lute,

lutes   frequency: 1   relative frequency: 0.00001
    p. 327 HORACE 2   484 Was said to move the stones, by his Lutes
                               powers,

luther's. See "lvthers."

luxurie   frequency: 2   relative frequency: 0.00002
    p.   48 EPIGRAMS 65   4 To a great image through thy luxurie.
    p. 111 FOREST 11   69 Peace, Luxurie, thou art like one of those

luxury. See "luxurie."

lvcan   frequency: 1   relative frequency: 0.00001
    p. 395 UNGATHERED 29   t2 The learned Translator of LVCAN,

lvcina's   frequency: 1   relative frequency: 0.00001
    p. 115 FOREST 12   66 Of all LVCINA'S traine; LVCY the
                                 bright,

lvcivs   frequency: 1   relative frequency: 0.00001
    p. 242 UNDERWOOD 70   t2 that noble paire, Sir LVCIVS CARY,

lvcklesse   frequency: 3   relative frequency: 0.00004
    p.   42 EPIGRAMS 46   3 'Tis LVCKLESSE he, that tooke vp one on
                                 band
    p.   42 EPIGRAMS 46   t1 TO SIR LVCKLESSE WOO-ALL.
    p.   42 EPIGRAMS 47   1 Sir LVCKLESSE, troth, for lucks sake
                                 passe by one:

lvcy   frequency: 7   relative frequency: 0.00010
    p.   52 EPIGRAMS 76   t1 ON LVCY COVNTESSE OF
                                 BEDFORD.
    p.   54 EPIGRAMS 84   t1 TO LVCY COVNTESSE OF
                                 BEDFORD.
    p.   60 EPIGRAMS 94   1 LVCY, you brightnesse of our spheare, who are
    p.   60 EPIGRAMS 94   t1 TO LVCY, COVNTESSE OF
                                 BEDFORD,
    p.   61 EPIGRAMS 94   15 LVCY, you brightnesse of our spheare, who are
    p. 115 FOREST 12   66 Of all LVCINA'S traine; LVCY the
                                 bright,
    p. 662 INSCRIPIS. 2   3 LVCY of BEDFORD; she, that Bounty

lvthers   frequency: 1   relative frequency: 0.00001
    p.   65 EPIGRAMS 101   34 Are all but LVTHERS beere, to this I
                                 sing.

lyaeus   frequency: 1   relative frequency: 0.00001
    p. 221 UNDERWOOD 48   18 Lyaeus, and defend him,

lybian   frequency: 1   relative frequency: 0.00001
    p. 408 UNGATHERED 36   7 The Lybian Lion hunts noe butter flyes,

lycense   frequency: 1   relative frequency: 0.00001
    p. 423 UNGATHERED 50   12 It is a lycense to doe ill, protectes

lycoris   frequency: 1   relative frequency: 0.00001
    p. 181 UNDERWOOD 27   15 With bright Lycoris, Gallus choice,

lyd.   frequency: 3   relative frequency: 0.00004
    p. 293 UNDERWOOD 87   5 LYD. Whilst Horace lov'd no Mistres more,
    p. 293 UNDERWOOD 87   13 LYD. And I, am mutually on fire
    p. 294 UNDERWOOD 87   21 LYD. Though he be fairer then a Starre;

lydia   frequency: 4   relative frequency: 0.00005
    See also "left-lydia," "lyd."
    p. 293 UNDERWOOD 87   1 HOR. Whilst, Lydia, I was lov'd of thee,
    p. 293 UNDERWOOD 87   6 Nor after C<h>loe did his Lydia sound;
    p. 293 UNDERWOOD 87   t1 Ode IX. 3 Booke, to Lydia.
    p. 293 UNDERWOOD 87   t2 Dialogue of Horace, and Lydia.

lye   frequency: 10 relative frequency: 0.00014
    p.   28 EPIGRAMS 3   5 To lye vpon thy stall, till it be sought;
    p.   35 EPIGRAMS 26   2 He'adulters still: his thoughts lye with a whore.
    p.   41 EPIGRAMS 45   9 Rest in soft peace, and, ask'd, say here doth lye
    p.   47 EPIGRAMS 63   11 Curst be his Muse, that could lye dumbe, or hid
    p.   65 EPIGRAMS 101   17 Ile tell you of more, and lye, so you will come:
    p.   69 EPIGRAMS 107   20 And then lye with you, closer, then a punque,
    p.   79 EPIGRAMS 124   3 Vnder-neath this stone doth lye
    p. 114 FOREST 12   40 And now lye lost in their forgotten dust.
    p. 391 UNGATHERED 26   20 Chaucer, or Spenser, or bid Beaumont lye
    p. 392 UNGATHERED 26   53 But antiquated, and deserted lye

lyer   frequency: 1   relative frequency: 0.00001
    p. 383 UNGATHERED 16   15 shall looke, & on hyme soe, then arte's a
                                 lyer

lyes   frequency: 7   relative frequency: 0.00010
   p.   33 EPIGRAMS 22   1 Here lyes to each her parents ruth,
   p.   38 EPIGRAMS 38   6 And lyes so farre from wit, 'tis impudence.
   p.   94 FOREST 2   29 The painted partrich lyes in euery field,
   p. 137 UNDERWOOD 2.5   34 Lyes the Valley, cal'd my nest,
   p. 174 UNDERWOOD 23   8 Dri'd up? lyes Thespia wast?
   p. 210 UNDERWOOD 43   174 Lyes there no Writ, out of the Chancerie,
   p. 248 UNDERWOOD 71   10 But lyes block'd up, and straightned, narrow'd
                                   in,

lyfe   frequency: 1   relative frequency: 0.00001
   p. 387 UNGATHERED 22   7 I made my lyfe my monument, & yours:

lying   frequency: 3   relative frequency: 0.00004
   p. 105 FOREST 8   32 Lying for the spirit of amber.
   p. 238 UNDERWOOD 66   t1 An Epigram to the Queene, then lying in.
   p. 380 UNGATHERED 12   31 Of lying, he feares so much the reproofe

lyke   frequency: 3   relative frequency: 0.00004
   p. 361 UNGATHERED 1   14 how lyke the Carbuncle in Aarons brest
   p. 405 UNGATHERED 34   79 How would he firke? lyke Adam ouerdooe
   p. 420 UNGATHERED 48   15 Whilest lyke a blaze of strawe,

lyly. See "lily."

lyne   frequency: 5   relative frequency: 0.00007
   p. 175 UNDERWOOD 23   27 With Japhets lyne, aspire
   p. 176 UNDERWOOD 24   12 Doth mete, whose lyne doth sound the depth of
                                   things:)
   p. 183 UNDERWOOD 29   29 Nor a lyne deserving praise,
   p. 193 UNDERWOOD 38   91 Forgiven him; And in that lyne stand I,
   p. 406 UNGATHERED 34   95 Expression for! wth that vnbounded lyne

lynes   frequency: 2   relative frequency: 0.00002
   p. 200 UNDERWOOD 42   8 His lynes, and hourely sits the Poets horse?
   p. 230 UNDERWOOD 56   3 A booke to a few lynes: but, it was fit

lyons   frequency: 1   relative frequency: 0.00001
   p. 327 HORACE 2   482 Was Tigers, said, and Lyons fierce, to tame.

lyre   frequency: 7   relative frequency: 0.00010
  *p. 493 TO HIMSELF   43 Or thine owne Horace, or Anacreons Lyre;
   p.   98 FOREST 3   51 APOLLO'S harpe, and HERMES lyre
                                   resound,
   p. 175 UNDERWOOD 23   25 Then take in hand thy Lyre,
   p. 177 UNDERWOOD 25   9 My bolder numbers to thy golden Lyre:
   p. 239 UNDERWOOD 67   16 Let every Lyre be strung,
   p. 263 UNDERWOOD 79   2 Lute, Lyre, Theorbo, all are call'd to day.
   p. 329 HORACE 2   502 Or Muse, upon the Lyre, thou chance
                                   b<e>'asham'd.

lyric. See "lyrick."

lyrick   frequency: 2   relative frequency: 0.00002
   p. 131 UNDERWOOD 2   t2 ten Lyrick Peeces.
   p. 309 HORACE 2   113 Unto the Lyrick Strings, the Muse gave grace

lyst   frequency: 1   relative frequency: 0.00001
   p. 156 UNDERWOOD 13   114 I have the lyst of mine owne faults to know,

lyue   frequency: 1   relative frequency: 0.00001
   p. 406 UNGATHERED 34 101 Lyue long ye ffeasting Roome. And ere thou
                                   burne

m.   frequency: 4   relative frequency: 0.00005
   p. 370 UNGATHERED 8   t1 To the worthy Author M.
   p. 396 UNGATHERED 30   t4 M. DRAYTON.
   p. 409 UNGATHERED 38   t3 the Author of this Work, M. RICH.
                                   BROME.
   p. 412 UNGATHERED 41   3 The M. the Myrtle, A. the Almonds clame,

ma'   frequency: 1   relative frequency: 0.00001

maas   frequency: 1   relative frequency: 0.00001
   p. 369 UNGATHERED 6   116 Scheldt, nor the Maas,

machine   frequency: 2   relative frequency: 0.00002
   p. 395 UNGATHERED 29   22 In the great masse, or machine there is stirr'd?
   p. 403 UNGATHERED 34   32 That doe cry vp ye Machine, & ye Showes!

mad   frequency: 5   relative frequency: 0.00007
        See also "mad-men," "madde."
        p. 164 UNDERWOOD 15   70 And then, leape mad on a neat Pickardill,
        p. 168 UNDERWOOD 15   194 More honour in him, 'cause we'<h>ave knowne him
                                  mad:
        p. 313 HORACE 2_   177 Poore Jo wandring; wild Orestes mad:
        p. 335 HORACE 2   646 The yellow Jaundies, or were furious mad
        p. 337 HORACE 2   673 (Defiled) touch'd; but certaine he was mad,

mad<e>   frequency: 1   relative frequency: 0.00001
        p. 207 UNDERWOOD 43   91 Was there mad<e> English: with a Grammar too,

mad-men   frequency: 1   relative frequency: 0.00001
        p. 27 EPIGRAMS 2   6 As mad-men stones: not caring whom they hit.

madam   frequency: 4   relative frequency: 0.00005
        See also "madame."
        p. 188 UNDERWOOD 34   10 Any beliefe, in Madam Baud-bees bath,
        p. 224 UNDERWOOD 50   1 The Wisdome, Madam, of your private Life,
        p. 230 UNDERWOOD 56   1 You won not Verses, Madam, you won mee,
        p. 231 UNDERWOOD 56   27 How many verses, Madam, are your Due!

madame   frequency: 12   relative frequency: 0.00017
        p. 46 EPIGRAMS 62   1 Fine MADAME WOVLD-BEE, wherefore
                                  should you feare,
        p. 51 EPIGRAMS 73   11 With which a learned Madame you belye.
        p. 54 EPIGRAMS 84   1 MADAME, I told you late how I repented,
        p. 55 EPIGRAMS 84   9 O Madame, if your grant did thus transferre mee,
        p. 67 EPIGRAMS 105   1 MADAME, had all antiquitie beene lost,
        p. 89 EPIGRAMS 133   180 And MADAME CAESAR, great
                                  PROSERPINA,
        p. 113 FOREST 12   t2+ MADAME,
        p. 114 FOREST 12   38 Riches thought most: But, Madame, thinke what
                                  store
        p. 117 FOREST 13   21 I, Madame, am become your praiser. Where,
        p. 118 FOREST 13   53 Wherewith, then, Madame, can you better pay
        p. 119 FOREST 13   89 You, Madame, yong haue learn'd to shunne these
                                  shelues,
        p. 120 FOREST 13   122 Madame, be bold to vse this truest glasse:

madames   frequency: 2   relative frequency: 0.00002
        p. 50 EPIGRAMS 72   3 At MADAMES table, where thou mak'st all
                                  wit
        p. 63 EPIGRAMS 97   14 Of any Madames, hath neadd squires, and must.

madam's. See "madames."

madde   frequency: 4   relative frequency: 0.00005
        p. 147 UNDERWOOD 7   10 But then if I grow jealous madde,
        p. 191 UNDERWOOD 38   2 Of Credit lost. And I am now run madde:
        p. 206 UNDERWOOD 43   70 All the madde Rolands, and sweet Oliveers;
        p. 208 UNDERWOOD 43   131 (Which, some are pleas'd to stile but thy madde
                                  pranck)

made   frequency: 97   relative frequency: 0.00140
        See also "ill-made," "mad<e>," "wel-made."
      *p. 492 TO HIMSELF   10 They were not made for thee, lesse, thou for
                                  them.
      *p. 493 TO HIMSELF   46 Ere yeares haue made thee old;
     **p. 115 PANEGYRE   66 And infants, that the houres had made such hast
     **p. 115 PANEGYRE   95 "She shewd him, who made wise, who honest acts;
     **p. 115 PANEGYRE   99 "Where lawes were made to serue the tyran' will;
     **p. 117 PANEGYRE   146 Brighter then all, hath yet made no one lesse;
        p. 27 EPIGRAMS 2   10 Made from the hazard of anothers shame:
        p. 28 EPIGRAMS 3   6 Not offer'd, as it made sute to be bought;
        p. 29 EPIGRAMS 10   2 But I haue my reuenge made, in thy name.
        p. 30 EPIGRAMS 11   4 It made me a great face, I ask'd the name.
        p. 41 EPIGRAMS 44   6 When he made him executor, might be heire.
        p. 45 EPIGRAMS 56   5 At first he made low shifts, would picke and
                                  gleane,
        p. 48 EPIGRAMS 65   3 Made me commit most fierce idolatrie
        p. 51 EPIGRAMS 73   20 Then had I made 'hem good, to fit your vaine.
        p. 52 EPIGRAMS 74   10 T<o>'our times return'd, hath made her heauen in
                                  thee.
        p. 53 EPIGRAMS 79   9 At which, shee happily displeas'd, made you:
        p. 56 EPIGRAMS 87   6 Since when, hee's sober againe, and all play's
                                  made.
        p. 56 EPIGRAMS 88   15 The new french-taylors motion, monthly made,
        p. 64 EPIGRAMS 99   9 From place, or fortune, are made high, or low,
        p. 67 EPIGRAMS 105   5 But euen their names were to be made a-new,

made (cont.)

p.	74	EPIGRAMS 114	5 Hath chang'd his soule, and made his obiect you:
p.	74	EPIGRAMS 114	8 But, in your loue, made all his seruants wise.
p.	79	EPIGRAMS 125	2 Made for what Nature could, or Vertue can;
p.	81	EPIGRAMS 129	7 That still th'art made the suppers flagge, the drum,
p.	86	EPIGRAMS 133	84 Made of the trull, that cut her fathers lock:
p.	93	FOREST 2	11 Where PAN, and BACCHVS their high feasts haue made,
p.	98	FOREST 3	45 The trees cut out in log; and those boughes made
p.	99	FOREST 3	93 Thy peace is made; and, when man's state is well,
p.	105	FOREST 8	20 And haue more diseases made.
p.	107	FOREST 10	8 Shall not giue out, that I haue made thee stay,
p.	114	FOREST 12	23 When gold was made no weapon to cut throtes,
p.	115	FOREST 12	61 Who made a lampe of BERENICES hayre?
p.	119	FOREST 13	95 Of your blest wombe, made fruitfull from aboue,
p.	120	FOREST 13	120 Each into other, and had now made one.
p.	129	UNDERWOOD 1.2	21 First made of nought;
p.	130	UNDERWOOD 1.3	17 The Word was now made Flesh indeed,
p.	130	UNDERWOOD 1.3	20 Who made himselfe the price of sinne,
p.	136	UNDERWOOD 2.5	15 Of her face, and made to rise,
p.	137	UNDERWOOD 2.5	32 Lovers, made into a Chaine!
p.	143	UNDERWOOD 3	3 Till each of us be made a Starre,
p.	145	UNDERWOOD 5	16 Then when 'tis made, why so will wee.
p.	155	UNDERWOOD 13	63 Their bounties forth, to him that last was made,
p.	159	UNDERWOOD 14	22 But 'twas with purpose to have made them such.
p.	163	UNDERWOOD 15	36 But more licentious made, and desperate!
p.	163	UNDERWOOD 15	43 As they are made! Pride, and stiffe Clownage mixt
p.	169	UNDERWOOD 17	17 Some grounds are made the richer, for the Rest;
p.	172	UNDERWOOD 20	18 Then all Ingredients made into one curse,
p.	180	UNDERWOOD 26	7 Have made their fairest flight,
p.	182	UNDERWOOD 27	28 Made Dian, not his notes refuse?
p.	186	UNDERWOOD 33	2 The Seat made of a more then civill warre;
p.	187	UNDERWOOD 33	14 Have made me to conceive a Lawyer new.
p.	189	UNDERWOOD 36	2 For Love in shadow best is made.
p.	197	UNDERWOOD 40	14 Of vowes so sacred, and in silence made;
p.	198	UNDERWOOD 40	47 (Made to blow up loves secrets) to discover
p.	200	UNDERWOOD 42	21 Made longer by our praises. Or, if not,
p.	203	UNDERWOOD 43	6 Nor made least line of love to thy loose Wife;
p.	206	UNDERWOOD 43	84 Had made a meale for Vulcan to lick up.
p.	208	UNDERWOOD 43	117 For none but Smiths would have made thee a God.
p.	208	UNDERWOOD 43	126 They made a Vulcan of a sheafe of Reedes,
p.	208	UNDERWOOD 43	130 Made thee beget that cruell Stratagem,
p.	212	UNDERWOOD 43	198 And there made Swords, Bills, Glaves, and Armes your fill;
p.	217	UNDERWOOD 46	8 Thy just defences made th'oppressor afraid.
p.	219	UNDERWOOD 47	58 Last it be justled, crack'd, made nought, or lesse:
p.	220	UNDERWOOD 48	4 Where now, thou art made Dweller;
p.	227	UNDERWOOD 52	15 You made it a brave piece, but not like me.
p.	230	UNDERWOOD 56	12 And that's made up as doth the purse abound.
p.	241	UNDERWOOD 69	3 Profit, or Chance had made us: But I know
p.	246	UNDERWOOD 70	100 Made, or indentur'd, or leas'd out t<o>'advance
p.	247	UNDERWOOD 70	107 This made you first to know the Why
p.	247	UNDERWOOD 70	114 And titles, by which all made claimes
p.	248	UNDERWOOD 71	7 And made those strong approaches, by False braies,
p.	249	UNDERWOOD 72	12 Made lighter with the Wine. All noises else,
p.	250	UNDERWOOD 73	t4 Hee was made Earle of Portland,
p.	250	UNDERWOOD 73	12 T<o>'effect it, feele, thou'ast made thine owne heart ake.
p.	257	UNDERWOOD 75	139 These two, now holy Church hath made them one,
p.	258	UNDERWOOD 75	183 By this Sun's Noone-sted's made
p.	268	UNDERWOOD 82	16 Her Rose, and Lilly, intertwind, have made.
p.	270	UNDERWOOD 83	60 Made her friends joyes to get above their feares!
p.	270	UNDERWOOD 83	65 Who saw the way was made it! and were sent
p.	284	U'WOOD 84.9	80 Have busie search made in his mysteries!
p.	307	HORACE 2	68 Are, by thy cunning placing, made meere new.
p.	321	HORACE 2	333 A royall Crowne, and purple, be made hop,
p.	323	HORACE 2	370 His power of foulely hurting made to cease.
p.	361	UNGATHERED 1	3 weare made the obiects to my weaker powers;
p.	361	UNGATHERED 1	10 Thy skill hath made of ranck dispised weedes;
p.	371	UNGATHERED 9	6 She might haue claym'd t'have made the Graces foure;
p.	383	UNGATHERED 16	12 made prospectiue, behould hym, hee must pas<s>e
p.	387	UNGATHERED 22	7 I made my lyfe my monument, & yours:
p.	389	UNGATHERED 23	10 Such Passage hast thou found, such Returnes made,
p.	392	UNGATHERED 26	64 For a good Poet's made, as well as borne.

made (cont.)
    p. 392 UNGATHERED 26   76 Aduanc'd, and made a Constellation there!
    p. 394 UNGATHERED 28   18 And her, she made her Inmate, to the End,
    p. 397 UNGATHERED 30   27 Which made me thinke, the old Theocritus,
    p. 397 UNGATHERED 30   48 Vnder one title. Thou hast made thy way
    p. 403 UNGATHERED 34   30 And all men eccho you haue made a Masque.
    p. 406 UNGATHERED 35   2 Hath made his Inigo Marquess, wouldst thou
                               fayne
    p. 415 UNGATHERED 42   23 Of wit, and a new made: a Warden then,

madest. See "mad'st."

madmen. See "mad-men."

madnesse   frequency: 2   relative frequency: 0.00002
    p. 36 EPIGRAMS 30   3 'Twere madnesse in thee, to betray thy fame,
    p. 163 UNDERWOOD 15   31 The whole world here leaven'd with madnesse
                               swells;

madrigal. See "madrigall."

madrigall   frequency: 1   relative frequency: 0.00001
    p. 201 UNDERWOOD 42   68 That (in pure Madrigall) unto his Mother

mad'st   frequency: 5   relative frequency: 0.00007
    p. 75 EPIGRAMS 116   5 Thou wert the first, mad'st merit know her
                               strength,
    p. 107 FOREST 10   14 That, at thy birth, mad'st the poore Smith
                               affraid,
    p. 242 UNDERWOOD 70   8 And mad'st thy Mothers wombe thine urne.
    p. 414 UNGATHERED 41   47 Who mad'st us happy all, in thy reflexe,
    p. 421 UNGATHERED 48   40 Thou mad'st in open ffeild

magic. See "magick."

magick   frequency: 1   relative frequency: 0.00001
    p. 85 EPIGRAMS 133   49 Or magick sacrifice, they past along!

magistrates   frequency: 1   relative frequency: 0.00001
    p. 32 EPIGRAMS 17   2 As guiltie men doe magistrates: glad I,

magnetic. See "magnetique."

magnetique   frequency: 1   relative frequency: 0.00001
    p. 399 UNGATHERED 31   19 Or else Magnetique in the force,

maid   frequency: 5   relative frequency: 0.00007
    See also "mayd."
  **p. 113 PANEGYRE   23 Beside her, stoup't on either hand, a maid,
    p. 107 FOREST 10   13 PALLAS, nor thee I call on, mankinde maid,
    p. 138 UNDERWOOD 2.6   8 That the Bride (allow'd a Maid)
    p. 207 UNDERWOOD 43   96 To speake the fate of the Sicilian Maid
    p. 238 UNDERWOOD 66   2 And by an Angell, to the blessed'st Maid,

maiden   frequency: 1   relative frequency: 0.00001
    See also "mayden."
    p. 254 UNDERWOOD 75   47 Nought of a Maiden Queene,

maidens   frequency: 1   relative frequency: 0.00001
    p. 253 UNDERWOOD 75   39 Of all the Maidens faire;

maides   frequency: 1   relative frequency: 0.00001
    p. 63 EPIGRAMS 97   18 Nor are the Queenes most honor'd maides by
                               th'eares

maids   frequency: 1   relative frequency: 0.00001
    See also "maides."
    p. 292 UNDERWOOD 86   26 The Youths and tender Maids shall sing thy
                               praise:

maim. See "maime."

maime   frequency: 1   relative frequency: 0.00001
    p. 162 UNDERWOOD 15   22 Till envie wound, or maime it at a blow!

maimed. See "maymed."

main. See "maine," "mayne."

maine   frequency: 6   relative frequency: 0.00008
    p. 35 EPIGRAMS 28   13 Which is maine greatnesse. And, at his still
                              boord,
    p. 76 EPIGRAMS 119   4 Shuns prease, for two maine causes, poxe, and
                              debt,
    p. 258 UNDERWOOD 75   181 Whilst the maine tree, still found
    p. 307 HORACE 2   48 But in the maine worke haplesse: since he knowes
    p. 367 UNGATHERED 6   42 Ouer Ierna maine,
    p. 368 UNGATHERED 6   90 Of thine, shall thinke the Maine

maintain. See "maintaine," "maintayne."

maintain'd   frequency: 2   relative frequency: 0.00002
    p. 209 UNDERWOOD 43   144 When Venus there maintain'd the Misterie.
    p. 212 UNDERWOOD 43   199 Maintain'd the trade at Bilbo, or else-where;

maintaine   frequency: 1   relative frequency: 0.00001
    p. 317 HORACE 2   277 Must maintaine manly; not be heard to sing,

maintains. See "maintaynes."

maintayne   frequency: 3   relative frequency: 0.00004
    p. 34 EPIGRAMS 23   8 Which might with halfe mankind maintayne a
                              strife.
    p. 105 FOREST 8   19 They maintayne the truest trade,
    p. 118 FOREST 13   72 Maintayne their liedgers forth, for forraine
                              wyres,

maintaynes   frequency: 1   relative frequency: 0.00001
    p. 51 EPIGRAMS 73   8 That yet maintaynes you, and your house in
                              laughter.

maior   frequency: 1   relative frequency: 0.00001
    p. 417 UNGATHERED 45   25 If there be a Coockold Maior,

maiors   frequency: 2   relative frequency: 0.00002
    p. 87 EPIGRAMS 133   120 And that is when it is the Lord Maiors foist.
    p. 96 FOREST 3   6 Of Sheriffes dinner, or Maiors feast.

maist   frequency: 8   relative frequency: 0.00011

maistring   frequency: 1   relative frequency: 0.00001
    p. 232 UNDERWOOD 59   3 The noble Science, and the maistring skill

maistry   frequency: 1   relative frequency: 0.00001
    p. 227 UNDERWOOD 52   16 O, had I now your manner, maistry, might,

majestie   frequency: 6   relative frequency: 0.00008
    p. 128 UNDERWOOD 1.1   38 All coeternall in your Majestie,
    p. 236 UNDERWOOD 64   6 For safetie of such Majestie, cry out?
    p. 259 UNDERWOOD 76   4 To your Majestie your Poet:
    p. 260 UNDERWOOD 76   25 Please your Majestie to make
    p. 270 UNDERWOOD 83   44 A dazling, yet inviting, Majestie:
    p. 286 U'WOOD 84.9   130 Will there revealed be in Majestie!

majesties   frequency: 2   relative frequency: 0.00002
    p. 239 UNDERWOOD 67   t2 In celebration of her Majesties birth-day.
    p. 254 UNDERWOOD 75   53 Whose Majesties appeare,

majesty   frequency: 1   relative frequency: 0.00001
    See also "majestie."
    p. 403 UNGATHERED 34   33 The majesty of Iuno in ye Cloudes,

major. See "maior."

make   frequency: 176   relative frequency: 0.00254
  **p. 113 PANEGYRE   14 And make their denne the slaughter-house of
                              soules:
  **p. 114 PANEGYRE   52 As our ambitious dames, when they make feast,
    p. 28 EPIGRAMS 3   8 Or in cleft-sticks, aduanced to make calls
    p. 31 EPIGRAMS 14   10 Man scarse can make that doubt, but thou canst
                              teach.
    p. 32 EPIGRAMS 16   8 Make good what thou dar'st doe in all the rest.
    p. 34 EPIGRAMS 24   1 There's reason good, that you good lawes should
                              make:
    p. 34 EPIGRAMS 25   8 Iust wife, and, to change me, make womans hast?
    p. 37 EPIGRAMS 33   4 Breathe to expect my when, and make my how.
    p. 41 EPIGRAMS 44   5 He meant they thither should make swift repaire,
    p. 42 EPIGRAMS 50   3 Arsenike would thee fit for societie make.
    p. 46 EPIGRAMS 62   2 That loue to make so well, a child to beare?

make (cont.)

p.	46 EPIGRAMS 62	8	To make amends, yo'are thought a wholesome creature.
p.	48 EPIGRAMS 65	9	Make him loose all his friends; and, which is worse,
p.	48 EPIGRAMS 66	6	Durst valour make, almost, but not a crime.
p.	50 EPIGRAMS 70	8	Though life be short, let vs not make it so.
p.	52 EPIGRAMS 76	5	I meant to make her faire, and free, and wise,
p.	53 EPIGRAMS 80	4	And hath it, in his powers, to make his way!
p.	54 EPIGRAMS 81	8	I must a libell make, and cosen both.
p.	55 EPIGRAMS 84	10	Make it your gift. See whither that will beare mee.
p.	55 EPIGRAMS 85	10	Till they be sure to make the foole their quarrie.
p.	59 EPIGRAMS 92	30	If the States make peace, how it will goe
p.	59 EPIGRAMS 92	34	And at the Pope, and Spaine slight faces make.
p.	62 EPIGRAMS 96	3	That so alone canst iudge, so'alone dost make:
p.	63 EPIGRAMS 97	12	Nor 'bout the beares, nor noyse to make lords sport.
p.	64 EPIGRAMS 101	5	With those that come; whose grace may make that seeme
p.	65 EPIGRAMS 101	37	Nor shall our cups make any guiltie men:
p.	65 EPIGRAMS 101	41	Shall make vs sad next morning: or affright
p.	67 EPIGRAMS 104	6	To make those faithfull, did the Fates send you?
p.	69 EPIGRAMS 107	19	Giue your yong States-men, (that first make you drunke,
p.	70 EPIGRAMS 109	11	To make thy lent life, good against the Fates:
p.	73 EPIGRAMS 112	22	There's no vexation, that can make thee prime.
p.	73 EPIGRAMS 113	10	Could make such men, and such a place repent:
p.	78 EPIGRAMS 121	6	If onely loue should make the action pris'd:
p.	80 EPIGRAMS 128	4	And those to turne to bloud, and make thine owne:
p.	81 EPIGRAMS 129	8	The very call, to make all others come:
p.	85 EPIGRAMS 133	66	Thorough her wombe they make their famous road,
p.	88 EPIGRAMS 133	144	That, with still-scalding steemes, make the place hell.
p.	95 FOREST 2	52	Some nuts, some apples; some that thinke they make
p.	95 FOREST 2	83	Did'st thou, then, make 'hem! and what praise was heap'd
p.	98 FOREST 3	65	And such since thou canst make thine owne content,
p.	100 FOREST 4	15	That onely fooles make thee a saint,
p.	100 FOREST 4	19	To take the weake, or make them stop:
p.	102 FOREST 4	67	But make my strengths, such as they are,
p.	105 FOREST 8	36	That, to make all pleasure theirs,
p.	108 FOREST 10	26	(Though they were crusht into one forme) could make
p.	108 FOREST 10 A	6	Could ne'er make prize of thy white Chastetye.
p.	109 FOREST 11	18	To make our sense our slaue.
p.	112 FOREST 11	94	Would make a day of night,
p.	113 FOREST 12	12	Of some grand peere, whose ayre doth make reioyce
p.	114 FOREST 12	48	That had no Muse to make their fame abide.
p.	115 FOREST 12	64	And such, or my hopes faile, shall make you shine.
p.	120 FOREST 14	22	Are iustly summ'd, that make you man;
p.	130 UNDERWOOD 1.3	11	The Word, which heaven, and earth did make;
p.	130 UNDERWOOD 1.3	21	To make us heires of glory!
p.	131 UNDERWOOD 2.1	20	She shall make the old man young,
p.	133 UNDERWOOD 2.3	10	At her hand, with oath, to make
p.	133 UNDERWOOD 2.3	26	Heare and make Example too.
p.	137 UNDERWOOD 2.5	48	Make in one, the same were shee.
p.	140 UNDERWOOD 2.8	29	Make accompt, unlesse you can,
p.	140 UNDERWOOD 2.9	6	And a woman God did make me:
p.	141 UNDERWOOD 2.9	24	And make Love or me afeard.
p.	141 UNDERWOOD 2.9	37	Yet no Taylor help to make him;
p.	143 UNDERWOOD 3	11	To make the Mountaine Quarries move,
p.	143 UNDERWOOD 3	16	But what those lips doe make.
p.	145 UNDERWOOD 5	3	To make us still sing o're, and o're,
p.	145 UNDERWOOD 5	11	Wee shall, at last, of parcells make
p.	145 UNDERWOOD 5	18	To make a new, and hang that by.
p.	146 UNDERWOOD 6	14	For what is better, or to make
p.	147 UNDERWOOD 7	23	As make away my doubt,
p.	150 UNDERWOOD 11	2	I must the true Relation make,
p.	153 UNDERWOOD 13	16	The smallest courtesies with thankes, I make
p.	154 UNDERWOOD 13	38	Must make me sad for what I have obtain'd.
p.	155 UNDERWOOD 13	84	Now, but command; make tribute, what was gift;
p.	156 UNDERWOOD 13	99	And almost deifie the Authors! make
p.	159 UNDERWOOD 14	35	Which Grace shall I make love to first? your skill,
p.	163 UNDERWOOD 15	44	To make up Greatnesse! and mans whole good fix'd

make (cont.)

p. 164	UNDERWOOD 15	62	Not make a verse; Anger; or laughter would,
p. 164	UNDERWOOD 15	64	How they may make some one that day an Asse;
p. 166	UNDERWOOD 15	128	But both fell prest under the load they make.
p. 166	UNDERWOOD 15	134	Goe make our selves the Usurers at a cast.
p. 168	UNDERWOOD 15	183	That fortune never make thee to complaine,
p. 171	UNDERWOOD 19	24	As would make shift, to make himselfe alone,
p. 175	UNDERWOOD 23	33	Make not thy selfe a Page,
p. 181	UNDERWOOD 26	21	Such thoughts wil make you more in love with truth.
p. 182	UNDERWOOD 28	14	For Venus Ceston, every line you make.
p. 186	UNDERWOOD 32	4	Then to make falshood blush, and fraud afraid:
p. 187	UNDERWOOD 33	21	And make the Scarre faire; If that will not be,
p. 188	UNDERWOOD 34	12	Spanish receipt, to make her teeth to rot.
p. 188	UNDERWOOD 34	15	That heaven should make no more; or should amisse,
p. 188	UNDERWOOD 34	16	Make all hereafter, had'st thou ruin'd this?
p. 192	UNDERWOOD 38	59	That were to wither all, and make a Grave
p. 193	UNDERWOOD 38	84	Of crueltie, lest they doe make you such.
p. 194	UNDERWOOD 38	106	And let your mercie make me asham'd t<o>'offend.
p. 197	UNDERWOOD 40	8	Shortly againe: and make our absence sweet.
p. 201	UNDERWOOD 42	53	An Officer there, did make most solemne love,
p. 205	UNDERWOOD 43	58	To make consumption, ever, where thou go'st;
p. 212	UNDERWOOD 43	206	Make your Petards, and Granats, all your fine
p. 213	UNDERWOOD 44	16	To see the Pride at Court, their Wives doe make:
p. 215	UNDERWOOD 44	90	What, to make legs? yes, and to smell most sweet,
p. 216	UNDERWOOD 45	14	No piece of money, but you know, or make
p. 218	UNDERWOOD 47	12	As make it their proficiencie, how much
p. 220	UNDERWOOD 48	12	And relish merry make him.
p. 221	UNDERWOOD 48	29	And thou make many a Poet,
p. 222	UNDERWOOD 49	12	Make State, Religion, Bawdrie, all a theame?
p. 224	UNDERWOOD 50	27	Or your Allies, you make your bookes your friends,
p. 225	UNDERWOOD 50	33	As they are hard, for them to make their owne,
p. 229	UNDERWOOD 54	6	An ill commoditie! 'T must make good weight.
p. 229	UNDERWOOD 54	17	And you shall make me good, in weight, and fashion,
p. 230	UNDERWOOD 56	21	To make you merry on the Dressing stoole,
p. 234	UNDERWOOD 61	14	My Lord, till felt griefe make our stone hearts soft,
p. 236	UNDERWOOD 63	11	That thought shall make, he will this losse supply
p. 236	UNDERWOOD 64	10	And what are bounds to her, you make your owne?
p. 238	UNDERWOOD 66	10	To make the hearts of a whole Nation smile,
p. 241	UNDERWOOD 68	8	Would make the very Greene-cloth to looke blew:
p. 244	UNDERWOOD 70	54	And make them yeares;
p. 245	UNDERWOOD 70	64	These make the lines of life, and that's her ayre.
p. 245	UNDERWOOD 70	66	In bulke, doth make man better bee;
p. 254	UNDERWOOD 75	54	To make more cleare
p. 257	UNDERWOOD 75	140	Doe long to make themselves, so, another way:
p. 259	UNDERWOOD 76	8	To make all the MUSES debters
p. 260	UNDERWOOD 76	25	Please your Majestie to make
p. 261	UNDERWOOD 77	19	Of murmuring Subjects; make the Nations know
p. 270	UNDERWOOD 83	35	And, calling truth to witnesse, make that good
p. 273	U'WOOD 84.1	11	A dedicated Ensigne make
p. 275	U'WOOD 84.3	2	What make these Velvets, Silkes, and Lawne,
p. 276	U'WOOD 84.3	14	And, out of that, make Day to breake;
p. 278	U'WOOD 84.4	9	You could make shift to paint an Eye,
p. 278	U'WOOD 84.4	21	I call you Muse; now make it true:
p. 282	U'WOOD 84.9	7	To hang a window, or make darke the roome,
p. 284	U'WOOD 84.9	72	That she is in, or, make it more compleat?
p. 286	U'WOOD 84.9	120	But make him All in All, their Theme, that Day:
p. 292	UNDERWOOD 86	11	There jest, and feast, make him thine host,
p. 292	UNDERWOOD 86	19	He'll thee a Marble Statue make
p. 294	UNDERWOOD 87	17	HOR. But, say old Love returne should make,
p. 295	UNDERWOOD 90	1	The Things that make the happier life, are these,
p. 295	UNDERWOOD 90	11	Sleepe, that will make the darkest howres swift-pac't;
p. 313	HORACE 2	175	Medea make brave with impetuous scorne;
p. 313	HORACE 2	187	Yet common matter thou thine owne maist make,
p. 317	HORACE 2	262	Much from the sight, which faire report will make
p. 321	HORACE 2	345	As not make difference, whether Davus speake,
p. 325	HORACE 2	454	On life, and manners, and make those his booke,
p. 329	HORACE 2	519	With honour make the farre-knowne Author live.
p. 331	HORACE 2	570	Yet who's most ignorant, dares Verses make.
p. 333	HORACE 2	593	But, now, it is enough to say; I make

make (cont.)

p.	333 HORACE 2	602	Make a great Supper; or for some poore man
p.	335 HORACE 2	655	For, if one should, and with a rope make haste
p.	354 HORACE 1	620	.... make ....
p.	362 UNGATHERED 2	11	Wants facultie to make a censure true:
p.	367 UNGATHERED 6	29	Nor Sunne could make to vary from the rest,
p.	372 UNGATHERED 9	14	Might make the Fable of Good Women true.
p.	384 UNGATHERED 18	12	Out-bee yt wife, in worth, thy freind did make:
p.	384 UNGATHERED 18	14	Hymens amends, to make it worth his fault.
p.	385 UNGATHERED 20	4	Least a false praise do make theyr dotage his.
p.	387 UNGATHERED 22	4	will all turne dust, & may not make me swell.
p.	388 UNGATHERED 23	6	To make thy honour, and our wealth the more!
p.	389 UNGATHERED 23	12	And who make thither else, rob, or inuade.
p.	391 UNGATHERED 26	21	A little further, to make thee a roome:
p.	392 UNGATHERED 26	73	And make those flights vpon the bankes of Thames,
p.	394 UNGATHERED 28	26	This second marriage, will aeternall make.
p.	396 UNGATHERED 30	3	Because, who make the question, haue not seene
p.	397 UNGATHERED 30	36	Like him, to make the ayre, one volary:
p.	398 UNGATHERED 30	64	Braue are the Musters, that the Muse will make.
p.	399 UNGATHERED 31	6	With pause vpon it; make this page your booke;
p.	401 UNGATHERED 32	15	Stay, till she make her vaine Approches. Then
p.	401 UNGATHERED 32'	18	But higher power, as spight could not make lesse,
p.	402 UNGATHERED 33	14	To make the Language sweet vpon her tongue.
p.	403 UNGATHERED 34	28	Though gold or Iuory haftes would make it good.
p.	404 UNGATHERED 34	49	Oh, to make Boardes to speake! There is a taske
p.	406 UNGATHERED 34	104	Wth all Remonstrance make an honest man.
p.	406 UNGATHERED 35	3	Our Charles should make thee such? T'will not become
p.	408 UNGATHERED 37	6	Is to make cheape, the Lord, the lines, the price.
p.	410 UNGATHERED 38	15	An honest Bilbo-Smith would make good blades,
p.	421 UNGATHERED 49	11	or Malyce to make ffaultes, wch nowe is skill.
p.	422 UNGATHERED 50	2	make many, hurt themselues; a praysed faith
p.	666 INSCRIPTS. 11	10	To make these good, and what comes after, better./

maker   frequency: 5   relative frequency: 0.00007

p.	128 UNDERWOOD 1.1	41	11. My Maker, Saviour, and my Sanctifier:
p.	163 UNDERWOOD 15	33	Against his Maker; high alone with weeds,
p.	271 UNDERWOOD 83	73	Beholds her Maker! and, in him, doth see
p.	325 HORACE 2	453	And I still bid the learned Maker looke
p.	404 UNGATHERED 34	61	The maker of ye Propertyes! in summe

makers   frequency: 2   relative frequency: 0.00002

p.	60 EPIGRAMS 94	5	But these, desir'd by you, the makers ends
p.	193 UNDERWOOD 38	85	But view the mildnesse of your Makers state,

makes   frequency: 56   relative frequency: 0.00081

**p.	115 PANEGYRE	72	That friendly temper'd, one pure taper makes.
p.	33 EPIGRAMS 22	4	It makes the father, lesse, to rue.
p.	34 EPIGRAMS 25	5	And now, her (hourely) her owne cucqueane makes,
p.	35 EPIGRAMS 28	3	Makes serious vse of all great trade he knowes.
p.	45 EPIGRAMS 56	8	He takes vp all, makes each mans wit his owne.
p.	50 EPIGRAMS 70	2	Then to begin, my ROE: He makes a state
p.	51 EPIGRAMS 73	1	What is't, fine GRAND, makes thee my friendship flye,
p.	63 EPIGRAMS 98	6	And what would hurt his vertue makes it still.
p.	70 EPIGRAMS 109	3	Where vertue makes them both, and that's in thee:
p.	71 EPIGRAMS 110	22	His life, but makes, that he can dye no more.
p.	72 EPIGRAMS 111	8	Nor to giue CAESAR this, makes ours the lesse.
p.	73 EPIGRAMS 113	1	So PHOEBVS makes me worthy of his bayes,
p.	73 EPIGRAMS 113	4	Where, what makes others great, doth keepe thee good!
p.	74 EPIGRAMS 115	17	Tell's of him, all the tales, it selfe then makes;
p.	76 EPIGRAMS 118	4	He makes himselfe a thorough-fare of vice.
p.	76 EPIGRAMS 119	16	Makes, the whole longer, then 'twas giuen him, much.
p.	84 EPIGRAMS 133	30	Makes the poore Banck-side creature wet it' shoone,
p.	97 FOREST 3	20	And makes sleepe softer then it is!
p.	97 FOREST 3	24	Who, for it, makes thy house his court;
p.	97 FOREST 3	27	In autumne, at the Partrich makes a flight,
p.	112 FOREST 11	86	Makes a most blessed gayne.
p.	112 FOREST 11	97	All taste of bitternesse, and makes the ayre
p.	113 FOREST 12	9	While it makes huishers seruiceable men,
p.	113 FOREST 12	17	Solders crackt friendship; makes loue last a day;
p.	118 FOREST 13	59	This makes, that wisely you decline your life,

makes (cont.)
p. 119 FOREST 13	118 This makes, that your affections still be new,
p. 145 UNDERWOOD 5	15 More pleasure while the thing he makes
p. 152 UNDERWOOD 12	40 Who makes the one, so't be first, makes both.
p. 157 UNDERWOOD 13	137 That makes the Arch. The rest that there were put
p. 163 UNDERWOOD 15	46 All which he makes the servants of the Groine,
p. 164 UNDERWOOD 15	56 The bravery makes, she can no honour leese:
p. 170 UNDERWOOD 18	7 That as the water makes things, put in't streight,
p. 176 UNDERWOOD 24	9 Which makes that (lighted by the beamie hand
p. 191 UNDERWOOD 38	4 This sadnesse makes no approaches, but to kill.
p. 193 UNDERWOOD 38	78 That makes us live, not that which calls to die.
p. 197 UNDERWOOD 40	9 This makes me, Mrs. that sometime by stealth,
p. 224 UNDERWOOD 50	20 As makes Penelopes old fable true,
p. 255 UNDERWOOD 75	89 It is their Grace, and favour, that makes seene,
p. 279 U'WOOD 84.4	31 It moveth all; and makes a flight
p. 291 UNDERWOOD 85	48 And unbought viands ready makes:
p. 295 UNDERWOOD 89	8 Makes his life longer then 'twas given him, much.
p. 307 HORACE 2	57 His matter to his power, in all he makes,
p. 327 HORACE 2	471 An ounce, what makes it then? The halfe pound just;
p. 331 HORACE 2	581 'Tis now inquir'd, which makes the nobler Verse,
p. 337 HORACE 2	678 And, there an end of him, reciting makes:
p. 355 HORACE 1	670 Here's one makes ...... but there's ....
	...
p. 363 UNGATHERED 3	12 And makes her supple feete, as swift as winde.
p. 366 UNGATHERED 6	10 How faire a flight he makes!
p. 369 UNGATHERED 6	102 (Which makes him sing
p. 385 UNGATHERED 20	1 It fits not onely him that makes a Booke,
p. 395 UNGATHERED 29	13 It makes me rauish'd with iust wonder, cry
p. 401 UNGATHERED 32	22 Of Ethnicisme, makes his Muse a Saint.
p. 403 UNGATHERED 34	23 What makes your Wretchednes to bray soe loud
p. 408 UNGATHERED 36	8 He makes ye Camell & dull Ass his prize.
p. 657 L. CONVIVALES	16 Clears the Brains, makes Wit the Quicker:

making   frequency: 12   relative frequency: 0.00017
p. 55 EPIGRAMS 86	4 In making thy friends bookes, and thy bookes friends:
p. 82 EPIGRAMS 130	2 Of building townes, and making wilde beasts tame,
p. 107 FOREST 10	18 Thou, nor thy loosenesse with my making sorts.
p. 112 FOREST 11	106 Making his fortunes swim
p. 155 UNDERWOOD 13	66 Their thoughts and meanes to making loude the cry;
p. 189 UNDERWOOD 37	2 Next to your selfe, for making your love true:
p. 232 UNDERWOOD 59	4 Of making just approaches, how to kill,
p. 251 UNDERWOOD 74	18 In making soft her aromatique bed.
p. 335 HORACE 2	670 His cause of making Verses none knowes why:
p. 361 UNGATHERED 1	19 still making that the greatest that is last
p. 386 UNGATHERED 20	7 Or skill of making matches in my life:
p. 402 UNGATHERED 34	12 Or making of ye Propertyes it meane?

makings   frequency: 1   relative frequency: 0.00001
| p. 215 UNDERWOOD 44 | 94 Of severall makings? helps, helps, t<o>'attire |

mak'st   frequency: 9   relative frequency: 0.00013
p. 27 EPIGRAMS 3	1 Thou, that mak'st gaine thy end, and wisely well,
p. 44 EPIGRAMS 55	5 At once thou mak'st me happie, and vnmak'st;
p. 50 EPIGRAMS 72	3 At MADAMES table, where thou mak'st all wit
p. 72 EPIGRAMS 112	12 Next morne, an Ode: Thou mak'st a song ere night.
p. 73 EPIGRAMS 113	3 So, where thou liu'st, thou mak'st life vnderstood!
p. 81 EPIGRAMS 129	4 To Braynford, Hackney, Bow, but thou mak'st one;
p. 168 UNDERWOOD 15	181 That by commanding first thy selfe, thou mak'st
p. 187 UNDERWOOD 33	16 Mak'st it religion to grow rich by Crimes!
p. 281 U'WOOD 84.4	72 But such a Mind, mak'st God thy Guest.

male   frequency: 2   relative frequency: 0.00002
| p. 53 EPIGRAMS 79 | 7 No male vnto him: who could so exceed |
| p. 378 UNGATHERED 11 | 92 Euer his thighes Male then, and his braines Shee. |

malice   frequency: 6   relative frequency: 0.00008
See also "malyce."
**p. 113 PANEGYRE	29 Till forraine malice, or vnnaturall spight
p. 27 EPIGRAMS 2	7 Deceiue their malice, who could wish it so.
p. 188 UNDERWOOD 34	18 And scorn'd, thou'<h>ast showne thy malice, but hast fail'd.

malice (cont.)
```
      p. 203 UNDERWOOD 43    19 But, on thy malice, tell me, didst thou spie
      p. 234 UNDERWOOD 60    15 Could stop the malice of this ill,
      p. 391 UNGATHERED 26   11 Or crafty Malice, might pretend this praise,
```

malicious   frequency: 1   relative frequency: 0.00001
```
     *p. 492 TO HIMSELF      t3 Play, by some malicious spectators,
```

mallowes   frequency: 1   relative frequency: 0.00001
```
      p. 291 UNDERWOOD 85    58 Or Mallowes loosing bodyes ill:
```

mallows. See "mallowes."

malt   frequency: 1   relative frequency: 0.00001
```
      p. 193 UNDERWOOD 38    95 The wit of Ale, and Genius of the Malt
```

malyce   frequency: 1   relative frequency: 0.00001
```
      p. 421 UNGATHERED 49   11 Or Malyce to make ffaultes, wch nowe is skill.
```

man   frequency: 131   relative frequency: 0.00189
```
      See also "coach-man," "fine-man," "foot-man,"
               "man's," "seruing-man," "states-man,"
               "tire-man," "towns-man," "truch-man,"
               "tyre-man."
    **p. 117 PANEGYRE       140 The temp'rance of a priuate man did bring,
      p.  30 EPIGRAMS 11      6 And such from whom let no man hope least good,
      p.  30 EPIGRAMS 12      3 Keepes himselfe, with halfe a man, and defrayes
      p.  31 EPIGRAMS 14     10 Man scarse can make that doubt, but thou canst
                                teach.
      p.  31 EPIGRAMS 15      1 All men are wormes: But this no man. In silke
      p.  35 EPIGRAMS 27      6 If any pious life ere lifted man
      p.  35 EPIGRAMS 28      2 Of a great man, and to be thought the same,
      p.  35 EPIGRAMS 28     14 He drinkes to no man: that's, too, like a lord.
      p.  36 EPIGRAMS 28     22 Stile thee a most great foole, but no great man.
      p.  38 EPIGRAMS 38      4 Any man else, you clap your hands, and rore,
      p.  40 EPIGRAMS 42     16 If, now, with man and wife, to will, and nill
      p.  41 EPIGRAMS 45      6 Will man lament the state he should enuie?
      p.  43 EPIGRAMS 53      2 When hauing pill'd a booke, which no man buyes,
      p.  45 EPIGRAMS 58      8 And, hood-wink'd, for a man, embrace a post.
      p.  57 EPIGRAMS 90      3 Was dull, and long, ere shee would goe to man:
      p.  58 EPIGRAMS 91     17 And best become the valiant man to weare,
    . p.  61 EPIGRAMS 95     27 We need a man that knowes the seuerall graces
      p.  62 EPIGRAMS 95     31 We need a man, can speake of the intents,
      p.  62 EPIGRAMS 96     12 A man should seeke great glorie, and not broad.
      p.  65 EPIGRAMS 101    20 Knat, raile, and ruffe too. How so ere, my man
      p.  68 EPIGRAMS 106     2 What man art thou, that art so many men,
      p.  74 EPIGRAMS 115    t1 ON THE TOWNES HONEST MAN.
      p.  75 EPIGRAMS 116     1 IEPHSON, thou man of men, to whose lou'd
                                name
      p.  76 EPIGRAMS 119     5 With me can merit more, then that good man,
      p.  79 EPIGRAMS 124     1 Would'st thou heare, what man can say
      p.  79 EPIGRAMS 125     1 VV'DALE, thou piece of the first times, a
                                man
      p.  80 EPIGRAMS 127     1 Is there a hope, that Man would thankefull bee,
      p.  81 EPIGRAMS 128    14 Came backe vntouch'd. This man hath trauail'd
                                well.
      p.  83 EPIGRAMS 131     9 Say, this, or that man they to thee preferre;
      p.  84 EPIGRAMS 133    26 But, in the action, greater man then hee:
      p.  86 EPIGRAMS 133    80 Man, that had neuer heard of a Chimaera.
      p.  95 FOREST 2        67 Here no man tells my cups; nor, standing by,
      p.  99 FOREST 3        73 Let this man sweat, and wrangle at the barre,
      p. 113 FOREST 11      116 Man may securely sinne, but safely neuer.
      p. 113 FOREST 12       16 Runs betweene man, and man; 'tweene dame, and
                                dame;
      p. 118 FOREST 13       79 Them, or their officers: and no man know,
      p. 119 FOREST 13       84 Boast, but how oft they haue gone wrong to man:
      p. 120 FOREST 14       22 Are iustly summ'd, that make you man;
      p. 128 UNDERWOOD 1.1   22 To take our nature; becam'st man, and dyd'st,
      p. 128 UNDERWOOD 1.1   27 Pure thoughts in man: with fiery zeale them
                                feeding
      p. 128 UNDERWOOD 1.1   35 The gladdest light, darke man can thinke upon;
      p. 130 UNDERWOOD 1.3   24 Can man forget this Storie?
      p. 131 UNDERWOOD 2.1   20 She shall make the old man young,
      p. 139 UNDERWOOD 2.8    4 What a man she could loue well:
      p. 140 UNDERWOOD 2.8   30 (And that quickly) speake your Man.
      p. 140 UNDERWOOD 2.9    2 I will tell what Man would please me.
      p. 140 UNDERWOOD 2.9   t1 Her man described by her owne Dictamen.
      p. 141 UNDERWOOD 2.9   10 Yet a man; with crisped haire
      p. 141 UNDERWOOD 2.9   38 Drest, you still for man should take him;
      p. 142 UNDERWOOD 2.9   53 Such a man, with every part,
```

man (cont.)

p. 143	UNDERWOOD 3	8	What man but must lose his?
p. 145	UNDERWOOD 5	9	Find some one good, in some one man;
p. 146	UNDERWOOD 6	8	Doe change, though man, and often fight,
p. 146	UNDERWOOD 6	24	To love one man, hee'd leave her first.
p. 153	UNDERWOOD 13	20	Deepest in Man, of which when he doth thinke,
p. 154	UNDERWOOD 13	58	Ha's Feathers, and will serve a man to pull.
p. 155	UNDERWOOD 13	83	Man out their Boates to th' Temple, and not shift
p. 156	UNDERWOOD 13	103	Cannot a man be reck'ned in the State
p. 156	UNDERWOOD 13	115	Looke to and cure; Hee's not a man hath none,
p. 158	UNDERWOOD 14	8	A pennance, where a man may not be free,
p. 162	UNDERWOOD 15	11	Looke on th'ambitious man, and see him nurse
p. 162	UNDERWOOD 15	15	Looke on the false, and cunning man, that loves
p. 162	UNDERWOOD 15	23	See him, that's call'd, and thought the happiest man,
p. 163	UNDERWOOD 15	27	No part or corner man can looke upon,
p. 163	UNDERWOOD 15	41	That kept man living! Pleasures only sought!
p. 165	UNDERWOOD 15	102	For man to spend his money on? his wit?
p. 165	UNDERWOOD 15	114	Is it that man pulls on himselfe Disease?
p. 166	UNDERWOOD 15	136	Now use the bones, we see doth hire a man
p. 168	UNDERWOOD 15	192	Man thought the valianter, 'cause he durst sweare,
p. 172	UNDERWOOD 21	1	Aske not to know this Man. If fame should speake
p. 190	UNDERWOOD 37	31	For no man lives so out of passions sway,
p. 192	UNDERWOOD 38	31	Thinke it was frailtie, Mistris, thinke me man,
p. 192	UNDERWOOD 38	44	No man inflicts that paine, till hope be spent:
p. 192	UNDERWOOD 38	66	In man, because man hath the flesh abus'd.
p. 193	UNDERWOOD 38	100	Of Contumelie, and urge a good man more
p. 194	UNDERWOOD 38	104	A man should flie from, as he would disdaine.
p. 198	UNDERWOOD 40	25	No, Mistris, no, the open merrie Man
p. 199	UNDERWOOD 41	4	Be idle words, though of a parting Man;
p. 200	UNDERWOOD 42	31	As any Mercer; or the whale-bone man,
p. 216	UNDERWOOD 45	23	For that is first requir'd, A man be his owne.
p. 217	UNDERWOOD 46	23	Of if Chance must, to each man that doth rise,
p. 219	UNDERWOOD 47	59	Live to that point I will, for which I am man,
p. 223	UNDERWOOD 49	28	To stuffes and Laces, those my Man can buy.
p. 223	UNDERWOOD 49	31	Indeed, her Dressing some man might delight,
p. 231	UNDERWOOD 56	25	By this, although you fancie not the man,
p. 232	UNDERWOOD 58	4	What each man sayes of it, and of what coat
p. 235	UNDERWOOD 61	20	He is the Man, and Favorite of God.
p. 243	UNDERWOOD 70	23	Or masked man, if valu'd by his face,
p. 245	UNDERWOOD 70	66	In bulke, doth make man better bee;
p. 249	UNDERWOOD 72	11	Three Kingdomes Mirth, in light, and aerie man,
p. 250	UNDERWOOD 73	5	WESTON! That waking man! that Eye of State!
p. 255	UNDERWOOD 75	82	Of Sex, to rob the Creature; but from Man,
p. 256	UNDERWOOD 75	111	What kind of waking Man
p. 261	UNDERWOOD 77	14	Discerne betweene a Statue, and a Man;
p. 262	UNDERWOOD 78	4	Court can call hers, or Man could call his Arts.
p. 288	U'WOOD 84.9	208	The kind of Man, on whom his doome should fall!
p. 288	U'WOOD 84.9	211	To him should be her Judge, true God, true Man,
p. 288	U'WOOD 84.9	217	As being the Sonne of Man) to shew his Power,
p. 292	UNDERWOOD 86	6	To bend a man, now at his fiftieth yeare
p. 309	HORACE 2	109	Were also clos'd: But, who the man should be,
p. 313	HORACE 2	162	Or an Heroe; if a ripe old man,
p. 315	HORACE 2	201	Speake to me, Muse, the Man, who, after Troy was sack't,
p. 315	HORACE 2	216	Falshood with truth, as no man can espie
p. 315	HORACE 2	237	These studies alter now, in one, growne man;
p. 315	HORACE 2	241	The old man many evils doe girt round;
p. 317	HORACE 2	275	Any fourth man, to speake at all, aspire.
p. 321	HORACE 2	350	And so, as every man may hope the same;
p. 325	HORACE 2	452	Indeed, give fitting dues to every man.
p. 331	HORACE 2	554	Yet, there's a value given to this man.
p. 331	HORACE 2	562	To bettring of the mind of man, in ought,
p. 333	HORACE 2	602	Make a great Supper; or for some poore man
p. 333	HORACE 2	605	I wonder how this happie man should know,
p. 333	HORACE 2	618	And rack, with Wine, the man whom they would try,
p. 335	HORACE 2	633	A wise, and honest man will cry out shame
p. 335	HORACE 2	642	The man once mock'd, and suffer'd wrong to tread.
p. 335	HORACE 2	644	And shun to touch him, as a man that were
p. 335	HORACE 2	665	Hee that preserves a man, against his will,
p. 335	HORACE 2	668	Recall him yet, hee'ld be no more a man:
p. 364	UNGATHERED 4	1	Now, after all, let no man
p. 370	UNGATHERED 8	3	(Compos'd of Gamester, Captaine, Knight, Knight's man,

man (cont.)
    p. 379 UNGATHERED 12   15 He sayes to the world, let any man mend it,
    p. 389 UNGATHERED 24   8 That an ill man dares not securely looke
    p. 389 UNGATHERED 24   23 When you behold me wish my selfe, the man
    p. 390 UNGATHERED 26   4 As neither Man, nor Muse, can praise too much.
    p. 397 UNGATHERED 30   32 With vs be call'd, the Naso, but this man?
    p. 402 UNGATHERED 34   2 From thirty pound in pipkins, to ye Man
    p. 406 UNGATHERED 34 104 Wth all Remonstrance make an honest man.
    p. 406 UNGATHERED 35   5 Besydes, his Man may merit it, and be
    p. 409 UNGATHERED 37   17 No man will tarry by thee, as hee goes,

man-kind   frequency: 8   relative frequency: 0.00011
    p.   66 EPIGRAMS 102   2 It is an Epigramme, on all man-kind;
    p. 167 UNDERWOOD 15 171 (Because th'are every where amongst Man-kind
    p. 172 UNDERWOOD 20   19 And that pour'd out upon Man-kind can be!
    p. 185 UNDERWOOD 30   1 If thou wouldst know the vertues of Man-kind,
    p. 212 UNDERWOOD 43 208 Of massacring Man-kind so many wayes.
    p. 238 UNDERWOOD 66   8 Whereby the safetie of Man-kind was wrought)
    p. 243 UNDERWOOD 70   9 How summ'd a circle didst thou leave man-kind
    p. 247 UNDERWOOD 70 121 Was left yet to Man-kind;

manage   frequency: 1   relative frequency: 0.00001
    p. 287 U'WOOD 84.9   167 And by the awfull manage of her Eye

manger   frequency: 2   relative frequency: 0.00002
    p. 130 UNDERWOCD 1.3 12 Was now laid in a Manger.
    p. 288 U'WOOD 84.9   200 Incarnate in the Manger, shining bright

mangers   frequency: 1   relative frequency: 0.00001
    p. 228 UNDERWOOD 53   20 At these Immortall Mangers Virgil fed.

manie   frequency: 1   relative frequency: 0.00001
    p. 361 UNGATHERED 1   6 that mongst so manie plants transplanted hether,

mankind   frequency: 5   relative frequency: 0.00007
See also "man-kind," "mankinde."
    p.   34 EPIGRAMS 23   8 Which might with halfe mankind maintayne a
                                   strife.
    p.   60 EPIGRAMS 94   7 Yet, Satyres, since the most of mankind bee
    p. 221 UNDERWOOD 48   23 To give mankind their eases,
    p. 271 UNDERWOOD 83   90 Whole Nations! nay, Mankind! the World, with
                                   all
    p. 289 UNDERWOOD 85   2 As the old race of Mankind were,

mankinde   frequency: 2   relative frequency: 0.00002
    p. 107 FOREST 10   13 PALLAS, nor thee I call on, mankinde maid,
    p. 119 FOREST 13   90 Whereon the most of mankinde wracke themselues,

mankinds   frequency: 1   relative frequency: 0.00001
    p. 289 U'WOOD 84.9   224 And giving dues to all Mankinds deserts!

manly   frequency: 5   relative frequency: 0.00007
    p.   48 EPIGRAMS 65   14 Things manly, and not smelling parasite.
    p.   52 EPIGRAMS 76   13 Onely a learned, and a manly soule
    p. 160 UNDERWOOD 14   56 And manly elocution, not one while
    p. 217 UNDERWOOD 46   13 And that thy strong and manly Eloquence
    p. 317 HORACE 2   277 Must maintaine manly; not be heard to sing,

mann'd   frequency: 1   relative frequency: 0.00001
    p. 105 FOREST 8   30 In decoctions; and are mann'd

manner   frequency: 4   relative frequency: 0.00005
    p. 154 UNDERWOOD 13   37 In that proud manner, as a good so gain'd,
    p. 227 UNDERWOOD 52   16 O, had I now your manner, maistry, might,
    p. 288 U'WOOD 84.9   210 In manner of a daily Apostrophe,
    p. 292 UNDERWOOD 86   27 And in the Salian manner meet

manners   frequency: 26   relative frequency: 0.00037
    p.   29 EPIGRAMS 9   3 'Tis 'gainst the manners of an Epigram:
    p.   34 EPIGRAMS 24   2 Mens manners ne're were viler, for your sake.
    p.   37 EPIGRAMS 35   3 Whose manners draw, more than thy powers
                                   constraine.
    p.   42 EPIGRAMS 49   5 PLAY-WRIGHT, I loath to haue thy
                                   manners knowne
    p.   73 EPIGRAMS 113   6 That the wit there, and manners might be sau'd:
    p.   78 EPIGRAMS 121   8 That striues, his manners should precede his wit.
    p.   80 EPIGRAMS 128   2 Countries, and climes, manners, and men to know,
    p.   96 FOREST 2   98 The mysteries of manners, armes, and arts.
    p. 119 FOREST 13   112 What your try'd manners are, what theirs should
                                   bee.

manners (cont.)
```
    p. 141 UNDERWOOD 2.9    8 And his Manners of that Nation.
    p. 152 UNDERWOOD 12    22 His very Manners taught t<o>'amend,
    p. 157 UNDERWOOD 13   134 Alone in money, but in manners too.
    p. 159 UNDERWOOD 14    33 Of generall knowledge; watch'd men, manners too,
    p. 160 UNDERWOOD 14    44 Times, manners, customes! Innovations spide!
    p. 164 UNDERWOOD 15    60 Who can behold their Manners, and not clowd-
    p. 187 UNDERWOOD 33    13 Thou art my Cause: whose manners since I knew,
    p. 188 UNDERWOOD 35     2 What manners prettie, Nature milde,
    p. 202 UNDERWOOD 42    88 More then of eithers manners, wit, or face!
    p. 224 UNDERWOOD 50    22 Countries, and Climes, manners, and men to know.
    p. 230 UNDERWOOD 56    19 Such, (if her manners like you) I doe send:
    p. 237 UNDERWOOD 64    17 O Times! O Manners! Surfet bred of ease,
    p. 246 UNDERWOOD 70   106 That knits brave minds, and manners, more then
                             blood.
    p. 261 UNDERWOOD 77    18 To compose men, and manners; stint the strife
    p. 315 HORACE 2       202 Saw many Townes, and Men, and could their
                             manners tract.
    p. 325 HORACE 2       454 On life, and manners, and make those his booke,
    p. 392 UNGATHERED 26   67 Of Shakespeares minde, and manners brightly
                             shines
```

mans   frequency: 18   relative frequency: 0.00026
```
    p.  45 EPIGRAMS 56      8 He takes vp all, makes each mans wit his owne.
    p.  49 EPIGRAMS 67     10 Before thou wert it, in each good mans heart.
    p.  94 FOREST 2        46 They'are rear'd with no mans ruine, no mans
                             grone,
    p. 127 UNDERWOOD 1.1    3 The faithfull mans beleeved Mysterie,
    p. 162 UNDERWOOD 15     7 Mans buried honour, in his sleepie life:
    p. 163 UNDERWOOD 15    44 To make up Greatnesse! and mans whole good fix'd
    p. 175 UNDERWOOD 24     2 The Mistresse of Mans life, grave Historie,
    p. 177 UNDERWOOD 25    32 Where only a mans birth is his offence,
    p. 186 UNDERWOOD 31    10 You favour Truth, and me, in this mans Cause.
    p. 193 UNDERWOOD 38    68 God lightens not at mans each fraile offence,
    p. 217 UNDERWOOD 46     7 When, being the Strangers helpe, the poore mans
                             aide,
    p. 218 UNDERWOOD 47    18 Like flies, or wormes, which mans corrupt parts
                             fed:
    p. 317 HORACE 2       250 Mans comming yeares much good with them doe
                             bring:
    p. 329 HORACE 2       539 As Painting, so is Poesie. Some mans hand
    p. 379 UNGATHERED 12   12 Since he treads in no other Mans steps but his
                             owne.
    p. 401 UNGATHERED 33    4 Of two, the choicest Paire of Mans delights,
    p. 414 UNGATHERED 41   44 And art the spotlesse Mirrour to Mans eyes.
```

man's   frequency: 3   relative frequency: 0.00004
    See also "bell-mans," "mans," "states-mans."
```
    p.  75 EPIGRAMS 115    34 Then, The townes honest Man's her errant'st
                             knaue.
    p.  99 FOREST 3        93 Thy peace is made; and, when man's state is well,
    p.  99 FOREST 3        96 To him, man's dearer, then t<o>'himselfe.
```

mansfeld. See "mansfield."

mansfield   frequency: 1   relative frequency: 0.00001
```
    p. 219 UNDERWOOD 47    44 Brunsfield, and Mansfield doe this yeare, my
                             fates
```

mansion   frequency: 1   relative frequency: 0.00001
```
    p. 281 U'WOOD 84.4    69 In thee, faire Mansion, let it rest,
```

many   frequency: 51   relative frequency: 0.00073
    See also "manie," "many'of."
```
  **p. 115 PANEGYRE         84 "Vnto as many enuies, there, as eyes.
  **p. 117 PANEGYRE        147 Though many greater: and the most, the best.
    p.  29 EPIGRAMS 7       1 Where lately harbour'd many a famous whore,
    p.  31 EPIGRAMS 14     13 Many of thine this better could, then I,
    p.  46 EPIGRAMS 60      9 My countries parents I haue many knowne;
    p.  50 EPIGRAMS 70      7 Then, since we (more then many) these truths
                             know:
    p.  57 EPIGRAMS 89     14 So many Poets life, by one should liue.
    p.  68 EPIGRAMS 106     2 What man art thou, that art so many men,
    p.  74 EPIGRAMS 115     3 Naming so many, too! But, this is one,
    p.  85 EPIGRAMS 133    47 The many perills of this Port, and how
    p.  86 EPIGRAMS 133    71 With famine, wants, and sorrowes many a dosen,
    p.  86 EPIGRAMS 133    73 But they vnfrighted passe, though many a priuie
    p.  86 EPIGRAMS 133    75 And many a sinke pour'd out her rage anenst 'hem;
    p.  87 EPIGRAMS 133   103 But many Moones there shall not wane (quoth hee)
    p.  94 FOREST 2        16 Of many a SYLVANE, taken with his flames.
```

many (cont.)

p.	105 FOREST 8	40	Bald, or blinde, or nere so many:
p.	109 FOREST 11	19	But this true course is not embrac'd by many:
p.	109 FOREST 11	20	By many? scarse by any.
p.	114 FOREST 12	49	How many equall with the Argiue Queene,
p.	117 FOREST 13	31	And so doe many more. All which can call
p.	133 UNDERWOOD 2.3	1	After many scornes like these,
p.	155 UNDERWOOD 13	78	Many a pound, and piece, will p<l>ace one well:
p.	159 UNDERWOOD 14	25	And what I write? and vexe it many dayes
p.	171 UNDERWOOD 20	3	Amongst my many other, that I may
p.	171 UNDERWOOD 20	11	Of many Colours; outward, fresh from spots,
p.	179 UNDERWOOD 25	55	Though many Gems be in your bosome stor'd,
p.	202 UNDERWOOD 43	4	So many my Yeares-labours in an houre?
p.	205 UNDERWOOD 43	62	Had tickled your large Nosthrill: many a Reame
p.	212 UNDERWOOD 43	208	Of massacring Man-kind so many wayes.
p.	216 UNDERWOOD 45	17	For there are many slips, and Counterfeits.
p.	220 UNDERWOOD 47	74	I would call mine, to which not many Staires
p.	221 UNDERWOOD 48	29	And thou make many a Poet,
p.	223 UNDERWOOD 49	21	What though she hath won on Trust, as many doe,
p.	225 UNDERWOOD 50	35	For when they find so many meet in one,
p.	225 UNDERWOOD 51	6	For whose returnes, and many, all these pray:
p.	231 UNDERWOOD 56	27	How many verses, Madam, are your Due!
p.	236 UNDERWOOD 64	3	How many times, Live long, CHARLES, would he say,
p.	269 UNDERWOOD 83	23	Had I a thousand Mouthes, as many Tongues,
p.	287 U'WOOD 84.9	173	She was, in one, a many parts of life:
p.	290 UNDERWOOD 85	31	Or hence, or thence, he drives with many a Hound
p.	292 UNDERWOOD 86	22	In many a Gumme, and for thy soft eares sake
p.	315 HORACE 2	202	Saw many Townes, and Men, and could their manners tract.
p.	315 HORACE 2	241	The old man many evils doe girt round;
p.	325 HORACE 2	416	To taxe that Verse, which many a day, and blot
p.	333 HORACE 2	617	Rich men are said with many cups to plie,
p.	380 UNGATHERED 12	44	How many learned men he haue drawne with his hooke
p.	385 UNGATHERED 19	3	Or, to so many, and so Broad-seales had,
p.	404 UNGATHERED 34	47	Of many Coulors! read them! & reueale
p.	422 UNGATHERED 50	2	make many, hurt themselues; a praysed faith
p.	660 INSCRIPTS. 11	9	Shall powre forth many a line, drop many a letter,

many-headed   frequency: 1   relative frequency: 0.00001
        p. 370 UNGATHERED 8   1 The wise, and many-headed Bench, that sits

many'of   frequency: 1   relative frequency: 0.00001
        p. 159 UNDERWOOD 14   15 A many'of bookes, even good judgements wound

map   frequency: 2   relative frequency: 0.00002
See also "mappe."
        p. 69 EPIGRAMS 107   18 Then can a flea at twise skip i'the Map.
        p. 288 U'WOOD 84.9   196 Poring, as on a Map, to find the wayes

mappe   frequency: 1   relative frequency: 0.00001
        p. 379 UNGATHERED 12 18 The Mappe of his iourney, and sees in his booke,

maps   frequency: 1   relative frequency: 0.00001
        p. 59 EPIGRAMS 92   9 Yet haue they seene the maps, and bought 'hem too,

marble   frequency: 6   relative frequency: 0.00008
        p. 39 EPIGRAMS 40   1 Marble, weepe, for thou dost couer
        p. 46 EPIGRAMS 60   4 Thy fact, in brasse or marble writ the same)
        p. 93 FOREST 2   2 Of touch, or marble; nor canst boast a row
        p. 114 FOREST 12   44 Inscrib'd in touch or marble, or the cotes
        p. 269 UNDERWOOD 83   13 Alas, I am all Marble! write the rest
        p. 292 UNDERWOOD 86   19 He'll thee a Marble Statue make

march   frequency: 2   relative frequency: 0.00002
      **p. 112 PANEGYRE   t10 March, 1603.
        p. 43 EPIGRAMS 51   t3 and twentieth day of March,

marching   frequency: 1   relative frequency: 0.00001
        p. 397 UNGATHERED 30 39 And Rouze, the Marching of a mighty force,

marchion: frequency: 1   relative frequency: 0.00001
        p. 268 UNDERWOOD 83   t3 Marchion: of Winton.

marchioness. See "marchion:," "marchionisse."

marchionisse   frequency: 1   relative frequency: 0.00001
        p. 269 UNDERWOOD 83   19 Shee was the Lady Jane, and Marchionisse

mard   frequency: 1   relative frequency: 0.00001
        p. 153 UNDERWOOD 13   24 Where any Deed is forc't, the Grace is mard.

mare. See "coach-mare."

mares   frequency: 1   relative frequency: 0.00001
        p. 94 FOREST 2   24 The middle grounds thy mares, and horses breed.

margaret   frequency: 2   relative frequency: 0.00002
        p. 39 EPIGRAMS 40   t1 ON MARGARET RATCLIFFE.
        p. 398 UNGATHERED 30   75 The miseries of Margaret the Queene

mariage   frequency: 4   relative frequency: 0.00005
        p. 253 UNDERWOOD 75   29 Mariage, the end of life,
        p. 257 UNDERWOOD 75   162 (The holy perfumes of the Mariage bed.)
        p. 327 HORACE 2   489 Wild ra<n>ging lusts; prescribe the mariage good;
        p. 384 UNGATHERED 18   18 And eue'ry ioy, in mariage, turne a fruite.

mariage-day   frequency: 1   relative frequency: 0.00001
        p. 380 UNGATHERED 20   12 Shee need not blush vpon the Mariage-Day.

mariage-horne   frequency: 1   relative frequency: 0.00001
        p. 165 UNDERWOOD 15   100 Ne're came to taste the plenteous Mariage-horne.

mariage-pledges   frequency: 1   relative frequency: 0.00001
        p. 384 UNGATHERED 18   19 So, may those Mariage-Pledges, comforts proue:

mariage-rites   frequency: 1   relative frequency: 0.00001
        p. 401 UNGATHERED 33   3 They are the Mariage-rites

marie   frequency: 1   relative frequency: 0.00001
        p. 412 UNGATHERED 41   t3 MARIE.

marish   frequency: 1   relative frequency: 0.00001
        p. 209 UNDERWOOD 43   134 Planck'd with a Ditch, and forc'd out of a
                                  Marish,

mark. See "marke."

mark'd   frequency: 5   relative frequency: 0.00007
        p. 58 EPIGRAMS 91   14 Nor lesse in practice; but lesse mark'd, lesse
                                  knowne:
        p. 62 EPIGRAMS 96   8 Mark'd by thy hand, and with the better stone,
        p. 134 UNDERWOOD 2.4   23 Have you mark'd but the fall o'the Snow
        p. 307 HORACE 2   51 To be that Smith; then live, mark'd one of
                                  those,
        p. 319 HORACE 2   323 How he could jest, because he mark'd and saw,

marke   frequency: 16   relative frequency: 0.00023
        p. 60 EPIGRAMS 93   2 For the great marke of vertue, those being gone
        p. 67 EPIGRAMS 104   12 The light, and marke vnto posteritie?
        p. 132 UNDERWOOD 2.2   8 Marke of glorie, come with me;
        p. 134 UNDERWOOD 2.4   15 Doe but marke, her forehead's smoother
        p. 144 UNDERWOOD 3   17 They say the Angells marke each Deed,
        p. 157 UNDERWOOD 13   139 Then stands it a triumphall marke! then Men
        p. 160 UNDERWOOD 14   47 Where is that nominall marke, or reall rite,
        p. 160 UNDERWOOD 14   55 To marke the excellent seas'ning of your Stile!
        p. 173 UNDERWOOD 22   1 Though Beautie be the Marke of praise,
        p. 205 UNDERWOOD 43   57 But that's a marke, wherof thy Rites doe boast,
        p. 255 UNDERWOOD 75   95 And set the marke upon,
        p. 331 HORACE 2   542 This, fearing not the subtlest Judges marke,
        p. 366 UNGATHERED 6   9 Marke, marke, but when his wing he takes,
        p. 383 UNGATHERED 17   6 Yet may as blind men sometimes hit the marke.
        p. 389 UNGATHERED 24   7 And hath the noblest marke of a good Booke,

markes   frequency: 6   relative frequency: 0.00008
        p. 45 EPIGRAMS 56   11 He markes not whose 'twas first: and after-times
        p. 93 FOREST 2   7 Thou ioy'st in better markes, of soyle, of ayre,
        p. 193 UNDERWOOD 38   83 Be not affected with these markes too much
        p. 213 UNDERWOOD 44   12 Nor markes of wealth so from our Nation fled,
        p. 259 UNDERWOOD 76   11 A large hundred Markes annuitie,
        p. 260 UNDERWOOD 76   27 Those your Fathers Markes, your Pounds;

market. See "mercat."

market-folkes   frequency: 1   relative frequency: 0.00001
        p. 155 UNDERWOOD 13   90 Or robbing the poore Market-folkes should nurse

marks. See "markes."

mar'le   frequency: 1   relative frequency: 0.00001
        p. 208 UNDERWOOD 43 116 No mar'le the Clownes of Lemnos tooke thee up,

marlowes   frequency: 1   relative frequency: 0.00001
        p. 391 UNGATHERED 26   30 Or sporting Kid, or Marlowes mighty line.

maro   frequency: 1   relative frequency: 0.00001
        p. 181 UNDERWOOD 27   8 As he whom Maro did rehearse?

marquess   frequency: 3   relative frequency: 0.00004
        p. 406 UNGATHERED 35   2 Hath made his Inigo Marquess, wouldst thou
                                  fayne
        p. 406 UNGATHERED 35   t1 To Inigo Marquess Would be
        p. 407 UNGATHERED 35   24 Wee'll haue thee styld ye Marquess of
                                  New-Ditch.

marquis. See "marquess."

marred. See "mard."

marriage   frequency: 2   relative frequency: 0.00002
        See also "mariage," words beginning "mariage-."
        p. 42 EPIGRAMS 46   4 To pay at's day of marriage. By my hand
        p. 394 UNGATHERED 28   26 This second marriage, will aeternall make.

marrie   frequency: 1   relative frequency: 0.00001
        p. 230 UNDERWOOD 56   13 Marrie the Muse is one, can tread the Aire,

married   frequency: 2   relative frequency: 0.00002
        p. 40 EPIGRAMS 42   3 Indeed, poore GILES repents he married euer.
        p. 384 UNGATHERED 18   26 Sure, this glad payre were married, but this day.

marrow   frequency: 2   relative frequency: 0.00002
        p. 393 UNGATHERED 27   14 The Marrow from the Bone,
        p. 408 UNGATHERED 36   5 The Marrow! Wretch, I quitt thee of thy paine

marry   frequency: 2   relative frequency: 0.00002
        See also "marrie."
        p. 57 EPIGRAMS 90   16 Longer a day, but with his MILL will marry.
        p. 378 UNGATHERED 11   83 Marry he sets it out at his owne charge;

marrying   frequency: 1   relative frequency: 0.00001
        p. 290 UNDERWOOD 85   9 The Poplar tall, he then doth marrying twine

mars   frequency: 5   relative frequency: 0.00007
        p. 93 FOREST 1   6 MARS, and my Mother, in their net:
        p. 107 FOREST 10   16 Goe, crampe dull MARS, light VENVS, when
                                  he snorts,
        p. 203 UNDERWOOD 43   10 And Mars, that gave thee a Lanthorne for a
                                  Crowne.
        p. 293 UNDERWOOD 86   39 Whether in Mars his field thou bee,
        p. 331 HORACE 2   566 His armes in Mars his field, he doth refuse;

marsh. See "mersh-lambeth."

mart   frequency: 1   relative frequency: 0.00001
        p. 59 EPIGRAMS 92   21 They meet in sixes, and at euery mart,

martial   frequency: 4   relative frequency: 0.00005
        p. 38 EPIGRAMS 36   1 MARTIAL, thou gau'st farre nobler
                                  Epigrammes
        p. 38 EPIGRAMS 36   t1 TO THE GHOST OF MARTIAL.
        p. 295 UNDERWOOD 90   2 Most pleasant Martial; Substance got with ease,
        p. 295 UNDERWOOD 90   t1 Martial.

martirdome   frequency: 1   relative frequency: 0.00001
        p. 371 UNGATHERED 8   13 In such a Martirdome; To vexe their eyes,

martyr   frequency: 1   relative frequency: 0.00001
        p. 130 UNDERWOOD 1.3   23 A Martyr borne in our defence;

martyrdom. See "martirdome."

martyrs   frequency: 3   relative frequency: 0.00004
        p. 218 UNDERWOOD 47   3 They meet the fire, the Test, as Martyrs would;
        p. 285 U'WOOD 84.9   85 Saints, Martyrs, Prophets, with those
                                  Hierarchies,
        p. 400 UNGATHERED 31   39 Both Saints, and Martyrs, by her loued Lord.

marvailes   frequency: 1   relative frequency: 0.00001
     p. 206 UNDERWOOD 43   71 To Merlins Marvailes, and his Caballs losse,

marvel. See "mar'le."

marvels. See "marvailes."

mary   frequency: 12   relative frequency: 0.00017
     See also "marie."
     p. 33 EPIGRAMS 22   2 MARY, the daughter of their youth:
     p. 66 EPIGRAMS 103   t1 TO MARY LADY WROTH.
     p. 67 EPIGRAMS 105   t1 TO MARY LADY WROTH.
     p. 182 UNDERWOOD 28   t3 MARY WORTH.
     p. 235 UNDERWOOD 63   t1 To K. CHARLES, and Q. MARY.
     p. 236 UNDERWOOD 63   7 Then, Royall CHARLES, and MARY, doe
                                 not grutch
     p. 238 UNDERWOOD 66   1 Haile Mary, full of grace, it once was said,
     p. 238 UNDERWOOD 66   5 Haile Mary, full of honours, to my Queene,
     p. 238 UNDERWOOD 66   7 (Except the joy that the first Mary brought,
     p. 238 UNDERWOOD 66   13 Glorie to God. Then, Haile to Mary! spring
     p. 240 UNDERWOOD 67   25 5. TERP. Behold the royall Mary,
     p. 240 UNDERWOOD 67   49 9. POLY. Sweet! happy Mary! All

masculine   frequency: 2   relative frequency: 0.00002
     p. 53 EPIGRAMS 79   6 (Saue that most masculine issue of his braine)
     p. 327 HORACE 2   494 On edge the Masculine spirits, and did whet

mask. See "maske."

mask'd   frequency: 1   relative frequency: 0.00001
     p. 163 UNDERWOOD 15   39 Friendship is now mask'd Hatred! Justice fled,

maske   frequency: 2   relative frequency: 0.00002
     p. 107 FOREST 10   20 Turne the stale prologue to some painted maske,
     p. 370 UNGATHERED 8   4 Lady, or Pusil, that weares maske, or fan,

masked   frequency: 1   relative frequency: 0.00001
     See also "mask'd."
     p. 243 UNDERWOOD 70   23 Or masked man, if valu'd by his face,

maskes   frequency: 2   relative frequency: 0.00002
     p. 118 FOREST 13   70 For truthes complexion, where they all weare
                                 maskes.
     p. 273 U'WOOD 84.1   22 Their painted Maskes, their paper Boates,

masks. See "maskes," "masques."

masque   frequency: 2   relative frequency: 0.00002
     See also "maske."
     p. 403 UNGATHERED 34 30 And all men eccho you haue made a Masque.
     p. 404 UNGATHERED 34 50 Painting & Carpentry are ye Soule of
                                 Masque.

masques   frequency: 2   relative frequency: 0.00002
     p. 216 UNDERWOOD 45   18 Deceit is fruitfull. Men have Masques and nets,
     p. 403 UNGATHERED 34 40 The Eloquence of Masques! What need of prose

masquing   frequency: 1   relative frequency: 0.00001
     p. 96 FOREST 3   9 Nor throng'st (when masquing is) to haue a sight

mass. See "christ-masse," "masse."

massacring   frequency: 1   relative frequency: 0.00001
     p. 212 UNDERWOOD 43 208 Of massacring Man-kind so many wayes.

masse   frequency: 5   relative frequency: 0.00007
     p. 88 EPIGRAMS 133 139 Or, that it lay, heap'd like an vsurers masse,
     p. 99 FOREST 3   81 Let that goe heape a masse of wretched wealth,
     p. 172 UNDERWOOD 21   5 A parcell of Court-durt, a heape, and masse
     p. 244 UNDERWOOD 70   55 Produce thy masse of miseries on the Stage,
     p. 395 UNGATHERED 29 22 In the great masse, or machine there is stirr'd?

mast   frequency: 1   relative frequency: 0.00001
     p. 98 FOREST 3   44 The hogs return'd home fat from mast;

master   frequency: 15   relative frequency: 0.00021
     See also "m.," "mr.," "muster-master,"
         "say-master."
     p. 61 EPIGRAMS 95   17 For who can master those great parts like thee,
     p. 72 EPIGRAMS 111   4 Beholding, to this master of the warre;

master (cont.)
        p. 151 UNDERWOOD 12   t1 An Epitaph on Master
        p. 158 UNDERWOOD 14   t1 An Epistle to Master
        p. 168 UNDERWOOD 16   t1 An Epitaph on Master
        p. 216 UNDERWOOD 45   t1 An Epistle to Master
        p. 220 UNDERWOOD 48   8 Of all to the great Master.
        p. 231 UNDERWOOD 57   t1 To Master Iohn Burges.
        p. 258 UNDERWOOD 75   187 Hee's Master of the Office; yet no more
        p. 333 HORACE 2   592 Did learne them first, and once a Master fear'd.
        p. 362 UNGATHERED 2   5 Looke here on Bretons worke, the master print:
        p. 401 UNGATHERED 33   t1 To my worthy Friend, Master Edward Filmer,
        p. 404 UNGATHERED 34   63 To be ye Musick Master! Fabler too!
        p. 409 UNGATHERED 38   8 Which I, your Master, first did teach the Age.
        p. 414 UNGATHERED 42   t2 Master JOSEPH RVTTER.

master-braine   frequency: 1   relative frequency: 0.00001
        p. 75 EPIGRAMS 116   4 That age, when thou stood'st vp the
                                    master-braine:

master-worker   frequency: 1   relative frequency: 0.00001
        p. 415 UNGATHERED 42   22 A Master-worker call'd, th'old standerd burst

mastering. See "maistring."

masters   frequency: 6   relative frequency: 0.00008
        p. 48 EPIGRAMS 65   5 Be thy next masters more vnluckie Muse,
        p. 87 EPIGRAMS 133   122 By which the Masters sweare, when, on the stoole
        p. 97 FOREST 3   23 In spring, oft roused for thy masters sport,
        p. 167 UNDERWOOD 15   164 Informers, Masters both of Arts and lies;
        p. 259 UNDERWOOD 76   2 To th'best of Monarchs, Masters, Men,
        p. 263 UNDERWOOD 79   7 We sing the best of Monarchs, Masters, Men;

mastery. See "maistry," "mastrie," "mastry."

mastrie   frequency: 1   relative frequency: 0.00001
        p. 235 UNDERWOOD 62   5 But thou wilt yet a Kinglier mastrie trie,

mastry   frequency: 1   relative frequency: 0.00001
        p. 206 UNDERWOOD 43   88 There were of search, and mastry in the Arts.

match   frequency: 8   relative frequency: 0.00011
        p. 67 EPIGRAMS 104   8 Of birth, of match, of forme, of chastitie?
        p. 117 FOREST 13   46 As bloud, and match. Wherein, how more then much
        p. 206 UNDERWOOD 43   77 With Nicholas Pasquill's, Meddle with your
                                    match,
        p. 219 UNDERWOOD 47   36 Or that the Match from Spaine was ever meant?
        p. 229 UNDERWOOD 54   5 Who, when shee heard the match, concluded
                                    streight,
        p. 272 UNDERWOOD 84   t15 Her happie MATCH.
        p. 394 UNGATHERED 28   4 In blood, in birth, by match, and by her seate;
        p. 401 UNGATHERED 33   10 Recelebrates the ioyfull Match with France.

match'd   frequency: 1   relative frequency: 0.00001
        p. 309 HORACE 2   107 In Verse vnequall match'd, first sowre Laments,

matches   frequency: 1   relative frequency: 0.00001
        p. 386 UNGATHERED 20   7 Or skill of making matches in my life:

matching. See "purple-matching."

mate. See "bed-mate."

material. See "materiall."

materiall   frequency: 1   relative frequency: 0.00001
        p. 387 UNGATHERED 22   8 to which there's no materiall that endures;

materialls   frequency: 1   relative frequency: 0.00001
        p. 406 UNGATHERED 34   100 See ye Materialls be of Purbeck stone!

materials. See "materialls."

matron   frequency: 1   relative frequency: 0.00001
        See also "matrone."
        p. 391 UNGATHERED 26   14 Should praise a Matron. What could hurt her
                                    more?

matrone   frequency: 1   relative frequency: 0.00001
        p. 321 HORACE 2   338 But, as a Matrone drawne at solemne times

matter   frequency: 18   relative frequency: 0.00026
    See also "meere-matter-lesse."
    p. 60 EPIGRAMS 94   11 They, then, that liuing where the matter is bred,
    p. 70 EPIGRAMS 109   9 Thou rather striu'st the matter to possesse,
    p. 86 EPIGRAMS 133   91 No matter, stinkards, row. What croaking sound
    p. 116 FOREST 12   89 But high, and noble matter, such as flies
    p. 157 UNDERWOOD 13 142 Meet some new matter to looke up and wonder!
    p. 160 UNDERWOOD 14   61 I yeeld, I yeeld, the matter of your praise
    p. 187 UNDERWOOD 33   15 So dost thou studie matter, men, and times,
    p. 200 UNDERWOOD 42   17 But is the Poets matter: And he must,
    p. 307 HORACE 2   53 Take, therefore, you that write, still, matter
                             fit
    p. 307 HORACE 2   57 His matter to his power, in all he makes,
    p. 311 HORACE 2   121 The Comick matter will not be exprest
    p. 313 HORACE 2   187 Yet common matter thou thine owne maist make,
    p. 315 HORACE 2   213 The middle of his matter: letting goe
    p. 325 HORACE 2   441 Is to be wise; thy matter first to know;
    p. 325 HORACE 2   443 And, where the matter is provided still,
    p. 379 UNGATHERED 12   3 Who, because his matter in all should be meete,
    p. 387 UNGATHERED 22 11 it will be matter lowd inoughe to tell
    p. 392 UNGATHERED 26 57 For though the Poets matter, Nature be,

mature   frequency: 1   relative frequency: 0.00001
    p. 368 UNGATHERED 6   88 Though slower Spaine; and Italy mature.

maurice   frequency: 1   relative frequency: 0.00001
    p. 214 UNDERWOOD 44   41 So acted to the life, as Maurice might,

maw   frequency: 2   relative frequency: 0.00002
    p. 329 HORACE 2   510 The Child, when Lamia'has din'd, out of her
                             maw.
    p. 374 UNGATHERED 10 11 All sorts of fish with Musicke of his maw.

maximus   frequency: 1   relative frequency: 0.00001
    p. 292 UNDERWOOD 86   10 With thy bright Swans, of Paulus Maximus:

may   frequency: 176   relative frequency: 0.00254
    See also "ma'," "may'admire," "may'any."
   *p. 493 TO HIMSELF   26 May keepe vp the Play-club:
   *p. 493 TO HIMSELF   50 May, blushing, sweare no palsey's in thy braine.
   *p. 494 TO HIMSELF   54 They may, blood-shaken, then,
  **p. 115 PANEGYRE   76 How he may triumph in his subiects brests,
    p. 29 EPIGRAMS 9   1 May none, whose scatter'd names honor my booke,
    p. 32 EPIGRAMS 17   1 May others feare, flie, and traduce thy name,
    p. 33 EPIGRAMS 21   8 The bodies stripes, I see, the soule may saue.
    p. 35 EPIGRAMS 27   8 Wee, sad for him, may glorie, and not sinne.
    p. 36 EPIGRAMS 28   20 May heare my Epigrammes, but like of none.
    p. 41 EPIGRAMS 43   8 Of adding to thy fame; thine may to me,
    p. 41 EPIGRAMS 45   12 As what he loues may neuer like too much.
    p. 45 EPIGRAMS 56   12 May iudge it to be his, as well as ours.
    p. 49 EPIGRAMS 66   16 It may be much, or little, in the cause.
    p. 64 EPIGRAMS 101   5 With those that come; whose grace may make that
                             seeme
    p. 65 EPIGRAMS 101 16 The skie not falling, thinke we may haue larkes.
    p. 65 EPIGRAMS 101 19 May yet be there; and godwit, if we can:
    p. 68 EPIGRAMS 105 10 You were the bright OENONE, FLORA, or
                             May?
    p. 78 EPIGRAMS 122 10 Who prou'st, all these were, and againe may bee.
    p. 81 EPIGRAMS 128   5 May windes as soft as breath of kissing friends,
    p. 81 EPIGRAMS 128   6 Attend thee hence; and there, may all thy ends,
    p. 81 EPIGRAMS 128 11 We each to other may this voyce enspire;
    p. 85 EPIGRAMS 133 42 Of some Bride-well, and may, in time, concerne
                             vs
    p. 94 FOREST 2   44 Hang on thy walls, that euery child may reach.
    p. 96 FOREST 2   91 His children thy great lord may call his owne:
    p. 96 FOREST 2   96 With the whole houshold, and may, euery day,
    p. 96 FOREST 2   102 May say, their lords haue built, but thy lord
                             dwells.
    p. 98 FOREST 3   70 That they may sleepe with scarres in age.
    p. 99 FOREST 3   97 And, howsoeuer we may thinke things sweet,
    p. 101 FOREST 4   55 That, what to all may happen here,
    p. 102 FOREST 5   2 While we may, the sports of loue;
    p. 102 FOREST 5   6 Sunnes, that set, may rise againe:
    p. 103 FOREST 6   19 That the curious may not know
    p. 113 FOREST 11   116 Man may securely sinne, but safely neuer.
    p. 114 FOREST 12   34 Almost you haue, or may haue, when you will?
    p. 116 FOREST 12   100 My best of wishes, may you beare a sonne.
    p. 117 FOREST 13   22 If it may stand with your soft blush to heare
    p. 117 FOREST 13   42 And raise not vertue; they may vice enhance.
    p. 118 FOREST 13   64 Which though the turning world may dis-esteeme,

may (cont.)

p.	118	FOREST 13	83 May they haue nothing left, whereof they can
p.	119	FOREST 13	111 Other great wiues may blush at: when they see
p.	120	FOREST 14	12 That I may tell to SYDNEY, what
p.	120	FOREST 14	15 And he may thinke on that
p.	121	FOREST 14	51 So may you liue in honor, as in name,
p.	121	FOREST 14	53 So may
p.	129	UNDERWOOD 1.2	5 That I may prove
p.	131	UNDERWOOD 2.1	24 All the world for love may die.
p.	132	UNDERWOOD 2.2	2 When her looke out-flourisht May:
p.	138	UNDERWOOD 2.6	36 May not claime another kisse.
p.	139	UNDERWOOD 2.7	9 Nay, you may erre in this,
p.	142	U'WOOD 2.10	7 What you please, you parts may call,
p.	143	UNDERWOOD 3	9 Mixe then your Notes, that we may prove
p.	144	UNDERWOOD 3	28 May wish us of their Quire.
p.	147	UNDERWOOD 7	9 They yet may envie me:
p.	147	UNDERWOOD 7	24 Where Love may all his Torches light,
p.	157	UNDERWOOD 13	157 That I may love your Person (as I doe)
p.	158	UNDERWOOD 13	161 May grow so great to be example, when
p.	158	UNDERWOOD 14	8 A pennance, where a man may not be free,
p.	158	UNDERWOOD 14	9 Rather then Office, when it doth or may
p.	164	UNDERWOOD 15	64 How they may make some one that day an Asse;
p.	165	UNDERWOOD 15	92 That may corrupt her, even in his eyes.
p.	167	UNDERWOOD 15	150 That may stand by, and hold my peace? will he,
p.	167	UNDERWOOD 15	157 That watch, and catch, at what they may applaud,
p.	169	UNDERWOOD 17	2 Debts when they can: good men may breake their day,
p.	170	UNDERWOOD 18	15 Oh how a Lover may mistake! to thinke,
p.	170	UNDERWOOD 19	10 Where men at once may plant, and gather blisses:
p.	170	UNDERWOOD 19	12 So well as I may tell in verse, 'tis so?
p.	171	UNDERWOOD 19	14 (Though they may number bodyes) or but one.
p.	171	UNDERWOOD 19	16 And so that either may example prove
p.	171	UNDERWOOD 19	18 Others, in time may love, as we doe now.
p.	171	UNDERWOOD 20	3 Amongst my many other, that I may
p.	177	UNDERWOOD 25	13 That I may sing my thoughts, in some unvulgar straine.
p.	177	UNDERWOOD 25	16 May shine (through every chincke) to every sight
p.	182	UNDERWOOD 27	32 Where men may see whom I doe sing?
p.	184	UNDERWOOD 29	50 May his joynts tormented bee,
p.	184	UNDERWOOD 29	52 Still may Syllabes jarre with time,
p.	184	UNDERWOOD 29	53 Stil may reason warre with rime,
p.	184	UNDERWOOD 29	55 May his Sense, when it would meet
p.	185	UNDERWOOD 31	1 So, justest Lord, may all your Judgements be
p.	185	UNDERWOOD 31	3 So, may the King proclaime your Conscience is
p.	186	UNDERWOOD 31	5 So, from all sicknesse, may you rise to health,
p.	186	UNDERWOOD 31	7 So may the gentler Muses, and good fame
p.	190	UNDERWOOD 37	14 So may the fruitfull Vine my temples steepe,
p.	191	UNDERWOOD 38	7 Or there to sterve it. Helpe, O you that may
p.	191	UNDERWOOD 38	13 There may some face or menace of a storme
p.	192	UNDERWOOD 38	35 Thinke that I once was yours, or may be now;
p.	192	UNDERWOOD 38	37 Errour and folly in me may have crost
p.	192	UNDERWOOD 38	51 You may so place me, and in such an ayre,
p.	193	UNDERWOOD 38	67 O may your wisdome take example hence,
p.	194	UNDERWOOD 38	118 I may dilate my selfe, but not depart.
p.	197	UNDERWOOD 40	15 For though Love thrive, and may grow up with cheare,
p.	198	UNDERWOOD 40	31 They may say Grace, and for Loves Chaplaines passe;
p.	198	UNDERWOOD 40	48 That Article, may not become <y>our lover:
p.	199	UNDERWOOD 41	22 Till I may see both it and you agen.
p.	200	UNDERWOOD 42	30 Where I may handle Silke, as free, and neere,
p.	208	UNDERWOOD 43	118 Some Alchimist there may be yet, or odde
p.	208	UNDERWOOD 43	120 May to thy name a Vulcanale say;
p.	208	UNDERWOOD 43	122 As th'other may his braines with Quicksilver.
p.	213	UNDERWOOD 44	9 They saw too store of feathers, and more may,
p.	213	UNDERWOOD 44	13 But they may see Gold-Chaines, and Pearle worne then,
p.	213	UNDERWOOD 44	27 These ten yeares day; As all may sweare that looke
p.	216	UNDERWOOD 44	98 I may no longer on these pictures stay,
p.	219	UNDERWOOD 47	51 But that's a blow, by which in time I may
p.	219	UNDERWOOD 47	55 Of earthen Jarres, there may molest me too:
p.	221	UNDERWOOD 48	25 So may the Muses follow
p.	221	UNDERWOOD 48	31 So may there never Quarrell
p.	222	UNDERWOOD 48	47 Whereby he may knit sure up
p.	225	UNDERWOOD 51	19 Give me a deep-crown'd-Bowle, that I may sing
p.	230	UNDERWOOD 56	7 And you may justly, being a tardie, cold,
p.	235	UNDERWOOD 62	13 What can the Poet wish his King may doe,
p.	237	UNDERWOOD 65	4 What Month then May, was fitter to disclose
p.	238	UNDERWOOD 66	3 The Mother of our Lord: why may not I

may (cont.)

p. 239	UNDERWOOD 67	20	The Harmony may pull
p. 239	UNDERWOOD 67	23	May wish it selfe a sense,
p. 245	UNDERWOOD 70	70	Is fairer farre, in May,
p. 245	UNDERWOOD 70	74	And in short measures, life may perfect bee.
p. 255	UNDERWOOD 75	92	And what of Dignitie, and Honour may
p. 257	UNDERWOOD 75	146	Some houres before it should, that these may know
p. 257	UNDERWOOD 75	158	We pray may grace
p. 257	UNDERWOOD 75	161	Yet, as we may, we will, with chast desires,
p. 258	UNDERWOOD 75	177	And never may there want one of the Stem,
p. 261	UNDERWOOD 77	28	Aloud; and (happ'ly) it may last as long.
p. 264	UNDERWOOD 79	26	Who walkes on Earth as May still went along,
p. 265	UNDERWOOD 79	53	That they may take it eccho'd by the Floods.
p. 268	UNDERWOOD 82	3	And by thy blessing, may thy People see
p. 269	UNDERWOOD 83	18	At least may beare th'inscription to her Tombe.
p. 269	UNDERWOOD 83	31	To touch these Mysteries! We may admire
p. 269	UNDERWOOD 83	34	T<o>'inlive posteritie, her Fame may tell!
p. 273	U'WOOD 84.1	15	May something by that twilight see
p. 276	U'WOOD 84.3	16	And Men may thinke, all light rose there.
p. 276	U'WOOD 84.3	20	May rather yet adore, then spy.
p. 277	U'WOOD 84.4	1	Painter, yo'are come, but may be gone,
p. 277	U'WOOD 84.4	6	But here I may no colours use.
p. 278	U'WOOD 84.4	22	Hence-forth may every line be you;
p. 278	U'WOOD 84.4	23	That all may say, that see the frame,
p. 280	U'WOOD 84.4	62	Where it may run to any good;
p. 290	UNDERWOOD 85	21	With which, Priapus, he may thanke thy hands,
p. 290	UNDERWOOD 85	23	Then now beneath some ancient Oke he may,
p. 305	HORACE 2	18	Ye have oft-times, that may ore-shine the rest,
p. 315	HORACE 2	204	But light from smoake; that he may draw his bright
p. 321	HORACE 2	350	And so, as every man may hope the same;
p. 321	HORACE 2	351	Yet he that offers at it, may sweat much,
p. 323	HORACE 2	392	Or rather, thinking all my faults may spie,
p. 325	HORACE 2	439	Whether truth may, and whether error bring,
p. 327	HORACE 2	469	A third of twelve, you may: foure ounces. Glad,
p. 329	HORACE 2	504	The docile mind may soone thy precepts know,
p. 329	HORACE 2	538	May, with some right, upon an Author creepe.
p. 331	HORACE 2	550	There may a Lawyer be, may not excell;
p. 331	HORACE 2	551	Or Pleader at the Barre, that may come short
p. 347	HORACE 1	354	... . Pulse there .. perhaps may ....
p. 370	UNGATHERED 7	14	Being tould there, Reason cannot, Sense may erre.
p. 371	UNGATHERED 8	7	That may iudge for his six-pence) had, before
p. 379	UNGATHERED 12	13	And that you may see he most luckily ment
p. 383	UNGATHERED 17	4	May aske, what Author would conceale his name?
p. 383	UNGATHERED 17	5	Who reads may roaue, and call the passage darke,
p. 383	UNGATHERED 17	6	Yet may as blind men sometimes hit the marke.
p. 383	UNGATHERED 17	8	May take thy volume to his vertuous hand.
p. 383	UNGATHERED 17	10	To vnderstand, hee may at length admire.
p. 384	UNGATHERED 18	11	May she, whome thou for spouse, to day, dost take,
p. 384	UNGATHERED 18	13	And thou to her, that Husband, may exalt
p. 384	UNGATHERED 18	19	So, may those Mariage-Pledges, comforts proue:
p. 384	UNGATHERED 18	21	So, in theyr number, may <you> neuer see
p. 384	UNGATHERED 18	25	That all, yt view you then, and late; may say,
p. 386	UNGATHERED 21	2	May hurt them more with praise, then Foes with spight.
p. 387	UNGATHERED 22	4	will all turne dust, & may not make me swell.
p. 389	UNGATHERED 24	13	And this hath met that one, that may be stil'd
p. 390	UNGATHERED 26	7	For seeliest Ignorance on these may light,
p. 392	UNGATHERED 26	63	Or for the lawrell, he may gaine a scorne,
p. 395	UNGATHERED 29	t3	THOMAS MAY,
p. 395	UNGATHERED 29	24	The Sunne translated, or the Sonne of May.
p. 396	UNGATHERED 30	12	Lend me thy voyce, O FAME, that I may draw
p. 398	UNGATHERED 30	73	That can but reade; who cannot, may in prose
p. 406	UNGATHERED 35	5	Besydes, his Man may merit it, and be
p. 406	UNGATHERED 35	7	He may haue skill & iudgment to designe
p. 418	UNGATHERED 46	5	Il may Ben Johnson slander so his feete,
p. 423	UNGATHERED 50	17	he that will honest be, may quitt the Court,

may'admire
                                 frequency: 1   relative frequency: 0.00001
   p. 36 EPIGRAMS 29   1 TILTER, the most may'admire thee, though not
                        I:

may'any
                                   frequency: 1   relative frequency: 0.00001
   p. 73 EPIGRAMS 113   11 Nor may'any feare, to loose of their degree,

mayd
                                   frequency: 1   relative frequency: 0.00001
   p. 413 UNGATHERED 41 37 Most holy, & pure Virgin, blessed Mayd,

mayden   frequency: 1   relative frequency: 0.00001
     p.   83 EPIGRAMS 132   14 No more, those mayden glories shee hath lost.

maymed   frequency: 1   relative frequency: 0.00001
     p. 401 UNGATHERED 32   16 If, maymed, she come off, 'tis not of men

mayne   frequency: 3   relative frequency: 0.00004
     p.   86 EPIGRAMS 133   78 Ploughing the mayne. When, see (the worst of all
                               lucks)
     p. 404 UNGATHERED 34   64 He is, or would be ye mayne Dominus doe
     p. 422 UNGATHERED 50   9 The mayne comaund of scepters, soone doth perishe

mayoress. See "mayresse."

mayor's. See "maiors."

mayresse   frequency: 1   relative frequency: 0.00001
     p. 201 UNDERWOOD 42   70 The Lady Mayresse pass'd in through the Towne,

mayst   frequency: 3   relative frequency: 0.00004
     See also "maist," "may'st."

may'st   frequency: 2   relative frequency: 0.00002

maze   frequency: 2   relative frequency: 0.00002
     p.   76 EPIGRAMS 119   13 And, in their errors maze, thine owne way know:
     p. 113 FOREST 13   60 Farre from the maze of custome, error, strife,

me   frequency: 199   relative frequency: 0.00288
     See also "dam'mee," "mee," "me'vp."

meades   frequency: 1   relative frequency: 0.00001
     p.   97 FOREST 3   17 Along'st the curled woods, and painted meades,

meadows   frequency: 1   relative frequency: 0.00001
     See also "meddowes."
     p. 291 UNDERWOOD 85   57 Or the herb Sorrell, that loves Meadows still,

meads. See "meades."

meal. See "meale."

meale   frequency: 7   relative frequency: 0.00010
    *p. 493 TO HIMSELF   28 As the best order'd meale.
     p.   69 EPIGRAMS 107   27 For your next meale: this you are sure of. Why
     p.   74 EPIGRAMS 115   10 Of newes, and noyse, to s<tr>ow out a long meale.
     p.   74 EPIGRAMS 115   23 At euery meale, where it doth dine, or sup,
     p. 206 UNDERWOOD 43   84 Had made a meale for Vulcan to lick up.
     p. 218 UNDERWOOD 47   28 Of newes they get, to strew out the long meale,
     p. 331 HORACE 2   560 These, the free meale might have beene well
                               drawne out:

meales   frequency: 1   relative frequency: 0.00001
     p.   35 EPIGRAMS 28   12 He doth, at meales, alone, his pheasant eate,

meals. See "meales."

mean   frequency: 1   relative frequency: 0.00001
     See also "meane."
     p. 657 L. CONVIVALES   11 Those dull Girls, no good can mean us,

meane   frequency: 13   relative frequency: 0.00018
    **p. 115 PANEGYRE   73 Meane while, the reuerend THEMIS drawes
                               aside
     p.   42 EPIGRAMS 49   3 I haue no salt: no bawdrie he doth meane.
     p.   87 EPIGRAMS 133   104 (In the meane time, let 'hem imprison mee)
     p. 111 FOREST 11   83 Nor meane we those, whom vowes and conscience
     p. 156 UNDERWOOD 13   105 I thought that Fortitude had beene a meane
     p. 159 UNDERWOOD 14   28 Meane what I speake: and still will keepe that
                               Vow.
     p. 263 UNDERWOOD 79   3 Your change of Notes, the flat, the meane, the
                               sharpe,
     p. 321 HORACE 2   360 The Roman Gentrie, men of birth, and meane,
     p. 331 HORACE 2   549 A meane, and toleration, which does well:
     p. 380 UNGATHERED 12   41 I meane that one paire, wherewith he so hobled
     p. 391 UNGATHERED 26   26 I meane with great, but disproportion'd Muses:
     p. 402 UNGATHERED 34   12 Or making of ye Propertyes it meane?
     p. 405 UNGATHERED 34   70 To be worth Enuy. Henceforth I doe meane

meanes   frequency: 5   relative frequency: 0.00007
    p.   30 EPIGRAMS 133   86 So huge, it seem'd, they could by no meanes quite
                                 her.
    p. 111 FOREST 11   78 Because lust's meanes are spent:
    p. 155 UNDERWOOD 13   66 Their thoughts and meanes to making loude the
                                 cry;
    p. 169 UNDERWOOD 18   2 Now threaten, with those meanes she did invite?
    p. 242 UNDERWOOD 69   15 At a Friends freedome, proves all circling
                                 meanes

meanest   frequency: 2   relative frequency: 0.00002
    p.   30 EPIGRAMS 12   1 SHIFT, here, in towne, not meanest among
                                 squires,
    p. 321 HORACE 2   354 There comes sometimes to things of meanest place.

means. See "meanes."

meant   frequency: 18   relative frequency: 0.00026
    See also "ment."
    p.   34 EPIGRAMS 23   9 All which I meant to praise, and, yet, I would;
    p.   41 EPIGRAMS 44   5 He meant they thither should make swift repaire,
    p.   48 EPIGRAMS 64   17 That whil'st I meant but thine to gratulate,
    p.   52 EPIGRAMS 76   5 I meant to make her faire, and free, and wise,
    p.   52 EPIGRAMS 76   7 I meant the day-starre should not brighter rise,
    p.   52 EPIGRAMS 76   9 I meant shee should be curteous, facile, sweet,
    p.   52 EPIGRAMS 76   11 I meant each softest vertue, there should meet,
    p.   52 EPIGRAMS 76   17 Such when I meant to faine, and wish'd to see,
    p. 153 UNDERWOOD 13   12 As I did feele it done, as soone as meant:
    p. 192 UNDERWOOD 38   43 That as the last of punishments is meant;
    p. 208 UNDERWOOD 43   115 And so did Jove, who ne're meant thee his Cup:
    p. 219 UNDERWOOD 47   36 Or that the Match from Spaine was ever meant?
    p. 246 UNDERWOOD 70   87 Or taste a part of that full joy he meant
    p. 256 UNDERWOOD 75   119 It is: to th' envious meant
    p. 307 HORACE 2   29 Was meant at first. Why, forcing still about
    p. 331 HORACE 2   555 But neither, Men, nor Gods, nor Pillars meant,
    p. 333 HORACE 2   612 Looke pale, distill a showre (was never meant)
    p. 390 UNGATHERED 26   6 Were not the paths I meant vnto thy praise:

measled. See "meazled."

measur'd   frequency: 3   relative frequency: 0.00004
    p. 233 UNDERWOOD 59   7 I hate such measur'd, give me mettall'd fire
    p. 243 UNDERWOOD 70   21 For, what is life, if measur'd by the space,
    p. 379 UNGATHERED 12   4 To his strength, hath measur'd it out with his
                                 feet.

measure   frequency: 7   relative frequency: 0.00010
    p. 164 UNDERWOOD 15   75 And laugh, and measure thighes, then squeake,
                                 spring, itch,
    p. 183 UNDERWOOD 29   5 Cosening Judgement with a measure,
    p. 184 UNDERWOOD 29   45 Of true measure,
    p. 240 UNDERWOOD 67   43 8. URA. This day the Court doth measure
    p. 244 UNDERWOOD 70   50 In weight, in measure, number, sound,
    p. 395 UNGATHERED 29   8 And those in number so, and measure rais'd,
    p. 399 UNGATHERED 31   23 In number, measure, or degree

measures   frequency: 2   relative frequency: 0.00002
    p. 245 UNDERWOOD 70   62 To light: her measures are, how well
    p. 245 UNDERWOOD 70   74 And in short measures, life may perfect bee.

meat   frequency: 1   relative frequency: 0.00001
    See also "meate," "meate-boate."
    p. 167 UNDERWOOD 15   159 Is nothing, such scarce meat and drinke he'le
                                 give,

meate   frequency: 6   relative frequency: 0.00008
    p.   65 EPIGRAMS 101   23 Of which wee'll speake our minds, amidst our
                                 meate;
    p.   69 EPIGRAMS 107   32 Doe what you come for Captayne, There's your
                                 meate.
    p.   76 EPIGRAMS 118   2 So all his meate he tasteth ouer, twise:
    p.   88 EPIGRAMS 133   167 Laxatiue lettuce, and such windie meate)
    p.   95 FOREST 2   62 Without his feare, and of thy lords owne meate:
    p.   95 FOREST 2   70 He knowes, below, he shall finde plentie of
                                 meate,

meate-boate   frequency: 1   relative frequency: 0.00001
    p.   87 EPIGRAMS 133   117 The meate-boate of Beares colledge,
                                 Paris-garden,

meats. See "sweet-meats."

meazled   frequency: 1   relative frequency: 0.00001
    p. 88 EPIGRAMS 133   145 The sinkes ran grease, and haire of meazled hogs,

mechanic. See "mechanick."

mechanick   frequency: 1   relative frequency: 0.00001
    p. 404 UNGATHERED 34   52 This is ye money-gett, Mechanick Age!

med'cin'd   frequency: 1   relative frequency: 0.00001
    p. 197 UNDERWOOD 40   4 In hast the bottome of a med'cin'd Cup,

meddle   frequency: 2   relative frequency: 0.00002
    p. 86 EPIGRAMS 133   82 (Who hath the hundred hands when he doth meddle)
    p. 206 UNDERWOOD 43   77 With Nicholas Pasquill's, Meddle with your
                              match,

meddowes   frequency: 1   relative frequency: 0.00001
    p. 97 FOREST 3   39 The mowed meddowes, with the fleeced sheepe,

medea   frequency: 2   relative frequency: 0.00002
    p. 313 HORACE 2   175 Medea make brave with impetuous scorne;
    p. 317 HORACE 2   263 Present anone: Medea must not kill

mediate   frequency: 1   relative frequency: 0.00001
    p. 128 UNDERWOOD 1.1   42 To heare, to mediate, sweeten my desire,

medicine   frequency: 1   relative frequency: 0.00001
    p. 192 UNDERWOOD 38   50 Before you prove a medicine, is unjust.

medicined. See "med'cin'd."

meditations   frequency: 2   relative frequency: 0.00002
    p. 411 UNGATHERED 40   2 your holy Meditations,
    p. 411 UNGATHERED 40   t3 her divine Meditations.

medway   frequency: 1   relative frequency: 0.00001
    p. 94 FOREST 2   31 And if the high-swolne Medway faile thy dish,

mee   frequency: 32   relative frequency: 0.00046

meeds   frequency: 1   relative frequency: 0.00001
    p. 53 EPIGRAMS 80   2 Through which, our merit leads vs to our meeds.

meek   frequency: 1   relative frequency: 0.00001
    p. 414 UNGATHERED 41   41 Great Queen of Queens, most mild, most meek,
                              most wise,

meere   frequency: 15   relative frequency: 0.00021
    p. 32 EPIGRAMS 18   t1 TO MY MEERE ENGLISH
                              CENSVRER.
    p. 51 EPIGRAMS 73   6 I lent you, on meere acquaintance, at a feast.
    p. 72 EPIGRAMS 112   3 Think'st thou it is meere fortune, that can win?
    p. 73 EPIGRAMS 114   4 In meere out-formes, vntill he lost his sight,
    p. 111 FOREST 11   82 Is meere necessitie.
    p. 154 UNDERWOOD 13   30 But by meere Chance? for interest? or to free
    p. 192 UNDERWOOD 38   64 Is natures meere obliquitie! as Heaven
    p. 208 UNDERWOOD 43 129 But, O those Reeds! thy meere disdaine of them,
    p. 256 UNDERWOOD 75 120 A meere upbraiding Griefe, and tort'ring
                              punishment.
    p. 307 HORACE 2   68 Are, by by cunning placing, made meere new.
    p. 313 HORACE 2   180 A meere new person, looke he keepe his state
    p. 321 HORACE 2   343 Meere raigning words: nor will I labour so
    p. 323 HORACE 2   374 But meere Iambicks all, from first to last.
    p. 331 HORACE 2   583 Into the Profits, what a meere rude braine
    p. 349 HORACE 1   460 .. empty Verses ... meere ....

meere-matter-lesse   frequency: 1   relative frequency: 0.00001
    p. 327 HORACE 2   460 Of verse meere-matter-lesse, and tinckling toies.

meerely   frequency: 1   relative frequency: 0.00001
    p. 218 UNDERWOOD 47   9 Let those that meerely talke, and never thinke,

meet   frequency: 30   relative frequency: 0.00043
    See also "meete."
    p. 52 EPIGRAMS 76   11 I meant each softest vertue, there should meet,
    p. 58 EPIGRAMS 92   4 At sixe and twentie, ripe. You shall 'hem meet,
    p. 59 EPIGRAMS 92   21 They meet in sixes, and at euery mart,
    p. 72 EPIGRAMS 111   9 Yet thou, perhaps, shalt meet some tongues will
                              grutch,
    p. 81 EPIGRAMS 128   8 And perfect in a circle alwayes meet.

meet (cont.)
```
p.  98 FOREST 3       69 Goe enter breaches, meet the cannons rage,
p.  99 FOREST 3       98 He alwayes giues what he knowes meet;
p. 127 UNDERWOOD 1.1  12 An offring meet
p. 129 UNDERWOOD 1.2  15 Untill they meet
p. 137 UNDERWOOD 2.5  28 Then when flowers, and West-winds meet.
p. 144 UNDERWOOD 3    26 To meet their high desire;
p. 149 UNDERWOOD 9     7 And every close did meet
p. 153 UNDERWOOD 13   10 The way to meet, what others would upbraid;
p. 157 UNDERWOOD 13  142 Meet some new matter to looke up and wonder!
p. 170 UNDERWOOD 18   20 Be brought by us to meet our Destinie.
p. 184 UNDERWOOD 29   55 May his Sense, when it would meet
p. 185 UNDERWOOD 30   16 Rather than meet him: And, before his eyes
p. 197 UNDERWOOD 40    7 Of parting, drowne it in the hope to meet
p. 215 UNDERWOOD 44   89 The Academie, where the Gallants meet --
p. 218 UNDERWOOD 47    3 They meet the fire, the Test, as Martyrs would;
p. 219 UNDERWOOD 47   33 Or the States Ships sent forth belike to meet
p. 225 UNDERWOOD 50   35 For when they find so many meet in one,
p. 233 UNDERWOOD 59   10 Of bodies, meet like rarified ayre!
p. 249 UNDERWOOD 72    5 Let Ireland meet it out at Sea, halfe way,
p. 252 UNDERWOOD 75    3 Thou canst not meet more Glory, on the way,
p. 262 UNDERWOOD 78   10 Where all heroique ample thoughts doe meet:
p. 285 U'WOOD 84.9   108 When shee departed? you will meet her there,
p. 285 U'WOOD 84.9   114 Shall meet with gladnesse in one Theatre;
p. 291 UNDERWOOD 85   39 But if, to boot with these, a chaste Wife meet
p. 292 UNDERWOOD 86   27 And in the Salian manner meet
```

meete   frequency: 4   relative frequency: 0.00005
```
p. 362 UNGATHERED 2   14 His proofe their praise, will meete, as in this
                         line.
p. 379 UNGATHERED 12   3 Who, because his matter in all should be meete,
p. 409 UNGATHERED 37  20 Out in the Dog-daies, least the killer meete
p. 418 UNGATHERED 46   6 for when the profitt with the payne doth meete,
```

meeting   frequency: 3   relative frequency: 0.00004
```
p. 221 UNDERWOOD 48   15 Of feast, and merry meeting,
p. 274 U'WOOD 84.2    10 Meeting of Graces, that so swell'd the flood
p. 365 UNGATHERED 5    8 When night their meeting couers.
```

meets   frequency: 4   relative frequency: 0.00005
```
p.  31 EPIGRAMS 12    19 To euery cause he meets, this voyce he brayes:
p. 165 UNDERWOOD 15  106 Is it for these that Fine-man meets the street
p. 254 UNDERWOOD 75   71 The Bridegroome meets the Bride
p. 407 UNGATHERED 35  12 Thou paint a Lane, where Thumb ye Pygmy meets!
```

meet'st   frequency: 1   relative frequency: 0.00001
```
p.  73 EPIGRAMS 112   13 I passe to Elegies; Thou meet'st me there:
```

mel.   frequency: 1   relative frequency: 0.00001
```
p. 239 UNDERWOOD 67    7 2. MEL. What, though the thriftie Tower
```

melancholic. See "melancholique."

melancholie   frequency: 1   relative frequency: 0.00001
```
p. 231 UNDERWOOD 56   24 Your Joane to passe her melancholie time.
```

melancholique   frequency: 1   relative frequency: 0.00001
```
p. 335 HORACE 2      662 Immortall, tooke a melancholique, odde
```

melancholy   frequency: 1   relative frequency: 0.00001
```
See also "melancholie."
p. 122 FOREST 15       2 But it must, straight, my melancholy bee?
```

meleager   frequency: 1   relative frequency: 0.00001
```
p. 315 HORACE 2      208 Of Meleager, brings he the returne
```

mellow   frequency: 2   relative frequency: 0.00002
```
p.  59 EPIGRAMS 92     7 And graue as ripe, like mellow as their faces.
p. 290 UNDERWOOD 85   18 His head, with mellow Apples crown'd,
```

melpomene. See "mel."

melt   frequency: 2   relative frequency: 0.00002
```
p. 108 FOREST 10 A     3 Thy thoughtes did neuer melt in amorous fire,
p. 118 FOREST 13      73 Melt downe their husbands land, to poure away
```

melted   frequency: 1   relative frequency: 0.00001
```
p.  88 EPIGRAMS 133  153 For, here they were throwne in wi'the melted
                         pewter,
```

```
melts                              frequency:    1   relative frequency: 0.00001
     p.   38 EPIGRAMS 37      3 And pleaseth both. For while he melts his greace

memorie                            frequency:    7   relative frequency: 0.00010
     p.   89 EPIGRAMS 133   193 In memorie of which most liquid deed,
     p.  153 UNDERWOOD 13     21 The memorie delights him more, from whom
     p.  176 UNDERWOOD 24     18 The light of Truth, and life of Memorie.
     p.  197 UNDERWOOD 40      6 To put all relish from my memorie
     p.  242 UNDERWOOD 70     t1 To the immortall memorie, and friendship of
     p.  246 UNDERWOOD 70     84 And there he lives with memorie; and Ben
     p.  416 UNGATHERED 43     5 How they doe keepe alive his memorie;

memory                             frequency:    1   relative frequency: 0.00001
     See also "memorie," "memorye."
     p.  390 UNGATHERED 26     t1 To the memory of my beloued,

memorye                            frequency:    1   relative frequency: 0.00001
     p.  394 UNGATHERED 28     t1 To ye memorye of that most honoured Ladie Jane,

men                                frequency:  137   relative frequency: 0.00198
     See also "car-men," "countrey-men,"
              "french-men," "mad-men," "states-men,"
              "veluet-men," "wise-men."
  *p.  494 TO HIMSELF      53 His zeale to God, and his iust awe o're men;
 **p.  113 PANEGYRE        10 Where men commit blacke incest with their faults;
 **p.  114 PANEGYRE        65 Old men were glad, their fates till now did last;
 **p.  115 PANEGYRE        81 "As they are men, then men. That all they doe,
 **p.  115 PANEGYRE        92 "Their lawes, their endes; the men she did
                              report:
 **p.  116 PANEGYRE       126 Then by their power; and men doe more obay
     p.   27 EPIGRAMS 2      8 And by thy wiser temper, let men know
     p.   31 EPIGRAMS 13     1 When men a dangerous disease did scape,
     p.   31 EPIGRAMS 15     1 All men are wormes: But this no man. In silke
     p.   32 EPIGRAMS 17     2 As guiltie men doe magistrates: glad I,
     p.   32 EPIGRAMS 18     8 When thou wert wont t<o>'admire, not censure men.
     p.   33 EPIGRAMS 21     7 What seuerall wayes men to their calling haue!
     p.   35 EPIGRAMS 28     4 He speakes to men with a Rhinocerotes nose,
     p.   35 EPIGRAMS 28     6 And, that is done, as he saw great men doe.
     p.   40 EPIGRAMS 43     5 'Tofore, great men were glad of Poets: Now,
     p.   41 EPIGRAMS 43     9 When, in my booke, men reade but CECILL'S
                              name,
     p.   44 EPIGRAMS 54     4 That quit'st the cause so oft, and rayl'st at
                              men?
     p.   49 EPIGRAMS 67     1 Since men haue left to doe praise-worthy things,
     p.   49 EPIGRAMS 67     5 Stand high, then, HOWARD, high in eyes of
                              men,
     p.   49 EPIGRAMS 68     1 PLAY-WRIGHT conuict of publike wrongs to
                              men,
     p.   54 EPIGRAMS 80     7 So to front death, as men might iudge vs past it.
     p.   54 EPIGRAMS 80     8 For good men but see death, the wicked tast it.
     p.   54 EPIGRAMS 81     3 Or that I'haue by, two good sufficient men,
     p.   55 EPIGRAMS 85     5 Shee doth instruct men by her gallant flight,
     p.   56 EPIGRAMS 89     3 As skilfull ROSCIVS, and graue
                              AESOPE, men,
     p.   62 EPIGRAMS 95    34 Can write the things, the causes, and the men.
     p.   64 EPIGRAMS 99     6 If time to facts, as vnto men would owe?
     p.   65 EPIGRAMS 101   37 Nor shall our cups make any guiltie men:
     p.   68 EPIGRAMS 106    1 If men get name, for some one vertue: Then,
     p.   68 EPIGRAMS 106    2 What man art thou, that art so many men,
     p.   73 EPIGRAMS 113   10 Could make such men, and such a place repent:
     p.   75 EPIGRAMS 115   29 Executes men in picture. By defect,
     p.   75 EPIGRAMS 116    1 IEPHSON, thou man of men, to whose lou'd
                              name
     p.   75 EPIGRAMS 116   10 In men, but euery brauest was the best:
     p.   77 EPIGRAMS 120   14 Old men so duely,
     p.   80 EPIGRAMS 128    2 Countries, and climes, manners, and men to know,
     p.   81 EPIGRAMS 129   18 Men loue thee not for this: They laugh at thee.
     p.   82 EPIGRAMS 130    9 T<o>'alledge, that greatest men were not asham'd,
     p.   83 EPIGRAMS 131    5 And though we could all men, all censures heare,
     p.   84 EPIGRAMS 133   16 And, for the cryes of Ghosts, women, and men,
     p.   86 EPIGRAMS 133   67 Betweene two walls: where, on one side, to scar
                              men,
     p.  104 FOREST 7        6 Stil'd but the shaddowes of vs men?
     p.  104 FOREST 7        9 So men at weakest, they are strongest,
     p.  104 FOREST 7       12 Stil'd but the shaddowes of vs men?
     p.  104 FOREST 8        3 Doe not men, ynow of rites
     p.  105 FOREST 8       14 Sicknesse; onely on vs men.
     p.  113 FOREST 12       9 While it makes huishers seruiceable men,
     p.  114 FOREST 12      53 Gaue killing strokes. There were braue men,
                              before
```

men (cont.)

p. 117 FOREST 13	18	Men are not iust, or keepe no holy lawes
p. 121 FOREST 14	43	And men
p. 121 FOREST 14	60	The Birth-day shines, when logs not burne, but men.
p. 131 UNDERWOOD 2.1	5	Poets, though divine, are men:
p. 136 UNDERWOOD 2.5	26	Where, you say, men gather blisses,
p. 145 UNDERWOOD 5	1	Men, if you love us, play no more
p. 150 UNDERWOOD 10	15	Seeke doubting Men to please,
p. 152 UNDERWOOD 12	28	It chid the vice, yet not the Men.
p. 153 UNDERWOOD 13	4	Lesse list of proud, hard, or ingratefull Men.
p. 154 UNDERWOOD 13	45	Lest Ayre, or Print, but flies it: Such men would
p. 155 UNDERWOOD 13	79	But these men ever want: their very trade
p. 156 UNDERWOOD 13	98	That men such reverence to such actions show!
p. 156 UNDERWOOD 13	124	Man have beene great, but never good by chance,
p. 157 UNDERWOOD 13	131	'Tis by degrees that men arrive at glad
p. 157 UNDERWOOD 13	139	Then stands it a triumphall marke! then Men
p. 157 UNDERWOOD 13	143	Such Notes are vertuous men! they live as fast
p. 158 UNDERWOOD 13	162	(As their true rule or lesson) either men,
p. 159 UNDERWOOD 14	21	Men past their termes, and prais'd some names too much,
p. 159 UNDERWOOD 14	26	Before men get a verse: much lesse a Praise;
p. 159 UNDERWOOD 14	33	Of generall knowledge; watch'd men, manners too,
p. 166 UNDERWOOD 15	146	To lose the formes, and dignities of men,
p. 168 UNDERWOOD 16	6	For, if such men as he could die,
p. 169 UNDERWOOD 17	2	Debts when they can: good men may breake their day,
p. 170 UNDERWOOD 18	12	Such Guides men use not, who their way would find,
p. 170 UNDERWOOD 18	17	To see men feare: or else for truth, and State,
p. 170 UNDERWOOD 19	10	Where men at once may plant, and gather blisses:
p. 173 UNDERWOOD 22	15	By whom he is restor'd to men:
p. 181 UNDERWOOD 26	23	For men to use their fortune reverently,
p. 182 UNDERWOOD 27	32	Where men may see whom I doe sing?
p. 187 UNDERWOOD 33	5	That, henceforth, I beleeve nor bookes, nor men,
p. 187 UNDERWOOD 33	15	So dost thou studie matter, men, and times,
p. 197 UNDERWOOD 40	3	And then I taste it. But as men drinke up
p. 199 UNDERWOOD 41	21	Or like a Ghost walke silent amongst men,
p. 210 UNDERWOOD 43	173	But say, all sixe good men, what answer yee?
p. 212 UNDERWOOD 43	211	So doth the King, and most of the Kings men
p. 213 UNDERWOOD 44	8	Launces, and men, and some a breaking force.
p. 213 UNDERWOOD 44	14	Lent by the London Dames, to the Lords men;
p. 214 UNDERWOOD 44	53	Insert thy Hodges, and those newer men,
p. 214 UNDERWOOD 44	57	And could (if our great men would let their Sonnes
p. 215 UNDERWOOD 44	75	We will beleeve, like men of our owne Ranke,
p. 216 UNDERWOOD 45	18	Deceit is fruitfull. Men have Masques and nets,
p. 218 UNDERWOOD 47	1	Men that are safe, and sure, in all they doe,
p. 218 UNDERWOOD 47	15	But for a Sealing: let these men protest.
p. 218 UNDERWOOD 47	25	Let these men have their wayes, and take their times
p. 224 UNDERWOOD 50	22	Countries, and Climes, manners, and men to know.
p. 225 UNDERWOOD 51	3	The fire, the wine, the men! and in the midst,
p. 242 UNDERWOOD 69	20	To judge; So all men comming neere can spie.
p. 244 UNDERWOOD 70	36	And had his noble name advanc'd with men:
p. 246 UNDERWOOD 70	83	Such truths, as we expect for happy men,
p. 247 UNDERWOOD 70	125	Of two so early men,
p. 250 UNDERWOOD 73	6	Who seldome sleepes! whom bad men only hate!
p. 256 UNDERWOOD 75	116	And by his Rise, in active men, his Name
p. 259 UNDERWOOD 76	2	To th'best of Monarchs, Masters, Men,
p. 261 UNDERWOOD 77	18	To compose men, and manners; stint the strife
p. 263 UNDERWOOD 79	7	We sing the best of Monarchs, Masters, Men;
p. 272 UNDERWOOD 83	97	Hee were the wretched'st of the race of men:
p. 276 U'WOOD 84.3	16	And Men may thinke, all light rose there.
p. 281 U'WOOD 84.8	17	Which all men doe, that urge not their owne deeds
p. 309 HORACE 2	72	Of the Cethegi; And all men will grace,
p. 309 HORACE 2	94	Once rowable, but now doth nourish men
p. 315 HORACE 2	202	Saw many Townes, and Men, and could their manners tract.
p. 317 HORACE 2	252	The parts of age to youth be given; or men
p. 317 HORACE 2	280	It still must favour good men, and to these
p. 321 HORACE 2	357	Like men street-borne, and neere the Hall, reherse
p. 321 HORACE 2	360	The Roman Gentrie, men of birth, and meane,
p. 327 HORACE 2	463	Being men were covetous of nought, but praise.
p. 327 HORACE 2	480	First frighted men, that wildly liv'd, at ods,
p. 329 HORACE 2	511	The Poems void of profit, our grave men
p. 331 HORACE 2	555	But neither, Men, nor Gods, nor Pillars meant,
p. 333 HORACE 2	617	Rich men are said with many cups to plie,

men (cont.)
```
    p. 380 UNGATHERED 12    44 How many learned men he haue drawne with his
                               hooke
    p. 382 UNGATHERED 16     3 vnto thee, king of men; their noblest partes
    p. 383 UNGATHERED 16    14 your Royal Eye which still creat[t]es new men
    p. 383 UNGATHERED 17     6 Yet may as blind men sometimes hit the marke.
    p. 386 UNGATHERED 21     1 Some men, of Bookes or Freinds not speaking
                               right,
    p. 389 UNGATHERED 23    11 As, now, of all men, it is call'd thy Trade:
    p. 389 UNGATHERED 24     2 Shall finde, that either hath read Bookes, and
                               Men:
    p. 395 UNGATHERED 29    18 Are still th'interpreters twixt godds, and men!
    p. 401 UNGATHERED 32    16 If, maymed, she come off, 'tis not of men
    p. 403 UNGATHERED 34    30 And all men eccho you haue made a Masque.
    p. 405 UNGATHERED 34    66 Be Inigo, ye Whistle, & his men!
    p. 409 UNGATHERED 37    22 Thy Dirty braines, Men smell thy want of worth.
    p. 410 UNGATHERED 38    13 It was not so of old: Men tooke vp trades
    p. 410 UNGATHERED 38    16 And the Physician teach men spue, or shite;
    p. 414 UNGATHERED 42     7 By those deepe-grounded, understanding men,
    p. 415 UNGATHERED 42    11 Such men I met withall, and so have you.
    p. 415 UNGATHERED 42    24 And a Comptroller, two most rigid men
    p. 419 UNGATHERED 48     1 Yff Men, and tymes were nowe
```

menace   frequency: 1   relative frequency: 0.00001
```
    p. 191 UNDERWOOD 38    13 There may some face or menace of a storme
```

menacings   frequency: 1   relative frequency: 0.00001
```
    p. 311 HORACE 2       149 Sad language fits sad lookes; stuff'd menacings,
```

mend   frequency: 5   relative frequency: 0.00007
```
    p. 139 UNDERWOOD 2.7   13 I will but mend the last, and tell
    p. 329 HORACE 2       530 Still in the same, and warned will not mend,
    p. 331 HORACE 2       579 To change, and mend, what you not forth doe set.
    p. 333 HORACE 2       624 Hee'd say, Mend this, good friend, and this;
                               'tis naught.
    p. 379 UNGATHERED 12   15 He sayes to the world, let any man mend it,
```

mended   frequency: 2   relative frequency: 0.00002
```
    p. 325 HORACE 2       413 Her language, if the Stay, and Care t'have
                               mended,
    p. 380 UNGATHERED 12   39 How well, and how often his shoes too were
                               mended,
```

mendicant   frequency: 1   relative frequency: 0.00001
```
    p. 248 UNDERWOOD 71    t3 An Epistle Mendicant.
```

mending   frequency: 2   relative frequency: 0.00002
```
    p. 139 UNDERWOOD 2.7   t1 Begging another, on colour of mending
    p. 192 UNDERWOOD 38    49 Doe not despaire my mending; to distrust
```

mends   frequency: 1   relative frequency: 0.00001
```
    p. 156 UNDERWOOD 13   116 But like to be, that every day mends one,
```

mens   frequency: 22   relative frequency: 0.00031
```
 **p. 113 PANEGYRE         16 Those dampes, that so offend all good mens eyes;
 **p. 117 PANEGYRE        143 Before mens hearts had crown'd him. Who (vnlike
 **p. 117 PANEGYRE        150 What all mens wishes did aspire vnto.
   p.  34 EPIGRAMS 24      2 Mens manners ne're were viler, for your sake.
   p.  35 EPIGRAMS 28      8 And, can forget mens names, with a great grace.
   p.  47 EPIGRAMS 64     11 Where good mens vertues them to honors bring,
   p.  49 EPIGRAMS 67      7 When, in mens wishes, so thy vertues wrought,
   p.  58 EPIGRAMS 91     18 Who more should seeke mens reuerence, then feare.
   p.  95 FOREST 2        66 At great mens tables) and yet dine away.
   p. 104 FOREST 7        t2 THAT WOMEN ARE BVT MENS
   p. 150 UNDERWOOD 10     8 On all mens Fruit, and flowers, as well as mine.
   p. 173 UNDERWOOD 22     7 And draw, and conquer all mens love,
   p. 199 UNDERWOOD 41     9 What fate is this, to change mens dayes and
                             houres,
   p. 217 UNDERWOOD 46    20 Of worthiest knowledge, that can take mens minds.
   p. 244 UNDERWOOD 70    38 Hee stoop'd in all mens sight
   p. 248 UNDERWOOD 71     3 Of Princes aides, or good mens Charities.
   p. 255 UNDERWOOD 75   104 Mens Loves unto the Lawes, and Lawes to love
                             the Crowne,
   p. 309 HORACE 2       108 After, mens Wishes, crown'd in their events,
   p. 311 HORACE 2       143 Mens faces, still, with such as laugh, are prone
   p. 321 HORACE 2       328 Yet so the scoffing Satyres to mens view,
   p. 338 HORACE 1         9 ..... ...... .... sick mens ...... ... form'd ..
                             ....
   p. 390 UNGATHERED 26    5 'Tis true, and all mens suffrage. But these
                             wayes
```

men's. See "great-mens," "mens," "sick-mens."

ment   frequency: 1   relative frequency: 0.00001
      p. 379 UNGATHERED 12   13 And that you may see he most luckily ment

mention   frequency: 1   relative frequency: 0.00001
      p. 67 EPIGRAMS 105   4 Least mention of a Nymph, a Muse, a Grace,

mentioned. See "glad-mention'd."

mercat   frequency: 1   relative frequency: 0.00001
      p. 234 UNDERWOOD 61   3 View'd there the mercat, read the wretched rate

mercer   frequency: 1   relative frequency: 0.00001
      p. 200 UNDERWOOD 42   31 As any Mercer; or the whale-bone man

merchant   frequency: 2   relative frequency: 0.00002
      p. 237 UNDERWOOD 64   19 'T is not alone the Merchant, but the Clowne,
      p. 313 HORACE 2   165 A ventring Merchant, or the Farmer free

merchants   frequency: 1   relative frequency: 0.00001
      p. 229 UNDERWOOD 54   4 A Merchants Wife is Regent of the Scale.

mercie   frequency: 2   relative frequency: 0.00002
      p. 191 UNDERWOOD 38   16 Of Graces, or your mercie here in me,
      p. 194 UNDERWOOD 38   106 And let your mercie make me asham'd t<o>'offend.

mercies   frequency: 1   relative frequency: 0.00001
      p. 191 UNDERWOOD 38   29 And (stil'd your mercies Creature) will live
                                     more

mercury   frequency: 1   relative frequency: 0.00001
      See also "mercvry."
      p. 392 UNGATHERED 26   46 Our eares, or like a Mercury to charme!

mercvry   frequency: 2   relative frequency: 0.00002
      p. 86 EPIGRAMS 133   96 Poore MERCVRY, crying out on
                                     PARACELSVS,
      p. 87 EPIGRAMS 133   111 Their MERCVRY did now. By this, the
                                     stemme

mercy   frequency: 1   relative frequency: 0.00001
      See also "mercie."
      p. 286 U'WOOD 84.9   138 What love with mercy mixed doth appeare?

mercy-seat   frequency: 1   relative frequency: 0.00001
      p. 288 U'WOOD 84.9   190 The doore of Grace, and found the Mercy-Seat.

merd-vrinous   frequency: 1   relative frequency: 0.00001
      p. 85 EPIGRAMS 133   65 Who shall discharge first his merd-vrinous load:

mere   frequency: 2   relative frequency: 0.00002
      See also "meere," "meere-matter-lesse."
      p. 291 UNDERWOOD 85   68 To turne mere farmer, had spoke out,
      p. 404 UNGATHERED 34   44 In ye mere perspectiue of an Inch board!

merely. See "meerely."

merit   frequency: 14   relative frequency: 0.00020
      p. 47 EPIGRAMS 64   10 Where merit is not sepulcher'd aliue.
      p. 53 EPIGRAMS 80   2 Through which, our merit leads vs to our meeds.
      p. 60 EPIGRAMS 93   10 And thine owne goodnesse to encrease thy merit,
      p. 61 EPIGRAMS 95   12 Onely to boast thy merit in supply.
      p. 75 EPIGRAMS 116   5 Thou wert the first, mad'st merit know her
                                     strength,
      p. 76 EPIGRAMS 119   5 With me can merit more, then that good man,
      p. 83 EPIGRAMS 132   2 Might then both thee, thy worke and merit raise:
      p. 99 FOREST 3   78 And each where boast it as his merit,
      p. 108 FOREST 10   27 A beautie of that merit, that should take
      p. 164 UNDERWOOD 15   57 To do't with Cloth, or Stuffes, lusts name
                                     might merit;
      p. 177 UNDERWOOD 25   21 And keepes your merit
      p. 230 UNDERWOOD 56   4 You won them too, your oddes did merit it.
      p. 323 HORACE 2   406 Nor did they merit the lesse Crowne to weare,
      p. 406 UNGATHERED 35   5 Besydes, his Man may merit it, and be

merited   frequency: 1   relative frequency: 0.00001
      p. 323 HORACE 2   396 But, in conclusion, merited no fame.

merkins. See "mirkins."

merlins   frequency: 1   relative frequency: 0.00001
    p. 206 UNDERWOOD 43   71 To Merlins Marvailes, and his Caballs losse,

mermaid   frequency: 1   relative frequency: 0.00001
    p. 85 EPIGRAMS 133   37 At Bread-streets Mermaid, hauing din'd, and
                              merry,

mermaides   frequency: 1   relative frequency: 0.00001
    p. 368 UNGATHERED 6   91 Hath sent her Mermaides in,

mermaids   frequency: 1   relative frequency: 0.00001
    See also "mermaides."
    p. 65 EPIGRAMS 101   30 Which is the Mermaids, now, but shall be mine:

merrie   frequency: 1   relative frequency: 0.00001
    p. 193 UNDERWOOD 40   25 No, Mistris, no, the open merrie Man

merry   frequency: 9   relative frequency: 0.00013
    See also "merrie."
    p. 85 EPIGRAMS 133   37 At Bread-streets Mermaid, hauing din'd, and
                              merry,
    p. 85 EPIGRAMS 133   54 Alwayes at hand, to aide the merry Muses.
    p. 89 EPIGRAMS 133   184 That had, so often, shew'd 'hem merry prankes.
    p. 220 UNDERWOOD 48   12 And relish merry make him.
    p. 221 UNDERWOOD 48   15 Of feast, and merry meeting,
    p. 230 UNDERWOOD 56   21 To make you merry on the Dressing stoole,
    p. 392 UNGATHERED 26   51 The merry Greeke, tart Aristophanes,
    p. 416 UNGATHERED 45   7 but a very merry wight
    p. 417 UNGATHERED 45   13 To the merry beards in Hall,

mersh-lambeth   frequency: 1   relative frequency: 0.00001
    p. 30 EPIGRAMS 12   2 That haunt Pickt-hatch, Mersh-Lambeth, and
                              White-fryers,

meschines   frequency: 1   relative frequency: 0.00001
    p. 274 U'WOOD 84.2   16 Meschines honour with the Cestrian fame

meschin's. See "meschines."

mess. See "messe."

messalla's   frequency: 1   relative frequency: 0.00001
    p. 331 HORACE 2   552 Of eloquent Messalla's power in Court,

messe   frequency: 1   relative frequency: 0.00001
    p. 94 FOREST 2   30 And, for thy messe, is willing to be kill'd.

met   frequency: 15   relative frequency: 0.00021
    See also "mett."
  **p. 114 PANEGYRE   64 With seuerall eyes, that in this obiect met.
    p. 30 EPIGRAMS 11   1 At court I met it, in clothes braue enough,
    p. 62 EPIGRAMS 97   8 Where ere he met me; now hee's dumbe, or proud.
    p. 65 EPIGRAMS 101   39 We innocently met. No simple word,
    p. 74 EPIGRAMS 114   6 Where finding so much beautie met with vertue,
    p. 86 EPIGRAMS 133   79 They met the second Prodigie, would feare a
    p. 94 FOREST 2   14 At his great birth, where all the Muses met.
    p. 212 UNDERWOOD 43   201 Or stay'd but where the Fryar, and you first
                              met,
    p. 243 UNDERWOOD 70   17 Sword, fire, and famine, with fell fury met;
    p. 270 UNDERWOOD 83   42 And pietie the Center, where all met.
    p. 291 UNDERWOOD 85   65 The wealthy houshold swarme of bondmen met,
    p. 319 HORACE 2   292 So over-thick, but, where the people met,
    p. 389 UNGATHERED 24   13 And this hath met that one, that may be stil'd
    p. 413 UNGATHERED 41   32 The glorious Trinity in Vnion met.
    p. 415 UNGATHERED 42   11 Such men I met withall, and so have you.

metal. See "mettall," "mettal's."

metals. See "mettalls."

mete   frequency: 1   relative frequency: 0.00001
    p. 176 UNDERWOOD 24   12 Doth mete, whose lyne doth sound the depth of
                              things:)

meticulous   frequency: 1   relative frequency: 0.00001
    p. 380 UNGATHERED 12   33 That he dares to informe you, but somewhat
                              meticulous,

metius   frequency: 1   relative frequency: 0.00001
    p. 331 HORACE 2   576 To send it to be judg'd by Metius eare,

mett   frequency: 1   relative frequency: 0.00001
     p. 403 UNGATHERED 34   31 I chyme that too: And I haue mett wth those

mettall   frequency: 3   relative frequency: 0.00004
  **p. 113 PANEGYRE   18 And in their vapor her bright mettall drowne.
     p. 172 UNDERWOOD 21   2 His name in any mettall, it would breake.
     p. 228 UNDERWOOD 53   2 Provoke his mettall, and command his force

mettall'd   frequency: 1   relative frequency: 0.00001
     p. 233 UNDERWOOD 59   7 I hate such measur'd, give me mettall'd fire

mettalls   frequency: 1   relative frequency: 0.00001
     p. 86 EPIGRAMS 133   100 And subtiltie of mettalls) they dispense

mettal's   frequency: 1   relative frequency: 0.00001
     p. 179 UNDERWOOD 25   43 Though but while mettal's heating:

mettle. See "mettall."

mettled. See "mettall'd."

me'vp   frequency: 1   relative frequency: 0.00001
     p. 72 EPIGRAMS 112   6 Art still at that, and think'st to blow me'vp
                               too?

mew'd   frequency: 1   relative frequency: 0.00001
     p. 88 EPIGRAMS 133   161 With great gray eyes, are lifted vp, and mew'd;

michael   frequency: 2   relative frequency: 0.00002
     See also "m."
     p. 260 UNDERWOOD 77   7 Titian, or Raphael, Michael Angelo,
     p. 396 UNGATHERED 30   1 It hath beene question'd, MICHAEL, if I
                               bee

mid-sun   frequency: 1   relative frequency: 0.00001
     p. 156 UNDERWOOD 13   95 Or feats of darknesse acted in Mid-Sun,

mid-wife   frequency: 1   relative frequency: 0.00001
     p. 107 FOREST 10   15 Who, with his axe, thy fathers mid-wife plaid.

mid-wives   frequency: 1   relative frequency: 0.00001
     p. 202 UNDERWOOD 42   83 Under that cover; an old Mid-wives hat!

midas   frequency: 1   relative frequency: 0.00001
     p. 197 UNDERWOOD 40   21 Not, like a Midas, shut up in himselfe,

middle   frequency: 3   relative frequency: 0.00004
     p. 94 FOREST 2   24 The middle grounds thy mares, and horses breed.
     p. 131 UNDERWOOD 2.1   21 Keepe the middle age at stay,
     p. 315 HORACE 2   213 The middle of his matter: letting goe

midst   frequency: 5   relative frequency: 0.00007
     p. 71 EPIGRAMS 110   14 And that, midst enuy' and parts; then fell by
                               rage:
     p. 122 FOREST 15   10 First, midst, and last, conuerted one, and three;
     p. 225 UNDERWOOD 51   3 The fire, the wine, the men! and in the midst,
     p. 315 HORACE 2   217 Where the midst differs from the first: or where
     p. 315 HORACE 2   218 The last doth from the midst dis-joyn'd appeare.

midwife. See "mid-wife."

midwife's. See "mid-wives."

might   frequency: 56   relative frequency: 0.00081
     See also "mought."
  **p. 114 PANEGYRE   51 That might her beauties heighten; but so drest,
  **p. 117 PANEGYRE   158 Saue, that shee might the same perpetuall see.
     p. 32 EPIGRAMS 18   6 As theirs did with thee, mine might credit get:
     p. 34 EPIGRAMS 23   8 Which might with halfe mankind maintayne a
                               strife.
     p. 39 EPIGRAMS 40   8 Then they might in her bright eyes.
     p. 41 EPIGRAMS 44   6 When he made him executor, might be heire.
     p. 43 EPIGRAMS 51   1 That we·thy losse might know, and thou our loue,
     p. 48 EPIGRAMS 66   1 That neither fame, nor loue might wanting be
     p. 48 EPIGRAMS 66   4 In onely thee, might be both great, and glad.
     p. 54 EPIGRAMS 80   7 So to front death, as men might iudge vs past it.
     p. 58 EPIGRAMS 91   10 Throughout, might flatt'rie seeme; and to be mute
     p. 66 EPIGRAMS 103   1 How well, faire crowne of your faire sexe, might
                               hee,
     p. 68 EPIGRAMS 106   4 Truth might spend all her voyce, Fame all her
                               art.

might (cont.)

p.	71 EPIGRAMS 110	7	And that so strong and deepe, as 't might be thought,
p.	73 EPIGRAMS 113	6	That the wit there, and manners might be sau'd:
p.	75 EPIGRAMS 116	8	Might be found out as good, and not my Lord.
p.	79 EPIGRAMS 125	3	Both whose dimensions, lost, the world might finde
p.	79 EPIGRAMS 125	6	Might loue the treasure for the cabinet.
p.	83 EPIGRAMS 132	2	Might then both thee, thy worke and merit raise:
p.	89 EPIGRAMS 133	182	Were you IOVE'S sonnes, or had ALCIDES might.
p.	106 FOREST 9	7	But might I of IOVE'S Nectar sup,
p.	119 FOREST 13	93	'Gainst stormes, or pyrats, that might charge your peace;
p.	132 UNDERWOOD 2.2	14	Sooner, then he lost his might,
p.	133 UNDERWOOD 2.3	9	Unto her; which Love might take
p.	134 UNDERWOOD 2.4	7	And enamour'd, doe wish, so they might
p.	138 UNDERWOOD 2.6	26	As might all the Graces lead,
p.	164 UNDERWOOD 15	57	To do't with Cloth, or Stuffes, lusts name might merit;
p.	168 UNDERWOOD 16	5	It might thy patience richly pay:
p.	172 UNDERWOOD 20	23	But she is such, as she might, yet, forestall
p.	176 UNDERWOOD 24	6	Might be defrauded, nor the great secur'd,
p.	176 UNDERWOOD 24	7	But both might know their wayes were understood,
p.	189 UNDERWOOD 36	12	And waste still, that they still might bee.
p.	201 UNDERWOOD 42	47	So I might dote upon thy Chaires, and Stooles,
p.	202 UNDERWOOD 43	2	What had I done that might call on thine ire?
p.	204 UNDERWOOD 43	45	Adulterate moneys, such as might not goe:
p.	209 UNDERWOOD 43	136	And raz'd, e're thought could urge, This might have bin!
p.	211 UNDERWOOD 43	182	Or lest that vapour might the Citie choake,
p.	212 UNDERWOOD 43	203	Or fixt in the Low-Countrey's, where you might
p.	214 UNDERWOOD 44	41	So acted to the life, as Maurice might,
p.	216 UNDERWOOD 45	3	My gentle Arthur; that it might be said
p.	223 UNDERWOOD 49	31	Indeed, her Dressing some man might delight,
p.	226 UNDERWOOD 52	3	But there are lines, wherewith I might b<e>'embrac'd.
p.	227 UNDERWOOD 52	16	O, had I now your manner, maistry, might,
p.	244 UNDERWOOD 70	51	As though his age imperfect might appeare,
p.	247 UNDERWOOD 70	122	Where they might read, and find
p.	257 UNDERWOOD 75	147	All that their Fathers, and their Mothers might
p.	273 U'WOOD 84.1	27	With Gold, or Claspes, which might be bought
p.	315 HORACE 2	214	What he despaires, being handled, might not show.
p.	319 HORACE 2	293	They might with ease be numbred, being a few
p.	319 HORACE 2	297	And they uncensur'd might at Feasts, and Playes
p.	331 HORACE 2	560	These, the free meale might have beene well drawne out:
p.	361 UNGATHERED 1	13	Next, that which rapt mee, was: I might behold
p.	371 UNGATHERED 9	6	She might haue claym'd t'have made the Graces foure;
p.	372 UNGATHERED 9	14	Might make the Fable of Good Women true.
p.	391 UNGATHERED 26	11	Or crafty Malice, might pretend this praise,
p.	406 UNGATHERED 34	98	That might compare wth thee? what story shall

mightiest   frequency: 2   relative frequency: 0.00002
   p. 261 UNDERWOOD 77   21 And mightiest Monarchs feele what large increase
   p. 271 UNDERWOOD 83   89 The Sunne! great Kings, and mightiest
                                      Kingdomes fall!

mightst   frequency: 2   relative frequency: 0.00002

mighty   frequency: 5   relative frequency: 0.00007
   p. 391 UNGATHERED 26   30 Or sporting Kid, or Marlowes mighty line.
   p. 395 UNGATHERED 29   1 When, Rome, I reade thee in thy mighty paire,
   p. 397 UNGATHERED 30   39 And Rouze, the Marching of a mighty force,
   p. 403 UNGATHERED 34   39 To hold her vp. O Showes! Showes! Mighty
                                      Showes!
   p. 406 UNGATHERED 35   1 But cause thou hearst ye mighty k. of Spaine

milan. See "millan."

mild   frequency: 3   relative frequency: 0.00004
   See also "milde."
   p. 189 UNDERWOOD 36   15 Now hot, now cold, now fierce, now mild.
   p. 192 UNDERWOOD 38   40 Of your compassion; Parents should be mild:
   p. 414 UNGATHERED 41   41 Great Queen of Queens, most mild, most meek,
                                      most wise,

milde   frequency: 1   relative frequency: 0.00001
   p. 188 UNDERWOOD 35   2 What manners prettie, Nature milde,

milder   frequency: 1   relative frequency: 0.00001
    p. 88 EPIGRAMS 133   163 Our braue Heroes with a milder glare,

mildnesse   frequency: 1   relative frequency: 0.00001
    p. 193 UNDERWOOD 38   85 But view the mildnesse of your Makers state,

mile   frequency: 2   relative frequency: 0.00002
    p. 222 UNDERWOOD 49   15 What though she ride two mile on Holy-dayes
    p. 379 UNGATHERED 12   9 And allow you for each particular mile,

militar   frequency: 1   relative frequency: 0.00001
    p. 214 UNDERWOOD 44   60 In Politique, and Militar Affaires.

militarie   frequency: 1   relative frequency: 0.00001
    p. 213 UNDERWOOD 44   26 Of London, in the Militarie truth,

military. See "militar," "militarie."

milk   frequency: 1   relative frequency: 0.00001
    See also "milke."
    p. 657 L. CONVIVALES 12 Wine it is the Milk of Venus,

milke   frequency: 5   relative frequency: 0.00007
    p. 31 EPIGRAMS 15   2 'Twas brought to court first wrapt, and white as
                              milke;
    p. 136 UNDERWOOD 2.5   22 In her cheekes, of Milke, and Roses;
    p. 170 UNDERWOOD 19   8 Where he doth steepe himselfe in Milke and
                              Roses;
    p. 264 UNDERWOOD 79   16 3. Our milke. 4. Our fells. 5. Our fleeces. 6.
                              And first Lambs.
    p. 313 HORACE 2   168 Or, with the milke of Thebes; or Argus, fed.

milkes   frequency: 1   relative frequency: 0.00001
    p. 265 UNDERWOOD 79   50 Your Milkes, your Fells, your Fleeces, and
                              first Lambes,

milks. See "milkes."

mill   frequency: 6   relative frequency: 0.00008
    p. 57 EPIGRAMS 90   1 When MILL first came to court, the
                              vnprofiting foole,
    p. 57 EPIGRAMS 90   t1 ON MILL MY LADIES WOMAN.
    p. 57 EPIGRAMS 90   11 Still MILL continu'd: Nay, his face growing
                              worse,
    p. 57 EPIGRAMS 90   13 MILL was the same. Since, both his body and
                              face
    p. 57 EPIGRAMS 90   16 Longer a day, but with his MILL will marry.
    p. 211 UNDERWOOD 43   184 foot (out in Sussex) to an iron Mill;

millan   frequency: 1   relative frequency: 0.00001
    p. 212 UNDERWOOD 43   200 Strooke in at Millan with the Cutlers there;

millar   frequency: 1   relative frequency: 0.00001
    p. 214 UNDERWOOD 44   54 As Stiles, Dike, Ditchfield, Millar, Crips,
                              and Fen:

milo   frequency: 1   relative frequency: 0.00001
    p. 57 EPIGRAMS 90   17 And it is hop'd, that shee, like MILO, wull,

mime   frequency: 2   relative frequency: 0.00002
    p. 81 EPIGRAMS 129   9 Think'st thou, MIME, this is great? or, that
                              they striue
    p. 81 EPIGRAMS 129   t1 TO MIME.

miming   frequency: 2   relative frequency: 0.00002
    p. 74 EPIGRAMS 115   28 Of miming, gets th'opinion of a wit.
    p. 81 EPIGRAMS 129   10 Whose noyse shall keepe thy miming most aliue,

mince   frequency: 1   relative frequency: 0.00001
    p. 88 EPIGRAMS 133   151 Then, selling not, a dish was tane to mince 'hem,

mind   frequency: 43   relative frequency: 0.00062
    See also "minde," "mynd," "mynde."
  **p. 115 PANEGYRE   75 In these vaine stirres, and to his mind suggests
    p. 37 EPIGRAMS 32   6 His often change of clime (though not of mind)
    p. 47 EPIGRAMS 63   8 By constant suffring of thy equall mind;
    p. 82 EPIGRAMS 130   8 No lesse a sou'raigne cure, then to the mind;
    p. 112 FOREST 11   111 Much more a noble, and right generous mind
    p. 117 FOREST 13   44 And takes, and giues the beauties of the mind.
    p. 137 UNDERWOOD 2.5   46 Call to mind the formes, that strove

mind (cont.)

p. 142 U'WOOD 2.10	1 For his Mind, I doe not care,
p. 150 UNDERWOOD 10	4 Nor have I yet the narrow mind
p. 151 UNDERWOOD 12	15 His Mind as pure, and neatly kept,
p. 153 UNDERWOOD 13	5 For benefits are ow'd with the same mind
p. 166 UNDERWOOD 15	133 And whilst our states, strength, body, and mind we waste,
p. 175 UNDERWOOD 24	t1 The mind of the Frontispice to a Booke.
p. 176 UNDERWOOD 25	5 High, as his mind, that doth advance
p. 179 UNDERWOOD 25	48 No Armour to the mind! he is shot-free
p. 180 UNDERWOOD 26	9 Yet doth some wholsome Physick for the mind,
p. 225 UNDERWOOD 50	29 Searching for knowledge, and to keepe your mind
p. 227 UNDERWOOD 52	23 A letter'd mind, and a large heart would place
p. 231 UNDERWOOD 57	14 Put him in mind
p. 234 UNDERWOOD 61	7 Yet are got off thence, with cleare mind, and hands
p. 260 UNDERWOOD 77	1 If to my mind, great Lord, I had a state,
p. 274 U'WOOD 84.2	3 For Mind, and Body, the most excellent
p. 277 U'WOOD 84.3	32 Next sitting we will draw her mind.
p. 277 U'WOOD 84.4	t1 The MIND.
p. 278 U'WOOD 84.4	12 But these are like a Mind, not it.
p. 278 U'WOOD 84.4	13 No, to expresse a Mind to sense,
p. 278 U'WOOD 84.4	17 Sweet Mind, then speake your selfe, and say,
p. 278 U'WOOD 84.4	25 A Mind so pure, so perfect fine,
p. 279 U'WOOD 84.4	41 But, that a Mind so rapt, so high,
p. 281 U'WOOD 84.4	72 But such a Mind, mak'st God thy Guest.
p. 283 U'WOOD 84.9	23 My wounded mind cannot sustaine this stroke,
p. 285 U'WOOD 84.9	104 That pure, that pretious, and exalted mind
p. 287 U'WOOD 84.9	163 She had a mind as calme, as she was faire;
p. 295 UNDERWOOD 90	6 A quiet mind; free powers; and body sound;
p. 315 HORACE 2	238 His better'd mind seekes wealth, and friendship: than
p. 317 HORACE 2	257 In at the eare, doe stirre the mind more slow
p. 329 HORACE 2	504 The docile mind may soone thy precepts know,
p. 329 HORACE 2	522 The hand, and mind would, but it will resound
p. 331 HORACE 2	547 And, of your selfe too, understand; yet mind
p. 331 HORACE 2	562 To bettring of the mind of man, in ought,
p. 333 HORACE 2	596 Or, of the things, that ne're came in my mind,
p. 333 HORACE 2	622 For praises, where the mind conceales a foxe.
p. 416 UNGATHERED 45	4 my mind vnto you,

minde   frequency: 9   relative frequency: 0.00013

p. 79 EPIGRAMS 125	4 Restored in thy body, and thy minde!
p. 99 FOREST 3	102 A body sound, with sounder minde;
p. 109 FOREST 11	9 At th'eye and eare (the ports vnto the minde)
p. 110 FOREST 11	29 Doe seuerall passions <still> inuade the minde,
p. 116 FOREST 13	2 Of any good minde, now: There are so few.
p. 120 FOREST 13	124 Because nor it can change, nor such a minde.
p. 362 UNGATHERED 2	2 And see a minde attir'd in perfect straines;
p. 392 UNGATHERED 26	67 Of Shakespeares minde, and manners brightly shines
p. 417 UNGATHERED 45	40 hir minde is eased.

mindes   frequency: 3   relative frequency: 0.00004

| p. 75 EPIGRAMS 116 | 11 That bloud not mindes, but mindes did bloud adorne: |
| p. 110 FOREST 11 | 50 The soft, and sweetest mindes |

minds   frequency: 10   relative frequency: 0.00014
See also "mindes."

p. 65 EPIGRAMS 101	23 Of which wee'll speake our minds, amidst our meate;
p. 129 UNDERWOOD 1.2	13 As minds ill bent
p. 156 UNDERWOOD 13	122 And my minds motion not? or have I none?
p. 174 UNDERWOOD 23	16 Minds that are great and free,
p. 217 UNDERWOOD 46	20 Of worthiest knowledge, that can take mens minds.
p. 246 UNDERWOOD 70	106 That knits brave minds, and manners, more then blood.
p. 311 HORACE 2	142 To worke the hearers minds, still, to their plight.
p. 313 HORACE 2	157 Her truch-man, she reports the minds each throw.
p. 327 HORACE 2	473 And care of getting, thus, our minds hath stain'd,
p. 329 HORACE 2	495 Their minds to Warres, with rimes they did rehearse;

mine   frequency: 35   relative frequency: 0.00050
See also "myne."

| p. 27 EPIGRAMS 3 | 3 Vse mine so, too: I giue thee leaue. But craue |
| p. 32 EPIGRAMS 18 | 5 And mine come nothing like. I hope so. Yet, |

mine (cont.)
```
p.   32  EPIGRAMS   18       6 As theirs did with thee, mine might credit get:
p.   37  EPIGRAMS   33       6 Who wets my graue, can be no friend of mine.
p.   38  EPIGRAMS   36       4 Thou flattered'st thine, mine cannot flatter'd
                               bee.
p.   44  EPIGRAMS   55       7 What fate is mine, that so it selfe bereaues?
p.   48  EPIGRAMS   65       6 And, as thou'hast mine, his houres, and youth
                               abuse.
p.   50  EPIGRAMS   71       1 To plucke downe mine, POLL sets vp new wits
                               still,
p.   65  EPIGRAMS  101      30 Which is the Mermaids, now, but shall be mine:
p.   67  EPIGRAMS  103       9 Forgiue me then, if mine but say you are
p.   95  FOREST     2      64 That is his Lordships, shall be also mine.
p.   95  FOREST     2      74 As if thou, then, wert mine, or I raign'd here:
p.  106  FOREST     9       2 And I will pledge with mine;
p.  116  FOREST    12      92 And your braue friend, and mine so well did loue.
p.  145  UNDERWOOD   4     12 Mine owne enough betray me.
p.  150  UNDERWOOD  10      8 On all mens Fruit, and flowers, as well as mine.
p.  156  UNDERWOOD  13    114 I have the lyst of mine owne faults to know,
p.  159  UNDERWOOD  14     20 And mine not least) I have too oft preferr'd
p.  174  UNDERWOOD  22     32 To light upon a Love of mine.
p.  182  UNDERWOOD  28      8 Both braines and hearts; and mine now best doe
                               know it:
p.  205  UNDERWOOD  43     63 To redeeme mine, I had sent in; Enough,
p.  211  UNDERWOOD  43    196 Losse, remaines yet, as unrepair'd as mine.
p.  219  UNDERWOOD  47     56 Well, with mine owne fraile Pitcher, what to doe
p.  220  UNDERWOOD  47     74 I would call mine, to which not many Staires
p.  223  UNDERWOOD  49     26 For bawdry, 'tis her language, and not mine.
p.  255  UNDERWOOD  75     98 That Mine of Wisdome, and of Counsells deep,
p.  283  U'WOOD  84.9      26 I summe up mine owne breaking, and wish all.
p.  293  UNDERWOOD  86     34 Flow my thin teares, downe these pale cheeks of
                               mine?
p.  331  HORACE     2     577 And, to your Fathers, and to mine; though 't be
p.  386  UNGATHERED 21      8 This thy worke forth: that iudgment mine
                               commends.
p.  388  UNGATHERED 23      3 Who hadst before wrought in rich Homers Mine?
p.  396  UNGATHERED 30      5 Thy Muse, and mine, as they expect. 'Tis true:
p.  398  UNGATHERED 30     77 I feele it by mine owne, that ouer flow,
p.  398  UNGATHERED 30     82 And with their grassie greene restor'd mine eyes.
p.  415  UNGATHERED 42     12 Now, for mine owne part, and it is but due,
```

mineruas   frequency: 1   relative frequency: 0.00001
```
p.  397  UNGATHERED 30     33 And looking vp, I saw Mineruas fowle,
```

minerva   frequency: 3   relative frequency: 0.00004
See also "mynerva."
```
p.  137  UNDERWOOD 2.5     54 And Minerva, when she talkes.
p.  203  UNDERWOOD  43     12 By Jove to have Minerva for thy Bride,
p.  208  UNDERWOOD  43    109 Thou woo Minerva! or to wit aspire!
```

minervaes   frequency: 1   relative frequency: 0.00001
```
p.   61  EPIGRAMS   95     16 MINERVAES loome was neuer richer spred.
```

minerva's   frequency: 2   relative frequency: 0.00002
See also "mineruas," "minervaes."
```
p.  141  UNDERWOOD 2.9     15 Venus, and Minerva's eyes,
p.  233  UNDERWOOD  60      4 Minerva's and the Muses care!
```

mines   frequency: 1   relative frequency: 0.00001
```
p.  161  UNDERWOOD  14     76 In the same Mines of knowledge; and thence
                               brought
```

mingle   frequency: 1   relative frequency: 0.00001
```
p.  240  UNDERWOOD  67     41 Doe mingle in a shout,
```

ministry   frequency: 1   relative frequency: 0.00001
```
p.  410  UNGATHERED 39      6 Nor Degradation from the Ministry,
```

minos   frequency: 1   relative frequency: 0.00001
```
p.   89  EPIGRAMS  133    189 Who kept an ale-house; with my little MINOS,
```

mint   frequency: 2   relative frequency: 0.00002
```
p.  415  UNGATHERED 42     20 Office of Wit, a Mint, and (this is true)
p.  415  UNGATHERED 42     28 Yo'have all the Mysteries of Wits new Mint,
```

minute   frequency: 1   relative frequency: 0.00001
```
p.  197  UNDERWOOD  40      2 Till the sower Minute comes of taking leave,
```

minutes   frequency: 1   relative frequency: 0.00001
```
p.  205  UNDERWOOD  43     56 Not ravish'd all hence in a minutes rage.
```

mira   frequency: 3   relative frequency: 0.00004
    p. 264 UNDERWOOD 79   18 9. See where he walkes <10> with MIRA by his side.

    p. 264 UNDERWOOD 79   24 Nym. Of brightest MIRA, doe we raise our
                             Song,
    p. 264 UNDERWOOD 79   32 Nymp. Of brightest MIRA, is our Song; the
                             grace

miracle   frequency: 3   relative frequency: 0.00004
    p. 101 FOREST 4   60 There should a miracle be wrought.
    p. 223 UNDERWOOD 49   41 And practise for a Miracle: take heed
    p. 405 UNGATHERED 34   89 Of thy dead Standards: or (wth miracle) see

miracles   frequency: 1   relative frequency: 0.00001
    p. 73 EPIGRAMS 114   1 I must beleeue some miracles still bee,

mirkins   frequency: 1   relative frequency: 0.00001
    p. 417 UNGATHERED 45   15 morts, and mirkins that wagg all,

mirror   frequency: 1   relative frequency: 0.00001
    See also "mirrour."
    p. 117 FOREST 13   43 My mirror is more subtile, cleere, refin'd,

mirrour   frequency: 2   relative frequency: 0.00002
    p. 255 UNDERWOOD 75   80 They are th'exampled Paire, and mirrour of their
                             kind.
    p. 414 UNGATHERED 41   44 And art the spotlesse Mirrour to Mans eyes.

mirth   frequency: 8   relative frequency: 0.00011
    p. 74 EPIGRAMS 115   14 Giue euery one his dose of mirth: and watches
    p. 82 EPIGRAMS 130   6 Doth sweeten mirth, and heighten pietie,
    p. 98 FOREST 3   49 And fills thy open hall with mirth, and cheere,
    p. 197 UNDERWOOD 40   18 As neither wine doe rack it out, or mirth.
    p. 231 UNDERWOOD 57   17 Mirth, fooling, nor wit,
    p. 249 UNDERWOOD 72   11 Three Kingdomes Mirth, in light, and aerie man,
    p. 398 UNGATHERED 30   84 Of thy strange Moon-Calfe, both thy straine of
                             mirth,
    p. 417 UNGATHERED 45   17 And as either newes or mirth

mirthfull   frequency: 1   relative frequency: 0.00001
    p. 65 EPIGRAMS 101   40 That shall be vtter'd at our mirthfull boord,

mis-apply   frequency: 1   relative frequency: 0.00001
    p. 180 UNDERWOOD 26   11 Which in the taking if you mis-apply,

mis-call't   frequency: 1   relative frequency: 0.00001
    p. 79 EPIGRAMS 125   9 Which (would the world not mis-call't flatterie)

misapply. See "mis-apply."

miscall. See "mis-call't."

miscalled. See "misse-call'd."

mischief. See "mischife."

mischiefes   frequency: 2   relative frequency: 0.00002
    p. 212 UNDERWOOD 43   204 On both sides doe your mischiefes with delight;
    p. 335 HORACE 2   641 These trifles into serious mischiefes lead

mischiefs. See "mischiefes."

mischife   frequency: 1   relative frequency: 0.00001
    p. 108 FOREST 10A   5 The skilfull mischife of a rovinge Eye

miserie   frequency: 2   relative frequency: 0.00002
    p. 41 EPIGRAMS 45   8 And, if no other miserie, yet age?
    p. 311 HORACE 2   137 That are Spectators, with their miserie,

miseries   frequency: 5   relative frequency: 0.00007
    p. 70 EPIGRAMS 109   5 Thou are not one, seek'st miseries with hope,
    p. 243 UNDERWOOD 70   19 As, could they but lifes miseries fore-see,
    p. 244 UNDERWOOD 70   55 Produce thy masse of miseries on the Stage,
    p. 363 UNGATHERED 3   3 Warres grea<t>est woes, and miseries increase,
    p. 398 UNGATHERED 30   75 The miseries of Margaret the Queene

misery. See "miserie."

misfortune   frequency: 1   relative frequency: 0.00001
    p. 102 FOREST 4   62 To age, misfortune, sicknesse, griefe:

miss. See "misse."

misse   frequency: 5   relative frequency: 0.00007
    p.   55 EPIGRAMS 85   8 Which if they misse, they yet should re-aduance
    p. 137 UNDERWOOD 2.6   1 Charis, guesse, and doe not misse,
    p. 182 UNDERWOOD 27   29 Have all these done (and yet I misse
    p. 285 U'WOOD 84.9   98 Put black, and mourning on? and say you misse
    p. 288 U'WOOD 84.9   185 Her broken sighes did never misse whole sense:

misse-call'd   frequency: 1   relative frequency: 0.00001
    p.   69 EPIGRAMS 108   2 Such as are misse-call'd Captaynes, and wrong
                               you;

missed. See "mist."

mist   frequency: 1   relative frequency: 0.00001
    p.   66 EPIGRAMS 102   5 Nor could the age haue mist thee, in this strife

mistake   frequency: 3   relative frequency: 0.00004
    p. 101 FOREST 4   57 Else, I my state should much mistake,
    p. 170 UNDERWOOD 18   15 Oh how a Lover may mistake! to thinke,
    p. 339 HORACE 1   60 ... . mistake,

mistaking   frequency: 1   relative frequency: 0.00001
    p. 144 UNDERWOOD 3   24 Mistaking earth for heaven.

misterie   frequency: 2   relative frequency: 0.00002
    p. 156 UNDERWOOD 13   97 Sure there is Misterie in it, I not know,
    p. 209 UNDERWOOD 43   144 When Venus there maintain'd the Misterie.

misteryes   frequency: 1   relative frequency: 0.00001
    p. 404 UNGATHERED 34   46 Eyes yt can pierce into ye Misteryes

mistook. See "mistocke."

mistooke   frequency: 1   relative frequency: 0.00001
    p. 402 UNGATHERED 34   8 With mistooke Names out of Vitruvius!

mistres   frequency: 2   relative frequency: 0.00002
    p. 189 UNDERWOOD 36   4+ MISTRES.
    p. 293 UNDERWOOD 87   5 LYD. Whilst Horace lov'd no Mistres more,

mistress. See "mistres," "mistresse," "mistris," "mrs."

mistresse   frequency: 4   relative frequency: 0.00005
    p. 165 UNDERWOOD 15   95 Lasse must not be thought on then Mistresse: or,
    p. 165 UNDERWOOD 15   97 Whom no great Mistresse hath as yet infam'd,
    p. 175 UNDERWOOD 24   2 The Mistresse of Mans life, grave Historie,
    p. 287 U'WOOD 84.9   175 A solemne Mistresse, and so good a Friend,

mistris   frequency: 11   relative frequency: 0.00015
    p.   51 EPIGRAMS 73   16 Item, your mistris anagram, i' your hilt.
    p.   51 EPIGRAMS 73   17 Item, your owne, sew'd in your mistris smock.
    p.   57 EPIGRAMS 90   2 Vnworthy such a mistris, such a schoole,
    p. 104 FOREST 7   3 So court a mistris, shee denyes you;
    p. 191 UNDERWOOD 38   9 Offended Mistris, you are yet so faire,
    p. 192 UNDERWOOD 38   31 Thinke it was frailtie, Mistris, thinke me man,
    p. 194 UNDERWOOD 38   105 Then Mistris, here, here let your rigour end,
    p. 198 UNDERWOOD 40   25 No, Mistris, no, the open merrie Man
    p. 199 UNDERWOOD 41   2 Heare, Mistris, your departing servant tell
    p. 199 UNDERWOOD 41   14 How shall I doe, sweet Mistris, for my heart?
    p. 364 UNGATHERED 4   7 Proue of his Mistris Feature,

mists   frequency: 1   relative frequency: 0.00001
    p.   87 EPIGRAMS 133   130 These be the cause of those thicke frequent mists

misus'd   frequency: 1   relative frequency: 0.00001
    p. 127 UNDERWOOD 1.1   6 By sinne, and Sathan; and my flesh misus'd,

mite   frequency: 1   relative frequency: 0.00001
    p. 229 UNDERWOOD 54   10 Within the ballance; and not want a mite;

mix. See "mixe."

mix'd   frequency: 2   relative frequency: 0.00002
    p. 319 HORACE 2   302 Clowne, Towns-man, base, and noble, mix'd, to
                               judge?
    p. 329 HORACE 2   515 Sweet mix'd with sowre, to his Reader, so

mixe   frequency: 4   relative frequency: 0.00005
    p. 107 FOREST 10   22 HERMES, the cheater, shall not mixe with vs,
    p. 143 UNDERWOOD 3   9 Mixe then your Notes, that we may prove
    p. 190 UNDERWOOD 37   12 In letters, that mixe spirits, thus to weave.
    p. 391 UNGATHERED 26   25 That I not mixe thee so, my braine excuses;

mixed   frequency: 1   relative frequency: 0.00001
    See also "mix'd," "mixt."
    p. 286 U'WOOD 84.9   138 What love with mercy mixed doth appeare?

mixeth   frequency: 1   relative frequency: 0.00001
    p. 315 HORACE 2   215 And so well faines, so mixeth cunningly

mixing   frequency: 1   relative frequency: 0.00001
    p. 327 HORACE 2   478 Or mixing sweet, and fit, teach life the right.

mixt   frequency: 5   relative frequency: 0.00007
    p. 98 FOREST 3   57 Sit mixt with losse of state, or reuerence.
    p. 118 FOREST 13   48 For such a lot! that mixt you with a state
    p. 162 UNDERWOOD 15   25 Be honour is so mixt) by such as would,
    p. 163 UNDERWOOD 15   43 As they are made! Pride, and stiffe Clownage
                              mixt
    p. 365 UNGATHERED 5   15 But mixt with sound, transcending

mixtures   frequency: 2   relative frequency: 0.00002
    p. 156 UNDERWOOD 13   110 That with these mixtures we put out her light.
    p. 415 UNGATHERED 42   29 The valuations, mixtures, and the same

moan.   See "mone."

moath   frequency: 1   relative frequency: 0.00001
    p. 174 UNDERWOOD 23   5 It is the common Moath,

moathes   frequency: 1   relative frequency: 0.00001
    p. 371 UNGATHERED 8   16 Or moathes shall eate, what all these Fooles
                              admire.

mocion   frequency: 1   relative frequency: 0.00001
    p. 361 UNGATHERED 1   23 which thoughts being circumvol<v>d in gyerlyk
                              mocion

mock'd   frequency: 2   relative frequency: 0.00002
    p. 132 UNDERWOOD 2.2   28 Mock'd of all: and call'd of one
    p. 335 HORACE 2   642 The man once mock'd, and suffer'd wrong to tread.

mocks   frequency: 2   relative frequency: 0.00002
    p. 216 UNDERWOOD 44   100 Cover'd with Tissue, whose prosperitie mocks
    p. 333 HORACE 2   621 Looke through him, and be sure, you take not
                              mocks

model. See "modell."

modell   frequency: 1   relative frequency: 0.00001
    p. 379 UNGATHERED 12   5 And that, say Philosophers, is the best modell.

moderately   frequency: 1   relative frequency: 0.00001
    p. 65 EPIGRAMS 101   35 Of this we will sup free, but moderately,

modern. See "moderne."

moderne   frequency: 2   relative frequency: 0.00002
    p. 72 EPIGRAMS 111   2 What th'antique souldiers were, the moderne bee?
    p. 214 UNDERWOOD 44   36 And the Greeke Discipline (with the moderne)
                              shed

modes. See "moodes."

modest   frequency: 4   relative frequency: 0.00005
    p. 59 EPIGRAMS 92   39 Others more modest, but contemne vs too,
    p. 161 UNDERWOOD 14   86 You both are modest. So am I. Farewell.
    p. 311 HORACE 2   130 Perversly modest, had I rather owe
    p. 319 HORACE 2   294 Chaste, thriftie, modest folke, that came to
                              view.

modestie   frequency: 6   relative frequency: 0.00008
 **p. 114 PANEGYRE   55 To her great sister: saue that modestie,
    p. 31 EPIGRAMS 14   11 Pardon free truth, and let thy modestie,
    p. 38 EPIGRAMS 38   8 I'le loose my modestie, and tell your name.
    p. 251 UNDERWOOD 74   21 With love, to heare your modestie relate
    p. 254 UNDERWOOD 75   48 With Modestie so crown'd, and Adoration seene.

modestie (cont.)
    p. 313 HORACE 2   193 From whence thy Modestie, or Poemes law

modestly   frequency: 3   relative frequency: 0.00004
    p. 46 EPIGRAMS 60   3 Or, if shee would but modestly haue prais'd
    p. 72 EPIGRAMS 112   11 I modestly quit that, and thinke to write,
    p. 309 HORACE 2   73 And give, being taken modestly, this leave,

modesty   frequency: 1   relative frequency: 0.00001
See also "modestie."
    p. 371 UNGATHERED 9   7 Taught Pallas language; Cynthia modesty;

modet   frequency: 1   relative frequency: 0.00001
    p. 164 UNDERWOOD 15   80 Where Pittes, or Wright, or Modet would not
        venter,

moist   frequency: 1   relative frequency: 0.00001
    p. 42 EPIGRAMS 50   2 Or fumie clysters, thy moist lungs to bake:

molest   frequency: 3   relative frequency: 0.00004
    p. 104 FOREST 8   1 Why, Disease, dost thou molest
    p. 106 FOREST 8   47 In thy iustice to molest
    p. 219 UNDERWOOD 47   55 Of earthen Jarres, there may molest me too:

mon. See "mone."

monarch   frequency: 1   relative frequency: 0.00001
    p. 160 UNDERWOOD 14   65 Monarch in Letters! 'Mongst thy Titles showne

monarchs   frequency: 3   relative frequency: 0.00004
    p. 259 UNDERWOOD 76   2 To th'best of Monarchs, Masters, Men,
    p. 261 UNDERWOOD 77   21 And mightiest Monarchs feele what large increase
    p. 263 UNDERWOOD 79   7 We sing the best of Monarchs, Masters, Men;

mone   frequency: 3   relative frequency: 0.00004
    p. 77 EPIGRAMS 120   13 And did act (what now we mone)
    p. 311 HORACE 2   144 To laughter; so they grieve with those that mone.
    p. 367 UNGATHERED 6   38 Salute old Mone,   .

moneths   frequency: 1   relative frequency: 0.00001
    p. 33 EPIGRAMS 22   5 At sixe moneths end, shee parted hence

money   frequency: 13   relative frequency: 0.00018
    p. 29 EPIGRAMS 8   3 But, for this money was a courtier found,
    p. 29 EPIGRAMS 8   5 Rob'd both of money, and the lawes reliefe,
    p. 30 EPIGRAMS 12   8 Shee must haue money: he returnes, god payes.
    p. 30 EPIGRAMS 12   12 At dice his borrow'd money: which, god payes.
    p. 65 EPIGRAMS 101   14 Is not to be despair'd of, for our money;
    p. 99 FOREST 3   76 Then either money, warre, or death:
    p. 157 UNDERWOOD 13   134 Alone in money, but in manners too.
    p. 165 UNDERWOOD 15   102 For man to spend his money on? his wit?
    p. 216 UNDERWOOD 45   14 No piece of money, but you know, or make
    p. 231 UNDERWOOD 57   21 If there be no money;
    p. 305 HORACE 2   26 What's this? if he whose money hireth thee
    p. 315 HORACE 2   235 Of money, haughtie, to desire soon mov'd,
    p. 329 HORACE 2   517 This booke will get the Sosii money; This

money-brokers   frequency: 2   relative frequency: 0.00002
    p. 155 UNDERWOOD 13   62 Like Money-brokers, after Names, and hire
    p. 386 UNGATHERED 21   10 Or, like our Money-Brokers, take vp names

money-gett   frequency: 1   relative frequency: 0.00001
    p. 404 UNGATHERED 34   52 This is ye money-gett, Mechanick Age!

moneyes   frequency: 1   relative frequency: 0.00001
    p. 85 EPIGRAMS 133   32 Of those, that put out moneyes, on returne

moneys   frequency: 3   relative frequency: 0.00004
See also "moneyes," "money's," "monyes."
    p. 204 UNDERWOOD 43   45 Adulterate moneys, such as might not goe:
    p. 215 UNDERWOOD 44   77 That turnes us so much moneys, at which rate
    p. 291 UNDERWOOD 85   69 'Gainst th'Ides, his moneys he gets in with
        paine;

money's   frequency: 1   relative frequency: 0.00001
    p. 333 HORACE 2   600 Or great in money's out at use, command

mongrel. See "mungrel," "mvng'," "mvngril."

mongst   frequency: 1   relative frequency: 0.00001
    p. 361 UNGATHERED 1   6 that mongst so manie plants transplanted hether,

'mongst   frequency: 8   relative frequency: 0.00011
    p. 61 EPIGRAMS 94   14 Be of the best: and 'mongst those, best are you.
    p. 80 EPIGRAMS 126   2 'Mongst Hampton shades, and PHOEBVS groue
                              of bayes,
    p. 97 FOREST 3   16 'Mongst loughing heards, and solide hoofes:
    p. 136 UNDERWOOD 2.5   7 'Mongst my Muses finding me,
    p. 160 UNDERWOOD 14   65 Monarch in Letters! 'Mongst thy Titles showne
    p. 220 UNDERWOOD 47   63 'Mongst which, if I have any friendships sent,
    p. 233 UNDERWOOD 59   21 Who durst live great, 'mongst all the colds, and
                              heates,
    p. 258 UNDERWOOD 75   179 But like an Arme of Eminence, 'mongst them,

'mong'st   frequency: 1   relative frequency: 0.00001
    p. 88 EPIGRAMS 133   155 But 'mong'st these Tiberts, who do'you thinke
                              there was?

moniment   frequency: 1   relative frequency: 0.00001
    p. 391 UNGATHERED 26   22 Thou art a Moniment, without a tombe,

monogram   frequency: 1   relative frequency: 0.00001
    p. 227 UNDERWOOD 52   11 To be describ'd <but> by a Monogram,

monsieur. See "movnsievr."

monsieur's. See "movnsievrs."

monster   frequency: 3   relative frequency: 0.00004
    p. 85 EPIGRAMS 133   61 In the first lawes appear'd that vgly monster,
    p. 204 UNDERWOOD 43   32 And so some goodlier monster had begot:
    p. 398 UNGATHERED 30   87 Empusa, Lamia, or some Monster, more

monsters   frequency: 1   relative frequency: 0.00001
    p. 164 UNDERWOOD 15   59 O, these so ignorant Monsters! light, as proud,

monteagle. See "movnteagle."

montgomery   frequency: 1   relative frequency: 0.00001
    p. 67 EPIGRAMS 104   t1 TO SVSAN COVNTESSE OF
                              MONTGOMERY.

month   frequency: 3   relative frequency: 0.00004
    p. 50 EPIGRAMS 87   2 HAZARD a month forsware his; and grew
                              drunke,
    p. 237 UNDERWOOD 65   4 What Month then May, was fitter to disclose
    p. 253 UNDERWOOD 75   26 The Month of youth, which calls all Creatures
                              forth

monthes   frequency: 2   relative frequency: 0.00002
    p. 379 UNGATHERED 12   16 In fiue monthes he went it, in fiue monthes he
                              pend it.

monthly   frequency: 1   relative frequency: 0.00001
    p. 56 EPIGRAMS 88   15 The new french-taylors motion, monthly made,

months. See "moneths," "monthes."

montioy   frequency: 1   relative frequency: 0.00001
    p. 367 UNGATHERED 6   50 (Charles Montioy) whose command

montrell   frequency: 2   relative frequency: 0.00002
    p. 374 UNGATHERED 10   13 Hee's carried 'twixt Montrell and Abbeuile.
    p. 380 UNGATHERED 12   53 In a Cart twixt Montrell and Abbeuile.

montreuil. See "montrell."

monument   frequency: 1   relative frequency: 0.00001
    See also "moniment."
    p. 387 UNGATHERED 22   7 I made my lyfe my monument, & yours:

monyes   frequency: 1   relative frequency: 0.00001
    p. 36 EPIGRAMS 31   2 His monyes trauaile for him, in and out:

mood   frequency: 1   relative frequency: 0.00001
    p. 40 EPIGRAMS 42   2 Th'obseruing neighbours no such mood can see.

moodes   frequency: 3   relative frequency: 0.00004
    p. 116 FOREST 12   91 Moodes, which the god-like SYDNEY oft did
                              proue,

moodes (cont.)
    p. 362 UNGATHERED 2   3 Not wearing moodes, as gallants doe a fashion,
    p. 395 UNGATHERED 29 15 Taught Lucan these true moodes! Replyes my
        sence

moods   frequency: 1   relative frequency: 0.00001
    See also "moodes."
    p. 112 FOREST 11   112 (To vertuous moods inclin'd)

moon. See "moone."

moon-calfe   frequency: 1   relative frequency: 0.00001
    p. 398 UNGATHERED 30 84 Of thy strange Moon-Calfe, both thy straine of
        mirth,

moone   frequency: 7   relative frequency: 0.00010
    p. 84 EPIGRAMS 133   29 It was the day, what time the powerfull Moone
    p. 136 UNDERWOOD 2.5   4 Then the various Moone the flood!
    p. 238 UNDERWOOD 65   9 And there to stand so. Hast now, envious Moone,
    p. 335 HORACE 2   647 According to the Moone. But, then the boyes
    p. 414 UNGATHERED 41 49 Thou Throne of glory, beauteous as the Moone,
    p. 417 UNGATHERED 45 12 The Moone comends hir
    p. 417 UNGATHERED 45 28 the Moone will beare it.

moones   frequency: 2   relative frequency: 0.00002
    p. 87 EPIGRAMS 133 103 But many Moones there shall not wane (quoth hee)
    p. 119 FOREST 13   102 Before the moones haue fill'd their tripple
        trine,

moons. See "halfe-moones," "moones."

moore-fields   frequency: 1   relative frequency: 0.00001
    p. 202 UNDERWOOD 42 73 Or in Moore-fields, this other night! sings one,

moorfields. See "moore-fields."

moral. See "morall."

morall   frequency: 1   relative frequency: 0.00001
    p. 405 UNGATHERED 34 83 Vnder ye Morall? shewe he had a pate

morauian   frequency: 1   relative frequency: 0.00001
    p. 69 EPIGRAMS 107   8 Of your Morauian horse, Venetian bull.

moravian. See "morauian."

more   frequency: 246   relative frequency: 0.00356
  *p. 492 TO HIMSELF   2 And the more lothsome age:
  **p. 114 PANEGYRE   48 His gladding looke, now long'd to see it more.
  **p. 115 PANEGYRE   68 To vnderstand the more, the more were rapt.
  **p. 115 PANEGYRE   80 "To rule like Heauen; and haue no more, their
        owne,
  **p. 115 PANEGYRE   87 "Betraid to fame, should take more care, and
        feare
  **p. 116 PANEGYRE   107 "All this she told, and more, with bleeding eyes;
  **p. 116 PANEGYRE   115 And that no wretch was more vnblest then he,
  **p. 116 PANEGYRE   125 That kings, by their example, more doe sway
  **p. 116 PANEGYRE   126 Then by their power; and men doe more obay
  **p. 117 PANEGYRE   156 Neuer had land more reason to reioyce.
  p. 28 EPIGRAMS 4   4 And gaue thee both, to shew they could no more.
  p. 28 EPIGRAMS 5   2 Or celebrated with more truth of state?
  p. 31 EPIGRAMS 14   5 Then thee the age sees not that thing more graue,
  p. 31 EPIGRAMS 14   6 More high, more holy, that shee more would craue.
  p. 32 EPIGRAMS 16   2 Thou more; that with it euery day, dar'st iest
  p. 32 EPIGRAMS 16   10 He that dares damne himselfe, dares more then
        fight.
  p. 35 EPIGRAMS 26   1 Then his chast wife, though BEAST now know
        no more,
  p. 36 EPIGRAMS 28   19 Nay more, for greatnesse sake, he will be one
  p. 37 EPIGRAMS 33   1 Ile not offend thee with a vaine teare more,
  p. 37 EPIGRAMS 35   2 A Prince, that rules by'example, more than sway?
  p. 37 EPIGRAMS 35   3 Whose manners draw, more than thy powers
        constraine.
  p. 38 EPIGRAMS 35   8 And than in them, how could we know god more?
  p. 39 EPIGRAMS 41   2 And get more gold, then all the colledge can:
  p. 40 EPIGRAMS 42   6 No more would IONE he should. GILES
        riseth early,
  p. 44 EPIGRAMS 55   6 And giuing largely to me, more thou tak'st.
  p. 48 EPIGRAMS 65   5 Be thy next masters more vnluckie Muse,
  p. 49 EPIGRAMS 66   7 Which deed I know not, whether were more high,

more (cont.)

p.	49 EPIGRAMS 66	8	Or thou more happie, it to iustifie
p.	50 EPIGRAMS 70	7	Then, since we (more then many) these truths know:
p.	51 EPIGRAMS 73	19	In most vile verses, and cost me more paine,
p.	51 EPIGRAMS 73	21	Fortie things more, deare GRAND, which you know true,
p.	52 EPIGRAMS 76	6	Of greatest bloud, and yet more good then great;
p.	53 EPIGRAMS 77	4	I'am more asham'd to haue thee thought my foe.
p.	57 EPIGRAMS 89	9	Who both their graces in thy selfe hast more
p.	58 EPIGRAMS 91	18	Who more should seeke mens reuerence, then feare.
p.	59 EPIGRAMS 92	39	Others more modest, but contemne vs too,
p.	60 EPIGRAMS 94	10	But, when they heard it tax'd, tooke more offence.
p.	61 EPIGRAMS 95	9	To thine owne proper I ascribe then more;
p.	61 EPIGRAMS 95	23	No more then SALVST in the Romane state!
p.	62 EPIGRAMS 97	3	But one more rare, and in the case so new:
p.	63 EPIGRAMS 97	17	Since he was gone, more then the one he weares.
p.	63 EPIGRAMS 98	2	And I know nothing more thou hast to doo.
p.	63 EPIGRAMS 98	10	And studie conscience, more then thou would'st fame.
p.	64 EPIGRAMS 99	12	Thy fact is more: let truth encourage thee.
p.	65 EPIGRAMS 101	17	Ile tell you of more, and lye, so you will come:
p.	66 EPIGRAMS 102	19	Thou must draw more: and they, that hope to see
p.	67 EPIGRAMS 103	14	Becomes none more then you, who need it least.
p.	67 EPIGRAMS 104	9	Or, more then borne for the comparison
p.	68 EPIGRAMS 105	8	Would call you more then CERES, if not that:
p.	68 EPIGRAMS 107	4	Not that I loue it, more, then I will you.
p.	69 EPIGRAMS 107	16	For which there must more sea, and land be leap'd,
p.	70 EPIGRAMS 108	8	No more, then I dare now doe, with my pen.
p.	71 EPIGRAMS 110	22	His life, but makes, that he can dye no more.
p.	72 EPIGRAMS 111	6	More, then to varie what our elders knew:
p.	74 EPIGRAMS 115	25	And, shifting of it's faces, doth play more
p.	76 EPIGRAMS 119	5	With me can merit more, then that good man,
p.	79 EPIGRAMS 124	6	To more vertue, then doth liue.
p.	80 EPIGRAMS 126	5	Said I wrong'd him, and (which was more) his loue.
p.	82 EPIGRAMS 130	13	Mou'd by her order, and the ninth more high,
p.	82 EPIGRAMS 131	4	The learn'd haue no more priuiledge, then the lay.
p.	83 EPIGRAMS 132	14	No more, those mayden glories shee hath lost.
p.	84 EPIGRAMS 133	1	No more let Greece her bolder fables tell
p.	84 EPIGRAMS 133	12	And in it, two more horride knaues, then CHARON.
p.	85 EPIGRAMS 133	40	Or his to Antwerpe. Therefore, once more, list ho'.
p.	85 EPIGRAMS 133	56	Still, with thy former labours; yet, once more,
p.	87 EPIGRAMS 133	116	Neuer did bottome more betray her burden;
p.	87 EPIGRAMS 133	126	White, black, blew, greene, and in more formes out-started,
p.	95 FOREST 2	57	But what can this (more then expresse their loue)
p.	97 FOREST 3	30	More for thy exercise, then fare;
p.	99 FOREST 3	77	Let him, then hardest sires, more disinherit,
p.	99 FOREST 3	85	Let thousands more goe flatter vice, and winne,
p.	101 FOREST 4	40	More hatred, then thou hast to mee.
p.	103 FOREST 6	11	Adde a thousand, and so more:
p.	105 FOREST 8	12	And this age will build no more:
p.	105 FOREST 8	20	And haue more diseases made.
p.	105 FOREST 8	34	More then citizens dare lend
p.	107 FOREST 10	3	For the more countenance to my actiue Muse?
p.	107 FOREST 10	5	With his old earthly labours. T<o>'exact more,
p.	110 FOREST 11	45	That is an essence, farre more gentle, softer,
p.	111 FOREST 11	57	A forme more fresh, then are the Eden bowers,
p.	111 FOREST 11	75	And yet (in this t<o>'expresse our selues more cleare)
p.	112 FOREST 11	88	Is more crowne-worthy still,
p.	112 FOREST 11	111	Much more a noble, and right generous mind
p.	114 FOREST 12	21	The truth of times) was once of more esteeme,
p.	114 FOREST 12	37	Beautie, I know, is good, and bloud is more;
p.	117 FOREST 13	31	And so doe many more. All which can call
p.	117 FOREST 13	43	My mirror is more subtile, cleere, refin'd,
p.	117 FOREST 13	46	As bloud, and match. Wherein, how more then much
p.	121 FOREST 14	36	And studie more:
p.	121 FOREST 14	55	Be more, and long desir'd:
p.	127 UNDERWOOD 1.1	16	To thee more sweet?
p.	129 UNDERWOOD 1.2	17	Who more can crave
p.	133 UNDERWOOD 2.3	4	Eyes and limbes; to hurt me more.
p.	136 UNDERWOOD 2.5	3	And doe governe more my blood,
p.	137 UNDERWOOD 2.5	27	Rip'ned with a breath more sweet,

more (cont.)

p. 137	UNDERWOOD 2.5	50	Something more then thou hast spi'd.
p. 138	UNDERWOOD 2.6	14	You were more the eye, and talke
p. 139	UNDERWOOD 2.7	7	Once more, and (faith) I will be gone,
p. 141	UNDERWOOD 2.9	13	Chestnut colour, or more slack
p. 142	UNDERWOOD 2.9	42	Shewing danger more then ire.
p. 145	UNDERWOOD 5	1	Men, if you love us, play no more
p. 145	UNDERWOOD 5	15	More pleasure while the thing he makes
p. 146	UNDERWOOD 6	21	Our pleasure; but preserves us more
p. 147	UNDERWOOD 7	21	And feare much more, that more of him be showne.
p. 148	UNDERWOOD 7	29	I'le tell no more, and yet I love,
p. 152	UNDERWOOD 12	30	And more, and more, I should have done,
p. 153	UNDERWOOD 13	21	The memorie delights him more, from whom
p. 153	UNDERWOOD 13	28	That they have more opprest me, then my want?
p. 154	UNDERWOOD 13	43	No more then he doth thanke, that will receive
p. 156	UNDERWOOD 13	96	And told of with more Licence then th'were done!
p. 156	UNDERWOOD 13	113	No more are these of us, let them then goe,
p. 157	UNDERWOOD 13	135	Yet we must more then move still, or goe on,
p. 158	UNDERWOOD 14	13	Then which there is not unto Studie'a more
p. 163	UNDERWOOD 15	36	But more licentious made, and desperate!
p. 163	UNDERWOOD 15	53	That all respect; She must lie downe: Nay more,
p. 166	UNDERWOOD 15	119	What reputation to beare one Glasse more?
p. 166	UNDERWOOD 15	127	More then themselves, or then our lives could take,
p. 166	UNDERWOOD 15	129	I'le bid thee looke no more, but flee, flee friend,
p. 166	UNDERWOOD 15	135	He that no more for Age, Cramps, Palsies, can
p. 167	UNDERWOOD 15	169	Boasters, and perjur'd, with the infinite more
p. 168	UNDERWOOD 15	179	That thou dost all things more for truth, then glory,
p. 168	UNDERWOOD 15	193	No more, then we should thinke a Lord had had
p. 168	UNDERWOOD 15	194	More honour in him, 'cause we'<h>ave knowne him mad:
p. 168	UNDERWOOD 16	2	And if I had no more to say,
p. 171	UNDERWOOD 19	15	I'le therefore aske no more, but bid you love;
p. 171	UNDERWOOD 20	4	No more, I am sorry for so fond cause, say,
p. 172	UNDERWOOD 20	22	Perjur'd! and painted! if she were no more --,
p. 177	UNDERWOOD 25	23	Of eyes more true,
p. 179	UNDERWOOD 25	52	Oft scape an Imputation, more through luck, then wit.
p. 180	UNDERWOOD 26	4	A gentler, and more agile hand, to tend
p. 180	UNDERWOOD 26	17	In one full Action; nor have you now more
p. 181	UNDERWOOD 26	21	Such thoughts wil make you more in love with truth.
p. 181	UNDERWOOD 27	12	Shine more, then she, the Stars among?
p. 185	UNDERWOOD 30	6	What is there more that can ennoble blood?
p. 186	UNDERWOOD 32	3	Without the pompe of Counsell; or more Aide,
p. 186	UNDERWOOD 33	2	The Seat made of a more then civill warre;
p. 188	UNDERWOOD 34	4	Of those that set by their false faces more
p. 188	UNDERWOOD 34	15	That heaven should make no more; or should amisse,
p. 189	UNDERWOOD 36	10	Who more they burne, they more desire,
p. 191	UNDERWOOD 38	29	And (stil'd your mercies Creature) will live more
p. 193	UNDERWOOD 38	70	And then his thunder frights more, then it kills.
p. 193	UNDERWOOD 38	73	And how more faire, and lovely lookes the world
p. 193	UNDERWOOD 38	92	Rather then once displease you more, to die
p. 193	UNDERWOOD 38	100	Of Contumelie, and urge a good man more
p. 194	UNDERWOOD 38	107	I will no more abuse my vowes to you,
p. 202	UNDERWOOD 42	88	More then of eithers manners, wit, or face!
p. 205	UNDERWOOD 43	50	With some more thrift, and more varietie:
p. 210	UNDERWOOD 43	154	Scap'd not his Justice any jot the more:
p. 210	UNDERWOOD 43	164	More then advanc'd the houses, and their rites?
p. 213	UNDERWOOD 44	9	They saw too store of feathers, and more may,
p. 213	UNDERWOOD 44	30	Would thinke no more of Vlushing, or the Brill:
p. 214	UNDERWOOD 44	48	More then the surfets, in thee, that day stood.
p. 214	UNDERWOOD 44	55	That keepe the warre, though now't be growne more tame,
p. 215	UNDERWOOD 44	71	More then to praise a Dog? or Horse? or speake
p. 217	UNDERWOOD 46	4	Whom Fortune aided lesse, or Vertue more.
p. 217	UNDERWOOD 46	12	More for thy Patronage, then for their Cause,
p. 217	UNDERWOOD 46	22	None Fortune aided lesse, or Vertue more.
p. 218	UNDERWOOD 47	5	I could say more of such, but that I flie
p. 218	UNDERWOOD 47	24	And know whose ignorance is more then theirs;
p. 219	UNDERWOOD 47	29	I studie other friendships, and more one,
p. 221	UNDERWOOD 48	27	And thinke thy streame more quicker
p. 222	UNDERWOOD 49	14	Doth labour with the Phrase more then the sense?
p. 223	UNDERWOOD 49	30	In Contract twice, what can shee perjure more?
p. 225	UNDERWOOD 51	12	Now with a Title more to the Degree;
p. 227	UNDERWOOD 52	20	A Poet hath no more but black and white,

more (cont.)

p. 229	UNDERWOOD 54	16	Lend me, deare Arthur, for a weeke five more,
p. 231	UNDERWOOD 56	30	And should grow rich, had I much more to pay.
p. 231	UNDERWOOD 57	13	And more is behind:
p. 235	UNDERWOOD 62	9	Nay, and in this, thou show'st to value more
p. 235	UNDERWOOD 63	4	Doth by his doubt, distrust his promise more.
p. 241	UNDERWOOD 69	7	His is more safe commoditie, or none:
p. 242	UNDERWOOD 69	22	More subtle workes, and finer pieces farre,
p. 246	UNDERWOOD 70	106	That knits brave minds, and manners, more then blood.
p. 249	UNDERWOOD 72	6	Repeating all Great Britain's joy, and more,
p. 252	UNDERWOOD 75	3	Thou canst not meet more Glory, on the way,
p. 254	UNDERWOOD 75	54	To make more cleare
p. 254	UNDERWOOD 75	59	The bright Brides paths, embelish'd more then thine
p. 256	UNDERWOOD 75	129	O happy bands! and thou more happy place,
p. 258	UNDERWOOD 75	187	Hee's Master of the Office; yet no more
p. 264	UNDERWOOD 79	22	And in the chase, more then SYLVANUS can,
p. 268	UNDERWOOD 82	14	Sate safe enough, but now secured more.
p. 269	UNDERWOOD 83	12	And e're I can aske more of her, shee's gone!
p. 274	U'WOOD 84.2	13	And tell thou, ALDE-LEGH, None can tell more true
p. 277	U'WOOD 84.4	4	And give you reasons more then one.
p. 283	U'WOOD 84.9	27	Thou hast no more blowes, Fate, to drive at one:
p. 284	U'WOOD 84.9	71	Nothing can more adorne it, then the seat
p. 284	U'WOOD 84.9	72	That she is in, or, make it more compleat?
p. 285	U'WOOD 84.9	109	Much more desir'd, and dearer then before,
p. 287	U'WOOD 84.9	158	As nature could not more increase the flood
p. 287	U'WOOD 84.9	180	She spent more time in teares her selfe to dresse
p. 290	UNDERWOOD 85	12	And sets more happy in the place:
p. 291	UNDERWOOD 85	49	Not Lucrine Oysters I could then more prize,
p. 291	UNDERWOOD 85	55	More sweet then Olives, that new gather'd be
p. 292	UNDERWOOD 86	9	More timely hie thee to the house,
p. 293	UNDERWOOD 87	3	His armes more acceptable free,
p. 293	UNDERWOOD 87	5	LYD. Whilst Horace lov'd no Mistres more,
p. 293	UNDERWOOD 87	8	The Roman Ilia was not more renown'd.
p. 295	UNDERWOOD 90	12	Will to bee, what thou art; and nothing more:
p. 307	HORACE 2	50	To forme a worke, I would no more desire
p. 317	HORACE 2	257	In at the eare, doe stirre the mind more slow
p. 317	HORACE 2	272	Have more or lesse then just five Acts: nor laid,
p. 319	HORACE 2	315	With lees of Wine. Next Eschylus, more late,
p. 321	HORACE 2	364	Receive, or give it an applause, the more.
p. 323	HORACE 2	378	More slow, and come more weightie to the eare:
p. 325	HORACE 2	411	Nor had our Italie more glorious bin
p. 327	HORACE 2	458	More strongly takes the people with delight,
p. 329	HORACE 2	535	Twice, or thrice good, I wonder: but am more
p. 331	HORACE 2	540	Will take you more, the neerer that you stand;
p. 333	HORACE 2	615	Cry, and doe more then the true Mourners: so
p. 335	HORACE 2	630	Then change; no word, or worke, more would he spend
p. 335	HORACE 2	668	Recall him yet, hee'ld be no more a man:
p. 350	HORACE 1	464	... . more thriving .....
p. 361	UNGATHERED 1	15	The seauen-fold flower of Arte (more rich then gold)
p. 364	UNGATHERED 5	1	Splendor! O more then mortall,
p. 365	UNGATHERED 5	6	As fire; and more delightfull
p. 367	UNGATHERED 6	52	And more hath wonne
p. 368	UNGATHERED 6	62	(But this more apt
p. 369	UNGATHERED 6	103	With more delight, and grace)
p. 371	UNGATHERED 8	8	They saw it halfe, damd thy whole play, and more;
p. 371	UNGATHERED 9	5	To fill an Epitaph. But she had more.
p. 378	UNGATHERED 11	85	Shewes he dares more then Paules Church-yard durst do.
p. 380	UNGATHERED 12	47	Nay more in his wardrobe, if you will laugh at a
p. 384	UNGATHERED 18	23	And when your yeares rise more, then would be told,
p. 386	UNGATHERED 21	2	May hurt them more with praise, then Foes with spight.
p. 386	UNGATHERED 21	12	By offring not more sureties, then inow,
p. 386	UNGATHERED 21	15	More of our writers would like thee, not swell
p. 388	UNGATHERED 23	6	To make thy honour, and our wealth the more!
p. 389	UNGATHERED 24	14	More then the Foster-father of this Child;
p. 391	UNGATHERED 26	14	Should praise a Matron. What could hurt her more?
p. 398	UNGATHERED 30	76	Of tender eyes will more be wept, then seene:
p. 398	UNGATHERED 30	87	Empusa, Lamia, or some Monster, more
p. 404	UNGATHERED 34	45	You aske noe more then certeyne politique Eyes,
p. 413	UNGATHERED 41	20	No faith's more firme, or flat, then where't doth creep.

more (cont.)
    p. 413 UNGATHERED 41   29 These Mysteries do point to three more great,
    p. 420 UNGATHERED 48   32 And once more stryke the eare of tyme wth those
                              ffresh straynes:
    p. 420 UNGATHERED 48   36 But vnto more dispayre to Imitate their sounde.
    p. 421 UNGATHERED 49   2 before, I wryte more verse, to bee more wyse.

morison   frequency: 3   relative frequency: 0.00004
    See also "morison's."
    p. 242 UNDERWOOD 70   t3 and Sir H. MORISON.
    p. 244 UNDERWOOD 70   43 Alas, but Morison fell young:
    p. 247 UNDERWOOD 70   116 But as a CARY, or a MORISON.

morison's   frequency: 1   relative frequency: 0.00001
    p. 245 UNDERWOOD 70   78 And thinke, nay know, thy Morison's not dead.

morn. See "morne."

morne   frequency: 4   relative frequency: 0.00005
    p. 72 EPIGRAMS 112   12 Next morne, an Ode: Thou mak'st a song ere
                              night.
    p. 96 FOREST 2   95 Each morne, and euen, they are taught to pray,
    p. 100 FOREST 4   2 That houre vpon my morne of age,
    p. 104 FOREST 7   7 At morne, and euen, shades are longest;

mornes   frequency: 1   relative frequency: 0.00001
    p. 193 UNDERWOOD 38   79 In darke, and sullen mornes, doe we not say,

morning   frequency: 6   relative frequency: 0.00008
    p. 52 EPIGRAMS 76   1 This morning, timely rapt with holy fire,
    p. 65 EPIGRAMS 101   41 Shall make vs sad next morning: or affright
    p. 137 UNDERWOOD 2.6   2 Since I drew a Morning kisse
    p. 147 UNDERWOOD 7   19 That were this morning blowne;
    p. 157 UNDERWOOD 13   126 Who was this Morning such a one, should be
    p. 414 UNGATHERED 41   50 The rosie Morning, or the rising Sun,

morning-star   frequency: 1   relative frequency: 0.00001
    p. 413 UNGATHERED 41   40 The Morning-star, whose light our Fal hath
                              stay'd.

morning-starre   frequency: 2   relative frequency: 0.00002
    p. 60 EPIGRAMS 94   2 Life of the Muses day, their morning-starre!
    p. 61 EPIGRAMS 94   16 The Muses euening, as their morning-starre.

mornings   frequency: 1   relative frequency: 0.00001
    p. 230 UNDERWOOD 56   22 A mornings, and at afternoones, to foole

morning's   frequency: 1   relative frequency: 0.00001
    p. 99 FOREST 3   100 Thy morning's, and thy euening's vow

morns. See "mornes."

morris. See "morrisse."

morrisse   frequency: 1   relative frequency: 0.00001
    p. 85 EPIGRAMS 133   36 Did dance the famous Morrisse, vnto Norwich)

morrow   frequency: 2   relative frequency: 0.00002
    See also "morrow'."
    p. 66 EPIGRAMS 102   10 To morrow vice, if shee giue better pay:
    p. 384 UNGATHERED 18   16 To rise wth eyther of you, on the morrow.

morrow'   frequency: 1   relative frequency: 0.00001
    p. 121 FOREST 14   50 To liue vntill to morrow' hath lost two dayes.

mortal. See "mortall."

mortalitie   frequency: 1   relative frequency: 0.00001
    p. 271 UNDERWOOD 83   67 'Twixt death and life! Where her mortalitie

mortality   frequency: 1   relative frequency: 0.00001
    See also "mortalitie."
    p. 384 UNGATHERED 18   22 Mortality, till you <im>mortall bee.

mortall   frequency: 2   relative frequency: 0.00002
    p. 309 HORACE 2   98 Being taught a better way. All mortall deeds
    p. 364 UNGATHERED 5   1 Splendor! O more then mortall,

morts   frequency: 1   relative frequency: 0.00001
    p. 417 UNGATHERED 45   15 morts, and mirkins that wagg all,

mosco   frequency: 1   relative frequency: 0.00001
      p.   37 EPIGRAMS 32   5 The cold of Mosco, and fat Irish ayre,

moscow. See "mosco."

moses   frequency: 1   relative frequency: 0.00001
      p.   413 UNGATHERED 41   24 In Moses bush, un-wasted in the fire.

most   frequency: 81   relative frequency: 0.00117
  **p.   115 PANEGYRE   78 "Are here on earth the most conspicuous things:
  **p.   117 PANEGYRE   147 Though many greater: and the most, the best.
    p.   29 EPIGRAMS 6   2 Sure, willing pouertie liues most in you.
    p.   31 EPIGRAMS 14   1 CAMDEN, most reuerend head, to whom I owe
    p.   31 EPIGRAMS 14   8 What sight in searching the most antique springs!
    p.   33 EPIGRAMS 20   1 Th'expence in odours is a most vaine sinne,
    p.   34 EPIGRAMS 23   3 Whose euery worke, of thy most earely wit,
    p.   34 EPIGRAMS 23   5 Longer a knowing, then most wits doe liue.
    p.   36 EPIGRAMS 28   22 Stile thee a most great foole, but no great man.
    p.   36 EPIGRAMS 29   1 TILTER, the most may'admire thee, though not
                                   I:
    p.   37 EPIGRAMS 33   5 Which if most gracious heauen grant like thine,
    p.   44 EPIGRAMS 55   9 When euen there, where most thou praysest mee,
    p.   48 EPIGRAMS 65   1 Away, and leaue me, thou thing most abhord,
    p.   48 EPIGRAMS 65   3 Made me commit most fierce idolatrie
    p.   49 EPIGRAMS 66   14 When they cost dearest, and are done most free,
    p.   49 EPIGRAMS 67   2 Most thinke all praises flatteries. But truth
                                   brings
    p.   51 EPIGRAMS 73   19 In most vile verses, and cost me more paine,
    p.   52 EPIGRAMS 76   3 What kinde of creature I could most desire,
    p.   53 EPIGRAMS 79   6 (Saue that most masculine issue of his braine)
    p.   54 EPIGRAMS 84   4 For your most noble offer had supply'd me.
    p.   55 EPIGRAMS 84   5 Straight went I home; and there most like a
                                   Poet,
    p.   59 EPIGRAMS 92   10 And vnderstand 'hem, as most chapmen doe.
    p.   60 EPIGRAMS 94   7 Yet, Satyres, since the most of mankind bee
    p.   61 EPIGRAMS 95   4 In thee, most weighty SAVILE, liu'd to vs:
    p.   62 EPIGRAMS 95   35 But most we need his faith (and all haue you)
    p.   63 EPIGRAMS 97   18 Nor are the Queenes most honor'd maides by
                                   th'eares
    p.   65 EPIGRAMS 101   28 But that, which most doth take my Muse, and mee,
    p.   78 EPIGRAMS 123   2 I know not which th'hast most, candor, or wit:
    p.   81 EPIGRAMS 129   10 Whose noyse shall keepe thy miming most aliue,
    p.   89 EPIGRAMS 133   193 In memorie of which most liquid deed,
    p.   106 FOREST 8   45 On their beds, most prostitute,
    p.   110 FOREST 11   33 Most frequent tumults, horrors, and vnrests,
    p.   112 FOREST 11   86 Makes a most blessed gayne.
    p.   114 FOREST 12   38 Riches thought most: But, Madame, thinke what
                                   store
    p.   118 FOREST 13   49 Of so great title, birth, but vertue most,
    p.   119 FOREST 13   90 Whereon the most of mankinde wracke themselues,
    p.   157 UNDERWOOD 13   128 Coriat, should rise the most sufficient head
    p.   158 UNDERWOOD 14   7 To aske it: though in most of workes it be
    p.   176 UNDERWOOD 24   10 Of Truth that searcheth the most <hidden>
                                   Springs,
    p.   179 UNDERWOOD 25   53 But to your selfe, most loyal Lord,
    p.   190 UNDERWOOD 37   13 Which, how most sacred I will ever keepe,
    p.   194 UNDERWOOD 38   113 You would be then most confident, that tho
    p.   201 UNDERWOOD 42   53 An Officer there, did make most solemne love,
    p.   203 UNDERWOOD 43   26 And my selfe most, in some selfe-boasting Rimes?
    p.   212 UNDERWOOD 43   211 So doth the King, and most of the Kings men
    p.   214 UNDERWOOD 44   44 Of bearing Armes! most civill Soldierie!
    p.   215 UNDERWOOD 44   90 What, to make legs? yes, and to smell most sweet,
    p.   232 UNDERWOOD 58   12 As if that part lay for a [   ] most fit!
    p.   236 UNDERWOOD 64   2 Most pious King, but his owne good in you!
    p.   244 UNDERWOOD 70   47 But most, a vertuous Sonne.
    p.   259 UNDERWOOD 76   3 Doth most humbly show it,
    p.   274 U'WOOD 84.2   3 For Mind, and Body, the most excellent
    p.   284 U'WOOD 84.9   74 Who violates the God-head, is most vitious
    p.   288 U'WOOD 84.9   187 For, Prayer is the Incense most perfumes
    p.   289 U'WOOD 84.9   223 And most his Justice, in the fitting parts,
    p.   295 U'WOOD 90   2 Most pleasant Martial; Substance got with ease,
    p.   307 HORACE 2   33 Most Writers, noble Sire, and either Sonne,
    p.   307 HORACE 2   67 Most worthie praise, when words that common grew,
    p.   331 HORACE 2   570 Yet who's most ignorant, dares Verses make.
    p.   361 UNGATHERED 1   8 Vnseason'd ffrostes, or the most enuyous weather.
    p.   361 UNGATHERED 1   12 the sweetest simples, and most soueraigne seedes.
    p.   363 UNGATHERED 3   8 The knottie heads of the most surly Groomes,
    p.   363 UNGATHERED 3   13 It thawes the frostiest, and most stiffe
                                   disdaine:
    p.   375 UNGATHERED 10   35 Beeing in teare to be robd, he most learnedly
                                   begs.

most (cont.)
```
    p.  379 UNGATHERED 12    13 And that you may see he most luckily ment
    p.  384 UNGATHERED 18    t1 To the most noble, and aboue his Titles,
    p.  386 UNGATHERED 21     6 I find thee write most worthy to be read.
    p.  386 UNGATHERED 21     9 And, where the most reade bookes, on Authors
                                famos,
    p.  393 UNGATHERED 27    20 Of the most worthie loue.
    p.  394 UNGATHERED 28    t1 To ye memorye of that most honoured Ladie Jane,
    p.  413 UNGATHERED 41    34 Alike of kin, to that most blessed Trine,
    p.  413 UNGATHERED 41    37 Most holy, & pure Virgin, blessed Mayd,
    p.  414 UNGATHERED 41    41 Great Queen of Queens, most mild, most meek,
                                most wise,
    p.  414 UNGATHERED 41    42 Most venerable. Cause of all our ioy.
    p.  414 UNGATHERED 41    45 The Seat of Sapience, the most lovely Mother,
    p.  414 UNGATHERED 41    46 And most to be admired of thy Sexe,
    p.  415 UNGATHERED 42    24 And a Comptroller, two most rigid men
    p.  416 UNGATHERED 44     6 We offer as a Circle the most fit
    p.  423 UNGATHERED 50    13 Euen states most hated, when no lawes resist
```

moth   frequency: 1   relative frequency: 0.00001
    See also "moath."
```
    p.  230 UNDERWOOD 55     7 Yet with a Dye, that feares no Moth,
```

mother   frequency: 14   relative frequency: 0.00020
```
    p.   36 EPIGRAMS 133     70 Hung stench, diseases, and old filth, their
                                mother,
    p.   93 FOREST 1          6 MARS, and my Mother, in their net:
    p.  136 UNDERWOOD 2.5    12 By description, but my Mother!
    p.  201 UNDERWOOD 42     68 That (in pure Madrigall) unto his Mother
    p.  208 UNDERWOOD 43    111 Sonne of the Wind! for so thy mother gone
    p.  221 UNDERWOOD 48     36 Then Cupid, and his Mother.
    p.  223 UNDERWOOD 49     40 They say you weekly invite with fits o'th'
                                Mother,
    p.  238 UNDERWOOD 66      3 The Mother of our Lord: why may not I
    p.  238 UNDERWOOD 66      6 The Mother of our Prince? When was there seene
    p.  287 U'WOOD 84.9     174 A tender Mother, a discreeter Wife,
    p.  292 UNDERWOOD 86      5 Sower Mother of sweet Loves, forbeare
    p.  413 UNGATHERED 41    33 Daughter, and Mother, and the Spouse of GOD,
    p.  414 UNGATHERED 41    45 The Seat of Sapience, the most lovely Mother,
    p.  414 UNGATHERED 41    56 Of being Daughter, Mother, Spouse of GOD!
```

mothers   frequency: 8   relative frequency: 0.00011
```
    p.   33 EPIGRAMS 22       8 In comfort of her mothers teares,
    p.  136 UNDERWOOD 2.5    20 Such my Mothers blushes be,
    p.  137 UNDERWOOD 2.5    31 Is my Mothers! Hearts of slaine
    p.  137 UNDERWOOD 2.5    38 With my Mothers is the same.
    p.  182 UNDERWOOD 28     12 But then his Mothers sweets you so apply,
    p.  223 UNDERWOOD 49     44 Both for the Mothers, and the Babes of grace,
    p.  242 UNDERWOOD 70      8 And mad'st thy Mothers wombe thine urne.
    p.  257 UNDERWOOD 75    147 All that their Fathers, and their Mothers might
```

moths. See "moathes."

motion   frequency: 8   relative frequency: 0.00011
    See also "mocion."
```
    p.   56 EPIGRAMS 88      15 The new french-taylors motion, monthly made,
    p.   62 EPIGRAMS 97       1 See you yond' Motion? Not the old Fa-ding,
    p.   62 EPIGRAMS 97      t1 ON THE NEW MOTION.
    p.  132 UNDERWOOD 2.2    26 And my motion from me quite;
    p.  138 UNDERWOOD 2.6    24 That at every motion sweld
    p.  156 UNDERWOOD 13    122 And my minds motion not? or have I none?
    p.  166 UNDERWOOD 15    124 But being in Motion still (or rather in race)
    p.  233 UNDERWOOD 59      9 A quick, and dazeling motion! when a paire
```

motions   frequency: 2   relative frequency: 0.00002
```
    p.   34 EPIGRAMS 25       3 Telling the motions of each petticote,
    p.  219 UNDERWOOD 47     50 That guides the Motions, and directs the beares.
```

motiue   frequency: 1   relative frequency: 0.00001
```
    p.  363 UNGATHERED 3     18 Where Gold's the Motiue, women haue no Nay.
```

motiues   frequency: 1   relative frequency: 0.00001
```
    p.  371 UNGATHERED 8      9 Their motiues were, since it had not to do
```

motive. See "motiue."

motives   frequency: 1   relative frequency: 0.00001
    See also "motiues."
```
    p.  411 UNGATHERED 40     5 The motives, and true Spurres
```

motley. See "motly."

motly   frequency: 1   relative frequency: 0.00001
   p.   44 EPIGRAMS 53   9 For, but thy selfe, where, out of motly, 's hee

mou'd   frequency: 2   relative frequency: 0.00002
   p.   34 EPIGRAMS 25   4 And how his GANIMEDE mou'd, and how his
                         goate,
   p.   82 EPIGRAMS 130   13 Mou'd by her order, and the ninth more high,

moue   frequency: 8   relative frequency: 0.00011
 **p. 114 PANEGYRE   45 And euery windore grieu'd it could not moue
   p.   55 EPIGRAMS 86   7 Where, though 't be loue, that to thy praise doth
                         moue,
   p.   56 EPIGRAMS 88   13 Or is it some french statue? No: 'T doth moue,
   p. 106 FOREST 8   46 Moue it, as their humblest sute,
   p. 110 FOREST 11   32 The first; as prone to moue
   p. 111 FOREST 11   71 Because they moue, the continent doth so:
   p. 115 FOREST 12   78 For I shall moue stocks, stones, no lesse then
                         he.
   p. 116 FOREST 13   8 With euery vertue, wheresoere it moue,

mought   frequency: 1   relative frequency: 0.00001

mouing   frequency: 2   relative frequency: 0.00002
 **p. 114 PANEGYRE   61 As with the murmure of a mouing wood;
 **p. 114 PANEGYRE   62 The ground beneath did seeme a mouing floud:

moulded   frequency: 2   relative frequency: 0.00002
   p. 280 U'WOOD 84.4   56 As it slid moulded off from Heaven.
   p. 405 UNGATHERED 34   84 Moulded or stroakt vp to suruey a State!

mouldie   frequency: 1   relative frequency: 0.00001
   p.   88 EPIGRAMS 133   150 And, after mouldie growne, againe were tosted,

moulds   frequency: 1   relative frequency: 0.00001
   p. 216 UNDERWOOD 44   102 Her broken Armes up, to their emptie moulds.

mouldy   frequency: 1   relative frequency: 0.00001
  See also "mouldie."
  *p. 492 TO HIMSELF   21 No doubt some mouldy tale,

mount   frequency: 3   relative frequency: 0.00004
   p.   93 FOREST 2   10 Thy Mount, to which the Dryads doe resort,
   p. 161 UNDERWOOD 14   80 Among my commings in, and see it mount,
   p. 366 UNGATHERED 6   21 The pale Pyrene, and the forked Mount:

mountain. See "mountaine."

mountaine   frequency: 3   relative frequency: 0.00004
   p. 143 UNDERWOOD 3   11 To make the Mountaine Quarries move,
   p. 150 UNDERWOOD 9   17 My mountaine belly, and my rockie face,
   p. 368 UNGATHERED 6   71 And ouer Grampius mountaine,

mountaines   frequency: 1   relative frequency: 0.00001
   p. 315 HORACE 2   198 Afford? The Mountaines travail'd, and brought
                         forth

mountains. See "mountaines."

mounte-banck   frequency: 1   relative frequency: 0.00001
   p. 402 UNGATHERED 34   16 Of Tyre-man, Mounte-banck & Iustice
                         Iones,

mountebank. See "mounte-banck."

mounted   frequency: 3   relative frequency: 0.00004
  See also "ymounted."
   p.   81 EPIGRAMS 129   13 Or (mounted on a stoole) thy face doth hit
   p. 228 UNDERWOOD 53   8 Or Castor mounted on his Cyllarus:
   p. 657 L. CONVIVALES   14 Ply it, and you all are mounted;

mounting   frequency: 1   relative frequency: 0.00001
  See also "lustie-mounting."
   p. 265 UNDERWOOD 79   51 Your teeming Ewes, aswell as mounting Rammes.

mountjoy. See "montioy."

mounts   frequency: 1   relative frequency: 0.00001
   p. 233 UNDERWOOD 59   8 That trembles in the blaze, but (then) mounts
                         higher!

mourn'd   frequency: 1   relative frequency: 0.00001
    p. 392 UNGATHERED 26   79 Which, since thy flight from hence, hath mourn'd
                              like night,

mourners   frequency: 1   relative frequency: 0.00001
    p. 333 HORACE 2   615 Cry, and doe more then the true Mourners: so

mournes   frequency: 1   relative frequency: 0.00001
    p. 37 EPIGRAMS 34   1 He that feares death, or mournes it, in the iust,

mourning   frequency: 1   relative frequency: 0.00001
    p. 285 U'WOOD 84.9   98 Put black, and mourning on? and say you misse

mourns. See "mournes."

mouse   frequency: 1   relative frequency: 0.00001
    p. 315 HORACE 2   199 A scorned Mouse! O, how much better this,

mouth   frequency: 2   relative frequency: 0.00002
    p. 111 FOREST 11   79 Or those, who doubt the common mouth of fame,
    p. 327 HORACE 2   462 But a well-compass'd mouth to utter it;

mouthes   frequency: 4   relative frequency: 0.00005
    p. 82 EPIGRAMS 131   3 For, then, all mouthes will iudge, and their owne
                              way:
    p. 187 UNDERWOOD 33   11 All mouthes, that dare entitle them (from hence)
    p. 232 UNDERWOOD 58   2 All mouthes are open, and all stomacks free:
    p. 269 UNDERWOOD 83   23 Had I a thousand Mouthes, as many Tongues,

mouths. See "mouthes."

mov'd   frequency: 4   relative frequency: 0.00005
    p. 148 UNDERWOOD 8   3 By Atomes mov'd;
    p. 256 UNDERWOOD 75   105 And this well mov'd the Judgement of the King
    p. 287 U'WOOD 84.9   166 Mov'd by the wind, so comely moved she.
    p. 315 HORACE 2   235 Of money, haughtie, to desire soon mov'd,

move   frequency: 12   relative frequency: 0.00017
    See also "moue."
    p. 131 UNDERWOOD 2.1   1 Let it not your wonder move,
    p. 138 UNDERWOOD 2.6   21 Or, if you did move to night
    p. 143 UNDERWOOD 3   11 To make the Mountaine Quarries move,
    p. 148 UNDERWOOD 7   31 One un-becomming thought doth move
    p. 157 UNDERWOOD 13   135 Yet we must more then move still, or goe on,
    p. 173 UNDERWOOD 22   6 Throughout your forme; as though that move,
    p. 190 UNDERWOOD 37   27 As flatt'ry with friends humours still to move.
    p. 194 UNDERWOOD 38   111 How all my Fibres by your Spirit doe move,
    p. 199 UNDERWOOD 42   3 No Poets verses yet did ever move,
    p. 202 UNDERWOOD 42   82 A Goat in Velvet; or some block could move
    p. 287 U'WOOD 84.9   170 To another, Move; he went; To a third, Go,
    p. 327 HORACE 2   484 Was said to move the stones, by his Lutes
                              powers,

moved   frequency: 1   relative frequency: 0.00001
    See also "mou'd," "mov'd."
    p. 287 U'WOOD 84.9   166 Mov'd by the wind, so comely moved she.

moves   frequency: 1   relative frequency: 0.00001
    p. 198 UNDERWOOD 40   26 Moves like a sprightly River, and yet can

movest. See "mov'st."

moveth   frequency: 1   relative frequency: 0.00001
    p. 279 U'WOOD 84.4   31 It moveth all; and makes a flight

moving. See "mouing."

movnsievr   frequency: 2   relative frequency: 0.00002
    p. 56 EPIGRAMS 88   1 Would you beleeue, when you this
                              MOVNSIEVR see,
    p. 56 EPIGRAMS 88   t1 ON ENGLISH MOVNSIEVR

movnsievrs   frequency: 1   relative frequency: 0.00001
    p. 56 EPIGRAMS 88   11 Or hung some MOVNSIEVRS picture on the
                              wall,

movnteagle   frequency: 1   relative frequency: 0.00001
    p. 46 EPIGRAMS 60   t1 TO WILLIAM LORD MOVNTEAGLE.

mov'st   frequency: 1   relative frequency: 0.00001
     p. 292 UNDERWOOD 86   1 Venus, againe thou mov'st a warre

mowed   frequency: 1   relative frequency: 0.00001
     p. 97 FOREST 3   39 The mowed meddowes, with the fleeced sheepe,

mr.   .   frequency: 12   relative frequency: 0.00017
     p. 60 EPIGRAMS 94   t2 WITH Mr. DONNES SATYRES.
     p. 83 EPIGRAMS 132   t1 TO Mr. IOSVAH SYLVESTER.
     p. 229 UNDERWOOD 54   t2 To Mr. ARTHUR SQUIB.
     p. 229 UNDERWOOD 55   t2 Mr. IOHN BURGES.
     p. 252 UNDERWOOD 75   t5 of that Noble Gentleman, Mr. HIEROME
                                 WESTON,
     p. 379 UNGATHERED 12   2 The height, let him learne of Mr. Tom.
                                 Coryate;
     p. 381 UNGATHERED 12 60 The height, let him learne of Mr. Tom Coryate.
     p. 386 UNGATHERED 21 t2 Mr. BROWNE:
     p. 388 UNGATHERED 23 t2 Mr George Chapman, on his Translation
     p. 390 UNGATHERED 26 t3 MR. WILLIAM SHAKESPEARE:
     p. 402 UNGATHERED 34   1 Mr Surueyr, you yt first begann
     p. 415 UNGATHERED 43 t2 Good Freind Mr. Robert Dover, on his great

mrs.   frequency: 5   relative frequency: 0.00007
     p. 73 EPIGRAMS 114   t1 TO Mrs. PHILIP SYDNEY.
     p. 80 EPIGRAMS 126   t1 TO HIS LADY, THEN Mrs. CARY.
     p. 149 UNDERWOOD 8   7 And in his Mrs. flame, playing like a flye,
     p. 197 UNDERWOOD 40   9 This makes me, Mrs. that sometime by stealth,
     p. 411 UNGATHERED 40 t2 Mrs. Alice Sutcliffe, on

much   frequency: 97   relative frequency: 0.00140
     See also "too-much."
    *p. 493 TO HIMSELF   31 And much good do't you then:
     p. 27 EPIGRAMS 2   11 Much lesse with lewd, prophane, and beastly
                                 phrase,
     p. 27 EPIGRAMS 3   4 For the lucks sake, it thus much fauour haue,
     p. 41 EPIGRAMS 45   2 My sinne was too much hope of thee, lou'd boy,
     p. 41 EPIGRAMS 45   12 As what he loues may neuer like too much.
     p. 46 EPIGRAMS 60   8 But thine, for which I doo't, so much exceeds!
     p. 49 EPIGRAMS 66   16 It may be much, or little, in the cause.
     p. 56 EPIGRAMS 88   3 That so much skarfe of France, and hat, and
                                 fether,
     p. 56 EPIGRAMS 88   7 That he, vntrauell'd, should be french so much,
     p. 59 EPIGRAMS 92   36 Much like those Brethren; thinking to preuaile
     p. 59 EPIGRAMS 92   40 That know not so much state, wrong, as they doo.
     p. 64 EPIGRAMS 99   5 How much of great example wert thou, ROE,
     p. 64 EPIGRAMS 99   7 But much it now auailes, what's done, of whom:
     p. 70 EPIGRAMS 108   9 He that not trusts me, hauing vow'd thus much,
     p. 72 EPIGRAMS 111   3 Wherein thou shew'st, how much the latter are
     p. 72 EPIGRAMS 111 10 That to the world thou should'st reueale so much,
     p. 74 EPIGRAMS 114   6 Where finding so much beautie met with vertue,
     p. 76 EPIGRAMS 119 16 Makes, the whole longer, then 'twas giuen him,
                                 much.
     p. 77 EPIGRAMS 120 23 But, being so much too good for earth,
     p. 79 EPIGRAMS 124   4 As much beautie, as could dye:
     p. 101 FOREST 4   57 Else, I my state should much mistake,
     p. 106 FOREST 9   10 Not so much honoring thee,
     p. 112 FOREST 11   111 Much more a noble, and right generous mind
     p. 117 FOREST 13   27 And this shall be no false one, but as much
     p. 117 FOREST 13   46 As bloud, and match. Wherein, how more then much
     p. 119 FOREST 13   108 Onely, thus much, out of a rauish'd zeale,
     p. 141 UNDERWOOD 2.9 23 Till he cherish'd too much beard,
     p. 142 UNDERWOOD 2.9 46 As to doe no thing too much.
     p. 147 UNDERWOOD 7   21 And feare much more, that more of him be showne.
     p. 149 UNDERWOOD 9   4 Whom I adore so much, should so slight me,
     p. 150 UNDERWOOD 9   16 Read so much wast, as she cannot imbrace
     p. 151 UNDERWOOD 12   3 Would say as much, as both have done
     p. 152 UNDERWOOD 12 29 Much from him I professe I wonne,
     p. 155 UNDERWOOD 13 73 O, is it so? knowes he so much? and will
     p. 157 UNDERWOOD 13 155 You know (without my flatt'ring you) too much
     p. 158 UNDERWOOD 14   5 Your Booke, my Selden, I have read, and much
     p. 159 UNDERWOOD 14 21 Men past their termes, and prais'd some names too
                                 much,
     p. 159 UNDERWOOD 14 26 Before men get a verse: much lesse a Praise;
     p. 161 UNDERWOOD 14 82 Selden! two Names that so much understand!
     p. 163 UNDERWOOD 15 47 Thither it flowes. How much did Stallion spend
     p. 169 UNDERWOOD 17 14 Now so much friend, as you would trust in me,
     p. 173 UNDERWOOD 22   3 As not the World can praise too much,
     p. 173 UNDERWOOD 22 22 With so much Loyalties expence,
     p. 182 UNDERWOOD 27 36 So much my Subject drownes the rest.
     p. 182 UNDERWOOD 28   4 A better lover, and much better Poet.

much (cont.)
p.	187 UNDERWOOD 33	24 What use, what strength of reason! and how much
p.	190 UNDERWOOD 37	21 How much they lame her in her propertie.
p.	193 UNDERWOOD 38	83 Be not affected with these markes too much
p.	194 UNDERWOOD 38	110 How much you are the better part of me;
p.	210 UNDERWOOD 43	160 Troy, though it were so much his Venus care.
p.	213 UNDERWOOD 44	3 And Ord'nance too: so much as from the Tower
p.	215 UNDERWOOD 44	76 In so much land a yeare, or such a Banke,
p.	215 UNDERWOOD 44	77 That turnes us so much moneys, at which rate
p.	216 UNDERWOOD 45	9 Much lesse a name would we bring up, or nurse,
p.	218 UNDERWOOD 47	12 As make it their proficiencie, how much
p.	221 UNDERWOOD 48	22 Then Phoebus; and much stronger
p.	223 UNDERWOOD 49	25 I am no States-man, and much lesse Divine,
p.	231 UNDERWOOD 56	30 And should grow rich, had I much more to pay.
p.	237 UNDERWOOD 64	22 How much to heaven for thee, great
		CHARLES, they owe!
p.	238 UNDERWOOD 66	14 Of so much safetie to the Realme, and King!
p.	249 UNDERWOOD 72	20 What prayers (People) can you thinke too much?
p.	268 UNDERWOOD 82	4 How much they are belov'd of God, in thee;
p.	269 UNDERWOOD 83	26 Thereof, no notion can expresse how much
p.	285 U'WOOD 84.9	109 Much more desir'd, and dearer then before,
p.	291 UNDERWOOD 85	51 If with bright floods, the Winter troubled much,
p.	295 UNDERWOOD 89	8 Makes his life longer then 'twas given him, much.
p.	307 HORACE 2	60 Or I am much deceiv'd, shall be to place
p.	307 HORACE 2	62 Much, that mought now be spoke: omitted here
p.	309 HORACE 2	76 And come not too much wrested. What's that
		thing,
p.	309 HORACE 2	81 Cato's and Ennius tongues have lent much worth,
p.	309 HORACE 2	101 Much phrase that now is dead, shall be reviv'd;
p.	309 HORACE 2	102 And much shall dye, that now is nobly liv'd,
p.	313 HORACE 2	161 It much will differ, if a God speake, than,
p.	315 HORACE 2	199 A scorned House! O, how much better this,
p.	317 HORACE 2	250 Mans comming yeares much good with them doe
		bring:
p.	317 HORACE 2	251 As his departing take much thence: lest, then,
p.	317 HORACE 2	262 Much from the sight, which faire report will make
p.	321 HORACE 2	351 Yet he that offers at it, may sweat much,
p.	321 HORACE 2	353 Of Order, and Connexion: so much grace
p.	321 HORACE 2	366 And not without much praise; till libertie
p.	323 HORACE 2	385 Of too much haste, and negligence in part,
p.	329 HORACE 2	526 Much in the Poeme shine, I will not bee
p.	329 HORACE 2	533 So he that flaggeth much, becomes to me
p.	333 HORACE 2	588 The wished goale, both did, and suffer'd much
p.	367 UNGATHERED 6	31 "So much doth Virtue hate,
p.	371 UNGATHERED 9	2 Read here a little, that thou mayst know much.
p.	372 UNGATHERED 9	13 Vp so much truth, as could I it pursue
p.	380 UNGATHERED 12	31 Of lying, he feares so much the reproofe
p.	383 UNGATHERED 17	t1 To his much and worthily esteemed
p.	386 UNGATHERED 21	16 With the how much they set forth, but th'how
		well.
p.	390 UNGATHERED 26	4 As neither Man, nor Muse, can praise too much.
p.	393 UNGATHERED 27	4 Refine it neere so much.
p.	402 UNGATHERED 34	10 How much Architectonice is your owne!
p.	403 UNGATHERED 34	21 Why much good doo't you! Be what beast you will,
p.	403 UNGATHERED 34	38 And Goody Sculpture, brought wth much adoe
p.	420 UNGATHERED 48	11 soe much the starte
p.	666 INSCRIPTS. 11	7 Till I, at much expense of Time, and Paper

mud
                           frequency: 1   relative frequency: 0.00001
    p. 85 EPIGRAMS 133   62 Ycleped Mud, which, when their oares did once
           stirre,

muffles
                           frequency: 1   relative frequency: 0.00001
    p. 363 UNGATHERED 3   14 Muffles the clearnesse of Election,

multipli'd
                           frequency: 1   relative frequency: 0.00001
    p. 251 UNDERWOOD 74   17 Have multipli'd their arts, and powers,

multitude
                           frequency: 1   relative frequency: 0.00001
    p. 187 UNDERWOOD 33   31 Against a multitude; and (with thy Stile

mungrel
                           frequency: 1   relative frequency: 0.00001
    p. 409 UNGATHERED 37   15 A Mungrel Curre? Thou should'st stinck forth,
           and dye

muniments
                           frequency: 1   relative frequency: 0.00001
    p. 400 UNGATHERED 32   9 And doth deserue all muniments of praise,

murder
                           frequency: 4   relative frequency: 0.00005
    See also "murther."

murder (cont.)
  **p. 113 PANEGYRE   12 Where Murder, Rapine, Lust, doe sit within,
    p. 72 EPIGRAMS 111   14 They murder him againe, that enuie thee.
    p. 212 UNDERWOOD 43 207 Engines of Murder, and receive the praise
    p. 363 UNGATHERED 3   t1 Murder.

murdered. See "murdred."

murdred   frequency: 1   relative frequency: 0.00001
    p. 371 UNGATHERED 8   14 Do crowne thy murdred Poeme: which shall rise

murmur. See "murmure."

murmure   frequency: 4   relative frequency: 0.00005
  **p. 114 PANEGYRE   61 As with the murmure of a mouing wood;
    p. 237 UNDERWOOD 64   14 And murmure cannot quarrell at your wayes?
    p. 283 U'WOOD 84.9   33 I murmure against God, for having ta'en
    p. 290 UNDERWOOD 85   27 The Fountaines murmure as the streames doe
                              creepe,

murmures   frequency: 1   relative frequency: 0.00001
    p. 258 UNDERWOOD 75 189 Strifes, murmures, or delay,

murmuring   frequency: 1   relative frequency: 0.00001
    p. 261 UNDERWOOD 77   19 Of murmuring Subjects; make the Nations know

murmurs. See "murmures."

murther   frequency: 1   relative frequency: 0.00001
    p. 110 FOREST 11   52 To murther different hearts,

muse   frequency: 69   relative frequency: 0.00099
    See also "mvse."
    p. 28 EPIGRAMS 4   9 Whom should my Muse then flie to, but the best
    p. 34 EPIGRAMS 23   1 DONNE, the delight of PHOEBVS, and
                              each Muse,
    p. 35 EPIGRAMS 27   4 If any Muse out-liue their spight, his can;
    p. 40 EPIGRAMS 43   1 What need hast thou of me? or of my Muse?
    p. 44 EPIGRAMS 55   1 How I doe loue thee BEAVMONT, and thy
                              Muse,
    p. 47 EPIGRAMS 63   11 Curst be his Muse, that could lye dumbe, or hid
    p. 48 EPIGRAMS 65   5 Be thy next masters more vnluckie Muse,
    p. 48 EPIGRAMS 65   11 With me thou leau'st an happier Muse then thee,
    p. 52 EPIGRAMS 76   2 I thought to forme vnto my zealous Muse,
    p. 52 EPIGRAMS 76   18 My Muse bad, Bedford write, and that was shee.
    p. 55 EPIGRAMS 84   7 I would haue spent: how euery Muse should know
                              it,
    p. 58 EPIGRAMS 91   4 Sung by a HORACE, or a Muse as free;
    p. 65 EPIGRAMS 101   28 But that, which most doth take my Muse, and mee,
    p. 67 EPIGRAMS 105   4 Least mention of a Nymph, a Muse, a Grace,
    p. 70 EPIGRAMS 108   5 I sweare by your true friend, my Muse, I loue
    p. 70 EPIGRAMS 109   1 Who now calls on thee, NEVIL, is a Muse,
    p. 78 EPIGRAMS 121   2 My lighter comes, to kisse thy learned Muse;
    p. 80 EPIGRAMS 127   7 I, and this Muse had beene, if thou hadst not
    p. 84 EPIGRAMS 133   3 ORPHEVS, VLYSSES: or the Latine
                              Muse,
    p. 89 EPIGRAMS 133 196 My Muse had plough'd with his, that sung
                              A-IAX.
    p. 107 FOREST 10   3 For the more countenance to my actiue Muse?
    p. 108 FOREST 10   28 My Muse vp by commission: No, I bring
    p. 108 FOREST 10A   1 An elegie? no, muse; yt askes a straine
    p. 108 FOREST 10A   15 the glories of yt ... or muse ....
    p. 114 FOREST 12   41 It is the Muse, alone, can raise to heauen,
    p. 114 FOREST 12   48 That had no Muse to make their fame abide.
    p. 115 FOREST 12   72 To my lesse sanguine Muse, wherein she'hath
                              wonne
    p. 115 FOREST 12   79 Then all, that haue but done my Muse least
                              grace,
    p. 138 UNDERWOOD 2.6   5 What my Muse and I have done:
    p. 159 UNDERWOOD 14   19 Though I confesse (as every Muse hath err'd,
    p. 161 UNDERWOOD 14   84 The Credit, what would furnish a tenth Muse!
    p. 176 UNDERWOOD 25   3 Wake, and put on the wings of Pindars Muse,
    p. 182 UNDERWOOD 27   27 Or Constables Ambrosiack Muse
    p. 182 UNDERWOOD 28   5 Nor is my Muse, or I asham'd to owe it
    p. 183 UNDERWOOD 29   20 At the Well[s] no Muse did stay,
    p. 200 UNDERWOOD 42   15 Of beautie; but the Muse hath interest in:
    p. 222 UNDERWOOD 49   7 What though with Tribade lust she force a Muse,
    p. 230 UNDERWOOD 56   5 So have you gain'd a Servant, and a Muse:
    p. 230 UNDERWOOD 56   13 Marrie the Muse is one, can tread the Aire,
    p. 231 UNDERWOOD 56   26 Accept his Muse; and tell, I know you can,

muse (cont.)

p. 232	UNDERWOOD 57	25	the Muse, or the Poet,
p. 241	UNDERWOOD 68	12	'T were better spare a Butt, then spill his Muse.
p. 248	UNDERWOOD 71	9	The Muse not peepes out, one of hundred dayes;
p. 255	UNDERWOOD 75	84	With Angels, Muse, to speake these: Nothing can
p. 259	UNDERWOOD 76	16	(For with both the MUSE was fed)
p. 262	UNDERWOOD 78	1	Tho', happy Muse, thou know my Digby well,
p. 262	UNDERWOOD 78	19	Goe, Muse, in, and salute him. Say he be
p. 263	UNDERWOOD 78	31	Wilt thou be, Muse, when this shall them befall?
p. 272	UNDERWOOD 84	t13	Her being chosen a MUSE.
p. 278	U'WOOD 84.4	21	I call you Muse; now make it true:
p. 282	U'WOOD 84.9	2	Who was my Muse, and life of all I sey'd,
p. 282	U'WOOD 84.9	t1	Elegie on my Muse.
p. 283	U'WOOD 84.9	28	What's left a Poet, when his Muse is gone?
p. 289	U'WOOD 84.9	228	To publish her a Saint. My Muse is gone.
p. 309	HORACE 2	113	Unto the Lyrick Strings, the Muse gave grace
p. 311	HORACE 2	140	'Tis not enough, th'elaborate Muse affords
p. 315	HORACE 2	201	Speake to me, Muse, the Man, who, after Troy was sack't,
p. 327	HORACE 2	461	The Muse not only gave the Greek's a wit,
p. 329	HORACE 2	502	Or Muse, upon the Lyre, thou chance b<e>'asham'd.
p. 339	HORACE 1	39	His Muse .... height, and ....
p. 390	UNGATHERED 26	4	As neither Man, nor Muse, can praise too much.
p. 395	UNGATHERED 29	14	What Muse, or rather God of harmony
p. 396	UNGATHERED 30	5	Thy Muse, and mine, as they expect. 'Tis true:
p. 398	UNGATHERED 30	64	Braue are the Musters, that the Muse will make.
p. 400	UNGATHERED 32	6	When they doe sweat to fortifie a Muse.
p. 401	UNGATHERED 32	22	Of Ethnicisme, makes his Muse a Saint.
p. 411	UNGATHERED 39	11	Thy blatant Muse abroad, and teach it rather
p. 415	UNGATHERED 43	1	I cannot bring my Muse to dropp <her> Vies
p. 662	INSCRIPTS. 2	5	Tell her, his Muse did inuent thee

muses   frequency: 29   relative frequency: 0.00041

p. 53	EPIGRAMS 79	3	Or then, or since, about our Muses springs,
p. 60	EPIGRAMS 94	2	Life of the Muses day, their morning-starre!
p. 61	EPIGRAMS 94	16	The Muses euening, as their morning-starre.
p. 66	EPIGRAMS 103	6	Need any Muses praise to giue it fame?
p. 85	EPIGRAMS 133	54	Alwayes at hand, to aide the merry Muses.
p. 94	FOREST 2	14	At his great birth, where all the Muses met.
p. 98	FOREST 3	52	Nor are the Muses strangers found:
p. 114	FOREST 12	33	His loue vnto the Muses, when his skill
p. 119	FOREST 13	100	Heare, what the Muses sing about thy roote,
p. 136	UNDERWOOD 2.5	7	'Mongst my Muses finding me,
p. 184	UNDERWOOD 29	41	And the Muses to their braine;
p. 186	UNDERWOOD 31	7	So may the gentler Muses, and good fame
p. 200	UNDERWOOD 42	7	That from the Muses fountaines doth indorse
p. 221	UNDERWOOD 48	25	So may the Muses follow
p. 228	UNDERWOOD 53	15	For never saw I yet the Muses dwell,
p. 231	UNDERWOOD 57	9	He lov'd the Muses;
p. 233	UNDERWOOD 60	4	Minerva's and the Muses care!
p. 239	UNDERWOOD 67	t1	An Ode, or Song, by all the Muses.
p. 259	UNDERWOOD 76	8	To make all the MUSES debters
p. 311	HORACE 2	128	Nor know t<o>'observe: why (i'the Muses name)
p. 329	HORACE 2	498	Attempted by the Muses tunes, and strings;
p. 339	HORACE 1	33	The greater part, that boast the Muses fire,
p. 353	HORACE 1	579	.... of the singer Apollo, and Muses fam'd
p. 371	UNGATHERED 8	12	And wish that all the Muses blood were spilt,
p. 391	UNGATHERED 26	26	I meane with great, but disproportion'd Muses:
p. 391	UNGATHERED 26	44	And all the Muses still were in their prime,
p. 392	UNGATHERED 26	61	Vpon the Muses anuile: turne the same,
p. 396	UNGATHERED 30	t3	MUSES OF HIS FRIEND
p. 657	I. CONVIVALES	10	That sits watering with the Muses.

music.   See "musick," "musicke," "musique."

musical.   See "musicall."

musicall   frequency: 1   relative frequency: 0.00001

p. 143	UNDERWOOD 3	t1	The Musicall strife; In a Pastorall Dialogue.

musick   frequency: 3   relative frequency: 0.00004

p. 82	EPIGRAMS 130	3	Which Musick had; or speake her knowne effects,
p. 404	UNGATHERED 34	53	To plant ye Musick where noe eare can reach!
p. 404	UNGATHERED 34	63	To be ye Musick Master! Fabler too!

musicke   frequency: 3   relative frequency: 0.00004
    p. 319 HORACE 2   306 In time to Tragedie, a Musicke new.
    p. 367 UNGATHERED 6   47 "Musicke hath power to draw,
    p. 374 UNGATHERED 10   11 All sorts of fish with Musicke of his maw.

musique   ·   frequency: 5   relative frequency: 0.00007
    p. 183 UNDERWOOD 29   23 And Apollo's Musique die,
    p. 279 U'WOOD 84.4   35 Of grace, and Musique to the eare,
    p. 286 U'WOOD 84.9   124 A Musique in the Eares, will ever last;
    p. 331 HORACE 2   557 As jarring Musique doth, at jolly feasts,
    p. 401 UNGATHERED 33   5 Musique and Poesie:

must   frequency: 96   relative frequency: 0.00138

muster   frequency: 1   relative frequency: 0.00001
    p.   85 EPIGRAMS 133   63 Belch'd forth an ayre, as hot, as at the muster

muster-master   frequency: 1   relative frequency: 0.00001
    p. 167 UNDERWOOD 15   .74 Though thou wert Muster-master of the Land.

musters   frequency: 1   relative frequency: 0.00001
    p. 398 UNGATHERED 30   64 Braue are the Musters, that the Muse will make.

mute   frequency: 4   relative frequency: 0.00005
  **p. 114 PANEGYRE   39 Vnto their zeales expression; they are mute:
    p.   58 EPIGRAMS 91   10 Throughout, might flatt'rie seeme; and to be mute
    p. 181 UNDERWOOD 27   4 So speake (as yet it is not mute)
    p. 384 UNGATHERED 18   17 So, be yor Concord, still, as deepe, as mute;

mutton   frequency: 1   relative frequency: 0.00001
    p.   64 EPIGRAMS 101   11 Vshring the mutton; with a short-leg'd hen,

mutual. See "mutuall."

mutuall   frequency: 2   relative frequency: 0.00002
    p. 186 UNDERWOOD 33   4 Where mutuall frauds are fought, and no side
                                  yeild;
    p. 293 UNDERWOOD 86   30 Delights, nor credulous hope of mutuall Joy,

mutually   frequency: 1   relative frequency: 0.00001
    p. 293 UNDERWOOD 87   13 LYD. And I, am mutually on fire

mvng'   frequency: 1   relative frequency: 0.00001
    p.   42 EPIGRAMS 48   1 His bought armes MVNG' not lik'd; for his
                                  first day

mvngril   frequency: 1   relative frequency: 0.00001
    p.   42 EPIGRAMS 48   t1 ON MVNGRIL ESQVIRE.

mvse   frequency: 2   relative frequency: 0.00002
    p.   48 EPIGRAMS 65   t1 TO MY MVSE.
    p. 262 UNDERWOOD 78   t2 To my MVSE, the Lady Digby, on her

my   frequency: 420   relative frequency: 0.00608

mynd   frequency: 1   relative frequency: 0.00001
    p. 403 UNGATHERED 34   25 your Trappings will not change you. Change yor
                                  mynd.

mynde   frequency: 1   relative frequency: 0.00001
    p. 405 UNGATHERED 34   75 What would he doe now, gi'ng his mynde yt waye

myne   frequency: 3   relative frequency: 0.00004
    p. 212 UNDERWOOD 43   205 Blow up, and ruine, myne, and countermyne,
    p. 421 UNGATHERED 49   3 Soe ended yor Epistle, myne beginns
    p. 421 UNGATHERED 49   10 deignes myne the power to ffinde, yett want I
                                  will

mynerva   frequency: 1   relative frequency: 0.00001
    p. 420 UNGATHERED 48   29 Mynerva deignes

myrtle   frequency: 2   relative frequency: 0.00002
    p. 412 UNGATHERED 41   3 The M. the Myrtle, A. the Almonds clame,
    p. 412 UNGATHERED 41   5 These forme thy Ghyrlond. Wherof Myrtle green,

mysterie   frequency: 7   relative frequency: 0.00010
    p. 119 FOREST 13   106 And greater rites, yet writ in mysterie,
    p. 127 UNDERWOOD 1.1   3 The faithfull mans beleeved Mysterie,
    p. 128 UNDERWOOD 1.1   31 Till I attaine the long'd-for mysterie
    p. 219 UNDERWOOD 47   48 Of the late Mysterie of reception,

mysterie (cont.)
    p. 225 UNDERWOOD 51   4 Thou stand'st as if some Mysterie thou did'st!
    p. 286 U'WOOD 84.9   129 That holy, great, and glorious Mysterie,
    p. 412 UNGATHERED 41   2 Which, chang'd, a five-fold mysterie designe,

mysteries   frequency: 6   relative frequency: 0.00008
    See also "misteryes."
    p. 96 FOREST 2   98 The mysteries of manners, armes, and arts.
    p. 269 UNDERWOOD 83   31 To touch these Mysteries! We may admire
    p. 284 U'WOOD 84.9   80 Have busie search made in his mysteries!
    p. 369 UNGATHERED 6   111 But these are Mysteries
    p. 413 UNGATHERED 41   29 These Mysteries do point to three more great,
    p. 415 UNGATHERED 42   28 Yo'have all the Mysteries of Wits new Mint,

mystery. See "misterie," "mysterie."

mystic. See "mystick."

mystick   frequency: 1   relative frequency: 0.00001
    p. 413 UNGATHERED 41   23 Inflam'd with ardor to that mystick Shine,

mythology   frequency: 1   relative frequency: 0.00001
    p. 404 UNGATHERED 34   48 Mythology there painted on slit deale!

n<e>'re   frequency: 1   relative frequency: 0.00001
    p. 150 UNDERWOOD 10   3 I n<e>'re was of thy kind;

nail. See "naile."

naile   frequency: 1   relative frequency: 0.00001
    p. 325 HORACE 2   418 Not, ten times o're, corrected to the naile.

nailes   frequency: 2   relative frequency: 0.00002
    p. 307 HORACE 2   47 The nailes, and every curled haire disclose;
    p. 325 HORACE 2   423 Their nailes, nor shave their beards, but to
                      by-paths

nails. See "nailes."

naked   frequency: 6   relative frequency: 0.00008
    p. 74 EPIGRAMS 115   22 'Twill see it's sister naked, ere a sword.
    p. 78 EPIGRAMS 122   7 If holiest friend-ship, naked to the touch,
    p. 158 UNDERWOOD 14   4 Truth, and the Graces best, when naked are.
    p. 288 U'WOOD 84.9   194 To cloath the naked, feed the hungry. Shee
    p. 319 HORACE 2   321 The rough rude Satyres naked; and would try,
    p. 365 UNGATHERED 5   11 Cleare as a naked vestall

nall   frequency: 1   relative frequency: 0.00001
    p. 410 UNGATHERED 38   17 The Cobler kept him to his nall; but, now

nam'd   frequency: 10   relative frequency: 0.00014
    p. 27 EPIGRAMS 2   2 Thy title, Epigrammes, and nam'd of mee,
    p. 66 EPIGRAMS 103   5 And, being nam'd, how little doth that name
    p. 67 EPIGRAMS 104   1 Were they that nam'd you, prophets? Did they
                      see,
    p. 83 EPIGRAMS 131   12 They were not to be nam'd on the same day.
    p. 94 FOREST 2   19 Thy copp's, too, nam'd of GAMAGE, thou hast
                      there,
    p. 165 UNDERWOOD 15   98 A fellow of course Letcherie, is nam'd,
    p. 180 UNDERWOOD 26   6 And doubtfull Dayes (which were nam'd
                      Criticall,)
    p. 329 HORACE 2   501 All which I tell, lest when Apollo's nam'd,
    p. 380 UNGATHERED 12   21 There nam'd to be trauell'd? For this our Tom
                      saith:
    p. 398 UNGATHERED 30   68 With bold Tyrtaeus verse, when thou art nam'd,

name   frequency: 90   relative frequency: 0.00130
    See also "name's."
**p. 116 PANEGYRE   114 To their voluptuous lustes, had lost their name;
    p. 29 EPIGRAMS 10   2 But I haue my reuenge made, in thy name.
    p. 30 EPIGRAMS 11   4 It made me a great face, I ask'd the name.
    p. 31 EPIGRAMS 14   4 The great renowne, and name wherewith shee goes.
    p. 31 EPIGRAMS 14   7 What name, what skill, what faith hast thou in
                      things!
    p. 32 EPIGRAMS 17   1 May others feare, flie, and traduce thy name,
    p. 33 EPIGRAMS 22   7 Whose soule heauens Queene, (whose name shee
                      beares)
    p. 35 EPIGRAMS 28   1 DON SVRLY, to aspire the glorious name
    p. 36 EPIGRAMS 30   4 And person to the world; ere I thy name.
    p. 38 EPIGRAMS 38   8 I'le loose my modestie, and tell your name.

name (cont.)

p.	41	EPIGRAMS 43	9 When, in my booke, men reade but CECILL'S name,
p.	41	EPIGRAMS 44	1 CHVFFE, lately rich in name, in chattels, goods,
p.	43	EPIGRAMS 53	3 Thou wert content the authors name to loose:
p.	46	EPIGRAMS 60	2 An obeliske, or columne to thy name,
p.	48	EPIGRAMS 64	16 Wherein what wonder see thy name hath wrought?
p.	49	EPIGRAMS 67	3 That sound, and that authoritie with her name,
p.	53	EPIGRAMS 77	2 That, any way, my booke should speake thy name:
p.	53	EPIGRAMS 77	t2 NAME HIM.
p.	57	EPIGRAMS 89	5 Who had no lesse a trumpet of their name,
p.	64	EPIGRAMS 99	11 Well, though thy name lesse then our great ones bee,
p.	66	EPIGRAMS 102	1 I doe but name thee PEMBROKE, and I find
p.	66	EPIGRAMS 103	5 And, being nam'd, how little doth that name
p.	68	EPIGRAMS 106	1 If men get name, for some one vertue: Then,
p.	70	EPIGRAMS 109	17 Thy deedes, vnto thy name, will proue new wombes,
p.	71	EPIGRAMS 110	3 The name of POMPEY for an enemie,
p.	73	EPIGRAMS 114	2 When SYDNYES name I heare, or face I see:
p.	74	EPIGRAMS 115	1 You wonder, who this is! and, why I name
p.	74	EPIGRAMS 115	4 Suffers no name, but a description:
p.	75	EPIGRAMS 116	1 IEPHSON, thou man of men, to whose lou'd name
p.	79	EPIGRAMS 124	9 One name was ELIZABETH,
p.	80	EPIGRAMS 127	9 So, all reward, or name, that growes to mee
p.	80	EPIGRAMS 128	1 ROE (and my ioy to name) th'art now, to goe
p.	107	FOREST 10	2 Or whose great name in Poets heauen vse,
p.	111	FOREST 11	80 And for their place, and name,
p.	117	FOREST 13	11 And, in this name, am giuen out dangerous
p.	119	FOREST 13	98 To CLIFTON'S bloud, that is deny'd their name.
p.	119	FOREST 13	109 Vnto your name, and goodnesse of your life,
p.	121	FOREST 14	41 'T will be exacted of your name, whose sonne,
p.	121	FOREST 14	51 So may you liue in honor, as in name,
p.	129	UNDERWOOD 1.2	24 His glorious Name
p.	136	UNDERWOOD 2.5	8 Where he chanc't your name to see
p.	137	UNDERWOOD 2.5	37 To my shafts! Her very Name,
p.	148	UNDERWOOD 7	35 If Love, or feare, would let me tell his name.
p.	152	UNDERWOOD 12	37 Reader, whose life, and name, did e're become
p.	153	UNDERWOOD 13	18 To have such doe me good, I durst not name:
p.	161	UNDERWOOD 14	69 In offering this thy worke to no great Name,
p.	164	UNDERWOOD 15	57 To do't with Cloth, or Stuffes, lusts name might merit;
p.	168	UNDERWOOD 15	190 Still pretious, with the odour of thy name.
p.	172	UNDERWOOD 21	2 His name in any mettall, it would breake.
p.	173	UNDERWOOD 22	24 Is gone himselfe into your Name.
p.	181	UNDERWOOD 27	17 Or hath Corynna, by the name
p.	185	UNDERWOOD 30	11 But stood unshaken in his Deeds, and Name,
p.	186	UNDERWOOD 31	8 Still flie about the Odour of your Name;
p.	187	UNDERWOCD 33	40 Alone, but all thy ranke a reverend Name.
p.	190	UNDERWOOD 37	10 But, as a friend, which name your selfe receave,
p.	193	UNDERWOCD 38	82 The name of Cruell weather, storme, and raine?
p.	197	UNDERWOCD 40	10 Under another Name, I take your health;
p.	198	UNDERWOOD 40	42 The Jewell of your name, as close as sleepe
p.	208	UNDERWOOD 43	120 May to thy name a Vulcanale say;
p.	214	UNDERWOOD 44	50 And keepe the Glorie of the English name,
p.	216	UNDERWOOD 45	9 Much lesse a name would we bring up, or nurse,
p.	224	UNDERWOOD 50	13 And though all praise bring nothing to your name,
p.	234	UNDERWOOD 60	10 Of Vertue, got above his name?
p.	241	UNDERWOOD 69	4 What, by that name, wee each to other owe,
p.	244	UNDERWOOD 70	36 And had his noble name advanc'd with men:
p.	252	UNDERWOOD 75	t12 of the same name.
p.	255	UNDERWOOD 75	96 To give a greater Name, and Title to! Their owne!
p.	256	UNDERWOOD 75	116 And by his Rise, in active men, his Name
p.	268	UNDERWOOD 82	11 Grow up, sweet Babe, as blessed, in thy Name,
p.	269	UNDERWOOD 83	7 To give your shade a name! Stay, stay, I feele
p.	269	UNDERWOOD 83	22 Sound thou her Vertues, give her soule a Name.
p.	274	U'WOOD 84.2	14 Thy Neeces line, then thou that gav'st thy Name
p.	282	U'WOOD 84.9	6 Spun out in name of some one of the old Nine!
p.	293	UNDERWOOD 87	7 In name, I went all names before,
p.	311	HORACE 2	128 Nor know t<o>'observe: why (i'the Muses name)
p.	323	HORACE 2	372 A foot, whose swiftnesse gave the Verse the name
p.	327	HORACE 2	491 And thus, at first, an honour, and a name
p.	362	UNGATHERED 1	30 Palmer thy trauayles well becum thy name,
p.	372	UNGATHERED 9	12 She was 'Sell Boulstred. In wch name, I call
p.	383	UNGATHERED 17	4 May aske, what Author would conceale his name?
p.	390	UNGATHERED 26	1 To draw no enuy (Shakespeare) on thy name,

name (cont.)
```
   p.  394  UNGATHERED 28   12 And Christian name too, with a Heralds witt.
   p.  399  UNGATHERED 31   17 All that was solid, in the name
   p.  400  UNGATHERED 31   30 Keeps warme the spice of her good name,
   p.  401  UNGATHERED 32   19 Nor flatt'ry! but secur'd, by the Authors Name,
   p.  404  UNGATHERED 34   60 His name is #Skeuopoios wee all knowe,
   p.  409  UNGATHERED 37   11 I now would write on thee? No, wretch; thy name
   p.  409  UNGATHERED 37   18 To aske thy name, if he haue half his Nose!
   p.  412  UNGATHERED 41    1 Here, are five letters in this blessed Name,
   p.  423  UNGATHERED 50   19 That prince that shames a tyrants name to beare,
```

nameless   frequency: 1   relative frequency: 0.00001
```
   p.  409  UNGATHERED 37   16 Nameless, and noysome, as thy infamy!
```

names   frequency: 27   relative frequency: 0.00039
```
   p.   28  EPIGRAMS 3       10 Who scarse can spell th'hard names: whose knight
                                lesse can.
   p.   29  EPIGRAMS 9        1 May none, whose scatter'd names honor my booke,
   p.   35  EPIGRAMS 28       8 And, can forget mens names, with a great grace.
   p.   58  EPIGRAMS 91       1 Which of thy names I take, not onely beares
   p.   59  EPIGRAMS 92      24 Or BILS, and there he buyes the names of
                                books.
   p.   67  EPIGRAMS 105      5 But euen their names were to be made a-new,
   p.   69  EPIGRAMS 107     24 That are your wordes of credit. Keepe your
                                Names
   p.   69  EPIGRAMS 108      3 And your high names: I doe desire, that thence
   p.   94  FOREST 2         15 There, in the writhed barke, are cut the names
   p.  155  UNDERWOOD 13     62 Like Money-brokers, after Names, and hire
   p.  156  UNDERWOOD 13    101 Reare-Suppers in their Names! and spend whole
                                nights
   p.  159  UNDERWOOD 14     21 Men past their termes, and prais'd some names too
                                much,
   p.  161  UNDERWOOD 14     82 Selden! two Names that so much understand!
   p.  169  UNDERWOOD 17      8 But that some greater names have broke with me,
   p.  187  UNDERWOOD 33      7 But when I read or heare the names so rife
   p.  204  UNDERWOOD 43     39 Acrostichs, and Telestichs, on jumpe names,
   p.  246  UNDERWOOD 70     98 Two names of friendship, but one Starre:
   p.  257  UNDERWOOD 75    149 To propagate their Names,
   p.  257  UNDERWOOD 75    155 Their names are not recorded on the File
   p.  258  UNDERWOOD 75    170 A Richard, and a Hierome, by their names
   p.  273  U'WOOD 84.1       6 Their names of being kept alive,
   p.  281  U'WOOD 84.8      12 When your owne Vertues, equall'd have their
                                Names,
   p.  293  UNDERWOOD 87      7 In name, I went all names before,
   p.  309  HORACE 2         83 New names of things. It hath beene ever free,
   p.  386  UNGATHERED 21    10 Or, like our Money-Brokers, take vp names
   p.  391  UNGATHERED 26    33 For names; but call forth thund'ring Aeschilus,
   p.  402  UNGATHERED 34     8 With mistooke Names out of Vitruvius!
```

name's   frequency: 1   relative frequency: 0.00001
```
   p.   74  EPIGRAMS 115     15 Whose name's vn-welcome to the present eare,
```

naming   frequency: 3   relative frequency: 0.00004
```
   p.   59  EPIGRAMS 92      33 At naming the French King, their heads they
                                shake,
   p.   74  EPIGRAMS 115      3 Naming so many, too! But, this is one,
   p.  191  UNDERWOOD 38     25 By naming in what companie 'twas in,
```

nard   frequency: 1   relative frequency: 0.00001
```
   p.  135  UNDERWOOD 2.4    28 Or the Nard i' the fire?
```

nare   frequency: 1   relative frequency: 0.00001
```
   p.   87  EPIGRAMS 133    133 And that ours did. For, yet, no nare was
                                tainted,
```

narrow   frequency: 7   relative frequency: 0.00010
```
   p.  100  FOREST 4         10 Thy subtle wayes, be narrow straits;
   p.  147  UNDERWOOD 7       7 For that's a narrow joy is but our owne.
   p.  150  UNDERWOOD 10      4 Nor have I yet the narrow mind
   p.  222  UNDERWOOD 48     53 The narrow Seas are shadie,
   p.  225  UNDERWOOD 51     18 For 't were a narrow gladnesse, kept thine owne.
   p.  250  UNDERWOOD 73      2 Thy faint, and narrow eyes, to reade the King
   p.  408  UNGATHERED 36    14 Thy Forehead is too narrow for my Brand.
```

narrow'd   frequency: 1   relative frequency: 0.00001
```
   p.  248  UNDERWOOD 71     10 But lyes block'd up, and straightned, narrow'd
                                in,
```

naso   frequency: 1   relative frequency: 0.00001
```
   p.  397  UNGATHERED 30    32 With vs be call'd, the Naso, but this man?
```

nastie   frequency: 1   relative frequency: 0.00001
    p.   88 EPIGRAMS 133   147 For, to say truth, what scullion is so nastie,

nasty
    See also "nastie."   frequency: 1   relative frequency: 0.00001
   *p. 493 TO HIMSELF   23 As the Shrieues crusts, and nasty as his fish-

nation   frequency: 4   relative frequency: 0.00005
    p. 141 UNDERWOOD 2.9   8 And his Manners of that Nation.
    p. 213 UNDERWOOD 44   12 Nor markes of wealth so from our Nation fled,
    p. 238 UNDERWOOD 66   10 To make the hearts of a whole Nation smile,
    p. 380 UNGATHERED 12   29 And therefore how euer the trauelling nation,

nations   frequency: 6   relative frequency: 0.00008
    p. 214 UNDERWOOD 44   51 Up among Nations. In the stead of bold
    p. 217 UNDERWOOD 46   14 Stood up thy Nations fame, her Crownes defence.
    p. 234 UNDERWOOD 61   12 A Nations sinne got pardon'd! 'twere a taske
    p. 261 UNDERWOOD 77   19 Of murmuring Subjects; make the Nations know
    p. 271 UNDERWOOD 83   90 Whole Nations! nay, Mankind! the World, with
                              all
    p. 411 UNGATHERED 40   6 to all good Nations.

native   frequency: 1   relative frequency: 0.00001
    p. 286 U'WOOD 84.9   142 Our native portions, and possessed rent;

nativitie   frequency: 1   relative frequency: 0.00001
    p. 130 UNDERWOOD 1.3   t2 On the Nativitie of my Saviour.

nativity. See "nativitie."

natural. See "naturall."

naturall   frequency: 1   relative frequency: 0.00001
    p. 117 FOREST 13   32 It perfect, proper, pure, and naturall,

natur'd   frequency: 1   relative frequency: 0.00001
    p. 317 HORACE 2   265 Natur'd, and wicked Atreus cooke, to th'eye,

nature
    See also "nature's."   frequency: 44   relative frequency: 0.00063
  **p. 117 PANEGYRE   159 Which when time, nature, and the fates deny'd,
    p.   39 EPIGRAMS 40   3 Rich, as nature could bequeath thee:
    p.   50 EPIGRAMS 70   1 When Nature bids vs leaue to liue, 'tis late
    p.   53 EPIGRAMS 79   8 Nature, they thought, in all, that he would
                              faine.
    p.   75 EPIGRAMS 116   9 That Nature no such difference had imprest
    p.   77 EPIGRAMS 120   7 As Heauen and Nature seem'd to striue
    p.   79 EPIGRAMS 125   2 Made for what Nature could, or Vertue can;
    p. 112 FOREST 11   100 As if Nature disclos'd
    p. 114 FOREST 12   35 Wherein wise Nature you a dowrie gaue,
    p. 117 FOREST 13   19 Of nature, and societie, I should faint;
    p. 128 UNDERWOOD 1.1   22 To take our nature; becam'st man, and dyd'st,
    p. 130 UNDERWOOD 1.3   18 And tooke on him our Nature.
    p. 160 UNDERWOOD 14   64 Large claspe of Nature, such a wit can bound.
    p. 162 UNDERWOOD 15   8 Quickning dead Nature, to her noblest strife.
    p. 164 UNDERWOOD 15   61 Like upon them lighten? If nature could
    p. 165 UNDERWOOD 15   90 Nature, that will not let his Wife be a whore;
    p. 169 UNDERWOOD 17   3 And yet the noble Nature never grudge;
    p. 173 UNDERWOOD 22   20 That envie wish'd, and Nature fear'd.
    p. 188 UNDERWOOD 34   6 Quarrell with Nature, or in ballance brought
    p. 188 UNDERWOOD 35   2 What manners prettie, Nature milde,
    p. 192 UNDERWOOD 38   60 Of that wise Nature would a Cradle have.
    p. 192 UNDERWOOD 38   62 Consumptions nature to destroy, and sterve.
    p. 243 UNDERWOOD 70   11 Did wiser Nature draw thee back,
    p. 262 UNDERWOOD 78   11 Where Nature such a large survey hath ta'en,
    p. 264 UNDERWOOD 79   33 Of all that Nature, yet, to life did bring;
    p. 270 UNDERWOOD 83   45 What Nature, Fortune, Institution, Fact
    p. 274 U'WOOD 84.2   4 That ever Nature, or the later Ayre
    p. 279 U'WOOD 84.4   30 As it another Nature were,
    p. 282 U'WOOD 84.9   13 On Nature, for her: who did let her lie,
    p. 282 U'WOOD 84.9   15 Sleepie, or stupid Nature, couldst thou part
    p. 284 U'WOOD 84.9   75 Against the Nature he would worship. Hee
    p. 286 U'WOOD 84.9   139 To style us Friends, who were, by Nature,
                              Foes?
    p. 287 U'WOOD 84.9   158 As nature could not more increase the flood
    p. 288 U'WOOD 84.9   214 Of lapsed Nature) best know what to doe,
    p. 311 HORACE 2   152 For Nature, first, within doth fashion us
    p. 329 HORACE 2   518 Will passe the Seas, and long as nature is,
    p. 331 HORACE 2   574 Wilt nothing against nature speake, or doe:
    p. 331 HORACE 2   582 Nature, or Art. My Judgement will not pierce

nature (cont.)
    p. 365 UNGATHERED 5   16 All Nature of commending.
    p. 390 UNGATHERED 25   4 With Nature, to out-doo the life:
    p. 392 UNGATHERED 26 47 Nature her selfe was proud of his designes,
    p. 392 UNGATHERED 26 55 Yet must I not giue Nature all: Thy Art,
    p. 392 UNGATHERED 26 57 For though the Poets matter, Nature be,
    p. 415 UNGATHERED 42 18 As it were spun by nature, off the fleece:

natures   frequency: 11 relative frequency: 0.00015
    p. 60 EPIGRAMS 93   12 Nor could I, had I seene all Natures roule,
    p. 68 EPIGRAMS 105   19 So are you Natures Index, and restore,
    p. 154 UNDERWOOD 13   60 That to such Natures let their full hands flow,
    p. 192 UNDERWOOD 38   64 Is natures meere obliquitie! as Heaven
    p. 250 UNDERWOOD 74   2 Doth take in easie Natures birth,
    p. 253 UNDERWOOD 75   27 To doe their Offices in Natures Chime,
    p. 271 UNDERWOOD 83   70 On Natures secrets, there, as her owne bookes:
    p. 284 U'WOOD 84.9   51 For, as there are three Natures, Schoolemen
                                   call
    p. 315 HORACE 2   224 And give their yeares, and natures, as they
                                   swerve,
    p. 364 UNGATHERED 4   6 That Natures fairest Creature,
    p. 392 UNGATHERED 26 54 As they were not of Natures family.

nature's   frequency: 1 relative frequency: 0.00001
  See also "natures."
    p. 256 UNDERWOOD 75 113 Stand there; for when a noble Nature's rais'd,

naught   frequency: 1 relative frequency: 0.00001
  See also "nought."
    p. 333 HORACE 2   624 Hee'd say, Mend this, good friend, and this;
                                 'tis naught.

navie   frequency: 1 relative frequency: 0.00001
    p. 309 HORACE 2   92 That from the North, the Navie safe doth store,

navy. See "navie."

nay   frequency: 23 relative frequency: 0.00033
    p. 36 EPIGRAMS 28   19 Nay more, for greatnesse sake, he will be one
    p. 57 EPIGRAMS 90   11 Still MILL continu'd: Nay, his face growing
                                   worse,
    p. 59 EPIGRAMS 92   18 Nay, aske you, how the day goes, in your eare.
    p. 69 EPIGRAMS 107   29 Nay, now you puffe, tuske, and draw vp your chin,
    p. 81 EPIGRAMS 129   16 Thou dost out-zany COKELY, POD; nay,
                                   GVE:
    p. 110 FOREST 11   46 Pure, perfect, nay diuine;
    p. 137 UNDERWOOD 2.5 29 Nay, her white and polish'd neck,
    p. 139 UNDERWOOD 2.7   9 Nay, you may erre in this,
    p. 140 UNDERWOOD 2.8 21 Nay, I will not let you sit
    p. 144 UNDERWOOD 3   25 Nay, rather both our soules bee strayn'd
    p. 163 UNDERWOOD 15   53 That all respect; She must lie downe: Nay more,
    p. 209 UNDERWOOD 43 148 Nay, sigh'd a Sister, 'twas the Nun, Kate
                                   Arden,
    p. 210 UNDERWOOD 43 156 Nay, let White-Hall with Revels have to doe,
    p. 228 UNDERWOOD 53   11 Nay, so your Seate his beauties did endorse,
    p. 235 UNDERWOOD 62   9 Nay, and in this, thou show'st to value more
    p. 241 UNDERWOOD 68   4 For want of knowing the Poet, to say him nay?
    p. 245 UNDERWOOD 70   78 And thinke, nay know, thy Morison's not dead.
    p. 271 UNDERWOOD 83   90 Whole Nations! nay, Mankind! the World, with
                                   all
    p. 363 UNGATHERED 3   18 Where Gold's the Motiue, women haue no Nay.
    p. 380 UNGATHERED 12 47 Nay more in his wardrobe, if you will laugh at a
    p. 394 UNGATHERED 28 11 Nay they will venter ones Descent to hitt,
    p. 399 UNGATHERED 31   7 Your booke? your volume! Nay, the state, and
                                   story!
    p. 408 UNGATHERED 37   2 And they were very good: yet thou think'st nay.

ne   frequency: 1 relative frequency: 0.00001
    p. 227 UNDERWOOD 52   21 Ne knowes he flatt'ring Colours, or false light.

neadd   frequency: 1 relative frequency: 0.00001
    p. 63 EPIGRAMS 97   14 Of any Madames, hath neadd squires, and must.

near. See "neare," "neere," "nere."

neare   frequency: 3 relative frequency: 0.00004
    p. 111 FOREST 11   66 Some vicious foole draw neare,
    p. 365 UNGATHERED 5   20 My selfe am so neare drowning?
    p. 397 UNGATHERED 30 49 And flight about the Ile, well neare, by this,

nearer   frequency: 1   relative frequency: 0.00001
     See also "neerer."
     p. 409 UNGATHERED 38   3 Now, you are got into a nearer roome,

neat   frequency: 3   relative frequency: 0.00004
     See also "neate."
     p. 142 U'WOOD 2.10   4 His Clothes rich, and band sit neat,
     p. 164 UNDERWOOD 15   70 And then, leape mad on a neat Pickardill,
     p. 392 UNGATHERED 26   52 Neat Terence, witty Plautus, now not please;

neate   frequency: 2   relative frequency: 0.00002
     p. 35 EPIGRAMS 28   11 That's greater, yet: to crie his owne vp neate.
     p. 387 UNGATHERED 22   3 which, did they neere so neate, or proudly dwell,

neatly   frequency: 1   relative frequency: 0.00001
     p. 151 UNDERWOOD 12   15 His Mind as pure, and neatly kept,

necessary   frequency: 1   relative frequency: 0.00001
    **p. 116 PANEGYRE   116 Whose necessary good 'twas now to be

necessitie   frequency: 4   relative frequency: 0.00005
     p. 41 EPIGRAMS 43   12 As thou stand'st cleere of the necessitie.
     p. 111 FOREST 11   82 Is meere necessitie.
     p. 231 UNDERWOOD 57   2 Necessitie urges
     p. 271 UNDERWOOD 83   93 T<o>'escape this common knowne necessitie,

necessities   frequency: 1   relative frequency: 0.00001
     p. 153 UNDERWOOD 13   8 To succour my necessities, tooke fire,

necessity. See "necessitie."

neck   frequency: 5   relative frequency: 0.00007
     See also "horse-neck," "necke."
     p. 33 EPIGRAMS 21   2 His neck fenc'd round with ruffe! his eyes halfe
                                shut!
     p. 137 UNDERWOOD 2.5   29 Nay, her white and polish'd neck,
     p. 276 U'WOOD 84.3   13 Draw first a Cloud: all save her neck;
     p. 293 UNDERWOOD 87   2 And ('bout thy Ivory neck,) no youth did fling
     p. 338 HORACE 1   2 . horse neck joyn . sundry plumes ore-fold

neck-stockt   frequency: 1   relative frequency: 0.00001
     p. 411 UNGATHERED 39   16 Cropt, branded, slit, neck-stockt; go, you are
                                stript.

necke   frequency: 1   relative frequency: 0.00001
     p. 101 FOREST 4   26 And thrust my necke into the noose,

necks   frequency: 1   relative frequency: 0.00001
     p. 291 UNDERWOOD 85   64 And fainting necks, the turned Share!

nectar   frequency: 4   relative frequency: 0.00005
     p. 39 EPIGRAMS 40   10 And like Nectar euer flowing:
     p. 65 EPIGRAMS 101   33 Tabacco, Nectar, or the Thespian spring,
     p. 106 FOREST 9   7 But might I of IOVE'S Nectar sup,
     p. 187 UNDERWOOD 33   36 Thy Hearers Nectar, and thy Clients Balme,

neeces   frequency: 1   relative frequency: 0.00001
     p. 274 U'WOOD 84.2   14 Thy Neeces line, then thou that gav'st thy Name

need   frequency: 23   relative frequency: 0.00033
     See also "neadd," "neede."
     p. 40 EPIGRAMS 43   1 What need hast thou of me? or of my Muse?
     p. 61 EPIGRAMS 95   27 We need a man that knowes the seuerall graces
     p. 62 EPIGRAMS 95   31 We need a man, can speake of the intents,
     p. 62 EPIGRAMS 95   33 Of state, and censure them: we need his pen
     p. 62 EPIGRAMS 95   35 But most we need his faith (and all haue you)
     p. 63 EPIGRAMS 98   4 Need seeke no other strength, no other height;
     p. 66 EPIGRAMS 103   6 Need any Muses praise to giue it fame?
     p. 67 EPIGRAMS 103   14 Becomes none more then you, who need it least.
     p. 78 EPIGRAMS 122   9 I need no other arts, but studie thee:
     p. 95 FOREST 2   72 Nor, when I take my lodging, need I pray
     p. 102 FOREST 4   64 As shall not need thy false reliefe.
     p. 117 FOREST 13   28 Remou'd, as you from need to haue it such.
     p. 143 UNDERWOOD 3   13 What need of mee? doe you but sing,
     p. 155 UNDERWOOD 13   75 I not deny it, but to helpe the need
     p. 157 UNDERWOOD 13   145 They need no stilts, nor rise upon their toes,
     p. 158 UNDERWOOD 14   11 Unto the Censure. Yours all need doth flie
     p. 215 UNDERWOOD 44   70 All licence in our lives? What need we know,
     p. 215 UNDERWOOD 44   83 Past any need of vertue. Let them care,
     p. 307 HORACE 2   70 Thou need new termes; thou maist, without excuse,

need (cont.)
    p. 385 UNGATHERED 19   5 To such a worke, as could not need theirs? Yet
    p. 386 UNGATHERED 20 12 Shee need not blush vpon the Mariage-Day.
    p. 391 UNGATHERED 26 16 Aboue th'ill fortune of them, or the need.
    p. 403 UNGATHERED 34 40 The Eloquence of Masques! What need of prose

neede   frequency: 1   relative frequency: 0.00001
    p. 95 FOREST 2   59 The neede of such? whose liberall boord doth
                   flow,

needfully   frequency: 1   relative frequency: 0.00001
    p. 61 EPIGRAMS 94   13 And like them too; must needfully, though few,

needs   frequency: 10   relative frequency: 0.00014
  *p. 493 TO HIMSELF   30 Needs set them, but, the almes-basket of wit.
    p. 56 EPIGRAMS 88   14 And stoupe, and cringe. O then, it needs must
                   proue
    p. 105 FOREST 8   15 Or if needs thy lust will tast
    p. 189 UNDERWOOD 36   5 Where Love doth shine, there needs no Sunne,
    p. 204 UNDERWOOD 43 48 Or if thou needs would'st trench upon her power,
    p. 208 UNDERWOOD 43 125 Against thy furie, when to serve their needs,
    p. 217 UNDERWOOD 46 24 Needs lend an aide, to thine she had her eyes.
    p. 275 U'WOOD 84.3   8 Needs nought to cloath it but the ayre.
    p. 393 UNGATHERED 27   2 And needs no other touch.
    p. 400 UNGATHERED 32   3 Hence, then, prophane: Here needs no words
                   expense

need'st   frequency: 2   relative frequency: 0.00002
    p. 32 EPIGRAMS 16   7 Nor need'st thou: for those few, by oath releast,
    p. 61 EPIGRAMS 95   20 Thou need'st not shrinke at voyce of after-times;

ne'er   frequency: 1 relative frequency: 0.00001
    p. 108 FOREST 10 A   6 Could ne'er make prize of thy white Chastetye.

neere   frequency: 17   relative frequency: 0.00024
    p. 30 EPIGRAMS 11   3 To seeme a statesman: as I neere it came,
    p. 86 EPIGRAMS 133 85 But, comming neere, they found it but a liter,
    p. 96 FOREST 3   3 And, though so neere the citie, and the court,
    p. 169 UNDERWOOD 18   5 Or was she gracious a-farre off? but neere
    p. 175 UNDERWOOD 24   1 From Death, and darke oblivion, neere the same,
    p. 200 UNDERWOOD 42 30 Where I may handle Silke, as free, and neere,
    p. 224 UNDERWOOD 50 26 And when you want those friends, or neere in
                   blood,
    p. 231 UNDERWOOD 57 15 Christmas is neere;
    p. 242 UNDERWOOD 69 17 Some of his formes, he lets him not come neere
    p. 242 UNDERWOOD 69 20 To judge; So all men comming neere can spie.
    p. 269 UNDERWOOD 83 29 It is too neere of kin to Heaven, the Soule,
    p. 292 UNDERWOOD 86 20 Beneath a Sweet-wood Roofe, neere Alba Lake:
    p. 321 HORACE 2   357 Like men street-borne, and neere the Hall,
                   reherse
    p. 329 HORACE 2   507 Let what thou fain'st for pleasures sake, be
                   neere
    p. 366 UNGATHERED 6   18 Neere which, the Thespiad's sing;
    p. 387 UNGATHERED 22   3 which, did they neere so neate, or proudly dwell,
    p. 393 UNGATHERED 27   4 Refine it neere so much.

neerer   frequency: 1   relative frequency: 0.00001
    p. 331 HORACE 2   540 Will take you more, the neerer that you stand;

neglect   frequency: 1   relative frequency: 0.00001
    p. 219 UNDERWOOD 47 54 I, and for this neglect, the courser sort

negligence   frequency: 2   relative frequency: 0.00002
    p. 323 HORACE 2   385 Of too much haste, and negligence in part,
    p. 329 HORACE 2   527 Offended with few spots, which negligence

neighbour   frequency: 1   relative frequency: 0.00001
    p. 417 UNGATHERED 45 35 'tis but the next neighbour ride

neighbour-townes   frequency: 1   relative frequency: 0.00001
    p. 309 HORACE 2   95 In neighbour-townes, and feeles the weightie
                   plough;

neighbourhood   frequency: 1   relative frequency: 0.00001
    p. 416 UNGATHERED 43   7 How they advance true Love, and neighbourhood,

neighbours   frequency: 1   relative frequency: 0.00001
  See also "countrie-neighbours."
    p. 40 EPIGRAMS 42   2 Th'obseruing neighbours no such mood can see.

neighing   frequency: 1   relative frequency: 0.00001
     p. 397 UNGATHERED 30   40 Drums against Drums, the neighing of the Horse,

neither   frequency: 23   relative frequency: 0.00033
     See also "neyther."
   **p. 115 PANEGYRE   96 "Who both, who neither: all the cunning tracts,
     p. 48 EPIGRAMS 66   1 That neither fame, nor loue might wanting be
     p. 63 EPIGRAMS 97   9 Know you the cause? H'has neither land, nor
                                lease,
     p. 99 FOREST 3   92 Shalt neither that, nor this enuy:
     p. 100 FOREST 3   104 That neither want doe thee affright,
     p. 140 UNDERWOOD 2.8   15 You shall neither eat, nor sleepe,
     p. 154 UNDERWOOD 13   41 He neither gives, or do's, that doth delay
     p. 157 UNDERWOOD 13   129 Of Christendome! And neither of these know,
     p. 157 UNDERWOOD 13   147 Are Dwarfes of Honour, and have neither weight
     p. 197 UNDERWOOD 40   18 As neither wine doe rack it out, or mirth.
     p. 215 UNDERWOOD 44   86 We neither love the Troubles, nor the harmes.
     p. 216 UNDERWOOD 45   5 I neither am, nor art thou one of those
     p. 219 UNDERWOOD 47   46 Though I doe neither heare these newes, nor tell
     p. 231 UNDERWOOD 57   16 And neither good Cheare,
     p. 305 HORACE 2   10 As neither head, nor foot, one forme retaine.
     p. 307 HORACE 2   37 Hath neither soule, nor sinewes. Loftie he
     p. 321 HORACE 2   331 As neither any God, were brought in there,
     p. 329 HORACE 2   521 For, neither doth the String still yeeld that
                                sound
     p. 331 HORACE 2   555 But neither, Men, nor Gods, nor Pillars meant,
     p. 367 UNGATHERED 6   48 "Where neither Force can bend, nor Feare can
                                awe.
     p. 375 UNGATHERED 10   34 Bvt here, neither trusting his hands, nor his
                                legs,
     p. 390 UNGATHERED 26   4 As neither Man, nor Muse, can praise too much.
     p. 395 UNGATHERED 29   9 As neither Pompey's popularitie,

neithers   frequency: 1   relative frequency: 0.00001
     p. 96 FOREST 3   4 Art tane with neithers vice, nor sport:

nephew   frequency: 1   relative frequency: 0.00001
     p. 121 FOREST 14   42 Whose nephew, whose grand-child you are;

nephewes   frequency: 3   relative frequency: 0.00004
     p. 238 UNDERWOOD 65   7 And long in changing. Let our Nephewes see
     p. 387 UNGATHERED 22   10 And teach your nephewes it to aemulate:
     p. 399 UNGATHERED 31   3 Transmitt it to your Nephewes, ffreinds,
                                Allies,

nephews   frequency: 1   relative frequency: 0.00001
     See also "nephewes."
     p. 317 HORACE 2   266 His Nephews entrailes; nor must Progne flie

ne'r   frequency: 1   relative frequency: 0.00001
     p. 382 UNGATHERED 16   8 his life, his loue, his honour, which ne'r dyes,

nere   frequency: 2   relative frequency: 0.00002
     p. 105 FOREST 8   40 Bald, or blinde, or nere so many:
     p. 422 UNGATHERED 50   4 whom fortune hath deprest; come nere the fates

ne're   frequency: 15   relative frequency: 0.00021
     p. 34 EPIGRAMS 24   2 Mens manners ne're were viler, for your sake.
     p. 93 FOREST 1   9 Into my ri'mes could ne're be got
     p. 150 UNDERWOOD 10   16 I ne're will owe my health to a disease.
     p. 161 UNDERWOOD 14   83 On whom I could take up, and ne're abuse
     p. 165 UNDERWOOD 15   100 Ne're came to taste the plenteous Mariage-horne.
     p. 171 UNDERWOOD 20   6 That ne're was knowne to last above a fit!
     p. 177 UNDERWOOD 25   26 True noblesse. Palme growes straight, though
                                handled ne're so rude.
     p. 188 UNDERWOOD 34   9 Her owne bloud gave her: Shee ne're had, nor
                                hath
     p. 197 UNDERWOOD 40   1 That Love's a bitter sweet, I ne're conceive
     p. 202 UNDERWOOD 43   5 I ne're attempted, Vulcan, 'gainst thy life:
     p. 208 UNDERWOOD 43   115 And so did Jove, who ne're meant thee his Cup:
     p. 323 HORACE 2   379 Provided, ne're to yeeld, in any case
     p. 331 HORACE 2   563 If ne're so little it depart the first,
     p. 333 HORACE 2   596 Or, of the things, that ne're came in my mind,
     p. 391 UNGATHERED 26   9 Or blinde Affection, which doth ne're aduance

nero   frequency: 1   relative frequency: 0.00001
     p. 61 EPIGRAMS 95   8 Where NERO falls, and GALBA is ador'd,

nerues   frequency: 1   relative frequency: 0.00001
    *p. 493 TO HIMSELF   45 And though thy nerues be shrunke, and blood be
                                cold,

nerves. See "nerues."

nest   frequency: 4   relative frequency: 0.00005
    p. 137 UNDERWOOD 2.5   34 Lyes the Valley, cal'd my nest,
    p. 198 UNDERWOOD 40   38 Farre from the Nest, and so himselfe belie
    p. 251 UNDERWOOD 74   13 The very verdure of her nest,
    p. 280 U'WOOD 84.4   64 A nest of odorous spice, and gummes.

net   frequency: 3   relative frequency: 0.00004
    p.   93 FOREST 1   6 MARS, and my Mother, in their net:
    p.   94 FOREST 2   33 Fat, aged carps, that runne into thy net.
    p. 164 UNDERWOOD 15   65 Planting their Purles, and Curles spread forth
                                 like Net,

nether   frequency: 1   relative frequency: 0.00001
    p. 338 HORACE 1   20 .... and .... nether

nets   frequency: 3   relative frequency: 0.00004
    p. 100 FOREST 4   8 From all the nets that thou canst spread.
    p. 216 UNDERWOOD 45   18 Deceit is fruitfull. Men have Masques and nets,
    p. 290 UNDERWOOD 85   33 Or straines on his small forke his subtill nets

neuer   frequency: 20   relative frequency: 0.00028
  **p. 117 PANEGYRE   156 Neuer had land more reason to reioyce.
    p.   40 EPIGRAMS 42   4 But that his IONE doth too. And GILES
                                 would neuer,
    p.   41 EPIGRAMS 45   12 As what he loues may neuer like too much.
    p.   42 EPIGRAMS 46   5 The knight-wright's cheated then: Hee'll neuer
                                 pay.
    p.   55 EPIGRAMS 85   7 And neuer stoupe, but to strike ignorance:
    p.   56 EPIGRAMS 88   5 And land on one, whose face durst neuer bee
    p.   61 EPIGRAMS 95   16 MINERVAES loome was neuer richer spred.
    p.   73 EPIGRAMS 112   19 And neuer art encounter'd, I confesse:
    p.   86 EPIGRAMS 133   80 Man, that had neuer heard of a Chimaera.
    p.   87 EPIGRAMS 133   116 Neuer did bottome more betray her burden;
    p.   94 FOREST 2   20 That neuer failes to serue thee season'd deere,
    p. 100 FOREST 4   23 And neuer will redeeme a day,
    p. 108 FOREST 10 A   3 Thy thoughtes did neuer melt in amorous fire,
    p. 113 FOREST 11   116 Man may securely sinne, but safely neuer.
    p. 113 FOREST 12   11 Though neuer after; whiles it gaynes the voyce
    p. 119 FOREST 13   87 And neuer thinke, how vice doth euery houre,
    p. 363 UNGATHERED 3   5 Gold is a sutor, neuer tooke repulse,
    p. 366 UNGATHERED 6   8 Did neuer dint the breast of Tamisis.
    p. 384 UNGATHERED 18   15 So, be there neuer discontent, or sorrow,
    p. 384 UNGATHERED 18   21 So, in theyr number, may <you> neuer see

never   frequency: 36   relative frequency: 0.00052
    See also "n<e>'re," "ne'er," "neere," "ne'r,"
             "nere," "ne're," "neuer."
    p. 131 UNDERWOOD 2.1   15 That you never knew till now,
    p. 151 UNDERWOOD 11   6 Whom never yet he durst attempt awake;
    p. 152 UNDERWOOD 12   18 That never came ill odour thence:
    p. 156 UNDERWOOD 13   124 Men have beene great, but never good by chance,
    p. 168 UNDERWOOD 15   180 And never but for doing wrong be sory;
    p. 168 UNDERWOOD 15   183 That fortune never make thee to complaine,
    p. 168 UNDERWOOD 15   191 And last, blaspheme not, we did never heare
    p. 169 UNDERWOOD 17   3 And yet the noble Nature never grudge;
    p. 181 UNDERWOOD 27   1 Helen, did Homer never see
    p. 181 UNDERWOOD 27   26 Where never Star shone brighter yet?
    p. 184 UNDERWOOD 29   54 Resting never.
    p. 185 UNDERWOOD 30   10 That in all tempests, never quit the helme,
    p. 188 UNDERWOOD 34   5 Then this did by her true? She never sought
    p. 189 UNDERWOOD 37   5 On which with profit, I shall never looke,
    p. 198 UNDERWOOD 40   44 And never be by time, or folly brought,
    p. 218 UNDERWOOD 47   9 Let those that meerely talke, and never thinke,
    p. 218 UNDERWOOD 47   14 That never yet did friend, or friendship seeke
    p. 221 UNDERWOOD 48   31 So may there never Quarrell
    p. 223 UNDERWOOD 49   23 I never stood for any place: my wit
    p. 228 UNDERWOOD 53   15 For never saw I yet the Muses dwell,
    p. 242 UNDERWOOD 69   25 Never so great to get them: and the ends,
    p. 244 UNDERWOOD 70   44 Hee never fell, thou fall'st, my tongue.
    p. 248 UNDERWOOD 71   12 Health, or scarce breath, as she had never bin,
    p. 257 UNDERWOOD 75   153 Th'Ignoble never liv'd, they were a-while
    p. 258 UNDERWOOD 75   177 And never may there want one of the Stem,
    p. 277 U'WOOD 84.4   7 Beside, your hand will never hit,
    p. 286 U'WOOD 84.9   121 That happy Day, that never shall see night!
    p. 288 U'WOOD 84.9   185 Her broken sighes did never misse whole sense:
    p. 294 UNDERWOOD 88   9 This hath pleas'd, doth please, and long will
                                 please; never
    p. 295 UNDERWOOD 90   5 Never at Law; seldome in office gown'd;

never (cont.)
p. 313 HORACE 2   178 If something strange, that never yet was had
p. 331 HORACE 2   580 The Writ, once out, never returned yet.
p. 333 HORACE 2   612 Looke pale, distill a showre (was never meant)
p. 349 HORACE 1   444 .... never ...... 'gainst ....
p. 414 UNGATHERED 42   4 You know, I never was of Truth afeard,
p. 423 UNGATHERED 5C 20 shall never dare do any thing but feare./

nevil   frequency: 2   relative frequency: 0.00002
p.   70 EPIGRAMS 109   1 Who now calls on thee, NEVIL, is a Muse,
p.   70 EPIGRAMS 109   t1 TO SIR HENRY NEVIL.

nevills. See "nevil."

nevilles. See "nevills."

nevills   frequency: 1   relative frequency: 0.00001
p. 214 UNDERWOOD 44   52 Beauchamps, and Nevills, Cliffords, Audleys
                            old:

new   frequency: 64   relative frequency: 0.00092
     See also "a-new."
p.   29 EPIGRAMS 7   t1 ON THE NEW HOT-HOVSE.
p.   30 EPIGRAMS 12   14 Signes to new bond, forfeits: and cryes, god
                            payes.
p.   32 EPIGRAMS 18   1 To thee, my way in Epigrammes seemes new,
p.   39 EPIGRAMS 41   1 GYPSEE, new baud, is turn'd physitian,
p.   47 EPIGRAMS 64   1 Not glad, like those that haue new hopes, or
                            sutes,
p.   47 EPIGRAMS 64   2 With thy new place, bring I these early fruits
p.   47 EPIGRAMS 64   6 To see thy fathers rites new laid on thee.
p.   50 EPIGRAMS 71   1 To plucke downe mine, POLL sets vp new wits
                            still,
p.   54 EPIGRAMS 82   1 SVRLY'S old whore in her new silkes doth
                            swim:
p.   56 EPIGRAMS 88   15 The new french-taylors motion, monthly made,
p.   58 EPIGRAMS 92   t1 THE NEW CRIE.
p.   62 EPIGRAMS 97   3 But one more rare, and in the case so new:
p.   62 EPIGRAMS 97   t1 ON THE NEW MOTION.
p.   67 EPIGRAMS 104   4 A new SVSANNA, equall to that old?
p.   70 EPIGRAMS 109   17 Thy deedes, vnto thy name, will proue new wombes,
p.   71 EPIGRAMS 110   18 (As by a new creation) part by part,
p.   72 EPIGRAMS 111   5 And that, in action, there is nothing new,
p.   77 EPIGRAMS 120   21 And haue sought (to giue new birth)
p.   80 EPIGRAMS 127   8 Lent timely succours, and new life begot:
p.   81 EPIGRAMS 129   14 On some new gesture, that 's imputed wit?
p.   94 FOREST 2   40 Fresh as the ayre, and new as are the houres.
p.   98 FOREST 3   48 COMVS puts in, for new delights;
p. 107 FOREST 10   17 Or, with thy Tribade trine, inuent new sports,
p. 116 FOREST 12   98 A vow as new, and ominous as the yeare,
p. 119 FOREST 13   118 This makes, that your affections still be new,
p. 121 FOREST 14   35 And great, must seeke for new,
p. 137 UNDERWOOD 2.5 36 After flight; and put new stings
p. 145 UNDERWOOD 5   18 To make a new, and hang that by.
p. 157 UNDERWOOD 13 142 Meet some new matter to looke up and wonder!
p. 175 UNDERWOOD 23   28 Sols Chariot for new fire,
p. 181 UNDERWOOD 27   23 His new Cassandra, 'bove the old;
p. 187 UNDERWOOD 33   14 Have made me to conceive a Lawyer new.
p. 220 UNDERWOOD 48   t1 The Dedication of the Kings new Cellar.
p. 222 UNDERWOOD 49   6 New in their stead, out of the Candidates?
p. 223 UNDERWOOD 49   20 As new rewards of her old secrecie?
p. 253 UNDERWOOD 75   35 As they had learn'd new changes, for the day,
p. 263 UNDERWOOD 79   1 New yeares, expect new gifts: Sister, your
                            Harpe,
p. 263 UNDERWOOD 79   5 Of the New Yeare, in a new silken warpe,
p. 263 UNDERWOOD 79   9 Rector Chori. To day old Janus opens the new
                            yeare,
p. 269 UNDERWOOD 83   16 And the disposure will be something new,
p. 270 UNDERWOOD 83   37 Else, who doth praise a person by a new,
p. 275 U'WOOD 84.3   10 Were fitly interpos'd; so new:
p. 285 U'WOOD 84.9   90 A new Song to his praise, and great I AM:
p. 291 UNDERWOOD 85   55 More sweet then Olives, that new gather'd be
p. 307 HORACE 2   65 In using also of new words, to be
p. 307 HORACE 2   68 Are, by thy cunning placing, made meere new.
p. 307 HORACE 2   70 Thou need new termes; thou maist, without excuse,
p. 309 HORACE 2   74 And those thy new, and late-coyn'd words receive,
p. 309 HORACE 2   83 New names of things. It hath beene ever free,
p. 313 HORACE 2   180 A meere new person, looke he keepe his state
p. 319 HORACE 2   306 In time to Tragedie, a Musicke new.
p. 321 HORACE 2   327 With something that was acceptably new.

new (cont.)
```
     p. 333 HORACE 2        628 Those ill-torn'd Verses, to new hammering.
     p. 383 UNGATHERED 16    14 your Royal Eye which still creat[t]es new men
     p. 389 UNGATHERED 24     4 When the old words doe strike on the new times,
     p. 394 UNGATHERED 28    13 But, I would haue, thee, to know something new,
     p. 405 UNGATHERED 34    87 On ye new priming of thy old Signe postes
     p. 415 UNGATHERED 42     9 Or why to like; they found, it all was new,
     p. 415 UNGATHERED 42    19 This is my censure. Now there is a new
     p. 415 UNGATHERED 42    23 Of wit, and a new made: a Warden then,
     p. 415 UNGATHERED 42    28 Yo'have all the Mysteries of Wits new Mint,
     p. 416 UNGATHERED 44     1 Fresh as the Day, and new as are the Howers,
```

new-come   frequency: 1   relative frequency: 0.00001
```
     p. 290 UNDERWOOD 85     35 And snares the fearfull Hare, and new-come
                                Crane,
```

new-ditch   frequency: 1   relative frequency: 0.00001
```
     p. 407 UNGATHERED 35    24 Wee'll haue thee styld ye Marquess of
                                New-Ditch.
```

new-yeares-gift   frequency: 1   relative frequency: 0.00001
```
     p. 263 UNDERWOOD 79     8+ A New-yeares-Gift sung to King
```

new-yeeres   frequency: 1   relative frequency: 0.00001
```
     p. 113 FOREST 13        74 On the close groome, and page, on new-yeeres day,
```

newcastle   frequency: 2   relative frequency: 0.00002
```
     p. 228 UNDERWOOD 53     t3 WILLIAM, Earle of Newcastle.
     p. 232 UNDERWOOD 59     t2 To WILLIAM Earle of Newcastle.
```

newer   frequency: 2   relative frequency: 0.00002
```
     p. 214 UNDERWOOD 44     53 Insert thy Hodges, and those newer men,
     p. 415 UNGATHERED 42    10 And newer, then could please them, by-cause trew.
```

newes   frequency: 10   relative frequency: 0.00014
```
     p.  68 EPIGRAMS 107      1 Doe what you come for, Captayne, with your
                                newes;
     p.  69 EPIGRAMS 107     21 For newes) your Ville-royes, and Silleries,
     p.  74 EPIGRAMS 115     10 Of newes, and noyse, to s<tr>ow out a long meale.
     p. 209 UNDERWOOD 43    139 The Brethren, they streight nois'd it out for
                                Newes,
     p. 218 UNDERWOOD 47     28 Of newes they get, to strew out the long meale,
     p. 219 UNDERWOOD 47     46 Though I doe neither heare these newes, nor tell
     p. 222 UNDERWOOD 49      8 And in an Epicoene fury can write newes
     p. 222 UNDERWOOD 49      9 Equall with that, which for the best newes goes,
     p. 417 UNGATHERED 45    17 And as either newes or mirth
     p. 417 UNGATHERED 45    21 Specially the newes of Darby;
```

newnesse   frequency: 1   relative frequency: 0.00001
```
     p. 160 UNDERWOOD 14     60 Newnesse of Sense, Antiquitie of voyce!
```

news. See "newes."

next   frequency: 19   relative frequency: 0.00027
```
     p.  48 EPIGRAMS 65       5 Be thy next masters more vnluckie Muse,
     p.  61 EPIGRAMS 95      26 It is the next deed, and a great one too.
     p.  65 EPIGRAMS 101     41 Shall make vs sad next morning: or affright
     p.  69 EPIGRAMS 107     27 For your next meale: this you are sure of. Why
     p.  72 EPIGRAMS 112     12 Next morne, an Ode: Thou mak'st a song ere
                                night.
     p.  95 FOREST 2         71 Thy tables hoord not vp for the next day,
     p. 109 FOREST 11         3 Next, to that vertue, is to know vice well,
     p. 133 UNDERWOOD 2.3    11 Mee, the scope of his next draught,
     p. 154 UNDERWOOD 13     56 Then turning unto him is next at hand,
     p. 189 UNDERWOOD 37      2 Next to your selfe, for making your love true:
     p. 260 UNDERWOOD 76     32 You'ld reade a Snake, in his next Song.
     p. 263 UNDERWOOD 78     24 Upon them, (next to Spenser's noble booke,)
     p. 276 U'WOOD 84.3      21 The Heaven design'd, draw next a Spring,
     p. 277 U'WOOD 84.3      32 Next sitting we will draw her mind.
     p. 319 HORACE 2        315 With lees of Wine. Next Eschylus, more late,
     p. 327 HORACE 2        493 Next these great Homer and Tyrtaeus set
     p. 361 UNGATHERED 1     13 Next, that which rapt mee, was: I might behold
     p. 394 UNGATHERED 28    25 Where spight of Death, next Life  for her
                                Loues sake,
     p. 417 UNGATHERED 45    35 'tis but the next neighbour ride
```

neyther   frequency: 1   relative frequency: 0.00001
```
     p. 384 UNGATHERED 18    24 Yet neyther of you seeme to th'other old.
```

nice   frequency: 2   relative frequency: 0.00002
   See also "nyce."
   p. 191 UNDERWOOD 38   23 Or in confessing of the Crime be nice,
   p. 365 UNGATHERED 5   23 Yet shee's nor nice to shew them,

nicer   frequency: 1   relative frequency: 0.00001
   p. 57 EPIGRAMS 90   5 The nicer thing to tast her ladies page;

nicholas   frequency: 2   relative frequency: 0.00002
   p. 87 EPIGRAMS 133   128 Whereof old DEMOCRITE, and HILL
                            NICHOLAS,
   p. 206 UNDERWOOD 43   77 With Nicholas Pasquill's, Meddle with your
                            match,

niece's. See "neeces."

nigh   frequency: 4   relative frequency: 0.00005
   p. 89 EPIGRAMS 133   188 A sope-boyler; and AEACVS him nigh,
   p. 96 FOREST 2   86 To haue her linnen, plate, and all things nigh,
   p. 200 UNDERWOOD 42   35 Of love, and hate: and came so nigh to know
   p. 279 U'WOOD 84.4   43 It selfe to us, and come so nigh

night   frequency: 29   relative frequency: 0.00041
   See also "good-night," "nights."
   p. 45 EPIGRAMS 58   1 IDEOT, last night, I pray'd thee but
                            forbeare
   p. 56 EPIGRAMS 87   3 Each night, to drowne his cares: But when the
                            gaine
   p. 64 EPIGRAMS 101   1 To night, graue sir, both my poore house, and I
   p. 65 EPIGRAMS 101   42 The libertie, that wee'll enioy to night.
   p. 72 EPIGRAMS 112   12 Next morne, an Ode: Thou mak'st a song ere
                            night.
   p. 76 EPIGRAMS 118   1 GVT eates all day, and lechers all the night,
   p. 96 FOREST 3   10 Of the short brauerie of the night;
   p. 97 FOREST 3   21 Or, if thou list the night in watch to breake,
   p. 102 FOREST 5   8 'Tis, with vs, perpetuall night.
   p. 112 FOREST 11   94 Would make a day of night,
   p. 130 UNDERWOOD 1.3   1 I sing the birth, was borne to night,
   p. 138 UNDERWOOD 2.6   18 Wisht the Bride were chang'd to night,
   p. 138 UNDERWOOD 2.6   21 Or, if you did move to night
   p. 150 UNDERWOOD 11   3 I am undone to night;
   p. 157 UNDERWOOD 13   127 Sydney e're night! or that did goe to bed
   p. 199 UNDERWOOD 41   5 It is as if a night should shade noone-day,
   p. 202 UNDERWOOD 42   73 Or in Moore-fields, this other night! sings one,
   p. 218 UNDERWOOD 47   21 Call every night to Supper in these fitts,
   p. 243 UNDERWOOD 70   14 Lay trampled on: the deeds of death, and night,
   p. 245 UNDERWOOD 70   71 Although it fall, and die that night;
   p. 257 UNDERWOOD 75   145 Haste, haste, officious Sun, and send them
                            Night
   p. 258 UNDERWOOD 75   191 Night, and the sheetes will show
   p. 271 UNDERWOOD 83   87 The Starres, that are the Jewels of the Night,
   p. 286 U'WOOD 84.9   121 That happy Day, that never shall see night!
   p. 293 UNDERWOOD 86   37 Hard-hearted, I dreame every Night
   p. 295 UNDERWOOD 90   9 Thy night not dronken, but from cares layd wast:
   p. 323 HORACE 2   398 In hand, and turne them over, day, and night.
   p. 365 UNGATHERED 5   8 When night their meeting couers.
   p. 392 UNGATHERED 26   79 Which, since thy flight from hence, hath mourn'd
                            like night,

night-sinnes   frequency: 1   relative frequency: 0.00001
   p. 39 EPIGRAMS 39   1 For all night-sinnes, with others wiues,
                            vnknowne,

night-tubs   frequency: 1   relative frequency: 0.00001
   p. 85 EPIGRAMS 133   64 Of all your night-tubs, when the carts doe
                            cluster,

nights   frequency: 5   relative frequency: 0.00007
   See also "sommer-nights."
   p. 104 FOREST 8   4 To thy altars, by their nights
   p. 104 FOREST 8   6 And nights too, in worser wayes?
   p. 156 UNDERWOOD 13   101 Reare-Suppers in their Names! and spend whole
                            nights
   p. 166 UNDERWOOD 15   132 Is not enough now, but the Nights to play:
   p. 197 UNDERWOOD 40   11 And turne the Ceremonies of those Nights

nill   frequency: 1   relative frequency: 0.00001
   p. 40 EPIGRAMS 42   16 If, now, with man and wife, to will, and nill

nimble   frequency: 2   relative frequency: 0.00002
    p. 230 UNDERWOOD 56   14 And stroke the water, nimble, chast, and faire,
    p. 368 UNGATHERED 6   84 The nimble French;

nine   frequency: 3   relative frequency: 0.00004
    p. 207 UNDERWOOD 43   98 Of our fift Henry, eight of his nine yeare;
    p. 282 U'WOOD 84.9   6 Spun out in name of some of the old Nine!
    p. 331 HORACE 2   578 Nine yeares kept in, your papers by, yo'are free

ninth   frequency: 1   relative frequency: 0.00001
    p.   82 EPIGRAMS 130   13 Mou'd by her order, and the ninth more high,

no   frequency: 288   relative frequency: 0.00416
    See also "no'," "noe."

no'   frequency: 1   relative frequency: 0.00001

nobilitie   frequency: 3   relative frequency: 0.00004
    p. 215 UNDERWOOD 44   79 Let poore Nobilitie be vertuous: Wee,
    p. 282 U'WOOD 84.8   21 'Tis Vertue alone, is true Nobilitie.
    p. 287 U'WOOD 84.9   159 Of title in her! All Nobilitie

nobility. See "nobilitie."

noble   frequency: 39   relative frequency: 0.00056
    See also "truly-noble."
    p.   54 EPIGRAMS 84   4 For your most noble offer had supply'd me.
    p.   58 EPIGRAMS 91   16 As noble in great chiefes, as they are rare.
    p.   96 FOREST 2   90 Thy lady's noble, fruitfull, chaste withall.
    p.   96 FOREST 2   97 Reade, in their vertuous parents noble parts,
    p. 100 FOREST 4   t3 and noble.
    p. 112 FOREST 11   111 Much more a noble, and right generous mind
    p. 114 FOREST 12   28 With noble ignorants, and let them still,
    p. 116 FOREST 12   89 But high, and noble matter, such as flies
    p. 119 FOREST 13   97 And raise a noble stemme, to giue the fame,
    p. 140 UNDERWOOD 2.9   4 Noble; or of greater Blood:
    p. 169 UNDERWOOD 17   3 And yet the noble Nature never grudge;
    p. 182 UNDERWOOD 28   t2 To the noble Lady, the Lady
    p. 191 UNDERWOOD 38   12 That you should be too noble to destroy.
    p. 194 UNDERWOOD 38 102 To carry noble danger in the face:
    p. 207 UNDERWOOD 43 100 Which noble Carew, Cotton, Selden lent:
    p. 213 UNDERWOOD 44   1 Why yet, my noble hearts, they cannot say,
    p. 214 UNDERWOOD 44   59 And there instruct the noble English heires
    p. 232 UNDERWOOD 59   3 The noble Science, and the maistring skill
    p. 234 UNDERWOOD 60   11 No noble furniture of parts,
    p. 242 UNDERWOOD 70   t2 that noble paire, Sir LVCIVS CARY,
    p. 244 UNDERWOOD 70   36 And had his noble name advanc'd with men:
    p. 244 UNDERWOOD 70   46 A perfect Patriot, and a noble friend,
    p. 245 UNDERWOOD 70   75 Call, noble Lucius, then for Wine,
    p. 252 UNDERWOOD 75   t5 of that Noble Gentleman, Mr. HIEROME
                              WESTON,
    p. 256 UNDERWOOD 75 106 To pay, with honours, to his noble Sonne,
    p. 256 UNDERWOOD 75 113 Stand there; for when a noble Nature's rais'd,
    p. 263 UNDERWOOD 78   24 Upon them, (next to Spenser's noble booke,)
    p. 284 U'WOOD 84.9   82 Out of her noble body, to this Feast,
    p. 287 U'WOOD 84.9   155 And best he knew her noble Character,
    p. 292 UNDERWOOD 86   13 For he's both noble, lovely, young,
    p. 307 HORACE 2   33 Most Writers, noble Sire, and either Sonne,
    p. 313 HORACE 2   196 I sing a noble Warre, and Priam's Fate.
    p. 319 HORACE 2   302 Clowne, Towns-man, base, and noble, mix'd, to
                              judge?
    p. 378 UNGATHERED 11 t1 To the Right Noble Tom, Tell-Troth of
    p. 382 UNGATHERED 16   1 Two noble knightes, whome true desire and zeale,
    p. 382 UNGATHERED 16 t2 behalfe of the two noble Brothers sr Robert
                              & sr Henrye
    p. 384 UNGATHERED 18 t1 To the most noble, and aboue his Titles,
    p. 394 UNGATHERED 28   3 To see (who' it is?) A noble Countesse, greate,
    p. 406 UNGATHERED 35   6 A Noble honest Soule! what's this to thee?

nobler   frequency: 3   relative frequency: 0.00004
    p.   38 EPIGRAMS 36   1 MARTIAL, thou gau'st farre nobler
                              Epigrammes
    p. 115 FOREST 12   67 Then which, a nobler heauen it selfe knowes not.
    p. 331 HORACE 2   581 'Tis now inquir'd, which makes the nobler Verse,

nobles   frequency: 2   relative frequency: 0.00002
  **p. 115 PANEGYRE   70 The Nobles zeale, yet either kept aliue
    p. 121 FOREST 14   32 Of nobles vertue, shew in you;

noblesse   frequency: 2   relative frequency: 0.00002
    p.   66 EPIGRAMS 102   13 But thou, whose noblesse keeps one stature still,
    p. 177 UNDERWOOD 25   26 True noblesse. Palme growes straight, though
                             handled ne're so rude.

noblest   frequency: 12   relative frequency: 0.00017
    p.   48 EPIGRAMS 64   15 These (noblest CECIL) labour'd in my
                             thought,
    p.   53 EPIGRAMS 79   2 Your noblest father prou'd: like whom, before,
    p.   98 FOREST 3   55 Thy noblest spouse affords them welcome grace;
    p. 136 UNDERWOOD 2.5   1 Noblest Charis, you that are
    p. 153 UNDERWOOD 13   19 They are the Noblest benefits, and sinke
    p. 162 UNDERWOOD 15   8 Quickning dead Nature, to her noblest strife.
    p. 173 UNDERWOOD 22   11 The noblest freedome, not to chuse
    p. 185 UNDERWOOD 30   18 And in the noblest Families tooke root
    p. 224 UNDERWOOD 50   28 And studie them unto the noblest ends,
    p. 382 UNGATHERED 16   3 vnto thee, king of men; their noblest partes
    p. 389 UNGATHERED 24   7 And hath the noblest marke of a good Booke,
    p. 402 UNGATHERED 34   6 The noblest Ingenyre that euer was!

noblier   frequency: 1   relative frequency: 0.00001
    p. 234 UNDERWOOD 60   18 Because it durst have noblier dy'd.

nobly   frequency: 3   relative frequency: 0.00004
    p.   63 EPIGRAMS 98   7 That thou at once, then, nobly maist defend
    p. 230 UNDERWOOD 56   2 When you would play so nobly, and so free.
    p. 309 HORACE 2   102 And much shall dye, that now is nobly liv'd,

noddell   frequency: 1   relative frequency: 0.00001
    p. 379 UNGATHERED 12   6 Yet who could haue hit on't but the wise noddell

nodding   frequency: 1   relative frequency: 0.00001
    p.   87 EPIGRAMS 133 123 Of worship, they their nodding chinnes doe hit

noddle   frequency: 1   relative frequency: 0.00001
    See also "noddell."
    p. 409 UNGATHERED 37 21 Thy Noddle, with his clubb; and dashing forth

noe   frequency: 7   relative frequency: 0.00010

nois'd   frequency: 1   relative frequency: 0.00001
    p. 209 UNDERWOOD 43 139 The Brethren, they streight nois'd it out for
                             Newes,

noise   frequency: 8   relative frequency: 0.00011
    See also "noyse," "pit-pat-noyse."
 **p. 114 PANEGYRE   41 Some cry from tops of houses; thinking noise
    p.   88 EPIGRAMS 133 170 Vrine, and plaisters? when the noise doth beate
    p. 151 UNDERWOOD 12   12 A life that knew nor noise, nor strife:
    p. 214 UNDERWOOD 44   56 Alive yet, in the noise; and still the same;
    p. 311 HORACE 2   120 On popular noise with, and doe businesse in.
    p. 327 HORACE 2   459 And better stayes them there, then all fine noise
    p. 335 HORACE 2   648 They vexe, and follow him with shouts, and noise.
    p. 411 UNGATHERED 39 14 But Tune and Noise the Eccho of thy Shame.

noises   frequency: 2   relative frequency: 0.00002
    See also "noyses."
    p. 239 UNDERWOOD 67   9 Their noises forth in Thunder:
    p. 249 UNDERWOOD 72   12 Made lighter with the Wine. All noises else,

noisome. See "noysome."

nominal. See "nominall."

nominall   frequency: 1   relative frequency: 0.00001
    p. 160 UNDERWOOD 14   47 Where is that nominall marke, or reall rite,

none   frequency: 48   relative frequency: 0.00069
    p.   29 EPIGRAMS 9   1 May none, whose scatter'd names honor my booke,
    p.   30 EPIGRAMS 11   7 For I will doe none: and as little ill,
    p.   30 EPIGRAMS 11   8 For I will dare none. Good Lord, walke dead
                             still.
    p.   32 EPIGRAMS 16   6 Some hundred quarrells, yet dost thou fight none;
    p.   36 EPIGRAMS 28   20 May heare my Epigrammes, but like of none.
    p.   40 EPIGRAMS 42   13 The children, that he keepes, GILES sweares
                             are none
    p.   42 EPIGRAMS 47   2 Hee that wooes euery widdow, will get none.
    p.   60 EPIGRAMS 94   9 For none ere tooke that pleasure in sinnes sense,
    p.   67 EPIGRAMS 103   14 Becomes none more then you, who need it least.
    p.   68 EPIGRAMS 105   15 There's none so dull, that for your stile would
                             aske

none (cont.)
p. 84 EPIGRAMS 133   11 Their wherry had no saile, too; ours had none:
p. 94 FOREST 2   47 There's none, that dwell about them, wish them
                           downe;
p. 99 FOREST 3   95 God wisheth, none should wracke on a strange
                           shelfe.
p. 104 FOREST 7   8 At noone, they are or short, or none:
p. 106 FOREST 8   48 None but them, and leaue the rest.
p. 113 FOREST 12   19 I, that haue none (to send you) send you verse.
p. 114 FOREST 12   50 Haue beautie knowne, yet none so famous seene?
p. 115 FOREST 12   55 That HOMER brought to Troy; yet none so
                           liue:
p. 116 FOREST 13   6 For others ill, ought none their good forget.
p. 118 FOREST 13   56 Without companions? 'Tis safe to haue none.
p. 118 FOREST 13   69 Your conscience, and not wonder, if none askes
p. 139 UNDERWOOD 2.7   3 Here's none to spie, or see;
p. 140 UNDERWOOD 2.8   12 We all feare, she loueth none.
p. 147 UNDERWOOD 7   6 The pleasure is as good as none,
p. 156 UNDERWOOD 13   115 Looke to and cure; Hee's not a man hath none,
p. 156 UNDERWOOD 13   122 And my minds motion not? or haue I none?
p. 171 UNDERWOOD 19   13 You blush, but doe not: friends are either none,
p. 189 UNDERWOOD 36   4 None brookes the Sun-light worse then he.
p. 202 UNDERWOOD 42   74 Another answers, 'Lasse, those Silkes are none,
p. 202 UNDERWOOD 42   86 None of their pleasures! nor will aske thee, why
p. 203 UNDERWOOD 43   27 If none of these, then why this fire? Or find
p. 208 UNDERWOOD 43   112 With lust conceiv'd thee; Father thou hadst
                           none:
p. 208 UNDERWOOD 43   117 For none but Smiths would have made thee a God.
p. 216 UNDERWOOD 45   24 But he that's too-much that, is friend of none.
p. 217 UNDERWOOD 46   22 None Fortune aided lesse, or Vertue more.
p. 219 UNDERWOOD 47   30 Then these can ever be; or else wish none.
p. 223 UNDERWOOD 49   32 Her face there's none can like by Candle light.
p. 225 UNDERWOOD 50   36 It will be shame for them, if they have none.
p. 231 UNDERWOOD 56   28 I can lose none in tendring these to you.
p. 237 UNDERWOOD 64   21 Are lost upon accompt! And none will know
p. 241 UNDERWOOD 69   7 His is more safe commoditie, or none:
p. 274 U'WOOD 84.2   13 And tell thou, ALDE-LEGH, None can tell
                           more true
p. 281 U'WOOD 84.8   11 (Brave Youths) th<ey>'are their possessions,
                           none of yours:
p. 329 HORACE 2   513 Our Gallants give them none, but passe them by:
p. 335 HORACE 2   654 There's none will take the care, to helpe him
                           then;
p. 335 HORACE 2   670 His cause of making Verses none knowes why:
p. 349 HORACE 1   430 ... . none ....
p. 403 UNGATHERED 34   35 Th'ascent of Lady Fame which none could spy

nook. See "nooke."

nooke   frequency: 1   relative frequency: 0.00001
**p. 113 PANEGYRE   6 To euery nooke and angle of his realme.

nookes   frequency: 1   relative frequency: 0.00001
p. 85 EPIGRAMS 133   51 Thou hast seene hell (some say) and know'st all
                            nookes there,

nooks. See "nookes."

noon. See "noone," "noone-day," "noone-sted's."

noone   frequency: 2   relative frequency: 0.00002
p. 104 FOREST 7   8 At noone, they are or short, or none:
p. 414 UNGATHERED 41   52 Till he hath reach'd his two-fold point of
                           Noone.

noone-day   frequency: 1   relative frequency: 0.00001
p. 199 UNDERWOOD 41   5 It is as if a night should shade noone-day,

noone-sted's   frequency: 1   relative frequency: 0.00001
p. 258 UNDERWOOD 75   183 By this Sun's Noone-sted's made

noose   frequency: 1   relative frequency: 0.00001
p. 101 FOREST 4   26 And thrust my necke into the noose,

nor   frequency: 206   relative frequency: 0.00298

norembery   frequency: 1   relative frequency: 0.00001
p. 260 UNDERWOOD 77   3 Of Noremberg, or Turkie; hang your roomes

north   frequency: 1   relative frequency: 0.00001
     p. 309 HORACE 2   92 That from the North, the Navie safe doth store,

northumberland   frequency: 1   relative frequency: 0.00001
     p. 274 U'WOOD 84.2   5 Gave two such Houses as
                                 NORTHUMBERLAND,

norwich   frequency: 1   relative frequency: 0.00001
     p.   85 EPIGRAMS 133   36 Did dance the famous Morrisse, vnto Norwich)

nose   frequency: 8   relative frequency: 0.00011
     p.   35 EPIGRAMS 28   4 He speakes to men with a Rhinocerotes nose,
     p.   85 EPIGRAMS 133   59 To this dire passage. Say, thou stop thy nose:
     p.   87 EPIGRAMS 133   132 Must trie the'vn-vsed valour of a nose:
     p.   89 EPIGRAMS 133   190 An ancient pur-blinde fletcher, with a high nose;
     p. 141 UNDERWOOD 2.9   19 Even nose, and cheeke (withall)
     p. 232 UNDERWOOD 58   10 That hang their richest jewells i' their nose;
     p. 307 HORACE 2   52 With faire black eyes, and haire; and a wry nose.
     p. 409 UNGATHERED 37   18 To aske thy name, if he haue half his Nose!

nosthrill   frequency: 1   relative frequency: 0.00001
     p. 205 UNDERWOOD 43   62 Had tickled your large Nosthrill: many a Reame

nostril. See "nosthrill," "nostrill."

nostrill   frequency: 1   relative frequency: 0.00001
     p. 292 UNDERWOOD 86   21 There shall thy dainty Nostrill take

nostrills   frequency: 1   relative frequency: 0.00001
     p.   88 EPIGRAMS 133   165 Your daintie nostrills (in so hot a season,

nostrils. See "nostrills."

not   frequency: 567   relative frequency: 0.00820
     See also "not>."

not>   frequency: 2   relative frequency: 0.00002
     p. 207 UNDERWOOD 43   92 To teach some that, their Nurses could <not>
                                 doe,
     p. 214 UNDERWOOD 44   63 Should he <not> heare of billow, wind, and
                                 storme,

note   frequency: 10   relative frequency: 0.00014
   **p. 115 PANEGYRE   97 "And thriuing statutes she could promptly note;
     p.   40 EPIGRAMS 42   17 The selfe-same things, a note of concord be:
     p.   71 EPIGRAMS 110   20 Action, or engine, worth a note of thine,
     p. 176 UNDERWOOD 24   15 Some note of which each varied Pillar beares,
     p. 232 UNDERWOOD 58   3 Bee thou my Bookes intelligencer, note
     p. 263 UNDERWOOD 78   22 Good Omen to him, in the note thou sing'st,
     p. 287 U'WOOD 84.9   178 As her whole life was now become one note
     p. 323 HORACE 2   388 To note, in Poemes, breach of harmonie;
     p. 335 HORACE 2   638 Reprove; and, what is to be changed, note:
     p. 366 UNGATHERED 6   4 Whose Note, and Hue,

noted   frequency: 3   relative frequency: 0.00004
     p.   66 EPIGRAMS 103   3 And noted for what flesh such soules were fram'd,
     p. 150 UNDERWOOD 10   14 Loves sicknesse, and his noted want of worth,
     p. 160 UNDERWOOD 14   46 And noted the beginnings and decayes!

notes   frequency: 9   relative frequency: 0.00013
     p. 114 FOREST 12   43 The soules, shee loues. Those other glorious
                                 notes,
     p. 115 FOREST 12   76 To curious light, the notes, I then shall sing,
     p. 143 UNDERWOOD 3   9 Mixe then your Notes, that we may prove
     p. 157 UNDERWOOD 13   143 Such Notes are vertuous men! they live as fast
     p. 182 UNDERWOOD 27   28 Made Dian, not his notes refuse?
     p. 263 UNDERWOOD 79   3 Your change of Notes, the flat, the meane, the
                                 sharpe,
     p. 273 U'WOOD 84.1   23 With Sayles of silke, as the first notes
     p. 367 UNGATHERED 6   45 With thy soft notes, and hold them within Pale
     p. 419 UNGATHERED 48   6 I then could rayse my notes

nothing   frequency: 37   relative frequency: 0.00053
     See also "nothing's."
     p.   32 EPIGRAMS 18   5 And mine come nothing like. I hope so. Yet,
     p.   33 EPIGRAMS 21   4 Forbidd' his side! and nothing, but the word
     p.   63 EPIGRAMS 98   2 And I know nothing more thou hast to doo.
     p.   66 EPIGRAMS 102   12 As nothing else discernes the vertue' or vice.
     p.   72 EPIGRAMS 111   5 And that, in action, there is nothing new,
     p.   82 EPIGRAMS 130   15 I, yet, had vtter'd nothing on thy part,

nothing (cont.)
```
  p.  95 FOREST 2         75 There's nothing I can wish, for which I stay.
  p.  96 FOREST 2        101 Those proud, ambitious heaps, and nothing else,
  p. 101 FOREST 4         49 Where nothing is examin'd, weigh'd,
  p. 118 FOREST 13        83 May they haue nothing left, whereof they can
  p. 127 UNDERWOOD 1.1    18 This All of nothing, gavest it forme, and fate,
  p. 131 UNDERWOOD 2.1    22 And let nothing high decay,
  p. 157 UNDERWOOD 13    138 Are nothing till that comes to bind and shut.
  p. 157 UNDERWOOD 13    153 And last, goe out in nothing: You that see
  p. 158 UNDERWOOD 13    164 Find you to reckon nothing, me owe all.
  p. 160 UNDERWOOD 14     63 A banke against it. Nothing but the round
  p. 167 UNDERWOOD 15    159 Is nothing, such scarce meat and drinke he'le
                            give,
  p. 168 UNDERWOOD 15    187 That thou thinke nothing great, but what is good,
  p. 169 UNDERWOOD 17      5 And he is not in friendship. Nothing there
  p. 179 UNDERWOOD 25     35 Nothing, but practise upon honours thrall.
  p. 191 UNDERWOOD 38     15 If there be nothing worthy you can see
  p. 192 UNDERWOOD 38     36 Nothing is vile, that is a part of you:
  p. 209 UNDERWOOD 43    137 See the worlds Ruines! nothing but the piles
  p. 215 UNDERWOOD 44     68 Live by their Scale, that dare doe nothing free?
  p. 216 UNDERWOOD 45     12 'Tis vertue alone, or nothing, that knits
                            friends.
  p. 224 UNDERWOOD 50     13 And though all praise bring nothing to your name,
  p. 237 UNDERWOOD 64     16 That nothing can her gratitude provoke!
  p. 247 UNDERWOOD 70    115 Unto the Vertue. Nothing perfect done,
  p. 255 UNDERWOOD 75     84 With Angels, Muse, to speake these: Nothing
                            can
  p. 263 UNDERWOOD 79      8 For, had we here said lesse, we had sung nothing
                            then.
  p. 278 U'WOOD 84.4      15 Since nothing can report that flame,
  p. 282 U'WOOD 84.9       9 Nothing, that could remaine, or yet can stirre
  p. 283 U'WOOD 84.9      30 Nothing I doe; but, like a heavie wheele,
  p. 284 U'WOOD 84.9      71 Nothing can more adorne it, then the seat
  p. 295 UNDERWOOD 90     12 Will to bee, what thou art; and nothing more:
  p. 329 HORACE 2        505 And hold them faithfully; For nothing rests,
  p. 331 HORACE 2        574 Wilt nothing against nature speake, or doe:
```

nothing's   frequency: 1   relative frequency: 0.00001
```
  p.  31 EPIGRAMS 14       3 (How nothing's that?) to whom my countrey owes
```

notion   frequency: 1   relative frequency: 0.00001
```
  p. 269 UNDERWOOD 83     26 Thereof, no notion can expresse how much
```

notions   frequency: 1   relative frequency: 0.00001
```
  p. 279 U'WOOD 84.4      33 Whose Notions when it will expresse
```

nought   frequency: 14   relative frequency: 0.00020
See also "naught."
```
  p. 129 UNDERWOOD 1.2    21 First made of nought;
  p. 154 UNDERWOOD 13     44 Nought but in corners; and is loath to leave
  p. 161 UNDERWOOD 14     71 But nought beyond. He thou hast given it to,
  p. 163 UNDERWOOD 15     32 And being a thing, blowne out of nought, rebells
  p. 219 UNDERWOOD 47     58 Lest it be justled, crack'd, made nought, or
                            lesse:
  p. 223 UNDERWOOD 49     24 Thinkes it selfe nought, though she should valew
                            it.
  p. 254 UNDERWOOD 75     47 Nought of a Maiden Queene,
  p. 275 U'WOOD 84.3       8 Needs nought to cloath it but the ayre.
  p. 313 HORACE 2        174 Be nought so'above him but his sword let claime.
  p. 315 HORACE 2        200 Who nought assaies unaptly, or amisse?
  p. 323 HORACE 2        405 Our Poets, too, left nought unproved here;
  p. 325 HORACE 2        435 I, writing nought my selfe, will teach them yet
  p. 327 HORACE 2        463 Being men were covetous of nought, but praise.
  p. 411 UNGATHERED 39    13 For thou hast nought <in thee> to cure his Fame,
```

nourceries   frequency: 1   relative frequency: 0.00001
```
  p. 151 UNDERWOOD 12     16 As were his Nourceries; and swept
```

nourish   frequency: 2   relative frequency: 0.00002
```
  p. 184 UNDERWOOD 29     38 Scarce the world a Wit doth nourish,
  p. 309 HORACE 2         94 Once rowable, but now doth nourish men
```

nourisheth   frequency: 1   relative frequency: 0.00001
```
  p. 325 HORACE 2        437 What nourisheth, what formed, what begot
```

nourse   frequency: 1   relative frequency: 0.00001
```
  p. 313 HORACE 2        164 Where some great Lady, or her diligent Nourse;
```

november   frequency: 1   relative frequency: 0.00001
   p. 239 UNDERWOOD 67   2 This sixteenth of November,

now   frequency: 202   relative frequency: 0.00292
      See also "nowe," "now's," "now't."
  **p. 113 PANEGYRE   1 Heau'n now not striues, alone, our brests to fill
  **p. 113 PANEGYRE   26 On earth, till now, they came to grace his
                              throne.
  **p. 114 PANEGYRE   48 His gladding looke, now long'd to see it more.
  **p. 114 PANEGYRE   65 Old men were glad, their fates till now did last;
  **p. 116 PANEGYRE   116 Whose necessary good 'twas now to be
  **p. 116 PANEGYRE   129 And now the dame had dried her dropping eyne,
  **p. 117 PANEGYRE   137 How deare a father they did now enioy
  **p. 117 PANEGYRE   157 Nor to her blisse, could ought now added bee,
    p. 29 EPIGRAMS 7   2 A purging bill, now fix'd vpon the dore,
    p. 29 EPIGRAMS 8   4 Beg'd RIDWAYES pardon: DVNCOTE,
                              now, doth crye,
    p. 34 EPIGRAMS 25   5 And now, her (hourely) her owne cucqueane makes,
    p. 35 EPIGRAMS 26   1 Then his chast wife, though BEAST now know
                              no more,
    p. 37 EPIGRAMS 33   3 Whither the world must follow. And I, now,
    p. 38 EPIGRAMS 35   5 Hast purg'd thy realmes, as we haue now no cause
    p. 39 EPIGRAMS 39   2 COLT, now, doth daily penance in his owne.
    p. 40 EPIGRAMS 42   16 If, now, with man and wife, to will, and nill
    p. 40 EPIGRAMS 43   5 'Tofore, great men were glad of Poets: Now,
    p. 41 EPIGRAMS 45   5 O, could I loose all father, now. For why
    p. 42 EPIGRAMS 46   6 Yes, now he weares his knight-hood euery day.
    p. 45 EPIGRAMS 56   6 Buy the reuersion of old playes; now growne
    p. 45 EPIGRAMS 58   2 To reade my verses; now I must to heare:
    p. 53 EPIGRAMS 79   10 On whom, if he were liuing now, to looke,
    p. 55 EPIGRAMS 85   11 Now, in whose pleasures I haue this discerned,
    p. 55 EPIGRAMS 86   5 Now, I must giue thy life, and deed, the voice
    p. 62 EPIGRAMS 97   8 Where ere he met me; now hee's dumbe, or proud.
    p. 64 EPIGRAMS 100   3 And I must now beleeue him: for, to day,
    p. 64 EPIGRAMS 99   7 But much it now auailes, what's done, of whom:
    p. 65 EPIGRAMS 101   15 And, though fowle, now, be scarce, yet there are
                              clarkes,
    p. 65 EPIGRAMS 101   30 Which is the Mermaids, now, but shall be mine:
    p. 65 EPIGRAMS 101   32 Their liues, as doe their lines, till now had
                              lasted.
    p. 69 EPIGRAMS 107   29 Nay, now you puffe, tuske, and draw vp your chin,
    p. 70 EPIGRAMS 108   8 No more, then I dare now doe, with my pen.
    p. 70 EPIGRAMS 109   1 Who now calls on thee, NEVIL, is a Muse,
    p. 70 EPIGRAMS 109   16 Now I haue sung thee thus, shall iudge of thee.
    p. 75 EPIGRAMS 116   13 These were thy knowing arts: which who doth now
    p. 77 EPIGRAMS 120   13 And did act (what now we mone)
    p. 80 EPIGRAMS 126   6 I answer'd, DAPHNE now no paine can proue.
    p. 80 EPIGRAMS 128   1 ROE (and my ioy to name) th'art now, to goe
    p. 83 EPIGRAMS 132   10 BARTAS doth wish thy English now were his.
    p. 83 EPIGRAMS 132   12 As his will now be the translation thought,
    p. 84 EPIGRAMS 133   28 His three for one. Now, lordings, listen well.
    p. 86 EPIGRAMS 133   101 His spirits, now, in pills, and eeke in potions,
    p. 87 EPIGRAMS 133   111 Their MERCVRY did now. By this, the
                              stemme
    p. 87 EPIGRAMS 133   114 The well-greas'd wherry now had got betweene,
    p. 88 EPIGRAMS 133   160 And, now, aboue the poole, a face right fat
    p. 89 EPIGRAMS 133   181 Is now from home. You lose your labours quite,
    p. 94 FOREST 2   34 And pikes, now weary their owne kinde to eat,
    p. 96 FOREST 2   99 Now, PENSHVRST, they that will
                              proportion thee
    p. 98 FOREST 3   46 A fire now, that lent a shade!
    p. 108 FOREST 10   29 My owne true fire. Now my thought takes wing,
    p. 108 FOREST 10   30 And now an Epode to deepe eares I sing.
    p. 110 FOREST 11   43 In a continuall tempest. Now, true Loue
    p. 113 FOREST 12   1 Whil'st that, for which, all vertue now is sold,
    p. 114 FOREST 12   40 And now lye lost in their forgotten dust.
    p. 116 FOREST 12   94 Now thincking on you, though to England lost,
    p. 116 FOREST 13   2 Of any good minde, now: There are so few.
    p. 120 FOREST 13   120 Each into other, and had now made one.
    p. 120 FOREST 14   1 Now that the harth is crown'd with smiling fire,
    p. 120 FOREST 14   24 Must now
    p. 121 FOREST 14   47 Which must be now,
    p. 122 FOREST 15   14 And whither rap'd, now thou but stoup'st to mee?
    p. 130 UNDERWOOD 1.3   12 Was now laid in a Manger.
    p. 130 UNDERWOOD 1.3   17 The Word was now made Flesh indeed,
    p. 131 UNDERWOOD 2.1   3 Though I now write fiftie yeares,
    p. 131 UNDERWOOD 2.1   15 That you never knew till now.
    p. 133 UNDERWOOD 2.3   21 Looser-like, now, all my wreake
    p. 149 UNDERWOOD 9   1 I now thinke, Love is rather deafe, then blind,
    p. 152 UNDERWOOD 12   32 Now I conceive him by my want,

now (cont.)

p. 153	UNDERWOOD 13	t2 now Earle of Dorset.
p. 154	UNDERWOOD 13	53 Now dam'mee, Sir, if you shall not command
p. 155	UNDERWOOD 13	84 Now, but command; make tribute, what was gift;
p. 159	UNDERWOOD 14	27 So that my Reader is assur'd, I now
p. 160	UNDERWOOD 14	50 Conjectures retriv'd! And a Storie now
p. 163	UNDERWOOD 15	35 Not to be checkt, or frighted now with fate,
p. 163	UNDERWOOD 15	39 Friendship is now mask'd Hatred! Justice fled,
p. 165	UNDERWOOD 15	85 Adulteries, now, are not so hid, or strange,
p. 166	UNDERWOOD 15	125 Tilt one upon another, and now beare
p. 166	UNDERWOOD 15	126 This way, now that, as if their number were
p. 166	UNDERWOOD 15	132 Is not enough now, but the Nights to play:
p. 166	UNDERWOOD 15	136 Now use the bones, we see doth hire a man
p. 168	UNDERWOOD 15	195 These take, and now goe seeke thy peace in Warre.
p. 169	UNDERWOOD 17	14 Now so much friend, as you would trust in me,
p. 169	UNDERWOOD 18	2 Now threaten, with those meanes she did invite?
p. 169	UNDERWOOD 18	4 Then like, then love; and now would they amaze?
p. 171	UNDERWOOD 19	18 Others, in time may love, as we doe now.
p. 172	UNDERWOOD 20	14 Were such as I will now relate, or worse?
p. 173	UNDERWOOD 22	4 Yet is't your vertue now I raise.
p. 174	UNDERWOOD 23	10 That not a Nymph now sings?
p. 180	UNDERWOOD 25	62 Doth now command;
p. 180	UNDERWOOD 25	65 As farre from all revolt, as you are now from Fortune.
p. 180	UNDERWOOD 26	8 And now are out of sight.
p. 180	UNDERWOOD 26	15 Must now be rayn'd.
p. 180	UNDERWOOD 26	17 In one full Action; nor have you now more
p. 182	UNDERWOOD 28	8 Both braines and hearts; and mine now best doe know it:
p. 185	UNDERWOOD 30	19 Of all the Land. Who now at such a Rate,
p. 187	UNDERWOOD 33	10 Upon the reverend Pleaders; doe now shut
p. 189	UNDERWOOD 36	14 Now swift, now slow, now tame, now wild;
p. 189	UNDERWOOD 36	15 Now hot, now cold, now fierce, now mild.
p. 191	UNDERWOOD 38	2 Of Credit lost. And I am now run madde:
p. 191	UNDERWOOD 38	30 Your honour now, then your disgrace before.
p. 192	UNDERWOOD 38	35 Thinke that I once was yours, or may be now;
p. 192	UNDERWOOD 38	39 I am regenerate now, become the child
p. 194	UNDERWOOD 38	114 Publike affaires command me now to goe
p. 200	UNDERWOOD 42	37 It is not likely I should now looke downe
p. 207	UNDERWOOD 43	107 I now begin to doubt, if ever Grace,
p. 214	UNDERWOOD 44	39 Were now the greater Captaine? for they saw
p. 215	UNDERWOOD 44	82 The Herald will. Our blood is now become
p. 217	UNDERWOOD 46	10 And skill in thee, now, grew Authoritie;
p. 217	UNDERWOOD 46	15 And now such is thy stand; while thou dost deale
p. 220	UNDERWOOD 47	77 As you have writ your selfe. Now stand, and then,
p. 220	UNDERWOOD 48	4 Where now, thou art made Dweller;
p. 223	UNDERWOOD 49	34 To his poore Instrument, now out of grace.
p. 223	UNDERWOOD 49	39 For Sermoneeres: of which now one, now other,
p. 225	UNDERWOOD 51	12 Now with a Title more to the Degree;
p. 227	UNDERWOOD 52	16 O, had I now your manner, maistry, might,
p. 229	UNDERWOOD 54	13 That's six in silver; now within the Socket
p. 231	UNDERWOOD 57	10 Though now he refuses
p. 236	UNDERWOOD 64	8 Then now, to love the Soveraigne, and the Lawes?
p. 238	UNDERWOOD 65	9 And there to stand so. Hast now, envious Moone,
p. 241	UNDERWOOD 68	14 The Kings fame lives. Go now, denie his Teirce.
p. 241	UNDERWOOD 69	10 Painted a Dog, that now his subtler skill
p. 242	UNDERWOOD 69	21 Though now of flattery, as of picture, are
p. 244	UNDERWOOD 70	53 Goe now, and tell out dayes summ'd up with feares,
p. 248	UNDERWOOD 71	6 Have cast a trench about mee, now, five yeares;
p. 254	UNDERWOOD 75	64 O, now thou smil'st, faire Sun, and shin'st, as thou wouldst stay!
p. 254	UNDERWOOD 75	73 Our Court, and all the Grandees; now, Sun, looke,
p. 256	UNDERWOOD 75	121 See, now the Chappell opens; where the King
p. 257	UNDERWOOD 75	138 Now, Sun, and post away the rest of day:
p. 257	UNDERWOOD 75	139 These two, now holy Church hath made them one,
p. 258	UNDERWOOD 75	184 So great; his Body now alone projects the shade.
p. 260	UNDERWOOD 76	28 Let their spite (which now abounds)
p. 260	UNDERWOOD 77	2 I would present you now with curious plate
p. 268	UNDERWOOD 82	14 Sate safe enough, but now secured more.
p. 271	UNDERWOOD 83	69 And now, through circumfused light, she lookes
p. 271	UNDERWOOD 83	77 Goe now, her happy Parents, and be sad,
p. 277	U'WOOD 84.4	2 Now I have better thought thereon,
p. 278	U'WOOD 84.4	21 I call you Muse; now make it true:
p. 282	U'WOOD 84.9	1 'Twere time that I dy'd too, now shee is dead,

now (cont.)

p. 283 U'WOOD 84.9	22	(For so thou art with me) now shee is gone.
p. 287 U'WOOD 84.9	178	As her whole life was now become one note
p. 288 U'WOOD 84.9	197	To that eternall Rest, where now sh'hath place
p. 290 UNDERWOOD 85	23	Then now beneath some ancient Oke he may,
p. 290 UNDERWOOD 85	24	Now in the rooted Grasse him lay,
p. 291 UNDERWOOD 85	67	These thoughts when Usurer Alphius, now about
p. 292 UNDERWOOD 86	6	To bend a man, now at his fiftieth yeare
p. 293 UNDERWOOD 86	29	Me now, nor Wench, nor wanton Boy,
p. 293 UNDERWOOD 86	31	Nor care I now healths to propound;
p. 294 UNDERWOOD 87	20	And to left-Lydia, now the gate stood ope.
p. 305 HORACE 2	23	Or Rainbow is describ'd. But here was now
p. 307 HORACE 2	61	Invention. Now, to speake; and then differ
p. 307 HORACE 2	62	Much, that mought now be spoke: omitted here
p. 307 HORACE 2	63	Till fitter season. Now, to like of this,
p. 309 HORACE 2	79	Or Varius? Why am I now envi'd so,
p. 309 HORACE 2	94	Once rowable, but now doth nourish men
p. 309 HORACE 2	96	Or the wilde river, who hath changed now
p. 309 HORACE 2	101	Much phrase that now is dead, shall be reviv'd;
p. 309 HORACE 2	102	And much shall dye, that now is nobly liv'd,
p. 311 HORACE 2	126	If now the turnes, the colours, and right hues
p. 313 HORACE 2	158	If now the phrase of him that speakes, shall flow,
p. 315 HORACE 2	225	Fit rites. The Child, that now knowes how to say,
p. 315 HORACE 2	237	These studies alter now, in one, growne man;
p. 319 HORACE 2	287	The Hau'-boy, not as now with latten bound,
p. 319 HORACE 2	310	Now differ'd not from Delphick riddling.
p. 321 HORACE 2	367	Fell into fault so farre, as now they saw
p. 327 HORACE 2	470	He cries, Good boy, thou'lt keepe thine owne. Now, adde
p. 331 HORACE 2	581	'Tis now inquir'd, which makes the nobler Verse,
p. 333 HORACE 2	593	But, now, it is enough to say; I make
p. 339 HORACE 1	61	Is ... . even now to ......
p. 353 HORACE 1	591	... now .. ..
p. 355 HORACE 1	668	Now, bring ... backe, he'le .. ..
p. 364 UNGATHERED 4	1	Now, after all, let no man
p. 368 UNGATHERED 6	64	Now must we plie our ayme; our Swan's on wing.
p. 369 UNGATHERED 6	101	Though, now by Loue transform'd, & dayly dying:
p. 370 UNGATHERED 7	9	But now, your Worke is done, if they that view
p. 378 UNGATHERED 11	t3	and his Booke now going to
p. 378 UNGATHERED 11	80	Trie and trust Roger, was the word, but now
p. 380 UNGATHERED 12	40	That sacred to Odcombe are there now suspended,
p. 381 UNGATHERED 12	57	Which he not denies. Now being so free,
p. 382 UNGATHERED 16	t3	Rich, now Earles of warwick and Hollande.
p. 389 UNGATHERED 23	11	As, now, of all men, it is call'd thy Trade:
p. 392 UNGATHERED 26	52	Neat Terence, witty Plautus, now not please;
p. 396 UNGATHERED 30	7	And, though I now begin, 'tis not to rub
p. 404 UNGATHERED 34	62	The Scene! the Engyne! but he now is come
p. 405 UNGATHERED 34	67	Hee's warme on his feet now he sayes, & can
p. 405 UNGATHERED 34	75	What would he doe now, gi'ng his mynde yt waye
p. 409 UNGATHERED 37	11	I now would write on thee? No, wretch; thy name
p. 409 UNGATHERED 38	3	Now, you are got into a nearer roome,
p. 410 UNGATHERED 38	10	A Prentise-ship: which few doe now a dayes.
p. 410 UNGATHERED 38	11	Now each Court-Hobby-horse will wince in rime;
p. 410 UNGATHERED 38	17	The Cobler kept him to his nall; but, now
p. 413 UNGATHERED 41	15	To top the fairest Lillie, now, that growes,
p. 415 UNGATHERED 42	12	Now, for mine owne part, and it is but due,
p. 415 UNGATHERED 42	19	This is my censure. Now there is a new
p. 416 UNGATHERED 44	4	Now, in a garland by the graces knit;
p. 420 UNGATHERED 48	12	Of Civill virtue, that hee now is not

nowe   frequency: 2   relative frequency: 0.00002

p. 419 UNGATHERED 48	1	Yff Men, and tymes were nowe
p. 421 UNGATHERED 49	11	Or Malyce to make ffaultes, wch nowe is skill.

now's   frequency: 2   relative frequency: 0.00002

p. 165 UNDERWOOD 15	89	The Husband now's call'd churlish, or a poore
p. 166 UNDERWOOD 15	144	That scratching now's our best Felicitie?

now't   frequency: 1   relative frequency: 0.00001

p. 214 UNDERWOOD 44	55	That keepe the warre, though now't be growne more tame,

noyse   frequency: 8   relative frequency: 0.00011

p. 63 EPIGRAMS.97	12	Nor 'bout the beares, nor noyse to make lords sport.
p. 74 EPIGRAMS 115	10	Of newes, and noyse, to s<tr>ow out a long meale.
p. 81 EPIGRAMS 129	10	Whose noyse shall keepe thy miming most aliue,

noyse (cont.)
   p. 84 EPIGRAMS 133   9 The filth, stench, noyse: saue only what was
                                   there
   p. 120 FOREST 14   17 When all the noyse
   p. 273 U'WOOD 84.1   18 Take little Infants with their noyse,
   p. 397 UNGATHERED 30   45 And caried, though with shoute, and noyse,
                                   confesse
   p. 408 UNGATHERED 37   8 That thou hast lost thy noyse, thy foame, thy
                                   stirre,

noyses   frequency: 1   relative frequency: 0.00001
   p. 341 HORACE 1   120 Of .... noyses, borne to actuate things.

noysome   frequency: 1   relative frequency: 0.00001
   p. 409 UNGATHERED 37   16 Nameless, and noysome, as thy infamy!

nullifie   frequency: 1   relative frequency: 0.00001
   p. 188 UNDERWOOD 34   14 Of Beautie, so to nullifie a face,

nullify. See "nullifie."

numb. See "numbe."

numbe   frequency: 1   relative frequency: 0.00001
   p. 317 HORACE 2   245 A great deferrer, long in hope, growne numbe

number   frequency: 14   relative frequency: 0.00020
   p. 103 FOREST 6   22 What their number is, be pin'd.
   p. 111 FOREST 11   76 We doe not number, here,
   p. 116 FOREST 13   3 The bad, by number, are so fortified,
   p. 120 FOREST 14   21 This day sayes, then, the number of glad yeeres
   p. 160 UNDERWOOD 15   126 This way, now that, as if their number were
   p. 167 UNDERWOOD 15   173 Then once to number, or bring forth to hand,
   p. 171 UNDERWOOD 19   14 (Though they may number bodyes) or but one.
   p. 193 UNDERWOOD 38   99 I number these as being of the Chore
   p. 244 UNDERWOOD 70   50 In weight, in measure, number, sound,
   p. 309 HORACE 2   106 What number best can fit, Homer declares.
   p. 384 UNGATHERED 18   21 So, in theyr number, may <you> neuer see
   p. 394 UNGATHERED 28   6 And number Attributes vnto a flood:
   p. 395 UNGATHERED 29   8 And those in number so, and measure rais'd,
   p. 399 UNGATHERED 31   23 In number, measure, or degree

numbered. See "numbred," "numbred-five."

numbers   frequency: 9   relative frequency: 0.00013
   p. 53 EPIGRAMS 79   11 He should those rare, and absolute numbers view,
   p. 61 EPIGRAMS 95   6 And all his numbers, both of sense, and sounds.
   p. 93 FOREST 1   11 That since, my numbers are so cold,
   p. 108 FOREST 10A   7 Then, leaue these lighter numbers, to light
                                     braines
   p. 177 UNDERWOOD 25   9 My bolder numbers to thy golden Lyre:
   p. 272 UNDERWOOD 84   t7 A Gentleman absolute in all Numbers;
   p. 311 HORACE 2   123 Abhorres low numbers, and the private straine
   p. 319 HORACE 2   300 And in their numbers; For, alas, what knew
   p. 323 HORACE 2   399 Our Ancestors did Plautus numbers praise,

numbred   frequency: 2   relative frequency: 0.00002
   p. 77 EPIGRAMS 120   9 Yeeres he numbred scarse thirteene
   p. 319 HORACE 2   293 They might with ease be numbred, being a few

numbred-five   frequency: 1   relative frequency: 0.00001
   p. 412 UNGATHERED 41   6 The gladdest ground to all the numbred-five,

numerous   frequency: 1   relative frequency: 0.00001
   p. 182 UNDERWOOD 28   6 To those true numerous Graces; whereof some,

nun   frequency: 1   relative frequency: 0.00001
   p. 209 UNDERWOOD 43   148 Nay, sigh'd a Sister, 'twas the Nun, Kate
                                     Arden,

nuncio's   frequency: 1   relative frequency: 0.00001
   p. 69 EPIGRAMS 107   22 Ianin's, your Nuncio's, and your Tuilleries,

nuptial. See "nuptiall."

nuptiall   frequency: 3   relative frequency: 0.00004
   p. 253 UNDERWOOD 75   24 To welcome home a Paire, and deck the nuptiall
                                     bower?
   p. 257 UNDERWOOD 75   133 And knit the Nuptiall knot,
   p. 257 UNDERWOOD 75   148 Of Nuptiall Sweets, at such a season, owe,

nuptials   frequency: 1   relative frequency: 0.00001
     See also "nvptials."
     p. 334 UNGATHERED 18   3 At these thy Nuptials; but, whose heart, and
                                 thought

nuremburg. See "ncremberg."

nurse   frequency: 4   relative frequency: 0.00005
     See also "nourse."
     p. 155 UNDERWOOD 13   90 Or robbing the poore Market-folkes should nurse
     p. 162 UNDERWOOD 15   11 Looke on th'ambitious man, and see him nurse
     p. 216 UNDERWOOD 45   9 Much lesse a name would we bring up, or nurse,
     p. 321 HORACE 2   348 Or old Silenus, Bacchus guard, and Nurse.

nurseries. See "ncurceries."

nurses   frequency: 1   relative frequency: 0.00001
     p. 207 UNDERWOOD 43   92 To teach some that, their Nurses could <not>
                                 doe,

nut   frequency: 1   relative frequency: 0.00001
     See also "chest-nut."
     p. 94 FOREST 2   13 That taller tree, which of a nut was set,

nut-crackers   frequency: 1   relative frequency: 0.00001
     p. 321 HORACE 2   363 The nut-crackers throughout, will they therefore

nuts   frequency: 1   relative frequency: 0.00001
     p. 95 FOREST 2   52 Some nuts, some apples; some that thinke they
                                 make

nvptials   frequency: 1   relative frequency: 0.00001
     p. 252 UNDERWOOD 75   t4 CELEBRATING THE NVPTIALS

nyce   frequency: 1   relative frequency: 0.00001
     p. 423 UNGATHERED 50   11 whole armyes fall, swayd by those nyce respects.

nym.   frequency: 1   relative frequency: 0.00001
     p. 264 UNDERWOOD 79   24 Nym. Of brightest MIRA, doe we raise our
                                 Song,

nymp.   frequency: 1   relative frequency: 0.00001
     p. 264 UNDERWOOD 79   32 Nymp. Of brightest MIRA, is our Song; the
                                 grace

nymph   frequency: 4   relative frequency: 0.00005
     p. 67 EPIGRAMS 105   4 Least mention of a Nymph, a Muse, a Grace,
     p. 148 UNDERWOOD 7   27 What Nymph so e're his voyce but heares,
     p. 174 UNDERWOOD 23   10 That not a Nymph now sings?
     p. 662 INSCRIPTS. 2   6 to CYNTHIAS fayrest Nymph hath sent thee,

nymphs   frequency: 2   relative frequency: 0.00002
     See also "nym.," "nymp."
     p. 147 UNDERWOOD 7   3 For if the Nymphs should know my Swaine,
     p. 147 UNDERWOOD 7   t1 A Nymphs Passion.

                                  frequency: 68   relative frequency: 0.00098
     See also "oh."
     p. 35 EPIGRAMS 27   7 To heauen; his hath: O happy state! wherein
     p. 41 EPIGRAMS 45   5 O, could I loose all father, now. For why
     p. 55 EPIGRAMS 84   9 O Madame, if your grant did thus transferre mee,
     p. 56 EPIGRAMS 88   14 And stoupe, and cringe. O then, it needs must
                                 proue
     p. 61 EPIGRAMS 95   13 O, would'st thou adde like hand, to all the rest!
     p. 73 EPIGRAMS 112   16 O, (thou cry'st out) that is thy proper game.
     p. 81 EPIGRAMS 129   15 O, runne not proud of this. Yet, take thy due.
     p. 110 FOREST 11   55 O, who is he, that (in this peace) enioyes
     p. 112 FOREST 11   102 O, so diuine a creature
     p. 122 FOREST 15   5 O, be thou witnesse, that the reynes dost know,
     p. 122 FOREST 15   15 Dwell, dwell here still: O, being euery-where,
     p. 127 UNDERWOOD 1.1   1 1. O holy, blessed, glorious Trinitie
     p. 127 UNDERWOOD 1.1   8 O take my gift.
     p. 127 UNDERWOOD 1.1   13 4. For thy acceptance. O, behold me right,
     p. 128 UNDERWOOD 1.1   29 8. Increase those acts, o glorious Trinitie
     p. 128 UNDERWOOD 1.1   36 O grant it me!
     p. 128 UNDERWOOD 1.1   44 O, then how blest,
     p. 129 UNDERWOOD 1.2   1 Heare mee, O God!
     p. 135 UNDERWOOD 2.4   30 O so white! O so soft! O so sweet is she!
     p. 144 UNDERWOOD 3   21 O sing not you then lest the best
     p. 144 UNDERWOOD 4   5 O, be not angry with those fires,

o (cont.)
```
    p. 145 UNDERWOOD 4      9 O, doe not steepe them in thy Teares,
    p. 155 UNDERWOOD 13    73 O, is it so? knowes he so much? and will
    p. 161 UNDERWOOD 14    79 Thy gift 'gainst envie. O how I doe count
    p. 164 UNDERWOOD 15    59 O, these so ignorant Monsters! light, as proud,
    p. 165 UNDERWOOD 15   113 For lesse Securitie? O         for these
    p. 167 UNDERWOOD 15   161 And be belov'd, while the Whores last. O times,
    p. 177 UNDERWOOD 25    10 O, then inspire
    p. 177 UNDERWOOD 25    31 But whisper; O glad Innocence,
    p. 179 UNDERWOOD 25    36 O vertues fall,
    p. 180 UNDERWOOD 25    63 O then (my best-best lov'd) let me importune,
    p. 191 UNDERWOOD 38     7 Or there to sterve it. Helpe, O you that may
    p. 193 UNDERWOOD 38    67 O may your wisdome take example hence,
    p. 193 UNDERWOOD 38    77 O imitate that sweet Serenitie
    p. 194 UNDERWOOD 38   109 O, that you could but by dissection see
    p. 199 UNDERWOOD 41    17 O, keepe it still; for it had rather be
    p. 201 UNDERWOOD 42    71 Unto the Spittle Sermon. O, what strange
    p. 208 UNDERWOOD 43   129 But, O those Reeds! thy meere disdaine of them,
    p. 209 UNDERWOOD 43   153 O no, cry'd all, Fortune, for being a whore,
    p. 214 UNDERWOOD 44    43 O happie Art! and wise Epitome
    p. 215 UNDERWOOD 44    91 All that they doe at Playes. O, but first here
    p. 227 UNDERWOOD 52    16 O, had I now your manner, maistry, might,
    p. 234 UNDERWOOD 61    13 Fit for a Bishops knees! O bow them oft,
    p. 235 UNDERWOOD 62    11 O pietie! so to weigh the poores estates!
    p. 235 UNDERWOOD 62    12 O bountie! so to difference the rates!
    p. 237 UNDERWOOD 64    17 O Times! O Manners! Surfet bred of ease,
    p. 251 UNDERWOOD 74    25 O how will then our Court be pleas'd,
    p. 254 UNDERWOOD 75    56 Although that thou, O Sun, at our intreaty
                              stay!
    p. 254 UNDERWOOD 75    64 O, now thou smil'st, faire Sun, and shin'st, as
                              thou wouldst stay!
    p. 256 UNDERWOOD 75   129 O happy bands! and thou more happy place,
    p. 263 UNDERWOOD 78    25 And praise them too. O! what a fame 't will be?
    p. 264 UNDERWOOD 79    23 Chor. Heare, o you Groves, and, Hills, resound
                              his praise.
    p. 264 UNDERWOOD 79    31 Chor. Heare, O you Groves, and, Hills,
                              resound his worth.
    p. 269 UNDERWOOD 83     6 You seeme a faire one! O that you had breath,
    p. 282 U'WOOD 84.9     11 O! had I seene her laid out a faire Corse,
    p. 284 U'WOOD 84.9     61 O Day of joy, and suretie to the just!
    p. 315 HORACE 2       199 A scorned Mouse! O, how much better this,
    p. 325 HORACE 2       429 O I left-witted, that purge every spring
    p. 327 HORACE 2       472 Sixe ounces. O, when once the canker'd rust,
    p. 364 UNGATHERED 5     1 Splendor! O more then mortall,
    p. 380 UNGATHERED 12   37 How faine for his venery he was to crie (Tergum
                              o)
    p. 390 UNGATHERED 25    5 O, could he but haue drawne his wit
    p. 396 UNGATHERED 30   12 Lend me thy voyce, O FAME, that I may draw
    p. 397 UNGATHERED 30   43 O, how in those, dost thou instruct these times,
    p. 403 UNGATHERED 34   39 To hold her vp. O Showes! Showes! Mighty
                              Showes!
```

o'   frequency: 3   relative frequency: 0.00004

oak. See "oake," "oke."

oake   frequency: 1   relative frequency: 0.00001
```
    p. 245 UNDERWOOD 70    67 Or standing long an Oake, three hundred yeare,
```

oares   frequency: 1   relative frequency: 0.00001
```
    p.  85 EPIGRAMS 133    62 Ycleped Mud, which, when their oares did once
                              stirre,
```

oars. See "oares."

oath   frequency: 4   relative frequency: 0.00005
```
    p.  32 EPIGRAMS 16      7 Nor need'st thou: for those few, by oath releast,
    p.  43 EPIGRAMS 53      5 It was as if thou printed had'st an oath,
    p. 133 UNDERWOOD 2.3   10 At her hand, with oath, to make
    p. 389 UNGATHERED 24   18 Finer then was his Spanish, if my Oath
```

oathes   frequency: 3   relative frequency: 0.00004
```
   *p. 493 TO HIMSELF      34 Dare quit, vpon your oathes,
    p.  35 EPIGRAMS 28      9 He will both argue, and discourse in oathes,
    p. 191 UNDERWOOD 38     1 'Tis true, I'm broke! Vowes, Oathes, and all
                              I had
```

oaths. See "oathes," "othes."

obay   frequency: 1   relative frequency: 0.00001
   **p. 116 PANEGYRE   126 Then by their power; and men doe more obay

obedience   frequency: 1   relative frequency: 0.00001
     p. 130 UNDERWOOD 1.3   14 The Sonnes obedience knew no No,

obelisk. See "obeliske."

obeliske   frequency: 2   relative frequency: 0.00002
     p. 46 EPIGRAMS 60   2 An obeliske, or columne to thy name,
     p. 416 UNGATHERED 44   5 Vpon this obeliske, advanc'd for it,

obey   frequency: 3   relative frequency: 0.00004
   See alsc "obay," "t<c>'obay," "t<o>'obey."
     p. 190 UNDERWOOD 37   32 But shall sometimes be tempted to obey
     p. 251 UNDERWOOD 74   9 The rudest Winds obey the calmest Ayre:
     p. 269 UNDERWOOD 83   5 I doe obey you, Beautie! for in death,

obeying   frequency: 1   relative frequency: 0.00001
   **p. 115 PANEGYRE   74 The Kings obeying will, from taking pride

obiect   frequency: 5   relative frequency: 0.00007
   **p. 114 PANEGYRE   64 With seuerall eyes, that in this obiect met.
     p. 74 EPIGRAMS 114   5 Hath chang'd his soule, and made his obiect you:
     p. 109 FOREST 11   11 Obiect arriue there, but the heart (our spie)
     p. 113 FOREST 11   115 And to his sense obiect this sentence euer,
     p. 362 UNGATHERED 2   8 The fault's not in the obiect, but their eyes.

obiectest   frequency: 1   relative frequency: 0.00001
     p. 408 UNGATHERED 37   3 ffor thou obiectest (as thou hast been told)

obiects   frequency: 2   relative frequency: 0.00002
     p. 118 FOREST 13   66 And after varyed, as fresh obiects goes,
     p. 361 UNGATHERED 1   3 weare made the obiects to my weaker powers;

object   frequency: 2   relative frequency: 0.00002
   See alsc "obiect."
     p. 132 UNDERWOOD 2.2   23 This my object. But she threw
     p. 159 UNDERWOOD 14   29 Stand forth my Object, then, you that have beene

objectest. See "obiectest."

objects   frequency: 3   relative frequency: 0.00004
   See alsc "obiects."
     p. 163 UNDERWOOD 15   28 But there are objects, bid him to be gone
     p. 165 UNDERWOOD 15   101 Thus they doe talke. And are these objects fit
     p. 173 UNDERWOOD 22   27 That would their better objects find:

oblations   frequency: 1   relative frequency: 0.00001
     p. 383 UNGATHERED 16   10 As true oblations; his Brothers Embleme sayes,

oblique   frequency: 1   relative frequency: 0.00001
     p. 224 UNDERWOOD 50   11 By all oblique Degrees, that killing height

obliquitie   frequency: 1   relative frequency: 0.00001
     p. 192 UNDERWOOD 38   64 Is natures meere obliquitie! as Heaven

obliquity. See "obliquitie."

oblivion   frequency: 1   relative frequency: 0.00001
     p. 175 UNDERWOOD 24   1 From Death, and darke oblivion, neere the same,

obscene   frequency: 2   relative frequency: 0.00002
   See also "th'obscene."
     p. 42 EPIGRAMS 49   4 For wittie, in his language, is obscene.
     p. 156 UNDERWOOD 13   106 'Twixt feare and rashnesse: not a lust obscene,

obscure   frequency: 2   relative frequency: 0.00002
     p. 158 UNDERWOOD 14   2 Though I am short, I cannot be obscure:
     p. 307 HORACE 2   36 Obscure. This, striving to run smooth, and flow,

obseruation   frequency: 2   relative frequency: 0.00002
     p. 363 UNGATHERED 3   7 Respect, and obseruation; it vncouers
     p. 409 UNGATHERED 38   7 By obseruation of those Comick Lawes

obserued   frequency: 1   relative frequency: 0.00001
     p. 71 EPIGRAMS 110   t2 CAESARS Commentaries obserued, and
                                     translated.

observation. See "obseruation."

observe   frequency: 2   relative frequency: 0.00002
    See also "t<o>'observe."
    p. 157 UNDERWOOD 13   140 Observe the strength, the height, the why, and
                              when,
    p. 315 HORACE 2   223 The customes of each age thou must observe,

observed. See "obserued."

observing. See "th'obseruing."

obtain. See "obtaine," "t<o>'obtaine."

obtain'd   frequency: 1   relative frequency: 0.00001
    p. 154 UNDERWOOD 13   38 Must make me sad for what I have obtain'd.

obtaine   frequency: 1   relative frequency: 0.00001
    p. 193 UNDERWOOD 38   81 And with the vulgar doth it not obtaine

occasion   frequency: 1   relative frequency: 0.00001
    p. 171 UNDERWOOD 19   19 Slip no occasion; As time stands not still,

occasions   frequency: 1   relative frequency: 0.00001
    p. 118 FOREST 13   63 Times, and occasions, to start forth, and seeme)

occupy   frequency: 1   relative frequency: 0.00001
    p. 75 EPIGRAMS 117   2 For his whore: GROYNE doth still occupy his
                              land.

ocean   frequency: 1   relative frequency: 0.00001
    p. 280 U'WOOD 84.4   57 Not swelling like the Ocean proud,

od   frequency: 1   relative frequency: 0.00001
    p. 85 EPIGRAMS 133   43 All, that are readers: but, me thinkes 'tis od,

odcombe   frequency: 3   relative frequency: 0.00004
    p. 378 UNGATHERED 11   t2 his trauailes, the Coryate of Odcombe,
    p. 378 UNGATHERED 11   87 Of Tom of Odcombe that odde Iouiall Author,
    p. 380 UNGATHERED 12   40 That sacred to Odcombe are there now suspended,

odcombian   frequency: 2   relative frequency: 0.00002
    p. 379 UNGATHERED 12   7 Of our Odcombian, that literate Elfe?
    p. 379 UNGATHERED 12   t1 To the London Reader, on the Odcombian writer,

odd. See "od," "odde."

odde   frequency: 3   relative frequency: 0.00004
    p. 208 UNDERWOOD 43   118 Some Alchimist there may be yet, or odde
    p. 335 HORACE 2   662 Immortall, tooke a melancholique, odde
    p. 378 UNGATHERED 11   87 Of Tom of Odcombe that odde Iouiall Author,

oddes   frequency: 2   relative frequency: 0.00002
    p. 138 UNDERWOOD 2.6   7 If by us, the odds were laid,
    p. 230 UNDERWOOD 56   4 You won them too, your oddes did merit it.

odds. See "oddes," "ods."

ode   frequency: 14   relative frequency: 0.00020
   *p. 492 TO HIMSELF   t4 begat this following Ode to
    p. 72 EPIGRAMS 112   12 Next morne, an Ode: Thou mak'st a song ere
                              night.
    p. 120 FOREST 14   t1 Ode.
    p. 174 UNDERWOOD 23   t1 An Ode. To himselfe.
    p. 176 UNDERWOOD 25   t1 An Ode to IAMES Earle of Desmond,
    p. 180 UNDERWOOD 26   t1 An Ode.
    p. 181 UNDERWOOD 27   t1 An Ode.
    p. 239 UNDERWOOD 67   t1 An Ode, or Song, by all the Muses.
    p. 250 UNDERWOOD 74   t2 An Ode gratulatorie,
    p. 292 UNDERWOOD 86   t1 Ode the first. The fourth Booke.
    p. 293 UNDERWOOD 87   t1 Ode IX. 3 Booke, to Lydia.
    p. 364 UNGATHERED 5   t1 Ode #enthousiastike.
    p. 366 UNGATHERED 6   t1 Ode. #allegorike.
    p. 419 UNGATHERED 48   t1 Ode:

odious   frequency: 1   relative frequency: 0.00001
    p. 207 UNDERWOOD 43   106 All soote, and embers odious, as thy worke

odorous   frequency: 1   relative frequency: 0.00001
    See also "od'rous."
    p. 280 U'WOOD 84.4   64 A nest of odorous spice, and gummes.

odour   frequency: 5   relative frequency: 0.00007
    p. 127 UNDERWOOD 1.1   15 What odour can be, then a heart contrite,
    p. 152 UNDERWOOD 12   18 That never came ill odour thence:
    p. 168 UNDERWOOD 15   190 Still pretious, with the odour of thy name.
    p. 186 UNDERWOOD 31   8 Still flie about the Odour of your Name;
    p. 220 UNDERWOOD 48   11 That both, their odour take him,

odours   frequency: 1   relative frequency: 0.00001
    p.   33 EPIGRAMS 20   1 Th'expence in odours is a most vaine sinne,

od'rous   frequency: 2   relative frequency: 0.00002
    p. 112 FOREST 11   96 Whose od'rous breath destroyes
    p. 413 UNGATHERED 41 27 With od'rous sweets and soft humilitie,

ods   frequency: 1   relative frequency: 0.00001
    p. 327 HORACE 2   480 First frighted men, that wildly liv'd, at ods,

oenone   frequency: 1   relative frequency: 0.00001
    p.   68 EPIGRAMS 105 10 You were the bright OENONE, FLORA, or
                            May?

of   frequency: 1554   relative frequency: 0.02249
    See also "many'of," "o'," "of>," "o'th',"
        "o'th'dcctors," "o'the."

of>   frequency: 1   relative frequency: 0.00001
  *p. 493 TO HIMSELF   24 scraps, out <of> euery dish,

off   frequency: 19   relative frequency: 0.00027
    See also "of."
    p. 154 UNDERWOOD 13   52 But then, fist-fill'd, to put me off the sent.
    p. 169 UNDERWOOD 18   5 Or was she gracious a-farre off? but neere
    p. 187 UNDERWOOD 33   35 Then com'st thou off with Victorie and Palme,
    p. 192 UNDERWOOD 38   46 We cut not off, till all Cures else doe faile:
    p. 193 UNDERWOOD 38   88 Streight puts off all his Anger, and doth kisse
    p. 201 UNDERWOOD 42   56 Or slipper was left off, and kisse it too,
    p. 234 UNDERWOOD 61   7 Yet are got off thence, with cleare mind, and
                            hands
    p. 242 UNDERWOOD 69   16 To keepe him off; and how-so-e're he gleanes
    p. 280 U'WOOD 84.4   56 As it slid moulded off from Heaven.
    p. 283 U'WOOD 84.9   43 From off her pillow, and deluded bed;
    p. 290 UNDERWOOD 85   11 And with his hooke lops off the fruitlesse race,
    p. 294 UNDERWOOD 87   19 That I bright C<h>loe off should shake;
    p. 309 HORACE 2   99 Shall perish: so farre off it is, the state,
    p. 323 HORACE 2   395 'Tis cleare, this way I have got off from blame,
    p. 331 HORACE 2   541 As some the farther off: This loves the darke:
    p. 335 HORACE 2   636 Cut off superfluous ornaments; and when
    p. 337 HORACE 2   680 Till he drop off, a Horse-leech, full of blood.
    p. 401 UNGATHERED 32 16 If, maymed, she come off, 'tis not of men
    p. 415 UNGATHERED 42 18 As it were spun by nature, off the fleece:

off-spring   frequency: 1   relative frequency: 0.00001
    p. 325 HORACE 2   415 But you, Pompilius off-spring, spare you not

offal. See "offall."

offall   frequency: 1   relative frequency: 0.00001
    p.   88 EPIGRAMS 133 148 To put the skins, and offall in a pastie?

offence   frequency: 8   relative frequency: 0.00011
    p.   60 EPIGRAMS 94   10 But, when they heard it tax'd, tooke more
                            offence.
    p.   69 EPIGRAMS 108   4 Be nor put on you, nor you take offence.
    p. 152 UNDERWOOD 12   17 So of uncleannesse, or offence,
    p. 177 UNDERWOOD 25   32 Where only a mans birth is his offence,
    p. 191 UNDERWOOD 38   6 And drives it in to eat on my offence,
    p. 193 UNDERWOOD 38   68 God lightens not at mans each fraile offence,
    p. 232 UNDERWOOD 59   6 As all defence, or offence, were a chime!
    p. 321 HORACE 2   361 Will take offence, at this: Nor, though it
                            strike

offend   frequency: 5   relative frequency: 0.00007
    See also "h<e>'offend," "t<o>'offend."
 **p. 113 PANEGYRE   16 Those dampes, that so offend all good mens eyes;
    p.   37 EPIGRAMS 33   1 Ile not offend thee with a vaine teare more,
    p. 112 FOREST 11   109 Would not be fearefull to offend a dame
    p. 192 UNDERWOOD 38   33 Where weaknesse doth offend, and vertue grieve,
    p. 331 HORACE 2   558 Or thick grosse ointment, but offend the Guests:

offended   frequency: 4   relative frequency: 0.00005
    p. 191 UNDERWOOD 38   9 Offended Mistris, you are yet so faire,
    p. 234 UNDERWOOD 60   9 Offended with the dazeling flame
    p. 325 HORACE 2   414 Had not our every Poet like offended.
    p. 329 HORACE 2   527 Offended with few spots, which negligence

offenders. See "they'offenders."

offending   frequency: 1   relative frequency: 0.00001
    p. 156 UNDERWOOD 13   107 Or appetite of offending, but a skill,

offer   frequency: 6   relative frequency: 0.00008
   *p. 492 TO HIMSELF   15 To offer them a surfet of pure bread,
  **p. 116 PANEGYRE   124 To offer cause of iniurie, or feare.
    p. 54 EPIGRAMS 84   4 For your most noble offer had supply'd me.
    p. 263 UNDERWOOD 79   12 And offer your just service on these plaines;
    p. 401 UNGATHERED 32   11 Yet, who dares offer a redoubt to reare?
    p. 416 UNGATHERED 44   6 We offer as a Circle the most fit

offer'd   frequency: 2   relative frequency: 0.00002
    p. 28 EPIGRAMS 3   6 Not offer'd, as it made sute to be bought;
    p. 157 UNDERWOOD 13   130 Were the Rack offer'd them, how they came so;

offering   frequency: 1   relative frequency: 0.00001
    See also "offring," "off'ring."
    p. 161 UNDERWOOD 14   69 In offering this thy worke to no great Name,

offers   frequency: 1   relative frequency: 0.00001
    p. 321 HORACE 2   351 Yet he that offers at it, may sweat much,

office   frequency: 12   relative frequency: 0.00017
  **p. 113 PANEGYRE   28 And in her office vow'd she would remaine,
    p. 63 EPIGRAMS 97   11 Nor office in the towne, nor place in court,
    p. 78 EPIGRAMS 121   5 Yet is the office not to be despis'd,
    p. 158 UNDERWOOD 14   9 Rather then Office, when it doth or may
    p. 216 UNDERWOOD 45   13 And as within your Office, you doe take
    p. 258 UNDERWOOD 75   187 Hee's Master of the Office; yet no more
    p. 295 UNDERWOOD 90   5 Never at Law; seldome in office gown'd;
    p. 307 HORACE 2   64 Lay that aside, the Epicks office is.
    p. 317 HORACE 2   276 An Actors parts, and Office too, the Quire
    p. 325 HORACE 2   436 Their Charge, and Office, whence their wealth
                               to fet,
    p. 325 HORACE 2   450 And office of a Judge are, what the parts
    p. 415 UNGATHERED 42   20 Office of Wit, a Mint, and (this is true)

officer   frequency: 1   relative frequency: 0.00001
    p. 201 UNDERWOOD 42   53 An Officer there, did make most solemne love,

officers   frequency: 2   relative frequency: 0.00002
    p. 105 FOREST 8   35 Them, and all their officers.
    p. 118 FOREST 13   79 Them, or their officers: and no man know,

offices   frequency: 4   relative frequency: 0.00005
    p. 185 UNDERWOOD 30   15 Whose Offices, and honours did surprize,
    p. 244 UNDERWOOD 70   48 All Offices were done
    p. 253 UNDERWOOD 75   27 To doe their Offices in Natures Chime,
    p. 272 UNDERWOOD 84   t14 Her faire OFFICES.

officious   frequency: 1   relative frequency: 0.00001
    p. 257 UNDERWOOD 75   145 Haste, haste, officious Sun, and send them
                               Night

officiously   frequency: 1   relative frequency: 0.00001
    p. 94 FOREST 2   36 Officiously, at first, themselues betray.

offring   frequency: 4   relative frequency: 0.00005
    p. 45 EPIGRAMS 58   3 For offring, with thy smiles, my wit to grace,
    p. 114 FOREST 12   30 With you, I know, my offring will find grace.
    p. 127 UNDERWOOD 1.1   12 An offring meet
    p. 386 UNGATHERED 21   12 By offring not more sureties, then inow,

off'ring   frequency: 1   relative frequency: 0.00001
    p. 174 UNDERWOOD 22   29 Who as an off'ring at your shrine,

offspring. See "off-spring."

oft   frequency: 17   relative frequency: 0.00024
    See also "oft>."
    p. 44 EPIGRAMS 54   4 That quit'st the cause so oft, and rayl'st at
                               men?

oft (cont.)
```
    p.   68 EPIGRAMS 107      3 I oft looke on false coyne, to know't from true:
    p.   73 EPIGRAMS 112     18 That both for wit, and sense, so oft dost plucke,
    p.   94 FOREST 2         17 And thence, the ruddy Satyres oft prouoke
    p.   97 FOREST 3         23 In spring, oft roused for thy masters sport,
    p.  116 FOREST 12        91 Moodes, which the god-like SYDNEY oft did
                                proue,
    p.  119 FOREST 13        84 Boast, but how oft they haue gone wrong to man:
    p.  136 UNDERWOOD 2.5    23 Such as oft I wanton in!
    p.  141 UNDERWOOD 2.9    26 As the Downe, and shew it oft;
    p.  159 UNDERWOOD 14     20 And mine not least) I have too oft preferr'd
    p.  166 UNDERWOOD 15    120 When oft the Bearer, is borne out of dore?
    p.  179 UNDERWOOD 25     52 Oft scape an Imputation, more through luck, then
                                wit.
    p.  189 UNDERWOOD 36      3 Though Envie oft his shadow be,
    p.  234 UNDERWOOD 61     13 Fit for a Bishops knees! O bow them oft,
    p.  311 HORACE 2        134 With swelling throat: and, oft, the tragick wight
    p.  380 UNGATHERED 12    30 Or builders of Story haue oft imputation
    p.  417 UNGATHERED 45    29 Though shee chainge as oft as shee,
```

oft-times   frequency: 4   relative frequency: 0.00005
```
  **p.  115 PANEGYRE         86 "Oft-times, to haue the secrets of their state
    p.   40 EPIGRAMS 42       9 And so is IONE. Oft-times, when GILES
                                doth find
    p.  305 HORACE 2         18 Ye have oft-times, that may ore-shine the rest,
    p.  329 HORACE 2        523 Oft-times a Sharpe, when we require a Flat:
```

oft>   frequency: 1   relative frequency: 0.00001
```
    p.  174 UNDERWOOD 23      6 That eats on wits, and Arts, and <oft> destroyes
                                them both.
```

often   frequency: 7   relative frequency: 0.00010
    See also "th'often."
```
    p.   37 EPIGRAMS 32       6 His often change of clime (though not of mind)
    p.   82 EPIGRAMS 130      7 And is t<o>'a body, often, ill inclin'd,
    p.   89 EPIGRAMS 133    184 That had, so often, shew'd 'hem merry prankes.
    p.   98 FOREST 3         59 The iolly wassall walkes the often round,
    p.  146 UNDERWOOD 6       8 Doe change, though man, and often fight,
    p.  146 UNDERWOOD 6      18 But as 'tis often vext and tri'd.
    p.  380 UNGATHERED 12    39 How well, and how often his shoes too were
                                mended,
```

oftener. See "oftner."

oftner   frequency: 1   relative frequency: 0.00001
```
    p.   99 FOREST 3         75 And change possessions, oftner with his breath,
```

ogle   frequency: 2   relative frequency: 0.00002
```
    p.  394 UNGATHERED 28    t2 eldest Daughter, to Cuthbert Lord Ogle:
    p.  400 UNGATHERED 31    33 For this did Katherine, Ladie Ogle, die
```

oh   frequency: 8   relative frequency: 0.00011
    See also "o."
```
    p.   46 EPIGRAMS 62       9 What should the cause be? Oh, you liue at court:
    p.  144 UNDERWOOD 4       1 Oh doe not wanton with those eyes,
    p.  149 UNDERWOOD 9      11 Oh, but my conscious feares,
    p.  170 UNDERWOOD 18     15 Oh how a Lover may mistake! to thinke,
    p.  293 UNDERWOOD 86     33 But, why, oh why, my Ligurine,
    p.  404 UNGATHERED 34    49 Oh, to make Boardes to speake! There is a taske
    p.  404 UNGATHERED 34    59 Whither? oh whither will this Tire-man growe?
    p.  405 UNGATHERED 34    85 Oh wise Surueyor! wyser Architect!
```

oil. See "cyle," "th'oyle."

oils. See "oyles."

oily. See "oylie."

ointment   frequency: 1   relative frequency: 0.00001
```
    p.  331 HORACE 2        558 Or thick grosse ointment, but offend the Guests;
```

oke   frequency: 2   relative frequency: 0.00002
```
    p.   94 FOREST 2         18 The lighter Faunes, to reach the Ladies oke.
    p.  290 UNDERWOOD 85     23 Then now beneath some ancient Oke he may,
```

old   frequency: 67   relative frequency: 0.00096
    See also "olde," "th'old."
```
   *p.  493 TO HIMSELF       46 Ere yeares haue made thee old;
  **p.  114 PANEGYRE         65 Old men were glad, their fates till now did last;
    p.   31 EPIGRAMS 13       2 Of old, they gaue a cock to AESCVLAPE;
```

old (cont.)
p.	32	EPIGRAMS 18	2 When both it is the old way, and the true.
p.	39	EPIGRAMS 39	t1 ON OLD COLT.
p.	45	EPIGRAMS 56	6 Buy the reuersion of old playes; now growne
p.	47	EPIGRAMS 64	5 Nor glad as those, that old dependents bee,
p.	50	EPIGRAMS 70	4 On the true causes, ere they grow too old.
p.	54	EPIGRAMS 82	1 SVRLY'S old whore in her new silkes doth swim:
p.	62	EPIGRAMS 97	1 See you yond' Motion? Not the old Fa-ding,
p.	67	EPIGRAMS 104	4 A new SVSANNA, equall to that old?
p.	74	EPIGRAMS 115	27 Acts old Iniquitie, and in the fit
p.	77	EPIGRAMS 120	14 Old men so duely,
p.	82	EPIGRAMS 130	10 Of old, euen by her practise, to be fam'd;
p.	86	EPIGRAMS 133	70 Hung stench, diseases, and old filth, their mother,
p.	87	EPIGRAMS 133	128 Whereof old DEMOCRITE, and HILL NICHOLAS,
p.	88	EPIGRAMS 133	156 Old BANKES the iuggler, our PYTHAGORAS,
p.	93	FOREST 1	12 When Loue is fled, and I grow old.
p.	98	FOREST 3	63 Such, and no other was that age, of old,
p.	100	FOREST 4	14 Yet art thou both shrunke vp, and old,
p.	107	FOREST 10	5 With his old earthly labours. T<o>'exact more,
p.	107	FOREST 10	19 Let the old boy, your sonne, ply his old taske,
p.	115	FOREST 12	77 Will proue old ORPHEVS act no tale to be:
p.	131	UNDERWOOD 2.1	6 Some have lov'd as old agen.
p.	131	UNDERWOOD 2.1	20 She shall make the old man young,
p.	181	UNDERWOOD 27	23 His new Cassandra, 'bove the old;
p.	199	UNDERWOOD 42	2 As Horace fat; or as Anacreon old;
p.	202	UNDERWOOD 42	83 Under that cover; an old Mid-wives hat!
p.	203	UNDERWOOD 43	11 Was it because thou wert of old denied
p.	207	UNDERWOOD 43	89 All the old Venusine, in Poetrie,
p.	213	UNDERWOOD 44	5 Old Aesope Gundomar: the French can tell,
p.	213	UNDERWOOD 44	21 What a strong Fort old Pimblicoe had bin!
p.	214	UNDERWOOD 44	52 Beauchamps, and Nevills, Cliffords, Audleys old;
p.	216	UNDERWOOD 45	20 They cannot last. No lie grew ever old.
p.	223	UNDERWOOD 49	20 As new rewards of her old secrecie?
p.	224	UNDERWOOD 50	20 As makes Penelopes old fable true,
p.	230	UNDERWOOD 56	8 Unprofitable Chattell, fat and old,
p.	241	UNDERWOOD 68	11 As the old Bard, should no Canary lack.
p.	258	UNDERWOOD 75	165 That when you both are old,
p.	260	UNDERWOOD 77	9 The old Greek-hands in picture, or in stone.
p.	263	UNDERWOOD 79	9 Rector Chori. To day old Janus opens the new yeare,
p.	263	UNDERWOOD 79	10 And shuts the old. Haste, haste, all loyall Swaines,
p.	282	U'WOOD 84.9	6 Spun out in name of some of the old Nine!
p.	289	UNDERWOOD 85	2 As the old race of Mankind were,
p.	291	UNDERWOOD 85	43 To deck the hallow'd Harth with old wood fir'd
p.	294	UNDERWOOD 87	17 HOR. But, say old Love returne should make,
p.	295	UNDERWOOD 89	5 Darke thy cleare glasse with old Falernian Wine;
p.	313	HORACE 2	162 Or an Heroe; if a ripe old man,
p.	315	HORACE 2	241 The old man many evils doe girt round;
p.	321	HORACE 2	348 Or old Silenus, Bacchus guard, and Nurse.
p.	321	HORACE 2	365 To these succeeded the old Comoedie,
p.	327	HORACE 2	486 This was the wisdome, that they had of old,
p.	348	HORACE 1	385 Your .... old .... prais'd
p.	367	UNGATHERED 6	38 Salute old Mone,
p.	369	UNGATHERED 6	109 In heau'n the Signe of old Eridanus:
p.	375	UNGATHERED 10	26 Old Hat here, torne Hose, with Shoes full of grauell,
p.	384	UNGATHERED 18	24 Yet neyther of you seeme to th'other old.
p.	389	UNGATHERED 24	4 When the old words doe strike on the new times,
p.	397	UNGATHERED 30	27 Which made me thinke, the old Theocritus,
p.	398	UNGATHERED 30	86 Thou hadst brought Lapland, or old Cobalus,
p.	405	UNGATHERED 34	87 On ye new priming of thy old Signe postes
p.	407	UNGATHERED 35	14 From ye fam'd pillars of old Hercules!
p.	409	UNGATHERED 38	4 Of Fellowship, professing my old Arts.
p.	409	UNGATHERED 38	t1 To my old Faithfull Seruant: and (by
p.	410	UNGATHERED 38	13 It was not so of old: Men tooke vp trades
p.	657	L. CONVIVALES	8 Cries Old Sym, the King of Skinkers;

old-end   frequency: 2   relative frequency: 0.00002
| p. | 43 | EPIGRAMS 53 | 1 Long-gathering OLD-END, I did feare thee wise, |
| p. | 43 | EPIGRAMS 53 | t1 TO OLD-END GATHERER. |

olde   frequency: 1   relative frequency: 0.00001
    p. 388 UNGATHERED 23   2 Olde Hesiods Ore, and giue it vs; but thine,

olimpicke   frequency: 1   relative frequency: 0.00001
    p. 415 UNGATHERED 43   2 Twixt Cotswold, and the Olimpicke exercise:

oliue   frequency: 1   relative frequency: 0.00001
    p. 64 EPIGRAMS 101   10 An oliue, capers, or some better sallade

olive   frequency: 1   relative frequency: 0.00001
    See also "oliue."
    p. 251 UNDERWOOD 74   28 Shoot up an Olive fruitfull, faire,

oliveers   frequency: 1   relative frequency: 0.00001
    p. 206 UNDERWOOD 43   70 All the madde Rolands, and sweet Oliveers;

olivers. See "cliveers."

olives   frequency: 1   relative frequency: 0.00001
    p. 291 UNDERWOOD 85   55 More sweet then Clives, that new gather'd be

olympic. See "climpicke."

omen   frequency: 1   relative frequency: 0.00001
    p. 263 UNDERWOOD 78   22 Good Omen to him, in the note thou sing'st,

ominous   frequency: 1   relative frequency: 0.00001
    p. 116 FOREST 12   98 A vow as new, and ominous as the yeare,

omitted   frequency: 1   relative frequency: 0.00001
    p. 307 HORACE 2   62 Much, that mought now be spoke: omitted here

omnipotent   frequency: 1   relative frequency: 0.00001
    p. 406 UNGATHERED 34   96 Aymd at in thy omnipotent Designe!

on   frequency: 305   relative frequency: 0.00441
    See also "on[e]," "on't."

on[e]   frequency: 1   relative frequency: 0.00001
    p. 383 UNGATHERED 16   9 hee freely bringes; and on[e] this Alter layes

once   frequency: 53   relative frequency: 0.00076
    See also "ones."
  **p. 115 PANEGYRE   83 "And, being once found out, discouer'd lies
  **p. 116 PANEGYRE   110 As once defend, what THEMIS did reproue.
  **p. 116 PANEGYRE   118 Who once haue got the habit to doe ill.
    p. 31 EPIGRAMS 14   12 Which conquers all, be once ouer-come by thee.
    p. 44 EPIGRAMS 55   5 At once thou mak'st me happie, and vnmak'st;
    p. 52 EPIGRAMS 74   7 Whil'st thou art certaine to thy words, once
                              gone,
  · p. 57 EPIGRAMS 90   9 Not though that haire grew browne, which once was
                              amber,
    p. 63 EPIGRAMS 98   7 That thou at once, then, nobly maist defend
    p. 70 EPIGRAMS 108   6 Your great profession; which I once, did proue:
    p. 85 EPIGRAMS 133   40 Or his to Antwerpe. Therefore, once more, list
                              ho'.
    p. 85 EPIGRAMS 133   56 Still, with thy former labours; yet, once more,
    p. 85 EPIGRAMS 133   62 Ycleped Mud, which, when their oares did once
                              stirre,
    p. 93 FOREST 1   5 It is enough, they once did get
    p. 100 FOREST 4   5 Doe not once hope, that thou canst tempt
    p. 102 FOREST 5   7 But if once we loose this light,
    p. 114 FOREST 12   21 The truth of times) was once of more esteeme,
    p. 118 FOREST 13   52 For he, that once is good, is euer great.
    p. 132 UNDERWOOD 2.2   19 Could be brought once back to looke.
    p. 139 UNDERWOOD 2.7   1 For Loves-sake, kisse me once againe,
    p. 139 UNDERWOOD 2.7   7 Once more, and (faith) I will be gone,
    p. 139 UNDERWOOD 2.7   12 What w'are but once to doe, we should doe long.
    p. 162 UNDERWOOD 15   24 Honour'd at once, and envi'd (if it can
    p. 167 UNDERWOOD 15   173 Then once to number, or bring forth to hand,
    p. 170 UNDERWOOD 18   10 And Fortune once, t<o>'assist the spirits that
                              dare.
    p. 170 UNDERWOOD 19   10 Where men at once may plant, and gather blisses:
    p. 181 UNDERWOOD 27   6 In whom Anacreon once did joy,
    p. 192 UNDERWOOD 38   35 Thinke that I once was yours, or may be now;
    p. 192 UNDERWOOD 38   47 And then with pause; for sever'd once, that's
                              gone,
    p. 192 UNDERWOOD 38   63 But to exact againe what once is given,
    p. 193 UNDERWOOD 38   92 Rather then once displease you more, to die
    p. 212 UNDERWOOD 43   212 That have good places: therefore once agen,

once (cont.)

p. 222 UNDERWOOD 49	11	What though she talke, and cannot once with them,
p. 223 UNDERWOOD 49	37	The wits will leave you, if they once perceive
p. 238 UNDERWOOD 66	1	Haile Mary, full of grace, it once was said,
p. 285 U'WOOD 84.9	105	You once enjoy'd: A short space severs yee,
p. 309 HORACE 2	94	Once rowable, but now doth nourish men
p. 315 HORACE 2	229	Th'unbearded Youth, his Guardian once being gone,
p. 317 HORACE 2	271	Once seene, to be againe call'd for, and plaid,
p. 327 HORACE 2	472	Sixe ounces. O, when once the canker'd rust,
p. 331 HORACE 2	543	Will in the light be view'd: This, once, the sight
p. 331 HORACE 2	580	The Writ, once out, never returned yet.
p. 333 HORACE 2	592	Did learne them first, and once a Master fear'd.
p. 335 HORACE 2	642	The man once mock'd, and suffer'd wrong to tread.
p. 335 HORACE 2	667	Nor did he doe this once; for if you can
p. 337 HORACE 2	677	Learn'd and unlearn'd; holding, whom once he takes;
p. 351 HORACE 1	512	..... if once . ...
p. 353 HORACE 1	597	Once ... .
p. 369 UNGATHERED 6	99	Were CYCNVS, once high flying
p. 380 UNGATHERED 12	52	Doth he once dissemble, but tels he did ride
p. 409 UNGATHERED 38	1	I had you for a Seruant, once, Dick Brome;
p. 420 UNGATHERED 48	32	And once more stryke the eare of tyme wth those ffresh straynes.
p. 421 UNGATHERED 48	44	And by their takeinge, lett it once appeare
p. 657 L. CONVIVALES	18	And at once, three Senses pleases.

one   frequency: 184   relative frequency: 0.00266

See also "one's," "th'one."

**p. 115 PANEGYRE	72	That friendly temper'd, one pure taper makes.
**p. 116 PANEGYRE	119	One wickednesse another must defend;
**p. 117 PANEGYRE	146	Brighter then all, hath yet made no one lesse;
p. 30 EPIGRAMS 12	5	By that one spell he liues, eates, drinkes, arrayes
p. 32 EPIGRAMS 16	4	Scarse thy weekes swearing brings thee of, of one.
p. 34 EPIGRAMS 23	2	Who, to thy one, all other braines refuse;
p. 36 EPIGRAMS 28	19	Nay more, for greatnesse sake, he will be one
p. 42 EPIGRAMS 46	3	'Tis LVCKLESSE he, that tooke vp one on band
p. 42 EPIGRAMS 47	1	Sir LVCKLESSE, troth, for lucks sake passe by one:
p. 45 EPIGRAMS 57	2	Baudrie', and vsurie were one kind of game.
p. 45 EPIGRAMS 58	7	So haue I seene at CHRIST-masse sports one lost,
p. 46 EPIGRAMS 61	2	One doth not stroke me, nor the other strike.
p. 50 EPIGRAMS 69	2	Yet by thy weapon liu'st! Th'hast one good part.
p. 51 EPIGRAMS 73	13	Your partie-per-pale picture, one halfe drawne
p. 51 EPIGRAMS 74	2	And know thee, then, a iudge, not of one yeare;
p. 52 EPIGRAMS 74	8	As is thy conscience, which is alwayes one:
p. 53 EPIGRAMS 77	t1	TO ONE THAT DESIRED ME NOT TO
p. 54 EPIGRAMS 80	6	And here, it should be one of our first strifes,
p. 56 EPIGRAMS 88	5	And land on one, whose face durst neuer bee
p. 57 EPIGRAMS 89	14	So many Poets life, by one should liue.
p. 58 EPIGRAMS 91	11	To any one, were enuie: which would liue
p. 58 EPIGRAMS 92	2	Vnto the cryes of London Ile adde one;
p. 59 EPIGRAMS 92	23	Or, euery day, some one at RIMEE'S looks,
p. 61 EPIGRAMS 95	26	It is the next deed, and a great one too.
p. 62 EPIGRAMS 96	7	Reade all I send: and, if I find but one
p. 62 EPIGRAMS 97	3	But one more rare, and in the case so new:
p. 63 EPIGRAMS 97	17	Since he was gone, more then the one he weares.
p. 66 EPIGRAMS 102	7	Almost, is exercis'd: and scarse one knowes,
p. 66 EPIGRAMS 102	13	But thou, whose noblesse keeps one stature still,
p. 66 EPIGRAMS 102	14	And one true posture, though besieg'd with ill
p. 67 EPIGRAMS 104	10	Of former age, or glorie of our one,
p. 68 EPIGRAMS 106	1	If men get name, for some one vertue: Then,
p. 70 EPIGRAMS 109	5	Thou art not one, seek'st miseries with hope,
p. 71 EPIGRAMS 110	13	For, where his person liu'd scarce one iust age,
p. 74 EPIGRAMS 115	3	Naming so many, too! But, this is one,
p. 74 EPIGRAMS 115	14	Giue euery one his dose of mirth: and watches
p. 74 EPIGRAMS 115	21	With such a one. And therein keepes it's word.
p. 77 EPIGRAMS 120	15	As, sooth, the Parcae thought him one,
p. 78 EPIGRAMS 122	6	And heare her speake with one, and her first tongue;
p. 79 EPIGRAMS 124	9	One name was ELIZABETH,
p. 81 EPIGRAMS 129	2	But the first question is, when one saw thee?
p. 81 EPIGRAMS 129	4	To Braynford, Hackney, Bow, but thou mak'st one;

one (cont.)

	p.	84	EPIGRAMS 133	8	COCYTVS, PHLEGETON, our haue prou'd in one;
	p.	84	EPIGRAMS 133	14	And for one CERBERVS, the whole coast was dogs.
	p.	84	EPIGRAMS 133	23	One was; and he, for brawne, and braine, right able
	p.	84	EPIGRAMS 133	28	His three for one. Now, lordings, listen well.
	p.	86	EPIGRAMS 133	67	Betweene two walls; where, on one side, to scar men,
	p.	86	EPIGRAMS 133	81	One said, it was bold BRIAREVS, or the beadle,
	p.	87	EPIGRAMS 133	119	Yet, one day in the yeere, for sweet 'tis voyc't,
	p.	87	EPIGRAMS 133	129	One said, the other swore, the world consists.
	p.	88	EPIGRAMS 133	158	Being, beyond sea, burned for one witch:
	p.	95	FOREST 2	49	And no one empty-handed, to salute
	p.	108	FOREST 10	26	(Though they were crusht into one forme) could make
	p.	111	FOREST 11	69	Peace, Luxurie, thou art like one of those
	p.	112	FOREST 11	101	All her best symmetrie in that one feature!
	p.	113	FOREST 12	10	And some one apteth to be trusted, then,
	p.	117	FOREST 13	27	And this shall be no false one, but as much
	p.	119	FOREST 13	88	Eate on her clients, and some one deuoure.
	p.	119	FOREST 13	113	How you loue one, and him you should; how still
	p.	120	FOREST 13	120	Each into other, and had now made one.
	p.	120	FOREST 13	121	Liue that one, still: and as long yeeres doe passe,
	p.	122	FOREST 15	10	First, midst, and last, conuerted one, and three;
	p.	127	UNDERWOOD 1.1	2	Of persons, still one God, in Unitie,
	p.	128	UNDERWOOD 1.1	30	Of persons, still one God in Unitie;
	p.	128	UNDERWOOD 1.1	33	9. Beholding one in three, and three in one,
	p.	128	UNDERWOOD 1.1	40	One God to see,
	p.	130	UNDERWOOD 1.3	15	Both wills were in one stature;
	p.	132	UNDERWOOD 2.2	28	Mock'd of all: and call'd of one
	p.	132	UNDERWOOD 2.2	31	Or else one that plaid his Ape,
	p.	137	UNDERWOOD 2.5	48	Make in one, the same were shee.
	p.	139	UNDERWOOD 2.7	8	Can he that loves, aske lesse then one?
	p.	139	UNDERWOOD 2.8	1	Charis one day in discourse
	p.	140	UNDERWOOD 2.8	11	As, untill she tell her one,
	p.	142	U'WOOD 2.10	8	'Tis one good part I'ld lie withall.
	p.	142	UNDERWOOD 2.9	55	But of one, if short he came,
	p.	145	UNDERWOOD 5	9	Find some one good, in some one man;
	p.	145	UNDERWOOD 5	12	One good enough for a songs sake.
	p.	146	UNDERWOOD 6	24	To love one man, hee'd leave her first.
	p.	148	UNDERWOOD 7	31	One un-becomming thought doth move
	p.	148	UNDERWOOD 8	6	Of one that lov'd?
	p.	152	UNDERWOOD 12	40	Who makes the one, so't be first, makes both.
	p.	154	UNDERWOOD 13	32	Of pressure, like one taken in a streight?
	p.	154	UNDERWOOD 13	39	No! Gifts and thankes should have one cheerefull face,
	p.	155	UNDERWOOD 13	67	But one is bitten by the Dog he fed,
	p.	155	UNDERWOOD 13	78	Many a pound, and piece, will p<l>ace one well;
	p.	156	UNDERWOOD 13	116	But like to be, that every day mends one,
	p.	157	UNDERWOOD 13	126	Who was this Morning such a one, should be
	p.	159	UNDERWOOD 14	31	And like a Compasse keeping one foot still
	p.	160	UNDERWOOD 14	56	And manly elocution, not one while
	p.	164	UNDERWOOD 15	55	Hee's one of blood, and fashion! and with these
	p.	164	UNDERWOOD 15	64	How they may make some one that day an Asse;
	p.	164	UNDERWOOD 15	69	Ready to cast, at one, whose band sits ill,
	p.	166	UNDERWOOD 15	119	What reputation to beare one Glasse more?
	p.	166	UNDERWOOD 15	125	Tilt one upon another, and now beare
	p.	168	UNDERWOOD 15	186	Thou shrinke or start not, but be alwayes one;
	p.	170	UNDERWOOD 18	23	That I must send one first, my Choyce assignes,
	p.	171	UNDERWOOD 19	14	(Though they may number bodyes) or but one.
	p.	171	UNDERWOOD 19	23	Of all that can be done him; Such a one
	p.	171	UNDERWOOD 20	2	Forgive me this one foolish deadly sin,
	p.	172	UNDERWOOD 20	18	Then all Ingredients made into one curse,
	p.	173	UNDERWOOD 22	8	This subjects you to love of one.
	p.	174	UNDERWOOD 22	31	One sparke of your Diviner heat
	p.	180	UNDERWOOD 26	17	In one full Action; nor have you now more
	p.	185	UNDERWOOD 30	2	Read here in one, what thou in all canst find,
	p.	185	UNDERWOOD 31	2	Lawes, and no change e're come to one decree:
	p.	188	UNDERWOOD 34	2	One beautie in an Age, and free from thee?
	p.	189	UNDERWOOD 36	6	All light[s] into his one doth run;
	p.	192	UNDERWOOD 38	41	There is no Father that for one demerit,
	p.	198	UNDERWOOD 40	33	Is fix'd upon one leg, and dares not come
	p.	198	UNDERWOOD 40	40	Due to that one, that doth believe him just.
	p.	201	UNDERWOOD 42	58	Lift up some one, and doe, I tell not what.
	p.	202	UNDERWOOD 42	73	Or in Moore-fields, this other night! sings one,
	p.	203	UNDERWOOD 43	28	A cause before; or leave me one behind.

one (cont.)
```
      p. 209 UNDERWOOD 43   149 Kindled the fire! But then, did one returne,
      p. 210 UNDERWOOD 43   172 Will be remembred by Six Clerkes, to one.
      p. 216 UNDERWOOD 45     4 One lesson we have both learn'd, and well read;
      p. 216 UNDERWOOD 45     5 I neither am, nor art thou one of those
      p. 218 UNDERWOOD 47    t1 An Epistle answering to one that
      p. 219 UNDERWOOD 47    29 I studie other friendships, and more one,
      p. 219 UNDERWOOD 47    47 Of Spaine or France; or were not prick'd downe
                                one
      p. 223 UNDERWOOD 49    39 For Sermoneeres: of which now one, now other,
      p. 225 UNDERWOOD 50    35 For when they find so many meet in one,
      p. 227 UNDERWOOD 52    12 With one great blot, yo'had form'd me as I am.
      p. 229 UNDERWOOD 54    15 It doe not come: One piece I have in store,
      p. 230 UNDERWOOD 56    13 Marrie the Muse is one, can tread the Aire,
      p. 235 UNDERWOOD 62    10 One Poet, then of other folke ten score.
      p. 243 UNDERWOOD 70    25 Here's one out-liv'd his Peeres,
      p. 246 UNDERWOOD 70    94 And keepe the one halfe from his Harry.
      p. 246 UNDERWOOD 70    98 Two names of friendship, but one Starre:
      p. 247 UNDERWOOD 70   109 That liking; and approach so one the tother,
      p. 248 UNDERWOOD 71     9 The Muse not peepes out, one of hundred dayes;
      p. 256 UNDERWOOD 75   125 One in the others hand,
      p. 257 UNDERWOOD 75   139 These two, now holy Church hath made them one,
      p. 257 UNDERWOOD 75   144 One to the other, long e're these to light were
                                brought.
      p. 258 UNDERWOOD 75   176 How each one playes his part, of the large
                                Pedigree.
      p. 258 UNDERWOOD 75   177 And never may there want one of the Stem,
      p. 260 UNDERWOOD 77    10 This I would doe, could I thinke Weston one
      p. 263 UNDERWOOD 78    32 Being sent to one, they will be read of all.
      p. 269 UNDERWOOD 83     6 You seeme a faire one! O that you had breath,
      p. 269 UNDERWOOD 83     9 Stiffe! starke! my joynts 'gainst one another
                                knock!
      p. 271 UNDERWOOD 83    92 With what injustice should one soule pretend
      p. 277 U'WOOD 84.4      4 And give you reasons more then one.
      p. 282 U'WOOD 84.8     20 Hang all your roomes, with one large Pedigree:
      p. 283 U'WOOD 84.9     27 Thou hast no more blowes, Fate, to drive at one:
      p. 284 U'WOOD 84.9     52 One corporall, only; th'other spirituall,
      p. 285 U'WOOD 84.9    114 Shall meet with gladnesse in one Theatre;
      p. 285 U'WOOD 84.9    115 And each shall know, there, one anothers face,
      p. 287 U'WOOD 84.9    169 To one she said, Doe this, he did it; So
      p. 287 U'WOOD 84.9    173 She was, in one, a many parts of life;
      p. 287 U'WOOD 84.9    178 As her whole life was now become one note
      p. 305 HORACE 2        10 As neither head, nor foot, one forme retaine.
      p. 307 HORACE 2        32 Be simple quite throughout, and wholly one.
      p. 307 HORACE 2        41 One thing prodigiously, paints in the woods
      p. 307 HORACE 2        51 To be that Smith; then live, mark'd one of
                                those,
      p. 315 HORACE 2       230 Loves Dogges, and Horses; and is ever one
      p. 315 HORACE 2       237 These studies alter now, in one, growne man;
      p. 329 HORACE 2       532 Is laugh'd at, that still jarreth on one string:
      p. 333 HORACE 2       585 So doth the one, the others helpe require,
      p. 333 HORACE 2       586 And friendly should unto one end conspire.
      p. 333 HORACE 2       609 You doe not bring, to judge your Verses, one,
      p. 335 HORACE 2       655 For, if one should, and with a rope make haste
      p. 355 HORACE 1       670 Here's one makes ...... but there's .... .....
                                  ...
      p. 361 UNGATHERED 1     7 not one but thriues; in spite of stormes &
                                thunder,
      p. 362 UNGATHERED 2     9 For, as one comming with a laterall viewe,
      p. 366 UNGATHERED 6     3 Behold, where one doth swim;
      p. 367 UNGATHERED 6    35 Nor let one Riuer boast
      p. 371 UNGATHERED 9     3 It couers, first, a Virgin; and then, one
      p. 380 UNGATHERED 12   41 I meane that one paire, wherewith he so hobled
      p. 380 UNGATHERED 12   48 Iest, he saies. Item one sute of blacke taffata
      p. 385 UNGATHERED 19    4 What can one witnesse, and a weake one, add
      p. 386 UNGATHERED 20   10 Was worthy of a Good one; And this, here,
      p. 389 UNGATHERED 24    3 To say but one, were single. Then it chimes,
      p. 389 UNGATHERED 24    6 But in one tongue, was form'd with the worlds
                                wit:
      p. 389 UNGATHERED 24   13 And this hath met that one, that may be stil'd
      p. 391 UNGATHERED 26   41 Triumph, my Britaine, thou hast one to showe,
      p. 393 UNGATHERED 27   16 Doth shew the Holy one.
      p. 394 UNGATHERED 28   16 But of one Husband; and since he left life,
      p. 397 UNGATHERED 30   36 Like him, to make the ayre, one volary:
      p. 397 UNGATHERED 30   48 Vnder one title. Thou hast made thy way
      p. 406 UNGATHERED 34   99 Of all ye Worthyes hope t'outlast thy one,
      p. 413 UNGATHERED 41   35 Of Persons, yet in Vnion (ONE) divine.
```

onely   frequency: 35   relative frequency: 0.00050
```
  **p. 113 PANEGYRE       7 His former rayes did onely cleare the skie;
```

onely (cont.)

p.	31	EPIGRAMS 12	20	His onely answere is to all, god payes.
p.	48	EPIGRAMS 66	4	In onely thee, might be both great, and glad.
p.	49	EPIGRAMS 67	4	As, to be rais'd by her, is onely fame.
p.	52	EPIGRAMS 76	13	Onely a learned, and a manly soule
p.	57	EPIGRAMS 89	12	As others speake, but onely thou dost act.
p.	58	EPIGRAMS 91	1	Which of thy names I take, not onely beares
p.	59	EPIGRAMS 92	38	On them: And therefore doe not onely shunne
p.	61	EPIGRAMS 95	12	Onely to boast thy merit in supply.
p.	63	EPIGRAMS 97	20	Onely his clothes haue ouer-leauen'd him.
p.	71	EPIGRAMS 110	21	T<o>'all future time, not onely doth restore
p.	74	EPIGRAMS 114	7	He hath not onely gain'd himselfe his eyes,
p.	78	EPIGRAMS 121	6	If onely loue should make the action pris'd:
p.	100	FOREST 4	15	That onely fooles make thee a saint,
p.	105	FOREST 8	14	Sicknesse; onely on vs men.
p.	106	FOREST 9	1	Drinke to me, onely, with thine eyes,
p.	106	FOREST 9	13	But thou thereon did'st onely breath,
p.	111	FOREST 11	77	Such spirits as are onely continent,
p.	112	FOREST 11	104	How onely shee bestowes
p.	113	FOREST 12	7	Well, or ill, onely, all the following yeere,
p.	115	FOREST 12	63	But onely Poets, rapt with rage diuine?
p.	118	FOREST 13	51	'Tis onely that can time, and chance defeat:
p.	119	FOREST 13	86	That doe sinne onely for the infamie:
p.	119	FOREST 13	108	Onely, thus much, out of a rauish'd zeale,
p.	261	UNDERWOOD 77	12	As farre as sense, and onely by the eyes.
p.	294	UNDERWOOD 88	4	Like lustfull beasts, that onely know to doe it:
p.	366	UNGATHERED 6	15	This Swanne is onely his,
p.	380	UNGATHERED 12	56	I writ he onely his taile there did waue;
p.	383	UNGATHERED 17	9	Who cannot reade, but onely doth desire
p.	385	UNGATHERED 20	1	It fits not onely him that makes a Booke,
p.	388	UNGATHERED 23	9	To the Greeke coast thine onely knew the way.
p.	389	UNGATHERED 24	24	That would haue done, that, which you onely can.
p.	398	UNGATHERED 30	91	Onely my losse is, that I am not there:
p.	412	UNGATHERED 41	11	As it, alone, (and onely it) had roome,
p.	414	UNGATHERED 41	48	By bringing forth GOD's onely Son, no other.

onely-gotten   frequency: 1   relative frequency: 0.00001
| p. | 288 | U'WOOD 84.9 | 212 | Jesus, the onely-gotten Christ! who can |

ones   frequency: 8   relative frequency: 0.00011
p.	49	EPIGRAMS 68	3	Two kindes of valour he doth shew, at ones;
p.	64	EPIGRAMS 99	11	Well, though thy name lesse then our great ones
				bee,
p.	78	EPIGRAMS 121	1	RVDYERD, as lesser dames, to great ones
				vse,
p.	200	UNDERWOOD 42	22	Wish, you had fowle ones, and deformed got;
p.	315	HORACE 2	220	If such a ones applause thou dost require,
p.	335	HORACE 2	634	On artlesse Verse; the hard ones he will blame;
p.	394	UNGATHERED 28	11	Nay they will venter ones Descent to hitt,
p.	402	UNGATHERED 34	15	By all your Titles, & whole style at ones

one's   frequency: 1   relative frequency: 0.00001
See also "ones."
| p. | 265 | UNDERWOOD 79 | 44 | Chorus Our great, our good. Where one's so |
| | | | | drest |

onions   frequency: 1   relative frequency: 0.00001
| p. | 59 | EPIGRAMS 92 | 28 | With iuyce of limons, onions, pisse, to write, |

only   frequency: 35   relative frequency: 0.00050
See also "onely," "onely-gotten."
**p.	114	PANEGYRE	40	And only with red silence him salute.
p.	36	EPIGRAMS 28	21	SVRLY, vse other arts, these only can
p.	50	EPIGRAMS 72	6	Thy person only, COVRTLING, is the vice.
p.	83	EPIGRAMS 132	6	Since they can only iudge, that can conferre.
p.	84	EPIGRAMS 133	9	The filth, stench, noyse: saue only what was
				there
p.	108	FOREST 10 A	10	only pursewinge Constancy, in Chainge;
p.	150	UNDERWOOD 10	10	Thou sai'st, thou only cam'st to prove
p.	153	UNDERWOOD 13	7	You then, whose will not only, but desire
p.	155	UNDERWOOD 13	88	Carryed and wrapt, I only am alow'd
p.	161	UNDERWOOD 14	73	It true respects. He will not only love,
p.	163	UNDERWOOD 15	41	That kept man living! Pleasures only sought!
p.	175	UNDERWOOD 23	24	And only pitious scorne, upon their folly waites.
p.	177	UNDERWOOD 25	32	Where only a mans birth is his offence,
p.	185	UNDERWOOD 30	9	The only faithfull Watchman for the Realme,
p.	191	UNDERWOOD 38	18	In will and power, only to defeat.
p.	210	UNDERWOOD 43	168	Which thou hast only vented, not enjoy'd.
p.	218	UNDERWOOD 47	11	Subject to quarrell only; or else such
p.	224	UNDERWOOD 50	5	Not only shunning by your act, to doe

only (cont.)

p. 224 UNDERWOOD 50	23	Only your time you better entertaine,
p. 230 UNDERWOOD 55	6	I only can the Paper staine;
p. 234 UNDERWOOD 60	17	And only, his great Soule envy'd,
p. 234 UNDERWOOD 61	6	But whisper'd Counsells, and those only thrive;
p. 250 UNDERWOOD 73	6	Who seldome sleepes! whom bad men only hate!
p. 253 UNDERWOOD 75	32	Through which not only we, but all our Species are.
p. 265 UNDERWOOD 79	43	PAN only our great Shep'ard is,
p. 265 UNDERWOOD 79	65	This only the great Shep'ard is.
p. 284 U'WOOD 84.9	52	One corporall, only; th'other spirituall,
p. 305 HORACE 2	25	Know'st only well to paint a Cipresse tree.
p. 325 HORACE 2	425	For so, they shall not only gaine the worth,
p. 327 HORACE 2	461	The Muse not only gave the Greek's a wit,
p. 362 UNGATHERED 2	4	In these pide times, only to shewe their braines,
p. 384 UNGATHERED 18	2	And clothes, and guifts, that only do thee grace
p. 384 UNGATHERED 18	9	Not only this, but euery day of thine,
p. 387 UNGATHERED 22	2	these only hide part of my flesh, and bones:
p. 422 UNGATHERED 50	5	and the immortall gods; loue only those

on't   frequency: 3   relative frequency: 0.00004

ope   frequency: 2   relative frequency: 0.00002

p. 201 UNDERWOOD 42	51	Then ope thy wardrobe, thinke me that poore Groome
p. 294 UNDERWOOD 87	20	And to left-Lydia, now the gate stood ope.

ope'   frequency: 2   relative frequency: 0.00002

p. 59 EPIGRAMS 92	27	To ope' the character. They'haue found the sleight
p. 274 U'WOOD 84.1	39	Of that eternall Port kept ope'

open   frequency: 9   relative frequency: 0.00013
See also "i'th'open," "ope," "ope'."

p. 87 EPIGRAMS 133	135	But open, and vn-arm'd encounter'd all:
p. 94 FOREST 2	27	To crowne thy open table, doth prouide
p. 98 FOREST 3	49	And fills thy open hall with mirth, and cheere,
p. 198 UNDERWOOD 40	25	No, Mistris, no, the open merrie Man
p. 232 UNDERWOOD 58	2	All mouthes are open, and all stomacks free:
p. 315 HORACE 2	231	I'the open field; is Waxe like to be wrought
p. 317 HORACE 2	284	Peace, and the open ports, that peace doth cause.
p. 354 HORACE 1	633	. good ... . open .....
p. 421 UNGATHERED 48	40	Thou mad'st in open ffeild

opens   frequency: 2   relative frequency: 0.00002

p. 256 UNDERWOOD 75	121	See, now the Chappell opens; where the King
p. 263 UNDERWOOD 79	9	Rector Chori. To day old Janus opens the new yeare,

opinion   frequency: 1   relative frequency: 0.00001
See also "th'opinion."

p. 218 UNDERWOOD 47	4	And though Opinion stampe them not, are gold.

opinions   frequency: 1   relative frequency: 0.00001

p. 160 UNDERWOOD 14	40	Antiquities search'd! Opinions dis-esteem'd!

oppose   frequency: 1   relative frequency: 0.00001

p. 186 UNDERWOOD 32	8	Both arm'd with wealth, and slander to oppose,

oppressed. See "opprest."

oppressor. See "th'oppressor."

opprest   frequency: 1   relative frequency: 0.00001

p. 153 UNDERWOOD 13	28	That they have more opprest me, then my want?

or   frequency: 739   relative frequency: 0.01069

oracle   frequency: 2   relative frequency: 0.00002

p. 657 L. CONVIVALES	2	To the Oracle of Apollo.
p. 657 L. CONVIVALES	20	To the Oracle of Apollo.

oracles   frequency: 1   relative frequency: 0.00001

p. 329 HORACE 2	496	The Oracles, too, were given out in Verse;

orb. See "orbe."

orbe   frequency: 3   relative frequency: 0.00004

p. 365 UNGATHERED 5	12	Closde in an orbe of Christall.
p. 396 UNGATHERED 30	19	And fill'd an Orbe as circular, as heauen!

orbe (cont.)
p. 396 UNGATHERED 30   20 The Orbe was cut forth into Regions seauen.

orcades   frequency: 1   relative frequency: 0.00001
p. 368 UNGATHERED 6   67 The scatter'd Orcades;

orchard   frequency: 1   relative frequency: 0.00001
p. 94 FOREST 2   39 Then hath thy orchard fruit, thy garden flowers,

ordain'd   frequency: 1   relative frequency: 0.00001
p. 272 U'WOOD 84.1   1 Faire FAME, who art ordain'd to crowne

order   frequency: 10   relative frequency: 0.00014
p. 82 EPIGRAMS 130   13 Mou'd by her order, and the ninth more high,
p. 151 UNDERWOOD 12   14 All order, and Disposure, still.
p. 192 UNDERWOOD 38   61 Her order is to cherish, and preserve,
p. 211 UNDERWOOD 43   176 No order? no Decree? Though we be gone
p. 251 UNDERWOOD 74   12 Because the order of the whole is faire!
p. 271 UNDERWOOD 83   72 To every Order, ev'ry Hierarchie!
p. 307 HORACE 2   58 Nor language, nor cleere order ere forsakes.
p. 307 HORACE 2   59 The vertue of which order, and true grace,
p. 321 HORACE 2   353 Of Order, and Connexion; so much grace
p. 415 UNGATHERED 42   25 For order, and for governing the pixe,

order'd   frequency: 1   relative frequency: 0.00001
*p. 493 TO HIMSELF   28 As the best order'd meale.

ordering. See "ord'ring."

orders   frequency: 1   relative frequency: 0.00001
p. 62 EPIGRAMS 95   32 The councells, actions, orders, and euents

ordinaries   frequency: 1   relative frequency: 0.00001
p. 30 EPIGRAMS 12   11 He steales to ordinaries; there he playes

ordnance. See "ord'nance."

ord'nance   frequency: 2   relative frequency: 0.00002
p. 213 UNDERWOOD 44   3 And Ord'nance too: so much as from the Tower
p. 249 UNDERWOOD 72   9 What Drums or Trumpets, or great Ord'nance
                           can,

ord'ring   frequency: 1   relative frequency: 0.00001
p. 273 U'WOOD 84.1   32 Of ord'ring all.

ore   frequency: 4   relative frequency: 0.00005
p. 73 EPIGRAMS 112   21 Pr'y thee, yet saue thy rest; giue ore in time:
p. 89 EPIGRAMS 133   177 Of Hol'borne (<the> three sergeants heads)
                           lookes ore,
p. 388 UNGATHERED 23   2 Olde Hesiods Ore, and giue it vs; but thine,
p. 400 UNGATHERED 31   29 And howrely brooding ore the same,

o're   frequency: 8   relative frequency: 0.00011
*p. 494 TO HIMSELF   53 His iust awe o're men;
p. 30 EPIGRAMS 12   10 Lookes o're the bill, likes it: and say's, god
                           payes.
p. 99 FOREST 3   83 And brooding o're it sit, with broadest eyes,
p. 145 UNDERWOOD 5   3 To make us still sing o're, and o're,
p. 234 UNDERWOOD 60   16 That spread his body o're, to kill:
p. 325 HORACE 2   418 Not, ten times o're, corrected to the naile.
p. 421 UNGATHERED 49   7 O're read, examin'd, try'd, and prou'd yor: Ryme

ore-blowne   frequency: 1   relative frequency: 0.00001
p. 62 EPIGRAMS 97   5 His rosie tyes and garters so ore-blowne,

ore-flow   frequency: 1   relative frequency: 0.00001
p. 117 FOREST 13   40 T<o>'aduance his doubtfull issue, and ore-flow

ore-flowne   frequency: 1   relative frequency: 0.00001
p. 368 UNGATHERED 6   65 Who (see) already hath ore-flowne

ore-fold   frequency: 1   relative frequency: 0.00001
p. 338 HORACE 1   2 . horse neck joyn . sundry plumes ore-fold

o're-joy'd   frequency: 1   relative frequency: 0.00001
p. 201 UNDERWOOD 42   59 Thou didst tell me; and wert o're-joy'd to peepe

o're-praise   frequency: 1   relative frequency: 0.00001
p. 142 UNDERWOOD 2.9   47 Nor o're-praise, nor yet condemne;

ore-shine   frequency: 1   relative frequency: 0.00001
     p. 305 HORACE 2   18 Ye have oft-times, that may ore-shine the rest,

ore-swelleth   frequency: 1   relative frequency: 0.00001
     p. 329 HORACE 2   506 But flowes out, that ore-swelleth in full brests.

orestes   frequency: 1   relative frequency: 0.00001
     p. 313 HORACE 2   177 Poore Jo wandring; wild Orestes mad:

o'rewhelm'd   frequency: 1   relative frequency: 0.00001
     p. 162 UNDERWOOD 15   4 Their vitious ease, and be o'rewhelm'd with it.

organes   frequency: 1   relative frequency: 0.00001
     p. 99 FOREST 3   86 By being organes to great sinne,

organs. See "organes."

orgies   frequency: 1   relative frequency: 0.00001
     p. 246 UNDERWOOD 70 104 Orgies of drinke, or fain'd protests:

orient   frequency: 1   relative frequency: 0.00001
     p. 62 EPIGRAMS 97   4 His cloke with orient veluet quite lin'd through,

original. See "originall."

originall   frequency: 4   relative frequency: 0.00005
     p. 83 EPIGRAMS 132   13 Thine the originall; and France shall boast,
     p. 202 UNDERWOOD 42   80 And all the originall riots of the place:
     p. 268 UNDERWOOD 82   9 As hath thy JAMES; cleans'd from originall
                              drosse,
     p. 270 UNDERWOOD 83   64 Her spirit home, to her originall!

ornament   frequency: 2   relative frequency: 0.00002
   **p. 114 PANEGYRE   50 The amorous Citie spar'd no ornament,
     p. 253 UNDERWOOD 75   40 In gracefull Ornament of Garland, Gemmes, and
                              Haire.

ornaments   frequency: 3   relative frequency: 0.00004
     p. 35 EPIGRAMS 27   2 Take better ornaments, my teares, and verse.
     p. 115 FOREST 12   85 Aboue your vnder-carued ornaments,
     p. 335 HORACE 2   636 Cut off superfluous ornaments; and when

orniths   frequency: 1   relative frequency: 0.00001
     p. 293 UNDERWOOD 87   14 With gentle Calais, Thurine Orniths Sonne;

orphanes   frequency: 1   relative frequency: 0.00001
     p. 99 FOREST 3   79 To blow vp orphanes, widdowes, and their states;

orphans   frequency: 1   relative frequency: 0.00001
     See also "orphanes."
     p. 185 UNDERWOOD 30   7 The Orphans Pillar, the true Subjects shield,

orpheus   frequency: 3   relative frequency: 0.00004
     See also "orphevs."
     p. 327 HORACE 2   479 Orpheus, a priest, and speaker for the Gods,
     p. 397 UNGATHERED 30 35 I thought thee then our Orpheus, that wouldst
                              try
     p. 397 UNGATHERED 30 37 And I had stil'd thee, Orpheus, but before

orphevs   frequency: 2   relative frequency: 0.00002
     p. 84 EPIGRAMS 133   3 ORPHEVS, VLYSSES: or the Latine
                              Muse,
     p. 115 FOREST 12   77 Will proue old ORPHEVS act no tale to be:

orts   frequency: 1   relative frequency: 0.00001
    *p. 493 TO HIMSELF   33 Can feed on orts: And safe in your
                              stage-clothes,

o'th'   frequency: 1   relative frequency: 0.00001

o'th'doctors   frequency: 1   relative frequency: 0.00001
     p. 117 FOREST 13   33 Not taken vp o'th'doctors, but as well

o'the   frequency: 4   relative frequency: 0.00005

other   frequency: 66   relative frequency: 0.00095
     See also "other>," "th'other," "tother,"
             "t'other."
     p. 34 EPIGRAMS 23   2 Who, to thy one, all other braines refuse;
     p. 36 EPIGRAMS 28   21 SVRLY, vse other arts, these only can

other (cont.)
p.	41 EPIGRAMS 45	8 And, if no other miserie, yet age?
p.	43 EPIGRAMS 52	5 This but thy iudgement fooles: the other way
p.	46 EPIGRAMS 61	2 One doth not stroke me, nor the other strike.
p.	48 EPIGRAMS 66	3 Whose house, if it no other honor had,
p.	51 EPIGRAMS 73	14 In solemne cypres, the other cob-web-lawne.
p.	54 EPIGRAMS 80	5 This world deaths region is, the other lifes:
p.	58 EPIGRAMS 91	13 I speake thy other graces, not lesse showne,
p.	63 EPIGRAMS 98	4 Need seeke no other strength, no other height;
p.	78 EPIGRAMS 122	9 I need no other arts, but studie thee:
p.	81 EPIGRAMS 128	11 We each to other may this voyce enspire;
p.	81 EPIGRAMS 129	1 That, not a paire of friends each other see,
p.	84 EPIGRAMS 133	25 The other was a squire, of faire degree;
p.	86 EPIGRAMS 133	69 Gorgonian scolds, and Harpyes: on the other
p.	86 EPIGRAMS 133	83 The other thought it HYDRA, or the rock
p.	87 EPIGRAMS 133	129 One said, the other swore, the world consists.
p.	96 FOREST 2	100 With other edifices, when they see
p.	98 FOREST 3	63 Such, and no other was that age, of old,
p.	114 FOREST 12	43 The soules, shee loues. Those other glorious notes,
p.	115 FOREST 12	65 You, and that other starre, that purest light,
p.	119 FOREST 13	111 Other great wiues may blush at: when they see
p.	120 FOREST 13	120 Each into other, and had now made one.
p.	122 FOREST 15	8 To ought but grace, or ayme at other end.
p.	136 UNDERWOOD 2.5	11 This, here sung, can be no other
p.	138 UNDERWOOD 2.6	20 To no other Grace but you!
p.	162 UNDERWOOD 15	9 All other Acts of Worldlings, are but toyle
p.	164 UNDERWOOD 15	73 And jealous each of other, yet thinke long
p.	171 UNDERWOOD 19	17 Unto the other; and live patternes, how
p.	171 UNDERWOOD 20	3 Amongst my many other, that I may
p.	184 UNDERWOOD 29	48 Other ceasure.
p.	188 UNDERWOOD 34	8 Was drawne to practise other hue, then that
p.	198 UNDERWOOD 40	34 Out with the other, for hee's still at home;
p.	198 UNDERWOOD 40	46 The sinne of Boast, or other countermine
p.	201 UNDERWOOD 42	67 And straight-way spent a Sonnet; with that other
p.	202 UNDERWOOD 42	73 Or in Moore-fields, this other night! sings one,
p.	215 UNDERWOOD 44	97 This other for his eye-browes; hence, away,
p.	219 UNDERWOOD 47	29 I studie other friendships, and more one,
p.	221 UNDERWOOD 48	35 And not a Song be other
p.	223 UNDERWOOD 49	39 For Sermoneeres: of which now one, now other,
p.	230 UNDERWOOD 56	20 And can for other Graces her commend,
p.	232 UNDERWOOD 58	6 Thanke him: if other, hee can give no Bayes.
p.	235 UNDERWOOD 62	10 One Poet, then of other folke ten score.
p.	241 UNDERWOOD 69	4 What, by that name, wee each to other owe,
p.	247 UNDERWOOD 70	110 Till either grew a portion of the other:
p.	249 UNDERWOOD 72	8 Like Eccho playing from the other shore.
p.	257 UNDERWOOD 75	144 One to the other, long e're these to light were brought.
p.	257 UNDERWOOD 75	154 Like Swine, or other Cattell here on earth:
p.	262 UNDERWOOD 78	12 As other soules, to his, dwell in a Lane:
p.	265 UNDERWOOD 79	42 1. Wee know no other power then his,
p.	265 UNDERWOOD 79	64 PAN knowes no other power then his,
p.	284 U'WOOD 84.9	55 Those other two; which must be judg'd, or crown'd:
p.	284 U'WOOD 84.9	67 All other gladnesse, with the thought is barr'd;
p.	288 U'WOOD 84.9	193 Or doing other deeds of Charitie,
p.	317 HORACE 2	278 Betweene the Acts, a quite cleane other thing
p.	339 HORACE 1	40 Downe close .. shore, this other creeping steales,
p.	361 UNGATHERED 1	11 Whilst other soules conuert to base abuse
p.	361 UNGATHERED 1	20 till th'one hath drownd the other in our sightes,
p.	364 UNGATHERED 5	2 For other formes come short all
p.	366 UNGATHERED 6	5 Besides the other Swannes admiring him,
p.	379 UNGATHERED 12	12 Since he treads in no other Mans steps but his owne.
p.	392 UNGATHERED 26	50 As, since, she will vouchsafe no other Wit.
p.	393 UNGATHERED 27	2 And needs no other touch.
p.	394 UNGATHERED 28	17 But Sorrow, she desir'd no other ffriend:
p.	414 UNGATHERED 41	48 By bringing forth GOD's onely Son, no other.

other>   frequency: 1   relative frequency: 0.00001
| p. | 420 UNGATHERED 48 | 27 And in this Age, canst hope no <other> grace. |

others   frequency: 28   relative frequency: 0.00040
**p.	114 PANEGYRE	37 Others would faine haue shew'ne it in their words:
**p.	114 PANEGYRE	43 Others on ground runne gazing by his side,
**p.	115 PANEGYRE	71 The others flame, as doth the wike and waxe,
p.	32 EPIGRAMS 17	1 May others feare, flie, and traduce thy name,
p.	39 EPIGRAMS 39	1 For all night-sinnes, with others wiues, vnknowne,

others (cont.)

p.	57 EPIGRAMS 89	12 As others speake, but onely thou dost act.
p.	59 EPIGRAMS 92	39 Others more modest, but contemne vs too,
p.	70 EPIGRAMS 109	18 Whil'st others toyle for titles to their tombes.
p.	73 EPIGRAMS 113	4 Where, what makes others great, doth keepe thee good!
p.	78 EPIGRAMS 123	1 Writing thy selfe, or iudging others writ,
p.	81 EPIGRAMS 129	8 The very call, to make all others come:
p.	98 FOREST 3	67 Let others watch in guiltie armes, and stand
p.	116 FOREST 13	6 For others ill, ought none their good forget.
p.	117 FOREST 13	20 Or feare to draw true lines, 'cause others paint:
p.	139 UNDERWOOD 2.7	16 Each suck <the> others breath.
p.	150 UNDERWOOD 10	6 That others should not warme them at my fire,
p.	153 UNDERWOOD 13	10 The way to meet, what others would upbraid;
p.	160 UNDERWOOD 14	66 Of others honours, thus, enjoy thine owne.
p.	171 UNDERWOOD 19	18 Others, in time may love, as we doe now.
p.	182 UNDERWOOD 28	7 But charme the Senses, others over-come
p.	194 UNDERWOOD 38	119 Others by common Stars their courses run,
p.	198 UNDERWOOD 40	39 To others, as he will deserve the Trust
p.	209 UNDERWOOD 43	145 But, others fell with that conceipt by the eares,
p.	217 UNDERWOOD 46	6 In others evill best was understood:
p.	222 UNDERWOOD 49	16 To Church, as others doe to Feasts and Playes,
p.	256 UNDERWOOD 75	125 One in the others hand,
p.	283 U'WOOD 84.9	31 Am turned with an others powers. My Passion
p.	333 HORACE 2	585 So doth the one, the others helpe require,

otherwise   frequency: 1   relative frequency: 0.00001
p. 159 UNDERWOOD 14   17 But I on yours farre otherwise shall doe,

othes   frequency: 1   relative frequency: 0.00001
p.   76 EPIGRAMS 119   2 At hunting railes, hauing no guift in othes,

ouer   frequency: 7   relative frequency: 0.00010

p.	76 EPIGRAMS 118	2 So all his meate he tasteth ouer, twise:
p.	86 EPIGRAMS 133	93 Ouer your heads: Well, row. At this a loud
p.	367 UNGATHERED 6	42 Ouer Ierna maine,
p.	368 UNGATHERED 6	71 And ouer Grampius mountaine,
p.	368 UNGATHERED 6	75 But ouer Land to Trent:
p.	397 UNGATHERED 30	34 Pearch'd ouer head, the wise Athenian Owle:
p.	398 UNGATHERED 30	77 I feele it by mine owne, that ouer flow,

ouer-blow   frequency: 1   relative frequency: 0.00001
p. 110 FOREST 11   36 Which thus we ouer-blow.

ouer-come   frequency: 1   relative frequency: 0.00001
p.   31 EPIGRAMS 14   12 Which conquers all, be once ouer-come by thee.

ouer-leauen'd   frequency: 1   relative frequency: 0.00001
p.   63 EPIGRAMS 97   20 Onely his clothes haue ouer-leauen'd him.

ouerbearing   frequency: 1   relative frequency: 0.00001
p. 402 UNGATHERED 34   7 Controll Ctesibius: ouerbearing vs

ouerdooe   frequency: 1   relative frequency: 0.00001
p. 405 UNGATHERED 34   79 How would he firke? lyke Adam ouerdooe

ought   frequency: 11   relative frequency: 0.00015

**p.	117 PANEGYRE	157 Nor to her blisse, could ought now added bee,
p.	65 EPIGRAMS 101	25 To this, if ought appeare, which I not know of,
p.	83 EPIGRAMS 131	6 We ought not giue them taste, we had an eare.
p.	116 FOREST 13	6 For others ill, ought none their good forget.
p.	119 FOREST 13	101 By me, their priest (if they can ought diuine)
p.	122 FOREST 15	8 To ought but grace, or ayme at other end.
p.	157 UNDERWOOD 13	132 Profit in ought; each day some little adde,
p.	224 UNDERWOOD 50	6 Ought that is ill, but the suspition too,
p.	331 HORACE 2	562 To bettring of the mind of man, in ought,
p.	333 HORACE 2	623 If to Quintilius, you recited ought:
p.	338 HORACE 1	12 .. .. ought ....

ounce   frequency: 2   relative frequency: 0.00002
p. 327 HORACE 2   467 There's Albin's sonne will say, Substract an ounce
p. 327 HORACE 2   471 An ounce, what makes it then? The halfe pound just;

ounces   frequency: 3   relative frequency: 0.00004
p. 327 HORACE 2   468 From the five ounces; what remaines? pronounce
p. 327 HORACE 2   469 A third of twelve, you may: foure ounces. Glad,
p. 327 HORACE 2   472 Sixe ounces. O, when once the canker'd rust,

our   frequency: 196   relative frequency: 0.00283
See also "or," "ovr," "t<o>'our."

ours   frequency: 11   relative frequency: 0.00015

ouse. See "owse."

out   frequency: 118   relative frequency: 0.00170
        See also words beginning "out=" and "out-,"
               "t<o>'out-strip."

out=liu'd   frequency: 1   relative frequency: 0.00001
        p. 387 UNGATHERED 22   5 Let such as iustly haue out=liu'd all prayse,

out-bee   frequency: 1   relative frequency: 0.00001
        p. 384 UNGATHERED 18   12 Out-bee yt Wife, in worth, thy freind did make:

out-boast   frequency: 1   relative frequency: 0.00001
        p. 81 EPIGRAMS 129   12 Out-dance the Babion, or out-boast the Braue;

out-brave   frequency: 1   relative frequency: 0.00001
        p. 132 UNDERWOOD 2.2   3 And her dressing did out-brave

out-cryes   frequency: 1   relative frequency: 0.00001
        p. 88 EPIGRAMS 133   172 And out-cryes of the damned in the Fleet?

out-dance   frequency: 1   relative frequency: 0.00001
        p. 81 EPIGRAMS 129   12 Out-dance the Babion, or out-boast the Braue;

out-did   frequency: 1   relative frequency: 0.00001
        p. 233 UNDERWOOD 59   12 As they out-did the lightning in the<ir> course;

out-doo   frequency: 1   relative frequency: 0.00001
        p. 390 UNGATHERED 25   4 With Nature, to out-doo the life:

out-flourisht   frequency: 1   relative frequency: 0.00001
        p. 132 UNDERWOOD 2.2   2 When her looke out-flourisht May:

out-formes   frequency: 1   relative frequency: 0.00001
        p. 73 EPIGRAMS 114   4 In meere out-formes, vntill he lost his sight,

out-goe   frequency: 2   relative frequency: 0.00002
        p. 260 UNDERWOOD 77   8 Have left in fame to equall, or out-goe
        p. 333 HORACE 2   616 The Scoffer, the true Praiser doth out-goe.

out-last   frequency: 1   relative frequency: 0.00001
        See also "t'outlast."
        p. 46 EPIGRAMS 60   6 And proud, my worke shall out-last common deeds,

out-lasts   frequency: 1   relative frequency: 0.00001
        p. 230 UNDERWOOD 55   8 But Scarlet-like out-lasts the Cloth.

out-liue   frequency: 2   relative frequency: 0.00002
        p. 32 EPIGRAMS 17   6 Shall out-liue gyrlands, stolne from the chast
                                  tree.
        p. 35 EPIGRAMS 27   4 If any Muse out-liue their spight, his can;

out-liv'd   frequency: 1   relative frequency: 0.00001
        See also "out=liu'd."
        p. 243 UNDERWOOD 70   25 Here's one out-liv'd his Peeres,

out-live   frequency: 2   relative frequency: 0.00002
        See also "out-liue."
        p. 179 UNDERWOOD 25   45 Gold, that is perfect, will out-live the fire.
        p. 229 UNDERWOOD 55   4 Verse, that should thee, and me out-live.

out-right   frequency: 1   relative frequency: 0.00001
        p. 311 HORACE 2   133 Her voyce, and angry Chremes chafes out-right

out-shine   frequency: 2   relative frequency: 0.00002
        p. 338 HORACE 1   18 You .... out-shine ... .
        p. 391 UNGATHERED 26   29 And tell, how farre thou didst our Lily
                                  out-shine,

out-spun   frequency: 1   relative frequency: 0.00001
        p. 40 EPIGRAMS 42   12 Were quite out-spun. The like wish hath his
                                  wife.

out-started   frequency: 1   relative frequency: 0.00001
        p. 87 EPIGRAMS 133   126 White, black, blew, greene, and in more formes
                                  out-started,

out-strip. See "t<o>'out-strip."

out-stript   frequency: 1   relative frequency: 0.00001
  p. 57 EPIGRAMS 89   10 Out-stript, then they did all that went before:

out-valew   frequency: 1   relative frequency: 0.00001
  p. 142 UNDERWOOD 2.9 48 Nor out-valew, nor contemne;

out-weare   frequency: 1   relative frequency: 0.00001
  p. 97 FOREST 3   35 Thou dost with some delight the day out-weare,

out-zany   frequency: 1   relative frequency: 0.00001
  p. 81 EPIGRAMS 129   16 Thou dost out-zany COKELY, POD; nay,
                           GVE:

outward   frequency: 4   relative frequency: 0.00005
  p. 117 FOREST 13   36 And, in those outward formes, all fooles are
                           wise.
  p. 137 UNDERWOOD 2.5 51 Outward Grace weake love beguiles:
  p. 162 UNDERWOOD 15   20 In outward face, but inward, light as Furre,
  p. 171 UNDERWOOD 20   11 Of many Colours; outward, fresh from spots,

ovens   frequency: 1   relative frequency: 0.00001
  p. 205 UNDERWOOD 43   54 Condemn'd me to the Ovens with the pies;

over   frequency: 5   relative frequency: 0.00007
    See also "ore," "o're," "ouer," words beginning
             "ore-," "o're-," "ouer-."
  p. 140 UNDERWOOD 2.8 23 To say over every purle
  p. 214 UNDERWOOD 44   31 But give them over to the common eare
  p. 288 U'WOOD 84.9   203 Shee saw him rise, triumphing over Death
  p. 323 HORACE 2   398 In hand, and turne them over, day, and night.
  p. 331 HORACE 2   544 Doth please; this, ten times over, will delight.

over-come   frequency: 1   relative frequency: 0.00001
  p. 182 UNDERWOOD 28   7 But charme the Senses, others over-come

over-gone   frequency: 1   relative frequency: 0.00001
  p. 333 HORACE 2   610 With joy of what is given him, over-gone:

over-safe   frequency: 1   relative frequency: 0.00001
  p. 339 HORACE 1   41 Being over-safe, and fearing .. the flaw:

over-seer   frequency: 1   relative frequency: 0.00001
  p. 221 UNDERWOOD 48   14 Of cares, and over-seer

over-thick   frequency: 1   relative frequency: 0.00001
  p. 319 HORACE 2   292 So over-thick, but, where the people met,

over-wanton   frequency: 1   relative frequency: 0.00001
  p. 321 HORACE 2   358 Their youthfull tricks in over-wanton verse:

overbearing. See "ouerbearing."

overblow. See "ouer-blow."

overblown. See "ore-blowne."

overbvry   frequency: 2   relative frequency: 0.00002
  p. 73 EPIGRAMS 113   2 As but to speake thee, OVERBVRY, is
                           praise:
  p. 73 EPIGRAMS 113   t1 TO SIR THOMAS OVERBVRY.

overcame   frequency: 1   relative frequency: 0.00001
  p. 129 UNDERWOOD 1.2 25 Quite overcame,

overcome. See "ouer-come," "over-come."

overdo. See "ouerdooe."

overflow. See "ore-flow."

overflown. See "ore-flowne."

overfold. See "ore-fold."

overgone. See "over-gone."

overjoyed. See "o're-joy'd."

overpraise. See "o're-praise."

overseer. See "over-seer."

overshine. See "ore-shine."

overswelleth. See "ore-swelleth."

overthrow   frequency: 1   relative frequency: 0.00001
    p. 182 UNDERWOOD 28   11 His very eyes are yours to overthrow.

overwhelmed. See "o'rewhelm'd."

ovid   frequency: 1   relative frequency: 0.00001
    p. 181 UNDERWOOD 27   18 Her Ovid gave her, dimn'd the fame

ovr   frequency: 1   relative frequency: 0.00001

ow'd   frequency: 1   relative frequency: 0.00001
    p. 153 UNDERWOOD 13   5 For benefits are ow'd with the same mind

owe   frequency: 21   relative frequency: 0.00030
    p. 31 EPIGRAMS 14   1 CAMDEN, most reuerend head, to whom I owe
    p. 51 EPIGRAMS 73   5 In-primis, GRAND, you owe me for a iest,
    p. 59 EPIGRAMS 92   12 And what each prince doth for intelligence owe,
    p. 64 EPIGRAMS 99   6 If time to facts, as vnto men would owe?
    p. 75 EPIGRAMS 116   2 All gentrie, yet, owe part of their best flame!
    p. 150 UNDERWOOD 10   16 I ne're will owe my health to a disease.
    p. 153 UNDERWOOD 13   14 This Good from you, as freely will it owe;
    p. 153 UNDERWOOD 13   25 Can I owe thankes, for Curtesies receiv'd
    p. 158 UNDERWOOD 13 164 Find you to reckon nothing, me owe all.
    p. 182 UNDERWOOD 28   5 Nor is my Muse, or I asham'd to owe it
    p. 197 UNDERWOOD 40   12 I give, or owe my friends, into your Rites,
    p. 237 UNDERWOOD 64   22 How much to heaven for thee, great
                            CHARLES, they owe!
    p. 238 UNDERWOOD 66   12 To compare small with great, as still we owe
    p. 241 UNDERWOOD 69   4 What, by that name, wee each to other owe,
    p. 257 UNDERWOOD 75 148 Of Nuptiall Sweets, at such a season, owe,
    p. 261 UNDERWOOD 77   20 What worlds of blessings to good Kings they owe:
    p. 264 UNDERWOOD 79   15 2. To him we owe all profits of our grounds.
    p. 265 UNDERWOOD 79   49 To whom you owe all duties of your grounds;
    p. 309 HORACE 2   90 Our selves, and all that's ours, to death we owe:
    p. 311 HORACE 2   130 Perversly modest, had I rather owe
    p. 391 UNGATHERED 26 42 To whom all Scenes of Europe homage owe.

owers   frequency: 1   relative frequency: 0.00001
    p. 169 UNDERWOOD 17   1 They are not, Sir, worst Owers, that doe pay

owes   frequency: 3   relative frequency: 0.00004
    p. 31 EPIGRAMS 14   3 (How nothing's that?) to whom my countrey owes
    p. 66 EPIGRAMS 102   8 To which, yet, of the sides himselfe he owes.
    p. 325 HORACE 2   446 What to his Countrey, what his friends he owes,

owing   frequency: 1   relative frequency: 0.00001
    p. 80 EPIGRAMS 127   10 By her attempt, shall still be owing thee.

owl. See "owle."

owle   frequency: 1   relative frequency: 0.00001
    p. 397 UNGATHERED 30 34 Pearch'd ouer head, the wise Athenian Owle:

own. See "owne."

own'd   frequency: 1   relative frequency: 0.00001
    See also "ownde."
    p. 77 EPIGRAMS 120   8 Which own'd the creature.

ownde   frequency: 1   relative frequency: 0.00001
  **p. 116 PANEGYRE   112 He ownde their crownes, he would not so their
                            crimes.

owne   frequency: 89   relative frequency: 0.00128
   *p. 493 TO HIMSELF   43 Or thine owne Horace, or Anacreons Lyre;
  **p. 115 PANEGYRE   80 "To rule like Heauen; and haue no more, their
                            owne,
    p. 27 EPIGRAMS 2   13 He that departs with his owne honesty
    p. 34 EPIGRAMS 25   5 And now, her (hourely) her owne cucqueane makes,
    p. 35 EPIGRAMS 28   11 That's greater, yet: to crie his owne vp neate.
    p. 36 EPIGRAMS 30   2 Be thine, I taxe, yet doe not owne my rimes:
    p. 39 EPIGRAMS 39   2 COLT, now, doth daily penance in his owne.
    p. 41 EPIGRAMS 44   3 Ere blacks were bought for his owne funerall,
    p. 42 EPIGRAMS 49   6 In my chast booke: professe them in thine owne.
    p. 45 EPIGRAMS 56   8 He takes vp all, makes each mans wit his owne.
    p. 48 EPIGRAMS 64   14 As her owne conscience, still, the same reward.

owne (cont.)

p.	51	EPIGRAMS 73	17	Item, your owne, sew'd in your mistris smock.
p.	52	EPIGRAMS 76	16	Of destinie, and spin her owne free houres.
p.	60	EPIGRAMS 93	10	And thine owne goodnesse to encrease thy merit,
p.	60	EPIGRAMS 94	3	If workes (not th'authors) their owne grace should looke,
p.	60	EPIGRAMS 94	6	Crowne with their owne. Rare poemes aske rare friends
p.	61	EPIGRAMS 95	9	To thine owne proper I ascribe then more;
p.	63	EPIGRAMS 98	8	With thine owne course the iudgement of thy friend,
p.	70	EPIGRAMS 109	12	And first to know thine owne state, then the States.
p.	71	EPIGRAMS 110	6	To haue engrau'd these acts, with his owne stile,
p.	75	EPIGRAMS 115	30	From friendship, is it's owne fames architect.
p.	76	EPIGRAMS 119	13	And, in their errors maze, thine owne way know:
p.	80	EPIGRAMS 128	4	And those to turne to bloud, and make thine owne:
p.	81	EPIGRAMS 129	17	And thine owne CORIAT too. But (would'st thou see)
p.	82	EPIGRAMS 131	2	A worke of ours, we part with our owne right;
p.	82	EPIGRAMS 131	3	For, then, all mouthes will iudge, and their owne way:
p.	83	EPIGRAMS 131	8	They should be fooles, for me, at their owne charge.
p.	85	EPIGRAMS 133	31	In it' owne hall; when these (in worthy scorne
p.	94	FOREST 2	34	And pikes, now weary their owne kinde to eat,
p.	95	FOREST 2	62	Without his feare, and of thy lords owne meate:
p.	96	FOREST 2	91	His children thy great lord may call his owne:
p.	98	FOREST 3	65	And such since thou canst make thine owne content,
p.	108	FOREST 10	29	My owne true fire. Now my thought takes wing,
p.	117	FOREST 13	14	For their owne cap'tall crimes, t<o>'indite my wit:
p.	118	FOREST 13	82	When their owne Parasites laugh at their fall,
p.	140	UNDERWOOD 2.9	t1	Her man described by her owne Dictamen.
p.	145	UNDERWOOD 4	12	Mine owne enough betray me.
p.	145	UNDERWOOD 5	4	Our owne false praises, for your ends:
p.	147	UNDERWOOD 7	7	For that's a narrow joy is but our owne.
p.	156	UNDERWOOD 13	114	I have the lyst of mine owne faults to know,
p.	160	UNDERWOOD 14	66	Of others honours, thus, enjoy thine owne.
p.	162	UNDERWOOD 15	14	Till he become both their, and his owne curse!
p.	165	UNDERWOOD 15	88	Is lov'd, though he let out his owne for life:
p.	170	UNDERWOOD 18	19	Vaile their owne eyes, and would impartially
p.	174	UNDERWOOD 23	18	'Tis crowne enough to vertue still, her owne applause.
p.	176	UNDERWOOD 24	14	Assisted by no strengths, but are her owne,
p.	180	UNDERWOOD 26	16	True valour doth her owne renowne command
p.	188	UNDERWOOD 34	9	Her owne bloud gave her: Shee ne're had, nor hath
p.	191	UNDERWOOD 38	17	Spare your owne goodnesse yet; and be not great
p.	200	UNDERWOOD 42	36	Whether their faces were their owne, or no:
p.	203	UNDERWOOD 43	22	By thy owne vote, a sacrifice to thee?
p.	207	UNDERWOOD 43	97	To our owne Ladyes; and in storie there
p.	209	UNDERWOOD 43	150	No Foole would his owne harvest spoile, or burne!
p.	215	UNDERWOOD 44	75	We will beleeve, like men of our owne Ranke,
p.	216	UNDERWOOD 45	23	For that is first requir'd, A man be his owne.
p.	219	UNDERWOOD 47	56	Well, with mine owne fraile Pitcher, what to doe
p.	224	UNDERWOOD 50	12	From whence they fall, cast downe with their owne weight.
p.	225	UNDERWOOD 50	33	As they are hard, for them to make their owne,
p.	225	UNDERWOOD 51	18	For 't were a narrow gladnesse, kept thine owne.
p.	236	UNDERWOOD 64	2	Most pious King, but his owne good in you!
p.	236	UNDERWOOD 64	10	And what are bounds to her, you make your owne?
p.	249	UNDERWOOD 72	7	Adding her owne glad accents, to this Day,
p.	250	UNDERWOOD 73	12	T<o>'effect it, feele, thou'ast made thine owne heart ake.
p.	251	UNDERWOOD 74	27	When he beholds a graft of his owne hand,
p.	255	UNDERWOOD 75	96	To give a greater Name, and Title to! Their owne!
p.	271	UNDERWOOD 83	70	On Natures secrets, there, as her owne bookes:
p.	271	UNDERWOOD 83	83	If you can envie your owne Daughters blisse,
p.	276	U'WOOD 84.3	12	Worke with my fancie, his owne hand.
p.	279	U'WOOD 84.4	48	Up to her owne sublimed hight?
p.	281	U'WOOD 84.8	12	When your owne Vertues, equall'd have their Names,
p.	281	U'WOOD 84.8	17	Which all men doe, that urge not their owne deeds
p.	283	U'WOOD 84.9	26	I summe up mine owne breaking, and wish all.
p.	289	UNDERWOOD 85	3	With his owne Oxen tills his Sires left lands,
p.	290	UNDERWOOD 85	19	How plucking Peares, his owne hand grafted had,

owne (cont.)
```
     p. 313 HORACE 2      185 Of Homers, forth in acts, then of thine owne,
     p. 313 HORACE 2      187 Yet common matter thou thine owne maist make,
     p. 315 HORACE 2      234 For his owne good, a carelesse letter-goe
     p. 323 HORACE 2      408 And celebrating our owne home-borne facts;
     p. 327 HORACE 2      470 He cries, Good boy, thou'lt keepe thine owne.
                              Now, adde
     p. 378 UNGATHERED 11   83 Marry he sets it out at his owne charge;
     p. 379 UNGATHERED 12   12 Since he treads in no other Mans steps but his
                              owne.
     p. 386 UNGATHERED 21    7 It must be thine owne iudgment, yet, that sends
     p. 386 UNGATHERED 21   13 Hold thyne owne worth vnbroke: which is so good
     p. 398 UNGATHERED 30   77 I feele it by mine owne, that ouer flow,
     p. 399 UNGATHERED 31    5 To veiw the truth and owne it. Doe but looke
     p. 402 UNGATHERED 34   10 How much Architectonice is your owne!
     p. 412 UNGATHERED 40   18 by our owne discerning
     p. 415 UNGATHERED 42   12 Now, for mine owne part, and it is but due,
     p. 422 UNGATHERED 50    3 Is her owne scourge, when it sustaines their
                              states
```

owse   frequency: 1   relative frequency: 0.00001
```
     p. 368 UNGATHERED 6    74 Humber, or Owse, decline;
```

ox. See "oxe."

oxe   frequency: 1   relative frequency: 0.00001
```
     p.  86 EPIGRAMS 133    74 Spake to 'hem louder, then the oxe in LIVIE;
```

oxen   frequency: 2   relative frequency: 0.00002
```
     p. 289 UNDERWOOD 85     3 With his owne Oxen tills his Sires left lands,
     p. 291 UNDERWOOD 85    63 To view the weary Oxen draw, with bare
```

oyle   frequency: 5   relative frequency: 0.00007
```
     p. 188 UNDERWOOD 34    11 Or Turners oyle of Talck. Nor ever got
     p. 207 UNDERWOOD 43    99 Wherein was oyle, beside the succour spent,
     p. 280 U'WOOD 84.4     59 As smooth as Oyle pour'd forth, and calme
     p. 285 U'WOOD 84.9    101 Her fellowes, with the oyle of gladnesse, bright
     p. 294 UNDERWOOD 89     3 If thou be'st wise, with 'Syrian Oyle let shine
```

oyles   frequency: 1   relative frequency: 0.00001
```
     p. 118 FOREST 13       77 Let 'hem on poulders, oyles, and paintings,
                              spend,
```

oylie   frequency: 1   relative frequency: 0.00001
```
     p. 220 UNDERWOOD 47    68 Oylie Expansions, or shrunke durtie folds,
```

oysters   frequency: 1   relative frequency: 0.00001
```
     p. 291 UNDERWOOD 85    49 Not Lucrine Oysters I could then more prize,
```

p<avy>   frequency: 1   relative frequency: 0.00001
```
     p.  77 EPIGRAMS 120    t1 EPITAPH ON S<ALOMON> P<AVY> A
                              CHILD
```

p<l>ace   frequency: 1   relative frequency: 0.00001
```
     p. 155 UNDERWOOD 13    78 Many a pound, and piece, will p<l>ace one well:
```

paccuuius   frequency: 1   relative frequency: 0.00001
```
     p. 391 UNGATHERED 26   35 Paccuuius, Accius, him of Cordoua dead,
```

paced. See "pas'd," "sixe-pac'd," "swift-pac't."

paceth   frequency: 1   relative frequency: 0.00001
```
     p. 253 UNDERWOOD 75    41 See, how she paceth forth in Virgin-white,
```

pack   frequency: 1   relative frequency: 0.00001
```
     p. 404 UNGATHERED 34   51 Pack wth your pedling Poetry to the Stage,
```

pacuvius. See "paccuuius."

page   frequency: 4   relative frequency: 0.00005
```
     p.  57 EPIGRAMS 90      5 The nicer thing to tast her ladies page;
     p. 118 FOREST 13       74 On the close groome, and page, on new-yeeres day,
     p. 175 UNDERWOOD 23    33 Make not thy selfe a Page,
     p. 399 UNGATHERED 31    6 With pause vpon it; make this page your booke;
```

pageant   frequency: 2   relative frequency: 0.00002
```
     p. 202 UNDERWOOD 42    77 And vouches both the Pageant, and the Day,
     p. 208 UNDERWOOD 43   119 Squire of the Squibs, against the Pageant day,
```

paid   frequency: 5   relative frequency: 0.00007
    See also "payd."
    p.   31 EPIGRAMS 12   24 Lent him a pockie whore. Shee hath paid him.
    p.   97 FOREST 3   12 There wasted, some not paid for yet!
    p. 155 UNDERWOOD 13   85 And it is paid 'hem with a trembling zeale,
    p. 229 UNDERWOOD 54   2 For a just wager, and that wager paid
    p. 271 UNDERWOOD 83   80 T'have paid againe a blessing was but lent,

pain. See "paine," "payne."

paine   frequency: 11   relative frequency: 0.00015
    p.   46 EPIGRAMS 62   5 Is it the paine affrights? that's soone forgot.
    p.   51 EPIGRAMS 73   19 In most vile verses, and cost me more paine,
    p.   80 EPIGRAMS 126   6 I answer'd, DAPHNE now no paine can proue.
    p. 145 UNDERWOOD 5   8 If wee would search with care, and paine,
    p. 159 UNDERWOOD 14   37 T<o>'instruct and teach? or your unweary'd paine
    p. 192 UNDERWOOD 38   44 No man inflicts that paine, till hope be spent:
    p. 194 UNDERWOOD 38   103 There is not any punishment, or paine,
    p. 203 UNDERWOOD 43   13 That since thou tak'st all envious care and
                                    paine,
    p. 251 UNDERWOOD 74   5 Shee lies deliver'd, without paine,
    p. 291 UNDERWOOD 85   69 'Gainst th'Ides, his moneys he gets in with
                                    paine,
    p. 408 UNGATHERED 36   5 The Marrow! Wretch, I quitt thee of thy paine

paines   frequency: 6   relative frequency: 0.00008
    p.   83 EPIGRAMS 132   5 How can I speake of thy great paines, but erre?
    p.   85 EPIGRAMS 133   60 'Tis but light paines: Indeede this Dock's no
                                    rose.
    p.   97 FOREST 3   11 To view the iewells, stuffes, the paines, the wit
    p. 105 FOREST 8   27 Any paines; yea, thinke it price,
    p. 161 UNDERWOOD 14   75 And estimate thy Paines; as having wrought
    p. 213 UNDERWOOD 44   15 Withall, the dirtie paines those Citizens take,

pains. See "paines."

paint   frequency: 8   relative frequency: 0.00011
    p. 100 FOREST 4   13 I know too, though thou strut, and paint,
    p. 117 FOREST 13   20 Or feare to draw true lines, 'cause others paint:
    p. 227 UNDERWOOD 52   19 But, you are he can paint; I can but write:
    p. 261 UNDERWOOD 77   16 And act the businesse, which they paint, or
                                    carve.
    p. 278 U'WOOD 84.4   9 You could make shift to paint an Eye,
    p. 305 HORACE 2   25 Know'st only well to paint a Cipresse tree.
    p. 305 HORACE 2   27 To paint him, hath by swimming, hopelesse,
                                    scap'd,
    p. 407 UNGATHERED 35   12 Thou paint a Lane, where Thumb ye Pygmy meets!

painted   frequency: 10   relative frequency: 0.00014
    See also "paynted."
    p.   94 FOREST 2   29 The painted partrich lyes in euery field,
    p.   97 FOREST 3   17 Along'st the curled woods, and painted meades,
    p. 107 FOREST 10   20 Turne the stale prologue to some painted maske,
    p. 114 FOREST 12   45 Painted, or caru'd vpon our great-mens tombs,
    p. 172 UNDERWOOD 20   22 Perjur'd! and painted! if she were no more --,
    p. 241 UNDERWOOD 69   10 Painted a Dog, that now his subtler skill
    p. 273 U'WOOD 84.1   22 Their painted Maskes, their paper Boates,
    p. 277 U'WOOD 84.3   28 And thou hast painted beauties world.
    p. 404 UNGATHERED 34   48 Mythology there painted on slit deale!
    p. 406 UNGATHERED 34   97 What Poesy ere was painted on a wall

painter   frequency: 9   relative frequency: 0.00013
    p. 145 UNDERWOOD 5   13 And as a cunning Painter takes
    p. 226 UNDERWOOD 52   t2 The Poet to the Painter.
    p. 241 UNDERWOOD 69   9 But as the wretched Painter, who so ill
    p. 277 U'WOOD 84.3   29 But, Painter, see thou doe not sell
    p. 277 U'WOOD 84.4   1 Painter, yo'are come, but may be gone,
    p. 305 HORACE 2   1 If to a Womans head a Painter would
    p. 305 HORACE 2   11 But equall power, to Painter, and to Poet,
    p. 305 HORACE 2   24 No place for these. And, Painter, hap'ly, thou
    p. 408 UNGATHERED 36   10 Seek out some hungry painter, yt for bread

painters   frequency: 2   relative frequency: 0.00002
    p. 227 UNDERWOOD 52   7 You were not tied, by any Painters Law,
    p. 275 U'WOOD 84.3   9 Yet something, to the Painters view,

painting   frequency: 3   relative frequency: 0.00004
    p. 242 UNDERWOOD 69   24 All is but web, and painting; be the strife
    p. 329 HORACE 2   539 As Painting, so is Poesie. Some mans hand
    p. 404 UNGATHERED 34   50 Painting & Carpentry are ye Soule of
                                    Masque.

paintings   frequency: 1   relative frequency: 0.00001
    p. 113 FOREST 13   77 Let 'hem on poulders, oyles, and paintings,
                                 spend,

paints   frequency: 1   relative frequency: 0.00001
    p. 307 HORACE 2   41 One thing prodigiously, paints in the woods

pair.   See "paire," "payre."

paire   frequency: 12   relative frequency: 0.00017
    p.   28 EPIGRAMS 5   4 The spoused paire two realmes, the sea the ring.
    p.   81 EPIGRAMS 129   1 That, not a paire of friends each other see,
    p. 204 UNDERWOOD 43   38 A paire of Scisars, and a Combe in verse;
    p. 233 UNDERWOOD 59   9 A quick, and dazeling motion! when a paire
    p. 242 UNDERWOOD 70   t2 that noble paire, Sir LVCIVS CARY,
    p. 253 UNDERWOOD 75   24 To welcome home a Paire, and deck the nuptiall
                                 bower?
    p. 254 UNDERWOOD 75   60 With light of love, this Paire doth intertexe!
    p. 254 UNDERWOOD 75   76 Saw'st thou that Paire, became these Rites so
                                 well,
    p. 255 UNDERWOOD 75   80 They are th'exampled Paire, and mirrour of their
                                 kind.
    p. 380 UNGATHERED 12   41 I meane that one paire, wherewith he so hobled
    p. 395 UNGATHERED 29   1 When, Rome, I reade thee in thy mighty paire,
    p. 401 UNGATHERED 33   4 Of two, the choicest Paire of Mans delights,

palace   frequency: 2   relative frequency: 0.00002
    See also "pallace."
    p. 262 UNDERWOOD 78   9 His brest is a brave Palace, a broad Street,
    p. 280 U'WOOD 84.4   50 Some Paradise, or Palace found

palate   frequency: 1   relative frequency: 0.00001
    See also "palate's," "pallat."
    p.   64 EPIGRAMS 101   9 Yet shall you haue, to rectifie your palate,

palate's   frequency: 1   relative frequency: 0.00001
   *p. 492 TO HIMSELF   20 Enuy them not, their palate's with the swine.

pale   frequency: 5   relative frequency: 0.00007
    See also "partie-per-pale."
    p. 293 UNDERWOOD 86   34 Flow my thin teares, downe these pale cheeks of
                                 mine?
    p. 333 HORACE 2   612 Looke pale, distill a showre (was never meant)
    p. 366 UNGATHERED 6   21 The pale Pyrene, and the forked Mount:
    p. 367 UNGATHERED 6   45 With thy soft notes, and hold them within Pale
    p. 405 UNGATHERED 34   88 Reuiuing wth fresh coulors ye pale Ghosts

pales   frequency: 2   relative frequency: 0.00002
    p. 264 UNDERWOOD 79   30 To better Pastures then great PALES can:
    p. 265 UNDERWOOD 79   61 Then ever PALES could, or PAN;

palindromes   frequency: 1   relative frequency: 0.00001
    p. 204 UNDERWOOD 43   34 Of Logogriphes, and curious Palindromes,

pallace   frequency: 1   relative frequency: 0.00001
    p. 407 UNGATHERED 35   9 Or Ale! He build a pallace! Thou a shopp

pallas   frequency: 6   relative frequency: 0.00008
    p.   68 EPIGRAMS 105   16 That saw you put on PALLAS plumed caske:
    p. 107 FOREST 10   13 PALLAS, nor thee I call on, mankinde maid,
    p. 183 UNDERWOOD 29   30 Pallas frowning.
    p. 371 UNGATHERED 9   7 Taught Pallas language; Cynthia modesty;
    p. 378 UNGATHERED 11   91 To be his Bacchus as his Pallas: bee
    p. 421 UNGATHERED 48   45 Whoe worthie wine, whoe not, to bee wyse Pallas
                                 guests.

pallat   frequency: 1   relative frequency: 0.00001
    p. 105 FOREST 8   21 What should, yet, thy pallat please?

palm.   See "palme."

palme   frequency: 5   relative frequency: 0.00007
    p. 177 UNDERWOOD 25   26 True noblesse. Palme growes straight, though
                                 handled ne're so rude.
    p. 187 UNDERWOOD 33   35 Then com'st thou off with Victorie and Palme,
    p. 285 U'WOOD 84.9   96 With boughs of Palme, a crowned Victrice stand!
    p. 286 U'WOOD 84.9   126 And to the Touch, a Flower, like soft as
                                 Palme.
    p. 363 UNGATHERED 3   6 It carries Palme with it, (where e're it goes)

palmer   frequency: 2   relative frequency: 0.00002
      p. 361 UNGATHERED 1   1 When late (graue Palmer) these thy graffs and
                                 flowers
      p. 362 UNGATHERED 1   30 Palmer thy trauayles well becum thy name,

palmerins   frequency: 1   relative frequency: 0.00001
      p. 203 UNDERWOOD 43   30 Th'Esplandians, Arthurs, Palmerins, and all

palsey's   frequency: 1   relative frequency: 0.00001
     *p. 493 TO HIMSELF   50 May, blushing, sweare no palsey's in thy braine.

palsgrave. See "paltzgrave."

palsies   frequency: 1   relative frequency: 0.00001
      p. 166 UNDERWOOD 15   135 He that no more for Age, Cramps, Palsies, can

palsy. See "palsey's."

paltzgrave   frequency: 1   relative frequency: 0.00001
      p. 418 UNGATHERED 47   2 The Paltzgrave, and the Lady Besse,

pamp<h>lets   frequency: 1   relative frequency: 0.00001
      p. 206 UNDERWOOD 43   79 Or Captaine Pamp<h>lets horse, and foot, that
                                 sallie

pan   frequency: 12   relative frequency: 0.00017
    See also "quick-warming-pan."
      p. 93 FOREST 2   11 Where PAN, and BACCHVS their high
                                 feasts haue made,
      p. 98 FOREST 3   47 Thus PAN, and SYLVANE, hauing had their
                                 rites,
      p. 264 UNDERWOOD 79   14 1. PAN is the great Preserver of our bounds.
      p. 264 UNDERWOOD 79   20 Shep. Of PAN wee sing, the best of Hunters,
                                 PAN,
      p. 264 UNDERWOOD 79   25 Sister of PAN, and glory of the Spring:
      p. 264 UNDERWOOD 79   28 Shep. Of PAN wee sing, the Chiefe of
                                 Leaders, PAN,
      p. 265 UNDERWOOD 79   43 PAN only our great Shep'ard is,
      p. 265 UNDERWOOD 79   55 And hunting, PAN, exceedeth thee.
      p. 265 UNDERWOOD 79   61 Then ever PALES could, or PAN;
      p. 265 UNDERWOOD 79   64 PAN knowes no other power then his,

pancharis   frequency: 2   relative frequency: 0.00002
      p. 182 UNDERWOOD 27   30 The Swan [that] so relish'd Pancharis)
      p. 369 UNGATHERED 6   98 Who warbleth PANCHARIS,

pancridge   frequency: 1   relative frequency: 0.00001
      p. 407 UNGATHERED 35   20 Content thee to be Pancridge Earle ye whyle;

pandects   frequency: 1   relative frequency: 0.00001
      p. 399 UNGATHERED 31   8 Code, Digests, Pandects of all faemale glory!

panders   frequency: 1   relative frequency: 0.00001
    **p. 116 PANEGYRE   103 "And with their ruines raise the panders bowers:

pandora's   frequency: 1   relative frequency: 0.00001
      p. 212 UNDERWOOD 43   213 Pox on thee, Vulcan, thy Pandora's pox,

panegyre   frequency: 1   relative frequency: 0.00001
    **p. 112 PANEGYRE   t2 PANEGYRE,

panic. See "panick."

panick   frequency: 1   relative frequency: 0.00001
      p. 43 EPIGRAMS 51   3 Which though it did but panick terror proue,

panton   frequency: 1   relative frequency: 0.00001
      p. 214 UNDERWOOD 44   34 Supplant bold Panton; and brought there to view

paper   frequency: 11   relative frequency: 0.00015
      p. 65 EPIGRAMS 101   26 That will the pastrie, not my paper, show of.
      p. 117 FOREST 13   25 You will not from the paper slightly passe:
      p. 180 UNDERWOOD 26   10 Wrapt in this paper lie,
      p. 203 UNDERWOOD 43   20 Any, least loose, or s<c>urrile paper, lie
      p. 205 UNDERWOOD 43   61 Especially in paper; that, that steame
      p. 213 UNDERWOOD 44   25 Powder, or paper, to bring up the youth
      p. 220 UNDERWOOD 47   65 Not built with Canvasse, paper, and false
                                 lights,
      p. 230 UNDERWOOD 55   6 I only can the Paper staine;
      p. 273 U'WOOD 84.1   22 Their painted Maskes, their paper Boates,

paper (cont.)
    p. 407 UNGATHERED 35   17 And stradling shews ye Boyes Brown paper fleet,
    p. 666 INSCRIPTS. 11   8 Wth Chequer Inke, vpon his guift, my paper,

papers   frequency: 2   relative frequency: 0.00002
    p. 30 EPIGRAMS 12   16 Takes physick, teares the papers: still god
                                payes.
    p. 331 HORACE 2   578 Nine yeares kept in, your papers by, yo'are free

paracelsvs   frequency: 1   relative frequency: 0.00001
    p. 86 EPIGRAMS 133   96 Poore MERCVRY, crying out on
                                PARACELSVS,

paradise   frequency: 2   relative frequency: 0.00002
    p. 276 U'WOOD 84.3   24 And Paradise confining these.
    p. 280 U'WOOD 84.4   50 Some Paradise, or Palace found

parasite   frequency: 1   relative frequency: 0.00001
    p. 48 EPIGRAMS 65   14 Things manly, and not smelling parasite.

parasites   frequency: 2   relative frequency: 0.00002
    p. 118 FOREST 13   82 When their owne Parasites laugh at their fall,
    p. 193 UNDERWOOD 38   94 What Fooles, and all their Parasites can apply;

parcae   frequency: 1   relative frequency: 0.00001
    p. 77 EPIGRAMS 120   15 As, sooth, the Parcae thought him one,

parcel. See "parcell."

parcell   frequency: 2   relative frequency: 0.00002
    p. 62 EPIGRAMS 97   6 By his each glorious parcell to be knowne!
    p. 172 UNDERWOOD 21   5 A parcell of Court-durt, a heape, and masse

parcells   frequency: 1   relative frequency: 0.00001
    p. 145 UNDERWOOD 5   11 Wee shall, at last, of parcells make

parcels   frequency: 1   relative frequency: 0.00001
    See also "parcells."
    p. 204 UNDERWOOD 43   43 And as false stampe there; parcels of a Play,

pardon   frequency: 8   relative frequency: 0.00011
    p. 29 EPIGRAMS 8   4 Beg'd RIDWAYES pardon: DVNCOTE,
                                now, doth crye,
    p. 31 EPIGRAMS 14   11 Pardon free truth, and let thy modestie,
    p. 155 UNDERWOOD 13   71 Pardon, sayes he, that were a way to see
    p. 167 UNDERWOOD 15   155 Pardon his Lordship. Flattry's growne so cheape
    p. 225 UNDERWOOD 51   5 Pardon, I read it in thy face, the day
    p. 289 U'WOOD 84.9   226 Who reades, will pardon my Intelligence,
    p. 329 HORACE 2   531 Deserves no pardon; or who'd play, and sing
    p. 410 UNGATHERED 39   1 Shall the prosperity of a Pardon still

pardon'd   frequency: 1   relative frequency: 0.00001
    p. 234 UNDERWOOD 61   12 A Nations sinne got pardon'd! 'twere a taske

pardoning   frequency: 1   relative frequency: 0.00001
    p. 191 UNDERWOOD 38   28 The Subject of your Grace in pardoning me,

pardons   frequency: 1   relative frequency: 0.00001
    p. 193 UNDERWOOD 38   69 He pardons slips, goes by a world of ills,

pare   frequency: 1   relative frequency: 0.00001
    p. 325 HORACE 2   422 In Helicon; a great sort will not pare

parent   frequency: 2   relative frequency: 0.00002
    p. 325 HORACE 2   447 What height of love, a Parent will fit best,
    p. 399 UNGATHERED 31   13 Or of a parent! or a freind!

parents   frequency: 9   relative frequency: 0.00013
    p. 33 EPIGRAMS 22   1 Here lyes to each her parents ruth,
    p. 46 EPIGRAMS 60   9 My countries parents I haue many knowne;
    p. 96 FOREST 2   97 Reade, in their vertuous parents noble parts,
    p. 192 UNDERWOOD 38   40 Of your compassion; Parents should be mild:
    p. 257 UNDERWOOD 75   143 Which their glad Parents taught
    p. 263 UNDERWOOD 82   7 To pious parents, who would have their blood
    p. 270 UNDERWOOD 83   59 With gladnesse temper'd her sad Parents teares!
    p. 271 UNDERWOOD 83   77 Goe now, her happy Parents, and be sad,
    p. 285 U'WOOD 84.9   118 And Sons, and Daughters, with their Parents
                                talke;

paris   frequency: 1   relative frequency: 0.00001
    p. 85 EPIGRAMS 133   33 From Venice, Paris, or some in-land passage

paris-garden   frequency: 1   relative frequency: 0.00001
   See also "parish-garden."
    p. 87 EPIGRAMS 133 117 The meate-boate of Beares colledge,
                      Paris-garden,

parish   frequency: 2   relative frequency: 0.00002
    p. 209 UNDERWOOD 43 133 Which, though it were the Fort of the whole
                      Parish,
    p. 232 UNDERWOOD 57   26 the Parish will know it.

parish-garden   frequency: 1   relative frequency: 0.00001
    p. 209 UNDERWOOD 43 147 And that accursed ground, the Parish-Garden:

parish-steeple   frequency: 1   relative frequency: 0.00001
    p. 239 UNDERWOOD 67   4 And though the Parish-steeple

paritie   frequency: 1   relative frequency: 0.00001
    p. 255 UNDERWOOD 75   83 The king of Creatures, take his paritie

parity. See "paritie."

park. See "hide-parke."

parliament   frequency: 4   relative frequency: 0.00005
   See also "parlyamt."
 **p. 112 PANEGYRE   t8 His first high Session of PARLIAMENT
    p. 34 EPIGRAMS 24   t1 TO THE PARLIAMENT.
    p. 87 EPIGRAMS 133 108 Of the graue fart, late let in parliament,
    p. 273 U'WOOD 84.1   30 And Call to the high Parliament

parlyamt   frequency: 1   relative frequency: 0.00001
    p. 406 UNGATHERED 34 103 Whom not ten fyres, nor a Parlyamt can

parnassus   frequency: 1   relative frequency: 0.00001
    p. 183 UNDERWOOD 29   17 All Parnassus Greene did wither,

parrot   frequency: 1   relative frequency: 0.00001
   See also "covrt-parrat."
    p. 65 EPIGRAMS 101   36 And we will haue no Pooly', or Parrot by;

part   frequency: 31   relative frequency: 0.00044
 **p. 114 PANEGYRE   59 That did not beare a part in this consent
    p. 50 EPIGRAMS 69   2 Yet by thy weapon liu'st! Th'hast one good part.
    p. 67 EPIGRAMS 103   12 For euery part a character assign'd.
    p. 68 EPIGRAMS 106   3 All-vertuous HERBERT! on whose euery part
    p. 69 EPIGRAMS 107   28 Will you part with them, here, vnthriftely?
    p. 71 EPIGRAMS 110   18 (As by a new creation) part by part,
    p. 75 EPIGRAMS 116   2 All gentrie, yet, owe part of their best flame!
    p. 82 EPIGRAMS 130   15 I, yet, had vtter'd nothing on thy part,
    p. 82 EPIGRAMS 131   2 A worke of ours, we part with our owne right;
    p. 100 FOREST 4   4 My part is ended on thy stage.
    p. 129 UNDERWOOD 1.2   3 Is my best part:
    p. 142 U'WOOD 2.10   8 'Tis one good part I'ld lie withall.
    p. 142 UNDERWOOD 2.9 53 Such a man, with every part,
    p. 163 UNDERWOOD 15   27 No part or corner man can looke upon,
    p. 192 UNDERWOOD 38   36 Nothing is vile, that is a part of you:
    p. 194 UNDERWOOD 38 110 How much you are the better part of me;
    p. 210 UNDERWOOD 43 170 And didst invade part of the Common-wealth,
    p. 232 UNDERWOOD 58   12 As if that part lay for a [   ] most fit!
    p. 246 UNDERWOOD 70   87 Or taste a part of that full joy he meant
    p. 258 UNDERWOOD 75 176 How each one playes his part, of the large
                      Pedigree.
    p. 269 UNDERWOOD 83   28 But rather I, should I of that part speake!
    p. 282 U'WOOD 84.9   15 Sleepie, or stupid Nature, couldst thou part
    p. 323 HORACE 2   385 Of too much haste, and negligence in part,
    p. 323 HORACE 2   403 To part scurrilitie from wit: or can
    p. 339 HORACE 1   33 The greater part, that boast the Muses fire,
    p. 345 HORACE 1   276 .. .. part ... .
    p. 366 UNGATHERED 6   28 That part nor Winde,
    p. 387 UNGATHERED 22   2 these only hide part of my flesh, and bones:
    p. 392 UNGATHERED 26 56 My gentle Shakespeare, must enioy a part.
    p. 415 UNGATHERED 42 12 Now, for mine owne part, and it is but due,

partakes   frequency: 1   relative frequency: 0.00001
    p. 34 EPIGRAMS 22   11 This graue partakes the fleshly birth.

parted   frequency: 2   relative frequency: 0.00002
    p.   33 EPIGRAMS 22   5 At sixe moneths end, shee parted hence
    p. 279 U'WOOD 84.4   39 And, though the sound were parted thence,

partes   frequency: 1   relative frequency: 0.00001
    p. 382 UNGATHERED 16   3 vnto thee, king of men; their noblest partes

particular   frequency: 1   relative frequency: 0.00001
    p. 379 UNGATHERED 12   9 And allow you for each particular mile,

partie-per-pale   frequency: 1   relative frequency: 0.00001
    p.   51 EPIGRAMS 73   13 Your partie-per-pale picture, one halfe drawne

parties   frequency: 1   relative frequency: 0.00001
    p. 284 U'WOOD 84.9   60 T<o>'accuse, or quit all Parties to be heard!

parting   frequency: 3   relative frequency: 0.00004
    p.   65 EPIGRAMS 101   38 But, at our parting, we will be, as when
    p. 197 UNDERWOOD 40   7 Of parting, drowne it in the hope to meet
    p. 199 UNDERWOOD 41   4 Be idle words, though of a parting Man;

partrich   frequency: 3   relative frequency: 0.00004
    p.   65 EPIGRAMS 101'   18 Of partrich, pheasant, wood-cock, of which some
    p.   94 FOREST 2   29 The painted partrich lyes in euery field,
    p.   97 FOREST 3   27 In autumne, at the Partrich makes a flight,

partridge. See "partrich."

parts   frequency: 23   relative frequency: 0.00033
   See also "partes," "west-parts."
  **p. 114 PANEGYRE   32 Breath'd in his way; and soules (their better
                                parts)
    p.   61 EPIGRAMS 95   17 For who can master those great parts like thee,
    p.   69 EPIGRAMS 107   9 Tell them, what parts yo'haue tane, whence run
                                away,
    p.   71 EPIGRAMS 110   14 And that, midst enuy' and parts; then fell by
                                rage:
    p.   74 EPIGRAMS 115   26 Parts, then th'Italian could doe, with his dore.
    p.   96 FOREST 2   97 Reade, in their vertuous parents noble parts,
    p. 142 U'WOOD 2.10   7 What you please, you parts may call,
    p. 206 UNDERWOOD 43   87 I dare not say a body, but some parts
    p. 218 UNDERWOOD 47   18 Like flies, or wormes, which mans corrupt parts
                                fed:
    p. 234 UNDERWOOD 60   11 No noble furniture of parts,
    p. 244 UNDERWOOD 70   33 Hee entred well, by vertuous parts,
    p. 259 UNDERWOOD 76   23 Parts of me (they judg'd) decay'd,
    p. 262 UNDERWOOD 78   3 In honour, courtesie, and all the parts
    p. 287 U'WOOD 84.9   173 She was, in one, a many parts of life:
    p. 289 U'WOOD 84.9   223 And most his Justice, in the fitting parts,
    p. 317 HORACE 2   252 The parts of age to youth be given; or men
    p. 317 HORACE 2   276 An Actors parts, and Office too, the Quire
    p. 325 HORACE 2   450 And office of a Judge are, what the parts
    p. 327 HORACE 2   465 How to divide, into a hundred parts,
    p. 370 UNGATHERED 7   4 All which are parts commend the cunning hand;
    p. 395 UNGATHERED 29   7 But when againe I veiw the parts so peiz'd,
    p. 396 UNGATHERED 30   21 And those so sweet, and well proportion'd parts,
    p. 409 UNGATHERED 38   2 And you perform'd a Seruants faithfull parts:

party-per-pale. See "partie-per-pale."

pas<s>e   frequency: 1   relative frequency: 0.00001
    p. 383 UNGATHERED 16   12 made prospectiue, behould hym, hee must pas<s>e

pas'd   frequency: 1   relative frequency: 0.00001
    p. 379 UNGATHERED 12   8 To line out no stride, but pas'd by himselfe?

pasquill's   frequency: 1   relative frequency: 0.00001
    p. 206 UNDERWOOD 43   77 With Nicholas Pasquill's, Meddle with your
                                match,

pass. See "pas<s>e," "passe."

passage   frequency: 7   relative frequency: 0.00010
    p.   85 EPIGRAMS 133   33 From Venice, Paris, or some in-land passage
    p.   85 EPIGRAMS 133   59 To this dire passage. Say, thou stop thy nose:
    p.   88 EPIGRAMS 133   168 Tempt such a passage? when each priuies seate
    p. 119 FOREST 13   92 Into your harbor, and all passage shut
    p. 221 UNDERWOOD 48   45 Or gratulates the passage
    p. 383 UNGATHERED 17   5 Who reads may roaue, and call the passage darke,
    p. 389 UNGATHERED 23   10 Such Passage hast thou found, such Returnes
                                made,

pass'd   frequency: 2   relative frequency: 0.00002
  See also "past."
**p. 113 PANEGYRE   31 With these he pass'd, and with his peoples hearts
  p. 201 UNDERWOOD 42   70 The Lady Mayresse pass'd in through the Towne,

passe   frequency: 14   relative frequency: 0.00020
  p. 38 EPIGRAMS 36   3 But in my royall subiect I passe thee,
  p. 42 EPIGRAMS 47   1 Sir LVCKLESSE, troth, for lucks sake
                            passe by one:
  p. 73 EPIGRAMS 112   13 I passe to Elegies; Thou meet'st me there:
  p. 86 EPIGRAMS 133   73 But they vnfrighted passe, though many a priuie
  p. 88 EPIGRAMS 133 140 All was to them the same, they were to passe,
  p. 117 FOREST 13   25 You will not from the paper slightly passe:
  p. 120 FOREST 13   121 Liue that one, still; and as long yeeres doe
                            passe,
  p. 165 UNDERWOOD 15 112 Sweet bags, sweet Powders, nor sweet words will
                            passe
  p. 198 UNDERWOOD 40   31 They may say Grace, and for Loves Chaplaines
                            passe;
  p. 231 UNDERWOOD 56   24 Your Joane to passe her melancholie time.
  p. 329 HORACE 2   513 Our Gallants give them none, but passe them by:
  p. 329 HORACE 2   518 Will passe the Seas, and long as nature is,
  p. 389 UNGATHERED 24   9 Vpon it, but will loath, or let it passe,
  p. 396 UNGATHERED 30   4 Those ambling visits, passe in verse, betweene

passenger   frequency: 1   relative frequency: 0.00001
  p. 233 UNDERWOOD 60   1 If, Passenger, thou canst but reade:

passer-by   frequency: 1   relative frequency: 0.00001
  p. 233 UNDERWOOD 60   t3 To the Passer-by.

passion   frequency: 8   relative frequency: 0.00011
  See also "passion's."
  p. 39 EPIGRAMS 40   16 For wit, feature, and true passion,
  p. 131 UNDERWOOD 2.1 11 With the Ardor, and the Passion,
  p. 147 UNDERWOOD 7   t1 A Nymphs Passion.
  p. 201 UNDERWOOD 42   49 Of race accompted, that no passion have
  p. 283 U'WOOD 84.9   31 Am turned with an others powers. My Passion
  p. 362 UNGATHERED 1   28 I struggled with this passion that did drowne
  p. 362 UNGATHERED 2   1 Thou, that wouldst finde the habit of true
                            passion,
  p. 370 UNGATHERED 7   7 Each subt'lest Passion, with her source, and
                            spring,

passions   frequency: 2   relative frequency: 0.00002
  p. 110 FOREST 11   29 Doe seuerall passions <still> inuade the minde,
  p. 190 UNDERWOOD 37   31 For no man lives so out of passions sway,

passion's   frequency: 1   relative frequency: 0.00001
  See also "passions."
  p. 370 UNGATHERED 7   11 To iudge which Passion's false, and which is
                            true,

passiue   frequency: 1   relative frequency: 0.00001
  p. 49 EPIGRAMS 68   4 Actiue in's braine, and passiue in his bones.

passive. See "passiue."

past   frequency: 16   relative frequency: 0.00023
  p. 34 EPIGRAMS 25   2 In the past pleasures of his sensuall life,
  p. 54 EPIGRAMS 80   7 So to front death, as men might iudge vs past it.
  p. 64 EPIGRAMS 100   4 Fiue of my iests, then stolne, past him a play.
  p. 67 EPIGRAMS 104   11 Were you aduanced, past those times, to be
  p. 81 EPIGRAMS 128   12 This is that good AENEAS, past through
                            fire,
  p. 85 EPIGRAMS 133   49 Or magick sacrifice, they past along!
  p. 89 EPIGRAMS 133 185 They laugh't, at his laugh-worthy fate. And past
  p. 140 UNDERWOOD 2.8 28 All your sweet of life is past,
  p. 159 UNDERWOOD 14   21 Men past their termes, and prais'd some names too
                            much,
  p. 159 UNDERWOOD 14   34 Heard what times past have said, seene what ours
                            doe:
  p. 162 UNDERWOOD 15   18 Crush'd in the snakie brakes, that he had past!
  p. 215 UNDERWOOD 44   83 Past any need of vertue. Let them care,
  p. 228 UNDERWOOD 53   5 And saw a Centaure, past those tales of Greece;
  p. 252 UNDERWOOD 75   1 Though thou hast past thy Summer standing, stay
  p. 317 HORACE 2   248 Of the times past, when he was a young lad;
  p. 385 UNGATHERED 19   8 Thy Richard, rais'd in song, past pulling downe.

pastie   frequency: 1   relative frequency: 0.00001
   p.   88 EPIGRAMS 133   148 To put the skins, and offall in a pastie?

pastoral.   See "pastorall."

pastorall   frequency: 1   relative frequency: 0.00001
   p. 143 UNDERWOOD 3   t1 The Musicall strife; In a Pastorall Dialogue.

pastorals   frequency: 1   relative frequency: 0.00001
   p. 386 UNGATHERED 21   t3 on his Pastorals.

pastrie   frequency: 1   relative frequency: 0.00001
   p.   65 EPIGRAMS 101   26 That will the pastrie, not my paper, show of.

pastry.   See "pastrie."

pastures   frequency: 2   relative frequency: 0.00002
   p. 264 UNDERWOOD 79   30 To better Pastures then great PALES can:
   p. 265 UNDERWOOD 79   60 To sweeter Pastures lead hee can,

pasty.   See "pastie."

pat.   See "pit-pat-noyse."

patched.   See "patch't."

patch't   frequency: 1   relative frequency: 0.00001
  *p. 493 TO HIMSELF   39 Which, if they are torne, and turn'd, &
                           patch't enough,

pate   frequency: 1   relative frequency: 0.00001
   p. 405 UNGATHERED 34   83 Vnder ye Morall? shewe he had a pate

path   frequency: 2   relative frequency: 0.00002
   p.   70 EPIGRAMS 119   12 Treading a better path, not contrary;
   p. 339 HORACE 1   46 If .. th'escape an .... path .. ..

pathes   frequency: 1   relative frequency: 0.00001
   p. 386 UNGATHERED 21   5 For, though but early in these pathes thou tread,

paths   frequency: 4   relative frequency: 0.00005
   See also "by-paths," "pathes."
   p. 118 FOREST 13   57 In single paths, dangers with ease are watch'd:
   p. 160 UNDERWOOD 14   45 Sought out the Fountaines, Sources, Creekes,
                           paths, wayes,
   p. 254 UNDERWOOD 75   59 The bright Brides paths, embelish'd more then
                           thine
   p. 390 UNGATHERED 26   6 Were not the paths I meant vnto thy praise:

patience   frequency: 3   relative frequency: 0.00004
   p. 168 UNDERWOOD 16   5 It might thy patience richly pay:
   p. 179 UNDERWOOD 25   47 As patience lasteth.
   p. 323 HORACE 2   375 Nor is't long since, they did with patience take

patient   frequency: 1   relative frequency: 0.00001
   p. 207 UNDERWOOD 43   108 Or Goddesse, could be patient of thy face.

patiently   frequency: 1   relative frequency: 0.00001
   p. 323 HORACE 2   401 Too patiently, that I not fondly say;

patriot   frequency: 1   relative frequency: 0.00001
   p. 244 UNDERWOOD 70   46 A perfect Patriot, and a noble friend,

patronage   frequency: 1   relative frequency: 0.00001
   p. 217 UNDERWOOD 46   12 More for thy Patronage, then for their Cause,

patrons   frequency: 2   relative frequency: 0.00002
   p.   43 EPIGRAMS 53   4 But when (in place) thou didst the patrons
                           choose,
   p. 113 FOREST 12   14 When his proud patrons fauours are asleepe;

patternes   frequency: 1   relative frequency: 0.00001
   p. 171 UNDERWOOD 19   17 Unto the other; and live patternes, how

patterns.   See "patternes."

paul.   See "pavl."

paules   frequency: 1   relative frequency: 0.00001
   p. 378 UNGATHERED 11   85 Shewes he dares more then Paules Church-yard
                           durst do.

paulet. See "pawlet."

pauls   frequency: 1   relative frequency: 0.00001
      See also "paules," "pavls."
      p. 206 UNDERWOOD 43   81 The weekly Corrants, with Pauls Seale; and all

pauls-steeple   frequency: 1   relative frequency: 0.00001
      p. 211 UNDERWOOD 43 193 And to Pauls-Steeple; which was unto us

paulus   frequency: 1   relative frequency: 0.00001
      p. 292 UNDERWOOD 86   10 With thy bright Swans, of Paulus Maximus:

pause   frequency: 5   relative frequency: 0.00007
      p.   43 EPIGRAMS 51   4 And farre beneath least pause of such a king,
      p.   57 EPIGRAMS 89   8 That ALLEN, I should pause to publish thee?
      p. 174 UNDERWOOD 23   17 Should not on fortune pause,
      p. 192 UNDERWOOD 38   47 And then with pause; for sever'd once, that's
                              gone,
      p. 399 UNGATHERED 31   6 With pause vpon it; make this page your booke;

pavl   frequency: 1   relative frequency: 0.00001
      p. 122 FOREST 15   24 With holy PAVL, lest it be thought the breath

pavls   frequency: 2   relative frequency: 0.00002
      p.   52 EPIGRAMS 75   3 Though LIPPE, at PAVLS, ranne from his
                              text away,
      p.   56 EPIGRAMS 88   16 Daily to turne in PAVLS, and helpe the
                              trade.

pavy. See "p<avy>."

pawlet   frequency: 1   relative frequency: 0.00001
      p. 268 UNDERWOOD 83   t2 On the Lady JANE PAWLET,

pawn. See "pawne."

pawne   frequency: 2   relative frequency: 0.00002
      p. 107 FOREST 10   24 And riffle him: or pawne his PETASVS.
      p. 417 UNGATHERED 45 38 each to pawne hir husbands capp,

pay   frequency: 21   relative frequency: 0.00030
      p.   41 EPIGRAMS 45   3 Seuen yeeres tho'wert lent to me, and I thee
                              pay,
      p.   42 EPIGRAMS 46   4 To pay at's day of marriage. By my hand
      p.   42 EPIGRAMS 46   5 The knight-wright's cheated then: Hee'll neuer
                              pay.
      p.   49 EPIGRAMS 66   17 Hee's valiant'st, that dares fight, and not for
                              pay;
      p.   51 EPIGRAMS 73   22 For which, or pay me quickly', or Ile pay you.
      p.   66 EPIGRAMS 102 10 To morrow vice, if shee giue better pay:
      p.   69 EPIGRAMS 107 10 What States yo'haue gull'd, and which yet keepes
                              yo'in pay.
      p.   80 EPIGRAMS 127 12 To thanke thy benefits: which is, to pay.
      p.   94 FOREST 2   32 Thou hast thy ponds, that pay thee tribute fish,
      p. 118 FOREST 13   53 Wherewith, then, Madame, can you better pay
      p. 119 FOREST 13   96 To pay your lord the pledges of chast loue:
      p. 128 UNDERWOOD 1.1 23 To pay our debts, upon thy Crosse, and cryd'st,
      p. 168 UNDERWOOD 16   5 It might thy patience richly pay:
      p. 169 UNDERWOOD 17   1 They are not, Sir, worst Owers, that doe pay
      p. 231 UNDERWOOD 56   30 And should grow rich, had I much more to pay.
      p. 236 UNDERWOOD 63   5 Hee can, he will, and with large int'rest pay,
      p. 241 UNDERWOOD 68   2 His Poet Sack, the House-hold will not pay?
      p. 256 UNDERWOOD 75 106 To pay, with honours, to his noble Sonne,
      p. 258 UNDERWOOD 75 188 Exacts then she is pleas'd to pay: no suits,
      p. 396 UNGATHERED 30   9 About the towne: this reck'ning I will pay,

payd   frequency: 1   relative frequency: 0.00001
      p. 405 UNGATHERED 34   90 Thy twice conceyud, thrice payd for Imagery?

payes   frequency: 11   relative frequency: 0.00015
      p.   30 EPIGRAMS 12   4 The charge of that state, with this charme, god
                              payes.
      p.   30 EPIGRAMS 12   6 Himselfe: his whole reuennue is, god payes.
      p.   30 EPIGRAMS 12   8 Shee must haue money: he returnes, god payes.
      p.   30 EPIGRAMS 12   10 Lookes o're the bill, likes it: and say's, god
                              payes.
      p.   30 EPIGRAMS 12   12 At dice his borrow'd money: which, god payes.
      p.   30 EPIGRAMS 12   14 Signes to new bond, forfeits: and cryes, god
                              payes.
      p.   30 EPIGRAMS 12   16 Takes physick, teares the papers: still god
                              payes.

payes (cont.)
    p. 30 EPIGRAMS 12   18 Calls for his stoole, adornes the stage: god
                                 payes.
    p. 31 EPIGRAMS 12   20 His onely answere is to all, god payes.
    p. 31 EPIGRAMS 12   22 Thus: and for his letcherie, scores, god payes.
    p. 164 UNDERWOOD 15   78 That payes, or what he will: The Dame is
                                 steele.

payne   frequency: 1   relative frequency: 0.00001
    p. 418 UNGATHERED 46   6 for when the profitt with the payne doth meete,

paynted   frequency: 1   relative frequency: 0.00001
    p. 406 UNGATHERED 34 93 A Goddess is, then paynted Cloth, Deal-boards,

payre   frequency: 1   relative frequency: 0.00001
    p. 384 UNGATHERED 18 26 Sure, this glad payre were married, but this day.

pays   frequency: 1   relative frequency: 0.00001
    See also "payes."
    p. 657 L. CONVIVALES 17 Pays all Debts, cures all Diseases,

peace   frequency: 28   relative frequency: 0.00040
  *p. 494 TO HIMSELF   57 In sound of peace, or warres,
    p. 38 EPIGRAMS 37   4 For this: that winnes, for whom he holds his
                                 peace.
    p. 41 EPIGRAMS 45   9 Rest in soft peace, and, ask'd, say here doth lye
    p. 59 EPIGRAMS 92   30 If the States make peace, how it will goe
    p. 60 EPIGRAMS 93   13 Thou yet remayn'st, vn-hurt in peace, or warre,
    p. 99 FOREST 3   93 Thy peace is made; and, when man's state is well,
    p. 102 FOREST 4   65 Nor for my peace will I goe farre,
    p. 110 FOREST 11   55 O, who is he, that (in this peace) enioyes
    p. 111 FOREST 11   69 Peace, Luxurie, thou art like one of those
    p. 119 FOREST 13   93 'Gainst stormes, or pyrats, that might charge
                                 your peace;
    p. 166 UNDERWOOD 15 121 This hath our ill-us'd freedome, and soft peace
    p. 167 UNDERWOOD 15 150 That may stand by, and hold my peace? will he,
    p. 168 UNDERWOOD 15 195 These take, and now goe seeke thy peace in
                                 Warre,
    p. 185 UNDERWOOD 30 17 Clos'd to their peace, he saw his branches shoot,
    p. 212 UNDERWOOD 43 209 We aske your absence here, we all love peace,
    p. 222 UNDERWOOD 48 48 The wished Peace of Europe:
    p. 261 UNDERWOOD 77 22 Of sweets, and safeties, they possesse by Peace.
    p. 264 UNDERWOOD 79 40 1. Hee is the Father of our peace;
    p. 265 UNDERWOOD 79 57 Hee is the author of our peace.
    p. 317 HORACE 2   284 Peace, and the open ports, that peace doth cause.
    p. 323 HORACE 2   369 Which law receiv'd, the Chorus held his peace,
    p. 363 UNGATHERED 3   4 Flowes fro the surfets which we take in peace.
    p. 363 UNGATHERED 3 2+ Peace.
    p. 382 UNGATHERED 16   6 presentes a Royall Alter of fayre peace,
    p. 411 UNGATHERED 40   7 The Peace of Conscience,
    p. 417 UNGATHERED 45 22 for if there, or peace or warr be,
    p. 418 UNGATHERED 45 42 or theire Ale, they break the peace,

peach   frequency: 2   relative frequency: 0.00002
    p. 94 FOREST 2   43 The blushing apricot, and woolly peach
    p. 141 UNDERWOOD 2.9 21 Chin, as woolly as the Peach;

peacock   frequency: 1   relative frequency: 0.00001
    p. 68 EPIGRAMS 105 18 There IVNO sate, and yet no Peacock by.

peak. See "peake."

peake   frequency: 2   relative frequency: 0.00002
    p. 416 UNGATHERED 45   1 To the wonders of the Peake,
    p. 417 UNGATHERED 45 23 to the Peake it is so hard-by,

peales   frequency: 1   relative frequency: 0.00001
    p. 401 UNGATHERED 33   1 What charming Peales are these,

peals. See "peales."

pear. See "peare."

pearch'd   frequency: 1   relative frequency: 0.00001
    p. 397 UNGATHERED 30 34 Pearch'd ouer head, the wise Athenian Owle:

peare   frequency: 1   relative frequency: 0.00001
    p. 95 FOREST 2   56 An embleme of themselues, in plum, or peare.

peares   frequency: 1   relative frequency: 0.00001
    p. 290 UNDERWOOD 85   19 How plucking Peares, his owne hand grafted had,

pearl. See "pearle."

pearle   frequency: 1   relative frequency: 0.00001
    p. 213 UNDERWOOD 44   13 But they may see Gold-Chaines, and Pearle
                  worne then,

pears. See "peares."

peas. See "peason."

peasants   frequency: 1   relative frequency: 0.00001
    p. 114 FOREST 12   26 Then, here, to giue pride fame, and peasants
                  birth.

peason   frequency: 1   relative frequency: 0.00001
    p.   88 EPIGRAMS 133   166 When euery clerke eates artichokes, and peason,

peddling. See "pedling."

pediculous   frequency: 1   relative frequency: 0.00001
    p. 380 UNGATHERED 12   34 How scabbed, how ragged, and how pediculous

pedigree   frequency: 3   relative frequency: 0.00004
    p.   70 EPIGRAMS 109   4 Where all is faire, beside thy pedigree.
    p. 258 UNDERWOOD 75   176 How each one playes his part, of the large
                  Pedigree.
    p. 282 U'WOOD 84.8   20 Hang all your roomes, with one large Pedigree:

pedling   frequency: 1   relative frequency: 0.00001
    p. 404 UNGATHERED 34   51 Pack wth your pedling Poetry to the Stage,

peece   frequency: 6   relative frequency: 0.00008
    p.   45 EPIGRAMS 56   14 From locks of wooll, or shreds from the whole
                  peece?
    p. 145 UNDERWOOD 5   14 In any curious peece you see
    p. 228 UNDERWOOD 53   6 So seem'd your horse and you, both of a peece!
    p. 277 U'WOOD 84.3   30 A Copie of this peece; nor tell
    p. 305 HORACE 2   8 This peece, my Piso's, and that booke agree,
    p. 305 HORACE 2   19 A Scarlet peece, or two, stitch'd in: when or

peeces   frequency: 4   relative frequency: 0.00005
    p. 127 UNDERWOOD 1.1   7 As my heart lies in peeces, all confus'd,
    p. 131 UNDERWOOD 2   t2 ten Lyrick Peeces.
    p. 187 UNDERWOOD 33   30 Arm'd at all peeces, as to keepe a Fort
    p. 398 UNGATHERED 30   74 Get broken peeces, and fight well by those.

peep. See "peepe."

peepe   frequency: 3   relative frequency: 0.00004
    p. 140 UNDERWOOD 2.8   16 No, nor forth your window peepe,
    p. 201 UNDERWOOD 42   59 Thou didst tell me; and wert o're-joy'd to peepe
    p. 258 UNDERWOOD 75   175 Peepe forth a Gemme; to see

peepes   frequency: 1   relative frequency: 0.00001
    p. 248 UNDERWOOD 71   9 The Muse not peepes out, one of hundred dayes;

peeps. See "peepes."

peer. See "peere."

peere   frequency: 1   relative frequency: 0.00001
    p. 113 FOREST 12   12 Of some grand peere, whose ayre doth make reioyce

peeres   frequency: 7   relative frequency: 0.00010
    *p. 493 TO HIMSELF   35 The stagers, and the stage-wrights too (your
                  peeres)
    p. 121 FOREST 14   26 T<o>'out-strip your peeres:
    p. 131 UNDERWOOD 2.1   4 I have had, and have my Peeres;
    p. 138 UNDERWOOD 2.6   23 Of your Peeres, you were beheld,
    p. 243 UNDERWOOD 70   25 Here's one out-liv'd his Peeres,
    p. 284 U'WOOD 84.9   84 Amongst her Peeres, those Princes of all good!
    p. 391 UNGATHERED 26   28 I should commit thee surely with thy peeres,

peering   frequency: 1   relative frequency: 0.00001
    p. 403 UNGATHERED 34   34 And peering forth of Iris in ye Shrowdes!

peers   frequency: 3   relative frequency: 0.00004
    See also "peeres."
    p. 206 UNDERWOOD 43   69 The Tristrams, Lanc'lots, Turpins, and the
                                  Peers,
    p. 403 UNGATHERED 34   19 Or are you soe ambitious 'boue your peers!
    p. 410 UNGATHERED 39   3 At libelling? Shall no Star-Chamber Peers,

pegasus   frequency: 2   relative frequency: 0.00002
    See also "pegasvs."
    p. 183 UNDERWOOD 29   19 Pegasus did flie away,
    p. 228 UNDERWOOD 53   7 You shew'd like Perseus upon Pegasus;

pegasvs   frequency: 1   relative frequency: 0.00001
    p. 107 FOREST 10   23 Though he would steale his sisters
                                  PEGASVS,

peirce   frequency: 1   relative frequency: 0.00001
    p. 420 UNGATHERED 48   23 Whose ayre will sooner Hell, then their dull
                                  senses peirce,

peised. See "peiz'd."

peiz'd   frequency: 1   relative frequency: 0.00001
    p. 395 UNGATHERED 29   7 But when againe I veiw the parts so peiz'd,

peleus   frequency: 2   relative frequency: 0.00002
    p. 311 HORACE 2   136 And Peleus, if they seeke to heart-strike us
    p. 311 HORACE 2   147 Peleus, or Telephus. If you speake vile

pelf. See "pelfe."

pelfe   frequency: 1   relative frequency: 0.00001
    p. 197 UNDERWOOD 40   22 And turning all he toucheth into pelfe,

pellets   frequency: 1   relative frequency: 0.00001
    p. 259 UNDERWOOD 76   22 With their pellets of small wit,

pelts   frequency: 1   relative frequency: 0.00001
    p. 375 UNGATHERED 10   18 A Punke here pelts him with egs. How so?

pem   frequency: 1   relative frequency: 0.00001
    p. 417 UNGATHERED 45   39 at Pem Wakers good ale Tapp,

pembroke   frequency: 2   relative frequency: 0.00002
    p. 66 EPIGRAMS 102   1 I doe but name thee PEMBROKE, and I find
    p. 66 EPIGRAMS 102   t1 TO WILLIAM EARLE OF
                                  PEMBROKE.

pen   frequency: 11   relative frequency: 0.00015
    See also "penne."
    p. 44 EPIGRAMS 55   4 The least indulgent thought thy pen drops forth!
    p. 54 EPIGRAMS 81   4 To be the wealthy witnesse of my pen:
    p. 62 EPIGRAMS 95   33 Of state, and censure them: we need his pen
    p. 63 EPIGRAMS 99   3 Hast taught thy selfe worthy thy pen to tread,
    p. 70 EPIGRAMS 108   8 No more, then I dare now doe, with my pen.
    p. 115 FOREST 12   56 Because they lack'd the sacred pen, could giue
    p. 247 UNDERWOOD 70   124 And with the heart, not pen,
    p. 284 U'WOOD 84.9   69 This being thus: why should my tongue, or pen
    p. 335 HORACE 2   635 Blot out the carelesse, with his turned pen;
    p. 389 UNGATHERED 24   1 Who tracks this Authors, or Translators Pen,
    p. 395 UNGATHERED 29   17 Phoebus, and Hermes? They whose tongue, or pen

penaltie   frequency: 1   relative frequency: 0.00001
    p. 112 FOREST 11   89 Then he, which for sinnes penaltie forbeares.

penalty. See "penaltie."

penance   frequency: 2   relative frequency: 0.00002
    See also "pennance."
    p. 39 EPIGRAMS 39   2 COLT, now, doth daily penance in his owne.
    p. 235 UNDERWOOD 61   19 And doe their penance, to avert Gods rod,

penates   frequency: 2   relative frequency: 0.00002
    p. 95 FOREST 2   79 Of thy Penates had beene set on flame,
    p. 274 U'WOOD 84.2   7 Speake it, you bold PENATES, you that
                                  stand

pence. See "six-pence."

pend   frequency: 1   relative frequency: 0.00001
    p. 379 UNGATHERED 12   16 In fiue monthes he went it, in fiue monthes he
                             pend it.

penelopes   frequency: 1   relative frequency: 0.00001
    p. 224 UNDERWOOD 50   20 As makes Penelopes old fable true,

penitent   frequency: 1   relative frequency: 0.00001
    p. 172 UNDERWOOD 20   16 How penitent I am, or I should be!

penitents   frequency: 1   relative frequency: 0.00001
    p. 193 UNDERWOOD 38   86 As I the penitents here emulate:

pennance   frequency: 1   relative frequency: 0.00001
    p. 158 UNDERWOOD 14   8 A pennance, where a man may not be free,

penne   frequency: 1   relative frequency: 0.00001
    p. 380 UNGATHERED 12   32 Of his foote, or his penne, his braine or his
                             hoofe,

penned. See "ill-penn'd," "pend."

penning   frequency: 1   relative frequency: 0.00001
    p. 291 UNDERWOOD 85   45 That penning the glad flock in hurdles by,

penshvrst   frequency: 4   relative frequency: 0.00005
    p. 93 FOREST 2   1 Thou art not, PENSHVRST, built to
                             enuious show,
    p. 93 FOREST 2   t1 TO PENSHVRST.
    p. 96 FOREST 2   89 These, PENSHVRST, are thy praise, and
                             yet not all.
    p. 96 FOREST 2   99 Now, PENSHVRST, they that will
                             proportion thee

pension   frequency: 2   relative frequency: 0.00002
    p. 231 UNDERWOOD 57   12 Of a yeares Pension,
    p. 259 UNDERWOOD 76   10 Of a free Poetique Pension,

penurie   frequency: 1   relative frequency: 0.00001
    p. 152 UNDERWOOD 12   39 Nor wants it here through penurie, or sloth,

penury. See "penurie."

people   frequency: 11   relative frequency: 0.00015
  **p. 116 PANEGYRE   133 She blest the people, that in shoales did swim
  **p. 117 PANEGYRE   151 Hereat, the people could no longer hold
    p. 235 UNDERWOOD 61   18 To teach the people, how to fast, and pray,
    p. 239 UNDERWOOD 67   5 Be silent, to the people
    p. 240 UNDERWOOD 67   50 The People her doe call.
    p. 249 UNDERWOOD 72   20 What prayers (People) can you thinke too much?
    p. 268 UNDERWOOD 82   3 And by thy blessing, may thy People see
    p. 315 HORACE 2   219 Heare, what it is the People, and I desire:
    p. 317 HORACE 2   264 Her Sonnes before the people; nor the ill-
    p. 319 HORACE 2   292 So over-thick, but, where the people met,
    p. 327 HORACE 2   458 More strongly takes the people with delight,

peoples   frequency: 4   relative frequency: 0.00005
  **p. 113 PANEGYRE   31 With these he pass'd, and with his peoples hearts
  **p. 115 PANEGYRE   69 This was the peoples loue, with which did striue
    p. 49 EPIGRAMS 67   12 Proues, that is gods, which was the peoples
                             voice.
    p. 235 UNDERWOOD 62   14 But, that he cure the Peoples Evill too?

per. See "partie-per-pale."

perceiv'd   frequency: 1   relative frequency: 0.00001
    p. 171 UNDERWOOD 20   9 Knew I all this afore? had I perceiv'd,

perceive   frequency: 1   relative frequency: 0.00001
    p. 223 UNDERWOOD 49   37 The wits will leave you, if they once perceive

perched. See "pearch'd."

perfect   frequency: 16   relative frequency: 0.00023
    p. 64 EPIGRAMS 101   8 The entertaynment perfect: not the cates.
    p. 81 EPIGRAMS 128   8 And perfect in a circle alwayes meet.
    p. 104 FOREST 7   10 But grant vs perfect, they're not knowne.
    p. 110 FOREST 11   46 Pure, perfect, nay diuine;
    p. 117 FOREST 13   32 It perfect, proper, pure, and naturall,
    p. 179 UNDERWOOD 25   45 Gold, that is perfect, will out-live the fire.

perfect (cont.)
    p. 188 UNDERWOOD 35   3 What wonder perfect, all were fil'd,
    p. 244 UNDERWOOD 70 46 A perfect Patriot, and a noble friend,
    p. 245 UNDERWOOD 70 74 And in short measures, life may perfect bee.
    p. 247 UNDERWOOD 70 115 Unto the Vertue. Nothing perfect done,
    p. 278 U'WOOD 84.4   25 A Mind so pure, so perfect fine,
    p. 280 U'WOOD 84.4   55 So polisht, perfect, round, and even,
    p. 288 U'WOOD 84.9 206 For his designed worke, the perfect end
    p. 362 UNGATHERED 2   2 And see a minde attir'd in perfect straines;
    p. 397 UNGATHERED 30 24 I found it pure, and perfect Poesy,
    p. 399 UNGATHERED 31 15 In her! and what could perfect bee,

perfection   frequency: 6   relative frequency: 0.00008
    p. 112 FOREST 11   107 In the full floud of her admir'd perfection?
    p. 146 UNDERWOOD 6   12 Is that which doth perfection breed.
    p. 253 UNDERWOOD 75 28 And celebrate (perfection at the worth)
    p. 270 UNDERWOOD 83 46 Could summe to a perfection, was her Act!
    p. 286 U'WOOD 84.9 127 Hee will all Glory, all Perfection be,
    p. 325 HORACE 2   417 Have not kept in; and (lest perfection faile)

perfections   frequency: 2   relative frequency: 0.00002
    p. 169 UNDERWOOD 18   3 Did her perfections call me on to gaze,
    p. 362 UNGATHERED 2   6 Where, such perfections to the life doe rise.

perform. See "performe."

perform'd   frequency: 1   relative frequency: 0.00001
    p. 409 UNGATHERED 38 2 And you perform'd a Seruants faithfull parts:

performe   frequency: 1   relative frequency: 0.00001
    p. 277 U'WOOD 84.4   3 This worke I can performe alone;

perfum'd   frequency: 1   relative frequency: 0.00001
    p. 232 UNDERWOOD 58 14 Their perfum'd judgements, let them kisse thy
                                 Wife.

perfumed. See "perfum'd," "perfvmed."

perfumes   frequency: 2   relative frequency: 0.00002
    p. 257 UNDERWOOD 75 162 (The holy perfumes of the Mariage bed.)
    p. 288 U'WOOD 84.9 187 For, Prayer is the Incense most perfumes

perfvmed   frequency: 1   relative frequency: 0.00001
    p. 33 EPIGRAMS 19   t1 ON SIR COD THE PERFVMED.

perhaps   frequency: 7   relative frequency: 0.00010
    p. 67 EPIGRAMS 103 11 As lowdest praisers, who perhaps would find
    p. 72 EPIGRAMS 111   9 Yet thou, perhaps, shalt meet some tongues will
                                grutch,
    p. 113 FOREST 12   18 Or perhaps lesse: whil'st gold beares all this
                                 sway,
    p. 161 UNDERWOOD 14 70 That would, perhaps, have prais'd, and thank'd
                                 the same,
    p. 167 UNDERWOOD 15 149 Although, perhaps it has, what's that to me,
    p. 203 UNDERWOOD 43 18 Perhaps, to have beene burned with my bookes.
    p. 347 HORACE 1   354 ... . Pulse there .. perhaps may ....

pericles   frequency: 1   relative frequency: 0.00001
  *p. 492 TO HIMSELF   22 Like Pericles; and stale

periegesis   frequency: 1   relative frequency: 0.00001
    p. 397 UNGATHERED 30 50 In thy admired Periegesis,

peril. See "perill."

perill   frequency: 1   relative frequency: 0.00001
    p. 43 EPIGRAMS 51   7 No lesse than if from perill; and deuout,

perills   frequency: 2   relative frequency: 0.00002
    p. 37 EPIGRAMS 32   1 What two braue perills of the priuate sword
    p. 85 EPIGRAMS 133 47 The many perills of this Port, and how

perils. See "perills."

period   frequency: 1   relative frequency: 0.00001
    p. 284 U'WOOD 84.9   66 Of joy the Circle, and sole Period!

perish   frequency: 3   relative frequency: 0.00004
    See also "perishe."
    p. 205 UNDERWOOD 43 51 Thou mightst have had me perish, piece, by piece,

perish (cont.)
    p. 309 HORACE 2   99 Shall perish: so farre off it is, the state,
    p. 335 HORACE 2   664 Let Poets perish, that will not be kept.

perishe   frequency: 1   relative frequency: 0.00001
    p. 422 UNGATHERED 50   9 The mayne comaund of scepters, soone doth perishe

perjur'd   frequency: 2   relative frequency: 0.00002
    p. 167 UNDERWOOD 15 169 Boasters, and perjur'd, with the infinite more
    p. 172 UNDERWOOD 20   22 Perjur'd! and painted! if she were no more --,

perjure   frequency: 1   relative frequency: 0.00001
    p. 223 UNDERWOOD 49   30 In Contract twice, what can shee perjure more?

perjurie   frequency: 1   relative frequency: 0.00001
    p. 186 UNDERWOOD 32   11 Who, though their guilt, and perjurie they know,

perjury. See "perjurie."

permanent   frequency: 1   relative frequency: 0.00001
    p. 220 UNDERWOOD 47   64 Such as are square, wel-tagde, and permanent,

pernicious. See "pernitious."

pernitious   frequency: 1   relative frequency: 0.00001
    p. 158 UNDERWOOD 14   14 Pernitious enemie; we see, before

perpetual. See "perpetuall."

perpetuall   frequency: 2   relative frequency: 0.00002
  **p. 117 PANEGYRE   158 Saue, that shee might the same perpetuall see.
    p. 102 FOREST 5   8 'Tis, with vs, perpetuall night.

perplexed   frequency: 1   relative frequency: 0.00001
    p. 139 UNDERWOOD 2.7 17 And whilst our tongues perplexed lie,

perseus   frequency: 1   relative frequency: 0.00001
    p. 228 UNDERWOOD 53   7 You shew'd like Perseus upon Pegasus;

persian   frequency: 2   relative frequency: 0.00002
    p. 260 UNDERWOOD 77   4 Not with the Arras, but the Persian Loomes.
    p. 293 UNDERWOOD 87   4 I thought me richer then the Persian King.

person   frequency: 14   relative frequency: 0.00020
    p. 36 EPIGRAMS 30   4 And person to the world; ere I thy name.
    p. 36 EPIGRAMS 30   t1 TO PERSON GVILTIE.
    p. 38 EPIGRAMS 38   t1 TO PERSON GVILTIE.
    p. 50 EPIGRAMS 72   6 Thy person only, COVRTLING, is the vice.
    p. 71 EPIGRAMS 110   13 For, where his person liu'd scarce one iust age,
    p. 74 EPIGRAMS 115   5 Being no vitious person, but the vice
    p. 112 FOREST 11   91 But we propose a person like our Doue,
    p. 145 UNDERWOOD 5   t1 In the person of Woman-kind.
    p. 157 UNDERWOOD 13 157 That I may love your Person (as I doe)
    p. 162 UNDERWOOD 15   16 No person, nor is lov'd: what wayes he proves
    p. 168 UNDERWOOD 15 182 Thy person fit for any charge thou tak'st;
    p. 235 UNDERWOOD 62   2 Annexed to thy Person, and thy place,
    p. 270 UNDERWOOD 83   37 Else, who doth praise a person by a new,
    p. 313 HORACE 2   180 A meere new person, looke he keepe his state

persons   frequency: 5   relative frequency: 0.00007
    p. 127 UNDERWOOD 1.1   2 Of persons, still one God, in Unitie.
    p. 128 UNDERWOOD 1.1 30 Of persons, still one God in Unitie;
    p. 128 UNDERWOOD 1.1 39 Distinct in persons, yet in Unitie
    p. 404 UNGATHERED 34 54 Attyre ye Persons as noe thought can teach
    p. 413 UNGATHERED 41 35 Of Persons, yet in Vnion (ONE) divine.

perspectiue   frequency: 2   relative frequency: 0.00002
    p. 362 UNGATHERED 2   10 Vnto a cunning piece wrought perspectiue,
    p. 404 UNGATHERED 34 44 In ye mere perspectiue of an Inch board!

perspective. See "perspectiue."

persuade. See "perswade."

persuades. See "perswades."

persuading. See "perswading."

perswade   frequency: 2   relative frequency: 0.00002
    p. 162 UNDERWOOD 15   t1 An Epistle to a Friend, to perswade

perswade (cont.)
    p. 214 UNDERWOOD 44   61 But he that should perswade, to have this done

perswades   frequency: 1   relative frequency: 0.00001
    p. 82 EPIGRAMS 130   5 Declineth anger, perswades clemencie,

perswading   frequency: 1   relative frequency: 0.00001
    p. 191 UNDERWOOD 38   11 And fills my powers with perswading joy,

pertinax   frequency: 1   relative frequency: 0.00001
    p. 50 EPIGRAMS 69   t1 TO PERTINAX COB.

peruerts   frequency: 1   relative frequency: 0.00001
    p. 38 EPIGRAMS 38   5 And crie good! good! This quite peruerts my
                              sense,

perversely. See "perversly."

perversly   frequency: 1   relative frequency: 0.00001
    p. 311 HORACE 2   130 Perversly modest, had I rather owe

perverts. See "peruerts."

pest   frequency: 1   relative frequency: 0.00001
    p. 409 UNGATHERED 37   19 But fly thee, like the Pest! Walke not the
                              street

pest-house   frequency: 1   relative frequency: 0.00001
    p. 104 FOREST 8   10 Spittles, pest-house, hospitalls,

petards   frequency: 1   relative frequency: 0.00001
    p. 212 UNDERWOOD 43   206 Make your Petards, and Granats, all your fine

petasvs   frequency: 1   relative frequency: 0.00001
    p. 107 FOREST 10   24 And riffle him: or pawne his PETASVS.

petite   frequency: 1   relative frequency: 0.00001
    p. 287 U'WOOD 84.9   177 In all her petite actions, so devote,

petition   frequency: 1   relative frequency: 0.00001
    p. 259 UNDERWOOD 76   1 The humble Petition of poore Ben.

petrarch   frequency: 1   relative frequency: 0.00001
    p. 181 UNDERWOOD 27   21 Hath Petrarch since his Laura rais'd

petticoat. See "petticote."

petticoats. See "petticotes."

petticote   frequency: 3   relative frequency: 0.00004
    p. 34 EPIGRAMS 25   3 Telling the motions of each petticote,
    p. 200 UNDERWOOD 42   38 Upon a Velvet Petticote, or a Gowne,
    p. 201 UNDERWOOD 42   54 To ev'ry Petticote he brush'd, and Glove

petticotes   frequency: 1   relative frequency: 0.00001
    p. 223 UNDERWOOD 49   19 And spangled Petticotes brought forth to eye,

pettie   frequency: 1   relative frequency: 0.00001
    p. 210 UNDERWOOD 43   163 And what hast thou done in these pettie spights,

petty. See "pettie."

petulant   frequency: 3   relative frequency: 0.00004
    p. 27 EPIGRAMS 2   5 Become a petulant thing, hurle inke, and wit,
    p. 44 EPIGRAMS 54   3 What are thy petulant pleadings, CHEV-RIL,
                              then,
    p. 321 HORACE 2   340 From what th'obscene, and petulant Satyres are.

pewter   frequency: 1   relative frequency: 0.00001
    p. 88 EPIGRAMS 133   153 For, here they were throwne in wi'the melted
                              pewter,

phao<n>s   frequency: 1   relative frequency: 0.00001
    p. 181 UNDERWOOD 27   5 Of Phao<n>s forme? or doth the Boy

pheasant   frequency: 3   relative frequency: 0.00004
    p. 35 EPIGRAMS 28   12 He doth, at meales, alone, his pheasant eate,
    p. 65 EPIGRAMS 101   18 Of partrich, pheasant, wood-cock, of which some
    p. 94 FOREST 2   28 The purpled pheasant, with the speckled side:

philip   frequency: 3   relative frequency: 0.00004
    p. 73 EPIGRAMS 114   t1 TO Mrs. PHILIP SYDNEY.
    p. 168 UNDERWOOD 16   4 All that is left of PHILIP GRAY,
    p. 168 UNDERWOOD 16   t2 PHILIP GRAY.

philosophers   frequency: 1   relative frequency: 0.00001
    p. 379 UNGATHERED 12   5 And that, say Philosophers, is the best modell.

philosophy. See "shop-philosophy."

phlebotomie   frequency: 1   relative frequency: 0.00001
    p. 179 UNDERWOOD 25   39 Is but a Statists theame, to read Phlebotomie.

phlebotomy. See "phlebotomie."

phlegethon. See "phlegeton."

phlegeton   frequency: 1   relative frequency: 0.00001
    p. 84 EPIGRAMS 133   8 COCYTVS, PHLEGETON, our haue
                             prou'd in one;

phoeb<e>'s   frequency: 1   relative frequency: 0.00001
    p. 179 UNDERWOOD 25   58 (As my hope tells) that our faire Phoeb<e>'s
                             shine,

phoebeian   frequency: 1   relative frequency: 0.00001
    p. 657 L. CONVIVALES   15 Tis the true Phoebeian Liquor,

phoebe's. See "phoeb<e>'s."

phoebus   frequency: 4   relative frequency: 0.00005
    See also "phoebvs," "phoebvs-selfe."
    p. 184 UNDERWOOD 29   40 Phoebus to his Crowne againe;
    p. 221 UNDERWOOD 48   22 Then Phoebus; and much stronger
    p. 366 UNGATHERED 6   16 And Phoebus loue cause of his blackenesse is.
    p. 395 UNGATHERED 29   17 Phoebus, and Hermes? They whose tongue, or pen

phoebvs   frequency: 5   relative frequency: 0.00007
    p. 34 EPIGRAMS 23   1 DONNE, the delight of PHOEBVS, and
                             each Muse,
    p. 73 EPIGRAMS 113   1 So PHOEBVS makes me worthy of his bayes,
    p. 80 EPIGRAMS 126   2 'Mongst Hampton shades, and PHOEBVS groue
                             of bayes,
    p. 80 EPIGRAMS 126   7 PHOEBVS replyed. Bold head, it is not
                             shee:
    p. 107 FOREST 10   7 PHOEBVS. No? tend thy cart still. Enuious
                             day

phoebvs-selfe   frequency: 1   relative frequency: 0.00001
    p. 55 EPIGRAMS 84   8 And PHOEBVS-selfe should be at eating it.

phoenix   frequency: 6   relative frequency: 0.00008
    p. 112 FOREST 11   92 Grac'd with a Phoenix loue;
    p. 255 UNDERWOOD 75   81 Force from the Phoenix, then, no raritie
    p. 283 U'WOOD 84.9   19 Thou wouldst have lost the Phoenix, had the kind
    p. 364 UNGATHERED 4   t1 The Phoenix Analysde.
    p. 365 UNGATHERED 5   14 The Phoenix place of breeding,
    p. 400 UNGATHERED 31 32 Into a Phoenix, which is shee.

phrase   frequency: 7   relative frequency: 0.00010
    See also "bombard-phrase."
    p. 27 EPIGRAMS 2   11 Much lesse with lewd, prophane, and beastly
                             phrase,
    p. 85 EPIGRAMS 133   46 And with both bombard-stile, and phrase, rehearse
    p. 222 UNDERWOOD 49   14 Doth labour with the Phrase more then the sense?
    p. 309 HORACE 2   101 Much phrase that now is dead, shall be reviv'd;
    p. 311 HORACE 2   135 Complaines in humble phrase. Both Telephus,
    p. 313 HORACE 2   158 If now the phrase of him that speakes, shall
                             flow,
    p. 321 HORACE 2   342 Plaine phrase, my Piso's, as alone, t<o>'approve

phrases   frequency: 1   relative frequency: 0.00001
    p. 309 HORACE 2   88 Of words decay, and phrases borne but late

phrygian   frequency: 1   relative frequency: 0.00001
    p. 292 UNDERWOOD 86   24 And Phrygian Hau'boy, not without the Flute.

physic. See "physick."

physician   frequency: 1   relative frequency: 0.00001
     See also "physitian."
     p. 410 UNGATHERED 38   16 And the Physician teach men spue, or shite;

physick   frequency: 2   relative frequency: 0.00002
     p.   30 EPIGRAMS 12   16 Takes physick, teares the papers: still god
                               payes.
     p. 180 UNDERWOOD 26   9 Yet doth some wholsome Physick for the mind,

physitian   frequency: 1   relative frequency: 0.00001
     p.   39 EPIGRAMS 41   1 GYPSEE, new baud, is turn'd physitian,

piccadill. See "pickardill."

pick. See "picke."

pickardill   frequency: 1   relative frequency: 0.00001
     p. 164 UNDERWOOD 15   70 And then, leape mad on a neat Pickardill,

picke   frequency: 1   relative frequency: 0.00001
     p.   45 EPIGRAMS 56   5 At first he made low shifts, would picke and
                               gleane,

pickt-natch   frequency: 1   relative frequency: 0.00001
     p.   30 EPIGRAMS 12   2 That haunt Pickt-hatch, Mersh-Lambeth, and
                               White-fryers,

picture   frequency: 11   relative frequency: 0.00015
     p.   51 EPIGRAMS 73   13 Your partie-per-pale picture, one halfe drawne
     p.   56 EPIGRAMS 88   11 Or hung some MOVNSIEVRS picture on the
                               wall,
     p.   67 EPIGRAMS 104   14 A picture, which the world for yours must know,
     p.   75 EPIGRAMS 115   29 Executes men in picture. By defect,
     p. 149 UNDERWOOD 9   t1 My Picture left in Scotland.
     p. 242 UNDERWOOD 69   21 Though now of flattery, as of picture, are
     p. 260 UNDERWOOD 77   9 The old Greek-hands in picture, or in stone.
     p. 275 U'WOOD 84.3   t1 The Picture of the BODY.
     p. 278 U'WOOD 84.4   24 This is no Picture, but the same.
     p. 370 UNGATHERED 7   1 In Picture, they which truly vnderstand,
     p. 390 UNGATHERED 25   10 Not on his Picture, but his Booke.

pictures   frequency: 1   relative frequency: 0.00001
     p. 216 UNDERWOOD 44   98 I may no longer on these pictures stay,

pide   frequency: 1   relative frequency: 0.00001
     p. 362 UNGATHERED 2   4 In these pide times, only to shewe their braines,

pie   frequency: 1   relative frequency: 0.00001
     p. 231 UNDERWOOD 57   4 To Sir Robert Pie:

piece   frequency: 14   relative frequency: 0.00020
     See also "peece."
     p.   41 EPIGRAMS 45   10 BEN. IONSON his best piece of poetrie.
     p.   61 EPIGRAMS 95   7 But when I read that speciall piece, restor'd,
     p.   65 EPIGRAMS 101   21 Shall reade a piece of VIRGIL,
                               TACITVS,
     p.   79 EPIGRAMS 125   1 VV'DALE, thou piece of the first times, a
                               man
     p. 155 UNDERWOOD 13   78 Many a pound, and piece, will p<l>ace one well:
     p. 205 UNDERWOOD 43   51 Thou mightst have had me perish, piece, by piece,
     p. 216 UNDERWOOD 45   14 No piece of money, but you know, or make
     p. 227 UNDERWOOD 52   15 You made it a brave piece, but not like me.
     p. 229 UNDERWOOD 54   15 It doe not come: One piece I have in store,
     p. 242 UNDERWOOD 69   13 Till he had sold his Piece, drawne so unlike:
     p. 327 HORACE 2   466 A pound, or piece, by their long compting arts:
     p. 362 UNGATHERED 2   10 Vnto a cunning piece wrought perspectiue,
     p. 415 UNGATHERED 42   17 So soft, and smooth it handles, the whole piece,

pieces   frequency: 5   relative frequency: 0.00007
     See also "peeces."
     p. 204 UNDERWOOD 43   42 There were some pieces of as base allay,
     p. 205 UNDERWOOD 43   66 With pieces of the Legend: The whole summe
     p. 242 UNDERWOOD 69   22 More subtle workes, and finer pieces farre,
     p. 272 UNDERWOOD 84   t8 Consisting of these Ten Pieces.

pied. See "pide."

pierce   frequency: 3   relative frequency: 0.00004
     See also "peirce."
     p. 331 HORACE 2   582 Nature, or Art. My Judgement will not pierce

pierce (cont.)
    p. 404 UNGATHERED 34 46 Eyes yt can pierce into ye Misteryes
    p. 407 UNGATHERED 36   4 Able to eat into his bones & pierce

pies   frequency: 3 relative frequency: 0.00004
    p. 174 UNDERWOOD 23 12 To see their Seats and Bowers by chattring
                  Pies defac't?
    p. 205 UNDERWOOD 43 54 Condemn'd me to the Ovens with the pies;
    p. 380 UNGATHERED 12 22 Pies on't, you haue his historicall faith.

pietie   frequency: 9 relative frequency: 0.00013
    p. 31 EPIGRAMS 14   14 But for their powers, accept my pietie.
    p. 58 EPIGRAMS 91   15 Humanitie, and pietie, which are
    p. 68 EPIGRAMS 106   8 Like straight, thy pietie to God, and friends:
    p. 82 EPIGRAMS 130   6 Doth sweeten mirth, and heighten pietie,
    p. 151 UNDERWOOD 12   1 I have my Pietie too, which could
    p. 235 UNDERWOOD 62   3 'T is not enough (thy pietie is such)
    p. 235 UNDERWOOD 62 11 O pietie! so to weigh the poores estates!
    p. 270 UNDERWOOD 83 42 And pietie the Center, where all met.
    p. 287 U'WOOD 84.9 179 Of Pietie, and private holinesse.

piety   frequency: 1 relative frequency: 0.00001
  See also "pietie."
    p. 401 UNGATHERED 32 20 Defies, what's crosse to Piety, or good Fame.

pigges   frequency: 1 relative frequency: 0.00001
    p. 205 UNDERWOOD 43 53 Sindge Capons, or poore Pigges, dropping their
                  eyes;

pigs. See "pigges."

pikes   frequency: 1 relative frequency: 0.00001
    p. 94 FOREST 2   34 And pikes, now weary their owne kinde to eat,

pile   frequency: 2 relative frequency: 0.00002
    p. 93 FOREST 2   5 Or stayre, or courts; but stand'st an ancient
                  pile,
    p. 225 UNDERWOOD 51   1 Haile, happie Genius of this antient pile!

piles   frequency: 2 relative frequency: 0.00002
    p. 209 UNDERWOOD 43 137 See the worlds Ruines! nothing but the piles
    p. 261 UNDERWOOD 77 26 In glorious Piles, or Pyramids erect

pillar   frequency: 2 relative frequency: 0.00002
    p. 176 UNDERWOOD 24 15 Some note of which each varied Pillar beares,
    p. 185 UNDERWOOD 30   7 The Orphans Pillar, the true Subjects shield,

pillars   frequency: 3 relative frequency: 0.00004
    p. 93 FOREST 2   3 Of polish'd pillars, or a roofe of gold:
    p. 331 HORACE 2 555 But neither, Men, nor Gods, nor Pillars meant,
    p. 407 UNGATHERED 35 14 From ye fam'd pillars of old Hercules!

pill'd   frequency: 1 relative frequency: 0.00001
    p. 43 EPIGRAMS 53   2 When hauing pill'd a booke, which no man buyes,

pillory   frequency: 1 relative frequency: 0.00001
    p. 410 UNGATHERED 39   4 Pillory nor Whip, nor want of Ears,

pillow   frequency: 1 relative frequency: 0.00001
    p. 283 U'WOOD 84.9 43 From off her pillow, and deluded bed;

pills   frequency: 1 relative frequency: 0.00001
    p. 80 EPIGRAMS 133 101 His spirits, now, in pills, and eeke in potions,

pilot   frequency: 1 relative frequency: 0.00001
    p. 410 UNGATHERED 38 18 Hee'll be a Pilot, scarce can guide a Plough.

pimblicoe   frequency: 1 relative frequency: 0.00001
    p. 213 UNDERWOOD 44 21 What a strong Fort old Pimblicoe had bin!

pimlico. See "pimblicoe."

pin   frequency: 1 relative frequency: 0.00001
  See also "pinn."
    p. 200 UNDERWOOD 42 16 There is not worne that lace, purle, knot or pin,

pin'd   frequency: 1 relative frequency: 0.00001
    p. 103 FOREST 6   22 What their number is, be pin'd.

pindar   frequency: 1   relative frequency: 0.00001
     p. 366 UNGATHERED 6   20 Where Pindar swamme;

pindares   frequency: 1   relative frequency: 0.00001
     *p. 493 TO HIMSELF   44 Warme thee, by Pindares fire:

pindars   frequency: 1   relative frequency: 0.00001
     See also "pindares."
     p. 176 UNDERWOOD 25   3 Wake, and put on the wings of Pindars Muse,

pinn   frequency: 1   relative frequency: 0.00001
     p. 395 UNGATHERED 29   5 At euery line some pinn thereof should slacke

pioneers. See "picners."

pioners   frequency: 1   relative frequency: 0.00001
     p. 400 UNGATHERED 32   5 Such, as the creeping common Pioners vse

pious   frequency: 4   relative frequency: 0.00005
     p. 35 EPIGRAMS 27   6 It any pious life ere lifted man
     p. 236 UNDERWOOD 64   2 Most pious King, but his owne good in you!
     p. 268 UNDERWOOD 82   7 To pious parents, who would have their blood
     p. 288 U'WOOD 84.9   191 In frequent speaking by the pious Psalmes

pipe   frequency: 1   relative frequency: 0.00001
     p. 397 UNGATHERED 30   28 Or Rurall Virgil come, to pipe to vs!

piper   frequency: 1   relative frequency: 0.00001
     p. 319 HORACE 2   303 Thus, to his antient Art the Piper lent

pipkins   frequency: 1   relative frequency: 0.00001
     p. 402 UNGATHERED 34   2 From thirty pound in pipkins, to ye Man

pirates. See "pyrats."

pirene. See "pyrene."

piso   frequency: 1   relative frequency: 0.00001
     p. 333 HORACE 2   607 But you, my Piso, carefully beware,

piso's   frequency: 3   relative frequency: 0.00004
     p. 305 HORACE 2   8 This peece, my Piso's, and that booke agree,
     p. 321 HORACE 2   342 Plaine phrase, my Piso's, as alone, t<o>'approve
     p. 338 HORACE 1   t4 PISO'S.

piss. See "pisse."

piss'd   frequency: 1   relative frequency: 0.00001
     p. 335 HORACE 2   671 Whether he piss'd upon his Fathers grave;

pisse   frequency: 2   relative frequency: 0.00002
     p. 59 EPIGRAMS 92   28 With iuyce of limons, onions, pisse, to write,
     p. 211 UNDERWOOD 43   186 Vile Tavernes, and the Drunkards pisse him out;

pistle   frequency: 1   relative frequency: 0.00001
     p. 380 UNGATHERED 12   43 Yes. And thanks God in his Pistle or his
                               Booke

pit   frequency: 3   relative frequency: 0.00004
     p. 222 UNDERWOOD 49   3 What though her Chamber be the very pit
     p. 278 U'WOOD 84.4   11 The Sunne, a Sea, or soundlesse Pit;
     p. 335 HORACE 2   652 Into a pit, or hole; although he call,

pit-falls   frequency: 1   relative frequency: 0.00001
     p. 290 UNDERWOOD 85   34 For th'eating Thrush, or Pit-falls sets:

pit-pat-noyse   frequency: 1   relative frequency: 0.00001
     p. 259 UNDERWOOD 76   19 And the ratling pit-pat-noyse,

pitch   frequency: 1   relative frequency: 0.00001
     p. 407 UNGATHERED 35   23 Or canst of truth ye least intrenchmt pitch,

pitch'd   frequency: 1   relative frequency: 0.00001
     p. 290 UNDERWOOD 85   32 Wild Bores into his toyles pitch'd round:

pitcher   frequency: 2   relative frequency: 0.00002
     p. 219 UNDERWOOD 47   56 Well, with mine owne fraile Pitcher, what to doe
     p. 307 HORACE 2   30 Thy labouring wheele, comes scarce a Pitcher
                               out?

piteous. See "pitious," "pittious."

pitfall   frequency: 1   relative frequency: 0.00001
    p. 164 UNDERWOOD 15   66 And every Dressing for a Pitfall set

pitfalls. See "pit-falls."

pitied. See "pittied."

pitious   frequency: 1   relative frequency: 0.00001
    p. 175 UNDERWOOD 23   24 And only pitious scorne, upon their folly waites.

pittes   frequency: 1   relative frequency: 0.00001
    p. 164 UNDERWOOD 15   80 Where Pittes, or Wright, or Modet would not
                              venter,

pittie   frequency: 4   relative frequency: 0.00005
    p. 44 EPIGRAMS 56   4 As we, the rob'd, leaue rage, and pittie it.
    p. 133 UNDERWOOD 2.3   20 But the Pittie comes too late.
    p. 150 UNDERWOOD 11   1 Or Scorne, or pittie on me take,
    p. 191 UNDERWOOD 38   20 The ignorant, and fooles, no pittie have.

pittied   frequency: 1   relative frequency: 0.00001
    p. 147 UNDERWOOD 7   11 And of them pittied be,

pittious   frequency: 1   relative frequency: 0.00001
    p. 88 EPIGRAMS 133   164 And, in a pittious tune, began. How dare

pitts. See "pittes."

pitty   frequency: 4   relative frequency: 0.00005
    p. 73 EPIGRAMS 112   17 Troth, if it be, I pitty thy ill lucke;
    p. 84 EPIGRAMS 133   22 And pitty 'tis, I cannot call 'hem knights:
    p. 405 UNGATHERED 34   71 To pitty him, as smiling at his ffeat
    p. 408 UNGATHERED 37   7 But bawle thou on; I pitty thee, poore Curre,

pity. See "pittie," "pitty."

pixe   frequency: 1   relative frequency: 0.00001
    p. 415 UNGATHERED 42   25 For order, and for governing the pixe,

pize. See "pies."

plac'd   frequency: 5   relative frequency: 0.00007
  **p. 115 PANEGYRE   79 "That they, by Heauen, are plac'd vpon his
                              throne,
    p. 34 EPIGRAMS 22   9 Hath plac'd amongst her virgin-traine:
    p. 114 FOREST 12   25 Were yet vnfound, and better plac'd in earth,
    p. 136 UNDERWOOD 2.5   25 Have you plac'd the banke of kisses,
    p. 284 U'WOOD 84.9   54 Of Body and Spirit together, plac'd betwixt

place   frequency: 48   relative frequency: 0.00069
    See also "p<l>ace."
  **p. 114 PANEGYRE   56 Her place, and yeares, gaue her precedencie.
  **p. 115 PANEGYRE   89 "She then remembred to his thought the place
    p. 35 EPIGRAMS 27   1 In place of scutcheons, that should decke thy
                              herse,
    p. 43 EPIGRAMS 53   4 But when (in place) thou didst the patrons
                              choose,
    p. 45 EPIGRAMS 58   4 Thy ignorance still laughs in the wrong place.
    p. 47 EPIGRAMS 64   2 With thy new place, bring I these early fruits
    p. 49 EPIGRAMS 67   6 High in thy bloud, thy place, but highest then,
    p. 57 EPIGRAMS 90   14 Blowne vp; and he (too'vnwieldie for that place)
    p. 63 EPIGRAMS 97   11 Nor office in the towne, nor place in court,
    p. 64 EPIGRAMS 99   9 From place, or fortune, are made high, or low,
    p. 67 EPIGRAMS 105   3 That we had left vs, nor by time, nor place,
    p. 73 EPIGRAMS 113   10 Could make such men, and such a place repent:
    p. 86 EPIGRAMS 133   89 How hight the place? a voyce was heard,
                              COCYTVS.
    p. 87 EPIGRAMS 133   131 Airising in that place, through which, who goes,
    p. 88 EPIGRAMS 133   144 That, with still-scalding steemes, make the place
                              hell.
    p. 99 FOREST 3   87 Get place, and honor, and be glad to keepe
    p. 111 FOREST 11   80 And for their place, and name,
    p. 115 FOREST 12   80 Shall thronging come, and boast the happy place
    p. 161 UNDERWOOD 14   85 But here's no time, nor place, my wealth to tell,
    p. 166 UNDERWOOD 15   123 Our vices doe not tarry in a place,
    p. 171 UNDERWOOD 19   27 As in his place, because he would not varie,
    p. 192 UNDERWOOD 38   51 You may so place me, and in such an ayre,
    p. 202 UNDERWOOD 42   80 And all the originall riots of the place:
    p. 209 UNDERWOOD 43   152 The place, that was thy Wives inheritance.
    p. 223 UNDERWOOD 49   23 I never stood for any place: my wit

place (cont.)
    p. 223 UNDERWOOD 49   43 Or if it would, the Court is the worst place,
    p. 227 UNDERWOOD 52   23 A letter'd mind, and a large heart would place
    p. 235 UNDERWOOD 62   2 Annexed to thy Person, and thy place,
    p. 256 UNDERWOOD 75   129 O happy bands! and thou more happy place,
    p. 264 UNDERWOOD 79   34 And were shee lost, could best supply her place,
    p. 283 U'WOOD 84.9   38 The glorie, and gaine of rest, which the place
                              gives!
    p. 284 U'WOOD 84.9   83 And give her place, according to her blood,
    p. 285 U'WOOD 84.9   116 By beatifick vertue of the Place.
    p. 288 U'WOOD 84.9   197 To that eternall Rest, where now sh'hath place
    p. 290 UNDERWOOD 85   12 And sets more happy in the place:
    p. 292 UNDERWOOD 86   18 With thee 'bove all his Rivals gifts take place,
    p. 305 HORACE 2   24 No place for these. And, Painter, hap'ly, thou
    p. 307 HORACE 2   60 Or I am much deceiv'd, shall be to place
    p. 311 HORACE 2   125 The place allotted it, with decent thewes.
    p. 321 HORACE 2   354 There comes sometimes to things of meanest place.
    p. 323 HORACE 2   380 Of fellowship, the fourth, or second place.
    p. 347 HORACE 1   349 .... Town-born ... ... place ....
    p. 365 UNGATHERED 5   14 The Phoenix place of breeding,
    p. 369 UNGATHERED 6   95 And (in the place) enuie
    p. 369 UNGATHERED 6   104 Or thought they, Leda's white Adult'rers place
    p. 380 UNGATHERED 12   25 He went out at each place, and at what he came
                              in,
    p. 385 UNGATHERED 19   2 What place is for my testimony void?
    p. 402 UNGATHERED 34   18 Will any of these express yor place? or witt?

placed   frequency: 2   relative frequency: 0.00002
See also "plac'd," "plac't."
    p. 115 FOREST 12   59 Who placed IASONS ARGO in the skie?
    p. 128 UNDERWOOD 1.1 46 And with thy Angels, placed side, by side,

places   frequency: 8   relative frequency: 0.00011
    p. 59 EPIGRAMS 92   8 They know the states of Christendome, not the
                              places:
    p. 61 EPIGRAMS 95   28 Of historie, and how to apt their places;
    p. 116 FOREST 12   88 Or common places, filch'd, that take these times,
    p. 179 UNDERWOOD 25   59 Shall light those places
    p. 212 UNDERWOOD 43 212 That have good places: therefore once agen,
    p. 221 UNDERWOOD 48   34 Pursue thee in all places,
    p. 327 HORACE 2   457 With specious places, and being humour'd right,
    p. 349 HORACE 1   424 In secret places, flee ... .

placing   frequency: 1   relative frequency: 0.00001
    p. 307 HORACE 2   68 Are, by thy cunning placing, made meere new.

plac't   frequency: 1   relative frequency: 0.00001
    p. 401 UNGATHERED 32 14 A Trench against it, nor a Battry plac't?

plagiary   frequency: 1   relative frequency: 0.00001
    p. 54 EPIGRAMS 81   t1 TO PROVLE THE PLAGIARY.

plague   frequency: 3   relative frequency: 0.00004
    p. 86 EPIGRAMS 133   72 The least of which was to the plague a cosen.
    p. 147 UNDERWOOD 7   12 It were a plague 'bove scorne,
    p. 172 UNDERWOOD 21   3 Two letters were enough the plague to teare

plague-bill   frequency: 1   relative frequency: 0.00001
    p. 88 EPIGRAMS 133 173 Cannot the Plague-bill keepe you backe? nor
                              bells

plague-sores   frequency: 1   relative frequency: 0.00001
    p. 84 EPIGRAMS 133   17 Laden with plague-sores, and their sinnes, were
                              heard,

plagues   frequency: 1   relative frequency: 0.00001
    p. 212 UNDERWOOD 43 215 Light on thee: Or if those plagues will not doo,

plaid   frequency: 4   relative frequency: 0.00005
    p. 107 FOREST 10   15 Who, with his axe, thy fathers mid-wife plaid.
    p. 132 UNDERWOOD 2.2 31 Or else one that plaid his Ape,
    p. 234 UNDERWOOD 61   2 And all the games of Fortune, plaid at Court;
    p. 317 HORACE 2   271 Once seene, to be againe call'd for, and plaid,

plai'd   frequency: 1   relative frequency: 0.00001
    p. 77 EPIGRAMS 120   16 He plai'd so truely.

plaies   frequency: 1   relative frequency: 0.00001
    p. 293 UNDERWOOD 87   10 Who sings so sweet, and with such cunning plaies,

plain. See "plaine."

plaine   frequency: 3   relative frequency: 0.00004
  p.   67 EPIGRAMS 103   13 My praise is plaine, and where so ere profest,
  p. 321 HORACE 2   342 Plaine phrase, my Piso's, as alone, t<o>'approve
  p. 374 UNGATHERED 10   16 Here, vp the Alpes (not so plaine as to
                              Dunstable)

plaines   frequency: 2   relative frequency: 0.00002
  p. 263 UNDERWOOD 79   12 And offer your just service on these plaines;
  p. 265 UNDERWOOD 79   47 That have a Flock, or Herd, upon these plaines;

plains. See "plaines."

plaisters   frequency: 1   relative frequency: 0.00001
  p.   88 EPIGRAMS 133   170 Vrine, and plaisters? when the noise doth beate

planets   frequency: 1   relative frequency: 0.00001
  p.   82 EPIGRAMS 130   12 That the eight spheare, no lesse, then planets
                              seauen,

plant   frequency: 6   relative frequency: 0.00008
  p. 109 FOREST 11   7 Some way of entrance) we must plant a guard
  p. 170 UNDERWOOD 19   10 Where men at once may plant, and gather blisses:
  p. 245 UNDERWOOD 70   72 It was the Plant, and flowre of light.
  p. 245 UNDERWOOD 70   77 Accept this garland, plant it on thy head,
  p. 251 UNDERWOOD 74   11 And ev'ry Plant the sense surprize,
  p. 404 UNGATHERED 34   53 To plant ye Musick where noe eare can reach!

planted   frequency: 4   relative frequency: 0.00005
  p. 101 FOREST 4   45 Then, in a soile hast planted me,
  p. 279 U'WOOD 84.4   36 As what it spoke, it planted there.
  p. 281 U'WOOD 84.8   19 By which yo'are planted, shew's your fruit shall
                              bide.
  p. 285 U'WOOD 84.9   89 That, planted round, there sing before the Lamb,

planting   frequency: 1   relative frequency: 0.00001
  p. 164 UNDERWOOD 15   65 Planting their Purles, and Curles spread forth
                              like Net,

plants   frequency: 2   relative frequency: 0.00002
  p. 251 UNDERWOOD 74   10 Rare Plants from ev'ry banke doe rise,
  p. 361 UNGATHERED 1   6 that mongst so manie plants transplanted hether,

plasters. See "plaisters."

plat   frequency: 1   relative frequency: 0.00001
  p. 188 UNDERWOOD 34   7 Art, her false servant; Nor, for Sir Hugh
                              Plat,

plate   frequency: 3   relative frequency: 0.00004
  See also "crowne-plate."
  p.   96 FOREST 2   86 To haue her linnen, plate, and all things nigh,
  p.   99 FOREST 3   89 And, so they ride in purple, eate in plate,
  p. 260 UNDERWOOD 77   2 I would present you now with curious plate

platt. See "plat."

plautus   frequency: 3   relative frequency: 0.00004
  p. 309 HORACE 2   78 Or Plautus, and in Virgil disauow,
  p. 323 HORACE 2   399 Our Ancestors did Plautus numbers praise,
  p. 392 UNGATHERED 26   52 Neat Terence, witty Plautus, now not please;

play   frequency: 23   relative frequency: 0.00033
  See also "play's."
  *p. 492 TO HIMSELF   6 Something they call a Play.
  *p. 492 TO HIMSELF   t3 Play, by some malicious spectators,
  p.   52 EPIGRAMS 75   4 T<o>'inueigh 'gainst playes: what did he then but
                              play?
  p.   56 EPIGRAMS 87   1 Touch'd with the sinne of false play, in his
                              punque,
  p.   57 EPIGRAMS 90   8 Discern'd no difference of his yeeres, or play,
  p.   64 EPIGRAMS 100   4 Fiue of my iests, then stolne, past him a play.
  p.   72 EPIGRAMS 112   8 Tragick, or Comick; but thou writ'st the Play.
  p.   74 EPIGRAMS 115   25 And, shifting of it's faces, doth play more
  p. 105 FOREST 8   42 Play away, health, wealth, and fame.
  p. 145 UNDERWOOD 5   1 Men, if you love us, play no more
  p. 166 UNDERWOOD 15   132 Is not enough now, but the Nights to play:
  p. 204 UNDERWOOD 43   43 And as false stampe there; parcels of a Play,
  p. 229 UNDERWOOD 54   8 Is, she will play Dame Justice, too severe;
  p. 230 UNDERWOOD 56   2 When you would play so nobly, and so free.
  p. 240 UNDERWOOD 67   46 The Revells, and the Play,

play (cont.)
```
     p. 253 UNDERWOOD 75    33 Harke how the Bells upon the waters play
     p. 315 HORACE 2        226 And can tread firme, longs with like lads to
                                play;
     p. 329 HORACE 2        531 Deserves no pardon; or who'd play, and sing
     p. 347 HORACE 1        350 Or play young ...... .. ............ .....
     p. 371 UNGATHERED 8      8 They saw it halfe, damd thy whole play, and more;
     p. 405 UNGATHERED 34    76 In presentacon of some puppet play!
     p. 414 UNGATHERED 42     2 Unto the world, in praise of your first Play:
     p. 415 UNGATHERED 42    14 And weigh'd your Play: untwisted ev'ry thread,
```

play-club   frequency: 1   relative frequency: 0.00001
```
    *p. 493 TO HIMSELF        26 May keepe vp the Play-club:
```

play-wright   frequency: 7   relative frequency: 0.00010
```
     p.  42 EPIGRAMS 49        1 PLAY-WRIGHT me reades, and still my
                                 verses damnes,
     p.  42 EPIGRAMS 49        5 PLAY-WRIGHT, I loath to haue thy
                                 manners knowne
     p.  42 EPIGRAMS 49       t1 TO PLAY-WRIGHT.
     p.  49 EPIGRAMS 68        1 PLAY-WRIGHT conuict of publike wrongs to
                                 men,
     p.  49 EPIGRAMS 68       t1 ON PLAY-WRIGHT.
     p.  64 EPIGRAMS 100       1 PLAY-WRIGHT, by chance, hearing some
                                 toyes I'had writ,
     p.  64 EPIGRAMS 100      t1 ON PLAY-WRIGHT.
```

play'd   frequency: 1   relative frequency: 0.00001
See also "plaid," "plai'd."
```
     p. 201 UNDERWOOD 42      61 From the poore wretch, which though he play'd in
                                 prose,
```

player   frequency: 1   relative frequency: 0.00001
```
     p.  81 EPIGRAMS 129      11 Whil'st thou dost rayse some Player, from the
                                 graue,
```

players   frequency: 2   relative frequency: 0.00002
```
     p.  52 EPIGRAMS 75        2 'Twixt puritanes, and players, as some cry;
     p.  62 EPIGRAMS 96       10 Let pui'nees, porters, players praise delight,
```

playes   frequency: 12   relative frequency: 0.00017
```
     p.  30 EPIGRAMS 12       11 He steales to ordinaries; there he playes
     p.  30 EPIGRAMS 12       17 Or else by water goes, and so to playes;
     p.  45 EPIGRAMS 56        6 Buy the reuersion of old playes; now growne
     p.  52 EPIGRAMS 75        4 T<o>'inueigh 'gainst playes: what did he then but
                                 play?
     p. 215 UNDERWOOD 44      91 All that they doe at Playes. O, but first here
     p. 222 UNDERWOOD 49      16 To Church, as others doe to Feasts and Playes,
     p. 258 UNDERWOOD 75     176 How each one playes his part, of the large
                                 Pedigree.
     p. 319 HORACE 2         297 And they uncensur'd might at Feasts, and Playes
     p. 329 HORACE 2         499 Playes were found out; and rest, the end, and
                                 crowne
     p. 370 UNGATHERED 8       2 Vpon the Life, and Death of Playes, and Wits,
     p. 410 UNGATHERED 38     12 Both learned, and vnlearned, all write Playes.
     p. 414 UNGATHERED 42      8 That sit to censure Playes, yet know not when,
```

playing   frequency: 2   relative frequency: 0.00002
```
     p. 149 UNDERWOOD 8        7 And in his Mrs. flame, playing like a flye,
     p. 249 UNDERWOOD 72       8 Like Eccho playing from the other shore.
```

plays. See "plaies," "playes."

play's   frequency: 1   relative frequency: 0.00001
```
     p.  56 EPIGRAMS 87        6 Since when, hee's sober againe, and all play's
                                 made.
```

play'st   frequency: 1   relative frequency: 0.00001
```
     p.  72 EPIGRAMS 112       2 At this so subtile sport: and play'st so ill?
```

playwright. See "play-wright."

plea   frequency: 1   relative frequency: 0.00001
```
     p. 288 U'WOOD 84.9      209 All this by Faith she saw, and fram'd a Plea,
```

plead   frequency: 1   relative frequency: 0.00001
```
     p.  36 EPIGRAMS 29        2 And thou, right guiltlesse, may'st plead to it,
                                 why?
```

pleaded   frequency: 1   relative frequency: 0.00001
    p. 186 UNDERWOOD 33   t2 pleaded, and carried the Cause.

pleader   frequency: 1   relative frequency: 0.00001
    p. 331 HORACE 2   551 Or Pleader at the Barre, that may come short

pleaders   frequency: 1   relative frequency: 0.00001
    p. 187 UNDERWOOD 33   10 Upon the reverend Pleaders; doe now shut

pleadings   frequency: 1   relative frequency: 0.00001
    p. 44 EPIGRAMS 54   3 What are thy petulant pleadings, CHEV-RIL,
                             then,

pleasant   frequency: 2   relative frequency: 0.00002
    p. 295 UNDERWOOD 90   2 Most pleasant Martial; Substance got with ease,
    p. 305 HORACE 2   22 The pleasant grounds, or when the River Rhine,

pleas'd   frequency: 9   relative frequency: 0.00013
    p. 145 UNDERWOOD 5   17 And having pleas'd our art, wee'll try
    p. 206 UNDERWOOD 43   83 These, had'st thou pleas'd either to dine, or
                             sup,
    p. 208 UNDERWOOD 43 131 (Which, some are pleas'd to stile but thy madde
                             pranck)
    p. 251 UNDERWOOD 74   25 O how will then our Court be pleas'd,
    p. 258 UNDERWOOD 75 188 Exacts then she is pleas'd to pay: no suits,
    p. 259 UNDERWOOD 76   6 JAMES the blessed, pleas'd the rather,
    p. 294 UNDERWOOD 88   9 This hath pleas'd, doth please, and long will
                             please; never
    p. 315 HORACE 2   227 Soone angry, and soone pleas'd, is sweet, or
                             sowre,
    p. 366 UNGATHERED 6   12 Whil'st pleas'd Apollo

please   frequency: 15   relative frequency: 0.00021
    p. 37 EPIGRAMS 32   9 Which shewes, where euer death doth please
                             t<o>'appeare,
    p. 105 FOREST 8   21 What should, yet, thy pallat please?
    p. 119 FOREST 13   116 But to please him, who is the dearer prise
    p. 133 UNDERWOOD 2.3   2 Which the prouder Beauties please,
    p. 140 UNDERWOOD 2.9   2 I will tell what Man would please me.
    p. 142 U'WOOD 2.10   7 What you please, you parts may call,
    p. 150 UNDERWOOD 10   15 Seeke doubting Men to please,
    p. 260 UNDERWOOD 76   25 Please your Majestie to make
    p. 294 UNDERWOOD 88   9 This hath pleas'd, doth please, and long will
                             please; never
    p. 309 HORACE 2   103 If Custome please; at whose disposing will
    p. 331 HORACE 2   544 Doth please; this, ten times over, will delight.
    p. 392 UNGATHERED 26 52 Neat Terence, witty Plautus, now not please;
    p. 401 UNGATHERED 33   2 That, while they bind the senses, doe so please?
    p. 415 UNGATHERED 42 10 And newer, then could please them, by-cause trew.

pleased   frequency: 1   relative frequency: 0.00001
    See also "pleas'd."
    p. 417 UNGATHERED 45 36 and she is pleased.

pleases   frequency: 1   relative frequency: 0.00001
    p. 657 L. CONVIVALES 18 And at once, three Senses pleases.

pleaseth   frequency: 1   relative frequency: 0.00001
    p. 38 EPIGRAMS 37   3 And pleaseth both. For while he melts his greace

pleasure   frequency: 13   relative frequency: 0.00018
    p. 60 EPIGRAMS 94   9 For none ere tooke that pleasure in sinnes sense,
    p. 105 FOREST 8   36 That, to make all pleasure theirs,
    p. 144 UNDERWOOD 3   19 And out of inward pleasure feed
    p. 145 UNDERWOOD 5   15 More pleasure while the thing he makes
    p. 146 UNDERWOOD 6   21 Our pleasure; but preserves us more
    p. 147 UNDERWOOD 7   6 The pleasure is as good as none,
    p. 240 UNDERWOOD 67   44 Her joy in state, and pleasure;
    p. 250 UNDERWOOD 74   1 Such pleasure as the teeming Earth
    p. 271 UNDERWOOD 83   82 At pleasure, to be call'd for, every day!
    p. 294 UNDERWOOD 88   1 Doing, a filthy pleasure is, and short;
    p. 329 HORACE 2   512 Cast out by voyces; want they pleasure, then
    p. 350 HORACE 1   483 ... . pleasure ....
    p. 363 UNGATHERED 3   1 Those that in blood such violent pleasure haue,

pleasures   frequency: 8   relative frequency: 0.00011
    p. 34 EPIGRAMS 25   2 In the past pleasures of his sensuall life,
    p. 55 EPIGRAMS 85   11 Now, in whose pleasures I haue this discerned,
    p. 163 UNDERWOOD 15   41 That kept man living! Pleasures only sought!
    p. 202 UNDERWOOD 42   86 None of their pleasures! nor will aske thee, why

pleasures (cont.)
    p. 224 UNDERWOOD 50   10 Are growne so fruitfull, and false pleasures
                            climbe,
    p. 246 UNDERWOOD 70 102 No pleasures vaine did chime,
    p. 329 HORACE 2   507 Let what thou fain'st for pleasures sake, be
                            neere
    p. 411 UNGATHERED 40 11 And the deceipt of pleasures,

pledge   frequency: 1   relative frequency: 0.00001
    p. 106 FOREST 9   2 And I will pledge with mine;

pledges   frequency: 1   relative frequency: 0.00001
    See also "mariage-pledges."
    p. 119 FOREST 13   96 To pay your lord the pledges of chast loue:

plenteous   frequency: 2   relative frequency: 0.00002
    p. 165 UNDERWOOD 15 100 Ne're came to taste the plenteous Mariage-horne.
    p. 254 UNDERWOOD 75 65 With what full hands, and in how plenteous
                            showers

plentie   frequency: 2   relative frequency: 0.00002
    p. 95 FOREST 2   70 He knowes, below, he shall finde plentie of
                            meate,
    p. 265 UNDERWOOD 79 56 Hee gives all plentie, and encrease,

plenty. See "plentie."

plie   frequency: 2   relative frequency: 0.00002
    p. 333 HORACE 2   617 Rich men are said with many cups to plie,
    p. 368 UNGATHERED 6   64 Now must we plie our ayme; our Swan's on wing.

plight   frequency: 2   relative frequency: 0.00002
    p. 127 UNDERWOOD 1.1 14 And take compassion on my grievous plight.
    p. 311 HORACE 2   142 To worke the hearers minds, still, to their
                            plight.

plights   frequency: 1   relative frequency: 0.00001
    p. 256 UNDERWOOD 75 124 Askes first, Who gives her (I Charles) then he
                            plights

plot. See "poulder-plot," "seed-plot."

plough   frequency: 2   relative frequency: 0.00002
    p. 309 HORACE 2   95 In neighbour-townes, and feeles the weightie
                            plough;
    p. 410 UNGATHERED 38 18 Hee'll be a Pilot, scarce can guide a Plough.

plough'd   frequency: 1   relative frequency: 0.00001
    p. 89 EPIGRAMS 133 196 My Muse had plough'd with his, that sung
                            A-IAX.

ploughing   frequency: 1   relative frequency: 0.00001
    p. 86 EPIGRAMS 133 78 Ploughing the mayne. When, see (the worst of all
                            lucks)

plover   frequency: 1   relative frequency: 0.00001
    p. 231 UNDERWOOD 57 22 No Plover, or Coney

pluck   frequency: 1   relative frequency: 0.00001
    See also "plucke."
    p. 268 UNDERWOOD 83   4 To pluck a Garland, for her selfe, or mee?

pluck'd   frequency: 1   relative frequency: 0.00001
    p. 80 EPIGRAMS 126   3 I pluck'd a branch; the iealous god did frowne,

plucke   frequency: 2   relative frequency: 0.00002
    p. 50 EPIGRAMS 71   1 To plucke downe mine, POLL sets vp new wits
                            still,
    p. 73 EPIGRAMS 112 18 That both for wit, and sense, so oft dost plucke,

plucking   frequency: 1   relative frequency: 0.00001
    p. 290 UNDERWOOD 85 19 How plucking Peares, his owne hand grafted had,

plum   frequency: 2   relative frequency: 0.00002
    p. 94 FOREST 2   41 The earely cherry, with the later plum,
    p. 95 FOREST 2   56 An embleme of themselues, in plum, or peare.

plumed   frequency: 1   relative frequency: 0.00001
    p. 68 EPIGRAMS 105 16 That saw you put on PALLAS plumed caske:

plumes   frequency: 2   relative frequency: 0.00002
     p. 338 HORACE 1   2 . horse neck joyn . sundry plumes ore-fold
     p. 368 UNGATHERED 6   76 There coole thy Plumes,

plush   frequency: 2   relative frequency: 0.00002
    *p. 493 TO HIMSELF   32 Braue plush, and veluet-men;
     p. 164 UNDERWOOD 15   58 With Velvet, Plush, and Tissues, it is spirit.

plushes   frequency: 1   relative frequency: 0.00001
     p. 202 UNDERWOOD 42   79 The Stuffes, the Velvets, Plushes, Fringes,
                                 Lace,

pluto. See "plvto."

pluto's. See "plvto's."

plvto   frequency: 1   relative frequency: 0.00001
     p. 89 EPIGRAMS 133   179 Tempt not his furie, PLVTO is away:

plvto's   frequency: 1   relative frequency: 0.00001
     p. 89 EPIGRAMS 133   175 But you will visit grisly PLVTO'S hall?

ply   frequency: 3   relative frequency: 0.00004
   See also "plie."
     p. 103 FOREST 6   18 When youths ply their stolne delights.
     p. 107 FOREST 10   19 Let the old boy, your sonne, ply his old taske,
     p. 657 L. CONVIVALES   14 Ply it, and you all are mounted;

po   frequency: 1   relative frequency: 0.00001
     p. 369 UNGATHERED 6   114 At their returne, nor Po,

pocket   frequency: 1   relative frequency: 0.00001
     p. 229 UNDERWOOD 54   14 Stinketh my credit, if into the Pocket

pockets   frequency: 1   relative frequency: 0.00001
     p. 59 EPIGRAMS 92   15 They carry in their pockets TACITVS,

pockie   frequency: 1   relative frequency: 0.00001
     p. 31 EPIGRAMS 12   24 Lent him a pockie whore. Shee hath paid him.

pocky. See "pockie."

pod   frequency: 2   relative frequency: 0.00002
     p. 62 EPIGRAMS 97   2 Nor Captayne POD, nor yet the Eltham-thing;
     p. 81 EPIGRAMS 129   16 Thou dost out-zany COKELY, POD; nay,
                                 GVE:

poem. See "poeme."

poeme   frequency: 5   relative frequency: 0.00007
     p. 72 EPIGRAMS 112   10 An Epick poeme; thou hast the same end.
     p. 327 HORACE 2   456 A Poeme, of no grace, weight, art, in rimes,
     p. 329 HORACE 2   526 Much in the Poeme shine, I will not bee
     p. 331 HORACE 2   561 So, any Poeme, fancied, or forth-brought
     p. 371 UNGATHERED 8   14 Do crowne thy murdred Poeme: which shall rise

poemes   frequency: 6   relative frequency: 0.00008
     p. 32 EPIGRAMS 17   3 That wish my poemes a legitimate fame,
     p. 60 EPIGRAMS 94   4 Whose poemes would not wish to be your booke?
     p. 60 EPIGRAMS 94   6 Crowne with their owne. Rare poemes aske rare
                                 friends
     p. 60 EPIGRAMS 94   12 Dare for these poemes, yet, both aske, and read,
     p. 313 HORACE 2   193 From whence thy Modestie, or Poemes law
     p. 323 HORACE 2   388 To note, in Poemes, breach of harmonie;

poems   frequency: 6   relative frequency: 0.00008
   See also "poemes," "poem's."
     p. 115 FOREST 12   81 They hold in my strange poems, which, as yet,
     p. 127 UNDERWOOD 1   t1 POEMS
     p. 311 HORACE 2   127 Of Poems here describ'd, I can, nor use,
     p. 325 HORACE 2   431 Out better Poems? But I cannot buy
     p. 329 HORACE 2   511 The Poems void of profit, our grave men
     p. 400 UNGATHERED 32   t1 On the honor'd Poems of his honored

poem's   frequency: 1   relative frequency: 0.00001
   See also "poemes."
     p. 311 HORACE 2   141 Her Poem's beautie, but a sweet delight

poesie   frequency: 4   relative frequency: 0.00005
     p. 51 EPIGRAMS 73   10 Item, a faire greeke poesie for a ring:

poesie (cont.)
    p. 175 UNDERWOOD 23   22 And thinke it Poesie?
    p. 329 HORACE 2   539 As Painting, so is Poesie. Some mans hand
    p. 401 UNGATHERED 33   5 Musique and Poesie:

poesy   frequency: 2   relative frequency: 0.00002
    See also "poesie."
    p. 397 UNGATHERED 30   24 I found it pure, and perfect Poesy,
    p. 406 UNGATHERED 34   97 What Poesy ere was painted on a wall

poet   frequency: 29   relative frequency: 0.00041
    See also "poet's."
    p.   28 EPIGRAMS 4   5 For such a Poet, while thy dayes were greene,
    p.   29 EPIGRAMS 10   1 Thou call'st me Poet, as a terme of shame:
    p.   29 EPIGRAMS 9   4 And, I a Poet here, no Herald am.
    p.   55 EPIGRAMS 84   5 Straight went I home; and there most like a
                             Poet,
    p.   62 EPIGRAMS 96   1 Who shall doubt, DONNE, where I a Poet
                             bee,
    p. 115 FOREST 12   69 (Or Poet, in the court account) then I,
    p. 182 UNDERWOOD 28   4 A better lover, and much better Poet.
    p. 183 UNDERWOOD 29   26 Not a Poet in an Age,
    p. 221 UNDERWOOD 48   29 And thou make many a Poet,
    p. 226 UNDERWOOD 52   t2 The Poet to the Painter.
    p. 227 UNDERWOOD 52   20 A Poet hath no more but black and white,
    p. 232 UNDERWOOD 57   25 the Muse, or the Poet,
    p. 235 UNDERWOOD 62   10 One Poet, then of other folke ten score.
    p. 235 UNDERWOOD 62   13 What can the Poet wish his King may doe,
    p. 238 UNDERWOOD 66   4 (Without prophanenesse) yet, a Poet, cry,
    p. 241 UNDERWOOD 68   2 His Poet Sack, the House-hold will not pay?
    p. 241 UNDERWOOD 68   4 For want of knowing the Poet, to say him nay?
    p. 241 UNDERWOOD 68   6 His Poet leave to sing his House-hold true;
    p. 259 UNDERWOOD 76   4 To your Majestie your Poet:
    p. 269 UNDERWOOD 83   17 When I, who would her Poet have become,
    p. 283 U'WOOD 84.9   28 What's left a Poet, when his Muse is gone?
    p. 305 HORACE 2   11 But equall power, to Painter, and to Poet,
    p. 311 HORACE 2   129 Am I call'd Poet? wherefore with wrong shame,
    p. 313 HORACE 2   189 For, being a Poet, thou maist feigne, create,
    p. 325 HORACE 2   414 Had not our every Poet like offended.
    p. 325 HORACE 2   438 The Poet, what becommeth, and what not:
    p. 333 HORACE 2   599 So doth the Poet, who is rich in land,
    p. 335 HORACE 2   643 Wise, sober folke, a frantick Poet feare,
    p. 335 HORACE 2   660 Of the Sicilian Poet Empedocles,

poet-ape   frequency: 2   relative frequency: 0.00002
    p.   44 EPIGRAMS 56   1 Poore POET-APE, that would be thought our
                             chiefe,
    p.   44 EPIGRAMS 56   t1 ON POET-APE.

poetic. See "lesse-poetique," "poetique."

poetique   frequency: 1   relative frequency: 0.00001
    p. 259 UNDERWOOD 76   10 Of a free Poetique Pension,

poetrie   frequency: 6   relative frequency: 0.00008
    p.   41 EPIGRAMS 45   10 BEN. IONSON his best piece of poetrie.
    p. 183 UNDERWOOD 29   14 All good Poetrie hence was flowne,
    p. 207 UNDERWOOD 43   89 All the old Venusine, in Poetrie,
    p. 249 UNDERWOOD 72   10 The Poetrie of Steeples, with the Bells,
    p. 305 HORACE 2   t5 POETRIE.
    p. 400 UNGATHERED 32   8 The Bound, and Frontire of our Poetrie;

poetry   frequency: 3   relative frequency: 0.00004
    See also "poetrie."
    p.   72 EPIGRAMS 112   t1 TO A WEAKE GAMSTER IN
                            POETRY.
    p. 403 UNGATHERED 34   36 Not they that sided her, Dame Poetry,
    p. 404 UNGATHERED 34   51 Pack wth your pedling Poetry to the Stage,

poets   frequency: 30   relative frequency: 0.00043
    p.   28 EPIGRAMS 4   2 How, best of Poets, do'st thou laurell weare!
    p.   28 EPIGRAMS 4   10 Of Kings for grace; of Poets for my test?
    p.   40 EPIGRAMS 43   5 'Tofore, great men were glad of Poets: Now,
    p.   41 EPIGRAMS 43   11 From seruile flatterie (common Poets shame)
    p.   52 EPIGRAMS 76   4 To honor, serue, and loue; as Poets vse.
    p.   53 EPIGRAMS 79   1 That Poets are far rarer births then kings,
    p.   57 EPIGRAMS 89   14 So many Poets life, by one should liue.
    p.   84 EPIGRAMS 133   20 Shee brought the Poets forth, but ours
                             th'aduenter.
    p.   93 FOREST 1   4 Can Poets hope to fetter mee?

poets (cont.)
```
    p. 107 FOREST 10        2 Or whose great name in Poets heauen vse,
    p. 115 FOREST 12       63 But onely Poets, rapt with rage diuine?
    p. 131 UNDERWOOD 2.1    5 Poets, though divine, are men:
    p. 199 UNDERWOOD 42     3 No Poets verses yet did ever move,
    p. 200 UNDERWOOD 42     8 His lynes, and hourely sits the Poets horse?
    p. 200 UNDERWOOD 42    17 But is the Poets matter: And he must,
    p. 235 UNDERWOOD 62     6 To cure the Poets Evill, Povertie:
    p. 241 UNDERWOOD 68    13 For in the Genius of a Poets Verse,
    p. 245 UNDERWOOD 70    82 Of which we Priests, and Poets say
    p. 260 UNDERWOOD 76    31 And so warme the Poets tongue
    p. 323 HORACE 2       390 To Roman Poets. Shall I therefore weave
    p. 323 HORACE 2       405 Our Poets, too, left nought unproved here;
    p. 325 HORACE 2       421 Exclude all sober Poets, from their share
    p. 325 HORACE 2       426 But fame of Poets, they thinke, if they come
                                 forth,
    p. 327 HORACE 2       477 Poets would either profit, or delight,
    p. 327 HORACE 2       492 To divine Poets, and their Verses came.
    p. 331 HORACE 2       556 Poets should ever be indifferent.
    p. 335 HORACE 2       664 Let Poets perish, that will not be kept.
    p. 392 UNGATHERED 26   57 For though the Poets matter, Nature be,
    p. 392 UNGATHERED 26   77 Shine forth, thou Starre of Poets, and with
                                 rage,
    p. 398 UNGATHERED 30   63 The Poets act! and for his Country's sake
```

poet's   frequency: 1   relative frequency: 0.00001
    See also "poets."
```
    p. 392 UNGATHERED 26   64 For a good Poet's made, as well as borne.
```

poets'   frequency: 1   relative frequency: 0.00001
    See also "poets."
```
    p. 657 L. CONVIVALES   13 And the Poets' Horse accounted.
```

point   frequency: 5   relative frequency: 0.00007
    See also "poynte."
```
    p. 219 UNDERWOOD 47    59 Live to that point I will, for which I am man,
    p. 229 UNDERWOOD 54     7 So that upon the point, my corporall feare
    p. 287 U'WOOD 84.9    152 Find all our Atomes from a point t<o>'a span!
    p. 413 UNGATHERED 41   29 These Mysteries do point to three more great,
    p. 414 UNGATHERED 41   52 Till he hath reach'd his two-fold point of
                                 Noone.
```

pointed   frequency: 1   relative frequency: 0.00001
```
    p. 240 UNDERWOOD 67    39 Upon his pointed Lance:
```

points   frequency: 2   relative frequency: 0.00002
    See also "poyntes."
```
    p.  45 EPIGRAMS 58      6 Then thou did'st late my sense, loosing my
                                 points.
    p. 155 UNDERWOOD 13    74 Feed those, at whom the Table points at still?
```

poison. See "poyson."

poland   frequency: 1   relative frequency: 0.00001
```
    p.  69 EPIGRAMS 107    13 In Hungary, and Poland, Turkie too;
```

poley. See "pooly'."

policie   frequency: 1   relative frequency: 0.00001
```
    p. 109 FOREST 11       17 'Tis the securest policie we haue,
```

policy. See "policie."

polish'd   frequency: 3   relative frequency: 0.00004
    See also "polisht."
```
    p.  93 FOREST 2         3 Of polish'd pillars, or a roofe of gold:
    p. 137 UNDERWOOD 2.5   29 Nay, her white and polish'd neck,
    p. 387 UNGATHERED 22    1 Sonnes, seeke not me amonge these polish'd
                                 stones:
```

polisht   frequency: 1   relative frequency: 0.00001
```
    p. 280 U'WOOD 84.4     55 So polisht, perfect, round, and even,
```

politic. See "politique."

politique   frequency: 3   relative frequency: 0.00004
```
    p. 177 UNDERWOOD 25    29 Of politique pretext, that wryes a State,
    p. 214 UNDERWOOD 44    60 In Politique, and Militar Affaires.
    p. 404 UNGATHERED 34   45 You aske noe more then certeyne politique Eyes,
```

poll   frequency: 1   relative frequency: 0.00001
    p.   50 EPIGRAMS 71   1 To plucke downe mine, POLL sets vp new wits
                                still,

polluted   frequency: 1   relative frequency: 0.00001
    p. 355 HORACE 1   673 Polluted .... certainly he's ...

pollvx   frequency: 1   relative frequency: 0.00001
    p.   86 EPIGRAMS 133   77 And, on they went, like CASTOR braue, and
                                POLLVX:

poly.   frequency: 1   relative frequency: 0.00001
    p. 240 UNDERWOOD 67   49 9. POLY. Sweet! happy Mary! All

poly-olbyon   frequency: 1   relative frequency: 0.00001
    p. 397 UNGATHERED 30   52 Of all that reade thy Poly-Olbyon.

polyhymnia. See "poly."

polypheme   frequency: 2   relative frequency: 0.00002
    p.   87 EPIGRAMS 133   112 Of the hulke touch'd, and, as by
                                POLYPHEME
    p. 315 HORACE 2   206 Scylla, Charybdis, Polypheme, with these.

polytopian   frequency: 1   relative frequency: 0.00001
    p. 379 UNGATHERED 12   t2 Polytopian Thomas the Traueller.

pomp. See "pompe."

pomp'd   frequency: 1   relative frequency: 0.00001
    p. 204 UNDERWOOD 43   35 Or pomp'd for those hard trifles, Anagrams,

pompe   frequency: 6   relative frequency: 0.00008
  **p. 115 PANEGYRE   77 "With better pompe. She tells him first, that
                                Kings
    p. 186 UNDERWOOD 32   3 Without the pompe of Counsell; or more Aide,
    p. 240 UNDERWOOD 67   28 Comes in the pompe, and glorie
    p. 254 UNDERWOOD 75   72 With all the pompe of Youth, and all our Court
                                beside.
    p. 287 U'WOOD 84.9   182 Of sorrow, then all pompe of gaudy daies:
    p. 403 UNGATHERED 34   29 What is ye cause you pompe it soe? I aske,

pompey   frequency: 1   relative frequency: 0.00001
    p.   71 EPIGRAMS 110   3 The name of POMPEY for an enemie,

pompey's   frequency: 1   relative frequency: 0.00001
    p. 395 UNGATHERED 29   9 As neither Pompey's popularitie,

pompilius   frequency: 1   relative frequency: 0.00001
    p. 325 HORACE 2   415 But you, Pompilius off-spring, spare you not

pompous   frequency: 1   relative frequency: 0.00001
    p.   69 EPIGRAMS 107   12 In Ireland, Holland, Sweden, pompous lies,

ponderous   frequency: 1   relative frequency: 0.00001
    p. 361 UNGATHERED 1   17 thus, as a ponderous thinge in water cast

ponds   frequency: 1   relative frequency: 0.00001
    p.   94 FOREST 2   32 Thou hast thy ponds, that pay thee tribute fish,

pool. See "poole."

poole   frequency: 2   relative frequency: 0.00002
    p.   87 EPIGRAMS 133   121 By this time had they reach'd the Stygian poole,
    p.   88 EPIGRAMS 133   160 And, now, aboue the poole, a face right fat

pooly'   frequency: 1   relative frequency: 0.00001
    p.   65 EPIGRAMS 101   36 And we will haue no Pooly', or Parrot by;

poor   frequency: 2   relative frequency: 0.00002
    See also "poore."
    p. 410 UNGATHERED 39   10 I'll laugh at thee poor wretched Tike, go send
    p. 657 L. CONVIVALES   7 Hang up all the poor Hop-Drinkers,

poore   frequency: 39   relative frequency: 0.00056
  **p. 114 PANEGYRE   38 But, when their speech so poore a helpe affords
    p.   31 EPIGRAMS 12   21 Not his poore cocatrice but he betrayes
    p.   33 EPIGRAMS 21   3 His clothes two fashions of, and poore! his sword
    p.   36 EPIGRAMS 28   17 Blaspheme god, greatly. Or some poore hinde
                                beat,

poore (cont.)

p.	40 EPIGRAMS 42	3 Indeed, poore GILES repents he married euer.
p.	44 EPIGRAMS 56	1 Poore POET-APE, that would be thought our chiefe,
p.	64 EPIGRAMS 101	1 To night, graue sir, both my poore house, and I
p.	69 EPIGRAMS 107	30 Twirle the poore chaine you run a feasting in.
p.	84 EPIGRAMS 133	30 Makes the poore Banck-side creature wet it' shoone,
p.	86 EPIGRAMS 133	96 Poore MERCVRY, crying out on PARACELSVS,
p.	102 FOREST 5	12 Of a few poore houshold spyes?
p.	107 FOREST 10	14 That, at thy birth, mad'st the poore Smith affraid,
p.	113 FOREST 12	15 While thus it buyes great grace, and hunts poore fame;
p.	150 UNDERWOOD 10	5 To vent that poore desire,
p.	154 UNDERWOOD 13	54 My Sword ('tis but a poore Sword, understand)
p.	154 UNDERWOOD 13	55 As farre as any poore Sword i' the Land.
p.	155 UNDERWOOD 13	90 Or robbing the poore Market-folkes should nurse
p.	163 UNDERWOOD 15	42 Honour and honestie, as poore things thought
p.	165 UNDERWOOD 15	89 The Husband now's call'd churlish, or a poore
p.	167 UNDERWOOD 15	158 As a poore single flatterer, without Baud,
p.	167 UNDERWOOD 15	167 Of the poore sufferers) where the envious, proud,
p.	201 UNDERWOOD 42	51 Then ope thy wardrobe, thinke me that poore Groome
p.	201 UNDERWOOD 42	61 From the poore wretch, which though he play'd in prose,
p.	202 UNDERWOOD 42	81 Let the poore fooles enjoy their follies, love
p.	205 UNDERWOOD 43	53 Sindge Capons, or poore Pigges, dropping their eyes;
p.	209 UNDERWOOD 43	135 I saw with two poore Chambers taken in,
p.	215 UNDERWOOD 44	79 Let poore Nobilitie be vertuous: Wee,
p.	216 UNDERWOOD 45	11 Those are poore Ties, depend on those false ends,
p.	217 UNDERWOOD 46	7 When, being the Strangers helpe, the poore mans aide,
p.	223 UNDERWOOD 49	34 To his poore Instrument, now out of grace.
p.	248 UNDERWOOD 71	1 Poore wretched states, prest by extremities,
p.	259 UNDERWOOD 76	1 The humble Petition of poore Ben.
p.	311 HORACE 2	138 When they are poore, and banish'd, must throw by
p.	313 HORACE 2	177 Poore Jo wandring; wild Orestes mad:
p.	319 HORACE 2	286 Fortune would love the poore, and leave the proud.
p.	321 HORACE 2	334 With poore base termes, through every baser shop:
p.	333 HORACE 2	602 Make a great Supper; or for some poore man
p.	381 UNGATHERED 12	58 Poore Tom haue we cause to suspect iust thee?
p.	408 UNGATHERED 37	7 But bawle thou on; I pitty thee, poore Curre,

poores   frequency: 2   relative frequency: 0.00002
    p. 185 UNDERWOOD 30   8 The poores full Store-house, and just servants field.
    p. 235 UNDERWOOD 62   11 O pietie! so to weigh the poores estates!

poor's. See "poores."

pope   frequency: 1   relative frequency: 0.00001
    p. 59 EPIGRAMS 92   34 And at the Pope, and Spaine slight faces make.

popenheim   frequency: 1   relative frequency: 0.00001
    p. 69 EPIGRAMS 107   25 Of Hannow, Shieter-huissen, Popenheim,

poperie   frequency: 1   relative frequency: 0.00001
    p. 209 UNDERWOOD 43   143 Bred on the Banck, in time of Poperie,

popery. See "poperie."

popes-head-alley   frequency: 1   relative frequency: 0.00001
    p. 206 UNDERWOOD 43   80 Upon th'Exchange, still, out of Popes-head-Alley;

poplar   frequency: 1   relative frequency: 0.00001
    p. 290 UNDERWOOD 85   9 The Poplar tall, he then doth marrying twine

poppie   frequency: 1   relative frequency: 0.00001
    p. 331 HORACE 2   559 As Poppie, and Sardane honey; 'cause without

poppy. See "poppie."

popular   frequency: 1   relative frequency: 0.00001
    p. 311 HORACE 2   120 On popular noise with, and doe businesse in.

popularitie   frequency: 1   relative frequency: 0.00001
     p. 395 UNGATHERED 29   9 As neither Pompey's popularitie,

popularity. See "popularitie."

porcelain. See "porc'lane."

porches   frequency: 1   relative frequency: 0.00001
     p. 97 FOREST 3   15 Free from proud porches, or their guilded roofes,

porc'lane   frequency: 1   relative frequency: 0.00001
     p. 219 UNDERWOOD 47   53 And animated Porc'lane of the Court,

poring   frequency: 1   relative frequency: 0.00001
     p. 288 U'WOOD 84.9   196 Poring, as on a Map, to find the wayes

port   frequency: 3   relative frequency: 0.00004
     p. 85 EPIGRAMS 133   47 The many perills of this Port, and how
     p. 250 UNDERWOOD 73   4 Hath rais'd to be the Port unto his Land!
     p. 274 U'WOOD 84.1   39 Of that eternall Port kept ope'

porta   frequency: 1   relative frequency: 0.00001
     p. 59 EPIGRAMS 92   25 They all get Porta, for the sundrie wayes

porters   frequency: 1   relative frequency: 0.00001
     p. 62 EPIGRAMS 96   10 Let pui'nees, porters, players praise delight,

porting   frequency: 1   relative frequency: 0.00001
     p. 254 UNDERWOOD 75   51 Porting the Ensignes of united Two,

portion   frequency: 3   relative frequency: 0.00004
     p. 218 UNDERWOOD 47   27 I have no portion in them, nor their deale
     p. 247 UNDERWOOD 70   110 Till either grew a portion of the other:
     p. 282 U'WOOD 84.9   14 And saw that portion of her selfe to die.

portions   frequency: 1   relative frequency: 0.00001
     p. 286 U'WOOD 84.9   142 Our native portions, and possessed rent;

portland   frequency: 1   relative frequency: 0.00001
     p. 250 UNDERWOOD 73   t4 Hee was made Earle of Portland,

ports   frequency: 3   relative frequency: 0.00004
     p. 53 EPIGRAMS 80   1 The ports of death are sinnes; of life, good
                                 deeds:
     p. 109 FOREST 11   9 At th'eye and eare (the ports vnto the minde)
     p. 317 HORACE 2   284 Peace, and the open ports, that peace doth cause.

possess. See "possesse."

possesse   frequency: 4   relative frequency: 0.00005
    *p. 494 TO HIMSELF   55 Feele such a flesh-quake to possesse their
                                 powers:
     p. 70 EPIGRAMS 109   9 Thou rather striu'st the matter to possesse,
     p. 151 UNDERWOOD 12   9 That though they did possesse each limbe,
     p. 261 UNDERWOOD 77   22 Of sweets, and safeties, they possesse by Peace.

possessed   frequency: 1   relative frequency: 0.00001
     See also "possest."
     p. 286 U'WOOD 84.9   142 Our native portions, and possessed rent;

possessions   frequency: 2   relative frequency: 0.00002
     p. 99 FOREST 3   75 And change possessions, oftner with his breath,
     p. 281 U'WOOD 84.8   11 (Brave Youths) th<ey>'are their possessions,
                                 none of yours:

possest   frequency: 4   relative frequency: 0.00005
     p. 187 UNDERWOOD 33   28 And not being borrow'd by thee, but possest.
     p. 245 UNDERWOOD 70   80 Possest with holy rage,
     p. 281 U'WOOD 84.4   70 Yet know, with what thou art possest,
     p. 399 UNGATHERED 31   25 Her soule possest her fleshes state

post   frequency: 2   relative frequency: 0.00002
     p. 45 EPIGRAMS 58   8 And, hood-wink'd, for a man, embrace a post.
     p. 257 UNDERWOOD 75   138 Now, Sun, and post away the rest of day:

posteritie   frequency: 13   relative frequency: 0.00018
     p. 67 EPIGRAMS 104   12 The light, and marke vnto posteritie?
     p. 70 EPIGRAMS 109   15 Goe on, and doubt not, what posteritie,
     p. 80 EPIGRAMS 127   4 No, I doe, therefore, call Posteritie
     p. 227 UNDERWOOD 52   24 To all posteritie; I will write Burlase.

posteritie (cont.)
       p. 236 UNDERWOOD 63   12 With a long, large, and blest posteritie!
       p. 256 UNDERWOOD 75   114 It brings Friends Joy, Foes Griefe,
                                 Posteritie Fame;
       p. 257 UNDERWOOD 75   152 For Fame keepes Vertue up, and it Posteritie.
       p. 262 UNDERWOOD 78   18 Which I have vow'd posteritie to give.
       p. 269 UNDERWOOD 83   34 T<o>'inlive posteritie, her Fame may tell!
       p. 272 UNDERWOOD 84   t4 LEFT TO POSTERITIE
       p. 273 U'WOOD 84.1   13 That all Posteritie, as wee,
       p. 387 UNGATHERED 22   t1 Charles Cauendish to his posteritie.
       p. 416 UNGATHERED 43   6 With the Glad Countrey, and Posteritie:

posterity. See "posteritie."

postes   frequency: 1   relative frequency: 0.00001
       p. 405 UNGATHERED 34   87 On ye new priming of thy old Signe postes

posts   frequency: 1   relative frequency: 0.00001
     See also "postes."
       p. 28 EPIGRAMS 3   7 Nor have my title-leafe on posts, or walls,

posture   frequency: 3   relative frequency: 0.00004
       p. 60 EPIGRAMS 102   14 And one true posture, though besieg'd with ill
       p. 213 UNDERWOOD 44   28 But on thy practise, and the Posture booke:
       p. 370 UNGATHERED 7   3 Light, Posture, Height'ning, Shadow,
                                 Culloring,

pot   frequency: 1   relative frequency: 0.00001
       p. 46 EPIGRAMS 62   6 Or your complexions losse? you haue a pot,

pot-guns   frequency: 1   relative frequency: 0.00001
       p. 259 UNDERWOOD 76   21 When their pot-guns ayme to hit,

'pothecarie   frequency: 1   relative frequency: 0.00001
       p. 46 EPIGRAMS 62   4 Your 'pothecarie, and his drug sayes no.

potions   frequency: 1   relative frequency: 0.00001
       p. 86 EPIGRAMS 133   101 His spirits, now, in pills, and eeke in potions,

pots   frequency: 1   relative frequency: 0.00001
       p. 290 UNDERWOOD 85   15 Or the prest honey in pure pots doth keepe

pottle   frequency: 1   relative frequency: 0.00001
       p. 657 L. CONVIVALES   3 Here he speaks out of his Pottle,

pouertie   frequency: 2   relative frequency: 0.00002
       p. 29 EPIGRAMS 6   2 Sure, willing pouertie liues most in you.
       p. 43 EPIGRAMS 65   12 And which thou brought'st me, welcome pouertie.

poulder-plot   frequency: 1   relative frequency: 0.00001
       p. 59 EPIGRAMS 92   32 And of the poulder-plot, they will talke yet.

poulders   frequency: 1   relative frequency: 0.00001
       p. 118 FOREST 13   77 Let 'hem on poulders, oyles, and paintings,
                                 spend,

pound   frequency: 10   relative frequency: 0.00014
       p. 29 EPIGRAMS 8   1 RIDWAY rob'd DVNCOTE of three hundred
                                 pound,
       p. 155 UNDERWOOD 13   78 Many a pound, and piece, will p<l>ace one well;
       p. 164 UNDERWOOD 15   67 To catch the flesh in, and to pound a Prick.
       p. 164 UNDERWOOD 15   77 For t'other pound of sweet-meats, he shall feele
       p. 229 UNDERWOOD 54   12 Full twentie stone; of which I lack two pound:
       p. 230 UNDERWOOD 56   11 His weight is twenty Stone within two pound;
       p. 327 HORACE 2   466 A pound, or piece, by their long compting arts:
       p. 327 HORACE 2   471 An ounce, what makes it then? The halfe pound
                                 just;
       p. 402 UNGATHERED 34   2 From thirty pound in pipkins, to ye Man
       p. 408 UNGATHERED 37   4 Th'enuy'd returne, of forty pound in gold.

pounds   frequency: 2   relative frequency: 0.00002
       p. 235 UNDERWOOD 62   t3 for a 100. pounds he sent me in my sicknesse.
       p. 260 UNDERWOOD 76   27 Those your Fathers Markes, your Pounds;

pour. See "poure," "powre."

pour'd   frequency: 3   relative frequency: 0.00004
       p. 86 EPIGRAMS 133   75 And many a sinke pour'd out her rage anenst 'hem;
       p. 172 UNDERWOOD 20   19 And that pour'd out upon Man-kind can be!
       p. 280 U'WOOD 84.4   59 As smooth as Oyle pour'd forth, and calme

poure   frequency: 2   relative frequency: 0.00002
     p. 118 FOREST 13   73 Melt downe their husbands land, to poure away
     p. 239 UNDERWOOD 67   8 And Gunnes there, spare to poure

pouring   frequency: 2   relative frequency: 0.00002
     p. 159 UNDERWOOD 14   38 Of Gathering? Bountie' in pouring out againe?
     p. 413 UNGATHERED 41 31 All, pouring their full showre of graces downe,

pour'st   frequency: 1   relative frequency: 0.00001
    *p. 492 TO HIMSELF   11 Say, that thou pour'st them wheat,

povertie   frequency: 1   relative frequency: 0.00001
     p. 235 UNDERWOOD 62   6 To cure the Poets Evill, Povertie:

poverty. See "pouertie," "povertie."

powder   frequency: 2   relative frequency: 0.00002
     See also "gun-powder," "poulder-plot."
     p. 213 UNDERWOOD 44   2 But we have Powder still for the Kings Day,
     p. 213 UNDERWOOD 44   25 Powder, or paper, to bring up the youth

powders   frequency: 1   relative frequency: 0.00001
     See also "poulders."
     p. 165 UNDERWOOD 15 112 Sweet bags, sweet Powders, nor sweet words will
                             passe

power   frequency: 25   relative frequency: 0.00036
   **p. 113 PANEGYRE   22 That fastneth heauenly power to earthly raigne:
   **p. 116 PANEGYRE   126 Then by their power; and men doe more obay
   **p. 117 PANEGYRE   139 And entring with the power of a king,
     p. 34 EPIGRAMS 133   6 Had power to act, what they to faine had not.
     p. 99 FOREST 3   80 And thinke his power doth equall Fates.
     p. 117 FOREST 13   38 Doe I reflect. Some alderman has power,
     p. 153 UNDERWOOD 13   1 If, Sackvile, all that have the power to doe
     p. 191 UNDERWOOD 38   18 In will and power, only to defeate.
     p. 204 UNDERWOOD 43   48 Or if thou needs would'st trench upon her power,
     p. 210 UNDERWOOD 43 157 Though but in daunces, it shall know his power;
     p. 227 UNDERWOOD 52   17 Your Power of handling shadow, ayre, and
                             spright,
     p. 265 UNDERWOOD 79   42 1. Wee know no other power then his,
     p. 265 UNDERWOOD 79   64 PAN knowes no other power then his,
     p. 288 U'WOOD 84.9   217 As being the Sonne of Man) to shew his Power,
     p. 289 U'WOOD 84.9   220 Where first his Power will appeare, by call
     p. 305 HORACE 2   11 But equall power, to Painter, and to Poet,
     p. 307 HORACE 2   57 His matter to his power, in all he makes,
     p. 309 HORACE 2   104 The power, and rule of speaking resteth still.
     p. 323 HORACE 2   370 His power of fouely hurting made to cease.
     p. 331 HORACE 2   552 Of eloquent Messalla's power in Court,
     p. 367 UNGATHERED 6   47 "Musicke hath power to draw,
     p. 393 UNGATHERED 27 11 As giues a power to faith, to tread
     p. 401 UNGATHERED 32 18 But higher power, as spight could not make lesse,
     p. 413 UNGATHERED 41 39 The House of gold, the Gate of heavens power,
     p. 421 UNGATHERED 49 10 deignes myne the power to ffinde, yett want I
                             will

powerfull   frequency: 1   relative frequency: 0.00001
     p. 84 EPIGRAMS 133   29 It was the day, what time the powerfull Moone

powers   frequency: 19   relative frequency: 0.00027
    *p. 494 TO HIMSELF   55 Feele such a flesh-quake to possesse their
                             powers:
   **p. 116 PANEGYRE   104 "When, publique iustice borrow'd all her powers
     p. 31 EPIGRAMS 14   14 But for their powers, accept my pietie.
     p. 37 EPIGRAMS 35   3 Whose manners draw, more than thy powers
                             constraine.
     p. 52 EPIGRAMS 76   14 I purpos'd her; that should, with euen powers,
     p. 53 EPIGRAMS 80   4 And hath it, in his powers, to make his way!
     p. 101 FOREST 4   28 With all my powers, my selfe to loose?
     p. 115 FOREST 12   73 My gratefull soule, the subiect of her powers,
     p. 166 UNDERWOOD 15 140 To be beholders, when their powers are spent.
     p. 189 UNDERWOOD 36   13 Such are his powers, whom time hath stil'd,
     p. 191 UNDERWOOD 38   11 And fills my powers with perswading joy,
     p. 199 UNDERWOOD 41   10 To shift their seasons, and destroy their powers!
     p. 251 UNDERWOOD 74   17 Have multipli'd their arts, and powers,
     p. 283 U'WOOD 84.9   31 Am turned with an others powers. My Passion
     p. 285 U'WOOD 84.9   87 The Dominations, Vertues, and the Powers,
     p. 295 UNDERWOOD 90   6 A quiet mind; free powers; and body sound;
     p. 327 HORACE 2   484 Was said to move the stones, by his Lutes
                             powers,
     p. 351 HORACE 1   528 .. .. powers .. ..

powers (cont.)
   p. 361 UNGATHERED 1   3 weare made the obiects to my weaker powers;

powre   frequency: 1   relative frequency: 0.00001
   p. 666 INSCRIPTS. 11   9 Shall powre forth many a line, drop many a
                   letter,

pox   frequency: 4   relative frequency: 0.00005
   See also "poxe."
   p. 211 UNDERWOOD 43   191 Pox on your flameship, Vulcan; if it be
   p. 212 UNDERWOOD 43   213 Pox on thee, Vulcan, thy Pandora's pox,
   p. 212 UNDERWOOD 43   216 Thy Wives pox on thee, and B<ess> B<roughton>s
                   too.

poxe   frequency: 2   relative frequency: 0.00002
   p. 76 EPIGRAMS 119   4 Shuns prease, for two maine causes, poxe, and
                   debt,
   p. 188 UNDERWOOD 34   t2 To the small Poxe.

poynte   frequency: 1   relative frequency: 0.00001
   p. 383 UNGATHERED 16   13 still that same little poynte hee was; but when

poyntes   frequency: 1   relative frequency: 0.00001
   p. 382 UNGATHERED 16   2 hath armde att all poyntes; charge mee humblye
                   kneele

poyson   frequency: 2   relative frequency: 0.00002
   p. 99 FOREST 3   90 Though poyson, thinke it a great fate.
   p. 172 UNDERWOOD 21   4 Out of his Grave, and poyson every eare.

practice   frequency: 1   relative frequency: 0.00001
   See also "practise."
   p. 58 EPIGRAMS 91   14 Nor lesse in practice; but lesse mark'd, lesse
                   knowne:

practices. See "practises."

practisd   frequency: 1   relative frequency: 0.00001
   p. 404 UNGATHERED 34   57 But in ye practisd truth Destruction is

practis'd   frequency: 1   relative frequency: 0.00001
   See also "practisd," "practiz'd."
   p. 225 UNDERWOOD 50   32 Not boasted in your life, but practis'd true,

practise   frequency: 13   relative frequency: 0.00018
   p. 39 EPIGRAMS 41   3 Such her quaint practise is, so it allures,
   p. 75 EPIGRAMS 116   14 Vertuously practise must at least allow
   p. 82 EPIGRAMS 130   10 Of old, euen by her practise, to be fam'd;
   p. 117 FOREST 13   12 By arts, and practise of the vicious,
   p. 158 UNDERWOOD 13   163 Donnor's or Donnee's, to their practise shall
   p. 179 UNDERWOOD 25   35 Nothing, but practise upon honours thrall.
   p. 187 UNDERWOOD 33   39 Thy sincere practise, breeds not thee a fame
   p. 188 UNDERWOOD 34   8 Was drawne to practise other hue, then that
   p. 213 UNDERWOOD 44   28 But on thy practise, and the Posture booke:
   p. 215 UNDERWOOD 44   92 They learne and studie; and then practise there.
   p. 223 UNDERWOOD 49   41 And practise for a Miracle; take heed
   p. 236 UNDERWOOD 64   11 When your assiduous practise doth secure
   p. 247 UNDERWOOD 70   119 The good, and durst not practise it, were glad

practises   frequency: 1   relative frequency: 0.00001
   p. 59 EPIGRAMS 92   11 The councels, proiects, practises they know,

practiz'd   frequency: 2   relative frequency: 0.00002
   p. 154 UNDERWOOD 13   48 Well knowne, and practiz'd borrowers on their
                   word,
   p. 190 UNDERWOOD 37   26 In practiz'd friendship wholly to reprove,

praeceding   frequency: 1   relative frequency: 0.00001
   **p. 115 PANEGYRE   91 "Of kings, praeceding him in that high court;

praecipice   frequency: 1   relative frequency: 0.00001
   p. 166 UNDERWOOD 15   130 This Praecipice, and Rocks that have no end,

praeoccupie   frequency: 1   relative frequency: 0.00001
   p. 201 UNDERWOOD 42   42 Being, the best clothes still to praeoccupie.

praevaricators   frequency: 1   relative frequency: 0.00001
   p. 167 UNDERWOOD 15   170 Praevaricators swarme. Of which the store,

prais'd   frequency: 9   relative frequency: 0.00013
p.   46 EPIGRAMS 60   3 Or, if shee would but modestly haue prais'd
p.   48 EPIGRAMS 65   16 For worth he has not, He is tax'd, not prais'd.
p. 116 FOREST 13   5 So both the prais'd, and praisers suffer: Yet,
p. 136 UNDERWOOD 2.5   13 So hath Homer prais'd her haire;
p. 159 UNDERWOOD 14   21 Men past their termes, and prais'd some names too
                           much,
p. 161 UNDERWOOD 14   70 That would, perhaps, have prais'd, and thank'd
                           the same,
p. 181 UNDERWOOD 27   22 Equall with her? or Ronsart prais'd
p. 256 UNDERWOOD 75   115 In him the times, no lesse then Prince, are
                           prais'd,
p. 348 HORACE 1   385 Your .... old .... prais'd

praise   frequency: 50   relative frequency: 0.00072
See also "o're-praise," "prayse."
p.   27 EPIGRAMS 2   14 For vulgar praise, doth it too dearely buy.
p.   34 EPIGRAMS 23   6 And which no' affection praise enough can giue!
p.   34 EPIGRAMS 23   9 All which I meant to praise, and, yet, I would;
p.   43 EPIGRAMS 52   2 Dispraise my worke, then praise it frostily:
p.   46 EPIGRAMS 61   1 Thy praise, or dispraise is to me alike,
p.   50 EPIGRAMS 71   2 Still, 'tis his lucke to praise me 'gainst his
                           will.
p.   55 EPIGRAMS 86   7 Where, though 't be loue, that to thy praise doth
                           moue,
p.   62 EPIGRAMS 96   10 Let pui'nees, porters, players praise delight,
p.   66 EPIGRAMS 102   16 Whose life, eu'n they, that enuie it, must
                           praise;
p.   66 EPIGRAMS 103   6 Need any Muses praise to giue it fame?
p.   67 EPIGRAMS 103   13 My praise is plaine, and where so ere profest,
p.   68 EPIGRAMS 106   9 Their latter praise would still the greatest bee,
p.   73 EPIGRAMS 113   2 As but to speake thee, OVERBVRY, is
                           praise:
p.   80 EPIGRAMS 126   1 Retyr'd, with purpose your faire worth to praise,
p.   83 EPIGRAMS 132   1 If to admire were to commend, my praise
p.   95 FOREST 2   83 Did'st thou, then, make 'hem! and what praise was
                           heap'd
p.   96 FOREST 2   89 These, PENSHVRST, are thy praise, and
                           yet not all.
p. 156 UNDERWOOD 13   102 Unto their praise, in certaine swearing rites!
p. 159 UNDERWOOD 14   26 Before men get a verse: much lesse a Praise;
p. 160 UNDERWOOD 14   61 I yeeld, I yeeld, the matter of your praise
p. 173 UNDERWOOD 22   1 Though Beautie be the Marke of praise,
p. 173 UNDERWOOD 22   3 As not the World can praise too much,
p. 183 UNDERWOOD 29   29 Nor a lyne deserving praise,
p. 212 UNDERWOOD 43   207 Engines of Murder, and receive the praise
p. 215 UNDERWOOD 44   71 More then to praise a Dog? or Horse? or speake
p. 217 UNDERWOOD 46   19 No lesse of praise, then readers in all kinds
p. 224 UNDERWOOD 50   13 And though all praise bring nothing to your name,
p. 232 UNDERWOOD 58   5 His judgement is; If he be wise, and praise,
p. 263 UNDERWOOD 78   25 And praise them too. O! what a fame 't will be?
p. 264 UNDERWOOD 79   23 Chor. Heare, o you Groves, and, Hills, resound
                           his praise.
p. 270 UNDERWOOD 83   37 Else, who doth praise a person by a new,
p. 285 U'WOOD 84.9   90 A new Song to his praise, and great I AM:
p. 292 UNDERWOOD 86   26 The Youths and tender Maids shall sing thy
                           praise:
p. 307 HORACE 2   67 Most worthie praise, when words that common grew,
p. 317 HORACE 2   283 Praise the spare diet, wholsome justice, lawes,
p. 321 HORACE 2   366 And not without much praise; till libertie
p. 323 HORACE 2   399 Our Ancestors did Plautus numbers praise,
p. 327 HORACE 2   463 Being men were covetous of nought, but praise.
p. 341 HORACE 1   131 ... . praise
p. 362 UNGATHERED 2   14 His proofe their praise, will meete, as in this
                           line.
p. 365 UNGATHERED 5   18 In thought to praise this Ladie;
p. 385 UNGATHERED 20   4 Least a false praise do make theyr dotage his.
p. 386 UNGATHERED 21   2 May hurt them more with praise, then Foes with
                           spight.
p. 390 UNGATHERED 26   4 As neither Man, nor Muse, can praise too much.
p. 390 UNGATHERED 26   6 Were not the paths I meant vnto thy praise:
p. 391 UNGATHERED 26   11 Or crafty Malice, might pretend this praise,
p. 391 UNGATHERED 26   14 Should praise a Matron. What could hurt her
                           more?
p. 391 UNGATHERED 26   24 And we haue wits to read, and praise to giue.
p. 400 UNGATHERED 32   9 And doth deserue all muniments of praise,
p. 414 UNGATHERED 42   2 Unto the world, in praise of your first Play:

praise-worthy   frequency: 1   relative frequency: 0.00001
p.   49 EPIGRAMS 67   1 Since men haue left to doe praise-worthy things,

praised.   See "prais'd," "praysed."

praiser   frequency: 2   relative frequency: 0.00002
    See also "prayser."
    p. 117 FOREST 13   21 I, Madame, am become your praiser. Where,
    p. 333 HORACE 2   616 The Scoffer, the true Praiser doth out-goe.

praisers   frequency: 4   relative frequency: 0.00005
    p.   64 EPIGRAMS 99   10 And euen the praisers iudgement suffers so.
    p.   67 EPIGRAMS 103   11 As lowdest praisers, who perhaps would find
    p. 116 FOREST 13   5 So both the prais'd, and praisers suffer: Yet,
    p. 353 HORACE 1   601 ... praisers .. ..

praises   frequency: 10   relative frequency: 0.00014
    See also "prayses."
    p.   49 EPIGRAMS 67   2 Most thinke all praises flatteries. But truth
                                 brings
    p.   82 EPIGRAMS 130   16 When these were but the praises of the Art.
    p. 145 UNDERWOOD 5   4 Our owne false praises, for your ends:
    p. 162 UNDERWOOD 15   12 His unjust hopes, with praises begg'd, or (worse)
    p. 200 UNDERWOOD 42   21 Made longer by our praises. Or, if not,
    p. 264 UNDERWOOD 79   19 Chor. Sound, sound his praises loud, and with
                                 his, hers divide.
    p. 265 UNDERWOOD 79   52 Whose praises let's report unto the Woods,
    p. 289 UNDERWOOD 85   t2 The praises of a Countrie life.
    p. 333 HORACE 2   622 For praises, where the mind conceales a foxe.
    p. 385 UNGATHERED 19   6 If Praises, when th'are full, heaping admit,

praisest.   See "praysest."

praiseworthy.   See "praise-worthy."

praising   frequency: 1   relative frequency: 0.00001
    p. 167 UNDERWOOD 15   151 When I am hoarse, with praising his each cast,

pranck   frequency: 1   relative frequency: 0.00001
    p. 208 UNDERWOOD 43   131 (Which, some are pleas'd to stile but thy madde
                                 pranck)

prank.   See "pranck."

prankes   frequency: 1   relative frequency: 0.00001
    p.   89 EPIGRAMS 133   184 That had, so often, shew'd 'hem merry prankes.

pranks.   See "prankes."

prating   frequency: 1   relative frequency: 0.00001
    p. 321 HORACE 2   329 And so their prating to present was best,

pratling   frequency: 1   relative frequency: 0.00001
    p. 346 HORACE 1   321 ... . pratling .. .. were ....

prattling.   See "pratling."

pray   frequency: 16   relative frequency: 0.00023
    See also "'pray," "p'ry."
    p.   27 EPIGRAMS 1   1 Pray thee, take care, that tak'st my booke in
                                 hand,
    p.   95 FOREST 2   72 Nor, when I take my lodging, need I pray
    p.   96 FOREST 2   95 Each morne, and euen, they are taught to pray,
    p. 152 UNDERWOOD 12   33 And pray who shall my sorrowes read,
    p. 212 UNDERWOOD 43   210 And pray the fruites thereof, and the increase;
    p. 219 UNDERWOOD 47   37 I wish all well, and pray high heaven conspire
    p. 225 UNDERWOOD 51   6 For whose returnes, and many, all these pray:
    p. 235 UNDERWOOD 61   18 To teach the people, how to fast, and pray,
    p. 249 UNDERWOOD 72   14 That cry that gladnesse, which their hearts would
                                 pray,
    p. 257 UNDERWOOD 75   158 We pray may grace
    p. 292 UNDERWOOD 86   2 Long intermitted, pray thee, pray thee spare:
    p. 319 HORACE 2   285 Hide faults, pray to the Gods, and wish aloud
    p. 384 UNGATHERED 18   8 And pray, thy ioyes as lasting bee, as great.
    p. 394 UNGATHERED 28   2 And pray thee Reader, bring thy weepinge Eyes
    p. 398 UNGATHERED 30   59 There, thou art Homer! Pray thee, vse the stile

'pray   frequency: 1   relative frequency: 0.00001
    p. 105 FOREST 8   13 'Pray thee, feed contented, then,

pray'd   frequency: 1   relative frequency: 0.00001
    p.   45 EPIGRAMS 58   1 IDEOT, last night, I pray'd thee but
                                 forbeare

prayer   frequency: 3   relative frequency: 0.00004
    p.   99 FOREST 3   101 Be thankes to him, and earnest prayer, to finde
    p. 260 UNDERWOOD 77   5 I would, if price, or prayer could them get,
    p. 288 U'WOOD 84.9   187 For, Prayer is the Incense most perfumes

prayers   frequency: 3   relative frequency: 0.00004
    p. 122 FOREST 15   25 Of discontent; or that these prayers bee
    p. 153 UNDERWOOD 13   9 Not at my prayers, but your sense; which laid
    p. 249 UNDERWOOD 72   20 What prayers (People) can you thinke too much?

prayes   frequency: 1   relative frequency: 0.00001
    p. 256 UNDERWOOD 75   123 The holy Prelate prayes, then takes the Ring,

prays. See "prayes."

prayse   frequency: 2   relative frequency: 0.00002
    p. 387 UNGATHERED 22   5 Let such as iustly haue out=liu'd all prayse,
    p. 394 UNGATHERED 28   8 A list of Epithites: And prayse this way.

praysed   frequency: 1   relative frequency: 0.00001
    p. 422 UNGATHERED 50   2 make many, hurt themselues; a praysed faith

prayser   frequency: 1   relative frequency: 0.00001
    p. 400 UNGATHERED 32   2 Aboue his Reader, or his Prayser, is.

prayses   frequency: 1   relative frequency: 0.00001
    p.   75 EPIGRAMS 115   32 That seeming prayses, are, yet accusations.

praysest   frequency: 1   relative frequency: 0.00001
    p.   44 EPIGRAMS 55   9 When euen there, where most thou praysest mee,

preach   frequency: 1   relative frequency: 0.00001
    p. 286 U'WOOD 84.9   133 In his humanitie! To heare him preach

prease   frequency: 2   relative frequency: 0.00002
    p.   76 EPIGRAMS 119   4 Shuns prease, for two maine causes, poxe, and
                                    debt,
    p. 118 FOREST 13   58 Contagion in the prease is soonest catch'd.

precede   frequency: 1   relative frequency: 0.00001
    p.   78 EPIGRAMS 121   8 That striues, his manners should precede his wit.

precedencie   frequency: 1   relative frequency: 0.00001
  **p. 114 PANEGYRE   56 Her place, and yeares, gaue her precedencie.

precedency. See "precedencie."

precedent   frequency: 1   relative frequency: 0.00001
    See also "president."
    p.   73 EPIGRAMS 113   9 Repent thee not of thy faire precedent,

precedents. See "presidents."

preceding   frequency: 1   relative frequency: 0.00001
    See also "praeceding."
    p. 255 UNDERWOOD 75   77 Save the preceding Two?

precepts   frequency: 1   relative frequency: 0.00001
    p. 329 HORACE 2   504 The docile mind may soone thy precepts know,

precious. See "prescious," "pretious."

precipice. See "praecipice."

precipitated   frequency: 1   relative frequency: 0.00001
    p.   87 EPIGRAMS 133   137 Or were precipitated downe the jakes,

predestin'd   frequency: 1   relative frequency: 0.00001
    p. 288 U'WOOD 84.9   198 By sure Election, and predestin'd grace!

preen. See "proyne."

prefer. See "preferre."

preferr'd   frequency: 1   relative frequency: 0.00001
    p. 159 UNDERWOOD 14   20 And mine not least) I have too oft preferr'd

preferre   frequency: 2   relative frequency: 0.00002
    p.   83 EPIGRAMS 131   9 Say, this, or that man they to thee preferre;
    p. 370 UNGATHERED 7   13 'Tis not your fault, if they shall sense
                                    preferre,

preiudice   frequency: 1   relative frequency: 0.00001
     p. 50 EPIGRAMS 72   5 'Tis not thy iudgement breeds the preiudice,

prejudice. See "preiudice."

prelate   frequency: 1   relative frequency: 0.00001
     p. 256 UNDERWOOD 75   123 The holy Prelate prayes, then takes the Ring,

prentise-ship   frequency: 1   relative frequency: 0.00001
     p. 410 UNGATHERED 38   10 A Prentise-ship: which few doe now a dayes.

preoccupy. See "praeoccupie."

prepar'd   frequency: 3   relative frequency: 0.00004
     p. 116 FOREST 12   96 I, that am gratefull for him, haue prepar'd
     p. 274 U'WOOD 84.1   35 As comming with his Harpe, prepar'd
     p. 284 U'WOOD 84.9   59 Who will be there, against that day prepar'd,

prepare   frequency: 1   relative frequency: 0.00001
     p. 131 UNDERWOCD 2.1   14 First, prepare you to be sorie,

prescious   frequency: 1   relative frequency: 0.00001
     p. 361 UNGATHERED 1   9 Then I admir'd, the rare and prescious vse

prescribe   frequency: 1   relative frequency: 0.00001
     p. 327 HORACE 2   489 Wild ra<n>ging lusts; prescribe the mariage good;

presence   frequency: 2   relative frequency: 0.00002
     p. 128 UNDERWOOD 1.1   47 But in thy presence, truly glorified,
     p. 265 UNDERWOOD 79   63 The theefe from spoyle, his presence holds.

present   frequency: 14   relative frequency: 0.00020
     p. 52 EPIGRAMS 74   5 That still th'art present to the better cause;
     p. 57 EPIGRAMS 89   11 And present worth in all dost so contract,
     p. 61 EPIGRAMS 95   19 That hast thy brest so cleere of present crimes,
     p. 74 EPIGRAMS 115   15 Whose name's vn-welcome to the present eare,
     p. 105 FOREST 8   11 Scarce will take our present store?
     p. 113 FOREST 12   20 A present, which (if elder writs reherse
     p. 142 U'WOOD 2.10   t1 Another Ladyes exception present at the hearing.
     p. 171 UNDERWOOD 19   21 To use the present, then, is not abuse,
     p. 176 UNDERWOOD 25   2 Thy present Aide: Arise Invention,
     p. 245 UNDERWOOD 70   79 Hee leap'd the present age,
     p. 260 UNDERWOOD 77   2 I would present you now with curious plate
     p. 317 HORACE 2   263 Present anone: Medea must not kill
     p. 321 HORACE 2   329 And so their prating to present was best,
     p. 384 UNGATHERED 18   1 They are not those, are present wth theyre face,

presentacon   frequency: 1   relative frequency: 0.00001
     p. 405 UNGATHERED 34   76 In presentacon of some puppet play!

presentation. See "presentacon."

presented   frequency: 1   relative frequency: 0.00001
     p. 382 UNGATHERED 16   t1 A speach presented vnto king James at a tylting
                               in the

presentes   frequency: 1   relative frequency: 0.00001
     p. 382 UNGATHERED 16   6 presentes a Royall Alter of fayre peace,

presenting   frequency: 2   relative frequency: 0.00002
     p. 305 HORACE 2   4 Presenting upwards, a faire female feature,
     p. 370 UNGATHERED 7   6 Will well confesse; presenting, limiting,

presently   frequency: 1   relative frequency: 0.00001
     p. 201 UNDERWOOD 42   44 Her presently? Or leape thy Wife of force,

presents   frequency: 1   relative frequency: 0.00001
     See also "dayes-presents," "presentes."
     p. 115 FOREST 12   86 And show, how, to the life, my soule presents

preseru'd   frequency: 1   relative frequency: 0.00001
     p. 38 EPIGRAMS 35   10 And since, the whole land was preseru'd for thee.

preserued   frequency: 1   relative frequency: 0.00001
     p. 38 EPIGRAMS 35   9 First thou preserued wert, our king to bee,

preserues   frequency: 1   relative frequency: 0.00001
     p. 110 FOREST 11   54 Preserues communitie.

preserve   frequency: 3   relative frequency: 0.00004
     p. 168 UNDERWOOD 15   189 So, 'live or dead, thou wilt preserve a fame
     p. 192 UNDERWOOD 38   61 Her order is to cherish, and preserve,
     p. 220 UNDERWOOD 47   72 And free it from all question to preserve.

preserved   frequency: 1   relative frequency: 0.00001
     See alsc "preseru'd," "preserued."
     p. 413 UNGATHERED 41   19 Preserved, in her antique bed of Vert,

preserver   frequency: 2   relative frequency: 0.00002
     p. 264 UNDERWOOD 79   14 1. PAN is the great Preserver of our bounds.
     p. 265 UNDERWOOD 79   48 This is the great Preserver of our bounds,

preserves   frequency: 2   relative frequency: 0.00002
     See alsc "preserues."
     p. 146 UNDERWOOD 6   21 Our pleasure; but preserves us more
     p. 335 HORACE 2   665 Hee that preserves a man, against his will,

president   frequency: 1   relative frequency: 0.00001
     p. 237 UNDERWOOD 64   13 When all your life's a president of dayes,

presidents   frequency: 1   relative frequency: 0.00001
     p. 187 UNDERWOOD 33   25 Of Bookes, of Presidents, hast thou at hand!

press. See "prease," "presse."

presse   frequency: 1   relative frequency: 0.00001
     p. 219 UNDERWOOD 47   57 I have decreed; keepe it from waves, and presse;

pressed. See "prest."

pressure   frequency: 1   relative frequency: 0.00001
     p. 154 UNDERWOOD 13   32 Of pressure, like one taken in a streight?

prest   frequency: 4   relative frequency: 0.00005
     p. 166 UNDERWOOD 15   128 But both fell prest under the load they make.
     p. 248 UNDERWOOD 71   1 Poore wretched states, prest by extremities,
     p. 290 UNDERWOOD 85   15 Or the prest honey in pure pots doth keepe
     p. 416 UNGATHERED 45   8 prest in to se you.

presume   frequency: 2   relative frequency: 0.00002
     p. 87 EPIGRAMS 133   110 Vanish'd away: as you must all presume
     p. 284 U'WOOD 84.9   70 Presume to interpell that fulnesse, when

presumes   frequency: 1   relative frequency: 0.00001
     p. 288 U'WOOD 84.9   188 The holy Altars, when it least presumes.

pretend   frequency: 3   relative frequency: 0.00004
     p. 122 FOREST 15   7 And iudge me after: if I dare pretend
     p. 271 UNDERWOOD 83   92 With what injustice should one soule pretend
     p. 391 UNGATHERED 26   11 Or crafty Malice, might pretend this praise,

pretext   frequency: 1   relative frequency: 0.00001
     p. 177 UNDERWOOD 25   29 Of politique pretext, that wryes a State,

pretious   frequency: 3   relative frequency: 0.00004
     p. 168 UNDERWOOD 15   190 Still pretious, with the odour of thy name.
     p. 285 U'WOOD 84.9   104 That pure, that pretious, and exalted mind
     p. 399 UNGATHERED 31   18 Of vertue, pretious in the frame:

prettie   frequency: 1   relative frequency: 0.00001
     p. 188 UNDERWOOD 35   2 What manners prettie, Nature milde,

pretty   frequency: 1   relative frequency: 0.00001
     See alsc "prettie."
     p. 258 UNDERWOOD 75   174 Like pretty Spies,

preuaile   frequency: 1   relative frequency: 0.00001
     p. 59 EPIGRAMS 92   36 Much like those Brethren; thinking to preuaile

preuented   frequency: 1   relative frequency: 0.00001
     p. 54 EPIGRAMS 84   3 And, ere I could aske you, I was preuented:

prevail. See "preuaile."

prevail'd   frequency: 1   relative frequency: 0.00001
     p. 188 UNDERWOOD 34   17 I, that thy Ayme was; but her fate prevail'd:

prevaricators. See "praevaricators."

prevent   frequency: 1   relative frequency: 0.00001
    p. 153 UNDERWOOD 13   11 And in the Act did so my blush prevent,

prevented. See "preuented."

priam's   frequency: 1   relative frequency: 0.00001
    p. 313 HORACE 2   196 I sing a noble Warre, and Priam's Fate.

priapus   frequency: 1   relative frequency: 0.00001
    p. 290 UNDERWOOD 85   21 With which, Priapus, he may thanke thy hands,

price   frequency: 9   relative frequency: 0.00013
    p. 60 EPIGRAMS 102   11 And are so good, and bad, iust at a price,
    p. 74 EPIGRAMS 115   6 About the towne; and knowne too, at that price.
    p. 99 FOREST 3   74 For euery price, in euery iarre,
    p. 105 FOREST 8   27 Any paines; yea, thinke it price,
    p. 114 FOREST 12   27 But let this drosse carry what price it will
    p. 130 UNDERWOOD 1.3   20 Who made himselfe the price of sinne,
    p. 260 UNDERWOOD 77   5 I would, if price, or prayer could them get,
    p. 286 U'WOOD 84.9   134 The price of our Redemption, and to teach
    p. 408 UNGATHERED 37   6 Is to make cheape, the Lord, the lines, the
        price.

prick   frequency: 1   relative frequency: 0.00001
    p. 164 UNDERWOOD 15   67 To catch the flesh in, and to pound a Prick.

prick'd   frequency: 1   relative frequency: 0.00001
    p. 219 UNDERWOOD 47   47 Of Spaine or France; or were not prick'd downe
        one

pride   frequency: 16   relative frequency: 0.00023
  *p. 492 TO HIMSELF   3 Where pride, and impudence (in faction knit)
  **p. 115 PANEGYRE   74 The Kings obeying will, from taking pride
    p. 52 EPIGRAMS 76   10 Hating that solemne vice of greatnesse, pride;
    p. 60 EPIGRAMS 93   6 Vpbraiding rebells armes, and barbarous pride:
    p. 60 EPIGRAMS 102   15 Of what ambition, faction, pride can raise;
    p. 73 EPIGRAMS 113   7 For since, what ignorance, what pride is fled!
    p. 101 FOREST 4   48 And pride, and ignorance the schooles,
    p. 114 FOREST 12   26 Then, here, to giue pride fame, and peasants
        birth.
    p. 132 UNDERWOOD 2.2   4 All the Pride the fields than have:
    p. 163 UNDERWOOD 15   43 As they are made! Pride, and stiffe Clownage
        mixt
    p. 213 UNDERWOOD 44   16 To see the Pride at Court, their Wives doe
        make:
    p. 234 UNDERWOOD 61   1 That you have seene the pride, beheld the sport,
    p. 287 U'WOOD 84.9   160 (But pride, that schisme of incivilitie)
    p. 365 UNGATHERED 5   24 Nor takes she pride to know them.
    p. 368 UNGATHERED 6   83 The choise of Europes pride;
    p. 420 UNGATHERED 48   10 Butt, Clownishe pride hath gott

prie   frequency: 1   relative frequency: 0.00001
  **p. 113 PANEGYRE   8 But these his searching beams are cast, to prie

priest   frequency: 4   relative frequency: 0.00005
    p. 28 EPIGRAMS 5   3 The world the temple was, the priest a king,
    p. 119 FOREST 13   101 By me, their priest (if they can ought diuine)
    p. 177 UNDERWOOD 25   11 Thy Priest in this strange rapture; heat my
        braine
    p. 327 HORACE 2   479 Orpheus, a priest, and speaker for the Gods,

priests   frequency: 1   relative frequency: 0.00001
    p. 245 UNDERWOOD 70   82 Of which we Priests, and Poets say

prime   frequency: 8   relative frequency: 0.00011
    p. 73 EPIGRAMS 112   22 There's no vexation, that can make thee prime.
    p. 199 UNDERWOOD 41   11 Alas I ha' lost my heat, my blood, my prime,
    p. 222 UNDERWOOD 49   4 Where fight the prime Cocks of the Game, for
        wit?
    p. 251 UNDERWOOD 74   6 Of the prime beautie of the yeare, the Spring.
    p. 273 U'WOOD 84.1   21 Their Corrals, Whistles, and prime Coates,
    p. 311 HORACE 2   115 The conqu'ring Champion, the prime Horse in
        course,
    p. 391 UNGATHERED 26   44 And all the Muses still were in their prime,
    p. 416 UNGATHERED 44   2 Our first of fruits, that is the prime of flowers

priming   frequency: 1   relative frequency: 0.00001
    p. 405 UNGATHERED 34   87 On ye new priming of thy old Signe postes

primis. See "in-primis."

prince   frequency: 16   relative frequency: 0.00023
```
 **p. 116 PANEGYRE      106 "Lawes, Iudges, co<u>nsellors, yea prince, and
                             state.
 **p. 116 PANEGYRE      128 In all these knowing artes our prince excell'd.
   p.  28 EPIGRAMS 4      7 And such a Prince thou art, wee daily see,
   p.  37 EPIGRAMS 35     2 A Prince, that rules by'example, more than sway?
   p.  59 EPIGRAMS 92    12 And what each prince doth for intelligence owe,
   p.  95 FOREST 2       77 With his braue sonne, the Prince, they saw thy
                             fires
   p. 215 UNDERWOOD 44   78 Our Ancestors impos'd on Prince and State.
   p. 234 UNDERWOOD 61    4 At which there are, would sell the Prince, and
                             State:
   p. 237 UNDERWOOD 65    5 This Prince of flowers? Soone shoot thou up,
                             and grow
   p. 238 UNDERWOOD 66    6 The Mother of our Prince? When was there seene
   p. 238 UNDERWOOD 66   11 As in this Prince? Let it be lawfull, so
   p. 249 UNDERWOOD 72   19 The wish is great; but where the Prince is such,
   p. 256 UNDERWOOD 75  115 In him the times, no lesse then Prince, are
                             prais'd,
   p. 271 UNDERWOOD 83   88 And Day, deceasing with the Prince of light,
   p. 419 UNGATH'D 47A    1 The ..... ye ...... ... Prince god ......
   p. 423 UNGATHERED 50  19 That prince that shames a tyrants name to beare,
```

princes   frequency: 9   relative frequency: 0.00013
```
 **p. 115 PANEGYRE       85 "That princes, since they know it is their fate,
 **p. 116 PANEGYRE      113 He knew that princes, who had sold their fame
   p.  69 EPIGRAMS 107    7 And yet are with their Princes: Fill them full
   p. 117 FOREST 13      41 A Princes fortune: These are gifts of chance,
   p. 219 UNDERWOOD 47   38 My Princes safetie, and my Kings desire,
   p. 237 UNDERWOOD 65   t1 An Epigram on the Princes birth.
   p. 248 UNDERWOOD 71    3 Of Princes aides, or good mens Charities.
   p. 268 UNDERWOOD 82    5 Would they would understand it! Princes are
   p. 284 U'WOOD 84.9    84 Amongst her Peeres, those Princes of all good!
```

principalities   frequency: 1   relative frequency: 0.00001
```
   p. 285 U'WOOD 84.9    86 Angels, Arch-angels, Principalities,
```

print   frequency: 3   relative frequency: 0.00004
```
   p. 154 UNDERWOOD 13   45 Lest Ayre, or Print, but flies it: Such men
                             would
   p. 362 UNGATHERED 2    5 Looke here on Bretons worke, the master print:
   p. 390 UNGATHERED 25   7 His face; the Print would then surpasse
```

printed   frequency: 1   relative frequency: 0.00001
```
   p.  43 EPIGRAMS 53     5 It was as if thou printed had'st an oath,
```

pris'd   frequency: 1   relative frequency: 0.00001
```
   p.  78 EPIGRAMS 121    6 If onely loue should make the action pris'd:
```

prise   frequency: 1   relative frequency: 0.00001
```
   p. 119 FOREST 13     116 But to please him, who is the dearer prise
```

priuate   frequency: 6   relative frequency: 0.00008
```
 **p. 116 PANEGYRE      105 "From priuate chambers; that could then create
 **p. 117 PANEGYRE      140 The temp'rance of a priuate man did bring,
   p.  37 EPIGRAMS 32     1 What two braue perills of the priuate sword
   p.  47 EPIGRAMS 63     6 Not from the publike voyce, but priuate fact;
   p.  49 EPIGRAMS 68     2 Takes priuate beatings, and begins againe.
   p.  70 EPIGRAMS 109    8 Is priuate gaine, which hath long guilt to
                             friend.
```

priuie   frequency: 1   relative frequency: 0.00001
```
   p.  86 EPIGRAMS 133   73 But they vnfrighted passe, though many a priuie
```

priuies   frequency: 1   relative frequency: 0.00001
```
   p.  88 EPIGRAMS 133  168 Tempt such a passage? when each priuies seate
```

priuiledge   frequency: 1   relative frequency: 0.00001
```
   p.  82 EPIGRAMS 131    4 The learn'd haue no more priuiledge, then the
                             lay.
```

private   frequency: 4   relative frequency: 0.00005
```
      See also "priuate."
   p. 224 UNDERWOOD 50    1 The Wisdome, Madam, of your private Life,
   p. 287 U'WOOD 84.9   179 Of Pietie, and private holinesse.
   p. 311 HORACE 2      123 Abhorres low numbers, and the private straine
   p. 327 HORACE 2      488 The publike, from the private; to abate
```

privilege. See "priuiledge."

privy. See "priuie."

privy's. See "priuies."

prize   frequency: 5   relative frequency: 0.00007
    See alsc "prise."
    p. 108 FOREST 10 A   6 Could ne'er make prize of thy white Chastetye.
    p. 127 UNDERWOOD 1.1   11 But 'bove the fat of rammes, or bulls, to prize
    p. 155 UNDERWOOD 13   81 All as their prize, turne Pyrats here at Land,
    p. 291 UNDERWOOD 85   49 Not Lucrine Oysters I could then more prize,
    p. 408 UNGATHERED 36   8 He makes ye Camell & dull Ass his prize.

prized. See "pris'd."

proceeding   frequency: 1   relative frequency: 0.00001
    p. 128 UNDERWOOD 1.1   25 7. Eternall Spirit, God from both proceeding,

process. See "processe."

processe   frequency: 1   relative frequency: 0.00001
    p. 217 UNDERWOOD 46   9 Such was thy Processe, when Integritie,

procession   frequency: 1   relative frequency: 0.00001
    p. 252 UNDERWOOD 75   9 See, the Procession! what a Holy day

proclaim. See "prcclaime."

proclaime   frequency: 4   relative frequency: 0.00005
  **p. 114 PANEGYRE   42 The fittest herald to proclaime true ioyes:
    p. 72 EPIGRAMS 111   13 By thy great helpe: and doth proclaime by mee,
    p. 185 UNDERWOOD 31   3 So, may the King proclaime your Conscience is
    p. 190 UNDERWOOD 37   16 Though you sometimes proclaime me too severe,

proclamation   frequency: 1   relative frequency: 0.00001
    p. 59 EPIGRAMS 92   20 And whisper what a Proclamation sayes.

procne. See "progne."

procure   frequency: 1   relative frequency: 0.00001
    p. 109 FOREST 11   6 Or safe, but shee'll procure

prodigally   frequency: 1   relative frequency: 0.00001
    p. 280 U'WOOD 84.9   141 Had lost our selves? and prodigally spent

prodigie   frequency: 1   relative frequency: 0.00001
    p. 86 EPIGRAMS 133   79 They met the second Prodigie, would feare a

prodigious   frequency: 2   relative frequency: 0.00002
    p. 226 UNDERWOOD 52   1 Why? though I seeme of a prodigious wast,
    p. 242 UNDERWOOD 70   3 When the Prodigious Hannibal did crowne

prodigiously   frequency: 1   relative frequency: 0.00001
    p. 307 HORACE 2   41 One thing prodigiously, paints in the woods

prodigy. See "prodigie."

produce   frequency: 3   relative frequency: 0.00004
    p. 193 UNDERWOOD 38   97 Produce; though threatning with a coale, or
                              chalke
    p. 244 UNDERWOOD 70   55 Produce thy masse of miseries on the Stage,
    p. 366 UNGATHERED 6   2 Produce vs a blacke Swan?

profane   frequency: 1   relative frequency: 0.00001
    See also "prophane."
    p. 327 HORACE 2   487 Things sacred, from profane to separate;

profaneness. See "prophanenesse."

profess. See "professe."

professe   frequency: 5   relative frequency: 0.00007
    p. 42 EPIGRAMS 49   6 In my chast booke: professe them in thine owne.
    p. 65 EPIGRAMS 101   24 And Ile professe no verses to repeate:
    p. 116 FOREST 13   7 I, therefore, who professe my selfe in loue
    p. 152 UNDERWOOD 12   29 Much from him I professe I wonne,
    p. 190 UNDERWOOD 37   19 Little know they, that professe Amitie,

professed   frequency: 1   relative frequency: 0.00001
    See alsc "profest."
    p. 101 FOREST 4   47 Where enuious arts professed be,

professeth   frequency: 1   relative frequency: 0.00001
    p. 236 UNDERWOOD 64   12 That Faith, which she professeth to be pure?

professing   frequency: 2   relative frequency: 0.00002
    p. 307 HORACE 2   38 Professing greatnesse, swells: That, low by lee
    p. 409 UNGATHERED 38   4 Of Fellowship, professing my old Arts.

profession   frequency: 2   relative frequency: 0.00002
    p.   70 EPIGRAMS 108   6 Your great profession; which I once, did proue:
    p. 146 UNDERWOOD 6   19 And this profession of a store

profest   frequency: 2   relative frequency: 0.00002
    p.   67 EPIGRAMS 103   13 My praise is plaine, and where so ere profest,
    p. 305 HORACE 2   17 In grave beginnings, and great things profest,

proffitt   frequency: 1   relative frequency: 0.00001
    p. 422 UNGATHERED 50   8 are distant, so is proffitt from iust aymes.

proficiencie   frequency: 1   relative frequency: 0.00001
    p. 218 UNDERWOOD 47   12 As make it their proficiencie, how much

proficiency. See "proficiencie."

profit   frequency: 6   relative frequency: 0.00008
    See also "proffitt," "profitt."
    p. 157 UNDERWOOD 13   132 Profit in ought; each day some little adde,
    p. 189 UNDERWOOD 37   5 On which with profit, I shall never looke,
    p. 241 UNDERWOOD 69   3 Profit, or Chance had made us: But I know
    p. 319 HORACE 2   309 That found out profit, and foretold each thing,
    p. 327 HORACE 2   477 Poets would either profit, or delight,
    p. 329 HORACE 2   511 The Poems void of profit, our grave men

profitable   frequency: 1   relative frequency: 0.00001
    p. 225 UNDERWOOD 50   34 So are they profitable to be knowne:

profits   frequency: 3   relative frequency: 0.00004
    p. 246 UNDERWOOD 70   101 The profits for a time.
    p. 264 UNDERWOOD 79   15 2. To him we owe all profits of our grounds.
    p. 331 HORACE 2   583 Into the Profits, what a meere rude braine

profitt   frequency: 1   relative frequency: 0.00001
    p. 418 UNGATHERED 46   6 for when the profitt with the payne doth meete,

progne   frequency: 1   relative frequency: 0.00001
    p. 317 HORACE 2   266 His Nephews entrailes; nor must Progne flie

proiects   frequency: 1   relative frequency: 0.00001
    p.   59 EPIGRAMS 92   11 The councels, proiects, practises they know,

projects   frequency: 1   relative frequency: 0.00001
    See also "proiects."
    p. 258 UNDERWOOD 75   184 So great; his Body now alone projects the shade.

prologue   frequency: 1   relative frequency: 0.00001
    p. 107 FOREST 10   20 Turne the stale prologue to some painted maske,

proludium   frequency: 1   relative frequency: 0.00001
    p. 108 FOREST 10A   t1 Proludium.

promethean   frequency: 1   relative frequency: 0.00001
    p.   71 EPIGRAMS 110   17 Thy learned hand, and true Promethean art

promis'd   frequency: 2   relative frequency: 0.00002
    p. 139 UNDERWOOD 2.8   3 Lightly promis'd, she would tell
    p. 237 UNDERWOOD 65   6 The same that thou art promis'd, but be slow,

promise   frequency: 6   relative frequency: 0.00008
    p.   28 EPIGRAMS 4   8 As chiefe of those still promise they will bee.
    p. 139 UNDERWOOD 2.8   5 And that promise set on fire
    p. 139 UNDERWOOD 2.8   t1 Urging her of a promise.
    p. 229 UNDERWOOD 55   3 Then would I promise here to give
    p. 235 UNDERWOOD 63   4 Doth by his doubt, distrust his promise more.
    p. 252 UNDERWOOD 75   10 (Bearing the promise of some better fate)

promiser   frequency: 1   relative frequency: 0.00001
    p. 313 HORACE 2   197 What doth this Promiser such gaping worth

prompt   frequency: 1   relative frequency: 0.00001
    p. 169 UNDERWOOD 18   1 Can Beautie that did prompt me first to write,

promptly   frequency: 1   relative frequency: 0.00001
  **p. 115 PANEGYRE   97 "And thriuing statutes she could promptly note;

prone   frequency: 2   relative frequency: 0.00002
    p. 110 FOREST 11   32 The first; as prone to moue
    p. 311 HORACE 2   143 Mens faces, still, with such as laugh, are prone

pronounce   frequency: 2   relative frequency: 0.00002
    p. 140 UNDERWOOD 2.8   19 And pronounce, which band, or lace,
    p. 327 HORACE 2   468 From the five ounces; what remaines? pronounce

proof. See "proofe."

proofe   frequency: 3   relative frequency: 0.00004
    p. 362 UNGATHERED 2   14 His proofe their praise, will meete, as in this
                               line.
    p. 367 UNGATHERED 6   49 Be proofe, the glory of his hand,
    p. 391 UNGATHERED 26   15 But thou art proofe against them, and indeed

proofes   frequency: 1   relative frequency: 0.00001
    p. 82 EPIGRAMS 130   17 But when I haue said, The proofes of all these
                               bee

proofs. See "proofes."

propagate   frequency: 1   relative frequency: 0.00001
    p. 257 UNDERWOOD 75   149 To propagate their Names,

proper   frequency: 8   relative frequency: 0.00011
    p. 61 EPIGRAMS 95   9 To thine owne proper I ascribe then more;
    p. 73 EPIGRAMS 112   16 O, (thou cry'st out) that is thy proper game.
    p. 117 FOREST 13   32 It perfect, proper, pure, and naturall,
    p. 146 UNDERWOOD 6   4 Our proper vertue is to range:
    p. 175 UNDERWOOD 23   26 Strike in thy proper straine,
    p. 176 UNDERWOOD 24   16 By which as proper titles, she is knowne
    p. 205 UNDERWOOD 43   64 Thou should'st have cry'd, and all beene proper
                               stuffe.
    p. 317 HORACE 2   254 In fitting proper adjuncts to each day.

properest. See "prop'rest."

properly   frequency: 1   relative frequency: 0.00001
    p. 313 HORACE 2   183 'Tis hard, to speake things common, properly:

propertie   frequency: 1   relative frequency: 0.00001
    p. 190 UNDERWOOD 37   21 How much they lame her in her propertie.

properties. See "propertyes."

propertius   frequency: 1   relative frequency: 0.00001
    p. 181 UNDERWOOD 27   11 Doth Cynthia, in Propertius song

property. See "propertie."

propertyes   frequency: 2   relative frequency: 0.00002
    p. 402 UNGATHERED 34   12 Or making of ye Propertyes it meane?
    p. 404 UNGATHERED 34   61 The maker of ye Propertyes! in summe

prophane   frequency: 4   relative frequency: 0.00005
    p. 27 EPIGRAMS 2   11 Much lesse with lewd, prophane, and beastly
                               phrase,
    p. 283 U'WOOD 84.9   39 Dare I prophane, so irreligious bee
    p. 284 U'WOOD 84.9   79 Dull, and prophane, weake, and imperfect eyes,
    p. 400 UNGATHERED 32   3 Hence, then, prophane: Here needs no words
                               expense

prophanenesse   frequency: 1   relative frequency: 0.00001
    p. 238 UNDERWOOD 66   4 (Without prophanenesse) yet, a Poet, cry,

prophet   frequency: 1   relative frequency: 0.00001
  See also "prophet's."
    p. 206 UNDERWOOD 43   82 Th'admir'd discourses of the Prophet Ball:
                               .

prophetic. See "propheticke."

propheticke   frequency: 1   relative frequency: 0.00001
    p. 369 UNGATHERED 6   112 Conceal'd from all but cleare Propheticke eyes.

prophets   frequency: 2   relative frequency: 0.00002
    p. 67 EPIGRAMS 104   1 Were they that nam'd you, prophets? Did they
                               see,

prophets (cont.)
   p. 285 U'WOOD 84.9   85 Saints, Martyrs, Prophets, with those
                                 Hierarchies,

prophet's   frequency: 1   relative frequency: 0.00001
   p. 223 UNDERWOOD 49   46 Will cal't a Bastard, when a Prophet's borne.

proportion   frequency: 4   relative frequency: 0.00005
   p. 96 FOREST 2   99 Now, PENSHVRST, they that will
                                   proportion thee
   p. 200 UNDERWOOD 42   14 No face, no hand, proportion, line, or Ayre
   p. 395 UNGATHERED 29   12 Keepe due proportion in the ample song,
   p. 399 UNGATHERED 31   21 What was proportion, or could bee

proportion'd   frequency: 1   relative frequency: 0.00001
   p. 396 UNGATHERED 30   21 And those so sweet, and well proportion'd parts,

proportions   frequency: 1   relative frequency: 0.00001
   p. 245 UNDERWOOD 70   73 In small proportions, we just beautie see:

propos'd   frequency: 1   relative frequency: 0.00001
   p. 85 EPIGRAMS 133   38 Propos'd to goe to Hol'borne in a wherry:

propose   frequency: 1   relative frequency: 0.00001
   p. 112 FOREST 11   91 But we propose a person like our Doue,

propound   frequency: 1   relative frequency: 0.00001
   p. 293 UNDERWOOD 86   31 Nor care I now healths to propound;

propping   frequency: 1   relative frequency: 0.00001
   p. 183 UNDERWOOD 29   8 Propping Verse, for feare of falling

prop'rest   frequency: 1   relative frequency: 0.00001
   p. 273 U'WOOD 84.1   19 As prop'rest gifts, to Girles, and Boyes,

prose   frequency: 4   relative frequency: 0.00005
   p. 133 UNDERWOOD 2.3   23 And in either Prose, or Song,
   p. 201 UNDERWOOD 42   61 From the poore wretch, which though he play'd in
                                   prose,
   p. 398 UNGATHERED 30   73 That can but reade; who cannot, may in prose
   p. 403 UNGATHERED 34   40 The Eloquence of Masques! What need of prose

prosecute. See "prosequute."

prosequute   frequency: 1   relative frequency: 0.00001
   p. 58 EPIGRAMS 91   9 I leaue thy acts, which should I prosequute

proserpina   frequency: 1   relative frequency: 0.00001
   p. 89 EPIGRAMS 133   180 And MADAME CAESAR, great
                                   PROSERPINA,

prospectiue   frequency: 1   relative frequency: 0.00001
   p. 383 UNGATHERED 16   12 made prospectiue, behould hym, hee must pas<s>e

prospective. See "prospectiue."

prosperitie   frequency: 2   relative frequency: 0.00002
   p. 186 UNDERWOOD 32   10 A right by the prosperitie of their Crimes;
   p. 216 UNDERWOOD 44   100 Cover'd with Tissue, whose prosperitie mocks

prosperity   frequency: 1   relative frequency: 0.00001
  See also "prosperitie."
   p. 410 UNGATHERED 39   1 Shall the prosperity of a Pardon still

prostitute   frequency: 2   relative frequency: 0.00002
  *p. 493 TO HIMSELF   41 Leaue things so prostitute,
   p. 106 FOREST 8   45 On their beds, most prostitute,

protectes   frequency: 1   relative frequency: 0.00001
   p. 423 UNGATHERED 50   12 It is a lycense to doe ill, protectes

protection   frequency: 1   relative frequency: 0.00001
   p. 184 UNDERWOOD 29   32 Happy Greeke, by this protection,

protects. See "protectes."

protest   frequency: 2   relative frequency: 0.00002
   p. 218 UNDERWOOD 47   15 But for a Sealing: let these men protest.
   p. 380 UNGATHERED 12   46 He there doth protest he saw of the eleuen.

protestation   frequency: 1   relative frequency: 0.00001
     p. 229 UNDERWOOD 54   18 And then to be return'd; on protestation

protested   frequency: 1   relative frequency: 0.00001
     p. 169 UNDERWOOD 17   7 Nor should I at this time protested be,

protests   frequency: 1   relative frequency: 0.00001
     p. 246 UNDERWOOD 70   104 Orgies of drinke, or fain'd protests:

proteus   frequency: 1   relative frequency: 0.00001
     p. 389 UNGATHERED 24   5 As in this Spanish Proteus; who, though writ

protraction   frequency: 1   relative frequency: 0.00001
     p. 39 EPIGRAMS 133   192 And so went brauely backe, without protraction.

proud   frequency: 18   relative frequency: 0.00026
     See also "prowde."
     p. 46 EPIGRAMS 60   6 And proud, my worke shall out-last common deeds,
     p. 62 EPIGRAMS 97   8 Where ere he met me; now hee's dumbe, or proud.
     p. 81 EPIGRAMS 129   15 O, runne not proud of this. Yet, take thy due.
     p. 96 FOREST 2   101 Those proud, ambitious heaps, and nothing else,
     p. 97 FOREST 3   15 Free from proud porches, or their guilded roofes,
     p. 113 FOREST 12   14 When his proud patrons fauours are asleepe;
     p. 153 UNDERWOOD 13   4 Lesse list of proud, hard, or ingratefull Men.
     p. 154 UNDERWOOD 13   37 In that proud manner, as a good so gain'd,
     p. 164 UNDERWOOD 15   59 O, these so ignorant Monsters! light, as proud,
     p. 164 UNDERWOOD 15   83 Nor is the title question'd with our proud,
     p. 167 UNDERWOOD 15   167 Of the poore sufferers) where the envious, proud,
     p. 172 UNDERWOOD 20   21 I could forgive her being proud! a whore!
     p. 172 UNDERWOOD 21   7 Proud, false, and trecherous, vindictive, all
     p. 280 U'WOOD 84.4   57 Not swelling like the Ocean proud,
     p. 289 UNDERWOOD 85   7 But flees the Barre and Courts, with the proud
                               bords,
     p. 319 HORACE 2   286 Fortune would love the poore, and leave the
                               proud.
     p. 392 UNGATHERED 26   47 Nature her selfe was proud of his designes,
     p. 403 UNGATHERED 34   24 In Towne & Court? Are you growne rich?
                               & proud?

prou'd   frequency: 3   relative frequency: 0.00004
     p. 53 EPIGRAMS 79   2 Your noblest father prou'd: like whom, before,
     p. 84 EPIGRAMS 133   8 COCYTVS, PHLEGETON, our haue
                               prou'd in one;
     p. 421 UNGATHERED 49   7 O're read, examin'd, try'd, and prou'd yor: Ryme

prouder   frequency: 1   relative frequency: 0.00001
     p. 133 UNDERWOOD 2.3   2 Which the prouder Beauties please,

proudly   frequency: 1   relative frequency: 0.00001
     p. 387 UNGATHERED 22   3 which, did they neere so neate, or proudly dwell,

proue   frequency: 16   relative frequency: 0.00023
   **p. 114 PANEGYRE   46 Along with him, and the same trouble proue.
     p. 43 EPIGRAMS 51   3 Which though it did but panick terror proue,
     p. 56 EPIGRAMS 88   14 And stoupe, and cringe. O then, it needs must
                               proue
     p. 70 EPIGRAMS 108   6 Your great profession; which I once, did proue:
     p. 70 EPIGRAMS 109   17 Thy deedes, vnto thy name, will proue new wombes,
     p. 80 EPIGRAMS 126   6 I answer'd, DAPHNE now no paine can proue.
     p. 81 EPIGRAMS 128   7 As the beginnings here, proue purely sweet,
     p. 102 FOREST 5   1 Come my CELIA, let vs proue,
     p. 110 FOREST 11   44 No such effects doth proue;
     p. 114 FOREST 12   46 Or in their windowes; doe but proue the wombs,
     p. 115 FOREST 12   77 Will proue old ORPHEVS act no tale to be:
     p. 116 FOREST 12   91 Moodes, which the god-like SYDNEY oft did
                               proue,
     p. 364 UNGATHERED 4   7 Proue of his Mistris Feature,
     p. 367 UNGATHERED 6   37 But proue the Aire, and saile from Coast to
                               Coast:
     p. 384 UNGATHERED 18   19 So, may those Mariage-Pledges, comforts proue:
     p. 393 UNGATHERED 27   18 Vnto the world doth proue.

proues   frequency: 1   relative frequency: 0.00001
     p. 49 EPIGRAMS 67   12 Proues, that is gods, which was the peoples
                               voice.

prouide   frequency: 1   relative frequency: 0.00001
     p. 94 FOREST 2   27 To crowne thy open table, doth prouide

prouing   frequency: 1   relative frequency: 0.00001
      p.   57 EPIGRAMS 90   7 Went on: and prouing him still, day by day,

prouision   frequency: 1   relative frequency: 0.00001
      p.   97 FOREST 3   14 Liue, with vn-bought prouision blest;

prouisions   frequency: 1   relative frequency: 0.00001
      p.   95 FOREST 2   58 Adde to thy free prouisions, farre aboue

prouoke   frequency: 1   relative frequency: 0.00001
      p.   94 FOREST 2   17 And thence, the ruddy Satyres oft prouoke

prou'st   frequency: 1   relative frequency: 0.00001
      p.   78 EPIGRAMS 122   10 Who prou'st, all these were, and againe may bee.

prov'd   frequency: 2   relative frequency: 0.00002
   See alsc "prou'd."
      p. 177 UNDERWOOD 25   25 (As prov'd in you)
      p. 255 UNDERWOOD 75   101 In all the prov'd assayes,

prove   frequency: 6   relative frequency: 0.00008
   See alsc "proue."
      p. 129 UNDERWOOD 1.2   5 That I may prove
      p. 143 UNDERWOOD 3   9 Mixe then your Notes, that we may prove
      p. 150 UNDERWOOD 10   10 Thou sai'st, thou only cam'st to prove
      p. 171 UNDERWOOD 19   16 And so that either may example prove
      p. 192 UNDERWOOD 38   50 Before you prove a medicine, is unjust.
      p. 307 HORACE 2   55 Upon your shoulders. Prove what they will beare,

proves   frequency: 3   relative frequency: 0.00004
   See alsc "proues."
      p. 158 UNDERWOOD 14   10 Chance that the Friends affection proves Allay
      p. 162 UNDERWOOD 15   16 No person, nor is lov'd: what wayes he proves
      p. 242 UNDERWOOD 69   15 At a Friends freedome, proves all circling
                                 meanes

provest. See "prou'st," "prov'st."

provide   frequency: 1   relative frequency: 0.00001
   See alsc "prouide."
      p. 208 UNDERWOOD 43   124 My friends, the Watermen! They could provide

provided   frequency: 2   relative frequency: 0.00002
      p. 323 HORACE 2   379 Provided, ne're to yeeld, in any case
      p. 325 HORACE 2   443 And, where the matter is provided still,

providence   frequency: 1   relative frequency: 0.00001
      p. 176 UNDERWOOD 24   5 Wise Providence would so; that nor the good

provider   frequency: 1   relative frequency: 0.00001
      p. 315 HORACE 2   233 To endure counsell: a Provider slow

proving. See "prouing."

provision. See "prouisicn."

provisions. See "prouisions."

provle   frequency: 3   relative frequency: 0.00004
      p.   54 EPIGRAMS 81   1 Forbeare to tempt me, PROVLE, I will not
                                 show
      p.   54 EPIGRAMS 81   6 Thy wit liues by it, PROVLE, and belly too.
      p.   54 EPIGRAMS 81   t1 TO PROVLE THE PLAGIARY.

provoke   frequency: 4   relative frequency: 0.00005
   See alsc "proucke."
      p. 228 UNDERWOOD 53   2 Provoke his mettall, and command his force
      p. 233 UNDERWOOD 59   18 To bend, to breake, provoke,or suffer it!
      p. 237 UNDERWOOD 64   16 That nothing can her gratitude provoke!
      p. 283 U'WOOD 84.9   24 It rages, runs, flies, stands, and would provoke

prov'st   frequency: 1   relative frequency: 0.00001
      p. 187 UNDERWOOD 33   20 Thou prov'st the gentler wayes, to clense the
                                 wound,

prowde   frequency: 2   relative frequency: 0.00002
      p. 368 UNGATHERED 6   80 From whose prowde bosome, thou began'st thy
                                 flight.
      p. 368 UNGATHERED 6   81 Tames, prowde of thee, and of his Fate

prowess. See "prowesse."

prowesse   frequency: 1   relative frequency: 0.00001
     p. 240 UNDERWOOD 67   30 And of her Fathers prowesse!

prowl. See "provle."

proyne   frequency: 1   relative frequency: 0.00001
     p. 137 UNDERWOOD 2.5   35 Where I sit and proyne my wings

prudent   frequency: 1   relative frequency: 0.00001
     p. 262 UNDERWOOD 78   5 Hee's prudent, valiant, just, and temperate;

pry. See "prie."

pr'y   frequency: 2   relative frequency: 0.00002
     p. 32 EPIGRAMS 18   9 Pr'y thee beleeue still, and not iudge so fast,
     p. 73 EPIGRAMS 112   21 Pr'y thee, yet saue thy rest; giue ore in time:

psalmes   frequency: 1   relative frequency: 0.00001
     p. 288 U'WOOD 84.9   191 In frequent speaking by the pious Psalmes

psalms. See "psalmes."

ptolemey   frequency: 1   relative frequency: 0.00001
     p. 422 UNGATHERED 50   1 Just and fit actions Ptolemey (he saith)

public. See "publike," "publique."

publike   frequency: 10   relative frequency: 0.00014
     p. 47 EPIGRAMS 63   6 Not from the publike voyce, but priuate fact;
     p. 49 EPIGRAMS 68   1 PLAY-WRIGHT conuict of publike wrongs to
                              men,
     p. 156 UNDERWOOD 13   111 Her ends are honestie, and publike good!
     p. 186 UNDERWOOD 31   6 The Care, and wish still of the publike wealth:
     p. 194 UNDERWOOD 38   114 Publike affaires command me now to goe
     p. 204 UNDERWOOD 43   46 Thou should'st have stay'd, till publike fame
                              said so.
     p. 234 UNDERWOOD 61   5 That scarce you heare a publike voyce alive,
     p. 239 UNDERWOOD 67   1 1. CLIO. Up publike joy, remember
     p. 325 HORACE 2   424 Retire themselves, avoid the publike baths;
     p. 327 HORACE 2   488 The publike, from the private; to abate

publique   frequency: 5   relative frequency: 0.00007
  **p. 115 PANEGYRE   88 "In publique acts what face and forme they beare.
  **p. 116 PANEGYRE   104 "When, publique iustice borrow'd all her powers
     p. 70 EPIGRAMS 109   7 Of seruice to the publique, when the end
     p. 217 UNDERWOOD 46   16 Desired Justice to the publique Weale,
     p. 268 UNDERWOOD 82   8 Should take first Seisin of the publique good,

publish   frequency: 5   relative frequency: 0.00007
     p. 57 EPIGRAMS 89   8 That ALLEN, I should pause to publish thee?
     p. 83 EPIGRAMS 132   9 That to the world I publish, for him, this;
     p. 289 U'WOOD 84.9   228 To publish her a Saint. My Muse is gone.
     p. 313 HORACE 2   186 First publish things unspoken, and unknowne.
     p. 368 UNGATHERED 6   61 With entheate rage, to publish their bright
                              tracts?

published   frequency: 1   relative frequency: 0.00001
     p. 401 UNGATHERED 33 t2 on his Worke published.

pucell   frequency: 2   relative frequency: 0.00002
     p. 222 UNDERWOOD 49   t3 The Court Pucell.
     p. 223 UNDERWOOD 49   35 Shall I advise thee, Pucell? steale away

pucelle. See "court-pucell," "pucell," "pusil."

puff. See "puffe."

puffe   frequency: 1   relative frequency: 0.00001
     p. 69 EPIGRAMS 107   29 Nay, now you puffe, tuske, and draw vp your chin,

pui'nees   frequency: 1   relative frequency: 0.00001
     p. 62 EPIGRAMS 96   10 Let pui'nees, porters, players praise delight,

puisnes'. See "pui'nees."

pukes   frequency: 1   relative frequency: 0.00001
     p. 375 UNGATHERED 10 31 Their hornes, and Germany pukes on his head.

pull   frequency: 3   relative frequency: 0.00004
     p. 154 UNDERWOOD 13   58 Ha's Feathers, and will serve a man to pull.

pull (cont.)
```
     p. 239 UNDERWOOD 67    20 The Harmony may pull
     p. 279 U'WOOD 84.4     46 And stuck in clay here, it would pull
```

pulling   frequency: 1   relative frequency: 0.00001
```
     p. 385 UNGATHERED 19    8 Thy Richard, rais'd in song, past pulling downe.
```

pulls   frequency: 1   relative frequency: 0.00001
```
     p. 165 UNDERWOOD 15   114 Is it that man pulls on himselfe Disease?
```

pulpit   frequency: 1   relative frequency: 0.00001
```
     p.  76 EPIGRAMS 119     6 Whose dice not doing well, to'a pulpit ran.
```

pulse   frequency: 1   relative frequency: 0.00001
     See also "jacks-pulse."
```
     p. 347 HORACE 1       354 ... .... ..... Pulse there .. perhaps may ....
```

pump. See "pumpe."

pumpe   frequency: 1   relative frequency: 0.00001
```
     p. 193 UNDERWOOD 38    96 Can pumpe for; or a Libell without salt
```

pumped. See "pomp'd."

punck   frequency: 1   relative frequency: 0.00001
```
     p. 155 UNDERWOOD 13    93 Such worship due to kicking of a Punck!
```

punishment   frequency: 4   relative frequency: 0.00005
```
     p. 129 UNDERWOOD 1.2   16 Their punishment.
     p. 186 UNDERWOOD 32    14 They will come of, and scape the Punishment.
     p. 194 UNDERWOOD 38   103 There is not any punishment, or paine,
     p. 256 UNDERWOOD 75   120 A meere upbraiding Griefe, and tort'ring
                              punishment.
```

punishments   frequency: 1   relative frequency: 0.00001
```
     p. 192 UNDERWOOD 38    43 That as the last of punishments is meant;
```

punk. See "punck," "punke," "punque."

punke   frequency: 2   relative frequency: 0.00002
```
     p. 375 UNGATHERED 10   18 A Punke here pelts him with egs. How so?
     p. 375 UNGATHERED 10   28 Here, finer then comming from his Punke you him
                              see,
```

punque   frequency: 2   relative frequency: 0.00002
```
     p.  56 EPIGRAMS 87      1 Touch'd with the sinne of false play, in his
                              punque,
     p.  69 EPIGRAMS 107    20 And then lye with you, closer, then a punque,
```

puppet   frequency: 1   relative frequency: 0.00001
```
     p. 405 UNGATHERED 34   76 In presentacon of some puppet play!
```

pur-blinde   frequency: 1   relative frequency: 0.00001
```
     p.  89 EPIGRAMS 133   190 An ancient pur-blinde fletcher, with a high nose;
```

purbeck   frequency: 1   relative frequency: 0.00001
```
     p. 406 UNGATHERED 34  100 Soe ye Materialls be of Purbeck stone!
```

purblind. See "pur-blinde."

purchas'd   frequency: 2   relative frequency: 0.00002
```
     p.  99 FOREST 3        82 Purchas'd by rapine, worse then stealth,
     p. 244 UNDERWOOD 70    35 He purchas'd friends, and fame, and honours then,
```

purchase   frequency: 2   relative frequency: 0.00002
```
     p. 216 UNDERWOOD 45    26 It is a richer Purchase then of land.
     p. 400 UNGATHERED 31   36 Her right, by gift, and purchase of the Lambe:
```

pure   frequency: 18   relative frequency: 0.00026
```
    *p. 492 TO HIMSELF      15 To offer them a surfet of pure bread,
   **p. 115 PANEGYRE        72 That friendly temper'd, one pure taper makes.
     p.  65 EPIGRAMS 101    29 Is a pure cup of rich Canary-wine,
     p.  78 EPIGRAMS 122     4 The world's pure gold, and wise simplicitie;
     p. 110 FOREST 11       46 Pure, perfect, nay diuine;
     p. 117 FOREST 13       32 It perfect, proper, pure, and naturall,
     p. 128 UNDERWOOD 1.1   27 Pure thoughts in man: with fiery zeale them
                              feeding
     p. 151 UNDERWOOD 12    15 His Mind as pure, and neatly kept,
     p. 170 UNDERWOOD 19     7 By those pure bathes your either cheeke
                              discloses,
```

pure (cont.)
    p. 201 UNDERWOOD 42   68 That (in pure Madrigall) unto his Mother
    p. 236 UNDERWOOD 64   12 That Faith, which she professeth to be pure?
    p. 278 U'WOOD 84.4   25 A Mind so pure, so perfect fine,
    p. 279 U'WOOD 84.4   42 So swift, so pure, should yet apply
    p. 285 U'WOOD 84.9   104 That pure, that pretious, and exalted mind
    p. 290 UNDERWOOD 85   15 Or the prest honey in pure pots doth keepe
    p. 367 UNGATHERED 6   40 The Vale, that bred thee pure, as her Hills
                              Snow.
    p. 397 UNGATHERED 30   24 I found it pure, and perfect Poesy,
    p. 413 UNGATHERED 41   37 Most holy, & pure Virgin, blessed Mayd,

purely   frequency: 1   relative frequency: 0.00001
    p. 81 EPIGRAMS 128   7 As the beginnings here, proue purely sweet,

purer   frequency: 1   relative frequency: 0.00001
    p. 393 UNGATHERED 27   3 And purer then the purest Gold,

purest   frequency: 3   relative frequency: 0.00004
    p. 51 EPIGRAMS 74   3 Whil'st I behold thee liue with purest hands;
    p. 115 FOREST 12   65 You, and that other starre, that purest light,
    p. 393 UNGATHERED 27   3 And purer then the purest Gold,

purg'd   frequency: 3   relative frequency: 0.00004
    p. 38 EPIGRAMS 35   5 Hast purg'd thy realmes, as we haue now no cause
    p. 160 UNDERWOOD 14   42 What blots and errours, have you watch'd and
                              purg'd
    p. 414 UNGATHERED 41   55 T'imprint in all purg'd hearts this virgin sence,

purge   frequency: 1   relative frequency: 0.00001
    p. 325 HORACE 2   429 O I left-witted, that purge every spring

purged   frequency: 1   relative frequency: 0.00001
    See also "purg'd."
    p. 147 UNDERWOOD 7   17 As Summers sky, or purged Ayre,

purging   frequency: 1   relative frequency: 0.00001
    p. 29 EPIGRAMS 7   2 A purging bill, now fix'd vpon the dore,

puritanes   frequency: 2   relative frequency: 0.00002
    p. 44 EPIGRAMS 53   7 And that, as puritanes at baptisme doo,
    p. 52 EPIGRAMS 75   2 'Twixt puritanes, and players, as some cry;

puritans. See "puritanes."

puritie   frequency: 1   relative frequency: 0.00001
    p. 207 UNDERWOOD 43   93 The puritie of Language; and among

purity. See "puritie."

purl. See "purle."

purle   frequency: 2   relative frequency: 0.00002
    p. 140 UNDERWOOD 2.8   23 To say over every purle
    p. 200 UNDERWOOD 42   16 There is not worne that lace, purle, knot or pin,

purles   frequency: 1   relative frequency: 0.00001
    p. 164 UNDERWOOD 15   65 Planting their Purles, and Curles spread forth
                              like Net,

purls. See "purles."

purple   frequency: 3   relative frequency: 0.00004
    p. 99 FOREST 3   89 And, so they ride in purple, eate in plate,
    p. 321 HORACE 2   333 A royall Crowne, and purple, be made hop,
    p. 338 HORACE 1   19 . purple .... either

purple-matching   frequency: 1   relative frequency: 0.00001
    p. 290 UNDERWOOD 85   20 And purple-matching Grapes, hee's glad!

purpled   frequency: 1   relative frequency: 0.00001
    p. 94 FOREST 2   28 The purpled pheasant, with the speckled side:

purpos'd   frequency: 1   relative frequency: 0.00001
    p. 52 EPIGRAMS 76   14 I purpos'd her; that should, with euen powers,

purpose   frequency: 3   relative frequency: 0.00004
    p. 80 EPIGRAMS 126   1 Retyr'd, with purpose your faire worth to praise,
    p. 159 UNDERWOOD 14   22 But 'twas with purpose to have made them such.
    p. 317 HORACE 2   279 Then to the purpose leades, and fitly 'grees.

```
purposely                              frequency:    1   relative frequency: 0.00001
     p. 335 HORACE 2       657 Himselfe there purposely, or no; and would

purse                                  frequency:    5   relative frequency: 0.00007
     p. 155 UNDERWOOD 13    89 My wonder, why the taking a Clownes purse,
     p. 162 UNDERWOOD 15    13 Bought Flatteries, the issue of his purse,
     p. 216 UNDERWOOD 45    10 That could but claime a kindred from the purse.
     p. 230 UNDERWOOD 56    12 And that's made up as doth the purse abound.
     p. 321 HORACE 2       347 Simo; and, of a talent vip'd his purse;

pursewinge                             frequency:    1   relative frequency: 0.00001
     p. 108 FOREST 10A      10 only pursewinge Constancy, in Chainge;

pursue                                 frequency:    4   relative frequency: 0.00005
     p.  73 EPIGRAMS 112    14 To Satyres; and thou dost pursue me. Where,
     p. 104 FOREST 7         2 Seeme to flye it, it will pursue:
     p. 221 UNDERWOOD 48    34 Pursue thee in all places,
     p. 372 UNGATHERED 9    13 Vp so much truth, as could I it pursue

pursues                                frequency:    2   relative frequency: 0.00002
     p. 166 UNDERWOOD 15   137 To take the box up for him; and pursues
     p. 186 UNDERWOOD 32    13 As though the Court pursues them on the sent,

pursuing.  See "pursewinge."

pusil                                  frequency:    1   relative frequency: 0.00001
     p. 370 UNGATHERED 8     4 Lady, or Pusil, that weares maske, or fan,

puss.  See "pvsse."

put                                    frequency:   35   relative frequency: 0.00050
   **p. 114 PANEGYRE        53 And would be courted: so this Towne put on
     p.  36 EPIGRAMS 29      6 But that's put in, thou'lt say. Why so is thine.
     p.  54 EPIGRAMS 83      1 To put out the word, whore, thou do'st me woo,
     p.  54 EPIGRAMS 83      2 Throughout my booke. 'Troth put out woman too.
     p.  68 EPIGRAMS 105    16 That saw you put on PALLAS plumed caske:
     p.  69 EPIGRAMS 108     4 Be nor put on you, nor you take offence.
     p.  71 EPIGRAMS 110    11 Not all these, EDMONDS, or what else put
                               too,
     p.  72 EPIGRAMS 112     4 Or thy ranke setting? that thou dar'st put in
     p.  85 EPIGRAMS 133    32 Of those, that put out moneyes, on returne
     p.  88 EPIGRAMS 133   148 To put the skins, and offall in a pastie?
     p. 114 FOREST 12       24 Or put to flight ASTREA, when her ingots
     p. 119 FOREST 13       91 And, keeping a iust course, haue earely put
     p. 137 UNDERWOOD 2.5   36 After flight; and put new stings
     p. 147 UNDERWOOD 7     25 Though hate had put them out;
     p. 154 UNDERWOOD 13    52 But then, fist-fill'd, to put me off the sent.
     p. 156 UNDERWOOD 13   110 That with these mixtures we put out her light.
     p. 157 UNDERWOOD 13   137 That makes the Arch. The rest that there were
                               put
     p. 170 UNDERWOOD 18     7 That as the water makes things, put in't
                               streight,
     p. 171 UNDERWOOD 20     8 Put on for fashion, and take up on trust:
     p. 176 UNDERWOOD 25     3 Wake, and put on the wings of Pindars Muse,
     p. 187 UNDERWOOD 33     9 Hook-handed Harpies, gowned Vultures, put
     p. 187 UNDERWOOD 33    22 Thou hast the brave scorne, to put back the fee!
     p. 197 UNDERWOOD 40     6 To put all relish from my memorie
     p. 200 UNDERWOOD 42     9 Put on my Ivy Garland, let me see
     p. 201 UNDERWOOD 42    39 Whose like I have knowne the Taylors Wife put
                               on
     p. 201 UNDERWOOD 42    43 Put a Coach-mare in Tissue, must I horse
     p. 218 UNDERWOOD 47     2 Care not what trials they are put unto;
     p. 218 UNDERWOOD 47     8 Put conscience and my right to compromise.
     p. 222 UNDERWOOD 48    50 To put his Court in dances,
     p. 231 UNDERWOOD 57    14 Put him in mind
     p. 270 UNDERWOOD 83    53 Stick on your Cupping-glasses, feare not, put
     p. 285 U'WOOD 84.9     95 And white, as that, put on: and in her hand,
     p. 285 U'WOOD 84.9     98 Put black, and mourning on? and say you misse
     p. 325 HORACE 2       433 Be like a Whet-stone, that an edge can put
     p. 390 UNGATHERED 25    1 This Figure, that thou here seest put,

putrid                                 frequency:    1   relative frequency: 0.00001
     p. 172 UNDERWOOD 21     9 Of putrid flesh alive! of blood, the sinke!

puts                                   frequency:    8   relative frequency: 0.00011
     p.  98 FOREST 3        48 COMVS puts in, for new delights;
     p. 154 UNDERWOOD 13    34 That puts it in his Debt-booke e're't be done;
     p. 168 UNDERWOOD 15   185 That whatsoever face thy fate puts on,
     p. 193 UNDERWOOD 38    88 Streight puts off all his Anger, and doth kisse
     p. 250 UNDERWOOD 74     3 When shee puts forth the life of ev'ry thing:
```

puts (cont.)
```
    p. 291 UNDERWOOD 85    70 At th'Calends, puts all out againe.
    p. 337 HORACE 2       676 All; So this grievous Writer puts to flight
    p. 378 UNGATHERED 11   81 Honest Tom Tell-Troth puts downe Roger, How?
```

pvsse   frequency: 1   relative frequency: 0.00001
```
    p.  89 EPIGRAMS 133   183 They cry'd out PVSSE. He told them he was
                             BANKES,
```

pye. See "pie."

pygmy   frequency: 1   relative frequency: 0.00001
```
    p. 407 UNGATHERED 35   12 Thou paint a Lane, where Thumb ye Pygmy meets!
```

pyracmon's   frequency: 1   relative frequency: 0.00001
```
    p. 179 UNDERWOOD 25    42 Pyracmon's houre will come to give them ease,
```

pyramede   frequency: 1   relative frequency: 0.00001
```
    p. 115 FOREST 12      83 There like a rich, and golden pyramede,
```

pyramid. See "pyramede," "pyramide."

pyramide   frequency: 1   relative frequency: 0.00001
```
    p.  89 EPIGRAMS 133   194 The citie since hath rais'd a Pyramide.
```

pyramids   frequency: 1   relative frequency: 0.00001
```
    p. 261 UNDERWOOD 77    26 In glorious Piles, or Pyramids erect
```

pyrats   frequency: 2   relative frequency: 0.00002
```
    p. 119 FOREST 13      93 'Gainst stormes, or pyrats, that might charge
                             your peace;
    p. 155 UNDERWOOD 13    81 All as their prize, turne Pyrats here at Land,
```

pyrene   frequency: 1   relative frequency: 0.00001
```
    p. 366 UNGATHERED 6    21 The pale Pyrene, and the forked Mount:
```

pythagoras   frequency: 2   relative frequency: 0.00002
```
    p.  61 EPIGRAMS 95     2 That stranger doctrine of PYTHAGORAS,
    p.  89 EPIGRAMS 133   156 Old BANKES the iuggler, our
                             PYTHAGORAS,
```

pythian   frequency: 1   relative frequency: 0.00001
```
    p. 333 HORACE 2       591 Who, since, to sing the Pythian rites is heard,
```

pythias   frequency: 1   relative frequency: 0.00001
```
    p. 321 HORACE 2       346 And the bold Pythias, having cheated weake
```

pyx. See "pixe."

q.   frequency: 2   relative frequency: 0.00002
```
    p.  77 EPIGRAMS 120   t2 OF Q. EL<IZABETHS> CHAPPEL.
    p. 235 UNDERWOOD 63   t1 To K. CHARLES, and Q. MARY.
```

quadriuiall   frequency: 1   relative frequency: 0.00001
```
    p. 407 UNGATHERED 35   11 He draw a Forum, wth quadriuiall Streets!
```

quadrivial. See "quadriuiall."

quaint   frequency: 1   relative frequency: 0.00001
```
    p.  39 EPIGRAMS 41     3 Such her quaint practise is, so it allures,
```

quake   frequency: 1   relative frequency: 0.00001
```
    See also "flesh-quake."
    p. 193 UNDERWOOD 38    71 He cannot angrie be, but all must quake,
```

qualitie   frequency: 1   relative frequency: 0.00001
```
    p. 369 UNGATHERED 6    96 So blacke a Bird, so bright a Qualitie.
```

qualities   frequency: 1   relative frequency: 0.00001
```
    p. 220 UNDERWOOD 48    10 Their Qualities, and races,
```

quality. See "qualitie."

quarrel   frequency: 1   relative frequency: 0.00001
```
    See also "quarrell."
    p. 166 UNDERWOOD 15   115 Surfet? and Quarrel? drinkes the tother health?
```

quarrell   frequency: 5   relative frequency: 0.00007
```
    p. 188 UNDERWOOD 34    6 Quarrell with Nature, or in ballance brought
    p. 218 UNDERWOOD 47    11 Subject to quarrell only; or else such
```

quarrell (cont.)
    p. 221 UNDERWOOD 48   31 So may there never Quarrell
    p. 237 UNDERWOOD 64   14 And murmure cannot quarrell at your wayes?
    p. 290 UNDERWOOD 85   26 The soft birds quarrell in the Woods,

quarrells   frequency: 1   relative frequency: 0.00001
    p. 32 EPIGRAMS 16   6 Some hundred quarrells, yet dost thou fight none;

quarrels   frequency: 1   relative frequency: 0.00001
  See also "quarrells."
    p. 397 UNGATHERED 30   30 Their loues, their quarrels, iealousies, and
                        wrongs,

quarrie   frequency: 1   relative frequency: 0.00001
    p. 55 EPIGRAMS 85   10 Till they be sure to make the foole their
                        quarrie.

quarries   frequency: 1   relative frequency: 0.00001
    p. 143 UNDERWOOD 3   11 To make the Mountaine Quarries move,

quarry. See "quarrie."

quarter   frequency: 2   relative frequency: 0.00002
    p. 30 EPIGRAMS 12   7 The quarter day is come; the hostesse sayes,
    p. 199 UNDERWOOD 41   12 Winter is come a Quarter e're his Time,

quarter-face   frequency: 1   relative frequency: 0.00001
    p. 114 FOREST 12   29 Turne, vpon scorned verse, their quarter-face:

quarters   frequency: 1   relative frequency: 0.00001
    p. 417 UNGATHERED 45   31 or hir quarters lighter bee,

queen   frequency: 3   relative frequency: 0.00004
  See also "q.," "queene."
    p. 405 UNGATHERED 34   68 Swim wthout Corke! Why, thank ye good Queen
                        Anne.
    p. 414 UNGATHERED 41   41 Great Queen of Queens, most mild, most meek,
                        most wise,
    p. 418 UNGATHERED 47   1 Our King and Queen the Lord-God blesse,

queene   frequency: 13   relative frequency: 0.00018
    p. 33 EPIGRAMS 22   7 Whose soule heauens Queene, (whose name shee
                        beares)
    p. 68 EPIGRAMS 105   11 If dancing, all would cry th'Idalian Queene,
    p. 114 FOREST 12   49 How many equall with the Argiue Queene,
    p. 138 UNDERWOOD 2.6   28 To be envi'd of the Queene.
    p. 176 UNDERWOOD 25   t2 writ in Queene ELIZABETHS time,
    p. 184 UNDERWOOD 29   34 Whilst the Latin, Queene of Tongues,
    p. 238 UNDERWOOD 66   5 Haile Mary, full of honours, to my Queene,
    p. 238 UNDERWOOD 66   t1 An Epigram to the Queene, then lying in.
    p. 240 UNDERWOOD 67   32 The fained Queene of Love,
    p. 252 UNDERWOOD 75   8 The bountie of a King, and beautie of his
                        Queene!
    p. 254 UNDERWOOD 75   47 Nought of a Maiden Queene,
    p. 255 UNDERWOOD 75   91 All is a story of the King and Queene!
    p. 398 UNGATHERED 30   75 The miseries of Margaret the Queene

queenes   frequency: 1   relative frequency: 0.00001
    p. 63 EPIGRAMS 97   18 Nor are the Queenes most honor'd maides by
                        th'eares

queens   frequency: 1   relative frequency: 0.00001
  See also "queenes."
    p. 414 UNGATHERED 41   41 Great Queen of Queens, most mild, most meek,
                        most wise,

quell   frequency: 1   relative frequency: 0.00001
    p. 341 HORACE 1   119 .. .. and quell the rings

question   frequency: 4   relative frequency: 0.00005
  See also "cittie-question."
    p. 81 EPIGRAMS 129   2 But the first question is, when one saw thee?
    p. 217 UNDERWOOD 46   11 That Clients strove, in Question of the Lawes,
    p. 220 UNDERWOOD 47   72 And free it from all question to preserve.
    p. 396 UNGATHERED 30   3 Because, who make the question, haue not seene

question'd   frequency: 3   relative frequency: 0.00004
    p. 74 EPIGRAMS 115   18 But, if it shall be question'd, vnder-takes,
    p. 164 UNDERWOOD 15   83 Nor is the title question'd with our proud,
    p. 396 UNGATHERED 30   1 It hath beene question'd, MICHAEL, if I
                        bee

quick   frequency: 3   relative frequency: 0.00004
    See also "quicke."
    p. 33 EPIGRAMS 21   5 Quick in his lips! Who hath this wonder wrought?
    p. 233 UNDERWOOD 59   9 A quick, and dazeling motion! when a paire
    p. 291 UNDERWOOD 85   42 Some lustie quick Apulians spouse,

quick-warming-pan   frequency: 1   relative frequency: 0.00001
    p. 232 UNDERWOOD 57   27 nor any quick-warming-pan helpe him to bed,

quicke   frequency: 1   relative frequency: 0.00001
    p. 365 UNGATHERED 5   5 Her wit as quicke, and sprightfull

quicken   frequency: 2   relative frequency: 0.00002
    p. 174 UNDERWOOD 23   15 Let this thought quicken thee,
    p. 288 U'WOOD 84.9   204 To justifie, and quicken us in breath!

quickening. See "quickning."

quicker   frequency: 3   relative frequency: 0.00004
    p. 56 EPIGRAMS 87   5 Vpon th'accompt, hers grew the quicker trade.
    p. 221 UNDERWOOD 48   27 And thinke thy streame more quicker
    p. 657 L. CONVIVALES   16 Clears the Brains, makes Wit the Quicker:

quickest-sighted   frequency: 1   relative frequency: 0.00001
    p. 363 UNGATHERED 3   16 And strikes the quickest-sighted Iudgement
                              blinde.

quickly   frequency: 5   relative frequency: 0.00007
    See also "quickly'."
    p. 109 FOREST 11   15 Will quickly taste the treason, and commit
    p. 140 UNDERWOOD 2.8   30 (And that quickly) speake your Man.
    p. 141 UNDERWOOD 2.9   31 Quickly fir'd, as in beginners
    p. 150 UNDERWOOD 10   13 Goe, get thee quickly forth,
    p. 238 UNDERWOOD 65   8 Thee quickly <come> the gardens eye to bee,

quickly'   frequency: 1   relative frequency: 0.00001
    p. 51 EPIGRAMS 73   22 For which, or pay me quickly', or Ile pay you.

quickning   frequency: 1   relative frequency: 0.00001
    p. 162 UNDERWOOD 15   8 Quickning dead Nature, to her noblest strife.

quicksilver   frequency: 1   relative frequency: 0.00001
    p. 208 UNDERWOOD 43   122 As th'other may his braines with Quicksilver.

quiet   frequency: 1   relative frequency: 0.00001
    p. 295 UNDERWOOD 90   6 A quiet mind; free powers; and body sound;

quills   frequency: 1   relative frequency: 0.00001
    p. 420 UNGATHERED 48   19 Breake then thie quills, blott out

quilts   frequency: 1   relative frequency: 0.00001
    p. 200 UNDERWOOD 42   32 That quilts those bodies, I have leave to span:

quince   frequency: 1   relative frequency: 0.00001
    p. 94 FOREST 2   42 Fig, grape, and quince, each in his time doth
                              come:

quintilius   frequency: 1   relative frequency: 0.00001
    p. 333 HORACE 2   623 If to Quintilius, you recited ought:

quintus   frequency: 1   relative frequency: 0.00001
    p. 338 HORACE 1   t1 Quintus Horatius Flaccus

quire   frequency: 4   relative frequency: 0.00005
    p. 144 UNDERWOOD 3   28 May wish us of their Quire.
    p. 239 UNDERWOOD 67   19 4. EVT. That when the Quire is full,
    p. 256 UNDERWOOD 75   128 The Solemne Quire cryes, Joy; and they
                              returne, Amen.
    p. 317 HORACE 2   276 An Actors parts, and Office too, the Quire

quit   frequency: 8   relative frequency: 0.00011
    See also "quite," "quitt."
   *p. 493 TO HIMSELF   34 Dare quit, vpon your oathes,
    p. 72 EPIGRAMS 112   11 I modestly quit that, and thinke to write,
    p. 100 FOREST 4   3 Hence-forth I quit thee from my thought,
    p. 132 UNDERWOOD 2.2   21 Both the Arrow he had quit,
    p. 162 UNDERWOOD 15   3 All that dare rowse: or are not loth to quit
    p. 167 UNDERWOOD 15   175 Goe, quit 'hem all. And take along with thee,
    p. 185 UNDERWOOD 30   10 That in all tempests, never quit the helme,
    p. 284 U'WOOD 84.9   60 T<o>'accuse, or quit all Parties to be heard!

quite   frequency: 13   relative frequency: 0.00018
    p.   38 EPIGRAMS 38   5 And crie good! good! This quite peruerts my
                               sense,
    p.   40 EPIGRAMS 42   12 Were quite out-spun. The like wish hath his
                               wife.
    p.   62 EPIGRAMS 97   4 His cloke with orient veluet quite lin'd through,
    p.   86 EPIGRAMS 133   86 So huge, it seem'd, they could by no meanes quite
                               her.
    p.   89 EPIGRAMS 133   181 Is now from home. You lose your labours quite,
    p. 129 UNDERWOOD 1.2   25 Quite overcame,
    p. 132 UNDERWOOD 2.2   26 And my motion from me quite;
    p. 155 UNDERWOOD 13   69 And spunge-like with it dry up the blood quite:
    p. 307 HORACE 2   32 Be simple quite throughout, and wholly one.
    p. 313 HORACE 2   159 In sound, quite from his fortune; both the rout,
    p. 317 HORACE 2   278 Betweene the Acts, a quite cleane other thing
    p. 321 HORACE 2   344 Quite from all face of Tragedie to goe,
    p. 662 INSCRIPTS. 2   7 And sworne, that he will quite discard thee

quit'st   frequency: 1   relative frequency: 0.00001
    p.   44 EPIGRAMS 54   4 That quit'st the cause so oft, and rayl'st at
                               men?

quitt   frequency: 2   relative frequency: 0.00002
    p. 408 UNGATHERED 36   5 The Marrow! Wretch, I quitt thee of thy paine
    p. 423 UNGATHERED 50   17 he that will honest be, may quitt the Court,

quittest. See "quit'st."

quiver   frequency: 2   relative frequency: 0.00002
    p. 132 UNDERWOOD 2.2   9 Where's thy Quiver? bend thy Bow:
    p. 182 UNDERWOOD 28   10 His flames, his shafts, his Quiver, and his
                               Bow,

quixote   frequency: 1   relative frequency: 0.00001
    p. 204 UNDERWOOD 43   31 The learned Librarie of Don Quixote;

quoit. See "coit."

quote   frequency: 1   relative frequency: 0.00001
  **p. 115 PANEGYRE   98 "The bloody, base, and barbarous she did quote;

quoth   frequency: 2   relative frequency: 0.00002
    p.   87 EPIGRAMS 133   103 But many Moones there shall not wane (quoth hee)
    p.   93 FOREST 1   3 Which when he felt, Away (quoth hee)

r.   frequency: 1   relative frequency: 0.00001
    p. 412 UNGATHERED 41   4 R. Rose, I. Ivy, E. sweet Eglantine.

ra<n>ging   frequency: 1   relative frequency: 0.00001
    p. 327 HORACE 2   489 Wild ra<n>ging lusts; prescribe the mariage good;

rabbin   frequency: 1   relative frequency: 0.00001
    p. 375 UNGATHERED 10   23 A Rabbin confutes him with the Bastinado.

race   frequency: 19   relative frequency: 0.00027
  **p. 115 PANEGYRE   90 "Where he was going; and the vpward race
    p.   41 EPIGRAMS 44   4 Saw all his race approch the blacker floods:
    p.   98 FOREST 3   56 And the great Heroes, of her race,
    p. 116 FOREST 12   99 Before his swift and circled race be run,
    p. 166 UNDERWOOD 15   124 But being in Motion still (or rather in race)
    p. 193 UNDERWOOD 38   101 Then sword, or fire, or what is of the race
    p. 201 UNDERWOOD 42   49 Of race accompted, that no passion have
    p. 228 UNDERWOOD 53   3 To all the uses of the field, and race,
    p. 257 UNDERWOOD 75   157 Alone, and such a race,
    p. 258 UNDERWOOD 75   169 Till you behold a race to fill your Hall,
    p. 270 UNDERWOOD 83   58 Chear'd her faire Sisters in her race to runne!
    p. 272 UNDERWOOD 83   97 Hee were the wretched'st of the race of men:
    p. 289 UNDERWOOD 85   2 As the old race of Mankind were,
    p. 290 UNDERWOOD 85   11 And with his hooke lops off the fruitlesse race,
    p. 309 HORACE 2   71 Faine words, unheard of to the well-truss'd race
    p. 311 HORACE 2   114 To chant the Gods, and all their God-like race,
    p. 333 HORACE 2   587 Hee, that's ambitious in the race to touch
    p. 369 UNGATHERED 6   118 With all the race
    p. 392 UNGATHERED 26   66 Liues in his issue, euen so, the race

races   frequency: 1   relative frequency: 0.00001
    p. 220 UNDERWOOD 48   10 Their Qualities, and races,

rack   frequency: 6   relative frequency: 0.00008
    p. 157 UNDERWOOD 13   130 Were the Rack offer'd them, how they came so;

ack (cont.)
   p. 163 UNDERWOOD 15   50 In admiration, stretch'd upon the rack
   p. 183 UNDERWOOD 29   1 Rime, the rack of finest wits,
   p. 197 UNDERWOOD 40   18 As neither wine doe rack it out, or mirth.
   p. 251 UNDERWOOD 74   8 The Clowdes rack cleare before the Sun,
   p. 333 HORACE 2   618 And rack, with Wine, the man whom they would
                        try,

adamanthvs   frequency: 1   relative frequency: 0.00001
   p. 89 EPIGRAMS 133 187 Calling for RADAMANTHVS, that dwelt
                        by,

adcliffe   frequency: 2   relative frequency: 0.00002
   See also "ratcliffe."
   p. 60 EPIGRAMS 93   1 How like a columne, RADCLIFFE, left
                        alone
   p. 60 EPIGRAMS 93   t1 TO SIR IOHN RADCLIFFE.

adiant   frequency: 2   relative frequency: 0.00002
 **p. 113 PANEGYRE   5 (To day) a thousand radiant lights, that stream
   p. 278 U'WOOD 84.4 26 As 'tis not radiant, but divine:

age   frequency: 12   relative frequency: 0.00017
 *p. 492 TO HIMSELF   9 Run on, and rage, sweat, censure, and condemn:
   p. 41 EPIGRAMS 45   7 To haue so soone scap'd worlds, and fleshes rage,
   p. 44 EPIGRAMS 56   4 As we, the rob'd, leaue rage, and pittie it.
   p. 71 EPIGRAMS 110 14 And that, midst enuy' and parts; then fell by
                        rage:
   p. 86 EPIGRAMS 133 75 And many a sinke pour'd out her rage anenst 'hem;
   p. 93 FOREST 3   69 Goe enter breaches, meet the cannons rage,
   p. 115 FOREST 12   63 But onely Poets, rapt with rage diuine?
   p. 205 UNDERWOOD 43 56 Not ravish'd all hence in a minutes rage.
   p. 242 UNDERWOOD 70   4 His rage, with razing your immortall Towne.
   p. 245 UNDERWOOD 70 80 Possest with holy rage,
   p. 368 UNGATHERED 6 61 With entheate rage, to publish their bright
                        tracts?
   p. 392 UNGATHERED 26 77 Shine forth, thou Starre of Poets, and with
                        rage,

ages   frequency: 1   relative frequency: 0.00001
   p. 283 U'WOOD 84.9 24 It rages, runs, flies, stands, and would provoke

agged   frequency: 1   relative frequency: 0.00001
   p. 380 UNGATHERED 12 34 How scabbed, how ragged, and how pediculous

aging   frequency: 1   relative frequency: 0.00001
   p. 193 UNDERWOOD 38 75 About in Cloudes, and wrapt in raging weather,

aign'd   frequency: 1   relative frequency: 0.00001
   p. 95 FOREST 2   74 As if thou, then, wert mine, or I raign'd here:

aigne   frequency: 5   relative frequency: 0.00007
 *p. 494 TO HIMSELF   59 In tuning forth the acts of his sweet raigne:
 **p. 113 PANEGYRE   22 That fastneth heauenly power to earthly raigne:
   p. 37 EPIGRAMS 35   4 And in this short time of thy happiest raigne,
   p. 98 FOREST 3   50 As if in SATVRNES raigne it were;
   p. 236 UNDERWOOD 64   9 When you that raigne, are her Example growne,

aignes   frequency: 1   relative frequency: 0.00001
   p. 108 FOREST 10A   8 in whom the flame of euery beauty raignes,

aigning   frequency: 2   relative frequency: 0.00002
   p. 240 UNDERWOOD 67 35 But, that shee raigning here,
   p. 321 HORACE 2   343 Meere raigning words: nor will I labour so

ail. See "raile."

aile   frequency: 3   relative frequency: 0.00004
   p. 59 EPIGRAMS 92   35 Or 'gainst the Bishops, for the Brethren,
                        raile,
   p. 65 EPIGRAMS 101 20 Knat, raile, and ruffe too. How so ere, my man
   p. 164 UNDERWOOD 15 72 And firke, and jerke, and for the Coach-man
                        raile,

ailes   frequency: 1   relative frequency: 0.00001
   p. 76 EPIGRAMS 119   2 At hunting railes, hauing no guift in othes,

ailest. See "rayl'st."

railing   frequency: 1   relative frequency: 0.00001
     p. 410 UNGATHERED 39   2 Secure thy railing Rhymes, infamous Gill,

rails. See "railes."

rain. See "raine."

rainbow   frequency: 1   relative frequency: 0.00001
     p. 305 HORACE 2   23 Or Rainbow is describ'd. But here was now

raine   frequency: 3   relative frequency: 0.00004
     p. 192 UNDERWOOD 38   56 Why was't? did e're the Cloudes aske back their
                                    raine?
     p. 193 UNDERWOOD 38   82 The name of Cruell weather, storme, and raine?
     p. 251 UNDERWOOD 74   4 And in a dew of sweetest Raine,

rainge   frequency: 1   relative frequency: 0.00001
     p. 108 FOREST 10A   9 Such, as in lustes wilde forrest loue to rainge,

rais'd   frequency: 12   relative frequency: 0.00017
     See also "ray'sd."
     p. 46 EPIGRAMS 60   1 Loe, what my countrey should haue done (haue
                                    rais'd
     p. 48 EPIGRAMS 65   15 But I repent me: Stay. Who e're is rais'd,
     p. 49 EPIGRAMS 67   4 As, to be rais'd by her, is onely fame.
     p. 67 EPIGRAMS 104   13 Iudge they, that can: Here I haue rais'd to
                                    show
     p. 89 EPIGRAMS 133   194 The citie since hath rais'd a Pyramide.
     p. 181 UNDERWOOD 27   21 Hath Petrarch since his Laura rais'd
     p. 217 UNDERWOOD 46   2 And steps of all rais'd servants of the Crowne,
     p. 250 UNDERWOOD 73   4 Hath rais'd to be the Port unto his Land!
     p. 256 UNDERWOOD 75   113 Stand there; for when a noble Nature's rais'd,
     p. 348 HORACE 1   386 ... . rais'd
     p. 385 UNGATHERED 19   8 Thy Richard, rais'd in song, past pulling downe.
     p. 395 UNGATHERED 29   8 And those in number so, and measure rais'd,

raise   frequency: 16   relative frequency: 0.00023
     See also "rayse."
   **p. 116 PANEGYRE   103 "And with their ruines raise the panders bowers:
     p. 66 EPIGRAMS 102   15 Of what ambition, faction, pride can raise;
     p. 83 EPIGRAMS 132   2 Might then both thee, thy worke and merit raise:
     p. 107 FOREST 10   11 To raise my spirits with thy coniuring wine,
     p. 114 FOREST 12   41 It is the Muse, alone, can raise to heauen,
     p. 117 FOREST 13   42 And raise not vertue; they may vice enhance.
     p. 119 FOREST 13   97 And raise a noble stemme, to giue the fame,
     p. 160 UNDERWOOD 14   62 Flowes in upon me, and I cannot raise
     p. 173 UNDERWOOD 22   4 Yet is't your vertue now I raise.
     p. 264 UNDERWOOD 79   24 Nym. Of brightest MIRA, doe we raise our
                                    Song,
     p. 269 UNDERWOOD 83   24 And voyce to raise them from my brazen Lungs,
     p. 323 HORACE 2   400 And jests; and both to admiration raise
     p. 341 HORACE 1   132 ... . both ... . raise
     p. 391 UNGATHERED 26   12 And thinke to ruine, where it seem'd to raise.
     p. 396 UNGATHERED 30   8 Hanch against Hanch, or raise a riming Club
     p. 400 UNGATHERED 32   10 That Art, or Ingine, on the strength can raise.

raising   frequency: 2   relative frequency: 0.00002
     See also "raysing."
     p. 175 UNDERWOOD 24   3 Raising the World to good or evill fame,
     p. 288 U'WOOD 84.9   207 Of raising, judging, and rewarding all

rak'd   frequency: 1   relative frequency: 0.00001
     See also "rak't."
     p. 209 UNDERWOOD 43   142 That was rak'd up in the Winchestrian Goose

rak't   frequency: 1   relative frequency: 0.00001
    *p. 493 TO HIMSELF   25 Throwne forth, and rak't into the common tub,

ralph. See "raph."

ram'd   frequency: 1   relative frequency: 0.00001
     p. 363 UNGATHERED 3   10 Were they as strong ram'd vp as Aetna gates.

rammed. See "ram'd."

rammes   frequency: 3   relative frequency: 0.00004
     p. 127 UNDERWOOD 1.1   11 But 'bove the fat of rammes, or bulls, to prize
     p. 264 UNDERWOOD 79   17 7. Our teeming Ewes, 8. and lustie-mounting
                                    Rammes. .
     p. 265 UNDERWOOD 79   51 Your teeming Ewes, aswell as mounting Rammes.

ramparts   frequency: 1   relative frequency: 0.00001
      p. 400 UNGATHERED 32   4 In Bulwarkes, Rau'lins, Ramparts, for defense,

rams. See "rammes.

ran   frequency: 5   relative frequency: 0.00007
      See also "ranne."
      p. 76 EPIGRAMS 119   6 Whose dice not doing well, to'a pulpit ran.
      p. 88 EPIGRAMS 133 145 The sinkes ran grease, and haire of meazled hogs,
      p. 132 UNDERWOOD 2.2   6 For I ran and call'd on Cupid;
      p. 132 UNDERWOOD 2.2 16 Strait hee ran, and durst not stay,
      p. 193 UNDERWOOD 38   76 As all with storme and tempest ran together.

ranck   frequency: 1   relative frequency: 0.00001
      p. 361 UNGATHERED 1   10 Thy skill hath made of ranck dispised weedes;

ranck'd   frequency: 1   relative frequency: 0.00001
      p. 53 EPIGRAMS 77   3 For, if thou shame, ranck'd with my friends, to
                              goe,

rancke   frequency: 1   relative frequency: 0.00001
      p. 110 FOREST 11   31 Of which vsurping rancke, some haue thought loue

random. See "randome."

randome   frequency: 1   relative frequency: 0.00001
      p. 323 HORACE 2   391 My Verse at randome, and licentiously?

range   frequency: 1   relative frequency: 0.00001
      See also "rainge."
      p. 146 UNDERWOOD 6   4 Our proper vertue is to range:

ranging. See "ra<n>ging."

rank. See "ranck," "rancke," "ranke."

rank'd   frequency: 1   relative frequency: 0.00001
      See also "ranck'd."
      p. 371 UNGATHERED 8   5 Veluet, or Taffata cap, rank'd in the darke

ranke   frequency: 4   relative frequency: 0.00005
      p. 29 EPIGRAMS 9   2 For strict degrees of ranke, or title looke:
      p. 72 EPIGRAMS 112   4 Or thy ranke setting? that thou dar'st put in
      p. 187 UNDERWOOD 33   40 Alone, but all thy ranke a reverend Name.
      p. 215 UNDERWOOD 44   75 We will beleeve, like men of our owne Ranke,

ranknesse   frequency: 2   relative frequency: 0.00002
      p. 88 EPIGRAMS 133 152 But still, it seem'd, the ranknesse did conuince
                              'hem.
      p. 163 UNDERWOOD 15   34 And impious ranknesse of all Sects and seeds:

ranne   frequency: 1   relative frequency: 0.00001
      p. 52 EPIGRAMS 75   3 Though LIPPE, at PAVLS, ranne from his
                              text away,

ranulph   frequency: 1   relative frequency: 0.00001
      p. 274 U'WOOD 84.2   18 By Ranulph -----

rap'd   frequency: 1   relative frequency: 0.00001
      p. 122 FOREST 15   14 And whither rap'd, now thou but stoup'st to mee?

rape   frequency: 1   relative frequency: 0.00001
      p. 366 UNGATHERED 6   24 From Zephyr's rape would close him with his
                              beames.

raph   frequency: 2   relative frequency: 0.00002
      p. 76 EPIGRAMS 119   t1 TO SIR RAPH SHELTON
      p. 419 UNGATHERED 47   8 And God blesse me, and God blesse Raph.

raphael   frequency: 1   relative frequency: 0.00001
      p. 260 UNDERWOOD 77   7 Titian, or Raphael, Michael Angelo,

rapine   frequency: 2   relative frequency: 0.00002
   **p. 113 PANEGYRE   12 Where Murder, Rapine, Lust, doe sit within,
      p. 99 FOREST 3   82 Purchas'd by rapine, worse then stealth,

rapps   frequency: 1   relative frequency: 0.00001
      p. 315 HORACE 2   212 (As if he knew it) rapps his hearer to

raps. See "rapps," "rap's."

rap's   frequency: 1   relative frequency: 0.0000
     p. 108 FOREST 10 A   13 wch rap's mee vp to the true heau'en of loue;

rapt   frequency: 6   relative frequency: 0.0000
     See also "rap'd," "rap't."
  **p. 115 PANEGYRE   68 To vnderstand the more, the more were rapt.
     p. 52 EPIGRAMS 76   1 This morning, timely rapt with holy fire,
     p. 115 FOREST 12   63 But onely Poets, rapt with rage diuine?
     p. 279 U'WOOD 84.4   41 But, that a Mind so rapt, so high,
     p. 289 U'WOOD 84.9   225 In this sweet Extasie, she was rapt hence.
     p. 361 UNGATHERED 1   13 Next, that which rapt mee, was: I might behold

rap't   frequency: 3   relative frequency: 0.0000
     p. 181 UNDERWOOD 27   14 Rap't from the Earth, as not to die?
     p. 367 UNGATHERED 6   60 And is not rap't
     p. 369 UNGATHERED 6   107 Or Tames be rap't from vs

rapture   frequency: 1   relative frequency: 0.0000
     p. 177 UNDERWOOD 25   11 Thy Priest in this strange rapture; heat my
                                braine

rare   frequency: 15   relative frequency: 0.0002
     p. 28 EPIGRAMS 4   3 But two things, rare, the FATES had in their
                                store,
     p. 39 EPIGRAMS 40   9 Rare, as wonder, was her wit;
     p. 53 EPIGRAMS 79   11 He should those rare, and absolute numbers view,
     p. 58 EPIGRAMS 91   16 As noble in great chiefes, as they are rare.
     p. 60 EPIGRAMS 94   6 Crowne with their owne. Rare poemes aske rare
                                friends
     p. 62 EPIGRAMS 97   3 But one more rare, and in the case so new:
     p. 111 FOREST 11   59 Richer then Time, and as Time's vertue, rare.
     p. 119 FOREST 13   110 They speake; since you are truly that rare wife,
     p. 242 UNDERWOOD 69   26 Rather to boast rich hangings, then rare friends.
     p. 251 UNDERWOOD 74   10 Rare Plants from ev'ry banke doe rise,
     p. 323 HORACE 2   382 Of Accius, and Ennius, rare appeares:
     p. 323 HORACE 2   383 So rare, as with some taxe it doth ingage
     p. 361 UNGATHERED 1   9 Then I admir'd, the rare and prescious vse
     p. 367 UNGATHERED 6   33 Be then both Rare, and Good; and long

rarefied. See "rarified."

rarely   frequency: 2   relative frequency: 0.0000
     p. 96 FOREST 2   92 A fortune, in this age, but rarely knowne.
     p. 129 UNDERWOOD 1.2   14 Rarely repent,

rarenesse   frequency: 1   relative frequency: 0.0000
     p. 367 UNGATHERED 6   32 "For stile of rarenesse, to degenerate.

rarer   frequency: 1   relative frequency: 0.0000
     p. 53 EPIGRAMS 79   1 That Poets are far rarer births then kings,

rarified   frequency: 2   relative frequency: 0.0000
     p. 197 UNDERWOOD 40   20 In all his Actions rarified to spright;
     p. 233 UNDERWOOD 59   10 Of bodies, meet like rarified ayre!

raritie   frequency: 2   relative frequency: 0.0000
     p. 255 UNDERWOOD 75   81 Force from the Phoenix, then, no raritie
     p. 282 U'WOOD 84.9   16 With such a Raritie, and not rowse Art

rarity. See "raritie."

rash   frequency: 2   relative frequency: 0.0000
     p. 98 FOREST 3   68 The furie of a rash command,
     p. 319 HORACE 2   307 The rash, and head-long eloquence brought forth

rashnesse   frequency: 1   relative frequency: 0.0000
     p. 156 UNDERWOOD 13   106 'Twixt feare and rashnesse: not a lust obscene,

ratcliffe   frequency: 1   relative frequency: 0.0000
     p. 39 EPIGRAMS 40   t1 ON MARGARET RATCLIFFE.

rate   frequency: 7   relative frequency: 0.0001
     p. 156 UNDERWOOD 13   104 Of Valour, but at this Idolatrous rate?
     p. 157 UNDERWOOD 13   158 Without your gift, though I can rate that too,
     p. 185 UNDERWOOD 30   19 Of all the Land. Who now at such a Rate,
     p. 215 UNDERWOOD 44   77 That turnes us so much moneys, at which rate
     p. 234 UNDERWOOD 61   3 View'd there the mercat, read the wretched rate
     p. 325 HORACE 2   432 My title, at the<ir> rate, I'<h>ad rather, I,
     p. 408 UNGATHERED 37   5 ffoole, doe not rate my Rymes; I'haue found thy
                                Vice

rated. See "easy-rated."

rates   frequency: 1   relative frequency: 0.00001
    p. 235 UNDERWOOD 62   12 O bountie! so to difference the rates!

rather   frequency: 31   relative frequency: 0.00044
    p. 43 EPIGRAMS 52   1 COVRTLING, I rather thou should'st
                                vtterly
    p. 70 EPIGRAMS 109   9 Thou rather striu'st the matter to possesse,
    p. 144 UNDERWOOD 3   25 Nay, rather both our soules bee strayn'd
    p. 149 UNDERWOOD 9   1 I now thinke, Love is rather deafe, then blind,
    p. 152 UNDERWOOD 12   36 I feele, I'm rather dead than he!
    p. 158 UNDERWOOD 14   9 Rather then Office, when it doth or may
    p. 163 UNDERWOOD 15   30 Rather then here so bogg'd in vices stay.
    p. 166 UNDERWOOD 15   124 But being in Motion still (or rather in race)
    p. 185 UNDERWOOD 30   16 Rather than meet him: And, before his eyes
    p. 193 UNDERWOOD 38   92 Rather then once displease you more, to die
    p. 194 UNDERWOOD 38   122 Rather then want your light, I wish a grave.
    p. 199 UNDERWOOD 41   17 O, keepe it still; for it had rather be
    p. 209 UNDERWOOD 43   151 If that were so, thou rather would'st advance
    p. 220 UNDERWOOD 48   2 Of Wines, to thee the rather
    p. 224 UNDERWOOD 50   9 The rather when the vices of the Time
    p. 229 UNDERWOOD 54   11 But rather with advantage to be found
    p. 241 UNDERWOOD 68   9 And rather wish, in their expence of Sack,
    p. 242 UNDERWOOD 69   26 Rather to boast rich hangings, then rare friends.
    p. 259 UNDERWOOD 76   6 JAMES the blessed, pleas'd the rather,
    p. 269 UNDERWOOD 83   28 But rather I, should I of that part speake!
    p. 276 U'WOOD 84.3   20 May rather yet adore, then spy.
    p. 288 U'WOOD 84.9   216 Hath given wholly to the Sonne (the rather
    p. 311 HORACE 2   130 Perversly modest, had I rather owe
    p. 323 HORACE 2   392 Or rather, thinking all my faults may spie,
    p. 325 HORACE 2   432 My title, at the<ir> rate, I'<h>ad rather, I,
    p. 335 HORACE 2   629 Then: If your fault you rather had defend
    p. 374 UNGATHERED 10   15 It should rather haue bene Tom that a horse did
                                lack.
    p. 378 UNGATHERED 11   88 Rather his sonne, I should haue cal'd thee, why?
    p. 395 UNGATHERED 29   14 What Muse, or rather God of harmony
    p. 411 UNGATHERED 39   11 Thy blatant Muse abroad, and teach it rather
    p. 420 UNGATHERED 48   21 And rather to the ffyre, then to the Rowte

ratling   frequency: 1   relative frequency: 0.00001
    p. 259 UNDERWOOD 76   19 And the ratling pit-pat-noyse,

rattles   frequency: 1   relative frequency: 0.00001
    p. 273 U'WOOD 84.1   17 For, though that Rattles, Timbrels, Toyes,

rattling   frequency: 1   relative frequency: 0.00001
    See also "ratling."
    p. 273 U'WOOD 84.1   16 'Bove rattling Rime.

rauish'd   frequency: 3   relative frequency: 0.00004
    p. 119 FOREST 13   108 Onely, thus much, out of a rauish'd zeale,
    p. 395 UNGATHERED 29   13 It makes me rauish'd with iust wonder, cry
    p. 397 UNGATHERED 30   53 That reade it? that are rauish'd! such was I

rauished   frequency: 1   relative frequency: 0.0000'
    p. 60 EPIGRAMS 93   8 The Belgick feuer rauished away.

rau'lins   frequency: 1   relative frequency: 0.0000'
    p. 400 UNGATHERED 32   4 In Bulwarkes, Rau'lins, Ramparts, for defense,

rave   frequency: 1   relative frequency: 0.0000'
    p. 311 HORACE 2   117 Th'Iambick arm'd Archilochus to rave,

ravelins. See "rau'lins."

ravenous   frequency: 1   relative frequency: 0.0000
    p. 206 UNDERWOOD 43   86 So ravenous, and vast an appetite?

ravish'd   frequency: 3   relative frequency: 0.0000
    p. 130 UNDERWOOD 1.3   4 And like the ravish'd Sheep'erds said,
    p. 205 UNDERWOOD 43   56 Not ravish'd all hence in a minutes rage.
    p. 240 UNDERWOOD 67   40 Whilst all the ravish'd rout

ravished. See "rauish'd," "rauished," "ravish'd."

rayes   frequency: 1   relative frequency: 0.0000
 **p. 113 PANEGYRE   7 His former rayes did onely cleare the skie;

rayl'st   frequency: 1   relative frequency: 0.00001
      p.   44 EPIGRAMS 54   4 That quit'st the cause so oft, and rayl'st at
                                  men?

rayn'd   frequency: 1   relative frequency: 0.00001
      p. 180 UNDERWOOD 26   15 Must now be rayn'd.

rays. See "rayes."

ray'sd   frequency: 1   relative frequency: 0.00001
      p. 108 FOREST 10A   12 A farther fury my ray'sd spirit Controules,

rayse   frequency: 3   relative frequency: 0.00004
      p.   81 EPIGRAMS 129   11 Whil'st thou dost rayse some Player, from the
                                  graue,
      p. 387 UNGATHERED 22   6 trust in the tombes, their care=full freinds do
                                  rayse;
      p. 419 UNGATHERED 48   6 I then could rayse my notes

raysing   frequency: 2   relative frequency: 0.00002
    *p. 494 TO HIMSELF   60 And raysing Charles his chariot, 'boue his
                                  Waine.
      p. 225 UNDERWOOD 51   20 In raysing him the wisdome of my King.

raz'd   frequency: 1   relative frequency: 0.00001
      p. 209 UNDERWOOD 43   136 And raz'd, e're thought could urge, This might
                                  have bin!

razing   frequency: 1   relative frequency: 0.00001
      p. 242 UNDERWOOD 70   4 His rage, with razing your immortall Towne.

re-aduance   frequency: 1   relative frequency: 0.00001
      p.   55 EPIGRAMS 85   8 Which if they misse, they yet should re-aduance

re-joyne   frequency: 1   relative frequency: 0.00001
      p. 285 U'WOOD 84.9   107 That shall re-joyne yee. Was she, then, so
                                  deare,

re-shine   frequency: 1   relative frequency: 0.00001
      p. 238 UNDERWOOD 65   12 Sol will re-shine. If not, CHARLES hath a
                                  Sonne.

reach   frequency: 5   relative frequency: 0.00007
      p.   94 FOREST 2   18 The lighter Faunes, to reach the Ladies oke.
      p.   94 FOREST 2   44 Hang on thy walls, that euery child may reach.
      p. 176 UNDERWOOD 25   6 Her upright head, above the reach of Chance,
      p. 232 UNDERWOOD 58   7 If his wit reach no higher, but to spring
      p. 404 UNGATHERED 34   53 To plant ye Musick where noe eare can reach!

reach'd   frequency: 3   relative frequency: 0.00004
      p.   37 EPIGRAMS 32   4 What not the enuie of the seas reach'd too,
      p.   87 EPIGRAMS 133   121 By this time had they reach'd the Stygian poole,
      p. 414 UNGATHERED 41   52 Till he hath reach'd his two-fold point of
                                  Noone.

reaching   frequency: 1   relative frequency: 0.00001
      p. 258 UNDERWOOD 75   180 Extend a reaching vertue, early and late:

read   frequency: 37   relative frequency: 0.00053
   See also "reade," "reed."
      p.   39 EPIGRAMS 40   6 Read not in faire heauens storie,
      p.   43 EPIGRAMS 52   3 When I am read, thou fain'st a weake applause,
      p.   60 EPIGRAMS 94   12 Dare for these poemes, yet, both aske, and read,
      p.   61 EPIGRAMS 95   7 But when I read that speciall piece, restor'd,
      p.   63 EPIGRAMS 99   4 And that to write things worthy to be read:
      p.   71 EPIGRAMS 110   16 How few haue read! how fewer vnderstood!)
      p.   77 EPIGRAMS 120   1 Weepe with me all you that read
      p. 131 UNDERWOOD 2.1   13 If you then will read the Storie,
      p. 150 UNDERWOOD 9   16 Read so much wast, as she cannot imbrace
      p. 152 UNDERWOOD 12   33 And pray who shall my sorrowes read,
      p. 158 UNDERWOOD 14   5 Your Booke, my Selden, I have read, and much
      p. 179 UNDERWOOD 25   39 Is but a Statists theame, to read Phlebotomie.
      p. 185 UNDERWOOD 30   2 Read here in one, what thou in all canst find,
      p. 187 UNDERWOOD 33   7 But when I read or heare the names so rife
      p. 214 UNDERWOOD 44   35 Translated Aelian<'s> tactickes to be read,
      p. 216 UNDERWOOD 45   4 One lesson we have both learn'd, and well read;
      p. 220 UNDERWOOD 47   73 So short you read my Character, and theirs
      p. 225 UNDERWOOD 51   5 Pardon, I read it in thy face, the day
      p. 228 UNDERWOOD 53   4 Me thought I read the ancient Art of Thrace,
      p. 234 UNDERWOOD 61   3 View'd there the mercat, read the wretched rate

read (cont.)
```
    p. 247 UNDERWOOD 70    122 Where they might read, and find
    p. 262 UNDERWOOD 78      2 Yet read him in these lines: He doth excell
    p. 263 UNDERWOOD 78     27 When hee shall read them at the Treasurers bord,
    p. 263 UNDERWOOD 78     32 Being sent to one, they will be read of all.
    p. 273 U'WOOD 84.1      14 Who read what the CREPUNDIA bee,
    p. 371 UNGATHERED 9      2 Read here a little, that thou mayst know much.
    p. 386 UNGATHERED 21     6 I find thee write most worthy to be read.
    p. 389 UNGATHERED 24     2 Shall finde, that either hath read Bookes, and
                               Men:
    p. 391 UNGATHERED 26    24 And we haue wits to read, and praise to giue.
    p. 397 UNGATHERED 30    25 There read I, streight, thy learned Legends
                               three,
    p. 397 UNGATHERED 30    42 I saw, and read, it was thy Barons Warres!
    p. 398 UNGATHERED 30    67 Looke, how we read the Spartans were inflam'd
    p. 404 UNGATHERED 34    47 Of many Coulors! read them! & reueale
    p. 408 UNGATHERED 36     9 If thou be soe desyrous to be read,
    p. 411 UNGATHERED 40     1 When I had read
    p. 415 UNGATHERED 42    13 (You have deserv'd it from me) I have read,
    p. 421 UNGATHERED 49     7 O're read, examin'd, try'd, and prou'd yor: Ryme
```

reade   frequency: 17   relative frequency: 0.00024
```
    p.  27 EPIGRAMS 1        2 To reade it well: that is, to vnderstand.
    p.  41 EPIGRAMS 43       9 When, in my booke, men reade but CECILL'S
                               name,
    p.  45 EPIGRAMS 58       2 To reade my verses; now I must to heare:
    p.  62 EPIGRAMS 96       7 Reade all I send: and, if I find but one
    p.  65 EPIGRAMS 101     21 Shall reade a piece of VIRGIL,
                               TACITVS,
    p.  96 FOREST 2         97 Reade, in their vertuous parents noble parts,
    p. 201 UNDERWOOD 42     64 Had he'had the facultie to reade, and write!
    p. 233 UNDERWOOD 60      1 If, Passenger, thou canst but reade:
    p. 250 UNDERWOOD 73      2 Thy faint, and narrow eyes, to reade the King
    p. 260 UNDERWOOD 76     32 You'ld reade a Snake, in his next Song.
    p. 383 UNGATHERED 17     9 Who cannot reade, but onely doth desire
    p. 386 UNGATHERED 21     9 And, where the most reade bookes, on Authors
                               fames,
    p. 395 UNGATHERED 29     1 When, Rome, I reade thee in thy mighty paire,
    p. 397 UNGATHERED 30    52 Of all that reade thy Poly-Olbyon.
    p. 397 UNGATHERED 30    53 That reade it? that are rauish'd! such was I
    p. 398 UNGATHERED 30    60 Thou hast deseru'd: And let me reade the while
    p. 398 UNGATHERED 30    73 That can but reade; who cannot, may in prose
```

reader   frequency: 11   relative frequency: 0.00015
```
    p.  27 EPIGRAMS 1       t1 TO THE READER.
    p.  79 EPIGRAMS 124      2 In a little? Reader, stay.
    p. 152 UNDERWOOD 12     37 Reader, whose life, and name, did e're become
    p. 159 UNDERWOOD 14     27 So that my Reader is assur'd, I now
    p. 168 UNDERWOOD 16      1 Reader, stay,
    p. 329 HORACE 2        515 Sweet mix'd with sowre, to his Reader, so
    p. 379 UNGATHERED 12    t1 To the London Reader, on the Odcombian writer,
    p. 390 UNGATHERED 25     9 But, since he cannot, Reader, looke
    p. 390 UNGATHERED 25    t1 To the Reader.
    p. 394 UNGATHERED 28     2 And pray thee Reader, bring thy weepinge Eyes
    p. 400 UNGATHERED 32     2 Aboue his Reader, or his Prayser, is.
```

readers   frequency: 5   relative frequency: 0.00007
```
    p.  85 EPIGRAMS 133     43 All, that are readers: but, me thinkes 'tis od,
    p. 182 UNDERWOOD 28     13 Her joyes, her smiles, her loves, as readers take
    p. 199 UNDERWOOD 42      4 Whose Readers did not thinke he was in love.
    p. 217 UNDERWOOD 46     19 No lesse of praise, then readers in all kinds
    p. 362 UNGATHERED 2     12 So with this Authors Readers will it thriue:
```

reades   frequency: 5   relative frequency: 0.00007
```
    p.  30 EPIGRAMS 12      15 That lost, he keepes his chamber, reades
                               Essayes,
    p.  35 EPIGRAMS 28       5 Which hee thinkes great; and so reades verses,
                               too:
    p.  42 EPIGRAMS 49       1 PLAY-WRIGHT me reades, and still my
                               verses damnes,
    p.  72 EPIGRAMS 111      1 Who EDMONDS, reades thy booke, and doth
                               not see
    p. 289 U'WOOD 84.9     226 Who reades, will pardon my Intelligence,
```

reading   frequency: 1   relative frequency: 0.00001
```
    p. 355 HORACE 1        678 ... ..... .. ... .. ... with reading .....
```

reads   frequency: 2   relative frequency: 0.00002
```
See also "reades."
    p. 383 UNGATHERED 17     5 Who reads may roaue, and call the passage darke,
```

reads (cont.)
    p. 383 UNGATHERED 17   7 Who reads, who roaues, who hopes to vnderstand,

readvance. See "re-aduance."

ready   frequency: 4   relative frequency: 0.0000
    p. 164 UNDERWOOD 15   69 Ready to cast, at one, whose band sits ill,
    p. 165 UNDERWOOD 15 108 To teach each suit he has, the ready way
    p. 275 U'WOOD 84.3   1 Sitting, and ready to be drawne,
    p. 291 UNDERWOOD 85   48 And unbought viands ready makes:

real. See "reall."

reall   frequency: 2   relative frequency: 0.0000
    p. 160 UNDERWOOD 14   47 Where is that nominall marke, or reall rite,
    p. 407 UNGATHERED 35 22 But when thou turnst a Reall Inigo;

realm. See "realme."

realme   frequency: 3   relative frequency: 0.0000
**p. 113 PANEGYRE   6 To euery nooke and angle of his realme.
    p. 185 UNDERWOOD 30   9 The only faithfull Watchman for the Realme,
    p. 238 UNDERWOOD 66 14 Of so much safetie to the Realme, and King!

realmes   frequency: 2   relative frequency: 0.0000
    p. 28 EPIGRAMS 5   4 The spoused paire two realmes, the sea the ring.
    p. 38 EPIGRAMS 35   5 Hast purg'd thy realmes, as we haue now no cause

realms. See "realmes."

ream. See "reame."

reame   frequency: 1   relative frequency: 0.0000
    p. 205 UNDERWOOD 43 62 Had tickled your large Nosthrill: many a Reame

reap'd   frequency: 1   relative frequency: 0.0000
    p. 95 FOREST 2   84 On thy good lady, then! who, therein, reap'd

rear. See "reare."

rear'd   frequency: 3   relative frequency: 0.0000
    p. 89 EPIGRAMS 133 176 Behold where CERBERVS, rear'd on the wall
    p. 94 FOREST 2   46 They'are rear'd with no mans ruine, no mans
                        grone,
    p. 173 UNDERWOOD 22 17 His falling Temples you have rear'd,

reare   frequency: 4   relative frequency: 0.0000
    p. 115 FOREST 12   84 Borne vp by statues, shall I reare your head,
    p. 116 FOREST 12   97 This hasty sacrifice, wherein I reare
    p. 307 HORACE 2   56 And what they will not. Him, whose choice doth
                        reare
    p. 401 UNGATHERED 32 11 Yet, who dares offer a redoubt to reare?

reare-suppers   frequency: 1   relative frequency: 0.0000
    p. 156 UNDERWOOD 13 101 Reare-Suppers in their Names! and spend whole
                        nights

reares   frequency: 1   relative frequency: 0.0000
    p. 176 UNDERWOOD 24 13 Shee chearfully supporteth what she reares,

rearing   frequency: 1   relative frequency: 0.0000
    p. 184 UNDERWOOD 29 59 That in rearing such a Schoole,

rears. See "reares."

reason   frequency: 10   relative frequency: 0.0001
    See also "reason'."
**p. 117 PANEGYRE   156 Neuer had land more reason to reioyce.
    p. 34 EPIGRAMS 24   1 There's reason good, that you good lawes should
                        make:
    p. 101 FOREST 4   35 Little, for me, had reason done,
    p. 109 FOREST 11   13 To wakefull reason, our affections king:
    p. 110 FOREST 11   30 And strike our reason blinde.
    p. 131 UNDERWOOD 2.1 23 Till she be the reason why,
    p. 143 UNDERWOOD 3   6 Of reason emptie is?
    p. 184 UNDERWOOD 29 53 Stil may reason warre with rime,
    p. 187 UNDERWOOD 33 24 What use, what strength of reason! and how much
    p. 370 UNGATHERED 7 14 Being tould there, Reason cannot, Sense may
                        erre.

reason'   frequency: 1   relative frequency: 0.00001
    p. 370 UNGATHERED 7   12 Betweene the doubtfull sway of Reason', and
                              sense;

reasons   frequency: 2   relative frequency: 0.00002
    p. 220 UNDERWOOD 47   69 But all so cleare, and led by reasons flame,
    p. 277 U'WOOD 84.4   4 And give you reasons more then one.

rebel. See "rebell."

rebell   frequency: 3   relative frequency: 0.00004
    p. 109 FOREST 11   21 For either our affections doe rebell,
    p. 129 UNDERWOOD 1.2   26 Yet I rebell,
    p. 421 UNGATHERED 48   41 The Rebell Gyantes stoope, and Gorgon Envye
                              yeild,

rebells   frequency: 3   relative frequency: 0.00004
    p. 60 EPIGRAMS 93   6 Vpbraiding rebells armes, and barbarous pride:
    p. 163 UNDERWOOD 15   32 And being a thing, blowne out of nought, rebells
    p. 397 UNGATHERED 30   44 That Rebells actions, are but valiant crimes!

rebels. See "rebells."

rebound   frequency: 1   relative frequency: 0.00001
    p. 350 HORACE 1   498 ... . rebound

rebuke   frequency: 1   relative frequency: 0.00001
    p. 253 UNDERWOOD 75   44 On all that come her Simplesse to rebuke!

recall   frequency: 1   relative frequency: 0.00001
    p. 335 HORACE 2   668 Recall him yet, hee'ld be no more a man:

receave   frequency: 2   relative frequency: 0.00002
    p. 142 UNDERWOOD 2.9   49 Nor doe wrongs, nor wrongs receave;
    p. 190 UNDERWOOD 37   10 But, as a friend, which name your selfe receave,

receipt   frequency: 2   relative frequency: 0.00002
    p. 188 UNDERWOOD 34   12 Spanish receipt, to make her teeth to rot.
    p. 280 U'WOOD 84.4   53 Thrice happy house, that hast receipt

receiu'd   frequency: 1   relative frequency: 0.00001
    p. 389 UNGATHERED 24   19 Will bee receiu'd in Court; If not, would I

receiue   frequency: 1   relative frequency: 0.0000
    p. 364 UNGATHERED 4   2 Receiue it for a Fable,

receiv'd   frequency: 4   relative frequency: 0.0000
    p. 153 UNDERWOOD 13   22 Then what he hath receiv'd. Gifts stinke from
                              some,
    p. 153 UNDERWOCD 13   25 Can I owe thankes, for Curtesies receiv'd
    p. 309 HORACE 2   91 Whether the Sea receiv'd into the shore,
    p. 323 HORACE 2   369 Which law receiv'd, the Chorus held his peace,

receive   frequency: 4   relative frequency: 0.0000
    See also "receave," "receiue."
    p. 154 UNDERWOOD 13   43 No more then he doth thanke, that will receive
    p. 212 UNDERWOOD 43   207 Engines of Murder, and receive the praise
    p. 309 HORACE 2   74 And those thy new, and late-coyn'd words receive,
    p. 321 HORACE 2   364 Receive, or give it an applause, the more.

received   frequency: 1   relative frequency: 0.0000
    See also "receiu'd," "receiv'd."
    p. 218 UNDERWOOD 47   22 And are received for the Covey of Witts;

recelebrates   frequency: 1   relative frequency: 0.0000
    p. 401 UNGATHERED 33   10 Recelebrates the ioyfull Match with France.

reception   frequency: 1   relative frequency: 0.0000
    p. 219 UNDERWOOD 47   48 Of the late Mysterie of reception,

recited   frequency: 1   relative frequency: 0.0000
    p. 333 HORACE 2   623 If to Quintilius, you recited ought:

reciting   frequency: 1   relative frequency: 0.0000
    p. 337 HORACE 2   678 And, there an end of him, reciting makes:

reck'ned   frequency: 1   relative frequency: 0.0000
    p. 156 UNDERWOOD 13   103 Cannot a man be reck'ned in the State

reck'ning   frequency: 1   relative frequency: 0.00001
    p. 396 UNGATHERED 30   9 About the towne: this reck'ning I will pay,

reckon   frequency: 2   relative frequency: 0.00002
    p. 80 EPIGRAMS 127   5 Into the debt; and reckon on her head,
    p. 158 UNDERWOOD 13   164 Find you to reckon nothing, me owe all.

reckoned. See "reck'ned."

reckoning. See "reck'ning."

reconcil'd   frequency: 2   relative frequency: 0.00002
    p. 48 EPIGRAMS 65   8 And, reconcil'd, keepe him suspected still.
    p. 133 UNDERWOOD 2.3   6 Reconcil'd to Love, and me.

record   frequency: 3   relative frequency: 0.00004
    p. 188 UNDERWOOD 35   4 Upon record, in this blest child.
    p. 399 UNGATHERED 31   1 T'is a Record in heauen. You, that were
    p. 400 UNGATHERED 31   40 And this a coppie is of the Record.

recorded   frequency: 1   relative frequency: 0.00001
    p. 257 UNDERWOOD 75   155 Their names are not recorded on the File

records   frequency: 3   relative frequency: 0.00004
    p. 160 UNDERWOOD 14   43 Records, and Authors of! how rectified
    p. 210 UNDERWOOD 43   171 In those Records, which, were all Chronicle<r>s
                               gone,
    p. 247 UNDERWOOD 70   126 Whose lines her rowles were, and records.

recovered   frequency: 1   relative frequency: 0.00001
    p. 176 UNDERWOOD 25   t3 since lost, and recovered.

recovery   frequency: 1   relative frequency: 0.00001
    p. 167 UNDERWOOD 15   154 For the recovery of my voyce? No, there

rectifie   frequency: 1   relative frequency: 0.00001
    p. 64 EPIGRAMS 101   9 Yet shall you haue, to rectifie your palate,

rectified   frequency: 1   relative frequency: 0.00001
    p. 160 UNDERWOOD 14   43 Records, and Authors of! how rectified

rectify. See "rectifie."

rector   frequency: 1   relative frequency: 0.00001
    p. 263 UNDERWOOD 79   9 Rector Chori. To day old Janus opens the new
                               yeare,

red   frequency: 1   relative frequency: 0.00001
  **p. 114 PANEGYRE   40 And only with red silence him salute.

redeem. See "redeeme."

redeem'd   frequency: 1   relative frequency: 0.00001
    p. 159 UNDERWOOD 14   39 What fables have you vext! what truth redeem'd!

redeeme   frequency: 3   relative frequency: 0.00004
    p. 100 FOREST 4   23 And neuer will redeeme a day,
    p. 205 UNDERWOOD 43   63 To redeeme mine, I had sent in; Enough,
    p. 288 U'WOOD 84.9   202 Suffring, and dying to redeeme our losse!

redeemer   frequency: 2   relative frequency: 0.00002
    p. 285 U'WOOD 84.9   100 Whom her Redeemer, honour'd hath above
    p. 288 U'WOOD 84.9   213 (As being Redeemer, and Repairer too

redemption   frequency: 1   relative frequency: 0.00001
    p. 286 U'WOOD 84.9   134 The price of our Redemption, and to teach

redoubt   frequency: 1   relative frequency: 0.00001
    p. 401 UNGATHERED 32   11 Yet, who dares offer a redoubt to reare?

reduicts   frequency: 1   relative frequency: 0.00001
    p. 248 UNDERWOOD 71   8 Reduicts, Halfe-moones, Horne-workes, and such
                               close wayes,

reduits. See "reduicts."

reed   frequency: 2   relative frequency: 0.00002
    p. 187 UNDERWOOD 33   34 They had, but were a Reed unto thy Sword.
    p. 399 UNGATHERED 31   2 Her Children, and Grand=children, reed it heere!

reedes   frequency: 2   relative frequency: 0.00002
    p. 208 UNDERWOOD 43   126 They made a Vulcan of a sheafe of Reedes,
    p. 281 U'WOOD 84.8   16 It is a wretched thing to trust to reedes;

reeds   frequency: 1   relative frequency: 0.00001
    See also "reedes."
    p. 208 UNDERWOOD 43   129 But, O those Reeds! thy meere disdaine of them,

reeking   frequency: 2   relative frequency: 0.00002
 **p. 113 PANEGYRE   15 From whose foule reeking cauernes first arise
    p. 368 UNGATHERED 6   78 Their reeking fumes;

refin'd   frequency: 2   relative frequency: 0.00002
    p. 117 FOREST 13   43 My mirror is more subtile, cleere, refin'd,
    p. 225 UNDERWOOD 50   30 The same it was inspir'd, rich, and refin'd.

refine   frequency: 2   relative frequency: 0.00002
    p. 388 UNGATHERED 23   1 Whose worke could this be, Chapman, to refine
    p. 393 UNGATHERED 27   4 Refine it neere so much.

reflect   frequency: 2   relative frequency: 0.00002
    p. 117 FOREST 13   38 Doe I reflect. Some alderman has power,
    p. 405 UNGATHERED 34   86 But wisest Inigo! who can reflect

reflection   frequency: 1   relative frequency: 0.00001
    p. 177 UNDERWOOD 25   17 Graced by your Reflection!

reflex. See "reflexe."

reflexe   frequency: 2   relative frequency: 0.00002
    p. 399 UNGATHERED 31   9 Shee was the light (without reflexe
    p. 414 UNGATHERED 41   47 Who mad'st us happy all, in thy reflexe,

reform. See "reforme."

reforme   frequency: 1   relative frequency: 0.00001
    p. 140 UNDERWOOD 2.8   24 There; or to reforme a curle;

reformed   frequency: 1   relative frequency: 0.00001
    p. 33 EPIGRAMS 21   t1 ON REFORMED GAM'STER.

refrain. See "refraine."

refraine   frequency: 2   relative frequency: 0.00002
    p. 112 FOREST 11   113 That knowes the waight of guilt: He will
                              refraine
    p. 292 UNDERWOOD 86   4 Of the good Cynara I was: Refraine,

refreshed   frequency: 1   relative frequency: 0.00001
    p. 398 UNGATHERED 30   79 But then refreshed, with thy Fayerie Court,

refuse   frequency: 6   relative frequency: 0.00008
    p. 34 EPIGRAMS 23   2 Who, to thy one, all other braines refuse;
    p. 40 EPIGRAMS 43   3 Which should thy countries loue to speake refuse,
    p. 182 UNDERWOOD 27   28 Made Dian, not his notes refuse?
    p. 230 UNDERWOOD 56   6 The first of which, I feare, you will refuse;
    p. 277 U'WOOD 84.4   5 Not, that your Art I doe refuse:
    p. 331 HORACE 2   566 His armes in Mars his field, he doth refuse;

refused   frequency: 1   relative frequency: 0.00001
    p. 184 UNDERWOOD 29   47 That they long since have refused

refuses   frequency: 1   relative frequency: 0.00001
    p. 231 UNDERWOOD 57   10 Though now he refuses

regard   frequency: 3   relative frequency: 0.00004
    p. 48 EPIGRAMS 64   13 Contends t'haue worth enioy, from his regard,
    p. 116 FOREST 12   95 For that firme grace he holdes in your regard,
    p. 243 UNDERWOOD 70   13 Where shame, faith, honour, and regard of right

regenerate   frequency: 1   relative frequency: 0.00001
    p. 192 UNDERWOOD 38   39 I am regenerate now, become the child

regent   frequency: 1   relative frequency: 0.00001
    p. 229 UNDERWOOD 54   4 A Merchants Wife is Regent of the Scale.

regiment   frequency: 1   relative frequency: 0.00001
    p. 413 UNGATHERED 41   16 With wonder on the thorny regiment.

region   frequency: 1   relative frequency: 0.00001
    p.   54 EPIGRAMS 80   5 This world deaths region is, the other lifes:

regions   frequency: 1   relative frequency: 0.00001
    p. 396 UNGATHERED 30   20 The Orbe was cut forth into Regions seauen.

regret. See "'greet."

rehearse   frequency: 3   relative frequency: 0.00004
    See also "reherse."
    p.   85 EPIGRAMS 133   46 And with both bombard-stile, and phrase, rehearse
    p. 181 UNDERWOOD 27   8 As he whom Maro did rehearse?
    p. 329 HORACE 2   495 Their minds to Warres, with rimes they did
                              rehearse;

reherse   frequency: 4   relative frequency: 0.00005
    p.   93 FOREST 1   1 Some act of Loue's bound to reherse,
    p. 113 FOREST 12   20 A present, which (if elder writs reherse
    p. 321 HORACE 2   357 Like men street-borne, and neere the Hall,
                              reherse
    p. 420 UNGATHERED 48   22 Their labour'd tunes reherse,

reiect   frequency: 1   relative frequency: 0.00001
    p. 117 FOREST 13   45 Though it reiect not those of FORTVNE:
                              such

reign. See "raigne," "reigne."

reigne   frequency: 1   relative frequency: 0.00001
    p. 292 UNDERWOOD 86   3 I am not such, as in the Reigne

reigned. See "raign'd."

reigning. See "raigning."

reigns. See "raignes."

reined. See "rayn'd."

reins. See "reynes."

reioyce   frequency: 2   relative frequency: 0.00002
    **p. 117 PANEGYRE   156 Neuer had land more reason to reioyce.
    p. 113 FOREST 12   12 Of some grand peere, whose ayre doth make reioyce

reject. See "reiect."

rejoice. See "reioyce."

rejoin. See "re-joyne."

relate   frequency: 2   relative frequency: 0.00002
    p. 172 UNDERWOOD 20   14 Were such as I will now relate, or worse?
    p. 251 UNDERWOOD 74   21 With love, to heare your modestie relate

relation   frequency: 2   relative frequency: 0.00002
    p. 150 UNDERWOOD 11   2 I must the true Relation make,
    p. 282 U'WOOD 84.9   t5 Her #APOTHEOSIS, or Relation to the Saints.

released. See "releast."

releast   frequency: 1   relative frequency: 0.00001
    p.   32 EPIGRAMS 16   7 Nor need'st thou: for those few, by oath releast,

relentlesse   frequency: 1   relative frequency: 0.00001
    p. 283 U'WOOD 84.9   18 Of Vulture death, and those relentlesse cleies?

relic. See "relique."

relief. See "reliefe."

reliefe   frequency: 2   relative frequency: 0.00002
    p.   29 EPIGRAMS 8   5 Rob'd both of money, and the lawes reliefe,
    p. 102 FOREST 4   64 As shall not need thy false reliefe.

relieve   frequency: 2   relative frequency: 0.00002
    p. 192 UNDERWOOD 38   34 There greatnesse takes a glorie to relieve.
    p. 248 UNDERWOOD 71   14 Dare thinke it, to relieve, no lesse renowne,

religion   frequency: 6   relative frequency: 0.00008
    p.   44 EPIGRAMS 55   2 That vnto me dost such religion vse!
    p.   61 EPIGRAMS 95   1 If, my religion safe, I durst embrace
    p.   96 FOREST 2   93 They are, and haue beene taught religion: Thence
    p. 187 UNDERWOOD 33   16 Mak'st it religion to grow rich by Crimes!
    p. 222 UNDERWOOD 49   12 Make State, Religion, Bawdrie, all a theame?
    p. 261 UNDERWOOD 77   24 And strike Religion in the standers-by;

religious   frequency: 5   relative frequency: 0.00007
    p. 155 UNDERWOOD 13   91 Such a religious horrour in the brests
    p. 287 U'WOOD 84.9   176 So charitable, to religious end,
    p. 372 UNGATHERED 9   10 The sole Religious house, and Votary,
    p. 394 UNGATHERED 28   5 Religious, wise, chast, louing, gratious, good;
    p. 422 UNGATHERED 50   10 if it begyn religious thoughts to cherish;

religiously   frequency: 1   relative frequency: 0.00001
    p. 375 UNGATHERED 10   20 Religiously here he bids, row from the stewes,

relique   frequency: 1   relative frequency: 0.00001
    p. 209 UNDERWOOD 43   140 'Twas verily some Relique of the Stewes:

relish   frequency: 3   relative frequency: 0.00004
    See also "rellish."
   *p. 493 TO HIMSELF   29 For, who the relish of these ghests will fit,
    p. 197 UNDERWOOD 40   6 To put all relish from my memorie
    p. 220 UNDERWOOD 48   12 And relish merry make him.

relish'd   frequency: 2   relative frequency: 0.00002
    p. 139 UNDERWOOD 2.7   14 Where, how it would have relish'd well;
    p. 182 UNDERWOOD 27   30 The Swan [that] so relish'd Pancharis)

rellish   frequency: 1   relative frequency: 0.00001
    p.   58 EPIGRAMS 91   8 Whose rellish to eternitie shall last.

remain. See "remaine."

remaine   frequency: 6   relative frequency: 0.00008
  **p. 113 PANEGYRE   28 And in her office vow'd she would remaine,
    p.   34 EPIGRAMS 22   10 Where, while that seuer'd doth remaine,
    p. 199 UNDERWOOD 41   18 Your sacrifice, then here remaine with me.
    p. 220 UNDERWOOD 48   7 That thou remaine here taster
    p. 278 U'WOOD 84.4   20 And yet remaine our wonder still.
    p. 282 U'WOOD 84.9   9 Nothing, that could remaine, or yet can stirre

remaines   frequency: 3   relative frequency: 0.00004
    p.   34 EPIGRAMS 23   4 Came forth example, and remaines so, yet:
    p. 211 UNDERWOOD 43   196 Losse, remaines yet, as unrepair'd as mine.
    p. 327 HORACE 2   468 From the five ounces; what remaines? pronounce

remainest. See "remayn'st."

remains. See "remaines."

remayn'st   frequency: 1   relative frequency: 0.00001
    p.   60 EPIGRAMS 93   13 Thou yet remayn'st, vn-hurt in peace, or warre,

remember   frequency: 1   relative frequency: 0.00001
    p. 239 UNDERWOOD 67   1 1. CLIO. Up publike joy, remember

remembered. See "remembred."

remembrance   frequency: 2   relative frequency: 0.00002
    p. 115 FOREST 12   75 To her remembrance; which when time shall bring
    p. 203 UNDERWOOD 43   7 Or in remembrance of thy afront, and scorne,

remembred   frequency: 2   relative frequency: 0.00002
  **p. 115 PANEGYRE   89 "She then remembred to his thought the place
    p. 210 UNDERWOOD 43   172 Will be remembred by Six Clerkes, to one.

remonstrance   frequency: 1   relative frequency: 0.00001
    p. 406 UNGATHERED 34 104 Wth all Remonstrance make an honest man.

remorse   frequency: 1   relative frequency: 0.00001
    p. 282 U'WOOD 84.9   12 By Death, on Earth, I should have had remorse

remou'd   frequency: 2   relative frequency: 0.00002
    p.   57 EPIGRAMS 90   12 And he remou'd to gent'man of the horse,
    p. 117 FOREST 13   28 Remou'd, as you from need to haue it such.

remoue   frequency: 1   relative frequency: 0.00001
    p.   39 EPIGRAMS 40   4 Grant then, no rude hand remoue her.

remoued   frequency: 1   relative frequency: 0.00001
    p. 102 FOREST 5   14 So remoued by our wile?

remoueth   frequency: 1   relative frequency: 0.00001
    p.   82 EPIGRAMS 130   4 That shee remoueth cares, sadnesse eiects,

remove. See "remoue."

removed. See "remou'd," "remoued."

removeth. See "remoueth."

render   frequency: 3   relative frequency: 0.00004
    p. 101 FOREST 4   32 Render his head in there againe?
    p. 313 HORACE 2   191 To render word for word: nor with thy sleight
    p. 317 HORACE 2   259 And the beholder to himselfe doth render.

rendered. See "rendred."

rendred   frequency: 1   relative frequency: 0.00001
    p.   61 EPIGRAMS 95   5 So hast thou rendred him in all his bounds,

renew   frequency: 1   relative frequency: 0.00001
    p. 415 UNGATHERED 43   4 Renew the Glories of our blessed Ieames:

renewed   frequency: 1   relative frequency: 0.00001
    p. 258 UNDERWOOD 75   167 There; but, renewed, say,

renewing   frequency: 1   relative frequency: 0.00001
    p. 268 UNDERWOOD 82   12 As in renewing thy good Grandsires fame;

renown. See "renowne."

renown'd   frequency: 1   relative frequency: 0.00001
    p. 293 UNDERWOOD 87   8 The Roman Ilia was not more renown'd.

renowne   frequency: 7   relative frequency: 0.00010
    p.   31 EPIGRAMS 14   4 The great renowne, and name wherewith shee goes.
    p.   49 EPIGRAMS 66   11 Loue thy great losse, which a renowne hath wonne,
    p.   57 EPIGRAMS 89   13 Weare this renowne. 'Tis iust, that who did giue
    p. 180 UNDERWOOD 26   16 True valour doth her owne renowne command
    p. 248 UNDERWOOD 71   14 Dare thinke it, to relieue, no lesse renowne,
    p. 272 U'WOOD 84.1   2 With ever-greene, and great renowne,
    p. 325 HORACE 2   412 In vertue, and renowne of armes, then in

renowning   frequency: 1   relative frequency: 0.00001
    p. 365 UNGATHERED 5   19 When seeking her renowning,

rent   frequency: 2   relative frequency: 0.00002
  **p. 114 PANEGYRE   60 Of hearts, and voices. All the aire was rent,
    p. 286 U'WOOD 84.9   142 Our native portions, and possessed rent;

repair. See "repaire."

repaire   frequency: 3   relative frequency: 0.00004
    p.   37 EPIGRAMS 32   7 What could not worke; at home in his repaire
    p.   41 EPIGRAMS 44   5 He meant they thither should make swift repaire,
    p. 215 UNDERWOOD 44   96 This, and that box his Beautie to repaire:

repairer   frequency: 1   relative frequency: 0.00001
    p. 288 U'WOOD 84.9   213 (As being Redeemer, and Repairer too

repeat   frequency: 1   relative frequency: 0.00001
    See also "repeate."
    p. 245 UNDERWOOD 70   57 Repeat of things a throng,

repeate   frequency: 2   relative frequency: 0.00002
    p.   65 EPIGRAMS 101   24 And Ile professe no verses to repeate:
    p.   66 EPIGRAMS 103   8 And glorie of them all, but to repeate!

repeating   frequency: 1   relative frequency: 0.00001
    p. 249 UNDERWOOD 72   6 Repeating all Great Britain's joy, and more,

repent   frequency: 7   relative frequency: 0.00010
    p.   48 EPIGRAMS 65   15 But I repent me: Stay. Who e're is rais'd,
    p.   73 EPIGRAMS 113   9 Repent thee not of thy faire precedent,
    p.   73 EPIGRAMS 113   10 Could make such men, and such a place repent:

repent (cont.)
    p. 129 UNDERWOOD 1.2   14 Rarely repent,
    p. 271 UNDERWOOD 83   79 If you dare grudge at Heaven, and repent
    p. 294 UNDERWOOD 88   2 And done, we straight repent us of the sport:
    p. 411 UNGATHERED 40   10 to Repent,

repented   frequency: 3   relative frequency: 0.00004
    p.   54 EPIGRAMS 84   1 MADAME, I told you late how I repented,
    p.   77 EPIGRAMS 120   20 They haue repented.
    p. 133 UNDERWOOD 2.3   18 She repented of the deed,

repents   frequency: 1   relative frequency: 0.00001
    p.   40 EPIGRAMS 42   3 Indeed, poore GILES repents he married euer.

replide   frequency: 1   relative frequency: 0.00001
    p. 137 UNDERWOOD 2.5   39 I confesse all, I replide,

replied. See "replide," "replyed."

replies. See "replyes."

replyed   frequency: 1   relative frequency: 0.00001
    p.   80 EPIGRAMS 126   7 PHOEBVS replyed. Bold head, it is not
                                  shee:

replyes   frequency: 1   relative frequency: 0.00001
    p. 395 UNGATHERED 29   15 Taught Lucan these true moodes! Replyes my
                                  sence

report   frequency: 8   relative frequency: 0.00011
 **p. 115 PANEGYRE   92 "Their lawes, their endes; the men she did
                                  report:
    p.   55 EPIGRAMS 85   1 GOODYERE, I'am glad, and gratefull to
                                  report,
    p.   86 EPIGRAMS 133   94 Crack did report it selfe, as if a cloud
    p. 113 FOREST 12   6 To euery squire, or groome, that will report
    p. 265 UNDERWOOD 79   52 Whose praises let's report unto the Woods,
    p. 278 U'WOOD 84.4   15 Since nothing can report that flame,
    p. 309 HORACE 2   112 Before the Judge, it hangs, and waites report.
    p. 317 HORACE 2   262 Much from the sight, which faire report will make

reports   frequency: 1   relative frequency: 0.00001
    p. 313 HORACE 2   157 Her truch-man, she reports the minds each throw.

reprehend   frequency: 1   relative frequency: 0.00001
    p. 152 UNDERWOOD 12   21 'Tis true, he could not reprehend;

reproof. See "reproofe."

reproofe   frequency: 2   relative frequency: 0.00002
    p. 175 UNDERWOOD 23   32 Cannot indure reproofe,
    p. 380 UNGATHERED 12   31 Of lying, he feares so much the reproofe

reproue   frequency: 1   relative frequency: 0.00001
 **p. 116 PANEGYRE   110 As once defend, what THEMIS did reproue.

reprove   frequency: 2   relative frequency: 0.00002
    See also "reproue."
    p. 190 UNDERWOOD 37   26 In practiz'd friendship wholly to reprove,
    p. 335 HORACE 2   638 Reprove; and, what is to be changed, note:

repulse   frequency: 1   relative frequency: 0.00001
    p. 363 UNGATHERED 3   5 Gold is a sutor, neuer tooke repulse,

reputation   frequency: 2   relative frequency: 0.00002
    p. 166 UNDERWOOD 15 119 What reputation to beare one Glasse more?
    p. 263 UNDERWOOD 78   26 What reputation to my lines, and me,

reputes   frequency: 1   relative frequency: 0.00001
    p.   46 EPIGRAMS 62   3 The world reputes you barren: but I know

requir'd   frequency: 2   relative frequency: 0.00002
    p.   62 EPIGRAMS 95   30 Where sweetnesse is requir'd, and where weight;
    p. 216 UNDERWOOD 45   23 For that is first requir'd, A man be his owne.

require   frequency: 5   relative frequency: 0.00007
    p.   67 EPIGRAMS 104   3 Or did our times require it, to behold
    p. 315 HORACE 2   220 If such a ones applause thou dost require,
    p. 329 HORACE 2   523 Oft-times a Sharpe, when we require a Flat:
    p. 333 HORACE 2   585 So doth the one, the others helpe require,

require (cont.)
       p. 370 UNGATHERED 7   2 Require (besides the likenesse of the thing)

requite   frequency: 1   relative frequency: 0.00001
       p. 236 UNDERWOOD 63   14 Cannot but heape that grace, he will requite.

rere-suppers. See "reare-suppers."

reseru'd   frequency: 1   relative frequency: 0.00001
       p. 59 EPIGRAMS 92   17 And talke reseru'd, lock'd vp, and full of feare,

reserv'd   frequency: 1   relative frequency: 0.00001
       See also "reseru'd."
       p. 198 UNDERWOOD 40   23 Keepe in reserv'd in his Dark-lanterne face,

reshine. See "re-shine."

reside   frequency: 1   relative frequency: 0.00001
       p. 52 EPIGRAMS 76   12 Fit in that softer bosome to reside.

resign'd   frequency: 1   relative frequency: 0.00001
       p. 369 UNGATHERED 6   105 Among the starres should be resign'd

resist   frequency: 1   relative frequency: 0.00001
       p. 423 UNGATHERED 50   13 Euen states most hated, when no lawes resist

resolu'd   frequency: 1   relative frequency: 0.00001
       p. 100 FOREST 4   6 A spirit so resolu'd to tread

resolved. See "resolu'd."

resort   frequency: 1   relative frequency: 0.00001
       p. 93 FOREST 2   10 Thy Mount, to which the Dryads doe resort,

resound   frequency: 4   relative frequency: 0.00005
       p. 98 FOREST 3   51 APOLLO'S harpe, and HERMES lyre
                                    resound,
       p. 264 UNDERWOOD 79   23 Chor. Heare, o you Groves, and, Hills, resound
                                    his praise.
       p. 264 UNDERWOOD 79   31 Chor. Heare, O you Groves, and, Hills,
                                    resound his worth.
       p. 329 HORACE 2   522 The hand, and mind would, but it will resound

respect   frequency: 3   relative frequency: 0.00004
       p. 79 EPIGRAMS 125   7 But I, no child, no foole, respect the kinde,
       p. 163 UNDERWOOD 15   53 That all respect; She must lie downe: Nay more,
       p. 363 UNGATHERED 3   7 Respect, and obseruation; it vncouers

respects   frequency: 2   relative frequency: 0.00002
       p. 161 UNDERWOOD 14   73 It true respects. He will not only love,
       p. 423 UNGATHERED 50   11 whole armyes fall, swayd by those nyce respects.

rest   frequency: 37   relative frequency: 0.00053
     **p. 117 PANEGYRE   148 Wherein, his choice was happie with the rest
       p. 32 EPIGRAMS 16   8 Make good what thou dar'st doe in all the rest.
       p. 41 EPIGRAMS 45   9 Rest in soft peace, and, ask'd, say here doth lye
       p. 61 EPIGRAMS 95   13 O, would'st thou adde like hand, to all the rest!
       p. 73 EPIGRAMS 112   21 Pr'y thee, yet saue thy rest; giue ore in time:
       p. 97 FOREST 3   13 But canst, at home, in thy securer rest,
       p. 106 FOREST 8   48 None but them, and leaue the rest.
       p. 118 FOREST 13   50 Without which, all the rest were sounds, or lost.
       p. 121 FOREST 14   37 Not weary, rest
       p. 128 UNDERWOOD 1.1   48 Shall I there rest!
       p. 140 UNDERWOOD 2.8   7 With the rest, I long expected,
       p. 142 UNDERWOOD 2.9   56 I can rest me where I am.
       p. 149 UNDERWOOD 8   11 Even ashes of lovers find no rest.
       p. 157 UNDERWOOD 13   137 That makes the Arch. The rest that there were
                                    put
       p. 169 UNDERWOOD 17   17 Some grounds are made the richer, for the Rest;
       p. 182 UNDERWOOD 27   36 So much my Subject drownes the rest.
       p. 207 UNDERWOOD 43   94 The rest, my journey into Scotland song,
       p. 216 UNDERWOOD 45   25 Then rest, and a friends value understand,
       p. 225 UNDERWOOD 50   31 These Graces, when the rest of Ladyes view
       p. 234 UNDERWOOD 61   10 To see you set apart, thus, from the rest,
       p. 246 UNDERWOOD 70   86 Himselfe to rest,
       p. 248 UNDERWOOD 71   5 Want, with the rest of his conceal'd compeeres,
       p. 253 UNDERWOOD 75   38 Above the rest
       p. 257 UNDERWOOD 75   138 Now, Sun, and post away the rest of day:
       p. 269 UNDERWOOD 83   13 Alas, I am all Marble! write the rest
       p. 280 U'WOOD 84.4   66 In rest, like spirits left behind

rest (cont.)
```
    p. 281 U'WOOD 84.4      69 In thee, faire Mansion, let it rest,
    p. 282 U'WOOD 84.9       5 And set it forth; the rest were Cobwebs fine,
    p. 283 U'WOOD 84.9      38 The glorie, and gaine of rest, which the place
                               gives!
    p. 284 U'WOOD 84.9      63 That great eternall Holy-day of rest,
    p. 288 U'WOOD 84.9     197 To that eternall Rest, where now sh'hath place
    p. 305 HORACE 2         18 Ye have oft-times, that may ore-shine the rest,
    p. 329 HORACE 2        499 Playes were found out; and rest, the end, and
                               crowne
    p. 361 UNGATHERED 1     16 did sparcle foorth in Center of the rest:
    p. 366 UNGATHERED 6     13 Smiles in his Sphaere, to see the rest affect,
    p. 367 UNGATHERED 6     29 Nor Sunne could make to vary from the rest,
    p. 412 UNGATHERED 41    12 To knit thy Crowne, and glorifie the rest.
```

resteth   frequency: 1   relative frequency: 0.00001
```
    p. 309 HORACE 2        104 The power, and rule of speaking resteth still.
```

resting   frequency: 1   relative frequency: 0.00001
```
    p. 184 UNDERWOOD 29     54 Resting never.
```

restitution   frequency: 1   relative frequency: 0.00001
```
    p. 283 U'WOOD 84.9      50 Expected with the fleshes restitution.
```

restor'd   frequency: 4   relative frequency: 0.00005
```
    p.  61 EPIGRAMS 95       7 But when I read that speciall piece, restor'd,
    p. 173 UNDERWOOD 22     15 By whom he is restor'd to men:
    p. 219 UNDERWOOD 47     40 And force back that, which will not be restor'd,
    p. 398 UNGATHERED 30    82 And with their grassie greene restor'd mine eyes.
```

restore   frequency: 9   relative frequency: 0.00013
```
    p.  35 EPIGRAMS 27       5 If any friends teares could restore, his would;
    p.  46 EPIGRAMS 62       7 That can restore that. Will it hurt your
                               feature?
    p.  68 EPIGRAMS 105     19 So are you Natures Index, and restore,
    p.  71 EPIGRAMS 110     21 T<o>'all future time, not onely doth restore
    p.  78 EPIGRAMS 122      8 I would restore, and keepe it euer such;
    p. 133 UNDERWOOD 2.3     3 She content was to restore
    p. 184 UNDERWOOD 29     39 To restore
    p. 199 UNDERWOOD 41     15 You would restore it? No, that's worth a feare,
    p. 235 UNDERWOOD 63      3 Who doubts, those fruits God can with gaine
                               restore,
```

restored   frequency: 1   relative frequency: 0.00001
```
    See also "restor'd."
    p.  79 EPIGRAMS 125      4 Restored in thy body, and thy minde!
```

restrain'd   frequency: 1   relative frequency: 0.00001
```
    p. 321 HORACE 2        368 Her licence fit to be restrain'd by law:
```

rests   frequency: 4   relative frequency: 0.00005
```
    p. 155 UNDERWOOD 13     92 Of our Towne Gallantry! or why there rests
    p. 184 UNDERWOOD 29     36 But rests foiled.
    p. 323 HORACE 2        371 Two rests, a short and long, th'Iambick frame;
    p. 329 HORACE 2        505 And hold them faithfully; For nothing rests,
```

resurrection   frequency: 2   relative frequency: 0.00002
```
    p.  37 EPIGRAMS 34       2 Shewes of the resurrection little trust.
    p. 284 U'WOOD 84.9      62 Who in that feast of Resurrection trust!
```

retain. See "retaine."

retain'd   frequency: 1   relative frequency: 0.00001
```
    p. 144 UNDERWOOD 3      27 So they in state of Grace retain'd,
```

retaine   frequency: 2   relative frequency: 0.00002
```
    p. 305 HORACE 2         10 As neither head, nor foot, one forme retaine.
    p. 311 HORACE 2        124 Fit for the sock: Each subject should retaine
```

retire   frequency: 2   relative frequency: 0.00002
```
    p. 325 HORACE 2        424 Retire themselves, avoid the publike baths;
    p. 365 UNGATHERED 5     21 Retire, and say; Her Graces
```

retired. See "retyr'd."

retorned   frequency: 1   relative frequency: 0.00001
```
    p. 400 UNGATHERED 31    31 Vntill the dust retorned bee
```

retract   frequency: 1   relative frequency: 0.00001
```
    p. 315 HORACE 2        240 What straight-way he must labour to retract.
```

retribution   frequency: 1   relative frequency: 0.00001
    p. 283 U'WOOD 84.9   49 To have that finall retribution,

retrieved. See "retriv'd."

retriv'd   frequency: 1   relative frequency: 0.00001
    p. 160 UNDERWOOD 14   50 Conjectures retriv'd! And a Storie now

return. See "returne."

return'd   frequency: 3   relative frequency: 0.00004
    p. 52 EPIGRAMS 74   10 T<o>'our times return'd, hath made her heauen in
                              thee.
    p. 98 FOREST 3   44 The hogs return'd home fat from mast;
    p. 229 UNDERWOOD 54   18 And then to be return'd; on protestation

returne   frequency: 15   relative frequency: 0.00021
    p. 81 EPIGRAMS 128   9 So, when we, blest with thy returne, shall see
    p. 84 EPIGRAMS 133   27 Who gaue, to take at his returne from Hell,
    p. 85 EPIGRAMS 133   32 Of those, that put out moneyes, on returne
    p. 101 FOREST 4   25 Or, hauing scap'd, shall I returne,
    p. 209 UNDERWOOD 43   149 Kindled the fire! But then, did one returne,
    p. 213 UNDERWOOD 44   17 And the returne those thankfull Courtiers yeeld,
    p. 242 UNDERWOOD 70   7 Wise child, did'st hastily returne,
    p. 243 UNDERWOOD 70   20 No doubt all Infants would returne like thee.
    p. 250 UNDERWOOD 74   t3 For his Returne from his Embassie.
    p. 251 UNDERWOOD 74   19 Such joyes, such sweet's doth your Returne
    p. 256 UNDERWOOD 75   128 The Solemne Quire cryes, Joy; and they
                              returne, Amen.
    p. 294 UNDERWOOD 87   17 HOR. But, say old Love returne should make,
    p. 315 HORACE 2   208 Of Meleager, brings he the returne
    p. 369 UNGATHERED 6   114 At their returne, nor Po,
    p. 408 UNGATHERED 37   4 Th'enuy'd returne, of forty pound in gold.

returned   frequency: 1   relative frequency: 0.00001
See also "retorned," "return'd."
    p. 331 HORACE 2   580 The Writ, once out, never returned yet.

returnes   frequency: 4   relative frequency: 0.00005
    p. 30 EPIGRAMS 12   8 Shee must haue money: he returnes, god payes.
    p. 153 UNDERWOOD 13   6 As they are done, and such returnes they find:
    p. 225 UNDERWOOD 51   6 For whose returnes, and many, all these pray:
    p. 389 UNGATHERED 23   10 Such Passage hast thou found, such Returnes
                              made,

returns. See "returnes."

retyr'd   frequency: 1   relative frequency: 0.00001
    p. 80 EPIGRAMS 126   1 Retyr'd, with purpose your faire worth to praise,

reueale   frequency: 4   relative frequency: 0.00005
    p. 72 EPIGRAMS 111   10 That to the world thou should'st reueale so much,
    p. 102 FOREST 5   16 But the sweet theft to reueale:
    p. 119 FOREST 13   107 But which the Fates forbid me to reueale.
    p. 404 UNGATHERED 34   47 Of many Coulors! read them! & reueale

reuenge   frequency: 1   relative frequency: 0.00001
    p. 29 EPIGRAMS 10   2 But I haue my reuenge made, in thy name.

reuennue   frequency: 1   relative frequency: 0.00001
    p. 30 EPIGRAMS 12   6 Himselfe: his whole reuennue is, god payes.

reuerenc'd   frequency: 2   relative frequency: 0.00002
    p. 66 EPIGRAMS 102   17 That art so reuerenc'd, as thy comming in,
    p. 93 FOREST 2   6 And these grudg'd at, art reuerenc'd the while.

reuerence   frequency: 2   relative frequency: 0.00002
    p. 58 EPIGRAMS 91   18 Who more should seeke mens reuerence, then feare.
    p. 98 FOREST 3   57 Sit mixt with losse of state, or reuerence.

reuerend   frequency: 4   relative frequency: 0.00005
  **p. 113 PANEGYRE   20 I saw, when reuerend THEMIS did descend
  **p. 115 PANEGYRE   73 Meane while, the reuerend THEMIS drawes
                              aside
    p. 31 EPIGRAMS 14   1 CAMDEN, most reuerend head, to whom I owe
    p. 83 EPIGRAMS 132   7 Behold! the reuerend shade of BARTAS stands

reuersion   frequency: 1   relative frequency: 0.00001
    p. 45 EPIGRAMS 56   6 Buy the reuersion of old playes; now growne

reuiuing   frequency: 1   relative frequency: 0.00001
        p. 405 UNGATHERED 34   88 Reuiuing wth fresh coulors ye pale Ghosts

reveal. See "reueale," "reveale."

reveale   frequency: 1   relative frequency: 0.00001
        p. 155 UNDERWOOD 13   86 And superstition I dare scarce reveale,

revealed   frequency: 1   relative frequency: 0.00001
        p. 286 U'WOOD 84.9   130 Will there revealed be in Majestie!

revells   frequency: 1   relative frequency: 0.00001
        p. 240 UNDERWOOD 67   46 The Revells, and the Play,

revels   frequency: 2   relative frequency: 0.00002
        See also "revells."
        p. 210 UNDERWOOD 43   155 He burnt that Idoll of the Revels too:
        p. 210 UNDERWOOD 43   156 Nay, let White-Hall with Revels have to doe,

revenge   frequency: 1   relative frequency: 0.00001
        See also "reuenge."
        p. 133 UNDERWOOD 2.3   24 To revenge me with my Tongue,

revenue. See "reuennue."

reverence   frequency: 4   relative frequency: 0.00005
        See also "reuerence."
        p. 156 UNDERWOOD 13   98 That men such reverence to such actions show!
        p. 219 UNDERWOOD 47   62 With reverence using all the gifts then<ce>
                                  given.
        p. 274 U'WOOD 84.1   34 Who claimes (of reverence) to be heard,
        p. 421 UNGATHERED 48   42 Cause Reverence, yf not ffeare,

reverenced. See "reuerenc'd."

reverend   frequency: 4   relative frequency: 0.00005
        See also "reuerend."
        p. 187 UNDERWOOD 33   10 Upon the reverend Pleaders; doe now shut
        p. 187 UNDERWOOD 33   40 Alone, but all thy ranke a reverend Name.
        p. 240 UNDERWOOD 67   45 And with a reverend feare,
        p. 270 UNDERWOOD 83   43 A reverend State she had, an awfull Eye,

reverent   frequency: 1   relative frequency: 0.00001
        p. 261 UNDERWOOD 77   23 These I looke up at, with a reverent eye,

reverently   frequency: 1   relative frequency: 0.00001
        p. 181 UNDERWOOD 26   23 For men to use their fortune reverently,

reverse   frequency: 2   relative frequency: 0.00002
        p. 413 UNGATHERED 41   30 On the reverse of this your circling crowne,
        p. 413 UNGATHERED 41   28+ THE REVERSE

reversion. See "reuersion."

reviv'd   frequency: 1   relative frequency: 0.00001
        p. 309 HORACE 2   101 Much phrase that now is dead, shall be reviv'd;

revive   frequency: 1   relative frequency: 0.00001
        p. 162 UNDERWOOD 15   6 That gaspe for action, and would yet revive

reviving. See "reuiuing."

revolt   frequency: 1   relative frequency: 0.00001
        p. 180 UNDERWOOD 25   65 As farre from all revolt, as you are now from
                                  Fortune.

reward   frequency: 11   relative frequency: 0.00015
        See also "rewarde."
        p. 47 EPIGRAMS 63   5 And that thou seek'st reward of thy each act,
        p. 48 EPIGRAMS 64   14 As her owne conscience, still, the same reward.
        p. 49 EPIGRAMS 66   18 That vertuous is, when the reward 's away.
        p. 66 EPIGRAMS 102   9 They follow vertue, for reward, to day;
        p. 80 EPIGRAMS 127   9 So, all reward, or name, that growes to mee
        p. 96 FOREST 2   85 The iust reward of her high huswifery;
        p. 185 UNDERWOOD 30   14 Upon reward, till the reward him sought.
        p. 232 UNDERWOOD 58   9 Will be reward enough: to weare like those,
        p. 284 U'WOOD 84.9   68 Hope, hath her end! and Faith hath her reward!
        p. 412 UNGATHERED 40   19 Our great reward,

rewarde   frequency: 1   relative frequency: 0.00001
     p. 662 INSCRIPTS. 2   8 if any way she do rewarde thee

rewarded   frequency: 1   relative frequency: 0.00001
     p. 224 UNDERWOOD 50   15 Are in your selfe rewarded; yet 'twill be

rewarding   frequency: 1   relative frequency: 0.00001
     p. 288 U'WOOD 84.9   207 Of raising, judging, and rewarding all

rewards   frequency: 2   relative frequency: 0.00002
     p. 223 UNDERWOOD 49   20 As new rewards of her old secrecie?
     p. 290 UNDERWOOD 85   36 And 'counts them sweet rewards so ta'en.

reynes   frequency: 2   relative frequency: 0.00002
   **p. 116 PANEGYRE   123 Sustaine the reynes, and in the checke forbeare
     p. 122 FOREST 15   5 O, be thou witnesse, that the reynes dost know,

rhadamanthus. See "radamanthvs."

rhapsody   frequency: 1   relative frequency: 0.00001
     p. 313 HORACE 2   184 And thou maist better bring a Rhapsody

rheine   frequency: 1   relative frequency: 0.00001
     p. 369 UNGATHERED 6   115 Iberus, Tagus, Rheine,

rhetia   frequency: 1   relative frequency: 0.00001
     p. 379 UNGATHERED 12   20 The Low-countries, Germany and Rhetia

rhine   frequency: 1   relative frequency: 0.00001
   See also "rheine."
     p. 305 HORACE 2   22 The pleasant grounds, or when the River Rhine,

rhinocerotes   frequency: 1   relative frequency: 0.00001
     p. 35 EPIGRAMS 28   4 He speakes to men with a Rhinocerotes nose,

rhoetia. See "rhetia."

rhone   frequency: 1   relative frequency: 0.00001
     p. 369 UNGATHERED 6   117 Slow Arar, nor swift Rhone; the Loyre, nor
                               Seine,

rhyme. See "rime," "ryme."

rhymes   frequency: 1   relative frequency: 0.00001
   See also "rimes," "ri'mes," "rymes."
     p. 410 UNGATHERED 39   2 Secure thy railing Rhymes, infamous Gill,

rhyming. See "riming," "ryming."

rhythm. See "rithme."

rhythms. See "rithmes."

rich   frequency: 22   relative frequency: 0.00031
   See also "riche."
   **p. 113 PANEGYRE   21 Vpon his state; let downe in that rich chaine,
     p. 39 EPIGRAMS 40   3 Rich, as nature could bequeath thee:
     p. 41 EPIGRAMS 44   1 CHVFFE, lately rich in name, in chattels,
                               goods,
     p. 41 EPIGRAMS 44   2 And rich in issue to inherit all,
     p. 65 EPIGRAMS 101   29 Is a pure cup of rich Canary-wine,
     p. 115 FOREST 12   83 There like a rich, and golden pyramede,
     p. 142 U'WOOD 2.10   4 His Clothes rich, and band sit neat,
     p. 163 UNDERWOOD 15   51 Of lust, to his rich Suit and Title, Lord?
     p. 177 UNDERWOOD 25   14 Rich beame of honour, shed your light
     p. 187 UNDERWOOD 33   16 Mak'st it religion to grow rich by Crimes!
     p. 215 UNDERWOOD 44   69 Why are we rich, or great, except to show
     p. 225 UNDERWOOD 50   30 The same it was inspir'd, rich, and refin'd.
     p. 231 UNDERWOOD 56   30 And should grow rich, had I much more to pay.
     p. 242 UNDERWOOD 69   26 Rather to boast rich hangings, then rare friends.
     p. 333 HORACE 2   599 So doth the Poet, who is rich in land,
     p. 333 HORACE 2   617 Rich men are said with many cups to plie,
     p. 361 UNGATHERED 1   15 The seauen-fold flower of Arte (more rich then
                               gold)
     p. 361 UNGATHERED 1   22 of thy rich labors worlds of thoughts created,
     p. 382 UNGATHERED 16   t3 Rich, now Earles of warwick and Hollande.
     p. 388 UNGATHERED 23   3 Who hadst before wrought in rich Homers Mine?
     p. 403 UNGATHERED 34   24 In Towne & Court? Are you growne rich?
                               & proud?
     p. 409 UNGATHERED 38   t3 the Author of this Work, M. RICH.
                               BROME.

richard   frequency: 3   relative frequency: 0.00004
    See also "rich."
    p. 258 UNDERWOOD 75 170 A Richard, and a Hierome, by their names
    p. 385 UNGATHERED 19   8 Thy Richard, rais'd in song, past pulling downe.
    p. 385 UNGATHERED 19 t2 his Richard.

riche   frequency: 1   relative frequency: 0.00001
    p. 382 UNGATHERED 16   5 The elder of these two, riche hopes Increase,

richer   frequency: 6   relative frequency: 0.00008
    p. 61 EPIGRAMS 95   16 MINERVAES loome was neuer richer spred.
    p. 96 FOREST 3   8 The richer hangings, or crowne-plate;
    p. 111 FOREST 11   59 Richer then Time, and as Time's vertue, rare.
    p. 169 UNDERWOOD 17   17 Some grounds are made the richer, for the Rest;
    p. 216 UNDERWOOD 45   26 It is a richer Purchase then of land.
    p. 293 UNDERWOOD 87   4 I thought me richer then the Persian King.

riches   frequency: 4   relative frequency: 0.00005
    p. 56 EPIGRAMS 89   4 Yet crown'd with honors, as with riches, then;
    p. 114 FOREST 12   38 Riches thought most: But, Madame, thinke what
                             store
    p. 206 UNDERWOOD 43   74 Their Jemme of Riches, and bright Stone, that
                             brings
    p. 303 UNGATHERED 3   4+ Riches.

richest   frequency: 2   relative frequency: 0.00002
    p. 232 UNDERWOOD 58   10 That hang their richest jewells i' their nose;
    p. 420 UNGATHERED 48 31 Wee'l rip our Richest veynes

richly   frequency: 3   relative frequency: 0.00004
    p. 168 UNDERWOOD 16   5 It might thy patience richly pay:
    p. 251 UNDERWOOD 74   14 Wherein she sits so richly drest,
    p. 392 UNGATHERED 26 49 Which were so richly spun, and wouen so fit,

richnesse   frequency: 1   relative frequency: 0.00001
    p. 160 UNDERWOOD 14   53 I wonder'd at the richnesse, but am lost,

rid. See "bed-rid."

riddles   frequency: 1   relative frequency: 0.00001
    p. 204 UNDERWOOD 43   33 Or spun out Riddles, and weav'd fiftie tomes

riddling   frequency: 1   relative frequency: 0.00001
    p. 319 HORACE 2   310 Now differ'd not from Delphick riddling.

ride   frequency: 7   relative frequency: 0.00010
    p. 99 FOREST 3   89 And, so they ride in purple, eate in plate,
    p. 134 UNDERWOOD 2.4 10 Th<o>rough Swords, th<o>rough Seas, whether she
                             would ride.
    p. 156 UNDERWOOD 13 121 Ride, saile, am coach'd, know I how farre I
                             have gone,
    p. 222 UNDERWOOD 49   15 What though she ride two mile on Holy-dayes
    p. 319 HORACE 2   313 Till then unknowne, in Carts, wherein did ride
    p. 380 UNGATHERED 12 52 Doth he once dissemble, but tels he did ride
    p. 417 UNGATHERED 45 35 'tis but the next neighbour ride

rides   frequency: 2   relative frequency: 0.00002
    p. 110 FOREST 11   41 With whom who sailes, rides on the surge of
                             feare,
    p. 272 UNDERWOOD 83 100 And, sure of Heaven, rides triumphing in.

rideth   frequency: 1   relative frequency: 0.00001
    p. 134 UNDERWOOD 2.4   2 Wherein my Lady rideth!

ridiculous   frequency: 1   relative frequency: 0.00001
    p. 87 EPIGRAMS 133 127 Then all those Atomi ridiculous,

ridway   frequency: 2   relative frequency: 0.00002
    p. 29 EPIGRAMS 8   1 RIDWAY rob'd DVNCOTE of three hundred
                             pound,
    p. 29 EPIGRAMS 8   2 RIDWAY was tane, arraign'd, condemn'd to
                             dye;

ridwayes   frequency: 1   relative frequency: 0.00001
    p. 29 EPIGRAMS 8   4 Beg'd RIDWAYES pardon: DVNCOTE,
                             now, doth crye,

ridway's. See "ridwayes."

rife   frequency: 1   relative frequency: 0.00001
    p. 187 UNDERWOOD 33   7 But when I read or heare the names so rife

riffle   frequency: 1   relative frequency: 0.00001
    p. 107 FOREST 10   24 And riffle him: or pawne his PETASVS.

rifle. See "riffle."

right   frequency: 44   relative frequency: 0.00063
    See also "birth-right," "out-right."
 **p. 113 PANEGYRE   30 (Which Fates auert) should force her from her
                            right.
 **p. 116 PANEGYRE   108 "For Right is as compassionate as wise.
 **p. 116 PANEGYRE   111 For though by right, and benefite of Times,
    p. 32 EPIGRAMS 16   9 Keepe thy selfe there, and thinke thy valure
                            right,
    p. 36 EPIGRAMS 29   2 And thou, right guiltlesse, may'st plead to it,
                            why?
    p. 41 EPIGRAMS 45   1 Farewell, thou child of my right hand, and ioy;
    p. 47 EPIGRAMS 63   1 Who can consider thy right courses run,
    p. 82 EPIGRAMS 131   2 A worke of ours, we part with our owne right;
    p. 83 EPIGRAMS 132   8 Before my thought, and (in thy right) commands
    p. 84 EPIGRAMS 133   23 One was; and he, for brawne, and braine, right
                            able
    p. 88 EPIGRAMS 133 160 And, now, aboue the poole, a face right fat
    p. 100 FOREST 3   103 To doe thy countrey seruice, thy selfe right;
    p. 112 FOREST 11   111 Much more a noble, and right generous mind
    p. 118 FOREST 13   68 Right, the right way: yet must your comfort bee
    p. 121 FOREST 14   25 Striue all right wayes it can,
    p. 127 UNDERWOOD 1.1 13 4. For thy acceptance. O, behold me right,
    p. 186 UNDERWOOD 32   10 A right by the prosperitie of their Crimes;
    p. 186 UNDERWOOD 32   16 He do's you wrong, that craves you to doe right.
    p. 200 UNDERWOOD 42   11 Fathers, and Husbands, I doe claime a right
    p. 211 UNDERWOOD 43 178 A Court of Equitie should doe us right,
    p. 218 UNDERWOOD 47   8 Put conscience and my right to compromise.
    p. 224 UNDERWOOD 50   3 And the right wayes you take unto the right,
    p. 243 UNDERWOOD 70   13 Where shame, faith, honour, and regard of right
    p. 244 UNDERWOOD 70   45 Hee stood, a Souldier to the last right end,
    p. 248 UNDERWOOD 71   t1 To the Right Honourable,
    p. 250 UNDERWOOD 73   t1 On the Right Honourable, and vertuous Lord
    p. 250 UNDERWOOD 74   t1 To the Right honble Hierome, L. Weston.
    p. 260 UNDERWOOD 77   t1 To the right Honourable, the Lord Treasurer
    p. 286 U'WOOD 84.9   144 B<y>'imputed right to an inheritance
    p. 307 HORACE 2   66 Right spare, and warie: then thou speak'st to mee
    p. 311 HORACE 2   126 If now the turnes, the colours, and right hues
    p. 323 HORACE 2   402 If either you, or I, know the right way
    p. 327 HORACE 2   457 With specious places, and being humour'd right,
    p. 327 HORACE 2   478 Or mixing sweet, and fit, teach life the right.
    p. 329 HORACE 2   538 May, with some right, upon an Author creepe.
    p. 339 HORACE 1   34 Father ... sons right worthy of your ....
    p. 378 UNGATHERED 11 t1 To the Right Noble Tom, Tell-Troth of
    p. 386 UNGATHERED 21   1 Some men, of Bookes or Freinds not speaking
                            right,
    p. 390 UNGATHERED 26   8 Which, when it sounds at best, but eccho's right;
    p. 397 UNGATHERED 30 58 Our right in France! if ritely vnderstood.
    p. 400 UNGATHERED 31 36 Her right, by gift, and purchase of the Lambe:
    p. 410 UNGATHERED 38 14 That knew the Crafts they had bin bred in,
                            right:

right-learned   frequency: 1   relative frequency: 0.00001
    p. 414 UNGATHERED 42 t1 To my deare Sonne, and right-learned Friend,

righteousnesse   frequency: 1   relative frequency: 0.00001
    p. 286 U'WOOD 84.9   135 Through his inherent righteousnesse, in death,

rightly   frequency: 1   relative frequency: 0.00001
    See also "ritely."
    p. 331 HORACE 2   546 Informed rightly, by your Fathers care,

rigid   frequency: 2   relative frequency: 0.00002
    p. 190 UNDERWOOD 37   17 Rigid, and harsh, which is a Drug austere
    p. 415 UNGATHERED 42 24 And a Comptroller, two most rigid men

rigour   frequency: 1   relative frequency: 0.00001
    p. 194 UNDERWOOD 38 105 Then Mistris, here, here let your rigour end,

rime   frequency: 9   relative frequency: 0.00013
    p. 183 UNDERWOOD 29   1 Rime, the rack of finest wits,
    p. 183 UNDERWOOD 29   t1 A Fit of Rime against Rime.
    p. 184 UNDERWOOD 29   46 Tyran Rime hath so abused,

rime (cont.)
    p. 184 UNDERWOOD 29   53 Stil may reason warre with rime,
    p. 231 UNDERWOOD 56   23 Away ill company, and helpe in rime
    p. 273 U'WOOD 84.1   16 'Bove rattling Rime.
    p. 319 HORACE 2   290 And tune too, fitted to the Chorus rime,
    p. 410 UNGATHERED 38   11 Now each Court-Hobby-horse will wince in rime;

rimee's   frequency: 1   relative frequency: 0.00001
    p.   59 EPIGRAMS 92   23 Or, euery day, some one at RIMEE'S looks,

rimes   frequency: 12   relative frequency: 0.00017
    p.   36 EPIGRAMS 30   2 Be thine, I taxe, yet doe not owne my rimes:
    p. 116 FOREST 12   87 Your forme imprest there: not with tickling
                                 rimes,
    p. 167 UNDERWOOD 15   162 Friend, flie from hence; and let these kindled
                                 rimes
    p. 183 UNDERWOOD 29   25 Starveling rimes did fill the Stage,
    p. 184 UNDERWOOD 29   31 Greeke was free from Rimes infection,
    p. 184 UNDERWOOD 29   35 Is not yet free from Rimes wrongs,
    p. 203 UNDERWOOD 43   26 And my selfe most, in some selfe-boasting Rimes?
    p. 218 UNDERWOOD 47   26 To vent their Libels, and to issue rimes,
    p. 246 UNDERWOOD 70   103 Of rimes, or ryots, at your feasts,
    p. 321 HORACE 2   337 And farre unworthy to blurt out light rimes;
    p. 327 HORACE 2   456 A Poeme, of no grace, weight, art, in rimes,
    p. 329 HORACE 2   495 Their minds to Warres, with rimes they did
                                 rehearse;

ri'mes   frequency: 1   relative frequency: 0.00001
    p.   93 FOREST 1   9 Into my ri'mes could ne're be got

riming   frequency: 1   relative frequency: 0.00001
    p. 396 UNGATHERED 30   8 Hanch against Hanch, or raise a riming Club

ring   frequency: 10   relative frequency: 0.00014
  See also "cramp-ring."
    p.   28 EPIGRAMS 5   4 The spoused paire two realmes, the sea the ring.
    p.   51 EPIGRAMS 73   10 Item, a faire greeke poesie for a ring:
    p. 109 FOREST 11   23 (That should ring larum to the heart) doth
                                 sleepe,
    p. 120 FOREST 14   3 Some ring,
    p. 239 UNDERWOOD 67   6 Ring thou it Holy-day.
    p. 240 UNDERWOOD 67   38 Hath taken twice the Ring
    p. 253 UNDERWOOD 75   36 And all did ring th'approches of the Bride;
    p. 256 UNDERWOOD 75   123 The holy Prelate prayes, then takes the Ring,
    p. 270 UNDERWOOD 83   41 Were like a ring of Vertues, 'bout her set,
    p. 313 HORACE 2   188 If thou the vile, broad-troden ring forsake.

rings   frequency: 5   relative frequency: 0.00007
    p. 141 UNDERWOOD 2.9   11 Cast in thousand snares, and rings
    p. 170 UNDERWOOD 19   5 By that tall Grove, your haire; whose globy
                                 rings
    p. 206 UNDERWOOD 43   73 Their Seales, their Characters, Hermetique
                                 rings,
    p. 341 HORACE 1   119 .. .. and quell the rings
    p. 352 HORACE 1   545 .... rings .... free ....
                                 ....

riot   frequency: 2   relative frequency: 0.00002
    p. 235 UNDERWOOD 61   17 Of riot, and consumption, knowes the way
    p. 319 HORACE 2   304 Gesture, and riot, whilst he swooping went

rioting   frequency: 1   relative frequency: 0.00001
    p. 160 UNDERWOOD 14   57 With horrour rough, then rioting with wit!

riots   frequency: 1   relative frequency: 0.00001
  See also "ryots."
    p. 202 UNDERWOOD 42   80 And all the originall riots of the place:

rip   frequency: 1   relative frequency: 0.00001
    p. 420 UNGATHERED 48   31 Wee'l rip our Richest veynes

ripe   frequency: 10   relative frequency: 0.00014
    p.   58 EPIGRAMS 92   1 Ere cherries ripe, and straw-berries be gone,
    p.   58 EPIGRAMS 92   3 Ripe statesmen, ripe: They grow in euery street.
    p.   58 EPIGRAMS 92   4 At sixe and twentie, ripe. You shall 'hem meet,
    p.   58 EPIGRAMS 92   6 Ripe are their ruffes, their cuffes, their
                                 beards, their gate,
    p.   59 EPIGRAMS 92   7 And graue as ripe, like mellow as their faces.
    p.   95 FOREST 2   54 By their ripe daughters, whom they would commend
    p. 119 FOREST 13   104 It shall a ripe and timely issue fall,

ripe (cont.)
    p. 282 U'WOOD 84.8   22 Which Vertue from your Father, ripe, will fall;
    p. 313 HORACE 2   162 Or an Heroe; if a ripe old man,

ripened   frequency: 1   relative frequency: 0.00001
    See also "rip'ned."
    p. 98 FOREST 3   41 The ripened eares, yet humble in their height,

riper   frequency: 1   relative frequency: 0.00001
  **p. 115 PANEGYRE   67 To bring them forth: Whil'st riper ag'd, and apt

rip'ned   frequency: 1   relative frequency: 0.00001
    p. 137 UNDERWOOD 2.5 27 Rip'ned with a breath more sweet,

rise   frequency: 23   relative frequency: 0.00033
    p. 52 EPIGRAMS 76   7 I meant the day-starre should not brighter rise,
    p. 102 FOREST 5   6 Sunnes, that set, may rise againe:
    p. 106 FOREST 9   5 The thirst, that from the soule doth rise,
    p. 136 UNDERWOOD 2.5 15 Of her face, and made to rise,
    p. 144 UNDERWOOD 4   3 Nor cast them downe, but let them rise,
    p. 157 UNDERWOOD 13 128 Coriat, should rise the most sufficient head
    p. 157 UNDERWOOD 13 145 They need no stilts, nor rise upon their toes,
    p. 157 UNDERWOOD 13 149 'Tis like light Canes, that first rise big and
                             brave,
    p. 168 UNDERWOOD 15 196 Who falls for love of God, shall rise a Starre.
    p. 186 UNDERWOOD 31   5 So, from all sicknesse, may you rise to health,
    p. 217 UNDERWOOD 46   23 Of if Chance must, to each man that doth rise,
    p. 251 UNDERWOOD 74   10 Rare Plants from ev'ry banke doe rise,
    p. 256 UNDERWOOD 75 116 And by his Rise, in active men, his Name
    p. 288 U'WOOD 84.9   203 Shee saw him rise, triumphing over Death
    p. 362 UNGATHERED 2   6 Where, such perfections to the life doe rise.
    p. 371 UNGATHERED 8   14 Do crowne thy murdred Poeme: which shall rise
    p. 383 UNGATHERED 16 16 yf from a little sparke hee rise not fier.
    p. 384 UNGATHERED 18 16 To rise wth eyther of you, on the morrow.
    p. 384 UNGATHERED 18 23 And when your yeares rise more, then would be
                             told,
    p. 391 UNGATHERED 26 19 My Shakespeare, rise; I will not lodge thee by
    p. 396 UNGATHERED 30 15 I saw a Beauty from the Sea to rise,
    p. 398 UNGATHERED 30 81 As, on two flowry Carpets, that did rise,
    p. 417 UNGATHERED 45 18 rise or fall vppon the earth,

riseth   frequency: 2   relative frequency: 0.00002
    p. 40 EPIGRAMS 42   6 No more would IONE he should. GILES
                             riseth early,
    p. 134 UNDERWOOD 2.4 14 As Loves starre when it riseth!

rising   frequency: 3   relative frequency: 0.00004
    p. 137 UNDERWOOD 2.5 33 And betweene each rising breast,
    p. 141 UNDERWOOD 2.9 29 Rising through it e're it came;
    p. 414 UNGATHERED 41 50 The rosie Morning, or the rising Sun,

rite   frequency: 1   relative frequency: 0.00001
    p. 160 UNDERWOOD 14   47 Where is that nominall marke, or reall rite,

ritely   frequency: 1   relative frequency: 0.00001
    p. 397 UNGATHERED 30 58 Our right in France! if ritely vnderstood.

rites   frequency: 19   relative frequency: 0.00027
    See also "mariage-rites."
    p. 47 EPIGRAMS 64   6 To see thy fathers rites new laid on thee.
    p. 78 EPIGRAMS 122   2 The aged SATVRNE'S age, and rites to
                             know;
    p. 98 FOREST 3   47 Thus PAN, and SYLVANE, hauing had their
                             rites,
    p. 104 FOREST 8   3 Doe not men, ynow of rites
    p. 119 FOREST 13   106 And greater rites, yet writ in mysterie,
    p. 138 UNDERWOOD 2.6 19 And did thinke, such Rites were due
    p. 156 UNDERWOOD 13 102 Unto their praise, in certaine swearing rites!
    p. 197 UNDERWOOD 40   12 I give, or owe my friends, into your Rites,
    p. 201 UNDERWOOD 42   40 To doe her Husbands rites in, e're 'twere gone
    p. 205 UNDERWOOD 43   57 But that's a marke, wherof thy Rites doe boast,
    p. 210 UNDERWOOD 43 164 More then advanc'd the houses, and their rites?
    p. 254 UNDERWOOD 75   49 Stay, thou wilt see what rites the Virgins doe!
    p. 254 UNDERWOOD 75   76 Saw'st thou that Paire, became these Rites so
                             well,
    p. 256 UNDERWOOD 75 122 And Bishop stay, to consummate the Rites:
    p. 263 UNDERWOOD 79   4 To shew the rites, and t<o>'usher forth the way
    p. 315 HORACE 2   225 Fit rites. The Child, that now knowes how to
                             say,
    p. 319 HORACE 2   325 Having well eat, and drunke (the rites being
                             done)

rites (cont.)
    p. 333 HORACE 2   591 Who, since, to sing the Pythian rites is heard,
    p. 372 UNGATHERED 9   11 Wth Rites not bound, but conscience. Wouldst
                             thou All?

rithme   frequency: 1   relative frequency: 0.00001
    p. 200 UNDERWOOD 42   5 Who shall forbid me then in Rithme to bee

rithmes   frequency: 1   relative frequency: 0.00001
    p. 182 UNDERWOOD 28   2 Though not in these, in rithmes not wholly dumbe,

riuer   frequency: 5   relative frequency: 0.00007
    p. 94 FOREST 2   22 The lower land, that to the riuer bends,
    p. 97 FOREST 3   18 Through which a serpent riuer leades
    p. 97 FOREST 3   33 Or hauking at the riuer, or the bush,
    p. 367 UNGATHERED 6   35 Nor let one Riuer boast
    p. 367 UNGATHERED 6   57 Who euer sipt at Baphyre riuer,

rival. See "rivall."

rivall   frequency: 3   relative frequency: 0.00004
    p. 148 UNDERWOOD 7   28 Will be my Rivall, though she have but eares.
    p. 319 HORACE 2   288 And rivall with the Trumpet for his sound,
    p. 335 HORACE 2   632 Alone, without a rivall, by his will.

rivals   frequency: 1   relative frequency: 0.00001
    p. 292 UNDERWOOD 86   18 With thee 'bove all his Rivals gifts take place,

river   frequency: 3   relative frequency: 0.00004
    See also "riuer."
    p. 198 UNDERWOOD 40   26 Moves like a sprightly River, and yet can
    p. 305 HORACE 2   22 The pleasant grounds, or when the River Rhine,
    p. 309 HORACE 2   96 Or the wilde river, who hath changed now

rivers   frequency: 6   relative frequency: 0.00008
    p. 251 UNDERWOOD 74   7 The Rivers in their shores doe run,
    p. 264 UNDERWOOD 79   27 Chor. Rivers, and Vallies, Eccho what wee
                             sing.
    p. 264 UNDERWOOD 79   35 Chor. Rivers, and Valleys, Eccho what wee
                             sing.
    p. 269 UNDERWOOD 83   21 Earle Rivers Grand-Child -- serve not formes,
                             good Fame,
    p. 276 U'WOOD 84.3   23 Foure Rivers branching forth like Seas,
    p. 281 U'WOOD 84.8   18 Up to their Ancestors; the rivers side,

road   frequency: 1   relative frequency: 0.00001
    p. 85 EPIGRAMS 133   66 Thorough her wombe they make their famous road,

roam. See "rome."

roar. See "rore."

roasted   frequency: 1   relative frequency: 0.00001
    See also "rosted."
    p. 205 UNDERWOOD 43   52 To light Tobacco, or save roasted Geese,

roaue   frequency: 1   relative frequency: 0.00001
    p. 383 UNGATHERED 17   5 Who reads may roaue, and call the passage darke,

roaues   frequency: 1   relative frequency: 0.00001
    p. 383 UNGATHERED 17   7 Who reads, who roaues, who hopes to vnderstand,

rob   frequency: 3   relative frequency: 0.00004
    p. 255 UNDERWOOD 75   82 Of Sex, to rob the Creature; but from Man,
    p. 270 UNDERWOOD 83   38 But a fain'd way, doth rob it of the true.
    p. 389 UNGATHERED 23 12 And who make thither else, rob, or inuade.

robbed. See "robd," "rob'd."

robbery   frequency: 1   relative frequency: 0.00001
    p. 29 EPIGRAMS 8   t1 ON A ROBBERY.

robbing   frequency: 1   relative frequency: 0.00001
    p. 155 UNDERWOOD 13   90 Or robbing the poore Market-folkes should nurse

robd   frequency: 1   relative frequency: 0.00001
    p. 375 UNGATHERED 10 35 Beeing in feare to be robd, he most learnedly
                             begs.

rob'd   frequency: 3   relative frequency: 0.00004
     p.   29 EPIGRAMS 8   1 RIDWAY rob'd DVNCOTE of three hundred
                               pound,
     p.   29 EPIGRAMS 8   5 Rob'd both of money, and the lawes reliefe,
     p.   44 EPIGRAMS 56   4 As we, the rob'd, leaue rage, and pittie it.

robe   frequency: 3   relative frequency: 0.00004
     p. 276 U'WOOD 84.3   26 And let there be a starry Robe
     p. 285 U'WOOD 84.9   102 In Heav'n<s> Empyrean, with a robe of light?
     p. 319 HORACE 2   316 Brought in the Visor, and the robe of State,

robert   frequency: 7   relative frequency: 0.00010
     p.   40 EPIGRAMS 43   t1 TO ROBERT EARLE OF
                               SALISBVRIE.
     p.   47 EPIGRAMS 63   t1 TO ROBERT EARLE OF
                               SALISBVRIE.
     p.   96 FOREST 3   t1 TO SIR ROBERT WROTH.
     p. 231 UNDERWOOD 57   4 To Sir Robert Pie:
     p. 382 UNGATHERED 16 t2 behalfe of the two noble Brothers sr Robert
                               & sr Henrye
     p. 384 UNGATHERED 18 t2 Robert, Earle of Somerset.
     p. 415 UNGATHERED 43 t2 Good Freind Mr. Robert Dover, on his great

robes   frequency: 1   relative frequency: 0.00001
     p. 384 UNGATHERED 18   5 Such weare true wedding robes, and are true
                               freindes,

rock   frequency: 3   relative frequency: 0.00004
     p.   52 EPIGRAMS 76   15 The rock, the spindle, and the sheeres controule
     p.   86 EPIGRAMS 133   83 The other thought it HYDRA, or the rock
     p. 269 UNDERWOOD 83   10 Whose Daughter? ha? Great Savage of the Rock?

rockets   frequency: 1   relative frequency: 0.00001
     p. 249 UNDERWOOD 72   13 At Bonefires, Rockets, Fire-workes, with the
                               Shoutes

rockie   frequency: 1   relative frequency: 0.00001
     p. 150 UNDERWOOD 9   17 My mountaine belly, and my rockie face,

rocks   frequency: 1   relative frequency: 0.00001
     p. 160 UNDERWOOD 15 130 This Praecipice, and Rocks that have no end,

rocky. See "rockie."

rod   frequency: 3   relative frequency: 0.00004
     p. 129 UNDERWOOD 1.2   4 Use still thy rod,
     p. 235 UNDERWOOD 61   19 And doe their penance, to avert Gods rod,
     p. 287 U'WOOD 84.9   183 And came forth ever cheered, with the rod

roe   frequency: 10   relative frequency: 0.00014
     p.   35 EPIGRAMS 27   t1 ON SIR IOHN ROE.
     p.   37 EPIGRAMS 32   t1 ON SIR IOHN ROE.
     p.   37 EPIGRAMS 33   2 Glad-mention'd ROE: thou art but gone before,
     p.   50 EPIGRAMS 70   2 Then to begin, my ROE: He makes a state
     p.   50 EPIGRAMS 70   t1 TO WILLIAM ROE.
     p.   63 EPIGRAMS 98   1 Thou hast begun well, ROE, which stand well
                               too,
     p.   63 EPIGRAMS 98   t1 TO SIR THOMAS ROE.
     p.   64 EPIGRAMS 99   5 How much of great example wert thou, ROE,
     p.   80 EPIGRAMS 128   1 ROE (and my ioy to name) th'art now, to goe
     p.   80 EPIGRAMS 128   t1 TO WILLIAM ROE.

roehampton. See "row-hampton."

roe's   frequency: 1   relative frequency: 0.00001
     p.   35 EPIGRAMS 27   3 If any sword could saue from Fates, ROE'S
                               could;

roger   frequency: 2   relative frequency: 0.00002
     p. 378 UNGATHERED 11 80 Trie and trust Roger, was the word, but now
     p. 378 UNGATHERED 11 81 Honest Tom Tell-Troth puts downe Roger, How?

rogue   frequency: 1   relative frequency: 0.00001
     See also "english-rogue."
     p. 411 UNGATHERED 39 15 A Rogue by Statute, censur'd to be whipt,

rogues   frequency: 1   relative frequency: 0.00001
     p.   86 EPIGRAMS 133   88 No going backe; on still you rogues, and row.

rolands   frequency: 1   relative frequency: 0.00001
     p. 206 UNDERWOOD 43   70 All the madde Rolands, and sweet Oliveers;

rol'd   frequency: 1   relative frequency: 0.00001
   **p. 117 PANEGYRE   152 Their bursting ioyes; but through the ayre was
                               rol'd

roll. See "roule," "rowle."

rolled. See "rol'd."

rolls   frequency: 1   relative frequency: 0.00001
     See also "rowles."
     p. 210 UNDERWOOD 43   169 So would'st th<ou>'have run upon the Rolls by
                               stealth,

roman   frequency: 6   relative frequency: 0.00008
     See also "romane."
     p. 293 UNDERWOOD 87   8 The Roman Ilia was not more renown'd.
     p. 309 HORACE 2   77 A Roman to Caecilius will allow,
     p. 313 HORACE 2   160 And Roman Gentrie, jearing, will laugh out.
     p. 321 HORACE 2   360 The Roman Gentrie, men of birth, and meane,
     p. 323 HORACE 2   390 To Roman Poets. Shall I therefore weave
     p. 327 HORACE 2   464 Our Roman Youths they learne the subtle wayes

romane   frequency: 3   relative frequency: 0.00004
     p. 58 EPIGRAMS 91   2 A romane sound, but romane vertue weares,
     p. 61 EPIGRAMS 95   23 No more then SALVST in the Romane state!

romano   frequency: 1   relative frequency: 0.00001
     p. 260 UNDERWOOD 77   6 Send in, what or Romano, Tintoret,

rome   frequency: 7   relative frequency: 0.00010
     p. 56 EPIGRAMS 89   1 If Rome so great, and in her wisest age,
     p. 69 EPIGRAMS 107   14 What at Ligorne, Rome, Florence you did doe:
     p. 71 EPIGRAMS 110   4 CATO'S to boote, Rome, and her libertie,
     p. 102 FOREST 4   66 As wandrers doe, that still doe rome,
     p. 210 UNDERWOOD 43   162 Did not she save from thence, to build a Rome?
     p. 391 UNGATHERED 26   39 Of all, that insolent Greece, or haughtie Rome
     p. 395 UNGATHERED 29   1 When, Rome, I reade thee in thy mighty paire,

romney. See "rumney."

ronsard. See "ronsart."

ronsart   frequency: 1   relative frequency: 0.00001
     p. 181 UNDERWOOD 27   22 Equall with her? or Ronsart prais'd

roof. See "roofe."

roofe   frequency: 2   relative frequency: 0.00002
     p. 93 FOREST 2   3 Of polish'd pillars, or a roofe of gold:
     p. 292 UNDERWOOD 86   20 Beneath a Sweet-wood Roofe, neere Alba Lake:

roofes   frequency: 2   relative frequency: 0.00002
   **p. 114 PANEGYRE   63 Walls, windores, roofes, towers, steeples, all
                               were set
     p. 97 FOREST 3   15 Free from proud porches, or their guilded roofes,

roofs. See "roofes."

room. See "roome."

roome   frequency: 8   relative frequency: 0.00011
     p. 90 FOREST 2   87 When shee was farre: and not a roome, but drest,
     p. 226 UNDERWOOD 53   17 So well! as when I saw the floore, and Roome,
     p. 262 UNDERWOOD 78   7 And he is built like some imperiall roome
     p. 282 U'WOOD 84.9   7 To hang a window, or make darke the roome,
     p. 391 UNGATHERED 26   21 A little further, to make thee a roome:
     p. 406 UNGATHERED 34 101 Lyue long ye ffeasting Roome. And ere thou
                               burne
     p. 409 UNGATHERED 38   3 Now, you are got into a nearer roome,
     p. 412 UNGATHERED 41   11 As it, alone, (and onely it) had roome,

roomes   frequency: 2   relative frequency: 0.00002
     p. 260 UNDERWOOD 77   3 Of Noremberg, or Turkie; hang your roomes
     p. 282 U'WOOD 84.8   20 Hang all your roomes, with one large Pedigree:

rooms. See "roomes."

roor   frequency: 1   relative frequency: 0.00001
    p.   49 EPIGRAMS 66   12 To liue when Broeck not stands, nor Roor doth
                                   runne.

root   frequency: 2   relative frequency: 0.00002
    See also "roote."
    p. 135 UNDERWOOD 30   18 And in the noblest Families tooke root
    p. 325 HORACE 2   440 The very root of writing well, and spring

roote   frequency: 2   relative frequency: 0.00002
    p.   70 EPIGRAMS 109   13 To be the same in roote, thou art in height;
    p. 119 FOREST 13   100 Heare, what the Muses sing about thy roote,

rooted   frequency: 2   relative frequency: 0.00002
    p. 157 UNDERWOOD 13   144 As they are high; are rooted, and will last.
    p. 290 UNDERWOOD 85   24 Now in the rooted Grasse him lay,

rootes   frequency: 1   relative frequency: 0.00001
    p. 274 U'WOOD 84.2   9 Run from your rootes; Tell, testifie the grand

roots. See "rootes."

rope   frequency: 2   relative frequency: 0.00002
    p. 215 UNDERWOOD 44   80 Descended in a rope of Titles, be
    p. 335 HORACE 2   655 For, if one should, and with a rope make haste

rore   frequency: 2   relative frequency: 0.00002
    p.   38 EPIGRAMS 38   4 Any man else, you clap your hands, and rore,
    p. 397 UNGATHERED 30   38 My lippes could forme the voyce, I heard that
                                   Rore,

roscivs   frequency: 1   relative frequency: 0.00001
    p.   56 EPIGRAMS 89   3 As skilfull ROSCIVS, and graue
                                   AESOPE, men,

rose   frequency: 8   relative frequency: 0.00011
    p.   72 EPIGRAMS 111   12 CAESAR stands vp, as from his vrne late
                                   rose.
    p.   85 EPIGRAMS 133   60 'Tis but light paines: Indeede this Dock's no
                                   rose.
    p. 237 UNDERWOOD 65   3 The bed of the chast Lilly, and the Rose!
    p. 268 UNDERWOOD 82   16 Her Rose, and Lilly, intertwind, have made.
    p. 270 U'WOOD 84.3   16 And Men may thinke, all light rose there.
    p. 401 UNGATHERED 33   8 Againe hath brought the Lillie to the Rose;
    p. 412 UNGATHERED 41   4 R. Rose, I. Ivy, E. sweet Eglantine.
    p. 413 UNGATHERED 41   13 The third, is from the garden cull'd, the Rose,

roses   frequency: 4   relative frequency: 0.00005
    p. 136 UNDERWOOD 2.5   22 In her cheekes, of Milke, and Roses;
    p. 170 UNDERWOOD 19   8 Where he doth steepe himselfe in Milke and
                                   Roses;
    p. 254 UNDERWOOD 75   57 See, how with Roses, and with Lillies shine,
    p. 254 UNDERWOOD 75   58 (Lillies and Roses, Flowers of either Sexe)

rosie   frequency: 4   relative frequency: 0.00005
    p.   62 EPIGRAMS 97   5 His rosie tyes and garters so ore-blowne,
    p. 106 FOREST 9   9 I sent thee, late, a rosie wreath,
    p. 294 UNDERWOOD 89   4 Thy locks, and rosie garlands crowne thy head;
    p. 414 UNGATHERED 41   50 The rosie Morning, or the rising Sun,

rosie-crosse   frequency: 1   relative frequency: 0.00001
    p. 206 UNDERWOOD 43   72 With the Chimaera of the Rosie-Crosse,

rosted   frequency: 1   relative frequency: 0.00001
    p.   88 EPIGRAMS 133   149 Cats there lay diuers had beene flead, and
                                   rosted,

rosy. See "rosie," "rosie-crosse."

rot   frequency: 1   relative frequency: 0.00001
    p. 188 UNDERWOOD 34   12 Spanish receipt, to make her teeth to rot.

rothenburg. See "rotteinberg."

rotteinberg   frequency: 1   relative frequency: 0.00001
    p.   69 EPIGRAMS 107   26 Hans-spiegle, Rotteinberg, and Boutersheim,

rotten   frequency: 1   relative frequency: 0.00001
    p. 408 UNGATHERED 36   11 Wth rotten chalk, or Cole vpon a wall,

rough   frequency: 5   relative frequency: 0.00007
  p. 110 FOREST 11   40 Rough, swelling, like a storme:
  p. 160 UNDERWOOD 14   57 With horrour rough, then rioting with wit!
  p. 289 UNDERWOOD 85   5 Nor Souldier-like started with rough alarmes,
  p. 294 UNDERWOOD 87   23 And then rough Adria, angrier, farre;
  p. 319 HORACE 2   321 The rough rude Satyres naked; and would try,

roule   frequency: 1   relative frequency: 0.00001
  p. 60 EPIGRAMS 93   12 Nor could I, had I seene all Natures roule,

round   frequency: 20   relative frequency: 0.00028
  See also "rounde."
  p. 33 EPIGRAMS 21   2 His neck fenc'd round with ruffe! his eyes halfe
                shut!
  p. 63 EPIGRAMS 98   3 He that is round within himselfe, and streight,
  p. 98 FOREST 3   59 The iolly wassall walkes the often round,
  p. 105 FOREST 8   17 Liuers, round about the towne.
  p. 147 UNDERWOOD 7   22 But he hath eyes so round, and bright,
  p. 160 UNDERWOOD 14   63 A banke against it. Nothing but the round
  p. 170 UNDERWOOD 19   4 His double Bow, and round his Arrowes sends;
  p. 225 UNDERWOOD 51   15 Whose even Thred the Fates spinne round, and
                full,
  p. 227 UNDERWOOD 52   5 And the whole lumpe growes round, deform'd, and
                droupes,
  p. 244 UNDERWOOD 70   49 By him, so ample, full, and round,
  p. 280 U'WOOD 84.4   55 So polisht, perfect, round, and even,
  p. 285 U'WOOD 84.9   89 That, planted round, there sing before the Lamb,
  p. 290 UNDERWOOD 85   17 Or when that Autumne, through the fields, lifts
                round
  p. 290 UNDERWOOD 85   32 Wild Bores into his toyles pitch'd round:
  p. 293 UNDERWOOD 86   32 Or with fresh flowers to girt my temple round.
  p. 315 HORACE 2   241 The old man many evils doe girt round;
  p. 319 HORACE 2   296 That wider Walls embrac'd their Citie round,
  p. 335 HORACE 2   650 And stalketh, like a Fowler, round about,
  p. 396 UNGATHERED 30   14 Hot from thy trumpet, round, about the world.
  p. 415 UNGATHERED 42   16 Where it runs round, and even: where so well,

rounde   frequency: 1   relative frequency: 0.00001
  p. 421 UNGATHERED 48   39 Aboute this Isle, and Charme the rounde, as
                when

rounds   frequency: 2   relative frequency: 0.00002
  p. 221 UNDERWOOD 48   41 Thy Circuits, and thy Rounds free,
  p. 230 UNDERWOOD 56   16 Run all the Rounds in a soft Ladyes eare,

rouse. See "rouze," "rowse."

roused   frequency: 1   relative frequency: 0.00001
  p. 97 FOREST 3   23 In spring, oft roused for thy masters sport,

rout   frequency: 4   relative frequency: 0.00005
  See also "rowte."
  p. 98 FOREST 3   53 The rout of rurall folke come thronging in,
  p. 240 UNDERWOOD 67   40 Whilst all the ravish'd rout
  p. 313 HORACE 2   159 In sound, quite from his fortune; both the rout,
  p. 367 UNGATHERED 6   44 There charme the rout

routes   frequency: 1   relative frequency: 0.00001
  p. 249 UNDERWOOD 72   15 Had they but grace, of thinking, at these routes,

routs. See "routes."

rouze   frequency: 1   relative frequency: 0.00001
  p. 397 UNGATHERED 30   39 And Rouze, the Marching of a mighty force,

rove. See "roaue."

roves. See "roaues."

roving. See "rovinge."

rovinge   frequency: 1   relative frequency: 0.00001
  p. 108 FOREST 10 A   5 The skilfull mischife of a rovinge Eye

row   frequency: 6   relative frequency: 0.00008
  p. 86 EPIGRAMS 133   88 No going backe; on still you rogues, and row.
  p. 86 EPIGRAMS 133   90 Row close then, slaues. Alas, they will beshite
                vs.
  p. 86 EPIGRAMS 133   91 No matter, stinkards, row. What croaking sound
  p. 86 EPIGRAMS 133   93 Ouer your heads: Well, row. At this a loud

row (cont.)
   p. 93 FOREST 2   2 Of touch, or marble; nor canst boast a row
   p. 375 UNGATHERED 10   20 Religiously here he bids, row from the stewes,

row-hampton   frequency: 1   relative frequency: 0.00001
   p. 252 UNDERWOOD 75   12 From Greenwich, hither, to Row-hampton gate!

rowable   frequency: 1   relative frequency: 0.00001
   p. 309 HORACE 2   94 Once rowable, but now doth nourish men

rowle   frequency: 1   relative frequency: 0.00001
   p. 188 UNDERWOOD 35   6 To fetch the flesh, we keepe the Rowle.

rowles   frequency: 1   relative frequency: 0.00001
   p. 247 UNDERWOOD 70   126 Whose lines her rowles were, and records.

rowse   frequency: 2   relative frequency: 0.00002
   p. 162 UNDERWOOD 15   3 All that dare rowse: or are not loth to quit
   p. 282 U'WOOD 84.9   16 With such a Raritie, and not rowse Art

rowte   frequency: 1   relative frequency: 0.00001
   p. 420 UNGATHERED 48   21 And rather to the ffyre, then to the Rowte

royal   frequency: 1   relative frequency: 0.00001
  See also "royall."
   p. 383 UNGATHERED 16   14 your Royal Eye which still creat[t]es new men

royall   frequency: 7   relative frequency: 0.00010
   p. 38 EPIGRAMS 36   3 But in my royall subiect I passe thee,
   p. 222 UNDERWOOD 48   52 When with his royall shipping
   p. 236 UNDERWOOD 63   7 Then, Royall CHARLES, and MARY, doe
                           not grutch
   p. 240 UNDERWOOD 67   25 5. TERP. Behold the royall Mary,
   p. 259 UNDERWOOD 76   5 That whereas your royall Father,
   p. 321 HORACE 2   333 A royall Crowne, and purple, be made hop,
   p. 382 UNGATHERED 16   6 presentes a Royall Alter of fayre peace,

rub   frequency: 1   relative frequency: 0.00001
   p. 396 UNGATHERED 30   7 And, though I now begin, 'tis not to rub

ruddy   frequency: 1   relative frequency: 0.00001
   p. 94 FOREST 2   17 And thence, the ruddy Satyres oft prouoke

rude   frequency: 6   relative frequency: 0.00008
   p. 39 EPIGRAMS 40   4 Grant then, no rude hand remoue her.
   p. 134 UNDERWOOD 2.4   22 Before rude hands have touch'd it?
   p. 177 UNDERWOOD 25   26 True noblesse. Palme growes straight, though
                           handled ne're so rude.
   p. 284 U'WOOD 84.9   78 With silence, and amazement! not with rude,
   p. 319 HORACE 2   321 The rough rude Satyres naked; and would try,
   p. 331 HORACE 2   583 Into the Profits, what a meere rude braine

ru'de   frequency: 1   relative frequency: 0.00001
   p. 39 EPIGRAMS 40   14 In these times. Few so haue ru'de

rudenesse   frequency: 1   relative frequency: 0.00001
   p. 98 FOREST 3   54 (Their rudenesse then is thought no sinne)

rudest   frequency: 1   relative frequency: 0.00001
   p. 251 UNDERWOOD 74   9 The rudest Winds obey the calmest Ayre:

rudyerd. See "rvdyerd."

rue   frequency: 1   relative frequency: 0.00001
   p. 33 EPIGRAMS 22   4 It makes the father, lesse, to rue.

rued. See "ru'de."

ruff. See "ruffe."

ruffe   frequency: 2   relative frequency: 0.00002
   p. 33 EPIGRAMS 21   2 His neck fenc'd round with ruffe! his eyes halfe
                           shut!
   p. 65 EPIGRAMS 101   20 Knat, raile, and ruffe too. How so ere, my man

ruffes   frequency: 1   relative frequency: 0.00001
   p. 58 EPIGRAMS 92   6 Ripe are their ruffes, their cuffes, their
                           beards, their gate,

ruffs. See "ruffes."

ruhr.   See "roor."

ruin.   See "ruine."

ruin'd   frequency: 1   relative frequency: 0.00001
     p. 188 UNDERWOOD 34   16 Make all hereafter, had'st thou ruin'd this?

ruine   frequency: 7   relative frequency: 0.00010
     p.   94 FOREST 2   46 They'are rear'd with no mans ruine, no mans
                                grone,
     p. 166 UNDERWOOD 15   131 Or side, but threatens Ruine. The whole Day
     p. 203 UNDERWOOD 43   14 To ruine any issue of the braine?
     p. 212 UNDERWOOD 43   205 Blow up, and ruine, myne, and countermyne,
     p. 243 UNDERWOOD 70   18 And all on utmost ruine set;
     p. 283 U'WOOD 84.9   25 The world to ruine with it; in her Fall,
     p. 391 UNGATHERED 26   12 And thinke to ruine, where it seem'd to raise.

ruines   frequency: 4   relative frequency: 0.00005
   **p. 116 PANEGYRE   103 "And with their ruines raise the panders bowers:
     p. 207 UNDERWOOD 43   105 How in these ruines, Vulcan, thou dost lurke,
     p. 209 UNDERWOOD 43   137 See the worlds Ruines! nothing but the piles
     p. 224 UNDERWOOD 50   17 Among the daily Ruines that fall foule,

ruins. See "ruines."

rule   frequency: 3   relative frequency: 0.00004
   **p. 115 PANEGYRE   80 "To rule like Heauen; and haue no more, their
                                owne,
     p. 158 UNDERWOOD 13   162 (As their true rule or lesson) either men,
     p. 309 HORACE 2   104 The power, and rule of speaking resteth still.

rules   frequency: 1   relative frequency: 0.00001
     p.   37 EPIGRAMS 35   2 A Prince, that rules by'example, more than sway?

rumney   frequency: 1   relative frequency: 0.00001
     p. 103 FOREST 6   13 All the grasse that Rumney yeelds,

rumor   frequency: 1   relative frequency: 0.00001
     p. 102 FOREST 5   10 Fame, and rumor are but toyes.

rumor'd   frequency: 1   relative frequency: 0.00001
     p. 101 FOREST 4   50 But, as 'tis rumor'd, so beleeu'd:

rumour   frequency: 3   relative frequency: 0.00004
     See also "rumor."
     p.   43 EPIGRAMS 51   6 Who this thy scape from rumour gratulate,
     p.   43 EPIGRAMS 51   t2 Vpon the happy false rumour of his death, the two
     p. 224 UNDERWOOD 50   4 To conquer rumour, and triumph on spight;

rumoured. See "rumor'd."

run   frequency: 20   relative frequency: 0.00028
     See also "runne."
    *p. 492 TO HIMSELF   9 Run on, and rage, sweat, censure, and condemn:
     p.   47 EPIGRAMS 63   1 Who can consider thy right courses run,
     p.   69 EPIGRAMS 107   9 Tell them, what parts yo'haue tane, whence run
                                away,
     p.   69 EPIGRAMS 107   30 Twirle the poore chaine you run a feasting in.
     p. 116 FOREST 12   99 Before his swift and circled race be run,
     p. 134 UNDERWOOD 2.4   9 That they still were to run by her side,
     p. 154 UNDERWOOD 13   46 Run from the Conscience of it, if they could.
     p. 189 UNDERWOOD 36   6 All light[s] into his one doth run;
     p. 191 UNDERWOOD 38   2 Of Credit lost. And I am now run madde:
     p. 194 UNDERWOOD 38   119 Others by common Stars their courses run,
     p. 210 UNDERWOOD 43   169 So would'st th<ou>'have run upon the Rolls by
                                stealth,
     p. 230 UNDERWOOD 56   16 Run all the Rounds in a soft Ladyes eare,
     p. 251 UNDERWOOD 74   7 The Rivers in their shores doe run,
     p. 274 U'WOOD 84.2   9 Run from your rootes; Tell, testifie the grand
     p. 280 U'WOOD 84.4   62 Where it may run to any good;
     p. 287 U'WOOD 84.9   171 He run; and all did strive with diligence
     p. 293 UNDERWOOD 87   16 So Fates would let the Boy a long thred run.
     p. 307 HORACE 2   36 Obscure. This, striving to run smooth, and flow,
     p. 317 HORACE 2   256 Or acted told. But, ever, things that run
     p. 414 UNGATHERED 41   51 Who like a Giant hasts his course to run,

rung   frequency: 1   relative frequency: 0.00001
     p. 232 UNDERWOOD 58   11 Like a rung Beare, or Swine: grunting out wit

runne   frequency: 10   relative frequency: 0.00014
  **p. 114 PANEGYRE   43 Others on ground runne gazing by his side,
    p.   36 EPIGRAMS 29   4 All braines, at times of triumph, should runne
                              wit.
    p.   36 EPIGRAMS 29   5 For then, our water-conduits doe runne wine;
    p.   49 EPIGRAMS 66   12 To liue when Broeck not stands, nor Roor doth
                              runne.
    p.   81 EPIGRAMS 129   15 O, runne not proud of this. Yet, take thy due.
    p.   94 FOREST 2   33 Fat, aged carps, that runne into thy net.
    p. 121 FOREST 14   30 Doth vrge him to runne wrong, or to stand still.
    p. 156 UNDERWOOD 13   120 And can I lesse of substance? When I runne,
    p. 238 UNDERWOOD 65   11 And threat' the great Eclipse. Two houres but
                              runne,
    p. 270 UNDERWOOD 83   58 Chear'd her faire Sisters in her race to runne!

running   frequency: 2   relative frequency: 0.00002
    p. 143 UNDERWOOD 3   10 To stay the running floods,
    p. 148 UNDERWOOD 8   2 Here running in the Glasse,

runs   frequency: 4   relative frequency: 0.00005
    p. 113 FOREST 12   16 Runs betweene man, and man; 'tweene dame, and
                              dame;
    p. 167 UNDERWOOD 15   148 Runs sweetly, as it had his Lordships Soule;
    p. 283 U'WOOD 84.9   24 It rages, runs, flies, stands, and would provoke
    p. 415 UNGATHERED 42   16 Where it runs round, and even: where so well,

rural. See "rurall."

rurall   frequency: 3   relative frequency: 0.00004
    p.   95 FOREST 2   51 Some bring a capon, some a rurall cake,
    p.   98 FOREST 3   53 The rout of rurall folke come thronging in,
    p. 397 UNGATHERED 30   28 Or Rurall Virgil come, to pipe to vs!

rush   frequency: 2   relative frequency: 0.00002
    p. 141 UNDERWOOD 2.9   27 Skin as smooth as any rush,
    p. 294 UNDERWOOD 88   3 Let us not then rush blindly on unto it,

rust   frequency: 1   relative frequency: 0.00001
    p. 327 HORACE 2   472 Sixe ounces. O, when once the canker'd rust,

ruth   frequency: 1   relative frequency: 0.00001
    p.   33 EPIGRAMS 22   1 Here lyes to each her parents ruth,

rutland. See "rvtland."

rutter. See "rvtter."

rvdyerd   frequency: 2   relative frequency: 0.00002
    p.   78 EPIGRAMS 121   1 RVDYERD, as lesser dames, to great ones
                              vse,
    p.   78 EPIGRAMS 121   t1 TO BENIAMIN RVDYERD.

rvtland   frequency: 2   relative frequency: 0.00002
    p.   53 EPIGRAMS 79   t1 TO ELIZABETH COVNTESSE OF
                              RVTLAND.
    p. 113 FOREST 12   t2 TO ELIZABETH COVNTESSE OF
                              RVTLAND.

rvtter   frequency: 1   relative frequency: 0.00001
    p. 414 UNGATHERED 42   t2 Master JOSEPH RVTTER.

ryme   frequency: 1   relative frequency: 0.00001
    p. 421 UNGATHERED 49   7 O're read, examin'd, try'd, and prou'd yor: Ryme

rymer's. See "rimee's."

rymes   frequency: 3   relative frequency: 0.00004
    p. 177 UNDERWOOD 25   15 On these darke rymes; that my affection
    p. 259 UNDERWOOD 76   18 All the envie of the Rymes,
    p. 408 UNGATHERED 37   5 ffoole, doe not rate my Rymes; I'haue found thy
                              Vice

ryming   frequency: 1   relative frequency: 0.00001
    p. 200 UNDERWOOD 42   27 It is a ryming Age, and Verses swarme

ryots   frequency: 1   relative frequency: 0.00001
    p. 246 UNDERWOOD 70   103 Of rimes, or ryots, at your feasts,

's   frequency: 7   relative frequency: 0.00010

s<alomon>   frequency: 1   relative frequency: 0.00001
    p. 77 EPIGRAMS 120   t1 EPITAPH ON S<ALOMON> P<AVY> A
                                CHILD

s<c>urrile   frequency: 1   relative frequency: 0.00001
    p. 203 UNDERWOOD 43   20 Any, least loose, or s<c>urrile paper, lie

s<tr>ow   frequency: 1   relative frequency: 0.00001
    p. 74 EPIGRAMS 115   10 Of newes, and noyse, to s<tr>ow out a long meale.

sabines   frequency: 1   relative frequency: 0.00001
    p. 291 UNDERWOOD 85   41 Such as the Sabines, or a Sun-burnt-blowse,

sack   frequency: 3   relative frequency: 0.00004
    p. 241 UNDERWOOD 68   2 His Poet Sack, the House-hold will not pay?
    p. 241 UNDERWOOD 68   9 And rather wish, in their expence of Sack,
    p. 243 UNDERWOOD 70   12 From out the horrour of that sack?

sackcloth   frequency: 1   relative frequency: 0.00001
    p. 200 UNDERWOOD 42   25 Yet keepe those up in sackcloth too, or lether,

sacked. See "sack't."

sack't   frequency: 1   relative frequency: 0.00001
    p. 315 HORACE 2   201 Speake to me, Muse, the Man, who, after Troy
                                was sack't,

sackvile   frequency: 1   relative frequency: 0.00001
    p. 153 UNDERWOOD 13   1 If, Sackvile, all that have the power to doe

sackville. See "sackvile," "sacvile."

sacred   frequency: 8   relative frequency: 0.00011
    p. 55 EPIGRAMS 85   4 And why that bird was sacred to APOLLO,
    p. 115 FOREST 12   56 Because they lack'd the sacred pen, could giue
    p. 190 UNDERWOOD 37   13 Which, how most sacred I will ever keepe,
    p. 197 UNDERWOOD 40   14 Of vowes so sacred, and in silence made;
    p. 257 UNDERWOOD 75   163 Be kept alive those Sweet, and Sacred fires
    p. 292 UNDERWOOD 86   25 There twice a day in sacred Laies,
    p. 327 HORACE 2   487 Things sacred, from profane to separate;
    p. 380 UNGATHERED 12   40 That sacred to Odcombe are there now suspended,

sacrifice   frequency: 9   relative frequency: 0.00013
    p. 85 EPIGRAMS 133   49 Or magick sacrifice, they past along!
    p. 105 FOREST 8   28 To become thy sacrifice.
    p. 116 FOREST 12   97 This hasty sacrifice, wherein I reare
    p. 127 UNDERWOOD 1.1   9 3. All-gracious God, the Sinners sacrifice,
    p. 127 UNDERWOOD 1.1   t1 The Sinners Sacrifice.
    p. 156 UNDERWOOD 13   100 Lowd sacrifice of drinke, for their health-sake!
    p. 199 UNDERWOOD 41   18 Your sacrifice, then here remaine with me.
    p. 203 UNDERWOOD 43   22 By thy owne vote, a sacrifice to thee?
    p. 382 UNGATHERED 16   7 And as an euer-lasting Sacrifice

sacvile   frequency: 1   relative frequency: 0.00001
    p. 153 UNDERWOOD 13   t1 An Epistle to Sir EDWARD SACVILE,

sad   frequency: 14   relative frequency: 0.00020
    p. 35 EPIGRAMS 27   8 Wee, sad for him, may glorie, and not sinne.
    p. 40 EPIGRAMS 42   8 The like is IONE. But turning home, is sad.
    p. 65 EPIGRAMS 101   41 Shall make vs sad next morning: or affright
    p. 122 FOREST 15   6 And hearts of all, if I be sad for show,
    p. 154 UNDERWOOD 13   38 Must make me sad for what I have obtain'd.
    p. 270 UNDERWOOD 83   59 With gladnesse temper'd her sad Parents teares!
    p. 271 UNDERWOOD 83   77 Goe now, her happy Parents, and be sad,
    p. 287 U'WOOD 84.9   181 For her devotions, and those sad essayes
    p. 309 HORACE 2   105 The gests of Kings, great Captaines, and sad
                                Warres,
    p. 311 HORACE 2   149 Sad language fits sad lookes; stuff'd menacings,
    p. 315 HORACE 2   209 Of Diomede; nor Troyes sad Warre begins
    p. 335 HORACE 2   672 Or the sad thunder-stroken thing he have
    p. 342 HORACE 1   177 .. still .... griev'd .... sad

saddest   frequency: 1   relative frequency: 0.00001
    p. 111 FOREST 11   60 Sober, as saddest care:

saddled. See "sadled."

sadled   frequency: 1   relative frequency: 0.00001
    p. 374 UNGATHERED 10   14 A Horse here is sadled, but no Tom him to
                                backe,

sadnesse   frequency: 4   relative frequency: 0.00005
    p. 82 EPIGRAMS 130   4 That shee remoueth cares, sadnesse eiects,
    p. 191 UNDERWOOD 38   4 This sadnesse makes no approaches, but to kill.
    p. 221 UNDERWOOD 48   20 From any thought like sadnesse.
    p. 414 UNGATHERED 41   43 Whose chearfull look our sadnesse doth destroy,

safe   frequency: 19   relative frequency: 0.00027
  See also "over-safe."
   *p. 493 TO HIMSELF   33 Can feed on orts: And safe in your
                  stage-clothes,
  **p. 116 PANEGYRE   120 For vice is safe, while she hath vice to friend.
    p. 53 EPIGRAMS 77   1 Be safe, nor feare thy selfe so good a fame,
    p. 61 EPIGRAMS 95   1 If, my religion safe, I durst embrace
    p. 66 EPIGRAMS 102   20 The common-wealth still safe, must studie thee.
    p. 76 EPIGRAMS 119   9 Dar'st breath in any ayre; and with safe skill,
    p. 109 FOREST 11   6 Or safe, but shee'll procure
    p. 118 FOREST 13   56 Without companions? 'Tis safe to haue none.
    p. 118 FOREST 13   76 (They finde it both so wittie, and safe to giue.)
    p. 175 UNDERWOOD 23   36 Safe from the wolves black jaw, and the dull
                  Asses hoofe.
    p. 186 UNDERWOOD 32   9 Who thus long safe, would gaine upon the times
    p. 218 UNDERWOOD 47   1 Men that are safe, and sure, in all they doe,
    p. 241 UNDERWOOD 69   7 His is more safe commoditie, or none:
    p. 268 UNDERWOOD 82   14 Sate safe enough, but now secured more.
    p. 307 HORACE 2   39 Creepes on the ground; too safe, too afraid of
                  storme.
    p. 309 HORACE 2   92 That from the North, the Navie safe doth store,
    p. 323 HORACE 2   393 Grow a safe Writer, and be warie-driven
    p. 419 UNGATHERED 47   7 God blesse them all, and keepe them safe:
    p. 423 UNGATHERED 50   16 not safe; but when thou dost them thoroughlie:

safely   frequency: 3   relative frequency: 0.00004
    p. 111 FOREST 11   81 Cannot so safely sinne. Their chastitie
    p. 113 FOREST 11   116 Man may securely sinne, but safely neuer.
    p. 208 UNDERWOOD 43 128 And safely trust to dresse, not burne their
                  Boates.

safetie   frequency: 8   relative frequency: 0.00011
    p. 33 EPIGRAMS 22   6 With safetie of her innocence;
    p. 186 UNDERWOOD 31   9 As with the safetie, and honour of the Lawes,
    p. 219 UNDERWOOD 47   38 My Princes safetie, and my Kings desire,
    p. 236 UNDERWOOD 64   6 For safetie of such Majestie, cry out?
    p. 238 UNDERWOOD 66   8 Whereby the safetie of Man-kind was wrought)
    p. 238 UNDERWOOD 66   14 Of so much safetie to the Realme, and King!
    p. 286 U'WOOD 84.9   136 The safetie of our soules, and forfeit breath!
    p. 319 HORACE 2   322 Though sower, with safetie of his gravitie,

safeties   frequency: 1   relative frequency: 0.00001
    p. 261 UNDERWOOD 77   22 Of sweets, and safeties, they possesse by Peace.

safety. See "safetie."

saguntum   frequency: 1   relative frequency: 0.00001
    p. 242 UNDERWOOD 70   1 Brave Infant of Saguntum, cleare

said   frequency: 19   relative frequency: 0.00027
  See also "sayd," "sey'd."
  **p. 113 PANEGYRE   24 Faire DICE, and EVNOMIA; who were said
    p. 28 EPIGRAMS 4   6 Thou wert, as chiefe of them are said t'haue
                  beene.
    p. 80 EPIGRAMS 126   5 Said I wrong'd him, and (which was more) his
                  loue.
    p. 82 EPIGRAMS 130   17 But when I haue said, The proofes of all these
                  bee
    p. 86 EPIGRAMS 133   81 One said, it was bold BRIAREVS, or the
                  beadle,
    p. 87 EPIGRAMS 133 129 One said, the other swore, the world consists.
    p. 130 UNDERWOOD 1.3   4 And like the ravish'd Sheep'erds said,
    p. 136 UNDERWOOD 2.5 10 Sure, said he, if I have Braine,
    p. 159 UNDERWOOD 14   34 Heard what times past have said, seene what ours
                  doe:
    p. 204 UNDERWOOD 43   46 Thou should'st have stay'd, till publike fame
                  said so.
    p. 216 UNDERWOOD 45   3 My gentle Arthur; that it might be said
    p. 238 UNDERWOOD 66   1 Haile Mary, full of grace, it once was said,
    p. 263 UNDERWOOD 79   8 For, had we here said lesse, we had sung nothing
                  then.
    p. 287 U'WOOD 84.9   169 To one she said, Doe this, he did it; So
    p. 319 HORACE 2   311 Thespis is said to be the first found out
    p. 327 HORACE 2   482 Was Tigers, said, and Lyons fierce, to tame.

said (cont.)
    p. 327 HORACE 2   484 Was said to move the stones, by his Lutes
                               powers,
    p. 333 HORACE 2   617 Rich men are said with many cups to plie,
    p. 381 UNGATHERED 12   59 No: as I first said, who would write a story at

saies   frequency: 2   relative frequency: 0.00002
    p. 315 HORACE 2   222 And sits, till th'Epilogue saies Clap, or
                               Crowne:
    p. 380 UNGATHERED 12   48 Iest, he saies. Item one sute of blacke taffata

sail. See "saile," "sayle."

saile   frequency: 3   relative frequency: 0.00004
    p. 84 EPIGRAMS 133   11 Their wherry had no saile, too; ours had none:
    p. 156 UNDERWOOD 13   121 Ride, saile, am coach'd, know I how farre I
                               have gone,
    p. 367 UNGATHERED 6   37 But proue the Aire, and saile from Coast to
                               Coast:

sailes   frequency: 1   relative frequency: 0.00001
    p. 110 FOREST 11   41 With whom who sailes, rides on the surge of
                               feare,

sails. See "sailes," "sayles."

saint   frequency: 5   relative frequency: 0.00007
    p. 100 FOREST 4   15 That onely fooles make thee a saint,
    p. 213 UNDERWOOD 44   10 If they stay here, but till Saint Georges Day.
    p. 221 UNDERWOOD 48   44 In great Saint Georges Union;
    p. 289 U'WOOD 84.9   228 To publish her a Saint. My Muse is gone.
    p. 401 UNGATHERED 32   22 Of Ethnicisme, makes his Muse a Saint.

saints   frequency: 5   relative frequency: 0.00007
    p. 128 UNDERWOOD 1.1   45 12. Among thy Saints elected to abide,
    p. 282 U'WOOD 84.9   t5 Her #APOTHEOSIS, or Relation to the Saints.
    p. 283 U'WOOD 84.9   37 The joy of Saints! the Crowne for which it
                               lives,
    p. 285 U'WOOD 84.9   85 Saints, Martyrs, Prophets, with those
                               Hierarchies,
    p. 400 UNGATHERED 31   39 Both Saints, and Martyrs, by her loued Lord.

saist   frequency: 1   relative frequency: 0.00001
    p. 32 EPIGRAMS 18   3 Thou saist, that cannot be: for thou hast seene

sai'st   frequency: 1   relative frequency: 0.00001
    p. 150 UNDERWOOD 10   10 Thou sai'st, thou only cam'st to prove

saith   frequency: 3   relative frequency: 0.00004
    p. 366 UNGATHERED 6   1 Who saith our Times nor haue, nor can
    p. 380 UNGATHERED 12   21 There nam'd to be trauell'd? For this our Tom
                               saith:
    p. 422 UNGATHERED 50   1 Just and fit actions Ptolemey (he saith)

sake   frequency: 18   relative frequency: 0.00026
    See also "health-sake," "loves-sake."
    p. 27 EPIGRAMS 3   4 For the lucks sake, it thus much fauour haue,
    p. 34 EPIGRAMS 24   2 Mens manners ne're were viler, for your sake.
    p. 36 EPIGRAMS 28   19 Nay more, for greatnesse sake, he will be one
    p. 41 EPIGRAMS 45   11 For whose sake, hence-forth, all his vowes be
                               such,
    p. 42 EPIGRAMS 47   1 Sir LVCKLESSE, troth, for lucks sake
                               passe by one:
    p. 101 FOREST 4   59 From all my kinde: that, for my sake,
    p. 105 FOREST 8   25 There are those, that, for thy sake,
    p. 145 UNDERWOOD 5   12 One good enough for a songs sake.
    p. 146 UNDERWOOD 6   16 Familiar, tor the uses sake;
    p. 151 UNDERWOOD 11   7 Nor will he tell me for whose sake
    p. 185 UNDERWOOD 30   13 That still was good for goodnesse sake, nor
                               thought
    p. 260 UNDERWOOD 76   26 Of your grace, for goodnesse sake,
    p. 273 U'WOOD 84.1   10 This CRADLE, and for Goodnesse sake,
    p. 292 UNDERWOOD 86   22 In many a Gumme, and for thy soft eares sake
    p. 323 HORACE 2   376 Into their birth-right, and for fitnesse sake,
    p. 329 HORACE 2   507 Let what thou fain'st for pleasures sake, be
                               neere
    p. 394 UNGATHERED 28   25 Wher   't of Death, next Life, for her
                               I
    p. 398 UNGATHERED 30   63 The   t! and for his Country's sake

```
sakes                          frequency:    1   relative frequency: 0.00001
      p.   89 EPIGRAMS 133    195 And I could wish for their eterniz'd sakes,

salad.  See "sallade."

sale                           frequency:    1   relative frequency: 0.00001
      p.  333 HORACE 2        598 That to the sale of Wares calls every Buyer;

salian                         frequency:    1   relative frequency: 0.00001
      p.  292 UNDERWOOD 86     27 And in the Salian manner meet

salisburie                     frequency:    1   relative frequency: 0.00001
      p.   47 EPIGRAMS 63       9 And can to these be silent, Salisburie,

salisbury.  See "salisburie," "salisbvrie."

salisbvrie                     frequency:    2   relative frequency: 0.00002
      p.   40 EPIGRAMS 43      t1 TO ROBERT EARLE OF
                                  SALISBVRIE.
      p.   47 EPIGRAMS 63      t1 TO ROBERT EARLE OF
                                  SALISBVRIE.

sallade                        frequency:    1   relative frequency: 0.00001
      p.   64 EPIGRAMS 101     10 An oliue, capers, or some better sallade

sallie                         frequency:    1   relative frequency: 0.00001
      p.  206 UNDERWOOD 43     79 Or Captaine Pamp<h>lets horse, and foot, that
                                  sallie

sallust.  See "salvst."

sally.  See "sallie."

salomon.  See "s<alomon>."

salt                           frequency:    2   relative frequency: 0.00002
  See also "saut."
      p.   42 EPIGRAMS 49       3 I haue no salt: no bawdrie he doth meane.
      p.  193 UNDERWOOD 38     96 Can pumpe for; or a Libell without salt

salute                         frequency:    7   relative frequency: 0.00010
  **p.  114 PANEGYRE           40 And only with red silence him salute.
      p.   63 EPIGRAMS 97      15 Nor did the king of Denmarke him salute,
      p.   95 FOREST 2         49 And no one empty-handed, to salute
      p.  161 UNDERWOOD 14     67 I first salute thee so; and gratulate,
      p.  262 UNDERWOOD 78     19 Goe, Muse, in, and salute him. Say he be
      p.  367 UNGATHERED 6     38 Salute old Mone,
      p.  402 UNGATHERED 34    17 I doe salute you! Are you fitted yet?

salvation                      frequency:    1   relative frequency: 0.00001
      p.  130 UNDERWOOD 1.3     8 That did us all salvation bring,

salvst                         frequency:    1   relative frequency: 0.00001
      p.   61 EPIGRAMS 95      23 No more then SALVST in the Romane state!

same                           frequency:   59   relative frequency: 0.00085
  See also "selfe-same."
  **p.  114 PANEGYRE           46 Along with him, and the same trouble proue.
  **p.  117 PANEGYRE          158 Saue, that shee might the same perpetuall see.
      p.   33 EPIGRAMS 20      t1 TO THE SAME SIR COD.
      p.   35 EPIGRAMS 26      t1 ON THE SAME BEAST.
      p.   35 EPIGRAMS 28       2 Of a great man, and to be thought the same,
      p.   37 EPIGRAMS 33      t1 TO THE SAME.
      p.   42 EPIGRAMS 47      t1 TO THE SAME.
      p.   45 EPIGRAMS 57       1 If, as their ends, their fruits were so, the
                                  same,
      p.   46 EPIGRAMS 60       4 Thy fact, in brasse or marble writ the same)
      p.   47 EPIGRAMS 64      t1 TO THE SAME.
      p.   48 EPIGRAMS 64      14 As her owne conscience, still, the same reward.
      p.   49 EPIGRAMS 67       9 And thou design'd to be the same thou art,
      p.   55 EPIGRAMS 86      t1 TO THE SAME.
      p.   57 EPIGRAMS 90      13 MILL was the same. Since, both his body and
                                  face
      p.   63 EPIGRAMS 98       9 Be alwayes to thy gather'd selfe the same:
      p.   63 EPIGRAMS 99      t1 TO THE SAME.
      p.   70 EPIGRAMS 109     13 To be the same in roote, thou art in height;
      p.   71 EPIGRAMS 110      8 He wrote, with the same spirit that he fought,
      p.   72 EPIGRAMS 111     t1 TO THE SAME; ON THE SAME.
      p.   72 EPIGRAMS 112     10 An Epick poeme; thou hast the same end.
      p.   78 EPIGRAMS 122     t1 TO THE SAME.
```

same (cont.)

p.	78	EPIGRAMS 123	t1 TO THE SAME.
p.	80	EPIGRAMS 127	11 And, than this same, I know no abler way
p.	82	EPIGRAMS 131	t1 TO THE SAME.
p.	83	EPIGRAMS 131	12 They were not to be nam'd on the same day.
p.	88	EPIGRAMS 133	140 All was to them the same, they were to passe,
p.	95	FOREST 2	63 Where the same beere, and bread, and selfe-same wine,
p.	103	FOREST 6	t1 TO THE SAME.
p.	120	FOREST 13	123 Wherein, your forme, you still the same shall finde;
p.	129	UNDERWOOD 1.2	27 And slight the same.
p.	137	UNDERWOOD 2.5	38 With my Mothers is the same.
p.	137	UNDERWOOD 2.5	48 Make in one, the same were shee.
p.	153	UNDERWOOD 13	5 For benefits are ow'd with the same mind
p.	161	UNDERWOOD 14	70 That would, perhaps, have prais'd, and thank'd the same,
p.	161	UNDERWOOD 14	76 In the same Mines of knowledge; and thence brought
p.	175	UNDERWOOD 24	1 From Death, and darke oblivion, neere the same,
p.	180	UNDERWOOD 26	20 This same which you have caught,
p.	214	UNDERWOOD 44	56 Alive yet, in the noise; and still the same;
p.	225	UNDERWOOD 50	30 The same it was inspir'd, rich, and refin'd.
p.	237	UNDERWOOD 65	6 The same that thou art promis'd, but be slow,
p.	241	UNDERWOOD 69	2 To mee; or beene the same to you; if show,
p.	252	UNDERWOOD 75	t12 of the same name.
p.	254	UNDERWOOD 75	70 On the same floore,
p.	256	UNDERWOOD 75	108 Him up, to doe the same himselfe had done.
p.	278	U'WOOD 84.4	24 This is no Picture, but the same.
p.	321	HORACE 2	350 And so, as every man may hope the same;
p.	327	HORACE 2	481 From slaughters, and foule life; and for the same
p.	329	HORACE 2	530 Still in the same, and warned will not mend,
p.	335	HORACE 2	666 Doth the same thing with him, that would him kill.
p.	379	UNGATHERED 12	14 To write it with the selfe same spirit he went,
p.	383	UNGATHERED 16	13 still that same little poynte hee was; but when
p.	383	UNGATHERED 17	3 Who bluntly doth but looke vpon the same,
p.	384	UNGATHERED 18	10 Wth the same looke, or wth a better, shine.
p.	392	UNGATHERED 26	61 Vpon the Muses anuile: turne the same,
p.	395	UNGATHERED 29	23 The selfe same Genius! so the worke will say.
p.	400	UNGATHERED 31	29 And howrely brooding ore the same,
p.	406	UNGATHERED 35	4 All kings to doe ye self same deeds wth some!
p.	415	UNGATHERED 42	29 The valuations, mixtures, and the same

sanctified   frequency: 1   relative frequency: 0.00001
**p. 113 PANEGYRE   19 To this so cleare and sanctified an end,

sanctifier   frequency: 1   relative frequency: 0.00001
p. 128 UNDERWOOD 1.1   41 11. My Maker, Saviour, and my Sanctifier:

sand   frequency: 1   relative frequency: 0.00001
p. 100 FOREST 3   105 Nor death; but when thy latest sand is spent,

sands   frequency: 1   relative frequency: 0.00001
p. 103 FOREST 6   14 Or the sands in Chelsey fields,

sanguine   frequency: 1   relative frequency: 0.00001
p. 115 FOREST 12   72 To my lesse sanguine Muse, wherein she'hath wonne

sans   frequency: 1   relative frequency: 0.00001
p. 85 EPIGRAMS 133   48 Sans helpe of SYBIL, or a golden bough,

sapience   frequency: 1   relative frequency: 0.00001
p. 414 UNGATHERED 41   45 The Seat of Sapience, the most lovely Mother,

sappho   frequency: 1   relative frequency: 0.00001
p. 181 UNDERWOOD 27   3 Did Sappho on her seven-tongu'd Lute,

sardane   frequency: 1   relative frequency: 0.00001
p. 331 HORACE 2   559 As Poppie, and Sardane honey; 'cause without

sardus   frequency: 1   relative frequency: 0.00001
p. 351 HORACE 1   535 ..... with .... of Sardus ....

sat. See "sate."

satan. See "sathan."

sate   frequency: 3   relative frequency: 0.00004
    p. 68 EPIGRAMS 105   18 There IVNO sate, and yet no Peacock by.
    p. 185 UNDERWOOD 31   t3 the last Terme he sate Chancellor.
    p. 268 UNDERWOOD 82   14 Sate safe enough, but now secured more.

sathan   frequency: 1   relative frequency: 0.00001
    p. 127 UNDERWOOD 1.1   6 By sinne, and Sathan; and my flesh misus'd,

satires. See "satyres."

satirical. See "satyricall."

saturn's. See "satvrnes," "satvrne's."

satvrnes   frequency: 1   relative frequency: 0.00001
    p. 98 FOREST 3   50 As if in SATVRNES raigne it were;

satvrne's   frequency: 1   relative frequency: 0.00001
    p. 78 EPIGRAMS 122   2 The aged SATVRNE'S age, and rites to
                             know;

satyres   frequency: 8   relative frequency: 0.00011
    p. 60 EPIGRAMS 94   7 Yet, Satyres, since the most of mankind bee
    p. 60 EPIGRAMS 94   t2 WITH Mr. DONNES SATYRES.
    p. 73 EPIGRAMS 112   14 To Satyres; and thou dost pursue me. Where,
    p. 94 FOREST 2   17 And thence, the ruddy Satyres oft prouoke
    p. 319 HORACE 2   321 The rough rude Satyres naked; and would try,
    p. 321 HORACE 2   328 Yet so the scoffing Satyres to mens view,
    p. 321 HORACE 2   340 From what th'obscene, and petulant Satyres are.
    p. 321 HORACE 2   341 Nor I, when I write Satyres, will so love

satyricall   frequency: 1   relative frequency: 0.00001
    p. 171 UNDERWOOD 20   t1 A Satyricall Shrub.

satyrs. See "satyres."

sauage   frequency: 1   relative frequency: 0.00001
    p. 112 FOREST 11   108 What sauage, brute affection,

sauce   frequency: 1   relative frequency: 0.00001
    p. 65 EPIGRAMS 101   13 Limons, and wine for sauce: to these, a coney

sau'd   frequency: 1   relative frequency: 0.00001
    p. 73 EPIGRAMS 113   6 That the wit there, and manners might be sau'd:

saue   frequency: 10   relative frequency: 0.00014
  **p. 114 PANEGYRE   55 To her great sister: saue that modestie,
  **p. 116 PANEGYRE   100 "Where sleeping they could saue, and waking kill;
  **p. 117 PANEGYRE   138 That came to saue, what discord would destroy:
  **p. 117 PANEGYRE   158 Saue, that shee might the same perpetuall see.
    p. 33 EPIGRAMS 21   8 The bodies stripes, I see, the soule may saue.
    p. 35 EPIGRAMS 27   3 If any sword could saue from Fates, ROE'S
                             could;
    p. 44 EPIGRAMS 53   10 Could saue that line to dedicate to thee?
    p. 53 EPIGRAMS 79   6 (Saue that most masculine issue of his braine)
    p. 73 EPIGRAMS 112 21 Pr'y thee, yet saue thy rest; giue ore in time:
    p. 84 EPIGRAMS 133   9 The filth, stench, noyse: saue only what was
                             there

sauer   frequency: 1   relative frequency: 0.00001
    p. 46 EPIGRAMS 60   10 But sauer of my countrey thee alone.

sauour   frequency: 1   relative frequency: 0.00001
    p. 58 EPIGRAMS 92   5 And haue'hem yeeld no sauour, but of state.

sauoy   frequency: 1   relative frequency: 0.00001
    p. 379 UNGATHERED 12 19 France, Sauoy, Italy, and Heluetia,

saut   frequency: 1   relative frequency: 0.00001
    p. 164 UNDERWOOD 15 76 Doe all the tricks of a saut Lady Bitch;

savage   frequency: 1   relative frequency: 0.00001
    See also "sauage."
    p. 269 UNDERWOOD 83 10 Whose Daughter? ha? Great Savage of the Rock?

sav'd   frequency: 1   relative frequency: 0.00001
    See also "sau'd."
    p. 335 HORACE 2   658 Not thence be sav'd, although indeed he could?

save   frequency: 7 relative frequency: 0.00010
     See also "saue."
     p. 137 UNDERWOOD 2.5   42 All is Venus: save unchaste.
     p. 191 UNDERWOOD 38   19 God, and the good, know to forgive, and save.
     p. 205 UNDERWOOD 43   52 To light Tobacco, or save roasted Geese,
     p. 210 UNDERWOOD 43   162 Did not she save from thence, to build a Rome?
     p. 255 UNDERWOOD 75   77 Save the preceding Two?
     p. 276 U'WOOD 84.3   13 Draw first a Cloud: all save her neck;
     p. 283 U'WOOD 84.9   17 With all her aydes, to save her from the seize

saver. See "sauer."

savile   frequency: 2 relative frequency: 0.00002
     p. 61 EPIGRAMS 95   4 In thee, most weighty SAVILE, liu'd to vs:
     p. 61 EPIGRAMS 95   t1 TO SIR HENRIE SAVILE.

saving-honour   frequency: 1 relative frequency: 0.00001
     p. 248 UNDERWOOD 71   13 Unlesse some saving-Honour of the Crowne,

saviour   frequency: 4 relative frequency: 0.00005
     p. 128 UNDERWOOD 1.1   41 11. My Maker, Saviour, and my Sanctifier:
     p. 130 UNDERWOOD 1.3   t2 On the Nativitie of my Saviour.
     p. 286 U'WOOD 84.9   132 The vision of our Saviour, face to face,
     p. 288 U'WOOD 84.9   199 Shee saw her Saviour, by an early light,

saviours   frequency: 1 relative frequency: 0.00001
     p. 268 UNDERWOOD 82   10 This day, by Baptisme, and his Saviours crosse:

savour   frequency: 1 relative frequency: 0.00001
     See also "sauour."
     p. 177 UNDERWOOD 25   34 Of such as savour

savoy. See "sauoy."

saw   frequency: 36 relative frequency: 0.00052
     See also "sawe."
   **p. 113 PANEGYRE   20 I saw, when reuerend THEMIS did descend
     p. 35 EPIGRAMS 28   6 And, that is done, as he saw great men doe.
     p. 41 EPIGRAMS 44   4 Saw all his race approch the blacker floods:
     p. 68 EPIGRAMS 105   7 He, that but saw you weare the wheaten hat,
     p. 68 EPIGRAMS 105   16 That saw you put on PALLAS plumed caske:
     p. 81 EPIGRAMS 129   2 But the first question is, when one saw thee?
     p. 95 FOREST 2   77 With his braue sonne, the Prince, they saw thy
                              fires
     p. 130 UNDERWOOD 1.3   5 Who saw the light, and were afraid,
     p. 132 UNDERWOOD 2.2 t1 How he saw her.
     p. 185 UNDERWOOD 30   17 Clos'd to their peace, he saw his branches shoot,
     p. 209 UNDERWOOD 43 135 I saw with two poore Chambers taken in,
     p. 213 UNDERWOOD 44   9 They saw too store of feathers, and more may,
     p. 213 UNDERWOOD 44   29 He that but saw thy curious Captaines drill,
     p. 214 UNDERWOOD 44   39 Were now the greater Captaine? for they 'saw
     p. 227 UNDERWOOD 52   9 My Superficies: that was all you saw.
     p. 228 UNDERWOOD 53   1 When first, my Lord, I saw you backe your
                              horse,
     p. 228 UNDERWOOD 53   5 And saw a Centaure, past those tales of Greece;
     p. 228 UNDERWOOD 53   15 For never saw I yet the Muses dwell,
     p. 228 UNDERWOOD 53   17 So well! as when I saw the floore, and Roome,
     p. 247 UNDERWOOD 70 118 As they that saw
     p. 270 UNDERWOOD 83   65 Who saw the way was made it! and were sent
     p. 282 U'WOOD 84.9   14 And saw that portion of her selfe to die.
     p. 288 U'WOOD 84.9   199 Shee saw her Saviour, by an early light,
     p. 288 U'WOOD 84.9   201 On all the world! She saw him on the Crosse
     p. 288 U'WOOD 84.9   203 Shee saw him rise, triumphing over Death
     p. 288 U'WOOD 84.9   205 Shee saw him too, in glory to ascend
     p. 288 U'WOOD 84.9   209 All this by Faith she saw, and fram'd a Plea,
     p. 315 HORACE 2   202 Saw many Townes, and Men, and could their
                              manners tract.
     p. 319 HORACE 2   323 How he could jest, because he mark'd and saw,
     p. 321 HORACE 2   367 Fell into fault so farre, as now they saw
     p. 371 UNGATHERED 8   8 They saw it halfe, damd thy whole play, and more;
     p. 380 UNGATHERED 12 46 He there doth protest he saw of the eleuen.
     p. 396 UNGATHERED 30 11 It was no Dreame! I was awake, and saw!
     p. 396 UNGATHERED 30 15 I saw a Beauty from the Sea to rise,
     p. 397 UNGATHERED 30 33 And looking vp, I saw Mineruas fowle,
     p. 397 UNGATHERED 30 42 I saw, and read, it was thy Barons Warres!

sawe   frequency: 1 relative frequency: 0.00001
     p. 420 UNGATHERED 48 17 To every sence, and scorne to those that sawe

saw'st   frequency: 1   relative frequency: 0.00001
     p. 254 UNDERWOOD 75   76 Saw'st thou that Paire, became these Rites so
                                well,

say   frequency: 70   relative frequency: 0.00101
    *p. 492 TO HIMSELF   11 Say, that thou pour'st them wheat,
     p. 34 EPIGRAMS 25   7 What doth he else, but say, leaue to be chast,
     p. 36 EPIGRAMS 29   3 For thy late sharpe deuice. I say 'tis fit
     p. 36 EPIGRAMS 29   6 But that's put in, thou'lt say. Why so is thine.
     p. 41 EPIGRAMS 45   9 Rest in soft peace, and, ask'd, say here doth lye
     p. 42 EPIGRAMS 48   3 And hath no honor lost, our Due'llists say.
     p. 67 EPIGRAMS 103   9 Forgiue me then, if mine but say you are
     p. 68 EPIGRAMS 105   9 And, drest in shepheards tyre, who would not say:
     p. 79 EPIGRAMS 124   1 Would'st thou heare, what man can say
     p. 82 EPIGRAMS 130   11 To say, indeed, shee were the soule of heauen,
     p. 83 EPIGRAMS 131   9 Say, this, or that man they to thee preferre;
     p. 83 EPIGRAMS 131   11 And would (being ask'd the truth) ashamed say,
     p. 85 EPIGRAMS 133   51 Thou hast seene hell (some say) and know'st all
                                nookes there,
     p. 85 EPIGRAMS 133   59 To this dire passage. Say, thou stop thy nose:
     p. 88 EPIGRAMS 133   147 For, to say truth, what scullion is so nastie,
     p. 95 FOREST 2   82 What (great, I will not say, but) sodayne cheare
     p. 96 FOREST 2   102 May say, their lords haue built, but thy lord
                                dwells.
     p. 104 FOREST 7   5 Say, are not women truely, then,
     p. 104 FOREST 7   11 Say, are not women truely, then,
     p. 117 FOREST 13   29 Looke then, and see your selfe. I will not say
     p. 117 FOREST 13   34 As I, can say, and see it doth excell.
     p. 120 FOREST 14   14 Doth say,
     p. 121 FOREST 14   45 Say you haue follow'd farre,
     p. 136 UNDERWOOD 2.5   26 Where, you say, men gather blisses,
     p. 140 UNDERWOOD 2.8   23 To say over every purle
     p. 144 UNDERWOOD 3   17 They say the Angells marke each Deed,
     p. 151 UNDERWOOD 12   3 Would say as much, as both have done
     p. 168 UNDERWOOD 16   2 And if I had no more to say,
     p. 171 UNDERWOOD 20   4 No more, I am sorry for so fond cause, say,
     p. 193 UNDERWOOD 38   79 In darke, and sullen mornes, doe we not say,
     p. 198 UNDERWOOD 40   31 They may say Grace, and for Loves Chaplaines
                                passe;
     p. 204 UNDERWOOD 43   41 On such my serious follies; But, thou'lt say,
     p. 206 UNDERWOOD 43   87 I dare not say a body, but some parts
     p. 208 UNDERWOOD 43   120 May to thy name a Vulcanale say;
     p. 210 UNDERWOOD 43   173 But say, all sixe good men, what answer yee?
     p. 213 UNDERWOOD 44   1 Why yet, my noble hearts, they cannot say,
     p. 213 UNDERWOOD 44   23 Well, I say, thrive, thrive brave Artillerie
                                yard,
     p. 218 UNDERWOOD 47   5 I could say more of such, but that I flie
     p. 223 UNDERWOOD 49   40 They say you weekly invite with fits o'th'
                                Mother,
     p. 236 UNDERWOOD 64   3 How many times, Live long, CHARLES, would
                                he say,
     p. 241 UNDERWOOD 68   4 For want of knowing the Poet, to say him nay?
     p. 245 UNDERWOOD 70   82 Of which we Priests, and Poets say
     p. 258 UNDERWOOD 75   167 There; but, renewed, say,
     p. 262 UNDERWOOD 78   19 Goe, Muse, in, and salute him. Say he be
     p. 270 UNDERWOOD 83   52 And to the Torturers (her Doctors) say,
     p. 278 U'WOOD 84.4   17 Sweet Mind, then speake your selfe, and say,
     p. 278 U'WOOD 84.4   23 That all may say, that see the frame,
     p. 285 U'WOOD 84.9   98 Put black, and mourning on? and say you misse
     p. 286 U'WOOD 84.9   119 But all of God; They still shall have to say,
     p. 294 UNDERWOOD 87   17 HOR. But, say old Love returne should make,
     p. 315 HORACE 2   225 Fit rites. The Child, that now knowes how to
                                say,
     p. 323 HORACE 2   401 Too patiently, that I not fondly say;
     p. 327 HORACE 2   467 There's Albin's sonne will say, Substract an
                                ounce
     p. 333 HORACE 2   593 But, now, it is enough to say; I make
     p. 333 HORACE 2   597 To say, I'm ignorant. Just as a Crier
     p. 333 HORACE 2   601 His flatterers to their gaine. But say, he can
     p. 333 HORACE 2   624 Hee'd say, Mend this, good friend, and this;
                                'tis naught.
     p. 335 HORACE 2   639 Become an Aristarchus. And, not say,
     p. 365 UNGATHERED 5   21 Retire, and say; Her Graces
     p. 379 UNGATHERED 12   5 And that, say Philosophers, is the best modell.
     p. 380 UNGATHERED 12   55 Some want, they say in a sort he did craue:
     p. 384 UNGATHERED 18   25 That all, yt view you then, and late; may say,
     p. 388 UNGATHERED 23   8 Were askt of thy Discoueries; They must say,
     p. 389 UNGATHERED 24   3 To say but one, were single. Then it chimes,
     p. 394 UNGATHERED 28   7 But euery Table in this Church can say,
     p. 395 UNGATHERED 29   23 The selfe same Genius! so the worke will say.

say (cont.)
    p. 408 UNGATHERED 37   1 My verses were commended, thou dar'st say,
    p. 414 UNGATHERED 42   1 You looke, my Joseph, I should something say
    p. 416 UNGATHERED 45   3 or as some would say to breake
    p. 417 UNGATHERED 45   9 I had somwhat else to say,

say-master   frequency: 2   relative frequency: 0.00002
    p. 255 UNDERWOOD 75   99 Great Say-Master of State, who cannot erre,
    p. 415 UNGATHERED 42   26 A Say-master, hath studied all the tricks

sayd   frequency: 2   relative frequency: 0.00002
    p. 403 UNGATHERED 34   22 you'l be as Langley sayd, an Inigo still.
    p. 412 UNGATHERED 40   21 I sayd, who'had supp'd so deepe

sayes   frequency: 11   relative frequency: 0.00015
    p.   30 EPIGRAMS 12   7 The quarter day is come; the hostesse sayes,
    p.   40 EPIGRAMS 42   1 Who sayes that GILES and IONE at discord
                             be?
    p.   42 EPIGRAMS 49   2 He sayes, I want the tongue of Epigrammes;
    p.   46 EPIGRAMS 62   4 Your 'pothecarie, and his drug sayes no.
    p.   59 EPIGRAMS 92   20 And whisper what a Proclamation sayes.
    p. 120 FOREST 14   21 This day sayes, then, the number of glad yeeres
    p. 155 UNDERWOOD 13   71 Pardon, sayes he, that were a way to see
    p. 232 UNDERWOOD 58   4 What each man sayes of it, and of what coat
    p. 379 UNGATHERED 12   15 He sayes to the world, let any man mend it,
    p. 383 UNGATHERED 16   10 As true oblations; his Brothers Embleme sayes,
    p. 405 UNGATHERED 34   67 Hee's warme on his feet now he sayes, & can

sayest. See "saist," "sai'st," "sayst."

saying   frequency: 1   relative frequency: 0.00001
    p. 331 HORACE 2   548 This saying: To some things there is assign'd

sayle   frequency: 1   relative frequency: 0.00001
    p. 407 UNGATHERED 35   18 yearly set out there, to sayle downe ye Street,

sayles   frequency: 1   relative frequency: 0.00001
    p. 273 U'WOOD 84.1   23 With Sayles of silke, as the first notes

says. See "saies," "sayes," "say's."

say's   frequency: 1   relative frequency: 0.00001
    p.   30 EPIGRAMS 12   10 Lookes o're the bill, likes it: and say's, god
                             payes.

sayst   frequency: 1   relative frequency: 0.00001
    p. 397 UNGATHERED 30   47 Sayst thou so, Lucan? But thou scornst to stay

scab   frequency: 1   relative frequency: 0.00001
    p. 353 HORACE 1   594 .. .. Scab ....

scabbard. See "scabberd."

scabbed   frequency: 1   relative frequency: 0.00001
    p. 380 UNGATHERED 12   34 How scabbed, how ragged, and how pediculous

scabberd   frequency: 1   relative frequency: 0.00001
    p. 202 UNDERWOOD 42   85 Bawd, in a Velvet scabberd! I envy

scabbes   frequency: 1   relative frequency: 0.00001
    p. 380 UNGATHERED 12   50 So that not them, his scabbes, lice, or the
                             stewes,

scabs. See "scabbes."

scalding. See "still-scalding."

scale   frequency: 3   relative frequency: 0.00004
    p. 215 UNDERWOOD 44   68 Live by their Scale, that dare doe nothing free?
    p. 229 UNDERWOOD 54   4 A Merchants Wife is Regent of the Scale.
    p. 379 UNGATHERED 12   10 By the scale of his booke, a yard of his stile?

scan   frequency: 1   relative frequency: 0.00001
    p. 323 HORACE 2   404 A lawfull Verse, by th'eare, or finger scan.

scan'd   frequency: 1   relative frequency: 0.00001
    p. 370 UNGATHERED 7   5 And all your Booke (when it is throughly scan'd)

scandero<o>ne   frequency: 1   relative frequency: 0.00001
    p. 262 UNDERWOOD 78   13 Witnesse his Action done at Scandero<o>ne;

scanderoon. See "scandero<o>ne."

scanned. See "scan'd."

scant   frequency: 5   relative frequency: 0.00007
    p. 152 UNDERWOOD 12   31 But that I understood him scant.
    p. 153 UNDERWOOD 13   27 Excuses, or Delayes? or done 'hem scant,
    p. 174 UNDERWOOD 22   33 Which if it kindle not, but scant
    p. 184 UNDERWOOD 29   44 Words, and sweetnesse, and be scant
    p. 190 UNDERWOOD 37   20 And seeke to scant her comelie libertie,

scanted   frequency: 1   relative frequency: 0.00001
    p. 241 UNDERWOOD 68   3 Are they so scanted in their store? or driven

scap'd   frequency: 5   relative frequency: 0.00007
    p. 41 EPIGRAMS 45   7 To haue so soone scap'd worlds, and fleshes rage,
    p. 101 FOREST 4   25 Or, hauing scap'd, shall I returne,
    p. 160 UNDERWOOD 14   48 Forme, Art or Ensigne, that hath scap'd your
                              sight?
    p. 210 UNDERWOOD 43   154 Scap'd not his Justice any jot the more:
    p. 305 HORACE 2   27 To paint him, hath by swimming, hopelesse,
                              scap'd,

scape   frequency: 5   relative frequency: 0.00007
    p. 31 EPIGRAMS 13   1 When men a dangerous disease did scape,
    p. 43 EPIGRAMS 51   6 Who this thy scape from rumour gratulate,
    p. 73 EPIGRAMS 112   15 Where shall I scape thee? in an Epigramme?
    p. 179 UNDERWOOD 25   52 Oft scape an Imputation, more through luck, then
                              wit.
    p. 186 UNDERWOOD 32   14 They will come of, and scape the Punishment.

scar   frequency: 1   relative frequency: 0.00001
    See also "scarre."
    p. 86 EPIGRAMS 133   67 Betweene two walls; where, on one side, to scar
                              men,

scarce   frequency: 16   relative frequency: 0.00023
    See also "scarse."
    p. 65 EPIGRAMS 101   15 And, though fowle, now, be scarce, yet there are
                              clarkes,
    p. 67 EPIGRAMS 104   5 Or, because some scarce thinke that storie true,
    p. 71 EPIGRAMS 110   13 For, where his person liu'd scarce one iust age,
    p. 73 EPIGRAMS 112   20 Nor scarce dost colour for it, which is lesse.
    p. 99 FOREST 3   84 Not doing good, scarce when he dyes.
    p. 105 FOREST 8   11 Scarce will take our present store?
    p. 122 FOREST 15   21 I feele my griefes too, and there scarce is
                              ground,
    p. 155 UNDERWOOD 13   86 And superstition I dare scarce reveale,
    p. 167 UNDERWOOD 15   159 Is nothing, such scarce meat and drinke he'le
                              give,
    p. 184 UNDERWOOD 29   37 Scarce the Hill againe doth flourish,
    p. 184 UNDERWOOD 29   38 Scarce the world a Wit doth nourish,
    p. 234 UNDERWOOD 61   5 That scarce you heare a publike voyce alive,
    p. 248 UNDERWOOD 71   12 Health, or scarce breath, as she had never bin,
    p. 307 HORACE 2   30 Thy labouring wheele, comes scarce a Pitcher
                              out?
    p. 410 UNGATHERED 38   18 Hee'll be a Pilot, scarce can guide a Plough.
    p. 414 UNGATHERED 42   6 How well I lov'd Truth: I was scarce allow'd

scare. See "scar."

scarf. See "skarfe."

scarlet   frequency: 3   relative frequency: 0.00004
    p. 201 UNDERWOOD 42   69 Commended the French-hood, and Scarlet gowne
    p. 305 HORACE 2   19 A Scarlet peece, or two, stitch'd in: when or
    p. 346 HORACE 1   325 . ... Scarlet .. ..

scarlet-like   frequency: 1   relative frequency: 0.00001
    p. 230 UNDERWOOD 55   8 But Scarlet-like out-lasts the Cloth.

scarre   frequency: 2   relative frequency: 0.00002
    p. 187 UNDERWOOD 33   21 And make the Scarre faire; If that will not be,
    p. 192 UNDERWOOD 38   52 As not alone the Cure, but scarre be faire.

scarres   frequency: 1   relative frequency: 0.00001
    p. 98 FOREST 3   70 That they may sleepe with scarres in age.

scars. See "scarres."

scarse   frequency: 7   relative frequency: 0.00010
    p.   28 EPIGRAMS 3   10 Who scarse can spell th'hard names: whose knight
                              lesse can.
    p.   31 EPIGRAMS 14   10 Man scarse can make that doubt, but thou canst
                              teach.
    p.   32 EPIGRAMS 16   4 Scarse thy weekes swearing brings thee of, of
                              one.
    p.   66 EPIGRAMS 102   7 Almost, is exercis'd: and scarse one knowes,
    p.   77 EPIGRAMS 120   9 Yeeres he numbred scarse thirteene
    p.   81 EPIGRAMS 129   5 That scarse the Towne designeth any feast
    p. 109 FOREST 11   20 By many? scarse by any.

scatter'd   frequency: 2   relative frequency: 0.00002
    p.   29 EPIGRAMS 9   1 May none, whose scatter'd names honor my booke,
    p. 368 UNGATHERED 6   67 The scatter'd Orcades;

scene   frequency: 5   relative frequency: 0.00007
    p.   45 EPIGRAMS 56   7 To'a little wealth, and credit in the scene,
    p.   67 EPIGRAMS 104   7 And to your Scene lent no lesse dignitie
    p. 313 HORACE 2   179 Unto the Scene thou bringst, and dar'st create
    p. 402 UNGATHERED 34   11 Whether ye buylding of ye Stage or Scene!
    p. 404 UNGATHERED 34   62 The Scene! the Engyne! but he now is come

scenes   frequency: 2   relative frequency: 0.00002
    p. 220 UNDERWOOD 47   66 As are the Glorious Scenes, at the great
                              sights;
    p. 391 UNGATHERED 26   42 To whom all Scenes of Europe homage owe.

scent   frequency: 1   relative frequency: 0.00001
    See also "sent."
    p. 413 UNGATHERED 41   14 The Eye of flowers, worthy, for his scent,

scepter   frequency: 1   relative frequency: 0.00001
    p.   28 EPIGRAMS 4   1 How, best of Kings, do'st thou a scepter beare!

scepters   frequency: 1   relative frequency: 0.00001
    p. 422 UNGATHERED 50   9 The mayne comaund of scepters, soone doth perishe

sceptre. See "scepter."

sceptred. See "glcomie-sceptred."

sceptres. See "scepters."

scheldt   frequency: 1   relative frequency: 0.00001
    p. 369 UNGATHERED 6   116 Scheldt, nor the Maas,

schism. See "schisme."

schisme   frequency: 2   relative frequency: 0.00002
    p. 246 UNDERWOOD 70   90 Where it were friendships schisme,
    p. 287 U'WOOD 84.9   160 (But pride, that schisme of incivilitie)

school   frequency: 1   relative frequency: 0.00001
    See also "schocle."
    p. 410 UNGATHERED 39   7 To be the Denis of thy Father's School,

schoole   frequency: 5   relative frequency: 0.00007
    p.   57 EPIGRAMS 90   2 Vnworthy such a mistris, such a schoole,
    p. 141 UNDERWOOD 2.9   32 In loves schoole, and yet no sinners.
    p. 184 UNDERWOOD 29   59 That in rearing such a Schoole,
    p. 307 HORACE 2   46 Th'Aemilian Schoole, in brasse can fashion out
    p. 402 UNGATHERED 33   11 They are a Schoole to win

schoolemen   frequency: 1   relative frequency: 0.00001
    p. 284 U'WOOD 84.9   51 For, as there are three Natures, Schoolemen
                              call

schooles   frequency: 2   relative frequency: 0.00002
    p. 101 FOREST 4   48 And pride, and ignorance the schooles,
    p. 214 UNDERWOOD 44   58 Come to their Schooles,) show 'hem the use of
                              Guns;

schoolmen. See "schoolemen."

schools. See "schooles."

science   frequency: 2   relative frequency: 0.00002
    p. 156 UNDERWOOD 13   108 Or Science of discerning Good and Ill.
    p. 232 UNDERWOOD 59   3 The noble Science, and the maistring skill

scisars   frequency: 1   relative frequency: 0.00001
      p. 204 UNDERWOOD 43   38 A paire of Scisars, and a Combe in verse;

scissors. See "scisars."

scoffer   frequency: 1   relative frequency: 0.00001
      p. 333 HORACE 2   616 The Scoffer, the true Praiser doth out-goe.

scoffing   frequency: 1   relative frequency: 0.00001
      p. 321 HORACE 2   328 Yet so the scoffing Satyres to mens view,

scold   frequency: 1   relative frequency: 0.00001
      p. 84 EPIGRAMS 133   15 Furies there wanted not: each scold was ten.

scolds   frequency: 1   relative frequency: 0.00001
      p. 86 EPIGRAMS 133   69 Gorgonian scolds, and Harpyes: on the other

scope   frequency: 2   relative frequency: 0.00002
      p. 70 EPIGRAMS 109   6 Wrestlest with dignities, or fain'st a scope
      p. 133 UNDERWOOD 2.3   11 Mee, the scope of his next draught,

score   frequency: 2   relative frequency: 0.00002
      See also "foure-score."
      p. 103 FOREST 6   6 Kisse, and score vp wealthy summes
      p. 235 UNDERWOOD 62   10 One Poet, then of other folke ten score.

scores   frequency: 1   relative frequency: 0.00001
      p. 31 EPIGRAMS 12   22 Thus: and for his letcherie, scores, god payes.

scorn. See "scorne."

scorn'd   frequency: 1   relative frequency: 0.00001
      p. 188 UNDERWOOD 34   18 And scorn'd, thou'<h>ast showne thy malice, but
                                   hast fail'd.

scorne   frequency: 16   relative frequency: 0.00023
      p. 85 EPIGRAMS 133   31 In it' owne hall: when these (in worthy scorne
      p. 102 FOREST 4   63 But I will beare these, with that scorne,
      p. 122 FOREST 15   17 I know my state, both full of shame, and scorne,
      p. 147 UNDERWOOD 7   12 It were a plague 'bove scorne,
      p. 150 UNDERWOOD 11   1 Or Scorne, or pittie on me take,
      p. 165 UNDERWOOD 15   99 The Servant of the Serving-woman, in scorne,
      p. 175 UNDERWOOD 23   24 And only pitious scorne, upon their folly waites.
      p. 187 UNDERWOOD 33   22 Thou hast the brave scorne, to put back the fee!
      p. 193 UNDERWOOD 38   93 To suffer tortures, scorne, and Infamie,
      p. 203 UNDERWOOD 43   7 Or in remembrance of thy afront, and scorne,
      p. 223 UNDERWOOD 49   45 For there the wicked in the Chaire of scorne,
      p. 313 HORACE 2   175 Medea make brave with impetuous scorne;
      p. 333 HORACE 2   595 Him that is last, I scorne to come behind,
      p. 392 UNGATHERED 26   63 Or for the lawrell, he may gaine a scorne,
      p. 420 UNGATHERED 48   17 To every sence, and scorne to those that sawe
      p. 421 UNGATHERED 49   5 The emptye Carper, scorne, not Creditt wynns.

scorned   frequency: 2   relative frequency: 0.00002
      See also "scorn'd."
      p. 114 FOREST 12   29 Turne, vpon scorned verse, their quarter-face:
      p. 315 HORACE 2   199 A scorned Mouse! O, how much better this,

scornes   frequency: 1   relative frequency: 0.00001
      p. 133 UNDERWOOD 2.3   1 After many scornes like these,

scorns. See "scornes."

scornst   frequency: 1   relative frequency: 0.00001
      p. 397 UNGATHERED 30   47 Sayst thou so, Lucan? But thou scornst to stay

scotland   frequency: 2   relative frequency: 0.00002
      p. 149 UNDERWOOD 9   t1 My Picture left in Scotland.
      p. 207 UNDERWOOD 43   94 The rest, my journey into Scotland song,

scourge   frequency: 1   relative frequency: 0.00001
      p. 422 UNGATHERED 50   3 Is her owne scourge, when it sustaines their
                                   states

scraps   frequency: 1   relative frequency: 0.00001
     *p. 493 TO HIMSELF   24 scraps, out <of> euery dish,

scratching   frequency: 1   relative frequency: 0.00001
      p. 166 UNDERWOOD 15   144 That scratching now's our best Felicitie?

scrivener   frequency: 1   relative frequency: 0.00001
    p. 329 HORACE 2   529 How then? Why, as a Scrivener, if h<e>'offend

scullion   frequency: 1   relative frequency: 0.00001
    p. 88 EPIGRAMS 133   147 For, to say truth, what scullion is so nastie,

sculpture   frequency: 1   relative frequency: 0.00001
    p. 403 UNGATHERED 34   38 And Goody Sculpture, brought wth much adoe

scurf. See "scurfe."

scurfe   frequency: 1   relative frequency: 0.00001
    p. 333 HORACE 2   594 An admirable Verse. The great Scurfe take

scurrile. See "s<c>urrile."

scurrilitie   frequency: 1   relative frequency: 0.00001
    p. 323 HORACE 2   403 To part scurrilitie from wit: or can

scurrility. See "scurrilitie."

scutcheons   frequency: 1   relative frequency: 0.00001
    p. 35 EPIGRAMS 27   1 In place of scutcheons, that should decke thy
                                herse,

scylla   frequency: 1   relative frequency: 0.00001
    p. 315 HORACE 2   206 Scylla, Charybdis, Polypheme, with these.

se   frequency: 1   relative frequency: 0.00001
    p. 416 UNGATHERED 45   8 prest in to se you.

sea   frequency: 12   relative frequency: 0.00017
    p. 28 EPIGRAMS 5   4 The spoused paire two realmes, the sea the ring.
    p. 56 EPIGRAMS 88   6 Toward the sea, farther then halfe-way tree?
    p. 69 EPIGRAMS 107   16 For which there must more sea, and land be
                                leap'd,
    p. 88 EPIGRAMS 133   158 Being, beyond sea, burned for one witch:
    p. 110 FOREST 11   39 Inconstant, like the sea, of whence 'tis borne,
    p. 111 FOREST 11   70 Who, being at sea, suppose,
    p. 244 UNDERWOOD 70   40 And sunke in that dead sea of life
    p. 249 UNDERWOOD 72   5 Let Ireland meet it out at Sea, halfe way,
    p. 268 UNDERWOOD 82   13 Me thought, Great Britaine in her Sea, before,
    p. 278 U'WOOD 84.4   11 The Sunne, a Sea, or soundlesse Pit;
    p. 309 HORACE 2   91 Whether the Sea receiv'd into the shore,
    p. 396 UNGATHERED 30   15 I saw a Beauty from the Sea to rise,

sea-coale   frequency: 1   relative frequency: 0.00001
    p. 211 UNDERWOOD 43   181 To live in Sea-coale, and goe forth in smoake;

sea-girt   frequency: 1   relative frequency: 0.00001
    p. 240 UNDERWOOD 67   33 This sea-girt Isle upon:

seal. See "seale."

seal'd   frequency: 3   relative frequency: 0.00004
    p. 62 EPIGRAMS 96   9 My title's seal'd. Those that for claps doe
                                write,
    p. 67 EPIGRAMS 105   2 All historie seal'd vp, and fables crost;
    p. 400 UNGATHERED 31   37 Seal'd, and deliuer'd to her, in the sight

seale   frequency: 3   relative frequency: 0.00004
    p. 206 UNDERWOOD 43   81 The weekly Corrants, with Pauls Seale; and all
    p. 220 UNDERWOOD 48   5 And seale thee thy Commission:
    p. 225 UNDERWOOD 51   9 Sonne to the grave wise Keeper of the Seale,

sealed   frequency: 2   relative frequency: 0.00002
    See also "seal'd."
    p. 218 UNDERWOOD 47   t2 asked to be Sealed of the
    p. 220 UNDERWOOD 47   78 Sir, you are Sealed of the Tribe of Ben.

seales   frequency: 2   relative frequency: 0.00002
    p. 59 EPIGRAMS 92   29 To breake vp seales, and close 'hem. And they
                                know,.
    p. 206 UNDERWOOD 43   73 Their Seales, their Characters, Hermetique
                                rings,

sealing   frequency: 1   relative frequency: 0.00001
    p. 218 UNDERWOOD 47   15 But for a Sealing: let these men protest.

seals. See "broad-seales," "seales."

search   frequency: 8   relative frequency: 0.00011
    p. 145 UNDERWOOD 5   8 If wee would search with care, and paine,
    p. 160 UNDERWOOD 14   59 In sharpnesse of all Search, wisdome of Choise,
    p. 177 UNDERWOOD 25   24 Who would with judgement search, searching
                              conclude
    p. 187 UNDERWOOD 33   19 But first dost vexe, and search it! If not
                              sound,
    p. 206 UNDERWOOD 43   88 There were of search, and mastry in the Arts.
    p. 217 UNDERWOOD 46   1 He that should search all Glories of the Gowne,
    p. 255 UNDERWOOD 75   79 Search, Sun, and thou wilt find,
    p. 284 U'WOOD 84.9   80 Have busie search made in his mysteries!

search'd   frequency: 3   relative frequency: 0.00004
  **p. 115 PANEGYRE   82 "Though hid at home, abroad is search'd into:
    p. 130 UNDERWOOD 1.3   6 Yet search'd, and true they found it.
    p. 160 UNDERWOOD 14   40 Antiquities search'd! Opinions dis-esteem'd!

searcheth   frequency: 1   relative frequency: 0.00001
    p. 176 UNDERWOOD 24   10 Of Truth that searcheth the most <hidden>
                              Springs,

searching   frequency: 5   relative frequency: 0.00007
  **p. 113 PANEGYRE   8 But these his searching beams are cast, to prie
    p. 31 EPIGRAMS 14   8 What sight in searching the most antique springs!
    p. 146 UNDERWOOD 6   15 (By searching) what before was strange,
    p. 177 UNDERWOOD 25   24 Who would with judgement search, searching
                              conclude
    p. 225 UNDERWOOD 50   29 Searching for knowledge, and to keepe your mind

seare   frequency: 1   relative frequency: 0.00001
    p. 245 UNDERWOOD 70   68 To fall a logge at last, dry, bald, and seare:

seas   frequency: 12   relative frequency: 0.00017
    p. 37 EPIGRAMS 32   4 What not the enuie of the seas reach'd too,
    p. 37 EPIGRAMS 32   10 Seas, serenes, swords, shot, sicknesse, all are
                              there.
    p. 81 EPIGRAMS 128   13 Through seas, stormes, tempests: and imbarqu'd
                              for hell,
    p. 134 UNDERWOOD 2.4   10 Th<o>rough Swords, th<o>rough Seas, whether she
                              would ride.
    p. 222 UNDERWOOD 48   53 The narrow Seas are shadie,
    p. 276 U'WOOD 84.3   23 Foure Rivers branching forth like Seas,
    p. 289 UNDERWOOD 85   6 Nor dreads the Seas inraged harmes:
    p. 291 UNDERWOOD 85   52 Into our Seas send any such:
    p. 329 HORACE 2   518 Will passe the Seas, and long as nature is,
    p. 368 UNGATHERED 6   69 To vtmost Thule: whence, he backes the Seas
    p. 407 UNGATHERED 35   13 He some Colossus to bestryde ye Seas,
    p. 422 UNGATHERED 50   7 Looke how the starres from earth, or seas from
                              flames

seas'ning   frequency: 1   relative frequency: 0.00001
    p. 160 UNDERWOOD 14   55 To marke the excellent seas'ning of your Stile!

season   frequency: 6   relative frequency: 0.00008
    p. 88 EPIGRAMS 133   165 Your daintie nostrills (in so hot a season,
    p. 245 UNDERWOOD 70   61 In season, and so brought
    p. 251 UNDERWOOD 74   15 As all the wealth of Season, there was spread;
    p. 253 UNDERWOOD 75   25 It is the kindly Season of the time,
    p. 257 UNDERWOOD 75   148 Of Nuptiall Sweets, at such a season, owe,
    p. 307 HORACE 2   63 Till fitter season. Now, to like of this,

season'd   frequency: 1   relative frequency: 0.00001
    p. 94 FOREST 2   20 That neuer failes to serue thee season'd deere,

seasoning   frequency: 1   relative frequency: 0.00001
  See also "seas'ning."
    p. 68 EPIGRAMS 106   6 Or valour, or thy iudgement seasoning it,

seasons   frequency: 3   relative frequency: 0.00004
    p. 97 FOREST 3   37 The whil'st, the seuerall seasons thou hast seene
    p. 199 UNDERWOOD 41   10 To shift their seasons, and destroy their powers!
    p. 263 UNDERWOOD 79   11 That know the times, and seasons when
                              t<o>'appeare,

seat   frequency: 4   relative frequency: 0.00005
  See also "mercy-seat," "seate."
    p. 52 EPIGRAMS 76   8 Nor lend like influence from his lucent seat.
    p. 186 UNDERWOOD 33   2 The Seat made of a more then civill warre;
    p. 284 U'WOOD 84.9   71 Nothing can more adorne it, then the seat
    p. 414 UNGATHERED 41   45 The Seat of Sapience, the most lovely Mother,

seate   frequency: 3   relative frequency: 0.00004
    p.   88 EPIGRAMS 133   168 Tempt such a passage? when each priuies seate
    p. 228 UNDERWOOD 53   11 Nay, so your Seate his beauties did endorse,
    p. 394 UNGATHERED 28   4 In blood, in birth, by match, and by her seate;

seates   frequency: 1   relative frequency: 0.00001
    p. 319 HORACE 2   291 As loud enough to fill the seates, not yet

seats   frequency: 1   relative frequency: 0.00001
    See also "seates."
    p. 174 UNDERWOOD 23   12 To see their Seats and Bowers by chattring
                                Pies defac't?

seauen   frequency: 2   relative frequency: 0.00002
    p.   82 EPIGRAMS 130   12 That the eight spheare, no lesse, then planets
                                seauen,
    p. 396 UNGATHERED 30   20 The Orbe was cut forth into Regions seauen.

seauen-fold   frequency: 1   relative frequency: 0.00001
    p. 361 UNGATHERED 1   15 The seauen-fold flower of Arte (more rich then
                                gold)

second   frequency: 11   relative frequency: 0.00015
    p.   86 EPIGRAMS 133   79 They met the second Prodigie, would feare a
    p.   94 FOREST 2   35 As loth, the second draught, or cast to stay,
    p. 137 UNDERWOOD 2.6   t1 Clayming a second kisse by Desert.
    p. 268 UNDERWOOD 82   2 Great King, thy having of a second Sonne:
    p. 268 UNDERWOOD 82   t3 His second Sonne IAMES.
    p. 323 HORACE 2   380 Of fellowship, the fourth, or second place.
    p. 369 UNGATHERED 6   120 Set out a like, or second to our Swan.
    p. 392 UNGATHERED 26   60 (Such as thine are) and strike the second heat
    p. 394 UNGATHERED 28   24 To lay her here, inclos'd, his second Bride.
    p. 394 UNGATHERED 28   26 This second marriage, will aeternall make.
    p. 412 UNGATHERED 41   9 The second string is the sweet Almond bloome

seconded   frequency: 1   relative frequency: 0.00001
    p.   87 EPIGRAMS 133   109 Had it beene seconded, and not in fume

secrecie   frequency: 1   relative frequency: 0.00001
    p. 223 UNDERWOOD 49   20 As new rewards of her old secrecie?

secrecy. See "secrecie."

secret   frequency: 2   relative frequency: 0.00002
    p. 198 UNDERWOOD 40   27 Keepe secret in his Channels what he breedes,
    p. 349 HORACE 1   424 In secret places, flee ... .

secretarie   frequency: 1   relative frequency: 0.00001
    p. 140 UNDERWOOD 2.8   25 Or with Secretarie Sis

secretary. See "secretarie."

secrets   frequency: 4   relative frequency: 0.00005
 **p. 115 PANEGYRE   86 "Oft-times, to haue the secrets of their state
    p.   99 FOREST 3   88 The secrets, that shall breake their sleepe:
    p. 198 UNDERWOOD 40   47 (Made to blow up loves secrets) to discover
    p. 271 UNDERWOOD 83   70 On Natures secrets, there, as her owne bookes:

sects   frequency: 1   relative frequency: 0.00001
    p. 163 UNDERWOOD 15   34 And impious ranknesse of all Sects and seeds:

secur'd   frequency: 2   relative frequency: 0.00002
    p. 176 UNDERWOOD 24   6 Might be defrauded, nor the great secur'd,
    p. 401 UNGATHERED 32   19 Nor flatt'ry! but secur'd, by the Authors Name,

secure   frequency: 2   relative frequency: 0.00002
    p. 236 UNDERWOOD 64   11 When your assiduous practise doth secure
    p. 410 UNGATHERED 39   2 Secure thy railing Rhymes, infamous Gill,

secured   frequency: 1   relative frequency: 0.00001
    See also "secur'd."
    p. 268 UNDERWOOD 82   14 Sate safe enough, but now secured more.

securely   frequency: 2   relative frequency: 0.00002
    p. 113 FOREST 11   116 Man may securely sinne, but safely neuer.
    p. 389 UNGATHERED 24   8 That an ill man dares not securely looke

securer   frequency: 1   relative frequency: 0.00001
    p.   97 FOREST 3   13 But canst, at home, in thy securer rest,

```
securest                            frequency:    1    relative frequency: 0.00001
     p.  109 FOREST 11          17 'Tis the securest policie we haue,


securitie                           frequency:    4    relative frequency: 0.00005
     p.   57 EPIGRAMS 90         6 And, finding good securitie in his age,
     p.  165 UNDERWOOD 15      113 For lesse Securitie? O        for these
     p.  174 UNDERWOOD 23        4 And this Securitie,
     p.  229 UNDERWOOD 54       20 For your securitie. I can no better.


security. See "securitie."


see                                 frequency:  128    relative frequency: 0.00185
     See also "fore-see," "se."
 **p.  114 PANEGYRE           48 His gladding looke, now long'd to see it more.
 **p.  117 PANEGYRE          149 Of his great actions, first to see, and do
 **p.  117 PANEGYRE          158 Saue, that shee might the same perpetuall see.
     p.   27 EPIGRAMS 2          1 It will be look'd for, booke, when some but see
     p.   28 EPIGRAMS 4          7 And such a Prince thou art, wee daily see,
     p.   31 EPIGRAMS 12        23 But see! th'old baud hath seru'd him in his trim,
     p.   33 EPIGRAMS 21         8 The bodies stripes, I see, the soule may saue.
     p.   40 EPIGRAMS 42         2 Th'obseruing neighbours no such mood can see.
     p.   47 EPIGRAMS 63         3 And not thy fortune; who can cleerely see
     p.   47 EPIGRAMS 64         6 To see thy fathers rites new laid on thee.
     p.   47 EPIGRAMS 64         9 But I am glad to see that time suruiue,
     p.   48 EPIGRAMS 64        16 Wherein what wonder see thy name hath wrought?
     p.   52 EPIGRAMS 74         9 The Virgin, long-since fled from earth, I see,
     p.   52 EPIGRAMS 76        17 Such when I meant to faine, and wish'd to see,
     p.   54 EPIGRAMS 80         8 For good men but see death, the wicked tast it.
     p.   55 EPIGRAMS 84        10 Make it your gift. See whither that will beare
                                      mee.
     p.   56 EPIGRAMS 88         1 Would you beleeue, when you this
                                      MOVNSIEVR see,
     p.   60 EPIGRAMS 94         8 Their vn-auoided subiect, fewest see:
     p.   62 EPIGRAMS 97         1 See you yond' Motion? Not the old Fa-ding,
     p.   66 EPIGRAMS 102       19 Thou must draw more: and they, that hope to see
     p.   66 EPIGRAMS 103        2 That but the twi-light of your sprite did see,
     p.   67 EPIGRAMS 104        1 Were they that nam'd you, prophets? Did they
                                      see,
     p.   72 EPIGRAMS 111        1 Who EDMONDS, reades thy booke, and doth
                                      not see
     p.   73 EPIGRAMS 114        2 When SYDNYES name I heare, or face I
                                      see:
     p.   74 EPIGRAMS 115       22 'Twill see it's sister naked, ere a sword.
     p.   81 EPIGRAMS 128        9 So, when we, blest with thy returne, shall see
     p.   81 EPIGRAMS 129        1 That, not a paire of friends each other see,
     p.   81 EPIGRAMS 129       17 And thine owne CORIAT too. But (would'st
                                      thou see)
     p.   86 EPIGRAMS 133       78 Ploughing the mayne. When, see (the worst of all
                                      lucks)
     p.   96 FOREST 2          100 With other edifices, when they see
     p.  117 FOREST 13          23 Your selfe but told vnto your selfe, and see
     p.  117 FOREST 13          29 Looke then, and see your selfe. I will not say
     p.  117 FOREST 13          30 Your beautie; for you see that euery day:
     p.  117 FOREST 13          34 As I, can say, and see it doth excell.
     p.  118 FOREST 13          67 Giddie with change, and therefore cannot see
     p.  119 FOREST 13         111 Other great wiues may blush at: when they see
     p.  128 UNDERWOOD 1.1      40 One God to see,
     p.  130 UNDERWOOD 1.3      22 To see this Babe, all innocence;
     p.  132 UNDERWOOD 2.2       7 Love, if thou wilt ever see
     p.  134 UNDERWOOD 2.4       1 See the Chariot at hand here of Love,
     p.  136 UNDERWOOD 2.5       8 Where he chanc't your name to see
     p.  136 UNDERWOOD 2.5      19 Which you call my Shafts. And see!
     p.  138 UNDERWOOD 2.6      25 So to see a Lady tread,
     p.  139 UNDERWOOD 2.7       3 Here's none to spie, or see:
     p.  141 UNDERWOOD 2.9      28 And so thin, to see a blush
     p.  145 UNDERWOOD 5        14 In any curious peece you see
     p.  155 UNDERWOOD 13       71 Pardon, sayes he, that were a way to see
     p.  157 UNDERWOOD 13      153 And last, goe out in nothing: You that see
     p.  158 UNDERWOOD 14       14 Pernitious enemie; we see, before
     p.  160 UNDERWOOD 14       54 To see the workmanship so'<e>xceed the cost!
     p.  161 UNDERWOOD 14       80 Among my commings in, and see it mount,
     p.  162 UNDERWOOD 15       11 Looke on th'ambitious man, and see him nurse
     p.  162 UNDERWOOD 15       19 See the grave, sower, and supercilious Sir
     p.  162 UNDERWOOD 15       23 See him, that's call'd, and thought the happiest
                                      man,
     p.  164 UNDERWOOD 15       63 To see 'hem aye discoursing with their Glasse,
     p.  164 UNDERWOOD 15       68 Be at their Visits, see 'hem squemish, sick,
     p.  166 UNDERWOOD 15      136 Now use the bones, we see doth hire a man
     p.  170 UNDERWOOD 18       17 To see men feare: or else for truth, and State,
     p.  172 UNDERWOOD 20       15 Knew I this Woman? yes; And you doe see,
```

see (cont.)

p. 174	UNDERWOOD 23	12	To see their Seats and Bowers by chattring Pies defac't?
p. 179	UNDERWOOD 25	51	So fooles, we see,
p. 181	UNDERWOOD 27	1	Helen, did Homer never see
p. 182	UNDERWOOD 27	32	Where men may see whom I doe sing?
p. 183	UNDERWOOD 29	22	So to see the Fountaine drie,
p. 189	UNDERWOOD 36	11	And have their being, their waste to see;
p. 191	UNDERWOOD 38	15	If there be nothing worthy you can see
p. 194	UNDERWOOD 38	109	O, that you could but by dissection see
p. 194	UNDERWOOD 38	120	When I see you, then I doe see my Sun,
p. 199	UNDERWOOD 41	22	Till I may see both it and you agen.
p. 200	UNDERWOOD 42	9	Put on my Ivy Garland, let me see
p. 201	UNDERWOOD 42	60	In at a hole, and see these Actions creepe
p. 201	UNDERWOOD 42	66	That chanc'd the lace, laid on a Smock, to see,
p. 204	UNDERWOOD 43	44	Fitter to see the fire-light, then the day;
p. 209	UNDERWOOD 43	137	See the worlds Ruines! nothing but the piles
p. 213	UNDERWOOD 44	6	For they did see it the last tilting well,
p. 213	UNDERWOOD 44	13	But they may see Gold-Chaines, and Pearle worne then,
p. 213	UNDERWOOD 44	16	To see the Pride at Court, their Wives doe make:
p. 216	UNDERWOOD 45	21	Turne him, and see his Threds: looke, if he be
p. 221	UNDERWOOD 48	17	See then thou dost attend him,
p. 222	UNDERWOOD 49	2	And thinkes I dare not her? let the world see.
p. 224	UNDERWOOD 50	16	A cheerefull worke to all good eyes, to see
p. 227	UNDERWOOD 52	14	An Archetype, for all the world to see,
p. 234	UNDERWOOD 61	10	To see you set apart, thus, from the rest,
p. 238	UNDERWOOD 65	7	And long in changing. Let our Nephewes see
p. 240	UNDERWOOD 67	37	7. CALLI. See, see our active King
p. 245	UNDERWOOD 70	73	In small proportions, we just beautie see:
p. 245	UNDERWOOD 70	81	To see that bright eternall Day:
p. 250	UNDERWOOD 73	8	Thou sluggish spawne, that canst, but wilt not see?
p. 251	UNDERWOOD 74	26	To see great Charles of Travaile eas'd,
p. 252	UNDERWOOD 75	5	Then thou shalt see to day:
p. 252	UNDERWOOD 75	7	And see, what can be seene,
p. 252	UNDERWOOD 75	9	See, the Procession! what a Holy day
p. 253	UNDERWOOD 75	20	As they came all to see, and to be seene!
p. 253	UNDERWOOD 75	41	See, how she paceth forth in Virgin-white,
p. 254	UNDERWOOD 75	49	Stay, thou wilt see what rites the Virgins doe!
p. 254	UNDERWOOD 75	57	See, how with Roses, and with Lillies shine,
p. 254	UNDERWOOD 75	61	Stay, see the Virgins sow,
p. 254	UNDERWOOD 75	69	See, at another doore,
p. 255	UNDERWOOD 75	88	All else we see beside, are Shadowes, and goe lesse.
p. 256	UNDERWOOD 75	121	See, now the Chappell opens; where the King
p. 258	UNDERWOOD 75	175	Peepe forth a Gemme; to see
p. 264	UNDERWOOD 79	18	9. See where he walkes <10> with MIRA by his side.
p. 268	UNDERWOOD 82	3	And by thy blessing, may thy People see
p. 271	UNDERWOOD 83	73	Beholds her Maker! and, in him, doth see
p. 271	UNDERWOOD 83	86	And see all dead here, or about to dye!
p. 273	U'WOOD 84.1	15	May something by that twilight see
p. 277	U'WOOD 84.3	29	But, Painter, see thou doe not sell
p. 278	U'WOOD 84.4	23	That all may say, that see the frame,
p. 286	U'WOOD 84.9	121	That happy Day, that never shall see night!
p. 305	HORACE 2	15	Together: not that we should Serpents see
p. 329	HORACE 2	525	Which it doth threaten. Therefore, where I see
p. 329	HORACE 2	534	A Choerilus, in whom if I but see
p. 362	UNGATHERED 2	2	And see a minde attir'd in perfect straines;
p. 366	UNGATHERED 6	13	Smiles in his Sphaere, to see the rest affect,
p. 368	UNGATHERED 6	65	Who (see) already hath ore-flowne
p. 375	UNGATHERED 10	28	Here, finer then comming from his Punke you him see,
p. 379	UNGATHERED 12	13	And that you may see he most luckily ment
p. 384	UNGATHERED 18	21	So, in theyr number, may <you> neuer see
p. 385	UNGATHERED 20	2	To see his worke be good; but that he looke
p. 386	UNGATHERED 21	11	On credit, and are cossen'd; see, that thou
p. 392	UNGATHERED 26	72	To see them in our waters yet appeare,
p. 392	UNGATHERED 26	75	But stay, I see thee in the Hemisphere
p. 394	UNGATHERED 28	3	To see (who' it is?) A noble Countesse, greate,
p. 395	UNGATHERED 29	2	And see both climing vp the slippery staire
p. 398	UNGATHERED 30	93	I call the world, that enuies mee, to see
p. 405	UNGATHERED 34	89	Of thy dead Standards: or (wth miracle) see

seed   frequency: 1   relative frequency: 0.00001
p. 250	UNDERWOOD 73	1	Looke up, thou seed of envie, and still bring

seed-plot   frequency: 1   relative frequency: 0.00001
    p. 213 UNDERWOOD 44   24 Thou Seed-plot of the warre, that hast not
                              spar'd

seedes   frequency: 2   relative frequency: 0.00002
    p. 309 HORACE 2   97 His course so hurtfull both to graine, and
                              seedes,
    p. 361 UNGATHERED 1   12 the sweetest simples, and most soueraigne seedes.

seeds   frequency: 1   relative frequency: 0.00001
    See also "seedes."
    p. 163 UNDERWOOD 15   34 And impious ranknesse of all Sects and seeds:

seeing   frequency: 2   relative frequency: 0.00002
    See also "farre-all-seeing."
    p. 128 UNDERWOOD 1.1   32 Of seeing your face,
    p. 144 UNDERWOOD 4   2 Lest I be sick with seeing;

seek   frequency: 2   relative frequency: 0.00002
    See also "seeke."
    p. 349 HORACE 1   423 .... seek
                              ....
    p. 408 UNGATHERED 36   10 Seek out some hungry painter, yt for bread

seeke   frequency: 17   relative frequency: 0.00024
    p. 58 EPIGRAMS 91   18 Who more should seeke mens reuerence, then feare.
    p. 62 EPIGRAMS 96   12 A man should seeke great glorie, and not broad.
    p. 63 EPIGRAMS 98   4 Need seeke no other strength, no other height;
    p. 83 EPIGRAMS 131   13 Then stand vnto thy selfe, not seeke without
    p. 121 FOREST 14   35 And great, must seeke for new,
    p. 122 FOREST 15   4 That, laden with my sinnes, I seeke for ease?
    p. 150 UNDERWOOD 10   15 Seeke doubting Men to please,
    p. 155 UNDERWOOD 13   61 And seeke not wants to succour: but enquire,
    p. 168 UNDERWOOD 15   195 These take, and now goe seeke thy peace in
                              Warre,
    p. 190 UNDERWOOD 37   20 And seeke to scant her comelie libertie,
    p. 218 UNDERWOOD 47   14 That never yet did friend, or friendship seeke
    p. 248 UNDERWOOD 71   2 Are faine to seeke for succours, and supplies
    p. 264 UNDERWOOD 79   21 That drives the Hart to seeke unused wayes,
    p. 292 UNDERWOOD 86   12 If a fit livor thou dost seeke to toast;
    p. 311 HORACE 2   136 And Peleus, if they seeke to heart-strike us
    p. 387 UNGATHERED 22   1 Sonnes, seeke not me amonge these polish'd
                              stones:
    p. 391 UNGATHERED 26   32 From thence to honour thee, I would not seeke

seekes   frequency: 2   relative frequency: 0.00002
    p. 315 HORACE 2   238 His better'd mind seekes wealth, and friendship:
                              than
    p. 317 HORACE 2   242 Either because he seekes, and, having found,

seeking   frequency: 2   relative frequency: 0.00002
    p. 307 HORACE 2   40 This, seeking, in a various kind, to forme
    p. 365 UNGATHERED 5   19 When seeking her renowning,

seeks   frequency: 1   relative frequency: 0.00001
    See also "seekes."
    p. 155 UNDERWOOD 13   68 And hurt seeks Cure, the Surgeon bids take
                              bread,

seek'st   frequency: 2   relative frequency: 0.00002
    p. 47 EPIGRAMS 63   5 And that thou seek'st reward of thy each act,
    p. 70 EPIGRAMS 109   5 Thou are not one, seek'st miseries with hope,

seeliest   frequency: 1   relative frequency: 0.00001
    p. 390 UNGATHERED 26   7 For seeliest Ignorance on these may light,

seem   frequency: 1   relative frequency: 0.00001
    See also "seeme."
    p. 407 UNGATHERED 36   2 (And labours to seem worthy of yt feare)

seem'd   frequency: 5   relative frequency: 0.00007
    p. 77 EPIGRAMS 120   7 As Heauen and Nature seem'd to striue
    p. 86 EPIGRAMS 133   86 So huge, it seem'd, they could by no meanes quite
                              her.
    p. 88 EPIGRAMS 133   152 But still, it seem'd, the ranknesse did conuince
                              'hem.
    p. 228 UNDERWOOD 53   6 So seem'd your horse and you, both of a peece!
    p. 391 UNGATHERED 26   12 And thinke to ruine, where it seem'd to raise.

seeme   frequency: 12   relative frequency: 0.00017
  **p. 114 PANEGYRE   62 The ground beneath did seeme a mouing floud:
  **p. 116 PANEGYRE   109 Nor did he seeme their vices so to loue,
    p.   30 EPIGRAMS 11   3 To seeme a statesman: as I neere it came,
    p.   56 EPIGRAMS 88   8 As french-men in his companie, should seeme
                                 dutch?
    p.   58 EPIGRAMS 91   10 Throughout, might flatt'rie seeme; and to be mute
    p.   64 EPIGRAMS 101   5 With those that come; whose grace may make that
                                 seeme
    p. 104 FOREST 7   2 Seeme to flye it, it will pursue:
    p. 118 FOREST 13   63 Times, and occasions, to start forth, and seeme)
    p. 226 UNDERWOOD 52   1 Why? though I seeme of a prodigious wast,
    p. 269 UNDERWOOD 83   6 You seeme a faire one! O that you had breath,
    p. 362 UNGATHERED 2   7 If they seeme wry, to such as looke asquint,
    p. 384 UNGATHERED 18   24 Yet neyther of you seeme to th'other old.

seemes   frequency: 3   relative frequency: 0.00004
    p.   32 EPIGRAMS 18   1 To thee, my way in Epigrammes seemes new,
    p.   61 EPIGRAMS 95   11 Which Fate (it seemes) caus'd in the historie,
    p. 392 UNGATHERED 26   69 In each of which, he seemes to shake a Lance,

seeming   frequency: 1   relative frequency: 0.00001
    p.   75 EPIGRAMS 115   32 That seeming prayses, are, yet accusations.

seems. See "seemes."

seen. See "seene."

seene   frequency: 30   relative frequency: 0.00043
  **p. 114 PANEGYRE   47 They that had seene, but foure short daies
                                 before,
    p.   32 EPIGRAMS 18   3 Thou saist, that cannot be: for thou hast seene
    p.   45 EPIGRAMS 58   7 So haue I seene at CHRIST-masse sports one
                                 lost,
    p.   59 EPIGRAMS 92   9 Yet haue they seene the maps, and bought 'hem
                                 too,
    p.   60 EPIGRAMS 93   12 Nor could I, had I seene all Natures roule,
    p.   85 EPIGRAMS 133   51 Thou hast seene hell (some say) and know'st all
                                 nookes there,
    p.   86 EPIGRAMS 133   68 Were seene your vgly Centaures, yee call
                                 Car-men,
    p.   97 FOREST 3   37 The whil'st, the seuerall seasons thou hast seene
    p. 102 FOREST 5   17 To be taken, to be seene,
    p. 114 FOREST 12   39 The world hath seene, which all these had in
                                 trust,
    p. 114 FOREST 12   50 Haue beautie knowne, yet none so famous seene?
    p. 134 UNDERWOOD 2.4   21 Have you seene but a bright Lillie grow,
    p. 138 UNDERWOOD 2.6   27 And was worthy (being so seene)
    p. 149 UNDERWOOD 9   13 Tell me that she hath seene
    p. 154 UNDERWOOD 13   47 As I have seene some Infants of the Sword,
    p. 159 UNDERWOOD 14   30 Ever at home: yet, have all Countries seene:
    p. 159 UNDERWOOD 14   34 Heard what times past have said, seene what ours
                                 doe:
    p. 228 UNDERWOOD 53   13 And surely had I but your Stable seene
    p. 234 UNDERWOOD 61   1 That you have seene the pride, beheld the sport,
    p. 238 UNDERWOOD 66   6 The Mother of our Prince? When was there seene
    p. 252 UNDERWOOD 75   7 And see, what can be seene,
    p. 253 UNDERWOOD 75   20 As they came all to see, and to be seene!
    p. 254 UNDERWOOD 75   48 With Modestie so crown'd, and Adoration seene.
    p. 255 UNDERWOOD 75   89 It is their Grace, and favour, that makes seene,
    p. 282 U'WOOD 84.9   11 O! had I seene her laid out a faire Corse,
    p. 317 HORACE 2   271 Once seene, to be againe call'd for, and plaid,
    p. 321 HORACE 2   332 Or Semi-god, that late was seene to weare
    p. 386 UNGATHERED 21   3 But I haue seene thy worke, and I know thee:
    p. 396 UNGATHERED 30   3 Because, who make the question, haue not seene
    p. 398 UNGATHERED 30   76 Of tender eyes will more be wept, then seene:

seer. See "over-seer."

sees   frequency: 6   relative frequency: 0.00008
    p.   31 EPIGRAMS 14   5 Then thee the age sees not that thing more graue,
    p.   79 EPIGRAMS 125   5 Who sees a soule, in such a body set,
    p. 193 UNDERWOOD 38   87 He when he sees a sorrow such as this,
    p. 262 UNDERWOOD 78   20 Busie, or frowne at first; when he sees thee,
    p. 279 U'WOOD 84.4   45 Is it because it sees us dull,
    p. 379 UNGATHERED 12   18 The Mappe of his iourney, and sees in his booke,

seest   frequency: 3   relative frequency: 0.00004
    p. 137 UNDERWOOD 2.5   43 But alas, thou seest the least
    p. 390 UNGATHERED 25   1 This Figure, that thou here seest put,

seest (cont.)
    p. 422 UNGATHERED 50   6 whom thou seest happy; wretches flee as foes:

seine   frequency: 1   relative frequency: 0.00001
    p. 369 UNGATHERED 6   117 Slow Arar, nor swift Rhone; the Loyre, nor
                              Seine,

seise   frequency: 1   relative frequency: 0.00001
    p. 418 UNGATHERED 45   44 shee will not seise it.

seisin   frequency: 1   relative frequency: 0.00001
    p. 268 UNDERWOOD 82   8 Should take first Seisin of the publique good,

seiz'd   frequency: 1   relative frequency: 0.00001
    p. 313 HORACE 2   171 Honour'd Achilles chance by thee be seiz'd,

seize   frequency: 1   relative frequency: 0.00001
See also "seise."
    p. 283 U'WOOD 84.9   17 With all her aydes, to save her from the seize

selden   frequency: 4   relative frequency: 0.00005
    p. 158 UNDERWOOD 14   5 Your Booke, my Selden, I have read, and much
    p. 158 UNDERWOOD 14   t2 IOHN SELDEN.
    p. 161 UNDERWOOD 14   82 Selden! two Names that so much understand!
    p. 207 UNDERWOOD 43 100 Which noble Carew, Cotton, Selden lent:

seldom. See "seldome."

seldome   frequency: 3   relative frequency: 0.00004
    p. 250 UNDERWOOD 73   6 Who seldome sleepes! whom bad men only hate!
    p. 295 UNDERWOOD 90   5 Never at Law; seldome in office gown'd;
    p. 363 UNGATHERED 3   2 Seldome descend but bleeding to their graue.

self   frequency: 1   relative frequency: 0.00001
See also "phoebvs-selfe," "selfe,"
           words beginning "selfe-."
    p. 406 UNGATHERED 35   4 All kings to doe ye self same deeds wth some!

selfe   frequency: 88   relative frequency: 0.00127
*p. 492 TO HIMSELF   13 'Twere simple fury, still, thy selfe to waste
 p. 32 EPIGRAMS 16   3 Thy selfe into fresh braules: when, call'd vpon,
 p. 32 EPIGRAMS 16   9 Keepe thy selfe there, and thinke thy valure
                            right,
 p. 44 EPIGRAMS 53   9 For, but thy selfe, where, out of motly, 's hee
 p. 44 EPIGRAMS 55   3 How I doe feare my selfe, that am not worth
 p. 44 EPIGRAMS 55   7 What fate is mine, that so it selfe bereaues?
 p. 47 EPIGRAMS 63   12 To so true worth, though thou thy selfe forbid.
 p. 53 EPIGRAMS 77   1 Be safe, nor feare thy selfe so good a fame,
 p. 53 EPIGRAMS 78   2 To draw thee custome: but her selfe gets all.
 p. 54 EPIGRAMS 81   5 For all thou hear'st, thou swear'st thy selfe
                            didst doo.
 p. 55 EPIGRAMS 84   6 I fancied to my selfe, what wine, what wit
 p. 55 EPIGRAMS 85   2 My selfe a witnesse of thy few dayes sport:
 p. 57 EPIGRAMS 89   9 Who both their graces in thy selfe hast more
 p. 58 EPIGRAMS 91   5 Which thou art to thy selfe: whose fame was wonne
 p. 63 EPIGRAMS 98   5 Fortune vpon him breakes her selfe, if ill,
 p. 63 EPIGRAMS 98   9 Be alwayes to thy gather'd selfe the same:
 p. 63 EPIGRAMS 99   3 Hast taught thy selfe worthy thy pen to tread,
 p. 66 EPIGRAMS 103   7 Which is, it selfe, the imprese of the great,
 p. 68 EPIGRAMS 105   20 I' your selfe, all treasure lost of th'age
                            before.
 p. 68 EPIGRAMS 106   7 Thy standing vpright to thy selfe, thy ends
 p. 74 EPIGRAMS 115   17 Tell's of him, all the tales, it selfe then
                            makes;
 p. 76 EPIGRAMS 119   11 That to the vulgar canst thy selfe apply,
 p. 77 EPIGRAMS 120   4 Death's selfe is sorry.
 p. 78 EPIGRAMS 123   1 Writing thy selfe, or iudging others writ,
 p. 81 EPIGRAMS 128   10 Thy selfe, with thy first thoughts, brought home
                            by thee,
 p. 83 EPIGRAMS 131   13 Then stand vnto thy selfe, not seeke without
 p. 84 EPIGRAMS 133   20+ THE VOYAGE IT SELFE.
 p. 86 EPIGRAMS 133   94 Crack did report it selfe, as if a cloud
 p. 100 FOREST 3   103 To doe thy countrey seruice, thy selfe right;
 p. 101 FOREST 4   28 With all my powers, my selfe to loose?
 p. 106 FOREST 9   16 Not of it selfe, but thee.
 p. 115 FOREST 12   67 Then which, a nobler heauen it selfe knowes not.
 p. 116 FOREST 13   7 I, therefore, who professe my selfe in loue
 p. 117 FOREST 13   17 Or so my selfe abandon'd, as because
 p. 117 FOREST, 13   23 Your selfe but told vnto your selfe, and see
 p. 117 FOREST 13   29 Looke then, and see your selfe. I will not say

selfe (cont.)
```
     p. 127 UNDERWOOD 1.1     5 2. My selfe up to thee, harrow'd, torne, and
                                  bruis'd
     p. 129 UNDERWOOD 1.2    11 My selfe and thee.
     p. 134 UNDERWOOD 2.4    18 Sheds it selfe through the face,
     p. 151 UNDERWOOD 12      2 It vent it selfe, but as it would,
     p. 159 UNDERWOOD 14     24 Upon my selfe, and aske to whom? and why?
     p. 168 UNDERWOOD 15    181 That by commanding first thy selfe, thou mak'st
     p. 173 UNDERWOOD 22     10 'Tis of your selfe, and that you use
     p. 175 UNDERWOOD 23     33 Make not thy selfe a Page,
     p. 177 UNDERWOOD 25     27 Nor thinke your selfe unfortunate,
     p. 179 UNDERWOOD 25     53 But to your selfe, most loyal Lord,
     p. 189 UNDERWOOD 37      2 Next to your selfe, for making your love true:
     p. 190 UNDERWOOD 37     10 But, as a friend, which name your selfe receave,
     p. 191 UNDERWOOD 38      3 Or doe upon my selfe some desperate ill;
     p. 192 UNDERWOOD 38     32 Thinke that your selfe like heaven forgive me
                                  can:
     p. 194 UNDERWOOD 38    118 I may dilate my selfe, but not depart.
     p. 203 UNDERWOOD 43     26 And my selfe most, in some selfe-boasting Rimes?
     p. 216 UNDERWOOD 45      2 Whilst I informe my selfe, I would teach thee,
     p. 217 UNDERWOOD 46     17 Like Solons selfe; explat'st the knottie Lawes
     p. 218 UNDERWOOD 47      6 To speake my selfe out too ambitiously,
     p. 220 UNDERWOOD 47     76 My selfe a little. I will take you so,
     p. 220 UNDERWOOD 47     77 As you have writ your selfe. Now stand, and
                                  then,
     p. 223 UNDERWOOD 49     24 Thinkes it selfe nought, though she should valew
                                  it.
     p. 224 UNDERWOOD 50     15 Are in your selfe rewarded; yet 'twill be
     p. 228 UNDERWOOD 53     12 As I began to wish my selfe a horse.
     p. 235 UNDERWOOD 62      7 And, in these Cures, do'st so thy selfe enlarge,
     p. 238 UNDERWOOD 65     10 And interpose thy selfe, ('care not how soone.)
     p. 239 UNDERWOOD 67     23 May wish it selfe a sense,
     p. 250 UNDERWOOD 73      9 Feed on thy selfe for spight, and shew thy Kind:
     p. 268 UNDERWOOD 83      4 To pluck a Garland, for her selfe, or mee?
     p. 278 U'WOOD 84.4      17 Sweet Mind, then speake your selfe, and say,
     p. 279 U'WOOD 84.4      43 It selfe to us, and come so nigh
     p. 282 U'WOOD 84.9      14 And saw that portion of her selfe to die.
     p. 283 U'WOOD 84.9      20 Beene trusted to thee: not to't selfe assign'd.
     p. 283 U'WOOD 84.9      21 Looke on thy sloth, and give thy selfe undone,
     p. 287 U'WOOD 84.9     180 She spent more time in teares her selfe to dresse
     p. 307 HORACE 2         35 My selfe for shortnesse labour; and I grow
     p. 311 HORACE 2        146 Thy selfe in teares, then me thy losse will
                                  wound,
     p. 325 HORACE 2        434 On steele, though 't selfe be dull, and cannot
                                  cut.
     p. 325 HORACE 2        435 I, writing nought my selfe, will teach them yet
     p. 331 HORACE 2        547 And, of your selfe too, understand; yet mind
     p. 365 UNGATHERED 5     20 My selfe am so neare drowning?
     p. 367 UNGATHERED 6     56 And conquers all things, yea it selfe, at length.
     p. 379 UNGATHERED 12    14 To write it with the selfe same spirit he went,
     p. 386 UNGATHERED 21     4 And, if thou list thy selfe, what thou canst bee.
     p. 389 UNGATHERED 24    23 When you behold me wish my selfe, the man
     p. 392 UNGATHERED 26    47 Nature her selfe was proud of his designes,
     p. 393 UNGATHERED 27     1 Truth is the triall of it selfe,
     p. 395 UNGATHERED 29    23 The selfe same Genius! so the worke will say.
     p. 399 UNGATHERED 31    10 Vpon her selfe) to all her sexe!
     p. 420 UNGATHERED 48    18 howe soone wth a selfe ticklinge hee was spent.
     p. 421 UNGATHERED 49     8 As Cleare, and distant, as yor: selfe from
                                  Cryme;
```

selfe-boasting   frequency: 1   relative frequency: 0.00001
```
     p. 203 UNDERWOOD 43     26 And my selfe most, in some selfe-boasting Rimes?
```

selfe-diuided   frequency: 1   relative frequency: 0.00001
```
     p.  37 EPIGRAMS 32       3 That selfe-diuided Belgia did afford;
```

selfe-fame   frequency: 1   relative frequency: 0.00001
```
     p.  27 EPIGRAMS 2        9 Thou are not couetous of least selfe-fame,
```

selfe-same   frequency: 4   relative frequency: 0.00005
```
     p.  40 EPIGRAMS 42      17 The selfe-same things, a note of concord be:
     p.  64 EPIGRAMS 99       8 The selfe-same deeds, as diuersly they come,
     p.  95 FOREST 2         63 Where the same beere, and bread, and selfe-same
                                  wine,
     p. 133 UNDERWOOD 2.3    12 Aymed with that selfe-same shaft.
```

selinis   frequency: 1   relative frequency: 0.00001
```
     p. 412 UNGATHERED 41    10 Ymounted high upon Selinis crest:
```

selinus'. See "selinis."

sell   frequency: 4   relative frequency: 0.00005
    p.   27 EPIGRAMS 3   2 Call'st a booke good, or bad, as it doth sell,
    p.   28 EPIGRAMS 3   11 If, without these vile arts, it will not sell,
    p. 234 UNDERWOOD 61   4 At which there are, would sell the Prince, and
                               State:
    p. 277 U'WOOD 84.3   29 But, Painter, see thou doe not sell

'sell   frequency: 1   relative frequency: 0.00001
    p. 372 UNGATHERED 9   12 She was 'Sell Boulstred. In wch name, I call

seller. See "book-seller," "booke-seller."

selling   frequency: 1   relative frequency: 0.00001
    p.   88 EPIGRAMS 133   151 Then, selling not, a dish was tane to mince 'hem,

selues   frequency: 2   relative frequency: 0.00002
    p.   45 EPIGRAMS 59   2 Who, when you'haue burnt your selues downe to the
                               snuffe,
    p. 111 FOREST 11   75 And yet (in this t<o>'expresse our selues more
                               cleare)

selues   frequency: 4   relative frequency: 0.00005
    See also "selues," "them-selues."
    p. 166 UNDERWOOD 15   134 Goe make our selues the Usurers at a cast.
    p. 200 UNDERWOOD 42   24 So to be sure you doe injoy your selues.
    p. 286 U'WOOD 84.9   141 Had lost our selues? and prodigally spent
    p. 309 HORACE 2   90 Our selues, and all that's ours, to death we owe:

semi-god   frequency: 1   relative frequency: 0.00001
    p. 321 HORACE 2   332 Or Semi-god, that late was seene to weare

sence   frequency: 4   relative frequency: 0.00005
    p. 361 UNGATHERED 1   5 ffirst: thy successe did strike my sence with
                               wonder;
    p. 395 UNGATHERED 29   15 Taught Lucan these true moodes! Replyes my
                               sence
    p. 414 UNGATHERED 41   55 T'imprint in all purg'd hearts this virgin sence,
    p. 420 UNGATHERED 48   17 To every sence, and scorne to those that sawe

send   frequency: 19   relative frequency: 0.00027
    p.   28 EPIGRAMS 3   12 Send it to Bucklers-bury, there 'twill, well.
    p.   62 EPIGRAMS 96   2 When I dare send my Epigrammes to thee?
    p.   62 EPIGRAMS 96   7 Reade all I send: and, if I find but one
    p.   67 EPIGRAMS 104   6 To make those faithfull, did the Fates send you?
    p.   95 FOREST 2   53 The better cheeses, bring 'hem; or else send
    p. 113 FOREST 12   19 I, that haue none (to send you) send you verse.
    p. 170 UNDERWOOD 18   23 That I must send one first, my Choyce assignes,
    p. 180 UNDERWOOD 26   2 I send nor Balmes, nor Cor'sives to your wound,
    p. 230 UNDERWOOD 56   19 Such, (if her manners like you) I doe send:
    p. 231 UNDERWOOD 57   6 To send my Debentur.
    p. 257 UNDERWOOD 75   145 Haste, haste, officious Sun, and send them
                               Night
    p. 260 UNDERWOOD 77   6 Send in, what or Romano, Tintoret,
    p. 275 U'WOOD 84.3   5 Send these suspected helpes, to aide
    p. 291 UNDERWOOD 85   52 Into our Seas send any such:
    p. 319 HORACE 2   320 For the vile Goat, soone after, forth did send
    p. 331 HORACE 2   576 To send it to be judg'd by Metius eare,
    p. 410 UNGATHERED 39   10 I'll laugh at thee poor wretched Tike, go send
    p. 417 UNGATHERED 45   20 some tast to send hir.

sends   frequency: 2   relative frequency: 0.00002
    p. 170 UNDERWOOD 19   4 His double Bow, and round his Arrowes sends;
    p. 386 UNGATHERED 21   7 It must be thine owne iudgment, yet, that sends

sense   frequency: 29   relative frequency: 0.00041
    See also "sence."
    p.   38 EPIGRAMS 38   5 And crie good! good! This quite peruerts my
                               sense,
    p.   45 EPIGRAMS 58   6 Then thou did'st late my sense, loosing my
                               points.
    p.   60 EPIGRAMS 94   9 For none ere tooke that pleasure in sinnes sense,
    p.   61 EPIGRAMS 95   6 And all his numbers, both of sense, and sounds.
    p.   73 EPIGRAMS 112   18 That both for wit, and sense, so oft dost plucke,
    p. 101 FOREST 4   33 If these, who haue but sense, can shun
    p. 109 FOREST 11   18 To make our sense our slaue.
    p. 113 FOREST 11   115 And to his sense obiect this sentence euer,
    p. 153 UNDERWOOD 13   9 Not at my prayers, but your sense; which laid
    p. 160 UNDERWOOD 14   60 Newnesse of Sense, Antiquitie of voyce!
    p. 184 UNDERWOOD 29   55 May his Sense, when it would meet
    p. 191 UNDERWOOD 38   5 It is a Darknesse hath blockt up my sense,

sense (cont.)
  p. 198 UNDERWOOD 40   43 Can lock the Sense up, or the heart a thought,
  p. 222 UNDERWOOD 49   14 Doth labour with the Phrase more then the sense?
  p. 239 UNDERWOOD 67   23 May wish it selfe a sense,
  p. 251 UNDERWOOD 74   11 And ev'ry Plant the sense surprize,
  p. 261 UNDERWOOD 77   12 As farre as sense, and onely by the eyes.
  p. 273 U'WOOD 84.1   24 Surprize their sense:
  p. 278 U'WOOD 84.4   13 No, to expresse a Mind to sense,
  p. 278 U'WOOD 84.4   19 Our sense you doe with knowledge fill,
  p. 279 U'WOOD 84.4   40 Still left an Eccho in the sense.
  p. 284 U'WOOD 84.9   57 Must come to take a sentence, by the sense
  p. 288 U'WOOD 84.9   185 Her broken sighes did never misse whole sense:
  p. 319 HORACE 2   308 Unwonted language; and that sense of worth
  p. 370 UNGATHERED 7   12 Betweene the doubtfull sway of Reason', and
                             sense;
  p. 370 UNGATHERED 7   13 'Tis not your fault, if they shall sense
                             preferre,
  p. 370 UNGATHERED 7   14 Being tould there, Reason cannot, Sense may
                             erre.
  p. 403 UNGATHERED 34   41 Or Verse, or Sense t'express Immortall you?
  p. 404 UNGATHERED 34   55 Sense, what they are! which by a specious fyne

senses   frequency: 5   relative frequency: 0.00007
  p. 182 UNDERWOOD 28   7 But charme the Senses, others over-come
  p. 183 UNDERWOOD 29   4 Spoyling Senses of their Treasure,
  p. 401 UNGATHERED 33   2 That, while they bind the senses, doe so please?
  p. 420 UNGATHERED 48   23 Whose ayre will sooner Hell, then their dull
                             senses peirce,
  p. 657 L. CONVIVALES   18 And at once, three Senses pleases.

sensual. See "sensuall."

sensuall   frequency: 1   relative frequency: 0.00001
  p. 34 EPIGRAMS 25   2 In the past pleasures of his sensuall life,

sent   frequency: 21   relative frequency: 0.00030
  p. 33 EPIGRAMS 19   2 I sent the cause: Hee wooes with an ill sprite.
  p. 106 FOREST 9   9 I sent thee, late, a rosie wreath,
  p. 154 UNDERWOOD 13   52 But then, fist-fill'd, to put me off the sent.
  p. 186 UNDERWOOD 32   13 As though the Court pursues them on the sent,
  p. 205 UNDERWOOD 43   63 To redeeme mine, I had sent in; Enough,
  p. 219 UNDERWOOD 47   33 Or the States Ships sent forth belike to meet
  p. 219 UNDERWOOD 47   35 Whether the Dispensation yet be sent,
  p. 220 UNDERWOOD 47   63 'Mongst which, if I have any friendships sent,
  p. 235 UNDERWOOD 62   t3 for a 100. pounds he sent me in my sicknesse.
  p. 263 UNDERWOOD 78   32 Being sent to one, they will be read of all.
  p. 270 UNDERWOOD 83   56 And I, into the world, all Soule, was sent!
  p. 270 UNDERWOOD 83   65 Who saw the way was made it! and were sent
  p. 286 U'WOOD 84.9   125 Unto the Sent, a Spicerie, or Balme;
  p. 309 HORACE 2   110 That first sent forth the dapper Elegie,
  p. 323 HORACE 2   384 Those heavie Verses, sent so to the Stage,
  p. 325 HORACE 2   451 Of a brave Chiefe sent to the warres: He can,
  p. 368 UNGATHERED 6   91 Hath sent her Mermaides in,
  p. 391 UNGATHERED 26   40 Sent forth, or since did from their ashes come.
  p. 393 UNGATHERED 27   10 That yeeld's a sent so sweete,
  p. 420 UNGATHERED 48   16 Hee dyes wth an Ill sent,
  p. 662 INSCRIPTS. 2   6 to CYNTHIAS fayrest Nymph hath sent thee,

sentence   frequency: 5   relative frequency: 0.00007
  p. 59 EPIGRAMS 92   19 Keepe a starre-chamber sentence close, twelue
                             dayes:
  p. 113 FOREST 11   115 And to his sense obiect this sentence euer,
  p. 149 UNDERWOOD 9   8 In sentence, of as subtile feet,
  p. 211 UNDERWOOD 43   189 I could invent a sentence, yet were worse;
  p. 284 U'WOOD 84.9   57 Must come to take a sentence, by the sense

sentinel. See "sentinell."

sentinell   frequency: 1   relative frequency: 0.00001
  p. 109 FOREST 11   22 Or else the sentinell

sent'st   frequency: 1   relative frequency: 0.00001
  p. 106 FOREST 9   14 And sent'st it backe to mee:

separate   frequency: 2   relative frequency: 0.00002
  p. 246 UNDERWOOD 70   92 To separate these twi-
  p. 327 HORACE 2   487 Things sacred, from profane to separate;

sepulcher'd   frequency: 1   relative frequency: 0.00001
  p. 47 EPIGRAMS 64   10 Where merit is not sepulcher'd aliue.

sepulchre's. See "sepvlchres."

sepvlchres   frequency: 1   relative frequency: 0.00001
     p. 89 EPIGRAMS 133   174 Of loud SEPVLCHRES with their hourely
                               knells,

seraphic. See "seraphick."

seraphick   frequency: 1   relative frequency: 0.00001
     p. 285 U'WOOD 84.9   88 The Thrones, the Cherube, and Seraphick
                               bowers,

seraphim   frequency: 1   relative frequency: 0.00001
     p. 273 U'WOOD 84.1   31 Of Heaven; where SERAPHIM take tent

sere. See "seare."

serenes   frequency: 1   relative frequency: 0.00001
     p. 37 EPIGRAMS 32   10 Seas, serenes, swords, shot, sicknesse, all are
                               there.

serenitie   frequency: 1   relative frequency: 0.00001
     p. 193 UNDERWOOD 38   77 O imitate that sweet Serenitie

serenity. See "serenitie."

sergeants   frequency: 1   relative frequency: 0.00001
     p. 89 EPIGRAMS 133   177 Of Hol'borne (<the> three sergeants heads)
                               lookes ore,

serious   frequency: 5   relative frequency: 0.00007
     p. 35 EPIGRAMS 28   3 Makes serious vse of all great trade he knowes.
     p. 55 EPIGRAMS 85   12 What would his serious actions me haue learned?
     p. 204 UNDERWOOD 43   41 On such my serious follies; But, thou'lt say,
     p. 311 HORACE 2   151 And the severe, speech ever serious.
     p. 335 HORACE 2   641 These trifles into serious mischiefes lead

sermon   frequency: 1   relative frequency: 0.00001
     p. 201 UNDERWOOD 42   71 Unto the Spittle Sermon. O, what strange

sermoneeres   frequency: 1   relative frequency: 0.00001
     p. 223 UNDERWOOD 49   39 For Sermoneeres: of which now one, now other,

sermoneers. See "sermoneeres."

serpent   frequency: 1   relative frequency: 0.00001
     p. 97 FOREST 3   18 Through which a serpent riuer leades

serpents   frequency: 2   relative frequency: 0.00002
     p. 272 UNDERWOOD 83   99 The Serpents head: Gets above Death, and
                               Sinne,
     p. 305 HORACE 2   15 Together: not that we should Serpents see

seruant   frequency: 2   relative frequency: 0.00002
     p. 409 UNGATHERED 38   1 I had you for a Seruant, once, Dick Brome;
     p. 409 UNGATHERED 38 t1 To my old Faithfull Seruant: and (by

seruants   frequency: 3   relative frequency: 0.00004
     p. 74 EPIGRAMS 114   8 But, in your loue, made all his seruants wise.
     p. 399 UNGATHERED 31   4 Tenants, and Seruants, haue they harts, and
                               eyes,
     p. 409 UNGATHERED 38   2 And you perform'd a Seruants faithfull parts:

seru'd   frequency: 2   relative frequency: 0.00002
     p. 31 EPIGRAMS 12   23 But see! th'old baud hath seru'd him in his trim,
     p. 410 UNGATHERED 38   9 You learn'd it well; and for it, seru'd your time

serue   frequency: 3   relative frequency: 0.00004
   **p. 115 PANEGYRE   99 "Where lawes were made to serue the tyran' will;
     p. 52 EPIGRAMS 76   4 To honor, serue, and loue; as Poets vse.
     p. 94 FOREST 2   20 That neuer failes to serue thee season'd deere,

serues   frequency: 1   relative frequency: 0.00001
     p. 70 EPIGRAMS 109   2 That serues nor fame, nor titles; but doth chuse

seruice   frequency: 2   relative frequency: 0.00002
     p. 70 EPIGRAMS 109   7 Of seruice to the publique, when the end
     p. 100 FOREST 3   103 To doe thy countrey seruice, thy selfe right;

seruiceable   frequency: 1   relative frequency: 0.00001
   p. 113 FOREST 12   9 While it makes huishers seruiceable men,

seruices   frequency: 1   relative frequency: 0.00001
   p. 69 EPIGRAMS 107   11 Giue them your seruices, and embassies

seruile   frequency: 1   relative frequency: 0.00001
   p. 41 EPIGRAMS 43   11 From seruile flatterie (common Poets shame)

seruing-man   frequency: 1   relative frequency: 0.00001
   p. 28 EPIGRAMS 3   9 For termers, or some clarke-like seruing-man,

servant   frequency: 7   relative frequency: 0.00010
   See also "seruant."
   p. 165 UNDERWOOD 15   99 The Servant of the Serving-woman, in scorne,
   p. 188 UNDERWOOD 34   7 Art, her false servant; Nor, for Sir Hugh
                             Plat,
   p. 198 UNDERWOOD 40   41 And such your Servant is, who vowes to keepe
   p. 199 UNDERWOOD 41   2 Heare, Mistris, your departing servant tell
   p. 230 UNDERWOOD 56   5 So have you gain'd a Servant, and a Muse:
   p. 230 UNDERWOOD 56   18 Of either Suitor, or a Servant by.
   p. 258 UNDERWOOD 75   178 To be a watchfull Servant for this State;

servants   frequency: 3   relative frequency: 0.00004
   See also "seruants."
   p. 163 UNDERWOOD 15   46 All which he makes the servants of the Groine,
   p. 185 UNDERWOOD 30   8 The poores full Store-house, and just servants
                             field.
   p. 217 UNDERWOOD 46   2 And steps of all rais'd servants of the Crowne,

serve   frequency: 7   relative frequency: 0.00010
   See also "serue."
   p. 154 UNDERWOOD 13   58 Ha's Feathers, and will serve a man to pull.
   p. 185 UNDERWOOD 30   20 Of divine blessing, would not serve a State?
   p. 208 UNDERWOOD 43   125 Against thy furie, when to serve their needs,
   p. 215 UNDERWOOD 44   85 To serve the State by Councels, and by Armes:
   p. 220 UNDERWOOD 47   71 These I will honour, love, embrace, and serve:
   p. 269 UNDERWOOD 83   21 Earle Rivers Grand-Child -- serve not formes,
                             good Fame,
   p. 287 U'WOOD 84.9   172 T<o>'obey, and serve her sweet Commandements.

served. See "seru'd."

serves. See "serues."

service   frequency: 3   relative frequency: 0.00004
   See also "seruice."
   p. 256 UNDERWOOD 75   107 To day, the Fathers service; who could bring
   p. 259 UNDERWOOD 76   13 For done service, and to come:
   p. 263 UNDERWOOD 79   12 And offer your just service on these plaines;

serviceable. See "seruiceable."

services. See "seruices."

servile. See "seruile."

serving-man. See "seruing-man."

serving-woman   frequency: 1   relative frequency: 0.00001
   p. 165 UNDERWOOD 15   99 The Servant of the Serving-woman, in scorne,

session   frequency: 1   relative frequency: 0.00001
 **p. 112 PANEGYRE   t8 His first high Session of PARLIAMENT

set   frequency: 32   relative frequency: 0.00046
  *p. 493 TO HIMSELF   30 Needs set them, but, the almes-basket of wit.
 **p. 114 PANEGYRE   63 Walls, windores, roofes, towers, steeples, all
                            were set
   p. 78 EPIGRAMS 122   5 If I would vertue set, as shee was yong,
   p. 79 EPIGRAMS 125   5 Who sees a soule, in such a body set,
   p. 81 EPIGRAMS 129   3 That there 's no iourney set, or thought vpon,
   p. 94 FOREST 2   13 That taller tree, which of a nut was set,
   p. 95 FOREST 2   79 Of thy Penates had beene set on flame,
   p. 102 FOREST 5   6 Sunnes, that set, may rise againe:
   p. 115 FOREST 12   60 Or set bright ARIADNES crowne so high?
   p. 136 UNDERWOOD 2.5   9 Set, and to this softer straine;
   p. 139 UNDERWOOD 2.8   5 And that promise set on fire
   p. 142 UNDERWOOD 2.9 40 Or were set up in a Brake.
   p. 164 UNDERWOOD 15   66 And every Dressing for a Pitfall set

set (cont.)
```
    p. 181 UNDERWOOD 27    25 Hath our great Sydney, Stella set,
    p. 188 UNDERWOOD 34     4 Of those that set by their false faces more
    p. 189 UNDERWOOD 36     9 A Sparke to set whole world<s> a-fire,
    p. 222 UNDERWOOD 48    51 And set us all on skipping,
    p. 234 UNDERWOOD 61    10 To see you set apart, thus, from the rest,
    p. 243 UNDERWOOD 70    18 And all on utmost ruine set;
    p. 255 UNDERWOOD 75    95 And set the marke upon,
    p. 256 UNDERWOOD 75   112 He had so highly set; and, in what Barbican.
    p. 270 UNDERWOOD 83    41 Were like a ring of Vertues, 'bout her set,
    p. 282 U'WOOD 84.9      5 And set it forth; the rest were Cobwebs fine,
    p. 291 UNDERWOOD 85    66 And 'bout the steeming Chimney set!
    p. 292 UNDERWOOD 86    23 Shall Verse be set to Harpe and Lute,
    p. 305 HORACE 2         2 Set a Horse-neck, and divers feathers fold
    p. 327 HORACE 2       493 Next these great Homer and Tyrtaeus set
    p. 329 HORACE 2       500 Of their long labours, was in Verse set downe:
    p. 331 HORACE 2       579 To change, and mend, what you not forth doe set.
    p. 369 UNGATHERED 6   120 Set out a like, or second to our Swan.
    p. 386 UNGATHERED 21   16 With the how much they set forth, but th'how
                             well.
    p. 407 UNGATHERED 35   18 yearly set out there, to sayle downe ye Street,
```

sets   frequency: 4   relative frequency: 0.00005
```
    p.  50 EPIGRAMS 71      1 To plucke downe mine, POLL sets vp new wits
                             still,
    p. 290 UNDERWOOD 85    12 And sets more happy in the place:
    p. 290 UNDERWOOD 85    34 For th'eating Thrush, or Pit-falls sets:
    p. 378 UNGATHERED 11   83 Marry he sets it out at his owne charge;
```

setting   frequency: 2   relative frequency: 0.00002
```
    p.  72 EPIGRAMS 112     4 Or thy ranke setting? that thou dar'st put in
    p. 405 UNGATHERED 34   78 In setting forth of such a solemne Toye!
```

seuen   frequency: 2   relative frequency: 0.00002
```
    p.  41 EPIGRAMS 45      3 Seuen yeeres tho'wert lent to me, and I thee
                             pay,
    p. 380 UNGATHERED 12   45 Of Latine and Greeke, to his friendship. And
                             seuen
```

seuer   frequency: 1   relative frequency: 0.00001
```
    p. 102 FOREST 5         4 He, at length, our good will seuer.
```

seuerall   frequency: 7   relative frequency: 0.00010
```
  **p. 114 PANEGYRE        64 With seuerall eyes, that in this obiect met.
    p.  33 EPIGRAMS 21      7 What seuerall wayes men to their calling haue!
    p.  59 EPIGRAMS 92     26 To write in cypher, and the seuerall keyes,
    p.  61 EPIGRAMS 95     27 We need a man that knowes the seuerall graces
    p.  97 FOREST 3        37 The whil'st, the seuerall seasons thou hast seene
    p. 110 FOREST 11       29 Doe seuerall passions <still> inuade the minde,
    p. 370 UNGATHERED 7    10 The seuerall figures, languish in suspence,
```

seuer'd   frequency: 1   relative frequency: 0.00001
```
    p.  34 EPIGRAMS 22     10 Where, while that seuer'd doth remaine,
```

seu'rall   frequency: 1   relative frequency: 0.00001
```
    p.  87 EPIGRAMS 133   124 Against their breasts. Here, seu'rall ghosts did
                             flit
```

seven   frequency: 1   relative frequency: 0.00001
    See also "seauen," "seuen."
```
    p. 150 UNDERWOOD 9     15 Told seven and fortie years,
```

seven-fold. See "seauen-fold."

seven-tongu'd   frequency: 1   relative frequency: 0.00001
```
    p. 181 UNDERWOOD 27     3 Did Sappho on her seven-tongu'd Lute,
```

sever. See "seuer."

several. See "seuerall," "seu'rall," "severall."

severall   frequency: 3   relative frequency: 0.00004
```
    p. 215 UNDERWOOD 44    94 Of severall makings? helps, helps, t<o>'attire
    p. 305 HORACE 2         3 On every limbe, ta'en from a severall creature,
    p. 341 HORACE 1       121 .. ... ... changes ... ... severall ....
```

sever'd   frequency: 1   relative frequency: 0.00001
    See also "seuer'd."
```
    p. 192 UNDERWOOD 38    47 And then with pause; for sever'd once, that's
                             gone,
```

severe   frequency: 3   relative frequency: 0.00004
    p. 190 UNDERWOOD 37   16 Though you sometimes proclaime me too severe,
    p. 229 UNDERWOOD 54   8 Is, she will play Dame Justice, too severe;
    p. 311 HORACE 2   151 And the severe, speech ever serious.

severs   frequency: 1   relative frequency: 0.00001
    p. 285 U'WOOD 84.9   105 You once enjoy'd: A short space severs yee,

sew'd   frequency: 1   relative frequency: 0.00001
    p.   51 EPIGRAMS 73   17 Item, your owne, sew'd in your mistris smock.

sex   frequency: 4   relative frequency: 0.00005
    See also "sexe."
  **p. 114 PANEGYRE   58 No age, nor sex, so weake, or strongly dull,
    p. 137 UNDERWOOD 2.5   45 Of her Sex; But could'st thou, Love,
    p. 172 UNDERWOOD 20   20 Thinke but the Sin of all her sex, 'tis she!
    p. 255 UNDERWOOD 75   82 Of Sex, to rob the Creature; but from Man,

sexe   frequency: 5   relative frequency: 0.00007
    p.   66 EPIGRAMS 103   1 How well, faire crowne of your faire sexe, might
                                   hee,
    p. 254 UNDERWOOD 75   58 (Lillies and Roses, Flowers of either Sexe)
    p. 274 U'WOOD 84.2   12 The wonder of her Sexe, and of your Blood.
    p. 399 UNGATHERED 31   10 Vpon her selfe) to all her sexe!
    p. 414 UNGATHERED 41   46 And most to be admired of thy Sexe,

sey'd   frequency: 1   relative frequency: 0.00001
    p. 282 U'WOOD 84.9   2 Who was my Muse, and life of all I sey'd,

shaddow   frequency: 1   relative frequency: 0.00001
    p. 104 FOREST 7   1 Follow a shaddow, it still flies you;

shaddowes   frequency: 3   relative frequency: 0.00004
    p. 104 FOREST 7   6 Stil'd but the shaddowes of vs men?
    p. 104 FOREST 7   t3 SHADDOWES.
    p. 104 FOREST 7   12 Stil'd but the shaddowes of vs men?

shade   frequency: 12   relative frequency: 0.00017
    p.   83 EPIGRAMS 132   7 Behold! the reuerend shade of BARTAS stands
    p.   93 FOREST 2   12 Beneath the broad beech, and the chest-nut shade;
    p.   97 FOREST 3   19 To some coole, courteous shade, which he calls
                                   his,
    p.   98 FOREST 3   46 A fire now, that lent a shade!
    p. 189 UNDERWOOD 36   1 Come, let us here enjoy the shade,
    p. 197 UNDERWOOD 40   13 But ever without blazon, or least shade
    p. 199 UNDERWOOD 41   5 It is as if a night should shade noone-day,
    p. 258 UNDERWOOD 75   184 So great; his Body now alone projects the shade.
    p. 268 UNDERWOOD 82   15 At land she triumphs in the triple shade,
    p. 269 UNDERWOOD 83   7 To give your shade a name! Stay, stay, I feele
    p. 272 U'WOOD 84.1   4 With her, in shade
    p. 285 U'WOOD 84.9   91 And she doth know, out of the shade of Death,

shades   frequency: 2   relative frequency: 0.00002
    p.   80 EPIGRAMS 126   2 'Mongst Hampton shades, and PHOEBVS groue
                                   of bayes,
    p. 104 FOREST 7   7 At morne, and euen, shades are longest;

shadie   frequency: 1   relative frequency: 0.00001
    p. 222 UNDERWOOD 48   53 The narrow Seas are shadie,

shadow   frequency: 6   relative frequency: 0.00008
    See also "shaddow."
    p. 149 UNDERWOOD 9   10 That sits in shadow of Apollo's tree.
    p. 189 UNDERWOOD 36   2 For Love in shadow best is made.
    p. 189 UNDERWOOD 36   3 Though Envie oft his shadow be,
    p. 227 UNDERWOOD 52   17 Your Power of handling shadow, ayre, and
                                   spright,
    p. 251 UNDERWOOD 74   29 To be a shadow to his Heire,
    p. 370 UNGATHERED 7   3 Light, Posture, Height'ning, Shadow,
                                   Culloring,

shadowes   frequency: 2   relative frequency: 0.00002
    p. 156 UNDERWOOD 13   118 Can I discerne how shadowes are decreast,
    p. 255 UNDERWOOD 75   88 All else we see beside, are Shadowes, and goe
                                   lesse.

shadows. See "shaddowes," "shadowes."

shady. See "shadie."

shaft   frequency: 3   relative frequency: 0.00004
    p. 132 UNDERWOOD 2.2   10 Here's a shaft, thou art to slow!
    p. 133 UNDERWOOD 2.3   8 Both the Bow, and shaft I held,
    p. 133 UNDERWOOD 2.3   12 Aymed with that selfe-same shaft.

shafts   frequency: 4   relative frequency: 0.00005
    p. 110 FOREST 11   38 Arm'd with bow, shafts, and fire;
    p. 136 UNDERWOOD 2.5   19 Which you call my Shafts. And see!
    p. 137 UNDERWOOD 2.5   37 To my shafts! Her very Name,
    p. 182 UNDERWOOD 28   10 His flames, his shafts, his Quiver, and his
                                Bow,

shake   frequency: 6   relative frequency: 0.00008
    p.   59 EPIGRAMS 92   33 At naming the French King, their heads they
                                shake,
    p. 193 UNDERWOOD 38   72 It shakes even him, that all things else doth
                                shake.
    p. 239 UNDERWOOD 67   11 This Citie, or to shake
    p. 294 UNDERWOOD 87   19 That I bright C<h>loe off should shake;
    p. 391 UNGATHERED 26   37 And shake a Stage: Or, when thy Sockes were
                                on,
    p. 392 UNGATHERED 26   69 In each of which, he seemes to shake a Lance,

shaken. See "blood-shaken."

shakes   frequency: 1   relative frequency: 0.00001
    p. 193 UNDERWOOD 38   72 It shakes even him, that all things else doth
                                shake.

shakespeare   frequency: 5   relative frequency: 0.00007
    p. 390 UNGATHERED 25   2 It was for gentle Shakespeare cut;
    p. 390 UNGATHERED 26   1 To draw no enuy (Shakespeare) on thy name,
    p. 390 UNGATHERED 26   t3 MR. WILLIAM SHAKESPEARE:
    p. 391 UNGATHERED 26   19 My Shakespeare, rise; I will not lodge thee by
    p. 392 UNGATHERED 26   56 My gentle Shakespeare, must enioy a part.

shakespeares   frequency: 1   relative frequency: 0.00001
    p. 392 UNGATHERED 26   67 Of Shakespeares minde, and manners brightly
                                shines

shall   frequency: 120   relative frequency: 0.00173

shalt   frequency: 5   relative frequency: 0.00007

shame   frequency: 16   relative frequency: 0.00023
    p.   27 EPIGRAMS 2   10 Made from the hazard of anothers shame:
    p.   29 EPIGRAMS 10   1 Thou call'st me Poet, as a terme of shame:
    p.   38 EPIGRAMS 38   7 Beleeue it, GVILTIE, if you loose your
                                shame,
    p.   41 EPIGRAMS 43   11 From seruile flatterie (common Poets shame)
    p.   53 EPIGRAMS 77   3 For, if thou shame, ranck'd with my friends, to
                                goe,
    p.   70 EPIGRAMS 108   7 And did not shame it with my actions, then,
    p. 122 FOREST 15   17 I know my state, both full of shame, and scorne,
    p. 144 UNDERWOOD 4   4 Lest shame destroy their being.
    p. 153 UNDERWOOD 13   17 Yet choyce from whom I take them; and would
                                shame
    p. 220 UNDERWOOD 47   70 As but to stumble in her sight were shame;
    p. 225 UNDERWOOD 50   36 It will be shame for them, if they have none.
    p. 243 UNDERWOOD 70   13 Where shame, faith, honour, and regard of right
    p. 294 UNDERWOOD 88   8 There is no labour, nor no shame in this;
    p. 311 HORACE 2   129 Am I call'd Poet? wherefore with wrong shame,
    p. 335 HORACE 2   633 A wise, and honest man will cry out shame
    p. 411 UNGATHERED 39   14 But Tune and Noise the Eccho of thy Shame.

shamefac'd   frequency: 1   relative frequency: 0.00001
    p. 321 HORACE 2   339 To Dance, so she should, shamefac'd, differ
                                farre

shamefastnesse   frequency: 1   relative frequency: 0.00001
    p. 163 UNDERWOOD 15   40 And shamefastnesse together! All lawes dead,

shamefull   frequency: 1   relative frequency: 0.00001
    p. 347 HORACE 1   351 .. .. shamefull .... or ....

shames   frequency: 1   relative frequency: 0.00001
    p. 423 UNGATHERED 50   19 That prince that shames a tyrants name to beare,

shap'd   frequency: 1   relative frequency: 0.00001
    p. 305 HORACE 2   28 The whole fleet wreck'd? A great jarre to be
                                shap'd,

shape   frequency: 1   relative frequency: 0.00001
     p. 132 UNDERWOOD 2.2   32 In a Hercules-his shape.

shapes   frequency: 2   relative frequency: 0.00002
     p. 34 EPIGRAMS 25   6 In varied shapes, which for his lust shee takes:
     p. 305 HORACE 2   9 Whose shapes, like sick-mens dreames, are fain'd
                                   so vaine,

share   frequency: 3   relative frequency: 0.00004
    *p. 493 TO HIMSELF   40 The gamesters share your guilt, and you their
                                   stuffe.
     p. 291 UNDERWOCD 85   64 And fainting necks, the turned Share!
     p. 325 HORACE 2   421 Exclude all sober Poets, from their share

sharp   frequency: 2   relative frequency: 0.00002
     See also "sharpe."
     p. 180 UNDERWOOD 32   15 When this appeares, just Lord, to your sharp
                                   sight,
     p. 407 UNGATHERED 36   3 That I should wryte vpon him some sharp verse,

sharpe   frequency: 5   relative frequency: 0.00007
     p. 27 EPIGRAMS 2   4 Wormewood, and sulphure, sharpe, and tooth'd
                                   withall;
     p. 36 EPIGRAMS 29   3 For thy late sharpe deuice. I say 'tis fit
     p. 263 UNDERWOOD 79   3 Your change of Notes, the flat, the meane, the
                                   sharpe,
     p. 313 HORACE 2   173 Sharpe, and contemning lawes, at him should aime,
     p. 329 HORACE 2   523 Oft-times a Sharpe, when we require a Flat:

sharper   frequency: 1   relative frequency: 0.00001
     p. 159 UNDERWOOD 14   23 Since, being deceiv'd, I turne a sharper eye

sharply. See "sharplye."

sharplye   frequency: 1   relative frequency: 0.00001
     p. 421 UNGATHERED 49   1 Censure, not sharplye then, but mee advise

sharpnesse   frequency: 2   relative frequency: 0.00002
     p. 45 EPIGRAMS 58   5 And so my sharpnesse thou no lesse dis-ioynts,
     p. 160 UNDERWOOD 14   59 In sharpnesse of all Search, wisdome of Choise,

shave   frequency: 1   relative frequency: 0.00001
     p. 325 HORACE 2   423 Their nailes, nor shave their beards, but to
                                   by-paths

she   frequency: 117   relative frequency: 0.00169
     See also "shee," "shee'll," "shee's,"
            "she'hath," "sh'had," "sh'hath."

sheaf. See "sheafe."

sheafe   frequency: 1   relative frequency: 0.00001
     p. 208 UNDERWOOD 43   126 They made a Vulcan of a sheafe of Reedes,

shearers   frequency: 1   relative frequency: 0.00001
     p. 97 FOREST 3   40 And feasts, that either shearers keepe;

sheares   frequency: 1   relative frequency: 0.00001
     p. 290 UNDERWOOD 85   16 Of Earth, and sheares the tender Sheepe:

shears. See "sheares," "sheeres."

sheath   frequency: 1   relative frequency: 0.00001
     p. 403 UNGATHERED 34   26 Noe veluet Sheath you weare, will alter kynde.

shed   frequency: 7   relative frequency: 0.00010
     p. 77 EPIGRAMS 120   3 And know, for whom a teare you shed,
     p. 82 EPIGRAMS 130   18 Shed in thy Songs; 'tis true: but short of thee.
     p. 152 UNDERWOOD 12   34 That they for me their teares will shed;
     p. 177 UNDERWOOD 25   14 Rich beame of honour, shed your light
     p. 214 UNDERWOOD 44   36 And the Greeke Discipline (with the moderne)
                                   shed ·
     p. 329 HORACE 2   528 Hath shed, or humane frailtie not kept thence.
     p. 375 UNGATHERED 10   30 Here France, and Italy both to him shed

sheds   frequency: 1   relative frequency: 0.00001
     p. 134 UNDERWOOD 2.4   18 Sheds it selfe through the face,

shee   frequency: 81   relative frequency: 0.00117

shee'll   frequency: 2   relative frequency: 0.00002 sheep. See "sheepe."

sheepe   frequency: 4   relative frequency: 0.00005
    p.   94 FOREST 2   23 Thy sheepe, thy bullocks, kine, and calues doe
                              feed:
    p.   97 FOREST 3   39 The mowed meddowes, with the fleeced sheepe,
    p. 283 U'WOOD 84.9   46 In earth, till the last Trumpe awake the Sheepe
    p. 290 UNDERWOOD 85   16 Of Earth, and sheares the tender Sheepe:

sheep'erds   frequency: 1   relative frequency: 0.00001
    p. 130 UNDERWOOD 1.3   4 And like the ravish'd Sheep'erds said,

sheepes-skin   frequency: 1   relative frequency: 0.00001
    p.   87 EPIGRAMS 133   113 The slie VLYSSES stole in a sheepes-skin,

sheepskin. See "sheepes-skin."

sheeres   frequency: 1   relative frequency: 0.00001
    p.   52 EPIGRAMS 76   15 The rock, the spindle, and the sheeres controule

shee's   frequency: 3   relative frequency: 0.00004

sheetes   frequency: 1   relative frequency: 0.00001
    p. 258 UNDERWOOD 75   191 Night, and the sheetes will show

sheets. See "sheetes."

she'hath   frequency: 1   relative frequency: 0.00001

sheild   frequency: 1   relative frequency: 0.00001
    p. 421 UNGATHERED 48   38 Thie Chrystall sheild

sheldon. See "shelton."

shelf. See "shelfe."

shelfe   frequency: 1   relative frequency: 0.00001
    p.   99 FOREST 3   95 God wisheth, none should wracke on a strange
                              shelfe.

shelton   frequency: 3   relative frequency: 0.00004
    p.   76 EPIGRAMS 119   7 No, SHELTON, giue me thee, canst want all
                              these,
    p.   76 EPIGRAMS 119   t1 TO SIR RAPH SHELTON
    p.   84 EPIGRAMS 133   5 We haue a SHELTON, and a HEYDEN got,

shelues   frequency: 1   relative frequency: 0.00001
    p. 119 FOREST 13   89 You, Madame, yong haue learn'd to shunne these
                              shelues,

shelves. See "shelues."

shep.   frequency: 2   relative frequency: 0.00002
    p. 264 UNDERWOOD 79   20 Shep. Of PAN wee sing, the best of Hunters,
                              PAN,
    p. 264 UNDERWOOD 79   28 Shep. Of PAN wee sing, the Chiefe of
                              Leaders, PAN,

shep'ard   frequency: 2   relative frequency: 0.00002
    p. 265 UNDERWOOD 79   43 PAN only our great Shep'ard is,
    p. 265 UNDERWOOD 79   65 This only the great Shep'ard is.

shepheards   frequency: 1   relative frequency: 0.00001
    p.   68 EPIGRAMS 105   9 And, drest in shepheards tyre, who would not say:

shepherd. See "shep'ard."

shepherds. See "sheep'erds," "shep.," "shepheards."

sheriffes   frequency: 1   relative frequency: 0.00001
    p.   96 FOREST 3   6 Of Sheriffes dinner, or Maiors feast.

sheriff's. See "sheriffes," "shrieues."

shew   frequency: 16   relative frequency: 0.00023
    p.   28 EPIGRAMS 4   4 And gaue thee both, to shew they could no more.
    p.   47 EPIGRAMS 64   7 Nor glad for fashion. Nor to shew a fit
    p.   49 EPIGRAMS 68   3 Two kindes of valour he doth shew, at ones;
    p.   60 EPIGRAMS 93   4 Stand'st thou, to shew the times what you all
                              were?

shew (cont.)
    p. 98 FOREST 3   71 And shew their feathers shot, and cullors torne,
    p. 101 FOREST 4   39 I know thou canst nor shew, nor beare
    p. 121 FOREST 14   32 Of nobles vertue, shew in you;
    p. 141 UNDERWOOD 2.9   26 As the Downe, and shew it oft;
    p. 182 UNDERWOOD 28   1 I that have beene a lover, and could shew it,
    p. 222 UNDERWOOD 49   17 To shew their Tires? to view, and to be view'd?
    p. 245 UNDERWOOD 70   58 To shew thou hast beene long,
    p. 250 UNDERWOOD 73   9 Feed on thy selfe for spight, and shew thy Kind:
    p. 263 UNDERWOOD 79   4 To shew the rites, and t<o>'usher forth the way
    p. 288 U'WOOD 84.9   217 As being the Sonne of Man) to shew his Power,
    p. 365 UNGATHERED 5   23 Yet shee's nor nice to shew them,
    p. 393 UNGATHERED 27   16 Doth shew the Holy one.

shewd   frequency: 1   relative frequency: 0.00001
  **p. 115 PANEGYRE   95 "She shewd him, who made wise, who honest acts;

shew'd   frequency: 3   relative frequency: 0.00004
    p. 89 EPIGRAMS 133   184 That had, so often, shew'd 'hem merry prankes.
    p. 228 UNDERWOOD 53   7 You shew'd like Perseus upon Pegasus;
    p. 366 UNGATHERED 6   17 He shew'd him first the hoofe-cleft Spring,

shewe   frequency: 2   relative frequency: 0.00002
    p. 362 UNGATHERED 2   4 In these pide times, only to shewe their braines,
    p. 405 UNGATHERED 34   83 Vnder ye Morall? shewe he had a pate

shewen   frequency: 1   relative frequency: 0.00001
    p. 329 HORACE 2   497 All way of life was shewen; the grace of Kings

shewes   frequency: 6   relative frequency: 0.00008
    p. 37 EPIGRAMS 32   9 Which shewes, where euer death doth please
                              t<o>'appeare,
    p. 37 EPIGRAMS 34   2 Shewes of the resurrection little trust.
    p. 60 EPIGRAMS 93   14 Though not vnprou'd: which shewes, thy fortunes
                              are
    p. 370 UNGATHERED 7   8 So bold, as shewes your Art you can command.
    p. 375 UNGATHERED 10   29 F. shewes what he was, K. what he will bee.
    p. 378 UNGATHERED 11   85 Shewes he dares more then Paules Church-yard
                              durst do.

shewing   frequency: 2   relative frequency: 0.00002
    p. 142 UNDERWOOD 2.9   42 Shewing danger more then ire.
    p. 218 UNDERWOOD 47   7 And shewing so weake an Act to vulgar eyes,

shew'n   frequency: 1   relative frequency: 0.00001
    p. 210 UNDERWOOD 43   158 There was a Judgement shew'n too in an houre.

shew'ne   frequency: 1   relative frequency: 0.00001
  **p. 114 PANEGYRE   37 Others would faine haue shew'ne it in their
                              words:

shews   frequency: 1   relative frequency: 0.00001
    p. 407 UNGATHERED 35   17 And stradling shews ye Boyes Brown paper fleet,

shew's   frequency: 1   relative frequency: 0.00001
    p. 281 U'WOOD 84.8   19 By which yo'are planted, shew's your fruit shall
                              bide.

shew'st   frequency: 1   relative frequency: 0.00001
    p. 72 EPIGRAMS 111   3 Wherein thou shew'st, how much the latter are

sh'had   frequency: 1   relative frequency: 0.00001

sh'hath   frequency: 1   relative frequency: 0.00001

shield   frequency: 1   relative frequency: 0.00001
    See also "sheild."
    p. 185 UNDERWOOD 30   7 The Orphans Pillar, the true Subjects shield,

shieter-huissen   frequency: 1   relative frequency: 0.00001
    p. 69 EPIGRAMS 107   25 Of Hannow, Shieter-huissen, Popenheim,

shift   frequency: 6   relative frequency: 0.00008
    p. 30 EPIGRAMS 12   1 SHIFT, here, in towne, not meanest among
                              squires,
    p. 30 EPIGRAMS 12   t1 ON LIEVTENANT SHIFT.
    p. 155 UNDERWOOD 13   83 Man out their Boates to th' Temple, and not
                              shift
    p. 171 UNDERWOOD 19   24 As would make shift, to make himselfe alone,
    p. 199 UNDERWOOD 41   10 To shift their seasons, and destroy their powers!

shift (cont.)
    p. 278 U'WOOD 84.4   9 You could make shift to paint an Eye,

shifting   frequency: 1   relative frequency: 0.00001
    p. 74 EPIGRAMS 115   25 And, shifting of it's faces, doth play more

shifts   frequency: 1   relative frequency: 0.00001
    p. 45 EPIGRAMS 56   5 At first he made low shifts, would picke and
                               gleane,

shine   frequency: 21   relative frequency: 0.00030
    See also "ore-shine," "out-shine," "re-shine."
  **p. 116 PANEGYRE   130 When, like an April Iris, flew her shine
    p. 47 EPIGRAMS 63   4 The iudgement of the king so shine in thee;
    p. 95 FOREST 2   78 Shine bright on euery harth as the desires
    p. 115 FOREST 12   64 And such, or my hopes faile, shall make you
                               shine.
    p. 128 UNDERWOOD 1.1   34 A Trinitie, to shine in Union;
    p. 150 UNDERWOOD 10   7 I wish the Sun should shine
    p. 177 UNDERWOOD 25   16 May shine (through every chincke) to every sight
    p. 179 UNDERWOOD 25   58 (As my hope tells) that our faire Phoeb<e>'s
                               shine,
    p. 181 UNDERWOOD 27   12 Shine more, then she, the Stars among?
    p. 189 UNDERWOOD 36   5 Where Love doth shine, there needs no Sunne,
    p. 245 UNDERWOOD 70   76 And let thy lookes with gladnesse shine:
    p. 246 UNDERWOOD 70   96 Whilst that in heav'n, this light on earth must
                               shine.
    p. 246 UNDERWOOD 70   97 And shine as you exalted are;
    p. 253 UNDERWOOD 75   22 Or so did shine,
    p. 254 UNDERWOOD 75   57 See, how with Roses, and with Lillies shine,
    p. 294 UNDERWOOD 89   3 If thou be'st wise, with 'Syrian Oyle let shine
    p. 329 HORACE 2   526 Much in the Poeme shine, I will not bee
    p. 365 UNGATHERED 5   10 Doth shine in her discerning,
    p. 384 UNGATHERED 18   10 Wth the same looke, or wth a better, shine.
    p. 392 UNGATHERED 26   77 Shine forth, thou Starre of Poets, and with
                               rage,
    p. 413 UNGATHERED 41   23 Inflam'd with ardor to that mystick Shine,

shines   frequency: 3   relative frequency: 0.00004
    p. 121 FOREST 14   60 The Birth-day shines, when logs not burne, but
                               men.
    p. 194 UNDERWOOD 38   117 Your forme shines here, here fixed in my heart:
    p. 392 UNGATHERED 26   67 Of Shakespeares minde, and manners brightly
                               shines

shineth   frequency: 1   relative frequency: 0.00001
    p. 393 UNGATHERED 27   6 The Sunne that euer shineth,

shining   frequency: 1   relative frequency: 0.00001
    p. 288 U'WOOD 84.9   200 Incarnate in the Manger, shining bright

shin'st   frequency: 1   relative frequency: 0.00001
    p. 254 UNDERWOOD 75   64 O, now thou smil'st, faire Sun, and shin'st, as
                               thou wouldst stay!

ship   frequency: 1   relative frequency: 0.00001
    p. 380 UNGATHERED 12   27 Besides he tried Ship, Cart, Waggon, and
                               Chayre,

shipping   frequency: 1   relative frequency: 0.00001
    p. 222 UNDERWOOD 48   52 When with his royall shipping

ships   frequency: 4   relative frequency: 0.00005
    p. 219 UNDERWOOD 47   33 Or the States Ships sent forth belike to meet
    p. 249 UNDERWOOD 72   2 Unto the Ships, and they from tier, to tier,
    p. 398 UNGATHERED 30   61 Thy Catalogue of Ships, exceeding his,
    p. 398 UNGATHERED 30   65 And when he ships them where to vse their Armes,

shit. See "beshite," "shite," "shitten."

shite   frequency: 1   relative frequency: 0.00001
    p. 410 UNGATHERED 38   16 And the Physician teach men spue, or shite;

shitten   frequency: 1   relative frequency: 0.00001
    p. 86 EPIGRAMS 133   98 And, in so shitten sort, so long had vs'd him:

shoales   frequency: 1   relative frequency: 0.00001
  **p. 116 PANEGYRE   133 She blest the people, that in shoales did swim

shoals. See "shoales."

shoe. See "shooe."

shoes   frequency: 2   relative frequency: 0.00002
    See also "shoone."
    p. 375 UNGATHERED 10   26 Old Hat here, torne Hose, with Shoes full of
                              grauell,
    p. 380 UNGATHERED 12   39 How well, and how often his shoes too were
                              mended,

shone   frequency: 2   relative frequency: 0.00002
    **p. 114 PANEGYRE   54 Her brightest tyre; and, in it, equall shone
    p. 181 UNDERWOOD 27   26 Where never Star shone brighter yet?

shooe   frequency: 2   relative frequency: 0.00002
    p. 50 EPIGRAMS 88   4 And shooe, and tye, and garter should come
                              hether,
    p. 201 UNDERWOOD 42   55 He did lay up, and would adore the shooe,

shoone   frequency: 1   relative frequency: 0.00001
    p. 84 EPIGRAMS 133   30 Makes the poore Banck-side creature wet it'
                              shoone,

shoot   frequency: 5   relative frequency: 0.00007
    See also "shoote."
    p. 157 UNDERWOOD 13   150 Shoot forth in smooth and comely spaces; have
    p. 185 UNDERWOOD 30   17 Clos'd to their peace, he saw his branches shoot,
    p. 237 UNDERWOOD 65   5 This Prince of flowers? Soone shoot thou up,
                              and grow
    p. 251 UNDERWOOD 74   28 Shoot up an Olive fruitfull, faire,
    p. 309 HORACE 2   89 Like tender buds shoot up, and freshly grow.

shoote   frequency: 1   relative frequency: 0.00001
    p. 119 FOREST 13   99 Grow, grow, faire tree, and as thy branches
                              shoote,

shooting   frequency: 1   relative frequency: 0.00001
    p. 97 FOREST 3   34 Or shooting at the greedie thrush,

shop   frequency: 2   relative frequency: 0.00002
    See also "shopp."
    p. 100 FOREST 4   17 I know thou whole art but a shop
    p. 321 HORACE 2   334 With poore base termes, through every baser shop:

shop-philosophy   frequency: 1   relative frequency: 0.00001
    p. 405 UNGATHERED 34   74 Suckt from ye Veynes of shop-philosophy.

shopp   frequency: 1   relative frequency: 0.00001
    p. 407 UNGATHERED 35   9 Or Ale! He build a pallace! Thou a shopp

shops   frequency: 3   relative frequency: 0.00004
    p. 202 UNDERWOOD 42   78 When not the Shops, but windowes doe display
    p. 241 UNDERWOOD 69   12 All live dogs from the lane, and his shops sight,
    p. 371 UNGATHERED 8   6 With the shops Foreman, or some such braue
                              sparke,

shore   frequency: 5   relative frequency: 0.00007
    p. 87 EPIGRAMS 133   125 About the shore, of farts, but late departed,
    p. 249 UNDERWOOD 72   8 Like Eccho playing from the other shore.
    p. 309 HORACE 2   91 Whether the Sea receiv'd into the shore,
    p. 339 HORACE 1   40 Downe close .. shore, this other creeping
                              steales,
    p. 388 UNGATHERED 23   5 Still, still, dost thou arriue with, at our
                              shore,

shores   frequency: 1   relative frequency: 0.00001
    p. 251 UNDERWOOD 74   7 The Rivers in their shores doe run,

short   frequency: 19   relative frequency: 0.00027
    **p. 114 PANEGYRE   47 They that had seene, but foure short daies
                              before,
    p. 32 EPIGRAMS 16   5 So, in short time, th'art in arrerage growne
    p. 37 EPIGRAMS 35   4 And in this short time of thy happiest raigne,
    p. 50 EPIGRAMS 70   8 Though life be short, let vs not make it so.
    p. 82 EPIGRAMS 130   18 Shed in thy Songs; 'tis true: but short of thee.
    p. 96 FOREST 3   10 Of the short brauerie of the night;
    p. 104 FOREST 7   8 At noone, they are or short, or none:
    p. 142 UNDERWOOD 2.9   55 But of one, if short he came,
    p. 158 UNDERWOOD 14   2 Though I am short, I cannot be obscure:
    p. 182 UNDERWOOD 27   34 Come short of all this learned throng,
    p. 220 UNDERWOOD 47   73 So short you read my Character, and theirs

short (cont.)
```
     p. 245 UNDERWOOD 70    74 And in short measures, life may perfect bee.
     p. 274 U'WOOD 84.2     11 Of vertues in her, as, in short, shee grew
     p. 285 U'WOOD 84.9    105 You once enjoy'd: A short space severs yee,
     p. 294 UNDERWOOD 88     1 Doing, a filthy pleasure is, and short;
     p. 307 HORACE 2        31 In short; I bid, Let what thou work'st upon,
     p. 323 HORACE 2       371 Two rests, a short and long, th'Iambick frame;
     p. 331 HORACE 2       551 Or Pleader at the Barre, that may come short
     p. 364 UNGATHERED 5     2 For other formes come short all
```

short-leg'd   frequency: 1   relative frequency: 0.00001
```
     p.  64 EPIGRAMS 101    11 Vshring the mutton; with a short-leg'd hen,
```

shortest   frequency: 1   relative frequency: 0.00001
```
     p. 174 UNDERWOOD 22    34 Appeare, and that to shortest view,
```

shortly   frequency: 1   relative frequency: 0.00001
```
     p. 197 UNDERWOOD 40     8 Shortly againe: and make our absence sweet.
```

shortnesse   frequency: 1   relative frequency: 0.00001
```
     p. 307 HORACE 2        35 My selfe for shortnesse labour; and I grow
```

shot   frequency: 3   relative frequency: 0.00004
```
     p.  37 EPIGRAMS 32     10 Seas, serenes, swords, shot, sicknesse, all are
                               there.
     p.  98 FOREST 3        71 And shew their feathers shot, and cullors torne,
     p. 233 UNDERWOOD 59    11 Their weapons shot out, with that flame, and
                               force,
```

shot-free   frequency: 1   relative frequency: 0.00001
```
     p. 179 UNDERWOOD 25    48 No Armour to the mind! he is shot-free
```

should   frequency: 143   relative frequency: 0.00207

shoulders   frequency: 1   relative frequency: 0.00001
```
     p. 307 HORACE 2        55 Upon your shoulders. Prove what they will beare,
```

should'st   frequency: 7   relative frequency: 0.00010

shout   frequency: 2   relative frequency: 0.00002
     See also "shoute," "showt."
```
     p. 240 UNDERWOOD 67    41 Doe mingle in a shout,
     p. 342 HORACE 1      160 ... ...... ....... .... with laughter shout.
```

shoute   frequency: 2   relative frequency: 0.00002
```
   **p. 117 PANEGYRE      160 With a twice louder shoute againe they cry'd,
     p. 397 UNGATHERED 30  45 And caried, though with shoute, and noyse,
                               confesse
```

shoutes   frequency: 1   relative frequency: 0.00001
```
     p. 249 UNDERWOOD 72    13 At Bonefires, Rockets, Fire-workes, with the
                               Shoutes
```

shouts   frequency: 2   relative frequency: 0.00002
     See also "shoutes."
```
   **p. 114 PANEGYRE       33 Hasting to follow forth in shouts, and cryes.
     p. 335 HORACE 2      648 They vexe, and follow him with shouts, and noise.
```

show   frequency: 22   relative frequency: 0.00031
     See also "shew," "shewe," "showe."
```
     p.  54 EPIGRAMS 81      1 Forbeare to tempt me, PROVLE, I will not
                               show
     p.  65 EPIGRAMS 101    26 That will the pastrie, not my paper, show of.
     p.  67 EPIGRAMS 104    13 Iudge they, that can: Here I haue rais'd to
                               show
     p.  76 EPIGRAMS 119    14 Which is to liue to conscience, not to show.
     p.  78 EPIGRAMS 122     1 If I would wish, for truth, and not for show,
     p.  93 FOREST 2         1 Thou art not, PENSHVRST, built to
                               enuious show,
     p. 115 FOREST 12       86 And show, how, to the life, my soule presents
     p. 122 FOREST 15        6 And hearts of all, if I be sad for show,
     p. 156 UNDERWOOD 13    98 That men such reverence to such actions show!
     p. 162 UNDERWOOD 15    21 Or Feathers: lay his fortune out to show,
     p. 214 UNDERWOOD 44    58 Come to their Schooles,) show 'hem the use of
                               Guns;
     p. 215 UNDERWOOD 44    69 Why are we rich, or great, except to show
     p. 241 UNDERWOOD 69     2 To mee; or beene the same to you; if show,
     p. 251 UNDERWOOD 74    16 Doth show, the Graces, and the Houres,
     p. 258 UNDERWOOD 75   191 Night, and the sheetes will show
     p. 259 UNDERWOOD 76     3 Doth most humbly show it,
```

show (cont.)
```
     p. 276 U'WOOD 84.3    18 The Cloud, and show the Universe;
     p. 289 U'WOOD 84.9   221 Of all are dead to life! His Wisdome show
     p. 315 HORACE 2      214 What he despaires, being handled, might not show.
     p. 317 HORACE 2      258 Then those the faithfull eyes take in by show,
     p. 325 HORACE 2      442 Which the Socratick writings best can show:
     p. 407 UNGATHERED 35  21 An Earle of show: for all thy worke is showe:
```

showe   frequency: 2   relative frequency: 0.00002
```
     p. 391 UNGATHERED 26  41 Triumph, my Britaine, thou hast one to showe,
     p. 407 UNGATHERED 35  21 An Earle of show: for all thy worke is showe:
```

showed. See "shewd," "shew'd."

shower. See "showre."

showers   frequency: 3   relative frequency: 0.00004
     See also "showres."
```
     p. 254 UNDERWOOD 75   65 With what full hands, and in how plenteous
                              showers
     p. 280 U'WOOD 84.4    60 As showers; and sweet as drops of Balme.
     p. 280 U'WOOD 84.4    68 Begotten by that wind, and showers.
```

showes   frequency: 6   relative frequency: 0.00008
```
     p. 118 FOREST 13      65 Because that studies spectacles, and showes,
     p. 240 UNDERWOOD 67   31 6. ERAT. Shee showes so farre above
     p. 403 UNGATHERED 34  32 That doe cry vp ye Machine, & ye Showes!
     p. 403 UNGATHERED 34  39 To hold her vp. O Showes! Showes! Mighty
                              Showes!
```

showest. See "shew'st," "show'st."

showing. See "shewing."

shown. See "shewen," "shew'n," "shew'ne," "showne."

showne   frequency: 6   relative frequency: 0.00008
```
     p.  58 EPIGRAMS 91    13 I speake thy other graces, not lesse showne,
     p. 147 UNDERWOOD 7    21 And feare much more, that more of him be showne.
     p. 160 UNDERWOOD 14   65 Monarch in Letters! 'Mongst thy Titles showne
     p. 188 UNDERWOOD 34   18 And scorn'd, thou'<h>ast showne thy malice, but
                              hast fail'd.
     p. 317 HORACE 2      269 What so is showne, I not beleeve, and hate.
     p. 402 UNGATHERED 34   9 Drawne Aristotle on vs! & thence showne
```

showre   frequency: 2   relative frequency: 0.00002
```
     p. 333 HORACE 2      612 Looke pale, distill a showre (was never meant)
     p. 413 UNGATHERED 41  31 All, pouring their full showre of graces downe,
```

showres   frequency: 1   relative frequency: 0.00001
```
     p. 290 UNDERWOOD 85   29 Then when the thundring Jove his Snow and
                              showres
```

shows. See "shewes," "shews," "shew's," "showes."

show'st   frequency: 1   relative frequency: 0.00001
```
     p. 235 UNDERWOOD 62    9 Nay, and in this, thou show'st to value more
```

showt   frequency: 1   relative frequency: 0.00001
```
   **p. 117 PANEGYRE      153 The length'ned showt, as when th'artillery
```

shreds   frequency: 1   relative frequency: 0.00001
```
     p.  45 EPIGRAMS 56    14 From locks of wooll, or shreds from the whole
                              peece?
```

shrewsbury   frequency: 1   relative frequency: 0.00001
```
     p. 394 UNGATHERED 28  t3 and Countesse of Shrewsbury:--
```

shrieues   frequency: 1   relative frequency: 0.00001
```
    *p. 493 TO HIMSELF     23 As the Shrieues crusts, and nasty as his fish-
```

shrin'd   frequency: 1   relative frequency: 0.00001
```
     p. 369 UNGATHERED 6  106 To him, and he there shrin'd;
```

shrine   frequency: 1   relative frequency: 0.00001
```
     p. 174 UNDERWOOD 22   29 Who as an off'ring at your shrine,
```

shrink. See "shrinke."

shrinke   frequency: 2   relative frequency: 0.00002
    p. 61 EPIGRAMS 95   20 Thou need'st not shrinke at voyce of after-times;
    p. 168 UNDERWOOD 15   186 Thou shrinke or start not, but be alwayes one;

shrouds. See "shrowdes."

shrowdes   frequency: 1   relative frequency: 0.00001
    p. 403 UNGATHERED 34   34 And peering forth of Iris in ye Shrowdes!

shrub   frequency: 2   relative frequency: 0.00002
    p. 171 UNDERWOOD 20   t1 A Satyricall Shrub.
    p. 172 UNDERWOOD 21   t1 A little Shrub growing by.

shrunk. See "shrunke."

shrunke   frequency: 3   relative frequency: 0.00004
   *p. 493 TO HIMSELF   45 And though thy nerues be shrunke, and blood be
                              cold,
    p. 100 FOREST 4   14 Yet art thou both shrunke vp, and old,
    p. 220 UNDERWOOD 47   68 Oylie Expansions, or shrunke durtie folds,

shun   frequency: 2   relative frequency: 0.00002
    See also "shunne."
    p. 101 FOREST 4   33 If these, who haue but sense, can shun
    p. 335 HORACE 2   644 And shun to touch him, as a man that were

shunne   frequency: 2   relative frequency: 0.00002
    p. 59 EPIGRAMS 92   38 On them: And therefore doe not onely shunne
    p. 119 FOREST 13   89 You, Madame, yong haue learn'd to shunne these
                              shelues,

shunnes   frequency: 1   relative frequency: 0.00001
    p. 341 HORACE 1   127 Yet .... shunnes to .. ..

shunning   frequency: 2   relative frequency: 0.00002
    p. 224 UNDERWOOD 50   5 Not only shunning by your act, to doe
    p. 307 HORACE 2   43 So, shunning faults, to greater fault doth lead,

shuns   frequency: 2   relative frequency: 0.00002
    See also "shunnes."
    p. 76 EPIGRAMS 119   4 Shuns prease, for two maine causes, poxe, and
                              debt,
    p. 321 HORACE 2   335 Or, whilst he shuns the Earth, to catch at Aire

shut   frequency: 7   relative frequency: 0.00010
    p. 33 EPIGRAMS 21   2 His neck fenc'd round with ruffe! his eyes halfe
                              shut!
    p. 119 FOREST 13   92 Into your harbor, and all passage shut
    p. 157 UNDERWOOD 13   138 Are nothing till that comes to bind and shut.
    p. 187 UNDERWOOD 33   10 Upon the reverend Pleaders; doe now shut
    p. 197 UNDERWOOD 40   21 Not, like a Midas, shut up in himselfe,
    p. 258 UNDERWOOD 75   185 They both are slip'd to Bed; Shut fast the
                              Doore,
    p. 400 UNGATHERED 31   27 And when the flesh, here, shut vp day,

shuts   frequency: 1   relative frequency: 0.00001
    p. 263 UNDERWOOD 79   10 And shuts the old. Haste, haste, all loyall
                              Swaines,

shutter   frequency: 1   relative frequency: 0.00001
    p. 289 U'WOOD 84.9   219 The last of houres, and shutter up of all;

sibyl. See "sybil."

sicilian   frequency: 2   relative frequency: 0.00002
    p. 207 UNDERWOOD 43   96 To speake the fate of the Sicilian Maid
    p. 335 HORACE 2   660 Of the Sicilian Poet Empedocles,

sick   frequency: 3   relative frequency: 0.00004
    p. 144 UNDERWOOD 4   2 Lest I be sick with seeing;
    p. 164 UNDERWOOD 15   68 Be at their Visits, see 'hem squemish, sick,
    p. 338 HORACE 1   9 .... sick mens .... form'd ..
                              ....

sick-mens   frequency: 1   relative frequency: 0.00001
    p. 305 HORACE 2   9 Whose shapes, like sick-mens dreames, are fain'd
                              so vaine,

sicknes   frequency: 1   relative frequency: 0.00001
    p. 394 UNGATHERED 28   19 To call on Sicknes still, to be her Guest,

sickness. See "sicknes," "sicknesse."

sicknesse   frequency: 8   relative frequency: 0.00011
    p.   37 EPIGRAMS 32   10 Seas, serenes, swords, shot, sicknesse, all are
                                  there.
    p. 102 FOREST 4   62 To age, misfortune, sicknesse, griefe:
    p. 104 FOREST 8   7 Take heed, Sicknesse, what you doe,
    p. 104 FOREST 8   t1 TO SICKNESSE.
    p. 105 FOREST 8   14 Sicknesse; onely on vs men.
    p. 150 UNDERWOOD 10   14 Loves sicknesse, and his noted want of worth,
    p. 186 UNDERWOOD 31   5 So, from all sicknesse, may you rise to health,
    p. 235 UNDERWOOD 62   t3 for a 100. pounds he sent me in my sicknesse.

side   frequency: 16   relative frequency: 0.00023
  **p. 114 PANEGYRE   43 Others on ground runne gazing by his side,
    p.   33 EPIGRAMS 21   4 Forbidd' his side! and nothing, but the word
    p.   86 EPIGRAMS 133   67 Betweene two walls; where, on one side, to scar
                                  men,
    p.   94 FOREST 2   28 The purpled pheasant, with the speckled side:
    p.   93 FOREST 3   61 They thinke not, then, which side the cause shall
                                  leese,
    p. 128 UNDERWOOD 1.1   46 And with thy Angels, placed side, by side,
    p. 134 UNDERWOOD 2.4   9 That still were to run by her side,
    p. 137 UNDERWOOD 2.5   40 And the Glasse hangs by her side,
    p. 166 UNDERWOOD 15   131 Or side, but threatens Ruine. The whole Day
    p. 186 UNDERWOOD 33   4 Where mutuall frauds are fought, and no side
                                  yeild;
    p. 253 UNDERWOOD 75   34 Their Sister-tunes, from Thames his either
                                  side,
    p. 264 UNDERWOOD 79   18 9. See where he walkes <10> with MIRA by his side.
    p. 281 U'WOOD 84.8   18 Up to their Ancestors; the rivers side,
    p. 394 UNGATHERED 28   23 Importune wish; and by her lou'd Lords side
    p. 413 UNGATHERED 41   997 on the backe side.

sided   frequency: 1   relative frequency: 0.00001
    p. 403 UNGATHERED 34   36 Not they that sided her, Dame Poetry,

sides   frequency: 4   relative frequency: 0.00005
    p.   38 EPIGRAMS 37   2 But as they come, on both sides he takes fees,
    p.   66 EPIGRAMS 102   8 To which, yet, of the sides himselfe he owes.
    p. 207 UNDERWOOD 43   104 Whom Faction had not drawne to studie sides.
    p. 212 UNDERWOOD 43   204 On both sides doe your mischiefes with delight;

sidney. See "sydney."

sidney's. See "sydney's," "sydnyes."

siege   frequency: 1   relative frequency: 0.00001
    p. 214 UNDERWOOD 44   40 The Berghen siege, and taking in Breda,

sigh'd   frequency: 1   relative frequency: 0.00001
    p. 209 UNDERWOOD 43   148 Nay, sigh'd a Sister, 'twas the Nun, Kate
                                  Arden,

sighes   frequency: 1   relative frequency: 0.00001
    p. 288 U'WOOD 84.9   185 Her broken sighes did never misse whole sense:

sighs. See "sighes."

sight   frequency: 33   relative frequency: 0.00047
    p.   31 EPIGRAMS 14   8 What sight in searching the most antique springs!
    p.   73 EPIGRAMS 114   4 In meere out-formes, vntill he lost his sight,
    p.   96 FOREST 3   9 Nor throng'st (when masquing is) to haue a sight
    p.   97 FOREST 3   28 And giu'st thy gladder guests the sight;
    p. 132 UNDERWOOD 2.2   13 But, he had not gain'd his sight
    p. 132 UNDERWOOD 2.2   25 At my face, that tooke my sight,
    p. 134 UNDERWOOD 2.4   8 But enjoy such a sight,
    p. 138 UNDERWOOD 2.6   17 So, as those that had your sight,
    p. 138 UNDERWOOD 2.6   32 Or have charg'd his sight of Crime,
    p. 138 UNDERWOOD 2.6   33 To have left all sight for you:
    p. 151 UNDERWOOD 11   14 As since he dares not come within my sight.
    p. 152 UNDERWOOD 12   26 As twice to trespasse in his sight,
    p. 160 UNDERWOOD 14   48 Forme, Art or Ensigne, that hath scap'd your
                                  sight?
    p. 177 UNDERWOOD 25   16 May shine (through every chincke) to every sight
    p. 180 UNDERWOOD 26   8 And now are out of sight.
    p. 186 UNDERWOOD 32   15 When this appeares, just Lord, to your sharp
                                  sight,
    p. 200 UNDERWOOD 42   12 In all that is call'd lovely: take my sight

sight (cont.)

p. 214 UNDERWOOD 44	42	And Spinola have blushed at the sight.
p. 220 UNDERWOOD 47	70	As but to stumble in her sight were shame;
p. 233 UNDERWOOD 59	13	This were a spectacle! A sight to draw
p. 241 UNDERWOOD 69	12	All live dogs from the lane, and his shops sight,
p. 244 UNDERWOOD 70	38	Hee stoop'd in all mens sight
p. 252 UNDERWOOD 75	4	Betweene thy Tropicks, to arrest thy sight,
p. 284 U'WOOD 84.9	65	And the whole Banquet is full sight of God!
p. 286 U'WOOD 84.9	122	Where Hee will be, all Beautie to the Sight;
p. 291 UNDERWOOD 85	61	Among these Cates how glad the sight doth come
p. 305 HORACE 2	6	Admitted to the sight, although his friends,
p. 317 HORACE 2	262	Much from the sight, which faire report will make
p. 331 HORACE 2	543	Will in the light be view'd: This, once, the sight
p. 366 UNGATHERED 6	26	As the whole heard in sight,
p. 392 UNGATHERED 26	71	Sweet Swan of Auon! what a sight it were
p. 398 UNGATHERED 30	78	And stop my sight, in euery line I goe.
p. 400 UNGATHERED 31	37	Seal'd, and deliuer'd to her, in the sight

sighted. See "quickest-sighted."

sightes   frequency: 1   relative frequency: 0.00001
    p. 361 UNGATHERED 1   20 till th'one hath drownd the other in our sightes,

sights   frequency: 2   relative frequency: 0.00002
    See alsc "sightes."
    p. 40 EPIGRAMS 42   10 Harsh sights at home, GILES wisheth he were
                              blind.
    p. 220 UNDERWOOD 47   66 As are the Glorious Scenes, at the great
                              sights;

sign. See "signe."

signe   frequency: 4   relative frequency: 0.00005
    p. 262 UNDERWOOD 78   17 In signe the Subject, and the Song will live,
    p. 369 UNGATHERED 6   109 In heau'n the Signe of old Eridanus:
    p. 380 UNGATHERED 12   26 How long he did stay, at what signe he did Inne.
    p. 405 UNGATHERED 34   87 On ye new priming of thy old Signe postes

signes   frequency: 1   relative frequency: 0.00001
    p. 30 EPIGRAMS 12   14 Signes to new bond, forfeits: and cryes, god
                              payes.

signs. See "signes."

silence   frequency: 5   relative frequency: 0.00007
  **p. 114 PANEGYRE   40 And only with red silence him salute.
    p. 174 UNDERWOOD 23   13 If hence thy silence be,
    p. 197 UNDERWOOD 40   14 Of vowes so sacred, and in silence made;
    p. 284 U'WOOD 84.9   78 With silence, and amazement! not with rude,
    p. 293 UNDERWOOD 86   36 With an uncomely silence failes my tongue?

silent   frequency: 6   relative frequency: 0.00008
    p. 47 EPIGRAMS 63   9 And can to these be silent, Salisburie,
    p. 103 FOREST 6   17 In the silent sommer-nights,
    p. 120 FOREST 14   8 Stand silent by,
    p. 199 UNDERWOOD 41   21 Or like a Ghost walke silent amongst men,.
    p. 224 UNDERWOOD 50   8 No friend to vertue, could be silent here.
    p. 239 UNDERWOOD 67   5 Be silent, to the people

silenus   frequency: 1   relative frequency: 0.00001
    p. 321 HORACE 2   348 Or old Silenus, Bacchus guard, and Nurse.

silk. See "silke."

silke   frequency: 4   relative frequency: 0.00005
    p. 31 EPIGRAMS 15   1 All men are wormes: But this no man. In silke
    p. 200 UNDERWOOD 42   26 For Silke will draw some sneaking Songster
                              thither.
    p. 200 UNDERWOOD 42   30 Where I may handle Silke, as free, and neere,
    p. 273 U'WOOD 84.1   23 With Sayles of silke, as the first notes

silken   frequency: 1   relative frequency: 0.00001
    p. 263 UNDERWOOD 79   5 Of the New Yeare, in a new silken warpe,

silkes   frequency: 4   relative frequency: 0.00005
    p. 54 EPIGRAMS 82   1 SVRLY'S old whore in her new silkes doth
                              swim:
    p. 202 UNDERWOOD 42   72 Varietie of Silkes were on th'Exchange!
    p. 202 UNDERWOOD 42   74 Another answers, 'Lasse, those Silkes are none,

silkes (cont.)
    p. 275 U'WOOD 84.3   2 What make these Velvets, Silkes, and Lawne,

silks. See "silkes."

silleries   frequency: 1   relative frequency: 0.00001
    p. 69 EPIGRAMS 107   21 For newes) your Ville-royes, and Silleries,

silliest. See "seeliest."

siluer   frequency: 1   relative frequency: 0.00001
    p. 103 FOREST 6   15 Or the drops in siluer Thames,

silvane. See "sylvane."

silvanus. See "sylvanus."

silver   frequency: 1   relative frequency: 0.00001
    See also "siluer."
    p. 229 UNDERWOOD 54   13 That's six in silver; now within the Socket

simo   frequency: 1   relative frequency: 0.00001
    p. 321 HORACE 2   347 Simo; and, of a talent wip'd his purse;

simple   frequency: 6   relative frequency: 0.00008
  *p. 492 TO HIMSELF   13 'Twere simple fury, still, thy selfe to waste
    p. 65 EPIGRAMS 101   39 We innocently met. No simple word,
    p. 101 FOREST 4   41 My tender, first, and simple yeeres
    p. 246 UNDERWOOD 70   105 But simple love of greatnesse, and of good;
    p. 307 HORACE 2   32 Be simple quite throughout, and wholly one.
    p. 319 HORACE 2   289 But soft, and simple, at few holes breath'd time

simples   frequency: 1   relative frequency: 0.00001
    p. 361 UNGATHERED 1   12 the sweetest simples, and most soueraigne seedes.

simplesse   frequency: 1   relative frequency: 0.00001
    p. 253 UNDERWOOD 75   44 On all that come her Simplesse to rebuke!

simplicitie   frequency: 4   relative frequency: 0.00005
    p. 62 EPIGRAMS 96   5 As free simplicitie, to dis-auow,
    p. 78 EPIGRAMS 122   4 The world's pure gold, and wise simplicitie;
    p. 270 UNDERWOOD 83   40 Her wary guardes, her wise simplicitie,
    p. 284 U'WOOD 84.9   76 Will honour'd be in all simplicitie!

simplicity   frequency: 1   relative frequency: 0.00001
    See also "simplicitie."
    p. 295 UNDERWOOD 90   7 A wise simplicity; freindes alike-stated;

simply   frequency: 1   relative frequency: 0.00001
    p. 169 UNDERWOOD 17   12 Simply my Band, his trust in me forsakes,

sin   frequency: 5   relative frequency: 0.00007
    See also "sinne," "sinne's," "sin's."
 **p. 113 PANEGYRE   11 And snore supinely in the stall of sin:
    p. 76 EPIGRAMS 118   5 Thus, in his belly, can he change a sin,
    p. 171 UNDERWOOD 20   2 Forgive me this one foolish deadly sin,
    p. 172 UNDERWOOD 20   20 Thinke but the Sin of all her sex, 'tis she!
    p. 193 UNDERWOOD 38   90 Upon the hope to have another sin

since   frequency: 52   relative frequency: 0.00075
    See also "long-since."
 **p. 115 PANEGYRE   85 "That princes, since they know it is their fate,
    p. 38 EPIGRAMS 35   10 And since, the whole land was preseru'd for thee.
    p. 49 EPIGRAMS 67   1 Since men haue left to doe praise-worthy things,
    p. 50 EPIGRAMS 70   7 Then, since we (more then many) these truths
                                know:
    p. 53 EPIGRAMS 79   3 Or then, or since, about our Muses springs,
    p. 56 EPIGRAMS 87   6 Since when, hee's sober againe, and all play's
                                made.
    p. 57 EPIGRAMS 90   13 MILL was the same. Since, both his body and
                                face
    p. 60 EPIGRAMS 94   7 Yet, Satyres, since the most of mankind bee
    p. 63 EPIGRAMS 97   17 Since he was gone, more then the one he weares.
    p. 73 EPIGRAMS 113   7 For since, what ignorance, what pride is fled!
    p. 76 EPIGRAMS 119   3 Cryes out 'gainst cocking, since he cannot bet,
    p. 77 EPIGRAMS 120   19 But viewing him since (alas, too late)
    p. 83 EPIGRAMS 132   6 Since they can only iudge, that can conferre.
    p. 89 EPIGRAMS 133   194 The citie since hath rais'd a Pyramide.
    p. 93 FOREST 1   11 That since, my numbers are so cold,
    p. 98 FOREST 3   65 And such since thou canst make thine owne
                                content,

since (cont.)

p. 100 FOREST 4	1	False world, good-night: since thou hast brought
p. 101 FOREST 4	43	Since stird'st vp iealousies and feares,
p. 106 FOREST 9	15	Since when it growes, and smells, I sweare,
p. 109 FOREST 11	5	Which to effect (since no brest is so sure,
p. 119 FOREST 13	110	They speake; since you are truly that rare wife,
p. 121 FOREST 14	27	Since he doth lacke
p. 129 UNDERWOOD 1.2	22	With all since bought.
p. 137 UNDERWOOD 2.6	2	Since I drew a Morning kisse
p. 151 UNDERWOOD 11	14	As since he dares not come within my sight.
p. 152 UNDERWOOD 12	35	For truly, since he left to be,
p. 159 UNDERWOOD 14	23	Since, being deceiv'd, I turne a sharper eye
p. 175 UNDERWOOD 23	31	And since our Daintie age,
p. 176 UNDERWOOD 25	t3	since lost, and recovered.
p. 181 UNDERWOOD 27	21	Hath Petrarch since his Laura rais'd
p. 182 UNDERWOOD 28	3	Since I exscribe your Sonnets, am become
p. 184 UNDERWOOD 29	47	That they long since have refused
p. 187 UNDERWOOD 33	13	Thou art my Cause: whose manners since I knew,
p. 199 UNDERWOOD 41	1	Since you must goe, and I must bid farewell,
p. 203 UNDERWOOD 43	13	That since thou tak'st all envious care and paine,
p. 209 UNDERWOOD 43	138	Left! and wit since to cover it with Tiles.
p. 220 UNDERWOOD 48	1	Since, Bacchus, thou art father
p. 225 UNDERWOOD 51	8	Since Bacon, and thy Lord was borne, and here;
p. 225 UNDERWOOD 51	11	What then his Father was, that since is hee,
p. 230 UNDERWOOD 55	5	But since the Wine hath steep'd my braine,
p. 278 U'WOOD 84.4	15	Since nothing can report that flame,
p. 307 HORACE 2	48	But in the maine worke haplesse: since he knowes
p. 323 HORACE 2	375	Nor is't long since, with patience take
p. 333 HORACE 2	591	Who, since, to sing the Pythian rites is heard,
p. 371 UNGATHERED 8	9	Their motiues were, since it had not to do
p. 379 UNGATHERED 12	12	Since he treads in no other Mans steps but his owne.
p. 390 UNGATHERED 25	9	But, since he cannot, Reader, looke
p. 391 UNGATHERED 26	40	Sent forth, or since did from their ashes come.
p. 392 UNGATHERED 26	50	As, since, she will vouchsafe no other Wit.
p. 392 UNGATHERED 26	79	Which, since thy flight from hence, hath mourn'd like night,
p. 394 UNGATHERED 28	16	But of one Husband; and since he left life,
p. 420 UNGATHERED 48	28	Yett: since the bright, and wyse,

sincere   frequency: 2   relative frequency: 0.00002
p. 169 UNDERWOOD 17	6	Is done for gaine: If't be, 'tis not sincere.
p. 187 UNDERWOOD 33	39	Thy sincere practise, breeds not thee a fame

sindge   frequency: 1   relative frequency: 0.00001
p. 205 UNDERWOOD 43	53	Sindge Capons, or poore Pigges, dropping their eyes;

sinewes   frequency: 1   relative frequency: 0.00001
p. 307 HORACE 2	37	Hath neither soule, nor sinewes. Loftie he

sinews.   See "sinewes."

sing   frequency: 40   relative frequency: 0.00057
*p. 494 TO HIMSELF	51	But, when they heare thee sing
p. 48 EPIGRAMS 66	2	To greatnesse, CARY, I sing that, and thee.
p. 51 EPIGRAMS 73	9	Item, the babylonian song you sing;
p. 65 EPIGRAMS 101	34	Are all but LVTHERS beere, to this I sing.
p. 74 EPIGRAMS 115	13	Except the duell. Can sing songs, and catches;
p. 84 EPIGRAMS 133	21	I sing the braue aduenture of two wights,
p. 107 FOREST 10	1	And must I sing? what subiect shall I chuse?
p. 108 FOREST 10	30	And now an Epode to deepe eares I sing.
p. 111 FOREST 11	68	As this chaste loue we sing.
p. 115 FOREST 12	76	To curious light, the notes, I then shall sing,
p. 119 FOREST 13	100	Heare, what the Muses sing about thy roote,
p. 120 FOREST 14	4	Some sing,
p. 130 UNDERWOOD 1.3	1	I sing the birth, was borne to night,
p. 143 UNDERWOOD 3	13	What need of mee? doe you but sing,
p. 144 UNDERWOOD 3	21	O sing not you then lest the best
p. 145 UNDERWOOD 5	3	To make us still sing o're, and o're,
p. 145 UNDERWOOD 5	6	And if wee must, let's sing of you.
p. 173 UNDERWOOD 22	2	And yours of whom I sing be such
p. 175 UNDERWOOD 23	35	But sing high and aloofe,
p. 177 UNDERWOOD 25	13	That I may sing my thoughts, in some unvulgar straine.
p. 182 UNDERWOOD 27	32	Where men may see whom I doe sing?
p. 225 UNDERWOOD 51	19	Give me a deep-crown'd-Bowle, that I may sing
p. 241 UNDERWOOD 68	6	His Poet leave to sing his House-hold true;

sing (cont.)
   p. 263 UNDERWOOD 79   7 We sing the best of Monarchs, Masters, Men;
   p. 264 UNDERWOOD 79   20 Shep. Of PAN wee sing, the best of Hunters,
                             PAN,
   p. 264 UNDERWOOD 79   27 Chor. Rivers, and Vallies, Eccho what wee
                             sing.
   p. 264 UNDERWOOD 79   28 Shep. Of PAN wee sing, the Chiefe of
                             Leaders, PAN,
   p. 264 UNDERWOOD 79   35 Chor. Rivers, and Valleys, Eccho what wee
                             sing.
   p. 270 UNDERWOOD 83   63 Let Angels sing her glories, who did call
   p. 274 U'WOOD 84.2   1 I sing the just, and uncontrol'd Descent
   p. 285 U'WOOD 84.9   89 That, planted round, there sing before the Lamb,
   p. 292 UNDERWOOD 86   26 The Youths and tender Maids shall sing thy
                             praise:
   p. 313 HORACE 2   196 I sing a noble Warre, and Priam's Fate.
   p. 317 HORACE 2   277 Must maintaine manly; not be heard to sing,
   p. 319 HORACE 2   314 Those that did sing, and act: their faces dy'd
   p. 329 HORACE 2   531 Deserves no pardon; or who'd play, and sing
   p. 333 HORACE 2   591 Who, since, to sing the Pythian rites is heard,
   p. 366 UNGATHERED 6   18 Neere which, the Thespiad's sing;
   p. 368 UNGATHERED 6   63 When him alone we sing)
   p. 369 UNGATHERED 6   102 (Which makes him sing

singe. See "sindge."

singer   frequency: 2   relative frequency: 0.00002
   p. 353 HORACE 1   579 .... of the singer Apollo, and Muses fam'd
   p. 368 UNGATHERED 6   73 Haste, Haste, sweete Singer: Nor to Tine,

singing   frequency: 1   relative frequency: 0.00001
   p. 265 UNDERWOOD 79   54 'Tis hee, 'tis hee, in singing hee,

single   frequency: 4   relative frequency: 0.00005
   p. 118 FOREST 13   57 In single paths, dangers with ease are watch'd:
   p. 167 UNDERWOOD 15   158 As a poore single flatterer, without Baud,
   p. 284 U'WOOD 84.9   53 Like single; so, there is a third, commixt,
   p. 389 UNGATHERED 24   3 To say but one, were single. Then it chimes,

sings   frequency: 3   relative frequency: 0.00004
   p. 174 UNDERWOOD 23   10 That not a Nymph now sings?
   p. 202 UNDERWOOD 42   73 Or in Moore-fields, this other night! sings one,
   p. 293 UNDERWOOD 87   10 Who sings so sweet, and with such cunning plaies,

sing'st   frequency: 1   relative frequency: 0.00001
   p. 263 UNDERWOOD 78   22 Good Omen to him, in the note thou sing'st,

sink. See "sinke."

sinke   frequency: 4   relative frequency: 0.00005
   p. 86 EPIGRAMS 133   75 And many a sinke pour'd out her rage anenst 'hem;
   p. 153 UNDERWOOD 13   19 They are the Noblest benefits, and sinke
   p. 172 UNDERWOOD 21   9 Of putrid flesh alive! of blood, the sinke!
   p. 177 UNDERWOOD 25   30 Sinke not beneath these terrors:

sinkes   frequency: 1   relative frequency: 0.00001
   p. 88 EPIGRAMS 133   145 The sinkes ran grease, and haire of meazled hogs,

sinketh   frequency: 1   relative frequency: 0.00001
   p. 331 HORACE 2   564 And highest; sinketh to the lowest, and worst.

sinks. See "sinkes."

sinne   frequency: 26   relative frequency: 0.00037
   p. 33 EPIGRAMS 20   1 Th'expence in odours is a most vaine sinne,
   p. 35 EPIGRAMS 27   8 Wee, sad for him, may glorie, and not sinne.
   p. 41 EPIGRAMS 45   2 My sinne was too much hope of thee, lou'd boy,
   p. 56 EPIGRAMS 87   1 Touch'd with the sinne of false play, in his
                             punque,
   p. 66 EPIGRAMS 102   18 But in the view, doth interrupt their sinne;
   p. 98 FOREST 3   54 (Their rudenesse then is thought no sinne)
   p. 99 FOREST 3   86 By being organes to great sinne,
   p. 102 FOREST 5   15 'Tis no'sinne, loues fruit to steale,
   p. 107 FOREST 10   6 Of his dull god-head, were sinne. Ile implore
   p. 111 FOREST 11   81 Cannot so safely sinne. Their chastitie
   p. 113 FOREST 11   116 Man may securely sinne, but safely neuer.
   p. 114 FOREST 12   31 For what a sinne 'gainst your great fathers
                             spirit,
   p. 116 FOREST 13   10 With sinne and vice, though with a throne
                             endew'd:

sinne (cont.)

p. 119 FOREST 13	85	And call it their braue sinne. For such there be
p. 119 FOREST 13	86	That doe sinne onely for the infamie:
p. 122 FOREST 15	18	Conceiu'd in sinne, and vnto labour borne,
p. 127 UNDERWOOD 1.1	6	By sinne, and Sathan; and my flesh misus'd,
p. 129 UNDERWOOD 1.2	23	Sinne, Death, and Hell,
p. 130 UNDERWOOD 1.3	20	Who made himselfe the price of sinne,
p. 191 UNDERWOOD 38	26	As I would urge Authoritie for sinne.
p. 198 UNDERWOOD 40	46	The sinne of Boast, or other countermine
p. 218 UNDERWOOD 47	19	That to speake well, thinke it above all sinne,
p. 234 UNDERWOOD 61	12	A Nations sinne got pardon'd! 'twere a taske
p. 234 UNDERWOOD 61	15	And wee doe weepe, to water, for our sinne.
p. 272 UNDERWOOD 83	99	The Serpents head: Gets above Death, and Sinne,
p. 375 UNGATHERED 10	21	He will expiate this sinne with conuerting the Iewes.

sinners   frequency: 3   relative frequency: 0.00004

p. 127 UNDERWOOD 1.1	9	3. All-gracious God, the Sinners sacrifice,
p. 127 UNDERWOOD 1.1	t1	The Sinners Sacrifice.
p. 141 UNDERWOOD 2.9	32	In loves schoole, and yet no sinners.

sinnes   frequency: 6   relative frequency: 0.00008

p. 53 EPIGRAMS 80	1	The ports of death are sinnes; of life, good deeds:
p. 60 EPIGRAMS 94	9	For none ere tooke that pleasure in sinnes sense,
p. 84 EPIGRAMS 133	17	Laden with plague-sores, and their sinnes, were heard,
p. 112 FOREST 11	89	Then he, which for sinnes penaltie forbeares.
p. 112 FOREST 11	90	His heart sinnes, though he feares.
p. 122 FOREST 15	4	That, laden with my sinnes, I seeke for ease?

sinne's   frequency: 1   relative frequency: 0.00001

p. 364 UNGATHERED 5	4	As farre as Sinne's from lightnesse.

sins. See "night-sinnes," "sinnes," "synns."

sin's   frequency: 1   relative frequency: 0.00001
See also "sinnes," "sinne's."

p. 129 UNDERWOOD 1.2	12	For, sin's so sweet,

sipped. See "sipt."

sipt   frequency: 1   relative frequency: 0.00001

p. 367 UNGATHERED 6	57	Who euer sipt at Baphyre riuer,

sir   frequency: 46   relative frequency: 0.00066
See also "sr," "surship."

p. 33 EPIGRAMS 19	t1	ON SIR COD THE PERFVMED.
p. 33 EPIGRAMS 20	2	Except thou could'st, Sir COD, weare them within.
p. 33 EPIGRAMS 20	t1	TO THE SAME SIR COD.
p. 34 EPIGRAMS 25	t1	ON SIR VOLVPTVOVS BEAST.
p. 35 EPIGRAMS 27	t1	ON SIR IOHN ROE.
p. 36 EPIGRAMS 29	t1	TO SIR ANNVAL TILTER.
p. 37 EPIGRAMS 32	t1	ON SIR IOHN ROE.
p. 42 EPIGRAMS 46	1	Is this the Sir, who, some wast wife to winne,
p. 42 EPIGRAMS 46	t1	TO SIR LVCKLESSE WOO-ALL.
p. 42 EPIGRAMS 47	1	Sir LVCKLESSE, troth, for lucks sake passe by one:
p. 42 EPIGRAMS 50	t1	TO SIR COD.
p. 48 EPIGRAMS 66	t1	TO SIR HENRIE CARY.
p. 55 EPIGRAMS 85	t1	TO SIR HENRY GOODYERE.
p. 58 EPIGRAMS 91	t1	TO SIR HORACE VERE.
p. 60 EPIGRAMS 93	t1	TO SIR IOHN RADCLIFFE.
p. 61 EPIGRAMS 95	t1	TO SIR HENRIE SAVILE.
p. 63 EPIGRAMS 98	t1	TO SIR THOMAS ROE.
p. 64 EPIGRAMS 101	1	To night, graue sir, both my poore house, and I
p. 64 EPIGRAMS 101	7	It is the faire acceptance, Sir, creates
p. 68 EPIGRAMS 106	t1	TO SIR EDWARD HERBERT.
p. 70 EPIGRAMS 109	t1	TO SIR HENRY NEVIL.
p. 73 EPIGRAMS 113	t1	TO SIR THOMAS OVERBVRY.
p. 75 EPIGRAMS 116	t1	TO SIR WILLIAM IEPHSON.
p. 76 EPIGRAMS 119	t1	TO SIR RAPH SHELTON
p. 79 EPIGRAMS 125	t1	TO SIR WILLIAM VVEDALE.
p. 96 FOREST 3	t1	TO SIR ROBERT WROTH.
p. 120 FOREST 14	t2	TO SIR WILLIAM SYDNEY, ON HIS
p. 153 UNDERWOOD 13	t1	An Epistle to Sir EDWARD SACVILE,
p. 154 UNDERWOOD 13	53	Now dam'mee, Sir, if you shall not command

sir (cont.)
```
     p. 156 UNDERWOOD 13    109 And you, Sir, know it well, to whom I write,
     p. 162 UNDERWOOD 15     19 See the grave, sower, and supercilious Sir
     p. 169 UNDERWOOD 17      1 They are not, Sir, worst Owers, that doe pay
     p. 188 UNDERWOOD 34      7 Art, her false servant; Nor, for Sir Hugh
                                Plat,
     p. 189 UNDERWOOD 37      1 Sir, I am thankfull, first, to heaven, for you;
     p. 214 UNDERWOOD 44     33 Well did thy craftie Clerke, and Knight, Sir
                                Hugh,
     p. 217 UNDERWOOD 46     t1 An Epigram on Sir Edward Coke, when he was
     p. 220 UNDERWOOD 47     78 Sir, you are Sealed of the Tribe of Ben.
     p. 228 UNDERWOOD 53     10 Of bold Sir Bevis, and his Arundell:
     p. 231 UNDERWOOD 57      4 To Sir Robert Pie:
     p. 242 UNDERWOOD 70     t2 that noble paire, Sir LVCIVS CARY,
     p. 242 UNDERWOOD 70     t3 and Sir H. MORISON.
     p. 262 UNDERWOOD 78     t3 Husband, Sir KENELME DIGBY.
     p. 272 UNDERWOOD 84     t6 late Wife of Sir KENELME DIGBY,
                                Knight:
     p. 285 U'WOOD 84.9      97 And will you, worthy Sonne, Sir, knowing this,
     p. 331 HORACE 2        545 You Sir, the elder brother, though you are
     p. 400 UNGATHERED 32    t2 Friend, Sir Iohn Beaumont, Baronet.
```

sire   frequency: 2   relative frequency: 0.00002
```
     p. 295 UNDERWOOD 90      3 Not labour'd for, but left thee by thy Sire;
     p. 307 HORACE 2         33 Most Writers, noble Sire, and either Sonne,
```

sirenas   frequency: 1   relative frequency: 0.00001
```
     p. 398 UNGATHERED 30    80 I looke on Cynthia, and Sirenas sport,
```

sires   frequency: 2   relative frequency: 0.00002
```
     p.  99 FOREST 3         77 Let him, then hardest sires, more disinherit,
     p. 289 UNDERWOOD 85      3 With his owne Oxen tills his Sires left lands,
```

sirrup   frequency: 1   relative frequency: 0.00001
```
     p. 197 UNDERWOOD 40      5 And take some sirrup after; so doe I,
```

sis   frequency: 1   relative frequency: 0.00001
```
     p. 140 UNDERWOOD 2.8    25 Or with Secretarie Sis
```

sister   frequency: 10   relative frequency: 0.00014
```
   **p. 114 PANEGYRE         55 To her great sister: saue that modestie,
     p.  74 EPIGRAMS 115     22 'Twill see it's sister naked, ere a sword.
     p. 165 UNDERWOOD 15     93 The brother trades a sister; and the friend
     p. 209 UNDERWOOD 43    148 Nay, sigh'd a Sister, 'twas the Nun, Kate
                                Arden,
     p. 240 UNDERWOOD 67     27 And Sister to just Lewis!
     p. 252 UNDERWOOD 75    t11 and Sister of the Surviving Duke
     p. 253 UNDERWOOD 75     43 And Sister: darting forth a dazling light
     p. 263 UNDERWOOD 79      1 New yeares, expect new gifts: Sister, your
                                Harpe,
     p. 264 UNDERWOOD 79     25 Sister of PAN, and glory of the Spring:
     p. 285 U'WOOD 84.9     117 There shall the Brother, with the Sister walke,
```

sister-tunes   frequency: 1   relative frequency: 0.00001
```
     p. 253 UNDERWOOD 75     34 Their Sister-tunes, from Thames his either
                                side,
```

sisters   frequency: 2   relative frequency: 0.00002
```
     p. 107 FOREST 10        23 Though he would steale his sisters
                                PEGASVS,
     p. 270 UNDERWOOD 83     58 Chear'd her faire Sisters in her race to runne!
```

sit   frequency: 16   relative frequency: 0.00023
```
   **p. 113 PANEGYRE         12 Where Murder, Rapine, Lust, doe sit within,
     p.  68 EPIGRAMS 107      2 That's, sit, and eate: doe not my eares abuse.
     p.  95 FOREST 2         65 And I not faine to sit (as some, this day,
     p.  98 FOREST 3         57 Sit mixt with losse of state, or reuerence.
     p.  99 FOREST 3         83 And brooding o're it sit, with broadest eyes,
     p. 137 UNDERWOOD 2.5    35 Where I sit and proyne my wings
     p. 138 UNDERWOOD 2.6    13 Or, that did you sit, or walke,
     p. 140 UNDERWOOD 2.8    21 Nay, I will not let you sit
     p. 142 U'WOOD 2.10       4 His Clothes rich, and band sit neat,
     p. 146 UNDERWOOD 6       3 We were not bred to sit on stooles,
     p. 277 U'WOOD 84.4       8 To draw a thing that cannot sit.
     p. 286 U'WOOD 84.9     145 In his eternall Kingdome, where we sit
     p. 288 U'WOOD 84.9     195 Would sit in an Infirmery, whole dayes
     p. 331 HORACE 2        568 Or trundling Wheele, he can sit still, from all;
     p. 408 UNGATHERED 36    13 That sit vpon ye Comon Draught: or Strand!
     p. 414 UNGATHERED 42     8 That sit to censure Playes, yet know not when,
```

sits   frequency: 7   relative frequency: 0.00010
    p. 149 UNDERWOOD 9   10 That sits in shadow of Apollo's tree.
    p. 164 UNDERWOOD 15   69 Ready to cast, at one, whose band sits ill,
    p. 200 UNDERWOOD 42   8 His lynes, and hourely sits the Poets horse?
    p. 251 UNDERWOOD 74   14 Wherein she sits so richly drest,
    p. 315 HORACE 2   222 And sits, till th'Epilogue saies Clap, or
                              Crowne:
    p. 370 UNGATHERED 8   1 The wise, and many-headed Bench, that sits
    p. 657 L. CONVIVALES   10 That sits watering with the Muses.

sitting   frequency: 2   relative frequency: 0.00002
    p. 275 U'WOOD 84.3   1 Sitting, and ready to be drawne,
    p. 277 U'WOOD 84.3   32 Next sitting we will draw her mind.

six   frequency: 2   relative frequency: 0.00002
    See also "sixe," "sixe-pac'd."
    p. 210 UNDERWOOD 43   172 Will be remembred by Six Clerkes, to one.
    p. 229 UNDERWOOD 54   13 That's six in silver; now within the Socket

six-pence   frequency: 1   relative frequency: 0.00001
    p. 371 UNGATHERED 8   7 That may iudge for his six-pence) had, before

sixe   frequency: 5   relative frequency: 0.00007
    p. 33 EPIGRAMS 22   5 At sixe moneths end, shee parted hence
    p. 58 EPIGRAMS 92   4 At sixe and twentie, ripe. You shall 'hem meet,
    p. 85 EPIGRAMS 133   34 Of sixe times to, and fro, without embassage,
    p. 210 UNDERWOOD 43   173 But say, all sixe good men, what answer yee?
    p. 327 HORACE 2   472 Sixe ounces. O, when once the canker'd rust,

sixe-pac'd   frequency: 1   relative frequency: 0.00001
    p. 323 HORACE 2   373 Of Trimeter, when yet it was sixe-pac'd,

sixes   frequency: 1   relative frequency: 0.00001
    p. 59 EPIGRAMS 92   21 They meet in sixes, and at euery mart,

sixteenth   frequency: 1   relative frequency: 0.00001
    p. 239 UNDERWOOD 67   2 This sixteenth of November,

sixtieth   frequency: 1   relative frequency: 0.00001
    p. 225 UNDERWOOD 51   7 And so doe I. This is the sixtieth yeare

skarfe   frequency: 1   relative frequency: 0.00001
    p. 56 EPIGRAMS 88   3 That so much skarfe of France, and hat, and
                              fether,

#skeuopoios   frequency: 1   relative frequency: 0.00001
    p. 404 UNGATHERED 34   60 His name is #Skeuopoios wee all knowe,

skie   frequency: 5   relative frequency: 0.00007
  **p. 113 PANEGYRE   7 His former rayes did onely cleare the skie;
  **p. 117 PANEGYRE   154 Of heauen is discharg'd along the skie:
    p. 65 EPIGRAMS 101   16 The skie not falling, thinke we may haue larkes.
    p. 115 FOREST 12   59 Who placed IASONS ARGO in the skie?
    p. 193 UNDERWOOD 38   74 In a calme skie, then when the heauen is horl'd

skies   frequency: 2   relative frequency: 0.00002
    p. 39 EPIGRAMS 40   5 All the gazers on the skies
    p. 368 UNGATHERED 6   77 And vp againe, in skies, and aire to vent

skilfull   frequency: 3   relative frequency: 0.00004
    p. 52 EPIGRAMS 74   6 And no lesse wise, then skilfull in the lawes;
    p. 56 EPIGRAMS 89   3 As skilfull ROSCIVS, and graue
                              AESOPE, men,
    p. 108 FOREST 10A   5 The skilfull mischife of a rovinge Eye

skill   frequency: 14   relative frequency: 0.00020
    p. 31 EPIGRAMS 14   7 What name, what skill, what faith hast thou in
                              things!
    p. 63 EPIGRAMS 99   2 Better'd thy trust to letters; that thy skill;
    p. 76 EPIGRAMS 119   9 Dar'st breath in any ayre; and with safe skill,
    p. 114 FOREST 12   33 His loue vnto the Muses, when his skill
    p. 156 UNDERWOOD 13   107 Or appetite of offending, but a skill,
    p. 159 UNDERWOOD 14   35 Which Grace shall I make love to first? your
                              skill,
    p. 187 UNDERWOOD 33   18 Or skill, to carry out an evill cause!
    p. 217 UNDERWOOD 46   10 And skill in thee, now, grew Authoritie;
    p. 232 UNDERWOOD 59   3 The noble Science, and the maistring skill
    p. 241 UNDERWOOD 69   10 Painted a Dog, that now his subtler skill
    p. 361 UNGATHERED 1   10 Thy skill hath made of ranck dispised weedes;
    p. 386 UNGATHERED 20   7 Or skill of making matches in my life:

skill (cont.)
    p. 406 UNGATHERED 35   7 He may haue skill & iudgment to designe
    p. 421 UNGATHERED 49   11 or Malyce to make ffaultes, wch nowe is skill.

skin   frequency: 2   relative frequency: 0.00002
    See also "sheepes-skin."
    p. 141 UNDERWOOD 2.9   27 Skin as smooth as any rush,
    p. 355 HORACE 1   679 ... . the skin ....

skinkers   frequency: 1   relative frequency: 0.00001
    p. 657 L. CONVIVALES   8 Cries Old Sym, the King of Skinkers;

skins   frequency: 1   relative frequency: 0.00001
    p. 88 EPIGRAMS 133 148 To put the skins, and offall in a pastie?

skip   frequency: 1   relative frequency: 0.00001
    p. 69 EPIGRAMS 107   18 Then can a flea at twise skip i'the Map.

skipping   frequency: 1   relative frequency: 0.00001
    p. 222 UNDERWOOD 48   51 And set us all on skipping,

sky   frequency: 2   relative frequency: 0.00002
    See also "skie," "skye."
  **p. 117 PANEGYRE   144 Those greater bodies of the sky, that strike
    p. 147 UNDERWOOD 7   17 As Summers sky, or purged Ayre,

skye   frequency: 1   relative frequency: 0.00001
    p. 278 U'WOOD 84.4   10 An Eagle towring in the skye,

slack   frequency: 2   relative frequency: 0.00002
    See also "slacke."
    p. 141 UNDERWOOD 2.9   13 Chestnut colour, or more slack
    p. 292 UNDERWOOD 86   7 Too stubborne for Commands so slack:

slacke   frequency: 1   relative frequency: 0.00001
    p. 395 UNGATHERED 29   5 At euery line some pinn thereof should slacke

slain. See "slaine."

slaine   frequency: 2   relative frequency: 0.00002
    p. 137 UNDERWOOD 2.5   31 Is my Mothers! Hearts of slaine
    p. 291 UNDERWOOD 85   59 Or at the Feast of Bounds, the Lambe then
                         slaine,

slander   frequency: 2   relative frequency: 0.00002
    p. 186 UNDERWOOD 32   8 Both arm'd with wealth, and slander to oppose,
    p. 418 UNGATHERED 46   5 Il may Ben Johnson slander so his feete,

slanderers   frequency: 1   relative frequency: 0.00001
    p. 167 UNDERWOOD 15 165 Lewd slanderers, soft whisperers that let blood

slanders   frequency: 1   relative frequency: 0.00001
    p. 75 EPIGRAMS 115   31 An inginer, in slanders, of all fashions,

slaue   frequency: 1   relative frequency: 0.00001
    p. 109 FOREST 11   18 To make our sense our slaue.

slaues   frequency: 1   relative frequency: 0.00001
    p. 86 EPIGRAMS 133   90 Row close then, slaues. Alas, they will beshite
                         vs.

slaughter-house   frequency: 1   relative frequency: 0.00001
  **p. 113 PANEGYRE   14 And make their denne the slaughter-house of
                         soules:

slaughters   frequency: 1   relative frequency: 0.00001
    p. 327 HORACE 2   481 From slaughters, and foule life; and for the same

slave   frequency: 2   relative frequency: 0.00002
    See also "slaue."
    p. 129 UNDERWOOD 1.2   20 To free a slave,
    p. 167 UNDERWOOD 15 160 But he that's both, and slave to boote, shall
                         live,

slaves. See "slaues."

slay   frequency: 1   relative frequency: 0.00001
    p. 145 UNDERWOOD 4   10 For so will sorrow slay me;

sleeked   frequency: 1   relative frequency: 0.00001
     p. 105 FOREST 8   23 Sleeked limmes, and finest blood?

sleep. See "sleepe."

sleepe   frequency: 18   relative frequency: 0.00026
     p. 79 EPIGRAMS 124   10 Th'other let it sleepe with death:
     p. 97 FOREST 3   20 And makes sleepe softer then it is!
     p. 98 FOREST 3   70 That they may sleepe with scarres in age.
     p. 99 FOREST 3   88 The secrets, that shall breake their sleepe:
     p. 109 FOREST 11   23 (That should ring larum to the heart) doth
                                 sleepe,
     p. 110 FOREST 11   49 That falls like sleepe on louers, and combines
     p. 140 UNDERWOOD 2.8   15 You shall neither eat, nor sleepe,
     p. 143 UNDERWOOD 3   14 Sleepe, and the Grave will wake.
     p. 151 UNDERWOOD 11   12 Of sleepe againe, who was his Aid:
     p. 151 UNDERWOOD 11   13 And sleepe so guiltie and afraid,
     p. 190 UNDERWOOD 37   15 And Fame wake for me, when I yeeld to sleepe.
     p. 198 UNDERWOOD 40   42 The Jewell of your name, as close as sleepe
     p. 230 UNDERWOOD 56   15 Sleepe in a Virgins bosome without feare,
     p. 283 U'WOOD 84.9   45 Indeed, she is not dead! but laid to sleepe
     p. 290 UNDERWOOD 85   28 And all invite to easie sleepe.
     p. 295 UNDERWOOD 90   11 Sleepe, that will make the darkest howres
                                 swift-pac't;
     p. 311 HORACE 2   148 And ill-penn'd things, I shall, or sleepe, or
                                 smile.
     p. 329 HORACE 2   537 But, I confesse, that, in a long worke, sleepe

sleepes   frequency: 2   relative frequency: 0.00002
     p. 174 UNDERWOOD 23   3 Knowledge, that sleepes, doth die;
     p. 250 UNDERWOOD 73   6 Who seldome sleepes! whom bad men only hate!

sleepie   frequency: 2   relative frequency: 0.00002
     p. 162 UNDERWOOD 15   7 Mans buried honour, in his sleepie life:
     p. 282 U'WOOD 84.9   15 Sleepie, or stupid Nature, couldst thou part

sleeping   frequency: 2   relative frequency: 0.00002
  **p. 116 PANEGYRE   100 "Where sleeping they could saue, and waking kill;
     p. 213 UNDERWOOD 44   4 T'have wak'd, if sleeping, Spaines Ambassadour,

sleeps. See "sleepes."

sleepy. See "sleepie."

sleight   frequency: 3   relative frequency: 0.00004
     See also "slight."
     p. 59 EPIGRAMS 92   27 To ope' the character. They'haue found the
                                 sleight
     p. 233 UNDERWOOD 59   16 Valour! to sleight it, being done to you!
     p. 313 HORACE 2   191 To render word for word: nor with thy sleight

slid   frequency: 1   relative frequency: 0.00001
     p. 280 U'WOOD 84.4   56 As it slid moulded off from Heaven.

slide   frequency: 1   relative frequency: 0.00001
     p. 290 UNDERWOOD 85   25 Whilst from the higher Bankes doe slide the
                                 floods;

slides. See "back-slides."

sliding   frequency: 1   relative frequency: 0.00001
     See also "slyding."
     p. 309 HORACE 2   86 Still in their leaves, throughout the sliding
                                 yeares,

slie   frequency: 1   relative frequency: 0.00001
     p. 87 EPIGRAMS 133   113 The slie VLYSSES stole in a sheepes-skin,

slight   frequency: 4   relative frequency: 0.00005
     See also "sleight."
     p. 59 EPIGRAMS 92   34 And at the Pope, and Spaine slight faces make.
     p. 129 UNDERWOOD 1.2   27 And slight the same.
     p. 149 UNDERWOOD 9   4 Whom I adore so much, should so slight me,
     p. 279 U'WOOD 84.4   47 Us forth, by some Celestiall slight

slightly   frequency: 1   relative frequency: 0.00001
     p. 117 FOREST 13   25 You will not from the paper slightly passe:

slights   frequency: 1   relative frequency: 0.00001
     p. 45 EPIGRAMS 56   9 And, told of this, he slights it. Tut, such
                                 crimes

slip   frequency: 1   relative frequency: 0.00001
   p. 171 UNDERWOOD 19   19 Slip no occasion; As time stands not still,

slip'd   frequency: 1   relative frequency: 0.00001
   p. 258 UNDERWOOD 75   185 They both are slip'd to Bed; Shut fast the
                                       Doore,

slipped. See "slip'd."

slipper   frequency: 1   relative frequency: 0.00001
   p. 201 UNDERWOOD 42   56 Or slipper was left off, and kisse it too,

slippery   frequency: 1   relative frequency: 0.00001
   p. 395 UNGATHERED 29   2 And see both climing vp the slippery staire

slips   frequency: 2   relative frequency: 0.00002
   p. 193 UNDERWOOD 38   69 He pardons slips, goes by a world of ills,
   p. 216 UNDERWOOD 45   17 For there are many slips, and Counterfeits.

slit   frequency: 2   relative frequency: 0.00002
   p. 404 UNGATHERED 34   48 Mythology there painted on slit deale!
   p. 411 UNGATHERED 39   16 Cropt, branded, slit, neck-stockt; go, you are
                                       stript.

sloth   frequency: 5   relative frequency: 0.00007
   p. 48 EPIGRAMS 66   5 Who, to vpbraid the sloth of this our time,
   p. 152 UNDERWOOD 12   39 Nor wants it here through penurie, or sloth,
   p. 174 UNDERWOOD 23   2 Buried in ease and sloth?
   p. 283 U'WOOD 84.9   21 Looke on thy sloth, and give thy selfe undone,
   p. 317 HORACE 2   246 With sloth, yet greedy still of what's to come:

slow   frequency: 7   relative frequency: 0.00010
   p. 132 UNDERWOOD 2.2   10 Here's a shaft, thou art to slow!
   p. 189 UNDERWOOD 36   14 Now swift, now slow, now tame, now wild;
   p. 237 UNDERWOOD 65   6 The same that thou art promis'd, but be slow,
   p. 315 HORACE 2   233 To endure counsell: a Provider slow
   p. 317 HORACE 2   257 In at the eare, doe stirre the mind more slow
   p. 323 HORACE 2   378 More slow, and come more weightie to the eare:
   p. 369 UNGATHERED 6   117 Slow Arar, nor swift Rhone; the Loyre, nor
                                       Seine,

slower   frequency: 1   relative frequency: 0.00001
   p. 368 UNGATHERED 6   88 Though slower Spaine; and Italy mature.

sluggish   frequency: 2   relative frequency: 0.00002
   p. 45 EPIGRAMS 56   10 The sluggish gaping auditor deuoures;
   p. 250 UNDERWOOD 73   8 Thou sluggish spawne, that canst, but wilt not
                                       see?

sly. See "slie."

slyding   frequency: 1   relative frequency: 0.00001
   p. 407 UNGATHERED 35   10 Wth slyding windowes, & false Lights a top!

small   frequency: 12   relative frequency: 0.00017
   p. 72 EPIGRAMS 112   1 With thy small stocke, why art thou ventring
                                       still,
   p. 148 UNDERWOOD 8   1 Doe but consider this small dust,
   p. 188 UNDERWOOD 34   t2 To the small Poxe.
   p. 211 UNDERWOOD 43   185 Or in small Fagots have him blaze about
   p. 223 UNDERWOOD 49   36 From Court, while yet thy fame hath some small
                                       day;
   p. 238 UNDERWOOD 66   12 To compare small with great, as still we owe
   p. 245 UNDERWOOD 70   73 In small proportions, we just beautie see:
   p. 259 UNDERWOOD 76   22 With their pellets of small wit,
   p. 290 UNDERWOOD 85   33 Or straines on his small forke his subtill nets
   p. 309 HORACE 2   80 If I can give some small increase? when, loe,
   p. 313 HORACE 2   166 Of some small thankfull land: whether he bee
   p. 391 UNGATHERED 26   31 And though thou hadst small Latine, and lesse
                                       Greeke,

small-timbred   frequency: 1   relative frequency: 0.00001
   p. 319 HORACE 2   317 Built a small-timbred Stage, and taught them
                                       talke

smallest   frequency: 3   relative frequency: 0.00004
   p. 153 UNDERWOOD 13   16 The smallest courtesies with thankes, I make
   p. 286 U'WOOD 84.9   151 The smallest Fibre of our flesh; he can
   p. 395 UNGATHERED 29   21 As not the smallest ioint, or gentlest word

smell   frequency: 2   relative frequency: 0.00002
     p. 215 UNDERWOOD 44   90 What, to make legs? yes, and to smell most sweet,
     p. 409 UNGATHERED 37   22 Thy Dirty braines, Men smell thy want of worth.

smelled. See "smelt."

smelling   frequency: 1   relative frequency: 0.00001
     p. 48 EPIGRAMS 65   14 Things manly, and not smelling parasite.

smells   frequency: 1   relative frequency: 0.00001
     p. 106 FOREST 9   15 Since when it growes, and smells, I sweare,

smelt   frequency: 1   relative frequency: 0.00001
     p. 135 UNDERWOOD 2.4   27 Or have smelt o'the bud o'the Brier?

smile   frequency: 3   relative frequency: 0.00004
     p. 225 UNDERWOOD 51   2 How comes it all things so about the<e> smile?
     p. 238 UNDERWOOD 66   10 To make the hearts of a whole Nation smile,
     p. 311 HORACE 2   148 And ill-penn'd things, I shall, or sleepe, or
                              smile.

smiles   frequency: 4   relative frequency: 0.00005
     p. 45 EPIGRAMS 58   3 For offring, with thy smiles, my wit to grace,
     p. 137 UNDERWOOD 2.5   52 Shee is Venus, when she smiles,
     p. 182 UNDERWOOD 28   13 Her joyes, her smiles, her loves, as readers take
     p. 366 UNGATHERED 6   13 Smiles in his Sphaere, to see the rest affect,

smiling   frequency: 4   relative frequency: 0.00005
     p. 120 FOREST 14   1 Now that the harth is crown'd with smiling fire,
     p. 202 UNDERWOOD 42   75 In smiling L'envoye, as he would deride
     p. 292 UNDERWOOD 86   17 And when he smiling finds his Grace
     p. 405 UNGATHERED 34   71 To pitty him, as smiling at his ffeat

smil'st   frequency: 1   relative frequency: 0.00001
     p. 254 UNDERWOOD 75   64 O, now thou smil'st, faire Sun, and shin'st, as
                              thou wouldst stay!

smith   frequency: 2   relative frequency: 0.00002
     See also "bilbo-smith."
     p. 107 FOREST 10   14 That, at thy birth, mad'st the poore Smith
                              affraid,
     p. 307 HORACE 2   51 To be that Smith; then live, mark'd one of
                              those,

smiths   frequency: 1   relative frequency: 0.00001
     p. 208 UNDERWOOD 43   117 For none but Smiths would have made thee a God.

smoake   frequency: 3   relative frequency: 0.00004
     p. 211 UNDERWOOD 43   181 To live in Sea-coale, and goe forth in smoake;
     p. 315 HORACE 2   203 Hee thinks not, how to give you smoake from
                              light,
     p. 315 HORACE 2   204 But light from smoake; that he may draw his
                              bright

smock   frequency: 2   relative frequency: 0.00002
     p. 51 EPIGRAMS 73   17 Item, your owne, sew'd in your mistris smock.
     p. 201 UNDERWOOD 42   66 That chanc'd the lace, laid on a Smock, to see,

smoke. See "smoake."

smooth   frequency: 8   relative frequency: 0.00011
     p. 141 UNDERWOOD 2.9   20 Smooth as is the Billiard Ball:
     p. 141 UNDERWOOD 2.9   27 Skin as smooth as any rush,
     p. 157 UNDERWOOD 13   150 Shoot forth in smooth and comely spaces; have
     p. 280 U'WOOD 84.4   59 As smooth as Oyle pour'd forth, and calme
     p. 280 U'WOOD 84.4   61 Smooth, soft, and sweet, in all a floud
     p. 307 HORACE 2   36 Obscure. This, striving to run smooth, and flow,
     p. 327 HORACE 2   476 And in smooth Cypresse boxes to be keep'd?
     p. 415 UNGATHERED 42   17 So soft, and smooth it handles, the whole piece,

smoother   frequency: 1   relative frequency: 0.00001
     p. 134 UNDERWOOD 2.4   15 Doe but marke, her forehead's smoother

smutch'd   frequency: 1   relative frequency: 0.00001
     p. 134 UNDERWOOD 2.4   24 Before the soyle hath smutch'd it?

snake   frequency: 2   relative frequency: 0.00002
     p. 260 UNDERWOOD 76   32 You'ld reade a Snake, in his next Song.
     p. 317 HORACE 2   268 Upon the Stage, the figure of a Snake.

snakie   frequency: 1   relative frequency: 0.00001
      p. 162 UNDERWOOD 15   18 Crush'd in the snakie brakes, that he had past!

snaky. See "snakie."

snares   frequency: 3   relative frequency: 0.00004
      p. 100 FOREST 4   18 Of toyes, and trifles, traps, and snares,
      p. 141 UNDERWOOD 2.9   11 Cast in thousand snares, and rings
      p. 290 UNDERWOOD 85   35 And snares the fearfull Hare, and new-come
                               Crane,

snatch   frequency: 1   relative frequency: 0.00001
      p. 155 UNDERWOOD 13   72 All the Towne-curs take each their snatch at me.

sneaking   frequency: 1   relative frequency: 0.00001
      p. 200 UNDERWOOD 42   26 For Silke will draw some sneaking Songster
                               thither.

snore   frequency: 2   relative frequency: 0.00002
    **p. 113 PANEGYRE   11 And snore supinely in the stall of sin:
      p. 329 HORACE 2   536 Angry. Sometimes, I heare good Homer snore.

snorts   frequency: 1   relative frequency: 0.00001
      p. 107 FOREST 10   16 Goe, crampe dull MARS, light VENVS, when
                               he snorts,

snout   frequency: 1   relative frequency: 0.00001
      p. 339 HORACE 1   54 .... some vile
                               snout.

snow   frequency: 4   relative frequency: 0.00005
      p. 134 UNDERWOOD 2.4   23 Have you mark'd but the fall o'the Snow
      p. 141 UNDERWOOD 2.9   18 Front, an ample field of snow;
      p. 290 UNDERWOOD 85   29 Then when the thundring Jove his Snow and
                               showres
      p. 367 UNGATHERED 6   40 The Vale, that bred thee pure, as her Hills
                               Snow.

snuff. See "snuffe."

snuffe   frequency: 2   relative frequency: 0.00002
      p. 45 EPIGRAMS 59   2 Who, when you'haue burnt your selues downe to the
                               snuffe,
      p. 211 UNDERWOOD 43   188 Burne to a snuffe, and then stinke out, and die:

so   frequency: 477   relative frequency: 0.00690
      See also "how-so-e're," "so'<e>xceed,"
            "so'above," "so'alone," "soe," "so't."

so'<e>xceed   frequency: 1   relative frequency: 0.00001
      p. 160 UNDERWOOD 14   54 To see the workmanship so'<e>xceed the cost!

so'above   frequency: 1   relative frequency: 0.00001
      p. 313 HORACE 2   174 Be nought so'above him but his sword let claime.

so'alone   frequency: 1   relative frequency: 0.00001
      p. 62 EPIGRAMS 96   3 That so alone canst iudge, so'alone dost make:

soap. See "sope-boyler."

soares   frequency: 1   relative frequency: 0.00001
      p. 272 UNDERWOOD 83   98 But as he soares at that, he bruiseth then

soars. See "soares."

sober   frequency: 4   relative frequency: 0.00005
      p. 56 EPIGRAMS 87   6 Since when, hee's sober againe, and all play's
                               made.
      p. 111 FOREST 11   60 Sober, as saddest care:
      p. 325 HORACE 2   421 Exclude all sober Poets, from their share
      p. 335 HORACE 2   643 Wise, sober folke, a frantick Poet feare,

societie   frequency: 3   relative frequency: 0.00004
      p. 42 EPIGRAMS 50   3 Arsenike would thee fit for societie make.
      p. 117 FOREST 13   19 Of nature, and societie, I should faint;
      p. 197 UNDERWOOD 40   16 And free societie, hee's borne else-where,

society. See "societie."

sock   frequency: 1   relative frequency: 0.00001
     p. 311 HORACE 2   124 Fit for the sock: Each subject should retaine

sockes   frequency: 1   relative frequency: 0.00001
     p. 391 UNGATHERED 26   37 And shake a Stage: Or, when thy Sockes were
                              on,

socket   frequency: 1   relative frequency: 0.00001
     p. 229 UNDERWOOD 54   13 That's six in silver; now within the Socket

socks   frequency: 2   relative frequency: 0.00002
     See also "sockes."
    *p. 493 TO HIMSELF   37 With their foule comick socks;
     p. 311 HORACE 2   118 This foot the socks tooke up, and buskins grave,

socratic. See "socratick."

socratick   frequency: 1   relative frequency: 0.00001
     p. 325 HORACE 2   442 Which the Socratick writings best can show:

sodaine   frequency: 1   relative frequency: 0.00001
     p. 100 FOREST 4   11 Thy curtesie but sodaine starts,

sodayne   frequency: 1   relative frequency: 0.00001
     p. 95 FOREST 2   82 What (great, I will not say, but) sodayne cheare

soe   frequency: 12   relative frequency: 0.00017

soft   frequency: 27   relative frequency: 0.00039
     p. 41 EPIGRAMS 45   9 Rest in soft peace, and, ask'd, say here doth lye
     p. 81 EPIGRAMS 128   5 May windes as soft as breath of kissing friends,
     p. 110 FOREST 11   50 The soft, and sweetest mindes
     p. 111 FOREST 11   65 Of all his happinesse? But soft: I heare
     p. 117 FOREST 13   22 If it may stand with your soft blush to heare
     p. 135 UNDERWOOD 2.4   30 O so white! O so soft! O so sweet is she!
     p. 141 UNDERWOOD 2.9   25 He would have a hand as soft
     p. 166 UNDERWOOD 15   121 This hath our ill-us'd freedome, and soft peace
     p. 167 UNDERWOOD 15   165 Lewd slanderers, soft whisperers that let blood
     p. 181 UNDERWOOD 27   7 Lie drawne to life, in his soft Verse,
     p. 225 UNDERWOOD 51   14 In his soft Cradle to his Fathers Chaire,
     p. 230 UNDERWOOD 56   16 Run all the Rounds in a soft Ladyes eare,
     p. 234 UNDERWOOD 61   14 My Lord, till felt griefe make our stone hearts
                              soft,
     p. 251 UNDERWOOD 74   18 In making soft her aromatique bed.
     p. 279 U'WOOD 84.4   38 As some soft chime had stroak'd the ayre;
     p. 280 U'WOOD 84.4   61 Smooth, soft, and sweet, in all a floud
     p. 283 U'WOOD 84.9   40 To 'greet, or grieve her soft Euthanasee?
     p. 286 U'WOOD 84.9   126 And to the Touch, a Flower, like soft as
                              Palme.
     p. 290 UNDERWOOD 85   26 The soft birds quarrell in the Woods,
     p. 292 UNDERWOOD 86   8 Goe where Youths soft intreaties call thee back.
     p. 292 UNDERWOOD 86   22 In many a Gumme, and for thy soft eares sake
     p. 319 HORACE 2   289 But soft, and simple, at few holes breath'd time
     p. 327 HORACE 2   485 And lead them with soft songs, where that he
                              would.
     p. 367 UNGATHERED 6   45 With thy soft notes, and hold them within Pale
     p. 397 UNGATHERED 30   26 Heard the soft ayres, between our swaynes &
                              thee,
     p. 413 UNGATHERED 41   27 With od'rous sweets and soft humilitie,
     p. 415 UNGATHERED 42   17 So soft, and smooth it handles, the whole piece,

softer   frequency: 5   relative frequency: 0.00007
     p. 52 EPIGRAMS 76   12 Fit in that softer bosome to reside.
     p. 97 FOREST 3   20 And makes sleepe softer then it is!
     p. 105 FOREST 8   22 Daintinesse, and softer ease,
     p. 136 UNDERWOOD 2.5   9 Set, and to this softer straine;
     p. 295 UNDERWOOD 89   6 And heat, with softest love, thy softer bed.

softest   frequency: 2   relative frequency: 0.00002
     p. 52 EPIGRAMS 76   11 I meant each softest vertue, there should meet,
     p. 295 UNDERWOOD 89   6 And heat, with softest love, thy softer bed.

softly   frequency: 1   relative frequency: 0.00001
     p. 199 UNDERWOOD 41   20 Of me, I'le softly tread unto my Tombe;

softnesse   frequency: 2   relative frequency: 0.00002
     p. 263 UNDERWOOD 79   6 To fit the softnesse of our Yeares-gift: when
     p. 270 UNDERWOOD 83   39 Her Sweetnesse, Softnesse, her faire
                              Courtesie,

softnesses   frequency: 1   relative frequency: 0.00001
    p. 321 HORACE 2   326 Were to be staid with softnesses, and wonne

soil. See "soile," "soyle."

soile   frequency: 1   relative frequency: 0.00001
    p. 101 FOREST 4   45 Then, in a soile hast planted me,

sol   frequency: 1   relative frequency: 0.00001
    p. 238 UNDERWOOD 65   12 Sol will re-shine. If not, CHARLES hath a
                              Sonne.

sold   frequency: 5   relative frequency: 0.00007
  **p. 116 PANEGYRE   113 He knew that princes, who had sold their fame
    p. 75 EPIGRAMS 117   1 GROYNE, come of age, his state sold out of
                              hand
    p. 100 FOREST 4   16 And all thy good is to be sold.
    p. 113 FOREST 12   1 Whil'st that, for which, all vertue now is sold,
    p. 242 UNDERWOOD 69   13 Till he had sold his Piece, drawne so unlike:

solders   frequency: 1   relative frequency: 0.00001
    p. 113 FOREST 12   17 Solders crackt friendship; makes loue last a day;

soldier. See "souldier," "souldier-like."

soldierie   frequency: 1   relative frequency: 0.00001
    p. 214 UNDERWOOD 44   44 Of bearing Armes! most civill Soldierie!

soldiers. See "souldiers," "sovldiers."

soldiery. See "soldierie."

sole   frequency: 3   relative frequency: 0.00004
    p. 32 EPIGRAMS 17   4 Charge them, for crowne, to thy sole censure hye.
    p. 284 U'WOOD 84.9   66 Of joy the Circle, and sole Period!
    p. 372 UNGATHERED 9   10 The sole Religious house, and Votary,

solecism. See "scloecisme."

solemn. See "solemne."

solemne   frequency: 9   relative frequency: 0.00013
    p. 36 EPIGRAMS 28   16 Of solemne greatnesse. And he dares, at dice,
    p. 51 EPIGRAMS 73   14 In solemne cypres, the other cob-web-lawne.
    p. 52 EPIGRAMS 76   10 Hating that solemne vice of greatnesse, pride;
    p. 201 UNDERWOOD 42   53 An Officer there, did make most solemne love,
    p. 256 UNDERWOOD 75   128 The Solemne Quire cryes, Joy; and they
                              returne, Amen.
    p. 287 U'WOOD 84.9   175 A solemne Mistresse, and so good a Friend,
    p. 288 U'WOOD 84.9   192 Her solemne houres she spent, or giving Almes,
    p. 321 HORACE 2   338 But, as a Matrone drawne at solemne times
    p. 405 UNGATHERED 34   78 In setting forth of such a solemne Toye!

solemnly   frequency: 1   relative frequency: 0.00001
    p. 268 UNDERWOOD 83   2 Hayles me, so solemnly, to yonder Yewgh?

solid   frequency: 1   relative frequency: 0.00001
    See also "solide."
    p. 399 UNGATHERED 31   17 All that was solid, in the name

solide   frequency: 1   relative frequency: 0.00001
    p. 97 FOREST 3   16 'Mongst loughing heards, and solide hoofes:

sollen   frequency: 1   relative frequency: 0.00001
    p. 295 UNDERWOOD 90   10 No sowre, or sollen bed-mate, yet a Chast;

soloecisme   frequency: 1   relative frequency: 0.00001
    p. 75 EPIGRAMS 116   16 A desperate soloecisme in truth and wit.

solons   frequency: 1   relative frequency: 0.00001
    p. 217 UNDERWOOD 46   17 Like Solons selfe; explat'st the knottie Lawes

sols   frequency: 1   relative frequency: 0.00001
    p. 175 UNDERWOOD 23   28 Sols Chariot for new fire,

some   frequency: 138   relative frequency: 0.00199
   *p. 492 TO HIMSELF   t3 Play, by some malicious spectators,
   *p. 492 TO HIMSELF   21 No doubt some mouldy tale,
  **p. 114 PANEGYRE   35 As on a wonder: some amazed stood,
  **p. 114 PANEGYRE   41 Some cry from tops of houses; thinking noise

some (cont.)

p.	27	EPIGRAMS 2	1 It will be look'd for, booke, when some but see
p.	28	EPIGRAMS 3	9 For termers, or some clarke-like seruing-man,
p.	32	EPIGRAMS 16	6 Some hundred quarrells, yet dost thou fight none;
p.	36	EPIGRAMS 28	17 Blaspheme god, greatly. Or some poore hinde beat,
p.	42	EPIGRAMS 46	1 Is this the Sir, who, some wast wife to winne,
p.	51	EPIGRAMS 73	7 Item, a tale or two, some fortnight after;
p.	52	EPIGRAMS 75	2 'Twixt puritanes, and players, as some cry;
p.	56	EPIGRAMS 88	11 Or hung some MOVNSIEVRS picture on the wall,
p.	56	EPIGRAMS 88	13 Or is it some french statue? No: 'T doth moue,
p.	59	EPIGRAMS 92	23 Or, euery day, some one at RIMEE'S looks,
p.	64	EPIGRAMS 100	1 PLAY-WRIGHT, by chance, hearing some toyes I'had writ,
p.	64	EPIGRAMS 101	10 An oliue, capers, or some better sallade
p.	65	EPIGRAMS 101	18 Of partrich, pheasant, wood-cock, of which some
p.	65	EPIGRAMS 101	22 LIVIE, or of some better booke to vs,
p.	67	EPIGRAMS 104	5 Or, because some scarce thinke that storie true,
p.	67	EPIGRAMS 104	16 If not, 'tis fit for you, some should enuy.
p.	68	EPIGRAMS 106	1 If men get name, for some one vertue: Then,
p.	69	EPIGRAMS 107	15 And, in some yeere, all these together heap'd,
p.	72	EPIGRAMS 111	9 Yet thou, perhaps, shalt meet some tongues will grutch,
p.	73	EPIGRAMS 114	1 I must beleeue some miracles still bee,
p.	75	EPIGRAMS 116	7 'Twas not entayl'd on title. That some word
p.	81	EPIGRAMS 129	11 Whil'st thou dost rayse some Player, from the graue,
p.	81	EPIGRAMS 129	14 On some new gesture, that 's imputed wit?
p.	85	EPIGRAMS 133	33 From Venice, Paris, or some in-land passage
p.	85	EPIGRAMS 133	42 Of some Bride-well, and may, in time, concerne vs
p.	85	EPIGRAMS 133	44 That all this while I haue forgot some god,
p.	85	EPIGRAMS 133	51 Thou hast seene hell (some say) and know'st all nookes there,
p.	93	FOREST 1	1 Some act of Loue's bound to reherse,
p.	95	FOREST 2	51 Some bring a capon, some a rurall cake,
p.	95	FOREST 2	52 Some nuts, some apples; some that thinke they make
p.	95	FOREST 2	65 And I not faine to sit (as some, this day,
p.	97	FOREST 3	12 There wasted, some not paid for yet!
p.	97	FOREST 3	19 To some coole, courteous shade, which he calls his,
p.	97	FOREST 3	35 Thou dost with some delight the day out-weare,
p.	107	FOREST 10	20 Turne the stale prologue to some painted maske,
p.	109	FOREST 11	7 Some way of entrance) we must plant a guard
p.	109	FOREST 11	24 Or some great thought doth keepe
p.	110	FOREST 11	31 Of which vsurping rancke, some haue thought loue
p.	111	FOREST 11	66 Some vicious foole draw neare,
p.	113	FOREST 12	10 And some one apteth to be trusted, then,
p.	113	FOREST 12	12 Of some grand peere, whose ayre doth make reioyce
p.	115	FOREST 12	74 I haue already vs'd some happy houres,
p.	117	FOREST 13	26 No lady, but, at some time, loues her glasse.
p.	117	FOREST 13	38 Doe I reflect. Some alderman has power,
p.	119	FOREST 13	88 Eate on her clients, and some one deuoure.
p.	120	FOREST 14	2 And some doe drinke, and some doe dance,
p.	120	FOREST 14	3 Some ring,
p.	120	FOREST 14	4 Some sing,
p.	131	UNDERWOOD 2.1	6 Some have lov'd as old agen.
p.	145	UNDERWOOD 5	9 Find some one good, or some one man;
p.	153	UNDERWOOD 13	22 Then what he hath receiv'd. Gifts stinke from some,
p.	154	UNDERWOOD 13	47 As I have seene some Infants of the Sword,
p.	157	UNDERWOOD 13	132 Profit in ought; each day some little adde,
p.	157	UNDERWOOD 13	142 Meet some new matter to looke up and wonder!
p.	159	UNDERWOOD 14	21 Men past their termes, and prais'd some names too much,
p.	164	UNDERWOOD 15	64 How they may make some one that day an Asse;
p.	164	UNDERWOOD 15	74 To be abroad chanting some baudie song,
p.	169	UNDERWOOD 17	8 But that some greater names have broke with me,
p.	169	UNDERWOOD 17	17 Some grounds are made the richer, for the Rest;
p.	176	UNDERWOOD 24	15 Some note of which each varied Pillar beares,
p.	177	UNDERWOOD 25	13 That I may sing my thoughts, in some unvulgar straine.
p.	180	UNDERWOOD 26	9 Yet doth some wholsome Physick for the mind,
p.	182	UNDERWOOD 28	6 To those true numerous Graces; whereof some,
p.	191	UNDERWOOD 38	3 Or doe upon my selfe some desperate ill;
p.	191	UNDERWOOD 38	13 There may some face or menace of a storme
p.	197	UNDERWOOD 40	5 And take some sirrup after; so doe I,
p.	200	UNDERWOOD 42	26 For Silke will draw some sneaking Songster thither.

some (cont.)
```
    p. 201 UNDERWOOD 42    58 Lift up some one, and doe, I tell not what.
    p. 202 UNDERWOOD 42    82 A Goat in Velvet; or some block could move
    p. 203 UNDERWOOD 43    26 And my selfe most, in some selfe-boasting Rimes?
    p. 204 UNDERWOOD 43    32 And so some goodlier monster had begot:
    p. 204 UNDERWOOD 43    40 Thou then hadst had some colour for thy flames,
    p. 204 UNDERWOOD 43    42 There were some pieces of as base allay,
    p. 205 UNDERWOOD 43    50 With some more thrift, and more varietie:
    p. 206 UNDERWOOD 43    87 I dare not say a body, but some parts
    p. 207 UNDERWOOD 43    92 To teach some that, their Nurses could <not>
                              doe,
    p. 208 UNDERWOOD 43   118 Some Alchimist there may be yet, or odde
    p. 208 UNDERWOOD 43   131 (Which, some are pleas'd to stile but thy madde
                              pranck)
    p. 209 UNDERWOOD 43   140 'Twas verily some Relique of the Stewes:
    p. 211 UNDERWOOD 43   183 Condemne him to the Brick-kills, or some Hill-
    p. 213 UNDERWOOD 44     8 Launces, and men, and some a breaking force.
    p. 219 UNDERWOOD 47    34 Some hopes of Spaine in their West-Indian
                              Fleet?
    p. 221 UNDERWOOD 48    46 Of some wel-wrought Embassage:
    p. 223 UNDERWOOD 49    31 Indeed, her Dressing some man might delight,
    p. 223 UNDERWOOD 49    36 From Court, while yet thy fame hath some small
                              day;
    p. 225 UNDERWOOD 51     4 Thou stand'st as if some Mysterie thou did'st!
    p. 239 UNDERWOOD 67     3 Some brave un-common way:
    p. 242 UNDERWOOD 69    17 Some of his formes, he lets him not come neere
    p. 248 UNDERWOOD 71    13 Unlesse some saving-Honour of the Crowne,
    p. 252 UNDERWOOD 75    10 (Bearing the promise of some better fate)
    p. 257 UNDERWOOD 75   146 Some houres before it should, that these may know
    p. 262 UNDERWOOD 78     7 And he is built like some imperiall roome
    p. 275 U'WOOD 84.3      6 Some Forme defective, or decay'd;
    p. 279 U'WOOD 84.4     38 As some soft chime had stroak'd the ayre;
    p. 279 U'WOOD 84.4     47 Us forth, by some Celestiall slight
    p. 280 U'WOOD 84.4     50 Some Paradise, or Palace found
    p. 282 U'WOOD 84.9      6 Spun out in name of some of the old Nine!
    p. 287 U'WOOD 84.9    165 But, kept an even gate, as some streight tree
    p. 290 UNDERWOOD 85    23 Then now beneath some ancient Oke he may,
    p. 291 UNDERWOOD 85    42 Some lustie quick Apulians spouse,
    p. 305 HORACE 2         5 Which in some swarthie fish uncomely ends:
    p. 309 HORACE 2        80 If I can give some small increase? when, loe,
    p. 313 HORACE 2       163 Or some hot youth, yet in his flourishing course;
    p. 313 HORACE 2       164 Where some great Lady, or her diligent Nourse;
    p. 313 HORACE 2       166 Of some small thankfull land: whether he bee
    p. 323 HORACE 2       383 So rare, as with some taxe it doth ingage
    p. 329 HORACE 2       538 May, with some right, upon an Author creepe.
    p. 329 HORACE 2       539 As Painting, so is Poesie. Some mans hand
    p. 331 HORACE 2       541 As some the farther off: This loves the darke;
    p. 331 HORACE 2       548 This saying: To some things there is assign'd
    p. 333 HORACE 2       602 Make a great Supper; or for some poore man
    p. 339 HORACE 1        54 .... ..... ..... .... ... .... ... some vile
                              snout.
    p. 371 UNGATHERED 8     6 With the shops Foreman, or some such braue
                              sparke,
    p. 380 UNGATHERED 12   55 Some want, they say in a sort he did craue:
    p. 386 UNGATHERED 21    1 Some men, of Bookes or Freinds not speaking
                              right,
    p. 391 UNGATHERED 26   13 These are, as some infamous Baud, or Whore,
    p. 395 UNGATHERED 29    5 At euery line some pinn thereof should slacke
    p. 396 UNGATHERED 30   18 Is fayre got vp, and day some houres begun!
    p. 398 UNGATHERED 30   87 Empusa, Lamia, or some Monster, more
    p. 405 UNGATHERED 34   76 In presentacon of some puppet play!
    p. 406 UNGATHERED 35    4 All kings to doe ye self same deeds wth some!
    p. 407 UNGATHERED 35   13 He some Colossus to bestryde ye Seas,
    p. 407 UNGATHERED 35   15 Thy Canuas Gyant, at some Channell aymes,
    p. 407 UNGATHERED 36    3 That I should wryte vpon him some sharp verse,
    p. 408 UNGATHERED 36   10 Seek out some hungry painter, yt for bread
    p. 416 UNGATHERED 45    3 or as some would say to breake
    p. 417 UNGATHERED 45   20 some tast to send hir.
    p. 420 UNGATHERED 48   35 Give cause to some of wonnder, some despite,
```

some-thing   frequency: 1   relative frequency: 0.00001
```
    p. 30 EPIGRAMS 11    t1 ON SOME-THING, THAT WALKES
```

some-where   frequency: 1   relative frequency: 0.00001
```
    p. 30 EPIGRAMS 11    t2 SOME-WHERE.
```

somerset   frequency: 2   relative frequency: 0.00002
```
    p. 384 UNGATHERED 18    7 Wch I do, early, vertuous Somerset,
    p. 384 UNGATHERED 18   t2 Robert, Earle of Somerset.
```

something   frequency: 11   relative frequency: 0.00015
   See also "some-thing."
  *p. 492 TO HIMSELF   6 Something they call a Play.
   p.   64 EPIGRAMS 101   6 Something, which, else, could hope for no
                              esteeme.
   p. 137 UNDERWOOD 2.5   50 Something more then thou hast spi'd.
   p. 269 UNDERWOOD 83   16 And the disposure will be something new,
   p. 273 U'WOOD 84.1   15 May something by that twilight see
   p. 275 U'WOOD 84.3   9 Yet something, to the Painters view,
   p. 313 HORACE 2   178 If something strange, that never yet was had
   p. 321 HORACE 2   327 With something that was acceptably new.
   p. 394 UNGATHERED 28   13 But, I would haue, thee, to know something new,
   p. 402 UNGATHERED 34   14 Something your Surship doth not yet intend!
   p. 414 UNGATHERED 42   1 You looke, my Joseph, I should something say

sometime   frequency: 2   relative frequency: 0.00002
   p. 197 UNDERWOOD 40   9 This makes me, Mrs. that sometime by stealth,
   p. 311 HORACE 2   132 Yet, sometime, doth the Comedie excite

sometimes   frequency: 6   relative frequency: 0.00008
   p. 190 UNDERWOOD 37   16 Though you sometimes proclaime me too severe,
   p. 190 UNDERWOOD 37   32 But shall sometimes be tempted to obey
   p. 321 HORACE 2   354 There comes sometimes to things of meanest place.
   p. 327 HORACE 2   455 Thence draw forth true expressions. For,
                              sometimes,
   p. 329 HORACE 2   536 Angry. Sometimes, I heare good Homer snore.
   p. 383 UNGATHERED 17   6 Yet may as blind men sometimes hit the marke.

somewhat   frequency: 1   relative frequency: 0.00001
   See also "somwhat."
   p. 380 UNGATHERED 12   33 That he dares to informe you, but somewhat
                              meticulous,

somewhere. See "some-where."

sommer-nights   frequency: 1   relative frequency: 0.00001
   p. 103 FOREST 6   17 In the silent sommer-nights,

somwhat   frequency: 1   relative frequency: 0.00001
   p. 417 UNGATHERED 45   9 I had somwhat else to say,

son   frequency: 2   relative frequency: 0.00002
   See also "sonne."
   p. 252 UNDERWOOD 75   t6 Son, and Heire, of the Lord WESTON,
   p. 414 UNGATHERED 41   48 By bringing forth GOD's onely Son, no other.

song   frequency: 32   relative frequency: 0.00046
   See also "songe."
   p.   51 EPIGRAMS 73   9 Item, the babylonian song you sing;
   p.   72 EPIGRAMS 112   12 Next morne, an Ode: Thou mak'st a song ere
                              night.
   p.   85 EPIGRAMS 133   50 ALCIDES, be thou succouring to my song.
   p. 102 FOREST 5   t1 Song.
   p. 104 FOREST 7   t1 Song.
   p. 106 FOREST 9   t1 Song.
   p. 133 UNDERWOOD 2.3   23 And in either Prose, or Song,
   p. 144 UNDERWOOD 4   t1 A SONG.
   p. 145 UNDERWOOD 5   t2 A Song Apologetique.
   p. 146 UNDERWOOD 6   t3 A Song.
   p. 164 UNDERWOOD 15   74 To be abroad chanting some baudie song,
   p. 181 UNDERWOOD 27   11 Doth Cynthia, in Propertius song
   p. 182 UNDERWOOD 27   33 Though I, in working of my song,
   p. 189 UNDERWOOD 36   t1 A Song.
   p. 207 UNDERWOOD 43   94 The rest, my journey into Scotland song,
   p. 221 UNDERWOOD 48   35 And not a Song be other
   p. 239 UNDERWOOD 67   t1 An Ode, or Song, by all the Muses.
   p. 249 UNDERWOOD 72   17 And ever close the burden of the Song,
   p. 252 UNDERWOOD 75   t3 A SONG:
   p. 260 UNDERWOOD 76   32 You'ld reade a Snake, in his next Song.
   p. 261 UNDERWOOD 77   27 Unto your honour: I can tune in song
   p. 262 UNDERWOOD 78   17 In signe the Subject, and the Song will live,
   p. 264 UNDERWOOD 79   24 Nym. Of brightest MIRA, doe we raise our
                              Song,
   p. 264 UNDERWOOD 79   32 Nymp. Of brightest MIRA, is our Song; the
                              grace
   p. 273 U'WOOD 84.1   29 But, here's a Song of her DESCENT;
   p. 274 U'WOOD 84.2   t1 The Song of her DESCENT.
   p. 285 U'WOOD 84.9   90 A new Song to his praise, and great I AM:
   p. 367 UNGATHERED 6   34 Continue thy sweete Song.
   p. 385 UNGATHERED 19   8 Thy Richard, rais'd in song, past pulling downe.

song (cont.)
 p. 395 UNGATHERED 29 12 Keepe due proportion in the ample song,
 p. 397 UNGATHERED 30 54 With euery song, I sweare, and so would dye:
 p. 402 UNGATHERED 33 13 And, graced with her song,

songe   frequency: 1 relative frequency: 0.00001
 p. 419 UNGATHERED 48 9 That were the happie subiect of my songe.

songs   frequency: 5 relative frequency: 0.00007
 p. 74 EPIGRAMS 115 13 Except the duell. Can sing songs, and catches;
 p. 82 EPIGRAMS 130 18 Shed in thy Songs; 'tis true: but short of thee.
 p. 145 UNDERWOOD 5 12 One good enough for a songs sake.
 p. 327 HORACE 2 485 And lead them with soft songs, where that he
        would.
 p. 397 UNGATHERED 30 29 But then, thy'epistolar Heroick Songs,

songster   frequency: 1 relative frequency: 0.00001
 p. 200 UNDERWOOD 42 26 For Silke will draw some sneaking Songster
        thither.

songsters   frequency: 1 relative frequency: 0.00001
 p. 201 UNDERWOOD 42 65 Such Songsters there are store of; witnesse he

sonne   frequency: 32 relative frequency: 0.00046
 p. 41 EPIGRAMS 45 t1 ON MY FIRST SONNE.
 p. 95 FOREST 2 77 With his braue sonne, the Prince, they saw thy
        fires
 p. 107 FOREST 10 19 Let the old boy, your sonne, ply his old taske,
 p. 116 FOREST 12 100 My best of wishes, may you beare a sonne.
 p. 121 FOREST 14 41 'T will be exacted of your name, whose sonne,
 p. 128 UNDERWOOD 1.1 21 6. Eternall God the Sonne, who not denyd'st
 p. 128 UNDERWOOD 1.1 26 Father and Sonne; the Comforter, inbreeding
 p. 128 UNDERWOOD 1.1 37 10. Father, and Sonne, and Holy Ghost, you three
 p. 129 UNDERWOOD 1.2 19 That gav'st a Sonne,
 p. 130 UNDERWOOD 1.3 7 The Sonne of God, th'Eternall King,
 p. 151 UNDERWOOD 12 4 Before me here, the Friend and Sonne;
 p. 192 UNDERWOOD 38 42 Or two, or three, a Sonne will dis-inherit,
 p. 208 UNDERWOOD 43 111 Sonne of the Wind! for so thy mother gone
 p. 225 UNDERWOOD 51 9 Sonne to the grave wise Keeper of the Seale,
 p. 238 UNDERWOOD 65 12 Sol will re-shine. If not, CHARLES hath a
        Sonne.
 p. 241 UNDERWOOD 69 1 Sonne, and my Friend, I had not call'd you so
 p. 241 UNDERWOOD 69 t2 To a Friend, and Sonne.
 p. 244 UNDERWOOD 70 47 But most, a vertuous Sonne.
 p. 256 UNDERWOOD 75 106 To pay, with honours, to his noble Sonne,
 p. 268 UNDERWOOD 82 2 Great King, thy having of a second Sonne:
 p. 268 UNDERWOOD 82 t3 His second Sonne IAMES.
 p. 270 UNDERWOOD 83 57 Then comforted her Lord! and blest her Sonne!
 p. 285 U'WOOD 84.9 97 And will you, worthy Sonne, Sir, knowing this,
 p. 285 U'WOOD 84.9 112 Of life, and light, the Sonne of God, the
        Word!
 p. 288 U'WOOD 84.9 216 Hath given wholly to the Sonne (the rather
 p. 288 U'WOOD 84.9 217 As being the Sonne of Man) to shew his Power,
 p. 293 UNDERWOOD 87 14 With gentle Calais, Thurine Orniths Sonne;
 p. 307 HORACE 2 33 Most Writers, noble Sire, and either Sonne,
 p. 327 HORACE 2 467 There's Albin's sonne will say, Substract an
        ounce
 p. 378 UNGATHERED 11 88 Rather his sonne, I should haue cal'd thee, why?
 p. 395 UNGATHERED 29 24 The Sunne translated, or the Sonne of May.
 p. 414 UNGATHERED 42 t1 To my deare Sonne, and right-learned Friend,

sonnes   frequency: 6 relative frequency: 0.00008
 p. 89 EPIGRAMS 133 182 Were you IOVE'S sonnes, or had
        ALCIDES might.
 p. 130 UNDERWOOD 1.3 14 The Sonnes obedience knew no No,
 p. 214 UNDERWOOD 44 57 And could (if our great men would let their
        Sonnes
 p. 215 UNDERWOOD 44 74 Their Sonnes to studie Arts, the Lawes, the
        Creed:
 p. 317 HORACE 2 264 Her Sonnes before the people; nor the ill-
 p. 387 UNGATHERED 22 1 Sonnes, seeke not me amonge these polish'd
        stones:

sonnet   frequency: 2 relative frequency: 0.00002
 p. 182 UNDERWOOD 28 t1 A Sonnet,
 p. 201 UNDERWOOD 42 67 And straight-way spent a Sonnet; with that other

sonnets   frequency: 1 relative frequency: 0.00001
 p. 182 UNDERWOOD 28 3 Since I exscribe your Sonnets, am become

sons   frequency: 2   relative frequency: 0.00002
    See also "sonnes."
    p. 285 U'WOOD 84.9   118 And Sons, and Daughters, with their Parents
                                 talke;
    p. 339 HORACE 1   34 Father ... sons right worthy of your ....

soon   frequency: 1   relative frequency: 0.00001
    See also "soone."
    p. 315 HORACE 2   235 Of money, haughtie, to desire soon mov'd,

soone   frequency: 22   relative frequency: 0.00031
    p.   36 EPIGRAMS 31   4 He toyles to be at hell, as soone as they.
    p.   41 EPIGRAMS 45   7 To haue so soone scap'd worlds, and fleshes rage,
    p.   46 EPIGRAMS 62   5 Is it the paine affrights? that's soone forgot.
    p.   54 EPIGRAMS 81   7 Which, if thou leaue not soone (though I am
                                 loth)
    p.   83 EPIGRAMS 131   14 For fame, with breath soone kindled, soone blowne
                                 out.
    p. 131 UNDERWOOD 2.1   17 But be glad, as soone with me,
    p. 153 UNDERWOOD 13   12 As I did feele it done, as soone as meant:
    p. 183 UNDERWOOD 29   13 Soone as lazie thou wert knowne,
    p. 198 UNDERWOOD 40   29 They looke at best like Creame-bowles, and you
                                 soone
    p. 214 UNDERWOOD 44   37 So, in that ground, as soone it grew to be
    p. 214 UNDERWOOD 44   62 For education of our Lordings; soone
    p. 237 UNDERWOOD 65   5 This Prince of flowers? Soone shoot thou up,
                                 and grow
    p. 238 UNDERWOOD 65   10 And interpose thy selfe, ('care not how soone.)
    p. 256 UNDERWOOD 75   110 Could soone espie
    p. 315 HORACE 2   227 Soone angry, and soone pleas'd, is sweet, or
                                 sowre,
    p. 319 HORACE 2   320 For the vile Goat, soone after, forth did send
    p. 329 HORACE 2   504 The docile mind may soone thy precepts know,
    p. 417 UNGATHERED 45   24 shee soone will heare it.
    p. 420 UNGATHERED 48   18 howe soone wth a selfe ticklinge hee was spent.
    p. 422 UNGATHERED 50   9 The mayne comaund of scepters, soone doth perishe

sooner   frequency: 5   relative frequency: 0.00007
    p.   74 EPIGRAMS 115   24 The cloth's no sooner gone, but it gets vp
    p. 132 UNDERWOOD 2.2   14 Sooner, then he lost his might,
    p. 133 UNDERWOOD 2.3   13 He no sooner heard the Law,
    p. 200 UNDERWOOD 42   13 Sooner then my affection from the faire.
    p. 420 UNGATHERED 48   23 Whose ayre will sooner Hell, then their dull
                                 senses peirce,

soonest   frequency: 1   relative frequency: 0.00001
    p. 118 FOREST 13   58 Contagion in the prease is soonest catch'd.

soot. See "soote."

soote   frequency: 1   relative frequency: 0.00001
    p. 207 UNDERWOOD 43   106 All soote, and embers! odious, as thy worke!

sooth   frequency: 2   relative frequency: 0.00002
    p.   77 EPIGRAMS 120   15 As, sooth, the Parcae thought him one,
    p. 134 UNDERWOOD 2.4   16 Then words that sooth her!

soothe. See "sooth."

soothing   frequency: 1   relative frequency: 0.00001
    p. 333 HORACE 2   606 Whether his soothing friend speake truth, or no.

sop   frequency: 1   relative frequency: 0.00001
    p.   89 EPIGRAMS 133 186 The tripple head without a sop. At last,

sope-boyler   frequency: 1   relative frequency: 0.00001
    p.   89 EPIGRAMS 133 188 A sope-boyler; and AEACVS him nigh,

sophocles   frequency: 1   relative frequency: 0.00001
    p. 391 UNGATHERED 26   34 Euripides, and Sophocles to vs,

sordid   frequency: 2   relative frequency: 0.00002
    p. 201 UNDERWOOD 42   45 When by thy sordid bountie she hath on
    p. 244 UNDERWOOD 70   39 To sordid flatteries, acts of strife,

sore   frequency: 2   relative frequency: 0.00002
    p.   85 EPIGRAMS 133   55 Great Club-fist, though thy backe, and bones be
                                 sore,
    p. 107 FOREST 10   4 HERCVLES? alas his bones are yet sore,

sores. See "plague-sores."

sorie   frequency: 1   relative frequency: 0.00001
    p. 131 UNDERWOOD 2.1   14 First, prepare you to be sorie,

sorrel. See "sorrell."

sorrell   frequency: 1   relative frequency: 0.00001
    p. 291 UNDERWOOD 85   57 Or the herb Sorrell, that loves Meadows still,

sorrow   frequency: 8   relative frequency: 0.00011
    p. 145 UNDERWOOD 4   10 For so will sorrow slay me;
    p. 193 UNDERWOOD 38   87 He when he sees a sorrow such as this,
    p. 282 U'WOOD 84.9   10 A sorrow in me, fit to wait to her!
    p. 287 U'WOOD 84.9   182 Of sorrow, then all pompe of gaudy daies:
    p. 311 HORACE 2   155 With weightie sorrow hurles us all along,
    p. 384 UNGATHERED 18 15 So, be there neuer discontent, or sorrow,
    p. 394 UNGATHERED 28 17 But Sorrow, she desir'd no other ffriend:
    p. 394 UNGATHERED 28 20 Whom shee, with Sorrow first did lodge, then
                             feast,

sorrowes   frequency: 3   relative frequency: 0.00004
    p. 86 EPIGRAMS 133   71 With famine, wants, and sorrowes many a dosen,
    p. 112 FOREST 11   95 And turne the blackest sorrowes to bright ioyes:
    p. 152 UNDERWOOD 12   33 And pray who shall my sorrowes read,

sorrows. See "sorrowes."

sorry   frequency: 2   relative frequency: 0.00002
    See also "sorie," "sory."
    p. 77 EPIGRAMS 120   4 Death's selfe is sorry.
    p. 171 UNDERWOOD 20   4 No more, I am sorry for so fond cause, say,

sort   frequency: 4   relative frequency: 0.00005
    p. 86 EPIGRAMS 133   98 And, in so shitten sort, so long had vs'd him:
    p. 219 UNDERWOOD 47   54 I, and for this neglect, the courser sort
    p. 325 HORACE 2   422 In Helicon; a great sort will not pare
    p. 380 UNGATHERED 12 55 Some want, they say in a sort he did craue:

sorts   frequency: 2   relative frequency: 0.00002
    p. 107 FOREST 10   18 Thou, nor thy loosenesse with my making sorts.
    p. 374 UNGATHERED 10 11 All sorts of fish with Musicke of his maw.

sory   frequency: 1   relative frequency: 0.00001
    p. 168 UNDERWOOD 15 180 And never but for doing wrong be sory;

sosii   frequency: 1   relative frequency: 0.00001
    p. 329 HORACE 2   517 This booke will get the Sosii money; This

so't   frequency: 2   relative frequency: 0.00002

soueraigne   frequency: 1   relative frequency: 0.00001
    p. 361 UNGATHERED 1   12 the sweetest simples, and most soueraigne seedes.

sough   frequency: 1   relative frequency: 0.00001
    p. 87 EPIGRAMS 133 115 And bad her fare-well sough, vnto the lurden:

sought   frequency: 7   relative frequency: 0.00010
    p. 28 EPIGRAMS 3   5 To lye vpon thy stall, till it be sought;
    p. 49 EPIGRAMS 67   8 As all thy honors were by them first sought:
    p. 77 EPIGRAMS 120 21 And haue sought (to giue new birth)
    p. 160 UNDERWOOD 14 45 Sought out the Fountaines, Sources, Creekes,
                             paths, wayes,
    p. 163 UNDERWOOD 15 41 That kept man living! Pleasures only sought!
    p. 185 UNDERWOOD 30 14 Upon reward, till the reward him sought.
    p. 188 UNDERWOOD 34   5 Then this did by her true? She never sought

soul. See "soule."

souldier   frequency: 2   relative frequency: 0.00002
    p. 50 EPIGRAMS 69   1 COB, thou nor souldier, thiefe, nor fencer art,
    p. 244 UNDERWOOD 70 45 Hee stood, a Souldier to the last right end,

souldier-like   frequency: 1   relative frequency: 0.00001
    p. 289 UNDERWOOD 85   5 Nor Souldier-like started with rough alarmes,

souldiers   frequency: 1   relative frequency: 0.00001
    p. 72 EPIGRAMS 111   2 What th'antique souldiers were, the moderne bee?

soule   frequency: 33   relative frequency: 0.00047
    p. 33 EPIGRAMS 21   8 The bodies stripes, I see, the soule may saue.
    p. 33 EPIGRAMS 22   7 Whose soule heauens Queene, (whose name shee
                             beares)

soule (cont.)

p.	52	EPIGRAMS 76	13	Onely a learned, and a manly soule
p.	53	EPIGRAMS 79	4	Came not that soule exhausted so their store.
p.	60	EPIGRAMS 93	11	Then whose I doe not know a whiter soule,
p.	61	EPIGRAMS 95	3	I should beleeue, the soule of TACITVS
p.	70	EPIGRAMS 109	14	And that thy soule should giue thy flesh her weight.
p.	74	EPIGRAMS 114	5	Hath chang'd his soule, and made his obiect you:
p.	79	EPIGRAMS 125	5	Who sees a soule, in such a body set,
p.	82	EPIGRAMS 130	11	To say, indeed, shee were the soule of heauen,
p.	106	FOREST 9	5	The thirst, that from the soule doth rise,
p.	115	FOREST 12	73	My gratefull soule, the subiect of her powers,
p.	115	FOREST 12	86	And show, how, to the life, my soule presents
p.	130	UNDERWOOD 1.3	9	And freed the soule from danger;
p.	143	UNDERWOOD 3	7	What Tree or stone doth want a soule?
p.	165	UNDERWOOD 15	103	His time? health? soule? will he for these goe throw
p.	167	UNDERWOOD 15	148	Runs sweetly, as it had his Lordships Soule;
p.	188	UNDERWOOD 35	5	And, till the comming of the Soule
p.	193	UNDERWOOD 38	89	The contrite Soule, who hath no thought to win
p.	224	UNDERWOOD 50	18	Of State, of fame, of body, and of soule,
p.	234	UNDERWOOD 60	17	And only, his great Soule envy'd,
p.	269	UNDERWOOD 83	22	Sound thou her Vertues, give her soule a Name.
p.	269	UNDERWOOD 83	29	It is too neere of kin to Heaven, the Soule,
p.	270	UNDERWOOD 83	50	Of her disease, how did her soule assure
p.	270	UNDERWOOD 83	56	And I, into the world, all Soule, was sent!
p.	271	UNDERWOOD 83	92	With what injustice should one soule pretend
p.	283	U'WOOD 84.9	34	Her blessed Soule, hence, forth this valley vane
p.	284	U'WOOD 84.9	64	To Body, and Soule! where Love is all the guest!
p.	307	HORACE 2	37	Hath neither soule, nor sinewes. Loftie he
p.	391	UNGATHERED 26	17	I, therefore will begin. Soule of the Age!
p.	399	UNGATHERED 31	25	Her soule possest her fleshes state
p.	404	UNGATHERED 34	50	Painting & Carpentry are ye Soule of Masque.
p.	406	UNGATHERED 35	6	A Noble honest Soule! what's this to thee?

soules   frequency: 13   relative frequency: 0.00018

**p.	113	PANEGYRE	14	And make their denne the slaughter-house of soules:
**p.	114	PANEGYRE	32	Breath'd in his way; and soules (their better parts)
p.	66	EPIGRAMS 103	3	And noted for what flesh such soules were fram'd,
p.	108	FOREST 10A	11	Let these in wanton feete daunce out their soules.
p.	113	FOREST 12	4	And, for it, life, conscience, yea, soules are giuen,
p.	114	FOREST 12	43	The soules, shee loues. Those other glorious notes,
p.	119	FOREST 13	119	And that your soules conspire, as they were gone
p.	144	UNDERWOOD 3	25	Nay, rather both our soules bee strayn'd
p.	218	UNDERWOOD 47	17	On all Soules that are absent; even the dead;
p.	262	UNDERWOOD 78	12	As other soules, to his, dwell in a Lane:
p.	285	U'WOOD 84.9	113	There, all the happy soules, that ever were,
p.	286	U'WOOD 84.9	136	The safetie of our soules, and forfeit breath!
p.	361	UNGATHERED 1	11	Whilst other soules conuert to base abuse

souls. See "soules."

sound   frequency: 24   relative frequency: 0.00034
See also "sounde."

*p.	494	TO HIMSELF	57	In sound of peace, or warres,
p.	49	EPIGRAMS 67	3	That sound, and that authoritie with her name,
p.	58	EPIGRAMS 91	2	A romane sound, but romane vertue weares,
p.	58	EPIGRAMS 91	7	When on thy trumpet shee did sound a blast,
p.	86	EPIGRAMS 133	91	No matter, stinkards, row. What croaking sound
p.	99	FOREST 3	102	A body sound, with sounder minde;
p.	130	UNDERWOOD 1.3	3	The Angels so did sound it,
p.	154	UNDERWOOD 13	35	Or that doth sound a Trumpet, and doth call
p.	176	UNDERWOOD 24	12	Doth mete, whose lyne doth sound the depth of things:)
p.	187	UNDERWOOD 33	19	But first dost vexe, and search it! If not sound,
p.	239	UNDERWOOD 67	13	3. THAL. Yet, let our Trumpets sound;
p.	244	UNDERWOOD 70	50	In weight, in measure, number, sound,
p.	258	UNDERWOOD 75	182	Upright and sound,
p.	264	UNDERWOOD 79	19	Chor. Sound, sound his praises loud, and with his, hers divide.
p.	269	UNDERWOOD 83	22	Sound thou her Vertues, give her soule a Name.
p.	279	U'WOOD 84.4	39	And, though the sound were parted thence,

sound (cont.)
    p. 293 UNDERWOOD 87   6 Nor after C<h>loe did his Lydia sound;
    p. 295 UNDERWOOD 90   6 A quiet mind; free powers; and body sound;
    p. 313 HORACE 2   159 In sound, quite from his fortune; both the rout,
    p. 319 HORACE 2   288 And rivall with the Trumpet for his sound,
    p. 329 HORACE 2   521 For, neither doth the String still yeeld that
                              sound
    p. 353 HORACE 1   614 .. .. sound
    p. 365 UNGATHERED 5   15 But mixt with sound, transcending

sounde   frequency: 1   relative frequency: 0.00001
    p. 420 UNGATHERED 48   36 But vnto more dispayre to Imitate their sounde.

sounded   frequency: 1   relative frequency: 0.00001
    p. 198 UNDERWOOD 40   30 Shall find their depth: they're sounded with a
                              spoone.

sounder   frequency: 1   relative frequency: 0.00001
    p. 99 FOREST 3   102 A body sound, with sounder minde;

soundest   frequency: 1   relative frequency: 0.00001
    p. 36 EPIGRAMS 31   3 And though the soundest legs goe euery day,

soundlesse   frequency: 1   relative frequency: 0.00001
    p. 278 U'WOOD 84.4   11 The Sunne, a Sea, or soundlesse Pit;

sounds   frequency: 3   relative frequency: 0.00004
    p. 61 EPIGRAMS 95   6 And all his numbers, both of sense, and sounds.
    p. 118 FOREST 13   50 Without which, all the rest were sounds, or lost.
    p. 390 UNGATHERED 26   8 Which, when it sounds at best, but eccho's right;

sour. See "sower," "sowre."

sou'raigne   frequency: 1   relative frequency: 0.00001
    p. 82 EPIGRAMS 130   8 No lesse a sou'raigne cure, then to the mind;

source   frequency: 2   relative frequency: 0.00002
    p. 311 HORACE 2   116 Fresh Lovers businesse, and the Wines free
                              source.
    p. 370 UNGATHERED 7   7 Each subt'lest Passion, with her source, and
                              spring,

sources   frequency: 1   relative frequency: 0.00001
    p. 160 UNDERWOOD 14   45 Sought out the Fountaines, Sources, Creekes,
                              paths, wayes,

soveraigne   frequency: 2   relative frequency: 0.00002
 **p. 112 PANEGYRE   t6 OVR SOVERAIGNE,
    p. 236 UNDERWOOD 64   8 Then now, to love the Soveraigne, and the
                              Lawes?

soveraigntie   frequency: 1   relative frequency: 0.00001
    p. 423 UNGATHERED 50   18 Virtue, and Soveraigntie, they not consort./

sovereign. See "soueraigne," "sou'raigne," "soveraigne."

sovereignty. See "soveraigntie."

sovldiers   frequency: 1   relative frequency: 0.00001
    p. 69 EPIGRAMS 108   t1 TO TRVE SOVLDIERS.

sow   frequency: 1   relative frequency: 0.00001
    p. 254 UNDERWOOD 75   61 Stay, see the Virgins sow,

sow'd   frequency: 1   relative frequency: 0.00001
    p. 247 UNDERWOOD 70   128 Had sow'd these fruits, and got the harvest in.

sower   frequency: 4   relative frequency: 0.00005
    p. 162 UNDERWOOD 15   19 See the grave, sower, and supercilious Sir
    p. 197 UNDERWOOD 40   2 Till the sower Minute comes of taking leave,
    p. 292 UNDERWOOD 86   5 Sower Mother of sweet Loves, forbeare
    p. 319 HORACE 2   322 Though sower, with safetie of his gravitie,

sowre   frequency: 4   relative frequency: 0.00005
    p. 295 UNDERWOOD 90   10 No sowre, or sollen bed-mate, yet a Chast;
    p. 309 HORACE 2   107 In Verse unequall match'd, first sowre Laments,
    p. 315 HORACE 2   227 Soone angry, and soone pleas'd, is sweet, or
                              sowre,
    p. 329 HORACE 2   515 Sweet mix'd with sowre, to his Reader, so

soyle   frequency: 3   relative frequency: 0.00004
    p.   93 FOREST 2   7 Thou ioy'st in better markes, of soyle, of ayre,
    p. 134 UNDERWOOD 2.4   24 Before the soyle hath smutch'd it?
    p. 295 UNDERWOOD 90   4 A Soyle, not barren; a continewall fire;

space   frequency: 2   relative frequency: 0.00002
    p. 243 UNDERWOOD 70   21 For, what is life, if measur'd by the space,
    p. 285 U'WOOD 84.9   105 You once enjoy'd: A short space severs yee,

spaces   frequency: 1   relative frequency: 0.00001
    p. 157 UNDERWOOD 13   150 Shoot forth in smooth and comely spaces; have

spain. See "spaine."

spaine   frequency: 7   relative frequency: 0.00010
    p.   59 EPIGRAMS 92   34 And at the Pope, and Spaine slight faces make.
    p. 219 UNDERWOOD 47   34 Some hopes of Spaine in their West-Indian
                               Fleet?
    p. 219 UNDERWOOD 47   36 Or that the Match from Spaine was ever meant?
    p. 219 UNDERWOOD 47   47 Of Spaine or France; or were not prick'd downe
                               one
    p. 368 UNGATHERED 6   88 Though slower Spaine; and Italy mature.
    p. 389 UNGATHERED 24   15 For though Spaine gaue him his first ayre and
                               Vogue,
    p. 406 UNGATHERED 35   1 But cause thou hearst ye mighty k. of Spaine

spaines   frequency: 1   relative frequency: 0.00001
    p. 213 UNDERWOOD 44   4 T'have wak'd, if sleeping, Spaines Ambassadour,

spain's. See "spaines."

spake   frequency: 1   relative frequency: 0.00001
    p.   86 EPIGRAMS 133   74 Spake to 'hem louder, then the oxe in LIVIE;

span   frequency: 2   relative frequency: 0.00002
    p. 200 UNDERWOOD 42   32 That quilts those bodies, I have leave to span:
    p. 287 U'WOOD 84.9   152 Find all our Atomes from a point t<o>'a span!

spangled   frequency: 1   relative frequency: 0.00001
    p. 223 UNDERWOOD 49   19 And spangled Petticotes brought forth to eye,

spanish   frequency: 3   relative frequency: 0.00004
    p. 188 UNDERWOOD 34   12 Spanish receipt, to make her teeth to rot.
    p. 389 UNGATHERED 24   5 As in this Spanish Proteus; who, though writ
    p. 389 UNGATHERED 24   18 Finer then was his Spanish, if my Oath

sparcle   frequency: 1   relative frequency: 0.00001
    p. 361 UNGATHERED 1   16 did sparcle foorth in Center of the rest:

spar'd   frequency: 2   relative frequency: 0.00002
 **p. 114 PANEGYRE   50 The amorous Citie spar'd no ornament,
    p. 213 UNDERWOOD 44   24 Thou Seed-plot of the warre, that hast not
                               spar'd

spare   frequency: 11   relative frequency: 0.00015
    p. 142 U'WOOD 2.10   2 That's a Toy, that I could spare:
    p. 191 UNDERWOOD 38   17 Spare your owne goodnesse yet; and be not great
    p. 199 UNDERWOOD 41   19 And so I spare it. Come what can become
    p. 210 UNDERWOOD 43   159 Hee is true Vulcan still! He did not spare
    p. 239 UNDERWOOD 67   8 And Gunnes there, spare to poure
    p. 241 UNDERWOOD 68   12 'T were better spare a Butt, then spill his
                               Muse.
    p. 292 UNDERWOOD 86   2 Long intermitted, pray thee, pray thee spare:
    p. 307 HORACE 2   66 Right spare, and warie: then thou speak'st to mee
    p. 317 HORACE 2   283 Praise the spare diet, wholsome justice, lawes,
    p. 325 HORACE 2   415 But you, Pompilius off-spring, spare you not
    p. 662 INSCRIPTS. 2   10 of her white Hand; or she can spare it.

spark. See "sparke."

sparke   frequency: 5   relative frequency: 0.00007
    p. 174 UNDERWOOD 22   31 One sparke of your Diviner heat
    p. 189 UNDERWOOD 36   8 Yet he himselfe is but a sparke.
    p. 189 UNDERWOOD 36   9 A Sparke to set whole world<s> a-fire,
    p. 371 UNGATHERED 8   6 With the shops Foreman, or some such braue
                               sparke,
    p. 383 UNGATHERED 16   16 yf from a little sparke hee rise not fier.

sparkle   frequency: 1   relative frequency: 0.00001
    See also "sparcle."

Sparkle (cont.)
   p. 209 UNDERWOOD 43   141 And this a Sparkle of that fire let loose

sparkling   frequency: 2   relative frequency: 0.00002
   p. 112 FOREST 11   93 A beautie of that cleere, and sparkling light,
   p. 136 UNDERWOOD 2.5   16 Just above her sparkling eyes,

sparrowes   frequency: 1   relative frequency: 0.00001
   p. 111 FOREST 11   73 Though thy wild thoughts with sparrowes wings doe
                     flye,

sparrows'. See "sparrowes."

spartans   frequency: 1   relative frequency: 0.00001
   p. 393 UNGATHERED 30   67 Looke, how we read the Spartans were inflam'd

spawn. See "spawne."

spawne   frequency: 1   relative frequency: 0.00001
   p. 250 UNDERWOOD 73   8 Thou sluggish spawne, that canst, but wilt not
                     see?

speach   frequency: 2   relative frequency: 0.00002
   p. 213 UNDERWOOD 44   t1 A speach according to Horace.
   p. 382 UNGATHERED 16   t1 A speach presented vnto king James at a tylting
                     in the

speak. See "speake."

speake   frequency: 44   relative frequency: 0.00063
   p. 40 EPIGRAMS 43   3 Which should thy countries loue to speake refuse,
   p. 53 EPIGRAMS 77   2 That, any way, my booke should speake thy name:
   p. 56 EPIGRAMS 88   2 That his whole body should speake french, not he?
   p. 57 EPIGRAMS 89   12 As others speake, but onely thou dost act.
   p. 58 EPIGRAMS 91   13 I speake thy other graces, not lesse showne,
   p. 62 EPIGRAMS 95   31 We need a man, can speake of the intents,
   p. 65 EPIGRAMS 101   23 Of which wee'll speake our minds, amidst our
                     meate:
   p. 71 EPIGRAMS 110   12 Can so speake CAESAR, as thy labours doe.
   p. 73 EPIGRAMS 113   2 As but to speake thee, OVERBVRY, is
                     praise:
   p. 78 EPIGRAMS 122   6 And heare her speake with one, and her first
                     tongue;
   p. 82 EPIGRAMS 130   3 Which Musick had; or speake her knowne effects,
   p. 83 EPIGRAMS 132   5 How can I speake of thy great paines, but erre?
   p. 87 EPIGRAMS 133   105 But I will speake (and know I shall be heard)
   p. 97 FOREST 3   22 A-bed canst heare the loud stag speake,
   p. 116 FOREST 13   1 'Tis growne almost a danger to speake true
   p. 119 FOREST 13   110 They speake; since you are truly that rare wife,
   p. 133 UNDERWOOD 2.3   22 Is, that I have leave to speake,
   p. 140 UNDERWOOD 2.8   30 (And that quickly) speake your Man.
   p. 141 UNDERWOOD 2.9   33 'Twere to<o> long, to speake of all:
   p. 159 UNDERWOOD 14   28 Meane what I speake: and still will keepe that
                     Vow.
   p. 172 UNDERWOOD 21   1 Aske not to know this Man. If fame should
                     speake
   p. 181 UNDERWOOD 27   4 So speake (as yet it is not mute)
   p. 207 UNDERWOOD 43   96 To speake the fate of the Sicilian Maid
   p. 215 UNDERWOOD 44   71 More then to praise a Dog? or Horse? or speake
   p. 218 UNDERWOOD 47   6 To speake my selfe out too ambitiously,
   p. 218 UNDERWOOD 47   19 That to speake well, thinke it above all sinne,
   p. 234 UNDERWOOD 61   9 Your happinesse, and doth not speake you blest,
   p. 249 UNDERWOOD 72   1 This is King CHARLES his Day. Speake
                     it, thou Towre,
   p. 255 UNDERWOOD 75   84 With Angels, Muse, to speake these: Nothing
                     can
   p. 269 UNDERWOOD 83   28 But rather I, should I of that part speake!
   p. 274 U'WOOD 84.2   7 Speake it, you bold PENATES, you that
                     stand
   p. 278 U'WOOD 84.4   17 Sweet Mind, then speake your selfe, and say,
   p. 307 HORACE 2   61 Invention. Now, to speake; and then differ
   p. 311 HORACE 2   147 Peleus, or Telephus. If you speake vile
   p. 313 HORACE 2   161 It much will differ, if a God speake, than,
   p. 313 HORACE 2   183 'Tis hard, to speake things common, properly:
   p. 315 HORACE 2   201 Speake to me, Muse, the Man, who, after Troy
                     was sack't,
   p. 317 HORACE 2   275 Any fourth man, to speake at all, aspire.
   p. 321 HORACE 2   345 As not make difference, whether Davus speake,
   p. 331 HORACE 2   574 Wilt nothing against nature speake, or doe:
   p. 333 HORACE 2   606 Whether his soothing friend speake truth, or no.

speake (cont.)
    p. 388 UNGATHERED 23   7 If all the vulgar Tongues, that speake this day,
    p. 404 UNGATHERED 34 49 Oh, to make Boardes to speake! There is a taske
    p. 416 UNGATHERED 45   2 I am come to Add, and speake,

speaker   frequency: 1   relative frequency: 0.00001
    p. 327 HORACE 2   479 Orpheus, a priest, and speaker for the Gods,

speakes   frequency: 3   relative frequency: 0.00004
    p. 35 EPIGRAMS 28   4 He speakes to men with a Rhinocerotes nose,
    p. 271 UNDERWOOD 83 71 Speakes Heavens Language! and discourseth free
    p. 313 HORACE 2   158 If now the phrase of him that speakes, shall
                           flow,

speaking   frequency: 5   relative frequency: 0.00007
    p. 74 EPIGRAMS 115   8 By speaking well o' the company' it 's in.
    p. 154 UNDERWOOD 13 51 And speaking worst of those, from whom they went
    p. 288 U'WOOD 84.9 191 In frequent speaking by the pious Psalmes
    p. 309 HORACE 2   104 The power, and rule of speaking resteth still.
    p. 336 UNGATHERED 21   1 Some men, of Bookes or Freinds not speaking
                           right,

speaks   frequency: 1   relative frequency: 0.00001
    See also "speakes."
    p. 657 L. CONVIVALES 3 Here he speaks out of his Pottle,

speak'st   frequency: 1   relative frequency: 0.00001
    p. 307 HORACE 2   66 Right spare, and warie: then thou speak'st to mee

special. See "speciall."

speciall   frequency: 3   relative frequency: 0.00004
    p. 61 EPIGRAMS 95   7 But when I read that speciall piece, restor'd,
    p. 259 UNDERWOOD 76   7 Of his speciall grace to Letters,
    p. 393 UNGATHERED 27   7 And spirit of that speciall Grace,

specially   frequency: 1   relative frequency: 0.00001
    p. 417 UNGATHERED 45 21 Specially the newes of Darby;

species   frequency: 1   relative frequency: 0.00001
    p. 253 UNDERWOOD 75 32 Through which not only we, but all our Species
                           are.

specious   frequency: 3   relative frequency: 0.00004
    p. 152 UNDERWOOD 12 20 They were as specious as his Trees.
    p. 327 HORACE 2   457 With specious places, and being humour'd right,
    p. 404 UNGATHERED 34 55 Sense, what they are! which by a specious fyne

speckled   frequency: 1   relative frequency: 0.00001
    p. 94 FOREST 2   28 The purpled pheasant, with the speckled side:

spectacle   frequency: 1   relative frequency: 0.00001
    p. 233 UNDERWOOD 59 13 This were a spectacle! A sight to draw

spectacles   frequency: 2   relative frequency: 0.00002
    p. 118 FOREST 13   65 Because that studies spectacles, and showes,
    p. 403 UNGATHERED 34 42 You are ye Spectacles of State! Tis true

spectators   frequency: 3   relative frequency: 0.00004
  *p. 492 TO HIMSELF   t3 Play, by some malicious spectators,
    p. 311 HORACE 2   137 That are Spectators, with their miserie,
    p. 319 HORACE 2   324 The free spectators, subject to no Law,

speech   frequency: 7   relative frequency: 0.00010
    See also "speach."
  **p. 114 PANEGYRE   38 But, when their speech so poore a helpe affords
  **p. 116 PANEGYRE   134 To heare her speech; which still began in him
    p. 31 EPIGRAMS 14   9 What weight, and what authoritie in thy speech!
    p. 279 U'WOOD 84.4 34 In speech; it is with that excesse
    p. 309 HORACE 2   100 Or grace of speech, should hope a lasting date.
    p. 311 HORACE 2   151 And the severe, speech ever serious.
    p. 422 UNGATHERED 50 t1 A speech out of Lucane.

speeches   frequency: 1   relative frequency: 0.00001
    p. 321 HORACE 2   359 Or crack out bawdie speeches, and uncleane.

spell   frequency: 3   relative frequency: 0.00004
    p. 28 EPIGRAMS 3   10 Who scarse can spell th'hard names: whose knight
                           lesse can.
    p. 30 EPIGRAMS 12   5 By that one spell he liues, eates, drinkes,
                           arrayes

spell (cont.)
   p. 245 UNDERWOOD 70   59 Not liv'd; for Life doth her great actions
                              spell,

spend   frequency: 9   relative frequency: 0.00013
   p. 68 EPIGRAMS 106   4 Truth might spend all her voyce, Fame all her
                              art.
   p. 102 FOREST 5   5 Spend not then his guifts in vaine.
   p. 105 FOREST 8   33 That for th'oyle of Talke, dare spend
   p. 118 FOREST 13   77 Let 'hem on poulders, oyles, and paintings,
                              spend,
   p. 156 UNDERWOOD 13   101 Reare-Suppers in their Names! and spend whole
                              nights
   p. 163 UNDERWOOD 15   47 Thither it flowes. How much did Stallion spend
   p. 165 UNDERWOOD 15   102 For man to spend his money on? his wit?
   p. 335 HORACE 2   630 Then change; no word, or worke, more would he
                              spend
   p. 420 UNGATHERED 48 24 Thou that doest spend thie dayes

spenser   frequency: 1   relative frequency: 0.00001
   p. 391 UNGATHERED 26 20 Chaucer, or Spenser, or bid Beaumont lye

spenser's   frequency: 1   relative frequency: 0.00001
   p. 263 UNDERWOOD 78 24 Upon them, (next to Spenser's noble booke,)

spent   frequency: 13   relative frequency: 0.00018
   p. 55 EPIGRAMS 84   7 I would haue spent: how euery Muse should know
                              it,
   p. 100 FOREST 3   105 Nor death; but when thy latest sand is spent,
   p. 104 FOREST 8   5 Spent in surfets: and their dayes,
   p. 111 FOREST 11   78 Because lust's meanes are spent:
   p. 166 UNDERWOOD 15   140 To be beholders, when their powers are spent.
   p. 192 UNDERWOOD 38   44 No man inflicts that paine, till hope be spent:
   p. 201 UNDERWOOD 42   67 And straight-way spent a Sonnet; with that other
   p. 207 UNDERWOOD 43   99 Wherein was oyle, beside the succour spent,
   p. 286 U'WOOD 84.9   141 Had lost our selves? and prodigally spent
   p. 287 U'WOOD 84.9   180 She spent more time in teares her selfe to dresse
   p. 288 U'WOOD 84.9   192 Her solemne houres she spent, or giving Almes,
   p. 361 UNGATHERED 1   24 wear spent with wonder as they weare delated,
   p. 420 UNGATHERED 48 18 howe soone wth a selfe ticklinge hee was spent.

spew. See "spue."

sphaere   frequency: 1   relative frequency: 0.00001
   p. 366 UNGATHERED 6   13 Smiles in his Sphaere, to see the rest affect,

spheare   frequency: 5   relative frequency: 0.00007
   p. 60 EPIGRAMS 94   1 LVCY, you brightnesse of our spheare, who are
   p. 61 EPIGRAMS 94   15 LVCY, you brightnesse of our spheare, who are
   p. 82 EPIGRAMS 130   12 That the eight spheare, no lesse, then planets
                              seauen,
   p. 244 UNDERWOOD 70   52 His life was of Humanitie the Spheare.
   p. 279 U'WOOD 84.4   29 There, high exalted in the Spheare,

spheares   frequency: 4   relative frequency: 0.00005
   p. 143 UNDERWOOD 3   2 And challenge all the Spheares,
   p. 239 UNDERWOOD 67   21 The Angels from their Spheares:
   p. 253 UNDERWOOD 75   16 By all the Spheares consent, so in the heart of
                              June?
   p. 372 UNGATHERED 9   9 Of Spheares, as light of starres; She was
                              earthes Eye:

sphere   frequency: 1   relative frequency: 0.00001
  See also "sphaere," "spheare."
   p. 179 UNDERWOOD 25   54 (Whose heart in that bright Sphere flames
                              clearest,

spheres. See "spheares."

spice   frequency: 3   relative frequency: 0.00004
   p. 36 EPIGRAMS 28   15 He keepes anothers wife, which is a spice
   p. 280 U'WOOD 84.4   64 A nest of odorous spice, and gummes.
   p. 400 UNGATHERED 31 30 Keeps warme the spice of her good name,

spicerie   frequency: 1   relative frequency: 0.00001
   p. 286 U'WOOD 84.9   125 Unto the Sent, a Spicerie, or Balme;

spicery. See "spicerie."

spi'd   frequency: 1   relative frequency: 0.00001
    p. 137 UNDERWOOD 2.5   50 Something more then thou hast spi'd.

spide   frequency: 1   relative frequency: 0.00001
    p. 160 UNDERWOOD 14   44 Times, manners, customes! Innovations spide!

spie   frequency: 7   relative frequency: 0.00010
    p. 109 FOREST 11   11 Obiect arriue there, but the heart (our spie)
    p. 139 UNDERWOOD 2.7   3 Here's none to spie, or see;
    p. 203 UNDERWOOD 43   19 But, on thy malice, tell me, didst thou spie
    p. 207 UNDERWOOD 43   90 And lighted by the Stagirite, could spie,
    p. 211 UNDERWOOD 43   187 Or in the Bell-Mans Lanthorne, like a spie,
    p. 242 UNDERWOOD 69   20 To judge; So all men comming neere can spie.
    p. 323 HORACE 2   392 Or rather, thinking all my faults may spie,

spied. See "spi'd," "spide."

spies   frequency: 4   relative frequency: 0.00005
  See also "spyes."
    p. 45 EPIGRAMS 59   1 SPIES, you are lights in state, but of base
                              stuffe,
    p. 45 EPIGRAMS 59   t1 ON SPIES.
    p. 167 UNDERWOOD 15   163 Light thee from hell on earth: where flatterers,
                              spies,
    p. 258 UNDERWOOD 75   174 Like pretty Spies,

spight   frequency: 15   relative frequency: 0.00021
  **p. 113 PANEGYRE   29 Till forraine malice, or vnnaturall spight
  **p. 115 PANEGYRE   94 "To heare the truth, from spight, or flattery
                              voyd.
    p. 35 EPIGRAMS 27   4 If any Muse out-liue their spight, his can;
    p. 109 FOREST 11   4 And her blacke spight expell.
    p. 138 UNDERWOOD 2.6   22 In the Daunces, with what spight
    p. 151 UNDERWOOD 11   9 Or Spight,
    p. 162 UNDERWOOD 15   26 For all their spight, be like him if they could:
    p. 188 UNDERWOOD 34   3 What did she worth thy spight? were there not
                              store
    p. 224 UNDERWOOD 50   4 To conquer rumour, and triumph on spight;
    p. 234 UNDERWOOD 60   5 What could their care doe 'gainst the spight
    p. 250 UNDERWOOD 73   9 Feed on thy selfe for spight, and shew thy Kind:
    p. 367 UNGATHERED 6   58 That heard but Spight deliuer
    p. 386 UNGATHERED 21   2 May hurt them more with praise, then Foes with
                              spight.
    p. 394 UNGATHERED 28   25 Where spight of Death, next Life, for her
                              Loues sake,
    p. 401 UNGATHERED 32   18 But higher power, as spight could not make lesse,

spights   frequency: 1   relative frequency: 0.00001
    p. 210 UNDERWOOD 43   163 And what hast thou done in these pettie spights,

spill   frequency: 2   relative frequency: 0.00002
    p. 144 UNDERWOOD 4   8 For then my hopes will spill me.
    p. 241 UNDERWOOD 68   12 'T were better spare a Butt, then spill his
                              Muse.

spilt   frequency: 1   relative frequency: 0.00001
    p. 371 UNGATHERED 8   12 And wish that all the Muses blood were spilt,

spin   frequency: 1   relative frequency: 0.00001
  See also "spinne."
    p. 52 EPIGRAMS 76   16 Of destinie, and spin her owne free houres.

spindle   frequency: 1   relative frequency: 0.00001
    p. 52 EPIGRAMS 76   15 The rock, the spindle, and the sheeres controule

spinne   frequency: 1   relative frequency: 0.00001
    p. 225 UNDERWOOD 51   15 Whose even Thred the Fates spinne round, and
                              full,

spinola   frequency: 1   relative frequency: 0.00001
    p. 214 UNDERWOOD 44   42 And Spinola have blushed at the sight.

spire   frequency: 1   relative frequency: 0.00001
    p. 111 FOREST 11   64 Cast himselfe from the spire

spirit   frequency: 20   relative frequency: 0.00028
    p. 60 EPIGRAMS 93   9 Thou, that art all their valour, all their
                              spirit,
    p. 71 EPIGRAMS 110   8 He wrote, with the same spirit that he fought,
    p. 100 FOREST 4   6 A spirit so resolu'd to tread

spirit (cont.)
p. 105 FOREST 8	32	Lying for the spirit of amber.
p. 108 FOREST 10A	12	A farther fury my ray'sd spirit Controules,
p. 114 FOREST 12	31	For what a sinne 'gainst your great fathers spirit,
p. 123 UNDERWOOD 1.1	25	7. Eternall Spirit, God from both proceeding,
p. 164 UNDERWOOD 15	58	With Velvet, Plush, and Tissues, it is spirit.
p. 164 UNDERWOOD 15	82	Of woman of fashion, and a Lady of spirit:
p. 177 UNDERWOOD 25	20	That hold<s> your spirit:
p. 192 UNDERWOOD 38	58	Or winds the Spirit, by which the flower so grew?
p. 194 UNDERWOOD 38	111	How all my fibres by your Spirit doe move,
p. 219 UNDERWOOD 47	41	I have a body, yet, that spirit drawes
p. 270 UNDERWOOD 83	64	Her spirit home, to her originall!
p. 282 U'WOOD 84.9	3	The Spirit that I wrote with, and conceiv'd;
p. 283 U'WOOD 84.9	42	As spirits had stolne her Spirit, in a kisse,
p. 284 U'WOOD 84.9	54	Of Body and Spirit together, plac'd betwixt
p. 285 U'WOOD 84.9	93	To have her captiv'd spirit freed from flesh,
p. 379 UNGATHERED 12	14	To write it with the selfe same spirit he went,
p. 393 UNGATHERED 27	7	And spirit of that speciall Grace,

spirited. See "high-spirited."

spirits   frequency: 13   relative frequency: 0.00018
See also "spirrites."
p. 86 EPIGRAMS 133	101	His spirits, now, in pills, and eeke in potions,
p. 88 EPIGRAMS 133	159	Their spirits transmigrated to a cat:
p. 96 FOREST 2	94	Their gentler spirits haue suck'd innocence.
p. 107 FOREST 10	11	To raise my spirits with thy coniuring wine,
p. 111 FOREST 11	77	Such spirits as are onely continent,
p. 162 UNDERWOOD 15	5	It is a call to keepe the spirits alive
p. 170 UNDERWOOD 18	10	And Fortune once, t<o>'assist the spirits that dare.
p. 190 UNDERWOOD 37	12	In letters, that mix spirits, thus to weave.
p. 192 UNDERWOOD 38	65	Should aske the blood, and spirits he hath infus'd
p. 280 U'WOOD 84.4	66	In rest, like spirits left behind
p. 283 U'WOOD 84.9	42	As spirits had stolne her Spirit, in a kisse,
p. 327 HORACE 2	494	On edge the Masculine spirits, and did whet
p. 339 HORACE 1	38	Wants strength, and .... as his spirits were done;

spiritual. See "spirituall."

spirituall   frequency: 2   relative frequency: 0.00002
p. 284 U'WOOD 84.9	52	One corporall, only; th'other spirituall,
p. 286 U'WOOD 84.9	131	By light, and comfort of spirituall Grace,

spirrites   frequency: 1   relative frequency: 0.00001
p. 419 UNGATHERED 48	5	By Cherissheinge the Spirrites yt gaue their greatnesse grace:

spit   frequency: 3   relative frequency: 0.00004
p. 88 EPIGRAMS 133	162	Thrise did it spit: thrise diu'd. At last, it view'd
p. 190 UNDERWOOD 37	9	Which is indeed but friendship of the spit:
p. 216 UNDERWOOD 45	8	Was issue of the Taverne, or the Spit:

spite   frequency: 4   relative frequency: 0.00005
See also "spight."
p. 43 EPIGRAMS 52	6	Would both thy folly, and thy spite betray.
p. 260 UNDERWOOD 76	28	Let their spite (which now abounds)
p. 361 UNGATHERED 1	7	not one but thriues; in spite of stormes & thunder,
p. 416 UNGATHERED 43	9	In spite of Hipocrites, who are the worst

spites. See "spights."

spittle   frequency: 1   relative frequency: 0.00001
p. 201 UNDERWOOD 42	71	Unto the Spittle Sermon. O, what strange

spittles   frequency: 1   relative frequency: 0.00001
p. 104 FOREST 8	10	Spittles, pest-house, hospitalls,

splendor   frequency: 3   relative frequency: 0.00004
p. 62 EPIGRAMS 95	29	Where breuitie, where splendor, and where height,
p. 269 UNDERWOOD 83	32	The blaze, and splendor, but not handle fire!
p. 364 UNGATHERED 5	1	Splendor! O more then mortall,

spoil. See "spoile," "spoyle."

spoile   frequency: 2   relative frequency: 0.00002
    p. 162 UNDERWOOD 15   10 In dreames, begun in hope, and end in spoile.
    p. 209 UNDERWOOD 43   150 No Foole would his owne harvest spoile, or
                             burne!

spoiled. See "spoyled."

spoiling. See "spoyling."

spoke   frequency: 3   relative frequency: 0.00004
    See also "spake."
    p. 279 U'WOOD 84.4   36 As what it spoke, it planted there.
    p. 291 UNDERWOOD 85   68 To turne mere farmer, had spoke out,
    p. 307 HORACE 2   62 Much, that mought now be spoke: omitted here

spondaees   frequency: 1   relative frequency: 0.00001
    p. 323 HORACE 2   377 The steadie Spondaees; so themselves to beare

spondees. See "spondaees."

sponge. See "spunge-like."

spoon. See "spoone."

spoone   frequency: 1   relative frequency: 0.00001
    p. 198 UNDERWOOD 40   30 Shall find their depth: they're sounded with a
                             spoone.

sport   frequency: 11   relative frequency: 0.00015
    p. 46 EPIGRAMS 62   10 And there's both losse of time, and losse of
                             sport
    p. 55 EPIGRAMS 85   2 My selfe a witnesse of thy few dayes sport:
    p. 63 EPIGRAMS 97   12 Nor 'bout the beares, nor noyse to make lords
                             sport.
    p. 72 EPIGRAMS 112   2 At this so subtile sport: and play'st so ill?
    p. 93 FOREST 2   9 Thou hast thy walkes for health, as well as
                             sport:
    p. 96 FOREST 3   4 Art tane with neithers vice, nor sport:
    p. 97 FOREST 3   23 In spring, oft roused for thy masters sport,
    p. 231 UNDERWOOD 57   19 Of gambol, or sport
    p. 234 UNDERWOOD 61   1 That you have seene the pride, beheld the sport,
    p. 294 UNDERWOOD 88   2 And done, we straight repent us of the sport:
    p. 398 UNGATHERED 30 80 I looke on Cynthia, and Sirenas sport,

sporting   frequency: 1   relative frequency: 0.00001
    p. 391 UNGATHERED 26   30 Or sporting Kid, or Marlowes mighty line.

sportive   frequency: 1   relative frequency: 0.00001
    p. 311 HORACE 2   150 The angry brow; the sportive, wanton things;

sports   frequency: 6   relative frequency: 0.00008
    p. 45 EPIGRAMS 58   7 So haue I seene at CHRIST-masse sports one
                             lost,
    p. 102 FOREST 5   2 While we may, the sports of loue;
    p. 107 FOREST 10   17 Or, with thy Tribade trine, inuent new sports,
    p. 163 UNDERWOOD 15   38 And even our sports are dangers! what we call
    p. 345 HORACE 1   284 ... . sports ....
    p. 365 UNGATHERED 5   7 Then the stolne sports of Louers,

spotlesse   frequency: 1   relative frequency: 0.00001
    p. 414 UNGATHERED 41   44 And art the spotlesse Mirrour to Mans eyes.

spots   frequency: 2   relative frequency: 0.00002
    p. 171 UNDERWOOD 20   11 Of many Colours; outward, fresh from spots,
    p. 329 HORACE 2   527 Offended with few spots, which negligence

spouse   frequency: 5   relative frequency: 0.00007
    p. 98 FOREST 3   55 Thy noblest spouse affords them welcome grace;
    p. 291 UNDERWOOD 85   42 Some lustie quick Apulians spouse,
    p. 384 UNGATHERED 18 11 May she, whome thou for spouse, to day, dost
                             take,
    p. 413 UNGATHERED 41 33 Daughter, and Mother, and the Spouse of GOD,
    p. 414 UNGATHERED 41 56 Of being Daughter, Mother, Spouse of GOD!

spoused   frequency: 1   relative frequency: 0.00001
    p. 28 EPIGRAMS 5   4 The spoused paire two realmes, the sea the ring.

spoyle   frequency: 1   relative frequency: 0.00001
    p. 265 UNDERWOOD 79   63 The theefe from spoyle, his presence holds.

spoyled   frequency: 1   relative frequency: 0.00001
    p. 184 UNDERWOOD 29   33 Was not spoyled.

spoyling   frequency: 1   relative frequency: 0.00001
    p. 183 UNDERWOOD 29   4 Spoyling Senses of their Treasure,

spread   frequency: 6   relative frequency: 0.00008
    See also "spred."
    p. 100 FOREST 4   8 From all the nets that thou canst spread.
    p. 145 UNDERWOOD 4   11 Nor spread them as distract with feares,
    p. 164 UNDERWOOD 15   65 Planting their Purles, and Curles spread forth
                               like Net,
    p. 167 UNDERWOOD 15   172 Spread through the World) is easier farre to
                               find,
    p. 234 UNDERWOOD 60   16 That spread his body o're, to kill:
    p. 251 UNDERWOOD 74   15 As all the wealth of Season, there was spread;

spreading   frequency: 1   relative frequency: 0.00001
    p. 257 UNDERWOOD 75   159 Your fruitfull spreading Vine,

spred   frequency: 1   relative frequency: 0.00001
    p. 61 EPIGRAMS 95   16 MINERVAES loome was neuer richer spred.

sprig. See "sprigge."

sprigge   frequency: 1   relative frequency: 0.00001
    p. 32 EPIGRAMS 17   5 And, but a sprigge of bayes, giuen by thee,

spright   frequency: 3   relative frequency: 0.00004
    p. 197 UNDERWOOD 40   20 In all his Actions rarified to spright;
    p. 227 UNDERWOOD 52   17 Your Power of handling shadow, ayre, and
                               spright,
    p. 416 UNGATHERED 45   6 at my back, I am no spright,

sprightfull   frequency: 1   relative frequency: 0.00001
    p. 365 UNGATHERED 5   5 Her wit as quicke, and sprightfull

sprightly   frequency: 1   relative frequency: 0.00001
    p. 198 UNDERWOOD 40   26 Moves like a sprightly River, and yet can

spring   frequency: 18   relative frequency: 0.00026
  **p. 116 PANEGYRE   131 About the streets, as it would force a spring
    p. 65 EPIGRAMS 101   33 Tabacco, Nectar, or the Thespian spring,
    p. 97 FOREST 3   23 In spring, oft roused for thy masters sport,
    p. 164 UNDERWOOD 15   75 And laugh, and measure thighes, then squeake,
                               spring, itch,
    p. 232 UNDERWOOD 58   7 If his wit reach no higher, but to spring
    p. 237 UNDERWOOD 65   2 That so hath crown'd our hopes, our spring, and
                               earth,
    p. 238 UNDERWOOD 66   13 Glorie to God. Then, Haile to Mary! spring
    p. 251 UNDERWOOD 74   6 Of the prime beautie of the yeare, the Spring.
    p. 254 UNDERWOOD 75   67 As if her ayrie steps did spring the flowers,
    p. 264 UNDERWOOD 79   25 Sister of PAN, and glory of the Spring:
    p. 276 U'WOOD 84.3   21 The Heaven design'd, draw next a Spring,
    p. 309 HORACE 2   75 So they fall gently from the Grecian spring,
    p. 325 HORACE 2   429 O I left-witted, that purge every spring
    p. 325 HORACE 2   440 The very root of writing well, and spring
    p. 366 UNGATHERED 6   17 He shew'd him first the hoofe-cleft Spring,
    p. 370 UNGATHERED 7   7 Each subt'lest Passion, with her source, and
                               spring,
    p. 399 UNGATHERED 31   14 All Circles had their spring and end
    p. 416 UNGATHERED 44   8 And you, with them, as Father of our spring.

springing. See "blacke-springing."

springs   frequency: 4   relative frequency: 0.00005
    p. 31 EPIGRAMS 14   8 What sight in searching the most antique springs!
    p. 53 EPIGRAMS 79   3 Or then, or since, about our Muses springs,
    p. 174 UNDERWOOD 23   7 Are all th'Aonian springs
    p. 176 UNDERWOOD 24   10 Of Truth that searcheth the most <hidden>
                               Springs,

sprite   frequency: 2   relative frequency: 0.00002
    See also "spright."
    p. 33 EPIGRAMS 19   2 I sent the cause: Hee wooes with an ill sprite.
    p. 66 EPIGRAMS 103   2 That but the twi-light of your sprite did see,

sprung   frequency: 1   relative frequency: 0.00001
    p. 239 UNDERWOOD 67   17 Harpe, Lute, Theorbo sprung,

spue   frequency: 1   relative frequency: 0.00001
    p. 410 UNGATHERED 38 16 And the Physician teach men spue, or shite;

spun   frequency: 5   relative frequency: 0.00007
    See also "out-spun."
    p. 140 UNDERWOOD 2.8 10 And excuse spun every day,
    p. 204 UNDERWOOD 43   33 Or spun out Riddles, and weav'd fiftie tomes
    p. 282 U'WOOD 84.9   6 Spun out in name of some of the old Nine!
    p. 392 UNGATHERED 26 49 Which were so richly spun, and wouen so fit,
    p. 415 UNGATHERED 42 18 As it were spun by nature, off the fleece:

spunge-like   frequency: 1   relative frequency: 0.00001
    p. 155 UNDERWOOD 13   69 And spunge-like with it dry up the blood quite:

spur   frequency: 1   relative frequency: 0.00001
    p. 256 UNDERWOOD 75 118 To th' dull, a Spur

spurres   frequency: 1   relative frequency: 0.00001
    p. 411 UNGATHERED 40   5 The motives, and true Spurres

spurs. See "spurres."

spy   frequency: 2   relative frequency: 0.00002
    See also "spie."
    p. 276 U'WOOD 84.3   20 May rather yet adore, then spy.
    p. 403 UNGATHERED 34 35 Th'ascent of Lady Fame which none could spy

spyes   frequency: 1   relative frequency: 0.00001
    p. 102 FOREST 5   12 Of a few poore houshold spyes?

square   frequency: 2   relative frequency: 0.00002
    p. 220 UNDERWOOD 47   64 Such as are square, wel-tagde, and permanent,
    p. 227 UNDERWOOD 52   8 To square my Circle, I confesse; but draw

squeak. See "squeake."

squeake   frequency: 1   relative frequency: 0.00001
    p. 164 UNDERWOOD 15   75 And laugh, and measure thighes, then squeake,
                             spring, itch,

squeamish. See "squemish."

squemish   frequency: 1   relative frequency: 0.00001
    p. 164 UNDERWOOD 15   68 Be at their Visits, see 'hem squemish, sick,

squib   frequency: 2   relative frequency: 0.00002
    p. 216 UNDERWOOD 45   t2 Arth: Squib.
    p. 229 UNDERWOOD 54   t2 To Mr. ARTHUR SQUIB.

squibs   frequency: 1   relative frequency: 0.00001
    p. 208 UNDERWOOD 43 119 Squire of the Squibs, against the Pageant day,

squire   frequency: 3   relative frequency: 0.00004
    p. 84 EPIGRAMS 133   25 The other was a squire, of faire degree;
    p. 113 FOREST 12   6 To euery squire, or groome, that will report
    p. 208 UNDERWOOD 43 119 Squire of the Squibs, against the Pageant day,

squires   frequency: 2   relative frequency: 0.00002
    p. 30 EPIGRAMS 12   1 SHIFT, here, in towne, not meanest among
                             squires,
    p. 63 EPIGRAMS 97   14 Of any Madames, hath neadd squires, and must.

sr   frequency: 3   relative frequency: 0.00004
    p. 382 UNGATHERED 16 t2 behalfe of the two noble Brothers sr Robert
                             & sr Henrye
    p. 407 UNGATHERED 36   1 Sr Inigo doth feare it as I heare

'ssayd   frequency: 1   relative frequency: 0.00001
    p. 333 HORACE 2   626 And twice, or thrice had 'ssayd it, still in
                             vaine:

ssayes   frequency: 1   relative frequency: 0.00001
    p. 30 EPIGRAMS 12   9 The taylor brings a suite home; he it ssayes,

stable   frequency: 1   relative frequency: 0.00001
    p. 228 UNDERWOOD 53   13 And surely had I but your Stable seene

stag   frequency: 1   relative frequency: 0.00001
    p. 97 FOREST 3   22 A-bed canst heare the loud stag speake,

stage   frequency: 22   relative frequency: 0.00031
*p. 492 TO HIMSELF   1 Come leaue the lothed stage,
 p.   30 EPIGRAMS 12   18 Calls for his stoole, adornes the stage: god
                            payes.
 p.   56 EPIGRAMS 89   2 Fear'd not to boast the glories of her stage,
 p.   72 EPIGRAMS 112   7 I cannot for the stage a Drama lay,
 p. 100 FOREST 4   4 My part is ended on thy stage.
 p. 165 UNDERWOOD 15   109 From Hide-Parke to the Stage, where at the
                            last
 p. 175 UNDERWOOD 23   34 To that strumpet the Stage,
 p. 183 UNDERWOOD 29   25 Starveling rimes did fill the Stage,
 p. 244 UNDERWOOD 70   55 Produce thy masse of miseries on the Stage,
 p. 317 HORACE 2   255 The businesse either on the Stage is done,
 p. 317 HORACE 2   260 Yet, to the Stage, at all thou maist not tender
 p. 317 HORACE 2   268 Upon the Stage, the figure of a Snake.
 p. 319 HORACE 2   305 In his train'd Gowne about the Stage: So grew
 p. 319 HORACE 2   317 Built a small-timbred Stage, and taught them
                            talke
 p. 323 HORACE 2   384 Those heavie Verses, sent so to the Stage,
 p. 342 HORACE 1   179 .... Stage ....
 p. 391 UNGATHERED 26   18 The applause! delight! the wonder of our Stage!
 p. 391 UNGATHERED 26   37 And shake a Stage: Or, when thy Sockes were
                            on,
 p. 392 UNGATHERED 26   78 Or influence, chide, or cheere the drooping
                            Stage;
 p. 402 UNGATHERED 34   11 Whether ye buylding of ye Stage or Scene!
 p. 404 UNGATHERED 34   51 Pack wth your pedling Poetry to the Stage,
 p. 409 UNGATHERED 38   6 Which you haue iustly gained from the Stage,

stage-clothes   frequency: 1   relative frequency: 0.00001
*p. 493 TO HIMSELF   33 Can feed on orts: And safe in your
                            stage-clothes,

stage-wrights   frequency: 1   relative frequency: 0.00001
*p. 493 TO HIMSELF   35 The stagers, and the stage-wrights too (your
                            peeres)

stagers   frequency: 1   relative frequency: 0.00001
*p. 493 TO HIMSELF   35 The stagers, and the stage-wrights too (your
                            peeres)

stages   frequency: 1   relative frequency: 0.00001
 p.   77 EPIGRAMS 120   12 The stages iewell;

stagirite   frequency: 1   relative frequency: 0.00001
 p. 207 UNDERWOOD 43   90 And lighted by the Stagirite, could spie,

staid   frequency: 1   relative frequency: 0.00001
 p. 321 HORACE 2   326 Were to be staid with softnesses, and wonne

stain. See "staine."

stain'd   frequency: 1   relative frequency: 0.00001
 p. 327 HORACE 2   473 And care of getting, thus, our minds hath
                            stain'd,

staine   frequency: 1   relative frequency: 0.00001
 p. 230 UNDERWOOD 55   6 I only can the Paper staine;

stair. See "staire," "stayre."

staire   frequency: 1   relative frequency: 0.00001
 p. 395 UNGATHERED 29   2 And see both climing vp the slippery staire

staires   frequency: 1   relative frequency: 0.00001
 p. 220 UNDERWOOD 47   74 I would call mine, to which not many Staires

stairs. See "staires."

stake   frequency: 2   relative frequency: 0.00002
 p. 142 UNDERWOOD 2.9   39 And not thinke h'had eat a stake,
 p. 401 UNGATHERED 32   12 To cut a Dike? or sticke a Stake vp, here,

stale   frequency: 2   relative frequency: 0.00002
*p. 492 TO HIMSELF   22 Like Pericles; and stale
 p. 107 FOREST 10   20 Turne the stale prologue to some painted maske,

stalk. See "stalke."

stalke   frequency: 1   relative frequency: 0.00001
     p. 319 HORACE 2   318 Loftie, and grave; and in the buskin stalke.

stalketh   frequency: 1   relative frequency: 0.00001
     p. 335 HORACE 2   650 And stalketh, like a Fowler, round about,

stall   frequency: 5   relative frequency: 0.00007
     See also "lay-stall."
   **p. 113 PANEGYRE   11 And snore supinely in the stall of sin:
     p. 28 EPIGRAMS 3   5 To lye vpon thy stall, till it be sought;
     p. 53 EPIGRAMS 78   1 HORNET, thou hast thy wife drest, for the
                               stall,
     p. 200 UNDERWOOD 42   28 At every stall: The Cittie Cap's a charme.
     p. 273 U'WOOD 84.1   28 On every Stall.

stallion   frequency: 1   relative frequency: 0.00001
     p. 163 UNDERWOOD 15   47 Thither it flowes. How much did Stallion spend

stalls   frequency: 1   relative frequency: 0.00001
     p. 104 FOREST 8   9 Liue not we, as, all thy stalls,

stamp.   See "stampe."

stamp'd   frequency: 1   relative frequency: 0.00001
     p. 309 HORACE 2   85 Stamp'd to the time. As woods whose change
                               appeares

stampe   frequency: 2   relative frequency: 0.00002
     p. 204 UNDERWOOD 43   43 And as false stampe there; parcels of a Play,
     p. 218 UNDERWOOD 47   4 And though Opinion stampe them not, are gold.

stand   frequency: 33   relative frequency: 0.00047
     p. 49 EPIGRAMS 67   5 Stand high, then, HOWARD, high in eyes of
                               men,
     p. 61 EPIGRAMS 95   21 Whose knowledge claymeth at the helme to stand;
     p. 63 EPIGRAMS 98   1 Thou hast begun well, ROE, which stand well
                               too,
     p. 83 EPIGRAMS 131   13 Then stand vnto thy selfe, not seeke without
     p. 98 FOREST 3   67 Let others watch in guiltie armes, and stand
     p. 117 FOREST 13   22 If it may stand with your soft blush to heare
     p. 120 FOREST 14   8 Stand silent by,
     p. 121 FOREST 14   30 Doth vrge him to runne wrong, or to stand still.
     p. 159 UNDERWOOD 14   29 Stand forth my Object, then, you that have beene
     p. 167 UNDERWOOD 15   150 That may stand by, and hold my peace? will he,
     p. 170 UNDERWOOD 19   3 By that faire Stand, your forehead, whence he
                               bends
     p. 180 UNDERWOOD 25   64 That you will stand
     p. 191 UNDERWOOD 38   21 I will not stand to justifie my fault,
     p. 191 UNDERWOOD 38   27 No, I will stand arraign'd, and cast, to be
     p. 193 UNDERWOOD 38   91 Forgiven him; And in that lyne stand I,
     p. 198 UNDERWOOD 40   36 Doth, while he keepes his watch, betray his
                               stand.
     p. 217 UNDERWOOD 46   15 And now such is thy stand; while thou dost deale
     p. 220 UNDERWOOD 47   77 As you have writ your selfe. Now stand, and
                               then,
     p. 224 UNDERWOOD 50   19 So great a Vertue stand upright to view,
     p. 229 UNDERWOOD 54   9 And hold me to it close; to stand upright
     p. 238 UNDERWOOD 65   9 And there to stand so. Hast now, envious Moone,
     p. 241 UNDERWOOD 69   11 Was, t'have a Boy stand with a Club, and fright
     p. 243 UNDERWOOD 70   20+ The Stand.
     p. 244 UNDERWOOD 70   52+ The Stand.
     p. 246 UNDERWOOD 70   84+ The Stand.
     p. 247 UNDERWOOD 70   116+ The Stand.
     p. 256 UNDERWOOD 75   113 Stand there; for when a noble Nature's rais'd,
     p. 256 UNDERWOOD 75   126 Whilst they both stand,
     p. 274 U'WOOD 84.2   7 Speake it, you bold PENATES, you that
                               stand
     p. 285 U'WOOD 84.9   96 With boughs of Palme, a crowned Victrice stand!
     p. 331 HORACE 2   540 Will take you more, the neerer that you stand;
     p. 361 UNGATHERED 1   4 I could not but in admiracon stand.
     p. 375 UNGATHERED 10   33 To lie at Liuory, while the Horses did stand.

standard   frequency: 1   relative frequency: 0.00001
     See also "standerd."
     p. 255 UNDERWOOD 75   100 But doth his Carract, and just Standard keepe

standards   frequency: 1   relative frequency: 0.00001
     p. 405 UNGATHERED 34   89 Of thy dead Standards: or (wth miracle) see

standerd   frequency: 2   relative frequency: 0.00002
   p. 415 UNGATHERED 42   22 A Master-worker call'd, th'old standerd burst
   p. 417 UNGATHERED 45   27 as the standerd shall engage him,

standers-by   frequency: 2   relative frequency: 0.00002
   p. 261 UNDERWOOD 77   24 And strike Religion in the standers-by;
   p. 270 UNDERWOOD 83   61 And, in her last act, taught the Standers-by,

standing   frequency: 7   relative frequency: 0.00010
   p. 68 EPIGRAMS 106   7 Thy standing vpright to thy selfe, thy ends
   p. 95 FOREST 2   67 Here no man tells my cups; nor, standing by,
   p. 122 FOREST 15   19 Standing with feare, and must with horror fall,
   p. 198 UNDERWOOD 40   28 'Bove all your standing waters, choak'd with
                weedes.
   p. 245 UNDERWOOD 70   67 Or standing long an Oake, three hundred yeare,
   p. 252 UNDERWOOD 75   1 Though thou hast past thy Summer standing, stay
   p. 397 UNGATHERED 30   23 When, by thy bright Ideas standing by,

stands   frequency: 7   relative frequency: 0.00010
   p. 49 EPIGRAMS 66   12 To liue when Broeck not stands, nor Roor doth
                runne.
   p. 72 EPIGRAMS 111   12 CAESAR stands vp, as from his vrne late
                rose,
   p. 83 EPIGRAMS 132   7 Behold! the reuerend shade of BARTAS stands
   p. 155 UNDERWOOD 13   64 Or stands to be'<i>n Commission o' the blade?
   p. 157 UNDERWOOD 13 139 Then stands it a triumphall marke! then Men
   p. 171 UNDERWOOD 19   19 Slip no occasion; As time stands not still,
   p. 283 U'WOOD 84.9   24 It rages, runs, flies, stands, and would provoke

stand'st   frequency: 4   relative frequency: 0.00005
   p. 41 EPIGRAMS 43   12 As thou stand'st cleere of the necessitie.
   p. 60 EPIGRAMS 93   4 Stand'st thou, to shew the times what you all
                were?
   p. 93 FOREST 2   5 Or stayre, or courts; but stand'st an ancient
                pile,
   p. 225 UNDERWOOD 51   4 Thou stand'st as if some Mysterie thou did'st!

stanley   frequency: 1   relative frequency: 0.00001
   p. 274 U'WOOD 84.2   6 And STANLEY, to the which shee was
                Co-heire.

star   frequency: 1   relative frequency: 0.00001
  See also "day-starre," "morning-star,"
      "morning-starre," "starre."
   p. 181 UNDERWOOD 27   26 Where never Star shone brighter yet?

star-chamber   frequency: 1   relative frequency: 0.00001
  See also "starre-chamber."
   p. 410 UNGATHERED 39   3 At libelling? Shall no Star-Chamber Peers,

starch   frequency: 1   relative frequency: 0.00001
   p. 163 UNDERWOOD 15   49 His Lace and Starch; And fall upon her back

stark. See "starke."

starke   frequency: 1   relative frequency: 0.00001
   p. 269 UNDERWOOD 83   9 Stiffe! starke! my joynts 'gainst one another
                knock!

starre   frequency: 9   relative frequency: 0.00013
   p. 115 FOREST 12   65 You, and that other starre, that purest light,
   p. 134 UNDERWOOD 2.4   14 As Loves starre when it riseth!
   p. 136 UNDERWOOD 2.5   2 Both my fortune, and my Starre!
   p. 143 UNDERWOOD 3   3 Till each of us be made a Starre,
   p. 168 UNDERWOOD 15 196 Who falls for love of God, shall rise a Starre.
   p. 234 UNDERWOOD 60   14 Ambition to become a Starre,
   p. 246 UNDERWOOD 70   98 Two names of friendship, but one Starre:
   p. 294 UNDERWOOD 87   21 LYD. Though he be fairer then a Starre;
   p. 392 UNGATHERED 26   77 Shine forth, thou Starre of Poets, and with
                rage,

starre-chamber   frequency: 2   relative frequency: 0.00002
   p. 44 EPIGRAMS 54   2 And threatens the starre-chamber, and the barre:
   p. 59 EPIGRAMS 92   19 Keepe a starre-chamber sentence close, twelve
                dayes:

starres   frequency: 8   relative frequency: 0.00011
  *p. 494 TO HIMSELF   58 No Harpe ere hit the starres;
   p. 103 FOREST 6   16 Or the starres, that guild his streames,
   p. 115 FOREST 12   58 Vnto the starres? or the Tyndarides?

starres (cont.)
 p. 118 FOREST 13   54 This blessing of your starres, then by that way
 p. 271 UNDERWOOD 83 87 The Starres, that are the Jewels of the Night,
 p. 369 UNGATHERED 6 105 Among the starres should be resign'd
 p. 372 UNGATHERED 9   9 Of Spheares, as light of starres; She was
               earthes Eye:
 p. 422 UNGATHERED 50 7 Looke how the starres from earth, or seas from
               flames

starry   frequency: 1 relative frequency: 0.00001
 p. 276 U'WOOD 84.3 26 And let there be a starry Robe

stars   frequency: 2 relative frequency: 0.00002
 See also "starres."
 p. 181 UNDERWOOD 27 12 Shine more, then she, the Stars among?
 p. 194 UNDERWOOD 38 119 Others by common Stars their courses run,

start   frequency: 3 relative frequency: 0.00004
 See also "starte."
 p. 118 FOREST 13   63 Times, and occasions, to start forth, and seeme)
 p. 168 UNDERWOOD 15 186 Thou shrinke or start not, but be alwayes one;
 p. 395 UNGATHERED 29 11 Calme Brutus tenor start; but all along

starte   frequency: 1 relative frequency: 0.00001
 p. 420 UNGATHERED 48 11 soe much the starte

started   frequency: 2 relative frequency: 0.00002
 See also "out-started."
 p. 50 EPIGRAMS 72   1 I grieue not, COVRTLING, thou are
               started vp
 p. 289 UNDERWOOD 85 5 Nor Souldier-like started with rough alarmes,

starts   frequency: 1 relative frequency: 0.00001
 p. 100 FOREST 4   11 Thy curtesie but sodaine starts,

starue   frequency: 1 relative frequency: 0.00001
 p. 106 FOREST 8   44 And will, long ere thou should'st starue,

starve. See "starue," "sterve."

starveling   frequency: 1 relative frequency: 0.00001
 p. 183 UNDERWOOD 29 25 Starveling rimes did fill the Stage,

state   frequency: 63 relative frequency: 0.00091
 See also "after-state," "estate."
**p. 113 PANEGYRE   21 Vpon his state; let downe in that rich chaine,
**p. 115 PANEGYRE   86 "Oft-times, to haue the secrets of their state
**p. 116 PANEGYRE 106 "Lawes, iudges, co<u>nsellors, yea prince, and
               state.
**p. 117 PANEGYRE 136 Was gently falne from heauen vpon this state;
 p. 28 EPIGRAMS 5   2 Or celebrated with more truth of state?
 p. 30 EPIGRAMS 12   4 The charge of that state, with this charme, god
               payes.
 p. 35 EPIGRAMS 27   7 To heauen; his hath: O happy state! wherein
 p. 41 EPIGRAMS 45   6 Will man lament the state he should enuie?
 p. 45 EPIGRAMS 59   1 SPIES, you are lights in state, but of base
               stuffe,
 p. 48 EPIGRAMS 64 18 I'haue sung the greater fortunes of our state.
 p. 50 EPIGRAMS 70   2 Then to begin, my ROE: He makes a state
 p. 58 EPIGRAMS 92   5 And haue'hem yeeld no sauour, but of state.
 p. 59 EPIGRAMS 92 14 For twelue yeeres yet to come, what each state
               lacks.
 p. 59 EPIGRAMS 92 40 That know not so much state, wrong, as they doo.
 p. 61 EPIGRAMS 95 23 No more then SALVST in the Romane state!
 p. 62 EPIGRAMS 95 33 Of state, and censure them: we need his pen
 p. 68 EPIGRAMS 105 17 Or, keeping your due state, that would not cry,
 p. 70 EPIGRAMS 109 12 And first to know thine owne state, then the
               States.
 p. 75 EPIGRAMS 117 1 GROYNE, come of age, his state sold out of
               hand
 p. 78 EPIGRAMS 123 3 But both th'hast so, as who affects the state
 p. 96 FOREST 3   7 Nor com'st to view the better cloth of state;
 p. 98 FOREST 3   57 Sit mixt with losse of state, or reuerence.
 p. 99 FOREST 3   93 Thy peace is made; and, when man's state is well,
 p. 101 FOREST 4   57 Else, I my state should much mistake,
 p. 109 FOREST 11   1 Not to know vice at all, and keepe true state,
 p. 118 FOREST 13   48 For such a lot! that mixt you with a state
 p. 118 FOREST 13   81 Let 'hem waste body, and state; and after all,
 p. 122 FOREST 15   11 My faith, my hope, my loue: and in this state,
 p. 122 FOREST 15   17 I know my state, both full of shame, and scorne,

state (cont.)
     p. 127 UNDERWOOD 1.1   19 And breath'st into it, life, and light, with
                                state
     p. 144 UNDERWOOD 3   27 So they in state of Grace retain'd,
     p. 156 UNDERWOOD 13   103 Cannot a man be reck'ned in the State
     p. 161 UNDERWOOD 14   68 With that thy Stile, thy keeping of thy State,
     p. 170 UNDERWOOD 18   17 To see men feare: or else for truth, and State,
     p. 177 UNDERWOOD 25   29 Of politique pretext, that wryes a State,
     p. 185 UNDERWOOD 30   20 Of divine blessing, would not serve a State?
     p. 193 UNDERWOOD 38   85 But view the mildnesse of your Makers state,
     p. 203 UNDERWOOD 43   25 Itch to defame the State? or brand the Times?
     p. 215 UNDERWOOD 44   78 Our Ancestors impos'd on Prince and State.
     p. 215 UNDERWOOD 44   85 To serve the State by Councels, and by Armes:
     p. 222 UNDERWOOD 49   12 Make State, Religion, Bawdrie, all a theame?
     p. 224 UNDERWOOD 50   18 Of State, of fame, of body, and of soule,
     p. 234 UNDERWOOD 61   4 At which there are, would sell the Prince, and
                                State:
     p. 240 UNDERWOOD 67   44 Her joy in state, and pleasure;
     p. 243 UNDERWOOD 70   27 He vexed time, and busied the whole State;
     p. 250 UNDERWOOD 73   5 WESTON! That waking man! that Eye of
                                State!
     p. 251 UNDERWOOD 74   24 Both to the honour of the King and State.
     p. 255 UNDERWOOD 75   99 Great Say-Master of State, who cannot erre,
     p. 258 UNDERWOOD 75   178 To be a watchfull Servant for this State;
     p. 260 UNDERWOOD 77   1 If to my mind, great Lord, I had a state,
     p. 262 UNDERWOOD 78   6 In him all vertue is beheld in State:
     p. 270 UNDERWOOD 83   43 A reverend State she had, an awfull Eye,
     p. 271 UNDERWOOD 83   84 And wish her state lesse happie then it is!
     p. 309 HORACE 2   87 The first-borne dying; so the aged state
     p. 309 HORACE 2   99 Shall perish: so farre off it is, the state,
     p. 311 HORACE 2   153 To every state of fortune; she helpes on,
     p. 313 HORACE 2   180 A meere new person, looke he keepe his state
     p. 319 HORACE 2   316 Brought in the Visor, and the robe of State,
     p. 399 UNGATHERED 31   7 Your booke? your volume! Nay, the state, and
                                story!
     p. 399 UNGATHERED 31   25 Her soule possess her fleshes state
     p. 403 UNGATHERED 34   42 You are ye Spectacles of State! Tis true
     p. 405 UNGATHERED 34   84 Moulded or stroakt vp to suruey a State!
     p. 419 UNGATH'D 47A   3 ... . and the State

stated. See "alike-stated."

states   frequency: 12   relative frequency: 0.00017
     p. 59 EPIGRAMS 92   8 They know the states of Christendome, not the
                                places:
     p. 59 EPIGRAMS 92   30 If the States make peace, how it will goe
     p. 69 EPIGRAMS 107   10 What States yo'haue gull'd, and which yet keepes
                                yo'in pay.
     p. 70 EPIGRAMS 109   12 And first to know thine owne state, then the
                                States.
     p. 78 EPIGRAMS 121   4 Shee learnes to know long difference of their
                                states.
     p. 99 FOREST 3   79 To blow vp orphanes, widdowes, and their states;
     p. 166 UNDERWOOD 15   133 And whilst our states, strength, body, and mind
                                we waste,
     p. 219 UNDERWOOD 47   33 Or the States Ships sent forth belike to meet
     p. 219 UNDERWOOD 47   43 So farre without inquirie what the States,
     p. 248 UNDERWOOD 71   1 Poore wretched states, prest by extremities,
     p. 422 UNGATHERED 50   3 Is her owne scourge, when it sustaines their
                                states
     p. 423 UNGATHERED 50   13 Euen states most hated, when no lawes resist

states-man   frequency: 1   relative frequency: 0.00001
     p. 223 UNDERWOOD 49   25 I am no States-man, and much lesse Divine,

states-mans   frequency: 1   relative frequency: 0.00001
     p. 325 HORACE 2   449 Can tell a States-mans dutie, what the arts

states-men   frequency: 1   relative frequency: 0.00001
     p. 69 EPIGRAMS 107   19 Giue your yong States-men, (that first make you
                                drunke,

statesman   frequency: 1   relative frequency: 0.00001
     See also "states-man."
     p. 30 EPIGRAMS 11   3 To seeme a statesman: as I neere it came,

statesman's. See "states-mans."

statesmen   frequency: 1   relative frequency: 0.00001
     See also "states-men."

statesmen (cont.)
p.   58 EPIGRAMS 92   3 Ripe statesmen, ripe: They grow in euery street.

statists   frequency: 1   relative frequency: 0.00001
p. 179 UNDERWOOD 25   39 Is but a Statists theame, to read Phlebotomie.

statuaries   frequency: 1   relative frequency: 0.00001
p. 307 HORACE 2   45 The worst of Statuaries, here about

statue   frequency: 4   relative frequency: 0.00005
p.   56 EPIGRAMS 88   13 Or is it some french statue? No: 'T doth moue,
p. 132 UNDERWOOD 2.2   30 Cupids Statue with a Beard,
p. 261 UNDERWOOD 77   14 Discerne betweene a Statue, and a Man;
p. 292 UNDERWOOD 86   19 He'll thee a Marble Statue make

statues   frequency: 2   relative frequency: 0.00002
p. 115 FOREST 12   84 Borne vp by statues, shall I reare your head,
p. 261 UNDERWOOD 77   15 Can doe the things that Statues doe deserve,

stature   frequency: 3   relative frequency: 0.00004
p.   66 EPIGRAMS 102   13 But thou, whose noblesse keeps one stature still,
p. 130 UNDERWOOD 1.3.   15 Both wills were in one stature;
p. 157 UNDERWOOD 13   146 As if they would belie their stature; those

statute   frequency: 1   relative frequency: 0.00001
p. 411 UNGATHERED 39   15 A Rogue by Statute, censur'd to be whipt,

statutes   frequency: 1   relative frequency: 0.00001
**p. 115 PANEGYRE   97 "And thriuing statutes she could promptly note;

stay   frequency: 34   relative frequency: 0.00049
p.   48 EPIGRAMS 65   15 But I repent me: Stay. Who e're is rais'd,
p.   79 EPIGRAMS 124   2 In a little? Reader, stay.
p.   94 FOREST 2   35 As loth, the second draught, or cast to stay,
p.   95 FOREST 2   75 There's nothing I can wish, for which I stay.
p. 100 FOREST 4   21 And, knowing this, should I yet stay,
p. 107 FOREST 10   8 Shall not giue out, that I haue made thee stay,
p. 131 UNDERWOOD 2.1   21 Keepe the middle age at stay,
p. 132 UNDERWOOD 2.2   16 Strait hee ran, and durst not stay,
p. 139 UNDERWOOD 2.7   4 Why doe you doubt, or stay?
p. 143 UNDERWOOD 3   10 To stay the running floods,
p. 163 UNDERWOOD 15   30 Rather then here so bogg'd in vices stay.
p. 168 UNDERWOOD 16   1 Reader, stay,
p. 183 UNDERWOOD 29   20 At the Well[s] no Muse did stay,
p. 191 UNDERWOOD 38   8 Alone lend succours, and this furie stay,
p. 213 UNDERWOOD 44   10 If they stay here, but till Saint Georges Day.
p. 216 UNDERWOOD 44   98 I may no longer on these pictures stay,
p. 233 UNDERWOOD 60   2 Stay, drop a teare for him that's dead,
p. 252 UNDERWOOD 75   1 Though thou hast past thy Summer standing, stay
p. 252 UNDERWOOD 75   6 We wooe thee, stay
p. 254 UNDERWOOD 75   49 Stay, thou wilt see what rites the Virgins doe!
p. 254 UNDERWOOD 75   56 Although/that thou, O Sun, at our intreaty
                           stay!
p. 254 UNDERWOOD 75   61 Stay, see the Virgins sow,
p. 254 UNDERWOOD 75   64 O, now thou smil'st, faire Sun, and shin'st, as
                           thou wouldst stay!
p. 256 UNDERWOOD 75   122 And Bishop stay, to consummate the Rites:.
p. 269 UNDERWOOD 83   7 To give your shade a name! Stay, stay, I feele
p. 317 HORACE 2   253 To children; we must alwayes dwell, and stay
p. 325 HORACE 2   413 Her language, if the Stay, and Care t'have
                           mended,
p. 371 UNGATHERED 9   1 Stay, view this stone: And, if thou beest not
                           such,
p. 380 UNGATHERED 12   26 How long he did stay, at what signe he did Inne.
p. 392 UNGATHERED 26   75 But stay, I see thee in the Hemisphere
p. 397 UNGATHERED 30   47 Sayst thou so, Lucan? But thou scornst to stay
p. 400 UNGATHERED 31   28 Fames heate vpon the graue did stay;
p. 401 UNGATHERED 32   15 Stay, till she make her vaine Approches. Then

stay'd   frequency: 4   relative frequency: 0.00005
See also "staid."
p. 138 UNDERWOOD 2.6   29 Or if you would yet have stay'd,
p. 204 UNDERWOOD 43   46 Thou should'st have stay'd, till publike fame
                           said so.
p. 212 UNDERWOOD 43   201 Or stay'd but where the Fryar, and you first
                           met,
p. 413 UNGATHERED 41   40 The Morning-star, whose light our Fal hath
                           stay'd.

stayes   frequency: 4   relative frequency: 0.00005
    p. 89 EPIGRAMS 133 178 And stayes but till you come vnto the dore!
    p. 121 FOREST 14   49 And he that stayes
    p. 280 U'WOOD 84.4   63 And where it stayes, it there becomes
    p. 327 HORACE 2   459 And better stayes them there, then all fine noise

stayre   frequency: 1   relative frequency: 0.00001
    p. 93 FOREST 2   5 Or stayre, or courts; but stand'st an ancient
                            pile,

stays. See "stayes."

stead   frequency: 4   relative frequency: 0.00005
    See also "noone-sted's."
    p. 73 EPIGRAMS 113   8 And letters and humanitie in the stead!
    p. 84 EPIGRAMS 133   13 Arses were heard to croake, in stead of frogs;
    p. 214 UNDERWOOD 44   51 Up among Nations. In the stead of bold
    p. 222 UNDERWOOD 49   6 New in their stead, out of the Candidates?

steadfast. See "stedfast."

steadie   frequency: 1   relative frequency: 0.00001
    p. 323 HORACE 2   377 The steadie Spondaees; so themselves to beare

steady. See "steadie."

steal. See "steale."

steale   frequency: 3   relative frequency: 0.00004
    p. 102 FOREST 5   15 'Tis no sinne, loues fruit to steale,
    p. 107 FOREST 10   23 Though he would steale his sisters
                            PEGASVS,
    p. 223 UNDERWOOD 49   35 Shall I advise thee, Pucell? steale away

steales   frequency: 2   relative frequency: 0.00002
    p. 30 EPIGRAMS 12   11 He steales to ordinaries; there he playes
    p. 339 HORACE 1   40 Downe close .. shore, this other creeping
                            steales,

steals. See "steales."

stealth   frequency: 5   relative frequency: 0.00007
    p. 99 FOREST 3   82 Purchas'd by rapine, worse then stealth,
    p. 154 UNDERWOOD 13   49 Give thankes by stealth, and whispering in the
                            eare,
    p. 166 UNDERWOOD 15 116 Or by Damnation voids it? or by stealth?
    p. 197 UNDERWOOD 40   9 This makes me, Mrs. that sometime by stealth,
    p. 210 UNDERWOOD 43 169 So would'st th<ou>'have run upon the Rolls by
                            stealth,

steam. See "steame."

steame   frequency: 1   relative frequency: 0.00001
    p. 205 UNDERWOOD 43   61 Especially in paper; that, that steame

steaming. See "steeming."

steams. See "steemes."

stedfast   frequency: 1   relative frequency: 0.00001
  **p. 116 PANEGYRE   122 Must with a tender (yet a stedfast) hand

steel. See "steele."

steele   frequency: 3   relative frequency: 0.00004
    p. 164 UNDERWOOD 15   78 That payes, or what he will: The Dame is
                            steele.
    p. 269 UNDERWOOD 83   8 A horrour in mee! all my blood is steele!
    p. 325 HORACE 2   434 On steele, though 't selfe be dull, and cannot
                            cut.

steemes   frequency: 1   relative frequency: 0.00001
    p. 88 EPIGRAMS 133 144 That, with still-scalding steemes, make the place
                            hell.

steeming   frequency: 1   relative frequency: 0.00001
    p. 291 UNDERWOOD 85   66 And 'bout the steeming Chimney set!

steep. See "steepe."

steep'd   frequency: 2   relative frequency: 0.00002
     p. 230 UNDERWOOD 55   5 But since the Wine hath steep'd my braine,
     p. 327 HORACE 2   475 In juyce of Cedar worthy to be steep'd,

steepe   frequency: 7   relative frequency: 0.00010
     p. 77 EPIGRAMS 120   22 In bathes to steepe him;
     p. 111 FOREST 11   63 Would, at suggestion of a steepe desire,
     p. 145 UNDERWOOD 4   9 O, doe not steepe them in thy Teares,
     p. 170 UNDERWOOD 19   8 Where he doth steepe himselfe in Milke and
                                Roses;
     p. 190 UNDERWOOD 37   14 So may the fruitfull Vine my temples steepe,
     p. 319 HORACE 2   298 Steepe the glad Genius in the Wine, whole
                                dayes,
     p. 374 UNGATHERED 10   12 Here, not vp Holdborne, but downe a steepe hill,

steeple. See "parish-steeple," "pauls-steeple."

steeples   frequency: 2   relative frequency: 0.00002
   **p. 114 PANEGYRE   63 Walls, windores, roofes, towers, steeples, all
                                were set
     p. 249 UNDERWOOD 72   10 The Poetrie of Steeples, with the Bells,

stella   frequency: 1   relative frequency: 0.00001
     p. 181 UNDERWOOD 27   25 Hath our great Sydney, Stella set,

stem   frequency: 1   relative frequency: 0.00001
   See also "stemme."
     p. 258 UNDERWOOD 75   177 And never may there want one of the Stem,

stemme   frequency: 3   relative frequency: 0.00004
     p. 87 EPIGRAMS 133   111 Their MERCVRY did now. By this, the
                                stemme
     p. 119 FOREST 13   97 And raise a noble stemme, to giue the fame,
     p. 274 U'WOOD 84.2   8 At either Stemme, and know the veines of good

stench   frequency: 2   relative frequency: 0.00002
     p. 84 EPIGRAMS 133   9 The filth, stench, noyse: saue only what was
                                there
     p. 86 EPIGRAMS 133   70 Hung stench, diseases, and old filth, their
                                mother,

steps   frequency: 4   relative frequency: 0.00005
   **p. 117 PANEGYRE   141 That wan affections, ere his steps wan ground;
     p. 217 UNDERWOOD 46   2 And steps of all rais'd servants of the Crowne,
     p. 254 UNDERWOOD 75   67 As if her ayrie steps did spring the flowers,
     p. 379 UNGATHERED 12   12 Since he treads in no other Mans steps but his
                                owne.

stern. See "sterne."

sterne   frequency: 1   relative frequency: 0.00001
     p. 129 UNDERWOOD 1.2   8 Beene sterne to mee,

steropes   frequency: 1   relative frequency: 0.00001
     p. 179 UNDERWOOD 25   40 Let Brontes, and black Steropes,

sterve   frequency: 2   relative frequency: 0.00002
     p. 191 UNDERWOOD 38   7 Or there to sterve it. Helpe, O you that may
     p. 192 UNDERWOOD 38   62 Consumptions nature to destroy, and sterve.

stew   frequency: 1   relative frequency: 0.00001
     p. 105 FOREST 8   38 Euery stew in towne to know;

stewards   frequency: 1   relative frequency: 0.00001
     p. 57 EPIGRAMS 90   15 Hath got the stewards chaire; he will not tarry

stewes   frequency: 3   relative frequency: 0.00004
     p. 209 UNDERWOOD 43   140 'Twas verily some Relique of the Stewes:
     p. 375 UNGATHERED 10   20 Religiously here he bids, row from the stewes,
     p. 380 UNGATHERED 12   50 So that not them, his scabbes, lice, or the
                                stewes,

stews. See "stewes."

stick   frequency: 1   relative frequency: 0.00001
   See also "sticke."
     p. 270 UNDERWOOD 83   53 Stick on your Cupping-glasses, feare not, put

sticke   frequency: 1   relative frequency: 0.00001
     p. 401 UNGATHERED 32   12 To cut a Dike? or sticke a Stake vp, here,

sticking   frequency: 1   relative frequency: 0.00001
    p. 133 UNDERWOOD 2.3   16 Left it sticking in my heart:

sticks. See "cleft-sticks."

stiff. See "stiffe."

stiffe   frequency: 4   relative frequency: 0.00005
    p. 152 UNDERWOOD 12   24 No stubbornnesse so stiffe, nor folly
    p. 163 UNDERWOOD 15   43 As they are made! Pride, and stiffe Clownage
                             mixt
    p. 269 UNDERWOOD 83   9 Stiffe! starke! my joynts 'gainst one another
                             knock!
    p. 363 UNGATHERED 3   13 It thawes the frostiest, and most stiffe
                             disdaine:

stil   frequency: 1   relative frequency: 0.00001
    p. 184 UNDERWOOD 29   53 Stil may reason warre with rime,

stil'd   frequency: 7   relative frequency: 0.00010
    p. 104 FOREST 7   6 Stil'd but the shaddowes of vs men?
    p. 104 FOREST 7   12 Stil'd but the shaddowes of vs men?
    p. 189 UNDERWOOD 36   13 Such are his powers, whom time hath stil'd,
    p. 191 UNDERWOOD 38   29 And (stil'd your mercies Creature) will live
                             more
    p. 339 HORACE 1   36 .. .. stil'd
    p. 389 UNGATHERED 24 13 And this hath met that one, that may be stil'd
    p. 397 UNGATHERED 30 37 And I had stil'd thee, Orpheus, but before

stilde   frequency: 1   relative frequency: 0.00001
    p. 188 UNDERWOOD 35   1 What Beautie would have lovely stilde,

stile   frequency: 11   relative frequency: 0.00015
    p. 36 EPIGRAMS 28   22 Stile thee a most great foole, but no great man.
    p. 68 EPIGRAMS 105   15 There's none so dull, that for your stile would
                             aske,
    p. 71 EPIGRAMS 110   6 To haue engrau'd these acts, with his owne stile,
    p. 160 UNDERWOOD 14   55 To marke the excellent seas'ning of your Stile!
    p. 161 UNDERWOOD 14   68 With that thy Stile, thy keeping of thy State,
    p. 164 UNDERWOOD 15   81 And comes by these Degrees, the Stile
                             t<o>'inherit
    p. 187 UNDERWOOD 33   31 Against a multitude; and (with thy Stile
    p. 208 UNDERWOOD 43 131 (Which, some are pleas'd to stile but thy madde
                             pranck)
    p. 367 UNGATHERED 6   32 "For stile of rarenesse, to degenerate.
    p. 379 UNGATHERED 12 10 By the scale of his booke, a yard of his stile?
    p. 398 UNGATHERED 30 59 There, thou art Homer! Pray thee, vse the stile

stiled   frequency: 2   relative frequency: 0.00002
    p. 84 EPIGRAMS 133   24 To haue beene stiled of King ARTHVRS
                             table.
    p. 247 UNDERWOOD 70 111 Each stiled, by his end,

stiles   frequency: 1   relative frequency: 0.00001
    p. 214 UNDERWOOD 44   54 As Stiles, Dike, Ditchfield, Millar, Crips,
                             and Fen:

still   frequency: 146   relative frequency: 0.00211
    See also "stil," "still>."
   *p. 492 TO HIMSELF   13 'Twere simple fury, still, thy selfe to waste
  **p. 113 PANEGYRE   2 With ioyes: but vrgeth his full fauors still.
  **p. 116 PANEGYRE   117 An euill king: And so must such be still,
  **p. 116 PANEGYRE   134 To heare her speech; which still began in him
  **p. 117 PANEGYRE   162 Still to haue such a king, and this king long.
    p. 28 EPIGRAMS 4   8 As chiefe of those still promise they will bee.
    p. 29 EPIGRAMS 7   4 And still be a whore-house. Th'are Synonima.
    p. 30 EPIGRAMS 11   8 For I will dare none. Good Lord, walke dead
                             still.
    p. 30 EPIGRAMS 12   16 Takes physick, teares the papers: still god
                             payes.
    p. 32 EPIGRAMS 18   9 Pr'y thee beleeue still, and not iudge so fast,
    p. 35 EPIGRAMS 26   2 He'adulters still: his thoughts lye with a whore.
    p. 35 EPIGRAMS 28   13 Which is maine greatnesse. And, at his still
                             boord,
    p. 40 EPIGRAMS 42   15 In all affections shee concurreth still.
    p. 42 EPIGRAMS 49   1 PLAY-WRIGHT me reades, and still my
                             verses damnes,
    p. 43 EPIGRAMS 51   9 For we, that haue our eyes still in our eares,
    p. 45 EPIGRAMS 58   4 Thy ignorance still laughs in the wrong place.
    p. 48 EPIGRAMS 64   14 As her owne conscience, still, the same reward.

still (cont.)

p.	48	EPIGRAMS 65	8	And, reconcil'd, keepe him suspected still.
p.	50	EPIGRAMS 71	1	To plucke downe mine, POLL sets vp new wits still,
p.	50	EPIGRAMS 71	2	Still, 'tis his lucke to praise me 'gainst his will.
p.	52	EPIGRAMS 74	5	That still th'art present to the better cause;
p.	57	EPIGRAMS 90	7	Went on: and prouing him still, day by day,
p.	57	EPIGRAMS 90	11	Still MILL continu'd: Nay, his face growing worse,
p.	63	EPIGRAMS 98	6	And what would hurt his vertue makes it still.
p.	66	EPIGRAMS 102	13	But thou, whose noblesse keeps one stature still,
p.	66	EPIGRAMS 102	20	The common-wealth still safe, must studie thee.
p.	68	EPIGRAMS 106	9	Their latter praise would still the greatest bee,
p.	70	EPIGRAMS 108	10	But 's angry for the Captayne, still: is such.
p.	72	EPIGRAMS 112	1	With thy small stocke, why art thou ventring still,
p.	72	EPIGRAMS 112	6	Art still at that, and think'st to blow me'vp too?
p.	73	EPIGRAMS 114	1	I must beleeue some miracles still bee,
p.	75	EPIGRAMS 117	2	For'his whore: GROYNE doth still occupy his land.
p.	80	EPIGRAMS 127	10	By her attempt, shall still be owing thee.
p.	81	EPIGRAMS 129	7	That still th'art made the suppers flagge, the drum,
p.	85	EPIGRAMS 133	56	Still, with thy former labours; yet, once more,
p.	86	EPIGRAMS 133	76	But still their valour, and their vertue fenc't 'hem,
p.	86	EPIGRAMS 133	88	No going backe: on still you rogues, and row.
p.	88	EPIGRAMS 133	152	But still, it seem'd, the ranknesse did conuince 'hem.
p.	102	FOREST 4	66	As wandrers doe, that still doe rome,
p.	104	FOREST 7	1	Follow a shaddow, it still flies you;
p.	107	FOREST 10	7	PHOEBVS. No? tend thy cart still. Enuious day
p.	112	FOREST 11	88	Is more crowne-worthy still,
p.	114	FOREST 12	28	With noble ignorants, and let them still,
p.	119	FOREST 13	113	How you loue one, and him you should; how still
p.	119	FOREST 13	118	This makes, that your affections still be new,
p.	120	FOREST 13	121	Liue that one, still; and as long yeeres doe passe,
p.	120	FOREST 13	123	Wherein, your forme, you still the same shall finde;
p.	121	FOREST 14	30	Doth vrge him to runne wrong, or to stand still.
p.	122	FOREST 15	15	Dwell, dwell here still: O, being euery-where,
p.	127	UNDERWOOD 1.1	2	Of persons, still one God, in Vnitie,
p.	128	UNDERWOOD 1.1	30	Of persons, still one God in Vnitie;
p.	129	UNDERWOOD 1.2	4	Use still thy rod,
p.	134	UNDERWOOD 2.4	9	That they still were to run by her side,
p.	141	UNDERWOOD 2.9	38	Drest, you still for man should take him;
p.	145	UNDERWOOD 5	3	To make us still sing o're, and o're,
p.	151	UNDERWOOD 12	14	All order, and Disposure, still.
p.	155	UNDERWOOD 13	65	Still, still, the hunters of false fame apply
p.	155	UNDERWOOD 13	74	Feed those, at whom the Table points at still?
p.	157	UNDERWOOD 13	135	Yet we must more then move still, or goe on,
p.	157	UNDERWOOD 13	141	It was erected; and still walking under
p.	159	UNDERWOOD 14	28	Meane what I speake: and still will keepe that Vow.
p.	159	UNDERWOOD 14	31	And like a Compasse keeping one foot still
p.	160	UNDERWOOD 14	58	But to the Subject, still the Colours fit
p.	166	UNDERWOOD 15	124	But being in Motion still (or rather in race)
p.	168	UNDERWOOD 15	190	Still pretious, with the odour of thy name.
p.	170	UNDERWOOD 18	14	And then the best are, still, the blindest friends!
p.	171	UNDERWOOD 19	19	Slip no occasion; As time stands not still,
p.	174	UNDERWOOD 23	18	'Tis crowne enough to vertue still, her owne applause.
p.	184	UNDERWOOD 29	52	Still may Syllabes jarre with time,
p.	185	UNDERWOOD 30	13	That still was good for goodnesse sake, nor thought
p.	186	UNDERWOOD 31	6	The Care, and wish still of the publike wealth:
p.	186	UNDERWOOD 31	8	Still flie about the Odour of your Name;
p.	187	UNDERWOOD 33	27	Of Argument, still drawing forth the best,
p.	189	UNDERWOOD 36	12	And waste still, that they still might bee.
p.	189	UNDERWOOD 36	16	The eldest God, yet still a Child.
p.	190	UNDERWOOD 37	27	As flatt'ry with friends humours still to move.
p.	192	UNDERWOOD 38	53	That is, if still your Favours you apply,
p.	197	UNDERWOOD 40	19	Yet should the Lover still be ayrie and light,
p.	198	UNDERWOOD 40	34	Out with the other, for hee's still at home;
p.	199	UNDERWOOD 41	17	O, keepe it still; for it had rather be

still (cont.)

p. 201 UNDERWOOD 42	42	Being, the best clothes still to praeoccupie.
p. 206 UNDERWOOD 43	80	Upon th'Exchange, still, out of Popes-head-Alley;
p. 210 UNDERWOOD 43	159	Hee is true Vulcan still! He did not spare
p. 212 UNDERWOOD 43	197	Would you had kept your Forge, at Aetna still,
p. 213 UNDERWOOD 44	2	But we have Powder still for the Kings Day,
p. 214 UNDERWOOD 44	56	Alive yet, in the noise; and still the same,
p. 219 UNDERWOOD 47	61	Still looking to, and ever loving heaven;
p. 221 UNDERWOOD 48	16	And still begin'st the greeting:
p. 221 UNDERWOOD 48	21	So mayst thou still be younger
p. 221 UNDERWOOD 48	26	Thee still, and leave Apollo,
p. 236 UNDERWOOD 63	10	And thinke all still the best, that he will doe.
p. 238 UNDERWOOD 66	12	To compare small with great, as still we owe
p. 249 UNDERWOOD 72	18	Still to have such a CHARLES, but this CHARLES long.
p. 250 UNDERWOOD 73	1	Looke up, thou seed of envie, and still bring
p. 258 UNDERWOOD 75	181	Whilst the maine tree, still found
p. 259 UNDERWOOD 76	24	But we last out, still unlay'd.
p. 262 UNDERWOOD 78	8	For that to dwell in, and be still at home.
p. 264 UNDERWOOD 79	26	Who walkes on Earth as May still went along,
p. 264 UNDERWOOD 79	39	Still waited on 'hem where they were.
p. 273 U'WOOD 84.1	9	Of Goodnesse still: Vouchsafe to take
p. 278 U'WOOD 84.4	20	And yet remaine our wonder still.
p. 279 U'WOOD 84.4	40	Still left an Eccho in the sense.
p. 286 U'WOOD 84.9	119	But all of God; They still shall have to say,
p. 291 UNDERWOOD 85	57	Or the herb Sorrell, that loves Meadows still,
p. 305 HORACE 2	12	Of daring all, hath still beene given; we know it:
p. 307 HORACE 2	29	Was meant at first. Why, forcing still about
p. 307 HORACE 2	53	Take, therefore, you that write, still, matter fit
p. 309 HORACE 2	86	Still in their leaves, throughout the sliding yeares,
p. 309 HORACE 2	104	The power, and rule of speaking resteth still.
p. 311 HORACE 2	131	To ignorance still, then either learne, or know?
p. 311 HORACE 2	142	To worke the hearers minds, still, to their plight.
p. 311 HORACE 2	143	Mens faces, still, with such as laugh, are prone
p. 313 HORACE 2	172	Keepe him still active, angry, un-appeas'd,
p. 313 HORACE 2	182	Still to be like himselfe, and hold his worth.
p. 317 HORACE 2	246	With sloth, yet greedy still of what's to come:
p. 317 HORACE 2	249	And still correcting youth, and censuring.
p. 317 HORACE 2	280	It still must favour good men, and to these
p. 325 HORACE 2	443	And, where the matter is provided still,
p. 325 HORACE 2	453	And I still bid the learned Maker looke
p. 329 HORACE 2	521	For, neither doth the String still yeeld that sound
p. 329 HORACE 2	530	Still in the same, and warned will not mend,
p. 329 HORACE 2	532	Is laugh'd at, that still jarreth on one string:
p. 331 HORACE 2	568	Or trundling Wheele, he can sit still, from all;
p. 333 HORACE 2	626	And twice, or thrice had 'ssayd it, still in vaine:
p. 335 HORACE 2	631	In vaine, but you, and yours, you should love still
p. 339 HORACE 1	42	So he that varying still affects .. draw
p. 342 HORACE 1	177	.. still .... griev'd .... sad
p. 361 UNGATHERED 1	19	still making that the greatest that is last
p. 366 UNGATHERED 6	27	And still is in the Brest:
p. 383 UNGATHERED 16	13	still that same little poynte hee was; but when
p. 383 UNGATHERED 16	14	your Royal Eye which still creat[t]es new men
p. 383 UNGATHERED 17	2	Must be intended still to vnderstand:
p. 384 UNGATHERED 18	17	So, be yor Concord, still, as deepe, as mute;
p. 388 UNGATHERED 23	5	Still, still, dost thou arriue with, at our shore,
p. 391 UNGATHERED 26	23	And art aliue still, while thy Booke doth liue,
p. 391 UNGATHERED 26	44	And all the Muses still were in their prime,
p. 394 UNGATHERED 28	19	To call on Sicknes still, to be her Guest,
p. 395 UNGATHERED 29	18	Are still th'interpreters twixt godds, and men!
p. 403 UNGATHERED 34	22	you'l be as Langley sayd, an Inigo still.
p. 404 UNGATHERED 34	65	All in ye Worke! And soe shall still for Ben:
p. 410 UNGATHERED 39	1	Shall the prosperity of a Pardon still
p. 421 UNGATHERED 49	9	And though yor virtue (as becomes it) still
p. 662 INSCRIPTS. 2	4	appropriates still vnto that County:

still-scalding   frequency: 1   relative frequency: 0.00001

p. 88 EPIGRAMS 133	144	That, with still-scalding steemes, make the place hell.

still>   frequency: 1   relative frequency: 0.00001
     p. 110 FOREST 11   29 Doe seuerall passions <still> inuade the minde,

stilts   frequency: 1   relative frequency: 0.00001
     p. 157 UNDERWOOD 13   145 They need no stilts, nor rise upon their toes,

stinck   frequency: 1   relative frequency: 0.00001
     p. 409 UNGATHERED 37   15 A Mungrel Curre? Thou should'st stinck forth,
                                and dye

sting   frequency: 1   relative frequency: 0.00001
     p. 143 UNDERWOOD 3   15 No tunes are sweet, nor words have sting,

stings   frequency: 1   relative frequency: 0.00001
     p. 137 UNDERWOOD 2.5   36 After flight; and put new stings

stink. See "stinck," "stinke."

stinkards   frequency: 1   relative frequency: 0.00001
     p. 86 EPIGRAMS 133   91 No matter, stinkards, row. What croaking sound

stinke   frequency: 4   relative frequency: 0.00005
     p. 45 EPIGRAMS 59   3 Stinke, and are throwne away. End faire enough.
     p. 153 UNDERWOOD 13   22 Then what he hath receiv'd. Gifts stinke from
                                some,
     p. 172 UNDERWOOD 21   10 And so I leave to stirre him, lest he stinke.
     p. 211 UNDERWOOD 43   188 Burne to a snuffe, and then stinke out, and die:

stinketh   frequency: 1   relative frequency: 0.00001
     p. 229 UNDERWOOD 54   14 Stinketh my credit, if into the Pocket

stint   frequency: 1   relative frequency: 0.00001
     p. 261 UNDERWOOD 77   18 To compose men, and manners; stint the strife

stir   frequency: 1   relative frequency: 0.00001
     See also "stirre."
     p. 410 UNGATHERED 39   9 Thinking to stir me, thou hast lost thy End,

stird'st   frequency: 1   relative frequency: 0.00001
     p. 101 FOREST 4   43 Since stird'st vp iealousies and feares,

stirr'd   frequency: 1   relative frequency: 0.00001
     p. 395 UNGATHERED 29   22 In the great masse, or machine there is stirr'd?

stirre   frequency: 7   relative frequency: 0.00010
     p. 85 EPIGRAMS 133   62 Ycleped Mud, which, when their oares did once
                                stirre,
     p. 172 UNDERWOOD 21   10 And so I leave to stirre him, lest he stinke.
     p. 250 UNDERWOOD 73   7 Why doe I irritate, or stirre up thee,
     p. 256 UNDERWOOD 75   117 Doth Emulation stirre;
     p. 282 U'WOOD 84.9   9 Nothing, that could remaine, or yet can stirre
     p. 317 HORACE 2   257 In at the eare, doe stirre the mind more slow
     p. 408 UNGATHERED 37   8 That thou hast lost thy noyse, thy foame, thy
                                stirre,

stirredest. See "stird'st."

stirrer   frequency: 1   relative frequency: 0.00001
     p. 243 UNDERWOOD 70   30 What did this Stirrer, but die late?

stirres   frequency: 1   relative frequency: 0.00001
   **p. 115 PANEGYRE   75 In these vaine stirres, and to his mind suggests

stirs. See "stirres."

stitch'd   frequency: 1   relative frequency: 0.00001
     p. 305 HORACE 2   19 A Scarlet peece, or two, stitch'd in: when or

stitchers-to   frequency: 1   relative frequency: 0.00001
     p. 187 UNDERWOOD 33   8 Of hirelings, wranglers, stitchers-to of strife,

stock   frequency: 1   relative frequency: 0.00001
     See also "stocke."
     p. 63 EPIGRAMS 97   10 Nor baudie stock, that trauells for encrease,

stocke   frequency: 1   relative frequency: 0.00001
     p. 72 EPIGRAMS 112   1 With thy small stocke, why art thou ventring
                                still,

stocked. See "neck-stockt."

stocks   frequency: 1   relative frequency: 0.00001
       p. 115 FOREST 12   78 For I shall moue stocks, stones, no lesse then
                                     he.

stole   frequency: 1   relative frequency: 0.00001
       p. 87 EPIGRAMS 133   113 The slie VLYSSES stole in a sheepes-skin,

stolen. See "stolne."

stolne   frequency: 5   relative frequency: 0.00007
       p. 32 EPIGRAMS 17   6 Shall out-liue gyrlands, stolne from the chast
                                     tree.
       p. 64 EPIGRAMS 100   4 Fiue of my iests, then stolne, past him a play.
       p. 103 FOREST 6   18 When youths ply their stolne delights.
       p. 283 U'WOOD 84.9   42 As spirits had stolne her Spirit, in a kisse,
       p. 365 UNGATHERED 5   7 Then the stolne sports of Louers,

stomachs. See "stomacks."

stomacks   frequency: 1   relative frequency: 0.00001
       p. 232 UNDERWOOD 58   2 All mouthes are open, and all stomacks free:

stone   frequency: 14   relative frequency: 0.00020
       See also "key-stone," "whet-stone."
       p. 62 EPIGRAMS 96   8 Mark'd by thy hand, and with the better stone,
       p. 79 EPIGRAMS 124   3 Vnder-neath this stone doth lye
       p. 94 FOREST 2   45 And though thy walls be of the countrey stone,
       p. 132 UNDERWOOD 2.2   27 So that, there, I stood a stone,
       p. 143 UNDERWOOD 3   7 What Tree or stone doth want a soule?
       p. 206 UNDERWOOD 43   74 Their Jemme of Riches, and bright Stone, that
                                     brings
       p. 229 UNDERWOOD 54   12 Full twentie stone; of which I lack two pound:
       p. 230 UNDERWOOD 56   11 His weight is twenty Stone within two pound;
       p. 234 UNDERWOOD 61   14 My Lord, till felt griefe make our stone hearts
                                     soft,
       p. 260 UNDERWOOD 77   9 The old Greek-hands in picture, or in stone.
       p. 269 UNDERWOOD 83   11 Hee's good, as great. I am almost a stone!
       p. 371 UNGATHERED 9   1 Stay, view this stone: And, if thou beest not
                                     such,
       p. 394 UNGATHERED 28   9 No stone in any wall here, but can tell
       p. 406 UNGATHERED 34   100 Soe ye Materialls be of Purbeck stone!

stones   frequency: 5   relative frequency: 0.00007
     **p. 116 PANEGYRE   132 From out the stones, to gratulate the king.
       p. 27 EPIGRAMS 2   6 As mad-men stones: not caring whom they hit.
       p. 115 FOREST 12   78 For I shall moue stocks, stones, no lesse then
                                     he.
       p. 327 HORACE 2   484 Was said to move the stones, by his Lutes
                                     powers,
       p. 387 UNGATHERED 22   1 Sonnes, seeke not me amonge these polish'd
                                     stones:

stonie   frequency: 1   relative frequency: 0.00001
       p. 177 UNDERWOOD 25   19 Breake the knit Circle of her Stonie Armes,

stony. See "stonie."

stood   frequency: 9   relative frequency: 0.00013
     **p. 114 PANEGYRE   35 As on a wonder: some amazed stood,
       p. 132 UNDERWOOD 2.2   27 So that, there, I stood a stone,
       p. 185 UNDERWOOD 30   11 But stood unshaken in his Deeds, and Name,
       p. 214 UNDERWOOD 44   48 More then the surfets, in thee, that day stood.
       p. 217 UNDERWOOD 46   14 Stood up thy Nations fame, her Crownes defence.
       p. 223 UNDERWOOD 49   23 I never stood for any place: my wit
       p. 243 UNDERWOOD 70   31 How well at twentie had he falne, or stood!
       p. 244 UNDERWOOD 70   45 Hee stood, a Souldier to the last right end,
       p. 294 UNDERWOOD 87   20 And to left-Lydia, now the gate stood ope.

stood'st   frequency: 1   relative frequency: 0.00001
       p. 75 EPIGRAMS 116   4 That age, when thou stood'st vp the
                                     master-braine:

stool. See "close-stoole," "stoole."

stoole   frequency: 4   relative frequency: 0.00005
       p. 30 EPIGRAMS 12   18 Calls for his stoole, adornes the stage: god
                                     payes.
       p. 81 EPIGRAMS 129   13 Or (mounted on a stoole) thy face doth hit
       p. 87 EPIGRAMS 133   122 By which the Masters sweare, when, on the stoole
       p. 230 UNDERWOOD 56   21 To make you merry on the Dressing stoole,

stooles   frequency: 3   relative frequency: 0.00004
     p.   74 EPIGRAMS 115   11 Can come from Tripoly, leape stooles, and winke,
     p. 146 UNDERWOOD 6   3 We were not bred to sit on stooles,
     p. 201 UNDERWOOD 42   47 So I might dote upon thy Chaires, and Stooles,

stools. See "stooles."

stoop. See "stoope," "stoupe."

stoop'd   frequency: 1   relative frequency: 0.00001
     See also "stoup't."
     p. 244 UNDERWOOD 70   38 Hee stoop'd in all mens sight

stoope   frequency: 2   relative frequency: 0.00002
     p. 367 UNGATHERED 6   39 But first to Cluid stoope low,
     p. 421 UNGATHERED 48 41 The Rebell Gyantes stoope, and Gorgon Envye
                               yeild,

stoopest. See "stoup'st."

stooping   frequency: 1   relative frequency: 0.00001
     p. 280 U'WOOD 84.4   58 But stooping gently, as a Cloud,

stoops. See "stoupes."

stop   frequency: 5   relative frequency: 0.00007
     p.   85 EPIGRAMS 133   59 To this dire passage. Say, thou stop thy nose:
     p.   87 EPIGRAMS 133 134 Nor thumbe, nor finger to the stop acquainted,
     p. 100 FOREST 4   19 To take the weake, or make them stop:
     p. 234 UNDERWOOD 60   15 Could stop the malice of this ill,
     p. 398 UNGATHERED 30 78 And stop my sight, in euery line I goe.

stopped. See "stopt."

stopt   frequency: 2   relative frequency: 0.00002
     p. 150 UNDERWOOD 9   18 And all these through her eyes, have stopt her
                               eares.
     p. 155 UNDERWOOD 13   80 Is borrowing; that but stopt, they doe invade

stor'd   frequency: 2   relative frequency: 0.00002
     p. 179 UNDERWOOD 25   55 Though many Gems be in your bosome stor'd,
     p. 207 UNDERWOOD 43 101 And twice-twelve-yeares stor'd up humanitie,

store   frequency: 23   relative frequency: 0.00033
     p.   28 EPIGRAMS 4   3 But two things, rare, the FATES had in their
                               store,
     p.   53 EPIGRAMS 79   4 Came not that soule exhausted so their store.
     p. 103 FOREST 6   12 Till you equall with the store,
     p. 105 FOREST 8   11 Scarce will take our present store?
     p. 114 FOREST 12   38 Riches thought most: But, Madame, thinke what
                               store
     p. 114 FOREST 12   54 AIAX, or IDOMEN, or all the store,
     p. 121 FOREST 14   31 Nor can a little of the common store,
     p. 146 UNDERWOOD 6   19 And this profession of a store
     p. 167 UNDERWOOD 15 170 Praevaricators swarme. Of which the store,
     p. 180 UNDERWOOD 26   18 To doe, then be a husband of that store.
     p. 187 UNDERWOOD 33   26 As if the generall store thou didst command
     p. 188 UNDERWOOD 34   3 What did she worth thy spight? were there not
                               store
     p. 189 UNDERWOOD 37   4 You have unto my Store added a booke,
     p. 201 UNDERWOOD 42   65 Such Songsters there are store of; witnesse he
     p. 213 UNDERWOOD 44   9 They saw too store of feathers, and more may,
     p. 217 UNDERWOOD 46   3 He could not find, then thee, of all that store
     p. 229 UNDERWOOD 54   15 It doe not come: One piece I have in store,
     p. 241 UNDERWOOD 68   3 Are they so scanted in their store? or driven
     p. 241 UNDERWOOD 68   7 Hae'ld frame such ditties of their store, and
                               want,
     p. 285 U'WOOD 84.9   110 By all the wealth of blessings, and the store
     p. 309 HORACE 2   92 That from the North, the Navie safe doth store,
     p. 388 UNGATHERED 23   4 What treasure hast thou brought vs! and what
                               store
     p. 398 UNGATHERED 30 88 Then Affricke knew, or the full Grecian store!

store-house   frequency: 1   relative frequency: 0.00001
     p. 185 UNDERWOOD 30   8 The poores full Store-house, and just servants
                               field.

storie   frequency: 9   relative frequency: 0.00013
     p.   39 EPIGRAMS 40   6 Read not in faire heauens storie,
     p.   61 EPIGRAMS 95   15 To haue her storie wouen in thy thred;

storie (cont.)
  p.   67 EPIGRAMS 104   5 Or, because some scarce thinke that storie true,
  p.   77 EPIGRAMS 120   2 This little storie:
  p. 130 UNDERWOOD 1.3   24 Can man forget this Storie?
  p. 131 UNDERWOOD 2.1   13 If you then will read the Storie,
  p. 160 UNDERWOOD 14   50 Conjectures retriv'd! And a Storie now
  p. 207 UNDERWOOD 43   97 To our owne Ladyes; and in storie there
  p. 240 UNDERWOOD 67   29 Of all her Brothers storie,

storm. See "storme."

                              frequency: 7   relative frequency: 0.00010
storme
  p.   86 EPIGRAMS 133   95 Had burst with storme, and downe fell, ab
                              excelsis,
  p. 110 FOREST 11   40 Rough, swelling, like a storme:
  p. 191 UNDERWOOD 38   13 There may some face or menace of a storme
  p. 193 UNDERWOOD 38   76 As all with storme and tempest ran together.
  p. 193 UNDERWOOD 38   82 The name of Cruell weather, storme, and raine?
  p. 214 UNDERWOOD 44   63 Should he <not> heare of billow, wind, and
                              storme,
  p. 307 HORACE 2   39 Creepes on the ground; too safe, too afraid of
                              storme.

                              frequency: 3   relative frequency: 0.00004
stormes
  p.   81 EPIGRAMS 128   13 Through seas, stormes, tempests: and imbarqu'd
                              for hell,
  p. 119 FOREST 13   93 'Gainst stormes, or pyrats, that might charge
                              your peace;
  p. 361 UNGATHERED 1   7 not one but thriues; in spite of stormes &
                              thunder,

storms. See "stormes."

                              frequency: 6   relative frequency: 0.00008
story
  See also "storie."
  p. 255 UNDERWOOD 75   91 All is a story of the King and Queene!
  p. 379 UNGATHERED 12   1 Who euer he be, would write a Story at
  p. 380 UNGATHERED 12   30 Or builders of Story haue oft imputation
  p. 381 UNGATHERED 12   59 No: as I first said, who would write a story at
  p. 399 UNGATHERED 31   7 Your booke? your volume! Nay, the state, and
                              story!
  p. 406 UNGATHERED 34   98 That might compare wth thee? what story shall

                              frequency: 2   relative frequency: 0.00002
stoupe
  p.   55 EPIGRAMS 85   7 And neuer stoupe, but to strike ignorance:
  p.   56 EPIGRAMS 88   14 And stoupe, and cringe. O then, it needs must
                              proue

                              frequency: 1   relative frequency: 0.00001
stoupes
  p. 227 UNDERWOOD 52   4 'Tis true, as my wombe swells, so my backe
                              stoupes,

                              frequency: 1   relative frequency: 0.00001
stoup'st
  p. 122 FOREST 15   14 And whither rap'd, now thou but stoup'st to mee?

                              frequency: 1   relative frequency: 0.00001
stoup't
 .**p. 113 PANEGYRE   23 Beside her, stoup't on either hand, a maid,

straddling. See "stradling."

                              frequency: 1   relative frequency: 0.00001
stradling
  p. 407 UNGATHERED 35   17 And stradling shews ye Boyes Brown paper fleet,

                              frequency: 5   relative frequency: 0.00007
straight
  See also "strait," "straite," "streight."
  p.   55 EPIGRAMS 84   5 Straight went I home; and there most like a
                              Poet,
  p.   68 EPIGRAMS 106   8 Like straight, thy pietie to God, and friends:
  p. 122 FOREST 15   2 But it must, straight, my melancholy bee?
  p. 177 UNDERWOOD 25   26 True noblesse. Palme growes straight, though
                              handled ne're so rude.
  p. 294 UNDERWOOD 88   2 And done, we straight repent us of the sport:

                              frequency: 2   relative frequency: 0.00002
straight-way
  p. 201 UNDERWOOD 42   67 And straight-way spent a Sonnet; with that other
  p. 315 HORACE 2   240 What straight-way he must labour to retract.

                              frequency: 1   relative frequency: 0.00001
straightned
  p. 248 UNDERWOOD 71   10 But lyes block'd up, and straightned, narrow'd
                              in,

straightway. See "straight-way."

strain. See "straine."

straine   frequency: 11   relative frequency: 0.00015
  *p. 493 TO HIMSELF   49 As curious fooles, and enuious of thy straine,
   p. 108 FOREST 10A   1 An elegie? no, muse; yt askes a straine
   p. 112 FOREST 11   114 From thoughts of such a straine.
   p. 136 UNDERWOOD 2.5   9 Set, and to this softer straine;
   p. 145 UNDERWOOD 5   10 So going thorow all your straine,
   p. 175 UNDERWOOD 23   26 Strike in thy proper straine,
   p. 177 UNDERWOOD 25   13 That I may sing my thoughts, in some unvulgar
                            straine.
   p. 311 HORACE 2   123 Abhorres low numbers, and the private straine
   p. 333 HORACE 2   625 If you denied, you had no better straine,
   p. 368 UNGATHERED 6   89 All which, when they but heare a straine
   p. 398 UNGATHERED 30 84 Of thy strange Moon-Calfe, both thy straine of
                            mirth,

strained. See "strayn'd."

straines   frequency: 4   relative frequency: 0.00005
   p. 289 U'WOOD 84.9   227 That thus have ventur'd these true straines upon;
   p. 290 UNDERWOOD 85   33 Or straines on his small forke his subtill nets
   p. 362 UNGATHERED 2   2 And see a minde attir'd in perfect straines;
   p. 363 UNGATHERED 3   15 Straines fancie vnto foule Apostacie,

strains. See "straines," "straynes."

strait   frequency: 1   relative frequency: 0.00001
  See also "streight."
   p. 132 UNDERWOOD 2.2 16 Strait hee ran, and durst not stay,

straite   frequency: 1   relative frequency: 0.00001
   p. 176 UNDERWOOD 24   11 And guided by Experience, whose straite wand

straitened. See "straightned," "streightned."

straits   frequency: 1   relative frequency: 0.00001
  See also "streights."
   p. 100 FOREST 4   10 Thy subtle wayes, be narrow straits;

strand   frequency: 2   relative frequency: 0.00002
   p. 155 UNDERWOOD 13   82 Ha' their Bermudas, and their streights i'th'
                            Strand:
   p. 408 UNGATHERED 36 13 That sit vpon ye Comon Draught: or Strand!

strange   frequency: 10   relative frequency: 0.00014
   p. 99 FOREST 3   95 God wisheth, none should wracke on a strange
                            shelfe.
   p. 109 FOREST 11   10 That no strange, or vnkinde
   p. 115 FOREST 12   81 They hold in my strange poems, which, as yet,
   p. 146 UNDERWOOD 6   15 (By searching) what before was strange,
   p. 156 UNDERWOOD 13 125 Or on the sudden. It were strange that he
   p. 165 UNDERWOOD 15   85 Adulteries, now, are not so hid, or strange,
   p. 177 UNDERWOOD 25   11 Thy Priest in this strange rapture; heat my
                            braine
   p. 201 UNDERWOOD 42   71 Unto the Spittle Sermon. O, what strange
   p. 313 HORACE 2   178 If something strange, that never yet was had
   p. 398 UNGATHERED 30 84 Of thy strange Moon-Calfe, both thy straine of
                            mirth,

stranger   frequency: 3   relative frequency: 0.00004
   p. 61 EPIGRAMS 95   2 That stranger doctrine of PYTHAGORAS,
   p. 83 EPIGRAMS 132   4 And vtter stranger to all ayre of France)
   p. 325 HORACE 2   448 What brethren, what a stranger, and his guest,

strangers   frequency: 3   relative frequency: 0.00004
   p. 98 FOREST 3   52 Nor are the Muses strangers found:
   p. 119 FOREST 13   115 Not fashion'd for the court, or strangers eyes;
   p. 217 UNDERWOOD 46   7 When, being the Strangers helpe, the poore mans
                            aide,

stratagem   frequency: 1   relative frequency: 0.00001
  See also "strategeme."
   p. 208 UNDERWOOD 43 130 Made thee beget that cruell Stratagem,

stratageme   frequency: 1   relative frequency: 0.00001
   p. 71 EPIGRAMS 110   19 In euery counsell, stratageme, designe,

straw   frequency: 1   relative frequency: 0.00001
    See also "strawe."
    p. 380 UNGATHERED 12   38 And lay in straw with the horses at Bergamo,

straw-berries   frequency: 1   relative frequency: 0.00001
    p. 58 EPIGRAMS 92   1 Ere cherries ripe, and straw-berries be gone,

strawe   frequency: 1   relative frequency: 0.00001
    p. 420 UNGATHERED 48   15 Whilest lyke a blaze of strawe,

stray   frequency: 1   relative frequency: 0.00001
    p. 53 EPIGRAMS 80   3 How wilfull blind is he then, that would stray,

strayn'd   frequency: 1   relative frequency: 0.00001
    p. 144 UNDERWOOD 3   25 Nay, rather both our soules bee strayn'd

straynes   frequency: 1   relative frequency: 0.00001
    p. 420 UNGATHERED 48   32 And once more stryke the eare of tyme wth those
                             ffresh straynes:

stream   frequency: 1   relative frequency: 0.00001
    See also "streame."
  **p. 113 PANEGYRE   5 (To day) a thousand radiant lights, that stream

streame   frequency: 1   relative frequency: 0.00001
    p. 221 UNDERWOOD 48   27 And thinke thy streame more quicker

streames   frequency: 4   relative frequency: 0.00005
    p. 103 FOREST 6   16 Or the starres, that guild his streames,
    p. 290 UNDERWOOD 85   27 The Fountaines murmure as the streames doe
                             creepe,
    p. 293 UNDERWOOD 86   40 Or Tybers winding streames, I follow thee.
    p. 366 UNGATHERED 6   23 To brookes, and broader streames,

streams. See "streames."

street   frequency: 5   relative frequency: 0.00007
    p. 58 EPIGRAMS 92   3 Ripe statesmen, ripe: They grow in euery street.
    p. 165 UNDERWOOD 15   106 Is it for these that Fine-man meets the street
    p. 262 UNDERWOOD 78   9 His brest is a brave Palace, a broad Street,
    p. 407 UNGATHERED 35   18 yearly set out there, to sayle downe ye Street,
    p. 409 UNGATHERED 37   19 But fly thee, like the Pest! Walke not the
                             street

street-borne   frequency: 1   relative frequency: 0.00001
    p. 321 HORACE 2   357 Like men street-borne, and neere the Hall,
                             reherse

streets   frequency: 2   relative frequency: 0.00002
    See also "bread-streets."
  **p. 116 PANEGYRE   131 About the streets, as it would force a spring
    p. 407 UNGATHERED 35   11 He draw a Forum, wth quadriuiall Streets!

streight   frequency: 11   relative frequency: 0.00015
    p. 63 EPIGRAMS 98   3 He that is round within himselfe, and streight,
    p. 154 UNDERWOOD 13   32 Of pressure, like one taken in a streight?
    p. 154 UNDERWOOD 13   50 For what they streight would to the world
                             forsweare;
    p. 170 UNDERWOOD 18   7 That as the water makes things, put in't
                             streight,
    p. 193 UNDERWOOD 38   88 Streight puts off all his Anger, and doth kisse
    p. 209 UNDERWOOD 43   139 The Brethren, they streight nois'd it out for
                             Newes,
    p. 229 UNDERWOOD 54   5 Who, when shee heard the match, concluded
                             streight,
    p. 280 U'WOOD 84.4   54 For this so loftie forme, so streight,
    p. 287 U'WOOD 84.9   165 But, kept an even gate, as some streight tree
    p. 313 HORACE 2   192 Of imitation, leape into a streight,
    p. 397 UNGATHERED 30   25 There read I, streight, thy learned Legends
                             three,

streightned   frequency: 1   relative frequency: 0.00001
    p. 157 UNDERWOOD 13   152 Aloft, grow lesse and streightned, full of knot;

streights   frequency: 1   relative frequency: 0.00001
    p. 155 UNDERWOOD 13   82 Ha' their Bermudas, and their streights i'th'
                             Strand:

strength   frequency: 17   relative frequency: 0.00024
    p. 63 EPIGRAMS 98   4 Need seeke no other strength, no other height;

strength (cont.)
p.	69 EPIGRAMS 108	1	Strength of my Countrey, whilst I bring to view
p.	75 EPIGRAMS 116	5	Thou wert the first, mad'st merit know her strength,
p.	157 UNDERWOOD 13	140	Observe the strength, the height, the why, and when,
p.	161 UNDERWOOD 14	78	And strength to be a Champion, and defend
p.	166 UNDERWOOD 15	133	And whilst our states, strength, body, and mind we waste,
p.	187 UNDERWOOD 33	24	What use, what strength of reason! and how much
p.	206 UNDERWOOD 43	75	Invisibilitie, and strength, and tongues:
p.	251 UNDERWOOD 74	30	And both a strength, and Beautie to his Land!
p.	307 HORACE 2	54	Unto your strength, and long examine it,
p.	337 HORACE 2	674	And, as a Beare, if he the strength but had
p.	339 HORACE 1	38	Wants strength, and .... as his spirits were done;
p.	367 UNGATHERED 6	55	Whose strength is aboue strength;
p.	379 UNGATHERED 12	4	To his strength, hath measur'd it out with his feet.
p.	400 UNGATHERED 32	10	That Art, or Ingine, on the strength can raise.
p.	413 UNGATHERED 41	38	Sweet Tree of Life, King Davids Strength and Tower,

strengths   frequency: 2   relative frequency: 0.00002
| p. | 102 FOREST 4 | 67 | But make my strengths, such as they are, |
| p. | 176 UNDERWOOD 24 | 14 | Assisted by no strengths, but are her owne, |

stretch'd   frequency: 1   relative frequency: 0.00001
| p. | 163 UNDERWOOD 15 | 50 | In admiration, stretch'd upon the rack |

strew   frequency: 1   relative frequency: 0.00001
   See also "s<tr>ow."
| p. | 218 UNDERWOOD 47 | 28 | Of newes they get, to strew out the long meale, |

strict   frequency: 2   relative frequency: 0.00002
| p. | 29 EPIGRAMS 9 | 2 | For strict degrees of ranke, or title looke: |
| p. | 421 UNGATHERED 49 | 6 | I haue, wth strict advantage of ffree tyme |

stricter   frequency: 1   relative frequency: 0.00001
| p. | 108 FOREST 10A | 2 | to loose, and Cap'ring, for thy stricter veyne. |

stride   frequency: 1   relative frequency: 0.00001
| p. | 379 UNGATHERED 12 | 8 | To line out no stride, but pas'd by himselfe? |

strife   frequency: 17   relative frequency: 0.00024
p.	34 EPIGRAMS 23	8	Which might with halfe mankind maintayne a strife.
p.	66 EPIGRAMS 102	5	Nor could the age haue mist thee, in this strife
p.	118 FOREST 13	60	Farre from the maze of custome, error, strife,
p.	134 UNDERWOOD 2.4	20	All the Gaine, all the Good, of the Elements strife.
p.	143 UNDERWOOD 3	t1	The Musicall strife; In a Pastorall Dialogue.
p.	151 UNDERWOOD 12	12	A life that knew nor noise, nor strife:
p.	158 UNDERWOOD 13	160	Which you will bury; but therein, the strife
p.	162 UNDERWOOD 15	8	Quickning dead Nature, to her noblest strife.
p.	187 UNDERWOOD 33	8	Of hirelings, wranglers, stitchers-to of strife,
p.	242 UNDERWOOD 69	24	All is but web, and painting; be the strife
p.	244 UNDERWOOD 70	39	To sordid flatteries, acts of strife,
p.	253 UNDERWOOD 75	30	That holy strife,
p.	261 UNDERWOOD 77	18	To compose men, and manners; stint the strife
p.	271 UNDERWOOD 83	95	And, but for that Contention, and brave strife
p.	390 UNGATHERED 25	3	Wherein the Grauer had a strife
p.	411 UNGATHERED 40	8	and the Godly's strife,
p.	417 UNGATHERED 45	33	Or if any strife bety'de

strifes   frequency: 2   relative frequency: 0.00002
| p. | 54 EPIGRAMS 80 | 6 | And here, it should be one of our first strifes, |
| p. | 258 UNDERWOOD 75 | 189 | Strifes, murmures, or delay, |

strike   frequency: 14   relative frequency: 0.00020
   See also "heart-strike," "stryke."
*p.	493 TO HIMSELF	47	Strike that disdaine-full heate
**p.	117 PANEGYRE	144	Those greater bodies of the sky, that strike
p.	46 EPIGRAMS 61	2	One doth not stroke me, nor the other strike.
p.	55 EPIGRAMS 85	7	And neuer stoupe, but to strike ignorance:
p.	110 FOREST 11	30	And strike our reason blinde.
p.	175 UNDERWOOD 23	26	Strike in thy proper straine,
p.	242 UNDERWOOD 69	14	So doth the flatt'rer with faire cunning strike
p.	261 UNDERWOOD 77	24	And strike Religion in the standers-by;
p.	321 HORACE 2	361	Will take offence, at this: Nor, though it strike

strike (cont.)
    p. 361 UNGATHERED 1   5 ffirst: thy successe did strike my sence with
                               wonder;
    p. 389 UNGATHERED 24   4 When the old words doe strike on the new times,
    p. 392 UNGATHERED 26   60 (Such as thine are) and strike the second heat
    p. 397 UNGATHERED 30   31 Did all so strike me, as I cry'd, who can
    p. 397 UNGATHERED 30   56 A better cause, and strike the brauest heate

strikes   frequency: 1   relative frequency: 0.00001
    p. 363 UNGATHERED 3   16 And strikes the quickest-sighted Iudgement
                               blinde.

string   frequency: 3   relative frequency: 0.00004
    p. 329 HORACE 2   521 For, neither doth the String still yeeld that
                               sound
    p. 329 HORACE 2   532 Is laugh'd at, that still jarreth on one string:
    p. 412 UNGATHERED 41   9 The second string is the sweet Almond bloome

strings   frequency: 3   relative frequency: 0.00004
    p. 174 UNDERWOOD 23   9 Doth Clarius Harp want strings,
    p. 309 HORACE 2   113 Unto the Lyrick Strings, the Muse gave grace
    p. 329 HORACE 2   498 Attempted by the Muses tunes, and strings;

strip. See "t<o>'out-strip."

stripes   frequency: 1   relative frequency: 0.00001
    p. 33 EPIGRAMS 21   8 The bodies stripes, I see, the soule may saue.

stripped. See "stript," "out-strip."

stript   frequency: 1   relative frequency: 0.00001
    p. 411 UNGATHERED 39   16 Cropt, branded, slit, neck-stockt; go, you are
                               stript.

striue   frequency: 7   relative frequency: 0.00010
  **p. 115 PANEGYRE   69 This was the peoples loue, with which did striue
    p. 77 EPIGRAMS 120   7 As Heauen and Nature seem'd to striue
    p. 78 EPIGRAMS 122   3 If I would striue to bring backe times, and trie
    p. 81 EPIGRAMS 129   9 Think'st thou, MIME, this is great? or, that
                               they striue
    p. 98 FOREST 3   66 Striue, WROTH, to liue long innocent.
    p. 120 FOREST 14   5 And all doe striue t<o>'aduance
    p. 121 FOREST 14   25 Striue all right wayes it can,

striues   frequency: 2   relative frequency: 0.00002
  **p. 113 PANEGYRE   1 Heau'n now not striues, alone, our brests to fill
    p. 78 EPIGRAMS 121   8 That striues, his manners should precede his wit.

striuing   frequency: 1   relative frequency: 0.00001
    p. 76 EPIGRAMS 118   3 And, striuing so to double his delight,

striu'st   frequency: 1   relative frequency: 0.00001
    p. 70 EPIGRAMS 109   9 Thou rather striu'st the matter to possesse,

strive   frequency: 3   relative frequency: 0.00004
    See also "striue."
    p. 168 UNDERWOOD 15   188 And from that thought strive to be understood.
    p. 287 U'WOOD 84.9   171 He run; and all did strive with diligence
    p. 309 HORACE 2   111 All the Grammarians strive; and yet in Court

strives. See "striues."

strivest. See "striu'st."

striving   frequency: 1   relative frequency: 0.00001
    See also "striuing."
    p. 307 HORACE 2   36 Obscure. This, striving to run smooth, and flow,

stroak'd   frequency: 1   relative frequency: 0.00001
    p. 279 U'WOOD 84.4   38 As some soft chime had stroak'd the ayre;

stroakt   frequency: 1   relative frequency: 0.00001
    p. 405 UNGATHERED 34   84 Moulded or stroakt vp to suruey a State!

stroke   frequency: 3   relative frequency: 0.00004
    p. 46 EPIGRAMS 61   2 One doth not stroke me, nor the other strike.
    p. 230 UNDERWOOD 56   14 And stroke the water, nimble, chast, and faire,
    p. 283 U'WOOD 84.9   23 My wounded mind cannot sustaine this stroke,

stroked. See "stroak'd," "stroakt."

strokes   frequency: 1   relative frequency: 0.00001
    p. 114 FOREST 12   53 Gaue killing strokes. There were braue men,
                                 before

strong   frequency: 11   relative frequency: 0.00015
    See also "stronge."
    p.   39 EPIGRAMS 40   11 Till time, strong by her bestowing,
    p.   71 EPIGRAMS 110   7 And that so strong and deepe, as 't might be
                                 thought,
    p. 114 FOREST 12   42 And, at her strong armes end, hold vp, and euen,
    p. 151 UNDERWOOD 12   8 Had wrestled with Diseases strong,
    p. 177 UNDERWOOD 25   18 Then shall my Verses, like strong Charmes,
    p. 206 UNDERWOOD 43   78 And the strong lines, that so the time doe catch:
    p. 213 UNDERWOOD 44   21 What a strong Fort old Pimblicoe had bin!
    p. 217 UNDERWOOD 46   13 And that thy strong and manly Eloquence
    p. 248 UNDERWOOD 71   7 And made those strong approaches, by False
                                 braies,
    p. 281 U'WOOD 84.8   14 For they are strong Supporters: But, till then,
    p. 363 UNGATHERED 3   10 Were they as strong ram'd vp as Aetna gates.

stronge   frequency: 1   relative frequency: 0.00001
    p. 361 UNGATHERED 1   21 So in my braine; the stronge impression

stronger   frequency: 1   relative frequency: 0.00001
    p. 221 UNDERWOOD 48   22 Then Phoebus; and much stronger

strongest   frequency: 1   relative frequency: 0.00001
    p. 104 FOREST 7   9 So men at weakest, they are strongest,

strongly   frequency: 2   relative frequency: 0.00002
  **p. 114 PANEGYRE   58 No age, nor sex, so weake, or strongly dull,
    p. 327 HORACE 2   458 More strongly takes the people with delight,

strooke   frequency: 2   relative frequency: 0.00002
    p. 212 UNDERWOOD 43   200 Strooke in at Millan with the Cutlers there;
    p. 222 UNDERWOOD 49   5 And that as any are strooke, her breath creates

strove   frequency: 2   relative frequency: 0.00002
    p. 137 UNDERWOOD 2.5   46 Call to mind the formes, that strove
    p. 217 UNDERWOOD 46   11 That Clients strove, in Question of the Lawes,

struck. See "strocke."

strucken. See "thunder-stroken."

struggled   frequency: 1   relative frequency: 0.00001
    p. 362 UNGATHERED 1   28 I struggled with this passion that did drowne

strumpet   frequency: 1   relative frequency: 0.00001
    p. 175 UNDERWOOD 23   34 To that strumpet the Stage,

strung   frequency: 1   relative frequency: 0.00001
    p. 239 UNDERWOOD 67   16 Let every Lyre be strung,

strut   frequency: 1   relative frequency: 0.00001
    p. 100 FOREST 4   13 I know too, though thou strut, and paint,

stryke   frequency: 1   relative frequency: 0.00001
    p. 420 UNGATHERED 48   32 And once more stryke the eare of tyme wth those
                                 ffresh straynes:

stuart   frequency: 1   relative frequency: 0.00001
    p. 252 UNDERWOOD 75   t9 FRANCES STUART,

stubborn. See "stubborne."

stubborne   frequency: 1   relative frequency: 0.00001
    p. 292 UNDERWOOD 86   7 Too stubborne for Commands so slack:

stubbornnesse   frequency: 1   relative frequency: 0.00001
    p. 152 UNDERWOOD 12   24 No stubbornnesse so stiffe, nor folly

stuck   frequency: 1   relative frequency: 0.00001
    See also "stucke."
    p. 279 U'WOOD 84.4   46 And stuck in clay here, it would pull

stucke   frequency: 1   relative frequency: 0.00001
    p.   87 EPIGRAMS 133   136 Whether it languishing stucke vpon the wall,

studie   frequency: 13   relative frequency: 0.00018
   p.   55 EPIGRAMS 86   6 Attending such a studie, such a choice.
   p.   63 EPIGRAMS 98   10 And studie conscience, more then thou would'st
                             fame.
   p.   66 EPIGRAMS 102   20 The common-wealth still safe, must studie thee.
   p.   78 EPIGRAMS 122   9 I need no other arts, but studie thee:
   p. 121 FOREST 14   36 And studie more:
   p. 187 UNDERWOOD 33   12 To the Wolves studie, or Dogs eloquence;
   p. 187 UNDERWOOD 33   15 So dost thou studie matter, men, and times,
   p. 194 UNDERWOOD 38   108 Then I will studie falshood, to be true.
   p. 207 UNDERWOOD 43   104 Whom Faction had not drawne to studie sides.
   p. 215 UNDERWOOD 44   74 Their Sonnes to studie Arts, the Lawes, the
                             Creed:
   p. 215 UNDERWOOD 44   92 They learne and studie; and then practise there.
   p. 219 UNDERWOOD 47   29 I studie other friendships, and more one,
   p. 224 UNDERWOOD 50   28 And studie them unto the noblest ends,

studie'a   frequency: 1   relative frequency: 0.00001
   p. 153 UNDERWOOD 14   13 Then which there is not unto Studie'a more

studied   frequency: 4   relative frequency: 0.00005
   See also "studyed."
   p. 261 UNDERWOOD 77   17 What you have studied are the arts of life;
   p. 325 HORACE 2   445 Hee, that hath studied well the debt, and knowes
   p. 412 UNGATHERED 41   8 As Love, here studied to keep Grace alive.
   p. 415 UNGATHERED 42   26 A Say-master, hath studied all the tricks

studies   frequency: 3   relative frequency: 0.00004
   p.   78 EPIGRAMS 121   3 Whose better studies while shee emulates,
   p. 118 FOREST 13   65 Because that studies spectacles, and showes,
   p. 315 HORACE 2   237 These studies alter now, in one, growne man;

study   frequency: 2   relative frequency: 0.00002
   See also "studie," "studie'a."
   p. 215 UNDERWOOD 44   87 What love you then? your whore. What study?
                             gate,
   p. 282 U'WOOD 84.8   23 Study illustrious Him and you have all.

studyed   frequency: 1   relative frequency: 0.00001
   p. 100 FOREST 4   9 I know thy formes are studyed arts,

studying   frequency: 1   relative frequency: 0.00001
   p. 224 UNDERWOOD 50   14 Who (herein studying conscience, and not fame)

stuff   frequency: 1   relative frequency: 0.00001
   See also "stuffe."
   p. 347 HORACE 1   341 . ... stuff . ...

stuff'd   frequency: 1   relative frequency: 0.00001
   p. 311 HORACE 2   149 Sad language fits sad lookes; stuff'd menacings,

stuffe   frequency: 4   relative frequency: 0.00005
  *p. 493 TO HIMSELF   40 The gamesters share your guilt, and you their
                             stuffe.
   p.   45 EPIGRAMS 59   1 SPIES, you are lights in state, but of base
                             stuffe,
   p.   85 EPIGRAMS 133   45 Or goddesse to inuoke, to stuffe my verse;
   p. 205 UNDERWOOD 43   64 Thou should'st have cry'd, and all beene proper
                             stuffe.

stuffes   frequency: 4   relative frequency: 0.00005
   p.   97 FOREST 3   11 To view the iewells, stuffes, the paines, the wit
   p. 164 UNDERWOOD 15   57 To do't with Cloth, or Stuffes, lusts name
                             might merit;
   p. 202 UNDERWOOD 42   79 The Stuffes, the Velvets, Plushes, Fringes,
                             Lace,
   p. 223 UNDERWOOD 49   28 To stuffes and Laces, those my Man can buy.

stuffs. See "stuffes."

stumble   frequency: 1   relative frequency: 0.00001
   p. 220 UNDERWOOD 47   70 As but to stumble in her sight were shame;

stunk. See "stunke."

stunke   frequency: 1   relative frequency: 0.00001
   p.   87 EPIGRAMS 133   118 Stunke not so ill; nor, when shee kist, KATE
                             ARDEN.

stupid   frequency: 2   relative frequency: 0.00002
    p. 132 UNDERWOOD 2.2   5 Farre I was from being stupid,
    p. 282 U'WOOD 84.9   15 Sleepie, or stupid Nature, couldst thou part

stygian   frequency: 1   relative frequency: 0.00001
    p. 87 EPIGRAMS 133   121 By this time had they reach'd the Stygian poole,

styld   frequency: 1   relative frequency: 0.00001
    p. 407 UNGATHERED 35   24 Wee'll haue thee styld ye Marquess of
                               New-Ditch.

styl'd   frequency: 2   relative frequency: 0.00002
    p. 181 UNDERWOOD 27   20 Which all the world then styl'd divine?
    p. 274 U'WOOD 84.2   2 Of Dame VENETIA DIGBY, styl'd The
                               Faire:

style   frequency: 3   relative frequency: 0.00004
    See also "bombard-stile," "stile."
    p. 286 U'WOOD 84.9   139 To style us Friends, who were, by Nature,
                               Foes?
    p. 402 UNGATHERED 34   15 By all your Titles, & whole style at ones
    p. 407 UNGATHERED 35   19 your workes thus differing, troth let soe yor
                               style:

styled. See "stil'd," "stilde," "stiled," "styld," "styl'd."

styles. See "stiles."

styx   frequency: 2   relative frequency: 0.00002
    p. 84 EPIGRAMS 133   7 All, that they boast of STYX, of
                               ACHERON,
    p. 88 EPIGRAMS 133   141 And so they did, from STYX, to
                               ACHERON:

subiect   frequency: 6   relative frequency: 0.00008
    p. 37 EPIGRAMS 35   1 Who would not be thy subiect, IAMES,
                               t<o>'obay
    p. 38 EPIGRAMS 36   3 But in my royall subiect I passe thee,
    p. 60 EPIGRAMS 94   8 Their vn-auoided subiect, fewest see:
    p. 107 FOREST 10   1 And must I sing? what subiect shall I chuse?
    p. 115 FOREST 12   73 My gratefull soule, the subiect of her powers,
    p. 419 UNGATHERED 48   9 That were the happie subiect of my songe.

subiects   frequency: 3   relative frequency: 0.00004
  **p. 115 PANEGYRE   76 How he may triumph in his subiects brests,
    p. 43 EPIGRAMS 51   5 Yet giue thy iealous subiects leaue to doubt:
    p. 416 UNGATHERED 43   10 Of Subiects; Let such envie, till they burst.

subject   frequency: 10   relative frequency: 0.00014
    See also "subiect."
    p. 160 UNDERWOOD 14   58 But to the Subject, still the Colours fit
    p. 177 UNDERWOOD 25   28 If subject to the jealous errors
    p. 182 UNDERWOOD 27   36 So much my Subject drownes the rest.
    p. 191 UNDERWOOD 38   28 The Subject of your Grace in pardoning me,
    p. 218 UNDERWOOD 47   11 Subject to quarrell only; or else such
    p. 236 UNDERWOOD 64   1 How happy were the Subject, if he knew,
    p. 262 UNDERWOOD 78   17 In signe the Subject, and the Song will live,
    p. 311 HORACE 2   124 Fit for the sock: Each subject should retaine
    p. 319 HORACE 2   324 The free spectators, subject to no Law,
    p. 339 HORACE 1   55 .... a subject ...

subjects   frequency: 3   relative frequency: 0.00004
    See also "subiects."
    p. 173 UNDERWOOD 22   8 This subjects you to love of one.
    p. 185 UNDERWOOD 30   7 The Orphans Pillar, the true Subjects shield,
    p. 261 UNDERWOOD 77   19 Of murmuring Subjects; make the Nations know

sublimed   frequency: 1   relative frequency: 0.00001
    p. 279 U'WOOD 84.4   48 Up to her owne sublimed hight?

substance   frequency: 2   relative frequency: 0.00002
    p. 156 UNDERWOOD 13   120 And can I lesse of substance? When I runne,
    p. 295 UNDERWOOD 90   2 Most pleasant Martial; Substance got with ease,

substract   frequency: 1   relative frequency: 0.00001
    p. 327 HORACE 2   467 There's Albin's sonne will say, Substract an
                               ounce

subtile   frequency: 4   relative frequency: 0.00005
    p. 72 EPIGRAMS 112   2 At this so subtile sport: and play'st so ill?
    p. 117 FOREST 13   43 My mirror is more subtile, cleere, refin'd,
    p. 149 UNDERWOOD 9   8 In sentence, of as subtile feet,
    p. 151 UNDERWOOD 11   4 Love in a subtile Dreame disguis'd,

subtill   frequency: 1   relative frequency: 0.00001
    p. 290 UNDERWOOD 85   33 Or straines on his small forke his subtill nets

subtiltie   frequency: 1   relative frequency: 0.00001
    p. 86 EPIGRAMS 133 100 And subtiltie of mettalls) they dispense

subtilty   frequency: 1 .relative frequency: 0.00001
    p. 405 UNGATHERED 34 73 Whirling his Whymseys, by a subtilty

subtle   frequency: 5   relative frequency: 0.00007
    See also "subtile," "subtill."
    p. 74 EPIGRAMS 115   7 A subtle thing, that doth affections win
    p. 100 FOREST 4   10 Thy subtle wayes, be narrow straits;
    p. 110 FOREST 11   28 Thus, by these subtle traines,
    p. 242 UNDERWOOD 69   22 More subtle workes, and finer pieces farre,
    p. 327 HORACE 2   464 Our Roman Youths they learne the subtle wayes

subtler   frequency: 1   relative frequency: 0.00001
    p. 241 UNDERWOOD 69   10 Painted a Dog, that now his subtler skill

subtlest   frequency: 1   relative frequency: 0.00001
    See also "subt'lest."
    p. 331 HORACE 2   542 This, fearing not the subtlest Judges marke,

subt'lest   frequency: 1   relative frequency: 0.00001
    p. 370 UNGATHERED 7   7 Each subt'lest Passion, with her source, and
                             spring,

subtlety. See "subtiltie," "subtilty."

subtly   frequency: 1   relative frequency: 0.00001
    p. 84 EPIGRAMS 133   10 Subtly distinguish'd, was confused here.

subtract   frequency: 1   relative frequency: 0.00001
    See also "substract."
    p. 350 HORACE 1   467 .... subtract .. ..

succeeded   frequency: 1   relative frequency: 0.00001
    p. 321 HORACE 2   365 To these succeeded the old Comoedie,

success. See "successe."

successe   frequency: 1   relative frequency: 0.00001
    p. 361 UNGATHERED 1   5 ffirst: thy successe did strike my sence with
                             wonder;

succour   frequency: 4   relative frequency: 0.00005
    p. 153 UNDERWOOD 13   8 To succour my necessities, tooke fire,
    p. 154 UNDERWOOD 13   29 Or if he did it not to succour me,
    p. 155 UNDERWOOD 13   61 And seeke not wants to succour: but enquire,
    p. 207 UNDERWOOD 43   99 Wherein was oyle, beside the succour spent,

succouring   frequency: 1   relative frequency: 0.00001
    p. 85 EPIGRAMS 133   50 ALCIDES, be thou succouring to my song.

succours   frequency: 3   relative frequency: 0.00004
    p. 80 EPIGRAMS 127   8 Lent timely succours, and new life begot:
    p. 191 UNDERWOOD 38   8 Alone lend succours, and this furie stay,
    p. 248 UNDERWOOD 71   2 Are faine to seeke for succours, and supplies

such   frequency: 177   relative frequency: 0.00256

suck   frequency: 1   relative frequency: 0.00001
    p. 139 UNDERWOOD 2.7 16 Each suck <the> others breath.

suck'd   frequency: 2   relative frequency: 0.00002
    See also "suckt."
    p. 96 FOREST 2   94 Their gentler spirits haue suck'd innocence.
    p. 137 UNDERWOOD 2.6   3 From your lips, and suck'd an ayre

suckt   frequency: 1   relative frequency: 0.00001
    p. 405 UNGATHERED 34 74 Suckt from ye Veynes of shop-philosophy.

sudden   frequency: 1   relative frequency: 0.00001
        See also "sodaine," "sodayne."
        p. 156 UNDERWOOD 13   125 Or on the sudden. It were strange that he

suffer   frequency: 3   relative frequency: 0.00004
        p. 116 FOREST 13   5 So both the prais'd, and praisers suffer: Yet,
        p. 193 UNDERWOOD 38   93 To suffer tortures, scorne, and Infamie,
        p. 233 UNDERWOOD 59   18 To bend, to breake, provoke,or suffer it!

suffer'd   frequency: 3   relative frequency: 0.00004
        p. 117 FOREST 13   15 I, that haue suffer'd this; and, though forsooke
        p. 333 HORACE 2   588 The wished goale, both did, and suffer'd much
        p. 335 HORACE 2   642 The man once mock'd, and suffer'd wrong to tread.

suffered   frequency: 1   relative frequency: 0.00001
        See also "suffer'd."
        p. 133 UNDERWOOD 2.3   t1 What hee suffered.

sufferers   frequency: 1   relative frequency: 0.00001
        p. 167 UNDERWOOD 15 167 Of the poore sufferers) where the envious, proud,

suffering. See "suffring."

sufferings. See "suffrings."

suffers   frequency: 2   relative frequency: 0.00002
        p. 64 EPIGRAMS 99   10 And euen the praisers iudgement suffers so.
        p. 74 EPIGRAMS 115   4 Suffers no name, but a description:

sufficient   frequency: 2   relative frequency: 0.00002
        p. 54 EPIGRAMS 81   3 Or that I'haue by, two good sufficient men,
        p. 157 UNDERWOOD 13 128 Coriat, should rise the most sufficient head

suffolk. See "svffclke."

suffrage   frequency: 3   relative frequency: 0.00004
        p. 329 HORACE 2   514 But he hath every suffrage, can apply
        p. 385 UNGATHERED 19   7 My suffrage brings thee all increase, to crowne
        p. 390 UNGATHERED 26   5 'Tis true, and all mens suffrage. But these
                                 wayes

suffring   frequency: 3   relative frequency: 0.00004
        p. 47 EPIGRAMS 63   8 By constant suffring of thy equall mind;
        p. 287 U'WOOD 84.9   162 T'have knowne no envy, but by suffring it!
        p. 288 U'WOOD 84.9   202 Suffring, and dying to redeeme our losse!

suffrings   frequency: 1   relative frequency: 0.00001
        p. 270 UNDERWOOD 83   51 Her suffrings, as the body had beene away!

sugar   frequency: 1   relative frequency: 0.00001
        p. 167 UNDERWOOD 15 153 In Sugar Candide, or in butter'd beere,

suggestion   frequency: 1   relative frequency: 0.00001
        p. 111 FOREST 11   63 Would, at suggestion of a steepe desire,

suggests   frequency: 1   relative frequency: 0.00001
        **p. 115 PANEGYRE   75 In these vaine stirres, and to his mind suggests

suit   frequency: 3   relative frequency: 0.00004
        See also "suite," "sute."
        p. 163 UNDERWOOD 15   51 Of lust, to his rich Suit and Title, Lord?
        p. 165 UNDERWOOD 15 108 To teach each suit he has, the ready way
        p. 333 HORACE 2   604 Of an entangling suit; and bring 't about:

suite   frequency: 1   relative frequency: 0.00001
        p. 30 EPIGRAMS 12   9 The taylor brings a suite home; he it ssayes,

suited. See "suted."

suitor   frequency: 1   relative frequency: 0.00001
        See also "sutor."
        p. 230 UNDERWOOD 56   18 Of either Suitor, or a Servant by.

suits   frequency: 1   relative frequency: 0.00001
        See also "sutes."
        p. 258 UNDERWOOD 75 188 Exacts then she is pleas'd to pay: no suits,

sullen   frequency: 1   relative frequency: 0.00001
        See also "sollen."
        p. 193 UNDERWOOD 38   79 In darke, and sullen mornes, doe we not say,

sulphur. See "sulphure."

sulphure   frequency: 1   relative frequency: 0.00001
    p. 27 EPIGRAMS 2   4 Wormewood, and sulphure, sharpe, and tooth'd
                            withall;

sun. See "sunne."

summ'd   frequency: 3   relative frequency: 0.00004
    p. 120 FOREST 14   22 Are iustly summ'd, that make you man;
    p. 243 UNDERWOOD 70   9 How summ'd a circle didst thou leave man-kind
    p. 244 UNDERWOOD 70   53 Goe now, and tell out dayes summ'd up with
                            feares,

summe   frequency: 6   relative frequency: 0.00008
    p. 205 UNDERWOOD 43   66 With pieces of the Legend; The whole summe
    p. 240 UNDERWOOD 67   47 Summe up this crowned day,
    p. 259 UNDERWOOD 76   14 And that this so accepted summe,
    p. 270 UNDERWOOD 83   46 Could summe to a perfection, was her Act!
    p. 283 U'WOOD 84.9   26 I summe up mine owne breaking, and wish all.
    p. 404 UNGATHERED 34 61 The maker of ye Propertyes! in summe

summer   frequency: 1   relative frequency: 0.00001
    See also "sommer-nights."
    p. 252 UNDERWOOD 75   1 Though thou hast past thy Summer standing, stay

summers   frequency: 2   relative frequency: 0.00002
    p. 147 UNDERWOOD 7   17 As Summers sky, or purged Ayre,
    p. 253 UNDERWOOD 75   18 Of Summers Liveries, and gladding greene;

summes   frequency: 2   relative frequency: 0.00002
    p. 103 FOREST 6   6 Kisse, and score vp wealthy summes
    p. 413 UNGATHERED 41 21 But, that which summes all, is the Eglantine,

sums. See "summes."

sun   frequency: 13   relative frequency: 0.00018
    See also "mid-sun," "sunne."
    p. 150 UNDERWOOD 10   7 I wish the Sun should shine
    p. 194 UNDERWOOD 38 120 When I see you, then I doe see my Sun,
    p. 199 UNDERWOOD 41   6 Or that the Sun was here, but forc't away;
    p. 251 UNDERWOOD 74   8 The Clowdes rack cleare before the Sun,
    p. 252 UNDERWOOD 75   2 A-while with us, bright Sun, and helpe our
                            light;
    p. 254 UNDERWOOD 75   56 Although that thou, O Sun, at our intreaty
                            stay!
    p. 254 UNDERWOOD 75   64 O, now thou smil'st, faire Sun, and shin'st, as
                            thou wouldst stay!
    p. 254 UNDERWOOD 75   73 Our Court, and all the Grandees; now, Sun,
                            looke,
    p. 255 UNDERWOOD 75   79 Search, Sun, and thou wilt find,
    p. 257 UNDERWOOD 75 138 Now, Sun, and post away the rest of day:
    p. 257 UNDERWOOD 75 145 Haste, haste, officious Sun, and send them
                            Night
    p. 396 UNGATHERED 30 17 It cast a beame as when the chear=full Sun
    p. 414 UNGATHERED 41 50 The rosie Morning, or the rising Sun,

sun-burnt-blowse   frequency: 1   relative frequency: 0.00001
    p. 291 UNDERWOOD 85   41 Such as the Sabines, or a Sun-burnt-blowse,

sun-light   frequency: 1   relative frequency: 0.00001
    p. 189 UNDERWOOD 36   4 None brookes the Sun-light worse then he.

sundered. See "sundred."

sundred   frequency: 1   relative frequency: 0.00001
    p. 103 FOREST 6   7 On my lips, thus hardly sundred,

sundrie   frequency: 1   relative frequency: 0.00001
    p. 59 EPIGRAMS 92   25 They all get Porta, for the sundrie wayes

sundry   frequency: 1   relative frequency: 0.00001
    See also "sundrie."
    p. 338 HORACE 1   2 . horse neck joyn . sundry plumes ore-fold

sung   frequency: 14   relative frequency: 0.00020
    See also "song."
    p. 48 EPIGRAMS 64   18 I'haue sung the greater fortunes of our state.
    p. 58 EPIGRAMS 91   4 Sung by a HORACE, or a Muse as free;
    p. 70 EPIGRAMS 109   16 Now I haue sung thee thus, shall iudge of thee.

sung (cont.)
   p. 89 EPIGRAMS 133 196 My Muse had plough'd with his, that sung
                                A-IAX.
   p. 131 UNDERWOOD 2.1 19 Of whose Beautie it was sung,
   p. 136 UNDERWOOD 2.5 11 This, here sung, can be no other
   p. 174 UNDERWOOD 22   30 Have sung this Hymne, and here intreat
   p. 181 UNDERWOOD 27   9 Was Lesbia sung by learn'd Catullus?
   p. 193 UNDERWOOD 38   98 On every wall, and sung where e're I walke.
   p. 217 UNDERWOOD 46   21 Such is thy All; that (as I sung before)
   p. 246 UNDERWOOD 70   85 Jonson, who sung this of him, e're he went
   p. 263 UNDERWOOD 79   8 For, had we here said lesse, we had sung nothing
                                then.
   p. 263 UNDERWOOD 79   8+ A New-yeares-Gift sung to King
   p. 274 U'WOOD 84.1   37 Is sung: as als<o>'her getting up

sunk. See "sunke."

sunke   frequency: 1   relative frequency: 0.00001
   p. 244 UNDERWOOD 70   40 And sunke in that dead sea of life

sunne   frequency: 8   relative frequency: 0.00011
   p. 156 UNDERWOOD 13 119 Or growne; by height or lownesse of the Sunne?
   p. 189 UNDERWOOD 36   5 Where Love doth shine, there needs no Sunne,
   p. 192 UNDERWOOD 38   57 The Sunne his heat, and light, the ayre his dew?
   p. 271 UNDERWOOD 83   89 The Sunne! great Kings, and mightiest
                                Kingdomes fall!
   p. 278 U'WOOD 84.4   11 The Sunne, a Sea, or soundlesse Pit;
   p. 367 UNGATHERED 6   29 Nor Sunne could make to vary from the rest,
   p. 393 UNGATHERED 27   6 The Sunne that euer shineth,
   p. 395 UNGATHERED 29   24 The Sunne translated, or the Sonne of May.

sunnes   frequency: 1   relative frequency: 0.00001
   p. 102 FOREST 5   6 Sunnes, that set, may rise againe:

suns. See "sunnes."

sun's   frequency: 1   relative frequency: 0.00001
   p. 258 UNDERWOOD 75 183 By this Sun's Noone-sted's made

sup   frequency: 6   relative frequency: 0.00008
   p. 50 EPIGRAMS 72   2 A chamber-critick, and dost dine, and sup
   p. 65 EPIGRAMS 101 35 Of this we will sup free, but moderately,
   p. 74 EPIGRAMS 115 23 At euery meale, where it doth dine, or sup,
   p. 106 FOREST 9   7 But might I of IOVE'S Nectar sup,
   p. 206 UNDERWOOD 43   83 These, had'st thou pleas'd either to dine, or
                                sup,
   p. 244 UNDERWOOD 70   41 So deep, as he did then death's waters sup;

supercilious   frequency: 1   relative frequency: 0.00001
   p. 162 UNDERWOOD 15   19 See the grave, sower, and supercilious Sir

superficies   frequency: 1   relative frequency: 0.00001
   p. 227 UNDERWOOD 52   9 My Superficies: that was all you saw.

superfluous   frequency: 1   relative frequency: 0.00001
   p. 335 HORACE 2   636 Cut off superfluous ornaments; and when

superstition   frequency: 1   relative frequency: 0.00001
   p. 155 UNDERWOOD 13   86 And superstition I dare scarce reveale,

superstitious   frequency: 2   relative frequency: 0.00002
   p. 167 UNDERWOOD 15 168 Ambitious, factious, superstitious, lowd
   p. 284 U'WOOD 84.9   73 Better be dumbe, then superstitious!

supinely   frequency: 1   relative frequency: 0.00001
**p. 113 PANEGYRE   11 And snore supinely in the stall of sin:

supp'd   frequency: 1   relative frequency: 0.00001
   p. 412 UNGATHERED 40 21 I sayd, who'had supp'd so deepe

supper   frequency: 2   relative frequency: 0.00002
  See also "svpper."
   p. 218 UNDERWOOD 47   21 Call every night to Supper in these fitts,
   p. 333 HORACE 2   602 Make a great Supper; or for some poore man

suppers   frequency: 1   relative frequency: 0.00001
  See also "reare-suppers."
   p. 81 EPIGRAMS 129 7 That still th'art made the suppers flagge, the
                                drum,

supplant   frequency: 1   relative frequency: 0.00001
    p. 214 UNDERWOOD 44   34 Supplant bold Panton; and brought there to view

supple   frequency: 1   relative frequency: 0.00001
    p. 363 UNGATHERED 3   12 And makes her supple feete, as swift as winde.

supplied. See "supply'd."

supplies   frequency: 1   relative frequency: 0.00001
    p. 248 UNDERWOOD 71   2 Are faine to seeke for succours, and supplies

supply   frequency: 4   relative frequency: 0.00005
    p. 61 EPIGRAMS 95   12 Onely to boast thy merit in supply.
    p. 236 UNDERWOOD 63   11 That thought shall make, he will this losse
                             supply
    p. 264 UNDERWOOD 79   34 And were shee lost, could best supply her place,
    p. 389 UNGATHERED 24 20 Had cloath'd him so. Here's all I can supply

supply'd   frequency: 1   relative frequency: 0.00001
    p. 54 EPIGRAMS 84   4 For your most noble offer had supply'd me.

supporters   frequency: 1   relative frequency: 0.00001
    p. 281 U'WOOD 84.8   14 For they are strong Supporters: But, till then,

supporteth   frequency: 1   relative frequency: 0.00001
    p. 176 UNDERWOOD 24   13 Shee chearfully supporteth what she reares,

suppose   frequency: 1   relative frequency: 0.00001
    p. 111 FOREST 11   70 Who, being at sea, suppose,

suppositories   frequency: 1   relative frequency: 0.00001
    p. 86 EPIGRAMS 133 102 Suppositories, cataplasmes, and lotions.

supreme   frequency: 1   relative frequency: 0.00001
    p. 286 U'WOOD 84.9   148 He that shall be our supreme Judge, should leave

surcoates   frequency: 1   relative frequency: 0.00001
    p. 273 U'WOOD 84.1   26 No cobweb Call's; no Surcoates wrought

surcoats. See "surcoates."

sure   frequency: 23   relative frequency: 0.00033
    p. 29 EPIGRAMS 6   2 Sure, willing pouertie liues most in you.
    p. 53 EPIGRAMS 85   10 Till they be sure to make the foole their
                             quarrie.
    p. 59 EPIGRAMS 92   22 Are sure to con the catalogue by hart;
    p. 65 EPIGRAMS 101   27 Digestiue cheese, and fruit there sure will bee;
    p. 69 EPIGRAMS 107   27 For your next meale: this you are sure of. Why
    p. 87 EPIGRAMS 133 107 To answere me. And sure, it was th'intent
    p. 109 FOREST 11   5 Which to effect (since no brest is so sure,
    p. 130 UNDERWOOD 1.2 31 As sure to win
    p. 136 UNDERWOOD 2.5 10 Sure, said he, if I have Braine,
    p. 149 UNDERWOOD 9   6 I'm sure my language to her, was as sweet,
    p. 156 UNDERWOOD 13   97 Sure there is Misterie in it, I not know,
    p. 158 UNDERWOOD 14   1 I know to whom I write. Here, I am sure,
    p. 182 UNDERWOOD 27   35 Yet sure my tunes will be the best,
    p. 200 UNDERWOOD 42   24 So to be sure you doe injoy your selves.
    p. 213 UNDERWOOD 47   1 Men that are safe, and sure, in all they doe,
    p. 222 UNDERWOOD 48   47 Whereby he may knit sure up
    p. 271 UNDERWOOD 83   76 Which they that have the Crowne are sure to
                             know!
    p. 272 UNDERWOOD 83 100 And, sure of Heaven, rides triumphing in.
    p. 283 U'WOOD 84.9   29 Sure, I am dead, and know it not! I feele
    p. 288 U'WOOD 84.9   198 By sure Election, and predestin'd grace!
    p. 333 HORACE 2   621 Looke through him, and be sure, you take not
                             mocks
    p. 363 UNGATHERED 6   87 Their cares in wine; with sure
    p. 384 UNGATHERED 18 26 Sure, this glad payre were married, but this day.

surely   frequency: 2   relative frequency: 0.00002
    p. 228 UNDERWOOD 53   13 And surely had I but your Stable seene
    p. 391 UNGATHERED 26 28 I should commit thee surely with thy peeres,

suretie   frequency: 3   relative frequency: 0.00004
    p. 108 UNDERWOOD 16   7 What suretie of life have thou, and I?
    p. 284 U'WOOD 84.9   61 O Day of joy, and suretie to the just!
    p. 333 HORACE 2   603 Will be a suretie; or can helpe him out

sureties   frequency: 1   relative frequency: 0.00001
    p. 386 UNGATHERED 21 12 By offring not more sureties, then inow,

surety. See "suretie."

surfeit. See "surfet."

surfeits. See "surfets."

surfet   frequency: 4   relative frequency: 0.00005
    *p. 492 TO HIMSELF   15 To offer them a surfet of pure bread,
     p. 104 FOREST 8   8 I shall feare, you'll surfet too.
     p. 166 UNDERWOOD 15 115 Surfet? and Quarrel? drinkes the tother health?
     p. 237 UNDERWOOD 64   17 O Times! O Manners! Surfet bred of ease,

surfets   frequency: 3   relative frequency: 0.00004
     p. 104 FOREST 8   5 Spent in surfets: and their dayes,
     p. 214 UNDERWOOD 44   48 More then the surfets, in thee, that day stood.
     p. 363 UNGATHERED 3   4 Flowes fro the surfets which we take in peace.

surge   frequency: 1   relative frequency: 0.00001
     p. 110 FOREST 11   41 With whom who sailes, rides on the surge of
                               feare,

surgeon   frequency: 1   relative frequency: 0.00001
     p. 155 UNDERWOOD 13   68 And hurt seeks Cure, the Surgeon bids take
                               bread,

surgeons   frequency: 1   relative frequency: 0.00001
     p. 179 UNDERWOOD 25   38 In Surgeons hall)

surly   frequency: 1   relative frequency: 0.00001
     See also "svrly."
     p. 363 UNGATHERED 3   8 The knottie heads of the most surly Groomes,

surly's. See "svrly's."

surnames   frequency: 1   relative frequency: 0.00001
     p. 247 UNDERWOOD 70 113 You liv'd to be the great surnames,

surpass. See "surpasse.

surpasse   frequency: 1   relative frequency: 0.00001
     p. 390 UNGATHERED 25   7 His face; the Print would then surpasse

surprise. See "surprize."

surprised. See "surpriz'd."

surpriz'd   frequency: 1   relative frequency: 0.00001
     p. 151 UNDERWOOD 11   5 Hath both my heart and me surpriz'd,

surprize   frequency: 3   relative frequency: 0.00004
     p. 185 UNDERWOOD 30   15 Whose Offices, and honours did surprize,
     p. 251 UNDERWOOD 74   11 And ev'ry Plant the sense surprize,
     p. 273 U'WOOD 84.1   24 Surprize their sense:

surrounding   frequency: 1   relative frequency: 0.00001
     p.   51 EPIGRAMS 73   12 Item, a charme surrounding fearefully

surship   frequency: 1   relative frequency: 0.00001
     p. 402 UNGATHERED 34   14 Something your Surship doth not yet intend!

suruey   frequency: 1   relative frequency: 0.00001
     p. 405 UNGATHERED 34   84 Moulded or stroakt vp to suruey a State!

surueyor   frequency: 1   relative frequency: 0.00001
     p. 405 UNGATHERED 34   85 Oh wise Surueyor! wyser Architect!

surueyr   frequency: 1   relative frequency: 0.00001
     p. 402 UNGATHERED 34   1 Mr Surueyr, you yt first begann

suruiue   frequency: 1   relative frequency: 0.00001
     p.   47 EPIGRAMS 64   9 But I am glad to see that time suruiue,

survey   frequency: 1   relative frequency: 0.00001
     See also "suruey."
     p. 262 UNDERWOOD 78   11 Where Nature such a large survey hath ta'en,

surveyor. See "surueyor," "surueyr."

survive. See "suruiue."

surviving   frequency: 1   relative frequency: 0.00001
     p. 252 UNDERWOOD 75   t11 and Sister of the Surviving Duke

susan. See "svsan."

susanna. See "svsanna."

suspect   frequency: 3   relative frequency: 0.00004
     p. 75 EPIGRAMS 116   6 And those that lack'd it, to suspect at length,
     p. 117 FOREST 13   13 Such as suspect them-selues, and thinke it fit
     p. 381 UNGATHERED 12 58 Poore Tom haue we cause to suspect iust thee?

suspected   frequency: 2   relative frequency: 0.00002
     p. 48 EPIGRAMS 65   8 And, reconcil'd, keepe him suspected still.
     p. 275 U'WOOD 84.3   5 Send these suspected helpes, to aide

suspence   frequency: 1   relative frequency: 0.00001
     p. 370 UNGATHERED 7   10 The seuerall figures, languish in suspence,

suspended   frequency: 1   relative frequency: 0.00001
     p. 380 UNGATHERED 12 40 That sacred to Odcombe are there now suspended,

suspense. See "suspence."

suspicion. See "suspition."

suspition   frequency: 2   relative frequency: 0.00002
     p. 159 UNDERWOOD 14   18 Not flie the Crime, but the Suspition too:
     p. 224 UNDERWOOD 50   6 Ought that is ill, but the suspition too,

sussex   frequency: 1   relative frequency: 0.00001
     p. 211 UNDERWOOD 43 184 foot (out in Sussex) to an iron Mill;

sustain. See "sustaine."

sustaine   frequency: 3   relative frequency: 0.00004
   **p. 116 PANEGYRE   123 Sustaine the reynes, and in the checke forbeare
     p. 75 EPIGRAMS 116   3 So did thy vertue'enforme, thy wit sustaine
     p. 283 U'WOOD 84.9   23 My wounded mind cannot sustaine this stroke,

sustaines   frequency: 1   relative frequency: 0.00001
     p. 422 UNGATHERED 50   3 Is her owne scourge, when it sustaines their
                             states

sustains. See "sustaines."

sutcliffe   frequency: 1   relative frequency: 0.00001
     p. 411 UNGATHERED 40   t2 Mrs. Alice Sutcliffe, on

sute   frequency: 5   relative frequency: 0.00007
     p. 28 EPIGRAMS 3   6 Not offer'd, as it made sute to be bought;
     p. 63 EPIGRAMS 97   16 When he was here. Nor hath he got a sute,
     p. 95 FOREST 2   50 Thy lord, and lady, though they haue no sute.
     p. 106 FOREST 8   46 Moue it, as their humblest sute,
     p. 380 UNGATHERED 12 48 Iest, he saies. Item one sute of blacke taffata

suted   frequency: 1   relative frequency: 0.00001
     p. 389 UNGATHERED 24 17 But that hee's too well suted, in a cloth,

sutes   frequency: 1   relative frequency: 0.00001
     p. 47 EPIGRAMS 64   1 Not glad, like those that haue new hopes, or
                             sutes,

sutor   frequency: 1   relative frequency: 0.00001
     p. 363 UNGATHERED 3   5 Gold is a sutor, neuer tooke repulse,

svffolke   frequency: 1   relative frequency: 0.00001
     p. 49 EPIGRAMS 67   t1 TO THOMAS EARLE OF
                              SVFFOLKE.

svpper   frequency: 1   relative frequency: 0.00001
     p. 64 EPIGRAMS 101   t1 INVITING A FRIEND TO
                              SVPPER.

svrly   frequency: 4   relative frequency: 0.00005
     p. 35 EPIGRAMS 28   1 DON SVRLY, to aspire the glorious name
     p. 35 EPIGRAMS 28   t1 ON DON SVRLY.
     p. 36 EPIGRAMS 28   21 SVRLY, vse other arts, these only can
     p. 54 EPIGRAMS 82   t1 ON CASHIERD CAPT. SVRLY.

svrly's   frequency: 1   relative frequency: 0.00001
    p.   54 EPIGRAMS 82   1 SVRLY'S old whore in her new silkes doth
                               swim:

svsan   frequency: 1   relative frequency: 0.00001
    p.   67 EPIGRAMS 104   t1 TO SVSAN COVNTESSE OF
                               MONTGOMERY.

svsanna   frequency: 1   relative frequency: 0.00001
    p.   67 EPIGRAMS 104   4 A new SVSANNA, equall to that old?

swaggering   frequency: 1   relative frequency: 0.00001
    p. 156 UNDERWOOD 13   94 Or swaggering with the Watch, or Drawer,
                               drunke;

swaid   frequency: 1   relative frequency: 0.00001
    p. 287 U'WOOD 84.9   168 She swaid all bus'nesse in the Familie!

swain. See "swaine."

swaine   frequency: 1   relative frequency: 0.00001
    p. 147 UNDERWOOD 7   3 For if the Nymphs should know my Swaine,

swaines   frequency: 2   relative frequency: 0.00002
    p. 263 UNDERWOOD 79   10 And shuts the old. Haste, haste, all loyall
                               Swaines,
    p. 265 UNDERWOOD 79   46 Haste, haste you hither, all you gentler
                               Swaines,

swains. See "swaines," "swaynes."

swallow   frequency: 1   relative frequency: 0.00001
    p. 317 HORACE 2   267 Into a Swallow there; Nor Cadmus take,

swallow'd   frequency: 1   relative frequency: 0.00001
    p. 80 EPIGRAMS 12   6 How full of want, how swallow'd vp, how dead

swam. See "swamme," "swom."

swamme   frequency: 1   relative frequency: 0.00001
    p. 366 UNGATHERED 6   20 Where Pindar swamme;

swan   frequency: 5   relative frequency: 0.00007
    See also "swanne," "swan's."
    p. 134 UNDERWOOD 2.4   3 Each that drawes, is a Swan, or a Dove,
    p. 182 UNDERWOOD 27   30 The Swan [that] so relish'd Pancharis)
    p. 366 UNGATHERED 6   2 Produce vs a blacke Swan?
    p. 369 UNGATHERED 6   120 Set out a like, or second to our Swan.
    p. 392 UNGATHERED 26   71 Sweet Swan of Auon! what a sight it were

swanne   frequency: 1   relative frequency: 0.00001
    p. 366 UNGATHERED 6   15 This Swanne is onely his,

swannes   frequency: 1   relative frequency: 0.00001
    p. 366 UNGATHERED 6   5 Besides the other Swannes admiring him,

swans   frequency: 2   relative frequency: 0.00002
    See also "swannes."
    p. 135 UNDERWOOD 2.4   26 Or Swans Downe ever?
    p. 292 UNDERWOOD 86   10 With thy bright Swans, of Paulus Maximus:

swan's   frequency: 1   relative frequency: 0.00001
    See also "swans."
    p. 368 UNGATHERED 6   64 Now must we plie our ayme; our Swan's on wing.

sware   frequency: 1   relative frequency: 0.00001
    p. 170 UNDERWOOD 18   9 I can helpe that with boldnesse; And Love
                               sware,

swarm. See "swarme."

swarme   frequency: 3   relative frequency: 0.00004
    p. 167 UNDERWOOD 15   170 Praevaricators swarme. Of which the store,
    p. 200 UNDERWOOD 42   27 It is a ryming Age, and Verses swarme
    p. 291 UNDERWOOD 85   65 The wealthy houshold swarme of bondmen met,

swarthie   frequency: 1   relative frequency: 0.00001
    p. 305 HORACE 2   5 Which in some swarthie fish uncomely ends:

swarthy. See "swarthie."

sway   frequency: 7   relative frequency: 0.00010
  **p. 116 PANEGYRE   125 That kings, by their example, more doe sway
    p. 37 EPIGRAMS 35   2 A Prince, that rules by'example, more than sway?
    p. 113 FOREST 12   18 Or perhaps lesse: whil'st gold beares all this
                             sway,
    p. 190 UNDERWOOD 37   31 For no man lives so out of passions sway,
    p. 317 HORACE 2   281 Be wonne a friend; it must both sway, and bend
    p. 342 HORACE 1   161 .. .. sway whether . ...
    p. 370 UNGATHERED 7   12 Betweene the doubtfull sway of Reason', and
                             sense;

swayd   frequency: 1   relative frequency: 0.00001
    p. 423 UNGATHERED 50 11 whole armyes fall, swayd by those nyce respects.

swayed. See "swaid," "swayd."

swaynes   frequency: 1   relative frequency: 0.00001
    p. 397 UNGATHERED 30 26 Heard the soft ayres, between our swaynes &
                             thee,

swear. See "sweare."

sweare   frequency: 9   relative frequency: 0.00013
  *p. 493 TO HIMSELF   50 May, blushing, sweare no palsey's in thy braine.
    p. 70 EPIGRAMS 108   5 I sweare by your true friend, my Muse, I loue
    p. 87 EPIGRAMS 133 122 By which the Masters sweare, when, on the stoole
    p. 106 FOREST 9   15 Since when it growes, and smells, I sweare,
    p. 168 UNDERWOOD 15 192 Man thought the valianter, 'cause he durst
                             sweare,
    p. 213 UNDERWOOD 44   27 These ten yeares day; As all may sweare that
                             looke
    p. 386 UNGATHERED 20   9 That went before, a Husband. Shee, Ile sweare,
    p. 397 UNGATHERED 30 54 With euery song, I sweare, and so would dye:
    p. 416 UNGATHERED 45   5 And I sweare by all the light

sweares   frequency: 4   relative frequency: 0.00005
    p. 40 EPIGRAMS 42   13 The children, that he keepes, GILES sweares
                             are none
    p. 40 EPIGRAMS 42   14 Of his begetting. And so sweares his IONE.
    p. 109 FOREST 11   25 Backe the intelligence, and falsely sweares,
    p. 111 FOREST 11   67 That cryes, we dreame, and sweares, there's no
                             such thing,

swearing   frequency: 2   relative frequency: 0.00002
    p. 32 EPIGRAMS 16   4 Scarse thy weekes swearing brings thee of, of
                             one.
    p. 156 UNDERWOOD 13 102 Unto their praise, in certaine swearing rites!

swears. See "sweares."

swear'st   frequency: 1   relative frequency: 0.00001
    p. 54 EPIGRAMS 81   5 For all thou hear'st, thou swear'st thy selfe
                             didst doo.

sweat   frequency: 7   relative frequency: 0.00010
    See also "sweate."
  *p. 492 TO HIMSELF   9 Run on, and rage, sweat, censure, and condemn:
    p. 99 FOREST 3   73 Let this man sweat, and wrangle at the barre,
    p. 179 UNDERWOOD 25   41 Sweat at the forge, their hammers beating;
    p. 321 HORACE 2   351 Yet he that offers at it, may sweat much,
    p. 333 HORACE 2   589 While he was young; he sweat; and freez'd againe:
    p. 392 UNGATHERED 26 59 Who casts to write a liuing line, must sweat,
    p. 400 UNGATHERED 32   6 When they doe sweat to fortifie a Muse.

sweate   frequency: 1   relative frequency: 0.00001
    p. 88 EPIGRAMS 133 169 Is fill'd with buttock? And the walls doe sweate

sweates   frequency: 1   relative frequency: 0.00001
    p. 233 UNDERWOOD 59   22 Of humane life! as all the frosts, and sweates

sweats. See "sweates."

sweden   frequency: 1   relative frequency: 0.00001
    p. 69 EPIGRAMS 107   12 In Ireland, Holland, Sweden, pompous lies,

sweepings   frequency: 1   relative frequency: 0.00001
  *p. 493 TO HIMSELF   27 There, sweepings doe as well

sweet   frequency: 52   relative frequency: 0.00075
    See also "sweete."

sweet (cont.)
```
 *p.  494 TO HIMSELF       59 In tuning forth the acts of his sweet raigne:
  p.   52 EPIGRAMS 76        9 I meant shee should be curteous, facile, sweet,
  p.   81 EPIGRAMS 128       7 As the beginnings here, proue purely sweet,
  p.   87 EPIGRAMS 133     119 Yet, one day in the yeere, for sweet 'tis voyc't,
  p.   99 FOREST 3          97 And, howsoeuer we may thinke things sweet,
  p.  102 FOREST 5          16 But the sweet theft to reueale:
  p.  103 FOREST 6           1 Kisse me, sweet: The warie louer
  p.  112 FOREST 11         98 As sweet, as shee is fayre.
  p.  127 UNDERWOOD 1.1     16 To thee more sweet?
  p.  129 UNDERWOOD 1.2     12 For, sin's so sweet,
  p.  135 UNDERWOOD 2.4     30 O so white! O so soft! O so sweet is she!
  p.  137 UNDERWOOD 2.5     27 Rip'ned with a breath more sweet,
  p.  137 UNDERWOOD 2.6      4 Thence, as sweet, as you are faire,
  p.  140 UNDERWOOD 2.8     28 All your sweet of life is past,
  p.  143 UNDERWOOD 3       15 No tunes are sweet, nor words have sting,
  p.  149 UNDERWOOD 9        6 I'm sure my language to her, was as sweet,
  p.  165 UNDERWOOD 15     112 Sweet bags, sweet Powders, nor sweet words will
                              passe
  p.  193 UNDERWOOD 38      77 O imitate that sweet Serenitie
  p.  197 UNDERWOOD 40       1 That Love's a bitter sweet, I ne're conceive
  p.  197 UNDERWOOD 40       8 Shortly againe: and make our absence sweet.
  p.  199 UNDERWOOD 41      14 How shall I doe, sweet Mistris, for my heart?
  p.  206 UNDERWOOD 43      70 All the madde Rolands, and sweet Oliveers;
  p.  215 UNDERWOOD 44      90 What, to make legs? yes, and to smell most sweet,
  p.  240 UNDERWOOD 67      49 9. POLY. Sweet! happy Mary! All
  p.  257 UNDERWOOD 75     163 Be kept alive those Sweet, and Sacred fires
  p.  268 UNDERWOOD 82      11 Grow up, sweet Babe, as blessed, in thy Name,
  p.  278 U'WOOD 84.4       17 Sweet Mind, then speake your selfe, and say,
  p.  279 U'WOOD 84.4       37 The Voyce so sweet, the words so faire,
  p.  280 U'WOOD 84.4       60 As showers; and sweet as drops of Balme.
  p.  280 U'WOOD 84.4       61 Smooth, soft, and sweet, in all a floud
  p.  287 U'WOOD 84.9      172 T<o>'obey, and serve her sweet Commandements.
  p.  289 U'WOOD 84.9      225 In this sweet Extasie, she was rapt hence.
  p.  290 UNDERWOOD 85      36 And 'counts them sweet rewards so ta'en.
  p.  291 UNDERWOOD 85      40 For houshold and, and Children sweet;
  p.  291 UNDERWOOD 85      47 And from the sweet Tub Wine of this yeare
                              takes,
  p.  291 UNDERWOOD 85      55 More sweet then Olives, that new gather'd be
  p.  292 UNDERWOOD 86       5 Sower Mother of sweet Loves, forbeare
  p.  293 UNDERWOOD 87      10 Who sings so sweet, and with such cunning plaies,
  p.  311 HORACE 2         141 Her Poem's beautie, but a sweet delight
  p.  315 HORACE 2         227 Soone angry, and soone pleas'd, is sweet, or
                              sowre,
  p.  327 HORACE 2         478 Or mixing sweet, and fit, teach life the right.
  p.  329 HORACE 2         515 Sweet mix'd with sowre, to his Reader, so
  p.  392 UNGATHERED 26     71 Sweet Swan of Auon! what a sight it were
  p.  396 UNGATHERED 30     21 And those so sweet, and well proportion'd parts,
  p.  399 UNGATHERED 31     20 Or sweet, or various, in the course!
  p.  402 UNGATHERED 33     14 To make the Language sweet vpon her tongue.
  p.  412 UNGATHERED 40     22 of this sweet Chalice,
  p.  412 UNGATHERED 41      4 R. Rose, I. Ivy, E. sweet Eglantine.
  p.  412 UNGATHERED 41      9 The second string is the sweet Almond bloome
  p.  413 UNGATHERED 41     38 Sweet Tree of Life, King Davids Strength and
                              Tower,
```

sweet-meats   frequency: 1   relative frequency: 0.00001
```
  p.  164 UNDERWOOD 15      77 For t'other pound of sweet-meats, he shall feele
```

sweet-wood   frequency: 1   relative frequency: 0.00001
```
  p.  292 UNDERWOOD 86      20 Beneath a Sweet-wood Roofe, neere Alba Lake:
```

sweete   frequency: 5   relative frequency: 0.00007
```
  p.  365 UNGATHERED 5      13 Her breath for sweete exceeding
  p.  367 UNGATHERED 6      34 Continue thy sweete Song.
  p.  368 UNGATHERED 6      73 Haste, Haste, sweete Singer: Nor to Tine,
  p.  393 UNGATHERED 27     10 That yeeld's a sent so sweete,
  p.  418 UNGATHERED 46      7 Although the gate were hard, the gayne is sweete.
```

sweeten   frequency: 2   relative frequency: 0.00002
```
  p.   82 EPIGRAMS 130       6 Doth sweeten mirth, and heighten pietie,
  p.  128 UNDERWOOD 1.1     42 To heare, to mediate, sweeten my desire,
```

sweetening. See "sweetning."

sweeter   frequency: 1   relative frequency: 0.00001
```
  p.  265 UNDERWOOD 79      60 To sweeter Pastures lead hee can,
```

sweetest   frequency: 5   relative frequency: 0.00007
```
  p.  110 FOREST.11         50 The soft, and sweetest mindes
```

sweetest (cont.)
p. 251 UNDERWOOD 74   4 And in a dew of sweetest Raine,
p. 294 UNDERWOOD 89   1 Liber, of all thy friends, thou sweetest care,
p. 361 UNGATHERED 1   12 the sweetest simples, and most soueraigne seedes.
p. 413 UNGATHERED 41   22 Which, of the field is clep'd the sweetest brier,

sweetly   frequency: 2   relative frequency: 0.00002
p. 167 UNDERWOOD 15   148 Runs sweetly, as it had his Lordships Soule;
p. 283 U'WOOD 84.9   41 So sweetly taken to the Court of blisse,

sweetnesse   frequency: 3   relative frequency: 0.00004
p. 62 EPIGRAMS 95   30 Where sweetnesse is requir'd, and where weight;
p. 184 UNDERWOOD 29   44 Words, and sweetnesse, and be scant
p. 270 UNDERWOOD 83   39 Her Sweetnesse, Softnesse, her faire
                          Courtesie,

sweetning   frequency: 1   relative frequency: 0.00001
p. 151 UNDERWOOD 12   13 But was by sweetning so his will,

sweets   frequency: 4   relative frequency: 0.00005
See also "sweet's.
p. 182 UNDERWOOD 28   12 But then his Mothers sweets you so apply,
p. 257 UNDERWOOD 75   148 Of Nuptiall Sweets, at such a season, owe,
p. 261 UNDERWOOD 77   22 Of sweets, and safeties, they possesse by Peace.
p. 413 UNGATHERED 41   27 With od'rous sweets and soft humilitie,

sweet's   frequency: 1   relative frequency: 0.00001
p. 251 UNDERWOOD 74   19 Such joyes, such sweet's doth your Returne

sweld   frequency: 1   relative frequency: 0.00001
p. 138 UNDERWOOD 2.6   24 That at every motion sweld

swell   frequency: 4   relative frequency: 0.00005
p. 121 FOREST 14   39 For they, that swell
p. 244 UNDERWOOD 70   56 To swell thine age;
p. 386 UNGATHERED 21   15 More of our writers would like thee, not swell
p. 387 UNGATHERED 22   4 will all turne dust, & may not make me swell.

swell'd   frequency: 1   relative frequency: 0.00001
See also "sweld."
p. 274 U'WOOD 84.2   10 Meeting of Graces, that so swell'd the flood

swelleth. See "ore-swelleth."

swelling   frequency: 4   relative frequency: 0.00005
p. 110 FOREST 11   40 Rough, swelling, like a storme:
p. 280 U'WOOD 84.4   57 Not swelling like the Ocean proud,
p. 291 UNDERWOOD 85   46 Their swelling udders doth draw dry:
p. 311 HORACE 2   134 With swelling throat: and, oft, the tragick wight

swells   frequency: 4   relative frequency: 0.00005
p. 63 EPIGRAMS 97   19 About his forme. What then so swells each lim?
p. 163 UNDERWOOD 15   31 The whole world here leaven'd with madnesse
                          swells;
p. 227 UNDERWOOD 52   4 'Tis true, as my wombe swells, so my backe
                          stoupes,
p. 307 HORACE 2   38 Professing greatnesse, swells: That, low by lee

swept   frequency: 2   relative frequency: 0.00002
p. 151 UNDERWOOD 12   16 As were his Nourceries; and swept
p. 282 U'WOOD 84.9   8 Till swept away, th<ey>'were cancell'd with a
                          broome!

swerve   frequency: 1   relative frequency: 0.00001
p. 315 HORACE 2   224 And give their yeares, and natures, as they
                          swerve,

swift   frequency: 9   relative frequency: 0.00013
p. 41 EPIGRAMS 44   5 He meant they thither should make swift repaire,
p. 116 FOREST 12   99 Before his swift and circled race be run,
p. 189 UNDERWOOD 36   14 Now swift, now slow, now tame, now wild;
p. 249 UNDERWOOD 72   4 As lowd'as Thunder, and as swift as fire.
p. 279 U'WOOD 84.4   42 So swift, so pure, should yet apply
p. 305 HORACE 2   21 Dring Circles of swift waters that intwine
p. 315 HORACE 2   236 And then as swift to leave what he hath lov'd.
p. 363 UNGATHERED 3   12 And makes her supple feete, as swift as winde.
p. 369 UNGATHERED 6   117 Slow Arar, nor swift Rhone; the Loyre, nor
                          Seine,

swift-pac't   frequency: 1   relative frequency: 0.00001
     p. 295 UNDERWOOD 90   11 Sleepe, that will make the darkest howres
                              swift-pac't;

swiftnesse   frequency: 1   relative frequency: 0.00001
     p. 323 HORACE 2   372 A foot, whose swiftnesse gave the Verse the name

swill   frequency: 1   relative frequency: 0.00001
    *p. 492 TO HIMSELF   18 Huskes, draffe to drinke, and swill.

swim   frequency: 5   relative frequency: 0.00007
   **p. 116 PANEGYRE   133 She blest the people, that in shoales did swim
     p. 54 EPIGRAMS 82   1 SVRLY'S old whore in her new silkes doth
                              swim:
     p. 112 FOREST 11   106 Making his fortunes swim
     p. 366 UNGATHERED 6   3 Behold, where one doth swim;
     p. 405 UNGATHERED 34   68 Swim wthout Corke! Why, thank ye good Queen
                              Anne.

swimming   frequency: 1   relative frequency: 0.00001
     p. 305 HORACE 2   27 To paint him, hath by swimming, hopelesse,
                              scap'd,

swine   frequency: 3   relative frequency: 0.00004
    *p. 492 TO HIMSELF   20 Enuy them not, their palate's with the swine.
     p. 232 UNDERWOOD 58   11 Like a rung Beare, or Swine: grunting out wit
     p. 257 UNDERWOOD 75   154 Like Swine, or other Cattell here on earth:

swinnerton. See "swynnerton."

swollen. See "high-swolne."

swom   frequency: 1   relative frequency: 0.00001
     p. 87 EPIGRAMS 133   138 And, after, swom abroad in ample flakes,

swoon. See "swoune."

swooping   frequency: 1   relative frequency: 0.00001
     p. 319 HORACE 2   304 Gesture, and riot, whilst he swooping went

sword   frequency: 15   relative frequency: 0.00021
     p. 33 EPIGRAMS 21   3 His clothes two fashions of, and poore! his sword
     p. 35 EPIGRAMS 27   3 If any sword could saue from Fates, ROE'S
                              could;
     p. 37 EPIGRAMS 32   1 What two braue perills of the priuate sword
     p. 74 EPIGRAMS 115   22 'Twill see it's sister naked, ere a sword.
     p. 154 UNDERWOOD 13   47 As I have seene some Infants of the Sword,
     p. 154 UNDERWOOD 13   54 My Sword ('tis but a poore Sword, understand)
     p. 154 UNDERWOOD 13   55 As farre as any poore Sword i' the Land.
     p. 187 UNDERWOOD 33   34 They had, but were a Reed unto thy Sword.
     p. 193 UNDERWOOD 38   101 Then sword, or fire, or what is of the race
     p. 219 UNDERWOOD 47   39 But if, for honour, we must draw the Sword,
     p. 243 UNDERWOOD 70   17 Sword, fire, and famine, with fell fury met;
     p. 313 HORACE 2   174 Be nought so'above him but his sword let claime.
     p. 393 UNGATHERED 27   13 It is the Sword that doth diuide
     p. 423 UNGATHERED 50   14 the sword, but that it acteth what it list.

swords   frequency: 3   relative frequency: 0.00004
     p. 37 EPIGRAMS 32   10 Seas, serenes, swords, shot, sicknesse, all are
                              there.
     p. 134 UNDERWOOD 2.4   10 Th<o>rough Swords, th<o>rough Seas, whether she
                              would ride.
     p. 212 UNDERWOOD 43   198 And there made Swords, Bills, Glaves, and
                              Armes your fill;

swore   frequency: 1   relative frequency: 0.00001
    See also "sware."
     p. 87 EPIGRAMS 133   129 One said, the other swore, the world consists.

sworn. See "sworne."

sworne   frequency: 1   relative frequency: 0.00001
     p. 662 INSCRIPTS. 2   7 And sworne, that he will quite discard thee

swoune   frequency: 1   relative frequency: 0.00001
     p. 333 HORACE 2   614 As those that hir'd to weepe at Funeralls,
                              swoune,

swynnerton   frequency: 1   relative frequency: 0.00001
     p. 213 UNDERWOOD 44   20 Under the Auspice of young Swynnerton.

sybil   frequency: 1   relative frequency: 0.00001
    p.   85 EPIGRAMS 133   48 Sans helpe of SYBIL, or a golden bough,

sydney   frequency: 8   relative frequency: 0.00011
    p.   66 EPIGRAMS 103   4 Know you to be a SYDNEY, though vn-nam'd?
    p.   67 EPIGRAMS 103   10 A SYDNEY: but in that extend as farre
    p.   73 EPIGRAMS 114   t1 TO Mrs. PHILIP SYDNEY.
    p. 116 FOREST 12   91 Moodes, which the god-like SYDNEY oft did
                              proue,
    p. 120 FOREST 14   t2 TO SIR WILLIAM SYDNEY, ON
                              HIS
    p. 120 FOREST 14   12 That I may tell to SYDNEY, what
    p. 157 UNDERWOOD 13   127 Sydney e're night! or that did goe to bed
    p. 181 UNDERWOOD 27   25 Hath our great Sydney, Stella set,

sydney's   frequency: 1   relative frequency: 0.00001
    p.   94 FOREST 2   26 Fertile of wood, ASHORE, and
                              SYDNEY'S copp's,

sydnyes   frequency: 1   relative frequency: 0.00001
    p.   73 EPIGRAMS 114   2 When SYDNYES name I heare, or face I
                              see:

syllab'e   frequency: 1   relative frequency: 0.00001
    p. 245 UNDERWOOD 70   63 Each syllab'e answer'd, and was form'd, how
                              faire;

syllabes   frequency: 2   relative frequency: 0.00002
    p. 183 UNDERWOOD 29   10 Joynting Syllabes, drowning Letters,
    p. 184 UNDERWOOD 29   52 Still may Syllabes jarre with time,

syllable. See "syllab'e."

syllables. See "syllabes."

sylvan. See "sylvane."

sylvane   frequency: 3   relative frequency: 0.00004
    p.   94 FOREST 2   16 Of many a SYLVANE, taken with his flames.
    p.   98 FOREST 3   47 Thus PAN, and SYLVANE, hauing had their
                              rites,
    p. 290 UNDERWOOD 85   22 And, Sylvane, thine, that keptst his Lands!

sylvanus   frequency: 1   relative frequency: 0.00001
    p. 264 UNDERWOOD 79   22 And in the chase, more then SYLVANUS can,

sylvester   frequency: 1   relative frequency: 0.00001
    p.   83 EPIGRAMS 132   t1 TO Mr. IOSVAH SYLVESTER.

sym   frequency: 1   relative frequency: 0.00001
    p. 657 L. CONVIVALES   8 Cries Old Sym, the King of Skinkers;

symboles   frequency: 1   relative frequency: 0.00001
    p. 396 UNGATHERED 30   10 Without conferring symboles. This's my day.

symbols. See "symboles."

symetry   frequency: 1   relative frequency: 0.00001
    p. 399 UNGATHERED 31   22 By warrant call'd iust Symetry,

symmetrie   frequency: 1   relative frequency: 0.00001
    p. 112 FOREST 11   101 All her best symmetrie in that one feature!

symmetry. See "symetry," "symmetrie."

synns   frequency: 1   relative frequency: 0.00001
    p. 421 UNGATHERED 49   4 Hee that soe Censureth, or adviseth synns,

synonima   frequency: 1   relative frequency: 0.00001
    p.   29 EPIGRAMS 7   4 And still be a whore-house. Th'are Synonima.

'syrian   frequency: 1   relative frequency: 0.00001
    p. 294 UNDERWOOD 89   3 If thou be'st wise, with 'Syrian Oyle let shine

syrup. See "sirrup."

't   frequency: 15   relative frequency: 0.00021

t<o>'a   frequency: 2   relative frequency: 0.00002
    p.   82 EPIGRAMS 130   7 And is t<o>'a body, often, ill inclin'd,

t<o>'a (cont.)
    p. 287 U'WOOD 84.9   152 Find all our Atomes from a point t<o>'a span!

t<o>'accuse   frequency: 1   relative frequency: 0.00001
    p. 284 U'WOOD 84.9   60 T<o>'accuse, or quit all Parties to be heard!

t<o>'admire   frequency: 1   relative frequency: 0.00001
    p. 32 EPIGRAMS 18   8 When thou wert wont t<o>'admire, not censure men.

t<o>'adore   frequency: 1   relative frequency: 0.00001
    p. 174 UNDERWOOD 22   35 Yet give me leave t<o>'adore in you

t<o>'aduance   frequency: 2   relative frequency: 0.00002
    p. 117 FOREST 13   40 T<o>'aduance his doubtfull issue, and ore-flow
    p. 120 FOREST 14   5 And all doe striue t<o>'aduance

t<o>'advance   frequency: 1   relative frequency: 0.00001
    p. 246 UNDERWOOD 70   100 Made, or indentur'd, or leas'd out t<o>'advance

t<o>'all   frequency: 1   relative frequency: 0.00001
    p. 71 EPIGRAMS 110   21 T<o>'all future time, not onely doth restore

t<o>'alledge   frequency: 1   relative frequency: 0.00001
    p. 82 EPIGRAMS 130   9 T<o>'alledge, that greatest men were not asham'd,

t<o>'allow   frequency: 1   relative frequency: 0.00001
    p. 62 EPIGRAMS 96   6 As thou hast best authoritie, t<o>'allow.

t<o>'amend   frequency: 1   relative frequency: 0.00001
    p. 152 UNDERWOOD 12   22 His very Manners taught t<o>'amend,

t<o>'appeare   frequency: 2   relative frequency: 0.00002
    p. 37 EPIGRAMS 32   9 Which shewes, where euer death doth please
                               t<o>'appeare,
    p. 263 UNDERWOOD 79   11 That know the times, and seasons when
                               t<o>'appeare,

t<o>'approue   frequency: 1   relative frequency: 0.00001
    p. 108 FOREST 10 A   14 and Coniures all my faculties t<o>'approue

t<o>'approve   frequency: 1   relative frequency: 0.00001
    p. 321 HORACE 2   342 Plaine phrase, my Piso's, as alone, t<o>'approve

t<o>'aquit   frequency: 1   relative frequency: 0.00001
    p. 173 UNDERWOOD 22   23 As Love, t<o>'aquit such excellence,

t<o>'assist   frequency: 1   relative frequency: 0.00001
    p. 170 UNDERWOOD 18   10 And Fortune once, t<o>'assist the spirits that
                               dare.

t<o>'attire   frequency: 1   relative frequency: 0.00001
    p. 215 UNDERWOOD 44   94 Of severall makings? helps, helps, t<o>'attire

t<o>'effect   frequency: 1   relative frequency: 0.00001
    p. 250 UNDERWOOD 73   12 T<o>'effect it, feele, thou'ast made thine owne
                               heart ake.

t<o>'enjoy   frequency: 2   relative frequency: 0.00002
    p. 271 UNDERWOOD 83   96 The Christian hath t<o>'enjoy the future life,
    p. 285 U'WOOD 84.9   92 What 'tis t<o>'enjoy an everlasting breath!

t<o>'escape   frequency: 1   relative frequency: 0.00001
    p. 271 UNDERWOOD 83   93 T<o>'escape this common knowne necessitie,

t<o>'exact   frequency: 1   relative frequency: 0.00001
    p. 107 FOREST 10   5 With his old earthly labours. T<o>'exact more,

t<o>'exchange   frequency: 1   relative frequency: 0.00001
    p. 311 HORACE 2   119 As fit t<o>'exchange discourse; a Verse to win

t<o>'expect   frequency: 2   relative frequency: 0.00002
    p. 116 FOREST 13   4 As what th'haue lost t<o>'expect, they dare
                               deride.
    p. 119 FOREST 13   105 T<o>'expect the honors of great 'AVBIGNY:

t<o>'expresse   frequency: 1   relative frequency: 0.00001
    p. 111 FOREST 11   75 And yet (in this t<o>'expresse our selues more
                               cleare)

t<o>'extract   frequency: 1   relative frequency: 0.00001
    p. 60 EPIGRAMS 128   3 T<o>'extract, and choose the best of all these
                             knowne,

t<o>'himselfe   frequency: 1   relative frequency: 0.00001
    p. 99 FOREST 3   96 To him, man's dearer, then t<o>'himselfe.

t<o>'idolatrie   frequency: 1   relative frequency: 0.00001
    p. 79 EPIGRAMS 125   10 I could adore, almost t<o>'idolatrie.

t<o>'increase   frequency: 1   relative frequency: 0.00001
    p. 148 UNDERWOOD 7   26 But then t<o>'increase my feares,

t<o>'indite   frequency: 1   relative frequency: 0.00001
    p. 117 FOREST 13   14 For their owne cap'tall crimes, t<o>'indite my
                             wit;

t<o>'inflict   frequency: 1   relative frequency: 0.00001
    p. 122 FOREST 15   22 Vpon my flesh t<o>'inflict another wound.

t<o>'inhabit   frequency: 1   relative frequency: 0.00001
    p. 280 U'WOOD 84.4   52 For her t<o>'inhabit? There is it.

t<o>'inherit   frequency: 1   relative frequency: 0.00001
    p. 164 UNDERWOOD 15   81 And comes by these Degrees, the Stile
                             t<o>'inherit

t<o>'inlive   frequency: 1   relative frequency: 0.00001
    p. 269 UNDERWOOD 83   34 T<o>'inlive posteritie, her Fame may tell!

t<o>'instruct   frequency: 1   relative frequency: 0.00001
    p. 159 UNDERWOOD 14   37 T<o>'instruct and teach? or your unweary'd paine

t<o>'inueigh   frequency: 1   relative frequency: 0.00001
    p. 52 EPIGRAMS 75   4 T<o>'inueigh 'gainst playes: what did he then but
                             play?

t<o>'obay   frequency: 1   relative frequency: 0.00001
    p. 37 EPIGRAMS 35   1 Who would not be thy subiect, IAMES,
                             t<o>'obay

t<o>'obey   frequency: 1   relative frequency: 0.00001
    p. 287 U'WOOD 84.9   172 T<o>'obey, and serve her sweet Commandements.

t<o>'observe   frequency: 1   relative frequency: 0.00001
    p. 311 HORACE 2   128 Nor know t<o>'observe: why (i'the Muses name)

t<o>'obtaine   frequency: 1   relative frequency: 0.00001
    p. 234 UNDERWOOD 61   11 T<o>'obtaine of God, what all the Land should
                             aske?

t<o>'offend   frequency: 2   relative frequency: 0.00002
    p. 194 UNDERWOOD 38 106 And let your mercie make me asham'd t<o>'offend.
    p. 317 HORACE 2   282 The angry, and love those that feare t<o>'offend.

t<o>'our   frequency: 1   relative frequency: 0.00001
    p. 52 EPIGRAMS 74   10 T<o>'our times return'd, hath made her heauen in
                             thee.

t<o>'out-strip   frequency: 1   relative frequency: 0.00001
    p. 121 FOREST 14   26 T<o>'out-strip your peeres:

t<o>'usher   frequency: 1   relative frequency: 0.00001
    p. 263 UNDERWOOD 79   4 To shew the rites, and t<o>'usher forth the way

tabacco   frequency: 1   relative frequency: 0.00001
    p. 65 EPIGRAMS 101   33 Tabacco, Nectar, or the Thespian spring,

tabacco-like   frequency: 1   relative frequency: 0.00001
    p. 42 EPIGRAMS 50   1 Leaue COD, tabacco-like, burnt gummes to take,

table   frequency: 8   relative frequency: 0.00011
    p. 50 EPIGRAMS 72   3 At MADAMES table, where thou mak'st all
                             wit
    p. 84 EPIGRAMS 133   24 To haue beene stiled of King ARTHVRS
                             table.
    p. 94 FOREST 2   27 To crowne thy open table, doth prouide
    p. 155 UNDERWOOD 13   74 Feed those, at whom the Table points at still?
    p. 232 UNDERWOOD 57   23 will come to the Table,
    p. 269 UNDERWOOD 83   15 It is a large faire table, and a true,

table (cont.)
    p. 295 UNDERWOOD 90   8 Thy table without art, and easy-rated:
    p. 394 UNGATHERED 28   7 But euery Table in this Church can say,

tables   frequency: 2   relative frequency: 0.00002
    p. 95 FOREST 2   66 At great mens tables) and yet dine away.
    p. 95 FOREST 2   71 Thy tables hoord not vp for the next day,

tacitvs   frequency: 3   relative frequency: 0.00004
    p. 59 EPIGRAMS 92   15 They carry in their pockets TACITVS,
    p. 61 EPIGRAMS 95   3 I should beleeue, the soule of TACITVS
    p. 65 EPIGRAMS 101   21 Shall reade a piece of VIRGIL,
                               TACITVS,

tactickes   frequency: 1   relative frequency: 0.00001
    p. 214 UNDERWOOD 44   35 Translated Aelian<'s> tactickes to be read,

tactics. See "tactickes."

ta'en   frequency: 5   relative frequency: 0.00007
    p. 262 UNDERWOOD 78   11 Where Nature such a large survey hath ta'en,
    p. 283 U'WOOD 84.9   33 I murmure against God, for having ta'en
    p. 290 UNDERWOOD 85   36 And 'counts them sweet rewards so ta'en.
    p. 305 HORACE 2   3 On every limbe, ta'en from a severall creature,
    p. 315 HORACE 2   221 That tarries till the hangings be ta'en downe,

taffata   frequency: 2   relative frequency: 0.00002
    p. 371 UNGATHERED 8   5 Veluet, or Taffata cap, rank'd in the darke
    p. 380 UNGATHERED 12   48 Iest, he saies. Item one sute of blacke taffata

taffeta. See "taffata."

tagged. See "wel-tagde."

tagus   frequency: 1   relative frequency: 0.00001
    p. 369 UNGATHERED 6   115 Iberus, Tagus, Rheine,

tail. See "taile," "tayle."

taile   frequency: 1   relative frequency: 0.00001
    p. 380 UNGATHERED 12   56 I writ he onely his taile there did waue;

tailor. See "taylor."

tailors. See "french-taylors," "taylors."

taint   frequency: 1   relative frequency: 0.00001
    p. 401 UNGATHERED 32   21 And like a hallow'd Temple, free from taint

tainted   frequency: 1   relative frequency: 0.00001
    See also "teynted."
    p. 87 EPIGRAMS 133   133 And that ours did. For, yet, no nare was
                               tainted,

take   frequency: 86   relative frequency: 0.00124
   *p. 493 TO HIMSELF   42 And take the Alcaick Lute;
  **p. 115 PANEGYRE   87 "Betraid to fame, should take more care, and
                              feare
    p. 27 EPIGRAMS 1   1 Pray thee, take care, that tak'st my booke in
                              hand,
    p. 35 EPIGRAMS 27   2 Take better ornaments, my teares, and verse.
    p. 42 EPIGRAMS 50   1 Leaue COD, tabacco-like, burnt gummes to take,
    p. 51 EPIGRAMS 73   2 Or take an Epigramme so fearefully:
    p. 58 EPIGRAMS 91   1 Which of thy names I take, not onely beares
    p. 62 EPIGRAMS 96   4 And, in thy censures, euenly, dost take
    p. 65 EPIGRAMS 101   28 But that, which most doth take my Muse, and mee,
    p. 68 EPIGRAMS 106   5 Whether thy learning they would take, or wit,
    p. 69 EPIGRAMS 108   4 Be nor put on you, nor you take offence.
    p. 81 EPIGRAMS 129   15 O, runne not proud of this. Yet, take thy due.
    p. 84 EPIGRAMS 133   27 Who gaue, to take at his returne from Hell,
    p. 95 FOREST 2   72 Nor, when I take my lodging, need I pray
    p. 100 FOREST 4   19 To take the weake, or make them stop:
    p. 104 FOREST 8   7 Take heed, Sicknesse, what you doe,
    p. 105 FOREST 8   11 Scarce will take our present store?
    p. 105 FOREST 8   26 Doe enough; and who would take
    p. 108 FOREST 10   27 A beautie of that merit, that should take
    p. 116 FOREST 12   88 Or common places, filch'd, that take these times,
    p. 127 UNDERWOOD 1.1   8 O take my gift.
    p. 127 UNDERWOOD 1.1   14 And take compassion on my grievous plight.
    p. 128 UNDERWOOD 1.1   22 To take our nature; becam'st man, and dyd'st,

take (cont.)

p. 130	UNDERWOOD 1.3	10	Hee whom the whole world could not take,
p. 133	UNDERWOOD 2.3	9	Unto her; which Love might take
p. 140	UNDERWOOD 2.9	5	Titles, I confesse, doe take me;
p. 141	UNDERWOOD 2.9	38	Drest, you still for man should take him;
p. 146	UNDERWOOD 6	5	Take that away, you take our lives,
p. 150	UNDERWOOD 11	1	Or Scorne, or pittie on me take,
p. 153	UNDERWOOD 13	15	And though my fortune humble me, to take
p. 153	UNDERWOOD 13	17	Yet choyce from whom I take them; and would shame
p. 155	UNDERWOOD 13	68	And hurt seeks Cure, the Surgeon bids take bread,
p. 155	UNDERWOOD 13	72	All the Towne-curs take each their snatch at me.
p. 161	UNDERWOOD 14	83	On whom I could take up, and ne're abuse
p. 166	UNDERWOOD 15	127	More then themselves, or then our lives could take,
p. 166	UNDERWOOD 15	137	To take the box up for him; and pursues
p. 167	UNDERWOOD 15	175	Goe, quit 'hem all. And take along with thee,
p. 168	UNDERWOOD 15	195	These take, and now goe seeke thy peace in Warre,
p. 171	UNDERWOOD 20	8	Put on for fashion, and take up on trust:
p. 175	UNDERWOOD 23	25	Then take in hand thy Lyre,
p. 182	UNDERWOOD 28	13	Her joyes, her smiles, her loves, as readers take
p. 193	UNDERWOOD 38	67	O may your wisdome take example hence,
p. 197	UNDERWOOD 40	5	And take some sirrup after; so doe I,
p. 197	UNDERWOOD 40	10	Under another Name, I take your health;
p. 200	UNDERWOOD 42	12	In all that is call'd lovely: take my sight
p. 213	UNDERWOOD 44	15	Withall, the dirtie paines those Citizens take,
p. 216	UNDERWOOD 45	13	And as within your Office, you doe take
p. 217	UNDERWOOD 46	20	Of worthiest knowledge, that can take mens minds.
p. 218	UNDERWOOD 47	25	Let these men have their wayes, and take their times
p. 220	UNDERWOOD 47	76	My selfe a little. I will take you so,
p. 220	UNDERWOOD 48	11	That both, their odour take him,
p. 223	UNDERWOOD 49	41	And practise for a Miracle; take heed
p. 224	UNDERWOOD 50	3	And the right wayes you take unto the right,
p. 227	UNDERWOOD 52	18	How I would draw, and take hold and delight.
p. 229	UNDERWOOD 54	19	To goe out after ----- till when take this letter
p. 231	UNDERWOOD 57	11	To take Apprehension
p. 236	UNDERWOOD 63	6	What (at his liking) he will take away.
p. 250	UNDERWOOD 74	2	Doth take in easie Natures birth,
p. 255	UNDERWOOD 75	83	The king of Creatures, take his paritie
p. 265	UNDERWOOD 79	53	That they may take it eccho'd by the Floods.
p. 268	UNDERWOOD 82	8	Should take first Seisin of the publique good,
p. 273	U'WOOD 84.1	9	Of Goodnesse still: Vouchsafe to take
p. 273	U'WOOD 84.1	18	Take little Infants with their noyse,
p. 273	U'WOOD 84.1	31	Of Heaven; where SERAPHIM take tent
p. 284	U'WOOD 84.9	57	Must come to take a sentence, by the sense
p. 292	UNDERWOOD 86	18	With thee 'bove all his Rivals gifts take place,
p. 292	UNDERWOOD 86	21	There shall thy dainty Nostrill take
p. 307	HORACE 2	53	Take, therefore, you that write, still, matter fit
p. 317	HORACE 2	251	As his departing take much thence: lest, then,
p. 317	HORACE 2	258	Then those the faithfull eyes take in by show,
p. 317	HORACE 2	261	Things worthy to be done within, but take
p. 317	HORACE 2	267	Into a Swallow there; Nor Cadmus take,
p. 321	HORACE 2	361	Will take offence, at this: Nor, though it strike
p. 323	HORACE 2	375	Nor is't long since, they did with patience take
p. 323	HORACE 2	397	Take you the Greeke Examples, for your light,
p. 331	HORACE 2	540	Will take you more, the neerer that you stand;
p. 331	HORACE 2	569	Lest the throng'd heapes should on a laughter take:
p. 333	HORACE 2	594	An admirable Verse. The great Scurfe take
p. 333	HORACE 2	621	Looke through him, and be sure, you take not mocks
p. 335	HORACE 2	654	There's none will take the care, to helpe him then;
p. 303	UNGATHERED 3	4	Flowes fro the surfets which we take in peace.
p. 383	UNGATHERED 17	8	May take thy volume to his vertuous hand.
p. 384	UNGATHERED 18	11	May she, whome thou for spouse, to day, dost take,
p. 386	UNGATHERED 21	10	Or, like our Money-Brokers, take vp names
p. 392	UNGATHERED 26	74	That so did take Eliza, and our Iames!

takeinge   frequency: 1   relative frequency: 0.00001

p. 421	UNGATHERED 48	44	And by their takeinge, lett it once appeare

taken   frequency: 10   relative frequency: 0.00014
    See also "ta'en," "tane," "ta'ne."

taken (cont.)
  p. 94 FOREST 2   16 Of many a SYLVANE, taken with his flames.
  p. 102 FOREST 5   17 To be taken, to be seene,
  p. 117 FOREST 13   33 Not taken vp o'th'doctors, but as well
  p. 154 UNDERWOOD 13   32 Of pressure, like one taken in a streight?
  p. 175 UNDERWOOD 23   20 Be taken with false Baytes
  p. 209 UNDERWOOD 43   135 I saw with two poore Chambers taken in,
  p. 213 UNDERWOOD 44   22 How it held out! how (last) 'twas taken in!
  p. 240 UNDERWOOD 67   38 Hath taken twice the Ring
  p. 283 U'WOOD 84.9   41 So sweetly taken to the Court of blisse,
  p. 309 HORACE 2   73 And give, being taken modestly, this leave,

takes   frequency: 20 relative frequency: 0.00028
  See also "vnder-takes."
  p. 30 EPIGRAMS 12   13 Then takes vp fresh commoditie, for dayes;
  p. 30 EPIGRAMS 12   16 Takes physick, teares the papers: still god
                            payes.
  p. 34 EPIGRAMS 25   6 In varied shapes, which for his lust shee takes:
  p. 38 EPIGRAMS 37   2 But as they come, on both sides he takes fees,
  p. 45 EPIGRAMS 56   8 He takes vp all, makes each mans wit his owne.
  p. 49 EPIGRAMS 68   2 Takes priuate beatings, and begins againe.
  p. 50 EPIGRAMS 70   3 In life, that can employ it; and takes hold
  p. 108 FOREST 10   29 My owne true fire. Now my thought takes wing,
  p. 117 FOREST 13   44 And takes, and giues the beauties of the mind.
  p. 145 UNDERWOOD 5   13 And as a cunning Painter takes
  p. 169 UNDERWOOD 17   11 That as the lesser breach: for he that takes
  p. 192 UNDERWOOD 38   34 There greatnesse takes a glorie to relieve.
  p. 256 UNDERWOOD 75   123 The holy Prelate prayes, then takes the Ring,
  p. 275 U'WOOD 84.3   4 Where every lim takes like a face?
  p. 291 UNDERWOOD 85   47 And from the sweet Tub Wine of this yeare
                            takes,
  p. 327 HORACE 2   458 More strongly takes the people with delight,
  p. 337 HORACE 2   677 Learn'd and unlearn'd; holding, whom once he
                            takes;
  p. 365 UNGATHERED 5   24 Nor takes she pride to know them.
  p. 366 UNGATHERED 6   9 Marke, marke, but when his wing he takes,
  p. 383 UNGATHERED 17   1 Who takes thy volume to his vertuous hand,

taking   frequency: 5 relative frequency: 0.00007
  See also "takeinge."
**p. 115 PANEGYRE   74 The Kings obeying will, from taking pride
  p. 155 UNDERWOOD 13   89 My wonder, why the taking a Clownes purse,
  p. 180 UNDERWOOD 26   11 Which in the taking if you mis-apply,
  p. 197 UNDERWOOD 40   2 Till the sower Minute comes of taking leave,
  p. 214 UNDERWOOD 44   40 The Berghen siege, and taking in Breda,

tak'st   frequency: 4 relative frequency: 0.00005
  p. 27 EPIGRAMS 1   1 Pray thee, take care, that tak'st my booke in
                            hand,
  p. 44 EPIGRAMS 55   6 And giuing largely to me, more thou tak'st.
  p. 168 UNDERWOOD 15   182 Thy person fit for any charge thou tak'st;
  p. 203 UNDERWOOD 43   13 That since thou tak'st all envious care and
                            paine,

talc. See "talck," "talke."

talck   frequency: 1 relative frequency: 0.00001
  p. 188 UNDERWOOD 34   11 Or Turners oyle of Talck. Nor ever got

tale   frequency: 4 relative frequency: 0.00005
 *p. 492 TO HIMSELF   21 No doubt some mouldy tale,
  p. 51 EPIGRAMS 73   7 Item, a tale or two, some fortnight after:
  p. 115 FOREST 12   77 Will proue old ORPHEVS act no tale to be:
  p. 229 UNDERWOOD 54   3 If I doe lose it: And, without a Tale,

talent   frequency: 1 relative frequency: 0.00001
  p. 321 HORACE 2   347 Simo; and, of a talent wip'd his purse;

tales   frequency: 6 relative frequency: 0.00008
  p. 68 EPIGRAMS 107   5 Tell the grosse Dutch those grosser tales of
                            yours,
  p. 74 EPIGRAMS 115   17 Tell's of him, all the tales, it selfe then
                            makes;
  p. 84 EPIGRAMS 133   4 With tales of Troyes iust knight, our faiths
                            abuse:
  p. 93 FOREST 2   4 Thou hast no lantherne, whereof tales are told;
  p. 221 UNDERWOOD 48   40 And have thy tales and jests too,
  p. 228 UNDERWOOD 53   5 And saw a Centaure, past those tales of Greece;

talk   frequency: 1   relative frequency: 0.00001
    See also "talke."
    p. 402 UNGATHERED 34   4 Able to talk of Euclide, and correct

talk'd   frequency: 1   relative frequency: 0.00001
    p. 287 U'WOOD 84.9   184 Of divine Comfort, when sh'had talk'd with God.

talke   frequency: 12   relative frequency: 0.00017
    p. 59 EPIGRAMS 92   17 And talke reseru'd, lock'd vp, and full of feare,
    p. 59 EPIGRAMS 92   32 And of the poulder-plot, they will talke yet.
    p. 83 EPIGRAMS 131   7 For, if the hum'rous world will talke at large,
    p. 105 FOREST 8   33 That for th'oyle of Talke, dare spend
    p. 138 UNDERWOOD 2.6   14 You were more the eye, and talke
    p. 146 UNDERWOCD 6   2 That talke abroad of Womans change,
    p. 165 UNDERWOOD 15   101 Thus they doe talke. And are these objects fit
    p. 213 UNDERWOOD 47   9 Let those that meerely talke, and never thinke,
    p. 222 UNDERWOOD 49   11 What though she talke, and cannot once with them,
    p. 232 UNDERWOOD 59   1 They talke of Fencing, and the use of Armes,
    p. 235 U'WOOD 84.9   118 And Sons, and Daughters, with their Parents
                              talke;
    p. 319 HORACE 2   317 Built a small-timbred Stage, and taught them
                              talke

talkes   frequency: 2   relative frequency: 0.00002
    p. 74 EPIGRAMS 115   9 Talkes loud, and baudy, has a gather'd deale
    p. 137 UNDERWOOD 2.5   54 And Minerva, when she talkes.

talks. See "talkes."

tall   frequency: 2   relative frequency: 0.00002
    p. 170 UNDERWOOD 19   5 By that tall Grove, your haire; whose globy
                              rings
    p. 290 UNDERWOOD 85   9 The Poplar tall, he then doth marrying twine

taller   frequency: 1   relative frequency: 0.00001
    p. 94 FOREST 2   13 That taller tree, which of a nut was set,

talmud   frequency: 1   relative frequency: 0.00001
    p. 205 UNDERWOOD 43   65 The Talmud, and the Alcoran had come,

tame   frequency: 5   relative frequency: 0.00007
    p. 82 EPIGRAMS 130   2 Of building townes, and making wilde beasts tame,
    p. 189 UNDERWOOD 36   14 Now swift, now slow, now tame, now wild;
    p. 214 UNDERWOOD 44   55 That keepe the warre, though now't be growne more
                              tame,
    p. 305 HORACE 2   14 Yet, not as therefore wild, and tame should
                              cleave
    p. 327 HORACE 2   482 Was Tigers, said, and Lyons fierce, to tame.

tames   frequency: 3   relative frequency: 0.00004
    p. 368 UNGATHERED 6   79 Till thou at Tames alight,
    p. 368 UNGATHERED 6   81 Tames, prowde of thee, and of his Fate
    p. 369 UNGATHERED 6   107 Or Tames be rap't from vs

tamisis   frequency: 1   relative frequency: 0.00001
    p. 366 UNGATHERED 6   8 Did neuer dint the breast of Tamisis.

tane   frequency: 7   relative frequency: 0.00010
    p. 29 EPIGRAMS 8   2 RIDWAY was tane, arraign'd, condemn'd to
                              dye;
    p. 33 EPIGRAMS 21   6 The late tane bastinado. So I thought.
    p. 69 EPIGRAMS 107   9 Tell them, what parts yo'haue tane, whence run
                              away,
    p. 88 EPIGRAMS 133   151 Then, selling not, a dish was tane to mince 'hem,
    p. 96 FOREST 3   4 Art tane with neithers vice, nor sport:
    p. 154 UNDERWOOD 13   40 So each, that's done, and tane, becomes a Brace.
    p. 173 UNDERWOOD 22   18 The withered Garlands tane away;

ta'ne   frequency: 1   relative frequency: 0.00001
    p. 224 UNDERWOOD 50   21 Whilst your Ulisses hath ta'ne leave to goe,

tap. See "tapp."

taper   frequency: 2   relative frequency: 0.00002
  **p. 115 PANEGYRE   72 That friendly temper'd, one pure taper makes.
    p. 666 INSCRIPTS. 11   7 Till I, at much expense of Time, and Taper

tapp   frequency: 1   relative frequency: 0.00001
    p. 417 UNGATHERED 45   39 at Pem Wakers good ale Tapp,

tardie   frequency: 1   relative frequency: 0.00001
     p. 230 UNDERWOOD 56   7 And you may justly, being a tardie, cold,

tardy. See "tardie."

tarrie   frequency: 1   relative frequency: 0.00001
     p. 55 EPIGRAMS 85   9 To former height, and there in circle tarrie,

tarries   frequency: 2   relative frequency: 0.00002
     p. 156 UNDERWOOD 13   117 And feeles it; Else he tarries by the Beast.
     p. 315 HORACE 2   221 That tarries till the hangings be ta'en downe,

tarry   frequency: 4   relative frequency: 0.00005
     See also "tarrie."
     p. 57 EPIGRAMS 90   15 Hath got the stewards chaire; he will not tarry
     p. 165 UNDERWOOD 15   123 Our vices doe not tarry in a place,
     p. 246 UNDERWOOD 70   91 (Were not his Lucius long with us to tarry)
     p. 409 UNGATHERED 37   17 No man will tarry by thee, as hee goes,

tart   frequency: 1   relative frequency: 0.00001
     p. 392 UNGATHERED 26 ,51 The merry Greeke, tart Aristophanes,

task. See "taske," "tasque."

taske   frequency: 3   relative frequency: 0.00004
     p. 107 FOREST 10   19 Let the old boy, your sonne, ply his old taske,
     p. 234 UNDERWOOD 61   12 A Nations sinne got pardon'd! 'twere a taske
     p. 404 UNGATHERED 34   49 Oh, to make Boardes to speake! There is a taske

tasque   frequency: 1   relative frequency: 0.00001
     p. 85 EPIGRAMS 133   39 A harder tasque, then either his to Bristo',

tast   frequency: 4   relative frequency: 0.00005
     p. 54 EPIGRAMS 80   8 For good men but see death, the wicked tast it.
     p. 57 EPIGRAMS 90   5 The nicer thing to tast her ladies page;
     p. 105 FOREST 8   15 Or if needs thy lust will tast
     p. 417 UNGATHERED 45   20 some tast to send hir.

taste   frequency: 9   relative frequency: 0.00013
     See also "tast."
    *p. 492 TO HIMSELF   14 On such as haue no taste!
     p. 83 EPIGRAMS 131   6 We ought not giue them taste, we had an eare.
     p. 109 FOREST 11   15 Will quickly taste the treason, and commit
     p. 112 FOREST 11   97 All taste of bitternesse, and makes the ayre
     p. 139 UNDERWOOD 2.7   5 I'le taste as lightly as the Bee,
     p. 165 UNDERWOOD 15   100 Ne're came to taste the plenteous Mariage-horne.
     p. 197 UNDERWOOD 40   3 And then I taste it. But as men drinke up
     p. 246 UNDERWOOD 70   87 Or taste a part of that full joy he meant
     p. 286 U'WOOD 84.9   123 Wine, or delicious fruits, unto the Taste;

tasted   frequency: 2   relative frequency: 0.00002
     p. 65 EPIGRAMS 101   31 Of which had HORACE, or ANACREON
                              tasted,
     p. 135 UNDERWOOD 2.4   29 Or have tasted the bag o'the Bee?

taster   frequency: 1   relative frequency: 0.00001
     p. 220 UNDERWOOD 48   7 That thou remaine here taster

tasteth   frequency: 1   relative frequency: 0.00001
     p. 76 EPIGRAMS 118   2 So all his meate he tasteth ouer, twise:

tasting   frequency: 1   relative frequency: 0.00001
     p. 101 FOREST 4   31 And tasting ayre, and freedome, wull

taught   frequency: 11   relative frequency: 0.00015
     p. 63 EPIGRAMS 99   3 Hast taught thy selfe worthy thy pen to tread,
     p. 96 FOREST 2   93 They are, and haue beene taught religion: Thence
     p. 96 FOREST 2   95 Each morne, and euen, they are taught to pray,
     p. 152 UNDERWOOD 12   22 His very Manners taught t<o>'amend,
     p. 257 UNDERWOOD 75   143 Which their glad Parents taught
     p. 270 UNDERWOOD 83   61 And, in her last act, taught the Standers-by,
     p. 309 HORACE 2   98 Being taught a better way. All mortall deeds
     p. 319 HORACE 2   317 Built a small-timbred Stage, and taught them
                              talke
     p. 323 HORACE 2   410 Or 'twere the gowned Comoedy they taught.
     p. 371 UNGATHERED 9   7 Taught Pallas language; Cynthia modesty;
     p. 395 UNGATHERED 29   15 Taught Lucan these true moodes! Replyes my
                              sence

tavern. See "taverne."

taverne   frequency: 1   relative frequency: 0.00001
   p. 216 UNDERWOOD 45   8 Was issue of the Taverne, or the Spit:

tavernes   frequency: 1   relative frequency: 0.00001
   p. 211 UNDERWOOD 43   186 Vile Tavernes, and the Drunkards pisse him out;

taverns. See "tavernes."

tax. See "taxe."

tax'd   frequency: 3   relative frequency: 0.00004
   p. 48 EPIGRAMS 65   16 For worth he has not, He is tax'd, not prais'd.
   p. 60 EPIGRAMS 94   10 But, when they heard it tax'd, tooke more
                   offence.
   p. 101 FOREST 4   52 And euery goodnesse tax'd, or grieu'd.

taxe   frequency: 4   relative frequency: 0.00005
   p. 36 EPIGRAMS 30   2 Be thine, I taxe, yet doe not owne my rimes:
   p. 203 UNDERWOOD 43   24 Or taxe the Glories of the Church, and Gowne?
   p. 323 HORACE 2   383 So rare, as with some taxe it doth ingage
   p. 325 HORACE 2   416 To taxe that Verse, which many a day, and blot

taxeth   frequency: 1   relative frequency: 0.00001
   p. 200 UNDERWOOD 42   10 Who frownes, who jealous is, who taxeth me.

tayle   frequency: 1   relative frequency: 0.00001
   p. 164 UNDERWOOD 15   71 As if a Brize were gotten i' their tayle;

taylor   frequency: 2   relative frequency: 0.00002
   p. 30 EPIGRAMS 12   9 The taylor brings a suite home; he it ssayes,
   p. 141 UNDERWOOD 2.9   37 Yet no Taylor help to make him;

taylors   frequency: 2   relative frequency: 0.00002
   p. 201 UNDERWOOD 42   39 Whose like I have knowne the Taylors Wife put
                   on
   p. 216 UNDERWOOD 44   99 These Carkasses of honour; Taylors blocks,

teach   frequency: 16   relative frequency: 0.00023
   p. 31 EPIGRAMS 14   10 Man scarse can make that doubt, but thou canst
                   teach.
   p. 121 FOREST 14   48 They teach you, how.
   p. 141 UNDERWOOD 2.9   22 And his lip should kissing teach,
   p. 159 UNDERWOOD 14   37 T<o>'instruct and teach? or your unweary'd paine
   p. 165 UNDERWOOD 15   108 To teach each suit he has, the ready way
   p. 207 UNDERWOOD 43   92 To teach some that, their Nurses could <not>
                   doe,
   p. 216 UNDERWOOD 45   2 Whilst I informe my selfe, I would teach thee,
   p. 235 UNDERWOOD 61   18 To teach the people, how to fast, and pray,
   p. 286 U'WOOD 84.9   134 The price of our Redemption, and to teach
   p. 325 HORACE 2   435 I, writing nought my selfe, will teach them yet
   p. 327 HORACE 2   478 Or mixing sweet, and fit, teach life the right.
   p. 387 UNGATHERED 22   10 And teach your nephewes it to aemulate:
   p. 404 UNGATHERED 34   54 Attyre ye Persons as noe thought can teach
   p. 409 UNGATHERED 38   8 Which I, your Master, first did teach the Age.
   p. 410 UNGATHERED 38   16 And the Physician teach men spue, or shite;
   p. 411 UNGATHERED 39   11 Thy blatant Muse abroad, and teach it rather

teacher   frequency: 1   relative frequency: 0.00001
   p. 52 EPIGRAMS 75   t1 ON LIPPE, THE TEACHER.

team. See "teame."

teame   frequency: 1   relative frequency: 0.00001
   p. 107 FOREST 10   9 And foundred thy hot teame, to tune my lay.

tear. See "teare."

teare   frequency: 4   relative frequency: 0.00005
   p. 37 EPIGRAMS 33   1 Ile not offend thee with a vaine teare more,
   p. 77 EPIGRAMS 120   3 And know, for whom a teare you shed,
   p. 172 UNDERWOOD 21   3 Two letters were enough the plague to teare
   p. 233 UNDERWOOD 60   2 Stay, drop a teare for him that's dead,

teares   frequency: 11   relative frequency: 0.00015
   p. 30 EPIGRAMS 12   16 Takes physick, teares the papers: still god
                   payes.
   p. 33 EPIGRAMS 22   8 In comfort of her mothers teares,
   p. 35 EPIGRAMS 27   2 Take better ornaments, my teares, and verse.
   p. 35 EPIGRAMS 27   5 If any friends teares could restore, his would;
   p. 145 UNDERWOOD 4   9 O, doe not steepe them in thy Teares,

teares (cont.)
p. 152 UNDERWOOD 12	34 That they for me their teares will shed;
p. 270 UNDERWOOD 83	59 With gladnesse temper'd her sad Parents teares!
p. 283 U'WOOD 84.9	35 Of teares, and dungeon of calamitie!
p. 287 U'WOOD 84.9	180 She spent more time in teares her selfe to dresse
p. 293 UNDERWOOD 86	34 Flow my thin teares, downe these pale cheeks of mine?
p. 311 HORACE 2	146 Thy selfe in teares, then me thy losse will wound,

tears. See "teares."

teeming   frequency: 3   relative frequency: 0.00004
p. 250 UNDERWOOD 74	1 Such pleasure as the teeming Earth
p. 264 UNDERWOOD 79	17 7. Our teeming Ewes, 8. and lustie-mounting Rammes. .
p. 265 UNDERWOOD 79	51 Your teeming Ewes, aswell as mounting Rammes.

teeth   frequency: 1   relative frequency: 0.00001
| p. 183 UNDERWOOD 34 | 12 Spanish receipt, to make her teeth to rot. |

teirce   frequency: 1   relative frequency: 0.00001
| p. 241 UNDERWOOD 68 | 14 The Kings fame lives. Go now, denie his Teirce. |

telephus   frequency: 2   relative frequency: 0.00002
| p. 311 HORACE 2 | 135 Complaines in humble phrase. Both Telephus, |
| p. 311 HORACE 2 | 147 Peleus, or Telephus. If you speake vile |

telestichs   frequency: 1   relative frequency: 0.00001
| p. 204 UNDERWOOD 43 | 39 Acrostichs, and Telestichs, on jumpe names, |

tell   frequency: 51   relative frequency: 0.00073
See also "tell'."
p. 33 EPIGRAMS 38	8 I'le loose my modestie, and tell your name.
p. 65 EPIGRAMS 101	17 Ile tell you of more, and lye, so you will come:
p. 68 EPIGRAMS 107	5 Tell the grosse Dutch those grosser tales of yours,
p. 69 EPIGRAMS 107	9 Tell them, what parts yo'haue tane, whence run away,
p. 79 EPIGRAMS 124	11 Fitter, where it dyed, to tell,
p. 84 EPIGRAMS 133	1 No more let Greece her bolder fables tell
p. 85 EPIGRAMS 133	52 Canst tell me best, how euery Furie lookes there,
p. 120 FOREST 14	12 That I may tell to SYDNEY, what
p. 120 FOREST 14	16 Which I doe tell:
p. 139 UNDERWOOD 2.7	13 I will but mend the last, and tell
p. 139 UNDERWOOD 2.8	3 Lightly promis'd, she would tell
p. 140 UNDERWOOD 2.8	11 As, untill she tell her one,
p. 140 UNDERWOOD 2.9	2 I will tell what Man would please me.
p. 147 UNDERWOOD 7	2 Yet dare I not tell who;
p. 147 UNDERWOOD 7	8 I'le tell, that if they be not glad,
p. 148 UNDERWOOD 7	29 I'le tell no more, and yet I love,
p. 148 UNDERWOOD 7	35 If Love, or feare, would let me tell his name.
p. 149 UNDERWOOD 9	13 Tell me that she hath seene
p. 151 UNDERWOOD 11	7 Nor will he tell me for whose sake
p. 155 UNDERWOOD 13	77 Yea, of th'ingratefull: and he forth must tell
p. 161 UNDERWOOD 14	85 But here's no time, nor place, my wealth to tell,
p. 170 UNDERWOOD 19	11 Tell me (my lov'd Friend) doe you love, or no,
p. 170 UNDERWOOD 19	12 So well as I may tell in verse, 'tis so?
p. 198 UNDERWOOD 40	49 Which in assurance to your brest I tell,
p. 199 UNDERWOOD 41	2 Heare, Mistris, your departing servant tell
p. 201 UNDERWOOD 42	58 Lift up some one, and doe, I tell not what.
p. 201 UNDERWOOD 42	59 Thou didst tell me; and wert o're-joy'd to peepe
p. 203 UNDERWOOD 43	19 But, on thy malice, tell me, didst thou spie
p. 213 UNDERWOOD 44	5 Old Aesope Gundomar: the French can tell,
p. 213 UNDERWOOD 44	19 And comming home, to tell what acts were done
p. 219 UNDERWOOD 47	46 Though I doe neither heare these newes, nor tell
p. 228 UNDERWOOD 53	9 Or what we heare our home-borne Legend tell,
p. 231 UNDERWOOD 56	26 Accept his Muse; and tell, I know you can,
p. 231 UNDERWOOD 57	7 Tell him his Ben
p. 244 UNDERWOOD 70	53 Goe now, and tell out dayes summ'd up with feares,
p. 254 UNDERWOOD 75	74 And looking with thy best Inquirie, tell,
p. 269 UNDERWOOD 83	20 Of Winchester; the Heralds can tell this:
p. 269 UNDERWOOD 83	34 T<o>'inlive posteritie, her Fame may tell!
p. 274 U'WOOD 84.2	9 Run from your rootes; Tell, testifie the grand
p. 274 U'WOOD 84.2	13 And tell thou, ALDE-LEGH, None can tell more true
p. 277 U'WOOD 84.3	30 A Copie of this peece; nor tell

tell (cont.)
    p. 329 HORACE 2   449 Can tell a States-mans dutie, what the arts
    p. 329 HORACE 2   501 All which I tell, lest when Apollo's nam'd,
    p. 333 HORACE 2   659 I'le tell you but the death, and the disease
    p. 337 UNGATHERED 22 11 it will be matter lowd inoughe to tell
    p. 391 UNGATHERED 26 29 And tell, how farre thou didst our Lily
                            out-shine,
    p. 394 UNGATHERED 28   9 No stone in any wall here, but can tell
    p. 415 UNGATHERED 42 15 And know the woofe, and warpe thereof; can tell
    p. 415 UNGATHERED 43   3 But I can tell thee, Dover, how thy Games
    p. 652 INSCRIPTS. 2   5 Tell her, his Muse that did inuent thee

tell-troth   frequency: 2   relative frequency: 0.00002
    p. 376 UNGATHERED 11 t1 To the Right Noble Tom, Tell-Troth of
    p. 378 UNGATHERED 11 81 Honest Tom Tell-Troth puts downe Roger, How?

tell'   frequency: 1   relative frequency: 0.00001
    p. 103 FOREST 6   20 How to tell' hem, as th<e>y flow,

telling   frequency: 1   relative frequency: 0.00001
    p. 34 EPIGRAMS 25   3 Telling the motions of each petticote,

tells   frequency: 5   relative frequency: 0.00007
    See also "tell's," "tels."
 **p. 115 PANEGYRE   77 "With better pompe. She tells him first, that
                            Kings
    p. 29 EPIGRAMS 7   3 Tells you it is a hot-house: So it ma',
    p. 95 FOREST 2   67 Here no man tells my cups; nor, standing by,
    p. 160 UNDERWOOD 14   52 Of what it tells us) weav'd in to instruct!
    p. 179 UNDERWOOD 25   58 (As my hope tells) that our faire Phoeb<e>'s
                            shine,

tell's   frequency: 2   relative frequency: 0.00002
    p. 74 EPIGRAMS 115   17 Tell's of him, all the tales, it selfe then
                            makes;
    p. 380 UNGATHERED 12 24 The truth of his heart there, and tell's what a
                            clocke

tels   frequency: 1   relative frequency: 0.00001
    p. 380 UNGATHERED 12 52 Doth he once dissemble, but tels he did ride

temper   frequency: 1   relative frequency: 0.00001
    p. 27 EPIGRAMS 2   8 And by thy wiser temper, let men know

temperance. See "temp'rance."

temperate   frequency: 1   relative frequency: 0.00001
    p. 262 UNDERWOOD 78   5 Hee's prudent, valiant, just, and temperate;

temper'd   frequency: 2   relative frequency: 0.00002
 **p. 115 PANEGYRE   72 That friendly temper'd, one pure taper makes.
    p. 270 UNDERWOOD 83   59 With gladnesse temper'd her sad Parents teares!

tempest   frequency: 2   relative frequency: 0.00002
    p. 110 FOREST 11   43 In a continuall tempest. Now, true Loue
    p. 193 UNDERWOOD 38   76 As all with storme and tempest ran together.

tempests   frequency: 2   relative frequency: 0.00002
    p. 81 EPIGRAMS 128   13 Through seas, stormes, tempests: and imbarqu'd
                            for hell,
    p. 185 UNDERWOOD 30   10 That in all tempests, never quit the helme,

tempestuous   frequency: 1   relative frequency: 0.00001
    p. 215 UNDERWOOD 44   64 From the Tempestuous Grandlings, Who'll
                            informe

temple   frequency: 4   relative frequency: 0.00005
    p. 28 EPIGRAMS 5   3 The world the temple was, the priest a king,
    p. 155 UNDERWOOD 13   83 Man out their Boates to th' Temple, and not
                            shift
    p. 293 UNDERWOOD 86   32 Or with fresh flowers to girt my temple round.
    p. 401 UNGATHERED 32 21 And like a hallow'd Temple, free from taint

temples   frequency: 3   relative frequency: 0.00004
    p. 173 UNDERWOOD 22   17 His falling Temples you have rear'd,
    p. 190 UNDERWOOD 37   14 So may the fruitfull Vine my temples steepe,
    p. 406 UNGATHERED 35   8 Cittyes & Temples! thou a Caue for Wyne,

temp'rance   frequency: 1   relative frequency: 0.00001
 **p. 117 PANEGYRE   140 The temp'rance of a priuate man did bring,

tempt   frequency: 4   relative frequency: 0.00005
    p.   54 EPIGRAMS 81   1 Forbeare to tempt me, PROVLE, I will not
                                show
    p.   88 EPIGRAMS 133   168 Tempt such a passage? when each priuies seate
    p.   89 EPIGRAMS 133   179 Tempt not his furie, PLVTO is away:
    p. 100 FOREST 4   5 Doe not once hope, that thou canst tempt

tempted   frequency: 1   relative frequency: 0.00001
    p. 190 UNDERWOOD 37   32 But shall sometimes be tempted to obey

ten   frequency: 10   relative frequency: 0.00014
    p.   84 EPIGRAMS 133   15 Furies there wanted not: each scold was ten.
    p. 105 FOREST 8   31 With ten Emp'ricks, in their chamber,
    p. 131 UNDERWOOD 2   t2 ten Lyrick Peeces.
    p. 213 UNDERWOOD 44   27 These ten yeares day; As all may sweare that
                                looke
    p. 235 UNDERWOOD 62   10 One Poet, then of other folke ten score.
    p. 272 UNDERWOOD 84   t8 Consisting of these Ten Pieces.
    p. 325 HORACE 2   418 Not, ten times o're, corrected to the naile.
    p. 331 HORACE 2   544 Doth please; this, ten times over, will delight.
    p. 406 UNGATHERED 34   103 Whom not ten fyres, nor a Parlyamt can

tenants   frequency: 1   relative frequency: 0.00001
    p. 399 UNGATHERED 31   4 Tenants, and Seruants, haue they harts, and
                                eyes,

tend   frequency: 2   relative frequency: 0.00002
    p. 107 FOREST 10   7 PHOEBVS. No? tend thy cart still. Enuious
                                day
    p. 180 UNDERWOOD 26   4 A gentler, and more agile hand, to tend

tender   frequency: 10   relative frequency: 0.00014
  **p. 116 PANEGYRE   122 Must with a tender (yet a stedfast) hand
    p. 101 FOREST 4   41 My tender, first, and simple yeeres
    p. 287 U'WOOD 84.9   174 A tend r Mother, a discreeter Wife,
    p. 290 UNDERWOOD 85   16 Of Earth, and sheares the tender Sheepe:
    p. 292 UNDERWOOD 86   26 The Youths and tender Maids shall sing thy
                                praise:
    p. 309 HORACE 2   89 Like tender buds shoot up, and freshly grow.
    p. 317 HORACE 2   260 Yet, to the Stage, at all thou maist not tender
    p. 382 UNGATHERED 16   4 to tender thus, their liues, their loues, their
                                hartes!
    p. 398 UNGATHERED 30   76 Of tender eyes will more be wept, then seene:
    p. 417 UNGATHERED 45   16 Tough, foule, or Tender.

tendering. See "tendring."

tendring   frequency: 1   relative frequency: 0.00001
    p. 231 UNDERWOOD 56   28 I can lose none in tendring these to you.

tenor   frequency: 1   relative frequency: 0.00001
    p. 395 UNGATHERED 29   11 Calme Brutus tenor start; but all along

tent   frequency: 1   relative frequency: 0.00001
    p. 273 U'WOOD 84.1   31 Of Heaven; where SERAPHIM take tent

tenth   frequency: 1   relative frequency: 0.00001
    p. 161 UNDERWOOD 14   84 The Credit, what would furnish a tenth Muse!

t'enuy   frequency: 1   relative frequency: 0.00001
    p. 405 UNGATHERED 34   69 I am too fat t'enuy him. He too leane

terence   frequency: 1   relative frequency: 0.00001
    p. 392 UNGATHERED 26   52 Neat Terence, witty Plautus, now not please;

tergum   frequency: 1   relative frequency: 0.00001
    p. 380 UNGATHERED 12   37 How faine for his venery he was to crie (Tergum
                                o)

term. See "terme."

terme   frequency: 3   relative frequency: 0.00004
    p.   29 EPIGRAMS 10   1 Thou call'st me Poet, as a terme of shame:
    p. 185 UNDERWOOD 31   t3 the last Terme he sate Chancellor.
    p. 404 UNGATHERED 34   56 Terme of ye Architects is called Designe!

termers   frequency: 1   relative frequency: 0.00001
    p.   26 EPIGRAMS 3   9 For termers, or some clarke-like seruing-man,

termes   frequency: 4   relative frequency: 0.00005
  p. 159 UNDERWOOD 14   21 Men past their termes, and prais'd some names too
                             much,
  p. 307 HORACE 2   70 Thou need new termes; thou maist, without excuse,
  p. 309 HORACE 2   84 And ever will, to utter termes that bee
  p. 321 HORACE 2   334 With poore base termes, through every baser shop:

terms. See "termes."

terp.   frequency: 1   relative frequency: 0.00001
  p. 240 UNDERWOOD 67   25 5. TERP. Behold the royall Mary,

terpsichore. See "terp."

terror   frequency: 2   relative frequency: 0.00002
  p. 43 EPIGRAMS 51   3 Which though it did but panick terror proue,
  p. 169 UNDERWOOD 18   6 A terror? or is all this but my feare?

terrors   frequency: 1   relative frequency: 0.00001
  p. 177 UNDERWOOD 25   30 Sinke not beneath these terrors:

test   frequency: 3   relative frequency: 0.00004
  p. 28 EPIGRAMS 4   10 Of Kings for grace; of Poets for my test?
  p. 218 UNDERWOOD 47   3 They meet the fire, the Test, as Martyrs would;
  p. 385 UNGATHERED 20   3 Who are his Test, and what their iudgement is:

testifie   frequency: 1   relative frequency: 0.00001
  p. 274 U'WOOD 84.2   9 Run from your rootes; Tell, testifie the grand

testify. See "testifie."

testimony   frequency: 1   relative frequency: 0.00001
  p. 385 UNGATHERED 19   2 What place is for my testimony void?

t'express   frequency: 1   relative frequency: 0.00001
  p. 403 UNGATHERED 34   41 Or Verse, or Sense t'express Immortall you?

text   frequency: 1   relative frequency: 0.00001
  p. 52 EPIGRAMS 75   3 Though LIPPE, at PAVLS, ranne from his
                             text away,

teynted   frequency: 1   relative frequency: 0.00001
  p. 190 UNDERWOOD 37   29 Yet if with eithers vice I teynted be,

th<e>y   frequency: 1   relative frequency: 0.00001
  p. 103 FOREST 6   20 How to tell' hem, as th<e>y flow,

th<ey>'are   frequency: 1   relative frequency: 0.00001
  p. 281 U'WOOD 84.8   11 (Brave Youths) th<ey>'are their possessions,
                             none of yours:

th<ey>'were   frequency: 1   relative frequency: 0.00001
  p. 282 U'WOOD 84.9   8 Till swept away, th<ey>'were cancell'd with a
                             broome!

th<o>rough   frequency: 2   relative frequency: 0.00002
  p. 134 UNDERWOOD 2.4   10 Th<o>rough Swords, th<o>rough Seas, whether she
                             would ride.

th<ou>'have   frequency: 1   relative frequency: 0.00001
  p. 210 UNDERWOOD 43   169 So would'st th<ou>'have run upon the Rolls by
                             stealth,

th'   frequency: 4   relative frequency: 0.00005

th'accompt   frequency: 1   relative frequency: 0.00001
  p. 56 EPIGRAMS 87   5 Vpon th'accompt, hers grew the quicker trade.

th'admir'd   frequency: 1   relative frequency: 0.00001
  p. 206 UNDERWOOD 43   82 Th'admir'd discourses of the Prophet Ball:

th'aduenter   frequency: 1   relative frequency: 0.00001
  p. 184 EPIGRAMS 133   20 Shee brought the Poets forth, but ours
                             th'aduenter.

th'advantage   frequency: 1   relative frequency: 0.00001
  p. 138 UNDERWOOD 2.6   10 With th'advantage of her haire,

th'adventures   frequency: 1   relative frequency: 0.00001
  p. 207 UNDERWOOD 43   95 With all th'adventures; Three bookes not afraid

th'aemilian   frequency: 1   relative frequency: 0.00001
    p. 307 HORACE 2   46 Th'Aemilian Schoole, in brasse can fashion out

th'aeternall   frequency: 1   relative frequency: 0.00001
    p. 412 UNGATHERED 40   20 th'aeternall Crown to win.

th'affaires   frequency: 1   relative frequency: 0.00001
    p. 218 UNDERWOOD 47   23 That censure all the Towne, and all th'affaires,

th'affrighted   frequency: 1   relative frequency: 0.00001
    p. 243 UNDERWOOD 70   16 Upon th'affrighted world:

th'age   frequency: 2   relative frequency: 0.00002
    p.   47 EPIGRAMS 64   4 A treasure, art: contemn'd in th'age of gold.
    p.   68 EPIGRAMS 105   20 I' your selfe, all treasure lost of th'age
                              before.

thal.   frequency: 1   relative frequency: 0.00001
    p. 239 UNDERWOOD 67   13 3. THAL. Yet, let our Trumpets sound:

thalia. See "thal."

th'ambitious   frequency: 1   relative frequency: 0.00001
    p. 162 UNDERWOOD 15   11 Looke on th'ambitious man, and see him nurse

thames   frequency: 4   relative frequency: 0.00005
    See also "tames."
    p. 103 FOREST 6   15 Or the drops in siluer Thames,
    p. 253 UNDERWOOD 75   34 Their Sister-tunes, from Thames his either
                              side,
    p. 392 UNGATHERED 26   73 And make those flights vpon the bankes of
                              Thames,
    p. 407 UNGATHERED 35   16 Or Dowgate Torrent falling into Thames,

than   frequency: 11   relative frequency: 0.00015
    See also "then."

thank   frequency: 1   relative frequency: 0.00001
    See also "tharke."
    p. 405 UNGATHERED 34   68 Swim wthout Corke! Why, thank ye good Queen
                              Anne.

thank'd   frequency: 1   relative frequency: 0.00001
    p. 161 UNDERWOOD 14   70 That would, perhaps, have prais'd, and thank'd
                              the same,

thanke   frequency: 5   relative frequency: 0.00007
    p.   80 EPIGRAMS 127   12 To thanke thy benefits: which is, to pay.
    p. 154 UNDERWOOD 13   43 No more then he doth thanke, that will receive
    p. 232 UNDERWOOD 58   6 Thanke him: if other, hee can give no Bayes.
    p. 236 UNDERWOOD 63   9 But thanke his greatnesse, and his goodnesse too:
    p. 290 UNDERWOOD 85   21 With which, Priapus, he may thanke thy hands,

thankefull   frequency: 1   relative frequency: 0.00001
    p.   80 EPIGRAMS 127   1 Is there a hope, that Man would thankefull bee,

thankes   frequency: 6   relative frequency: 0.00008
    p.   99 FOREST 3   101 Be thankes to him, and earnest prayer, to finde
    p. 153 UNDERWOOD 13   16 The smallest courtesies with thankes, I make
    p. 153 UNDERWOOD 13   25 Can I owe thankes, for Curtesies receiv'd
    p. 154 UNDERWOOD 13   33 All this corrupts the thankes; lesse hath he
                              wonne,
    p. 154 UNDERWOOD 13   39 No! Gifts and thankes should have one cheerefull
                              face,
    p. 154 UNDERWOOD 13   49 Give thankes by stealth, and whispering in the
                              eare,

thankful. See "thankefull," "thankfull."

thankfull   frequency: 3   relative frequency: 0.00004
    p. 189 UNDERWOOD 37   1 Sir, I am thankfull, first, to heaven, for you;
    p. 213 UNDERWOOD 44   17 And the returne those thankfull Courtiers yeeld,
    p. 313 HORACE 2   166 Of some small thankfull land: whether he bee

thanking   frequency: 1   relative frequency: 0.00001
    p. 158 UNDERWOOD 13   159 By thanking thus the curtesie to life,

thanks   frequency: 1   relative frequency: 0.00001
    See also "thankes."
    p. 380 UNGATHERED 12   43 Yes. And thanks God in his Pistle or his
                              Booke

th'antique   frequency: 1   relative frequency: 0.00001
     p. 72 EPIGRAMS 111   2 What th'antique souldiers were, the moderne bee?

th'aonian   frequency: 1   relative frequency: 0.00001
     p. 174 UNDERWOOD 23   7 Are all th'Aonian springs

th'approches   frequency: 1   relative frequency: 0.00001
     p. 253 UNDERWOOD 75   36 And all did ring th'approches of the Bride;

th'are   frequency: 5   relative frequency: 0.00007

th'art   frequency: 4   relative frequency: 0.00005

th'artillery   frequency: 1   relative frequency: 0.00001
   **p. 117 PANEGYRE   153 The length'ned showt, as when th'artillery

th'ascent   frequency: 1   relative frequency: 0.00001
     p. 403 UNGATHERED 34   35 Th'ascent of Lady Fame which none could spy

th'assembly   frequency: 1   relative frequency: 0.00001
     p. 138 UNDERWOOD 2.6   12 Of th'Assembly, as did you!

that   frequency: 1059   relative frequency: 0.01533
     See also "that]," "that's," "yt."

that]   frequency: 1   relative frequency: 0.00001
     p. 182 UNDERWOOD 27   30 The Swan [that] so relish'd Pancharis)

that's   frequency: 24   relative frequency: 0.00034

t'haue   frequency: 3   relative frequency: 0.00004

th'authors   frequency: 1   relative frequency: 0.00001
     p. 60 EPIGRAMS 94   3 If workes (not th'authors) their owne grace
                            should looke,

t'have   frequency: 7   relative frequency: 0.00010

thawes   frequency: 1   relative frequency: 0.00001
     p. 363 UNGATHERED 3   13 It thawes the frostiest, and most stiffe disdaine:

thaws.   See "thawes."

th'best   frequency: 1   relative frequency: 0.00001
     p. 259 UNDERWOOD 76   2 To th'best of Monarchs, Masters, Men,

th'calends   frequency: 1   relative frequency: 0.00001
     p. 291 UNDERWOOD 85   70 At th'Calends, puts all out againe.

the   frequency: 2787   relative frequency: 0.04034
     See also "i'th'," "i'the," "i'th'open," "o'th',"
              "o'th'doctors," "o'the," "th',"
              "th'accompt," "th'admir'd,"
              "th'aduenter," "th'advantage,"
              "th'adventures," "th'aemilian,"
              "th'aeternall," "th'affaires,"
              "th'affrighted," "th'age,"
              "th'ambitious," "th'antique,"
              "th'aonian," "th'approches,"
              "th'artillery," "th'ascent,"
              "th'assembly," "th'authors," "th'best,"
              "th'calends," "the>," "th'eare,"
              "th'eares," "th'eating," "the'chequer,"
              "the'elixir," "th'elaborate,"
              "th'elixir," "th'enamour'd,"
              "th'enuy'd," "th'epilogue,"
              "th'escape," "th'esplandians,"
              "th'eternall," "the'vn-vsed,"
              "th'examining," "th'exampled,"
              "th'exchange," "th'expence," "th'eye,"
              "th'hard," "th'how," "th'iambick,"
              "th'idalian," "th'ides," "th'ignoble,"
              "th'ill," "th'ingratefull,"
              "th'inscription," "th'intent,"
              "th'interpreters," "th'ionian,"
              "th'italian," "th'obscene,"
              "th'obseruing," "th'often," "th'old,"
              "th'one," "th'opinion," "th'oppressor,"
              "th'other," "th'oyle," "th'unbearded,"
              "th'uncertainty," "th'vsurped,"
              "t'other," "wi'the," "ye."

the<e>   frequency: 2   relative frequency: 0.00002
      p. 225 UNDERWOOD 51   2 How comes it all things so about the<e> smile?
      p. 420 UNGATHERED 48   25 to gett the<e> a leane fface,

the<ir>   frequency: 6   relative frequency: 0.00008
      p. 110 FOREST 11   35 But this doth from the<ir> cloud of error grow,
      p. 205 UNDERWOOD 43   67 Of errant Knight-hood, with the<ir> Dames, and
                                 Dwarfes,
      p. 205 UNDERWOOD 43   68 The<ir> charmed Boates, and the<ir> inchanted
                                 Wharfes;
      p. 233 UNDERWOOD 59   12 As they out-did the lightning in the<ir> course;
      p. 325 HORACE 2   432 My title, at the<ir> rate, I'<h>ad rather, I,

the>   frequency: 2   relative frequency: 0.00002
      p. 89 EPIGRAMS 133   177 Of Hol'borne (<the> three sergeants heads)
                                  lookes ore,
      p. 139 UNDERWOOD 2.7   16 Each suck <the> others breath.

theame   frequency: 2   relative frequency: 0.00002
      p. 179 UNDERWOOD 25   39 Is but a Statists theame, to read Phlebotomie.
      p. 222 UNDERWOOD 49   ·12 Make State, Religion, Bawdrie, all a theame?

th'eare   frequency: 1   relative frequency: 0.00001
      p. 323 HORACE 2   404 A lawfull Verse, by th'eare, or finger scan.

th'eares   frequency: 1   relative frequency: 0.00001
      p. 63 EPIGRAMS 97   18 Nor are the Queenes most honor'd maides by
                                 th'eares

th'eating   frequency: 1   relative frequency: 0.00001
      p. 290 UNDERWOOD 85   34 For th'eating Thrush, or Pit-falls sets:

theatre   frequency: 1   relative frequency: 0.00001
      p. 285 U'WOOD 84.9   114 Shall meet with gladnesse in one Theatre;

theban   frequency: 1   relative frequency: 0.00001
      p. 327 HORACE 2   483 Amphion, too, that built the Theban towres,

thebes   frequency: 1   relative frequency: 0.00001
      p. 313 HORACE 2   168 Or, with the milke of Thebes; or Argus, fed.

the'chequer   frequency: 1   relative frequency: 0.00001
      p. 232 UNDERWOOD 57   28 if the'Chequer be emptie, so will be his Head.

thee   frequency: 229   relative frequency: 0.00331
      See also "the<e>," "thee>."

thee>   frequency: 1   relative frequency: 0.00001
      p. 411 UNGATHERED 39   13 For thou hast nought <in thee> to cure his Fame,

theefe   frequency: 1   relative frequency: 0.00001
      p. 265 UNDERWOOD 79   63 The theefe from spoyle, his presence holds.

the'elixir   frequency: 1   relative frequency: 0.00001
      p. 110 FOREST 11   56 The'Elixir of all ioyes?

theft   frequency: 1   relative frequency: 0.00001
      p. 102 FOREST 5   16 But the sweet theft to reueale:

their   frequency: 394   relative frequency: 0.00570
      See also "the<ir>," "theire," "theyr," "theyre."

theire   frequency: 1   relative frequency: 0.00001

theirs   frequency: 6   relative frequency: 0.00008

th'elaborate   frequency: 1   relative frequency: 0.00001
      p. 311 HORACE 2   140 'Tis not enough, th'elaborate Muse affords

th'elixir   frequency: 1   relative frequency: 0.00001
      p. 64 EPIGRAMS 100   2 Cry'd to my face, they were th'elixir of wit:

them   frequency: 122   relative frequency: 0.00176
      See also "haue'hem," "hem," "'hem."

them-selues   frequency: 1   relative frequency: 0.00001
      p. 117 FOREST 13   13 Such as suspect them-selues, and thinke it fit

theme   frequency: 1   relative frequency: 0.00001
      See also "theame."
      p. 286 U'WOOD 84.9   120 But make him All in All, their Theme, that
                                  Day:

themis   frequency: 3   relative frequency: 0.00004
   **p. 113 PANEGYRE   20 I saw, when reuerend THEMIS did descend
   **p. 115 PANEGYRE   73 Meane while, the reuerend THEMIS drawes
                                  aside
   **p. 116 PANEGYRE   110 As once defend, what THEMIS did reproue.

themselues   frequency: 5   relative frequency: 0.00007
      p. 40 EPIGRAMS 43   2 Whose actions so themselues doe celebrate;
      p. 94 FOREST 2   36 Officiously, at first, themselues betray.
      p. 95 FOREST 2   56 An embleme of themselues, in plum, or peare.
      p. 119 FOREST 13   90 Whereon the most of mankinde wracke themselues,
      p. 422 UNGATHERED 50   2 make many, hurt themselues; a praysed faith

themselves   frequency: 8   relative frequency: 0.00011
      See also "them-selues," "themselues."
      p. 159 UNDERWOOD 14   16 Themselves through favouring what is there not
                                  found:
      p. 166 UNDERWOOD 15   127 More then themselves, or then our lives could
                                  take,
      p. 216 UNDERWOOD 45   19 But these with wearing will themselves unfold:
      p. 255 UNDERWOOD 75   86 Themselves to day,
      p. 257 UNDERWOOD 75   140 Doe long to make themselves, so, another way:
      p. 313 HORACE 2   170 Things in themselves agreeing: If againe
      p. 323 HORACE 2   377 The steadie Spondaees; so themselves to beare
      p. 325 HORACE 2   424 Retire themselves, avoid the publike baths;

then   frequency: 404   relative frequency: 0.00584
      See also "than."

then<ce>   frequency: 1   relative frequency: 0.00001
      p. 219 UNDERWOOD 47   62 With reverence using all the gifts then<ce>
                                  given.

th'enamour'd   frequency: 1   relative frequency: 0.00001
      p. 264 UNDERWOOD 79   36 1. Where ere they tread th'enamour'd ground,

thence   frequency: 22   relative frequency: 0.00031
      See also "then<ce>."
      p. 69 EPIGRAMS 108   3 And your high names: I doe desire, that thence
      p. 72 EPIGRAMS 111   11 And thence, depraue thee, and thy worke. To
                                  those
      p. 82 EPIGRAMS 130   14 Including all, were thence call'd harmonie:
      p. 94 FOREST 2   17 And thence, the ruddy Satyres oft prouoke
      p. 96 FOREST 2   93 They are, and haue beene taught religion: Thence
      p. 137 UNDERWOOD 2.6   4 Thence, as sweet, as you are faire,
      p. 152 UNDERWOOD 12   18 That never came ill odour thence:
      p. 161 UNDERWOOD 14   76 In the same Mines of knowledge; and thence
                                  brought
      p. 210 UNDERWOOD 43   162 Did not she save from thence, to build a Rome?
      p. 234 UNDERWOOD 61   7 Yet are got off thence, with cleare mind, and
                                  hands
      p. 271 UNDERWOOD 83   75 And all beatitudes, that thence doe flow:
      p. 279 U'WOOD 84.4   39 And, though the sound were parted thence,
      p. 290 UNDERWOOD 85   31 Or hence, or thence, he drives with many a Hound
      p. 317 HORACE 2   251 As his departing take much thence: lest, then,
      p. 327 HORACE 2   455 Thence draw forth true expressions. For,
                                  sometimes,
      p. 329 HORACE 2   528 Hath shed, or humane frailtie not kept thence.
      p. 335 HORACE 2   658 Not thence be sav'd, although indeed he could?
      p. 367 UNGATHERED 6   41 From thence, display thy wing againe
      p. 368 UNGATHERED 6   68 From thence is gon
      p. 391 UNGATHERED 26   32 From thence to honour thee, I would not seeke
      p. 402 UNGATHERED 34   9 Drawne Aristotle on vs! & thence showne
      p. 405 UNGATHERED 34   81 Disguisd? and thence drag forth Enormity?

th'enuy'd   frequency: 1   relative frequency: 0.00001
      p. 408 UNGATHERED 37   4 Th'enuy'd returne, of forty pound in gold.

theocritus   frequency: 1   relative frequency: 0.00001
      p. 397 UNGATHERED 30   27 Which made me thinke, the old Theocritus,

theorbo   frequency: 2   relative frequency: 0.00002
      p. 239 UNDERWOOD 67   17 Harpe, Lute, Theorbo sprung,
      p. 263 UNDERWOOD 79   2 Lute, Lyre, Theorbo, all are call'd to day.

th'epilogue   frequency: 1   relative frequency: 0.00001
     p. 315 HORACE 2   222 And sits, till th'Epilogue saies Clap, or
                                Crowne:

there   frequency: 183   relative frequency: 0.00264
     See also "there's."

thereby   frequency: 1   relative frequency: 0.00001
     p. 378 UNGATHERED 11   90 As well as from his braines, and claimest thereby

therefore   frequency: 17   relative frequency: 0.00024
     See also "therfore."
     p. 59 EPIGRAMS 92   38 On them: And therefore doe not onely shunne
     p. 80 EPIGRAMS 127   4 No, I doe, therefore, call Posteritie
     p. 85 EPIGRAMS 133   40 Or his to Antwerpe. Therefore, once more, list
                                ho'.
     p. 99 FOREST 3   72 And brag, that they were therefore borne.
     p. 116 FOREST 13   7 I, therefore, who professe my selfe in loue
     p. 118 FOREST 13   67 Giddie with change, and therefore cannot see
     p. 140 UNDERWOOD 2.8   13 Therefore, Charis, you must do't,
     p. 171 UNDERWOOD 19   15 I'le therefore aske no more, but bid you love;
     p. 212 UNDERWOOD 43   212 That have good places: therefore once agen,
     p. 305 HORACE 2   14 Yet, not as therefore wild, and tame should
                                cleave
     p. 307 HORACE 2   53 Take, therefore, you that write, still, matter
                                fit
     p. 321 HORACE 2   363 The nut-crackers throughout, will they therefore
     p. 323 HORACE 2   390 To Roman Poets. Shall I therefore weave
     p. 329 HORACE 2   525 Which it doth threaten. Therefore, where I see
     p. 380 UNGATHERED 12   29 And therefore how euer the trauelling nation,
     p. 386 UNGATHERED 20   8 And therefore I commend vnto the Wife,
     p. 391 UNGATHERED 26   17 I, therefore will begin. Soule of the Age!

therein   frequency: 6   relative frequency: 0.00008
     p. 74 EPIGRAMS 115   21 With such a one. And therein keepes it's word.
     p. 93 FOREST 2   8 Of wood, of water: therein thou art faire.
     p. 95 FOREST 2   84 On thy good lady, then! who, therein, reap'd
     p. 129 UNDERWOOD 1.2   6 Therein, thy Love.
     p. 158 UNDERWOOD 13   160 Which you will bury; but therein, the strife
     p. 378 UNGATHERED 11   84 And therein (which is worth his valour too)

thereof   frequency: 6   relative frequency: 0.00008
     p. 41 EPIGRAMS 43   10 And what I write thereof find farre, and free
     p. 212 UNDERWOOD 43   210 And pray the fruites thereof, and the increase;
     p. 269 UNDERWOOD 83   26 Thereof, no notion can expresse how much
     p. 273 U'WOOD 84.1   12 Thereof, to TIME.
     p. 395 UNGATHERED 29   5 At euery line some pinn thereof should slacke
     p. 415 UNGATHERED 42   15 And know the woofe, and warpe thereof; can tell

thereon   frequency: 2   relative frequency: 0.00002
     p. 106 FOREST 9   13 But thou thereon did'st onely breath,
     p. 277 U'WOOD 84.4   2 Now I have better thought thereon,

there's   frequency: 16   relative frequency: 0.00023

therfore   frequency: 1   relative frequency: 0.00001
     p. 295 UNDERWOOD 90   13 Nor feare thy latest day, nor wish therfore.

th'escape   frequency: 1   relative frequency: 0.00001
     p. 339 HORACE 1   46 If .. th'escape an .... path .. ..

these   frequency: 149   relative frequency: 0.00215

thesevs   frequency: 1   relative frequency: 0.00001
     p. 84 EPIGRAMS 133   2 Of HERCVLES, or THESEVS going to
                                hell,

thespia   frequency: 1   relative frequency: 0.00001
     p. 174 UNDERWOOD 23   8 Dri'd up? lyes Thespia wast?

thespiades. See "thespiad's."

thespiad's   frequency: 1   relative frequency: 0.00001
     p. 366 UNGATHERED 6   18 Neere which, the Thespiad's sing;

thespian   frequency: 3   relative frequency: 0.00004
     p. 65 EPIGRAMS 101   33 Tabacco, Nectar, or the Thespian spring,
     p. 108 FOREST 10   25 Nor all the ladies of the Thespian lake,
     p. 120 FOREST 14   11 Giue me my cup, but from the Thespian well,

thespis   frequency: 1   relative frequency: 0.00001
    p. 319 HORACE 2   311 Thespis is said to be the first found out

th'esplandians   frequency: 1   relative frequency: 0.00001
    p. 203 UNDERWOOD 43   30 Th'Esplandians, Arthurs, Palmerins, and all

th'eternall   frequency: 1   relative frequency: 0.00001
    p. 130 UNDERWOOD 1.3   7 The Sonne of God, th'Eternall King,

the'vn-vsed   frequency: 1   relative frequency: 0.00001
    p. 87 EPIGRAMS 133 132 Must trie the'vn-vsed valour of a nose:

thewes   frequency: 1   relative frequency: 0.00001
    p. 311 HORACE 2   125 The place allotted it, with decent thewes.

thews. See "thewes."

th'examining   frequency: 1   relative frequency: 0.00001
    p. 109 FOREST 11   14 Who (in th'examining)

th'exampled   frequency: 1   relative frequency: 0.00001
    p. 255 UNDERWOOD 75   80 They are th'exampled Paire, and mirrour of their
                             kind.

th'exchange   frequency: 3   relative frequency: 0.00004
    p. 202 UNDERWOOD 42   72 Varietie of Silkes were on th'Exchange!
    p. 206 UNDERWOOD 43   80 Upon th'Exchange, still, out of
                             Popes-head-Alley;
    p. 386 UNGATHERED 21 14 Vpon th'Exchange of Letters, as I wou'd

th'expence   frequency: 1   relative frequency: 0.00001
    p. 33 EPIGRAMS 20   1 Th'expence in odours is a most vaine sinne,

they   frequency: 344   relative frequency: 0.00497
    See also "th<e>y," "th<ey>'are," "th<ey>'were,"
             "th'are," "they'," "they'<h>ave,"
             "they'are," "they'd," "they'haue,"
             "they'offenders," "they're," "th'haue,"
             "th'were."

they'<h>ave   frequency: 1   relative frequency: 0.00001
    p. 218 UNDERWOOD 47   13 They'<h>ave glutted in, and letcher'd out that
                             weeke,

they'   frequency: 1   relative frequency: 0.00001

they'are   frequency: 1   relative frequency: 0.00001

they'd   frequency: 1   relative frequency: 0.00001

th'eye   frequency: 3   relative frequency: 0.00004
    p. 58 EPIGRAMS 91   6 In th'eye of Europe, where thy deeds were done,
    p. 109 FOREST 11   9 At th'eye and eare (the ports vnto the minde)
    p. 317 HORACE 2   265 Natur'd, and wicked Atreus cooke, to th'eye,

they'haue   frequency: 1   relative frequency: 0.00001

they'offenders   frequency: 1   relative frequency: 0.00001
    p. 60 EPIGRAMS 93   16 Wherewith, against thy bloud, they'offenders bee.

theyr   frequency: 2   relative frequency: 0.00002

theyre   frequency: 2   relative frequency: 0.00002

they're   frequency: 4   relative frequency: 0.00005

th'hard   frequency: 1   relative frequency: 0.00001
    p. 28 EPIGRAMS 3   10 Who scarse can spell th'hard names: whose knight
                             lesse can.

th'hast   frequency: 3   relative frequency: 0.00004

th'haue   frequency: 1   relative frequency: 0.00001

th'how   frequency: 1   relative frequency: 0.00001

th'iambick   frequency: 2   relative frequency: 0.00002
    p. 311 HORACE 2   117 Th'Iambick arm'd Archilochus to rave,
    p. 323 HORACE 2   371 Two rests, a short and long, th'Iambick frame;

thick   frequency: 1   relative frequency: 0.00001
     See also "over-thick," "thicke."
     p. 331 HORACE 2   558 Or thick grosse ointment, but offend the Guests:

thicke   frequency: 1   relative frequency: 0.00001
     p. 87 EPIGRAMS 133   130 These be the cause of those thicke frequent mists

th'idalian   frequency: 1   relative frequency: 0.00001
     p. 63 EPIGRAMS 105   11 If dancing, all would cry th'Idalian Queene,

th'ides   frequency: 1   relative frequency: 0.00001
     p. 291 UNDERWOOD 85   69 'Gainst th'Ides, his moneys he gets in with
                               paine,

thie   frequency: 4   relative frequency: 0.00005

thief. See "theefe," "thiefe."

thiefe   frequency: 3   relative frequency: 0.00004
     p. 29 EPIGRAMS 8   6 The courtier is become the greater thiefe.
     p. 44 EPIGRAMS 56   3 From brocage is become so bold a thiefe,
     p. 50 EPIGRAMS 69   1 COB, thou nor souldier, thiefe, nor fencer art,

thigh   frequency: 1   relative frequency: 0.00001
     p. 378 UNGATHERED 11   89 Yes thou wert borne out of his trauelling thigh

thighes   frequency: 3   relative frequency: 0.00004
     p. 164 UNDERWOOD 15   75 And laugh, and measure thighes, then squeake,
                               spring, itch,
     p. 258 UNDERWOOD 75   173 And 'tweene their Grandsires thighes,
     p. 378 UNGATHERED 11   92 Euer his thighes Male then, and his braines
                               Shee.

thighs. See "thighes."

th'ignoble   frequency: 1   relative frequency: 0.00001
     p. 257 UNDERWOOD 75   153 Th'Ignoble never liv'd, they were a-while

th'ill   frequency: 1   relative frequency: 0.00001
     p. 391 UNGATHERED 26   16 Aboue th'ill fortune of them, or the need.

thin   frequency: 2   relative frequency: 0.00002
     p. 141 UNDERWOOD 2.9   28 And so thin, to see a blush
     p. 293 UNDERWOOD 86   34 Flow my thin teares, downe these pale cheeks of
                               mine?

thincking   frequency: 1   relative frequency: 0.00001
     p. 116 FOREST 12   94 Now thincking on you, though to England lost,

thine   frequency: 44   relative frequency: 0.00063
     See also "thyne."

thing   frequency: 24   relative frequency: 0.00034
     See also "eltham-thing," "some-thing," "thinge."
     p. 27 EPIGRAMS 2   5 Become a petulant thing, hurle inke, and wit,
     p. 31 EPIGRAMS 14   5 Then thee the age sees not that thing more graue,
     p. 48 EPIGRAMS 65   1 Away, and leaue me, thou thing most abhord,
     p. 57 EPIGRAMS 90   5 The nicer thing to tast her ladies page;
     p. 74 EPIGRAMS 115   7 A subtle thing, that doth affections win
     p. 100 FOREST 3   106 Thou maist thinke life, a thing but lent.
     p. 110 FOREST 11   37 The thing, they here call Loue, is blinde
                               Desire,
     p. 111 FOREST 11   67 That cryes, we dreame, and sweares, there's no
                               such thing,
     p. 142 UNDERWOOD 2.9   46 As to doe no thing too much.
     p. 145 UNDERWOOD 5   15 More pleasure while the thing he makes
     p. 163 UNDERWOOD 15   32 And being a thing, blowne out of nought, rebells
     p. 250 UNDERWOOD 74   3 When shee puts forth the life of ev'ry thing:
     p. 277 U'WOOD 84.4   8 To draw a thing that cannot sit.
     p. 281 U'WOOD 84.8   16 It is a wretched thing to trust to reedes;
     p. 307 HORACE 2   41 One thing prodigiously, paints in the woods
     p. 309 HORACE 2   76 And come not too much wrested. What's that
                               thing,
     p. 317 HORACE 2   278 Betweene the Acts, a quite cleane other thing
     p. 319 HORACE 2   309 That found out profit, and foretold each thing,
     p. 335 HORACE 2   666 Doth the same thing with him, that would him
                               kill.
     p. 335 HORACE 2   672 Or the sad thunder-stroken thing he have
     p. 370 UNGATHERED 7   2 Require (besides the likenesse of the thing)
     p. 380 UNGATHERED 12   51 Or any thing else that another should hide,

thing (cont.)
```
    p.  418 UNGATHERED 47    3 And God blesse every living thing,
    p.  423 UNGATHERED 50   20 shall never dare do any thing but feare./
```

thinge   frequency: 1   relative frequency: 0.00001
```
    p.  361 UNGATHERED 1     17 thus, as a ponderous thinge in water cast
```

th'ingratefull   frequency: 1   relative frequency: 0.00001
```
    p.  155 UNDERWOOD 13     77 Yea, of th'ingratefull: and he forth must tell
```

things   frequency: 45   relative frequency: 0.00065
```
   *p.  493 TO HIMSELF        41 Leaue things so prostitute,
  **p.  115 PANEGYRE          78 "Are here on earth the most conspicuous things:
    p.   28 EPIGRAMS 4         3 But two things, rare, the FATES had in their
                                   store,
    p.   31 EPIGRAMS 14        7 What name, what skill, what faith hast thou in
                                   things!
    p.   40 EPIGRAMS 42       17 The selfe-same things, a note of concord be:
    p.   48 EPIGRAMS 65       14 Things manly, and not smelling parasite.
    p.   49 EPIGRAMS 67        1 Since men haue left to doe praise-worthy things,
    p.   51 EPIGRAMS 73       21 Fortie things more, deare GRAND, which you
                                   know true,
    p.   62 EPIGRAMS 95       34 Can write the things, the causes, and the men.
    p.   62 EPIGRAMS 95       36 That dares nor write things false, nor hide
                                   things true.
    p.   63 EPIGRAMS 99        4 And that to write things worthy to be read:
    p.   96 FOREST 2          86 To haue her linnen, plate, and all things nigh,
    p.   99 FOREST 3          97 And, howsoeuer we may thinke things sweet,
    p.  159 UNDERWOOD 14      36 Or faith in things? or is't your wealth and will
    p.  163 UNDERWOOD 15      42 Honour and honestie, as poore things thought
    p.  168 UNDERWOOD 15     179 That thou dost all things more for truth, then
                                   glory,
    p.  170 UNDERWOOD 18       7 That as the water makes things, put in't
                                   streight,
    p.  176 UNDERWOOD 24      12 Doth mete, whose lyne doth sound the depth of
                                   things:)
    p.  193 UNDERWOOD 38      72 It shakes even him, that all things else doth
                                   shake.
    p.  216 UNDERWOOD 44     101 The fate of things: whilst totter'd vertue holds
    p.  225 UNDERWOOD 51       2 How comes it all things so about the<e> smile?
    p.  245 UNDERWOOD 70      57 Repeat of things a throng,
    p.  261 UNDERWOOD 77      15 Can doe the things that Statues doe deserve,
    p.  295 UNDERWOOD 90       1 The Things that make the happier life, are
                                   these,
    p.  305 HORACE 2          17 In grave beginnings, and great things profest,
    p.  307 HORACE 2          69 Yet, if by chance, in utt'ring things abstruse,
    p.  309 HORACE 2          83 New names of things. It hath beene ever free,
    p.  311 HORACE 2         148 And ill-penn'd things, I shall, or sleepe, or
                                   smile.
    p.  311 HORACE 2         150 The angry brow; the sportive, wanton things;
    p.  313 HORACE 2         170 Things in themselves agreeing: If againe
    p.  313 HORACE 2         183 'Tis hard, to speake things common, properly:
    p.  313 HORACE 2         186 First publish things unspoken, and unknowne.
    p.  317 HORACE 2         243 Doth wretchedly the use of things forbeare,
    p.  317 HORACE 2         256 Or acted told. But, ever, things that run
    p.  317 HORACE 2         261 Things worthy to be done within, but take
    p.  321 HORACE 2         354 There comes sometimes to things of meanest place.
    p.  327 HORACE 2         487 Things sacred, from profane to separate;
    p.  331 HORACE 2         548 This saying: To some things there is assign'd
    p.  333 HORACE 2         596 Or, of the things, that ne're came in my mind,
    p.  338 HORACE 1          14 ... ... .. ......... cruell things ...... ......
    p.  341 HORACE 1         120 Of ....... noyses, borne to actuate things.
    p.  367 UNGATHERED 6      56 And conquers all things, yea it selfe, at length.
    p.  394 UNGATHERED 28     10 Such things, of euery body, and as well.
    p.  423 UNGATHERED 50     15 Yet ware; thou mayst do all things cruellie:
```

think   frequency: 1   relative frequency: 0.00001
```
    See also "thinke."
    p.  417 UNGATHERED 45     11 I shall think on't ere't be day.
```

thinke   frequency: 66   relative frequency: 0.00095
```
    p.   32 EPIGRAMS 16        9 Keepe thy selfe there, and thinke thy valure
                                   right,
    p.   46 EPIGRAMS 60        7 Durst thinke it great, and worthy wonder too,
    p.   49 EPIGRAMS 67        2 Most thinke all praises flatteries. But truth
                                   brings
    p.   52 EPIGRAMS 75        1 I Cannot thinke there's that antipathy
    p.   64 EPIGRAMS 101       3 Not that we thinke vs worthy such a ghest,
    p.   65 EPIGRAMS 101      16 The skie not falling, thinke we may haue larkes.
    p.   67 EPIGRAMS 104       5 Or, because some scarce thinke that storie true,
```

thinke (cont.)

p.	72 EPIGRAMS 112	11	I modestly quit that, and thinke to write,
p.	73 EPIGRAMS 113	5	I thinke, the Fate of court thy comming crau'd,
p.	88 EPIGRAMS 133	155	But 'mong'st these Tiberts, who do'you thinke there was?
p.	95 FOREST 2	52	Some nuts, some apples; some that thinke they make
p.	98 FOREST 3	61	They thinke not, then, which side the cause shall leese,
p.	99 FOREST 3	80	And thinke his power doth equall Fates.
p.	99 FOREST 3	90	Though poyson, thinke it a great fate.
p.	99 FOREST 3	97	And, howsoeuer we may thinke things sweet,
p.	100 FOREST 3	106	Thou maist thinke life, a thing but lent.
p.	105 FOREST 8	27	Any paines; yea, thinke it price,
p.	114 FOREST 12	32	Were it to thinke, that you should not inherit
p.	114 FOREST 12	38	Riches thought most: But, Madame, thinke what store
p.	117 FOREST 13	13	Such as suspect them-selues, and thinke it fit
p.	119 FOREST 13	87	And neuer thinke, how vice doth euery houre,
p.	120 FOREST 14	15	And he may thinke on that
p.	122 FOREST 15	1	Good, and great GOD, can I not thinke of thee,
p.	128 UNDERWOOD 1.1	35	The gladdest light, darke man can thinke upon;
p.	138 UNDERWOOD 2.6	19	And did thinke, such Rites were due
p.	139 UNDERWOOD 2.7	18	Let who will thinke us dead, or wish our death.
p.	142 UNDERWOOD 2.9	39	And not thinke h'had eat a stake,
p.	149 UNDERWOOD 9	1	I now thinke, Love is rather deafe, then blind,
p.	153 UNDERWOOD 13	20	Deepest in Man, of which when he doth thinke,
p.	164 UNDERWOOD 15	73	And jealous each of other, yet thinke long
p.	168 UNDERWOOD 15	187	That thou thinke nothing great, but what is good,
p.	168 UNDERWOOD 15	193	No more, then we should thinke a Lord had had
p.	170 UNDERWOOD 18	15	Oh how a Lover may mistake! to thinke,
p.	172 UNDERWOOD 20	20	Thinke but the Sin of all her sex, 'tis she!
p.	175 UNDERWOOD 23	22	And thinke it Poesie?
p.	177 UNDERWOOD 25	27	Nor thinke your selfe unfortunate,
p.	180 UNDERWOOD 26	19	Thinke but how deare you bought
p.	185 UNDERWOOD 31	4	Law, to his Law; and thinke your enemies his:
p.	186 UNDERWOOD 32	12	Thinke, yea and boast, that they have done it so
p.	186 UNDERWOOD 33	1	That I, hereafter, doe not thinke the Barre,
p.	192 UNDERWOOD 38	31	Thinke it was frailtie, Mistris, thinke me man,
p.	192 UNDERWOOD 38	32	Thinke that your selfe like heaven forgive me can:
p.	192 UNDERWOOD 38	35	Thinke that I once was yours, or may be now;
p.	199 UNDERWOOD 41	3	What it is like: And doe not thinke they can
p.	199 UNDERWOOD 42	4	Whose Readers did not thinke he was in love.
p.	201 UNDERWOOD 42	51	Then ope thy wardrobe, thinke me that poore Groome
p.	213 UNDERWOOD 44	30	Would thinke no more of Vlushing, or the Brill:
p.	218 UNDERWOOD 47	9	Let those that meerely talke, and never thinke,
p.	218 UNDERWOOD 47	19	That to speake well, thinke it above all sinne,
p.	221 UNDERWOOD 48	27	And thinke thy streame more quicker
p.	228 UNDERWOOD 53	14	Before, I thinke my wish absolv'd had beene.
p.	229 UNDERWOOD 55	1	Would God, my Burges, I could thinke
p.	236 UNDERWOOD 63	10	And thinke all still the best, that he will doe.
p.	245 UNDERWOOD 70	78	And thinke, nay know, thy Morison's not dead.
p.	248 UNDERWOOD 71	14	Dare thinke it, to relieve, no lesse renowne,
p.	249 UNDERWOOD 72	20	What prayers (People) can you thinke too much?
p.	260 UNDERWOOD 77	10	This I would doe, could I thinke Weston one
p.	263 UNDERWOOD 78	21	He will cleare up his forehead, thinke thou bring'st
p.	276 U'WOOD 84.3	16	And Men may thinke, all light rose there.
p.	325 HORACE 2	426	But fame of Poets, they thinke, if they come forth,
p.	327 HORACE 2	474	Thinke wee, or hope, there can be Verses fain'd
p.	329 HORACE 2	508	The truth; nor let thy Fable thinke, what e're
p.	368 UNGATHERED 6	90	Of thine, shall thinke the Maine
p.	391 UNGATHERED 26	12	And thinke to ruine, where it seem'd to raise.
p.	397 UNGATHERED 30	27	Which made me thinke, the old Theocritus,

thinkes   frequency: 7   relative frequency: 0.00010

p.	35 EPIGRAMS 28	5	Which hee thinkes great; and so reades verses, too:
p.	88 EPIGRAMS 133	43	All, that are readers: but, me thinkes 'tis od,
p.	211 UNDERWOOD 43	177	At Common-Law: me thinkes in his despight
p.	222 UNDERWOOD 49	2	And thinkes I dare not her? let the world see.
p.	223 UNDERWOOD 49	24	Thinkes it selfe nought, though she should valew it.
p.	315 HORACE 2	203	Hee thinkes not, how to give you smoake from light,
p.	392 UNGATHERED 26	62	(And himselfe with it) that he thinkes to frame;

thinking   frequency: 5   relative frequency: 0.00007
    See also "thincking."
   **p. 114 PANEGYRE   41 Some cry from tops of houses; thinking noise
     p. 59 EPIGRAMS 92   36 Much like those Brethren; thinking to preuaile
     p. 249 UNDERWOOD 72 15 Had they but grace, of thinking, at these routes,
     p. 323 HORACE 2   392 Or rather, thinking all my faults may spie,
     p. 410 UNGATHERED 39 9 Thinking to stir me, thou hast lost thy End,

thinks. See "thinkes."

think'st   frequency: 5   relative frequency: 0.00007
     p. 72 EPIGRAMS 112   3 Think'st thou it is meere fortune, that can win?
     p. 72 EPIGRAMS 112   6 Art still at that, and think'st to blow me'vp
                             too?
     p. 81 EPIGRAMS 129   9 Think'st thou, MIME, this is great? or, that
                             they striue
     p. 150 UNDERWOOD 10 12 Think'st thou that love is help'd by feare?
     p. 408 UNGATHERED 37 2 And they were very good: yet thou think'st nay.

th'inscription   frequency: 1   relative frequency: 0.00001
     p. 269 UNDERWOOD 83 18 At least may beare th'inscription to her Tombe.

th'intent   frequency: 1   relative frequency: 0.00001
     p. 87 EPIGRAMS 133 107 To answere me. And sure, it was th'intent

th'interpreters   frequency: 1   relative frequency: 0.00001
     p. 395 UNGATHERED 29 18 Are still th'interpreters twixt godds, and men!

th'ionian   frequency: 1   relative frequency: 0.00001
     p. 291 UNDERWOOD 85 53 Th'Ionian God-wit, nor the Ginny hen

third   frequency: 5   relative frequency: 0.00007
   **p. 113 PANEGYRE   27 Her third, IRENE, help'd to beare his
                             traine;
     p. 284 U'WOOD 84.9   53 Like single; so, there is a third, commixt,
     p. 287 U'WOOD 84.9 170 To another, Move; he went; To a third, Go,
     p. 327 HORACE 2   469 A third of twelve, you may: foure ounces. Glad,
     p. 413 UNGATHERED 41 13 The third, is from the garden cull'd, the Rose,

thirst   frequency: 1   relative frequency: 0.00001
     p. 106 FOREST 9   5 The thirst, that from the soule doth rise,

thirsty. See "lip-thirstie."

thirteene   frequency: 1   relative frequency: 0.00001
     p. 77 EPIGRAMS 120   9 Yeeres he numbred scarse thirteene

thirty   frequency: 1   relative frequency: 0.00001
     p. 402 UNGATHERED 34 2 From thirty pound in pipkins, to ye Man

this   frequency: 338   relative frequency: 0.00489
    See also "this's."

this's   frequency: 1   relative frequency: 0.00001

th'italian   frequency: 1   relative frequency: 0.00001
     p. 74 EPIGRAMS 115 26 Parts, then th'Italian could doe, with his dore.

thither   frequency: 5   relative frequency: 0.00007
     p. 41 EPIGRAMS 44   5 He meant they thither should make swift repaire,
     p. 163 UNDERWOOD 15 47 Thither it flowes. How much did Stallion spend
     p. 200 UNDERWOOD 42 26 For Silke will draw some sneaking Songster
                             thither.
     p. 285 U'WOOD 84.9 103 Thither, you hope to come; and there to find
     p. 389 UNGATHERED 23 12 And who make thither else, rob, or inuade.

tho   frequency: 1   relative frequency: 0.00001
     p. 194 UNDERWOOD 38 113 You would be then most confident, that tho

tho'   frequency: 1   relative frequency: 0.00001
     p. 252 UNDERWOOD 78   1 Tho', happy Muse, thou know my Digby well,

th'obscene   frequency: 1   relative frequency: 0.00001
     p. 321 HORACE 2   340 From what th'obscene, and petulant Satyres are.

th'obseruing   frequency: 1   relative frequency: 0.00001
     p. 40 EPIGRAMS 42   2 Th'obseruing neighbours no such mood can see.

th'often   frequency: 1   relative frequency: 0.00001
     p. 249 UNDERWOOD 72 16 On th'often comming of this Holy-day:

```
th'old                        frequency:    2  relative frequency: 0.00002
    p.   31 EPIGRAMS 12    23 But see! th'old baud hath seru'd him in his trim,
    p.  415 UNGATHERED 42  22 A Master-worker call'd, th'old standerd burst

thomas                        frequency:    8  relative frequency: 0.00011
    See also "tom."
    p.   49 EPIGRAMS 67    t1 TO THOMAS EARLE OF
                              SVFFOLKE.
    p.   51 EPIGRAMS 74    t1 TO THOMAS LORD CHANCELOR.
    p.   63 EPIGRAMS 98    t1 TO SIR THOMAS ROE.
    p.   73 EPIGRAMS 113   t1 TO SIR THOMAS OVERBVRY.
    p.  185 UNDERWOOD 31   t2 To THOMAS Lo: ELSMERE,
    p.  258 UNDERWOOD 75  171 Upon a Thomas, or a Francis call;
    p.  379 UNGATHERED 12  t2 Polytopian Thomas the Traueller.
    p.  395 UNGATHERED 29  t3 THOMAS MAY,

th'one                        frequency:    1  relative frequency: 0.00001
    p.  361 UNGATHERED 1   20 till th'one hath drownd the other in our sightes,

th'opinion                    frequency:    1  relative frequency: 0.00001
    p.   74 EPIGRAMS 115   28 Of miming, gets th'opinion of a wit.

th'oppressor                  frequency:    1  relative frequency: 0.00001
    p.  217 UNDERWOOD 46    8 Thy just defences made th'oppressor afraid.

thorny                        frequency:    1  relative frequency: 0.00001
    p.  413 UNGATHERED 41  16 With wonder on the thorny regiment.

thorough                      frequency:    1  relative frequency: 0.00001
    p.   85 EPIGRAMS 133   66 Thorough her wombe they make their famous road,

thorough-fare                 frequency:    1  relative frequency: 0.00001
    p.   76 EPIGRAMS 118    4 He makes himselfe a thorough-fare of vice.

thoroughlie                   frequency:    1  relative frequency: 0.00001
    p.  423 UNGATHERED 50  16 not safe; but when thou dost them thoroughlie:

thoroughly. See "thoroughlie," "throughly."

thorow                        frequency:    1  relative frequency: 0.00001
    p.  145 UNDERWOOD 5    10 So going thorow all your straine,

those                         frequency:  127  relative frequency: 0.00183

th'other                      frequency:    5  relative frequency: 0.00007
    p.   79 EPIGRAMS 124   10 Th'other let it sleepe with death:
    p.  208 UNDERWOOD 43  122 As th'other may his braines with Quicksilver.
    p.  218 UNDERWOOD 47   16 Or th'other on their borders, that will jeast
    p.  284 U'WOOD 84.9    52 One corporall, only; th'other spirituall,
    p.  384 UNGATHERED 18  24 Yet neyther of you seeme to th'other old.

thou                          frequency:  377  relative frequency: 0.00545
    See also "th<ou>'have," "th'art," "th'hast,"
             "thou'<h>ast," "thou'ast," "thou'hast,"
             "thou'ldst," "thou'lt," "thou'rt,"
             "tho'wert."

thou'<h>ast                   frequency:    1  relative frequency: 0.00001
    p.  188 UNDERWOOD 34   18 And scorn'd, thou'<h>ast showne thy malice, but
                              hast fail'd.

thou'ast                      frequency:    1  relative frequency: 0.00001

though                        frequency:  124  relative frequency: 0.00179
    See also "tho," "tho'," "though't."
  *p.  493 TO HIMSELF    45 And though thy nerues be shrunke, and blood be
                              cold,
 **p.  115 PANEGYRE      82 "Though hid at home, abroad is search'd into:
 **p.  116 PANEGYRE     111 For though by right, and benefite of Times,
 **p.  117 PANEGYRE     147 Though many greater: and the most, the best.
   p.   35 EPIGRAMS 26    1 Then his chast wife, though BEAST now know
                              no more,
   p.   36 EPIGRAMS 29    1 TILTER, the most may'admire thee, though not
                              I:
   p.   36 EPIGRAMS 30    1 GVILTIE, be wise; and though thou know'st
                              the crimes
   p.   36 EPIGRAMS 31    3 And though the soundest legs goe euery day,
   p.   37 EPIGRAMS 32    6 His often change of clime (though not of mind)
   p.   43 EPIGRAMS 51    3 Which though it did but panick terror proue,
   p.   47 EPIGRAMS 63   12 To so true worth, though thou thy selfe forbid.
```

though (cont.)

p.	49 EPIGRAMS 66	15	Though euery fortitude deserues applause,
p.	50 EPIGRAMS 70	8	Though life be short, let vs not make it so.
p.	52 EPIGRAMS 75	3	Though LIPPE, at PAVLS, ranne from his text away,
p.	54 EPIGRAMS 81	7	Which, if thou leaue not soone (though I am loth)
p.	55 EPIGRAMS 86	7	Where, though 't be loue, that to thy praise doth moue,
p.	57 EPIGRAMS 90	9	Not though that haire grew browne, which once was amber,
p.	60 EPIGRAMS 93	14	Though not vnprou'd: which shewes, thy fortunes are
p.	61 EPIGRAMS 94	13	And like them too; must needfully, though few,
p.	63 EPIGRAMS 98	11	Though both be good, the latter yet is worst,
p.	64 EPIGRAMS 99	11	Well, though thy name lesse then our great ones bee,
p.	65 EPIGRAMS 101	15	And, though fowle, now, be scarce, yet there are clarkes,
p.	66 EPIGRAMS 102	14	And one true posture, though besieg'd with ill
p.	66 EPIGRAMS 103	4	Know you to be a SYDNEY, though vn-nam'd?
p.	83 EPIGRAMS 131	5	And though we could all men, all censures heare,
p.	85 EPIGRAMS 133	55	Great Club-fist, though thy backe, and bones be sore,
p.	86 EPIGRAMS 133	73	But they vnfrighted passe, though many a priuie
p.	94 FOREST 2	45	And though thy walls be of the countrey stone,
p.	95 FOREST 2	50	Thy lord, and lady, though they haue no sute.
p.	96 FOREST 3	3	And, though so neere the citie, and the court,
p.	99 FOREST 3	90	Though poyson, thinke it a great fate.
p.	100 FOREST 4	13	I know too, though thou strut, and paint,
p.	107 FOREST 10	23	Though he would steale his sisters PEGASVS,
p.	108 FOREST 10	26	(Though they were crusht into one forme) could make
p.	111 FOREST 11	73	Though thy wild thoughts with sparrowes wings doe flye,
p.	112 FOREST 11	85	Though we acknowledge, who can so abstayne,
p.	112 FOREST 11	90	His heart sinnes, though he feares.
p.	113 FOREST 12	11	Though neuer after; whiles it gaynes the voyce
p.	115 FOREST 12	68	Who, though shee haue a better verser got,
p.	115 FOREST 12	70	And, who doth me (though I not him) enuy,
p.	116 FOREST 12	94	Now thincking on you, though to England lost,
p.	116 FOREST 13	10	With sinne and vice, though with a throne endew'd;
p.	117 FOREST 13	15	I, that haue suffer'd this; and, though forsooke
p.	117 FOREST 13	45	Though it reiect not those of FORTVNE: such
p.	118 FOREST 13	64	Which though the turning world may dis-esteeme,
p.	131 UNDERWOOD 2.1	3	Though I now write fiftie yeares,
p.	131 UNDERWOOD 2.1	5	Poets, though divine, are men:
p.	146 UNDERWOOD 6	8	Doe change, though man, and often fight,
p.	147 UNDERWOOD 7	25	Though hate had put them out;
p.	148 UNDERWOOD 7	28	Will be my Rivall, though she have but eares.
p.	151 UNDERWOOD 12	9	That though they did possesse each limbe,
p.	153 UNDERWOOD 13	15	And though my fortune humble me, to take
p.	157 UNDERWOOD 13	158	Without your gift, though I can rate that too,
p.	158 UNDERWOOD 14	2	Though I am short, I cannot be obscure:
p.	158 UNDERWOOD 14	7	To aske it: though in most of workes it be
p.	159 UNDERWOOD 14	19	Though I confesse (as every Muse hath err'd,
p.	165 UNDERWOOD 15	88	Is lov'd, though he let out his owne for life:
p.	167 UNDERWOOD 15	174	Though thou wert Muster-master of the Land.
p.	171 UNDERWOOD 19	14	(Though they may number bodyes) or but one.
p.	171 UNDERWOOD 20	10	That their whole life was wickednesse, though weav'd
p.	173 UNDERWOOD 22	1	Though Beautie be the Marke of praise,
p.	173 UNDERWOOD 22	6	Throughout your forme; as though that move,
p.	175 UNDERWOOD 23	19	That though the greedie Frie
p.	177 UNDERWOOD 25	26	True noblesse. Palme growes straight, though handled ne're so rude.
p.	179 UNDERWOOD 25	43	Though but while mettal's heating:
p.	179 UNDERWOOD 25	55	Though many Gems be in your bosome stor'd,
p.	182 UNDERWOOD 27	33	Though I, in working of my song,
p.	182 UNDERWOOD 28	2	Though not in these, in rithmes not wholly dumbe,
p.	185 UNDERWOOD 30	4	Thy Universe, though his Epitome.
p.	186 UNDERWOOD 32	11	Who, though their guilt, and perjurie they know,
p.	186 UNDERWOOD 32	13	As though the Court pursues them on the sent,
p.	189 UNDERWOOD 36	3	Though Envie oft his shadow be,
p.	190 UNDERWOOD 37	16	Though you sometimes proclaime me too severe,
p.	193 UNDERWOOD 38	97	Produce; though threatning with a coale, or chalke

though (cont.)

p. 197 UNDERWOOD 40	15	For though Love thrive, and may grow up with cheare,
p. 199 UNDERWOOD 41	4	Be idle words, though of a parting Man;
p. 201 UNDERWOOD 42	61	From the poore wretch, which though he play'd in prose,
p. 209 UNDERWOOD 43	133	Which, though it were the Fort of the whole Parish,
p. 210 UNDERWOOD 43	157	Though but in daunces, it shall know his power;
p. 210 UNDERWOOD 43	160	Troy, though it were so much his Venus care.
p. 211 UNDERWOOD 43	176	No order? no Decree? Though we be gone
p. 211 UNDERWOOD 43	195	Or Alexandria; and though a Divine
p. 214 UNDERWOOD 44	55	That keepe the warre, though now't be growne more tame,
p. 218 UNDERWOOD 47	4	And though Opinion stampe them not, are gold.
p. 219 UNDERWOOD 47	46	Though I doe neither heare these newes, nor tell
p. 222 UNDERWOOD 49	3	What though her Chamber be the very pit
p. 222 UNDERWOOD 49	7	What though with Tribade lust she force a Muse,
p. 222 UNDERWOOD 49	11	What though she talke, and cannot once with them,
p. 222 UNDERWOOD 49	15	What though she ride two mile on Holy-dayes
p. 222 UNDERWOOD 49	18	What though she be with Velvet gownes indu'd,
p. 223 UNDERWOOD 49	21	What though she hath won on Trust, as many doe,
p. 223 UNDERWOOD 49	24	Thinkes it selfe nought, though she should valew it.
p. 224 UNDERWOOD 50	13	And though all praise bring nothing to your name,
p. 226 UNDERWOOD 52	1	Why? though I seeme of a prodigious wast,
p. 231 UNDERWOOD 57	10	Though now he refuses
p. 239 UNDERWOOD 67	4	And though the Parish-steeple
p. 239 UNDERWOOD 67	7	2. MEL. What, though the thriftie Tower
p. 242 UNDERWOOD 69	21	Though now of flattery, as of picture, are
p. 244 UNDERWOOD 70	51	As though his age imperfect might appeare,
p. 252 UNDERWOOD 75	1	Though thou hast past thy Summer standing, stay
p. 261 UNDERWOOD 77	25	Which, though I cannot as an Architect
p. 273 U'WOOD 84.1	17	For, though that Rattles, Timbrels, Toyes,
p. 279 U'WOOD 84.4	39	And, though the sound were parted thence,
p. 294 UNDERWOOD 87	21	LYD. Though he be fairer then a Starre;
p. 313 HORACE 2	322	Though sower, with safetie of his gravitie,
p. 321 HORACE 2	361	Will take offence, at this: Nor, though it strike
p. 325 HORACE 2	434	On steele, though 't selfe be dull, and cannot cut.
p. 331 HORACE 2	545	You Sir, the elder brother, though you are
p. 331 HORACE 2	577	And, to your Fathers, and to mine; though 't be
p. 351 HORACE 1	513	Though . . . .
p. 368 UNGATHERED 6	88	Though slower Spaine; and Italy mature.
p. 369 UNGATHERED 6	101	Though, now by Loue transform'd, & dayly dying:
p. 386 UNGATHERED 21	5	For, though but early in these pathes thou tread,
p. 389 UNGATHERED 24	5	As in this Spanish Proteus; who, though writ
p. 389 UNGATHERED 24	15	For though Spaine gaue him his first ayre and Vogue,
p. 391 UNGATHERED 26	31	And though thou hadst small Latine, and lesse Greeke,
p. 392 UNGATHERED 26	57	For though the Poets matter, Nature be,
p. 396 UNGATHERED 30	7	And, though I now begin, 'tis not to rub
p. 397 UNGATHERED 30	45	And caried, though with shoute, and noyse, confesse
p. 400 UNGATHERED 32	7	Though I confesse a Beaumonts Booke to bee
p. 403 UNGATHERED 34	28	Though gold or Iuory haftes would make it good.
p. 417 UNGATHERED 45	29	Though shee chainge as oft as shee,
p. 421 UNGATHERED 49	9	And though yor: virtue (as becomes it) still
p. 422 UNGATHERED 49	26	. . . . though . . . . hee . . . .

thought   frequency: 61   relative frequency: 0.00088

**p. 115 PANEGYRE	89	"She then remembred to his thought the place
p. 33 EPIGRAMS 21	6	The late tane bastinado. So I thought.
p. 35 EPIGRAMS 28	2	Of a great man, and to be thought the same,
p. 41 EPIGRAMS 43	7	Yet dare not, to my thought, lest hope allow
p. 44 EPIGRAMS 55	4	The least indulgent thought thy pen drops forth!
p. 44 EPIGRAMS 56	1	Poore POET-APE, that would be thought our chiefe,
p. 46 EPIGRAMS 62	8	To make amends, yo'are thought a wholesome creature.
p. 48 EPIGRAMS 64	15	These (noblest CECIL) labour'd in my thought,
p. 52 EPIGRAMS 76	2	I thought to forme vnto my zealous Muse,
p. 53 EPIGRAMS 77	4	I'am more asham'd to haue thee thought my foe.
p. 53 EPIGRAMS 79	8	Nature, they thought, in all, that he would faine.
p. 55 EPIGRAMS 86	1	When I would know thee GOODYERE, my thought lookes

thought (cont.)

p.	71 EPIGRAMS 110	7 And that so strong and deepe, as 't might be thought,
p.	77 EPIGRAMS 120	15 As, sooth, the Parcae thought him one,
p.	78 EPIGRAMS 121	7 Nor he, for friendship, to be thought vnfit,
p.	81 EPIGRAMS 129	3 That there 's no iourney set, or thought vpon,
p.	83 EPIGRAMS 132	8 Before my thought, and (in thy right) commands
p.	83 EPIGRAMS 132	12 As his will now be the translation thought,
p.	86 EPIGRAMS 133	83 The other thought it HYDRA, or the rock
p.	93 FOREST 1	2 I thought to binde him, in my verse:
p.	98 FOREST 3	54 (Their rudenesse then is thought no sinne)
p.	100 FOREST 4	3 Hence-forth I quit thee from my thought,
p.	101 FOREST 4	58 To harbour a diuided thought
p.	108 FOREST 10	29 My owne true fire. Now my thought takes wing,
p.	109 FOREST 11	24 Or some great thought doth keepe
p.	110 FOREST 11	31 Of which vsurping rancke, some haue thought loue
p.	111 FOREST 11	61 A fixed thought, an eye vn-taught to glance;
p.	113 FOREST 12	3 That which, to boote with hell, is thought worth heauen,
p.	114 FOREST 12	38 Riches thought most: But, Madame, thinke what store
p.	122 FOREST 15	24 With holy PAVL, lest it be thought the breath
p.	132 UNDERWOOD 2.2	22 And the Bow: with thought to hit
p.	147 UNDERWOOD 7	14 Unlesse my heart would as my thought be torne.
p.	148 UNDERWOOD 7	31 One un-becomming thought doth move
p.	156 UNDERWOOD 13	105 I thought that Fortitude had beene a meane
p.	158 UNDERWOOD 14	6 Was trusted, that you thought my judgement such
p.	162 UNDERWOOD 15	23 See him, that's call'd, and thought the happiest man,
p.	163 UNDERWOOD 15	42 Honour and honestie, as poore things thought
p.	165 UNDERWOOD 15	95 Lesse must not be thought on then Mistresse: or,
p.	165 UNDERWOOD 15	96 If it be thought, kild like her Embrions; for,
p.	168 UNDERWOOD 15	188 And from that thought strive to be understood.
p.	168 UNDERWOOD 15	192 Man thought the valianter, 'cause he durst sweare,
p.	172 UNDERWOOD 21	8 That thought can adde, unthankfull, the lay-stall
p.	174 UNDERWOOD 23	15 Let this thought quicken thee,
p.	185 UNDERWOOD 30	13 That still was good for goodnesse sake, nor thought
p.	193 UNDERWOOD 38	89 The contrite Soule, who hath no thought to win
p.	198 UNDERWOOD 40	43 Can lock the Sense up, or the heart a thought,
p.	209 UNDERWOOD 43	136 And raz'd, e're thought could urge, This might have bin!
p.	221 UNDERWOOD 48	20 From any thought like sadnesse.
p.	228 UNDERWOOD 53	4 Me thought I read the ancient Art of Thrace,
p.	236 UNDERWOOD 63	11 That thought shall make, he will this losse supply
p.	268 UNDERWOOD 82	13 Me thought, Great Britaine in her Sea, before,
p.	277 U'WOOD 84.4	2 Now I have better thought thereon,
p.	284 U'WOOD 84.9	67 All other gladnesse, with the thought is barr'd;
p.	293 UNDERWOOD 87	4 I thought me richer then the Persian King.
p.	335 HORACE 2	661 Hee, while he labour'd to be thought a God
p.	363 UNGATHERED 5	18 In thought to praise this Ladie,
p.	369 UNGATHERED 6	104 Or thought they, Leda's white Adult'rers place
p.	384 UNGATHERED 18	3 At these thy Nuptials; but, whose heart, and thought
p.	391 UNGATHERED 26	27 For, if I thought my iudgement were of yeeres,
p.	397 UNGATHERED 30	35 I thought thee then our Orpheus, that wouldst try
p.	404 UNGATHERED 34	54 Attyre ye Persons as noe thought can teach

though't   frequency: 1   relative frequency: 0.00001

    p. 352 HORACE 1   553 ... . though't ..

thoughtes   frequency: 1   relative frequency: 0.00001

    p. 108 FOREST 10 A   3 Thy thoughtes did neuer melt in amorous fire,

thoughts   frequency: 16   relative frequency: 0.00023

See also "after-thoughts," "thoughtes."

    p. 35 EPIGRAMS 26   2 He'adulters still: his thoughts lye with a whore.
    p. 81 EPIGRAMS 128   10 Thy selfe, with thy first thoughts, brought home by thee,
    p. 109 FOREST 11   8 Of thoughts to watch, and ward
    p. 111 FOREST 11   73 Though thy wild thoughts with sparrowes wings doe flye,
    p. 112 FOREST 11   114 From thoughts of such a straine.
    p. 128 UNDERWOOD 1.1   27 Pure thoughts in man: with fiery zeale them feeding
    p. 149 UNDERWOOD 9   12 That flie my thoughts betweene,
    p. 155 UNDERWOOD 13   66 Their thoughts and meanes to making loude the cry;

thoughts (cont.)
    p. 177 UNDERWOOD 25   13 That I may sing my thoughts, in some unvulgar
                                    straine.
    p. 181 UNDERWOOD 26   21 Such thoughts wil make you more in love with
                                    truth.
    p. 229 UNDERWOOD 55   2 Thoughts worthy of thy gift, this Inke,
    p. 262 UNDERWOOD 78   10 Where all heroique ample thoughts doe meet:
    p. 291 UNDERWOOD 85   67 These thoughts when Usurer Alphius, now about
    p. 361 UNGATHERED 1   22 of thy rich labors worlds of thoughts created,
    p. 361 UNGATHERED 1   23 which thoughts being circumvol<v>d in gyerlyk
                                      mocion
    p. 422 UNGATHERED 50   10 if it begyn religious thoughts to cherish;

thought'st   frequency: 1   relative frequency: 0.00001
    p. 188 UNDERWOOD 34   13 What was the cause then? Thought'st thou in
                                      disgrace

thou'hast   frequency: 1   relative frequency: 0.00001

thou'lust   frequency: 1   relative frequency: 0.00001

thou'lt   frequency: 3   relative frequency: 0.00004

thou'rt   frequency: 2   relative frequency: 0.00002

thousand   frequency: 6   relative frequency: 0.00008
  **p. 113 PANEGYRE   5 (To day) a thousand radiant lights, that stream
    p. 103 FOREST 6   9 Then a thousand, then another
    p. 103 FOREST 6   11 Adde a thousand, and so more:
    p. 141 UNDERWOOD 2.9   11 Cast in thousand snares, and rings
    p. 183 UNDERWOOD 29   16 For a thousand yeares together,
    p. 269 UNDERWOOD 83   23 Had I a thousand Mouthes, as many Tongues,

thousands   frequency: 2   relative frequency: 0.00002
    p. 99 FOREST 3   85 Let thousands more goe flatter vice, and winne,
    p. 165 UNDERWOOD 15   104 Those thousands on his back, shall after blow

tho'wert   frequency: 1   relative frequency: 0.00001

th'oyle   frequency: 1   relative frequency: 0.00001
    p. 105 FOREST 8   33 That for th'oyle of Talke, dare spend

thrace   frequency: 1   relative frequency: 0.00001
    p. 228 UNDERWOOD 53   4 Me thought I read the ancient Art of Thrace,

thracian   frequency: 1   relative frequency: 0.00001
    p. 293 UNDERWOOD 87   9 HOR. 'Tis true, I'am Thracian Chloes, I,

thrall   frequency: 1   relative frequency: 0.00001
    p. 179 UNDERWOOD 25   35 Nothing, but practise upon honours thrall.

thread   frequency: 1   relative frequency: 0.00001
  See also "thred."
    p. 415 UNGATHERED 42   14 And weigh'd your Play: untwisted ev'ry thread,

threads. See "threds."

threat   frequency: 1   relative frequency: 0.00001
    p. 132 UNDERWOOD 2.2   18 Nor for any threat, or call,

threat'   frequency: 1   relative frequency: 0.00001
    p. 238 UNDERWOOD 65   11 And threat' the great Eclipse. Two houres but
                                      runne,

threaten   frequency: 3   relative frequency: 0.00004
  See also "threat'."
    p. 101 FOREST 4   37 Yes, threaten, doe. Alas I feare
    p. 169 UNDERWOOD 18   2 Now threaten, with those meanes she did invite?
    p. 329 HORACE 2   525 Which it doth threaten. Therefore, where I see

threatening. See "threatning."

threatens   frequency: 2   relative frequency: 0.00002
    p. 44 EPIGRAMS 54   2 And threatens the starre-chamber, and the barre:
    p. 166 UNDERWOOD 15   131 Or side, but threatens Ruine. The whole Day

threatning   frequency: 2   relative frequency: 0.00002
    p. 193 UNDERWOOD 38   97 Produce; though threatning with a coale, or
                                    chalke
    p. 209 UNDERWOOD 43   146 And cry'd, it was a threatning to the beares;

threats   frequency: 1   relative frequency: 0.00001
    p. 144 UNDERWOOD 4   6 For then their threats will kill me;

thred   frequency: 3   relative frequency: 0.00004
    p. 61 EPIGRAMS 95   15 To haue her storie wouen in thy thred;
    p. 225 UNDERWOOD 51   15 Whose even Thred the Fates spinne round, and
                              full,
    p. 293 UNDERWOOD 87   16 So Fates would let the Boy a long thred run.

threds   frequency: 1   relative frequency: 0.00001
    p. 216 UNDERWOOD 45   21 Turne him, and see his Threds: looke, if he be

three   frequency: 19   relative frequency: 0.00027
    p. 29 EPIGRAMS 8   1 RIDWAY rob'd DVNCOTE of three hundred
                              pound,
    p. 77 EPIGRAMS 120   11 Yet three till'd Zodiackes had he beene
    p. 84 EPIGRAMS 133   28 His three for one. Now, lordings, listen well.
    p. 89 EPIGRAMS 133   177 Of Hol'borne (<the> three sergeants heads)
                              lookes ore,
    p. 122 FOREST 15   10 First, midst, and last, conuerted one, and three;
    p. 128 UNDERWOOD 1.1   33 9. Beholding one in three, and three in one,
    p. 128 UNDERWOOD 1.1   37 10. Father, and Sonne, and Holy Ghost, you three
    p. 137 UNDERWOOD 2.5   47 For the Apple, and those three
    p. 192 UNDERWOOD 38   42 Or two, or three, a Sonne will dis-inherit,
    p. 207 UNDERWOOD 43   95 With all th'adventures; Three bookes not afraid
    p. 243 UNDERWOOD 70   32 For three of his foure-score, he did no good.
    p. 245 UNDERWOOD 70   67 Or standing long an Oake, three hundred yeare,
    p. 249 UNDERWOOD 72   11 Three Kingdomes Mirth, in light, and aerie man,
    p. 284 U'WOOD 84.9   51 For, as there are three Natures, Schoolemen
                              call
    p. 325 HORACE 2   428 Their heads, which three Anticyra's cannot
                              heale.
    p. 397 UNGATHERED 30   25 There read I, streight, thy learned Legends
                              three,
    p. 413 UNGATHERED 41   29 These Mysteries do point to three more great,
    p. 657 L. CONVIVALES   18 And at once, three Senses pleases.

threw   frequency: 3   relative frequency: 0.00004
 **p. 114 PANEGYRE   34 Vpon his face all threw their couetous eyes,
    p. 42 EPIGRAMS 48   2 Of bearing them in field, he threw 'hem away:
    p. 132 UNDERWOOD 2.2   23 This my object. But she threw

thrice   frequency: 6   relative frequency: 0.00008
See also "thrise."
    p. 165 UNDERWOOD 15   107 Coach'd, or on foot-cloth, thrice chang'd every
                              day,
    p. 280 U'WOOD 84.4   53 Thrice happy house, that hast receipt
    p. 292 UNDERWOOD 86   28 Thrice 'bout thy Altar with their Ivory feet.
    p. 329 HORACE 2   535 Twice, or thrice good, I wonder: but am more
    p. 333 HORACE 2   626 And twice, or thrice had 'ssayd it, still in
                              vaine:
    p. 405 UNGATHERED 34   90 Thy twice conceyud, thrice payd for Imagery?

thrift   frequency: 1   relative frequency: 0.00001
    p. 205 UNDERWOOD 43   50 With some more thrift, and more varietie:

thriftie   frequency: 2   relative frequency: 0.00002
    p. 239 UNDERWOOD 67   7 2. MEL. What, though the thriftie Tower
    p. 319 HORACE 2   294 Chaste, thriftie, modest folke, that came to
                              view.

thrifty. See "thriftie."

thrise   frequency: 2   relative frequency: 0.00002
    p. 88 EPIGRAMS 133   162 Thrise did it spit: thrise diu'd. At last, it
                              view'd

thriue   frequency: 2   relative frequency: 0.00002
    p. 77 EPIGRAMS 120   5 'Twas a child, that so did thriue
    p. 362 UNGATHERED 2   12 So with this Authors Readers will it thriue:

thriues   frequency: 1   relative frequency: 0.00001
    p. 361 UNGATHERED 1   7 not one but thriues; in spite of stormes &
                              thunder,

thriuing   frequency: 1   relative frequency: 0.00001
 **p. 115 PANEGYRE   97 "And thriuing statutes she could promptly note;

thriv'd   frequency: 1   relative frequency: 0.00001
    p. 244 UNDERWOOD 70   34 Got up and thriv'd with honest arts:

thrive   frequency: 5   relative frequency: 0.00007
    See also "thriue."
    p. 197 UNDERWOOD 40   15 For though Love thrive, and may grow up with
                             cheare,
    p. 213 UNDERWOOD 44   23 Well, I say, thrive, thrive brave Artillerie
                             yard,
    p. 234 UNDERWOOD 61   6 But whisper'd Counsells, and those only thrive:
    p. 273 U'WOOD 84.1   7 By THEE, and CONSCIENCE, both who
                             thrive

thrives. See "thriues."

thriving   frequency: 1   relative frequency: 0.00001
    See also "thriuing."
    p. 350 HORACE 1   464 ... . more thriving .....

throat   frequency: 1   relative frequency: 0.00001
    See also "throate."
    p. 311 HORACE 2   134 With swelling throat: and, oft, the tragick wight

throate   frequency: 1   relative frequency: 0.00001
    p. 100 FOREST 4   7 Vpon thy throate, and liue exempt

throats. See "throtes."

throe. See "throw."

throne   frequency: 4   relative frequency: 0.00005
 **p. 113 PANEGYRE   26 On earth, till now, they came to grace his
                             throne.
 **p. 115 PANEGYRE   79 "That they, by Heauen, are plac'd vpon his
                             throne,
    p. 116 FOREST 13   10 With sinne and vice, though with a throne
                             endew'd;
    p. 414 UNGATHERED 41 49 Thou Throne of glory, beauteous as the Moone,

thrones   frequency: 1   relative frequency: 0.00001
    p. 285 U'WOOD 84.9   88 The Thrones, the Cherube, and Seraphick
                             bowers,

throng   frequency: 2   relative frequency: 0.00002
    See also "thronge."
    p. 182 UNDERWOOD 27 34 Come short of all this learned throng,
    p. 245 UNDERWOOD 70 57 Repeat of things a throng,

throng'd   frequency: 1   relative frequency: 0.00001
    p. 331 HORACE 2   569 Lest the throng'd heapes should on a laughter
                             take:

thronge   frequency: 1   relative frequency: 0.00001
    p. 419 UNGATHERED 48 7 Lowd to the wondringe thronge

thronging   frequency: 2   relative frequency: 0.00002
    p. 98 FOREST 3   53 The rout of rurall folke come thronging in,
    p. 115 FOREST 12   80 Shall thronging come, and boast the happy place

throng'st   frequency: 1   relative frequency: 0.00001
    p. 96 FOREST 3   9 Nor throng'st (when masquing is) to haue a sight

throtes   frequency: 1   relative frequency: 0.00001
    p. 114 FOREST 12   23 When gold was made no weapon to cut throtes,

through   frequency: 27   relative frequency: 0.00039
    See also "th<o>rough," "thorough," "thorow."
 **p. 114 PANEGYRE   49 And as of late, when he through London went,
 **p. 117 PANEGYRE   152 Their bursting ioyes: but through the ayre was
                             rol'd
    p. 48 EPIGRAMS 65   4 To a great image through thy luxurie.
    p. 53 EPIGRAMS 80   2 Through which, our merit leads vs to our meeds.
    p. 62 EPIGRAMS 97   4 His cloke with orient veluet quite lin'd through,
    p. 81 EPIGRAMS 128 12 This is that good AENEAS, past through
                             fire,
    p. 81 EPIGRAMS 128 13 Through seas, stormes, tempests: and imbarqu'd
                             for hell,
    p. 87 EPIGRAMS 133 131 Airising in that place, through which, who goes,
    p. 97 FOREST 3   18 Through which a serpent riuer leades
    p. 134 UNDERWOOD 2.4 18 Sheds it selfe through the face,

through (cont.)
```
     p. 141 UNDERWOOD 2.9   29 Rising through it e're it came;
     p. 150 UNDERWOOD 9     18 And all these through her eyes, have stopt her
                               eares.
     p. 152 UNDERWOOD 12    39 Nor wants it here through penurie, or sloth,
     p. 159 UNDERWOOD 14    16 Themselves through favouring what is there not
                               found:
     p. 167 UNDERWOOD 15   172 Spread through the World) is easier farre to
                               find,
     p. 177 UNDERWOOD 25    16 May shine (through every chincke) to every sight
     p. 179 UNDERWOOD 25    52 Oft scape an Imputation, more through luck, then
                               wit.
     p. 201 UNDERWOOD 42    70 The Lady Mayresse pass'd in through the Towne,
     p. 234 UNDERWOOD 60     8 But crept like darknesse through his blood?
     p. 253 UNDERWOOD 75    32 Through which not only we, but all our Species
                               are.
     p. 271 UNDERWOOD 83    69 And now, through circumfused light, she lookes
     p. 286 U'WOOD 84.9    135 Through his inherent righteousnesse, in death,
     p. 290 UNDERWOOD 85    17 Or when that Autumne, through the fields, lifts
                               round
     p. 321 HORACE 2       334 With poore base termes, through every baser shop:
     p. 333 HORACE 2       621 Looke through him, and be sure, you take not
                               mocks
     p. 383 UNGATHERED 16   11 Except your Gratious Eye as through a Glass
     p. 414 UNGATHERED 41   54 Through all the lines of this circumference,
```

throughly   frequency: 1   relative frequency: 0.00001
```
     p. 370 UNGATHERED 7     5 And all your Booke (when it is throughly scan'd)
```

throughout   frequency: 8   relative frequency: 0.00011
```
    *p. 493 TO HIMSELF     48 Throughout, to their defeate:
     p.  54 EPIGRAMS 83     2 Throughout my booke. 'Troth put out woman too.
     p.  58 EPIGRAMS 91    10 Throughout, might flatt'rie seeme; and to be mute
     p. 173 UNDERWOOD 22    6 Throughout your forme; as though that move,
     p. 307 HORACE 2       32 Be simple quite throughout, and wholly one.
     p. 309 HORACE 2       86 Still in their leaves, throughout the sliding
                               yeares,
     p. 321 HORACE 2      363 The nut-crackers throughout, will they therefore
     p. 421 UNGATHERED 48  43 Throughout their generall breastes,
```

throw   frequency: 4   relative frequency: 0.00005
     See also "throwe."
```
     p. 154 UNDERWOOD 13   42 A Benefit; or that doth throw 't away:
     p. 165 UNDERWOOD 15  103 His time? health? soule? will he for these goe
                               throw
     p. 311 HORACE 2      138 When they are poore, and banish'd, must throw by
     p. 313 HORACE 2      157 Her truch-man, she reports the minds each throw.
```

throwe   frequency: 1   relative frequency: 0.00001
```
     p. 421 UNGATHERED 48  37 Throwe, Holye Virgin, then
```

throwes   frequency: 1   relative frequency: 0.00001
```
     p. 166 UNDERWOOD 15  139 Of what he throwes: Like letchers growne content
```

thrown.   See "throwne."

throwne   frequency: 3   relative frequency: 0.00004
```
    *p. 493 TO HIMSELF     25 Throwne forth, and rak't into the common tub,
     p.  45 EPIGRAMS 59     3 Stinke, and are throwne away. End faire enough.
     p.  88 EPIGRAMS 133  153 For, here they were throwne in wi'the melted
                               pewter,
```

throws.   See "throwes."

thrush   frequency: 2   relative frequency: 0.00002
```
     p.  97 FOREST 3       34 Or shooting at the greedie thrush,
     p. 290 UNDERWOOD 85   34 For th'eating Thrush, or Pit-falls sets:
```

thrust   frequency: 1   relative frequency: 0.00001
```
     p. 101 FOREST 4       26 And thrust my necke into the noose,
```

thrusts   frequency: 1   relative frequency: 0.00001
```
     p.  61 EPIGRAMS 95    22 But, wisely, thrusts not forth a forward hand,
```

thule   frequency: 1   relative frequency: 0.00001
```
     p. 368 UNGATHERED 6   69 To vtmost Thule: whence, he backes the Seas
```

thumb   frequency: 1   relative frequency: 0.00001
     See also "thumbe."
```
     p. 407 UNGATHERED 35  12 Thou paint a Lane, where Thumb ye Pygmy meets!
```

thumbe   frequency: 1   relative frequency: 0.00001
    p. 87 EPIGRAMS 133   134 Nor thumbe, nor finger to the stop acquainted,

thumbs. See "thum's."

thum's   frequency: 1   relative frequency: 0.00001
    p. 239 UNDERWOOD 67   18 With touch of daintie thum's!

th'unbearded   frequency: 1   relative frequency: 0.00001
    p. 315 HORACE 2   229 Th'unbearded Youth, his Guardian once being
                              gone,

th'uncertainty   frequency: 1   relative frequency: 0.00001
    p. 411 UNGATHERED 40   4 th'uncertainty of Life,

thunder   frequency: 4   relative frequency: 0.00005
    p. 193 UNDERWOOD 38   70 And then his thunder frights more, then it kills.
    p. 239 UNDERWOOD 67   9 Their noises forth in Thunder:
         UNDERWOOD 72   4 As lowd as Thunder, and as swift as fire.
         UNGATHERED 1   7 not one but thriues; in spite of stormes &
                              thunder,

   thunder-stroken   frequency: 1   relative frequency: 0.00001
         HORACE 2   672 Or the sad thunder-stroken thing he have

     See "thundring," "thund'ring."

thundring   frequency: 1   relative frequency: 0.00001
         UNDERWOOD 85   29 Then when the thundring Jove his Snow and
                              showres

thund'ring   frequency: 1   relative frequency: 0.00001
    p. 391 UNGATHERED 26   33 For names; but call forth thund'ring Aeschilus,

Thurine   frequency: 1   relative frequency: 0.00001
    p. 293 UNDERWOOD 87   14 With gentle Calais, Thurine Orniths Sonne;

thus   frequency: 38   relative frequency: 0.00055
    p. 27 EPIGRAMS 3   4 For the lucks sake, it thus much fauour haue,
    p. 31 EPIGRAMS 12   22 Thus: and for his letcherie, scores, god payes.
    p. 55 EPIGRAMS 84   9 O Madame, if your grant did thus transferre mee,
    p. 70 EPIGRAMS 108   9 He that not trusts me, hauing vow'd thus much,
    p. 70 EPIGRAMS 109   16 Now I haue sung thee thus, shall iudge of thee.
    p. 75 EPIGRAMS 115   33 Describ'd, it 's thus: Defin'd would you it
                              haue?
    p. 76 EPIGRAMS 118   5 Thus, in his belly, can he change a sin,
    p. 98 FOREST 3   47 Thus PAN, and SYLVANE, hauing had their
                              rites,
    p. 103 FOREST 6   7 On my lips, thus hardly sundred,
    p. 110 FOREST 11   28 Thus, by these subtle traines,
    p. 110 FOREST 11   36 Which thus we ouer-blow.
    p. 113 FOREST 12   15 While thus it buyes great grace, and hunts poore
                              fame;
    p. 119 FOREST 13   108 Onely, thus much, out of a rauish'd zeale,
    p. 150 UNDERWOOD 10   2 How cam'st thou thus to enter me?
    p. 158 UNDERWOOD 13   159 By thanking thus the curtesie to life,
    p. 160 UNDERWOOD 14   66 Of others honours, thus, enjoy thine owne.
    p. 165 UNDERWOOD 15   101 Thus they doe talke. And are these objects fit
    p. 170 UNDERWOOD 18   21 If it be thus; Come Love, and Fortune goe,
    p. 186 UNDERWOOD 32   9 Who thus long safe, would gaine upon the times
    p. 190 UNDERWOOD 37   12 In letters, that mixe spirits, thus to weave.
    p. 202 UNDERWOOD 43   3 Or urge thy Greedie flame, thus to devoure
    p. 215 UNDERWOOD 44   65 Us, in our bearing, that are thus, and thus,
    p. 234 UNDERWOOD 61   10 To see you set apart, thus, from the rest,
    p. 284 U'WOOD 84.9   69 This being thus: why should my tongue, or pen
    p. 289 U'WOOD 84.9   227 That thus have ventur'd these true straines upon;
    p. 294 UNDERWOOD 88   6 But thus, keeping endlesse Holy-day,
    p. 319 HORACE 2   303 Thus, to his antient Art the Piper lent
    p. 327 HORACE 2   473 And care of getting, thus, our minds hath
                              stain'd,
    p. 327 HORACE 2   491 And thus, at first, an honour, and a name
    p. 346 HORACE 1   305 .. .. thus ....
    p. 361 UNGATHERED 1   17 thus, as a ponderous thinge in water cast
    p. 362 UNGATHERED 1   29 my abler faculties; and thus brake foorth
    p. 382 UNGATHERED 16   4 to tender thus, their liues, their loues, their
                              hartes!
    p. 390 UNGATHERED 26   2 Am I thus ample to thy Booke, and Fame:
    p. 407 UNGATHERED 35   19 your workes thus differing, troth let see yor
                              style:
    p. 413 UNGATHERED 41   25 Thus, Love, and Hope, and burning Charitie,

th'vsurped   frequency: 1   relative frequency: 0.00001
    p. 80 EPIGRAMS 126   4 And bad me lay th'vsurped laurell downe:

th'were   frequency: 1   relative frequency: 0.00001

thy   frequency: 523   relative frequency: 0.00757
    See also "thie," "thy'epistolar."

thy'epistolar   frequency: 1   relative frequency: 0.00001
    p. 397 UNGATHERED 30   29 But then, thy'epistolar Heroick Songs,

thyestes   frequency: 1   relative frequency: 0.00001
    p. 311 HORACE 2   122 In tragick Verse; no lesse Thyestes feast

thyne   frequency: 1   relative frequency: 0.00001

tiber's. See "tybers."

tiberts   frequency: 1   relative frequency: 0.00001
    p. 88 EPIGRAMS 133   155 But 'mong'st these Tiberts, who do'you thinke
                             there was?

tibullus   frequency: 1   relative frequency: 0.00001
    p. 181 UNDERWOOD 27   10 Or Delia's Graces, by Tibullus?

tickled   frequency: 1   relative frequency: 0.00001
    p. 205 UNDERWOOD 43   62 Had tickled your large Nosthrill: many a Reame

tickling   frequency: 1   relative frequency: 0.00001
    See also "ticklinge."
    p. 116 FOREST 12   87 Your forme imprest there: not with tickling
                             rimes,

ticklinge   frequency: 1   relative frequency: 0.00001
    p. 420 UNGATHERED 48   18 howe soone wth a selfe ticklinge hee was spent.

tie   frequency: 1   relative frequency: 0.00001
    See also "tye."
    p. 142 UNDERWOOD 2.9   50 Nor tie knots, nor knots unweave;

tied   frequency: 1   relative frequency: 0.00001
    p. 227 UNDERWOOD 52   7 You were not tied, by any Painters Law,

tier   frequency: 2   relative frequency: 0.00002
    p. 249 UNDERWOOD 72   2 Unto the Ships, and they from tier, to tier,

tierce. See "teirce."

ties   frequency: 1   relative frequency: 0.00001
    See also "tyes."
    p. 216 UNDERWOOD 45   11 Those are poore Ties, depend on those false
                             ends,

tigers   frequency: 1   relative frequency: 0.00001
    See also "tygres."
    p. 327 HORACE 2   482 Was Tigers, said, and Lyons fierce, to tame.

tike   frequency: 1   relative frequency: 0.00001
    p. 410 UNGATHERED 39   10 I'll laugh at thee poor wretched Tike, go send

tiles   frequency: 1   relative frequency: 0.00001
    p. 209 UNDERWOOD 43   138 Left! and wit since to cover it with Tiles.

till   frequency: 57   relative frequency: 0.00082
   **p. 113 PANEGYRE   26 On earth, till now, they came to grace his
                             throne.
   **p. 113 PANEGYRE   29 Till forraine malice, or vnnaturall spight
   **p. 114 PANEGYRE   65 Old men were glad, their fates till now did last;
     p. 28 EPIGRAMS 3   5 To lye vpon thy stall, till it be sought;
     p. 39 EPIGRAMS 40   11 Till time, strong by her bestowing,
     p. 54 EPIGRAMS 81   2 A line vnto thee, till the world it know;
     p. 55 EPIGRAMS 85   10 Till they be sure to make the foole their
                             quarrie.
     p. 62 EPIGRAMS 96   11 And, till they burst, their backs, like asses
                             load:
     p. 65 EPIGRAMS 101   32 Their liues, as doe their lines, till now had
                             lasted.
     p. 76 EPIGRAMS 119   10 Till thou canst finde the best, choose the least
                             ill.
     p. 89 EPIGRAMS 133 178 And stayes but till you come vnto the dore!

till (cont.)
p. 103 FOREST 6	12	Till you equall with the store,
p. 118 FOREST 13	78	Till that no vsurer, nor his bawds dare lend
p. 128 UNDERWOOD 1.1	31	Till I attaine the long'd-for mysterie
p. 131 UNDERWOOD 2.1	15	That you never knew till now,
p. 131 UNDERWOOD 2.1	23	Till she be the reason why,
p. 141 UNDERWOOD 2.9	23	Till he cherish'd too much beard,
p. 143 UNDERWOOD 3	3	Till each of us be made a Starre,
p. 157 UNDERWOOD 13	138	Are nothing till that comes to bind and shut.
p. 162 UNDERWOOD 15	14	Till he become both their, and his owne curse!
p. 162 UNDERWOOD 15	22	Till envie wound, or maime it at a blow!
p. 168 UNDERWOOD 16	3	But here doth lie, till the last Day,
p. 185 UNDERWOOD 30	14	Upon reward, till the reward him sought.
p. 188 UNDERWOOD 35	5	And, till the comming of the Soule
p. 192 UNDERWOOD 38	44	No man inflicts that paine, till hope be spent:
p. 192 UNDERWOOD 38	46	We cut not off, till all Cures else doe faile:
p. 194 UNDERWOOD 38	121	Till then 'tis all but darknesse, that I have;
p. 197 UNDERWOOD 40	2	Till the sower Minute comes of taking leave,
p. 199 UNDERWOOD 41	22	Till I may see both it and you agen.
p. 204 UNDERWOOD 43	46	Thou should'st have stay'd, till publike fame said so.
p. 213 UNDERWOOD 44	10	If they stay here, but till Saint Georges Day.
p. 229 UNDERWOOD 54	19	To goe out after ----- till when take this letter
p. 234 UNDERWOOD 61	14	My Lord, till felt griefe make our stone hearts soft,
p. 242 UNDERWOOD 69	13	Till he had sold his Piece, drawne so unlike:
p. 247 UNDERWOOD 70	110	Till either grew a portion of the other:
p. 258 UNDERWOOD 75	169	Till you behold a race to fill your Hall,
p. 258 UNDERWOOD 75	190	Will last till day;
p. 276 U'WOOD 84.3	15	Till, like her face, it doe appeare,
p. 281 U'WOOD 84.8	14	For they are strong Supporters: But, till then,
p. 282 U'WOOD 84.9	8	Till swept away, th\<ey>'were cancell'd with a broome!
p. 283 U'WOOD 84.9	46	In earth, till the last Trumpe awake the Sheepe
p. 307 HORACE 2	63	Till fitter season. Now, to like of this,
p. 315 HORACE 2	221	That tarries till the hangings be ta'en downe,
p. 315 HORACE 2	222	And sits, till th'Epilogue saies Clap, or Crowne:
p. 319 HORACE 2	313	Till then unknowne, in Carts, wherein did ride
p. 321 HORACE 2	366	And not without much praise; till libertie
p. 337 HORACE 2	680	Till he drop off, a Horse-leech, full of blood.
p. 361 UNGATHERED 1	20	till th'one hath drownd the other in our sightes,
p. 361 UNGATHERED 1	25	till giddie with amazement I fell downe
p. 366 UNGATHERED 6	25	This change'd his Downe; till this, as white
p. 368 UNGATHERED 6	79	Till thou at Tames alight,
p. 384 UNGATHERED 18	22	Mortality, till you \<im>mortall bee.
p. 398 UNGATHERED 30	92	And, till I worthy am to wish I were,
p. 401 UNGATHERED 32	15	Stay, till she make her vaine Approches. Then
p. 414 UNGATHERED 41	52	Till he hath reach'd his two-fold point of Noone.
p. 416 UNGATHERED 43	10	Of Subiects; Let such envie, till they burst.
p. 666 INSCRIPTS. 11	7	Till I, at much expense of Time, and Taper

tills   frequency: 1   relative frequency: 0.00001
        p. 289 UNDERWOOD 85   3 With his owne Oxen tills his Sires left lands,

tilly   frequency: 1   relative frequency: 0.00001
        p. 214 UNDERWOOD 44   38 The Cittie-Question, whether Tilly, or he,

tilt   frequency: 2   relative frequency: 0.00002
        p. 51 EPIGRAMS 73   15 Item, a gulling imprese for you, at tilt.
        p. 166 UNDERWOOD 15   125 Tilt one upon another, and now beare   ◆

tilter   frequency: 2   relative frequency: 0.00002
        p. 36 EPIGRAMS 29   1 TILTER, the most may'admire thee, though not I:
        p. 36 EPIGRAMS 29   t1 TO SIR ANNVAL TILTER.

tilting   frequency: 1   relative frequency: 0.00001
        See also "tylting."
        p. 213 UNDERWOOD 44   6 For they did see it the last tilting well,

timbered. See "small-timbred."

timbrels   frequency: 1   relative frequency: 0.00001
        p. 273 U'WOOD 84.1   17 For, though that Rattles, Timbrels, Toyes,

time   frequency: 61   relative frequency: 0.00088
        See also "tyme."
      **p. 117 PANEGYRE   159 Which when time, nature, and the fates deny'd,

time (cont.)

p.	32 EPIGRAMS 16	5	So, in short time, th'art in arrerage growne
p.	37 EPIGRAMS 35	4	And in this short time of thy happiest raigne,
p.	39 EPIGRAMS 40	11	Till time, strong by her bestowing,
p.	46 EPIGRAMS 62	10	And there's both losse of time, and losse of sport
p.	47 EPIGRAMS 64	9	But I am glad to see that time suruiue,
p.	48 EPIGRAMS 66	5	Who, to vpbraid the sloth of this our time,
p.	58 EPIGRAMS 91	12	Against my graue, and time could not forgiue.
p.	64 EPIGRAMS 99	6	If time to facts, as vnto men would owe?
p.	67 EPIGRAMS 105	3	That we had left vs, nor by time, nor place,
p.	71 EPIGRAMS 110	21	T<o>'all future time, not onely doth restore
p.	73 EPIGRAMS 112	21	Pr'y thee, yet saue thy rest; giue ore in time:
p.	84 EPIGRAMS 133	29	It was the day, what time the powerfull Moone
p.	85 EPIGRAMS 133	42	Of some Bride-well, and may, in time, concerne vs
p.	87 EPIGRAMS 133	104	(In the meane time, let 'hem imprison mee)
p.	87 EPIGRAMS 133	121	By this time had they reach'd the Stygian poole,
p.	94 FOREST 2	42	Fig, grape, and quince, each in his time doth come:
p.	102 FOREST 5	3	Time will not be ours, for euer:
p.	111 FOREST 11	59	Richer then Time, and as Time's vertue, rare.
p.	115 FOREST 12	75	To her remembrance; which when time shall bring
p.	117 FOREST 13	26	No lady, but, at some time, loues her glasse.
p.	118 FOREST 13	51	'Tis onely that can time, and chance defeat:
p.	138 UNDERWOOD 2.6	31	To himselfe his losse of Time;
p.	153 UNDERWOOD 13	2	Great and good turns, as wel could time them too,
p.	157 UNDERWOOD 13	133	In time 'twill be a heape; This is not true
p.	161 UNDERWOOD 14	85	But here's no time, nor place, my wealth to tell,
p.	165 UNDERWOOD 15	103	His time? health? soule? will he for these goe throw
p.	169 UNDERWOOD 17	7	Nor should I at this time protested be,
p.	169 UNDERWOOD 17	15	Venter a longer time, and willingly:
p.	171 UNDERWOOD 19	18	Others, in time may love, as we doe now.
p.	171 UNDERWOOD 19	19	Slip no occasion; As time stands not still,
p.	176 UNDERWOOD 24	8	When Vice alike in time with vertue dur'd.
p.	176 UNDERWOOD 25	t2	writ in Queene ELIZABETHS time,
p.	184 UNDERWOOD 29	52	Still may Syllabes jarre with time,
p.	189 UNDERWOOD 36	13	Such are his powers, whom time hath stil'd,
p.	198 UNDERWOOD 40	44	And never be by time, or folly brought,
p.	199 UNDERWOOD 41	12	Winter is come a Quarter e're his Time,
p.	206 UNDERWOOD 43	78	And the strong lines, that so the time doe catch:
p.	209 UNDERWOOD 43	143	Bred on the Banck, in time of Poperie,
p.	219 UNDERWOOD 47	51	But that's a blow, by which in time I may
p.	224 UNDERWOOD 50	9	The rather when the vices of the Time
p.	224 UNDERWOOD 50	23	Only your time you better entertaine,
p.	231 UNDERWOOD 56	24	Your Joane to passe her melancholie time.
p.	231 UNDERWOOD 57	8	Knew the time, when
p.	232 UNDERWOOD 59	5	To hit in angles, and to clash with time:
p.	243 UNDERWOOD 70	27	He vexed time, and busied the whole State;
p.	246 UNDERWOOD 70	101	The profits for a time.
p.	253 UNDERWOOD 75	25	It is the kindly Season of the time,
p.	257 UNDERWOOD 75	134	Which Time shall not,
p.	273 U'WOOD 84.1	12	Thereof, to TIME.
p.	282 U'WOOD 84.9	1	'Twere time that I dy'd too, now shee is dead,
p.	287 U'WOOD 84.9	180	She spent more time in teares her selfe to dresse
p.	309 HORACE 2	85	Stamp'd to the time. As woods whose change appeares
p.	319 HORACE 2	289	But soft, and simple, at few holes breath'd time
p.	319 HORACE 2	306	In time to Tragedie, a Musicke new.
p.	321 HORACE 2	356	Be I their Judge, they doe at no time dare
p.	367 UNGATHERED 6	54	Then Time hath donne,
p.	371 UNGATHERED 8	15	A glorified worke to Time, when Fire,
p.	391 UNGATHERED 26	43	He was not of an age, but for all time!
p.	410 UNGATHERED 38	9	You learn'd it well; and for it, seru'd your time
p.	666 INSCRIPTS. 11	7	Till I, at much expense of Time, and Taper

timely   frequency: 6   relative frequency: 0.00008

p.	52 EPIGRAMS 76	1	This morning, timely rapt with holy fire,
p.	80 EPIGRAMS 127	8	Lent timely succours, and new life begot:
p.	115 FOREST 12	71	Yet, for the timely fauours shee hath done,
p.	119 FOREST 13	104	It shall a ripe and timely issue fall,
p.	186 UNDERWOOD 32	1	The Judge his favour timely then extends,
p.	292 UNDERWOOD 86	9	More timely hie thee to the house,

times   frequency: 40   relative frequency: 0.00057

See also "after-times," "oft-times," "tymes."

**p.	116 PANEGYRE	111	For though by right, and benefite of Times,
p.	36 EPIGRAMS 29	4	All braines, at times of triumph, should runne wit.

times (cont.)
```
       p.  39 EPIGRAMS 40     14 In these times. Few so haue ru'de
       p.  47 EPIGRAMS 63      2 With what thy vertue on the times hath won,
       p.  47 EPIGRAMS 63     10 Without his, thine, and all times iniurie?
       p.  48 EPIGRAMS 65      7 Get him the times long grudge, the courts ill
                                 will;
       p.  52 EPIGRAMS 74     10 T<o>'our times return'd, hath made her heauen in
                                 thee.
       p.  60 EPIGRAMS 93      4 Stand'st thou, to shew the times what you all
                                 were?
       p.  67 EPIGRAMS 104     3 Or did our times require it, to behold
       p.  67 EPIGRAMS 104    11 Were you aduanced, past those times, to be
       p.  78 EPIGRAMS 122     3 If I would striue to bring backe times, and trie
       p.  79 EPIGRAMS 125     1 VV'DALE, thou piece of the first times, a
                                 man
       p.  85 EPIGRAMS 133    34 Of sixe times to, and fro, without embassage,
       p.  96 FOREST 3         5 That at great times, art no ambitious guest
       p. 114 FOREST 12       21 The truth of times) was once of more esteeme,
       p. 116 FOREST 12       88 Or common places, filch'd, that take these times,
       p. 118 FOREST 13       63 Times, and occasions, to start forth, and seeme)
       p. 159 UNDERWOOD 14    34 Heard what times past have said, seene what ours
                                 doe:
       p. 160 UNDERWOOD 14    44 Times, manners, customes! Innovations spide!
       p. 160 UNDERWOOD 14    51 And then of times (besides the bare Conduct
       p. 167 UNDERWOOD 15   161 And be belov'd, while the Whores last. O times,
       p. 176 UNDERWOOD 24    17 Times witnesse, herald of Antiquitie,
       p. 176 UNDERWOOD 25     7 Or the times envie:
       p. 186 UNDERWOOD 32     9 Who thus long safe, would gaine upon the times
       p. 187 UNDERWOOD 33    15 So dost thou studie matter, men, and times,
       p. 203 UNDERWOOD 43    25 Itch to defame the State? or brand the Times?
       p. 218 UNDERWOOD 47    25 Let these men have their wayes, and take their
                                 times
       p. 236 UNDERWOOD 64     3 How many times, Live long, CHARLES, would
                                 he say,
       p. 237 UNDERWOOD 64    17 O Times! O Manners! Surfet bred of ease,
       p. 256 UNDERWOOD 75   115 In him the times, no lesse then Prince, are
                                 prais'd,
       p. 259 UNDERWOOD 76    17 Hath drawne on me, from the times,
       p. 263 UNDERWOOD 79    11 That know the times, and seasons when
                                 t<o>'appeare,
       p. 317 HORACE 2       248 Of the times past, when he was a young lad;
       p. 321 HORACE 2       338 But, as a Matrone drawne at solemne times
       p. 325 HORACE 2       418 Not, ten times o're, corrected to the naile.
       p. 331 HORACE 2       544 Doth please; this, ten times over, will delight.
       p. 362 UNGATHERED 2     4 In these pide times, only to shewe their braines,
       p. 366 UNGATHERED 6     1 Who saith our Times nor haue, nor can
       p. 389 UNGATHERED 24    4 When the old words doe strike on the new times,
       p. 397 UNGATHERED 30   43 O, how in those, dost thou instruct these times,
```

time's   frequency: 1   relative frequency: 0.00001
    See also "times."
```
       p. 111 FOREST 11       59 Richer then Time, and as Time's vertue, rare.
```

t'imprint   frequency: 1   relative frequency: 0.00001
```
       p. 414 UNGATHERED 41   55 T'imprint in all purg'd hearts this virgin sence,
```

tinckling   frequency: 1   relative frequency: 0.00001
```
       p. 327 HORACE 2       460 Of verse meere-matter-lesse, and tinckling toies.
```

tine   frequency: 1   relative frequency: 0.00001
```
       p. 368 UNGATHERED 6    73 Haste, Haste, sweete Singer: Nor to Tine,
```

tinkling. See "tinckling."

tintoret   frequency: 1   relative frequency: 0.00001
```
       p. 260 UNDERWOOD 77     6 Send in, what or Romano, Tintoret,
```

tir'd   frequency: 1   relative frequency: 0.00001
```
       p. 291 UNDERWOOD 85    44 Against the Husband comes home tir'd;
```

tire. See "tier."

tire-man   frequency: 1   relative frequency: 0.00001
```
       p. 404 UNGATHERED 34   59 Whither? oh whither will this Tire-man growe?
```

tires   frequency: 1   relative frequency: 0.00001
```
       p. 222 UNDERWOOD 49    17 To shew their Tires? to view, and to be view'd?
```

tis   frequency: 2   relative frequency: 0.00002

t'is   frequency: 1   relative frequency: 0.00001 'tis   frequency: 72   relative frequency: 0.00104

tissue   frequency: 2   relative frequency: 0.00002
    p. 201 UNDERWOOD 42   43 Put a Coach-mare in Tissue, must I horse
    p. 216 UNDERWOOD 44   100 Cover'd with Tissue, whose prosperitie mocks

tissues   frequency: 1   relative frequency: 0.00001
    p. 164 UNDERWOOD 15   58 With Velvet, Plush, and Tissues, it is spirit.

titian   frequency: 1   relative frequency: 0.00001
    p. 260 UNDERWOOD 77   7 Titian, or Raphael, Michael Angelo,

title   frequency: 14   relative frequency: 0.00020
    See also "title's."
    p. 27 EPIGRAMS 2   2 Thy title, Epigrammes, and nam'd of mee,
    p. 29 EPIGRAMS 9   2 For strict degrees of ranke, or title looke:
    p. 75 EPIGRAMS 116   7 'Twas not entayl'd on title. That some word
    p. 118 FOREST 13   49 Of so great title, birth, but vertue most,
    p. 142 U'WOOD 2.10   3 Let his Title be but great,
    p. 163 UNDERWOOD 15   51 Of lust, to his rich Suit and Title, Lord?
    p. 164 UNDERWOOD 15   83 Nor is the title question'd with our proud,
    p. 184 UNDERWOOD 29   58 And his Title be long foole,
    p. 225 UNDERWOOD 51   12 Now with a Title more to the Degree;
    p. 244 UNDERWOOD 70   42 But that the Corke of Title boy'd him up.
    p. 255 UNDERWOOD 75   96 To give a greater Name, and Title to! Their
                              owne!
    p. 287 U'WOOD 84.9   159 Of title in her! All Nobilitie
    p. 325 HORACE 2   432 My title, at the<ir> rate, I'<h>ad rather, I,
    p. 397 UNGATHERED 30   48 Vnder one title. Thou hast made thy way

title-leafe   frequency: 1   relative frequency: 0.00001
    p. 28 EPIGRAMS 3   7 Nor have my title-leafe on posts, or walls,

titles   frequency: 11   relative frequency: 0.00015
    p. 47 EPIGRAMS 64   8 Of flatterie to thy titles. Nor of wit.
    p. 70 EPIGRAMS 109   2 That serues nor fame, nor titles; but doth chuse
    p. 70 EPIGRAMS 109   18 Whil'st others toyle for titles to their tombes.
    p. 140 UNDERWOOD 2.9   5 Titles, I confesse, doe take me;
    p. 160 UNDERWOOD 14   65 Monarch in Letters! 'Mongst thy Titles showne
    p. 176 UNDERWOOD 24   16 By which as proper titles, she is knowne
    p. 215 UNDERWOOD 44   80 Descended in a rope of Titles, be
    p. 247 UNDERWOOD 70   114 And titles, by which all made claimes
    p. 281 U'WOOD 84.8   10 Boast not these Titles of your Ancestors;
    p. 384 UNGATHERED 18   t1 To the most noble, and aboue his Titles,
    p. 402 UNGATHERED 34   15 By all your Titles, & whole style at ones

title's   frequency: 1   relative frequency: 0.00001
    p. 62 EPIGRAMS 96   9 My title's seal'd. Those that for claps doe
                              write,

to   frequency: 1832   relative frequency: 0.02652
    See also "stitchers-to," words beginning
             "t<o>'," "t'enuy," "t'express,"
             "t'haue," "t'have," "t'imprint,"
             "to'<h>ave," "to'a," "too," "to't,"
             "t'outlast."

to'<h>ave   frequency: 1   relative frequency: 0.00001
    p. 271 UNDERWOOD 83   91 That ever had beginning there, to'<h>ave end!

to<o>   frequency: 3   relative frequency: 0.00004
    p. 141 UNDERWOOD 2.9   9 Young I'ld have him to<o>, and faire,
    p. 141 UNDERWOOD 2.9   33 'Twere to<o> long, to speake of all:
    p. 141 UNDERWOOD 2.9   36 Well he should his clothes to<o> weare;

to'a   frequency: 2   relative frequency: 0.00002

toast   frequency: 1   relative frequency: 0.00001
    p. 292 UNDERWOOD 86   12 If a fit livor thou dost seeke to toast;

toasted. See "tosted."

tobacco   frequency: 1   relative frequency: 0.00001
    See also "tabacco," "tabacco-like."
    p. 205 UNDERWOOD 43   52 To light Tobacco, or save roasted Geese,

toes   frequency: 1   relative frequency: 0.00001
    p. 157 UNDERWOOD 13   145 They need no stilts, nor rise upon their toes,

'tofore   frequency: 1   relative frequency: 0.00001
    p.   40 EPIGRAMS 43   5 'Tofore, great men were glad of Poets: Now,

together   frequency: 11   relative frequency: 0.00015
    p.   68 EPIGRAMS 106   10 And yet, they, all together, lesse then thee.
    p.   69 EPIGRAMS 107   15 And, in some yeere, all these together heap'd,
    p. 163 UNDERWOOD 15   40 And shamefastnesse together! All lawes dead,
    p. 172 UNDERWOOD 21   6 Of all vice hurld together, there he was,
    p. 183 UNDERWOOD 29   16 For a thousand yeares together,
    p. 193 UNDERWOOD 38   76 As all with storme and tempest ran together.
    p. 283 U'WOOD 84.9   47 And Goates together, whither they must come
    p. 284 U'WOOD 84.9   54 Of Body and Spirit together, plac'd betwixt
    p. 294 UNDERWOOD 88   7 Let us together closely lie, and kisse,
    p. 305 HORACE 2   15 Together: not that we should Serpents see
    p. 329 HORACE 2   516 As doctrine, and delight together go.

toies   frequency: 1   relative frequency: 0.00001
    p. 327 HORACE 2   460 Of verse meere-matter-lesse, and tinckling toies.

toil. See "toile," "toyle."

toile   frequency: 2   relative frequency: 0.00002
    p. 321 HORACE 2   352 And toile in vaine: the excellence is such
    p. 331 HORACE 2   584 Can; or all toile, without a wealthie veine:

toils. See "toyles."

told   frequency: 14   relative frequency: 0.00020
    See also "tould."
  **p. 116 PANEGYRE   107 "All this she told, and more, with bleeding eyes;
  **p. 117 PANEGYRE   135 And ceas'd in them. She told them, what a fate
    p.   45 EPIGRAMS 56   9 And, told of this, he slights it. Tut, such
                               crimes
    p.   54 EPIGRAMS 84   1 MADAME, I told you late how I repented,
    p.   89 EPIGRAMS 133   183 They cry'd out PVSSE. He told them he was
                               BANKES,
    p.   93 FOREST 2   4 Thou hast no lantherne, whereof tales are told;
    p. 117 FOREST 13   23 Your selfe but told vnto your selfe, and see
    p. 150 UNDERWOOD 9   15 Told seven and fortie yeares,
    p. 156 UNDERWOOD 13   96 And told of with more Licence then th'were done!
    p. 243 UNDERWOOD 70   26 And told forth fourescore yeares;
    p. 317 HORACE 2   256 Or acted told. But, ever, things that run
    p. 384 UNGATHERED 18 23 And when your yeares rise more, then would be
                               told,
    p. 408 UNGATHERED 37   3 ffor thou obiectest (as thou hast been told)
    p. 414 UNGATHERED 42   5 And lesse asham'd; not when I told the crowd

toleration   frequency: 1   relative frequency: 0.00001
    p. 331 HORACE 2   549 A meane, and toleration, which does well:

tom   frequency: 9   relative frequency: 0.00013
    p. 374 UNGATHERED 10 14 A Horse here is sadled, but no Tom him to
                               backe,
    p. 374 UNGATHERED 10 15 It should rather haue bene Tom that a horse did
                               lack.
    p. 378 UNGATHERED 11 t1 To the Right Noble Tom, Tell-Troth of
    p. 378 UNGATHERED 11 81 Honest Tom Tell-Troth puts downe Roger, How?
    p. 378 UNGATHERED 11 87 Of Tom of Odcombe that odde Iouiall Author,
    p. 379 UNGATHERED 12   2 The height, let him learne of Mr. Tom.
                               Coryate;
    p. 380 UNGATHERED 12 21 There nam'd to be trauell'd? For this our Tom
                               saith:
    p. 381 UNGATHERED 12 58 Poore Tom haue we cause to suspect iust thee?
    p. 381 UNGATHERED 12 60 The height, let him learne of Mr. Tom Coryate.

tomb. See "tombe."

tombe   frequency: 5   relative frequency: 0.00007
    p.   46 EPIGRAMS 62   12 Of the not borne, yet buried, here's the tombe.
    p. 152 UNDERWOOD 12   38 An Epitaph, deserv'd a Tombe:
    p. 199 UNDERWOOD 41   20 Of me, I'le softly tread unto my Tombe;
    p. 269 UNDERWOOD 83   18 At least may beare th'inscription to her Tombe.
    p. 391 UNGATHERED 26 22 Thou art a Moniment, without a tombe,

tombes   frequency: 2   relative frequency: 0.00002
    p.   70 EPIGRAMS 109   18 Whil'st others toyle for titles to their tombes.
    p. 387 UNGATHERED 22   6 trust in the tombes, their care=full freinds do
                               rayse;

tombs   frequency: 1   relative frequency: 0.00001
  See also "tombes."
  p. 114 FOREST 12   45 Painted, or caru'd vpon our great-mens tombs,

tomes   frequency: 1   relative frequency: 0.00001
  p. 204 UNDERWOOD 43   33 Or spun out Riddles, and weav'd fiftie tomes

tongue   frequency: 12   relative frequency: 0.00017
  p.   42 EPIGRAMS 49   2 He sayes, I want the tongue of Epigrammes;
  p.   78 EPIGRAMS 122   6 And heare her speake with one, and her first
                             tongue;
  p. 133 UNDERWOOD 2.3   24 To revenge me with my Tongue,
  p. 244 UNDERWOOD 70   44 Hee never fell, thou fall'st, my tongue.
  p. 260 UNDERWOOD 76   31 And so warme the Poets tongue
  p. 284 U'WOOD 84.9   69 This being thus: why should my tongue, or pen
  p. 292 UNDERWOOD 86   14 And for the troubled Clyent fyl's his tongue,
  p. 293 UNDERWOOD 86   36 With an uncomely silence failes my tongue?
  p. 311 HORACE 2   156 And tortures us: and, after, by the tongue
  p. 389 UNGATHERED 24   6 But in one tongue, was form'd with the worlds
                             wit:
  p. 395 UNGATHERED 29   17 Phoebus, and Hermes? They whose tongue, or pen
  p. 402 UNGATHERED 33   14 To make the Language sweet vpon her tongue.

tongued. See "seven-tongu'd."

tongues   frequency: 7   relative frequency: 0.00010
  p.   72 EPIGRAMS 111   9 Yet thou, perhaps, shalt meet some tongues will
                             grutch,
  p. 139 UNDERWOOD 2.7   17 And whilst our tongues perplexed lie,
  p. 184 UNDERWOOD 29   34 Whilst the Latin, Queene of Tongues,
  p. 206 UNDERWOOD 43   75 Invisibilitie, and strength, and tongues:
  p. 269 UNDERWOOD 83   23 Had I a thousand Mouthes, as many Tongues,
  p. 309 HORACE 2   81 Cato's and Ennius tongues have lent much worth,
  p. 388 UNGATHERED 23   7 If all the vulgar Tongues, that speake this day,

too   frequency: 115   relative frequency: 0.00166
  See also "to," "to<o>," "too'vnwieldie."

too-much   frequency: 1   relative frequency: 0.00001
  p. 216 UNDERWOOD 45   24 But he that's too-much that, is friend of none.

took. See "tooke," "up-tooke."

tooke   frequency: 17   relative frequency: 0.00024
 *p. 492 TO HIMSELF   t2 tooke at the vulgar censure of his
  p.   42 EPIGRAMS 46   3 'Tis LVCKLESSE he, that tooke vp one on
                             band
  p.   60 EPIGRAMS 94   9 For none ere tooke that pleasure in sinnes sense,
  p.   60 EPIGRAMS 94   10 But, when they heard it tax'd, tooke more
                             offence.
  p.   73 EPIGRAMS 114   3 For CVPID, who (at first) tooke vaine
                             delight,
  p.   89 EPIGRAMS 133   191 They tooke 'hem all to witnesse of their action:
  p. 130 UNDERWOOD 1.3   18 And tooke on him our Nature.
  p. 132 UNDERWOOD 2.2   25 At my face, that tooke my sight,
  p. 153 UNDERWOOD 13   8 To succour my necessities, tooke fire,
  p. 185 UNDERWOOD 30   18 And in the noblest Families tooke root
  p. 189 UNDERWOOD 37   6 But must confesse from whom what gift I tooke.
  p. 208 UNDERWOOD 43   116 No mar'le the Clownes of Lemnos tooke thee up,
  p. 254 UNDERWOOD 75   75 In all thy age of Journals thou hast tooke,
  p. 311 HORACE 2   118 This foot the socks tooke up, and buskins grave,
  p. 335 HORACE 2   662 Immortall, tooke a melancholique, odde
  p. 363 UNGATHERED 3   5 Gold is a sutor, neuer tooke repulse,
  p. 410 UNGATHERED 38   13 It was not so of old: Men tooke vp trades

tooth'd   frequency: 1   relative frequency: 0.00001
  p.   27 EPIGRAMS 2   4 Wormewood, and sulphure, sharpe, and tooth'd
                             withall;

too'vnwieldie   frequency: 1   relative frequency: 0.00001
  p.   57 EPIGRAMS 90   14 Blowne vp; and he (too'vnwieldie for that place)

top   frequency: 3   relative frequency: 0.00004
  p. 274 U'WOOD 84.1   38 By JACOBS Ladder, to the top
  p. 407 UNGATHERED 35   10 Wth slyding windowes, & false Lights a top!
  p. 413 UNGATHERED 41   15 To top the fairest Lillie, now, that growes,

topps   frequency: 1   relative frequency: 0.00001
  p.   94 FOREST 2   25 Each banke doth yeeld thee coneyes; and the topps

tops   frequency: 1   relative frequency: 0.00001
    See also "topps."
  **p. 114 PANEGYRE   41 Some cry from tops of houses; thinking noise

torch   frequency: 1   relative frequency: 0.00001
    p.   85 EPIGRAMS 133   58 But hold my torch, while I describe the entry

torches   frequency: 2   relative frequency: 0.00002
    p. 147 UNDERWOOD 7   24 Where Love may all his Torches light,
    p. 170 UNDERWOOD 19   2 Love lights his torches to inflame desires;

torment   frequency: 1   relative frequency: 0.00001
    p. 270 UNDERWOOD 83   55 'Tis but a body which you can torment,

tormented   frequency: 1   relative frequency: 0.00001
    p. 184 UNDERWOOD 29   50 May his joynts tormented bee,

torn. See "torne."

torne   frequency: 5   relative frequency: 0.00007
   *p. 493 TO HIMSELF   ,39 Which, if they are torne, and turn'd, &
                              patch't enough,
    p.   98 FOREST 3   71 And shew their feathers shot, and cullors torne,
    p. 127 UNDERWOOD 1.1   5 2. My selfe up to thee, harrow'd, torne, and
                              bruis'd
    p. 147 UNDERWOOD 7   14 Unlesse my heart would as my thought be torne.
    p. 375 UNGATHERED 10   26 Old Hat here, torne Hose, with Shoes full of
                              grauell,

torned   frequency: 1   relative frequency: 0.00001
    p. 392 UNGATHERED 26   68 In his well torned, and true-filed lines:

torrent   frequency: 1   relative frequency: 0.00001
    p. 407 UNGATHERED 35   16 Or Dowgate Torrent falling into Thames,

tort'ring   frequency: 1   relative frequency: 0.00001
    p. 256 UNDERWOOD 75   120 A meere upbraiding Griefe, and tort'ring
                              punishment.

torturers   frequency: 1   relative frequency: 0.00001
    p. 270 UNDERWOOD 83   52 And to the Torturers (her Doctors) say,

tortures   frequency: 2   relative frequency: 0.00002
    p. 193 UNDERWOOD 38   93 To suffer tortures, scorne, and Infamie,
    p. 311 HORACE 2   156 And tortures us: and, after, by the tongue

torturing. See "tort'ring."

toss. See "tosse."

tosse   frequency: 1   relative frequency: 0.00001
    p. 129 UNDERWOOD 1.2   30 Me farther tosse

tossed. See "tost."

tost   frequency: 1   relative frequency: 0.00001
    p. 287 U'WOOD 84.9   164 Not tost or troubled with light Lady-aire;

tosted   frequency: 1   relative frequency: 0.00001
    p.   88 EPIGRAMS 133 150 And, after mouldie growne, againe were tosted,

to't   frequency: 2   relative frequency: 0.00002

tother   frequency: 3   relative frequency: 0.00004
    p. 103 FOREST 6   10 Hundred, then vnto the tother
    p. 166 UNDERWOOD 15 115 Surfet? and Quarrel? drinkes the tother health?
    p. 247 UNDERWOOD 70 109 That liking; and approach so one the tother,

t'other   frequency: 1   relative frequency: 0.00001
    p. 164 UNDERWOOD 15   77 For t'other pound of sweet-meats, he shall feele

totter'd   frequency: 1   relative frequency: 0.00001
    p. 216 UNDERWOOD 44 101 The fate of things: whilst totter'd vertue holds

touch   frequency: 13   relative frequency: 0.00018
    p.   78 EPIGRAMS 122   7 If holiest friend-ship, naked to the touch,
    p.   93 FOREST 2   2 Of touch, or marble; nor canst boast a row
    p. 114 FOREST 12   44 Inscrib'd in touch or marble, or the cotes
    p. 139 UNDERWOOD 2.7   6 That doth but touch his flower, and flies away.
    p. 187 UNDERWOOD 33   23 But in a businesse, that will bide the Touch,

touch (cont.)
     p. 216 UNDERWOOD 45   16 First weigh a friend, then touch, and trie him
                                  too:
     p. 235 UNDERWOOD 62   4 To cure the call'd Kings Evill with thy touch;
     p. 239 UNDERWOOD 67   18 With touch of daintie thum's!
     p. 269 UNDERWOOD 83   31 To touch these Mysteries! We may admire
     p. 286 U'WOOD 84.9   126 And to the Touch, a Flower, like soft as
                                  Palme.
     p. 333 HORACE 2   587 Hee, that's ambitious in the race to touch
     p. 335 HORACE 2   644 And shun to touch him, as a man that were
     p. 393 UNGATHERED 27   2 And needs no other touch.

touch'd   frequency: 6   relative frequency: 0.00008
     p.   38 EPIGRAMS 38   3 You laugh when you are touch'd, and long before
     p.   56 EPIGRAMS 87   1 Touch'd with the sinne of false play, in his
                                  punque,
     p.   87 EPIGRAMS 133 112 Of the hulke touch'd, and, as by
                                  POLYPHEME
     p. 115 FOREST 12   82 Had not their forme touch'd by an English wit.
     p. 134 UNDERWOOD 2.4 22 Before rude hands have touch'd it?
     p. 337 HORACE 2   673 (Defiled) touch'd; but certaine he was mad,

toucheth   frequency: 1   relative frequency: 0.00001
     p. 197 UNDERWOOD 40   22 And turning all he toucheth into pelfe,

touching   frequency: 1   relative frequency: 0.00001
     p.   87 EPIGRAMS 133 106 Touching this cause, where they will be affeard

tough   frequency: 1   relative frequency: 0.00001
     p. 417 UNGATHERED 45 16 Tough, foule, or Tender.

tould   frequency: 1   relative frequency: 0.00001
     p. 370 UNGATHERED 7   14 Being tould there, Reason cannot, Sense may
                                  erre.

toure   frequency: 1   relative frequency: 0.00001
     p.   55 EPIGRAMS 85   6 That they to knowledge so should toure vpright,

t'outlast   frequency: 1   relative frequency: 0.00001
     p. 406 UNGATHERED 34 99 Of all ye Worthyes hope t'outlast thy one,

toward   frequency: 1   relative frequency: 0.00001
     p.   56 EPIGRAMS 88   6 Toward the sea, farther then halfe-way tree?

tower   frequency: 4   relative frequency: 0.00005
     See also "toure," "towre."
     p. 213 UNDERWOOD 44   3 And Ord'nance too: so much as from the Tower
     p. 239 UNDERWOOD 67   7 2. MEL. What, though the thriftie Tower
     p. 413 UNGATHERED 41 38 Sweet Tree of Life, King Davids Strength and
                                  Tower,
     p. 657 L. CONVIVALES   4 Or the Tripos, his Tower Bottle:

towering. See "towring."

towers   frequency: 1   relative frequency: 0.00001
     See also "towres."
  **p. 114 PANEGYRE   63 Walls, windores, roofes, towers, steeples, all
                                  were set

town. See "towne," "towne-curs."

town-born   frequency: 1   relative frequency: 0.00001
     p. 347 HORACE 1   349 .... Town-born ... . place ....

towne   frequency: 14   relative frequency: 0.00020
  **p. 114 PANEGYRE   53 And would be courted: so this Towne put on
     p.   30 EPIGRAMS 12   1 SHIFT, here, in towne, not meanest among
                                  squires,
     p.   63 EPIGRAMS 97   11 Nor office in the towne, nor place in court,
     p.   74 EPIGRAMS 115   6 About the towne; and knowne too, at that price.
     p.   81 EPIGRAMS 129   5 That scarse the Towne designeth any feast
     p. 105 FOREST 8   17 Liuers, round about the towne.
     p. 105 FOREST 8   38 Euery stew in towne to know;
     p. 155 UNDERWOOD 13   92 Of our Towne Gallantry! or why there rests
     p. 201 UNDERWOOD 42   70 The Lady Mayresse pass'd in through the Towne,
     p. 218 UNDERWOOD 47   23 That censure all the Towne, and all th'affaires,
     p. 242 UNDERWOOD 70   4 His rage, with razing your immortall Towne.
     p. 248 UNDERWOOD 71   15 A Bed-rid Wit, then a besieged Towne.
     p. 396 UNGATHERED 30   9 About the towne: this reck'ning I will pay,
     p. 403 UNGATHERED 34 24 In Towne & Court? Are you growne rich?
                                  & proud?

towne-curs   frequency: 1   relative frequency: 0.00001
    p. 155 UNDERWOOD 13   72 All the Towne-curs take each their snatch at me.

townes   frequency: 5   relative frequency: 0.00007
    p. 74 EPIGRAMS 115   t1 ON THE TOWNES HONEST MAN.
    p. 75 EPIGRAMS 115   34 Then, The townes honest Man's her errant'st
                              knaue.
    p. 82 EPIGRAMS 130   2 Of building townes, and making wilde beasts tame,
    p. 315 HORACE 2   202 Saw many Townes, and Men, and could their
                              manners tract.
    p. 327 HORACE 2   490 Build Townes, and carve the Lawes in leaves of
                              wood.

towns. See "neighbour-townes," "townes."

towns-man   frequency: 1   relative frequency: 0.00001
    p. 319 HORACE 2   302 Clowne, Towns-man, base, and noble, mix'd, to
                              judge?

towre   frequency: 2   relative frequency: 0.00002
    p. 176 UNDERWOOD 25   4 To towre with my intention
    p. 249 UNDERWOOD 72   1 This is King CHARLES his Day. Speake
                              it, thou Towre,

towres   frequency: 1   relative frequency: 0.00001
    p. 327 HORACE 2   483 Amphion, too, that built the Theban towres,

towring   frequency: 1   relative frequency: 0.00001
    p. 278 U'WOOD 84.4   10 An Eagle towring in the skye,

toy   frequency: 1   relative frequency: 0.00001
    See also "toye."
    p. 142 U'WOOD 2.10   2 That's a Toy, that I could spare:

toye   frequency: 1   relative frequency: 0.00001
    p. 405 UNGATHERED 34 78 In setting forth of such a solemne Toye!

toyes   frequency: 4   relative frequency: 0.00005
    p. 64 EPIGRAMS 100   1 PLAY-WRIGHT, by chance, hearing some
                              toyes I'had writ,
    p. 100 FOREST 4   18 Of toyes, and trifles, traps, and snares,
    p. 102 FOREST 5   10 Fame, and rumor are but toyes.
    p. 273 U'WOOD 84.1   17 For, though that Rattles, Timbrels, Toyes,

toyle   frequency: 2   relative frequency: 0.00002
    p. 70 EPIGRAMS 109   18 Whil'st others toyle for titles to their tombes.
    p. 162 UNDERWOOD 15   9 All other Acts of Worldlings, are but toyle

toyles   frequency: 3   relative frequency: 0.00004
    p. 36 EPIGRAMS 31   4 He toyles to be at hell, as soone as they.
    p. 113 FOREST 12   5 Toyles, by graue custome, vp and downe the court,
    p. 290 UNDERWOOD 85   32 Wild Bores into his toyles pitch'd round:

toys. See "toies," "toyes."

trace   frequency: 1   relative frequency: 0.00001
    p. 287 U'WOOD 84.9   153 Our closest Creekes, and Corners, and can trace

tracks   frequency: 1   relative frequency: 0.00001
    p. 389 UNGATHERED 24   1 Who tracks this Authors, or Translators Pen,

tract   frequency: 1   relative frequency: 0.00001
    p. 315 HORACE 2   202 Saw many Townes, and Men, and could their
                              manners tract.

tracts   frequency: 3   relative frequency: 0.00004
  **p. 115 PANEGYRE   96 "Who both, who neither: all the cunning tracts,
    p. 323 HORACE 2   407 In daring to forsake the Grecian tracts,
    p. 368 UNGATHERED 6   61 With entheate rage, to publish their bright
                              tracts?

trade   frequency: 8   relative frequency: 0.00011
    p. 35 EPIGRAMS 28   3 Makes serious vse of all great trade he knowes.
    p. 56 EPIGRAMS 87   5 Vpon th'accompt, hers grew the quicker trade.
    p. 56 EPIGRAMS 88   16 Daily to turne in PAVLS, and helpe the
                              trade.
    p. 105 FOREST 8   19 They maintayne the truest trade,
    p. 155 UNDERWOOD 13   79 But these men ever want: their very trade
    p. 212 UNDERWOOD 43 199 Maintain'd the trade at Bilbo, or else-where;
    p. 273 U'WOOD 84.1   8 By the just trade

trade (cont.)
   p. 389 UNGATHERED 23   11 As, now, of all men, it is call'd thy Trade:

trades   frequency: 2   relative frequency: 0.00002
   p. 165 UNDERWOOD 15   93 The brother trades a sister; and the friend
   p. 410 UNGATHERED 38   13 It was not so of old: Men tooke vp trades

tradesmen   frequency: 2   relative frequency: 0.00002
   p. 203 UNDERWOOD 43   8 With Clownes, and Tradesmen, kept thee clos'd
                in horne.
   p. 215 UNDERWOOD 44   73 With Citizens? let Clownes, and Tradesmen
                breed

traditions   frequency: 1   relative frequency: 0.00001
   p. 160 UNDERWOOD 14   49 How are Traditions there examin'd: how

traduce   frequency: 1   relative frequency: 0.00001
   p. 32 EPIGRAMS 17   1 May others feare, flie, and traduce thy name,

tragedie   frequency: 5   relative frequency: 0.00007
   p. 319 HORACE 2   306 In time to Tragedie, a Musicke new.
   p. 319 HORACE 2   312 The Tragedie, and carried it about,
   p. 321 HORACE 2   336 And emptie Clowdes. For Tragedie is faire,
   p. 321 HORACE 2   344 Quite from all face of Tragedie to goe,
   p. 323 HORACE 2   409 Whether the guarded Tragedie they wrought,

tragedy. See "tragedie."

tragic. See "tragick."

tragick   frequency: 4   relative frequency: 0.00005
   p. 72 EPIGRAMS 112   8 Tragick, or Comick; but thou writ'st the play.
   p. 311 HORACE 2   122 In tragick Verse; no lesse Thyestes feast
   p. 311 HORACE 2   134 With swelling throat: and, oft, the tragick wight
   p. 319 HORACE 2   319 Hee too, that did in Tragick Verse contend

train. See "traine," "virgin-traine."

train'd   frequency: 1   relative frequency: 0.00001
   p. 319 HORACE 2   305 In his train'd Gowne about the Stage: So grew

traine   frequency: 2   relative frequency: 0.00002
**p. 113 PANEGYRE   27 Her third, IRENE, help'd to beare his
                traine;
   p. 115 FOREST 12   66 Of all LVCINA'S traine; LVCY the
                bright,

traines   frequency: 1   relative frequency: 0.00001
   p. 110 FOREST 11   28 Thus, by these subtle traines,

trains. See "traines."

trampled   frequency: 1   relative frequency: 0.00001
   p. 243 UNDERWOOD 70   14 Lay trampled on: the deeds of death, and night,

trance   frequency: 1   relative frequency: 0.00001
   p. 361 UNGATHERED 1   26 in a deepe trance;

transcending   frequency: 1   relative frequency: 0.00001
   p. 365 UNGATHERED 5   15 But mixt with sound, transcending

transcripts   frequency: 1   relative frequency: 0.00001
   p. 263 UNDERWOOD 78   30 What transcripts begg'd? how cry'd up, and how
                glad,

transfer. See "transferre."

transferre   frequency: 1   relative frequency: 0.00001
   p. 55 EPIGRAMS 84   9 O Madame, if your grant did thus transferre mee,

transform'd   frequency: 1   relative frequency: 0.00001
   p. 369 UNGATHERED 6 101 Though, now by Loue transform'd, & dayly
                dying:

translate   frequency: 1   relative frequency: 0.00001
   p. 313 HORACE 2   190 Not care, as thou wouldst faithfully translate,

translated   frequency: 3   relative frequency: 0.00004
   p. 71 EPIGRAMS 110   t2 CAESARS Commentaries obserued, and
                translated.

translated (cont.)
    p. 214 UNDERWOOD 44   35 Translated Aelian<'s> tactickes to be read,
    p. 395 UNGATHERED 29   24 The Sunne translated, or the Sonne of May.

translation   frequency: 2   relative frequency: 0.00002
    p. 83 EPIGRAMS 132   12 As his will now be the translation thought,
    p. 388 UNGATHERED 23   t2 Mr George Chapman, on his Translation

translator   frequency: 2   relative frequency: 0.00002
    p. 389 UNGATHERED 24   t1 On the Author, Worke, and Translator.
    p. 395 UNGATHERED 29   t2 The learned Translator of LVCAN,

translators   frequency: 2   relative frequency: 0.00002
    p. 389 UNGATHERED 24   1 Who tracks this Authors, or Translators Pen,
    p. 389 UNGATHERED 24   11 Such Bookes deserue Translators, of like coate

transmigrated   frequency: 1   relative frequency: 0.00001
    p. 88 EPIGRAMS 133   159 Their spirits transmigrated to a cat:

transmit. See "transmitt."

transmitt   frequency: 1   relative frequency: 0.00001
    p. 399 UNGATHERED 31   3 Transmitt it to your Nephewes, ffreinds,
                               Allies,

transplanted   frequency: 1   relative frequency: 0.00001
    p. 361 UNGATHERED 1   6 that mongst so manie plants transplanted hether,

trappings   frequency: 1   relative frequency: 0.00001
    p. 403 UNGATHERED 34   25 your Trappings will not change you. Change yor
                                 mynd.

traps   frequency: 1   relative frequency: 0.00001
    p. 100 FOREST 4   18 Of toyes, and trifles, traps, and snares,

trauail'd   frequency: 1   relative frequency: 0.00001
    p. 81 EPIGRAMS 128   14 Came backe vntouch'd. This man hath trauail'd
                                 well.

trauaile   frequency: 2   relative frequency: 0.00002
    p. 36 EPIGRAMS 31   2 His monyes trauaile for him, in and out:
    p. 380 UNGATHERED 12   35 He was in his trauaile, how like to be beaten,

trauailes   frequency: 1   relative frequency: 0.00001
    p. 378 UNGATHERED 11   t2 his trauailes, the Coryate of Odcombe,

trauayles   frequency: 1   relative frequency: 0.00001
    p. 362 UNGATHERED 1   30 Palmer thy trauayles well becum thy name,

trauell   frequency: 3   relative frequency: 0.00004
    p. 375 UNGATHERED 10   27 And louse-dropping Case, are the Armes of his
                                 trauell.
    p. 378 UNGATHERED 11   t4 trauell
    p. 378 UNGATHERED 11   82 Of trauell he discourseth so at large,

trauell'd   frequency: 1   relative frequency: 0.00001
    p. 380 UNGATHERED 12   21 There nam'd to be trauell'd? For this our Tom
                                 saith:

traueller   frequency: 1   relative frequency: 0.00001
    p. 379 UNGATHERED 12   t2 Polytopian Thomas the Traueller.

trauelling   frequency: 2   relative frequency: 0.00002
    p. 378 UNGATHERED 11   89 Yes thou wert borne out of his trauelling thigh
    p. 380 UNGATHERED 12   29 And therefore how euer the trauelling nation,

trauells   frequency: 1   relative frequency: 0.00001
    p. 63 EPIGRAMS 97   10 Nor baudie stock, that trauells for encrease,

travail. See "trauaile," "travaile."

travail'd   frequency: 1   relative frequency: 0.00001
  See also "trauail'd."
    p. 315 HORACE 2   198 Afford? The Mountaines travail'd, and brought
                               forth

travaile   frequency: 1   relative frequency: 0.00001
    p. 251 UNDERWOOD 74   26 To see great Charles of Travaile eas'd,

travails. See "trauailes," "trauayles."

travel. See "trauaile," "trauell."

travelled. See "trauell'd."

traveller. See "traueller."

travelling. See "trauelling."

travels. See "trauells."

treacherous. See "trecherous."

tread   frequency: 14   relative frequency: 0.00020
    p.   63 EPIGRAMS 99   3 Hast taught thy selfe worthy thy pen to tread,
    p. 100 FOREST 4   6 A spirit so resolu'd to tread
    p. 118 FOREST 13   55 Of vertue, which you tread? what if alone?
    p. 138 UNDERWOOD 2.6   25 So to see a Lady tread,
    p. 199 UNDERWOOD 41   20 Of me, I'le softly tread unto my Tombe;
    p. 230 UNDERWOOD 56   13 Marrie the Muse is one, can tread the Aire,
    p. 254 UNDERWOOD 75   66 Have they bedew'd the Earth, where she doth
                                   tread,
    p. 264 UNDERWOOD 79   36 1. Where ere they tread th'enamour'd ground,
    p. 307 HORACE 2   44 When in a wrong, and artlesse way we tread.
    p. 315 HORACE 2   226 And can tread firme, longs with like lads to
                                   play;
    p. 335 HORACE 2   642 The man once mock'd, and suffer'd wrong to tread.
    p. 386 UNGATHERED 21   5 For, though but early in these pathes thou tread,
    p. 391 UNGATHERED 26   36 To life againe, to heare thy Buskin tread,
    p. 393 UNGATHERED 27   11 As giues a power to faith, to tread

treading   frequency: 1   relative frequency: 0.00001
    p.   76 EPIGRAMS 119   12 Treading a better path, not contrary;

treads   frequency: 1   relative frequency: 0.00001
    p. 379 UNGATHERED 12   12 Since he treads in no other Mans steps but his
                                   owne.

treason   frequency: 2   relative frequency: 0.00002
    p. 109 FOREST 11   15 Will quickly taste the treason, and commit
    p. 203 UNDERWOOD 43   15 Had I wrote treason there, or heresie,

treasons   frequency: 1   relative frequency: 0.00001
    p.   38 EPIGRAMS 35   7 Like aydes gainst treasons who hath found before?

treasure   frequency: 7   relative frequency: 0.00010
    p.   47 EPIGRAMS 64   4 A treasure, art: contemn'd in th'age of gold.
    p.   68 EPIGRAMS 105   20 I' your selfe, all treasure lost of th'age
                                   before.
    p.   79 EPIGRAMS 125   6 Might loue the treasure for the cabinet.
    p. 112 FOREST 11   105 The wealthy treasure of her loue on him;
    p. 183 UNDERWOOD 29   4 Spoyling Senses of their Treasure,
    p. 255 UNDERWOOD 75   97 Weston, their Treasure, as their Treasurer,
    p. 388 UNGATHERED 23   4 What treasure hast thou brought vs! and what
                                   store

treasurer   frequency: 6   relative frequency: 0.00008
    p. 185 UNDERWOOD 30   t3 Lo: high Treasurer of England.
    p. 248 UNDERWOOD 71   t2 the Lord high Treasurer of England.
    p. 250 UNDERWOOD 73   t2 Weston, L. high Treasurer of England,
    p. 252 UNDERWOOD 75   t7 Lord high Treasurer of England,
    p. 255 UNDERWOOD 75   97 Weston, their Treasure, as their Treasurer,
    p. 260 UNDERWOOD 77   t1 To the right Honourable, the Lord Treasurer

treasurer-ship   frequency: 1   relative frequency: 0.00001
    p.   47 EPIGRAMS 64   t2 Vpon the accession of the Treasurer-ship to him.

treasurers   frequency: 1   relative frequency: 0.00001
    p. 263 UNDERWOOD 78   27 When hee shall read them at the Treasurers bord,

treble   frequency: 1   relative frequency: 0.00001
    p. 114 FOREST 12   36 Worth an estate, treble to that you haue.

trecherous   frequency: 2   relative frequency: 0.00002
    p. 172 UNDERWOOD 21   7 Proud, false, and trecherous, vindictive, all
    p. 342 HORACE 1   176 ... . trecherous

tree   frequency: 15   relative frequency: 0.00021
    p.   32 EPIGRAMS 17   6 Shall out-liue gyrlands, stolne from the chast
                                   tree.
    p.   56 EPIGRAMS 88   6 Toward the sea, farther then halfe-way tree?

tree (cont.)
p.	80	EPIGRAMS 126	8 CARY my loue is, DAPHNE but my tree.
p.	94	FOREST 2	13 That taller tree, which of a nut was set,
p.	119	FOREST 13	99 Grow, grow, faire tree, and as thy branches shoote,
p.	143	UNDERWOOD 3	7 What Tree or stone doth want a soule?
p.	149	UNDERWOOD 9	10 That sits in shadow of Apollo's tree.
p.	245	UNDERWOOD 70	65 It is not growing like a tree
p.	258	UNDERWOOD 75	181 Whilst the maine tree, still found
p.	268	UNDERWOOD 83	3 And beckning wooes me, from the fatall tree
p.	287	U'WOOD 84.9	165 But, kept an even gate, as some streight tree
p.	291	UNDERWOOD 85	56 From fattest branches of the Tree:
p.	294	UNDERWOOD 87	22 Thou lighter then the barke of any tree,
p.	305	HORACE 2	25 Know'st only well to paint a Cipresse tree.
p.	413	UNGATHERED 41	38 Sweet Tree of Life, King Davids Strength and Tower,

trees   frequency: 2   relative frequency: 0.00002
p.	98	FOREST 3	45 The trees cut out in log; and those boughes made
p.	152	UNDERWOOD 12	20 They were as specious as his Trees.

trembles   frequency: 1   relative frequency: 0.00001
          p. 233 UNDERWOOD 59   8 That trembles in the blaze, but (then) mounts higher!

trembling   frequency: 1   relative frequency: 0.00001
          p. 155 UNDERWOOD 13   85 And it is paid 'hem with a trembling zeale,

trench   frequency: 3   relative frequency: 0.00004
p.	204	UNDERWOOD 43	48 Or if thou needs would'st trench upon her power,
p.	248	UNDERWOOD 71	6 Have cast a trench about mee, now, five yeares;
p.	401	UNGATHERED 32	14 A Trench against it, nor a Battry plac't?

trent   frequency: 1   relative frequency: 0.00001
          p. 368 UNGATHERED 6   75 But ouer Land to Trent:

trespass. See "trespasse."

trespasse   frequency: 1   relative frequency: 0.00001
          p. 152 UNDERWOOD 12   26 As twice to trespasse in his sight,

tresses   frequency: 1   relative frequency: 0.00001
          p. 254 UNDERWOOD 75   45 Her tresses trim her back,

trew   frequency: 1   relative frequency: 0.00001
          p. 415 UNGATHERED 42   10 And newer, then could please them, by-cause trew.

trial. See "triall."

triall   frequency: 1   relative frequency: 0.00001
          p. 393 UNGATHERED 27   1 Truth is the triall of it selfe,

trials   frequency: 1   relative frequency: 0.00001
     See also "tryals."
          p. 218 UNDERWOOD 47   2 Care not what trials they are put unto;

tribade   frequency: 2   relative frequency: 0.00002
p.	107	FOREST 10	17 Or, with thy Tribade trine, inuent new sports,
p.	222	UNDERWOOD 49	7 What though with Tribade lust she force a Muse,

tribe   frequency: 2   relative frequency: 0.00002
p.	218	UNDERWOOD 47	t3 Tribe of BEN.
p.	220	UNDERWOOD 47	78 Sir, you are Sealed of the Tribe of Ben.

tribute   frequency: 2   relative frequency: 0.00002
p.	94	FOREST 2	32 Thou hast thy ponds, that pay thee tribute fish,
p.	155	UNDERWOOD 13	84 Now, but command; make tribute, what was gift;

tricks   frequency: 3   relative frequency: 0.00004
p.	164	UNDERWOOD 15	76 Doe all the tricks of a saut Lady Bitch;
p.	321	HORACE 2	358 Their youthfull tricks in over-wanton verse:
p.	415	UNGATHERED 42	26 A Say-master, hath studied all the tricks

tri'd   frequency: 1   relative frequency: 0.00001
          p. 146 UNDERWOOD 6   18 But as 'tis often vext and tri'd.

trie   frequency: 5   relative frequency: 0.00007
p.	78	EPIGRAMS 122	3 If I would striue to bring backe times, and trie
p.	87	EPIGRAMS 133	132 Must trie the'vn-vsed valour of a nose:
p.	216	UNDERWOOD 45	16 First weigh a friend, then touch, and trie him too:

trie (cont.)
    p. 235 UNDERWOOD 62   5 But thou wilt yet a Kinglier mastrie trie,
    p. 378 UNGATHERED 11 80 Trie and trust Roger, was the word, but now

tried   frequency: 1   relative frequency: 0.00001
   See also "tri'd," "try'd."
    p. 380 UNGATHERED 12 27 Besides he tried Ship, Cart, Waggon, and
                      Chayre,

trier. See "tryer."

trifles   frequency: 4   relative frequency: 0.00005
    p. 100 FOREST 4   18 Of toyes, and trifles, traps, and snares,
    p. 204 UNDERWOOD 43   35 Or pomp'd for those hard trifles, Anagrams,
    p. 273 U'WOOD 84.1   25 Yet, here are no such Trifles brought,
    p. 335 HORACE 2   641 These trifles into serious mischiefes lead

trifling   frequency: 2   relative frequency: 0.00002
    p. 335 HORACE 2   640 Why should I grieve my friend, this trifling
                      way?
    p. 343 HORACE 1   199 . trifling ....

trim   frequency: 2   relative frequency: 0.00002
    p. 31 EPIGRAMS 12   23 But see! th'old baud hath seru'd him in his trim,
    p. 254 UNDERWOOD 75   45 Her tresses trim her back,

trimeter   frequency: 1   relative frequency: 0.00001
    p. 323 HORACE 2   373 Of Trimeter, when yet it was sixe-pac'd,

trimeters   frequency: 1   relative frequency: 0.00001
    p. 323 HORACE 2   381 This foot yet, in the famous Trimeters

trine   frequency: 3   relative frequency: 0.00004
    p. 107 FOREST 10   17 Or, with thy Tribade trine, inuent new sports,
    p. 119 FOREST 13   102 Before the moones haue fill'd their tripple
                      trine,
    p. 413 UNGATHERED 41 34 Alike of kin, to that most blessed Trine,

trinitie   frequency: 5   relative frequency: 0.00007
    p. 127 UNDERWOOD 1.1 1 1. O holy, blessed, glorious Trinitie
    p. 127 UNDERWOOD 1.1 t2 To the Holy Trinitie.
    p. 128 UNDERWOOD 1.1 29 8. Increase those acts, o glorious Trinitie
    p. 128 UNDERWOOD 1.1 34 A Trinitie, to shine in Union;
    p. 286 U'WOOD 84.9 128 God, in the Union, and the Trinitie!

trinity   frequency: 1   relative frequency: 0.00001
   See also "trinitie."
    p. 413 UNGATHERED 41 32 The glorious Trinity in Vnion met.

triple   frequency: 1   relative frequency: 0.00001
   See also "tripple."
    p. 268 UNDERWOOD 82   15 At land she triumphs in the triple shade,

tripoly   frequency: 1   relative frequency: 0.00001
    p. 74 EPIGRAMS 115 11 Can come from Tripoly, leape stooles, and winke,

tripos   frequency: 1   relative frequency: 0.00001
    p. 657 L. CONVIVALES 4 Or the Tripos, his Tower Bottle:

tripple   frequency: 2   relative frequency: 0.00002
    p. 89 EPIGRAMS 133 186 The tripple head without a sop. At last,
    p. 119 FOREST 13   102 Before the moones haue fill'd their tripple
                      trine,

tristrams   frequency: 1   relative frequency: 0.00001
    p. 206 UNDERWOOD 43   69 The Tristrams, Lanc'lots, Turpins, and the
                      Peers,

triumph   frequency: 7   relative frequency: 0.00010
  **p. 115 PANEGYRE   76 How he may triumph in his subiects brests,
    p. 36 EPIGRAMS 29   4 All braines, at times of triumph, should runne
                      wit.
    p. 134 UNDERWOOD 2.4 t1 Her Triumph.
    p. 173 UNDERWOOD 22   9 Wherein you triumph yet: because
    p. 205 UNDERWOOD 43   60 T'have held a Triumph, or a feast of fire,
    p. 224 UNDERWOOD 50   4 To conquer rumour, and triumph on spight;
    p. 391 UNGATHERED 26 41 Triumph, my Britaine, thou hast one to showe,

triumphal. See "triumphall."

triumphall   frequency: 1   relative frequency: 0.00001
      p. 157 UNDERWOOD 13   139 Then stands it a triumphall marke! then Men

triumphing   frequency: 2   relative frequency: 0.00002
      p. 272 UNDERWOOD 83   100 And, sure of Heaven, rides triumphing in.
      p. 288 U'WOOD 84.9   203 Shee saw him rise, triumphing over Death

triumphs   frequency: 2   relative frequency: 0.00002
      p. 134 UNDERWOOD 2.4   19 As alone there triumphs to the life
      p. 268 UNDERWOOD 82   15 At land she triumphs in the triple shade,

trodden. See "broad-troden."

troop. See "troope," "virgin-troup."

troope   frequency: 1   relative frequency: 0.00001
      p. 173 UNDERWOOD 22   28 Among which faithful troope am I.

tropicks   frequency: 1   relative frequency: 0.00001
      p. 252 UNDERWOOD 75   4 Betweene thy Tropicks, to arrest thy sight,

tropics. See "tropicks."

troth   frequency: 3   relative frequency: 0.00004
   See also "tell-troth," "'troth."
      p. 42 EPIGRAMS 47   1 Sir LVCKLESSE, troth, for lucks sake
                                 passe by one:
      p. 73 EPIGRAMS 112   17 Troth, if it be, I pitty thy ill lucke;
      p. 407 UNGATHERED 35   19 your workes thus differing, troth let soe yor
                                 style:

'troth   frequency: 1   relative frequency: 0.00001
      p. 54 EPIGRAMS 83   2 Throughout my booke. 'Troth put out woman too.

trouble   frequency: 3   relative frequency: 0.00004
    **p. 114 PANEGYRE   46 Along with him, and the same trouble proue.
      p. 140 UNDERWOOD 2.9   1 Of your Trouble, Ben, to ease me,
      p. 154 UNDERWOOD 13   31 Himselfe of farther trouble, or the weight

troubled   frequency: 4   relative frequency: 0.00005
      p. 243 UNDERWOOD 70   28 Troubled both foes, and friends;
      p. 287 U'WOOD 84.9   164 Not tost or troubled with light Lady-aire;
      p. 291 UNDERWOOD 85   51 If with bright floods, the Winter troubled much,
      p. 292 UNDERWOOD 86   14 And for the troubled Clyent fyl's his tongue,

troubles   frequency: 1   relative frequency: 0.00001
      p. 215 UNDERWOOD 44   86 We neither love the Troubles, nor the harmes.

troy   frequency: 4   relative frequency: 0.00005
      p. 115 FOREST 12   55 That HOMER brought to Troy; yet none so
                                 liue:
      p. 181 UNDERWOOD 27   24 Which all the Fate of Troy foretold?
      p. 210 UNDERWOOD 43   160 Troy, though it were so much his Venus care.
      p. 315 HORACE 2   201 Speake to me, Muse, the Man, who, after Troy
                                 was sack't,

troyes   frequency: 2   relative frequency: 0.00002
      p. 84 EPIGRAMS 133   4 With tales of Troyes iust knight, our faiths
                                 abuse:
      p. 315 HORACE 2   209 Of Diomede; nor Troyes sad Warre begins

troy's. See "troyes."

truch-man   frequency: 1   relative frequency: 0.00001
      p. 313 HORACE 2   157 Her truch-man, she reports the minds each throw.

true   frequency: 87   relative frequency: 0.00125
   See also "trew," "trve."
    **p. 114 PANEGYRE   42 The fittest herald to proclaime true ioyes:
      p. 29 EPIGRAMS 6   1 If all you boast of your great art be true;
      p. 32 EPIGRAMS 18   2 When both it is the old way, and the true.
      p. 39 EPIGRAMS 40   16 For wit, feature, and true passion,
      p. 47 EPIGRAMS 63   12 To so true worth, though thou thy selfe forbid.
      p. 50 EPIGRAMS 70   4 On the true causes, ere they grow too old.
      p. 51 EPIGRAMS 73   21 Fortie things more, deare GRAND, which you
                                 know true,
      p. 62 EPIGRAMS 95   36 That dares nor write things false, nor hide
                                 things true.
      p. 66 EPIGRAMS 102   14 And one true posture, though besieg'd with ill
      p. 67 EPIGRAMS 104   5 Or, because some scarce thinke that storie true,

true (cont.)

p.	68 EPIGRAMS 107	3	I oft looke on false coyne, to know't from true:
p.	70 EPIGRAMS 108	5	I sweare by your true friend, my Muse, I loue
p.	71 EPIGRAMS 110	17	Thy learned hand, and true Promethean art
p.	82 EPIGRAMS 130	18	Shed in thy Songs; 'tis true: but short of thee.
p.	108 FOREST 10	29	My owne true fire. Now my thought takes wing,
p.	108 FOREST 10 A	13	wch rap's mee vp to the true heau'en of loue;
p.	109 FOREST 11	1	Not to know vice at all, and keepe true state,
p.	109 FOREST 11	19	But this true course is not embrac'd by many:
p.	110 FOREST 11	43	In a continuall tempest. Now, true Loue
p.	116 FOREST 13	1	'Tis growne almost a danger to speake true
p.	117 FOREST 13	20	Or feare to draw true lines, 'cause others paint:
p.	130 UNDERWOOD 1.3	6	Yet search'd, and true they found it.
p.	136 UNDERWOOD 2.5	6	Love, and I have had; and true.
p.	138 UNDERWOOD 2.6	34	Guesse of these, which is the true;
p.	150 UNDERWOOD 11	2	I must the true Relation make,
p.	152 UNDERWOOD 12	21	'Tis true, he could not reprehend;
p.	157 UNDERWOOD 13	133	In time 'twill be a heape; This is not true
p.	158 UNDERWOOD 13	162	(As their true rule or lesson) either men,
p.	161 UNDERWOOD 14	73	It true respects. He will not only love,
p.	167 UNDERWOOD 15	176	Thy true friends wishes, Colby, which shall be,
p.	173 UNDERWOOD 22	16	And kept, and bred, and brought up true.
p.	177 UNDERWOOD 25	23	Of eyes more true,
p.	177 UNDERWOOD 25	26	True noblesse. Palme growes straight, though handled ne're so rude.
p.	180 UNDERWOOD 26	16	True valour doth her owne renowne command
p.	182 UNDERWOOD 28	6	To those true numerous Graces; whereof some,
p.	183 UNDERWOOD 29	3	True Conceipt,
p.	183 UNDERWOOD 29	7	Wresting words, from their true calling;
p.	184 UNDERWOOD 29	45	Of true measure,
p.	185 UNDERWOOD 30	7	The Orphans Pillar, the true Subjects shield,
p.	188 UNDERWOOD 34	5	Then this did by her true? She never sought
p.	189 UNDERWOOD 37	2	Next to your selfe, for making your love true:
p.	191 UNDERWOOD 38	1	'Tis true, I'm broke! Vowes, Oathes, and all I had
p.	194 UNDERWOOD 38	108	Then I will studie falshood, to be true.
p.	206 UNDERWOOD 43	76	The art of kindling the true Coale, by Lungs:
p.	210 UNDERWOOD 43	159	Hee is true Vulcan still! He did not spare
p.	210 UNDERWOOD 43	167	'Tis true, that in thy wish they were destroy'd,
p.	224 UNDERWOOD 50	20	As makes Penelopes old fable true,
p.	225 UNDERWOOD 50	32	Not boasted in your life, but practis'd true,
p.	227 UNDERWOOD 52	4	'Tis true, as my wombe swells, so my backe stoupes,
p.	233 UNDERWOOD 59	15	Of daring not to doe a wrong, is true
p.	235 UNDERWOOD 63	2	To God, denies the God-head to be true:
p.	241 UNDERWOOD 68	6	His Poet leave to sing his House-hold true;
p.	250 UNDERWOOD 73	10	To vertue, and true worth, be ever blind.
p.	269 UNDERWOOD 83	15	It is a large faire table, and a true,
p.	270 UNDERWOOD 83	38	But a fain'd way, doth rob it of the true.
p.	274 U'WOOD 84.2	13	And tell thou, ALDE-LEGH, None can tell more true
p.	278 U'WOOD 84.4	21	I call you Muse; now make it true:
p.	282 U'WOOD 84.8	21	'Tis Vertue alone, is true Nobilitie.
p.	288 U'WOOD 84.9	211	To him should be her Judge, true God, true Man,
p.	289 U'WOOD 84.9	227	That thus have ventur'd these true straines upon;
p.	293 UNDERWOOD 87	9	HOR. 'Tis true, I'am Thracian Chloes, I,
p.	307 HORACE 2	59	The vertue of which order, and true grace,
p.	327 HORACE 2	455	Thence draw forth true expressions. For, sometimes,
p.	333 HORACE 2	615	Cry, and doe more then the true Mourners: so
p.	333 HORACE 2	616	The Scoffer, the true Praiser doth out-goe.
p.	362 UNGATHERED 2	1	Thou, that wouldst finde the habit of true passion,
p.	362 UNGATHERED 2	11	Wants facultie to make a censure true:
p.	366 UNGATHERED 6	6	Betray it true:
p.	370 UNGATHERED 7	11	To iudge which Passion's false, and which is true,
p.	372 UNGATHERED 9	14	Might make the Fable of Good Women true.
p.	382 UNGATHERED 16	1	Two noble knightes, whome true desire and zeale,
p.	383 UNGATHERED 16	10	As true oblations; his Brothers Embleme sayes,
p.	384 UNGATHERED 18	5	Such weare true wedding robes, and are true freindes,
p.	389 UNGATHERED 24	10	As a deformed face doth a true glasse.
p.	390 UNGATHERED 26	5	'Tis true, and all mens suffrage. But these wayes
p.	394 UNGATHERED 28	14	Not vsuall in a Lady; and yet true:
p.	395 UNGATHERED 29	15	Taught Lucan these true moodes! Replyes my sence
p.	395 UNGATHERED 29	25	Your true freind in Iudgement and Choise

true (cont.)
    p. 396 UNGATHERED 30   5 Thy Muse, and mine, as they expect. 'Tis true:
    p. 403 UNGATHERED 34 42 You are ye Spectacles of State! Tis true
    p. 411 UNGATHERED 40   5 The motives, and true Spurres
    p. 415 UNGATHERED 42 20 Office of Wit, a Mint, and (this is true)
    p. 416 UNGATHERED 43   7 How they advance true Love, and neighbourhood,
    p. 419 UNGATHERED 48   2 Of that true fface
    p. 657 L. CONVIVALES 15 Tis the true Phoebeian Liquor,

true-filed   frequency: 1   relative frequency: 0.00001
    p. 392 UNGATHERED 26 68 In his well torned, and true-filed lines:

truely   frequency: 5   relative frequency: 0.00007
    p. 77 EPIGRAMS 120   16 He plai'd so truely.
    p. 104 FOREST 7   5 Say, are not women truely, then,
    p. 104 FOREST 7   11 Say, are not women truely, then,
    p. 354 HORACE 1   646 ... . truely ...
    p. 414 UNGATHERED 42   3 And truely, so I would, could I be heard.

truer   frequency: 2   relative frequency: 0.00002
    p. 39 EPIGRAMS 40   7 Expresser truth, or truer glorie,
    p. 166 UNDERWOOD 15 142 Is that the truer excuse? or have we got

truest   frequency: 2   relative frequency: 0.00002
    p. 105 FOREST 8   19 They maintayne the truest trade,
    p. 120 FOREST 13   122 Madame, be bold to vse this truest glasse:

trull   frequency: 1   relative frequency: 0.00001
    p. 86 EPIGRAMS 133   84 Made of the trull, that cut her fathers lock:

truly   frequency: 6   relative frequency: 0.00008
    See also "truely."
    p. 119 FOREST 13   110 They speake; since you are truly that rare wife,
    p. 128 UNDERWOOD 1.1 47 But in thy presence, truly glorified,
    p. 152 UNDERWOOD 12   35 For truly, since he left to be,
    p. 237 UNDERWOOD 64   18 The truly Epidemicall disease!
    p. 282 U'WOOD 84.9   t2 The truly honoured Lady, the Lady
                             VENETIA DIGBY;
    p. 370 UNGATHERED 7   1 In Picture, they which truly vnderstand,

truly-belou'd   frequency: 1   relative frequency: 0.00001
    p. 386 UNGATHERED 21 t1 To my truly-belou'd Freind,

truly-noble   frequency: 1   relative frequency: 0.00001
    p. 272 UNDERWOOD 84   t5 Of that truly-noble Lady, the Lady
                             VENETIA DIGBY,

trump   frequency: 1   relative frequency: 0.00001
    See also "trumpe."
    p. 269 UNDERWOOD 83   27 Their Carract was! I, or my trump must breake,

trumpe   frequency: 1   relative frequency: 0.00001
    p. 283 U'WOOD 84.9   46 In earth, till the last Trumpe awake the Sheepe

trumpet   frequency: 5   relative frequency: 0.00007
    p. 57 EPIGRAMS 89   5 Who had no lesse a trumpet of their name,
    p. 58 EPIGRAMS 91   7 When on thy trumpet shee did sound a blast,
    p. 154 UNDERWOOD 13   35 Or that doth sound a Trumpet, and doth call
    p. 319 HORACE 2   288 And rivall with the Trumpet for his sound,
    p. 396 UNGATHERED 30 14 Hot from thy trumpet, round, about the world.

trumpets   frequency: 4   relative frequency: 0.00005
    p. 213 UNDERWOOD 44   7 That we have Trumpets, Armour, and great
                             Horse,
    p. 239 UNDERWOOD 67   13 3. THAL. Yet, let our Trumpets sound;
    p. 249 UNDERWOOD 72   9 What Drums or Trumpets, or great Ord'nance
                             can,
    p. 396 UNGATHERED 30 66 How do his trumpets breath! What loud alarmes!

trundling   frequency: 1   relative frequency: 0.00001
    p. 331 HORACE 2   568 Or trundling Wheele, he can sit still, from all;

trussed. See "well-truss'd."

trust   frequency: 16   relative frequency: 0.00023
    p. 37 EPIGRAMS 34   2 Shewes of the resurrection little trust.
    p. 63 EPIGRAMS 97   13 He is no fauourites fauourite, no deare trust
    p. 63 EPIGRAMS 99   2 Better'd thy trust to letters; that thy skill;
    p. 114 FOREST 12   39 The world hath seene, which all these had in
                             trust,

trust (cont.)
```
   p. 169 UNDERWOOD 17     12 Simply my Band, his trust in me forsakes,
   p. 169 UNDERWOOD 17     14 Now so much friend, as you would trust in me,
   p. 171 UNDERWOOD 20      1 A Womans friendship! God whom I trust in,
   p. 171 UNDERWOOD 20      8 Put on for fashion, and take up on trust:
   p. 198 UNDERWOOD 40     39 To others, as he will deserve the Trust
   p. 203 UNDERWOOD 43    128 And safely trust to dresse, not burne their
                             Boates.
   p. 223 UNDERWOOD 49     21 What though she hath won on Trust, as many doe,
   p. 223 UNDERWOOD 49     29 And trust her I would least, that hath forswore
   p. 281 U'WOOD 84.8      16 It is a wretched thing to trust to reedes;
   p. 284 U'WOOD 84.9      62 Who in that feast of Resurrection trust!
   p. 378 UNGATHERED 11    80 Trie and trust Roger, was the word, but now
   p. 387 UNGATHERED 22     6 trust in the tombes, their care=full freinds do
                             rayse;
```

trusted   frequency: 5   relative frequency: 0.00007
```
   p. 113 FOREST 12        10 And some one apteth to be trusted, then,
   p. 158 UNDERWOOD 14      6 Was trusted, that you thought my judgement such
   p. 216 UNDERWOOD 45      7 Nor ever trusted to that friendship yet,
   p. 271 UNDERWOOD 83     81 And trusted so, as it deposited lay
   p. 283 U'WOOD 84.9      20 Beene trusted to thee: not to't selfe assign'd.
```

truster   frequency: 1   relative frequency: 0.00001
```
   p. 223 UNDERWOOD 49     22 And that her truster feares her? Must I too?
```

trusting   frequency: 1   relative frequency: 0.00001
```
   p. 375 UNGATHERED 10    34 Bvt here, neither trusting his hands, nor his
                             legs,
```

trusts   frequency: 1   relative frequency: 0.00001
```
   p.  70 EPIGRAMS 108      9 He that not trusts me, hauing vow'd thus much,
```

truth   frequency: 44   relative frequency: 0.00063
  See also "tell-troth."
```
 **p. 115 PANEGYRE         94 "To heare the truth, from spight, or flattery
                             voyd.
   p.  28 EPIGRAMS 5        2 Or celebrated with more truth of state?
   p.  31 EPIGRAMS 14      11 Pardon free truth, and let thy modestie,
   p.  39 EPIGRAMS 40       7 Expresser truth, or truer glorie,
   p.  49 EPIGRAMS 67       2 Most thinke all praises flatteries. But truth
                             brings
   p.  64 EPIGRAMS 99      12 Thy fact is more: let truth encourage thee.
   p.  68 EPIGRAMS 106      4 Truth might spend all her voyce, Fame all her
                             art.
   p.  75 EPIGRAMS 116     16 A desperate soloecisme in truth and wit.
   p.  78 EPIGRAMS 122      1 If I would wish, for truth, and not for show,
   p.  83 EPIGRAMS 131     11 And would (being ask'd the truth) ashamed say,
   p.  88 EPIGRAMS 133    147 For, to say truth, what scullion is so nastie,
   p.  99 FOREST 3         91 But thou, my WROTH, if I can truth apply,
   p. 114 FOREST 12        21 The truth of times) was once of more esteeme,
   p. 121 FOREST 14        52 If with this truth you be inspir'd,
   p. 131 UNDERWOOD 2.1    10 But the Language, and the Truth,
   p. 142 UNDERWOOD 2.9    52 As he durst love Truth and me.
   p. 158 UNDERWOOD 14      4 Truth, and the Graces best, when naked are.
   p. 159 UNDERWOOD 14     39 What fables have you vext! what truth redeem'd!
   p. 168 UNDERWOOD 15    179 That thou dost all things more for truth, then
                             glory,
   p. 170 UNDERWOOD 18     17 To see men feare: or else for truth, and State,
   p. 176 UNDERWOOD 24     10 Of Truth that searcheth the most <hidden>
                             Springs,
   p. 176 UNDERWOOD 24     18 The light of Truth, and life of Memorie.
   p. 181 UNDERWOOD 26     21 Such thoughts wil make you more in love with
                             truth.
   p. 186 UNDERWOOD 31     10 You favour Truth, and me, in this mans Cause.
   p. 213 UNDERWOOD 44     26 Of London, in the Militarie truth,
   p. 241 UNDERWOOD 69      5 Freedome, and Truth; with love from those begot:
   p. 265 UNDERWOOD 79     45 In truth of colours, both are best.
   p. 270 UNDERWOOD 83     35 And, calling truth to witnesse, make that good
   p. 307 HORACE 2         34 Are, with the likenesse of the truth, undone.
   p. 315 HORACE 2        216 Falshood with truth, as no man can espie
   p. 325 HORACE 2        439 Whether truth may, and whether error bring.
   p. 329 HORACE 2        508 The truth; nor let thy Fable thinke, what e're
   p. 333 HORACE 2        606 Whether his soothing friend speake truth, or no.
   p. 372 UNGATHERED 9     13 Vp so much truth, as could I it pursue
   p. 380 UNGATHERED 12    24 The truth of his heart there, and tell's what a
                             clocke
   p. 391 UNGATHERED 26    10 The truth, but gropes, and vrgeth all by chance;
   p. 393 UNGATHERED 27     1 Truth is the triall of it selfe,
   p. 396 UNGATHERED 30    13 Wonder to truth! and haue my Vision hoorld,
```

truth (cont.)
```
    p. 399 UNGATHERED 31     5 To veiw the truth and owne it. Doe but looke
    p. 404 UNGATHERED 34    57 But in ye practisd truth Destruction is
    p. 407 UNGATHERED 35    23 Or canst of truth ye least intrenchmt pitch,
    p. 414 UNGATHERED 42     4 You know, I never was of Truth afeard,
    p. 414 UNGATHERED 42     6 How well I lov'd Truth: I was scarce allow'd
    p. 657 L. CONVIVALES     6 Truth itself doth flow in Wine.
```

truthes   frequency: 1   relative frequency: 0.00001
```
    p. 118 FOREST 13        70 For truthes complexion, where they all weare
                               maskes.
```

truths   frequency: 2   relative frequency: 0.00002
See also "truthes."
```
    p.  50 EPIGRAMS 70       7 Then, since we (more then many) these truths
                               know:
    p. 246 UNDERWOOD 70     83 Such truths, as we expect for happy men,
```

trve   frequency: 1   relative frequency: 0.00001
```
    p.  69 EPIGRAMS 108     t1 TO TRVE SOVLDIERS.
```

try   frequency: 6   relative frequency: 0.00008
See also "trie."
```
    p. 139 UNDERWOOD 2.7    15 Joyne lip to lip, and try:
    p. 145 UNDERWOOD 5      17 And having pleas'd our art, wee'll try
    p. 278 U'WOOD 84.4      28 'Tis got where it can try the fire.
    p. 319 HORACE 2        321 The rough rude Satyres naked; and would try,
    p. 333 HORACE 2        618 And rack, with Wine, the man whom they would
                               try,
    p. 397 UNGATHERED 30    35 I thought thee then our Orpheus, that wouldst
                               try
```

tryals   frequency: 1   relative frequency: 0.00001
```
    p. 255 UNDERWOOD 75    103 Of Tryals, to worke downe
```

try'd   frequency: 2   relative frequency: 0.00002
```
    p. 119 FOREST 13       112 What your try'd manners are, what theirs should
                               bee.
    p. 421 UNGATHERED 49     7 O're read, examin'd, try'd, and prou'd yor: Ryme
```

tryer   frequency: 1   relative frequency: 0.00001
```
    p. 278 U'WOOD 84.4      27 And so disdaining any tryer;
```

tub   frequency: 2   relative frequency: 0.00002
```
   *p. 493 TO HIMSELF       25 Throwne forth, and rak't into the common tub,
    p. 291 UNDERWOOD 85     47 And from the sweet Tub Wine of this yeare
                               takes,
```

tubs. See "night-tubs."

tuileries. See "tuilleries."

tuilleries   frequency: 1   relative frequency: 0.00001
```
    p.  69 EPIGRAMS 107     22 Ianin's, your Nuncio's, and your Tuilleries,
```

tumor   frequency: 1   relative frequency: 0.00001
```
    p. 184 UNDERWOOD 29     56 The cold tumor in his feet,
```

tumults   frequency: 1   relative frequency: 0.00001
```
    p. 110 FOREST 11        33 Most frequent tumults, horrors, and vnrests,
```

tun   frequency: 1   relative frequency: 0.00001
```
    p. 227 UNDERWOOD 52      6 But yet the Tun at Heidelberg had houpes.
```

tune   frequency: 7   relative frequency: 0.00010
```
    p.  88 EPIGRAMS 133    164 And, in a pittious tune, began. How dare
    p. 107 FOREST 10         9 And foundred thy hot teame, to tune my lay.
    p. 253 UNDERWOOD 75     15 Or were Affaires in tune,
    p. 261 UNDERWOOD 77     27 Unto your honour: I can tune in song
    p. 319 HORACE 2        290 And tune too, fitted to the Chorus rime,
    p. 411 UNGATHERED 39    12 A Tune to drown the Ballads of thy Father:
    p. 411 UNGATHERED 39    14 But Tune and Noise the Eccho of thy Shame.
```

tunes   frequency: 6   relative frequency: 0.00008
See also "sister-tunes."
```
    p. 143 UNDERWOOD 3      15 No tunes are sweet, nor words have sting,
    p. 182 UNDERWOOD 27     35 Yet sure my tunes will be the best,
    p. 319 HORACE 2        299 Both in their tunes, the licence greater grew,
    p. 329 HORACE 2        498 Attempted by the Muses tunes, and strings;
    p. 367 UNGATHERED 6     36 Thy tunes alone;
```

tunes (cont.)
    p. 420 UNGATHERED 48   22 Their labour'd tunes reherse,

tuning   frequency: 1   relative frequency: 0.00001
    *p. 494 TO HIMSELF   59 In tuning forth the acts of his sweet raigne:

turbot   frequency: 1   relative frequency: 0.00001
    p. 291 UNDERWOOD 85   50 Nor Turbot, nor bright Golden-eyes:

turkey. See "turkie."

turkie   frequency: 2   relative frequency: 0.00002
    p. 69 EPIGRAMS 107   13 In Hungary, and Poland, Turkie too;
    p. 260 UNDERWOOD 77   3 Of Noremberg, or Turkie; hang your roomes

turn. See "counter-turne," "turne."

turnd   frequency: 1   relative frequency: 0.00001
    p. 417 UNGATHERED 45   14 those turnd vp, and those that fall,

turn'd   frequency: 5   relative frequency: 0.00007
    *p. 493 TO HIMSELF   39 Which, if they are torne, and turn'd, &
                       patch't enough,
    p. 39 EPIGRAMS 41   1 GYPSEE, new baud, is turn'd physitian,
    p. 77 EPIGRAMS 120   10 When Fates turn'd cruell,
    p. 149 UNDERWOOD 8   8 Turn'd to cinders by her eye?
    p. 237 UNDERWOOD 64   20 Is Banke-rupt turn'd! the Cassock, Cloake, and
                       Gowne,

turne   frequency: 22   relative frequency: 0.00031
    p. 56 EPIGRAMS 88   16 Daily to turne in PAVLS, and helpe the
                       trade.
    p. 80 EPIGRAMS 128   4 And those to turne to bloud, and make thine owne:
    p. 107 FOREST 10   20 Turne the stale prologue to some painted maske,
    p. 112 FOREST 11   95 And turne the blackest sorrowes to bright ioyes:
    p. 114 FOREST 12   29 Turne, vpon scorned verse, their quarter-face:
    p. 143 UNDERWOOD 3   4 And all the world turne Eares.
    p. 155 UNDERWOOD 13   81 All as their prize, turne Pyrats here at Land,
    p. 159 UNDERWOOD 14   23 Since, being deceiv'd, I turne a sharper eye
    p. 197 UNDERWOOD 40   11 And turne the Ceremonies of those Nights
    p. 216 UNDERWOOD 45   21 Turne him, and see his Threds: looke, if he be
    p. 242 UNDERWOOD 70   t3+ The Turne.
    p. 244 UNDERWOOD 70   32+ The Turne.
    p. 245 UNDERWOOD 70   64+ The Turne.
    p. 246 UNDERWOOD 70   96+ The Turne.
    p. 291 UNDERWOOD 85   68 To turne mere farmer, had spoke out,
    p. 321 HORACE 2   330 And so to turne all earnest into jest,
    p. 323 HORACE 2   398 In hand, and turne them over, day, and night.
    p. 364 UNGATHERED 4   4 Do turne into a Woman.
    p. 384 UNGATHERED 18   18 And eue'ry ioy, in mariage, turne a fruite.
    p. 387 UNGATHERED 22   4 will all turne dust, & may not make me swell.
    p. 392 UNGATHERED 26   61 Vpon the Muses anuile: turne the same,
    p. 406 UNGATHERED 34   102 Againe, thy Architect to ashes turne!

turned   frequency: 3   relative frequency: 0.00004
    See also "ill-torn'd," "torned," "turnd,"
            "turn'd."
    p. 283 U'WOOD 84.9   31 Am turned with an others powers. My Passion
    p. 291 UNDERWOOD 85   64 And fainting necks, the turned Share!
    p. 335 HORACE 2   635 Blot out the carelesse, with his turned pen;

turners   frequency: 1   relative frequency: 0.00001
    p. 188 UNDERWOOD 34   11 Or Turners oyle of Talck. Nor ever got

turnes   frequency: 3   relative frequency: 0.00004
    p. 215 UNDERWOOD 44   77 That turnes us so much moneys, at which rate
    p. 236 UNDERWOOD 64   5 And as it turnes our joyfull yeare about,
    p. 311 HORACE 2   126 If now the turnes, the colours, and right hues

turning   frequency: 5   relative frequency: 0.00007
    p. 40 EPIGRAMS 42   8 The like is IONE. But turning home, is sad.
    p. 118 FOREST 13   64 Which though the turning world may dis-esteeme,
    p. 154 UNDERWOOD 13   56 Then turning unto him is next at hand,
    p. 197 UNDERWOOD 40   22 And turning all he toucheth into pelfe,
    p. 339 HORACE 1   56 .... be turning ..

turns   frequency: 1   relative frequency: 0.00001
    See also "turnes."
    p. 153 UNDERWOOD 13   2 Great and good turns, as wel could time them too,

turnst   frequency: 1   relative frequency: 0.00001
    p. 407 UNGATHERED 35   22 But when thou turnst a Reall Inigo;

turpins   frequency: 1   relative frequency: 0.00001
    p. 206 UNDERWOOD 43   69 The Tristrams, Lanc'lots, Turpins, and the
                              Peers,

turtles   frequency: 2   relative frequency: 0.00002
    p. 111 FOREST 11   74 Turtles can chastly dye;
    p. 364 UNGATHERED 4   5 Or (by our Turtles Augure)

tusk. See "tuske."

tuske   frequency: 1   relative frequency: 0.00001
    p. 69 EPIGRAMS 107   29 Nay, now you puffe, tuske, and draw vp your chin,

tut   frequency: 1   relative frequency: 0.00001
    p. 45 EPIGRAMS 56   9 And, told of this, he slights it. Tut, such
                              crimes

tutor   frequency: 2   relative frequency: 0.00002
    p. 88 EPIGRAMS 133   157 Graue tutor to the learned horse. Both which,
    p. 215 UNDERWOOD 44   66 Borne, bred, allied? what's he dare tutor us?

'twas   frequency: 14   relative frequency: 0.00020

twedes   frequency: 1   relative frequency: 0.00001
    p. 368 UNGATHERED 6   72 To Loumond lake, and Twedes blacke-springing
                              fountaine.

tweed's. See "twedes."

'tweene   frequency: 2   relative frequency: 0.00002
    p. 113 FOREST 12   16 Runs betweene man, and man; 'tweene dame, and
                              dame;
    p. 258 UNDERWOOD 75   173 And 'tweene their Grandsires thighes,

twelue   frequency: 2   relative frequency: 0.00002
    p. 59 EPIGRAMS 92   14 For twelue yeeres yet to come, what each state
                              lacks.
    p. 59 EPIGRAMS 92   19 Keepe a starre-chamber sentence close, twelue
                              dayes:

twelve   frequency: 1   relative frequency: 0.00001
See also "twelue," "twice-twelve-yeares."
    p. 327 HORACE 2   469 A third of twelve, you may: foure ounces. Glad,

twentie   frequency: 4   relative frequency: 0.00005
    p. 58 EPIGRAMS 92   4 At sixe and twentie, ripe. You shall 'hem meet,
    p. 200 UNDERWOOD 42   29 But I who live, and have liv'd twentie yeare
    p. 229 UNDERWOOD 54   12 Full twentie stone; of which I lack two pound:
    p. 243 UNDERWOOD 70   31 How well at twentie had he falne, or stood!

twentieth   frequency: 1   relative frequency: 0.00001
See also "twenti'th."
    p. 43 EPIGRAMS 51   t3 and twentieth day of March,

twenti'th   frequency: 1   relative frequency: 0.00001
    p. 240 UNDERWOOD 67   48 Her two and twenti'th yeare!

twenty   frequency: 2   relative frequency: 0.00002
See also "twentie."
  *p. 493 TO HIMSELF   38 Wrought vpon twenty blocks:
    p. 230 UNDERWOOD 56   11 His weight is twenty Stone within two pound;

'twere   frequency: 7   relative frequency: 0.00010

twi-   frequency: 1   relative frequency: 0.00001
    p. 246 UNDERWOOD 70   92 To separate these twi-

twi-light   frequency: 1   relative frequency: 0.00001
    p. 66 EPIGRAMS 103   2 That but the twi-light of your sprite did see,

twice   frequency: 8   relative frequency: 0.00011
    See also "twise."
 **p. 117 PANEGYRE   160 With a twice louder shoute againe they cry'd,
    p. 152 UNDERWOOD 12   26 As twice to trespasse in his sight,
    p. 223 UNDERWOOD 49   30 In Contract twice, what can shee perjure more?
    p. 240 UNDERWOOD 67   38 Hath taken twice the Ring
    p. 292 UNDERWOOD 86   25 There twice a day in sacred Laies,

twice (cont.)
    p. 329 HORACE 2   535 Twice, or thrice good, I wonder: but am more
    p. 333 HORACE 2   626 And twice, or thrice had 'ssayd it, still in
                                vaine:
    p. 405 UNGATHERED 34   90 Thy twice conceyud, thrice payd for Imagery?

twice-twelve-yeares   frequency: 1   relative frequency: 0.00001
    p. 207 UNDERWOOD 43   101 And twice-twelve-yeares stor'd up humanitie,

twilight   frequency: 1   relative frequency: 0.00001
    See also "twi-light."
    p. 273 U'WOOD 84.1   15 May something by that twilight see

twilights. See "twi-."

t'will   frequency: 1   relative frequency: 0.00001

'twill   frequency: 5   relative frequency: 0.00007

twine   frequency: 2   relative frequency: 0.00002
    p. 107 FOREST 10   12 In the greene circle of thy Iuy twine.
    p. 290 UNDERWOOD 85   9 The Poplar tall, he then doth marrying twine

twins   frequency: 1   relative frequency: 0.00001
    p. 315 HORACE 2   210 From the two Egges, that did disclose the twins.

twirl. See "twirle."

twirle   frequency: 1   relative frequency: 0.00001
    p.   69 EPIGRAMS 107   30 Twirle the poore chaine you run a feasting in.

twise   frequency: 2   relative frequency: 0.00002
    p.   69 EPIGRAMS 107   18 Then can a flea at twise skip i'the Map.
    p.   76 EPIGRAMS 118   2 So all his meate he tasteth ouer, twise:

twixt   frequency: 3   relative frequency: 0.00004
    p. 380 UNGATHERED 12   53 In a Cart twixt Montrell and Abbeuile.
    p. 395 UNGATHERED 29   18 Are still th'interpreters twixt godds, and men!
    p. 415 UNGATHERED 43   2 Twixt Cotswold, and the Olimpicke exercise:

'twixt   frequency: 4   relative frequency: 0.00005
    p.   52 EPIGRAMS 75   2 'Twixt puritanes, and players, as some cry;
    p. 156 UNDERWOOD 13   106 'Twixt feare and rashnesse: not a lust obscene,
    p. 271 UNDERWOOD 83   67 'Twixt death and life! Where her mortalitie
    p. 374 UNGATHERED 10   13 Hee's carried 'twixt Montrell and Abbeuile.

two   frequency: 44   relative frequency: 0.00063
    p.   28 EPIGRAMS 4   3 But two things, rare, the FATES had in their
                                store,
    p.   28 EPIGRAMS 5   4 The spoused paire two realmes, the sea the ring.
    p.   31 EPIGRAMS 13   3 Let me giue two: that doubly am got free,
    p.   33 EPIGRAMS 21   3 His clothes two fashions of, and poore! his sword
    p.   37 EPIGRAMS 32   1 What two braue perills of the priuate sword
    p.   43 EPIGRAMS 51   t2 Vpon the happy false rumour of his death, the two
    p.   49 EPIGRAMS 68   3 Two kindes of valour he doth shew, at ones;
    p.   51 EPIGRAMS 73   7 Item, a tale or two, some fortnight after;
    p.   54 EPIGRAMS 81   3 Or that I'haue by, two good sufficient men,
    p.   60 EPIGRAMS 93   5 Two brauely in the battaile fell, and dy'd,
    p.   60 EPIGRAMS 93   7 And two, that would haue falne as great, as they,
    p.   68 EPIGRAMS 107   6 How great you were with their two Emperours;
    p.   76 EPIGRAMS 119   4 Shuns prease, for two maine causes, poxe, and
                                debt,
    p.   84 EPIGRAMS 133   12 And in it, two more horride knaues, then
                                CHARON.
    p.   84 EPIGRAMS 133   21 I sing the braue aduenture of two wights,
    p.   86 EPIGRAMS 133   67 Betweene two walls; where, on one side, to scar
                                men,
    p. 121 FOREST 14   50 To liue vntill to morrow' hath lost two dayes.
    p. 161 UNDERWOOD 14   81 The Gaine of your two friendships! Hayward and
    p. 161 UNDERWOOD 14   82 Selden! two Names that so much understand!
    p. 172 UNDERWOOD 21   3 Two letters were enough the plague to teare
    p. 192 UNDERWOOD 38   42 Or two, 'or three, a Sonne will dis-inherit,
    p. 209 UNDERWOOD 43   135 I saw with two poore Chambers taken in,
    p. 222 UNDERWOOD 49   15 What though she ride two mile on Holy-dayes
    p. 229 UNDERWOOD 54   12 Full twentie stone; of which I lack two pound:
    p. 230 UNDERWOOD 56   11 His weight is twenty Stone within two pound.
    p. 238 UNDERWOOD 65   11 And threat' the great Eclipse. Two houres but
                                runne,
    p. 240 UNDERWOOD 67   48 Her two and twenti'th yeare!
    p. 246 UNDERWOOD 70   98 Two names of friendship, but one Starre:

two (cont.)
    p. 247 UNDERWOOD 70   125 Of two so early men,
    p. 254 UNDERWOOD 75   51 Porting the Ensignes of united Two,
    p. 255 UNDERWOOD 75   77 Save the preceding Two?
    p. 257 UNDERWOOD 75   139 These two, now holy Church hath made them one,
    p. 274 U'WOOD 84.2   5 Gave two such Houses as
                              NORTHUMBERLAND,
    p. 284 U'WOOD 84.9   55 Those other two; which must be judg'd, or
                              crown'd:
    p. 287 U'WOOD 84.9   157 And to that forme, lent two such veines of blood
    p. 305 HORACE 2   19 A Scarlet peece, or two, stitch'd in: when or
    p. 315 HORACE 2   210 From the two Egges, that did disclose the twins.
    p. 323 HORACE 2   371 Two rests, a short and long, th'Iambick frame;
    p. 382 UNGATHERED 16   1 Two noble knightes, whome true desire and zeale,
    p. 382 UNGATHERED 16   5 The elder of these two, riche hopes Increase,
    p. 382 UNGATHERED 16   t2 behalfe of the two noble Brothers sr Robert
                              & sr Henrye
    p. 398 UNGATHERED 30   81 As, on two flowry Carpets, that did rise,
    p. 401 UNGATHERED 33   4 Of two, the choicest Paire of Mans delights,
    p. 415 UNGATHERED 42   24 And a Comptroller, two most rigid men

two-fold   frequency: 1   relative frequency: 0.00001
    p. 414 UNGATHERED 41   52 Till he hath reach'd his two-fold point of
                              Noone.

tybers   frequency: 1   relative frequency: 0.00001
    p. 293 UNDERWOOD 86   40 Or Tybers winding streames, I follow thee.

tye   frequency: 1   relative frequency: 0.00001
    p. 50 EPIGRAMS 88   4 And shooe, and tye, and garter should come
                              hether,

tyes   frequency: 1   relative frequency: 0.00001
    p. 62 EPIGRAMS 97   5 His rosie tyes and garters so ore-blowne,

tygres   frequency: 1   relative frequency: 0.00001
    p. 305 HORACE 2   16 With Doves; or Lambes, with Tygres coupled be.

tyke   frequency: 1   relative frequency: 0.00001
See also "tike."
    p. 409 UNGATHERED 37   14 If such a Tyke as thou, er'e wer't, or noe?

tylting   frequency: 1   relative frequency: 0.00001
    p. 382 UNGATHERED 16   t1 A speach presented vnto king James at a tylting
                              in the

tyme   frequency: 2   relative frequency: 0.00002
    p. 420 UNGATHERED 48   32 And once more stryke the eare of tyme wth those
                              ffresh straynes:
    p. 421 UNGATHERED 49   6 I haue, wth strict advantage of ffree tyme

tymes   frequency: 1   relative frequency: 0.00001
    p. 419 UNGATHERED 48   1 Yff Men, and tymes were nowe

tympanies   frequency: 1   relative frequency: 0.00001
    p. 35 EPIGRAMS 28   7 H'has tympanies of businesse, in his face,

tyndarides   frequency: 1   relative frequency: 0.00001
    p. 115 FOREST 12   58 Vnto the starres? or the Tyndarides?

tyne. See "tine."

type   frequency: 1   relative frequency: 0.00001
    p. 364 UNGATHERED 4   8 But a bare Type and Figure.

tyran   frequency: 1   relative frequency: 0.00001
    p. 184 UNDERWOOD 29   46 Tyran Rime hath so abused,

tyran'   frequency: 1   relative frequency: 0.00001
  **p. 115 PANEGYRE   99 "Where lawes were made to serue the tyran' will;

tyrannie   frequency: 1   relative frequency: 0.00001
    p. 190 UNDERWOOD 37   25 It is an Act of tyrannie, not love,

tyranny. See "tyrannie."

tyrant. See "tyran," "tyran'."

tyrants   frequency: 2   relative frequency: 0.00002
    p. 145 UNDERWOOD 5   2 The fooles, or Tyrants with your friends,

tyrants (cont.)
    p. 423 UNGATHERED 50   19 That prince that shames a tyrants name to beare,

tyre   frequency: 2   relative frequency: 0.00002
  **p. 114 PANEGYRE   54 Her brightest tyre; and, in it, equall shone
    p. 68 EPIGRAMS 105   9 And, drest in shepheards tyre, who would not say:

tyre-man   frequency: 1   relative frequency: 0.00001
    p. 402 UNGATHERED 34   16 Of Tyre-man, Mounte-banck & Iustice
                                Iones,

tyrtaeus   frequency: 2   relative frequency: 0.00002
    p. 327 HORACE 2   493 Next these great Homer and Tyrtaeus set
    p. 398 UNGATHERED 30   68 With bold Tyrtaeus verse, when thou art nam'd,

udders   frequency: 1   relative frequency: 0.00001
    p. 291 UNDERWOOD 85   46 Their swelling udders doth draw dry:

ugly. See "vgly."

ulcers. See "vlcers."

ulisses   frequency: 1   relative frequency: 0.00001
    p. 224 UNDERWOOD 50   21 Whilst your Ulisses hath ta'ne leave to goe,

ulysses. See "ulisses," "vlysses."

un-appeas'd   frequency: 1   relative frequency: 0.00001
    p. 313 HORACE 2   172 Keepe him still active, angry, un-appeas'd,

un-becomming   frequency: 1   relative frequency: 0.00001
    p. 148 UNDERWOOD 7   31 One un-becomming thought doth move

un-common   frequency: 1   relative frequency: 0.00001
    p. 239 UNDERWOOD 67   3 Some brave un-common way:

un-inform'd   frequency: 1   relative frequency: 0.00001
    p. 286 U'WOOD 84.9   149 Himselfe so un-inform'd of his elect,

un-wasted   frequency: 1   relative frequency: 0.00001
    p. 413 UNGATHERED 41   24 In Moses bush, un-wasted in the fire.

unaltered. See "vnalter'd."

unappeased. See "un-appeas'd."

unaptly   frequency: 1   relative frequency: 0.00001
    p. 315 HORACE 2   200 Who nought assaies unaptly, or amisse?

unargued. See "vn-argued."

unarmed. See "vn-arm'd."

unavoided. See "vn-auoided."

unbearded   frequency: 1   relative frequency: 0.00001
    See also "th'unbearded."
    p. 344 HORACE 1   229 The unbearded ....

unbecoming. See "un-becomming."

unblessed. See "unblest," "vnblest."

unblest   frequency: 1   relative frequency: 0.00001
    p. 149 UNDERWOOD 8   9 Yes; and in death, as life, unblest,

unbought   frequency: 1   relative frequency: 0.00001
    See also "vn-bought."
    p. 291 UNDERWOOD 85   48 And unbought viands ready makes:

unbounded. See "vnbounded."

unbroke. See "vnbroke."

uncensur'd   frequency: 1   relative frequency: 0.00001
    p. 319 HORACE 2   297 And they uncensur'd might at Feasts, and Playes

uncertainty. See "th'uncertainty."

unchaste   frequency: 1   relative frequency: 0.00001
    p. 137 UNDERWOOD 2.5   42 All is Venus: save unchaste.

unclean. See "uncleane."

uncleane   frequency: 1   relative frequency: 0.00001
    p. 321 HORACE 2   359 Or crack out bawdie speeches, and uncleane.

uncleannesse   frequency: 1   relative frequency: 0.00001
    p. 152 UNDERWOOD 12   17 So of uncleannesse, or offence,

uncomely   frequency: 2   relative frequency: 0.00002
    p. 293 UNDERWOOD 86   36 With an uncomely silence failes my tongue?
    p. 305 HORACE 2   5 Which in some swarthie fish uncomely ends:

uncommon. See "un-common."

uncontrol'd   frequency: 1   relative frequency: 0.00001
    p. 274 U'WOOD 84.2   1 I sing the just, and uncontrol'd Descent

uncontrolled. See "uncontrol'd."

uncovers. See "vncouers."

under   frequency: 10   relative frequency: 0.00014
    See also "vnder," "vnder-carued."
    p. 130 UNDERWOOD 1.2   32 Under his Crosse.
    p. 150 UNDERWOOD 10   9 But under the Disguise of love,
    p. 157 UNDERWOOD 13   141 It was erected; and still walking under
    p. 166 UNDERWOOD 15   128 But both fell prest under the load they make.
    p. 197 UNDERWOOD 40   10 Under another Name, I take your health;
    p. 199 UNDERWOOD 41   7 And we were left under that Hemisphere,
    p. 202 UNDERWOOD 42   83 Under that cover; an old Mid-wives hat!
    p. 213 UNDERWOOD 44   20 Under the Auspice of young Swynnerton.
    p. 286 U'WOOD 84.9   147 Nor dare we under blasphemy conceive
    p. 354 HORACE 1   647 Under ... angry ....

under-heares   frequency: 1   relative frequency: 0.00001
    p. 219 UNDERWOOD 47   49 Although my Fame, to his, not under-heares,

underneath. See "vnder-reath."

understand   frequency: 8   relative frequency: 0.00011
    See also "vnderstand."
    p. 154 UNDERWOOD 13   54 My Sword ('tis but a poore Sword, understand)
    p. 161 UNDERWOOD 14   82 Selden! two Names that so much understand!
    p. 169 UNDERWOOD 17   10 I adde that (but) because I understand
    p. 216 UNDERWOOD 45   25 Then rest, and a friends value understand,
    p. 268 UNDERWOOD 82   5 Would they would understand it! Princes are
    p. 271 UNDERWOOD 83   78 If you not understand, what Child you had.
    p. 276 U'WOOD 84.3   11 Hee shall, if he can understand,
    p. 331 HORACE 2   547 And, of your selfe too, understand; yet mind

understanding   frequency: 1   relative frequency: 0.00001
    p. 414 UNGATHERED 42   7 By those deepe-grounded, understanding men,

understands   frequency: 1   relative frequency: 0.00001
    p. 234 UNDERWOOD 61   8 To lift to heaven: who is't not understands

understood   frequency: 7   relative frequency: 0.00010
    See also "vnderstood."
    p. 142 U'WOOD 2.10   6 All I wish is understood.
    p. 152 UNDERWOOD 12   31 But that I understood him scant.
    p. 156 UNDERWOOD 13   112 And where they want, she is not understood.
    p. 167 UNDERWOOD 15   166 The life, and fame-vaynes (yet not understood
    p. 168 UNDERWOOD 15   188 And from that thought strive to be understood.
    p. 176 UNDERWOOD 24   7 But both might know their wayes were understood,
    p. 217 UNDERWOOD 46   6 In others evill best was understood:

undertakes. See "vnder-takes."

underwood. See "vnder-wood."

undone   frequency: 3   relative frequency: 0.00004
    p. 150 UNDERWOOD 11   3 I am undone to night;
    p. 283 U'WOOD 84.9   21 Looke on thy sloth, and give thy selfe undone,
    p. 307 HORACE 2   34 Are, with the likenesse of the truth, undone.

unequal. See "unequall."

unequall   frequency: 1   relative frequency: 0.00001
    p. 309 HORACE 2   107 In Verse unequall match'd, first sowre Laments,

unfit. See "vnfit."

unfold   frequency: 1   relative frequency: 0.00001
    p. 216 UNDERWOOD 45   19 But these with wearing will themselves unfold:

unfolds. See "vnfolds."

unfortunate   frequency: 1   relative frequency: 0.00001
    p. 177 UNDERWOOD 25   27 Nor thinke your selfe unfortunate,

unfound. See "vnfound."

unfrighted. See "vnfrighted."

ungrateful. See "ingratefull," "th'ingratefull."

unheard   frequency: 1   relative frequency: 0.00001
    p. 309 HORACE 2   71 Faine words, unheard of to the well-truss'd race

unhurt. See "vn-hurt."

uninformed. See "un-inform'd."

union   frequency: 4   relative frequency: 0.00005
    See also "vnion."
    p. 128 UNDERWOOD 1.1   34 A Trinitie, to shine in Union;
    p. 221 UNDERWOOD 48   44 In great Saint Georges Union;
    p. 246 UNDERWOOD 70   99 Of hearts the union. And those not by chance
    p. 286 U'WOOD 84.9   128 God, in the Union, and the Trinitie!

united   frequency: 1   relative frequency: 0.00001
    p. 254 UNDERWOOD 75   51 Porting the Ensignes of united Two,

unitie   frequency: 3   relative frequency: 0.00004
    p. 127 UNDERWOOD 1.1   2 Of persons, still one God, in Unitie,
    p. 128 UNDERWOOD 1.1   30 Of persons, still one God in Unitie;
    p. 128 UNDERWOOD 1.1   39 Distinct in persons, yet in Unitie

unity. See "unitie," "vnitie."

universal. See "vniuersall."

universe   frequency: 2   relative frequency: 0.00002
    p. 185 UNDERWOOD 30   4 Thy Universe, though his Epitome.
    p. 276 U'WOOD 84.3   18 The Cloud, and show the Universe;

unjust   frequency: 2   relative frequency: 0.00002
    p. 162 UNDERWOOD 15   12 His unjust hopes, with praises begg'd, or (worse)
    p. 192 UNDERWOOD 38   50 Before you prove a medicine, is unjust.

unkind   frequency: 1   relative frequency: 0.00001
    See also "vnkinde."
    p. 180 UNDERWOOD 26   12 You are unkind.

unknown. See "unknowne," "vnknowne."

unknowne   frequency: 3   relative frequency: 0.00004
    p. 179 UNDERWOOD 25   56 Unknowne which is the Dearest)
    p. 313 HORACE 2   186 First publish things unspoken, and unknowne.
    p. 319 HORACE 2   313 Till then unknowne, in Carts, wherein did ride

unlaid. See "unlay'd."

unlay'd   frequency: 1   relative frequency: 0.00001
    p. 259 UNDERWOOD 76   24 But we last out, still unlay'd.

unlearn'd   frequency: 1   relative frequency: 0.00001
    p. 337 HORACE 2   677 Learn'd and unlearn'd; holding, whom once he
                              takes;

unlearned. See "unlearn'd," "vnlearned."

unless. See "unlesse."

unlesse   frequency: 3   relative frequency: 0.00004
    p. 140 UNDERWOOD 2.8   29 Make accompt, unlesse you can,
    p. 147 UNDERWOOD 7   14 Unlesse my heart would as my thought be torne.

unlesse (cont.)
   p. 248 UNDERWOOD 71   13 Unlesse some saving-Honour of the Crowne,

unlike   frequency: 2   relative frequency: 0.00002
   See also "vnlike."
   p. 242 UNDERWOOD 69   13 Till he had sold his Piece, drawne so unlike:
   p. 248 UNDERWOOD 71   11 Fix'd to the bed, and boords, unlike to win

unlock. See "vnlocke."

unlucky. See "vnluckie."

unmakest. See "vnmak'st."

unnamed. See "vn-nam'd."

unnatural. See "vnnaturall."

unnecessarie   frequency: 1   relative frequency: 0.00001
   p. 214 UNDERWOOD 44   32 For that unnecessarie Charge they were.

unnecessary. See "unnecessarie."

unprofitable   frequency: 1   relative frequency: 0.00001
   p. 230 UNDERWOOD 56   8 Unprofitable Chattell, fat and old,

unprofiting. See "vnprofiting."

unproved   frequency: 1   relative frequency: 0.00001
   See also "vnprou'd."
   p. 323 HORACE 2   405 Our Poets, too, left nought unproved here;

unrepair'd   frequency: 1   relative frequency: 0.00001
   p. 211 UNDERWOOD 43   196 Losse, remaines yet, as unrepair'd as mine.

unrests. See "vnrests."

unsatisfied. See "vnsatisfied."

unseasoned. See "vnseason'd."

unshaken   frequency: 1   relative frequency: 0.00001
   p. 185 UNDERWOOD 30   11 But stood unshaken in his Deeds, and Name,

unskilfull   frequency: 1   relative frequency: 0.00001
   p. 331 HORACE 2   567 Or, who's unskilfull at the Coit, or Ball,

unsounder   frequency: 1   relative frequency: 0.00001
   p. 184 UNDERWOOD 29   57 Grow unsounder.

unspoken   frequency: 1   relative frequency: 0.00001
   p. 313 HORACE 2   186 First publish things unspoken, and unknowne.

unsweet. See "vn-sweet."

untaught. See "vn-taught."

unthankfull   frequency: 1   relative frequency: 0.00001
   p. 172 UNDERWOOD 21   8 That thought can adde, unthankfull, the lay-stall

unthought   frequency: 1   relative frequency: 0.00001
   p. 283 U'WOOD 84.9   44 And left her lovely body unthought dead!

unthrittily. See "vnthriftely."

untie   frequency: 2   relative frequency: 0.00002
   p. 132 UNDERWOOD 2.2   11 And (withall) I did untie
   p. 257 UNDERWOOD 75   136 With all corroding Arts, be able to untie!

until. See "untill," "vntill."

untill   frequency: 2   relative frequency: 0.00002
   p. 129 UNDERWOOD 1.2   15 Untill they meet
   p. 140 UNDERWOOD 2.8   11 As, untill she tell her one,

unto   frequency: 39 relative frequency: 0.00056
   See also "vnto."

untouched. See "vntouch'd."

untravelled. See "vntrauell'd."

untwisted   frequency: 1   relative frequency: 0.00001
    p. 415 UNGATHERED 42   14 And weigh'd your Play: untwisted ev'ry thread,

untying   frequency: 1   relative frequency: 0.00001
    p. 317 HORACE 2   274 Worth his untying happen there: And not

unused   frequency: 1   relative frequency: 0.00001
    See also "the'vn-vsed."
    p. 264 UNDERWOOD 79   21 That drives the Hart to seeke unused wayes,

unvulgar   frequency: 1   relative frequency: 0.00001
    p. 177 UNDERWOOD 25   13 That I may sing my thoughts, in some unvulgar
                              straine.

unwasted. See "un-wasted."

unwearied. See "unweary'd," "vnwearied."

unweary'd   frequency: 1   relative frequency: 0.00001
    p. 159 UNDERWOOD 14   37 T<o>'instruct and teach? or your unweary'd paine

unweave   frequency: 1   relative frequency: 0.00001
    p. 142 UNDERWOOD 2.9   50 Nor tie knots, nor knots unweave;

unwelcome. See "vn-welccme."

unwieldy. See "too'vnwieldie."

unwonted   frequency: 1   relative frequency: 0.00001
    p. 319 HORACE 2   308 Unwonted language; and that sense of worth

unworthy   frequency: 2   relative frequency: 0.00002
    See also "vnworthy."
    p. 321 HORACE 2   337 And farre unworthy to blurt out light rimes;
    p. 323 HORACE 2   389 And there is given too unworthy leave

up   frequency: 58   relative frequency: 0.00083
    See also "me'vp," "vp," "vp-beare."
    p. 127 UNDERWOOD 1.1   5 2. My selfe up to thee, harrow'd, torne, and
                              bruis'd
    p. 142 UNDERWOOD 2.9   40 Or were set up in a Brake.
    p. 146 UNDERWOOD 6   1 Hang up those dull, and envious fooles,
    p. 155 UNDERWOOD 13   69 And spunge-like with it dry up the blood quite:
    p. 157 UNDERWOOD 13   142 Meet some new matter to looke up and wonder!
    p. 161 UNDERWOOD 14   83 On whom I could take up, and ne're abuse
    p. 163 UNDERWOOD 15   44 To make up Greatnesse! and mans whole good fix'd
    p. 166 UNDERWOOD 15   137 To take the box up for him; and pursues
    p. 171 UNDERWOOD 20   8 Put on for fashion, and take up on trust:
    p. 173 UNDERWOOD 22   16 And kept, and bred, and brought up true.
    p. 174 UNDERWOOD 23   8 Dri'd up? lyes Thespia wast?
    p. 191 UNDERWOOD 38   5 It is a Darknesse hath blockt up my sense,
    p. 197 UNDERWOOD 40   3 And then I taste it. But as men drinke up
    p. 197 UNDERWOOD 40   15 For though Love thrive, and may grow up with
                              cheare,
    p. 197 UNDERWOOD 40   21 Not, like a Midas, shut up in himselfe,
    p. 198 UNDERWOOD 40   43 Can lock the Sense up, or the heart a thought,
    p. 198 UNDERWOOD 40   47 (Made to blow up loves secrets) to discover
    p. 200 UNDERWOOD 42   25 Yet keepe those up in sackcloth too, or lether,
    p. 201 UNDERWOOD 42   55 He did lay up, and would adore the shooe,
    p. 201 UNDERWOOD 42   58 Lift up some one, and doe, I tell not what.
    p. 206 UNDERWOOD 43   84 Had made a meale for Vulcan to lick up.
    p. 207 UNDERWOOD 43   101 And twice-twelve-yeares stor'd up humanitie,
    p. 208 UNDERWOOD 43   116 No mar'le the Clownes of Lemnos tooke thee up,
    p. 209 UNDERWOOD 43   142 That was rak'd up in the Winchestrian Goose
    p. 212 UNDERWOOD 43   205 Blow up, and ruine, myne, and countermyne,
    p. 213 UNDERWOOD 44   25 Powder, or paper, to bring up the youth
    p. 214 UNDERWOOD 44   51 Up among Nations. In the stead of bold
    p. 215 UNDERWOOD 44   88 Carriage, and dressing. There is up of late
    p. 216 UNDERWOOD 44   102 Her broken Armes up, to their emptie moulds.
    p. 216 UNDERWOOD 45   9 Much lesse a name would we bring up, or nurse,
    p. 217 UNDERWOOD 46   14 Stood up thy Nations fame, her Crownes defence.
    p. 222 UNDERWOOD 48   47 Whereby he may knit sure up
    p. 230 UNDERWOOD 56   12 And that's made up as doth the purse abound.
    p. 237 UNDERWOOD 65   5 This Prince of flowers? Soone shoot thou up,
                              and grow
    p. 239 UNDERWOOD 67   1 1. CLIO. Up publike joy, remember
    p. 240 UNDERWOOD 67   47 Summe up this crowned day,
    p. 244 UNDERWOOD 70   34 Got up and thriv'd with honest arts:
    p. 244 UNDERWOOD 70   42 But that the Corke of Title boy'd him up.
    p. 244 UNDERWOOD 70   53 Goe now, and tell out dayes summ'd up with
                              feares,

up (cont.)
    p. 248 UNDERWOOD 71   10 But lyes block'd up, and straightned, narrow'd
                               in,
    p. 250 UNDERWOOD 73   1 Looke up, thou seed of envie, and still bring
    p. 250 UNDERWOOD 73   7 Why doe I irritate, or stirre up thee,
    p. 251 UNDERWOOD 74   28 Shoot up an Olive fruitfull, faire,
    p. 256 UNDERWOOD 75   108 Him up, to doe the same himselfe had done.
    p. 257 UNDERWOOD 75   152 For Fame keepes Vertue up, and it Posteritie.
    p. 261 UNDERWOOD 77   23 These I looke up at, with a reverent eye,
    p. 263 UNDERWOOD 78   21 He will cleare up his forehead, thinke thou
                               bring'st
    p. 263 UNDERWOOD 78   30 What transcripts begg'd? how cry'd up, and how
                               glad,
    p. 268 UNDERWOOD 82   11 Grow up, sweet Babe, as blessed, in thy Name,
    p. 274 U'WOOD 84.1   37 Is sung: as als<o>'her getting up
    p. 279 U'WOOD 84.4   48 Up to her owne sublimed hight?
    p. 281 U'WOOD 84.8   18 Up to their Ancestors; the rivers side,
    p. 283 U'WOOD 84.9   26 I summe up mine owne breaking, and wish all.
    p. 289 U'WOOD 84.9   219 The last of houres, and shutter up of all;
    p. 309 HORACE 2   89 Like tender buds shoot up, and freshly grow.
    p. 311 HORACE 2   118 This foot the socks tooke up, and buskins grave,
    p. 415 UNGATHERED 42   21 Cry'd up of late: Whereto there must be first
    p. 657 L. CONVIVALES   7 Hang up all the poor Hop-Drinkers,

up-braid   frequency: 1   relative frequency: 0.00001
    p. 138 UNDERWOOD 2.6   30 Whether any would up-braid

up-tooke   frequency: 1   relative frequency: 0.00001
    p. 132 UNDERWOOD 2.2   20 I foole-hardie, there up-tooke

upbraid   frequency: 1   relative frequency: 0.00001
    See also "up-braid," "vpbraid."
    p. 153 UNDERWOOD 13   10 The way to meet, what others would upbraid;

upbraiding   frequency: 1   relative frequency: 0.00001
    See also "vpbraiding."
    p. 256 UNDERWOOD 75   120 A meere upbraiding Griefe, and tort'ring
                               punishment.

upon   frequency: 57   relative frequency: 0.00082
    See also "vpon," "vppon."

upright   frequency: 4   relative frequency: 0.00005
    See also "vpright."
    p. 176 UNDERWOOD 25   6 Her upright head, above the reach of Chance,
    p. 224 UNDERWOOD 50   19 So great a Vertue stand upright to view,
    p. 229 UNDERWOOD 54   9 And hold me to it close; to stand upright
    p. 258 UNDERWOOD 75   182 Upright and sound,

upward. See "vpward."

upwards   frequency: 1   relative frequency: 0.00001
    p. 305 HORACE 2   4 Presenting upwards, a faire female feature,

ura.   frequency: 1   relative frequency: 0.00001
    p. 240 UNDERWOOD 67   43 8. URA. This day the Court doth measure

urania. See "ura."

urg'd   frequency: 3   relative frequency: 0.00004
    p. 160 UNDERWOOD 14   41 Impostures branded! and Authorities urg'd!
    p. 243 UNDERWOOD 70   15 Urg'd, hurried forth, and horld
    p. 270 UNDERWOOD 83   49 From all affection! when they urg'd the Cure

urge   frequency: 6   relative frequency: 0.00008
    See also "vrge."
    p. 140 UNDERWOOD 2.8   14 For I will so urge you to't,
    p. 191 UNDERWOOD 38   26 As I would urge Authoritie for sinne.
    p. 193 UNDERWOOD 38   100 Of Contumelie, and urge a good man more
    p. 202 UNDERWOOD 43   3 Or urge thy Greedie flame, thus to devoure
    p. 209 UNDERWOOD 43   136 And raz'd, e're thought could urge, This might
                               have bin!
    p. 281 U'WOOD 84.8   17 Which all men doe, that urge not their owne deeds

urges   frequency: 1   relative frequency: 0.00001
    p. 231 UNDERWOOD 57   2 Necessitie urges

urgeth   frequency: 1   relative frequency: 0.00001
    See also "vrgeth."
    p. 311 HORACE 2   154 Or urgeth us to anger; and anon

urging   frequency: 2   relative frequency: 0.00002
    p. 139 UNDERWOOD 2.8   t1 Urging her of a promise.
    p. 232 UNDERWOOD 59   2 The art of urging, and avoyding harmes,

urine. See "vrine."

urinous. See "merd-vrinous."

urn. See "urne," "vrne."

urne   frequency: 1   relative frequency: 0.00001
    p. 242 UNDERWOOD 70   8 And mad'st thy Mothers wombe thine urne.

us   frequency: 46   relative frequency: 0.00066
    See also "let's," "vs."

use   frequency: 19   relative frequency: 0.00027
    See also "vse."
    p. 129 UNDERWOOD 1.2   4 Use still thy rod,
    p. 165 UNDERWOOD 15   91 Or use all arts, or haunt all Companies
    p. 166 UNDERWOOD 15   136 Now use the bones, we see doth hire a man
    p. 170 UNDERWOOD 18   12 Such Guides men use not, who their way would
                             find,
    p. 171 UNDERWOOD 19   21 To use the present, then, is not abuse,
    p. 173 UNDERWOOD 22   10 'Tis of your selfe, and that you use
    p. 176 UNDERWOOD 25   1 Where art thou, Genius? I should use
    p. 181 UNDERWOOD 26   23 For men to use their fortune reverently,
    p. 187 UNDERWOOD 33   24 What use, what strength of reason! and how much
    p. 190 UNDERWOOD 37   22 And lesse they know, who being free to use
    p. 214 UNDERWOOD 44   58 Come to their Schooles,) show 'hem the use of
                             Guns;
    p. 232 UNDERWOOD 59   1 They talke of Fencing, and the use of Armes,
    p. 241 UNDERWOOD 68   10 So, the allowance from the King to use,
    p. 256 UNDERWOOD 75   130 Which to this use, wert built and consecrate!
    p. 277 U'WOOD 84.4   6 But here I may no colours use.
    p. 311 HORACE 2   127 Of Poems here describ'd, I can, nor use,
    p. 317 HORACE 2   243 Doth wretchedly the use of things forbeare,
    p. 331 HORACE 2   565 Hee, that not knowes the games, nor how to use
    p. 333 HORACE 2   600 Or great in money's out at use, command

used. See "ill-us'd," "vs'd."

uses   frequency: 2   relative frequency: 0.00002
    p. 146 UNDERWOOD 6   16 Familiar, for the uses sake;
    p. 228 UNDERWOOD 53   3 To all the uses of the field, and race,

usher. See "t<o>'usher."

ushering. See "vshring."

ushers. See "huishers."

using   frequency: 2   relative frequency: 0.00002
    p. 219 UNDERWOOD 47   62 With reverence using all the gifts then<ce>
                             given.
    p. 307 HORACE 2   65 In using also of new words, to be

usual. See "vsuall."

usurer   frequency: 2   relative frequency: 0.00002
    See also "vsurer," "vsvrer."
    p. 169 UNDERWOOD 17   4 'Tis then a crime, when the Usurer is Judge.
    p. 291 UNDERWOOD 85   67 These thoughts when Usurer Alphius, now about

usurers   frequency: 2   relative frequency: 0.00002
    See also "vsvrers."
    p. 166 UNDERWOOD 15   134 Goe make our selves the Usurers at a cast.
    p. 289 UNDERWOOD 85   4 And is not in the Usurers bands:

usurer's. See "usurers," "vsurers," "vsvrer's."

usurp. See "vsurpe."

usurped. See "th'vsurped."

usurping. See "vsurping."

usury. See "vsurie."

utmost   frequency: 1   relative frequency: 0.00001
    See also "vtmost."
    p. 243 UNDERWOOD 70   18 And all on utmost ruine set;

utter   frequency: 2   relative frequency: 0.00002
    See also "vtter."
    p. 309 HORACE 2   84 And ever will, to utter termes that bee
    p. 327 HORACE 2   462 But a well-compass'd mouth to utter it;

utter'd   frequency: 1   relative frequency: 0.00001
    See also "vtter'd."
    p. 274 U'WOOD 84.1   33 This, utter'd by an antient BARD,

uttering   frequency: 1   relative frequency: 0.00001
    See also "utt'ring," "vttring."
    p. 340 HORACE 1   69 ... . uttering ....

utterly. See "vtterly."

utt'ring   frequency: 1   relative frequency: 0.00001
    p. 307 HORACE 2   69 Yet, if by chance, in utt'ring things abstruse,

uvedale. See "vv'dale," "vvedale."

vaile   frequency: 1   relative frequency: 0.00001
    p. 170 UNDERWOOD 18   19 Vaile their owne eyes, and would impartially

vain. See "vaine," "vane."

vaine   frequency: 18   relative frequency: 0.00026
   *p. 492 TO HIMSELF   7 Let their fastidious, vaine
  **p. 115 PANEGYRE   75 In these vaine stirres, and to his mind suggests
    p. 27 EPIGRAMS 2   12 To catch the worlds loose laughter, or vaine
                             gaze.
    p. 33 EPIGRAMS 20   1 Th'expence in odours is a most vaine sinne,
    p. 37 EPIGRAMS 33   1 Ile not offend thee with a vaine teare more,
    p. 51 EPIGRAMS 73   20 Then had I made 'hem good, to fit your vaine.
    p. 73 EPIGRAMS 114   3 For CVPID, who (at first) tooke vaine
                             delight,
    p. 93 FOREST 1   7 I weare not these my wings in vaine.
    p. 102 FOREST 5   5 Spend not then his guifts in vaine.
    p. 139 UNDERWOOD 2.7   2 I long, and should not beg in vaine,
    p. 246 UNDERWOOD 70   102 No pleasures vaine did chime,
    p. 305 HORACE 2   9 Whose shapes, like sick-mens dreames, are fain'd
                             so vaine,
    p. 321 HORACE 2   352 And toile in vaine: the excellence is such
    p. 333 HORACE 2   626 And twice, or thrice had 'ssayd it, still in
                             vaine:
    p. 335 HORACE 2   631 In vaine, but you, and yours, you should love
                             still
    p. 366 UNGATHERED 6   14 In vaine to follow:
    p. 401 UNGATHERED 32   15 Stay, till she make her vaine Approches. Then
    p. 408 UNGATHERED 36   6 Thou'rt too ambitious: and dost fear in vaine!

val-telline   frequency: 1   relative frequency: 0.00001
    p. 219 UNDERWOOD 47   32 Be, or be not, to get the Val-telline?

vale   frequency: 2   relative frequency: 0.00002
    p. 290 UNDERWOOD 85   13 Or in the bending Vale beholds a-farre
    p. 367 UNGATHERED 6   40 The Vale, that bred thee pure, as her Hills
                             Snow.

valew   frequency: 1   relative frequency: 0.00001
    p. 223 UNDERWOOD 49   24 Thinkes it selfe nought, though she should valew
                             it.

valiant   frequency: 7   relative frequency: 0.00010
    p. 32 EPIGRAMS 16   1 HARDIE, thy braine is valiant, 'tis confest,
    p. 58 EPIGRAMS 91   17 And best become the valiant man to weare,
    p. 114 FOREST 12   51 ACHILLES was not first, that valiant was,
    p. 142 UNDERWOOD 2.9   41 Valiant he should be as fire,
    p. 233 UNDERWOOD 59   24 And valiant were, with, or without their hands.
    p. 262 UNDERWOOD 78   5 Hee's prudent, valiant, just, and temperate;
    p. 397 UNGATHERED 30   44 That Rebells actions, are but valiant crimes!

valianter   frequency: 1   relative frequency: 0.00001
    p. 168 UNDERWOOD 15   192 Man thought the valianter, 'cause he durst
                             sweare,

valiant'st   frequency: 1   relative frequency: 0.00001
   p.   49 EPIGRAMS 66   17 Hee's valiant'st, that dares fight, and not for
                       pay;

valley   frequency: 2   relative frequency: 0.00002
   p. 137 UNDERWOOD 2.5   34 Lyes the Valley, cal'd my nest,
   p. 283 U'WOOD 84.9   34 Her blessed Soule, hence, forth this valley vane

valleys   frequency: 1   relative frequency: 0.00001
   See also "vallies."
   p. 264 UNDERWOOD 79   35 Chor. Rivers, and Valleys, Eccho what wee
                       sing.

vallies   frequency: 1   relative frequency: 0.00001
   p. 264 UNDERWOOD 79   27 Chor. Rivers, and Vallies, Eccho what wee
                       sing.

valour   frequency: 13   relative frequency: 0.00018
   See also "valure."
   p.   48 EPIGRAMS 66   6 Durst valour make, almost, but not a crime.
   p.   49 EPIGRAMS 68   3 Two kindes of valour he doth shew, at ones;
   p.   60 EPIGRAMS 93   9 Thou, that art all their valour, all their
                       spirit,
   p.   68 EPIGRAMS 106   6 Or valour, or thy iudgement seasoning it,
   p.   86 EPIGRAMS 133   76 But still their valour, and their vertue fenc't
                       'hem,
   p.   87 EPIGRAMS 133   132 Must trie the'vn-vsed valour of a nose:
   p. 146 UNDERWOOD 6   7 Such as in valour would excell,
   p. 156 UNDERWOOD 13   104 Of Valour, but at this Idolatrous rate?
   p. 180 UNDERWOOD 26   16 True valour doth her owne renowne command
   p. 233 UNDERWOOD 59   14 Wonder to Valour! No, it is the Law
   p. 233 UNDERWOOD 59   16 Valour! to sleight it, being done to you!
   p. 233 UNDERWOOD 59   19 All this (my Lord) is Valour! This is yours!
   p. 378 UNGATHERED 11   84 And therein (which is worth his valour too)

valtelline. See "val-telline."

valuations   frequency: 1   relative frequency: 0.00001
   p. 415 UNGATHERED 42   29 The valuations, mixtures, and the same

valu'd   frequency: 1   relative frequency: 0.00001
   p. 243 UNDERWOOD 70   23 Or masked man, if valu'd by his face,

value   frequency: 5   relative frequency: 0.00007
   See also "out-valew," "valew."
   p.   50 EPIGRAMS 72   4 Goe high, or low, as thou wilt value it.
   p. 171 UNDERWOOD 20   5 At fifty yeares, almost, to value it,
   p. 216 UNDERWOOD 45   25 Then rest, and a friends value understand,
   p. 235 UNDERWOOD 62   9 Nay, and in this, thou show'st to value more
   p. 331 HORACE 2   554 Yet, there's a value given to this man.

valure   frequency: 1   relative frequency: 0.00001
   p.   32 EPIGRAMS 16   9 Keepe thy selfe there, and thinke thy valure
                       right,

vane   frequency: 1   relative frequency: 0.00001
   p. 283 U'WOOD 84.9   34 Her blessed Soule, hence, forth this valley vane

vanish'd   frequency: 2   relative frequency: 0.00002
   p.   87 EPIGRAMS 133   110 Vanish'd away: as you must all presume
   p. 183 UNDERWOOD 29   18 And wit vanish'd.

vanitie   frequency: 1   relative frequency: 0.00001
   p. 166 UNDERWOOD 15   143 In this, and like, an itch of Vanitie,

vanity. See "vanitie."

vapor   frequency: 1   relative frequency: 0.00001
  **p. 113 PANEGYRE   18 And in their vapor her bright mettall drowne.

vapour   frequency: 1   relative frequency: 0.00001
   See also "vapor."
   p. 211 UNDERWOOD 43   182 Or lest that vapour might the Citie choake,

varie   frequency: 2   relative frequency: 0.00002
   p.   72 EPIGRAMS 111   6 More, then to varie what our elders knew:
   p. 171 UNDERWOOD 19   27 As in his place, because he would not varie,

varied   frequency: 2   relative frequency: 0.00002
   See also "varyed."

varied (cont.)
   p. 34 EPIGRAMS 25   6 In varied shapes, which for his lust shee takes:
   p. 176 UNDERWOOD 24   15 Some note of which each varied Pillar beares,

varietie   frequency: 2   relative frequency: 0.00002
   p. 202 UNDERWOOD 42   72 Varietie of Silkes were on th'Exchange!
   p. 205 UNDERWOOD 43   50 With some more thrift, and more varietie:

variety. See "varietie."

various   frequency: 3   relative frequency: 0.00004
   p. 136 UNDERWOOD 2.5   4 Then the various Moone the flood!
   p. 307 HORACE 2   40 This, seeking, in a various kind, to forme
   p. 399 UNGATHERED 31   20 Or sweet, or various, in the course!

varius   frequency: 1   relative frequency: 0.00001
   p. 309 HORACE 2   79 Or Varius? Why am I now envi'd so,

vary   frequency: 1   relative frequency: 0.00001
   See also "varie."
   p. 367 UNGATHERED 6   29 Nor Sunne could make to vary from the rest,

varyed   frequency: 1   relative frequency: 0.00001
   p. 118 FOREST 13   66 And after varyed, as fresh obiects goes,

varying   frequency: 2   relative frequency: 0.00002
   p. 146 UNDERWOOD 6   11 The frequent varying of the deed,
   p. 339 HORACE 1   42 So he that varying still affects .. draw

vast   frequency: 2   relative frequency: 0.00002
   p. 206 UNDERWOOD 43   86 So ravenous, and vast an appetite?
   p. 226 UNDERWOOD 52   2 I am not so voluminous, and vast,

vats. See "dye-fats."

vault   frequency: 2   relative frequency: 0.00002
   p. 79 EPIGRAMS 124   8 Leaue it buryed in this vault.
   p. 191 UNDERWOOD 38   22 Or lay the excuse upon the Vintners vault:

vaults   frequency: 1   relative frequency: 0.00001
  **p. 113 PANEGYRE   9 Into those darke and deepe concealed vaults,

veil. See "vaile."

vein. See "veine," "veyne."

veine   frequency: 1   relative frequency: 0.00001
   p. 331 HORACE 2   584 Can; or all toile, without a wealthie veine:

veines   frequency: 2   relative frequency: 0.00002
   p. 274 U'WOOD 84.2   8 At either Stemme, and know the veines of good
   p. 287 U'WOOD 84.9   157 And to that forme, lent two such veines of blood

veins. See "fame-vaynes," "veines," "veynes."

veiw   frequency: 2   relative frequency: 0.00002
   p. 395 UNGATHERED 29   7 But when againe I veiw the parts so poi'd,
   p. 399 UNGATHERED 31   5 To veiw the truth and owne it. Doe but looke

veluet   frequency: 3   relative frequency: 0.00004
   p. 62 EPIGRAMS 97   4 His cloke with orient veluet quite lin'd through,
   p. 371 UNGATHERED 8   5 Veluet, or Taffata cap, rank'd in the darke
   p. 403 UNGATHERED 34   26 Noe veluet Sheath you weare, will alter kynde.

veluet-men   frequency: 1   relative frequency: 0.00001
  *p. 493 TO HIMSELF   32 Braue plush, and veluet-men;

velvet   frequency: 5   relative frequency: 0.00007
   See also "veluet," "veluet-men."
   p. 164 UNDERWOOD 15   58 With Velvet, Plush, and Tissues, it is spirit.
   p. 200 UNDERWOOD 42   38 Upon a Velvet Petticote, or a Gowne,
   p. 202 UNDERWOOD 42   82 A Goat in Velvet: or some block could move
   p. 202 UNDERWOOD 42   85 Bawd, in a Velvet scabberd! I envy
   p. 222 UNDERWOOD 49   18 What though she be with Velvet gownes indu'd,

velvets   frequency: 2   relative frequency: 0.00002
   p. 202 UNDERWOOD 42   79 The Stuffes, the Velvets, Plushes, Fringes,
                    Lace,
   p. 275 U'WOOD 84.3   2 What make these Velvets, Silkes, and Lawne,

venerable   frequency: 1   relative frequency: 0.00001
    p. 414 UNGATHERED 41 42 Most venerable. Cause of all our ioy.

venery   frequency: 1   relative frequency: 0.00001
    p. 380 UNGATHERED 12 37 How faine for his venery he was to crie (Tergum
                             o)

venetia   frequency: 3   relative frequency: 0.00004
    p. 272 UNDERWOOD 84   t5 Of that truly-noble Lady, the Lady
                             VENETIA DIGBY,
    p. 274 U'WOOD 84.2   2 Of Dame VENETIA DIGBY, styl'd The
                             Faire:
    p. 282 U'WOOD 84.9   t2 The truly honoured Lady, the Lady
                             VENETIA DIGBY;

venetian   frequency: 1   relative frequency: 0.00001
    p. 69 EPIGRAMS 107   8 Of your Morauian horse, Venetian bull.

venice   frequency: 2   relative frequency: 0.00002
    p. 85 EPIGRAMS 133   33 From Venice, Paris, or some in-land passage
    p. 380 UNGATHERED 12 42 From Venice to Flushing, were not they well
                             cobled?

vent   frequency: 4   relative frequency: 0.00005
    p. 150 UNDERWOOD 10   5 To vent that poore desire,
    p. 151 UNDERWOOD 12   2 It vent it selfe, but as it would,
    p. 218 UNDERWOOD 47   26 To vent their Libels, and to issue rimes,
    p. 368 UNGATHERED 6   77 And vp againe, in skies, and aire to vent

vented   frequency: 1   relative frequency: 0.00001
    p. 210 UNDERWOOD 43 168 Which thou hast only vented, not enjoy'd.

venter   frequency: 4   relative frequency: 0.00005
    p. 164 UNDERWOOD 15   80 Where Pittes, or Wright, or Modet would not
                             venter,
    p. 169 UNDERWOOD 17   15 Venter a longer time, and willingly:
    p. 231 UNDERWOOD 57   5 And that he will venter
    p. 394 UNGATHERED 28 11 Nay they will venter ones Descent to hitt,

ventring   frequency: 2   relative frequency: 0.00002
    p. 72 EPIGRAMS 112   1 With thy small stocke, why art thou ventring
                             still,
    p. 313 HORACE 2   165 A ventring Merchant, or the Farmer free

ventur'd   frequency: 1   relative frequency: 0.00001
    p. 289 U'WOOD 84.9   227 That thus have ventur'd these true straines upon;

venture. See "venter."

ventures   frequency: 1   relative frequency: 0.00001
    p. 241 UNDERWOOD 69   6 Wise-crafts, on which the flatterer ventures not.

venturing. See "ventring."

venus   frequency: 11   relative frequency: 0.00015
    See also "venvs."
    p. 137 UNDERWOOD 2.5 42 All is Venus: save unchaste.
    p. 137 UNDERWOOD 2.5 52 Shee is Venus, when she smiles,
    p. 141 UNDERWOOD 2.9 15 Venus, and Minerva's eyes,
    p. 182 UNDERWOOD 28   14 For Venus Ceston, every line you make.
    p. 209 UNDERWOOD 43 144 When Venus there maintain'd the Misterie.
    p. 210 UNDERWOOD 43 160 Troy, though it were so much his Venus care.
    p. 221 UNDERWOOD 48   33 But Venus and the Graces
    p. 240 UNDERWOOD 67   34 As here no Venus were;
    p. 292 UNDERWOOD 86   1 Venus, againe thou mov'st a warre
    p. 292 UNDERWOOD 86   t2 To Venus.
    p. 657 I. CONVIVALES 12 Wine it is the Milk of Venus,

venusine   frequency: 1   relative frequency: 0.00001
    p. 207 UNDERWOOD 43   89 All the old Venusine, in Poetrie,

venvs   frequency: 1   relative frequency: 0.00001
    p. 107 FOREST 10   16 Goe, crampe dull MARS, light VENVS, when
                             he snorts,

verdure   frequency: 1   relative frequency: 0.00001
    p. 251 UNDERWOOD 74   13 The very verdure of her nest,

vere   frequency: 2   relative frequency: 0.00002
    p. 58 EPIGRAMS 91   3 Illustrous VERE, or HORACE; fit to be

vere (cont.)
    p. 58 EPIGRAMS 91   t1 TO SIR HORACE VERE.

veriest   frequency: 1   relative frequency: 0.00001
    p. 154 UNDERWOOD 13   57 Dam's whom he damn'd to, as the veriest Gull,

verily   frequency: 1   relative frequency: 0.00001
    p. 209 UNDERWOOD 43   140 'Twas verily some Relique of the Stewes:

vermilion   frequency: 1   relative frequency: 0.00001
    p. 406 UNGATHERED 34   94 Vermilion, Lake, or Cinnopar affoards

verse   frequency: 41   relative frequency: 0.00059
    p. 35 EPIGRAMS 27   2 Take better ornaments, my teares, and verse.
    p. 85 EPIGRAMS 133   45 Or goddesse to inuoke, to stuffe my verse;
    p. 93 FOREST 1   2 I thought to binde him, in my verse:
    p. 107 FOREST 10   21 His absence in my verse, is all I aske.
    p. 113 FOREST 12   19 I, that haue none (to send you) send you verse.
    p. 114 FOREST 12   29 Turne, vpon scorned verse, their quarter-face:
    p. 136 UNDERWOOD 2.5   21 As the Bath your verse discloses
    p. 138 UNDERWOOD 2.6   35 And, if such a verse as this,
    p. 159 UNDERWOOD 14   26 Before men get a verse: much lesse a Praise;
    p. 164 UNDERWOOD 15   62 Not make a verse; Anger; or laughter would,
    p. 170 UNDERWOOD 19   12 So well as I may tell in verse, 'tis so?
    p. 181 UNDERWOOD 27   7 Lie drawne to life, in his soft Verse,
    p. 182 UNDERWOOD 28   9 For in your verse all Cupids Armorie,
    p. 183 UNDERWOOD 29   8 Propping Verse, for feare of falling
    p. 201 UNDERWOOD 42   62 He would have done in verse, with any of those
    p. 204 UNDERWOOD 43   38 A paire of Scisars, and a Combe in verse;
    p. 229 UNDERWOOD 55   4 Verse, that should thee, and me out-live.
    p. 241 UNDERWOOD 68   13 For in the Genius of a Poets Verse,
    p. 292 UNDERWOOD 86   23 Shall Verse be set to Harpe and Lute,
    p. 309 HORACE 2   107 In Verse unequall match'd, first sowre Laments,
    p. 311 HORACE 2   119 As fit t<o>'exchange discourse; a Verse to win
    p. 311 HORACE 2   122 In tragick Verse; no lesse Thyestes feast
    p. 319 HORACE 2   319 Hee too, that did in Tragick Verse contend
    p. 321 HORACE 2   358 Their youthfull tricks in over-wanton verse:
    p. 323 HORACE 2   372 A foot, whose swiftnesse gave the Verse the name
    p. 323 HORACE 2   391 My Verse at randome, and licentiously?
    p. 323 HORACE 2   404 A lawfull Verse, by th'eare, or finger scan.
    p. 325 HORACE 2   416 To taxe that Verse, which many a day, and blot
    p. 327 HORACE 2   460 Of verse meere-matter-lesse, and tinckling toies.
    p. 329 HORACE 2   496 The Oracles, too, were given out in Verse;
    p. 329 HORACE 2   500 Of their long labours, was in Verse set downe:
    p. 331 HORACE 2   581 'Tis now inquir'd, which makes the nobler Verse,
    p. 333 HORACE 2   594 An admirable Verse. The great Scurfe take
    p. 335 HORACE 2   634 On artlesse Verse; the hard ones he will blame;
    p. 396 UNGATHERED 30   4 Those ambling visits, passe in verse, betweene
    p. 398 UNGATHERED 30   68 With bold Tyrtaeus verse, when thou art nam'd,
    p. 401 UNGATHERED 33   6 French Aire and English Verse here Wedded
                             lie.
    p. 403 UNGATHERED 34   41 Or Verse, or Sense t'express Immortall you?
    p. 407 UNGATHERED 36   3 That I should wryte vpon him some sharp verse,
    p. 420 UNGATHERED 48   20 This long watch'<d> verse
    p. 421 UNGATHERED 49   2 before, I wryte more verse, to bee more wyse.

verser   frequency: 1   relative frequency: 0.00001
    p. 115 FOREST 12   68 Who, though shee haue a better verser got,

verses   frequency: 23   relative frequency: 0.00033
    p. 35 EPIGRAMS 28   5 Which hee thinkes great; and so reades verses,
                             too:
    p. 42 EPIGRAMS 49   1 PLAY-WRIGHT me reades, and still my
                             verses damnes,
    p. 44 EPIGRAMS 54   1 CHEV'RIL cryes out, my verses libells are;
    p. 45 EPIGRAMS 58   2 To reade my verses; now I must to heare:
    p. 51 EPIGRAMS 73   19 In most vile verses, and cost me more paine,
    p. 65 EPIGRAMS 101   24 And Ile professe no verses to repeate:
    p. 177 UNDERWOOD 25   18 Then shall my Verses, like strong Charmes,
    p. 199 UNDERWOOD 42   3 No Poets verses yet did ever move,
    p. 200 UNDERWOOD 42   27 It is a ryming Age, and Verses swarme
    p. 230 UNDERWOOD 56   1 You won not Verses, Madam, you won mee,
    p. 231 UNDERWOOD 56   27 How many verses, Madam, are your Due!
    p. 263 UNDERWOOD 78   23 For he doth love my Verses, and will looke
    p. 323 HORACE 2   384 Those heavie Verses, sent so to the Stage,
    p. 327 HORACE 2   474 Thinke wee, or hope, there can be Verses fain'd
    p. 327 HORACE 2   492 To divine Poets, and their Verses came.
    p. 331 HORACE 2   570 Yet who's most ignorant, dares Verses make.
    p. 333 HORACE 2   609 You doe not bring, to judge your Verses, one,
    p. 333 HORACE 2   620 When you write Verses, with your judge do so:

verses (cont.)
```
     p. 333 HORACE 2      628 Those ill-torn'd Verses, to new hammering.
     p. 335 HORACE 2      649 The while he belcheth loftie Verses out,
     p. 335 HORACE 2      670 His cause of making Verses none knowes why:
     p. 349 HORACE 1      460 .. empty Verses ... meere ......... ......
     p. 408 UNGATHERED 37   1 My verses were commended, thou dar'st say,
```

vert   frequency: 1 relative frequency: 0.00001
```
     p. 413 UNGATHERED 41  19 Preserved, in her antique bed of Vert,
```

vertu'   frequency: 1 relative frequency: 0.00001
```
     p. 371 UNGATHERED 9    4 That durst be that in Court: a vertu' alone
```

vertue   frequency: 50 relative frequency: 0.00072
```
     p.  47 EPIGRAMS 63     2 With what thy vertue on the times hath won,
     p.  52 EPIGRAMS 76    11 I meant each softest vertue, there should meet,
     p.  58 EPIGRAMS 91     2 A romane sound, but romane vertue weares,
     p.  60 EPIGRAMS 93     2 For the great marke of vertue, those being gone
     p.  63 EPIGRAMS 98     6 And what would hurt his vertue makes it still.
     p.  66 EPIGRAMS 102    6 Of vice, and vertue; wherein all great life
     p.  66 EPIGRAMS 102    9 They follow vertue, for reward, to day;
     p.  68 EPIGRAMS 106    1 If men get name, for some one vertue: Then,
     p.  70 EPIGRAMS 109    3 Where vertue makes them both, and that's in thee:
     p.  74 EPIGRAMS 114    6 Where finding so much beautie met with vertue,
     p.  78 EPIGRAMS 122    5 If I would vertue set, as shee was yong,
     p.  79 EPIGRAMS 124    6 To more vertue, then doth liue.
     p.  79 EPIGRAMS 125    2 Made for what Nature could, or Vertue can;
     p.  86 EPIGRAMS 133   76 But still their valour, and their vertue fenc't
                              'hem,
     p. 109 FOREST 11       2 Is vertue, and not Fate:
     p. 109 FOREST 11       3 Next, to that vertue, is to know vice well,
     p. 111 FOREST 11      59 Richer then Time, and as Time's vertue, rare.
     p. 113 FOREST 12       1 Whil'st that, for which, all vertue now is sold,
     p. 116 FOREST 13       8 With euery vertue, wheresoere it moue,
     p. 117 FOREST 13      42 And raise not vertue; they may vice enhance.
     p. 118 FOREST 13      49 Of so great title, birth, but vertue most,
     p. 118 FOREST 13      55 Of vertue, which you tread? what if alone?
     p. 121 FOREST 14      32 Of nobles vertue, shew in you;
     p. 146 UNDERWOOD 6     4 Our proper vertue is to range:
     p. 173 UNDERWOOD 22    4 Yet is't your vertue now I raise.
     p. 173 UNDERWOOD 22    5 A vertue, like Allay, so gone
     p. 174 UNDERWOOD 23   18 'Tis crowne enough to vertue still, her owne
                              applause.
     p. 176 UNDERWOOD 24    8 When Vice alike in time with vertue dur'd.
     p. 192 UNDERWOOD 38   33 Where weaknesse doth offend, and vertue grieve,
     p. 214 UNDERWOOD 44   49 Goe on, increase in vertue; and in fame:
     p. 215 UNDERWOOD 44   83 Past any need of vertue. Let them care,
     p. 216 UNDERWOOD 44  101 The fate of things: whilst totter'd vertue holds
     p. 216 UNDERWOOD 45   12 'Tis vertue alone, or nothing, that knits
                              friends:
     p. 217 UNDERWOOD 46    4 Whom Fortune aided lesse, or Vertue more.
     p. 217 UNDERWOOD 46   22 None Fortune aided lesse, or Vertue more.
     p. 224 UNDERWOOD 50    8 No friend to vertue, could be silent here.
     p. 224 UNDERWOOD 50   19 So great a Vertue stand upright to view,
     p. 234 UNDERWOOD 60   10 Of Vertue, got above his name?
     p. 247 UNDERWOOD 70  115 Unto the Vertue. Nothing perfect done,
     p. 250 UNDERWOOD 73   10 To vertue, and true worth, be ever blind.
     p. 257 UNDERWOOD 75  152 For Fame keepes Vertue up, and it Posteritie.
     p. 258 UNDERWOOD 75  180 Extend a reaching vertue, early and late:
     p. 262 UNDERWOOD 78    6 In him all vertue is beheld in State:
     p. 282 U'WOOD 84.8    21 'Tis Vertue alone, is true Nobilitie.
     p. 282 U'WOOD 84.8    22 Which Vertue from your Father, ripe, will fall;
     p. 285 U'WOOD 84.9   116 By beatifick vertue of the Place.
     p. 307 HORACE 2       59 The vertue of which order, and true grace,
     p. 325 HORACE 2      412 In vertue, and renowne of armes, then in
     p. 399 UNGATHERED 31  18 Of vertue, pretious in the frame:
     p. 409 UNGATHERED 38  t2 his continu'd Vertue) my louing Friend:
```

vertue'   frequency: 1 relative frequency: 0.00001
```
     p.  66 EPIGRAMS 102   12 As nothing else discernes the vertue' or vice.
```

vertue'enforme   frequency: 1 relative frequency: 0.00001
```
     p.  75 EPIGRAMS 116    3 So did thy vertue'enforme, thy wit sustaine
```

vertues   frequency: 9 relative frequency: 0.00013
```
     p.  47 EPIGRAMS 64    11 Where good mens vertues them to honors bring,
     p.  49 EPIGRAMS 67     7 When, in mens wishes, so thy vertues wrought,
     p. 179 UNDERWOOD 25   36 O vertues fall,
     p. 185 UNDERWOOD 30    1 If thou wouldst know the vertues of Man-kind,
     p. 209 UNDERWOOD 83   22 Sound thou her Vertues, give her soule a Name.
```

vertues (cont.)
    p. 270 UNDERWOOD 83   41 Were like a ring of Vertues, 'bout her set,
    p. 274 U'WOOD 84.2   11 Of vertues in her, as, in short, shee grew
    p. 281 U'WOOD 84.8   12 When your owne Vertues, equall'd have their
                               Names,
    p. 285 U'WOOD 84.9   87 The Dominations, Vertues, and the Powers,

vertuous   frequency: 13   relative frequency: 0.00018
    p. 49 EPIGRAMS 66   18 That vertuous is, when the reward 's away.
    p. 96 FOREST 2   97 Reade, in their vertuous parents noble parts,
    p. 100 FOREST 4   t2 A farewell for a Gentle-woman, vertuous
    p. 112 FOREST 11   112 (To vertuous moods inclin'd)
    p. 157 UNDERWOOD 13   143 Such Notes are vertuous men! they live as fast
    p. 215 UNDERWOOD 44   79 Let poore Nobilitie be vertuous: Wee,
    p. 244 UNDERWOOD 70   33 Hee entred well, by vertuous parts,
    p. 244 UNDERWOOD 70   47 But most, a vertuous Sonne.
    p. 250 UNDERWOOD 73   t1 On the Right Honourable, and vertuous Lord
    p. 383 UNGATHERED 17   1 Who takes thy volume to his vertuous hand,
    p. 383 UNGATHERED 17   8 May take thy volume to his vertuous hand.
    p. 384 UNGATHERED 18   7 Wch I do, early, vertuous Somerset,
    p. 398 UNGATHERED 30   90 To all thy vertuous, and well chosen Friends,

vertuously   frequency: 1   relative frequency: 0.00001
    p. 75 EPIGRAMS 116   14 Vertuously practise must at least allow

very   frequency: 12   relative frequency: 0.00017
    p. 81 EPIGRAMS 129   8 The very call, to make all others come:
    p. 137 UNDERWOOD 2.5   37 To my shafts! Her very Name,
    p. 142 UNDERWOOD 2.9   54 I could give my very heart;
    p. 152 UNDERWOOD 12   22 His very Manners taught t<o>'amend,
    p. 155 UNDERWOOD 13   79 But these men ever want: their very trade
    p. 182 UNDERWOOD 28   11 His very eyes are yours to overthrow.
    p. 222 UNDERWOOD 49   3 What though her Chamber be the very pit
    p. 241 UNDERWOOD 68   8 Would make the very Greene-cloth to looke blew:
    p. 251 UNDERWOOD 74   13 The very verdure of her nest,
    p. 325 HORACE 2   440 The very root of writing well, and spring
    p. 408 UNGATHERED 37   2 And they were very good: yet thou think'st nay.
    p. 416 UNGATHERED 45   7 but a very merry wight

vestal. See "vestall."

vestall   frequency: 1   relative frequency: 0.00001
    p. 365 UNGATHERED 5   11 Cleare as a naked vestall

vex. See "vexe."

vexation   frequency: 1   relative frequency: 0.00001
    p. 73 EPIGRAMS 112   22 There's no vexation, that can make thee prime.

vexe   frequency: 4   relative frequency: 0.00005
    p. 159 UNDERWOOD 14   25 And what I write? and vexe it many dayes
    p. 187 UNDERWOOD 33   19 But first dost vexe, and search it! If not
                               sound,
    p. 335 HORACE 2   648 They vexe, and follow him with shouts, and noise.
    p. 371 UNGATHERED 8   13 In such a Martirdome; To vexe their eyes,

vexed   frequency: 1   relative frequency: 0.00001
    See also "vext."
    p. 243 UNDERWOOD 70   27 He vexed time, and busied the whole State;

vext   frequency: 2   relative frequency: 0.00002
    p. 146 UNDERWOOD 6   18 But as 'tis often vext and tri'd.
    p. 159 UNDERWOOD 14   39 What fables have you vext! what truth redeem'd!

veyne   frequency: 1   relative frequency: 0.00001
    p. 108 FOREST 10A   2 to loose, and Cap'ring, for thy stricter veyne.

veynes   frequency: 2   relative frequency: 0.00002
    p. 405 UNGATHERED 34   74 Suckt from ye Veynes of shop-philosophy.
    p. 420 UNGATHERED 48   31 Wee'l rip our Richest veynes

vgly   frequency: 2   relative frequency: 0.00002
    p. 85 EPIGRAMS 133   61 In the first iawes appear'd that vgly monster,
    p. 86 EPIGRAMS 133   68 Were seene your vgly Centaures, yee call
                               Car-men,

viands   frequency: 1   relative frequency: 0.00001
    p. 291 UNDERWOOD 85   48 And unbought viands ready makes:

vice			frequency: 30 relative frequency: 0.00043
**p.	116	PANEGYRE	120 For vice is safe, while she hath vice to friend.
p.	50	EPIGRAMS 72	6 Thy person only, COVRTLING, is the vice.
p.	52	EPIGRAMS 76	10 Hating that solemne vice of greatnesse, pride;
p.	66	EPIGRAMS 102	6 Of vice, and vertue; wherein all great life
p.	66	EPIGRAMS 102	10 To morrow vice, if shee giue better pay:
p.	66	EPIGRAMS 102	12 As nothing else discernes the vertue' or vice.
p.	74	EPIGRAMS 115	5 Being no vitious person, but the vice
p.	76	EPIGRAMS 118	4 He makes himselfe a thorough-fare of vice.
p.	96	FOREST 3	4 Art tane with neithers vice, nor sport:
p.	99	FOREST 3	85 Let thousands more goe flatter vice, and winne,
p.	109	FOREST 11	1 Not to know vice at all, and keepe true state,
p.	109	FOREST 11	3 Next, to that vertue, is to know vice well,
p.	111	FOREST 11	72 No, vice, we let thee know,
p.	113	FOREST 12	2 And almost euery vice, almightie gold,
p.	116	FOREST 13	10 With sinne and vice, though with a throne endew'd;
p.	117	FOREST 13	42 And raise not vertue; they may vice enhance.
p.	119	FOREST 13	87 And neuer thinke, how vice doth euery houre,
p.	152	UNDERWOOD 12	28 It chid the vice, yet not the Men.
p.	172	UNDERWOOD 21	6 Of all vice hurld together, there he was,
p.	176	UNDERWOOD 24	8 When Vice alike in time with vertue dur'd.
p.	190	UNDERWOOD 37	8 Their vice of loving for a Christmasse fit;
p.	190	UNDERWOOD 37	29 Yet if with eithers vice I teynted be,
p.	191	UNDERWOOD 38	24 Or goe about to countenance the vice,
p.	315	HORACE 2	232 To every vice, as hardly to be brought
p.	331	HORACE 2	572 Vice, and, am knowne to have a Knights estate.
p.	339	HORACE 1	45 The .... vice .. .. vice ....
p.	405	UNGATHERED 34	82 Discouer Vice? Commit Absurdity?
p.	408	UNGATHERED 37	5 ffoole, doe not rate my Rymes; I'haue found thy Vice

vices			frequency: 5 relative frequency: 0.00007
**p.	116	PANEGYRE	109 Nor did he seeme their vices so to loue,
p.	163	UNDERWOOD 15	30 Rather then here so bogg'd in vices stay.
p.	166	UNDERWOOD 15	123 Our vices doe not tarry in a place,
p.	224	UNDERWOOD 50	9 The rather when the vices of the Time
p.	371	UNGATHERED 8	10 With vices, which they look'd for, and came to.

vicious			frequency: 2 relative frequency: 0.00002
See also "viticus."			
p.	111	FOREST 11	66 Some vicious foole draw neare,
p.	117	FOREST 13	12 By arts, and practise of the vicious,

victorie			frequency: 1 relative frequency: 0.00001
p.	187	UNDERWOOD 33	35 Then com'st thou off with Victorie and Palme,

victory. See "victorie."

victrice			frequency: 1 relative frequency: 0.00001
p.	285	U'WOOD 84.9	96 With boughs of Palme, a crowned Victrice stand!

victrix. See "victrice."

vies			frequency: 1 relative frequency: 0.00001
p.	415	UNGATHERED 43	1 I cannot bring my Muse to dropp <her> Vies

view			frequency: 21 relative frequency: 0.00030
See also "veiw," "viewe."			
p.	53	EPIGRAMS 79	11 He should those rare, and absolute numbers view,
p.	66	EPIGRAMS 102	18 But in the view, doth interrupt their sinne;
p.	69	EPIGRAMS 108	1 Strength of my Countrey, whilst I bring to view
p.	96	FOREST 3	7 Nor com'st to view the better cloth of state;
p.	97	FOREST 3	11 To view the iewells, stuffes, the paines, the wit
p.	138	UNDERWOOD 2.6	11 And her Jewels, to the view
p.	174	UNDERWOOD 22	34 Appeare, and that to shortest view,
p.	177	UNDERWOOD 25	22 Lock't in her cold embraces, from the view
p.	193	UNDERWOOD 38	85 But view the mildnesse of your Makers state,
p.	214	UNDERWOOD 44	34 Supplant bold Panton; and brought there to view
p.	222	UNDERWOOD 49	17 To shew their Tires? to view, and to be view'd?
p.	224	UNDERWOOD 50	19 So great a Vertue stand upright to view,
p.	225	UNDERWOOD 50	31 These Graces, when the rest of Ladyes view
p.	250	UNDERWOOD 73	3 In his great Actions: view whom his large hand
p.	275	U'WOOD 84.3	9 Yet something, to the Painters view,
p.	291	UNDERWOOD 85	63 To view the weary Oxen draw, with bare
p.	319	HORACE 2	294 Chaste, thriftie, modest folke, that came to view.
p.	321	HORACE 2	328 Yet so the scoffing Satyres to mens view,
p.	370	UNGATHERED 7	9 But now, your Worke is done, if they that view
p.	371	UNGATHERED 9	1 Stay, view this stone: And, if thou beest not such,

view (cont.)
     p. 384 UNGATHERED 18   25 That all, yt view you then, and late; may say,

viewd   frequency: 1 relative frequency: 0.00001
     p. 408 UNGATHERED 36   12 Will well designe thee, to be viewd of all

view'd   frequency: 6 relative frequency: 0.00008
     See also "viewd."
     p. 88 EPIGRAMS 133   162 Thrise did it spit: thrise diu'd. At last, it
                                view'd
     p. 222 UNDERWOOD 49   17 To shew their Tires? to view, and to be view'd?
     p. 234 UNDERWOOD 61   3 View'd there the mercat, read the wretched rate
     p. 284 U'WOOD 84.9   77 Have all his actions wondred at, and view'd
     p. 331 HORACE 2   543 Will in the light be view'd: This, once, the
                                sight
     p. 411 UNGATHERED 40   3 And in them view'd

viewe   frequency: 1 relative frequency: 0.00001
     p. 362 UNGATHERED 2   9 For, as one comming with a laterall viewe,

viewes   frequency: 1 relative frequency: 0.00001
     p. 166 UNDERWOOD 15   138 The Dice with glassen eyes, to the glad viewes

viewing   frequency: 2 relative frequency: 0.00002
     p. 77 EPIGRAMS 120   19 But viewing him since (alas, too late)
     p. 144 UNDERWOOD 3   20 On what they viewing know.

views. See "viewes."

vigilance   frequency: 1 relative frequency: 0.00001
     p. 363 UNGATHERED 3   11 It bends the hams of Gossip Vigilance,

vile   frequency: 8 relative frequency: 0.00011
     p. 28 EPIGRAMS 3   11 If, without these vile arts, it will not sell,
     p. 51 EPIGRAMS 73   19 In most vile verses, and cost me more paine,
     p. 192 UNDERWOOD 38   36 Nothing is vile, that is a part of you:
     p. 211 UNDERWOOD 43   186 Vile Tavernes, and the Drunkards pisse him out;
     p. 311 HORACE 2   147 Peleus, or Telephus. If you speake vile
     p. 313 HORACE 2   188 If thou the vile, broad-troden ring forsake.
     p. 319 HORACE 2   320 For the vile Goat, soone after, forth did send
     p. 339 HORACE 1   54 .... some vile
                                snout.

viler   frequency: 1 relative frequency: 0.00001
     p. 34 EPIGRAMS 24   2 Mens manners ne're were viler, for your sake.

ville-royes   frequency: 1 relative frequency: 0.00001
     p. 69 EPIGRAMS 107   21 For newes) your Ville-royes, and Silleries,

villeroys. See "ville-royes."

vincent   frequency: 2 relative frequency: 0.00002
     p. 151 UNDERWOOD 12   7 Deare Vincent Corbet, who so long
     p. 151 UNDERWOOD 12   t2 VINCENT CORBET.

vindicate   frequency: 1 relative frequency: 0.00001
     p. 175 UNDERWOOD 24   4 Doth vindicate it to eternitie.

vindictive   frequency: 1 relative frequency: 0.00001
     p. 172 UNDERWOOD 21   7 Proud, false, and trecherous, vindictive, all

vine   frequency: 4 relative frequency: 0.00005
     p. 107 FOREST 10   10 Nor will I beg of thee, Lord of the vine,
     p. 190 UNDERWOOD 37   14 So may the fruitfull Vine my temples steepe,
     p. 257 UNDERWOOD 75   159 Your fruitfull spreading Vine,
     p. 290 UNDERWOOD 85   10 With the growne issue of the Vine;

vintners   frequency: 1 relative frequency: 0.00001
     p. 191 UNDERWOOD 38   22 Or lay the excuse upon the Vintners vault;

viol. See "violl."

violates   frequency: 1 relative frequency: 0.00001
     p. 284 U'WOOD 84.9   74 Who violates the God-head, is most vitious

violent   frequency: 1 relative frequency: 0.00001
     p. 363 UNGATHERED 3   1 Those that in blood such violent pleasure haue,

violl   frequency: 1 relative frequency: 0.00001
     p. 346 HORACE 1   306 .. the grave Harp, and Violl voyces ...

virgil   frequency: 5   relative frequency: 0.00007
    p. 65 EPIGRAMS 101   21 Shall reade a piece of VIRGIL,
                              TACITVS,
    p. 199 UNDERWOOD 42   1 Let me be what I am, as Virgil cold;
    p. 228 UNDERWOOD 53   20 At these Immortall Mangers Virgil fed.
    p. 309 HORACE 2   78 Or Plautus, and in Virgil disavow,
    p. 397 UNGATHERED 30   28 Or Rurall Virgil come, to pipe to vs!

virgin   frequency: 6   relative frequency: 0.00008
    p. 52 EPIGRAMS 74   9 The Virgin, long-since fled from earth, I see,
    p. 371 UNGATHERED 9   3 It couers, first, a Virgin; and then, one
    p. 412 UNGATHERED 41   t2 of the blessed Virgin
    p. 413 UNGATHERED 41   37 Most holy, & pure Virgin, blessed Mayd,
    p. 414 UNGATHERED 41   55 T'imprint in all purg'd hearts this virgin sence,
    p. 421 UNGATHERED 48   37 Throwe, Holye Virgin, then

virgin-traine   frequency: 1   relative frequency: 0.00001
    p. 34 EPIGRAMS 22   9 Hath plac'd amongst her virgin-traine:

virgin-troup   frequency: 1   relative frequency: 0.00001
    p. 254 UNDERWOOD 75   50 The choisest Virgin-troup of all the Land!

virgin-white   frequency: 1   relative frequency: 0.00001
    p. 253 UNDERWOOD 75   41 See, how she paceth forth in Virgin-white,

virgins   frequency: 3   relative frequency: 0.00004
    p. 230 UNDERWOOD 56   15 Sleepe in a Virgins bosome without feare,
    p. 254 UNDERWOOD 75   49 Stay, thou wilt see what rites the Virgins doe!
    p. 254 UNDERWOOD 75   61 Stay, see the Virgins sow,

virtue   frequency: 4   relative frequency: 0.00005
    See also "vertu'," "vertue," "vertue',"
             "vertue'enforme."
    p. 367 UNGATHERED 6   31 "So much doth Virtue hate,
    p. 420 UNGATHERED 48   12 Of Civill virtue, that hee now is not
    p. 421 UNGATHERED 49   9 And though yor: virtue (as becomes it) still
    p. 423 UNGATHERED 50   18 Virtue, and Soveraigntie, they not consort./

virtues. See "vertues."

virtuous. See "all-vertuous," "vertuous."

virtuously. See "vertuously."

vision   frequency: 3   relative frequency: 0.00004
    p. 286 U'WOOD 84.9   132 The vision of our Saviour, face to face,
    p. 396 UNGATHERED 30   t1 THE VISION OF
    p. 396 UNGATHERED 30   13 Wonder to truth! and haue my Vision hoorld,

visit   frequency: 1   relative frequency: 0.00001
    p. 89 EPIGRAMS 133   175 But you will visit grisly PLVTO'S hall?

visits   frequency: 2   relative frequency: 0.00002
    p. 164 UNDERWOOD 15   68 Be at their Visits, see 'hem squemish, sick,
    p. 396 UNGATHERED 30   4 Those ambling visits, passe in verse, betweene

visor   frequency: 1   relative frequency: 0.00001
    p. 319 HORACE 2   316 Brought in the Visor, and the robe of State,

visors. See "vizors."

vitious   frequency: 4   relative frequency: 0.00005
    p. 74 EPIGRAMS 115   5 Being no vitious person, but the vice
    p. 158 UNDERWOOD 14   12 Of this so vitious Humanitie.
    p. 162 UNDERWOOD 15   4 Their vitious ease, and be o'rewhelm'd with it.
    p. 284 U'WOOD 84.9   74 Who violates the God-head, is most vitious

vitruvius   frequency: 1   relative frequency: 0.00001
    p. 402 UNGATHERED 34   8 With mistooke Names out of Vitruvius!

vizors   frequency: 1   relative frequency: 0.00001
    p. 402 UNGATHERED 34   13 Vizors or Anticks? or it comprhend

vlcers   frequency: 1   relative frequency: 0.00001
    p. 38 EPIGRAMS 38   2 And to conceale your vlcers, did aduise,

vlushing   frequency: 1   relative frequency: 0.00001
    p. 213 UNDERWOOD 44   30 Would thinke no more of Vlushing, or the Brill:

vlysses   frequency: 2   relative frequency: 0.00002
    p.   84 EPIGRAMS 133   3 ORPHEVS, VLYSSES: or the Latine
                               Muse,
    p.   87 EPIGRAMS 133   113 The slie VLYSSES stole in a sheepes-skin,

vn-argued   frequency: 1   relative frequency: 0.00001
    p.   71 EPIGRAMS 110   10 Vn-argued then, and yet hath fame from those;

vn-arm'd   frequency: 1   relative frequency: 0.00001
    p.   87 EPIGRAMS 133   135 But open, and vn-arm'd encounter'd all:

vn-auoided   frequency: 1   relative frequency: 0.00001
    p.   60 EPIGRAMS 94   8 Their vn-auoided subiect, fewest see:

vn-bought   frequency: 1   relative frequency: 0.00001
    p.   97 FOREST 3   14 Liue, with vn-bought prouision blest;

vn-hurt   frequency: 1   relative frequency: 0.00001
    p.   60 EPIGRAMS 93   13 Thou yet remayn'st, vn-hurt in peace, or warre,

vn-nam'd   frequency: 1   relative frequency: 0.00001
    p.   66 EPIGRAMS 103   4 Know you to be a SYDNEY, though vn-nam'd?

vn-sweet   frequency: 1   relative frequency: 0.00001
    p.   88 EPIGRAMS 133   171 Vpon your eares, of discords so vn-sweet?

vn-taught   frequency: 1   relative frequency: 0.00001
    p. 111 FOREST 11   61 A fixed thought, an eye vn-taught to glance;

vn-welcome   frequency: 1   relative frequency: 0.00001
    p.   74 EPIGRAMS 115   15 Whose name's vn-welcome to the present eare,

vnalter'd   frequency: 1   relative frequency: 0.00001
    p. 118 FOREST 13   61 And keepe an euen, and vnalter'd gaite;

vnblest   frequency: 1   relative frequency: 0.00001
  **p. 116 PANEGYRE   115 And that no wretch was more vnblest then he,

vnbounded   frequency: 1   relative frequency: 0.00001
    p. 406 UNGATHERED 34   95 Expression for! wth that vnbounded lyne

vnbroke   frequency: 1   relative frequency: 0.00001
    p. 386 UNGATHERED 21   13 Hold thyne owne worth vnbroke: which is so good

vncouers   frequency: 1   relative frequency: 0.00001
    p. 363 UNGATHERED 3   7 Respect, and obseruation; it vncouers

vnder   frequency: 3   relative frequency: 0.00004
    p. 393 UNGATHERED 27   12 All false-hood vnder feete.
    p. 397 UNGATHERED 30   48 Vnder one title. Thou hast made thy way
    p. 405 UNGATHERED 34   83 Vnder ye Morall? shewe he had a pate

vnder-carued   frequency: 1   relative frequency: 0.00001
    p. 115 FOREST 12   85 Aboue your vnder-carued ornaments,

vnder-neath   frequency: 2   relative frequency: 0.00002
    p.   39 EPIGRAMS 40   2 A dead beautie vnder-neath thee,
    p.   79 EPIGRAMS 124   3 Vnder-neath this stone doth lye

vnder-takes   frequency: 1   relative frequency: 0.00001
    p.   74 EPIGRAMS 115   18 But, if it shall be question'd, vnder-takes,

vnder-wood   frequency: 1   relative frequency: 0.00001
    p. 127 GENERAL TITLE t1 VNDER-WOOD.

vnderstand   frequency: 7   relative frequency: 0.00010
  **p. 115 PANEGYRE   68 To vnderstand the more, the more were rapt.
    p.   27 EPIGRAMS 1   2 To reade it well: that is, to vnderstand.
    p.   59 EPIGRAMS 92   10 And vnderstand 'hem, as most chapmen doe.
    p. 370 UNGATHERED 7   1 In Picture, they which truly vnderstand,
    p. 383 UNGATHERED 17   2 Must be intended still to vnderstand:
    p. 383 UNGATHERED 17   7 Who reads, who roaues, who hopes to vnderstand,
    p. 383 UNGATHERED 17 10 To vnderstand, hee may at length admire.

vnderstood   frequency: 4   relative frequency: 0.00005
    p.   66 EPIGRAMS 102   4 Both which are ask'd, to haue thee vnderstood.
    p.   71 EPIGRAMS 110   16 How few haue read! how fewer vnderstood!)
    p.   73 EPIGRAMS 113   3 So, where thou liu'st, thou mak'st life
                               vnderstood!
    p. 397 UNGATHERED 30   58 Our right in France! if ritely vnderstood. .

vnfit   frequency: 1   relative frequency: 0.00001
     p. 78 EPIGRAMS 121   7 Nor he, for friendship, to be thought vnfit,

vnfolds   frequency: 1   relative frequency: 0.00001
     **p. 113 PANEGYRE   4 Vnfolds himself: & from his eyes are hoorl'd

vnfound   frequency: 1   relative frequency: 0.00001
     p. 114 FOREST 12   25 Were yet vnfound, and better plac'd in earth,

vnfrighted   frequency: 1   relative frequency: 0.00001
     p. 80 EPIGRAMS 133   73 But they vnfrighted passe, though many a priuie

vnion   frequency: 3   relative frequency: 0.00004
     p. 28 EPIGRAMS 5   +1 ON THE VNION.
     p. 413 UNGATHERED 41 32 The glorious Trinity in Vnion met.
     p. 413 UNGATHERED 41 35 Of Persons, yet in Vnion (ONE) divine.

vnitie   frequency: 1   relative frequency: 0.00001
     p. 110 FOREST 11   53 But, in a calme, and god-like vnitie,

vniuersall   frequency: 1   relative frequency: 0.00001
     p. 397 UNGATHERED 30 51 Or vniuersall circumduction

vnkinde   frequency: 1   relative frequency: 0.00001
     p. 109 FOREST 11   10 That no strange, or vnkinde

vnknowne   frequency: 1   relative frequency: 0.00001
     p. 39 EPIGRAMS 39   1 For all night-sinnes, with others wiues,
                              vnknowne,

vnlearned   frequency: 1   relative frequency: 0.00001
     p. 410 UNGATHERED 38 12 Both learned, and vnlearned, all write Playes.

vnlike   frequency: 1   relative frequency: 0.00001
     **p. 117 PANEGYRE   143 Before mens hearts had crown'd him. Who (vnlike

vnlocke   frequency: 1   relative frequency: 0.00001
     p. 380 UNGATHERED 12 23 Each leafe of his iournall, and line doth vnlocke

vnluckie   frequency: 1   relative frequency: 0.00001
     p. 43 EPIGRAMS 65   5 Be thy next masters more vnluckie Muse,

vnmak'st   frequency: 1   relative frequency: 0.00001
     p. 44 EPIGRAMS 66   5 At once thou mak'st me happie, and vnmak'st;

vnnaturall   frequency: 1   relative frequency: 0.00001
     **p. 113 PANEGYRE   29 Till forraine malice, or vnnaturall spight

vnprofiting   frequency: 1   relative frequency: 0.00001
     p. 57 EPIGRAMS 90   1 When MILL first came to court, the
                              vnprofiting foole,

vnprou'd   frequency: 1   relative frequency: 0.00001
     p. 60 EPIGRAMS 93   14 Though not vnprou'd: which shewes, thy fortunes
                              are

vnrests   frequency: 1   relative frequency: 0.00001
     p. 110 FOREST 11   33 Most frequent tumults, horrors, and vnrests,

vnsatisfied   frequency: 1   relative frequency: 0.00001
     **p. 114 PANEGYRE   44 All, as vnwearied, as vnsatisfied:

vnseason'd   frequency: 1   relative frequency: 0.00001
     p. 361 UNGATHERED 1   8 Vnseason'd ffrostes, or the most enuyous weather.

vnthriftely   frequency: 1   relative frequency: 0.00001
     p. 69 EPIGRAMS 107   28 Will you part with them, here, vnthriftely?

vntill   frequency: 3   relative frequency: 0.00004
     p. 73 EPIGRAMS 114   4 In meere out-formes, vntill he lost his sight,
     p. 121 FOREST 14   56 To liue vntill to morrow' hath lost   dayes.
     p. 400 UNGATHERED 31 31 Vntill the dust retorned bee

vnto   frequency: 42   relative frequency: 0.00060

vntouch'd   frequency: 1   relative frequency: 0.00001
     p. 81 EPIGRAMS 128   14 Came backe vntouch'd. This man hath trauail'd
                              well.

vntrauell'd   frequency: 1   relative frequency: 0.00001
     p.   56 EPIGRAMS 88   7 That he, vntrauell'd, should be french so much,

vnwearied   frequency: 1   relative frequency: 0.00001
  **p. 114 PANEGYRE   44 All, as vnwearied, as vnsatisfied:

vnworthy   frequency: 1   relative frequency: 0.00001
     p.   57 EPIGRAMS 90   2 Vnworthy such a mistris, such a schoole,

vogue   frequency: 1   relative frequency: 0.00001
     p. 383 UNGATHERED 24 15 For though Spaine gaue him his first ayre and
                              Vogue,

voice   frequency: 3   relative frequency: 0.00004
     See also "voyce."
     p.   49 EPIGRAMS 67   12 Proues, that is gods, which was the peoples
                              voice.
     p.   55 EPIGRAMS 86   5 Now, I must giue thy life, and deed, the voice
     p. 181 UNDERWOOD 27   16 Whose fame hath an eternall voice?

voiced. See "voyc't."

voices   frequency: 2   relative frequency: 0.00002
     See also "voyces."
  **p. 114 PANEGYRE   60 Of hearts, and voices. All the aire was rent,
     p. 385 UNGATHERED 19   1 When these, and such, their voices haue employd;

void   frequency: 2   relative frequency: 0.00002
     See also "voyd."
     p. 329 HORACE 2   511 The Poems void of profit, our grave men
     p. 385 UNGATHERED 19   2 What place is for my testimony void?

voids   frequency: 1   relative frequency: 0.00001
     p. 166 UNDERWOOD 15 116 Or by Damnation voids it? or by stealth?

volary   frequency: 1   relative frequency: 0.00001
     p. 397 UNGATHERED 30 36 Like him, to make the ayre, one volary:

volume   frequency: 3   relative frequency: 0.00004
     p. 383 UNGATHERED 17   1 Who takes thy volume to his vertuous hand,
     p. 383 UNGATHERED 17   8 May take thy volume to his vertuous hand.
     p. 399 UNGATHERED 31   7 Your booke? your volume! Nay, the state, and
                              story!

volumes   frequency: 1   relative frequency: 0.00001
     p. 392 UNGATHERED 26 80 And despaires day, but for thy Volumes light.

voluminous   frequency: 1   relative frequency: 0.00001
     p. 225 UNDERWOOD 52   2 I am not so voluminous, and vast,

voluptuous   frequency: 1   relative frequency: 0.00001
     See also "volvptvovs."
  **p. 116 PANEGYRE   114 To their voluptuous lustes, had lost their name;

volvptvovs   frequency: 1   relative frequency: 0.00001
     p.   34 EPIGRAMS 25   t1 ON SIR VOLVPTVOVS BEAST.

votary   frequency: 1   relative frequency: 0.00001
     p. 372 UNGATHERED 9   10 The sole Religious house, and Votary,

vote   frequency: 1   relative frequency: 0.00001
     p. 203 UNDERWOOD 43   22 By thy owne vote, a sacrifice to thee?

vouches   frequency: 1   relative frequency: 0.00001
     p. 202 UNDERWOOD 42   77 And vouches both the Pageant, and the Day,

vouchsafe   frequency: 2   relative frequency: 0.00002
     p. 273 U'WOOD 84.1   9 Of Goodnesse still: Vouchsafe to take
     p. 392 UNGATHERED 26 50 As, since, she will vouchsafe no other Wit.

vow   frequency: 4   relative frequency: 0.00005
     p.   99 FOREST 3   100 Thy morning's, and thy euening's vow
     p. 116 FOREST 12   98 A vow as new, and ominous as the yeare,
     p. 120 FOREST 14   23 Your vow
     p. 159 UNDERWOOD 14   28 Meane what I speake: and still will keepe that
                              Vow.

vow'd   frequency: 3   relative frequency: 0.00004
  **p. 113 PANEGYRE   28 And in her office vow'd she would remaine,
     p.   70 EPIGRAMS 108   9 He that not trusts me, hauing vow'd thus much,

vow'd (cont.)
p. 202 UNDERWOOD 78   18 Which I have vow'd posteritie to give.

vowells   frequency: 1   relative frequency: 0.00001
p. 183 UNDERWOOD 29   11 Fastning Vowells, as with fetters

vowels. See "vowells."

vowes   frequency: 7   relative frequency: 0.00010
p. 41 EPIGRAMS 45   11 For whose sake, hence-forth, all his vowes be
                           such,
p. 77 EPIGRAMS 120   24 Heauen vowes to keepe him.
p. 111 FOREST 11   83 Nor meane we those, whom vowes and conscience
p. 191 UNDERWOOD 38   1 'Tis true, I'm broke! Vowes, Oathes, and all
                           I had
p. 194 UNDERWOOD 38   107 I will no more abuse my vowes to you,
p. 197 UNDERWOOD 40   14 Of vowes so sacred, and in silence made;
p. 198 UNDERWOOD 40   41 And such your Servant is, who vowes to keepe

vows. See "vowes."

voyage   frequency: 2   relative frequency: 0.00002
p. 84 EPIGRAMS 133   +1 ON THE FAMOVS VOYAGE.
p. 84 EPIGRAMS 133   20+ THE VOYAGE IT SELFE.

voyce   frequency: 18   relative frequency: 0.00026
**p. 117 PANEGYRE   155 And this confession flew from euery voyce:
p. 31 EPIGRAMS 12   19 To euery cause he meets, this voyce he brayes:
p. 47 EPIGRAMS 63   6 Not from the publike voyce, but priuate fact:
p. 51 EPIGRAMS 74   4 That no affection in thy voyce commands;
p. 61 EPIGRAMS 95   20 Thou need'st not shrinke at voyce of after-times;
p. 66 EPIGRAMS 106   4 Truth might spend all her voyce, Fame all her
                           art.
p. 81 EPIGRAMS 128   11 We each to other may this voyce enspire;
p. 86 EPIGRAMS 133   89 How hight the place? a voyce was heard,
                           COCYTVS.
p. 113 FOREST 12   11 Though neuer after; whiles it gaynes the voyce
p. 145 UNDERWOOD 7   27 What Nymph so e're his voyce but heares,
p. 160 UNDERWOOD 14   60 Newnesse of Sense, Antiquitie of voyce!
p. 167 UNDERWOOD 15   154 For the recovery of my voyce? No, there
p. 234 UNDERWOOD 61   5 That scarce you heare a publike voyce alive,
p. 209 UNDERWOOD 83   24 And voyce to raise them from my brazen Lungs,
p. 273 U'WOOD 84.4   37 The Voyce so sweet, the words so faire,
p. 311 HORACE 2   133 Her voyce, and angry Chremes chafes out-right
p. 396 UNGATHERED 30   12 Lend me thy voyce, O FAME, that I may draw
p. 397 UNGATHERED 30   38 My lippes could forme the voyce, I heard that
                           Rore,

voyces   frequency: 3   relative frequency: 0.00004
p. 143 UNDERWOOD 3   1 Come, with our Voyces, let us warre,
p. 329 HORACE 2   512 Cast out by voyces; want they pleasure, then
p. 340 HORACE 1   306 .. the graue Harp, and Violl voyces ...

voyc't   frequency: 1   relative frequency: 0.00001
p. 87 EPIGRAMS 133   119 Yet, one day in the yeere, for sweet 'tis voyc't,

voyd   frequency: 1   relative frequency: 0.00001
**p. 115 PANEGYRE   94 "To heare the truth, from spight, or flattery
                           voyd.

vp   frequency: 46   relative frequency: 0.00066
*p. 433 TO HIMSELF   26 May keepe vp the Play-club:
p. 30 EPIGRAMS 12   13 Then takes vp fresh commoditie, for dayes;
p. 35 EPIGRAMS 28   11 That's greater, yet: to crie his owne vp neate.
p. 42 EPIGRAMS 46   3 'Tis LVCKLESSE he, that tooke vp one on
                           band
p. 45 EPIGRAMS 56   8 He takes vp all, makes each mans wit his owne.
p. 50 EPIGRAMS 71   1 To plucke downe mine, POLL sets vp new wits
                           still,
p. 50 EPIGRAMS 72   1 I grieue not, COVRTLING, thou are
                           started vp
p. 57 EPIGRAMS 90   14 Blowne vp; and he (too'vnwieldie for that place)
p. 59 EPIGRAMS 92   17 And talke reseru'd, lock'd vp, and full of feare,
p. 59 EPIGRAMS 92   29 To breake vp seales, and close 'hem. And they
                           know,
p. 67 EPIGRAMS 105   2 All historie seal'd vp, and fables crost;
p. 69 EPIGRAMS 107   29 Nay, now you puffe, tuske, and draw vp your chin,
p. 72 EPIGRAMS 111   12 CAESAR stands vp, as from his vrne late
                           rose,
p. 74 EPIGRAMS 115   24 The cloth's no sooner gone, but it gets vp

vp (cont.)
p.	75	EPIGRAMS	116	4 That age, when thou stood'st vp the master-braine:
p.	80	EPIGRAMS	127	6 How full of want, how swallow'd vp, how dead
p.	88	EPIGRAMS	133	161 With great gray eyes, are lifted vp, and mew'd;
p.	95	FOREST	2	71 Thy tables hoord not vp for the next day,
p.	99	FOREST	3	79 To blow vp orphanes, widdowes, and their states;
p.	100	FOREST	4	14 Yet art thou both shrunke vp, and old,
p.	101	FOREST	4	43 Since stird'st vp iealousies and feares,
p.	103	FOREST	6	6 Kisse, and score vp wealthy summes
p.	108	FOREST	10	28 My Muse vp by commission: No, I bring
p.	108	FOREST	10 A	4 like glasse, blowne vp, and fashion'd by desire.
p.	108	FOREST	10 A	13 wch rap's mee vp to the true heau'en of loue;
p.	113	FOREST	12	5 Toyles, by graue custome, vp and downe the court,
p.	114	FOREST	12	42 And, at her strong armes end, hold vp, and euen,
p.	115	FOREST	12	84 Borne vp by statues, shall I reare your head,
p.	117	FOREST	13	33 Not taken vp o'th'doctors, but as well
p.	363	UNGATHERED	3	10 Were they as strong ram'd vp as Aetna gates.
p.	368	UNGATHERED	6	77 And vp againe, in skies, and aire to vent
p.	372	UNGATHERED	9	13 Vp so much truth, as could I it pursue
p.	374	UNGATHERED	10	12 Here, not vp Holdborne, but downe a steepe hill,
p.	374	UNGATHERED	10	16 Here, vp the Alpes (not so plaine as to Dunstable)
p.	386	UNGATHERED	21	10 Or, like our Money-Brokers, take vp names
p.	395	UNGATHERED	29	2 And see both climing vp the slippery staire
p.	396	UNGATHERED	30	18 Is fayre got vp, and day some houres begun!
p.	397	UNGATHERED	30	33 And looking vp, I saw Mineruas fowle,
p.	400	UNGATHERED	31	27 And when the flesh, here, shut vp day,
p.	401	UNGATHERED	32	12 To cut a Dike? or sticke a Stake vp, here,
p.	403	UNGATHERED	34	32 That doe cry vp ye Machine, & ye Showes!
p.	403	UNGATHERED	34	39 To hold her vp. O Showes! Showes! Mighty Showes!
p.	405	UNGATHERED	34	80 Vp & about? Dyue into Cellars too
p.	405	UNGATHERED	34	84 Moulded or stroakt vp to suruey a State!
p.	410	UNGATHERED	38	13 It was not so of old: Men tooke vp trades
p.	417	UNGATHERED	45	14 those turnd vp, and those that fall,

vp-beare   frequency: 1   relative frequency: 0.00001
    p.   60 EPIGRAMS 93   3 Who did, alike with thee, thy house vp-beare,

vpbraid   frequency: 1   relative frequency: 0.00001
    p.   48 EPIGRAMS 66   5 Who, to vpbraid the sloth of this our time,

vpbraiding   frequency: 1   relative frequency: 0.00001
    p.   60 EPIGRAMS 93   6 Vpbraiding rebells armes, and barbarous pride:

vpon   frequency: 45   relative frequency: 0.00065

vppon   frequency: 2   relative frequency: 0.00002

vpright   frequency: 2   relative frequency: 0.00002
    p.   55 EPIGRAMS 85   6 That they to knowledge so should toure vpright,
    p.   68 EPIGRAMS 106   7 Thy standing vpright to thy selfe, thy ends

vpward   frequency: 2   relative frequency: 0.00002
  **p. 115 PANEGYRE   90 "Where he was going; and the vpward race
    p. 366 UNGATHERED 6   11 How vpward, and direct!

vrge   frequency: 3   relative frequency: 0.00004
    p.   82 EPIGRAMS 130   1 To vrge, my lou'd ALPHONSO, that bold fame
    p. 121 FOREST   14   30 Doth vrge him to runne wrong, or to stand still.
    p. 398 UNGATHERED 30   69 So shall our English Youth vrge on, and cry

vrgeth   frequency: 2   relative frequency: 0.00002
  **p. 113 PANEGYRE   2 With ioyes: but vrgeth his full fauors still.
    p. 391 UNGATHERED 26   10 The truth, but gropes, and vrgeth all by chance;

vrine   frequency: 1   relative frequency: 0.00001
    p.   88 EPIGRAMS 133   170 Vrine, and plaisters? when the noise doth beate

vrne   frequency: 1   relative frequency: 0.00001
    p.   72 EPIGRAMS 111   12 CAESAR stands vp, as from his vrne late rose,

vs   frequency: 35   relative frequency: 0.00050

vs'd   frequency: 2   relative frequency: 0.00002
    p.   80 EPIGRAMS 133   98 And, in so shitten sort, so long had vs'd him:
    p. 115 FOREST   12   74 I haue already vs'd some happy houres,

vse   frequency: 14   relative frequency: 0.00020
     p.   27 EPIGRAMS 3   3 Vse mine so, too: I giue thee leaue. But craue
     p.   32 EPIGRAMS 18   7 If thou'ldst but vse thy faith, as thou didst
                                then,
     p.   35 EPIGRAMS 28   3 Makes serious vse of all great trade he knowes.
     p.   36 EPIGRAMS 28   21 SVRLY, vse other arts, these only can
     p.   44 EPIGRAMS 55   2 That vnto me dost such religion vse!
     p.   52 EPIGRAMS 76   4 To honor, serue, and loue; as Poets vse.
     p.   78 EPIGRAMS 121   1 RVDYERD, as lesser dames, to great ones
                                vse,
     p.   99 FOREST 3   99 Which who can vse is happy: Such be thou.
     p. 107 FOREST 10   2 Or whose great name in Poets heauen vse,
     p. 120 FOREST 13   122 Madame, be bold to vse this truest glasse:
     p. 361 UNGATHERED 1   9 Then I admir'd, the rare and prescious vse
     p. 398 UNGATHERED 30   59 There, thou art Homer! Pray thee, vse the stile
     p. 398 UNGATHERED 30   65 And when he ships them where to vse their Armes,
     p. 400 UNGATHERED 32   5 Such, as the creeping common Pioners vse

vshring   frequency: 1   relative frequency: 0.00001
     p.   64 EPIGRAMS 101   11 Vshring the mutton; with a short-leg'd hen,

vsuall   frequency: 1   relative frequency: 0.00001
     p. 394 UNGATHERED 28   14 Not vsuall in a Lady; and yet true:

vsurer   frequency: 1   relative frequency: 0.00001
     p. 118 FOREST 13   78 Till that no vsurer, nor his bawds dare lend

vsurers   frequency: 1   relative frequency: 0.00001
     p.   88 EPIGRAMS 133   139 Or, that it lay, heap'd like an vsurers masse,

vsurie   frequency: 1   relative frequency: 0.00001
     p.   45 EPIGRAMS 57   2 Baudrie', and vsurie were one kind of game.

vsurpe   frequency: 1   relative frequency: 0.00001
    *p. 492 TO HIMSELF   4 Vsurpe the chaire of wit!

vsurping   frequency: 1   relative frequency: 0.00001
     p. 110 FOREST 11   31 Of which vsurping rancke, some haue thought loue

vsvrer   frequency: 1   relative frequency: 0.00001
     p.   36 EPIGRAMS 31   t1 ON BANCK THE VSVRER.

vsvrers   frequency: 1   relative frequency: 0.00001
     p.   45 EPIGRAMS 57   t1 ON BAVDES, AND VSVRERS.

vsvrer's   frequency: 1   relative frequency: 0.00001
     p.   41 EPIGRAMS 44   t1 ON CHVFFE, BANCKS THE
                                VSVRER'S

vtmost   frequency: 1   relative frequency: 0.00001
     p. 368 UNGATHERED 6   69 To vtmost Thule: whence, he backes the Seas

vtter   frequency: 1   relative frequency: 0.00001
     p.   83 EPIGRAMS 132   4 And vtter stranger to all ayre of France)

vtter'd   frequency: 2   relative frequency: 0.00002
     p.   65 EPIGRAMS 101   40 That shall be vtter'd at our mirthfull boord,
     p.   82 EPIGRAMS 130   15 I, yet, had vtter'd nothing on thy part,

vtterly   frequency: 1   relative frequency: 0.00001
     p.   43 EPIGRAMS 52   1 COVRTLING, I rather thou should'st
                                vtterly

vttring   frequency: 1   relative frequency: 0.00001
     p. 385 UNGATHERED 20   6 The art of vttring wares, if they were bad;

vulcan   frequency: 9   relative frequency: 0.00013
     p. 202 UNDERWOOD 43   5 I ne're attempted, Vulcan, 'gainst thy life;
     p. 202 UNDERWOOD 43   t1 An Execration upon Vulcan.
     p. 206 UNDERWOOD 43   84 Had made a meale for Vulcan to lick up.
     p. 207 UNDERWOOD 43   105 How in these ruines, Vulcan, thou dost lurke,
     p. 208 UNDERWOOD 43   126 They made a Vulcan of a sheafe of Reedes,
     p. 210 UNDERWOOD 43   159 Hee is true Vulcan still! He did not spare
     p. 210 UNDERWOOD 43   175 Against this Vulcan? No Injunction?
     p. 211 UNDERWOOD 43   191 Pox on your flameship, Vulcan; if it be
     p. 212 UNDERWOOD 43   213 Pox on thee, Vulcan, thy Pandora's pox,

vulcanale   frequency: 1   relative frequency: 0.00001
     p. 208 UNDERWOOD 43   120 May to thy name a Vulcanale say;

vulgar   frequency: 8   relative frequency: 0.00011
  *p. 492 TO HIMSELF   t2 tooke at the vulgar censure of his
   p.   27 EPIGRAMS 2   14 For vulgar praise, doth it too dearely buy.
   p.   76 EPIGRAMS 119   11 That to the vulgar canst thy selfe apply,
   p. 184 UNDERWOOD 29   43 Vulgar Languages that want
   p. 193 UNDERWOOD 38   81 And with the vulgar doth it not obtaine
   p. 218 UNDERWOOD 47   7 And shewing so weake an Act to vulgar eyes,
   p. 340 HORACE 1   67 .... vulgar ....
   p. 388 UNGATHERED 23   7 If all the vulgar Tongues, that speake this day,

vulture   frequency: 1   relative frequency: 0.00001
   p. 283 U'WOOD 84.9   18 Of Vulture death, and those relentlesse cleies?

vultures   frequency: 1   relative frequency: 0.00001
   p. 187 UNDERWOOD 33   9 Hook-handed Harpies, gowned Vultures, put

vv'dale   frequency: 1   relative frequency: 0.00001
   p.   79 EPIGRAMS 125   1 VV'DALE, thou piece of the first times, a
                              man

vvedale   frequency: 1   relative frequency: 0.00001
   p.   79 EPIGRAMS 125   t1 TO SIR WILLIAM VVEDALE.

wade   frequency: 1   relative frequency: 0.00001
   p. 365 UNGATHERED 5   17 Alas: then whither wade I,

wag. See "wagg."

wager   frequency: 3   relative frequency: 0.00004
   p. 229 UNDERWOOD 54   2 For a just wager, and that wager paid
   p. 417 UNGATHERED 45   26 that the wife heades for a wager

wagg   frequency: 1   relative frequency: 0.00001
   p. 417 UNGATHERED 45   15 morts, and mirkins that wagg all,

waggon   frequency: 1   relative frequency: 0.00001
   p. 380 UNGATHERED 12   27 Besides he tried Ship, Cart, Waggon, and
                              Chayre,

wagon. See "waggon."

waigh   frequency: 1   relative frequency: 0.00001
   p. 386 UNGATHERED 20   11 I know for such, as (if my word will waigh)

waight   frequency: 2   relative frequency: 0.00002
   p. 112 FOREST 11   113 That knowes the waight of guilt: He will
                              refraine
   p. 113 FOREST 12   8 Iust to the waight their this dayes-presents
                              beare;

wain. See "waine."

waine   frequency: 1   relative frequency: 0.00001
  *p. 494 TO HIMSELF   60 And raysing Charles his chariot, 'boue his
                              Waine.

waist. See "wast," "waste."

wait   frequency: 1   relative frequency: 0.00001
    See also "waite," "wayte."
   p. 282 U'WOOD 84.9   10 A sorrow in me, fit to wait to her!

waite   frequency: 1   relative frequency: 0.00001
   p. 118 FOREST 13   62 Not looking by, or backe (like those, that waite

waited   frequency: 1   relative frequency: 0.00001
   p. 204 UNDERWOOD 79   39 Still waited on 'hem where they were.

waiter   frequency: 1   relative frequency: 0.00001
   p.   95 FOREST 2   68 A waiter, doth my gluttony enuy:

waites   frequency: 2   relative frequency: 0.00002
   p. 175 UNDERWOOD 23   24 And only pitious scorne, upon their folly waites.
   p. 309 HORACE 2   112 Before the Judge, it hangs, and waites report.

waiting   frequency: 1   relative frequency: 0.00001
   p. 289 UNDERWOOD 85   8 And waiting Chambers of great Lords.

waits. See "waites."

wak'd   frequency: 2   relative frequency: 0.00002
    p.   56 EPIGRAMS 87   4 Of what shee had wrought came in, and wak'd his
                                 braine,
    p. 213 UNDERWOOD 44   4 T'have wak'd, if sleeping, Spaines Ambassadour,

wake   frequency: 5   relative frequency: 0.00007
    p. 143 UNDERWOOD 3   14 Sleepe, and the Grave will wake.
    p. 162 UNDERWOOD 15   1 Wake, friend, from forth thy Lethargie: the
                                 Drum
    p. 176 UNDERWOOD 25   3 Wake, and put on the wings of Pindars Muse,
    p. 190 UNDERWOOD 37   15 And Fame wake for me, when I yeeld to sleepe.
    p. 250 UNDERWOOD 73   11 Dreame thou could'st hurt it; but before thou
                                 wake

wakefull   frequency: 1   relative frequency: 0.00001
    p. 109 FOREST 11   13 To wakefull reason, our affections king:

wakers   frequency: 1   relative frequency: 0.00001
    p. 417 UNGATHERED 45   39 at Pem Wakers good ale Tapp,

waking   frequency: 3   relative frequency: 0.00004
  **p. 116 PANEGYRE   100 "Where sleeping they could saue, and waking kill;
    p. 250 UNDERWOOD 73   5 WESTON! That waking man! that Eye of
                                 State!
    p. 256 UNDERWOOD 75   111 What kind of waking Man

walk   frequency: 1   relative frequency: 0.00001
    See also "walke."
    p. 348 HORACE 1   398 .... great ... . walk

walke   frequency: 6   relative frequency: 0.00008
    p.   30 EPIGRAMS 11   8 For I will dare none. Good Lord, walke dead
                                 still.
    p. 138 UNDERWOOD 2.6   13 Or, that did you sit, or walke,
    p. 193 UNDERWOOD 38   98 On every wall, and sung where e're I walke.
    p. 199 UNDERWOOD 41   21 Or like a Ghost walke silent amongst men,
    p. 285 U'WOOD 84.9   117 There shall the Brother, with the Sister walke,
    p. 409 UNGATHERED 37   19 But fly thee, like the Pest! Walke not the
                                 street

walkes   frequency: 6   relative frequency: 0.00008
    p.   30 I GRAMS 11   t1 ON SOME-THING, THAT WALKES
    p.   93 F ?ST 2   9 Thou hast thy walkes for health, as well as
                                 sport:
    p.   98 FC ;T 3   59 The iolly wassall walkes the often round,
    p. 137 UN. WOOD 2.5   53 But shee's Juno, when she walkes,
    p. 264 UN. WOOD 79   ·18 9. See where he walkes <10> with MIRA by his side.
    p. 264 UND WOOD 79   26 Who walkes on Earth as May still went along,

walking   frequency: 2   relative frequency: 0.00002
    p. 143 UNDER WOOD 3   12 And call the walking woods.
    p. 157 UNDERWOOD 13   141 It was erected; and still walking under

walks. See "walkes."

wall   frequency: 7   relative frequency: 0.00010
    p.   56 EPIGRAMS 88   11 Or hung some MOVNSIEVRS picture on the
                                 wall,
    p.   87 EPIGRAMS 133   136 Whether it languishing stucke vpon the wall,
    p.   89 EPIGRAMS 133   176 Behold where CERBERVS, rear'd on the wall
    p. 193 UNDERWOOD 38   98 On every wall, and sung where e're I walke.
    p. 394 UNGATHERED 28   9 No stone in any wall here, but can tell
    p. 406 UNGATHERED 34   97 What Poesy ere was painted on a wall
    p. 408 UNGATHERED 36   11 Wth rotten chalk, or Cole vpon a wall,

walls   frequency: 7   relative frequency: 0.00010
  **p. 114 PANEGYRE   63 Walls, windores, roofes, towers, steeples, all
                                 were set
    p.   28 EPIGRAMS 3   7 Nor have my title-leafe on posts, or walls,
    p.   86 EPIGRAMS 133   67 Betweene two walls; where, on one side, to scar
                                 men,
    p.   88 EPIGRAMS 133   169 Is fill'd with buttock? And the walls doe sweate
    p.   94 FOREST 2   44 Hang on thy walls, that euery child may reach.
    p.   94 FOREST 2   45 And though thy walls be of the countrey stone,
    p. 319 HORACE 2   296 That wider Walls embrac'd their Citie round,

wan   frequency: 3   relative frequency: 0.00004
  **p. 117 PANEGYRE   141 That wan affections, ere his steps wan ground;
    p.   57 EPIGRAMS 90   4 At last, ease, appetite, and example wan

wand   frequency: 1   relative frequency: 0.00001
    p. 176 UNDERWOOD 24   11 And guided by Experience, whose straite wand

wanderers. See "wandrers."

wandering. See "wandring."

wandrers   frequency: 1   relative frequency: 0.00001
    p. 102 FOREST 4   66 As wandrers doe, that still doe rome,

wandring   frequency: 2   relative frequency: 0.00002
    p. 313 HORACE 2   177 Poore Jo wandring; wild Orestes mad:
    p. 346 HORACE 1   304 .... wandring ....

wane   frequency: 1   relative frequency: 0.00001
    p. 87 EPIGRAMS 133   103 But many Moones there shall not wane (quoth hee)

want   frequency: 28   relative frequency: 0.00040
    p. 42 EPIGRAMS 49   2 He sayes, I want the tongue of Epigrammes;
    p. 76 EPIGRAMS 119   1 Not he that flies the court for want of clothes,
    p. 76 EPIGRAMS 119   7 No, SHELTON, giue me thee, canst want all
                             these,
    p. 80 EPIGRAMS 127   6 How full of want, how swallow'd vp, how dead
    p. 100 FOREST 3   104 That neither want doe thee affright,
    p. 113 FOREST 12   13 The foole that gaue it; who will want, and weepe,
    p. 143 UNDERWOOD 3   7 What Tree or stone doth want a soule?
    p. 150 UNDERWOOD 10   14 Loves sicknesse, and his noted want of worth,
    p. 152 UNDERWOOD 12   32 Now I conceive him by my want,
    p. 153 UNDERWOOD 13   28 That they have more opprest me, then my want?
    p. 155 UNDERWOOD 13   79 But these men ever want: their very trade
    p. 156 UNDERWOOD 13   112 And where they want, she is not understood.
    p. 174 UNDERWOOD 22   36 What I, in her, am griev'd to want.
    p. 174 UNDERWOOD 23   9 Doth Clarius Harp want strings,
    p. 184 UNDERWOOD 29   43 Vulgar Languages that want
    p. 194 UNDERWOOD 38   122 Rather then want your light, I wish a grave.
    p. 224 UNDERWOOD 50   26 And when you want those friends, or neere in
                             blood,
    p. 229 UNDERWOOD 54   10 Within the ballance; and not want a mite;
    p. 241 UNDERWOOD 68   4 For want of knowing the Poet, to say him nay?
    p. 241 UNDERWOOD 68   7 Hee'ld frame such ditties of their store, and
                             want,
    p. 248 UNDERWOOD 71   5 Want, with the rest of his conceal'd compeeres,
    p. 258 UNDERWOOD 75   177 And never may there want one of the Stem,
    p. 288 U'WOOD 84.9   186 Nor can the bruised heart want eloquence:
    p. 329 HORACE 2   512 Cast out by voyces; want they pleasure, then
    p. 380 UNGATHERED 12   55 Some want, they say in a sort he did craue:
    p. 409 UNGATHERED 37   22 Thy Dirty braines, Men smell thy want of worth.
    p. 410 UNGATHERED 39   4 Pillory nor Whip, nor want of Ears,
    p. 421 UNGATHERED 49   10 deignes myne the power to ffinde, yett want I
                             will

wanted   frequency: 2   relative frequency: 0.00002
    p. 84 EPIGRAMS 133   15 Furies there wanted not: each scold was ten.
    p. 117 FOREST 13   37 Nor that your beautie wanted not a dower,

wanting   frequency: 1   relative frequency: 0.00001
    p. 48 EPIGRAMS 66   1 That neither fame, nor loue might wanting be

wanton   frequency: 5   relative frequency: 0.00007
    See also "over-wanton."
    p. 108 FOREST 10A   11 Let these in wanton feete daunce out their
                             soules.
    p. 136 UNDERWOOD 2.5   23 Such as oft I wanton in!
    p. 144 UNDERWOOD 4   1 Oh doe not wanton with those eyes,
    p. 293 UNDERWOOD 86   29 Me now, nor Wench, nor wanton Boy,
    p. 311 HORACE 2   150 The angry brow; the sportive, wanton things;

wanton-wise   frequency: 1   relative frequency: 0.00001
    p. 141 UNDERWOOD 2.9   16 For he must looke wanton-wise.

wants   frequency: 5   relative frequency: 0.00007
    p. 80 EPIGRAMS 133   71 With famine, wants, and sorrowes many a dosen,
    p. 152 UNDERWOOD 12   39 Nor wants it here through penurie, or sloth,
    p. 155 UNDERWOOD 13   61 And seeke not wants to succour: but enquire,
    p. 339 HORACE 1   38 Wants strength, and .... as his spirits were
                             done;
    p. 362 UNGATHERED 2   11 Wants facultie to make a censure true:

war. See "warr," "warre."

warbleth   frequency: 1   relative frequency: 0.00001
    p. 369 UNGATHERED 6   98 Who warbleth PANCHARIS,

ward   frequency: 1   relative frequency: 0.00001
    p. 109 FOREST 11   8 Of thoughts to watch, and ward

warden   frequency: 1   relative frequency: 0.00001
    p. 415 UNGATHERED 42   23 Of wit, and a new made: a Warden then,

wardrobe   frequency: 2   relative frequency: 0.00002
    p. 201 UNDERWOOD 42   51 Then ope thy wardrobe, thinke me that poore
                             Groome
    p. 380 UNGATHERED 12   47 Nay more in his wardrobe, if you will laugh at a

ware   frequency: 1   relative frequency: 0.00001
    p. 423 UNGATHERED 50   15 Yet ware; thou mayst do all things cruellie:

w'are   frequency: 1   relative frequency: 0.00001

wares   frequency: 3   relative frequency: 0.00004
    p. 100 FOREST 4   20 Yet art thou falser then thy wares.
    p. 333 HORACE 2   598 That to the sale of Wares calls every Buyer;
    p. 385 UNGATHERED 20   6 The art of vttring wares, if they were bad;

warie   frequency: 2   relative frequency: 0.00002
    p. 103 FOREST 6   1 Kisse me, sweet: The warie louer
    p. 307 HORACE 2   66 Right spare, and warie: then thou speak'st to mee

warie-driven   frequency: 1   relative frequency: 0.00001
    p. 323 HORACE 2   393 Grow a safe Writer, and be warie-driven

warm. See "warme."

warme   frequency: 7   relative frequency: 0.00010
   *p. 493 TO HIMSELF   44 Warme thee, by Pindares fire:
    p. 95 FOREST 2   81 With all their zeale, to warme their welcome
                             here.
    p. 150 UNDERWOOD 10   6 That others should not warme them at my fire,
    p. 260 UNDERWOOD 76   31 And so warme the Poets tongue
    p. 392 UNGATHERED 26   45 When like Apollo he came forth to warme
    p. 400 UNGATHERED 31   30 Keeps warme the spice of her good name,
    p. 405 UNGATHERED 34   67 Hee's warme on his feet now he sayes, & can

warming. See "quick-warming-pan."

warned   frequency: 1   relative frequency: 0.00001
    p. 329 HORACE 2   530 Still in the same, and warned will not mend,

warning   frequency: 1   relative frequency: 0.00001
    p. 411 UNGATHERED 40   14 with their warning,

warp. See "warpe."

warpe   frequency: 2   relative frequency: 0.00002
    p. 263 UNDERWOOD 79   5 Of the New Yeare, in a new silken warpe,
    p. 415 UNGATHERED 42   15 And know the woofe, and warpe thereof; can tell

warr   frequency: 1   relative frequency: 0.00001
    See also "la-ware."
    p. 417 UNGATHERED 45   22 for if there, or peace or warr be,

warrant   frequency: 2   relative frequency: 0.00002
    p. 393 UNGATHERED 27   9 It is the Warrant of the Word,
    p. 399 UNGATHERED 31   22 By warrant call'd iust Symetry,

warre   frequency: 18   relative frequency: 0.00026
    p. 60 EPIGRAMS 93   13 Thou yet remayn'st, vn-hurt in peace, or warre,
    p. 71 EPIGRAMS 110   2 In these west-parts, nor when that warre was
                             done,
    p. 72 EPIGRAMS 111   4 Beholding, to this master of the warre;
    p. 99 FOREST 3   76 Then either money, warre, or death:
    p. 143 UNDERWOOD 3   1 Come, with our Voyces, let us warre,
    p. 168 UNDERWOOD 15   195 These take, and now goe seeke thy peace in
                             Warre,
    p. 184 UNDERWOOD 29   53 Stil may reason warre with rime,
    p. 186 UNDERWOOD 33   2 The Seat made of a more then civill warre;
    p. 213 UNDERWOOD 44   11 All Ensignes of a Warre, are not yet dead,
    p. 213 UNDERWOOD 44   24 Thou Seed-plot of the warre, that hast not
                             spar'd
    p. 214 UNDERWOOD 44   55 That keepe the warre, though now't be growne more
                             tame,

warre (cont.)
    p. 234 UNDERWOOD 60   13 No aime at glorie, or, in warre,
    p. 253 UNDERWOOD 75   31 And the allowed warre:
    p. 292 UNDERWOOD 86   1 Venus, againe thou mov'st a warre
    p. 292 UNDERWOOD 86   16 Will he display the Ensignes of thy warre.
    p. 313 HORACE 2   196 I sing a noble Warre, and Priam's Fate.
    p. 315 HORACE 2   209 Of Diomede; nor Troyes sad Warre begins
    p. 393 UNGATHERED 27   17 This, blessed Warre, thy blessed Booke

warres   frequency: 7   relative frequency: 0.00010
   *p. 494 TO HIMSELF   57 In sound of peace, or warres,
    p. 162 UNDERWOOD 15   t2 him to the Warres.
    p. 309 HORACE 2   105 The gests of Kings, great Captaines, and sad
                             Warres,
    p. 325 HORACE 2   451 Of a brave Chiefe sent to the warres: He can,
    p. 329 HORACE 2   495 Their minds to Warres, with rimes they did
                             rehearse;
    p. 363 UNGATHERED 3   3 Warres grea<t>est woes, and miseries increase,
    p. 397 UNGATHERED 30 42 I saw, and read, it was thy Barons Warres!

wars   frequency: 1   relative frequency: 0.00001
    See also "warres."
    p. 343 HORACE 1   209 .. .. wars ......

warwick   frequency: 1   relative frequency: 0.00001
    p. 382 UNGATHERED 16 t3 Rich, now Earles of warwick and Hollande.

wary   frequency: 1   relative frequency: 0.00001
    See also "warie," "warie-driven."
    p. 270 UNDERWOOD 83   40 Her wary guardes, her wise simplicitie,

was   frequency: 218   relative frequency: 0.00315
    See also "'twas," "was't."

wassail. See "wassall."

wassall   frequency: 1   relative frequency: 0.00001
    p. 98 FOREST 3   59 The iolly wassall walkes the often round,

wast   frequency: 7   relative frequency: 0.00010
    p. 42 EPIGRAMS 46   1 Is this the Sir, who, some wast wife to winne,
    p. 105 FOREST 8   16 Woman-kinde; deuoure the wast
    p. 150 UNDERWOOD 9   16 Read so much wast, as she cannot imbrace
    p. 167 UNDERWOOD 15 152 Give me but that againe, that I must wast
    p. 174 UNDERWOOD 23   8 Dri'd up? lyes Thespia wast?
    p. 226 UNDERWOOD 52   1 Why? though I seeme of a prodigious wast,
    p. 295 UNDERWOOD 90   9 Thy night not dronken, but from cares layd wast;

was't   frequency: 1   relative frequency: 0.00001

waste   frequency: 6   relative frequency: 0.00008
    See also "wast."
   *p. 492 TO HIMSELF   13 'Twere simple fury, still, thy selfe to waste
    p. 118 FOREST 13   81 Let 'hem waste body, and state; and after all,
    p. 137 UNDERWOOD 2.5 41 And the Girdle 'bout her waste,
    p. 166 UNDERWOOD 15 133 And whilst our states, strength, body, and mind
                             we waste,
    p. 189 UNDERWOOD 36   11 And have their being, their waste to see;
    p. 189 UNDERWOOD 36   12 And waste still, that they still might bee.

wasted   frequency: 1   relative frequency: 0.00001
    p. 97 FOREST 3   12 There wasted, some not paid for yet!

wasteth   frequency: 1   relative frequency: 0.00001
    p. 179 UNDERWOOD 25   46 For fury wasteth,

watch   frequency: 6   relative frequency: 0.00008
    p. 97 FOREST 3   21 Or, if thou list the night in watch to breake,
    p. 98 FOREST 3   67 Let others watch in guiltie armes, and stand
    p. 109 FOREST 11   8 Of thoughts to watch, and ward
    p. 156 UNDERWOOD 13   94 Or swaggering with the Watch, or Drawer,
                             drunke;
    p. 167 UNDERWOOD 15 157 That watch, and catch, at what they may applaud,
    p. 198 UNDERWOOD 40   36 Doth, while he keepes his watch, betray his
                             stand.

watch'<d>   frequency: 1   relative frequency: 0.00001
    p. 420 UNGATHERED 48 20 Thie long watch'<d> verse

watch'd   frequency: 3   relative frequency: 0.00004
    See also "watch'<d>."
    p. 118 FOREST 13   57 In single paths, dangers with ease are watch'd:
    p. 159 UNDERWOOD 14   33 Of generall knowledge; watch'd men, manners too,
    p. 160 UNDERWOOD 14   42 What blots and errours, have you watch'd and
                              purg'd

watches   frequency: 1   relative frequency: 0.00001
    p. 74 EPIGRAMS 115   14 Giue euery one his dose of mirth: and watches

watchfull   frequency: 1   relative frequency: 0.00001
    p. 258 UNDERWOOD 75   178 To be a watchfull Servant for this State;

watchman   frequency: 1   relative frequency: 0.00001
    p. 185 UNDERWOOD 30   9 The only faithfull Watchman for the Realme,

water   frequency: 7   relative frequency: 0.00010
    p. 30 EPIGRAMS 12   17 Or else by water goes, and so to playes;
    p. 93 FOREST 2   8 Of wood, of water: therein thou art faire.
    p. 105 FOREST 8   37 Will by coach, and water goe,
    p. 170 UNDERWOOD 18   7 That as the water makes things, put in't
                              streight,
    p. 230 UNDERWOOD 56   14 And stroke the water, nimble, chast, and faire,
    p. 234 UNDERWOOD 61   15 And wee doe weepe, to water, for our sinne.
    p. 361 UNGATHERED 1   17 thus, as a ponderous thinge in water cast

water-conduits   frequency: 1   relative frequency: 0.00001
    p. 36 EPIGRAMS 29   5 For then, our water-conduits doe runne wine;

watering   frequency: 1   relative frequency: 0.00001
    p. 657 L. CONVIVALES   10 That sits watering with the Muses.

watermen   frequency: 1   relative frequency: 0.00001
    p. 208 UNDERWOOD 43   124 My friends, the Watermen! They could provide

waters   frequency: 6   relative frequency: 0.00008
    p. 198 UNDERWOOD 40   28 'Bove all your standing waters, choak'd with
                              weedes.
    p. 244 UNDERWOOD 70   41 So deep, as he did then death's waters sup;
    p. 253 UNDERWOOD 75   33 Harke how the Bells upon the waters play
    p. 305 HORACE 2   21 Dring Circles of swift waters that intwine
    p. 369 UNGATHERED 6   119 Of Europes waters can
    p. 392 UNGATHERED 26   72 To see thee in our waters yet appeare,

waue   frequency: 1   relative frequency: 0.00001
    p. 380 UNGATHERED 12   56 I writ he onely his taile there did waue;

wave. See "waue."

waves   frequency: 1   relative frequency: 0.00001
    p. 219 UNDERWOOD 47   57 I have decreed; keepe it from waves, and presse;

wax. See "waxe," "waxe-like."

waxe   frequency: 2   relative frequency: 0.00002
  **p. 115 PANEGYRE   71 The others flame, as doth the wike and waxe,
    p. 315 HORACE 2   231 I'the open field; is Waxe like to be wrought

waxe-like   frequency: 1   relative frequency: 0.00001
    p. 344 HORACE 1   231 I'th'open .... waxe-like .. ..

way   frequency: 45   relative frequency: 0.00065
    See also "halfe-way," "straight-way," "waye."
  **p. 114 PANEGYRE   32 Breath'd in his way; and soules (their better
                              parts)
    p. 32 EPIGRAMS 18   1 To thee, my way in Epigrammes seemes new,
    p. 32 EPIGRAMS 18   2 When both it is the old way, and the true.
    p. 36 EPIGRAMS 28   18 That breathes in his dogs way: and this is great.
    p. 43 EPIGRAMS 52   5 This but thy iudgement fooles: the other way
    p. 53 EPIGRAMS 77   2 That, any way, my booke should speake thy name:
    p. 53 EPIGRAMS 80   4 And hath it, in his powers, to make his way!
    p. 72 EPIGRAMS 112   9 I leaue thee there, and giuing way, entend
    p. 76 EPIGRAMS 119   13 And, in their errors maze, thine owne way know:
    p. 80 EPIGRAMS 127   11 And, than this same, I know no abler way
    p. 82 EPIGRAMS 131   3 For, then, all mouthes will iudge, and their owne
                              way:
    p. 95 FOREST 2   55 This way to husbands; and whose baskets beare
    p. 95 FOREST 2   76 That found King IAMES, when hunting late,
                              this way,
    p. 109 FOREST 11   7 Some way of entrance) we must plant a guard

way (cont.)

p.	118 FOREST 13	54	This blessing of your starres, then by that way
p.	118 FOREST 13	68	Right, the right way: yet must your comfort \bee
p.	153 UNDERWOOD 13	10	The way to meet, what others would upbraid;
p.	155 UNDERWOOD 13	71	Pardon, sayes he, that were a way to see
p.	165 UNDERWOOD 15	108	To teach each suit he has, the ready way
p.	166 UNDERWOOD 15	126	This way, now that, as if their number were
p.	170 UNDERWOOD 18	12	Such Guides men use not, who their way would find,
p.	170 UNDERWOOD 18	13	Except the way be errour to those ends:
p.	235 UNDERWOOD 61	17	Of riot, and consumption, knowes the way
p.	239 UNDERWOOD 67	3	Some brave un-common way:
p.	249 UNDERWOOD 72	5	Let Ireland meet it out at Sea, halfe way,
p.	252 UNDERWOOD 75	3	Thou canst not meet more Glory, on the way,
p.	252 UNDERWOOD 75	11	Hath fil<l>ed, with Caroches, all the way,
p.	254 UNDERWOOD 75	63	The Emblemes of their way.
p.	257 UNDERWOOD 75	140	Doe long to make themselves, so, another way:
p.	263 UNDERWOOD 79	4	To shew the rites, and t<o>'usher forth the way
p.	270 UNDERWOOD 83	38	But a fain'd way, doth rob it of the true.
p.	270 UNDERWOOD 83	65	Who saw the way was made it! and were sent
p.	278 U'WOOD 84.4	18	As you goe on, by what brave way
p.	307 HORACE 2	44	When in a wrong, and artlesse way we tread.
p.	309 HORACE 2	98	Being taught a better way. All mortall deeds
p.	323 HORACE 2	395	'Tis cleare, this way I have got off from blame,
p.	323 HORACE 2	402	If either you, or I, know the right way
p.	329 HORACE 2	497	All way of life was shewen; the grace of Kings
p.	335 HORACE 2	640	Why should I grieve my friend, this trifling way?
p.	363 UNGATHERED 3	9	Enforcing yron doores to yeeld it way,
p.	388 UNGATHERED 23	9	To the Greeke coast thine onely knew the way.
p.	394 UNGATHERED 28	8	A list of Epithites: And prayse this way.
p.	397 UNGATHERED 30	48	Vnder one title. Thou hast made thy way
p.	417 UNGATHERED 45	10	but haue lost it by the way,
p.	662 INSCRIPTS. 2	8	if any way she do rewarde thee

waye   frequency: 1   relative frequency: 0.00001
    p. 405 UNGATHERED 34   75 What would he doe now, gi'ng his mynde yt waye

wayes   frequency: 20   relative frequency: 0.00028

p.	33 EPIGRAMS 21	7	What seuerall wayes men to their calling haue!
p.	48 EPIGRAMS 65	10	Almost all wayes, to any better course.
p.	59 EPIGRAMS 92	25	They all get Porta, for the sundrie wayes
p.	100 FOREST 4	10	Thy subtle wayes, be narrow straits;
p.	104 FOREST 8	6	And nights too, in worser wayes?
p.	121 FOREST 14	25	Striue all right wayes it can,
p.	160 UNDERWOOD 14	45	Sought out the Fountaines, Sources, Creekes, paths, wayes,
p.	162 UNDERWOOD 15	16	No person, nor is lov'd: what wayes he proves
p.	176 UNDERWOOD 24	7	But both might know their wayes were understood,
p.	187 UNDERWOOD 33	20	Thou prov'st the gentler wayes, to clense the wound,
p.	212 UNDERWOOD 43	208	Of massacring Man-kind so many wayes.
p.	218 UNDERWOOD 47	25	Let these men have their wayes, and take their times
p.	224 UNDERWOOD 50	3	And the right wayes you take unto the right,
p.	237 UNDERWOOD 64	14	And murmure cannot quarrell at your wayes?
p.	248 UNDERWOOD 71	8	Reduicts, Halfe-moones, Horne-workes, and such close wayes,
p.	255 UNDERWOOD 75	102	And legall wayes
p.	264 UNDERWOOD 79	21	That drives the Hart to seeke unused wayes,
p.	288 U'WOOD 84.9	196	Poring, as on a Map, to find the wayes
p.	327 HORACE 2	464	Our Roman Youths they learne the subtle wayes
p.	390 UNGATHERED 26	5	'Tis true, and all mens suffrage. But these wayes

ways. See "wayes."

wayte   frequency: 1   relative frequency: 0.00001
    p. 384 UNGATHERED 18   4 Do wayte vpon thee: and theyre Loue not bought.

wch   frequency: 4   relative frequency: 0.00005

we   frequency: 136   relative frequency: 0.00196
    See also "w'are," "we'<h>ave," "we'are," "wee,"
             "wee'l," "wee'll."

we'<h>ave   frequency: 1   relative frequency: 0.00001
    p. 168 UNDERWOOD 15   194 More honour in him, 'cause we'<h>ave knowne him mad:

weak. See "weake."

weake   frequency: 10   relative frequency: 0.00014
   **p. 114 PANEGYRE   58 No age, nor sex, so weake, or strongly dull,
     p. 43 EPIGRAMS 52   3 When I am read, thou fain'st a weake applause,
     p. 72 EPIGRAMS 112   t1 TO A WEAKE GAMSTER IN
                               POETRY.
     p. 100 FOREST 4   19 To take the weake, or make them stop:
     p. 137 UNDERWOOD 2.5   51 Outward Grace weake love beguiles:
     p. 218 UNDERWOOD 47   7 And shewing so weake an Act to vulgar eyes,
     p. 284 U'WOOD 84.9   79 Dull, and prophane, weake, and imperfect eyes,
     p. 321 HORACE 2   346 And the bold Pythias, having cheated weake
     p. 385 UNGATHERED 19   4 What can one witnesse, and a weake one, add
     p. 411 UNGATHERED 40   13 The comfort of weake Christians,

weaker   frequency: 1   relative frequency: 0.00001
     p. 361 UNGATHERED 1   3 weare made the obiects to my weaker powers;

weakest   frequency: 1   relative frequency: 0.00001
     p. 104 FOREST 7   9 So men at weakest, they are strongest,

weaknesse   frequency: 2   relative frequency: 0.00002
     p. 192 UNDERWOOD 38   33 Where weaknesse doth offend, and vertue grieve,
     p. 198 UNDERWOOD 40   45 Weaknesse of braine, or any charme of Wine,

weal. See "weale."

weale   frequency: 2   relative frequency: 0.00002
     p. 217 UNDERWOOD 46   16 Desired Justice to the publique Weale,
     p. 225 UNDERWOOD 51   10 Fame, and foundation of the English Weale.

wealth   frequency: 15   relative frequency: 0.00021
     See also "common-wealth."
     p. 45 EPIGRAMS 56   7 To'a little wealth, and credit in the scene,
     p. 99 FOREST 3   81 Let that goe heape a masse of wretched wealth,
     p. 105 FOREST 8   42 Play away, health, wealth, and fame.
     p. 159 UNDERWOOD 14   36 Or faith in things? or is't your wealth and will
     p. 161 UNDERWOOD 14   85 But here's no time, nor place, my wealth to tell,
     p. 186 UNDERWOOD 31   6 The Care, and wish still of the publike wealth:
     p. 186 UNDERWOOD 32   8 Both arm'd with wealth, and slander to oppose,
     p. 213 UNDERWOOD 44   12 Nor markes of wealth so from our Nation fled,
     p. 251 UNDERWOOD 74   15 As all the wealth of Season, there was spread;
     p. 285 U'WOOD 84.9   110 By all the wealth of blessings, and the store
     p. 309 HORACE 2   82 And wealth unto our language; and brought forth
     p. 315 HORACE 2   238 His better'd mind seekes wealth, and friendship:
                               than
     p. 325 HORACE 2   436 Their Charge, and Office, whence their wealth
                               to fet,
     p. 368 UNGATHERED 6   85 The Dutch whom Wealth (not Hatred) doth
                               diuide;
     p. 388 UNGATHERED 23   6 To make thy honour, and our wealth the more!

wealthie   frequency: 1   relative frequency: 0.00001
     p. 331 HORACE 2   584 Can; or all toile, without a wealthie veine:

wealthy   frequency: 5   relative frequency: 0.00007
     See also "wealthie."
     p. 54 EPIGRAMS 81   4 To be the wealthy witnesse of my pen:
     p. 103 FOREST 6   6 Kisse, and score vp wealthy summes
     p. 112 FOREST 11   105 The wealthy treasure of her loue on him;
     p. 291 UNDERWOOD 85   65 The wealthy houshold swarme of bondmen met,
     p. 353 HORACE 1   600 .. wealthy .. ..

weapon   frequency: 2   relative frequency: 0.00002
     p. 50 EPIGRAMS 69   2 Yet by thy weapon liu'st! Th'hast one good part.
     p. 114 FOREST 12   23 When gold was made no weapon to cut throtes,

weapons   frequency: 1   relative frequency: 0.00001
     p. 233 UNDERWOOD 59   11 Their weapons shot out, with that flame, and
                               force,

wear   frequency: 1   relative frequency: 0.00001
     See also "out-weare," "weare."
     p. 361 UNGATHERED 1   24 wear spent with wonder as they weare delated,

weare   frequency: 17   relative frequency: 0.00024
     p. 28 EPIGRAMS 4   2 How, best of Poets, do'st thou laurell weare!
     p. 33 EPIGRAMS 20   2 Except thou could'st, Sir COD, weare them
                               within.
     p. 57 EPIGRAMS 89   13 Weare this renowne. 'Tis iust, that who did giue
     p. 58 EPIGRAMS 91   17 And best become the valiant man to weare,
     p. 68 EPIGRAMS 105   7 He, that but saw you weare the wheaten hat,

weare (cont.)
     p. 93 FOREST 1   7 I weare not these my wings in vaine.
     p. 118 FOREST 13   70 For truthes complexion, where they all weare
                             maskes.
     p. 118 FOREST 13   80 Whether it be a face they weare, or no.
     p. 141 UNDERWOOD 2.9 36 Well he should his clothes to<o> weare;
     p. 232 UNDERWOOD 58   9 Will be reward enough: to weare like those,
     p. 321 HORACE 2   332 Or Semi-god, that late was seene to weare
     p. 323 HORACE 2   406 Nor did they merit the lesse Crowne to weare,
     p. 361 UNGATHERED 1   3 weare made the obiects to my weaker powers;
     p. 361 UNGATHERED 1   24 wear spent with wonder as they weare delated,
     p. 384 UNGATHERED 18   5 Such weare true wedding robes, and are true
                             freindes,
     p. 392 UNGATHERED 26 48 And ioy'd to weare the dressing of his lines!
     p. 403 UNGATHERED 34 26 Noe veluet Sheath you weare, will alter kynde.

we're   frequency: 2   relative frequency: 0.00002

weares   frequency: 4   relative frequency: 0.00005
     p. 42 EPIGRAMS 46   6 Yes, now he weares his knight-hood euery day.
     p. 58 EPIGRAMS 91   •2 A romane sound, but romane vertue weares,
     p. 63 EPIGRAMS 97   17 Since he was gone, more then the one he weares.
     p. 370 UNGATHERED 8   4 Lady, or Pusil, that weares maske, or fan,

wearied   frequency: 1   relative frequency: 0.00001
     p. 198 UNDERWOOD 40   35 Like the dull wearied Crane that (come on land)

wearinesse   frequency: 1   relative frequency: 0.00001
     p. 122 FOREST 15   26 For wearinesse of life, not loue of thee.

wearing   frequency: 2   relative frequency: 0.00002
     p. 216 UNDERWOOD 45   19 But these with wearing will themselves unfold:
     p. 362 UNGATHERED 2   3 Not wearing moodes, as gallants doe a fashion,

wears. See "weares."

weary   frequency: 4   relative frequency: 0.00005
     p. 94 FOREST 2   34 And pikes, now weary their owne kinde to eat,
     p. 121 FOREST 14   37 Not weary, rest
     p. 244 UNDERWOOD 70   37 But weary of that flight,
     p. 291 UNDERWOOD 85   63 To view the weary Oxen draw, with bare

weather   frequency: 3   relative frequency: 0.00004
     p. 193 UNDERWOOD 38   75 About in Cloudes, and wrapt in raging weather,
     p. 193 UNDERWOOD 38   82 The name of Cruell weather, storme, and raine?
     p. 361 UNGATHERED 1   8 Vnseason'd ffrostes, or the most enuyous weather.

weav'd   frequency: 5   relative frequency: 0.00007
     p. 153 UNDERWOOD 13   26 Against his will that do's 'hem? that hath weav'd
     p. 160 UNDERWOOD 14   52 Of what it tells us) weav'd in to instruct!
     p. 171 UNDERWOOD 20   10 That their whole life was wickednesse, though
                             weav'd
     p. 204 UNDERWOOD 43   33 Or spun out Riddles, and weav'd fiftie tomes
     p. 282 U'WOOD 84.9   4 All that was good, or great in me she weav'd,

weave   frequency: 3   relative frequency: 0.00004
     p. 187 UNDERWOOD 33   6 Who 'gainst the Law, weave Calumnies, my
                             <BENN:>
     p. 190 UNDERWOOD 37   12 In letters, that mixe spirits, thus to weave.
     p. 323 HORACE 2   390 To Roman Poets. Shall I therefore weave

web   frequency: 1   relative frequency: 0.00001
     See also "cob-web-lawne."
     p. 242 UNDERWOOD 69   24 All is but web, and painting; be the strife

wedded   frequency: 1   relative frequency: 0.00001
     p. 401 UNGATHERED 33   6 French Aire and English Verse here Wedded
                             lie.

wedding   frequency: 2   relative frequency: 0.00002
     p. 258 UNDERWOOD 75 168 (After the last child borne;) This is our
                             wedding day.
     p. 384 UNGATHERED 18   5 Such weare true wedding robes, and are true
                             freindes,

wee   frequency: 20   relative frequency: 0.00028

weedes   frequency: 2   relative frequency: 0.00002
     p. 198 UNDERWOOD 40   28 'Bove all your standing waters, choak'd with
                             weedes.

weedes (cont.)
  p. 361 UNGATHERED 1   10 Thy skill hath made of ranck dispised weedes;

weeds   frequency: 1   relative frequency: 0.00001
    See also "weedes."
  p. 163 UNDERWOOD 15   33 Against his Maker; high alone with weeds,

week. See "weeke."

weeke   frequency: 3   relative frequency: 0.00004
  p. 81 EPIGRAMS 129   6 To which thou'rt not a weeke, bespoke a guest;
  p. 218 UNDERWOOD 47   13 They'<h>ave glutted in, and letcher'd out that
                             weeke,
  p. 229 UNDERWOOD 54   16 Lend me, deare Arthur, for a weeke five more,

weekes   frequency: 1   relative frequency: 0.00001
  p. 32 EPIGRAMS 16   4 Scarse thy weekes swearing brings thee of, of
                             one.

weekly   frequency: 2   relative frequency: 0.00002
  p. 206 UNDERWOOD 43   81 The weekly Corrants, with Pauls Seale; and all
  p. 223 UNDERWOOD 49   40 They say you weekly invite with fits o'th'
                             Mother,

week's. See "weekes."

wee'l   frequency: 1   relative frequency: 0.00001

wee'll   frequency: 4   relative frequency: 0.00005

weep. See "weepe."

weepe   frequency: 6   relative frequency: 0.00008
  p. 39 EPIGRAMS 40   1 Marble, weepe, for thou dost couer
  p. 77 EPIGRAMS 120   1 Weepe with me all you that read
  p. 113 FOREST 12   13 The foole that gaue it; who will want, and weepe,
  p. 234 UNDERWOOD 61   15 And wee doe weepe, to water, for our sinne.
  p. 311 HORACE 2   145 If thou would'st have me weepe, be thou first
                             drown'd
  p. 333 HORACE 2   614 As those that hir'd to weepe at Funeralls,
                             swoune,

weeping. See "weepinge."

weepinge   frequency: 1   relative frequency: 0.00001
  p. 394 UNGATHERED 28   2 And pray thee Reader, bring thy weepinge Eyes

weever   frequency: 1   relative frequency: 0.00001
  p. 32 EPIGRAMS 18   4 DAVIS, and WEEVER, and the best haue
                             beene,

weigh   frequency: 2   relative frequency: 0.00002
    See also "waigh."
  p. 216 UNDERWOOD 45   16 First weigh a friend, then touch, and trie him
                             too:
  p. 235 UNDERWOOD 62   11 O pietie! so to weigh the poores estates!

weigh'd   frequency: 5   relative frequency: 0.00007
  p. 51 EPIGRAMS 74   1 Whil'st thy weigh'd iudgements, EGERTON,
                             I heare,
  p. 101 FOREST 4   49 Where nothing is examin'd, weigh'd,
  p. 229 UNDERWOOD 54   1 I am to dine, Friend, where I must be weigh'd
  p. 236 UNDERWOOD 64   4 If he but weigh'd the blessings of this day?
  p. 415 UNGATHERED 42   14 And weigh'd your Play: untwisted ev'ry thread,

weight   frequency: 15   relative frequency: 0.00021
    See also "waight."
  p. 31 EPIGRAMS 14   9 What weight, and what authoritie in thy speech!
  p. 62 EPIGRAMS 95   30 Where sweetnesse is requir'd, and where weight;
  p. 70 EPIGRAMS 109   14 And that thy soule should giue thy flesh her
                             weight.
  p. 98 FOREST 3   42 And furrowes laden with their weight;
  p. 131 UNDERWOOD 2.1   12 Gives the Lover weight, and fashion.
  p. 154 UNDERWOOD 13   31 Himselfe of farther trouble, or the weight
  p. 157 UNDERWOOD 13   147 Are Dwarfes of Honour, and have neither weight
  p. 183 UNDERWOOD 29   6 But false weight.
  p. 224 UNDERWOOD 50   12 From whence they fall, cast downe with their owne
                             weight.
  p. 229 UNDERWOOD 54   6 An ill commoditie! 'T must make good weight.
  p. 229 UNDERWOOD 54   17 And you shall make me good, in weight, and
                             fashion,

weight (cont.)
    p. 230 UNDERWOOD 56   11 His weight is twenty Stone within two pound;
    p. 244 UNDERWOOD 70   50 In weight, in measure, number, sound,
    p. 327 HORACE 2   456 A Poeme, of no grace, weight, art, in rimes,
    p. 399 UNGATHERED 31   24 Of weight, or fashion, it was shee.

weightie   frequency: 3   relative frequency: 0.00004
    p. 309 HORACE 2   95 In neighbour-townes, and feeles the weightie
                    plough;
    p. 311 HORACE 2   155 With weightie sorrow hurles us all along,
    p. 323 HORACE 2   378 More slow, and come more weightie to the eare:

weighty   frequency: 1   relative frequency: 0.00001
    See also "weightie."
    p. 61 EPIGRAMS 95   4 In thee, most weighty SAVILE, liu'd to vs:

wel   frequency: 1   relative frequency: 0.00001
    p. 153 UNDERWOOD 13   2 Great and good turns, as wel could time them too,

wel-made   frequency: 1   relative frequency: 0.00001
    p. 55 EPIGRAMS 86   2 Vpon thy wel-made choise of friends, and bookes;

wel-tagde   frequency: 1   relative frequency: 0.00001
    p. 220 UNDERWOOD 47   64 Such as are square, wel-tagde, and permanent,

wel-wrought   frequency: 1   relative frequency: 0.00001
    p. 221 UNDERWOOD 48   46 Of some wel-wrought Embassage:

welcome   frequency: 6   relative frequency: 0.00008
    p. 48 EPIGRAMS 65   12 And which thou brought'st me, welcome pouertie.
    p. 95 FOREST 2   81 With all their zeale, to warme their welcome
                    here.
    p. 98 FOREST 3   55 Thy noblest spouse affords them welcome grace;
    p. 253 UNDERWOOD 75   24 To welcome home a Paire, and deck the nuptiall
                    bower?
    p. 657 L. CONVIVALES   1 Welcome all, who lead or follow,
    p. 657 L. CONVIVALES   19 Welcome all, who lead or follow,

well   frequency: 85   relative frequency: 0.00123
    See also "aswell," "wel," "well[s],"
        words beginning "wel-" and "well-."
  *p. 493 TO HIMSELF   27 There, sweepings doe as well
    p. 27 EPIGRAMS 1   2 To reade it well: that is, to vnderstand.
    p. 27 EPIGRAMS 3   1 Thou, that mak'st gaine thy end, and wisely well,
    p. 28 EPIGRAMS 3   12 Send it to Bucklers-bury, there 'twill, well.
    p. 43 EPIGRAMS 51   2 Great heau'n did well, to giue ill fame free
                    wing;
    p. 45 EPIGRAMS 56   12 May iudge it to be his, as well as ours.
    p. 46 EPIGRAMS 62   2 That loue to make so well, a child to beare?
    p. 54 EPIGRAMS 82   2 He cast, yet keeps her well! No, shee keeps him.
    p. 63 EPIGRAMS 98   1 Thou hast begun well, ROE, which stand well
                    too,
    p. 64 EPIGRAMS 99   11 Well, though thy name lesse then our great ones
                    bee,
    p. 66 EPIGRAMS 103   1 How well, faire crowne of your faire sexe, might
                    hee,
    p. 74 EPIGRAMS 115   8 By speaking well o' the company' it 's in.
    p. 76 EPIGRAMS 119   6 Whose dice not doing well, to'a pulpit ran.
    p. 81 EPIGRAMS 128   14 Came backe vntouch'd. This man hath trauail'd
                    well.
    p. 83 EPIGRAMS 132   11 So well in that are his inuentions wrought,
    p. 84 EPIGRAMS 133   28 His three for one. Now, lordings, listen well.
    p. 86 EPIGRAMS 133   93 Ouer your heads: Well, row. At this a loud
    p. 93 FOREST 2   9 Thou hast thy walkes for health, as well as
                    sport:
    p. 99 FOREST 3   93 Thy peace is made; and, when man's state is well,
    p. 109 FOREST 11   3 Next, to that vertue, is to know vice well,
    p. 113 FOREST 12   7 Well, or ill, onely, all the following yeere,
    p. 116 FOREST 12   92 And your braue friend, and mine so well did loue.
    p. 117 FOREST 13   33 Not taken vp o'th'doctors, but as well
    p. 120 FOREST 14   11 Giue me my cup, but from the Thespian well,
    p. 121 FOREST 14   46 When well begunne:
    p. 134 UNDERWOOD 2.4   4 And well the Carre Love guideth.
    p. 139 UNDERWOOD 2.7   14 Where, how it would have relish'd well;
    p. 139 UNDERWOOD 2.8   4 What a man she could love well:
    p. 141 UNDERWOOD 2.9   36 Well he should his clothes to<o> weare;
    p. 150 UNDERWOOD 10   8 On all mens Fruit, and flowers, as well as mine.
    p. 154 UNDERWOOD 13   48 Well knowne, and practiz'd borrowers on their
                    word,
    p. 155 UNDERWOOD 13   78 Many a pound, and piece, will p<l>ace one well;

well (cont.)

p. 156 UNDERWOOD 13	109 And you, Sir, know it well, to whom I write,
p. 166 UNDERWOOD 15	145 Well, let it goe. Yet this is better, then
p. 170 UNDERWOOD 19	12 So well as I may tell in verse, 'tis so?
p. 208 UNDERWOOD 43	123 Well fare the wise-men yet, on the Banckside,
p. 213 UNDERWOOD 44	6 For they did see it the last tilting well,
p. 213 UNDERWOOD 44	23 Well, I say, thrive, thrive brave Artillerie yard,
p. 214 UNDERWOOD 44	33 Well did thy craftie Clerke, and Knight, Sir Hugh,
p. 216 UNDERWOOD 45	4 One lesson we have both learn'd, and well read;
p. 218 UNDERWOOD 47	19 That to speake well, thinke it above all sinne,
p. 219 UNDERWOOD 47	37 I wish all well, and pray high heaven conspire
p. 219 UNDERWOOD 47	45 Shall carry me at Call; and I'le be well,
p. 219 UNDERWOOD 47	56 Well, with mine owne fraile Pitcher, what to doe
p. 228 UNDERWOOD 53	16 Nor any of their houshold, halfe so well.
p. 228 UNDERWOOD 53	17 So well! as when I saw the floore, and Roome,
p. 241 UNDERWOOD 68	5 Well, they should know him, would the K<ing> but grant
p. 243 UNDERWOOD 70	31 How well at twentie had he falne, or stood!
p. 244 UNDERWOOD 70	33 Hee entred well, by vertuous parts,
p. 245 UNDERWOOD 70	62 To light: her measures are, how well
p. 254 UNDERWOOD 75	76 Saw'st thou that Paire, became these Rites so well,
p. 256 UNDERWOOD 75	105 And this well mov'd the Judgement of the King
p. 262 UNDERWOOD 78	1 Tho', happy Muse, thou know my Digby well,
p. 269 UNDERWOOD 83	33 What she did here, by great example, well,
p. 305 HORACE 2	25 Know'st only well to paint a Cipresse tree.
p. 315 HORACE 2	215 And so well faines, so mixeth cunningly
p. 319 HORACE 2	325 Having well eat, and drunke (the rites being done)
p. 325 HORACE 2	440 The very root of writing well, and spring
p. 325 HORACE 2	445 Hee, that hath studied well the debt, and knowes
p. 329 HORACE 2	520 There are yet faults, which we would well forgive,
p. 331 HORACE 2	549 A meane, and toleration, which does well:
p. 331 HORACE 2	560 These, the free meale might have beene well drawne out:
p. 361 UNGATHERED 1	2 (so well dispos'd by thy auspicious hand)
p. 362 UNGATHERED 1	30 Palmer thy trauayles well becum thy name,
p. 370 UNGATHERED 7	6 Will well confesse; presenting, limiting,
p. 378 UNGATHERED 11	90 As well as from his braines, and claimest thereby
p. 380 UNGATHERED 12	39 How well, and how often his shoes too were mended,
p. 380 UNGATHERED 12	42 From Venice to Flushing, were not they well cobled?
p. 386 UNGATHERED 21	16 With the how much they set forth, but th'how well.
p. 389 UNGATHERED 24	17 But that hee's too well suted, in a cloth,
p. 390 UNGATHERED 25	6 As well in brasse, as he hath hit
p. 392 UNGATHERED 26	64 For a good Poet's made, as well as borne.
p. 392 UNGATHERED 26	68 In his well torned, and true-filed lines:
p. 393 UNGATHERED 27	19 A worthy worke, and worthy well
p. 394 UNGATHERED 28	10 Such things, of euery body, and as well.
p. 396 UNGATHERED 30	21 And those so sweet, and well proportion'd parts,
p. 397 UNGATHERED 30	49 And flight about the Ile, well neare, by this,
p. 398 UNGATHERED 30	74 Get broken peeces, and fight well by those.
p. 398 UNGATHERED 30	90 To all thy vertuous, and well chosen Friends,
p. 408 UNGATHERED 36	12 Will well designe thee, to be viewd of all
p. 409 UNGATHERED 38	5 And you doe doe them well, with good applause,
p. 410 UNGATHERED 38	9 You learn'd it well; and for it, seru'd your time
p. 414 UNGATHERED 42	6 How well I lov'd Truth: I was scarce allow'd
p. 415 UNGATHERED 42	16 Where it runs round, and even: where so well,

well[s]   frequency: 1   relative frequency: 0.00001
p. 183 UNDERWOOD 29   20 At the Well[s] no Muse did stay,

well-compass'd   frequency: 1   relative frequency: 0.00001
p. 327 HORACE 2   462 But a well-compass'd mouth to utter it;

well-grac'd   frequency: 1   relative frequency: 0.00001
p. 293 UNDERWOOD 86   35 Or why, my well-grac'd words among,

well-greas'd   frequency: 1   relative frequency: 0.00001
p. 87 EPIGRAMS 133   114 The well-greas'd wherry now had got betweene,

well-truss'd   frequency: 1   relative frequency: 0.00001
p. 309 HORACE 2   71 Faine words, unheard of to the well-truss'd race

wench   frequency: 1   relative frequency: 0.00001
      p. 293 UNDERWOOD 86   29 Me now, nor Wench, nor wanton Boy,

went   frequency: 19   relative frequency: 0.00027
    **p. 114 PANEGYRE   49 And as of late, when he through London went,
      p.   55 EPIGRAMS 84   5 Straight went I home; and there most like a
                                 Poet,
      p.   57 EPIGRAMS 89   10 Out-stript, then they did all that went before:
      p.   57 EPIGRAMS 90   7 Went on: and prouing him still, day by day,
      p.   76 EPIGRAMS 118   6 Lust it comes out, that gluttony went in.
      p.   85 EPIGRAMS 133   35 Or him that backward went to Berwicke, or which
      p.   86 EPIGRAMS 133   77 And, on they went, like CASTOR braue, and
                                 POLLVX:
      p.   89 EPIGRAMS 133   192 And so went brauely backe, without protraction.
      p. 154 UNDERWOOD 13   51 And speaking worst of those, from whom they went
      p. 246 UNDERWOOD 70   85 Jonson, who sung this of him, e're he went
      p. 264 UNDERWOOD 79   26 Who walkes on Earth as May still went along,
      p. 287 U'WOOD 84.9   170 To another, Move; he went; To a third, Go,
      p. 293 UNDERWOOD 87   7 In name, I went all names before,
      p. 313 HORACE 2   181 Unto the last, as when he first went forth,
      p. 319 HORACE 2   304 Gesture, and riot, whilst he swooping went
      p. 379 UNGATHERED 12   14 To write it with the selfe same spirit he went,
      p. 379 UNGATHERED 12   16 In fiue monthes he went it, in fiue monthes he
                                 pend it.
      p. 380 UNGATHERED 12   25 He went out at each place, and at what he came
                                 in,
      p. 386 UNGATHERED 20   9 That went before, a Husband. Shee, Ile sweare,

wept   frequency: 1   relative frequency: 0.00001
      p. 398 UNGATHERED 30   76 Of tender eyes will more be wept, then seene:

were   frequency: 193   relative frequency: 0.00279
      See also "th<ey>'were," "th'were," "'twere,"
            "wear," "weare."

wert   frequency: 20   relative frequency: 0.00028
      See also "tho'wert," "wer't."

wer't   frequency: 1   relative frequency: 0.00001

west-indian   frequency: 1   relative frequency: 0.00001
      p. 219 UNDERWOOD 47   34 Some hopes of Spaine in their West-Indian
                                 Fleet?

west-parts   frequency: 1   relative frequency: 0.00001
      p.   71 EPIGRAMS 110   2 In these west-parts, nor when that warre was
                                 done,

west-winds   frequency: 1   relative frequency: 0.00001
      p. 137 UNDERWOOD 2.5   28 Then when flowers, and West-winds meet.

western.   See "westerne."

westerne   frequency: 1   relative frequency: 0.00001
    **p. 113 PANEGYRE   3 Againe, the glory of our Westerne world

westminster   frequency: 1   relative frequency: 0.00001
      p. 186 UNDERWOOD 33   3 Or the great Hall at Westminster, the field

weston   frequency: 8   relative frequency: 0.00011
      p. 250 UNDERWOOD 73   5 WESTON! That waking man! that Eye of
                                 State!
      p. 250 UNDERWOOD 73   t2 Weston, L. high Treasurer of England,
      p. 250 UNDERWOOD 74   t1 To the Right honble Hierome, L. Weston.
      p. 252 UNDERWOOD 75   t5 of that Noble Gentleman, Mr. HIEROME
                                 WESTON,
      p. 252 UNDERWOOD 75   t6 Son, and Heire, of the Lord WESTON,
      p. 255 UNDERWOOD 75   97 Weston, their Treasure, as their Treasurer,
      p. 260 UNDERWOOD 77   10 This I would doe, could I thinke Weston one
      p. 263 UNDERWOOD 78   28 The knowing Weston, and that learned Lord

wet   frequency: 1   relative frequency: 0.00001
      p.   84 EPIGRAMS 133   30 Makes the poore Banck-side creature wet it'
                                 shoone,

wets   frequency: 1   relative frequency: 0.00001
      p.   37 EPIGRAMS 33   6 Who wets my graue, can be no friend of mine.

whale-bone   frequency: 1   relative frequency: 0.00001
      p. 200 UNDERWOOD 42   31 As any Mercer; or the whale-bone man

wharfes   frequency: 1   relative frequency: 0.00001
    p. 205 UNDERWOOD 43   68 The\<ir> charmed Boates, and the\<ir> inchanted
                     Wharfes;

wharfs. See "wharfes."

what   frequency: 311   relative frequency: 0.00450
    See also "what's."

what's   frequency: 11   relative frequency: 0.00015

whatsoever   frequency: 1   relative frequency: 0.00001
    p. 168 UNDERWOOD 15 185 That whatsoever face thy fate puts on,

wheat   frequency: 1   relative frequency: 0.00001
  *p. 492 TO HIMSELF   11 Say, that thou pour'st them wheat,

wheaten   frequency: 1   relative frequency: 0.00001
    p. 68 EPIGRAMS 105   7 He, that but saw you weare the wheaten hat,

wheel. See "wheele."

wheele   frequency: 4   relative frequency: 0.00005
    p. 283 U'WOOD 84.9   30 Nothing I doe; but, like a heavie wheele,
    p. 307 HORACE 2   30 Thy labouring wheele, comes scarce a Pitcher
                     out?
    p. 331 HORACE 2   568 Or trundling Wheele, he can sit still, from all;
    p. 395 UNGATHERED 29   3 Of Fortunes wheele by Lucan driu'n about,

when   frequency: 253   relative frequency: 0.00366

whence   frequency: 10   relative frequency: 0.00014
    p. 69 EPIGRAMS 107   9 Tell them, what parts yo'haue tane, whence run
                     away,
    p. 101 FOREST 4   27 From whence, so lately, I did burne,
    p. 110 FOREST 11   39 Inconstant, like the sea, of whence 'tis borne,
    p. 170 UNDERWOOD 19   3 By that faire Stand, your forehead, whence he
                     bends
    p. 224 UNDERWOOD 50 12 From whence they fall, cast downe with their owne
                     weight.
    p. 274 U'WOOD 84.2   15 Into the Kindred, whence thy Adam drew
    p. 278 U'WOOD 84.4   16 But what's of kinne to whence it came.
    p. 313 HORACE 2   193 From whence thy Modestie, or Poemes law
    p. 325 HORACE 2   436 Their Charge, and Office, whence their wealth
                     to fet,
    p. 368 UNGATHERED 6   69 To vtmost Thule: whence, he backes the Seas

where   frequency: 148   relative frequency: 0.00214
    See also "else-where," "euery-where,"
           "some-where," "where's," "where't."

whereas   frequency: 1   relative frequency: 0.00001
    p. 259 UNDERWOOD 76   5 That whereas your royall Father,

whereby   frequency: 2   relative frequency: 0.00002
    p. 222 UNDERWOOD 48 47 Whereby he may knit sure up
    p. 238 UNDERWOOD 66   8 Whereby the safetie of Man-kind was wrought)

wherefore   frequency: 3   relative frequency: 0.00004
    p. 46 EPIGRAMS 62   1 Fine MADAME WOVLD-BEE, wherefore
                     should you feare,
    p. 120 FOREST 14   7 Wherefore should I
    p. 311 HORACE 2   129 Am I call'd Poet? wherefore with wrong shame,

wherein   frequency: 17   relative frequency: 0.00024
  **p. 117 PANEGYRE   148 Wherein, his choice was happie with the rest
    p. 35 EPIGRAMS 27   7 To heauen; his hath: O happy state! wherein
    p. 48 EPIGRAMS 64   16 Wherein what wonder see thy name hath wrought?
    p. 66 EPIGRAMS 102   6 Of vice, and vertue; wherein all great life
    p. 72 EPIGRAMS 111   3 Wherein thou shew'st, how much the latter are
    p. 114 FOREST 12   35 Wherein wise Nature you a dowrie gaue,
    p. 115 FOREST 12   72 To my lesse sanguine Muse, wherein she'hath
                     wonne
    p. 116 FOREST 12   97 This hasty sacrifice, wherein I reare
    p. 117 FOREST 13   46 As bloud, and match. Wherein, how more then much
    p. 120 FOREST 13   123 Wherein, your forme, you still the same shall
                     finde;
    p. 134 UNDERWOOD 2.4 2 Wherein my Lady rideth!
    p. 173 UNDERWOOD 22   9 Wherein you triumph yet: because
    p. 207 UNDERWOOD 43 99 Wherein was oyle, beside the succour spent,

wherein (cont.)
```
    p. 251 UNDERWOOD 74     14 Wherein she sits so richly drest,
    p. 261 UNDERWOOD 77     11 Catch'd with these Arts, wherein the Judge is
                               wise
    p. 319 HORACE 2        313 Till then unknowne, in Carts, wherein did ride
    p. 390 UNGATHERED 25     3 Wherein the Grauer had a strife
```

whereof   frequency: 5   relative frequency: 0.00007
    See also "wherof."
```
    p.  87 EPIGRAMS 133    128 Whereof old DEMOCRITE, and HILL
                               NICHOLAS,
    p.  93 FOREST 2          4 Thou hast no lantherne, whereof tales are told;
    p. 110 FOREST 11        27 Whereof the loyall conscience so complaines.
    p. 118 FOREST 13        83 May they haue nothing left, whereof they can
    p. 182 UNDERWOOD 28      6 To those true numerous Graces; whereof some,
```

whereon   frequency: 1   relative frequency: 0.00001
    See also "wheron."
```
    p. 119 FOREST 13        90 Whereon the most of mankinde wracke themselues,
```

where's   frequency: 1   relative frequency: 0.00001

wheresoere   frequency: 2   relative frequency: 0.00002
```
    p. 116 FOREST 12        93 Who, wheresoere he be, on what dear coast,
    p. 116 FOREST 13         8 With euery vertue, wheresoere it moue,
```

where't   frequency: 1   relative frequency: 0.00001

whereto   frequency: 1   relative frequency: 0.00001
```
    p. 415 UNGATHERED 42    21 Cry'd up of late: Whereto there must be first
```

wherewith   frequency: 7   relative frequency: 0.00010
```
    p.  31 EPIGRAMS 14       4 The great renowne, and name wherewith shee goes.
    p.  60 EPIGRAMS 93      16 Wherewith, against thy bloud, they'offenders bee.
    p. 118 FOREST 13        53 Wherewith, then, Madame, can you better pay
    p. 224 UNDERWOOD 50      2 Wherewith this while you live a widow'd wife,
    p. 226 UNDERWOOD 52      3 But there are lines, wherewith I might
                               b<e>'embrac'd.
    p. 380 UNGATHERED 12    41 I meane that one paire, wherewith he so hobled
    p. 389 UNGATHERED 24    12 As was the Genius wherewith they were wrote;
```

wherof   frequency: 2   relative frequency: 0.00002
```
    p. 205 UNDERWOOD 43     57 But that's a marke, wherof thy Rites doe boast,
    p. 412 UNGATHERED 41     5 These forme thy Ghyrlond. Wherof Myrtle green,
```

wheron   frequency: 1   relative frequency: 0.00001
```
    p. 413 UNGATHERED 41    28 As if they' ador'd the Head, wheron th'are fixt.
```

wherry   frequency: 3   relative frequency: 0.00004
```
    p.  84 EPIGRAMS 133     11 Their wherry had no saile, too; ours had none:
    p.  85 EPIGRAMS 133     38 Propos'd to goe to Hol'borne in a wherry:
    p.  87 EPIGRAMS 133    114 The well-greas'd wherry now had got betweene,
```

whet   frequency: 1   relative frequency: 0.00001
```
    p. 327 HORACE 2        494 On edge the Masculine spirits, and did whet
```

whet-stone   frequency: 1   relative frequency: 0.00001
```
    p. 325 HORACE 2        433 Be like a Whet-stone, that an edge can put
```

whether   frequency: 24   relative frequency: 0.00034
    See also "where."
```
    p.  49 EPIGRAMS 66       7 Which deed I know not, whether were more high,
    p.  68 EPIGRAMS 106      5 Whether thy learning they would take, or wit,
    p.  87 EPIGRAMS 133    136 Whether it languishing stucke vpon the wall,
    p.  96 FOREST 3          2 Whether by choice, or fate, or both;
    p. 118 FOREST 13        80 Whether it be a face they weare, or no.
    p. 134 UNDERWOOD 2.4    10 Th<o>rough Swords, th<o>rough Seas, whether she
                               would ride.
    p. 138 UNDERWOOD 2.6     6 Whether we have lost, or wonne,
    p. 138 UNDERWOOD 2.6    30 Whether any would up-braid
    p. 200 UNDERWOOD 42     36 Whether their faces were their owne, or no:
    p. 214 UNDERWOOD 44     38 The Cittie-Question, whether Tilly, or he,
    p. 219 UNDERWOOD 47     31 What is't to me whether the French Designe
    p. 219 UNDERWOOD 47     35 Whether the Dispensation yet be sent,
    p. 293 UNDERWOOD 86     39 Whether in Mars his field thou bee,
    p. 309 HORACE 2         91 Whether the Sea receiv'd into the shore,
    p. 313 HORACE 2        166 Of some small thankfull land: whether he bee
    p. 321 HORACE 2        345 As not make difference, whether Davus speake,
    p. 323 HORACE 2        409 Whether the guarded Tragedie they wrought,
    p. 325 HORACE 2        439 Whether truth may, and whether error bring.
```

whether (cont.)
```
     p. 333 HORACE 2     606 Whether his soothing friend speake truth, or no.
     p. 333 HORACE 2     608 (Whether yo'are given to, or giver are)
     p. 335 HORACE 2     671 Whether he piss'd upon his Fathers grave;
     p. 342 HORACE 1     161 .. .... .... sway whether . ... ..... ....
     p. 402 UNGATHERED 34  11 Whether ye buylding of ye Stage or Scene!
```

which   frequency: 263   relative frequency: 0.00380
    See also "wch."

while   frequency: 36   relative frequency: 0.00052
    See also "a-while," "whyle."
```
  **p. 115 PANEGYRE      73 Meane while, the reuerend THEMIS drawes
                            aside
  **p. 116 PANEGYRE     120 For vice is safe, while she hath vice to friend.
     p.  28 EPIGRAMS 4     5 For such a Poet, while thy dayes were greene,
     p.  34 EPIGRAMS 22   10 Where, while that seuer'd doth remaine,
     p.  34 EPIGRAMS 25    1 While BEAST instructs his faire, and
                            innocent wife,
     p.  38 EPIGRAMS 37    3 And pleaseth both. For while he melts his greace
     p.  71 EPIGRAMS 110   5 All yeelding to his fortune, nor, the while,
     p.  78 EPIGRAMS 121   3 Whose better studies while shee emulates,
     p.  85 EPIGRAMS 133  44 That all this while I haue forgot some god,
     p.  85 EPIGRAMS 133  58 But hold my torch, while I describe the entry
     p.  93 FOREST 2       6 And these grudg'd at, art reuerenc'd the while.
     p.  97 FOREST 3      31 While all, that follow, their glad eares apply
     p. 102 FOREST 5       2 While we may, the sports of loue;
     p. 103 FOREST 6       8 While you breath. First giue a hundred,
     p. 113 FOREST 12      9 While it makes huishers seruiceable men,
     p. 113 FOREST 12     15 While thus it buyes great grace, and hunts poore
                            fame;
     p. 118 FOREST 13     75 And almost, all dayes after, while they liue;
     p. 122 FOREST 15     13 Where haue I beene this while exil'd from thee?
     p. 145 UNDERWOOD 5   15 More pleasure while the thing he makes
     p. 160 UNDERWOOD 14  56 And manly elocution, not one while
     p. 167 UNDERWOOD 15 161 And be belov'd, while the Whores last. O times,
     p. 179 UNDERWOOD 25  43 Though but while mettal's heating:
     p. 187 UNDERWOOD 33  32 So brightly brandish'd) wound'st, defend'st! the
                            while
     p. 198 UNDERWOOD 40  36 Doth, while he keepes his watch, betray his
                            stand.
     p. 217 UNDERWOOD 46  15 And now such is thy stand; while thou dost deale
     p. 223 UNDERWOOD 49  36 From Court, while yet thy fame hath some small
                            day;
     p. 224 UNDERWOOD 50   2 Wherewith this while you live a widow'd wife,
     p. 333 HORACE 2     589 While he was young; he sweat; and freez'd againe:
     p. 335 HORACE 2     649 The while he belcheth loftie Verses out,
     p. 335 HORACE 2     661 Hee, while he labour'd to be thought a God
     p. 375 UNGATHERED 10 22 And there, while he giues the zealous Brauado,
     p. 375 UNGATHERED 10 33 To lie at Liuory, while the Horses did stand.
     p. 390 UNGATHERED 26  3 While I confesse thy writings to be such,
     p. 391 UNGATHERED 26 23 And art aliue still, while thy Booke doth liue,
     p. 398 UNGATHERED 30 60 Thou hast deseru'd: And let me reade the while
     p. 401 UNGATHERED 33  2 That, while they bind the senses, doe so please?
```

whiles   frequency: 1   relative frequency: 0.00001
```
     p. 113 FOREST 12     11 Though neuer after; whiles it gaynes the voyce
```

whilest   frequency: 1   relative frequency: 0.00001
```
     p. 420 UNGATHERED 48 15 Whilest lyke a blaze of strawe,
```

whilst   frequency: 20   relative frequency: 0.00028
    See also "whilest," "whil'st."
```
     p.  69 EPIGRAMS 108   1 Strength of my Countrey, whilst I bring to view
     p. 139 UNDERWOOD 2.7 17 And whilst our tongues perplexed lie,
     p. 160 UNDERWOOD 15 133 And whilst our states, strength, body, and mind
                            we waste,
     p. 184 UNDERWOOD 29  34 Whilst the Latin, Queene of Tongues,
     p. 216 UNDERWOOD 44 101 The fate of things: whilst totter'd vertue holds
     p. 216 UNDERWOOD 45   2 Whilst I informe my selfe, I would teach thee,
     p. 217 UNDERWOOD 46  18 With endlesse labours, whilst thy learning drawes
     p. 224 UNDERWOOD 50  21 Whilst your Ulisses hath ta'ne leave to goe,
     p. 227 UNDERWOOD 52  13 But whilst you curious were to have it be
     p. 239 UNDERWOOD 67  24 Whilst it the Dittie heares.
     p. 240 UNDERWOOD 67  40 Whilst all the ravish'd rout
     p. 246 UNDERWOOD 70  96 Whilst that in heav'n, this light on earth must
                            shine.
     p. 256 UNDERWOOD 75 126 Whilst they both stand,
     p. 258 UNDERWOOD 75 181 Whilst the maine tree, still found
     p. 290 UNDERWOOD 85  25 Whilst from the higher Bankes doe slide the
                            floods;
```

whilst (cont.)
    p. 293 UNDERWOOD 87   1 HOR. Whilst, Lydia, I was lov'd of thee,
    p. 293 UNDERWOOD 87   5 LYD. Whilst Horace lov'd no Mistres more,
    p. 319 HORACE 2   304 Gesture, and riot, whilst he swooping went
    p. 321 HORACE 2   335 Or, whilst he shuns the Earth, to catch at Aire
    p. 361 UNGATHERED 1   11 Whilst other soules conuert to base abuse

whil'st   frequency: 11   relative frequency: 0.00015
  **p. 115 PANEGYRE   67 To bring them forth: Whil'st riper ag'd, and apt
    p. 48 EPIGRAMS 64   17 That whil'st I meant but thine to gratulate,
    p. 51 EPIGRAMS 74   1 Whil'st thy weigh'd iudgements, EGERTON,
                              I heare,
    p. 51 EPIGRAMS 74   3 Whil'st I behold thee liue with purest hands;
    p. 52 EPIGRAMS 74   7 Whil'st thou art certaine to thy words, once
                              gone,
    p. 70 EPIGRAMS 109   18 Whil'st others toyle for titles to their tombes.
    p. 81 EPIGRAMS 129   11 Whil'st thou dost rayse some Player, from the
                              graue,
    p. 97 FOREST 3   37 The whil'st, the seuerall seasons thou hast seene
    p. 113 FOREST 12   1 Whil'st that, for which, all vertue now is sold,
    p. 113 FOREST 12   18 Or perhaps lesse: whil'st gold beares all this
                              sway,
    p. 366 UNGATHERED 6   12 Whil'st pleas'd Apollo

whimsies. See "whymseys."

whip   frequency: 1   relative frequency: 0.00001
    p. 410 UNGATHERED 39   4 Pillory nor Whip, nor want of Ears,

whipped. See "whipt."

whipt   frequency: 1   relative frequency: 0.00001
    p. 411 UNGATHERED 39   15 A Rogue by Statute, censur'd to be whipt,

whirling   frequency: 1   relative frequency: 0.00001
    p. 405 UNGATHERED 34   73 Whirling his Whymseys, by a subtilty

whirls. See "whoorles."

whisper   frequency: 2   relative frequency: 0.00002
    p. 59 EPIGRAMS 92   20 And whisper what a Proclamation sayes.
    p. 177 UNDERWOOD 25   31 But whisper; O glad Innocence,

whisper'd   frequency: 1   relative frequency: 0.00001
    p. 234 UNDERWOOD 61   6 But whisper'd Counsells, and those only thrive;

whisperers   frequency: 1   relative frequency: 0.00001
    p. 167 UNDERWOOD 15   165 Lewd slanderers, soft whisperers that let blood

whispering   frequency: 1   relative frequency: 0.00001
    p. 154 UNDERWOOD 13   49 Give thankes by stealth, and whispering in the
                              eare,

whistle   frequency: 1   relative frequency: 0.00001
    p. 405 UNGATHERED 34   66 Be Inigo, ye Whistle, & his men!

whistles   frequency: 1   relative frequency: 0.00001
    p. 273 U'WOOD 84.1   21 Their Corrals, Whistles, and prime Coates,

whit   frequency: 1   relative frequency: 0.00001
    p. 140 UNDERWOOD 2.8   22 'Fore your Idoll Glasse a whit,

white   frequency: 10   relative frequency: 0.00014
  See also "virgin-white."
    p. 31 EPIGRAMS 15   2 'Twas brought to court first wrapt, and white as
                              milke;
    p. 87 EPIGRAMS 133   126 White, black, blew, greene, and in more formes
                              out-started,
    p. 108 FOREST 10A   6 Could ne'er make prize of thy white Chastetye.
    p. 135 UNDERWOOD 2.4   30 O so white! O so soft! O so sweet is she!
    p. 137 UNDERWOOD 2.5   29 Nay, her white and polish'd neck,
    p. 227 UNDERWOOD 52   20 A Poet hath no more but black and white,
    p. 285 U'WOOD 84.9   95 And white, as that, put on: and in her hand,
    p. 360 UNGATHERED 6   25 This change'd his Downe; till this, as white
    p. 369 UNGATHERED 6   104 Or thought they, Leda's white Adult'rers place
    p. 662 INSCRIPTS. 2   10 of her white Hand; or she can spare it.

white-fryers   frequency: 1   relative frequency: 0.00001
    p. 30 EPIGRAMS 12   2 That haunt Pickt-hatch, Mersh-Lambeth, and
                              White-fryers,

white-hall   frequency: 2   relative frequency: 0.00002
   p. 138 UNDERWOOD 2.6   16 Else that glister'd in White-hall;
   p. 210 UNDERWOOD 43   156 Nay, let White-Hall with Revels have to doe,

whitefriars. See "white-fryers."

whitehall. See "white-hall."

whiter   frequency: 1   relative frequency: 0.00001
   p. 60 EPIGRAMS 93   11 Then whose I doe not know a whiter soule,

whitest   frequency: 1   relative frequency: 0.00001
   p. 225 UNDERWOOD 51   16 Out of their Choysest, and their whitest wooll.

whither   frequency: 7   relative frequency: 0.00010
   See also "whether."
   p. 37 EPIGRAMS 33   3 Whither the world must follow. And I, now,
   p. 55 EPIGRAMS 84   10 Make it your gift. See whither that will beare
                    mee.
   p. 122 FOREST 15   14 And whither rap'd, now thou but stoup'st to mee?
   p. 283 U'WOOD 84.9   47 And Goates together, whither they must come
   p. 365 UNGATHERED 5   17 Alas: then whither wade I,
   p. 404 UNGATHERED 34   59 Whither? oh whither will this Tire-man growe?

who   frequency: 201   relative frequency: 0.00290
   See also "who'd," "whoe," "who'had," "who'haue,"
          "who'in," "who'it," "who'll," "who's."

who'd   frequency: 1   relative frequency: 0.00001

whoe   frequency: 2   relative frequency: 0.00002

who'had   frequency: 1   relative frequency: 0.00001

who'haue   frequency: 1   relative frequency: 0.00001

who'in   frequency: 1   relative frequency: 0.00001

who'it   frequency: 1   relative frequency: 0.00001

whole   frequency: 39   relative frequency: 0.00056
   p. 30 EPIGRAMS 12   6 Himselfe: his whole reuennue is, god payes.
   p. 38 EPIGRAMS 35   10 And since, the whole land was preseru'd for thee.
   p. 45 EPIGRAMS 56   14 From locks of wooll, or shreds from the whole
                    peece?
   p. 56 EPIGRAMS 88   2 That his whole body should speake french, not he?
   p. 76 EPIGRAMS 119   16 Makes, the whole longer, then 'twas giuen him,
                    much.
   p. 84 EPIGRAMS 133   14 And for one CERBERVS, the whole coast was
                    dogs.
   p. 96 FOREST 2   96 With the whole houshold, and may, euery day,
   p. 100 FOREST 4   17 I know thou whole art but a shop
   p. 130 UNDERWOOD 1.3   10 Hee whom the whole world could not take,
   p. 156 UNDERWOOD 13   101 Reare-Suppers in their Names! and spend whole
                    nights
   p. 163 UNDERWOOD 15   31 The whole world here leaven'd with madnesse
                    swells;
   p. 163 UNDERWOOD 15   44 To make up Greatnesse! and mans whole good fix'd
   p. 166 UNDERWOOD 15   131 Or side, but threatens Ruine. The whole Day
   p. 171 UNDERWOOD 20   10 That their whole life was wickednesse, though
                    weav'd
   p. 171 UNDERWOOD 20   12 But their whole inside full of ends, and knots?
   p. 189 UNDERWOOD 36   9 A Sparke to set whole world<s> a-fire,
   p. 205 UNDERWOOD 43   55 And so, have kept me dying a whole age,
   p. 205 UNDERWOOD 43   66 With pieces of the Legend; The whole summe
   p. 209 UNDERWOOD 43   133 Which, though it were the Fort of the whole
                    Parish,
   p. 227 UNDERWOOD 52   5 And the whole lumpe growes round, deform'd, and
                    droupes,
   p. 238 UNDERWOOD 66   10 To make the hearts of a whole Nation smile,
   p. 243 UNDERWOOD 70   27 He vexed time, and busied the whole State;
   p. 251 UNDERWOOD 74   12 Because the order of the whole is faire!
   p. 255 UNDERWOOD 75   87 Who the whole Act expresse;
   p. 271 UNDERWOOD 83   90 Whole Nations! nay, Mankind! the World, with
                    all
   p. 284 U'WOOD 84.9   65 And the whole Banquet is full sight of God!
   p. 287 U'WOOD 84.9   178 As her whole life was now become one note
   p. 288 U'WOOD 84.9   185 Her broken sighes did never misse whole sense:
   p. 288 U'WOOD 84.9   195 Would sit in an Infirmery, whole dayes
   p. 305 HORACE 2   28 The whole fleet wreck'd? A great jarre to be
                    shap'd,

whole (cont.)
    p. 307 HORACE 2   49 Not to designe the whole. Should I aspire
    p. 319 HORACE 2   298 Steepe the glad Genius in the Wine, whole
                             dayes,
    p. 366 UNGATHERED 6   26 As the whole heard in sight,
    p. 371 UNGATHERED 8   8 They saw it halfe, damd thy whole play, and more;
    p. 395 UNGATHERED 29   20 Lucans whole frame vnto vs, and so wrought,
    p. 399 UNGATHERED 31   11 The best of Woemen! her whole life
    p. 402 UNGATHERED 34   15 By all your Titles, & whole style at ones
    p. 415 UNGATHERED 42   17 So soft, and smooth it handles, the whole piece,
    p. 423 UNGATHERED 50   11 whole armyes fall, swayd by those nyce respects.

wholesome   frequency: 1   relative frequency: 0.00001
    See also "wholsome."
    p. 46 EPIGRAMS 62   8 To make amends, yo'are thought a wholesome
                             creature.

who'll   frequency: 1   relative frequency: 0.00001

wholly   frequency: 4   relative frequency: 0.00005
    p. 182 UNDERWOOD 28   2 Though not in these, in rithmes not wholly dumbe,
    p. 190 UNDERWOOD 37   26 In practiz'd friendship wholly to reprove,
    p. 288 U'WOOD 84.9   216 Hath given wholly to the Sonne (the rather
    p. 307 HORACE 2   32 Be simple quite throughout, and wholly one.

wholsome   frequency: 2   relative frequency: 0.00002
    p. 180 UNDERWOOD 26   9 Yet doth some wholsome Physick for the mind,
    p. 317 HORACE 2   283 Praise the spare diet, wholsome justice, lawes,

whom   frequency: 63   relative frequency: 0.00091
    See also "whome."

whome   frequency: 2   relative frequency: 0.00002

whoorles   frequency: 1   relative frequency: 0.00001
    p. 283 U'WOOD 84.9   32 Whoorles me about, and to blaspheme in fashion!

whore   frequency: 13   relative frequency: 0.00018
    p. 29 EPIGRAMS 7   1 Where lately harbour'd many a famous whore,
    p. 31 EPIGRAMS 12   24 Lent him a pockie whore. Shee hath paid him.
    p. 35 EPIGRAMS 26   2 He'adulters still: his thoughts lye with a whore.
    p. 39 EPIGRAMS 41   4 For what shee gaue, a whore; a baud, shee cures.
    p. 54 EPIGRAMS 82   1 SVRLY'S old whore in her new silkes doth
                             swim:
    p. 54 EPIGRAMS 83   1 To put out the word, whore, thou do'st me woo,
    p. 75 EPIGRAMS 117   2 For'his whore: GROYNE doth still occupy his
                             land.
    p. 163 UNDERWOOD 15   54 'Tis there civilitie to be a whore;
    p. 165 UNDERWOOD 15   90 Nature, that will not let his Wife be a whore;
    p. 172 UNDERWOOD 20   21 I could forgive her being proud! a whore!
    p. 209 UNDERWOOD 43   153 O no, cry'd all, Fortune, for being a whore,
    p. 215 UNDERWOOD 44   87 What love you then? your whore. What study?
                             gate,
    p. 391 UNGATHERED 26   13 These are, as some infamous Baud, or Whore,

whore-house   frequency: 1   relative frequency: 0.00001
    p. 29 EPIGRAMS 7   4 And still be a whore-house. Th'are Synonima.

whores   frequency: 1   relative frequency: 0.00001
    p. 167 UNDERWOOD 15   161 And be belov'd, while the Whores last. O times,

who's   frequency: 2   relative frequency: 0.00002

whose   frequency: 88   relative frequency: 0.00127

why   frequency: 47   relative frequency: 0.00068

whyle   frequency: 1   relative frequency: 0.00001
    p. 407 UNGATHERED 35   20 Content thee to be Pancridge Earle ye whyle;

whymseys   frequency: 1   relative frequency: 0.00001
    p. 405 UNGATHERED 34   73 Whirling his Whymseys, by a subtilty

wick. See "wike."

wicked   frequency: 3   relative frequency: 0.00004
    p. 54 EPIGRAMS 80   8 For good men but see death, the wicked tast it.
    p. 223 UNDERWOOD 49   45 For there the wicked in the Chaire of scorne,
    p. 317 HORACE 2   265 Natur'd, and wicked Atreus cooke, to th'eye,

wickednesse   frequency: 3   relative frequency: 0.00004
  **p. 116 PANEGYRE   119 One wickednesse another must defend;
    p. 171 UNDERWOOD 20   10 That their whole life was wickednesse, though
                              weav'd
    p. 397 UNGATHERED 30   46 A wild, and an authoriz'd wickednesse!

widdow   frequency: 2   relative frequency: 0.00002
    p. 33 EPIGRAMS 19   1 That COD can get no widdow, yet a knight,
    p. 42 EPIGRAMS 47   2 Hee that wooes euery widdow, will get none.

widdowes   frequency: 1   relative frequency: 0.00001
    p. 99 FOREST 3   79 To blow vp orphanes, widdowes, and their states;

wider   frequency: 1   relative frequency: 0.00001
    p. 319 HORACE 2   296 That wider Walls embrac'd their Citie round,

widow   frequency: 1   relative frequency: 0.00001
    See also "widdow."
    p. 230 UNDERWOOD 56   17 Widow or Wife, without the jealousie

widow'd   frequency: 1   relative frequency: 0.00001
    p. 224 UNDERWOOD 50   2 Wherewith this while you live a widow'd wife,

widows. See "widdowes."

wife   frequency: 30   relative frequency: 0.00043
    See also "mid-wife."
    p. 34 EPIGRAMS 25   1 While BEAST instructs his faire, and
                              innocent wife,
    p. 34 EPIGRAMS 25   8 Iust wife, and, to change me, make womans hast?
    p. 35 EPIGRAMS 26   1 Then his chast wife, though BEAST now know
                              no more,
    p. 36 EPIGRAMS 28   15 He keepes anothers wife, which is a spice
    p. 40 EPIGRAMS 42   12 Were quite out-spun. The like wish hath his
                              wife.
    p. 40 EPIGRAMS 42   16 If, now, with man and wife, to will, and nill
    p. 42 EPIGRAMS 46   1 Is this the Sir, who, some wast wife to winne,
    p. 53 EPIGRAMS 78   1 HORNET, thou hast thy wife drest, for the
                              stall,
    p. 119 FOREST 13   110 They speake; since you are truly that rare wife,
    p. 165 UNDERWOOD 15   87 He that will follow but anothers wife,
    p. 165 UNDERWOOD 15   90 Nature, that will not let his Wife be a whore;
    p. 171 UNDERWOOD 19   25 That which we can, who both in you, his Wife,
    p. 201 UNDERWOOD 42   39 Whose like I have knowne the Taylors Wife put
                              on
    p. 201 UNDERWOOD 42   44 Her presently? Or leape thy Wife of force,
    p. 201 UNDERWOOD 42   50 But when thy Wife (as thou conceiv'st) is brave?
    p. 203 UNDERWOOD 43   6 Nor made least line of love to thy loose Wife;
    p. 224 UNDERWOOD 50   2 Wherewith this while you live a widow'd wife,
    p. 229 UNDERWOOD 54   4 A Merchants Wife is Regent of the Scale.
    p. 230 UNDERWOOD 56   17 Widow or Wife, without the jealousie
    p. 232 UNDERWOOD 58   8 Thy Wife a fit of laughter; a Cramp-ring
    p. 232 UNDERWOOD 58   14 Their perfum'd judgements, let them kisse thy
                              Wife.
    p. 272 UNDERWOOD 84   t6 late Wife of Sir KENELME DIGBY,
                              Knight:
    p. 285 U'WOOD 84.9   99 A Wife, a Friend, a Lady, or a Love;
    p. 287 U'WOOD 84.9   174 A tender Mother, a discreeter Wife,
    p. 291 UNDERWOOD 85   39 But if, to boot with these, a chaste Wife meet
    p. 384 UNGATHERED 18   12 Out-bee yt Wife, in worth, thy freind did make:
    p. 386 UNGATHERED 20   8 And therefore I commend vnto the Wife,
    p. 394 UNGATHERED 28   15 At least so great a Lady. She was wife
    p. 399 UNGATHERED 31   12 Was the example of a wife!
    p. 417 UNGATHERED 45   26 that the wife heades for a wager

wifes   frequency: 1   relative frequency: 0.00001
    p. 202 UNDERWOOD 42   87 Thou art jealous of thy Wifes, or Daughters
                              Case:

wife's. See "mid-wives," "wifes," "wives."

wight   frequency: 2   relative frequency: 0.00002
    p. 311 HORACE 2   134 With swelling throat: and, oft, the tragick wight
    p. 416 UNGATHERED 45   7 but a very merry wight

wights   frequency: 1   relative frequency: 0.00001
    p. 84 EPIGRAMS 133   21 I sing the braue aduenture of two wights,

wike   frequency: 1   relative frequency: 0.00001
  **p. 115 PANEGYRE   71 The others flame, as doth the wike and waxe,

wil   frequency: 1   relative frequency: 0.00001

wild   frequency: 10   relative frequency: 0.00014
      See also "wilde."
      p. 111 FOREST 11   73 Though thy wild thoughts with sparrowes wings doe
                                 flye,
      p. 151 UNDERWOOD 11   11 In all my wild desire,
      p. 189 UNDERWOOD 36   14 Now swift, now slow, now tame, now wild;
      p. 218 UNDERWOOD 47   10 That live in the wild Anarchie of Drinke,
      p. 290 UNDERWOOD 85   32 Wild Bores into his toyles pitch'd round:
      p. 305 HORACE 2   14 Yet, not as therefore wild, and tame should
                                 cleave
      p. 313 HORACE 2   177 Poore Jo wandring; wild Orestes mad:
      p. 327 HORACE 2   489 Wild ra<n>ging lusts; prescribe the mariage good;
      p. 342 HORACE 1   175 .... wild, fierce ....
      p. 397 UNGATHERED 30   46 A wild, and an authoriz'd wickednesse!

wilde   frequency: 3   relative frequency: 0.00004
      p. 82 EPIGRAMS 130   2 Of building townes, and making wilde beasts tame,
      p. 108 FOREST 10A   9 Such, as in lustes wilde forrest loue to rainge,
      p. 309 HORACE 2   96 Or the wilde river, who hath changed now

wildest   frequency: 1   relative frequency: 0.00001
      p. 367 UNGATHERED 6   53 Vpon the Kerne, and wildest Irishry,

wildly   frequency: 1   relative frequency: 0.00001
      p. 327 HORACE 2   480 First frighted men, that wildly liv'd, at ods,

wile   frequency: 1   relative frequency: 0.00001
      p. 102 FOREST 5   14 So remoued by our wile?

wilfull   frequency: 1   relative frequency: 0.00001
      p. 53 EPIGRAMS 80   3 How wilfull blind is he then, that would stray,

will   frequency: 288   relative frequency: 0.00416
      See also "hee'll," "he'le," "he'll," "ile,"
              "i'le," "i'll," "shee'll," "t'will,"
              "'twill," "wee'l," "wee'll," "who'll,"
              "wil," "wull," "you'l," "you'll."
   *p. 492 TO HIMSELF   12 And they will acornes eat:
   *p. 493 TO HIMSELF   29 For, who the relish of these ghests will fit,
  **p. 115 PANEGYRE   74 The Kings obeying will, from taking pride
  **p. 115 PANEGYRE   99 "Where lawes were made to serue the tyran' will;
    p. 27 EPIGRAMS 2   1 It will be look'd for, booke, when some but see
    p. 28 EPIGRAMS 3   11 If, without these vile arts, it will not sell,
    p. 28 EPIGRAMS 4   8 As chiefe of those still promise they will bee.
    p. 30 EPIGRAMS 11   7 For I will doe none: and as little ill,
    p. 30 EPIGRAMS 11   8 For I will dare none. Good Lord, walke dead
                                still.
    p. 31 EPIGRAMS 15   4 Which was a cater-piller. So't will dye.
    p. 35 EPIGRAMS 28   9 He will both argue, and discourse in oathes,
    p. 36 EPIGRAMS 28   19 Nay more, for greatnesse sake, he will be one
    p. 38 EPIGRAMS 37   1 No cause, nor client fat, will CHEV'RILL
                                leese,
    p. 40 EPIGRAMS 42   5 By his free will, be in IONES company.
    p. 40 EPIGRAMS 42   16 If, now, with man and wife, to will, and nill
    p. 41 EPIGRAMS 45   6 Will man lament the state he should enuie?
    p. 42 EPIGRAMS 47   2 Hee that wooes euery widdow, will get none.
    p. 45 EPIGRAMS 56   13 Foole, as if halfe eyes will not know a fleece
    p. 46 EPIGRAMS 62   7 That can restore that. Will it hurt your
                                feature?
    p. 48 EPIGRAMS 65   7 Get him the times long grudge, the courts ill
                                will;
    p. 50 EPIGRAMS 71   2 Still, 'tis his lucke to praise me 'gainst his
                                will.
    p. 54 EPIGRAMS 81   1 Forbeare to tempt me, PROVLE, I will not
                                show
    p. 55 EPIGRAMS 84   10 Make it your gift. See whither that will beare
                                mee.
    p. 57 EPIGRAMS 90   15 Hath got the stewards chaire; he will not tarry
    p. 57 EPIGRAMS 90   16 Longer a day, but with his MILL will marry.
    p. 59 EPIGRAMS 92   30 If the States make peace, how it will goe
    p. 59 EPIGRAMS 92   32 And of the poulder-plot, they will talke yet.
    p. 63 EPIGRAMS 99   1 That thou hast kept thy loue, encreast thy will,
    p. 64 EPIGRAMS 101   4 But that your worth will dignifie our feast,
    p. 65 EPIGRAMS 101   17 Ile tell you of more, and lye, so you will come:
    p. 65 EPIGRAMS 101   26 That will the pastrie, not my paper, show of.
    p. 65 EPIGRAMS 101   27 Digestiue cheese, and fruit there sure will bee;
    p. 65 EPIGRAMS 101   35 Of this we will sup free, but moderately,
    p. 65 EPIGRAMS 101   36 And we will haue no Pooly', or Parrot by;

will (cont.)

p.	65	EPIGRAMS 101	38	But, at our parting, we will be, as when
p.	68	EPIGRAMS 107	4	Not that I loue it, more, then I will you.
p.	69	EPIGRAMS 107	28	Will you part with them, here, vnthriftely?
p.	70	EPIGRAMS 109	17	Thy deedes, vnto thy name, will proue new wombes,
p.	72	EPIGRAMS 111	7	Which all, but ignorant Captaynes, will confesse:
p.	72	EPIGRAMS 111	9	Yet thou, perhaps, shalt meet some tongues will grutch,
p.	74	EPIGRAMS 115	19	It will deny all; and forsweare it too:
p.	74	EPIGRAMS 115	20	Not that it feares, but will not haue to doo
p.	82	EPIGRAMS 131	3	For, then, all mouthes will iudge, and their owne way:
p.	83	EPIGRAMS 131	7	For, if the hum'rous world will talke at large,
p.	83	EPIGRAMS 132	12	As his will now be the translation thought,
p.	86	EPIGRAMS 133	90	Row close then, slaues. Alas, they will beshite vs.
p.	87	EPIGRAMS 133	105	But I will speake (and know I shall be heard)
p.	87	EPIGRAMS 133	106	Touching this cause, where they will be affeard
p.	89	EPIGRAMS 133	175	But you will visit grisly PLVTO'S hall?
p.	95	FOREST 2	82	What (great, I will not say, but) sodayne cheare
p.	96	FOREST 2	99	Now, PENSHVRST, they that will proportion thee
p.	100	FOREST 4	23	And neuer will redeeme a day,
p.	102	FOREST 4	63	But I will beare these, with that scorne,
p.	102	FOREST 4	65	Nor for my peace will I goe farre,
p.	102	FOREST 5	3	Time will not be ours, for euer:
p.	102	FOREST 5	4	He, at length, our good will seuer.
p.	103	FOREST 6	4	All your bounties will betray.
p.	104	FOREST 7	2	Seeme to flye it, it will pursue:
p.	104	FOREST 7	4	Let her alone, shee will court you.
p.	105	FOREST 8	11	Scarce will take our present store?
p.	105	FOREST 8	12	And this age will build no more:
p.	105	FOREST 8	15	Or if needs thy lust will tast
p.	105	FOREST 8	37	Will by coach, and water goe,
p.	106	FOREST 8	43	These, disease, will thee deserue:
p.	106	FOREST 8	44	And will, long ere thou should'st starue,
p.	106	FOREST 9	2	And I will pledge with mine;
p.	107	FOREST 10	10	Nor will I beg of thee, Lord of the vine,
p.	109	FOREST 11	15	Will quickly taste the treason, and commit
p.	112	FOREST 11	113	That knowes the waight of guilt: He will refraine
p.	113	FOREST 12	6	To euery squire, or groome, that will report
p.	113	FOREST 12	13	The foole that gaue it; who will want, and weepe,
p.	114	FOREST 12	27	But let this drosse carry what price it will
p.	114	FOREST 12	30	With you, I know, my offring will find grace.
p.	114	FOREST 12	34	Almost you haue, or may haue, when you will?
p.	115	FOREST 12	77	Will proue old ORPHEVS act no tale to be:
p.	117	FOREST 13	25	You will not from the paper slightly passe:
p.	117	FOREST 13	29	Looke then, and see your selfe. I will not say
p.	118	FOREST 13	71	Let who will follow fashions, and attyres,
p.	119	FOREST 13	114	You are depending on his word, and will;
p.	121	FOREST 14	29	Little, whose will
p.	121	FOREST 14	41	'T will be exacted of your name, whose sonne,
p.	121	FOREST 14	44	Will, then,
p.	131	UNDERWOOD 2.1	13	If you then will read the Storie,
p.	139	UNDERWOOD 2.7	7	Once more, and (faith) I will be gone,
p.	139	UNDERWOOD 2.7	13	I will but mend the last, and tell
p.	139	UNDERWOOD 2.7	18	Let who will thinke us dead, or wish our death.
p.	140	UNDERWOOD 2.8	14	For I will so urge you to't,
p.	140	UNDERWOOD 2.8	21	Nay, I will not let you sit
p.	140	UNDERWOOD 2.9	2	I will tell what Man would please me.
p.	143	UNDERWOOD 3	14	Sleepe, and the Grave will wake.
p.	144	UNDERWOOD 4	6	For then their threats will kill me;
p.	144	UNDERWOOD 4	8	For then my hopes will spill me.
p.	145	UNDERWOOD 4	10	For so will sorrow slay me;
p.	145	UNDERWOOD 5	16	Then when 'tis made, why so will wee.
p.	146	UNDERWOOD 6	10	If ever we will love aright.
p.	148	UNDERWOOD 7	28	Will be my Rivall, though she have but eares.
p.	150	UNDERWOOD 10	16	I ne're will owe my health to a disease.
p.	151	UNDERWOOD 11	7	Nor will he tell me for whose sake
p.	151	UNDERWOOD 12	13	But was by sweetning so his will,
p.	152	UNDERWOOD 12	34	That they for me their teares will shed;
p.	153	UNDERWOOD 13	7	You then, whose will not only, but desire
p.	153	UNDERWOOD 13	14	This Good from you, as freely will it owe;
p.	153	UNDERWOOD 13	26	Against his will that do's 'hem? that hath weav'd
p.	154	UNDERWOOD 13	43	No more then he doth thanke, that will receive
p.	154	UNDERWOOD 13	58	Ha's Feathers, and will serve a man to pull.
p.	155	UNDERWOOD 13	73	O, is it so? knowes he so much? and will
p.	155	UNDERWOOD 13	78	Many a pound, and piece, will p<l>ace one well;

will (cont.)

p. 156	UNDERWOOD	13	123	No! he must feele and know, that will advance.
p. 157	UNDERWOOD	13	144	As they are high; are rooted, and will last.
p. 157	UNDERWOOD	13	154	Their difference, cannot choose which you will be.
p. 158	UNDERWOOD	13	160	Which you will bury; but therein, the strife
p. 159	UNDERWOOD	14	28	Meane what I speake: and still will keepe that Vow.
p. 159	UNDERWOOD	14	36	Or faith in things? or is't your wealth and will
p. 161	UNDERWOOD	14	73	It true respects. He will not only love,
p. 164	UNDERWOOD	15	78	That payes, or what he will: The Dame is steele.
p. 165	UNDERWOOD	15	87	He that will follow but anothers wife,
p. 165	UNDERWOOD	15	90	Nature, that will not let his Wife be a whore;
p. 165	UNDERWOOD	15	103	His time? health? soule? will he for these goe throw
p. 165	UNDERWOOD	15	112	Sweet bags, sweet Powders, nor sweet words will passe
p. 166	UNDERWOOD	15	122	Brought on us, and will every houre increase.
p. 166	UNDERWOOD	15	141	Can we not leave this worme? or will we not?
p. 167	UNDERWOOD	15	150	That may stand by, and hold my peace? will he,
p. 169	UNDERWOOD	17	18	And I will bring a Crop, if not the best.
p. 170	UNDERWOOD	18	22	I'le lead you on; or if my fate will so,
p. 171	UNDERWOOD	19	20	I know no beautie, nor no youth that will.
p. 172	UNDERWOOD	20	14	Were such as I will now relate, or worse?
p. 175	UNDERWOOD	23	30	Who aided him, will thee, the issue of Joves braine.
p. 179	UNDERWOOD	25	42	Pyracmon's houre will come to give them ease,
p. 179	UNDERWOOD	25	45	Gold, that is perfect, will out-live the fire.
p. 180	UNDERWOOD	25	64	That you will stand
p. 182	UNDERWOOD	27	35	Yet sure my tunes will be the best,
p. 186	UNDERWOOD	32	14	They will come of, and scape the Punishment.
p. 187	UNDERWOOD	33	21	And make the Scarre faire; If that will not be,
p. 187	UNDERWOOD	33	23	But in a businesse, that will bide the Touch,
p. 190	UNDERWOOD	37	13	Which, how most sacred I will ever keepe,
p. 190	UNDERWOOD	37	24	Will unto Licence that faire leave abuse.
p. 191	UNDERWOOD	38	18	In will and power, only to defeat.
p. 191	UNDERWOOD	38	21	I will not stand to justifie my fault,
p. 191	UNDERWOOD	38	27	No, I will stand arraign'd, and cast, to be
p. 191	UNDERWOOD	38	29	And (stil'd your mercies Creature) will live more
p. 192	UNDERWOOD	38	42	Or two, or three, a Sonne will dis-inherit,
p. 194	UNDERWOOD	38	107	I will no more abuse my vowes to you,
p. 194	UNDERWOOD	38	108	Then I will studie falshood, to be true.
p. 198	UNDERWOOD	40	37	Where he that knowes will, like a Lapwing, flie
p. 198	UNDERWOOD	40	39	To others, as he will deserve the Trust
p. 199	UNDERWOOD	41	13	My health will leave me; and when you depart,
p. 200	UNDERWOOD	42	26	For Silke will draw some sneaking Songster thither.
p. 202	UNDERWOOD	42	86	None of their pleasures! nor will aske thee, why
p. 210	UNDERWOOD	43	165	I will not argue thee, from those, of guilt,
p. 210	UNDERWOOD	43	172	Will be remembred by Six Clerkes, to one.
p. 212	UNDERWOOD	43	215	Light on thee: Or if those plagues will not doo,
p. 215	UNDERWOOD	44	75	We will beleeve, like men of our owne Ranke,
p. 215	UNDERWOOD	44	82	The Herald will. Our blood is now become
p. 216	UNDERWOOD	45	19	But these with wearing will themselves unfold:
p. 218	UNDERWOOD	47	16	Or th'other on their borders, that will jeast
p. 219	UNDERWOOD	47	40	And force back that, which will not be restor'd,
p. 219	UNDERWOOD	47	59	Live to that point I will, for which I am man,
p. 220	UNDERWOOD	47	71	These I will honour, love, embrace, and serve:
p. 220	UNDERWOOD	47	76	My selfe a little. I will take you so,
p. 223	UNDERWOOD	49	37	The wits will leave you, if they once perceive
p. 223	UNDERWOOD	49	46	Will cal't a Bastard, when a Prophet's borne.
p. 225	UNDERWOOD	50	36	It will be shame for them, if they have none.
p. 227	UNDERWOOD	52	24	To all posteritie; I will write Burlase.
p. 229	UNDERWOOD	54	8	Is, she will play Dame Justice, too severe;
p. 230	UNDERWOOD	56	6	The first of which, I feare, you will refuse;
p. 231	UNDERWOOD	57	5	And that he will venter
p. 231	UNDERWOOD	57	20	Will come at the Court,
p. 232	UNDERWOOD	57	23	will come to the Table,
p. 232	UNDERWOOD	57	26	the Parish will know it.
p. 232	UNDERWOOD	57	28	if the'Chequer be emptie, so will be his Head.
p. 232	UNDERWOOD	58	9	Will be reward enough: to weare like those,
p. 236	UNDERWOOD	63	5	Hee can, he will, and with large int'rest pay,
p. 236	UNDERWOOD	63	6	What (at his liking) he will take away.
p. 236	UNDERWOOD	63	8	That the Almighties will to you is such:
p. 236	UNDERWOOD	63	10	And thinke all still the best, that he will doe.
p. 236	UNDERWOOD	63	11	That thought shall make, he will this losse supply
p. 236	UNDERWOOD	63	14	Cannot but heape that grace, he will requite.

will (cont.)

p. 237	UNDERWOOD 64	21 Are lost upon accompt! And none will know
p. 238	UNDERWOOD 65	12 Sol will re-shine. If not, CHARLES hath a Sonne.
p. 241	UNDERWOOD 68	2 His Poet Sack, the House-hold will not pay?
p. 251	UNDERWOOD 74	25 O how will then our Court be pleas'd,
p. 257	UNDERWOOD 75	161 Yet, as we may, we will, with chast desires,
p. 258	UNDERWOOD 75	190 Will last till day;
p. 258	UNDERWOOD 75	191 Night, and the sheetes will show
p. 262	UNDERWOOD 78	17 In signe the Subject, and the Song will live,
p. 263	UNDERWOOD 78	21 He will cleare up his forehead, thinke thou bring'st
p. 263	UNDERWOOD 78	23 For he doth love my Verses, and will looke
p. 263	UNDERWOOD 78	25 And praise them too. O! what a fame 't will be?
p. 263	UNDERWOOD 78	32 Being sent to one, they will be read of all.
p. 269	UNDERWOOD 83	16 And the disposure will be something new,
p. 277	U'WOOD 84.3	32 Next sitting we will draw her mind.
p. 277	U'WOOD 84.4	7 Beside, your hand will never hit,
p. 279	U'WOOD 84.4	33 Whose Notions when it will expresse
p. 282	U'WOOD 84.8	22 Which Vertue from your Father, ripe, will fall;
p. 284	U'WOOD 84.9	59 Who will be there, against that day prepar'd,
p. 284	U'WOOD 84.9	76 Will honour'd be in all simplicitie!
p. 285	U'WOOD 84.9	97 And will you, worthy Sonne, Sir, knowing this,
p. 285	U'WOOD 84.9	108 When shee departed? you will meet her there,
p. 286	U'WOOD 84.9	122 Where Hee will be, all Beautie to the Sight;
p. 286	U'WOOD 84.9	124 A Musique in the Eares, will ever last;
p. 286	U'WOOD 84.9	127 Hee will all Glory, all Perfection be,
p. 286	U'WOOD 84.9	130 Will there revealed be in Majestie!
p. 289	U'WOOD 84.9	220 Where first his Power will appeare, by call
p. 289	U'WOOD 84.9	226 Who reades, will pardon my Intelligence,
p. 292	UNDERWOOD 86	16 Will he display the Ensignes of thy warre.
p. 294	UNDERWOOD 88	5 For lust will languish, and that heat decay.
p. 294	UNDERWOOD 88	9 This hath pleas'd, doth please, and long will please; never
p. 295	UNDERWOOD 90	11 Sleepe, that will make the darkest howres swift-pac't;
p. 295	UNDERWOOD 90	12 Will to bee, what thou art; and nothing more:
p. 307	HORACE 2	55 Upon your shoulders. Prove what they will beare,
p. 307	HORACE 2	56 And what they will not. Him, whose choice doth reare
p. 309	HORACE 2	72 Of the Cethegi; And all men will grace,
p. 309	HORACE 2	77 A Roman to Caecilius will allow,
p. 309	HORACE 2	84 And ever will, to utter termes that bee
p. 309	HORACE 2	103 If Custome please; at whose disposing will
p. 311	HORACE 2	121 The Comick matter will not be exprest
p. 311	HORACE 2	146 Thy selfe in teares, then me thy losse will wound,
p. 313	HORACE 2	160 And Roman Gentrie, jearing, will laugh out.
p. 313	HORACE 2	161 It much will differ, if a God speake, than,
p. 317	HORACE 2	262 Much from the sight, which faire report will make
p. 321	HORACE 2	341 Nor I, when I write Satyres, will so love
p. 321	HORACE 2	343 Meere raigning words: nor will I labour so
p. 321	HORACE 2	361 Will take offence, at this: Nor, though it strike
p. 321	HORACE 2	363 The nut-crackers throughout, will they therefore
p. 325	HORACE 2	422 In Helicon; a great sort will not pare
p. 325	HORACE 2	435 I, writing nought my selfe, will teach them yet
p. 325	HORACE 2	444 There words will follow, not against their will.
p. 325	HORACE 2	447 What height of love, a Parent will fit best,
p. 327	HORACE 2	467 There's Albin's sonne will say, Substract an ounce
p. 329	HORACE 2	517 This booke will get the Sosii money; This
p. 329	HORACE 2	518 Will passe the Seas, and long as nature is,
p. 329	HORACE 2	522 The hand, and mind would, but it will resound
p. 329	HORACE 2	526 Much in the Poeme shine, I will not bee
p. 329	HORACE 2	530 Still in the same, and warned will not mend,
p. 331	HORACE 2	540 Will take you more, the neerer that you stand;
p. 331	HORACE 2	543 Will in the light be view'd: This, once, the sight
p. 331	HORACE 2	544 Doth please; this, ten times over, will delight.
p. 331	HORACE 2	582 Nature, or Art. My Judgement will not pierce
p. 333	HORACE 2	603 Will be a suretie; or can helpe him out
p. 335	HORACE 2	632 Alone, without a rivall, by his will.
p. 335	HORACE 2	633 A wise, and honest man will cry out shame
p. 335	HORACE 2	634 On artlesse Verse; the hard ones he will blame;
p. 335	HORACE 2	654 There's none will take the care, to helpe him then;
p. 335	HORACE 2	664 Let Poets perish, that will not be kept.
p. 335	HORACE 2	665 Hee that preserves a man, against his will,
p. 339	HORACE 1	59 ... . will forsake:

will (cont.)
    p. 349 HORACE 1   439 .... will ... .
    p. 362 UNGATHERED 2   12 So with this Authors Readers will it thriue:
    p. 362 UNGATHERED 2   14 His proofe their praise, will meete, as in this
                                       line.
    p. 370 UNGATHERED 7   6 Will well confesse; presenting, limiting,
    p. 375 UNGATHERED 10   21 He will expiate this sinne with conuerting the
                                       Iewes.
    p. 375 UNGATHERED 10   29 P. shewes what he was, K. what he will bee.
    p. 379 UNGATHERED 12   11 Which, vnto all Ages, for his will be knowne,
    p. 379 UNGATHERED 12   17 But who will beleeue this, that chanceth to looke
    p. 380 UNGATHERED 12   47 Nay more in his wardrobe, if you will laugh at a
    p. 386 UNGATHERED 20   11 I know for such, as (if my word will waigh)
    p. 387 UNGATHERED 22   4 will all turne dust, & may not make me swell.
    p. 387 UNGATHERED 22   11 it will be matter lowd inoughe to tell
    p. 389 UNGATHERED 24   9 Vpon it, but will loath, or let it passe,
    p. 389 UNGATHERED 24   19 Will bee receiu'd in Court; If not, would I
    p. 391 UNGATHERED 26   17 I, therefore will begin. Soule of the Age!
    p. 391 UNGATHERED 26   19 My Shakespeare, rise; I will not lodge thee by
    p. 392 UNGATHERED 26   50 As, since, she will vouchsafe no other Wit.
    p. 394 UNGATHERED 28   11 Nay they will venter ones Descent to hitt,
    p. 394 UNGATHERED 28   26 This second marriage, will aeternall make.
    p. 395 UNGATHERED 29   23 The selfe same Genius! so the worke will say.
    p. 396 UNGATHERED 30   9 About the towne: this reck'ning I will pay,
    p. 398 UNGATHERED 30   64 Braue are the Musters, that the Muse will make.
    p. 398 UNGATHERED 30   72 And will be bought of euery Lord, and Knight,
    p. 398 UNGATHERED 30   76 Of tender eyes will more be wept, then seene:
    p. 400 UNGATHERED 32   1 This Booke will liue; It hath a Genius: This
    p. 402 UNGATHERED 34   18 Will any of these express yor place? or witt?
    p. 403 UNGATHERED 34   21 Why much good doo't you! Be what beast you will,
    p. 403 UNGATHERED 34   25 your Trappings will not change you. Change yor
                                       mynd.
    p. 403 UNGATHERED 34   26 Noe veluet Sheath you weare, will alter kynde.
    p. 404 UNGATHERED 34   59 Whither? oh whither will this Tire-man growe?
    p. 408 UNGATHERED 36   12 Will well designe thee, to be viewd of all
    p. 409 UNGATHERED 37   13 Thou art not worth it. Who will care to knowe
    p. 409 UNGATHERED 37   17 No man will tarry by thee, as hee goes,
    p. 410 UNGATHERED 38   11 Now each Court-Hobby-horse will wince in rime;
    p. 417 UNGATHERED 45   24 shee soone will heare it.
    p. 417 UNGATHERED 45   28 the Moone will beare it.
    p. 418 UNGATHERED 45   44 shee will not seise it.
    p. 420 UNGATHERED 48   23 Whose ayre will sooner Hell, then their dull
                                       senses peirce,
    p. 421 UNGATHERED 49   10 deignes myne the power to ffinde, yett want I
                                       will
    p. 423 UNGATHERED 50   17 he that will honest be, may quitt the Court,
    p. 662 INSCRIPTS. 2   7 And sworne, that he will quite discard thee

will<i>am   frequency: 1   relative frequency: 0.00001
    p. 185 UNDERWOOD 30   t2 On WILL<I>AM Lord Burl<eigh,>

will'd   frequency: 1   relative frequency: 0.00001
    p. 130 UNDERWOOD 1.3   13 The Fathers wisedome will'd it so,

william   frequency: 11   relative frequency: 0.00015
    See also "will<i>am."
    p.   31 EPIGRAMS 14   t1 TO WILLIAM CAMDEN.
    p.   46 EPIGRAMS 60   t1 TO WILLIAM LORD MOVNTEAGLE.
    p.   50 EPIGRAMS 70   t1 TO WILLIAM ROE.
    p.   66 EPIGRAMS 102   t1 TO WILLIAM EARLE OF
                                       PEMBROKE.
    p.   75 EPIGRAMS 116   t1 TO SIR WILLIAM IEPHSON.
    p.   79 EPIGRAMS 125   t1 TO SIR WILLIAM VVEDALE.
    p.   80 EPIGRAMS 128   t1 TO WILLIAM ROE.
    p. 120 FOREST 14   t2 TO SIR WILLIAM SYDNEY, ON
                                       HIS
    p. 228 UNDERWOOD 53   t3 WILLIAM, Earle of Newcastle.
    p. 232 UNDERWOOD 59   t2 To WILLIAM Earle of Newcastle.
    p. 390 UNGATHERED 26   t3 MR. WILLIAM SHAKESPEARE:

willing   frequency: 3   relative frequency: 0.00004
    p.   29 EPIGRAMS 6   2 Sure, willing pouertie liues most in you.
    p.   60 EPIGRAMS 93   15 Willing to expiate the fault in thee,
    p.   94 FOREST 2   30 And, for thy messe, is willing to be kill'd.

willingly   frequency: 1   relative frequency: 0.00001
    p. 169 UNDERWOOD 17   15 Venter a longer time, and willingly:

wills   frequency: 1   relative frequency: 0.00001
    p. 130 UNDERWOOD 1.3   15 Both wills were in one stature;

wilt   frequency: 11   relative frequency: 0.00015
     See also "thou'lt."

win   frequency: 8   relative frequency: 0.00011
     See also "wine," "winne."
     p. 72 EPIGRAMS 112   3 Think'st thou it is meere fortune, that can win?
     p. 74 EPIGRAMS 115   7 A subtle thing, that doth affections win
     p. 130 UNDERWOOD 1.2   31 As sure to win
     p. 193 UNDERWOOD 38   89 The contrite Soule, who hath no thought to win
     p. 248 UNDERWOOD 71   11 Fix'd to the bed, and boords, unlike to win
     p. 311 HORACE 2   119 As fit t<o>'exchange discourse; a Verse to win
     p. 402 UNGATHERED 33   11 They are a Schoole to win
     p. 412 UNGATHERED 40   20 th'aeternall Crown to win.

wince   frequency: 1   relative frequency: 0.00001
     p. 410 UNGATHERED 38   11 Now each Court-Hobby-horse will wince in rime;

winchester   frequency: 1   relative frequency: 0.00001
     p. 269 UNDERWOOD 83   20 Of Winchester; the Heralds can tell this:

winchestrian   frequency: 1   relative frequency: 0.00001
     p. 209 UNDERWOOD 43   142 That was rak'd up in the Winchestrian Goose

wind   frequency: 5   relative frequency: 0.00007
     See also "winde."
     p. 208 UNDERWOOD 43   111 Sonne of the Wind! for so thy mother gone
     p. 214 UNDERWOOD 44   63 Should he <not> heare of billow, wind, and
                               storme,
     p. 280 U'WOOD 84.4   65 In action, winged as the wind,
     p. 280 U'WOOD 84.4   68 Begotten by that wind, and showers.
     p. 287 U'WOOD 84.9   166 Mov'd by the wind, so comely moved she.

wind-bound   frequency: 1   relative frequency: 0.00001
     p. 86 EPIGRAMS 133   92 Is this we heare? of frogs? No, guts wind-bound,

winde   frequency: 2   relative frequency: 0.00002
     p. 363 UNGATHERED 3   12 And makes her supple feete, as swift as winde.
     p. 360 UNGATHERED 6   28 That part nor Winde,

windes   frequency: 1   relative frequency: 0.00001
     p. 81 EPIGRAMS 128   5 May windes as soft as breath of kissing friends,

windie   frequency: 1   relative frequency: 0.00001
     p. 88 EPIGRAMS 133   167 Laxatiue lettuce, and such windie meate)

winding   frequency: 1   relative frequency: 0.00001
     p. 293 UNDERWOOD 86   40 Or Tybers winding streames, I follow thee.

windore   frequency: 1   relative frequency: 0.00001
   **p. 114 PANEGYRE   45 And euery windore grieu'd it could not moue

windores   frequency: 1   relative frequency: 0.00001
   **p. 114 PANEGYRE   63 Walls, windores, roofes, towers, steeples, all
                               were set

window   frequency: 2   relative frequency: 0.00002
     See also "windore."
     p. 140 UNDERWOOD 2.8   16 No, nor forth your window peepe,
     p. 282 U'WOOD 84.9   7 To hang a window, or make darke the roome,

windowes   frequency: 3   relative frequency: 0.00004
     p. 114 FOREST 12   46 Or in their windowes; doe but proue the wombs,
     p. 202 UNDERWOOD 42   78 When not the Shops, but windowes doe display
     p. 407 UNGATHERED 35   10 Wth slyding windowes, & false Lights a top!

windows. See "windores," "windowes."

winds   frequency: 2   relative frequency: 0.00002
     See also "west-winds," "windes."
     p. 192 UNDERWOOD 38   58 Or winds the Spirit, by which the flower so
                               grew?
     p. 251 UNDERWOOD 74   9 The rudest Winds obey the calmest Ayre:

windy. See "windie."

wine   frequency: 25   relative frequency: 0.00036
     See also "canary-wine," "wyne."
    *p. 492 TO HIMSELF   19 If they loue lees, and leaue the lusty wine,
     p. 36 EPIGRAMS 29   5 For then, our water-conduits doe runne wine;
     p. 55 EPIGRAMS 84   6 I fancied to my selfe, what wine, what wit

wine (cont.)
p.	65 EPIGRAMS 101	13	Limons, and wine for sauce: to these, a coney
p.	95 FOREST 2	63	Where the same beere, and bread, and selfe-same wine,
p.	106 FOREST 9	4	And Ile not looke for wine.
p.	107 FOREST 10	11	To raise my spirits with thy coniuring wine,
p.	197 UNDERWOOD 40	18	As neither wine doe rack it out, or mirth.
p.	198 UNDERWOOD 40	45	Weaknesse of braine, or any charme of Wine,
p.	225 UNDERWOOD 51	3	The fire, the wine, the men! and in the midst,
p.	230 UNDERWOOD 55	5	But since the Wine hath steep'd my braine,
p.	232 UNDERWOOD 57	24	or Wine to enable
p.	245 UNDERWOOD 70	75	Call, noble Lucius, then for Wine,
p.	249 UNDERWOOD 72	12	Made lighter with the Wine. All noises else,
p.	286 U'WOOD 84.9	123	Wine, or delicious fruits, unto the Taste;
p.	291 UNDERWOOD 85	47	And from the sweet Tub Wine of this yeare takes,
p.	295 UNDERWOOD 89	5	Darke thy cleare glasse with old Falernian Wine:
p.	319 HORACE 2	298	Steepe the glad Genius in the Wine, whole dayes,
p.	319 HORACE 2	315	With lees of Wine. Next Eschylus, more late,
p.	333 HORACE 2	590	And both from Wine, and Women did abstaine.
p.	333 HORACE 2	618	And rack, with Wine, the man whom they would try,
p.	368 UNGATHERED 6	87	Their cares in wine; with sure
p.	421 UNGATHERED 48	45	Whoe worthie wine, whoe not, to bee wyse Pallas guests.
p.	657 L. CONVIVALES	6	Truth itself doth flow in Wine.
p.	657 L. CONVIVALES	12	Wine it is the Milk of Venus,

wines   frequency: 2   relative frequency: 0.00002
p.	220 UNDERWOOD 48	2	Of Wines, to thee the rather
p.	311 HORACE 2	116	Fresh Lovers businesse, and the Wines free source.

wing   frequency: 6   relative frequency: 0.00008
p.	43 EPIGRAMS 51	2	Great heau'n did well, to giue ill fame free wing;
p.	108 FOREST 10	29	My owne true fire. Now my thought takes wing,
p.	366 UNGATHERED 6	9	Marke, marke, but when his wing he takes,
p.	367 UNGATHERED 6	41	From thence, display thy wing againe
p.	368 UNGATHERED 6	64	Now must we plie our ayme; our Swan's on wing.
p.	369 UNGATHERED 6	100	With Cupids wing;

winged   frequency: 1   relative frequency: 0.00001
p.	280 U'WOOD 84.4	65	In action, winged as the wind,

wings   frequency: 6   relative frequency: 0.00008
p.	93 FOREST 1	7	I weare not these my wings in vaine.
p.	111 FOREST 11	73	Though thy wild thoughts with sparrowes wings doe flye,
p.	137 UNDERWOOD 2.5	35	Where I sit and proyne my wings
p.	141 UNDERWOOD 2.9	12	For Loves fingers, and his wings:
p.	170 UNDERWOOD 19	6	He flying curles, and crispeth, with his wings;
p.	176 UNDERWOOD 25	3	Wake, and put on the wings of Pindars Muse,

wink. See "winke."

winke   frequency: 2   relative frequency: 0.00002
p.	74 EPIGRAMS 115	11	Can come from Tripoly, leape stooles, and winke,
p.	170 UNDERWOOD 18	16	Or Love, or Fortune blind, when they but winke

winked. See "hood-wink'd."

winne   frequency: 3   relative frequency: 0.00004
p.	42 EPIGRAMS 46	1	Is this the Sir, who, some wast wife to winne,
p.	99 FOREST 3	85	Let thousands more goe flatter vice, and winne,
p.	130 UNDERWOOD 1.3	19	What comfort by him doe wee winne,

winnes   frequency: 1   relative frequency: 0.00001
p.	38 EPIGRAMS 37	4	For this: that winnes, for whom he holds his peace.

wins. See "winnes," "wynns."

winter   frequency: 3   relative frequency: 0.00004
p.	97 FOREST 3	29	And, in the winter, hunt'st the flying hare,
p.	199 UNDERWOOD 41	12	Winter is come a Quarter e're his Time,
p.	291 UNDERWOOD 85	51	If with bright floods, the Winter troubled much,

winton   frequency: 1   relative frequency: 0.00001
      p. 208 UNDERWOOD 83   t3 Marchion: of Winton.

wintry   frequency: 1   relative frequency: 0.00001
      p. 290 UNDERWOOD 85   30 Are gathering by the Wintry houres;

wip'd   frequency: 1   relative frequency: 0.00001
      p. 321 HORACE 2   347 Simo; and, of a talent wip'd his purse;

wires. See "wyres."

wisdom. See "wisdcme," "wisedome."

wisdome   frequency: 10   relative frequency: 0.00014
      p. 160 UNDERWOOD 14   59 In sharpnesse of all Search, wisdome of Choise,
      p. 181 UNDERWOOD 26   22 'Tis wisdome, and that high,
      p. 187 UNDERWOOD 33   17 Dar'st not abuse thy wisdome, in the Lawes,
      p. 193 UNDERWOOD 38   67 O may your wisdome take example hence,
      p. 224 UNDERWOOD 50   1 The Wisdome, Madam, of your private Life,
      p. 225 UNDERWOOD 51   20 In raysing him the wisdome of my King.
      p. 255 UNDERWOOD 75   98 That Mine of Wisdome, and of Counsells deep,
      p. 288 U'WOOD 84.9   218 His Wisdome, and his Justice, in that houre,
      p. 289 U'WOOD 84.9   221 Of all are dead to life! His Wisdome show
      p. 327 HORACE 2   486 This was the wisdome, that they had of old,

wise   frequency: 32   relative frequency: 0.00046
      See also "wantcn-wise," "wyse."
    **p. 115 PANEGYRE   95 "She shewd him, who made wise, who honest acts;
    **p. 116 PANEGYRE   108 "For Right is as compassionate as wise.
      p. 36 EPIGRAMS 30   1 GVILTIE, be wise; and though thou know'st
                               the crimes
      p. 38 EPIGRAMS 38   1 GVILTIE, because I bad you late be wise,
      p. 43 EPIGRAMS 53   1 Long-gathering OLD-END, I did feare thee
                               wise,
      p. 47 EPIGRAMS 64   12 And not to dangers. When so wise a king
      p. 52 EPIGRAMS 74   6 And no lesse wise, then skilfull in the lawes;
      p. 52 EPIGRAMS 76   5 I meant to make her faire, and free, and wise.
      p. 74 EPIGRAMS 114   8 But, in your loue, made all his seruants wise.
      p. 78 EPIGRAMS 122   4 The world's pure gold, and wise simplicitie;
      p. 114 FOREST 12   35 Wherein wise Nature you a dowrie gaue,
      p. 117 FOREST 13   36 And, in those outward formes, all fooles are
                               wise.
      p. 176 UNDERWOOD 24   5 Wise Providence would so; that nor the good
      p. 185 UNDERWOOD 30   5 Cecill, the grave, the wise, the great, the good,
      p. 192 UNDERWOOD 38   60 Of that wise Nature would a Cradle have.
      p. 214 UNDERWOOD 44   43 O happie Art! and wise Epitome
      p. 225 UNDERWOOD 51   9 Sonne to the grave wise Keeper of the Seale,
      p. 232 UNDERWOOD 58   5 His judgement is; If he be wise, and praise,
      p. 242 UNDERWOOD 70   7 Wise child, did'st hastily returne,
      p. 261 UNDERWOOD 77   11 Catch'd with these Arts, wherein the Judge is
                               wise
      p. 270 UNDERWOOD 83   40 Her wary guardes, her wise simplicitie,
      p. 294 UNDERWOOD 89   3 If thou be'st wise, with 'Syrian Oyle let shine
      p. 295 UNDERWOOD 90   7 A wise simplicity; freindes alike-stated;
      p. 325 HORACE 2   441 Is to be wise; thy matter first to know;
      p. 335 HORACE 2   633 A wise, and honest man will cry out shame
      p. 335 HORACE 2   643 Wise, sober folke, a frantick Poet feare,
      p. 370 UNGATHERED 8   1 The wise, and many-headed Bench, that sits
      p. 379 UNGATHERED 12   6 Yet who could haue hit on't but the wise noddell
      p. 394 UNGATHERED 28   5 Religious, wise, chast, louing, gratious, good;
      p. 397 UNGATHERED 30 34 Pearch'd ouer head, the wise Athenian Owle:
      p. 405 UNGATHERED 34 85 Oh wise Surueyor! wyser Architect!
      p. 414 UNGATHERED 41 41 Great Queen of Queens, most mild, most meek,
                               most wise,

wise-crafts   frequency: 1   relative frequency: 0.00001
      p. 241 UNDERWOOD 69   6 Wise-crafts, on which the flatterer ventures not.

wise-men   frequency: 2   relative frequency: 0.00002
      p. 55 EPIGRAMS 85   3 Where I both learn'd, why wise-men hawking
                               follow,
      p. 208 UNDERWOOD 43 123 Well fare the wise-men yet, on the Banckside,

wisedome   frequency: 2   relative frequency: 0.00002
      p. 130 UNDERWOOD 1.3 13 The Fathers wisedome will'd it so,
      p. 130 UNDERWOOD 1.3 16 And as that wisedome had decreed,

wisely   frequency: 3   relative frequency: 0.00004
      p. 27 EPIGRAMS 3   1 Thou, that mak'st gaine thy end, and wisely well,
      p. 61 EPIGRAMS 95   22 But, wisely, thrusts not forth a forward hand,

wisely (cont.)
      p. 118 FOREST 13   59 This makes, that wisely you decline your life,

wiser   frequency: 3   relative frequency: 0.00004
      See also "wyser."
      p.   27 EPIGRAMS 2   8 And by thy wiser temper, let men know
      p. 207 UNDERWOOD 43   103 After the Fathers, and those wiser Guides
      p. 243 UNDERWOOD 70   11 Did wiser Nature draw thee back,

wisest   frequency: 2   relative frequency: 0.00002
      p.   56 EPIGRAMS 89   1 If Rome so great, and in her wisest age,
      p. 405 UNGATHERED 34   86 But wisest Inigo! who can reflect

wish   frequency: 37   relative frequency: 0.00053
      p.   27 EPIGRAMS 2   7 Deceiue their malice, who could wish it so.
      p.   32 EPIGRAMS 17   3 That wish my poemes a legitimate fame,
      p.   40 EPIGRAMS 42   12 Were quite out-spun. The like wish hath his
                                    wife.
      p.   60 EPIGRAMS 94   4 Whose poemes would not wish to be your booke?
      p.   78 EPIGRAMS 122   1 If I would wish, for truth, and not for show,
      p.   83 EPIGRAMS 132   10 BARTAS doth wish thy English now were his.
      p.   89 EPIGRAMS 133   195 And I could wish for their eterniz'd sakes,
      p.   94 FOREST 2   47 There's none, that dwell about them, wish them
                                    downe;
      p.   95 FOREST 2   75 There's nothing I can wish, for which I stay.
      p. 122 FOREST 15   23 Yet dare I not complaine, or wish for death
      p. 134 UNDERWOOD 2.4   7 And enamour'd, doe wish, so they might
      p. 139 UNDERWOOD 2.7   18 Let who will thinke us dead, or wish our death.
      p. 142 U'WOOD 2.10   6 All I wish is understood.
      p. 144 UNDERWOOD 3   28 May wish us of their Quire.
      p. 150 UNDERWOOD 10   7 I wish the Sun should shine
      p. 186 UNDERWOOD 31   6 The Care, and wish still of the publike wealth:
      p. 194 UNDERWOOD 38   122 Rather then want your light, I wish a grave.
      p. 200 UNDERWOOD 42   22 Wish, you had fowle ones, and deformed got;
      p. 210 UNDERWOOD 43   167 'Tis true, that in thy wish they were destroy'd,
      p. 219 UNDERWOOD 47   30 Then these can ever be; or else wish none.
      p. 219 UNDERWOOD 47   37 I wish all well, and pray high heaven conspire
      p. 228 UNDERWOOD 53   12 As I began to wish my selfe a horse.
      p. 228 UNDERWOOD 53   14 Before, I thinke my wish absolv'd had beene.
      p. 235 UNDERWOOD 62   13 What can the Poet wish his King may doe,
      p. 239 UNDERWOOD 67   23 May wish it selfe a sense,
      p. 241 UNDERWOOD 68   9 And rather wish, in their expence of Sack,
      p. 249 UNDERWOOD 72   19 The wish is great; but where the Prince is such,
      p. 257 UNDERWOOD 75   160 But dare not aske our wish in Language
                                    fescennine:
      p. 271 UNDERWOOD 83   84 And wish her state lesse happie then it is!
      p. 283 U'WOOD 84.9   26 I summe up mine owne breaking, and wish all.
      p. 294 UNDERWOOD 87   24 Yet would I wish to love, live, die with thee.
      p. 295 UNDERWOOD 90   13 Nor feare thy latest day, nor wish therfore.
      p. 319 HORACE 2   285 Hide faults, pray to the Gods, and wish aloud
      p. 371 UNGATHERED 8   12 And wish that all the Muses blood were spilt,
      p. 389 UNGATHERED 24   23 When you behold me wish my selfe, the man
      p. 394 UNGATHERED 28   23 Importune wish; and by her lou'd Lords side
      p. 398 UNGATHERED 30   92 And, till I worthy am to wish I were,

wish'd   frequency: 2   relative frequency: 0.00002
      p.   52 EPIGRAMS 76   17 Such when I meant to faine, and wish'd to see,
      p. 173 UNDERWOOD 22   20 That envie wish'd, and Nature fear'd.

wished   frequency: 2   relative frequency: 0.00002
      See also "wish'd," "wisht."
      p. 222 UNDERWOOD 48   48 The wished Peace of Europe:
      p. 333 HORACE 2   588 The wished goale, both did, and suffer'd much

wishes   frequency: 5   relative frequency: 0.00007
   **p. 117 PANEGYRE   150 What all mens wishes did aspire vnto.
      p.   49 EPIGRAMS 67   7 When, in mens wishes, so thy vertues wrought,
      p. 116 FOREST 12   100 My best of wishes, may you beare a sonne.
      p. 167 UNDERWOOD 15   176 Thy true friends wishes, Colby, which shall be,
      p. 309 HORACE 2   108 After, mens Wishes, crown'd in their events,

wisheth   frequency: 2   relative frequency: 0.00002
      p.   40 EPIGRAMS 42   10 Harsh sights at home, GILES wisheth he were
                                    blind.
      p.   99 FOREST 3   95 God wisheth, none should wracke on a strange
                                    shelfe.

wisht   frequency: 1   relative frequency: 0.00001
      p. 138 UNDERWOOD 2.6   18 Wisht the Bride were chang'd to night,

wit   frequency: 59   relative frequency: 0.00085
      See also "witt."
  *p. 492 TO HIMSELF   4 Vsurpe the chaire of wit!
  *p. 493 TO HIMSELF   30 Needs set them, but, the almes-basket of wit.
   p.   27 EPIGRAMS 2   5 Become a petulant thing, hurle inke, and wit,
   p.   34 EPIGRAMS 23   3 Whose euery worke, of thy most earely wit,
   p.   36 EPIGRAMS 29   4 All braines, at times of triumph, should runne
                              wit.
   p.   38 EPIGRAMS 38   6 And lyes so farre from wit, 'tis impudence.
   p.   39 EPIGRAMS 40   9 Rare, as wonder, was her wit;
   p.   39 EPIGRAMS 40   16 For wit, feature, and true passion,
   p.   44 EPIGRAMS 56   2 Whose workes are eene the fripperie of wit,
   p.   45 EPIGRAMS 56   8 He takes vp all, makes each mans wit his owne.
   p.   45 EPIGRAMS 58   3 For offring, with thy smiles, my wit to grace,
   p.   47 EPIGRAMS 64   8 Of flatterie to thy titles. Nor of wit.
   p.   50 EPIGRAMS 72   3 At MADAMES table, where thou mak'st all
                              wit
   p.   54 EPIGRAMS 81   6 Thy wit liues by it, PROVLE, and belly too.
   p.   55 EPIGRAMS 84   6 I fancied to my selfe, what wine, what wit
   p.   64 EPIGRAMS 100   2 Cry'd to my face, they were th'elixir of wit:
   p.   68 EPIGRAMS 106   5 Whether thy learning they would take, or wit,
   p.   73 EPIGRAMS 112   18 That both for wit, and sense, so oft dost plucke,
   p.   73 EPIGRAMS 113   6 That the wit there, and manners might be sau'd:
   p.   74 EPIGRAMS 115   28 Of miming, gets th'opinion of a wit.
   p.   75 EPIGRAMS 116   3 So did thy vertue'enforme, thy wit sustaine
   p.   75 EPIGRAMS 116   16 A desperate soloecisme in truth and wit.
   p.   78 EPIGRAMS 121   8 That striues, his manners should precede his wit.
   p.   78 EPIGRAMS 123   2 I know not which th'hast most, candor, or wit:
   p.   81 EPIGRAMS 129   14 On some new gesture, that 's imputed wit?
   p.   97 FOREST 3   11 To view the iewells, stuffes, the paines, the wit
   p. 115 FOREST 12   82 Had not their forme touch'd by an English wit.
   p. 117 FOREST 13   14 For their owne cap'tall crimes, t<o>'indite my
                              wit;
   p. 160 UNDERWOOD 14   57 With horrour rough, then rioting with wit!
   p. 160 UNDERWOOD 14   64 Large claspe of Nature, such a wit can bound.
   p. 165 UNDERWOOD 15   102 For man to spend his money on? his wit?
   p. 179 UNDERWOOD 25   52 Oft scape an Imputation, more through luck, then
                              wit.
   p. 183 UNDERWOOD 29   18 And wit vanish'd.
   p. 184 UNDERWOOD 29   38 Scarce the world a Wit doth nourish,
   p. 193 UNDERWOOD 38   95 The wit of Ale, and Genius of the Malt
   p. 202 UNDERWOOD 42   88 More then of eithers manners, wit, or face!
   p. 208 UNDERWOOD 43   109 Thou woo Minerva! or to wit aspire!
   p. 209 UNDERWOOD 43   138 Left! and wit since to cover it with Tiles.
   p. 222 UNDERWOOD 49   4 Where fight the prime Cocks of the Game, for
                              wit?
   p. 222 UNDERWOOD 49   10 As aerie light, and as like wit as those?
   p. 223 UNDERWOOD 49   23 I never stood for any place: my wit
   p. 224 UNDERWOOD 50   24 Then the great Homers wit, for her, could faine;
   p. 231 UNDERWOOD 57   17 Mirth, fooling, nor wit,
   p. 232 UNDERWOOD 58   7 If his wit reach no higher, but to spring
   p. 232 UNDERWOOD 58   11 Like a rung Beare, or Swine: grunting out wit
   p. 248 UNDERWOOD 71   15 A Bed-rid Wit, then a besieged Towne.
   p. 251 UNDERWOOD 74   22 The bus'nesse of your blooming wit,
   p. 259 UNDERWOOD 76   22 With their pellets of small wit,
   p. 323 HORACE 2   403 To part scurrilitie from wit: or can
   p. 325 HORACE 2   419 Because Democritus beleeves a wit
   p. 327 HORACE 2   461 The Muse not only gave the Greek's a wit,
   p. 365 UNGATHERED 5   5 Her wit as quicke, and sprightfull
   p. 389 UNGATHERED 24   6 But in one tongue, was form'd with the worlds
                              wit:
   p. 390 UNGATHERED 25   5 O, could he but haue drawne his wit
   p. 392 UNGATHERED 26   50 As, since, she will vouchsafe no other Wit.
   p. 410 UNGATHERED 39   8 Keep in thy barking Wit, thou bawling Fool?
   p. 415 UNGATHERED 42   20 Office of Wit, a Mint, and (this is true)
   p. 415 UNGATHERED 42   23 Of wit, and a new made: a Warden then,
   p. 657 L. CONVIVALES   16 Clears the Brains, makes Wit the Quicker:

witch   frequency: 1   relative frequency: 0.00001
   p.   83 EPIGRAMS 133   158 Being, beyond sea, burned for one witch:

witchcraft   frequency: 1   relative frequency: 0.00001
   p. 203 UNDERWOOD 43   16 Imposture, witchcraft, charmes, or blasphemie,

with   frequency: 572   relative frequency: 0.00823
      See also "wi'the," "wth."

withal. See "withall."

```
withall                              frequency:    8  relative frequency: 0.00011
   p.   27 EPIGRAMS 2        4 Wormewood, and sulphure, sharpe, and tooth'd
                              withall;
   p.   96 FOREST 2         90 Thy lady's noble, fruitfull, chaste withall.
   p.  119 FOREST 13       103 To crowne the burthen which you goe withall,
   p.  132 UNDERWOOD 2.2    11 And (withall) I did untie
   p.  141 UNDERWOOD 2.9    19 Even nose, and cheeke (withall)
   p.  142 U'WOOD 2.10       8 'Tis one good part I'ld lie withall.
   p.  213 UNDERWOOD 44     15 Withall, the dirtie paines those Citizens take,
   p.  415 UNGATHERED 42    11 Such men I met withall, and so have you.

wi'the                               frequency:    1  relative frequency: 0.00001

wither                               frequency:    2  relative frequency: 0.00002
   p.  183 UNDERWOOD 29     17 All Parnassus Greene did wither,
   p.  192 UNDERWOOD 38     59 That were to wither all, and make a Grave

withered                             frequency:    2  relative frequency: 0.00002
   p.  100 FOREST 9         12 It could not withered bee.
   p.  173 UNDERWOOD 22     18 The withered Garlands tane away;

withers                              frequency:    1  relative frequency: 0.00001
   p.  201 UNDERWOOD 42     63 Wrung on the Withers, by Lord Loves despight,

within                               frequency:   12  relative frequency: 0.00017
 **p.  113 PANEGYRE        12 Where Murder, Rapine, Lust, doe sit within,
   p.   33 EPIGRAMS 20      2 Except thou could'st, Sir COD, weare them
                              within.
   p.   63 EPIGRAMS 98      3 He that is round within himselfe, and streight,
   p.  151 UNDERWOOD 11     14 As since he dares not come within my sight.
   p.  216 UNDERWOOD 45     13 And as within your Office, you doe take
   p.  229 UNDERWOOD 54     10 Within the ballance; and not want a mite;
   p.  229 UNDERWOOD 54     13 That's six in silver; now within the Socket
   p.  230 UNDERWOOD 56     11 His weight is twenty Stone within two pound;
   p.  311 HORACE 2        152 For Nature, first, within doth fashion us
   p.  317 HORACE 2        261 Things worthy to be done within, but take
   p.  323 HORACE 2        394 Within the hope of having all forgiven?
   p.  367 UNGATHERED 6     45 With thy soft notes, and hold them within Pale

without                              frequency:   38  relative frequency: 0.00055
   See also "wthout."
 **p.  117 PANEGYRE       161 Yet, let blest Brit[t]aine aske (without your
                              wrong)
   p.   28 EPIGRAMS 3      11 If, without these vile arts, it will not sell,
   p.   47 EPIGRAMS 63     10 Without his, thine, and all times iniurie?
   p.   63 EPIGRAMS 98     12 And euer is ill got without the first.
   p.   83 EPIGRAMS 131    13 Then stand vnto thy selfe, not seeke without
   p.   85 EPIGRAMS 133    34 Of sixe times to, and fro, without embassage,
   p.   89 EPIGRAMS 133   186 The tripple head without a sop. At last,
   p.   89 EPIGRAMS 133   192 And so went brauely backe, without protraction.
   p.   95 FOREST 2        62 Without his feare, and of thy lords owne meate:
   p.  118 FOREST 13       50 Without which, all the rest were sounds, or lost.
   p.  118 FOREST 13       56 Without companions? 'Tis safe to haue none.
   p.  157 UNDERWOOD 13   155 You know (without my flatt'ring you) too much
   p.  157 UNDERWOOD 13   158 Without your gift, though I can rate that too,
   p.  167 UNDERWOOD 15   158 As a poore single flatterer, without Baud,
   p.  186 UNDERWOOD 32     3 Without the pompe of Counsell; or more Aide,
   p.  189 UNDERWOOD 36     7 Without which all the world were darke;
   p.  193 UNDERWOOD 38    96 Can pumpe for; or a Libell without salt
   p.  197 UNDERWOOD 40    13 But ever without blazon, or least shade
   p.  214 UNDERWOOD 44    47 Without the hazard of a drop of blood,
   p.  219 UNDERWOOD 47    43 So farre without inquirie what the States,
   p.  229 UNDERWOOD 54     3 If I doe lose it: And, without a Tale,
   p.  230 UNDERWOOD 56    15 Sleepe in a Virgins bosome without feare,
   p.  230 UNDERWOOD 56    17 Widow or Wife, without the jealousie
   p.  233 UNDERWOOD 59    24 And valiant were, with, or without their hands.
   p.  238 UNDERWOOD 66     4 (Without prophanenesse) yet, a Poet, cry,
   p.  251 UNDERWOOD 74     5 Shee lies deliver'd, without paine,
   p.  275 U'WOOD 84.3      7 This beautie without falshood fayre,
   p.  292 UNDERWOOD 86    24 And Phrygian Hau'boy, not without the Flute.
   p.  295 UNDERWOOD 90     8 Thy table without art, and easy-rated:
   p.  307 HORACE 2        70 Thou need new termes; thou maist, without excuse,
   p.  321 HORACE 2       366 And not without much praise; till libertie
   p.  331 HORACE 2       559 As Poppie, and Sardane honey; 'cause without
   p.  331 HORACE 2       584 Can; or all toile, without a wealthie veine:
   p.  335 HORACE 2       632 Alone, without a rivall, by his will.
   p.  391 UNGATHERED 26   22 Thou art a Moniment, without a tombe,
   p.  396 UNGATHERED 30   10 Without conferring symboles. This's my day.
   p.  399 UNGATHERED 31    9 Shee was the light (without reflexe
   p.  399 UNGATHERED 31   16 Or without angles, it was shee!
```

witness. See "witnesse."

witnesse   frequency: 12   relative frequency: 0.00017
    p.   44 EPIGRAMS 53   8 Thou art the father, and the witnesse too.
    p.   54 EPIGRAMS 81   4 To be the wealthy witnesse of my pen:
    p.   55 EPIGRAMS 85   2 My selfe a witnesse of thy few dayes sport:
    p.   89 EPIGRAMS 133   191 They tooke 'hem all to witnesse of their action:
    p. 122 FOREST 15   5 O, be thou witnesse, that the reynes dost know,
    p. 122 FOREST 15   12 My iudge, my witnesse, and my aduocate.
    p. 154 UNDERWOOD 13   36 His Groomes to witnesse; or else lets it fall
    p. 176 UNDERWOOD 24   17 Times witnesse, herald of Antiquitie,
    p. 201 UNDERWOOD 42   65 Such Songsters there are store of; witnesse he
    p. 262 UNDERWOOD 78   13 Witnesse his Action done at Scandero<o>ne;
    p. 270 UNDERWOOD 83   35 And, calling truth to witnesse, make that good
    p. 385 UNGATHERED 19   4 What can one witnesse, and a weake one, add

witnesses   frequency: 1   relative frequency: 0.00001
    p. 400 UNGATHERED 31   38 Of Angelis, and all witnesses of light,

wits   frequency: 10   relative frequency: 0.00014
    See also "witts."
    p.   34 EPIGRAMS 23   5 Longer a knowing, then most wits doe liue.
    p.   50 EPIGRAMS 71   1 To plucke downe mine, POLL sets vp new wits
                              still,
    p. 145 UNDERWOOD 5   5 Wee have both wits, and fancies too,
    p. 174 UNDERWOOD 23   6 That eats on wits, and Arts, and <oft> destroyes
                              them both.
    p. 183 UNDERWOOD 29   1 Rime, the rack of finest wits,
    p. 200 UNDERWOOD 42   33 Have eaten with the Beauties, and the wits,
    p. 223 UNDERWOOD 49   37 The wits will leave you, if they once perceive
    p. 370 UNGATHERED 8   2 Vpon the Life, and Death of Playes, and Wits,
    p. 391 UNGATHERED 26   24 And we haue wits to read, and praise to giue.
    p. 415 UNGATHERED 42   28 Yo'have all the Mysteries of Wits new Mint,

witt   frequency: 2   relative frequency: 0.00002
    p. 394 UNGATHERED 28   12 And Christian name too, with a Heralds witt.
    p. 402 UNGATHERED 34   18 Will any of these express yor place? or witt?

witted. See "left-witted."

wittie   frequency: 2   relative frequency: 0.00002
    p.   42 EPIGRAMS 49   4 For wittie, in his language, is obscene.
    p. 118 FOREST 13   76 (They finde it both so wittie, and safe to giue.)

witts   frequency: 1   relative frequency: 0.00001
    p. 218 UNDERWOOD 47   22 And are received for the Covey of Witts;

witty   frequency: 1   relative frequency: 0.00001
    See also "wittie."
    p. 392 UNGATHERED 26   52 Neat Terence, witty Plautus, now not please;

wiues   frequency: 2   relative frequency: 0.00002
    p.   39 EPIGRAMS 39   1 For all night-sinnes, with others wiues,
                              vnknowne,
    p. 119 FOREST 13   111 Other great wiues may blush at: when they see

wives   frequency: 5   relative frequency: 0.00007
    See also "wiues."
    p. 146 UNDERWOOD 6   6 We are no women then, but wives.
    p. 200 UNDERWOOD 42   19 But then consent, your Daughters and your
                              Wives,
    p. 209 UNDERWOOD 43   152 The place, that was thy Wives inheritance.
    p. 212 UNDERWOOD 43   216 Thy Wives pox on thee, and B<ess> B<roughton>s
                              too.
    p. 213 UNDERWOOD 44   16 To see the Pride at Court, their Wives doe
                              make:

wodden   frequency: 1   relative frequency: 0.00001
    p. 403 UNGATHERED 34   27 A wodden Dagger, is a Dagger of wood

woeful. See "wofull."

woemen   frequency: 1   relative frequency: 0.00001
    p. 399 UNGATHERED 31   11 The best of Woemen! her whole life

woes   frequency: 2   relative frequency: 0.00002
    p. 342 HORACE 1   155 .... woes she ....
    p. 363 UNGATHERED 3   3 Warres grea<t>est woes, and miseries increase,

wofull   frequency: 1   relative frequency: 0.00001
     p. 231 UNDERWOOD 57   3 My wofull crie,

wolf. See "wolfe."

wolfe   frequency: 1   relative frequency: 0.00001
     p. 291 UNDERWOOD 85   60 Or Kid forc't from the Wolfe againe.

wolves   frequency: 2   relative frequency: 0.00002
     p. 175 UNDERWOOD 23   36 Safe from the wolves black jaw, and the dull
                              Asses hoofe.
     p. 187 UNDERWOOD 33   12 To the Wolves studie, or Dogs eloquence;

woman   frequency: 7   relative frequency: 0.00010
     See also "gentle-woman," "serving-woman."
     p. 54 EPIGRAMS 83   2 Throughout my booke. 'Troth put out woman too.
     p. 57 EPIGRAMS 90   t1 ON MILL MY LADIES WOMAN.
     p. 140 UNDERWOOD 2.9   6 And a woman God did make me:
     p. 146 UNDERWOOD 6   23 For were the worthiest woman curst
     p. 164 UNDERWOOD 15   82 Of woman of fashion, and a Lady of spirit:
     p. 172 UNDERWOOD 20   15 Knew I this Woman? yes; And you doe see,
     p. 364 UNGATHERED 4   4 Do turne into a Woman.

woman-kind   frequency: 1   relative frequency: 0.00001
     p. 145 UNDERWOOD 5   t1 In the person of Woman-kind.

woman-kinde   frequency: 1   relative frequency: 0.00001
     p. 105 FOREST 8   16 Woman-kinde; deuoure the wast

womans   frequency: 4   relative frequency: 0.00005
     p. 34 EPIGRAMS 25   8 Iust wife, and, to change me, make womans hast?
     p. 146 UNDERWOOD 6   2 That talke abroad of Womans change,
     p. 171 UNDERWOOD 20   1 A Womans friendship! God whom I trust in,
     p. 305 HORACE 2   1 If to a Womans head a Painter would

womb. See "wombe."

wombe   frequency: 6   relative frequency: 0.00008
     p. 46 EPIGRAMS 62   11 In a great belly. Write, then on thy wombe,
     p. 85 EPIGRAMS 133   66 Thorough her wombe they make their famous road,
     p. 119 FOREST 13   95 Of your blest wombe, made fruitfull from aboue,
     p. 227 UNDERWOOD 52   4 'Tis true, as my wombe swells, so my backe
                              stoupes,
     p. 240 UNDERWOOD 67   51 And this the wombe divine,
     p. 242 UNDERWOOD 70   8 And mad'st thy Mothers wombe thine urne.

wombes   frequency: 1   relative frequency: 0.00001
     p. 70 EPIGRAMS 109   17 Thy deedes, vnto thy name, will proue new wombes,

wombs   frequency: 1   relative frequency: 0.00001
     See also "wombes."
     p. 114 FOREST 12   46 Or in their windowes; doe but proue the wombs,

women   frequency: 8   relative frequency: 0.00011
     See also "woemen."
     p. 84 EPIGRAMS 133   16 And, for the cryes of Ghosts, women, and men,
     p. 104 FOREST 7   5 Say, are not women truely, then,
     p. 104 FOREST 7   t2 THAT WOMEN ARE BVT MENS
     p. 104 FOREST 7   11 Say, are not women truely, then,
     p. 146 UNDERWOOD 6   6 We are no women then, but wives.
     p. 333 HORACE 2   590 And both from Wine, and Women did abstaine.
     p. 363 UNGATHERED 3   18 Where Gold's the Motiue, women haue no Nay.
     p. 372 UNGATHERED 9   14 Might make the Fable of Good Women true.

won   frequency: 5   relative frequency: 0.00007
     See also "wan," "wonne."
     p. 47 EPIGRAMS 63   2 With what thy vertue on the times hath won,
     p. 223 UNDERWOOD 49   21 What though she hath won on Trust, as many doe,
     p. 230 UNDERWOOD 56   1 You won not Verses, Madam, you won mee,
     p. 230 UNDERWOOD 56   4 You won them too, your oddes did merit it.

wonder   frequency: 24   relative frequency: 0.00034
     See also "wonnder."
   **p. 114 PANEGYRE   35 As on a wonder: some amazed stood,
     p. 33 EPIGRAMS 21   5 Quick in his lips! Who hath this wonder wrought?
     p. 39 EPIGRAMS 40   9 Rare, as wonder, was her wit;
     p. 46 EPIGRAMS 60   7 Durst thinke it great, and worthy wonder too,
     p. 48 EPIGRAMS 64   16 Wherein what wonder see thy name hath wrought?
     p. 74 EPIGRAMS 115   1 You wonder, who this is! and, why I name
     p. 93 FOREST 1   10 By any arte. Then wonder not,

wonder (cont.)
```
     p.  118 FOREST 13        69 Your conscience, and not wonder, if none askes
     p.  131 UNDERWOOD 2.1      1 Let it not your wonder move,
     p.  155 UNDERWOOD 13      89 My wonder, why the taking a Clownes purse,
     p.  157 UNDERWOOD 13     142 Meet some new matter to looke up and wonder!
     p.  188 UNDERWOOD 35       3 What wonder perfect, all were fil'd,
     p.  233 UNDERWOOD 59      14 Wonder to Valour! No, it is the Law
     p.  274 U'WOOD 84.2       12 The wonder of her Sexe, and of your Blood.
     p.  278 U'WOOD 84.4       20 And yet remaine our wonder still.
     p.  329 HORACE 2         535 Twice, or thrice good, I wonder: but am more
     p.  333 HORACE 2         605 I wonder how this happie man should know,
     p.  361 UNGATHERED 1       5 ffirst: thy successe did strike my sence with
                                  wonder;
     p.  361 UNGATHERED 1      24 wear spent with wonder as they weare delated,
     p.  391 UNGATHERED 26     18 The applause! delight! the wonder of our Stage!
     p.  395 UNGATHERED 29     13 It makes me rauish'd with iust wonder, cry
     p.  396 UNGATHERED 30     13 Wonder to truth! and haue my Vision hoorld,
     p.  398 UNGATHERED 30     83 Yet giue mee leaue, to wonder at the birth
     p.  413 UNGATHERED 41     16 With wonder on the thorny regiment.
```

wonder'd   frequency: 2   relative frequency: 0.00002
     See also "wondred."
```
     p.  160 UNDERWOOD 14      53 I wonder'd at the richnesse, but am lost,
     p.  255 UNDERWOOD 75      90 And wonder'd at, the bounties of this day:
```

wondering. See "wondring," "wondringe."

wonders   frequency: 2   relative frequency: 0.00002
```
     p.  315 HORACE 2         205 Wonders forth after: As Antiphates,
     p.  416 UNGATHERED 45      1 To the wonders of the Peake,
```

wondred   frequency: 1   relative frequency: 0.00001
```
     p.  284 U'WOOD 84.9       77 Have all his actions wondred at, and view'd
```

wondring   frequency: 1   relative frequency: 0.00001
```
     p.  397 UNGATHERED 30     41 The Fights, the Cryes, and wondring at the
                                  Iarres
```

wondringe   frequency: 1   relative frequency: 0.00001
```
     p.  419 UNGATHERED 48      7 Lowd to the wondringe thronge
```

wonnder   frequency: 1   relative frequency: 0.00001
```
     p.  420 UNGATHERED 48     35 Give cause to some of wonnder, some despite,
```

wonne   frequency: 11   relative frequency: 0.00015
```
     p.   49 EPIGRAMS 66       11 Loue thy great losse, which a renowne hath wonne,
     p.   58 EPIGRAMS 91        5 Which thou art to thy selfe: whose fame was wonne
     p.   71 EPIGRAMS 110       1 Not CAESARS deeds, nor all his honors
                                  wonne,
     p.  115 FOREST 12         72 To my lesse sanguine Muse, wherein she'hath
                                  wonne
     p.  138 UNDERWOOD 2.6      6 Whether we have lost, or wonne,
     p.  152 UNDERWOOD 12      29 Much from him I professe I wonne,
     p.  154 UNDERWOOD 13      33 All this corrupts the thankes: lesse hath he
                                  wonne,
     p.  317 HORACE 2         281 Be wonne a friend; it must both sway, and bend
     p.  321 HORACE 2         326 Were to be staid with softnesses, and wonne
     p.  367 UNGATHERED 6      52 And more hath wonne
     p.  394 UNGATHERED 28     22 So wood at last, that he was wonne to her
```

wont   frequency: 3   relative frequency: 0.00004
```
     p.   32 EPIGRAMS 18        8 When thou wert wont t<o>'admire, not censure men.
     p.   62 EPIGRAMS 97        7 He wont was to encounter me, aloud,
     p.  127 UNDERWOOD 1.1     10 A broken heart thou wert not wont despise,
```

woo   frequency: 2   relative frequency: 0.00002
     See also "wooe."
```
     p.   54 EPIGRAMS 83        1 To put out the word, whore, thou do'st me woo,
     p.  208 UNDERWOOD 43     109 Thou woo Minerva! or to wit aspire!
```

woo-all   frequency: 1   relative frequency: 0.00001
```
     p.   42 EPIGRAMS 46       t1 TO SIR LVCKLESSE WOO-ALL.
```

wood   frequency: 7   relative frequency: 0.00010
     See also "sweet-wood," "vnder-wood."
```
   **p.  114 PANEGYRE         61 As with the murmure of a mouing wood;
     p.   93 FOREST 2          8 Of wood, of water: therein thou art faire.
     p.   94 FOREST 2         26 Fertile of wood, ASHORE, and
                                  SYDNEY'S copp's,
     p.  291 UNDERWOOD 85     43 To deck the hallow'd Harth with old wood fir'd
```

wood (cont.)
    p. 327 HORACE 2   490 Build Townes, and carve the Lawes in leaves of
                               wood.
    p. 394 UNGATHERED 28   22 So wood at last, that he was wonne to her
    p. 403 UNGATHERED 34   27 A wodden Dagger, is a Dagger of wood

wood-cock   frequency: 1   relative frequency: 0.00001
    p. 65 EPIGRAMS 101   18 Of partrich, pheasant, wood-cock, of which some

wooden. See "wodden."

woods   frequency: 7   relative frequency: 0.00010
    p. 97 FOREST 3   17 Along'st the curled woods, and painted meades,
    p. 143 UNDERWOOD 3   12 And call the walking woods.
    p. 265 UNDERWOOD 79   52 Whose praises let's report unto the Woods,
    p. 290 UNDERWOOD 85   26 The soft birds quarrell in the Woods,
    p. 307 HORACE 2   41 One thing prodigiously, paints in the woods
    p. 309 HORACE 2   85 Stamp'd to the time. As woods whose change
                               appeares
    p. 352 HORACE 1   558 .... in woods

wooe   frequency: 1   relative frequency: 0.00001
    p. 252 UNDERWOOD 75   6 We wooe thee, stay

wooed. See "wood."

wooes   frequency: 3   relative frequency: 0.00004
    p. 33 EPIGRAMS 19   2 I sent the cause: Hee wooes with an ill sprite.
    p. 42 EPIGRAMS 47   2 Hee that wooes euery widdow, will get none.
    p. 268 UNDERWOOD 83   3 And beckning wooes me, from the fatall tree

woof. See "woofe."

woofe   frequency: 1   relative frequency: 0.00001
    p. 415 UNGATHERED 42   15 And know the woofe, and warpe thereof; can tell

wooing   frequency: 1   relative frequency: 0.00001
    p. 42 EPIGRAMS 46   2 A knight-hood bought, to goe a wooing in?

wool. See "wooll."

wooll   frequency: 3   relative frequency: 0.00004
    p. 45 EPIGRAMS 56   14 From locks of wooll, or shreds from the whole
                               peece?
    p. 135 UNDERWOOD 2.4   25 Have you felt the wooll o' the Bever?
    p. 225 UNDERWOOD 51   16 Out of their Choysest, and their whitest wooll.

woolly   frequency: 2   relative frequency: 0.00002
    p. 94 FOREST 2   43 The blushing apricot, and woolly peach
    p. 141 UNDERWOOD 2.9   21 Chin, as woolly as the Peach;

woos. See "wooes."

word   frequency: 20   relative frequency: 0.00028
    p. 33 EPIGRAMS 21   4 Forbidd' his side! and nothing, but the word
    p. 54 EPIGRAMS 83   1 To put out the word, whore, thou do'st me woo,
    p. 65 EPIGRAMS 101   39 We innocently met. No simple word,
    p. 74 EPIGRAMS 115   21 With such a one. And therein keepes it's word.
    p. 75 EPIGRAMS 116   7 'Twas not entayl'd on title. That some word
    p. 119 FOREST 13   114 You are depending on his word, and will;
    p. 130 UNDERWOOD 1.3   11 The Word, which heaven, and earth did make;
    p. 130 UNDERWOOD 1.3   17 The Word was now made Flesh indeed,
    p. 154 UNDERWOOD 13   48 Well knowne, and practiz'd borrowers on their
                               word,
    p. 187 UNDERWOOD 33   33 Thy Adversaries fall, as not a word
    p. 198 UNDERWOOD 40   50 If I had writ no word, but Deare, farewell.
    p. 285 U'WOOD 84.9   112 Of life, and light, the Sonne of God, the
                               Word!
    p. 313 HORACE 2   191 To render word for word: nor with thy sleight
    p. 335 HORACE 2   630 Then change; no word, or worke, more would he
                               spend
    p. 352 HORACE 1   556 ... word ....
    p. 378 UNGATHERED 11   80 Trie and trust Roger, was the word, but now
    p. 386 UNGATHERED 20   11 I know for such, as (if my word will waigh)
    p. 393 UNGATHERED 27   9 It is the Warrant of the Word,
    p. 395 UNGATHERED 29   21 As not the smallest ioint, or gentlest word

worded   frequency: 1   relative frequency: 0.00001
    p. 173 UNDERWOOD 23   21 Of worded Balladrie,

wordes   frequency: 1   relative frequency: 0.00001
    p.   69 EPIGRAMS 107   24 That are your wordes of credit. Keepe your
                            Names

words   frequency: 23   relative frequency: 0.00033
   See also "wordes."
 **p. 114 PANEGYRE   37 Others would faine haue shew'ne it in their
                            words:
    p.   52 EPIGRAMS 74   7 Whil'st thou art certaine to thy words, once
                            gone,
    p. 134 UNDERWOOD 2.4   16 Then words that sooth her!
    p. 143 UNDERWOOD 3   15 No tunes are sweet, nor words have sting,
    p. 165 UNDERWOOD 15   112 Sweet bags, sweet Powders, nor sweet words will
                            passe
    p. 169 UNDERWOOD 17   9 And their words too; where I but breake my
                            Band.
    p. 183 UNDERWOOD 29   7 Wresting words, from their true calling;
    p. 184 UNDERWOOD 29   44 Words, and sweetnesse, and be scant
    p. 199 UNDERWOOD 41   4 Be idle words, though of a parting Man;
    p. 222 UNDERWOOD 49   13 And as lip-thirstie, in each words expence,
    p. 247 UNDERWOOD 70   123 Friendship, in deed, was written, not in words:
    p. 279 U'WOOD 84.4   37 The Voyce so sweet, the words so faire,
    p. 293 UNDERWOOD 86   35 Or why, my well-grac'd words among,
    p. 307 HORACE 2   65 In using also of new words, to be
    p. 307 HORACE 2   67 Most worthie praise, when words that common grew,
    p. 309 HORACE 2   71 Faine words, unheard of to the well-truss'd race,
    p. 309 HORACE 2   74 And those thy new, and late-coyn'd words receive,
    p. 309 HORACE 2   88 Of words decay, and phrases borne but late
    p. 311 HORACE 2   139 Their bombard-phrase, and foot-and-halfe-foot
                            words.
    p. 321 HORACE 2   343 Meere raigning words: nor will I labour so
    p. 325 HORACE 2   444 There words will follow, not against their will.
    p. 389 UNGATHERED 24   4 When the old words doe strike on the new times,
    p. 400 UNGATHERED 32   3 Hence, then, prophane: Here needs no words
                            expense

work   frequency: 1   relative frequency: 0.00001
   See also "worke."
    p. 409 UNGATHERED 38   t3 the Author of this Work, M. RICH.
                            BROME.

worke   frequency: 44   relative frequency: 0.00063
    p.   34 EPIGRAMS 23   3 Whose euery worke, of thy most earely wit,
    p.   37 EPIGRAMS 32   7 What could not worke; at home in his repaire
    p.   43 EPIGRAMS 52   2 Dispraise my worke, then praise it frostily:
    p.   46 EPIGRAMS 60   6 And proud, my worke shall out-last common deeds,
    p.   61 EPIGRAMS 95   14 Or, better worke! were thy glad countrey blest,
    p.   71 EPIGRAMS 110   9 Nor that his worke liu'd in the hands of foes,
    p.   72 EPIGRAMS 111   11 And thence, depraue thee, and thy worke. To
                            those
    p.   82 EPIGRAMS 131   2 A worke of ours, we part with our owne right;
    p.   83 EPIGRAMS 132   2 Might then both thee, thy worke and merit raise:
    p.   85 EPIGRAMS 133   57 Act a braue worke, call it thy last aduentry:
    p. 140 UNDERWOOD 2.8   8 When the worke would be effected:
    p. 161 UNDERWOOD 14   69 In offering this thy worke to no great Name,
    p. 183 UNDERWOOD 29   28 Not a worke deserving Baies,
    p. 185 UNDERWOOD 30   12 And labour'd in the worke; not with the fame:
    p. 207 UNDERWOOD 43   106 All soote, and embers! odious, as thy worke!
    p. 224 UNDERWOOD 50   16 A cheerefull worke to all good eyes, to see
    p. 255 UNDERWOOD 75   103 Of Tryals, to worke downe
    p. 268 UNDERWOOD 82   1 That thou art lov'd of God, this worke is done,
    p. 276 U'WOOD 84.3   12 Worke with my fancie, his owne hand.
    p. 277 U'WOOD 84.4   3 This worke I can performe alone;
    p. 284 U'WOOD 84.9   81 Hee knowes, what worke h'hath done, to call this
                            Guest,
    p. 288 U'WOOD 84.9   206 For his designed worke, the perfect end
    p. 307 HORACE 2   48 But in the maine worke haplesse: since he knowes
    p. 307 HORACE 2   50 To forme a worke, I would no more desire
    p. 309 HORACE 2   93 A kingly worke; or that long barren fen
    p. 311 HORACE 2   142 To worke the hearers minds, still, to their
                            plight.
    p. 329 HORACE 2   537 But, I confesse, that, in a long worke, sleepe
    p. 335 HORACE 2   630 Then change; no word, or worke, more would he
                            spend
    p. 362 UNGATHERED 2   5 Looke here on Bretons worke, the master print:
    p. 370 UNGATHERED 7   9 But now, your Worke is done, if they that view
    p. 371 UNGATHERED 8   15 A glorified worke to Time, when Fire,
    p. 385 UNGATHERED 19   5 To such a worke, as could not need theirs? Yet
    p. 385 UNGATHERED 20   2 To see his worke be good; but that he looke
    p. 386 UNGATHERED 21   3 But I haue seene thy worke, and I know thee:

worke (cont.)
```
    p. 386 UNGATHERED 21    8 This thy worke forth: that iudgment mine
                              commends.
    p. 388 UNGATHERED 23    1 Whose worke could this be, Chapman, to refine
    p. 389 UNGATHERED 24   t1 On the Author, Worke, and Translator.
    p. 393 UNGATHERED 27   19 A worthy worke, and worthy well
    p. 395 UNGATHERED 29   23 The selfe same Genius! so the worke will say.
    p. 401 UNGATHERED 32   13 Before this worke? where Enuy hath not cast
    p. 401 UNGATHERED 33   t2 on his Worke published.
    p. 404 UNGATHERED 34   65 All in ye Worke! And soe shall still for Ben:
    p. 407 UNGATHERED 35   21 An Earle of show: for all thy worke is showe:
    p. 409 UNGATHERED 37   12 Shall not worke out vnto it, such a fame.
```

worker.   See "master-worker."

workes   frequency: 5   relative frequency: 0.00007
```
    p.  44 EPIGRAMS 56     2 Whose workes are eene the fripperie of wit,
    p.  60 EPIGRAMS 94     3 If workes (not th'authors) their owne grace
                             should looke,
    p. 158 UNDERWOOD 14    7 To aske it: though in most of workes it be
    p. 242 UNDERWOOD 69   22 More subtle workes, and finer pieces farre,
    p. 407 UNGATHERED 35  19 your workes thus differing, troth let soe yor
                             style:
```

working   frequency: 1   relative frequency: 0.00001
```
    p. 182 UNDERWOOD 27   33 Though I, in working of my song,
```

workmanship   frequency: 1   relative frequency: 0.00001
```
    p. 160 UNDERWOOD 14   54 To see the workmanship so'<e>xceed the cost!
```

works   frequency: 1   relative frequency: 0.00001
```
    See also "fire-workes," "horne-workes,"
             "workes."
    p. 388 UNGATHERED 23  t3 of Hesiods Works, & Dayes.
```

work'st   frequency: 1   relative frequency: 0.00001
```
    p. 307 HORACE 2       31 In short; I bid, Let what thou work'st upon,
```

world   frequency: 50   relative frequency: 0.00072
```
  **p. 113 PANEGYRE        3 Againe, the glory of our Westerne world
    p.  28 EPIGRAMS 5      3 The world the temple was, the priest a king,
    p.  36 EPIGRAMS 30     4 And person to the world; ere I thy name.
    p.  37 EPIGRAMS 33     3 Whither the world must follow. And I, now,
    p.  43 EPIGRAMS 53     6 To giue the world assurance thou wert both;
    p.  46 EPIGRAMS 62     3 The world reputes you barren: but I know
    p.  51 EPIGRAMS 73     4 The world must know your greatnesse is my debter.
    p.  54 EPIGRAMS 80     5 This world deaths region is, the other lifes:
    p.  54 EPIGRAMS 81     2 A line vnto thee, till the world it know;
    p.  67 EPIGRAMS 104   14 A picture, which the world for yours must know,
    p.  72 EPIGRAMS 111   10 That to the world thou should'st reueale so much,
    p.  79 EPIGRAMS 125    3 Both whose dimensions, lost, the world might
                             finde
    p.  79 EPIGRAMS 125    9 Which (would the world not mis-call't flatterie)
    p.  83 EPIGRAMS 131    7 For, if the hum'rous world will talke at large,
    p.  83 EPIGRAMS 132    9 That to the world I publish, for him, this;
    p.  87 EPIGRAMS 133  129 One said, the other swore, the world consists.
    p. 100 FOREST 4        1 False world, good-night: since thou hast brought
    p. 100 FOREST 4       t1 TO THE WORLD.
    p. 114 FOREST 12      39 The world hath seene, which all these had in
                             +rust,
    p. 118 FOREST 13      64 Which though the turning world may dis-esteeme,
    p. 130 UNDERWOOD 1.3  10 Hee whom the whole world could not take,
    p. 131 UNDERWOOD 2.1  24 All the world for love may die.
    p. 134 UNDERWOOD 2.4  12 All that Loves world compriseth!
    p. 143 UNDERWOOD 3     4 And all the world turne Eares.
    p. 154 UNDERWOOD 13   50 For what they streight would to the world
                             forsweare;
    p. 163 UNDERWOOD 15   31 The whole world here leaven'd with madnesse
                             swells;
    p. 167 UNDERWOOD 15  172 Spread through the World) is easier farre to
                             find,
    p. 173 UNDERWOOD 22    3 As not the World can praise too much,
    p. 175 UNDERWOOD 23   29 To give the world againe:
    p. 175 UNDERWOOD 24    3 Raising the World to good or evill fame,
    p. 181 UNDERWOOD 27   20 Which all the world then styl'd divine?
    p. 184 UNDERWOOD 29   38 Scarce the world a Wit doth nourish,
    p. 189 UNDERWOOD 36    7 Without which all the world were darke;
    p. 193 UNDERWOOD 38   69 He pardons slips, goes by a world of ills,
    p. 193 UNDERWOOD 38   73 And how more faire, and lovely lookes the world
    p. 222 UNDERWOOD 49    2 And thinkes I dare not her? let the world see.
```

world (cont.)
    p. 227 UNDERWOOD 52   14 An Archetype, for all the world to see,
    p. 243 UNDERWOOD 70   16 Upon th'affrighted world:
    p. 270 UNDERWOOD 83   47 How did she leave the world? with what contempt?
    p. 270 UNDERWOOD 83   56 And I, into the world, all Soule, was sent!
    p. 271 UNDERWOOD 83   90 Whole Nations! nay, Mankind! the World, with
                              all
    p. 277 U'WOOD 84.3   28 And thou hast painted beauties world.
    p. 283 U'WOOD 84.9   25 The world to ruine with it; in her Fall,
    p. 288 U'WOOD 84.9·   201 On all the world! She saw him on the Crosse
    p. 379 UNGATHERED 12   15 He sayes to the world, let any man mend it,
    p. 393 UNGATHERED 27   18 Vnto the world doth proue.
    p. 395 UNGATHERED 29   4 And the world in it, I begin to doubt,
    p. 396 UNGATHERED 30   14 Hot from thy trumpet, round, about the world.
    p. 398 UNGATHERED 30   93 I call the world, that enuies mee, to see
    p. 414 UNGATHERED 42   2 Unto the world, in praise of your first Play:

world<s>   frequency: 1   relative frequency: 0.00001
    p. 189 UNDERWOOD 36   9 A Sparke to set whole world<s> a-fire,

worldlings   frequency: 1   relative frequency: 0.00001
    p. 162 UNDERWOOD 15   9 All other Acts of Worldlings, are but toyle

worlds   frequency: 7   relative frequency: 0.00010
    See also "world<s>."
    p. 27 EPIGRAMS 2   12 To catch the worlds loose laughter, or vaine
                              gaze.
    p. 41 EPIGRAMS 45   7 To haue so soone scap'd worlds, and fleshes rage,
    p. 209 UNDERWOOD 43   137 See the worlds Ruines! nothing but the piles
    p. 221 UNDERWOOD 48   24 And cure the Worlds diseases:
    p. 261 UNDERWOOD 77   20 What worlds of blessings to good Kings they owe:
    p. 361 UNGATHERED 1   22 of thy rich labors worlds of thoughts created,
    p. 389 UNGATHERED 24   6 But in one tongue, was form'd with the worlds
                              wit:

world's   frequency: 1   relative frequency: 0.00001
    See also "worlds."
    p. 78 EPIGRAMS 122   4 The world's pure gold, and wise simplicitie;

worm. See "covrt-worme," "worme."

worme   frequency: 1   relative frequency: 0.00001
    p. 166 UNDERWOOD 15   141 Can we not leave this worme? or will we not?

wormes   frequency: 2   relative frequency: 0.00002
    p. 31 EPIGRAMS 15   1 All men are wormes: But this no man. In silke
    p. 218 UNDERWOOD 47   18 Like flies, or wormes, which mans corrupt parts
                              fed:

wormewood   frequency: 1   relative frequency: 0.00001
    p. 27 EPIGRAMS 2   4 Wormewood, and sulphure, sharpe, and tooth'd
                              withall;

worms. See "booke-wormes," "wormes."

wormwood. See "wormewood."

worn. See "worne."

worne   frequency: 2   relative frequency: 0.00002
    p. 200 UNDERWOOD 42   16 There is not worne that lace, purle, knot or pin,
    p. 213 UNDERWOOD 44   13 But they may see Gold-Chaines, and Pearle
                              worne then,

worse   frequency: 10   relative frequency: 0.00014
    p. 48 EPIGRAMS 65   9 Make him loose all his friends; and, which is
                              worse,
    p. 50 EPIGRAMS 70   5 Delay is bad, doubt worse, depending worst;
    p. 57 EPIGRAMS 90   11 Still MILL continu'd: Nay, his face growing
                              worse,
    p. 99 FOREST 3   82 Purchas'd by rapine, worse then stealth,
    p. 162 UNDERWOOD 15   12 His unjust hopes, with praises begg'd, or (worse)
    p. 172 UNDERWOOD 20   14 Were such as I will now relate, or worse?
    p. 172 UNDERWOOD 20   17 Doe not you aske to know her, she is worse
    p. 189 UNDERWOOD 36   4 None brookes the Sun-light worse then he.
    p. 211 UNDERWOOD 43   189 I could invent a sentence, yet were worse;
    p. 323 HORACE 2   386 Or a worse Crime, the ignorance of art.

worser   frequency: 1   relative frequency: 0.00001
    p. 104 FOREST 8   6 And nights too, in worser wayes?

worship   frequency: 4   relative frequency: 0.00005
    p.   87 EPIGRAMS 133   123 Of worship, they their nodding chinnes doe hit
    p. 127 UNDERWOOD 1.1   20 To worship thee.
    p. 155 UNDERWOOD 13   93 Such worship due to kicking of a Punck!
    p. 284 U'WOOD 84.9   75 Against the Nature he would worship. Hee

worst   frequency: 11   relative frequency: 0.00015
    p.   40 EPIGRAMS 43   6 I, not the worst, am couetous of thee.
    p.   50 EPIGRAMS 70   5 Delay is bad, doubt worse, depending worst;
    p.   63 EPIGRAMS 98   11 Though both be good, the latter yet is worst,
    p.   86 EPIGRAMS 133   78 Ploughing the mayne. When, see (the worst of all
                               lucks)
    p. 154 UNDERWOOD 13   51 And speaking worst of those, from whom they went
    p. 169 UNDERWOOD 17   1 They are not, Sir, worst Owers, that doe pay
    p. 223 UNDERWOOD 49   43 Or if it would, the Court is the worst place,
    p. 260 UNDERWOOD 76   29 Then goe on, and doe its worst;
    p. 307 HORACE 2   45 The worst of Statuaries, here about
    p. 331 HORACE 2   564 And highest; sinketh to the lowest, and worst.
    p. 416 UNGATHERED 43   9 In spite of Hipocrites, who are the worst

worth   frequency: 35   relative frequency: 0.00050
    See also "wroth."
    p.   44 EPIGRAMS 55   3 How I doe feare my selfe, that am not worth
    p.   47 EPIGRAMS 63   12 To so true worth, though thou thy selfe forbid.
    p.   48 EPIGRAMS 64   13 Contends t'haue worth enioy, from his regard,
    p.   48 EPIGRAMS 65   16 For worth he has not, He is tax'd, not prais'd.
    p.   57 EPIGRAMS 89   11 And present worth in all dost so contract,
    p.   64 EPIGRAMS 101   4 But that your worth will dignifie our feast,
    p.   71 EPIGRAMS 110   20 Action, or engine, worth a note of thine,
    p.   80 EPIGRAMS 126   1 Retyr'd, with purpose your faire worth to praise,
    p. 113 FOREST 12   3 That which, to boote with hell, is thought worth
                               heauen,
    p. 114 FOREST 12   36 Worth an estate, treble to that you haue.
    p. 146 UNDERWOOD 6   22 From being forsaken, then doth worth:
    p. 150 UNDERWOOD 10   14 Loves sicknesse, and his noted want of worth,
    p. 182 UNDERWOOD 28   t3 MARY WORTH.
    p. 183 UNDERWOOD 29   27 Worth <a> crowning.
    p. 188 UNDERWOOD 34   3 What did she worth thy spight? were there not
                               store
    p. 199 UNDERWOOD 41   15 You would restore it? No, that's worth a feare,
    p. 200 UNDERWOOD 42   20 (If they be faire and worth it) have their lives
    p. 216 UNDERWOOD 45   15 Inquirie of the worth: So must we doe,
    p. 250 UNDERWOOD 73   10 To vertue, and true worth, be ever blind.
    p. 253 UNDERWOOD 75   28 And celebrate (perfection at the worth)
    p. 264 UNDERWOOD 79   31 Chor. Heare, O you Groves, and, Hills,
                               resound his worth.
    p. 309 HORACE 2   81 Cato's and Ennius tongues have lent much worth,
    p. 313 HORACE 2   182 Still to be like himselfe, and hold his worth.
    p. 313 HORACE 2   197 What doth this Promiser such gaping worth
    p. 317 HORACE 2   274 Worth his untying happen there: And not
    p. 319 HORACE 2   308 Unwonted language; and that sense of worth
    p. 325 HORACE 2   425 For so, they shall not only gaine the worth,
    p. 361 UNGATHERED 1   27 When loe to crowne thy worth
    p. 378 UNGATHERED 11   84 And therein (which is worth his valour too)
    p. 384 UNGATHERED 18   12 Out-bee yt Wife, in worth, thy freind did make:
    p. 384 UNGATHERED 18   14 Hymens amends, to make it worth his fault.
    p. 386 UNGATHERED 21   13 Hold thyne owne worth vnbroke: which is so good
    p. 405 UNGATHERED 34   70 To be worth Enuy. Henceforth I doe meane
    p. 409 UNGATHERED 37   13 Thou art not worth it. Who will care to knowe
    p. 409 UNGATHERED 37   22 Thy Dirty braines, Men smell thy want of worth.

worthie   frequency: 4   relative frequency: 0.00005
    p. 307 HORACE 2   67 Most worthie praise, when words that common grew,
    p. 393 UNGATHERED 27   20 Of the most worthie loue.
    p. 420 UNGATHERED 48   26 And come fforth worthie Ivye, or the Bayes,
    p. 421 UNGATHERED 48   45 Whoe worthie wine, whoe not, to bee wyse Pallas
                               guests.

worthier   frequency: 1   relative frequency: 0.00001
    p. 190 UNDERWOOD 37   11 And which you (being the worthier) gave me leave

worthies. See "worthyes."

worthiest   frequency: 2   relative frequency: 0.00002
    p. 146 UNDERWOOD 6   23 For were the worthiest woman curst
    p. 217 UNDERWOOD 46   20 Of worthiest knowledge, that can take mens minds.

worthily   frequency: 1   relative frequency: 0.00001
    p. 383 UNGATHERED 17   t1 To his much and worthily esteemed

worthlesse   frequency: 1   relative frequency: 0.00001
   p. 48 EPIGRAMS 65   2 That hast betray'd me to a worthlesse lord;

worthy   .   frequency: 29   relative frequency: 0.00041
   See also "crowne-worthy," "laugh-worthy,"
          "praise-worthy," "worthie."
   p. 46 EPIGRAMS 60   7 Durst thinke it great, and worthy wonder too,
   p. 63 EPIGRAMS 99   3 Hast taught thy selfe worthy thy pen to tread,
   p. 63 EPIGRAMS 99   4 And that to write things worthy to be read:
   p. 64 EPIGRAMS 101   3 Not that we thinke vs worthy such a ghest,
   p. 73 EPIGRAMS 113   1 So PHOEBVS makes me worthy of his bayes,
   p. 85 EPIGRAMS 133   31 In it' owne hall; when these (in worthy scorne
   p. 119 FOREST 13   94 For which you worthy are the glad encrease
   p. 138 UNDERWOOD 2.6   27 And was worthy (being so seene)
   p. 154 UNDERWOOD 13   59 Are they not worthy to be answer'd so,
   p. 191 UNDERWOOD 38   15 If there be nothing worthy you can see
   p. 199 UNDERWOOD 41   16 As if it were not worthy to be there:
   p. 229 UNDERWOOD 55   2 Thoughts worthy of thy gift, this Inke,
   p. 285 U'WOOD 84.9   97 And will you, worthy Sonne, Sir, knowing this,
   p. 294 UNDERWOOD 89   2 Thou worthy in eternall Flower to fare,
   p. 317 HORACE 2   261 Things worthy to be done within, but take
   p. 327 HORACE 2   475 In juyce of Cedar worthy to be steep'd,
   p. 333 HORACE 2   619 If of their friendship he be worthy, or no:
   p. 339 HORACE 1   34 Father ... sons right worthy of your ....
   p. 370 UNGATHERED 8   t1 To the worthy Author M.
   p. 385 UNGATHERED 20   t1 To the worthy Author on
   p. 386 UNGATHERED 20   10 Was worthy of a Good one; And this, here,
   p. 386 UNGATHERED 21   6 I find thee write most worthy to be read.
   p. 388 UNGATHERED 23   t1 To my worthy and honour'd Friend,
   p. 393 UNGATHERED 27   19 A worthy worke, and worthy well
   p. 398 UNGATHERED 30   92 And, till I worthy am to wish I were,
   p. 401 UNGATHERED 33   t1 To my worthy Friend, Master Edward Filmer,
   p. 407 UNGATHERED 36   2 (And labours to seem worthy of yt feare)
   p. 413 UNGATHERED 41   14 The Eye of flowers, worthy, for his scent,

worthyes   frequency: 1   relative frequency: 0.00001
   p. 406 UNGATHERED 34   99 Of all ye Worthyes hope t'outlast thy one,

wou'd   frequency: 1   relative frequency: 0.00001

wouen   frequency: 2   relative frequency: 0.00002
   p. 61 EPIGRAMS 95   15 To haue her storie wouen in thy thred;
   p. 392 UNGATHERED 26   49 Which were so richly spun, and wouen so fit,

would   frequency: 199   relative frequency: 0.00288
   See also "hee'd," "hee'ld," "i'ld,"
          "they'd," "who'd," "wou'd,"
          "you'ld."

would-be. See "wovld-bee."

wouldst   frequency: 10   relative frequency: 0.00014
   See also "thou'ldst," "would'st."

would'st   frequency: 9   relative frequency: 0.00013

wound   frequency: 8   relative frequency: 0.00011
   p. 122 FOREST 15   22 Vpon my flesh t<o>'inflict another wound.
   p. 159 UNDERWOOD 14   15 A many'of bookes, even good judgements wound
   p. 162 UNDERWOOD 15   22 Till envie wound, or maime it at a blow!
   p. 168 UNDERWOOD 15   178 Not wound thy conscience, when thy body bleeds;
   p. 180 UNDERWOOD 26   2 I send nor Balmes, nor Cor'sives to your wound,
   p. 187 UNDERWOOD 33   20 Thou prov'st the gentler wayes, to clense the
                             wound,
   p. 203 UNDERWOOD 43   23 Did I there wound the honour of the Crowne?
   p. 311 HORACE 2   146 Thy selfe in teares, then me thy losse will
                             wound,

wounded   frequency: 1   relative frequency: 0.00001
   p. 283 U'WOOD 84.9   23 My wounded mind cannot sustaine this stroke,
                                    .
wound'st   frequency: 1   relative frequency: 0.00001
   p. 187 UNDERWOOD 33   32 So brightly brandish'd) wound'st, defend'st! the
                             while

woven. See "wouen."

wovld-bee   frequency: 2   relative frequency: 0.00002
   p. 46 EPIGRAMS 62   1 Fine MADAME WOVLD-BEE, wherefore
                             should you feare,

wovld-bee (cont.)
    p. 40 EPIGRAMS 62   t1 TO FINE LADY WOVLD-BEE.

wrack. See "wracke."

wrack'd   frequency: 1 relative frequency: 0.00001
    p. 339 HORACE 1   28 ... . wrack'd . ...

wracke   frequency: 2 relative frequency: 0.00002
    p. 99 FOREST 3   95 God wisheth, none should wracke on a strange
                              shelfe.
    p. 119 FOREST 13   90 Whereon the most of mankinde wracke themselues,

wrangle   frequency: 1 relative frequency: 0.00001
    p. 99 FOREST 3   73 Let this man sweat, and wrangle at the barre,

wranglers   frequency: 1 relative frequency: 0.00001
    p. 187 UNDERWOOD 33   8 Of hirelings, wranglers, stitchers-to of strife,

wrapped. See "wrapt."

wrapt   frequency: 4 relative frequency: 0.00005
    p. 31 EPIGRAMS 15   2 'Twas brought to court first wrapt, and white as
                              milke;
    p. 155 UNDERWOOD 13   88 Carryed and wrapt, I only am alow'd
    p. 180 UNDERWOOD 26   10 Wrapt in this paper lie,
    p. 193 UNDERWOOD 38   75 About in Cloudes, and wrapt in raging weather,

wrath   frequency: 1 relative frequency: 0.00001
    p. 132 UNDERWOOD 2.2   29 (Which with griefe and wrath I heard)

wreak. See "wreake."

wreake   frequency: 1 relative frequency: 0.00001
    p. 133 UNDERWOOD 2.3   21 Looser-like, now, all my wreake

wreath   frequency: 1 relative frequency: 0.00001
    p. 106 FOREST 9   9 I sent thee, late, a rosie wreath,

wreck. See "wracke."

wreck'd   frequency: 1 relative frequency: 0.00001
    See also "wrack'd."
    p. 305 HORACE 2   28 The whole fleet wreck'd? A great jarre to be
                              shap'd,

wrested   frequency: 1 relative frequency: 0.00001
    p. 309 HORACE 2   76 And come not too much wrested. What's that
                              thing,

wresting   frequency: 1 relative frequency: 0.00001
    p. 183 UNDERWOOD 29   7 Wresting words, from their true calling;

wrestled   frequency: 1 relative frequency: 0.00001
    p. 151 UNDERWOOD 12   8 Had wrestled with Diseases strong,

wrestlest   frequency: 1 relative frequency: 0.00001
    p. 70 EPIGRAMS 109   6 Wrestlest with dignities, or fain'st a scope

wretch   frequency: 4 relative frequency: 0.00005
  **p. 116 PANEGYRE   115 And that no wretch was more vnblest then he,
    p. 201 UNDERWOOD 42   61 From the poore wretch, which though he play'd in
                              prose,
    p. 408 UNGATHERED 36   5 The Marrow! Wretch, I quitt thee of thy paine
    p. 409 UNGATHERED 37   11 I now would write on thee? No, wretch; thy name

wretched   frequency: 8 relative frequency: 0.00011
    p. 99 FOREST 3   81 Let that goe heape a masse of wretched wealth,
    p. 150 UNDERWOOD 10   1 Wretched and foolish Jealousie,
    p. 234 UNDERWOOD 61   3 View'd there the mercat, read the wretched rate
    p. 241 UNDERWOOD 69   9 But as the wretched Painter, who so ill
    p. 248 UNDERWOOD 71   1 Poore wretched states, prest by extremities,
    p. 281 U'WOOD 84.8   16 It is a wretched thing to trust to reedes;
    p. 325 HORACE 2   420 Happier then wretched art, and doth, by it,
    p. 410 UNGATHERED 39   10 I'll laugh at thee poor wretched Tike, go send

wretchedly   frequency: 1 relative frequency: 0.00001
    p. 317 HORACE 2   243 Doth wretchedly the use of things forbeare,

wretchednes   frequency: 1   relative frequency: 0.00001
    p. 403 UNGATHERED 34   23 What makes your Wretchednes to bray soe loud

wretched'st   frequency: 1   relative frequency: 0.00001
    p. 272 UNDERWOOD 83   97 Hee were the wretched'st of the race of men:

wretches   frequency: 1   relative frequency: 0.00001
    p. 422 UNGATHERED 50   6 whom thou seest happy; wretches flee as foes:

wries. See "wryes."

wright   frequency: 1   relative frequency: 0.00001
    See also "knight-wright's," "play-wright."
    p. 164 UNDERWOOD 15   80 Where Pittes, or Wright, or Modet would not
                              venter,

wrights. See "stage-wrights."

writ   frequency: 13   relative frequency: 0.00018
    p. 46 EPIGRAMS 60   4 Thy fact, in brasse or marble writ the same)
    p. 64 EPIGRAMS 100   1 PLAY-WRIGHT, by chance, hearing some
                              toyes I'had writ,
    p. 78 EPIGRAMS 123   1 Writing thy selfe, or iudging others writ,
    p. 119 FOREST 13   106 And greater rites, yet writ in mysterie,
    p. 176 UNDERWOOD 25   t2 writ in Queene ELIZABETHS time,
    p. 198 UNDERWOOD 40   50 If I had writ no word, but Deare, farewell.
    p. 210 UNDERWOOD 43   174 Lyes there no Writ, out of the Chancerie,
    p. 220 UNDERWOOD 47   77 As you have writ your selfe. Now stand, and
                              then,
    p. 331 HORACE 2   580 The Writ, once out, never returned yet.
    p. 380 UNGATHERED 12   56 I writ he onely his taile there did waue;
    p. 389 UNGATHERED 24   5 As in this Spanish Proteus; who, though writ
    p. 390 UNGATHERED 25   8 All, that was euer writ in brasse.
    p. 390 UNGATHERED 30   6 You haue not writ to me, nor I to you;

write   frequency: 38   relative frequency: 0.00055
    See also "wryte."
    p. 29 EPIGRAMS 9   t1 TO ALL, TO WHOM I WRITE.
    p. 41 EPIGRAMS 43   10 And what I write thereof find farre, and free
    p. 46 EPIGRAMS 62   11 In a great belly. Write, then on thy wombe,
    p. 48 EPIGRAMS 65   13 Shee shall instruct my after-thoughts to write
    p. 52 EPIGRAMS 76   18 My Muse bad, Bedford write, and that was shee.
    p. 59 EPIGRAMS 92   26 To write in cypher, and the seuerall keyes,
    p. 59 EPIGRAMS 92   28 With iuyce of limons, onions, pisse, to write,
    p. 61 EPIGRAMS 95   25 Although to write be lesser then to doo,
    p. 62 EPIGRAMS 95   34 Can write the things, the causes, and the men.
    p. 62 EPIGRAMS 95   36 That dares nor write things false, nor hide
                              things true.
    p. 62 EPIGRAMS 96   9 My title's seal'd. Those that for claps doe
                              write,
    p. 63 EPIGRAMS 99   4 And that to write things worthy to be read:
    p. 72 EPIGRAMS 112   11 I modestly quit that, and thinke to write,
    p. 93 FOREST 1   t1 WHY I WRITE NOT OF LOVE.
    p. 131 UNDERWOOD 2.1   3 Though I now write fiftie yeares,
    p. 156 UNDERWOOD 13   109 And you, Sir, know it well, to whom I write,
    p. 158 UNDERWOOD 14   1 I know to whom I write. Here, I am sure,
    p. 159 UNDERWOOD 14   25 And what I write? and vexe it many dayes
    p. 169 UNDERWOOD 18   1 Can Beautie that did prompt me first to write,
    p. 181 UNDERWOOD 27   2 Thy beauties, yet could write of thee?
    p. 201 UNDERWOOD 42 . 64 Had he'had the facultie to reade, and write!
    p. 222 UNDERWOOD 49   8 And in an Epicoene fury can write newes
    p. 227 UNDERWOOD 52   19 But, you are he can paint; I can but write:
    p. 227 UNDERWOOD 52   24 To all posteritie; I will write Burlase.
    p. 269 UNDERWOOD 83   13 Alas, I am all Marble! write the rest
    p. 307 HORACE 2   53 Take, therefore, you that write, still, matter
                              fit
    p. 313 HORACE 2   169 Or follow fame, thou that dost write, or faine
    p. 321 HORACE 2   341 Nor I, when I write Satyrs, will so love
    p. 331 HORACE 2   575 But, if hereafter thou shalt write, not feare
    p. 333 HORACE 2   620 When you write Verses, with your judge do so:
    p. 379 UNGATHERED 12   1 Who euer he be, would write a Story at
    p. 379 UNGATHERED 12   14 To write it with the selfe same spirit he went,
    p. 381 UNGATHERED 12   59 No: as I first said, who would write a story at
    p. 386 UNGATHERED 21   6 I find thee write most worthy to be read.
    p. 387 UNGATHERED 22   9 nor yet inscription like it. Write but that;
    p. 392 UNGATHERED 26   59 Who casts to write a liuing line, must sweat,
    p. 409 UNGATHERED 37   11 I now would write on thee? No, wretch; thy name
    p. 410 UNGATHERED 38   12 Both learned, and vnlearned, all write Playes.

writer   frequency: 4   relative frequency: 0.00005
     p.   78 EPIGRAMS 123   4 Of the best writer, and iudge, should emulate.
     p. 323 HORACE 2   393 Grow a safe Writer, and be warie-driven
     p. 337 HORACE 2   676 All; So this grievous Writer puts to flight
     p. 379 UNGATHERED 12   t1 To the London Reader, on the Odcombian writer,

writers   frequency: 2   relative frequency: 0.00002
     p. 307 HORACE 2   33 Most Writers, noble Sire, and either Sonne,
     p. 386 UNGATHERED 21   15 More of our writers would like thee, not swell

writhed   frequency: 1   relative frequency: 0.00001
     p.   94 FOREST 2   15 There, in the writhed barke, are cut the names

writing   frequency: 5   relative frequency: 0.00007
     p.   44 EPIGRAMS 55   10 For writing better, I must enuie thee.
     p.   78 EPIGRAMS 123   1 Writing thy selfe, or iudging others writ,
     p. 325 HORACE 2   435 I, writing nought my selfe, will teach them yet
     p. 325 HORACE 2   440 The very root of writing well, and spring
     p. 349 HORACE 1   442 .... writing ....

writings   frequency: 2   relative frequency: 0.00002
     p. 325 HORACE 2   442 Which the Socratick writings best can show:
     p. 390 UNGATHERED 26   3 While I confesse thy writings to be such,

writs   frequency: 1   relative frequency: 0.00001
     p. 113 FOREST 12   20 A present, which (if elder writs reherse

writ'st   frequency: 1   relative frequency: 0.00001
     p.   72 EPIGRAMS 112   8 Tragick, or Comick; but thou writ'st the play.

written   frequency: 2   relative frequency: 0.00002
     p. 247 UNDERWOOD 70   123 Friendship, in deed, was written, not in words:
     p. 269 UNDERWOOD 83   14 Thou wouldst have written, Fame, upon my brest:

wrong   frequency: 13   relative frequency: 0.00018
  **p. 117 PANEGYRE   161 Yet, let blest Brit[t]aine aske (without your
                                    wrong)
     p.   45 EPIGRAMS 58   4 Thy ignorance still laughs in the wrong place.
     p.   59 EPIGRAMS 92   40 That know not so much state, wrong, as they doo.
     p.   69 EPIGRAMS 108   2 Such as are misse-call'd Captaynes, and wrong
                                    you;
     p. 119 FOREST 13   84 Boast, but how oft they haue gone wrong to man:
     p. 121 FOREST 14   30 Doth vrge him to runne wrong, or to stand still.
     p. 139 UNDERWOOD 2.7   10 And all your bountie wrong:
     p. 168 UNDERWOOD 15   180 And never but for doing wrong be sory;
     p. 186 UNDERWOOD 32   16 He do's you wrong, that craves you to doe right.
     p. 233 UNDERWOOD 59   15 Of daring not to doe a wrong, is true
     p. 307 HORACE 2   44 When in a wrong, and artlesse way we tread.
     p. 311 HORACE 2   129 Am I call'd Poet? wherefore with wrong shame,
     p. 335 HORACE 2   642 The man once mock'd, and suffer'd wrong to tread.

wrong'd   frequency: 1   relative frequency: 0.00001
     p.   80 EPIGRAMS 126   5 Said I wrong'd him, and (which was more) his
                                    loue.

wrongs   frequency: 5   relative frequency: 0.00007
     p.   49 EPIGRAMS 68   1 PLAY-WRIGHT conuict of publike wrongs to
                                    men,
     p. 142 UNDERWOOD 2.9   49 Nor doe wrongs, nor wrongs receave;
     p. 184 UNDERWOOD 29   35 Is not yet free from Rimes wrongs,
     p. 397 UNGATHERED 30   30 Their loues, their quarrels, iealousies, and
                                    wrongs,

wrote   frequency: 5   relative frequency: 0.00007
     p.   71 EPIGRAMS 110   8 He wrote, with the same spirit that he fought,
     p. 203 UNDERWOOD 43   15 Had I wrote treason there, or heresie,
     p. 282 U'WOOD 84.9   3 The Spirit that I wrote with, and conceiv'd;
     p. 335 HORACE 2   637 They're darke, bid cleare this: all that's
                                    doubtfull wrote
     p. 389 UNGATHERED 24   12 As was the Genius wherewith they were wrote;

wroth   frequency: 6   relative frequency: 0.00008
  See also "worth."
     p.   66 EPIGRAMS 103   t1 TO MARY LADY WROTH.
     p.   67 EPIGRAMS 105   t1 TO MARY LADY WROTH.
     p.   96 FOREST 3   1 How blest art thou, canst loue the countrey,
                                    WROTH,
     p.   96 FOREST 3   t1 TO SIR ROBERT WROTH.
     p.   96 FOREST 3   66 Striue, WROTH, to liue long innocent.
     p.   99 FOREST 3   91 But thou, my WROTH, if I can truth apply,

wrought   frequency: 16   relative frequency: 0.00023
    See also "wel-wrought."
    *p. 493 TO HIMSELF   38 Wrought vpon twenty blocks:
     p. 33 EPIGRAMS 21   5 Quick in his lips! Who hath this wonder wrought?
     p. 48 EPIGRAMS 64   16 Wherein what wonder see thy name hath wrought?
     p. 49 EPIGRAMS 67   7 When, in mens wishes, so thy vertues wrought,
     p. 56 EPIGRAMS 87   4 Of what shee had wrought came in, and wak'd his
                                braine,
     p. 83 EPIGRAMS 132   11 So well in that are his inuentions wrought,
     p. 101 FOREST 4   60 There should a miracle be wrought.
     p. 161 UNDERWOOD 14   75 And estimate thy Paines; as having wrought
     p. 238 UNDERWOOD 66   8 Whereby the safetie of Man-kind was wrought)
     p. 245 UNDERWOOD 70   60 By what was done and wrought
     p. 273 U'WOOD 84.1   26 No cobweb Call's; no Surcoates wrought
     p. 315 HORACE 2   231 I'the open field; is Waxe like to be wrought
     p. 323 HORACE 2   409 Whether the guarded Tragedie they vrought,
     p. 362 UNGATHERED 2   10 Vnto a cunning piece wrought perspectiue,
     p. 388 UNGATHERED 23   3 Who hadst before wrought in rich Homers Mine?
     p. 395 UNGATHERED 29   20 Lucans whole frame vnto vs, and so wrought,

wrung   frequency: 1   relative frequency: 0.00001
     p. 201 UNDERWOOD 42   63 Wrung on the Withers, by Lord Loves despight,

wry   frequency: 2   relative frequency: 0.00002
     p. 307 HORACE 2   52 With faire black eyes, and haire; and a wry nose.
     p. 362 UNGATHERED 2   7 If they seeme wry, to such as looke asquint,

wryes   frequency: 1   relative frequency: 0.00001
     p. 177 UNDERWOOD 25   29 Of politique pretext, that wryes a State,

wryte   frequency: 2   relative frequency: 0.00002
     p. 407 UNGATHERED 36   3 That I should wryte vpon him some sharp verse,
     p. 421 UNGATHERED 49   2 before, I wryte more verse, to bee more wyse.

wth   frequency: 24   relative frequency: 0.00034

wthout   frequency: 1   relative frequency: 0.00001
     p. 405 UNGATHERED 34   68 Swim wthout Corke! Why, thank ye good Queen
                                Anne.

wull   frequency: 2   relative frequency: 0.00002

wyne   frequency: 1   relative frequency: 0.00001
     p. 406 UNGATHERED 35   8 Cittyes & Temples! thou a Caue for Wyne,

wynns   frequency: 1   relative frequency: 0.00001
     p. 421 UNGATHERED 49   5 The emptye Carper, scorne, not Creditt wynns.

wyres   frequency: 1   relative frequency: 0.00001
     p. 118 FOREST 13   72 Maintayne their liedgers forth, for forraine
                                wyres,

wyse   frequency: 3   relative frequency: 0.00004
     p. 420 UNGATHERED 48   28 Yett: since the bright, and wyse,
     p. 421 UNGATHERED 48   45 Whoe worthie wine, whoe not, to bee wyse Pallas
                                guests.
     p. 421 UNGATHERED 49   2 before, I wryte more verse, to bee more wyse.

wyser   frequency: 1   relative frequency: 0.00001
     p. 405 UNGATHERED 34   85 Oh wise Surueyor! wyser Architect!

y>our   frequency: 1   relative frequency: 0.00001
     p. 198 UNDERWOOD 40   48 That Article, may not become <y>our lover:

yard   frequency: 2   relative frequency: 0.00002
    See also "church-yard."
     p. 213 UNDERWOOD 44   23 Well, I say, thrive, thrive brave Artillerie
                                yard,
     p. 379 UNGATHERED 12   10 By the scale of his booke, a yard of his stile?

yarned. See "long-yearn'd."

ycleped   frequency: 1   relative frequency: 0.00001
     p. 85 EPIGRAMS 133   62 Ycleped Mud, which, when their oares did once
                                stirre,

ye   frequency: 47   relative frequency: 0.00068
    See also "yee."
     p. 305 HORACE 2   18 Ye have oft-times, that may ore-shine the rest,
     p. 394 UNGATHERED 28   t1 To ye memorye of that most honoured Ladie Jane,

ye (cont.)
```
      p.  402  UNGATHERED 34     2  From thirty pound in pipkins, to ye Man
      p.  402  UNGATHERED 34    11  Whether ye buylding of ye Stage or Scene!
      p.  402  UNGATHERED 34    12  Or making of ye Propertyes it meane?
      p.  403  UNGATHERED 34    29  What is ye cause you pompe it soe? I aske,
      p.  403  UNGATHERED 34    32  That doe cry vp ye Machine, & ye Showes!
      p.  403  UNGATHERED 34    33  The majesty of Iuno in ye Cloudes,
      p.  403  UNGATHERED 34    34  And peering forth of Iris in ye Shrowdes!
      p.  403  UNGATHERED 34    42  You are ye Spectacles of State! Tis true
      p.  404  UNGATHERED 34    44  In ye mere perspectiue of an Inch board!
      p.  404  UNGATHERED 34    46  Eyes yt can pierce into ye Misteryes
      p.  404  UNGATHERED 34    50  Painting & Carpentry are ye Soule of
                                       Masque.
      p.  404  UNGATHERED 34    52  This is ye money-gett, Mechanick Age!
      p.  404  UNGATHERED 34    53  To plant ye Musick where noe eare can reach!
      p.  404  UNGATHERED 34    54  Attyre ye Persons as noe thought can teach
      p.  404  UNGATHERED 34    56  Terme of ye Architects is called Designe!
      p.  404  UNGATHERED 34    57  But in ye practisd truth Destruction is
      p.  404  UNGATHERED 34    61  The maker of ye Propertyes! in summe
      p.  404  UNGATHERED 34    63  To be ye Musick Master! Fabler too!
      p.  404  UNGATHERED 34    64  He is, or would be ye mayne Dominus doe
      p.  404  UNGATHERED 34    65  All in ye Worke! And soe shall still for Ben:
      p.  405  UNGATHERED 34    66  Be Inigo, ye Whistle, & his men!
      p.  405  UNGATHERED 34    68  Swim wthout Corke! Why, thank ye good Queen
                                       Anne.
      p.  405  UNGATHERED 34    74  Suckt from ye Veynes of shop-philosophy.
      p.  405  UNGATHERED 34    77  Should but ye king his Iustice-hood employ
      p.  405  UNGATHERED 34    83  Vnder ye Morall? shewe he had a pate
      p.  405  UNGATHERED 34    87  On ye new priming of thy old Signe postes
      p.  405  UNGATHERED 34    88  Reuiuing wth fresh coulors ye pale Ghosts
      p.  406  UNGATHERED 34    99  Of all ye Worthyes hope t'outlast thy one,
      p.  406  UNGATHERED 34   100  Soe ye Materialls be of Purbeck stone!
      p.  406  UNGATHERED 34   101  Lyue long ye ffeasting Roome. And ere thou
                                       burne
      p.  406  UNGATHERED 35     1  But cause thou hearst ye mighty k. of Spaine
      p.  406  UNGATHERED 35     4  All kings to doe ye self same deeds wth some!
      p.  407  UNGATHERED 35    12  Thou paint a Lane, where Thumb ye Pygmy meets!
      p.  407  UNGATHERED 35    13  He some Colossus to bestryde ye Seas,
      p.  407  UNGATHERED 35    14  From ye fam'd pillars of old Hercules!
      p.  407  UNGATHERED 35    17  And stradling shews ye Boyes Brown paper fleet,
      p.  407  UNGATHERED 35    18  yearly set out there, to sayle downe ye Street,
      p.  407  UNGATHERED 35    20  Content thee to be Pancridge Earle ye whyle;
      p.  407  UNGATHERED 35    23  Or canst of truth ye least intrenchmt pitch,
      p.  407  UNGATHERED 35    24  Wee'll haue thee styld ye Marquess of
                                       New-Ditch.
      p.  408  UNGATHERED 36     8  He makes ye Camell & dull Ass his prize.
      p.  408  UNGATHERED 36    13  That sit vpon ye Comon Draught: or Strand!
      p.  419  UNGATH'D 47A      1  The ..... ye ....... ... Prince god ......
```

yea   frequency: 6   relative frequency: 0.00008
```
   **p.  116  PANEGYRE        106  "Lawes, iudges, co<u>nsellors, yea prince, and
                                       state.
      p.  105  FOREST 8         27  Any paines; yea, thinke it price,
      p.  113  FOREST 12         4  And, for it, life, conscience, yea, soules are
                                       giuen,
      p.  155  UNDERWOOD 13     77  Yea, of th'ingratefull: and he forth must tell
      p.  186  UNDERWOOD 32     12  Thinke, yea and boast, that they have done it so
      p.  367  UNGATHERED 6     56  And conquers all things, yea it selfe, at length.
```

year. See "yeare," "yeere."

yeare   frequency: 20   relative frequency: 0.00028
```
      p.   51  EPIGRAMS 74       2  And know thee, then, a iudge, not of one yeare;
      p.  116  FOREST 12         98 A vow as new, and ominous as the yeare,
      p.  199  UNDERWOOD 41       8 Where we must feele it Darke for halfe a yeare.
      p.  200  UNDERWOOD 42      29 But I who live, and have liv'd twentie yeare
      p.  207  UNDERWOOD 43      98 Of our fift Henry, eight of his nine yeare;
      p.  215  UNDERWOOD 44      76 In so much land a yeare, or such a Banke,
      p.  219  UNDERWOOD 47      44 Brunsfield, and Mansfield doe this yeare, my
                                       fates
      p.  225  UNDERWOOD 51       7 And so doe I. This is the sixtieth yeare
      p.  236  UNDERWOOD 64       5 And as it turnes our joyfull yeare about,
      p.  240  UNDERWOOD 67      48 Her two and twenti'th yeare!
      p.  242  UNDERWOOD 70       2 Thy comming forth in that great yeare,
      p.  245  UNDERWOOD 70      67 Or standing long an Oake, three hundred yeare,
      p.  251  UNDERWOOD 74       6 Of the prime beautie of the yeare, the Spring.
      p.  253  UNDERWOOD 75      13 When look'd the yeare, at best,
      p.  262  UNDERWOOD 78      16 Unto our yeare doth give the longest light.
      p.  263  UNDERWOOD 79       5 Of the New Yeare, in a new silken warpe,
      p.  263  UNDERWOOD 79       9 Rector Chori. To day old Janus opens the new
                                       yeare,
```

yeare (cont.)
    p. 264 UNDERWOOD 79   38 2. As if the beauties of the yeare,
    p. 291 UNDERWOOD 85   47 And from the sweet Tub Wine of this yeare
                              takes,
    p. 292 UNDERWOOD 86   6 To bend a man, now at his fiftieth yeare

yeares   frequency: 16   relative frequency: 0.00023
   *p. 493 TO HIMSELF   46 Ere yeares haue made thee old;
  **p. 114 PANEGYRE   56 Her place, and yeares, gaue her precedencie.
    p. 131 UNDERWOOD 2.1   3 Though I now write fiftie yeares,
    p. 171 UNDERWOOD 20   5 At fifty yeares, almost, to value it,
    p. 183 UNDERWOOD 29   16 For a thousand yeares together,
    p. 213 UNDERWOOD 44   27 These ten yeares day; As all may sweare that
                              looke
    p. 231 UNDERWOOD 57   12 Of a yeares Pension,
    p. 243 UNDERWOOD 70   26 And told forth fourescore yeares;
    p. 244 UNDERWOOD 70   54 And make them yeares;
    p. 248 UNDERWOOD 71   6 Have cast a trench about mee, now, five yeares;
    p. 263 UNDERWOOD 79   1 New yeares, expect new gifts: Sister, your
                              Harpe,
    p. 309 HORACE 2   86 Still in their leaves, throughout the sliding
                              yeares,
    p. 315 HORACE 2   224 And give their yeares, and natures, as they
                              swerve,
    p. 317 HORACE 2   250 Mans comming yeares much good with them doe
                              bring:
    p. 331 HORACE 2   578 Nine yeares kept in, your papers by, yo'are free
    p. 384 UNGATHERED 18   23 And when your yeares rise more, then would be
                              told,

yeares-gift   frequency: 1   relative frequency: 0.00001
    p. 263 UNDERWOOD 79   6 To fit the softnesse of our Yeares-gift: when

yeares-labours   frequency: 1   relative frequency: 0.00001
    p. 202 UNDERWOOD 43   4 So many my Yeares-labours in an houre?

yearly   frequency: 1   relative frequency: 0.00001
    p. 407 UNGATHERED 35   18 yearly set out there, to sayle downe ye Street,

years   frequency: 2   relative frequency: 0.00002
    See also "new-yeares-gift," "new-yeeres,"
             "twice-twelve-yeares," "yeares,"
             "yeares-gift," "yeares-labours,"
             "yeeres."
    p. 150 UNDERWOOD 9   15 Told seven and fortie years,
    p. 416 UNGATHERED 44   7 To Crowne the years, which you begin, great
                              king,

yee   frequency: 4   relative frequency: 0.00005
    p. 86 EPIGRAMS 133   68 Were seene your vgly Centaures, yee call
                              Car-men,
    p. 210 UNDERWOOD 43   173 But say, all sixe good men, what answer yee?
    p. 285 U'WOOD 84.9   105 You once enjoy'd: A short space severs yee,
    p. 285 U'WOOD 84.9   107 That shall re-joyne yee. Was she, then, so
                              deare,

yeeld   frequency: 10   relative frequency: 0.00014
    p. 58 EPIGRAMS 92   5 And haue'hem yeeld no sauour, but of state.
    p. 94 FOREST 2   25 Each banke doth yeeld thee coneyes; and the topps
    p. 133 UNDERWOOD 2.3   7 First, that I must kneeling yeeld
    p. 160 UNDERWOOD 14   61 I yeeld, I yeeld, the matter of your praise
    p. 190 UNDERWOOD 37   15 And Fame wake for me, when I yeeld to sleepe.
    p. 213 UNDERWOOD 44   17 And the returne those thankfull Courtiers yeeld,
    p. 323 HORACE 2   379 Provided, ne're to yeeld, in any case
    p. 329 HORACE 2   521 For, neither doth the String still yeeld that
                              sound
    p. 363 UNGATHERED 3   9 Enforcing yron doores to yeeld it way,

yeelding   frequency: 1   relative frequency: 0.00001
    p. 71 EPIGRAMS 110   5 All yeelding to his fortune, nor, the while,

yeelds   frequency: 1   relative frequency: 0.00001
    p. 103 FOREST 6   13 All the grasse that Rumney yeelds,

yeeld's   frequency: 1   relative frequency: 0.00001
    p. 393 UNGATHERED 27   10 That yeeld's a sent so sweete,

yeere   frequency: 5   relative frequency: 0.00007
    p. 69 EPIGRAMS 107   15 And, in some yeere, all these together heap'd,
    p. 87 EPIGRAMS 133   119 Yet, one day in t e yeere, for sweet 'tis voyc't,

yeere (cont.)
```
      p.  97 FOREST 3        25 Or with thy friends, the heart of all the yeere,
      p.  97 FOREST 3        36 Although the coldest of the yeere!
      p. 113 FOREST 12        7 Well, or ill, onely, all the following yeere,
```

yeeres   frequency: 8 relative frequency: 0.00011
```
      p.  41 EPIGRAMS 45      3 Seuen yeeres tho'wert lent to me, and I thee
                                pay,
      p.  57 EPIGRAMS 90      8 Discern'd no difference of his yeeres, or play,
      p.  59 EPIGRAMS 92     14 For twelue yeeres yet to come, what each state
                                lacks.
      p.  77 EPIGRAMS 120     9 Yeeres he numbred scarse thirteene
      p. 101 FOREST 4        41 My tender, first, and simple yeeres
      p. 120 FOREST 13      121 Liue that one, still; and as long yeeres doe
                                passe,
      p. 120 FOREST 14       21 This day sayes, then, the number of glad yeeres
      p. 391 UNGATHERED 26   27 For, if I thought my iudgement were of yeeres,
```

yeild   frequency: 2 relative frequency: 0.00002
```
      p. 186 UNDERWOOD 33     4 Where mutuall frauds are fought, and no side
                                yeild;
      p. 421 UNGATHERED 48   41 The Rebell Gyantes stoope, and Gorgon Envye
                                yeild,
```

yellow   frequency: 1 relative frequency: 0.00001
```
      p. 335 HORACE 2       646 The yellow Jaundies, or were furious mad
```

yes   frequency: 7 relative frequency: 0.00010
```
      p.  42 EPIGRAMS 46      6 Yes, now he weares his knight-hood euery day.
      p. 101 FOREST 4        37 Yes, threaten, doe. Alas I feare
      p. 149 UNDERWOOD 8      9 Yes; and in death, as life, unblest,
      p. 172 UNDERWOOD 20    15 Knew I this Woman? yes; And you doe see,
      p. 215 UNDERWOOD 44    90 What, to make legs? yes, and to smell most sweet,
      p. 378 UNGATHERED 11   89 Yes thou wert borne out of his trauelling thigh
      p. 380 UNGATHERED 12   43 Yes. And thanks God in his Pistle or his
                                Booke
```

yet   frequency: 210 relative frequency: 0.00304
```
      See also "yett."
    **p. 115 PANEGYRE        70 The Nobles zeale, yet either kept aliue
    **p. 116 PANEGYRE       122 Must with a tender (yet a stedfast) hand
    **p. 117 PANEGYRE       146 Brighter then all, hath yet made no one lesse;
    **p. 117 PANEGYRE       161 Yet, let blest Brit[t]aine aske (without your
                                wrong)
      p.  32 EPIGRAMS 16      6 Some hundred quarrells, yet dost thou fight none;
      p.  32 EPIGRAMS 18      5 And mine come nothing like. I hope so. Yet,
      p.  33 EPIGRAMS 19      1 That COD can get no widdow, yet a knight,
      p.  33 EPIGRAMS 22      3 Yet, all heauens gifts, being heauens due,
      p.  34 EPIGRAMS 23      4 Came forth example, and remaines so, yet:
      p.  34 EPIGRAMS 23      9 All which I meant to praise, and, yet, I would;
      p.  35 EPIGRAMS 28     11 That's greater, yet: to crie his owne vp neate.
      p.  36 EPIGRAMS 30      2 Be thine, I taxe, yet doe not owne my rimes:
      p.  41 EPIGRAMS 43      7 Yet dare not, to my thought, lest hope allow
      p.  41 EPIGRAMS 45      8 And, if no other miserie, yet age?
      p.  43 EPIGRAMS 51      5 Yet giue thy iealous subiects leaue to doubt:
      p.  46 EPIGRAMS 62     12 Of the not borne, yet buried, here's the tombe.
      p.  50 EPIGRAMS 69      2 Yet by thy weapon liu'st! Th'hast one good part.
      p.  51 EPIGRAMS 73      8 That yet maintaynes you, and your house in
                                laughter.
      p.  52 EPIGRAMS 76      6 Of greatest bloud, and yet more good then great;
      p.  54 EPIGRAMS 82      2 He cast, yet keeps her well! No, shee keeps him.
      p.  55 EPIGRAMS 85      8 Which if they misse, they yet should re-aduance
      p.  56 EPIGRAMS 88     10 The french disease, with which he labours yet?
      p.  56 EPIGRAMS 89      4 Yet crown'd with honors, as with riches, then;
      p.  59 EPIGRAMS 92      9 Yet haue they seene the maps, and bought 'hem
                                too,
      p.  59 EPIGRAMS 92     14 For twelue yeeres yet to come, what each state
                                lacks.
      p.  59 EPIGRAMS 92     32 And of the poulder-plot, they will talke yet.
      p.  60 EPIGRAMS 93     13 Thou yet remayn'st, vn-hurt in peace, or warre,
      p.  60 EPIGRAMS 94      7 Yet, Satyres, since the most of mankind bee
      p.  60 EPIGRAMS 94     12 Dare for these poemes, yet, both aske, and read,
      p.  62 EPIGRAMS 97      2 Nor Captayne POD, nor yet the Eltham-thing:
      p.  63 EPIGRAMS 98     11 Though both be good, the latter yet is worst,
      p.  64 EPIGRAMS 101     9 Yet shall you haue, to rectifie your palate,
      p.  65 EPIGRAMS 101    15 And, though fowle, now, be scarce, yet there are
                                clarkes,
      p.  65 EPIGRAMS 101    19 May yet be there; and godwit, if we can:
      p.  66 EPIGRAMS 102     8 To which, yet, of the sides himselfe he owes.
      p.  68 EPIGRAMS 105    18 There IVNO sate, and yet no Peacock by.
```

yet (cont.)

p.	68	EPIGRAMS 106	10	And yet, they, all together, lesse then thee.
p.	69	EPIGRAMS 107	7	And yet are with their Princes: Fill them full
p.	69	EPIGRAMS 107	10	What States yo'haue gull'd, and which yet keepes yo'in pay.
p.	71	EPIGRAMS 110	10	Vn-argued then, and yet hath fame from those;
p.	72	EPIGRAMS 111	9	Yet thou, perhaps, shalt meet some tongues will grutch,
p.	73	EPIGRAMS 112	21	Pr'y thee, yet saue thy rest; giue ore in time:
p.	75	EPIGRAMS 115	32	That seeming prayses, are, yet accusations.
p.	75	EPIGRAMS 116	2	All gentrie, yet, owe part of their best flame!
p.	77	EPIGRAMS 120	11	Yet three fill'd Zodiackes had he beene
p.	78	EPIGRAMS 121	5	Yet is the office not to be despis'd,
p.	81	EPIGRAMS 129	15	O, runne not proud of this. Yet, take thy due.
p.	82	EPIGRAMS 130	15	I, yet, had vtter'd nothing on thy part,
p.	85	EPIGRAMS 133	56	Still, with thy former labours; yet, once more,
p.	87	EPIGRAMS 133	119	Yet, one day in the yeere, for sweet 'tis voyc't,
p.	87	EPIGRAMS 133	133	And that ours did. For, yet, no nare was tainted,
p.	88	EPIGRAMS 133	154	Yet drown'd they not. They had fiue liues in future.
p.	95	FOREST 2	66	At great mens tables) and yet dine away.
p.	96	FOREST 2	89	These, PENSHVRST, are thy praise, and yet not all.
p.	97	FOREST 3	12	There wasted, some not paid for yet!
p.	98	FOREST 3	41	The ripened eares, yet humble in their height,
p.	100	FOREST 4	14	Yet art thou both shrunke vp, and old,
p.	100	FOREST 4	20	Yet art thou falser then thy wares.
p.	100	FOREST 4	21	And, knowing this, should I yet stay,
p.	105	FOREST 8	21	What should, yet, thy pallat please?
p.	107	FOREST 10	4	HERCVLES? alas his bones are yet sore,
p.	111	FOREST 11	75	And yet (in this t<o>'expresse our selues more cleare)
p.	114	FOREST 12	25	Were yet vnfound, and better plac'd in earth,
p.	114	FOREST 12	50	Haue beautie knowne, yet none so famous seene?
p.	115	FOREST 12	55	That HOMER brought to Troy; yet none so liue:
p.	115	FOREST 12	71	Yet, for the timely fauours shee hath done,
p.	115	FOREST 12	81	They hold in my strange poems, which, as yet,
p.	116	FOREST 13	5	So both the prais'd, and praisers suffer: Yet,
p.	117	FOREST 13	16	Of Fortune, haue not alter'd yet my looke,
p.	118	FOREST 13	68	Right, the right way: yet must your comfort bee
p.	119	FOREST 13	106	And greater rites, yet writ in mysterie:
p.	122	FOREST 15	23	Yet dare I not complaine, or wish for death
p.	128	UNDERWOOD 1.1	39	Distinct in persons, yet in Vnitie
p.	129	UNDERWOOD 1.2	26	Yet I rebell,
p.	130	UNDERWOOD 1.3	6	Yet search'd, and true they found it.
p.	137	UNDERWOOD 2.5	49	For this Beauty yet doth hide
p.	138	UNDERWOOD 2.6	29	Or if you would yet have stay'd,
p.	141	UNDERWOOD 2.9	10	Yet a man; with crisped haire
p.	141	UNDERWOOD 2.9	32	In loves schoole, or yet no sinners.
p.	141	UNDERWOOD 2.9	37	Yet no Taylor help to make him;
p.	142	UNDERWOOD 2.9	47	Nor o're-praise, nor yet condemne;
p.	147	UNDERWOOD 7	2	Yet dare I not tell who;
p.	147	UNDERWOOD 7	5	Yet if it be not knowne,
p.	147	UNDERWOOD 7	9	They yet may envie me:
p.	147	UNDERWOOD 7	13	And yet it cannot be forborne,
p.	147	UNDERWOOD 7	20	Yet, yet I doubt he is not knowne,
p.	148	UNDERWOOD 7	29	I'le tell no more, and yet I love,
p.	148	UNDERWOOD 7	30	And he loves me; yet no
p.	150	UNDERWOOD 10	4	Nor have I yet the narrow mind
p.	151	UNDERWOOD 11	6	Whom never yet he durst attempt awake;
p.	151	UNDERWOOD 12	10	Yet he broke them, e're they could him,
p.	152	UNDERWOOD 12	28	It chid the vice, yet not the Men.
p.	153	UNDERWOOD 13	17	Yet choyce from whom I take them; and would shame
p.	157	UNDERWOOD 13	135	Yet we must more then move still, or goe on,
p.	159	UNDERWOOD 14	30	Ever at home: yet, have all Countries seene:
p.	162	UNDERWOOD 15	6	That gaspe for action, and would yet revive
p.	164	UNDERWOOD 15	73	And jealous each of other, yet thinke long
p.	165	UNDERWOOD 15	97	Whom no great Mistresse hath as yet infam'd,
p.	166	UNDERWOOD 15	145	Well, let it goe. Yet this is better, then
p.	167	UNDERWOOD 15	166	The life, and fame-vaynes (yet not understood
p.	169	UNDERWOOD 17	3	And yet the noble Nature never grudge;
p.	172	UNDERWOOD 20	23	But she is such, as she might, yet, forestall
p.	173	UNDERWOOD 22	4	Yet is't your vertue now I raise.
p.	173	UNDERWOOD 22	9	Wherein you triumph yet: because
p.	174	UNDERWOOD 22	35	Yet give me leave t<o>'adore in you
p.	180	UNDERWOOD 26	9	Yet doth some wholsome Physick for the mind,
p.	181	UNDERWOOD 27	2	Thy beauties, yet could write of thee?

yet (cont.)

p.	181 UNDERWOOD 27	4	So speake (as yet it is not mute)
p.	181 UNDERWOOD 27	26	Where never Star shone brighter yet?
p.	182 UNDERWOOD 27	29	Have all these done (and yet I misse
p.	182 UNDERWOOD 27	35	Yet sure my tunes will be the best,
p.	184 UNDERWOOD 29	35	Is not yet free from Rimes wrongs,
p.	189 UNDERWOOD 36	8	Yet he himselfe is but a sparke.
p.	189 UNDERWOOD 36	16	The eldest God, yet still a Child.
p.	190 UNDERWOOD 37	29	Yet if with eithers vice I teynted be,
p.	190 UNDERWOOD 37	33	Her furie, yet no friendship to betray.
p.	191 UNDERWOOD 38	9	Offended Mistris, you are yet so faire,
p.	191 UNDERWOOD 38	17	Spare your owne goodnesse yet; and be not great
p.	192 UNDERWOOD 38	38	Your just commands; yet those, not I, be lost.
p.	197 UNDERWOOD 40	19	Yet should the Lover still be ayrie and light,
p.	198 UNDERWOOD 40	26	Moves like a sprightly River, and yet can
p.	199 UNDERWOOD 42	3	No Poets verses yet did ever move,
p.	200 UNDERWOOD 42	25	Yet keepe those up in sackcloth too, or lether,
p.	204 UNDERWOOD 43	49	Thou mightst have yet enjoy'd thy crueltie
p.	208 UNDERWOOD 43	118	Some Alchimist there may be yet, or odde
p.	208 UNDERWOOD 43	123	Well fare the wise-men yet, on the Banckside,
p.	211 UNDERWOOD 43	189	I could invent a sentence, yet were worse;
p.	211 UNDERWOOD 43	196	Losse, remaines yet, as unrepair'd as mine.
p.	213 UNDERWOOD 44	1	Why yet, my noble hearts, they cannot say,
p.	213 UNDERWOOD 44	11	All Ensignes of a Warre, are not yet dead,
p.	214 UNDERWOOD 44	56	Alive yet, in the noise; and still the same;
p.	216 UNDERWOOD 45	7	Nor ever trusted to that friendship yet,
p.	218 UNDERWOOD 47	14	That never yet did friend, or friendship seeke
p.	219 UNDERWOOD 47	35	Whether the Dispensation yet be sent,
p.	219 UNDERWOOD 47	41	I have a body, yet, that spirit drawes
p.	223 UNDERWOOD 49	36	From Court, while yet thy fame hath some small day;
p.	224 UNDERWOOD 50	15	Are in your selfe rewarded; yet 'twill be
p.	227 UNDERWOOD 52	6	But yet the Tun at Heidelberg had houpes.
p.	227 UNDERWOOD 52	22	Yet when of friendship I would draw the face,
p.	228 UNDERWOOD 53	15	For never saw I yet the Muses dwell,
p.	230 UNDERWOOD 55	7	Yet with a Dye, that feares no Moth,
p.	234 UNDERWOOD 61	7	Yet are got off thence, with cleare mind, and hands
p.	235 UNDERWOOD 62	5	But thou wilt yet a Kinglier mastrie trie,
p.	238 UNDERWOOD 66	4	(Without prophanenesse) yet, a Poet, cry,
p.	239 UNDERWOOD 67	13	3. THAL. Yet, let our Trumpets sound;
p.	242 UNDERWOOD 69	23	Then knew the former ages: yet to life,
p.	247 UNDERWOOD 70	121	Was left yet to Man-kind;
p.	257 UNDERWOOD 75	161	Yet, as we may, we will, with chast desires,
p.	258 UNDERWOOD 75	187	Hee's Master of the Office; yet no more
p.	262 UNDERWOOD 78	2	Yet read him in these lines: He doth excell
p.	264 UNDERWOOD 79	33	Of all that Nature, yet, to life did bring;
p.	270 UNDERWOOD 83	44	A dazling, yet inviting, Majestie:
p.	273 U'WOOD 84.1	25	Yet, here are no such Trifles brought,
p.	275 U'WOOD 84.3	9	Yet something, to the Painters view,
p.	276 U'WOOD 84.3	20	May rather yet adore, then spy.
p.	278 U'WOOD 84.4	20	And yet remaine our wonder still.
p.	279 U'WOOD 84.4	42	So swift, so pure, should yet apply
p.	281 U'WOOD 84.4	70	Yet know, with what thou art possest,
p.	282 U'WOOD 84.9	9	Nothing, that could remaine, or yet can stirre
p.	286 U'WOOD 84.9	143	Yet have all debts forgiven us, and advance
p.	294 UNDERWOOD 87	24	Yet would I wish to love, live, die with thee.
p.	295 UNDERWOOD 90	10	No sowre, or sollen bed-mate, yet a Chast;
p.	305 HORACE 2	14	Yet, not as therefore wild, and tame should cleave
p.	307 HORACE 2	69	Yet, if by chance, in utt'ring things abstruse,
p.	309 HORACE 2	111	All the Grammarians strive; and yet in Court
p.	311 HORACE 2	132	Yet, sometime, doth the Comedie excite
p.	313 HORACE 2	163	Or some hot youth, yet in his flourishing course;
p.	313 HORACE 2	178	If something strange, that never yet was had
p.	313 HORACE 2	187	Yet common matter thou thine owne maist make.
p.	317 HORACE 2	246	With sloth, yet greedy still of what's to come:
p.	317 HORACE 2	260	Yet, to the Stage, at all thou maist not tender
p.	319 HORACE 2	291	As loud enough to fill the seates, not yet
p.	321 HORACE 2	328	Yet so the scoffing Satyres to mens view,
p.	321 HORACE 2	351	Yet he that offers at it, may sweat much,
p.	323 HORACE 2	373	Of Trimeter, when yet it was sixe-pac'd,
p.	323 HORACE 2	381	This foot yet, in the famous Trimeters
p.	325 HORACE 2	435	I, writing nought my selfe, will teach them yet
p.	329 HORACE 2	520	There are yet faults, which we would well forgive,
p.	331 HORACE 2	547	And, of your selfe too, understand; yet mind
p.	331 HORACE 2	554	Yet, there's a value given to this man.
p.	331 HORACE 2	570	Yet who's most ignorant, dares Verses make.
p.	331 HORACE 2	580	The Writ, once out, never returned yet.

yet (cont.)
    p. 335 HORACE 2   668 Recall him yet, hee'ld be no more a man:
    p. 339 HORACE 1   50 Yet .. ..
    p. 341 HORACE 1   126 .. .. yet to ....
    p. 341 HORACE 1   127 Yet .... shunnes to .. ..
    p. 355 HORACE 1   667 ... ... yet ... ...
    p. 365 UNGATHERED 5   23 Yet shee's nor nice to shew them,
    p. 369 UNGATHERED 6   93 Yet, looking in thy face, they shall begin
    p. 379 UNGATHERED 12   6 Yet who could haue hit on't but the wise noddell
    p. 383 UNGATHERED 17   6 Yet may as blind men sometimes hit the marke.
    p. 384 UNGATHERED 18   24 Yet neyther of you seeme to th'other old.
    p. 385 UNGATHERED 19   5 To such a worke, as could not need theirs? Yet
    p. 385 UNGATHERED 20   5 I do not feele that euer yet I had
    p. 386 UNGATHERED 21   7 It must be thine owne iudgment, yet, that sends
    p. 387 UNGATHERED 22   9 nor yet inscription like it. Write but that;
    p. 392 UNGATHERED 26   55 Yet must I not giue Nature all: Thy Art,
    p. 392 UNGATHERED 26   72 To see thee in our waters yet appeare,
    p. 394 UNGATHERED 28   14 Not vsuall in a Lady; and yet true:
    p. 397 UNGATHERED 30   57 That euer yet did fire the English blood!
    p. 398 UNGATHERED 30   83 Yet giue mee leaue, to wonder at the birth
    p. 401 UNGATHERED 32   11 Yet, who dares offer a redoubt to reare?
    p. 402 UNGATHERED 34   14 Something your Surship doth not yet intend!
    p. 402 UNGATHERED 34   17 I doe salute you! Are you fitted yet?
    p. 408 UNGATHERED 37   2 And they were very good: yet thou think'st nay.
    p. 413 UNGATHERED 41   35 Of Persons, yet in Vnion (ONE) divine.
    p. 414 UNGATHERED 42   8 That sit to censure Playes, yet know not when,
    p. 417 UNGATHERED 45   32 yet doe not feare it.
    p. 423 UNGATHERED 50   15 Yet ware; thou mayst do all things cruellie:

yett   frequency: 2   relative frequency: 0.00002
    p. 420 UNGATHERED 48   28 Yett: since the bright, and wyse,
    p. 421 UNGATHERED 49   10 deignes myne the power to ffinde, yett want I
                         will

yew. See "yewgh."

yewgh   frequency: 1   relative frequency: 0.00001
    p. 268 UNDERWOOD 83   2 Hayles me, so solemnly, to yonder Yewgh?

yf   frequency: 2   relative frequency: 0.00002

yff   frequency: 1   relative frequency: 0.00001

yield. See "yeeld," "yeild."

yielding. See "yeelding."

yields. See "yeelds," "yeeld's."

ymounted   frequency: 1   relative frequency: 0.00001
    p. 412 UNGATHERED 41   10 Ymounted high upon Selinis crest:

ynow   frequency: 1   relative frequency: 0.00001
    p. 104 FOREST 8   3 Doe not men, ynow of rites

yo'are   frequency: 5   relative frequency: 0.00007

yo'had   frequency: 1   relative frequency: 0.00001

yo'haue   frequency: 2   relative frequency: 0.00002

yo'have   frequency: 1   relative frequency: 0.00001

yo'in   frequency: 1   relative frequency: 0.00001

yoke   frequency: 1   relative frequency: 0.00001
    p. 294 UNDERWOOD 87   18 And us dis-joyn'd force to her brazen yoke,

yond'   frequency: 1   relative frequency: 0.00001
    p. 62 EPIGRAMS 97   1 See you yond' Motion? Not the old Fa-ding,

yonder   frequency: 1   relative frequency: 0.00001
    See also "yond'."
    p. 268 UNDERWOOD 83   2 Hayles me, so solemnly, to yonder Yewgh?

yong   frequency: 3   relative frequency: 0.00004
    p. 69 EPIGRAMS 107   19 Giue your yong States-men, (that first make you
                         drunke,
    p. 78 EPIGRAMS 122   5 If I would vertue set, as shee was yong,
    p. 119 FOREST 13   89 You, Madame, yong haue learn'd to shunne these
                         shelues,

```
yor                               frequency:     8   relative frequency: 0.00011

you                               frequency:   413   relative frequency: 0.00597
     See alsc "do'you," "ye," "yee," "yo'are,"
               "yo'had," "yo'haue," "yo'have,"
               "yo'in," "ycu>," "you'haue," "you'l,"
               "you'ld," "you'll."

you>                              frequency:     1   relative frequency: 0.00001
     p. 334 UNGATHERED 18  21 So, in theyr number, may <you> neuer see

you'haue                          frequency:     1   relative frequency: 0.00001

you'l                             frequency:     1   relative frequency: 0.00001

you'ld                            frequency:     1   relative frequency: 0.00001

you'll                            frequency:     1   relative frequency: 0.00001

young                             frequency:    11   relative frequency: 0.00015
     See alsc "yong."
     p. 131 UNDERWOOD 2.1   20 She shall make the old man young,
     p. 141 UNDERWOOD 2.9    9 Young I'ld have him to<o>, and faire,
     p. 142 U'WOOD 2.10      5 Himselfe young, and face be good,
     p. 164 UNDERWOOD 15    79 For these with her young Companie shee'll enter,
     p. 213 UNDERWOOD 44    20 Under the Auspice of young Swynnerton.
     p. 233 UNDERWOOD 60     3 Henry, the brave young Lord La-ware,
     p. 244 UNDERWOOD 70    43 Alas, but Morison fell young:
     p. 292 UNDERWOOD 86    13 For he's both noble, lovely, young,
     p. 317 HORACE 2       248 Of the times past, when he was a young lad;
     p. 333 HORACE 2       589 While he was young; he sweat; and freez'd againe:
     p. 347 HORACE 1       350 Or play young ...... .. ............. .....

younger                           frequency:     1   relative frequency: 0.00001
     p. 221 UNDERWOOD 48    21 So mayst thou still be younger

youngest                          frequency:     2   relative frequency: 0.00002
     p. 149 UNDERWOOD 9      9 As hath the youngest Hee,
     p. 200 UNDERWOOD 42     6 As light, and active as the youngest hee

your                              frequency:   323   relative frequency: 0.00467
     See alsc "y>our," "yor."

yours                             frequency:    11   relative frequency: 0.00015

youth                             frequency:    16   relative frequency: 0.00023
     p.  33 EPIGRAMS 22      2 MARY, the daughter of their youth:
     p.  48 EPIGRAMS 65      6 And, as thou'hast mine, his houres, and youth
                               abuse.
     p.  57 EPIGRAMS 90     10 And he growne youth, was call'd to his ladies
                               chamber.
     p. 131 UNDERWOOD 2.1    9 Or the feature, or the youth:
     p. 171 UNDERWOOD 19    20 I know no beautie, nor no youth that will.
     p. 181 UNDERWOOD 26    24 Even in youth.
     p. 213 UNDERWOOD 44    25 Powder, or paper, to bring up the youth
     p. 253 UNDERWOOD 75    26 The Month of youth, which calls all Creatures
                               forth
     p. 254 UNDERWOOD 75    72 With all the pompe of Youth, and all our Court
                               beside.
     p. 276 U'WOOD 84.3     22 With all that Youth, or it can bring:
     p. 293 UNDERWOOD 87     2 And ('bout thy Ivory neck,) no youth did fling
     p. 313 HORACE 2       163 Or some hot youth, yet in his flourishing course;
     p. 315 HORACE 2       229 Th'unbearded Youth, his Guardian once being
                               gone,
     p. 317 HORACE 2       249 And still correcting youth, and censuring.
     p. 317 HORACE 2       252 The parts of age to youth be given; or men
     p. 398 UNGATHERED 30   69 So shall our English Youth vrge on, and cry

youthfull                         frequency:     1   relative frequency: 0.00001
     p. 321 HORACE 2       358 Their youthfull tricks in over-wanton verse:

youths                            frequency:     6   relative frequency: 0.00008
     p. 103 FOREST 6        18 When youths ply their stolne delights.
     p. 253 UNDERWOOD 75    17 What Beavie of beauties, and bright youths at
                               charge
     p. 281 U'WOOD 84.8     11 (Brave Youths) th<ey>'are their possessions,
                               none of yours:
     p. 292 UNDERWOOD 86     8 Goe where Youths soft intreaties call thee back.
     p. 292 UNDERWOOD 86    26 The Youths and tender Maids shall sing thy
                               praise:
```

youths (cont.)
    p. 327 HORACE 2   464 Our Roman Youths they learne the subtle wayes

yron   frequency: 2   relative frequency: 0.00002
  **p. 113 PANEGYRE   13 Carowsing humane bloud in yron bowles,
    p. 363 UNGATHERED 3   9 Enforcing yron doores to yeeld it way,

yt   frequency: 10   relative frequency: 0.00014
    p. 108 FOREST 10A   1 An elegie? no, muse; yt askes a straine
    p. 108 FOREST 10A   15 the glories of yt ... or muse ....
    p. 384 UNGATHERED 18 12 Out-bee yt Wife, in worth, thy freind did make:
    p. 384 UNGATHERED 18 25 That all, yt view you then, and late; may say,
    p. 402 UNGATHERED 34   1 Mr Surueyr, you yt first begann
    p. 404 UNGATHERED 34 46 Eyes yt can pierce into ye Misteryes
    p. 405 UNGATHERED 34 75 What would he doe now, gi'ng his mynde yt waye
    p. 407 UNGATHERED 36   2 (And labours to seem worthy of yt feare)
    p. 408 UNGATHERED 36 10 Seek out some hungry painter, yt for bread
    p. 419 UNGATHERED 48   5 By Cherissheinge the Spirrites yt gaue their
                             greatnesse grace:

zany. See "out-zany."

zeal. See "zeale."

zeale   frequency: 7   relative frequency: 0.00010
   *p. 494 TO HIMSELF   53 His zeale to God, and his iust awe o're men;
  **p. 115 PANEGYRE   70 The Nobles zeale, yet either kept aliue
    p. 95 FOREST 2   81 With all their zeale, to warme their welcome
                             here.
    p. 119 FOREST 13   108 Onely, thus much, out of a rauish'd zeale,
    p. 128 UNDERWOOD 1.1 27 Pure thoughts in man: with fiery zeale them
                             feeding
    p. 155 UNDERWOOD 13   85 And it is paid 'hem with a trembling zeale,
    p. 382 UNGATHERED 16   1 Two noble knightes, whome true desire and zeale,

zeales   frequency: 1   relative frequency: 0.00001
  **p. 114 PANEGYRE   39 Vnto their zeales expression; they are mute:

zealous   frequency: 2   relative frequency: 0.00002
    p. 52 EPIGRAMS 76   2 I thought to forme vnto my zealous Muse,
    p. 375 UNGATHERED 10 22 And there, while he giues the zealous Brauado,

zeal's. See "zeales."

zephyr's   frequency: 1   relative frequency: 0.00001
    p. 366 UNGATHERED 6   24 From Zephyr's rape would close him with his
                             beames.

zodiackes   frequency: 1   relative frequency: 0.00001
    p. 77 EPIGRAMS 120   11 Yet three fill'd Zodiackes had he beene

zodiacs. See "zodiackes."

1   frequency: 6
    p. 127 UNDERWOOD 1.1   1 1. O holy, blessed, glorious Trinitie
    p. 239 UNDERWOOD 67   1 1. CLIO. Up publike joy, remember
    p. 264 UNDERWOOD 79   14 1. PAN is the great Preserver of our bounds.
    p. 264 UNDERWOOD 79   36 1. Where ere they tread th'enamour'd ground,
    p. 264 UNDERWOOD 79   40 1. Hee is the Father of our peace;
    p. 265 UNDERWOOD 79   42 1. Wee know no other power then his,

2   frequency: 5
    p. 127 UNDERWOOD 1.1   5 2. My selfe up to thee, harrow'd, torne, and
                             bruis'd
    p. 239 UNDERWOOD 67   7 2. MEL. What, though the thriftie Tower
    p. 264 UNDERWOOD 79   15 2. To him we owe all profits of our grounds.
    p. 264 UNDERWOOD 79   38 2. As if the beauties of the yeare,
    p. 264 UNDERWOOD 79   41 2. Shee, to the Crowne, hath brought encrease.

3   frequency: 4
    p. 127 UNDERWOOD 1.1   9 3. All-gracious God, the Sinners sacrifice,
    p. 239 UNDERWOOD 67   13 3. THAL. Yet, let our Trumpets sound;
    p. 264 UNDERWOOD 79   16 3. Our milke. 4. Our fells. 5. Our fleeces. 6.
                             And first Lambs.
    p. 293 UNDERWOOD 87   t1 Ode IX. 3 Booke, to Lydia.

4   frequency: 3
    p. 127 UNDERWOOD 1.1   13 4. For thy acceptance. O, behold me right,
    p. 239 UNDERWOOD 67   19 4. EVT. That when the Quire is full,
    p. 264 UNDERWOOD 79   16 3. Our milke. 4. Our fells. 5. Our fleeces. 6.
                             And first Lambs.

5   frequency: 3
    p. 127 UNDERWOOD 1.1   17 5. Eternall Father, God, who did'st create
    p. 240 UNDERWOOD 67   25 5. TERP. Behold the royall Mary,
    p. 264 UNDERWOOD 79   16 3. Our milke. 4. Our fells. 5. Our fleeces. 6.
                             And first Lambs.

6   frequency: 3
    p. 128 UNDERWOOD 1.1   21 6. Eternall God the Sonne, who not denyd'st
    p. 240 UNDERWOOD 67   31 6. ERAT. Shee showes so farre above
    p. 264 UNDERWOOD 79   16 3. Our milke. 4. Our fells. 5. Our fleeces. 6.
                             And first Lambs.

7   frequency: 3
    p. 128 UNDERWOOD 1.1   25 7. Eternall Spirit, God from both proceeding,
    p. 240 UNDERWOOD 67   37 7. CALLI. See, see our active King
    p. 264 UNDERWOOD 79   17 7. Our teeming Ewes, 8. and lustie-mounting
                             Rammes.

8   frequency: 3
    p. 128 UNDERWOOD 1.1   29 8. Increase those acts, o glorious Trinitie
    p. 240 UNDERWOOD 67   43 8. URA. This day the Court doth measure
    p. 264 UNDERWOOD 79   17 7. Our teeming Ewes, 8. and lustie-mounting
                             Rammes.

9   frequency: 3
See also "ix" (which follows).
    p. 128 UNDERWOOD 1.1   33 9. Beholding one in three, and three in one,
    p. 240 UNDERWOOD 67   49 9. POLY. Sweet happy Mary All
    p. 264 UNDERWOOD 79   18 9. See where he walkes <10> with MIRA by his side.

ix   frequency: 1
    p. 293 UNDERWOOD 87   t1 Cde IX. 3 Booke, to Lydia.

10   frequency: 1
See also "10>."
    p. 128 UNDERWOOD 1.1   37 10. Father, and Sonne, and Holy Ghost, you three

10>   frequency: 1
    p. 264 UNDERWOOD 79   18 9. See where he walkes <10> with MIRA by his side.

11   frequency: 1
    p. 128 UNDERWOOD 1.1   41 11. My Maker, Saviour, and my Sanctifier:

12   frequency: 1
    p. 128 UNDERWOOD 1.1   45 12. Among thy Saints elected to abide,

19   frequency: 1
  **p. 112 PANEGYRE   t9 in this his Kingdome, the 19. of

100   frequency: 1
    p. 235 UNDERWOOD 62   t3 for a 100. pounds he sent me in my sicknesse.

1603   frequency: 1
  **p. 112 PANEGYRE   t10 March, 1603.

1607   frequency: 1
    p. 43 EPIGRAMS 51   t4 1607.

1635   frequency: 1
    p. 263 UNDERWOOD 79   8++ CHARLES, 1635.

Tokens (number of words, numerals omitted): 69078

Types (number of different words, numerals omitted): 9804

Words in order of frequency:

2787 the	394 their	199 me would	127 those
2674 and	377 thou	196 our	126 hath
1832 to	364 her	194 doth	124 though
1554 of	344 they	193 were	123 haue
1116 a	338 this	184 one	122 could them
1059 that	323 your	183 there	120 shall
996 in	311 what	180 him	118 out
750 i	305 on	177 such	117 she
739 or	301 by	176 did make may	115 too
668 but	288 no will	163	106 day
663 his	267 are	have	104 let
608 as	263 which	162 had	100 both
572 with	260 if	159 an	99 love
569 all	259 at	157 great	97 made much
567 not	253 when	149 how these	96 here must
547 it	246 more	148 where	94 first
523 thy	230 doe	146 still	93 life
478 for	from	143 should	90 name
477 so	229 thee	138 some	89 owne
469 be	218 was	137 men	88 selfe whose
468 is	210 yet	136 good we	87 true
447 he	209 can	134 like	86 take
420 my	206 nor	131 man	85 well
413 you	202 now	128 know see	
404 then	201 who		

83
art

81
most
shee

74
forth

72
'tis

71
light

70
fame
god
say

69
muse

68
come
o

67
old

66
other
thinke

65
any

64
new

63
state
whom

62
each
faire
hee

61
thought
time

60
am

59
grace
loue
same
wit

58
up

57
bee
best
eyes
till
upon

56
being
friend
makes
might

55
hast

54
looke

53
better
goe
lesse
once

52
king
since
sweet

51
lord
many
tell

50
long
praise
vertue
world

49
done

48
before
euery
feare
none
place

47
call
free
into
why
ye

46
face
last
sir
us
vp

45
keepe
things
vpon
way

44
booke
nature
right
speake
thine
truth
two
worke

43
court
mind

42
every
hand
heare
vnto

41
age
cause
verse

40
againe
fit
sing
times

39
fire
noble
poore
unto
whole

38
cannot
friends
thus
without
write

37
high
nothing
read
rest
wish

36
ever
giue
glad
never
saw
while

35
bright
downe
give
mine
onely
only
put
vs
worth

34
crowne
fate
stay

33
away
draw
farre
sight
soule
stand

32
about
alone
bring
death
dost
find
fortune
himselfe
lady
mee
set
song
sonne
wise

31
beene
brought
dare
either
full
hope
part
rather

30
arts
ayre
blood
ill
knowne
late
meet
poets
seene
vice
wife

29
&
after
against
body
earth
else
'hem
honour
least
lost
muses
night
poet
sense
worthy

28
land
others
peace
want

27
beautie
just
leave
left
names
soft
through

26
aske
borne
came
end
fall
false
found
gone
got
heart
manners
sinne

25
power
wine

24
because
canst
dead
epigram
forme
graces

knowes
lawes
little
sound
that's
thing
whether
wonder
wth

23
care
father
get
loves
nay
need
neither
parts
play
rise
store
sure
verses
words

22
beare
chance
enough
ere
e're
eye
home
liue
mens
rich
show
soone
stage
thence
turne

21
brave
cast
charles
desire
follow
friendship
happy
head
kept
owe
pay
sent
shine
view

20
act
another
birth
breath
call'd
feast
heard
hold
holy
kings
knew
leaue
live
neuer
round
run
spirit
takes
wayes
wee

wert
whilst
word
yeare

19
become
braine
dayes
die
grow
next
off
powers
race
rites
safe
said
send
short
three
use
went

18
bookes
change
conscience
cry
euer
faith
force
gold
growne
heaven
horse
kisse
mans
matter
meant
proud
pure
sake
sleepe
spring
vaine
voyce
warre

17
boast
child
cleare
do
doubt
durst
fathers
grave
halfe
heauen
helpe
iust
lay
line
neere
oft
reade
seeke
strength
strife
therefore
tooke
weare
wherein

16
actions
acts
armes
backe

common
delight
dull
example
gaine
graue
hee's
hence
joy
language
large
learned
marke
past
perfect
pray
pride
prince
proue
raise
scarce
scorne
shame
shew
side
sit
teach
there's
thoughts
trust
wrought
yeares
youth

15
blest
drawne
eare
eares
ends
even
fashion
few
given
greater
ground
hearts
judge
lest
lookes
losse
master
meere
met
ne're
please
rare
returne
spight
sword
't
tree
wealth
weight

14
above
author
bold
braue
breake
close
comes
dares
disease
euen
fates
feares
feele
flesh

flowers
fooles
fresh
'gainst
hit
issue
iudge
lent
lie
loose
merit
mother
nought
number
ode
passe
person
piece
present
sad
skill
stone
strike
sung
title
told
towne
tread
'twas
vse

13
behold
bow
command
comming
confesse
darke
deeds
divine
earle
epistle
flame
flie
gifts
glorie
greatnesse
grew
height
honest
houres
iudgement
lines
lov'd
meane
money
pleasure
posteritie
practise
queene
quite
soules
spent
spirits
studie
sun
touch
valour
vertuous
whore
writ
wrong

12
although
among
bad
blessed
bought
bred

burne	lust	publike	restore
censure	mistris	reason	rime
charge	natures	ring	sacrifice
circle	ought	ripe	solemne
course	ours	roe	spend
cure	paine	runne	starre
cut	paper	saue	stood
deare	payes	sister	storie
dwell	pen	strange	sweare
dye	people	subject	swift
english	picture	taken	taste
envie	reader	ten	tom
equall	reward	tender	vertues
faine	sayes	under	vulcan
field	second	weake	would'st
flight	something	whence	
foole	spare	white	**8**
glory	sport	wild	aboue
goes	stile	wisdome	affection
haire	straine	wits	applause
i'le	streight	worse	authors
knowledge	strong	wouldst	banke
law	taught	yeeld	blow
madame	teares	yt	bound
making	than		'bout
mary	titles		'bove
move	together	**9**	brings
mr.	venus	adde	built
noblest	what's	angels	businesse
office	whil'st	angry	cunning
paire	william	beares	curious
pan	wilt	beast	dar'st
playes	wonne	begin	doo
rage	worst	brest	drest
rais'd	young	calls	eate
rimes	yours	charme	england
sea		credit	enuie
seas	**10**	crown'd	except
seeme	abuse	cryes	fault
shade	action	designe	feasts
small	alas	didst	fight
soe	alive	drinke	foes
states	apply	enuy	foot
talke	back	faces	fruitfull
tongue	beauties	finde	giles
very	bed	fled	glories
within	bid	flow	gowne
witnesse	braines	formes	greene
	chast	foule	hall
11	cold	frame	hang
almost	creature	france	hard
alwayes	crimes	genius	hate
appeare	dame	gift	heads
ben	epitaph	greeke	heat
betray	fat	guest	here's
betweene	fell	having	honours
bloud	fill	houre	hopes
clothes	fine	house	hot
countrey	gladnesse	hurt	inigo
cry'd	haste	ile	ione
daughter	health	item	ioyes
deed	hell	judgement	justice
due	husband	keepes	labours
ease	iames	laugh	learn'd
elegie	increase	laughter	lend
eternall	indeed	lead	liues
french	kind	lords	loud
gaue	laid	loues	lover
gave	letters	mak'st	maist
gentle	longer	merry	man-kind
glasse	lye	minde	match
gloricus	minds	notes	mirth
goodnesse	nam'd	numbers	'mongst
hands	needs	open	mothers
happie	newes	painter	motion
horace	note	parents	moue
hundred	order	pietie	noise
ignorance	painted	pleas'd	nose
iohn	pound	prais'd	noyse
lives	praises	price	offence
		princes	

oh
ones
o're
paint
pardon
passion
places
pleasures
prime
proper
puts
quit
report
roome
rose
sacred
safetie
satyres
search
sicknesse
smooth
sorrow
starres
sunne
sydney
table
themselves
thomas
throughout
trade
twice
understand
vile
vulgar
weston
win
withall
women
wound
wretched
yeeres
yor

7

affections
along
ambitious
apollo
aspire
band
base
beleeue
birth-day
black
blesse
blind
blush
bones
boy
bride
cares
chang'd
chiefe
cloud
commit
danger
did'st
digby
diseases
dressing
early
eat
eloquence
envious
epigrammes
evill
fable
farewell
feature
feed

flies
former
freedome
furie
gate
gives
gods
golden
griefe
guilt
hadst
hauing
hir
homer
honor
humanitie
husbands
i'
immortall
is't
kill
knight
knowing
labour
lace
ladies
learne
licence
lights
list
liv'd
look'd
lose
low
lvcy
lyes
lyre
meale
measure
memorie
moone
mysterie
narrow
noe
often
ouer
passage
peeres
perhaps
phrase
play-wright
rate
renowne
repent
ride
robert
rome
royall
ruine
's
salute
save
scarse
servant
serue
seuerall
shed
should'st
shut
sits
slow
sought
spaine
speech
spie
standing
stands
steepe
stil'd
stirre

storme
striue
sway
sweat
tane
t'have
thinkes
tongues
treasure
triumph
tune
'twere
understood
valiant
vnderstand
vowes
wall
walls
warme
warres
wast
water
wherewith
whither
woman
wood
woods
worlds
yes
zeale

6

abroad
afraid
aide
aire
amongst
ample
asham'd
bedford
behind
belly
beneath
beside
blacke
bounds
bread
carry
cary
catch
choice
citie
cleere
cod
colours
comfort
commend
companie
content
covntesse
crime
darknesse
daughters
decay
deepe
defend
delights
destroy
difference
discourse
diuine
dreame
dust
eccho
encrease
ev'ry
excuse
expect
faithfull
fames

famous
farther
faults
feathers
fed
fill'd
fits
floods
flower
forgive
fruit
fruits
gentler
go
going
grand
grant
gratulate
grounds
harpe
holy-day
honors
honour'd
humble
ignorant
innocence
ioy
keeping
knit
leape
lies
lighter
looking
lovely
maine
majestie
malice
marble
markes
masters
meate
mill
modestie
morning
mysteries
naked
nations
offer
paines
pallas
peece
perfection
phoenix
plant
poemes
poems
poetrie
pompe
priuate
profit
promise
prove
rack
rapt
refuse
religion
remaine
richer
rivers
roman
row
rude
season
sees
shadow
shake
sheues
shift
showes
showne

silent	center	lesser	silence
simple	chaine	libertie	sin
sinnes	character	lips	sixe
sometimes	charis	london	skie
sonnes	chaste	lou'd	sloth
sports	children	lovers	softer
spread	chor.	lowd	sold
story	church	lute	songs
subiect	cloth	lyne	sooner
summe	coast	mad	sparke
sup	countries	mad'st	speaking
tales	cradle	maid	spheare
thankes	create	maker	spouse
the<ir>	crie	mankind	spun
theirs	crosse	manly	stall
therein	cup	mark'd	stealth
therecf	daily	mars	stolne
thousand	degree	masse	stones
thrice	describ'd	meanes	stop
timely	desires	mend	straight
touch'd	dice	midst	street
treasurer	dine	mighty	subtle
truly	dogs	milke	sute
try	doing	miseries	swan
tunes	donne	misse	sweete
urge	do's	mixt	sweetest
view'd	do'st	mrs.	swim
virgin	drawes	musique	ta'en
walke	drowne	neck	taking
walkes	dying	nights	tame
waste	edward	obiect	tells
watch	enuious	odour	thanke
waters	erre	offend	th'are
weepe	expresse	over	themselues
welcome	fact	oyle	thinking
wing	faile	paid	think'st
wings	fast	pale	third
wombe	favour	palme	thither
wroth	feet	pause	th'other
yea	felt	persons	thrive
youths	five	phoebvs	tombe
	flames	pieces	torne
5	fleet	plac'd	townes
advance	flood	poeme	tragedie
alike	flye	point	trie
aloud	folke	prize	trinitie
alter	folly	professe	truely
ancestors	forbeare	publique	trumpet
architect	form'd	publish	trusted
ask'd	fortunes	purse	turn'd
authoritie	freind	quarrell	turning
bacchus	friendships	quickly	'twill
bankes	fury	raigne	value
barre	gain'd	ran	velvet
barren	garland	reach	vices
baud	gather'd	readers	virgil
bayes	generall	reades	wake
bearing	gets	religious	wanton
becomes	giues	require	wants
beginnings	greatest	rings	wealthy
beheld	groome	riuer	weav'd
bend	growes	rough	weigh'd
besides	guests	saint	wherecf
bin	gviltie	saints	wind
bird	has	scant	wishes
blinde	heape	scap'd	wives
blowne	heire	scape	won
bosome	henry	scene	workes
bountie	hide	schoole	writing
brasse	higher	searching	wrongs
brests	houshold	seem'd	wrote
broke	i'm	senses	yeere
broken	instruct	sentence	yo'are
burst	intelligence	serious	
calme	jealcus	sexe	4
captayne	k.	shakespeare	able
case	kinde	shalt	absence
'cause	knot	sharpe	active
causes	l.	shoot	admire
celia	labour'd	shore	adore

agen	dames	hers	prophane
ale	dance	historie	proportion
aliue	dangers	horrour	prose
allow	deale	horses	provoke
allow'd	debt	hunting	punishment
ambition	debts	infants	pursue
anacreon	defence	it's	question
ancient	degrees	iustice	quire
anger	delay	iustly	ranke
anothers	descent	james	ready
apollo's	desir'd	keep	reare
arm'd	dew	keeps	receiv'd
arthur	discerning	knots	receive
askes	dore	lack	reherse
awake	doubtfull	laden	resound
ayme	drives	ladie	restor'd
bare	drop	ladyes	rests
beauty	drums	lake	returnes
became	drunke	lawyer	reueale
began	dumbe	length	reuerend
begot	dy'd	lillie	reverence
beleeve	dyes	liu'd	reverend
bids	elder	liuing	riches
blaze	elizabeth	living	roses
blessing	embrace	loftie	rosie
blot	emptie	lydia	rout
boates	emulate	m.	ruines
bodies	enioy	madam	runs
boote	enjoy	madde	sadnesse
borrow'd	error	manner	saviour
bounties	eternitie	mariage	seat
bowers	europe	martial	secrets
boyes	excell	meete	securitie
breed	exercise	meets	selden
brethren	expence	mistresse	selfe-same
brother	faction	mixe	sell
build	facultie	modest	selves
burges	fain'd	morne	sence
buried	fairest	mouthes	sets
burnt	falling	mov'd	sex
buy	falshood	murder	shafts
buyes	farmer	murmure	sheepe
caesar	fayre	mute	ships
calling	feete	nation	sides
captaine	fields	necessitie	signe
carelesse	fierce	nectar	silke
carried	figure	nest	silkes
chaire	finer	nigh	simplicitie
chamber	fires	nurse	single
chime	fitter	nymph	sinke
chin	fiue	oath	slight
choise	fix'd	offended	smiles
choose	flee	offices	smiling
chosen	floud	offring	snow
chuse	flowes	oft-times	sober
circles	flying	ore	sort
civill	forget	originall	sower
claime	fort	o'the	sowre
clownes	foure	outward	spheares
colour	fourth	page	spies
comick	fowle	parliament	spite
commands	freely	paths	springs
commission	frequent	peeces	stand'st
commoditie	game	penshvrst	statue
comparison	gather	peoples	stay'd
conceale	gentrie	phoebus	stayes
conceipt	ghost	pious	stead
conceive	giuen	pittie	steps
conclude	gray	pitty	stiffe
consent	grieve	plaid	stinke
coryate	growing	planted	stoole
couetous	guiltie	poesie	straines
counter-turne	haile	possesse	streames
courts	harmony	possest	studied
covrtling	hat	pox	stuffe
cruell	hazard	praisers	stuffes
cupids	heate	prest	subtile
cups	heauens	priest	succour
cures	held	private	supply
custome	herald	proclaime	surfet

svrly	arrow	dearer	fountaines
sweares	arte	deck	fraile
sweets	ashes	decreed	frailtie
swell	assign'd	deny	friendly
swelling	aydes	depart	frowne
swells	babe	desert	furies
tak'st	ball	deserue	furious
tale	balme	deserv'd	future
tarry	banck	design'd	gallants
tast	bands	desperate	games
taxe	beards	differ	garden
teare	beat	disclose	gently
temple	beere	disdaine	ghosts
tempt	beg	dish	giuing
termes	begun	display	gluttony
th'	beholds	distance	god-head
thames	bells	dog	god-like
th'art	bends	don	goodyere
they're	benefits	doore	grapes
thie	bent	do't	grasse
throne	blame	draught	gratefull
throw	blaspheme	dresse	grecian
thunder	blessings	drew	greece
tower	blisse	drinkes	greedie
toyes	boord	drops	grieu'd
tragick	box	drown'd	groues
trifles	branches	drum	groyne
troubled	brand	dry	grudge
troy	bravery	dues	grutch
trumpets	breach	dutch	guides
twentie	brighter	earely	ha'
'twixt	brightest	eaten	habit
union	brightnesse	eates	had'st
upright	britaine	edmonds	handle
vent	broad	effect	hangings
venter	brothers	enemie	happier
vexe	busie	enjoy'd	hardly
vine	caesars	ensignes	harmes
virtue	call'st	enter	harmonie
vitious	carract	envi'd	harth
vnderstood	cart	envy	hatred
vow	cato's	epigramme	heap'd
wch	celebrate	essence	hearing
weares	censures	estate	heau'n
weary	certaine	exalted	heavens
wee'll	chambers	examin'd	hee'd
wheele	chariot	excellent	hee'll
wholly	charitie	exempt	heires
womans	cheare	expected	hence-forth
worship	cherish	exprest	henceforth
worthie	chorus	fables	hercvles
wrapt	citizens	fain'st	hereafter
wretch	clients	falls	hermes
writer	clos'd	falne	hid
yee	cloudes	fam'd	hierome
	clowne	fancie	hill
3	coates	fare	hills
accept	common-wealth	fashion'd	holds
according	conceal'd	fashions	homers
acted	conquer	fauours	honourable
admiration	conspire	fear'd	hor.
advanc'd	contract	feeles	hourely
aetna	corporall	finding	house-hold
affaires	cost	firme	houses
afford	couer	first-fruits	humane
affords	could'st	fish	hymne
aged	counsell	fitting	i'am
aided	countesse	flat	iest
aime	courtier	flatterie	if't
allay	craue	flatteries	i'haue
alphonso	creepe	fleshes	i'ld
also	crownes	flew	imitate
altars	cupid	forbid	impudence
answer'd	curse	forc't	infinite
antient	curst	forehead	informe
antiquitie	customes	forgiue	inke
appeares	cynthia	forgiven	inquirie
appetite	daies	forgot	invite
approaches	daintie	forraine	iones
apt	daring	forsake	ionson

ire	month	purpose	sleight
isle	moodes	queen	smallest
italy	moriscn	question'd	smile
itch	mount	quick	smoake
i'the	mountaine	quicker	snares
iudgment	mounted	raile	societie
ivy	musick	raine	sole
jane	musicke	rammes	sorrowes
jealousie	myne	rap't	sounds
jest	naming	rauish'd	soyle
jove	neare	ravish'd	spanish
joyes	neat	rayse	speakes
judg'd	nephewes	reach'd	speciall
judgements	net	realme	specious
kate	nets	rear'd	spectators
kenelme	nine	rebell	spell
kindled	nobilitie	rebells	spice
kingdomes	nobler	record	spit
knight-hood	nobly	records	splendor
knottie	noted	redeeme	spoke
know'st	nuptiall	regard	spright
lance	o'	rehearse	squire
lane	oathes	relish	sr
lasting	obey	remaines	start
lately	objects	render	stature
latine	odcombe	repaire	steale
latter	odde	repented	steele
leades	on't	respect	stemme
leane	orbe	return'd	stewes
leap'd	ornaments	richard	stooles
learning	orpheus	richly	stormes
leaves	ounces	rising	stranger
led	owes	rivall	strangers
leese	painting	river	string
legs	parting	rob	strings
letcherie	partrich	rob'd	strive
lets	patience	robe	stroke
letter	pedigree	rock	studies
letting	peepe	rod	style
lift	peers	romane	subiects
lifted	perish	rule	subjects
lightly	petticote	rumour	succours
lillies	petulant	rurall	suffer
limbe	pheasant	rymes	suffer'd
lip	philip	sack	suffrage
liu'st	pierce	safely	suffring
load	pies	saile	suit
loath	pillars	saith	summ'd
loe	piso's	sate	suretie
loth	pit	scale	surfets
loving	plague	scarlet	surprize
lucan	plaine	seal'd	suspect
lucks	plate	seale	sustaine
lungs	plautus	search'd	swarme
lvcklesse	ply	seasons	sweetnesse
lyd.	poetry	seate	swine
lying	polish'd	seemes	swords
lyke	politique	seest	sylvane
maintayne	port	seldome	tacitvs
man's	portion	seruants	tames
marquess	ports	serue	taske
martyrs	posture	servants	tax'd
mayne	pour'd	service	teeming
mayst	prayer	severall	temples
measur'd	prayers	severe	terme
meeting	prepar'd	shaddowes	test
mettall	preserve	shaft	thankfull
middle	pretend	share	t'haue
mild	preticus	shee's	themis
mindes	print	shelton	thespian
minerva	produce	shew'd	th'exchange
mira	profits	shines	th'eye
miracle	proofe	shops	th'hast
mistake	prou'd	shot	thiefe
modestly	proves	showers	thighes
molest	provle	shrunke	thou'lt
monarchs	pull	sick	threaten
none	purest	sings	thred
moneys	purg'd	sinners	threw
monster	purple	skilfull	throwne

to<o>	added	bald	burning
top	adding	ballance	bury
tother	admir'd	banish'd	bush
toyles	admired	baptisme	buskin
tracts	admit	barbarous	bus'nesse
translated	ador'd	bard	butt
trauell	adorne	barke	bvt
trench	aduanced	barking	c<h>lce
tricks	advantage	bartas	cal'd
trine	advise	bastinado	called
troth	aerie	bath	camden
trouble	aesope	bathes	cam'st
turned	afeard	baudie	canker'd
turnes	affeard	bawdrie	captaines
twixt	affects	beame	captaynes
undone	affright	beames	carts
unitie	affrights	beard	carve
unknowne	after-times	beasts	castor
unlesse	ages	beate	catalogue
urg'd	agincourt	beaten	catch'd
various	agree	beating	cates
veluet	aid	beaumont	celebrating
venetia	aides	beavmont	celebration
virgins	alarmes	begat	cellar
vision	alcides	beget	censur'd
vnder	alice	begg'd	cerbervs
vnion	allen	beginning	ceston
vntill	allies	begins	chainge
voice	all's	beholding	chaires
volume	already	beleeu'd	challenge
vow'd	altar	belie	champion
voyces	amazement	belov'd	chancellor
vrge	amber	below	changed
wager	amends	betray'd	changes
waking	amiable	better'd	chant
wan	amidst	between	chapman
wares	amisse	bevis	chappell
watch'd	amitie	beware	charmes
weather	amorous	beyond	chase
weave	anagram	bide	chastitie
weeke	angells	bill	chayre
weightie	angles	bind	cheape
wherefore	angrie	bishop	cheated
wherry	answer	bishops	cheater
wicked	answere	blatant	cheeke
wickednesse	answers	blaz'd	cheere
wilde	antique	bleeding	cheerefull
willing	appear'd	blew	chev'ril
windowes	apples	blisses	chev'rill
winne	approach	blocks	chimaera
winter	april	bloome	choyce
wisely	architecture	blushing	christendome
wiser	arden	boasts	christian
wont	ardor	bodyes	christians
wooes	argue	bolder	christmas
wooll	arise	borrowers	chvffe
wyse	armour	bottome	circling
yong	arraign'd	'boue	circular
	arriue	brace	claimes
2	artes	brake	clap
a-farre	artlesse	branded	clay
a-while	aside	brauely	cleans'd
a>	asked	brauest	cleave
abbeuile	asse	brazen	clerke
abide	asses	breakes	climbe
abler	assurance	breaking	climes
absolute	aswell	breast	cloath
abus'd	atomes	breath'd	cloath'd
abuses	att	breathe	clowdes
acceptance	attempt	breeds	club
accesse	attempted	brier	coach
accius	attend	brightly	coach'd
accompt	autumne	brome	coale
accounted	avbigny	brooding	cob
acheron	'avbigny	brookes	cock
achilles	avthor	browes	cocytvs
acquaintance	awe	browne	coke
actiue	awfull	bull	cclds
adam	aymes	burden	colledge
add	ayrie	burned	colt

columne	deaths	easier	fire-workes
comely	death's	edge	firke
commended	decay'd	effects	first-borne
company	deceiv'd	egges	fitly
compare	decline	eglantine	fitted
compasse	decree	egs	fixed
compassion	dedicate	eight	fixt
complaine	dedication	eithers	flatter
complaines	deedes	eldest	flatterer
compos'd	deep	election	flatterers
compose	deepest	elements	flattery
com'st	deere	else-where	flatt'ring
conceiu'd	defeat	embassage	flatt'ry
conceiv'd	deformed	embleme	fleece
concluded	deignes	embrac'd	fleeces
concord	delphick	employ	fletcher
condemn'd	denie	encounter'd	flock
condemne	denied	ended	flocks
condition	denies	endes	floore
conduct	deny'd	endlesse	flowing
coney	departed	engine	flowre
conquer'd	departing	engines	flushing
conquers	depending	ennius	foe
consider	depth	ensigne	folds
consisting	deride	entertaine	follies
constable	descend	entertaining	follow'd
constant	description	entrailes	following
consumption	deserve	entrance	food
contemne	deserving	enuies	foolish
continent	desired	epitome	foorth
continu'd	despaire	epode	foote
contrite	despaires	equally	forc'd
coole	despight	errors	foretold
copie	destin'd	errour	forfeit
copp's	destinie	esme	forge
corbet	destroyes	espie	forgotten
coriat	deuoure	essayes	forrest
corke	dialogue	esteeme	forsakes
corners	dignitie	europes	forsweare
correct	dignities	evils	fortie
corrupt	dike	ewes	fortitude
cosen	din'd	exacted	fought
cotswold	dis-joyn'd	exceeding	fountaine
couers	discerne	excellence	fram'd
coulors	discharge	excuses	frances
councels	discloses	expense	francis
counsells	discontent	expiate	freed
countenance	discord	expression	freindes
couple	discourseth	extend	freinds
courses	disgrace	facts	fright
courtesie	dispaire	faculties	frighted
cover	dispense	failes	fringes
covetous	disposure	faint	fro
coyne	dispraise	fairer	frogs
crack	distant	faithfully	front
cracke	distill	familie	fulnesse
cradles	distrust	famine	gam'ster
crane	diuide	fancied	gaping
crave	divide	fatall	garlands
creates	doctrine	faunes	gates
creatures	doome	fearefull	gathering
creekes	doores	fearefully	gav'st
creeping	doo't	fearfull	gayne
crept	double	fearing	gaze
cries	doubly	fee	generous
crost	dover	fees	gentleman
crowned	dreames	fellow	george
crueltie	drie	fellowship	georges
curled	driven	fells	germany
curles	dropping	fen	gesture
curre	drosse	fetch	getting
curtesie	drowning	fface	ghyrlond
dagger	drug	ffree	giddie
damne	duke	fiftie	girt
dangerous	dvncote	fills	giving
daphne	dwarfes	filth	gladdest
daunces	earnest	finest	gladding
dazeling	ears	finger	globe
dazling	earthly	fingers	glorified
dearest	easie	fir'd	goat

goddesse	honestie	kissing	maske
jodds	honey	knights	maskes
gowned	honor'd	knits	masque
graced	honoured	knowe	masques
gracious	hoofe	la-ware	maw
grand-child	hooke	labouring	may'st
grandsires	horld	lack'd	maze
graticus	hornet	lambe	meanest
gratitude	hound	lambes	measures
graues	howe	lame	meddle
grease	howsoeuer	lands	medea
greate	hue	languish	meditations
griev'd	hugh	lanthorne	mellow
grievous	humilitie	later	melt
groomes	hung	latest	mended
grosse	hungry	laurell	mending
grove	hunters	lawfull	merchant
guard	hunts	layes	mercie
guarded	hvngry	lease	mercvry
guesse	ideot	lees	mere
guift	idle	legend	michael
guifts	idolatrie	lesson	mightiest
guiltlesse	idoll	let's	mightst
gummes	iealous	lewd	mile
guns	iealousies	libell	mime
gvt	iephson	licentious	miming
gypsee	iewes	lifes	minerva's
h.	illustrate	lighted	mint
half	imbrace	lightning	mirrour
hallow'd	imperfect	lik'd	mischiefes
hanch	impetuous	likenesse	miserie
handled	importune	liking	misterie
hangs	imprese	lilly	mistres
happen	imprest	lim	mix'd
happiest	imputation	limons	mixtures
happinesse	inclin'd	lippe	mock'd
harbour	inconstancie	liquor	mocks
hare	infamie	livie	moderne
harp	infamous	lo	money-brckers
harry	inflam'd	lock	monthes
harsh	influence	locks	montrell
hart	inherent	lodge	moones
harvest	inherit	longest	morning-starre
haughtie	inheritance	longs	morrow
haunt	iniurie	look'st	mortall
hawking	inmate	loosing	motions
hearers	innocent	lordings	mou'd
heares	inscription	lordship	mouing
heauenly	inspir'd	lordships	moulded
heavie	interest	lot	mouth
heed	interpreted	loude	movnsievr
hee'ld	inuade	louder	mutuall
heighten	inuent	louers	mvse
he'le	invade	louing	myrtle
helme	invention	loyall	nailes
help	inviting	lucius	neate
help'd	inward	lucke	need'st
helpes	iourney	lustes	negligence
helps	iove's	lusts	nere
hemisphere	ioy'd	luxurie	nevil
hen	ireland	lynes	newcastle
henrie	iris	lyrick	newer
heralds	it'	machine	nice
herbert	ivory	madames	nicholas
hercules	jarre	madnesse	nimble
heroes	jests	maintain'd	nobles
herse	jewels	maiors	noblesse
he's	joseph	majesties	noises
hesiods	joynts	makers	noone
hether	judges	male	not>
h'has	june	manger	nourish
h'hath	justifie	mankinde	nowe
highest	k<ing>	map	now's
hight	katherine	march	numbred
hire	kid	margaret	nymphs
hither	killing	marriage	obeliske
hogs	kin	married	obiects
hol'borne	kindred	marrow	object
hole	kingdome	marry	obscene
home-borne	kisses	masculine	obscure

obseruation	plush	redeemer	seeing
observe	pod	reed	seek
odcombian	poesy	reedes	seekes
oddes	poet-ape	reeking	seeking
od'rous	points	refin'd	seek'st
offer'd	polypheme	refine	selues
officers	poole	reflect	sends
ogle	poor	reflexe	separate
oke	poores	refraine	serpents
old-end	possessions	reioyce	seruant
ope	post	relate	seru'd
ope'	pouertie	relation	seruice
opens	pounds	reliefe	setting
oracle	poure	relieve	seuen
ord'nance	pouring	relish'd	shades
ornament	powder	remembrance	shadowes
orphevs	poxe	remembred	shapes
ounce	poyson	remou'd	sharp
out-goe	practiz'd	rent	sharpnesse
out-liue	praiser	repeate	shee'll
out-live	prayse	reproofe	shep.
out-shine	prease	reprove	shep'ard
overbvry	preferre	reputation	shewe
oxen	presence	requir'd	shewing
pageant	presenting	respects	shoes
painters	preserver	resurrection	shone
palace	preserves	retaine	shooe
pales	presume	retire	shop
palmer	prodigious	reuerenc'd	shout
pancharis	professing	reuerence	shoute
papers	profession	revels	shouts
paradise	profest	reverse	showe
parasites	promis'd	rewards	showre
parcell	prone	reynes	shrinke
parent	pronounce	richest	shrub
parish	propertyes	rides	shun
parted	prophets	ridway	shunne
pass'd	prosperitie	rigid	shunning
passions	prostitute	riot	shuns
pastures	protest	riseth	sicilian
path	prov'd	roger	sights
patrons	provided	roofe	sincere
pavls	prowde	roofes	singer
pawne	pr'y	roomes	sire
peach	pucell	root	sires
peake	punke	roote	sisters
pegasus	punque	rooted	sitting
peleus	purchas'd	rope	six
pembroke	purchase	rore	skies
penance	puritanes	rounds	skin
penates	purle	rowse	sky
pension	pursues	ruffe	slack
perfections	pyrats	running	slaine
perfumes	pythagoras	rush	slander
perills	q.	rvdyerd	slave
perjur'd	quarter	rvtland	sleepes
perpetuall	quicken	saies	sleepie
persian	quitt	salisbvrie	sleeping
perspectiue	quiver	salt	slips
perswade	quoth	savile	slit
physick	radcliffe	say-master	sluggish
pile	radiant	sayd	smell
piles	raigning	scarre	smith
pillar	raising	scatter'd	smock
pisse	ranknesse	scenes	snake
pitcher	raph	schisme	snore
placed	rapine	schooles	snuffe
plaines	rarely	science	socks
plants	rarified	scope	softest
players	raritie	score	softnesse
playing	rash	scorned	somerset
pleasant	raysing	scotland	sometime
plenteous	reads	sealed	son
plentie	reall	seales	sonnet
plie	realmes	seauen	sons
plight	reasons	secret	sooth
plough	receave	secur'd	sordid
plucke	receipt	secure	sore
plum	reckon	securely	sorry
plumes	reconcil'd	seedes	sorts

so't	taper	twise	who's
souldier	tarries	tyme	widdow
source	tasted	tyrants	wight
soveraigne	taylor	tyre	winde
space	taylors	tyrtaeus	window
span	telephus	uncomely	winds
spar'd	tell-troth	universe	wines
sparkling	tell's	unjust	winke
speach	temper'd	unlike	wise-men
spectacles	tempest	untie	wisedcme
spill	tempests	untill	wisest
spirituall	tend	unworthy	wish'd
spoile	terror	urging	wished
spots	th<o>rough	uses	wisheth
sprite	th'age	using	wither
spy	the<e>	usurer	withered
square	the>	usurers	witt
squib	theame	utter	wittie
squires	theorbo	vale	wiues
stake	thereon	valley	woes
stale	theyr	vanish'd	wolves
stampe	theyre	varie	wonder'd
standerd	th'iambick	varied	wonders
standers-by	thin	varietie	woo
starre-chamber	th'old	varying	woolly
stars	thou'rt	vast	wormes
started	thousands	vault	worne
statues	threatens	veines	worthiest
steales	threatning	veiw	wouen
steep'd	thriftie	velvets	wovld-bee
steeples	thrise	venice	wracke
stench	thriue	ventring	writers
sterve	throng	vere	writings
stiled	thronging	vext	written
stoope	thrush	veynes	wry
stopt	tier	vgly	wryte
stor'd	tilt	vicious	wull
stoupe	tilter	viewing	yard
straight-way	tis	vincent	years
strand	tissue	visits	yeild
streets	to'a	vlysses	yett
strengths	toile	vnder-neath	yf
strict	tombes	voices	yo'haue
strifes	torches	void	youngest
striues	tortures	vouchsafe	yron
strongly	to't	voyage	zealous
strooke	towre	vppon	
strove	toyle	vpright	1
study	trades	vpward	&c.
stupid	tradesmen	vrgeth	a-bed
styl'd	traine	vs'd	a-fire
styx	translation	vtter'd	a-iax
substance	translator	waight	a-life
suck'd	translators	waites	a-new
suffers	trauaile	wak'd	aarons
sufficient	trauelling	walking	ab
summers	treason	wandring	abandcn'd
summes	trecherous	wanted	abate
superstitious	trees	wardrobe	abhord
supper	tribade	warie	abhorres
surely	tribe	warpe	abound
suspected	tribute	warrant	abounds
suspition	trifling	waxe	aboute
swaines	trim	weaknesse	abro'd
swans	tripple	weale	absent
swearing	triumphing	weapon	absolv'd
sweeten	triumphs	we'are	abstaine
sweetly	troyes	wearing	abstayne
swert	truer	wedding	abstinence
syllabes	truest	weedes	abstruse
t<o>'a	truths	weekly	absurdity
t<o>'aduance	try'd	weigh	abused
t<o>'appeare	tub	wherety	academie
t<o>'enjoy	turkie	wheresoere	accents
t<o>'expect	turtles	wherof	acceptable
t<o>'offend	tutor	whisper	acceptably
tables	'tweene	white-hall	accepted
taffata	twelue	whoe	accession
talkes	twenty	wholscme	accite
tall	twine	whome	accomplish

accompted	all-gracious	apple-haruest	atchievements
account	all-vertuous	applie	athenian
accumulated	#allegorike	apprehension	atomi
accursed	allied	approaching	atreus
accusations	allmighty	approch	at's
acknowledge	allotted	approches	attaine
acornes	allowance	appropriates	attending
acquainted	allowed	approve	attir'd
acrostichs	allowes	apricot	attributes
acteth	alloy	apteth	attyre
actors	allures	apulians	attyres
actuate	almanacks	arar	auailes
ad	almes	arbiter	auditcr
adjuncts	almes-basket	arch	audleys
admirable	almightie	arch-angels	auert
admiracon	almighties	arch-dukes	augure
admiring	almond	arched	aulus
admitted	almonds	archetype	auon
adoe	aloft	archilochus	auoyd
adopt	along'st	archimede	auspice
adoration	aloofe	architas	auspicious
adornd	alow'd	architectonice	auspitiously
adornes	alpes	architects	austere
adria	alphius	argiue	authorem
aduanc'd	als<o>'her	argo	authorities
aduance	alter'd	argument	authoriz'd
aduentry	alternate	argus	avernvs
aduenture	amadis	ariadnes	avert
aduise	amaze	aright	avoid
adulterate	amazed	arion	avoyding
adulteries	ambassadour	aristarchus	awde
adult'rers	ambitiously	aristophanes	awhile
aduocate	ambling	aristctle	axe
advances	ambrosiack	armde	aye
adversaries	amen	arme	aymd
adviseth	amid'	armed	aymed
aeacvs	amonge	armies	ayres
aelian<'s>	amphion	armorie	b<e>'asham'd
aemulate	anacreons	armyes	b<e>'embrac'd
aemulation	anagrams	aromatique	b<ess>
aeneas	analysde	arraigning	b<roughton>s
aeschilus	anarchie	arras	b<y>'imputed
aescvlape	anarchy	arrayes	babes
aeternall	anatomie	arrerage	babion
aeternities	ancestours	arrest	babylonian
aetnean	anenst	arrive	bacchvs
affect	angell	arrowes	back-slides
affected	angelo	arsenike	backes
affoards	angle	arses	backs
affoord	angrier	arte's	backward
affraid	animated	arth:	bacon
affricke	anne	arthurs	+bacons
afore	annexed	arthvrs	bag
afront	anniversarie	artichokes	bags
after-state	anniversary	article	baies
after-thoughts	annoy'd	artillerie	baits
afternoones	annuitie	arundell	bake
afterwards	annval	ascend	balladrie
ag'd	anon	ascribe	ballads
agents	anone	ashamed	balmes
agile	answering	ashore	banck-side
agreeing	anticks	asinigo	bancke
agrees	anticyra's	askt	bancks
aiax	antipathy	asleep	banckside
aile	antiphates	asleepe	banke-rupt
airising	antiquated	asquint	banquet
ake	antiquities	ass	baphyre
alba	antwerpe	assaies	barber
albin's	anuile	assay'd	barbican
alcaick	anvile	assayes	barnabee
alchimist	apart	assiduous	baronet
alchymists	ape	assignes	barons
alcoran	apologetique	assisted	barr'd
alde-legh	apostacie	assur'd	barrell
alderman	apostle	assure	basenesse
aldermanitie	apostrophe	assyria	baser
ale-house	#apotheosis	as't	basest
alexandria	appetites	asterisme	baskets
alight	applaud	astrea	bastard
alike-stated	apple	asunder	baths

battaile	benn>	blushes	brew-houses
battells	bequeath	board	briarevs
battry	bereaues	boardes	brick-kills
baud-bees	berenices	boare	bride-well
baudrie'	bergamo	boasted	bridegrocme
baudy	berghen	boasters	brides
bavdes	beringhams	bogg'd	briefe
bawd	bermudas	boldnesse	brill
bawdie	berwicke	bcmbard-phrase	bringes
bawdry	beshite	bombard-stile	bringing
bawds	besieg'd	bond	bringst
bawle	besieged	bondmen	bring'st
bawling	bespoke	bone	bring't
baytes	besprent	bone-fires	bristo'
be'<i>n	besse	bonefires	brit[t]aine
beadle	be'st	bonnie	britain's
beamie	best-best	book	brize
beams	bestowes	book-seller	broad-seales
bearer	bestowing	booke-seller	broad-troden
beastly	bestryde	booke-wormes	broader
beates	besyde	books	broadest
beatifick	besydes	boords	brocage
beatings	bet	boore	broeck
beatitude	betraid	boot	brontes
beatitudes	betrayes	bor-	broome
beauchamps	bettring	bord	brought'st
beaumonts	betwixt	borders	brow
beauteous	bety'de	bords	brown
beavie	bever	bores	bruis'd
becam'st	bewail<e>d	borrowing	bruised
beckning	bewaild	bottle	bruiseth
becommeth	bewares	bough	brunsfield
becum	big	boughes	brush'd
bed-mate	bilbo	boughs	brute
bed-rid	bilbo-smith	boulstred	brutus
bedew'd	billiard	bouncing	buck
beds	billcw	bounteous	buckingham
beech	bills	bountie'	bucklers-bury
beeing	bils	bounty	bud
been	binde	boutersheim	buds
beest	birds	bouts	builders
befall	birth-right	bower	building
begann	births	bowle	bulke
began'st	bitch	bowles	bullocks
beg'd	bite	boxes	bulls
begetting	bitten	boy'd	bulwarkes
begging	bitter	bcyles	burl<eigh>
beginners	bitternesse	brag	burlase
beginns	black-bird	braies	bursting
begin'st	blacke-springing	brains	burthen
begotten	blackenesse	brakes	buryed
begs	blacker	branch	busied
beguil'd	blackest	branching	buskins
beguile	blacks	brandish'd	but>
beguiles	blade	brandish't	butter
begunne	blades	brands	butter-flye
begyn	blanch't	brauado	butter'd
behalfe	blason	brauerie	buttock
beholder	blasphemie	braules	buyer
beholders	blasphemy	braveries	buylding
behould	blast	brav'ries	by-cause
belch'd	blazon	brawne	by-paths
belcheth	bleed	bray	by'example
beleeved	bleeds	brayes	caballs
beleeves	blessed'st	brayne-hardie	cabinet
belgia	blindest	braynford	cadmus
belgick	blindly	breaches	caecilius
beliefe	block	bread-streets	caesarian
believe	block'd	break	caesar's
belike	blockt	breastes	cage
bell-mans	blood-shaken	breasts	cake
bellie	bloody	breathes	calais
beloued	bloomed	breath's	calamitie
belye	blooming	breath'st	caledon
bench	blots	breda	calfe
bending	blott	breeches	calli.
bene	blowes	breedes	call's
benefit	bluntly	breeding	calmest
benefite	blurt	bretons	cal't
beniamin	blusted	breuitie	calues

calumnies	cellars	chincke	closer
camell	censoriovs	chinnes	closest
canary	censureth	chloes	cloth's
canary-wine	censuring	choak'd	clouds
cancell'd	censvrer	choake	clowd-
candidates	centaure	choerilus	clownage
candide	centaures	choicest	clownishe
candle	ceremonies	choisest	club-fist
candor	ceres	choller	clubb
canes	certainly	chore	cluid
cann	certeyne	chori	cluster
cannons	cestrian	chorvs	clyent
canon	cethegi	chose	clysters
canuas	chafes	choyse	co<u>nsellors
canvasse	chained	choysest	co-heire
cap	chalice	chremes	co-heires
caparison	chalk	christ	coach-man
capers	chalke	christ-masse	coach-mare
capitall	chamber-critick	christall	coat
capon	chamber-fellow	christmasse	coate
capons	chanc'd	christning	cob-web-lawne
capp	chancelor	chronicle<r>s	cobalus
cap'ring	chancerie	chrystall	cobled
cap's	chanceth	church-yard	cobler
capt.	chanc't	churches	cobwet
cap'tall	change'd	churlish	cobwets
captiv'd	changeth	chyme	cocatrice
car-men	changing	cicero	cocking
carbuncle	channell	cinders	cocks
'care	channels	cinnopar	code
care=full	chanting	cipresse	coeternall
carefully	chaplaines	circled	coit
carew	chapmen	circler	cokely
caried	chappel	circuits	colby
caring	characters	circumduction	colchis
carkasse	charg'd	circumference	coldest
carkasses	charitable	circumfused	coldly
caroches	charities	circumstance	cole
caroline	charmed	circumvol<v>d	colossus
carowsing	charming	cittie	comaund
carpentry	charon	cittie-question	combe
carper	charons	cittyes	combes
carpets	charter	civilitie	combines
carps	charybdis	claimest	come>
carre	chastetye	clame	comedie
carriage	chastly	claps	comelie
carries	chattell	clarius	comends
carryed	chattels	clarke-like	comforted
caru'd	chattring	clarkes	comforter
cas'd	chaucer	clash	comforts
cashierd	cheap-side	claspe	commandements
caske	chear=full	claspes	commanding
cassandra	chear'd	claym'd	commender
cassellius	chearfull	claymeth	commending
cassiopea	chearfully	clayming	commends
cassock	checke	cleane	commentaries
casts	checkt	clearest	commings
cat	cheekes	clearnesse	commixt
cataplasmes	cheeks	clears	common-law
catches	cheered	cleerely	comm'st
catechisme	cheese	cleft-sticks	communion
cater-piller	cheeses	cleies	communitie
cats	chelsey	clemencie	comoedie
cattell	chequer	clement	comoedy
catullus	cherish'd	clense	comon
caue	cherishing	clep'd	companies
cauendish	cherissheinge	clerkes	companions
cauernes	cherries	client	company'
caught	cherry	cliffcrds .	compar'd
caus'd	cherube	clifton's	compassionate
causticks	chest-nut	clime	compeeres
ceas'd	chestnut	climing	compell'd
cease	chev-ril	cling	compil'd
ceasure	chiches	clio	complaining
cecil	chid	cloake	compleat
cecill	chide	clocke	complement
cecill's	chiefes	cloke	complexicn
cedar	chiefly	closde	complexions
celebrated	chimes	close-stocle	comprhend
celestiall	chimney	closely	compriseth

compromise	corner	criticall	dayly
compting	corollary	critick	de
comptroller	corrals	croake	deadly
comvs	corrants	croaking	deafe
con	corrected	crooked	deal-boards
concealed	correcting	crop	dear
conceales	corroding	cropt	dearely
conceits	corrupts	crowd	deaw
conceiv'st	corse	crown	debentur
concerne	cor'sives	crowne-plate	debt-booke
conceyud	corynna	crowne-worthy	debter
conclusion	cosening	crowning	debters
concurreth	cos'ning	cruellie	decayes
condemn	cossen'd	crush'd	deceased
conditions	cotes	crusht	deceasing
coneyes	cotton	crusts	deceast
conferre	couldst	cryd'st	deceipt
conferring	councell	crye	daceit
confess	councellour	cryed	deceiue
confessing	councells	crying	deceiues
confession	count	cryme	decent
confest	counterfeits	cry'st	decke
confident	countermine	ctesibius	declares
confine	countermyne	cucqueane	declin'd
confining	counters	cuffes	declineth
confirm'd	count'nances	cull'd	decoctions
confus'd	countrey-men	culloring	decreast
confused	countrie	cullors	dedicated
confutes	countrie-neighbours	cunninge	deeme
coniures	countrye	cunningly	deep-crown'd-bowle
coniuring	country's	cupping-glasses	deepe-grounded
conjectures	'counts	curle	deeper
connexion	county	curling-irons	defac't
conqu'ring	coupled	curteous	defame
consciences	courage	curtesies	defeate
conscious	courser	customer	defect
consecrate	court-bred-fillie	cuthbert	defective
consented	court-durt	cutlers	defences
consists	court-hobby-horse	cvpid	defenders
consolatorie	court-pucell	cycnvs	defend'st
consort	courted	cyllarus	defense
conspicuous	courteous	cynara	deferre
constables	courtesies	cynthias	deferrer
constancy	courtiers	cynthius	defies
constellation	courting	cypher	defiled
constellations	covell	cypres	defin'd
constraine	cover'd	cypresse	defineth
consult	covey	d.	deform'd
consuming	covrt-ling	daintinesse	defrauded
consummate	covrt-parrat	dainty	defrayes
consumptions	covrt-worme	dale	degenerate
contagion	crack'd	damd	degradation
containe	crackt	damme	deifie
contemn'd	craftie	dam'mee	delated
contemning	crafts	damnation	delayes
contempt	crafty	damn'd	delaying
contend	cramp-ring	damned	dalia's
contends	cramp'd	dannes	delicacies
contented	crampe	damning	delicious
contention	cramps	dampes	delightfull
continewall	crau'd	dam's	deliuer
continuall	craves	dances	deliuer'd
continue	creame-bowles	dancing	deliver'd
contrary	creat[t]es	danes	delude
controll	created	dapper	deluded
controule	creation	darby	delyght
controules	creditt	dark-lanterne	demand
contumelie	credulous	darkest	demerit
conuert	creed	darting	democrite
conuerted	creep	darts	democritus
conuerting	creepes	dashing	denis
conuict	crepundia	date	denmarke
conuince	crest	daunce	denne
coockold	cri'd	dauncing	denyd'st
cooke	crier	davghter	denyed
cookes	cringe	davids	denyes
cop'ces	cripple	davis	departs
copies	crips	davus	depend
coppie	crisped	day-starre	dependents
cordoua	crispeth	dayes-presents	deposited

depraue	disavow	dote	eeles
deprest	discard	dotes	eene
deprive	discern'd	doubting	effected
descended	discerned	doubts	egerton
describe	discernes	doue	eiects
described	discharg'd	dove	el\<izabeths\>
descride	discipline	doves	elders
deserted	disclos'd	dower	elect
deserts	discords	dowgate	elected
deseru'd	discouer	dowrie	elegies
deseruedly	discouer'd	do'you	eleuen
deserues	discoueries	draffe	eleventh
deserves	discourses	drag	elfe
designed	discoursing	drama	eliza
designes	discover	dramme	alizabeths
designeth	discreeter	drawer	elocution
deske	disdaine-full	drawing	eloquent
desmond	disdained	drayton	elsmere
despair'd	disdaining	dreads	eltham-thing
despis'd	disgrac't	drench	elves
despise	disguisd	dri'd	embassie
despite	disguis'd	dried	embassies
destinies	disguise	drill	embelish'd
destitute	disinherit	dring	embers
destrcy'd	dispayre	drinking	emblemes
destruction	dispenc'd	driuen	embraces
desyrous	dispensation	driu'n	embricns
detractor	dispers'd	drive	embroderies
deuice	disperse	dronken	eminence
deuoures	dispised	droop	emissarie
deuout	displeas'd	drooping	empedocles
devote	displease	dropp	emperours
devotion	dispos'd	droupes	empire
devotions	disposing	drown	empirick
devoure	disproportion'd	drownd	employd
dexterously	dispute	drownes	emp'ricks
dialogues	dissect	drrinke	empties
dian	dissection	drudge	empty
diana'alone	dissemble	drunkards	empty-handed
diana's	distinct	drunkennest	emptye
dick	distinctions	dryads	empusa
dictamen	distinguish'd	dublet	empyrean
di'd	distract	duell	emulates
die'd	ditch	due'llists	emulation
dies	ditchfield	duely	enable
diet	dittie	dulnesse	enamor'd
dietie	ditties	duly	enamour'd
differ'd	diu'd	dungeon	encounter
different	diuers	dunstable	encourage
differing	diuersly	dur'd	encreas'd
differrer	diuided	durtie	encreast
differs	diuid'st	dutie	endew'd
digestiue	divell	duties	endorse
digests	divels-arse	duty	endure
dignifie	divers	dweller	endures
dilate	diviner	dwells	enemies
diligence	divinest	dwelt	enflamed
diligent	divinitie	dyd'st	enforced
dim	divisions	dye-fats	enforcing
dimensions	docile	dyed	engage
dimme	docke	dyue	engaged
dimn'd	dock's	e.	englands
dinner	doctor	eagle	english-rogue
dint	doctors	earles	engrau'd
diomede	does	earthen	engyne
dioscuri	doest	earthes	enhance
dip\<h\>thera	dog-daies	earths	enioyes
dircaean	dogges	eas'd	enlarg'd
dire	dolphin	eased	enlarge
direct	dominations	eases	ennoble
directly	dominus	easy-rated	enormity
directs	domitian	eating	enquire
dirtie	donnee's	eats	enshrin'd
dirty	donnes	eccho'd	enspire
dis-auow	donnor's	eccho's	entangling
dis-esteem'd	dorrels	eclipse	entayl'd
dis-esteeme	dorset	eden	entayle
dis-favour	dose	edifices	entend
dis-inherit	dosen	education	entermixt
dis-ioynts	dotage	eeke	entertayne

entertaynment	exchange	fauour	fixe
entheate	excite	fauourite	flaccus
#enthcusiastike	exclude	fauourites	flagge
entitle	execration	favorite	flaggeth
entranc'd	executes	favouring	flakes
entred	execution	favours	flameship
entring	executioner	fayerie	flammes
entry	executor	fayne	flanck'd
enuy'	exercis'd	fayrest	flatter'd
enuyous	exhausted	fear	flattered'st
envy'd	exil'd	feasting	flatt'rer
envye	ex'lent	feats	flatt'rie
ephesus	expansions	features	flattry's
epick	expell	feeding	flaw
epicks	experience	feigne	flea
epicoene	expire	felicitie	flead
epidemicall	explat'st	fellowes	fleeced
epilogue	expostulacon	female	flees
epithalamion	express	fenc'd	fleet-lane
epithites	expresser	fencer	fleete
equall'd	expresseth	fencing	flesh-quake
equitie	expressions	fenc't	fleshly
erat.	exscribe	ferrabosco	flights
erect	extasie	fertile	fling
erected	extasies	fescennine	flit
ere't	extendeth	fet	flora
e're't	extends	fether	florence
eridanus	extension	fetter	flourish
errant	extraordinarie	fetters	flourishing
errant'st	extremities	feuer	flowne
err'd	eye-browes	fev'ry	flowrie
errours	eye-brows	fewd	flowry
escapes	eyed	fewer	flung
eschylus	eyne	fewest	flute
especially	eyther	ffaultes	fly
esquire	f.	ffeare	flyes
esqvire	fa-ding	ffeasting	foame
estates	fabler	ffeat	foiled
esteemed	facile	ffeild	foist
estimate	factious	ffinde	fold
eteostichs	faemale	ffirst	followers
eterniz'd	fagots	ffoole	fond
ethnicisme	fail'd	ffor	fondly
euclide	failed	fforth	fool
euening	fained	ffortune	foole-hardie
euening's	faines	ffreind	fooling
euenly	fainting	ffreinds	foot-and-halfe-foot
euents	faintly	ffresh	foot-cloth
euer-boyling	faithful	ffriend	foot-man
euer-lasting	faiths	ffrostes	forbeares
eue'ry	faith's	ffyre	forbidd'
euery-where	fal	fibre	forbidden
eugenian	falernian	fibres	forbids
euill	fallow	fier	forborne
eu'n	fall'st	fiers	forces
eupheme	false-hood	fiery	forcing
euripides	falsely	fift	'fore
eu'ry	falser	fiftieth	fore-knowne
euthanasee	fame-vaynes	fifty	fore-see
events	familiar	fig	forehead's
ever-greene	families	fights	foreman
ever>	family	figures	forestall
everlasting	famovs	fil<l>ed	forfeitinge
evidence	fan	filch'd	forfeits
evil	fancies	fil'd	for'his
evnomia	far	file	forke
evt.	fare-well	filmer	forked
exact	farre-admired	filthy	formed
exacts	farre-all-seeing	finall	fornaces
exalt	farre-knowne	finds	forsaken
examine	fart	fine-man	forsooke
examples	farthest	finenesse	forsware
exceed	farts	fire-light	forswore
exceedeth	fastidious	fish-	forsworne
exceeds	fastneth	fisher	forth-brought
excell'd	fastning	fist-fill'd	fortifie
excelling	father's	fitnesse	fortified
excelsis	fattest	fittest	fortnight
exception	fault's	fitts	fortunate
excesse	fauors	five-fold	fortvne

forty	gaule	graffs	haires
forum	gau'st	graft	halberds
forward	gavest	grafted	halfe-mocnes
foster-father	gaynes	graine	halfe-way
foulely	gazers	graines	halt
foundation	gazetti	grammar	hammering
founder	gazing	grammarians	hammers
foundred	geare	grampius	hamptcn
fount	geese	granats	hams
foure-score	gemme	grand=children	handles
fourescore	gemmes	grand-dames	handling
fowler	gems	grandees	hanging
foxe	gentle-wcman	grandlings	hannibal
fragrant	gentlemen	grape	hannow
frank	gentlest	graphick	hans-spiegle
frantick	gent'man	grassie	hap
fraud	gests	grates	haplesse
frauds	gett	gratuitie	hap'ly
free-borne	ghest	gratulates	happ
freehould	ghests	gratulatorie	happily
freer	giant	grauell	happ'ly
freez'd	gill	grauer	harbinger
french-hood	gi'ng	gravitie	harbor
french-men	ginnes	grazing	harbour'd
french-taylors	ginny	grea<t>est	harbours
freshly	girded	greace	hard-by
frie	girdle	great-mens	hard-hearted
friend-ship	girles	greatly	harder
frights	girls	'gree	hardest
fripperie	giu'st	greedy	hardie
frontire	giver	greek-hands	harke
frontispice	glad-menticn'd	greeks	harmoniously
frostiest	gladder	greek's	harms
frostily	glance	green	harpies
frosts	glare	greene-cloth	harpyes
froward	glass	greenwich	harrow'd
frownes	glasse-house	'grees	hartes
frowning	glassen	'greet	harts
fruite	glaves	greeting	ha's
fruites	gleane	griefes	hastens
fruitlesse	gleanes	grieue	hastily
fryar	gleanings	grisly	hasting
fucus	glister'd	groine	hasts
fuliginous	globy	grone	hasty
fume	gloomie-sceptred	gropes	hated
fumes	glorifie	grosser	hateth
fumie	glove	grossnesse	hating
funerall	glutted	groue	hau'-boy
funeralls	goale	groun'	hau'boy
furnish	goate	growe	haue'hem
furniture	goates	grownde	hauking
furre	god-wit	grudg'd	have't
furrowes	goddess	grunting	hay
further	godly's	guardes	hayles
fyl's	god's	guardian	hayre
fyne	godwit	guide	hayward
fyres	gold-chaines	guided	head-long
gained	golden-eyes	guideth	heades
gaines	gold's	guild	headlong
gainst	gon	guilded	he'adulters
gaite	good-night	guilty	heale
galba	goodlier	gull	health-sake
gall	goods	gull'd	healths
gallant	goody	gulling	heapes
gallantry	goose	gumme	heaping
gallo-belgicvs	gorgon	gun-powder	heaps
gallus	gorgonian	gundomar	heards
gamage	gossip	gunnes	hearer
gambol	gossip-got	juts	hearkens
gamester	gossipps	guy	hearst
gamesters	go'st	gve	hear'st
gamster	gott	gyant	heart-strike
ganimede	gotten	gyantes	heates
jardens	gout	gyerlyk	heating
garment	governe	gyrlands	heats
garter	governing	gyues	heau'd
garters	gown'd	h<e>'offend	heau'en
gaspe	gownes	ha	heav'n
gatherer	grac'd	hackney	heav'n<s>
gaudy	gracefull	haftes	hebrid

heere	horatius	iland	injustice
he'had	horl'd	ilia	inne
heidelberg	horne	i'll	innocently
height'ning	horne-workes	ill-	innovaticns
helen	hornes	ill-affected	ino
helicon	horride	ill-made	inough
he'll	horror	ill-penn'd	inoughe
heluetia	horrors	ill-torn'd	inow
hem	horse-leech	ill-us'd	inquir'd
henrye	horse-leech-like	ills	inquire
her>	horse-neck	illustrious	inraged
herb	hose	illustrous	in's
hercules-his	hospitalitie	im>mcrtall	inscrib'd
herd	hospitalls	image	insert
herds	host	imagery	inside
hereat	hostesse	imbarqu'd	insolent
herein	hot-house	imitation	inspire
heresie	hot-hovse	immortalitye	instantly
hermetique	hottest	impartially	instauration
heroe	houghs	imperiall	institution
heroick	houpes	impious	instructs
heroique	houre-glasse	implexed	instrument
heyden	how-sc-e're	implore	in't
h'had	howard	impos'd	integritie
hidden>	howers	imposture	intelligencer
hide-parke	howrely	impostures	intend
hides	howres	impregnable	intended
hie	hues	impression	intention
hierarchie	huge	imprison	intents
hierarchies	huishers	imputed	intermitted
hieroglyphicks	hulke	in-land	interpell
high-spirited	humber	in-primis	interpos'd
high-swclne	humbled	in>	interpose
highly	humblest	inbreeding	interrupt
hill-	humbly	incarnate	intersert
hilt	humblye	incense	intertexe
himself	humour'd	incest	intertwind
hinde	humours	inch	intertwine
hint	hum'rcus	inchanted	intire
hipocrites	hungary	incivilitie	intreat
hippocrenes	hunted	inclos'd	intreaties
hir'd	hunt'st	including	intreaty
hirelings	hurdles	inconstant	intrenchmt
hireth	hurld	incurr'd	int'rest
historicall	hurl'd	indeede	intwine
history	hurle	indentur'd	inuentions
hitt	hurles	index	inuoke
ho'	hurried	indice	invent
hoarse	hurtfull	indicting	invented
hobled	hurting	indifferent	invisibilitie
hodges	huskes	indignation	ioint
hold<s>	huswifery	indorse	iolly
holdborne	hydra	indu'd	iosvah
holdes	hye	indulgent	iouiall
holdeth	hym	indure	iouis
holding	hyme	infam'd	iournall
holes	hymens	infamy	iouiall
holiest	i'<h>ad	infant	ioyfull
holinesse	iambicke	infect	ioy'st
holland	iambicks	infected	irene
hollande	ianin's	infection	irish
holy-dayes	iarre	infinits	irishry
hclye	iarres	infirmery	iron
homage	iasons	inflame	irons
honble	iawes	inflicts	irreligious
honesty	iay	informed	irritate
honored	iberus	informers	isles
honoring	ideas	infus'd	italie
hood-wink'd	idiot	ingage	i'th'
hoofe-cleft	idolatrous	ingenyre	i'th'open
hoofes	idomen	ingine	its
hook-handed	iealousie	ingineeres	itself
hoord	ieames	ingirer	iudgements
hoorld	ierna	ingots	iudges
hoorl'd	iests	ingratefull	iudging
hop	iewell	ingredients	iuggler
hop-drinkers	iewells	iniquitie	iuno
hop'd	ignorants	injoy	iuory
hopefull	i'had	injunction	iustice-hood
hopelesse	il	injurie	iustifie

iuy
iuyce
ivno
ivye
ixion
jacks-pulse
jacobs
jakes
janus
japhets
jarres
jarreth
jarring
jaundies
jaw
jearing
jeast
jemme
jerke
jesus
jewell
jewells
jo
joane
john
johnson
jolly
jonson
jot
journals
journey
joves
joyfull
joyn
joyne
joynting
judging
jumpe
juno
jupiter
justest
justled
justly
juyce
keep'd
keeper
keptst
kerne
key-stone
keyes
kicking
kild
kill'd
killer
kills
kindes
kindle
kindling
kindly
kinds
kine
kinge
kinglier
kingly
kinne
kinsman
kist
knat
knaue
knaues
knave
kneele
kneeling
knees
knells
knewe
knight-wright's
knightes
knight's
knock

know't
kynde
labors
laces
lack'dst
lacke
lacks
lad
ladder
lads
lady-aire
lady's
laies
lamb
lambs
lamenesse
lament
laments
lamia
lamia'has
lampe
lanc'lots
langley
languages
languishing
lanterne-lerry
lantherne
lapland
lapsed
lapwing
larding
largely
larkes
larum
lash'd
'lasse
lasted
lasteth
lastly
late-coyn'd
laterall
latin
latten
laugh-worthy
laugh'd
laughe
laughs
laugh't
launces
laura
lawne
lawrell
laxatiue
lay-stall
layd
lazie
leaders
leading
leads
leafe
leanenesse
leapt
learnedly
learnes
leas'd
leau'st
leaven'd
lechers
leda's
lee
left-lydia
left-witted
leg
legall
legends
legitimate
lemnos
length'ned
lenox
l'envoye

leprosie
lesbia
less
lesse-poetique
letcher'd
letchers
lethargie
lether
lett
letter-goe
letter'd
lettuce
lewis
libelling
libells
libels
liber
liberall
librarie
librum
lice
licentiously
licinus
lick
liedgers
lievtenant
life's
lifts
light[s]
lighten
lightens
lightnesse
ligorne
ligurine
likely
likes
lily
limbes
limiting
limmes
lin'd
linkes
linnen
lion
lip-thirstie
lippes
liquid
listen
liter
literate
liud
liuers
liuorie
liuory
'live
liveries
livor
lock'd
lockt
lock't
lodging
log
logge
logogriphes
logs
long-gathering
long-since
long-yearn'd
long'd
long'd-for
longe
longing
look
looketh
looks
loome
loomes
loosed
loosenesse
looser-like

lops
lord-god
lore
lothed
lothsome
lotions
loued
louer
loue's
loughing
loumond
louse-dropping
lovely-head
love's
loves-sake
loveth
lov'st
low-countrey's
low-ccuntries
lowdest
lower
lowest
lowing
lowlie
lownesse
loyal
loyalties
loyre
lucane
lucans
lucent
luck
luckily
lucrine
lumpe
lupus
lurden
lurke
lustfull
lustie
lustie-mounting
lustrous
lust's
lusty
lutes
lvcan
lvcina's
lvcivs
lvthers
lyaeus
lybian
lycense
lycoris
lyer
lyfe
lyons
lyst
lyue
ma'
maas
mad<e>
mad-men
madrigall
magick
magistrates
magnetique
maiden
maidens
maides
maids
maime
maintaine
maintaynes
maior
maistring
maistry
majesty
makings
malicious
mallowes

malt	meleager	moath	mutton
malyce	melted	moathes	mutually
manage	melts	mocion	mvng'
mangers	memory	modell	mvngril
manie	memorye	moderately	mynd
mankinds	menace	modesty	mynde
mann'd	menacings	modet	mynerva
mansfield	mendicant	moist	mystick
mansion	mends	monarch	mythclogy
many-headed	ment	moneths	n<e>'re
many'of	mention	money-gett	naile
mappe	mercat	moneyes	nall
maps	mercer	money's	nameless
marching	merchants	mongst	name's
marchion:	mercies	'mong'st	nard
marchionisse	mercury	moniment	nare
mard	mercy	monogram	narrow'd
mares	mercy-seat	monsters	naso
mariage-day	merd-vrinous	montgomery	nastie
mariage-horne	merited	monthly	nasty
mariage-pledges	merlins	monticy	native
mariage-rites	mermaid	monument	nativitie
marie	mermaides	monyes	naturall
marish	mermaids	mood	natur'd
market-folkes	merrie	moods	nature's
mar'le	mersh-lambeth	moon-calfe	naught
marlowes	meschines	moore-fields	navie
maro	messalla's	morall	ne
marrie	messe	morauian	neadd
marrying	mete	morison's	nearer
mart	meticulous	mornes	neatly
martirdome	metius	morning-star	necessary
martyr	mett	mornings	necessities
marvailes	mettall'd	morning's	neck-stockt
mask'd	mettalls	morrisse	necke
masked	mettal's	morrow'	necks
masquing	me'vp	mortalitie	neeces
massacring	mew'd	mortality	neede
mast	mid-sun	morts	needfully
master-braine	mid-wife	mosco	ne'er
master-worker	mid-wives	moses	neerer
mastrie	midas	moth	neglect
mastry	milde	motiue	neighbour
match'd	milder	motiues	neighbour-towne
matches	mildnesse	motives	neighbourhood
materiall	militar	motly	neighbours
materialls	militarie	mought	neighing
matron	milk	mouldie	neithers
matrone	milkes	moulds	nephew
mature	millan	mouldy	nephews
maurice	millar	mountaines	ne'r
maximus	milo	mounte-banck	nero
may'admire	mince	mounting	nerues
may'any	mineruas	mounts	nether
mayd	minervaes	mourn'd	nevills
mayden	mines	mourners	new-come
maymed	mingle	mournes	new-ditch
mayresse	ministry	mourning	new-yeares-gift
meades	minos	mouse	new-yeeres
meadows	minute	moved	newnesse
meales	minutes	moves	neyther
mean	miracles	moveth	nicer
meat	mirkins	movnsievrs	night-sinnes
meate-boate	mirror	movnteagle	night-tubs
meazled	mirthfull	mov'st	nill
mechanick	mis-apply	mowed	ninth
med'cin'd	mis-call't	mud	no'
meddowes	mischife	muffles	noblier
mediate	misfortune	multipli'd	noddell
medicine	misse-call'd	multitude	nodding
medway	mist	mungrel	noddle
meeds	mistaking	muniments	nois'd
meek	misteryes	murdred	nominall
meere-matter-lesse	mistooke	murmures	nooke
meerely	mists	murmuring	nookes
meet'st	misus'd	murther	noone-day
mel.	mite	musicall	noone-sted's
melancholie	mixed	muster	noose
melancholique	mixeth	muster-master	noremberg
melancholy	mixing	musters	north

northumberland
norwich
nosthrill
nostrill
nostrills
nothing's
notion
notions
nourceries
nourisheth
nourse
november
now't
noyses
noyscme
nullifie
numbe
numbred-five
numercus
nun
nuncic's
nuptials
nurses
nut
nut-crackers
nuts
nvptials
nyce
nym.
nymp.
oake
oares
obay
obedience
obeying
obiectest
oblations
oblique
obliquitie
oblivion
obserued
obtain'd
obtaine
occasion
occasions
occupy
ocean
od
odious
odorous
odours
ods
oenone
of>
off-spring
offall
offending
offering
offers
officer
officious
officiously
off'ring
oft>
oftner
ointment
clde
olimpicke
cliue
olive
oliveers
olives
cmen
cminous
cmitted
cmnipotent
on[e]
onely-gotten
cne's
onions

opinion
opinions
oppose
opprest
oracles
orcades
orchard
ordain'd
order'd
orders
ordinaries
ord'ring
ore-blowne
ore-flow
ore-flowne
ore-fold
o're-joy'd
o're-praise
ore-shine
ore-swelleth
orestes
o'rewhelm'd
organes
orgies
orient
orniths
orphanes
orphans
orts
o'th'
o'th'doctors
other>
otherwise
othes
ouer-blow
ouer-come
ouer-leauen'd
ouerbearing
ouerdooe
out=liu'd
out-bee
out-boast
out-brave
out-cryes
out-dance
out-did
out-doo
out-flourisht
out-formes
out-last
out-lasts
out-liv'd
out-right
out-spun
out-started
out-stript
out-valew
out-weare
out-zany
ovens
over-come
over-gone
over-safe
over-seer
over-thick
over-wanton
overcame
overthrow
ovid
ovr
ow'd
owers
owing
owle
own'd
ownde
owse
oxe
oyles
oylie

oysters
p<avy>
p<l>ace
paccuuius
paceth
pack
paintings
paints
palate
palate's
palindromes
pallace
pallat
palmerins
palsey's
palsies
paltzgrave
pamp<h>lets
pancridge
pandects
panders
pandora's
panegyre
panick
panton
paracelsvs
parasite
parcae
parcells
parcels
pardon'd
pardoning
pardons
pare
paris
paris-garden
parish-garden
parish-steeple
paritie
parlyamt
parnassus
parrot
partakes
partes
particular
partie-per-pale
parties
pas<s>e
pas'd
pasquill's
passenger
passer-by
passion's
passiue
pastie
pastorall
pastorals
pastrie
patch't
pate
pathes
patient
patiently
patriot
patronage
patternes
paules
pauls
pauls-steeple
paulus
pavl
pawlet
payd
payne
paynted
payre
pays
pea~ock
pea_es
pearch'd

peare
peares
pearle
peasants
peason
pediculous
pedling
peepes
peere
peering
pegasvs
peirce
peiz'd
pelfe
pellets
pelts
pem
penaltie
pend
penelopes
penitent
penitents
pennance
penne
penning
penurie
perceiv'd
perceive
perform'd
performe
perfum'd
perfvmed
pericles
periegesis
perill
period
perishe
perjure
perjurie
permanent
pernitious
perplexed
perseus
perswades
perswading
pertinax
peruerts
perversly
pest
pest-house
petards
petasvs
petite
petition
petrarch
petticotes
pettie
pewter
phao<n>s
philosophers
phlebotomie
phlegeton
phoeb<e>'s
phoebeian
phoebvs-selfe
phrases
phrygian
physician
physitian
pickardill
picke
pickt-hatch
pictures
pide
pie
piety
pigges
pikes
pill'd
pillory

pillow	pollux	prescious	prosperity
pills	poly.	prescribe	protectes
pilot	poly-clbyon	presentacon	protection
pimblicoe	polytopian	presented	protestation
pin	pomp'd	presentes	protested
pin'd	pompey	presently	protests
pindar	pompey's	presents	proteus
pindares	pompilius	preseru'd	protraction
pindars	pompous	preserued	prouder
pinn	ponderous	preserues	proudly
pioners	ponds	preserved	proues
pipe	pooly'	president	prouide
piper	pope	presidents	prouing
pipkins	popenheim	presse	prouision
piso	poperie	pressure	prouisions
piss'd	popes-head-alley	presumes	prouoke
pistle	poplar	pretext	prou'st
pit-falls	poppie	prettie	provide
pit-pat-noyse	popular	pretty	providence
pitch	popularitie	preuaile	provider
pitch'd	porches	preuented	prov'st
pitfall	porc'lane	prevail'd	prowesse
pitious	poring	prevent	proyne
pittes	porta	priam's	prudent
pittied	porters	priapus	psalmes
pittious	porting	prick	ptolemey
pixe	portions	prick'd	published
placing	portland	prie	puffe
plac't	possessed	priests	pui'nees
plagiary	postes	priming	pukes
plague-bill	posts	principalities	pulling
plague-sores	pot	printed	pulls
plagues	pot-guns	pris'd	pulpit
plai'd	'pothecarie	prise	pulse
plaies	potions	priuie	pumpe
plaisters	pots	priuies	punck
planets	pottle	priuiledge	punishments
planting	poulder-plot	proceeding	puppet
plat	poulders	processe	pur-blinde
play-club	pour'st	procession	purbeck
play'd	povertie	proclamation	purely
player	powders	procure	purer
play's	powerfull	prodigally	purge
play'st	powre	prodigie	purged
plea	poynte	prodigiously	purging
plead	poyntes	profane	puritie
pleaded	practice	professed	purles
pleader	practisd	professeth	purple-matching
pleaders	practis'd	proffitt	purpled
pleadings	practises	proficiencie	purpos'd
pleased	praeceding	profitable	purposely
pleases	praecipice	profitt	pursewinge
pleaseth	praeoccupie	progne	pusil
pledge	praevaricators	proiects	putrid
pledges	praise-worthy	projects	pvsse
plights	praising	prologue	pygmy
plough'd	pranck	proludium	pyracmon's
ploughing	prankes	promethean	pyramede
plover	prating	promiser	pyramide
pluck	pratling	prompt	pyramids
pluck'd	'pray	promptly	pyrene
plucking	pray'd	proofes	pythian
plumed	prayes	propagate	pythias
plushes	praysed	properly	quadriuiall
plvto	prayser	propertie	quaint
plvto's	prayses	propertius	quake
po	praysest	prophanenesse	qualitie
pocket	preach	prophet	qualities
pockets	precede	propheticke	quarrel
pockie	precedencie	prophet's	quarrells
poem's	precedent	proportion'd	quarrels
poetique	preceding	proportions	quarrie
poet's	precepts	propos'd	quarries
poets'	precipitated	propose	quarter-face
pointed	predestin'd	propound	quarters
poland	preferr'd	propping	queenes
policie	preiudice	prop'rest	queens
polisht	prelate	prosequute	quell
poll	prentise-ship	proserpina	quick-warming-pan
polluted	prepare	prospectiue	quicke

quickest-sighted
quickly'
quickning
quicksilver
quiet
quills
quilts
quince
quintilius
quintus
quit'st
quixote
quote
r.
ra<n>ging
rabbin
races
radamanthvs
rages
ragged
raging
raign'd
raignes
railes
railing
rainbow
rainge
rak'd
rak't
ram'd
ramparts
ranck
ranck'd
rancke
randome
range
rank'd
ranne
ranulph
rap'd
rape
raphael
rapps
rap's
rapture
rarenesse
rarer
rashnesse
ratcliffe
rates
ratling
rattles
rattling
rauished
rau'lins
rave
ravenous
rayes
rayl'st
rayn'd
ray'sd
raz'd
razing
re-aduance
re-joyne
re-shine
reaching
reading
reame
reap'd
reare-suppers
reares
rearing
reason'
rebound
rebuke
recall
receiu'd
receiue
received

recelebrates
reception
recited
reciting
reck'ned
reck'ning
recorded
recovered
recovery
rectifie
rectified
rector
red
redeem'd
redemption
redoubt
reduicts
reeds
reflection
reforme
reformed
refreshed
refused
refuses
regenerate
regent
regiment
region
regions
reiect
reigne
releast
relentlesse
religiously
relique
rellish
remayn'st
remember
remonstrance
remorse
remoue
remoued
remoueth
rendred
renew
renewed
renewing
renown'd
renowning
repairer
repeat
repeating
repents
replide
replyed
replyes
reports
reprehend
reproue
repulse
reputes
requite
reseru'd
reserv'd
reside
resign'd
resist
resolu'd
resort
resteth
resting
restitution
restored
restrain'd
retain'd
retorned
retract
retribution
retriv'd
returned

retyr'd
reuenge
reuennue
reuersion
reuiuing
reveale
revealed
revells
revenge
reverent
reverently
reviv'd
revive
revolt
rewarde
rewarded
rewarding
rhapsody
rheine
rhetia
rhine
rhinocerotes
rhone
rhymes
riche
richnesse
riddles
riddling
rideth
ridiculous
ridwayes
rife
riffle
right-learned
righteousnesse
rightly
rigour
rimee's
ri'mes
riming
rioting
riots
rip
ripened
riper
rip'ned
rite
ritely
rithme
rithmes
rivals
road
roasted
roaue
roaues
robbery
robbing
robd
robes
rockets
rockie
rocks
roe's
rogue
rogues
rolands
rol'd
rolls
romano
ronsart
roor
rootes
roscivs
rosie-crosse
rosted
rot
rotteinberg
rotten
roule
rounde

roused
routes
rouze
rovinge
row-hampton
rowable
rowle
rowles
rowte
royal
rub
ruddy
ru'de
rudenesse
rudest
rue
ruffes
ruin'd
rules
rumney
rumor
rumor'd
rung
rust
ruth
rvtter
ryme
ryming
ryots
s<alomon>
s<c>urrile
s<tr>ow
sabines
sackcloth
sack't
sackvile
sacvile
saddest
sadled
safeties
saguntum
sailes
saist
sai'st
sakes
sale
salian
salisburie
sallade
sallie
salvation
salvst
sanctified
sanctifier
sand
sands
sanguine
sans
sapience
sappho
sardane
sardus
sathan
satvrnes
satvrne's
satyricall
sauage
sauce
sau'd
sauer
sauour
sauoy
saut
savage
sav'd
saving-honour
saviours
savour
sawe
saw'st

saying	sensuall	shooting	slights
sayle	sentinell	shop-philosophy	slip
sayles	sent'st	shopp	slip'd
say's	sepulcher'd	shores	slipper
sayst	sepvlchres	short-leg'd	slippery
scab	seraphick	shortest	slower
scabbed	seraphim	shortly	slyding
scabberd	serenes	shortnesse	small-timbred
scabbes	serenitie	shot-free	smelling
scan	sergeants	shoulders	smells
scan'd	sermon	shoutes	smelt
scandero<o>ne	sermoneeres	showres	smil'st
scanted	serpent	show'st	smiths
scar	serues	showt	smoother
scarlet-like	seruiceable	shreds	smutch'd
scarres	seruices	shrewsbury	snakie
scent	seruile	shrieues	snatch
scepter	seruing-man	shrin'd	sneaking
scepters	serving-wcman	shrine	snorts
scheldt	session	shrowdes	snout
school	seuer	shunnes	so'<e>xceed
schoolemen	seuer'd	shuts	so'above
scisars	seu'rall	shutter	so'alcne
scoffer	seven	sick-mens	soares
scoffing	seven-tongu'd	sicknes	sock
scold	sever'd	sided	sockes
scolds	severs	siege	socket
scores	sew'd	sigh'd	socratick
scorn'd	sey'd	sighes	sodaine
scornes	shaddow	sightes	sodayne
scornst	shadie	signes	softly
scourge	shakes	silenus	softnesses
scraps	shakespeares	silken	soile
scratching	shamefac'd	silleries	sol
scrivener	shamefastnesse	siluer	solders
scullion	shamefull	silver	soldierie
sculpture	shames	simo	sclemnly
scurfe	shap'd	simples	solid
scurrilitie	shape	simplesse	sclide
scutcheons	sharper	simplicity	sollen
scylla	sharplye	simply	soloecisme
se	shave	sindge	solons
sea-coale	sheafe	sinewes	sols
sea-girt	shearers	singing	some-thing
sealing	sheares	sing'st	some-where
searcheth	sheath	sinkes	somewhat
seare	sheds	sinketh	sommer-nights
seas'ning	sheep'erds	sinne's	somwhat
season'd	sheepes-skin	sin's	songe
seasoning	sheeres	sipt	songster
seates	sheetes	sirenas	songsters
seats	she'hath	sirrup	sonnets
seauen-fcld	sheild	sis	soon
seconded	shelfe	sister-tunes	soonest
secrecie	shelues	six-pence	soote
secretarie	shepheards	sixe-pac'd	soothing
sects	sheriffes	sixes	sop
secured	shewd	sixteenth	sope-boyler
securer	shewen	sixtieth	sophocles
securest	shew'n	skarfe	sorie
seed	shew'ne	‡skeuopoios	sorrell
seed-plot	shews	skinkers	sory
seeds	shew's	skins	sosii
seeks	shew'st	skip	soueraigne
seeliest	sh'had	skipping	sough
seem	sh'hath	skye	souldier-like
seeming	shield	slacke	souldiers
seine	shieter-huissen	slanderers	sounde
seise	shifting	slanders	sounded
seisin	shifts	slaue	sounder
seiz'd	shineth	slaues	soundest
seize	shining	slaughter-house	soundlesse
self	shin'st	slaughters	sou'raigne
selfe-boasting	ship	slay	sources
selfe-diuided	shipping	sleeked	soueraigntie
selfe-fame	shite	slid	sovldiers
selinis	shitten	slide	sow
'sell	shoales	sliding	sow'd
selling	shoone	slie	spaces
semi-god	shoote	slightly	spaines

spake	starke	stretch'd	supplies
spangled	starry	strew	supply'd
sparcle	starte	stricter	supporters
sparkle	starts	stride	supporteth
sparrowes	starue	strikes	suppose
spartans	starveling	stripes	suppositories
spawne	states-man	stript	supreme
speaker	states-mans	striuing	surcoates
speaks	states-men	striu'st	sureties
speak'st	statesman	striving	surge
specially	statesmen	stroak'd	surgeon
species	statists	stroakt	surgeons
speckled	statuaries	strokes	surly
spectacle	statute	stronge	surnames
speeches	statutes	stronger	surpasse
spenser	stayre	strongest	surpriz'd
spenser's	steadie	struggled	surrounding
sphaere	steame	strumpet	surship
sphere	stedfast	strung	suruey
spicerie	steemes	strut	surueyor
spi'd	steeming	stryke	surueyr
spide	stella	stuart	suruiue
spights	stem	stubborne	survey
spilt	sterne	stubbornnesse	surviving
spin	steropes	stuck	suspence
spindle	stew	stucke	suspended
spinne	stewards	studie'a	sussex
spinola	stick	studyed	sustaines
spire	sticke	studying	sutcliffe
spirrites	sticking	stuff	suted
spittle	stil	stuff'd	sutes
spittles	stilde	stumble	sutor
spondaees	stiles	stunke	svffolke
spoone	still-scalding	stygian	svpper
sporting	still>	styld	svrly's
sportive	stilts	sublimed	svsan
spotlesse	stinck	substract	svsanna
spoused	sting	subtill	swaggering
spoyle	stings	subtiltie	swaid
spoyled	stinkards	subtilty	swaine
spoyling	stinketh	subtler	swallow
spreading	stint	subtlest	swallow'd
spred	stir	subt'lest	swamme
sprigge	stird'st	subtly	swanne
sprightfull	stirr'd	subtract	swannes
sprightly	stirrer	succeeded	swan's
sprung	stirres	successe	sware
spue	stitch'd	succouring	swarthie
spunge-like	stitchers-to	suck	swayd
spur	stock	suckt	swaynes
spurres	stocke	sudden	swear'st
spyes	stocks	suffered	sweate
squeake	stole	sufferers	sweates
squemish	stomacks	suffrings	sweden
squibs	stonie	sugar	sweepings
'ssayd	stood'st	suggestion	sweet-meats
ssayes	stoop'd	suggests	sweet-wood
stable	stooping	suite	sweeter
stag	store-house	suitor	sweetning
stage-clothes	stoupes	suits	sweet's
stage-wrights	stoup'st	sullen	sweld
stagers	stoup't	sulphure	swell'd
stages	stradling	summer	swerve
stagirite	straightned	sun-burnt-blowse	swift-pac't
staid	strait	sun-light	swiftnesse
stain'd	straite	sundred	swill
staine	straits	sundrie	swimming
staire	stratagem	sundry	swom
staires	stratageme	sunke	swooping
stalke	straw	sunnes	swore
stalketh	straw-berries	sun's	sworne
stallion	strawe	supercilicus	swoune
stalls	stray	superficies	swynnerton
stamp'd	strayn'd	superfluous	sybil
standard	straynes	superstition	sydney's
standards	stream	supinely	sydnyes
stanley	streame	supp'd	syllab'e
star	street-borne	suppers	sylvanus
star-chamber	streightned	supplant	sylvester
starch	streights	supple	sym

symboles
symetry
symmetrie
synns
synonima
'syrian
t<o>'accuse
t<o>'admire
t<o>'adore
t<o>'advance
t<o>'all
t<o>'alledge
t<o>'allow
t<o>'amend
t<o>'approue
t<o>'approve
t<o>'aquit
t<o>'assist
t<o>'attire
t<o>'effect
t<o>'escape
t<o>'exact
t<o>'exchange
t<o>'expresse
t<o>'extract
t<o>'himselfe
t<o>'idolatrie
t<o>'increase
t<o>'indite
t<o>'inflict
t<o>'inhabit
t<o>'inherit
t<o>'inlive
t<o>'instruct
t<o>'inueigh
t<o>'obay
t<o>'obey
t<o>'observe
t<o>'obtaine
t<o>'our
t<o>'out-strip
t<o>'usher
tabacco
tabacco-like
tactickes
tagus
taile
taint
tainted
takeinge
talck
talent
talk
talk'd
taller
talmud
tamisis
ta'ne
tapp
tardie
tarrie
tart
tasque
taster
tasteth
tasting
taverne
tavernes
taxeth
ta/le
teacher
teame
teeth
teirce
telestichs
tell'
telling
tels
temper
temperate

tempestuous
temp'rance
tempted
tenants
tendring
tenor
tent
tenth
t'enuy
terence
tergum
termers
terp.
terrors
testifie
testimony
t'express
text
teynted
th<e>y
th<ey>'are
th<ey>'were
th<ou>'have
th'accompt
th'admir'd
th'aduenter
th'advantage
th'adventures
th'aemilian
th'aeternall
th'affaires
th'affrighted
thal.
th'ambitious
thank
thank'd
thankefull
thanking
thanks
th'antique
th'aonian
th'approches
th'artillery
th'ascent
th'assembly
that]
th'authors
thawes
th'best
th'calends
th'eare
th'eares
th'eating
theatre
theban
thebes
the'chequer
thee>
theefe
the'elixir
theft
theire
th'elaborate
th'elixir
them-selues
theme
then<ce>
th'enamour'd
th'enuy'd
theocritus
th'epilogue
thereby
therfore
th'escape
thesevs
thespia
thespiad's
thespis
th'esplandians
th'eternall

the'vn-vsed
thewes
th'examining
th'exampled
th'expence
they'<h>ave
they'
they'are
they'd
they'haue
they'offenders
th'hard
th'haue
th'how
thick
thicke
th'idalian
th'ides
thigh
th'ignoble
th'ill
thincking
thinge
th'ingratefull
think
th'inscription
th'intent
th'interpreters
th'ionian
thirst
thirteene
thirty
this's
th'italian
tho
tho'
th'obscene
th'obseruing
th'often
th'one
th'opinion
th'oppressor
thorny
thorough
thorough-fare
thoroughlie
thorow
thou'<h>ast
thou'ast
though't
thoughtes
thought'st
thou'hast
thou'ldst
tho'wert
th'oyle
thrace
thracian
thrall
thread
threat
threat'
threats
threds
thrift
thriues
thriuing
thriv'd
thriving
throat
throate
thrones
throng'd
thronge
throng'st
throtes
throughly
throwe
throwes
thrust

thrusts
thule
thumb
thumbe
thum's
th'unbearded
th'uncertainty
thunder-stroken
thundring
thund'ring
thurine
th'vsurped
th'were
thy'epistolar
thyestes
thyne
tiberts
tibullus
tickled
tickling
ticklinge
tie
tied
ties
tigers
tike
tiles
tills
tilly
tilting
timbrels
time's
t'imprint
tinckling
tine
tintoret
tir'd
tire-man
tires
t'is
tissues
titian
title-leafe
title's
to'<h>ave
toast
tobacco
toes
'tofore
toies
toleration
tombs
tomes
too-much
tooth'd
too'vnwieldie
topps
tops
torch
torment
tormented
torned
torrent
tort'ring
torturers
tosse
tost
tosted
t'other
totter'd
toucheth
touching
tough
tould
toure
t'outlast
toward
towers
town-born
towne-curs

towns-man	turbot	upbraid	vn-auoided
towres	turnd	upbraiding	vn-bought
towring	turners	upwards	vn-hurt
toy	turns	ura.	vn-nam'd
toye	turnst	urges	vn-sweet
trace	turpins	urgeth	vn-taught
tracks	tuske	urne	vn-welcome
tract	tut	utmost	vnalter'd
traditions	twedes	utter'd	vnblest
traduce	twelve	uttering	vnbounded
train'd	twentieth	utt'ring	vnbroke
traines	twenti'th	vaile	vncouers
trampled	twi-	val-telline	vnder-carued
trance	twi-light	valew	vnder-takes
transcending	twice-twelve-yeares	valianter	vnder-wood
transcripts	twilight	valiant'st	vnfit
transferre	t'will	valleys	vnfolds
transform'd	twins	vallies	vnfound
translate	twirle	valuations	vnfrighted
transmigrated	two-fold	valu'd	vnitie
transmitt	tybers	valure	vniuersall
transplanted	tye	vane	vnkinde
trappings	tyes	vanitie	vnknowne
traps	tygres	vapor	vnlearned
trauail'd	tyke	vapour	vnlike
trauailes	tylting	varius	vnlocke
trauayles	tymes	vary	vnluckie
trauell'd	tympanies	varyed	vnmak'st
traueller	tyndarides	vaults	vnnaturall
trauells	type	veine	vnprofiting
travail'd	tyran	veluet-men	vnprou'd
travaile	tyran'	venerable	vnrests
treading	tyrannie	venery	vnsatisfied
treads	tyre-man	venetian	vnseason'd
treasons	udders	vented	vnthriftely
treasurer-ship	ulisses	ventur'd	vntouch'd
treasurers	un-appeas'd	ventures	vntrauell'd
treble	un-becomming	venusine	vnwearied
trembles	un-common	venvs	vnworthy
trembling	un-inform'd	verdure	vogue
trent	un-wasted	veriest	voids
trespasse	unaptly	verily	volary
tresses	unbearded	vermilion	volumes
trew	unblest	verser	voluminous
triall	unbought	vert	voluptuous
trials	uncensur'd	vertu'	volvptvovs
tri'd	unchaste	vertue'	votary
tried	uncleane	vertue'enforme	vote
trimeter	uncleannesse	vertuously	vouches
trimeters	uncontrol'd	vestall	vowells
trinity	under-heares	vexation	voyc't
triple	understanding	vexed	voyd
tripoly	understands	veyne	vp-beare
tripos	unequall	viands	vpbraid
tristrams	unfold	victorie	vpbraiding
triumphall	unfortunate	victrice	vrine
troope	unheard	vies	vrne
tropicks	united	viewd	vshring
'troth	unkind	viewe	vsuall
troubles	unlay'd	viewes	vsurer
truch-man	unlearn'd	vigilance	vsurers
true-filed	unnecessarie	viler	vsurie
trull	unprofitable	ville-royes	vsurpe
truly-belou'd	unproved	vindicate	vsurping
truly-noble	unrepair'd	vindictive	vsvrer
trump	unshaken	vintners	vsvrers
trumpe	unskilfull	violates	vsvrer's
trundling	unsounder	violent	vtmost
truster	unspoken	violl	vtter
trusting	unthankfull	virgin-traine	vtterly
trusts	unthought	virgin-troup	vttring
truthes	untwisted	virgin-white	vulcanale
trve	untying	visit	vulture
tryals	unused	visor	vultures
tryer	unvulgar	vitruvius	vv'dale
tuilleries	unweary'd	vizors	vvedale
tumor	unweave	vlcers	wade
tumults	unwonted	vlushing	wagg
tun	up-braid	vn-argued	waggon
tuning	up-tooke	vn-arm'd	waigh

waine	well[s]	wildest	worthily
wait	well-compass'd	wildly	worthlesse
waite	well-grac'd	wile	worthyes
waited	well-greas'd	wilfull	wou'd
waiter	well-truss'd	will<i>am	wounded
waiting	wench	will'd	wound'st
wakefull	wept	willingly	wrack'd
wakers	wer't	wills	wrangle
walk	west-indian	wince	wranglers
wand	west-parts	winchester	wrath
wandrers	west-winds	winchestrian	wreake
wane	westerne	wind-bound	wreath
wanting	westminster	windes	wreck'd
wanton-wise	wet	windie	wrested
warbleth	wets	winding	wresting
ward	whale-bone	windore	wrestled
warden	wharfes	windores	wrestlest
ware	whatscever	winged	wretchedly
w'are	wheat	winnes	wretchednes
warie-driven	wheaten	winton	wretched'st
warned	whereas	wintry	wretches
warning	whereon	wip'd	wright
warr	where's	wise-crafts	writhed
wars	where't	wisht	writs
warwick	whereto	witch	writ'st
wary	wheron	witchcraft	wrong'd
wassall	whet	wi'the	wrung
was't	whet-stone	withers	wryes
wasted	whiles	witnesses	wthout
wasteth	whilest	witts	wyne
watch'<d>	whip	witty	wynns
watches	whipt	wodden	wyres
watchfull	whirling	woemen	wyser
watchman	whisper'd	wofull	y>our
water-conduits	whisperers	wolfe	ycleped
watering	whispering	woman-kind	yeares-gift
watermen	whistle	woman-kinde	yeares-labours
waue	whistles	wombes	yearly
waves	whit	wombs	yeelding
waxe-like	white-fryers	wondred	yeelds
waye	whiter	wondring	yeeld's
wayte	whitest	wondringe	yellow
we'<h>ave	who'd	wonnder	yewgh
weaker	who'had	woo-all	yff
weakest	who'haue	wood-cock	ymounted
wealthie	who'in	wooe	ynow
weapons	who'it	woofe	yo'had
wear	wholesome	wooing	yo'have
wearied	who'll	worded	yo'in
wearinesse	whoorles	wordes	yoke
web	whore-house	work	yond'
wedded	whores	working	yonder
weeds	whyle	workmanship	you>
weekes	whymseys	works	you'haue
wee'l	widdowes	work'st	you'l
weepinge	wider	world<s>	you'ld
weever	widow	worldlings	you'll
weighty	widow'd	world's	younger
wel	wifes	worme	youthfull
wel-made	wights	wormewood	zeales
wel-tagde	wike	worser	zephyr's
wel-wrought	wil	worthier	zodiackes

RITTER LIBRARY
BALDWIN-WALLACE COLLEGE